The Complete Resource Guide for Pediatric Disorders

2023/24
Twelfth Edition

The Complete Resource Guide for Pediatric Disorders

- Disorder Descriptions
- Body Systems Descriptions
- National & State Associations
- Libraries & Resource Centers
- Support Groups & Hotlines
- Books & Periodicals
- Research Centers
- Web Sites

PUBLISHER: Leslie Mackenzie
EDITORIAL DIRECTOR & COMPOSITION: Stuart Paterson
MARKETING DIRECTOR: Jessica Moody
EDITORIAL ASSISTANT: Olivia Parsonson

Grey House Publishing, Inc.
4919 Route 22
Amenia, NY 12501
518.789.8700
Fax: 845.373.6390
www.greyhouse.com
books@greyhouse.com

While every effort has been made to ensure the reliability of the information presented in this publication, Grey House Publishing neither guarantees the accuracy of the data contained herein nor assumes any responsibility for errors, omissions or discrepancies. Grey House accepts no payment for listing; inclusion in the publication of any organization, agency, institution, publication, service or individual does not imply endorsement of the editors or publisher.

Errors brought to the attention of the publisher and verified to the satisfaction of the publisher will be corrected in future editions.

Except by express prior written permission of the Copyright Proprietor no part of this work may be copied by any means of publication or communication now known or developed hereafter including, but not limited to, use in any directory or compilation or other print publication, in any information storage and retrieval system, in any other electronic device, or in any visual or audio-visual device or product.

This publication is an original and creative work, copyrighted by Grey House Publishing, Inc. and is fully protected by all applicable copyright laws, as well as by laws covering misappropriation, trade secrets and unfair competition.

Grey House has added value to the underlying factual material through one or more of the following efforts: unique and original selection; expression; arrangement; coordination; and classification.

Grey House Publishing, Inc. will defend its rights in this publication.

Copyright © 2023 Grey House Publishing, Inc.
All rights reserved

Names: Grey House Publishing, Inc., publisher.
Title: The complete resource guide for pediatric disorders.

Description: Amenia, NY : Grey House Publishing, 2023- | "Disorder Descriptions, Body Systems Descriptions, National & State Associations, Libraries & Resource Centers, Support Groups & Hotlines, Books & Periodicals, Research Centers, Web Sites."

Subjects: LCSH: Pediatrics—Directories. | Children—Diseases—Treatment—Directories. | Pediatrics—Periodicals. | Children—Diseases—Treatment—Periodicals.

Classification: LCC RJ61 .C728 | DDC 618.92—dc23

ISBN: 978-1-63700-546-0
ISSN: 1537-7180

Printed in the United States

Table of Contents

Introduction xi
Glossary xiii
Glossary of Acronyms xvii
Guidelines for Additional Information and Resources xix
Disorders by Biologic System Affected xxiii
America's Children in Brief: Key National Indicators of Well-Being xxxi

Section I: Pediatric Disorders

Achondroplasia 1
Acute Gastrointestinal Infections 4
Acute Lymphoblastic Leukemia 9
Acute Myeloid Leukemia 16
Albinism 22
Alopecia Areata 25
Alpha-1-Antitrypsin Deficiency 27
Anencephaly 29
Aniridia 31
Ankylosing Spondylitis 33
Anorectal Malformations 35
Aortic Stenosis 38
Apnea of Prematurity 40
Arnold-Chiari Malformation 42
Arrhythmias 44
Arthrogryposis Multiplex Congenita 47
Asperger Syndrome 49
Asthma 55
Ataxia 64
Atrial Septal Defects 73
Attention Deficit Hyperactivity Disorder 75
Autistic Disorder 85
Bell's Palsy 110
Biliary Atresia 112
Bipolar Disorder 114
Brain Tumors 119
Bronchopulmonary Dysplasia 133
Burn Injuries 135
Celiac Disease 138
Cerebral Palsy 141
Charcot-Marie-Tooth Disease 156
Childhood Dermatomyositis 159
Childhood Schizophrenia 163
Chorea 169
Cleft Lip and Cleft Palate 171
Clubfoot 175
Coarctation of the Aorta 177
Colic 179
Conduct Disorder 181
Congenital Adrenal Hyperplasia 186
Congenital Cataracts 188
Congenital Diaphragmatic Hernia 198

Table of Contents

Congenital Dysplasia of the Hip	200
Congenital Glaucoma	202
Conjunctivitis	213
Cornelia de Lange Syndrome	215
Craniosynostosis	217
Crohn's Disease	220
Cryptorchidism	229
Cushing's Syndrome	231
Cystic Fibrosis	233
Cytomegalovirus	244
Dental Conditions	246
Depression	251
Diabetes Mellitus	260
DiGeorge Syndrome	267
Down Syndrome	269
Dyslexia	281
Dystonia	285
Eating Disorders	289
Ectodermal Dysplasias	302
Eczema	305
Ehlers-Danlos Syndrome	309
Encephalocele	311
Encopresis	313
Epidermolysis Bullosa	315
Erb's Palsy	317
Erythema Infectiosum	318
Esophageal Atresia	320
Ewing's Sarcoma	322
Familial Dysautonomia	325
Fetal Alcohol Syndrome	326
Fetal Retinoid Syndrome	329
Fragile X Syndrome	331
Galactosemia	333
Gaucher's Disease	335
Growth Hormone Deficiency	337
Guillain-Barre Syndrome	342
HIV Infection	344
Head Injuries	351
Hearing Impairment/Deafness	363
Hemangiomas and Lymphangiomas	406
Hemolytic Disease of the Newborn	408
Hemophilia	410
Hepatitis	424
Hereditary Fructose Intolerance	428
Herpes Simplex	430
Hirschsprung Disease	432
Histiocytosis	434
Hodgkin's Disease	436
Homocystinuria	439
Hydrocephalus	441
Hypertrophic Cardiomyopathy	446
Hypoplastic Left Heart Syndrome	448
Hypothyroidism	451
Ichthyosis	453

Table of Contents

Intellectual Disabilities 455
Intraventricular Hemorrhage 460
Juvenile Rheumatoid Arthritis 461
Kawasaki Disease 465
Keloids 467
Kernicterus 469
Klinefelter Syndrome 471
Klippel-Feil Syndrome 473
Lazy Eye 475
Lead Poisoning 478
Learning Disability/Reading Dyslexia 479
Legg-Calve-Perthes Disease 485
Leukodystrophies 487
Lissencephaly 489
Lyme Disease 491
Macrocephaly 494
Maple Syrup Urine Disease 496
Marfan Syndrome 498
McCune-Albright Syndrome 500
Meningitis 502
Microcephaly 504
Microdontia 506
Migraine Headaches 507
Milk Protein Allergy/Lactose Intolerance 510
Mucolipidoses 512
Mucopolysaccharidoses 514
Muscular Dystrophies 516
Narcolepsy 523
Neonatal Herpes Simplex 530
Neonatal Jaundice 532
Nephrotic Syndrome 534
Neurofibromatosis 536
Neuroblastoma 539
Neutropenia 542
Nightmares 544
Night Terrors 547
Nocturnal Enuresis 550
Non-Hodgkin's Lymphoma 552
Noonan Syndrome 556
Nystagmus 558
Obesity 568
Obsessive-Compulsive Disorder 573
Omphalocele 578
Oppositional Defiant Disorder 580
Osteogenesis Imperfecta 582
Otitis Media 586
Passive-Aggressive Behavior 588
Patent Ductus Arteriosus 591
Pemphigus 593
Phenylketonuria (PKU) 595
Phobias 597
Photosensitivity 602
Physical & Sexual Abuse 605
PICA 611

Table of Contents

Pinworm (Enterobius Vermicularis)	613
Pityriasis Rosea	614
Pneumonia	616
Polydactyly	618
Porphyria	620
Post-Traumatic Stress Disorder	622
Prader-Willi Syndrome	626
Precocious Puberty	630
Prematurity	632
Preventable Childhood Infections	635
Protein C Deficiency	643
Psoriasis	645
Ptosis	650
Pulmonary Hypertension	652
Pulmonary Valve Stenosis	654
Pyloric Stenosis	656
Refraction Disturbances	658
Respiratory Distress Syndrome of the Newborn	668
Respiratory Syncytial Virus Infection	670
Retinitis Pigmentosa	672
Retinoblastoma	674
Retinopathy of Prematurity	677
Rhinitis	679
Sarcoidosis	683
Scleroderma	688
Scoliosis	692
Seizures	695
Sickle Cell Disease	706
Sleep Apnea	711
Sleepwalking	714
Social Anxiety Disorder	717
Speech Impairment	721
Spina Bifida	727
Spinal Muscular Atrophies	737
Strabismus	740
Stuttering	742
Subacute Sclerosing Panencephalitis (SSPE)	744
Sudden Infant Death Syndrome	746
Syncope	754
Syndactyly	756
Systemic Lupus Erythematosus	758
Tay-Sachs Disease	760
Telangiectasia	763
Tetralogy of Fallot	766
Thalassemias	768
Thrombocytopenias	773
Thumbsucking	775
Tics	777
Tourette Syndrome	781
Toxoplasmosis	792
Transposition of the Great Arteries	794
Trisomy 18 Syndrome	796
Trisomy 13 Syndrome	798
Tuberculosis	799

Table of Contents

Tuberous Sclerosis 802
Turner Syndrome 804
Ulcerative Colitis 809
Urticaria 813
Ventricular Septal Defects 815
Violence by Children & Teenagers 816
Williams Syndrome 825
Wilms Tumor 827
Wilson Disease 830

Section II: General Resources

Government Agencies 833
National Associations & Support Groups 835
State Agencies & Support Groups 848
Libraries & Resource Centers 877
Research Centers 887
Conferences 889
Audio Video 889
Web Sites 891
Book Publishers 895
Magazines 895
Journals 896
Newsletters 896
Pamphlets 897
Camps 898
Grant a Wish Foundations 908

Section III: The Human Body

Cardiovascular System 911
Cells 913
Dermatologic System 916
Digestive System 918
Endocrine System 921
Growth and Development 923
Hematologic System 925
Immune System 927
Musculoskeletal System 929
Nervous System 930
Reproductive System 934
Respiratory System 936
Sensory Organs 938
Urologic System 940

Section IV: Indexes

Entry Index 941
Geographic Index 981
Disorder & Related Term Index 999

Introduction

This twelfth edition of *The Complete Resource Guide for Pediatric Disorders* provides current, understandable medical information, resources and support services for 213 pediatric disorders. A repeat winner of the National Health Information Awards, this resource guide provides vital information for afflicted children and their support network, including family, friends, and medical professionals.

The disorders and issues covered in this directory have been determined to be most prevalent in the pediatric population, ages 0-18. They include both physical and mental conditions, and range from cancer to nightmares.

The front matter for *The Complete Resource Guide for Pediatric Disorders* includes:

- Two glossaries. The first is a guide to medical terminology that provides important navigational tips and more than 200 commonly used medical prefixes, roots and suffixes. The second includes medical acronyms, especially as they relate to vaccines;

- Guidelines for Obtaining Additional Information and Research. These updated guidelines assist parents and caregivers with information on pediatric specialists, accredited hospitals, approved drugs or medical devices, and clinical trials that are investigating new therapies;

- A valuable list of Disorders by Biologic System;

- *American's Children in Brief,* a report from the national Forum on Child and Family Statistics, details demographics, physical environments, economic conditions, social and cultural factors, community resources, and health and wellness of America's children. In more than 30 pages, the 2022 data is easy-to-understand, and supported by graphs and charts.

This reference work includes 7,823 listings. Each listing has updated contact data—address, phone, fax, web site, e-mail—and helpful descriptions. You will find 4,812 fax numbers, 4,464 e-mail addresses, 6,938 web sites and 12,331 key executives.

This one-stop resource, for professionals and the families they serve, is organized in the following six sections:

Section I — Disorders

This section includes 213 major disorder chapters that comprise more than 266 specific disorders, diseases, or conditions. They are arranged in alphabetical order, from Achondroplasia to Wilson Disease. Each chapter begins with an extensive description, written in understandable language. The descriptions in this eleventh edition have been reviewed by medical professionals to include the most up-to-date methods of diagnoses and treatment. Each description includes: Disorder name and synonyms; Primary symptoms; Physical findings; Related Disorders; Cause: Body system affected; Standard treatment.

Following each description are *disorder-specific resources*, including Associations, Federal and State Agencies, Support Groups, Libraries, Resource Centers, Research Centers, Web sites, Media Resources and Camps. The more prevalent a disorder is, the more resources there are available.

The Complete Resource Guide for Pediatric Disorders also includes care centers, medical organizations, and advocacy groups that offer extended information on a great variety of conditions. These combined resources offer the most comprehensive coverage available of the most prevalent pediatric disorders being diagnosed in pediatrician's offices around the country.

Introduction

Section II — General Resources
This section includes 1,020 resources, including Government Agencies, National Associations, State Agencies, Support Groups, Newsletters, Books, Magazines, Camps and Wish Foundations. These may not be limited to a specific disorder, but offer information and support for categories of disorders.

Users will find resources on not only physical pediatric disorders, but also on mental and emotional conditions that affect our younger population. There are also resources that deal with multi-disorder conditions.

Section III — The Human Body
This educational element is comprised of 14 detailed descriptions of body systems or medical categories. This section is designed to provide a comprehensive overview of the human body, enabling readers to broaden understanding of how a particular disorder affects a specific body system(s) and further, how it may relate to the body as a whole. It includes twelve specific body systems, from Cardiovascular to Urologic, plus two additional chapters: Human Cells and Child Growth & Development.

Section IV — Indexes
The Complete Resource Guide for Pediatric Disorders contains three indexes to help readers access the information from several places:

- **Entry Index** is an alphabetical listing of all entry names.

- **Geographic Index** groups listings by state.

- **Disorder & Related Term Index** is an alphabetical list of pediatric disorders, condition names, synonyms, and related disorders.

Praise for previous editions:

> *"The strength of this source is in the information referral portion for each entry: the wide range of resources and organizations presented that can assist with additional information and support."*
> —ARBA

> *"...thousands of resources are provided covering a diverse range of services... All entries offer resource descriptions, as well as full contact information. Three indexes assist readers in locating specific information..."*
> —Against the Grain

> *"...It will be particularly useful for libraries serving parents of young children and youth, and for medical professionals working in the pediatrics field...the information is comprehensive and current."*
> —Choice

The Complete Resource Guide for Pediatric Disorders is available for subscription online at http://gold.greyhouse.com, for even faster, easier access to this vast array of information. With a subscription, users can search by disorder, keyword, geographic area, bodily system, and much more. Visit the site or call (800) 562-2139 to set up a free trial of the Online Database.

Glossary
A Concise Guide to Medical Terminology

This Guide is designed to help the reader decipher some unfamiliar terms used in the disorder descriptions. It is helpful to divide medical terms into their basic elements: prefix, root, and suffix. Following these examples are 249 commonly used medical prefixes, roots, and suffixes—over a dozen more than last edition.

Example 1: The medical term *microcephaly* is a combination of "micr(o)," meaning small, and "cephal(o)," which means head. Therefore, microcephaly denotes an abnormally small head. In contrast, "macr(o)" means large. Thus, *macrocephaly* indicates an unusually large head.

Example 2: The word *polydactyly* includes "poly," meaning much or many, and "dactyl," which refers to fingers or toes. Thus, the medical term *polydactyly* means the presence of extra fingers or toes. Accordingly, because "brachy" means short, the word *brachydactyly* indicates abnormally short fingers or toes.

Example 3: The term *myositis* is a combination of "my(o)," which denotes muscle, and "itis," meaning inflammation. Therefore, *myositis* means muscle inflammation. When "cardi(o)," meaning heart, is added, forming the term *myocarditis*, the meaning becomes inflammation of heart muscle.

Medical Prefixes, Roots, and Suffixes

A	absence of, without	-cele	hernia, protrusion, tumor
Ab	away from	cent.	one hundred
Acou	hear	centr(o)	center
aden(o)	gland	cephal(o)	head
-algia	pain	cerebr(o)	brain
all(o)	other, different	cervic	neck
andr(o)	man	chole	bile
angi(o)	vessel	chondr(o)	cartilage
ankyl(o)	bent, crooked	circum	around
ante	before	-coele	body/organ cavity
anti	against, counter	contra	against, counter
arteri(o)	artery	cost(o)	rib
arthr(o)	joint	crani(o)	skull
audio	hearing, sound	cry(o)	cold
auri	ear	crypt(o)	conceal, hide
aut(o)	self	cyan	blue
bacteri(o)	bacteria	cyst(o)	bladder
bio	life	cyt(o)	cell
blast(o)	bud, early embryonic budding	de	away from, down
-blast	formative cell, germinal layer	dent(o)	tooth
blephar(o)	eyelid	dermat(o)	skin
brachi(o)	arm	di	two
brachy	short	dia	apart, through
brady	slow	digit	finger or toe
bronch(o)	bronchi	dipl(o)	double
bucc(o)	cheek	dors(o)	back
carcin(o)	cancer	dys	abnormal, bad
cardi(o)	heart	ect(o)	outside, out of place

Glossary

-emia	blood
en	in, on
end(o)	inside, within
enter(o)	intestine
epi	above, upon
erythr(o)	red
eso	inside, within
esthesi(o)	feel, perceive
eu	normal, well
ex	away from, outside
extra	beyond, in addition, outside of
flav(o)	yellow
galact(o)	milk
gastr(o)	stomach
gen(o)	gene or reproduction
gloss(o)	tongue
glyc(o)	sweet
gnath(o)	jaw
gram	draw, record, write
graph(o)	record, write
gynec(o)	woman
hemat(o)	blood
hemi	half
hepat(o)	liver
hex	six
hidr(o)	sweat
hist(o)	tissue
hom(o)	common, same
hydr(o)	water
hyper	above, beyond, excessive
hypn(o)	sleep
hyp(o)	below, deficient, low
hyster(o)	uterus
iatr(o)	physician
idi(o)	distinct, separate
ili(o)	intestines
inter	among, between
intra	inside, within
ischi(o)	hip
-itis	inflammation
kary(o)	nucleus
kilo	one thousand
kinet(o)	move
labio	lips
lact(o)	milk
lapar(o)	flank, loin
laryng(o)	larynx
latero	side
leuc(o)	white
leuk(o)	white
lien(o)	spleen
lingu(o)	tongue
lip(o)	fat
lith(o)	stone
lymph(o)	water
macr(o)	large
mal	abnormal, bad
malac(o)	soft
mamm(o)	breast
mast(o)	breast
medi	middle
mega	great, large
megal(o)	great, large
melan(o)	black
mening(o)	membrane
mes(o)	middle
meta	after, beyond
metr(o)	uterus
micr(o)	small
mill(i)	one thousand
mon(o)	only, single, sole
morph(o)	form, shape, structure
myel(o)	marrow
my(o)	muscle
myx(o)	mucus
narc(o)	stupor
nas(o)	nose
necr(o)	corpse, death
neo	new
nephr(o)	kidney
neur(o)	nerve
noci	pain
noso	disease
ocul(o)	eye
odont(o)	tooth
-odyn(o)	distress, pain
olig(o)	deficient, few, little
-oma neoplasm	tumor
omphal(o)	navel
onc(o)	mass, tumor
onych(o)	nail
oo	egg
ophthalm(o)	eye
orchi(o)	testicle
oro	mouth
-osis	process, disease from

Glossary

osse(o)	bone	retr(o)	backward, behind
oste(o)	bone	rheo	flow
ot(o)	ear	rhin(o)	nose
ovari(o)	ovary	sangui	blood
oxy	sharp	sarc(o)	flesh
pachy	thick	scler(o)	hard
pan	whole, all	-scope	instrument for examining
para	beside, beyond, resembling	semi	half
path(o)	disease	sial(o)	saliva
ped(o)	child	somat(o)	body
pen	around	somn(i)	sleep
penia	abnormal reduction, deficiency	spasm(o)	spasm
pent(a)	five	spermat(o)	seed
per	through	splen(o)	spleen
phag(o)	consume, eat	spondyl(o)	vertebra
pharmaco	drug, medicine	spor(o)	spore
pharyng(o)	throat	steat(o)	fat
phleb(o)	vein	sten(o)	compressed, narrow
phon(o)	sound	stomat(o)	mouth, opening
phot(o)	light	sub	below, near, under
physi(o)	natural, physical	super	above, beyond, excessive
pil(o)	hair	syn	together, with
-plasia	development, formation	tachy	fast, rapid
platy	broad, flat	tel(o)	end
pleur(o)	rib, side	tetra	four
-pnea	breathing	therm(o)	heat
pneumat(o)	air, breathing	thorac(o)	chest
pneum(o)	air, breath, lung	thromb(o)	clot
pod(o)	foot	-tome	instrument for cutting
poly	many, much	tox(o)	poison
post	after, behind	trans	through, across
pre	before, in front of	traumat(o)	wound
pro	before, in front of	tri	three
proct(o)	rectum	trich(o)	hair
pseud(o)	false	troph(o)	food, nourishment
psych(o)	mind	-uria	urine
pulmon(o)	lung	vas(o)	vessel
pyel(o)	pelvis	vertebr(o)	vertebrae
pyr(o)	fire, heat	vesic(o)	bladder or blister
quadri	four	xanth(o)	yellow
rachi(o)	spine	xen(o)	foreign, different
radio	radiation	xer(o)	dry
re	again, back	zyg(o)	junction, union
ren(o)	kidneys		

GLOSSARY OF ACRONYMS

Note: Compound acronyms denote vaccine combinations. 'DTPHibHepIPV', for example, denotes DTP, Hib, HepB and IPV vaccines combined.

AMC	advanced market commitment
aP	acellular pertussis vaccine
BCG	bacille Calmette-Guérin (vaccine against tuberculosis)
CBAW	childbearing-aged women; refers to ages 15-45 unless otherwise noted
Dip	diphtheria toxoid vaccine
DT	diphtheria toxoid
DTaP	diphtheria and tetanus toxoid with acellular pertussis vaccine
DTP	diphtheria and tetanus toxoid with pertussis vaccine
DTP1	first dose of diphtheria and tetanus toxoid with pertussis vaccine
DTP3	third dose of diphtheria and tetanus toxoid with pertussis vaccine
DTwP	diphtheria and tetanus toxoid with whole-cell pertussis vaccine
EPI	Expanded Programme on Immunization
GAVI	Global Alliance for Vaccines and Immunisation
GNI	gross national income (US)
H1N1	monovalent vaccine against the 2009 influenza A (H1N1) virus
HepA	hepatitis A vaccine
HepB	hepatitis B vaccine
HepB3	third dose of hepatitis B vaccine
HFRS	hemorrhagic fever with renal syndrome (hantavirus) vaccine
Hib	Haemophilus influenzae type b vaccine
Hib3	third dose of Haemophilus influenzae type b vaccine
HPV	human papilloma virus vaccine
IPV	inactivated polio vaccine
JE	Japanese encephalitis
MCV	measles-containing vaccine
MCV2	second dose of measles-containing vaccine
MenA	meningococcal A vaccine; this monovalent vaccine protects against meningitis serogroup A

Glossary of Acronyms

MenAC	meningococcal AC vaccine; this bivalent vaccine protects against meningitis serogroups A and C
MenACW	meningococcal ACWY vaccine; this quadrivalent vaccine protects against meningitis serogroups A, C and W-135
MenACWY	meningococcal ACWY vaccine; this quadrivalent vaccine protects against meningitis serogroups A, C, Y and W-135
MenBC	meningococcal BC vaccine; this bivalent vaccine protects against meningitis serogroups B and C
MenC	meningococcal C vaccine; this monovalent vaccine protects against meningitis serogroup C
MenC_conj	meningococcal C conjugate vaccine
MM	measles and mumps vaccine
MMR	measles-mumps-rubella vaccine
MMRV	measles-mumps-rubella-varicella vaccine
MR	measles and rubella vaccine
OPV	oral polio vaccine
PAB	protected at birth against tetanus
Pneumo_conj	pneumococcal conjugate vaccine
Pneumo_ps	pneumococcal polisaccharide vaccine
Pol3	third dose of poliomyelitis vaccine
PPP	purchasing power parity
Pw	whole-cell pertussis vaccine
TBE	tick-borne encephalitis vaccine
TBD	to be determined
Td	tetanus toxoid with reduced amount of diphtheria toxoid
Tdap	tetanus toxoid vaccine (full dose) with acellular pertussis vaccine (reduced dose)
TT	tetanus toxoid

Source: http://www.unicef.org and www.who.int

Guidelines for Obtaining Additional Information and Resources

Many parents and caregivers are interested in obtaining information regarding *physicians* who specialize in certain pediatric disorders, accredited *hospitals, approved drugs or medical devices* for certain pediatric conditions, or current *clinical trials* that are investigating possible new therapies for particular diseases. In addition, some individuals may wish to have access to medical journal articles and other medical literature that may be available on their child's disorder, disease, or condition. Following are several tips that may be shared with parents and caregivers in their efforts to obtain such information and resources.

Disease-Specific Resources: Many of the disease-specific resources in this *Directory* maintain listings of physicians who are experts in a particular pediatric disorder. They may also offer information on accredited hospitals with appropriate specialty departments. In addition, many may provide information on standard therapies for certain pediatric conditions and ongoing clinical trials that are investigating possible new therapies. Some of these organizations, such as certain national voluntary health associations (NVHAs) or support groups, function as patient registries, working closely with expert physicians, researchers, and university medical centers specializing in specific pediatric disorders.

Online "Physician Finder" Services: Several professional medical associations provide searchable databases on the Internet as a public service for individuals who wish to obtain information on physicians.

Example: The *American Medical Association (AMA) Physician Select* database provides information on licensed physicians in the United States, including credential data that has been verified by medical schools, residency training programs, certifying and licensing boards, and accrediting agencies. AMA Physician Select enables online visitors to search for physicians by name, medical specialty, or geographic location. This online service is located at https://doctorfinder.ama-assn.org/doctorfinder/home.jsp.

Example: The *American Board of Medical Specialties (ABMS) Public Education Program* offers an online physician locator and information service. This service, which lists all physicians certified by ABMS Member Boards, allows online visitors to verify board certification status, specialty, and location of physicians who are certified by one or more of the ABMS Member Boards. The ABMS also provides the *Certified/Doctor Locator Service,* which lists physicians certified by ABMS Member Boards who have subscribed to the service. Such listings include board certification(s), address, telephone number, and hospital affiliation(s). These online services may be accessed at www.abms.org.

Example: The U.S. federal government has an online service known as *healthfinder*® that serves as a Web portal or directory for those who are interested in locating current, high quality health information and resources on the Internet. The site is located at www.healthfinder.gov.

Hospital Accreditation: Individuals who are interested in learning about a particular medical facility's accreditation status may consider contacting the *Joint Commission,* which is the United States' leading health care quality evaluator and accredits approximately 15,000 health care facilities, organizations, and programs. Accreditation is recognized as a *"Gold Seal of Approval"* indicating that the hospital meets certain standards of performance and is committed to meeting state-of-the-art performance expectations. The Joint Commission offers an online service known as *Quality Check* that enables online visitors to obtain information about an organization's accreditation, such as how it was rated during its most recent quality report. This service is located at www.qualitycheck.org. Interested individuals may also receive information concerning a hospital's accreditation status by calling (630) 792-5800 or visiting www.jointcommission.org.

Local Hospitals: Your local hospital can be a good source of information on services available in your area and may provide online physician directories; publish newsletters, research reports, press releases, and other materials; and offer a variety of additional information. See hospital rankings by U.S. News at https://health.usnews.com/best-hospitals.

Academic Hospitals: If children have been diagnosed with a chronic, difficult-to-treat, or relatively uncommon disorder or if they remain undiagnosed after visits to several primary care or specialist pediatricians, parents or other caregivers may wish to consider taking their children to a major academic

Guidelines

medical center. Generally, such teaching hospitals use state-of-the-art testing techniques, have comprehensive evaluation centers, and follow multidisciplinary approaches to diagnosis and treatment. In addition, such centers are often affiliated with medical schools where clinical research is conducted.

Food and Drug Administration: Individuals who are interested in learning more about approved drug therapies or medical devices for certain pediatric disorders may wish to contact the *U. S. Food and Drug Administration (FDA)*. The FDA is the U.S. agency that enforces federal regulations to prevent the sale and distribution of dangerous or impure substances, such as unsafe foods, impure cosmetics, or unsafe or ineffective drugs or medical devices. For example, according to the FDA Modernization Act of 1997, one of the agency's primary objectives is "to promote the public health by promptly and efficiently reviewing clinical research and taking appropriate action on the marketing of regulated products in a timely manner." The agency is a branch of the U.S. Department of Health and Human Services. The FDA's Web site provides: FAQs (Frequently Asked Questions) areas; Consumer Drug Information Sheets; information on new and generic drug approvals, medical device product approvals, and drug labeling changes; health advisories; and access to MedWatch, the FDA's *Safety Information and Adverse Event Reporting Program*. MedWatch enables consumers and health care professionals to report adverse reactions to approved medical products directly to the FDA and/or the manufacturers. The primary purpose of MedWatch is to ensure the rapid identification of potential health hazards associated with approved medical products and the prompt communication of safety information to the health care and medical communities. The FDA's Web site is located at www.fda.gov/medwatch. Its address is 10903 New Hampshire Ave. Silver Spring, MD 20993-0002 Toll-free: (888) INFO-FDA or (888) 463-6332

Clinical Research: A clinical protocol is a scientific study that evaluates the safety or effectiveness (efficacy) of a particular drug therapy or medical device in humans. Clinical studies enable researchers and physicians to determine new and more effective ways to prevent, diagnose, manage, and treat disease. Medications and treatments that are found to be safe and effective during laboratory and animal testing must then prove safe and effective in humans before they are approved for use by the general public. Participation in clinical studies may only occur if individuals volunteer and are fully informed and understanding of both the potential benefits and risks of such participation ("informed consent"). Participants may voluntarily leave a clinical study at any time. Research on new drugs, which are known as *investigational new drug applications* or *INDS,* is conducted in three phases:

Phase I Study — The main objective of a Phase I study is to establish the *safety* of the investigational new drug. Such studies:

- may take several months

- typically involve a relatively small number of participants who are healthy volunteers

- are designed to evaluate the INDs biologic activities in the human body (e.g., absorption, metabolism, etc.) and its potential side effects as drug dosages are raised

Phase II Study — The purpose of a Phase II study is to establish the *safety and efficacy* of the investigational new drug in treating a specific disease. Such studies:

- may take from several months to a few years

- may include a relatively small number or up to several hundred patients

- usually involve randomized, double-blind trials. During such studies, one group of participants receives the drug (experimental group) and the other group is given a harmless, unmedicated substance (placebo) or a standard, well-established therapy (control group). The information concerning which patients are included in which group is hidden from both the patients and the researchers.

- *Phase III Study* — The purpose of a Phase III study is to evaluate the overall *safety, efficacy, possible adverse effects, and benefits* of the investigational new drug in a large number of patients and to compare such therapy with the use of well-established treatments or with an untreated disease course. Such studies:

- may last for several years

- may involve hundreds or thousands of patients

- may include research teams from multiple national or international clinical centers

- typically involve randomized, double-blind trials

If an investigational new drug application successfully completes Phase III studies, the drug's sponsor may request FDA approval for marketing to the public, which is known as a *New Drug Approval* (NDA). In some cases, additional clinical research may be conducted:

Phase IV Study — The purpose of a Phase IV study may be to:

- monitor the drug's long-term efficacy

- compare the drug with other medications that have been available for longer periods

As mentioned above, disease-specific organizations and registries, support groups, and online services may serve as essential sources of information concerning clinical studies for a particular disease. There are also several additional, more general resources that promote and provide information on clinical trials:

Example: The *NIH Clinical Center,* which is part of the National Institutes of Health (NIH), is a federally funded biomedical research hospital. The Clinical Center was designed to support studies conducted by the NIH. Only individuals with conditions or disorders under NIH investigation are admitted for treatment, and all patients must be referred by their physicians. The Clinical Center's Web site includes a clinical research database that enables online visitors to search for current research studies by certain predefined parameters, such as primary disease category, or specific diagnosis, symptom, sign, or other keywords. The Clinical Center's Web site is located at www.cc.nih.gov and its Protocol Database may be accessed at http://clinicalstudies.info.nih.gov. The Clinical Center's address follows:

The Center and its Patient Recruitment and Referral Center is at 10 Center Drive, Bethesda, MD 20892. They can be reached at:

Toll-free: (800) 411-1222
Facebook: https://www.facebook.com/NIHClinicalCenter
Twitter: @NIHClinicalCntr
YouTube Channel: https://www.youtube.com/c/nihclinicalcenter
E-mail: prpl@mail.cc.nih.gov

Example: *WCG CenterWatch, Inc.* provides a *Clinical Trials Listing Service*™ on its Web site for patients and research professionals. The site provides listings of more than 54,000 active trials listed and searchable by geographic region and therapeutic area. Interested individuals may also sign up for CenterWatch's confidential *Patient Notification Service,* which provides notification via e-mail of future clinical trial postings in a certain therapeutic area. CenterWatch's Clinical Trials Service also provides: a listing of NIH-funded clinical research programs that are currently being conducted at the NIH Clinical Center; a general explanation of clinical trials, profiles of clinical research centers; listings of medications recently approved by the FDA; and linkage to health-related sites for patients and patient advocates. The Clinical Trials Listing Service™ is located at www.centerwatch.com. CenterWatch's address follows:

CenterWatch, Inc.
300 N. Washington St., Suite 200
Falls Church, VA 22046, USA
Phone: (617) 948-5100
Fax: (617) 948-5101
Toll-Free: 866-219-3440
Twitter: @CWPatient

Guidelines

The *National Cancer Institute (NCI)* offers an online service known as *CancerNet*™ that provides information for patients and family members, health professionals, and researchers. The site offers: information on current clinical trials; summaries on cancer prevention, screening, treatment, and supportive care; cancer fact sheets; and linkage to the *Physician Data Query* or *PDQ® Cancer Information Service,* the NCI's cancer database. PDQ contains a registry of open and closed cancer clinical trials as well as directories of organizations, physicians, and genetic counselors who provide cancer care. The NCI also offers a Cancer Information Service (CIS) for callers Monday through Friday from 9 a.m. to 9 p.m., Eastern Standard Time. The CIS may be reached at (800) 422-6237. Individuals with hearing impairment who have TTY equipment may call (800) 332-8615.

OncoLink, the first cancer information site on the Internet, was launched in 1994 and remains one of the largest. Affiliated with the University of Pennsylvania, the site provides: information on cancer clinical trials; symptom management; personal experiences and psychosocial support; cancer causes, prevention, and screening; financial issues for cancer patients; and additional topics. The site is located at www.oncolink.org.

Medical Journal Articles. Individuals who are interested in accessing abstracts summarizing medical journal articles may visit the National Library of Medicine's (NLM's) *PubMed*. The PubMed search service provides free access to the more than 32 million medical journal citations within NLM's *MEDLINE*. MEDLINE is essentially the online version of *Index Medicus,* a monthly subject/author guide to articles in thousands of medical journals. Online visitors to PubMed may conduct searches for medical journal citations and abstracts by journal title and date, author, and topic. In addition to providing access to selected journal abstracts, PubMed offers links to participating online journals and enables registered users to order full-text articles for a fee. PubMed may be accessed at www.pubmed.gov. In addition, several general medical sites provide access to PubMed and enable users to order full-text journal articles for a fee.

Online Mendelian Inheritance in Man (OMIM). Individuals who wish to access comprehensive and timely medical information on genetic disorders may be interested in visiting OMIM™ or *Online Mendelian Inheritance in Man,* a database of genetic disorders and human genes. This searchable database is authored and edited at the McKusick-Nathans Institute of Genetic Medicine at the Johns Hopkins University School of Medicine. OMIM™ contains entries on genetic diseases, clinical synopses, links to relevant MEDLINE citations, and more. OMIM™ is located at www.ncbi.nlm.nih.gov/omim.

Disorders by Biologic System Affected

Cardiovascular Disorders; see also *Cardiovascular System*, page 911.
Aortic Stenosis
Arrhythmias
Atrial Septal Defects
Coarctation of the Aorta
Hypertrophic Cardiomyopathy
Hypoplastic Left Heart Syndrome (HLHS)
Kawasaki Disease
Marfan Syndrome
Noonan's Syndrome
Patent Ductus Arteriosus
Pulmonary Hypertension
Pulmonary Valve Stenosis
Syncope
Tetralogy of Fallot
Transposition of the Great Arteries
Ventricular Septal Defects
Williams Syndrome

Connective Tissue Disorders; see also *Cells*, page 913.
Childhood Dermatomyositis
Ehlers-Danlos Syndrome
Sarcoidosis
Scleroderma

Dental Disorders; see also *Digestive System*, page 918.
Dental Conditions
Ectodermal Dysplasia
Microdontia

Dermatologic Disorders; see also *Dermatologic System*, page 916.
Albinism
Alopecia Areata
Burn Injuries
Childhood Dermatomyositis
Cleft Life and Cleft Palate
Ectodermal Dysplasia
Eczema
Epidermolysis Bullosa
Hemangiomas and Lymphangiomas
Icthyosis
Keloids
Neurofibromatosis
Pemphigus
Photosensitivity
Pityriasis Rosea
Tuberous Sclerosis
Psoriasis

Disorders by Biologic System Affected

Telangiectasia
Urticaria

Developmental, Behavioral and Psychiatric Disorders; see also *Growth and Development*, page 923.
Asperger Syndrome
Attention Deficit Hyperactivity Disorder
Autistic Disorder
Bipolar Disorder
Childhood Schizophrenia
Conduct Disorder
Depression
Eating Disorders
Encopresis
Lead Poisoning
Learning Disability, Reading Disability Dyslexia
Mental Retardation
Migraine Headaches
Nightmares
Night Terrors
Nocturnal Enuresis
Obesity
Obsessive-Compulsive Disorder
Oppositional Defiant Behavior
Passive-Aggressive Behavior
Phobias
Physical and Sexual Abuse
PICA
Post-Traumatic Stress Disorder
Sleepwalking
Stuttering
Thumbsucking
Violence by Children & Teenagers

Endocrinologic Disorders; see also *Endocrine System*, page 921.
Congenital Adrenal Hyperplasia
Cushing's Syndrome
Diabetes Mellitus
Growth Hormone Deficiency
Hypothyroidism
McCune-Albright Syndrome
Obesity
Prader-Willi Syndrome
Precocious Puberty

Gastrointestinal Disorders; see also *Digestive System*, page 918.
Acute Gastrointestinal Infections
Alpha-1-Antitrypsin Deficiency
Anorectal Malformations
Biliary Atresia

Disorders by Biologic System Affected

Celiac Disease
Colic
Congenital Diaphragmatic Hernia
Crohn's Disease
Encopresis
Esophageal Atresia
Galactosemia
Hepatitis
Hirschsprung Disease
Milk Protein Allergy and Lactose Intolerance
Omphalocele
Pyloric Stenosis
Ulcerative Colitis
Wilson's Disease

Genetic/Chromosomal/Syndrome/Metabolic Disorders; see also *Growth and Development*, page 923.
Achondroplasia
Albinism
Alpha-1-Antitrypsin Deficiency
Asperger Syndrome
Congenital Cataracts
Cornelia de Lange Syndrome
DiGeorge Syndrome
Down Syndrome
Familial Dysautonomia
Fetal Alcohol Syndrome
Fragile X Syndrome
Galactosemia
Gaucher's Disease
Hereditary Fructose Intolerance
Homocystinuria
Klinefelter Syndrome
Klipple-Feil Syndrome
Leukodystrophies
Maple Syrup Urine Disease
Marfan Syndrome
McCune-Albright Syndrome
Mucolipidoses
Mucopolysaccharidoses
Noonan's Syndrome
Osteogenesis Imperfecta
Phenylketonuria
Polydactyly
Prader-Willi Syndrome
Tay-Sachs Disease
Trisomy 18 Syndrome
Trisomy 13 Syndrome
Turner Syndrome
Williams Syndrome

Disorders by Biologic System Affected

Hematologic and Oncologic Disorders; see also *Hematologic System*, page 925.
Acute Lymphoblastic Leukemia
Acute Myeloid Leukemia
Ewing's Sarcoma
Hemolytic Disease of the Newborn
Hemophilia
Histiocytosis
Hodgkins Disease
Neuroblastoma
Neutropenia
Non-Hodgkins Lymphoma
Porphyria
Protein C Deficiency
Retinoblastoma
Sickle Cell Disease
Thalasemias
Thrombocytopenias
Wilm's Tumor

Immunologic and Rheumatologic Disorders; see also *Immune System*, page 927.
Alopecia Areata
DiGeorge Syndrome
HIV Infection
Juvenile Rheumatoid Arthritis
Kawasaki Disease
Subacute Sclerosing Panencephalitis (SSPE)
Systemic Lupus Erythematosus

Infectious Diseases; see also *Immune System*, page 927.
Acute Gastrointestinal Infections
Conjunctivitis
Cytomegalovirus
Erythema Infectiosum
HIV Infection
Hepatitis
Herpes Simplex
Lyme Disease
Meningitis
Neonatal Herpes Simplex
Otitis Media
Pinworm
Pityriasis Rosea
Pneumonia
Preventable Childhood Infections
Respiratory Syncytial Virus
Toxoplasmosis
Tuberculosis

Disorders by Biologic System Affected

Neonatal and Infant Disorders; see also *Growth and Development*, page 923.
Apnea of Prematurity
Bronchopulmonary Dysplasia
Colic
Congenital Dysplasia of the Hip
Hemolytic Disease of the Newborn
Interventricular Hemorrhage
Kernicterus
Neonatal Herpes Simplex
Neonatal Jaundice
Omphalocele
Prematurity
Respiratory Distress Syndrome of the Newborn
Retinopathy of Prematurity
Sudden Infant Death Syndrome

Neurologic Disorders; see also *Nervous System*, page 930.
Anencephaly
Arnold-Chiari Malformation
Asperger Syndrome
Ataxia
Autistic Disorder
Brain Tumors
Bell's Palsy
Cerebral Palsy
Chorea
Dyslexia
Dystonia
Encephalocele
Erb's Palsy
Familial Dysautonomia
Guillain-Barre Syndrome
Head Injuries
Hearing Impairment/Deafness
Hydrocephalus
Interventricular Hemorrhage
Lead Poisoning
Leukodystrophies
Lissencephaly
Macrocephaly
Meningitis
Mental Retardation
Microcephaly
Muscular Dystrophies
Narcolepsy
Nystagmus
Ptosis
Seizures
Speech Impairment
Spina Bifida

Disorders by Biologic System Affected

Spinal Muscular Atrophies
Strabismus
Stuttering
Subacute Sclerosing Panencephalitis (SSPE)
Tics
Tourette Syndrome
Tuberous Sclerosis

Ophthalmologic Disorders; see also *Sensory Organs*, page 938.
Aniridia
Congenital Cataracts
Congenital Glaucoma
Conjunctivitis
Lazy Eye
Nystagmus
Ptosis
Refraction Disturbances
Retinitis Pigmentosa
Retinoblastoma
Retinopathy of Prematurity
Strabismus

Orthopedic and Muscle Disorders; see also *Musculoskeletal System*, page 929.
Achondroplasia
Ankylosing Spondylitis
Arthorogryposis Multiplex Congenita
Cerebral Palsy
Charcot-Marie-Tooth Disease
Childhood Dermatomyositis
Cleft Lip and Cleft Palate
Clubfoot
Congenital Dysplasia of the Hip
Craniosynostosis
Dystonia
Ewing's Sarcoma
Legg-Calve-Perthes Disease
Marfan Syndrome
Muscular Dystrophies
Neurofibromatosis
Osteogenesis Imperfecta
Polydactyly
Scoliosis
Spina Bifida
Spinal Muscular Atrophies
Strabismus
Syndactyly

Disorders by Biologic System Affected

Renal and Urologic Disorders; see also *Urologic System*, page 940.
Cryptorchidism
Nephrotic Syndrome
Nocturnal Enuresis

Respiratory Disorders; see also *Respiratory System*, page 936.
Alpha-1-Antitrypsin Deficiency
Apnea of Prematurity
Asthma
Bronchopulmonary Dysplasia
Congenital Diaphragmatic Hernia
Cystic Fibrosis
Pneumonia
Pulmonary Hypertension
Respiratory Distress Syndrome of the Newborn
Respiratory Syncytial Virus Infection
Rhinitis
Sleep Apnea
Tuberculosis

Introduction

This year's America's Children in Brief: Key National Indicators of Well-Being *continues a tradition of collaboration by agencies across the Federal Government to advance the understanding of what our Nation's children and families may need to help ensure bright, healthy futures.*

Office of the Chief Statistician, U.S. Office of Management and Budget

About This Report

The Federal Interagency Forum on Child and Family Statistics (Forum) was chartered in 1997 by Executive Order No. 13045. The Forum fosters collaboration among 23 Federal agencies that produce and use statistics on children and families and seeks to improve these Federal data. The Forum annually updates all 41 key indicators of well-being for children on its website (https://www.childstats.gov/), depending on data availability. The Forum alternates publishing a detailed report of these 41 indicators, *America's Children: Key National Indicators of Well-Being*, with a summary version, *America's Children in Brief*, which highlights selected indicators.

America's Children in Brief, 2022

This year's *America's Children in Brief* highlights selected special feature indicators related to COVID-19 to address the impact of this pandemic on child well-being. Indicator titles are COVID-19 Immunization, Child Food Insufficiency, Housing Instability, Pandemic Health Care and Child Care, How Schools Adapted to Pandemic Response, Summer Enrichment Programs, Child and Adolescent Mortality, and Substance Use and Mental Health of Adolescents. In addition to the focus on COVID-19, this brief provides a snapshot of the overall well-being of America's children through the At-a-Glance summary table displaying the most recent data for all 41 regular indicators.

Three special feature indicators in this brief rely on the Household Pulse Survey (HPS) as a data source.[1] The HPS was developed by the U.S. Census Bureau in collaboration with multiple Federal agencies in response to the COVID-19 pandemic. It is designed to collect data quickly and efficiently from U.S. households to produce timely information on the effects of the COVID-19 pandemic on the population. The survey asks respondents about educational, employment, health, housing, and food-related outcomes, as well as other topics, and offers an important new way to monitor the impact of COVID-19 on America's families with children. The HPS is different from other surveys traditionally used to provide data for *America's Children*. The survey was designed to go into the field quickly, be administered via the internet, and produce data for the public in near realtime. As such, data from the HPS may not meet some of the Census Bureau's traditional statistical quality standards. Readers should also be aware that this survey has several brief data collection phases. Where applicable, breaks in trend lines and data collection dates are shown in indicator figures to help ensure accurate data interpretation. Findings reported for early in the month corresponds to the 1st–10th, middle of the month to the 11th–20th, and end of the month to the 21st–last day of the month. Otherwise, indicator figure notes address specific details about the way data are displayed.

Conceptual Framework for Key National Indicators

The key national indicators of child well-being identified by the Forum are featured in an alternate full report publication and span seven domains: Family and Social Environment, Economic Circumstances, Health Care, Physical Environment and Safety, Behavior, Education, and Health. The indicators also must meet the following criteria:

- *Easy to understand* by broad audiences;
- *Objectively* based on reliable data;
- *Balanced*, so that no single area dominates the report;
- *Measured regularly* so that they can be updated and show trends; and
- *Representative* of large segments of the population.

Introduction

Race and Ethnicity

Every effort is made to include data breakouts by race and ethnicity for regular indicators in the full *America's Children* report and for selected indicators in this year's brief. Unless otherwise noted, data by race and ethnicity in this report have implemented the *Revisions to the Standards for the Classification of Federal Data on Race and Ethnicity* (hereafter referred to as standards on race and ethnicity) issued in 1997 by the Office of Management and Budget (https://www.gpo.gov/fdsys/pkg/FR-1997-10-30/pdf/97-28653.pdf). The 1997 standards on race and ethnicity allow for observer or proxy identification of race but clearly state a preference for self-classification. Persons of Hispanic origin may be of any race. Data on race and Hispanic origin are collected separately and presented in the greatest detail possible considering the quality of the data, the amount of missing data, and the number of observations. Data in this report are generally presented for the following six race and Hispanic origin groups: American Indian or Alaska Native, non-Hispanic; Asian, non-Hispanic; Black or African American, non-Hispanic; Native Hawaiian or Other Pacific Islander, non-Hispanic; White, non-Hispanic; and Hispanic or Latino. On the charts, shortened labels often are used because of limited space.

The 1997 standards on race and ethnicity also offer an opportunity for respondents to select more than one of the five race groups, leading to many possible multiple-race categories. These standards allow for two basic ways of defining a race group. A group such as Black may be defined as those who reported Black and no other race (the race-alone or single-race concept) or those who reported Black regardless of whether they also reported another race (the race-alone or in-combination concept). In this report, indicators present data using the first approach (single race). Use of the single-race population does not imply that it is the preferred method of presenting or analyzing data. Generally, a small percentage of people report two or more races. When possible, estimates for this group are shown separately. All groups not shown separately are included in the totals.

Statistical Significance

Most data in this report are estimates based on a sample of the population and are therefore subject to sampling error. Differences between estimates are tested for statistical significance at either the 0.05 or 0.10 cutoff level, according to agency standards; all differences discussed in the report are statistically significant according to the standards of the agency responsible for the data. Agency details about statistical reporting standards for indicators included in the *America's Children* report and standard error tables for select indicators are available online at https://www.childstats.gov.

For Further Information on the Forum

The Forum's website (https://www.childstats.gov) also includes this additional information:

- Detailed data for indicators discussed in this brief as well as trend data and other *America's Children* indicators not discussed here.
- Data source descriptions and agency contact information.
- *America's Children* reports from 1997 to the present and other Forum reports.
- Links to Forum agencies, their online data tools, and various international data sources.
- Forum news and information on the Forum's overall structure and organization.

COVID-19 Immunization

As of November 2021, the Centers for Disease Control and Prevention recommended the Pfizer COVID-19 vaccine for all children ages 5–17 to protect against severe illness.[2] Data on vaccination coverage can be used to identify groups of children who may be more likely to be unvaccinated and at a greater risk for severe COVID-19 illness.[3]

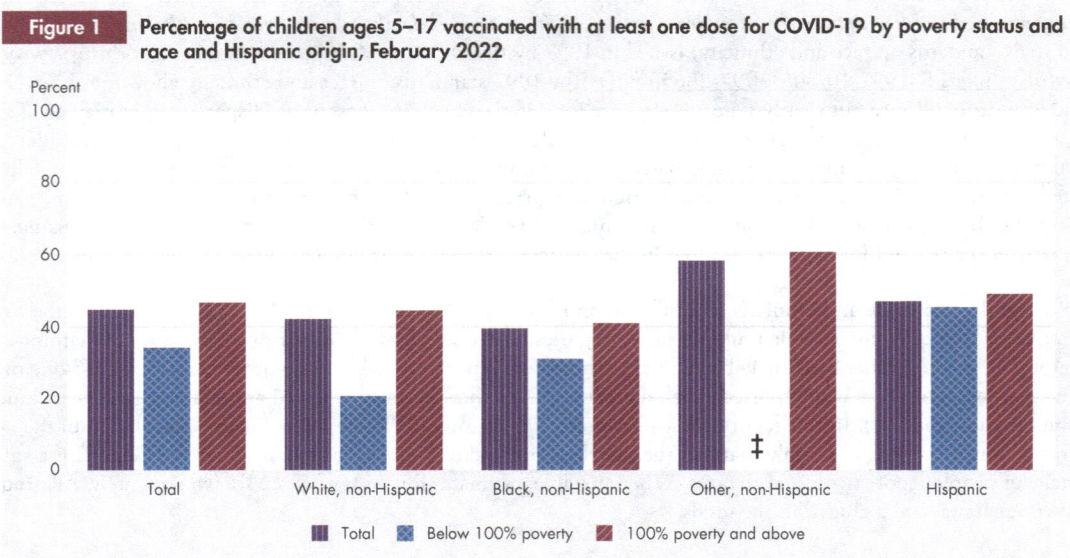

Figure 1 Percentage of children ages 5–17 vaccinated with at least one dose for COVID-19 by poverty status and race and Hispanic origin, February 2022

‡ Reporting standards not met.

NOTE: As of June 19, 2022, COVID-19 vaccination is recommended for all children ages 6 months–17 years. The data for the indicator in this report was collected during the time when COVID-19 vaccination was recommended for children ages 5–17 years. The recommendations are available at: https://www.cdc.gov/vaccines/covid-19/index.html. Poverty status is based on family income and household size using 2020 U.S. Census Bureau poverty thresholds. The revised 1997 U.S. Office of Management and Budget standards on race and ethnicity were used to classify persons into one of the following five racial groups: White, Black or African American, American Indian or Alaska Native, Asian, or Native Hawaiian or Other Pacific Islander. Those reporting more than one race were classified as "Two or more races." Data on race and Hispanic origin are collected separately but combined for reporting. Persons of Hispanic origin may be of any race. Included as "Other, non-Hispanic" but not shown separately are American Indian or Alaska Native, Asian, Native Hawaiian or Other Pacific Islander, and "Two or more races," due to the small sample size.

SOURCE: Centers for Disease Control and Prevention, National Center for Immunization and Respiratory Diseases, National Immunization Survey–Child COVID Module.

- In February 2022, approximately 45% of children ages 5–17 had received at least one dose of the COVID-19 vaccine.

- Overall, children in families with incomes below the poverty threshold had lower one-dose COVID-19 vaccination coverage (34%) than did children in families with incomes at or above the poverty level (47%).

- Among White, non-Hispanic children, those in families with incomes above the poverty threshold had higher one-dose COVID-19 vaccination coverage (45%) than did those in families with incomes below the poverty threshold (21%).

- Among children in families with incomes below the poverty threshold, one-dose COVID-19 vaccination coverage was greater for Hispanic children (45%) than for White, non-Hispanic children (21%). There were no statistically significant differences in coverage between Hispanic or White, non-Hispanic children and Black, non-Hispanic children.

- Among children in families with incomes above the poverty threshold, children of an Other, non-Hispanic race or ethnicity had greater one-dose COVID-19 vaccination coverage (61%) than did Hispanic children (49%), White, non-Hispanic children (45%), and Black, non-Hispanic children (41%).

Endnotes begin on page 27.

America's Children in Brief

Child Food Insufficiency

The U.S. Department of Agriculture's Economic Research Service monitors the annual prevalence of food insecurity in U.S. households with data from the Current Population Survey Food Security Supplement. Food insecurity means that households were, at times, unable to acquire adequate food for one or more household members because the households had insufficient money and other resources for food.

Food insufficiency is a simpler measure of whether or not there was enough to eat in the last 7 days. It is related to food insecurity but is often considered to be a more severe form as households that suffer from food insufficiency are likely to also have very low food security. Food insufficiency has been measured during the COVID-19 pandemic with the use of the Household Pulse Survey.[4] Child food insufficiency means a household's children were not eating enough food sometimes or often in the last 7 days because the household could not afford enough food. Food insufficiency is related to children's health and well-being. Studies have shown that food insecurity contributes to poorer physical and mental health and developmental outcomes and is negatively associated with education outcomes.[5]

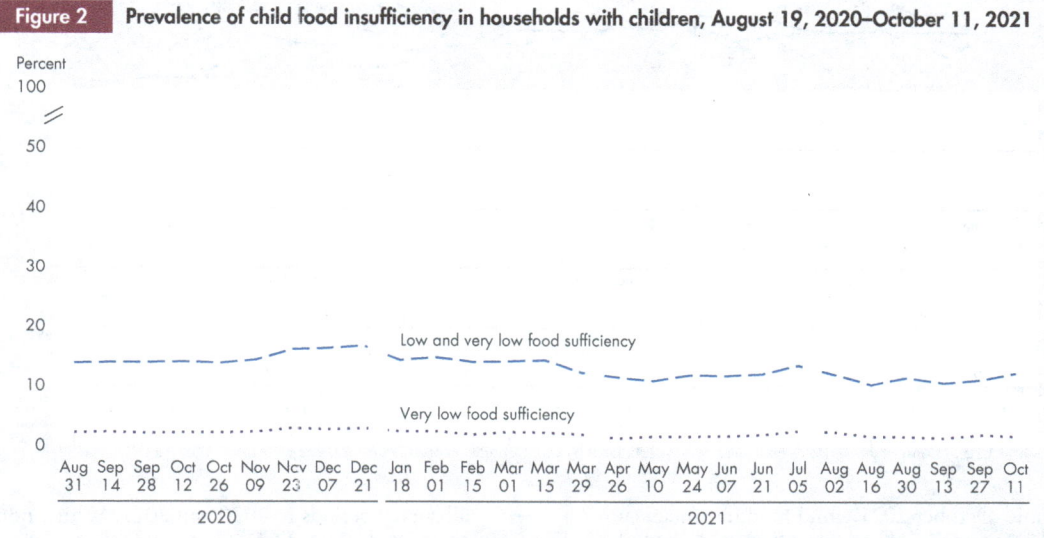

Figure 2 Prevalence of child food insufficiency in households with children, August 19, 2020–October 11, 2021

NOTE: Dates shown are the last day of each Household Pulse Survey (HPS) 13-day data collection period. Adult respondents were asked to indicate whether this statement was often true, sometimes true, or never true in the last 7 days for the children living in the household who are under age 18: "The children were not eating enough because we just couldn't afford enough food." Responses of "often true" indicate very low food sufficiency, and "sometimes true" indicates low food sufficiency, while "never true" indicates food sufficient. Child food insufficiency includes low and very low food sufficiency. The child food insufficiency question was not included in the HPS data collection until week 6; therefore, the above figure presents data for Phase 2 through Phase 3.2. These phases encompass four data collection periods from August 19, 2020, to October 11, 2021. Data were not collected during December 22, 2020–January 5, 2021, March 30–April 13, 2021, and July 6–20, 2021.
SOURCE: U.S. Census Bureau, Household Pulse Survey. Tabulated by U.S. Department of Agriculture, Economic Research Service.

- As of mid-October 2021, the prevalence of child food insufficiency (low and very low food sufficiency) was 13%, meaning 13% of households with children reported that children in the household sometimes or often did not have enough to eat in the last 7 days. The prevalence of very low child food sufficiency was 2%, meaning 2% of households with children reported that children often did not have enough to eat in the same time period.

- The prevalence rates of child food sufficiency varied across the pandemic. Child food insufficiency peaked at 17% in December 2020, meaning 17% of households with children reported that children in the household sometimes or often did not have enough to eat in the last 7 days. Child food insufficiency decreased to 11% in mid-August 2021, the lowest prevalence rate reported during 2020 and 2021.

- Very low child food sufficiency followed a similar pattern. The prevalence of very low food sufficiency peaked at 4% in November and December 2020, meaning that 4% of households with children reported that their children often did not have enough to eat in the last 7 days. Very low child food sufficiency decreased to a low of 2% in mid-August 2021.

America's Children in Brief

Child Food Insufficiency—Continued

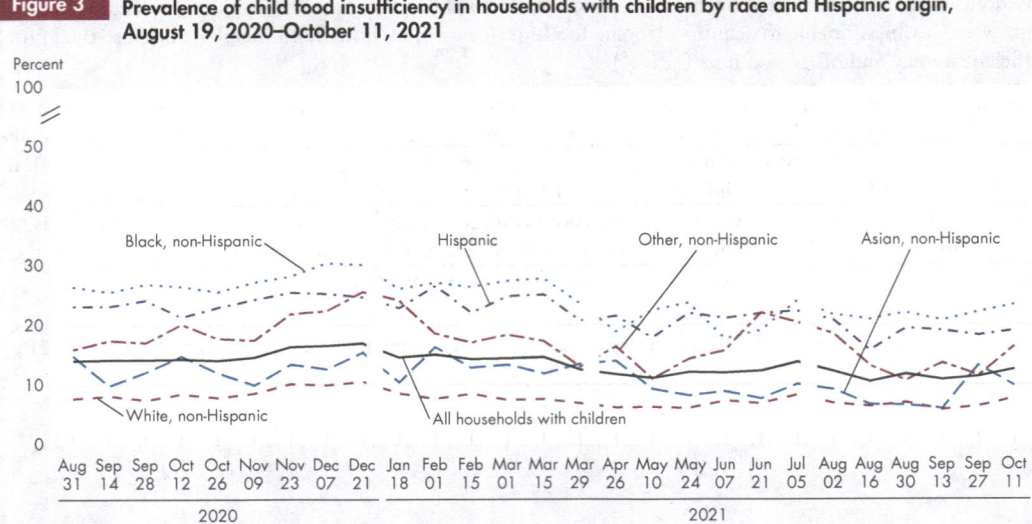

Figure 3. Prevalence of child food insufficiency in households with children by race and Hispanic origin, August 19, 2020–October 11, 2021

NOTE: Dates shown are the last day of each Household Pulse Survey (HPS) 13-day data collection period. Adult respondents were asked to indicate whether this statement was often true, sometimes true, or never true in the last 7 days for the children living in the household who are under age 18: "The children were not eating enough because we just couldn't afford enough food." Responses of "often true" indicate very low food sufficiency, and "sometimes true" indicates low food sufficiency, while "never true" indicates food sufficient. Child food insufficiency includes low and very low food sufficiency. The child food insufficiency question was not included in the HPS data collection until week 6; therefore, the above figure presents data for Phase 2 through Phase 3.2. These phases encompass four data collection periods from August 19, 2020, to October 11, 2021. Data were not collected during December 22, 2020–January 5, 2021, March 30–April 13, 2021, and July 6–20, 2021. The revised 1997 U.S. Office of Management and Budget standards on race and ethnicity were used to classify persons into one of the following five racial groups: White, Black or African American, American Indian or Alaska Native, Asian, or Native Hawaiian or Other Pacific Islander. Those reporting more than one race were classified as "Two or more races." Data on race and Hispanic origin are collected separately. Persons of Hispanic origin may be of any race. Included as "Other, non-Hispanic" but not shown separately are American Indian or Alaska Native, Asian, Native Hawaiian or Other Pacific Islander, and "Two or more races," due to the small sample size.
SOURCE: U.S. Census Bureau, Household Pulse Survey. Tabulated by U.S. Department of Agriculture, Economic Research Service.

- In mid-October 2021, child food insufficiency affected 23% of Black, non-Hispanic households, 19% of Hispanic households, and 17% of Other, non-Hispanic households—compared with 8% of White, non-Hispanic households and 10% of Asian, non-Hispanic households.

- Black, non-Hispanic and Hispanic households experienced higher rates of child food insufficiency as compared to All Households with Children for all survey periods in 2020 and 2021. White, non-Hispanic households experienced lower prevalence rates of child food insufficiency than All Households with Children in all survey periods in 2020 and 2021.

- Other, non-Hispanic and Asian, non-Hispanic households were not consistently above or below the prevalence rates for All Households with Children.

Endnotes begin on page 27.

Housing Instability

The COVID-19 pandemic and associated economic disruption of 2020–2021 posed severe challenges for national housing markets. The Centers for Disease Control and Prevention imposed national eviction moratoria as public health measures for most of a year-long period beginning September 4, 2020. Numerous government agencies took parallel actions, including federal, state, and local foreclosure moratoria that affected homeowners, renters, landlords, and financial institutions. Housing instability associated with financial difficulties, family instability, or health problems poses substantial risk to children and their caregivers, including risk of homelessness and increased risk of COVID-19 infection.[6,7,8,9]

The most recent available data from the American Housing Survey show that, in 2019, there were an estimated 12.8 million renter households with children. There were another 22.9 million owner households with children, of which 17.7 million households had mortgages.[10] Financial difficulties reported include being behind on payments, lacking confidence in ability to make payments during the next 2 months, and perceiving a risk of eviction or foreclosure within 2 months.

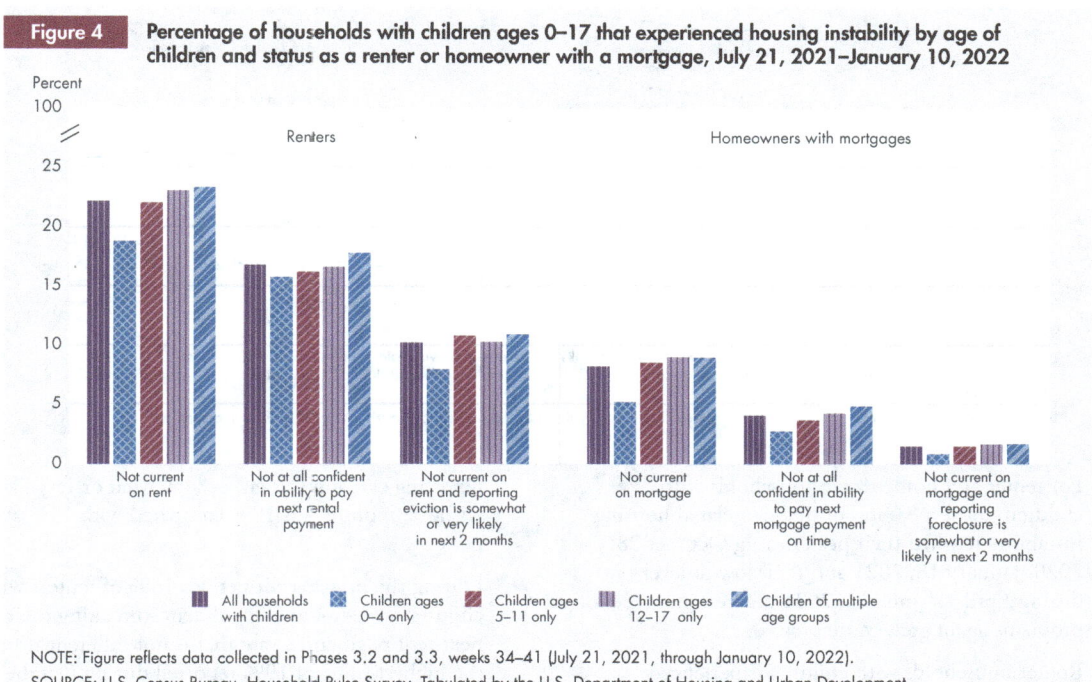

Figure 4. Percentage of households with children ages 0–17 that experienced housing instability by age of children and status as a renter or homeowner with a mortgage, July 21, 2021–January 10, 2022

NOTE: Figure reflects data collected in Phases 3.2 and 3.3, weeks 34–41 (July 21, 2021, through January 10, 2022).
SOURCE: U.S. Census Bureau, Household Pulse Survey. Tabulated by the U.S. Department of Housing and Urban Development.

- About 22% of renter households with children were not current on rent during July 21, 2021–January 10, 2022. About 17% anticipated future housing instability, reporting that they were not at all confident they could make the next rent payment.

- About 10% of renter households with children reported that eviction was somewhat or very likely within the next 2 months.

- Among homeowners with children and a mortgage, 4% were not at all confident in making the next mortgage payment and 2% reported that foreclosure was somewhat or very likely in the next 2 months.

- Homeowner households with children reported housing instability at lower rates than renter households with children. Among homeowners with children and a mortgage, 8% reported being behind on their mortgage payments during July 21, 2021–January 10, 2022.

- Both homeowner and renter families were less likely to experience several types of housing instability if they have only preschool-age children ages 0–4 rather than older children for whom school disruptions may create increased caregiver demands and for whom expenditures for housing, food, medical care, and transportation are generally greater.[11]

America's Children in Brief

Housing Instability—Continued

Over the course of the pandemic, the economic downturn, employment layoffs, health problems, and child care needs caused significant financial distress that households may have experienced in waves. Several courses of Federal stimulus and transfer payments during 2020 and early 2021, including child tax credit payments in 2021, may at various points have helped reduce housing payment difficulties and housing instability.[12]

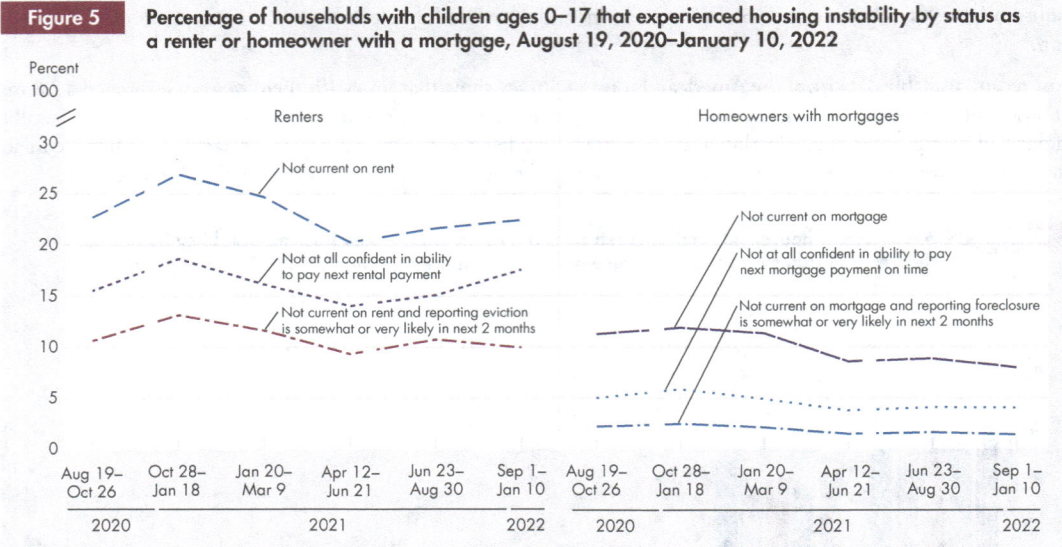

Figure 5. Percentage of households with children ages 0–17 that experienced housing instability by status as a renter or homeowner with a mortgage, August 19, 2020–January 10, 2022

NOTE: Figure presents data from pooled Household Pulse Survey weeks for the dates shown. Data were collected during Phases 2, 3, 3.1, 3.2, and 3.3, Weeks 13–41 (August 19, 2020, through January 10, 2022). Data were not collected during December 22, 2020–January 5, 2021, and July 6–20, 2021.
SOURCE: U.S. Census Bureau, Household Pulse Survey. Tabulated by the U.S. Department of Housing and Urban Development.

- For renter and homeowner households with children, most measures of finance-related housing instability reached their peak during October 28, 2020–January 18, 2021 and their lowest level during April 12–June 21, 2021 before some types of problems again grew more prevalent.

- Renter households with children experienced improvements in each measure of housing instability between October 28, 2020–January 18, 2021 and April 12–June 21, 2021. For example, the percentage of households who were not at all confident in their ability to pay their next rent payment decreased from 19% in the earlier period to 14% during the later period.

- Renter households with children experienced renewed housing instability by several measures during late 2021, but problems were not as severe as previously. During the most recent period of September 1, 2021–January 10, 2022, the percentage not current on rent was 22% compared with 27% at the peak levels of a year earlier, and the percentage behind on rent and reporting eviction was either somewhat or very likely within 2 months was 10% compared with 13% at the peak.

- During the most recent period, 18% of renters with children were not at all confident in making their next rent payment, a rate that is not different from the highest value of 19% reported during October 28, 2020–January 18, 2021.

- Among homeowner households with children and mortgage debt, the prevalence of housing instability during the most recent period was improved by all three measures relative to the peak levels observed during October 28, 2020–January 18, 2021. For example, by September 1, 2021–January 10, 2022, some 8% of homeowner households with children were not up to date on mortgage payments, compared with 12% in late 2020; 4% were not at all confident in making their next mortgage payment, down from 6% in late 2020; and 1% thought foreclosure was somewhat or very likely during the next 2 months, down from 3% in late 2020.

America's Children in Brief

Housing Instability—Continued

Among renters, those from racial and ethnic minority groups and those in single-female-headed households may experience additional risk. There are substantial disparities in housing instability for these populations and varying experiences during the pandemic.

The risk of housing instability among families with children is strongly associated with household income. Federal Poverty Guidelines provide a benchmark for material deprivation that adjusts for family size. In 2021, the poverty level for a family of four was $26,500.[13] About 8.7 million renters with children had incomes less than 200% of the poverty level in 2021, more than twice the 4.1 million renters with children that had incomes greater than 200% of the poverty level. There are substantial disparities in the rate of housing instability among renters with children with incomes above and below 200% of the poverty level. These data were collected during the period that the labor market was regaining strength and restrictions on eviction were ending.

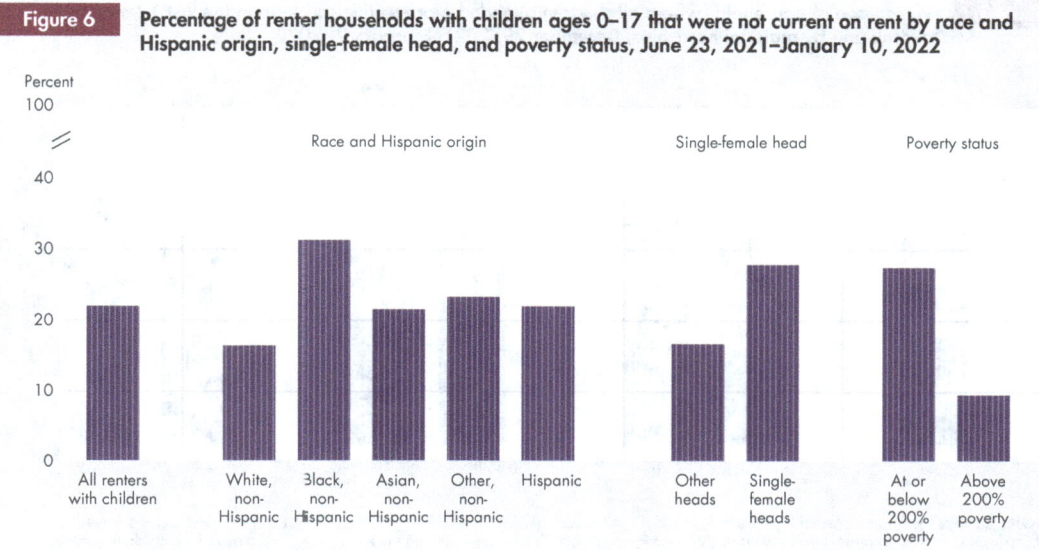

Figure 6 Percentage of renter households with children ages 0–17 that were not current on rent by race and Hispanic origin, single-female head, and poverty status, June 23, 2021–January 10, 2022

NOTE: Figure reflects data collected in Phases 3.2 and 3.3, Weeks 33–41 (June 23, 2021, through January 10, 2022), except for poverty status, which reflects data collected in Weeks 34–41 (July 21, 2021, through January 10, 2022). Data were not collected during July 6–20, 2021. Households are categorized by income as a percentage of Federal Poverty Guidelines. Categorization is subject to minor error because incomes in Household Pulse Survey data are grouped into ranges. The 1997 U.S. Office of Management and Budget standards on race and ethnicity were used to classify persons into one of the following four racial groups: White, Black, Asian, and Other. The "Other, non-Hispanic" category may include persons of the following races: American Indian or Alaska Native, Native Hawaiian or Other Pacific Islander or a combination of "Two or more races." Data on race and Hispanic origin are collected separately. Persons of Hispanic origin may be of any race.

SOURCE: U.S. Census Bureau, Household Pulse Survey. Tabulated by the U.S. Department of Housing and Urban Development.

- Among renter households with children, households of racial and ethnic minority groups were more likely than White, non-Hispanic households to be behind on rent during June 21, 2021–January 10, 2022.
- Being behind on rent was more likely to be reported by Black, Non-Hispanic (32%), Hispanic (22%), and Other, non-Hispanic (24%) households than for White, Non-Hispanic households (16%). The prevalence for Asian, Non-Hispanic (22%) was not significantly different from that of White, Non-Hispanic households.
- Single-female-headed renter households with children also were more likely to be behind on rent (28%) than were other heads of households (17%).
- During the same period, 22% of renter households with children were behind on rent. Those with incomes at or below 200% poverty were more likely to be behind on rent (28%) compared to those with incomes above 200% poverty (10%).

Endnotes begin on page 27.

America's Children in Brief

Pandemic Health Care and Child Care

The COVID-19 pandemic has posed a number of challenges for accessing health care and child care. Disruption of preventive health care can lead to challenges in the identification of health conditions, providing routine vaccinations, tracking developmental milestones, intervening early on identified health concerns, and providing support to families.[14] Telemedicine was widely adopted during the pandemic, which provided easier access to both sick and preventive care, while also protecting against the spread of disease. Recent Household Pulse Survey research shows that households experiencing material hardships—such as difficulty paying rent or mortgage, food insufficiency, or difficulty paying household expenses—were more likely to report missed/delayed preventive visits than those who did not experience material hardships.[14] Working from home or workplace closures were also experienced by many parents or caregivers. Because of these workplace changes, parents or caregivers often experienced material hardships and/or lost the access to child care, which contributed to work-related disruptions.

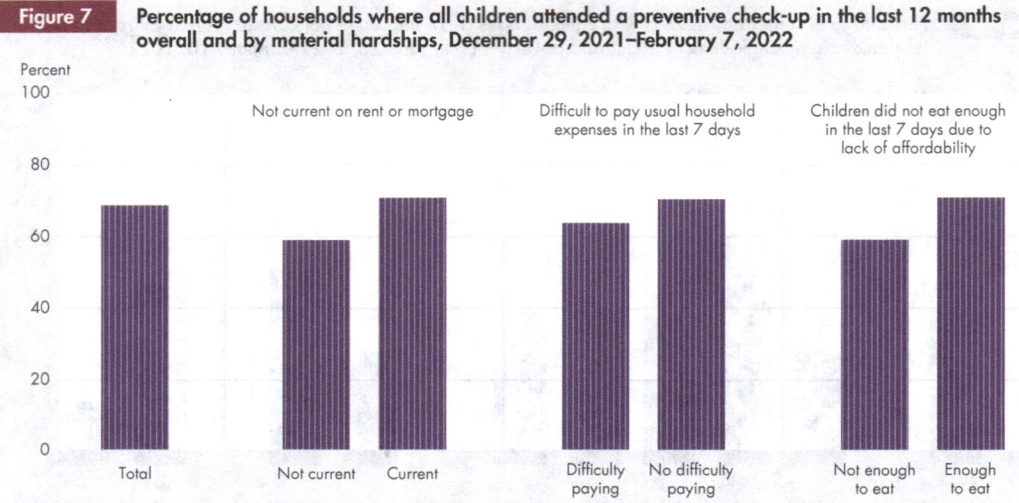

Figure 7 Percentage of households where all children attended a preventive check-up in the last 12 months overall and by material hardships, December 29, 2021–February 7, 2022

NOTE: Figure reflects data collected in Phase 3.3, weeks 41–42 (December 29, 2021, through February 7, 2022), the most recent 2 weeks of Phase 3.3, in order to present the most current information available. Survey item: "During the last 12 months did any of the children in the household have a PREVENTIVE check-up? Select only one answer: (1) Yes, all children had a preventive check-up, (2) Some, but not all, children had a preventive check-up, (3) None of the children had a preventive check-up." Figure shows the percentage of households with children who reported that all children had a preventive check-up.
SOURCE: U.S. Census Bureau, Household Pulse Survey. Tabulated by the Health Resources and Services Administration's Maternal and Child Health Bureau.

- From late December 2021 to early February 2022, approximately 68% of households with children reported that all children had a preventive check-up in the past 12 months.

- The percentage of households with all children having a preventive check-up was lower in households experiencing material hardship than in households that did not experience material hardships, including not being current on rent or mortgage (58% versus 70%), difficulty paying usual household expenses (64% versus 71%), and children not eating enough because of lack of affordability (58% versus 70%).

- According to poverty and insurance status, the percentage of households with all children having a preventive check-up was highest among households with a poverty status equal to or greater than 400% (78%) and those with privately insured adults (73%), and lowest among households with a poverty status of less than 138% (61%) and those with uninsured adults (53%), respectively.

Pandemic Health Care and Child Care—Continued

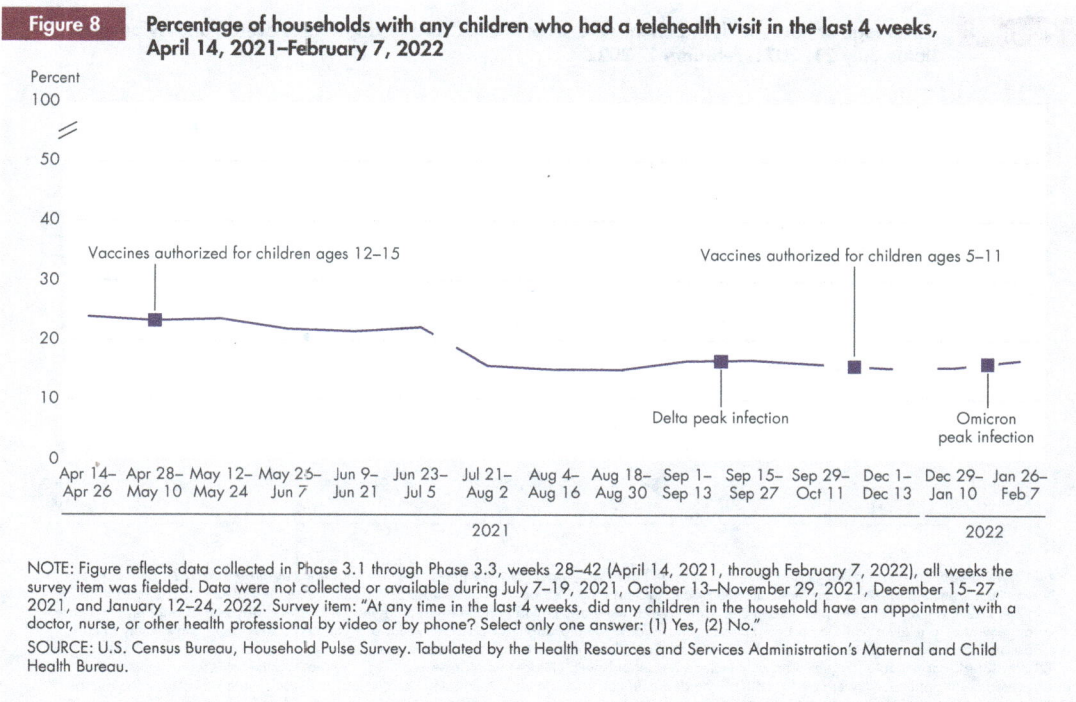

Figure 8. Percentage of households with any children who had a telehealth visit in the last 4 weeks, April 14, 2021–February 7, 2022

NOTE: Figure reflects data collected in Phase 3.1 through Phase 3.3, weeks 28–42 (April 14, 2021, through February 7, 2022), all weeks the survey item was fielded. Data were not collected or available during July 7–19, 2021, October 13–November 29, 2021, December 15–27, 2021, and January 12–24, 2022. Survey item: "At any time in the last 4 weeks, did any children in the household have an appointment with a doctor, nurse, or other health professional by video or by phone? Select only one answer: (1) Yes, (2) No."

SOURCE: U.S. Census Bureau, Household Pulse Survey. Tabulated by the Health Resources and Services Administration's Maternal and Child Health Bureau.

- The percentage of households with any children who had a telehealth visit in the last 4 weeks decreased from 24% (mid- to late April 2021) to 17% (late January–early February 2022).

- According to race/ethnicity and insurance status, children's telehealth visits were highest among households with adults who identified as Hispanic (18%) and adults with public insurance (19%), and lowest among households with adults who identified as White, non-Hispanic (15%) and adults with no insurance (14%).

Pandemic Health Care and Child Care—Continued

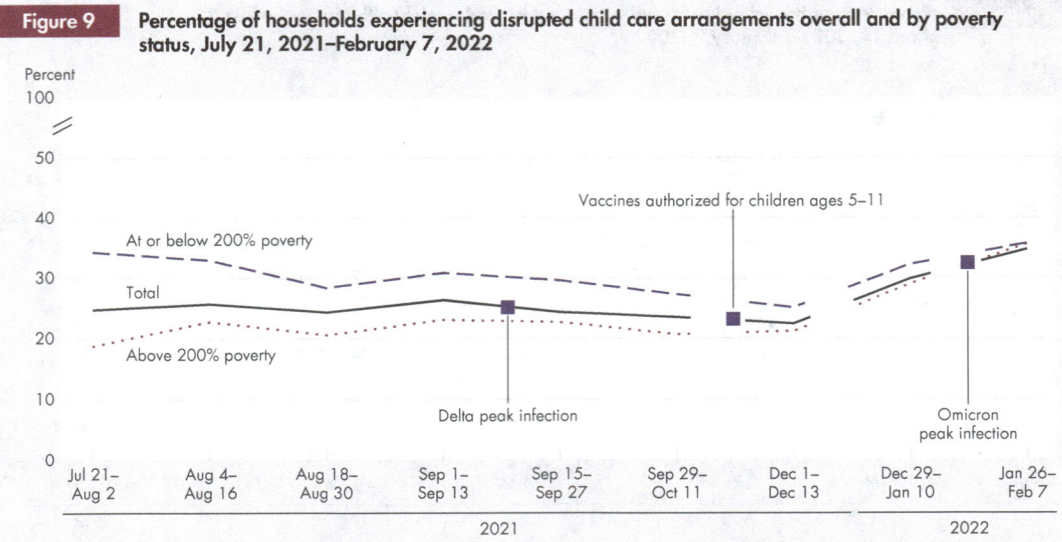

Figure 9. Percentage of households experiencing disrupted child care arrangements overall and by poverty status, July 21, 2021–February 7, 2022

NOTE: Figure reflects data collected in Phase 3.2 through Phase 3.3, weeks 34–42 (July 21, 2021, through February 7, 2022), all weeks the survey item was fielded. Data were not collected or available during October 13–November 29, 2021, December 15–27, 2021, and January 12–24, 2022. Survey item: "At any time in the last 4 weeks, were any children in the household unable to attend daycare or another child care arrangement as a result of child care being closed, unavailable, unaffordable, or because you are concerned about your child's safety in care? Please include before school care, after school care, and all other forms of child care that were unavailable. Select only one answer: (1) Yes, (2) No, (3) Not applicable." Figure data only include households with children who answered "Yes" or "No." Households with children who answered "Not applicable" were excluded from the denominator. Households with missing data on poverty status were included in the overall estimates of disrupted child care, but excluded from the estimates by poverty status. Poverty status is based on family income and household size using 2020 U.S. Census Bureau poverty thresholds.

SOURCE: U.S. Census Bureau, Household Pulse Survey. Tabulated by the Health Resources and Services Administration's Maternal and Child Health Bureau.

- Disrupted child care among households with children in a child care arrangement ranged from 25% of households (late July 2021) to 35% (early February 2022).

- With the exception of the last data collection period (early February 2022), the percentage of households reporting disrupted child care was higher among households with incomes at or below 200% poverty (25% to 34%), compared with households with incomes above 200% poverty (19% to 29%). During the period ending with February 7, 2022, both income groups had the same prevalence of disrupted child care (36%).

- Reports of disrupted child care were highest among households with adults who identified as Black, non-Hispanic or Other, non-Hispanic (36%) and Hispanic (32%), and lowest among households with adults who identified as Asian or Pacific Islander, non-Hispanic (27%). Additionally, reports of disrupted child care were highest among households with adults who had a bachelor's degree or higher (36%) and lowest among adults who had less than a high school diploma or an alternative credential such as a General Educational Development (GED) certificate (27%).

Pandemic Health Care and Child Care—Continued

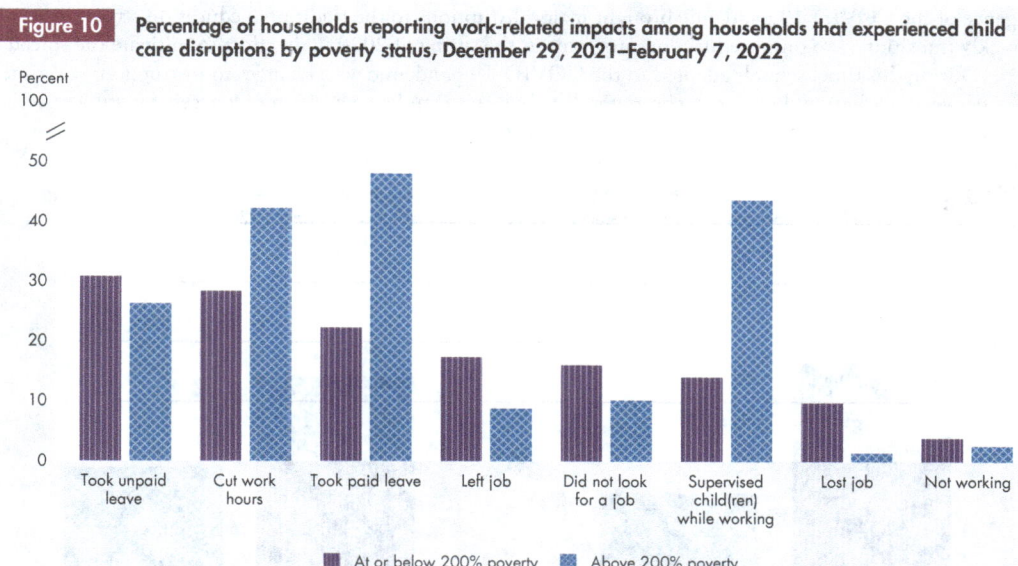

Figure 10. Percentage of households reporting work-related impacts among households that experienced child care disruptions by poverty status, December 29, 2021–February 7, 2022

NOTE: Figure reflects data collected in Phase 3.3, weeks 41–42 (December 29, 2021, through February 7, 2022), the most recent 2 weeks of Phase 3.3, in order to present the most current information available. Survey item: "Which if any of the following occurred in the last 4 weeks as a result of child care being closed, unavailable, unaffordable, or because you are concerned about your child's safety in care? Select all that apply: (1) You (or another adult) took unpaid leave to care for the children, (2) You (or another adult) used vacation, or sick days, or other paid leave in order to care for the children, (3) You (or another adult) cut your work hours in order to care for the children, (4) You (or another adult) left a job in order to care for the children, (5) You (or another adult) lost a job because of time away to care for the children, (6) You (or another adult) did not look for a job in order to care for the children, (7) You (or another adult) supervised one or more children while working, (8) Other (specify), (9) None of the above." Figure data only include households with children who reported any child care disruptions in the last 4 weeks. Poverty status is based on family income and household size using 2020 U.S. Census Bureau poverty thresholds.
SOURCE: U.S. Census Bureau, Household Pulse Survey. Tabulated by the Health Resources and Services Administration's Maternal and Child Health Bureau.

- As a result of child care disruptions, many households with children experienced work-related impacts, with notable differences by income level: Households with incomes at or below 200% poverty more frequently took unpaid leave (31%), left a job (18%), did not look for a job (16%), or lost a job (10%), while households with incomes above 200% poverty more frequently took paid leave (48%), cut work hours (43%), and supervised children while working (44%).

Endnotes begin on page 27.

America's Children in Brief

How Schools Adapted to Pandemic Response

The emergence of the COVID-19 pandemic brought major disruptions to the traditional education structure as schools quickly transitioned to online education programs in the spring of 2020 in an effort to mitigate the spread of COVID-19. During this time, schools adapted to the COVID-19 pandemic with changes to instruction; real-time interactions between teachers and students; computer distribution to students; and internet access for students. These data were collected in the National Teacher and Principal Survey.[15]

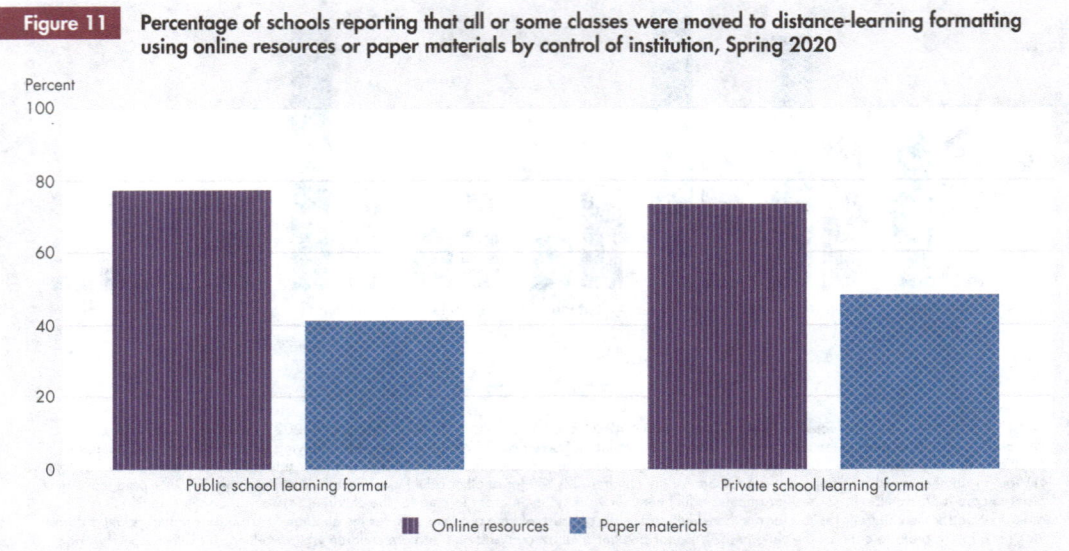

Figure 11 Percentage of schools reporting that all or some classes were moved to distance-learning formatting using online resources or paper materials by control of institution, Spring 2020

NOTE: The survey includes other response options on changes to instruction (such as "all or some classes were cancelled"), which are not included in this figure. Respondents could select more than one way in which the pandemic affected instruction. For additional information, see *Impact of the Coronavirus (COVID-19) Pandemic on Public and Private Elementary and Secondary Education in the United States (Preliminary Data): First Look*.
SOURCE: U.S. Department of Education, National Center for Education Statistics, National Teacher and Principal Survey.

- During the COVID-19 pandemic in the spring of 2020, a higher percentage of public schools than of private schools (77% versus 73%) reported moving classes to online distance-learning formats. Conversely, a lower percentage of public schools than of private schools (41% versus 48%) reported moving classes to a distance-learning format using paper materials. There was no measurable difference in the rates of cancelling classes between public and private schools (9% and 10%).

- Eighty-four percent each of public schools in cities and suburban areas moved classes to online distance-learning formats. These were higher than the rates in towns and rural areas (70% and 67%). A similar pattern was observed for private schools, where private schools located in cities and suburban areas (both 79%) had higher rates of moving classes to online distance-learning formats than did private schools in towns and rural areas (64% and 59%).

- Among public schools, both middle schools and high schools (80% and 81%) had higher rates of moving classes to online distance-learning formats than primary schools (76%). Among private schools, no measurable difference in the rates of moving classes to online distance-learning formats was observed by school level.[16]

- About 32% of public schools with less than 35% of students who were approved for Free or Reduced Price Lunch (FRPL) reported moving classes to a distance-learning format using paper materials. This rate was lower than public schools with higher percentages of students who were approved for FRPL. For example, 48% of public schools with 75% or more of students who were approved for FRPL reported moving classes to a distance-learning format using paper materials.

How Schools Adapted to Pandemic Response—Continued

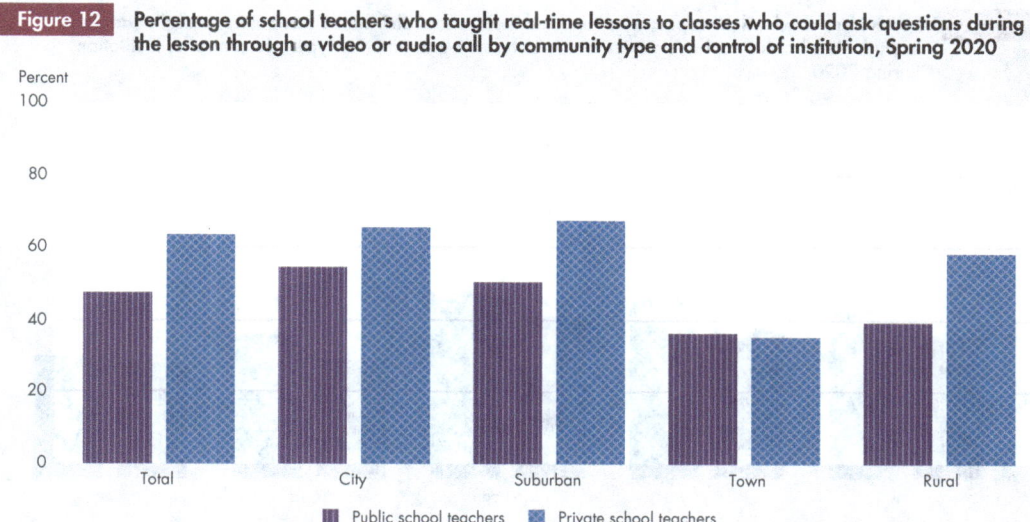

Figure 12. Percentage of school teachers who taught real-time lessons to classes who could ask questions during the lesson through a video or audio call by community type and control of institution, Spring 2020

NOTE: The survey includes other response options on types of real-time interaction (such as having "unscheduled sessions with students as needed through a video or audio call"), which are not included in this figure. Respondents could select more than one type of real-time interaction. For additional information, see *Impact of the Coronavirus (COVID-19) Pandemic on Public and Private Elementary and Secondary Education in the United States (Preliminary Data): First Look*.

SOURCE: U.S. Department of Education, National Center for Education Statistics, National Teacher and Principal Survey.

- During the COVID-19 pandemic in the spring of 2020, public school teachers (47%) reported that they taught real-time lessons to classes who could ask questions through a video or audio call at a lower rate than private school teachers (63%).

- The percentage of school teachers who taught real-time lessons to classes who could ask questions through a video varied by community type. The rate for public school teachers was higher for those in city schools (54%) than those in suburban schools (50%), rural schools (39%), and schools located within towns (36%).

- Among private schools, the rate was lower for teachers in towns (38%) than those teaching at suburban schools (67%), city schools (65%), and rural schools (58%).

How Schools Adapted to Pandemic Response—Continued

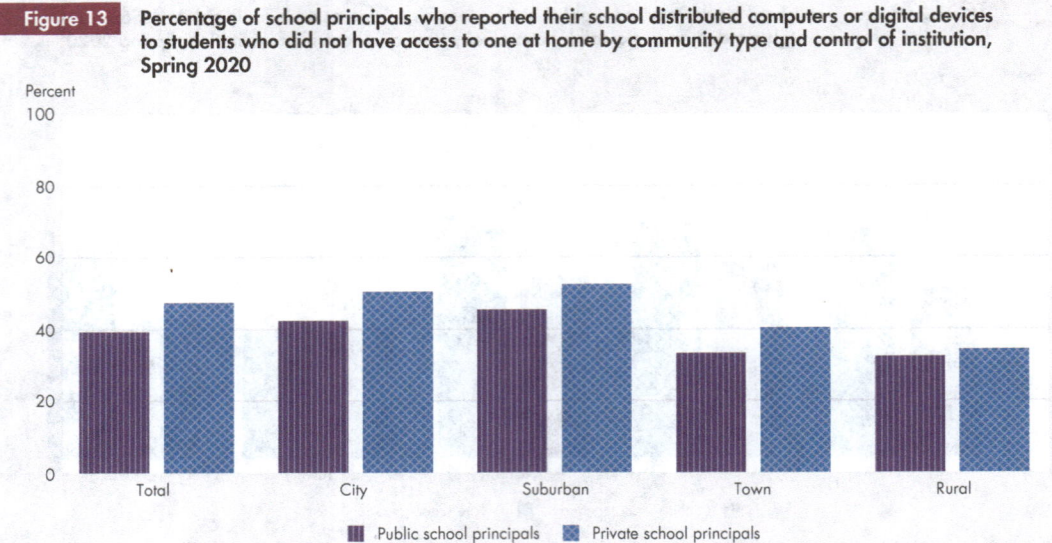

Figure 13. Percentage of school principals who reported their school distributed computers or digital devices to students who did not have access to one at home by community type and control of institution, Spring 2020

NOTE: The survey includes one additional response option ("we did not distribute any computers or digital devices to any students to take home"), which is not included in this figure. For additional information, see *Impact of the Coronavirus (COVID-19) Pandemic on Public and Private Elementary and Secondary Education in the United States (Preliminary Data): First Look*.

SOURCE: U.S. Department of Education, National Center for Education Statistics, National Teacher and Principal Survey.

- In the spring of 2020, during the COVID-19 pandemic, a lower percentage of public school principals than of private school principals (39% versus 47%) reported distributing computers to students who did not have access to computers or digital devices at home.[17]

- About 42% and 45% of public school principals in city and suburban schools, respectively, reported that their school distributed computers to students who did not have access to computers or digital devices at home. These percentages were higher than the percentages for public school principals in town and rural schools (33% and 32%). Private school principals reported a similar pattern. Private school principals in city and suburban schools (50% and 52%) reported higher rates of their school distributing computers to students who did not have access to one at home than did private school principals in rural schools only (34%).

- Among principals of smaller public schools (those with less than 200 students enrolled), 33% reported that their school distributed computers to students who did not have access to computers or digital devices at home. This was lower than the percentages for principals of larger public schools (ranging from 38% to 42%).[18]

How Schools Adapted to Pandemic Response—Continued

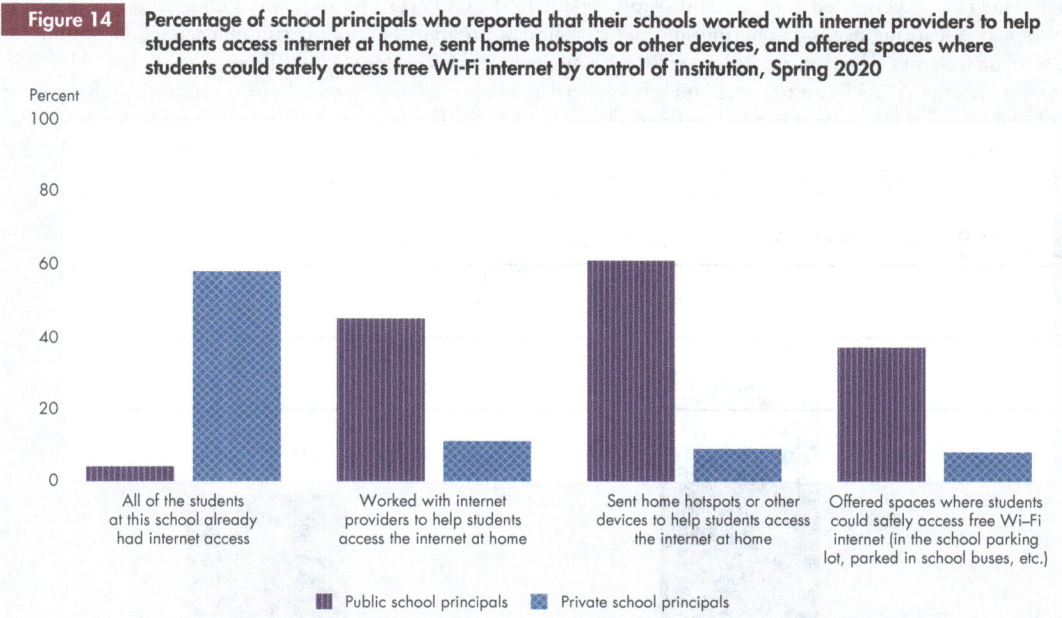

Figure 14. Percentage of school principals who reported that their schools worked with internet providers to help students access internet at home, sent home hotspots or other devices, and offered spaces where students could safely access free Wi-Fi internet by control of institution, Spring 2020

NOTE: The survey includes other response options on ways of helping students with their internet access (such as "other" and "did not take any steps to help students access the internet"), which are not included in this figure. Respondents could select more than one way of helping students. For additional information, see *Impact of the Coronavirus (COVID-19) Pandemic on Public and Private Elementary and Secondary Education in the United States (Preliminary Data): First Look*.

SOURCE: U.S. Department of Education, National Center for Education Statistics, National Teacher and Principal Survey.

- During the COVID-19 pandemic in the spring of 2020, internet access at home varied across students attending public and private schools. Public school principals reported 4% of students at their school already had internet access at home. Private school principals reported 58% of students at their schools already had internet access at home.

- School principals reported taking various steps to help students access the internet at home at higher rates than private school principals.[15] For example, 61% of public school principals responded that their school sent hotspots or other devices to students at home, compared to 9% of private school principals. Public school principals also reported working with internet providers to help students access the internet at home and offering spaces where students could safely access free Wi-Fi at higher rates than private school principals.

- About 52% of public school principals in city schools and 49% in suburban schools reported that their school worked with internet providers to help students access the internet at home. These percentages were higher than the percentages for public school principals in town and rural schools (42% and 36%).

- Public school principals in city and suburban schools (75% and 69%) also reported that their school sent home hotspots or other internet devices at higher rates than those in town and rural schools (both 49%). Public school principals in town and rural schools reported offering spaces where students could access free Wi-Fi at higher rates (47% and 46%) than those in city and suburban schools (30% and 27%).

Endnotes begin on page 27.

Summer Enrichment Programs

Many students have experienced enrollment disruptions due to the COVID-19 pandemic. Public schools can address pandemic-related learning needs by offering summer enrichment programs, including summer school and summer camps, to their students. The American Rescue Plan Elementary and Secondary School Emergency Relief (ARP ESSER) fund provides nearly $122 billion to states and school districts to help safely reopen schools, sustain the safe operation of schools, and address the impact of the pandemic. The ARP ESSER fund specifically requires that states invest in evidence-based initiatives to address the impact of lost instructional time, such as summer programs.[20] The School Pulse Panel survey collected data on schools' offering of summer enrichment programs in 2021.[21]

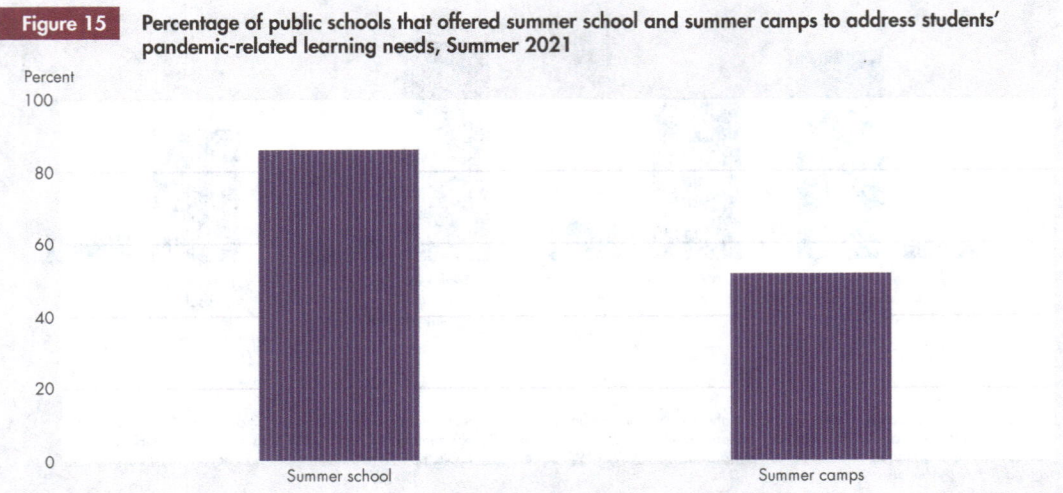

Figure 15. Percentage of public schools that offered summer school and summer camps to address students' pandemic-related learning needs, Summer 2021

NOTE: This figure is based on experimental data. While estimates have been weighted and adjusted for non-response, these experimental data should be interpreted with caution.
SOURCE: U.S. Department of Education, Institute of Education Sciences, National Center for Education Statistics, School Pulse Panel.

- During the summer of 2021, about 85% of public schools offered summer programs and 51% offered summer camps to their students to address pandemic-related learning needs.

Endnotes begin on page 27.

America's Children in Brief

Child and Adolescent Mortality

Although illness and hospitalization are lower among children and adolescents with COVID-19 compared with adults, COVID-19 can lead to severe symptoms that might require admission to an intensive care unit or result in death.[22,23,24,25] Children and adolescents with one or more underlying medical conditions are at greater risk of severe symptoms.[26] In the United States, one in four children has a chronic condition, including asthma, obesity, diabetes, or neurodevelopmental disorders.[27,28]

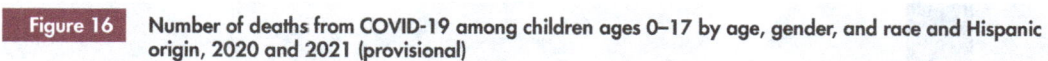

Figure 16. Number of deaths from COVID-19 among children ages 0–17 by age, gender, and race and Hispanic origin, 2020 and 2021 (provisional)

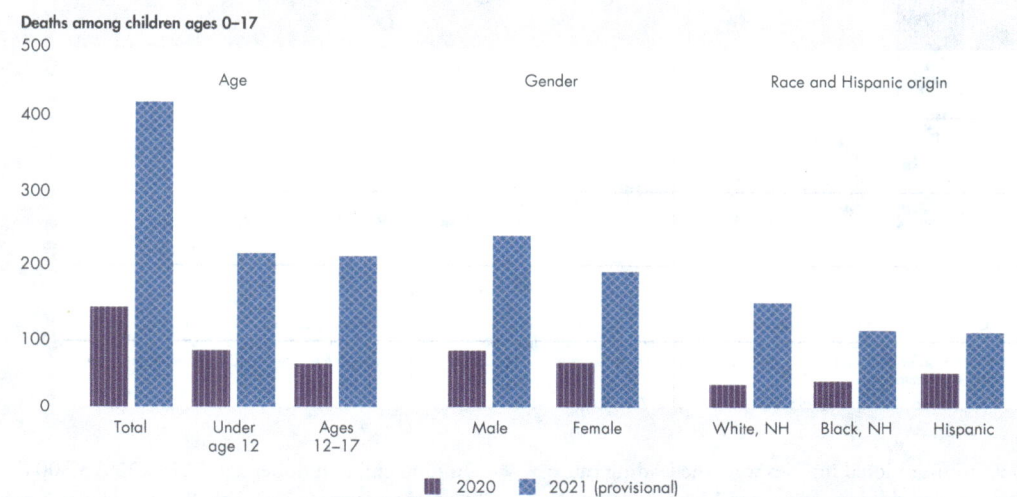

NOTE: NH = non-Hispanic origin. Deaths from COVID-19 are classified according to the underlying cause-of-death code *U07.1 from the *International Classification of Diseases, 10th Revision*. It can take several weeks for death records to be submitted to the National Center for Health Statistics, processed, and tabulated. Therefore, the data shown in this figure may be incomplete and will likely not include all deaths that occurred during the given time periods, especially data for 2021. Provisional deaths for 2021 are based on a current flow of mortality data in the National Vital Statistics System. Provisional counts include deaths occurring in the 50 states and the District of Columbia that have been received through April 16, 2022, as of May 1, 2022. Data on race and Hispanic origin are collected and reported separately. The race categories are based on the 1997 U.S. Office of Management and Budget standards on race and ethnicity and all categories are single race. Persons of Hispanic origin may be of any race. The "Total" includes children who classify as American Indian or Alaska Native, Asian, Native Hawaiian or Other Pacific Islander, and "Two or more races." The number of deaths for these race groups are not shown separately because the number of deaths are too small to meet reporting standards.

SOURCE: National Center for Health Statistics, National Vital Statistics System.

- In 2020, 141 children ages 0–17 died from COVID-19 (0.2 deaths per 100,000 population). In 2021, deaths from COVID-19 among children increased to 434 (0.6).

- In both 2020 and 2021, the number of deaths due to COVID-19 among children under age 12 were higher than the number among adolescents ages 12–17. However, the rates were higher among adolescents.

- Males were more likely to die from COVID-19 than females in both 2020 and 2021 based on number of deaths and rates. Among males, deaths increased from 79 in 2020 to 241 in 2021. Among females, deaths increased from 62 in 2020 to 193 in 2021.

- From 2020 to 2021, deaths from COVID-19 increased for all race and Hispanic-origin groups shown.

- In both 2020 and 2021, Black, non-Hispanic children had higher death rates from COVID-19 (0.4 and 1.2) than Hispanic (0.3 and 0.6) and White, non-Hispanic (0.1 and 0.4) children.

America's Children in Brief

Child and Adolescent Mortality—Continued

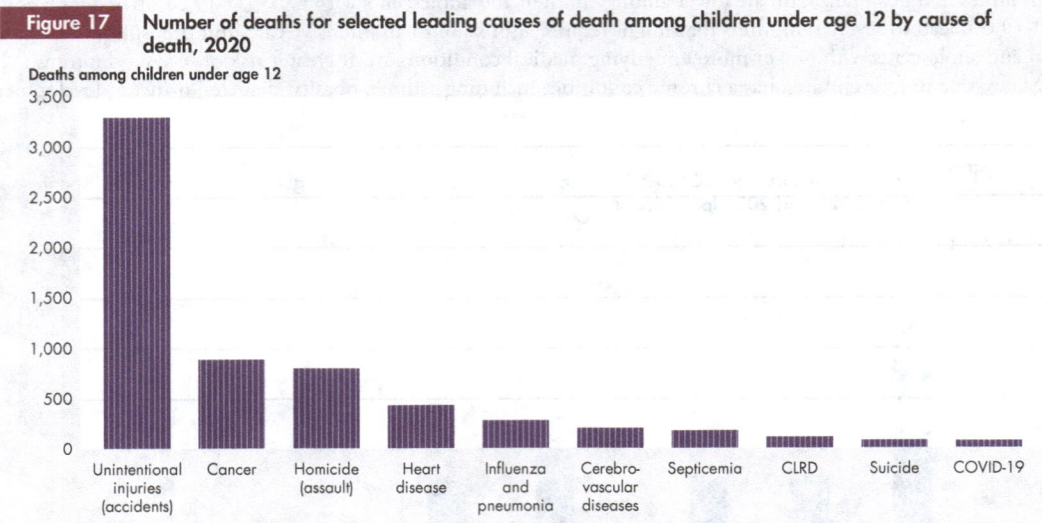

Figure 17. Number of deaths for selected leading causes of death among children under age 12 by cause of death, 2020

NOTE: CLRD = chronic lower respiratory diseases. Cause of death is classified according to the *International Classification of Diseases, 10th Revision*. Provisional 2021 data are not used for leading causes of death because any reclassifications of cause of death in final data may affect the rank order of causes. Rates are less likely to change due to a few reclassified deaths because they are based on the number of deaths per 100,000 population.

SOURCE: National Center for Health Statistics, National Vital Statistics System.

- In 2020, unintentional injuries were the leading cause of death among children under age 12, accounting for 12.5% of deaths. Deaths from COVID-19 accounted for only 0.3% of deaths among children.

- Among children under age 12 in 2020, 3,300 died from unintentional injuries; 893 died from cancer; 806 died from homicide; 438 died from heart disease; 284 died from influenza and pneumonia; 208 died from cerebrovascular diseases; 185 died from septicemia; 120 died from chronic lower respiratory diseases; 87 died from suicide; and 80 died from COVID-19.

America's Children in Brief

Child and Adolescent Mortality—Continued

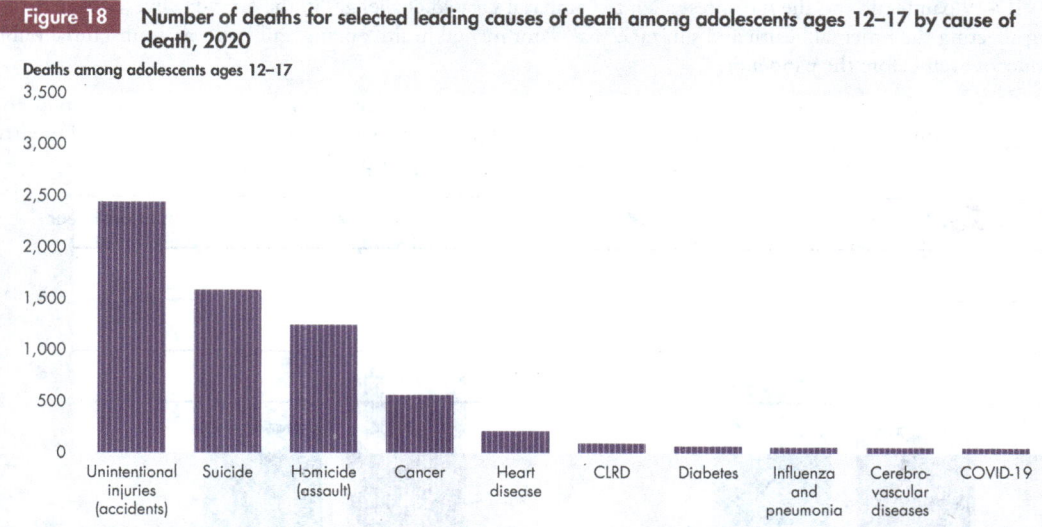

Figure 18. Number of deaths for selected leading causes of death among adolescents ages 12–17 by cause of death, 2020

NOTE: CLRD = chronic lower respiratory diseases. Cause of death is classified according to the *International Classification of Diseases, 10th Revision*. Provisional 2021 data are not used for leading causes of death because any reclassifications of cause of death in final data may affect the rank order of causes. Rates are less likely to change due to a few reclassified deaths because they are based on the number of deaths per 100,000 population.
SOURCE: National Center for Health Statistics, National Vital Statistics System.

- In 2020, unintentional injuries accounted for 31.4% of deaths among adolescents ages 12–17, followed by suicide (20.4%) and homicide (16.1%). Deaths from COVID-19 accounted for only 0.8% of deaths among adolescents.

- Among adolescents ages 12–17 in 2020, 2,446 died from unintentional injuries; 1,592 died from suicide; 1,253 died from homicide; 568 died from cancer; 219 died from heart disease; 102 died from chronic lower respiratory diseases; 75 died from diabetes; 66 died from influenza and pneumonia; 64 died from cerebrovascular diseases; and 61 died from COVID-19.

Endnotes begin on page 27.

Substance Use and Mental Health of Adolescents

The COVID-19 pandemic and the measures taken to combat it created challenges in the everyday lives of Americans, including affecting their mental health and substance use. Poor mental health among children was a substantial public health concern even before the pandemic.[29]

The COVID-19 pandemic may also have affected access to substance use treatment in different ways. In response to the COVID-19 pandemic, for example, health care providers (including behavioral health care providers) turned to virtual (or telehealth) services as a means of delivering services while also limiting in-person contact.

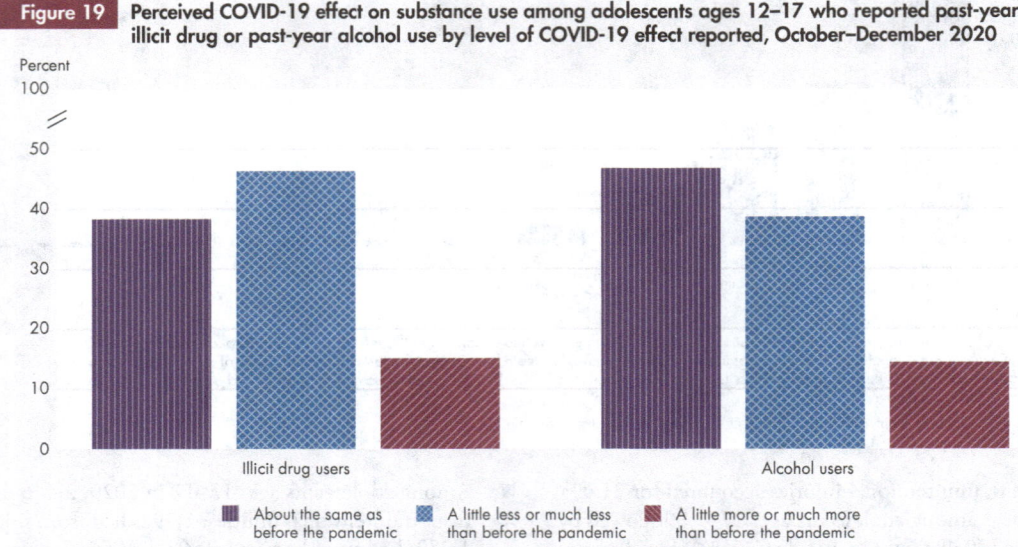

Figure 19. Perceived COVID-19 effect on substance use among adolescents ages 12–17 who reported past-year illicit drug or past-year alcohol use by level of COVID-19 effect reported, October–December 2020

NOTE: Respondents with unknown information on their perception of the COVID-19 pandemic's effect on their substance use were excluded. Respondents were asked how much, if at all, the COVID-19 pandemic affected their substance use. Potential responses were "much less," "a little less," "about the same," "a little more," or "much more" as compared to before the pandemic.
SOURCE: Substance Abuse and Mental Health Services Administration, National Survey on Drug Use and Health.

- In October–December 2020, about 46% of adolescents ages 12–17 who used illicit drugs in the past year perceived that they were using those substances "a little less or much less" than they did before the COVID-19 pandemic began. This is compared with 15% of adolescents ages 12–17 who perceived that they were using those substances "a little more or much more."

- About 39% of adolescents ages 12–17 who drank alcohol in the past year perceived that they were drinking "a little less or much less" than they did before the COVID-19 pandemic began. This is compared with 15% of adolescents ages 12–17 who perceived that they were drinking "a little more or much more."

Substance Use and Mental Health of Adolescents—Continued

Depression has a significant impact on adolescent development and well-being.[30] Adolescent depression can adversely affect school and work performance, impair peer and family relationships, and exacerbate the severity of other health conditions such as asthma and obesity.[31,32,33] Depressive episodes often persist, recur, or continue into adulthood.[34] Youth who have had a major depressive episode (MDE) in the past year are at greater risk for suicide and are more likely than other youth to initiate alcohol and other drug use, experience concurrent substance use disorders, and smoke daily.[35,36,37] The COVID-19 pandemic may have exacerbated the effect of MDE on adolescents.[38]

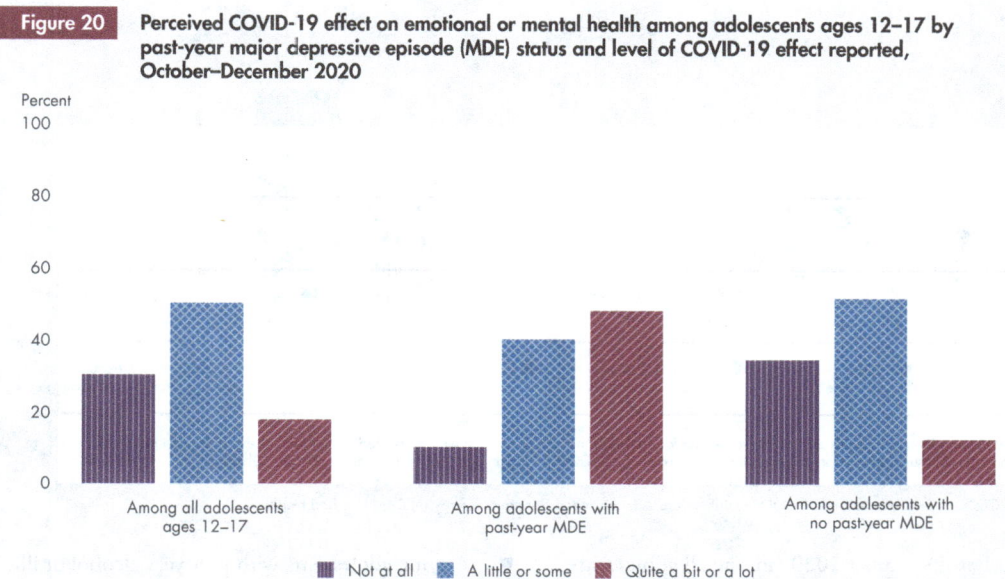

Figure 20. Perceived COVID-19 effect on emotional or mental health among adolescents ages 12–17 by past-year major depressive episode (MDE) status and level of COVID-19 effect reported, October–December 2020

NOTE: Respondents with unknown information on their perception of the COVID-19 pandemic's negative effect on their emotional or mental health, with unknown past-year major depressive episode (MDE) data, and with unknown impairment data were excluded. Respondents were asked how much, if at all, the COVID-19 pandemic affected their mental health. Potential responses were "not at all," "a little," "some," "quite a bit," or "a lot."
SOURCE: Substance Abuse and Mental Health Services Administration, National Survey on Drug Use and Health.

- In October–December 2020, almost 1 in 5 adolescents (18%) perceived that the COVID-19 pandemic negatively affected their mental health "quite a bit or a lot," and an additional 51% perceived "a little or some" negative effect on their mental health.

- Adolescents ages 12–17 who had a past-year MDE or a past-year MDE with severe impairment were more likely than those without a past-year MDE to perceive that the COVID-19 pandemic negatively affected their mental health "quite a bit or a lot" (49% and 55%, respectively). In comparison, 13% of adolescents without a past-year MDE perceived the COVID-19 pandemic negatively affected their mental health "quite a bit or a lot."

Substance Use and Mental Health of Adolescents—Continued

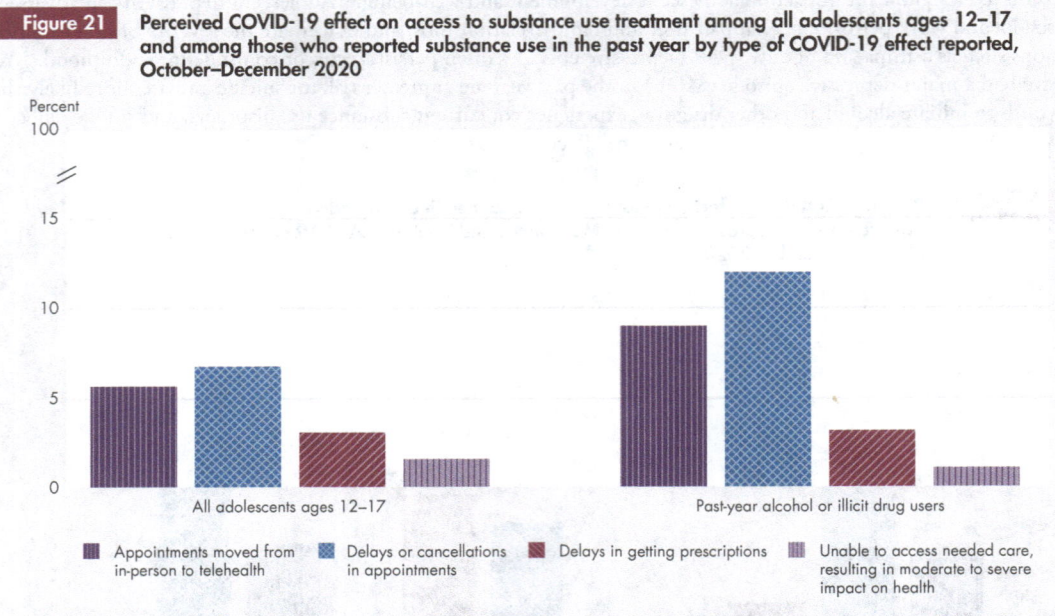

Figure 21. Perceived COVID-19 effect on access to substance use treatment among all adolescents ages 12–17 and among those who reported substance use in the past year by type of COVID-19 effect reported, October–December 2020

NOTE: Respondents who reported that the respective question did not apply to them were classified as not having experienced that effect. Respondents with unknown information on their perception of the COVID-19 pandemic's effect on their access to substance use treatment were excluded.

SOURCE: Substance Abuse and Mental Health Services Administration, National Survey on Drug Use and Health.

- In October–December 2020, among all adolescents ages 12–17, about 6% had their substance use treatment appointments moved from in-person to telehealth, 7% experienced delays or cancellations in appointments, 3% experienced delays in getting prescriptions, and 2% were unable to access needed care, resulting in a moderate to severe impact on health.

- Among adolescents with past-year alcohol or illicit drug use, 9% had their substance use treatment appointments moved from in-person to telehealth, 12% experienced delays or cancellations in appointments, 3% experienced delays in getting prescriptions, and 1% were unable to access needed care, resulting in a moderate to severe impact on health.

Endnotes begin on page 27.

America's Children in Brief

Notes to Indicators

1. For more information see https://www.census.gov/data/experimental-data-products/household-pulse-survey.html.

2. Centers for Disease Control and Prevention. (2022, January 11). *COVID-19 vaccines for children and teens.* https://www.cdc.gov/coronavirus/2019-ncov/vaccines/recommendations/children-teens.html

3. Centers for Disease Control and Prevention. (2021, November 2). *COVID-19 vaccine equity for racial and ethnic minority groups.* https://www.cdc.gov/coronavirus/2019-ncov/community/health-equity/vaccine-equity.html

4. The Household Pulse Survey (HPS) includes an indicator of child food insufficiency for U.S. households, defined as follows: Child food insufficiency means a household's children were not eating enough food sometimes or often in the last 7 days because the household could not afford enough food (based on a self-report to a single item). Low food sufficiency among children means a child did not have enough to eat sometimes in the last 7 days. Very low food sufficiency among children means a child did not have enough to eat often in the last 7 days. The food-sufficiency item in the HPS asks about the food eaten in the household in the last 7 days to assess rapid changes in food sufficiency. Household adults are asked the following: "In the last 7 days, which of these statements best describes the food eaten in your household? Select only one answer. (1) Enough of the kinds of food (I/we) wanted to eat; (2) Enough, but not always the kinds of food (I/we) wanted to eat; (3) Sometimes not enough to eat; (4) Often not enough to eat." Adults who select (1) are classified as living in households with full food sufficiency, while those who select (2) are classified as living in households with marginal food sufficiency. Those who select (3) or (4) are counted as having low and very low food sufficiency, respectively. Those who respond with (3) or (4) are classified as food insufficient, which means that a household did not have enough to eat in the last 7 days. Adults who select (2), (3), or (4) and have children under age 18 living in the household are then asked to indicate whether the next statement was often true, sometimes true, or never true in the last 7 days for the children living in the household who are under age 18: "The children were not eating enough because we just couldn't afford enough food. (1) Often true; (2) Sometimes true; (3) Never true." Adults who respond with (1) are classified as having children with full food sufficiency. Adults who select (2) are classified as having children with low food sufficiency, while those who select (3) are classified as having children with very low food sufficiency. Food insufficiency includes both low and very low food sufficiency. Data from the HPS and other sources are not entirely comparable. As such, there is not a directly comparable measure of food insufficiency prior to the COVID-19 pandemic. Technical information about how food insufficiency is measured in the HPS can be found at https://www.ers.usda.gov/topics/food-nutrition-assistance/foodsecurity-in-the-us/measurement/#insufficiency.

5. Coleman-Jensen, A., McFall, W., & Nord, M. (2013). *Food insecurity in households with children: Prevalence, severity, and household characteristics, 2010-11*(EIB-113). U.S. Department of Agriculture, Economic Research Service. https://www.ers.usda.gov/publications/pub-details/?pubid=43765

6. Clark, R. E., Weinreb, L., Flahive, J. M., & Seifert, R. W. (2019). Infants exposed to homelessness: Health, health care use, and health spending from birth to age six. *Health Affairs, 38*(5), 721–728. https://doi.org/10.1377/hlthaff.2019.00090

7. Collinson, R., & Reed, D. (2019). Retrieved from *The Effects of Evictions on Low-Income Households.* Unpublished manuscript. https://www.law.nyu.edu/sites/default/files/upload_documents/evictions_collinson_reed.pdf

8. Benfer, E. A., Vlahov, D., Long, M. Y., Walker-Wells, E., Pottenger, J. L., Jr., Gonsalves, G., & Keene, D. E. (2021). Eviction, health inequity, and the spread of COVID-19: Housing policy as a primary pandemic mitigation strategy. *Journal of Urban Health: Bulletin of the New York Academy of Medicine, 98*(1), 1–12. https://doi.org/10.1007/s11524-020-00502-1

9. Leifheit, K. M., Linton, S. L., Raifman, J., Schwartz, G. L., Benfer, E. A., Zimmerman, F. J., & Pollack, C. E. (2021). Expiring eviction moratoriums and COVID-19 incidence and mortality. *American Journal of Epidemiology, 190*(12), 2503–2510. https://doi.org/10.1093/aje/kwab196

10. Estimates of households with children by housing tenure are from the 2019 American Housing Survey (AHS). The AHS includes homeowners who do not report mortgage information among those who do not have a mortgage.

11. Lino, M., Kuczynski, K., Rodriguez, N., & Schap, T. (2017). *Expenditures on children by families, 2015*(Miscellaneous Publication No. 1528-2015). U.S. Department of Agriculture, Center for Nutrition Policy and Promotion. https://www.fns.usda.gov/resource/2015-expenditures-children-families

12. Weinstock, L. R. (2021). *COVID-19 and the U.S. economy* (CRS Report No. R46606). Congressional Research Service. https://crsreports.congress.gov/product/pdf/R/R46606

13. Federal Poverty Guidelines, informally Federal Poverty Levels, are found at https://aspe.hhs.gov/topics/poverty-economicmobility/poverty-guidelines/prior-hhs-poverty-guidelines-federal-register-references/2021-poverty-guidelines.

14. Lebrun-Harris, L. A., Sappenfield, O. R., & Warren, M. D. (2021). Missed and delayed preventive health care visits among US children due to the COVID-19 pandemic. *Public Health Reports.* https://doi.org/10.1177/00333549211061322

America's Children in Brief

Notes to Indicator—Continued

[15] For additional information, see *Impact of the Coronavirus (COVID-19) Pandemic on Public and Private Elementary and Secondary Education in the United States (Preliminary Data): First Look*.

[16] School levels for public schools are reported as primary, middle, high, or combined, while school levels for private schools are reported as elementary, secondary, or combined.

[17] The survey includes two other response options: "we distributed computers or digital devices to all students to take home" and "we did not distribute any computers or digital devices to any students to take home." Forty-five percent of public school principals, compared with 20% of private school principals, reported that their school distributed computers to all students. Sixteen percent of public school principals reported that their schools did not distribute computers to any students, while 34% of private school principals reported that their schools did not distribute computers to any students. For additional information on the full range of pandemic-related questions and topics covered in the 2020–21 NTPS, see *Impact of the Coronavirus (COVID-19) Pandemic on Public and Private Elementary and Secondary Education in the United States (Preliminary Data): First Look*.

[18] Enrollment levels for public schools are reported as fewer than 200 students, 200–499, 500–749, 750–999, and 1,000 or more, while enrollment levels for private schools are reported as fewer than 200, 200–499, 500–749, and 750 or more.

[19] Four percent of public school principals reported that all students at their school already had internet access, while 58% of private school principals reported so. For additional information on the full range of pandemic-related questions and topics covered in the 2020–21 NTPS, see *Impact of the Coronavirus (COVID-19) Pandemic on Public and Private Elementary and Secondary Education in the United States (Preliminary Data): First Look*.

[20] More information about the American Rescue Plan Elementary and Secondary School Emergency Relief Fund is available on the U.S. Department of Education, Office of Elementary and Secondary Education's website at https://oese.ed.gov/offices/american-rescue-plan/american-rescue-plan-elementary-and-secondary-school-emergency-relief/.

[21] Full results from the 2021 School Pulse Panel Summer survey are available on the Institute of Education Sciences website at https://ies.ed.gov/schoolsurvey/sppsummer/spp_summer.xlsx.

[22] Siegel, D. A., Reses, H. E., Cool, A. J., Shapiro, C. N., Hsu, J., Boehmer, T. K., … & Raizes, E. (2021). Trends in COVID-19 cases, emergency department visits, and hospital admissions among children and adolescents aged 0–17 years—United States, August 2020–August 2021. *Morbidity and Mortality Weekly Report, 70*(36), 1249.

[23] Kim, L., Whitaker, M., O'Halloran, A., Kambhampati, A., Chai, S. J., Reingold, A., … & COVID-NET Surveillance Team. (2020). Hospitalization rates and characteristics of children aged< 18 years hospitalized with laboratory-confirmed COVID-19—COVID-NET, 14 States, March 1–July 25, 2020. *Morbidity and Mortality Weekly Report, 69*(32), 1081.

[24] Bialek, S., Gierke, R., Hughes, M., McNamara, L. A., Pilishvili, T., & Skoff, T. (2020). Coronavirus disease 2019 in children—United States, February 12–April 2, 2020. *Morbidity and Mortality Weekly Report, 69*(14), 422.

[25] Fernandes, D. M., Oliveira, C. R., Guerguis, S., Eisenberg, R., Choi, J., Kim, M., … & Research Consortium. (2021). Severe acute respiratory syndrome coronavirus 2 clinical syndromes and predictors of disease severity in hospitalized children and youth. *Journal of Pediatrics, 230*, 23–31.

[26] Kompaniyets, L., Agathis, N. T., Nelson, J. M., Preston, L. E., Ko, J. Y., Belay, B., … & Goodman, A. B. (2021). Underlying medical conditions associated with severe COVID-19 illness among children. *JAMA Network Open, 4*(6), Article e2111182.

[27] Van Cleave, J., Gortmaker, S. L., & Perrin, J. M. (2010). Dynamics of obesity and chronic health conditions among children and youth. *JAMA, 303*(7), 623–630.

[28] Lawrence, J. M., Divers, J., Isom, S., Saydah, S., Imperatore, G., Pihoker, C., … & SEARCH for Diabetes in Youth Study Group. (2021). Trends in prevalence of type 1 and type 2 diabetes in children and adolescents in the US, 2001–2017. *JAMA, 326*(8), 717–727.

[29] Bitsko, R. H., Claussen A. H., Lichstein, J., … & Ghandour, R. M. (2022). Mental health surveillance among children—United States, 2013–2019. *MMWR Surveillance Summaries, 71*(2), 1–42.

[30] Mojtabai, R., Olfson, M., & Han, B. (2016). National trends in the prevalence and treatment of depression in adolescents and young adults. *Pediatrics, 138*(6), Article e20161878.

[31] Office of Applied Studies. (2008). *Major depressive episode among youths aged 12 to 17 in the United States: 2004 to 2006*. Substance Abuse and Mental Health Services Administration. https://ntrl.ntis.gov/NTRL/dashboard/searchResults/titleDetail/PB2009115665.xhtml

[32] Van Lieshout, R. J., & MacQueen, G. (2008). Psychological factors in asthma. *Allergy, Asthma and Clinical Immunology, 4*(1), 12–28.

Notes to Indicator—Continued

[33] Goodman, E., & Whitaker, R. C. (2007). A prospective study of the role of depression in the development and persistence of adolescent obesity. *Pediatrics, 110*(3), 497–504.

[34] Weissman, M. M., Wolk, S., Goldstein, R. B., Moreau, D., Adams, P., Greenwald, S., & Wickramaratne, P. (1999). Depressed adolescents grown up. *Journal of the American Medical Association, 282*, 1701–1713.

[35] Substance Abuse and Mental Health Services Administration. (2020). *Key substance use and mental health indicators in the United States: Results from the 2019 National Survey on Drug Use and Health* (HHS Publication No. PEP20-07-01-001, NSDUH Series H-55). Center for Behavioral Health Statistics and Quality. https://store.samhsa.gov/sites/default/files/ SAMHSA_Digital_Download/PEP20-07-01-001-PDF.pdf

[36] Shaffer, D., Gould, M. S., Fisher, P., Trautman, P., Moreau, D., Kleinman, M., & Flory, M. (1996). Psychiatric diagnosis in child and adolescent suicide. *Archives of General Psychiatry, 53*, 339–348. http://archpsyc.ama-assn.org/cgi/content/abstract/53/4/339

[37] Office of Applied Studies. (2007). *The NSDUH report: Depression and the initiation of alcohol and other drug use among youths aged 12 to 17*. Substance Abuse and Mental Health Services Administration.

[38] Guessoum, S. B., Lachal, J., Radjack, R., Carretier, E., Minassian, S., Benoit, L., & Moro, M. R. (2020). Adolescent psychiatric disorders during the COVID-19 pandemic and lockdown. *Psychiatry Research, 291*, Article 113264. https://doi.org/10.1016/j.psychres.2020.113264

America's Children at a Glance

	Previous Value (Year)	Most Recent Value (Year)	Change Between Years
Demographic Background			
Child population[a]			
Children ages 0–17 in the United States	74.2 million (2020)	73.6 million (2021)	↓
Children as a percentage of the population[a]			
Children ages 0–17 in the United States	22.4% (2020)	22.2% (2021)	↓
Racial and ethnic composition[a]			
Children ages 0–17 by race and Hispanic origin[b]			
White, non-Hispanic	49.7% (2020)	49.4% (2021)	↓
Black, non-Hispanic	13.7% (2020)	13.8% (2021)	↑
American Indian or Alaska Native, non-Hispanic	0.8% (2020)	0.8% (2021)	NS
Asian, non-Hispanic	5.4% (2020)	5.4% (2021)	NS
Native Hawaiian or Other Pacific Islander, non-Hispanic	0.2% (2020)	0.2% (2021)	NS
Two or more races, non-Hispanic	4.6% (2020)	4.7% (2021)	↑
Hispanic	25.6% (2020)	25.7% (2021)	↑
Family and Social Environment			
Family structure and children's living arrangements			
Children ages 0–17 living with two married parents	67% (2020)	65% (2021)	↓
Births to unmarried women			
Births to unmarried women ages 15–44	40 per 1,000 (2019)	39 per 1,000 (2020)	↓
Births to unmarried women among all births	40% (2019)	41% (2020)	↑
Child care			
Children ages 3–5, not yet enrolled in kindergarten with employed mothers, whose primary child care arrangement was nonparental care on a regular basis	85% (2016)	86% (2019)	NS
Children ages 3–5, not yet enrolled in kindergarten with employed mothers, who were in center-based care arrangements for any amount of time	70% (2016)	69% (2019)	NS
Children of at least one foreign-born parent			
Children ages 0–17 living with at least one foreign-born parent	25% (2020)	25% (2021)	NS
Language spoken at home and difficulty speaking English			
Children ages 5–17 who speak a language other than English at home	23% (2018)	23% (2019)	NS
Children ages 5–17 who speak a language other than English at home and who have difficulty speaking English	4% (2018)	4% (2019)	NS
Adolescent births			
Births to females ages 15–17	7 per 1,000 (2019)	6 per 1,000 (2020)	↓
Child maltreatment[a]			
Substantiated reports of maltreatment of children ages 0–17	8.9 per 1,000 (2019)	8.4 per 1,000 (2020)	↓

See notes at end of table.

Legend: NC = Not calculated   NS = No statistically significant change   ↑ = Statistically significant increase   ↓ = Statistically significant decrease

America's Children at a Glance—Continued

	Previous Value (Year)	Most Recent Value (Year)	Change Between Years
Economic Circumstances			
Child poverty and family income			
Children ages 0–17 in poverty	14.4% (2019)	16.1% (2020)	↑
Children living in families in extreme poverty	6.2% (2019)	7.6% (2020)	↑
Secure parental employment			
Children ages 0–17 living with at least one parent employed year-round, full-time	80.2% (2019)	71.7% (2020)	↓
Food insecurity			
Children ages 0–17 in households classified by the USDA as "food insecure"	15% (2019)	16% (2020)	↑
Health Care			
Health insurance coverage			
Children ages 0–17 who were uninsured at the time of interview	5% (2019)	5% (2020)	NS
Usual source of health care			
Children ages 0–17 with no usual source of health care	3% (2019)	2% (2020)	NS
Immunization			
Children ages 24 months with the combined 7-vaccine series	70% (2016)[c]	70% (2017)[c]	NS
Oral health			
Children ages 5–17 with a dental visit in the past year	91% (2019)	89% (2020)	↓
Physical Environment and Safety			
Outdoor air quality			
Children ages 0–17 living in counties with pollutant concentrations above the levels of the current air quality standards	64.1% (2018)	50.5% (2019)	↓
Secondhand smoke			
Children ages 4–11 with any detectable blood cotinine level, a measure for recent exposure to secondhand smoke	37% (2015–2016)	36% (2017–2018)	NS
Drinking water quality			
Children served by community water systems that did not meet all applicable health-based drinking water standards	9% (2018)	7% (2019)	NS
Lead in the blood of children			
Children ages 1–5 with blood lead greater than or equal to 5 µg/dL	2.6% (2007–2010)	0.8% (2013–2018)	↓
Housing problems			
Households with children ages 0–17 reporting shelter cost burden, crowding, and/or physically inadequate housing	39% (2017)	38% (2018)	↓
Youth victims of serious violent crimes[d]			
Serious violent crime victimization of youth ages 12–17	6 per 1,000 (2019)	4 per 1,000 (2020)	NS
Child injury and mortality			
Injury deaths of children ages 1–4	9 per 100,000 (2019)	10 per 100,000 (2020)	↑

See notes at end of table.

Legend: NC = Not calculated   NS = No statistically significant change   ↑ = Statistically significant increase   ↓ = Statistically significant decrease

America's Children at a Glance—Continued

	Previous Value (Year)	Most Recent Value (Year)	Change Between Years
Physical Environment and Safety—cont.			
Child injury and mortality—cont.			
Injury deaths of children ages 5–14	6 per 100,000 (2019)	7 per 100,000 (2020)	↑
Adolescent injury and mortality			
Injury deaths of adolescents ages 15–19	37 per 100,000 (2019)	46 per 100,000 (2020)	↑
Behavior			
Regular cigarette smoking			
Students who reported smoking daily in the past 30 days			
8th grade	0.8% (2020)	0.4% (2021)	NS
10th grade	1% (2020)	1% (2021)	NS
12th grade	3% (2020)	2% (2021)	NS
Alcohol use			
Students who reported having 5 or more alcoholic beverages in a row in the past 2 weeks			
8th grade	5% (2020)	3% (2021)	↓
10th grade	10% (2020)	6% (2021)	↓
12th grade	17% (2020)	12% (2021)	↓
Illicit drug use			
Students who reported using illicit drugs in the past 30 days			
8th grade	9% (2020)	6% (2021)	↓
10th grade	18% (2020)	11% (2021)	↓
12th grade	22% (2020)	21% (2021)	NS
Sexual activity			
High school students who reported ever having had sexual intercourse	40% (2017)	38% (2019)	NS
Youth perpetrators of serious violent crimes[d]			
Youth offenders ages 12–17 involved in serious violent crimes	5 per 1,000 (2019)	4 per 1,000 (2020)	NS
Education			
Family reading to young children			
Children ages 3–5 who were read to 3 or more times in the last week	81% (2016)	85% (2019)	↑
Mathematics and reading achievement			
Average mathematics scale score of			
4th graders (0–500 scale)	240 (2017)	241 (2019)	↑
8th graders (0–500 scale)	283 (2017)	282 (2019)	↓
12th graders (0–300 scale)	152 (2015)	150 (2019)	NS

See notes at end of table.

Legend: NC = Not calculated   NS = No statistically significant change   ↑ = Statistically significant increase   ↓ = Statistically significant decrease

America's Children at a Glance—Continued

	Previous Value (Year)	Most Recent Value (Year)	Change Between Years
Education—cont.			
Mathematics and reading achievement—cont.			
Average reading scale score of			
4th graders (0–500 scale)	222 (2017)	220 (2019)	↓
8th graders (0–500 scale)	267 (2017)	263 (2019)	↓
12th graders (0–500 scale)	287 (2015)	285 (2019)	↓
High school completion			
Young adults ages 18–24 who have completed high school	94% (2019)	94% (2020)	NS
Youth neither enrolled in school[e] nor working			
Youth ages 16–19 who are neither enrolled in school nor working	10% (2020)	9% (2021)	↓
College enrollment			
Recent high school completers enrolled in college the October immediately after completing high school	66% (2019)	63% (2020)	NS
Health			
Preterm birth and low birthweight			
Infants less than 37 completed weeks of gestation at birth	10.2% (2019)	10.1% (2020)	↓
Infants weighing less than 5 lb 8 oz at birth	8.3% (2019)	8.2% (2020)	↓
Infant mortality			
Deaths before first birthday	6 per 1,000 (2018)	6 per 1,000 (2019)	NS
Emotional and behavioral difficulties			
Children ages 4–17 reported by a parent to have serious difficulties with emotions, concentration, behavior, or getting along with other people	6% (2018)	6%* (2019)	NC
Adolescent depression			
Youth ages 12–17 with past-year major depressive episode	16% (2019)	17%** (2020)	NC
Activity limitation			
Children ages 5–17 with activity limitation resulting from one or more chronic health conditions	11% (2017)	10% (2018)	NS
Obesity			
Children ages 6–17 with obesity	20% (2011–2014)	20% (2015–2018)	NS
Asthma			
Children ages 0–17 who currently have asthma	8% (2018)	7%* (2019)	NC

*Caution: Due to survey redesign, 2019 estimates should not be compared with data from earlier years.
** Due to methodological changes between 2019 and 2020, exercise caution when comparing estimates from 2020 with prior years.
[a] Population estimates are not sample derived and thus not subject to statistical testing. Change between years identifies differences in the proportionate size of these estimates.
[b] Percentages may not sum to 100 because of rounding.
[c] Data years refer to birth years of children receiving vaccinations.
[d] The 2020 National Crime Victimization Survey (NCVS) weights include an additional adjustment to address the impact of modified field operations due to COVID-19. For more information on the weighting adjustments applied in 2020, see the Source and Accuracy Statement for the 2020 NCVS in the NCVS 2020 Codebook (https://www.icpsr.umich.edu/web/NACJD/series/95) and *Criminal Victimization, 2020* (NCJ 301775, BJS, October 2021).
[e] School refers to high school and college.

Legend: NC = Not calculated   NS = No statistically significant change   ↑ = Statistically significant increase   ↓ = Statistically significant decrease

Section I
Pediatric Disorders

Description

2 **ACHONDROPLASIA**
Synonyms: Chondrodystrophy, Fetal Rickets
Involves the following Biologic System(s):
Genetic/Chromosomal/Syndrome/Metabolic Disorders, Orthopedic and Muscle Disorders

Achondroplasia is a disorder of the skeletal system that occurs in about one of every 20,000 newborn infants. It belongs to a group of disorders known as chondrodystrophies. These disorders involve a disturbance in the cartilage at the ends of the body's long bones (arms and legs). In Achondroplasia, this disturbance interferes with the conversion of cartilage into bone in the regions known as epiphyses, where these bones normally grow in length. This occurs in infancy and childhood, preventing the bones from growing normally and resulting in shortened limbs and a short stature. Achondroplasia does not affect intelligence.

Achondroplasia is caused by a defect in a single, specific gene that permits the body to make a protein known as fibroblast growth factor-3 (FGF3). Normally, FGF3 limits bone growth, and a decline in the production of this protein is what permits growth during childhood and adolescence. The genetic defect in Achondroplasia, however, causes the body to continue to produce FGF3, leading to an excess of this protein that sharply limits growth. Genetically, Achondroplasia is called an autosomal dominant disorder, because the defective FGF3 gene needs to be inherited from only one parent for Achondroplasia to be present.

Symptoms and characteristic findings include a disproportionately large head with a protruding and prominent forehead (frontal bossing); a flattened nasal bridge; an underdeveloped upper jaw and prominent lower jaw (prognothism); a well-developed but shortened trunk; and short, bowed arms and legs. The upper portions of the arms and legs are proportionately shorter than the lower parts of these limbs, and the elbows may have a limited range of motion. Usually, the fingers and toes are also short, with a V-shaped gap between the third and fourth fingers, and the hands are relatively wide. As children with Achondroplasia grow, their pelvis tilts forward, resulting in a pronounced spinal curvature known as lumbar lordosis, that causes prominence of the abdomen and buttocks. Other effects of Achondroplasia can include decreased muscle tone and muscle weakness.

Diagnosis of Acondroplasia is made from physical examination and findings on X-ray images of the skeleton. Identification of this condition early in life facilitates family and medical planning for treatment and care.

Complications associated with Achondroplasia may include dental problems such as malocclusion, in which the upper and lower teeth do not meet in the proper alignment, and chronic and severe middle ear infections (otitis media) that can result in a loss of conductive hearing. Potentially life-threatening complications include temporary cessations of breathing during sleep, known as sleep apnea, caused by obstruction of the airways by the craniofacial abnormalities in Achondroplasia, and/or from compression of the spinal cord at the point where the cord passes from the spine into the skull. Additionally, this may obstruct the normal flow of cerebrospinal fluid (CSF) between the brain and spinal cord, resulting in hydrocephalus, a condition in which the cerebrospinal fluid collects in and around the brain, with potentially life-threatening effects.

Treatment with human growth hormone (HGH) is often used to improve growth and height in persons with Achondroplasia, and the availability of recombinant human growth hormone, or somatotropin, has revolutionized the treatment of short stature. Surgical lengthening of the limbs can produce improvement in some patients. Other treatment is directed at preventing or correcting complications of the condition. Monitoring head growth during infancy to insure normal growth limits is effective for detecting hydrocephalus. Physiotherapy, dental treatment and orthopedic appliances such as braces can correct or prevent a number of the complications caused by Achondroplasia. Appropriate counseling can provide emotional and psychological support to persons with the condition and their family members.

Government Agencies

3 **NIH/National Institute of Arthritis and Musculoskeletal and Skin Diseases**
1 AMS Circle
Bethesda, MD 20892
301-495-4484
877-226-4267
Fax: 301-718-6366
TTY: 301-565-2966
niamsinfo@mail.nih.gov
www.niams.nih.gov

The mission of the NIAMS, a part of the NIH, is to support research into the causes, treatment and prevention of arthritis and musculosketal and skin diseases, the training of basic and clinical scientists to carry out this research, and the dissemination of information on research progress in these diseases.
Lindsey A. Criswell, MD, Director
Rick Phillips, Executive Officer

4 **NIH/National Institute of Environmental Health Sciences (NIEHS)**
PO Box 12233
Durham, NC 27709
984-287-3815
www.niehs.nih.gov

NIEHS reduces the burden of human illness and dysfunction from environmental causes by defining how environmental exposures, genetics and age interact to affect an individual's health.
Chris Long, MPA, Executive Officer
Mitch Williams, Deputy Executive Officer

5 **NIH/National Institute on Drug Abuse (NIDA)**
301 N Stonestreet Avenue
Bethesda, MD 20892
301-443-1124
www.drugabuse.gov

NIDA leads the nation in bringing the power of science to bear on drug abuse and addiction through support and conduct of research across all disciplines and rapid and effective dissemination of results of that research to improve drug abuse and addiction prevention and treatment.
Nora D. Volkow MD, Director
Wilson Compton, MD, MPE, Deputy Director
Joellen Austin, MP, Associate Director for Management

National Associations & Support Groups

6 **American Academy of Pediatrics**
345 Park Blvd
Itasca, IL 60143
800-433-9016
Fax: 847-434-8000
mcc@aap.org
www.aap.org

The American Academy of Pediatrics and its member pediatricians are committed to the attainment of optimal physical, mental and social health and well-being for all infants, children, adolescents, and young adults.
Mark Del Monte, JD, CEO/Executive VP
Lynn Olson, PhD, Vice President, Research
Vera Tait, MD, FAAP, Chief Medical Officer

Achondroplasia / Libraries & Resource Centers

7   **Human Growth Foundation**
997 Glen Cove Avenue, Suite 5
Glen Head, NY 11545
800-451-6434
Fax: 516-671-4055
hgf1@hgfound.org
www.hgfound.org

A voluntary, nonprofit organization whose mission is to help children and adults with disorders of growth and growth hormones through research, education, support and advocacy. The foundation is dedicated to helping medical science to better understand the process of growth. It is composed of concerned parents and friends of children and adults with growth problems; and interested health professionals.

Joel Steelman, MD, President
Emily Germain-Lee, MD, Vice President

8   **Little People of America**
617 Broadway #518
Sonoma, CA 95476
714-368-3689
888-572-2001
Fax: 707-721-1896
info@lpaonline.org
www.lpaonline.org

A nonprofit organization that provides support and information to people of short stature and their families.

Deb Himsel, Executive Director
Mark Povinelli, President

9   **MAGIC Foundation: Major Aspects of Growth in Children**
4200 Cantera Drive, #106
Warrenville, IL 60555
630-836-8200
800-362-4423
Fax: 630-836-8181
contactus@magicfoundation.org
www.magicfoundation.org

A national nonprofit organization providing support and education regarding growth disorders in children and related adult disorders. Provides educational information, networking, a national conference, a kids' program and an extensive medical library.

10,000 members

Dianne Kremidas, Executive Director
Mary Andrews, CEO
Teresa Tucker, Patient Advocacy

Libraries & Resource Centers

10   **NIH/National Library of Medicine (NLM)**
8600 Rockville Pike
Bethesda, MD 20894
301-594-5983
888-346-3656
Fax: 301-402-1384
TDD: 800-735-2258
custserv@nlm.nih.gov
www.nlm.nih.gov

NLM collects, organizes and makes available biomedical science information to scientists, health professionals and the public. The library's databases, including PubMed/Medline and MedlinePlus, are used extensively around the world. NLM conducts and supports research in biometric communications; creates information resources for molecular biology, biotechnology, toxicology, and environmental health; and provides grant support for training, medical library resources, and biomedical informatics.

Patricia Flatley Brennan, Director
Betsy Humphreys, Deputy Director
Paul Kiehl, Deputy Executive Officer

Conferences

11   **Adult Endocrine Disorders/GHD Educational Convention**
Magic Foundation
4200 Cantera Drive, #106
Warrenville, IL 60555
630-836-8200
800-362-4423
Fax: 630-836-8181
contactus@magicfoundation.org
www.magicfoundation.org

An educational program for adults who are affected with Growth Hormone Deficiency and/or other endocrine disorders.

June

Dianne Kremidas, Executive Director
Rich Buckley, Chairman
Mary Andrews, Chief Executive Officer

12   **LPA National Conference**
Little People of America
617 Broadway #518
Sonoma, CA 95476
714-368-3689
888-572-2001
Fax: 707-721-1896
info@lpaonline.org
www.lpaonline.org

July

Deb Himsel, Executive Director
Mark Povinelli, President
Cuquis Robledo, Public Relations Director

Web Sites

13   **Achondroplasia UK**
52 Vernham Grove
Odd down, Bath, Avon, BA2 2
admin@achondroplasia.co.uk
www.achondroplasia.co.uk

Offers information on health supervision for children of all ages, divided into the following growth stages: newborn; infancy; early childhood; late childhood; and adolescence to early adulthood.

14   **Human Growth Foundation**
997 Glen Cove Avenue, Suite 5
Glen Head, NY 11545
800-451-6434
Fax: 516-671-4055
hgf1@hgfound.org
www.hgfound.org

The Human Growth Foundation is a voluntary, non-profit organization whose mission is to help children and adults with disorders of growth and growth horomone through research, education, support, and advocacy.

Joel Steelman, MD, President
Emily Germain-Lee, MD, Vice President

15   **Little People of America**
617 Broadway #518
Sonoma, CA 95476
714-368-3689
888-572-2001
Fax: 707-721-1896
info@lpaonline.org
www.lpaonline.org

A nonprofit organization that provides support and information to people of short stature and their families.

Deb Himsel, Executive Director
Mark Povinelli, President
Cuquis Robledo, Public Relations Director

16   **MAGIC Foundation: Major Aspects of Growth in Children**
4200 Cantera Drive, #106
Warrenville, IL 60555
630-836-8200
800-362-4423
Fax: 630-836-8181
ContactUs@magicfoundation.org
www.magicfoundation.org

Provides educational information regarding growth disorders.

Dianne Kremidas, Executive Director
Mary Andrews, Chief Executive Officer
Teresa Tucker, Patient Advocacy

17 Medical College of Wisconsin
8701 Watertown Plank Road
Milwaukee, WI 53226
414-955-8296
www.mcw.edu

A private, academic institution dedicated to leadership and excellence in education, research, patient care, and service.

John R. Raymond, Sr., MD, President/ CEO
Joseph E. Kerschner, MD, Dean/ EVP
Ravi Misra, PhD, Dean/ Professor of Biochemistry

18 National Center for Biotechnology Information
National Library of Medicine, 8600 Rockville Pike
Bethesda, MD 20894
888-346-3656
info@ncbi.nlm.nih.gov
www.ncbi.nlm.nih.gov

NCBI's mission is to develop new information technologoes to aid in the understanding of fundamental molecular and genetic processes that control health and disease.

Patricia Flatley Brennan, RN, PhD, Director
James Ostell, PhD, Executive Secretary

19 Online Mendelian Inheritance in Man
McKusick-Nathans Institue of Genetic Medicine-JHU
Baltimore, MD 21205
www.omim.org

This database is a catalog of human genes and genetic disorders.

Ada Hamosh, MD, Scientific Director

20 Restricted Growth Association
www.rgaonline.org.uk

www.rgaonline.org.uk

Provides medical advice, welfare and counseling services with the support of Regional Coordinators, and offers contact with others and the sharing of helpful information through an information magazine, advisory booklets, meetings, social events and conventions.

Pamphlets

21 Achondroplasia
Human Growth Foundation
977 Glen Cove Avenue, Suite 5
Glen Head, NY 11545
516-671-4041
800-451-6434

Signs, causes, and prevention of achondroplasia.

Acute Gastrointestinal Infections / Description

Description

22 ACUTE GASTROINTESTINAL INFECTIONS
Covers these related disorders: Acute infectious diarrhea, Gastroenteritis
Involves the following Biologic System(s):
Gastrointestinal Disorders, Infectious Disorders

Acute gastrointestinal infections are conditions of the gastrointestinal tract caused by various microorganisms such as certain bacteria, viruses, and parasites (more common outside the U.S.) and are usually characterized by diarrhea and vomiting. Such microorganisms may be transmitted through fecal-oral contamination or contamination of food or water. Bacterial gastrointestinal infection may result from the release of toxins by bacteria or by bacterial growth inside or outside the walls of the intestines. Viral infection by gastroenteritis viruses, especially the rotavirus, is a major source of diarrhea-causing infection in the U.S. Although infectious gastroenteritis often resolves on its own, some patients experience acute or prolonged symptoms that may require treatment, as well as identification of the causative agent.

Symptoms and findings associated with infectious gastroenteritis depend upon the cause of the infection and the age and general health of the patient. The most common manifestation of infection is watery or bloody diarrhea that usually appears suddenly and lasts from a few days to two weeks or longer. Other symptoms may include nausea, vomiting, loss of appetite, and abdominal cramping or distress. Infants and those with compromised immune systems are at risk for potentially severe illness. Diarrhea and vomiting in infants younger than six months, and severe episodes in any child, may result in a potentially life-threatening and excessive fluid loss (dehydration) as well as the loss of essential substances, known as electrolytes, in the fluid portion of the blood (e.g., sodium, potassium, and calcium). Symptoms associated with dehydration may include fever, thirst, less-than-average urinary output, dry mouth, and poor feeding. In addition, severely dehydrated infants and children may become weak, listless, or sleepy and their eyes may have a sunken, dry appearance. Bacteria associated with gastroenteritis sometimes cause infection outside the gastrointestinal tract and may involve the urinary tract, eyes, vaginal areas in females, as well as inflammation of the membranes surrounding the brain and spinal cord (meningitis), the liver (hepatitis), the lungs (pneumonia), the bone and bone marrow (osteomyelitis), and other tissues. In addition, certain food-borne or water-borne infections caused by bacterial or other toxins may produce severe, sudden, and potentially life-threatening symptoms including neurologic involvement such as numbness and paralysis.

Acute infectious diarrhea symptoms are similar to those associated with infectious gastroenteritis. In addition, a temporary inability to properly digest milk may result from damage to the mucosal lining of the small intestine.

Prevention of some types of infectious gastroenteritis may include vaccination against certain infectious diseases when traveling to countries in which these illnesses are widespread. In addition, care in handling and preparing foods may help to alleviate certain types of food-borne illness. Treatment for both infectious gastroenteritis and acute infectious diarrhea is first directed toward the replacement of body fluids and electrolytes through oral preparations or, in the case of more severe dehydration, intravenously. Once dehydration is corrected, breast-feeding, or feeding with lactose-free formula, gradually followed by regular formula, may resume. If indicated, identification of the cause may then be established through evaluation of family history including recent travels, foods eaten, other similar family illness as well as physical examination and testing of stool specimens. Although some cases of acute infectious diarrhea will resolve spontaneously, other treatment may be directed at the underlying cause. Bacterial infections may be treated with appropriate antibiotics. Prevention of this potentially severe condition may often be accomplished by attention to good hygienics such as frequent hand washing, etc. Other treatment is symptomatic and supportive.

Government Agencies

23 NIH/National Institute of Diabetes and Digestive and Kidney Diseases
9000 Rockville Pike
Bethesda, MD 20892
800-860-8747
TTY: 866-569-1162
healthinfo@niddk.nih.gov
www.niddk.nih.gov

Conducts and supports basic and applied research and provides leadership for a national program in diabetes, endocrinology, and metabolic diseases; digestive diseases and nutrition and kidney, urologic and hematologic diseases.
Griffin P. Rodgers, MD, Director
Gregory G. Germino, MD, Deputy Director

National Associations & Support Groups

24 American Academy of Pediatrics
345 Park Blvd
Itasca, IL 60143
800-433-9016
Fax: 847-434-8000
mcc@aap.org
www.aap.org

The American Academy of Pediatrics and its member pediatricians are committed to the attainment of optimal physical, mental and social health and well-being for all infants, children, adolescents, and young adults.
Mark Del Monte, JD, CEO/Executive VP
Lynn Olson, PhD, Vice President, Research
Vera Tait, MD, FAAP, Chief Medical Officer

25 American College of Gastroenterology
6400 Goldsboro Road
Bethesda, MD 20817
301-263-9000
www.gi.org

The American College of Gastroenterology was founded in 1932 to advance the scientific study and medical practice of diseases of the GI tract.
13,000 members

26 American Gastroenterological Association
4930 Del Ray Avenue
Bethesda, MD 20814
301-654-2055
Fax: 301-654-5920
member@gastro.org
www.gastro.org

Society of physicians, surgeons, scientists and other individuals within the healthcare community interested in the functions and disorders of the digestive system.
Tom Serena, CEO
Stacie Miller, Senior Director

27 Digestive Disease National Coalition
507 Capitol Court NE, Suite 200
Washington, DC 20002
202-544-7497
Fax: 202-546-7105
www.ddnc.org

Advocacy organization comprised of over 30 voluntary and professional societies concerned with the many diseases of the digestive tract and liver.

Ceciel Rooker, Chairperson
Bryan Green, MD, President
Cathy Griffith, Vice Chairperson

28 **International Foundation for Functional Gastrointestinal Disorders (IFFGD)**
3015 Dunes W Boulevard, Suite 512
Mount Pleasant, SC 29466   414-964-1799
                                  www.iffgd.org

The organization offers responses to those commonly asked questions for families and individuals whose lives have been touched by gastrointestinal disorders.

Nancy J. Norton, Founder
Ceciel T. Rooker, President

29 **North American Society for Pediatric Gastroenterology/Hepatology/Nutrition**
714 N Bethlehem Pike, Suite 300
Ambler, PA 19002   215-641-9800
                             Fax: 215-641-1995
                                  www.naspghan.org

Strives to improve the care of infants, children and adolescents with digestive disorders by promoting advances in clinical care of children with chronic abdominal pain, diarrhea, constipation, vomiting, bleeding from the GI tract, inflammatory bowel disease, liver diseases, diseases of the pancreas, poor weight gain and nutritional problems.

Margaret K Stallings, Executive Director
Kim Rose, Associate Director
Gina Brown, Membership

30 **Oley Foundation**
99 Delaware Avenue, MC-28 Albany Medical Ctr
Delmar, NY 12054   518-262-5079
                             Fax: 518-262-5528
                                  info@oley.org
                                  www.oley.org

Strives to enrich the lives of those living with home intravenous nutrition (parenteral) and tube feeding (enteral) through education, advocacy, and networking.

Joan Bishop, Executive Director
Roslyn Dahl, Director, Communications/Dvlpmnt
Lisa Crosby Metzger, Director, Community Engagement

31 **World Health Organization**
Avenue Appia 20
1202 Geneva,
Switzerland   www.who.int

WHO is the directing and coordinating authority for health within the United Nations system. WHO operates in more than 150 countries around the world.

Dr. Tedros Adhanom Ghebreyesus, Director General
Dr. Zsuzsanna Jakab, Deputy Director General
Stewart Simonson, Asst Director General, UN NYC

Libraries & Resource Centers

32 **National Digestive Diseases Information Clearinghouse (NDDIC)**
NIH
2 Information Way
Bethesda, MD 20892   301-654-3810
                                  800-891-5389
                             Fax: 301-907-8906
                             nddic@info.niddk.nih.gov
                             www.digestive.niddk.nih.gov

The National Institute of Diabetes and Digestive and Kidney Diseases conducts and supports research on many of the most serious diseases affecting public health. The Institute supports much of the clinical research on the diseases of internal medicine and related subspecialty fields as well as many basic science disciplines.

Griffin P. Rodgers, MD, Director
Gregory G. Germino, MD, Deputy Director
Kathy Kranzfelder, Communications Director

Conferences

33 **IFFGD Professional Symposia**
3015 Dunes W Boulevard, Suite 512
Mount Pleasant, SC 29466   414-964-1799
                                  www.iffgd.org

Aimed at promoting education and awareness among professionals from multiple disciplines who treat gastrointestinal disorders and incontinence.

April

Nancy J. Norton, Founder
Ceciel T. Rooker, President

34 **NASPGHAN Annual Meeting**
NASPGHAN
714 N. Bethlehem Pike, Ste 300
Ambler, PA 19002   215-641-9800
                             Fax: 215-641-1995
                                  www.naspghan.org

Strives to improve the care of infants, children and adolescents with digestive disorders by promoting advances in clinical care of children with chronic abdominal pain, diarrhea, constipation, vomiting, bleeding from the GI tract, inflammatory bowel disease, liver diseases, diseases of the pancreas, poor weight gain and nutritional problems.

Fall

Margaret K Stallings, Executive Director
Kim Rose, Associate Director
Gina Brown, Membership

35 **Oley Foundation Annual Conference**
99 Delaware Ave, MC-28, Albany Medical Center
Delmar, NY 12054   518-262-5079
                             Fax: 518-262-5528
                                  info@oley.org
                                  www.oley.org

The event includes formal presentations and informal discussions bringing the Oley Foundation community together for learning and connecting.

July

Joan Bishop, Executive Director

Computer Software

36 **Digestive Diseases Self-Education Program (DDSEP 9)**
American Gastroenterological Association
4930 Del Ray Avenue
Bethesda, MD 20814   301-654-2055
                             Fax: 301-654-5920
                                  member@gastro.org
                                  www.gastro.org

Provides an in-depth review of core topics in gastroenterology and hepatology. gastroenterologists use this software to assess and update their knowledge and earn CME credit.

Seth R. Sweetser, MD, Editor
Jennifer A. Christie, MD, Associate Editor
Amy S. Oxentenko, MD, Associate Editor

Web Sites

37 **American Gastroenterological Association**
4930 Del Ray Avenue
Bethesda, MD 20814   301-654-2055
                             Fax: 301-654-5920
                                  member@gastro.org
                                  www.gastro.org

Information regarding prevention, treatment and cure of digestive diseases.

Tom Serena, CEO

38 **Baby Center**
163 Freelon Street
San Francisco, CA 94107   www.babycenter.com

The Academy is committed to the attainment of optimal physical, mental and social health for all infants, children, adolescents, and young adults. To this end, the members of the Academy dedicate their efforts and resources.

Colleen Hancock, SVP/ Global COO
Linda J. Murray, SVP/ Global Editor-in-Chief
Clarence Wilhelm, Chief Information Officer

39 **Health Research Program (HaRP)**
www.harpnet.org

www.harpnet.org

A program by USAID, the project strives to improve the health status of infants, children, mothers and families through the development and research of new tools, technologies, policies and approaches.

40 **Hepatitis A**
NIDDK Health Information Center
Bethesda, MD 20892

800-860-8747
TTY: 866-569-1162
healthinfo@niddk.nih.gov
www.niddk.nih.gov

Explains the prevention, causes, symptoms, modes of transmission, and treatment of Hepatitis A.

Dr. Griffin P. Rodgers, Director
Dr. Gregory G. Germino, Deputy Director

41 **Hepatitis B**
NIDDK Health Information Center
Bethesda, MD 20892

800-860-8747
TTY: 866-569-1162
healthinfo@niddk.nih.gov
www.niddk.nih.gov

Explains the prevention, causes, symptoms, modes of transmission, and treatment of Hepatitis B.

Dr. Griffin P. Rodgers, Director
Dr. Gregory G. Germino, Deputy Director

42 **Hepatitis C**
NIDDK Health Information Center
Bethesda, MD 20892

800-860-8747
TTY: 866-569-1162
healthinfo@niddk.nih.gov
www.niddk.nih.gov

Explains the prevention, causes, symptoms, modes of transmission, and treatment of Hepatitis C.

Dr. Griffin P. Rodgers, Director
Dr. Gregory G. Germino, Deputy Director

43 **National Digestive Diseases Information Clearinghouse (NDDIC)**
NIH
2 Information Way
Bethesda, MD 20892

301-654-3810
800-891-5389
nddic@info.niddk.nih.gov
www.digestive.niddk.nih.gov

Information regarding digestive and kidney diseases.

Griffin P. Rodgers, MD, Director
Gregory G. Germino, MD, Deputy Director
Kathy Kranzfelder, Communications Director

Book Publishers

44 **Digestive Diseases Dictionary**
NIDDK Health Information Center
Bethesda, MD 20892

800-860-8747
TTY: 866-569-1162
healthinfo@niddk.nih.gov
catalog.niddk.nih.gov/catalog/

Defines words that are often used when talking or writing about digestive diseases.

Dr. Griffin P. Rodgers, Director
Dr. Gregory G. Germino, Deputy Director
Camille M. Hoover, Executive Officer

Journals

45 **American Journal of Gastroenterology**
American College of Gastroenterology
6400 Goldsboro Rd, Ste 200
Bethesda, MD 20817

301-263-9000
gi.org

Publishes scientific papers relevant to the practice of clinical gastroenterology, Features outstanding original research, review articles and consensus papers related to new drugs and therapeutic modalities.

Stephen B. Hanauer, MD, FACG, President
Carol A. Burke, MD, FACG, Vice President
Sunanda V. Kane, MD, MSPH, FACG, Secretary

46 **Journal of Pediatric Gastroenterology and Nutrition**
Lippincott Williams & Wilkins
Two Commerce Square, 2001 Market Street
Philadelphia, PA 19103

215-521-8300
Fax: 215-521-8902
www.wolterskluwerhealth.com

Provides a forum for original papers and reviews dealing with nutrition in normal and abnormal functions of the alimentary tract and its associated organs including the salivary glands, pancreas, gallbladder, and liver. Particular emphasis is on development and its relation to infant and childhood nutrition.

Bob Becker, President/ CEO
Susan Yules, Chief Financial Officer
Cathy Wolfe, President/ CEO, Medical Research

Newsletters

47 **LifelineLetter**
Oley Foundation
99 Delaware Ave, MC-28, Albany Medical Center
Delmar, NY 12054

518-262-5079
Fax: 518-262-5528
info@oley.org
www.oley.org

Strives to enrich the lives of those living with home intravenous nutrition (parenteral) and tube feeding (enteral) through education, advocacy, and networking.

July

Joan Bishop, Executive Director
Roslyn Dahl, Director, Communications/Dvlpmnt
Lisa Crosby Metzger, Director, Community Engagement

48 **NASPGHAN News**
714 N. Bethlehem Pike, Ste 300
Ambler, PA 19002

215-641-9800
Fax: 215-641-1995
www.naspghan.org

Publication of the North American Society for Pediatric Gastroenterolgy, Hepatology and Nutrition, which strives to improve the care of infants, children and adolescents with digestive disorders by promoting advances in clinical care of children with chronic abdominal pain, diarrhea, constipation, vomiting, bleeding from the GI tract, inflammatory bowel disease, liver diseases, diseases of the pancreas, poor weight gain and nutritional problems.

Margaret K Stallings, Executive Director
Kim Rose, Associate Director
Gina Brown, Membership

Acute Gastrointestinal Infections / Pamphlets

Pamphlets

49 Bleeding in the Digestive Tract
NIDDK Publications Catalog
1 Information Way
Bethesda, MD 20892
800-860-8747
TTY: 866-569-1162
healthinfo@niddk.nih.gov
catalog.niddk.nih.gov

Includes information on the causes of bleeding in the digestive tract and how the bleeding is recognized, diagnosed, and treated.

6 pages Spanish
Griffin P. Rodgers, M.D., Director

50 Cyclic Vomiting Syndrome
NDDIC
2 Information Way
Bethesda, MD 20892
301-654-3810
800-891-5389
Fax: 703-738-4929
TTY: 866-569-1162
nddic@info.niddk.nih.gov
www.niddk.nih.gov

Describes the four phases of cyclic vomiting syndrome and the current treatment options available. Outlines the complications associated with the disorder and provides additional resources.

4 pages
Griffin P. Rodgers, M.D., M.A.C.P, Director
Kevin Abbott, Program Director
Kristin Abraham, Program Director

51 Diagnostic Tests
NDDIC
2 Information Way
Bethesda, MD 20892
301-654-3810
800-891-5389
Fax: 703-738-4929
TTY: 866-569-1162
nddic@info.niddk.nih.gov
www.niddk.nih.gov

Contains patient education fact sheets on seven diagnostic tests for gastrointestinal disorders (Colonoscopy, Sigmoidoscopy, Upper Endoscopy, Lower GI Series, ERCP, Liver Biopsy). Designed to be photocopy masters for health professionals to copy and distribute to patients.

Griffin P. Rodgers, M.D., M.A.C.P, Director
Kevin Abbott, Program Director
Kristin Abraham, Program Director

52 Diarrhea
NDDIC
2 Information Way
Bethesda, MD 20892
301-654-3810
800-891-5389
Fax: 703-738-4929
TTY: 866-569-1162
nddic@info.niddk.nih.gov
www.niddk.nih.gov

Includes general information on diarrhea and what can cause it. Also provides information about diagnosis, treatment, and prevention.

6 pages
Griffin P. Rodgers, M.D., M.A.C.P, Director
Kevin Abbott, Program Director
Kristin Abraham, Program Director

53 Diverticular Disease
NIDDK Health Information Center
1 Information Way
Bethesda, MD 20892
800-860-8747
TTY: 866-569-1162
healthinfo@niddk.nih.gov
catalog.niddk.nih.gov

Provides clear definitions of diverticulosis and diverticulitis, along with information on symptoms, causes, complications, and treatments.

6 pages
Griffin P. Rodgers, M.D., Director

54 Facts & Fallacies About Digestive Diseases
NDDIC
2 Information Way
Bethesda, MD 20892
301-654-3810
800-891-5389
Fax: 703-738-4929
TTY: 866-569-1162
nddic@info.niddk.nih.gov
www.niddk.nih.gov

Provides information about common digestive disorders, including ulcers, inflammatory bowel disease, and constipation, in true/false format.

4 pages
Griffin P. Rodgers, M.D., M.A.C.P, Director
Kevin Abbott, Program Director
Kristin Abraham, Program Director

55 Gallstones
NDDIC
2 Information Way
Bethesda, MD 20892
301-654-3810
800-891-5389
Fax: 703-738-4929
TTY: 866-569-1162
nddic@info.niddk.nih.gov
www.niddk.nih.gov

Provides general information on gallstones, including what causes them, who is at risk, and how they are diagnosed and treated.

6 pages
Griffin P. Rodgers, M.D., M.A.C.P, Director
Kevin Abbott, Program Director
Kristin Abraham, Program Director

56 Gas in the Digestive Tract
NDDIC
2 Information Way
Bethesda, MD 20892
301-654-3810
800-891-5389
Fax: 703-738-4929
TTY: 866-569-1162
nddic@info.niddk.nih.gov
www.niddk.nih.gov

Describes what causes gas, discusses the symptoms and the problems they cause, and provides information on treatment.

8 pages
Griffin P. Rodgers, M.D., M.A.C.P, Director
Kevin Abbott, Program Director
Kristin Abraham, Program Director

57 Gastroesophageal Reflux Disease in Children
NDDIC
2 Information Way
Bethesda, MD 20892
301-654-3810
800-891-5389
Fax: 703-738-4929
TTY: 866-569-1162
nddic@info.niddk.nih.gov
www.niddk.nih.gov

Describes gastroesophageal reflux (GER) in children and adolescents, including information about the causes, symptoms, and diagnosis of this condition, as well as its treatment.

4 pages
Griffin P. Rodgers, M.D., M.A.C.P, Director
Kevin Abbott, Program Director
Kristin Abraham, Program Director

Acute Gastrointestinal Infections / Pamphlets

58   **Heart Burn, Hiatal Hernia, and Gastroesophageal Reflux Disease**
NDDIC
2 Information Way
Bethesda, MD 20892

301-654-3810
800-891-5389
Fax: 703-738-4929
TTY: 866-569-1162
nddic@info.niddk.nih.gov
www.niddk.nih.gov

Defines gastroesophageal reflux disease (GERD) and describes the role of hiatal hernia. Provides general information on heartburn, as well as treatments for GERD, including surgery.

6 pages

Griffin P. Rodgers, M.D., M.A.C.P, Director
Kevin Abbott, Program Director
Kristin Abraham, Program Director

59   **Hemochromatosis**
NDDIC
2 Information Way
Bethesda, MD 20892

301-654-3810
800-891-5389
Fax: 703-738-4929
TTY: 866-569-1162
nddic@info.niddk.nih.gov
www.niddk.nih.gov

Provides information about the causes, risk factors, symptoms, diagnosis, treatment, diagnostic tests for, and current research about hemochromatosis. Includes a list of additional resources.

6 pages

Griffin P. Rodgers, M.D., M.A.C.P, Director
Kevin Abbott, Program Director
Kristin Abraham, Program Director

60   **Irritable Bowel Syndrome**
NDDIC
2 Information Way
Bethesda, MD 20892

301-654-3810
800-891-5389
Fax: 703-738-4929
TTY: 866-569-1162
nddic@info.niddk.nih.gov
www.niddk.nih.gov

Describes causes, symptoms, tests to rule out more serious intestinal diseases, and lifestyle and medical approaches to syptom management.

4 pages

Griffin P. Rodgers, M.D., M.A.C.P, Director
Kevin Abbott, Program Director
Kristin Abraham, Program Director

61   **Ulcerative Colitis**
NDDIC
2 Information Way
Bethesda, MD 20892

301-654-3810
800-891-5389
Fax: 703-738-4929
TTY: 866-569-1162
nddic@info.niddk.nih.gov
www.niddk.nih.gov

Outlines the symptoms, diagnostic procedures, and risks and benefits of several drugs and kinds of surgery to treat this disease.

6 pages

Griffin P. Rodgers, M.D., M.A.C.P, Director
Kevin Abbott, Program Director
Kristin Abraham, Program Director

62   **Your Digestive System & How it Works**
NDDIC
2 Information Way
Bethesda, MD 20892

301-654-3810
800-891-5389
Fax: 703-738-4929
TTY: 866-569-1162
nddic@info.niddk.nih.gov
www.niddk.nih.gov

Providees general information about the organs of the digestive system, the digestive process, and the absorption of nutrients. Includes a list of additional readings.

6 pages

Griffin P. Rodgers, M.D., M.A.C.P, Director
Kevin Abbott, Program Director
Kristin Abraham, Program Director

Description

63 ACUTE LYMPHOBLASTIC LEUKEMIA
Synonyms: Acute lymphocytic leukemia, ALL
Involves the following Biologic System(s):
Hematologic and Oncologic Disorders

Acute lymphoblastic leukemia (ALL) is a malignant disease characterized by excessive production of immature white blood cells known as lymphoblasts. ALL is the most common type of leukemia in children, having a slightly greater incidence, or rate of occurrence, in boys than in girls. Although ALL may develop during adolescence or occasionally in adulthood, it occurs most commonly in children between 3 and 7 years of age. The outcome in childhood ALL is related to a multitude of factors, including age, numbers of lymphoblasts and other blood cells found in the blood and bone marrow, and various genetic factors.

The lymphoblasts involved in ALL are produced in the bone marrow, and normally go on to develop into the white blood cells called lymphocytes, which are primarily responsible for fighting infection. In ALL, these lymphoblasts go through an uncontrolled proliferation that results in their accumulation in huge numbers in the bone marrow, impairing its ability to produce the other types of blood cells that originate in the marrow. The lymphoblasts responsible for ALL also proliferate in organs other than the marrow, particularly the liver, spleen, and lymph nodes.

The lymphoblasts affected by ALL evolve into either of two types of mature lymphocytes. One of these types are T-lymphocytes, which migrate from the bone marrow to the thymus gland in the neck, where they complete their maturation. The second type of lymphocytes, called B-lymphocytes mature entirely within the bone marrow. Because of this difference, ALL itself is divided into two categories — T-cell and B-cell. The technique used for differentiating the two kinds of ALL is known as "immunophenotyping." B-cell ALL is more common than T-cell, which tends to occur more often in boys, after the age of 10 years. Treatment of the two types of ALL may also differ, depending upon age, results of clinical and laboratory tests, and other factors.

All forms of ALL originate from abnormalities in the genetic structure of the cells that give rise to lymphoblasts. These abnormalities include changes in the structure of specific genes, breaks in the chainlike strands of genes known as chromosomes, with the broken parts joining other parts of the same chromosome or to other chromosomes where they do not belong, and other kinds of damage to the chromosomes or genes.

The chromosomal or genetic abnormalities in ALL are responsible for both the uncontrolled proliferation of lymphocytes and a cessation in the development of these cells, preventing them from maturing normally into lymphocytes.

Factors that may increase the risk for developing childhood ALL include Trisomy 21, the chromosomal abnormality responsible for Down syndrome; certain genetic disorders, such as Fanconi's anemia; presence of the aberrant chromosome known as the Philadelphia chromosome, created by the breakage of a specific chromosome and entry of its broken part into another; exposure to radiation, some drugs used for chemotherapy, and certain chemicals such as benzene.

Many of the symptoms and effects of ALL in children and young adults are related to their uncontrolled proliferation of leukemic cells in the marrow or other organs. Overpopulation of the marrow by the diseased lymphoblasts in ALL may impede the formation of red blood cells, which also develop in the marrow; of the cells known as platelets, which are essential to blood clotting; and of the cells known as granulocytes, that normally team up with lymphocytes to fight off infection. The resulting symptoms typically include pallor, loss of appetite (anorexia), weight loss, and a generalized feeling of ill health (malaise); fatigue and weakness, from decreased numbers of the circulating red blood cells that carry oxygen to the body's tissues (anemia); bleeding from the gums or nose, easy bruising, and the development of small red or purple spots on the skin (petechiae) from decreased levels of the blood platelets responsible for blood clotting; and infection and fever from decreased numbers of mature white blood cells and granulocytes. Other symptoms of ALL may include headache and bone or joint pain. In many cases, effects of ALL include swollen lymph glands and an enlarged spleen (splenomegaly).

The diagnosis of ALL is established by the presence of lymphoblasts in a bone marrow sample obtained through biopsy. Treatment of ALL is directed toward destroying leukemic cells through the use of specific drugs, known as chemotherapy, which is sometimes given together with treatment delivered by high-energy radiation, such as that of X-rays. Treatment of ALL typically involves several stages, or "phases," and may cover a period of many months. The first stage of treatment, known as the "induction phase," is directed at maximum destruction of leukemic cells in the blood and bone marrow. This is commonly followed by what is known as "remission," in which the activity and effects of ALL are markedly reduced. The second phase of treatment, known as the "consolidation phase," is begun during remission and designed to eradicate any residual leukemic cells that may remain anywhere in the body and become reactivated, causing a recurrence or relapse of ALL. The third phase of therapy is known as "maintenance" or "continuation" therapy. The eradication of leukemic cells that have entered the brain, the membranes surrounding the brain and spinal cord (meninges), or the cerebrospinal fluid that surrounds these organs may require direct injection of a chemotherapeutic agent into the cerebrospinal fluid (intrathecal injection). Alternatively, X-ray or other irradiation may be focused on the brain or spinal cord to eliminate residual leukemic cells (intrathecal radiation). In some cases, immature blood cells are taken from the bone marrow of a donor and given to children with ALL to replace cells destroyed by chemotherapy or radiation therapy, with the goal of allowing these immature cells to grow to maturity and restore the patient's production of red and white blood cells and platelets.

Supportive measures in the treatment of ALL may include blood transfusions to alleviate anemia and bleeding irregularities, as well as the administration of antibiotics to treat infections resulting from the white cell abnormalities associated with both ALL and its treatment. Relapse of ALL after successful initial remission therapy usually results from lymphoblasts that have remained in the bone marrow and brain, and may require one or more additional courses of chemotherapy.

Government Agencies

64 NIH/National Cancer Institute
Bethesda, MD 20892

800-422-6237
NCIinfo@nih.gov
www.cancer.gov

Acute Lymphoblastic Leukemia / National Associations & Support Groups

The National Cancer Institute coordinates the National Cancer Program, which conducts and supports research, training, health information dissemination, and other programs with respect to the cause, diagnosis, prevention, and treatment of cancer, rehabilitation from cancer, and the continuing care of cancer patients and the families of cancer patients.

Norman E. Sharpless, MD, Director
Douglas R. Lowy, MD, Principal Deputy Director

65 **NIH/National Heart, Lung and Blood Institute**
31 Center Drive, Bldg 31
Bethesda, MD 20892
877-645-2448
www.nhlbi.nih.gov

Primary responsibility of this organization is the scientific investigation of heart, blood vessel, lung and blood disorders. Oversees research, demonstration, prevention, education, control and training activities in these fields and emphasizes the prevention and control of heart diseases.

Gary H. Gibbons, MD, Director
Kate O'Sullivan, Executive Officer

National Associations & Support Groups

66 **American Academy of Pediatrics**
345 Park Blvd
Itasca, IL 60143
800-433-9016
Fax: 847-434-8000
mcc@aap.org
www.aap.org

The American Academy of Pediatrics and its member pediatricians are committed to the attainment of optimal physical, mental and social health and well-being for all infants, children, adolescents, and young adults.

Mark Del Monte, JD, CEO/Executive VP
Lynn Olson, PhD, Vice President, Research
Vera Tait, MD, FAAP, Chief Medical Officer

67 **American Childhood Cancer Organization**
P.O. Box 498
Kensington, MD 20895
301-962-3520
855-858-2226
Fax: 310-962-3521
staff@acco.org
www.acco.org

The American Childhood Cancer Organization (ACCO) was founded in 1970 by a group of parents whose children had been diagnosed with cancer. Today ACCO is one of the largest grassroots, national organizations dedicated to improving the lives of children and adolescents with cancer and their families.

Ruth I. Hoffman, MPH, CEO
Krista Novak, Programs Manager
Blair Scroggs, Public Relations Coordinator

68 **Association of Child Life Professionals**
1820 N Fort Myer Drive, Ste 520
Arlington, VA 22209
501-483-4500
800-252-4515
Fax: 501-483-4482
aclpadmin@childlife.org
www.childlife.org

Professionals who strive to reduce the impact of stressful or traumatic life events and situations which affect the development, health and well being of infants, children, youth and families. They embrace the value of play as a healing modality while working to enhance the normal growth and development of children through assessment, intervention, prevention, advocacy and education. The council offers publications, annual conferences, professional certification and more.

Bailey Kasten, COO & Interim CEO
Yvonne Kassimatis, Marketing & Communications
Ramona Spencer, Director, Professional Development

69 **B.A.S.E. Camp Children's Cancer Foundation**
650 North Wymore Rd, #103
Winter Park, FL 32789
407-673-5060
Fax: 407-673-5095
info@basecamp.org
www.basecamp.org

Provides a year round base of support for children and families facing the challenge of living with cancer, hemophilia and other blood related illnesses.

Terri Jones, President
Cindy Whitaker, Parent & Program Coordinator
Rachel Perez, Office Administrator

70 **Believe In Tomorrow Children's Foundation**
6601 Frederick Road
Baltimore, MD 21228
410-744-1032
Fax: 410-744-1984
www.believeintomorrow.org

Provides housing services and a variety of special services and programs (such as beach and mountain retreats or attending Orioles games) to any child up to 18 years of age who is being treated for cancer. Services are provided free of charge and are available on an ongoing basis throughout treatment.

Brian Morrison, Founder & CEO
Richard E. McCready, Chairman
David Reymann, Vice Chairman

71 **CancerCare**
275 7th Avenue
New York, NY 10001
212-712-8400
800-813-4673
Fax: 212-712-8495
info@cancercare.org
www.cancercare.org

Dedicated to providing emotional support, information, and practical help to people with cancer and their loved ones. CancerCare is the oldest, largest, nonprofit agency devoted to offering professional services.

Patricia J Goldsmith, CEO
Christine Verini, RPh, COO

72 **Childhood Cancer Canada Foundation**
20 Queen Street W, Unit 702
Toronto, Ontario,
Canada
416-489-6440
800-363-1062
Fax: 416-489-9812
info@childhoodcancer.ca
www.childhoodcancer.ca

Founded in 1987, Childhood Cancer Canada (CCC) is the country's leading Foundation dedicated entirely to the fight against childhood cancer. Through their unique partnership will all of Canada's 17 childhood cancer hospitals and treatment centres, CCC can ensure that children with cancer are exposed to kinder and gentler treatments that will not only cure them but leave them with an improved quality of life into adulthood.

Glenn Fraser, Chair
Kathy Motton, Director, Marketing/Communication
Sandi Hancox, VP, Fundraising

73 **Childhood Leukemia Foundation**
807 Mantoloking Road
Brick, NJ 08723
732-920-8860
888-253-7109
www.clf4kids.org

Childhood Leukemia Foundation proudly promotes patient education, advocacy and self-esteem.

74 **Children's Cancer & Blood Foundation**
466 Lexington Avenue, 16th Floor
New York, NY 10017
info@childrenscbf.org
www.childrenscbf.org

The foundation's major emphasis is on blood diseases affecting children: leukemia, thalassemia, hemophilia, sickle cell anemia, platelet disorders, retinoblastoma and cancer.

Les J. Lieberman, Co-Chairman & Co-President
Ronald J. Iervolino, Co-Chairman & Co-President

75 **Children's Leukemia Research Association**
585 Stewart Avenue, Suite 520
Garden City, NY 11530
516-222-1944
Fax: 516-222-0457
www.childrensleukemia.org

A not-for-profit organization dedicated to raising funds to support research efforts towards finding the causes and cure for Leukemia.

Angela Russo, Executive Director

76 CureSearch for Children's Cancer
P.O. Box 45781
Baltimore, MD 21297
800-458-6223
Fax: 301-718-0047
info@curesearch.org
www.curesearch.org

CureSearch for Children's Cancer is a national non-profit foundation that accelerates the cure for children's cancer by driving innovation, eliminating research barriers and solving the field's most challenging problems.

Kay Koehler, CEO
Katharine A. Burke, COO & VP, Financing
Caitlyn W. Barrett, National Director, Research/Prgms

77 HairClub
www.hairclub.com
800-290-5511
www.hairclub.com

Since 1992, HairClub has offered free hair restoration services to children who suffer from diseases that lead to hair loss or alopecia. HairClub is a non-profit program that's available at no charge to children ages 6-17.

Sy Sperling, Founder

78 Just In Time
1737 Chestnut Street, #600
Philadelphia, PA 19103
215-977-7777
Fax: 215-247-0956
tome@softhats.com
www.softhats.com

All cotton headwear for girls and women who have experienced hair loss.

Verley Platt, President

79 Leukemia & Lymphoma Society
3 International Drive, Ste 200
Rye Brook, NY 10573
888-557-7177
www.lls.org

Large voluntary health organization dedicated to funding blood cancer research, education and patient services.

Louis J. DeGennaro, PhD, President & CEO
Troy Dunmire, COO
Gwen Nichols, MD, Chief Medical Officer

80 National Bone Marrow Transplant Link
2900 Union Lake Road, Ste 213
Commerce, MI 48382
800-546-5268
info@nbmtlink.org
www.nbmtlink.org

The mission of the National Bone Marrow Transplant Link is to help patients, caregivers, and families cope with the social and emotional challenges of bone marrow/stem cell transplant from diagnosis through survivorship by providing vital information and personalized support services.

Donna Posluszny, Board President
Peggy Burkhard, Executive Director
Cindy Burke, Director, Finance & Operations

81 National Coalition for Cancer Survivorship
8455 Colesville Road, Ste 930
Silver Spring, MD 20910
877-622-7937
info@canceradvocacy.org
www.canceradvocacy.org

NCCS advocates for quality cancer care for all people touched by cancer and provides tools that empower people to advocate for themselves. Founded by and for cancer survivors, NCCS created the widely accepted definition of survivorship and defines someone as a cancer survivor from the time of diagnosis and for the balance of life.

Samira K. Beckwith, Acting Chair
Shelley Fuld Nasso, CEO
Elena Jeannotte, VP, External Affairs

State Agencies & Support Groups

Alaska

82 Leukemia & Lymphoma Society - Washington/ Alaska Chapter
Leukemia & Lymphoma Society
5601 6th Avenue, Ste 182
Seattle, WA 98108
206-628-0777
anne.gillingham@lls.org
www.lls.org/washingtonalaska

Dedicated to finding cures for leukemia and related cancers and to improving the quality of life for patients and their families.

Anne Gillingham, Executive Director
Courtney Hale, Operations Director
Victoria Wenick, Senior Campaign Director

North Carolina

83 Leukemia & Lymphoma Society - North Carolina Chapter
Leukemia & Lymphoma Society
401 Harrison Oaks Blvd, Ste 200
Cary, NC 27513
919-367-4100
800-888-9934
Fax: 704-998-5010
emily.blust@lls.org
www.lls.org/north-carolina

The mission of The Leukemia & Lymphoma Society (LLS) is to Cure leukemia, lymphoma, Hodgkin's disease and myeloma, and improve the quality of life of patients and their families. LLS is the world's largest voluntary health agency dedicated to blood cancer. LLS funds lifesaving blood cancer research around the world and provides free information and support services.

Emily Blust, Executive Director

Ohio

84 Leukemia & Lymphoma Society - Central Ohio Chapter
2215 Citygate Drive, Suite A
Columbus, OH 43219
614-476-7194
800-686-CURE
Fax: 614-476-7189
breana.shawver@lls.org
www.lls.org/central-ohio

Dedicated to finding cures for leukemia and related cancers and to improving the quality of life for patients and their families.

Breana Shawver, Executive Director
Dan Swisher, Operations Manager

85 Leukemia & Lymphoma Society - Northern Ohio Chapter
5700 Brecksville Road 3rd Floor
Independence, OH 44131
216-264-5680
800-589-5721
Fax: 440-617-2879
lindsay.silverstein@lls.org
www.lls.org/northern-ohio

Dedicated to finding cures for leukemia and related cancers and to improving the quality of life for patients and their families.

Lindsay Silverstein, Executive Director
Deborah Kending, Patient Services Manager

86 Leukemia & Lymphoma Society - Tri-State Southern Ohio Chapter
4370 Glendale Milford Road
Cincinnati, OH 45242
513-698-2828
Fax: 513-351-5386
tom.carleton@lls.org
www.lls.org/tri-state-southern-ohio

Acute Lymphoblastic Leukemia / State Agencies & Support Groups

Dedicated to finding cures for leukemia and related cancers and to improving the quality of life for patients and their families. This chapter serves a 22-county geographic area that includes Adams, Brown, Butler, Clermont, Clinton, Darke, Gallia, Greene, Hamilton, Highland, Jackson, Lawrence, Meigs, Miami, Montgomery, Pike, Preble, Scioto and Warren counties in Ohio and Boone, Campbell and Kenton counties in Kentucky.

Tom Carleton, Executive Director
Cris Peterson, Dayton Area Director

Oklahoma

87 **Leukemia & Lymphoma Society - Oklahoma Chapter**
Leukemia & Lymphoma Society
500 N Broadway, Suite 250
Oklahoma City, OK 73102
405-943-8888
888-828-4572
Fax: 405-945-8355
jeannine.laughlin@lls.org
www.lls.org/oklahoma

Our Mission: Cure leukemia, lymphoma, Hodgkin's disease and myeloma, and improve the quality of life for patients and their families.

Jeannine Laughlin, Business Developmnt Mgr In Training

Oregon

88 **Leukemia & Lymphoma Society - Oregon Chapter**
9320 SW Barbur Boulevard Suite 350
Portland, OR 97219
503-245-9866
800-466-6572
Fax: 503-245-9865
stephanie.carlson@lls.org
www.lls.org

Dedicated to finding cures for leukemia and related cancers and to improving the quality of life for patients and their families.

Stephanie Carlson, Executive Director

Pennsylvania

89 **Leukemia & Lymphoma Society - Western Pennsylvania/West Virginia Chapter**
333 E. Carson Street, Ste, 441
Pittsburgh, PA 15219
412-263-2873
800-726-2873
Fax: 412-395-2888
christina.massari@lls.org
www.lls.org

Dedicated to finding cures for leukemia and related cancers and to improving the quality of life for patients and their families.

Tina Massari-Thompson, Executive Director
Jeanne Caliguiri, Director of Development
Robert Stout, Operations Director

Tennessee

90 **Leukemia & Lymphoma Society, Tennessee Chapter**
404 BNA Drive, Suite 102
Nashville, TN 37217
615-331-2980
800-332-2980
Fax: 615-331-2941
jeff.parsley@lls.org
www.lls.org/tennessee

To better serve the needs of Tennesseans - offers contribution-funded community services, family support groups, free educational materials and financial assistance for those affected by leukemia, Hodgkin's disease, myeloma and the lymphomas.

Jeff Parsley, Executive Director

Texas

91 **Leukemia & Lymphoma Society - North Texas Chapter**
8111 LBJ Freeway, Suite 425
Dallas, TX 75251
972-996-5900
800-800-6702
Fax: 972-239-0892
carol.withers@lls.org
www.lls.org

Dedicated to finding cures for leukemia and related cancers and to improving the quality of life for patients and their families.

Patricia Thomson, Executive Director
Stacey Russell, Deputy Executive Director
Kacy Lowe, Senior Director

92 **Leukemia & Lymphoma Society - South Central Texas - San Antonio Chapter**
1218 Arion Parkway, Ste 102
San Antonio, TX 78216
210-998-5400
800-683-2458
clarissa.flores@lls.org
www.lls.org/south-central-texas

Dedicated to finding cures for leukemia and related cancers and to improving the quality of life for patients and their families.

Clarissa Flores, Executive Director
Alana Seger, Area Director
Linda Juarez, Director, Operations

93 **Leukemia & Lymphoma Society - Texas Gulf Coast Chapter**
5433 Westheimer Suite 300
Houston, TX 77056
713-840-0483
Fax: 281-683-9504
billiesue.parris@lls.org
www.lls.org/texas-gulf-coast

Dedicated to finding cures for leukemia and related cancers and to improving the quality of life for patients and their families.

Billie Sue Parris, Executive Director
Charley Tauer, Development Director

Virginia

94 **Leukemia & Lymphoma Society - National Capital Area Chapter**
Leukemia & Lymphoma Society
3601 Eisenhower Avenue, Ste 450
Alexandria, VA 22304
703-399-2900
Fax: 703-960-0920
beth.gorman@lls.org
www.lls.org/national-capital-area

Serves the greater Washington DC metropolitan area, including Northern Virginia, Prince George's and Montgomery counties.

Beth Gorman, Executive Director
Jaclyn Toll, Deputy Executive Director
Mary Angelo, Sr Campaign Director, Special Event

Washington

95 **Leukemia & Lymphoma Society - Washington/ Alaska Chapter**
Leukemia & Lymphoma Society
5601 6th Avenue, Ste 182
Seattle, WA 98108
206-628-0777
anne.gillingham@lls.org
www.lls.org/washingtonalaska

Dedicated to finding cures for leukemia and related cancers and to improving the quality of life for patients and their families.

Anne Gillingham, Executive Director
Courtney Hale, Operations Director
Victoria Wenick, Senior Campaign Director

Wisconsin

96 **Leukemia & Lymphoma Society - Wisconsin Chapter**
4125 North 124th Street, No A
Brookfield, WI 53005
262-790-4701
800-261-7399
Fax: 262-790-4706
liz.klug@lls.org
www.lls.org/wisconsin

To serve Wisconsites touched by leukemia, lymphoma, Hodgkin's disease and myeloma.

Liz Klug, Executive Director
Karen Ropel, Deputy Executive Director
Naomi Gould, Director, Light The Night

Libraries & Resource Centers

97 **Children's National Health System**
George Washington University
111 Michigan Avenue NW
Washington, DC 20010
202-476-5000
888-884-2327
tbear@childrensnational.org
www.childrensnational.org

Children's National serves as the regional referral center for pediatric emergency, cancer, trauma, cardiac and critical care as well as neonatology, orthopaedic surgery, neurology, and neurosurgery.

Kurt Newman, MD, President and CEO
Vittorio Gallo, PhD, Chief Research Officer
Mark Batshaw, Executive VP & CAO

Research Centers

98 **International Bone Marrow Transplant Registry**
Medical College of Wisconsin
9200 W Wisconsin Avenue Suite C5500
Milwaukee, WI 53226
414-805-0700
Fax: 414-805-0714
contactus@cibmtr.org
www.cibmtr.org/pages/index.aspx

CIBMTR collaborates with the global scientific community to advance hematopoietic cell transplantation and cellular therapy research worldwide.

Jeffery Chell MD, Executive Leader
Mary Horowitz MD, Executive Leader
J. Douglas Rizzo MD, MS, Executive Leader

Conferences

99 **ACLP Annual Conference**
Association of Child Life Professionals
1820 N Fort Myer Drive, Ste 520
Arlington, VA 22209
501-483-4500
800-252-4515
Fax: 501-483-4482
aclpadmin@childlife.org
www.childlife.org

The premier educational experience for child life professionals. The largest gathering of child life specialists of the year, offers ample opportunities for both formal and informal networking with peers.

1,000 May

Bailey Kasten, COO & Interim CEO
Ramona Spencer, Manager, Professional Development
Yvonne Kassimatis, Marketing & Communications

Audio Video

100 **Coping with Childhood Cancer**
Films for the Humanities and Sciences
132 West 31st Street
New York, NY 10001
800-257-5126
Fax: 609-275-0266
custserv@films.com
www.ffh.films.com

Coping with chronic and perhaps fatal disease and gaining control over their lives is something that childhood cancer victims must learn. This program presents open and honest interviews with five family members of childhood cancer patients. The stress on the family is intense; the brothers and sisters of children with cancer or any chronic life-threatening illness are most severely affected emotionally.

28 minutes
ISBN: 1-421320-42-7

Web Sites

101 **ALL Kids**
www.all-kids.org/

www.all-kids.org/

ALL Kids is an Internet mailing list providing support for families and caregivers of children with Acute Lymphoblastic Leukemia.

102 **CancerCare**
275 7th Avenue
New York, NY 10001
212-712-8400
800-813-4673
Fax: 212-712-8495
info@cancercare.org
www.cancercare.org

Dedicated to providing emotional support, information, and practical help to people with cancer and their loved ones. CancerCare is the oldest, largest, nonprofit agency devoted to offering professional services.

Patricia J Goldsmith, CEO
Christine Verini, RPh, COO

103 **Children's Cancer Web**
www.cancerindex.org/ccw

www.cancerindex.org/ccw

An independent nonprofit site, established to provide a directory of childhood cancer resources.

104 **Leukemia & Lymphoma Society**
3 International Drive, Ste 200
Rye Brook, NY 10573
888-557-7177
www.lls.org

Large voluntary health organization dedicated to funding blood cancer research, education and patient services.

Louis J. DeGennaro, Ph.D., President/ CEO

Book Publishers

105 **Blood & Circulatory Disorders Sourcebook 4th Edition**
Omnigraphics
615 Griswold Street, Ste 520
Detroit, MI 48226
610-461-3548
800-234-1340
Fax: 800-875-1340
contact@omnigraphics.com
www.omnigraphics.com

Basic consumer health information on blood and its components, anemias, leukemias, bleeding disorders, and circulatory system disorders, including aplastic anemia, thrombophilia, RH disease and hemophilia.

Acute Lymphoblastic Leukemia / Magazines

664 pages
ISBN: 0-780814-76-9

106 Cancer Information for Teens, 4th Edition
Omnigraphics
615 Griswold Street, Ste 520
Detroit, MI 48226
610-461-3548
800-234-1340
Fax: 800-875-1340
contact@omnigraphics.com
www.omnigraphics.com

Updated information and facts about cancer causes, diagnosis, prevention and treatment especially for teens.

480 pages
ISBN: 0-780816-15-2

107 Cancer Sourcebook
Angela L. Williams, author
Omnigraphics
615 Griswold Street, Ste 520
Detroit, MI 48226
610-461-3548
800-234-1340
Fax: 800-875-1340
contact@omnigraphics.com
www.omnigraphics.com

Updated information and facts about cancer causes, diagnosis, prevention and treatment. Nearly 1.5 million people in the US are diagnosed with cancer every year.

1224 pages 8th Edition
ISBN: 0-780816-22-0

108 Childhood Diseases and Disorders Sourcebook, 4th Edition
Omnigraphics
615 Griswold Street, Ste 520
Detroit, MI 48226
610-461-3548
800-234-1340
Fax: 800-875-1340
contact@omnigraphics.com
www.omnigraphics.com

Basic and up to date consumer health information about common disorders that affect the physical, mental, and developmental health of school-age children.

792 pages
ISBN: 0-780815-38-4

109 Childhood Leukemia: A Guide for Families, Friends & Caregivers
O'Reilly & Associates
1005 Gravenstein Highway North
Sebastopol, CA 95472
707-827-7019
800-889-8969
Fax: 707-824-8268
orders@oreilly.com
www.oreilly.com

Features a wealth of tools to help parents become strong advocates for their child, detailed and precise medical information, and day-to-day practical advice to help cope with procedures, hospitalization, family and friends, schools, social, emotional and financial issues.

528 pages Softcover
ISBN: 0-596500-15-7

Tim O'Reilly, Founder/CEO

110 Draw Me a Picture
Cancervive
11636 Chayote Street
Los Angeles, CA 90049
310-203-9232
800-486-2873
Fax: 310-471-4618
cancervivr@aol.com
www.cancervive.org

A fun coloring book for children with cancer (ages three to six). Marty Bunny talks about how it was when he was in the hospital for cancer and invites readers to draw about their experiences.

111 Having Leukemia Isn't So Bad, of Course, It Wouldn't Be My First Choice
Sargasso Enterprises
18 Ginn Road
Winchester, MA 01890
781-729-9037
Fax: 781-729-2726
cak@krumme.com

Personal story of Catherine Krumme, diagnosed with leukemia at age four, relapsed at age seven, finished treatment at age ten. Catherine graduated from college in 1998 and went on to graduate school. The book is a supportive resource for families with cancer, for their friends, and for teachers working with children with health issues.

149 pages Softcover
ISBN: 0-963555-44-8

Ann Combs

112 Kathy's Hats: A Story of Hope
Albert Whitman and Company
250 South Northwest Highway, Suite 320
Park Ridge, IL 60068
847-232-2800
800-255-7675
Fax: 847-581-0039
mail@albertwhitman.com
www.albertwhitman.com

A charming book for ages five to ten about chemotherapy and the loss of Kathy's hair.

32 pages Hardcover
ISBN: 0-807541-16-8

Trudy Krisher, Author

113 Let's Talk About Going to the Hospital
Rosen Publishing Group's PowerKids Press
29 E 21st Street
New York, NY 10010
212-777-3017
800-237-9932
Fax: 888-436-4643
rosenpub@tribeca.ios.com
www.rosenpublishing.com

If a child has to check into the hospital, chances are he or she is already upset about being ill. Knowing how a hospital functions and what the procedures are, such as when family members can visit, will help in what is already a stressful situation. Grades K-5.

24 pages
ISBN: 0-823950-36-0

Roger Rosen, President

114 Surviving Childhood Cancer: A Guide for Families
New Harbinger Publications
5674 Shattuck Avenue
Oakland, CA 94609
510-652-0215
800-748-6273
Fax: 800-652-1613
customerservice@newharbinger.com
newharbinger.com

Cancer in a child is an overwhelming experience for a family. This book explains common medical procedures and offers readers practical advice about how to cope with emotions and stress during this time.

1998 215 pages
ISBN: 1-572241-02-0

Magazines

115 Coping with Cancer Magazine
PO Box 682268
Franklin, TN 37068
615-790-2400
Fax: 615-614-3986
info@copingmag.com
www.copingmag.com

A bimonthly publication devoted to people whose lives have been touched by cancer.

Paula Chadwell, Vice President

Acute Lymphoblastic Leukemia / Camps

Pamphlets

116 Resource Center for the American Alliance of Cancer - Pain Initiatives
Wisconsin Cancer Pain Initiative
1300 University Avenue, Room 4720
Madison, WI 53706
608-262-0978
Fax: 608-265-4014
trc@mailplus.wisc.edu
www.aacpi.org

A booklet that helps parents determine if their child is in pain and provides methods to manage the pain. Single copy free. Also available, a Handbook of Cancer Pain Management, 5th edition.

12 pages Paperback

Camps

117 Arizona Camp Sunrise & Sidekicks
PO Box 27872
Tempe, AZ 85285
480-382-8564
melissa@azcampsunrise.org
www.azcampsunrise.org

The camp is dedicated to provide an exciting, medically safe camp program for children whose families have been affected by cancer.

Melissa Lee, Camp Director

118 Big Sky Kids Cancer Camp
6901 Goldenstein Lane
Bozeman, MT 59715
406-586-1781
Fax: 406-586-5794
bigskykids@eaglemount.org
www.eaglemount.org

Provides a positive environment and give children, teens, and their parents emotional support, a sense of normalcy, and a network of friends who share similar experiences.

Mary Peterson, Executive Director
Chad Biggerstaff, Big Sky Program Director
Kara Erickson, Director

119 Camp Catch-A-Rainbow
American Cancer Society
1755 Abbey Rd
East Lansing, MI 48823
517-332-3300
kwilson@ymcastorercamps.org
www.cancer.org

Open to any child, ages 7 thru 15, who has, or has had, cancer.

Katie Wilson, Coordinator

120 Camp Fantastic
Special Love
117 Youth Development Court
Winchester, VA 22602
504-667-3774
888-930-2707
Fax: 540-667-8144
www.specialove.org

Nonprofit organization that provides enriching programs for children with cancer, including Camp Fantastic.

Dave Smith, CEO
Angela Ashman, Program Director

121 Camp Sunshine Dreams
PO Box 28232
Fresno, CA 93729
contact@campsunshinedreams.com
www.campsunshinedreams.com

Summer camp for children with cancer.

Anthony Aiello, Board Member

122 Des Moines YMCA Camp
1192 166th Drive
Boone, IA 50036
515-432-7558
Fax: 515-432-5414
ycamp@dmymca.org
www.y-camp.org

For boys and girls with cancer, diabetes, asthma, cystic fibrosis, hearing impaired and other disabilities.

David Sherry, Executive Director
Alex Kretzinger, Program Director

123 Okizu Foundation Camps
16 Digital Drive, Suite 130
Novato, CA 94949
415-382-9083
Fax: 415-382-8384
info@okizu.org
www.okizu.org

This foundation runs family camp programs for children who have cancer and their families, and for children who have or had a parent with cancer.

Lori Sparrow, Executive Director
Heather Ferrier, Camp Director of Operations

Description

124 ACUTE MYELOID LEUKEMIA

Synonyms: Acute granulocytic leukemia, Acute myeloblastic leukemia, Acute myelocytic leukemia, Acute myelogenous leukemia, Acute myelomonocytic leukemia, AML

Involves the following Biologic System(s):
Hematologic and Oncologic Disorders

Acute myeloid leukemia (AML) is a malignant disease, or cancer, characterized by excessive production in the bone marrow of the white blood cells called myelocytes, sometimes also known as granulocytes, which are vital in helping the body to combat and prevent infection. Although AML is primarily a disease of adulthood (median age at onset is 60 years), it is responsible for about 20% of all childhood leukemias.

The symptoms and characteristic findings associated with AML result from the accumulation of myelocytes in the bone marrow, eventually impairing the ability of the marrow to produce mature blood cells. In addition, myelocytes are released into the general blood circulation and carried to other organs, where they continue to grow at a rapid rate.

Children and young adults with AML exhibit fatigue, fever, lethargy, headache and bone or joint pain. In older adults, AML tends to have a slow, progressive onset, with lethargy, loss of appetite, and shortness of breath. Other findings may include enlargement of the liver and spleen (hepatosplenomegaly) and swollen lymph glands. Some children with AML may have swollen gums, as well as swelling of the salivary glands, which are located in front of the ears. Other effects of AML can include small leukemic cell tumors (chloromas) that develop under the skin or on the membranes surrounding the brain and spinal cord, and are followed by inflammation of these membranes (meningitis). Most children with AML develop irregularities in the blood, such as an abnormal deficiency in the numbers of circulating red blood cells (anemia) and platelets (thrombocytopenia), although the white blood cell count may range from low to high. Because AML directly affects cells that enable the body to fight off infection, one of its most serious effects is an increased susceptibility to severe, frequent infections.

AML results from mutations in the genes of myeloblasts or myelocytes, or from damage to these genes or chromosomes. This damage distorts the functions of the affected genes in such a way as to cause uncontrolled cell division and a subsequent rapid increase in the numbers of leukemic blood cells. Factors that may increase the risk for developing AML include genetic disorders such as trisomy 21 (the chromosome abnormality responsible for Down syndrome), Bloom syndrome (caused by a gene mutation and marked by small red lesions and sensitivity to light), Fanconi anemia (caused by any of several gene mutations), and certain other inherited disorders. Chemotherapy or radiation for earlier malignancies, as well as exposure to benzene or cigarette smoke, can also increase the risk of developing AML.

The diagnosis of AML is confirmed from a bone marrow sample obtained through biopsy. Treatment of AML is directed initially toward destroying leukemic cells through the use of drugs (chemotherapy) in an initial, induction phase intended to destroy leukemic cells and induce remission. This is followed with a second phase of chemotherapy to destroy any remaining leukemic cells, and by a further, "remission" phase of therapy to ensure lasting destruction of such cells. The chemotherapy used against AML may be given intravenously by infusion into the blood, or by infusion into the spinal canal. In some cases, radiation is directed at the brain and spinal cord to destroy leukemic cells. Chemotherapy or radiation directed at the brain and spinal cord is known as "intrathecal therapy." In some cases, bone marrow from a suitable donor is given to patients with AML to "reconstitute" or restore their capacity to produce normal myelocytes, and better enable them to defend themselves against infection and other effects of the disease.

Because the potent drugs used in chemotherapy also suppress white blood cell production, thus increasing susceptibility to infection, antibiotic therapy is often given to prevent infection. In some patients, transfusions of red blood cells and platelets are given to ease anemia and bleeding irregularities. Greater than 70% of adults younger than 60 achieve complete remission with treatment for AML. For some patients, a bone marrow or cord blood transplant may offer the best chance for a long-term remission.

Government Agencies

125 NIH/National Cancer Institute
Bethesda, MD 20892

800-422-6237
NCIinfo@nih.gov
www.cancer.gov

The National Cancer Institute coordinates the National Cancer Program, which conducts and supports research, training, health information dissemination, and other programs with respect to the cause, diagnosis, prevention, and treatment of cancer, rehabilitation from cancer, and the continuing care of cancer patients and the families of cancer patients.
Norman E. Sharpless, MD, Director
Douglas R. Lowy, MD, Principal Deputy Director

126 NIH/National Heart, Lung and Blood Institute
31 Center Drive, Bldg 31
Bethesda, MD 20892

877-645-2448
www.nhlbi.nih.gov

The National Heart, Lung, and Blood Institute (NHLBI) provides global leadership for a research, training, and education program to promote the prevention and treatment of heart, lung, and blood diseases and enhance the health of all individuals so that they can live longer and more fulfilling lives.
Gary H. Gibbons, MD, Director
Kate O'Sullivan, Executive Officer

National Associations & Support Groups

127 American Academy of Pediatrics
345 Park Blvd
Itasca, IL 60143

800-433-9016
Fax: 847-434-8000
mcc@aap.org
www.aap.org

The American Academy of Pediatrics and its member pediatricians are committed to the attainment of optimal physical, mental and social health and well-being for all infants, children, adolescents, and young adults.
Mark Del Monte, JD, CEO/Executive VP
Lynn Olson, PhD, Vice President, Research
Vera Tait, MD, FAAP, Chief Medical Officer

128 American Childhood Cancer Organization
P.O. Box 498
Kensington, MD 20895

301-962-3520
855-858-2226
Fax: 310-962-3521
staff@acco.org
www.acco.org

The American Childhood Cancer Organization (ACCO) was founded in 1970 by a group of parents whose children had been diagnosed with cancer. Today ACCO is one of the largest grassroots, national organizations dedicated to improving the lives of children and adolescents with cancer and their families.

Ruth I. Hoffman, MPH, CEO
Krista Novak, Programs Manager
Blair Scroggs, Public Relations Coordinator

129 Association of Child Life Professionals
1820 N Fort Myer Drive, Ste 520
Arlington, MD 22209
501-483-4500
800-252-4515
Fax: 501-483-4482
aclpadmin@childlife.org
www.childlife.org

Professionals who strive to reduce the impact of stressful or traumatic life events and situations which affect the development, health and well being of infants, children, youth and families. They embrace the value of play as a healing modality while working to enhance the normal growth and development of children through assessment, intervention, prevention, advocacy and education. The council offers publications, annual conferences, professional certification and more.

Bailey Kasten, COO & Interim CEO
Yvonne Kassimatis, Marketing & Communications
Ramona Spencer, Director, Professional Development

130 B.A.S.E. Camp Children's Cancer Foundation
650 North Wymore Rd, #103
Winter Park, FL 32789
407-673-5060
Fax: 407-673-5095
info@basecamp.org
www.basecamp.org

Provides a year round base of support for children and families facing the challenge of living with cancer, hemophilia and other blood related illnesses.

Terri Jones, President
Cindy Whitaker, Program Coordinator
Rachel Perez, Office Administrator

131 Believe In Tomorrow Children's Foundation
6601 Frederick Road
Baltimore, MD 21228
410-744-1032
Fax: 410-744-1984
www.believeintomorrow.org

Provides housing services and a variety of special services and programs (such as beach and mountain retreats or attending Orioles games) to any child up to 18 years of age who is being treated for cancer. Services are provided free of charge and are available on an ongoing basis throughout treatment.

Brian Morrison, Founder and CEO
Richard E McCready, Chairman
David Reymann, Vice Chairman

132 CancerCare
275 7th Avenue
New York, NY 10001
212-712-8400
800-813-4673
Fax: 212-712-8495
info@cancercare.org
www.cancercare.org

Dedicated to providing emotional support, information, and practical help to people with cancer and their loved ones. CancerCare is the oldest, largest, nonprofit agency devoted to offering professional services.

Patricia J Goldsmith, CEO
Christine Verini, RPh, COO

133 Childhood Leukemia Foundation
807 Mantoloking Road
Brick, NJ 08723
732-920-8860
888-253-7109
www.clf4kids.org

Childhood Leukemia Foundation proudly promotes patient education, advocacy and self-esteem.

134 Children's Cancer & Blood Foundation
466 Lexington Avenue, 16th Floor
New York, NY 10017
info@childrenscbf.org
www.childrenscbf.org

The foundation's major emphasis is on blood diseases affecting children: leukemia, thalassemia, hemophilia, sickle cell anemia, platelet disorders, retinoblastoma and cancer.

Les J. Lieberman, Co-Chairman & Co-President
Ronald J. Iervolino, Co-Chairman & Co-President

135 Children's Leukemia Research Association
585 Stewart Avenue, Suite 520
Garden City, NY 11530
516-222-1944
Fax: 516-222-0457
www.childrensleukemia.org

A not-for-profit organization dedicated to raising funds to support research efforts towards finding the causes and cure for Leukemia.

Angela Russo, Executive Director

136 HairClub
www.hairclub.com
800-290-5511
www.hairclub.com

Since 1992, HairClub has offered free hair restoration services to children who suffer from diseases that lead to hair loss or alopecia. HairClub is a non-profit program that's available at no charge to children ages 6-17.

Sy Sperling, Founder

137 ICARE
10421 Motor City Drive
Bethesda, MD 20827
301-512-7522
contact@icare.org
www.icare.org

The International Care Alliance for Research and Education (ICARE) is a nonprofit organization which provides high-quality, focused, user-friendly, cancer information to each patient as well as their physician on an on-going, and person to person basis.

138 Just In Time
1737 Chestnut Street, #600
Philadelphia, PA 19103
215-977-7777
Fax: 215-247-0956
tome@softhats.com
www.softhats.com

All cotton headwear for girls and women who have experienced hair loss.

Verley Platt, President

139 Leukemia & Lymphoma Society
3 International Drive, Ste 200
Rye Brook, NY 10573
888-557-7177
www.lls.org

Large voluntary health organization dedicated to funding blood cancer research, education and patient services.

Louis J. DeGennaro, PhD, President & CEO
Troy Dunmire, COO
Gwen Nichols, MD, Chief Medical Officer

140 National Bone Marrow Transplant Link
2900 Union Lake Road, Ste 213
Commerce, MI 48382
800-546-5268
info@nbmtlink.org
www.nbmtlink.org

The mission of the National Bone Marrow Transplant Link is to help patients, caregivers, and families cope with the social and emotional challenges of bone marrow/stem cell transplant from diagnosis through survivorship by providing vital information and personalized support services.

Donna Posluszny, Board President
Peggy Burkhard, Executive Director
Cindy Burke, Director, Finance & Operations

Acute Myeloid Leukemia / State Agencies & Support Groups

141 **National Coalition for Cancer Survivorship**
8455 Colesville Road, Ste 930
Silver Spring, MD 20910
877-622-7937
info@canceradvocacy.org
www.canceradvocacy.org

NCCS advocates for quality cancer care for all people touched by cancer and provides tools that empower people to advocate for themselves. Founded by and for cancer survivors, NCCS created the widely accepted definition of survivorship and defines someone as a cancer survivor from the time of diagnosis and for the balance of life.

Samira K. Beckwith, Acting Chair
Shelley Fuld Nasso, CEO
Elena Jeannotte, VP, External Affairs

State Agencies & Support Groups

New York

142 **Leukemia & Lymphoma Society - Westchester/Connecticut/Hudson Valley Chapter**
3 Landmark Square, Suite 330
Stamford, CT 06901
203-388-9160
deborah.barker@lls.org
www.lls.org

Cure leukemia, lymphoma, Hodgkin's disease and myeloma and improve the quality of life of patients and their families.

Deborah Barker, Executive Director
Brandy Sinisi, Operations Manager

143 **Leukemia & Lymphoma Society - Western & Central New York Chapter**
4043 Maple Road, Suite 105
Amherst, NY 14226
716-834-2578
800-955-4572
nancy.hails@lls.org
www.lls.org/western-central-new-york

Dedicated to finding cures for leukemia and related cancers and to improving the quality of life for patients and their families.

Nancy Hails, Executive Director
Luann Burgio, Deputy Executive Director
Sue Michalak, Operations Manager

North Carolina

144 **Leukemia & Lymphoma Society - North Carolina Chapter**
Leukemia & Lymphoma Society
401 Harrison Oaks Blvd, Ste 200
Cary, NC 27513
919-367-4100
800-888-9934
emily.blust@lls.org
www.lls.org/north-carolina

Dedicated to finding cures for leukemia and related cancers and to improving the quality of life for patients and their families.

Emily Blust, Executive Director

Ohio

145 **Leukemia & Lymphoma Society - Central Ohio Chapter**
2215 Citygate Drive, Suite A
Columbus, OH 43219
614-476-7194
800-686-CURE
Fax: 614-476-7189
breana.shawver@lls.org
www.lls.org/central-ohio

Dedicated to finding cures for leukemia and related cancers and to improving the quality of life for patients and their families.

Breana Shawver, Executive Director
Dan Swisher, Operations Manager

146 **Leukemia & Lymphoma Society - Northern Ohio Chapter**
5700 Brecksville Road 3rd Floor
Independence, OH 44131
216-264-5680
800-589-5721
Fax: 440-617-2879
lindsay.silverstein@lls.org
www.lls.org/northern-ohio

Dedicated to finding cures for leukemia and related cancers and to improving the quality of life for patients and their families.

Lindsay Silverstein, Executive Director
Deborah Kending, Patient Services Manager

147 **Leukemia & Lymphoma Society - Tri-State Southern Ohio Chapter**
4370 Glendale Milford Road
Cincinnati, OH 45242
513-698-2828
Fax: 513-351-5386
tom.carleton@lls.org
www.lls.org/tri-state-southern-ohio

Dedicated to finding cures for leukemia and related cancers and to improving the quality of life for patients and their families. This chapter serves a 22-county geographic area that includes Adams, Brown, Butler, Clermont, Clinton, Darke, Gallia, Greene, Hamilton, Highland, Jackson, Lawrence, Meigs, Miami, Montgomery, Pike, Preble, Scioto and Warren counties in Ohio and Boone, Campbell and Kenton counties in Kentucky.

Tom Carleton, Executive Director
Cris Peterson, Dayton Area Director
Roseann Hayes, Campaign Director, Special Events

Oklahoma

148 **Leukemia & Lymphoma Society - Oklahoma Chapter**
Leukemia & Lymphoma Society
500 N Broadway, Suite 250
Oklahoma City, OK 73102
405-943-8888
888-828-4572
Fax: 405-945-8355
jeannine.laughlin@lls.org
www.lls.org/oklahoma

Our Mission: Cure leukemia, lymphoma, Hodgkin's disease and myeloma, and improve the quality of life for patients and their families.

Jeannine Laughlin, Business Developmnt Mgr In Training

Oregon

149 **Leukemia & Lymphoma Society - Oregon Chapter**
9320 SW Barbur Boulevard Suite 350
Portland, OR 97219
503-245-9866
800-466-6572
Fax: 503-245-9865
stephanie.carlson@lls.org
www.lls.org

Dedicated to finding cures for leukemia and related cancers and to improving the quality of life for patients and their families.

Stephanie Carlson, Executive Director

Pennsylvania

150 **Leukemia & Lymphoma Society - Western Pennsylvania/West Virginia Chapter**
333 E. Carson Street, Ste. 441
Pittsburgh, PA 15219
412-263-2873
800-726-2873
Fax: 412-395-2888
christina.massari@lls.org
www.lls.org

Dedicated to finding cures for leukemia and related cancers and to improving the quality of life for patients and their families.

Tina Massari, Executive Director
Jeanne Caliguiri, Director of Development
Robert Stout, Operations Director

Acute Myeloid Leukemia / Web Sites

Tennessee

151   **Leukemia & Lymphoma Society, Tennessee Chapter**
404 BNA Drive, Suite 102
Nashville, TN 37217
615-331-2980
800-332-2980
Fax: 615-331-2941
jeff.parsley@lls.org
www.lls.org/tennessee

To better serve the needs of Tennesseans - offers contribution-funded community services, family support groups, free educational materials and financial assistance for those affected by leukemia, Hodgkin's disease, myeloma and the lymphomas.

Jeff Parsley, Executive Director

Texas

152   **Leukemia & Lymphoma Society - North Texas Chapter**
8111 LBJ Freeway, Suite 425
Dallas, TX 75251
972-996-5900
800-800-6702
Fax: 972-239-0892
carol.withers@lls.org
www.lls.org

Dedicated to finding cures for leukemia and related cancers and to improving the quality of life for patients and their families.

Patricia Thomson, Executive Director
Stacey Russell, Deputy Executive Director
Kacy Lowe, Senior Director

153   **Leukemia & Lymphoma Society - South Central Texas - San Antonio Chapter**
1218 Arion Parkway, Ste 102
San Antonio, TX 78216
210-998-5400
800-683-2458
clarissa.flores@lls.org
www.lls.org/south-central-texas

Dedicated to finding cures for leukemia and related cancers and to improving the quality of life for patients and their families.

Clarissa Flores, Executive Director
Alana Seger, Area Director
Linda Juarez, Director, Operations

154   **Leukemia & Lymphoma Society - Texas Gulf Coast Chapter**
5433 Westheimer Suite 300
Houston, TX 77056
713-840-0483
Fax: 281-683-9504
billiesue.parris@lls.org
www.lls.org/texas-gulf-coast

Dedicated to finding cures for leukemia and related cancers and to improving the quality of life for patients and their families.

Billie Sue Parris, Executive Director
Charley Tauer, Development Director

Virginia

155   **Leukemia & Lymphoma Society - National Capital Area Chapter**
3601 Eisenhower Avenue, Ste 450
Alexandria, VA 22304
703-399-2900
Fax: 703-960-0920
beth.gorman@lls.org
www.lls.org/national-capital-area

Serves the greater Washington DC metropolitan area, including Northern Virginia, Prince George's and Montgomery counties.

Beth Gorman, Executive Director
Jaclyn Toll, Deputy Executive Director
Mary Angelo, Sr Campaign Dir, Special Events

Wisconsin

156   **Leukemia & Lymphoma Society - Wisconsin Chapter**
200 S. Executive Drive Suite 203
Brookfield, WI 53005
262-790-4701
800-261-7399
Fax: 262-790-4706
liz.klug@lls.org
www.lls.org/wisconsin

To serve Wisconsites touched by leukemia, lymphoma, Hodgkin's disease and myeloma.

Liz Klug, Executive Director
Karen Ropel, Deputy Executive Director
Naomi Gould, Director, Light The Night

Libraries & Resource Centers

157   **Children's National Health System**
George Washington University
111 Michigan Avenue NW
Washington, DC 20010
202-476-5000
888-884-2327
tbear@childrensnational.org
www.childrensnational.org

Children's National serves as the regional referral center for pediatric emergency, cancer, trauma, cardiac and critical care as well as neonatology, orthopaedic surgery, neurology, and neurosurgery.

Kurt Newman, MD, President/CEO
Vittorio Gallo, PhD, Chief Research Officer
Mark Batshaw, Executive VP & CAO

Audio Video

158   **Coping with Childhood Cancer**
Films for the Humanities and Sciences
132 West 31st Street
New York, NY 10001
800-257-5126
Fax: 609-275-0266
custserv@films.com
www.ffh.films.com

Coping with chronic and perhaps fatal disease and gaining control over their lives is something that childhood cancer victims must learn. This program presents open and honest interviews with five family members of childhood cancer patients. The stress on the family is intense; the brothers and sisters of children with cancer or any chronic life-threatening illness are most severely affected emotionally.

28 minutes
ISBN: 1-421320-42-7

Web Sites

159   **CancerCare**
275 7th Avenue
New York, NY 10001
800-813-4673
info@cancercare.org
www.cancercare.org

Dedicated to providing emotional support, information, and practical help to people with cancer and their loved ones. CancerCare is the oldest, largest, nonprofit agency devoted to offering professional services.

Patricia J Goldsmith, CEO
Christine Verini, RPh, COO

160   **Children's Cancer Web**
www.cancerindex.org/ccw

www.cancerindex.org/ccw

An independent nonprofit site, established to provide a directory of childhood cancer resources.

Acute Myeloid Leukemia / Book Publishers

161 **Leukemia & Lymphoma Society**
3 International Drive, Ste 200
Rye Brook, NY 10573
888-557-7177
www.lls.org

Large voluntary health organization dedicated to funding blood cancer research, education and patient services.

Louis J. DeGennaro, Ph.D., President/ CEO

162 **Mediconsult**
www.mediconsult.com

www.mediconsult.com

We are committed to provide excellent and professional services to our business partners. Through a team approach we will develop, provide and continuously improve our knowledge and competency. We work towards the betterment of healthcare delivery systems for the community.

Book Publishers

163 **Blood & Circulatory Disorders Sourcebook 4th Edition**
Omnigraphics
615 Griswold Street, Ste 520
Detroit, MI 48226
610-461-3548
800-234-1340
Fax: 800-875-1340
contact@omnigraphics.com
www.omnigraphics.com

Basic consumer health information on blood and its components, anemias, leukemias, bleeding disorders, and circulatory system disorders, including aplastic anemia, thrombophilia, RH disease and hemophilia.

664 pages
ISBN: 0-780814-76-9

164 **Cancer Information for Teens, 4th Edition**
Omnigraphics
615 Griswold Street, Ste 520
Detroit, MI 48226
610-461-3548
800-234-1340
Fax: 800-875-1340
contact@omnigraphics.com
www.omnigraphics.com

Updated information and facts about cancer causes, diagnosis, prevention and treatment especially for teens.

480 pages
ISBN: 0-780816-15-2

165 **Cancer Sourcebook**

Angela L. Williams, author

Omnigraphics
615 Griswold Street, Ste 520
Detroit, MI 48226
610-461-3548
800-234-1340
Fax: 800-875-1340
contact@omnigraphics.com
www.omnigraphics.com

Updated information and facts about cancer causes, diagnosis, prevention and treatment. Nearly 1.5 million people in the US are diagnosed with cancer every year.

1224 pages 8th Edition
ISBN: 0-780816-22-0

166 **Childhood Diseases and Disorders Sourcebook, 4th Edition**
Omnigraphics
615 Griswold Street, Ste 520
Detroit, MI 48226
610-461-3548
800-234-1340
Fax: 800-875-1340
contact@omnigraphics.com
www.omnigraphics.com

Basic and up to date consumer health information about common disorders that affect the physical, mental, and developmental health of school-age children.

792 pages
ISBN: 0-780815-38-4

167 **Let's Talk About Going to the Hospital**
Rosen Publishing Group's PowerKids Press
29 E 21st Street
New York, NY 10010
212-777-3017
800-237-9932
Fax: 888-436-4643
rosenpub@tribeca.ios.com
www.rosenpublishing.com

If a child has to check into the hospital, chances are he or she is already upset about being ill. Knowing how a hospital functions and what the procedures are, such as when family members can visit, will help in what is already a stressful situation. Grades K-5.

24 pages
ISBN: 0-823950-36-0

Roger Rosen, President

168 **Let's Talk About When Kids Have Cancer**
Rosen Publishing Group's PowerKids Press
29 E 21st Street
New York, NY 10010
212-777-3017
800-237-9932
Fax: 888-436-4643
customerservice@rosenpub.com
www.rosenpublishing.com

In a straightforward yet comforting way, this book explains what cancer is, what kinds of treatments surround the disease and how to cope if a child has cancer. K-5.

24 pages Paperback
ISBN: 0-823951-95-6

169 **Surviving Childhood Cancer: A Guide for Families**
New Harbinger Publications
5674 Shattuck Avenue
Oakland, CA 94609
510-652-0215
800-748-6273
Fax: 800-652-1613
customerservice@newharbinger.com
newharbinger.com

Cancer in a child is an overwhelming experience for a family. This book explains common medical procedures and offers readers practical advice about how to cope with emotions and stress during this time.

1998 215 pages
ISBN: 1-572241-02-0

Pamphlets

170 **Acute Lymphocytic Leukemia**
Leukemia & Lymphoma Society
3 International Drive, Ste 200
Rye Brook, NY 10573
914-949-5213
Fax: 914-949-6691
www.lls.org

Information about acute lymphocytic leukemia for patients and their families and a glossary of terms to help readers understand technical terms.

16 pages

Louis J. DeGennaro, Ph.D., President/ CEO
Rosemarie Loffredo, CAO/ CFO
Mark Roithmyr, Chief Development Officer

Camps

171 **Arizona Camp Sunrise & Sidekicks**
PO Box 27872
Tempe, AZ 85285
480-382-8564
928-478-4564
melissa@azcampsunrise.org
www.azcampsunrise.org

The camp is dedicated to provide an exciting, medically safe camp program for children whose families have been affected by cancer.

Melissa Lee, Camp Director

172 Camp Catch-A-Rainbow
American Cancer Society
1205 E Saginaw Street
Lansing, MI 48906

517-371-2920
800-227-2345
kwilson@ymcastorercamps.org
www.cancer.org/camprainbow

Open to any child, age 7 thru 15, who has, or has had, cancer.

Katie Wilson, Coordinator

173 Camp Fantastic
Special Love
117 Youth Development Court
Winchester, VA 22602

703-667-3774
888-930-2707
www.specialove.org

Nonprofit organization that provides enriching programs for children with cancer, including Camp Fantastic.

Dave Smith, CEO
Angela Ashman, Program Director

174 Camp Sunshine Dreams
PO Box 28232
Fresno, CA 93729

contact@campsunshinedreams.com
www.campsunshinedreams.com

Summer camp for children with cancer.

Anthony Aiello, Board Member

175 Des Moines YMCA Camp
1192 166th Drive
Boone, IA 50036

515-432-7558
Fax: 515-432-5414
ycamp@dmymca.org
www.y-camp.org

For boys and girls with cancer, diabetes, asthma, cystic fibrosis, hearing impaired and other disabilities.

David Sherry, Executive Director
Mike Havlik, Program Director
Alex Kretzinger, Program Director- Summer Camp

176 Okizu Foundation Camps
16 Digital Drive, Suite 130
Novato, CA 94949

415-382-9083
Fax: 415-382-8384
info@okizu.org
www.okizu.org

This foundation runs family camp programs for children who have cancer and their families, and for children who have or had a parent with cancer.

Lori Sparrow, Executive Director
Heather Ferrier, Camp Director of Operations

Albinism / Description

Description

177 ALBINISM
Covers these related disorders: Tyrosinase negative albinism, Oculocutaneous albinism, Waardenburg syndrome
Involves the following Biologic System(s):
Dermatologic Disorders,
Genetic/Chromosomal/Syndrome/Metabolic Disorders

Albinism refers to a condition that is present at birth (congenital) and results from an inability of the body to produce and distribute the pigment melanin, which normally gives the skin, hair, and eyes their coloration. Albinism occurs in all races and in about one in 20,000 individuals worldwide.

Although there are several types of albinism, and all are caused by genetic defects, two major forms of the condition - tyrosinase-negative, and tyrosinase-positive - have been identified.

Tyrosinase-negative, or type I, albinism is the most severe form of generalized oculocutaneous albinism, or OCA. It results from a genetic defect that reduces or eliminates the activity of tyrosinase, an enzyme essential to the proper metabolism of melanin. Because of the absence of this enzyme, type I is characterized by a complete lack of melanin in the hair, skin, and eyes, resulting in pink or white skin, white hair, and eyes that may appear pink or bluish-gray. Other eye-related or optical irregularities also occur in type I, such as involuntary, flickering-type movements of the eyes (nystagmus), nearsightedness (myopia), and sensitivity or intolerance to bright light (photophobia). OCA type 1 is an autosomal recessive condition, meaning that it develops only when both parents carry the gene responsible for OCA type 1. A variant form of OCA type 1, in which some pigmentation develops in the skin, hair, and eyes with age, occurs in Amish communities in the United States. The optical irregularities in this variant form of OCA type 1 are usually less severe than in the more common form of the condition.

Tyrosinase-positive, or type II OCA is more common and less severe than type I. Rather than being caused by an absence of the enzyme tyrosinase, this type of albinism is thought to result from an inborn error in the transport of the substance known as tyrosinea which the body normally transforms into melanin. Newborns with OCA type II may have little to no melanin at birth, but it may accumulate in their skin, hair, and eyes as these children grow, producing some darkening of skin color during the course of childhood. Moreover, ocular abnormalities present at birth may ease over the course of childhood. Like OCA type I, OCA type II is caused by a genetic defect and is inherited as an autosomal recessive trait. Several variant forms of tyrosinase-positive albinism may be present as a part of several syndromes that affect other organs or systems of the body in addition to its pigmentation. Among these syndromes are Hermansky-Pudlak syndrome, Chediak-Higashi syndrome, and Cross-McKusick-Breen syndrome.

Types of albinism other than OCA types I and II may include ocular albinism that chiefly affects the pigmentation of the eyes and is characterized by photophobia; nystagmus; and decreased visual acuity. The hair and eyes of such persons may be of lighter than average color, but not excessively so. In what are known as Nettleship-Falls type ocular albinism and Forsius-Eriksson syndrome, ocular albinism may be inherited as a trait, or characteristic, that is associated with or "linked to" the X chromosome, which is inherited from an individual's mother. Ocular albinism may also be inherited as an autosomal dominant trait, in which it results from only a single copy of a defective gene, inherited from either a mother or a father.

Besides these various types of albinism, some individuals may have partial albinism, sometimes called piebaldism, which is characterized by patchy, unpigmented areas of hair or skin. In some individuals this type of albinism may be manifested only by a lock of white hair near the forehead. Piebaldism is inherited as an autosomal dominant trait, and may be part of the condition known as Waardenburg syndrome, which is also characterized by hearing impairment.

Because people with albinism have an increased risk of developing skin cancer from exposure to the sun, protection of their skin is highly important. This may be accomplished with suitable clothing and the use of an appropriate sunscreen of SPF 15 or greater. The deficit in pigmentation of the eyes in albinism may require the use of tinted or dark glasses to reduce light sensitivity. Children with albinism should have early evaluation and treatment for any visual irregularities caused by the condition, to minimize any difficulties at school. Other treatment is symptomatic and supportive.

Government Agencies

178 NIH/ Eunice Kennedy Shriver National Institute of Child Health & Human Development
P.O. Box 3006
Rockville, MD 20847

800-370-2943
Fax: 866-760-5947
www.nichd.nih.gov

Conducts and supports laboratory research, clinical trials, and epidemiological studies that explore health processes; examines the impact of disabilities, diseases, and variations on the lives of individuals; and sponsors training programs for scientists, health care providers, and researchers to ensure that NICHD research can continue.

Diana W. Bianchi, Director
Alison Cernich, PhD, Deputy Director

National Associations & Support Groups

179 American Academy of Pediatrics
345 Park Blvd
Itasca, IL 60143

800-433-9016
Fax: 847-434-8000
mcc@aap.org
www.aap.org

The American Academy of Pediatrics and its member pediatricians are committed to the attainment of optimal physical, mental and social health and well-being for all infants, children, adolescents, and young adults.

Mark Del Monte, JD, CEO/Executive VP
Lynn Olson, PhD, Vice President, Research
Vera Tait, MD, FAAP, Chief Medical Officer

180 American Council of the Blind
1703 N Beauregard Street, Ste 420
Alexandria, VA 22311

202-467-5081
800-424-8666
Fax: 703-465-5085
info@acb.org
www.acb.org

The council strives to improve the well being of all blind and visually impaired people by serving as a representative national organization of blind people, elevating the social, economic and cultural levels of blind people, improving educational and rehabilitation facilities and opportunities and cooperating with the public and private institutions and organizations concerned with blind services.

Eric Bridges, Executive Director
Clark Rachfal, Director, Advocacy/Govt'l Affairs
Nancy Marks-Becker, CFO

Albinism / Conferences

181 **American Foundation for the Blind**
1401 South Clark Street, Ste 730
Arlington, VA 22202
212-502-7600
info@afb.net
www.afb.org

The American Foundation of the Blind, has been eliminating barriers the prevent people who are blind or visually impaired from reaching their potential. AFB is dedicated to addressing the most critical issues of facing this growing population: independent living, literacy, employment, and technology.

Kirk Adams, President & CEO
Elizabeth Neal, Director, Communications
Adrianna Montague, Chief Community Engagement Officer

182 **American School Counselor Association**
1101 King Street, Ste 310
Alexandria, VA 22314
703-683-2722
asca@schoolcounselor.org
www.schoolcounselor.org

The mission of ASCA is to represent professional school counselors and to promote professionalism and ethical practices.

Jill Cook, Executive Director
Amanda Fitzgerald, Assistant Deputy Executive Director
Kathleen M Rakestraw, Director of Communications

183 **Genetic Alliance**
426400 Woodfield Road, Ste 189
Damascus, MD 20872
202-966-5557
Fax: 202-966-8553
info@geneticalliance.org
www.geneticalliance.org

World's leading nonprofit health advocacy organization committed to transforming health through genetics and promoting an environment of openness centered on the health of individuals, families, and communities.

Sharon Terry, CEO
Ruth Child, CFO
Natasha Bonhomme, Chief Strategy Officer

184 **Hermansky-Pudlak Syndrome Network**
One South Road
Oyster Bay, NY 11771
800-789-9477
Fax: 516-922-0640
info@hpsnetwork.org
www.hpsnetwork.org

A volunteer, support group for people and families dealing with Hermansky-Pudlak Syndrome (HPS) and related disorders such as Chediak Higashi Syndrome.

Donna Jean Appell, Founder & President
Heather Kirkwood, VP, Director of Outreach

185 **National Mental Health Consumers' Self-Help Clearinghouse**
1211 Chestnut Street, Suite 1207
Philadelphia, PA 19107
215-751-1810
800-553-4539
Fax: 215-636-6312
selfhelpclearinghouse@gmail.com
www.mhselfhelp.org

The Clearinghouse works to foster peer empowerment through our website, up-to-date news and information announcements, a directory of peer-driven services, electronic and printed publications, training packages, and individual and onsite consultation

Joseph Rogers, Founder/Executive Director
Susan Rogers, Director

186 **National Organization for Albinism and Hypopigmentation**
PO Box 959
East Hampstead, NH 03826
603-887-2310
800-473-2310
Fax: 603-887-6049
info@albinism.org
www.albinism.org

NOAH is a volunteer organization for persons and families involved with the condition of albinism. It does not diagnose, treat, or provide genetic counseling. It is involved in self-help, while trying to promote research and education.

Diana McCown, Interim Executive Director

187 **Positive Exposure**
14 E 109th Street
New York, NY 10029
212-420-1931
rick@positiveexposure.org
positiveexposure.org

Utilizes photography and video interviews to investigate the social and psychological experiences of people with albinism of all ages and ethnocultural heritages. This innovative program challenges the stigma associated with difference, attacks public fears about difference and celebrates the richness of genetic variation.

Rick Guidotti, Founder and Director

188 **Society for Pediatric Dermatology**
8365 Keystone Crossing, Ste 107
Indianapolis, IN 46240
317-202-0224
Fax: 317-205-9481
info@pedsderm.net
www.pedsderm.net

The objective of the Society is to promote, develop and advance education, research and care of skin disease in all pediatric age groups.

Kent Lindeman, Executive Director

189 **Vision of Children Foundation**
4310 Genesee Ave, Suite 101
San Diego, CA 92117
858-560-5181
Fax: 858-560-1926
www.familyvisioncaresd.com

Provides information, promotes research and assists the families of blind and visually impaired children, including those with ocular albinism, in locating organizations and service providers who can give support.

Gary Sneag, Manager

Conferences

190 **American School Counselor Association Annual Conference**
1101 King Street, Suite 310
Alexandria, VA 22314
703-683-2722
800-306-4722
Fax: 703-997-7572
asca@schoolcounselor.org
www.schoolcounselor.org

The mission of ASCA is to represent professional school counselors and to promote professionalism and ethical practices.

3,000 Attendees

Richard Wong, Executive Director
Jennifer Walsh, Director, Education & Training
Kathleen M Rakestraw, Director of Communications

191 **Annual World Symposium on Ocular Albinism**
11975 El Camino Real, Suite 104
San Diego, CA 92130
858-314-7917
Fax: 858-314-7920
info@visionofchildren.org
www.visionofchildren.org

The Vision of Children Foundation's team of doctors, scientists and researchers will collaborate on their research efforts in Ocular Albinism.

March

Samuel A Hardage, Chairman & Co-Founder
Vivian L Hardage, Co-Founder
Debora B Farber, Chief Scientific Advisor

192 **Hermansky-Pudlak Syndrome Network Annual Family Conference**
One South Road
Oyster Bay, NY 11771
516-922-3440
800-789-9477
Fax: 516-922-4022
appell@worldnet.att.net
www.medhelp.org/web/hpsn.htm

A volunteer, nonprofit, self-help support group for persons and families dealing with the syndrome. Assists in networking families and doctors, maintains a bibliography of materials and promotes research.

Albinism / Audio Video

Donna Jean Appell, Founder & President

193 **NFB National Convention**
American Foundation for the Blind
2 Penn Plaza, Suite 1102
New York, NY 10121
212-502-7600
800-232-5463
Fax: 212-502-7777
afbinfo@afb.net
www.afb.org

The largest disability conference of its kind.

3000

Carl R Augusto, President/CEO
Paul Schroeder, Vice President
Rick Bozeman, CFO

194 **Society for Pediatric Dermatology Annual Meeting**
8365 Keystone Crossing, Suite 107
Indianapolis, IN 46240
317-202-0224
Fax: 317-205-9481
info@pedsderm.net
www.pedsderm.net

Kent Lindeman, Executive Director
Stephanie Garwood, Meetings Manager

Audio Video

195 **Assistive Media**
400 Maynard Street, Suite 404
Ann Arbor, MI 48104
734-332-0369
info@assistivemedia.org
www.assistivemedia.org/

The mission of Assistive Media is to heighten the educational, cultural, and quality-of-living standard for people with disabilities and help achieve independence and become better integrated within the mainstream of society and community life in general. Assistve Media accomplishes this by providing free-of-charge, copyright-approved, high caliber audio literary works to the world-wide disability community via the internet effectively, inexpensively, and efficiently.

David Henry Erdody, Founder

Web Sites

196 **International Albinism Center**
www.cbc.umn.edu/iac/

www.cbc.umn.edu/iac/

IAC is a team of dedicated research professionals interested in understanding the basis of albinism in humans. We are a munlti-disciplinary group of researchers that include interests in clinical genetics, molecular biology, ophthalmology, dermatology, and biochemistry, all with a central theme of understnading the cause and effect of albinism and other forms of pigment loss in humans.

Journals

197 **Pediatric Dermatology Journal**
Society for Pediatric Dermatology
8365 Keystone Crossing, Suite 107
Indianapolis, IN 46240
317-202-0224
Fax: 317-205-9481
info@pedsderm.net
www.pedsderm.net

Answers the need for new ideas and strategies for today's pediatrician or dermatologist.

6 issues/yr

Kent Lindeman, Executive Director

Newsletters

198 **Hermansky-Pudlak Syndrome Network Newsletter**
One South Road
Oyster Bay, NY 11771
800-789-9477
Fax: 516-624-0640
info@hpsnetwork.org
www.hpsnetwork.org

A volunteer, nonprofit, self-help support group for persons and families dealing with the syndrome. Assists in networking families and doctors, maintains a bibliography of materials and promotes research.

Donna Jean Appell, R.N., Founder/President
Heather Kirkwood, VP/ Director of Outreach

Camps

199 **Camp Discovery**
American Academy of Dermatology
9500 W. Bryn Mawr Avenue, Ste 500
Rosemont, IL 60018
847-240-1737
Fax: 847-240-1859
jmueller@aad.org
www.campdiscovery.org

A camp for young people with chronic skin conditions. There is no fee and transportation is provided. Five locations: Camp Victory in Millville, PA, Camp Knutson in Crosslake, MN, Camp For All in Burton, TX, Channel 3 Kids Camp in Andover, CT, and Camp Seymour in Gig harbor, WA.

J Mueller, Camp Contact
Irvin Bomberger, Interim Executive Director

Description

200 ALOPECIA AREATA

Synonyms: Alopecia circumscripta, Androgenetic alopecia, Pelade

Involves the following Biologic System(s):

Dermatologic Disorders, Immunologic and Rheumatologic Disorders

Alopecia is partial or complete loss of hair (baldness) and may result from genetic factors, aging or local or systemic disease. Alopecia areata is characterized by the sudden, localized loss of patches of scalp hair and other areas of hair growth, such as the eyelashes and eyebrows. These patches are usually well-defined, round or oval in shape, and most often appear on the scalp or beard area. On rare occasions, progression of hair loss may result in the total loss of scalp hair in a condition called alopecia totalis. If the disease progresses to include the total loss of both scalp and body hair, the condition is called alopecia universalis. Another uncommon form of alopecia areata called ophiasis involves the loss of hair in a continuous band around the head. If hair loss associated with alopecia areata is not widespread, the condition is usually reversible, with most patients exhibiting new hair growth within a few months to a year; however, recurrences are quite common. Children who develop this condition at a very young age, patients who experience recurring episodes, and those who have extensive involvement are less likely to experience spontaneous remission. Although this disease occurs most commonly in the adult population, approximately 20 percent of those affected develop the disorder between birth and 20 years of age. This type of hair loss is different than male pattern baldness, an inherited condition.

Although the skin in the area of hair loss may appear unremarkable, microscopic examination may reveal the presence of inflammation. In addition, some individual hairs that appear at the margins of the bald, patchy areas may be easily removed and, upon microscopic examination, reveal a lightly-pigmented, tapered hair shaft that ends in a hair root that is reduced in size (exclamation hairs). Symptoms or characteristic findings sometimes associated with alopecia areata include the development of irregularities such as nail pitting and ridging, allergic or hypersensitivity reactions, and opacities of the lenses of the eye (cataracts). Alopecia areata may also be associated with certain autoimmune diseases such as Addison disease, Hashimoto thyroiditis, vitiligo, and others. In addition, approximately seven percent of children with Trisomy 21 exhibit the symptoms associated with alopecia areata.

The exact cause of alopecia areata is not known; however, approximately 25 percent of those affected are believed to inherit the disease through autosomal dominant transmission. Other suggested causes include autoimmune responses or emotional factors related to stress. Because alopecia areata so often resolves spontaneously, treatment for this disease in young children may simply include ongoing observation. A variety of treatments can be tried. Steroid injections and cream to the scalp have been used for many years. Other medications include minoxidil, irritants (anthralin or topical coal tar), and topical immunotherapy (cyclosporine), each of which are sometimes used in different combinations. The use of hairpieces and other cosmetic considerations may be beneficial to the emotional well-being of children, especially adolescents, with alopecia areata.

National Associations & Support Groups

201 American Academy of Dermatology
P.O. Box 1968
Des Plaines, IL 60017

847-240-1280
888-462-3376
mrc@aad.org
www.aad.org

To promote and advance the art of medicine and surgery of the skin; promote the highest possible standards in clinical practice, education and research in dermatology and related disciplines.

202 American Academy of Pediatrics
345 Park Blvd
Itasca, IL 60143

800-433-9016
Fax: 847-434-8000
mcc@aap.org
www.aap.org

The American Academy of Pediatrics and its member pediatricians are committed to the attainment of optimal physical, mental and social health and well-being for all infants, children, adolescents, and young adults.

Mark Del Monte, JD, CEO/Executive VP
Lynn Olson, PhD, Vice President, Research
Vera Tait, MD, FAAP, Chief Medical Officer

203 American Autoimmune Related Diseases Association
19176 Hall Road, Suite 130
Clinton, MI 48038

586-776-3900
aarda@aarda.org
www.aarda.org

The American Autoimmune Related Diseases Association is dedicated to the eradication of autoimmune diseases and the alleviation of suffering and the socioeconomic impact of autoimmunity through fostering and facilitating collaboration in the areas of education, public awareness, research, and patient services in an effective, ethical and efficient manner.

Lilly Stairs, Interim President/CEO
Laura Simpson, COO

204 American Hair Loss Association
23679 Calabasas Road, Suite 682
Calabasas, CA 91301

info-ahla@americanhairloss.org
www.americanhairloss.org

The American Hair Loss Association is committed to educating and improving the lives of all those affected by hair loss. It is their goal to create public awareness of this devastating disease of the spirit, and to legitimize hair loss of all forms in the eyes of our medical community, the media and society as a whole.

205 Children's Alopecia Project
906 Penn Avenue, First Floor
Wyomissing, PA 19610

610-468-1011
www.childrensalopeciaproject.org

The mission is to help any child in need who is living with hair loss due to all forms of Alopecia.

Jeff Woytovich, Founder
Jeffrey Miller, MD, Medical Director

206 National Alopecia Areata Foundation
65 Mitchell Boulevard, Suite 200-B
San Rafael, CA 94903

415-472-3780
Fax: 415-480-1800
info@naaf.org
www.naaf.org

NAAF supports research to find a cure or acceptable treatment for alopecia areata, supports those with the disease, and educates the public about alopecia areata. NAAF is widely regarded as the largest, most influential and most representative foundation associated with alopecia areata.

Andy Bryant, Acting CEO
Jeanne Rappoport, Chief Administrative Officer
Gary Sherwood, Communications Director

Alopecia Areata / Conferences

207 **Society for Pediatric Dermatology**
8365 Keystone Crossing, Ste 107
Indianapolis, IN 46240

317-202-0224
Fax: 317-205-9481
info@pedsderm.net
www.pedsderm.net

The objective of the Society is to promote, develop and advance education, research and care of skin disease in all pediatric age groups.

Kent Lindeman, Executive Director

Conferences

208 **National Alopecia Areata Foundation Annual Conference**
National Alopecia Areata Foundation
65 Mitchell Boulevard, Suite 200-B
San Rafael, CA 94903

415-472-3780
Fax: 415-480-1800
info@naaf.org
www.naaf.org

A four day conference for people of all ages who have alopecia areata or care about someone who has alopecia areata. Provides the attendee with the latest medical and research updates, to better understand and manage alopecia areata, and also provides them with a wealth of support.

June

Andy Bryant, Acting CEO
Jeanne Rappoport, Chief Administrative Officer
Gary Sherwood, Communications Director

Web Sites

209 **Children's Alopecia Project**
www.childrensalopeciaproject.org

www.childrensalopeciaproject.org

The mission is to help any child in need who is living with hair loss due to all forms of Alopecia.

Jeff Woytovich, Founder/Director
Betsy Woytovich, Co-Founder

Journals

210 **Pediatric Dermatology Journal**
Society for Pediatric Dermatology
8365 Keystone Crossing, Suite 107
Indianapolis, IN 46240

317-202-0224
Fax: 317-205-9481
info@pedsderm.net
www.pedsderm.net

Answers the need for new ideas and strategies for today's pediatrician or dermatologist.

6 issues/yr

Kent Lindeman, Executive Director

Newsletters

211 **Infocus Newsletter**
American Autoimmune Related Diseases Associaion
19176 Hall Road, Suite 130
Clinton, MI 48038

586-776-3900
aarda@aarda.org
www.aarda.org

The national newsletter of AARDA.

Alpha-1-Antitrypsin Deficiency / National Associations & Support Groups

Description

212 ALPHA-1-ANTITRYPSIN DEFICIENCY
Involves the following Biologic System(s):
Gastrointestinal Disorders,
Genetic/Chromosomal/Syndrome/Metabolic Disorders,
Respiratory Disorders

Alpha-1-antitrypsin (AAT) deficiency is a hereditary metabolic disorder characterized by deficiency of alpha-1-antitrypsin, an enzyme that is produced by the liver and inhibits the actions of other enzymes that break down certain proteins. Deficiency of alpha-1-antitrypsin may result in emphysema, a progressive destructive change in the lungs. In addition, some patients may experience liver disease that is thought to result from abnormal retention of the alpha-1-antitrypsin enzyme in liver cells. Alpha-1-antitrypsin deficiency is caused by certain changes (mutations) of a gene known as Pi (protease inhibitor). Alpha-1-antitrypsin deficiency is typically inherited as an autosomal recessive trait due to inheritance of two deficiency-causing genes (homozygosity).

The specific symptoms associated with alpha-1-antitrypsin deficiency as well as the age of onset vary from patient to patient. Shortly after birth, a small percentage of affected children may develop suppression or cessation of the flow of bile (neonatal cholestasis). Bile, a liquid secreted by the liver, carries waste products away from the liver and assists in the digestion of fats in the small intestine. During the first week of life, affected infants may have yellowish discoloration of the skin, whites of the eyes, and mucous membranes (jaundice); abnormal enlargement of the liver (hepatomegaly); and the presence of unabsorbed fat in the feces. Jaundice often spontaneously resolves within two to four months after birth. Affected infants and children may appear to have no further associated symptoms (asymptomatic), may have chronic liver disease, or, in the most severe cases, may experience scarring of the liver and gradual impairment of liver function (cirrhosis). Older children may develop chronic liver disease or cirrhosis and associated high blood pressure within veins from the spleen and intestines to the liver (portal hypertension). In some patients with portal hypertension, there may be a diversion of portal circulation to veins in the walls of the stomach and esophagus, causing abnormal widening of such blood vessels (esophageal varices). Without treatment, some patients with liver disease may experience potentially life-threatening complications.

In general, AAT deficiency leads to emphysema, progressive degeneration of and destructive changes in the air sacs (alveoli) of the lungs in the fourth decade of life in smokers and a decade later in nonsmokers. (emphysema).

In children with alpha-1-antitrypsin deficiency, the treatment of associated liver disease is primarily symptomatic and supportive. AAT deficiency is the main cause of liver transplantation in children. Preventing or slowing the progression of lung disease is the major goal of AAT deficiency management. No treatment for emphysema has a greater effect on survival than quitting smoking. Other options include prompt, aggressive treatment of respiratory infections and provision of oxygen therapy. Medications are available to improve lung function. In addition, patients should avoid exposure to tobacco smoke, aerosol sprays, and other lung irritants. Alpha-1-antitrypsin enzyme replacement therapy (e.g., prolastin therapy) is also available. Two surgical approaches may help selected patients with AAT deficiency - volume-reduction surgery and lung transplantation.

National Associations & Support Groups

213 AlphaNet, Inc.
www.alphanet.org

www.alphanet.org

Founded to improve the lives of individuals affected by Alpha-1 Antitrypsin Deficiency. AlphaNet provides a wide range of specialized programs and services designed to meet the specific needs of the Alphas it serves.
Mark Delvaux, President/CEO
Christine Lanser Yllanes, Director of Communications

214 American Academy of Pediatrics
345 Park Blvd
Itasca, IL 60143
800-433-9016
Fax: 847-434-8000
mcc@aap.org
www.aap.org

The American Academy of Pediatrics and its member pediatricians are committed to the attainment of optimal physical, mental and social health and well-being for all infants, children, adolescents, and young adults.
Mark Del Monte, JD, CEO/Executive VP
Lynn Olson, PhD, VP, Research
Vera Tait, MD, FAAP, Chief Medical Officer

215 American Liver Foundation
P.O. Box 299
West Orange, NJ 07052
800-465-4837
www.liverfoundation.org

The American Liver Foundation is the nation's leading nonprofit organization promoting liver health and disease prevention. ALF provides research, education and advocacy for those affected by liver-related diseases, including hepatitis.
Lorraine Stiehl, CEO
David Ticker, Executive VP & CFO

216 American Lung Association
55 W. Wacker Drive, Suite 1150
Chicago, IL 60601
800-586-4872
info@lung.org
www.lung.org

The American Lung Association fights lung disease in all its forms, with special emphasis on asthma, tobacco control and environmental health. The American Lung Association is funded with contributions from the public, along with gifts and grants from corporations, foundations and government agencies. The association achieves its many successes through the work of thousands of committed volunteers and staff.
Harold P. Wimmer, National President & CEO
Albert Rizzo, MD, Chief Medical Officer
Sue Swan, Chief Development Officer

217 Children's Liver Association for Support Services
PO Box 186
Monaca, PA 15061
724-581-5527
classkidscares@gmail.com
www.classkids.org

CLASS is an all volunteer, nonprofit organization dedicated to serving the emotional, educational and financial needs of families coping with childhood liver disease and transplantation. Its goal is to be both a service to families and a valuable resource for the medical community.
Stephan Circle, Co-President
Tamara Circle, Co-President

218 Genetic Alliance
426400 Woodfield Road, Ste 189
Damascus, MD 20872
202-966-5557
Fax: 202-966-8553
info@geneticalliance.org
www.geneticalliance.org

World's leading nonprofit health advocacy organization committed to transforming health through genetics and promoting an environment of openness centered on the health of individuals, families, and communities.

Sharon Terry, CEO
Ruth Child, CFO
Natasha Bonhomme, Chief Strategy Officer

219 March of Dimes Foundation
1550 Crystal Drive, Ste 1300
Arlington, VA 22202
888-663-4637
www.marchofdimes.org

March of Dimes help moms have full-term pregnancies and research the problems that threaten the health of babies. The March of Dimes also acts globally: sharing best practices in perinatal health and helping improve birth outcomes where the needs are the most urgent.

Stacey D. Stewart, President/CEO
Alan Brogdon, SVP/COO/Board Officer
Rahul Gupta, MD, SVP & Chief Medical/Health Officer

Web Sites

220 Children's Liver Association for Support Services
www.classkids.org
724-581-5527
classkidscares@gmail.com
www.classkids.org

CLASS is an all volunteer, nonprofit organization dedicated to serving the emotional, educational and financial needs of families coping with childhood liver disease and transplantation. Its goal is to be both a service to families and a valuable resource for the medical community.

221 National Center for Biotechnology Information
National Library of Medicine, 8600 Rockville Pike
Bethesda, MD 20894
888-346-3656
info@ncbi.nlm.nih.gov
www.ncbi.nlm.nih.gov

NCBI's mission is to develop new information technologoes to aid in the understanding of fundamental molecular and genetic processes that control health and disease.

Patricia Flatley Brennan, RN, PhD, Director
James Ostell, PhD, Executive Secretary

222 Online Mendelian Inheritance in Man
McKusick-Nathans Institue of Genetic Medicine-JHU
Baltimore, MD 21205
www.omim.org

This database is a catalog of human genes and genetic disorders.

Ada Hamosh, MD, Scientific Director

Book Publishers

223 Let's Talk About Going to the Hospital
Rosen Publishing Group's PowerKids Press
29 E 21st Street
New York, NY 10010
212-777-3017
800-237-9932
Fax: 888-436-4643
rosenpub@tribeca.ios.com
www.rosenpublishing.com

If a child has to check into the hospital, chances are he or she is already upset about being ill. Knowing how a hospital functions and what the procedures are, such as when family members can visit, will help in what is already a stressful situation. Grades K-5.

24 pages
ISBN: 0-823950-36-0

Roger Rosen, President

Description

224 ANENCEPHALY

Involves the following Biologic System(s):

Neurologic Disorders

Anencephaly is an abnormality that is present at birth (congenital) and belongs to a group of birth defects known as neural tube defects. This condition is characterized by the absence of a major portion of the brain, skull, and scalp. Approximately one of 1,000 infants is born with anencephaly.

During the early stages of pregnancy, a specialized layer of tissue extends along the back portion of the developing embryo. As the embryo grows, this tissue, known as the neural plate, forms a groove that is bordered by folds. This groove eventually deepens and closes to form the neural tube. Later in development, the neural tube gives rise to tissue that later forms the brain and spinal cord. The neural tube is surrounded and protected by the bones of the back (vertebrae). Failure in this sequence of developmental events results in a neural tube defect.

Anencephaly represents a type of neural tube defect that is incompatible with life. Infants with this disorder are born without a forebrain, the largest part of the brain consisting mainly of the cerebral hemispheres which are responsible for higher level cognition, i.e., thinking. The remaining brain tissue is often exposed - not covered by bone or skin. Infants born with anencephaly are usually blind, deaf, unconscious, and unable to feel pain. Additional physical findings associated with this abnormality include folded ears, incomplete closure of the palate (cleft palate), and congenital heart defects. The cause of anencephaly is unknown, although it is thought to occur as the result of genetic or environmental factors, alone or in combination. Neural tube defects do not follow direct patterns of heredity. However, the theory of a genetic predisposition to anencephaly is supported by the fact that the risk of additional children being born with this defect rises with each pregnancy.

Supplementation with high-dose folic acid, initiated before and given during pregnancy, reduces the risk of neural tube defects to 1%.

Government Agencies

225 NIH/ Eunice Kennedy Shriver National Institute of Child Health & Human Development
P.O. Box 3006
Rockville, MD 20847
800-370-2943
Fax: 866-760-5947
www.nichd.nih.gov

Conducts and supports laboratory research, clinical trials, and epidemiological studies that explore health processes; examines the impact of disabilities, diseases, and variations on the lives of individuals; and sponsors training programs for scientists, health care providers, and researchers to ensure that NICHD research can continue.

Diana W. Bianchi, Director
Alison Cernich, PhD, Deputy Director

National Associations & Support Groups

226 American Academy of Pediatrics
345 Park Blvd
Itasca, IL 60143
800-433-9016
Fax: 847-434-8000
mcc@aap.org
www.aap.org

The American Academy of Pediatrics and its member pediatricians are committed to the attainment of optimal physical, mental and social health and well-being for all infants, children, adolescents, and young adults.

Mark Del Monte, JD, CEO/Executive VP
Lynn Olson, PhD, VP, Research
Vera Tait, MD, FAAP, Chief Medical Officer

227 Birth Defect Research for Children
976 Lake Baldwin Lane, Suite 104
Orlando, FL 32814
407-895-0802
staff@birthdefects.org
www.birthdefects.org

Birth Defect Research for Children is a non-profit organization that provides parents and expectant parents with information about birth defects and support services for their children.

Betty Mekdeci, Executive Director

228 Center for Parent Information and Resources (CPIR)
c/o SPAN, 35 Halsey Street, 4th Floor
Newark, NJ 07102
973-642-8100
malizo@spanadvocacy.org
www.parentcenterhub.org

Family-friendly information and research-based materials on key topics for Parent Centers. Private workspaces for Parent Centers to exchange resources, discuss high-priority topics, and solve mutual challenges. Coordination of parent training efforts throughout the network.

Myriam Alizo, Project Assistant

229 Fetal Health Foundation
9786 S Holland Street
Littleton, CO 80127
980-224-0398
www.fetalhealthfoundation.org

Supports families receiving a fetal syndrome diagnosis, funds research, increases fetal syndrome awareness, and shares leading medical information on fetal syndromes.

Talitha McGuinness, Founder & Executive Director
Lonnie Somers, Founder & Chairman
Michelle Somers, Founder

230 Genetic Alliance
426400 Woodfield Road, Ste 189
Damascus, MD 20872
202-966-5557
Fax: 202-966-8553
info@geneticalliance.org
www.geneticalliance.org

World's leading nonprofit health advocacy organization committed to transforming health through genetics and promoting an environment of openness centered on the health of individuals, families, and communities.

Sharon Terry, CEO
Ruth Child, CFO
Natasha Bonhomme, Chief Strategy Officer

231 March of Dimes Foundation
1550 Crystal Drive, Ste 1300
Arlington, VA 22202
888-663-4637
www.marchofdimes.org

March of Dimes help moms have full-term pregnancies and research the problems that threaten the health of babies. The March of Dimes also acts globally: sharing best practices in perinatal health and helping improve birth outcomes where the needs are the most urgent.

Stacey D. Stewart, President
Alan Brogdon, SVP/COO/Board Officer
Rahul Gupta, MD, SVP & Chief Medical/Health Officer

Web Sites

232 Clinical Genetic Services-Department of Pediatrics
Hassenfeld Children's Hospital at NYU Langone
424 East 34th Street
New York, NY 10016
212-263-7300
Fax: 646-754-2250
nyulangone.org

Offers evaluations, genetic counseling and testing. Clinical services include carrier testing, prenatal counseling, and complete genetic evaluations for children and adults.

John G. Pappas, MD, Pediatric Genetic Associate
Naomi Yachelevich, MD, Pediatric Genetic Associate

233 National Center for Biotechnology Information
National Library of Medicine, 8600 Rockville Pike
Bethesda, MD 20894
888-346-3656
info@ncbi.nlm.nih.gov
www.ncbi.nlm.nih.gov

NCBI's mission is to develop new information technologoes to aid in the understanding of fundamental molecular and genetic processes that control health and disease.

Patricia Flatley Brennan, RN, PhD, Director
James Ostell, PhD, Executive Secretary

234 Online Mendelian Inheritance in Man
McKusick-Nathans Institue of Genetic Medicine-JHU
Baltimore, MD 21205
www.omim.org

This database is a catalog of human genes and genetic disorders.

Ada Hamosh, MD, Scientific Director

Description

235 ANIRIDIA
Synonym: Hypoplasia of iris
Involves the following Biologic System(s):
Ophthalmologic Disorders

Aniridia is a birth defect characterized by absence of all or a portion of the colored area of the eye (iris). Both eyes are typically affected (bilateral aniridia). The term aniridia may be a misnomer, since an undeveloped (vestigial) portion of the iris is usually present (i.e., apparent upon slit-lamp examination or gonioscopy). The iris is an involuntary circular muscle that is visible through the transparent, front portion of the eye (cornea). When certain fibers in the iris contract, the hole in the center of the iris (pupil) either widens or constricts, allowing in additional or less light.

In some infants with aniridia, the corneas of the eyes are also abnormally small. In addition, many affected infants and children experience loss of transparency of the lenses of the eyes (cataracts) or displacement of the lenses, which are located behind the pupils. Aniridia is often associated with underdevelopment (hypoplasia) of the macula, the central portion of the retina that distinguishes detail in the central field of vision.

Additional eye abnormalities often associated with aniridia include rapid, involuntary movements of the eyes (nystagmus); reduced fields of vision; abnormally increased sensitivity to light (photophobia); and progressively increased fluid pressure within the eyes (glaucoma). In most cases, glaucoma is not apparent during the first month of life (neonatal period).

Depending upon the range and severity of associated eye abnormalities, children with aniridia may have varying levels of visual impairment. However, in most cases, affected children may have visual acuity of approximately 20/200 or even further reductions in vision. The clearness or sharpness of vision (i.e., visual acuity) is typically measured on a scale comparing a patient's vision at 20 feet with that of an unaffected individual with full visual acuity. Thus, a person with 20/200 vision sees at 20 feet what someone with full visual acuity sees at 200 feet.

Aniridia may be an isolated condition or may occur in association with certain syndromes, such as WAGR syndrome, a rare disorder characterized by kidney tumors (Wilms tumor), aniridia, genitourinary anomalies (abnormalities of the reproductive and urinary tracts), due to spontaneous genetic changes (mutations), and intellectual disabilities. WAGR is inherited as an autosomal dominant trait; in very rare cases, aniridia is inherited as an autosomal recessive trait (e.g., aniridia-cerebellar ataxia-mental deficiency). Medical care for aniridia is directed toward prevention of glaucoma and control of intraocular pressure (fluid pressure inside the eye. Other measures focus on specific problems, such as nystagmus, sensitivity to light (photophobia) and supportive measures, such as removal of cataracts. Visual aids, such as artificial pupil contact lenses, may also be used.

Government Agencies

236 NIH/National Eye Institute
31 Center Drive MSC 2510
Bethesda, MD 20892

301-496-5248
2020@nei.nih.gov
www.nei.nih.gov

Conducts and supports research that helps prevent and treat eye diseases and other disorders of vision. This research leads to sight-saving treatments, reduces visual impairment and blindness, and improves the quality of life for people of all ages. NEI-supported research has advanced our knowledge of how the eye functions in health and disease.
Michael F. Chiang, MD, Director
Santa Tumminia, Deputy Director

National Associations & Support Groups

237 American Academy of Pediatrics
345 Park Blvd
Itasca, IL 60143

800-433-9016
Fax: 847-434-8000
mcc@aap.org
www.aap.org

The American Academy of Pediatrics and its member pediatricians are committed to the attainment of optimal physical, mental and social health and well-being for all infants, children, adolescents, and young adults.
Mark Del Monte, JD, CEO/Executive VP
Lynn Olson, PhD, VP, Research
Vera Tait, MD, FAAP, Chief Medical Officer

238 Genetic Alliance
426400 Woodfield Road, Ste 189
Damascus, MD 20872

202-966-5557
Fax: 202-966-8553
info@geneticalliance.org
www.geneticalliance.org

World's leading nonprofit health advocacy organization committed to transforming health through genetics and promoting an environment of openness centered on the health of individuals, families, and communities.
Sharon Terry, CEO
Ruth Child, CFO
Natasha Bonhomme, Chief Strategy Officer

239 Lighthouse Guild
250 West 64th Street
New York, NY 10023

800-284-4422
info@lighthouseguild.org
www.lighthouseguild.org

Lighthouse Guild is dedicated to providing exceptional services that inspire people who are visually impaired to attain their goals.
James M. Dubin, Chair
Calvin W. Roberts, President & CEO
Maura J. Sweeney, SVP, Programs & Services

240 March of Dimes Foundation
1550 Crystal Drive, Ste 1300
Arlington, VA 22202

888-663-4637
www.marchofdimes.org

March of Dimes help moms have full-term pregnancies and research the problems that threaten the health of babies. The March of Dimes also acts globally: sharing best practices in perinatal health and helping improve birth outcomes where the needs are the most urgent.
Stacey D. Stewart, President
Alan Brogdon, SVP/COO/Board Officer
Rahul Gupta, MD, SVP & Chief Medical/Health Officer

Web Sites

241 Aniridia Network
22 Cornish House, Adelaide Lane
Sheffield, S3 8B

077-2 8-7 94
info@aniridia.org.uk
aniridia.org.uk

We are an international support group which aims to bring people with aniridia closer together as well as providing practical support and information.

242　Aniridia Web Site
22 Cornish House, Adelaide Lane
Sheffield, S3 8B

077-2 8-7 94
info@aniridia.org.uk
aniridia.org.uk

The Aniridia Network is an international nonprofit organization dedicated to supporting people with aniridia and their families, increasing awareness of aniridia and improving the quality of information about aniridia around the world.

243　Lighthouse Guild
250 West 64th Street
New York, NY 10023

800-284-4422
info@lighthouseguild.org
www.lighthouseguild.org

Lighthouse Guild is dedicated to providing exceptional services that inspire people who are visually impaired to attain their goals.

244　Online Mendelian Inheritance in Man
McKusick-Nathans Institue of Genetic Medicine-JHU
Baltimore, MD 21205

www.omim.org

This database is a catalog of human genes and genetic disorders.

Ada Hamosh, MD, Scientific Director

Book Publishers

245　Children with Visual Impairments: A Parents' Guide
Peytral Publications
PO Box 1162
Minnetonka, MN 55345

952-949-8707
877-739-8725
Fax: 952-906-9777
help@peytral.com
www.peytral.com

Covers visual impairments ranging from low vision to total blindness. Offers authoritative information and empathy, parental insight on diagnosis and treatment, orientation and mobility, literacy, legal issues and more. Valuable to parents, educators and support staff.

395 pages

M Cay Holbrook PhD, Editor

246　Let's Talk About Going to the Hospital
Rosen Publishing Group's PowerKids Press
29 E 21st Street
New York, NY 10010

212-777-3017
800-237-9932
Fax: 888-436-4643
rosenpub@tribeca.ios.com
www.rosenpublishing.com

If a child has to check into the hospital, chances are he or she is already upset about being ill. Knowing how a hospital functions and what the procedures are, such as when family members can visit, will help in what is already a stressful situation. Grades K-5.

24 pages
ISBN: 0-823950-36-0

Roger Rosen, President

Ankylosing Spondylitis / National Associations & Support Groups

Description

247 ANKYLOSING SPONDYLITIS
Synonyms: AS, Marie-Strumpell spondylitis
Involves the following Biologic System(s):
Orthopedic and Muscle Disorders

Ankylosing spondylitis (AS) is a chronic, progressive, inflammatory disease that affects joints of the spine and results in pain, stiffness, and possible loss of spinal mobility. In most patients, the joints between the spine and the hipbones (sacroiliac joints) are affected. In addition, joints in the spinal column of the lower back (lumbosacral spine) and the neck (cervical spine) may be involved to varying degrees. Although the disease usually becomes apparent during young adulthood or middle age, it may also begin during childhood. Males are more commonly affected than females.

In most cases, children initially present with periodic inflammation and discomfort in the joints of the arms and legs (transient peripheral arthritis), particularly the large joints of the legs. Many also experience arthritis in the shoulders, the lower jaw bone (i.e., temporomandibular joints), and the feet. Such inflammation results in swelling, pain, abnormal warmth (erythema), and possible limited movement of affected joints. In children with AS, involvement of the sacroiliac joints may be apparent at the disorder's onset or may develop over several months or years. The different regions of the spine may then be progressively affected, usually beginning in the spinal column of the lower back (lumbar spine) and eventually involving the upper back (thoracic spine) and the cervical spine. Children with the disease experience periodic pain and stiffness that may be alleviated by movement. Many have hip, thigh, and lower back pain that is more severe at night and experience stiffness of affected areas in the mornings. In addition, some children have involvement of the joints that connect the ribs to the spine (costovertebral joints). The resulting inflammation, pain, and stiffness may limit expansion of the chest when taking deep breaths. Disease progression may spontaneously cease at any stage; however, in some cases, all regions of the spine may gradually be affected, potentially resulting in severely impaired spinal mobility.

Other symptoms associated with ankylosing spondylitis include fatigue, low-grade fever, lack of appetite (anorexia), low levels ofred blood cells (anemia), stunted growth, and repeated inflammation of the colored region of the eye (iritis) and its muscle (iridocyclitis). Inflammation of the aorta, the largest artery of the body (aoritis), is a finding that is often seen in adults with ankylosing spondylitis, but is rarely seen in affected children.

Research has shown that approximately 95 percent of affected individuals have a specific human leukocyte antigen or HLA. Antigens are proteins that stimulate the body to produce certain antibodies in response to invading microorganisms or foreign tissues. Most individuals with ankylosing spondylitis have a specific genetically determined HLA known as HLA-B27. The possible role of HLA-B27 in predisposing an individual to the disorder has not been determined. Anklosing spondylitis is thought to be an autosomal dominant disorder. In some cases, individuals with a defective gene for AS may not experience symptoms and findings associated with the disorder (reduced penetrance). AS is thought to have a higher penetrance among males.

Although HLA-B27 is present in most individuals with ankylosing spondylitis, it is not considered diagnostic for the disorder. AS is typically diagnosed based upon a complete patient and family history, characteristic physical findings, and specialized x-ray techniques. Treatment of children is primarily directed toward relieving pain and ensuring proper posture to help preserve spinal mobility. Certain medications may be prescribed to help alleviate or manage pain (e.g., indomethacin or other nonsteroidal antiinflammatory medications [NSAIDs]). Special exercises may be recommended to help strengthen back muscles and maintain proper posture. In addition, certain lifestyle changes may be suggested, including avoiding thick pillows and using a firm mattress. Additional treatment is usually symptomatic and supportive.

Government Agencies

248 NIH/National Institute of Arthritis and Musculoskeletal and Skin Diseases
1 AMS Circle
Bethesda, MD 20892
301-495-4484
877-226-4267
Fax: 301-718-6366
TTY: 301-565-2966
niamsinfo@mail.nih.gov
www.niams.nih.gov

The mission of the NIAMS, a part of the NIH, is to support research into the causes, treatment and prevention of arthritis and musculoskeletal and skin diseases, the training of basic and clinical scientists to carry out this research, and the dissemination of information on research progress in these diseases.

Lindsey A. Criswell, MD, Director
Rick Phillips, Executive Officer

National Associations & Support Groups

249 American Academy of Pediatrics
345 Park Blvd
Itasca, IL 60143
800-433-9016
Fax: 847-434-8000
mcc@aap.org
www.aap.org

The American Academy of Pediatrics and its member pediatricians are committed to the attainment of optimal physical, mental and social health and well-being for all infants, children, adolescents, and young adults.

Mark Del Monte, JD, CEO/Executive VP
Lynn Olson, PhD, VP, Research
Vera Tait, MD, FAAP, Chief Medical Officer

250 American Autoimmune Related Diseases Association
19176 Hall Road, Suite 130
Clinton, MI 48038
586-776-3900
aarda@aarda.org
www.aarda.org

The American Autoimmune Related Diseases Association is dedicated to the eradication of autoimmune diseases and the alleviation of suffering and the socioeconomic impact of autoimmunity through fostering and facilitating collaboration in the areas of education, public awareness, research, and patient services in an effective, ethical and efficient manner.

Lilly Stairs, Interim President/CEO
Laura Simpson, COO

251 Arthritis Foundation
1335 Peachtree Street NE, Suite 600
Atlanta, GA 30309
800-283-7800
www.arthritis.org

The Arthritis Foundation is committed to raising awareness and reducing the unacceptable impact of arthritis, a disease which must be taken as seriously as other chronic diseases because of its devastatng consequences.

Ann M. Palmer, President & CEO
Robin Kinard, SVP, Operations
Sabrina Sexton, SVP, Marketing & Communications

Ankylosing Spondylitis / Research Centers

252 March of Dimes Foundation
1550 Crystal Drive, Ste 1300
Arlington, VA 22202
888-663-4637
www.marchofdimes.org

March of Dimes help moms have full-term pregnancies and research the problems that threaten the health of babies. The March of Dimes also acts globally: sharing best practices in perinatal health and helping improve birth outcomes where the needs are the most urgent.

Stacey D. Stewart, President
Alan Brogdon, SVP/COO/Board Officer
Rahul Gupta, MD, SVP & Chief Medical/Health Officer

253 Spondylitis Association of America
16430 Ventura Blvd, Suite 300
Encino, CA 91436
818-892-1616
800-777-8189
Fax: 818-892-1611
info@spondylitis.org
www.spondylitis.org

SAA is committed to research, from funding scientific meetings to launching the first genetic research study in the United States on ankylosing spondylitis and related diseases. SAA has funded a spondyloarthritis patient registry, studies on the microbiome in spondyloarthritis, life impact studies, as well as a health care professional educational CME programs such as the MRI (magnetic resonance imaging) program to help radiologists and rheumatologists work together.

Cassie Shafer, CEO
Elin Aslanyan, Director of Programs
Kristine Callender, Programs Manager

Research Centers

254 John Hopkins Arthritis Center
5200 Eastern Avenue, Suite 4100
Baltimore, MD 21224
410-550-0545
Fax: 410-550-2090
arthritis@jhmi.edu
www.hopkins-arthritis.org

The Johns Hopkins Arthritis Center has assembled a team of some of the world's leading experts and specializes in the care of inflammatory arthritis. This includes, most notably, osteoarthritis and rheumatoid arthritis.

Penny Athanasiou, Clinic Coordinator

Web Sites

255 American Autoimmune Related Diseases Association
www.aarda.org
586-776-3900
aarda@aarda.org
www.aarda.org

The American Autoimmune Related Diseases Association is dedicated to the eradication of autoimmune diseases and the alleviation of suffering and the socioeconomic impact of autoimmunity through fostering and facilitating collaboration in the areas of education, public awareness, research, and patient services in an effective, ethical and efficient manner.

256 Online Mendelian Inheritance in Man
McKusick-Nathans Institue of Genetic Medicine-JHU
Baltimore, MD 21205
www.omim.org

This database is a catalog of human genes and genetic disorders.

Ada Hamosh, MD, Scientific Director

Pamphlets

257 Ankylosing Spondylitis
Arthritis Foundation
1335 Peachtree Street NE, Suite 600
Atlanta, GA 30309
404-872-7100
800-283-7800
www.arthritis.org

An informative pamphlet published by the Arthritis Foundation.

Ann M. Palmer, President & CEO
Melissa Honabach, SVP, Marketing & Communications
David McLoughlin, COO

Anorectal Malformations / National Associations & Support Groups

Description

258 ANORECTAL MALFORMATIONS
Covers these related disorders: Anal atresia, Anal fistula, Anal stenosis, Ectopic anus, Imperforate anus
Involves the following Biologic System(s):
Gastrointestinal Disorders

Anorectal malformations are a group of birth defects affecting the rectum, the anus, or both. The rectum is the final straight portion of the large intestine that terminates at an external opening known as the anus. Anorectal malformations are birth defects in which the anus and rectum do not develop normally and vary in severity. For example, the anal opening may be in its normal location but may be unusually small or narrow (e.g., anal stenosis or imperforate anus). Some anorectal malformations may not be apparent upon physical examination (e.g., imperforate anus or anal atresia). In infants with imperforate anus, the anal opening is partially or completely closed due to the presence of a thin membrane (i.e., cloacal membrane). In anal atresia, the rectum may end blindly due to absence (atresia) of the anal canal. In addition, in many affected infants, an abnormal channel (fistula) may be present between the rectum and certain other unusual locations. Anorectal malformations affect approximately one in 4,000 newborns.

Most newborns with anorectal malformations experience lower intestinal obstruction within 24 hours after birth due to incomplete passage of meconium, the thick, darkish green material that accumulates in the fetal intestines and forms a newborn's first stool. Newborns normally pass meconium during the first 24 to 48 hours after birth. Affected infants may also have incomplete or infrequent bowel movements or experience difficulty passing stools (constipation) within days or weeks after birth. Associated findings may include rectal bleeding; periodic episodes of diarrhea following constipation and associated abrasions of the skin (e.g., of the perineum and the buttocks); and abnormal enlargement of a segment of the large intestine (megacolon). In affected males with a channel between the rectum and the urinary tract, there can be passage of gas (pneumaturia) and meconium in the urine.

When newborns are diagnosed with anorectal malformations, physicians may consider surgical measures to prevent intestinal or urinary obstruction. Therapies for affected newborns or infants depend upon the nature and location of the anorectal malformation and, in some cases, other associated birth defects that may be present. Treatment measures, which may be conducted during the newborn period or later during infancy, may include surgical correction of anorectal malformations (e.g., anoplasty) and widening (dilatation) of the anal opening or other supportive measures; a colostomy is often needed.

Anorectal malformations are thought to result from abnormalities in the development of the embryonic structures that form the rectum and portions of the urinary tract. In cases in which anorectal malformations occur as isolated findings, such malformations are thought to result from abnormal changes (mutations) of one or several different genes, possibly in association with certain environmental factors (multifactorial). However, familial cases have also been reported that appear to have autosomal dominant, autosomal recessive, X-linked, or multifactorial inheritance. In approximately 50 percent of affected infants, anorectal malformations occur in association with other birth defects or underlying malformation syndromes, such as VACTERL association, a rare disorder that may be characterized by (V)ertebral abnormalities, (A)nal atresia, (C)ardiac defects, (T)racheo(E)sophageal fistula, (R)enal malformations, and (L)imb defects. Therefore, it is essential that newborns diagnosed with anorectal malformations are thoroughly examined and carefully monitored to ensure the detection and appropriate treatment of associated abnormalities.

National Associations & Support Groups

259 American Academy of Pediatrics
345 Park Blvd
Itasca, IL 60143
800-433-9016
Fax: 847-434-8000
mcc@aap.org
www.aap.org

The American Academy of Pediatrics and its member pediatricians are committed to the attainment of optimal physical, mental and social health and well-being for all infants, children, adolescents, and young adults.

Mark Del Monte, JD, CEO/Executive VP
Lynn Olson, PhD, VP, Research
Vera Tait, MD, FAAP, Chief Medical Officer

260 American College of Gastroenterology
6400 Goldsboro Road
Bethesda, MD 20817
301-263-9000
www.gi.org

The American College of Gastroenterology was founded in 1932 to advance the scientific study and medical practice of diseases of the GI tract.

13,000 members

261 Center for Parent Information and Resources (CPIR)
c/o SPAN, 35 Halsey Street, 4th Floor
Newark, NJ 07102
973-642-8100
malizo@spanadvocacy.org
www.parentcenterhub.org

Family-friendly information and research-based materials on key topics for Parent Centers. Private workspaces for Parent Centers to exchange resources, discuss high-priority topics, and solve mutual challenges. Coordination of parent training efforts throughout the network.

Myriam Alizo, Project Assistant

262 Digestive Disease National Coalition
507 Capitol Court NE, Suite 200
Washington, DC 20002
202-544-7497
Fax: 202-546-7105
www.ddnc.org

Advocacy organization comprised of over 30 voluntary and professional societies concerned with the many diseases of the digestive tract and liver.

Ceciel Rooker, Chairperson
Bryan Green, MD, President
Cathy Griffith, Vice Chairperson

263 International Foundation for Functional Gastrointestinal Disorders (IFFGD)
3015 Dunes W Boulevard, Suite 512
Mount Pleasant, SC 29466
414-964-1799
www.iffgd.org

The organization offers responses to those commonly asked questions for families and individuals whose lives have been touched by gastrointestinal disorders.

Nancy J. Norton, Founder
Ceciel T. Rooker, President

264 March of Dimes Foundation
1550 Crystal Drive, Ste 1300
Arlington, VA 22202
888-663-4637
www.marchofdimes.org

March of Dimes help moms have full-term pregnancies and research the problems that threaten the health of babies. The March of Dimes also acts globally: sharing best practices in perinatal health and helping improve birth outcomes where the needs are the most urgent.

Stacey D. Stewart, President
Alan Brogdon, SVP/COO/Board Officer
Rahul Gupta, MD, SVP & Chief Medical/Health Officer

265 North American Society for Pediatric Gastroenterology/Hepatology/Nutrition
714 N Bethlehem Pike, Suite 300
Ambler, PA 19002
215-641-9800
Fax: 215-641-1995
www.naspghan.org

Strives to improve the care of infants, children and adolescents with digestive disorders by promoting advances in clinical care of children with chronic abdominal pain, diarrhea, constipation, vomiting, bleeding from the GI tract, inflammatory bowel disease, liver diseases, diseases of the pancreas, poor weight gain and nutritional problems.

Margaret K Stallings, Executive Director
Kim Rose, Associate Director
Gina Brown, Membership

266 Oley Foundation
99 Delaware Avenue, MC-28, Albany Medical Ctr
Delmar, NY 12054
518-262-5079
Fax: 518-262-5528
info@oley.org
www.oley.org

Strives to enrich the lives of those living with home intravenous nutrition (parenteral) and tube feeding (enteral) through education, advocacy, and networking.

Joan Bishop, Executive Director
Roslyn Dahl, Director, Communications/Dvlpmnt
Lisa Crosby Metzger, Director, Community Engagement

267 Pull-Thru Network
Normal, IL 61761
pullthrunetwork@gmail.com
www.pullthrunetwork.org

Pull-thru Network (PTN) was founded in 1988 and has grown to be one of the largest organizations in the world dedicated to the needs of those born with an anorectal malformation or colon disease and any of the associated diagnoses.

Lori Parker, Executive Director
Hollie Filce, Associate Director
Carmell Burns, Director

Libraries & Resource Centers

268 National Digestive Diseases Information Clearinghouse (NDDIC)
NIH
2 Information Way
Bethesda, MD 20892
301-654-3810
800-891-5389
Fax: 301-907-8906
nddic@info.niddk.nih.gov
www.digestive.niddk.nih.gov

The National Institute of Diabetes and Digestive and Kidney Diseases conducts and supports research on many of the most serious diseases affecting public health. The Institute supports much of the clinical research on the diseases of internal medicine and related subspecialty fields as well as many basic science disciplines.

Griffin P. Rodgers, MD, Director
Gregory G. Germino, MD, Deputy Director
Kathy Kranzfelder, Communications Director

Conferences

269 IFFGD Professional Symposia
3015 Dunes W Boulevard, Suite 512
Mount Pleasant, SC 29466
414-964-1799
www.iffgd.org

Aimed at promoting education and awareness among professionals from multiple disciplines who treat gastrointestinal disorders and incontinence.

April
Nancy J. Norton, Founder
Ceciel T. Rooker, President

270 NASPGHAN Annual Meeting
NASPGHAN
714 N. Bethlehem Pike, Ste 300
Ambler, PA 19002
215-641-9800
Fax: 215-641-1995
www.naspghan.org

Strives to improve the care of infants, children and adolescents with digestive disorders by promoting advances in clinical care of children with chronic abdominal pain, diarrhea, constipation, vomiting, bleeding from the GI tract, inflammatory bowel disease, liver diseases, diseases of the pancreas, poor weight gain and nutritional problems.

Fall
Margaret K Stallings, Executive Director
Kim Rose, Associate Director
Gina Brown, Membership

271 Oley Foundation Annual Conference
Oley Foundation
99 Delaware Avenue, MC-28, Albany Medical Center
Delmar, NY 12054
518-262-5079
Fax: 518-262-5528
info@oley.org
www.oley.org

The event includes formal presentations and informal discussions bringing the Oley Foundation community together for learning and connecting.

July
Joan Bishop, Executive Director

272 PTN National Conference
Pull-Thru Network
Normal, IL 61761
pullthrunetwork@gmail.com
www.pullthrunetwork.org

Pull-thru Network (PTN) is one of the largest organizations in the world dedicated to the needs of those born with an anorectal malformation or colon disease and any of the associated diagnoses.

June
Lori Parker, Executive Director
Hollie Filce, Associate Director
Carmell Burns, Director

Web Sites

273 Baby Center
163 Freelon Street
San Francisco, CA 94107
www.babycenter.com

The Academy is committed to the attainment of optimal physical, mental and social health for all infants, children, adolescents, and young adults. To this end, the members of the Academy dedicate their efforts and resources.

Colleen Hancock, SVP/Global COO
Linda J. Murray, SVP/Global Editor-in-Chief
Clarence Wilhelm, Chief Information Officer

274 Health Research Program (HaRP)
www.harpnet.org

www.harpnet.org

A program by USAID, the project strives to improve the health status of infants, children, mothers and families through the development and research of new tools, technologies, policies and approaches.

275 National Digestive Diseases Information Clearinghouse (NDDIC)
2 Information Way
301-654-3810
800-891-5389
nddic@info.niddk.nih.gov
www.digestive.niddk.nih.gov

Supports clinical research on the diseases of internal medicine and related subspecialty fields as well as many basic science disciplines.

Journals

276 Journal of Pediatric Gastroenterology and Nutrition (NASPGHAN)
Lippincott Williams & Wilkins
Two Commerce Square, 2001 Market Street
Philadelphia, PA 19103
215-521-8300
Fax: 215-521-8902
www.wolterskluwerhealth.com

Publication of the North American Society for Pediatric Gastroenterolgy, Hepatology and Nutrition, which strives to improve the care of infants, children and adolescents with digestive disorders by promoting advances in clinical care of children with chronic abdominal pain, diarrhea, constipation, vomiting, bleeding from the GI tract, inflammatory bowel disease, liver diseases, diseases of the pancreas, poor weight gain and nutritional problems.

Bob Becker, President/ CEO
Susan Yules, Chief Financial Officer
Cathy Wolfe, President/ CEO, Medical Research

Newsletters

277 LifelineLetter
Oley Foundation
99 Delaware Avenue, MC-28, Albany Medical Center
Delmar, NY 12054
518-262-5079
Fax: 518-262-5528
www.oley.org

Strives to enrich the lives of those living with home intravenous nutrition (parenteral) and tube feeding (enteral) through education, advocacy, and networking.

July

Joan Bishop, Executive Director
Roslyn Dahl, Director, Communications/Dvlpmnt
Lisa Crosby Metzger, Director, Community Engagement

278 NASPGHAN News
714 N. Bethlehem Pike, Ste 300
Ambler, PA 19002
215-641-9800
Fax: 215-641-1995
www.naspghan.org

Publication of the North American Society for Pediatric Gastroenterolgy, Hepatology and Nutrition, which strives to improve the care of infants, children and adolescents with digestive disorders by promoting advances in clinical care of children with chronic abdominal pain, diarrhea, constipation, vomiting, bleeding from the GI tract, inflammatory bowel disease, liver diseases, diseases of the pancreas, poor weight gain and nutritional problems.

Margaret K Stallings, Executive Director
Kim Rose, Associate Director
Gina Brown, Membership

279 PTN News
Normal, IL 61761
pullthrunetwork@gmail.com
www.pullthrunetwork.org

Newsletter of the Pull-thru Network, one of the largest organizations in the world dedicated to the needs of those born with an anorectal malformation or colon disease and any of the associated diagnoses.

Quarterly

Aortic Stenosis / Description

Description

280 AORTIC STENOSIS

Synonym: Aortic stenosis

Involves the following Biologic System(s):

Cardiovascular Disorders

Aortic stenosis is a condition characterized by abnormal narrowing (stenosis) of the aortic valve, through which blood flows from the left ventricle of the heart to the aorta, the major artery of the body. Such stenosis may occur alone, as a sole abnormality, or together with other inborn abnormalities within or outside the heart. Narrowing of the aortic valve prevents the left ventricle from pumping its full load of blood into the aorta and therefore throughout the body. Effects of the diminished blood flow resulting from aortic stenosis include a deficient supply of blood-borne oxygen and nutrients to the body's tissues, including the muscle tissue of the ventricle, damaging these tissues. In an attempt to overcome this reduced blood supply by pumping blood more forcefully through a narrowed or stenotic aortic value and into the aorta, the muscular wall of the left ventricle may gradually thicken (hypertrophy). With its continued effort to pump blood through a stenotic aortic value, the left ventricle can eventually become enlarged and weakened, reducing its ability to pump blood and thereby leaving an increasing volume of residual blood and an increased blood pressure within the heart. Congestive heart failure, in which the heart ultimately becomes unable to pump blood, is a potentially life-threatening effect of aortic valve stenosis.

Normally, the aortic valve consists of three leaflets (cusps) that meet along their outer edges and overlap one another to prevent blood that is in the aorta from pushing back into the heart between heartbeats. These valves open when the heart contracts, permitting the left ventricle to pump blood out of itself and into the aorta. Most cases of aortic stenosis result from abnormalities in the leaflets or cusps of the valve. One such abnormality is an aortic valve that has only a single leaflet rather than the usual three leaflets. Such a monocuspid valve can occur either as an inherited, genetic effect or as the result of fusion of the valve's leaflets with one another. The inborn or congenital abnormality known as a bicuspid aortic valve is characterized by a valve that has only two cusps or leaflets instead of the usual three, and while many such valves work reasonably well, they are more often narrower than the normal aortic valve. Aortic stenosis can also result from genetic or inherited narrowing of the aortic valve, degenerative diseases, and inflammatory diseases that affect the heart, such as rheumatic fever.

Aortic valve stenosis is identified in as many as 15% of patients before the age of 1 year. Among other persons, the condition presents during childhood, adolescence, or adulthood. Congestive heart failure can be a major effect of aortic valve stenosis in newborns. In older children, a heart murmur is often the first indication of such stenosis. Fatigue soon after beginning a physical activity, dizziness, and chest pain may be other indications of aortic valve stenosis in older children.

Symptoms of aortic valve stenosis depend upon the severity of the abnormality. Valve obstruction that occurs in early infancy may be characterized by a weak pulse, a low output of urine difficulty in breathing, enlargement of the heart (cardiomegaly), congestive heart failure, and abnormal accumulation of fluid in the lungs (pulmonary edema). Severe aortic valve stenosis may be life-threatening to infants and older children. Children with less severe aortic stenosis may have no symptoms other than a heart murmur detected during a physical examination, while those with more severe involvement may experience fatigue, dizziness, and chest pain.

Treatment for aortic valve stenosis depends upon the severity of the obstruction. In some cases it is successfully corrected through the procedure known as balloon valvuloplasty, in which a thin, hollow tube (catheter), with a small balloon attached at its tip, is passed into the valve and the balloon is then inflated, increasing the size of the valve opening. The most frequent treatment for aortic satenosis is surgery to repair the valve if possible or to replace it if necessary. During such surgery, a heart bypass machine takes the place of the heart and lungs, oxygenating the patient's blood and pumping it through the body. In the procedure known as valvotomy, the aortic valve is surgically rebuilt so as to allow it to effectively pass blood from the ventricle into the aorta. In the technique known as the Ross procedure, achild's own pulmonary valve, which normally controls the flow of blood from the heart's right ventricle to the lungs, is used to replace a stenotic aortic valve, and is itself then replaced with a surgically implanted pulmonary valve.

Government Agencies

281 NIH/ Eunice Kennedy Shriver National Institute of Child Health & Human Development
P.O. Box 3006
Rockville, MD 20847

800-370-2943
Fax: 866-760-5947
www.nichd.nih.gov

Conducts and supports laboratory research, clinical trials, and epidemiological studies that explore health processes; examines the impact of disabilities, diseases, and variations on the lives of individuals; and sponsors training programs for scientists, health care providers, and researchers to ensure that NICHD research can continue.

Diana W. Bianchi, Director
Alison Cernich, PhD, Deputy Director

282 NIH/National Heart, Lung and Blood Institute
31 Center Drive, Bldg 31
Bethesda, MD 20892

877-645-2448
www.nhlbi.nih.gov

The National Heart, Lung, and Blood Institute (NHLBI) provides global leadership for a research, training, and education program to promote the prevention and treatment of heart, lung, and blood diseases and enhance the health of all individuals so that they can live longer and more fulfilling lives.

Gary H. Gibbons, MD, Director
Kate O'Sullivan, Executive Officer

National Associations & Support Groups

283 American Academy of Pediatrics
345 Park Blvd
Itasca, IL 60143

800-433-9016
Fax: 847-434-8000
mcc@aap.org
www.aap.org

The American Academy of Pediatrics and its member pediatricians are committed to the attainment of optimal physical, mental and social health and well-being for all infants, children, adolescents, and young adults.

Mark Del Monte, JD, CEO/Executive VP
Lynn Olson, PhD, VP, Research
Vera Tait, MD, FAAP, Chief Medical Officer

284 American Heart Association
7272 Greenville Avenue
Dallas, TX 75231

214-570-5978
800-242-8721
www.heart.org

The mission of the American Heart Associate is to build healthier lives, free of cardiovascular diseases and stroke.

Nancy Brown, CEO
Mitchell S.V. Elkin, President
Suzie Upton, Chief Operating Officer

285 Genetic Alliance
426400 Woodfield Road, Ste 189
Damascus, MD 20872
202-966-5557
Fax: 202-966-8553
info@geneticalliance.org
www.geneticalliance.org

World's leading nonprofit health advocacy organization committed to transforming health through genetics and promoting an environment of openness centered on the health of individuals, families, and communities.

Sharon Terry, CEO
Ruth Child, CFO
Natasha Bonhomme, Chief Strategy Officer

286 March of Dimes Foundation
1550 Crystal Drive, Ste 1300
Arlington, VA 22202
888-663-4637
www.marchofdimes.org

March of Dimes help moms have full-term pregnancies and research the problems that threaten the health of babies. The March of Dimes also acts globally: sharing best practices in perinatal health and helping improve birth outcomes where the needs are the most urgent.

Stacey D. Stewart, President
Alan Brogdon, SVP/COO/Board Officer
Rahul Gupta, MD, SVP & Chief Medical/Health Officer

Web Sites

287 Southern Illinois University School of Medicine
PO Box 19639
Springfield, IL 62794
217-545-8000
800-342-5748
TDD: 217-545-8038
admin@siuhealthcare.org
www.siumed.edu/peds/index.htm

Mission is to meet the health care needs of children and their families in Central and Southern Illinois through the provision of high quality, coordinated care of children with acute and chronic heart conditions with inpatient, ambulatory, and community-based programs.

288 Yale University School of Medicine
333 Cedar Street
New Haven, CT 6510
203-432-4771
medicine.yale.edu

Information on congenital heart conditions, including Aortic Stenosis — symptoms, treatments and support.

Peter Salovey, President of the University
Richard Belitsky, M.D., Deputy Dean for Education
Benjamin Polak, B.A., M.A., Ph.D., Provost of the University

Book Publishers

289 Congenital Disorders Sourcebook

Greg Mullin, author

Omnigraphics
615 Griswold Street, Ste 520
Detroit, MI 48226
610-461-3548
800-234-1340
Fax: 800-875-1340
contact@omnigraphics.com
www.omnigraphics.com

Provides basic consumer health information about the most common types of nonhereditary birth defects and disorders related to prematurity, gestational injuries, congenital infections, and birth complications, including disorders of the heart, brain, gastrointestinal tract, musculoskeletal system, urinary tract, and reproductive system, craniofacial disorders, cerebral palsy, spina bifida, and fetal alcohol syndrome, and detailing the causes, diagnostic tests, and treatments for each.

664 pages
ISBN: 0-780816-13-8

Apnea of Prematurity / Description

Description

290 APNEA OF PREMATURITY
Synonym: Idiopathic apnea of prematurity
Involves the following Biologic System(s):
Neonatal and Infant Disorders, Respiratory Disorders

Apnea is a condition characterized by a temporary cessation of breathing. Newborns may experience episodes of apnea due to several underlying disorders or conditions, including certain respiratory, neurologic, digestive, cardiovascular, metabolic, or infectious diseases. However, in newborns with apnea of prematurity, apneic episodes occur in the absence of identifiable, underlying disorders (idiopathic). The condition primarily affects premature infants who are born before 34 weeks of pregnancy (gestation). In general, the greater the degree of prematurity, the greater the frequency of the condition.

Apnea of prematurity is thought to occur due to immaturity of the region of the brain that controls breathing (respiratory centers of the medulla), causing failed stimulation of respiratory muscles. Resulting episodes of apnea, which are referred to as central apnea, are characterized by an absence of airflow as well as of chest wall movements. Apnea of prematurity may also be caused by obstruction of the upper airways due to improper coordination of the tongue and upper airway muscles, instability of the throat (pharynx), or other factors. Resulting episodes of apnea, known as obstructive apnea, are characterized by absence of airflow but ongoing chest wall movements. Most infants with apnea of prematurity experience both central and obstructive apnea.

With infant apnea, more appropriately called an apparent life-threatening event, initial episodes of apnea typically occur on the second to the seventh day of life. Such episodes are defined as serious if breathing spontaneously ceases for more than 15 to 20 seconds or if they result in decreased levels of oxygen in the blood and associated bluish discoloration of the skin and mucous membranes (cyanosis) and slowing of the heart rate (bradycardia).

The frequency of apnea episodes typically increases during the cycle of sleep that is associated with rapid eye movements (REMs), dreaming, increased levels of brain activity, and involuntary muscle jerks. During REM sleep, infants are more likely to experience abnormal chest wall movements during breathing, such as relaxation of the chest muscles while inhaling rather than exhaling. Abnormal chest wall movements as well as inhibition of muscle tone (particularly of the throat) during REM sleep contribute to the increased frequency of apneic episodes.

Infants at risk for episodes of apnea should be monitored with devices that detect abnormal changes in chest wall movements, heart rate, and respiratory activity. These devices, known as apnea monitors, sound an alarm when spontaneous breathing temporarily ceases. In infants who experience mild, occasional episodes of apnea, supportive measures may be sufficient, such as gentle skin stimulation and massage. In patients with severe, prolonged, and recurrent apnea episodes, treatment should include close monitoring, immediate measures to assist breathing (e.g., bag and maskentilation) and oxygen therapy to ensure sufficient oxygen supply to body tissues. Infants with apnea may be monitored at home which can have a significant impact on caregivers. In general, as the child matures, the cause of the ALTE is diagnosed and treated or spontaneously resolves.

Government Agencies

291 NIH/ Eunice Kennedy Shriver National Institute of Child Health & Human Development
P.O. Box 3006
Rockville, MD 20847

800-370-2943
Fax: 866-760-5947
www.nichd.nih.gov

Conducts and supports laboratory research, clinical trials, and epidemiological studies that explore health processes; examines the impact of disabilities, diseases, and variations on the lives of individuals; and sponsors training programs for scientists, health care providers, and researchers to ensure that NICHD research can continue.

Diana W. Bianchi, Director
Alison Cernich, PhD, Deputy Director

292 NIH/National Institute of Neurological Disorders and Stroke (NINDS)
PO Box 5801
Bethesda, MD 20824

800-352-9424
www.ninds.nih.gov

Works to reduce the burden of neurological disease by conducting, fostering, coordinating and guiding research on the causes, prevention, diagnosis and treatment of neurological disorders and stroke, while supporting basic research in related scientific areas.

Walter J. Koroshetz, MD, Director

National Associations & Support Groups

293 American Academy of Pediatrics
345 Park Blvd
Itasca, IL 60143

800-433-9016
Fax: 847-434-8000
mcc@aap.org
www.aap.org

The American Academy of Pediatrics and its member pediatricians are committed to the attainment of optimal physical, mental and social health and well-being for all infants, children, adolescents, and young adults.

Mark Del Monte, JD, CEO/Executive VP
Lynn Olson, PhD, VP, Research
Vera Tait, MD, FAAP, Chief Medical Officer

294 American Sleep Apnea Association
1250 Connecticut Ave NW, Ste 700
Washington, DC 20036

888-293-3650
Fax: 888-293-3650
asaa@sleepapnea.org
www.sleepapnea.org

Dedicated to reducing injury, disability and death from sleep apnea and to enhancing the well-being of those affected by this common disorder. They promote education and awareness. Network of voluntary mutual support groups, research, and continuous improvement of care.

Will Headapohl, Chair (Emeritus)
Justine Amdur, Program Coordinator, AWAKE
Valerie Danielson, Program Coordinator, CPAP

295 Child Neurology Foundation
601 W Short Street
Lexington, KY 40508

888-417-3435
info@childneurologyfoundation.org
childneurologyfoundation.org

The Child Neurology Foundation connects partners from all areas of the child neurology community so those navigating the journey of disease diagnosis, management, and care have the ongoing support from those dedicated to treatments and cures.

Amy Brin, Executive Director
Katie Hentges, Director, Programs
Brea McCormley, Director, Development

296 National Sleep Foundation
1414 NE 42nd St, Ste 400
Seattle, WA 98105

contact@sleepfoundation.org
www.sleepfoundation.org

Works to improve the quality of life for millions of Americans who suffer from sleep disorders, and to prevent the catastrophic accidents that are related to poor or disordered sleep through research, education and the dissemination of information towards the cause of the Narcolepsy Project. Seeks patients to aid new research project targeting the cause of the disorder.

Bill Fish, General Manager

Web Sites

297 **Apnea of Prematurity**
395 Hudson Street, 3rd Floor
New York, NY 10014   212-301-6700
emedicine.medscape.com/article/974971-overview

Provides information on how to tell if an unborn baby has sleep apnea.

Dharmendra J. Nimavat, MD, FAAP, Author
Ted Rosenkrantz, MD, Chief Editor

Camps

298 **VACC Camp**
Nicklaus Children's Hospital
3200 SW 60th Court, Suite 203
Miami, FL 33155   305-662-8222
                                   Fax: 786-268-1765
                                bela.florentin@mch.com
                                   www.vacccamp.com

Free, week-long, overnight camp for ventilation assisted children (children needing a tracheotomy ventilator, C-PAP, BiPAP, or oxygen to support breathing) and their families. Gives families a fun oppourtinity to socialize with peers and enjoy activities not readily accessible to technology dependent children.

Bela Florentin, Camp Coordinator
Rose Ann Farrell, Volunteer Assistants Coordinator
Alyssa Garcia, Operations

Arnold-Chiari Malformation / Description

Description

299 ARNOLD-CHIARI MALFORMATION
Synonyms: ACM, Arnold-Chiari deformity, Arnold-Chiari syndrome, Chiari malformation
Covers these related disorders: Arnold-Chiari malformation type I, Arnold-Chiari malformation type II
Involves the following Biologic System(s):
Neurologic Disorders

Arnold-Chiari malformation is a developmental abnormality characterized by deformities at the base of the brain that are present at birth (congenital). Such deformities typically include abnormal elongation of a portion of the cerebellum (cerebellar tonsils) and the lowest region of the brain stem (medulla oblongata), resulting in protrusion of these regions through the large opening (foramen magnum) in the base of the skull and into the upper spinal canal (cervical canal). The cerebellum is a region of the brain that plays an essential role in coordinating voluntary movement and maintaining posture and balance. The brain stem, which is the lowest section of the brain and connects it with the spinal cord, helps to relay motor and sensory impulses between other regions of the brain and the spinal cord, and connects with most of the cranial nerves, which conduct impulses involved in such functions as taste, vision, swallowing, and facial expression, as well as movements of the tongue, head, and shoulders. Although the exact cause of Arnold-Chiari malformation is unknown, researchers have suggested that it may result from the interaction of several genes, environmental influences, or both (multifactorial inheritance).

In some affected newborns, Arnold-Chiari malformation occurs in association with myelomeningocele, a developmental abnormality characterized by protrusion (herniation) of a portion of the spinal cord and its protective membranes (meninges) through an abnormal opening in the bone of the spinal column. Arnold-Chiari malformation without a myelomeningocele is termed Arnold-Chiari malformation type I. When it is accompanied by a myelomeningocele, the condition is known as Arnold-Chiari malformation type II. In both types of the condition, the foramen magnum is abnormally large. Additionally, the base of the skull is flattened and may be pushed upward by the upper vertebrae (cervical vertebrae) surrounding the spinal cord.

Infants and children with Arnold-Chiari malformation type II experience progressive hydrocephalus, a condition characterized by the abnormal accumulation of cerebrospinal fluid (CSF) in the brain. This accumulation of CSF, which comes from obstruction of the normal flow of this fluid between the brain and spine, or its impaired absorption results in increased fluid pressure within cavities (ventricles) of the brain. Other findings in Arnold-Chiari malformation type II may include abnormal enlargement of the chambers within the brain that contain its CSF, known as the ventricles, potential enlargement of the head, and other associated symptoms and findings. Some infants with Arnold-Chiari malformation type II may also experience abnormalities due to pressure or damage to lower cranial nerves. Such abnormalities, which vary in range and severity, include uncontrollable twitching (fasciculations) of the tongue, a high-pitched sound upon inhalation (i.e., laryngeal stridor), facial weakness, hearing impairment, lagging of the head (sternomastoid paralysis), or weakness or impaired control of muscles that turn the eyes outward (bilateral abducens palsies). During later childhood, some patients with Arnold-Chiari malformation type II may experience increased stiffness (rigidity), causing restriction of movement (spasticity); abnormalities in walking (abnormal gait); and progressive lack of coordination. During later childhood or adolescence, individuals with this condition may also experience symptoms and findings often associated with Arnold-Chiari malformation type I.

These symptoms may also first occur in adolescence or adulthood rather than in childhood, and often occur without hydrocephalus. Associated symptoms and findings may include recurrent headaches; neck pain; impaired control of voluntary movements (ataxia); or progressive muscle weakness, degeneration (atrophy), spasticity, and potential sensory loss affecting the lower, in some cases, the upper limbs.

Treatment of Arnold-Chiari malformation depends on the severity of the malformation and associated symptoms and findings. If symptoms are only mild, treatment includes regular monitoring and symptomatic and supportive measures as required, such as the use of medication to relieve pain. However, surgery is the only means of correcting the structural problem in Arnold-Chiari malformation, and is required in more severe cases of this condition. The surgery for Arnold-Chiari malformation is directed at uncrowding the area at the base of the cerebellum where this part of the brain is pushing against the brain stem and spinal cord. This is done by removing a small portion of bone at the base of the skull, and often also by removing a part of the back of the first and occasionally other upper segments of the spinal column (e.g., upper cervical laminectomy).

Government Agencies

300 NIH/ Eunice Kennedy Shriver National Institute of Child Health & Human Development
P.O. Box 3006
Rockville, MD 20847
800-370-2943
Fax: 866-760-5947
www.nichd.nih.gov

Conducts and supports laboratory research, clinical trials, and epidemiological studies that explore health processes; examines the impact of disabilities, diseases, and variations on the lives of individuals; and sponsors training programs for scientists, health care providers, and researchers to ensure that NICHD research can continue.

Diana W. Bianchi, Director
Alison Cernich, PhD, Deputy Director

National Associations & Support Groups

301 American Academy of Pediatrics
345 Park Blvd
Itasca, IL 60143
800-433-9016
Fax: 847-434-8000
mcc@aap.org
www.aap.org

The American Academy of Pediatrics and its member pediatricians are committed to the attainment of optimal physical, mental and social health and well-being for all infants, children, adolescents, and young adults.

Mark Del Monte, JD, CEO/Executive VP
Lynn Olson, PhD, VP, Research
Vera Tait, MD, FAAP, Chief Medical Officer

302 Genetic Alliance
426400 Woodfield Road, Ste 189
Damascus, MD 20872
202-966-5557
Fax: 202-966-8553
info@geneticalliance.org
www.geneticalliance.org

World's leading nonprofit health advocacy organization committed to transforming health through genetics and promoting an environment of openness centered on the health of individuals, families, and communities.

Sharon Terry, CEO
Ruth Child, CFO
Natasha Bonhomme, Chief Strategy Officer

303 March of Dimes Foundation
1550 Crystal Drive, Ste 1300
Arlington, VA 22202
888-663-4637
www.marchofdimes.org

March of Dimes help moms have full-term pregnancies and research the problems that threaten the health of babies. The March of Dimes also acts globally: sharing best practices in perinatal health and helping improve birth outcomes where the needs are the most urgent.

Stacey D. Stewart, President
Alan Brogdon, SVP/COO/Board Officer
Rahul Gupta, MD, SVP & Chief Medical/Health Officer

Web Sites

304 Clinical Genetic Services-Department of Pediatrics
Hassenfeld Children's Hospital at NYU Langone
424 East 34th Street
New York, NY 10016
212-263-7300
Fax: 646-754-2250
nyulangone.org

Offers evaluations, genetic counseling and testing. Clinical services include carrier testing, prenatal counseling, and complete genetic evaluations for children and adults.

John G. Pappas, MD, Pediatric Genetic Associate
Naomi Yachelevich, MD, Pediatric Genetic Associate

305 National Institute of Health NINDS Information Page
PO Box 5801
Bethesda, MD 20824
301-496-5751
800-352-9424
www.ninds.nih.gov

The mission is to reduce the burden of neurological disease — a burden born by every age group, by every segment of society, by people all over the world.

Walter J. Koroshetz, M.D., Director

306 Online Mendelian Inheritance in Man
McKusick-Nathans Institue of Genetic Medicine-JHU
Baltimore, MD 21205
www.omim.org

This database is a catalog of human genes and genetic disorders.

Ada Hamosh, MD, Scientific Director

Book Publishers

307 Let's Talk About Going to the Hospital
Rosen Publishing Group's PowerKids Press
29 E 21st Street
New York, NY 10010
212-777-3017
800-237-9932
Fax: 888-436-4643
rosenpub@tribeca.ios.com
www.rosenpublishing.com

If a child has to check into the hospital, chances are he or she is already upset about being ill. Knowing how a hospital functions and what the procedures are, such as when family members can visit, will help in what is already a stressful situation. Grades K-5.

24 pages
ISBN: 0-823950-36-0

Roger Rosen, President

Arrhythmias / National Associations & Support Groups

Description

308 ARRHYTHMIAS
Covers these related disorders: Supraventricular Tachycardia (SVT), Wolff-Parkinson-White Syndrome (WPW)
Involves the following Biologic System(s):
Cardiovascular Disorders

The term arrhythmia refers to an abnormality in the rhythm of the heartbeat. It may take the form of an abnormally slow or abnormally fast heartbeat or another disturbance in heart rhythm. Any such problem can interfere with the ability of the heart to effectively pump blood to the body's organs and tissues. Many such problems can, however, be treated medically, surgically, or in other ways.

Arrhythmias result from disturbances in the electrical conduction system of the heart, also called the cardiac conduction system. This system consists of pathways, made up of specialized tissues that conduct electrical impulses to the muscle cells of the heart, prompting them to contract and pump blood. Within the cardiac conduction system are also several tissue structures known as nodes, which act as pacemakers, coordinating the sequence of muscle contractions by which the heart pumps blood from each of its four chambers into the next chamber and out into the lungs and body. This coordinated pumping begins in the right atrium or upper right chamber of the heart, which collects blood that re-enters the heart after circulating through the body. The muscle tissue of the right atrium then contracts, pumping this blood downward and into the right ventricle, the chamber of the heart that is located immediately below the right atrium. The right ventricle pumps this blood to the lungs, which supply the blood with oxygen and return it to the left atrium of the heart, which pumps this oxygenated blood downward and into the most muscular of the heart's four chambers, the left ventricle. The left ventricle then pumps the oxygenated blood out of itself and into the body by way of the large main artery known as the aorta.

Most of the arrhythmias caused by aberrations in the cardiac conduction system can be detected with the diagnostic procedure known as electrocardiography. In this procedure, small electrodes that sense the electrical impulses that accompany each heartbeat are pasted to the skin at locations on the chest, arms, and legs. The impulses pass into the electrodes and through wires to an instrument that records, on paper or on a computer screen, the visible tracing known as an electrocardiogram (ECG or EKG), which indicates the intensity, rhythm, and other features of the heartbeat.

Normally, the heart contracts at a rate of 60 to 80 beats per minute when the body is at rest, and this rate increases with exercise to meet the body's increased need for oxygen and blood-borne nutrients. An increased heartbeat rate is known as a tachycardia, while a heartbeat that falls below the normal rate is called a bradycardia. In many instances, both tachycardias and bradycardias are temporary, passing events without serious or dangerous effects. Thus, exercise, excitement, and fever can all cause the typically harmless tachycardia known as sinus tachycardia. The most frequent type of medically important tachycardia in infants and children under the age of 12 is known as supraventricular tachycardia (SVT), sometimes also called paroxysmal supraventricular tachycardia (PSVT) or paroxysmal atrial tachycardia (PAT). As its name indicates, this type of tachycardia comes from a disturbance in the cardiac conduction system that originates at some point above the ventricles. It is characterized by a heart rate of more than 220 beats per minute, but is not typically life-threatening. Infants experiencing an instance of SVT may seem restless, have rapid breathing, or be especially sleepy. SVT requires treatment only if it is frequent or its episodes are long-lasting. Treatment of SVT is based on the specific mechanism responsible for the tachycardia and the age of the patient. A variety of medications (anti-arrhythmia agents) are available for controlling SVT.

More potentially serious than SVT is ventricular tachycardia (VT), caused by an aberration in conduction at some point below the atria of the heart. Although it may occur in the absence of any apparent source, VT is most often the result of damage to or an inborn defect in the conduction system or in another component of the heart. If it occurs in the right ventricle, VT can interfere with pumping of blood to the lungs, and in the left ventricle can interfere with pumping of blood through the entire body. One way in which VT may disrupt the heart's pumping of blood is by triggering the condition known as ventricular fibrillation, in which a weak, flaccid pattern of ventricular contraction replaces the normally forceful, coordinated contractions of these chambers of the heart, preventing them from effectively pumping blood.

A cause of serious disturbances in heart rhythm is the condition known as Wolff-Parkinson-White (WPW) syndrome. This results from an aberration in the cardiac conduction system at some point between the atria and ventricles, and can cause the sudden, complete, and life-threatening cessation of heartbeat known as cardiac arrest. In many cases, WPW syndrome shows no outward signs of its existence, and is first identified only on an electrocardiogram. WPW syndrome often responds to medical treatment with drugs. Destruction or ablation of its source within the cardiac conduction system often corrects WPW syndrome. This technique, known as radiofrequency ablation, involves the passage of an electrical current through a catheter and directly into the source of the syndrome. In other instances surgery is often effective in eliminating WPW syndrome.

Also serious is the condition known as complete heart block, which can occur during childhood and even prenatally. This disorder results from a genetic defect or other damage to the cardiac conduction system that interrupts electrical conduction within the heart, interfering with the pumping of blood from the atria into the ventricles. When this happens, a naturally occurring pacemaker within the ventricles sustains their contraction and pumping of blood, but at a reduced heart rate. If this natural process does not restore an adequate heart rate, heart block may be corrected by implantation of an artificial pacemaker.

Another source of interference with normal heart rhythm is sick sinus syndrome. In this condition, the sinus node, one of the natural pacemakers within the cardiac conduction system, is damaged by illness, injury, or accidentally during heart surgery, triggering intermittent episodes of either tachycardia or of the slowed heartbeat rate known as bradycardia. Symptoms of this condition may include fatigue or faintness. The condition can be treated medically, with drugs, and if necessary by implantation of an artificial pacemaker.

National Associations & Support Groups

309 American Academy of Pediatrics
345 Park Blvd
Itasca, IL 60143

800-433-9016
Fax: 847-434-8000
mcc@aap.org
www.aap.org

Arrhythmias / Journals

The American Academy of Pediatrics and its member pediatricians are committed to the attainment of optimal physical, mental and social health and well-being for all infants, children, adolescents, and young adults.

Mark Del Monte, JD, CEO/Executive VP
Lynn Olson, PhD, VP, Research
Vera Tait, MD, FAAP, Chief Medical Officer

310 American College of Cardiology
2400 N Street, NW
Washington, DC 20037
202-375-6000
800-253-4636
Fax: 202-375-7000
membercare@acc.org
www.acc.org

The mission of the American College of Cardiology is to advocate for quality cardiovascular care, through education, research promotion, development and application of standards and guidelines, and to influence health care policy.

Cathleen C. Gates, CEO
Janice B. Sibley, Executive VP
Brendan Mullen, Executive VP

311 American Heart Association
7272 Greenville Avenue
Dallas, TX 75231
214-570-5978
800-242-8721
www.heart.org

The mission of the American Heart Associate is to build healthier lives, free of cardiovascular diseases and stroke.

Nancy Brown, CEO
Mitchell S.V. Elkind, President
Suzie Upton, Chief Operating Officer

312 Heart Failure Society of America
9211 Corporate Blvd, Suite 270
Rockville, MD 20850
301-312-8635
info@hfsa.org
www.hfsa.org

The Heart Failure Society of America, Inc. (HFSA) represents the first organized effort by heart failure experts from the Americas to provide a forum for all those interested in heart function, heart failure, and congestive heart failure (CHF) research and patient care.

John D. Barnes, CEO
Jamie Abreu, EVP, CME & Educational Programs
Joori Jeon, COO

313 Rush Children's Heart Center
1653 W Congress Parkway
Chicago, IL 60612
312-942-5000
888-352-7874
contact_rush@rush.edu
www.rush.edu/kids/services-conditions/

Rush Children's Hospital, part of at Rush University Medical Center in Chicago, Illinois, provides complete clinical services for the diagnosis and treatment of congenital and acquired heart disease in children and young adults.

Larry J Goodman MD, CEO
Susan Crown, Chairperson

314 Sudden Arrhythmia Death Syndromes Foundation
4527 South 2300 East, Suite 104
Salt Lake City, UT 84117
801-948-0654
www.sads.org

To save the lives and support the families of children and young adults who are genetically predisposed to sudden death due to heart rhythm abnormalities.

Alice Lara, RN, President/CEO
Marcia Baker, Program Director
Jan Schiller, Director, Development/Marketing

Research Centers

315 Cardiovascular Research Foundation
1700 Broadway, 9th Floor
New York, NY 10019
646-434-4500
info@crf.org
www.crf.org

A nonprofit organization with a mission to improve the survival and quality of life for people with cardiovascular disease through research and education.

Gary S Mintz MD, Chief Medical Officer
Eric B Woldenberg Esq, Chairman

Conferences

316 HFSA Annual Scientific Meeting
Heart Failure Society of America
9211 Corporate Blvd, Suite 270
Rockville, MD 20850
301-312-8635
info@hfsa.org
meeting.hfsa.org

The Heart Failure Society of America, Inc. (HFSA) represents the first organized effort by heart failure experts from the Americas to provide a forum for all those interested in heart function, heart failure, and congestive heart failure (CHF) research and patient care.

September

Jamie Abreu, EVP, CME & Educational Programs
Cynthia Miranda, Manager, Meetings & Education

Web Sites

317 Heart Center Online
495 East Waterfront Drive Suite 200
Homestead, PA 15120
412-326-0330
www.theheartcenteronline.com

The mission of the Heart Center Online is to be the premier cardiovascular specialized health care site on the Internet, to provide cardiovascular patients, their families and site visitors with tools they need to better understand the complex nature of heart-related conditions, treatments and preventive care, and to provide services and applications that deliver value to cardiovascullar practices.

318 Rush Children's Heart Center
www.rush.edu

www.rush.edu

Provides complete clinical services for the diagnosis and treatment of congenital and acquired heart disease in children and young adults.

319 Yale University School of Medicine
333 Cedar Street
New Haven, CT 6510
203-432-4771
medicine.yale.edu

Information on heart conditions, including arrhythmias.

Peter Salovey, President of the University
Richard Belitsky M.D., Deputy Dean for Education
Benjamin Polak, B.A., M.A., Ph.D., Provost of the University

Journals

320 Journal of Cardiac Failure
Heart Failure Society of America
9211 Corporate Blvd, Suite 270
Rockville, MD 20850
301-312-8635
info@hfsa.org
www.onlinejcf.com; www.hfsa.org

Contains review articles on clinical research, basic human studies, animal studies, and bench research with potential clinical applications to heart failure, pathogenesis, etiology, epidemiology, pathophysiological mechanisms, assessment, prevention and treatment.

Arrhythmias / Newsletters

6x year
Robert J. Mentz, MD, Editor-in-Chief

321 Texas Heart Institute Journal
Texas Heart Institute
6770 Bertner Avenue
Houston, TX 77030
    832-355-3792
    Fax: 832-355-3714
    webmaster@texasheart.org
    www.texasheartinstitute.org

The purpose of the Texas Heart Institute Journal is to educate, with emphasis on the dissemination of information to physicians in practice.

Quaterly
Denton A. Cooley, MD, Founder
L. Maximilian Buja, MD, Chief
C. David Collard, MD, Chief

Newsletters

322 Heart Failure Society Newsletter
9211 Corporate Blvd, Suite 270
Rockville, MD 20850
    301-312-8635
    info@hfsa.org
    www.hfsa.org

Provides information on the society and also on different aspects of heart failure.

Quaterly
John D. Barnes, CEO
Jamie Abreu, EVP, CME & Educational Programs
Joori Joen, COO

Arthrogryposis Multiplex Congenita / National Associations & Support Groups

Description

323 **ARTHROGRYPOSIS MULTIPLEX CONGENITA**
Synonym: AMC
Covers these related disorders: Amyoplasia
Involves the following Biologic System(s):
Orthopedic and Muscle Disorders

Arthrogryposis multiplex congenita (AMC) refers to a group of disorders present at birth (congenital) that are characterized by limited movement or immobility of multiple joints and partial or complete replacement of involved muscle with fibrous or fatty tissue. Affected joints may be permanently flexed or extended in various fixed postures (joint contractures). Approximately 150 syndromes have been identified that are characterized by the presence of congenital multiple contractures. The most common form of arthrogryposis multiplex congenita is known as amyoplasia. This classic form of AMC affects approximately one in 10,000 newborns.

In newborns with amyoplasia, multiple congenital contractures are present that typically affect the upper and lower extremities. In most newborns who are affected, such contractures include abnormal flexion or extension of the elbows; flexion of the wrists toward either the thumb side or pinky side of the hands (radial or ulnar deviation); cupping of the hands; and internal rotation of the shoulders. Many newborns with amyoplasia also have severe deformities of the feet (clubfoot or talipes equinovarus) in which the heels are turned inward and the soles of the feet are flexed (plantar flexion). Additional musculoskeletal deformities are also typically present including abnormal rigidity of the joints between the bones of the thumbs and other fingers (interphalangeal joints); deformities of the palms of the hands; fixed flexion or extension of the knees; and abnormal flexion, extension, rotation, and possible dislocation of the hips. These abnormalities are usually similar from one side of the body to the other (symmetric). Amyoplasia is also characterized by a susceptibility to bone fractures (i.e., perinatal fractures) and progressive abnormal sideways curvature of the spine (scoliosis) that varies in severity and in age at onset. Most newborns with amyoplasia also have distinctive facial abnormalities including short, upturned (anteverted) nostrils; a rounded face; a slightly small jaw (mild micrognathia); and a benign, reddish, purple growth in the midportion of the face (midline frontal hemangioma). Amyoplasia appears to occur randomly for unknown reasons (sporadically), and the underlying causes of amyoplasia and other forms of AMC are not fully understood.

All newborns with multiple congenital joint contractures should receive a thorough neuromuscular evaluation to help detect, confirm, or rule out potential underlying muscular or neurologic abnormalities. The treatment of infants and children with amyoplasia includes symptomatic and supportive measures. The presence of fractures should be ruled out or confirmed (e.g., with x-ray studies) and treated as necessary (e.g., with appropriate immobilization) before physical therapy is begun. Other treatment measures for congenital contractures and associated abnormalities include physical therapy (e.g., passive range of motion exercises) and splinting of extremities to improve the range of motion; the use of casts or other orthopedic appliances; and possible surgical interventions. In addition, orthopedic appliances may be used to help slow the progression of scoliosis. In most patients with severe scoliosis, surgical measures may also be required.

Government Agencies

324 **NIH/National Institute of Arthritis and Musculoskeletal and Skin Diseases**
1 AMS Circle
Bethesda, MD 20892
301-495-4484
877-226-4267
Fax: 301-718-6366
TTY: 301-565-2966
niamsinfo@mail.nih.gov
www.niams.nih.gov

The mission of the NIAMS, a part of the NIH, is to support research into the causes, treatment and prevention of arthritis and musculoskeletal and skin diseases, the training of basic and clinical scientists to carry out this research, and the dissemination of information on research progress in these diseases.
Lindsey A. Criswell, MD, Director
Rick Phillips, Executive Officer

National Associations & Support Groups

325 **American Academy of Pediatrics**
345 Park Blvd
Itasca, IL 60143
800-433-9016
Fax: 847-434-8000
mcc@aap.org
www.aap.org

The American Academy of Pediatrics and its member pediatricians are committed to the attainment of optimal physical, mental and social health and well-being for all infants, children, adolescents, and young adults.
Mark Del Monte, JD, CEO/Executive VP
Lynn Olson, PhD, VP, Research
Vera Tait, MD, FAAP, Chief Medical Officer

326 **Genetic Alliance**
426400 Woodfield Road, Ste 189
Damascus, MD 20872
202-966-5557
Fax: 202-966-8553
info@geneticalliance.org
www.geneticalliance.org

World's leading nonprofit health advocacy organization committed to transforming health through genetics and promoting an environment of openness centered on the health of individuals, families, and communities.
Sharon Terry, CEO
Ruth Child, CFO
Natasha Bonhomme, Chief Strategy Officer

327 **Human Growth Foundation**
997 Glen Cove Avenue, Suite 5
Glen Head, NY 10069
800-451-6434
Fax: 516-671-4055
hgf1@hgfound.org
www.hgfound.org

A voluntary, nonprofit organization whose mission is to help children and adults with disorders of growth and growth hormones through research, education, support and advocacy. The foundation is dedicated to helping medical science to better understand the process of growth. It is composed of concerned parents and friends of children and adults with growth problems and interested health professionals.
Joel Steelman, MD, President
Emily Germain-Lee MD, Vice President

328 **MAGIC Foundation: Major Aspects of Growth in Children**
4200 Cantera Drive, #106
Warrenville, IL 60555
630-836-8200
800-362-4423
Fax: 630-836-8181
contactus@magicfoundation.org
www.magicfoundation.org

A national nonprofit organization providing support and education regarding growth disorders in children and related adult disorders. Provides educational information, networking, a national conference, a kids' program and an extensive medical library.

Dianne Kremidas, Executive Director
Mary Andrews, Chief Executive Officer
Teresa Tucker, Patient Advocacy

329 March of Dimes Foundation
1550 Crystal Drive, Ste 1300
Arlington, VA 22202
888-663-4637
www.marchofdimes.org

March of Dimes help moms have full-term pregnancies and research the problems that threaten the health of babies. The March of Dimes also acts globally: sharing best practices in perinatal health and helping improve birth outcomes where the needs are the most urgent.

Stacey D. Stewart, President
Alan Brogdon, SVP/COO/Board Officer
Rahul Gupta, MD, SVP & Chief Medical/Health Officer

Conferences

330 Adult Endocrine Disorders/GHD Educational Convention
Magic Foundation
4200 Cantera Drive, #106
Warrenville, IL 60555
630-836-8200
800-362-4423
Fax: 630-836-8181
contactus@magicfoundation.org
www.magicfoundation.org

An educational program for adults who are affected with Growth Hormone Deficiency and/or other endocrine disorders.

June

Rick Buckley, Chairman
Ken Dickard, Vice Chairman
Courtney Lance, Secretary

Web Sites

331 National Center for Biotechnology Information
National Library of Medicine, 8600 Rockville Pike
Bethesda, MD 20894
888-346-3656
info@ncbi.nlm.nih.gov
www.ncbi.nlm.nih.gov

NCBI's mission is to develop new information technologoes to aid in the understanding of fundamental molecular and genetic processes that control health and disease.

Patricia Flatley Brennan, RN, PhD, Director
James Ostell, PhD, Executive Secretary

332 Online Mendelian Inheritance in Man
McKusick-Nathans Institue of Genetic Medicine-JHU
Baltimore, MD 21205
www.omim.org

This database is a catalog of human genes and genetic disorders.

Ada Hamosh, MD, Scientific Director

333 Wheeless' Textbook of Orthopaedics
www.wheelessonline.com

www.wheelessonline.com

Comprehensive, unparalleled, dynamic online medical textbook that is updated daily.

Clifford R. Wheeless, III, M.D., Author

Book Publishers

334 Let's Talk About Going to the Hospital
Rosen Publishing Group's PowerKids Press
29 E 21st Street
New York, NY 10010
212-777-3017
800-237-9932
Fax: 888-436-4643
rosenpub@tribeca.ios.com
www.rosenpublishing.com

If a child has to check into the hospital, chances are he or she is already upset about being ill. Knowing how a hospital functions and what the procedures are, such as when family members can visit, will help in what is already a stressful situation. Grades K-5.

24 pages
ISBN: 0-823950-36-0

Roger Rosen, President

Asperger Syndrome / National Associations & Support Groups

Description

335 ASPERGER SYNDROME
Involves the following Biologic System(s):
Developmental/Behavioral/Psychiatric Disorders, Genetic/Chromosomal/Syndrome/Metabolic Disorders, Neurologic Disorders

Asperger syndrome (AS) is a developmental disorder belonging to the group of neurological conditions known as autism spectrum disorders (ASDs), which are marked by problems in language and communications and confined patterns of thought and behavior. AS usually manifests itself by the age of 3 years, and in some cases may be apparent in infancy through clumsiness and delayed crawling or walking. Children with AS have no difficulty with intelligence or language skills, but may speak in a monotone or in an excessively formal manner or have difficulties with the subtleties of language, such as the slight variations in rhythm and pitch that help to communicate different shades of meaning (prosody). Children with AS also exhibit repetitive or ritualistic behavior; tend to be preoccupied with a single activity or area of personal interest to the exclusion of other activities or interests; have difficulty in their gestures and motor movements, such as those needed for ballplaying or playground activities; and interact poorly with other children of their age group and usually also with adults, manifesting motor symptoms of the syndrome or focusing on their own interests rather than engaging in dialogue. In some cases, AS in children is followed by other psychological problems and symptoms in adolescence and adulthood.

AS occurs in about 2 of every 10,000 children and is more likely to affect boys than girls. Although its precise cause remains unknown, studies suggest that AS stems from aberrations in the structure and function of several regions of the brain, which may come from irregularities in the fetal development and growth of the brain. Recent studies suggest that susceptibility to AS, and the severity with which it affects an individual, may be related to one or more aberrations in a specific group of genes.

The absence of standardized, universally accepted diagnostic criteria for AS has complicated its diagnosis. Currently, several verbal and behavioral procedures are used in diagnostic testing for AS. Because each of these procedures has its own standards, the various procedures can yield different diagnostic results. Moreover, different specialists have different viewpoints about the nature and characteristics of AS, with some considering it a mild form of autism known as high-functioning autism rather than a distinct disorder. In identifying AS, most physicians use a set of criteria based on abnormal eye contact; failure of a child to respond to its name; failure to use gestures to point or indicate an object or item; and a lack of interest in and play with other children of the same age.

The complete examination of a child with suspected AS typically requires a psychologist, psychiatrist, neurologist, and speech therapist, with other professionals called upon as needed. Diagnosis of the syndrome includes testing of intelligence, language and communication skills, motor and other neurologic function, and genetics.

The treatment of AS similarly requires professionals specialized in improving the communications skills, easing the obsessive or repetitive behavioral patterns, and reducing the physical clumsiness of children with the syndrome. This typically involves strengthening the child's interests, actively involving the child in structured activities, and reinforcing socially adaptive behavior through the use of supervised group therapy. Physical and occupational therapy can be used to improve affected childrens' motor skills. Although they usually require these special educational services, children with Asperger syndrome are typically educated in the traditional community setting. If needed, medication can be used to alleviate anxiety and depression in children with AS.

Government Agencies

336 NIH/National Institute of Mental Health
6001 Executive Blvd, Rm 6200, MSC 9663
Bethesda, MD 20892
866-615-6464
Fax: 301-443-4279
TTY: 301-443-8431
nimhinfo@nih.gov
www.nimh.nih.gov

The mission of NIMH is to transform the understanding and treatment of mental illnesses through basic and clinical research, paving the way for prevention, recovery, and cure.
Joshua A. Gordon, MD, PhD, Director
Shelli Avenevoli, PhD, Deputy Director

337 NIH/National Institute of Neurological Disorders and Stroke (NINDS)
PO Box 5801
Bethesda, MD 20824
800-352-9424
www.ninds.nih.gov

Works to reduce the burden of neurological disease by conducting, fostering, coordinating and guiding research on the causes, prevention, diagnosis and treatment of neurological disorders and stroke, while supporting basic research in related scientific areas.
Walter J. Koroshetz, MD, Director

338 NIH/National Institute on Deafness and Other Communication Disorders (NIDCD)
31 Center Drive, MSC 2320
Bethesda, MD 20892
800-241-1044
TTY: 800-241-1055
nidcdinfo@nidcd.nih.gov
www.nidcd.nih.gov

Conducts and supports biomedical research and research training on normal mechanisms, as well as diseases and disorders of hearing, balance, smell, taste, voice, speech and language.
Debara L. Tucci, MD, Director
Judith A. Cooper, PhD, Deputy Director
Timothy J. Wheeles, Executive Officer

National Associations & Support Groups

339 AASCEND
P.O. Box 591011
San Francisco, CA 94159
info@aascend.org
www.aascend.org

Adults of all ages on the autism spectrum, their families and friends, academics and professionals in the autism field unite as a community in AASCEND.
Greg Yates, Co-Chair
Camilla Bixler, Co-Chair

340 America's Special Kidz
P.O. Box 2098
Woodland Park, NJ 07424
973-521-0433

America's Special Kidz A.S.K understands the importance of healthy families. With a large population of families with special kids-especially single parents-they serve these struggling families.

Asperger Syndrome / National Associations & Support Groups

341 **American Academy of Pediatrics**
345 Park Blvd
Itasca, IL 60143
800-433-9016
Fax: 847-434-8000
mcc@aap.org
www.aap.org

The American Academy of Pediatrics and its member pediatricians are committed to the attainment of optimal physical, mental and social health and well-being for all infants, children, adolescents, and young adults.

Mark Del Monte, JD, CEO/Executive VP
Lynn Olson, PhD, VP, Research
Vera Tait, MD, FAAP, Chief Medical Officer

342 **American Association for Marriage and Family Therapy**
112 South Alfred Street
Alexandria, VA 22314
703-838-9808
Fax: 703-838-9805
www.aamft.org

The American Association for Marriage and Family Therapy (AAMFT) is the professional association for the field of marriage and family therapy.

Shelley Hanson, MA, President
Tracy Todd, PhD, Executive Director
Chris Michaels, Chief Operations Officer

343 **American School Counselor Association**
1101 King Street, Ste 310
Alexandria, VA 22314
703-683-2722
asca@schoolcounselor.org
www.schoolcounselor.org

The mission of ASCA is to represent professional school counselors and to promote professionalism and ethical practices.

Jill Cook, Executive Director
Amanda Fitzgerald, Assistant Deputy Executive Director
Kathleen M Rakestraw, Director of Communications

344 **Asperger Autism Spectrum Education Network (ASPEN)**
P.O. Box 109
Oceanport, NJ 07757
732-321-0880
aspennj.org

ASPEN provides families and individuals whose lives are affected by Autism Spectrum Disorders (Asperger Syndrome, Pervasive Developmental Disorder-NOS, High Functioning Autism), and Nonverbal Learning Disabilities with education, support & advocacy.

Lori Shery, President/Executive Director
Rich Meleo, Vice President

345 **Asperger's Network Support for Well-being Education and Research**
www.aspergersmn.org
763-227-5059
tnamie@aspergersmn.org
www.aspergersmn.org

ANSWER is a group of advocates for improving awareness, research, education and support of individuals and families impacted by Asperger's Syndrome.

Theresa Namie, Executive Director/Co-Founder
Kathy Hoffman, Chair
James Namie, Treasurer

346 **Asperger/Autism Network**
51 Water Street, Suite 206
Watertown, MA 02472
617-393-3824
info@aane.org
www.aane.org

The Asperger/Autism Network (AANE) works with individuals, families, and professionals to help people with Asperger Syndrome and similar autism spectrum profiles build meaningful, connected lives.

Dania Jekel, Executive Director
Brenda Dater, Associate Director
Marcia Robinson, Volunteer Coordinator

347 **Aspergers Women's Association**
NOP-ONE-

AWA serves to educate the public on issues unique to women and girls on the spectrum, as well as their families.

Charlotte Eades-Willis, Director

348 **Autism New Jersey**
500 Horizon Drive, Suite 530
Robbinsville, NJ 08691
609-588-8200
800-428-8476
www.autismnj.org

Autism New Jersey is a nonprofit agency committed to ensuring safe and fulfilling lives for individuals with autism, their families, and the professionals who support them. Through awareness, credible information, education, and public policy initiatives, Autism New Jersey leads the way to lifelong individualized services provided with skill and compassion.

Suzanne Buchanan, Executive Director
Ellen Schisler, Associate Executive Director

349 **Autism Society of America**
6110 Executive Boulevard, Ste 305
Rockville, MD 20852
800-328-8476
www.autism-society.org

The Autism Society, the nation's leading grassroots autism organization, exists to improve the lives of all affected by autism. We do this by increasing public awareness about the day-to-day issues faced by people on the spectrum, advocating for appropriate services for individuals across the lifespan, and providing the latest information regarding treatment, education, research and advocacy.

Christopher Banks, President & CEO
John Dabrowski, CFO/COO

350 **Autism Spectrum Connection**
PO Box 524
Crown Point, IN 46308
219-789-9874
MAAPatOasis@gmail.com
www.aspergersyndrome.org

Autism Spectrum Coalition is a nonprofit organization providing information, networking, referrals and printed materials for families, challenged individuals and professionals concerned with the autism spectrum. Founded in 1984, MAAP Services, adheres to the basic principal that all individuals with autism spectrum challenges have the ability to learn, grow and enjoy a good quality of life.

Susan Moreno, Founder & President

351 **Bridges4Kids**
www.bridges4kids.org
info@bridges4kids.org
www.bridges4kids.org

A non-profit organization providing a comprehensive system of information and referral for parents and professionals seeking help for children from birth through transition to adult life.

352 **Center for Autism and Related Disorders**
21600 Oxnard St., Ste 1800
Woodland Hills, CA 91367
818-345-2345
877-448-4747
info@centerforautism.com
www.centerforautism.com

The Center for Autism and Related Disorders (CARD) uses applied behavior analysis (ABA) in the treatment of autism spectrum disorder.

Doreen Granpeesheh, Founder/Executive Director

353 **Child Neurology Foundation**
601 W Short Street
Lexington, KY 40508
888-417-3435
info@childneurologyfoundation.org
childneurologyfoundation.org

The Child Neurology Foundation connects partners from all areas of the child neurology community so those navigating the journey of disease diagnosis, management, and care have the ongoing support from those dedicated to treatments and cures.

Asperger Syndrome / Conferences

Amy Brin, Executive Director
Katie Hentges, Director, Programs
Brea McCormley, Director, Development

354 Global and Regional Asperger Syndrome Partnership
369 Lexington Avenue
New York, NY 10017
888-474-7277
info@grasp.org
grasp.org

GRASP works to improve the lives of teens and adults with autism spectrum disorder (ASD). It offers in-school programs to help students with autism learn advocacy skills and improve social skills. Through its website, it educates the public about autism, while also offering free online resources and networking opportunities for individuals with ASD and their families.

355 NIH/ Eunice Kennedy Shriver National Institute of Child Health & Human Development
P.O. Box 3006
Rockville, MD 20847
800-370-2943
Fax: 866-760-5947
www.nichd.nih.gov

NICHD conducts and supports laboratory research, clinical trials, and epidemiological studies that explore health processes; examines the impact of disabilities, diseases, and variations on the lives of individuals; and sponsors training programs for scientists, health care providers, and researchers to ensure that NICHD research can continue.

Diana W. Bianchi, Director
Alison Cernich, PhD, Deputy Director

356 NIH/National Institute of Environmental Health Sciences (NIEHS)
PO Box 12233
Durham, NC 27709
984-287-3815
www.niehs.nih.gov

NIEHS reduces the burden of human illness and dysfunction from environmental causes by defining how environmental exposures, genetics and age interact to affect an individual's health.

Chris Long, MPA, Executive Officer
Mitch Williams, Deputy Executive Officer

357 National Alliance on Mental Illness (NAMI)
4301 Wilson Blvd., Suite 300
Arlington, VA 22203
703-524-7600
800-999-6264
info@nami.org
www.nami.org

NAMI provides advocacy, education, support and public awareness so that all individuals and families affected by mental illness can build better lives.

Daniel H. Gillison, CEO
Ken Duckworth, Chief Medical Officer
David Levy, CFO

358 National Association of Special Education Teachers
1250 Connecticut Avenue, NW, Suite 200
Washington, DC 20036
800-754-4421
Fax: 800-754-4421
contactus@naset.org
www.naset.org

A membership organization dedicated solely to meeting the needs of special education teachers and those preparing for the field of special education teaching.

Dr. Roger Pierangelo, Co-Executive Director
Dr. George Giuliani, Co-Executive Director

359 National Autism Association
One Park Avenue, Suite 1
Portsmouth, RI 02871
401-293-5551
877-622-2884
Fax: 401-293-5342
naa@nationalautism.org
nationalautismassociation.org

NAA is a parent-run advocacy organization and the leading voice on urgent issues related to severe autism, regressive autism, autism safety, autism abuse, and crisis prevention.

Wendy Fournier, President
Krystal Higgins, Executive Director

360 National Mental Health Consumers' Self-Help Clearinghouse
1211 Chestnut Street, Suite 1207
Philadelphia, PA 19107
215-751-1810
800-553-4539
Fax: 215-636-6312
selfhelpclearinghouse@gmail.com
www.mhselfhelp.org

The Clearinghouse works to foster peer empowerment through our website, up-to-date news and information announcements, a directory of peer-driven services, electronic and printed publications, training packages, and individual and onsite consultation

Joseph Rogers, Founder/Executive Director
Susan Rogers, Director

361 US Autism Association
www.usautism.org

888-928-8476
www.usautism.org

Provides opportunity for all individuals with Autism Spectrum Disorders to achieve their fullest potential by expanding and enriching the ASD community through education, online training, published and electronic information and resources, and partnerships with local and national projects.

Jennifer Grace, CEO
Marlo Payne Thurman, PhD, President
Phillip C. DeMio, MD, Chief Medical Officer Emeritus

Conferences

362 ASPEN Annual Spring Conference
Asperger Autism Spectrum Education Network
P.O. Box 109
Oceanport, NJ 07757
732-321-0880
info@aspennj.org
www.aspennj.org

Practical strategies for teachers and parents of students with autism spectrum disorders for navigating school, home and life

Lori Shery, President/Executive Director
Rich Meleo, Vice President

363 American School Counselor Association Annual Conference
1101 King Street, Suite 310
Alexandria, VA 22314
703-683-2722
800-306-4722
Fax: 703-997-7572
asca@schoolcounselor.org
www.schoolcounselor.org

The mission of ASCA is to represent professional school counselors and to promote professionalism and ethical practices.

3,000 Attendees

Richard Wong, Executive Director
Jennifer Walsh, Director, Education & Training
Kathleen M Rakestraw, Director of Communications

364 Autism Society National Conference and Exposition
Autism Society of America
4340 East-West Hwy, Suite 350
Bethesda, MD 20814
301-657-0881
800-328-8476
info@autism-society.org
www.autism-society.org

Addresses the range of issues affecting people with autism including early intervention, education, employment, behavior, communication, social skills, biomedical interventions and others, across the entire lifespan.

July

Scott Badesch, President/CEO
Matthew Asner, VP Development
Selena Hernandez, Manager, Support Services

Asperger Syndrome / Audio Video

Audio Video

365 Asperger's Syndrome: Autism and Obsessive Behavior
Films for the Humanities and Sciences
132 West 31st Street
New York, NY 10001
800-257-5126
Fax: 609-275-0266
custserv@films.com
www.ffh.films.com

This program profiles the symptoms of Asperger's Syndrome and what sufferers and their families can do to overcome the limitations that it imposes.

28 minutes
ISBN: 1-421387-67-3

366 The Boy Inside
Fanlight Productions
32 Court Street, 21st Floor
Brooklyn, NY 11201
718-488-8900
800-876-1710
Fax: 718-488-8642
info@fanlight.com
www.fanlight.com

The harrowing story of the filmaker's son Adam, a 12-year-old with Asperger Syndrome, during a tumultuous year in the life of their family. AS makes Adam's life in seventh grade a minefield, where he finds himself isollated and bullied. As he struggles to find a place for himself, his troublees escalate, both at school and at home. ISBN: DVD: 1-57295-838-3; VHS: 1-57295-449-3

47 minutes DVD or VHS

Web Sites

367 Autism Resources
www.autism-resources.com

www.autism-resources.com

Offers information and links regarding the developemental disabilities autism and Asperger's Syndrom.

368 Autism Spectrum Connection
P.O. Box 524
Crown Point, IN 46308
219-789-9874
MAAPatOasis@gmail.com
www.aspergersyndrome.org

Provides parents, professionals and person with the links they need to research anything.

369 University Students with Autism and Asperger's Syndrome Web Site
www.users.dircon.co.uk/~cns/

www.users.dircon.co.uk/~cns/

Helps to develop an understanding of the difficulties people with Asperger Syndrome may face. We also work on a one to one basis with the student and liase with staff and peers. Help is also given in setting up support networks such as mentors and providing effective strategies to aid independent learning.

Book Publishers

370 Asperger Syndrome
A Klin, F Volkmar, S Sparrow, author

Guilford Publications
72 Spring Street
New York, NY 10012
212-431-9800
800-365-7006
Fax: 212-966-6708
info@guilford.com
www.guilford.com

Brings together preeminent scholars and practitioners to offer a definitive statement of what is currently known about Asperger syndrome and to highlight promising leads in research and clinical practice. Sifts through the latest developments in theory and research, discussing key diagnostic and conceptual issues and reviewing what is known about behavioral features and neurobiology. The effects of Asperger syndrome on social development, learning and communication are examined.

Jan 2000 489 pages
ISBN: 1-572305-34-2

371 Asperger Syndrome and Your Child: A Parent's Guide
Autism Society of North Carolina Bookstore
505 Oberlin Road, Suite 230
Raleigh, NC 27605
919-743-0204
800-442-2762
Fax: 919-743-0208
books@autismsociety-nc.org
www.autismbookstore.com

Written primarily for parents, this book provides a clinician's view of Asperger Syndrome.

372 Asperger Syndrome: A Practical Guide for Teachers
ADD WareHouse
300 NW 70th Avenue, Suite 102
Plantation, FL 33317
954-792-8100
800-233-9273
Fax: 954-792-8545
websales@addwarehouse.com
www.addwarehouse.com

A clear and concise guide to effective classroom practice for teachers and support assistants working with children with Asperger Syndrome in school. The authors explain characteristics of children with Asperger Syndrome, discuss methods of assessment and offer practical strategies for effective classroom interventions.

90 pages
ISBN: 1-853464-99-6

373 Asperger Syndrome: Guide for Educators and Parents, Second Edition
Pro-Ed
8700 Shoal Creek Boulevard
Austin, TX 78757
512-451-3246
800-897-3202
Fax: 800-397-7633
info@proedinc.com
www.proedinc.com

A ground-breaking resource on Asperger Syndrome, this text outlines, in lay terms, the characteristics of the syndrome sometimes referred to as higher-functioning autism.

215 pages
ISBN: 0-890798-98-2

374 Asperger's Syndrome: A Guide for Parents and Professionals
ADD WareHouse
300 NW 70th Avenue, Suite 102
Plantation, FL 33317
954-792-8100
800-233-9273
Fax: 954-792-8545
websales@addwarehouse.com
addwarehouse.com

Providing a description and analysis of the unusual characteristics of Asperger's Syndrome, with strategies to reduce those that are most conspicuous or debilitating. This guide brings together the most relevant and useful information on all aspects of the syndrome, from language and social behavior to motor clumsiness.

240 pages
ISBN: 1-853025-77-1

375 Autism and Asperger Syndrome
Autism Society of North Carolina Bookstore
505 Oberlin Road, Suite 230
Raleigh, NC 27605
919-743-0204
800-442-2762
info@autismsociety-nc.org
www.austismsociety-nc.org

Asperger Syndrome / Camps

Chapters include topics such as the relationship of autism and Asperger Syndrome, living with the syndrome and Asperger Syndrome in adulthood.

247 pages

Beverly Moore, Chairman
Sharon Jeffries-Jones, Vice Chair
Darryl R Marsch, Secretary

376 Can I Tell You About Asperger Syndrome?: A Guide for Friends and Family
Autism Society of North Carolina Bookstore
505 Oberlin Road, Suite 230
Raleigh, NC 27605
919-743-0204
800-442-2762
Fax: 919-743-0208
books@autismsociety-nc.org
www.autismbookstore.com

Written for young people so that they can better understand the challenges faced by a sibling, friend, or classmate who has Asperger Syndrome. For readers ages 7-15.

377 Oasis Guide to Asperger Syndrome
Autism Society of North Carolina Bookstore
505 Oberlin Road, Suite 230
Raleigh, NC 27605
919-743-0204
800-442-2762
Fax: 919-743-0208
books@autismsociety-nc.org
www.autismbookstore.com

Combining the most current information about Asperger Syndrome (AS) diagnosis and treatment with hundreds of practical tips and resource listings, this guide is comprehensive in scope.

378 Out-of-Sync Child: Recognizing and Coping with Sensory Processing Disorder
Autism Society of North Carolina Bookstore
505 Oberlin Road, Suite 230
Raleigh, NC 27605
919-743-0204
800-442-2762
Fax: 919-743-0208
books@autismsociety-nc.org
www.autismbookstore.com

The author provides, readers with information on the symptoms and diagnosis of sensory processing disorder (SPD), as well as treatment approach based on early intervention.

379 To Be Me: Understanding What It's Like to Have Asperger's Syndrome
Autism Society of North Carolina Bookstore
505 Oberlin Road, Suite 230
Raleigh, NC 27605
919-743-0204
800-442-2762
Fax: 919-743-0208
books@autismsociety-nc.org
www.autismbookstore.com

Colorfully illustrated book is about a boy named David, who has Asperger Syndrome (AS). Told from David's point of view, the story focuses on his social difficulties, as he struggles to fit in with his classmates at school. For readers ages 9-12.

Pamphlets

380 Asperger Syndrome
NINDS
PO Box 5801
Bethesda, MD 20824
301-496-5751
800-352-9424
www.ninds.nih.gov

Information sheet.

Walter J. Koroshetz, M.D., Acting Director
Alan L. Willard, Ph.D., Acting Deputy Director
Caroline Lewis, Executive Officer

381 Autism Fact Sheet
NINDS
PO Box 5801
Bethesda, MD 20824
301-496-5751
800-352-9424
TTY: 301-468-5981
www.ninds.nih.gov

Also available in Spanish.

Walter J. Koroshetz, M.D., Acting Director
Alan L. Willard, Ph.D., Acting Deputy Director
Caroline Lewis, Executive Officer

Camps

382 Camp Akeela
1 Thoreau Way
Thetford Center, VT 05075
866-680-4744
Fax: 866-462-2828
info@campakeela.com
www.campakeela.com

A co-ed, overnight camp in Vermont. Within a well-rounded and traditional program we emphasize the social growth of our campers, many of whom have been diagnosed with Asperger's Syndrome or a non verbal learning disability.

Debbie Sasson, Director

383 Camp Northwood
132 State Route 365
Remsen, NY 13438
315-831-3621
Fax: 315-831-5867
northwoodprograms@hotmail.com
www.nwood.com

Specialize in working with non-aggressive children ranging in age from 8-18 classified with Asperger's Syndrome, HFA, Attention Deficits, Language Processing Weaknesses and children with other forms of minimal learning issues.

Gordon Felt, Director

384 Charis Hills
498 Faulkner Road
Sunset, TX 76270
940-964-2145
888-681-2173
Fax: 940-964-2147
info@charishills.org
www.charishills.org

Residential Christian summer camp which helps kids with learning differences build confidence and find success. We welcome kids with ADHD, PDD, Asperger's Syndrome and High Functioning Autism.

Rand Soulhard, President

385 Frontier Travel Camp
2000 NE 197 Terrace
Miami, FL 33179
305-895-1123
866-750-2267
Fax: 305-402-0900
info@frontiertravelcamp.com
www.frontiertravelcamp.com

Established in 1997 as a summer camp alternative for individuals with special needs. We believe that group trips are an ideal way to experience independence, improve social skills, and increase self-esteem in a secure and exciting environment.

Scott Fineman, Director

386 Summer Experience
Vanguard School
PO Box 730
Paoli, PA 19301
610-296-6700
Fax: 610-640-0132
info@vanguardschool-pa.org
www.vanguardschool-pa.org

For students who are experiencing learning difficulties due to neurological impairment, social/emotional disturbance and/or autism/pervasive developmental disorder.

Asperger Syndrome / Camps

Susan Snyder, Admissions Director
John D Wilson, Education Director

387 Summit Camp
168 Duck Harbor Road
Honesdale, PA 18431

570-253-4381
800-323-9908
Fax: 570-253-2937
info@summitcamp.com
www.summitcamp.com

Provides a summer camp experience for boys and girls, ages 7-17, who have issues of attention. These may include ADD, verbal or non-verbal disabilities, mild social or emotional concerns, and/or Aspergers syndrome.

Eugene Bell, Senior Director

388 Wesley Woods
1001 Fiddlersgreen Rd
Grand Valley, PA 16420

814-430-7802
Fax: 814-436-7669
www.wesleywoods.com

Exceptional children's camp for children with emotional and intellectual handicaps.

Herb West

Description

389 ASTHMA
Synonym: Bronchial asthma
Involves the following Biologic System(s):
Respiratory Disorders

Asthma is a chronic respiratory disorder in which abnormal sensitivity (hyperresponsiveness) to certain stimuli causes inflammation and associated narrowing of the lungs' large and small airways, resulting in shortness of breath and other symptoms. Approximately 14 million adults and 6 million children have asthma. It is the primary cause of chronic illness in children. Up to 10 percent of girls and 15 percent of boys are affected by asthma at some point during childhood. Initial symptoms occur during the first year of life in about 30 percent of patients and before the age of four to five years in approximately 80 to 90 percent.

Episodes may be triggered by exposure to many different stimuli, such as certain foreign substances (allergens) including pollen, mold, house dust, or animal hair. Asthma attacks may also be triggered by respiratory infections or exposure to smoke, certain chemicals or medications, strong odors, cold air, vigorous exercise, or stress. Exposure to such stimuli or precipitating factors may prompt certain cells within the lungs' airways (e.g., mast cells) to release particular substances that may cause spasms of the smooth muscles lining the airways, inflammation and swelling of the airway walls, excessive secretion of mucus, and associated airway narrowing (bronchoconstriction) and obstruction.

Asthma episodes may vary greatly in frequency, severity, and duration. For example, attacks may subside after minutes or have a duration of hours or even days. Some patients may have only occasional, mild episodes of shortness of breath. Others may regularly cough and produce a high-pitched whistling sound while breathing (wheezing) and experience severe asthma episodes upon exposure to certain triggering stimuli. Most children with asthma have only periodic episodes that are mild to moderate in severity. However, a small percentage of children have severe asthma that interferes with regular daily functioning. Interestingly, most patients become relatively free of symptoms within 10 to 20 years after disease onset; however, many may have recurrences at some time during adulthood. Children with severe asthma may experience chronic disease through adulthood.

Asthma episodes may begin suddenly or gradually and are initially characterized by signs of air hunger, such as sighing, yawning, wheezing that may be most apparent while exhaling. Other symptoms include shortness of breath and a hacking, nonproductive cough. As mucus secretions increase, exhaling may become abnormally prolonged; however, this finding may not be obvious in infants and young children. Shortness of breath may become so severe that patients have difficulty walking and become unable to speak other than in a panting manner. These patients may assume a hunched over position in an attempt to make breathing easier. Additional symptoms may include chest tightness, profuse sweating due to exertion and anxiety, nausea, and vomiting. During extremely severe episodes, wheezing may diminish due to lack of airflow in the airways; breathing may become irregular and shallow; and patients may become listless (lethargic), appear confused due to lack of oxygen, and develop abnormal bluish discoloration of the skin and mucous membranes (cyanosis) due to abnormally diminished oxygen levels in the blood. Without immediate treatment, such patients may experience life-threatening complications.

Asthma is classified according to frequency of symptoms and the result of lung (pulmonary) tests. Classification and monitoring assists with the management of asthma and includes minimizing exposure to possible precipitating factors, such as avoiding rapid changes in humidity or temperature and reducing exposure to tobacco smoke, pollen, strong odors, fumes, or other possible irritants. In some cases, specialized tests may help to determine specific triggering stimuli that should be avoided. Asthma medications can be divided into long-term control and quick relief medications. Treatment choices are based on the severity of the patient's underlying asthma and the severity of asthma exacerbations. Treatment should be administered as quickly as possible to open the airways and restore normal breathing and proper oxygen levels in the blood. Drug therapy may include medications that relax and widen the airways (bronchodilators), such as albuterol. Depending upon the specific drugs prescribed or the severity of an episode, such medications may be administered by a metered dose inhaler with a spacer, or by a nebulizer, which produces a mist for inhalation. Inhaled steroids are the most effective anti-inflammatory medications for management of chronic asthma. Intravenous medications may be used in the hospitalized patient. If a patient is unable to be managed at home, or has progression of symptoms requiring intervention more often than every 4 hours, they should seek emergency care. Emergency treatment may include IV corticosteroids, IV bronchodilators, continuous nebulizer treatments and, in the most severe cases, possibly intubation with mechanical ventilation.

Government Agencies

390 NIH/National Heart, Lung and Blood Institute
31 Center Drive, Bldg 31
Bethesda, MD 20824
877-645-2448
www.nhlbi.nih.gov

The National Heart, Lung, and Blood Institute (NHLBI) provides global leadership for a research, training, and education program to promote the prevention and treatment of heart, lung, and blood diseases and enhance the health of all individuals so that they can live longer and more fulfilling lives.
Gary H. Gibbons, MD, Director
Kate O'Sullivan, Executive Officer

391 NIH/National Institute of Allergy and Disease Council
5601 Fishers Lane, MSC 9806
Bethesda, MD 20892
301-496-5717
866-284-4107
Fax: 301-402-3573
TDD: 800-877-8339
ocpostoffice@niaid.nih.gov
www.niaid.nih.gov

The principal advisory board of the NIAID. The council is composed of physicians, scientists and representatives of the public and advises on the conduct and support or research, training and dissemination of health information regarding allergies and infectious diseases.
Anthony S. Fauci MD, Director

392 National Advisory Allergic and Infectious Disease Council
5601 Fishers Lane, MSC 9806
Bethesda, MD 20892
301-496-5717
866-284-4107
Fax: 301-402-3573
TDD: 800-877-8339
ocpostoffice@niaid.nih.gov
www.niaid.nih.gov

The principal advisory board of the NIAID. The council is composed of physicians, scientists and representatives of the public and advises on the conduct and support or research, training and dissemination of health information regarding allergies and infectious diseases.
Dr. Anthony S. Fauci, M.D., Director

Asthma / National Associations & Support Groups

National Associations & Support Groups

393 **Allergy & Asthma Network Mothers of Asthmatics**
8229 Boone Boulevard, Suite 260
Vienna, VA 22182
800-878-4403
Fax: 703-288-5271
info@aanma.org
www.allergyasthmanetwork.org

A nonprofit family health organization dedicated to eliminating suffering and death due to asthma, allergies and related conditions.
Tonya Winders, President & CEO
Charmayne Anderson, Director of Advocacy
Marcela Gieminiani, Director of Outreach

394 **American Academy of Allergy, Asthma & Immunology**
555 East Wells Street, Suite 1100
Milwaukee, WI 53202
414-272-6071
Fax: 414-272-6070
info@aaaai.org
www.aaaai.org

The American Academy of Allergy, Asthma & Immunology is dedicated to the advancement of the knowledge and practice of allergy, asthma and immunology for optimal patient care.
David Lang, MD, President
Mary-Beth Fasano, MD, President-Elect
Giselle S. Mosnaim, MD, Secretary-Treasurer

395 **American Academy of Pediatrics**
345 Park Blvd
Itasca, IL 60143
800-433-9016
Fax: 847-434-8000
mcc@aap.org
www.aap.org

The American Academy of Pediatrics and its member pediatricians are committed to the attainment of optimal physical, mental and social health and well-being for all infants, children, adolescents, and young adults.
Mark Del Monte, JD, CEO/Executive VP
Lynn Olson, PhD, VP, Research
Vera Tait, MD, FAAP, Chief Medical Officer

396 **American Association for Respiratory Care**
9425 N. MacArthur Blvd. Suite 100
Irving, TX 75063
972-243-2272
Fax: 972-484-2720
info@aarc.org
www.aarc.org

The AARC encourages and promotes professional excellence, advances the science and practice of respiratory care, and serves as an advocate for patients and their families, the public, the profession and the respiratory therapist.
Tom Kallstrom, Executive Director
Shawna Strickland, Associate Executive Director
Heather Willden, Communications Coordinator

397 **American College of Allergy, Asthma and Immunology**
85 W Algonquin Road, Suite 550
Arlington Heights, IL 60005
847-427-1200
800-842-7777
Fax: 847-427-9656
mail@acaai.org
www.acaai.org

The association provides its members with continuing medical education, publications, and representation to managed care organizations, medical organizations, consumer and patient groups, and government and regulatory agencies. The College also develops and disseminates educational information to patients, other physicians, health professionals and health plan administrators.
Rick Slawny, Executive Director
Nancy Ryan, Associate Executive Director
Hollis Heavenrich-Jones, Public Relations Manager

398 **American Lung Association**
55 W. Wacker Drive, Suite 1150
Chicago, IL 60601
800-586-4872
info@lung.org
www.lung.org

The American Lung Association fights lung disease in all its forms, with special emphasis on asthma, tobacco control and environmental health. The American Lung Association is funded with contributions from the public, along with gifts and grants from corporations, foundations and government agencies. The association achieves its many successes through the work of thousands of committed volunteers and staff.
Harold P. Wimmer, National President & CEO
Albert Rizzo, MD, Chief Medical Officer
Sue Swan, Chief Development Officer

399 **American Medical Association**
AMA Plaza, 330 North Wabash Ave., Suite 39300
Chicago, IL 60611
312-464-4782
800-262-3211
www.ama-assn.org

AMA is dedicated to ensuring sustainable physician practices that result in better health outcomes for patients.
James L. Madara, MD, CEO/EVP
Bernard L. Hengesbaugh, Chief Operating Officer
Kenneth J. Sharigian, SVP

400 **American School Counselor Association**
1101 King Street, Ste 310
Alexandria, VA 22314
703-683-2722
asca@schoolcounselor.org
www.schoolcounselor.org

The mission of ASCA is to represent professional school counselors and to promote professionalism and ethical practices.
Jill Cook, Executive Director
Amanda Fitzgerald, Assistant Deputy Executive Director
Kathleen M Rakestraw, Director of Communications

401 **American Thoracic Society**
25 Broadway
New York, NY 10004
212-315-8600
Fax: 212-315-6498
atsinfo@Thoracic.org
www.thoracic.org

The American Thoracic Society improves global health by advancing research, patient care, and public health in pulmonary disease, critical illness, and sleep disorders. Founded in 1905 to combat TB, the ATS has grown to tackle asthma, COPD, lung cancer, sepsis, acute respiratory distress, and sleep apnea, among other diseases.
Karen J. Collishaw, MPP, CEO
Stephen Altobelli, COO

402 **Association of Asthma Educators**
70 Buckwalter Rd., Ste 900, #330
Royersford, PA 19468
888-988-7747
admin@asthmaeducators.org
www.asthmaeducators.org

The Association of Asthma Educators is the premier inter-professional organization striving for excellence to raise the competency of diverse individuals who educate patients and families living with asthma.
Teresa Summe, President
Kevin Collins, Vice-President
Julio Rebollebo, Treasurer

403 **Asthma and Allergy Foundation of America**
8201 Corporate Drive, Suite 1000
Landover, MD 20785
800-727-8462
info@aafa.org
www.aafa.org

AAFA is dedicated to improving the quality of life for people with asthma and allergic diseases through education, advocacy and research.
Richard Murray, Chair
Mary Ellen Conley, RN, Chair, Governance
Colette Martin, Chair, Communications & Marketing

404 **Breathing Association (The)**
788 Mount Vernon Avenue
Columbus, OH 43203
614-457-4570
Fax: 614-457-3777
info@breathingassociation.org
www.breathingassociation.org

Asthma / State Agencies & Support Groups

The Breathing Association serves the community as the leading resource for promoting lung health and preventing lung disease through education, detection, service, and treatment.

Susan Cornish, Chair
Ed Frantz, Treasurer
Matthew Curtis, Secretary

405 **Environmental Protection Agency**
1200 Pennsylvania Avenue, N.W.
Washington, DC 20004
202-564-4700
www.epa.gov

EPA promotes scientific understanding of environmental asthma triggers and ways to manage asthma in community settings through research, education and outreach.

Michael S. Regan, Administrator

406 **Genetic Alliance**
426400 Woodfield Road, Ste 189
Damascus, MD 20872
202-966-5557
Fax: 202-966-8553
info@geneticalliance.org
www.geneticalliance.org

World's leading nonprofit health advocacy organization committed to transforming health through genetics and promoting an environment of openness centered on the health of individuals, families, and communities.

Sharon Terry, CEO
Ruth Child, CFO
Natasha Bonhomme, Chief Strategy Officer

407 **Get a Grip on Asthma Programs**
8229 Boone Boulevard, Suite 260
Vienna, VA 22182
800-878-4403
800-878-4403
Fax: 703-288-5271
info@aanma.org
www.allergyasthmanetwork.org

Allergy & Asthma Network Mothers of Asthmatics (AANMA) is the leading nonprofit family health organization dedicated to eliminating suffering and death due to asthma, allergies and related conditions. From diagnosis to control, from diapers to college - AANMA is your one-stop, family-to-family support network.

Tonya Winders, President & CEO
Charmayne Anderson, Director of Advocacy
Marcela Gieminiani, Director of Outreach

408 **NIH/National Institute of Environmental Health Sciences (NIEHS)**
PO Box 12233
Durham, NC 27709
984-287-3815
www.niehs.nih.gov

NIEHS reduces the burden of human illness and dysfunction from environmental causes by defining how environmental exposures, genetics and age interact to affect an individual's health.

Chris Long, MPA, Executive Officer
Mitch Williams, Deputy Executive Officer

409 **National Association of School Nurses**
1100 Wayne Avenue, Suite 925
Silver Spring, MD 20910
240-821-1130
nasn@nasn.org
www.nasn.org

The mission is to advance school nurse practice to keep students healthy, safe and ready to learn.

Donna J. Mazyck, Executive Director
Nichole K. Bobo, Nursing Education Director
Jen McNally, Marketing/Communications Director

410 **National Asthma Educator Certification Board**
4227 South Meridian C662
Puyallup, WA 98373
877-408-0072
info@naecb.org
www.naecb.com

The mission of the National Asthma Educator Certification Board is to promote optimal asthma management and quality of life among individuals with asthma, their families and communities, by advancing excellence in asthma education through the certified asthma educator (AE-Cr) process.

411 **National Environmental Education Foundation**
4301 Connecticut Avenue NW, Suite 160
Washington, DC 20008
202-833-2933
www.neefusa.org

NEEF provides lifelong environmental learning, connecting people to knowledge they use to improve the quality of their lives and the health of the planet.

Meri-Margaret Deoudes, President/CEO
Sara Espinoza, VP, Programs

412 **National Medical Association**
8403 Colesville Road, Suite 820
Silver Spring, MD 20910
202-347-1895
www.nmanet.org

The National Medical Association (NMA) is the collective voice of African American physicians and the leading force for parity and justice in medicine and the elimination of disparities in health.

Martin Hamelette, JD, MHA, Executive Director

413 **Respiratory Health Association**
1440 W. Washington Blvd.
Chicago, IL 60607
312-243-2000
Fax: 312-243-3954
info@lungchicago.org
www.lungchicago.org

The association addresses asthma, COPD, lung cancer, tobacco control and air quality with a comprehensive approach involving research, education and advocacy activities.

Joel Africk, President/CEO
Avanthi Chatrathi, Program Coordinator
Gina Schwieger, Senior Director, Special Events

State Agencies & Support Groups

Alaska

414 **Alaska Chapter of Asthma and Allergy Foundation of America**
PO Box 201927
Anchorage, AK 99520
907-349-0637
800-651-4914
Fax: 907-696-4810
aafaalaska@gci.net
www.aafaalaska.com

The mission of AAFA Alaska is to serve people affected by asthma and allergies through education, community resources, research and support.

Jodyne Butto, MD, Chair
Kathleen Bell, Secretary
Mark Glore, CPA, Treasurer

Colorado

415 **Parents of Asthmatic/Allergic Children, Inc.**
1024 S. Lemay Avenue
Fort Collins, CO 80524
970-495-8153
Fax: 970-495-7608
cmc@pvhs.org
www.coloradoallergy.com

Support group for parents and children ages 6 and older, focusing on asthma, and issues such as allergic and non-allergic rhinitis.

Cindy Coopersmith, Coordinator

Asthma / Libraries & Resource Centers

Massachusetts

416 **Asthma & Allergy Foundation of America New England Chapter**
25 Braintree Hill Office Park, Suite 200
Braintree, MA 02184
781-444-7778
800-227-8462
Fax: 781-444-7718
aafane@aafane.org
www.asthmaandallergies.org

The Foundation was formed to alleviate suffering and loss from asthma and allergy disorders. The Foundation offers a nationwide network of chapters and support groups, and provides education and emotional support for persons with allergies and asthma. Also funds research for improved treatments and ultimately a cure.

Jan Hanson, Board President
David Guydan, Executive Director

Michigan

417 **Michigan Chapter of Allergy and Asthma Foundation of America**
26111 West 14 Mile, Suite LL1
Franklin, MI 48025
248-406-4254
888-444-0333
Fax: 248-757-2102
aafamich@sbcglobal.net
www.aafamich.org

Our mission is to improve the quality of life for individuals affected with asthma and allergic diseases by promoting awareness through education and training.

Kathleen Felice Slonager, Executive Director

Missouri

418 **Allergy and Pulmonary Medicine**
Saint Louis Children's Hospital
One Children's Place
Saint Louis, MO 63110
314-454-6000
Fax: 314-454-2515
www.stlouischildrens.org

Evaluating and treating a child's allergy or pulmonary disorder is only part of the care provided by the professionals at St. Louis Children's Hospital. Many of the difficulties children endure also require extensive treatment at home, therefore, educating parents and caregivers about home care and progress monitoring is a primary concern for the Allergy and Pulmonary Medicine staff. In most cases, the staff works with other team members throughout the hospital.

Stuart C Sweet MD PhD, Secretary

419 **Asthma and Allergy Foundation of America St Louis Chapter**
1500 South Big Bend, Suite 1S
St Louis, MO 63117
314-645-2422
888-542-8252
Fax: 314-645-2022
aafa@aafastl.org
aafastl.org

The Asthma and Allergy Foundation of America, St. Louis Chapter is committed to enhancing and saving the lives of asthma and allergy sufferers through support, advocacy, education, research and access to treatment.

Marjorie Moore, Executive Director
Brittany Van Almsick, Events/Public Awareness/Volunteer
Reagan Nelson, Program Director

Libraries & Resource Centers

420 **National Jewish Health**
National Jewish Health
1400 Jackson Street
Denver, CO 80206
877-225-5654
800-423-8891
lungline@njhealth.org
www.nationaljewish.org

A free information service answering questions, sending literature and giving advice to patients with immunologic or respiratory illnesses. The Line is an educational service and not a substitute for medical care. Diagnosis or suggested treatment will not be provided for a caller's specific condition. The Line does suggest topics that a patient might want to discuss with his or her doctor.

Michael Salem, MD, President & CEO
Richard Baer, Board Chair
Pamela L. Zeitlin, MD, PhD, Chair, Pediatrics Department

421 **Physician Referral and Information Line**
American Academy of Allergy, Asthma & Immunology
555 E Wells Street, Suite 1100
Milwaukee, WI 53202
414-272-6071
800-822-2762
Fax: 414-272-6070
info@aaaai.org
www.aaaai.org

Referral line offering information on allergy and asthma, referral to an allergy/immunology specialist.

Kay Whalen, Executive Director
Joy Blackburn, President
Dennis Ledfored, President-Elect

Research Centers

422 **Brigham and Women's Hospital, Asthma and Allergic Disease Research Center**
75 Francis Street
Boston, MA 10103
617-732-5500
800-294-9999
TTY: 617-732-6458
www.brighamandwomens.org

Brigham and Women's Hospital is world-renowned in virtually every area of adult medicine. As a teaching hospital of Harvard Medical School, our leadership in patient quality and safety, development of state-of-the-art treatments and technologies, and robust research programs have improved the health of people around the world.

Amy Yunes, President
Peter Helms, Vice President
Mary Montuori, Vice President

423 **Center for Interdisciplinary Research on Immunologic Diseases**
Children's Hospital Medical Center
300 Longwood Avenue
Boston, MA 10104
617-355-6000
800-355-7944
TTY: 617-730-0152
www.childrenshospital.org

Boston Children's community mission is to Provide the best quality care to our patients and serve as a safety net hospital, Develop and support community programs to make an impact and address the most pressing community health needs-asthma, obesity, mental health and child development and Work with partners to address health and non-health issues that affect the entire community

James Mandell, CEO/Trustee
Sandra Fenwick, President
Margaret Coughlin, Senior Vice President & Chief Admin

424 **National Jewish Health**
1400 Jackson Street
Denver, CO 10107
877-225-5654
800-423-8891
lungline@njhealth.org
www.nationaljewish.org

Asthma / Audio Video

Since 1899 we have been at the forefront of research and medicine. We integrate the latest scientific research discoveries with coordinated care for lung, heart and immune diseases.

Michael Salem, MD, President & CEO
Richard Baer, Board Chair
Pamela L. Zeitlin, MD, PhD, Chair, Pediatrics Department

425 Northwestern University Asthma and Allergy Disease Center
420 East Superior Street
Chicago, IL 60611
312-503-8194
Fax: 312-503-0994
medcommunications@northwestern.edu
www.feinberg.northwestern.edu/clinical-services/inde

The school has earned recognition for its research in genetic medicine, nanotechnology, biochemistry, neuroscience, cancer research, and materials sciences. NU partners with the Argonne National Laboratory, Fermilab, and local universities.

Eric G Neilson, MD, Vice President for Medical Affairs
William L. Lowe, Jr., MD, Vice Dean Academic Affairs
Raymond H. Curry, MD Curry, MD, Vice Dean Education

426 Tulane University Clinical Immunology Section
1430 Tulane Avenue Box SL-57
New Orleans, LA 10110
504-988-5578
800-355-7944
Fax: 504-988-3686
medsch@tulane.edu
www.tulane.edu/som/departments/medicine/medciar/

Tulane Medical Center, an acclaimed teaching, research and medical facility, serving the greater New Orleans area.

Laurianne G Wild, M.D., Director
Mary Brown, MBA, Vice President Health Sciences Syst

427 University of Texas Southwestern Medical Center/Asthma & Allergic Diseases
5323 Harry Hines Boulevard
Dallas, TX 10111
214-648-3111
Fax: 214-648-2102
www.utsouthwestern.edu

Among the nation's best performers in biology and biochemistry basic science research in achieving clinical breakthroughs.

Daniel K. Podolsky, President
J. Gregory Fitz MD, Executive Vice President
Bruce A Meyer MD MBA, Executive Vice President

428 University of Virginia General Clinical Research Center
1215 Lee Street
Charlottesville, VA 10112
434-924-5000
Fax: 434-924-9960
www.healthsystem.virginia.edu

To provide excellence, innovation and superlative quality in the care of patients, the training of health professionals, and the creation and sharing of health knowledge.

David R Jones, Program Director

429 University of Wisconsin Asthma and Allergic Disease Center
600 Highland Avenue
Madison, WI 10113
608-263-6100
877-942-7846
wiasthma@medicine.wisc.edu
www2.medicine.wisc.edu/home/asthma/asthmamain

The University of Wisconsin is known for its strong research environment, and the Department of Medicine has a rich history of academic achievement.

Carl J Getto, Head
Richard Page, Chair

Conferences

430 AAAAI Annual Meeting
American Academy of Allergy, Asthma & Immunology
555 East Wells Street, Suite 1100
Milwaukee, WI 53202
414-272-6071
Fax: 414-272-6070
annualmeeting@aaaai.org
annualmeeting.aaaai.org

The world's premier gathering of allergy and immunology experts. Attendees include clinicians, academicians, allied health professionals and others interested in allergic and immunologic disease.

Spring

431 ACAAI Annual Meeting
American College Of Allergy, Asthma & Immunology
86 W Algonquin Road, Suite 550
Arlington Heights, IL 60005
847-427-1200
800-842-7777
Fax: 847-427-9656
mail@acaai.org
www.acaai.org

Offers an array of educational sessions for physicians, allied health professionals, office managers and asthma educators, as well as some fantastic social events.

November

Rick Slawny, Executive Director
Gina Seegers, Director, Meetings & Conventions

432 American School Counselor Association Annual Conference
1101 King Street, Suite 310
Alexandria, VA 22314
703-683-2722
800-306-4722
Fax: 703-997-7572
asca@schoolcounselor.org
www.schoolcounselor.org

The mission of ASCA is to represent professional school counselors and to promote professionalism and ethical practices.

3,000 Attendees

Richard Wong, Executive Director
Jennifer Walsh, Director, Education & Training
Kathleen M Rakestraw, Director of Communications

Audio Video

433 A Regular Kid
American Lung Association
55 W. Wacker Drive, Suite 1150
Chicago, IL 60601
312-801-7630
800-LUN-USA
Fax: 202-452-1805
info@lungusa.org
www.lungusa.org

This film shows how families and children cope with asthma problems. Proven asthma management strategies are presented through the experiences of four children with asthma, ranging in age from toddler to teenager.

Film

Kathryn A. Forbes, CPA, Chair
John F. Emanuel, JD, Vice Chair
Penny J. Siewert, Secretary/Treasurer

434 AAAAI Impact
American Academy of Allergy, Asthma & Immunology
555 E Wells Street, Suite 1100
Milwaukee, WI 53202
414-272-6071
Fax: 414-272-6070
media@aaaai.org
www.aaaai.org

Patient newsletter covering issues for allergy and asthma patients throughout the year. Articles discuss and advise on flus, inhalers, allergins, climate change effects on allergins, astham attacks in pregnancy, and much more. Available free online.

Asthma / Web Sites

Quarterly

435 Allergy Control Begins at Home: House Dust Allergy
Allergy Control Products
1620-D Satellite Blvd
Duluth, GA 30097
800-255-3749
Fax: 800-395-9303
info@allergycontrol.com
www.allergycontrol.com

Shows simple steps to decrease your level of dust mite exposure.

1993 35 minutes

436 Asthma - Understanding and Control
American Academy of Allergy, Asthma & Immunology
555 E Wells Street, Suite 1100
Milwaukee, WI 53202
414-272-6071
Fax: 414-272-6070
info@aaaai.org
www.aaaai.org

This 20 minute public education tool helps patients understand asthma diagnosis, allergic and non-allergic triggers, risk factors, and guidelines for control of the disease. It is a great addition to physician waiting rooms and for patient use at home. This DVD format includes a Spanish version.

Melissa Graham, Media & Member Comm Manager
Megan Brown, Senior Media & Member Comm Manager

437 Baby Breaths: How to Get Babies to Sit Still During Nebulizer Treatments
Allergy and Asthma Network/Mothers of Asthmatics
8229 Boone Boulevard, Suite 260
Vienna, VA 22182
800-878-4403
800-878-4403
Fax: 703-288-5271
www.allergyasthmanetwork.org

10 minute video shows babies and toddlers taking a nebulizer treatment.

2009 Video

Tonya Winders, President & CEO
Charmayne Anderson, Director of Advocacy
Marcela Gieminiani, Director of Outreach

438 Childhood Asthma
Films for the Humanities and Sciences
132 West 31st Street
New York, NY 10001
800-257-5126
Fax: 609-275-0266
custserv@films.com
www.ffh.films.com

This program deals with the nature of bronchial and allergic asthma and with the diagnosis and treatment of childhood allergies. It explains how asthma attacks can be triggered by allergies, respiratory infections, exervise, and emotional stress; shows by means of animation how the bronchial tubes of asthmatics become inflamed and constricted during an attack; stresses the early diagnosis and treatment of childhood asthma; and explains what treatments are recommended.

28 minutes
ISBN: 1-421339-06-1

439 Managing Childhood Asthma
American Lung Association
50 East Huron Street
Chicago, IL 60611
312-944-6780
800-545-2433
Fax: 312-440-9374
ala@ala.org
www.ala.org

What parents need to know to manage asthma. 22 minutes.

Video

Keith Michael Fiels, Executive Director
Willie Glispie, Senior Administrative Assistant
Lois Ann Gregory-Wood, Secretariat

440 Mastering Asthma
Aquarius Health Care Videos
18 North Main Street
Sherborn, MA 1770
508-650-1616
888-440-2963
Fax: 508-650-1665
www.aquariusproductions.com

Mastering Asthma, so it doesn't master you, is an entertaining and informative video for both parents and children that takes viewers into the lives of three different families learning about and living with childhood asthma. Learn what is Asthma and what causes it. Everything from allergens and triggers to peak flow meters and bronchodilators and more is discussed. Closed captioned.

ISBN: 1-581402-93-7

441 Pharmacologic Therapy of Pediatric Asthma
American Lung Association
1740 Broadway
New York, NY 10019
212-315-8700

A Learning Resource Program developed by a joint committee of the American Thoracic Society and the ALA.

Film

442 What School Personnel Should Know About Asthma
American Lung Association
1740 Broadway
New York, NY 10019
212-315-8700

Professionally produced videotape discussing the triggers, symptoms and management of childhood asthma.

Videotape

Web Sites

443 Allergy & Asthma Network Mothers of Asthmatics
8229 Boone Boulevard, Suite 260
Vienna, VA 22182
800-878-4403
Fax: 703-288-5271
www.allergyasthmanetwork.org

A national nonprofit network of families whose desire is to overcome not to cope with allergies and asthma.

444 American Academy of Allergy, Asthma & Immunology
555 East Wells Street, Suite 1100
Milwaukee, WI 53202
414-272-6071
Fax: 414-272-6070
info@aaaai.org
www.aaaai.org

The mission of the American Academy of Allergy, Asthma and Immunology, is the advancement of the knowledge and practice of allergy, asthma and immunology for optimal patient care: by discussion at meetings, by fostering the education of students and the public, by encouraging union and cooperation among those engaged in the field, and by promoting and stimulating research and study in allergy, asthma and immunology.

David Lang, MD, President
Mary-Beth Fasano, MD, President-Elect
Giselle S. Mosnaim, MD, Secretary-Treasurer

445 American Lung Association
55 W. Wacker Drive, Suite 1150
Chicago, IL 60601
800-586-4872
info@lung.org
www.lung.org

The American Lung Association fights lung disease in all its forms, with special emphasis on asthma, tobacco control and environmental health. The American Lung Association is funded with contributions from the public, along with gifts and grants from corporations, foundations and government agencies. The association achieves its many successes through the work of thousands of committed volunteers and staff.

Harold P. Wimmer, National President & CEO
Albert Rizzo, MD, Chief Medical Officer
Sue Swan, Chief Development Officer

Asthma / Book Publishers

446 **Asthma and Allergy FAQs**
www.cs.unc.edu/~kupstas/FAQ.html

www.cs.unc.edu/~kupstas/FAQ.html

The Allergy and Asthma FAQ is an informal gathering of the net wisdom on allergies and asthma. It includes links to various (Web and non-Web) sources of information. This started as the misc.kids Allergy and Asthma FAQ, so a certain amount of this information is geared towards parents, but there is plenty of information for adults, too.

447 **Asthma and Allergy Foundation of America**
8201 Corporate Drive, Suite 1000
Landover, MD 20785
800-727-8462
info@aafa.org
www.aafa.org

Provides information, support and referrals through a national network of chapters and educational support groups.

Richard Murray, Chair
Mary Ellen Conley, RN, Chair, Governance
Colette Martin, Chair, Communications & Marketing

448 **Gazoontite**
www.gazoontite.com

www.gazoontite.com

We are an employee-owned company of allergy sufferers, dedicated to providing you with the very best allergen control products.

449 **NIH/National Institute of Allergy and Infectious Diseases**
5601 Fishers Lane, MSC 9806
Bethesda, MD 20892
301-496-5717
866-284-4107
Fax: 301-402-3573
TDD: 800-877-8339
ocpostoffice@niaid.nih.gov
www.niaid.nih.gov/

The National Institute of Allergy and Infectous Diseases is a component of the National Institutes of Health. NIAID conducts and supports research that strives to understand, treat, and ultimately prevent the myriad infectious, immunologic, and allergic diseases that threaten hundreds of millions of people worldwide.

Anthony S. Fauci, MD, Director
Hugh Auchincloss, MD, Principal Deputy Director

450 **Online Mendelian Inheritance in Man**
McKusick-Nathans Institue of Genetic Medicine-JHU
Baltimore, MD 21205
www.omim.org

This database is a catalog of human genes and genetic disorders.

Ada Hamosh, MD, Scientific Director

Book Publishers

451 **Asthma**
Franklin Watts c/o Grolier
90 Old Sherman Turnpike
Danbury, CT 06816
203-797-3500
Fax: 203-797-3197
http://librarypublishing.scholastic.com

This book offers vital information on causes and treatments, plus advice on how to prevent flare-ups.

128 pages Grades 9 12
ISBN: 0-531113-31-0

452 **Asthma Self Help Book**
Allergy Control Products
1620-D Satellite Blvd
Duluth, GA 30097
203-438-9580
800-255-3749
Fax: 203-431-8963
TTY: 123-019-99
info@allergycontrol.com
www.allergycontrol.com

A comprehensive manual on the management of asthma for parents of asthmatic children, adult asthmatics, and for health professionals.

Softcover

453 **Best of Superstuff Activity Booklet**
American Lung Association
1740 Broadway
New York, NY 10019
212-315-8700

For young children with asthma featuring a series of activities designed to help youngsters cope with asthma.

32 pages Ages 6-8

454 **Let's Talk About Going to the Hospital**
Rosen Publishing Group's PowerKids Press
29 E 21st Street
New York, NY 10010
212-777-3017
800-237-9932
Fax: 888-436-4643
rosenpub@tribeca.ios.com
www.rosenpublishing.com

If a child has to check into the hospital, chances are he or she is already upset about being ill. Knowing how a hospital functions and what the procedures are, such as when family members can visit, will help in what is already a stressful situation. Grades K-5.

24 pages
ISBN: 0-823950-36-0

Roger Rosen, President

455 **Let's Talk About Having Asthma**
Rosen Publishing Group's PowerKids Press
29 E 21st Street
New York, NY 10010
212-777-3017
800-237-9932
Fax: 888-436-4643
rosenpub@tribeca.ios.com
www.rosenpublishing.com

This book talks about the cause and treatments for asthma as well as the precautions sufferers should take. Recommended for grades K-4.

1997 24 pages
ISBN: 0-823950-32-8

456 **Living with Asthma**
Walker & Company
1385 Broadway 5th Floor
New York, NY 10018
212-419-5300
Fax: 212-727-0984
contact@bloomsbury.com
www.bloomsbury.com/us/childrens

Dispels the myths surrounding this disease and introduces readers to famous athletes and public figures who deal with it on a daily basis. Explains what asthma is, how to cope with it, what triggers an attack, and what to do if you or somone you are with is having an attack.

2000 112 pages
ISBN: 0-802775-85-3

457 **Respiratory Disorders Sourcebook, 4th Edition**
Omnigraphics
615 Griswold Street, Ste 520
Detroit, MI 48226
610-461-3548
800-234-1340
Fax: 800-875-1340
contact@omnigraphics.com
www.omnigraphics.com

Basic consumer health information on lung disorders including tuberculosis, asthma and cystic fibrosis.

720 pages
ISBN: 0-780815-36-0

458 **Understanding Asthma**
University Press of Mississippi
3825 Ridgewood Road
Jackson, MS 39211
601-432-6205
800-737-7788
Fax: 601-432-6217
press@ihl.state.ms.us
www.upress.state.ms.us

Asthma / Magazines

Noting that understanding and education are key to halting the rise in numbers of asthma cases, Dr. Phil Lieberman has written this book for families and the individual sufferer. Subjects include lungs of an asthmatic, allergies which trigger the disease, and measures used to control asthma. A Choice outstanding book for 2000, and American Journal of Nursing Book of the Year award for 2001.

120 pages Hardcover/Ppbck
ISBN: 1-578061-42-3

459 You Can Control Asthma - Books for the Family & Kids
Asthma and Allergy Foundation of America
8201 Corporate Drive, Suite 1000
Landover, MD 20785
202-466-7643
800-727-8462
Fax: 202-466-8940
info@aafa.org
www.aafa.org

Here is a set of easy to read workbooks, one for the family and one for children, ages 6-12, to help learn everything one needs to know about asthma. Learn how to keep asthma episodes from starting, what to do when an asthma episode starts, how to use flow meters, spacers, and inhalers through the use of pictures, captions and activities. Kids have their own workbook that helps them to make choices and to feel more in control of their asthma. Workbooks are available in English or Spanish.

45-61 pages

Lynn Hanessian, Chairman
Nancy Kercher, Secretary

Magazines

460 Allergy & Asthma Today
Allergy and Asthma Network/Mothers of Asthmatics
8229 Boone Boulevard, Suite 260
Vienna, VA 22182
800-878-4403
800-878-4403
Fax: 703-288-5271
info@aanma.org
www.allergyasthmanetwork.org

Communicates practical advice and support for the benefit of all people affected by allergies, asthma and related conditions. Seeks to improve health outcomes by providing information in a consumer-friendly format with strategies for implementing behavior changes. Free to AANMA members.

Quarterly

Tonya Winders, President & CEO
Charmayne Anderson, Director of Advocacy
Sally Schoessler, Director of Education

461 Controlling Asthma
American Lung Association
1740 Broadway
New York, NY 10019
212-315-8700

For parents of children with asthma, this newsmagazine tells how parents can help their child deal with the many problems presented by asthma.

16 pages

462 Coping with Allergies and Asthma
PO Box 682268
Franklin, TN 37068
615-790-2400
Fax: 615-614-3986
info@copingmag.com
www.copingmag.com

A bimonthly publication devoted to people whose lives are affected by difficult breathing conditions.

Paula Chadwell, Vice President

Pamphlets

463 Asthma and Allergy Answers: Patient Education Library
Asthma and Allergy Foundation of America
8201 Corporate Drive, Suite 1000
Landover, MD 20785
202-466-7643
800-727-8462
Fax: 202-466-8940
Info@aafa.org
www.aafa.org

This resource tool has information on more than forty topics of interest to patients. These reproducible camera ready answers are written in a patient friendly question and answer format. There is space to personalize the handy patient education materials with your practice or facility information. Topics covered are adult onset of asthma and allergies, food allergies, latex allergies, asthma medications, peak flow meters and managing your asthma.

In binder form

Cary Sennett, President/ CEO
Lynda Mitchell, SVP, Community Services
Yolanda Miller, SVP/ COO/ CFO

464 Childhood Asthma: A Matter of Control
American Lung Association
1740 Broadway
New York, NY 10019
212-315-8700

A guide for parents of children with asthma, this booklet covers topics such as identifying asthma signs and symptoms as well as controlling the condition.

28 pages

465 Living with Asthma and Allergies Brochure Series
Asthma and Allergy Foundation of America
8201 Corporate Drive, Suite 1000
Landover, MD 20785
202-466-7643
800-727-8462
Fax: 202-466-8940
Info@aafa.org
www.aafa.org

This informative series was developed to provide up-to-date, accurate information on common topics. Written in easy to understand language, with helpful illustrations, the brochures covers some of the most commonly asked questions about asthma and allergies. Perfect for individuals, whether newly diagnosed or more experienced, and for distribution to patients. Titles include, Allergy Basics, Seasonal Allergies: Pollens and Molds, Asthma Basics, Exercise and Asthma, and more.

Cary Sennett, President/ CEO
Lynda Mitchell, SVP, Community Services
Yolanda Miller, SVP/ COO/ CFO

466 Superstuff
American Lung Association
1740 Broadway
New York, NY 10019
212-315-8700

Kit specifically designed to help the elementary school child with asthma to learn how to manage the condition. The kit contains teaching tools, puzzles, riddles, stories and games.

467 Teens Talk to Teens About Asthma
Asthma and Allergy Foundation of America
8201 Corporate Drive, Suite 1000
Landover, MD 20785
202-466-7643
800-727-8462
Fax: 202-466-8940
Info@aafa.org
www.aafa.org

This brochure is a great gift of support to a teen you care about. Includes quotes and thoughts from teens that capture the essenceof what it feels like to live with asthma. Perfect for newly diagnosed teens. Single copies free with two first class stamps on a business-sized, self-addressed envelope.(Order #P-012) Quantities available, please call for prices.

Cary Sennett, President/ CEO
Lynda Mitchell, SVP, Community Services
Yolanda Miller, SVP/ COO/ CFO

468 There are Solutions for the Student with Asthma
American Lung Association
1740 Broadway
New York, NY 10017　　　　　　　212-315-8700

Leaflet telling how parents and school personnel can work together to make life easier for children with asthma.

4 pages

469 Your Child and Asthma
National Jewish Health
1400 Jackson Street
Denver, CO 80206　　　　　　　303-388-4461
　　　　　　　　　　　　　　　877-225-5654
　　　　　　　　　　　　　www.nationaljewish.org

A booklet offering information to parents and family about their child with asthma. Offers information on diagnosis, treatments, triggers and family concerns.

Michael Salem, MD, President & CEO

Camps

470 Camp Vacamas
256 Macopin Road
West Milford, NJ 7480　　　　　973-838-0942
　　　　　　　　　　　　　Fax: 973-838-7534
　　　　　　　　　　　　　info@vacamas.org
　　　　　　　　　　　　　www.vacamas.org

Disadvantaged children with asthma or sickle cell anemia, ages 8-16, are offered special programs in canoeing, backpacking, camping, music and leadership training. Sliding scale tuition. Year round programs for groups.

Michael Friedman, Executive Director
Philip Smith, Camp Director

471 Des Moines YMCA Camp
1192 166th Drive
Boone, IA 50036　　　　　　　515-432-7558
　　　　　　　　　　　　　Fax: 515-432-5414
　　　　　　　　　　　　　ycamp@dmymca.org
　　　　　　　　　　　　　www.y-camp.org

For boys and girls with cancer, diabetes, asthma, cystic fibrosis, hearing impaired and other disabilities.

David Sherry, Executive Director
Alex Kretzinger, Program Director Camps

472 VACC Camp
Nicklaus Children's Hospital
3200 SW 60th Court, Suite 203
Miami, FL 33155　　　　　　　305-662-8222
　　　　　　　　　　　　　Fax: 786-268-1765
　　　　　　　　　　　　　bela.florentin@mch.com
　　　　　　　　　　　　　www.vacccamp.com

Free, week-long, overnight camp for ventilation assisted children (children needing a tracheotomy ventilator, C-PAP, BiPAP, or oxygen to support breathing) and their families. Gives families a fun oppourtinity to socialize with peers and enjoy activities not readily accessible to technology dependent children.

Bela Florentin, Camp Coordinator
Rose Ann Farrell, Volunteer Assistants Coordinator
Alyssa Garcia, Operations

Description

473 ATAXIA

Involves the following Biologic System(s):
Neurologic Disorders

Ataxia is a neuromuscular condition characterized by an impaired ability to coordinate voluntary movements. The condition is caused by abnormalities of or damage to the region of the brain known as the cerebellum, nerve pathways that transmit messages to and from the cerebellum, or certain regions of the spinal cord. The cerebellum plays an essential role in regulating the maintenance of normal postures, sustaining balance, and producing smooth and coordinated movements. The spinal cord conducts sensory and motor impulses to and from the brain. The symptoms associated with ataxia vary, depending upon the specific regions of the brain that are affected; however, symptoms may often include imbalance and an abnormal staggering manner of walking (gait). Ataxia may be the result of certain infection, malformations of the cerebellum of spinal cord that are present at birth (congenital), head injury, brain tumors, exposure to particular medications, or certain genetic disorders. The primary infectious causes of ataxia during childhood include the formation of pus-filled pockets of infection in the cerebellum (cerebellar abscesses); sudden, severe inflammation of the passages within the inner ear (acute labyrinthitis): or acute cerebellar ataxia. Acute labyrinthitis typically occurs due to middle ear infections and may be characterized by vomiting and a sense that one's body or environment is spinning (vertigo). Acute cerebellar ataxia occurs subsequent to certain viral infections, such as chicken pox, and is thought to result from an abnormal immune response causing inflammation of the brain. Acute cerebellar ataxia typically occurs suddenly and may be characterized by impaired control of voluntary movements of the torso (truncal ataxia) and difficulties sitting or standing; involuntary, rapid eye movements (nystagmus); and severe slurring of speech or an inability to speak. Although the condition typically improves within a few weeks, it sometimes is present for up to two months. Most children have a complete recovery; however, some may have residual speech abnormalities and lack of coordination.

Abnormalities present at birth (congenital) that may cause ataxia include absence of the region of the brain between the two sides or hemispheres of the cerebellum (agensis of cerebellar vermis); protrusion of part of the brain through an opening in the skull (encephalocele); or protrusion of certain, malformed regions of the brain through the opening at the base of the skull (foramen magnum) into the upper spinal canal (Arnold-Chiari malformation). Infants and children with such birth defects develop ataxia due to malformation of or damage to certain regions of the cerebellum.

Ataxia may also be an initial symptom associated with certain brain tumors, including tumors affecting the cerebellum or a particular area of the cerebrum where it joins with the cerebellum (i.e., frontal lobe). In addition, brain tumors known as neuroblastomasmay result in progressive ataxia. Neuroblastomas are solid, malignant tumors that may originate in any part of the sympathetic nervous system, which is that part of the nervous system that regulates certain involuntary activities during times of stress, such as raising blood pressure and increasing the heart rate.

In some children, ataxia may result from the administration of certain drugs, such as anticonvulsant medications, particularly phenytoin. In addition, the condition may be caused by exposure to a household pesticide that is commonly used as a rat poison (thallium).

Ataxia may also occur in association with certain inborn errors of metabolism and is a primary feature of many hereditary degenerative disorders of the brain and spinal cord. These degenerative disorders, which may be referred to as hereditay ataxias, include ataxia-telangiectasia and Friedreich's ataxia.

Ataxia-telangiectasia (AT) is a multisystem disorder that is inherited as an autosomal recessive trait. Affected children typically develop ataxia at approximately two years of age, eventually leading to an inability to walk. Friedreich's ataxia is a genetic disorder that is usually inherited as an autosomal recessive trait. The disorder is characterized by degenerative changes of certain regions of the spinal cord and is categorized as a spinocerebellar ataxia. Children with Friedreich's ataxia typically develop ataxia before age 10. The ataxia is slowly progressive and usually affects the legs and feet more severely than the arms and hands. Patients develop unusual high arching and severe muscle weakness of the feet and progressive difficulties walking, typically resulting in the need of a wheelchair. Additional hereditary spinocerebellar ataxia of childhood, such as Roussy-Levy syndrome, cause symptoms and findings similar to those associated with Friedreich's ataxia. Roussy-Levy syndrome often becomes apparent during infancy and is characterized by loss of joint position sensation (sensory ataxia), causing poorly judged, uncoordinated movements. Such ataxia initially affects the legs, causing difficulty walking, and later progresses to affect the hands. Roussy-Levy syndrome is transmitted as an autosomal dominant trait.

Another group of hereditary disorders, known as the olivopontocerebellar atrophics (OPCAs) are associated with ataxia. These disorders are characterized by progressive degeneration of the cerebellum as well as other areas of the brain. Although associated symptoms of most forms of OPCA become apparent during adolescence or adulthood, one form of the disorder is known to occur during infancy (OPCA of neonatal onset). Symptoms may include severely diminished muscle tone; rapidly progressive ataxia; involuntary, rapid eye movements; episodes of abnormally increased electrical activity in the brain (seizures); failure to grow and gain weight at the expected rate (failure to thrive); abnormalities in the structure and function of heart muscle (hypertrophic cardiomyopathy); and other symptoms and findings. Methods used in the management of ataxia may vary and depend upon the condition's underlying cause, the specific form of ataxia present, and other factors. Such measures are typically symptomatic and supportive.

Government Agencies

474 NIH/National Institute of Neurological Disorders and Stroke (NINDS)
PO Box 5801
Bethesda, MD 20824
800-352-9424
www.ninds.nih.gov

Works to reduce the burden of neurological disease by conducting, fostering, coordinating and guiding research on the causes, prevention, diagnosis and treatment of neurological disorders and stroke, while supporting basic research in related scientific areas.

Walter J. Koroshetz, MD, Director

Ataxia / State Agencies & Support Groups

National Associations & Support Groups

475 **American Academy of Pediatrics**
345 Park Blvd
Itasca, IL 60143
800-433-9016
Fax: 847-434-8000
mcc@aap.org
www.aap.org

The American Academy of Pediatrics and its member pediatricians are committed to the attainment of optimal physical, mental and social health and well-being for all infants, children, adolescents, and young adults.

Mark Del Monte, JD, CEO/Executive VP
Lynn Olson, PhD, VP, Research
Vera Tait, MD, FAAP, Chief Medical Officer

476 **Child Neurology Foundation**
601 W Short Street
Lexington, KY 40508
888-417-3435
info@childneurologyfoundation.org
childneurologyfoundation.org

The Child Neurology Foundation connects partners from all areas of the child neurology community so those navigating the journey of disease diagnosis, management, and care have the ongoing support from those dedicated to treatments and cures.

Amy Brin, Executive Director
Katie Hentges, Director, Programs
Brea McCormley, Director, Development

477 **National Ataxia Foundation**
600 Highway 169 South, Ste 1725
Minneapolis, MN 55426
763-553-0020
Fax: 763-553-0167
naf@ataxia.org
ataxia.org

The National Ataxia Foundation is dedicated to improving the lives of persons affected by ataxia through support, education, and research.

William P. Sweeney, Board President
Andrew Rosen, Executive Director
Lori Shogren, Community Program/Services Director

State Agencies & Support Groups

Alabama

478 **Birmingham Support Group**
National Ataxia Foundation
16 The Oaks Circle
Birmingham, AL 10116
205-987-2883
Fax: 763-553-0167
donnelly613b@aol.com
www.ataxia.org

The primary mission is to encourage and support research into Hereditary Ataxia, a group of neurological disorders which are chronic and progressive conditions affecting coordination.

Fred Donnelly, Contact
Becky Donnelly, Contact

Arizona

479 **Arizona Ataxia Support Group**
National Ataxia Foundation
7665 E Placita Luna Preciosa
Tucson, AZ 10117
520-885-8326
Fax: 763-553-0167
bbeck15@cox.net
www.ataxia.org/chapters/Tucson/default.aspx

The primary mission is to encourage and support research into Hereditary Ataxia, a group of neurological disorders which are chronic and progressive conditions affecting coordination.

Bart Beck, SG Leader

California

480 **Greater North Valley California Support Group**
4335 Bourdeaux Drive
Oakley, CA 10118
925-625-0738
www.geocites.com/hotsprings/

The primary mission is to encourage and support research into Hereditary Ataxia, a group of neurological disorders which are chronic and progressive conditions affecting coordination.

Debra Kellerman, Contact

481 **Los Angeles Ataxia Support Group**
National Ataxia Foundation
339 W Palmer, Apartment A
Glendale, CA 10119
818-246-5758
Fax: 763-553-0167
ccherilynmc@yahoo.com
www.ataxia.org/chapters/losangeles/default.aspx

The primary mission is to encourage and support research into Hereditary Ataxia, a group of neurological disorders which are chronic and progressive conditions affecting coordination.

Sherry McLaughlin, Contact

482 **Northern California Support Group**
National Ataxia Foundation
1980 Saint George Rd
Danville, CA 10120
925-735-7037
Fax: 763-553-0167
joanneloveland@gmail.com
www.ataxia.org/chapters/northerncalifornia/default.a

The primary mission is to encourage and support research into Hereditary Ataxia, a group of neurological disorders which are chronic and progressive conditions affecting coordination.

Joanne Loveland, Contact

483 **Orange County Support Group**
National Ataxia Foundation
829 W Gary Ave
Montebello, CA 10121
323-788-7751
Fax: 763-553-0167
danieln27@gmail.com
www.ataxia.org/chapters/orangecounty/default.aspx

The primary mission is to encourage and support research into Hereditary Ataxia, a group of neurological disorders which are chronic and progressive conditions affecting coordination.

Daniel Navar, Leader

484 **Pacific Southwest Regional Genetics Group**
2151 Berkeley Way
Berkeley, CA 10122
510-540-2696
Fax: 510-540-2966
www.hgen.pitt.edu/counseling/resources/regional04.ht

Coordinates genetic services; promotes communication among genetic professionals and consumers through network newsletter, meetings, and other events; share resources; and promote education and awareness of genetic disorders.

George C Cunningham, Director

485 **San Diego Support Group**
National Ataxia Foundation
2087 Granite Hills Drive
El Cajon, CA 92019
619-447-3753
Fax: 763-553-0167
www.ataxia.org

The primary mission is to encourage and support research into Hereditary Ataxia, a group of neurological disorders which are chronic and progressive conditions affecting coordination.

Earl McLaughlin, Contact

486 **San Fernando Valley Support Group**
19450 Turtle Ridge Lane
Northridge, CA 10124
818-363-5335
www.ataxia.org

Ataxia / State Agencies & Support Groups

The primary mission is to encourage and support research into Hereditary Ataxia, a group of neurological disorders which are chronic and progressive conditions affecting coordination.

Darneal J Myers, Contact

Colorado

487 Colorado Support Group
National Ataxia Foundation
5902 W Maplewood Drive
Littleton, CO 10125
303-794-6351
Fax: 763-553-0167
tom_sathre@acm.org
www.ataxia.org

The primary mission is to encourage and support research into Hereditary Ataxia, a group of neurological disorders which are chronic and progressive conditions affecting coordination.

Donna Sathre, Leader
Tom Sathre, Leader

488 Mountain States Regional Genetics Services Network
4300 Cherry Creek Drive S
Denver, CO 10126
303-692-2423
Fax: 303-782-5576
www.hgen.pitt.edu/counseling/resources/regional04.ht

Coordinates genetic services; promotes communication among genetic professional and consumers through network newsletters, meetings, and other events; share resources; and promote education and awareness of genetic disorders.

George C Cunningham, Director

Florida

489 Broward County Support Group
10603 NW 49th Place
Coral Springs, FL 10127
954-341-8565
Fax: 954-753-6761
pathamilto@aol.com
community.insidecentralflorida.com/bcfasg/

The primary mission is to encourage and support research into Hereditary Ataxia, a group of neurological disorders which are chronic and progressive conditions affecting coordination.

Patricia B Hamilton, Contact

490 Clearwater, FL Support Group
2363 Mary Lane
Clearwater, FL 10128
727-799-2852
joyous7@mciworld.com
www.ataxia.org

The primary mission is to encourage and support research into Hereditary Ataxia, a group of neurological disorders which are chronic and progressive conditions affecting coordination.

Joyce Robbins, Contact

491 NE Florida Support Group
National Ataxia Foundation
8925 Adams Walk Dr
Jacksonville, FL 10129
904-314-2061
Fax: 763-553-0167
coryhannan@hotmail.com
www.ataxia.org

The primary mission is to encourage and support research into Hereditary Ataxia, a group of neurological disorders which are chronic and progressive conditions affecting coordination.

Cory Hannan, Leader

492 Tampa Support Group
National Ataxia Foundation
306 Caloosa Palm St
Son City Center, FL 10130
www.ataxia.org

The primary mission is to encourage and support research into Hereditary Ataxia, a group of neurological disorders which are chronic and progressive conditions affecting coordination.

Charlie Kirchner, Contact

Georgia

493 Georgia Ataxia Support Group
National Ataxia Foundation
320 Peters Street, Unit 12
Atlanta, GA 10131
404-822-7451
rooksgj@yahoo.com
www.ataxia.org

The primary mission is to encourage and support research into Hereditary Ataxia, a group of neurological disorders which are chronic and progressive conditions affecting coordination.

Greg Rooks, Contact

494 Greater Atlanta Area Support Group
National Ataxia Foundation
320 Peters Street, Unit 12
Atlanta, GA 10132
404-822-7451
rookssgj@yahoo.com
www.geocities.com/atlantaataxia

The primary mission is to encourage and support research into Hereditary Ataxia, a group of neurological disorders which are chronic and progressive conditions affecting coordination.

Greg Rooks, Contact

495 Macon Support Group
116 Summerfield Drive
Macon, GA 10133
912-757-9454
rookssgj@yahoo.com
www.ataxia.org

The primary mission is to encourage and support research into Hereditary Ataxia, a group of neurological disorders which are chronic and progressive conditions affecting coordination.

Millard H McWhorter III, MD, Contact

496 Southeast Regional Genetics Group
PO Box 1642
Decatur, GA 10134
404-778-8551
Fax: 404-778-8562
mlane@sergg.org
www.sergginc.org

SERGG addresses the inequities in genetic service and resources in the region and to expand existing regional capabilities and resources and to develop new regional systems to address these gaps. Another goal is to improve the existing regional communication infrastructure and to facilitate information sharing among providers of genetic services and consumers and to establish collaborative partnerships with other professional organizations.

Hans Andersson, MD, President
Mary Rose Simpson, BS, Secretary/Treasurer

Illinois

497 Chicago, IL Area Ataxia Support Group
National Ataxia Foundation
3400 Wellington Court, #302
Rolling Meadows, IL 10135
847-797-9398
caasgz@aol.com
www.ataxia.org

The primary mission is to encourage and support research into Hereditary Ataxia, a group of neurological disorders which are chronic and progressive conditions affecting coordination.

Craig Lisack, Contact

Indiana

498 Central Indiana Support Group
5716 N 225 W
W Lafayette, IN 10136
765-463-3973
Fax: 765-463-3972
www.ataxia.org

Ataxia / State Agencies & Support Groups

The primary mission is to encourage and support research into Hereditary Ataxia, a group of neurological disorders which are chronic and progressive conditions affecting coordination.

Judy Marten, Contact

499 NE Indiana Support Group
4522 Shenandoah Circle W
Fort Wayne, IN 10137
219-485-0965
Fax: 763-553-0167
naf@ataxia.org
www.ataxia.org

The primary mission is to encourage and support research into Hereditary Ataxia, a group of neurological disorders which are chronic and progressive conditions affecting coordination.

Don & Jenny Roemke, Contact

Louisiana

500 Louisiana Chapter
National Ataxia Foundation
1720 Parker St.
Baton Rouge, LA 10138
985-643-0783
louisiananaf@yahoo.com
www.angelfire.com/la/ataxiachapter/

The primary mission is to encourage and support research into Hereditary Ataxia, a group of neurological disorders which are chronic and progressive conditions affecting coordination.

Elizabeth Tanner, Contact

501 Louisiana Support Group
National Ataxia Foundation
1720 Parker St.
Baton Rouge, LA 10139
985-643-0783
Fax: 763-553-0167
louisiananaf@yahoo.com
www.angelfire.com/la/ataxiachapter/

The primary mission is to encourage and support research into Hereditary Ataxia, a group of neurological disorders which are chronic and progressive conditions affecting coordination.

Elizabeth Tanner, Contact

Maine

502 Maine Support
National Ataxia Foundation
PO Box 113
Bowdoinham, ME 10140
763-553-0020
Fax: 763-553-0167
Kelley3902@myfairpoint.net
www.ataxia.org

The primary mission is to encourage and support research into Hereditary Ataxia, a group of neurological disorders which are chronic and progressive conditions affecting coordination.

Kelly Rollins, Contact

503 New England Regional Genetics Group
PO Box 920288
Needham, MA 10141
781-444-0126
Fax: 781-444-0127
mfgnergg@verizon.net
www.nergg.org

To provide a forum for collaboration among genetic professionals, consumers of genetic services and the Public Health Community in New England by Raising awareness about the impact of genetics on health throughout the lifespan and Promoting and facilitating access to genetic services, education and resources

Lisa Demers MS, CGC, President
Marinell Newton, President Elect
Lisa Brailey MD, Service Provider

Maryland

504 Chesapeake Chapter
National Ataxia Foundation
5938 Rossmore Drive
Bethesda, MD 10142
301-530-4989
Fax: 301-530-2480
www.geocities.com/Hotsprings/Oasis/4988/

The primary mission is to encourage and support research into Hereditary Ataxia, a group of neurological disorders which are chronic and progressive conditions affecting coordination.

Carl J Lauter, President

Massachusetts

505 New England Support Group
National Ataxia Foundation
45 Juliette Street
Andover, MA 10143
978-475-8072
Fax: 763-553-0167
naf@ataxia.org
www.ataxia.org

The primary mission is to encourage and support research into Hereditary Ataxia, a group of neurological disorders which are chronic and progressive conditions affecting coordination.

Donna Gorzela, Leader
Richard Gorzela, Leader

Michigan

506 Detroit Michigian Ataxia Support Group
National Ataxia Foundation
20217 Wyoming
Detroit, MI 10144
313-397-7858
Fax: 763-553-0167
tinyt48221@yahoo.com
www.ataxia.org

The primary mission is to encourage and support research into Hereditary Ataxia, a group of neurological disorders which are chronic and progressive conditions affecting coordination.

Tany Tunstull, Leader

Minnesota

507 Minneapolis, MN Support Group
National Ataxia Foundation
2549 32nd Avenue S
Minneapolis, MN 10145
612-724-3784
Fax: 763-553-0167
schultz.lenore@yahoo.com
www.ataxia.org

The primary mission is to encourage and support research into Hereditary Ataxia, a group of neurological disorders which are chronic and progressive conditions affecting coordination.

Lenore Healey Schultz, Contact

Mississippi

508 Mississippi Chapter
National Ataxia Foundation
PO Box 17005
Hattiesburg, MS 10146
763-553-0020
Fax: 763-553-0167
daglio1@bellsouth.net
www.ataxia.org

The primary mission is to encourage and support research into Hereditary Ataxia, a group of neurological disorders which are chronic and progressive conditions affecting coordination.

Camille Daglio, President

Ataxia / State Agencies & Support Groups

Missouri

509 Central Missouri Area Support Group
National Ataxia Foundation
1609 Cocoa Court
Columbia, MO 10147
572-474-7232
Fax: 763-553-0167
rogercooley@localnet.com
www.ataxia.org

The primary mission is to encourage and support research into Hereditary Ataxia, a group of neurological disorders which are chronic and progressive conditions affecting coordination.

Roger Colley, Leader

510 Kansas City, Missouri Support Group
National Ataxia Foundation
17700 East 17th Terrace Ct. S #102
Independence, MO 10148
816-257-2428
Fax: 763-553-0167
clarkstone9348@sbcglobal.net
www.ataxia.org/chapters/kansascity/default.aspx

The primary mission is to encourage and support research into Hereditary Ataxia, a group of neurological disorders which are chronic and progressive conditions affecting coordination.

Jim Clark, Contact

511 Springfield Area Support Group
12 Jackson St, Apt 811-B
Jefferson City, MO 10149
www.ataxia.org/chapters/strode/default.aspx

The primary mission is to encourage and support research into Hereditary Ataxia, a group of neurological disorders which are chronic and progressive conditions affecting coordination.

Susan Strode, PhD, Contact

New York

512 Genetic Network of the Empire State
Laboratory of Human Genetics
Empire State Plaza
Albany, NY 10150
518-474-7148
Fax: 518-474-8590
www.sergginc.org

Coordinates genetic services; promotes communication among genetic professionals and consumers through network newsletters, meetings, and other events; share resources; and promote education and awareness of genetic disorders.

Karen Greendale, Coordinator

513 New York City Area Support Group
National Ataxia Foundation
36 West Redoubt Road
Fishkill, NY 10151
845-897-5632
vrabsolutely@aol.com
www.ataxia.org/chapters/valerieruggiero/default.aspx

The primary mission is to encourage and support research into Hereditary Ataxia, a group of neurological disorders which are chronic and progressive conditions affecting coordination.

Valerie Ruggiero, Contact

514 New York Support Group
National Ataxia Foundation
423 Church Street
North Syracuse, NY 10152
315-683-9486
jtarrants@aol.com
www.ataxia.org/chapters/centralnewyork/default.aspx

Primary mission is to encourage and support research into Hereditary Ataxia, a group of neurological disorders which are chronic and progressive conditions affecting coordination.

Mary Jane Damiano, Contact

515 Tri-State Support Group
National Ataxia Foundation
Northgate 6C
Bronxville, NY 10153
914-720-2179
Fax: 763-553-0167
markmeghan2@gmail.com
www.ataxia.org/chapters/tri-state/default.aspx

The primary mission is to encourage and support research into Hereditary Ataxia, a group of neurological disorders which are chronic and progressive conditions affecting coordination.

Denise Mitchell, Leader
Mark Mitchell, Contact

Ohio

516 Ohio Support Group
National Ataxia Foundation
7852 Country Court
Mentor, OH 10154
440-255-8284
wurbanski@oh.rr.com
www.ataxia.org/chapters/centralohio/default.aspx

The primary mission is to encourage and support research into Hereditary Ataxia, a group of neurological disorders which are chronic and progressive conditions affecting coordination.

Cecelia Urbanski, Contact

Oklahoma

517 North Central Oklahoma Support Group
915 Thislewood
Norman, OK 10155
405-447-6085
czechmarkmhd@yahoo.com
www.ataxia.org/chapters/Ambassador/default.aspx

The primary mission is to encourage and support research into Hereditary Ataxia, a group of neurological disorders which are chronic and progressive conditions affecting coordination.

Mark Dvorak, Contact

Oregon

518 Pacific Northwest Regional Genetics Group
PO Box 574
Portland, OR 10156
503-494-8342
Fax: 503-494-4447
www.sergginc.org

Coordinates genetics services; promotes communication among genetic professional and consumers through network newsletters, meetings, and other events; share resources; and promote education and awareness of genetic disorders.

Jonathan Zonana, MD, Director

519 Willamette Valley Ataxia Support Group
Albany General Hospital-National Ataxia Foundation
1046 6th Avenue SW
Albany, OR 10157
541-812-4162
Fax: 541-812-4614
www.ataxia.org/chapters/Willamette/default.aspx

The primary mission is to encourage and support research into Hereditary Ataxia, a group of neurological disorders which are chronic and progressive conditions affecting coordination.

Ivy Stilwell, Contact

Pennsylvania

520 Central Pennsylvania Area Support Group
3844 West Linden Street
Allentown, PA 18104
610-395-6905
www.ataxia.org/chapters/rakshys/default.aspx

The primary mission is to encourage and support research into Hereditary Ataxia, a group of neurological disorders which are chronic and progressive conditions affecting coordination.

Christina Rakshys, Contact

521 Mid-Atlantic Regional Human Genetics Network
260 S Broad Street
Philadelphia, PA 10158
215-456-7910
Fax: 215-456-7911
www.sergginc.org

Coordinates genetics services; promotes communication among genetic professional and consumers through network newsletters, meeting, and other events; share resources; and promote education and awareness of genetic disorders.

Deborah Eunpu, MS, President

522 Southeast Pennsylvania Support Group
National Ataxia Foundation
220 Beechwood Road
Norristown, PA 10159
610-272-1502
lizout@aol.com
www.ataxia.org/chapters/sepennsylvania/default.aspx

The primary mission is to encourage and support research into Hereditary Ataxia, a group of neurological disorders which are chronic and progressive conditions affecting coordination.

Liz Nussear, Contact

South Carolina

523 Carolinas Support Group
National Ataxia Foundation
1305 Cely Road
Easley, SC 10160
864-220-3395
www.ataxia.org/chapters/Carolinas/default.aspx

The primary mission is to encourage and support research into Hereditary Ataxia, a group of neurological disorders which are chronic and progressive conditions affecting coordination.

Cece Russell, Contact

Texas

524 Houston Support Group
National Ataxia Foundation
9405 Hwy 6 South
Houston, TX 10161
281-693-1826
angelahcloud@aol.com
www.ataxia.org/chapters/houston/default.aspx

The primary mission is to encourage and support research into Hereditary Ataxia, a group of neurological disorders which are chronic and progressive conditions affecting coordination.

Angela Cloud, Contact

525 North Texas Support Group
National Ataxia Foundation
7 Wentworth Court
Trophy Club, TX 10162
903-785-7058
chevelle@sbcglobal.net
www.ataxia.org/chapters/northtexas/default.aspx

The primary mission is to encourage and support research into Hereditary Ataxia, a group of neurological disorders which are chronic and progressive conditions affecting coordination.

David Henry Jr, Contact

Utah

526 Utah Support Group National Ataxia Foundation
University of Utah - Moran Eye Clinic
65 Mario Copecchi Dr.
Salt Lake City, UT 84132
801-587-3020
Lisa.ord@hsc.utah.edu
www.ataxia.org/chapters/Utah/default.aspx

The primary mission is to encourage and support research into Hereditary Ataxia, a group of neurological disorders which are chronic and progressive conditions affecting coordination.

Lisa Ord PhD, Contact

Washington

527 Seattle Area Support Group
National Ataxia Foundation
14104 107th Avenue NE
Kirkland, WA 10164
425-823-6239
www.ataxia.org/chapters/Seattle/default.aspx

The primary mission is to encourage and support research into Hereditary Ataxia, a group of neurological disorders which are chronic and progressive conditions affecting coordination.

Milly Lewendon, Contact

Research Centers

528 Ataxia Telangiectasia Medical Research Foundation
16224 Elisa Place
Encino, CA 91436
818-906-2861
Fax: 818-906-2870
atmrf@aol.com
www.ninds.nih.gov/find_people/voluntary_orgs/volorg1

Private nonprofit organization dedicated to finding a cure for ataxia-telangiectasia.

Story C Landis, PhD, Director
Walter J Koroshetz, MD, Deputy Director
Joellen Harper Austin, Associate Director

529 Ataxia Telangiectasia Project
3002 Enfield Road
Austin, TX 10166
512-472-4892
www.atproject.org

Nonprofit foundation that supports basic scientific research into treatments for neurological deterioration and cancer in children with ataia-telangiectasia.

Conferences

530 National Ataxia Foundation Annual Membership Meeting
National Ataxia Foundation
600 Highway 169 South, Ste 1725
Minneapolis, MN 55426
763-553-0020
Fax: 763-553-0167
naf@ataxia.org
ataxia.org

Brings together NAF members and their families to meet and learn from world leading ataxia researchers and neurologists, but also to build new friendships and reunite with old friends.

William P. Sweeney, Board President
Andrew Rosen, Executive Director
Lori Shogren, Community Program/Services Director

Audio Video

531 Diagnostic Approach to the Dysmorphic Patient
Southeastern Resgional Genetics Group, Inc SERGG
PO Box 1642
Decatur, GA 30031
404-778-8551
Fax: 404-778-8562
mlane@sergginc.org
www.sergginc.org

This 2-hour video focuses on learning how to approach, categorize, and conceptualize the patient with multiple congenital anomalies (MCA). Critical terminology is illustrated. Patients are seen in hospital and clinic settings. Emphasis is placed in prioritizing clinical features and weighing each feature's value in reaching a diagnosis. An outline is included with time frames and detailed explanations of what each statement, definition and categorization means.

Ataxia / Web Sites

Timothy C. Wood, PhD, President
Mary Rose Simpson, Administrator

532 Pearls of Dysmorphology
Southeastern Resgional Genetics Group, Inc SERGG
PO Box 1642
Decatur, GA 30031
404-778-8551
Fax: 404-778-8562
mlane@sergginc.org
www.sergginc.org

This 1 1/2-hour video which contains 87 individual features considered 'pearls' or 'semi-pearls' relative to their value in reaching or suspecting a specific diagnosis. Many additional features are commented on as the formal 'pearls' are presented. There is an exercise at the end of the tape for helping viewers understand how dysmorphology pearls can be used to prioritize the diagnostic value of individual features. A handout accompanies this tape, to help make this exercise fun and educational.

Timothy C. Wood, PhD, President
Mary Rose Simpson, Administrator

533 Syndromes Associated with Multiple Congenital Anomalies
Southeastern Resgional Genetics Group, Inc SERGG
PO Box 1642
Decatur, GA 30031
404-778-8551
Fax: 404-778-8562
mlane@sergginc.org
www.sergginc.org

This 2-hour video includes 30 of the more common malformation syndromes within the categories of single gene, chromosomal, teratogens, associations, and sequences. Each disorder is preceded by a Table of Features and each disorder is shown at different ages and often includes some verbal interaction. The vast majority of the cases are within the hospital or clinic setting. There is minimal use of slides.

Timothy C. Wood, PhD, President
Mary Rose Simpson, Administrator

534 Together...There Is Hope
National Ataxia Foundation
600 Highway 169 South, Suite 1725
Minneapolis, MN 55426
763-553-0020
Fax: 763-553-0167
naf@ataxia.org
www.ataxia.org

A video discussing ataxias genetic patterns of inheritance and the National Ataxia Foundation and its research efforts.

Andrew Rosen, Executive Director
Stephanie Lucas, Communications Manager
Lori Shogren, Community Program & Service Dir.

Web Sites

535 Gene Clinics
481B Edward H. Ross Drive
Elmwood Park, NJ 7407
888-729-1204
Fax: 201-212-6457
genetests@genetests.org
www.geneclinics.org

By providing current, authoritative information on genetic testing and its use in diagnosis, management, and genetic counseling, GeneTests promotes the appropriate use of genetic services in patient care and personal decision making.

Roberta A Pagon, Founder
Amar Kamath, Commercial Director
Deb Eunpu, Program Manager

536 Health Answers Education Sudler-WPP Health Practice
700 Dresher Road
Horsham, PA 19044
215-442-9010
www.healthanswers.com

HealthAnswers offers a breadth of services in medical education, sales force training, patient support solutions, professional promotion and consumer solutions.

Mike Hudnall, CEO

537 International Network of Ataxia Friends
www.internaf.org
www.internaf.org

Website mailing list which is maintained by volunteers who have some form of ataxia.

538 National Ataxia Foundation
600 Highway 169 South, Ste 1725
Minneapolis, MN 55426
763-553-0020
Fax: 763-553-0167
naf@ataxia.org
ataxia.org

Information regarding support, education, and research for dominant ataxia, recessive ataxia, and sporatic ataxia.

William P. Sweeney, Board President
Andrew Rosen, Executive Director
Lori Shogren, Community Program/Services Director

Book Publishers

539 A Balancing Act: Living with Spinal Cerebellar Ataxia
8600 Rockville Pike
Bethesda, MD 20894
301-594-5983
888-346-3656
Fax: 301-402-1384
TDD: 800-735-2258
custserv@nlm.nih.gov
www.nlm.nih.gov

Describes living with Spinocerebellar Ataxia. Available from Amazon.com only.

ISBN: 1-889826-00-6

Patricia B Hamilton

540 Directory of National Genetic Voluntary Organizations
Genetic Alliance
4301 Connecticut Avenue NW, Suite 404
Washington, DC 20008
202-966-5557
Fax: 202-966-8553
www.genticalliance.orgtm

Lists hundreds of organizations and associations dealing with genetic conditions.

Sharon F. Terry, President/CEO
Natasha Bonhomme, Vice President
Lisa Wise, Chief Operating Officer

541 Hereditary Ataxia: A Guidebook for Managing Speech & Swallowing
National Ataxia Foundation
600 Highway 169 South, Suite 1725
Minneapolis, MN 55426
763-553-0020
Fax: 763-553-0167
naf@ataxia.org
www.ataxia.org

Andrew Rosen, Executive Director
Stephanie Lucas, Communications Manager
Lori Shogren, Community Program & Service Dir.

542 Living with Ataxia
National Ataxia Foundation
600 Highway 169 South, Suite 1725
Minneapolis, MN 55426
763-553-0020
Fax: 763-553-0167
naf@ataxia.org
www.ataxia.org

A compassionate resource for people who have or may be at risk of having ataxia, and for their families. This book explains the nature and causes of ataxia, the basic genetics that underlie many kinds of ataxia, discusses medical management of ataxia, provides practical advice for everyday living, points the way to many useful resources and assures that living a good life is an entirely reasonable aspiration, even with ataxia.

112 pages

Andrew Rosen, Executive Director
Stephanie Lucas, Communications Manager
Lori Shogren, Community Program & Service Dir.

543 **Ten Years to Live**
National Ataxia Foundation
600 Highway 169 South, Suite 1725
Minneapolis, MN 55426
763-553-0020
Fax: 763-553-0167
naf@ataxia.org
www.ataxia.org

Struggles of the Schut family with hereditary ataxia.
ISBN: 0-962716-63-1
Andrew Rosen, Executive Director
Stephanie Lucas, Communications Manager
Lori Shogren, Community Program & Service Dir.

Newsletters

544 **A-TMRF Newsletter**
A-T Medical Research Foundation
5241 Round Meadow Road
Hidden Hills, CA 91302
818-704-8146
Fax: 818-704-8310

Reports on the two major labs that are supported and funded by us.

545 **Alert**
Alliance of Genetic Support Groups
4301 Connecticut Ave NW, Suite 404
Washington, DC 20008
202-966-5557
Fax: 202-966-8553
info@geneticalliance.org
www.geneticalliance.org

Functions as a vehicle of communication between the Alliance and its constituency. Provides timely and useful information on genetics research.
Monthly
Sharon Terry, MA, President/ CEO
Natasha Bonhomme, VP, Strategic Development
Ruth Evans, Director of Accounting

546 **Generations**
National Ataxia Foundation
600 Highway 169 South, Suite 1725
Minneapolis, MN 55426
763-553-0020
Fax: 763-553-0167
naf@ataxia.org
www.ataxia.org

Contains reports on the organization and its chapters, offers research, advice and guides to other resources available.
Andrew Rosen, Executive Director
Stephanie Lucas, Communications Manager
Lori Shogren, Community Program & Service Dir.

547 **MSRGSN Newsletter**
Mountain States Regional Genetics Service Network
4300 Cherry Creek Drive S
Denver, CO 80222
303-692-2423
Fax: 303-782-5576

Joyce Hooker, Coordinator

548 **NERG News**
New England Regional Genetics Group
PO Box 670
Mount Desert, ME 4660
207-288-2701
Fax: 207-288-2705

549 **SERGG Regional News**
Southeast Regional Genetics Group
PO Box 1642
Decatur, GA 30031
404-775-8551
Fax: 404-775-8562
mlane@sergginc.org
www.sergginc.org

Provides information on genetics services, public health departments, consumers, and related laboratory services.

Timothy C. Wood, PhD, President
Mary Rose Simpson, Administrator

Pamphlets

550 **Alliance Brochure**
Alliance of Genetic Support Groups
4301 Connecticut Ave NW, Suite 404
Washington, DC 20008
202-966-5557
Fax: 202-966-8553
info@geneticalliance.org
www.geneticalliance.org

Explains the services and programs offered by the Alliance.
Sharon Terry, MA, President/ CEO
Natasha Bonhomme, VP, Strategic Development
Ruth Evans, Director of Accounting

551 **Ataxia Fact Sheet**
National Ataxia Foundation
600 Highway 169 South, Suite 1725
Minneapolis, MN 55426
763-553-0020
Fax: 763-553-0167
naf@ataxia.org
www.ataxia.org

Describes ataxia as a symptom and its association with other medical problems as well as the hereditary types.
Andrew Rosen, Executive Director
Stephanie Lucas, Communications Manager
Lori Shogren, Community Program & Service Dir.

552 **Consumer Indicators of Quality Genetic Services**
Alliance of Genetic Support Groups
4301 Connecticut Avenue NW, #404
Washington, DC 20008
202-966-5557
800-336-4363
Fax: 202-966-8553
info@geneticalliance.org
www.geneticalliance.org

Describes the Alliance of Genetic Support Groups Partnership Program, which strives to increase provider awareness of the unique needs and resources of genetic consumers, improve provider access to quality, consumer-oriented support group resources, and develop replacable educational materials for other programs.
Sharon Terry, MA, President/ CEO
Natasha Bonhomme, VP, Strategic Development
Ruth Evans, Director of Accounting

553 **Facts About Friedreich's Ataxia**
Muscular Dystrophy Association
222 S. Riverside Plaza, Suite 1500
Chicago, IL 60606
520-529-2000
800-572-1717
Fax: 520-529-5300
mda@mdausa.org
mda.org

Explains Friedreich's ataxia in layman's terms and answers commonly asked questions about the disease. Also in Spanish and online.
2006
Kristine Welker, Interim President/CEO
Valerie A. Cwik, MD, EVP, Chief Medical & Scientific
Julie Faber, EVP, CFO

554 **Friedrich's Ataxia**
National Ataxia Foundation
600 Highway 169 South, Suite 1725
Minneapolis, MN 55426
763-553-0020
Fax: 763-553-0167
naf@ataxia.org
www.ataxia.org

Describes symptoms, diagnosis, genetics and hints on coping.
Andrew Rosen, Executive Director
Stephanie Lucas, Communications Manager
Lori Shogren, Community Program & Service Dir.

Ataxia / Pamphlets

555 **Gene Testing for Ataxia**
National Ataxia Foundation
600 Highway 169 South, Suite 1725
Minneapolis, MN 55426

763-553-0020
Fax: 763-553-0167
naf@ataxia.org
www.ataxia.org

Describes the latest information about who should consider it and where to have it done.

Andrew Rosen, Executive Director
Stephanie Lucas, Communications Manager
Lori Shogren, Community Program & Service Dir.

556 **Hereditary Ataxia: The Facts**
National Ataxia Foundation
600 Highway 169 South, Suite 1725
Minneapolis, MN 55426

763-553-0020
Fax: 763-553-0167
naf@ataxia.org
www.ataxia.org

Describes recessive and dominant ataxias, information on how hereditary ataxia is transmitted and explanations of the NAF's role in education, service and prevention.

Andrew Rosen, Executive Director
Stephanie Lucas, Communications Manager
Lori Shogren, Community Program & Service Dir.

557 **Incorporating Consumers into Regional Genetics Networks**
Alliance of Genetic Support Groups
4301 Connecticut Avenue NW, Suite 404
Washington, DC 20008

301-652-5553
Fax: 202-966-8553
medhelp.org/www/agsg.htm

558 **Informed Consent: Participation in Genetic Research Studies**
Alliance of Genetic Support Groups
4301 Connecticut Avenue NW, Suite 404
Washington, DC 20008

202-966-5557
800-336-4363
Fax: 202-966-8553
info@geneticalliance.org
www.geneticalliance.org

This booklet explains the nature of genetic research with its benefits and risks.

Sharon Terry, MA, President/ CEO
Natasha Bonhomme, VP, Strategic Development
Ruth Evans, Director of Accounting

559 **Pen-Pal Directory**
National Ataxia Foundation
600 Highway 169 South, Suite 1725
Minneapolis, MN 55426

763-553-0020
Fax: 763-553-0167
naf@ataxia.org
www.ataxia.org

National, state and international directory of others who are affected by ataxia. Available to NAF Pen-Pal members only.

Andrew Rosen, Executive Director
Stephanie Lucas, Communications Manager
Lori Shogren, Community Program & Service Dir.

Atrial Septal Defects / Web Sites

Description

560 **ATRIAL SEPTAL DEFECTS**
Synonyms: ASD, Atrioseptal defects
Involves the following Biologic System(s):
Cardiovascular Disorders

The term atrial septal defect, or ASD, refers to a group of congenital abnormalities characterized by the presence of a hole in the wall (septum) that separates the two upper chambers of the heart (atria). Atrial septal defects are classified according to their location and may occur as a single anomaly or in association with other heart (cardiac) defects. These types of abnormalities occur in approximately 2000 of every 100,000 births.

The upper left chamber of the heart (left atrium) receives blood that is rich with oxygen (oxygenated) from the lungs. The blood then passes into the lower left chamber (left ventricle) from which it is then pumped through the arteries of the body into the general circulation. The right atrium receives blood that has been depleted of oxygen (deoxygenated) that then passes into the right ventricle and is pumped to the lungs where it once again receives oxygen. Atrial septal defects may allow the passage of some oxygenated blood from the upper left side of the heart into the upper right side of the heart where it mixes with blood that is oxygen depleted. In some patients, this results in a reduced oxygen supply to the body and an increase in blood flow to the lungs. Physical findings associated with ASDs may include enlargement of the right atrium, the right ventricle, or both, and characteristic heart sounds. In some patients, symptoms may be completely absent, especially in early childhood. ASDs are often discovered during routine physical examination by the pressure of a systolic heart murmur. Some affected individuals may experience fatigue upon exertion or exercise. Other findings or symptoms may become apparent after the age of 30 years or when an affected woman becomes pregnant. In these patients, symptoms may include fatigue upon exercise (exercise intolerance), valve insufficiencies, and other, more serious problems such as heart failure and or arrhythmias.

The standard method for closure of atrial septal defects has been open-heart surgery. However, a new nonsurgical procedure has been developed and is done in the heart catheterization laboratory, thus avoiding the need for surgery. A patch, usually resembling a small umbrella, is inserted into the damaged area through a catheter. It is then put into place to close the hole.

Government Agencies

561 **NIH/ Eunice Kennedy Shriver National Institute of Child Health & Human Development**
P.O. Box 3006
Rockville, MD 20847

800-370-2943
Fax: 866-760-5947
www.nichd.nih.gov

Conducts and supports laboratory research, clinical trials, and epidemiological studies that explore health processes; examines the impact of disabilities, diseases, and variations on the lives of individuals; and sponsors training programs for scientists, health care providers, and researchers to ensure that NICHD research can continue.

Diana W. Bianchi, Director
Alison Cernich, PhD, Deputy Director

562 **NIH/National Heart, Lung and Blood Institute**
31 Center Drive, Bldg 31
Bethesda, MD 20892

877-645-2448
www.nhlbi.nih.gov

The National Heart, Lung, and Blood Institute (NHLBI) provides global leadership for a research, training, and education program to promote the prevention and treatment of heart, lung, and blood diseases and enhance the health of all individuals so that they can live longer and more fulfilling lives.

Gary H. Gibbons, MD, Director
Kate O'Sullivan, Executive Officer

National Associations & Support Groups

563 **American Academy of Pediatrics**
345 Park Blvd
Itasca, IL 60143

800-433-9016
Fax: 847-434-8000
mcc@aap.org
www.aap.org

The American Academy of Pediatrics and its member pediatricians are committed to the attainment of optimal physical, mental and social health and well-being for all infants, children, adolescents, and young adults.

Mark Del Monte, JD, CEO/Executive VP
Lynn Olson, PhD, VP, Research
Vera Tait, MD, FAAP, Chief Medical Officer

564 **American Heart Association**
7272 Greenville Avenue
Dallas, TX 75231

214-570-5978
800-242-8721
www.heart.org

The mission of the American Heart Associate is to build healthier lives, free of cardiovascular diseases and stroke.

Nancy Brown, CEO
Mitchelle S.V. Elkind, President
Suzie Upton, Chief Operating Officer

565 **Genetic Alliance**
426400 Woodfield Road, Ste 189
Damascus, MD 20872

202-966-5557
Fax: 202-966-8553
info@geneticalliance.org
www.geneticalliance.org

World's leading nonprofit health advocacy organization committed to transforming health through genetics and promoting an environment of openness centered on the health of individuals, families, and communities.

Sharon Terry, CEO
Ruth Child, CFO
Natasha Bonhomme, Chief Strategy Officer

566 **March of Dimes Foundation**
1550 Crystal Drive, Ste 1300
Arlington, VA 22202

888-663-4637
www.marchofdimes.org

March of Dimes help moms have full-term pregnancies and research the problems that threaten the health of babies. The March of Dimes also acts globally: sharing best practices in perinatal health and helping improve birth outcomes where the needs are the most urgent.

Stacey D. Stewart, President
Alan Brogdon, SVP/COO/Board Officer
Rahul Gupta, MD, SVP & Chief Medical/Health Officer

Web Sites

567 **Southern Illinois University School of Medicine**
P O Box 19658
Springfield, IL 62794

217-545-8000
www.siumed.edu/peds/index.htm

Mission is to meet the health care needs of children and their families in Central and Southern Illinois through provision of high quality, coordinated care of children with acute and chronic conditions with inpatient, ambulatory, and community-based programs.

Atrial Septal Defects / Book Publishers

568 **Yale University School of Medicine**
333 Cedar Street
New Haven, CT 6510

203-432-4771
medicine.yale.edu

Offers information on congential heart conditions such as Atrial Septal Defects, including symptoms, causes and treatments.

Peter Salovey, President of the University
Richard Belitsky M.D., Deputy Dean for Education
Benjamin Polak B.A., M.A., Ph.D., Provost of the University

Book Publishers

569 **Congenital Disorders Sourcebook**

Greg Mullin, author

Omnigraphics
615 Griswold Street, Ste 520
Detroit, MI 48226

610-461-3548
800-234-1340
Fax: 800-875-1340
contact@omnigraphics.com
www.omnigraphics.com

Provides basic consumer health information about the most common types of nonhereditary birth defects and disorders related to prematurity, gestational injuries, congenital infections, and birth complications, including disorders of the heart, brain, gastrointestinal tract, musculoskeletal system, urinary tract, and reproductive system craniofacial disorders, cerebral palsy, spina bifida, and fetal alcohol syndrome, and detailing the causes, diagnostic tests, and treatments for each.

664 pages
ISBN: 0-780816-13-8

Attention Deficit Hyperactivity Disorder / National Associations & Support Groups

Description

570 ATTENTION DEFICIT HYPERACTIVITY DISORDER
Synonyms: ADHD, Hyperactive child syndrome, Hyperkinetic syndrome
Involves the following Biologic System(s):
Developmental/Behavioral/Psychiatric Disorders

Attention deficit hyperactivity disorder, or ADHD, is a syndrome of childhood and adolescence characterized by impulsive behavior, motor-related overactivity (hyperactivity), and inattention. The short attention span results in a decreased ability or inability to complete chores, assignments, or other tasks. ADHD is four to six times more prevalent among boys than it is in girls. In approximately 50 percent of cases, this disorder develops before the age of four years, while in others it appears before seven years of age. Over the last decade, it has been increasingly diagnosed in adults. Some behavioral symptoms associated with this disorder may be present at times in children with ADHD or in children with certain other disorders (e.g., conduct disorder, learning disabilities, hearing impairment, etc.). Therefore, specialists often base their diagnosis on the frequent presence of eight or more characteristic findings. Among these are restlessness, difficulty in remaining seated, difficulty in waiting for a turn in group activities, inclination to be easily distracted, impulsively answering questions before they are completed, difficulty following instructions, inability to sustain concentration while performing tasks or playing, shifting to other tasks before completing others, talking excessively, poor ability to play quietly, interrupting or butting in on others, not appearing to listen when others speak, losing things, and frequently taking part in dangerous physical activities. Evaluation of an individual with ADHD involves taking a detailed family and medical history, paying careful attention to such things as activity level, behavior, and temperament during the early years of the life of the affected child. Obtaining this information may be helpful in determining the extent of the disorder and the presence of additional difficulties (e.g., learning disabilities, anxiety disorders, conduct disorders, etc.).

ADHD is currently considered to be a persistent and chronic condition for which no medical cure is available. Although the cause of ADHD is not known, genetic influences may be a factor in the development of this disorder. In addition, children with neurological disorders and other abnormalities related to the central nervous system may be predisposed to the development of ADHD. Treatment of attention deficit hyperactivity disorder may include an ongoing behavioral and psychosocial therapeutic plan that includes the cooperation of school personnel, the child, and the child's parents or caregivers. In addition, psychostimulant drugs or other medications may be prescribed and carefully monitored. Affected children may also benefit from a structured environment at home and in school. Studies show that, in many phases children who receive multifaceted treatment are better able to cope with ADHD through their adolescent years and into adulthood. Other treatment is supportive.

Government Agencies

571 NIH/National Institute of Mental Health
6001 Executive Blvd, Rm 6200, MSC 9663
Bethesda, MD 20892
866-615-6464
Fax: 301-443-4279
TTY: 301-443-8431
nimhinfo@nih.gov
www.nimh.nih.gov

The mission of NIMH is to transform the understanding and treatment of mental illnesses through basic and clinical research, paving the way for prevention, recovery, and cure.
Joshua A. Gordon, MD, PhD, Director
Shelli Avenevoli, PhD, Deputy Director

572 NIH/National Institute of Neurological Disorders and Stroke (NINDS)
PO Box 5801
Bethesda, MD 20824
800-352-9424
www.ninds.nih.gov

Works to reduce the burden of neurological disease by conducting, fostering, coordinating and guiding research on the causes, prevention, diagnosis and treatment of neurological disorders and stroke, while supporting basic research in related scientific areas.
Walter J. Koroshetz, MD, Director

National Associations & Support Groups

573 American Academy of Pediatrics
345 Park Blvd
Itasca, IL 60143
800-433-9016
Fax: 847-434-8000
mcc@aap.org
www.aap.org

The American Academy of Pediatrics and its member pediatricians are committed to the attainment of optimal physical, mental and social health and well-being for all infants, children, adolescents, and young adults.
Mark Del Monte, JD, CEO/Executive VP
Lynn Olson, PhD, VP, Research
Vera Tait, MD, FAAP, Chief Medical Officer

574 Arc of the United States
1825 K Street NW, Ste 1200
Washington, DC 20006
202-534-3700
800-433-5255
Fax: 202-534-3731
info@thearc.org
www.thearc.org

The Arc of the United States advocates for the rights and full participation of all children and adults with intellectual and developmental disabilities. Together with a network of members and affiliated chapters, they improve systems of support and services; connect families; inspire communities and influence public policy.
Peter V. Berns, CEO

575 Attention Deficit Disorder Association
www.add.org
800-939-1019
Fax: 800-939-1019
info@add.org
www.add.org

The Attention Deficit Disorder Association provides information, resources and networking opportunities to help adults with Attention Deficit Hyperactivity Disorder lead better lives.
Duane Gordon, President
Melissa Reskof, Community Outreach Committee Chair
Annette Tabor, Education Committee Chair

576 CHADD: Children and Adults with Attention Deficit/Hyperactivity Disorders
4221 Forbes Blvd, Suite 270
Lanham, MD 20706
301-306-7070
Fax: 301-306-7090
www.chadd.org

Children and Adults with Attention-Deficit/Hyperactivity Disorder (CHADD) was founded in 1987 in response to the frustration and sense of isolation experienced by parents and their children with ADHD.
Robert Cattoi, CEO
April Gower, COO

Attention Deficit Hyperactivity Disorder / Conferences

577 Child Neurology Foundation
601 W Short Street
Lexington, KY 40508
888-417-3435
info@childneurologyfoundation.org
childneurologyfoundation.org

The Child Neurology Foundation connects partners from all areas of the child neurology community so those navigating the journey of disease diagnosis, management, and care have the ongoing support from those dedicated to treatments and cures.

Amy Brin, Executive Director
Katie Hentges, Director, Programs
Brea McCormley, Director, Development

578 Feingold Association of the US
10955 Windjammer Drive S
Indianapolis, IN 46256
631-369-9340
www.feingold.org

Helps families of children with learning and behavior problems, including attention deficit disorder. Also helps chemically-sensitive and salicylate-sensitive adults. Program is based upon a diet which primarily eliminates certain synthetic food additives.

579 Genetic Alliance
426400 Woodfield Road, Ste 189
Damascus, MD 20872
202-966-5557
Fax: 202-966-8553
info@geneticalliance.org
www.geneticalliance.org

World's leading nonprofit health advocacy organization committed to transforming health through genetics and promoting an environment of openness centered on the health of individuals, families, and communities.

Sharon Terry, CEO
Ruth Child, CFO
Natasha Bonhomme, Chief Strategy Officer

580 Learning Disabilities Association of America
PO Box 10369, 4156 Library Road
Pittsburgh, PA 15234
412-341-1515
888-300-6710
Fax: 412-344-0224
info@LDAAmerica.org
www.ldaamerica.org

Helps families of the affected individual through information and referral to professionals in their area. A membership organization with affiliates across the country.

Stephanie Fedro-Byrom, Operations Manager
Maureen Swanson, Director, Healthy Children Project
Ericka Pardun, Communications Coordinator

581 March of Dimes Foundation
1550 Crystal Drive, Ste 1300
Arlington, VA 22202
888-663-4637
www.marchofdimes.org

March of Dimes help moms have full-term pregnancies and research the problems that threaten the health of babies. The March of Dimes also acts globally: sharing best practices in perinatal health and helping improve birth outcomes where the needs are the most urgent.

Stacey D. Stewart, President
Alan Brogdon, SVP/COO/Board Officer
Rahul Gupta, MD, SVP & Chief Medical/Health Officer

582 Mental Health America
500 Montgomery Street, Ste 820
Alexandria, VA 22314
703-684-7722
800-969-6642
Fax: 703-684-5968
www.mentalhealthamerica.net

MHA, the leading advocacy organization addressing the full spectrum of mental and substance use conditions and their effects nationwide, works to inform, advocate and enable access to quality behavioral health services for all Americans.

Paul Gionfriddo, President/CEO
Whitney Ball, Assoc. Dir., Marketing/Outreach
Sachin Doshi, Sr. Dir, Finance/Operations

583 National Alliance on Mental Illness (NAMI)
4301 Wilson Blvd., Suite 300
Arlington, VA 22203
703-525-7600
800-999-6264
info@nami.org
www.nami.org

NAMI provides advocacy, education, support and public awareness so that all individuals and families affected by mental illness can build better lives.

Daniel H. Gillison, CEO
Davi Levy, CFO
Ken Duckworth, Chief Medical Officer

584 National Center for Learning Disabilities
1 Thomas Circle NW, #700
Washington, DC 20005
212-545-7510
888-575-7373
Fax: 212-545-9665
ncld@ncld.org
www.ncld.org

The National Center for Learning Disabilities improves the lives of all people with learning difficulties and disabilities by empowering parents, enabling young adults, transforming schools, and creating policy and advocacy impact.

Lindsay E. Jones, Esq., CEO
Quinn Bradlee, Youth Engagement Associate
Meghan Whittaker, Esq., Director of Policy

585 National Mental Health Consumers' Self-Help Clearinghouse
1211 Chestnut Street, Suite 1207
Philadelphia, PA 19107
215-751-1810
800-553-4539
Fax: 215-636-6312
selfhelpclearinghouse@gmail.com
www.mhselfhelp.org

The Clearinghouse works to foster peer empowerment through our website, up-to-date news and information announcements, a directory of peer-driven services, electronic and printed publications, training packages, and individual and onsite consultation

Joseph Rogers, Founder/Executive Director
Susan Rogers, Director

586 Option Institute: Son Rise Program
Autism Treatment Center of America
2080 S Undermountain Road
Sheffield, MA 01257
800-714-2779
information@son-rise.org
www.son-rise.org

Describes an effective, loving and respectful method for treating children with autism. It teaches parents and healing professionals how to set up a home based program using the child's motivation to reach their special child.

Barry Neil Kaufman, Co-Founder/Co-Creator
Samahria Lyte Kaufman, Co-Founder/Co-Creator

587 The Council For Exceptional Children
3100 Clarendon Blvd, Suite 600
Arlington, VA 22201
888-232-7733
service@exceptionalchildren.org
exceptionalchildren.org

Advocates appropriate policies, standards and development for students with special needs.

Chad Rummel, Executive Director

Conferences

588 Annual International Conference on ADHD
CHADD
4221 Forbes Blvd, Suite 270
Lanham, MD 20706
301-306-7070
Fax: 301-306-7090
www.chadd.org

Offers presentations from keynote speakers, ADHD Professional Institutes, cutting-edge research through speaker and poster sessions, workshops, networking, peer-to-peer meetings, and a virtual exhibit hall.
November

589 Arc Annual National Convention
Arc of the United States
1825 K Street NW, Ste 1200
Washington, DC 20006
202-534-3700
800-433-5255
Fax: 202-534-3731
mckiernan@thearc.org
www.thearc.org

Where members, staff, volunteers, professionals, experts, self advocates and their families gather for a dynamic convention to meet each other, learn from each other, and tackle the tough issues facing the intellectual and developmental disability (I/DD) community together.
Peter V. Berns, CEO
Kristen McKiernan, Sr Exec. Offcr, Comms & Marketing
Liz Mahar, Director, Family/Sibling Initiative

590 CEC Convention & Expo
Council for Exceptional Children
2900 Crystal Drive Suite 1000
Arlington, VA 22202
703-243-0446
888-232-7733
Fax: 703-264-9494
TTY: 866-915-5000
service@cec.sped.org
exceptionalchildren.org

Offers an unparalleled experience with more than 800 sessions to help you learn the latest in evidence-based practices; explore innovative technologies, products, and services; and network with other professionals working with children with exceptionalities and their families.
April
Bruce Ramirez, Executive Director

591 NAMI Convention
National Alliance on Mental Illness
3803 N Fairfax Drive, Suite 100
Arlington, VA 22203
703-524-7600
888-999-6264
Fax: 703-524-9094
TDD: 703-516-7227
info@nami.org
www.nami.org

The NAMI Convention is packed with information, chances to network, leadership development opportunities, and lots more.
Summer
Richele Keas, Senior Mgr, Media Relations

Audio Video

592 ADD From A To Z-Understanding The Diagnosis & Treatment of ADD in Children & Adult
Connecticut Association for Children with LD
25 Van Zant Street, Suite 15-5
East Norwalk, CT 6855
203-838-5010
Fax: 203-866-6108
cacld@optonline.net
www.cacld.org

Provides a comprehensive overview of this complicated and often misunderstood subject. Informative, authorative, and entertaining, this video will be useful to anyone who wants a clear understanding of what ADD is and what is not.
107 Minutes

593 ADHD: What Can We Do?
ADD WareHouse
300 NW 70th Avenue, Suite 102
Plantation, FL 33317
954-792-8100
800-233-9273
Fax: 954-792-8545
websales@addwarehouse.com
www.addwarehouse.com

Can serve as a companion to ADHD: What Do We Know. This video focuses on the most effective ways to manage ADHD, both in the home and in the classroom. Scenes depict the use of behavior management at home and accommodations and interventions in the classroom which have proven to be effective in the treatment of ADHD. Thirty seven minutes.
1993
ISBN: 0-898629-82-1

594 ADHD: What Do We Know?
Russell A Barkley, author

Guilford Publications
370 Seventh Avenue, Suite 1200
New York, NY 10001
212-431-9800
800-365-7006
Fax: 212-966-6708
info@guilford.com
www.guilford.com

An introduction for teachers and special education practitioners, school psychologists and parents of ADHD children. Topics outlined in this video include the causes and prevalence of ADHD, ways children with ADHD behave, other conditions that may accompany ADHD and long-term prospects for children with ADHD. DVD 36 minutes, Manual 31 pages.
Oct 2006 31 pages DVD & Manual

595 Concentration Video
Learning disAbilities Resources
PO Box 716
Bryn Mawr, PA 19010
610-525-8336
Fax: 610-525-8337

An instructional video which provides a perspective about attention problems, possible causes and solutions.
Video

596 Educating Inattentive Children
ADD WareHouse
300 NW 70th Avenue, Suite 102
Plantation, FL 33317
954-792-8100
800-233-9273
Fax: 954-792-8545
websales@addwarehouse.com
www.addwarehouse.com

An excellent resources for teachers who encounter inattention and hyperactivity in the classroom. It helps teachers distinguish deliberate misbehavior from the incompetent, nonpurposeful behavior of the inattentive child.
1990 Video

597 How to Help Your Child Succeed in School
Peytral Publications
PO Box 1162
Minnetonka, MN 55345
952-949-8707
877-739-8725
Fax: 952-906-9777
help@peytral.com
www.peytral.com

In this deeply powerful video, Sandra Reif presents the essential information needed by those who work with ADHD and/or Learning Disabilities to help children in school. The focus is on the key for success, a strong partnership in education between home and school.
56 Minutes
Donna Kaufman

598 Medication for ADHD
ADD WareHouse
300 NW 70th Avenue, Suite 102
Plantation, FL 33317
954-792-8100
800-233-9273
Fax: 954-792-8545
websales@addwarehouse.com
www.addwarehouse.com

Attention Deficit Hyperactivity Disorder / Web Sites

This comprehensive DVD program addresses the critical questions regarding the use of medicati in the treatment of ADD or ADHD. WGN-TV medical reporter Dina Bair interviews two long-time ADHD experts: psychiatrist Dr Jonathan Bloomberg and clinical psychologist Dr Thomas Phelan.

ISBN: 1-889140-18-X

599 Understanding Attention Deficit Disorder
Connecticut Association for Children with LD
25 Van Zant Street, Suite 15-5
East Norwalk, CT 6855
203-838-5010
Fax: 203-866-6108
cacld@optonline.net
www.cacld.org

A video in an interview format for parents and professionals providing the history, symptoms, methods of diagnosis and three approaches used to ease the effects of attention deficit disorder.

45 minutes

600 Understanding Hyperactivity
Psychiatric Support Services
Houston, TX
281-580-0046

Designed for parents and teachers, a video explaining the symptoms and consequences of attention deficit hyperactivity disorder.

Video

601 Why Can't Michael Pay Attention?
Learning Seed
P.O. Box 617880
Chicago, IL 60661
800-634-4941
Fax: 800-998-0854
info@learningseed.com
www.learningseed.com

After a multi-faceted assessment, six year old, Michael is diagnosed with Attention Deficit Hyperactivity Disorder. Michael's parents learn techniques such as consistent schedules, docking systems, star charts, and self-monitoring to help organize home life. ISBN: DVD 1-55740-973-0; VHS 1-55740-896-3

21 minutes

602 Why Won't My Child Pay Attention?
Wiley Publishing Inc
111 River Street
Hoboken, NJ 07030
317-572-3000
201-748-6000
Fax: 201-748-6088
info@wiley.com
as.wiley.com/WileyCDA/Section/index.html

Practical and reassuring videotape. Noted child psychologist tells parents about two of the most common and complex problems of childhood: inattention and hyperactivity.

1993 Video
ISBN: 0-471303-19-4

Stephen M. Smith, President & CEO
John Kritzmacher, Executive Vice President
Edward J. May, Corporate Secretary

Web Sites

603 Attention Deficit Disorder Association
www.add.org

www.add.org

Provides children, adolescents and adults with ADD information, support groups, publications, videos, and referrals.

604 Attention Deficit Disorder and Parenting Site
www.LD-ADD.com

www.LD-ADD.com

Website has been created for parents to help them recognize and manage ADHD/LD in children.

605 CHADD: Children and Adults with Attention Deficit Disorders
4221 Forbes Blvd, Suite 270
Lanham, MD 20706
301-306-7070
Fax: 301-306-7090
www.chadd.org

Children and Adults with Attention Deficit Disorders) provides parents, professionals and adults diagnosed with ADD information, support and educational material dealing with this disorder.

Robert Cattoi, CEO
April Gower, COO

606 Feingold Association of the US
10955 Windjammer Drive S
Indianapolis, IN 46256
631-369-9340
www.feingold.org

Helps families of children with learning and behavior problems, including attention deficit disorder. Also helps chemically-sensitive and salicylate-sensitive adults. Program is based upon a diet which primarily eliminates certain synthetic food additives.

607 Health Answers Education Sudler-WPP Health Practice
700 Dresher Road
Horsham, PA 19044
215-442-9010
www.healthanswers.com

HealthAnswers offers a breadth of services in medical education, sales force training, patient support solutions, professional promotion and consumer solutions.

Mike Hudnall, CEO

608 Learning Disabilities Association of America
PO Box 10369, 4156 Library Road
Pittsburgh, PA 15234
412-341-1515
888-300-6710
Fax: 412-344-0224
info@LDAAmerica.org
www.ldaamerica.org

Helps families of the affected individual through information and referral to professionals in their area. A membership organization with affiliates across the country.

Stephanie Fedro-Byrom, Operations Manager
Maureen Swanson, Director, Healthy Children Project
Ericka Pardun, Communications Coordinator

609 National Center for Learning Disabilities
32 Laight Street, Second Floor
New York, NY 10013
212-545-7510
888-575-7373
Fax: 212-545-9665
help@ncld.org
www.ld.org

The mission of the NCLD is to increase opportunities for all individuals with learning disabilities to achieve their potential. NCLD accomplishes this by increasing public awareness and understanding of learning disabilities, conducting educational programs and services that promote research-based knowledge and providing national leadership in shaping public policy.

Frederic M Poses, Chairman
Mary Kalikow, Vice Chairman
William Haney, Secretary

Book Publishers

610 ADD & Learning Disabilities
Bantam Doubleday Dell Publishing
1745 Broadway, 10th Floor
New York, NY 10019
212-572-6066
Fax: 212-782-9700
webmaster@randomhouse.com
www.randomhouse.com

For parents of children with learning disabilities and attention deficit disorder - and for educational and medical professionals who encounter these children - two experts in the field have devised a handbook to help identify the very best treatments.

Attention Deficit Hyperactivity Disorder / Book Publishers

256 pages
ISBN: 0-385469-31-4

611 ADD: Helping Your Child
Warner Books
1271 Avenue of the Americas
New York, NY 10020
212-484-2900
Fax: 617-263-2854

1994 224 pages Paperback
ISBN: 0-446670-13-8

612 ADHD Parenting Handbook: Practical Advice for Parents from Parents
Taylor Publishing
1550 W Mockingbird Lane
Dallas, TX 75235
214-637-2800
Fax: 214-819-8141

Provides guidelines, suggestions, and advice to help parents interact with their children who have ADHD.

1994 224 pages Paperback
ISBN: 0-878338-62-4

613 ADHD Survival Guide for Parents and Teachers
Hope Press
PO Box 188
Duarte, CA 91009
818-303-0644
800-321-4039
Fax: 626-358-3520
dcomings@earthlink.net
hopepress.com

Guide for parents and teacher and other caretakers of ADHD children.

ISBN: 1-878267-43-4

614 ADHD in Schools: Assessment and Intervention Strategies
George DuPaul, Gary Stoner, author

Guilford Publications
72 Spring Street
New York, NY 10012
212-431-9800
800-365-7006
Fax: 212-966-6708
info@guilford.com
www.guilford.com

Comprehensive and practical, the book includes several reproducible assessment tools and handouts, and emphasizes a team-based approach to intervention. This is a popular reference providing essential guidance for school-based professionals meeting the challenges of ADHD at any grade level. Available in paperback or hardcover.

Oct 2004 330 pages Paperback
ISBN: 1-593850-89-0

615 ADHD in the Young Child
ADD WareHouse
300 NW 70th Avenue, Suite 102
Plantation, FL 33317
954-792-8100
800-233-9273
Fax: 954-792-8545
websales@addwarehouse.com
www.addwarehouse.com

The authors sensitively and effectively describe what life is like living with a young child with ADHD. With the help of over 75 cartoon illustrations they provide practical solutions to common problems found at home, in school and elsewhere.

2006 202 pages
ISBN: 1-886941-32-7

616 ADHD: Handbook for Diagnosis & Treatment
Guilford Press
72 Spring Street
New York, NY 10012
800-365-7006
Fax: 212-966-6708
info@guilford.com
www.guilford.com

This second edition helps clinicians diagnose and treat Attention Deficit Hyperactivity Disorder. Written by an internationally recognized authority in the field, it covers the history of ADHD, its primary symptoms, associated conditions, developmental course and outcome, and family context. A workbook companion manual is also available.

2005 770 pages
ISBN: 1-593852-10-8

617 All Kinds of Minds
ADD WareHouse
300 NW 70th Avenue, Suite 102
Plantation, FL 33317
954-792-8100
800-233-9273
Fax: 954-792-8545
websales@addwarehouse.com
www.addwarehouse.com

Primary and elementary students with learning disorders can now gain insight into the difficulties they face in school. This book helps all children understand and respect all kinds of minds and can encourage children with learning disorders to maintain their motivation and keep from developing behavior problems stemming from their learning disorders.

1993 283 pages
ISBN: 0-838820-90-5

618 Alphabet Soup: A Recipe for Understanding & Treating ADD
Minerva Books
137 W 14th Street
New York, NY 10011
212-343-6100
Fax: 212-343-6934

1994 50 pages Paperback
ISBN: 0-934695-00-8

619 Attention Deficit Disorder and Learning Disabilities
Random House
1745 Broadway
New York, NY 10019
212-572-6066
webmaster@randomhouse.com
www.randomhouse.com

Realities, myths, and controversial treatments. Section I tries to dispel the myths and discusses proven treatments for ADHD and LD. Section II explains how the scientific community evaluates new treatment methods, and Section III summarizes alternative treatments and discusses scientific evidence pertaining to its usefulness.

256 pages
ISBN: 0-385469-31-4

620 Attention Deficit Disorder: Concise Source of Information for Parents
Temeron Books
6531 111th Street NW
Edmonton, AB T6H 4
Canada
403-283-0900
855-283-0900
Fax: 403-283-6947
contact@brusheducation.ca
www.brusheducation.ca

Help with a frustrating situation that many parents face.

2006 112 pages
ISBN: 1-550590-82-0

Glenn Rollans, Partner
Lauri Seidlitz, Managing Editor

621 Attention Deficit Hyperactivity Disorder: What Every Parent Wants to Know
Paul H Brookes & Company
PO Box 10624
Baltimore, MD 21285
301-337-9580
800-638-3775
Fax: 410-337-8539
www.brookespublishing.com

The new edition breaks down the complex issues surrounding ADHD today into easy-to-understand, non-technical terms. Now you can quickly get the information you need to help your child with ADHD, without taking the time to wade through heavy research or statistics.

Attention Deficit Hyperactivity Disorder / Book Publishers

2000 304 pages Paperback
ISBN: 1-557663-98-X

622 Beyond Ritalin: Facts About Medication and Other Strategies for Helping Children
ADD WareHouse
300 NW 70th Avenue, Suite 102
Plantation, FL 33317 954-792-8100
800-233-9273
Fax: 954-792-8545
websales@addwarehouse.com
www.addwarehouse.com

The authors respond to concerns all parents and individuals have about using medication to treat disorders such as ADHD, explain the importance of a treatment program for those with this condition and discuss fads and fallacies in current treatments.

1996 272 pages
ISBN: 0-060977-25-6

623 Distant Drums, Different Drummers: A Guide for Young People with ADHD
ADD WareHouse
300 NW 70th Avenue, Suite 102
Plantation, FL 33317 954-792-8100
800-233-9273
Fax: 954-792-8545
websales@addwarehouse.com
www.addwarehouse.com

This book presents a positive perspective of ADHD - one that stresses the value of individual differences. Written for children and adolescents struggling with ADHD, it offers young readers the opportunity to see themselves in a positive light and motivates them to face challenging problems. Ages 8-14.

1995 39 pages
ISBN: 0-964854-80-5

Barbara Ingersoll, PhD

624 Don't Give Up Kid
ADD WareHouse
300 NW 70th Avenue, Suite 102
Plantation, FL 33317 954-792-8100
800-233-9273
Fax: 954-792-8545
websales@addwarehouse.com
www.addwarehouse.com

Alex, the hero of this book, is one of two million children in the US who have learning disabilities. This book gives children with reading problems and learning disabilities a clear understanding of their difficulties and the necessary courage to learn to live with them. Ages 5-12.

ISBN: 1-884281-10-9

625 Eagle Eyes A Child's View od Attention Deficit Disorder
Connecticut Association for Children with LD
25 Van Zant Street, Suite 15-5
East Norwalk, CT 06855 203-838-5010
Fax: 203-866-6108
cacld@optonline.net
www.cacld.org

Story about a boy with ADHD. A valuable tool for parents and teachers to use with elementary school age children with ADHD, their siblings and classmates to help them understand the strengths as well as weaknesses of this population.

30 pages

626 Eagle Eyes: A Child's View of Attention Deficit Disorder
ADD WareHouse
300 NW 70th Avenue, Suite 102
Plantation, FL 33317 954-792-8100
800-233-9273
Fax: 954-792-8545
websales@addwarehouse.com
www.addwarehouse.com

This book helps readers of all ages understand ADD and gives practical suggestions for organization, social cues and self calming. Expressive illustrations enhance the book and encourage reluctant readers. Ages 5-12.

ISBN: 1-884281-11-7

Jeanne Gehret

627 Eukee the Jumpy, Jumpy Elephant
ADD WareHouse
300 NW 70th Avenue, Suite 102
Plantation, FL 33317 954-792-8100
800-233-9273
Fax: 954-792-8545
websales@addwarehouse.com
www.addwarehouse.com

A story about a bright young elephant who is not like all the other elephants. Eukee moves through the jungle like a tornado, unable to pay attention to the other elephants. He begins to feel sad, but gets help after a visit to the doctor who explains why Eukee is so jumpy and hyperactive. With love, support and help, Eukee learns ways to help himself and gain renewed self-esteem. Ideal for ages 3-8.

1995 22 pages
ISBN: 0-962162-98-1

Cliff Corman, MD
Esther Trevino

628 Getting a Grip on ADD: A Kid's Guide to Understanding & Coping with ADD
Educational Media Corporation
6021 Wish Avenue
Encino, CA 91316 818-708-0962

1994 64 pages Paperback
ISBN: 0-932796-60-3

629 Give Your ADD Teen a Chance: A Guide for Parents of Teenagers with ADD
ADD WareHouse
300 NW 70th Avenue, Suite 102
Plantation, FL 33317 954-792-8100
800-233-9273
Fax: 954-792-8545
websales@addwarehouse.com
www.addwarehouse.com

Parenting teenagers is never easy, especially if your teen suffers from ADD. This book provides parents with expert help by showing them how to determine which issues are caused by 'normal' teenager development and which are caused by ADD.

1996 299 pages
ISBN: 0-891099-77-8

Lynn Weiss, PhD

630 Hyperactive Child, Adolescent, and Adult: ADD Through the Lifespan
Connecticut Association for Children with LD
25 Van Zant Street, Suite 15-5
East Norwalk, CT 06855 203-838-5010
Fax: 203-866-6108
cacld@optonline.net
www.cacld.org

Comprehensive general review. Update on previous research by the author, offering a basic text.

162 pages

631 Hyperactivity: Why Won't My Child Pay Attention?
John Wiley & Sons
1 Wiley Drive
Somerset, NJ 08875 732-469-4400
Fax: 732-302-2300
custserv@wiley.com
www.wiley.com

Deals with children who experience problems paying attention, controlling their emotions and physical actions and acting without forethought. Helps parents and professionals to accept the hyperactive child's behavior and find ways to help the child succeed. Provides and accurate understanding of the current state of science concerning the cause, developmental course, evaluation and outcome of this problem.

Attention Deficit Hyperactivity Disorder / Book Publishers

224 pages
ISBN: 0-471533-07-6

632 It's So Much Work to Be Your Friend
Active Parenting Publishers
1220 Kennestone Circle, Suite 130
Marietta, GA 30066
770-429-0565
800-825-0060
Fax: 770-429-0334
cservice@activeparenting.com
www.activeparenting.com

Offers practical strategies to help learning disabled children ages six through seventeen navigate the treacherous social waters of their school, home, and community.
448 pages

633 Jumpin' Johnny Get Back to Work! A Child's Guide to ADHD/Hyperactivity
Connecticut Association for Children with LD
25 Van Zant Street, Suite 15-5
East Norwalk, CT 06855
203-838-5010
Fax: 203-866-6108
cacld@optonline.net
www.cacld.org

Written primarily for elementary age youngsters with ADHD to help them understand their disability. Also valuable as an educational tool for parents, siblings, friends, and classmates. Includes two pages on medication.
24 pages

634 Kids With Incredible Potential Parent's Guide
Active Parenting Publishers
1220 Kennestone Circle, Suite 130
Marietta, GA 30066
770-429-0565
800-825-0060
Fax: 770-429-0334
cservice@activeparenting.com
www.activeparenting.com

The guide for parents of ADHD children is designed as an add-on to the Active Parenting Now video and discussion program. Adds an ADHD emphasis that makes the parenting information more immediate and practical for these parents' special needs.

635 Kids with Incredible Potential Leader's Guide
Active Parenting Publishers
1220 Kennestone Circle, Suite 130
Marietta, GA 30066
770-429-0565
800-825-0060
Fax: 770-429-0334
cservice@activeparenting.com
www.activeparenting.com

Allows the facilitator to give parents specialized information that is more immediate and practical to these parents' needs.

636 Learning To Slow Down and Pay Attention
Connecticut Association for Children with LD
25 Van Zant Street, Suite 15-5
East Norwalk, CT 06855
203-838-5010
Fax: 203-866-6108
cacld@optonline.net
www.cacld.org

Written for elementary school age children with ADHD to read with their parents. A checklist helps families decide if attention and concentration are problems. Interventions are given for parents, doctors and teachers. Includes practical strategies for paying better attention, getting more organized and problem solving.
62 pages

637 Managing Attention Deficit Hyperactivity Disorder in Children
John Wiley & Sons
1 Wiley Drive
Somerset, NJ 08875
732-469-4400
Fax: 732-302-2300
custserv@wiley.com
www.wiley.com

This book explores symptoms of ADHD, the crossover into adulthood with such a disorder, and the latest and most controversial treatments.
1998 896 pages
ISBN: 0-471121-58-4

638 Maybe You Know My Kid: A Parent's Guide to Identifying ADHD
Birch Lane Press
120 Enterprise Avenue S
Secaucus, NJ 07094
212-407-1500
Fax: 212-935-0699

The author writes about her family experiences with their son, David, who has attention deficit disorder. Contains a comprehensive review of important issues plus descriptions of some helpful management techniques.
222 pages

639 My Brother's a World Class Pain: A Sibling's Guide To ADHD/Hyperactivity
Connecticut Association for Children with LD
25 Van Zant Street, Suite 15-5
East Norwalk, CT 06855
203-838-5010
Fax: 203-866-6108
cacld@optonline.net
www.cacld.org

A young girl tells what it's like to have a little brother with ADHD. She expresses the frustration, anger, embarrassment and resentment that often develop living with a sibling who has attention deficit. Her parents seek professional help to understand the disability and enlisted in trying to bring about positive changes in the family.
34 pages

640 Otto Learns About His Medicine A Story About Medication for Hyperative Children
Connecticut Association for Children with LD
25 Van Zant Street, Suite 15-5
East Norwalk, CT 06855
203-838-5010
Fax: 203-866-6108
cacld@optonline.net
www.cacld.org

A book about Otto, a young, hyperactive car. Otto has difficulty paying attention in school, so his parents take him to a mechanic who prescribes medication that will help him control his behavior.
28 pages

641 Parenting Children with ADHD: Lessons That Medicine Cannot Teach
Active Parenting Publishers
1220 Kennestone Circle, Suite 130
Marietta, GA 30066
770-429-0565
800-825-0060
Fax: 770-429-0334
cservice@activeparenting.com
www.activeparenting.com

Gives parents a framework for building a successful parenting program at home. Presents a series of ten lessons that are essential for promoting the success of kids with ADHD.
261 pages

642 Parents' Hyperactivity Handbook: Helping the Fidgety Child
Plenum Press
233 Spring Street
New York, NY 10013
212-620-8000
Fax: 212-463-0742
info@plenum.com

1993 306 pages
ISBN: 0-306444-65-8

643 Putting On The Brakes - Young People's Guide To Understanding ADHD
Connecticut Association for Children with LD
25 Van Zant Street, Suite 15-5
East Norwalk, CT 06855
203-838-5010
Fax: 203-866-6108
cacld@optonline.net
www.cacld.org

Attention Deficit Hyperactivity Disorder / Newsletters

Written from both a medical and educational perspective. Reviews what it is like to have ADHD. It explains what's going on in the brain, discusses feelings and tries to help children gain some control of their lives.

64 pages

644 Putting on the Brakes
Courage To Change
PO Box 486
Wilkes-Barres, PA 18703
800-440-4003
Fax: 800-772-6499
www.couragetochange.com

This book written for kids ages eight to thirteen tells all they need to know about ADHD. Also available is a companion activity book that teaches organizing, setting priorities, problem solving, maintaining control and other life management skills. The activity book is 88 pages and sells for $14.95.

645 Rethinking Attention Deficit Disorders
Brookline Books
8 Trumbell Rd, Suite B-001
Northampton, MA 01060
413-584-0184
800-666-2665
Fax: 413-584-6184
brbooks@yahoo.com
www.brooklinebooks.com

Gives the classroom teacher useful information that provides ideas and strategies for working with children suffering from ADD.

ISBN: 1-571290-37-0

646 Ritalin is Not the Answer
Jossey-Bass
111 River Street
Hoboken, NJ 07030
201-748-6000
800-956-7739
Fax: 201-748-6088
www.josseybass.com

A healthy, drug-free alternative to Ritalin and an absolute must read for every physician before prescribing it.

224 pages
ISBN: 0-787945-14-5

647 Self-Control Games & Workbook
Western Psychological Services
12031 Wilshire Boulevard
Los Angeles, CA 90025
310-478-2061
Fax: 310-478-7838

This game is designed to teach self-control in academic and social situations. Addresses a total of 24 impulsive, inattentive and hyperactive behaviors. The companion workbook reinforces the use of positive self-statements, and problem-solving techniques, instead of expressing anger.

Game

648 Shelley The Hyperactive Turtle
Connecticut Association for Children with LD
25 Van Zant Street, Suite 15-5
East Norwalk, CT 06855
203-838-5010
Fax: 203-866-6108
cacld@optonline.net
www.cacld.org

Delightful picture book for use with very young children. Sensitive text and wonderful colored illustrations help little ones understand ADHD.

20 pages

649 Taking Charge of ADHD: The Complete, Authoritative Guide for Parents
Guilford Press
72 Spring Street
New York, NY 10012
800-365-7006
Fax: 212-966-6708
info@guilford.com
www.guilford.com

Provides a guide to understanding attention-deficit/hyperactivity disorder and relating to the children whose behavior can be frustrating and confusing. Hardcover, paperback, e-book.

2005 321 pages Paperback
ISBN: 1-572305-60-1

650 Teaching the Tiger
Hope Press
PO Box 188
Duarte, CA 91009
800-321-4039
Fax: 626-358-3520
dcomings@earthlink.net
www.hopepress.com

A handbook for individuals involved in the education of students with Attention Deficit Disorder, Tourette Syndrome, or Obsessive Compulsive Disorder.

ISBN: 1-878267-34-5

David E Comings MD, Presenter

651 The 'Putting On The Brakes' Activity Book For Young People With ADHD
Connecticut Association for Children with LD
25 Van Zant Street, Suite 15-5
East Norwalk, CT 06855
203-838-5010
Fax: 203-866-6108
cacld@optonline.net
www.cacld.org

A companion to the book 'Putting On The Brakes: Young People's Guide To Understanfing Attention Deficit Hyperactivity Disorder (ADHD)'. Offers various exercises to help children with ADHD learn to deal with their problems in a positive way. Some activities can be done independently, others need the collaboration of an adult.

88 pages

652 The ADHD Book of Lists
Courage To Change
PO Box 486
Wilkes-Barres, PA 18703
800-440-4003
Fax: 800-772-6499
www.couragetochange.com

Presented in list format and created for parents, school psychologists, and mental health professionals. A reliable source of answers, strategies, tools, interventions, support, and additional resources.

653 The LD Child and the ADHD Child: Ways Parents and Professionals Can Help
John F Blair Publishers
1406 Plaza Drive
Winston-Salem, NC 27103
336-768-1374
800-222-9796
Fax: 336-768-9194
editorial@blairpub.com
www.blairpub.com

The author recommends other options that can be explored to treat LD and ADHD children without drugs.

261 pages Paperback
ISBN: 0-895871-42-4

Carolyn Sakowski, President
Steve Kirk, Editor In Chief

654 You and Your ADD Child
Nelson Publications
1 Gateway Plaza
Port Chester, NY 10573
914-937-8400
Fax: 914-937-8676

1995 252 pages Paperback
ISBN: 0-785278-95-8

Newsletters

655 ADHD Report
Guilford Publications
370 Seventh Avenue, Suite 1200
New York, NY 10001
212-431-9800
800-365-7006
Fax: 212-966-6708
info@guilford.com
www.guilford.com

Presents the most up-to-date information on the evaluation, diagnosis and management of ADHD in children, adolescents and adults. This important newsletter is an invaluable resource for all professionals interested in ADHD. 6 issues per year; content available online.

16 pages Subscription
ISBN: 1-065802-5 -

Russell A. Barkley, PhD, Editor

656 Chadder
CHADD
BOX.8181 Professional Place, Suite 201
Landover, MD 20785
301-306-7070
Fax: 301-306-7090
TTY: 301-429-0641
disabilityresourcejs.weebly.com/adhd.html

Quarterly

Pamphlets

657 ADHD
Learning Disabilities Association of America
PO Box 10369, 4156 Library Road
Pittsburgh, PA 15234
412-341-1515
Fax: 412-344-0224
info@LDAAmerica.org
ldaamerica.org

A booklet for parents offering information on Attention Deficit-Hyperactivity Disorders and learning disabilities.

Stephanie Fedro-Byrom, Operations Manager

658 Attention Deficit Disorders and Hyperactivity
ERIC Clearinghouse on Disabled and Gifted Children
1920 Association Drive
Reston, VA 20191
703-620-3660
Fax: 703-620-2521

Dedicated to improving educational outcomes for individuals with exceptionalities, students with disabilities, and/or the gifted.

659 Attention Deficit-Hyperactivity Disorder: Is it a Learning Disability?
Georgetown University, School of Medicine
3800 Reservoir Road NW, Main Hospital Building, Fi
Washington, DC 20007
202-444-3960
Fax: 202-687-2387
www.medstarhealth.org

Offers information on learning disabilities and related disorders.

Stephen Ray Mitchell, MD, MBA, Dean for Medical Education
Mikey Cassidy, Executive Assistant to the Dean
Diana Kassar, Sr. Associate Dean for Fin & Admin

660 COGREHAB
Life Science Associates
1 Fenimore Road
Bayport, NY 11705
631-472-2111
Fax: 631-472-8146
www.lifesciassoc.home.pipeline.com

Divided into six groups for diagnosis and treatment of attention, memory and perceptual disorders to be used by and under the guidance of a professional.

$95 - $1,950

Frank Manoriota, Vice President

661 Children with ADD: A Shared Responsibility
Council for Exceptional Children
2900 Crystal Drive, Suite 1000
Arlington, VA 22202
703-264-9494
888-232-7733
TTY: 866-915-5000
service@cec.sped.org
www.cec.sped.org

This book represents a consensus of what professionals and parents believe ADD is all about and how children with ADD may best be served. Reviews the evaluation process under IDEA and 504 and presents effective classroom strategies.

35 pages
ISBN: 0-865862-33-8

James P. Heiden, President
Antonis Katsiyannis, President Elect
Sharon Raimondi, Treasurer

662 Coping with Your Inattentive Child
Connecticut Association for Children with LD
25 Van Zant Street, Suite 15-5
East Norwalk, CT 6855
203-838-5010
Fax: 203-866-6108
cacld@optonline.net
www.cacld.org

Lists signs of ADHD and discusses managing the problems of children with ADHD from infancy through elementary school.

13 pages

663 Identification and Treatment of Attention Deficit Disorders
Therapro
225 Arlington Street
Framingham, MA 1701
508-872-9494
800-257-5376
Fax: 508-875-2062

This handbook contains information that is based on research and offers practical suggestions for parents, teachers and other professionals.

664 Out of Darkness
Connecticut Association for Children with LD
25 Van Zant Street, Suite 15-5
East Norwalk, CT 6855
203-838-5010
Fax: 203-866-6108
cacld@optonline.net
www.cacld.org

Article by an adult who discovers at age 30 that he has ADD.

4 pages

665 Parenting Attention Deficit Disordered Teens
Connecticut Association for Children with LD
25 Van Zant Street, Suite 15-5
East Norwalk, CT 6855
203-838-5010
Fax: 203-866-6108
cacld@optonline.net
www.cacld.org

Detailed outline of the various problems of adolescents with ADHD.

14 pages

666 School Based Assessment of Attention Deficit Disorders
National Clearinghouse of Rehabilitation Materials
5202 N Richmond Hill Drive
Stillwater, OK 74078
405-624-7650
800-223-5219
Fax: 405-624-0695
TDD: 405-624-3156
www.nchrtm.okstate.edu

The 1992 OSEP ruling, placing more responsibility on schools for the assessment of students who may have attention deficit disorders, has raised questions concerning the assessment process. This guide was developed to help states formulate new policies. The paper seeks to: present an overview of current thoughts concerning ADD from an educational perspective, contrast traditional assessment strategies with an alternative model, and describe phases of evaluation.

David Brooks, Director
Carolyn Cain

Camps

667 Camp Buckskin
4124 Quebec Ave N, Ste 300
Minneapolis, MN 55427
763-208-4805
Fax: 952-938-6996
info@campbuckskin.com
www.campbuckskin.com

LD and ADD/ADHD youth have often experienced frustration and a lack of success. Buckskin assists these individuals to realize and develop the potentials and abilities which they possess.

Attention Deficit Hyperactivity Disorder / Camps

Thomas R Bauer, CCD, Camp Director

668 Camp Nuhop
404 Hillcrest Drive
Ashland, OH 44805

419-289-2227
Fax: 419-289-2227
info@campnuhop.org
www.campnuhop.org

A summer residential program for any youngster from 6 to 18 with a learning disability, behavior disorder or Attention Deficit Disorder. Sixty two campers and 35 staff members live on site in groups of 7 campers to every 3 counselors. Activities focus on positive self-concept and behaviors and teach children to learn how to find their strengths, abilities and talents from a positive, yet realistic viewpoint.

Jerry Dunlap, Director

669 Dallas Academy
950 Tiffany Way
Dallas, TX 75218

214-324-1481
Fax: 214-327-8537
www.dallas-academy.com

7-week summer session for students who are having difficulty in regular school classes.

Jim Richardson, Director

670 Developmental Center
6710 86th Avenue N
Pinellas Park, FL 33782

727-541-5716
Fax: 727-544-8186
infopp@centeracademy.com
www.centeracademy.com

Specifically designed for the learning disabled child and other children with difficulties in concentration, strategy, social skills, impulsivity, distractibility and study strategies. Programs offered include: attention training, visual-motor remediation, socialization skills training, relaxation training, horseback riding and more. The day camp meets weekdays from 9-3 for 3,4 or 5 week sessions.

Dr. Eric Larson

671 Eagle Hill School - Summer Program
242 Old Petersham Road, PO Box 116
Hardwick, MA 01037

413-477-6000
Fax: 413-477-6837
admission@eaglehillschool.com
www.ehs1.org

For the child, age 9-19, with a specific learning disability or Attention Deficit Disorder, this summer program offers a structured curriculum designed to build a basic foundation of academic competence. Extracurricular and outdoor activities complement the educational program.

Erin E Wynne, Dean of Admission

672 Groves Academy
3200 Highway 100 South
Saint Louis Park, MN 55416

952-920-6377
Fax: 952-920-2068
www.grovesacademy.org

A nonprofit day school in Minnesota designed especially for children with learning differences. The Center has a full day academic program from September through June, as well as an 8 week summer program. Groves also offers community services such as: psychoeducational testing for children and adults, consulting services, workshops on learning disabilities and other special learning needs, and afternoon/evening tutorial services for children and adults.

John Alexander, Head of School

673 Hill School of Fort Worth
4817 Odessa Avenue
Fort Worth, TX 76133

817-923-9482
Fax: 817-923-4894
admission@hillschool.org
www.hillschool.org

Provides an alternative learning environment for students having average or above-average intelligence with learning differences. Hill school is an established leader in North Texas with a 25 year history of effectively serving LD children. Beginning in 1961 as a tutorial service, Hill became a formal school in 1973. Our mission is to help those who learn differently develop skills and strategies to succeed. We do this by developing academic/study skills, and self-discipline.

Lucille H Helton, Principal
Cathy Allen, Admissions Director
Grey Owens, Principal

674 Lab School of Washington Summer Program
4759 Reservoir Road NW
Washington, DC 20007

202-965-6600
Fax: 202-965-5106
www.labschool.org

The Lab School 5-week summer session includes individualized reading, spelling, writing, study skills, and math programs. A multisensory approach addresses the needs of bright learning disabled children. Related services such as speech/language therapy and occupational therapy are integrated into the curriculum. Elementary/Intermediate; Junior High/High School.

Sally Smith, Founder
Susan Feeley, Admissions Director

675 Maplebrook School
5142 Route 22
Amenia, NY 12501

845-373-8191
Fax: 845-373-7029
jscully@maplebrookschool.org
www.maplebrookschool.org

A coeducational boarding school for students with learning differences and ADD. A New York State registered high school servicing ages 11-18. Post secondary options offered to 18-21.

Donna M Konkolios, Head of School
Jennifer Scully, Director Admissions

676 Round Lake Camp
21 Plymouth Street
Fairfield, NJ 7004

973-575-3333
800-776-5657
Fax: 973-575-4188
rlc@njycamps.org
www.njycamps.org

For ages 7-18, this camp provides individualized academics in reading, language development and math for children with mild learning disabilities. Round Lake also offers therapeutic recreation and Jewish cultural values to its participants.

Sheira Director, Asst. Director

677 Tourette Syndrome Camp Organization
6933 N Kedzie, Ste 816
Chicago, IL 60640

773-465-7536
info@tourettecamp.com
www.tourettecamp.com

Dedicated to promoting camping opportunities for children with Tourette Syndrome and its associated disorders, Obsessive Compulsive Disorder (OCD) and Attention Deficit/Hyperactivity Disorder (ADD/ADHD).

Monica Newman, Camp Director

Description

678 **AUTISTIC DISORDER**
Synonyms: Infantile autism, Kanner's syndrome
Involves the following Biologic System(s):
Developmental/Behavioral/Psychiatric Disorders, Neurologic Disorders

Autistic disorder, also known as infantile autism, is classified as a developmental disability that results from a disorder of the human central nervous system. It usually becomes apparent by three years of age. It is thought to affect approximately four in 10,000 children and is about three to four times more common in males than females. Autistic disorder is characterized by deficient verbal and nonverbal communication, impaired social interactions, and a restricted range of interests and activities.

Children with autistic disorder may fail to acquire or have poorly developed verbal and nonverbal communication skills. If children do communicate verbally, abnormal speech patterns are typically present, such as repetition of another's words or phrases (echolalia); reversal of the proper use of pronouns, such as use of the term "you" rather than "I" when referring to themselves; and nonsensical rhyming. In addition, affected children may be withdrawn, make little or no eye contact, resist cuddling, lack awareness of others' thoughts or feelings, or fail to seek comfort when distressed. Children also typically engage in solitary play for hours, perform ritualistic behaviors and repeated body movements (e.g., rocking, flicking fingers) and have a strong need for a predictable, consistent environment. Certain behaviors (e.g., rubbing an object or surface) may demonstrate a heightened awareness of particular stimuli, whereas others, such as a lack of reaction to sudden, loud noises, may indicate a lowered sensitivity to other stimuli. In many children with autistic disorder, disruptions of rituals or routines may result in tantrum-like outbursts or rages. In addition, some children may exhibit self-injurious or outwardly aggressive behaviors. Because of impairment of language and socialization skills, it may be difficult to obtain accurate estimates of overall intelligence levels and potential. Although such testing often demonstrates intellectual disabilities, some affected children perform adequately in nonverbal areas, such as spatial and motor skills, and those with speech skills may perform adequately in all test areas.

In most patients, the symptoms and findings associated with autistic disorder continue to affect them throughout life. The Food and Drug Administration (FDA) recently approved the use of an antipsychotic, risperidone, for the treatment of irritability associated with autistic disorder, including symptoms of aggression, deliberate self-injury, temper tantrums, and quickly changing moods. This is the first time the FDA has approved any medication for use in children and adolescents with autism. In addition, the management and treatment of affected children may include integrated, multidisciplinary techniques, such as language therapy, structured play and interpersonal exercises, and other behavioral therapies. Some patients, particularly those with speech development, may lead somewhat independent lives with proper support. However, other individuals with autistic disorder may require special, ongoing care.

The cause of autistic disorder is unknown. However, according to the medical literature, several underlying neurologic, infectious, and other disorders are known to produce or to increase a predisposition toward autistic-like behaviors in children. Genetic abnormalities are also thought to play some role in causing or resulting in susceptibility for the disorder. For example, some researchers theorize that autistic disorder may result from certain brain abnormalities during infancy (e.g., particular biochemical abnormalities, brain injury, etc.), potentially in combination with a genetic predisposition for the condition (multifactorial).

Government Agencies

679 **NIH/National Institute of Neurological Disorders and Stroke (NINDS)**
PO Box 5801
Bethesda, MD 20824
800-352-9424
www.ninds.nih.gov

Works to reduce the burden of neurological disease by conducting, fostering, coordinating and guiding research on the causes, prevention, diagnosis and treatment of neurological disorders and stroke, while supporting basic research in related scientific areas.
Walter J. Koroshetz, MD, Director

680 **NIH/National Institute on Deafness and Other Communication Disorders (NIDCD)**
31 Center Drive, MSC 2320
Bethesda, MD 20892
800-241-1044
TTY: 800-241-1055
nidcdinfo@nidcd.nih.gov
www.nidcd.nih.gov

Conducts and supports biomedical research and research training on normal mechanisms, as well as diseases and disorders of hearing, balance, smell, taste, voice, speech and language.
Debara L. Tucci, MD, Director
Judith A. Cooper, PhD, Deputy Director
Timothy J. Wheeles, Executive Officer

National Associations & Support Groups

681 **Achieve Beyond**
7000 Austin Street, Suite 200
Forest Hills, NY 11375
718-762-7633
Fax: 718-886-8694
info@achievebeyondusa.com
www.achievebeyondusa.com

Achieve Beyond was founded in 1995 to meet the needs of developmentally delayed and disabled children and their families, particularly children with bilingual needs.
Trudy Font Padron, Founder/Programs Executive Director
Robert Padron, Executive Director

682 **American Academy of Pediatrics**
345 Park Blvd
Itasca, IL 60143
800-433-9016
Fax: 847-434-8000
mcc@aap.org
www.aap.org

The American Academy of Pediatrics and its member pediatricians are committed to the attainment of optimal physical, mental and social health and well-being for all infants, children, adolescents, and young adults.
Mark Del Monte, JD, CEO/Executive VP
Lynn Olson, PhD, VP, Research
Vera Tait, MD, FAAP, Chief Medical Officer

683 **American Psychological Association**
750 First St. NE
Washington, DC 20002
202-336-5500
800-374-2721
TTY: 202-336-6123
www.apa.org

The mission is to advance the creation, communication and application of psychological knowledge to benefit society and improve people's lives.
Arthur C. Evans Jr, PhD, CEO/EVP

Autistic Disorder / National Associations & Support Groups

684 **American School Counselor Association**
1101 King Street, Ste 310
Alexandria, VA 22314
703-683-2722
asca@schoolcounselor.org
www.schoolcounselor.org

The mission of ASCA is to represent professional school counselors and to promote professionalism and ethical practices.

Jill Cook, Executive Director
Amanda Fitzgerald, Assistant Deputy Executive Director
Kathleen M Rakestraw, Director of Communications

685 **Asperger/Autism Network**
51 Water Street, Suite 206
Watertown, MA 02472
617-393-3824
info@aane.org
www.aane.org

The Asperger/Autism Network (AANE) works with individuals, families, and professionals to help people with Asperger Syndrome and similar autism spectrum profiles build meaningful, connected lives.

Dania Jekel, Executive Director
Brenda Dater, Associate Director
Marcia Robinson, Volunteer Coordinator

686 **Association for Science in Autism Treatment**
P.O. Box 1447
Hoboken, NJ 07030
info@asatonline.org
asatonline.org

To disseminate accurate information about autism and treatments, and to improve access to effective, science-based treatments for all people with autism.

David Celiberti, PhD, BCBA, Executive Director

687 **Autism National Committee**
www.autcom.org

info@autcom.org
www.autcom.org

Organization dedicated to social justice for all citizens with autism through a shared vision and a commitment to positive approaches.

688 **Autism Research Foundation**
72 East Concord Street, R-1010
Boston, MA 02118
hello@theautismresearchfoundation.org
www.theautismresearchfoundation.org

A nonprofit organization dedicated to brain-based research and inclusion programs in the community. Focuses on fundraise for continuous brain-based research, while providing tangible resources for families and providers managing autism right now.

Margaret Bauman MD, Fouding Director

689 **Autism Science Foundation**
3 Continental Road
Scarsdale, NY 10583
914-810-9100
contactus@autismsciencefoundation.org
autismsciencefoundation.org

The Autism Science Foundation's mission is to support autism research by providing funding and other assistance to scientists and organizations conducting, facilitating, publicizing and disseminating autism research. The organization also provides information about autism to the general public and serves to increase awareness of autism spectrum disorders and the needs of individuals and families affected by autism.

Alison Singer, Co-Founder/President
Alycia Halladay, Chief Scientific Officer

690 **Autism Services Center**
10 6th Avenue W
Huntington, WV 25710
304-525-8014
Fax: 304-525-8026
www.autismservicescenter.org

Autism Services Center (ASC) is a nonprofit, licensed behavioral health center that was founded in 1979 by Ruth C. Sullivan, Ph.D. to provide services in Cabell, Wayne, Lincoln and Mason counties in the state of West Virginia. Though specializing in autism, ASC provides comprehensive, community-integrated services to all individuals with intellectual and developmental disabilities.

Jimmie Beirne, CEO

691 **Autism Society of America**
6110 Executive Boulevard, Ste 305
Rockville, MD 20852
800-328-8476
www.autism-society.org

The Autism Society, the nation's leading grassroots autism organization, exists to improve the lives of all affected by autism. We do this by increasing public awareness about the day-to-day issues faced by people on the spectrum, advocating for appropriate services for individuals across the lifespan, and providing the latest information regarding treatment, education, research and advocacy.

Christopher Banks, President & CEO
John Dabrowski, CFO/COO

692 **Autism Speaks**
1 East 33rd Street, 4th Floor
New York, NY 10016
646-385-8500
Fax: 212-252-8676
help@autismspeaks.org
www.autismspeaks.org

At Autism Speaks, the goal is to change the future for all who struggle with autism spectrum disorder. Dedicated to funding global biomedical research into the causes, prevention, treatments, and cure for autism; to raising public awareness about autism and its effects on individuals, families, and society; and to bringing hope to all who deal with the hardships of this disorder.

Angela Timashenka Geiger, President/CEO
Thomas Frazier, II, Chief Scientific Officer
Lisa Goring, Chief Strategic Officer

693 **Autism Spectrum Connection**
PO Box 524
Crown Point, IN 46308
219-789-9874
MAAPatOasis@gmail.com
www.aspergersyndrome.org

Autism Spectrum Coalition is a nonprofit organization providing information, networking, referrals and printed materials for families, challenged individuals and professionals concerned with the autism spectrum. Founded in 1984, MAAP Services, adheres to the basic principal that all individuals with autism spectrum challenges have the ability to learn, grow and enjoy a good quality of life.

Susan Moreno, Founder & President

694 **Autism Treatment Center of America**
2080 S Undermountain Road
Sheffield, MA 01257
877-766-7473
www.autismtreatmentcenter.org

Since 1974, the Autism Treatment Center of America has taught the unique and effective approach of The Son-Rise Program to help over 35,000 families worldwide.

Barry Neil Kaufman, Co-Founder
Samahria Lyte Kaufman, Co-Founder

695 **Autistic Services**
40 Hazelwood Drive
Amherst, NY 14228
716-631-5777
888-288-4764
Fax: 716-565-0671
vfedericoni@autism-services-inc.org
www.autisticservices.org

Agency exclusively dedicated to serving the unique lifelong needs of autistic individuals. Also a regional resource for parents, school districts, physicians and other professionals.

Veronica Federiconi, Executive Director

696 **Center for Autism and Related Disorders**
21600 Oxnard St., Ste 1800
Woodland Hills, CA 91367
818-345-2345
877-448-4747
info@centerforautism.com
www.centerforautism.com

The Center for Autism and Related Disorders (CARD) uses applied behavior analysis (ABA) in the treatment of autism spectrum disorder.

Doreen Granpeesheh, Founder/Executive Director

Autistic Disorder / National Associations & Support Groups

697 Center for Parent Information and Resources (CPIR)
c/o SPAN, 35 Halsey Street, 4th Floor
Newark, NJ 07102   973-642-8100
malizo@spanadvocacy.org
www.parentcenterhub.org

Family-friendly information and research-based materials on key topics for Parent Centers. Private workspaces for Parent Centers to exchange resources, discuss high-priority topics, and solve mutual challenges. Coordination of parent training efforts throughout the network.

Myriam Alizo, Project Assistant

698 Center on Disability and Inclusion
370 Huntington Hall
Syracuse, NY 13244   cdi@syr.edu
disabilityinclusioncenter.syr.edu

The Center on Disability and Inclusion (CDI) at Syracuse University is a disability-related research center that works to develop and implement initiatives promoting the inclusion of people with disabilities in all aspects of school and society both locally and globally.

Christy Ashby, PhD, Director

699 Child Neurology Foundation
601 W Short Street
Lexington, KY 40508   888-417-3435
info@childneurologyfoundation.org
childneurologyfoundation.org

The Child Neurology Foundation connects partners from all areas of the child neurology community so those navigating the journey of disease diagnosis, management, and care have the ongoing support from those dedicated to treatments and cures.

Amy Brin, Executive Director
Katie Hentges, Director, Programs
Brea McCormley, Director, Development

700 Community Services for Autistic Adults & Children (CSAAC)
8615 East Village Avenue
Montgomery Village, MD 20886   204-912-2220
Fax: 301-926-9384
csaac@csaac.org
www.csaac.org

To enable individuals with autism to achieve their highest potential and contribute as confident individuals to their community.

Eric Salzano, Executive Director
Eva Muiruri, Assistant Executive Director

701 Developmental Delay Resources
5801 Beacon Street
Pittsburgh, PA 15217   800-497-0944
Fax: 412-422-1374
www.devdelay.org

A nonprofit organization dedicated to meeting the needs of those working with children who have developmental delays in sensory motor, language, social, and emotional areas. DDR provides a network for parents and professionals and current information after the diagnosis to support children with special needs.

Patricia Lemer, Executive Director

702 Families for Early Autism Treatment
PO Box 255722
Sacramento, CA 95865   916-303-7405
Fax: 916-303-7405
feat@feat.org
www.feat.org

A nonprofit organization of parents and professionals, designed to help families with children who are diagnosed with autism or pervasive developmental disorder. It offers a network of support for families.

703 Genetic Alliance
426400 Woodfield Road, Ste 189
Damascus, MD 20872   202-966-5557
Fax: 202-966-8553
info@geneticalliance.org
www.geneticalliance.org

World's leading nonprofit health advocacy organization committed to transforming health through genetics and promoting an environment of openness centered on the health of individuals, families, and communities.

Sharon Terry, CEO
Ruth Child, CFO
Natasha Bonhomme, Chief Strategy Officer

704 Global and Regional Asperger Syndrome Partnership
369 Lexington Avenue
New York, NY 10017   888-474-7277
info@grasp.org
grasp.org

GRASP works to improve the lives of teens and adults with autism spectrum disorder (ASD). It offers in-school programs to help students with autism learn advocacy skills and improve social skills. Through its website, it educates the public about autism, while also offering free online resources and networking opportunities for individuals with ASD and their families.

705 Groupworks West
3272 Motor Avenue, Suite I
Los Angeles, CA 90034   310-287-1640
chrismulligan@groupworkswest.com
groupworkswestla.com

GroupWorks West utilizes innovative intervention programs designed to improve the quality of life of children, teens and young adults challenged by developmental, psychiatric, and behavior disorders.

Christopher Mulligan, L.C.S.W., Founder/Clinical Director

706 Lovaas Institute
5601 W Slauson Avenue, Suite 266
Culver City, CA 90230   310-410-4450
Fax: 310-410-4455
info@lovaas.com
www.lovaas.com

Committed to providing the highest quality treatment available to children diagnosed with autism or a related disorder.

Scott Wright, President & CEO
Simone Stevens, Chief Operating Officer
Matthew Sands, Chief Financial Officer

707 March of Dimes Foundation
1550 Crystal Drive, Ste 1300
Arlington, VA 22202   888-663-4637
www.marchofdimes.org

March of Dimes help moms have full-term pregnancies and research the problems that threaten the health of babies. The March of Dimes also acts globally: sharing best practices in perinatal health and helping improve birth outcomes where the needs are the most urgent.

Stacey D. Stewart, President
Alan Brogdon, SVP/COO/Board Officer
Rahul Gupta, MD, SVP & Chief Medical/Health Officer

708 Mental Health America
500 Montgomery Street, Ste 820
Alexandria, VA 22314   703-684-7722
800-969-6642
Fax: 703-684-5968
www.mentalhealthamerica.net

MHA, the leading advocacy organization addressing the full spectrum of mental and substance use conditions and their effects nationwide, works to inform, advocate and enable access to quality behavioral health services for all Americans.

Paul Gionfriddo, President/CEO
Whitney Ball, Assoc. Dir., Marketing/Outreach
Sachin Doshi, Sr. Dir, Finance/Operations

709 National Association of Special Education Teachers
1250 Connecticut Avenue, NW, Suite 200
Washington, DC 20036   800-754-4421
Fax: 800-754-4421
contactus@naset.org
www.naset.org

A membership organization dedicated solely to meeting the needs of special education teachers and those preparing for the field of special education teaching.

Autistic Disorder / National Associations & Support Groups

Dr. Roger Pierangelo, Co-Executive Director
Dr. George Giuliani, Co-Executive Director

710 **National Autism Association**
One Park Avenue, Suite 1
Portsmouth, RI 02871
401-293-5551
877-622-2884
Fax: 401-293-5342
naa@nationalautism.org
nationalautismassociation.org

NAA is a parent-run advocacy organization and the leading voice on urgent issues related to severe autism, regressive autism, autism safety, autism abuse, and crisis prevention.

Wendy Fournier, President
Krystal Higgins, Executive Director

711 **National Federation of Families**
15800 Crabbs Branch Way, Suite 300
Rockville, MD 20855
240-403-1901
ffcmh@ffcmh.org
www.ffcmh.org

The National family run organization is dedicated exclusively to helping children with mental health needs and their families achieve a better quality of life.

Lynda Gargan, PhD, Executive Director

712 **National Mental Health Consumers' Self-Help Clearinghouse**
1211 Chestnut Street, Suite 1207
Philadelphia, PA 19107
215-751-1810
800-553-4539
Fax: 215-636-6312
selfhelpclearinghouse@gmail.com
www.mhselfhelp.org

The Clearinghouse works to foster peer empowerment through our website, up-to-date news and information announcements, a directory of peer-driven services, electronic and printed publications, training packages, and individual and onsite consultation

Joseph Rogers, Founder/Executive Director
Susan Rogers, Director

713 **New England Center for Children**
33 Turnpike Road
Southborough, MA 10213
508-481-1015
Fax: 508-485-3421
www.necc.org

Serving students between the ages of 3 and 22 diagnosed with autism, learning disabilities, language delays, behavior disorders and related disabilities; educational curriculum encompasses both the teaching of functional life skills and traditional academics; communication skills are taught throughout all activities in the school, residence, and community. Tuition and fees are set by the state. Consulting services also available.

Vincent Strully, Jr, President & CEO
Michaels S Downey, EVP & CFO
Susan Langer, Chief Program Officer

714 **Oak-Leyden Developmental Services**
411 Chicago Avenue
Oak Park, IL 60302
708-524-1050
Fax: 708-524-2469
info@oak-leyden.org
www.oak-leyden.org

The mission of Oak-Leyden Developmental Services is to serve people with developmental disabilities and their families in a manner which recognizes their dignity, is supportive of their personal choices and promotes their inclusion in the larger community.

R.J. McMahon, CEO
Nancy Thomas, Director of Human Resources
Melissa Ehmann, Director of Children's Services

715 **Option Institute: Son Rise Program**
Autism Treatment Center of America
2080 S Undermountain Road
Sheffield, MA 01257
800-714-2779
information@son-rise.org
www.son-rise.org

Describes an effective, loving and respectful method for treating children with autism. It teaches parents and healing professionals how to set up a home based program using the child's motivation to reach their special child.

Barry Neil Kaufman, Co-Founder/Co-Creator
Samahria Lyte Kaufman, Co-Founder/Co-Creator

716 **Organization for Autism Research**
2111 Wilson Blvd, Suite 401
Arlington, VA 22201
866-366-9710
info@researchautism.org
www.researchautism.org

The Organization for Autism Research (OAR) was created in December 2001-the product of the shared vision and unique life experiences of OAR's seven founders. Led by these parents and grandparents of children and adults on the autism spectrum, OAR set out to use applied science to answer questions that parents, families, individuals with autism, teachers and caregivers confront daily. No other autism organization has this singular focus.

Kristen Essex, Executive Director
Kimberly Ha, Sr Director, Research & Programs
Cate Hickman, Community Outreach Associate

717 **Raleigh TEACCH Center**
University of North Carolina at Chapel Hill
100 Renee Lynne Court
Carrboro, NC 27510
919-966-2174
Fax: 919-966-4127
TEACCH@unc.edu
www.teacch.com

The University of North Carolina TEACCH Autism Program creates and cultivates the development of exemplary community-based services, training programs, and research to enhance the quality of life for individuals with Autism Spectrum Disorder and for their families across the lifespan.

Dr. Laura G Klinger, Executive Director

718 **Rethink autism**
49 W 27th Street, 8th Floor
New York, NY 10001
www.rethinkfirst.com

Offers parents and professionals immediate access to effective and affordable Applied Behavior Analysis-based treatment tools for the growing population affected by autism spectrum disorders.

Daniel A. Etra, Co-Founder & CEO
Eran Rosenthal, Co-Founder, President & COO
Patty Mah, Chief Financial Officer

719 **The Autism Community in Action**
2222 Martin St., Suite 140
Irvine, CA 92612
949-640-4401
tacanow.org

The Autism Community in Action (TACA) provides education, support and hope to families living with autism.

Lisa Ackerman, Founder & Executive Director

720 **The Daniel Jordan Fiddle Foundation**
www.djfiddlefoundation.org

The Daniel Jordan Fiddle Foundation is a national organization focused on adults living with Autism Spectrum Disorders (ASD). The mission of the volunteer-run organization is to develop, advocate for and fund our Signature Programs that create innovative blueprints for grassroots organizations and service providers to develop their own programs for the diverse population of adults living with ASD.

Linda J. Walder, Esq., Founder & Executive Director
Fred Fiddle, Founder & Treasurer
Howard Fiddle, Founder & Secretary

721 **The Doug Flutie, Jr. Foundation for Autism**
PO Box 2157
Framingham, MA 01703
www.flutiefoundation.org

The goal of the Flutie Foundation is to help families affected by autism live life to the fullest.

Nick Savarese, Executive Director

Autistic Disorder / State Agencies & Support Groups

722 **The Golden Fund for Autism**
Cold Spring Harbor, NY
admin@goldenfundautism.org
www.goldenfundautism.org

The Golden Fund for Autism is a 501(c)(3) tax-exempt organization dedicated to raising funds for children diagnosed with Autism Spectrum Disorders and their families.

Joelle A. Perez, Executive Director
Liam B. Golden, Secretary
Brian B. Golden, Treasurer

723 **The Help Group**
13130 Burbank Blvd.
Sherman Oaks, CA 91401
818-781-0360
www.thehelpgroup.org

Serves children with special needs related to autism spectrum disorder, learning disabilities, ADHD, developmental delays, abuse and emotional problems.

Barbara Firestone, PhD, Founder, President & CEO
Susan Berman, PhD, Founder & COO
Barry N Nagoshiner, CPA, Vice Chair & CFO

724 **US Autism Association**
www.usautism.org
888-298-8476
www.usautism.org

Provides opportunity for all individuals with Autism Spectrum Disorders to achieve their fullest potential by expanding and enriching the ASD community through education, online training, published and electronic information and resources, and partnerships with local and national projects.

Jennifer Grace, CEO
Marlo Payne Thurman, PhD, President
Phillip C. DeMio, MD, Chief Medical Officer Emeritus

725 **iCanShine**
PO Box 541
Paoli, PA 19301
info@icanshine.org
icanshine.org

iCan Shine (formerly, Lose The Training Wheels) is a national charitable nonprofit organization. Movement and Play are the basis for all iCan Shine programs. Recreational skills can be difficult to master for individuals with disabilities. iCan Shine offers positive encouragement and guidance from well-trained, energized instructors and volunteers allow each participant to discover and develop their "iCan" mantra in a safe, supportive and fun environment.

Lisa Ruby, Founder & Executive Director
Jeff Sullivan, Founder, Dir of Finance & Admin
Andrea Patrick, Manager of Operations

State Agencies & Support Groups

Alabama

726 **Autism Society of Alabama**
Autism Society of America
4217 Dolly Ridge Rd
Birmingham, AL 10219
205-951-1364
877-428-8476
Fax: 205-951-1366
melanie@autism-alabama.org
www.autism-alabama.org

To improve services for persons with Autism Spectrum Disorders and their families through education and advocacy.

Melanie Jones, Executive Director
Michelle McDaniel, Community & Program Coordinator
Bama Hager, PhD, Program Director

727 **Autism Society of North Alabama**
Autism Society of America
PO Box 2902
Huntsville, AL 10220
256-773-0549
www.autism-alabama.org

To improve services for persons with Autism Spectrum Disorders and their families through education and advocacy.

Todd Tomerlin, Community/Program Coordinator

Arizona

728 **Autism Society of America Greater Phoenix Chapter**
PO Box 10543
Phoenix, AZ 10221
480-940-1093
cynthia.macluskie@phxautism.org
www.phxautism.org

The Autism Society of Greater Phoenix provides information, resources, and support to families affected by autism and helps families who have just received the autism diagnosis by providing information on effective treatments.

James B Adams, President
Catina Hoffman, Co-Chair

729 **Autism Society of America Southern Arizona Chapter**
2600 N Wyatt DR
Tucson, AZ 85712
520-770-1541
Fax: 520-319-5979
info@as-az.org
www.as-az.org

Volunteer organization of parents, professionals, and friends of persons with autism, designed to promote the general welfare of persons with autism.

Jared Perkins, President
Jared Perrine, Treasurer
Lynda Weigel-Firor, Secretary

California

730 **Autism Society of America Coachella Valley**
Autism Society of America
77564 Country Club Dr. Building B Suite 363
Palm Desert, CA 92211
760-772-1000
coordinator@cvasa.org
www.cvasa.org

The Coachella Valley Autism Society of America (CVASA) exists to provide support for families of individuals with autism in the Coachella Valley and surrounding desert areas.

Thomas Lister-Looker, President
Donna Redman-Bentley, Secretary
Kristen Alvarez, Treasurer

731 **Autism Society of America Greater Long Beach/San Gabriel Valley**
Autism Society of America
8635 Greenleaf Ave, Unit B
Long Beach, CA 90602
562-943-3335
562-941-1931
Fax: 562-943-3335
www.greaterlongbeach-asa.org

We provide information and referrals about behavior problems, education and treatment programs, your child's right to a free appropriate public education (FAPE), inclusion, how and where to obtain an evaluation and diagnosis, specialized facilities such as camps or residential programs, federal and state legislation, how to be an advocate for your child and more.

Regina Moreno, President
Penne Fode, Vice President
Roman Castro, Jr, Treasurer

732 **Autism Society of America Inland Empire Chapter**
Autism Society of America
2276 Griffin Way, Suite 105-194
Corona, CA 10227
909-220-6922
ieautism@att.net
www.ieautism.org

Autistic Disorder / State Agencies & Support Groups

The mission of the Autism Society Inland Empire is to improve the lives of all affected by an autism spectrum disorder. We do this by increasing public awareness about the day-to-day issues faced by people on the spectrum, advocating for appropriate services for individuals across the lifespan, and providing the latest information regarding treatment, education, research, support and advocacy.

Beth Burt, President
Lillian Vasquez, Vice President
Philip Hannawi, Treasurer

733 Autism Society of America Los Angeles Chapter
Autism Society of America
21250 Hawthorne Blvd, Ste 500
Los Angeles, CA 90503
562-804-5556
Fax: 562-425-4940
info@autismla.org
www.autismla.org/

To improve the lives of all affected by autism in Los Angeles County by empowering individuals with autism, their families, and professionals through advocacy, education, support, and community collaboration.

Andy Kopito, President
Mari-Anne Kehler, VP

734 Autism Society of America North San Diego County Chapter
Autism Society of America
4699 Murphy Canyon Road
San Diego, CA 10230
858-715-0678
Fax: 858-712-1510
info@autismsocietysandiego.org
www.autismsocietysandiego.org/Home.php

Offers chapter meetings, local groups for support and information, family events, and a lending library.

Amy Munera, President
Paul James, Treasurer
Kay Freeman, Administrator

735 Autism Society of America Orange County Chapter
Autism Society of America
582 N. Waverly
Orange, CA 10231
714-282-9005
paulap@mailcity.com
www.asaoc.tripod.com/Index.htm

The Autism Society of Orange County, in unison with the Autism Society of America, strives to promote lifelong access and opportunities for persons within the autistic spectrum and their families, to be fully included, participating members of their communities through advocacy, public awareness, education, and research related to autism.

Paula Peterson, President
Linda Molyneux, Vice President

736 Autism Society of America San Diego Chapter
Autism Society of America
PO Box 420908
San Diego, CA 10232
858-715-0678
Fax: 858-712-1510
info@autismsocietysandiego.org
www.autismsocietysandiego.org/Home.php

Promotes lifelong access and opportunities for persons within the autism spectrum and their families, to be fully included, participating members of their communities through advocacy, public awareness, education, and research related to autism.

Shirley Fett, President
Nichole Hope Moore, President Elect
Tina Huston, Treasurer

737 Autism Society of America San Francisco Bay Chapter
Autism Society of America
PO Box 249
San Mateo, CA 94401
650-637-7772
info@sfautismsociety.org
http://sfautismsociety.virtualave.net

Promotes lifelong access and opportunities for persons within the autism spectrum and their families, to be fully included, participating members of their communities through advocacy, public awareness, education, and research related to autism.

Connie Boyar, President
Sue Swezey, Secretary
Irma Velasquez, Treasurer

738 Autism Society of America San Gabriel Valley Chapter
Autism Society of America
PO Box 15247
Glendora, CA 10234
626-388-2134
www.greaterlongbeach-asa.org/

We provide information and referrals about behavior problems, education and treatment programs, your child's right to a free appropriate public education (FAPE), inclusion, how and where to obtain an evaluation and diagnosis, specialized facilities such as camps or residential programs, federal and state legislation, how to be an advocate for your child and more.

Regina Moreno, President
Bronwyn Estephan, Vice President
Joe McNiel, Treasurer

739 Autism Society of America Santa Barbara Chapter
Autism Society of America
PO Box 30364
Santa Barbara, CA 93130
805-560-3762
sdshove@cox.net
www.asasb.org

Promote lifelong access and opportunity for all individuals within the autism spectrum, and their families, to be fully participating, included members of their community. Support, education, advocacy, and an active public awareness from the cornerstones of ASA Santa Barbara's efforts to carry forth its mission.

Marcia Eichelberger, Co-President
Patti Gaultney, Co-President

740 Autism Society of America Tulare County Chapter
Autism Society of America
3201 West Payson Avenue
Visalia, CA 93291
559-747-2126
lori10677@aol.com
www.autism-society.org

Promote lifelong access and opportunity for all individuals within the autism spectrum, and their families, to be fully participating, included members of their community. Support, education, advocacy, and an active public awareness from the cornerstones of ASA Santa Barbara's efforts to carry forth its mission.

Lori Collins, President

741 Autism Society of California
Autism Society of America
PO Box 1355
Glendora, CA 10236
800-869-7069
www.autismsocietyca.org

The mission of the Autism Society of California is to promote lifelong access and opportunities for persons within the autism spectrum and their families, and to be fully included, participating members of their communities through advocacy, public awareness, education and research related to autism.

Marcia Eichelberger, President
Beth Burt, First Vice President
Sandra Shove, 2nd Vice President

742 Kern Autism Network
Autism Society of America
8200 Stockdale Hwy, M-10#171
Bakersfield, CA 10237
661-588-4235
661-762-7528
Fax: 661-588-4235
kernautism@gmail.com
www.kernautism.org

Autism Society Chapter-Kern Autism Network provides support, awareness, information and education to families, professionals and the public throughout Kern County.

Ramona Puget, parent and advocate
Carl Twisselman, Honorary Lifetime Board Member
Carol Baker-Willey, Parent

Autistic Disorder / State Agencies & Support Groups

Colorado

743 **Autism Society of America Larimer County Chapter**
3331 Lochwood Dr
Fort Collins, CO 10238   970-377-9640
www.autismlarimer.org

The ASLC is a volunteer group of dedicated well-informed parents and professionals working together to increase public awareness about autism and the day-to-day issues faced by individuals with autism, their families and the professionals with whom they interact.

Phyllis Zimmerman, President
Tina Boyer, Vice President
Jennifer Cotton, Treasurer

744 **Autism Society of America Pikes Peak Chapter**
918 Crown Ridge Drive
Colorado Springs, CO 80904   719-630-7072
www.asappr.org

Sponsors training opportunities for educators and parents in Southern Colorado to learn best practice strategies that will help students with autism be successful in inclusive classrooms and communities.

Alison Seyler, President

745 **Autism Society of America: Colorado Chapter**
550 S. Wadsworth Boulevard, Suite 100
Lakewood, CO 10240   720-214-0794
Fax: 720-274-2744
www.autismcolorado.org

To improve the lives of all affected by Autism.

Kevin Custer, President
John Sheldon, Vice President
Jeffery Nickless, Treasurer

746 **Autism Society of American Boulder County Chapter**
P.O. Box 270300
Louisville, CO 10241   720-272-8231
Fax: 303-604-6656
info@autismboulder.org
www.autismboulder.org

The Autism Society of Boulder County is an all-volunteer 501(c)(3) non-profit organization that offers all of its services for free to individuals and families affected by autism in Boulder and Broomfield Counties.

Lynn Wysolmierski, President
Allen Richardson, Secretary
Jill Sheldon, Treasurer

Connecticut

747 **Autism Society of America Connecticut Chapter**
PO Box 1404
Guilford, CT 10242   888-453-4975
www.asconn.org

Worked with parents, educators, state government, and therapeutic and medical professionals to enhance the lives of those touched by Autism Spectrum Disorders. ASCONN serves the entire autism spectrum, across specific diagnosis, needs, challenges, and age ranges.

Sara Reed, Executive Director
Kim Newgass, President
Jonathan Stein, Treasurer

Delaware

748 **Autism Society of Delaware**
Autism Society of America
924 Old Harmony Road, Suite 201
Newark, DE 10243   302-224-6020
302-472-2639
Fax: 302-224-6014
delautism@delautism.org
www.delautism.org

The Autism Delaware Mission: to create better lives for people with autism and their families in Delaware.

Marcy kempner, President
John Willey II, Vice President
Scott Young, Treasurer

District of Columbia

749 **Autism Society of America District of Columbia Chapter**
5167 7th Street NE
Washington, DC 10244   202-561-5300
202-561-8634
sondrakcunningham@verizon.net
www.autism-society.org/chapter130

Provides information and referrals for families affected by autism and related disabilities. Advocate for appropriate services in education, medical and other areas.

Ronald Hampton, President
Rhoda Mcleese Smith, Vice President
Franklin Davis SR, Treasurer

Florida

750 **Autism Society of America Broward Chapter**
10250 NW 53rd
Sunrise, FL 10245   954-577-4141
954-474-5333
www.asabroward.org

ASB's full range of family support, children's programming, public outreach and autism awareness campaigns are available to all interested in the betterment of life for not only individuals and families with autism, but to the community of South Florida as a whole

Hugh J Keough Esq, President
Fabiola Anna Torrez, Vice President
Brent Boucaud, Treasurer

751 **Autism Society of America Emerald Coast Chapter**
8668 Navarre Parkway Suite # 216
Navarre, FL 10246   850-736-0879
www.ecautismsociety.com

Provides information and support.

Myra Fowler, President
Kristen Bowen, Vice-President
Greg Hasty, Treasurer

752 **Autism Society of America Florida Chapter**
PO Box 450476
Sunrise, FL 10247   954-577-4141
855-529-6807
Fax: 954-571-2136
ven@autismfl.com
www.autismfl.com

The Autism Society of Florida is a statewide organization that supports individuals with autism, their families, and caregivers. It includes individuals with autism and volunteers (including family members, professionals, and other interested persons). The Autism Society of Florida coordinates activities on behalf of people with autism on a statewide basis.

753 **Autism Society of America Jacksonville Chapter**
1526 University Blvd W #235
Jacksonville, FL 32217   904-399-4490
www.autism-society.org/chapter1003

Mission is to support, inform and empower the families of Jacksonville.

Jeenifer Nunes, President

754 **Autism Society of America Manasota Chapter**
2380 Wycliff Street, Suite 102
St Paul, MN 10249   651-647-1083
941-780-5237
Fax: 651-642-1230
info@ausm.org
www.ausm.org

Autistic Disorder / State Agencies & Support Groups

Established in 1971, the Autism Society of Minnesota (AuSM) is a self-funded organization committed to education, support and advocacy designed to enhance the lives of those affected by autism from birth through retirement.

Todd Schwartzberg, President
Jean Bender, Vice President
Aaron R Deris, Treasurer

755 Autism Society of America Panhandle Chapter
P.O. Box 30213
Pensacola, FL 32503
850-450-0656
info@autismpensacola.org
www.autismpensacola.org

A nonprofit, tax-exempt association of parents, professionals and other concerned community members dedicated to the education and welfare of children and adults with autism and related disorders of communication and behavior.

Fred Donovan, President
Julian Irby, Vice President
Bonnie Sferes, Treasurer

756 Autism Society of Greater Orlando
Autism Society of America
12720 S. Orange Blossom Trail Suite 8
Orlando, FL 10251
407-855-0235
Fax: 407-855-5129
contact@asgo.org
www.asgo.org

ASGO was founded in 1996 by a group of volunteer parents to better assist families of children and adults with autism in the Central Florida area. The mission or goal of the ASGO is that all individuals within the autism spectrum will be provided a lifetime network of opportunities to become fully accepted, included, and actively participating members of our community, through family support, education, and advocacy, and public awareness.

Donna Lorman, President
Lorienda Crawford, Vice President
Angelica Taylor, Treasurer

Georgia

757 Autism Society of America Greater Georgia Chapter
P.O. Box 3707
Suwanee, GA 10252
770-904-4474
Fax: 678-935-1152
www.asaga.com

Chapter of ASA, we offer resource info to individuals and their families and to professionals about autism, add, add and other developmental disabilities

Gailynn Gluth, President
Jason Cavin, 1st Vice President
Jon Basinger, 2nd Vice President

Hawaii

758 Autism Society of Hawaii
Autism Society of America
1600 Kapiolani Blvd. #620
Honolulu, HI 10253
808-282-3676
808-228-0122
autismhi@gmail.com
www.autismhi.org

The Autism Society of Hawaii is a 501(c)(3) organization serving families and individuals touched by autism and autism spectrum disorders.

Dr William Bolman, President
Jessica Wong, Executive Director
John P Dellera, Board Member

Idaho

759 Autism Society of America Treasure Valley Chapter
P.O. Box 44831
Boise, ID 10254
208-336-5676
autism.asatvc@yahoo.com
www.asatvc.org

Top provide advocacy, support and information to individuals with autism, their families, professionals, and communities throughout Treasure Valley Chapter.

Illinois

760 Autism Society of Illinois
Autism Society of America
2200 South Main Street, # 205
Lombard, IL 10255
630-691-1270
888-691-1270
Fax: 630-932-5620
info@autismillinois.org
www.autismillinois.org

Partnering with families and communities living with autism in Illinois by generating awareness and providing education, training, support, and guidance as a compassionate and caring authority.

Mary K Betz, Executive Director
Jean C Thomas, Associate Executive Director
Dave Geslak, Treasurer

Indiana

761 Autism Society of Indiana
Autism Society of America
13295 Illinois Street Suite 213
Carmel, IN 10256
317-695-0252
800-609-8449
info@inautism.org
www.autismsocietyofindiana.org

Since 1998, the Autism Society of America - Indiana (ASI) has worked to raise awareness about autism, to promote early diagnosis and early intervention thereby helping people on the autism spectrum have the fullest and most successful journey possible.

Joshua Carr, Executive Board President
Kylee Hope, Executive Board Vice President
Kelli McKinzie, Executive Board Treasurer

Iowa

762 Autism Society of Iowa
Autism Society of America
4340 East-West Hwy, Suite 350
Bethesda, ML 10257
301-657-0881
800-328-8476
autism50ia@aol.com
www.autism-society.org

The Autism Society, the nation's leading grassroots autism organization, exists to improve the lives of all affected by autism.

Kris Steinmantz, Manager

763 The Link
Autism Society of Iowa
4549 Waterford Drive
West Des Moines, IA 50265
515-327-9075
888-457-7225
autism50ia@aol.com
www.autismia.org

Provides information for parents, professionals and care givers on autism spectrum disorders.

Kris Steinmantz, Manager

Autistic Disorder / State Agencies & Support Groups

Kansas

764 **Autism Society of the Heartland**
Autism Society of America
PO Box 4455
Olathe, KS 66063
913-706-0042
info@asaheartland.org
www.asaheartland.org

To provide advocacy, support and information to individuals with autism, their families, professionals, and communities throughout state Kansas.

Kathy Bennett, Office Manager

Kentucky

765 **Autism Society of America Bluegrass Chapter**
Autism Society of America
243 Shady Lane
Lexington, KY 40503
859-299-9000
www.asbg.org

A resource and support group for families and professionals in the Central Kentucky area who are involved with autism.

Sara Spragens, President

Louisiana

766 **Autism Society of Louisiana**
Autism Society of America
PO Box 80162
Baton Rouge, LA 70898
800-955-3760
autismsociety_lastatechapter@yahoo.com
www.lastateautism.org

To provide information and referrals, advocacy and support for individuals with ASD and their families; to help families identify qualified professionals in their communities; to assist families in securing benefits and services provided by law; and, to promote lifelong opportunities for persons with autism spectrum disorder in order to be fully included members of their communities.

Pat Giamanco, President

Maine

767 **Autism Society of Maine**
Autism Society of America
72 Main Street, Suite B
Winthrop, ME 04364
207-377-9603
800-273-5200
Fax: 207-377-9434
info@asmonline.org
www.asmonline.org

The Autism Society of Maine provides education and resources to support the valued lives of individuals on the autism spectrum and their families.

Janine Collins, President
Laurie Raymond', Vice President
Michael Lamoreau, Treasurer

Maryland

768 **Autism Society of America Baltimore Chesapeake Chapter**
PO Box 10822
Parkville, MD 21234
410-655-7933
info@baltimoreautismsociety.org
www.bcc-asa.org

Serves families of children and adults with autism spectrum disorders in Baltimore County, Maryland, Baltimore City, and the State of Maryland by providing information, advocacy, and support for families and individuals with autism.

Debbie Page, Co-President
David Savick, Co-President
Kay Holman, Vice President

Massachusetts

769 **Autism Society of America Massachusetts Chapter**
Autism Society of America
47 Walnut Street
Wellesley Hills, MA 02481
781-237-0272
Fax: 781-237-5020
asamasschapter@hotmail.com
www.massautism.org

Mission is to promote lifelong access and opportunity for all individuals within the autism spectrum and their families to be fully participating, included members of their community.

Barry Neil Kaufman, Co-Founder/Co-Creator
Samahria Lyte Kaufman, Co-Founder/Co-Creator

Michigan

770 **Autism Society of Michigan**
Autism Society of America
2178 Commons Parkway
Okemos, MI 48864
517-882-2800
800-223-6722
Fax: 517-862-2816
www.autism-mi.org

The Autism Society of Michigan is committed to empowering individuals with autism and their families by offering educational resources and materials, workshops, seminars and other services. ASM advocates that making human connections in a supportive, integrated community is a right of all persons.

Bob Opsommer, President

Minnesota

771 **Autism Society of Minnesota**
Autism Society of America
2380 Wycliff Street, Suite 102
Saint Paul, MN 55114
651-647-1083
Fax: 651-642-1230
info@ausm.org
www.ausm.org

The Autism Society of Minnesota exists to enhance the lives of individuals with autism spectrum disorders. AuSM seeks to realize its mission through education support, collaboration, and advocacy.

Todd Schwartzberg, President
Jean Bender, Vice President
Aaron R Deris, Treasurer

Mississippi

772 **Autism Society of Mississippi**
Autism Society of America
5908 Tolar Road
Moss Point, MS 39562
www.autismnow.org/local/autism-society-of-mississipp

Offers information, referrals, and support to parents, professionals and caregivers.

Cathy Pratt, Chairman
Joan Zaro, Executive Director
Lee Grossman, CEO

Missouri

773 **Autism Society of America Gateway Chapter**
Autism Society of America
7777 Bonhomme Avenue, Suite 1600
St Louis, MO 63105
314-721-0042
Fax: 314-863-7494
pegisues@aol.com

Autistic Disorder / State Agencies & Support Groups

Provides information and support.

Pegi Price, President

Nebraska

774 **Autism Society of Nebraska**
Autism Society of America
PO Box 83559
Lincoln, NE 68501

402-637-5670
800-580-9279
autismsociety@autismnebraska.org
www.autismnebraska.org

Supports and advocates for individuals with autism and their families through increasing education and awareness, fundraising, and facilitating community involvement for persons with autism spectrum disorders to achieve their potential by becoming a productive, accepted, and integral part of society.

Megan Misegadis, President
Wendy Hamilton, Vice President
Robyn Roberts, Treasurer

Nevada

775 **Autism Society of Northern Nevada Chapter**
Autism Society of America
3490 Southampton Drive
Reno, NV 89509

775-786-9315
Fax: 775-786-0984
pd1989@yahoo.com
www.nnasa.org

Promote and advocate for the general welfare of persons with autism. To further the education and training of parents and professional personnel for training, educating, and caring for persons with autism.

Dinah Deane, President
Paul Deane, Vice President
Guy McKillip, Web Master

New Hampshire

776 **Autism Society of New Hampshire**
Autism Society of America
PO Box 68
Concord, NH 03302

603-679-2424
Fax: 301-657-0869
www.autismnow.org/local/autism-society-of-new-hampsh

The Autism Society of New Hampshire is dedicated to individuals with Autism and Pervasive Developmental Disorders.

Stacey Shannon, President

New Mexico

777 **New Mexico Autism Society**
Autism Society of America
PO Box 30955
Albuquerque, NM 87190

505-332-0306
www.nmautismsociety.org

Our mission is to promote lifelong access and opportunities for persons within the autism spectrum, and their families, to be fully included participating members of their communities.

Roger Riley,, President
Sarah Baca, Executive Director
Pauline Riley, Treasurer

New York

778 **Center for Family Support**
333 7th Avenue, #901
New York, NY 10001

212-629-7939
Fax: 212-239-2211
svernikoff@cfsny.org
www.cfsny.org

The Center for Family Support is committed to providing support and assistance to individuals with developmental and related disabilities, and to the family members who care for them.

Steven Vernikoff, Executive Director
Linda Schellenberg, Director, Community Service
Barbara Greenwald, Associate Executive Director

779 **New York Autism Network**
Autism Society of America
101 State Street
Schenectady, NY 12305

518-355-2191
Fax: 518-355-2191
info@albanyautism.org
www.albanyautism.org

Provide ongoing support to families and professionals, develop regional networks, provide technical assistance, and conduct conferences related to pervasive developmental disorders.

Gordon Zuckerman, President
Jenny DeBellis, Treasurer
Haley Knox, Secretary

North Carolina

780 **Autism Society of North Carolina**
Autism Society of America
505 Oberlin Road Suite 230
Raleigh, NC 27605

800-442-2762
Fax: 919-743-0204
info@autismsociety-nc.org
www.autismsociety-nc.org

For over 43 years, the Autism Society of North Carolina (ASNC) has worked to address areas of need and expand services for the autism community in North Carolina. ASNC is a statewide organization, supporting North Carolinians affected by autism

Beverly Moore, Chair
Sharon Jeffries-Jones, Vice Chair
Elizabeth Phillippi, Treasurer

Ohio

781 **Autism Society of Greater Cincinatti**
Autism Society of America
PO Box 58385
Cincinnati, OH 45258

513-561-2300
Fax: 513-561-4748
info@autismcincy.org
www.autismcincy.org

The mission of the Autism Society of Greater Cincinnati is to improve the quality of life for all people with autism spectrum disorders and their families.

Kay Brown, President
Sue Radabaugh, Vice President
James Keller, Treasurer

782 **Autism Society of Ohio Tri-County Chapter**
Autism Society of America
25 East Boardman Street, Suite 230
Youngstown, OH 44503

330-501-7553
Fax: 614-754-6332
www.autismohio.org

To improve the quality of life for all people with autism spectrum disorders and their families.

Aundrea Cika, Director

Oklahoma

783 **Autism Society of Oklahoma**
Autism Society of America
PO Box 720103
Norman, OK 73070

405-370-3220
www.asofok.org

Dedicated to the education and welfare of all people with autism and other pervasive developmental disorders.

Autistic Disorder / State Agencies & Support Groups

Oregon

784 **Autism Society of Oregon**
Autism Society of America
PO Box 396
Marylhurst, OR 97036
503-636-1676
888-288-4761
Fax: 503-636-1696
www.autismsocietyoregon.org

Promote mutual communication, autism awareness and better service delivery across Oregon.

Tobi Burch, Executive Director
Leigh Ann Chapman, President
Brad Volchok, Treasurer

Pennsylvania

785 **Autism Society of America Greater Harrisburg Area Chapter**
PO Box 101
Enola, PA 17025
717-732-8400
800-244-2425
www.autismharrisburg.org

To promote opportunities for individuals with autism spectrum disorders, to participate in the same value life experiences as do other citizens.

Esther Feirick, President
Kathleen Haigh, Vice President
Diana Fishlock, Treasurer

Rhode Island

786 **Autism Society of Rhode Island**
Autism Society of America
PO Box 16603
Rumford, RI 02916
401-595-3241
www.asa-ri.org

Provides information and support.

Lisa Rego, President
Claudia Swiader, Vice President

South Carolina

787 **Autism Society of South Carolina**
Autism Society of America
806 12th Street
West Columbia, SC 29169
803-750-6988
800-438-4790
Fax: 803-750-8121
scas@scautism.org
www.scautism.org

The purpose of the South Carolina Autism Society is to enable all individuals with autism spectrum disorders to reach their maximum potential.

Susan Kastner, Chair
Alex Holbert, Vice Chair
Mitchell Yell, Treasurer

South Dakota

788 **Autism Society of South Dakota Black Hills Chapter**
Autism Society of America
3650 Range Road
Rapid City, SD 57702
605-415-3739
info@autismsd.org
www.autismsd.org

We have joined to enable all families and others associated with an autistic, Asperger's or Pervasive Development Disorder individual to have access to support groups, meetings, additional information and resources.

Tennessee

789 **Autism Society of America East Tennessee Chapter**
PO Box 30015
Knoxville, TN 37930
865-637-3914
info@asaetc.org
www.asaetc.org

To promote lifelong access and opportunity of all individuals within the autism spectrum, and their families, to be fully participating, included members of their community.

Mike Manfredo, President
Roddey M. Coe, Vice President
Sara Hirtz, Treasurer

Texas

790 **Autism Society of America Greater Austin Chapter**
Autism Society of America
PO Box 160841
Austin, TX 78716
512-479-4199
austinautismsociety@gmail.com
www.autism-society.org/chapter244

Mission is to promote lifelong access and opportunities for person within the autism spectrum, and their families, to be fully included, participating members of their communities through advocacy, public awareness, education, and research related to Autism.

Ann Hart, President
Sandra Batlouni, Vice President
Tom Ibis, Treasurer

Vermont

791 **Autism Society of Vermont**
Autism Society of America
PO Box 978
White River Junction, VT 05001
800-559-7398
www.asvermont.org

The ASVT is a non-profit corporation serving the needs of Vermont's Autism community.

Cathy Pratt, Chairman
Joan Zaro, Executive Director
Lee Grossman, CEO

Virginia

792 **Autism Society of America Northern Virginia Chapter**
98 N. Washington Street
Falls Church, VA 22046
703-495-8444
Fax: 703-563-6099
info@asanv.org
www.asanv.org

Provides information and support to individuals with autism and their families in Northern Virginia area.

Scott Campbell, President
Ray Nelson, Vice President
John J Wall, CPA, Treasurer

Washington

793 **Autism Society of Washington**
Autism Society of America
PO Box 503
Olympia, WA 98507
360-515-8910
888-279-4968
Fax: 253-503-1557
info@autismsocietyofwa.org
www.autismsocietyofwa.org

Autistic Disorder / Libraries & Resource Centers

The mission of the Autism Society of Washington is to promote life-long access and opportunities for persons within the autism spectrum and their families, and to be fully included, participating members of their communities through advocacy, public awareness, education, and research related to autism.

Jeffrey Foster, President
Teresa McCann, Vice President
Stephen Peters, Treasurer

West Virginia

794 Autism Society of West Virginia
PO Box 7
Huntington, WV 25706
304-748-1331
jfair3@comcast.net
http://autismwv.blogspot.com

ASA-WV is dedicated to increasing public awareness about autism and the day-to-day issues faced by individuals with autism, their families and the professionals with whom they interact. The Society's mission is to provide information and education, support research and advocate for programs and services for the autism population

Christina Lee Fair, President

Wisconsin

795 Autism Society of Wisconsin
Autism Society of America
1477 Kenwood Dr.
Menasha, WI 54952
920-558-4602
888-428-8476
Fax: 920-558-4611
asw@asw4autism.org
www.asw4autism.org

To promote lifelong opportunities for persons within the autism spectrum and their families to be fully included, participating members of their communities through information and referral, advocacy, public awareness, and education and support for local Autism Society of America chapters, professionals and others who support individuals with autism in Wisconsin.

Kristen Cooper, Executive Director
Kelly Brodhagen, Office Manager
Melissa Vande Velden, Events Coordinator/WALN Project Coo

Libraries & Resource Centers

Georgia

796 Emory Autism Resource Center
Emory University
101 Woodruff Circle, Suite 4000
Atlanta, GA 30322
404-727-8382
Fax: 404-727-3969
jsheikh@emory.edu
www.psychiatry.emory.edu/clinical_sites_autism_cente

Offers online bulletin boards which are relevant to autism.

Mark Hyman Rapaport, Chairman

Indiana

797 Indiana Resource Center for Autism
Inst. for the Study of Developmental Disabilities
2853 E 10th Street
Bloomington, IN 47408
812-855-6508
Fax: 812-855-9630
TTY: 812-855-9396
iidc@indiana.edu
www.iidc.indiana.edu/irca

Conducts outreach training and consultation, engage in research, and develops and disseminate information on behalf of individuals across the autism spectrum, including autism, asperger's syndrome, and other pervasive developmental disorders.

Dr. Cathy Pratt, Director

Michigan

798 Burger School for the Autistic
30922 Beechwood Street
Garden City, MI 48135
734-762-8420
Fax: 734-762-8533
www.resa.net/gardencity/burger.htm

Committed to maximizing the potential of each student to gain independence and self-fulfillment.

Mary O'Neill, Manager

Missouri

799 Judevine Center for Autism
1101 Olivette Executive Parkway
Saint Louis, MO 63132
314-432-6200
800-780-6545
Fax: 314-849-2721
contactus@judevine.org
www.judevine.org

Rooted in principles of applied behavior analysis within a social exchange framework, the Judevine Center has provided effective training and treatment to thousands of families locally, nationally and globally.

New York

800 Institute for Basic Research in Developmental Disabilities
1050 Forest Hill Road
Staten Island, NY 10314
718-494-0600
Fax: 718-698-3803
www.omr.state.ny.us

To conduct basic and clinical research in order to further the prevention and early detection and treatment of intellectual and developmental disabilities.

W Ted Brown, Manager

801 State University of New York Health Sciences Center
450 Clarkson Avenue, Box 32
Brooklyn, NY 11203
718-270-1000
Fax: 718-778-5397
www.downstate.edu

Child psychiatry research programs.

Richard Kream, Manager

North Carolina

802 Autism Society of North Carolina
505 Oberlin Road, Suite 230
Raleigh, NC 27605
919-743-0204
800-442-2762
Fax: 919-743-0208
books@autismsociety-nc.org
www.autismbookstore.com

Offers a library that carries one of the largest selections of books about autism.

David Lax, Manager

West Virginia

803 Autism Services Center
10 6th Avenue W
Huntington, WV 25710
304-525-8014
Fax: 304-525-8026
www.autismservicescenter.org

Works to improve appropriate and professional training, advocacy, consulting and information for individuals responsible for the welfare and care of autistic individuals and others with developmental disabilities.

Jimmie Beirne, CEO

Autistic Disorder / Conferences

804 **Autism Training Center**
Marshall University
1 John Marshall Drive, Suite 316
Huntington, WV 25755
304-696-2332
800-344-5115
Fax: 304-696-2846
www.marshall.edu/atc/

To provide education, training and treatment programs for West Virginians who have autism, pervasive developmental disorders or Asperger's disorders and have been formally registered with the center.

Barbara Cottrill, Executive Director

Research Centers

805 **Autism Research Foundation**
72 East Concord Street, R-1010
Boston, MA 02118
hello@theautismresearchfoundation.org
www.theautismresearchfoundation.org

A nonprofit organization dedicated to brain-based research and inclusion programs in the community. Focuses on fundraise for continuous brain-based research, while providing tangible resources for families and providers managing autism right now.

Margaret Bauman, MD, Founding Director

806 **Autism Speaks**
1 East 33rd Street, 4th Floor
New York, NY 10016
212-252-8584
Fax: 212-252-8676
help@autismspeaks.org
www.autismspeaks.org

At Autism Speaks, its goal is to change the future for all who struggle with autism spectrum disorder. Dedicated to funding global biomedical research into the causes, prevention, treatments, and cure for autism; to raising public awareness about autism and its effects on individuals, families, and society; and to bringing hope to all who deal with the hardships of this disorder.

Angela Timashenka Geiger, President/CEO
Thomas Frazier, II, Chief Scientific Officer
Lisa Goring, Chief Strategic Officer

807 **Children's Center for Neurodevelopmental Studies**
5430 West Glenn Drive
Glendale, AZ 85301
623-915-0345
Fax: 623-937-5425
admin@ccnsaz.org
www.thechildrenscenteraz.org

The Children's Center is a full service non-profit corporation (501-c3) offering comprehensive educational, therapeutic, and habilitative programs for children and adults

Kent Rideout, Director
Dawna Sterner, Preschool & Education Information
Catherine Orsak, Therapy Information

808 **Facilitated Communication Institute at Syracuse University**
230 Huntington Hall
Syracuse, NY 13244
315-443-4752
Fax: 315-443-2258
www.soe.syr.edu/about/

Facilitated Communication Institute, the new name, the Institute on Communication and Inclusion, represents a broadened focus developed over the past 20 years, reflecting lines of research, training and public dissemination that focus on school and community inclusion, narratives of disability and ability, and disability rights. Its initiatives stress the important relationship of communication to inclusion.

Robert Bogdan, Distinguished Professor Emeritus
Joan Burstyn, Professor Emerita
John Centra, Professor Emeritus

809 **Institute on Communication and Inclusion**
203 Huntington Hall
Syracuse, NY 13244
315-443-4752
Fax: 315-443-2258
icistaff@syr.edu
www.soe.syr.edu/about/

Facilitated Communication Institute, the new name, the Institute on Communication and Inclusion, represents a broadened focus developed over the past 20 years, reflecting lines of research, training and public dissemination that focus on school and community inclusion, narratives of disability and ability, and disability rights. Its initiatives stress the important relationship of communication to inclusion.

Robert Bogdan, Distinguished Professor Emeritus
Joan Burstyn, Professor Emerita
John Centra, Professor Emeritus

810 **State University of New York Health Sciences Center**
450 Clarkson Avenue
Brooklyn, NY 11203
718-270-1568
Fax: 718-778-5397
www.downstate.edu

Child psychiatry research programs.

Robert Furchgott, President

811 **University of North Carolina at Chapel Hill, Brain Research Center**
Matthew Gfeller Center 2207 Stallings-Evans Sports
Chapel Hill, NC 8700
919-962-0409
Fax: 919-962-7060
tbicenter@unc.edu
www.tbicenter.unc.edu/MAG_Center/Home.html

The Matthew Gfeller Sport-Related Traumatic Brain Injury Research Center demonstrates its commitment to providing the highest level of care for athletes of all ages suffering from sport-related brain injuries, and to assist parents, coaches, and medical professionals in managing these student-athletes.

Kevin M. Guskiewicz, Faculty
Jason P. Mihalik, Faculty
Stephen W. Marshall, Faculty

Conferences

812 **American School Counselor Association Annual Conference**
1101 King Street, Suite 310
Alexandria, VA 22314
703-683-2722
800-306-4722
Fax: 703-997-7572
asca@schoolcounselor.org
www.schoolcounselor.org

The mission of ASCA is to represent professional school counselors and to promote professionalism and ethical practices.

3,000 Attendees

Richard Wong, Executive Director
Jennifer Walsh, Director, Education & Training
Kathleen M Rakestraw, Director of Communications

813 **Autism National Committee Conference**
Autism National Committee
www.autcom.org

info@autcom.org
www.autcom.org

Organization dedicated to social justice for all citizens with autism through a shared vision and a commitment to positive approaches.

October

814 **Autism Society National Conference & Expo**
Austim Society
4340 East-West Way, Suite 350
Bethesda, MD 20814
301-657-0881
800-328-8476
info@autism-society.org
www.autism-society.org

Addresses the range of issues affecting people with autism including early intervention, education, employment, behavior, communication, social skills, biomedical interventions and others, across the entire lifespan. Bringing together the expertise and experiences of family members, professionals and individuals on the spectrum, attendees are able to learn how to more effectively advocate and obtain supports for the individual with ASD.

July

James Ball, Executive Chair
Ron E Simmons, Vice Chair
Sergio Mariaca, Treasurer

815 FFCMH Annual Conference
National Federation of Families
15800 Crabbs Branch Way, Suite 300
Rockville, MD 20855

240-403-1901
ffcmh@ffcmh.org
www.ffcmh.org

The only national conference dedicated solely to supporting families whose children - of any age - experience mental health and/or substance use challenges during their lifetime.

November

Lynda Gargan, PhD, Executive Director

Audio Video

816 A Sense of Belonging: Including Students with Autism in their School Community
Indiana Resource Center for Autism
1905 North Range Rd.
Bloomington, IN 47408

812-855-6508
Fax: 812-855-9630
TTY: 812-855-9396
iidc@indiana.edu
www.iidc.indiana.edu

Highlights the efforts of two elementary and one middle school in Indiana in teaching students with autism in general education settings. Truly involving students in their school community requires teamwork, the adoption of effective instructional practices, and a school committed to supporting a diverse range of students.

David Mank, Director

817 Autism
Fanflight Productions
32 Court Street, 21st Floor
Brooklyn, NY 11201

718-488-8900
800-876-1710
Fax: 718-488-8642
info@fanlight.com
www.fanlight.com

The stories of three families show us what the textbooks and studies cannot — what it's really like to love and care for children with autism.

28 minutes

Kelli English, Publicity Coordinator

818 Autism Is a World
Syracuse University, Institute on Communication
370 Huntington Hall
Syracuse, NY 13244

315-443-9657
Fax: 315-443-2274
http://suedweb.syr.edu/thefci

Documentary that takes the viewer on a journey into the mind of 13 year old girl, into her world and her obsessions. Explores Sue's world world, her writings, and the remarkable friendships she has created while in college.

Videotape

819 Autism: A Strange, Silent World
Filmakers Library
3212 Duke Street
Alexandria, VA 22314

212-808-4980
703-212-8520
Fax: 212-808-4983
sales@alexanderstreet.com
www.academicvideostore.com/filmakers

British educators and medical personnel offer insight into autism's characteristics and treatment approaches through the cameos of three children.

52 Minute

Sue Oscar, Co-President

820 Autism: A World Apart
Fanlight Productions
32 Court Street, 21st Floor
Brooklyn, NY 11201

718-488-8900
800-876-1710
Fax: 718-488-8642
info@fanlight.com
www.fanlight.com

In this documentary, three families show us what the textbooks and studies cannot, what it's like to live with autism day after day, raise and love children who may be withdrawn and violent and unable to make personal connections with their families. ISBN: DVD: 1-57295-950-9; VHS: 1-57295-039-0

29 Minutes DVD or VHS

821 Autism: Being Friends
Indiana Resource Center for Autism
1905 North Range Rd.
Bloomington, IN 47408

812-855-6508
800-280-7010
Fax: 812-855-9630
TTY: 812-855-9396
iidc@indiana.edu
www.iidc.indiana.edu

This autism awareness videotape was produced specifically for use with young children. The program portrays the abilities of the child with autism and describes ways in which peers can help the child to be a part of the everyday world.

David Mank, Director

822 Autism: The Child Who Couldn't Play
Films for the Humanities and Sciences
132 West 31st Street, 16th Floor
New York, NY 10001

800-257-5126
Fax: 609-275-0266
custserv@films.com
www.ffh.films.com

This program is a comprehensive overview of autism, the mysterious disorder that impedes normal child development. It was once believed that autism was caused by remote, cold parents; most often the mother was blamed. The program explores the frontiers of our understanding of autism, which today is recognized as a partly genetic biological disorder.

1996 46 minutes
ISBN: 1-421373-28-7

823 Autism: The Unfolding Mystery
Aquarius Health Care Videos
Lot 2/12 Willmott Ave
Margaret River, WA 6285

508-650-1616
888-440-2963
Fax: 508-650-1665
aquarius33@bigpond.com
www.Aquariusproductions.com

Explores what it means to be autistic, how you can recognize the signs of autism in your child, and hear about new tretments and programs to help children learn to deal with the disorder.

26 Minutes

824 Children and Autism: Time is Brain
Aquarius Health Care Videos
Lot 2/12 Willmott Ave
Margaret River, WA 6285

508-650-1616
888-440-2963
Fax: 508-650-1665
aquarius33@bigpond.com
www.Aquariusproductions.com

A mother of an autistic child implores parents who suspect their child may be autisitc not to 'wait and see.' Don't wait, don't be afraid of that diagnosis, diagnosis is a tool, not a stigma. The term 'time is brain' is absolutely accurate for children with autism, because the sooner diagnosed, the sooner they can get excellent care.

27 Minutes
ISBN: 1-581404-44-1

825 Children of the Stars
Fanlight Productions
32 Court Street, 21st Floor
Brooklyn, NY 11201
718-488-8900
800-876-1710
Fax: 718-488-8642
info@fanlight.com
www.fanlight.com

This film explores the harsh reality of raising children with autism in modern day China. It prodives moving insights into the hardships parents face and reminds us painfully of conditions that prevailed in the United States not so very many years ago.

49 Minutes DVD
ISBN: 1-572955-07-4

826 Developing Friendships: Wonderful People to Get to Know
Indiana Resource Center for Autism
1905 North Range Rd.
Bloomington, IN 47408
812-855-6508
Fax: 812-855-9630
TTY: 812-855-9396
iidc@indiana.edu
www.iidc.indiana.edu

Individuals discuss the various social difficulties they experience, such as being bullied, missing subtle social cues, and following and maintaining conversations. Strategies for supporting social interactions are highlighted.

David Mank, Director

827 Developing and Writing IEPs Under the New IDEA
LRP Publications
P.O. Box 24668
West Palm Beach, FL 33416
215-784-0860
800-515-4577
Fax: 215-784-9639
TTY: 215-658-0938
custserve@lrp.com
www.lrp.com

Addresses the new IEP content and IEP team requirements by explaining the new provisions, providing context and background to the changes, and predicting their potential impact on special education programs.

2005 90 minutes

Kenneth F. Kahn, President

828 Educating Students with Autism: Implementation of Applied Bahavior Analysis
LRP Publications
P.O. Box 24668
West Palm Beach, FL 33416
215-784-0860
800-515-4577
Fax: 215-784-9639
TTY: 215-658-0938
custserve@lrp.com
www.lrp.com

During this taped audio conference, behavior and autism consultant Dr Susan Catlett discusses the practical aspects of using ABA in your public school programs for students with autism spectrum disorders.

2006 90 Minutes

Kenneth F. Kahn, President

829 Getting Started with Facilitated Communication
Syracuse University, Institute On Communication
230 Huntington Hall
Syracuse, NY 13244
315-443-4752
Fax: 315-443-2258
ICIstaff@syr.edu
soe.syr.edu/centers_institutes/institute_communicati

Describes in detail how to help individuals with autism and/or severe communication difficulties to get started with facilitated communication.

Videotape
Christine Ashby, Director
Douglas Biklen, Senior Researcher
Dani Weinstein, Administrative Secretary

830 How I Am (Wie Ich Bin)
Fanlight Productions
32 Court Street, 21st Floor
Brooklyn, NY 11201
718-488-8900
800-876-1710
Fax: 718-488-8642
info@fanlight.com
www.fanlight.com

With the dreams and fears of a teenager, but wisdom beyond his years, Patrick takes us into his emotional world through the words he painstakingly types into his computer.

49 Minutes DVD
ISBN: 1-572955-05-8

831 Sense of Belonging: Including Students with Autism in Their School Community
Indiana Resource Center for Autism
1905 North Range Rd.
Bloomington, IN 47408
812-855-9630
Fax: 812-855-6508
iidc@indiana.edu
www.iidc.indiana.edu

Highlights the efforts of two elementary and one middle school in Indiana in teaching students with autism in general education settings.

20 minutes

David Mank, Director

832 Two Worlds - One Planet
Fanlight Productions
32 Court Street, 21st Floor
Brooklyn, NY 11201
718-488-8900
800-876-1710
Fax: 718-488-8642
info@fanlight.com
www.fanlight.com

This documentary brings Autism syndrome out of the shadows, stressing that young people with developmental disabilities can learn and grow, if their individual needs, styles, and abilities are respected. It takes an upbeat look at students attending a private day school.

62 minutes DVD
ISBN: 1-572954-99-X

833 Understanding Autism
Fanlight Productions
32 Court Street, 21st Floor
Brooklyn, NY 11201
718-488-8900
800-876-1710
Fax: 718-488-8642
info@fanlight.com
www.fanlight.com

Parents of children with autism discuss the nature and symptoms of this lifelong disability, and outline a treatment program based on behavior modification principles. ISBN: DVD: 1-57295-951-7; VHS: 1-572951-11-1

19 minutes DVD or VHS

Kelli English, Publicity Coordinator

834 We've Climbed Mountains: Increasing Our Understanding of Autism Spectrum Disorders
Indiana Resource Center for Autism
1905 North Range Rd.
Bloomington, IN 47408
812-855-6508
Fax: 812-855-9630
TTY: 812-855-9396
iidc@indiana.edu
www.iidc.indiana.edu

Provides general information about autism spectrum disorders with the hope of increasing overall awareness, especially about those with high-functioning autism/Asperger's syndrome. Specific topics addressed include sensory challenges, social understanding, and responses to the diagnosis.

Autistic Disorder / Web Sites

David Mank, Director

Web Sites

835　Asperger Autism Spectrum Education Network (ASPEN)
P.O. Box 109
Oceanport, NJ 07757
732-321-0880
www.aspennj.org

ASPEN provides families and individuals whose lives are affected by Autism Spectrum Disorders (Asperger Syndrome, Pervasive Developmental Disorder-NOS, High Functioning Autism), and Nonverbal Learning Disabilities with education, support & advocacy.

Lori Shery, President/Executive Director
Rich Meleo, Vice President

836　Autism Network for Dietary Intervention
www.autismndi.com

www.autismndi.com

Providing help and support for families using a gluten and casein free diet in the treatment of autism and related developmental disabilities.

837　Autism Resources
www.autism-resources.com

www.autism-resources.com

Offers information and links regarding the developmental dsabilities of autism and aspergers syndrome.

838　Autism Society of America
6110 Executive Boulevard, Ste 305
Rockville, MD 20852
800-328-8476
www.autism-society.org

The Autism Society, the nation's leading grassroots autism organization, exists to improve the lives of all affected by autism. We do this by increasing public awareness about the day-to-day issues faced by people on the spectrum, advocating for appropriate services for individuals across the lifespan, and providing the latest information regarding treatment, education, research and advocacy.

Christopher Banks, President & CEO
John Dabrowski, CFO/COO

839　Autism Speaks
1 East 33rd Street, 4th Floor
New York, NY 10016
212-252-8584
Fax: 212-252-8676
help@autismspeaks.org
www.autismspeaks.org

Information about Autism Research.

Angela Timashenka Geiger, President/CEO
Lisa Goring, Chief Strategic Officer
Thomas Frazier, II, Chief Scientific Officer

840　Center for the Study of Autism
www.autism.org

www.autism.org

Information about autism to parents and professionals.

841　Community Services for Autistic Adults & Children (CSAAC)
8615 East Village Avenue
Montgomery Village, MD 20886
240-912-2220
Fax: 301-926-9384
csaac@csaac.org
www.csaac.org

To enable individuals with autism to achieve their highest potential and contribute as confident individuals to their community.

Eric Salzano, Executive Director
Eva Muiruri, Assistant Executive Director

842　Families for Early Autism Treatment
PO Box 255722
Sacramento, CA 95865
916-303-7405
Fax: 916-303-7405
feat@feat.org
www.feat.org

A nonprofit organization of parents and professionals, designed to help families with children who are diagnosed with autism or pervasive developmental disorder. It offers a network of support for families.

843　Institute on Communication and Inclusion
230 Huntington Hall
Syracuse, NY 13244
315-443-4752
Fax: 315-443-2258
ICIstaff@syr.edu
soe.syr.edu/centers_institutes/institute_communicati

College offering facilitated learning research into communication with persons who have autism or severe disabilities. Offers books, videos and public awareness information on the research projects.

Christine Ashby, Director
Douglas Biklen, Senior Researcher
Dani Weinstein, Administrative Secretary

844　National Center for Biotechnology Information
National Library of Medicine, 8600 Rockville Pike
Bethesda, MD 20894
888-346-3656
info@ncbi.nlm.nih.gov
www.ncbi.nlm.nih.gov

NCBI's mission is to develop new information technologoes to aid in the understanding of fundamental molecular and genetic processes that control health and disease.

Patricia Flatley Brennan, RN, PhD, Director
James Ostell, PhD, Executive Secretary

845　Online Mendelian Inheritance in Man
McKusick-Nathans Institue of Genetic Medicine-JHU
Baltimore, MD 21205
www.omim.org

This database is a catalog of human genes and genetic disorders.

Ada Hamosh, MD, Scientific Director

846　University Students with Autism and Asperger's Syndrome Web Site
www.users.dircon.co.uk/~cns
207-704-7450
77- 56- 774
Fax: 207-359-9440
judith.kerem@nas.org.uk
www.users.dircon.co.uk/~cns

Helps to develop and understanding of the difficulties people with Asperger Syndrome may face. We also work on a one to one basis with the student and liase with staff and peers. help is also given in setting up support networks such as mentors and providing effective strategies to aid independent learning.

Book Publishers

847　ABA Program Companion
Autism Society of North Carolina Bookstore
505 Oberlin Road, Suite 230
Raleigh, NC 27605
919-743-0204
800-442-2762
Fax: 919-743-0208
books@autismsociety-nc.org
www.autismbookstore.com

A guide developed to help educational teams organize an implement Applied Behavior Analysis (ABA) programs, including home, school, and center-based programs.

Autistic Disorder / Book Publishers

848 **Activity Schedules for Children with Autism**
Autism Society of North Carolina Bookstore
505 Oberlin Road, Suite 230
Raleigh, NC 27605
919-743-0204
800-442-2762
Fax: 919-743-0208
books@autismsociety-nc.org
www.autismbookstore.com

Written to help parents and professionals utilize activity schedules to promote independence in children in a variety of settings.

849 **Al Capone Does My Shirts: A Novel**
Autism Society of North Carolina Bookstore
505 Oberlin Road, Suite 230
Raleigh, NC 27605
919-743-0204
800-442-2762
Fax: 919-743-0208
books@autismsociety-nc.org
www.autismbookstore.com

Set in 1935, this colorful novels tells the story of Matthew 'Moose' Flanagan, a 12-year-old boy who moves with his family (including sister with autism) to Alcatraz Island. For readers age 12 and up.

850 **Autism Acceptance Book: Being A Friend to Someone With Autism**
Autism Society of North Carolina Bookstore
505 Oberlin Road, Suite 230
Raleigh, NC 27605
919-743-0204
800-442-2762
Fax: 919-743-0208
books@autismsociety-nc.org
www.autismbookstore.com

Colorfully illustrated activity book was created to help neurotypical children learn about autism spectrum disorder (ASD) and the characteristics that make kids with ASD unique. For readers age 6 and up.

851 **Autism Spectrum Disorders: The Complete Guide**
Autism Society of North Carolina Bookstore
505 Oberlin Road, Suite 230
Raleigh, NC 27605
919-743-0204
800-442-2762
Fax: 919-743-0208
books@autismsociety-nc.org
www.autismbookstore.com

Written to help parents, professionals, and other members of the community learn more about autism spectrum disorder (ASD), and it presents a thorough overview of the disorder, from diagnosis through adulthood.

852 **Autism and Learning**
David Fulton Publishers
2 Park Square, Milton Park
Abingdon, 0X14 4RN,
United Kingdom
207-017-7913
Fax: 207-017-6707
http://catalogue.fultonpublishers.co.uk

This book is about how a cognitive perception on the way in which individuals with autism think and learn may be applied to particular curriculum areas.

1997 180 pages Paperback
ISBN: 1-853464-21-X

853 **Autism and the Family: Problems, Prospects and Coping with the Disorder**
Charles C Thomas Publishing
2600 S 1st Street
Springfield, IL 62704
217-789-8980
800-258-8980
Fax: 217-789-9130
books@ccthomas.com
www.ccthomas.com

Examination of certain issues such as stress, coping and stigma. Contains 33 interviews with parents whose children attended an autistic treatment center. An excellent resource text.

1998 210 pages Softcover
ISBN: 0-398068-43-7

854 **Autism as an Executive Director**
Oxford University Press
2001 Evans Road
Cary, NC 27513
919-677-0977
800-445-9714
Fax: 919-677-1303
custserv.us@oup.com
www.us.oup.com

Provides a new and conroversial perspective from some of the leading researchers in this field.

1998 328 pages
ISBN: 0-198523-49-1

855 **Autism: Effective Biomedical Treatments**
Autism Society of North Carolina Bookstore
505 Oberlin Road, Suite 230
Raleigh, NC 27605
919-743-0204
Fax: 919-743-0208
books@autismsociety-nc.org
www.autismbookstore.com

Written for clinicians, professionals, and parents who would like to understand more about specific biomedical treatments for autism spectrum disorder (ASD).

856 **Autism: From Tragedy to Triumph**
Branden Publishing Company
17 Station Street
Brookline Village, MA 02447
617-734-2045
Fax: 617-734-2046
www.branden.com

A book that deals with the Lovaas method and includes a foreward by Dr. Ivar Lovaas. The book is broken down into two parts — the long road to diagnosis and then treatment.

ISBN: 0-828319-65-0

857 **Autism: Mind and Brain**
Oxford University Press
2001 Evans Road
Cary, NC 27513
919-677-0977
800-445-9714
Fax: 919-677-1303
custserv.us@oup.com
www.us.oup.com

An important work describing the latest advances in autism research.

2004 320 pages
ISBN: 0-198529-24-4

858 **Autism: The Facts**
Oxford University Press
2001 Evans Road
Cary, NC 27513
919-677-0977
800-445-9714
Fax: 919-677-1303
custserv.us@oup.com
www.us.oup.com

Contains valuable information for families and those afflicted with this condition.

1994 124 pages
ISBN: 0-192623-27-3

859 **Beyond the Autism Diagnosis: A Professional's Guide to Helping Families**
Autism Society of North Carolina Bookstore
505 Oberlin Road, Suite 230
Raleigh, NC 27605
919-743-0204
Fax: 919-743-0208
books@autismsociety-nc.org
www.autismbookstore.com

Helps to change the way professionals communicate with parents of children with autism spectrum disorder (ASD), making the experience more effective and meaningful for all involved.

Autistic Disorder / Book Publishers

860 Children With Autism: A Parents Guide
Peytral Publications
P.O. Box 1162
Minnetonka, MN 55345
952-949-8707
877-739-8725
Fax: 952-906-9777
help@peytral.com
www.peytral.com

Informative handbook for parents of children and teens; covers medical, educational, legal, family life, daily care, emotional issues and more.

456 pages

861 Children with Autism and Asperger Syndrome A Guide for Practitioners and Carers
John Wiley & Sons
10475 Crosspoint Blvd
Indianapolis, IN 46256
877-762-2974
Fax: 800-597-3299
www.wiley.com

Covers the disorders of autism, understanding the causes and the different approaches of treatment for autistic children.

1999 342 pages
ISBN: 0-471983-28-4

862 Children with Autism: A Developmental Perspective
Harvard University Press
79 Garden Street
Cambridge, MA 02138
401-531-2800
800-405-1619
Fax: 401-531-2801
hup@harvard.edu
www.hup.harvard.edu

Offers a rare close look at the mysterious condition that afflicts approximately 350,000 Americans and millions more.

1997
ISBN: 0-674053-13-3

863 Children with Starving Brains
Autism Society of North Carolina Bookstore
505 Oberlin Road, Suite 230
Raleigh, NC 27605
919-743-0204
800-442-2762
Fax: 919-743-0208
books@autismsociety-nc.org
www.autismbookstore.com

Written by an experienced physician who is the grandmother of a child with autism spectrum disorder (ASD), this book takes a biomedical approach toward the treatment of ASD.

Eric Schopler, Editor
Gary Mesibov, Co-Editor

864 Cowden Preautism Observation Inventory
Jo E. Cowden, author

Charles C Thomas Publisher
2600 S 1st Street
Springfield, IL 62704
217-789-8980
800-258-8980
Fax: 217-789-9130
books@ccthomas.com
www.ccthomas.com

Contains effective intervention activities for sensory motor stimulation and joint attention.

226 pages
ISBN: 0-398086-43-5

Sue F V Rakow, Co-Author
Carol B Carpenter, Co-Author

865 Diagnosis Autism: Now What? 10 Steps to Improve Treatment Outcomes
Autism Society of North Carolina Bookstore
505 Oberlin Road, Suite 230
Raleigh, NC 27605
919-743-0204
800-442-2762
Fax: 919-743-0208
books@autismsociety-nc.org
www.autismbookstore.com

Practical guide was written to help parents of children with autism spectrum disorder (ASD) form successful pediatric partnerships with physicians and other healthcare practitioners involved in their child's diagnosis and treatment.

866 Different Like Me: My Book of Autism Heroe s
Autism Society of North Carolina Bookstore
505 Oberlin Road, Suite 230
Raleigh, NC 27605
919-743-0204
800-442-2762
Fax: 919-743-0208
books@autismsociety-nc.org
www.autismbookstore.com

This beautifully illustrated children's book tells the tales of many famous people throughout history who all had on thing in common: they didn't fit in. It's also possible they may have had autism spectrum disorder (ASD). For readers ages 7-12.

867 Does My Child Have Autism?
Autism Society of North Carolina Bookstore
505 Oberlin Road, Suite 230
Raleigh, NC 27605
919-743-0204
800-442-2762
Fax: 919-743-0208
books@autismsociety-nc.org
www.autismbookstore.com

Written for parents of children age three and younger who have concerns about their child's development.

868 Education and Care for Adolescents and Adults with Autism
Kate Wall, author

Hamill Institute on Disabilities
2455 Teller Road
Thousand Oaks, CA 91320
800-818-7243
Fax: 800-583-2665
info@sagepub.com
www.sagepub.com

Uses case studies and examples that show the reader how to put theory into practice in multi-disciplinary settings, this book clearly explains how changes in policy and provision have affected how young people and adults with autism are cared for and educated. With highlights of up-to-date and accessible information on the nature and affects of ASD, legislation information, family issues, positive intervention programs, and strategies. Hardcover or paperback.

2007 168 pages Paperback
ISBN: 1-412923-82-8

Sara Miller McCune, Founder/Chairman
Blaise R Simqu, President/CEO
Chris Hickok, Senior Vice President/CFO

869 Everybody is Different: A Book for Young P eople
Autism Society of North Carolina Bookstore
505 Oberlin Road, Suite 230
Raleigh, NC 27605
919-743-0204
800-442-2762
Fax: 919-743-0208
books@autismsociety-nc.org
www.autismbookstore.com

Written for brothers and sisters of young persons with autism spectrum disorder (ASD). It not only explains the basic characterisitics of ASD, but also answers the questions often asked by a sibling of a child with ASD. For readers ages 8-16.

Autistic Disorder / Book Publishers

Hardbound

870 Everyday Solutions: A Practical Guide for Families of Children with Autism
Autism Society of North Carolina Bookstore
505 Oberlin Road, Suite 230
Raleigh, NC 27605
919-743-0204
800-442-2762
Fax: 919-743-0208
books@autismsociety-nc.org
www.autismbookstore.com

Presents 37 everyday situations that may present difficulties for a child with autism spectrum disorder (ASD), along with recommendations and strategies.

871 Functional Behavior Assessment for People with Autism
Autism Society of North Carolina Bookstore
505 Oberlin Road, Suite 230
Raleigh, NC 27605
919-743-0204
800-442-2762
Fax: 919-743-0208
books@autismsociety-nc.org
www.autismbookstore.com

provides and introduction to functional behavior assessment (FBA). FBA is a valuable tool that can be used by parents and professionals to understand and address the challenging behaviors of persons with autism spectrum disorder (ASD).

872 Handbook of Autism and Pervasive Developmental Disorders
Autism Society of North Carolina Bookstore
505 Oberlin Road, Suite 230
Raleigh, NC 27605
919-743-0204
800-442-2762
Fax: 919-743-0208
books@autismsociety-nc.org
www.autismbookstore.com

Two-volume scholarly resource presents the latest scientific research on autism spectrum disorders (ASD).

873 Healthcare for Children on the Autism Spectrum
Autism Society of North Carolina Bookstore
505 Oberlin Road, Suite 230
Raleigh, NC 27605
919-743-0204
800-442-2762
Fax: 919-743-0208
books@autismsociety-nc.org
www.autismbookstore.com

The first publication of its kind to focus on the health and medical care of children with autism spectrum disorder (ASD).

874 Helping Children with Autism Learn
Oxford University Press
2001 Evans Road
Cary, NC 27513
919-677-0977
800-445-9714
Fax: 919-677-1303
custserv.us@oup.com
www.us.oup.com

A leading authority on autism offers practical, reliable advice on coping with learning disorders associated with autism.

2003 512 pages
ISBN: 0-195138-11-2

875 Ian's Walk: A Story About Autism
Autism Society of North Carolina Bookstore
505 Oberlin Road, Suite 230
Raleigh, NC 27605
919-743-0204
800-442-2762
Fax: 919-743-0208
books@autismsociety-nc.org
www.autismbookstore.com

In this moving fictional story, a young girl named Julie realizes how much she cares for her brother, Ian, who has autism spectrum disorder (ASD). For readers ages 4-8.

876 Incredible 5-Point Scale
Autism Society of North Carolina Bookstore
505 Oberlin Road, Suite 230
Raleigh, NC 27605
919-743-0204
800-442-2762
Fax: 919-743-0208
books@autismsociety-nc.org
www.autismbookstore.com

Shows parents and professionals how to implement a simple 5-point scale to help students with sutism spectrum disorder (ASD) understand and control their emotional responses and behavior.

877 Just Take a Bite: Easy, Effective Answers to Food Aversions and Eating Challenges
Autism Society of North Carolina Bookstore
505 Oberlin Road, Suite 230
Raleigh, NC 27605
919-743-0204
800-442-2762
Fax: 919-743-0208
books@autismsociety-nc.org
www.autismbookstore.com

A much-need resource that specifically addresses the eating challenges of children who may have autism spectrum disorder (ASD), sensory processing disorder (SPD), or other developmental delays.

878 Kids In the Syndrome Mix
Autism Society of North Carolina Bookstore
505 Oberlin Road, Suite 230
Raleigh, NC 27605
919-743-0204
800-442-2762
Fax: 919-743-0208
books@autismsociety-nc.org
www.autismbookstore.com

Children with autism spectrum disorder (ASD) often have coexisting neuropsychiatric diagnoses, and this handbook focuses on the most common neuropsychiatric disorders and their symptoms.

879 Looking After Louis
Autism Society of North Carolina
505 Oberlin Road, Suite 230
Raleigh, NC 27605
919-743-0204
800-442-2762
Fax: 919-743-0208
books@autismsociety-nc.org
www.autismbookstore.com

Colrfully illustrated fictional story introduces readers to Louis, a new boy in school who has autism spectrum disorder (ASD). Told from the perspective of a female classmate, the story describes how Louis plays and interacts with students and teachers in a general education classroom. For readers ages 4-8.

880 Mindblindness: An Essay on Autism & Theory of Mind
MIT Press
55 Hayward Street
Cambridge, MA 02142
617-253-5646
800-405-1619
Fax: 617-258-6779
mitpress-order-inq@mit.edu
http://mitpress.mit.edu

Interpretations and research into the theory of mindblindness in children with autism.

1995 208 pages
ISBN: 0-262023-84-9
Ellen W Faran, Director
Rebecca Schrader, Associate Director

881 Miracle to Believe In
Fawcett

NOP-ONE-

A group of people from all walks of life come together and are transformed as they reach out, under the direction of the Kaufmans, to help a little boy the medical world has given up as hopeless. The heartwarming journey of loving a child back to life will not only inspire you, the reader, but presents a compelling new way to deal with life's traumas and difficulties.

Autistic Disorder / Book Publishers

1982 384 pages
ISBN: 0-449201-08-2

882 My Brother Sammy
Autism Society of North Carolina Bookstore
505 Oberlin Road, Suite 230
Raleigh, NC 27605
919-743-0204
800-442-2762
Fax: 919-743-0208
books@autismsociety-nc.org
www.autismbookstore.com

Filled with beautiful watercolor illustrations, this book tells the fictional story of Sammy, a young boy with autism spectrum disorder (ASD). The story is told from the perspective of Sammy's older brother, who is sometimes frustrated by Sammy's behavior. For readers ages 4-8.

883 My Friend With Autism
Autism Society of North Carolina Bookstore
505 Oberlin Road, Suite 230
Raleigh, NC 27605
919-743-0204
800-442-2762
Fax: 919-743-0208
books@autismsociety-nc.org
www.autismbookstore.com

Created for teachers and students in her son's elementary school class. The book is a valuable tool for helping typical children understand the traits and behaviors of their classmates with autism spectrum disorder (ASD). For readers ages 4-10.

884 My Social Stories Book
Autism Society of North Carolina Bookstore
505 Oberlin Road, Suite 230
Raleigh, NC 27605
919-743-0204
800-442-2762
Fax: 919-743-0208
books@autismsociety-nc.org
www.autismbookstore.com

The Social Stones in this book are written for children with autism spectrum disorder (ASD) ages 2 to 6, and they include over 150 everyday situations that are frequently encountered in early childhood.

885 Neurobiology of Autism
Johns Hopkins University Press
2715 N Charles Street
Baltimore, MD 21218
410-516-6900
800-537-5487
Fax: 410-516-6998
webmaster@press.jhu.edu
www.press.jhu.edu

This book discusses recent advances in scientific research that point to a neurobiological basis for autism and examines the clinical implications of this research.

2006 424 pages
ISBN: 0-801880-47-5

Alfred R Berkeley, Chairman

886 Parenting Across the Autism Spectrum
Autism Society of North Carolina Bookstore
505 Oberlin Road, Suite 230
Raleigh, NC 27605
919-743-0204
800-442-2762
Fax: 919-743-0208
books@autismsociety-nc.org
www.autismbookstore.com

Two mothers who have children on the opposite ends of the autism spectrum wrote this poignant and insightful book, and the book also provides a look at what lies beyond the early intervention and elementary school years.

887 Positive Behavioral Strategies to Support Children & Young People with Autism
Martin Hanbury, author
Hamill Institute on Disabilities/Sage Publications
2455 Teller Road
Thousand Oaks, CA 91320
800-818-7243
Fax: 800-583-2665
info@sagepub.com
www.sagepub.com

Offers advice on understanding and managing childrens' often challenging actions. Covering a range from birth to 19 years, this resource provides: practical advice on developing an appropriate learning environement; INSET materials for developing behavior management practices; self-audit tools for practioners; and reproducables and practical resources. Hardcover or paperback.

2007 120 pages Paperback
ISBN: 1-412929-11-0

Sara Miller McCune, Founder/Chairman
Blaise R Simqu, President/CEO
Chris Hickok, Senior Vice President/CFO

888 Preschool Issues in Autism
Plenum Publishing Corporation
233 Spring Street
New York, NY 10013
212-620-8000
Fax: 212-463-0742
www.springer.com

Combines some of the most important theory and data related to the early identification and intervention in autism and related disorders. Addresses clinical aspects, parental concerns and legal issues. Helps professionals understand and implement state-of-the-art services for young children and their families.

294 pages
ISBN: 0-306444-40-2

Derk Haank, CEO
Ulrich Vest, CFO
Martin Mos, COO

889 Prescription for Success
Autism Society of North Carolina Bookstore
505 Oberlin Road, Suite 230
Raleigh, NC 27605
919-743-0204
800-442-2762
Fax: 919-743-0208
books@autismsociety-nc.org
www.autismbookstore.com

Written for medical professionals who work with patients who have autism spectrum disorder.

890 Reaching the Autistic Child: A Parent Training Program
Brookline Books/Lumen Editions
8 Trumbell Rd, Suite B-001
Northampton, MA 01060
413-584-0184
800-666-2665
Fax: 413-584-6184
brbooks@yahoo.com
www.brooklinebooks.com

Detailed case studies of social and behavioral change in autistic children and their families show parents how to implement the principles for improved socialization and behavior.

1998 Softcover
ISBN: 1-571290-56-7

891 Riddle of Autism: A Psychological Analysis
Jason Aronson
4501 Forbes Blvd, Suite 200
Lanham, MD 20706
301-459-3366
800-462-6420
Fax: 301-429-5748
custserv@rowman.com
www.aronson.com

Dr. Victor examines the myths that cloud an understanding of this disorder and describes the meanings of its specific behavioral symptoms.

356 pages Softcover
ISBN: 1-568215-73-8

892 **Social Skills Picture Book**
Autism Society of North Carolina Bookstore
505 Oberlin Road, Suite 230
Raleigh, NC 27605
919-743-0204
800-442-2762
Fax: 919-743-0208
books@autismsociety-nc.org
www.autismbookstore.com

(Teaching Play, Emotions, and Communication to Children with Autism). Through photographs and conversation bubbles, the author demonstrates approximately 30 social skills in the areas of communication, play, and emotion.

893 **Solving Behavior Problems in Autism**
Autism Society of North Carolina Bookstore
505 Oberlin Road, Suite 230
Raleigh, NC 27605
919-743-0204
800-442-2762
Fax: 919-743-0208
books@autismsociety-nc.org
www.autismbookstore.com

In this guide, the author explains how to use effective communication techniques to reduce problem behaviors in persons with autism spectrum disorder (ASD).

894 **Son-Rise: The Miracle Continues**

NOP-ONE-

Describes an effective, loving and respectful method for treating children with autism. It documents the development of the Son Rise Program throught the record of Raun Kaufman's astonishing development from a lifeless autistic child into a highly verbal, loveable youngster with no traces of his former condition. It further details Raun's extraordinary progress from the age of four into young adulthood. It also shares moving accounts of five families who successfully used the program.
1995 384 pages
ISBN: 0-915811-61-8

895 **Stress and Coping in Autism**
Oxford University Press
2001 Evans Road
Cary, NC 27513
919-677-0977
800-445-9714
Fax: 919-677-1303
custserv.us@oup.com
www.us.oup.com

Provides a theoretical framework for the usefukness of the stress construct in understanding and treating autism.
2006 472 pages
ISBN: 0-195182-26-X

896 **Taking Autism to School**
Autism Society of North Carolina Bookstore
505 Oberlin Road, Suite 230
Raleigh, NC 27605
919-743-0204
800-442-2762
Fax: 919-743-0208
books@autismsociety-nc.org
www.autismbookstore.com

A fictional story about a girl named Angel and her friendship woth Sam, a classmate who has autism spectrum disorder (ASD). From her own point of view, Angel explains how Sam thinks and behaves in school and at home. For readers ages 5-10.

897 **Teaching Children with Autism to Mind-Read A Pratical Guide for Teachers & Parents**
John Wiley & Sons
10475 Crosspoint Blvd
Indianapolis, IN 46256
877-762-2974
Fax: 800-597-3299
www.wiley.com

This book explains the Theory of Mind, which is the ability to infer other's mental states and then interpret their speech and actions based on this information. The author applies this theory to autistic children to help their social and communicative abnormalities.
1999 302 pages
ISBN: 0-471976-23-7

898 **Teaching Coversations to Children With Autism: Scripts and Script Fading**
Autism Society of North Carolina Bookstore
505 Oberlin Road, Suite 230
Raleigh, NC 27605
919-743-0204
800-442-2762
Fax: 919-743-0208
books@autismsociety-nc.org
www.autismbookstore.com

Uses the principles of Apllied Behavior Analysis (ABA) to create strategies that facilitate communication in children who have autism spectrum disorder.

899 **Ten Things Every Child With Autism Wishes You Know**
Autism Society of North Carolina Bookstore
505 Oberlin Road, Suite 230
Raleigh, NC 27605
919-743-0204
800-442-2762
Fax: 919-743-0208
books@autismsociety-nc.org
www.autismbookstore.com

Describes how children with autism spectrum disorder (ASD) function and what they are trying to say to the world when they cannot always express it in a conventional way.

900 **The Neurology of Autism**
Oxford University Press
2001 Evans Road
Cary, NC 27513
919-677-0977
800-445-9714
Fax: 919-677-1303
custserv.us@oup.com
www.us.oup.com

A valuable resource for both the latest information from basic-science research and its application to the diagnosis and treatment of autism.
2005 272 pages
ISBN: 0-195182-22-7

901 **Toilet Training for Individuals with Autism and Related Disorders**
Autism Society of North Carolina Bookstore
505 Oberlin Road, Suite 230
Raleigh, NC 27605
919-743-0204
800-442-2762
Fax: 919-743-0208
books@autismsociety-nc.org
www.autismbookstore.com

Comprehensive guide for parents and professionals provides over 200 toilet training tips and more than 40 helpful case examples.

902 **Treasure Chest of Behavioral Strategies for Individuals with Autism**
Autism Society of North Carolina Bookstore
505 Oberlin Road, Suite 230
Raleigh, NC 27605
919-743-0204
800-442-2762
Fax: 919-743-0208
books@autismsociety-nc.org
www.autismbookstore.com

Comprehensive resource manual provides parents and teachers with numerous behavior management strategies for individuals with autism spectrum disorder (ASD).

903 **Understanding and Treating Children with Autism**
John Wiley & Sons
10475 Crosspoint Blvd
Indianapolis, IN 46256
877-762-2974
Fax: 800-597-3299
www.wiley.com

Autistic Disorder / Magazines

Aimed at those concerned with the education and welfare of the children with autism, particularly at teachers in Special education and the psychologists and care professionals who work with teachers and parents of children with autism.

1995 188 pages
ISBN: 0-471958-88-3

904 Visual Strategies for Improving Communication
Autism Society of North Carolina Bookstore
505 Oberlin Road, Suite 230
Raleigh, NC 27605
919-743-0204
800-442-2762
Fax: 919-743-0208
books@autismsociety-nc.org
www.autismbookstore.com

This how-to manual describes a communication intervention strategy for teaching persons with autism spectrum disorder (ASD) that evolved from learning style research.

905 World of the Autistic Child
Oxford University Press
2001 Evans Road
Cary, NC 27513
919-677-0977
800-445-9714
Fax: 919-677-1303
custserv.us@oup.com
www.us.oup.com

Comprehensive guide for parents with children diagnosed or suspected of being autistic. Includes current thinking on causes, diagnosis, and treatment, using illustrative case studies.

1998 368 pages
ISBN: 0-195119-17-7

Magazines

906 Newslink
Autism Society Ontario
6110 Executive Boulevard, Ste 305
Rockville, MD 20852
800-328-8476
www.autism-society.org

Covers society activities and contains information on autism. Recurring features include news of research, a calendar of events, reports of meetings, and book reviews.

10 pages

Christopher Banks, President & CEO
John Dabrowski, CFO/COO

Journals

907 Focus on Autism and Other Developmental Disabilities
Hammill Institute on Disabilities/Sage Publication
2455 Teller Road
Thousand Oaks, CA 91320
800-818-7243
Fax: 800-583-2665
journals@sagepub.com
www.sagepub.com

Practical elements of management, treatment, planning and education for persons with autism or other pervasive developmental disabilities. FOCUS publishes articles representing diverse philosophical and theoretical positions and reflecting a wide range of disciplines, including, education, psychology, psychiatry, medicine, physical therapy, occupational therapy, speech/language pathology and related areas. ISSN: Print: 0885-7288; Electronic: 1538-4837

Quarterly

908 The Journal of Positive Behavior Interventions
Hamill Institute on Disabilities/Sage Publications
2455 Teller Road
Thousand Oaks, CA 91320
800-818-7243
Fax: 800-583-2665
journals@sagepub.com
www.sagepub.com

The JPBI offers sound, research-based principles of positive behavior support for use in school, home, and community settings with people with challenges in bahvior adaptations. JPBI is an official journal of the Association of Positive Behavior Support. Subscriptions: Institutional - Print Only $146, Institutional - Print & E-access $149, Individual - Print & E-access $57.

Quarterly

V Mark Durand, PhD, Co-Editor
Robert L Koegel, PhD, Co-Editor

909 The Journal of Special Education
Hamill Institute on Disabilities/Sage Publications
2455 Teller Road
Thousand Oaks, CA 91320
800-818-7243
Fax: 800-583-2665
journals@sagepub.com
www.sagepub.com

For four decades professionals have relied on the JSE'for timely, sound research in the area of special education. JSE provides reseach articles and scholarly review by expert authors in all subspecialties of special education for individuals with disabilities ranging from mild to severe. JSE is an official journal of the Division for Research of the CEC. Subscriptions: Institutional - Print Only $172, Institutional - Print & E-access $176, Individual - Print & E-access $57.

Quarterly

Bob Algozzine, PhD, Co-Editor
Fred Spooner, PhD, Co-Editor

Newsletters

910 MAAP Newsletter
PO Box 524
Crown Point, IN 46308
219-662-1311
Fax: 219-662-0638
chart@netnitco.net
www.maapservices.org

Shares information that are not find in textbooks or read in other sources.

Pamphlets

911 Autism Fact Sheet
NINDS
PO Box 5801
Bethesda, MD 20824
301-496-5751
800-352-9424
TTY: 301-468-5981
www.ninds.nih.gov

Also available in Spanish.

Walter J. Koroshetz, M.D., Acting Director
Alan L. Willard, Ph.D., Acting Deputy Director
Caroline Lewis, Executive Officer

912 Facts About Autism
Indiana Institute on Disability and Community
1905 North Range Rd.
Bloomington, IN 47408
812-855-6508
800-280-7010
Fax: 812-855-9630
TTY: 812-855-9396
iidc@indiana.edu
www.iidc.indiana.edu

Provides concise information describing autism, diagnosis, needs of the person with autism from diagnosis through adulthood. Information on the Autism Society of America chapters in Indiana is listed in the back, along with a description of the Indiana Resource Center for Autism and suggested books to look for in the local library. Also available in Spanish.

17 pages

David Mank, Director
Suzie Rimstidt
Susan Gray

Autistic Disorder / Camps

913 **Pervasive Developmental Disorders**
National Inst. of Neurological Disorders/Stroke
31 Center Drive, MSC 2540, Building 31, Room 8A06
Bethesda, MD 20892
301-496-5751
800-352-9424

Detailed booklet that describes symptoms, causes, and treatments, with information on getting help and coping.

Camps

914 **Beech Brook**
3737 Lander Road
Cleveland, OH 44124
216-831-2255
877-546-1225
Fax: 216-831-0436
www.beechbrook.org

A year-round residential and day treatment center, accepts summer residents when there are openings in the regular enrollment. The program is designed for emotionally disturbed, learning disabled and autistic children, providing therapeutically oriented teaching and programming techniques in a camp setting.

Don Harris, Director

915 **Big Crystal Camp**
8533 Williams Road
DeWitt, MI 48820
517-669-9367

One week residential camp sponsored by Lansing Area Chapter of Michigan Association for Children with Learning Disabilities.

Florence Curtis

916 **Camp Buckskin**
4124 Quebec Ave N, Ste 300
Minneapolis, MN 55427
763-208-4805
Fax: 952-938-6996
info@campbuckskin.com
www.campbuckskin.com

LD and ADD/ADHD youth have often experienced frustration and a lack of success. Buckskin assists these individuals to realize and develop the potentials and abilities which they possess.

Thomas R Bauer, CCD, Camp Director

917 **Camp Friendship**
Friendship Ventures
10509 108th Street NW
Annandale, MN 55302
952-852-0101
800-450-8376
Fax: 952-852-0123
info@friendshipventures.org
www.friendshipventures.org

Camp Friendship offers kids, teens, and adults the chance to have the time of their lives. The program focuses on building self-esteem and independence, and practicing social skills; and we nurture each person's strengths and abilities and encourage participation in activies at their own pace. Specially designed for persons with developmental, physical or multiple disabilities, special medical conditions, Down syndrome, autism or other conditions. Weekend camps and longer available.

Georgann Rumsey, Vice President, Programs
Laurie Tschetter, Program Director

918 **Camp Krem**
102 Brook Lane
Boulder Creek, CA 95006
510-222-6662
campkrem@gmail.com
www.campingunlimited.com

Camp with year-around recreational activities and summer camping for children and adults with developmental disabilities.

919 **Camp Lotsafun**
3660 Baker Lane, Suite 103
Reno, NV 89509
775-827-3866
Fax: 775-827-0334
www.camplotsafun.com

Provides recreational, therapeutic, and educational opportunities for individuals with developmental disabilities, while providing respite care for their families.

Jill Gabel, Program Director

920 **Camp Merrimack**
3320 Triana Boulevard
Huntsville, AL 35805
256-534-6455
ksimari@merrimackhall.com
www.merrimackhall.com

A unique arts half-day camp for children ages 3 through 12; open to children with special needs including Cerebral Palsy, Down Syndrome, autism and others.

Ashley Dinges, Executive Director
Kim Simari, Managing Director

921 **Camp New Hope**
Friendship Ventures
53035 Lake Avenue
McGregor, MN 55760
952-852-0101
800-450-8376
Fax: 952-852-0123
fv@friendshipventures.org
www.friendshipventures.org

Camp New Hope is a great place for children, teens, and adults to have the time of their lives. The program provides a unique opportunity for having fun, learning skills, boosting confidence, and making friends. Services are specifically designed for persons with developmental, phyisical or multiple disabilities, special medical needs, Down syndrome, autism, or other conditions. Weekend camps and longer available. Other services available throughout the year.

Georgann Rumsey, Vice President, Programs
Laurie Tschetter, Program Director

922 **Camp Nuhop**
404 Hillcrest Drive
Ashland, OH 44805
419-289-2227
Fax: 419-289-2227
www.campnuhop.org

A summer residential program for any youngster from 6 to 18 with a learning disability, behavior disorder or Attention Deficit Disorder. Sixty two campers and 35 staff members live on site in groups of 7 campers to every 3 counselors. Activities focus on positive self-concept and behaviors and teach children to learn how to find their strengths, abilities and talents from a positive, yet realistic viewpoint.

Jerry Dunlap, Director

923 **Camp Ramah in New England Tikvah Program**
39 Bennett Street
Palmer, MA 01609
413-283-9771
Fax: 413-283-6661
info@campramahne.org
www.campramahne.org

The Tikvah program is one of the first summer programs for Jewish children with special needs. It continues to grow and evolve as it strives to serve campers with a wide range of special needs including, but not limited to, congitive impairments, autism, cerebral palsy and seizure disorder.

Howard Blas, Tikvah Program Director
Talya Kalender, Director, Camper Care
Benjamin Greene, Director of Education

924 **Crotched Mountain School & Rehabilitation Center**
1 Verney Drive
Greenfield, NH 03047
603-547-3311
800-800-966
Fax: 603-547-3232
info@crotchedmountain.org
www.cmf.org

Currently serves children ages 6-22 with multiple-handicaps including: Cerebral Palsy, Spina Bifida, visual and hearing impairments and neurological disabilities, developmental disorders, autism, behavioral and emotional disorders, seizure disorders, spinal cord and head injuries. Member of the National Association of Independent Schools and accredited with the NE Association of Schools and Colleges, Independent Schools of Northern NE.

Autistic Disorder / Camps

Rita Phinney, Director Admissions
John Young, Registrar

925 Dallas Academy
950 Tiffany Way
Dallas, TX 75218
214-324-1481
Fax: 214-327-8537
www.dallas-academy.com

7-week summer session for students who are having difficulty in regular school classes.

Jim Richardson, Director

926 Developmental Center
6710 86th Avenue N
Pinellas Park, FL 33782
727-541-5716
Fax: 727-544-8186
infopp@centeracademy.com
www.centeracademy.com

Specifically designed for the learning disabled child and other children with difficulties in concentration, strategy, social skills, impulsivity, distractibility and study strategies. Programs offered include: attention training, visual-motor remediation, socialization skills training, relaxation training, horseback riding and more. The day camp meets weekdays from 9-3 for 3,4 or 5 week sessions.

Dr. Eric Larson

927 Eagle Hill School - Summer Program
242 Old Petersham Road, PO Box 116
Hardwick, MA 01037
413-477-6000
Fax: 413-477-6837
admission@eaglehillschool.com
www.ehs1.org

For the child, age 9-19, with a specific learning disability or Attention Deficit Disorder, this summer program offers a structured curriculum designed to build a basic foundation of academic competence. Extracurricular and outdoor activities complement the educational program.

Erin E Wynne, Dean of Admission

928 Groves Academy
3200 Highway 100 South
Saint Louis Park, MN 55416
952-920-6377
Fax: 952-920-2068
www.grovesacademy.org

A nonprofit day school in Minnesota designed especially for children with learning differences. The Center has a full day academic program from September through June, as well as an 8 week summer program. Groves also offers community services such as: psychoeducational testing for children and adults, consulting services, workshops on learning disabilities and other special learning needs, and afternoon/evening tutorial services for children and adults.

John Alexander, Head of School

929 Hill School of Fort Worth
4817 Odessa Avenue
Fort Worth, TX
817-923-9482
Fax: 817-923-4894
hillschool@hillschool.org
www.hillschool.org

Provides an alternative learning environment for students having average or above-average intelligence with learning differences. Hill school is an established leader in North Texas with a 25 year history of effectively serving LD children. Beginning in 1961 as a tutorial service, Hill became a formal school in 1973. Our mission is to help those who learn differently develop skills and strategies to succeed. We do this by developing academic/study skills, and self-discipline.

John W. Wright, Chairman
Randall Canedy, Vice Chairman
Audrey Boda-Davis, Executive Director

930 Kris' Camp
1132 Green Hill Trace
Tallahassee, FL 32317
801-942-1750
Fax: 877-267-9451
info@kriscamp.org
www.kriscamp.org

Therapy intensive/respite camp for children with special needs (thus far focusing on children with autism/autistic-like challenges) and their families.

Michelle Hardy, Program Director
Leidy Van Ispelen, Assistant Director

931 Lab School of Washington Summer Program
4759 Reservoir Road NW
Washington, DC 20007
202-965-6600
Fax: 202-965-5106
alexandra.freeman@labschool.org
www.labschool.org

The Lab School 5-week summer session includes individualized reading, spelling, writing, study skills, and math programs. A multisensory approach addresses the needs of bright learning disabled children. Related services such as speech/language therapy and occupational therapy are integrated into the curriculum. Elementary/Intermediate; Junior High/High School.

Sally Smith, Founder
Susan Feeley, Admissions Director

932 Maplebrook School
5142 Route 22
Amenia, NY 12501
845-373-8191
Fax: 845-373-7029
jscully@maplebrookschool.org
www.maplbrookschool.org

A coeductional boarding school for students with learning differences and ADD. A New York State registered high school servicing ages 11-18. Post secondary options offered to 18-21.

Donna M Konkolios, Head of School
Jennifer Scully, Director Admissions

933 Round Lake Camp
21 Plymouth Street
Fairfield, NJ
973-575-3333
800-776-5657
Fax: 973-575-4188
rlc@njycamps.org
www.njycamps.org

For ages 7-18, this camp provides individualized academics in reading, language development and math for children with mild learning disabilities, Round Lake also offers therapeutic recreation and Jewish cultural values to its participants.

Sheira Director, Asst. Director

934 Squirrel Hollow
5665 Milam Road
Fairburn, GA 30213
770-774-8001
Fax: 770-774-8005
bbox@thebedfordschool.org
www.thebedfordschool.org

A remedial summer program of The Bedford School; serves children with academic needs due to learning difficulties. For students ages 6-16 and held on the campus of The Bedford School in Fairburn, GA. Campers participate in an individualized academic program as well as recreational activities. Students receive the proper academic remediation as well as specific remedial help with physical skills, peer interaction and self-esteem.

Betsy E Box, Director
Jeff James, Assistant Director
Bonnie Sides, Administrative Secretary

935 Summer Experience
Vanguard School
PO Box 730
Paoli, PA 19301
610-296-6700
Fax: 610-640-0132
www.vanguardschool-pa.org

For students who are experiencing learning difficulties due to neurological impairment, social/emotional disturbance and/or autism/pervasive developmental disorder.

Susan Snyder, Admissions Director
John D Wilson, Education Director

936　Wesley Woods
1001 Fiddlersgreen Rd
Grand Valley, PA 16420
814-430-7802
Fax: 814-436-7669
www.wesleywoods.com

Exceptional children's camp for children with emotional and intellectual handicaps.

Herb West

937　Worthmore Academy
3535 Kessler Blvd East Drive
Indianapolis, IN 46220
877-700-6516
Fax: 317-251-6516
bjackson@worthmoreacademy.org
www.worthmoreacademy.org

A K-12 non-profit school for children with learning differences providing educational assessments, alternative educational programs, academic guidance and public awareness services.

Brenda J Jackson, Director
Diana Buser, Assistant

Description

938 BELL'S PALSY
Involves the following Biologic System(s):
Neurologic Disorders

Bell's palsy is the most common form of facial nerve paralysis and may affect children at any age from infancy through adolescence. The facial nerve, also known as the seventh cranial nerve, arises from a certain area of the brain (i.e., brainstem) and divides into several branches that supply (innervate) the forehead, scalp, eyelids, cheeks, jaws, and muscles of facial expression. The facial nerve also conveys taste sensations from the front two thirds of the tongue. Bell's palsy is a temporary form of facial paralysis that usually develops suddenly approximately two weeks after a widespread viral infection, such as Epstein-Barr virus, herpesvirus, or mumps virus. It is thought to represent a postinfectious demyelination of the facial nerve (neuritis) due to allergic or immune responses.

Bell's palsy typically affects one side of the face and may involve upper and lower areas on the affected side. Symptoms of Bell's palsy usually begin suddenly and reach their peak within 48 hours. Children with the condition may experience weakness or slight paralysis of the upper and lower face; drooping of the corner of the mouth; an inability to close the eye; loss of taste sensations from the front two thirds of the tongue; or abnormal sensitivity to loud sounds (hyperacusis). Because the affected eye may be overexposed to the air, some patients may develop inflammation (exposure keratitis) of the transparent, front region of the eye (cornea). In addition, saliva may dribble from the corner of the mouth and food may tend to collect between the teeth and lips.

There is no cure or standard course of treatment for Bell's palsy. Some cases are mild and do not require treatment since the symptoms usually subside on their own within 2 weeks. For others, treatment may include medications such as acyclovir, used to fight viral infections, combined with an anti-inflammatory drug such as the steroid prednisone, used to reduce inflammation and swelling. Pain medications, such as aspirin, acetaminophen, or ibuprofen may be helpful. Other treatment of children with Bell's palsy is supportive, including eye drops to lubricate the cornea, particularly at night. In over 85 percent of affected children, Bell's palsy spontaneously resolves with no remaining facial weakness. About 10 percent may have mild longstanding weakness, and approximately five percent may experience severe, permanent facial weakness.

Government Agencies

939 NIH/National Institute of Neurological Disorders and Stroke (NINDS)
PO Box 5801
Bethesda, MD 20824
800-352-9424
www.ninds.nih.gov

Works to reduce the burden of neurological disease by conducting, fostering, coordinating and guiding research on the causes, prevention, diagnosis and treatment of neurological disorders and stroke, while supporting basic research in related scientific areas.

Walter J. Koroshetz, MD, Director

National Associations & Support Groups

940 American Academy of Otolaryngology-Head and Neck Surgery
1650 Diagonal Road
Alexandria, VA 22314
703-836-4444
www.entnet.org

The missions of the AAO-HNS and its foundation are to advance the art and science of otolaryngology-head and neck surgery through state-of-the-art education, research and learning; and to unite, serve and represent the interests of its members and their patients to the public, government, other medical specialists and related organizations. Founded in 1896, the AAO-HNS is the world's largest organization of otolaryngologist-head and neck surgeons.

11,600 Members

James C Denneny III, MD, Chief Executive Officer

941 American Academy of Pediatrics
345 Park Blvd
Itasca, IL 60143
800-433-9016
Fax: 847-434-8000
mcc@aap.org
www.aap.org

The American Academy of Pediatrics and its member pediatricians are committed to the attainment of optimal physical, mental and social health and well-being for all infants, children, adolescents, and young adults.

Lynn Olson, PhD, VP, Research
Mark Del Monte, JD, CEO/Executive VP
Vera Tait, MD, FAAP, Chief Medical Officer

942 Child Neurology Foundation
601 W Short Street
Lexington, KY 40508
888-417-3435
info@childneurologyfoundation.org
childneurologyfoundation.org

The Child Neurology Foundation connects partners from all areas of the child neurology community so those navigating the journey of disease diagnosis, management, and care have the ongoing support from those dedicated to treatments and cures.

Amy Brin, Executive Director
Katie Hentges, Director, Programs
Brea McCormley, Director, Development

943 March of Dimes Foundation
1550 Crystal Drive, Ste 1300
Arlington, VA 22202
888-663-4637
www.marchofdimes.org

March of Dimes help moms have full-term pregnancies and research the problems that threaten the health of babies. The March of Dimes also acts globally: sharing best practices in perinatal health and helping improve birth outcomes where the needs are the most urgent.

Stacey D. Stewart, President
Alan Brogdon, SVP/COO/Board Officer
Rahul Gupta, MD, SVP & Chief Medical/Health Officer

Conferences

944 Annual Meeting & OTO Experience
American Academy of Otolaryngology
1650 Diagonal Road
Alexandria, VA 22314
703-836-4444
www.entnet.org

Held each fall, with thousands of Academy members, non-member physicians, allied health professionals, administrators, and exhibiting companies attending. It draws more than 6,000 medical experts and professionals from around the world. The conference will feature instruction courses, miniseminars, scientific oral presentations, honorary guest lectures, and numerous scientific posters.

September

James C Denneny III, MD, Chief Executive Officer

Web Sites

945 American Academy of Otolaryngology-Head and Neck Surgery
www.entnet.org

703-836-4444
www.entnet.org

The missions of the AAO-HNS and its foundation are to advance the art and science of otolaryngology-head and neck surgery through state-of-the-art education, research and learning; and to unite, serve and represent the interests of its members and their patients to the public, government, other medical specialists and related organizations. Founded in 1896, the AAO-HNS is the world's largest organization of otolaryngologist-head and neck surgeons.

946 Bell's Palsy Network
www.bellspalsy.net/

www.bellspalsy.net/

Provides information on facial paralysis, Bell's Palsy, Ramsey Hunt Syndrome and other forms of facial paralysis. We were the first dedicated web portal for Bell's palsy and facial paralysis informaton and host the largest and most popular forum about bell's palsy and facial palsy information.

947 Bell's Palsy Research Foundation
www.bellspalsyresearch.com

www.bellspalsyresearch.com

Online support foundation for facial palsy patients, providing information and supprt to patients worldwide.

948 NIH/National Institute of Neurological Disorders and Stroke (NINDS)
PO Box 5801
Bethesda, MD 20824

301-496-5751
800-352-9424
www.ninds.nih.gov

Mission is to reduce the burden of neurological disease-a burden borne by every age group, by every segment of society, by people all over the world.

Walter J. Koroshetz, MD, Director

Biliary Atresia / Description

Description

949 BILIARY ATRESIA

Involves the following Biologic System(s):

Gastrointestinal Disorders

Biliary atresia is a rare condition that is present at birth (congenital) in approximately 1 in 12,500 births, and is characterized by the absence of or the abnormal or incomplete development (hypoplasia) of the bile ducts. These ducts carry bile from the liver and gallbladder into the small intestine. Bile, which is secreted by the liver, is a yellowish or greenish fluid that aids in the digestion of fats. Bile passes through the common bile duct and into the upper portion of the small intestine (duodenum). Absence or underdevelopment of the bile ducts interferes with or prevents the passage of bile into the intestine and, as a result, characteristic findings and symptoms may be noticed within the first few weeks of life.

Symptoms may include progressively darkening urine; pale stools (acholic); a persistent yellowing of the skin, eyes, and mucous membranes (jaundice); and enlargement of the liver (hepatomegaly). If untreated, additional symptoms and findings may become apparent within two or three months. These may include stunted growth, increased irritability, and itching (pruritus). A potential complication of biliary atresia involves an increase in pressure in the vein that conveys blood from the spleen, stomach, pancreas, and intestine to the liver (portal hypertension). In addition, untreated biliary atresia may result in a life-threatening condition known as biliary cirrhosis, in which the liver's function is impaired and, eventually, the liverbecomes irreversibly damaged.

Treatment for biliary atresia is often determined by the site of the obstruction and includes various surgical procedures. In some infants, surgery may be performed as a means to help postpone cirrhosis and stunted growth until liver transplantation is feasible.

National Associations & Support Groups

950 American Academy of Pediatrics
345 Park Blvd
Itasca, IL 60143
800-433-9016
Fax: 847-434-8000
mcc@aap.org
www.aap.org

The American Academy of Pediatrics and its member pediatricians are committed to the attainment of optimal physical, mental and social health and well-being for all infants, children, adolescents, and young adults.

Lynn Olson, PhD, VP, Research
Mark Del Monte, JD, CEO/Executive VP
Vera Tait, MD, FAAP, Chief Medical Officer

951 American Association for the Study of Liver Diseases
1001 North Fairfax Street Suite 400
Alexandria, VA 22314
703-299-9766
Fax: 703-299-9622
www.aasld.org

To Advance the Science and Practice of Hepatology, Liver Transplantation and Hepatobiliary Surgery, Thereby Promoting Liver Health and Optimal Care of Patients with Liver and Biliary Tract Diseases.

Matthew R D'Uva, Chief Executive Officer
Julie Deal, Deputy Chief Executive Officer
Julia Merrill, Director, Grants & Programs

952 CHARGE Syndrome Foundation
318 Half Day Rd, #305
Buffalo Grove, IL 60089
516-684-4720
800-442-7604
info@chargesyndrome.org
www.chargesyndrome.org

The mission of the CHARGE Syndrome Foundation is to provide support to individuals with CHARGE syndrome and their families; to gather, develop, maintain and distribute information about CHARGE syndrome; and to promote awareness and research regarding its identification, cause and management.

Lisa Cunningham, Executive Director
Lourdes E Quintana Baez, Outreach & Engagement Manager
Ameli Leech, Development & Database Coordinator

953 Children's Liver Association for Support Services
PO Box 186
Monaca, PA 15061
724-581-5527
classkidscares@gmail.com
www.classkids.org

CLASS is an all volunteer, nonprofit organization dedicated to serving the emotional, educational and financial needs of families coping with childhood liver disease and transplantation. Its goal is to be both a service to families and a valuable resource for the medical community.

Stephan Circle, Co-President
Tamara Circle, Co-President

954 Genetic Alliance
426400 Woodfield Road, Ste 189
Damascus, MD 20872
202-966-5557
Fax: 202-966-8553
info@geneticalliance.org
www.geneticalliance.org

World's leading nonprofit health advocacy organization committed to transforming health through genetics and promoting an environment of openness centered on the health of individuals, families, and communities.

Sharon Terry, CEO
Ruth Child, CFO
Natasha Bonhomme, Chief Strategy Officer

Research Centers

955 Clinical Research Center, Pediatrics
Children's Hospital Research Foundation
3333 Burnett Avenue
Cincinnati, OH 45229
513-636-4200
800-344-2462
Fax: 513-636-7151
TTY: 513-636-4900
www.cincinnatichildrens.org

Cincinnati Children's will improve child health and transform delivery of care through fully integrated, globally recognized research, education and innovation

Michael Fisher, President and CEO
Steve Davis, COO
Margaret Hostetter, MD, Pediatrics Chair/Dir, Research Fdtn

956 Univ. of Texas-Southwestern Med. Ctr. at Dallas - Clinical Ctr. for Liver Disease
5323 Harry Hines Boulevard
Dallas, TX 75390
214-648-3111
Fax: 214-648-3715
LIVER@UTSouthwestern.edu
www.utsouthwestern.edu/about-us/contact-us.html

To achieve optimal outcomes for patients with a variety of liver disorders, including but not limited to Hepatitis B, C, and acute liver failure.

Dr. William Lee, Director
Dr Marlyn Mayo, Specialist

Web Sites

957 Children's Liver Association for Support Services
www.classkids.org

724-581-5527
classkidscares@gmail.com
www.classkids.org

CLASS is an all volunteer, nonprofit organization dedicated to serving the emotional, educational and financial needs of families coping with childhood liver disease and transplantation. Its goal is to be both a service to families and a valuable resource for the medical community.

958 Online Mendelian Inheritance in Man
McKusick-Nathans Institue of Genetic Medicine-JHU
Baltimore, MD 21205   www.omim.org

This database is a catalog of human genes and genetic disorders.

Ada Hamosh, MD, Scientific Director

Book Publishers

959 Liver Disease in Children
Lippincott Williams & Wilkins
530 Walnut Street
Philadelphia, PA 19106

215-521-8300
Fax: 215-521-8902
www.lww.com

This is a difinitive book on pediatric liver disease, providing extensive, well-edited information that is not easily accessible or available in other textbooks. A must-have for those interested in this rapidly growing subspecialty in pediatrics.

2000 1008 pages
ISBN: 0-781720-98-2

Pamphlets

960 Biliary Atresia
American Liver Foundation
39 Broadway, Suite 2700
New York, NY 10006

212-668-1000
Fax: 212-483-8179
www.liverfoundation.org

Pamphlet with information and symptoms on biliary atresia

Tom Nealon, Chair
David Ticker, Chief Financial Officer
Lynn Seim, Chief Operating Officer

961 Facts on Liver Transplantation
American Liver Foundation
39 Broadway, Suite 2700
New York, NY 10006

212-668-1000
800-223-0179
Fax: 212-483-8179
www.liverfoundation.org

Provides information on liver transplantation, and the effects.

Tom Nealon, Chair
David Ticker, Chief Financial Officer
Lynn Seim, Chief Operating Officer

Bipolar Disorder / Description

Description

962 BIPOLAR DISORDER

Synonyms: Manic-depressive disorder, Manic-depressive illness, Manic-depressive psychosis

Involves the following Biologic System(s):

Developmental/Behavioral/Psychiatric Disorders

Bipolar disorder, also known as manic-depressive disorder, is a condition characterized by alternating depression and mania or, in rare cases, mania alone. The disorder is thought to affect less than two percent of the general population. Although bipolar disorder usually becomes apparent during the third or fourth decade of life, a significant proportion of individuals are initially affected in childhood, adolescence, or early adulthood. Individuals with bipolar disorder may initially experience either a depressive or a manic episode. In some affected children and adolescents, manic episodes may be more frequent than depressive episodes during the first years of their illness. However, as the disease progresses, episodes of depression may become more frequent than manic episodes. Bipolar disorder is often further classified as unipolar in cases in which only depression is experienced and bipolar when mania occurs, with or without depression. In addition, mixed affected states are characterized by the occurrence of depressive and manic symptoms during a single episode.

In children and adolescents with bipolar disorder, associated symptoms resemble those seen in affected adults. Depressive states usually emerge gradually and may be characterized by feelings of sadness, despair, hopelessness, and discouragement; loss of self-esteem; physical and emotional exhaustion; and lack of interest of formerly enjoyed activities. In severe cases, affected individuals may have suicidal tendencies, and hospitalization in a pediatric, general, or psychiatric facility may be essential. In such cases, consultation with child psychiatrists is important for ongoing support and decision-making regarding treatment options.

In affected children and adolescents, manic states may be characterized by overactivity (hyperactivity); excessive talking; inability to sleep (insomnia); impulsive behavior and impaired judgment that may result in reckless spending; elation that may quickly change to irritability and anger; personal neglect that may result in poor hygiene; and, in some cases, delusions of grandeur and persecution (paranoid delusions). Initial episodes of depression or mania often last approximately six months without treatment. Although most manic or depressive episodes usually cease in months, some individuals may be affected for longer periods.

Adolescents with bipolar disorder may be misdiagnosed, e.g., with a psychotic disorder characterized by disturbances in behavior, cognition, and emotional reactions (schizophrenia) or a maladjusted reaction to a stressful life event (adjustment disorder). However, most affected individuals are correctly diagnosed with bipolar disorder during adulthood. According to reports in the literature, the earlier the onset of bipolar disorder, the more susceptible affected individuals may be to frequent episodes, rapid cycling between depressive and manic states, and severe episodes that may result in suicidal tendencies. In addition, earlier onset of the disorder is often associated with an increased incidence of depression and bipolar disorder in immediate (first-degree) relatives.

The treatment of children and adolescents with bipolar disorder may include therapy with certain medications (e.g., lithium carbonate, carbamazepine) and integrated, multidisciplinary management (e.g., behavioral therapy; individual, family, or group psychodynamic therapy; etc.). In children and adolescents with the disorder, thorough patient and family histories and specific medical evaluations are typically conducted before medications are prescribed. Pretreatment evaluation for lithium may include assessment of electrolyte levels, and kidney (renal) and thyroid function. Pretreatment evaluation for tricyclic antidepressants may include a cardiovascular examination including electrocardiography. If such medications are prescribed, regular blood levels should be taken until an adequate dose is determined.

Other treatment options include antipsychotics or tranquilizers if agitation or psychotic symptoms are present, especially at the initiation of treatment when acute manic episodes are likely. Recent studies have shown that about 75% of patients treated with electroconvulsive therapy (ECT) experienced improvement, and for some, it was the only treatment that worked. The exact cause of bipolar disorder is unknown. However, many researchers agree that genetic abnormalities may play some role in the etiology of the disorder.

Government Agencies

963 Center for Mental Health Services
5600 Fishers Lane
Rockville, MD 20857
240-276-1310
www.samhsa.gov

Encourages a range of programs such as systems of care to respond to the increasing number of mental, emotional, and behavioral problems among children. Supports outreach and case management programs for the thousands of Americans who are homeless and the improvement of these services.

Anita Everett, MD, Director

964 NIH/National Institute of Mental Health
6001 Executive Blvd, Rm 6200, MSC 9663
Bethesda, MD 20892
866-615-6464
Fax: 301-443-4279
TTY: 301-443-8431
nimhinfo@nih.gov
www.nimh.nih.gov

The mission of NIMH is to transform the understanding and treatment of mental illnesses through basic and clinical research, paving the way for prevention, recovery, and cure.

Joshua A. Gordon, MD, PhD, Director
Shelli Avenevoli, PhD, Deputy Director

National Associations & Support Groups

965 American Academy of Pediatrics
345 Park Blvd
Itasca, IL 60143
800-433-9016
Fax: 847-434-8000
mcc@aap.org
www.aap.org

The American Academy of Pediatrics and its member pediatricians are committed to the attainment of optimal physical, mental and social health and well-being for all infants, children, adolescents, and young adults.

Lynn Olson, PhD, VP, Research
Mark Del Monte, JD, CEO/Executive VP
Vera Tait, MD, FAAP, Chief Medical Officer

966 American Association Of Psychiatric Pharmacists
8055 O Street, Suite S113
Lincoln, NE 68510
402-476-1677
info@aapp.org
aapp.org

Bipolar Disorder / National Associations & Support Groups

The American Association of Psychiatric Pharmacists (AAPP) works to advance the reach and practice of psychiatric pharmacy and serve as the voice of the specialty. Formerly known as the College of Psychiatric and Neurologic Pharmacists (CPNP).

Brenda K. Schimenti, Executive Director
Robert Haight, PharmD, President
Sarah Melton, PharmD, BCPP, Treasurer

967 American Counseling Association
PO Box 31110
Alexandria, VA 22310
800-347-6647
Fax: 800-473-2329
ACAMemberServices@counseling.org
www.counseling.org

Represents professional counselors in various practice settings, and stands ready to serve more than 55,000 members with the resources they need to make a difference. From webinars, publications, and journals to Conference education sessions and legislative action alerts, ACA is where counseling professionals turn for powerful, credible content and support.

Shawn Boynes, Chief Executive Officer

968 American Group Psychotherapy Association
344 Lexington Ave, 15th Floor
New York, NY 10017
212-297-2190
Fax: 212-297-2158
info@agpa.org
www.agpa.org

The American Group Psychotherapy Association is a dynamic, thriving community of mental health professionals of all disciplines dedicated to advancing knowledge and research, and providing quality training in group psychotherapy and other group interventions, consultation and direct services nationally and internationally.

Angela Moore Stephens, CAE, Chief Executive Director

969 American Mental Health Counselors Association
107 S West Street, Suite 779
Alexandria, VA 22314
703-548-6002
www.amhca.org

The American Mental Health Counselors Association (AMHCA) is a national organization for licensed clinical mental health counselors. AMHCA strives to be the go-to organization for LCMHCs for education, advocacy, leadership and collaboration.

Dr. Beverly Smith, Interim Executive Director & CEO
Melissa McShepard, Director, Operations & Finance
Whitney Meyerhoeffer, Director, Communications

970 American Psychiatric Association
800 Maine Avenue SW, Suite 900
Washington, DC 20024
202-559-3900
apa@psych.org
www.psychiatry.org

It is a medical specialty society representing growing membership of more than 36,000 psychiatrists.

Saul Levin, MD, CEO & Medical Director

971 American Psychiatric Nurses Association
3141 Fairview Park Drive, Suite 625
Falls Church, VA 22042
571-533-1919
855-863-2762
Fax: 855-883-2762
inform@apna.org
www.apna.org

The American Psychiatric Nurses Association (APNA) is a professional association organized to advance the science and education of psychiatric-mental health nursing. It is committed to the specialty practice of psychiatric-mental health nursing, health, wellness and recovery promotion through identification of mental health issues, prevention of mental health problems and the care and treatment of persons with psychiatric disorders.

Lisa Deffenbaugh Nguyen, Executive Director
Patricia L. Black, PhD, RN, Associate Executive Director
Leslie Hoopengardner, Director of Operations

972 American Psychoanalytic Association
122 E 42nd Street, Suite 2310
New York, NY 10168
212-752-0450
info@apsa.org
www.apsa.org

APsaA as a professional organization for psychoanalysts, focuses on education, research and membership development.

Tom Newman, Executive Director
Tina Faison, Administrative Coordinator

973 American Psychological Association
750 First St. NE
Washington, DC 20002
202-336-5500
800-374-2721
TTY: 202-336-6123
www.apa.org

The mission is to advance the creation, communication and application of psychological knowledge to benefit society and improve people's lives.

Arthur C. Evans Jr, PhD, CEO/EVP

974 Anxiety and Depression Association of America
8701 Georgia Ave., Suite 412
Silver Spring, MD 20910
240-485-1018
information@adaa.org
www.adaa.org

ADAA is a national nonprofit organization dedicated to the prevention, treatment, and cure of anxiety, depression, OCD, PTSD, and related disorders and to improving the lives of all people who suffer from them through education, practice, and research.

Susan K Gurley, Executive Director
Lise Bram, Deputy Executive Director
Katie Russo, Senior Director, Operations

975 Association for Psychological Science
1800 Massachusetts Avenue NW, Suite 402
Washington, DC 20036
202-293-9300
Fax: 202-293-9350
www.psychologicalscience.org

The Association for Psychological Science (previously the American Psychological Society) is a nonprofit organization dedicated to the advancement of scientific psychology and its representation at the national and international level.

Robert Gropp, Chief Executive Director
Aime Ballard-Wood, Chief Operating Officer

976 Brain & Behavior Research Foundation
747 Third Avenue, 33rd Floor
New York, NY 10017
646-681-4888
800-829-8289
info@bbrfoundation.org
bbrfoundation.org

The Brain & Behavior Research Foundation is committed to alleviating the suffering caused by mental illness by awarding grants that will lead to advances and breakthroughs in scientific research.

Jeffrey Borenstein, MD, President & CEO

977 Center for Psychiatric Rehabilitation
940 Commonwealth Avenue W
Boston, MA 02215
psyrehab@bu.edu
cpr.bu.edu

The Center is a research, training, and service organization dedicated to improving the lives of persons who have psychiatric disabilities.

Dori Hutchinson, Executive Director

978 Depression and Bipolar Support Alliance
55 E Jackson Boulevard, Suite 490
Chicago, IL 60604
800-826-3632
Fax: 312-642-7243
www.dbsalliance.org

Patient-directed organization focusing on the most prevalent mental illnesses- depression and bipolar disorder. Fosters an understanding about the impact and management of these life-threatening illnesses by providing up-to-date, scientifically-based tools and information written in language the general public can understand.

Bipolar Disorder / State Agencies & Support Groups

Michael Pollock, Chief Executive Officer
John Quinn, Chief Financial Officer

979 Families for Depression Awareness
391 Totten Pond Road, Suite 101
Waltham, MA 02451
781-890-0220
Fax: 781-890-2411
info@familyaware.org
www.familyaware.org

Families for Depression Awareness is a national nonprofit organization helping families recognize and cope with depression and bipolar disorder to get people well and prevent suicides.

Arielle Cohen, Programs Manager
Valerie Cordero, Co-Executive Director
Susan Weinstein, Co-Executive Director

980 Juvenile Bipolar Research Foundation
17595 Harvard Avenue, Suite C-616
Irvine, CA 96214
www.jbrf.org

JBRF is a 501(c)(3) organization that actively promotes and supports scientific research focused on the cause of and treatments for bipolar disorder in children.

Demitri Papolos, Research Director

981 Mental Health America
500 Montgomery Street, Ste 820
Alexandria, VA 22314
703-684-7722
800-969-6642
Fax: 703-684-5968
www.mentalhealthamerica.net

MHA, the leading advocacy organization addressing the full spectrum of mental and substance use conditions and their effects nationwide, works to inform, advocate and enable access to quality behavioral health services for all Americans.

Paul Gionfriddo, President/CEO
Whitney Ball, Assoc. Dir., Marketing/Outreach
Sachin Doshi, Sr. Dir, Finance/Operations

982 National Alliance on Mental Illness (NAMI)
4301 Wilson Blvd., Suite 300
Arlington, VA 22203
703-525-7600
800-999-6264
info@nami.org
www.nami.org

NAMI provides advocacy, education, support and public awareness so that all individuals and families affected by mental illness can build better lives.

Daniel H. Gillison, CEO
Ken Levy, CFO
Ken Duckworth, Chief Medical Officer

983 National Association of State Mental Health Program Directors
675 N Washington Street, Suite 470
Alexandria, VA 22314
703-739-9333
www.nasmhpd.org

National Association of State Mental Health Program Directors (NASMHPD) represents the $37.6 billion public mental health service delivery system serving 7.1 million people annually in all 50 states, 4 territories, and the District of Columbia.

Brian Hepburn, MD, Executive Director
Christy Malik, MSW, Project Director
David Miller, MPAff, Sr. Operations & Project Director

984 National Council for Behavioral Health
1400 K Street NW, Suite 400
Washington, DC 20005
202-684-7457
www.thenationalcouncil.org

The National Council for Behavioral Health (National Council) is the unifying voice of America's community mental health and addictions treatment organizations.

Charles Ingoglia, President & CEO
Mohini Venkatesh, Chief of Staff
Deanna Roepke, Chief Program Officer

985 National Federation of Families
15800 Crabbs Branch Way, Suite 300
Rockville, MD 20855
240-403-1901
ffcmh@ffcmh.org
www.ffcmh.org

The National family run organization is dedicated exclusively to helping children with mental health needs and their families achieve a better quality of life.

Lynda Gargan, PhD, Executive Director

986 The Jed Foundation
530 7th Avenue, Suite 801
New York, NY 10018
212-647-7544
Fax: 212-647-7542
www.jedfoundation.org

The Jed Foundation is a nonprofit that protects emotional health and prevents suicide for our nation's teens and young adults, giving them the skills and support they need to thrive today and tomorrow.

John MacPhee, Chief Executive Director
Rebecca Benghiat, President & Chief Operating Officer
Laura Erickson-Schroth, MD, Chief Medical Officer

987 The Ryan Licht Sang Bipolar Foundation
875 N. Michigan Avenue, Suite 3100
Chicago, IL 60611
888-944-4408
www.ryanlichtsangbipolarfoundation.org

The Ryan Licht Sang Bipolar Foundation is dedicated to fostering awareness, understanding and research for early-onset Bipolar Disorder.

Joyce Licht Sang, President
Sarah Myers, Secretary & Treasurer
Kelly Ring, Events Coordinator

State Agencies & Support Groups

988 Center for Family Support
333 7th Avenue, #901
New York, NY 10001
212-629-7939
Fax: 212-239-2211
svernikoff@cfsny.org
www.cfsny.org

The Center for Family (CFS) is a not-for-profit human service agency providing support and assistance to individuals with developmental disabilities and traumatic brain injuries throughout New York City, Long Island, the lower Hudson Valley region and New Jersey.

Steven Vernikoff, Executive Director
Linda Schellenberg, Director, Community Service
Barbara Greenwald, Associate Executive Director

989 Depressive and Manic-Depressive Assocation of Mount Sinai
100 LaSalle Street, Suite 5A
New York, NY 10027
917-445-2399
jgg17@columbia.edu
www.columbia.edu/~jgg17/DMDA/PAGE_1.html

The NYC Depressive and Manic-Depressive Group is a support group for persons with mood disorders, depression and bipolar disorder, as well as their family members and friends.

Conferences

990 FFCMH Annual Conference
National Federation of Families
15800 Crabbs Branch Way, Suite 300
Rockville, MD 20855
240-403-1901
ffcmh@ffcmh.org
www.ffcmh.org

The only national conference dedicated solely to supporting families whose children - of any age - experience mental health and/or substance use challenges during their lifetime.

November

Lynda Gargan, PhD, Executive Director

991 **NAMI Convention**
National Alliance on Mental Illness
3803 N Fairfax Drive, Suite 100
Arlington, VA 22203

703-524-7600
888-999-6264
Fax: 703-524-9094
TDD: 703-516-7227
info@nami.org
www.nami.org

The NAMI Convention is packed with information, chances to network, leadership development opportunities, and lots more.
Summer
Richele Keas, Senior Mgr, Media Relations

Audio Video

992 **Families Coping with Mental Illness**
Mental Illness Education Project
25 West Street
Westborough, MA 1581
USA

617-562-1111
800-343-5540
Fax: 617-779-0061
info@miepvideos.org
miepvideos.org

Ten family members share their experiences of having a family member with schizophrenia or bipolar disorder. Designed to provide insights and support to other families, the tape also profoundly conveys to professionals the needs of families when mental illness strikes. In two versions: a 22-minute version ideal for short classes and workshops, and a richer 43-minute version with more examples and details. Discounted price for families/consumers.
Video
Michael M Faenza, Executive Director

Web Sites

993 **Bipolar World**
www.bipolarworld.net

www.bipolarworld.net

A support and educational web site for individuals diagnosed with Bipolar Affective Disorder and for the families and friends who care for them.

994 **CyberPsych**
www.cyberpsych.org

www.cyberpsych.org

CyberPsych presents information about psychoanalysis, psychotherapy, and special topics such as anxiety disorder, the problematic use of alcohol, homophobia, and the traumatic effects of racism. CyberPsych is a nonprofit network which offers free web hosting and technical support for internet communication to nonprofit groups and individuals.
Carol Lindemann, Ph.D., Contact

995 **Internet Mental Health**
www.mentalhealth.com

www.mentalhealth.com

Our goal is to improve understanding, diagnosis, and treatment of mental illness throughout the world.
Phillip W. Long, M.D., Psychiatrist

996 **Mental Health Net**
P.O. Box 20709
Columbus, OH 43220

614-448-4055
info@centersite.net
www.mentalhelp.net

We wish to provide the following: to discuss, develop and debate in an open forum the future of the mental health field in America and throughout the world. To help coordinate various components of the mental health field so as to bring about greater communication between them.

Book Publishers

997 **Bipolar Disorders: A Guide to Helping Children & Adolescents**
O'Reilly and Associates
1005 Gravenstein Highway N
Sebastopol, CA 95472

707-827-7019
800-998-8969
Fax: 707-824-8268
patientguides@oreilly.com
www.patientcenters.com

A million children and adolescents in the US may have childhood-onset bipolar disorder, including an estimated 23 percent of those currently diagnosed with ADHD. Bipolar Disorders helps parents and professionals recognize, treat, and cope with bipolar disorders in children and adolescents. It covers diagnosis, family life, medications, talk therapies, other interventions (improving sleep patterns, diet, preventing seasonal mood swings), insurance and school.
1999 460 pages
ISBN: 1-565926-56-0

998 **Bipolar Puzzle Solutions**
Taylor & Francis
7625 Empire Drive
Florence, KT 41042

800-634-7064
Fax: 800-248-4724
orders@taylorandfrancis.com
www.taylorandfrancis.com

187 answers to questions asked by support group members about living with manic depressive illness.
ISBN: 1-560324-93-7

999 **Covert Modeling and Reinforcement**
New Harbinger Publications
5674 Shattuck Avenue
Oakland, CA 94609

510-652-0215
800-748-6273
Fax: 800-652-1613
customreservice@newharbinger.com
www.newharbinger.com

Audio programs based on our essential book of cognitive behavioral techniques for effecting change in your life, Thoughts & Feelings. Listeners learn step-by-step protocols for controlling destructive behaviors such anxiety, obessional thinking, uncontrolled anger, and depression.
ISBN: 0-934986-29-0

1000 **Touched with Fire-Manic Depressive Illness & the Artistic Temperament**
Free Press
866 3rd Avenue
New York, NY 10022
USA

212-832-2101
800-323-7445
Fax: 800-943-9831
www.simonsays.com

Describing and discussing the markedly increased rates of severe mood disorders and suicides among the artistically creative and the reasons why.
384 pages
ISBN: 0-684831-83-X

Pamphlets

1001 **Bipolar Disorder**
National Institutes of Health
9000 Rockville Pike
Bethesda, MD 20892

301-443-3706
Fax: 301-443-6349
www.nih.gov

Bipolar Disorder / Pamphlets

A short booklet offering a concise description of this disorder, which is also called manic-depressive illness.

Francis S. Collins, Director

1002 Child and Adolescent Bipolar Disorder
Child and Adolescent Bipolar Foundation
730 N. Franklin Street, Suite 501
Chicago, IL 60654
312-642-0049
Fax: 847-920-9498
www.thebalancedmind.org

To educate families, professsionals and the public about early onset bipolar disorder.

Julia Small, Staff Leader
Karen Cruise, Volunteer Leaders
Kathy Karle, Support Network Coordinator

1003 Mood Disorders
Center for Mental Health Services
PO Box 42557
Washington, DC 20015
800-789-2647
Fax: 240-747-5470
TDD: 866-889-2647
http://mentalhealth.samhsa.gov

This fact sheet provides basic information on the symptoms, formal diagnosis, and treatment for bipolar disorder.

3 pages

Description

1004 BRAIN TUMORS
Involves the following Biologic System(s):
Neurologic Disorders

Brain tumors are abnormal growths in or on the brain. They may be cancerous (malignant) or noncancerous (benign), and may be classified as primary tumors that arise directly from brain tissue or as secondary tumors, which are almost always malignant and have spread or metastasized to the brain from cancers in other parts of the body. By contrast, tumors that begin in the brain or spinal cord rarely spread to other parts of the body.

All types of brain tumors, whether they are primary tumors that begin within the brain or secondary tumors that spread to the brain, originate from aberrations or mutations in the genes of a cell, causing the cell to divide and replicate itself into the large numbers of identical cells that constitute a tumor.

Space-occupying benign tumors may also present complications resulting from increasing intracranial pressure. Symptoms and characteristic findings associated with brain tumors depend upon their location as well as their size and rate of growth. However, many symptoms are common to most types of brain tumors and may include recurrent or constant headache, irregularities of vision, difficulties in balance and the coordination of voluntary movements, muscle weakness, speech difficulties, and sometimes seizures. Nausea, vomiting, fever, and fluctuations in pulse rate, breathing rate, and blood pressure may be later and more foreboding manifestations. Although there are many different types of brain tumors, children are most commonly affected by primary tumors, especially those that develop toward the back of the brain (posterior fossa tumor).

The most common of the posterior fossa tumors in children is the cerebellar astrocytoma. This type of tumor may be fluid-filled (cystic) or relatively solid and may often have a low grade of malignancy. However, cerebellar astrocytomas may sometimes invade the fibers on each side of the cerebellum that connect with other areas of the brain as well as the spinal cord (cerebellar peduncles). Symptoms and findings may include an abnormal accumulation of cerebrospinal fluid, often under increased pressure, within the skull (hydrocephalus) that is characterized by an increase in head size in infants as well as irritability, vomiting, lethargy, irregular reflex action, and leg rigidity followed by drowsiness and seizures. Older children may have a headache and may vomit, lose coordination, and exhibit deteriorating mental capabilities. Effective treatment for low-grade cerebellar astrocytoma includes surgical removal. Radiation treatment may be indicated for children with cerebellar astrocytoma of high-grade malignancy or in children who exhibit evidence of tumor growth after surgery.

Medulloblastoma is the second most common of the posterior fossa tumors in children and, in children younger than seven years of age, is the most common brain tumor. This type of malignant tumor usually grows relatively fast and spreads to other parts of the brain, the spinal cord, and sometimes other areas of the body. Symptoms associated with medulloblastoma may include headache, recurrent vomiting, and frequent falling. Diagnosis is achieved through imaging studies such as magnetic resonance imaging (MRI) or computer tomography (CT scan) which give a detailed picture of the size and extent of the tumor. Treatment may include surgical excision. In addition, children older than four years of age may receive radiation therapy, especially if the tumor is small and has not yet spread. Children who have evidence of some remaining tumor growth after surgery and those whose tumor has spread may benefit from chemotherapy in addition to further surgery and radiation therapy. Due to the possibility of adverse effects on the brain, radiation is delayed in very young children with medulloblastoma.

Craniopharyngioma is a tumor that appears most often in children and adolescents, and arises from the pituitary, an endocrine gland that is located at the base of the skull. This type of tumor may sometimes interfere with pituitary gland and other endocrine functions as well as cause compression resulting in hydrocephalus and its associated symptoms. Other findings may include headache, vomiting, irregularities in vision, and short stature resulting from hormonal irregularities. Treatment for craniopharyngioma includes surgical excision. Additional treatment with radiation may be indicated for those children whose tumor is not able to be completely removed through surgery or who experience a recurrence. Subsequent to surgery, some children may develop such hormonal abnormalities as an underactive thyroid (hypothyroidism), growth hormone deficiency, diabetes insipidus, and other problems. Evaluation for these hormonal disorders is indicated and treatment is dependent upon the particular abnormality.

Government Agencies

1005 NIH/National Cancer Institute
Bethesda, MD 20892
800-422-6237
NCIinfo@nih.gov
www.cancer.gov

The National Cancer Institute coordinates the National Cancer Program, which conducts and supports research, training, health information dissemination, and other programs with respect to the cause, diagnosis, prevention, and treatment of cancer, rehabilitation from cancer, and the continuing care of cancer patients and the families of cancer patients.

Norman E. Sharpless, MD, Director
Douglas R. Lowy, MD, Principal Deputy Director

1006 NIH/National Institute of Neurological Disorders and Stroke (NINDS)
PO Box 5801
Bethesda, MD 20824
800-352-9424
www.ninds.nih.gov

Works to reduce the burden of neurological disease by conducting, fostering, coordinating and guiding research on the causes, prevention, diagnosis and treatment of neurological disorders and stroke, while supporting basic research in related scientific areas.

Walter J. Koroshetz, MD, Director

National Associations & Support Groups

1007 American Academy of Pediatrics
345 Park Blvd
Itasca, IL 60143
800-433-9016
Fax: 847-434-8000
mcc@aap.org
www.aap.org

The American Academy of Pediatrics and its member pediatricians are committed to the attainment of optimal physical, mental and social health and well-being for all infants, children, adolescents, and young adults.

Lynn Olson, PhD, VP, Research
Mark Del Monte, JD, CEO/Executive VP
Vera Tait, MD, FAAP, Chief Medical Officer

Brain Tumors / National Associations & Support Groups

1008 American Association for Cancer Research
615 Chestnut St., 17th Floor
Philadelphia, PA 19106
215-440-9300
aacr@aacr.org
www.aacr.org

Helps prevent and cure cancer through research, education, communication, and collaboration.

Margaret Foti, Chief Executive Officer

1009 American Association of Neurological Surgeons
5550 Meadowbrook Drive
Rolling Meadows, IL 60008
847-378-0500
888-566-2267
Fax: 847-378-0600
info@aans.org
www.aans.org

The AANS is dedicated to advancing the specialty of neurological surgery in order to promote the highest quality of patient care.

Kathleen T Craig, Chief Executive Officer

1010 American Brain Tumor Association
8550 W. Bryn Mawr Ave. Ste 550
Chicago, IL 60631
773-577-8750
800-886-2282
Fax: 773-577-8738
info@abta.org
www.abta.org

Services include over 10 publications which address brain tumors, their treatment, and coping with the disease. Materials address brain tumors in all age groups. Provides free social service consultations; a mentorship program for new brain tumor support group leaders; a nationwide database of established support groups; the Connections support program; networking with organizations that provide services to patients and families; a resource listing of physicians offering investigative treatments

Ralph DeVitto, President & CEO
Nicole Willmarth, PhD, Chief Mission Officer
Kelly Sitkin, Chief Development Officer

1011 American Cancer Society
3380 Chastain Meadows Parkway NW, Suite 200
Kennesaw, GA 30144
800-227-2345
www.cancer.org

The American Cancer Society is the leading cancer-fighting organization with a vision of ending cancer as we know it, for everyone. We are the only organization working to improve the lives of people with cancer and their families through advocacy, research, and patient support, to ensure everyone has an opportunity to prevent, detect, treat, and survive cancer.

Karen E Knudsen, Chief Executive Officer
William L Dahut, MD, Chief Scientific Officer
Kymm Martinez, Chief Marketing Officer

1012 American Childhood Cancer Organization
P.O. Box 498
Kensington, MD 20895
301-962-3520
855-858-2226
Fax: 310-962-3521
staff@acco.org
www.acco.org

The American Childhood Cancer Organization (ACCO) was founded in 1970 by a group of parents whose children had been diagnosed with cancer. Today ACCO is one of the largest grassroots, national organizations dedicated to improving the lives of children and adolescents with cancer and their families.

Ruth I. Hoffman, MPH, CEO
Krista Novak, Programs Manager
Blair Scroggs, Public Relations Coordinator

1013 Ben and Catherine Ivy Foundation
6710 N Scottsdale Road, Suite 235
Scottsdale, AZ 85253
480-659-9621
Fax: 480-659-9651
www.ivyfoundation.org

At the Ivy Foundation, the long-term, ultimate goal is to cure brain cancer.

Catherine E. Ivy, Founder and Board President
Stephanie A. McRae, Secretary
Megan Edwards, Treasurer

1014 CERN Foundation
PO Box 217
Zionsville, IL 46077
844-237-6674
administrator@cern-foundation.org
cern-foundation.org

the CERN Foundation is now a designated program of the National Brain Tumor Society dedicated to improving the lives of those affected with ependymoma. Thanks to the efforts of an international network of collaborators, the CERN Foundation has been responsible for the publication of over 50 peer-reviewed papers in leading medical journals. This body of research has greatly advanced our understanding of ependymoma and has left a lasting legacy for future investigators to build upon.

Kimberly Wallgren, Executive Director

1015 CancerCare
275 7th Avenue
New York, NY 10001
212-712-8400
800-813-4673
Fax: 212-712-8495
info@cancercare.org
www.cancercare.org

Dedicated to providing emotional support, information, and practical help to people with cancer and their loved ones. CancerCare is the oldest, largest, nonprofit agency devoted to offering professional services.

Patricia J Goldsmith, CEO
Christine Verini, RPh, COO

1016 Central Brain Tumor Registry of the United States
www.cbtrus.org

CBTRUS serves as a resource for gathering and disseminating current epidemiological data on all primary brain tumors. CBTRUS data are available to assist in research projects that intend to describe incidence and survival patterns of brain tumor cases, to evaluate diagnosis and treatment, and to conduct etiologic studies.

Carol Kruchko, President & Chief Mission Officer

1017 Child Neurology Foundation
601 W Short Street
Lexington, KY 40508
888-417-3435
info@childneurologyfoundation.org
childneurologyfoundation.org

The Child Neurology Foundation connects partners from all areas of the child neurology community so those navigating the journey of disease diagnosis, management, and care have the ongoing support from those dedicated to treatments and cures.

Amy Brin, Executive Director
Katie Hentges, Director, Programs
Brea McCormley, Director, Development

1018 Children's Brain Tumor Foundation
274 Madison Avenue Suite 1004
New York, NY 10016
866-228-4673
info@cbtf.org
www.cbtf.org

To improve the treatment, quality of life and the long term outlook for children with brain and spinal cord tumors through research.

Robert Budlow, President
Eric Snyder, Vice President
Miriam Barry, Secretary

1019 CureSearch for Children's Cancer
P.O. Box 45781
Baltimore, MD 21297
800-458-6223
Fax: 301-718-0047
info@curesearch.org
www.curesearch.org

CureSearch for Children's Cancer is a national non-profit foundation that accelerates the cure for children's cancer by driving innovation, eliminating research barriers and solving the field's most challenging problems.

Brain Tumors / National Associations & Support Groups

Kay Koehler, CEO
Katharine A. Burke, COO & VP, Financing
Caitlyn W. Barrett, National Director, Research & Prgms

1020 Cushing's Support and Research Foundation
csrf.net

404-791-5483
csrf.net

CSRF aims to provide information and support for Cushing's Disease and Cushing's Syndrome patients and their families; to increase awareness in the medical community and the general public about Cushing's Disease and Cushing's Syndrome; and to be a resource for information and support to health care professionals.

Louise Pace, Founder
Leslie Edwin, President
Elissa Kline, Treasurer & Director

1021 Glenn Garcelon Foundation
PO Box 3142
Coppell, TX 75019

503-969-7651
ggf@glenngarcelonfoundation.org
glenngarcelonfoundation.org

Exists to improve the quality of life of brain tumor survivors, caregivers and their families by providing emotional and financial support.

Gail Garcelon, President
Danielle Hess, Vice President
Nicole Smith, Secretary

1022 Healing Exchange Brain Trust
459 Broadway, Suite 302
Everett, MA 02149

877-252-8480
www.braintrust.org

The mission of The Healing Exchange Brain Trust is to improve quality of life for people living with brain tumors and related conditions.

Samantha J Scolamiero, President & Founding Director

1023 Hope for Hypothalamic Hamartomas
PO Box 941
Eagle, ID 83616

info@hopeforhh.org
hopeforhh.org

A volunteer-based nonprofit organization founded by parents of children with hypothalamic hamartomas.

Erica Webster, Co-Founder & President
Lisa Dunn Soeby, Co-Founder & Vice-President
Kimberly Ranson, Treasurer

1024 James S. McDonnell Foundation
1034 S. Brentwood Blvd. Suite 1850
St. Louis, MO 63117

314-721-1532
info@jsmf.org
www.jsmf.org

The James S. McDonnell Foundation is a St. Louis, Missouri based private philanthropic institution established in 1950 by aerospace pioneer James S. McDonnell to "improve the quality of life." It does so by contributing to the generation of new knowledge through support of research and scholarship, and by encouraging knowledge-based solutions to important societal issues, especially in the St. Louis region.

Jason Q. Purnell, President
M. Brent Dolezalek, Vice President of Operations
Sarah Paterson, Senior Program Officer

1025 Musella Foundation for Brain Tumor Research and Information
1100 Peninsula Blvd
Hewlett, NY 11557

888-295-4740
musella@virtualtrials.org
www.virtualtrials.com

Nonprofit public charity dedicated to helping brain tumor patients through emotional and financial support, education, advocacy and raising money for brain tumor research.

Al Musella, President

1026 National Association for Proton Therapy
PO Box 7801
McLean, VA 22106

202-919-4536
www.proton-therapy.org

The National Association for Proton Therapy (NAPT) is registered as an independent, non-profit, public benefit corporation providing education and awareness for the public, professional and governmental communities.

Jennifer Maggiore, Executive Director

1027 National Brain Tumor Society
55 Chapel Street, Suite 006
Newton, MA 02458

617-924-9997
www.braintumor.org

The Brain Tumor Society exists to find a cure for brain tumors. It strives to improve the quality of life of brain tumor patients and their families. It disseminates educational information and provides access to psychosocial support. It raises funds to advance carefully selected scientific research projects, improve clinical care and find a cure.

David F Arons, JD, President & CEO
Katie Germain, Chief Marketing Officer
Dorothy Whalen, CPA, CGMA, MBA, Chief Financial Officer

1028 National Children's Cancer Society
500 North Broadway, Suite 1850
St Louis, MO 63102

314-241-1600
800-532-6459
Fax: 314-241-1996
www.thenccs.org

The National Children's Cancer Society (NCCS) provides emotional, financial and educational support to children with cancer, their families and survivors.

Mark Stolze, President & CEO
Julie Komanetsky, VP Patient & Family Services

1029 National Comprehensive Cancer Network
3025 Chemical Road, Suite 100
Plymouth Meeting, PA 19462

215-690-0300
Fax: 215-690-0280
www.nccn.org

Devoted to patient care, research, and education, is dedicated to improving the quality, effectiveness, and efficiency of cancer care so that patients can live better lives.

Robert W. Carlson, MD, Chief Executive Officer
Gary J. Weyhmuller, Executive VP & COO
Wui-Jin Koh, MD, Senior VP & Chief Medical Officer

1030 Nevus Outreach
361 Southwest Drive, Suite 353
Jonesboro, AR 72404

501-500-1932
www.nevus.org

Nevus Outreach is dedicated to improving awareness and providing support for people affected by congenital melanocytic nevi and finding a cure.

Lauren Isbell, Chief Executive Officer

1031 Pediatric Brain Tumor Foundation
6065 Roswell Road NE, Suite 505
Atlanta, GA 30328

800-253-6530
Fax: 404-252-4108
www.curethekids.org

Since 1991, the Pediatric Brain Tumor Foundation's family support, research funding, and advocacy have led the way in ending the childhood cancer community's biggest crisis: pediatric brain tumors. Dedicated wholly to addressing this rare but devastating disease and guided by the experiences of patients, survivors, their parents, and siblings, we are the only organization to meet families' needs along every step of their cancer journey.

Courtney Davies, President & CEO
Geoff Still, Chief Financial & Operating Officer
Ian Joyce, Chief Marketing Officer

Brain Tumors / State Agencies & Support Groups

1032 **Pituitary Network Association**
P.O. Box 1958
Thousand Oaks, CA 91358
805-499-9973
Fax: 805-480-0633
info@pituitary.org
www.pituitary.org

The PNA is an international non-profit organization for patients with pituitary tumors and disorders, their families, loved ones, and the physicians and health care providers who treat them.

Jackie Hubbard, Executive Director & President

1033 **Preuss Foundation**
2223 Avenida de la Playa, Suite 220
La Jolla, CA 92037
858-454-0200
www.thepreussfoundation.org

The goal of the foundation is to provide forums for medical researchers, leading to an increase in communication and collaboration among them. To facilitate this goal, The Preuss Foundation holds a series of research communication seminars in specific fields of scientific investigation. These seminars are designed to enhance future directions of research through communication, and to be a catalyst for new collaborations among its participants.

1034 **Society for NeuroOncology**
PO Box 273296
Houston, TX 77277
713-526-0269
caroline@soc-neuro-onc.org
www.soc-neuro-onc.org

Multi-disciplinary organization dedicated to promoting advances in neuro-oncology through research and education.

J. Charles Haynes, JD, Executive Director
Shelley Pressley, Director of Administration
Gabrielle Griffin, Marketing/Communications Specialist

1035 **Sontag Foundation**
816 A1A North, Suite 201
Ponte Verda Beach, FL 32082
904-273-8755
info@sontagfoundation.org
sontagfoundation.org

The Sontag Foundation is dedicated to advancing brain cancer research by investing in brilliant scientists who are committed to the pursuit of bold, innovative, and transformative ideas.

Hilary Keeley, Executive Director
Shandra Koler, Senior Program Officer
Carlos Granados, Director of Finance

1036 **Students Supporting Brain Tumor Research**
8390 E. Via de Ventura, F-110
Scottsdale, AZ 85258
844-840-4465
www.ssbtr.org

Students Supporting Brain Tumor Research (SSBTR) is about creating future leaders and team players among our young people. It is about stimulating their interest in philanthropy and selfless giving. It is about connecting with and supporting their friends and classmates who are currently in the process of fighting brain tumors and often struggling for their lives.

1037 **Tug McGraw Foundation**
100 California Drive
Yountville, CA 94599
707-947-7124
707-676-4398
info@tugmcgraw.org
www.tugmcgraw.org

To provide resources and hands-on support, foster understanding, promote awareness, and stimulate research.

Tom Higgins, Chair
Jennifer Brusstar, President & CEO
Tim McGraw, Honorary Chair

State Agencies & Support Groups

Alabama

1038 **Pediatric Brain Tumor Support Group**
Children's Hospital
1600 7th Avenue S
Birmingham, AL 35233
205-939-9090
Fax: 205-939-9010
info@braintumorkids.org
www.braintumorkids.org

Groups for parents and siblings of brain tumor patients. Related to Children's Hospital of Alabama. Babysitting available.

Pamela B Ellis, President
Robert Flamini MD, Vice President
William A Guzak, Treasurer

Arizona

1039 **Brain Tumor Support Group at NovaCare Rehabilitation Institute of Tucson**
2650 N Wyatt Drive
Tucson, AZ 85712
520-293-8040
www.tmcaz.com

Scott Gulbrandsen

1040 **Brain Tumor Support Group at Phoenix**
350 W Thomas Road
Phoenix, AZ 85013
602-873-2757
www.braintumorsupportgroup.com/hospital/children/pho

The Jaydie Lynn King Neuro-oncology Program at Phoenix Children's Hospital is the only comprehensive pediatric program of its kind in Arizona, combining the expertise of subspecialists in the Children's Neuroscience Institute and the Center for Cancer and Blood Disorders (CCBD).

Steve Westerhoff

California

1041 **Brain Tumor Patient & Family Support Group**
Saint Jude Medical Center
2151 N Harbor Blvd, St Jude Medical Plaza, Rm 2266
Fullerton, CA 92635
714-446-7182
www.stjudemedicalcenter.org

Periodic guest presentations.

Robert Merlino

1042 **Brain Tumor Support Group at Newport Beach**
301 Newport Blvd.
Newport Beach, CA 92658
949-760-2350
www.bettyclooneyfoundation.org

Speakers once a month, education materials available.

Kris O'Neal

1043 **Brain Tumor Support Group at San Diego**
8555 Aero Drive #340
San Diego, CA 92103
858-467-1065
www.bettyclooneyfoundation.org

Speakers once a month, education materials available.

Donna Gilpatrick RN, MS, FNP

1044 **Brain Tumor Support Group at San Luis Obispo**
1911 Johnson Avenue
San Luis Obispo, CA 93401
805-461-3989
www.bettyclooneyfoundation.org

Speakers once a month, education materials available.

Becky Nunez

Brain Tumors / State Agencies & Support Groups

1045 Brain Tumor Support Group at Santa Monica
2200 Colorado Boulevard
Santa Monica, CA 90404   310-453-2200
www.bettyclooneyfoundation.org

Speakers once a month, education materials available.
Michael Slater, Program Director

1046 Brain Tumor Support Program Cedars-Sinai Neurosurgical Inst. & Wellness Communit
8631 W 3rd Street, Suite 800 E
Los Angeles, CA 90048   310-855-7900
Fax: 310-423-0777
www.bettyclooneyfoundation.org

Last Wednesday of month 6-7:30 pm with an RSVP.
Jennice Vilhauer, Contact

1047 Inland Empire Brain Tumor Support Group
Medical Annex Building
Riverside Community Hospital, 4445 Magnolia Avenue
Riverside, CA 92502   951-222-8090
http://events.pe.com/riverside-ca

Meets third Saturday, once a month.
Sue Melton, Contact

1048 Neuroscience Institute Brain Tumor Support Group
637 S Lucas Avenue, Suite 501
Los Angeles, CA 90017   213-977-2234
800-762-1692
www.mhmni.com/support/

The group meets the second Wednesday of every month at 6 p.m. in the Heart & Vascular Institute, 3rd floor, conference room A.
Cherrie Valacruz, Manager

1049 Northridge Hospital: Leavey Cancer Center
18300 Roscoe Boulevard
Northridge, CA 91328   818-885-5431
www.northridgehospital.org

We are fully-accredited by the American College of Surgeons Commission on Cancer as a Comprehensive Cancer Center since 1980.
Marylou Perelmutter, Manager

1050 Palo Alto Brain Tumor Support Group
920 Bryant Street, 2nd Floor Room B
Palo Alto, CA 94301   415-284-0208
www.pamf.org

Joanie Taylor, RN

1051 Peninsula Support & Education Group for Parents of Children with Brain Tumors
3041 Olcott
Santa Clara, CA 95054   650-325-4523
www.supportforfamilies.org

Sheri Sobrato, MA, MFC

1052 Sacramento Area Brain Tumor Support Group Lawrence J Ellison Ambulatory Care Ctr
UC Davis Medical Center, Camellia Cottage
4860 Y Street Suite 3740
Sacramento, CA 95817   916-734-3658
Fax: 916-703-5368
kksmith@ucdavis.edu
www.ucdmc.ucdavis.edu/neurosurg/contactus/contact_in

First Thursday of month 6:30-8:30 pm.
J. Paul . Muizelaar, M.D., Ph.D, Program Director
James E Boggan MD, Professor and Acting Chair
Kee D Kim MD, Associate Professor

1053 San Francisco Brain Tumor Support Group
UC San Francisco, Clinical Sciences Building
521 Parnassus Avenue, Room C130
San Francisco, CA 94188   415-990-4461
mary.lovely@sbcglobal.net
www.ucsfhealth.org/support_groups/neurology/

First Wednesday of each month, 7:00 - 8:30 pm
Sharon Lamb, Contact
Mary Lovely, Contact

1054 Vital Options
4419 Coldwater Canyon Ave., Suite I
Studio City, CA 91604   818-508-5657
Fax: 818-788-5260
info@vitaloptions.org
www.vitaloptions.org

Vital Options International is a 501(c)(3) not-for-profit cancer communications organization with a mission, to facilitate a global cancer dialogue
Selma R Schimmel, CEO and Founder
Derek Alpert, President
Terry Merrill Wilcox, Creative Director and Supervising P

1055 Wellness Community San Francisco/East Bay
3276 McNutt Avenue
Walnut Creek, CA 94597   925-933-0107
Fax: 925-933-0249
www.twc-bayarea.org

To help people affected by cancer enhance their health and well-being through participation in a professional program of emotional support, education, and hope.
James R Bouquin, Executive Director
Margaret Stauffer MFT, Program Director
Amy Alanes, Development Manager

Florida

1056 Angels in the Sun Brain Tumor Support Group
3251 Proctor Road
Sarasota, FL 34231   941-364-9105
www.braintumorkids.org

Anna Browder
Jeffrey Kolodin, Chair
Michael Nathanson, Vice Chair

1057 Cancer Support Group for Children
3501 Johnson Street, 4th Floor
Hollywood, FL 33021   954-987-2000
www.ped-onc.org/resources/supportorg.html

Sub-groups for children with brain tumors and their parents. Contact at ext. 4193.
Suzanne Baxter RN

1058 South Florida Brain Tumor Association Lynn Regional Cancer Center
Boca Raton Community Hospital
800 Meadows Road, Education Center
Boca Raton, FL 33486   561-955-7100
561-955-5897
www.brrh.com/Cancer_Institute.aspx

Neuropsychologist Dr. Laurence Miller and therapist Marjorie O'Sullivan are present to facilitate the meetings. Second and Fourth Thursdays of each month, 7:30-8:30 pm.
Jerry Fedele, President and Chief Executive Offic
Karen Poole, FACHE, Vice President, Chief Operating Off
Dawn P Javersack, Vice President and Chief Financial

Georgia

1059 All Ages Support Group
1835 Savoy Drive, Suite 316
Atlanta, GA 30341   770-458-5554
btfc@bellsouth.net
www.braintumorkids.org

Contact for details.
Mary Campbell, Contact

123

Brain Tumors / State Agencies & Support Groups

1060 Brain Tumor Foundation for Children
6065 Roswell Road NE, Suite 505
Atlanta, GA 30328
404-252-4107
Fax: 404-252-4108
www.braintumorkids.org

The mission of the Brain Tumor Foundation for Children is to provide financial assistance, social support, and information for families of children with brain and spinal cord tumors; fund research projects that improve treatment options and search for a cure; and raise public awareness of the disease and advocate on behalf of children who are affected.

Pamela B Ellis, President
Robert Flamini MD, Vice President
William A Guzak, Treasurer

1061 Southeastern Brain Tumor Foundation Brain Tumor Support Group
Wellness Community, Peachtree Dunwoody Pavillion
PO Box 422471
Atlanta, GA 30342
404-843-3700
info@sbtf.org
www.sbtf.org/home.html

Second Monday of each month, 7:00-8:30 pm.

Costas G. Hadjipanayis, MD, PhD, President
Jennifer Keenan Giliberto, Vice President
Suzanne Boeren, Treasurer

Idaho

1062 Treasure Valley Brain Injury Support Group
Idaho Elks Rehabilitation Hospital
600 North Robbins Road
Boise, ID 83702
208-489-4558
bjaundalderis@elksrehab.org
www.idahoelksrehab.org

Through our expertise in rehab and uncompromising commitment to care, education and research, we help you live life to its fullest. Fourth Tuesday of each month 7:00-9:00 pm.

Bob Jaundalderis, Marketing Director
Katie McCurdy, Brain Injury Program Director

Illinois

1063 Parents of Children with Brain Tumors (PCBT)
Children's Memorial Hospital
2300 Children's Plaza
Chicago, IL 60614
773-880-4553
www.cbtrf.org/

Monthly newsletter. Library available at meetings (at CMH). Educational speakers and family functions. Call to confirm meetings.

Teresa Berry, Contact

Indiana

1064 Primary Brain Cancer Support Group
Women's Cancer Center at Lutheran Hospital
7910 W Jefferson Boulevard, Suite 112
Fort Wayne, IN 46804
260-435-7959
www.cancercenter.com/

First Tuesday of every month, 6:00 pm.

Linda Jordan RN, Contact

Kentucky

1065 Brain Injury Support Group
2050 Versailles Road
Lexington, KY 40504
859-254-5701
www.braininjuryguide.org/braininjurysupportgroups.ht

First Thursday of each month at 6:00 pm. Meeting will be held in Conference Room A or B in the Center of Learning.

Tonia Wells, Contact

Louisiana

1066 Brain Injury Support And Education Group
Touro Infirmary
1401 Foucher Street
New Orleans, LA 70115
504-897-7011
www.touro.com

Second and fourth Wednesday and families are every Third Monday. Offers outreach programs for survivors of brain injuries as well as their family members and caregivers.

Ruth Kullman, Chair
Hugh W Long, Vice Chairman
Joy Braun, Treasurer

1067 Brain Injury Support Group
West Jefferson Medical Center
1101 Medical Center Boulevard 4th Floor Rehab
Marrero, LA 70072
504-349-6396
www.biala.org/support-groups-1

Second Wednesday, 2:00 pm.

Tammy , Contact

1068 Tlane Cancer Center
1430 Tulane Avenue, SL-68
New Orleans, LA 70112
504-988-6592
Fax: 504-988-6077
mcross@tulane.edu
www.tulane.edu/som/cancer/cancer-center-history.cfm

Every other Wednesday, 6-8 pm.

Melanie N Cross, Contact

Maine

1069 Open Support Group-All Kinds of Cancer Care of Maine
489 State Street
Bangor, ME 04401
207-973-7000
877-366-3662
www.emmc.org/splash_cancercareofmaine.aspx

Wednesdays at 10:30 AM - 12 Noon. For families and patients.

Liane Judd, Chair

Maryland

1070 Brain Tumor Networking Group
410-832-2719

Fourth Monday of each month, 7:00-8:30 pm.

Carol Sharp, Contact

1071 Johns Hopkins Brain Tumor Education Group
Weinberg Building
Phipps Building, Room 123 600 N. Wolfe Street
Baltimore, MD 21287
410-614-1627
Fax: 410-502-4954
mlim3@jhmi.edu

First Wednesday of the month, 10:30-11:30 am. All are welcome at this group. Each meeting includes a speaker followed by discussion.

Dr Michael Lim, Contact

Massachusetts

1072 Brain Center Brain Tumor Support Group
Promontory Point
Mashpee, MA 02649
508-477-5300

Last Sunday of each month, 3:00 pm. Call to confirm.

Eleanor Grace, Contact
Dick Grace, Contact

Brain Tumors / State Agencies & Support Groups

1073 Brain Tumor Support Group
Dana Farber Cancer Center
Dana Building, 16th Floor, Room D-1635
Boston, MA 02155
617-632-3769
617-732-6826

First and Third Thursday of each month, 12:00-1:30 pm. Free parking is available in the Smith Garage at Dana Farber.

Nancy Olson RN, MBA, Contact
Genevieve Mason LCSW, Contact

1074 Brain Tumor Support Group at Burlington
Lahey Clinic Medical Center
Cancer Center, 3W Conference Room Lahey Hospital &
Burlington, MA 01805
781-744-8113

First and Third Monday of each month, 7:00-9:00 pm. 5 Central Clinic Conference Room.

Pam Reznick LICSW, Contact

1075 Brain Tumor Support Group at Worcester
University of Massachusetts Medical Center
Dept of Surgery Waiting Area, 55 Lake Avenue N
Worcester, MA 01655
508-334-3515

This group meets for 2 hours once a month and occasionally has speakers. Second Tuesday of every month, 6:00-8:00 pm.

Alexis Van Horn RN, Contact

1076 Brain Tumor Survivor Support Group
196 Main Street
Andover, MA 01810
617-543-1709
ddemella@hotmail.com

Second Saturday of the month, 10:00 am - 12 Noon. This is a Mutual Help support group that is peer led. It is an informal opportunity to share experiences, information, resources, and challenges as we learn to LIVE with brain tumors.

Debbie DeMella, Contact

1077 Parent Education/Support Group
Dana Farber Cancer Institute, Smith Family Room
44 Binney Street Yawkey 306
Boston, MA 02115
617-632-3578
617-632-4386

For parents of children with brain tumors. Call for details.

Kelly Birdsey, Contact
Laura Myerburg, LICSW, Contact
Nancy Bailey, RN, Contact

Michigan

1078 Brain Tumor Networking Club
Gilda's Club Metropolitan Center
Gilda's Club 3517 Rochester Road
Royal Oak, MI 48073
248-577-0800
Fax: 248-577-0898
www.gildasclubdetroit.org/

Second Monday of each month 6:00-8:00 pm.

Christin Bernat, Contact

1079 Brain Tumor Support Group
Henry Ford Hospital
6777 West Maple
West Bloomfield, MI 48322
313-916-1796

Third Saturday of each month, 10:00 am - 12 Noon. Call for location.

Sandy Remer, Contact

1080 Brain Tumor Support Group at Ann Arbor
St Joseph Mercy Hospital, Cancer Care Center
5301 E Huron River Drive
Ann Arbor, MI 48106
734-712-3658

Fourth Tuesday of each month, 7:00-8:30 pm.

Paula Nedela RN, Contact

1081 Brain Tumor Support Group for Patients & Families: University of Michigan Med Ctr
De Jong Neuro-Oncology Library, Taubman Ctr
1500 E Medical Center Dr, Reception Area C, 1st Lv
Ann Arbor, MI 48109
734-647-8906

Third Tuesday of each month, 7:00-8:30 pm.

Michaelyn Page MS RN OCN CNS, Contact

1082 Spectrum Brain Tumor Support Group
Spectrum Health East
1840 Wealthy SE
Grand Rapids, MI 49506
616-774-7278

Second Monday of each month, 7:00-9:00 pm.

Nancy Rude, Contact

1083 West Michigan Cancer Center Support Group
Lower Level Resource Room
200 North Park Street
Kalamazoo, MI 49007
269-373-7442
TTY: 269-382-2500
helpdesk@wmcc.org
www.wmcc.org

First Thursday of each month, 2:30-4:00 pm. Call to confirm.

Linda Diane Grossheim, Contact

Minnesota

1084 Abbott Northwestern Brain Tumor Support Group at Abbott Northwestern Hospital
800 East 28th Street
Minneapolis, MN 55407
612-863-4996

Second and Fourth Thursday of each month, 5:30-8:00 pm. Call to verify time.

Kathy Gilliland RN, Contact
Margaret Callan, Contact

1085 Brain Injury Support Group at Abbott Northwestern Hospital
Abbott Northwestern Board Room 1st Floor
800 East 28th Street
Minneapolis, MN 55407
612-863-4996
susan.newman@allinia.com

Second Wednesday of the month, 6:30-8:00 pm. This group has speakers that address group concerns. New members always welcome.

Sue Newman, Contact

1086 Brain Tumor Support Group at Duluth
St Mary's Medical Center
407 E 3rd Street, Michiras Room
Duluth, MN 55805
218-726-4230

Third Monday of the month at 6:30 pm.

Jan Stevens RN, Contact

1087 Brain Tumor Support Group at Robbinside
North Memorial Medical Center North Ed Ctr
3300 Oakdale Avenue N
Robbinside, MN 55422
612-520-5158

Facilitated by Radiation RN, social worker, rehab staff, chaplain and physician. Third Wednesday of each month, 7:00-8:30 pm.

Judy Zak, Contact

1088 Brain Tumor Support Group at United Hospital
St Luke's Room, Conference B & C
255 North Smith Avenue
Saint Paul, MN 55102
651-241-8575

Second Monday each month, 7:00-8:30 pm.

Kathy Maiers, Contact
Cathy Maiers RN, Contact

Brain Tumors / State Agencies & Support Groups

1089 Non-Malignant Brain Tumor Support Group
800 East 28th Street
Minneapolis, MN 55407 — 612-775-4681
Second Thursday, 7:00-8:30 pm.
Jerry , Contact

Missouri

1090 AMOR - A Cancer Support Group for Patients & Their Families
Brain Tumor Institute of Kansas City
2316 E Meyers Boulevard, Dining Room 3
Kansas City, MO 64132 — 816-235-5960
Every other Wednesday, 2:00-3:00 pm.
Peggy Smith MS, RN, Contact

1091 Brain Cancer Support Group at Mid-America Cancer Center
Saint John's Regional Health Center
2055 S Fremont, Room 116, 1st Floor
Springfield, MO 65804 — 417-885-3324
800-432-2273
Fax: 417-888-8761
Primary and metastatic brain tumors; patients, families, and friends welcome. Second and Fourth Tuesday of each month, 2:00-3:30 pm. Light refreshments provided.
Connie Zimmerman, Contact

1092 Brain Tumor Support Group
Saint Luke's Hospital of Kansas City
44th & Wornall Road, Spencer Bldg, 2nd Floor
Kansas City, MO 64141 — 816-932-6220
Educational materials, telephone help line, newsletter, lectures, bereavement support group. Second Tuesday of each month, 7:00-8:30 pm.

1093 Brain Tumor Support Group of Greater St Louis
The Wellness Community of Greater St Louis
Cancer Support Community, 1058 Old Des Peres Road
Saint Louis, MO 63131 — 314-238-2000
Third Thursday of each month, 6:30-8:30 pm.
Amy Eilers MSW LCSW, Program Director

Nebraska

1094 Brain Tumor Support Group at the Nebraska Medical Center
981130 Nebraska Medical Center
Omaha, NE 68198 — 402-559-4420
800-922-0000
www.nebraskamed.com/neuro/brain-spine-cancer-center/
Meets monthly. Call for more information. Please contact the Social Work Department at The Nebraska Medical Center for further information regarding this monthly support group.
Sue Stensland, Contact

Nevada

1095 Southern Nevada 'Grey Matters' Valley Hospital Medical Center
Medical Executive Conference Room
620 Shadow Lane
Las Vegas, NV 89106 — 702-204-1907
Third Tuesday of each month, 5:30-7:00 pm.
Janet Leinen RN, Contact

New Hampshire

1096 Angels of Hope
Derry Public Library
64 East Broadway
Derry, NH 03038 — 603-425-2822
Second Monday of each month, 5:30-7:00 pm. Downstairs in the Paul Collette Conference Room A.
Urszula Mansur, Contact

New Jersey

1097 Brain Tumor Support Group
Saint Barnabas Medical Center
PO Box 221
Martinsville, NJ 08836 — 908-685-0917
sshrodo@optonline.net
www.njbt.org/startCNJBTSG.cfm
Third Wednesday of each month, 6:30-8:00 pm.
Stan , Contact
Virginia , Contact

1098 Brain Tumor Support Group at Plainfield Muhlenberg Medical Center, Neuroscience
Saint Luke's Roman Catholic Church
300 Clinton Avenue
North Plainfield, NJ 07063 — 732-321-7000
sshrodo@optonline.net
www.njbt.org/startCNJBTSG.htm
First Thursday of each month, 7:00-8:30 pm.
Stan , Contact
Virginia Shrodo, Contact

New Mexico

1099 NM Alliance for the Neurologically Impaired
531 Harkle Road, Suite B
Santa Fe, NM 87505 — 505-992-3126
505-670-0274
traumatic brain injury program but no support group.
Terry Lucero, Contact

1100 People Living Through Cancer
3411 Candelaria Rd. NE Suite M
Albuquerque, NM 87107 — 505-242-3263
888-441-4439
Fax: 505-242-6756
info@pltc.org
www.pltc.org
To connect and support cancer survivors and caregivers by transforming shared individual experiences into enduring hope.
Kathleen Raskob, Executive Committee Chair/President
Nancy Hoing, Vice-President
Sara J Lynch, Treasurer

New York

1101 Brain Tumor Support Group
Albany Medical Center
47 New Scotland Avenue, D Building, Room D105
Albany, NY 12208 — 518-262-6696
First Monday of the month, 5:30-7:30 pm.
Susan Weaver MD, Contact

1102 Brain Tumor Support Group at South Nassau Community Hospital
One Healthy Way
Oceanside, NY 11572 — 516-632-3310
maddybrisman@aol.com

Brain Tumors / State Agencies & Support Groups

Third Wednesday of each month at 7:00 pm. We have just started this support group. We welcome patients, family members, and friends to join us and share feelings, concerns, and wuestions about brain tumors and treatments available.

Maddy Singer CSW, Contact
Kathy Garizio RN, Contact

1103 Long Island Adult Brain Tumor Support Group
Plainview-Old Bethpage Public Library
999 Old Country Road
Plainview, NY 11803
516-747-8749
bcrescenzo@lancer-ins.com

First Thursday of the month, 7:00-9:00 pm, but call for information.

Bob Crescenzo, Contact

1104 Making Headway Foundation-Family Support Program
115 King Street
Chappaqua, NY 10514
914-238-8384
Fax: 914-238-1693
info@makingheadway.org
www.makingheadway.org

Call for scheduling. Dedicated to the Care, Comfort and Cure of Children with Brain and Spinal Cord Tumors. The program offers free, short-term individual counseling and educational remediational services.

Edward Manley, President
Catherine Lepone, Executive Director
Linda Mudford-Lewis, Administrator

1105 New York Brain Tumor Support Group
525 East 68th Street, Room 5-106
New York, NY 10021
212-746-3986
wem9011@nyp.org

First Wednesdady of the month, 6:00 pm. Open to patients with brain tumors of any kind and their families, caregivers, and friends.

Wendy Mitchell LMSW, Contact

1106 People Treated for Brain Tumors and Their Caregivers
Memorial Sloan-Kettering Cancer Center
Rockefeller Research Lab, 430 East 67th Street
New York, NY 10065
212-717-3527

Fourth Wednesday of each month, 6:00-7:30 pm.

Clarissa Potter, Contact

1107 Support for Parents of Children with Brain Tumors, Siblings and Young Adults
19 E 88 Street, Suite 1D
New York, NY 10128
212-534-8877

Call for specific times.

Marcia Greenleaf MD, Contact

1108 WNY Brain Tumor Support Group
3980 Sheriddan Drive
Amherst, NY 14226
716-250-2000

Third Tuesday of the month, 6:30 pm. This group has been in existence since 2000(We also facilitate the Orchard Park, NY group). We have at least 3 speakers a year, usually doctors, and we focus on positive ways to sope with living with a brain tumor or caring for a loved one with a brain tumor.

Maria Caserta, Contact

North Carolina

1109 Brain Tumor Support Group of the Carolinas and Virginia Cancer Services
Wake Forest University-Baptist Medical Center
Wake Forest University Baptist Medical Center/Canc
Winston-Salem, NC 27157
336-716-4137
www.wfubmc.edu

Second Tuesday of each month, 6:30-8:00 pm.

Rayetta Johnson RN, MSN, Contact

1110 Duke Brain Tumor Support Group
Duke University Medical Center
3000 Erwin Road
Durham, NC 27710
919-681-1687
calho006@mc.duke.edu

First Wednesday of the month, 3:00-4:00 pm.

Roberta Calhoun-Eagan LCSW, Clinical Social Worker

1111 Duke Pediatric Brain Tumor Family Support Program
Duke University Medical Center
Durham, NC 27710
919-684-2913

First and Third Tuesday, Second and Fourth Thursday, 12:00-1:00 pm. Teen group meets on the 1st Thursday of the month from 5:00-6:30 pm.

Jean Hartford-Todd, Contact

1112 Western North Carolina Brain Tumor Support Group
West Asheville Presbyterian Church
West Presbyterian Church 690 Haywood Road
Asheville, NC 28806
828-253-0726
wncbt@cs.com

Third Thursday of each month, 6:15-8:00 pm. We will have guest speakers occasionally. This group os for adults and their caregivers/family. Please call for location and details. Refreshments provided.

George Plym, Contact

Ohio

1113 Brain Tumor Support Group
Cleveland Clinic Foundation
9500 Euclid Avenue, Conference Room R3-003
Cleveland, OH 44101
216-445-6910
800-223-2273
Fax: 216-444-9170

Fourth Wednesday of each month, 5:00-6:30 pm.

Kathy Lupica RN, MSN, Contact

1114 Central Ohio Brain Tumor Support Group
Arthur James Cancer Hospital & Research Institute
4918 Cooper Road
Cincinnati, OH 45242
513-791-4060
bcrawford@cancer-support.org

Call for times.

Bonnie Crawford

1115 Cleveland Brain Tumor Patient Network - Adult and Pediatric
Univ Hospitals of Cleveland, Neurosurgery Conf Rm
2065 Abington, Lakeside Room, 5218
Cleveland, OH 44101
216-932-8510
info@clevlandclinic.org
www.clevlandclinic.org

This group does not currently meet, but does offer support through networking. Please call and leave a message.

Lynn Szakacs, Contact

1116 Southwest Ohio Brain Tumor Support Group
Kettering Hospital
3535 Southern Boulevard, Dining Room 2B
Dayton, OH 45429
937-687-3325
937-298-4331

Second Monday each month, 7:00-8:30 pm.

Darlene Carroll, Contact
Jean Ruppert, Contact

1117 Support Group for Parents of Children with a Brain Tumor
Children's Hospital Medical Center
Cincinnati, OH 45229
513-559-4726

Call for specific times.

Karen Burkett CNS, Contact
Susan Mcgee CNS, Contact

Brain Tumors / State Agencies & Support Groups

Oregon

1118 Bend Support Group
St Charles Medical Center
St. Charles Medical Center MS Support Group 2500 N
Bend, OR 97701   541-617-2617

Second Saturday of every month.

1119 Brain Tumor Education & Support Group
Comprehensive Cancer Center
1130 NW 22nd Avenue, 2nd Floor, Conference Room#21
Portland, OR 97210   503-413-7921

First and Third Wednesday of each month, 4:00-5:30 pm. Parking is available in the garage #3-enter between NW 21st and NW 22nd on NW Marshall.

Dawn Brucker LCSW, Contact

1120 Klamath Falls Support Group
2200 Eldorado Ave
Klamath Falls, OR 97601   541-274-2696
                                        www.spokeunlimited.org

Third week of every month. Meets at the office, with a monthly fliar, and focuses on traumatic brain injuries.

Cornelea Coffman, Contact

Pennsylvania

1121 Brain Tumor Support Group at Philadelphia
Hospital of University of Pennsylvania Hospital
3400 Spruce Street, 1 Rhoads Conference Room
Philadelphia, PA 19104   215-746-7742

Third Tuesday of each month, 6:30-8:00 pm.

Stacy Oppleman, Contact

1122 Brain Tumor Support Group at Pittsburgh
4117 Liberty Avenue- Bloomfield Center
Pittsburgh, PA 15224   412-522-1212
                                        Fax: 412-622-1216
                                        info@cancercaring.org
                                        www.cancercaring.org

Brain tumor group offered for aduly patients and family members.

Judy Joyce, Contact

1123 Camelot For Children
Pediatric Cancer Foundation of the Lehigh Valley
2354 W Emmaus Ave
Allentown, PA 18103   610-791-5683
                                        Fax: 610-791-5256
                                        www.camelotforchildren.org

Mission Statement: The mission of Camelot for Children, Inc., a non-profit organization, is to be a gathering place for seriously, chronically, and terminally ill, handicapped or disabled children; to foster an environment of emotional support among these special children and their families; to provide opportunities for these special children to interact with each other in a family/home setting; and to help to develop their physical and mental abilities. Fourth Tuesday of each month at 6:30 pm.

Jo Ellen Moll, Executive Director
Cassie Kemmerer, Volunteer Coordinator

Rhode Island

1124 Brain Tumor Support Group at Providence
Brown University Campus
Brown University Biomedical Center
Providence, RI 02940   401-789-0126
                                              401-647-2935

First and Third Tuesday of each month, 6:30-8:00 pm.

Judy Allenson, Contact
Betty Bentley, Contact

South Carolina

1125 Newberry County Memorial Hospital Brain Tumor Support Group
2669 Kinard Street, Education Room
Newberry, SC 29108   803-276-7570
                                        info@newberryhospital.org
                                        www.angelfire.com/sc2/sctumor/

First Thursday of each month, 7:00-8:30 pm.

Joel S Sexton, Contact

Tennessee

1126 Memphis Regional Brain Tumor Survivors Group
Colonial Park United Methodist Church
Colonial Park United Methodist Church 5330 Park Av
Memphis, TN 38119   901-757-0806
                                        www.semmes-murphey.com/support_group.php

First THursday of every month at 6:30 pm.

Cherry Welborn, Contact

Texas

1127 Brain Tumor Support Group at Dallas
American Cancer Society
8900 Carpenter Freeway
Dallas, TX 75247   214-977-7969

Second Wednesday of each month, 7:00-8:30 pm.

Alice Anderson, Contact

1128 Brain Tumor Support Group at Plano
Health South Rehab Hospital
PO Box 867084
Plano, TX 75086   972-335-4948
                                              972-867-3431
                                        GreyMattersNorthTexas@yahoo.com
                                        www.greymatters.us

Second Tuesday of each month, 7:00-9:00 pm.

J Hoffman, CEO
S. Kuryla, President
P Griffith, Treasurer

1129 Central Texas Brain Tumor Support Group
Health South Rehab Hospital
1215 Red River Street
Austin, TX 78701   512-479-3509
                                        tennistoml@hotmail.com

Second Thursday of the month, 6:30 pm.

Thomas Lewman, Contact
Joam Lewman, Contact

1130 HOPE (Helping Oncology Parents Endure) Brain Tumor Foundation of the Southwest
Children's Medical Center of Dallas
1935 Motor Street
Dallas, TX 75235   214-456-6139

Call for meeting times.

Shane Valles, Contact

1131 Houston Area Brain Tumor Network
University of Texas MD Anderson Cancer Center
Place of Wellness, 1515 Holcombe Boulevard
Houston, TX 77030   713-792-0772
                                              800-392-1611

First Tuesday of each month, 6:00-8:00 pm.

Suki Gibson, Contact
Rebecca Savoie, Contact

Brain Tumors / Web Sites

Virginia

1132 Brain Tumor Support Group
Saint Mary's Hospital
5801 Bremo Road, Room 159
Richmond, VA 23226
877-284-3905
curebt@hotmail.com
www.curebt.org

Second Tuesday of the month, 7:00-9:00 pm.
Carol Roberts RN MS, Contact

Washington

1133 Adult Brain Tumor Support Group
Virginia Mason Medical Center
1201 Terry Ave, Lindeman Pavillion, 10th Floor
Seattle, WA 98101
206-341-0420

Third Tuesday of every month, 2:30-4:00 pm.
Rick Edwards, Contact

1134 Brain Tumor Support Group University of Washington Medical Center
1959 NE Pacific Street, Box 356043
Seattle, WA 98195
206-598-4108

Meets first Wednesday of each month, 5:30-7:30 pm.
Stephanie Martin MSW LICSW, Contact

Wisconsin

1135 Brain Tumor Support Group
Luther Hospital
1221 Whipple Street, Conference Rooms 2 & 3
Eau Claire, WI 54703
206-598-4108

Second Tuesday of the Month, 6:30-7:30 pm.
Karen Snoble, Contact

1136 Brain Tumor Support Group at Milwaukee
St Lukes Medical Center
2900 W Oklahoma Avenue
Milwaukee, WI 53215
414-649-7200
800-252-2990

Second Wednesday of the month, 5:00-6:30 pm.
Linda Piacentine RN, MS, CNRN

1137 Brain Tumor Support Group at Wauwatosa Froederdt Memorial Lutheran Hospital
Administrative Board Room
9200 W Wisconsin Avenue
Wauwatosa, WI 53226
414-805-2629

Third Tuesday of each month, 6:30-8:30 pm.
Celeste Volcesek, Contact

1138 John Sierzant Brain Tumor Support Group
Gunderson Lutheran Medical Center
Gundersen Lutheran Medical Center 1900 South Avenu
LaCrosse, WI 54601
608-775-2952

First Tuesday of each month, 7:00-9:00 pm.
Polly Davenport-Fortune, Contact

Research Centers

1139 Brain Research Center
Children's Hospital National Medical Center
111 Michigan Avenue NW
Washington, DC 20010
202-476-5000
800-787-0021
tbear@childrensnational.org
www.cnmc.org

Barbara Herman, Chief

1140 Brain Research Foundation
111 West Washington Street, Suite 1710
Chicago, IL 60602
312-759-5150
Fax: 312-759-5151
info@theBRF.org
www.brainresearchfdn.org

Provides support to scinetists who are working to undersatnd the functioning of the brain. It establishes and provides financial assistance for research at the Brain Research Foundation. It also funds professional and scientific education.

Nathan T. Hansen, President
Normal R Bobins, Vice President
David H Fishburn, Treasurer

Web Sites

1141 American Brain Tumor Association
8550 W. Bryn Mawr Ave. Ste 550
Chicago, IL 60631
773-577-875
800-886-2282
Fax: 773-577-8738
info@abta.org
www.abta.org

Information about brain tumors.
Ralp DeVitto, President & CEO
Nicole Willmarth, PhD, Chief Mission Officer
Kelly Sitkin, Chief Development Officer

1142 CancerCare
275 7th Avenue
New York, NY 10001
800-813-4673
info@cancercare.org
www.cancercare.org

Dedicated to providing emotional support, information, and practical help to people with cancer and their loved ones. CancerCare is the oldest, largest, nonprofit agency devoted to offering professional services.

Patricia J Goldsmith, CEO
Christine Verini, RPh, COO

1143 Online Mendelian Inheritance in Man
McKusick-Nathans Institue of Genetic Medicine-JHU
Baltimore, MD 21205
www.omim.org

This database is a catalog of human genes and genetic disorders.
Ada Hamosh, MD, Scientific Director

1144 Starting Point: To Connect with Resources Related to Pediatric Neuro-oncology
www.med.miami.edu/neurosurgery/start_intro.htm

www.med.miami.edu/neurosurgery/start_intro.htm

Specializes in the management of patients with surgically treatable neurological diseases. The scope of practice includes the care of patients with disorders of the brain, spinal cord and nerves including cerebrovascular disease, intracranial and spinal tumors, disorders of the spinal cord and vertebral column, pediatric neurosurgical problems, movement disorders, medically intractable seizure disorders, and head and spinal injuries.

Illinois

1145 Caregiver Brain Tumor Support Group
www.cancercare.org/support_groups/100-brain_tumor_ca

Brain Tumors / Book Publishers

www.cancercare.org/support_groups/100-brain_tumor_ca

This 15-week online support group is for people caring for a loved one with a malignant brain tumor. Fourth Wednesday of each month, 7:00-8:30 pm. Contact for location.

Book Publishers

1146 Alex's Journey: The Story of a Child with a Brain Tumor
American Brain Tumor Association
8550 W Bryn Mawr Ave. Ste 550
Chicago, IL 60631
773-577-8750
800-886-2282
Fax: 773-577-8738
info@abta.org
www.abta.org

DVD

1147 Cancer Information for Teens, 4th Edition
Omnigraphics
615 Griswold Street, Ste 520
Detroit, MI 48226
610-461-3548
800-234-1340
Fax: 800-875-1340
contact@omnigraphics.com
www.omnigraphics.com

Updated information and facts about cancer causes, diagnosis, prevention and treatment especially for teens.

480 pages
ISBN: 0-780816-15-2

1148 Cancer Sourcebook
Angela L. Williams, author
Omnigraphics
615 Griswold Street, Ste 520
Detroit, MI 48226
610-461-3548
800-234-1340
Fax: 800-875-1340
contact@omnigraphics.com
www.omnigraphics.com

Updated information and facts about cancer causes, diagnosis, prevention and treatment. Nearly 1.5 million people in the US are diagnosed with cancer every year.

1224 pages 8th Edition
ISBN: 0-780816-22-0

1149 Childhood Diseases and Disorders Sourcebook, 4th Edition
Omnigraphics
615 Griswold Street, Ste 520
Detroit, MI 48226
610-461-3548
800-234-1340
Fax: 800-875-1340
contact@omnigraphics.com
www.omnigraphics.com

Basic and up to date consumer health information about common disorders that affect the physical, mental, and developmental health of school-age children.

792 pages
ISBN: 0-780815-38-4

1150 Let's Talk About Going to the Hospital
Rosen Publishing Group's PowerKids Press
29 E 21st Street
New York, NY 10010
212-777-3017
800-237-9932
Fax: 888-436-4643
rosenpub@tribeca.ios.com
www.rosenpublishing.com

If a child has to check into the hospital, chances are he or she is already upset about being ill. Knowing how a hospital functions and what the procedures are, such as when family members can visit, will help in what is already a stressful situation. Grades K-5.

24 pages
ISBN: 0-823950-36-0

Roger Rosen, President

1151 Let's Talk About When Kids Have Cancer
Rosen Publishing Group's PowerKids Press
29 E 21st Street
New York, NY 10010
212-777-3017
800-237-9932
Fax: 888-436-4643
customerservice@rosenpub.com
www.rosenpublishing.com

In a straightforward yet comforting way, this book explains what cancer is, what kinds of treatments surround the disease and how to cope if a child or the friend of a child has cancer. K-5.

24 pages Paperback
ISBN: 0-823951-95-6

Pamphlets

1152 About Brain Tumors: A Primer for Patients & Caregivers
American Brain Tumor Association
8550 W. Bryn Mawr Ave. Ste 550
Chicago, IL 60631
773-577-875
800-886-2282
Fax: 773-577-8738
info@abta.org
www.abta.org

A patient's reference manual offering information on brain tumors.

Booklet

1153 About Meningioma
American Brain Tumor Association
8550 W. Bryn Mawr Ave. Ste 550
Chicago, IL 60631
773-577-875
800-886-2282
Fax: 773-577-8738
info@abta.org
www.abta.org

Pamphlet

Elizabeth M. Wilson, MNA, President/ CEO
Kerri Mink, Chief Operating Officer
Meg Schneider, Chief Advancement Officer

1154 About Metastatic Tumors to the Brain and Spine
American Brain Tumor Association
8550 W. Bryn Mawr Ave. Ste 550
Chicago, IL 60631
773-577-875
800-886-2282
Fax: 773-577-8738
info@abta.org
www.abta.org

Pamphlet

Elizabeth M. Wilson, MNA, President/ CEO
Kerri Mink, Chief Operating Officer
Meg Schneider, Chief Advancement Officer

1155 About Pituitary Tumors
American Brain Tumor Association
8550 W. Bryn Mawr Ave. Ste 550
Chicago, IL 60631
773-577-875
800-886-2282
Fax: 773-577-8738
info@abta.org
www.abta.org

Pamphlet

Elizabeth M. Wilson, MNA, President/ CEO
Kerri Mink, Chief Operating Officer
Meg Schneider, Chief Advancement Officer

1156 About the American Brain Tumor Association
American Brain Tumor Association
8550 W. Bryn Mawr Ave. Ste 550
Chicago, IL 60631
773-577-875
800-886-2282
Fax: 773-577-8738
info@abta.org
www.abta.org

Brain Tumors / Camps

Pamphlet

Elizabeth M. Wilson, MNA, President/ CEO
Kerri Mink, Chief Operating Officer
Meg Schneider, Chief Advancement Officer

1157 Brain Tumor Dictionary
American Brain Tumor Association
8550 W. Bryn Mawr Ave. Ste 550
Chicago, IL 60631
773-577-875
800-886-2282
Fax: 773-577-8738
info@abta.org
www.abta.org

Offers a dictionary of more than 1,200 terms used in the diagnosis and everyday living with brain tumors.

128 pages

1158 Chemotherapy
American Brain Tumor Association
8550 W. Bryn Mawr Ave. Ste 550
Chicago, IL 60631
773-577-875
800-886-2282
Fax: 773-577-8738
info@abta.org
www.abta.org

Provides information that will help you understand and participate in your chemotherapy treatment, such as drugs and methods of delivering them to the brain, and suggestions for managing potential side effects.

1159 Conventional Radiation Therapy
American Brain Tumor Association
8550 W. Bryn Mawr Ave. Ste 550
Chicago, IL 60631
773-577-875
800-886-2282
Fax: 773-577-8738
info@abta.org
www.abta.org

Elizabeth M. Wilson, MNA, President/ CEO
Kerri Mink, Chief Operating Officer
Meg Schneider, Chief Advancement Officer

1160 Ependymoma
American Brain Tumor Association
8550 W. Bryn Mawr Ave. Ste 550
Chicago, IL 60631
773-577-875
800-886-2282
Fax: 773-577-8738
info@abta.org
www.abta.org

An overview of the diagnosis and treatment of ependymoma in children and adults.

Pamphlet

1161 Glioblastoma and Anaplastic Astrocytoma
American Brain Tumor Association
8550 W. Bryn Mawr Ave. Ste 550
Chicago, IL 60631
773-577-875
800-886-2282
Fax: 773-577-8738
info@abta.org
www.abta.org

Pamphlet

1162 Medulloblastoma
American Brain Tumor Association
8550 W. Bryn Mawr Ave. Ste 550
Chicago, IL 60631
773-577-875
800-886-2282
Fax: 773-577-8738
info@abta.org
www.abta.org

An overview of the diagnosis and treatment of medullablastoma and PNETs in the cerebellum of children and adults.

Pamphlet

1163 Oligodendrogliomas and Oligoastrocytomas
American Brain Tumor Association
8550 W. Bryn Mawr Ave. Ste 550
Chicago, IL 60631
773-577-8750
800-886-2282
Fax: 773-577-8738
info@abta.org
www.abta.org

Pamphlet

1164 Organizing and Facilitating a Support Group
American Brain Tumor Association
8550 W. Bryn Mawr Ave. Ste 550
Chicago, IL 60631
773-577-875
800-886-2282
Fax: 773-577-8738
info@abta.org
www.abta.org

Elizabeth M. Wilson, MNA, President/ CEO
Kerri Mink, Chief Operating Officer
Meg Schneider, Chief Advancement Officer

1165 Stereotactic Radiosurgery
American Brain Tumor Association
8550 W. Bryn Mawr Ave. Ste 550
Chicago, IL 60631
773-577-875
800-886-2282
Fax: 773-577-8738
info@abta.org
www.abta.org

Explains this type of surgery, pictures, and a typical day of treatment.

1166 What You Need to Know About Brain Tumors
National Cancer Institute
BG 9609 MSC 9760, 9609 Medical Center Drive
Bethesda, MD 20892
800-422-6237
www.cancer.gov

Offers factual information about brain tumors, possible causes, primary and secondary tumors, symptoms, diagnosis, treatment, side effects, follow up care, support and medical terms.

1167 When Your Child is Ready to Return to School
American Brain Tumor Association
8550 W. Bryn Mawr Ave. Ste 550
Chicago, IL 60631
773-577-875
800-886-2282
Fax: 773-577-8738
info@abta.org
www.abta.org

Guides parents and teachers through a successful return to school when a child has had a brain tumor.

Paperback

Elizabeth M. Wilson, MNA, President/ CEO
Kerri Mink, Chief Operating Officer
Meg Schneider, Chief Advancement Officer

Camps

1168 Arizona Camp Sunrise & Sidekicks
PO Box 27872
Tempe, AZ 85285
480-382-8564
928-478-4564
melissa@azcampsunrise.org
www.azcampsunrise.org

The camp is dedicated to provide an exciting, medically safe camp program for children whose families have been affected by cancer.

Melissa Lee, Camp Director

Brain Tumors / Camps

1169 Camp Catch-A-Rainbow
American Cancer Society
1205 E Saginaw Street
Lansing, MI 48906

517-371-2920
800-227-2345
kwilson@ymcastorercamps.org
www.cancer.gov/camprainbow

Open to any child (ages 7 thru 15) who has, or has had, cancer.

Katie Wilson, Coordinator

1170 Camp Fantastic
Special Love
117 Youth Development Court
Winchester, VA 22602

703-667-3774
888-930-2707
www.specialove.org

Nonprofit organization that provides enriching programs for children with cancer, including Camp Fantastic.

Dave Smith, CEO
Angela Ashman, Program Director

1171 Camp Sunshine Dreams
PO Box 28232
Fresno, CA 93729

contact@campsunshinedreams.com
www.campsunshinedreams.com

Summer camp for children with cancer.

Anthony Aiello, Board Member

1172 Des Moines YMCA Camp
1192 166th Drive
Boone, IA 50036

515-432-7558
Fax: 515-432-5414
ycamp@dmymca.org
www.y-camp.org

For boys and girls with cancer, diabetes, asthma, cystic fibrosis, hearing impaired and other disabilities.

David Sherry, Executive Director
Alex Kretzinger, Program Director Camps

1173 Okizu Foundation Camps
16 Digital Drive, Suite 130
Novato, CA 94949

415-382-9083
Fax: 415-382-8384
info@okizu.org
www.okizu.org

This foundation runs family camp programs for children who have cancer and their families, and for children who have or had a parent with cancer.

Lori Sparrow, Executive Director
Heather Ferrier, Camp Director of Operations

Bronchopulmonary Dysplasia / National Associations & Support Groups

Description

1174 BRONCHOPULMONARY DYSPLASIA
Synonym: BPD
Involves the following Biologic System(s):
Neonatal and Infant Disorders, Respiratory Disorders

Bronchopulmonary dysplasia (BPD) is a chronic lung disease of infancy that is characterized by injury to the lung's airways, causing abnormal tissue changes, inflammation, and eventual scarring of lung tissue. BPD often affects infants who have become dependent on the long-term use of ventilators to mechanically assist their breathing. In these infants with BPD, lung injury is thought to result from prolonged breathing of high concentrations of oxygen under abnormally high pressure and volume (oxygen toxicity, barotrauma, and volutrauma). BPD affects infants who are born prior to 37 weeks of pregnancy (premature newborns) and are affected by severe respiratory distress syndrome of the newborn (RDS). RDS is characterized by insufficient production of a substance (surfactant) that is produced as the lungs mature during fetal development. Surfactant reduces the surface tension of fluids lining the air sacs (alveoli) of the lungs, enabling the air sacs to remain open between breaths. Due to insufficient surfactant in premature newborns with RDS, greater pressure is required to expand the lungs' airways and air sacs. As a result, the air sacs may collapse and the lungs may become unable to properly provide oxygenated blood to the body. Within minutes or hours after birth, newborns with RDS experience increasing difficulty breathing (dyspnea), characterized by rapid, labored, shallow breaths (tachypnea); grunting upon exhalation; drawing in of the chest wall during inhalation; and bluish discoloration of the skin and mucous membranes (cyanosis) due to lack of sufficient oxygen supply to bodily tissues (hypoxia). In infants with severe RDS, treatment typically includes prolonged support with a ventilator to keep the aveoli open (positive pressure ventilator). BPD is said to exist if lung disease persists, usually with an oxygen requirement, beyond the first month of life.

Despite receiving increasing concentrations of oxygen and other treatment measures, newborns with RDS and subsequent bronchopulmonary dysplasia continue to experience severe respiratory symptoms rather than improve as expected. These infants have ongoing respiratory distress associated with hypoxia, abnormally high levels of carbon dioxide in the blood (hypercarbia), a reduced ability of the right side of the heart to pump blood efficiently (right-sided heart failure), and continued oxygen dependency. Approximately two to three weeks after continued ventilation support, x-ray examination and other diagnostic techniques may demonstrate the abnormal tissue changes (bronchiolar metaplasia) and scarring of lung tissue associated with bronchopulmonary dysplasia.

The treatment of infants with BPD may include gradual weaning off mechanical ventilation; prescription of corticosteroid medications (e.g., dexamethasone) to reduce inflammation, administration of medications to help expand the airways of the lungs (bronchodilators) and drugs to promote the excretion of fluid from the body (diuretics); restriction of fluid intake; and therapies to help prevent or treat certain respiratory infections (e.g., respiratory syncytial virus). Maturation of the lungs is the most important treatment and most patients recover by approximately six to 12 months. However, these children may have an increased susceptibility to inflammation and infection of the lungs (pneumonia) or other potential complications, such as temporary growth failure. In some patients with severe BPD, prolonged hospitalization may be necessary.

Government Agencies

1175 NIH/ Eunice Kennedy Shriver National Institute of Child Health & Human Development
P.O. Box 3006
Rockville, MD 20847

800-370-2943
Fax: 866-760-5947
www.nichd.nih.gov

Conducts and supports laboratory research, clinical trials, and epidemiological studies that explore health processes; examines the impact of disabilities, diseases, and variations on the lives of individuals; and sponsors training programs for scientists, health care providers, and researchers to ensure that NICHD research can continue.

Diana W. Bianchi, Director
Alison Cernich, PhD, Deputy Director

1176 NIH/National Heart, Lung and Blood Institute
31 Center Drive, Bldg 31
Bethesda, MD 20892

877-645-2448
www.nhlbi.nih.gov

The National Heart, Lung, and Blood Institute (NHLBI) provides global leadership for a research, training, and education program to promote the prevention and treatment of heart, lung, and blood diseases and enhance the health of all individuals so that they can live longer and more fulfilling lives.

Gary H. Gibbons, MD, Director
Kate O'Sullivan, Executive Officer

National Associations & Support Groups

1177 American Academy of Pediatrics
345 Park Blvd
Itasca, IL 60143

800-433-9016
Fax: 847-434-8000
mcc@aap.org
www.aap.org

The American Academy of Pediatrics and its member pediatricians are committed to the attainment of optimal physical, mental and social health and well-being for all infants, children, adolescents, and young adults.

Lynn Olson, PhD, VP, Research
Mark Del Monte, JD, CEO/Executive VP
Vera Tait, MD, FAAP, Chief Medical Officer

1178 American Lung Association
55 W. Wacker Drive, Suite 1150
Chicago, IL 60601

800-586-4872
info@lung.org
www.lung.org

The American Lung Association fights lung disease in all its forms, with special emphasis on asthma, tobacco control and environmental health. The American Lung Association is funded with contributions from the public, along with gifts and grants from corporations, foundations and government agencies. The association achieves its many successes through the work of thousands of committed volunteers and staff.

Harold P. Wimmer, National President & CEO
Alert Rizzo, MD, Chief Medical Officer
Sue Swan, Chief Development Officer

1179 Genetic Alliance
426400 Woodfield Road, Ste 189
Damascus, MD 20872

202-966-5557
Fax: 202-966-8553
info@geneticalliance.org
www.geneticalliance.org

World's leading nonprofit health advocacy organization committed to transforming health through genetics and promoting an environment of openness centered on the health of individuals, families, and communities.

Sharon Terry, CEO
Ruth Child, CFO
Natasha Bonhomme, Chief Strategy Officer

1180 March of Dimes Foundation
1550 Crystal Drive, Ste 1300
Arlington, VA 22202
888-663-4637
www.marchofdimes.org

March of Dimes help moms have full-term pregnancies and research the problems that threaten the health of babies. The March of Dimes also acts globally: sharing best practices in perinatal health and helping improve birth outcomes where the needs are the most urgent.

Stacey D. Stewart, President
Alan Brogdon, SVP/COO/Board Officer
Rahul Gupta, MD, SVP & Chief Medical/Health Officer

Web Sites

1181 American Lung Association
55 W. Wacker Drive, Suite 1150
Chicago, IL 60601
800-586-4872
info@lung.org
www.lung.org

The American Lung Association fights lung disease in all its forms, with special emphasis on asthma, tobacco control and environmental health. The American Lung Association is funded with contributions from the public, along with gifts and grants from corporations, foundations and government agencies. The association achieves its many successes through the work of thousands of committed volunteers and staff.

Harold P. Wimmer, National President & CEO
Albert Rizzo, MD, Chief Medical Officer
Sue Swan, Chief Development Officer

Camps

1182 VACC Camp
Nicklaus Children's Hospital
3200 SW 60th Court, Suite 203
Miami, FL 33155
305-662-8222
Fax: 786-268-1765
bela.florentin@mch.com
www.vacccamp.com

Free, week-long, overnight camp for ventilation assisted children (children needing a tracheotomy ventilator, C-PAP, BiPAP, or oxygen to support breathing) and their families. Gives families a fun oppourtinity to socialize with peers and enjoy activities not readily accessible to technology dependent children.

Bela Florentin, Camp Coordinator
Rose Ann Farrell, Volunteer Assistants Coordinator
Alyssa Garcia, Operations

Burn Injuries / National Associations & Support Groups

Description

1183 BURN INJURIES

Involves the following Biologic System(s):
Dermatologic Disorders

Burn injuries account for approximately 6,000 deaths per year in the United States. Among children, it follows only automobile accidents as a leading cause of accidental fatalities. Burns may be caused by heat, chemicals, or electrical current and are classified as first degree burns, second degree burns, or third degree burns, according to the severity and depth of the injury.

First degree burns, the least severe, affect the surface of the skin (superficial) and are characterized by a sensitive or painful reddened area of skin that sometimes swells and, in some cases, peels off. These types of burns affect only the top layer of skin (epidermis), do not blister, and, in most cases, heal spontaneously with no complications.

Second degree burns affect both the upper layer of skin and varying degrees of the underlying layer (dermis). This type of burn causes blistering. Even if the burn is relatively superficial, the pain may be intense as a result of exposed nerve endings. Superficial second degree burns usually heal within one to two weeks with no residual effects. Deeper second degree burns may actually be less painful and, if kept clean and free of infection, also heal with no complications. Second degree burns that cover more than 30 percent of the body surface area are considered critical.

Third degree burns destroy the upper layer of the skin and the underlying tissues; therefore, this type of burn typically requires skin grafting or other special treatment. Third degree burns are usually characterized by either a white or charred appearance; however, the burned area may appear bright red. Third degree burns that cover more than 10 percent of the body surface area or that involve the face or extremities are considered critical.

Burns that are chracterized by significant charring and exposure of muscle and bone are sometimes referred to as fourth degree burns. Hospitalization for first and second degree burn injuries is largely determined by the amount of the body surface area that is affected. As a general rule, if there is less than 10 percent involvement, treatment may be provided at home or on an outpatient basis. Treatment may include thorough cleansing of the wounds and topical application of antibacterial ointments to small burn areas. Blister management may be provided through cream dressings. If blisters break, thorough cleansing (debridement) to prevent infection is indicated. Bandage or gauze dressings may be applied to keep the injured areas clean to avoid infection. Skin grafting may be indicated for extensive second degree burns. Other treatment may include the administration of antibiotics and analgesics, aswell as injection of a tetanus booster, if necessary.

Third degree or other severe burns may be life-threatening and usually require hospitalization. Smoke and injury due to inhalation can be severe yet go unrecognized. Facials burns should raise the suspicion that there may be damage to the respiratory tract, requiring special vigilance. Emergency intervention may include the administration of oxygen and use of a ventilator to assist in breathing. Vital signs are routinely checked. To prevent kidney failure and other serious complications such as shock, other treatment usually includes intravenous replacement of proteins, body fluids, and essential elements in the fluid portion of the blood (electrolytes such as sodium, potassium, and calcium) lost as a result of extensive injury. The wounds are meticulously cleaned and dressed, and antibiotics are usually administered intravenously to prevent infection. As with less severe burns, tetanus immunization is updated. Extreme vigilance is required in order to preserve the integrity of surrounding tissue, sometimes necessitating the surgical removal of crusted dead skin (escharotomy) that may interfere with circulation. If injured, arms or legs are elevated. In order to help avoid the tightening and contracting of skin and muscles, the limbs may be splinted. Temporary skin grafting may be performed until permanent grafting is possible. In addition, nutritional considerations may necessitate the administration of supplements or, in the case of those unable to eat or drink, insertion of a tube through the nose to deliver nutrition directly into the stomach. Burns sustained through chemical and electrical influences may involve other systems of the body and, as such, are treated symptomatically. Psychological support by a team of professionals is an extremely important element in the recovery of individuals with burn injuries. Other treatment is symptomatic and supportive.

National Associations & Support Groups

1184 American Academy of Pediatrics
345 Park Blvd
Itasca, IL 60143

800-433-9016
Fax: 847-434-8000
mcc@aap.org
www.aap.org

The American Academy of Pediatrics and its member pediatricians are committed to the attainment of optimal physical, mental and social health and well-being for all infants, children, adolescents, and young adults.

Lynn Olson, PhD, VP, Research
Mark Del Monte, JD, CEO/Executive VP
Vera Tait, MD, FAAP, Chief Medical Officer

1185 Burn Institute
8825 Aero Drive, Suite 200
San Diego, CA 92123

858-541-2277
Fax: 858-541-7179
info@burninstitute.org
www.burninstitute.org

A nonprofit health agency dedicated to reducing burn injuries and deaths through fire and burn prevention education, burn survivor support programs and the funding of burn care research and treatment.

Susan Day, Executive Director
Benjamin Hemmings, Director of Operations
Whitney Cartwright, Administrative Coordinator

1186 Burn Prevention Foundation
1275 Glenlivet Drive, Suite 100-628
Allentown, PA 18106

484-224-2948
www.burnprevention.org

The mission of the Burn Foundation is to provide burn injury prevention education and advocacy for those at greatest risk.

Corissa Rolon, Executive Director/CEO
Jessica Banks, Associate Executive Director
Lori Young, Controller

1187 Burn Survivors Throughout the World
16193 Lone Star Ranch Drive
Conroe, TX 77302

936-483-9014
Fax: 936-570-1179
info@burnsurvivorsttw.org
www.burnsurvivorsttw.org

An international nonprofit organization working to rebuild the lives of the current and future burn survivors worldwide. Offers membership, a peer support team, education, advocacy, medical referrals, a free medical treatment program, medical equipment, legal referrals, healing weekends, and public awareness for the burn survivor community and the public worldwide.

Michael Appleman, Founder & CEO

Burn Injuries / Conferences

1188 **International Society for Burn Injuries**
www.worldburn.org

346-505-3528
info@worldburn.org
www.worldburn.org

Our society acknowledges the importance of all of these specialists in burn care and had intelligently admitted those professionals as members since its foundation. We must mention there are very few, in fact almost no other medical societies like ours which bring together such a number of different specialists, including nurses. One of the main purposes and aims of our society is to disseminate knowledge and to stimulate prevention in the field of burns.

Folke Sjoberg, MD, President
Dr. Rajeev B. Harrington, President-Elect
Michael A. Serghiou, Executive Director

1189 **National Fire Protection Association**
1 Batterymach Park
Quincy, MA 02169

617-770-3000
800-344-3555
Fax: 617-984-7055
www.nfpa.org

The mission of the international nonprofit NFPA is to reduce the worldwide burden of providing and advocating scientifically-based consensus codes and standards, research, training and education.

Jim Pauley, President & CEO
Melinda Collins, Executive Assistant
Paul DeFronzo, Chief Financial Officer

1190 **Society for Pediatric Dermatology**
8365 Keystone Crossing, Ste 107
Indianapolis, IN 46240

317-202-0224
Fax: 317-205-9481
info@pedsderm.net
www.pedsderm.net

The objective of the society is to promote, develop and advance education, research and care of skin disease in all pediatric age groups.

Kent Lindeman, Executive Director

Conferences

1191 **Society for Pediatric Dermatology Annual Meeting**
Society for Pediatric Dermatology
8365 Keystone Crossing, Suite 107
Indianapolis, IN 46240

317-202-0224
Fax: 317-205-9481
info@pedsderm.net
www.pedsderm.net

Kent Lindeman, Executive Director
Stephanie Garwood, Meetings Manager

Web Sites

1192 **Burn Institute**
8825 Aero Drive, Suite 200
San Diego, CA 92123

858-541-2277
Fax: 858-541-7179
www.burninstitute.org

A nonprofit health agency dedicated to reducing burn injuries and deaths through fire and burn prevention education, burn survivor support programs and the funding of burn care research treatment.

Susan Day, Executive Director
Benjamin Hemmings, Director of Operations
Whitney Cartwright, Administrative Coordinator

1193 **Burn Prevention Foundation**
1275 Glenlivet Drive, Suite 100-628
Allentown, PA 18106

484-224-2948
www.burnprevention.org

The mission of the Burn Foundation is to provide burn injury prevention education and advocacy for those at greatest risk.

Corissa Rolon, Executive Director & CEO
Jessica Banks, Associate Executive Director
Lori Young, Controller

1194 **Burn Survivors Throughout the World**
16193 Lone Star Ranch Drive
Conroe, TX 77302

936-483-9014
Fax: 936-570-1179
www.burnsurvivorsttw.org

An international nonprofit organization working to rebuild the lives of the current and future burn survivors worldwide. Offers membership, a peer support team, education, advocacy, medical referrals, a free medical treatment program, medical equipment, legal referrals, healing weekends, and public awareness for the burn survivor community and the public worldwide.

Michael Appleman, Founder & CEO

1195 **Consumer Products Safety Commission**
4330 East West Highway
Bethesda, MD 20814

301-504-7923
800-638-2772
Fax: 301-504-0124
www.cpsc.gov

The U.S. Comsumer Product Safety Commission is committed to providing access to its web pages for individuals with disabilities.

Elliot F. Kaye, Chairman
Robert S. Adler, Commissioner
Ann Marie Buerkle, Commissioner

1196 **Cool the Burn**
640 Jackson Street
St. Paul, MN 55101

651-254-3456
www.regionshospital.com

Cool the Burn is a unique resource for children whose lives have been affected by a burn injury. Whether you, a family member or a friend have been burned, this section will help you better understand burn unjuries.

1197 **International Society for Burn Injuries**
www.worldburn.org

346-505-3528
info@worldburn.org
www.worldburn.org

Information on prevention of burn injuries.

Michael A. Serghiou, Executive Director

1198 **National Fire Protection Association**
1 Batterymarch Park
Quincy, MA 02169

617-770-3000
800-344-3555
Fax: 617-984-7055
www.nfpa.org

Providing and advocating scientifically-based consensus codes and standards, research, training and education.

Jim Pauley, President & CEO
Melinda Collins, Executive Assistant
Paul DeFronzo, Chief Financial Officer

1199 **Society for Pediatric Dermatology**
8365 Keystone Crossing, Suite 107
Indianapolis, IN 46240

317-202-0224
Fax: 317-205-9481
info@pedsderm.net
www.pedsderm.net

Promotes, develop and advance education, research and care of skin disease in all pediatric age groups.

Karen Wiss, President
Andrea Zaenglen, President-Elect
Stephanie Lander, Membership/Communications Manager

Book Publishers

1200 Pain Sourcebook
Siva Ganesh Maharaja, author

Omnigraphics
615 Griswold Street, Ste 520
Detroit, MI 48226
610-461-3548
800-234-1340
Fax: 800-875-1340
contact@omnigraphics.com
www.omnigraphics.com

Basic consumer health information on various types of pain including musculoskeletal pain and many other pain related disorders and injuries.

776 pages 5th Ed.
ISBN: 0-780815-71-1

Journals

1201 Pediatric Dermatology Journal
Society for Pediatric Dermatology
8365 Keystone Crossing, Suite 107
Indianapolis, IN 46240
317-202-0224
Fax: 317-205-9481
info@pedsderm.net
www.pedsderm.net

Answers the need for new ideas and strategies for today's pediatrician or dermatologist.

6 issues/yr

Kent Lindeman, Executive Director

Camps

1202 Firefighters Kids Camp Camp Concord
1000 Mount Tallac Road
South Lake Tahoe, CA 96150
916-739-8525
www.ffburn.org

One-week program to benefit young burn survivors who are age six to age seventeen. Our mission is to provide young burn survivors with a fun and safe camp environment that encourages healing, personal growth and character development within a natural setting.

Catharine Shaw, Director

Celiac Disease / Description

Description

1203 CELIAC DISEASE

Synonyms: CD, Celiac sprue, Gluten-sensitive enteropathy, GSE, Nontropical sprue

Involves the following Biologic System(s):

Gastrointestinal Disorders

Celiac disease (CD) is a digestive disorder in which the lining of the small intestine is damaged by gluten, a protein found in wheat, barley, rye, and oats. People with CD are thought to have an abnormal immune response to dietary gluten, resulting in the body's own immune system attacks and causes degeneration (atrophy) and flattening of the tiny projections (villi) that line the small intestine. These villi play a vital role in absorbing fats and other nutrients from food products (malabsorption). This damage to the intestinal villi seriously impairs their ability to absorb these nutrients. Although the specific cause of CD is unknown, it is thought to be multifactorial, resulting from interactions between multiple genes (polygenic) and certain environmental factors. CD may affect both children and adults. The frequency with which it occurs varies greatly among countries and among different populations, and more cases occur in Europe than in the United States. Approximately one in 10,000 infants is thought to be affected by CD in the U.S. Celiac disease is genetic, meaning it runs in families. Diagnosis is usually made by a gastroenterologist, through special blood tests and the testing of tissue from the small intestine.

The symptoms associated with celiac disease do not become apparent until gluten is introduced into the diet, and its symptoms may occur in the digestive system or elsewhere in the body. In most children with CD, symptoms begin between the ages of one to five years. Although the symptoms and findings in CD may vary, many children initially have diarrhea, and their stools become abnormally bulky, pale, frothy, and offensive smelling, the result of an abnormally increased fat content (steatorrhea). Other abnormalities in CD may include excessive gas (flatulence); a failure to grow and gain weight at the expected rate (failure to thrive), the result of a decreased intake of nutrients; lack of appetite (anorexia); hair loss; weight loss; vomiting; and swelling (distension) of the abdomen. Many children also experience muscle wasting, are unusually clingy and irritable, and have abnormally pale skin (pallor). As a result of the malabsorption of fats and other nutrients, children with this condition typically have deficiencies of certain vitamins, and some may have abnormally reduced levels of the oxygen-carrying protein hemoglobin in the blood, because of deficient intestinal absorption of iron (iron-deficiency anemia), which is an important component of hemoglobin.

The key step in treating celiac disease is eliminating gluten from the diet. Wheat and rye products must be completely eliminated, although some children with CD may be able to tolerate barley and oat products. Because gluten is widely used in various food products, parents and children may initially require assistance and guidance from an experienced dietitian in avoiding foods that contain it. Specially manufactured, gluten-free food products are available commercially, including gluten-free pasta, bread, and flour. Treatment may also include iron and vitamin supplementation as required.

National Associations & Support Groups

1204 Academy of Nutrition and Dietetics
120 South Riverside Plaza, Suite 2190
Chicago, IL 60606
312-899-0040
foundation@eatright.org
www.eatright.org

Representing more than 112,000 credentialed nutrition and dietetics practitioners, the Academy of Nutrition and Dietetics is the world's largest organization of food and nutrition professionals. The Academy is committed to improving the nation's health and advancing the profession of dietetics through research, education and advocacy.

1205 American Academy of Pediatrics
345 Park Blvd
Itasca, IL 60143
800-433-9016
Fax: 847-434-8000
mcc@aap.org
www.aap.org

The American Academy of Pediatrics and its member pediatricians are committed to the attainment of optimal physical, mental and social health and well-being for all infants, children, adolescents, and young adults.

Lynn Olson, PhD, VP, Research
Mark Del Monte, JD, CEO/Executive VP
Vera Tait, MD, FAAP, Chief Medical Officer

1206 American Autoimmune Related Diseases Association
19176 Hall Road, Suite 130
Clinton, MI 48038
586-776-3900
aarda@aarda.org
www.aarda.org

The American Autoimmune Related Diseases Association is dedicated to the eradication of autoimmune diseases and the alleviation of suffering and the socioeconomic impact of autoimmunity through fostering and facilitating collaboration in the areas of education, public awareness, research, and patient services in an effective, ethical and efficient manner.

Lilly Stairs, Interim President/CEO
Laura Simpson, COO

1207 American Celiac Disease Alliance
20 Pickering Street
Needham, MA 02492
617-262-5422
888-423-5422
nationalceliac.org

A non-profit organization dedicated to educating and advocating for individuals with celiac disease and non-celiac gluten sensitivities, their families, and communities throughout the country.

Wendie Trubow, MD, President
Lee Graham, Executive Director
Kimberly Buckton, Managing Director

1208 American Society for Gastrointestinal Endoscopy
3300 Woodcreek Dr.
Downers Grove, IL 60515
630-573-0600
866-353-2743
Fax: 630-963-8332
info@asge.org
www.asge.org

ASGE has been dedicated to advancing patient care and digestive health by promoting excellence and innovation in gastrointestinal endoscopy.

Bret T. Petersen, President
Jennifer A. Christie, President Elect
Amitabh Chak, Secretary

1209 Association of Gastrointestinal Motility Disorders
140 Pleasant Street
Lexington, MA 02421
781-275-1300
info@agmdhope.org
agmdhope.org

AGMD is a non-profit organizations in existence with a focus on digestive motility diseases and disorders.

Celiac Disease / Web Sites

1210 Asthma & Allergy Foundation of America
8201 Corporate Drive, Suite 1000
Landover, MD 20785
800-727-8462
info@aafa.org
www.aafa.org

AAFA is a patient organization for people with asthma and allergies, and the oldest asthma and allergy patient group in the world.

Richard Murray, Chair
Mary Ellen Conley, RN, Chair, Governance
Colette Martin, Chair, Communications & Marketing

1211 Beyond Celiac
PO Box 544
Ambler, PA 19002
215-325-1306
844-856-6692
info@beyondceliac.org
www.beyondceliac.org

Since 2003, Beyond Celiac has been the leading patient advocacy and research-driven celiac disease organization working to drive diagnosis, advance research and accelerate the discovery of new treatments and a cure.

Alice Bast, President & Ceo
Salvatore Alesci, MD, Phd, Chief Scientific/Strategy Officer
Claire Baker, Senior Director of Communications

1212 Celiac Disease Foundation
20350 Ventura Blvd Ste 240
Woodland Hills, CA 91364
818-716-1513
Fax: 818-267-5577
www.celiac.org

Provides services and support to persons with celiac disease and dermatitus herpetiformis, through programs of awareness, education, advocacy and research; telephone information and referral services; medical advisory board; and special educational seminars and quarterly meetings.

Marilyn Grunzweig Geller, Chief Executive Officer
Deborah J. Ceizler, Chief Development Officer
Lisa Shaevitz, Director of Finance

1213 Children's National Health System
111 Michigan Avenue, NW
Washington, DC 20010
202-476-5000
888-884-2327
childrensnational.org

At Children's National, we are champions for children, with our entire team focused on pediatric care.

Kurt Newman, President & CEO
Vittorio Gallo, PhD, Chief Research Officer
Mark Batshaw, Executive VP & CAO

1214 Food Allergy Research & Education
7901 Jones Branch Dr., Suite 240
McLean, VA 22102
703-691-3179
Fax: 703-691-2713
www.foodallergy.org

FARE works on behalf of the 15 million Americans with food allergies, including all those at risk for life-threatening anaphylaxis.

Sung Poblete, PhD, RN, President

1215 Gluten Intolerance Group of North America (GIG)
31214 124th Ave SE
Auburn, WA 98092
253-833-6655
Fax: 206-833-6675
CustomerService@gluten.net
www.gluten.net

The mission of the Gluten Intolerance Group of North America™ is to provide support to persons with gluten intolerances, including celiac disease, dermatitis herpetiformis, and other gluten sensitivities, in order to live healthy lives.

Cynthia Kupper, Chief Executive Director
Channon Quinn, Chief Operating Officer
Jeanne Reid, Marketing Manager

1216 Kids with Food Allergies
1235 South Clark Street, Suite 305
Arlington, VA 22202
800-727-8462
www.kidswithfoodallergies.org

Helps to mprove the day-to-day lives of families raising children with food allergies and empower them to create a safe and healthy future for their children.

Conferences

1217 GLC Annual Education Conference
Gluten Intolerance Group
31214 124th Ave SE
Auburn, WA 98092
253-833-6655
Fax: 206-833-6675
CustomerService@gluten.net
www.gluten.net

For individuals that are following a gluten-free diet, or want to know all you need about it.

July

David Kline, President
Joe Spancic, Vice President of Business Administ
Kim Kelly, Vice President of Programs

Audio Video

1218 Unmarking Celiac Disease
American Celiac Society
PO Box 23455
New Orleans, LA 70183
504-737-3293
Fax: 504-737-3283

Annette Bentley, President
James Bentley, Vice President

Web Sites

1219 Celiac Disease Foundation
20350 Ventura Boulevard, Suite 240
Woodland Hills, CA 91364
818-716-1513
Fax: 818-267-5577
www.celiac.org

Provides services and support to persons with celiac disease and dermatitus herpetiformis, through programs of awareness, education, advocacy and research; telephone information and referral services; medical advisory board; and special education seminars and quarterly meetings.

Marilyn Grunzweig Geller, Chief Executive Officer
Deborah J. Ceizler, Chief Development Officer
Lisa Shaevitz, Director of Finance

1220 Celiac Support Page
20350 Ventura Boulevard, Suite 240
Woodland Hills, CA 91364
818-716-1513
www.celiac.com

To help as many people as possibe with celiac disease get diagnosed and live happy, healthy gluten-free lives.

Elaine Monarch, Founder
Marc Riches, Chair
Chad Hines, Vice Chair

1221 Gluten-Free Page
donwiss.com

donwiss.com

Offers links about Gluten Free Pages about the Celiac Disease/ Gluten Intolerance, gluten free food vendors, and other types of gluten free food sites.

1222 Health Answers Education Sudler-WPP Health Practice
700 Dresher Road
Horsham, PA 19044
215-442-9010
www.healthanswers.com

The vision was to provide a breadth of services to clients through the formation of a network of companies. Each company plays a key role in meeting out clients' needs.

Mike Hudnall, CEO

Book Publishers

1223 Gastrointestinal Diseases and Disorders Sourcebook, 4th Edition
Omnigraphics
615 Griswold Street, Ste 520
Detroit, MI 48226
610-461-3548
800-234-1340
Fax: 800-875-1340
contact@omnigraphics.com
www.omnigraphics.com

Basic consumer health information including celiac disease, Crohn's disease, diarrhea, hernias, irritable bowel syndrome and ulcers.

816 pages
ISBN: 0-780816-50-3

Newsletters

1224 Whoo's Report
PO Box 23455
New Orleans, LA 70183
504-737-3293
Fax: 504-737-3283

Provides practical assistance to members and individuals with celiac disease and information about the disease to the public.

Annette Bentley, President
James Bentley, Vice President

Pamphlets

1225 Diet Instruction
Gluten Intolerance Group of North America
31214 124th Avenue SE
Auburn, WA 98092
253-833-6655
Fax: 253-833-6675

1226 Introductory Packet Brochure
Gluten Intolerance Group of North America
31214 124th Avenue SE
Auburn, WA 98092
253-833-6655
Fax: 253-833-6675

Offers facts and statistics on celiac sprue and dermatitis herpetiformis.

1227 Patient Packets For Celiac Disease
Gluten Intolerance Group of North America
31214 124th Avenue SE
Auburn, WA 98092
253-833-6655
Fax: 253-833-6675

Includes various brochures and research reports on celiac sprue, recipes, diet instruction and more.

Cerebral Palsy / National Associations & Support Groups

Description

1228 **CEREBRAL PALSY**
Synonym: CP
Covers these related disorders: Ataxic cerebral palsy, Choreoathetoid cerebral palsy, Mixed cerebral palsy, Spastic cerebral palsy
Involves the following Biologic System(s):
Neurologic Disorders, Orthopedic and Muscle Disorders

Cerebral palsy (CP) is a nonprogressive condition characterized by stiff, rigid, and awkward movements (spasticity); involuntary, slow writhing movements (athetosis); and poor balance and coordination of voluntary movement (ataxia). Approximately two of every 1,000 infants are affected with cerebral palsy. Both premature and low birth weight infants are particularly at risk for this condition. Cerebral palsy may occur as the result of an injury to the brain during pregnancy, birth, or the early childhood years. Such brain injuries may be caused by a decrease in the supply of oxygen to the brain during the birthing period; an infection passed from the mother to the fetus during pregnancy; or an excess of bile pigment (bilirubin) in the developing fetus, usually arising from a blood incompatibility between mother and child. After birth, cerebral palsy may result from head trauma, an infection of the brain (e.g., encephalitis), an infection of the membranes surrounding the brain (meningitis), or other insult to the brain or surrounding tissue.

This condition is divided into four main types, based on the movement disorder. These include spastic, choreoathetoid, ataxic, and mixed cerebral palsy. Spastic cerebral palsy is the most common type of this condition and is characterized by stiff and weak muscles in the arms and legs on one or both sides of the body. Choreoathetoid cerebral palsy is characterized by poorly controlled, spontaneous slow movements of the muscles and accounts for approximately 20 percent of affected children. Ataxic cerebral palsy affects approximately 10 percent of all those with cerebral palsy and is characterized by poor coordination and shaky movements. Mixed cerebral palsy is a combination of two or more types of this abnormality and is characterized by the physical characteristics of the types. Although some children with cerebral palsy have below-average intelligence or are intellectually disabled, others are of average or above-average intelligence.

There is no cure for cerebral palsy, but the disabilities associated with CP can be reduced. The type and extent of treatment depends upon the degree and type of disability experienced by the individual child. Medications are prescribed to reduce spasticity and abnormal movements and to prevent seizures. Surgery can also be used to reduce spasticity. Occupational and physical therapy may aid affected children with walking and muscle coordination and control. Some children may benefit from the use of braces or other orthopedic intervention. Speech therapy may be useful for improvement of speech and eating difficulties. Physical and emotional stimulation and support are very important aspects of treatment and will aid in helping children with cerebral palsy to realize their full potential.

Government Agencies

1229 **NIH/ Eunice Kennedy Shriver National Institute of Child Health & Human Development**
P.O. Box 3006
Rockville, MD 20847
800-370-2943
Fax: 866-760-5947
www.nichd.nih.gov

Conducts and supports laboratory research, clinical trials, and epidemiological studies that explore health processes; examines the impact of disabilities, diseases, and variations on the lives of individuals; and sponsors training programs for scientists, health care providers, and researchers to ensure that NICHD research can continue
Diana W. Bianchi, Director
Alison Cernich, PhD, Deputy Director

1230 **NIH/National Institute of Neurological Disorders and Stroke (NINDS)**
PO Box 5801
Bethesda, MD 20824
800-352-9424
www.ninds.nih.gov

Works to reduce the burden of neurological disease by conducting, fostering, coordinating and guiding research on the causes, prevention, diagnosis and treatment of neurological disorders and stroke, while supporting basic research in related scientific areas.
Walter J. Koroshetz, MD, Director

National Associations & Support Groups

1231 **American Academy for Cerebral Palsy and Developmental Medicine**
555 E Wells Street, Suite 1100
Milwaukee, WI 53202
414-918-3014
Fax: 414-276-2146
info@aacpdm.org
www.aacpdm.org

The American Academy for Cerebral Palsy and Developmental Medicine is a multidisciplinary scientific society devoted to the study of cerebral palsy and other childhood onset disabilities, to promoting professional education for the treatment and management of these conditions, and to improving the quality of life for people with these disabilities.
Anniekay Erby, Executive Director
Kay Whalen, Managing Partner

1232 **American Academy of Pediatrics**
345 Park Blvd
Itasca, IL 60143
800-433-9016
Fax: 847-434-8000
mcc@aap.org
www.aap.org

The American Academy of Pediatrics and its member pediatricians are committed to the attainment of optimal physical, mental and social health and well-being for all infants, children, adolescents, and young adults.
Lynn Olson, PhD, VP, Research
Mark Del Monte, JD, CEO/Executive VP
Vera Tait, MD, FAAP, Chief Medical Officer

1233 **American School Counselor Association**
1101 King Street, Ste 310
Alexandria, VA 22314
703-683-2722
asca@schoolcounselor.org
www.schoolcounselor.org

The mission of ASCA is to represent professional school counselors and to promote professionalism and ethical practices.
Jill Cook, Executive Director
Amanda Fitzgerald, Assistant Deputy Executive Director
Kathleen M Rakestraw, Director of Communications

Cerebral Palsy / National Associations & Support Groups

1234 Center for Disabilities and Development
University of Iowa Stead Family Children's Hosp.
100 Hawkins Drive
Iowa City, IA 52242
319-353-6900
877-686-0031
Fax: 319-356-7700
cdd-webmaster@uiowa.edu
www.uichildrens.org/cdd/

A trusted resource for healthcare, training, research and information for people with disabilities that include: behavior disorders, brain injury, cerebral palsy, diabetes, down syndrome, learning disabilities, sleep disorders and spina bifida.

Dianne McBrien, MD, Medical Director

1235 Center for Parent Information and Resources (CPIR)
c/o SPAN, 35 Halsey Street, 4th Floor
Newark, NJ 07102
973-642-8100
malizo@spanadvocacy.org
www.parentcenterhub.org

Family-friendly information and research-based materials on key topics for Parent Centers. Private workspaces for Parent Centers to exchange resources, discuss high-priority topics, and solve mutual challenges. Coordination of parent training efforts throughout the network.

Myriam Alizo, Project Assistant

1236 Child Neurology Foundation
601 W Short Street
Lexington, KY 40508
888-417-3435
info@childneurologyfoundation.org
childneurologyfoundation.org

The Child Neurology Foundation connects partners from all areas of the child neurology community so those navigating the journey of disease diagnosis, management, and care have the ongoing support from those dedicated to treatments and cures.

Amy Brin, Executive Director
Katie Hentges, Director, Programs
Brea McCormley, Director, Development

1237 Easter Seals
141 W Jackson Boulevard, Suite 1400A
Chicago, IL 60604
312-726-6200
800-221-6827
Fax: 312-726-1494
info@easterseals.com
www.easterseals.com

Easter Seals' mission is to create solutions that change lives for children and adults with disabilities and to provide appropriate developmental and rehabilitation services. Services provided include early intervention, after-school programs, preschool, tutoring, medical rehabilitation, vocational services, adult and senior day services, respite and in home care, camping and recreation, residential housing, support services, support groups, transportation, and referrals.

Kendra Davenport, President & CEO

1238 Epilepsy Foundation
8301 Professional Place West, Ste 230
Landover, MD 20785
301-459-3700
800-332-1000
Fax: 301-577-2684
ContactUs@efa.org
www.epilepsy.org

Nationwide organization dedicated to help those living with epilepsy pursue seizure freedom through community services, public education, advocacy and research funding.

18,000 members

Phil Gattone, President & CEO
Ellen Hobby, COO
Steve Owens, VP, Programs & Services

1239 March of Dimes Foundation
1550 Crystal Drive, Ste 1300
Arlington, VA 22202
888-663-4637
www.marchofdimes.org

March of Dimes help moms have full-term pregnancies and research the problems that threaten the health of babies. The March of Dimes also acts globally: sharing best practices in perinatal health and helping improve birth outcomes where the needs are the most urgent.

Stacey D. Stewart, President
Alan Brogdon, SVP/COO/Board Officer
Rahul Gupta, MD, SVP & Chief Medical/Health Officer

1240 Mid-Atlantic ADA Center
12300 Twinbrook Parkway, Suite 350
Rockville, MD 20852
301-217-0124
800-949-4232
www.adainfo.org

The Mid-Atlantic ADA Center provides information, guidance, and training on the Americans with Disabilities Act (ADA), tailored to meet the needs of businesses, government entities, organizations, and individuals in the Mid-Atlantic Region (DC, DE, MD, PA, VA, and WV).

Ann Deschamps, Director
Nancy Horton, Assistant Director

1241 Pediatric Brain Foundation
2144 E. Republic Road, Bldg B, Ste 201
Springfield, MO 65804
417-887-4242
866-267-5580
Fax: 805-965-8838
madison@pediatricbrainfoundation.org
www.pediatricbrainfoundation.org

Formerly Children's Neurobiological Solutions, the Foundation is a national, nonprofit organization committed to the goal of making sure every family with children suffering from all neurological disorders are provided with financial support.

Rochette Dahler, President
Matt Dahler, VP
Gillian Harrington, Director, Asset Allocation

1242 TSC Alliance
8737 Colesville Road, Suite 400
Silver Spring, MD 20910
301-562-9890
800-225-6872
info@tscalliance.org
www.tscalliance.org

The TSC Alliance is an internationally recognized nonprofit that does everything it takes to improve the lives of people with TSC. We drive research, improve quality care and access and advocate for all affected by the disease. The TSC community is our strongest ally. The collaboration of individuals and families, along with the partnership of other organizations, fuels our work to ensure people navigating TSC have supportand hopeevery step of the way.

Kari Luther Rosbeck, President & CEO
Cynthia Arcuri, CPA, Chief Financial Officer
Steven L. Roberds, PhD, Chief Scientific Officer

1243 United Cerebral Palsy (UCP)
1825 K Street NW Suite 600
Washington, DC 20006
202-776-0406
800-872-5827
Fax: 202-776-0414
TTY: 202-973-7197
info@ucp.org
www.ucp.org

For almost 70 years United Cerebral Palsy (UCP) has worked to ensure individuals with disabilities are included and involved in every facet of society. It has 64 nationwide affiliates with the shared mission to advance the independence, productivity and full citizenship of those with cerebral palsy, intellectual and developmental disabilities, and other conditions.

Armando Contreras, President & CEO
Anita Porco, VP, Affiliate Network
Michael Ludgaro, Manager of Development

1244 WE MOVE (Worldwide Education and Awareness of Movement Disorders)
204 West 84th Street
New York, NY 10024
wemove@wemove.org

Cerebral Palsy / State Agencies & Support Groups

WE MOVE provides movement disorder information and educational materials to physicians, patients and families, the media, and the public via its comprehensive Web sites, training courses, and more. Its goal is to make early diagnosis, up-to-date treatment and patient support a reality for all people living with movement disorders.

Susan Bressman, MD, President

State Agencies & Support Groups

Alabama

1245 **United Ability**
100 Oslo Circle
Birmingham, AL 35211
205-944-3900
Fax: 205-226-9112
info@unitedability.org
www.unitedability.org

Provides services that connects people with disabilities to their communities.

Gary Edwards, CEO
Tina Shaddix, COO
Dr. Charlie Law, Chief Medical Officer

1246 **United Cerebral Palsy of Alabama**
c/o UCP of East Central Alabama
415 Castle Avenue
Anniston, AL 36205
256-237-8203
Fax: 256-235-2388
www.ecaucp.org

For almost 70 years United Cerebral Palsy (UCP) has worked to ensure individuals with disabilities are included and involved in every facet of society. It has 64 nationwide affiliates with the shared mission to advance the independence, productivity and full citizenship of those with cerebral palsy, intellectual and developmental disabilities, and other conditions.

Katrina L. Lipscomb, General Information & Programs

1247 **United Cerebral Palsy of Huntsville & Tennessee Valley**
2075 Max Luther Drive NW
Huntsville, AL 35810
256-852-5600
256-852-5673
Fax: 256-852-6722
therapy@ucphuntsville.org
www.ucphuntsville.org

For almost 70 years United Cerebral Palsy (UCP) has worked to ensure individuals with disabilities are included and involved in every facet of society. It has 64 nationwide affiliates with the shared mission to advance the independence, productivity and full citizenship of those with cerebral palsy, intellectual and developmental disabilities, and other conditions.

Cheryl Smith, CEO
Suzanne Price, COO/CFO
Leslie Walker, Community Engagement Manager

1248 **United Cerebral Palsy of Mobile**
3058 Dauphin Square Connector
Mobile, AL 36607
251-479-4900
Fax: 251-479-4998
info@ucpmobile.org
www.ucpmobile.org

For almost 70 years United Cerebral Palsy (UCP) has worked to ensure individuals with disabilities are included and involved in every facet of society. It has 64 nationwide affiliates with the shared mission to advance the independence, productivity and full citizenship of those with cerebral palsy, intellectual and developmental disabilities, and other conditions.

Glenn Harger, President & CEO
Benita Battiste, VP/CFO
Todd Perkins, VP, Programs

1249 **United Cerebral Palsy of Northwest Alabama**
507 N. Hook Street
Tuscumbia, AL 35674
256-381-4310
Fax: 256-381-4378
alison@ucpshoals.org
www.ucpshoals.org

For almost 70 years United Cerebral Palsy (UCP) has worked to ensure individuals with disabilities are included and involved in every facet of society. It has 64 nationwide affiliates with the shared mission to advance the independence, productivity and full citizenship of those with cerebral palsy, intellectual and developmental disabilities, and other conditions.

Alison Isbell, Executive Director
Martha Holcomb, Office Manager

1250 **United Cerebral Palsy of West Alabama**
1100 UCP Parkway
Northport, AL 35476
205-345-3031
Fax: 205-345-3035
www.ucpwa.org

Provides early intervention for birth through age 3, preschool services, afternoon and summer CARE services, (child and adult respite/education), Start on Success Alabama (high school transition to work program), Adult Day Habilitation Program, UCP Miracle Riders (equestrian physical therapy program).

LaMonica Herron-McCoy, Executive Director
Eric McIntyre, Director, Programs & Services
Randy Mecredy, Marketing & Fundraising

Alaska

1251 **United Cerebral Palsy of Alaska/PARENTS**
4743 E Northern Lights Boulevard
Anchorage, AK 99508
907-337-7678
Fax: 907-337-7671
www.parentsinc.org

United Cerebral Palsy provides information, advocacy, referral services for persons with disabilities and/or their families. UCP also operates an equipment loan program, conducts parent workshops, disseminates written literature on topics of interest to people with disabilities.

Sanja Bolling, Executive Director

Arizona

1252 **United Cerebral Palsy of Central Arizona**
1802 W Parkside Lane
Phoenix, AZ 85027
602-943-5472
888-943-5472
Fax: 602-943-4936
info@ucpofcentralaz.org
ucpofcentralaz.org

For almost 70 years United Cerebral Palsy (UCP) has worked to ensure individuals with disabilities are included and involved in every facet of society. It has 64 nationwide affiliates with the shared mission to advance the independence, productivity and full citizenship of those with cerebral palsy, intellectual and developmental disabilities, and other conditions.

Brenda Hansend, CEO
Adrienne Diga, Director, Human Resources
Katy Hansen, Director, Development

1253 **United Cerebral Palsy of Southern Arizona**
635 N. Craycroft Road
Tucson, AZ 85711
520-795-3108
888-433-3629
Fax: 520-795-3196
staff@ucpsa.org
ucpsa.org

For almost 70 years United Cerebral Palsy (UCP) has worked to ensure individuals with disabilities are included and involved in every facet of society. It has 64 nationwide affiliates with the shared mission to advance the independence, productivity and full citizenship of those with cerebral palsy, intellectual and developmental disabilities, and other conditions.

Cindy Mars, PhD, Executive Director

Cerebral Palsy / State Agencies & Support Groups

Arkansas

1254 United Cerebral Palsy of Central Arkansas
9720 N Rodney Parham Road
Little Rock, AR 72227

501-224-6067
Fax: 501-227-5591
info@ucpcark.org
www.ucpcark.org

For almost 70 years United Cerebral Palsy (UCP) has worked to ensure individuals with disabilities are included and involved in every facet of society. It has 64 nationwide affiliates with the shared mission to advance the independence, productivity and full citizenship of those with cerebral palsy, intellectual and developmental disabilities, and other conditions.

Paula Rader, CEO
Shelly Yielding, Director of Development
Louis Dillard, Plant Operations

California

1255 United Cerebral Palsy of Central California
4224 N Cedar Avenue
Fresno, CA 93726

559-221-8272
Fax: 559-221-9347
www.ucpcc.org

United Cerebral Palsy provides information, advocacy, referral services for persons with disabilities and/or their families. UCP also operates an adult day program - the Center for Arts and Technology in Fresno, CA, and services to children and their parents in Kings County, CA.

Roger Slingerman, Executive Director
Debbie Gibson, Director, Children's Programs
Natalie DiBuduo Pimentel, Director, Development/Marketing

1256 United Cerebral Palsy of Greater Sacramento & Northern California
4350 Auburn Blvd.
Sacramento, CA 95841

916-565-7700
Fax: 916-565-7773
ucp@ucpsacto.org
www.ucpsacto.org

For almost 70 years United Cerebral Palsy (UCP) has worked to ensure individuals with disabilities are included and involved in every facet of society. It has 64 nationwide affiliates with the shared mission to advance the independence, productivity and full citizenship of those with cerebral palsy, intellectual and developmental disabilities, and other conditions.

Doug Begman, President & CEO
Eric Ciampa, COO
Steve Horton, Director, Marketing & Development

1257 United Cerebral Palsy of Los Angeles, Ventura and Santa Barbara Counties
6430 Independence Avenue
Woodland Hills, CA 91367

818-782-2211
Fax: 818-909-9106
mail@ucpla.org
www.ucpla.org

Serving Los Angeles, Ventura and Santa Barbara counties. Serves hundreds of adults and children with disabilities every day with housing, education programs and professional and personal support for people with disabilities and their families. In addition to the high volume of people assisted, UCP is known for a caring, personal approach to each family's individual situation and choices.

Lori Anderson, President & CEO
Kimberly Lee, Chief Program Officer
Shelly Briggs, Director, Client Services

1258 United Cerebral Palsy of Orange County
980 Roosevelt, Suite 100
Irvine, CA 92620

949-333-6400
Fax: 949-333-6440
info@ucpoc.org
www.ucpoc.org

United Cerebral Palsy of Orange County operaptes an infant stimulation program with physical, occupational and speech therapy consultation. Aditionally, UCP provides information and referral services for the families of children having developmental disabilities as well as an equiptment loan program, Respitality program, parent support groups and individualized support, respite/babysitter programs, and consultation/training to childcare providers.

Ramin Baschshi, President & CEO
Elizabeth Beas, Director, Community Engagement
Wendy Wood, VP, Operations

1259 United Cerebral Palsy of San Diego County
8525 Gibbs Drive, #209
San Diego, CA 92123

858-571-7803
Fax: 858-571-0919
info@ucpsd.org
www.ucpsd.org

For almost 70 years United Cerebral Palsy (UCP) has worked to ensure individuals with disabilities are included and involved in every facet of society. It has 64 nationwide affiliates with the shared mission to advance the independence, productivity and full citizenship of those with cerebral palsy, intellectual and developmental disabilities, and other conditions.

David Carucci, Executive Director
Marc Carucci, Director of Public Relations
Gillian Hennessey, Managing Director, Adult/Cmty Prgms

1260 United Cerebral Palsy of San Joaquin, Calaveras & Amador Counties
333 W Benjamin Holt Drive, Suite 1
Stockton, CA 95207

209-956-0290
Fax: 209-956-0294
sbelasco@ucpsj.org
www.ucpsj.org

United Cerebral Palsy provides early intervention, information, advocacy, assistive technology and referral services for persons with disabilities and/or their families. UCP also operates an equipment loan program, conducts parent workshops, disseminates written literature on topics of interest to people with disabilities.

Lynn Hogue, CEO
Debbie Link, Director, Clinical/Family Services
Corinne Seaton, Director, Adult Program & Services

1261 United Cerebral Palsy of San Luis Obispo
3620 Sacramento Drive, Suite 201C
San Luis Obispo, CA 93401

805-543-2039
Fax: 805-543-2045
contact@ucp-slo.org
www.ucp-slo.org

For almost 70 years United Cerebral Palsy (UCP) has worked to ensure individuals with disabilities are included and involved in every facet of society. It has 64 nationwide affiliates with the shared mission to advance the independence, productivity and full citizenship of those with cerebral palsy, intellectual and developmental disabilities, and other conditions.

Mark Shaffer, Executive Director
Jason Portugal, Technology Coordinator
Danielle Nelson, Program Manager

1262 United Cerebral Palsy of Stanislaus County
4265 Spyres Way #2
Modesto, CA 95356

209-577-2122
Fax: 209-577-2392
info@ucpstan.org
www.ucpstan.org

United Cerebral Palsy provides information, advocacy, referral services for persons with disabilities and/or their families. Conducts parent workshops, disseminates written literature on topics of interest to people with disabilities.

Jan Halloran, President
Keenon Krick, Executive Director
Celise R. Krick, Development/Communications Director

1263 **United Cerebral Palsy of the Golden Gate**
1521 Webster Street
Oakland, CA 94612
510-832-7430
Fax: 510-839-1329
info@ucpgg.org
www.ucpgg.org

For almost 70 years United Cerebral Palsy (UCP) has worked to ensure individuals with disabilities are included and involved in every facet of society. It has 64 nationwide affiliates with the shared mission to advance the independence, productivity and full citizenship of those with cerebral palsy, intellectual and developmental disabilities, and other conditions.

Barry N Gardin, President
Joanne Murphy, Vice President
Henry Gusman, Treasurer

1264 **United Cerebral Palsy of the Inland Empire**
70017 Highway 111, Ste 5
Rancho Mirage, CA 92270
760-321-8184
877-512-2224
Fax: 760-321-8284
info@ucpie.org
www.ucpie.org

United Cerebral Palsy provides information, advocacy, referral services for persons with disabilities and/or their families. UCP conducts parent workshops, disseminates written literature on topics of interest to people with disabilities.

Greg Wetmore, President/CEO
Sofia Campos, Director of Operations
Gaby Ayala-Reyes, Outreach Coordinator

1265 **United Cerebral Palsy of the North Bay**
3835 Cypress Drive, #103
Petaluma, CA 94954
707-766-9990
jwhalen@ucpnb.org
ucpnb.org

For almost 70 years United Cerebral Palsy (UCP) has worked to ensure individuals with disabilities are included and involved in every facet of society. It has 64 nationwide affiliates with the shared mission to advance the independence, productivity and full citizenship of those with cerebral palsy, intellectual and developmental disabilities, and other conditions.

Margaret Farman, CEO
Ron Hamilton, Chief of Operations
Janet Hart, Treasurer

Connecticut

1266 **United Cerebral Palsy of Eastern Connecticut**
42 Norwich Road
Quaker Hill, CT 06375
860-443-3800
Fax: 860-443-8272
info@ucpect.org
www.ucpect.org

For almost 70 years United Cerebral Palsy (UCF) has worked to ensure individuals with disabilities are included and involved in every facet of society. It has 64 nationwide affiliates with the shared mission to advance the independence, productivity and full citizenship of those with cerebral palsy, intellectual and developmental disabilities, and other conditions.

Jennifer Keatley, Executive Director
Christine Olbrys, Director, Community Programs/Scvs

1267 **United Cerebral Palsy of Greater Hartford**
80 Whitney Street
Hartford, CT 06105
860-236-6201
Fax: 860-218-2454
preid@sunrisegroup.org
www.ucphartford.org/

For almost 70 years United Cerebral Palsy (UCP) has worked to ensure individuals with disabilities are included and involved in every facet of society. It has 64 nationwide affiliates with the shared mission to advance the independence, productivity and full citizenship of those with cerebral palsy, intellectual and developmental disabilities, and other conditions.

Scott Stafford, Regional Administrator
Sarah Winiarski, Director, Dvlpment & Communications
Peter Cavanagh, Camp Coordinator

Delaware

1268 **United Cerebral Palsy of Delaware**
700A River Road
Wilmington, DE 19809
302-764-2400
Fax: 302-764-8713
ucpde@ucpde.org
www.ucpde.org

For almost 70 years United Cerebral Palsy (UCP) has worked to ensure individuals with disabilities are included and involved in every facet of society. It has 64 nationwide affiliates with the shared mission to advance the independence, productivity and full citizenship of those with cerebral palsy, intellectual and developmental disabilities, and other conditions.

Linda J. Royal, Acting Executive Director
Robert Layton Reed, President
D. Bruce McClenathan, Vice President

District of Columbia

1269 **United Cerebral Palsy of Washington DC & Northern Virginia**
3135 8th Street NE
Washington, DC 20017
202-269-1500
Fax: 202-526-0519
webmaster@ucpdc.org
www.ucpdc.org

For almost 70 years United Cerebral Palsy (UCP) has worked to ensure individuals with disabilities are included and involved in every facet of society. It has 64 nationwide affiliates with the shared mission to advance the independence, productivity and full citizenship of those with cerebral palsy, intellectual and developmental disabilities, and other conditions.

Dawn Gillom-Carter, Executive Director
Tola Akinmade, Director, Health Services

Florida

1270 **Tender Love and Care PPEC and Early Learning Center**
1241 N East Avenue
Panama City, FL 32401
850-769-7960
Fax: 850-769-1060

1271 **United Cerebral Palsy of Central Florida**
3305 S Orange Avenue
Orlando, FL 32806
407-852-3300
Fax: 407-480-4094
info@ucpcfl.org
www.ucpcfl.org

For almost 70 years United Cerebral Palsy (UCP) has worked to ensure individuals with disabilities are included and involved in every facet of society. It has 64 nationwide affiliates with the shared mission to advance the independence, productivity and full citizenship of those with cerebral palsy, intellectual and developmental disabilities, and other conditions.

Dr. Ilene Wilkins, President & CEO
Steve Judy, Senior Director, Operations
JP Soto, Senior Director, Mktg/Communication

1272 **United Cerebral Palsy of Southwest Florida**
6915 15th Street Unit 202
Sarasota, FL 34243
941-251-4956
Fax: 941-251-4959
sarasota@sunrisegroup.org
sarasotamanatee.ucpswfl.org

For almost 70 years United Cerebral Palsy (UCP) has worked to ensure individuals with disabilities are included and involved in every facet of society. It has 64 nationwide affiliates with the shared mission to advance the independence, productivity and full citizenship of those with cerebral palsy, intellectual and developmental disabilities, and other conditions.

Cerebral Palsy / State Agencies & Support Groups

Victoria DeWaters, Director of Operations
Caitlin Seeley, Director of Programs

1273 **United Cerebral Palsy of Tampa Bay**
300 East Sligh Avenue, Building B
Tampa, FL 33604
813-239-1179
Fax: 813-237-3091
lwhite@sunrisegroup.org
www.ucptampa.org

For almost 70 years United Cerebral Palsy (UCP) has worked to ensure individuals with disabilities are included and involved in every facet of society. It has 64 nationwide affiliates with the shared mission to advance the independence, productivity and full citizenship of those with cerebral palsy, intellectual and developmental disabilities, and other conditions.

Laura White, Executive Director
Debbie Trenker, Early Childhood Education Director

1274 **United Community Options of South Florida**
2700 W. 81 Street
Hialeah, FL 33016
305-325-1080
Fax: 850-922-1258
ucoinfo@uco-ucpsfl.org
www.unitedcommunityoptionssfl.org

Formerly United Cerebral Palsy (UCP) of South Florida. Provides information, advocacy, referral services for persons with disabilities and/or their families.

Joseph A. Aniello, Ed.D., President
Linda Gluck, CEO
Leigh Kapps, PhD, COO

Georgia

1275 **United Cerebral Palsy of Georgia**
3300 NE Expressway, Building 9
Atlanta, GA 30341
770-676-2000
888-827-9455
Fax: 770-455-8040
info@ucpga.org
www.ucpga.org

For almost 70 years United Cerebral Palsy (UCP) has worked to ensure individuals with disabilities are included and involved in every facet of society. It has 64 nationwide affiliates with the shared mission to advance the independence, productivity and full citizenship of those with cerebral palsy, intellectual and developmental disabilities, and other conditions.

Diane Wilush, President & CEO
Jonessa Alexander, COO
Kevin Walton, Chief Program Officer

Hawaii

1276 **United Cerebral Palsy of Hawaii**
414 Kuwili Street, Suite 105
Honolulu, HI 96817
808-532-6744
800-606-5654
Fax: 808-532-6747
info@unitedcerebralpalsyhawaii.org
www.unitedcerebralpalsyhawaii.org

United Cerebral Palsy provides information, advocacy, referral services for persons with disabilities and/or their families. UCP also operates an equipment loan program, conducts parent workshops, disseminates written literature on topics of interest to people with disabilities.

Illinois

1277 **Center for Disability Services**
311 South Reed Street
Joliet, IL 60436
815-744-3500
Fax: 815-744-3504
cdsil@cdsil.org
www.cdsil.org

The center is dedicated to advancing the independence of those with disabilities.

Larry Burich, Interim President & CEO
Brittany Jones, Community Support Services
Gina Wysocki, Development Coordinator

1278 **UCP Seguin of Greater Chicago**
3100 South Central Avenue
Cicero, IL 60804
708-863-3803
Fax: 708-863-3863
info@seguin.org
ucpseguin.org

For almost 70 years United Cerebral Palsy (UCP) has worked to ensure individuals with disabilities are included and involved in every facet of society. It has 64 nationwide affiliates with the shared mission to advance the independence, productivity and full citizenship of those with cerebral palsy, intellectual and developmental disabilities, and other conditions.

John Voit, President & CEO
Tom Foley, Executive Vice President
Michelle Sanders, VP, Organizational Management

1279 **United Cerebral Palsy Land of Lincoln**
101 North 16th Street
Springfield, IL 62703
217-525-6522
Fax: 217-525-9017
www.ucpll.org

For almost 70 years United Cerebral Palsy (UCP) has worked to ensure individuals with disabilities are included and involved in every facet of society. It has 64 nationwide affiliates with the shared mission to advance the independence, productivity and full citizenship of those with cerebral palsy, intellectual and developmental disabilities, and other conditions.

Kathy Leuelling, President & CEO
Jenny Niebrugge, COO
Jenny Dawson, Chief Marketing Officer

Indiana

1280 **United Cerebral Palsy of Greater Indiana**
6270 Corporate Drive
Indianapolis, IN 46278
317-871-4032
mfoddrill@ucpaindy.org
www.ucpaindy.org

For almost 70 years United Cerebral Palsy (UCP) has worked to ensure individuals with disabilities are included and involved in every facet of society. It has 64 nationwide affiliates with the shared mission to advance the independence, productivity and full citizenship of those with cerebral palsy, intellectual and developmental disabilities, and other conditions.

Mike Foddrill, Executive Direcror
Lee White, Board President

Kansas

1281 **Cerebral Palsy Research Foundation**
5111 East 21st Street N
Wichita, KS 67208
316-688-1888
Fax: 316-688-5687
www.cprf.org

A national leader in the development of rehabilitation engineering, advocacy, training, and specialized services for people with all types of disabilities.

Daniel M. Carney, Chairman
Deryl K. Schuster, Vice Chairman
Michael C. Burrus, Secretary

Louisiana

1282 **United Cerebral Palsy of Baton Rouge McMains Children's Developmental Center**
1805 College Drive
Baton Rouge, LA 70808
225-923-3420
Fax: 225-922-9316
info@mcmainscdc.org
www.mcmainscdc.org

Cerebral Palsy / State Agencies & Support Groups

United Cerebral Palsy provides information, advocacy, referral services for persons with disabilities and/or their families. UCP also operates an equipment loan program, conducts parent workshops, disseminates written literature on topics of interest to people with disabilities.

Anne Hindrichs, Executive Director
Hilary Collis, Director of Development
Janel Page, Communications/Marketing Manager

1283 United Cerebral Palsy of Greater New Orleans
2200 Veterans Memorial Boulevard, Suite 103
New Orleans, LA 70062
504-461-4266
Fax: 504-461-9976

United Cerebral Palsy provides information, advocacy, referral services for persons with disabilities and/or their families. UCP also operates an equipment loan program, conducts parent workshops, disseminates written literature on topics of interest to people with disabilities.

PJ Augustine, Director, Program Services

Maine

1284 United Cerebral Palsy of Maine
700 Mount Hope Avenue, Suite 320
Bangor, ME 04401
207-941-2952
Fax: 207-941-2955
www.ucpofmaine.org

For almost 70 years United Cerebral Palsy (UCP) has worked to ensure individuals with disabilities are included and involved in every facet of society. It has 64 nationwide affiliates with the shared mission to advance the independence, productivity and full citizenship of those with cerebral palsy, intellectual and developmental disabilities, and other conditions.

Scott Tash, Chief Executive Officer
Marianne Berube, Director of Operations
Andrea Richards, Early Childhood Services Director

Maryland

1285 Bay Community Support Services
908 Commerce Road
Annapolis, MD 21401
410-224-4205
Fax: 410-224-0763
somdprograms@baycss.org
www.baycss.org

Ike Puzon, President
Catherine Raines, CEO
Becki Mbure, Operations Manager, Northern Region

1286 Unified Community Connections
11350 McCormick Rd, Executive Plaza, Ste 1100
Hunt Valley, MD 21031
410-484-4540
Fax: 410-486-3825
info@unified.org
unified.org

Provides programs and services for children and adults with a wide array of disabilities and chronic health issues throughout Maryland.

Massachusetts

1287 United Cerebral Palsy of Berkshire County
208 West Street
Pittsfield, MA 01201
413-442-1562
Fax: 413-499-4077
info@ucpberkshire.org
ucpberkshire.org

For almost 70 years United Cerebral Palsy (UCP) has worked to ensure individuals with disabilities are included and involved in every facet of society. It has 64 nationwide affiliates with the shared mission to advance the independence, productivity and full citizenship of those with cerebral palsy, intellectual and developmental disabilities, and other conditions.

Sal Garozzo, Executive Director
Maren Jacobs, Board President

1288 United Cerebral Palsy of MetroBoston
71 Arsenal Street
Watertown, MA 02472
617-926-5480
Fax: 617-926-3059
ucpboston@ucpboston.org
www.ucpboston.org

For almost 70 years United Cerebral Palsy (UCP) has worked to ensure individuals with disabilities are included and involved in every facet of society. It has 64 nationwide affiliates with the shared mission to advance the independence, productivity and full citizenship of those with cerebral palsy, intellectual and developmental disabilities, and other conditions.

Todd Kates, PhD, CEO
Lynn McHugh, COO
Peter Vo, Director of Media Relations

Michigan

1289 United Cerebral Palsy Detroit
23077 Greenfield Rd, Suite 205
Southfield, MI 48075
248-557-5070
Fax: 248-557-0224
main@ucpdetroit.org
www.ucpdetroit.org

For almost 70 years United Cerebral Palsy (UCP) has worked to ensure individuals with disabilities are included and involved in every facet of society. It has 64 nationwide affiliates with the shared mission to advance the independence, productivity and full citizenship of those with cerebral palsy, intellectual and developmental disabilities, and other conditions.

Leslynn Angel, President & CEO

1290 United Cerebral Palsy Michigan
3496 East Lake Lansing Rd, #170
East Lansing, MI 48823
517-203-1200
Fax: 517-203-1203
ucp@ucpmichigan.org
www.ucpmichigan.org

For almost 70 years United Cerebral Palsy (UCP) has worked to ensure individuals with disabilities are included and involved in every facet of society. It has 64 nationwide affiliates with the shared mission to advance the independence, productivity and full citizenship of those with cerebral palsy, intellectual and developmental disabilities, and other conditions.

Leslynn Angel, President & CEO

Minnesota

1291 United Cerebral Palsy of Central Minnesota
24707 County Rd 5
St Augusta, MN 56301
320-253-0765
Fax: 320-253-6753
info@ucpcentralmn.org
www.ucpcentralmn.org

For almost 70 years United Cerebral Palsy (UCP) has worked to ensure individuals with disabilities are included and involved in every facet of society. It has 64 nationwide affiliates with the shared mission to advance the independence, productivity and full citizenship of those with cerebral palsy, intellectual and developmental disabilities, and other conditions.

Jenna Berger, Executive Director
Kat Harrison, VP, Operations & Finance
Jennifer Josephs, Program Director

1292 United Cerebral Palsy of Minnesota
200 University Avenue East
Saint Paul, MN 55101
651-265-7361
Fax: 651-229-1743
info@ucpmn.org
ucpmn.org

Cerebral Palsy / State Agencies & Support Groups

For almost 70 years United Cerebral Palsy (UCP) has worked to ensure individuals with disabilities are included and involved in every facet of society. It has 64 nationwide affiliates with the shared mission to advance the independence, productivity and full citizenship of those with cerebral palsy, intellectual and developmental disabilities, and other conditions.

MaryBeth Fitzgerald, Executive Director
Tara Swedberg, Administration & Resources

Missouri

1293 United Cerebral Palsy Heartland
13975 Manchester Road
Manchester, MO 63011
636-227-6030
Fax: 636-779-2270
www.ucpheartland.org

For almost 70 years United Cerebral Palsy (UCP) has worked to ensure individuals with disabilities are included and involved in every facet of society. It has 64 nationwide affiliates with the shared mission to advance the independence, productivity and full citizenship of those with cerebral palsy, intellectual and developmental disabilities, and other conditions.

Brenda Wrench, President & CEO
Judy Grainger, Senior VP of Programs
Christy Weisel, Director, Child Development Center

1294 United Cerebral Palsy of Northwest Missouri
3303 Frederick Avenue
Saint Joseph, MO 64506
816-364-3836
Fax: 816-390-8546
ucp@ucpnwmo.org
www.ucpnwmo.org

For almost 70 years United Cerebral Palsy (UCP) has worked to ensure individuals with disabilities are included and involved in every facet of society. It has 64 nationwide affiliates with the shared mission to advance the independence, productivity and full citizenship of those with cerebral palsy, intellectual and developmental disabilities, and other conditions.

Teresa Gagliano, Executive Director
Josh Emberton, President
Heather Weddle, Director of Children's Programs

Nebraska

1295 United Cerebral Palsy of Nebraska
920 S. 107th Avenue, Suite 302
Omaha, NE 68114
402-502-3572
800-729-2556
Fax: 402-502-6791
ucp@ucpnebraska.org
www.ucpnebraska.org

For almost 70 years United Cerebral Palsy (UCP) has worked to ensure individuals with disabilities are included and involved in every facet of society. It has 64 nationwide affiliates with the shared mission to advance the independence, productivity and full citizenship of those with cerebral palsy, intellectual and developmental disabilities, and other conditions.

Anne Brodin, Executive Director
Richard Troia, President
Timothy Mollak, Treasurer

New Jersey

1296 United Cerebral Palsy of Hudson County
721 Broadway
Bayonne, NJ 07002
201-436-2200
Fax: 201-436-6642
info@ucpofhudsoncounty.org
ucpofhudsoncounty.org

For almost 70 years United Cerebral Palsy (UCP) has worked to ensure individuals with disabilities are included and involved in every facet of society. It has 64 nationwide affiliates with the shared mission to advance the independence, productivity and full citizenship of those with cerebral palsy, intellectual and developmental disabilities, and other conditions.

Keith Kearney, Executive Director
Norma Garcia, Director, Community Supports

New York

1297 ADAPT Community Network
80 Maiden Lane, 8th Floor
New York, NY 10038
212-683-6700
Fax: 212-685-8394
info@adaptcommunitynetwork.org
www.adaptcommunitynetwork.org

Formerly United Cerebral Palsy of New York City. Provides information, advocacy, referral services for persons with disabilities and/or their families.

Edward R Matthews, CEO
Linda B. Laul, COO
Marianne Giordano, Senior VP, Program Services

1298 Aspire of WNY
2356 N Forest Road
Getzville, NY 14068
716-838-0047
Fax: 716-894-8257
info@aspirewny.org
www.aspirewny.org

Aspire of WNY is a provider of comprehensive programs and services for developmentally disabled children and adults in Western New York. Services areas include residential, vocational, therapeutic, clinical, habilitative and educational services amoung others. Aspire also offers advocacy, case management, work shops and referral services for the disabled and their families.

Thomas Sy, President & CEO
Maria Torgalski, COO

1299 Center for Disability Services
314 S Manning Boulevard
Albany, NY 12208
518-437-5700
Fax: 518-437-5931
www.cfdsny.org

Offers a wide variety of medical dental and therapy services provided in an outpatient practice setting, serving individuals with developmental disabilities and chronic disabling conditions. In addition, educational diagnostic and evaluation services are offered to children of different ages. parent workshops and support groups are conducted throughout the year.

Gregory J. Sorrentino, President & CEO
Brian Cregin, COO
Rosemary Lorello, Chief Program Officer

1300 Cerebral Palsy Associations of New York State
330 West 34th Street, 15th floor
New York, NY 10001
212-947-5770
Fax: 212-594-4538
information@cpofnys.org
www.cpofnys.org

CP of NYS provides information, advocacy, and services for persons with disabilities and/or their families. CP also operates an equipment loan program, conducts parent workshops, disseminates written literature on topics of interest to people with disabilities.

Susan Constantino, President & CEO
Mike Alvaro, Executive Director
Al Shibley, VP, Communications

1301 Cerebral Palsy of Nassau County
380 Washington Avenue
Roosevelt, NY 11575
516-378-2000
Fax: 516-378-0357
www.cpnassau.org

Provides information, advocacy, referral services for persons with disabilities and/or families. UCP also operates an equipment loan program, conducts parent workshops, disseminates written literature on topics of interest to people with disabilities.

Robert McGuire, Executive Director
Karen Geller-Hittleman, Children's Learning Center

Cerebral Palsy / State Agencies & Support Groups

1302 **Inspire - Cerebral Palsy Center**
2 Fletcher Street
Goshen, NY 10924
845-294-8806
Fax: 845-294-8650
www.inspirecp.org

An affiliate of Cerebral Palsy Associations of New York, provides information, advocacy, referral services for persons with disabilities and/or their families. Inspire runs a rehabilitative clinic and special needs preschool, conducts parent workshops, disseminates written literature on topics of interest to people with disabilities.

Marcel Martino, President & CEO
Allen Zick, Chairman

1303 **UCP of Long Island**
250 Marcus Boulevard, PO Box 18045
Hauppauge, NY 11788
631-232-0011
Fax: 631-232-4422
www.ucp-li.org

UCP LI provides information, advocacy, referral services for persons with disabilities and/or their families.

Stephen H Friedman, President & CEO
Janine Klein, CFO
Camille Schramm, Director, Development & PR

Ohio

1304 **UCP Norwood Stepping Stones**
2300 Drex Avenue
Cincinnati, OH 45212
513-831-4660
Fax: 513-831-5918
steppingstonesohio.org

Stepping Stones provides services that support the entire family of those with disabilities. Activities include camps, fun activities, weekend and evening programs, and more.

Chris Adams, Executive Director
Sam Browne Allen, Director, Programs & Operations
Jeannie Ludwig, Children's Services

1305 **United Cerebral Palsy of Greater Cleveland**
10011 Euclid Avenue
Cleveland, OH 44106
216-791-8363
Fax: 216-721-3372
info@ucpcleveland.org
www.ucpcleveland.org

For almost 70 years United Cerebral Palsy (UCF) has worked to ensure individuals with disabilities are included and involved in every facet of society. It has 64 nationwide affiliates with the shared mission to advance the independence, productivity and full citizenship of those with cerebral palsy, intellectual and developmental disabilities, and other conditions.

Patricia S. Otter, President & CEO
Beth A. Lucas, COO

Oklahoma

1306 **Ability Connection Oklahoma**
10400 Greenbriar Place, Suite 102
Oklahoma City, OK 73159
405-759-3562
800-827-2289
Fax: 405-917-7082
okc@acok.org
www.acok.org

(Formerly United Cerebral Palsy of Oklahoma) Provides information, advocacy, referral services for persons with disabilities and/or their families. UCP also operates an equipment loan program, disseminates written literature on topics of interest to people with disabilities.

Michelle Bartodej-Jackson, CEO & Executive Director
William Blochowiak, Board Chair

Oregon

1307 **United Cerebral Palsy Oregon**
305 NE 102nd Ave, Suite 100
Portland, OR 97220
503-777-4166
800-473-4581
Fax: 503-771-8048
ucpa@ucpaorwa.org
www.ucpaorwa.org

For almost 70 years United Cerebral Palsy (UCP) has worked to ensure individuals with disabilities are included and involved in every facet of society. It has 64 nationwide affiliates with the shared mission to advance the independence, productivity and full citizenship of those with cerebral palsy, intellectual and developmental disabilities, and other conditions.

Ann Coffey, Executive Director
John Goff, Community Services Director
Susan Cushman, Family Support Director

Pennsylvania

1308 **Alleghenies United Cerebral Palsy**
119 Jari Drive
Johnstown, PA 15904
814-619-3398
844-819-4455
Fax: 814-262-7174
info@scalucp.org
scalucp.org

For almost 70 years United Cerebral Palsy (UCP) has worked to ensure individuals with disabilities are included and involved in every facet of society. It has 64 nationwide affiliates with the shared mission to advance the independence, productivity and full citizenship of those with cerebral palsy, intellectual and developmental disabilities, and other conditions.

Tammy Rhodes, CEO
Kala Penrose, Service Coordination Director

1309 **United Cerebral Palsy Central Pennsylvania**
55 Utley Drive
Camp Hill, PA 17011
717-737-3477
800-998-4827
Fax: 717-975-3333
TTY: 717-737-0158
mainoffice@ucpcentralpa.org
www.ucpcentralpa.org

For almost 70 years United Cerebral Palsy (UCP) has worked to ensure individuals with disabilities are included and involved in every facet of society. It has 64 nationwide affiliates with the shared mission to advance the independence, productivity and full citizenship of those with cerebral palsy, intellectual and developmental disabilities, and other conditions.

Judith A. McCowan, President & CEO
Janeen M. Martin, COO
Marci Walborn, Director, Childhood Services

1310 **United Cerebral Palsy of Northeastern Pennsylvania**
425 Wyoming Avenue
Scranton, PA 18503
570-347-3117
Fax: 570-341-5308
TTY: 570-347-3117
info@ucpnepa.org
www.ucpnepa.org

For almost 70 years United Cerebral Palsy (UCP) has worked to ensure individuals with disabilities are included and involved in every facet of society. It has 64 nationwide affiliates with the shared mission to advance the independence, productivity and full citizenship of those with cerebral palsy, intellectual and developmental disabilities, and other conditions.

Sarah A. Drob, Chief Executive Officer
Tim McHugh, COO
Rae D. Baldino, Director, Communications & Dvlpmnt

Cerebral Palsy / State Agencies & Support Groups

Rhode Island

1311 **United Cerebral Palsy of Rhode Island**
200 Main Street, Suite 210, PO Box 36
Pawtucket, RI 02862
401-728-1800
Fax: 401-728-0182
info@ucpri.org
www.ucpri.org

For almost 70 years United Cerebral Palsy (UCP) has worked to ensure individuals with disabilities are included and involved in every facet of society. It has 64 nationwide affiliates with the shared mission to advance the independence, productivity and full citizenship of those with cerebral palsy, intellectual and developmental disabilities, and other conditions.

Peter Quattromani, Executive Director & CEO
Robert Winters, Director of Operations

South Carolina

1312 **United Cerebral Palsy of South Carolina**
1101 Harbor Drive
West Columbia, SC 29169
803-926-8878
888-827-7277
Fax: 803-926-1272
info@ucpsc.org
www.ucpsc.org

For almost 70 years United Cerebral Palsy (UCP) has worked to ensure individuals with disabilities are included and involved in every facet of society. It has 64 nationwide affiliates with the shared mission to advance the independence, productivity and full citizenship of those with cerebral palsy, intellectual and developmental disabilities, and other conditions.

Diane Wilush, President & CEO
Brad Beasley, Executive Director
Alanna Boozer, Development Coordinator

Tennessee

1313 **LIVITUP, Inc.**
4189 Leroy Avenue
Memphis, TN 38108
901-761-4277
Fax: 901-761-7876
www.livitupinc.org

Formerly United Cerebral Palsy (UCP) Mid-South. Provides information, advocacy, referral services for persons with disabilities and/or their families.

Kelly Burrow, Executive Director
Stephanie Greer, Program Director
Teresa Caruthers, Program Coordinator

1314 **United Cerebral Palsy of Middle Tennessee**
1200 9th Avenue North Suite 110
Nashville, TN 37208
615-242-4091
Fax: 615-242-3582
request_info@ucpnashville.org
www.ucpmidtn.org

For almost 70 years United Cerebral Palsy (UCP) has worked to ensure individuals with disabilities are included and involved in every facet of society. It has 64 nationwide affiliates with the shared mission to advance the independence, productivity and full citizenship of those with cerebral palsy, intellectual and developmental disabilities, and other conditions.

Deana Claiborne, Executive Director
Jo Ver Mulm, Family Support Program Coordinator

Texas

1315 **Easter Seals of Greater Houston**
4888 Loop Central Drive, Ste 200
Houston, TX 77081
713-838-9050
Fax: 713-838-9098
info@eastersealshouston.org
www.eastersealshouston.org

Provides information, advocacy, referral services for persons with disabilities and/or their families.

Elise Hough, CEO
Kelly Klein, Development Director
Dena Day, ECI Infant Program

Virginia

1316 **United Cerebral Palsy of Washington DC & Northern Virginia**
3135 8th Street NE
Washington, DC 20017
202-269-1500
webmaster@ucpdc.org
www.ucpdc.org

For almost 70 years United Cerebral Palsy (UCP) has worked to ensure individuals with disabilities are included and involved in every facet of society. It has 64 nationwide affiliates with the shared mission to advance the independence, productivity and full citizenship of those with cerebral palsy, intellectual and developmental disabilities, and other conditions.

Dawn Gillom-Carter, Executive Director
Tola Akinmade, Director, Health Services

Wisconsin

1317 **Broadscope Disability Services**
6102 W. Layton Avenue
Greenfield, WI 53220
414-329-4500
888-482-7739
Fax: 414-329-4510
info@broadscope.org
www.ucpsew.org

Formerly United Cerebral Palsy of SE Wisconsin. Provides information, advocacy, referral services for persons with disabilities and/or their families. UCP also operates an equipment loan program, conducts parent workshops, disseminates written literature on topics of interest to people with disabilities.

Mary Schinkowitch, Executive Director
Debra Boehner, Community Support Coordinator

1318 **United Cerebral Palsy of Greater Dane County**
2801 Coho Street, Suite 100
Madison, WI 53713
608-237-8512
Fax: 608-273-3426
gingers@ucpdane.org
www.ucpdane.org

United Cerebral Palsy provides information, advocacy, referral services for persons with disabilities and/or their families. UCP also conducts parent workshops and disseminates written literature on topics of interest to people with disabilities.

Ginger Schwahn, Executive Director
Anna Stern, President

1319 **United Cerebral Palsy of West Central Wisconsin**
206 Water Street
Eau Claire, WI 54703
715-832-1782
Fax: 715-832-8203
ucp1dave@sbcglobal.net
www.ucpwcw.org

For almost 70 years United Cerebral Palsy (UCP) has worked to ensure individuals with disabilities are included and involved in every facet of society. It has 64 nationwide affiliates with the shared mission to advance the independence, productivity and full citizenship of those with cerebral palsy, intellectual and developmental disabilities, and other conditions.

Todd Breaker, Executive Director
Measha Vieth, Programs Manager
Martha Woodworth, Program Coordinator

Cerebral Palsy / Web Sites

Libraries & Resource Centers

1320 National Rehabilitation Information Center
8400 Corporate Drive, Suite 500
Landover, MD 20785
800-346-2742
Fax: 301-459-4263
TTY: 301-459-5984
naricinfo@heitechservices.com
www.naric.com

Committed to providing direct, personal and information services to anyone interested in disability rehabilitation issues; Committed to serving consumers, researchers, family members, health professionals, educators, counselors, students, librarians and the administrators.

Mark X. Odum, Project Director
Jessica H. Chaiken, Media/Information Services Manager
Natalie J. Collier, Library and Acquisitions Manager

Research Centers

1321 Orthopaedic Biomechanics Laboratory
Shriners Hospital for Crippled Children
1701 19th Avenue
San Francisco, CA 94122
415-665-1100
Fax: 415-661-3615

Offers research and studies into cerebral palsy.

Stephen R Skinner, Clinical Director

1322 United Cerebral Palsy Research and Educational Foundation
186 Princeton Hightstown Road Building 4 2nd Floor
Princeton Junction, NJ 08550
609-452-1200
800-872-5827
Fax: 609-452-1201
cpirf@cpirf.org
www.cpirf.org

Provides research grants to prevent cerebral palsy and to improve treatment, management and functioning of persons with cerebral palsy.

Glenn R Tringali, Chief Executive Officer/President
James A Blackman, M.D., M.P.H, Medical Director
Jacqueline M Carmosino, Manager of Administration

Conferences

1323 American Academy for Cerebral Palsy and Developmental Medicine Annual Meeting
555 E Wells Street, Suite 1100
Milwaukee, WI 53202
414-918-3014
Fax: 414-276-2146
info@aacpdm.org
www.aacpdm.org

October

Anniekay Erby, Executive Director
Erin Trimmer, Senior Meetings Manager
Elizabeth Mueller, Meetings Coordinator

1324 American School Counselor Association Annual Conference
1101 King Street, Suite 310
Alexandria, VA 22314
703-683-2722
800-306-4722
Fax: 703-997-7572
asca@schoolcounselor.org
www.schoolcounselor.org

The mission of ASCA is to represent professional school counselors and to promote professionalism and ethical practices.

3,000 Attendees

Richard Wong, Executive Director
Jennifer Walsh, Director, Education & Training
Kathleen M Rakestraw, Director of Communications

Audio Video

1325 Accidents of Nature
Random House
1745 Broadway
New York, NY 10019
212-782-9000
rhkidspublicity@randomhouse.com
www.randomhouse.com

About a girl who goes to a camp and has experiences that will change her life forever. Audio book feature.

2006
ISBN: 0-739335-30-8

1326 Cerebral Palsy: What Every Parent Should Know
Films for the Humanities and Sciences
132 West 31st Street, 16th Floor
New York, NY 10001
800-257-5126
Fax: 609-275-0266
custserv@films.com
ffh.films.com

This program covers the causes, symptoms, and range of possible treatments of cerebral palsy, including the relationship between physical and mental handicaps, and the role of medications and physical therapy treatment.

1991 19 minutes
ISBN: 1-421336-41-1

Web Sites

1327 American Academy for Cerebral Palsy and Developmental Medicine
555 E Wells Street, Suite 1100
Milwaukee, WI 53202
414-918-3014
Fax: 414-276-2146
info@aacpdm.org
www.aacpdm.org

Organization of professionals involved in the care of people with Cerebral Palsy, developmental disorders, and related diseases.

Anniekay Erby, Executive Director

1328 Center for Parent Information and Resources (CPIR)
c/o SPAN, 35 Halsey Street, 4th Floor
Newark, NJ 07102
973-642-8100
malizo@spanadvocacy.org
www.parentcenterhub.org

Family-friendly information and research-based materials on key topics for Parent Centers. Private workspaces for Parent Centers to exchange resources, discuss high-priority topics, and solve mutual challenges. Coordination of parent training efforts throughout the network.

Myriam Alizo, Project Assistant

1329 Easter Seals
141 W Jackson Boulevard, Suite 1400A
Chicago, IL 60604
312-726-6200
800-221-6827
Fax: 312-726-1494
info@easterseals.com
www.easterseals.com

Easter Seals' mission is to create solutions that change lives for children and adults with disabilities and to provide appropriate developmental and rehabilitation services. Services provided include early intervention, after-school programs, preschool, tutoring, medical rehabilitation, vocational services, adult and senior day services, respite and in home care, camping and recreation, residential housing, support services, support groups, transportation, and referrals.

Kendra Davenport, President & CEO

1330 Health Answers Education Sudler-WPP Health Practice
700 Dresher Road
Horsham, PA 19044
215-442-9010
www.healthanswers.com

The vision was to provide a breadth of services to clients through the formation of a network of companies. Each company plays a key role in meeting out clients' needs.

Cerebral Palsy / Book Publishers

Mike Hudnall, CEO

1331 Infinitec
547 W. Jackson Street, Suite 225
Chicago, IL 60661
312-765-0419
Fax: 312-765-0503
mbettlach@ucpnet.org
www.infinitec.org

The mission of Infinitec is to advance independence and promote inclusive opportunities for children and adults with disabilities throught technology.

Mary Bettlach, Managing Director

1332 My Child Without Limits
www.mychildwithoutlimits.org

www.mychildwithoutlimits.org

An authoritative early intervention resource for families of young children ages 0-5 with developmental delays or disabilities, and professionals looking for a single, trusted, aggregate source of information that relates to their needs and interests. All medical information is reviewed by the My Child Without Limits medical advisory board, a panel composed of doctors in the fields of developmental disability and delay.

1333 Pediatric Brain Foundation
2144 E. Republic Road, Bldg B, Ste 201
Springfield, MO 65804
417-887-4242
madison@pediatricbrainfoundation.org
www.pediatricbrainfoundation.org

Formerly Children's Neurobiological Solutions, the Foundation is a national, nonprofit organization committed to the goal of making sure every family with children suffering from all neurological disorders are provided with financial support.

Rochette Dahler, President
Matt Dahler, VP
Gillian Harrington, Director, Asset Allocation

1334 Scope (UK)
www.scope.org.uk/

www.scope.org.uk/

Our aim is that disabled people achieve equality: a society in which they are as valued and have the same human and civil rights as everyone else.

Andrew McDonald, Chair
John Gilbert, Treasurer
Richard Hawkes, Chief Executive

1335 United Cerebral Palsy (UCP)
1825 K Street NW Suite 600
Washington, DC 20006
202-776-0406
800-872-5827
www.ucp.org

The UCP is the leading source of information on cerebral palsy and is a pivitol advocate for the rights of persons with any disability. As one of the largest health charities in America, UCP's mission is to advance the independence, productivity and full citizenship of people with Cerebral Palsy and other diabilities.

Armando Contreras, President & CEO
Anita Porco, VP, Affiliate Network
Michael Ludgaro, Manager of Development

1336 WE MOVE (Worldwide Education and Awareness of Movement Disorders)
204 West 84th Street
New York, NY 10024
wemove@wemove.org

WE MOVE provides movement disorder information and educational materials to physicians, patients and families, the media, and the public via its comprehensive Web sites, training courses, and more. Its goal is to make early diagnosis, up-to-date treatment and patient support a reality for all people living with movement disorders.

Book Publishers

1337 A Mother's Touch: The Tiffany Callo Story
United Cerebral Palsy
1825 K Street NW, Suite 600
Washington, DC 20006
202-776-0406
800-872-5827
Fax: 202-776-0414
info@ucp.org
www.ucp.org

A vivid portrayal of a woman with cerebral palsy who faced discrimination because of her disability.

Woody Connette, Chair
Ian Ridlon, Vice Chair
Pamela Talkin, Secretary

1338 After the Tears: Parents Talk About Raising a Child with a Disability
United Cerebral Palsy
1825 K Street NW, Suite 600
Washington, DC 20006
202-776-0406
800-872-5827
Fax: 202-776-0414
info@ucp.org
www.ucp.org

Book draws on stories of parents who have struggled, learned and grown in the years since their child was born with a disability.

89 pages Softcover

Woody Connette, Chair
Ian Ridlon, Vice Chair
Pamela Talkin, Secretary

1339 An Introduction to Your Child Who Has Cerebral Palsy
Medic Publishing Company
PO Box 89
Redmond, WA 98073
425-881-2883

Information and answers to questions for parents of children with cerebral palsy.

1340 Breaking Ground: Ten Families Building Opportunities Through Integration
United Cerebral Palsy
1825 K Street NW, Suite 600
Washington, DC 20006
202-776-0406
800-872-5827
Fax: 202-776-0414
info@ucp.org
www.ucp.org

Gives examples of strategies families have used to integrate the children fully into their schools and communities.

75 pages Softcover

Woody Connette, Chair
Ian Ridlon, Vice Chair
Pamela Talkin, Secretary

1341 Can't You be Still?
Gemma B Publishing
101-478 River Avenue, #779
Winnipeg, Manitoba, R3L 0
Canada
204-452-7566
Fax: 204-475-9903
gempub@shaw.ca
www.gemmab.ca

This wonderfully written children's book features a heroine, Ann, with cerebral palsy who goes to school for the first time. First in a trilogy, the book is written in the first person since Ann cannot speak out loud intelligibly but has lots of words inside her head.

28 pages Softcover

Sarah Yates
Anne Allan

Cerebral Palsy / Book Publishers

1342 Children With Cerebral Palsy: A Parents Guide
Peytral Publications
PO Box 1162
Minnetonka, MN 55345
952-949-8707
877-739-8725
Fax: 952-906-9777
help@peytral.com
www.peytral.com

Informative handbook for parents of children and teens; covers medical, educational, legal, family life, daily care, emotional issues and more.

470 pages

1343 Congenital Disorders Sourcebook
Greg Mullin, author
Omnigraphics
615 Griswold Street, Ste 520
Detroit, MI 48226
610-461-3548
800-234-1340
Fax: 800-875-1340
contact@omnigraphics.com
www.omnigraphics.com

Provides basic consumer health information about the most common types of nonhereditary birth defects and disorders related to prematurity, gestational injuries, congenital infections, and birth complications, including disorders of the heart, brain, gastrointestinal tract, musculoskeletal system, urinary tract, and reproductive system, craniofacial disorders, cerebral palsy, spina bifida, and fetal alcohol syndrome, and detailing the causes, diagnostic tests, and treatments for each.

664 pages
ISBN: 0-780816-13-8

1344 Connecting Students: A Guide to Thoughtful Friendship Facilitation
United Cerebral Palsy
1660 L Street NW, Suite 700
Washington, DC 20036
202-776-0406
800-872-5823
Fax: 202-776-0414
info@ucp.org
www.ucp.org

Contains helpful strategies on real-life experiences on building friendships.

48 pages Softcover

Woody Connette, Chair
Ian Ridlon, Vice Chair
Pamela Talkin, Secretary

1345 Discovery Book
United Cerebral Palsy
1825 K Street NW, Suite 600
Washington, DC 20006
202-776-0406
800-872-5827
Fax: 202-776-0414
info@ucp.org
www.ucp.org

Created within a United Cerebral Palsy group for childern with physical disabilities, The Discovery Book is an exploration of social and psychological aspects of childhood disability. Accompanied by their artwork, children speak in their own words about important areas of life such as: What about friends?; Doctors and hospitals; Problems and challenges; and Goals, wishes & dreams.

96 pages

Woody Connette, Chair
Ian Ridlon, Vice Chair
Pamela Talkin, Secretary

1346 Each of Us Remembers: Parents of Children With Cerebral Palsy
United Cerebral Palsy
1825 K Street NW, Suite 600
Washington, DC 20006
202-776-0406
800-872-5827
Fax: 202-776-0414
info@ucp.org
www.ucp.org

Parents of children with cerebral palsy answer questions that people really need to know.

Woody Connette, Chair
Ian Ridlon, Vice Chair
Pamela Talkin, Secretary

1347 Gemma B Publishing
101-478 River Avenue, Suite 779
Winnipeg, MB R3L 0
Canada
204-452-7566
Fax: 204-475-9903
gempub@shaw.ca
www.gemmab.ca

Gemma B Publishing was formed to develop literary heroines for the disabled, emphasizing their active participation in life.

Sarah Yates, Founder

1348 Handling the Young Cerebral Palsied Child at Home
United Cerebral Palsy
1825 K Street NW, Suite 600
Washington, DC 20006
202-776-0406
800-872-5827
Fax: 202-776-0414
info@ucp.org
www.ucp.org

Offers chapters on bathing, feeding, dressing and play for parents of children with cerebral palsy.

337 pages Softcover

Woody Connette, Chair
Ian Ridlon, Vice Chair
Pamela Talkin, Secretary

1349 Here's What I Mean to Say
Gemma B Publishing
101-478 River Avenue, #779
Winnipeg, Manitoba, R3L 0
Canada
204-452-7566
Fax: 204-475-9903
gempub@shaw.ca
www.gemmab.ca

Third in the Ann trilogy, Ann learns to read and uncovers the magic of literacy. She uses a speech program in her computer and wonders, when she succeeds in reading, 'Is it me or is it my angel?'

24 pages
ISBN: 0-969647-72-7

Sarah Yates
Anne Allan

1350 Lucky Lou Gets Game
Gemma B Publishing
101-478 River Avenue, #779
Winnipeg, Manitoba, R3L 0
Canada
204-452-7566
Fax: 204-475-9903
gempub@shaw.ca
www.gemmab.ca

A coming of age young adult novel about 17-year old Lucky Lou who takes on a neighborhood, learns how to play baseball, and meets the boy who was never in her dreams. In this funny and insightful book, Lou gets game and the results are unexpected.

24 pages
ISBN: 0-969647-71-9

Sarah Yates, Autor
Anne Allan

Cerebral Palsy / Newsletters

1351 Natural Supports in School/Work/Community for the Severely Disabled
United Cerebral Palsy
1825 K Street NW, Suite 600
Washington, DC 20006
202-776-0406
800-872-5827
Fax: 202-776-0414
info@ucp.org
www.ucp.org

Promotes the position that assistance must be defined by the needs of individuals rather than the requirements of the service systems.

361 pages Softcover

Woody Connette, Chair
Ian Ridlon, Vice Chair
Pamela Talkin, Secretary

1352 No Time for Jello: One Family's Experience
Brookline Books
8 Trumbell Rd, Suite B-001
Northampton, MA 01060
413-584-0184
Fax: 413-584-6184
brbooks@yahoo.com
http://brooklinebooks.com

One family's story of their attempts to remediate and cure the effects of cerebral palsied condition the oldest son was born with. The Bratts traveled traditional routes, through distinguished medical centers in Boston, and nontraditional routes in a search for treatments that would help their son.

Softcover
ISBN: 0-253363-65-9

1353 Nobody Knows
Gemma B Publishing
101-478 River Avenue, #779
Winnipeg, Manitoba, R3L 0
Canada
204-452-7566
Fax: 204-475-9903
gempub@shaw.ca
www.gemmab.ca

Sequel to 'Can't You Be Still,' Ann gets frustrated that nobody knows what she wants and is trying to say; they find it hard to understand her. She goes out to find someone who can understand and in the process, learns that there are many ways to communicate.

24 pages
ISBN: 0-969647-71-9

Sarah Yates
Anne Allan

1354 Opening Doors: Strategies for Including All Students in Regular Education
United Cerebral Palsy
1825 K Street NW, Suite 600
Washington, DC 20006
202-776-0406
800-872-5827
Fax: 202-776-0414
info@ucp.org
www.ucp.org

Contains practical information for including and supporting all students in regular classes.

55 pages Softcover

Woody Connette, Chair
Ian Ridlon, Vice Chair
Pamela Talkin, Secretary

1355 Teaching Motor Skills to Children with Cerebral Palsy & Similar Movement Disorders
Woodbine House
6510 Bells Mill Road
Bethesda, MD 20817
301-897-3570
800-843-7323
Fax: 301-897-5838
info@woodbinehouse.com
www.woodbinehouse.com

The resource that parents, therapists, and other caregivers can consult to help children with gross motor delays learn and practice motor skills outside of therapy sessions.

2006 275 pages
ISBN: 1-890627-72-0

1356 Walk with Me
United Cerebral Palsy
1825 K Sreet NW, Suite 600
Washington, DC 20006
202-776-0406
800-872-5827
Fax: 202-776-0414
info@ucp.org
www.ucp.org

A story written by eight-year-old Eric Grimm covering his thoughts on living with cerebral palsy.

Woody Connette, Chair
Ian Ridlon, Vice Chair
Pamela Talkin, Secretary

Newsletters

1357 Family Support Bulletin
United Cerebral Palsy
1825 K Street NW Suite 600
Washington, DC 20006
202-776-0406
800-872-5827
Fax: 202-776-0414
info@ucp.org
www.ucp.org

A detailed quarterly journal that takes a comprehensive look at the latest policies, resources and legislative information enacted in Washington and state capitals.

Quarterly

Stephen Bennett, President/ CEO
Connie Garner, EVP, Public Policy
Anita Porco, VP, Affiliate Network

1358 My Child Without Limits Newsletter
United Cerebral Palsy
1825 K Street NW Suite 600
Washington, DC 20006
202-776-0406
800-872-5827
Fax: 202-776-0414
info@ucp.org
www.ucp.org

A monthly publication that highlights new and relevant content from the 'My Child Without Limits' web site and online community, which provides an early intervention resource for families of young children ages 0-5 with developmental delays or disabilities, and the professionals who serve them.

Stephen Bennett, President & CEO
Connie Garner, EVP, Public Policy
Anita Porco, VP, Affiliate Network

1359 Networker
United Cerebral Palsy
1825 K Street NW Suite 600
Washington, DC 20006
202-776-0406
800-872-5827
Fax: 202-776-0414
info@ucp.org
www.ucp.org

Offers the latest information on the newest technology available for persons with cerebral palsy.

Quarterly

Stephen Bennett, President/ CEO
Connie Garner, EVP, Public Policy
Anita Porco, VP, Affiliate Network

Cerebral Palsy / Camps

1360 UCP Washington Wire
United Cerebral Palsy
1825 K Street NW Suite 600
Washington, DC 20006
202-776-0406
800-872-5827
Fax: 202-776-0414
info@ucp.org
www.ucp.org

A weekly publication that provides a comprehensive source of information on federal legislation, agency regulations, court decisions and other issues of interest to the disability community.

Stephen Bennett, President & CEO
Connie Garner, EVP, Public Policy
Anita Porco, VP, Affiliate Network

Pamphlets

1361 Cerebral Palsy-Facts & Figures
United Cerebral Palsy
1825 K Street NW Suite 600
Washington, DC 20006
202-776-0406
800-872-5827
Fax: 202-776-0414
www.ucp.org

Offers information on what cerebral palsy is, the effects, causes, types, and prevention.

Stephen Bennett, President/ CEO
Connie Garner, EVP, Public Policy
Anita Porco, VP, Affiliate Network

Camps

1362 Camp Merrimack
3320 Triana Boulevard
Huntsville, AL 35805
256-534-6455
ksimari@merrimackhall.com
www.merrimackhall.com

A unique arts half-day camp for children ages 3 through 12; open to children with special needs including Cerebral Palsy, Down Syndrome, autism and others.

Ashley Dinges, Executive Director
Kim Simari, Managing Director

1363 Camp Ramah in New England Tikvah Program
39 Bennett Street
Palmer, MA 01609
413-283-9771
Fax: 413-283-6661
info@campramahne.org
www.campramahne.org

The Tikvah program is one of the first summer programs for Jewish children with special needs. It continues to grow and evolve as it strives to serve campers with a wide range of special needs including, but not limited to, congitive impairments, autism, cerebral palsy and seizure disorder.

Howard Blas, Tikvah Program Director
Talya Kalender, Director, Camper Care
Benjamin Greene, Director of Education

1364 Cerebral Palsy Center Summer Program
7 Sanford Avenue
Belleville, NJ
201-751-0200
info@kidscamps.com
www.kidscamps.com

1365 Charles Campbell Children's Camp
PO Box 23342
Billings, MT 59104
campbellcamp@msn.com
www.billingslions.org

Camp for children with physical disabilities including but not limited to: sight or hearing impairment, cerebral palsy, spina bifida, amputee, gross motor skill impairments, and other disabilities.

Doug Hanson, Director

1366 Crotched Mountain School & Rehabilitation Center
1 Verney Drive
Greenfield, NH 03047
603-547-3311
800-800-966
Fax: 603-547-3232
info@crotchedmountain.org
www.cmf.org

Currently serves children ages 6-22 with multiple-handicaps including: Cerebral Palsy, Spina Bifida, visual and hearing impairments and neurological disabilities, developmental disorders, autism, behavioral and emotional disorders, seizure disorders, spinal cord and head injuries. Member of the National Association of Independent Schools and accredited with the NE Association of Schools and Colleges, Independent Schools of Northern NE.

Rita Phinney, Director Admissions
John Young, Registrar

1367 Easter Seals Wisconsin Camp Respite
1550 Waubeek Road
Wisconsin Dells, WI 53965
608-254-2502
Fax: 608-253-0327
www.eastersealswisconsin.com

Camp for individuals age 3 to adult with moderate to severe disabilities. The campers have a variety of different diagnosis such as: autism, cerebral palsy, traumatic brain injury, developmental disabilities, and behavioral issues.

Dan Fournes, Camp Director

1368 Eric RicStar Winter Music Therapy Summer Camp
4930 S Hagadorn Rd
East Lansing, MI 48823
517-353-7661
Fax: 517-355-3292
commusic@msu.edu
www.cms.msu.edu

The purpose of this camp is to provide opportunities for musical expression, enjoyment and interaction for all people with special needs and their siblings.

Cindy Edgerton, Director
Judy Winter, Co-Chair

Charcot-Marie-Tooth Disease / Description

Description

1369 CHARCOT-MARIE-TOOTH DISEASE

Charcot-Marie-Tooth (CMT) disease belongs to a group of disorders known as hereditary motor-sensory neuropathies or HMSNs. The HMSNs are progressive disorders of nerves outside of the central nervous system that extend from the brain and spinal cord to particular areas of the body (peripheral nervous system). Symptoms and findings associated with these disorders are primarily the result of involvement of motor nerve fibers (those that affect motion). These nerves transmit various nerve impulses away from the brain and spinal cord to their termination (e.g., muscle tissue). As these disorders progress, affected individuals may experience some symptoms due to sensory and autonomic involvement. Sensory nerve fibers carry impulses to the brain and spinal cord. The autonomic nervous system is the portion of the peripheral nervous system that regulates involuntary functioning of particular tissues and organs.

There are different types of Charcot-Marie-Tooth disease that have varying modes of inheritance. Charcot-Marie-Tooth disease (in all its forms) is the most prevalent hereditary peripheral neuropathy, affecting approximately one in 2,500 individuals. The most common form of the disease, known as Charcot-Marie-Tooth disease type 1A or CMT1A, is inherited as an autosomal dominant trait. A disease gene for CMT1A is located on the short arm of chromosome 17.

Children with CMT type 1A usually do not have associated symptoms until late childhood or early adolescence. However, some may experience abnormalities in their manner of walking (gait disturbances) as early as the second year of life. In other, rare instances, associated symptoms may not become apparent until middle adulthood. CMT1A initially affects muscles supplied by nerves of the lower legs (peroneal and tibial nerves), causing muscle degeneration (atrophy) in the lower legs and feet. This is accompanied by muscle weakness and a distinctive stork-like contour of the legs. Bending movements of the ankles become progressively weaker, eventually resulting in footdrop, a condition in which the foot does not flex or bend upward. In addition, the arch of the foot becomes unusually increased in height (pescavus deformities). An unstable gait may develop, and children may appear clumsy, easily tripping or falling. Although muscles of both legs are affected, disease progression and associated findings usually differ slightly from one side of the body to the other.

As the disorder progresses, individuals with CMT1A also usually develop a loss of muscle tissue mass and weakness in the forearms and hands. These areas seem to be less severely affected than the lower legs. However, patients may eventually develop permanent fixation of certain joints in a bend position. This typically occurs in the fingers and wrists. Some patients also experience gradual sensory involvement, such as abnormal burning or tingling sensations (paresthesias) in the feet. Associated autonomic abnormalities may include unusual paleness (pallor) or blotching of the skin, especially of the feet. In individuals with CMT1A, specialized testing typically reveals a marked reduction in the transmission of motor and sensory nerve signals to affected muscles (reduced conduction velocities).

Although CMT1A is progressive, most affected individuals maintain the ability to walk. However, the use of special orthopedic appliances, such as stiff boots that reach to the midcalf, plastic splints, or light leg braces, are typically necessary to help stabilize the ankles. Surgical measures may be considered, such as surgical fusion of the ankles. In addition, certain medications may help to alleviate burning sensations in the feet (e.g., carbamazepine or phenytoin). Other treatment is symptomatic and supportive.

In addition to Charcot-Marie-Tooth disease type 1A, additional autosomal dominant, autosomal recessive, and X-linked forms of the disease have been identified. Specific symptoms and findings and the nature of the disorder progression may vary, depending upon the specific form of the disease.

National Associations & Support Groups

1370 American Academy of Pediatrics
345 Park Blvd
Itasca, IL 60143
800-433-9016
Fax: 847-434-8000
mcc@aap.org
www.aap.org

The American Academy of Pediatrics and its member pediatricians are committed to the attainment of optimal physical, mental and social health and well-being for all infants, children, adolescents, and young adults.

Lynn Olson, PhD, VP, Research
Mark Del Monte, JD, CEO/Executive VP
Vera Tait, MD, FAAP, Chief Medical Officer

State Agencies & Support Groups

New York

1371 CMTA Chapter - New York (Greater)
CMT Association
333 East 34th StreetSuite 1J
Manhattan, NY 10016
212-535-4314
Fax: 212-535-6392
www.cmtnyc.org

Every other month (Third Saturday from 1:00 - 3:00 p.m.) - check website

Dr David Younger, Contact

Ohio

1372 CMTA Chapter - Ohio
CMT Association
405 Wagner Avenue
Greenville, OH 45331
937-548-3963
www.charcot-marie-tooth.org

Fourth Thursday, April - October

Dot Cain, Contact

Pennsylvania

1373 CMTA Chapter - Pennsylvania
CMT Association
PO Box 105
Glenolden, PA 19036
610-499-9264
800-606-2682
Fax: 610-499-9267
www.cmtausa.org

Bi-monthly (3rd Saturday, 10:00 a.m. - 12:00 p.m.)

Herbert Beron, Chairman
Gary J Gasper, Treasurer
Elizabeth Ouellette, Secretary

Charcot-Marie-Tooth Disease / Pamphlets

Web Sites

1374 **CMT Net**
275 Madison Ave (corner of 40th St)
New York, NY 10016
www.rcn.com

CMTNet is intended to provide information for both the medical and non-medical communities.

1375 **Charcot-Marie-Tooth Association**
PO Box 105
Glenolden, PA 19036
610-499-9264
800-606-2682
Fax: 610-499-9267
info@cmtausa.org
www.cmtausa.org

Information regarding patient support, public education, promotion of research and ultimately the treatment and cure of CMT.

Patrick A. Livney, Chief Executive Officer
Kim Magee, Director of Finance
Susan Ruediger, Director of Development

1376 **Health Answers Education Sudler-WPP Health Practice**
700 Dresher Road
Horsham, PA 19044
215-442-9010
www.healthanswers.com

The vision was to provide a breadth of services to clients through the formation of a network of companies. Each company plays a key role in meeting our clients' needs.

Mike Hudnall, CEO

1377 **Muscular Dystrophy Association**
16 N Clark, Ste 3550
Chicago, IL 60601
800-572-1717
resourcecenter@mda.org
www.mda.org

Information regarding neuromuscular diseases through programs of worldwide research, comprehensive medical and community services, and far-reaching professional and public health education; including publications.

R. Rodney Howell, MD, Chairman
Lynn O'Connor Vos, President & CEO
Mary Fiance, Director, PR & Communications

Book Publishers

1378 **Charcot-Marie-Tooth Disorders: A Handbook for Primary Care Physicians**
Charcot-Marie-Tooth Association
PO Box 105
Glenolden, PA 19036
610-499-9264
800-606-2682
Fax: 610-499-9267
info@cmtausa.org
www.cmtausa.org

Excellent source of information about the causes, symptoms, and treatment/management of CMT.

1995 130 pages

Patrick A Livney, CEO
Patricia Dreibelbis, Director Of Program Services
Kim Magee, Director Of Finance

1379 **Let's Talk About Going to the Hospital**
Rosen Publishing Group's PowerKids Press
29 E 21st Street
New York, NY 10010
212-777-3017
800-237-9932
Fax: 888-436-4643
rosenpub@tribeca.ios.com
www.rosenpublishing.com

If a child has to check into the hospital, chances are he or she is already upset about being ill. Knowing how a hospital functions and what the procedures are, such as when family members can visit, will help in what is already a stressful situation. Grades K-5.

24 pages
ISBN: 0-823950-36-0

Roger Rosen, President

Magazines

1380 **Quest Magazine**
MDA Publications
222 S. Riverside Plaza, Suite 1500
Chicago, IL 60606
520-529-2000
800-572-1717
Fax: 520-529-5300
mda@mdausa.org
mda.org

A national magazine that goes out to everyone registered with MDA, MDA clinics, researchers and subscribers. It presents news related to muscular dystrophy and other neuromuscular diseases including research, personal profiles, fund raising activities, patient services, and lifestyle information including products and trends.

Bimonthly

Steven M. Derks, President/ CEO
Valerie A. Cwik, M.D., EVP/ CMO/ CSO
Julie Faber, EVP/ CFO

Newsletters

1381 **CMTA Report**
CMT Association
PO Box 105
Glenolden, PA 19036
610-499-9264
800-606-2682
Fax: 610-499-9267
info@charcot-marie-tooth.org
www.cmtausa.org

Contains articles on CMT topics, research news and patient profiles. Free with membership.

Bi-Monthly

Patrick A. Livney, Chief Executive Officer
Kim Magee, Director of Finance
Susan Ruediger, Director of Development

Pamphlets

1382 **CMT Brochure**
Charcot-Marie-Tooth Association
PO Box 105
Glenolden, PA 19036
610-499-9264
800-606-2682
Fax: 610-499-9267
info@charcot-marie-tooth.org
www.cmtausa.org

Provides a quick overview of CMT.

2005 8 pages

Patrick A. Livney, Chief Executive Officer
Kim Magee, Director of Finance
Susan Ruediger, Director of Development

1383 **CMT Facts I**
Charcot-Marie-Tooth Association
PO Box 105
Glenolden, PA 19036
610-499-9264
800-606-2682
Fax: 610-499-9267
info@charcot-marie-tooth.org
www.cmtausa.org

Offers information on the neurotrophic drugs, genetics and therapies for CMT, surgical options and an overview of the disorder.

1993 16 pages

Patrick A. Livney, Chief Executive Officer
Kim Magee, Director of Finance
Susan Ruediger, Director of Development

Charcot-Marie-Tooth Disease / Pamphlets

1384 CMT Facts II
Charcot-Marie-Tooth Association
PO Box 105
Glenolden, PA 19036
610-499-9264
800-606-2682
Fax: 610-499-9267
info@charcot-marie-tooth.org
www.cmtausa.org

Offers information on adaptive devices, feature specialists and the Americans with disabilities act.

1993 24 pages

Patrick A. Livney, Chief Executive Officer
Kim Magee, Director of Finance
Susan Ruediger, Director of Development

1385 CMT Facts III
Charcot-Marie-Tooth Association
PO Box 105
Glenolden, PA 19036
610-499-9264
800-606-2682
Fax: 610-499-9267
info@charcot-marie-tooth.org
www.cmtausa.org

Offers information on neurotrophic drugs, neuromuscular disorders, genetic news and doctor's questions and answers.

1995 24 pages

Patrick A. Livney, Chief Executive Officer
Kim Magee, Director of Finance
Susan Ruediger, Director of Development

1386 CMT Facts IV
Charcot-Marie-Tooth Association
PO Box 105
Glenolden, PA 19036
610-499-9264
800-606-2682
Fax: 610-499-9267
info@charcot-marie-tooth.org
www.cmtausa.org

Provides information for Charcot-Marie-Tooth patients.

1998 32 pages

Patrick A. Livney, Chief Executive Officer
Kim Magee, Director of Finance
Susan Ruediger, Director of Development

1387 CMT Facts V
Charcot-Marie-Tooth Association
PO Box 105
Glenolden, PA 19036
610-499-9264
800-606-2682
Fax: 610-499-9267
info@charcot-marie-tooth.org
www.cmtausa.org

Source for information on orthotics, pain, emotional, HNPP, physical and occupational therapy, Social Security Disability and more.

2002 56 pages

Patrick A. Livney, Chief Executive Officer
Kim Magee, Director of Finance
Susan Ruediger, Director of Development

1388 Charcot-Marie-Tooth Disorders: A Guide abo ut Genetics for Patients
Charcot-Marie-Tooth Association
PO Box 105
Glenolden, PA 19036
610-499-9264
800-606-2682
Fax: 610-499-9267
www.cmtausa.org

Illustrated with easy-to-understand diagrams, this booklet outlines the basics of genetics inheritance and CMT.

2000 21 pages

Patrick A. Livney, Chief Executive Officer
Kim Magee, Director of Finance
Susan Ruediger, Director of Development

1389 Facts About Charcot-Marie-Tooth Disease an d Dejerine-Sottas
Muscular Dystrophy Association
222 S. Riverside Plaza, Suite 1500
Chicago, IL 60606
520-529-2000
800-572-1717
Fax: 520-529-5300
mda@mdausa.org
mda.org

This booklet has been prepared to give you the basic knowledge about CMT and Dejerine-Sottas disease that you'll need in order to help you prepare for changed that may offur in your future. It cover research, explaining the causes, treatments, and cures. Also available in Spanish and online.

2009 15 pages Paperback

Kristine Welker, Interim President/CEO
Valerie A. Cwik, MD, EVP, Chief Medical & Scientific
Julie Faber, EVP, CFO

1390 MDA Fact Sheet
Muscular Dystrophy Association
222 S. Riverside Plaza, Suite 1500
Chicago, IL 60606
520-529-2000
800-572-1717
Fax: 520-529-5300
mda@mdausa.org
mda.org

Provides information about the association, how it got started, and what muscular dystrophy can affect the body. Also in Spanish and online.

2008

Kristine Welker, Interim President/CEO
Valerie A. Cwik, MD, EVP, Chief Medical & Scientific
Julie Faber, EVP, CFO

Description

1391 CHILDHOOD DERMATOMYOSITIS
Synonym: Juvenile dermatomyositis (JDMS)
Involves the following Biologic System(s):
Connective Tissue Disorders, Dermatologic Disorders, Orthopedic and Muscle Disorders

Dermatomyositis is a connective tissue disorder characterized by inflammatory and degenerative changes of the muscles and distinctive lesions of the skin. Although the disorder may become apparent at any time, it most commonly occurs in children between five to 15 years of age or adults between the ages of 40 to 60 years. In children, the average age at onset is eight or nine years. More females than males are affected by dermatomyositis.

The cause of dermatomyositis is unknown. However, immune, genetic, and environmental factors are thought to play some role. Many researchers suggest that dermatomyositis is an autoimmune disorder resulting from abnormal immune responses directed against the body's own tissues.

The symptoms and findings associated with childhood dermatomyositis are similar to those seen in the adult form of the disease. However, involvement of the gastrointestinal (GI) tract and the development of abnormal calcium deposits (calcifications) within skin and muscle tissues are more frequent and widespread in childhood dermatomyositis. Affected children usually have widespread inflammation of small blood vessels (vasculitis) within connective tissues of the skin, muscles, tissues beneath the skin (subcutaneous tissues), and tissues underlying the nails (nail beds). In addition, cancerous growths (malignancies) occur in approximately 20 percent of affected adults; malignancies are rarely seen in those with childhood dermatomyositis.

In most patients with childhood dermatomyositis, the onset of symptoms is relatively gradual and subtle. Children initially experience slowly progressive muscle weakness affecting the upper arms, shoulders, hips, and thighs (proximal muscles) as well as the trunk. Involved muscles tend to be sore, stiff, tender, or abnormally hard. Affected children may develop an awkward manner of walking and gradually lose the ability to perform certain tasks, such as lifting the arms above the shoulders, combing their hair, dressing, climbing stairs, or rising from the floor unassisted. Involved muscles may eventually show varying degrees of degeneration (atrophy) and, in severe cases, permanent bending or extension in various fixed postures (joint contractures). Although muscles of the upper arms or legs are typically most severely affected, any muscle may become involved. In severe cases, affected muscles may include those of the roof of the mouth and those involved in respiration, resulting in a nasal quality to the voice; breathing difficulties; hyperventilation; inadvertent breathing of foreign materials into the respiratory passages (bronchial aspiration); and potentially life-threatening complications. In addition, involvement of muscles of the gastrointestinal tract may cause difficulties swallowing; abdominal pain; passage of dark, tarry stools containing digested blood (melena); and infrequent bowel movements or difficulty passing stools (constipation). In severe cases, gastrointestinal bleeding (hemorrhage) or other associated abnormalities (e.g., intestinal perforations) may cause potentially life-threatening conditions.

Patients with childhood dermatomyositis also develop characteristic skin changes, such as a reddish-purple rash of the upper eyelids (heliotrope rash); an abnormal accumulation of fluid in body tissues surrounding the eyes and in other facial areas (periorbital and facial edema); a reddish rash across the skin of the nose and cheeks (butterfly rash); and reddish-purple, raised, scaling skin lesions (papules) on the surfaces of certain joints, particularly the knuckles (Gottron's sign), elbows, and knees. These scaling lesions develop a central area of tissue loss (atrophy) that lacks color (vitiligo) or has increased pigmentation (hyperpigmentation). Patients may also have a dusky reddish rash covering the upper arms and legs and the upper trunk.

Approximately 20 to 50 percent of affected children also develop abnormal calcium deposits (calcifications) within muscle, skin, and subcutaneous tissues. These deposits may contribute to localized areas of muscle loss or the freezing of joints in permanently bent positions. Some patients may also experience additional symptoms and findings, such as a low-grade fever, joint inflammation (arthritis), enlargement of the liver and spleen (hepatosplenomegaly), or other abnormalities. In most patients, childhood dermatomyositis gradually becomes inactive over several years.

The treatment of patients with childhood dermatomyositis requires early, aggressive measures to help prevent potentially life-threatening complications. Such measures include evaluation to detect possible involvement of the respiratory or gastrointestinal systems and provision of ongoing nursing care for those with such involvement. Such care may include mechanical suctioning of the throat by way of the nose (nasopharyngeal suction), the creation of a temporary opening in the throat to ease breathing difficulties (tracheostomy), or mechanical breathing support (e.g., endotracheal intubation or respirator). In addition, the treatment of patients typically includes the use of corticosteroids (e.g., prednisone) to help suppress the inflammatory process of the disease. Blood levels of certain muscle enzymes are regularly measured to help gauge the effectiveness of such therapy. Once such enzyme levels are reduced to normal ranges, the steroid dosage may gradually be decreased to as low as possible while still being effective, owing to the numerous problems associated with prolonged administration or high-dose steroids. After about two years, such treatment may be discontinued without the reemergence of symptoms. In patients who do not respond to steroid therapy, certain immunosuppressant drugs such as methotrexate, azathioprine, or cyclosporine or, in some patients, intravenous immunoglobulin therapy may be beneficial. In addition, treatment may include surgical removal of calcium deposits. Physical therapy (e.g., passive exercises, eventual progression to active exercises) is important in helping to rebuild muscle strength and prevent permanent, disabling contractures. Splints may be required to help ensure proper positioning of certain limbs. Proper skin hygiene is also important in patients with childhood dermatomyositis.

National Associations & Support Groups

1392 American Academy of Pediatrics
345 Park Blvd
Itasca, IL 60143

800-433-9016
Fax: 847-434-8000
mcc@aap.org
www.aap.org

The American Academy of Pediatrics and its member pediatricians are committed to the attainment of optimal physical, mental and social health and well-being for all infants, children, adolescents, and young adults.

Lynn Olson, PhD, VP, Research
Mark Del Monte, JD, CEO/Executive VP
Vera Tait, MD, FAAP, Chief Medical Officer

1393 American Autoimmune Related Diseases Association
19176 Hall Road, Suite 130
Clinton, MI 48038
586-776-3900
aarda@aarda.org
www.aarda.org

The American Autoimmune Related Diseases Association is dedicated to the eradication of autoimmune diseases and the alleviation of suffering and the socioeconomic impact of autoimmunity through fostering and facilitating collaboration in the areas of education, public awareness, research, and patient services in an effective, ethical and efficient manner.

Lilly Stairs, Interim President/CEO
Laura Simpson, COO

1394 American Osteopathic College of Dermatology
2902 N Baltimore Street, PO Box 7525
Kirksville, MO 63501
660-665-2184
Fax: 660-627-2623
www.aocd.org

Strives to improve the standards of the practice of dermatology, to stimulate the study and extend knowledge in the field of dermatology, and to promote a more general understanding of the nature and scope of services rendered by osteopathic dermatologists to other divisions of practice, hospitals, clinics and the public.

Marsha Wise, Executive Director
John Wise, Director of Events
John C. Crogan, Member Services Coordinator

1395 Arthritis Foundation
1335 Peachtree Street NE, Suite 600
Atlanta, GA 30309
800-283-7800
www.arthritis.org

The Arthritis Foundation is committed to raising awareness and reducing the unacceptable impact of arthritis, a disease which must be taken as seriously as other chronic diseases because of its devastating consequences.

Ann M. Palmer, President & CEO
Sabrina Sexton, SVP, Marketing & Communications
Robin Kinard, SVP, Operations

1396 Myositis Association
6950 Columbia Gateway Drive, Suite 370
Columbia, MD 21046
800-821-7356
tma@myositis.org
www.myositis.org

The mission of The Myositis Association is to find a cure for inflammatory and other related myopathies, while serving those affected by these diseases.

Rhonda Buckley-Bishop, Interim Executive Director
Aisha Morrow, Senior Manager, Operations
Rachel Bromley, Senior Manager, Patient Education

1397 Society for Pediatric Dermatology
8365 Keystone Crossing, Ste 107
Indianapolis, IN 46240
317-202-0224
Fax: 317-205-9481
info@pedsderm.net
www.pedsderm.net

The objective of the Society is to promote, develop and advance education, research and care of skin disease in all pediatric age groups.

Kent Lindeman, Executive Director

Libraries & Resource Centers

California

1398 University of California, San Francisco Dermatology Drug Research
515 Spruce
San Francisco, CA 94143
415-476-2001
Fax: 415-476-6014
cc.ucsf.edu/people

Conducts clinical testing of new or existing pharmalogic agents used in the treatment of skin disorders.

John Koo, MD, Director

Delaware

1399 Delaware Division of Libraries for the Blind and Physically Handicapped
43 S Dupont Highway
Dover, DE 19901
302-736-4748
800-282-8676
Fax: 302-736-6787
TDD: 302-739-4748
bedpg@lib.de.us

Braille readers receive service from Philadelphia and Pennsylvania, summer reading program, braille writer and cassettes.

Beth Landon, Librarian

Illinois

1400 Dermatology Information Network (DERMINFONET)
American Academy of Dermatology
9500 W. Bryn Mawr Avenue, Ste 500
Rosemont, IL 60018
847-240-1737
888-462-3376
Fax: 847-240-1859
info@aad.org

Consists of a collection of dermatologic databases that are available to members on a subscription and/or purchase basis. These databases are designed to run on a wide variety of personal computers.

Irvin Bomberger, Interim Executive Director

1401 National Library of Dermatologic Teaching Slides
American Academy of Dermatology
9500 W. Bryn Mawr Avenue, Ste 500
Rosemont, IL 60018
847-240-1737
888-462-3376
Fax: 847-240-1859
info@aad.org
www.aad.org

A collection of dermatologic teaching slides offering the most comprehensive series ever assembled. Each set offers a realistic presentation of classic clinical skin conditions encountered by the dermatologist.

Irvin Bomberger, Interim Executive Director

New York

1402 Laboratory of Dermatology Research
Memorial Sloan-Kettering Cancer Center
1275 York Avenue
New York, NY 10065
212-639-2000
Fax: 212-639-3576
www.mskcc.org

Specific studies on the identification of skin disorders and dermatology.

Craig B Thompson, President/CEO

1403 Rockefeller University Laboratory for Investigative Dermatology
1230 York Avenue
New York, NY 10065
212-327-7490
Fax: 212-327-7459

Research into skin disorders and the whole specialty of dermatology in general.

Barry Coller, Head

Research Centers

1404 **University of California, San Francisco Dermatology Drug Research**
515 Spruce Street
San Francisco, CA 94115
41-76-701
Fax: 415-502-4126
www.dermatology.ucsf.edu/research/areasofresearch.as

Conducts clinical testing of new or existing pharmacologic agents used in the treatment of skin disorders.

Mounira Kenaani, MBA, Department Manager
Darrell Young, Associate Director of Development
Leslie Chau, Assistant to Chair

Conferences

1405 **Society for Pediatric Dermatology Annual Meeting**
8365 Keystone Crossing, Suite 107
Indianapolis, IN 46240
317-202-0224
Fax: 317-205-9481
info@pedsderm.net
www.pedsderm.net

Kent Lindeman, Executive Director
Stephanie Garwood, Meetings Manager

1406 **TMA Annual Patient Conference**
Myositis Association
6950 Columbia Gateway Drive, Suite 370
Columbia, MD 21046
800-821-7356
tma@myositis.org
www.myositis.org

To meet other myositis patients, hear from TMA's medical advisors about myositis research, and benefit from the support and practical ideas of others with your disease. The Conference regularly includes sessions on research, exercise, advocacy and coping skills, and disease-specific question and answer sessions as well as new and interesting sessions each year.

Rhonda Buckley-Bishop, Interim Executive Director
Aisha Morrow, Senior Manager, Operations
Rachel Bromley, Senior Manager, Patient Education

Web Sites

1407 **American Autoimmune Related Diseases Association**
www.aarda.org
586-776-3900
aarda@aarda.org
www.aarda.org

The American Autoimmune Related Diseases Association is dedicated to the eradication of autoimmune diseases and the alleviation of suffering and the socioeconomic impact of autoimmunity through fostering and facilitating collaboration in the areas of education, public awareness, research, and patient services in an effective, ethical and efficient manner.

1408 **American Osteopathic College of Dermatology**
2902 North Baltimore Street, PO Box 7525
Kirksville, MI 63501
660-665-2184
Fax: 660-627-2623
www.aocd.org

Improving the standards of the practice of dermatology, to stimulate the study and extend knowledge in the field of dermatology, and to promote a more general understanding of the nature and scope of services rendered by osteopathic dermatologists to other divisions of practice, hospitals, clinics and the public.

Marsha Wise, Executive Director
John Wise, Director of Events
John C. Crogan, Member Services Coordinator

1409 **Arthritis Foundation**
1335 Peachtree Street NE, Suite 600
Atlanta, GA 30309
800-283-7800
www.arthritis.org

The Arthritis Foundation is committed to raising awareness and reducing the unacceptable impact of arthritis, a disease which must be taken as seriously as other chronic diseases because of its devastating consequences.

Ann M. Palmer, President & CEO
Sabrina Sexton, SVP, Marketing & Communications
Robin Kinard, SVP, Operations

1410 **Myositis Association**
6950 Columbia Gateway Drive, Suite 370
Columbia, MD 21046
800-821-7356
www.myositis.org

Mission is to find a cure for inflammatory and other related myopathies, while serving those affected by these diseases.

Rhonda Buckley-Bishop, Interim Executive Director
Aisha Morrow, Senior Manager, Operations
Rachel Bromley, Senior Manager, Patient Education

1411 **Society for Pediatric Dermatology**
8365 Keystone Crossing, Suite 107
Indianapolis, IN 46240
317-202-0224
Fax: 317-205-9481
info@pedsderm.net
www.pedsderm.net

Objective is to promote, develop and advance education, research and care of skin disease in all pediatric age groups.

Karen Wiss, President
Kent Lindeman, Executive Director
Stephanie Garwood, Meeting Manager

Book Publishers

1412 **Let's Talk About Going to the Hospital**
Rosen Publishing Group's PowerKids Press
29 E 21st Street
New York, NY 10010
212-777-3017
800-237-9932
Fax: 888-436-4643
rosenpub@tribeca.ios.com
www.rosenpublishing.com

If a child has to check into the hospital, chances are he or she is already upset about being ill. Knowing how a hospital functions and what the procedures are, such as when family members can visit, will help in what is already a stressful situation. Grades K-5.

24 pages
ISBN: 0-823950-36-0

Roger Rosen, President

Magazines

1413 **International Journal of Dermatology**
International Society of Dermatology
2323 North State Street #30
Bunnell, FL 32110
386-437-4405
Fax: 386-437-4427
info@intsocdermatol.org
www.intsocderm.org

Focuses on information for dermatologists and the whole specialty of dermatology research and education.

10 times a year

Evangeline Handog, President
Nellie Konnikov, Secretary-General
Marcia˜ Ramos-e-Silva, Assistant Secretary-General

1414 **Journal of Dermatologic Surgery and Oncology**
International Society for Dermatologic Surgery
350 Main Street
Malden, MA 2148
781-388-8598
800-835-6770
Fax: 847-330-1135
cs-journals@wiley.com
onlinelibrary.wiley.com

Focuses on medical updates and information on dermatology.

Childhood Dermatomyositis / Journals

Monthly

Journals

1415 **Pediatric Dermatology Journal**
Society for Pediatric Dermatology
8365 Keystone Crossing, Suite 107
Indianapolis, IN 46240

317-202-0224
Fax: 317-205-9481
info@pedsderm.net
www.pedsderm.net

Answers the need for new ideas and strategies for today's pediatrician or dermatologist.

6 issues/yr

Kent Lindeman, Executive Director

Newsletters

1416 **DVH Quarterly**
University of Arkansas at Little Rock
2801 S University Avenue
Little Rock, AR 72204

Fax: 501-663-3536

Offers information on upcoming events, conferences and workshops on and for visual disabilities. Book reviews, information on the newest resources and technology, educational programs, want ads and more.

Quarterly

Bob Brasher, Editor

1417 **Dermatology Focus**
Dermatology Foundation
1560 Sherman Avenue, Suite 870
Evanston, IL 60201

847-328-2256
Fax: 847-328-0509
dfgen@dermatologyfoundation.org
dermatologyfoundation.org

Includes membership activities, research articles and lists recipients of foundation awards.

Quarterly

Bruce U. Wintroub, Chairman
Michael D. Tharp, President
Stuart R. Lessin, Vice President

1418 **Dermatology World**
American Academy of Dermatology
9500 W. Bryn Mawr Avenue, Ste 500
Rosemont, IL 60018

847-240-1737
888-462-3376
Fax: 847-240-1859
info@aad.org
www.aad.org

Offers Academy members information outside the clinical realm. It carries news of government actions, reports of socioeconomic issues, societal trends and other events which impinge on the practice of dermatology.

Monthly

Irvin Bomberger, Interim Executive Director

1419 **Progress in Dermatology**
Dermatology Foundation
1560 Sherman Avenue, Suite 870
Evanston, IL 60201

847-328-2256
Fax: 847-328-0509
dfgen@dermatologyfoundation.org
dermatologyfoundation.org

Bulletin offering information on research reports and clinical trials.

Quarterly

Bruce U. Wintroub, Chairman
Michael D. Tharp, President
Stuart R. Lessin, Vice President

Pamphlets

1420 **Arthritis in Children**
Arthritis Foundation
1335 Peachtree Street NE, Suite 600
Atlanta, GA 30309

404-872-7100
800-283-7800
www.arthritis.org

Includes definitions of nine types of juvenile arthritis and related conditions, diagnosis, treatment options, emotional coping, school issues, federal laws and financial assistance.

28 pages

Ann M. Palmer, President & CEO
Melissa Honabach, SVP, Marketing & Communications
David McLoughlin, COO

1421 **Juvenile Dermatomyositis**
Arthritis Foundation
PO Box 7669
Atlanta, GA 30357

404-872-7100
Fax: 404-872-0457
info@jdfcure.com
www.jdfcure.com

Camps

1422 **Camp Discovery**
American Academy of Dermatology
9500 W. Bryn Mawr Avenue, Ste 500
Rosemont, IL 60018

847-240-1737
Fax: 847-240-1859
jmueller@aad.org
www.campdiscovery.org

A camp for young people with chronic skin conditions. There is no fee and transportation is provided. Five locations: Camp Victory in Millville, PA, Camp Knutson in Crosslake, MN, Camp For All in Burton, TX, Channel 3 Kids Camp in Andover, CT, and Camp Seymour in Gig harbor, WA.

J Mueller, Camp Contact
Irvin Bomberger, Interim Executive Director

Childhood Schizophrenia / National Associations & Support Groups

Description

1423 CHILDHOOD SCHIZOPHRENIA
Involves the following Biologic System(s):
Developmental/Behavioral/Psychiatric Disorders

Childhood schizophrenia is characterized by disturbances in behavior, thought, and emotional reactions. These changes initially become apparent between approximately seven years of age and the onset of adolescence. Affected children may become increasingly withdrawn, have flat or blunted emotions that do not appear to change in response to environmental or external stimuli, experience episodes of unexplained silliness (hebephrenic silliness), exhibit aggressive behaviors, and have distortions in thinking. For example, some children may regularly repeat the same responses to different questions; experience sudden blockages in thought; perceive sights, sounds, or other sensations in the absence of external stimuli (hallucinations); and hold false beliefs in spite of evidence to the contrary (psychotic delusions), such as delusions of persecution (paranoid delusions). Affected children often appear to be chaotic in their emotions, thought, and behavioral patterns.

The relationship of childhood schizophrenia and adult schizophrenia remains unclear. Because schizophrenia typically becomes apparent during late adolescence or early adulthood and affects approximately one percent of the general population, only a small percentage of children exhibit symptoms that meet the criteria for a diagnosis of schizophrenia. In addition, many children who are diagnosed with schizophrenia before puberty are later diagnosed with mood disorders, such as bipolar disorder, or other conditions, such as intellectual disabilities or a metabolic disorder. Although there is no clear relationship between childhood and adult schizophrenia, childhood symptoms that most likely predict adult psychotic disorders appear to include social withdrawal, disturbed interpersonal relationships, and blunted emotions. Though the specific underlying abnormalities that may contribute to childhood schizoid behaviors are unknown, genetic factors and certain biochemical abnormalities of the brain play some role in their development.

The treatment of children with schizoid behaviors may include therapy with certain medications known as neuroleptics to manage psychotic delusions, hallucinations, and severe agitation. In addition, an integrated, multidisciplinary approach may include individual therapy or parental training to help modify the child's behavior. In severe cases, hospitalization may be required to ensure appropriate medication adjustments, to prevent children from harming themselves, or to prevent them from hurting others if they exhibit aggressive or violent behavior.

Although certain medications can help treat children with schizoid behaviors, these drugs should be prescribed with great caution due to the potential for side effects. For example, such therapy may result in tardive dyskinesia (TD), a usually nonreversible condition characterized by tics or spasms of facial muscles and involuntary, rapid or writhing movements of the limbs (choreoathetoid movements). In other cases, therapy may cause abnormally slow movement (bradykinesis); involuntary hand movements; abnormal twisting of the neck (torticollis); drooling; and other findings. If TD develops, treatment with other medications may be indicated and the neuroleptic medication may be decreased or discontinued.

Government Agencies

1424 Center for Mental Health Services
5600 Fishers Lane
Rockville, MD 20857
240-276-1310
www.samhsa.gov

Encourages a range of programs such as systems of care to respond to the increasing number of mental, emotional, and behavioral problems among children. Supports outreach and case management programs for the thousands of Americans who are homeless and the improvement of these services.

Anita Everett, MD, Director

1425 NIH/National Institute of Mental Health
6001 Executive Blvd, Rm 6200, MSC 9663
Bethesda, MD 20892
866-615-6464
Fax: 301-443-4279
TTY: 301-443-8431
nimhinfo@nih.gov
www.nimh.nih.gov

The mission of NIMH is to transform the understanding and treatment of mental illnesses through basic and clinical research, paving the way for prevention, recovery, and cure.

Joshua A. Gordon, MD, PhD, Director
Shelli Avenevoli, PhD, Deputy Director

National Associations & Support Groups

1426 American Academy of Pediatrics
345 Park Blvd
Itasca, IL 60143
800-433-9016
Fax: 847-434-8000
mcc@aap.org
www.aap.org

The American Academy of Pediatrics and its member pediatricians are committed to the attainment of optimal physical, mental and social health and well-being for all infants, children, adolescents, and young adults.

Lynn Olson, PhD, VP, Research
Mark Del Monte, JD, CEO/Executive VP
Vera Tait, MD, FAAP, Chief Medical Officer

1427 American Mental Health Foundation (AMHF)
PO Box 3
Riverdale, NY 10471
212-737-9027
elomke@americanmentalhealthfoundation.or
americanmentalhealthfoundation.org

Dedicated to the extensive and intensive research in the theories and techniques of treatment of emotional illness and to the implementation of reforms in the mental health system. Efforts have resulted in development of better and less expensive treatment methods. Findings are disseminated in English and other major languages.

Sister Joan Curtin. CND, Director
Evander Lomke, President & Executive Director
Eugene Gollogly, Vice President

1428 Brain & Behavior Research Foundation
747 Third Avenue, 33rd Floor
New York, NY 10017
646-681-4888
800-829-8289
info@bbrfoundation.org
www.bbrfoundation.org

The Brain & Behavior Research Foundation is committed to alleviating the suffering caused by mental illness by awarding grants that will lead to advances and breakthroughs in scientific research.

Jeffrey Borenstein, MD, President & CEO

1429 Child Neurology Foundation
601 W Short Street
Lexington, KY 40508
888-417-3435
info@childneurologyfoundation.org
childneurologyfoundation.org

Childhood Schizophrenia / State Agencies & Support Groups

The Child Neurology Foundation connects partners from all areas of the child neurology community so those navigating the journey of disease diagnosis, management, and care have the ongoing support from those dedicated to treatments and cures.

Amy Brin, Executive Director
Katie Hentges, Director, Programs
Brea McCormley, Director, Development

1430 Mental Health America
500 Montgomery Street, Ste 820
Alexandria, VA 22314
703-684-7722
800-969-6642
Fax: 703-684-5968
www.mentalhealthamerica.net

MHA, the leading advocacy organization addressing the full spectrum of mental and substance use conditions and their effects nationwide, works to inform, advocate and enable access to quality behavioral health services for all Americans.

Paul Gionfriddo, President/CEO
Whitney Ball, Assoc. Dir., Marketing/Outreach
Sachin Doshi, Sr. Dir, Finance/Operations

1431 NADD: National Association for the Dually Diagnosed
12 Hurley Avenue
Kingston, NY 12401
845-331-4336
800-331-5362
Fax: 845-331-4569
info@thenadd.org
www.thenadd.org

Nonprofit organization designed to promote the interests of professional and care providers for individuals who have the coexistence of mental illness and intellectual disabilities. NADD provides conferences, educational services and training materials to professionals, parents, concerned citizens and service organizations.

Jeanne Farr, CEO
Michelle Jordan, Office Manager
Edward Seliger, Project Coordinator

1432 National Alliance on Mental Illness (NAMI)
4301 Wilson Blvd., Suite 300
Arlington, VA 22203
703-525-7600
800-999-6264
info@nami.org
www.nami.org

NAMI provides advocacy, education, support and public awareness so that all individuals and families affected by mental illness can build better lives.

Daniel H. Gillison, CEO
David Levy, CFO
Ken Duckworth, Chief Medical Officer

1433 National Federation of Families
15800 Crabbs Branch Way, Suite 300
Rockville, MD 20855
240-403-1901
ffcmh@ffcmh.org
www.ffcmh.org

The National family run organization is dedicated exclusively to helping children with mental health needs and their families achieve a better quality of life.

Lynda Gargan, PhD, Executive Director

1434 National Mental Health Consumers' Self-Help Clearinghouse
1211 Chestnut Street, Suite 1207
Philadelphia, PA 19107
215-751-1810
800-553-4539
Fax: 215-636-6312
selfhelpclearinghouse@gmail.com
www.mhselfhelp.org

The Clearinghouse works to foster peer empowerment through our website, up-to-date news and information announcements, a directory of peer-driven services, electronic and printed publications, training packages, and individual and onsite consultation

Joseph Rogers, Founder/Executive Director
Susan Rogers, Director

State Agencies & Support Groups

1435 Center for Family Support
333 7th Avenue, #901
New York, NY 10001
212-629-7939
Fax: 212-239-2211
svernikoff@cfsny.org
www.cfsny.org

The Center for Family Support is committed to providing support and assistance to individuals with developmental and related disabilities, and to the family members who care for them.

Steven Vernikoff, Executive Director
Linda Schellenberg, Director, Community Service
Barbara Greenwald, Associate Executive Director

Libraries & Resource Centers

1436 National Alliance for Research on Schizophrenia and Depression
50 West Hawthorne Avenue
Valley Stream, NY 11580
516-569-6600
800-829-8289
Fax: 516-374-2261
info@narsad.org
www.pccli.org

Largest private 501 (c) (3) not for profit corporation and registered public charity. Raises and distributes funds for scientific research into the causes, cures, treatments and prevention of brain disorders.

David Schimel, President

Research Centers

1437 Suncoast Residential Training Center/Developmental Services Program
Goodwill Industries-Suncoast
10596 Gandy Boulevard
Saint Petersburg, FL 33702
727-523-1512
888-279-1988
Fax: 727-563-9300
TTY: 727-579-1068
www.goodwill-suncoast.org

A large group home which serves individuals with intellectual disabilities with a secondary diagnosis of psychiatric difficulties as evidenced by problem behavior. Providing residential, behavioral and instructional support and services that will promote the development of adaptive, socially appropriate behavior. Each individual is assessed to determine, socialization, basic academics and recreation. The primary intervention strategy is applied behavior analysis.

Oscar J. Horton, Chair
Martin W. Gladysz, Sr. Vice Chair
Steven M Erickson, Vice Chair

Conferences

1438 FFCMH Annual Conference
National Federation of Families
15800 Crabbs Branch Way, Suite 300
Rockville, MD 20855
240-403-1901
ffcmh@ffcmh.org
www.ffcmh.org

The only national conference dedicated solely to supporting families whose children - of any age - experience mental health and/or substance use challenges during their lifetime.

November

Lynda Gargan, PhD, Executive Director

1439 NAMI Convention
National Alliance on Mental Illness
3803 N Fairfax Drive, Suite 100
Arlington, VA 22203
703-524-7600
888-999-6264
Fax: 703-524-9094
TDD: 703-516-7227
info@nami.org
www.nami.org

The NAMI Convention is packed with information, chances to network, leadership development opportunities, and lots more.

Summer

Richele Keas, Senior Mgr, Media Relations

Audio Video

1440 Bonnie Tapes
Mental Illness Education Project
25 West Street
Westborough, MA 1581
617-562-1111
800-343-5540
Fax: 617-779-0061
info@miepvideos.org
www.miepvideos.org

Bonnie's account of coping with schizophrenia will be a relevation to people whose view of mental illness has been shaped by the popular media. She and her family provide an intimate view of the frequently feared, often misrepresented and much stigmatized illness and the human side of learning to live with a psychiatric disability. Tape 1: Mental Illness in the Family (26 minutes); Tape 2: Recovering from Mental Illness (27 minutes); Tape 3: My Sister Is Mentally Ill (22 minutes) $99.95 each

1997 $143.88 for 3

1441 Families Coping with Mental Illness
Mental Illness Education Project
25 West Street
Westborough, MA 1581
617-562-1111
800-343-5540
Fax: 617-779-0061
miepvideos.org

10 family members share their experiences of having a family member with schizophrenia or bipolar disorder. Designed to provide insights and support to other families, the tape also profoundly conveys to professionals the needs of families when mental illness strikes. In two versions: a twenty two minute version ideal for short classes and workshops, and a richer forty three minute version with more examples and details. Discounted price for families/consumers.

Michael M Faenza, Executive Director

1442 Living with Schizophrenia
Guilford Press
370 Seventh Avenue, Suite 1200
New York, NY 10001
800-365-7006
Fax: 212-966-6708
info@guilford.com
www.guilford.com

Offers essential information and huidance for individuals and families coping with schizophrenia diagnosis. Features illuminating first-hand accounts from three people with schizophrenia and one person with schizoaffective disorder, along with commentary from treatment expert Dr Andy Campbell. Learn clear steps to take to lead fuller, more successful lives.

2006 DVD, 39 minutes
ISBN: 1-593853-86-6

1443 Pharmacotherapy of Schizophrenia
American Psychiatric Publishing
1000 Wilson Boulevard, Suite 1825
Arlington, VA 22209
703-907-7322
800-368-5777
Fax: 703-907-1091
appi@psych.org
www.appi.org

Presented by John M Kane MD, Chairman of Psychiatry at LI Jewish Medical Center, and Professor of Psychiatry at Albert Einstein College of Medicine. Illustrates the major issues and treatment considerations, and the latest findings on the effectiveness as well as on the side effects of the many and varied psychopharmacological agents are carefully illustrated and discussed. 75 minutes. ISBN # 9780880483803

1995

Robert E. Hales, Editor-in-Chief
Rebecca D. Rinehart, Publisher
John McDuffie, Associate Publisher

Web Sites

1444 CyberPsych
www.cyberpsych.org

www.cyberpsych.org

CyberPsych presents information about psychoanalysis, psychotherapy, and special topics such as anxiety disorder, the problematic use of alcohol, homophobia, and the traumatic effects of racism. CyberPsych is a nonprofit network which offers free web hosting and technical support for internet communication to nonprofit groups and individuals.

Carol Lindemann, Ph.D., Contact

1445 Internet Mental Health
www.mentalhealth.com

www.mentalhealth.com

Our goal is to improve understanding, diagnosis, and treatment of mental illness throughout the world.

Phillip W. Long, M.D., Psychiatrist

1446 Mental Health Net
P.O. Box 20709
Columbus, OH 43220
614-448-4055
www.mentalhelp.net

We wish to provide the following: to discuss, develope and debate in an open forum the future of the mental health field in America and throughout the world. To help coordinate various components of the mental health field so as to bring about greater communication between them. To educate the public about mental health issues, to promote active collaboration between professionals in all segments of mental health development, implementation and policy.

1447 Mental Wellness
www.choicesinrecovery.com
800-526-7736
www.choicesinrecovery.com

Mental Wellness is an online resource for bipolar disorder, schizophrenia and general mental health information.

1448 NADD: National Association for the Dually Diagnosed
12 Hurley Avenue
Kingston, NY 12401
www.thenadd.org

Nonprofit organization designed to promote the interests of professional and care providers for individuals who have the coexistence of mental illness and intellectual disabilities. NADD provides conferences, educational services and training materials to professionals, parents, concerned citizens and service organizations.

Jeanne Farr, CEO
Michelle Jordan, Office Manager
Edward Seliger, Project Coordinator

1449 Online Mendelian Inheritance in Man
McKusick-Nathans Institue of Genetic Medicine-JHU
Baltimore, MD 21205
www.omim.org

This database is a catalog of human genes and genetic disorders.

Ada Hamosh, MD, Scientific Director

1450 Psych Central
55 Pleasant St., Suite 207
Newburyport, MA 1950
talkback@psychcentral.com
www.psychcentral.com

Offers free informational and educational articles and resources on psychology, support and mental health online.

John M. Grohol, CEO & Founder

1451 Schizophrenia Support Organizations
www.members.aol.com/leonardjk/USA.htm

www.members.aol.com/leonardjk/USA.htm

Contains a listing of support organizations for people with schizophrenia and their families.

1452 Schizophrenia.com
www.schizophrenia.com

www.schizophrenia.com

Is a leading web commuity dedicated to providing high quality information, support and education to the family members, caregivers and individuals who's lives have been impacted by schizophrenia.

Brain Chiko, Executive Director
J. Megginson Hollister, Editor

1453 Schizophrenia.com Home Page
www.schizophrenia.com/discuss/Disc3.html

www.schizophrenia.com/discuss/Disc3.html

On-line support for patients and families.

Brain Chiko, Executive Director
J. Megginson Hollister, Editor

1454 Schizophrenia: Handbook for Families
www.mentalhealth.com/book/p40-sc01.html

www.mentalhealth.com/book/p40-sc01.html

This handbook is dedicated to the families and to their loved ones who carry the burden of schizophrenia, a major psychiatric disorder.

Phillip W. Long, M.D., Psychiatrist

Book Publishers

1455 Biology of Schizophrenia and Affective Disease
American Psychiatric Publishing
1000 Wilson Boulevard, Suite 1825
Arlington, VA 22209
703-907-7322
800-368-5777
Fax: 703-907-1091
appi@psych.org
www.appi.org

Provides a state-of-the-art look at the biological bases of severe mental illness from the perspective of the researchers making these exceptional discoveries. ISBN # 9780880487467

1995 560 pages

Stanley J Watson PhD MD, Author

1456 Contemporary Issues in the Treatment of Schizophrenia
American Psychiatric Press
1000 Wilson Boulevard, Suite 1825
Arlington, VA 22209
703-907-7322
800-368-5777
Fax: 703-907-1091
appi@psych.org
www.appi.org

Covers approaches to the patient by investigating biological, pharmacological, and psychological treatments. ISBN #: 9780880486811

1995 889 pages

Christian L Shriqui, MD, Editor
Henry A Nasrallah, MD, Editor

1457 Diagnosis Schizophrenia: A Comprehensive Resource
Columbia University Press
116th and Broadway
New York, NY 10027
212-854-1754
Fax: 212-459-3678
www.columbia.edu/cu/cup

Has alot of consumers' stories in the first person and sketches of their faces sprinkled throughout.

2002

Rachel Miller, Author
Susan E Mason, Author

1458 Encyclopedia of Schizophrenia and the Psychotic Disorders
Facts on File
11 Penn Plaza
New York, NY 10001
212-290-8090
800-322-8755
Fax: 212-678-3633

This volume details recent theories and research findings on schizophrenia and psychotic disorders, together with a complete overview of the field's history.

368 pages

1459 Getting Your Life Back Together When You Have Schizophrenia
New Harbinger Publications
5674 Shattuck Ave
Oakland, CA 94609
800-748-6273
Fax: 800-652-1613
customerservice@newharbinger.com
www.newharbinger.com

Provides good information for someone who has just been diagnosed with schiophrenia.

2002

Roberta Temes PhD, Author

1460 Medical Illness and Schizophrenia
American Psychiatric Publishing
1000 Wilson Boulevard, Suite 1825
Arlington, VA 22209
703-907-7322
800-368-5777
Fax: 703-907-1091
appi@psych.org
www.appi.org

Examines the links between medical conditions and severe chronic mental illness, with a focus on the need for better medical assessment and treatment to improve outcomes in patients; links between schizophrenia and conditions such as obesity, cardiovascular disease, diabetes, HIV and hepatitis C, endocrine-related diorders, and others; the association between therapy with certain antipsychotics and adverse health outcomes; the importance of improving community health. ISBN # 9781585621064

2003 256 pages

Jonathan M Meyer MD, Author
Henry A Nasrallah MD, Author

1461 Negative Symptom and Cognitive Deficit Tre atment Response in Schizophrenia
American Psychiatric Publishing
1000 Wilson Boulevard, Suite 1825
Arlington, VA 22209
703-907-7322
800-368-5777
Fax: 703-907-1091
appi@psych.org
www.appi.org

Addresses the complex issues-issues rarely confronted in empirical studies of patients with schizophrenia-and controversial research surrounding the assessment of negative symptoms and cognitive deficits in patients with schizophrenia. ISBN # 9780880487856

2001 216 pages

Richard S E Keefe PhD, Author
Joseph P McEvoy MD, Author

1462 New Pharmacotherapy of Schizophrenia
American Psychiatric Press
1000 Wilson Boulevard, Suite 1825
Arlington, VA 22209
703-907-7322
800-368-5777
Fax: 703-907-1091
appi@psych.org
www.appi.org

Discusses the new class of antipsychotic agents that promises superior efficiency and more favorable side-effects; offers an improved understanding of how to employ exsisting pharmachotherapeutic agents. ISBN # 9780880484916

1996 264 pages

1463 **Plasma Homovanillic Asid in Schhizophrenia**
American Psychiatric Publishing
1000 Wilson Boulevard, Suite 1825
Arlington, VA 22209
703-907-7322
800-368-5777
Fax: 703-907-1091
appi@psych.org
www.appi.org

Provides the most comprehensive and current collection of information on plasma HVA levels to be found anywhere. Provides a consice synthesis and critique of current data as well as interesting proposals for future research. ISBN # 9780880484893

1997 216 pages

Arnold J Friedhoff MD, Author
Farooq Amin MD, Author

1464 **Prenatal Exposures in Schizophrenia**
American Psychiatric Press
1000 Wilson Boulevard, Suite 1825
Arlington, VA 22209
703-907-7322
800-368-5777
Fax: 703-907-1091
appi@psych.org
www.appi.org

Considers a range of epigenetic elements thought to interact with abnormal genes to produce the onset of illness. Attention to the evidence implicating obstetric complications, prenatal infection, autoimmunity and prenatal malnutrition in brain disorders. ISBN # 9780880484992

1999 296 pages Hardcover

Ezra S Susser MD, Author
Alan S Brown MD, Author
Jack M Gorman MD, Author

1465 **Schizophrenia**
American Psychiatric Publishing
1000 Wilson Boulevard, Suite 1825
Arlington, VA 22209
703-907-7322
800-368-5777
Fax: 703-907-1091
appi@psych.org
www.appi.org

Ideas in treating the disease, and how many patients can lead productive lives without relapse. ISBN # 9780880489508

1994 294 pages

Nancy C Andleasen MD, Author

1466 **Schizophrenia Into Later Life: Treatment, Research, and Policy**
American Psychiatric Publishing
1000 Wilson Boulevard, Suite 1825
Arlington, VA 22209
703-907-7322
800-368-5777
Fax: 703-907-1091
appi@psych.org
www.appi.org

Multidisciplinary reference on this important topic-a landmark work for researchers, service providers, and policy makers. ISBN # 9781585620371

2003 344 pages

Carl I Cohen MD, Author

1467 **Schizophrenia Revealed: From Neurons to Social Interactions**
W.W. Norton
500 Fifth Avenue
New York, NY 10110
212-354-5500
800-233-4830
Fax: 212-869-0856
www.wwnorton.com

Educational, informational, scientific and yet readable.

2003

1468 **Schizophrenia and Comorbid Conditions Diagnosis and Treatment**
American Psychiatric Publishing
1000 Wilson Boulevard, Suite 1825
Arlington, VA 22209
703-907-7322
800-368-5777
Fax: 703-907-1091
appi@psych.org
www.appi.org

Lays diagnostic oversimplification of schizophrenia to rest once and for all. Editors are criticizing the reductionist view of schizophrenia as a single unitary disorder- a view that has led many psychiatrists and mental health care professionals to overlook potentially important syndromes. ISBN # 9780880487719

2001 256 pages

1469 **Scizophrenia in a Molecular Age**
American Psychiatric Publishing
1000 Wilson Boulevard, Suite 1825
Arlington, VA 22209
703-907-7322
800-368-5777
Fax: 703-907-1091
appi@psych.org
www.appi.org

Reviews neuroscience mechanisms and analyzes genetic determinants. ISBN # 9780880489614

1999 204 pages

Carol A Tamminga MD, Author

1470 **Surviving Schizophrenia: A Manual for Families, Consumers and Providers**
Harper Collins
10 E 53rd Street
New York, NY 10022
212-207-7528
800-242-7737
Fax: 212-207-2586
orders@harpercollins.com
harpercollins.com

The third edition of this indispensable manual throughly details everything patients, families and mental health professionals need to know about one of the most widespread and misunderstood illnesses. Paperback.

464 pages
ISBN: 0-060950-76-5

1471 **The American Psychiatric Publishing Text book of Schizophrenia**
American Psychiatric Publishing
1000 Wilson Boulevard, Suite 1825
Arlington, VA 22209
703-907-7322
800-368-5777
Fax: 703-907-1091
appi@psych.org
www.appi.org

Offers broad coverage that encompasses the current state of knowledge the cause, nature, and treatment of schizophrenia. ISBN # 9781585621910

2006 453 pages

Jeffrey A Lieberman MD, Author
T Scott Stroup MD MPH, Author
Diana O Perkins MD MPH, Author

1472 **The Complete Family Guide to Schizophrenia**
Kim Mueser, Susan Gingerich, author

Guilford Press
72 Spring Street
New York, NY 10012
800-365-7006
Fax: 212-966-6708
info@guilford.com
www.guilford.com

The authors, noted therapists, deepen the reader's understanding of the illness and discuss a wide range of effective treatments. This volume walks the reader through a range of treatment and support options that can lead to a better life for the entire family. Topics include prioritizing needs, solving everyday problems, life-goals, symptoms, and the life-long journey of recovery. Hardcover, paperback, e-book.

2006 480 pages Paperback
ISBN: 1-593851-80-4

Kim T Mueser, Author
Susan Gingerich, Author

1473 The Early Stages of Schizophrenia
American Psychiatric Publishing
1000 Wilson Boulevard, Suite 1825
Arlington, VA 22209

703-907-7322
800-368-5777
Fax: 703-907-1091
appi@psych.org
www.appi.org

Divided into three major parts: Early Intervention, Epidemiology, and Natural History of Schizophrenia; Management of the Early Stages of Schizophrenia; and Neurobiological Investigations of the Early Stages of Schizophrenia. ISBN # 9780880488402

2002 280 pages

Robert B Zipursky MD, Author
S Charles Schulz MD, Author

1474 The Natural History of Mania, Depression, and Schizophrenia
American Psychiatric Publishing
1000 Wilson Boulevard, Suite 1825
Arlington, VA 22209

703-907-7322
800-368-5777
Fax: 703-907-1091
appi@psych.org
www.appi.org

Takes an unusual look at the course of mental illness, based on data from the Iowa 500 Research Project. This project involved the long-term (30-40 yrs) follow-up of patients diagnosed with schizophrenia, depression, and bipolar illness. ISBN # 9780880487269

1996 384 pages

George Winokur MD, Author
Ming T Tsuang MD PhD, Author

1475 Water Balance in Schizophrenia
American Psychiatric Publishing
1000 Wilson Boulevard, Suite 1825
Arlington, VA 22209

703-907-7322
800-368-5777
Fax: 703-907-1091
appi@psych.org
www.appi.org

Represents the first attempt to provide clinicians with a consolidated guide to polydipsia-hyponatremia, associated with schizophrenia. ISBN # 9780880484855

1996 360 pages

David B Schnur MD, Author
Darrell G Kirch MD, Author

Newsletters

1476 NADD Bulletin
NADD Press
12 Hurley Avenue
Kingston, NY 12401

845-331-4336
800-331-5362
Fax: 845-331-4569
info@thenadd.org
www.thenadd.org

Official publication of the National Association for the Dually Diagnosed. It features articles that address clinical, programmatic, research or family oriented issues concerning mental health aspects in persons with disabilities.

20 pages Bimonthly

Jeanne Farr, CEO
Lucy Esralew, Co Editor
Bob Klaehn, Co Editor

Pamphlets

1477 Schizophrenia
National Institute of Mental Health
PO Box 5801
Bethesda, MD 20824

301-496-5751
800-352-9424
Fax: 301-443-4279
TTY: 866-415-8051
nimhinfo@nih.gov
www.nimh.nih.gov

This booklet answers many common questions about schizophrenia, one of the most chronic, severe and disabling mental disorders. Current research-based information is provided for people with schizophrenia, their family members, friends and the general public about the symptoms and diagnosis of schizophrenia, possible causes, treatments and treatment resources.

2006 28 pages

Walter J. Koroshetz, M.D., Acting Director
Alan L. Willard, Ph.D., Acting Deputy Director
Caroline Lewis, Executive Officer

1478 Schizophrenia Fact Sheet
Center for Mental Health Services
PO Box 42557
Washington, DC 20015

800-789-2647
Fax: 240-747-5470
TDD: 866-889-2647
mentalhealth.samhsa.gov

This fact sheet provides information on the symptoms, diagnosis, and treatment for schizophrenia.

2 pages

Phillip W. Long, M.D., Psychiatrist

1479 Understanding Schizophrenia
National Alliance on Mental Illness
3803 N. Fairfax Drive, Suite 100
Arlington, VA 22203

703-524-7600
800-950-6264
Fax: 703-524-9094
TDD: 703-516-7227
www.nami.org

An excellent introduction to schizophrenia. Appropriate for supprt groups, physicians offices, coventions, health fairs, and the workplace.

Jim Payne, President
Ralph E. Nelson, 1st Vice President
Marilyn Ricci, 2nd Vice President

Description

1480 CHOREA

Covers these related disorders: Benign familial chorea, Drug-induced chorea, Sydenham's chorea

Involves the following Biologic System(s):
Neurologic Disorders

Chorea is a neuromuscular condition characterized by irregular, rapid, jerky movements that may appear to be well coordinated but actually occur involuntarily. These movements may be simple or highly complex. In addition, the arms and legs may have abnormally diminished muscle tone (hypotonia) and therefore may be abnormally loose or slack. Choreic movements are often subtle. However, if several of these movements are present, they may essentially flow into one another, causing them to appear relatively slow, sinuous, and writhing in nature (athetosis).

The specific underlying cause of chorea is unknown. However, some researchers suspect that it may result due to overactivity of certain neurotransmitters (dopamine) in the brain. Neurotransmitters are naturally produced chemicals that regulate the transmission of messages between certain nerve cells (neurons). In some children, chorea may result from the use of particular drugs, such as certain antiseizure medications, particularly phenytoin, or antipsychotic (neuroleptic) drugs, such as haloperidol or phenothiazines. Chorea may also occur in association with certain underlying disorders, such as systemic lupus erythematosus (lupus) or Wilson's disease, a disorder of copper metabolism. In addition, chorea is a primary feature of a rare genetic disorder known as benign familial chorea in which nonprogressive chorea begins in infancy or early childhood in the absence of other neurologic abnormalities. Associated symptoms and findings include delays in attaining certain motor milestones during childhood and poorly coordinated movements of the arms and legs. Benign familial chorea is likely inherited as an autosomal dominant trait.

In addition, chorea is the dominant feature of a disorder known as Sydenham's chorea. This disorder is the most common cause of acquired chorea during childhood. Sydenham's chorea occurs in association with rheumatic fever, which is an inflammatory disease following throat infection with certain strains of streptococcal bacteria. Patients with rheumatic fever may experience fever, inflammation and swelling of one or more large joints, or inflammation of the heart (carditis), potentially causing thickening, scarring, and associated disease of heart valves. If rheumatic fever affects the nervous system, Sydenham's chorea may result. Although Sydenham's chorea previously occurred in as many as half of those with rheumatic fever, recent studies suggest that it more likely affects approximately 10 percent of rheumatic patients in the United States.

Sydenham's chorea most commonly occurs in children between ages five and 15. The condition may begin subtly and gradually, sometimes as long as several months after other symptoms associated with rheumatic fever have resolved. Patients may initially experience increasing clumsiness. As symptoms progress, involuntary movements may become prominent in the face, trunk, and arms and legs; move from one muscle group to another; and eventually affect all motor movements, including walking and speech. In some patients, chorea may be restricted to one side of the body (hemichorea). If children have severe chorea and abnormally diminished muscle tone (hypotonia), they may become unable to dress, feed themselves, or walk. Many children with the condition also experience rapid mood swings and episodes of uncontrollable crying (emotional lability).

Sydenham's chorea is usually a self-limited disorder that subsides in weeks or months. However, in some patients, the condition may persist for up to one to two years. In approximately 20 percent of children, the condition may recur within two years of the initial episode. If patients experience mild symptoms, treatment may include symptomatic and supportive measures, including minimizing stress as much as possible. In children with more severe symptoms, treatment may be attempted with the drug diazepam.

Government Agencies

1481 NIH/National Institute of Neurological Disorders and Stroke (NINDS)
PO Box 5801
Bethesda, MD 20824
800-352-9424
www.ninds.nih.gov

Works to reduce the burden of neurological disease by conducting, fostering, coordinating and guiding research on the causes, prevention, diagnosis and treatment of neurological disorders and stroke, while supporting basic research in related scientific areas.

Walter J. Koroshetz, MD, Director

National Associations & Support Groups

1482 American Academy of Child and Adolescent Psychiatry
3615 Wisconsin Avenue NW
Washington, DC 20016
202-966-7300
Fax: 202-464-0131
www.aacap.org

The AACAP (American Academy of Child and Adolescent Psychiatry) is the leading national professional medical association dedicated to the promotion of healthy development for children, adolescents, and families.

Heidi B. Fordi, Executive Director

1483 American Academy of Pediatrics
345 Park Blvd
Itasca, IL 60143
800-433-9016
Fax: 847-434-8000
mcc@aap.org
www.aap.org

The American Academy of Pediatrics and its member pediatricians are committed to the attainment of optimal physical, mental and social health and well-being for all infants, children, adolescents, and young adults.

Lynn Olson, PhD, VP, Research
Mark Del Monte, JD, CEO/Executive VP
Vera Tait, MD, FAAP, Chief Medical Officer

1484 Child Neurology Foundation
601 W Short Street
Lexington, KY 40508
888-417-3435
info@childneurologyfoundation.org
childneurologyfoundation.org

The Child Neurology Foundation connects partners from all areas of the child neurology community so those navigating the journey of disease diagnosis, management, and care have the ongoing support from those dedicated to treatments and cures.

Amy Brin, Executive Director
Katie Hentges, Director, Programs
Brea McCormley, Director, Development

Chorea / Web Sites

1485 **Genetic Alliance**
426400 Woodfield Road, Ste 189
Damascus, MD 20872
202-966-5557
Fax: 202-966-8553
info@geneticalliance.org
www.geneticalliance.org

World's leading nonprofit health advocacy organization committed to transforming health through genetics and promoting an environment of openness centered on the health of individuals, families, and communities.

Sharon Terry, /CEO
Ruth Child, CFO
Natasha Bonhomme, Chief Strategy Officer

1486 **March of Dimes Foundation**
1550 Crystal Drive, Ste 1300
Arlington, VA 22202
888-663-4637
www.marchofdimes.org

March of Dimes help moms have full-term pregnancies and research the problems that threaten the health of babies. The March of Dimes also acts globally: sharing best practices in perinatal health and helping improve birth outcomes where the needs are the most urgent.

Stacey D. Stewart, President
Alan Brogdon, SVP/COO/Board Officer
Rahul Gupta, MD, SVP & Chief Medical/Health Officer

1487 **Muscular Dystrophy Association**
16 N Clark, Ste 3550
Chicago, IL 60601
646-992-2908
800-572-1717
resourcecenter@mda.org
www.mda.org

Voluntary health agency aimed at conquering neuromuscular diseases. The diseases in MDA's program include muscular dystrophy, ALS and numerous related muscle-debilitating diseases. With almost 100 field offices and over 150 affiliated MDA Care Centers nationwide, MDA conducts research, provides medical and community services, clinics, support groups, summer camps for youngsters and much more.

R. Rodney Howell, MD, Chairman
Lynn O'Connor Vos, President & CEO
Mary Fiance, Director, PR & Communications

1488 **WE MOVE (Worldwide Education and Awareness of Movement Disorders)**
204 West 84th Street
New York, NY 10024
wemove@wemove.org

Gives the general public the knowledge that they desire regarding any disorder involving movement difficulties.

Susan Bressman, MD, President

Web Sites

1489 **Online Mendelian Inheritance in Man**
McKusick-Nathans Institue of Genetic Medicine-JHU
Baltimore, MD 21205
www.omim.org

This database is a catalog of human genes and genetic disorders.

Ada Hamosh, MD, Scientific Director

Book Publishers

1490 **Diagnostic and Statistical Manual of Mental Disorders**
American Psychiatric Association
1000 Wilson Boulevard, Suite 1825
Arlington, VA 22209
703-907-7300
888-357-7924
apa@psych.org
www.psych.org

Includes updated information on diagnoses, etiology, and research on mental illness.

1491 **Merck Manual of Diagnosis and Therapy 18th Edition**
Wiley Publishers
10475 Crosspoint Boulevard
Indianapolis, IN 46256
317-572-3000
877-762-2974
Fax: 800-597-3299
consumer@wiley.com
www.wiley.com

Packed with essential information on diagnosing and treating medical disorders to help health care professionals and medical students deliver the best care.

2006
ISBN: 0-911910-18-2

1492 **Neuroanatomy: Text and Atlas 3rd Edition**
McGraw-Hill Medical
860 Taylor Station Road
Blacklick, OH 43004
877-833-5524
Fax: 614-759-3823
pbg.ecommerce_custserv@mcgraw-hill.com
http://books.mcgraw-hill.com

Comprehensive approach to neuroanatomy from both functional and regional perspective! Examines how parts of the nervous system work together to regulate body systems and produce behavior.

2003 532 pages
ISBN: 0-071381-83-X

Pamphlets

1493 **Sydenham Chorea Information Page**
National Inst. of Neurological Disorders/Stroke
PO Box 5801
Bethesda, MD 20824
301-496-5751
800-352-9424
TTY: 301-468-5981
www.ninds.nih.gov/disorders/sydenham/sydenham.htm

Provides information on the disease, treatment options, and the prognosis, as well as provides some research centers regarding the disease.

Walter J. Koroshetz, M.D., Acting Director
Alan L. Willard, Ph.D., Acting Deputy Director
Caroline Lewis, Executive Officer

Cleft Lip and Cleft Palate / National Associations & Support Groups

Description

1494 CLEFT LIP AND CLEFT PALATE
Involves the following Biologic System(s):
Dermatologic Disorders, Orthopedic and Muscle Disorders

Cleft lip and cleft palate are birth defects that may occur together or as isolated conditions. Newborns with cleft lip have a groove in the upper lip that may be a small notch or, in more severe cases, may be deep and extend up to the nose. Cleft palate is characterized by incomplete closure of the roof of the mouth (palate). In affected newborns, an abnormal gap runs along the midline of the soft, fleshy area of the palate (soft palate) and, in some patients, extends into one or both sides of the bony, front region of the palate (hard palate). As a result, the nasal cavity may open into the palate. Cleft lip with or without cleft palate affects approximately one in 600 newborns, whereas cleft palate alone occurs in about one in 1,000 births.

In newborns with cleft lip, the defect may occur on one or both sides of the upper lip and typically affects the bony ridge of the upper jaw (upper alveolar ridge). This ridge contains the sockets in which the roots of the teeth are held (dental alveoli). As a result, affected children often experience improper development of certain teeth, potentially resulting in absent, malformed, improperly positioned, or extra teeth and increased risk of dental decay (dental caries). In addition, infants with cleft lip and cleft palate typically have feeding difficulties associated with poor suckling capability and excessive swallowing of air. Affected children with cleft palate are also prone to repeated infections of the middle ear (otitis media) that, in some cases, may contribute to associated hearing loss. Many children also experience speech defects that may be due to inadequate functioning of certain muscles of the throat and palate (pharyngeal and palatal muscles).

In affected newborns, treatment initially consists of measures to ensure improved feeding and proper intake of nutrients. In many patients, a plastic device (a prosthetic known as an obturator) may be fitted that covers the gap in the palate, thereby improving suction and intake of fluids, milk, and or formula. The obturator is typically replaced every few weeks due to rapid growth during infancy. In addition, in those with cleft palate, modified artificial nipples may help to improve feeding. In many cases, cleft lip may be surgically closed by approximately two months of age and additional corrective surgery may be performed later during childhood. If affected children do not have associated physical abnormalities, surgical correction of cleft palate may be performed before the age of one year to help improve normal speech development. However, if surgery is delayed until the age of three years or later, a device (such as a contoured speech bulb) may be used to help close off the uppermost portion of the throat (nasopharynx) during the production of certain sounds. This helps children to develop understandable speech. Treatment may also include dental procedures to correct improperly positioned teeth or to replace absent teeth (e.g., with prosthetic devices). Speech therapy may be beneficial for some affected children. Additional treatment for infants and children with cleft lip and cleft palate is symptomatic and supportive.

Cleft lip and cleft palate may occur as isolated conditions or in association with several underlying chromosomal disorders or malformation syndromes. Isolated cleft lip and/or cleft palate may potentially result due to certain environmental factors, occur randomly for unknown reasons (sporadically), or be familial. Many cases have been reported in which several individuals in multigenerational families (kindreds) have been affected by isolated cleft lip and cleft palate. In such cases, the specific modes of inheritance are not understood. The frequent association of cleft lip and cleft palate is thought to result from certain developmental abnormalities during embryonic growth.

National Associations & Support Groups

1495 AmeriFace
PO Box 751112
Las Vegas, NV 89136
702-341-5351
888-486-1209
Fax: 702-341-5351
info@ameriface.org
www.ameriface.org

Provides information, services, emotional support and educational programs for and on behalf of individuals with facial differences and their families. Working to increase understanding through public awareness and education.

3M members

Debbie Oliver, Executive Director
Robin Remele, Program Driector
Joyce Bentz, National Action Team Coordinator

1496 American Academy of Pediatrics
345 Park Blvd
Itasca, IL 60143
800-433-9016
Fax: 847-434-8000
mcc@aap.org
www.aap.org

The American Academy of Pediatrics and its member pediatricians are committed to the attainment of optimal physical, mental and social health and well-being for all infants, children, adolescents, and young adults.

Lynn Olson, PhD, VP, Research
Mark Del Monte, JD, CEO/Executive VP
Vera Tait, MD, FAAP, Chief Medical Officer

1497 American Cleft Palate Craniofacial Association
510 Meadowmont Village Circle, Suite 377
Chapel Hill, NC 27517
919-933-9044
acpacares.org

The American Cleft Palate Craniofacial Association (ACPA) is a non-profit of individuals and healthcare professionals who are interested in clinical care and research advancements for those affected by cleft and craniofacial conditions. ACPA works to support the care of individuals affected by cleft and craniofacial conditions.

Adam Levy, CAE, Executive Director
Erin Brenneman, Manager, Member Programs/Engagement
Caitlyn Reinauer, Senior Manager, Education Programs

1498 FACES: National Craniofacial Association
PO Box 11082
Chattanooga, TN 37401
423-266-1632
800-332-2373
info@faces-cranio.org
www.faces-cranio.org

Assists individuals with facial disfigurations and their families They maintain a registry of centers offering corrective surgery for craniofacial deformities and financial assistance to qualified applicants.

Kim Teems Fox, President
Emily McKay, Communications Director
Ashley Rhodes, FACES Camp Director

1499 Genetic Alliance
426400 Woodfield Road, Ste 189
Damascus, MD 20872
202-966-5557
Fax: 202-966-8553
info@geneticalliance.org
www.geneticalliance.org

World's leading nonprofit health advocacy organization committed to transforming health through genetics and promoting an environment of openness centered on the health of individuals, families, and communities.

Cleft Lip and Cleft Palate / Conferences

Sharon Terry, CEO
Ruth Child, CFO
Natasha Bonhomme, Chief Strategy Officer

1500 **March of Dimes Foundation**
1550 Crystal Drive, Ste 1300
Arlington, VA 22202
888-663-4637
www.marchofdimes.org

March of Dimes help moms have full-term pregnancies and research the problems that threaten the health of babies. The March of Dimes also acts globally: sharing best practices in perinatal health and helping improve birth outcomes where the needs are the most urgent.

Stacey D. Stewart, President
Alan Brogdon, SVP/COO/Board Officer
Rahul Gupta, MD, SVP & Chief Medical/Health Officer

Conferences

1501 **Connections Conference**
Cleft Palate Foundation
1504 East Franklin Street, Suite 102
Chapel Hill, NC 27514
919-933-9044
800-242-5338
Fax: 919-933-9604
info@cleftline.org
www.cleftline.org

Nancy Smythe, Executive Director
Samantha Jennings, MSW, Director of Family Services
Emily Kiser, Foundation Administrator

Web Sites

1502 **AboutFace USA**
1057 Steeles Ave. West
North York, ON M2R 3
416-597-2229
800-597-3223
Fax: 416-597-8494
info@aboutface.ca
www.aboutface.ca

Provides information, services, emotional support and educational programs for and on behalf of individuals with facial differences and their families. Working to increase understanding through public awareness and education.

Anna Pileggi, Executive Director
Colleen Wheatley, Manager, Programs & Services
Emily Rivers, Manager, Communications

1503 **Cleft Palate/Craniofacial Birth Defects: Cleft Palate Foundation**
1504 East Franklin Street, Suite 102
Chapel Hill, NC 27514
919-933-9044
800-242-5338
Fax: 919-933-9604
www.cleftline.org

The Cleft Palate Foundation operates a toll-free CLEFTLINE for parents with children born with cleft lip, palate and other craniofacial birth defects. Referrals are made to cleft palate/craniofacial healthcare teams and to parent-support groups. Free information is available to parents.

Marilyn A. Cohen, LSLP, President
Nichelle Berry Weintraub, Secretary
Emily Kiser, Administrator

1504 **FACES: National Craniofacial Association**
PO Box 11082
Chattanooga, TN 37401
423-266-1632
800-332-2373
info@faces-cranio.org
www.faces-cranio.org

Assists individuals with facial disfigurations and their families They maintain a registry of centers offering corrective surgery for craniofacial deformities and financial assistance to qualified applicants.

Kim Teems Fox, President
Emily McKay, Communications Director
Ashley Rhodes, FACES Camp Director

1505 **March of Dimes Foundation**
1550 Crystal Drive, Ste 1300
Arlington, VA 22202
888-663-4637
www.marchofdimes.org

March of Dimes help moms have full-term pregnancies and research the problems that threaten the health of babies. The March of Dimes also acts globally: sharing best practices in perinatal health and helping improve birth outcomes where the needs are the most urgent.

Stacey D. Stewart, President
Alan Brogdon, SVP/COO/Board Officer
Rahul Gupta, MD, SVP & Chief Medical/Health Officer

1506 **Online Mendelian Inheritance in Man**
McKusick-Nathans Institue of Genetic Medicine-JHU
Baltimore, MD 21205
www.omim.org

This database is a catalog of human genes and genetic disorders.

Ada Hamosh, MD, Scientific Director

1507 **Prescription Parents**
www.samizdat.com/pp1.html

www.samizdat.com/pp1.html

Organization that gives information and support to children with cleft lip and cleft palate through its educational and support materials, including its directory, newsletter and brochures.

1508 **Wide Smiles**
P.O. Box 5153
Stockton, CA 95205
209-942-2812
Fax: 209-464-1497
josmiles@yahoo.com
www.widesmiles2.org

Wide Smiles was formed to ensure that parents of cleft-affected children do not have to feel alone. We offer support, inspiration, information and networking for families everywhere who may be dealing with the challenges associated with clefting.

Pamphlets

1509 **As You Get Older**
Cleft Palate Foundation
1504 East Franklin Street, Suite 102
Chapel Hill, NC 27514
919-933-9044
800-242-5338
Fax: 919-933-9604
info@cleftline.org
www.cleftline.org

Describes medical treatment and social skills that may be necessary for teens born with clefts. There are sections on surgery, braces, speech and ear/nose/throat concerns, as well as social relationships and planning for the future.

2002 17 pages

Marilyn A. Cohen, LSLP, President
Nichelle Berry Weintraub, Secretary
Emily Kiser, Administrator

1510 **CPF Teddy Bears**
Cleft Palate Foundation
1504 East Franklin Street, Suite 102
Chapel Hill, NC 27514
919-933-9044
800-242-5338
Fax: 919-933-9604
info@cleftline.org
www.cleftline.org

Marilyn A. Cohen, LSLP, President
Nichelle Berry Weintraub, Secretary
Emily Kiser, Administrator

Cleft Lip and Cleft Palate / Pamphlets

1511 Cleft Lip & Palate
March of Dimes Foundation
1550 Crystal Drive, Ste 1300
Arlington, VA 22202
914-977-4488
888-663-4637
Fax: 914-997-4763
answers@marchofdimes.org
www.marchofdimes.org

Discusses how oral-palate clefts affect a baby's face, when and why they develop, special challenges that arise due to clefts, and repair oprtions.

1512 Cleft Surgery
Cleft Palate Foundation
1504 East Franklin Street, Suite 102
Chapel Hill, NC 27514
919-933-9044
800-242-5338
Fax: 919-933-9604
info@cleftline.org
www.cleftline.org

Provides general information about primary cleft lip and cleft palate surgeries. Complete with drawing explaining the surgical procedures and before and after photos, this brochure addresses general considerations about surgery, post-operative care, and a list of questions to ask your surgeon. Available for newborns, toddlers, preschoolers and school-aged children, teens, and adults. Available in Spanish (Preparando para la Cirug a).

2001 8 pages

Marilyn A. Cohen, LSLP, President
Nichelle Berry Weintraub, Secretary
Emily Kiser, Administrator

1513 Developing Good Speech
Cleft Palate Foundation
1504 East Franklin Street, Suite 102
Chapel Hill, NC 27514
919-933-9044
800-242-5338
Fax: 919-933-9604
info@cleftline.org
www.cleftline.org

Describes additional procedures that may be needed to improve speech in people with repaired cleft palate. Explains surgical procedures including palate lengthening, pharyngeal flap, spincter pharyngoplasty, and pharyngeal wall augmentation. Non-surgical prosthetic treatments are also described. (This information is most relevant to patients ages 4 to adult). Also available in Spanish (Desarrollando Bien el Habla).

2004 10 pages

Marilyn A. Cohen, LSLP, President
Nichelle Berry Weintraub, Secretary
Emily Kiser, Administrator

1514 Feeding Your Baby
Cleft Palate Foundation
1504 East Franklin Street, Suite 102
Chapel Hill, NC 27514
919-933-9044
800-242-5338
Fax: 919-933-9604
info@cleftline.org
www.cleftline.org

Provides information on how best to feed your baby. Intended for use by parents, caregivers, and nurses caring for infants with cleft lip and/or cleft palate, not for infants with more complicated craniofacial conditions. Also avaible in Spanish (Alimentando a su BebS).

1999 15 pages

Marilyn A. Cohen, LSLP, President
Nichelle Berry Weintraub, Secretary
Emily Kiser, Administrator

1515 Genetics and You
Cleft Palate Foundation
1504 East Franklin Street, Suite 102
Chapel Hill, NC 27514
919-933-9044
800-242-5338
Fax: 919-933-9604
info@cleftline.org
www.cleftline.org

Contains a brief overview of genetic biology and a summary of what is known about the causes of clefting. Features a graph for affected individuals, parents, and siblings, showing each group's approximate chances of having a child with a cleft. Details the steps involved i a genetic evaluation, which can help a family to determine its own particular recurrence risks. (The information presented is only applicable to patients with isolated cleft lip and/or palate).

2001 11 pages

Marilyn A. Cohen, LSLP, President
Nichelle Berry Weintraub, Secretary
Emily Kiser, Administrator

1516 Helping with Hearing
Cleft Palate Foundation
1504 East Franklin Street, Suite 102
Chapel Hill, NC 27514
919-933-9044
800-242-5338
Fax: 919-933-9604
info@cleftline.org
www.cleftline.org

Provides information on types of hearing loss, middle ear disease and its treatment, and speech concerns resulting from hearing problems. Also available in Spanish (Ayuda con el Oido).

2002 9 pages

Marilyn A. Cohen, LSLP, President
Nichelle Berry Weintraub, Secretary
Emily Kiser, Administrator

1517 Information for Adults
Cleft Palate Foundation
1504 East Franklin Street, Suite 102
Chapel Hill, NC 27514
919-933-9044
800-242-5338
Fax: 919-933-9604
info@cleftline.org
www.cleftline.org

Designed to empower adults to make informed decisions about what additional treatment, if any, they want to seek out in relation to their clefts.

2000 25 pages

Marilyn A. Cohen, LSLP, President
Nichelle Berry Weintraub, Secretary
Emily Kiser, Administrator

1518 The First Year
Cleft Palate Foundation
1504 East Franklin Street, Suite 102
Chapel Hill, NC 27514
919-933-9044
800-242-5338
Fax: 919-933-9604
info@cleftline.org
www.cleftline.org

Also available in Spanish (Los Cuatro Primeros Aos).

Marilyn A. Cohen, LSLP, President
Nichelle Berry Weintraub, Secretary
Emily Kiser, Administrator

1519 The School-Aged Child
Cleft Palate Foundation
1504 East Franklin Street, Suite 102
Chapel Hill, NC 27514
919-933-9044
800-242-5338
Fax: 919-933-9604
info@cleftline.org
www.cleftline.org

Divided into two sections, one addressing the medical concerns of a school-aged child born with a cleft and other providing information about the school experience for these children. The medical section contains information about surgery, dental care, and speech providing simple diagrams of how the speech mechanism may be affected by cleft palate. Also available in Spanish (Los nios de Edad Escolar).

1995 29 pages

Marilyn A. Cohen, LSLP, President
Nichelle Berry Weintraub, Secretary
Emily Kiser, Administrator

Cleft Lip and Cleft Palate / Pamphlets

1520 Toddlers and Preschoolers
Cleft Palate Foundation
1504 East Franklin Street, Suite 102
Chapel Hill, NC 27514

919-933-9044
800-242-5338
Fax: 919-933-9604
info@cleftline.org
www.cleftline.org

Marilyn A. Cohen, LSLP, President
Nichelle Berry Weintraub, Secretary
Emily Kiser, Administrator

Description

1521 CLUBFOOT
Synonym: Talipes
Covers these related disorders: Talipes equinovarus
Involves the following Biologic System(s):
Orthopedic and Muscle Disorders

The term clubfoot describes a deformity in which the foot is rotated inward and downward, rather than being in its normal position. The deformity in clubfoot is congenital or inborn, and is present at birth. It has several variants, all of which are referred to collectively under the Latin name "talipes" because they stem from structural aberrations in the anklebone, or talus, and dislocation of the ankle (i.e., talonavicular joint). In the most common type of clubfoot, known as congenital talipes equinovarus, the foot is abnormally twisted inward and the toes point downward (plantar flexion). Other deformities classified as types of clubfoot include defects in which the inner portion of the foot is raised with the sole turned inward (metatarsus varus), or the front area of the foot is raised and the heel is turned outward (talipes calcaneovalgus).

In about half of all cases of clubfoot, both feet are affected. A clubfoot tends to be smaller than an unaffected foot, and muscles of the foot and calf are typically underdeveloped, which may become more apparent with advancing age, and depending upon the severity of the deformity, the affected foot may have varying levels of stiffness and inflexibility.

Talipes equinovarus occurs in about 1 of every 1000 births, and is approximately twice as common in males as in females, and may be familiar or idiopathic, occurring as an isolated condition of unknown cause. In infants in whom the condition affects only one foot, the right side is most often involved. Familial talipes equinovarus is thought to result from the interaction of an abnormal (mutated) gene with other genes or certain environmental factors (multifactorial inheritance). Although deformity of the ankle bone was once considered the primary abnormality in talipes, researchers speculate that a neuromuscular abnormality may be the underlying cause of the talus deformities and associated findings.

In some cases, talipes may occur in association with a neuromuscular disorder (e.g., arthrogryposis multiplex congenita) or with other underlying disorders or syndromes.

The treatment of talipes usually begins soon after birth, since failure to correct this deformity can result in walking on the edge of the foot rather than with the sole of the foot flat on the floor, and in reduced size and strength of muscles in the affected leg. Treatment typically involves the use of taping, casting, or splinting (e.g., malleable splints, serial plaster casts) to move the foot and ankle toward their normal positions. This is often done gradually and over a period of months, through successive, repeated taping, splinting, or casting procedures that each provide a small degree of correction until the proper position of the foot and ankle is achieved. The treatment may involve the use of other orthopedic appliances and corrective shoes to assist with walking. If the use of taping, splints, or casts does not result inappropriate correction, or if a clubfoot is rigid, with shortness or tightness of the Achilles tendon or other structural deformities in the connective tissues or bones of the foot and ankle, corrective surgery may be needed. This is typically delayed until at least the age of 4 months in order to allow natural growth and strengthening of these structures. Regular monitoring of children with a clubfoot is needed to ensure their continued improvement.

Although clubfoot is not always completely correctible, treatment can improve both the appearance and function of the foot, and in most cases the prognosis for children with a clubfoot is good.

Government Agencies

1522 National Center for Environmental Health
4770 Buford Hwy NE
Atlanta, GA 30341
800-232-4636
TTY: 888-232-6348
www.cdc.gov/nceh

Strives to promote health and quality of life by preventing or controlling those diseases or deaths that result from interactions between people and their enviroment.

National Associations & Support Groups

1523 American Academy of Pediatrics
345 Park Blvd
Itasca, IL 60143
800-433-9016
Fax: 847-434-8000
mcc@aap.org
www.aap.org

The American Academy of Pediatrics and its member pediatricians are committed to the attainment of optimal physical, mental and social health and well-being for all infants, children, adolescents, and young adults.

Lynn Olson, PhD, VP, Research
Mark Del Monte, JD, CEO/Executive VP
Vera Tait, MD, FAAP, Chief Medical Officer

1524 Genetic Alliance
426400 Woodfield Road, Ste 189
Damascus, MD 20872
202-966-5557
Fax: 202-966-8553
info@geneticalliance.org
www.geneticalliance.org

World's leading nonprofit health advocacy organization committed to transforming health through genetics and promoting an environment of openness centered on the health of individuals, families, and communities.

Sharon Terry, CEO
Ruth Child, CFO
Natasha Bonhomme, Chief Strategy Officer

1525 March of Dimes Foundation
1550 Crystal Drive, Ste 1300
Arlington, VA 22202
888-663-4637
www.marchofdimes.org

March of Dimes help moms have full-term pregnancies and research the problems that threaten the health of babies. The March of Dimes also acts globally: sharing best practices in perinatal health and helping improve birth outcomes where the needs are the most urgent.

Stacey D. Stewart, President
Alan Brogdon, SVP/COO/Board Officer
Rahul Gupta, MD, SVP & Chief Medical/Health Officer

Web Sites

1526 CLIPS: Clubfoot Information and Parental Support
ixprss.com/clubfoot

ixprss.com/clubfoot

A web site dedicated to providing clubfoot information and parental support, created by a parent as a resource for information, support and understanding.

1527 Children with Talipes (Clubfoot)
www.clubfoot.co.uk

Clubfoot / Pamphlets

www.clubfoot.co.uk

Created by a parent of a child with talipes, the web site offers a first-hand account of treatment and description of clubfoot, as well as links to other sites.

1528 Johns Hopkins Department of Orthopaedic Surgery
601 North Caroline Street , JHOC #5215
Baltimore, MD 21287
443-997-2663
hopkinsortho@jhmi.edu
www.hopkinsmedicine.org/orthopedicsurgery

A web site serving as a learning resource for patients and physicians alike, offering insight into the services provided by the university's professional staff members.

John V. Ingari, MD, Associate Professor
Adam S. Levin, Othopaedic Oncology
Carrol D. Morris, MD, MS, Division Chief,Othopaedic Oncology

1529 Orthoseek
www.orthoseek.com/articles/clubfoot.html

admin@orthoseek.com
www.orthoseek.com/articles/clubfoot.html

A source of authoritative information on pediatric orthopedics and pediatric sports medicine.

Andrew Chong, MD, Founder

1530 TIPS: Talipes Information and Parental Support
www.clubfootaustralia.com/about-us

www.clubfootaustralia.com/about-us

A support group run by parents whose children have, or had, talipes, offering comprehensive information and many web links, as well as a bi-monthly newletter, stories from parents, email correspondence, and emotional support.

1531 Virtual Children's Hospital: Treatment of Congenital Clubfoot
200 Hawkins Drive
Iowa City, IA 52242
800-777-8442
www.vh.org/pediatric/provider/orthopaedics/clubfoot

A digital library of pediatric information committed to educating patients, healthcare providers and students for the purpose of improving patients' care, outcome and lives; uses current, authoritative, trustworthy health information created by the University of Iowa, while serving as a platform for research into the challenges facing world-wide information distribution.

Jean E. Robillard, MD, UI VP for Medical Affairs
Theresa Brennan, MD, Chief Medical Officer
Sabi Singh, MS, MA, Co-Chief Operating Officer

1532 Wheeless' Textbook of Orthopaedics
www.wheelessonline.com

www.wheelessonline.com

Derives from a variety of sources, including journals, articles, national meetings, lectures and other textbooks.

Clifford R. Wheeless, III, M.D., Author

Pamphlets

1533 Club Foot & Other Physical Deformities
March of Dimes Foundation
1550 Crystal Drive, Ste 1300
Arlington, VA 22202
914-977-4488
888-663-4637
Fax: 914-997-4763
answers@marchofdimes.org
www.marchofdimes.org/complications/clubfoot.aspx

Provides information on Club Foot and other deformities, discussing the affects on the child, diagnoses, causes, prevention, and treatment. Online.

1534 Club Foot and Other Foot Deformities
March of Dimes Resource Center
1550 Crystal Drive, Ste 1300
Arlington, VA 22202
914-977-4488
888-663-4637
Fax: 914-997-4763
TTY: 914-997-4764
answers@marchofdimes.org
www.marchofdimes.org/complications/clubfoot.aspx

Fact Sheets: one to two page review written for the general public. Also available electronically from our website www.modimes.org. Brochures: 3 panel color brochures written for the general public.

Description

1535 COARCTATION OF THE AORTA
Involves the following Biologic System(s):
Cardiovascular Disorders

Coarctation of the aorta is a congenital heart defect characterized by a narrowing or constriction of the body's main artery. This artery, known as the aorta, carries blood away from the heart to nourish the tissues of the body. Most of these defects are located just below the origin of the artery that supplies blood to the left arm, (left subclavian artery). Because this constriction reduces blood flow to the lower portion of the body, affected individuals may have unusually low blood pressure and weak or absent pulses in their legs. In addition, there may be higher blood pressure and strong pulses in the arms.

The severity of associated symptoms relates to the degree of pressure changes resulting from aortic narrowing. Although some children have no symptoms, others may experience dizziness, headache, weakness, fainting, nosebleeds, cold legs, and leg pain or cramps. Some affected infants may develop heart failure within the first few days or weeks of life. In some newborns, heart failure may result in decreased blood flow and abnormally high levels of acid in the blood (metabolic acidosis), sometimes accompanied by severe diarrhea and kidney (renal) failure. This life-threatening situation requires immediate treatment. Treatment of coarctation in a newborn requires surgery. (As these infants age, the narrowing may recur [restenosis] necessitating dilation or opening of the vessel through a procedure called balloon angioplasty, during which a balloon-tipped tube [catheter] is inflated inside the aorta, thus helping to expand the narrowed area of the vessel) Correction of coarctation of the aorta through surgery or balloon catheterization may be recommended in older children with significant impairment. Because coarctation of the aorta is very often accompanied by other heart defects, early intervention is crucial. Other cardiac anomalies often associated with this defect include bicuspid aortic valve (i.e., the heart valve between the left ventricle and the aorta is composed of only two leaflets, or cusps, instead of the normal three); abnormalities of the mitral valve (located between the left atrium and the left ventricle); and an abnormal opening in the wall between the left and right ventricles (ventricular septal defect).

The cause of coarctation of the aorta is unknown. Some researchers think that it develops in the fetus in association with certain types of cardiac abnormalities. Coarctation of the aorta is more prevalent in males than in females by a ratio of about two to one.

Government Agencies

1536 NIH/ Eunice Kennedy Shriver National Institute of Child Health & Human Development
P.O. Box 3006
Rockville, MD 20847
800-370-2943
Fax: 866-760-5947
www.nichd.nih.gov

Conducts and supports laboratory research, clinical trials, and epidemiological studies that explore health processes; examines the impact of disabilities, diseases, and variations on the lives of individuals; and sponsors training programs for scientists, health care providers, and researchers to ensure that NICHD research can continue

Diana W. Bianchi, Director
Alison Cernich, PhD, Deputy Director

1537 NIH/National Heart, Lung and Blood Institute
31 Center Drive, Bldg 31
Bethesda, MD 20892
877-645-2448
www.nhlbi.nih.gov

The National Heart, Lung, and Blood Institute (NHLBI) provides global leadership for a research, training, and education program to promote the prevention and treatment of heart, lung, and blood diseases and enhance the health of all individuals so that they can live longer and more fulfilling lives.

Gary H. Gibbons, MD, Director
Kate O'Sullivan, Executive Officer

National Associations & Support Groups

1538 American Academy of Pediatrics
345 Park Blvd
Itasca, IL 60143
800-433-9016
Fax: 847-434-8000
mcc@aap.org
www.aap.org

The American Academy of Pediatrics and its member pediatricians are committed to the attainment of optimal physical, mental and social health and well-being for all infants, children, adolescents, and young adults.

Lynn Olson, PhD, VP, Research
Mark Del Monte, JD, CEO/Executive VP
Vera Tait, MD, FAAP, Chief Medical Officer

1539 American Heart Association
7272 Greenville Avenue
Dallas, TX 75231
214-570-5978
800-242-8721
www.heart.org

The mission of the American Heart Associate is to build healthier lives, free of cardiovascular diseases and stroke.

Nancy Brown, CEO
Mitchell S.V. Elkind, President
Suzie Upton, Chief Operating Officer

1540 Genetic Alliance
426400 Woodfield Road, Ste 189
Damascus, MD 20872
202-966-5557
Fax: 202-966-8553
info@geneticalliance.org
www.geneticalliance.org

World's leading nonprofit health advocacy organization committed to transforming health through genetics and promoting an environment of openness centered on the health of individuals, families, and communities.

Sharon Terry, CEO
Ruth Child, CFO
Natasha Bonhomme, Chief Strategy Officer

1541 March of Dimes Foundation
1550 Crystal Drive, Ste 1300
Arlington, VA 22202
888-663-4637
www.marchofdimes.org

March of Dimes help moms have full-term pregnancies and research the problems that threaten the health of babies. The March of Dimes also acts globally: sharing best practices in perinatal health and helping improve birth outcomes where the needs are the most urgent.

Stacey D. Stewart, President
Alan Brogdon, SVP/COO/Board Officer
Rahul Gupta, MD, SVP & Chief Medical/Health Officer

Research Centers

1542 Children's Hospital: Academic Pediatric Surgery Department
1056 E 19th Avenue
Denver, CO 80218
303-493-8333
800-624-6553
Fax: 303-764-5997
www.chipteam.org

Strives to improve the health of children through the provision of high quality, coordinated programs of patient care, education, research and advocacy.

Emily L Dobyns

Web Sites

1543 Southern Illinois University School of Medicine
PO Box 19658
Springfield, IL 62794
217-545-8000
www.siumed.edu/peds/index.htm

Mission is to meet the health care needs of children and their families in central and Southern Illinois through provision of high quality, coordinated care of children with acute and chronic conditions with inpatient, ambulatory, and community-based programs.

1544 Yale University School of Medicine
333 Cedar St.
New Haven, CT 6510
203-737-1770
medicine.yale.edu

A site that offers information on congential heart conditions including Coarctation of the Aorta.

Peter Salovey, AB, MA, PhD, President
Richard Belitsky, MD, Deputy Dean of Education
Benjamin Polak, MA, MA, PhD, Provost

Book Publishers

1545 Congenital Disorders Sourcebook

Greg Mullin, author

Omnigraphics
615 Griswold Street, Ste 520
Detroit, MI 48226
610-461-3548
800-234-1340
Fax: 800-875-1340
contact@omnigraphics.com
www.omnigraphics.com

Basic consumer health information on disorders aquired during gestation, including spina bifida, hydrocephalus, cerebral palsy, heart defects, craniofacial abnormalities and fetal alcohol syndrome.

664 pages
ISBN: 0-780816-13-8

Description

1546 COLIC

Synonyms: Infantile colic, Three-month colic

Involves the following Biologic System(s):

Gastrointestinal Disorders, Neonatal and Infant Disorders

Colic refers to a condition in which infants experience frequent episodes of abdominal pain, accompanied by irritability and intense crying. These episodes usually begin suddenly and continue for several hours. Symptoms and physical findings of colic may also include flushing of the face, swelling of the abdomen, repeated extending or flexing of the legs, and unusually cold feet.

It is suspected that colic is intestinal in origin, however, its exact cause is not known. Contributing factors may include the excessive swallowing of air during episodes of unceasing crying, overfeeding, hunger, certain foods, intestinal allergy, and environmental stress. Attacks of colic usually commence within the first few weeks of life and occur most often in the afternoon or evening. Colic often resolves spontaneously within three or four months, without residual effects.

Infants with symptoms associated with colic should be evaluated to determine if another, perhaps more serious disorder, is causing the pain and discomfort. The treatment of colic may include soothing, comforting gestures such as holding, patting, stroking, rocking, and other repetitive movements. Some affected infants may benefit from white noise or other comforting background sounds; the application of a warm wash cloth, hot water bottle, or warm heating pad under the stomach when the child is lying prone; or a ride in the car. Some episodes of colic may resolve with the passing of gas or stool. In addition, parents and caregivers may be advised to refrain from overstimulating, overfeeding, or underfeeding babies with colic. The toll colic takes on parents can be considerable. Physicians often advise that parents or caregivers try to get enough sleep as fatigue, may sometimes add to the already stressful situation.

National Associations & Support Groups

1547 American Academy of Pediatrics
345 Park Blvd
Itasca, IL 60143
800-433-9016
Fax: 847-434-8000
mcc@aap.org
www.aap.org

The American Academy of Pediatrics and its member pediatricians are committed to the attainment of optimal physical, mental and social health and well-being for all infants, children, adolescents, and young adults.

Lynn Olson, PhD, VP, Research
Mark Del Monte, JD, CEO/Executive VP
Vera Tait, MD, FAAP, Chief Medical Officer

1548 American College of Gastroenterology
6400 Goldsboro Road
Bethesda, MD 20817
301-263-9000
www.gi.org

The American College of Gastroenterology was founded in 1932 to advance the scientific study and medical practice of diseases of the GI tract.

13,000 members

1549 American Medical Association
AMA Plaza, 330 North Wabash Ave., Suite 39300
Chicago, IL 60611
312-464-4782
800-262-3211
www.ama-assn.org

AMA is dedicated to ensuring sustainable physician practices that result in better health outcomes for patients.

James L. Madara, MD, CEO/EVP
Bernard L. Hengesbaugh, Chief Operating Officer
Kenneth J. Sharigian, SVP

1550 American Pregnancy Association
3007 Skyway Circle N., Ste 800
Irving, TX 75038
800-672-2296
info@americanpregnancy.org
americanpregnancy.org

The American Pregnancy Association is a 501(c)(3) nonprofit organization committed to promoting pregnancy wellness through education, advocacy and community awareness.

1551 American Urological Association
1000 Corporate Boulevard
Linthicum, MD 21090
410-689-3700
800-828-7866
Fax: 410-689-3800
aua@AUAnet.org
www.auanet.org

Urology is a surgical specialty which deals with diseases of the male and female urinary tract and the male reproductive organs.

Mike Sheppard, CPA, CAE, Chief Executive Officer
Patricia Banks, Chief Marketing Officer
Maureen Cones, Esq., Chief Legal & Policy Officer

1552 Digestive Disease National Coalition
507 Capitol Court NE, Suite 200
Washington, DC 20002
202-544-7497
Fax: 202-546-7105
www.ddnc.org

Advocacy organization comprised of over 30 voluntary and professional societies concerned with the many diseases of the digestive tract and liver.

Ceciel Rooker, Chairperson
Bryan Green, MD, President
Cathy Griffith, Vice Chairperson

1553 ICPA
327 N. Middletown Road
Media, PA 19063
610-565-2360
support@icpa4kids.com
icpa4kids.org

ICPA is a non-profit organization of chiropractic family practitioners dedicated to advancing public awareness and attainment of the chiropractic family wellness lifestyle.

Justin Ohm, DC, Executive Director
Peter Kevorkian, DC, President

1554 North American Society for Pediatric Gastroenterology/Hepatology/Nutrition
714 N Bethlehem Pike, Suite 300
Ambler, PA 19002
215-641-9800
Fax: 215-641-1995
www.naspghan.org

Strives to improve the care of infants, children and adolescents with digestive disorders by promoting advances in clinical care of children with chronic abdominal pain, diarrhea, constipation, vomiting, bleeding from the GI tract, inflammatory bowel disease, liver diseases, diseases of the pancreas, poor weight gain and nutritional problems.

Margaret K Stallings, Executive Director
Kim Rose, Associate Director
Gina Brown, Membership

Colic / Libraries & Resource Centers

Libraries & Resource Centers

1555 **Family Resource Center at Lucile Packard Children's Hospital**
725 Welch Road
Palo Alto, CA 94304
650-497-8102
www.lpch.org/healthLibrary

Provides hospital patients, their families and staff with access to a wide variety of information about child and maternal health and well-being. The FRC collection includes books, periodicals and pamphlets on a variety of topics from coping with chronic illness such as colic to parenting skills and child development. The Family Resource Center also maintains a large collection of recreational reading materials and video tapes.

1556 **National Digestive Diseases Information Clearinghouse (NDDIC)**
NIH
2 Information Way
Bethesda, MD 20892
301-654-3810
800-891-5389
Fax: 301-907-8906
nddic@info.niddk.nih.gov
www.digestive.niddk.nih.gov

The National Institute of Diabetes and Digestive and Kidney Diseases conducts and supports research on many of the most serious diseases affecting public health. The Institute supports much of the clinical research on the diseases of internal medicine and related subspecialty fields as well as many basic science disciplines.

Griffin P. Rodgers, MD, Director
Gregory G. Germino, MD, Deputy Director
Kathy Kranzfelder, Communications Director

Research Centers

1557 **CRI Worldwide Pediatric Center for Excellence**
CRI Worldwide
130 White Horse Pike
Clementon, NJ 08021
856-566-9000
Fax: 856-566-4302
www.cnsresearchinstitute.com

Formerly called CNS Research Institute; Psychiatrists and Child Psychologists maintains a major emphasis in the area of pediatric research. Working hard with parents and their children to educate and treat the entire family.

Dr David Krefetz, Director

1558 **Central DuPage Hospital Center for Digestive Disorders**
25 N Winfield Road
Winfield, IL 60190
630-933-1600
Fax: 630-933-1300
TTY: 630-933-4833
www.cdh.org

Bringing together the best research about colic and weighed up the evidence about how to treat it.

Michael Vivoda, President/CEO
Brian Lemon, President of Delnor Hospital, Execu
Brian Lemon, President of Central DuPage Hospita

1559 **Cincinnati Digestive Health Center**
Cincinnati Children's Hospital Medical Center
3333 Burnet Avenue
Cincinnati, OH 45229
513-636-4200
800-344-2462
TTY: 513-636-4900
jorge.bezerra@cchmc.org
www.cincinnatichildrens.org

Promote research that will yield insights into the fundamental processes of growth and development in the digestive tract and lead to novel or improved therapies.

Michael Fisher, President/CEO
Jorge Bezerra, MD, Director, Digestive Health Center

1560 **Infant Behavior, Cry and Sleep Clinic**
Women & Infants Hospital of Rhode Island
50 Holden Street, 1st Floor
Providence, RI 02908
401-453-7690
Fax: 401-453-7697
Barry_Lester@brown.edu
www.womenandinfants.org/Services/Infant-Behavior-Cry

A clinical service developed to diagnose and treat infants with crying, sleeping, feeding and associated early behavior problems by helping parents understand and manage their infant and to adjust to the disruption caused by having an infant who has behavioral problems in the first few months of life.

Constance A. Howes, FACHE, President/CEO of Women & Infants Ho

Conferences

1561 **NASPGHAN Annual Meeting**
NASPGHAN
714 N. Bethlehem Pike, Ste 300
Ambler, PA 19002
215-641-9800
Fax: 215-641-1995
www.naspghan.org

Strives to improve the care of infants, children and adolescents with digestive disorders by promoting advances in clinical care of children with chronic abdominal pain, diarrhea, constipation, vomiting, bleeding from the GI tract, inflammatory bowel disease, liver diseases, diseases of the pancreas, poor weight gain and nutritional problems.

Fall

Margaret K Stallings, Executive Director
Kim Rose, Associate Director
Gina Brown, Membership

Journals

1562 **Journal of Pediatric Gastroenterology and Nutrition**
NASPGHAN, author

Lippincott Williams & Wilkins
Two Commerce Square, 2001 Market Street
Philadelphia, PA 19103
215-521-8300
Fax: 215-521-8902
www.wolterskluwerhealth.com

Publication of the North American Society for Pediatric Gastroenterolgy, Hepatology and Nutrition, which strives to improve the care of infants, children and adolescents with digestive disorders by promoting advances in clinical care of children with chronic abdominal pain, diarrhea, constipation, vomiting, bleeding from the GI tract, inflammatory bowel disease, liver diseases, diseases of the pancreas, poor weight gain and nutritional problems.

Bob Becker, President/ CEO
Susan Yules, Chief Financial Officer
Cathy Wolfe, President/ CEO, Medical Research

Newsletters

1563 **NASPGHAN News**
714 N. Bethlehem Pike, Ste 300
Ambler, PA 19002
215-641-9800
Fax: 215-641-1995
www.naspghan.org

Publication of the North American Society for Pediatric Gastroenterolgy, Hepatology and Nutrition, which strives to improve the care of infants, children and adolescents with digestive disorders by promoting advances in clinical care of children with chronic abdominal pain, diarrhea, constipation, vomiting, bleeding from the GI tract, inflammatory bowel disease, liver diseases, diseases of the pancreas, poor weight gain and nutritional problems.

Margaret K Stallings, Executive Director
Kim Rose, Associate Director
Gina Brown, Membership

Conduct Disorder / National Associations & Support Groups

Description

1564 CONDUCT DISORDER
Covers these related disorders: Group conduct disorder, Solitary aggressive conduct disorder, Undifferentiated conduct disorder
Involves the following Biologic System(s):
Developmental/Behavioral/Psychiatric Disorders

Conduct disorder refers to a group of distinct behavioral abnormalities characterized by the repetition of certain types of disruptive or antisocial behaviors. Children or adolescents with conduct disorder may often lie, steal, skip school, run away from home, use drugs or alcohol, hurt animals, commit arson or vandalism, engage in physical violence, use weapons, and commit other criminal acts. Those affected with solitary aggressive conduct disorder are usually selfish, rarely get along with or relate well to others, and often lack remorse for their behavior. Children and adolescents with group conduct disorder, however, may be attached and faithful to a particular clique, gang, or other group of friends while at the same time violating the rights of or displaying antisocial behavior toward those outside of the group. In some cases, affected individuals may display behavior characteristic of both solitary aggressive and group conduct disorders and, subsequently, may be diagnosed with undifferentiated conduct disorder.

Conduct disorder may be caused by a variety of factors including genetic as well as environmental influences (e.g., childrearing, etc.). In many cases, children with this type of behavioral irregularity have parents or caregivers who display similar patterns of conduct. In addition, parents or caregivers often have inconsistent parenting skills or may be overly aggressive in punishing or disciplining. Some parents or caregivers may be unsupportive of the child, or may lack other basic skills that help the child to develop a sense of self-worth, respect for others, etc. Several factors may influence whether affected children carry these characteristic patterns of behavior into adulthood. Some factors include parental or caregiver influences, the age of onset, the severity and type of behavior, the number of different types of antisocial behaviors exhibited, and whether the episodes of disruptive behavior continue to increase.

Treatment of conduct disorder may include individual, group, and family therapy, as well as parental or caregiver management training. In some cases, children with severe conduct disorder may benefit from hospitalization for psychiatric evaluation and treatment. Medication is, in most cases, not indicated for the treatment of conduct disorder; however, it is sometimes prescribed to treat other underlying disorders (e.g, depression, attention deficit hyperactivity disorder, etc.). Other treatment is supportive.

Government Agencies

1565 NIH/National Institute of Mental Health
6001 Executive Blvd, Rm 6200, MSC 9663
Bethesda, MD 20892
866-615-6464
Fax: 301-443-4279
TTY: 301-443-8431
nimhinfo@nih.gov
www.nimh.nih.gov

The mission of NIMH is to transform the understanding and treatment of mental illnesses through basic and clinical research, paving the way for prevention, recovery, and cure.
Joshua A. Gordon, MD, PhD, Director
Shelli Avenevoli, PhD, Deputy Director

National Associations & Support Groups

1566 American Academy of Pediatrics
345 Park Blvd
Itasca, IL 60143
800-433-9016
Fax: 847-434-8000
mcc@aap.org
www.aap.org

The American Academy of Pediatrics and its member pediatricians are committed to the attainment of optimal physical, mental and social health and well-being for all infants, children, adolescents, and young adults.
Lynn Olson, PhD, VP, Research
Mark Del Monte, JD, CEO/Executive VP
Vera Tait, MD, FAAP, Chief Medical Officer

1567 American Mental Health Foundation (AMHF)
PO Box 3
Riverdale,, NY 10471
USA
212-737-9027
elomke@americanmentalhealthfoundation.or
americanmentalhealthfoundation.org

Dedicated to the extensive and intensive research in the theories and techniques of treatment of emotional illness and to the implementation of reforms in the mental health system. Efforts have resulted in development of better and less expensive treatment methods. Findings are disseminated in English and other major languages.
Sister Joan Curtin. CND, Director
Evander Lomke, President/Executive Director
Eugene Gollogly, Vice President

1568 Association for Behavioral and Cognitive Therapies
305 7th Avenue, 16th Floor
New York, NY 10001
212-647-1890
Fax: 212-647-1865
www.abct.org

Formerly known as the Association for Advancement of Behavior Therapy; this organization is concerned with the application of behavioral and cognitive sciences to understanding human behavior, developing interventions to enhance the human condition, and promoting the appropriate utilization of these interventions.
Mary Jane Eimer, CAE, Executive Director
Rachel Lamb, Membership & Marketing Manager
Ewan Johnson, Senior Communications Manager

1569 Center for Disabilities and Development
University of Iowa Stead Family Children's Hospita
100 Hawkins Drive
Iowa City, IA 52242
319-353-6900
877-686-0031
Fax: 319-356-7700
cdd-webmaster@uiowa.edu
www.uichildrens.org/cdd/

A trusted resource for healthcare, training, research and information for people with disabilities that include: behavior disorders, brain injury, cerebral palsy, diabetes, down syndrome, learning disabilities, sleep disorders and spina bifida.
Dianne McBrien, MD, Medical Director

1570 Center for Mental Health Services
5600 Fishers Lane
Rockville, MD 20857
240-276-1310
www.samhsa.gov

Encourages a range of programs such as systems of care to respond to the increasing number of mental, emotional, and behavioral problems among children. Supports outreach and case management programs for the thousands of Americans who are homeless and the improvement of these services.
Anita Everett, MD, Director

1571 Mental Health America
500 Montgomery Street, Ste 820
Alexandria, VA 22314
703-684-7722
800-969-6642
Fax: 703-684-5968
www.mentalhealthamerica.net

Conduct Disorder / Research Centers

MHA, the leading advocacy organization addressing the full spectrum of mental and substance use conditions and their effects nationwide, works to inform, advocate and enable access to quality behavioral health services for all Americans.

Paul Gionfriddo, President/CEO
Whitney Ball, Assoc. Dir., Marketing/Outreach
Sachin Doshi, Sr. Dir, Finance/Operations

1572 NADD: National Association for the Dually Diagnosed
12 Hurley Avenue
Kingston, NY 12401
845-331-4336
800-331-5362
Fax: 845-331-4569
info@thenadd.org
www.thenadd.org

Nonprofit organization designed to promote the interests of professional and care providers for individuals who have the coexistence of mental illness and intellectual disabilities. NADD provides conferences, educational services and training materials to professionals, parents, concerned citizens and service organizations.

Jeanne Farr, CEO
Michelle Jordan, Office Manager
Edward Seliger, Project Coordinator

1573 National Alliance on Mental Illness (NAMI)
4301 Wilson Blvd., Suite 300
Arlington, VA 22203
703-525-7600
800-999-6264
info@nami.org
www.nami.org

NAMI provides advocacy, education, support and public awareness so that all individuals and families affected by mental illness can build better lives.

Daniel H. Gillison, CEO
David Levy, CFO
Ken Duckworth, Chief Medical Officer

1574 National Federation of Families
15800 Crabbs Branch Way, Suite 300
Rockville, MD 20855
240-403-1901
ffcmh@ffcmh.org
www.ffcmh.org

The National family run organization is dedicated exclusively to helping children with mental health needs and their families achieve a better quality of life.

Lynda Gargan, PhD, Executive Director

1575 National Mental Health Consumers' Self-Help Clearinghouse
1211 Chestnut Street, Suite 1207
Philadelphia, PA 19107
215-751-1810
800-553-4539
Fax: 215-636-6312
selfhelpclearinghouse@gmail.com
www.mhselfhelp.org

The Clearinghouse works to foster peer empowerment through our website, up-to-date news and information announcements, a directory of peer-driven services, electronic and printed publications, training packages, and individual and onsite consultation

Joseph Rogers, Founder/Executive Director
Susan Rogers, Director

Research Centers

1576 Menninger Child & Family Program
Menninger Clinic
2801 Gessner Drive, PO Box 809045
Houston, TX 77280
713-275-5000
800-351-9058
Fax: 713-275-5117
www.menninger.edu

Menninger's research strategies are developed through the Menninger Child & Family Program. Projects are designed to develop a better understanding of the mind in order to more effectively treat mental disorders.

Ian Aitken, Ceo

1577 National Technical Assistance Center for Children's Mental Health
Georgetown University
Center for Child and Human Development Georgetown
Washington, DC 20057
202-687-5000
Fax: 202-687-8899
TDD: 202-687-5503
gucdc@georgetown.edu
www.gucchd.georgetown.edu/67211.html

Devoted to helping states, tribes, territories, and communities discover, apply, and sustain innovative and collaborative solutions that improve the social, emotional, and behavioral well being of children and families.

James Wotring MSW, Director

1578 Research & Training Center for Children's Mental Health at University of South FL
Louis de la Parte Florida Mental Health Institute
13301 Bruce B. Downs Boulevard
Tampa, FL 33612
813-974-3154
Fax: 813-974-3078
friedman@fmhi.usf.edu
www.rtckids.fmhi.usf.edu/default.cfm

Working towards increasing the effectiveness of service systems by strengthening the empirical base for such systems through research and dissemination to key audiences. With its new, five-year research program, the Center expands its mission with an integrated research, training, and dissemination program targeted specifically at implementation issues for developing effective systems of care.

Robert M. Friedman, Ph.D, Center Director
Albert Duchnowski, Ph.D, Deputy Director
Krista Kutash, Ph.D, Deputy Director

1579 Research and Training Center on Family Support and Children's Mental Health
1600 SW 4th Avenue, Suite 900
Portland, OR 97201
503-725-4040
Fax: 503-725-4180
flemingd@pdx.edu
www.rtc.pdx.edu

Funded to pursue an integrated set of research, training, technical assistance, and dissemination activities. The center's work will focus on two related themes; community integration for children and adolescents with emotional and behavioral disorders and their families; and strengthening family and youth participation in child and adolescent mental health services.

Donna Flemming, Information Director

1580 Technical Assistance Partnership for Child and Family Mental Health
1000 Thomas Jefferson Street NW, Suite 400
Washington, DC 20007
202-403-6827
Fax: 202-342-5007
tapartnership@air.org
www.tapartnership.org

A staff of family members and professionals with extensive practice experience, grounded in an organization with vast research experience in children with serious emotional disturbance and their families.

Sharon Hunt, Deputy Director of Operations
Jeffrey Poirier, Continuous Quality Improvement
Regenia Hicks, Project Director Continuous Quality

Conferences

1581 FFCMH Annual Conference
National Federation of Families
15800 Crabbs Branch Way, Suite 300
Rockville, MD 20855
240-403-1901
ffcmh@ffcmh.org
www.ffcmh.org

The only national conference dedicated solely to supporting families whose children - of any age - experience mental health and/or substance use challenges during their lifetime.

November

Lynda Gargan, PhD, Executive Director

1582 NADD Annual Conference & Exhibit Show
National Association for the Dually Diagnosed
12 Hurley Avenue
Kingston, NY 12401
845-331-4336
800-331-5362
Fax: 845-331-4569
info@thenadd.org
www.thenadd.org

Educating professionals, families and clients of services on standard and state-of-the-art information across many specialties; Enhancing specific skills required to provide maximum benefit to individuals with special or specific cognitive and/or developmental needs; Providing a forum for an exchange of ideas and information among professionals, families and those who may receive services.

Fall

Jeanne Farr, CEO
Michelle Jordan, Office Manager
Edward Seliger, Project Coordinator

1583 NAMI Convention
National Alliance on Mental Illness
3803 N Fairfax Drive, Suite 100
Arlington, VA 22203
703-524-7600
888-999-6264
Fax: 703-524-9094
TDD: 703-516-7227
info@nami.org
www.nami.org

The NAMI Convention is packed with information, chances to network, leadership development opportunities, and lots more

Summer

Richele Keas, Senior Mgr, Media Relations

Audio Video

1584 Managing the Defiant Child
Courage To Change Publishing
PO Box 486
Wilkes-Barres, PA 18703
800-440-4003
Fax: 800-772-6499
www.couragetochange.com

An information-packed video brings to life a proven approach to behavior management. Shows clinicians, school practitioners, teachers, parents and students how enhanced parenting skills can dramatically improve the parent-child relationship.

Russell A Barkley, Editor

1585 Understanding and Treating the Hereditary Psychiatric Spectrum Disorders
Hope Press
PO Box 188
Duarte, CA 91009
818-303-0644
800-321-4039
Fax: 818-358-3520
hopepress.com

Learn with ten hours of audio tapes from a two day seminar given in May 1997 by David E Comings MD. Tapes cover: ADHD, Tourette syndrome, Obsessive-Compulsive Disorder, Conduct Disorder, Oppositional Defiant Disorder, Autism and other Hereditary Psychiatric Spectrum Disorders. Eight audio tapes.

David E Comings, MD, Presenter

1586 Understanding the Defiant Child
Courage To Change
PO Box 486
Wilkes-Barres, PA 18703
800-440-4003
Fax: 800-772-6499
www.couragetochange.com

Provides a vivid picture of what we know about Oppositional Defiant Disorder and presents real-life scenes of family interactions and commentary from parents. Illuminates the nature and causes of ODD, why it should be dealt with early, and what can be done. Ideal viewing for school practitioners, clinical child psychologists, counselors and parents coping with a defiant child.

Russell A Barkley, Editor

Web Sites

1587 Conductdisorders.com
www.conductdisorders.com

www.conductdisorders.com

Site for parents, teachers, and family members who deal with a child with one of the defined behavioral disorders.

1588 Internet Mental Health
www.mentalhealth.com

internetmentalhealth@shaw.ca
www.mentalhealth.com

Our goal is to improve understanding, diagnosis, and treatment of mental illness throughout the world.

Phillip W. Long, M.D., Psychiatrist

1589 NADD: National Association for the Dually Diagnosed
12 Hurley Avenue
Kingston, NY 12401
845-331-4336
800-331-5362
Fax: 845-331-4569
info@thenadd.org
www.thenadd.org

Nonprofit organization designed to promote the interests of professional and care providers for individuals who have the coexistence of mental illness and intellectual disabilities. NADD provides conferences, educational services and training materials to professionals, parents, concerned citizens and service organizations.

Jeanne Farr, CEO
Michelle Jordan, Office Manager
Edward Seliger, Project Coordinator

1590 Online Mendelian Inheritance in Man
McKusick-Nathans Institue of Genetic Medicine-JHU
Baltimore, MD 21205
www.omim.org

This database is a catalog of human genes and genetic disorders.

Ada Hamosh, MD, Scientific Director

Book Publishers

1591 Aggression and Violence Throughout the Life Span
Sage Publications
2455 Teller Road
Thousand Oaks, CA 91320
800-818-7243
Fax: 800-583-2665
info@sagepub.com
www.sagepub.com

A unique life span developmental perspective on some of society's most perplexing and pernicious problems, aggressive and violent behaviors. Examines issues in the development of aggressive behaviors in young children, the progression of these behaviors to older children and adolescents and cause, effect and treatment of aggressive and violent behaviors in adults. Integrates empirical research with clinical applications.

360 pages Softcover
ISBN: 0-803945-51-5

Sara Miller McCune, Founder/Chairman
Blaise R Simqu, President/CEO
Chris Hickok, Senior Vice President/CFO

Conduct Disorder / Pamphlets

1592 Antisocial Behavior by Young People
Cambridge University Press
32 Avenue of the Americas
New York, NY 10013

617-264-2300
Fax: 617-264-2323
info@cambridge.com
www.cambridge.org

Written by a child psychiatrist, a criminologist and a social psychologist, this book is a major international review of research evidence on anti-social behavior. Covers all aspects of the field, including descriptions of different types of delinquency and time trends, the state of knowledge on the individuals, social-psychological and cultural factors involved and recent advances in prevention and intervention.

490 pages Paperback
ISBN: 0-521646-08-1

Michael Rutter, Editor
Ann Hagell, Editor
Henri Giller, Editor

1593 Conduct Disorders in Childhood and Adolescence (Developmental Clinical)
Sage Publications
2455 Teller Road
Thousand Oaks, CA 91320

800-818-7243
800-818-7243
Fax: 800-583-2665
info@sagepub.com
www.sagepub.com

Conduct disorder is a clinical problem among children and adolescents that includes aggressive acts, theft, vandalism, firesetting, running away, truancy, defying authority and other antisocial behaviors. This book describes the nature of conduct disorder and what is currently known from research and clinical work. Topics include psychiatric diagnosis, parent psychopathology and child-rearing processes.

192 pages Hardcover
ISBN: 0-803971-81-8

Sara Miller McCune, Founder/Chairman
Blaise R Simqu, President/CEO
Chris Hickok, Senior Vice President/CFO

1594 Conduct Disorders in Children and Adolescents
American Psychiatric Publishing
1000 Wilson Boulevard, Suite 1825
Arlington, VA 22009

703-907-7322
800-368-5777
Fax: 703-907-1091
appi@psych.org
www.appi.org

Examines the phenomenology, etiology, and diagnosis of conduct disorders, and describes therapeutic and preventive interventions. Includes the range of treatments now available, including individual, family, group, and behavior therapy; hospitalization; and residential treatment.

1995 414 pages Hardcover
ISBN: 0-880485-17-5

G Pirooz Sholevar, MD, Editor

1595 Conduct Problem/Emotional Problem Interventions: A Holistic Perspective
Slosson Educational Publications
PO Box 544
East Aurora, NY 14052

716-625-0930
888-756-7766
Fax: 800-655-3840
slosson@slosson.com
www.slosson.com

This innovative book is broad in scope and addresses the now what sensation that many professionals get when charged with the education or treatment of individuals with conduct disorders or emotional disturbance. Distinct intervention and screening strategies and patient involvement strategies are offered in clear and practical terms.

Edward J Kelly, Editor

1596 Difficult Child
Random House
1745 Broadway
New York, NY 10019

212-782-9000
Fax: 212-572-6066
www.randomhouse.com

One of the nation's most respected experts on children and discipline; Dr. Stanley Turecki a father of a once difficult child offers compassionate and practical advice to parents of hard-to-raise children.

320 pages Paperback

Stanley Turecki, Writer

1597 Disruptive Behavior Disorders in Children and Adolescents
Robert L Hendren, DO, author

American Psychiatric Publishing
1000 Wilson Boulevard, Suite 1825
Arlington, VA 22209

703-907-7322
800-368-5777
Fax: 703-907-1091
appi@psych.org
www.appi.org

Discusses attention deficit hyperactivity disorder, conduct disorder, substance abuse and disruptive behavior disorders. Examines the relationship between violence and mental illness in adolescence.

1999 216 pages Paperback
ISBN: 0-880489-60-7

1598 Preventing Antisocial Behavior: Interventions
Guilford Press
72 Spring Street
New York, NY 10012

212-431-9800
800-365-7006
Fax: 212-966-6708
info@guilford.com
www.guilford.com

Establishes the crucial link between theory, measurement and intervention. Brings together a collection of studies that utilize experimental approaches for evaluating intervention programs, both the feasibility, and necessity of independent evaluation. Also shows how the information obtained in such studies can be used to test and refine prevailing theories about human behavior in general, and behavior changes in particular.

1992 391 pages
ISBN: 0-898628-82-1

Joan McCord, Editor
Richard Tremblay, Editor

1599 Skills Training for Children with Behavior Disorders
Courage To Change
PO Box 486
Wilkes-Barres, PA 18703

800-440-4003
Fax: 800-772-6499
www.couragetochange.com

Designed for use by both parents and therapists, provides background information, step-by-step instructions and many useful, reproducible worksheets. Techniques offered help children with anger management, compliance and following rules, academic success, emotional well-being and self-esteem and much more.

272 pages

Michael L Bloomquist, Editor

Pamphlets

1600 Conduct Disorder in Children and Adolescents
National Mental Health Information Center
PO Box 42557
Washington, DC 20015

800-789-2647
Fax: 240-747-5470
TDD: 866-889-2647
ken@mentalhealth.org
www.mentalhealth.samhsa.gov

This fact sheet defines conduct disorder, identifies risk factors, discusses types of help available, and suggests what parents or other caregivers can do.

1997 2 pages

1601 Mental, Emotional, and Behavior Disorders in Children and Adolescents
National Mental Health Information
PO Box 42557
Washington, DC 20015
240-747-5484
800-789-2647
Fax: 240-747-5470
mentalhealth.samhsa.gov

This fact sheet describes mental, emotional, and behavioral problems that can occur during childhood and adolescence and discusses related treatment, support services, and research.

4 pages

1602 Treatment of Children with Mental Disorder
National Institute of Mental Health
PO Box 5801
Bethesda, MD 20824
301-496-5751
800-352-9424
Fax: 301-443-4279
TTY: 301-443-8431
nimhinfo@nih.gov
www.nimh.nih.gov

A short booklet that contains questions and answers about therapy for children with mental disorders. Includes a chart of mental disorders and medications used.

Walter J. Koroshetz, M.D., Acting Director
Alan L. Willard, Ph.D., Acting Deputy Director
Caroline Lewis, Executive Officer

Camps

1603 Adventure Learning Center Camp Programs
Eagle Village
4507 170th Avenue
Hersey, MI 49639
231-832-2234
800-748-0061
Fax: 231-832-1468
summercamp@eaglevillage.org
www.eaglevillage.org

Offers a variety of fun camp experiences for children, including those with emotional and/or behavioral impairments. A low staff-to-camper ratio and exciting, challenging activities make the camps rewarding experiences. As funding is available, we will offer camp scholarships to eligible participants.

Sara Kofal, Camp Director

1604 Life Adventure Center
Life Adventure Center of the Bluegrass
PO Box 447
Versailles, KY 40383
859-873-3271
Fax: 859-873-2410
www.lifeadventurecamp.org

A unique experience of discovery and development where lifelong lessons are learned. Through purposeful play, using a combination of physical and mental problem-solving exercises, participants engage in opportunities to make positive choices, gain self-confidence, improve decision making, build on group strengths and much more.

1605 Talisman Summer Camps
Talisman Schools
64 Gap Creek Road
Zirconia, NC 28790
855-588-8254
Fax: 828-669-2521
summer@talismancamps.com
www.talismansummercamp.com/

Camps for children ages 6 to 17 and young adults 18-21 with LD, ADD and ADHD, Asperger's Syndrome, and high functioning autism. Talisman has been offering such experiences since 1980 and is ACA accredited. The unique summer camps specialize in creating camps that offer not only adventure, but learning experiences, for children and teenagers with learning disabilities, attention deficit hyperactivity disorder, Asperger's syndrome and high-functioning autism.

Linda Tatsapaugh, Director
Aaron McGinley, Base Camp Program Manager

Congenital Adrenal Hyperplasia / Description

Description

1606 CONGENITAL ADRENAL HYPERPLASIA

Synonyms: CAH, Androgenital syndrome, Congenital virilizing adrenal hyper, 21-hydroxylase deficiency, 11-beta-hydroxylase deficiency

Involves the following Biologic System(s):

Endocrinologic Disorders

Congenital adrenal hyperplasia (CAH) refers to a group of genetic diseases that leads to the inability of the adrenal glands to make cortisol. Cortisol is a steroid hormone needed to maintain metabolism, energy, blood pressure, and a normal responses to stress or injury. There are many different steps in the production of cortisol; each step requires an enzyme for completion and as a result, a deficiency in any enzyme along the path leads to one of the forms of CAH. The inability to make cortisol leads to symptoms from both the lack of cortisol as well as from the build-up of the cortisol precursors. In CAH, male hormones (androgens) are made in excess and this will lead to exaggerated male characteristics in these patients. Some people with CAH also have deficiency in another hormone, aldosterone. Aldosterone regulates salt (sodium)levels in the body.

Symptoms of CAH can vary in girls and boys, and also may vary according to the specific type of CAH. In girls, the excess of androgens leads to masculinization of the female external genitalia (ambiguous genitalia). Symptoms in girls with milder forms of CAH include irregular menstrual periods, excessive or male pattern hair growth, or infertility. In boys, symptoms of salt-wasting CAH include adrenal crisis which typically consists of low blood pressure and sodium abnormalities. Girls can also have salt abnormalities, but are often diagnosed before an adrenal crisis because of their ambiguous external genitalia can be seen. In boys with non-salt wasting CAH, the effect of excess androgens leads to pubertal changes earlier than expected (precocious puberty).

The treatment of CAH is replacement of cortisol with glucocorticoid medications, and if needed, replacement of aldosterone with mineralocorticoid medications. It is important to remember to give extra medication (stress dose steroids during times of stress, illness, or injury because of the body's greater demand for steroids during those times.)

National Associations & Support Groups

1607 American Academy of Pediatrics
345 Park Blvd
Itasca, IL 60143
800-433-9016
Fax: 847-434-8000
mcc@aap.org
www.aap.org

The American Academy of Pediatrics and its member pediatricians are committed to the attainment of optimal physical, mental and social health and well-being for all infants, children, adolescents, and young adults.

Lynn Olson, PhD, VP, Research
Mark Del Monte, JD, CEO/Executive VP
Vera Tait, MD, FAAP, Chief Medical Officer

1608 CARES Foundation
2414 Morris Avenue, Suite 110
Union, NJ 07083
908-364-0272
866-227-3737
Fax: 908-686-2019
www.caresfoundation.org

CARES Foundation is a nonprofit, educational organization. Its purpose is to educate the public and physicians about all forms of Congenital Adrenal Hyerplasia, its symptoms, diagnostic protocols, treatment, genetic frequency, the necessity for early intervention and benefits of newborn screening. It is also dedicated to providing support and information to affected individuals and their families.

Dina Matos, Executive Director
Bea Pereira, Director of Finance and Operations
Karen Lin Su, MD, Medical Director

1609 MAGIC Foundation: Major Aspects of Growth in Children
4200 Cantera Drive, #106
Warrenville, IL 60555
630-836-8200
800-362-4423
Fax: 630-836-8181
contactus@magicfoundation.org
www.magicfoundation.org

A national nonprofit organization providing support and education regarding growth disorders in children and related adult disorders. Provides educational information, networking, a national conference, a kids' program and an extensive medical library.

10,000 members

Dianne Kremidas, Executive Director
Mary Andrews, Chief Executive Officer
Teresa Tucker, Patient Advocacy

1610 National Adrenal Diseases Foundation
PO Box 95149
Newton, MA 02495
847-726-9010
nadfsupport@nadf.us
www.nadf.us

NADF is committed to bringing information regarding adrenal diseases into the public's awareness to facilitate early diagnosis and treatment.NADF sponsors support groups across the countrty allowing for an exchange of ideas and feelings by individuals who share a common illness. NADF members receive quaterly newsletters, educational materials, and access to a library of related information.

Kalina Warren, Co-President
Erin A. Foley-Moudry, MPH, Co-President
Lori Engler, Executive Director

Libraries & Resource Centers

1611 University of Iowa Birth Defects and Genetic Disorders Unit
2614 JCP
Iowa City, IA 52242
319-335-9901
James M Smith, Director

Conferences

1612 Adult Endocrine Disorders/GHD Educational Convention
Magic Foundation
4200 Cantera Drive, #106
Warrenville, IL 60555
630-836-8200
800-362-4423
Fax: 630-836-8181
contactus@magicfoundation.org
www.magicfoundation.org

An educational program for adults who are affected with Growth Hormone Deficiency and/or other endocrine disorders.

June

Dianne Kremidas, Executive Director
Mary Andrews, CEO
Teresa Tucker, Patient Advocacy

Web Sites

1613 CARES Foundation
2414 Morris Ave., Suite 110
Union, NJ 7083
908-364-0272
866-227-3737
Fax: 908-686-2019
contact@caresfoundation.org
www.caresfoundation.org

Provides education to the public and physicians about all forms of Congenital Adrenal Hyerplasia — symptoms, diagnostic protocols, treatment, genetic frequency, the necessity for early intervention and benefits of newborn screening. The web site also provides support and information to affected individuals and their families.

Katherine L. Fowler, President
Chad Lapp, Vice President
Alexandra Dubois, Secretary

1614 MAGIC Foundation: Major Aspects of Growth in Children
4200 Cantera Drive, #106
Warrenville, IL 60555
630-836-8200
800-362-4423
Fax: 630-836-8181
contactus@magicfoundation.org
www.magicfoundation.org

Created to provide support services for the families of children afflicted with a wide variety of chronic and/or critical disorders, syndromes, and diseases that affect a child's growth.

Dianne Kremidas, Executive Director
Mary Andrews, CEO
Teresa Tucker, Patient Advocacy

1615 National Adrenal Diseases Foundation
PO Box 95149
Newton, MA 02495
847-726-9010
info@nadf.us
www.nadf.us

Committed to bringing information regarding rare diseases to the publics awareness to facilitate early diagnosis and treatment.

Kalina Warren, Co-President
Erin A. Foley-Moudry, MPH, Co-President
Lori Engler, Executive Director

Newsletters

1616 CARES Foundation Newsletter
2414 Morris Avenue, Suite 110
Union, NJ 7083
973-912-3895
866-227-3737
kelly@caresfoundation.org
www.caresfoundation.org

Provides support and information to affected individuals and their families.

3x year

Kelly R Leight, Executive Director

1617 NADF News
505 Northern Boulevard
Great Neck, NY 11021
516-487-4992
nadfsupport@nadf.us
www.nadf.us

Features important information on adrenal disorders, support groups and the latest research.

quaterly

Kalina Warren, President
Melanie G Wong, Executive Director
Paul Margulies, MD, FACP, Medical Director

Congenital Cataracts / Description

Description

1618 CONGENITAL CATARACTS
Involves the following Biologic System(s):
Genetic/Chromosomal/Syndrome/Metabolic Disorders,
Ophthalmologic Disorders

Congenital cataracts refers to a condition in which cloudiness or opacities in the lens of the eye or eyes are present at birth. These opacities may vary in severity, with some resolving spontaneously as in cataracts of prematurity. Other congenital cataracts, if left untreated, may result in loss of transparency of the lens and subsequent visual impairment. In addition, in some newborns, remnants of other eye tissues may contribute to the formation of a stationary opacity of the cornea. In most instances, this type of stationary cloudiness does not contribute to visual impairment.

Congenital cataracts may occur as the result of many different factors (multifactorial), including genetic influences, associated metabolic and chromosomal disorders, congenital infections, and toxic exposure. If inherited as an isolated event, congenital cataracts are usually transmitted as an autosomal dominant or autosomal recessive trait. Several metabolic disorders are characterized by congenital cataracts, including galactosemia, in which an enzyme deficiency results in the inability to process the simple sugar galactose; oculocerebrorenal syndrome (Lowe's syndrome), an X-linked metabolic disorder that affects many systems of the body; certain metabolic diseases known as lyosomal storage disorders; and several other diseases related to inborn errors of metabolism. Other contributing metabolic factors may include low blood levels of calcium (hypocalcemia) or glucose (hypoglycemia). In addition, cataracts are sometimes diagnosed in newborns whose mothers have diabetes mellitus. Several chromosomal disorders are also characterized by congenital opacities including Down's syndrome (trisomy 21), trisomy 13 syndrome, Turner's syndrome (45XO), and others. Congenital cataracts are sometimes the result of maternal infections that occur during pregnancy. Such infections may include German measles (rubella), syphilis, measles, influenza, certain herpes infections, and others. Additional contributing factors may include toxic influences from drug substances taken by the mother during pregnancy.

Treatment for congenital cataracts depends upon the extent of the defect and its influence on vision. To restore lost transparency of the lens resulting from cataracts, surgery may be performed in which the cataract and lens are removed. To reestablish the ability of the eye to deflect light that was lost with lens removal, special contact lenses or implants are then fitted to the eye. In some cases, additional surgery may be indicated. Because congenital opacities of the lens are so often associated with other eye irregularities (e.g., amblyopia, glaucoma, strabismus, etc.) and in order to obtain the best outcome, treatment may also be directed toward any associated abnormalities. In addition, patients are followed carefully after surgery in order to prevent, correct, or treat any possible complications.

Government Agencies

1619 NIH/National Eye Institute
31 Center Drive MSC 2510
Bethesda, MD 20892

301-496-5248
2020@nei.nih.gov
www.nei.nih.gov

Conducts and supports research that helps prevent and treat eye diseases and other disorders of vision. This research leads to sight-saving treatments, reduces visual impairment and blindness, and improves the quality of life for people of all ages. NEI-supported research has advanced our knowledge of how the eye functions in health and disease.

Michael F. Chiang, MD, Director
Santa Tumminia, Deputy Director

National Associations & Support Groups

1620 American Academy of Pediatrics
345 Park Blvd
Itasca, IL 60143

800-433-9016
Fax: 847-434-8000
mcc@aap.org
www.aap.org

The American Academy of Pediatrics and its member pediatricians are committed to the attainment of optimal physical, mental and social health and well-being for all infants, children, adolescents, and young adults.

Lynn Olson, PhD, VP, Research
Mark Del Monte, JD, CEO/Executive VP
Vera Tait, MD, FAAP, Chief Medical Officer

1621 American Council of the Blind
1703 N Beauregard Street, Ste 420
Alexandria, VA 22311

202-467-5081
800-424-8666
Fax: 703-465-5085
info@acb.org
www.acb.org

The council strives to improve the well being of all blind and visually impaired people by serving as a representative national organization of blind people, elevating the social, economic and cultural levels of blind people, improving educational and rehabilitation facilities and opportunities and cooperating with the public and private institutions and organizations concerned with blind services.

Eric Bridges, Executive Director
Clark Rachfal, Director, Advocacy/Govt'l Affairs
Nancy Marks-Becker, CFO

1622 Association for Education & Rehabilitation of the Blind & Visually Impaired
5680 King Centre Drive, Suite 600
Alexandria, VA 22315

703-671-4500
aer@aerbvi.org
www.aerbvi.org

The Association for Education and Rehabilitation of the Blind and Visually Impaired (AER) is the only international membership organization dedicated to rendering all possible support and assistance to the professionals who work in all phases of education and rehabilitation of blind and visually impaired children and adults. Our membership is comprised of more than 4,200 professionals who provide services to people with visual impairment.

Lee Sonnenberg, Executive Director
Michele Basham, Membership & Community Engagement
Elly du Pre, Manager, Accreditation Program

1623 Genetic Alliance
426400 Woodfield Road, Ste 189
Damascus, MD 20872

202-966-5557
Fax: 202-966-8553
info@geneticalliance.org
www.geneticalliance.org

World's leading nonprofit health advocacy organization committed to transforming health through genetics and promoting an environment of openness centered on the health of individuals, families, and communities.

Sharon Terry, CEO
Ruth Child, CFO
Natasha Bonhomme, Chief Strategy Officer

1624 **Lighthouse Guild**
250 West 64th Street
New York, NY 10023
800-284-4422
info@lighthouseguild.org
www.lighthouseguild.org

Lighthouse Guild is dedicated to providing exceptional services that inspire people who are visually impaired to attain their goals.

James M. Dubin, Chair
Calvin W. Roberts, President & CEO
Maura J. Sweeney, SVP, Programs & Services

1625 **National Association of Blind Students**
200 East Wells Street, Jernigan Place
Baltimore, MD 21230
410-659-9314
nfb@nfb.org
nabslink.org

For over 50 years, the National Association of Blind Students has worked, as an integral part of the National Federation of the Blind, to promote the equality of the blind by serving as a source of information, forum for networking and vehicle for collective action for blind students. Our work on the local, state, and national levels is firmly rooted in the conviction that blindness need not prevent one from excelling in a chosen field of study or living a full and productive life.

State Agencies & Support Groups

Alabama

1626 **Alabama Institute for the Deaf & Blind**
PO Box 698 (35161) 205 East South Street
Talladega, AL 35160
256-761-3331
Fax: 256-761-3344
www.aidb.org

Services include central directory, representatives of agencies, service providers, families, and coordinators of infant, toddler, and preschool special education programs.

Charlotte Lowry, Principal
Martha Waites, Director, Academic Department
Teresa Lacy, Director, Library and Resource Cent

Pennsylvania

1627 **East Central Region-Helen Keller National Center**
4351 Garden City Drive
New Carrollton, MD 20785
301-459-5474
Fax: 301-459-5070
hkncreg3cl@aol.com
www.helenkeller.org

Christopher D Maher, Chairman
Richard T. Arkwright, Vice-Chairman
John R Caughey, Treasurer

South Carolina

1628 **Region 4 of the National Association for Parents of the Visually Impaired**
1032 Trail Road
Belton, SC 29627
864-338-9593

Washington

1629 **Northwestern Region-Helen Keller National Center**
1620 18th Ave Suite 201
Seattle, WA 98122
206-324-9120
Fax: 206-324-9159
TTY: 206-324-1133
nwhknc@juno.com
www.hknc.org/FieldServicesREGREPADD.htm

The Regional Representatives of HKNC are located in ten offices across the country. They are responsible for assessing the needs of individuals, communities and states within their regions; developing strategies of collaboration, coordination and cooperation to help meet those needs; advocating for those who are deaf-blind in local, state, national and international forums.

Libraries & Resource Centers

Arizona

1630 **Educational Services for the Visually Impaired**
PO Box 668
Little Rock, AR 72203
501-371-5710

Offers textbooks, braille books and more to the visually impaired grades K-12 in the Arkansas area.

David Beavers, Director

Arkansas

1631 **Arkansas Regional Library for the Blind and Physically Handicapped**
900 W Capitol, Suite 100
Little Rock, AR 72201
501-682-2053
Fax: 501-682-1533
TDD: 501-682-1002
nlsbooks@asl.lib.ar.us
www.asl.lib.ar.us/ASL_LBPH.htm

Public library books in recorded or braille format. Popular fiction and nonfiction books for all ages, books and players are on free loan, sent to patrons by mail and may be returned postage free. Anyone who cannot see well enough to read regular print with glasses on or who has a disability that makes it difficult to hold a book or turn the pages is eligible.

John D Hall, Director

California

1632 **American Action Fund for Blind Children and Adults**
1800 Johnson Street
Baltimore, MD 21230
410-659-9315
Fax: 818-343-3219
lucyabba@aol.com
www.actionfund.org

A lending library for the visually impaired. We send out a weekly Braille newspaper for the deaf-blind (worldwide), we also send out pocket-sized Braille calendars. Our lending library is for pre-school thru high school. All of our services are free.

Barbara Loos, President
Ramona Walhof, Vice President
Gary Mackenstadt, Secretary

1633 **Blind Children's Center**
4120 Marathon Street
Los Angeles, CA 90029
323-664-2153
Fax: 323-665-3828
www.blindchildrenscenter.org

Offers support and informational groups.

Midge Horton, Executive Director

1634 **Braille Institute Desert Center**
741 N Vermont Avenue
Los Angeles, CA 90029
323-663-1111
Fax: 323-663-0867
la@brailleinstitute.org
www.brailleinstitute.org

Dedicated to providing blind and visually impaired men, women and children with the training, programs and services they need to enjoy productive lives. Services offered include child development, youth programs, library services and adult education.

Lars Hansen, Manager

Congenital Cataracts / Libraries & Resource Centers

1635 **Braille Institute Sight Center**
741 N Vermont Avenue
Los Angeles, CA 90029
323-663-1111
Fax: 323-663-0867
la@brailleinstitute.org
www.brailleinstitute.org

Offers help, programs, services and information to the blind and visually impaired children and adults.

Les Stocker, President

1636 **Braille Institute Youth Center**
3450 Cahuenga Boulevard W
Los Angeles, CA 90068
213-851-5695

Offers various youth programs and services for the blind and visually impaired youngster.

1637 **New Beginnings - Blind Children's Center**
4120 Marathon, Street
Los Angeles, CA 90029
323-664-2153
800-222-3566
Fax: 323-665-3828

Helps children and their families become independent by creating a climate of safety and trust. Services include an infant stimulation program, educational preschool, interdisciplinary assessment services, family services, correspondence program, toll-free national hotline and a publication and research service.

1638 **San Francisco Public Library for the Blind and Print Disabled**
PO Box 9428327
Sacramento, CA 94237
916-654-0261
Fax: 415-557-4252
lbphmgr@sfpl.lib.ca.us
www.library.ca.us

Foreign-language books on cassette, children's books on cassettes and more.

Luis Herrera, Manager

1639 **Variety Audio**
PO Box 5731
San Jose, CA 95150
408-277-4839

Summer reading programs, braille writer, magnifiers, closed-circuit TV, large-print photocopier, cassette books and magazines, children's books on cassette, home visits and other reference materials on blindness and other handicaps.

Louisa Griehshammer

Florida

1640 **Florida Bureau of Braille and Talking Book Library Services**
420 Platt Street
Daytona Beach, FL 32114
386-239-6000
Fax: 386-239-6069
TDD: 800-226-6079
mike_gunde@dbs.doe.state.fl.us
www.state.fl.us/dbs/lswel.html

Discs, cassettes, closed-circuit TV, large-print photocopier, films, children's books on cassettes and more.

Michael Gunde, Librarian

1641 **Talking Book Library, Jacksonville Public Library**
2233 Park Avenue, Suite 402
Orange Park, FL 32073
904-278-5620
Fax: 904-278-5625
TDD: 904-768-7822
jerryr@coj.net
www.neflin.org

Discs, cassettes and reference materials on blindness and other disabilities.

Jerry Reynolds, Librarian Senior

1642 **Talking Book Service - Manatee County Central Library**
1112 Manatee Avenue West
Bradenton, FL 34205
941-748-4501
Fax: 941-751-7089
TDD: 941-742-5951
webmaster@mymanatee.org
www.mymanatee.org

Offers children's books on disc and cassette and more reference materials for the blind and physically handicapped.

Patricia Schubert, Librarian

Georgia

1643 **Albany Library for the Blind and Physical Handicapped**
300 Pine Avenue
Albany, GA 31701
229-420-3220
Fax: 229-420-3215
sinquefk@mail.dougherty.public.lib.ga.us
www.docolib.org/LBPH/index.html

Offers discs, cassettes, reference materials on blindness and other handicaps, large-print photocopiers, summer reading programs, cassette books and more.

Katy Sinquefield, Manager

1644 **Bainbridge Subregional Library for the Blind and Physically Handicapped**
215 Sycamore Street
Decatur, GA 30030
404-370-8450
800-795-2680
Fax: 404-370-8469
TDD: 912-248-2665
lbph@mail.deccatur.public.lib.ga.us
www.dekalblibrary.org

Discs, cassettes, summer reading programs, closed-circuit TV, magnifiers and more.

Jon Abercrombie, Chairman
Julia H Jones, Vice Chairman
Elizabeth Joyner, Treasurer

1645 **CEL Subregional Library for the Blind and Physically Handicapped**
2708 Mechanics
Savannah, GA 31404
912-354-5864
Fax: 912-354-5534
TDD: 912-652-3635
stokesl@cel.co.chatman.ga.us

Summer reading programs, braille writer, magnifiers, closed-circuit TV, large-print photocopier, cassette books and magazines, children's books on cassette, home visits and other reference materials on blindness and other handicaps.

Linda Stokes, Librarian

Idaho

1646 **Idaho State Talking Book Library**
325 W State Street
Boise, ID 83702
208-334-2150
800-458-3271
Fax: 208-334-4016
TDD: 800-377-1363
tblbooks@isl.state.id.us
www.lili.org/isl/tblinfo.htm

Summer reading programs, braille writer, magnifiers, closed-circuit TV, large-print photocopier, cassette books and magazines, children's books on cassette, home visits and other reference materials on blindness and other handicaps.

Sue Walker, Manager

Illinois

1647 Chicago Library Service for the Blind
1055 W Roosevelt Road
Chicago, IL 60608   312-746-9210

Summer reading programs, braille writer, magnifiers, closed-circuit TV, large-print photocopier, cassette books and magazines, children's books on cassette, home visits and other reference materials on blindness and other handicaps.

Carol Pellish, Librarian

1648 Illinois State Library, Talkng Book and Braille Service
213 State Capitol
Springfield, IL 62756   217-785-5600
Fax: 217-785-4326
TDD: 800-665-5576
sruda@ilsos.net
www.cyberdriveillinois.com

Summer reading programs, braille writer, magnifiers, closed-circuit TV, large-print photocopier, cassette books and magazines, descriptive videos, children's books on cassette, home visits and other reference materials on blindness and other handicaps.

Anne Craig, Executive Director

1649 Mid Illinois Talking Book System
515 York Street
Quincy, IL 62301   217-224-6619
Fax: 217-224-9818

Summer reading programs, braille writer, magnifiers, closed-circuit TV, large-print photocopier, cassette books and magazines, children's books on cassette, home visits and other reference materials on blindness and other handicaps.

1650 Mid-Illinois Talking Book Center
600 High Point Lane
East Peoria, IL 61611   309-353-4110
800-426-0709
Fax: 309-353-8281
hitbc@darkstar.rsa.lib.il.us
www.mitbc.org

Summer reading programs, braille writer, magnifiers, closed-circuit TV, large-print photocopier, cassette books and magazines, children's books on cassette, home visits and other reference materials on blindness and other handicaps.

Eileen Sheppard, Librarian

1651 Talking Book Center of Northwest Illinois
Ste 2
East Peoria, IL 61611   309-694-9200
Fax: 309-799-7916
kodean@libby.rbls.lib.il.us
www.rbls.lib.il.us

Subregional library provides Talking Book and Braille Book programs to eligible persons unable to use standard print materials due to visual or physical disabilities. Includes cassette books and magazines; summer reading program.

Indiana

1652 Northwest Indiana Subregional Library for Blind and Physically Handicapped
1919 W Lincoln Highway
Merrillville, IN 46410   219-769-3541
Fax: 219-769-0690

Summer reading programs, braille writer, magnifiers, closed-circuit TV, large-print photocopier, cassette books and magazines, children's books on cassette, home visits and other reference materials on blindness and other handicaps.

Renee Lewis

Iowa

1653 Iowa Library for the Blind and Physically Handicapped
Iowa Department for the Blind
524 4th Street
Des Moines, IA 50309   515-281-1333
Fax: 515-281-1378
TDD: 515-281-1355
www.blind.state.ia.us

Summer reading programs, magnifiers, closed-circuit TV, large-print photocopier, children's books on cassette, children's books in Braille and Print Braille, cassette magazines, home visits and reference materials on blindness and other handicaps.

Karen Keninger, Program Manager/Librarian

1654 University of Iowa Birth Defects and Genetic Disorders Unit
2614 JCP
Iowa City, IA 52242   319-335-9901
James M Smith, Director

Kansas

1655 CKLS Headquarters
PO Box 515
Northampton, MA 01061   413-268-7660
888-622-8527
Fax: 316-792-5495
www.macular.org

Summer reading programs, braille writer, magnifiers, closed-circuit TV, large-print photocopier, cassette books and magazines, children's books on cassette, home visits and other reference materials on blindness and other handicaps.

Chip Goehring, President/Treasurer
Mark E Torrey, Vice President
Paul F Gariepy, Secretary

1656 Services for the Visually Disabled
629 Poyntz Avenue
Manhattan, KS 66502   785-776-4741
Fax: 785-776-1545
marionr@manhattan.lib.ks.us

Summer reading programs, braille writer, magnifiers, closed-circuit TV, large-print photocopier, cassette books and magazines, children's books on cassette, home visits and other reference materials on blindness and other handicaps.

Marion Rice, Librarian

Kentucky

1657 Kentucky Library for the Blind and Physically Handicapped
PO Box 818
Frankfort, KY 40602   502-564-8300
800-372-2968
Fax: 502-564-5773
richard.feindel@kdla.net
www.kdla.net/libserv/ktbl.htm

Large-print photocopier, cassette books and magazines, children's books on cassette, and other reference materials on blindness and other handicaps.

5,200 members

Richard Feindel, Librarian

Maryland

1658 Maryland State Library for the Blind and Physically Handicapped
415 Park Avenue
Baltimore, MD 21201
410-230-2424
Fax: 410-333-2095
TTY: 800-934-2541
TDD: 410-333-8679
recept@lbta.lib.md.us
www.lbph.lib.md.us

Summer reading programs, braille writer, magnifiers, large-print photocopier, cassette books and magazines, children's books on cassette, and other reference materials on blindness and other handicaps.

Jill Lewis, Manager

1659 Prince George's County Memorial Library Talking Book Center
6530 Adelphi Road
Hyattsville, MD 20782
301-779-9330

Summer reading programs, braille writer, magnifiers, closed-circuit TV, large-print photocopier, cassette books and magazines, children's books on cassette, home visits and other reference materials on blindness and other handicaps.

Shirley Tuthill, Librarian

Massachusetts

1660 Braille and Talking Book Library Perkins School for the Blind
175 N Beacon Street
Watertown, MA 02472
617-924-3434
Fax: 617-972-7315
info@perkins.org
www.perkins.org

Steven M Rothstein, President
Micheal Schnitman, Secretary
Charles C J Platt, Treasurer

Michigan

1661 Downtown Detroit Subregional Library for the Blind and Handicapped
5201 Woodward Avenue
Detroit, MI 48202
313-224-0580
Fax: 313-965-1977
TDD: 313-224-0584
dir@detroitpubliclibrary.org
www.detroit.lib.mi.us

Summer reading programs, braille writer, magnifiers, closed-circuit TV, large-print photocopier, cassette books and magazines, children's books on cassette, home visits and other reference materials on blindness and other handicaps.

Russell Bellant, President
Gregory Hicks, Vice President
Jonathan C Kinloch, Secretary

1662 Kent County Library for the Blind
775 Ball Avenue NE
Grand Rapids, MI 49503
616-336-3250
Fax: 616-336-3201
kdlem@lakeland.lib.mi.us

Summer reading programs, braille writer, magnifiers, closed-circuit TV, large-print photocopier, cassette books and magazines, children's books on cassette, home visits and other reference materials on blindness and other handicaps.

Claudya Muller, Librarian

1663 Library of Michigan Service for the Blind
PO Box 30007
Lansing, MI 48909
517-373-1300
Fax: 517-373-5700
info@sbph.libomich.lib.mi.us

Summer reading programs, braille writer, magnifiers, closed-circuit TV, large-print photocopier, cassette books and magazines, children's books on cassette, home visits and other reference materials on blindness and other handicaps.

Nancy Robertson, Manager

1664 Macomb Library for the Blind and Physically Handicapped
16480 Hall Road
Clinton Township, MI 48038
586-286-1580
Fax: 586-286-0634
TDD: 810-869-40
macbld@libcoop.net
www.macomb.lib.mi.us/macspe/

Summer reading programs, braille writer, closed-circuit TV, cassette books and magazines, children's books on cassette, reference materials on blindness and other handicaps.

Beverlee Babcock, Executive Director

1665 Mideastern Michigan Library Co-op
G-4195 W Pasadena Avenue
Flint, MI 48504
810-732-1120
Fax: 810-732-1715
cnash@genesse.freeret.org
www.fakon.edu/gdl/talking.htm

Summer reading programs, braille writer, magnifiers, closed-circuit TV, large-print photocopier, cassette books and magazines, children's books on cassette, home visits and other reference materials on blindness and other handicaps.

Carolyn Nash, Librarian

1666 Muskegon County Library for the Blind
635 Ottawa Street
Muskegon, MI 49442
231-724-6361
Fax: 231-724-6675
TDD: 231-722-4103
www.muskcolib.org

Summer reading programs, braille typewriter, magnifiers, closed-circuit TV, large-print photocopier, cassette books and magazines, children's books on cassette, home visits and other reference materials on blindness and other handicaps, The Reading Edge, Perkins Brailler and large print books.

Linda Clapp, Librarian

1667 Upper Peninsula Library for the Blind Physically Handicapped
1615 Presque Isle Avenue
Marquette, MI 49855
906-228-7697
Fax: 906-228-5627
uproc.lib.mi.us
www.upesc.lib.mi.us/uplbph

Summer reading programs, braille writer, magnifiers, closed-circuit TV, large-print photocopier, cassette books and magazines, children's books on cassette, home visits and other reference materials on blindness and other handicaps.

Suzanne Dees, Executive Director

1668 Washtenaw County Library
PO Box 8645
Ann Arbor, MI 48107
734-994-4912
Fax: 734-663-2430
contact us@ewashtenaw.org
www.ewashtenaw.org

Summer reading programs, braille writer, magnifiers, closed-circuit TV, large-print photocopier, cassette books and magazines, children's books on cassette, home visits and other reference materials on blindness and other handicaps.

Kyeena Slater, Executive Director

1669 Washtenaw County Library for the Blind and Physically Disabled
PO Box 8645
Ann Arbor, MI 48107
734-222-4357
Fax: 734-222-6850
lbpd@co.washtennaw.mi.us
www.ewashtenaw.org

Book lovers club.adaptive technology,cassette equipment, cassette books and magazines, described videos, low vision aids reference and referral services.

Kyeena Slater, Executive Director

Missouri

1670 Adriene Resource Center for Blind Children
1445 N. Boonville Avenue
Springfield, MO 65802
417-862-2781
800-641-4310
Fax: 417-862-7566
blind@ag.org
www.gospelpublishing.com

Offers braille and cassette lending library, braille and cassette Sunday school materials for all ages, braille and cassette periodicals and resource assistance, and resources for blind children and children of blind parents.

Paul Weingariner, Director

1671 Assemblies of God National Center for the Blind
1445 N. Boonville Avenue
Springfield, MO 65802
417-862-2781
877-840-4800
Fax: 417-863-6614
www.ag.org

Offers braille and cassette lending library, braille and cassette Sunday school materials for all ages, braille and cassette periodicals and resource assistance, and resources for blind children and children of blind parents.

Thomas Trask, Manager
Greg Mundis, Executive Director

Nebraska

1672 Nebraska Library Commission Talking Book & Braille Services
1200 N Street
Lincoln, NE 68508
402-471-2045
800-742-7691
Fax: 402-471-2083
TDD: 402-471-4038
david.oertli@nebraska.gov
www.nlc.nebraska.gov

Free loan of books and magazines on cartridge, cassette, and in Braille, including children's materials, along with specially designed playback equipment. Summer reading program for children, Braille embossing, closed circuit TV, large-print copier. Reference materials on blindness and other disabilities.

David Oerti, Librarian

New Jersey

1673 New Jersey State Library Talking Book and Braille Center
185 West State Street
Trenton, NJ 08625
609-278-2640
800-792-8322
Fax: 609-278-2647
TDD: 877-882-5593
njlbh@njstatelib.org
www.njstatelib.org

Free home delivery of large-print, audio, and braille books and magazines, children's books on cassettes in braille and other reference materials on blindness and other handicaps. Services are for New Jersey residents with print disabilities.

Adan Szczepaniak, Director
Anne McArthur, Head of Outreach and Audiovision

New Mexico

1674 New Mexico State Library for the Blind and Physically Handicapped
1209 Camino Carlos Ray
Santa Fe, NM 87507
505-476-9700
Fax: 505-476-9761
jbrewstr@stlib.state.nm.us
www.stlib.state.nm.us

Summer reading programs, braille writer, magnifiers, closed-circuit TV, large-print photocopier, cassette books and magazines, children's books on cassette, home visits and other reference materials on blindness and other handicaps.

Susan Overland, Manager

New York

1675 New York State Talking Book & Braille Library
National Library Service/NYS Library
Empire State Plaza, CEC
Albany, NY 12230
518-474-5935
800-342-3688
Fax: 518-486-1957
tbbl@mail.nysed.gov
www.nysl.nysed.gov/tbbl

Recorded books and players, recorded magazines, braille books, braille writers, magnifiers, closed-circuit TV, children's books on cassette, reference materials on blindness and other disabilities. Service is completely free to eligible borrowers, including loan of equipment to listen to books. Over 60,000 titles available.

Sharon B Phillips, Library Program Director

Ohio

1676 American Council of Blind Parents
34400 Cedar Road, Apartment 108
University Heights, OH 44121
800-424-8666

Members are sighted parents of blind or visually impaired children. Offers a forum for support and outreach, sharing of experiences in parent-child relationships, and educational and cultural information about child development. Monitors developments in technical and legislative arenas.

Nola Webb, President

Oregon

1677 Oregon State Library, Talking Book and Braille Services
250 Winter Street NE
Salem, OR 97301
503-378-5389
800-452-0292
Fax: 503-585-8059
TDD: 503-378-4276
tbabs@sparkie.osl.state.or.us
www.tbabs.org

Cassette books and magazines, children's books on cassette, home visits and other reference materials on blindness and other handicaps.

Susan Westin, Manager

Virginia

1678 Alexandria Library Talking Book Service
5005 Duke Street
Alexandria, VA 22304
703-746-1702
Fax: 703-519-5916
TDD: 703-838-4568
emccaffr@lea.eda
www.alexandria.lib.va.us

Summer reading programs, braille writer, magnifiers, closed-circuit TV, large-print photocopier, cassette books and magazines, children's books on cassette, home visits and other reference materials on blindness and other handicaps.

Congenital Cataracts / Research Centers

Karen Russell, Manager

1679 Division for the Visually Handicapped
1920 Association Drive
Reston, VA 20191 703-620-3660

Members are teachers, college faculty members, administrators, supervisors and others concerned with the education and welfare of visually handicapped and blind children and youth. This is a division of the Council For Exceptional Children.

Dr. Kay Ferrell, President

1680 Division on Visual Impairments
Council for Exceptional Children
1110 North Glebe Road, Suite 300
Arlington, VA 22201 800-224-6830
Fax: 703-264-9494
TTY: 866-915-5000
www.ed.arizona.edu/dvi/welcome.htm; www.cec.sped.org

A division within the CEC, it handles concerns for Federal, state and local issues and policies related to education of youths, children and infants with visual impairments.

Ellyn Ross, President
Shirley J Wilson, Secretary
Phyllis T Simmons, President Elect

1681 Virginia State Library for the Visually and Physically Handicapped
1901 Roane Street
Richmond, VA 23222 804-367-0014

Summer reading programs, braille writer, magnifiers, closed-circuit TV, large-print photocopier, cassette books and magazines, children's books on cassette, home visits and other reference materials on blindness and other handicaps.

Mary Ruth Halapatz, Librarian

Washington

1682 Washington Library for the Blind and Physically Handicapped
1000 Fourth Avenue
Seattle, WA 98104 206-386-4636
Fax: 206-386-4685
wtbbl@spl.lib.wa.us
www.spl.lib.wa.us

Summer reading programs, braille writer, magnifiers, closed-circuit TV, large-print photocopier, cassette books and magazines, children's books on cassette, home visits and other reference materials on blindness and other handicaps.

Jan Ames, Librarian

West Virginia

1683 West Virginia School for the Blind
301 E Main Street
Romney, WV 26757 304-822-4801
Fax: 304-822-3370
cjohn@access.mountain.net

Summer reading programs, braille writer, magnifiers, closed-circuit TV, large-print photocopier, cassette books and magazines, children's books on cassette, home visits and other reference materials on blindness and other handicaps.

Patsy Shank, Administrator

Research Centers

1684 Center for the Partially Sighted
7462 North Figueroa Boulevard Suite 103
Los Angeles, CA 90041 310-988-1970
Fax: 310-988-1980
info@low-vision.org
www.low-vision.org

Our mission is to provide the tools and techniques that maximize the ability of partially sighted children and adults to live successful and independent lives

James Adler, Esq., Board
Steve Edwards, Board
Brenda Premo, Board

1685 Mobile Association for the Blind
2440 Gordon Smith Drive
Mobile, AL 36617 251-473-3585
877-292-5463
Fax: 251-470-8622
sales@mobile.blind.com
www.mobileblind.org

The American Foundation for the Blind removes barriers, creates solutions, and expands possibilities so people with vision loss can achieve their full potential

Jim Bullock, Executive Director

1686 New Beginnings - The Blind Children's Center
4120 Marathon Street
Los Angeles, CA 90029 213-664-2153
Fax: 323-665-3828
www.blindchildrenscenter.org/about.html

The purpose of the Center is to turn initial fears into hope. Helps children and their families become independent by creating a climate of safety and trust. Children learn to develop self confidence and to master a wide range of skills. Services include an infant stimulation program, educational preschool, interdisciplinary assessment services, family services, correspondence program, toll free national hotline and a publication and research service.

1687 Pediatric Ophathalmology and Adult Strabis mus Service Research
Indiana University
702 Rotary Circle
Indianapolis, IN 46202 317-274-2128
Fax: 317-274-2277
dplager@iupui.edu
www.iupui.edu/~ophthal/

Improve techniques and treatment modalities for children with eye and vision problems, such as cataracts, glaucoma, retinopathy of prematurity, and for both children and adults with eye muscle abnormalities.

David A Plager, MD, Director

1688 Research to Prevent Blindness
645 Madison Avenue Floor 21
New York, NY 10022 212-752-4333
800-621-0026
Fax: 212-688-6231
inforequest@rpbusa.org
www.rpbusa.org/rpb/about/overview/

Provides research grants to scientists interested in eye disease and vision disorders.

David F Weeks, Chairman Emeritus
Brian F. Hofland, PhD, President/Secretary
John I Bloomberg, Vice President

Audio Video

1689 Heart to Heart
Blind Children's Center
4120 Marathon Street
Los Angeles, CA 90029 323-644-2153
Fax: 323-665-3828
www.blindcntr.org

Parents of blind and partially sighted children talk about their feelings.

Videotape

1690 Let's Eat
Blind Children's Center
4120 Marathon Street
Los Angeles, CA 90029
323-664-2153
Fax: 323-665-3828
www.blindchildrenscenter.org

Teaches competent feeding skills to children with visual impairments.

Videotape

1691 See What I Feel
Britannica Film Co.
345 4th Street
San Francisco, CA 94107
415-597-5555

A blind child tells her friends about her trip to the zoo. Each experience was explained as a blind child would experience it. A teacher's guide comes with this video.

Films

Web Sites

1692 Lighthouse Guild
250 West 64th Street
New York, NY 10023
800-284-4422
info@lighthouseguild.org
www.lighthouseguild.org

Lighthouse Guild is dedicated to providing exceptional services that inspire people who are visually impaired to attain their goals.

James M. Dubin, Chair
Calvin W. Roberts, President & CEO
Maura J. Sweeney, SVP, Programs & Services

1693 National Association of Blind Students
200 East Wells Street, Jernigan Place
Baltimore, MD 21230
410-659-9314
nfb@nfb.org
nabslink.org

For over 50 years, the National Association of Blind Students has worked, as an integral part of the National Federation of the Blind, to promote the equality of the blind by serving as a source of information, forum for networking and vehicle for collective action for blind students. Our work on the local, state, and national levels is firmly rooted in the conviction that blindness need not prevent one from excelling in a chosen field of study or living a full and productive life.

1694 Online Mendelian Inheritance in Man
McKusick-Nathans Institue of Genetic Medicine-JHU
Baltimore, MD 21205
www.omim.org

This database is a catalog of human genes and genetic disorders.

Ada Hamosh, MD, Scientific Director

1695 Royal National Institute of Blind People
www.rnib.org.uk
303-123-9999
helpline@rnib.org.uk
www.rnib.org.uk

Offering information, support and advice to people with sight problems.

Matt Stringer, Chief Executive
Keith Valentine, Director of Development
David Clarke, Director of Services

Book Publishers

1696 Children with Visual Impairments: A Parents' Guide
Peytral Publications
PO Box 1162
Minnetonka, MN 55345
952-949-8707
877-739-8725
Fax: 952-906-9777
www.peytral.com

Covers visual impairments ranging from low vision to total blindness. Offers authoritative information and empathy, parental insight on diagnosis and treatment, orientation and mobility, literacy, legal issues and more. Valuable to parents, educators and support staff.

395 pages

M Cay Holbrook PhD, Editor

1697 Eye Care Sourcebook
Omnigraphics
615 Griswold Street, Ste 520
Detroit, MI 48226
610-461-3548
800-234-1340
Fax: 800-875-1340
contact@omnigraphics.comom
www.omnigraphics.com

Basic consumer information about glaucoma, cataracts, macular degeneration, strabismus, refractive disorders and more.

2017 656 pages Hardcover
ISBN: 0-780815-32-2

Magazines

1698 Journal of Visual Impairment and Blindness
American Foundation for the Blind
2 Penn Plaza, Suite 1102
New York, NY 10121
212-502-7600
Fax: 888-545-8331
contributions@afb.net
www.afb.org

Published in braille, regular print and on cassette this journal contains a wide variety of subjects including rehabilitation, psychology, education, legislation, medicine, technology, employment, sensory aids and childhood development as they relate to visual impairments.

10x Year

Larry Kimbler, Chair
James H. McLaughlin, Vice Chair
Carl S. Augusto, President & CEO

1699 Reaching, Crawling, Walking - Let's Get Moving
Blind Children's Center
4120 Marathon Street
Los Angeles, CA 90029
323-664-2153
Fax: 323-665-3828
info@blindchildrenscenter.org
www.blindchildrenscenter.org

Orientation and mobility for visually impaired preschool children.

24 pages

1700 Tactic
Clovernook Home and School for the Blind
7000 Hamilton Avenue
Cincinnati, OH 45231
513-522-3860
Fax: 513-728-3950
clovernook@aol.com

Quarterly

Newsletters

1701 Gleams
Glaucoma Research Foundation
251 Post Street, Suite 600
San Francisco, CA 94108
415-986-3162
800-826-6693
Fax: 415-986-3763
question@glaucoma.org
www.glaucoma.org

Includes information about glaucoma, new treatments, updates on research findings, and more.

3x/year

Thomas M. Brunner, President & CEO
Sunita Radhakrishnan, MD, Editor in Chief
Andrew L. Jackson, Director of Communications

Congenital Cataracts / Pamphlets

1702 **National Library Service for the Blind & Physically Handicapped**
Library of Congress
1291 Taylor Street NW
Washington, DC 20542
202-707-5100
800-424-8567
Fax: 202-707-0712
nls@loc.gov
www.loc.gov/nls

Provides information and advocacy resources for families and professionals, including listings of organizations focusing on more specific areas of concern to families and young adults who have disabilities. Administers a natural library service that provides recorded and braille reading materials to eligible children and adults who cannot read standard print.

12 pages Quarterly
ISSN: 1046-1663

1703 **Talking Book Topics**
National Library Services for the Blind
1291 Taylor Street NW
Washington, DC 20542
202-707-5100
Fax: 202-707-0712
TDD: 202-707-0744
nls@loc.gov
www.loc.gov/nls

Offers hundreds of listings of books, fiction and nonfiction, for adults and children who cannot read regular print material. Also offers foreign language books, talking magazines and reviews.

Bimonthly

Pamphlets

1704 **Dancing Cheek to Cheek**
Blind Children's Center
4120 Marathon Street
Los Angeles, CA 90029
323-664-2153
Fax: 323-665-3828
www.blindchildrenscenter.org

Discusses beginning social, play and language interactions.

33 pages

1705 **Family Guide - Growth and Development of the Partially Seeing Child**
Lighthouse Guild
250 West 64th Street
New York, NY 10023
800-284-4422
info@lighthouseguild.org
www.lighthouseguild.org

Offers information for parents and guidelines in raising a partially seeing child.

1706 **Family Guide to Vision Care**
American Optometric Association
243 N Lindbergh Boulevard
Saint Louis, MO 63141
314-991-4100
Fax: 314-991-4101
www.aoanet.org

Offers information on the early developmental years of your vision, finding a family optometrist and how to take care of your eyesight through the learning years, the working years and the mature years.

1707 **Heart to Heart**
Blind Children's Center
4120 Marathon Street
Los Angeles, CA 90029
323-664-2153
Fax: 323-665-3828
www.blindchildrenscenter.org

Parents of blind and partially sighted children talk about their feelings.

12 pages

1708 **Learning to Play**
Blind Children's Center
4120 Marathon Street
Los Angeles, CA 90029
323-664-2153
Fax: 323-665-3828
www.blindchildrenscenter.org

Discusses how to present play activities to the visually impaired preschool child.

12 pages

1709 **Let's Eat**
Blind Children's Center
4120 Marathon Street
Los Angeles, CA 90029
323-664-2153
Fax: 323-665-3828
www.blindchildrenscenter.org

Teaches competent feeding skills to children with visual impairments.

28 pages

1710 **Move with Me**
Blind Children's Center
4120 Marathon Street
Los Angeles, CA 90029
323-664-2153
Fax: 323-665-3828
www.blindchildrenscenter.org

A parent's guide to movement development for visually impaired babies.

12 pages

1711 **Selecting a Program**
Blind Children's Center
4120 Marathon Street
Los Angeles, CA 90029
323-664-2153
Fax: 323-665-3828
www.blindchildrenscenter.org

A guide for parents of infants and preschoolers with visual impairments.

28 pages

1712 **Standing on My Own Two Feet**
Blind Children's Center
4120 Marathon Street
Los Angeles, CA 90029
323-664-2153
Fax: 323-665-3828
info@blindchildrenscenter.org
www.blindchildrenscenter.org

A step-by-step guide to designing and constructing simple, individually tailored adaptive mobility devices for preschool-age children who are visually impaired.

36 pages

1713 **Talk to Me**
Blind Children's Center
4120 Marathon Street
Los Angeles, CA 90029
323-664-2153
Fax: 323-665-3828
www.blindchildrenscenter.org

A language guide for parents of deaf children.

11 pages

1714 **Talk to Me II**
Blind Children's Center
4120 Marathon Street
Los Angeles, CA 90029
323-664-2153
Fax: 323-665-3828
www.blindchildrenscenter.org

A sequel to Talk To Me, available in English and Spanish.

Congenital Cataracts / Camps

15 pages

Camps

1715 Bloomfield
5300 Angeles Vista Boulevard
Los Angeles, CA 90043
323-295-4555
800-352-2290
Fax: 323-296-0424
info@juniorblind.org
www.juniorblind.org

This camp is dedicated to serving blind and developmentally disabled children and adults.

Miki Jordan, President

1716 Camp Civitan
3519 East Shea Blvd # 133
Phoenix, AZ 85028
602-953-2944
Fax: 602-953-2946
info@campcivitan.org
www.campcivitan.org

A 501c3 non-profit organization, that has been providing multiple ever-changing programs to meet the needs of children and adults who are developmentally disabled.

Shannon Valenzuela, Director
Jane Armstrong, Director

1717 Camp Tushmehata
10500 Lincoln Lake Rd, PO Box 46
Greenville, MI 48838
616-754-5410
www.campt.org

Mission is to create and foster unlimited opportunities for blind and partially sighted people throughout Michigan and the world. The camp is comprised mainly of blind adults who have a passion for blind youth. The camp gained the opportunity to implement longer camping sessions, hire a large number of blind role models and steer the camp program into a bright, determined and promising future.

Gwen Botting, Director

1718 Enchanted Hills Camp
Lighthouse
214 Van Ness Avenue
San Francisco, CA 94102
415-694-7319
Fax: 415-863-7568
TTY: 415-431-4572
afletcher@lighthouse-sf.org
www.lighthouse-sf.org

For blind, deaf/blind children and adults, ages 5 and up. This program offers a basic camping experience. Activities include music, art, dance, hiking and riding. Camperships are available to California residents.

Tony Fletcher, Camp Director

1719 Florida School-Deaf and Blind Summer Camp
207 N San Marco Avenue
Saint Augustine, FL 32084
904-827-2200
800-344-3732
info@fsdb.k12.fl.us
www.fsdb.k12.fl.us

The Florida School for the Deaf and the Blind hosts summer campers from all over teh state of Florida for a week of fun and adventure. FSDB's 80 acre campus is where campers participate in a variety of activities including rock climbing, archery, swimming, kayaking, team games, arts and crafts, dance music, and much more.

L Daniel Hutto, President
Cindy Day, Executive Director of Parent Svcs
Terri Wiseman, Administrator of Business Services

1720 Highbrook Lodge Camp
12944 Aquilla Road
Chardon, OH 44024
216-791-8118
Fax: 216-791-1101
camp@clevelandsightcenter.org
www.clevelandsightcenter.org

A summer residential camp for blind and disabled children, adults and families.

Mike Mullin, Director

1721 National Camps for Blind Children
Christian Record
4444 S 52nd Street
Lincoln, NE 68516
402-488-0981
Fax: 402-488-7582
info@christianrecord.org
www.christianrecord.org

Camps throughout the US and Canada are offered at no cost to the legally blind, ages 9-65. Activities include archery, beeper basketball, water sports, hiking and rock climbing and horseback riding.

Peggy Hansen, Director

1722 Texas Lions Camp
Lions Clubs of Texas
PO Box 290247
Kerrville, TX 78029
830-896-8500
830-896-8500
Fax: 830-896-3666
tlc@ktc.com
www.lionscamp.com

The primary purpose of Texas Lions camp is to provide, without charge, a camp for physically disabled, hearing/vision impaired and diabetic children from the State of Texas, regardless of race, religion, or national origin. Our goal is to create an atmosphere wherein campers will learn the can do philosophy and be allowed to achieve maximum personal growth and self esteem. The camp welcomes boys and girls ages 7-16.

Stephen Mabry, Executive Director
Doug Parker, Business Manager
Steven King, Program/Client Service Director

1723 VISIONS/Vacation Camp for the Blind
500 Greenwich Street, 3rd Floor
New York, NY 10013
212-625-1616
888-245-8333
Fax: 212-219-4078
info@visions.org
www.visions.org

Family programs at Vacation Camp for the Blind in Rockland County, NY for children who are blind, severely visually impaired or multi-handicapped. Parent or guardian must attend winter weekends and summer session.

Thomas M Decker, Camp Director
Nancy D Miller, Executive Director

1724 Wisconsin Lions Camp
3834 County Road A
Rosholt, WI 54473
715-677-4969
Fax: 715-677-3297
TTY: 715-677-6999
info@wisconsinlionscamp.org
www.wisconsinlionscamp.com

Serves children who have either a visual, hearing or mild cognitive disability. Many of the children also have multiple disabilities or medical conditions. Program activities include sailing, ropes course, bike and canoe trips, environmental education, swimming, camping, canoeing, outdoor living skills and handicrafts. ACA accredited, located in central Wisconsin, near Stevens Point.

Russell Link, Camp Director

Congenital Diaphragmatic Hernia / Description

Description

1725 CONGENITAL DIAPHRAGMATIC HERNIA
Synonym: CDH
Involves the following Biologic System(s):
Gastrointestinal Disorders, Respiratory Disorders

Congenital diaphragmatic hernia (CDH) is a birth defect characterized by projection or bulging of organs of the abdomen into the chest cavity. This occurs as a result of an abnormal opening in the diaphragm, the dome-shaped muscle that separates the abdomen from the chest and plays an essential role in breathing. Approximately one in 5,000 newborns are affected by the condition. CDH is thought to result due to failed closure of a certain area of the embryonic diaphragm (i.e., the foramen of Bochdalek) during fetal development. In some cases, disrupted development in other areas of the growing fetus may also cause CDH. This birth defect may occur as an isolated condition or, in about 20 to 30 percent of patients, in association with other abnormalities or underlying malformation syndromes, such as Down syndrome (trisomy 21), trisomy 18 syndrome, or trisomy 13 syndrome. There are reports of several infants with isolated CDH in certain families (kindreds). In such cases, the condition is thought to result from abnormal changes (mutations) of different genes, possibly in association with certain environmental factors (multifactorial inheritance).

In newborns with CDH, the diaphragmatic defect may be small or can affect up to half of the diaphragm. The left side of the diaphragm is most commonly involved. The lungs may also be unusually small and underdeveloped (pulmonary hypoplasia), and abnormalities of the blood vessels supplying the lungs may also be present. In addition, the intestines may not be positioned properly (intestinal malformation). Most newborns with CDH experience increasing difficulties breathing (respiratory distress) within the first 24 hours after birth. Associated symptoms include labored breathing (dyspnea), grunting upon exhalation, drawing in of the chest wall during inhalation, and a bluish discoloration of the skin and mucous membranes (cyanosis). These findings may potentially result in life-threatening complications. In addition, in some affected newborns, air may collect in the chest cavity, causing the lung(s) to collapse (pneumothorax). Symptoms associated with CDH may not become apparent until after the first few weeks of life. These infants may experience mild respiratory symptoms or intestinal obstruction and associated vomiting (emesis).

In newborns with CDH, immediate measures may be necessary to prevent or treat potentially life-threatening complications. Surgery to repair the diaphragmatic defect is deferred until the newborn's respiratory status has been stabilized. Ongoing supportive measures may be employed before surgery, such as use of a device known as an extracorporeal membrane oxygenator (ECMO). This device supplies oxygen to the infant's blood and returns this oxygenated blood to the body. In addition, certain medications may also be used (e.g., surfactant therapy to help improve oxygenation, etc.).

Government Agencies

1726 NIH/ Eunice Kennedy Shriver National Institute of Child Health & Human Development
P.O. Box 3006
Rockville, MD 20847
800-370-2943
Fax: 866-760-5947
www.nichd.nih.gov

Conducts and supports laboratory research, clinical trials, and epidemiological studies that explore health processes; examines the impact of disabilities, diseases, and variations on the lives of individuals; and sponsors training programs for scientists, health care providers, and researchers to ensure that NICHD research can continue.

Diana W. Bianchi, Director
Alison Cernich, PhD, Deputy Director

National Associations & Support Groups

1727 American Academy of Pediatrics
345 Park Blvd
Itasca, IL 60143
800-433-9016
Fax: 847-434-8000
mcc@aap.org
www.aap.org

The American Academy of Pediatrics and its member pediatricians are committed to the attainment of optimal physical, mental and social health and well-being for all infants, children, adolescents, and young adults.

Lynn Olson, PhD, VP, Research
Mark Del Monte, JD, CEO/Executive VP
Vera Tait, MD, FAAP, Chief Medical Officer

1728 CDH International
3650 Rogers Rd Suite 290
Wake Forest, NC 27587
919-610-0129
info@cdhi.org
cdhi.org

The world's oldest, largest and leading Congenital Diaphragmatic Hernia charity. Created to help families of babies born with Congenital Diaphragmatic Hernia by providing support services, raising awareness and furthering research.

Dawn Ireland, President
Rachael Eller, Office & Operations Manager
Josh Hensley, Research Director

1729 Digestive Disease National Coalition
507 Capitol Court NE, Suite 200
Washington, DC 20002
202-544-7497
Fax: 202-546-7105
www.ddnc.org

Advocacy organization comprised of over 30 voluntary and professional societies concerned with the many diseases of the digestive tract and liver.

Ceciel Rooker, Chairperson
Bryan Green, MD, President
Cathy Griffith, Vice Chairperson

1730 Genetic Alliance
426400 Woodfield Road, Ste 189
Damascus, MD 20872
202-966-5557
Fax: 202-966-8553
info@geneticalliance.org
www.geneticalliance.org

World's leading nonprofit health advocacy organization committed to transforming health through genetics and promoting an environment of openness centered on the health of individuals, families, and communities.

Sharon Terry, CEO
Ruth Child, CFO
Natasha Bonhomme, Chief Strategy Officer

Libraries & Resource Centers

1731 National Digestive Diseases Information Clearinghouse (NDDIC)
NIH
2 Information Way
Bethesda, MD 20892
301-654-3810
800-891-5389
Fax: 301-907-8906
nddic@info.niddk.nih.gov
www.digestive.niddk.nih.gov

The National Institute of Diabetes and Digestive and Kidney Diseases conducts and supports research on many of the most serious diseases affecting public health. The Institute supports much of the clinical research on the diseases of internal medicine and related subspecialty fields as well as many basic science disciplines.

Griffin P. Rodgers, MD, Director
Gregory G. Germino, MD, Deputy Director
Kathy Kranzfelder, Communications Director

1732 University of Iowa Birth Defects and Genetic Disorders Unit
2614 JCP
Iowa City, IA 52242   319-335-9901
James M Smith, Director

Book Publishers

1733 Gastrointestinal Diseases and Disorders Sourcebook, 4th Edition
Omnigraphics
615 Griswold Street, Ste 520
Detroit, MI 48226   610-461-3548
                              800-234-1340
                              Fax: 800-875-1340
                              contact@omnigraphics.comom
                              www.omnigraphics.com

Provides basic information for the layperson about common disorders of the upper and lower digestive tract. It also includes information about medications and recommendations for maintaining a healthy digestive tract. A glossary of important terms and a directory of digestive diseases organizations are also provided.

816 pages Hardcover
ISBN: 0-780816-50-3

Congenital Dysplasia of the Hip / Description

Description

1734 CONGENITAL DYSPLASIA OF THE HIP

Synonyms: CDH, Congenital dislocation of the hip, DDH, Developmental dysplasia of the hip

Covers these related disorders: Teratologic congenital dysplasia of the hip, Typical congenital dysplasia of the hip (Developmental dysplasia)

Involves the following Biologic System(s):

Neonatal and Infant Disorders, Orthopedic and Muscle Disorders

Congenital dysplasia of the hip (CDH) refers to a condition present at birth or soon thereafter in which one or both hips are dislocated. This occurs when the ball-shaped head of the upper thigh bone (femur) does not fit appropriately into the hip socket of the pelvis (acetabulum). Congenital hip dysplasia may be classified as typical, which occurs shortly after birth in infants with no underlying neurologic irregularities, or teratologic, which develops before birth. The typical form of this condition is commonly referred to as developmental dysplasia of the hip.

The cause of CDH is unknown, although it is more prevalent in newborns who were surrounded by an unusually small amount of amniotic fluid during the gestational period (oligohydramnios). Those infants who present in a breech position; those with other close family members with this condition may also be at increased risk for CDH. In addition, it is more predominant in girls than it is in boys by a ratio of nine to one. Teratologic dysplasia of the hip in the developing fetus may occur as part of a pattern of abnormalities associated with certain underlying disorders affecting the neuromuscular system such as arthrogryposis multiplex congenita and myelodysplasia.

Assessment of the hips is part of the newborn physical exam. The Ortalani and Barlow maneuvers help to detect both anterior and posterior dislocations for the femoral head. Children with certain risk factors (i.e. breech delivery) should have a hip ultrasound at 3 months.

Treatment during infancy may include manipulation of the hip joint into its proper position followed by immobilization and splinting of the thigh for a period of several months. Some infants may benefit from wearing two or three diapers at a time. In some patients, delayed detection of this birth defect may necessitate the use of traction to restore the femoral head to its correct position. However, if the dislocation is not discovered until late childhood, surgery followed by fitting with a plaster cast may be necessary to correct this condition. Delayed treatment may result in chronic difficulties with walking. Untreated dysplasia of the hip may result in degenerative changes in the joint (osteoarthritis). Approximately 4 of every 1,000 infants are affected by congenital dysplasia of the hip; however, in approximately 70 percent of these children, the dislocation corrects itself.

Government Agencies

1735 NIH/ Eunice Kennedy Shriver National Institute of Child Health & Human Development
P.O. Box 3006
Rockville, MD 20847
800-370-2943
Fax: 866-760-5947
www.nichd.nih.gov

Conducts and supports laboratory research, clinical trials, and epidemiological studies that explore health processes; examines the impact of disabilities, diseases, and variations on the lives of individuals; and sponsors training programs for scientists, health care providers, and researchers to ensure that NICHD research can continue.

Diana W. Bianchi, Director
Alison Cernich, PhD, Deputy Director

1736 NIH/National Institute of Arthritis and Musculoskeletal and Skin Diseases
National Institutes of Health
1 AMS Circle
Bethesda, MD 20892
301-495-4484
877-226-4267
Fax: 301-718-6366
TTY: 301-565-2966
niamsinfo@mail.nih.gov
www.niams.nih.gov

The mission of the NIAMS, a part of the NIH, is to support research into the causes, treatment and prevention of arthritis and musculoskeletal and skin diseases, the training of basic and clinical scientists to carry out this research, and the dissemination of information on research progress in these diseases.

Lindsey A. Criswell, MD, Director
Rick Phillips, Executive Officer

National Associations & Support Groups

1737 American Academy of Pediatrics
345 Park Blvd
Itasca, IL 60143
800-433-9016
Fax: 847-434-8000
mcc@aap.org
www.aap.org

The American Academy of Pediatrics and its member pediatricians are committed to the attainment of optimal physical, mental and social health and well-being for all infants, children, adolescents, and young adults.

Lynn Olson, PhD, VP, Research
Mark Del Monte, JD, CEO/Executive VP
Vera Tait, MD, FAAP, Chief Medical Officer

1738 Center for Parent Information and Resources (CPIR)
c/o SPAN, 35 Halsey Street, 4th Floor
Newark, NJ 07102
973-642-8100
malizo@spanadvocacy.org
www.parentcenterhub.org

Family-friendly information and research-based materials on key topics for Parent Centers. Private workspaces for Parent Centers to exchange resources, discuss high-priority topics, and solve mutual challenges. Coordination of parent training efforts throughout the network.

Myriam Alizo, Project Assistant

1739 Genetic Alliance
426400 Woodfield Road, Ste 189
Damascus, MD 20872
202-966-5557
Fax: 202-966-8553
info@geneticalliance.org
www.geneticalliance.org

World's leading nonprofit health advocacy organization committed to transforming health through genetics and promoting an environment of openness centered on the health of individuals, families, and communities.

Sharon Terry, CEO
Ruth Child, CFO
Natasha Bonhomme, Chief Strategy Officer

1740 March of Dimes Foundation
1550 Crystal Drive, Ste 1300
Arlington, VA 22202
888-663-4637
www.marchofdimes.org

March of Dimes help moms have full-term pregnancies and research the problems that threaten the health of babies. The March of Dimes also acts globally: sharing best practices in perinatal health and helping improve birth outcomes where the needs are the most urgent.

Stacey D. Stewart, President
Alan Brogdon, SVP/COO/Board Officer
Rahul Gupta, MD, SVP & Chief Medical/Health Officer

Libraries & Resource Centers

1741 **University of Iowa Birth Defects and Genetic Disorders Unit**
2614 JCP
Iowa City, IA 52242   319-335-9901
James M Smith, Director

Web Sites

1742 **Dr. Koop**
www.drkoop.com/

www.drkoop.com/

Information on the condition, causes, symptoms, tests and treatment.

Book Publishers

1743 **Let's Talk About Going to the Hospital**
Rosen Publishing Group's PowerKids Press
29 E 21st Street
New York, NY 10010   212-777-3017
                                  800-237-9932
                             Fax: 888-436-4643
                        rosenpub@tribeca.ios.com
                        www.rosenpublishing.com

If a child has to check into the hospital, chances are he or she is already upset about being ill. Knowing how a hospital functions and what the procedures are, such as when family members can visit, will help in what is already a stressful situation. Grades K-5.

24 pages
ISBN: 0-823950-36-0

Roger Rosen, President

Congenital Glaucoma / Description

Description

1744 CONGENITAL GLAUCOMA

Synonym: Infantile glaucoma

Covers these related disorders: Primary glaucoma, Secondary glaucoma

Involves the following Biologic System(s):

Ophthalmologic Disorders

Glaucoma refers to a condition in which the fluid pressure within the eyes (intraocular pressure) is abnormally elevated. This may occur as a result of the buildup of fluid (aqueous humor) due to obstruction or other problems with the eyes. Glaucoma that develops by the third year of life is referred to as congenital or infantile glaucoma, which is a very rare occurrence. Primary glaucoma refers to the condition as it relates to an irregularity in the mechanism that drains the eye. Secondary glaucoma refers to increased intraocular pressure that results from other types of irregularities that may or may not be accompanied by a drainage deficit.

Symptoms associated with congenital glaucoma may include an abnormal sensitivity to light (photophobia), involuntary, repeated squeezing and closing of the eyelids (blepharospasm), abnormal tearing, swelling and enlargement of the cornea, difficulty in seeing, and other ocular irregularities. Affected infants under three months of age are at additional risk of incurring tissue damage due to heightened sensitivity of the cornea to elevated fluid pressure within the eye. Eye irregularities may be observed by a physician upon ophthalmic examination.

Congenital glaucoma may develop subsequent to certain congenital problems such as trauma, bleeding (hemorrhage) within the eye, or tumors and inflammation. Other associated abnormalities may include the lack of transparency (opacity) of the lenses of the eye (cataracts), displacement of the lenses (ectopia lentis), partial absence of the iris (aniridia), and other abnormalities. Disorders often associated with congenital glaucoma include certain chromosomal disorders that may affect various systems of the body such as Sturge-Weber syndrome, oculocerebrorenal syndrome, neurofibromatosis, and Marfan syndrome.

Treatment for congenital glaucoma includes surgery to relieve the pressure within the eye to prevent optic nerve damage and preserve vision. In some cases, more than one surgery may be necessary and follow-up therapy may be required. Additional treatment is directed toward associated irregularities and complications.

Government Agencies

1745 NIH/National Eye Institute
31 Center Drive MSC 2510
Bethesda, MD 20892

301-496-5248
2020@nei.nih.gov
www.nei.nih.gov

Conducts and supports research that helps prevent and treat eye diseases and other disorders of vision. This research leads to sight-saving treatments, reduces visual impairment and blindness, and improves the quality of life for people of all ages. NEI-supported research has advanced our knowledge of how the eye functions in health and disease.

Michael F. Chiang, MD, Director
Santa Tumminia, Deputy Director

National Associations & Support Groups

1746 American Academy of Pediatrics
345 Park Blvd
Itasca, IL 60143

800-433-9016
Fax: 847-434-8000
mcc@aap.org
www.aap.org

The American Academy of Pediatrics and its member pediatricians are committed to the attainment of optimal physical, mental and social health and well-being for all infants, children, adolescents, and young adults.

Lynn Olson, PhD, VP, Research
Mark Del Monte, JD, CEO/Executive VP
Vera Tait, MD, FAAP, Chief Medical Officer

1747 Children's Glaucoma Foundation
2 Longfellow Place, Suite 201
Boston, MA 02114

617-227-3011
Fax: 617-227-9538
info@childrensglaucomafoundation.org
www.childrensglaucoma.com

A nonprofit organization dedicated to supporting programs for children with glaucoma. Serves to increase awareness of the symptoms and encourage parents and doctors to screen infants and children for glaucoma, and supports research programs.

David S Walton, MD, President

1748 Genetic Alliance
426400 Woodfield Road, Ste 189
Damascus, MD 20872

202-966-5557
Fax: 202-966-8553
info@geneticalliance.org
www.geneticalliance.org

World's leading nonprofit health advocacy organization committed to transforming health through genetics and promoting an environment of openness centered on the health of individuals, families, and communities.

Sharon Terry, CEO
Ruth Child, CFO
Natasha Bonhomme, Chief Strategy Officer

1749 Glaucoma Research Foundation
251 Post Street, Suite 600
San Francisco, CA 94108

415-986-3162
800-826-6693
Fax: 415-986-3763
question@glaucoma.org
www.glaucoma.org

Mission is to preserve the sight and independence of individuals with glaucoma through research and education with the ultimate goal of finding a cure.

Thomas M. Brunner, President & CEO
Nancy Graydon, COO/Executive Director, Development
Andrew L. Jackson, Director of Communications

1750 Lighthouse Guild
250 West 64th Street
New York, NY 10023

800-284-4422
info@lighthouseguild.org
www.lighthouseguild.org

Lighthouse Guild is dedicated to providing exceptional services that inspire people who are visually impaired to attain their goals.

James M. Dubin, Chair
Calvin W. Roberts, President & CEO
Maura J. Sweeney, SVP, Programs & Services

1751 National Association of Blind Students
200 East Wells Street, Jernigan Place
Baltimore, MD 21230

410-659-9314
nfb@nfb.org
nabslink.org

For over 50 years, the National Association of Blind Students has worked, as an integral part of the National Federation of the Blind, to promote the equality of the blind by serving as a source of information, forum for networking and vehicle for collective action for blind students. Our work on the local, state, and national levels is firmly rooted in the conviction that blindness need not prevent one from excelling in a chosen field of study or living a full and productive life.

1752 **Prevent Blindness America**
225 West Wacker Drive, Suite 400
Chicago, IL 60606
800-331-2020
info@preventblindness.org
www.preventblindness.org

A volunteer eye health and safety organization dedicated to fighting blindness and saving sight. Focused on promoting a continuum of vision care, Prevent Blindness America touches the lives of millions of people each year through public and professional education, advocacy, certified vision screening training, community and patient service programs and research.

Jeff Todd, President & CEO
Karen Hartman, Vice President & COO
Kay Nottingham Chaplin, Education & Outreach Director

State Agencies & Support Groups

Alabama

1753 **Alabama Institute for the Deaf & Blind**
205 East South Street, PO Box 698
Talladega, AL 35160
256-761-3331
Fax: 256-761-3344
www.aidb.org

Services include central directory, representatives of agencies, service providers, families, and coordinators of infant, toddler, and preschool special education programs.

Dr. John Mascia, President

Ohio

1754 **Region 2 of the National Association for Parents of the Visually Impaired**
3910 Pocahontas Avenue
Cincinnati, OH 45227
513-561-8542
Victoria Gorman Miller

Pennsylvania

1755 **East Central Region-Helen Keller National Center**
141 Middle Neck Road
Sands Point, NY 11050
516-944-8900
Fax: 516-944-7302
HKNCinfo@hknc.org
www.helenkeller.org

Christopher D Maher, Chairman
Richard T Arkwright, Vice Chairman
John R. Caughey, Treasurer

South Carolina

1756 **Region 4 of the National Association for Parents of the Visually Impaired**
1032 Trail Road
Belton, SC 29627
864-338-9593

Washington

1757 **Northwestern Region-Helen Keller National Center**
141 Middle Neck Road
Sands Point, NY 11050
516-944-8900
Fax: 516-944-7302
HKNCinfo@hknc.org
www.helenkeller.org

Christopher D Maher, Chairman
Richard T Arkwright, Vice Chairman
John R. Caughey, Treasurer

Libraries & Resource Centers

Alabama

1758 **Mobile Association for the Blind**
2440 Gordon Smith Drive
Mobile, AL 36617
251-473-3585
Fax: 251-470-8622
www.mobileblind.org

Offers work adjustment training, activities of daily living, mobility, communication skills and sheltered employment for adults and children who are visually impaired.

Jim Bullock, Executive Director

Arizona

1759 **Educational Services for the Visually Impaired**
PO Box 668
Little Rock, AR 72203
501-371-5710

Offers textbooks, braille books and more to the visually impaired grades K-12 in the Arkansas area.

David Beavers, Director

Arkansas

1760 **Arkansas Regional Library for the Blind and Physically Handicapped**
900 W. Capitol, Suite 100
Little Rock, AR 72201
501-682-2053
Fax: 501-682-1533
TDD: 501-682-1002
nlsbooks@asl.lib.ar.us
www.asl.lib.ar.us/ASL_LBPH.htm

Public library books in recorded or braille format. Popular fiction and nonfiction books for all ages, books and players are on free loan, sent to patrons by mail and may be returned postage free. Anyone who cannot see well enough to read regular print with glasses on or who has a disability that makes it difficult to hold a book or turn the pages is eligible.

John D Hall, Director

California

1761 **American Action Fund for Blind Children and Adults**
18440 Oxnard Street
Tarzana, CA 91356
818-343-2022
Fax: 818-343-3219
lucyabba@aol.com
www.actinfund.org

A lending library for the visually impaired. We send out a weekly Braille newspaper for the deaf-blind (worldwide), we also send out pocket-sized Braille calendars. Our lending library is for pre-school thru high school. All of our services are free.

Lucille Abbazia, Manager

1762 **Blind Children's Center**
4120 Marathon Street
Los Angeles, CA 90029
323-664-2153
Fax: 323-665-3828
www.blindchildrenscenter.org

Offers support and informational groups.

Midge Horton, Executive Director

1763 **Braille Institute Desert Center**
741 N Vermont Avenue
Los Angeles, CA 90029
323-663-1111
Fax: 323-663-0867
la@brailleinstitute.org
www.brailleinstitute.org

Dedicated to providing blind and visually impaired men, women and children with the training, programs and services they need to enjoy productive lives. Services offered include child development, youth programs, library services and adult education.

Lars Hansen, Manager

1764 **Braille Institute Sight Center**
741 N Vermont Avenue
Los Angeles, CA 90029
323-663-1111
Fax: 323-663-0867
la@brailleinstitute.org
www.brailleinstitute.org

Offers help, programs, services and information to the blind and visually impaired children and adults.

Les Stocker, President

1765 **Braille Institute Youth Center**
3450 Cahuenga Boulevard W
Los Angeles, CA 90068
213-851-5695

Offers various youth programs and services for the blind and visually impaired youngster.

1766 **New Beginnings - Blind Children's Center**
4120 Marathon, Street
Los Angeles, CA 90029
323-664-2153
800-222-3566
Fax: 323-665-3828

Helps children and their families become independent by creating a climate of safety and trust. Services include an infant stimulation program, educational preschool, interdisciplinary assessment services, family services, correspondence program, toll-free national hotline and a publication and research service.

1767 **San Francisco Public Library for the Blind and Print Disabled**
P.O Box 942837
Sacramento, CA 94237
415-557-4400
800-952-5666
Fax: 415-557-4252
lbphmgr@sfpl.lib.ca.us
www.library.ca.gov

Foreign-language books on cassette, children's books on cassettes and more.

Luis Herrera, Manager

1768 **Variety Audio**
PO Box 5731
San Jose, CA 95150
408-277-4839

Summer reading programs, braille writer, magnifiers, closed-circuit TV, large-print photocopier, cassette books and magazines, children's books on cassette, home visits and other reference materials on blindness and other handicaps.

Louisa Griehshammer

Florida

1769 **Florida Bureau of Braille and Talking Book Library Services**
421 Platt Street
Daytona Beach, FL 32114
386-239-6000
800-226-6075
Fax: 386-239-6069
TDD: 800-226-6079
mike_gunde@dbs.doe.state.fl.us
www.state.fl.us/dbs/lswel.html

Discs, cassettes, closed-circuit TV, large-print photocopier, films, children's books on cassettes and more.

Michael Gunde, Librarian

1770 **Talking Book Library, Jacksonville Public Library**
1755 Edgewood Avenue W, Suite 1
Jacksonville, FL 32208
904-765-5588
Fax: 904-768-7404
TDD: 904-768-7822
jerryr@coj.net
www.neflin.org/neflin/members/jackspub.html

Discs, cassettes and reference materials on blindness and other disabilities.

Jerry Reynolds, Librarian Senior

1771 **Talking Book Service - Manatee County Central Library**
6081 26th Street W
Bradenton, FL 34207
941-742-5914
Fax: 941-751-7089
TDD: 941-742-5951
patricia.schubert@co.manatee.fl.us
www.co.manatee.fl.us

Offers children's books on disc and cassette and more reference materials for the blind and physically handicapped.

Patricia Schubert, Librarian

Georgia

1772 **Albany Library for the Blind and Physical Handicapped**
300 Pine Avenue
Albany, GA 31701
229-420-3220
Fax: 229-420-3215
sinquefk@mail.dougherty.public.lib.ga.us
www.docolib.org/LBPH/index.html

Offers discs, cassettes, reference materials on blindness and other handicaps, large-print photocopiers, summer reading programs, cassette books and more.

Katy Sinquefield, Manager

1773 **Bainbridge Subregional Library for the Blind and Physically Handicapped**
301 S Monroe Street
Bainbridge, GA 39819
912-248-2680
800-795-2680
Fax: 912-248-2670
TDD: 912-248-2665
lbph@mail.deccatur.public.lib.ga.us
www.decatur.public.lib.ga.us/local/lbph/lbph1.htm

Discs, cassettes, summer reading programs, closed-circuit TV, magnifiers and more.

Kathy Hutchins, Librarian

1774 **CEL Subregional Library for the Blind and Physically Handicapped**
2708 Mechanics
Savannah, GA 31404
912-354-5864
Fax: 912-354-5534
TDD: 912-652-3635
stokesl@cel.co.chatman.ga.us

Summer reading programs, braille writer, magnifiers, closed-circuit TV, large-print photocopier, cassette books and magazines, children's books on cassette, home visits and other reference materials on blindness and other handicaps.

Linda Stokes, Librarian

Idaho

1775 **Idaho State Talking Book Library**
325 W State Street
Boise, ID 83702
208-334-2117
Fax: 208-334-4016
TDD: 800-377-1363
tblbooks@isl.state.id.us
www.lili.org/isl/tblinfo.htm

Summer reading programs, braille writer, magnifiers, closed-circuit TV, large-print photocopier, cassette books and magazines, children's books on cassette, home visits and other reference materials on blindness and other handicaps.

Sue Walker, Manager

Illinois

1776 **Chicago Library Service for the Blind**
1055 W Roosevelt Road
Chicago, IL 60608
312-746-9210

Summer reading programs, braille writer, magnifiers, closed-circuit TV, large-print photocopier, cassette books and magazines, children's books on cassette, home visits and other reference materials on blindness and other handicaps.

Carol Pellish, Librarian

1777 **Illinois State Library, Talkng Book and Braille Service**
213 State Capitol
Springfield, IL 62756
217-785-5600
800-252-980
Fax: 217-785-4326
TDD: 800-665-5576
sruda@ilsos.net
www.cyberdriveillinois.com

Summer reading programs, braille writer, magnifiers, closed-circuit TV, large-print photocopier, cassette books and magazines, descriptive videos, children's books on cassette, home visits and other reference materials on blindness and other handicaps.

Anne Craig, Executive Director

1778 **Mid Illinois Talking Book System**
515 York Street
Quincy, IL 62301
217-224-6619
Fax: 217-224-9818

Summer reading programs, braille writer, magnifiers, closed-circuit TV, large-print photocopier, cassette books and magazines, children's books on cassette, home visits and other reference materials on blindness and other handicaps.

1779 **Mid-Illinois Talking Book Center**
600 High Point Lane
East Peoria, IL 61611
309-353-4110
800-426-0709
Fax: 309-353-8281
hitbc@darkstar.rsa.lib.il.us
www.mitbc.org

Summer reading programs, braille writer, magnifiers, closed-circuit TV, large-print photocopier, cassette books and magazines, children's books on cassette, home visits and other reference materials on blindness and other handicaps.

Eileen Sheppard, Librarian
Chenoweth Rose, Director
Boucher Nancy, Reader Advisor

1780 **Talking Book Center of Northwest Illinois**
PO Box 125
Coal Valley, IL 61240
309-799-3137
800-747-3137
Fax: 309-799-7916
kocean@libby.rbls.lib.il.us
www.rbls.lib.il.us

Subregional library provides Talking Book and Braille Book programs to eligible persons unable to use standard print materials due to visual or physical disabilities. Includes cassette books and magazines; summer reading program.

Indiana

1781 **Northwest Indiana Subregional Library for Blind and Physically Handicapped**
1919 W Lincoln Highway
Merrillville, IN 46410
219-769-3541
Fax: 219-769-0690

Summer reading programs, braille writer, magnifiers, closed-circuit TV, large-print photocopier, cassette books and magazines, children's books on cassette, home visits and other reference materials on blindness and other handicaps.

Renee Lewis

Iowa

1782 **Iowa Library for the Blind and Physically Handicapped**
Iowa Department for the Blind
524 4th Street
Des Moines, IA 50309
515-281-1333
800-362-2587
Fax: 515-281-1263
TTY: 515-281-1355
TDD: 515-281-1355
information@blind.state.ia.us
www.blind.state.ia.us

Summer reading programs, magnifiers, closed-circuit TV, large-print photocopier, children's books on cassette, children's books in Braille and Print Braille, cassette magazines, home visits and reference materials on blindness and other handicaps.

Eis Karen, Program Manager/Librarian
Richard Sorey, Director
Aldini Jodi, Library Support Staff

1783 **University of Iowa Birth Defects and Genetic Disorders Unit**
2614 JCP
Iowa City, IA 52242
319-335-9901
James M Smith, Director

Kansas

1784 **CKLS Headquarters**
1409 Williams Street
Great Bend, KS 67530
620-792-4865
800-362-2642
Fax: 620-792-5495
cenks@ink.org
www.ckls.org

Summer reading programs, braille writer, magnifiers, closed-circuit TV, large-print photocopier, cassette books and magazines, children's books on cassette, home visits and other reference materials on blindness and other handicaps.

Jerri Robinson, Librarian

1785 **Services for the Visually Disabled**
629 Poyntz Avenue
Manhattan, KS 66502
785-776-4741
Fax: 785-776-1545
marionr@manhattan.lib.ks.us

Summer reading programs, braille writer, magnifiers, closed-circuit TV, large-print photocopier, cassette books and magazines, children's books on cassette, home visits and other reference materials on blindness and other handicaps.

Marion Rice, Librarian

Kentucky

1786 Kentucky Library for the Blind and Physically Handicapped
PO Box 818
Frankfort, KY 40602
502-564-8300
800-372-2968
Fax: 502-564-5773
richard.feindel@kdla.net
www.kdla.net/libserv/ktbl.htm

Large-print photocopier, cassette books and magazines, children's books on cassette, and other reference materials on blindness and other handicaps.

5,200 members

Richard Feindel, Librarian

Maryland

1787 Maryland State Library for the Blind and Physically Handicapped
415 Park Avenue
Baltimore, MD 21201
410-230-2424
Fax: 410-333-2095
TTY: 800-934-2541
TDD: 410-333-8679
recept@lbta.lib.md.us
www.lbph.lib.md.us

Summer reading programs, braille writer, magnifiers, large-print photocopier, cassette books and magazines, children's books on cassette, and other reference materials on blindness and other handicaps.

Jill Lewis, Manager

1788 Prince George's County Memorial Library Talking Book Center
6530 Adelphi Road
Hyattsville, MD 20782
301-779-9330

Summer reading programs, braille writer, magnifiers, closed-circuit TV, large-print photocopier, cassette books and magazines, children's books on cassette, home visits and other reference materials on blindness and other handicaps.

Shirley Tuthill, Librarian

Massachusetts

1789 Braille and Talking Book Library Perkins School for the Blind
175 N Beacon Street
Watertown, MA 02472
617-924-3434
Fax: 617-926-2027
perkins@bpl.org
www.perkins.org

Patricia Kirk

1790 Carroll Center for the Blind
770 Centre Street
Newton, MA 02458
617-969-6200
800-852-3131
Fax: 617-969-6204
www.carroll.org

Assists blind and visually impaired adults and adolescents to adjust to loss of vision. The goal of this dynamic program is to help the person become more independent, to restore self-confidence, prepare for employment and improve the quality of life. Programs of individual counseling are offered as part of the program.

Rachel Rosenbaum, President

Michigan

1791 Downtown Detroit Subregional Library for the Blind and Handicapped
5201 Woodward Avenue
Detroit, MI 48202
313-224-0580
Fax: 313-965-1977
TDD: 313-224-0584
deveans@cms.xx.wayne.edu
www.detroit.lib.mi.us

Summer reading programs, braille writer, magnifiers, closed-circuit TV, large-print photocopier, cassette books and magazines, children's books on cassette, home visits and other reference materials on blindness and other handicaps.

Deborah Evans, Librarian
Jo Anne Mondowney, Library Director

1792 Kent County Library for the Blind
775 Ball Avenue NE
Grand Rapids, MI 49503
616-336-3250
Fax: 616-336-3201
kdlem@lakeland.lib.mi.us

Summer reading programs, braille writer, magnifiers, closed-circuit TV, large-print photocopier, cassette books and magazines, children's books on cassette, home visits and other reference materials on blindness and other handicaps.

Claudya Muller, Librarian

1793 Macomb Library for the Blind and Physically Handicapped
16480 Hall Road
Clinton Township, MI 48038
586-286-1580
Fax: 586-286-0634
TDD: 810-869-40
macbld@libcoop.net
www.macomb.lib.mi.us/macspe/

Summer reading programs, braille writer, closed-circuit TV, cassette books and magazines, children's books on cassette, reference materials on blindness and other handicaps.

Beverlee Babcock, Executive Director

1794 Mideastern Michigan Library Co-op
G-4195 W Pasadena Avenue
Flint, MI 48504
810-732-1120
Fax: 810-732-1715
cnash@genesse.freeret.org
www.fakon.edu/gdl/talking.htm

Summer reading programs, braille writer, magnifiers, closed-circuit TV, large-print photocopier, cassette books and magazines, children's books on cassette, home visits and other reference materials on blindness and other handicaps.

Carolyn Nash, Librarian

1795 Muskegon County Library for the Blind
635 Ottawa Street
Muskegon, MI 49442
231-724-6361
Fax: 231-724-6675
TDD: 231-722-4103
www.muskcolib.org

Summer reading programs, braille typewriter, magnifiers, closed-circuit TV, large-print photocopier, cassette books and magazines, children's books on cassette, home visits and other reference materials on blindness and other handicaps, The Reading Edge, Perkins Brailler and large print books.

Linda Clapp, Librarian

1796 Upper Peninsula Library for the Blind Physically Handicapped
1615 Presque Isle Avenue
Marquette, MI 49855
906-228-7697
Fax: 906-228-5627
www.upesc.lib.mi.us/uplbph

Summer reading programs, braille writer, magnifiers, closed-circuit TV, large-print photocopier, cassette books and magazines, children's books on cassette, home visits and other reference materials on blindness and other handicaps.

Suzanne Dees, Executive Director

1797 Washtenaw County Library
PO Box 8645
Ann Arbor, MI 48107
734-994-4912
Fax: 734-663-2430
www.ewashtenaw.org

Summer reading programs, braille writer, magnifiers, closed-circuit TV, large-print photocopier, cassette books and magazines, children's books on cassette, home visits and other reference materials on blindness and other handicaps.

Kyeena Slater, Executive Director

1798 Washtenaw County Library for the Blind and Physically Disabled
PO Box 8645
Ann Arbor, MI 48107
734-994-4912
Fax: 734-663-2430
lbpd@co.washtennaw.mi.us
www.ewashtenaw.org

Book lovers club.adaptive technology,cassette equipment, cassette books and magazines, described videos, low vision aids reference and referral services.

Kyeena Slater, Executive Director

Missouri

1799 Adriene Resource Center for Blind Children
1445 N. Boonville Avenue
Springfield, MO 65802
417-862-2781
Fax: 417-862-7566
blind@ag.org
www.gospelpublishing.com

Offers braille and cassette lending library, braille and cassette Sunday school materials for all ages, braille and cassette periodicals and resource assistance, and resources for blind children and children of blind parents.

Paul Weingariner, Director

1800 Assemblies of God National Center for the Blind
1445 Boonville Avenue
Springfield, MO 65802
417-862-2781
Fax: 417-863-6614
blind@ag.org
www.ag.org

Offers braille and cassette lending library, braille and cassette Sunday school materials for all ages, braille and cassette periodicals and resource assistance, and resources for blind children and children of blind parents.

Thomas Trask, Manager
George O Wood, General Superintendent

Nebraska

1801 Nebraska Library Commission Talking Book & Braille Services
1200 N Street
Lincoln, NE 68508
402-471-2045
800-742-7691
Fax: 402-471-2083
TDD: 402-471-4038
david.oertli@nebraska.gov
www.nlc.nebraska.gov

Free loan of books and magazines on cartridge, cassette, and in Braille, including children's materials, along with specially designed playback equipment. Summer reading program for children, Braille embossing, closed circuit TV, large-print copier. Reference materials on blindness and other disabilities.

David Oerti, Librarian

New Jersey

1802 New Jersey State Library Talking Book and Braille Center
185 West State Street
Trenton, NJ 08625
609-278-2640
800-792-8322
Fax: 609-278-2647
TDD: 877-882-5593
njlbh@njstatelib.org
www.njstatelib.org

Free home delivery of large-print, audio, and braille books and magazines, children's books on cassettes in braille and other reference materials on blindness and other handicaps. Services are for New Jersey residents with print disabilities.

Adanrah Szczepaniak, Director
Anne McArthur, Head of Outreach and Audiovision

New Mexico

1803 New Mexico State Library for the Blind and Physically Handicapped
1209 Camino Carlos Ray
Santa Fe, NM 87507
505-476-9700
Fax: 505-476-9761
jbrewstr@stlib.state.nm.us
www.stlib.state.nm.us

Summer reading programs, braille writer, magnifiers, closed-circuit TV, large-print photocopier, cassette books and magazines, children's books on cassette, home visits and other reference materials on blindness and other handicaps.

Susan Overland, Manager

New York

1804 New York State Talking Book & Braille Library
CEC, 222 Madison Avenue
Albany, NY 12230
518-474-5935
800-342-3688
Fax: 518-474-5786
TDD: 518-474-7121
tbbl@mail.nysed.gov
www.nysl.nysed.gov/contact.htm

Books on audio cassette, cassette players, Braille books, summer reading programs, Braille writer, magnifiers, closed-circuit TV, large-print photocopier, cassette books and magazines, children's books on cassette, reference materials on blindness and other handicaps.

loretta ebert, Director
Bernard A Margolis, State Librarian

North Carolina

1805 North Carolina Library for the Blind
1841 Capital Boulevard
Raleigh, NC 27635
919-733-4376
888-388-2460
Fax: 919-733-6910
TDD: 919-733-1462
nclbph@ncdcr.gov
http://statelibrary.ncdcr.gov/lbph/

Summer reading programs, Braille writer, magnifiers, closed-circuit TV, large-print photocopier, cassette books and magazines, children's books on cassette, home visits and other reference materials on blindness and other handicaps.

Mary Boone, State Librarian

Ohio

1806 American Council of Blind Parents
14400 Cedar Road, Apartment 108
University Heights, OH 44121
216-791-8118
800-424-8666

Members are sighted parents of blind or visually impaired children. Offers a forum for support and outreach, sharing of experiences in parent-child relationships, and educational and cultural information about child development. Monitors developments in technical and legislative arenas.

Nola Webb, President

Oregon

1807 Oregon State Library, Talking Book and Braille Services
250 Winter Street NE
Salem, OR 97301
503-378-5389
800-452-0292
Fax: 503-585-8059
TDD: 503-378-4276
tbabs@sparkie.osl.state.or.us
www.tbabs.org

Cassette books and magazines, children's books on cassette, home visits and other reference materials on blindness and other handicaps.

Susan Westin, Manager

Virginia

1808 Alexandria Library Talking Book Service
5005 Duke Street
Alexandria, VA 22304
703-746-1702
Fax: 703-746-1747
TDD: 703-838-4568
rdawson@alexandria.lib.va.us
www.alexandria.lib.va.us

Summer reading programs, Braille writer, magnifiers, closed-circuit TV, large-print photocopier, cassette books and magazines, children's books on cassette, home visits and other reference materials on blindness and other handicaps.

Rose Dawson, Director
Linden Renner, Deputy Director

1809 Division for the Visually Handicapped
1920 Association Drive
Reston, VA 20191
703-620-3660
Fax: 703-264-9494
cec@cec.sped.org
www.cecp.air.org/teams/stratpart/cec.asp

Members are teachers, college faculty members, administrators, supervisors and others concerned with the education and welfare of visually handicapped and blind children and youth. This is a division of the Council For Exceptional Children.

Dr. Kay Ferrell, President

1810 Division on Visual Impairments
Council for Exceptional Children
2900 Crystal Drive Suite 1000
Arlington, VA 22202
888-233-7733
Fax: 703-264-9494
TTY: 866-915-5000
www.cec.sped.org/AM/

A division within the CEC, it handles concerns for Federal, state and local issues and policies related to education of youths, children and infants with visual impairments.

Ellyn Ross, President
Shirley J Wilson, Secretary
Phyllis T Simmons, President Elect

1811 Virginia State Library for the Visually and Physically Handicapped
395 Azalea Ave
Richmond, VA 23227
804-371-3661
800-552-7015
Fax: 804-371-3328
www.vdbvi.org/lrcservices.htm

Summer reading programs, Braille writer, magnifiers, closed-circuit TV, large-print photocopier, cassette books and magazines, children's books on cassette, home visits and other reference materials on blindness and other handicaps.

Barbara McCarthy, Librarian

Washington

1812 Washington Library for the Blind and Physically Handicapped
2021 9th Ave
Seattle, WA 98121
206-615-0400
800-542-0866
Fax: 206-615-0437
TTY: 206-615-0418
wtbbl@sos.wa.gov
www.wtbbl.org/

Summer reading programs, Braille writer, magnifiers, closed-circuit TV, large-print photocopier, cassette books and magazines, children's books on cassette, home visits and other reference materials on blindness and other handicaps.

Danielle Miller, Librarian

West Virginia

1813 West Virginia School for the Blind
301 E Main Street
Romney, WV 26757
304-822-4800
Fax: 304-822-3370
www.sdb2.state.k12.wv.us/About%20WVSDB.htm

Summer reading programs, Braille writer, magnifiers, closed-circuit TV, large-print photocopier, cassette books and magazines, children's books on cassette, home visits and other reference materials on blindness and other handicaps.

Patsy Shank, Administrator

Research Centers

1814 Center for the Partially Sighted
6101 W. Centinela Ave, Suite 150
Culver City, CA 90230
310-988-1970
Fax: 310-988-1980
info@low-vision.org
www.low-vision.org

Provides professional, comprehensive vision rehabilitation services to visually impaired people of all ages. For those whose sight is severely limited due to macular degeneration, diabetic retinopathy, glaucoma, retinal detachment, stroke or other conditions not correctable medically or surgically.

La Donna Ringering, President
Phillis Amaral, Director
Marc Gerberick, IT Manager

1815 Florida Ophthalmic Institute
7106 NW 11th Place Suite B
Gainesville, FL 32605
352-377-8364

Nonprofit organization that understands and treats ocular diseases including glaucoma.

Norman S Levy, Director

1816 Glaucoma Laser Trabeculoplasty Study
29275 Northwestern Highway
Southfield, MI 48034
248-493-5157

Examines the effectiveness and safety of the treatments of glaucoma.

Hugh Beckman, Chairman

1817 Glaucoma Research Foundation
251 Post Street, Suite 600
San Francisco, CA 94108
415-986-3162
800-826-6693
Fax: 415-986-3763
question@glaucoma.org
www.glaucoma.org

Conducts patient education activities, maintains eye donor network, provides multi-disciplinary seminars and conducts collaborative studies.

Thomas M. Brunner, President & CEO
Nancy Graydon, COO/Executive Director, Development
Andrew L. Jackson, Director of Communications

1818 Mobile Association for the Blind
2440 Gordon Smith Drive
Mobile, AL 36617
251-473-3585
877-292-5463
Fax: 251-470-8622
www.mobileblind.org

Offers work adjustment training, activities of daily living, mobility, communication skills and sheltered employment for adults and children who are visually impaired.

Jim Bullock, Executive Director

1819 National Eye Research Foundation
910 Skokie Boulevard, Suite 207A
Northbrook, IL 60662
847-564-4652
800-621-2258
Fax: 847-564-0807
info@nerf.org
www.nerf.com

Devoted to the enhancement of care and study of eye related diseases.

Andrew Kim

1820 National Ophthalmic Research Institute
Retina Consultants of Southwest, Florida
6901 International Center Boulevard
Ft. Myers, FL 33912
239-938-1284
800-282-8281
Fax: 239-938-1270
NORI@eye.md
www.nori.md/index.htm

A physician-owned clinical research center specializing in innovative investigational treatments for ophthalmic, retinal and vitreous diseases.

Glen Wing MD, Research Director
Eileen Knips, RN, Clinical Research Coordinator
Glenn L Wing, MD, Medical Director

1821 New Beginnings - The Blind Children's Center
4120 Marathon Street
Los Angeles, CA 90029
323-664-2153
Fax: 323-665-3828
www.blindchildrenscenter.org/

The purpose of the Center is to turn initial fears into hope. Helps children and their families become independent by creating a climate of safety and trust. Children learn to develop self confidence and to master a wide range of skills. Services include an infant stimulation program, educational preschool, interdisciplinary assessment services, family services, correspondence program, toll free national hotline and a publication and research service.

1822 Research to Prevent Blindness
645 Madison Avenue, Floor 21
New York, NY 10022
212-752-4333
800-621-0026
Fax: 212-688-6231
inforequest@rpbusa.org
www.rpbusa.org

Provides research grants to scientists interested in eye disease and vision disorders.

Diane Swift, President
David Weeks, Chairman

Audio Video

1823 Heart to Heart
Blind Children's Center
4120 Marathon Street
Los Angeles, CA 90029
323-644-2153
Fax: 323-665-3828
www.blindcntr.org

Parents of blind and partially sighted children talk about their feelings.

Videotape

1824 Let's Eat
Blind Children's Center
4120 Marathon Street
Los Angeles, CA 90029
323-664-2153
Fax: 323-665-3828
www.blindchildrenscenter.org

Teaches competent feeding skills to children with visual impairments.

Videotape

1825 See What I Feel
Britannica Film Co.
345 4th Street
San Francisco, CA 94107
415-597-5555

A blind child tells her friends about her trip to the zoo. Each experience was explained as a blind child would experience it. A teacher's guide comes with this video.

Films

Web Sites

1826 Glaucoma Research Foundation
251 Post Street, Suite 600
San Francisco, CA 94108
question@glaucoma.org
www.glaucoma.org

Mission is to preserve the sight and independence of individuals with glaucoma through research and education with the ultimate goal of finding a cure.

Thomas M. Brunner, President & CEO
Nancy Graydon, COO/Executive Director, Development
Andrew L. Jackson, Director of Communications

1827 Lighthouse Guild
250 West 64th Street
New York, NY 10023
800-284-4422
info@lighthouseguild.org
www.lighthouseguild.org

Lighthouse Guild is dedicated to providing exceptional services that inspire people who are visually impaired to attain their goals.

James M. Dubin, Chair
Calvin W. Roberts, President & CEO
Maura J. Sweeney, SVP, Programs & Services

1828 National Association of Blind Students
200 East Wells Street, Jernigan Place
Baltimore, MD 21230
410-659-9314
nfb@nfb.org
nabslink.org

For over 50 years, the National Association of Blind Students has worked, as an integral part of the National Federation of the Blind, to promote the equality of the blind by serving as a source of information, forum for networking and vehicle for collective action for blind students. Our work on the local, state, and national levels is firmly rooted in the conviction that blindness need not prevent one from excelling in a chosen field of study or living a full and productive life.

1829 New York Glaucoma Research Institute
310 East 14th Street
New York, NY 10003
212-477-7540
Fax: 212-420-8743
www.glaucoma.net

Developed to promote research into the basic causes of Glaucoma, develop new treatments for Glaucoma, and to develop public education into the treatment of Glaucoma.

Dr. Robert Ritch, Principal Investigator

1830 Online Mendelian Inheritance in Man
McKusick-Nathans Institue of Genetic Medicine-JHU
Baltimore, MD 21205
www.omim.org

This database is a catalog of human genes and genetic disorders.

Ada Hamosh, MD, Scientific Director

Congenital Glaucoma / Book Publishers

1831 **Royal National Institute of Blind People**
www.rnib.org.uk

303-123-9999
helpline@rnib.org.uk
www.rnib.org.uk

Offering information, support and advice to over two million people with sight problems.

Matt Stringer, Chief Executive
Keith Valentine, Director of Development
David Clarke, Director of Services

Book Publishers

1832 **Children with Visual Impairments: A Parents' Guide**
Peytral Publications
PO Box 1162
Minnetonka, MN 55345

952-949-8707
877-739-8725
Fax: 952-906-9777
www.peytral.com

Covers visual impairments ranging from low vision to total blindness. Offers authoritative information and empathy, parental insight on diagnosis and treatment, orientation and mobility, literacy, legal issues and more. Valuable to parents, educators and support staff.

395 pages

M Cay Holbrook PhD, Editor

1833 **Eye Care Sourcebook**
Omnigraphics
615 Griswold Street, Ste 520
Detroit, MI 48226

610-461-3548
800-234-1340
Fax: 800-875-1340
www.omnigraphics.com

Basic Information about glaucoma, cataracts, macular degeneration, strabismus, refractive disorders, and more.

2017 656 pages
ISBN: 0-780815-32-2

Magazines

1834 **Journal of Visual Impairment and Blindness**
American Foundation for the Blind
2 Penn Plaza, Suite 1102
New York, NY 10121

212-502-7600
Fax: 888-545-8331
contributions@afb.net
www.afb.org

Published in braille, regular print and on cassette this journal contains a wide variety of subjects including rehabilitation, psychology, education, legislation, medicine, technology, employment, sensory aids and childhood development as they relate to visual impairments.

10x Year

Larry Kimbler, Chair
James H. McLaughlin, Vice Chair
Carl S. Augusto, President & CEO

1835 **Reaching, Crawling, Walking - Let's Get Moving**
Blind Children's Center
4120 Marathon Street
Los Angeles, CA 90029

323-664-2153
Fax: 323-665-3828
info@blindchildrenscenter.org
www.blindchildrenscenter.org

Orientation and mobility for visually impaired preschool children.

24 pages

1836 **Tactic**
Clovernook Home and School for the Blind
7000 Hamilton Avenue
Cincinnati, OH 45231

513-522-3860
Fax: 513-728-3950
clovernook@aol.com

Quarterly

Newsletters

1837 **National Library Service for the Blind & Physically Handicapped**
Library of Congress
1291 Taylor Street NW
Washington, DC 20542

202-707-5100
800-424-8567
Fax: 202-707-0712
nls@loc.gov
www.loc.gov/nls

Provides information and advocacy resources for families and professionals, including listings of organizations focusing on more specific areas of concern to families and young adults who have disabilities. Administers a natural library service that provides recorded and braille reading materials to eligible children and adults who cannot read standard print.

12 pages Quarterly
ISSN: 1046-1663

1838 **Talking Book Topics**
National Library Services for the Blind
1291 Taylor Street NW
Washington, DC 20542

202-707-5100
Fax: 202-707-0712
TDD: 202-707-0744
nls@loc.gov
www.loc.gov/nls

Offers hundreds of listings of books, fiction and nonfiction, for adults and children who cannot read regular print material. Also offers foreign language books, talking magazines and reviews.

Bimonthly

Pamphlets

1839 **Dancing Cheek to Cheek**
Blind Children's Center
4120 Marathon Street
Los Angeles, CA 90029

323-664-2153
Fax: 323-665-3828
www.blindchildrenscenter.org

Discusses beginning social, play and language interactions.

33 pages

1840 **Family Guide - Growth and Development of the Partially Seeing Child**
Lighthouse Guild
250 West 64th Street
New York, NY 10023

800-284-4422
info@lighthouseguild.org
www.lighthouseguild.org

Offers information for parents and guidelines in raising a partially seeing child.

1841 **Family Guide to Vision Care**
American Optometric Association
243 N Lindbergh Boulevard
Saint Louis, MO 63141

314-991-4100
Fax: 314-991-4101
www.aoanet.org

Offers information on the early developmental years of your vision, finding a family optometrist and how to take care of your eyesight through the learning years, the working years and the mature years.

1842 **Glaucoma**
Glaucoma Research Foundation
251 Post Street, Suite 600
San Francisco, CA 94108

415-986-3162
800-826-6693
Fax: 415-986-3763
question@glaucoma.org
www.glaucoma.org

Offers information on what glaucoma is, the causes, treatments, types of glaucoma, eye exams and prevention.

Thomas M. Brunner, President & CEO
Nancy Graydon, COO/Executive Director, Development
Andrew L. Jackson, Director of Communications

1843 **Glaucoma: The Sneak Thief of Sight**
Lighthouse Guild
250 West 64th Street
New York, NY 10023

800-284-4422
info@lighthouseguild.org
www.lighthouseguild.org

A pamphlet describing the disease, treatment and medications.

1844 **Heart to Heart**
Blind Children's Center
4120 Marathon Street
Los Angeles, CA 90029

323-664-2153
Fax: 323-665-3828
www.blindchildrenscenter.org

Parents of blind and partially sighted children talk about their feelings.

12 pages

1845 **Learning to Play**
Blind Children's Center
4120 Marathon Street
Los Angeles, CA 90029

323-664-2153
Fax: 323-665-3828
www.blindchildrenscenter.org

Discusses how to present play activities to the visually impaired pre-school child.

12 pages

1846 **Let's Eat**
Blind Children's Center
4120 Marathon Street
Los Angeles, CA 90029

323-664-2153
Fax: 323-665-3828
www.blindchildrenscenter.org

Teaches competent feeding skills to children with visual impairments.

28 pages

1847 **Move with Me**
Blind Children's Center
4120 Marathon Street
Los Angeles, CA 90029

323-664-2153
Fax: 323-665-3828
www.blindchildrenscenter.org

A parent's guide to movement development for visually impaired babies.

12 pages

1848 **Selecting a Program**
Blind Children's Center
4120 Marathon Street
Los Angeles, CA 90029

323-664-2153
Fax: 323-665-3828
www.blindchildrenscenter.org

A guide for parents of infants and preschoolers with visual impairments.

28 pages

1849 **Standing on My Own Two Feet**
Blind Children's Center
4120 Marathon Street
Los Angeles, CA 90029

323-664-2153
Fax: 323-665-3828
info@blindchildrenscenter.org
www.blindchildrenscenter.org

A step-by-step guide to designing and constructing simple, individually tailored adaptive mobility devices for preschool-age children who are visually impaired.

36 pages

1850 **Talk to Me**
Blind Children's Center
4120 Marathon Street
Los Angeles, CA 90029

323-664-2153
Fax: 323-665-3828
www.blindchildrenscenter.org

A language guide for parents of deaf children.

11 pages

1851 **Talk to Me II**
Blind Children's Center
4120 Marathon Street
Los Angeles, CA 90029

323-664-2153
Fax: 323-665-3828
www.blindchildrenscenter.org

A sequel to Talk To Me, available in English and Spanish.

15 pages

Camps

1852 **Bloomfield**
5300 Angeles Vista Boulevard
Los Angeles, CA 90043

323-295-4555
800-352-2290
Fax: 323-296-0424
info@juniorblind.org
www.juniorblind.org

This camp is dedicated to serving blind and developmentally disabled children and adults.

Miki Jordan, President

1853 **Camp Civitan**
3519 East Shea Blvd # 133
Phoenix, AZ 85028

602-953-2944
Fax: 602-953-2946
info@campcivitan.org
www.campcivitan.org

A 501c3 non-profit organization, that has been providing multiple ever-changing programs to meet the needs of children and adults who are developmentally disabled.

Shannon Valenzuela, Director
Jane Armstrong, Director

1854 **Enchanted Hills Camp**
Lighthouse
214 Van Ness Avenue
San Francisco, CA 94102

415-694-7319
Fax: 415-863-7568
TTY: 415-431-4572
afletcher@lighthouse-sf.org
www.lighthouse-sf.org

For blind, deaf/blind children and adults, ages 5 and up. This program offers a basic camping experience. Activities include music, art, dance, hiking and riding. Camperships are available to California residents.

Tony Fletcher, Camp Director

Congenital Glaucoma / Camps

1855 Florida School-Deaf and Blind Summer Camp
207 San Marco Avenue
Saint Augustine, FL 32084
904-827-2200
800-800-344
info@fsdb.k12.fl.us
www.fsdb.k12.fl.us

The Florida School for the Deaf and the Blind hosts summer campers from all over teh state of Florida for a week of fun and adventure. FSDB's 80 acre campus is where campers participate in a variety of activities including rock climbing, archery, swimming, kayaking, team games, arts and crafts, dance music, and much more.

L Daniel Hutto, President
Cindy Day, Executive Director of Parent Svcs
Terri Wiseman, Administrator of Business Services

1856 Highbrook Lodge Camp
12944 Aquilla Road
Chardon, OH 44024
216-791-8118
Fax: 216-791-1101
camp@clevelandsightcenter.org
www.clevelandsightcenter.org

A summer residential camp for blind and disabled children, adults and families.

Mike Mullin, Director

1857 National Camps for Blind Children
Christian Record
4444 S 52nd Street
Lincoln, NE 68516
402-488-0981
Fax: 402-488-7582
info@christianrecord.org
www.christianrecord.org

Camps throughout the US and Canada are offered at no cost to the legally blind, ages 9-65. Activities include archery, beeper basketball, water sports, hiking and rock climbing and horseback riding.

Peggy Hansen, Director

1858 Texas Lions Camp
Lions Clubs of Texas
PO Box 290247
Kerrville, TX 78029
830-896-8500
Fax: 830-896-3666
tlc@ktc.com
www.lionscamp.com

The primary purpose of Texas Lions camp is to provide, without charge, a camp for physically disabled, hearing/vision impaired and diabetic children from the State of Texas, regardless of race, religion, or national origin. Our goal is to create an atmosphere wherein campers will learn the can do philosophy and be allowed to achieve maximum personal growth and self esteem. The camp welcomes boys and girls ages 7-16.

Stephen Mabry, Executive Director
Doug Parker, Business Manager
Steven King, Program/Client Service Director

1859 VISIONS/Vacation Camp for the Blind
500 Greenwich Street, 3rd Floor
New York, NY 10013
212-625-1616
888-245-8333
Fax: 212-219-4078
info@visions.org
www.visions.org

Family programs at Vacation Camp for the Blind in Rockland County, NY for children who are blind, severely visually impaired or multi-handicapped. Parent or guardian must attend winter weekends and summer session.

Thomas M Decker, Camp Director
Nancy D Miller, Executive Director

1860 Wisconsin Lions Camp
3834 County Road A
Rosholt, WI 54473
715-677-4969
Fax: 715-677-3297
TTY: 715-677-6999
www.wisconlinlionscamp.com

Serves children who have either a visual, hearing or mild cognitive disability. Many of the children also have multiple disabilities or medical conditions. Program activities include sailing, ropes course, bike and canoe trips, environmental education, swimming, camping, canoeing, outdoor living skills and handicrafts. ACA accredited, located in central Wisconsin, near Stevens Point.

Russell Link, Camp Director

Description

1861 CONJUNCTIVITIS
Synonym: Pinkeye
Covers these related disorders: Infectious conjunctivitis, Noninfectious conjunctivitis
Involves the following Biologic System(s):
Infectious Disorders, Ophthalmologic Disorders

Conjunctivitis refers to a condition characterized by acute inflammation of the delicate mucous membranes (conjunctiva) that line the inside of the eyelids and the whites of the eyes (sclerae). This condition may be caused by a virus or bacterium. Allergic reactions or exposure to certain chemicals and other environmental factors may also play a role in certain types of conjunctivitis. Neonatal conjunctivitis (also known as neonatal ophthalmia or ophthalmia neonatorum) becomes apparent during the first four weeks of life and is considered an infectious disease resulting from bacterial or viral infections carried by the mother and passed to the child during the birthing process. Bacteria responsible for neonatal conjunctivitis infections may be common disease-causing organisms (pathogens) or may include Chlamydia trachomatis, the bacteria that causes the sexually transmitted disease (STD) chlamydia or Neisseria gonorrhoeae, responsible for the STD gonorrhea. In addition, viral transmission may be caused by herpes simplex type 2 virus, which is responsible for genital herpes. In addition, bacterial contamination may occur in a hospital nursery (Pseudomonas aeruginosa) and may, in some cases, cause severe infection.

The characteristic symptoms associated with infectious neonatal conjunctivitis include redness and severe swelling of the conjunctiva, including the eyelids and whites of the eyes, and a discharge from the eyes that may or may not contain pus (purulent). Symptoms of neonatal infection resulting from transmission during the birthing process may be present at birth or may appear during the second week of life, depending on the bacterium or virus responsible. Any early conjunctival infection should be evaluated as soon as possible to determine its cause and, subsequently, the appropriate course of treatment in order to prevent complications that could potentially lead to impaired vision or blindness.

Soon after delivery, erythromycin, or tetracycline drops or ointment are routinely administered to the eyes of the newborn to prevent gonococcal (gonorrheal) conjunctivitis. The use of 1% silver nitrate drops as prophylaxis (prevention) against gonococcal ophthalmia soon after birth has reduced its incidence in the United States to less than 0.03% of infants. Although silver nitrate is effective, it also may cause a chemical conjunctival inflammation that typically resolves on its own within 48 hours. Other preventive measures are directed toward identification and treatment of pregnant women with gonococcal infection.

Treatment for bacteria-caused neonatal conjunctivitis includes the use of particular antibiotics. In addition, washing (irrigating) the eye with a solution containing salt (saline) or direct application of antibiotic ointment to the eyes is often effective in relieving itching and discomfort and clearing up the discharge. Conjunctivitis caused by viral transmission may be treated with antiviral eye drops or ointment. Sometimes the antiviral drug acyclovir may be administered to prevent viral spread.

Additional causes of conjunctivitis in children may include other viruses associated with systemic diseases such as measles, some viruses of the adenovirus family, and intestinal viruses of the enterovirus family. This type of conjunctivitis is usually characterized by a watery discharge from the eyes, is usually self-limited, and treatment is symptomatic. However, one such adenovirus may cause severe itching and burning of the eyes, sensitivity to light (photophobia), and involvement of the cornea. This type of conjunctivitis is known as keratoconjunctivitis and affects the membranes lining the eyelids as well as the corneas. This virus is transmitted by direct contact. Conjunctivitis caused by allergies is usually seasonal and is characterized by swelling, tearing, and itching. Treatment is symptomatic and may include the application of antihistamine eye drops. Certain chemicals or environmental factors may also cause noninfectious, allergic-type conjunctivitis. In addition to silver nitrate used in preventive treatment in newborns, other irritating substances may include cleaning products, different types of sprays, smoke, pollen, and other materials. Treatment is directed toward prevention and relief of symptoms.

In the United States, as mentioned, the occurrence of neonatal conjunctivitis caused by Neisseria gonorrhoeae is extremely rare, while that caused by Chlamydia trachomatis is slightly more than eight out of every 1,000 births.

Government Agencies

1862 NIH/National Eye Institute
31 Center Drive MSC 2510
Bethesda, MD 20892
301-496-5248
2020@nei.nih.gov
www.nei.nih.gov

Conducts and supports research that helps prevent and treat eye diseases and other disorders of vision. This research leads to sight-saving treatments, reduces visual impairment and blindness, and improves the quality of life for people of all ages. NEI-supported research has advanced our knowledge of how the eye functions in health and disease.
Michael F. Chiang, MD, Director
Santa Tumminia, Deputy Director

1863 NIH/National Institute of Allergy and Infectious Diseases
5601 Fishers Lane, MSC 9806
Bethesda, MD 20892
301-496-5717
866-284-4107
Fax: 301-402-3573
TDD: 800-877-8339
ocpostoffice@niaid.nih.gov
www.niaid.nih.gov

The principal advisory board of the NIAID. The council is composed of physicians, scientists and representatives of the public and advises on the conduct and support or research, training and dissemination of health information regarding allergies and infectious diseases.
Anthony S. Fauci, MD, Director

National Associations & Support Groups

1864 American Academy of Pediatrics
345 Park Blvd
Itasca, IL 60143
800-433-9016
Fax: 847-434-8000
mcc@aap.org
www.aap.org

The American Academy of Pediatrics and its member pediatricians are committed to the attainment of optimal physical, mental and social health and well-being for all infants, children, adolescents, and young adults.
Lynn Olson, PhD, VP, Research
Mark Del Monte, JD, CEO/Executive VP
Vera Tait, MD, FAAP, Chief Medical Officer

Conjunctivitis / Web Sites

1865 **American Institute for Preventive Medicine**
Farmington Hills, MI

248-539-1800
800-345-2476
Fax: 248-539-1808
aipm@healthylife.com
www.healthylife.com

An internationally recognized authority on the development and implementation of health promotion, wellness, medical self-care, and disease management programs and publications.

Don R. Powell, PhD, President & CEO
Susan Schooley, MD, Medical Director
Hope Lawless, Senior Vice President & COO

1866 **World Health Organization**
Avenue Appia 20
1202 Geneva,
Switzerland

www.who.int

WHO is the directing and coordinating authority for health within the United Nations system. WHO operates in more than 150 countries around the world.

Dr. Tedros Adhanom Ghebreyesus, Director General
Dr. Zsuzsanna Jakab, Deputy Director General
Stewart Simonson, Asst Director General, UN NYC

Web Sites

1867 **Dr. Koop**
www.drkoop.com

www.drkoop.com

Information on the condition, causes, symptoms, tests and treatment.

1868 **LSU Health Sciences Center**
433 Bolivar Street
New Orleans, LA 70112

504-568-4808
webmaster@lsuhsc.edu
www.lsuhsc.edu

An online library of resources.

Larry H. Hollier, MD, FACS, FACC, Chancellor
Evana Morales, Staff Accountant
Martha Hotard, Collections Manager

1869 **MedicineNet.com**
www.medicinenet.com

www.medicinenet.com

An online, healthcare media publishing company providing easy-to-read, in-depth, authoritative medical information for consumers via its user-friendly, interactive web site. MedicineNet.com has had a highly accomplished, uniquely experienced team of qualified executives in the fields of medicine, healthcare, internet tehnology, and business to bring you the most comprehensive, sought after healthcare information anywhere.

1870 **Virtual Children's Hospital**
200 Hawkins Drive
Iowa City, IA 52242

800-777-8442
www.vh.org

Mission is to educate patients, healthcare providers, and students in a free and anonymous manner, for the purpose of improving patients' care, outcome and lives.

Jean E. Robillard, MD, UI VP for Medical Affairs
Theresa Brennan, MD, Chief Medical Officer
Sabi Singh, MS, MA, Co-Chief Operating Officer

Description

1871 CORNELIA DE LANGE SYNDROME
Synonyms: BDLS, Brachmann-de Lange syndrome, CdLS, De Lange syndrome
Involves the following Biologic System(s):
Genetic/Chromosomal/Syndrome/Metabolic Disorders

Cornelia de Lange syndrome is a genetic disorder characterized by growth delays before and after birth; delays in the acquisition of skills that require the coordination of physical and mental activities, and mild to severe intellectual disabilities. Characteristic physical abnormalities include delays in the maturation of bone; malformations of the head and facial (craniofacial) area that result in a distinctive facial appearance; abnormalities of the arms, legs, hands, and feet (limbs); or other abnormalities. Associated symptoms and findings may vary in range and severity from case to case.

Infants with Cornelia de Lange syndrome often have feeding difficulties (e.g., projectile vomiting, regurgitation, swallowing difficulties); fail to grow and gain weight at the expected rate (failure to thrive); and have a weak, growling cry. Affected infants usually experience breathing problems, such as episodes in which there is temporary cessation of breathing (apnea), inhalation (aspiration) of food into the air passages of the lungs, and increased susceptibility to repeated respiratory infections. Affected infants and children also typically have arched, bushy eyebrows that grow together (synophrys); unusually long, curly eyelashes; a low hair line; and generalized excessive hair growth (hirsutism). Characteristic craniofacial abnormalities may include an abnormally prominent vertical groove in the center of the upper lip (philtrum); thin, downturned lips; and a small jaw (micrognathia). In addition, in many affected children, the teeth may erupt later than expected and are widely spaced.

Many infants and children with Cornelia de Lange syndrome also have malformations of the upper limbs, such as small hands or abnormal positioning of the fifth fingers (clinodactyly) or thumbs. In rare cases, the forearms, hands, and fingers may be absent (phocomelia and oligodactyly). Many affected infants and children also may have abnormally small, short feet with webbing of the second and third toes (syndactyly).

In many cases, additional symptoms and findings are present. For example, in most affected males, the testes may fail to descend into the scrotum (cryptorchidism). Some affected infants may also have digestive abnormalities (e.g., gastroesophageal reflux, pyloric stenosis, bowel obstruction); heart defects (e.g., ventricular septal defects); episodes of uncontrolled electrical activity in the brain (seizures); or other physical abnormalities. In addition, many affected children experience hearing loss and speech delays and may demonstrate behavioral problems, such as self-destructive tendencies.

Treatment of infants and children with Cornelia de Lange syndrome includes symptomatic and supportive measures, such as the prescription of certain medications to help prevent or control seizures (i.e., anticonvulsants); supportive therapies to ensure the proper intake of nutrients and to help prevent or treat respiratory problems; and surgical or other appropriate methods to treat heart or digestive defects.

In most cases, Cornelia de Lange syndrome appears to occur randomly for unknown reasons. However, in a few reported cases, autosomal dominant inheritance has been suggested. The disorder is thought to affect approximately one in 10,000 newborns.

National Associations & Support Groups

1872 American Academy of Pediatrics
345 Park Blvd
Itasca, IL 60143
800-433-9016
Fax: 847-434-8000
mcc@aap.org
www.aap.org

The American Academy of Pediatrics and its member pediatricians are committed to the attainment of optimal physical, mental and social health and well-being for all infants, children, adolescents, and young adults.

Lynn Olson, PhD, VP, Research
Mark Del Monte, JD, CEO/Executive VP
Vera Tait, MD, FAAP, Chief Medical Officer

1873 Children's Craniofacial Association
13140 Coit Road, Suite 517
Dallas, TX 75240
214-570-9099
800-535-3643
contactCCA@ccakids.com
www.ccakids.com

A national, nonprofit organization dedicated to improving the quality of life for people with facial differences and their families. CCA's mission is to empower and give hope to facially disfigured children and their families.

Erica Klauber, Executive Director
Annie Reeves, Program Director
Khadija Z. Moten, Outreach Director

1874 Cornelia de Lange Syndrome Foundation
30 Tower Lane, Suite 400
Avon, CT 06001
860-676-8166
800-753-8166
Fax: 860-676-8337
info@cdlsusa.org
www.cdlsusa.org

Provides a host of services that attract, educate, and unite families touched by this rare birth disorder which causes individuals to develop at a slower rate, both physically and mentally.

Bonnie Royster, Executive Director
Antonie Kline, MD, Medical Director
Deirdre Summa, Family Services Manager

1875 FACES: National Craniofacial Association
PO Box 11082
Chattanooga, TN 37401
423-266-1632
800-332-2373
info@faces-cranio.org
www.faces-cranio.org

Assists individuals with facial disfigurations and their families They maintain a registry of centers offering corrective surgery for craniofacial deformities and financial assistance to qualified applicants.

Kim Teems Fox, President
Emily McKay, Communications Director
Ashley Rhodes, FACES Camp Director

1876 Genetic Alliance
426400 Woodfield Road, Ste 189
Damascus, MD 20872
202-966-5557
Fax: 202-966-8553
info@geneticalliance.org
www.geneticalliance.org

World's leading nonprofit health advocacy organization committed to transforming health through genetics and promoting an environment of openness centered on the health of individuals, families, and communities.

Sharon Terry, CEO
Ruth Child, CFO
Natasha Bonhomme, Chief Strategy Officer

Cornelia de Lange Syndrome / Conferences

1877 March of Dimes Foundation
1550 Crystal Drive, Ste 1300
Arlington, VA 22202
888-663-4637
www.marchofdimes.org

March of Dimes help moms have full-term pregnancies and research the problems that threaten the health of babies. The March of Dimes also acts globally: sharing best practices in perinatal health and helping improve birth outcomes where the needs are the most urgent.

Stacey D. Stewart, President
Alan Brogdon, SVP/COO/Board Officer
Rahul Gupta, MD, SVP & Chief Medical/Health Officer

Conferences

1878 CdLS Biennial Conference
30 Tower Lane, Suite 400
Avon, CT 06001
860-676-8166
800-753-8166
Fax: 860-676-8337
info@cdlsusa.org
www.cdlsusa.org

Provides education and support to families of individuals with CdLS. Attendees receive free head-to-toe consultations with experts from a range of medical and educational fields; attend workshops on legal concerns, educational issues and medical/behaviors challenges; and have opportunities to meet other families facing similar challenges.

June

Bonnie Royster, Executive Director
Antonie Kline, MD, Medical Director
Deirdre Summa, Family Services Manager

Web Sites

1879 Online Mendelian Inheritance in Man
McKusick-Nathans Institue of Genetic Medicine-JHU
Baltimore, MD 21205
www.omim.org

This database is a catalog of human genes and genetic disorders.

Ada Hamosh, MD, Scientific Director

Description

1880 CRANIOSYNOSTOSIS

Synonyms: Craniostenosis, Craniostosis

Covers these related disorders: Frontal plagiocephaly, Kleeblattschadel deformity, Scaphocephaly, Trigonocephaly, Turricephaly (oxycephaly or acrocephaly)

Involves the following Biologic System(s):
Orthopedic and Muscle Disorders

Craniosynostosis is a developmental abnormality in which early closure of one or more of the fibrous joints (sutures) between bones of the skull results in deformity of the skull and an abnormally shaped head. The severity of the deformity depends upon which fibrous joint or joints close prematurely as well as the ability of other joints in the skull to expand and compensate for the other closed joint or joints. Craniosynostosis may occur as an isolated condition or in association with certain chromosomal or malformation syndromes. In most instances of isolated craniosynostosis, the condition appears to occur randomly for unknown reasons. However, there have been reports of isolated craniosynostosis in members of several multigenerational families (kindreds), indicating autosomal dominant or autosomal recessive inheritance. Many genetic malformation syndromes have been identified in the medical literature that are associated with craniosynostosis. The specific underlying cause of craniosynostosis is not fully understood. Craniosynostosis occurs in approximately one in every 1,000 to 2,000 births and is more prevalent in males than females.

In infants with craniosynostosis, because the skull is unable to enlarge in certain directions relative to the affected fibrous joint in the skull, there is compensatory growth and enlargement in other directions at the sites of open joints. This causes deformity of the skull and an abnormally shaped head. For example, in the most common form of craniosynostosis, there is premature closure of the joint between the upper sides of the skull (sagittal suture), causing the head to appear abnormally long and narrow (scaphocephaly). Affected infants also tend to have a broad forehead and a prominent back portion of the head (occiput). This condition appears to be more common in males than females.

In the form of craniosynostosis known as frontal plagiocephaly, there is early closure of a suture between the upper sides of the head and one of the bones of the forehead (e.g., coronal suture). This results in flattening of one side of the forehead, prominence of the ear, and elevation of the eyebrow and eye on the affected side. Frontal plagiocephaly appears to affect females more commonly than males.

Trigonocephaly, another form of craniosynstosis, is characterized by premature fusion of the suture between the bones forming the forehead (metopic suture). Affected infants have a keel-shaped forehead and closely spaced eyes (hypotelorism). In infants with the form of craniosynostosis known as turricephaly (also called oxycephaly or acrocephaly), premature fusion of coronal and sagittal sutures causes the head to have an abnormally long, narrow, cone-like appearance. In addition, a rare form of craniosynostosis, known as Kleeblattschadel deformity, is characterized by premature closure of multiple cranial sutures, causing the skull to appear cloverleaf-like in shape. Affected infants have a high forehead, marked protrusion of the eyes (proptosis), abnormal prominence of the lower sides of the skull (temporal bones), and other associated abnormalities. Many affected infants also experience hydrocephalus, a condition in which obstruction or impaired absorption of the fluid surrounding the brain and spinal cord (cerebrospinal fluid) causes fluid accumulation under increasing pressure within the brain, resulting in abnormal enlargement of the brain.

In infants with craniosynostosis, premature closure of one suture is rarely associated with increased pressure within the skull or associated neurologic abnormalities, such as intellectual disabilities. In such patients, surgery may be considered for cosmetic purposes. Premature closure of two or more sutures is more likely to cause increased pressure within the skull, potentially resulting in brain damage and associated intellectual disabilities. Additional findings associated with increased pressure may include vomiting, headaches, and swelling of the area where the optic nerve enters the eye and joins with the nerve-rich membrane at the back of the eye (papilledema). In these infants, surgery is necessary to increase the capacity of the skull in order to prevent excessive pressure within the skull. If craniosynostosis is diagnosed before three months of age, surgery may be conducted to create artificial cranial joints in the skull, allowing skull growth and preventing abnormal shaping of the head.

National Associations & Support Groups

1881 AmeriFace
PO Box 751112
Las Vegas, NV 89136
702-341-5351
888-486-1209
Fax: 702-341-5351
info@ameriface.org
www.ameriface.org

Provides information, services, emotional support and educational programs for and on behalf of individuals with facial differences and their families. Working to increase understanding through public awareness and education.

3M members

Debbie Oliver, Executive Director

1882 American Academy of Pediatrics
345 Park Blvd
Itasca, IL 60143
800-433-9016
Fax: 847-434-8000
mcc@aap.org
www.aap.org

The American Academy of Pediatrics and its member pediatricians are committed to the attainment of optimal physical, mental and social health and well-being for all infants, children, adolescents, and young adults.

Lynn Olson, PhD, VP, Research
Mark Del Monte, JD, CEO/Executive VP
Vera Tait, MD, FAAP, Chief Medical Officer

1883 Children's Craniofacial Association
13140 Coit Road, Suite 307
Dallas, TX 75240
214-570-9099
800-535-3643
contactCCA@ccakids.com
www.ccakids.com

A national, nonprofit organization dedicated to improving the quality of life for people with facial differences and their families. CCA's mission is to empower and give hope to facially disfigured children and their families.

Erica Klauber, Executive Director
Annie Reeves, Program Director
Khadija Z. Moten, Outreach Director

1884 Craniosynostosis and Positional Plagiocephaly Support
www.cappskids.org

888-572-5526
info@cappskids.org
www.cappskids.org

Craniosynostosis / Libraries & Resource Centers

The mission of CAPPSKIDS is to support families, assist with expedited consultations so that more surgical options are available to the families, create awareness which will enable early detection and treatment, educate families, primary care providers, and the public, enhance treatment opportunities and to create a standard of care.

Amy Galm, Director

1885 FACES: National Craniofacial Association
PO Box 11082
Chattanooga, TN 37401
423-266-1632
800-332-2373
info@faces-cranio.org
www.faces-cranio.org

Assists individuals with facial disfigurations and their families They maintain a registry of centers offering corrective surgery for craniofacial deformities and financial assistance to qualified applicants.

Kim Teems Fox, President
Emily McKay, Communications Director
Ashley Rhodes, FACES Camp Director

1886 Genetic Alliance
426400 Woodfield Road, Ste 189
Damascus, MD 20872
202-966-5557
Fax: 202-966-8553
info@geneticalliance.org
www.geneticalliance.org

World's leading nonprofit health advocacy organization committed to transforming health through genetics and promoting an environment of openness centered on the health of individuals, families, and communities.

Sharon Terry, CEO
Ruth Child, CFO
Natasha Bonhomme, Chief Strategy Officer

1887 March of Dimes Foundation
1550 Crystal Drive, Ste 1300
Arlington, VA 22202
888-663-4637
www.marchofdimes.org

March of Dimes help moms have full-term pregnancies and research the problems that threaten the health of babies. The March of Dimes also acts globally: sharing best practices in perinatal health and helping improve birth outcomes where the needs are the most urgent.

Stacey D. Stewart, President
Alan Brogdon, SVP/COO/Board Officer
Rahul Gupta, MD, SVP & Chief Medical/Health Officer

1888 MyFace
333 East 30th Street, Lobby Unit
New York, NY 10016
917-720-4701
info@myface.org
myface.org

MyFace is a non-profit organization dedicated to changing the faces and transforming the lives of children and adults with facial differences.

Stephanie Paul, Executive Director
Dina Zuckerberg, Director of Family Programs
Katie Bazyluk, Communications Manager

1889 National Hydrocephalus Foundation
12413 Centralia Road
Lakewood, CA 90715
562-924-6666
info@nhfonline.org
www.nhfonline.org

Nonprofit public service organization that assembles and disseminates information about Hydrocephalus. Promotes communication networks among those affected and their families, helps others gain a deeper understanding of those areas affected by Hydrocephalus, such as education, tax and estate planning, employment and family. Also promotes and supports research on the causes, treatment and prevention of Hydrocephalus.

Debbi Fields, Executive Director

Libraries & Resource Centers

1890 University of Illinois at Chicago, Craniofacial Center
College of Medicine
808 S Wood Street
Chicago, IL 60612
312-996-7870
Fax: 312-413-1526
www.medicine.uic.edu

Richard M Novak, Director

Research Centers

1891 Craniofacial Center at University of Illinois, Chicago
811 S Paulina
Chicago, IL 60612
312-996-7546
Fax: 312-413-1157
uic.edu/com/surgery/plastic/craniofacial_cntr.htm

Maya Shahani, Director
Mimis Cohen, Professor of Surgery

Audio Video

1892 Face First
Fanlight Productions
32 Court Street, 21st Floor
Brooklyn, NY 11201
718-488-8900
800-876-1710
Fax: 718-488-8642
info@fanlight.com
www.fanlight.com

Profiles of several people born with facial deformities; they chronicle both physical pain and the pain of rejection, as well as the strengths that have enabled them to achieve successful adult lives. ISBN: DVD: 1-57295-886-3; VHS: 1-572952-59-8

29 minutes DVD or VHS

Nicole Johnson, Publicity Coordinator

Web Sites

1893 National Hydrocephalus Foundation
www.nhfonline.org
562-924-6666
info@nhfonline.org
www.nhfonline.org

Promotes information and educational assistance. Establishes and facilitates a communication network and works to increase public awareness. Promote and support research.

Book Publishers

1894 Congenital Disorders Sourcebook

Greg Mullin, author

Omnigraphics
615 Griswold Street, Ste 520
Detroit, MI 48226
610-461-3548
800-234-1340
Fax: 800-875-1340
contact@omnigraphics.com
www.omnigraphics.com

Basic consumer health information on disorders aquired during gestation, including spina bifida, hydrocephalus, cerebral palsy, heart defects, craniofacial abnormalities and fetal alcohol syndrome.

664 pages
ISBN: 0-780816-13-8

Camps

1895 Camp About Face
Riley Hospital # 2514, 702 Barnhill Drive
Indianapolis, IN 46202   317-274-2489
www.headsupfoundation.org/camp_about_face.htm

Camp designed to benefit youth ages 8-18 with craniofacial anomalies.

Crohn's Disease / Description

Description

1896 CROHN'S DISEASE

Synonym: Regional enteritis

Involves the following Biologic System(s):

Gastrointestinal Disorders

Crohn's disease is an inflammatory bowel disease (IBD) characterized by chronic inflammation of any region of the digestive (gastrointestinal) tract from the mouth to the anus. The disease most commonly involves the lower region of the small intestine (ileum) and the major part of the large intestine (colon). Chronic inflammation of these areas causes thickening and scarring of the intestinal wall. The range and severity of Crohn's disease is extremely variable and depends on the intestinal region affected, the severity of symptoms and findings of inflammation, and associated complications. In children, Crohn's disease usually becomes apparent during the late teens; however, symptoms may begin during early childhood. In developed countries, inflammatory bowel disease, including Crohn's disease, is the most common cause of chronic intestinal inflammation during mid-childhood. Crohn's disease affects males and females in equal numbers. In the U.S., the disease affects approximately 30 to 100 per 100,000 individuals in the general population and occurs more frequently among Caucasians and African-Americans, (and is more common in Jewish individuals than in Hispanic-Americans and Asian-Americans. Although the exact cause of Crohn's disease is unknown, genetic, immune, and environmental factors are thought to play a role. Some researchers suspect that the disorder may result from an exaggerated immune response to an invading microorganism, such as a particular virus or bacterium.

In most children, Crohn's disease initially involves both the lower region of the small intestine and the major part of the large intestine (ileocolitis). However, initial inflammation may be restricted to the small intestine or the colon. The inflammatory process tends to be segmental in nature, and diseased regions of the intestine are often separated by apparently normal segments (skip lesions). Chronic inflammation causes thickening, ulceration, and scarring of affected areas of the intestinal walls and may lead to the development of abnormal channels (fistulas) between regions of the colon, the intestine and the urinary bladder, or the intestine and the surface of the skin. Additional complications may include the development of pus-filled pockets of infection (abscesses) or intestinal obstruction due to abnormal narrowing of certain intestinal regions.

Many children with Crohn's disease experience episodes of cramping; abdominal discomfort and pain; diarrhea that may contain blood; persistent spasms of the rectum (tenesmus); and a compelling urge to defecate. Additional symptoms and findings typically include fever, chills, easy fatigability, a general feeling of ill health (malaise), lack of appetite (anorexia), weight loss, and malnutrition due to impaired intestinal absorption of fats and nutrients (malabsorption). Many patients also develop deep grooves or cracks (fissures) in the mucous membranes of the anus. Some children have delayed bone maturation, stunted physical growth, or delayed sexual development as much as one to two years before the onset of other symptoms.

Many patients with Crohn's disease may also develop more generalized, systemic symptoms. These may include joint swelling and inflammation (arthritis); inflammation of the outermost layers of the eye's tough, white, outer coat (episcleritis); eruption of multiple, inflamed, reddish-purplish swellings on the legs and possibly the arms (erythema nodosum); and abnormal concentrations of mineral salts (calculi or stones) in the kidneys or the muscular sac (gall bladder) that stores and concentrates bile from the liver. Patients may also be prone to developing ankylosing spondylitis, a chronic, progressive, inflammatory disease that affects joints of the spine and results in pain, stiffness, and possible loss of spinal mobility. In addition, it is suspected that patients who have Crohn's disease for many years may have an increased risk of colon cancer as compared with the general population.

Symptoms typically flare up at irregular intervals throughout life. These episodes may be mild or severe and last for relatively short or prolonged periods. The treatment of Crohn's disease is directed at minimizing symptoms. Therapy may include the use of certain medication, such as sulfasalazine, azathioprine, or metronidazole. For example, azathioprine or metronidazole may be helpful in treating anal fistulas, and metronidazole has been beneficial in treating some patients who have not responded to other medications. Oral steroids may be added if needed. They are highly effective in reducing symptoms but should be used for short-term treatment only. Steroids should be tapered as soon as possible to reduce the risk of long-term side effects. In many children, treatment may include the administration of nutrients in liquid form (total parenteral nutrition) via a tube through the nose to the stomach (nasogastric tube). Some patients who experience severe, sudden episodes may require hospitalization to ensure proper intake of nutrients and fluids and to receive appropriate medical therapy. In addition, some patients may eventually require surgery to remove diseased portions of the intestine. However, such surgery is reserved for very specific indications, because the recurrence rate is high and the risk of needing additional surgery increases after such a procedure. Additional treatment is symptomatic and supportive.

National Associations & Support Groups

1897 American Academy of Pediatrics
345 Park Blvd
Itasca, IL 60143
800-433-9016
Fax: 847-434-8000
mcc@aap.org
www.aap.org

The American Academy of Pediatrics and its member pediatricians are committed to the attainment of optimal physical, mental and social health and well-being for all infants, children, adolescents, and young adults.

Lynn Olson, PhD, VP, Research
Mark Del Monte, JD, CEO/Executive VP
Vera Tait, MD, FAAP, Chief Medical Officer

1898 American Autoimmune Related Diseases Association
19176 Hall Road, Suite 130
Clinton, MI 48038
586-776-3900
aarda@aarda.org
www.aarda.org

The American Autoimmune Related Diseases Association is dedicated to the eradication of autoimmune diseases and the alleviation of suffering and the socioeconomic impact of autoimmunity through fostering and facilitating collaboration in the areas of education, public awareness, research, and patient services in an effective, ethical and efficient manner.

Lilly Stairs, Interim President/CEO
Laura Simpson, COO

1899 Crohn's & Colitis Foundation
733 Third Avenue, Ste 510
New York, NY 10017
800-932-2423
info@crohnscolitisfoundation.org
www.crohnscolitisfoundation.org

Crohn's Disease / State Agencies & Support Groups

The mission of the Crohn's & Colitis Foundation is to cure and prevent Crohn's disease and ulcerative colitis through research and improve the quality of life of children and adults affected by these digestive diseases through education and support.

John Crosson, Chair
Michael Osso, President & CEO
Robert Territo, COO/CFO

1900 Digestive Disease National Coalition
507 Capitol Court NE, Suite 200
Washington, DC 20002
202-544-7497
Fax: 202-546-7105
www.ddnc.org

Advocacy organization comprised of over 30 voluntary and professional societies concerned with the many diseases of the digestive tract and liver.

Ceciel Rooker, Chairperson
Bryan Green, MD, President
Cathy Griffith, Vice Chairperson

1901 Genetic Alliance
426400 Woodfield Road, Ste 189
Damascus, MD 20872
202-966-5557
Fax: 202-966-8553
info@geneticalliance.org
www.geneticalliance.org

World's leading nonprofit health advocacy organization committed to transforming health through genetics and promoting an environment of openness centered on the health of individuals, families, and communities.

Sharon Terry, CEO
Ruth Child, CFO
Natasha Bonhomme, Chief Strategy Officer

1902 International Foundation for Functional Gastrointestinal Disorders (IFFGD)
3015 Dunes W Boulevard, Suite 512
Mount Pleasant, SC 29466
414-964-1799
www.iffgd.org

The organization offers responses to those commonly asked questions for families and individuals whose lives have been touched by gastrointestinal disorders.

Nancy J. Norton, Founder
Ceciel T. Rooker, President

1903 March of Dimes Foundation
1550 Crystal Drive, Ste 1300
Arlington, VA 22202
888-663-4637
www.marchofdimes.org

March of Dimes help moms have full-term pregnancies and research the problems that threaten the health of babies. The March of Dimes also acts globally: sharing best practices in perinatal health and helping improve birth outcomes where the needs are the most urgent.

Stacey D. Stewart, President
Alan Brogdon, SVP/COO/Board Officer
Rahul Gupta, MD, SVP & Chief Medical/Health Officer

State Agencies & Support Groups

Alabama

1904 Alabama/Northwest Florida Chapter of Crohn s Colitis Foundation of America
244 Goodwin Crest Drive, Suite 120
Birmingham, AL 35259
646-387-2149
800-249-1993
Fax: 205-941-1411
jshugart@ccfa.org
www.crohnscolitisfoundation.org

Each of the more than 40 chapters of the Crohn's & Colitis Foundation are either staffed or volunteer chapters in order to bring the Foundation's work and mission to local communities through support services, education and research programs, advocacy and quality care.

Pat Talty, Executive Director
Maura Breen, Chairman

Arizona

1905 Arizona Chapter of Crohn's & Colitis Foundation of America
8098 Via de Negocio, Suite 201
Scottsdale, AZ 85258
480-246-3676
877-259-2104
Fax: 480-246-3679
southwest@ccfa.org
www.crohnscolitisfoundation.org

Each of the more than 40 chapters of the Crohn's & Colitis Foundation are either staffed or volunteer chapters in order to bring the Foundation's work and mission to local communities through support services, education and research programs, advocacy and quality care.

Bridgette Haley, Executive Director
Maura Breen, Chairman

California

1906 Greater Los Angeles/Orange County Chapter of Chron's & Colitis Foundation
1640 S Sepulveda Boulevard, Suite 214
Los Angeles, CA 90025
310-478-4500
866-831-9157
Fax: 310-478-4546
losangeles@ccfa.org
www.crohnscolitisfoundation.org

Each of the more than 40 chapters of the Crohn's & Colitis Foundation are either staffed or volunteer chapters in order to bring the Foundation's work and mission to local communities through support services, education and research programs, advocacy and quality care.

Ronni Epstein, Executive Director
Lindsay Brown, Support Manager

1907 Greater San Diego/Desert Chapter of Crohn' s & Colitis Foundation of America
7850 Mission Center Ct. Suite 100
San Diego, CA 92108
619-497-1300
Fax: 619-497-1304
sandiego@ccfa.org
www.crohnscolitisfoundation.org

Each of the more than 40 chapters of the Crohn's & Colitis Foundation are either staffed or volunteer chapters in order to bring the Foundation's work and mission to local communities through support services, education and research programs, advocacy and quality care.

Pamela Meistrell, Executive Director

1908 Northern California Chapter of Crohn's and Colitis Foundation
5 Third Street, Suite 625
San Francisco, CA 94103
415-356-2232
800-241-0758
Fax: 415-356-0880
ncal@ccfa.org
www.crohnscolitisfoundation.org

Each of the more than 40 chapters of the Crohn's & Colitis Foundation are either staffed or volunteer chapters in order to bring the Foundation's work and mission to local communities through support services, education and research programs, advocacy and quality care.

Tamara Block, Executive Director

Colorado

1909 Rocky Mountain Chapter of Crohn's & Colitis Foundation of America
1777 S Bellaire Street, Suite 230
Denver, CO 80222
303-639-9163
800-768-2232
Fax: 303-639-9166
rockymountain@ccfa.org
www.crohnscolitisfoundation.org

Crohn's Disease / State Agencies & Support Groups

Each of the more than 40 chapters of the Crohn's & Colitis Foundation are either staffed or volunteer chapters in order to bring the Foundation's work and mission to local communities through support services, education and research programs, advocacy and quality care.

Michele L Basche, Executive Director
Maura Breen, Chairman

Connecticut

1910 Central Connecticut Chapter of Crohn's & Colitis Foundation of America
PO Box 34
New London, CT 06320
646-499-0159
mbfecteau@ccfa.org
www.crohnscolitisfoundation.org

Each of the more than 40 chapters of the Crohn's & Colitis Foundation are either staffed or volunteer chapters in order to bring the Foundation's work and mission to local communities through support services, education and research programs, advocacy and quality care.

Maura Breen, Chairman

1911 Fairfield/Westchester Chapter of Crohn's & Colitis Foundation of America
200 Bloomingdale Road
White Plains, NY 10603
914-328-2874
Fax: 914-468-2133
westfield@ccfa.org
www.crohnscolitisfoundation.org

Each of the more than 40 chapters of the Crohn's & Colitis Foundation are either staffed or volunteer chapters in order to bring the Foundation's work and mission to local communities through support services, education and research programs, advocacy and quality care.

Russell P Girolamo, Board President
Maura Breen, Chairman

1912 Northern Connecticut Affiliate Chapter of Crohn's & Colitis Foundation of America
PO Box 370614
West Hartford, CT 06137
www.crohnscolitisfoundation.org

Each of the more than 40 chapters of the Crohn's & Colitis Foundation are either staffed or volunteer chapters in order to bring the Foundation's work and mission to local communities through support services, education and research programs, advocacy and quality care.

Maura Breen, Chairman

Florida

1913 Florida Chapter of Crohn's & Colitis Found ation of America
21301 Powerline Road #301
21301 Powerline Rd., Suite 301
Boca Raton, FL 33433
561-218-2929
877-664-2929
Fax: 561-218-2240
florida@ccfa.org
www.crohnscolitisfoundation.org

Each of the more than 40 chapters of the Crohn's & Colitis Foundation are either staffed or volunteer chapters in order to bring the Foundation's work and mission to local communities through support services, education and research programs, advocacy and quality care.

Amy Gray, Executive Director
Maura Breen, Chairman

Georgia

1914 Georgia Chapter of Crohn's & Colitis Foundation of America
2250 N Druid Hills Road, Suite 250
Atlanta, GA 30329
404-982-0616
800-472-6795
Fax: 404-982-0656
sprimm@ccfa.org
www.crohnscolitisfoundation.org

Each of the more than 40 chapters of the Crohn's & Colitis Foundation are either staffed or volunteer chapters in order to bring the Foundation's work and mission to local communities through support services, education and research programs, advocacy and quality care.

Marcia Greenburg, Regional Executive Director
Karen Rittenbaum, Deputy Director

Illinois

1915 Crohn's & Colitis Foundation Carol Fisher Chapter
2200 E Devon Avenue, Suite 392
Des Plaines, IL 60018
847-827-0404
Fax: 847-827-6563
illinois@crohnscolitisfoundation.org
www.crohnscolitisfoundation.org

Crohn's & Colitis Foundation is a nonprofit, voluntary health organizaiton dedicated to finding the cause of, and cure for Crohn's disease and ulcerative colitis. The foundation is committed to conquering these devastating diseases.

$25.00 Dues

Brandon Combs, Executive Director
Lauren Erbach Barnfield, Education Manager

Indiana

1916 Indiana Chapter of Crohn's & Colitis Found ation of America
931 e. 86th St Suite 210
Indianapolis, IN 46240
317-259-8071
800-332-6029
Fax: 317-259-8091
jbender@ccfa.org
www.crohnscolitisfoundation.org

Each of the more than 40 chapters of the Crohn's & Colitis Foundation are either staffed or volunteer chapters in order to bring the Foundation's work and mission to local communities through support services, education and research programs, advocacy and quality care.

Jo Bender, Community Development Director
Maura Breen, Chairman

Iowa

1917 Iowa Chapter of Crohn's Colitis Foundation of America
8031 West Center Rd Suite 322
Omaha, NE 68124
402-505-9901
iowa@ccfa.org
www.crohnscolitisfoundation.org

Each of the more than 40 chapters of the Crohn's & Colitis Foundation are either staffed or volunteer chapters in order to bring the Foundation's work and mission to local communities through support services, education and research programs, advocacy and quality care.

Melissa Cupich, Development Manager
Maura Breen, Chairman

Kansas

1918 Mid-America Chapter of Crohn's & Colitis F oundation of America
1034 S. Brentwood Suite 1510
St. Louis, MO 63117
314-863-4747
800-783-8006
Fax: 314-863-4749
awillet@ccfa.org
www.crohnscolitisfoundation.org

Each of the more than 40 chapters of the Crohn's & Colitis Foundation are either staffed or volunteer chapters in order to bring the Foundation's work and mission to local communities through support services, education and research programs, advocacy and quality care.

Steve Skodak, Development Director
Maura Breen, Chairman

Kentucky

1919 **Kentucky Chapter of Crohn's & Colitis Foundation of America**
PO Box 573
Prospect, KY 40059
646-623-2620
kentucky@ccfa.org
www.crohnscolitisfoundation.org

Each of the more than 40 chapters of the Crohn's & Colitis Foundation are either staffed or volunteer chapters in order to bring the Foundation's work and mission to local communities through support services, education and research programs, advocacy and quality care.

Jenny Silberisen, Community Development Manager
Maura Breen, Chairman

Louisiana

1920 **Louisiana/Mississippi Chapter of Crohn's & Colitis Foundation of America**
8019 Maple Street
New Orleans, LA 70175
504-861-3433
866-382-2232
Fax: 504-861-3466
lams@ccfa.org
www.crohnscolitisfoundation.org

Each of the more than 40 chapters of the Crohn's & Colitis Foundation are either staffed or volunteer chapters in order to bring the Foundation's work and mission to local communities through support services, education and research programs, advocacy and quality care.

David Lee Thomas, Executive Director
Maura Breen, Chairman

Maryland

1921 **Maryland/South Delaware Chapter of Crohn's & Colitis Foundation of America**
10400 Little Patuxent Parkway, Suite 270
Columbia, MD 21044
443-276-0861
800-618-5583
Fax: 443-276-0865
maryland@ccfa.org
www.crohnscolitisfoundation.org

Each of the more than 40 chapters of the Crohn's & Colitis Foundation are either staffed or volunteer chapters in order to bring the Foundation's work and mission to local communities through support services, education and research programs, advocacy and quality care.

Allison Coffey, Community Development Director
Maura Breen, Chairman

Massachusetts

1922 **New England Chapter of Crohn's & Colitis Foundation of America**
280 Hillside Avenue
Needham, MA 02494
781-449-0324
800-314-3459
Fax: 781-449-0325
ne@ccfa.org
www.crohnscolitisfoundation.org

Each of the more than 40 chapters of the Crohn's & Colitis Foundation are either staffed or volunteer chapters in order to bring the Foundation's work and mission to local communities through support services, education and research programs, advocacy and quality care.

Craig Comins, Regional Executive Director
Maura Breen, Chairman

Michigan

1923 **Michigan Chapter of Crohn's & Colitis Foundation of America**
31313 Northwestern Highway, Suite 204
Farmington Hills, MI 48334
248-737-0900
Fax: 248-737-0904
michigan@ccfa.org
www.crohnscolitisfoundation.org

Each of the more than 40 chapters of the Crohn's & Colitis Foundation are either staffed or volunteer chapters in order to bring the Foundation's work and mission to local communities through support services, education and research programs, advocacy and quality care.

Anthonie Burke, Community Development Director
Maura Breen, Chairman

Minnesota

1924 **Minnesota/Dakotas Chapter of Crohn's & Colitis Foundation of America**
1885 University Avenue W, Suite 355
Saint Paul, MN 55104
651-917-2424
888-422-3266
Fax: 651-917-2425
minnesota@ccfa.org
www.crohnscolitisfoundation.org

Each of the more than 40 chapters of the Crohn's & Colitis Foundation are either staffed or volunteer chapters in order to bring the Foundation's work and mission to local communities through support services, education and research programs, advocacy and quality care.

Danielle L Baxter, Executive Director
Ruby Lanoux, Development Coordinator

Mississippi

1925 **Louisiana/Mississippi Chapter of Crohn's & Colitis Foundation of America**
8019 Maple Street
New Orleans, LA 70175
504-861-3433
866-382-2232
Fax: 504-861-3466
lams@ccfa.org
www.crohnscolitisfoundation.org

Each of the more than 40 chapters of the Crohn's & Colitis Foundation are either staffed or volunteer chapters in order to bring the Foundation's work and mission to local communities through support services, education and research programs, advocacy and quality care.

David Lee Thomas, Executive Director
Maura Breen, Chairman

Missouri

1926 **Saint Louis Chapter of Crohn's & Colitis Foundation of America**
8420 Delmar Boulevard, Suite 303
Saint Louis, MO 63124
314-997-4466
Fax: 314-991-8756
missouri@ccfa.org
www.crohnscolitisfoundation.org

Each of the more than 40 chapters of the Crohn's & Colitis Foundation are either staffed or volunteer chapters in order to bring the Foundation's work and mission to local communities through support services, education and research programs, advocacy and quality care.

Charise Cross, Owner
Maura Breen, Chairman

Crohn's Disease / State Agencies & Support Groups

New Jersey

1927 New Jersey Chapter of Crohn's & Colitis Foundation of America
45 Wilson Avenue
Manalapan, NJ 07726
732-786-9960
Fax: 732-786-9964
newjersey@ccfa.org
www.crohnscolitisfoundation.org

Each of the more than 40 chapters of the Crohn's & Colitis Foundation are either staffed or volunteer chapters in order to bring the Foundation's work and mission to local communities through support services, education and research programs, advocacy and quality care.

Rosemarie Golombos, Executive Director
Maura Breen, Chairman

New Mexico

1928 Southwest Chapter of Crohn's & Colitis Foundation of America
8098 Via de Negocio, Suite 201
Scottsdale, AZ 85254
480-246-3676
877-259-2104
Fax: 480-246-3679
southwest@ccfa.org
www.crohnscolitisfoundation.org

Each of the more than 40 chapters of the Crohn's & Colitis Foundation are either staffed or volunteer chapters in order to bring the Foundation's work and mission to local communities through support services, education and research programs, advocacy and quality care.

Cindy Sorensen, Regional Edu. & Support Manager
Maura Breen, Chairman

New York

1929 Central New York Chapter of Crohn's & Colitis Foundation of America
2117 Buffalo Rd Suite 299
Rochester, NY 14624
585-617-4771
smassaro@ccfa.org
www.crohnscolitisfoundation.org

Each of the more than 40 chapters of the Crohn's & Colitis Foundation are either staffed or volunteer chapters in order to bring the Foundation's work and mission to local communities through support services, education and research programs, advocacy and quality care.

Maura Breen, Chairman

1930 Fairfield/Westchester Chapter of Crohn's & Colitis Foundation of America
200 Bloomingdale Road
White Plains, NY 10605
914-328-2874
Fax: 914-328-2946
westfield@ccfa.org
www.crohnscolitisfoundation.org

Each of the more than 40 chapters of the Crohn's & Colitis Foundation are either staffed or volunteer chapters in order to bring the Foundation's work and mission to local communities through support services, education and research programs, advocacy and quality care.

Russell P Girolamo, Board President
Maura Breen, Chairman

1931 Greater New York Chapter of Crohn's & Colitis Foundation of America
386 Park Avenue S, 14th Floor
New York, NY 10016
212-679-1570
Fax: 212-679-3567
newyork@ccfa.org
www.crohnscolitisfoundation.org

Each of the more than 40 chapters of the Crohn's & Colitis Foundation are either staffed or volunteer chapters in order to bring the Foundation's work and mission to local communities through support services, education and research programs, advocacy and quality care.

Stacy Clark, Manager
Maura Breen, Chairman

1932 Long Island Chapter of Crohn's & Colitis Foundation of America
585 Stewart Avenue, Suite 580
Garden City, NY 11530
516-222-5530
Fax: 516-222-5535
longisland@ccfa.org
www.crohnscolitisfoundation.org

Each of the more than 40 chapters of the Crohn's & Colitis Foundation are either staffed or volunteer chapters in order to bring the Foundation's work and mission to local communities through support services, education and research programs, advocacy and quality care.

Edda Ramsdell, Executive Director
Maura Breen, Chairman

1933 Rochester Chapter of Crohn's & Colitis Foundation of America
2117 Buffalo Rd Suite 299
Rochester, NY 14624
585-617-4771
smassaro@ccfa.org
www.crohnscolitisfoundation.org

Each of the more than 40 chapters of the Crohn's & Colitis Foundation are either staffed or volunteer chapters in order to bring the Foundation's work and mission to local communities through support services, education and research programs, advocacy and quality care.

Adam Urbanski, President
Maura Breen, Chairman

1934 Upstate/Northeast New York Chapter of Crohn's & Colitis Foundation of America
103 Patroon Dr 10
Guilderland, NY 12084
518-608-5069
upstateny@ccfa.org
www.crohnscolitisfoundation.org

Each of the more than 40 chapters of the Crohn's & Colitis Foundation are either staffed or volunteer chapters in order to bring the Foundation's work and mission to local communities through support services, education and research programs, advocacy and quality care.

Linda Winston, Community Development Director
Maura Breen, Chairman

1935 Western New York Chapter of Crohn's & Colitis Foundation of America
651 Deleware Ave Suite 214
Buffalo, NY 14202
716-362-1232
jpetri@ccfa.org
www.crohnscolitisfoundation.org

Each of the more than 40 chapters of the Crohn's & Colitis Foundation are either staffed or volunteer chapters in order to bring the Foundation's work and mission to local communities through support services, education and research programs, advocacy and quality care.

Jeanenne Petri, Development Manager
Maura Breen, Chairman

North Carolina

1936 Carolinas Chapter of Crohn's & Colitis Foundation of America
2424 N. Davidson St, Suite 110
Charlotte, NC 28205
704-332-1611
Fax: 704-332-1612
jgolombos@ccfa.org
www.crohnscolitisfoundation.org

Each of the more than 40 chapters of the Crohn's & Colitis Foundation are either staffed or volunteer chapters in order to bring the Foundation's work and mission to local communities through support services, education and research programs, advocacy and quality care.

Joanne Colombos, National Walk Specialist
Maura Breen, Chairman

Crohn's Disease / State Agencies & Support Groups

Ohio

1937 Central Ohio Chapter of Crohn's & Colitis Foundation of America
5500 Frantz Rd, Suite 155
Dublin, OH 43017
614-889-6060
Fax: 614-889-6655
centralohio@ccfa.org
www.crohnscolitisfoundation.org

Each of the more than 40 chapters of the Crohn's & Colitis Foundation are either staffed or volunteer chapters in order to bring the Foundation's work and mission to local communities through support services, education and research programs, advocacy and quality care.

Deborah Shub, Community Development Director
Maura Breen, Chairman

1938 Northeast Ohio Chapter of Crohn's & Colitis Foundation of America
4700 Rockside Rd. #425
Independence, OH 44131
216-524-7700
866-345-2232
Fax: 216-524-7701
neohio@aol.com
www.crohnscolitisfoundation.org

Each of the more than 40 chapters of the Crohn's & Colitis Foundation are either staffed or volunteer chapters in order to bring the Foundation's work and mission to local communities through support services, education and research programs, advocacy and quality care.

Lesley Hoover, Chapter Director
Maura Breen, Chairman

1939 Southwest Ohio Chapter of Crohn's & Colitis Foundation of America
8 Triangle Park Drive, Suite 800
Cincinnati, OH 45246
513-772-3550
877-283-7513
Fax: 513-772-7599
swohio@ccfa.org
www.crohnscolitisfoundation.org

Each of the more than 40 chapters of the Crohn's & Colitis Foundation are either staffed or volunteer chapters in order to bring the Foundation's work and mission to local communities through support services, education and research programs, advocacy and quality care.

Jenny Southers, Development Director
Rachel Miller, Take Steps Walk Mgr

Oklahoma

1940 Oklahoma Chapter of Crohn's & Colitis Foundation of America
4504 E 67th Street, Suite 125
Tulsa, OK 74136
918-523-8540
Fax: 918-523-8560
oklahoma@ccfa.org
www.crohnscolitisfoundation.org

Each of the more than 40 chapters of the Crohn's & Colitis Foundation are either staffed or volunteer chapters in order to bring the Foundation's work and mission to local communities through support services, education and research programs, advocacy and quality care.

Mike Gramm, Board of Trustees
Maura Breen, Chairman

Pennsylvania

1941 Pennsylvania/Delaware Valley Chapter of Crohn's & Colitis Foundation of America
367 E Street Road
Trevose, PA 19053
215-396-9100
888-340-4744
Fax: 215-396-1170
philadelphia@ccfa.org
www.crohnscolitisfoundation.org

Each of the more than 40 chapters of the Crohn's & Colitis Foundation are either staffed or volunteer chapters in order to bring the Foundation's work and mission to local communities through support services, education and research programs, advocacy and quality care.

Barbara Berman, Executive Director
Maura Breen, Chairman

1942 Western Pennsylvania Chapter of Crohn's & Colitis Foundation of America
300 Penn Center Suite 401
Pittsburgh, PA 15235
412-823-8272
877-823-8272
Fax: 412-823-8276
wpawv@ccfa.org
www.crohnscolitisfoundation.org

Each of the more than 40 chapters of the Crohn's & Colitis Foundation are either staffed or volunteer chapters in order to bring the Foundation's work and mission to local communities through support services, education and research programs, advocacy and quality care.

600 Members

Susan Kukic, Executive Director

South Carolina

1943 South Carolina Chapter of Crohn's & Colitis Foundation of America
2424 N. Davidson St, Suite 110
Charlotte, NC 28205
704-332-1611
877-632-1611
Fax: 704-332-1612
carolinas@ccfa.org
www.crohnscolitisfoundation.org

Each of the more than 40 chapters of the Crohn's & Colitis Foundation are either staffed or volunteer chapters in order to bring the Foundation's work and mission to local communities through support services, education and research programs, advocacy and quality care.

Kelli King, Development Director
Maura Breen, Chairman

Tennessee

1944 Tennessee Chapter of Crohn's & Colitis Foundation of America
95 White Bridge Rd Suite 209
Nashville, TN 37205
615-356-0444
866-814-2232
Fax: 615-356-0445
tennessee@ccfa.org
www.crohnscolitisfoundation.org

Each of the more than 40 chapters of the Crohn's & Colitis Foundation are either staffed or volunteer chapters in order to bring the Foundation's work and mission to local communities through support services, education and research programs, advocacy and quality care.

Steve Wallace, Executive Director
Maura Breen, Chairman

Texas

1945 Houston-Gulf Coast/South Texas Chapter of Crohn's & Colitis Foundation of America
5120 Woodway, Suite 8008
Houston, TX 77056
713-752-2232
800-785-2232
Fax: 713-572-2433
infohouston@ccfa.org
www.crohnscolitisfoundation.org

Each of the more than 40 chapters of the Crohn's & Colitis Foundation are either staffed or volunteer chapters in order to bring the Foundation's work and mission to local communities through support services, education and research programs, advocacy and quality care.

Charles Weiss, IOM, Executive Director
Maura Breen, Chairman

Crohn's Disease / Libraries & Resource Centers

1946 **North Texas Chapter of Crohn's & Colitis Foundation of America**
12801 N Central Expressway Suite 270
Dallas, TX 75243
972-386-0607
Fax: 972-386-0509
ntexas@ccfa.org
www.crohnscolitisfoundation.org

Each of the more than 40 chapters of the Crohn's & Colitis Foundation are either staffed or volunteer chapters in order to bring the Foundation's work and mission to local communities through support services, education and research programs, advocacy and quality care.

Teresa Sheffield, Executive Director
Maura Breen, Chairman

Washington

1947 **Washington State Chapter of Crohn's & Colitis Foundation of America**
9 Lake Bellevue Drive, Suite 203
Bellevue, WA 98005
425-451-8455
Fax: 425-451-1708
northwest@ccfa.org
www.crohnscolitisfoundation.org

Each of the more than 40 chapters of the Crohn's & Colitis Foundation are either staffed or volunteer chapters in order to bring the Foundation's work and mission to local communities through support services, education and research programs, advocacy and quality care.

Linda Huse, Regional Director
Maura Breen, Chairman

Wisconsin

1948 **Wisconsin Chapter of Crohn's & Colitis Foundation of America**
1126 S 70th Street, Suite S210A
West Allis, WI 53214
414-475-5520
877-586-5588
Fax: 414-475-5502
wisconsin@ccfa.org
www.crohnscolitisfoundation.org

Each of the more than 40 chapters of the Crohn's & Colitis Foundation are either staffed or volunteer chapters in order to bring the Foundation's work and mission to local communities through support services, education and research programs, advocacy and quality care.

Tyler Hillstrom, Executive Director
Maura Breen, Chairman

Libraries & Resource Centers

1949 **National Digestive Diseases Information Clearinghouse (NDDIC)**
NIH
2 Information Way
Bethesda, MD 20892
301-654-3810
800-891-5389
Fax: 703-738-4929
nddic@info.niddk.nih.gov
www.digestive.niddk.nih.gov

The National Institute of Diabetes and Digestive and Kidney Diseases conducts and supports research on many of the most serious diseases affecting public health. The Institute supports much of the clinical research on the diseases of internal medicine and related subspecialty fields as well as many basic science disciplines.

Griffin P. Rodgers, MD, Director
Gregory G. Germino, MD, Deputy Director
Kathy Kranzfelder, Communications Director

Research Centers

1950 **Crohn's & Colitis Foundation**
733 Third Avenue, Ste 510
New York, NY 10017
800-932-2423
info@crohnscolitisfoundation.org
www.crohnscolitisfoundation.org

The mission of the Crohn's & Colitis Foundation is to cure and prevent Crohn's disease and ulcerative colitis through research and improve the quality of life of children and adults affected by these digestive diseases through education and support.

John Crosson, Chair
Michael Osso, President & CEO
Robert Territo, COO/CFO

1951 **Kranser Center for Inflammatory Bowel Disease Research**
Hahnemann University
Broad & Vine Streets
Philadelphia, PA 19102
215-762-8618
Fax: 215-762-1998

Research into the causes and treatments of ulcerative colitis and Crohn's disease.

Harris Clearfield, Director

Conferences

1952 **IFFGD Professional Symposia**
3015 Dunes W Boulevard, Suite 512
Mount Pleasant, SC 29466
414-964-1799
www.iffgd.org

Aimed at promoting education and awareness among professionals from multiple disciplines who treat gastrointestinal disorders and incontinence.

April

Nancy J. Norton, Founder
Ceciel T. Rooker, President

Web Sites

1953 **Crohn's & Colitis Foundation**
733 Third Avenue, Ste 510
New York, NY 10017
800-932-2423
info@crohnscolitisfoundation.org
www.crohnscolitisfoundation.org

The mission of the Crohn's & Colitis Foundation is to cure and prevent Crohn's disease and ulcerative colitis through research and improve the quality of life of children and adults affected by these digestive diseases through education and support.

John Crosson, Chair
Michael Osso, President & CEO
Robert Territo, COO/CFO

1954 **Health Answers Education Sudler-WPP Health Practice**
700 Dresher Road
Horsham, PA 19044
215-442-9010
www.healthanswers.com

HealthAnswers offers a breadth of services in medical education, sales force training, patient support, solutions, professional promotion and consumer solutions.

Mike Hudnall, CEO

Book Publishers

1955 **Crohn's Disease and Ulcerative Colitis Fact Book**
Crohn's & Colitis Foundation
733 Third Avenue, Ste 510
New York, NY 10017
800-932-2423
info@crohnscolitisfoundation.org
www.crohnscolitisfoundation.org

Written in layman's language, this first, complete guide is helpful in understanding and coping with inflammatory bowel diseases.

John Crosson, Chair
Michael Osso, President & CEO
Robert Territo, COO/CFO

1956 Gastrointestinal Diseases and Disorders Sourcebook, 4th Edition
Omnigraphics
615 Griswold Street, Ste 520
Detroit, MI 48226
610-461-3548
800-234-1340
Fax: 800-875-1340
contact@omnigraphics.com
www.omnigraphics.com

Basic consumer health information including celiac disease, Crohn's disease, diarrhea, hernias, irritable bowel syndrome and ulcers.

816 pages
ISBN: 0-780816-50-3

1957 Let's Talk About Going to the Hospital
Rosen Publishing Group's PowerKids Press
29 E 21st Street
New York, NY 10010
212-777-3017
800-237-9932
Fax: 888-436-4643
rosenpub@tribeca.ios.com
www.rosenpublishing.com

If a child has to check into the hospital, chances are he or she is already upset about being ill. Knowing how a hospital functions and what the procedures are, such as when family members can visit, will help in what is already a stressful situation. Grades K-5.

24 pages
ISBN: 0-823950-36-0

Roger Rosen, President

1958 Managing Your Child's Crohn's Disease or Ulcerative Colitis
Crohn's & Colitis Foundation
733 Third Avenue, Ste 510
New York, NY 10017
212-685-3440
800-932-2423
Fax: 212-779-4098
info@crohnscolitisfoundation.org
www.crohnscolitisfoundation.org

This first full-length book on Crohn's disease and ulcerative colitis, specifically targeted for parents of children and teenagers, includes topics on cause and diagnosis, treatment, surgery, hospitalization, diet and nutrition, school and social issues, and resources for the patient.

$16.95 Members

John Crosson, Chair
Michael Osso, President & CEO
Robert Territo, COO/CFO

1959 New People...Not Patients: a Source Book for Living with Bowel Disease
Crohn's & Colitis Foundation
733 Third Avenue, Ste 510
New York, NY 10017
212-685-3440
800-932-2423
Fax: 212-779-4098
info@crohnscolitisfoundation.org
www.crohnscolitisfoundation.org

This book contains the essential information you need to help you cope with Crohn's disease and ulcerative colitis after you leave the doctor's office.

John Crosson, Chair
Michael Osso, President & CEO
Robert Territo, COO/CFO

1960 Treating IBD
Crohn's & Colitis Foundation
733 Third Avenue, Ste 510
New York, NY 10017
212-685-3440
800-932-2423
info@crohnscolitisfoundation.org
www.crohnscolitisfoundation.org

A patient's guide to the medical and surgical management of Inflammatory Bowel Disease, this book gives information on treating Crohn's disease and ulcerative colitis, including drug therapies, advances in nutritional care, and recently developed surgical alternatives.

John Crosson, Chair
Michael Osso, President & CEO
Robert Territo, COO/CFO

1961 Understanding Crohn Disease and Ulcerative Colitis
University Press of Mississippi
3825 Ridgewood Road, Unit 9
Jackson, MS 39211
601-432-6205
800-737-7788
Fax: 601-432-6246
press@ihl.state.ms.us
www.upress.state.ms.us

For patients and caregivers, an overview of the nature and treatments of inflammatory bowel disease.

128 pages Paperback
ISBN: 1-578062-03-9

Leila W Salisbury Director

Magazines

1962 Take Charge
Crohn's & Colitis Foundation
733 Third Avenue, Ste 510
New York, NY 10017
800-932-2423
info@crohnscolitisfoundation.org
www.crohnscolitisfoundation.org

Offers the most up-to-date information on IBD research, treatment, and legislative initiatives for patients, families, and friends.

John Crosson, Chair
Michael Osso, President & CEO
Robert Territo, COO/CFO

Newsletters

1963 Under the Microscope
Crohn's & Colitis Foundation
733 Third Avenue, Ste 510
New York, NY 10017
800-932-2423
800-932-2423
Fax: 212-779-4098
info@crohnscolitisfoundation.org
www.crohnscolitisfoundation.org

Includes a variety of relevant information such as information on new research projects, clinical trials, conference notes, and breaking news about partnerships and grants.

John Crosson, Chair
Michael Osso, President & CEO
Robert Territo, COO/CFO

Pamphlets

1964 Coping with Crohn's and Colitis is Tough
Crohn's & Colitis Foundation
733 Third Avenue, Ste 510
New York, NY 10017
800-932-2423
800-932-2423
Fax: 212-779-4098
info@crohnscolitisfoundation.org
www.crohnscolitisfoundation.org

Offers information on the Crohn's and Colitis Association. Also offers factual information and statistics on the diseases.

John Crosson, Chair
Michael Osso, President & CEO
Robert Territo, COO/CFO

Crohn's Disease / Pamphlets

1965 **Crohn's Disaese and Ulcerative Colitis: Emotional Factors Q & A**
Crohn's & Colitis Foundation
733 Third Avenue, Ste 510
New York, NY 10017
800-932-2423
800-932-2423
Fax: 212-779-4098
info@crohnscolitisfoundation.org
www.crohnscolitisfoundation.org

Answers some of the most commonly asked questions about ileitis and colitis and the role of emotional factors in their cause and course.

John Crosson, Chair
Michael Osso, President & CEO
Robert Territo, COO/CFO

1966 **Crohn's Disease & Ulcerative Colitis: A Guide for Teachers & Other Personnel**
Crohn's & Colitis Foundation
733 Third Avenue, Ste 510
New York, NY 10017
800-932-2423
800-932-2423
Fax: 212-779-4098
info@crohnscolitisfoundation.org
www.crohnscolitisfoundation.org

John Crosson, Chair
Michael Osso, President & CEO
Robert Territo, COO/CFO

1967 **Crohn's Disease & Ulcerative Colitis: A Guide for Parents**
Crohn's & Colitis Foundation
733 Third Avenue, Ste 510
New York, NY 10017
800-932-2423
info@crohnscolitisfoundation.org
www.crohnscolitisfoundation.org

Answers questions about IBD in children, providing information on early signs, growth and developments, treatments and special problems in school.

John Crosson, Chair
Michael Osso, President & CEO
Robert Territo, COO/CFO

1968 **Diagnosing and Managing IBD**
Crohn's & Colitis Foundation
733 Third Avenue, Ste 510
New York, NY 10017
800-932-2423
info@crohnscolitisfoundation.org
www.crohnscolitisfoundation.org

Reviews the work of the Crohn's and Colitis Foundation of America, sponsors a nationally recognized research program, which seeks to improve treatment, and ultimately find the cure for inflammatory bowel disease.

John Crosson, Chair
Michael Osso, President & CEO
Robert Territo, COO/CFO

1969 **Facts About Inflammatory Bowel Disease**
Crohn's & Colitis Foundation
733 Third Avenue, Ste 510
New York, NY 10017
800-932-2423
800-932-2423
Fax: 212-779-4098
info@crohnscolitisfoundation.org
www.crohnscolitisfoundation.org

Offers information on the illness and answers the most frequently asked questions about Crohn's Disease. Also includes a glossary of IBD terms.

John Crosson, Chair
Michael Osso, President & CEO
Robert Territo, COO/CFO

1970 **IBD & Me: Activity Book for Kids!**
Crohn's & Colitis Foundation
733 Third Avenue, Ste 510
New York, NY 10017
800-932-2423
800-932-2423
Fax: 212-779-4098
info@crohnscolitisfoundation.org
www.crohnscolitisfoundation.org

Information and activities for children ages 8-12 to learn about IBD.

John Crosson, Chair
Michael Osso, President & CEO
Robert Territo, COO/CFO

1971 **Intestinal Complications**
Crohn's & Colitis Foundation
733 Third Avenue, Ste 510
New York, NY 10017
800-932-2423
800-932-2423
Fax: 212-779-4098
info@crohnscolitisfoundation.org
www.crohnscolitisfoundation.org

Medical facts and complications from surgery.

John Crosson, Chair
Michael Osso, President & CEO
Robert Territo, COO/CFO

1972 **Managing Inflammatory Bowel Disease as a Young Adult**
Crohn's & Colitis Foundation
733 Third Avenue, Ste 510
New York, NY 10017
800-932-2423
800-932-2423
Fax: 212-779-4098
info@crohnscolitisfoundation.org
www.crohnscolitisfoundation.org

Offers important information on these illnesses to children and teens.

John Crosson, Chair
Michael Osso, President & CEO
Robert Territo, COO/CFO

Cryptorchidism / Web Sites

Description

1973 CRYPTORCHIDISM

Synonyms: Cryptorchidy, Cryptorchism

Covers these related disorders: Ectopic (maldescended) testes, True undescended testes

Involves the following Biologic System(s):

Renal and Urologic Disorders

Cryptorchidism is characterized by failure of one or both testes to descend into the pouch-like structure known as the scrotum. The testes are the paired, oval-shaped glands that produce the male reproductive cells (sperm). Early during male fetal growth, the testes develop within the abdomen near the kidneys. The testes then descend into the scrotum through a tubular canal that passes through lower muscular layers of the abdominal wall (inguinal canal). In males with cryptorchidism, one or both testes fail to complete their descent into the scrotum. Undescended testes that are located along the proper path of descent are known as true undescended testes, whereas those that have completed their descent through the inguinal canal yet have become located in areas other than the scrotum are referred to as ectopic or maldescended testes.

In most cases, one testis is affected (unilateral cryptorchidism); however, both testes may fail to descend (bilateral cryptorchidism) in up to 30 percent of affected male infants. In many cases, undescended testes may move down into the scrotum before one year of age. However, testes that fail to spontaneously descend during the first year of life typically fail to develop properly, may decrease in size, and have decreased numbers of reproductive cells. Without treatment, affected males are at an increased risk of infertility; malignant tumor development in affected testes during the third or fourth decade of life; or pain, swelling, and, in some cases, localized areas of tissue loss (necrosis).

Treatment of cryptorchidism often includes early surgery to relocate undescended testes into the scrotum (i.e., orchiopexy) and to correct inguinal hernias, which typically occur in association with true undescended testes and ectopic testes. Inguinal hernias are characterized by bulging of portions of the intestine into the inguinal canal. Surgical correction of cryptorchidism is typically recommended in the first years of life to help improve proper testicular development and fertility in adulthood.

Cryptorchidism affects about three and a half percent of full-term male newborns and increases in incidence in newborns who are born before 37 weeks of pregnancy (preterm). The condition may occur as an isolated abnormality or, in some cases, due to or in association with a number of different underlying syndromes or conditions.

Government Agencies

1974 NIH/ Eunice Kennedy Shriver National Institute of Child Health & Human Development
P.O. Box 3006
Rockville, MD 20847
800-370-2943
Fax: 866-760-5947
www.nichd.nih.gov

Conducts and supports research on topics related to the health of children, adults, families and populations. Some of these topics include: developmental disabilities, growth and development, infant death, reproductive health and birth defects.

Diana W. Bianchi, Director
Alison Cernich, PhD, Deputy Director

National Associations & Support Groups

1975 American Academy of Pediatrics
345 Park Blvd
Itasca, IL 60143
800-433-9016
Fax: 847-434-8000
mcc@aap.org
www.aap.org

The American Academy of Pediatrics and its member pediatricians are committed to the attainment of optimal physical, mental and social health and well-being for all infants, children, adolescents, and young adults.

Lynn Olson, PhD, VP, Research
Mark Del Monte, JD, CEO/Executive VP
Vera Tait, MD, FAAP, Chief Medical Officer

1976 Genetic Alliance
426400 Woodfield Road, Ste 189
Damascus, MD 20872
202-966-5557
Fax: 202-966-8553
info@geneticalliance.org
www.geneticalliance.org

World's leading nonprofit health advocacy organization committed to transforming health through genetics and promoting an environment of openness centered on the health of individuals, families, and communities.

Sharon Terry, CEO
Ruth Child, CFO
Natasha Bonhomme, Chief Strategy Officer

1977 March of Dimes Foundation
1550 Crystal Drive, Ste 1300
Arlington, VA 22202
888-663-4637
www.marchofdimes.org

March of Dimes help moms have full-term pregnancies and research the problems that threaten the health of babies. The March of Dimes also acts globally: sharing best practices in perinatal health and helping improve birth outcomes where the needs are the most urgent.

Stacey D. Stewart, President
Alan Brogdon, SVP/COO/Board Officer
Rahul Gupta, MD, SVP & Chief Medical/Health Officer

1978 NIH/National Institute of Mental Health
6001 Executive Blvd, Rm 6200, MSC 9663
Bethesda, MD 20892
866-615-6464
Fax: 301-443-4279
TTY: 301-443-8431
nimhinfo@nih.gov
www.nimh.nih.gov

The mission of NIMH is to transform the understanding and treatment of mental illnesses through basic and clinical research, paving the way for prevention, recovery, and cure.

Joshua A. Gordon, MD, PhD, Director
Shelli Avenevoli, PhD, Deputy Director

Web Sites

1979 European Society for Pediatric Urology
www.espu.org
025-503-8690
Fax: 025-503-2546
president@espu.org
www.espu.org

A nonprofit society whose main purpose is to promote pediatric urology, appropriate practice, education as well as exchanges between practitioners involved in the treatment of genito urinary disorders in children.

Ramnath Subramaniam, Chairman, Educational Committee
Gianantonio Manzoni, President
Dr. Emilio Merlini, Treasurer

1980 National Center for Biotechnology Information
National Library of Medicine, 8600 Rockville Pike
Bethesda, MD 20894   888-346-3656
info@ncbi.nlm.nih.gov
www.ncbi.nlm.nih.gov

NCBI's mission is to develop new information technologoes to aid in the understanding of fundamental molecular and genetic processes that control health and disease.

Patricia Flatley Brennan, RN, PhD, Director
James Ostell, PhD, Executive Secretary

1981 Online Mendelian Inheritance in Man
McKusick-Nathans Institue of Genetic Medicine-JHU
Baltimore, MD 21205   www.omim.org

This database is a catalog of human genes and genetic disorders.

Ada Hamosh, MD, Scientific Director

Description

1982 CUSHING'S SYNDROME

Synonyms: Cushing's basophilism, Hyperadrenocorticism, Pituitary basophilism

Involves the following Biologic System(s):

Endocrinologic Disorders

Cushing's syndrome refers to a condition characterized by excessive levels of the corticosteroid hormone, cortisol, in the blood. Cortisol is produced in the outer portion (cortex) of the adrenal glands in response to the secretion of adrenocorticotropic hormone (ACTH; corticotropin). ACTH stimulates the growth of the adrenal cortex and thus the production of cortisol. Cushing's syndrome may be caused by a variety of factors including tumors of the adrenal glands or the pituitary gland, tumors of certain other organs, and excessive intake of corticosteroid drugs. In the very young, Cushing's syndrome occurs in more girls than boys by a ratio of approximately three to one.

Because cortisol assists in the metabolism of fat, protein, and glucose, many characteristic symptoms and findings associated with this disorder are related to the levels and distribution of body fat. For example, children with Cushing's syndrome may be somewhat obese with very full cheeks, a reddish moonface appearance, double chin, and excessive fat deposits on the back of the neck. In addition, the adrenal glands may be stimulated to secrete excessive amounts of other hormones that are converted in the liver to testosterone and estrogen. Overproduction of these androgenic hormones may result in symptoms such as increased amounts of hair on the face and trunk (hypertrichosis), the development of acne, and deepening of the voice as well as other masculine traits. Other findings that may appear over a period of time include elevated blood pressure (hypertension), kidney (renal) stones, and increased vulnerability to infection. Children with Cushing's syndrome may also experience growth delays or may not achieve height (short stature). However, those children who develop masculinization symptoms may reach average or above average height. Older children may experience a delay in onset of puberty and develop purplish stretch marks (striae) on the abdomen, breasts, hips, and thighs. In addition, their skin may become thin and fragile, leading to easy tissue injury. Affected children may develop headaches and weakness, experience increasing difficulty with school work, or become depressed or experience other emotional disturbances.

Treatment of Cushing's syndrome is dependent upon the underlying cause. If the disease results from a benign or malignant tumor or enlargement of the adrenal gland, surgical removal of the tumor or the adrenal gland (adrenalectomy) may be advised. A tumor in the pituitary gland may either be surgically removed or treated with radiation. Subsequent management of surgical or other procedures often includes appropriate hormone replacement therapy. Cushing's syndrome associated with prolonged or excessive intake of corticosteroids may be reversed by a monitored and gradual (tapered) withdrawal of the medication. Other treatment is symptomatic and supportive.

National Associations & Support Groups

1983 American Academy of Pediatrics
345 Park Blvd
Itasca, IL 60143
800-433-9016
Fax: 847-434-8000
mcc@aap.org
www.aap.org

The American Academy of Pediatrics and its member pediatricians are committed to the attainment of optimal physical, mental and social health and well-being for all infants, children, adolescents, and young adults.

Lynn Olson, PhD, VP, Research
Mark Del Monte, JD, CEO/Executive VP
Vera Tait, MD, FAAP, Chief Medical Officer

1984 American Association of Clinical Endocrinologists
245 Riverside Avenue, Suite 200
Jacksonville, FL 32202
904-353-7878
www.aace.com

A professional medical organization aimed at promoting the quality of clinical endocrinology research and improving the knowledge base for the diagnosis, prognosis, prevention and treatment of health conditions through the advancement and application of innovative methods.

1985 Cushing's Support and Research Foundation
csrf.net
404-791-5483
csrf.net

CSRF aims to provide information and support for Cushing's Disease and Cushing's Syndrome patients and their families; to increase awareness in the medical community and the general public about Cushing's Disease and Cushing's Syndrome; and to be a resource for information and support to health care professionals.

Louise Pace, Founder
Leslie Edwin, President
Elissa Kline, Treasurer & Director

1986 Human Growth Foundation
997 Glen Cove Avenue, Suite 5
Glen Head, NY 11545
800-451-6434
Fax: 516-671-4055
hgfl@hgfound.org
www.hgfound.org

A voluntary, nonprofit organization whose mission is to help children and adults with disorders of growth and growth hormones through research, education, support and advocacy. The foundation is dedicated to helping medical science to better understand the process of growth. It is composed of concerned parents and friends of children and adults with growth problems and interested health professionals.

Joel Steelman, MD, President
Emily Germain-Lee, MD, Vice President

1987 National Adrenal Diseases Foundation
PO Box 95149
Newton, MA 02495
847-726-9010
info@nadf.us
www.nadf.us

A nonprofit organization dedicated to providing support, information and education to individuals having Addison's disease as well as related diseases such as Cushing's Syndrome and Congenital Adrenal Hyperplasia. Promotes early diagnosis and treatment, and sponsors support groups and offers a quarterly newsletter, educational materials and access to a library of related information.

Kalina Warren, Co-President
Erin A. Foley-Moudry, MPH, Co-President
Lori Engler, Executive Director

Web Sites

1988 Cushing's Support and Research Foundation
csrf.net
404-791-5483
csrf.net

CSRF aims to provide information and support for Cushing's Disease and Cushing's Syndrome patients and their families; to increase awareness in the medical community and the general public about Cushing's Disease and Cushing's Syndrome; and to be a resource for information and support to health care professionals.

Louise Pace, Founder
Leslie Edwin, President
Elissa Kline, Treasurer & Director

Cushing's Syndrome / Book Publishers

Book Publishers

1989 Endocrine & Metabolic Disorders Sourcebook 3rd Edition
Keith Jones, author

Omnigraphics
615 Griswold Street, Ste 520
Detroit, MI 48226

610-461-3548
800-234-1340
Fax: 800-875-1340
contact@omnigraphics.com
www.omnigraphics.com

Basic information for the lay person about pancreatic and insulin-related disorders such as pancreatitis, diabetes and hypoglycemia; adrenal gland disorders such as Cushing's syndrome, Addison's disease and congenital adrenal hyperplasia; pituitary gland disorders such as growth hormone deficiency, acromegaly and pituitary tumors; and thyroid disorders such as hypothyroidism, Grave's disease, Hashimoto's disease and goiter.

560 pages hardcover
ISBN: 0-780815-43-8

1990 Let's Talk About Going to the Hospital
Rosen Publishing Group's PowerKids Press
29 E 21st Street
New York, NY 10010

212-777-3017
800-237-9932
Fax: 888-436-4643
rosenpub@tribeca.ios.com
www.rosenpublishing.com

If a child has to check into the hospital, chances are he or she is already upset about being ill. Knowing how a hospital functions and what the procedures are, such as when family members can visit, will help in what is already a stressful situation. Grades K-5.

24 pages
ISBN: 0-823950-36-0

Roger Rosen, President

Newsletters

1991 NADF News
National Adrenal Diseases Foundation
505 Northern Boulevard
Great Neck, NY 11021

516-487-4992
nadfsupport@nadf.us
www.nadf.us

Provides support and information to those living with adrenal diseases.

Kalina Warren, President
Melanie G. Wong, Executive Director
Edward A. Wong, Executive Director's Assistant

Description

1992 CYSTIC FIBROSIS

Synonyms: CF, Mucoviscidosis

Involves the following Biologic System(s):
Respiratory Disorders

Cystic fibrosis (CF) is an inherited multisystem disorder that results in the abnormal production of mucus by almost all exocrine glands, causing obstruction of those glands and ducts. Glands of the respiratory and reproductive systems as well as pancreatic glands and sweat glands are affected. CF is considered one of the most common autosomal recessive disorders affecting Caucasians. Cystic fibrosis occurs in approximately one in 2,500 to 3,000 Caucasian infants and about one in 17,000 African-American infants. It is considered extremely rare in other populations. The disorder results from abnormal changes (mutations) of a gene on the long arm (q) of chromosome 7 (7q31.2). More than 400 different mutations of the CF gene have been identified.

In infants, children, and adults with cystic fibrosis, mucus-secreting glands within the air passages of the lungs (bronchi) produce unusually thick secretions, clogging and obstructing the airways and promoting the growth of certain bacteria. As a result, affected individuals may experience chronic obstruction and infection of the airways. In addition, the pancreas lacks sufficient digestive enzymes to break down food materials (malabsorption). Other exocrine gland abnormalities may also be present. For example, the sweat glands produce secretions containing abnormally high levels of salt; glands of the neck of the uterus (cervix) in affected females may produce abnormally increased, thickened secretions of mucus; and certain ducts of the male reproductive system (e.g., epididymis, ductus [vas] deferens, seminal vesicles) may be absent (atretic).

During the first or second day of life, some newborns with cystic fibrosis may experience bloating of the abdomen (abdominal distension), vomiting (emesis), and abnormal blockage of the lower region of the small intestine with meconium (meconium ileus). Meconium is the thick, sticky, darkish green material that accumulates in the fetal intestines and forms a newborn's first stools. Infants with cystic fibrosis also usually fail to grow and gain weight at the expected rate (failure to thrive). Additional symptoms and findings may include abnormally decreased muscle mass; a protruding abdomen; and loose, foul-smelling stools that contain an excessive amount of fat (steatorrhea). Children with cystic fibrosis often have respiratory abnormalities including wheezing; a chronic cough that may be accompanied by gagging and vomiting; recurrent inflammation of the air passages (bronchiolitis); and an increased susceptibility to lower respiratory infections (e.g., pneumonia). Affected adolescents may experience abnormally slow growth and delayed sexual development (i.e., average delay of two years); in addition, affected males may be infertile due to lack of sperm development (azoospermia). As the disease progresses, individuals with cystic fibrosis tend to experience increasingly severe respiratory abnormalities that may result in life-threatening complications.

Cystic fibrosis may be diagnosed based upon characteristic physical findings (e.g., chronic obstructive pulmonary disease, exocrine pancreatic insufficiency), specialized laboratory tests (e.g., sweat testing), and a positive family history (including DNA analysis). The treatment of cystic fibrosis is symptomatic and supportive and includes early intervention, ongoing monitoring, preventive measures, the use of certain medications, and other specialized treatment techniques. Approaches to treatment may include physical therapy, a high protein, high calorie diet, pancreatic enzyme replacement therapy, vitamin supplementation, specialized respiratory therapy, medications to help clean mucus from the airways and prevent or treat respiratory infections (e.g., antibiotic therapy). Median survival is about 44 years of age.

National Associations & Support Groups

1993 American Academy of Pediatrics
345 Park Blvd
Itasca, IL 60143
800-433-9016
Fax: 847-434-8000
mcc@aap.org
www.aap.org

The American Academy of Pediatrics and its member pediatricians are committed to the attainment of optimal physical, mental and social health and well-being for all infants, children, adolescents, and young adults.

Lynn Olson, PhD, VP, Research
Mark Del Monte, JD, CEO/Executive VP
Vera Tait, MD, FAAP, Chief Medical Officer

1994 American Lung Association
55 W. Wacker Drive, Suite 1150
Chicago, IL 60601
800-586-4872
info@lung.org
www.lung.org

The American Lung Association fights lung disease in all its forms, with special emphasis on asthma, tobacco control and environmental health. The American Lung Association is funded with contributions from the public, along with gifts and grants from corporations, foundations and government agencies. The association achieves its many successes through the work of thousands of committed volunteers and staff.

Harold P. Wimmer, National President & CEO
Albert Rizzo, MD, Chief Medical Officer
Sue Swan, Chief Development Officer

1995 Cystic Fibrosis Foundation
4550 Montgomery Avenue, Suite 1100 N
Bethesda, MD 20814
800-344-4823
info@cff.org
www.cff.org

The mission of CF Foundation is to assure the development of means to cure and control CF and to improve the quality of life for those with the disease. It funds medical research and care programs which are improving the length and quality of life for people with cystic fibrosis.

Michael Boyle, MD, President & CEO

1996 Cystic Fibrosis Research, Inc.
1731 Embarcadero Road, Ste 210
Palo Alto, CA 94303
650-665-7576
855-237-4669
Fax: 650-561-4074
cfri@cfri.org
www.cfri.org

Cystic Fibrosis Research Inc.'s mission is to fund CF research, to provide educational and personal support and to spread awareness of Cystic Fibroses, a life threatening genetic disease.

Sri Vaeth, Executive Director
Sabine Brants, Programs & Outreach Associate
William Hult, Board President

1997 Genetic Alliance
426400 Woodfield Road, Ste 189
Damascus, MD 20872
202-966-5557
Fax: 202-966-8553
info@geneticalliance.org
www.geneticalliance.org

World's leading nonprofit health advocacy organization committed to transforming health through genetics and promoting an environment of openness centered on the health of individuals, families, and communities.

Cystic Fibrosis / Libraries & Resource Centers

Sharon Terry, CEO
Ruth Child, CFO
Natasha Bonhomme, Chief Strategy Officer

1998 March of Dimes Foundation
1550 Crystal Drive, Ste 1300
Arlington, VA 22202
888-663-4637
www.marchofdimes.org

March of Dimes help moms have full-term pregnancies and research the problems that threaten the health of babies. The March of Dimes also acts globally: sharing best practices in perinatal health and helping improve birth outcomes where the needs are the most urgent.

Stacey D. Stewart, President
Alan Brogdon, SVP/COO/Board Officer
Rahul Gupta, MD, SVP & Chief Medical/Health Officer

Libraries & Resource Centers

1999 National Digestive Diseases Information Clearinghouse (NDDIC)
NIH
2 Information Way
Bethesda, MD 20892
301-654-3810
800-891-5389
Fax: 301-907-8906
nddic@info.niddk.nih.gov
www.digestive.niddk.nih.gov

The National Institute of Diabetes and Digestive and Kidney Diseases conducts and supports research on many of the most serious diseases affecting public health. The Institute supports much of the clinical research on the diseases of internal medicine and related subspecialty fields as well as many basic science disciplines.

Griffin P. Rodgers, MD, Director
Gregory G. Germino, MD, Deputy Director
Kathy Kranzfelder, Communications Director

Research Centers

Alabama

2000 Gregory Fleming James Cystic Fibrosis Center
790 McCallum Basic Health Sciences Bldg
Birmingham, AL 35294
205-934-9640
Fax: 205-934-7593
sorscher@uab.edu
www.cfcenter.uab.edu

Eric J Sorscher MD, Director

Arizona

2001 Cystic Fibrosis Center: Phoenix Children's Hospital
1919 E Thomas Road
Phoenix, AZ 85016
602-546-0985
888-908-5437
www.phxchildrens.com

Wayne J Morgan MD, Director

California

2002 Brian Wesley Ray Cystic Fibrosis Center
San Bernadino County Medical Center
780 E Gilbert Street
San Bernardino, CA 92415
909-387-8111
Gerald Greene, MD

2003 Children's Hospital of Los Angeles
4650 W Sunset Boulevard
Los Angeles, CA 90027
323-660-2450
888-631-2452
webmaster@chla.usc.edu
www.chla.org

Elisabeth L Raab, Contact

2004 Children's Hospital of Orange County: Department of Pulmonology - Cystic Fibrosis
1201 W. La Veta Ave
Orange, CA 92868
714-997-3000
Fax: 714-516-4348
www.choc.org

Ivan I Kirov

2005 Children's Hospital: Pediatric Pulmonary Center
747 52nd Street
Oakland, CA 94609
510-428-3259
Kevan McCarten-Gibbs

2006 Cystic Fibrosis Center: Cedars-Sinai Medical Center
8700 Beverly Boulevard, N Tower, Fourth Floor
Los Angeles, CA 90048
800-233-2771
Fax: 310-423-1402

2007 Cystic Fibrosis Center: University of California at San Francisco
8700 Beverly Boulevard, N Tower, Fourth Floor
San Francisco, CA 94143
800-233-2771
Fax: 310-423-1402

2008 Cystic Fibrosis Research, Inc.
1731 Embarcadero Road, Ste 210
Palo Alto, CA 94303
650-665-7576
855-237-4669
Fax: 650-561-4074
cfri@cfri.org
www.cfri.org

Cystic Fibrosis Research Inc.'s mission is to fund CF research, to provide educational and personal support and to spread awareness of Cystic Fibroses, a life threatening genetic disease.

Sri Vaeth, Executive Director
Sabine Brants, Programs & Outreach Associate
William Hult, Board President

2009 Cystic Fibrosis and Pediatric Respiratory Diseases Center
University of California at Davis
2315 Stockton Boulevard
Sacramento, CA 95817
800-282-3284
Fax: 916-734-0491
children@ucdavis.edu
www.ucdmc.ucdavis.edu/children

2010 Kaiser Permanente Medical Center
Kaiser Permanente Oakland Medical Center
280 W MacArthur Boulevard
Oakland, CA 94611
510-752-1000
www.kaiserpermanente.org

Linda C Armstrong

2011 Memorial Miller Children's Hospital Cystic Fibrosis Center
2801 Atlantic Avenue
Long Beach, CA 90806
562-933-2000
Fax: 562-933-8539
www.memorialcare.org

Barry Arbuckle, President

2012 Pulmonary Care and Cystic Fibrosis Center
Lucille Packard Children's Hospital
725 Welch Road, Suite 350
Palo Alto, CA 94304
650-497-8000
Fax: 650-498-4209
www.lpch.org

Deals with children's breathing in all its aspects.

Richard B Boss MD, Director

2013 Stanford CF Center
Packard Children's Hospital At Stanford
730 Welch Road
Palo Alto, CA 94304
650-725-9302
cfcenter.stanford.edu

Kim Standridge, Manager

Cystic Fibrosis / Research Centers

Colorado

2014 Denver Children's Hospital
1056 E 19th Avenue
Denver, CO 80218
303-837-2680
Fax: 303-837-2924

Martin A Koyle, Pulmonology Pediatrics

Connecticut

2015 University of Connecticut Health Center
282 Washington Street
Hartford, CT 06106
860-545-9440
Fax: 860-545-9445

Karen Daigle MD, Pediatric Pulmonary Division

2016 Yale University Cystic Fibrosis Research Center
School of Medicine Department
333 Cedar Street, PO Box 208064
New Haven, CT 06520
203-785-4648
Fax: 203-688-7864
www.med.yale.edu

Respiratory Medicine in the Department of Pediatrics at Yale University and Yale-New Haven Hospital is a multi-disiplinary section that has developed considerably since the early 90's and continues to develop and refine its clinical and research activities. We have also reorganized our Cystic Fibrosis Care Center, increased the clinical research activities pertaining to the care of CF patients and organized a number of CF family group meetings to dissimenate new knowledge of care of patients.

Marie E Egan MD, Cystic Fibrosis Center

Florida

2017 CF & Pediatric Pulmonary Disease Center
University of Florida
PO Box 100225
Gainesville, FL 32610
352-392-3261
Fax: 352-392-0821

Eric L Olson, Director Adult CF Program

2018 Cystic Fibrosis Center - All Children's Hospital
801 6th Street S
St Petersburg, FL 33701
727-898-7451
800-456-4543

2019 Miami Children's Hospital, Division of Pulmonology
3100 SW 62nd Street
Miami, FL 33155
305-666-6511
800-432-6837
www.mch.com

Deise Granado-Villar, Director

2020 Pulmonary Wellness Program
Orlando Regional Medical Center
92 W. Miller St.
Orlando, FL 32806
321-841-4194
www.arnoldpalmerhospital.org

Our staff is trained in all diagnostic tests as well as a variety of Cystic Fibrosis therapies, including therapy vest treatments. Our professionals will work with your child and your family to create a more enriched diet including vitamin and enzyme supplements to help counteract the effects of Cystic Fibrosis. We also administer antibiotics in pill form as well as intravenously and through medicated vapors.

Georgia

2021 Department of Pediatrics, Medical College of Georgia
1120 15th Street, BT-1852
Augusta, GA 30912
706-721-2809
Fax: 706-721-7311
www.georgiahealth.edu

Tracy Chavous, Manager

2022 Egleston Cystic Fibrosis Center: Departmen t of Pediatrics
Emory University
201 Dowman
Atlanta, GA 30322
404-727-6123
Fax: 404-727-4828
www.emory.edu

Daniel Caplan MD, Director

Illinois

2023 Cystic Fibrosis Center: Children's Memoria l Hospital
Northwestern University
2300 N Children's Plaza, #43
Chicago, IL 60614
773-880-4382

Susanna McColley MD, Head, Pulmonary Medicine

2024 Loyola University Medical Center/ Department of Pediatrics
2160 S First Avenue
Maywood, IL 60153
708-216-8563
888-584-7888
www.loyolamedicine.org

Sergio L Gonzalez, Pediatric Pulmonary

2025 Park Ridge, Cystic Fibrosis Center
Advocate Lutheran General Hospital
1775 Dempster Street
Park Ridge, IL 60068
423-622-6848
800-242-5662
www.parkridgemedicalcenter.com

Darell Moore, CEO

2026 Saint Francis Medical Center Specialty Clinics, CF Center
Hillcrest Medical Plaza
530 NE Glen Oak Avenue
Peoria, IL 61637
309-655-7171
www.childrenshospitalofil.org

2027 University of Chicago Children's Hospital, Department of Pediatrics
University of Chicago Hospitals and Clinics
5721 S Maryland Avenue
Chicago, IL 60637
773-702-6176
888-824-0200
Fax: 773-702-4753
www.uchicagokidshospital.org

Provides comprehensive, innovative medical care to children of all social and economic backgrounds. Dedicated to enhancing the health and wellness through patient care, education and research into the causes and cure of childhood diseases. Immediate access to the full resources of The University of Chicago Hospitals and to faculty of the division of Biological Sciences. The hospital sees children from the Chicago area, the Midwest and around the world who have the most complex medical problems.

Shannon Smith, Manager

Indiana

2028 Cystic Fibrosis and Chronic Pulmonary Disease Clinic
Saint Joseph's Regional Medical Center
801 E LaSalle Avenue
South Bend, IN 46617
574-239-6126
800-206-0879
Fax: 574-472-6067

2029 Riley Cystic Fibrosis Center
Riley Hospital for Children
702 Barnhill Drive
Indianapolis, IN 46202
317-274-5000

Cystic Fibrosis / Research Centers

Iowa

2030 **Blank Children's Hospital: Department of Pulmonology**
1212 Pleasant Street, Suite 300
Des Moines, IA 50309
515-241-8336
Fax: 515-241-6465

Carissa Schneider, Manager

2031 **University of Iowa Hospitals & Clinics**
Allergy and Pulmonary Division: Cystic Fibrosis Ct
200 Hawkins Drive
Iowa City, IA 52242
319-356-1616
www.uihealthcare.org

Ronald Strauss, Director

Kansas

2032 **Kansas University Medical Center: Department of Pulmonology**
Department of Pediatrics
3901 Rainbow Boulevard
Kansas City, KS 66160
913-588-5000
TDD: 913-588-7963
www.kumc.edu

Raymond Franklin, Manager

2033 **Via Christi Specialty Clinics: Cystic Fibrosis, Adult and Pediatrics**
St Joseph Campus
3600 E Harry Street
Wichita, KS 67218
316-689-5735
Fax: 316-291-7963

Kentucky

2034 **University of Kentucky: Pediatric Pulmonary Medicine**
Department of Pediatrics
740 S Limestone
Lexington, KY 40536
859-323-6426
Fax: 859-257-7706

Michael I Anstead MD, Director

Louisiana

2035 **Louisiana State University Health Sciences Center**
Department of Pediatrics: Critical Care/Pulmonary
200 Henry Clay Avenue
New Orleans, LA 70118
504-896-2723
Fax: 504-896-2720
dhoppe@lsuhsc.edu

Robert Hopkins MD, Professor of Clinical Pediatrics

Maine

2036 **Central Maine Medical Center**
Department of Pediatrics
300 Main Street
Lewiston, ME 04240
207-795-0111
Fax: 207-797-7241
www.cmmc.org

Focuses special attention on the services that it provides to Cystic Fibrosis patients. In microbiology, for example, the lab employs a number of techniques supporting the special needs of CF patients. The CMMC pathology departments's chemistry section provides quantitative sweat analysis for the diagnosis of patients to other laboratories in the region, thereby assisting in diagnosis.

Marly L Larrabee, Special Interst: Cystic Fibrosis

2037 **Eastern Maine Medical Center: Cystic Fibrosis Center**
489 State Street
Bangor, ME 04401
207-973-7000
www.emmc.org

Shad Deering

2038 **Pediatric Cystic Fibrosis Center**
Maine Medical Center: Dept. of Resp. Care
22 Bramhall Street
Portland, ME 04102
207-662-0111
Fax: 207-775-6024
www.mmc.org

Services offered: pediatric pulmonary consultation, flexible bronchoscopy of the pediatric airway, full pediatric and infant pulmonary function testing, including exercise testing, bronchopulmonary challenge, and accredited sleep lab. Also offered, full-time inpatient consultation service for neonates through adolescence, a bimonthly Cystic Fibrosis Clinic, and a biweekly outpatient pulmonary clinic.

Maryland

2039 **John Hopkins Children's Hospital**
Division of Pulmonary
600 N Wolfe Street
Baltimore, MD 21287
410-955-5089
Fax: 410-955-0761
www.hopkinschildren.org

Edward Chambers, Administrator

Massachusetts

2040 **Baystate Medical Center**
280 Chestnut Street
Springfield, MA 01199
413-794-0000
Fax: 413-794-7408
www.baystatehealth.com

Gordon M Saperia, Chief, Pediatric Pulmonary

2041 **Children's Hospital Boston**
Pulmonary and Critical Care Unit
300 Longwood Avenue
Boston, MA 02115
617-355-6000
800-355-7944
Fax: 617-724-9948
TTY: 617-730-0152
www.childrenshospital.org

James Mandell, CEO
Sandra Fenwick, President & COO
Dick Argys, Chief Administrative Officer

2042 **Massachusetts General Hospital**
Pulmonary and Critical Care Unit
55 Fruit Street
Boston, MA 02114
617-726-2000
TDD: 617-724-8800
www.umass.org

Mass General aims to deliver the very best health care in a safe, compassionate environment; to advance that care through innovative research and education; and to improve the health and well-being of the diverse communities we serve.

Cathy Minehan, Chair
Peter Slavin, President & Trustee
Ronald Kleinman, Physician-in-Chief, Hospital for Ch

2043 **Tufts New England Medical Center Floating Hospital for Children**
Division of Pulmonary, Critical Care and Sleep
755 Washington Street
Boston, MA 02111
617-636-5000
www.tuftsmedicalcenter.org

Joseph Campanelli, Chairman
Richard Freeman, Chair, Organ Transplantation
Brien Barnewolt, Chairman, Chief of Emergency Medici

Cystic Fibrosis / Research Centers

Michigan

2044 Butterworth Hospital, Cystic Fibrosis Center
426 Michigan Street NE
Grand Rapids, MI 49503   616-454-1509
John Schuen, MD, Director

2045 Children's Hospital of Michigan Cystic Fibrosis Care, Teaching & Resource
Children's Hospital of Michigan
3901 Beaubien Boulevard
Detroit, MI 48201   313-745-5437
                           888-362-2500
                           www.childrensdmc.org
Herman Gray, Jr., President
Shawn Levitt, COO
Joseph Scallen, Jr., VP Finance

2046 Cystic Fibrosis Center/Pediatric Pulmonary and Sleep Medicine
330 Barclay Avenue NE, Suite 200
Grand Rapids, MI 49503   616-391-2125
                                Fax: 616-391-2131
John Schuen, MD, Director
Susan Millard, MD, Director

2047 Kalamazoo Center for Medical Studies
Michigan State University
1000 Oakland Drive
Kalamazoo, MI 49008   269-337-4400
                             www.kcms.msu.edu/
Robert Carter, CEO
Peter Ziemkowski, Family Practitioner

2048 University of Michigan, Cystic Fibrosis Center
1500 E. Medical Center Drive
Ann Arbor, MI 48109   734-936-4000
                             800-962-3555
                             Fax: 734-936-7635
           www.med.umich.edu/mott/cysticfibrosiscenter/

The University of Michigan Cystic Fibrosis Program mission is to provide excellence and leadership in patient care, services, research and education.
Samya Z. Nasr, MD, Director, Cystic Fibrosis Center

Minnesota

2049 Minnesota Cystic Fibrosis Center
Fairview University Medical Center
420 Delaware Street SE, MMC 742
Minneapolis, MN 55455   612-624-0962
                               Fax: 612-624-0696
                               www.med umn.edu/peds/cfcenter/

Comprehensive and coordinated care approach that is designed to prevent and slow the rate of disease progression. Since 1961, this care approach used by the University of Minnesota physicians has led to an increase in the average age of survival for patients with Cystic Fibrosis from 2 1/2 to 39 years.
Warren E. Regelmann, Co-Director, Ped CF Program
Carlye Tomczyk, CF Educator

Mississippi

2050 University of Mississippi Medical Center
2500 N State Street
Jackson, MS 39216   601-984-5820
                           www.umc.edu/
Thomas H. Fortner, Chief Public Affairs and Communicat
John E. Hall, Associate Vice Chancellor for Resea
James M. Lightsey, Chief Financial Officer

Missouri

2051 Children's Mercy Hospital, University of Missouri
Kansas City School of Medicine
2401 Gillham Road
Kansas City, MO 64108   816-234-3000
                               866-512-2168
                               TTY: 816-234-3816
                               webmaster@cmh.edu
                               www.childrensmercy.org
Ed Connolly, Jr., Chairman
Randall O'Donnell, President, CEO, and Director

2052 Cystic Fibrosis, Pediatric Pulmonary and Pediatric Gastrointestinal Center
Cardinal Glennon Memorial Hospital for Children
1465 S Grand
Saint Louis, MO 63104   314-577-5600
Anthony J Rejent, MD, Center Director

2053 University of Missouri-Columbia Cystic Fibrosis Center
University of Missouri/Department of Child Health
404 Keene Street
Columbia, MO 65203   573-875-9000
                            www.muhealth.org

University of Missouri Children's Hospital seves patients from every county in Missouri. With over 30 pediatric subspecialties, a pediatric ICU, adolescent unit and child life therapy, MU Children's Hospital is mid-Missouri's largest and most comprehensive pediatric health care facility.
James Ross, Chief Executive Officer
Anita Larsen, Chief Operating Officer
Jeri Doty, Chief Planning Officer

2054 Washington University Cystic Fibrosis Center
Saint Louis Children's Hospital
1 Childrens Place
Saint Louis, MO 63110   314-454-2694
                               888-503-2237
                               Fax: 314-454-2515
           peds.wustl.edu/pulmonary/CysticFibrosisCenter/tabid/
Thomas Ferkol, MD, Director

Nebraska

2055 University of Nebraska at Omaha Pediatric Pulmonary/Cystic Fibrosis Center
42nd and Emile
Omaha, NE 68198   402-559-6400
                         Fax: 402-559-7062
                         www.unmc.edu/pediatrics/
John W. Sparks, MD, Chairman

Nevada

2056 Children's Lung Specialists
3820 Meadows Lane
Las Vegas, NV 89107   702-598-4411
                             Fax: 702-598-1988
Kris Hissung, Manager
Brian Woo, Pediatric Pulmonologist

New Hampshire

2057 New Hampshire Cystic Fibrosis Care and Teaching Center
Dartmouth Hitchcock Medical Center
1 Medical Center Drive
Lebanon, NH 03756   603-650-6244
                           Fax: 603-650-8601
William Boyle Jr, MD, Director

Cystic Fibrosis / Research Centers

New Jersey

2058 Monmouth Medical Center, Cystic Fibrosis & Pediatric Pulmonary Center
300 Second Avenue
Long Branch, NJ 07740
732-222-5200
Fax: 908-222-4472
http://www.saintbarnabas.com/hospitals/monmouth_medi
Carol Foster, Manager

2059 New Jersey Medical School
185 S Orange Avenue
Newark, NJ 07103
973-972-4871
800-482-3627
Fax: 201-982-7597
njms.umdnj.edu

Robert Wieder, Director

New Mexico

2060 University of New Mexico School of Medicine
2400 Tucker Ne 4th Fl
Albuquerque, NM 87131
505-272-0518
Fax: 505-272-0329
somadmin@salud.unm.edu
www.som.unm.edu

The School of Medicine is committed to remain a world-leading institution in three equally valued and inter-related missions of patient care, education, and research.

Paul Roth, MD, Dean, School of Medicine
David Sklar, Emergency Medicine

New York

2061 Albany Medical College Pediatric Pulmonary & Cystic Fibrosis Center
Department of Pediatrics
47 New Scotland Avenue
Albany, NY 12208
518-262-6008
Fax: 518-262-6472
www.amc.edu

Vincent P Verdile, Exec Vp

2062 Armond V. Mascia CF Center
NY Medical College
Munger Pavillion, Room 106
Valhalla, NY 10595
914-493-7585
Fax: 914-594-4336
pedpulm@nymc.edu
www.nymc.edu/depthome/peds/pedspulm/CFCenter.asp

The mission of our CF Center is to enable our patients with cystic fibrosis to fulfill their maximal potential with the support of their families by providing state-of-the-art clinical care.~ To further this goal, our center is dedicated to the education of all patients, their families, healthcare professionals and the community, the pursuit of rigorous research and continuous quality improvement.

Allen Dozer, MD, Director

2063 CF & Pediatric Pulmonary Care Center
Mt. Sinai School of Medicine
5th Avenue at 100th Street
New York, NY 10029
212-241-7788
Richard J Bonforte, MD, Director

2064 CF, Pediatric Pulmonary & GI Center
Saint Vincent's Hospital & Medical Center of NY
36 7th Avenue
New York, NY 10011
212-604-8895
Joan DeGelie-Germana, MD, Director

2065 Children's Lung and Cystic Fibrosis Center
Children's Hospital of Buffalo
219 Bryant Street
Buffalo, NY 14222
716-878-7524
Fax: 716-888-3945
www.wchob.org/services/services_display.asp?PType=L

Services for infants, children and teenagers with cystic fibrosis and other chronic respiratory conditions.

Drucy Borowitz, MD, Director
David Sheehan, Medical Director

2066 Long Island College Hospital
350 Henry Street
Brooklyn, NY 11201
718-780-1071
www.futurenurselich.org/

Robert Giusti, MD, Director

2067 Pediatric Pulmonary Center
Babies Hospital & Columbia Presbyterian Med Center
750 East Adams Street
Syracuse, NY 13210
315-464-6323
Fax: 212-805-6103

Ran D Anbar, Medical Director
Mary Ann Russo, Dietician
Karen Watkins, Secretary

2068 Schneider Children's Hospital of Long Island
Albert Einstein College of Medicine
New Hyde Park, NY 14040
716-470-3250
Jack D Gorvoy, MD

2069 State University Hospital/Upstate Medical University
750 E Adams Street
Syracuse, NY 13210
315-464-8668
877-464-5540
Fax: 315-464-5158
www.upstate.edu/uh/

David Smith, President
Steven Brady, SVP Finance & Administration
Teresa Wagner, CIO

2070 University of Rochester Medical Center
Strong Memorial Hospital/Division of Pediatrics
601 Elmwood Avenue
Rochester, NY 14642
585-275-2838
www.urmc.rochester.edu/

Karen Z Voter, MD, Director

North Carolina

2071 Duke University Medical Center/ CF Center
350 Hanes House
Durham, NC 10236
919-684-3364
Fax: 919-684-2292
www.pediatrics.duke.edu

Marc Majure, MD, Director

2072 UNC CF Center
Department of Pediatrics
509 Burnett-Womack Building
Chapel Hill, NC 27599
919-966-1055
Gerald W Fernald, MD, Director

North Dakota

2073 Saint Alexius Medical Center/CF Center
311 N 9th Street
Bismarck, ND 58501
701-224-7500
Fax: 701-224-7560

Allan Stillerman, MD, Director

Cystic Fibrosis / Research Centers

Ohio

2074 Case Western Reserve University Cystic Fibrosis Center
2101 Adelbert Road
Cleveland, OH 44106
216-844-3264
Fax: 216-844-5916

Pamela B Davis, MD, Director

2075 Columbus Children's Hospital, Cystic Fibrosis Center
700 Childrens Drive
Columbus, OH 43205
614-722-4766
Fax: 614-722-4755

Karen S McCoy, MD, Director

2076 Lewis H. Walker, MD, Cystic Fibrosis Center
Children's Hospital Medical Center of Akron
1 Perkins Square
Akron, OH 44308
330-543-1000
ywebmaster@chmca.org
www.alchonchildrens.org

Part of the Robert T Stone Respiratory Center, one of six centers in the state of Ohio providing comprehensive care for patients who suffer from this disease. Caused by a defective gene, CF is characterized by a thick, sticky mucus in the lungs, intestines and other excretory organs that leads to severe respiratory and digestive problems.

Robert T Stone, MD, Director

2077 Pediatric Pulmonary Center
Children's Medical Center
1 Childrens Plaza
Dayton, OH 45404
937-641-3376
Fax: 937-463-5390

Michael E Steffan, MD, Director

2078 University of Cincinnati College of Medicine/Division of Pediatrics
Children's Hospital Medical Center
3333 Burnet Avenue
Cincinnati, OH 45229
513-636-0180
800-344-2462
TTY: 513-636-4900
www.cincinnatichildrens.org

Edward Donovan, Director, Child Policy Rsch Ctr

Oklahoma

2079 University of Oklahoma Cystic Fibrosis Center
940 NW 13th Street
Oklahoma City, OK 73106
405-271-6390
Fax: 405-271-7866

John E Grunow, MD, Director

Oregon

2080 Oregon Health Sciences Unit
3181 S.W. Sam Jackson Park Rd.
Portland, OR 97239
503-220-3405
Michael Heinrich, Research Director

Pennsylvania

2081 CF Center at The Children's Hospital of Philadelphia
34th & Civic Center Boulevard
Philadelphia, PA 19104
215-590-1000
Fax: 215-590-4298

The CF center consists of pediatric and adult specialists who collaborate to provide multidisciplinary care for CF patients through their entire life span. The interdisciplinary health care team forms the core of our Centerand meets regularly to assess the clinical, educational and psychosocial needs of the family and to plan and evaluate the care provided. The CF center also provides educational programs for health professionals and reserch focused on improved treatments.

Aaron A Chambers, Director
LeeAnn Webb CRNP, Coordinator
Thelma Gary BA, Clinical Research Specialist

2082 Cystic Fibrosis Center at Polyclinic Medical Center
Polyclinic Medical Center
2601 N 3rd Street
Harrisburg, PA 17110
717-782-4105
800-334-1007
Fax: 717-782-2597

Muttiah Ganeshananthan, MD, Director

2083 Pediatric Pulmonary and Cystic Fibrosis Center
Saint Christopher's Hospital For Children
Erie Avenue at Front Street
Philadelphia, PA 19134
215-427-5183

Daniel Schidlow, MD, Director

2084 University of Pittsburgh Cystic Fibrosis Center/Children's Hospital
3705 5th Avenue
Pittsburgh, PA 15213
412-692-7280
www.wpahs.org

Julie R Fuchs, Director

Rhode Island

2085 Rhode Island Hospital, Cystic Fibrosis Center
CDC-APC
593 Eddy Street
Providence, RI 02903
401-444-5171
Fax: 401-444-6115

Edwin N Forman, Director

South Carolina

2086 CF Center/Medical University of South Carolina
158 Rutledge Avenue
Charleston, SC 29425
803-792-3561
Fax: 803-792-0732

Robert Baker, MD, Director

South Dakota

2087 Sioux Valley Hospital, South Dakota Cystic Fibrosis Center
1100 S Euclid Avenue, PO Box 5039
Sioux Falls, SD 57117
605-333-1000
Rodney Parry, MD, Director

Tennessee

2088 Memphis Cystic Fibrosis Center
LeBonheur Children's Medical Center
One Children's Plaza
Memphis, TN 38103
901-572-5222
Fax: 901-572-3337

Robert Schoumacher, MD, Director

2089 Pediatric Pulmonary Medicine
2200 Children's Way
Nashville, TN 37232
615-936-1000
Fax: 615-343-7727
www.vanderbiltchildrens.com

Texas

2090 CF Center, Pulmonary Section
Baylor College of Medicine/Dept. of Pediatrics
1 Baylor Plaza
Houston, TX 77030
713-798-4945
Peter W Hiatt, MD, Director

Cystic Fibrosis / Conferences

2091 Cook-Ft. Worth Medical Center, CF Center
801 7th Avenue
Fort Worth, TX 76104
817-885-4207
Fax: 817-885-1090

James C Cunningham, MD, Director

2092 Cystic Fibrosis Care, Teaching and Research Center
Children's Medical Center
1935 Medical District
Dallas, TX 75235
214-456-7000
www.portal.childrens.com

Claude Prestidge, MD, Director

2093 Cystic Fibrosis-Lung Disease Center Santa Rosa Children's Hospital
519 W Houston Street
San Antonio, TX 78207
210-228-2058
Fax: 210-224-2132

2094 Tri-Services Military CF Center
Brooke Army Medical Center
3851 Roger Brooke Drive
Fort Sam Houston, TX 78234
210-916-3400
www.grmc.amed d.army.nil/

Stephen Inscore, LTC, MC, Director

Utah

2095 University of Utah Intermountain Cystic Fibrosis Center
50 N Medical Drive
Salt Lake City, UT 84132
801-581-2121
Fax: 801-581-2177
www.healthcare.utah.edu

Jeffrey R Saffle, Center Co-Director

Vermont

2096 Medical Center Hospital of Vermont
Cystic Fibrosis Center
50 Timber Lane
South Burlington, VT 05403
802-862-5529
Fax: 802-864-0294

Donald Swartz, MD, Director

Virginia

2097 Cystic Fibrosis Center/University of Virginia Health System
Department of Pediatrics
1215 Lee Street
Charlottesville, VA 22908
434-924-0211
Fax: 434-243-6618
www.healthsystem.virginia.edu

Comprehensive care for children and adults with cystic fibrosis.

Deborah K Froh, MD, Director Children's Program
Mark Robbins, MD, Director Adult Program

2098 Cystic Fibrosis Program of the Medical College of Virginia
9000 Stony Point Parkway
Richmond, VA 23235
804-786-9445
Fax: 804-560-7347

David Draper, MD, Director

2099 Eastern Virginia Medical Center
Children's Hospital of The King's Daughters
601 Childrens Lane
Norfolk, VA 23507
757-668-7243
Fax: 804-668-9767

William C Owen, Director

Washington

2100 University of Washington CF Center
4800 Sand Point Way NE
Seattle, WA 98105
206-987-2174
Fax: 206-987-2024
depts.washington.edu

Rohit K Khosla, Director

West Virginia

2101 West Virginia University Cystic Fibrosis Center
PO Box 9214
Morgantown, WV 26506
304-293-7332
Fax: 304-293-4341

Marybeth Hummel, Director

2102 West Virginia University Mountain State Cystic Fibrosis Center
PO Box 9214
Morgantown, WV 26506
304-293-7332
800-982-8242
Fax: 304-293-1216
kmoffett@hsc.wvu.edu

Marybeth Hummel, Director

Wisconsin

2103 Medical College of Wisconsin Cystic Fibrosis Center
Children's Hospital of Wisconsin
9000 W Wisconsin Avenue, MS #777A
Milwaukee, WI 53226
414-266-2412
Fax: 414-266-2653

William G Raasch, Director

2104 University of Wisconsin-Madison Cystic Fibrosis/Pulmonary Center
Clinical Science Center H4/430
600 Highland Avenue
Madison, WI 53792
608-263-6100
Fax: 608-263-0440
www.uwppc.org

Carl J Getto, Director

Conferences

2105 National Cystic Fibrosis Education Conference
Cystic Fibrosis Research Institute
1731 Embarcadero Road, Ste 210
Palo Alto, CA 94303
650-665-7576
855-237-4669
Fax: 650-561-4074
cfri@cfri.org
www.cfri.org

Brings together adults with cystic fibrosis, caregivers, experts and researchers for three days where a variety of CF topics are explored through presentations, panel discussions and support groups.

Sri Vaeth, Executive Director
Sabine Brants, Programs & Outreach Associate
William Hult, Board President

Audio Video

2106 Living with Cystic Fibrosis
Aquarius Health Care Videos
5 Powderhouse Lane, PO Box 1159
Sherborn, MA 1770
508-651-2963
888-440-2963
Fax: 508-650-4216
info@aquariusproductions.com
www.aquariusproductions.com

People diagnosed with this genetic disorder are surviving longer than ever. Many patients live well into their thirties and beyond. This film looks at the hope that current research offers to those with cystic fibrosis, their caregivers and families.

Donna Kaufman

Web Sites

2107 American Lung Association of the City of New York
21 West 38th Street, 3rd Floor
New York, NY 10018
212-889-3370
800-LUN-USA
Fax: 212-889-3375
www.lungusa.org

The American Lung Association fights lung disease in all its forms, with special emphasis on asthma, tobacco control and environmental health. The American Lung Association is funded by contributions from the public, along with gifts and grants from corporations, foundations and government agencies. The association achieves its many successes through the work of thousands of committed volunteers and staff.

2108 CF Index of Online Resources
vmsb.csd.mu.edu/~541lukasr/cystic.html

vmsb.csd.mu.edu/~541lukasr/cystic.html

2109 CF Web
cf-web.mit.edu

cf-web.mit.edu

2110 Healing Well
www.healingwell.com

admin@healingwell.com
www.healingwell.com

An online health resource guide to medical news, chat, information and articles, newsgroups and message boards, books, disease-related web sites, medical directories, and more for patients, friends, and family coping with disabling diseases, disorders, or chronic illnesses.

Peter Waite, Founder & CEO

2111 Onhealth
www.onhealth.com

www.onhealth.com

Provides over 50 links to information on cystic fibrosis.

2112 Online Mendelian Inheritance in Man
McKusick-Nathans Institue of Genetic Medicine-JHU
Baltimore, MD 21205
www.omim.org

This database is a catalog of human genes and genetic disorders.

Ada Hamosh, MD, Scientific Director

Book Publishers

2113 Alex: The Life of a Child Rutledge Press

Frank Deford, author

7625 Empire Drive
Florence, KY 41042
800-634-7064
Fax: 800-248-4724

Paperback
ISBN: 1-558535-52-7

2114 Cystic Fibrosis
Franklin Watts
90 Old Sherman Turnpike
Danbury, CT 06816
203-797-3500
Fax: 203-797-3197
www.grolier.com

1994 128 pages
ISBN: 0-531125-52-1

2115 Cystic Fibrosis: A Guide for Patient and Family
Raven Press
1185 Avenue of the Americas
New York, NY 10036
212-930-9500

253 pages Softcover
ISBN: 0-397516-53-3

2116 Cystic Fibrosis: The Facts
Oxford University Press
2001 Evans Road
Cary, NC 27513
212-726-6000
800-445-9714
Fax: 919-677-1303
custserv.us@oup.com
www.oup-usa.org

1995 128 pages Paperback
ISBN: 0-192625-43-8

2117 Give Me One Wish
Norton Publishers
500 5th Avenue
New York, NY 10110
212-354-5500
www.scholastic.com/

This book reads like a novel because it reenacts the author's daughter's bout with cystic fibrosis.

Grades 10-12

2118 Let's Talk About Going to the Hospital
Rosen Publishing Group's PowerKids Press
29 E 21st Street
New York, NY 10010
212-777-3017
800-237-9932
Fax: 888-436-4643
rosenpub@tribeca.ios.com
www.rosenpublishing.com

If a child has to check into the hospital, chances are he or she is already upset about being ill. Knowing how a hospital functions and what the procedures are, such as when family members can visit, will help in what is already a stressful situation. Grades K-5.

24 pages
ISBN: 0-823950-36-0

Roger Rosen, President

2119 Respiratory Disorders Sourcebook, 4th Edition
Omnigraphics
615 Griswold Street, Ste 520
Detroit, MI 48226
610-461-3548
800-234-1340
Fax: 800-875-1340
contact@omnigraphics.com
www.omnigraphics.com

Basic consumer health information on lung disorders including tuberculosis, asthma and cystic fibrosis.

720 pages
ISBN: 0-780815-36-0

2120 Robyn's Book: A True Diary
Scholastic
730 Broadway
New York, NY 10003
212-505-3000

This book chronicles the life of the author and her battle with cystic fibrosis.

Grades 7-12

2121 Toothpick
Holiday
40 E 49th Street
New York, NY 10017
212-688-0085

This book uses relationships between two different teenagers to parallel the life of a person with cystic fibrosis.

Cystic Fibrosis / Newsletters

Grades 6-9

2122 Understanding Cystic Fibrosis
University Press of Mississippi
3825 Ridgewood Road, Unit 9
Jackson, MS 39211

601-982-6205
Fax: 601-982-6217

This book charts the progress that has been made in identifying the mutations that cause CF and understanding how these genetic errors cause a disease whose symptoms can range from mild respiratory distress to life-threatening lung infections.

128 pages Hardcover
ISBN: 0-878059-66-0

Newsletters

2123 Commitment
Cystic Fibrosis Foundation
6931 Arlington Road, 2nd Floor
Bethesda, MD 20814

301-951-4422
800-344-4823
Fax: 301-951-6378
info@cff.org
www.cff.org

Offers medical news, fund-raising features, public policy and news from across the nation on cystic fibrosis.
Catherine C. McLoud, Chair
Robert J. Beall, Ph.D., President & CEO
C. Richard Mattingly, EVP & COO

Pamphlets

2124 An Introduction to Cystic Fibrosis for Patients and Families
Cystic Fibrosis Foundation
6931 Arlington Road, 2nd Floor
Bethesda, MD 20814

301-951-4422
800-344-4823
Fax: 301-951-6378
info@cff.org
www.cff.org

Offers up-dated medical information, the latest news on assistive technology and treatments, answers to some frequently asked questions on the illness and more.

94 pages
Catherine C. McLoud, Chair
Robert J. Beall, Ph.D., President & CEO
C. Richard Mattingly, EVP & COO

2125 Consumer Fact Sheet
Cystic Fibrosis Foundation
6931 Arlington Road, 2nd Floor
Bethesda, MD 20814

301-951-4422
800-344-4823
Fax: 301-951-6378
info@cff.org
www.cff.org

Offers a brief introduction to cystic fibrosis, symptoms, causes, treatments and offers illustrations pertaining to drainage positions.
Catherine C. McLoud, Chair
Robert J. Beall, Ph.D., President & CEO
C. Richard Mattingly, EVP & COO

2126 Cystic Fibrosis: Guide for Parents
American Lung Association
55 W. Wacker Drive, Suite 1150
Chicago, IL 60601

312-801-7630
800-LUN-USA
Fax: 202-452-1805
info@lungusa.org
www.lungusa.org

Comprehensive booklet covering topics such as treatment, social aspects, inheritance, genetics and outlook for the future.

24 pages
Kathryn A. Forbes, Chair
John F. Emanuel, JD, Vice Chair
Harold Wimmer, President & CEO

2127 Here's Everything You'll Need to Save Money with the CFF Health Services
CFF Home Health & Pharmacy Services
6931 Arlington Road, 2nd Floor
Bethesda, MD 20814

301-951-4422
800-344-4823
Fax: 301-951-6378
info@cff.org
www.cff.org

Offers information on the Cystic Fibrosis Foundation's home health services.
Catherine C. McLoud, Chair
Robert J. Beall, Ph.D., President & CEO
C. Richard Mattingly, EVP & COO

2128 Here's Everything You'll Need to Start Saving Money with the CFF Pharmacy
CFF Home Health And Pharmacy Services
6931 Arlington Road, 2nd Floor
Bethesda, MD 20814

301-951-4422
800-344-4823
Fax: 301-951-6378
info@cff.org
www.cff.org

Offers information on money-saving medications and patient information for the Cystic Fibrosis Pharmacy.
Catherine C. McLoud, Chair
Robert J. Beall, Ph.D., President & CEO
C. Richard Mattingly, EVP & COO

2129 Home Line
Cystic Fibrosis Foundation
6931 Arlington Road, 2nd Floor
Bethesda, MD 20814

301-951-4422
800-344-4823
Fax: 301-951-6378
info@cff.org
www.cff.org

This bimonthly newsletter offers information on services and programs offered by the Foundation.
Bimonhtly
Catherine C. McLoud, Chair
Robert J. Beall, Ph.D., President & CEO
C. Richard Mattingly, EVP & COO

2130 On the Threshold of a Cure...You Can Make the Difference!
Cystic Fibrosis Foundation
6931 Arlington Road, 2nd Floor
Bethesda, MD 20814

301-951-4422
800-344-4823
Fax: 301-951-6378
info@cff.org
www.cff.org

Offers information on what Cystic Fibrosis is and what people can do to help support the foundation's research.
Catherine C. McLoud, Chair
Robert J. Beall, Ph.D., President & CEO
C. Richard Mattingly, EVP & COO

Camps

2131 Camp Funshine
PO Box 576
Pea Ridge, AR 72751

832-541-9276
www.campfunshine.com

Summer camp for children with cystic fibrosis and their families.
Jeff Brown, Director

2132 Des Moines YMCA Camp
1192 166th Drive
Boone, IA 50036

515-432-7558
Fax: 515-432-5414
ycamp@dmymca.org
www.y-camp.org

For boys and girls with cancer, diabetes, asthma, cystic fibrosis, hearing impaired and other disabilities.

David Sherry, Executive Director
Alex Kretzinger, Program Director

2133 LA Lions Camp Pelican
PO Box 10235
New Orleans, LA 70181

504-466-7124
800-348-6567
Fax: 866-295-3803
www.lionscamp.org

Provides residential camp for children with lung disorders.

Troy Ricard

Cytomegalovirus / Description

Description

2134 CYTOMEGALOVIRUS

Synonyms: Child care virus, CMV, Cytomegalic inclusion disease
Involves the following Biologic System(s):
Infectious Disorders

Cytomegalovirus (CMV) is a member of the herpesvirus family. This very common, worldwide viral infection often causes no apparent disease; however, in some patients, CMV infection results in symptoms and physical findings that may range from mild to potentially life-threatening.

Cytomegalovirus may be transmitted from mother to child before birth through the placenta, during birth through genital tract secretions, or after birth through breast milk. CMV is present in the environment; therefore, infection may be acquired at virtually any age. Because this virus may be shed in the urine and saliva for months or years after infection, children and adults who work in child-care settings are especially vulnerable. This is such a common occurrence that CMV infection is sometimes called the child-care virus. CMV may also be excreted in feces or transmitted through blood transfusions and in transplanted organs such as the kidneys, heart, and bone marrow. In the case of transmission through donated organs, CMV symptoms may be particularly severe due to immune suppression that occurs with the use of immune-suppressive drugs used to prevent organ rejection. In this way, these individuals are less capable of mounting a defense against the virus. Other individuals with impaired immune systems, such as the elderly and those with acquired immunodeficiency syndrome (AIDS), are also at increased risk of potentially life-threatening complications.

Fetal infection is more common when the mother is infected by CMV for the first time as opposed to recurrent infection. The majority of CMV-infected infants have no symptoms at birth; however, approximately five to 10 percent may exhibit symptoms and physical findings involving different organs of the body. Symptomatic CMV infection in the newborn (congenital CMV) may include such characteristic findings as an unusually small head (microcephaly); accumulations of calcium salts in the tissues of the brain; enlargement of the liver and spleen (hepatosplenomegaly); yellowish discoloration of the skin, eyes, and mucous membranes (jaundice); purplish skin lesions; eye abnormalities (i.e., chorioretinitis); and other irregularities of the central nervous system that may result in loss of sight and hearing, paralysis, and intellectual disabilities. Approximately 10 to 20 percent of asymptomatic newborns later develop similar difficulties associated with the central nervous system. Infants who contract CMV infection after birth may have enlargement of the liver and spleen, inflammation of the liver (hepatitis), or pneumonia. In addition, premature, low birth weight infants who acquire CMV infection through blood transfusion may develop inflammation of the lungs (pneumonitis), jaundice, enlargement of the liver and spleen, grayish skin coloring, and irregularities of the blood. CMV-infected children with AIDS or transplanted organs may develop potentially life-threatening conditions, including pneumonitis, inflammation of the retinas of the eyes (retinitis), and gastrointestinal abnormalities. Primary cytomegalovirus infections in children receiving transplants are more likely to have more severe symptoms than those of recurrent infection.

Older affected children and adults with cytomegalovirus infection may develop symptoms and physical findings similar to those of mononucleosis. These findings usually last about two to three weeks and may include fever, rash, headache, fatigue, muscle pain, and hepatosplenomegaly. In addition, mild CMV infections in many children and adults often subside with no treatment.

In some cases, preventive treatment for CMV infection includes administration of intravenous immunoglobulin. Although this therapy is not usually effective in preventing disease acquired through most types of organ transplantation, it may be beneficial to bone marrow recipients whose compromised immune systems may not be capable of preventing a primary CMV infection. Other preventive measures may include screening of blood and organ donors for cytomegalovirus. In addition, pregnant child-care workers are urged to practice good hygiene, including frequent and thorough handwashing. Certain antiviral drugs (e.g., gancyclovir) are sometimes used to treat symptoms associated with life-threatening disease. However, symptoms tend to recur after treatment is stopped and serious side effects associated with this type of treatment are common. Separate studies on vaccine development and the use of antiviral drugs in the treatment of congenital cytomegalovirus are ongoing. Other treatment is supportive.

Government Agencies

2135 NIH/ Eunice Kennedy Shriver National Institute of Child Health & Human Development
P.O. Box 3006
Rockville, MD 20847

800-370-2943
Fax: 866-760-5947
www.nichd.nih.gov

Conducts and supports research on topics related to the health of children, adults, families and populations. Some of these topics include: developmental disabilities, growth and development, infant death, reproductive health and birth defects.

Diana W. Bianchi, Director
Alison Cernich, PhD, Deputy Director

2136 NIH/National Institute of Allergy and Infectious Diseases
5601 Fishers Lane, MSC 9806
Bethesda, MD 20892

301-496-5717
866-284-4107
Fax: 301-402-3573
TDD: 800-877-8339
ocpostoffice@niaid.nih.gov
www.niaid.nih.gov

The principal advisory board of the NIAID. The council is composed of physicians, scientists and representatives of the public and advises on the conduct and support or research, training and dissemination of health information regarding allergies and infectious diseases.

Anthony S. Fauci, MD, Director

National Associations & Support Groups

2137 American Academy of Pediatrics
345 Park Blvd
Itasca, IL 60143

800-433-9016
Fax: 847-434-8000
mcc@aap.org
www.aap.org

The American Academy of Pediatrics and its member pediatricians are committed to the attainment of optimal physical, mental and social health and well-being for all infants, children, adolescents, and young adults.

Lynn Olson, PhD, VP, Research
Mark Del Monte, JD, CEO/Executive VP
Vera Tait, MD, FAAP, Chief Medical Officer

2138 March of Dimes Foundation
1550 Crystal Drive, Ste 1300
Arlington, VA 22202

888-663-4637
www.marchofdimes.org

March of Dimes help moms have full-term pregnancies and research the problems that threaten the health of babies. The March of Dimes also acts globally: sharing best practices in perinatal health and helping improve birth outcomes where the needs are the most urgent.

Stacey D. Stewart, President
Alan Brogdon, SVP/COO/Board Officer
Rahul Gupta, MD, SVP & Chief Medical/Health Officer

2139 **National Congenital CMV Disease Registry**
Feigin Center
1102 Bates St., Suite 1150
Houston, TX 77030
832-824-4387
Fax: 832-825-4347
cvm@bcm.edu
www.bcm.edu/departments/pediatrics/

This national surveillance program tracks trends over time, identifies risk groups, and lays groundwork for evaluation of future intervention programs.

Web Sites

2140 **Kid's Health**
kidshealth.org

kidshealth.org

KidsHealth provides doctor-approved health information about children from before birth through adolescence. Kids health provides families with accurate, up to date and jargon free health information they can use.

Neil Izenberg, MD, Editor-in-Chief & Founder

Book Publishers

2141 **Let's Talk About Going to the Hospital**
Rosen Publishing Group's PowerKids Press
29 E 21st Street
New York, NY 10010
212-777-3017
800-237-9932
Fax: 888-436-4643
rosenpub@tribeca.ios.com
www.rosenpublishing.com

If a child has to check into the hospital, chances are he or she is already upset about being ill. Knowing how a hospital functions and what the procedures are, such as when family members can visit, will help in what is already a stressful situation. Grades K-5.

24 pages
ISBN: 0-823950-36-0

Roger Rosen, President

Dental Conditions / Description

Description

2142 DENTAL CONDITIONS

Covers these related disorders: Anodontia, Dental Caries, Discoloration of the Teeth, Malocclusion, Supernumerary Teeth

Involves the following Biologic System(s):

Dental Disorders

This chapter will discuss the following pediatric dental conditions: anodontia; dental caries; discoloration of the teeth; malocclusion; supernumerary teeth; teeth grinding.

Anodontia refers to a condition in which some or all of the teeth are missing as the result of a congenital defect or of damage sustained from disease. Ectodermal dysplasias are a group of congenital disorders characterized by abnormalities of the teeth, hair, nails, skin glands, the skin, nervous system, ears and eyes, and the membranes that line the anus and the mouth. Partial anodontia may also result from a common birth defect such as cleft palate, in which the roof of the mouth does not close completely. Partial anodontia is often a component of certain disorders or syndromes including pseudohypoparathyroidism, cleidocranial dysplasia, and other disorders affecting the face and skull. The absence of some teeth may result in malocclusion, or misalignment, of the upper and lower teeth.

Treatment of anodontia may include the use of full or partial dentures, other dental prosthetics (bridgework), and dental implants. These approaches may be delayed until underlying structural deficits, such as cleft palate, are surgically corrected.

Dental caries, or tooth decay, is a common condition characterized by the gradual destruction (erosion) of the enamel and, potentially, the dentin and interior pulp of a tooth. The main cause of dental caries is plaque, a sticky film consisting of food debris, saliva and mucus. Certain bacteria that reside in the mouth break down dietary carbohydrates within plaque, creating acids that gradually wear down the outer tooth surfaces. Dental caries initially appear as whitish spots. As loss of dental tissue progresses, the enamel is gradually destroyed. Without treatment, the dentin and pulp may erode, causing pain, infection, and eventual tooth loss. In affected infants or children, dental caries typically appear on the minute grooves on the grinding surfaces of the back molars, or on the contact surfaces between adjacent teeth.

Dental caries are thought to be caused more by the frequency of carbohydrate consumption than by the quantity of carbohydrates consumed. For example, baby bottle tooth decay, which becomes apparent between 1 and 2 years, is extensive decay due to sleeping with, and constant use of, bottles with milk, juice and other sugary liquids. The same amount of such liquids consumed during a single meal is much less likely to cause decay. The frequency of dental caries has decreased 35 to 50 percent during the past 20 years due to fluorinated water and toothpaste. Dental caries are treated by drilling out the decayed area and filling the cavity with a dental material. Treatment of advanced decay may include removal of the pulp (root canal), restoration (crown), or extraction of the tooth.

Permanent discoloration of the teeth is caused by the incorporation of particular substances into developing tooth enamel, such as taking certain antibiotic medications (e.g. tetracyclines), excessive fluoride consumption, particular pediatric conditions or disorders, or other factors. Since tetracycline medications are highly absorbed into the teeth and bones, taking such medications during the development of enamel may result in thin, deficient tooth enamel (hyypoplasia) that is permanently stained yellowish brown. The risk for this condition is from the fourth month of fetal development to 10 months for primary teeth and from four months to 16 years for secondary teeth. Risk varies with type of medication, dose, and duration of treatment. Excessive fluoride may also result in tooth discoloration known as mottling. This primarily affects children in areas with higher-than-recommended levels of fluoride in the water supply. Permanent discoloration may also result from certain vitamin deficiencies, infectious disorders, or certain pediatric conditions. The use of certain specialized dental procedures and devices may help to minimize or cover discolored teeth. Children may also experience temporary tooth staining on the surface of teeth due to certain bacteria or food dyes. These may be removed by professional tooth polishing.

Malocclusion is a dental condition in which there is improper positioning of the teeth of the upper jaw in relation to those of the lower jaw. There are three main classes of malocclusion. In proper contact of the teeth (occlusion) the front teeth of the upper jaw slightly overlap the front teeth of the lower jaw and the ridges (cusps) of the back teeth (premolars and molars) in the lower jaw interlock slightly ahead and inside the cusps of the corresponding teeth in the upper jaw. In class I malocclusion, certain upper and lower teeth do not have appropriate contact due to crowding. In class II malocclusion (retrognathism), the most common, the cusps of the back teeth in the lower jaw are positioned behind and inside the cusps of the corresponding teeth in the upper jaw. In class III malocclusion (prognathism), the cusps of the back teeth in the lower jaw are abnormally positioned in front of corresponding maxillary teeth and the front teeth of the lower jaw meet or protrude beyond the upper front teeth. Malocclusion usually occurs during childhood as the bones of the jaws grow and the teeth develop and, in most cases, is genetic. Some cases of malocclusion may result due to other dental abnormalities, such as improper development or crowding of teeth, or constant thumbsucking. Treating malocclusion may avoid strain, stiffness, or pain that may result from an abnormal bite, may improve facial appearance, and may prevent tooth decay and loss. Treatment may include a variety of measures: tooth extraction in cases of dental crowding; orthodontic appliances to correct the positioning of teeth; or, in severe cases, surgical correction of abnormal protrusion or recession of the lower jaw.

Supernumerary teeth refers to the presence of one or more teeth in excess of the normal 20 primary teeth or 32 secondary teeth. These teeth are usually abnormal in shape and size and may erupt through the gums or may remain impacted in the gums or the jaw bone. In addition, a primary or secondary tooth is typically not present to replace the supernumerary (super = "extra") tooth. In most cases, only one supernumerary tooth is present; however, instances of multiple supernumerary teeth have been reported. The presence of supernumerary teeth may cause delayed eruption, abnormal positioning, or impaction of nearby teeth. Therefore, early diagnosis is important in removal or extraction of the extra tooth, or in regular monitoring to assess the need for possible extraction. Natal teeth, which are teeth that are present at birth, may be supernumerary or primary teeth that have erupted unusually early. Natal teeth usually have little bony support or root formation and are typically loose and mobile. If natal teeth are determined to be supernumerary, they are often extracted; if they are primary teeth, attempts may be made to maintain them. Supernumerary teeth develop in different locations in the mouth, and have different names: mesiodens develop between the central front teeth in the upper jaw; paramolars form between molars in the upper jaw; disomolars, also known as retromolars, develop in the back of the third molars (widsom teeth); peridens erupt outside the dental arches, such as in the roofof the mouth. Supernumerary teeth may be the result of abnormalities during embryonic development, and may occur with other conditions, such as cleft lip and palate. There have been reports that suggest supernumerary teeth are inherited.

Teeth grinding, or bruxism, refers to compulsive, involuntary, rhythmic, and nonfunctional grinding, clenching, or gnashing of the teeth. This habitual grinding is most evident during sleep, so the individual may be oblivious to it, but family members may notice. Affected individuals may also unconsciously grind their teeth during the day as well. Daytime teeth grinding is known as bruxomania. In some, teeth grinding may be considered a habit or habit disorder, depending upon the degree of severity and the impact upon daily functioning. Bruxism most often results from unresolved or unexpressed anger, aggression, fear, frustration, resentment, or other negative emotions. Teeth grinding that occurs during sleep exerts more force than that of normal daytime chewing or grinding. For this reason, bruxism may cause muscle pain or tightness in the jaw area, headache, earache as well as irregularities in the surface contact between the upper and lower teeth. In addition, bruxism may wear down or loosen the teeth. The goals of treatment are to reduce pain, prevent permanent damage to the teeth, and reduce clenching behaviors as much as possible.Treatment for teeth grinding may include stress management and behavior therapy. Other treatment is symptomatic, and involves a dental appliance, such as a mouthguard, worn at night to help reduce associated dental injury.

Government Agencies

2143 NIH/ Eunice Kennedy Shriver National Institute of Child Health & Human Development
P.O. Box 3006
Rockville, MD 20847
800-370-2943
Fax: 866-760-5947
www.nichd.nih.gov

Conducts and supports research on topics related to the health of children, adults, families and populations. Some of these topics include: developmental disabilities, growth and development, infant death, reproductive health and birth defects.

Diana W. Bianchi, Director
Alison Cernich, PhD, Deputy Director

2144 NIH/National Institute of Dental and Craniofacial Research (NIDCR)
National Institutes of Health
Bldg 31, Rm 2C39, 31 Center Drive, MSC 2560
Bethesda, MD 20892
866-232-4528
nidcrinfo@mail.nih.gov
www.nidcr.nih.gov

The Institute promotes the general health of the American people by improving their oral, dental and craniofacial health. The NIDCR aims to promote health, to prevent diseases and conditions, and to develop new diagnostics and therapeutics.

Rena D'Souza, DDS, PhD, Director
Jonathan Horsford, PhD, Acting Deputy Director

National Associations & Support Groups

2145 Academy for Sports Dentistry
PO Box 358
Isanti, MN 55040
612-440-7125
info@academyforsportsdentistry.org
www.academyforsportsdentistry.org

The Academy for Sports Dentistry was founded in 1983 in San Antonio, Texas, as a forum for dentists, physicians, athletic trainers, coaches, dental technicians, and educators interested in exchanging ideas related to Sports Dentistry and the dental needs of athletes at risk to sports' injuries.

Jim Whitehead, Chief Executive Officer
Xavier Gutierrez, DDS, FASD, President
David Dowsett, DMD, Secretary

2146 Academy of General Dentistry
560 W. Lake St., Sixth Floor
Chicago, IL 60661
888-243-3368
Fax: 312-335-3443
membership@agd.org
www.agd.org

The mission of the AGD is to serve the needs and represent the interests of general dentists, to promote the oral health of the public, and to foster continued proficiency of general dentists through quality continuing dental education in order to better serve the public.

2147 Academy of Operative Dentistry
www.academyofoperativedentistry.com

The objective of the Academy of Operative Dentistry is to promote excellence in Operative Dentistry by exerting our influence in the practice of health professions, in organized dentistry.

Yana Nedvetsky, President
Chris Griffin, Vice President
Richard G. Stevenson III, Secretary

2148 Academy of Osseointegration
85 W. Algonquin Road, Suite 550
Arlington Heights, IL 60005
847-439-1919
800-656-7736
Fax: 847-427-9656
academy@osseo.org
www.osseo.org

The Academy of Osseointegration's dedication to the highest standards in patient care.

Kevin P. Smith, Executive Director
Kevin Bragaw, Chief Financial Officer
Karla Kaschub, Director of Membership

2149 Alpha Omega International Dental Society
PO Box 30847
Clarksville, TN 37040
301-738-6400
877-368-6326
Fax: 301-738-6403
www.ao.org

An international Jewish dental organization striving to enrich the lives of its members.

Heidi Weber, Executive Director

2150 American Academy of Cosmetic Dentistry
200 River Place, Suite 150
Monona, WI 53716
608-222-8583
800-543-9220
Fax: 608-222-9540
www.aacd.com

AACD is dedicated to advancing excellence in the art and science of comprehensive cosmetic dentistry and encouraging the highest standards of ethical conduct and responsible patient care.

Barbara Kachelski, Executive Director

2151 American Academy of Dental Hygiene
311 - 14th Street, Suite 2
Union City, NJ 07087
201-429-3002
admin@aadh.org
www.aadh.org

Advancing Individual Professional Growth through Leadership, Mentorship, and Fellowship.

Danni Gomes, Executive Director
Jane Cotter, Secretary
Valoree Althoff, Treasurer

Dental Conditions / National Associations & Support Groups

2152 American Academy of Dental Practice Administration
03 Navajo Trail
McGregor, TX 76657
254-563-5354
aadp.execdir@gmail.com
aadpa.org

Promotes leadership, life balance & success in dentistry.

Karen Edds, Executive Director

2153 American Academy of Esthetic Dentistry
233 S. Wacker Dr., Suite 4400
Chicago, IL 60606
312-981-6770
Fax: 312-265-2908
info@estheticacademy.org
www.estheticacademy.org

Established in 1975, the AAED promotes the integration of dental esthetics into the total spectrum of oral health care.

Joseph Jackson, CAE, Executive Director

2154 American Academy of Pediatric Dentistry
211 E Chicago Avenue, Suite 1600
Chicago, IL 60611
312-337-2169
Fax: 312-337-6329
www.aapd.org

The AAPD is the membership organization representing the specialty of pediatric dentistry. Our over 10,000 members serve as primary care providers for millions of children from infancy through adolescence.

4500 members

Jade Miller, D.D.S., President
John Rutkauskas, D.D.S., CEO

2155 American Academy of Pediatrics
345 Park Blvd
Itasca, IL 60143
800-433-9016
Fax: 847-434-8000
mcc@aap.org
www.aap.org

The American Academy of Pediatrics and its member pediatricians are committed to the attainment of optimal physical, mental and social health and well-being for all infants, children, adolescents, and young adults.

Lynn Olson, PhD, VP, Research
Mark Del Monte, JD, CEO/Executive VP
Vera Tait, MD, FAAP, Chief Medical Officer

2156 American Academy of Periodontology
737 N. Michigan Ave., Suite 800
Chicago, IL 60611
312-787-5518
www.perio.org

The American Academy of Periodontology (AAP) is an 8,400-member professional organization for periodontists - specialists in the prevention, diagnosis, and treatment of diseases affecting the gums and supporting structures of the teeth, and in the placement of dental implants.

David K. Okano, President
Mia L. Geisinger, Vice President
Ana Becil Giglio, Secretary & Treasurer

2157 American Association for Dental, Oral, and Craniofacial Research
1619 Duke Street
Alexandria, VA 22314
703-548-0066
Fax: 703-548-1883
www.aadocr.org

The American Association for Dental, Oral, and Craniofacial Research (AADOCR) is the leading professional community for multidisciplinary scientists who advance dental, oral, and craniofacial research. Previously the American Association for Dental Research, the 3,000-member organization connects the scientific community of professionals who champion research that contributes to overall health and well-being.

Christopher Fox, Chief Executive Officer

2158 American Association of Endodontists
180 N Stetson Avenue, Suite 1500
Chicago, IL 60601
312-266-7255
800-872-3636
Fax: 866-451-9020
info@aae.org
www.aae.org

The American Association of Endodontists is dedicated to excellence in the art and science of endodontics and to the highest standard of patient care. The Association inspires its members to pursue professional advancement and personal fulfillment through education, research, advocacy, leadership, communication and service.

Kenneth J. Widelka, Executive Director
Trina Andresen Coe, Deputy Executive Director
Jamie Jaglal, Executive Coordinator

2159 American Association of Oral and Maxillofacial Surgeons
9700 West Bryn Mawr Avenue
Rosemont, IL 60018
847-678-6200
800-822-6637
www.aaoms.org

The American Association of Oral and Maxillofacial Surgeons (AAOMS) represents more than 9,000 oral and maxillofacial surgeons in the United States, supporting specialized education, research and advocacy.

2160 American Association of Orthodontists
401 N Lindbergh Boulevard
St. Louis, MO 63141
314-993-1700
Fax: 314-997-1745
info@aaortho.org
www2.aaoinfo.org

A professional association of educationally qualified orthodontic specialists dedicated to advancing the art and science of orthodontics and dentofacial orthopedics, improving the health of the public by promoting quality orthodontic care, and supporting the successful practice of orthodontics.

2161 American Association of Public Health Dentistry
136 Everett Road
Albany, NY 12205
518-694-5525
info@aaphd.org
www.aaphd.org

Founded in 1937, the American Association of Public Health Dentistry (AAPHD) provides a focus for meeting the challenge to improve oral health.

Frances Kim, DDS, MPH, DrPH, Executive Director

2162 American Cleft Palate Craniofacial Association
510 Meadowmount Village Circle, Suite 377
Chapel Hill, NC 27517
919-933-9044
acpacares.org

The American Cleft Palate-Craniofacial Association (ACPA) is an international non-profit medical society of health care professionals who treat and/or perform research on birth defects of the head and face.

Adam Levy, CAE, Executive Director
Erin Brenneman, Manager, Member Programs/Engagement
Caitlyn Reinauer, Senior Manager, Education Programs

2163 American College of Dentists
103 N Adams Street
Rockville, MD 20850
301-977-3223
office@acd.org
www.acd.org

The American College of Dentists is the oldest major honorary organization for dentists. The mission of the American College of Dentists is to advance excellence, ethics, professionalism, and leadership in dentistry.

Suzan Pitman, Managing Director

2164 American Dental Assistants Association
529 - 14th Street NW, Suite 1280
Washington, DC 20045
410-940-6584
www.adaausa.org

Dental Conditions / National Associations & Support Groups

They work to advance the careers of dental assistants and to promote the dental assisting profession in matters of education, legislation, credentialing and professional activities which enhance the delivery of quality dental health care to the public.

Sheila O'Neal, Executive Director

2165 American Dental Association
211 E Chicago Avenue
Chicago, IL 60610
312-440-2500
msc@ada.org
www.ada.org

Founded in 1859, the American Dental Association is the oldest and largest national dental society in the world. Since then, the ADA has grown to become the leading source of oral health related information for dentists and their patients.

Raymond A. Cohlmia, Executive Director

2166 American Dental Education Association
655 K Street, NW, Suite 800
Washington, DC 20001
202-289-7201
Fax: 202-289-7204
membership@adea.org
www.adea.org

The American Dental Education Association (ADEA) is The Voice of Dental Education. The mission of ADEA is to lead individuals and institutions of the dental education community to address contemporary issues influencing education, research and the delivery of oral health care for the health of the public.

Karen P. West, President & CEO
Jason Lee, Chief of Staff
Chris Carr, Chief Financial Officer

2167 American Dental Hygienists Association
444 N Michigan Avenue, Suite 400
Chicago, IL 60611
312-440-8900
askADHA@adha.net
www.adha.org

ADHA believes in helping dental hygienists achieve their full potential as they seek to improve the public's oral health. We support your goals by helping to ensure access to quality oral health care; promoting dental hygiene education, licensure, practice and research; and representing your legislative interests at the local, state and federal levels.

Ann Battrell, MSDH, Chief Executive Officer

2168 American Dental Society of Anesthesiology
211 E. Chicago Avenue
Chicago, IL 60611
312-664-8270
adsa@adsahome.org
www.adsahome.org

The mission of the American Dental Society of Anesthesiology is to provide a forum for education, research, and recognition of achievement in order to promote safe and effective patient care for all dentists who have an interest in anesthesiology, edation and the control of anxiety and pain.

David L. Rothman, DDS, President
Edward C. Adlesic, DMD, Vice President
Robert C. Bosack, DDS, Treasurer

2169 American Society for Dental Aesthetics
1080 Polaris Parkway
Columbus, OH 43240
888-988-ASDA
info@asdatoday.com
www.asdatoday.com

Founded in 1976, the American Society for Dental Aesthetics (ASDA) is made up of members who share a lifelong commitment to learning and providing exceptional care.

2170 American Society of Forensic Odontology
Brookesmith, TX 76827
asfo.org

Founded in 1970, the American Society of Forensic Odontology (ASFO) was established to promote interest and research in the field of forensic odontology.

2171 American Student Dental Association
211 E. Chicago Avenue, Suite 700
Chicago, IL 60611
www.asdanet.org

ASDA protects and advances the rights, interests and welfare of dental students across the nation.

Nancy Honeycutt, CAE, Executive Director

2172 Christian Dental Society
PO Box 296
Sumner, IA 50674
563-578-8887
cdssent@netins.net
www.christiandental.org

There mission is to show the love of Christ by offering dental relief to those in need around the world. Since its inception in 1963, CDS has provided volunteers, equipment and supplies with the objective of serving Christ.

Robert Meyer, DMD, Executive Director

2173 Christian Medical & Dental Associations
PO Box 7500
Bristol, TN 37621
888-230-2637
Fax: 423-844-1005
Main@cmda.org
cmda.org

Christian Medical & Dental Associations exists to glorify God by motivating, educating and equipping Christian healthcare professionals and students.

Mike Chupp, MD, Chief Executive Officer
Scott Ledford, Chief Operating Officer
Mick Williams, Chief Information Officer

2174 Hispanic Dental Association
2 Talon Court
Sewell, NJ 08080
856-353-9459
www.hdassoc.org

Founded in 1990, the history of HDA is one of inclusive nature driven by our mission. Incorporated in Texas with a national scope, the HDA's founding members shared a common commitment to improve the oral health of the Hispanic community.

Manuel A. Cordero, Executive Director & CEO

2175 Holistic Dental Association
holisticdental.org
305-356-7338
director@holisticdental.org
holisticdental.org

Since 1978, the Holistic Dental Association has been providing support and guidance to practitioners of holistic and alternative dentistry, as well as informing the public of the benefits of holistic dentistry for their health and wellbeing. There purpose is to provide information and guidance to those persons seeking to participate in their own health care and to help in the continuing education of practitioners who have a desire to expand their knowledge and awareness.

Roberta Glasser, Executive Director

2176 International Association for Orthodontics
750 N Lincoln Memorial Dr., Suite 422
Milwaukee, WI 53202
414-272-2757
800-447-8770
Fax: 414-272-2754
WorldHeadquarters@iaortho.org
www.iaortho.org

The International Association for Orthodontics (IAO) was established in the United States in 1961 to promote international cooperation in the orthodontic field of dentistry. The IAO is a progressive and dynamic organization of general dentists, pediatric dentists and other dentists that provide orthodontic care to patients.

2177 International Association of Dental Research
1619 Duke Street
Alexandria, VA 22314
703-548-0066
Fax: 703-548-1883
memberservice@iadr.org
www.iadr.com

To advance research and increase knowledge for the improvement of oral health worldwide. Through the Divisions and Sections, establish and support programs to promote oral health research and IADR activities. Regions with less developed research programs will be identified for specific support.

Dental Conditions / Libraries & Resource Centers

Christopher Fox, Executive Director

2178 National Dental Association
3060 Mitchellville Road, Suite 215
Bowie, MD 20716
240-241-4448
ndaonline.org

The National Dental Association promotes oral health equity among people of color by harnessing the collective power of its members, advocating for the needs of and mentoring dental students of color, and raising the profile of the profession in communities.

Keith Andrew Perry, Executive Director

2179 Oral Cancer Foundation
1211 E State Street
Boise, ID 83712
949-723-4400
oralcancerfoundation.org

The Oral Cancer Foundation is a national public service, non-profit entity designed to reduce suffering and save lives through prevention, education, research, advocacy, and patient support activities.

Brian Hill, Founder & Executive Director
Ingrid Hill, Co-Founder & Operations Director
Natalie Riggs, Special Projects Director

2180 Special Care Dentistry Association
2800 West Higgins Road, Suite 440
Hoffman Estate, IL 60169
312-527-6764
Fax: 847-885-8393
scda@scdaonline.org
www.scdaonline.org

The Special Care Dentistry Association serves as a resource to all oral health care professionals who serve or are interested in serving patients with special needs through education and networking to increase access to oral healthcare for patients with special needs.

Dennis Bozzi, Executive Director

Libraries & Resource Centers

2181 University of Illinois at Chicago, Craniofacial Center
College of Medicine
1740 West Taylor Street
Chicago, IL 60612
312-996-6933
Fax: 312-355-4173
dreisber@uic.edu
www.uic.edu/com/craniofacial/

The Craniofacial Center is one of the oldest and largest facilities in the world, dedicated to the evaluation and treatment of infants, children, adolescents, and adults with cleft lip and palate and other congenital craniofacial conditions.

David J Reisberg, DDS, Medical Director

2182 University of Mississippi Medical Center
2500 N State Street
Jackson, MS 39216
601-984-5820
www.umc.edu

The health sciences campus of the University of Mississippi. It houses schools of Medicine, Nursing, Health Related Professions and Dentistry.

Lawrence Hornsby, Director

Audio Video

2183 Face First
Fanlight Productions
32 Court Street, 21st Floor
Brooklyn, NY 11201
718-488-8900
800-876-1710
Fax: 718-488-8642
info@fanlight.com, orders@fanlight.com
www.fanlight.com

Profiles of several people born with facial deformities; they chronicle both physical pain and the pain of rejection, as well as the strengths that have enabled them to achieve successful adult lives. ISBN: DVD: 1-57295-886-3; VHS: 1-572952-59-8

29 minutes DVD or VHS
Nicole Johnson, Publicity Coordinator

Web Sites

2184 American Academy of Pediatric Dentistry Foundation
211 East Chicago Avenue, Suite 1600
Chicago, IL 60611
312-337-2169
Fax: 312-337-6329
www.aapd.org

Supports and promotes education, research, service and policy development that advances the oral health of infants and children through adolescence, including those with special healthcare needs.

Jade Miller, D.D.S, President
Kristi Casale, Director, Meeting Services
John S. Rutkauskas, D.D.S., M.B., CEO

2185 Dental Consumer Advisory
www.toothinfo.com/

www.toothinfo.com/

The purpose of this site is to provide uselful and pracitcal information for the public concerning issues of dental care.

2186 Dental Resources on the Web
www.dental-resources.com

www.dental-resources.com

Dental sites for education, practices, laboratories, office supplies, dental care and associations.

Book Publishers

2187 Understanding Dental Health
University Press of Mississippi
3825 Ridgewood Road
Jackson, MS 39211
601-432-6205
800-737-7788
Fax: 601-432-6217
press@ihl.state.ms.us
www.upress.stat.ms.us

A user friendly manual on the basics of dental health.

128 pages Hard/Soft cover
ISBN: 1-578060-09-5

Description

2188 DEPRESSION
Involves the following Biologic System(s):
Developmental/Behavioral/Psychiatric Disorders

Depression refers to an emotional state characterized by exaggerated feelings of sadness, discouragement, loneliness, low self-esteem, and despair. These feelings may follow a recent loss or other tragic event. However, if feelings of depression worsen and are prolonged, or occur for no apparent reason, this may indicate a chronic (formerly called "endogenous") depressive disorder. Although clinical depression occurs more commonly among the adult population (2-3 times more common in females than in males, depression may be evident as early as infancy and is increasingly common among adolescents.

Symptoms and findings associated with depression are variable. It has a chronic course with relapses. The mood is typically depressed, irritable, and/or anxious, often accompanied by preoccupation with guilt, decreased ability to concentrate, diminished interest in usual activities (anhedonia), social withdrawal, hopelessness, and recurrent thoughts of death and suicide. Symptoms associated with depression in school-age children are similar to those seen in adults and include overwhelming feelings of sadness, crying, loss of interest in pleasurable activities, eating and sleeping irregularities, and, in some cases, suicidal thoughts (ideation). Some affected children may exhibit symptoms that belie a diagnosis of depression, such as overactivity and aggression. Adolescents with depression may have feelings of hopelessness and helplessness with no corresponding periods of happiness or well-being. However, inappropiate displays of euphoria together with such behavior as truancy, substance abuse, or other antisocial behaviors may also be symptomatic of depression. Other symptoms and findings associated with adolescent depression may include a decline in school grades, boredom, repetitive accidents, drug or alcohol abuse, absenteeism, feelings or delusions of guilt, and thoughts of suicide. Physical symptoms may sometimes include fatigue, headaches, and abdominal pain. Those who are psychotically depressed may experience delusions and hallucinations.

Depression in infants may be precipitated by such events as sudden separation from the mother or caregiver after six months of age (anaclitic depression of infancy) and may be manifested by ceaseless crying, panic, apprehension, withdrawal, and eating and sleeping disturbances. Eventually, indifference and unresponsiveness may develop and result in deficiencies in intellectual, physical, and social development. Endogenous depression may be caused by many different factors including genetic influences, hormonal disturbances, certain medications, infectious or neurologic disorders, physical conditions (i.e., stroke, etc.), certain tumors, nutritional influences, and psychosocial factors. In addition, depression may occur in association with other psychological disorders such as bipolar or other mood disorders (e.g., schizoaffective disorder).

Most persons with depression get treated as outpatients. Treatment of depression most often includes the administration of certain antidepressant medications. Most studies indicate that cognitive, interpersonal, and behavior therapy are effective, especially in combination with antidepressant medications. Electroconvulsive therapy (ECT) is effective but is usually reserved for severely depressed patients or patients who do not respond to or are not tolerant of medications. Children and adolescents with this disorder also often require individual psychotherapy and, in many cases, group and family therapy. Overall, the suicide rate is estimated at 15%. All patients with depression should be asked gently but directly about suicidal ideas or plans. All communications about self-destruction should be taken seriously.

Government Agencies

2189 NIH/National Institute of Mental Health
6001 Executive Blvd, Rm 6200, MSC 9663
Bethesda, MD 20892
866-615-6464
Fax: 301-443-4279
TTY: 301-443-8431
nimhinfo@nih.gov
www.nimh.nih.gov

The mission of NIMH is to transform the understanding and treatment of mental illnesses through basic and clinical research, paving the way for prevention, recovery, and cure.

Joshua A. Gordon, MD, PhD, Director
Shelli Avenevoli, PhD, Deputy Director

National Associations & Support Groups

2190 Agency for Healthcare Research & Quality
5600 Fishers Lane
Rockville, MD 20857
301-427-1364
howard.holland@ahrq.hhs.gov
www.ahrq.gov

The Agency for Healthcare Research and Quality's (AHRQ) mission is to produce evidence to make health care safer, higher quality, more accessible, equitable, and affordable, and to work within the U.S. Department of Health and Human Services and with other partners to make sure that the evidence is understood and used.

David Meyers, Director
Howard E. Holland, Communications Director

2191 American Academy of Pediatrics
345 Park Blvd
Itasca, IL 60143
800-433-9016
Fax: 847-434-8000
mcc@aap.org
www.aap.org

The American Academy of Pediatrics and its member pediatricians are committed to the attainment of optimal physical, mental and social health and well-being for all infants, children, adolescents, and young adults.

Lynn Olson, PhD, VP, Research
Mark Del Monte, JD, CEO/Executive VP
Vera Tait, MD, FAAP, Chief Medical Officer

2192 American Association of Suicidology
448 Walton Avenue, Suite 790
Hummelstown, PA 17036
www.suicidology.org

AAS is a membership organization for all those involved in suicide prevention and intervention, or touched by suicide. AAS is a leader in the advancement of scientific and programmatic efforts in suicide prevention through research, education and training, the development of standards and resources, and survivor support services.

Leeanne Sherman, President & CEO
Bonnie Benetti, Director of Finance
Rachael Ng, Director of Membership

2193 American College Counseling Association
1101 N Delaware Street
Indianapolis, IN 46202
855-220-8760
office@collegecounseling.org
www.collegecounseling.org

The American College Counseling Association is made up of diverse mental health professionals from the fields of counseling, psychology, and social work. Our common theme is working within higher education settings.

Becca Smith, President
Derrick Paladino, Treasurer
Lee Bard, III, Secretary

Depression / National Associations & Support Groups

2194 American College Health Association
8455 Colesville Road, Suite 740
Silver Spring, MD 20910
410-859-1500
Fax: 410-859-1510
contact@acha.org
www.acha.org

To serve as the principal leadership organization for advancing the health of college students and campus communities through advocacy, education, and research.

James Wilkinson, Executive Director

2195 American Foundation for Suicide Prevention
199 Water Street, 11th Floor
New York, NY 10038
212-363-3500
888-333-AFSP
Fax: 212-363-6237
info@afsp.org
www.afsp.org

The American Foundation for Suicide Prevention (AFSP) is the leader in the fight against suicide. We fund research, create educational programs, advocate for public policy, and support survivors of suicide loss.

Robert Gebbia, Chief Executive Officer
Christine Yu Moutier, MD, Chief Medical Officer
Daniel Killpack, Executive Vice President & CFO

2196 American Psychiatric Association
800 Maine Avenue SW, Suite 900
Washington, DC 20024
202-559-3900
apa@psych.org
www.psychiatry.org

It is a medical specialty society representing growing membership of more than 36,000 psychiatrists.

Saul Levin, MD, CEO & Medical Director

2197 American Psychological Association
750 First St. NE
Washington, DC 20002
202-336-5500
800-374-2721
TTY: 202-336-6123
www.apa.org

The mission is to advance the creation, communication and application of psychological knowledge to benefit society and improve people's lives.

Arthur C. Evans Jr, PhD, CEO/EVP

2198 American Public Health Association
800 I Street, NW
Washington, DC 20001
202-777-2742
Fax: 202-777-2534
TTY: 202-777-2500
www.apha.org

APHA champions the health of all people and all communities. They aim to strengthen the public health profession and speak out for public health issues and policies backed by science.

Georges C. Benjamin, MD, Executive Director
Kemi Oluwafemi, MBA, CPA, Chief Financial Officer
Susan Polan, PhD, Associate Executive Director

2199 American School Counselor Association
1101 King Street, Ste 310
Alexandria, VA 22314
703-683-2722
asca@schoolcounselor.org
www.schoolcounselor.org

The mission of ASCA is to represent professional school counselors and to promote professionalism and ethical practices.

Jill Cook, Executive Director
Amanda Fitzgerald, Assistant Deputy Executive Director
Kathleen M Rakestraw, Director of Communications

2200 American Society of Clinical Psychopharmacology
5034-A Thoroughbred Lane
Brentwood, NJ 37027
615-649-3085
Fax: 888-417-3311
www.ascpp.org

The American Society of Clinical Psychopharmacology (ASCP) was founded in 1992 to advance the science and practice of clinical psychopharmacology. Its nearly 800 members are physicians who study and practice psychopharmacology, as well as doctoral level investigators of clinical psychopharmacology or of pharmacology. ASCP members are advocates for clinical psychopharmacology and for clinical research.

Leslie Citrome, MD, President

2201 Anxiety and Depression Association of America
8701 Georgia Ave., Suite 412
Silver Spring, MD 20910
240-485-1018
information@adaa.org
www.adaa.org

ADAA is a national nonprofit organization dedicated to the prevention, treatment, and cure of anxiety, depression, OCD, PTSD, and related disorders and to improving the lives of all people who suffer from them through education, practice, and research.

Susan K Gurley, Executive Director
Lise Bram, Deputy Executive Director
Katie Russo, Senior Director, Operations

2202 Depressed Anonymous
depressedanon.com

depanon@netpenny.net
depressedanon.com

Individuals suffering from depression or anxiety. A self-help organization with meetings and sharing of experiences. Conducts research and offers classes. Disseminates information. Publications: Newsletter, three-four times a year. Brochures and pamphlets.

2203 Depression and Bipolar Support Alliance
55 E Jackson Boulevard, Suite 490
Chicago, IL 60604
800-826-3632
Fax: 312-642-7243
www.dbsalliance.org

Patient-directed organization focusing on the most prevalent mental illnesses- depression and bipolar disorder. Fosters an understanding about the impact and management of these life-threatening illnesses by providing up-to-date, scientifically-based tools and information written in language the general public can understand.

Michael Pollock, Chief Executive Officer
John Quinn, Chief Financial Officer

2204 Families for Depression Awareness
391 Totten Pond Road, Suite 101
Waltham, MA 02451
781-890-0220
Fax: 781-890-2411
www.familyaware.org

Families for Depression Awareness is a national nonprofit organization helping families recognize and cope with depression and bipolar disorder to get people well and prevent suicides.

Arielle Cohen, Programs Manager
Valerie Cordero, Co-Executive Director
Susan Weinstein, Co-Executive Director

2205 International Foundation for Research and Education on Depression (IFred)
PO Box 17598
Baltimore, MD 21297
Fax: 443-782-0739
info@ifred.org
www.ifred.org

iFred is a 501c3 organization aiming to shed a positive light on depression throughout the world in order to prevent the onset, research causes and treatments, and rebrand the disease in a positive way.

Tom Dean, Chair
Susan Minamyer, Secretary
Kathryn Goetzke, Founder

2206 NADD: National Association for the Dually Diagnosed
12 Hurley Avenue
Kingston, NY 12401
845-331-4336
800-331-5362
Fax: 845-331-4569
info@thenadd.org
www.thenadd.org

Depression / Research Centers

NADD is the leading North American expert in providing professionals, educators, policy makers, and families with education, training, and information on mental health issues relating to persons with intellectual or developmental disabilities.

Jeanne Farr, CEO
Michelle Jordan, Office Manager
Edward Seliger, Project Coordinator

2207 **National Alliance on Mental Illness (NAMI)**
4301 Wilson Blvd., Suite 300
Arlington, VA 22203

703-524-7600
800-999-6264
info@nami.org
www.nami.org

NAMI provides advocacy, education, support and public awareness so that all individuals and families affected by mental illness can build better lives.

Daniel H. Gillison, CEO
David Levy, CFO
Ken Duckworth, Chief Medical Officer

2208 **National Anxiety Foundation**
3135 Custer Drive
Lexington, KY 40517

859-272-7166
www.nationalanxietyfoundation.org

Offers information and help to persons with panic disorders, manic and depressive disorders and mental illness.

Stephen Cox, MD, President & Medical Director
Linda Vernon Blair, VP
C. Todd Strecker, Secretary-Treasurer

2209 **National Education Alliance for Borderline Personality Disorder**
www.borderlinepersonalitydisorder.com

NEA.BPD National Education Alliance for Borderline Personality Disorder is a nationally recognized organization dedicated to building better lives for millions of Americans affected by Borderline Personality Disorder.

Abby Ingber, Executive Director
Denice Whiteley, Administrative Coordinator

2210 **National Federation of Families**
15800 Crabbs Branch Way, Suite 300
Rockville, MD 20855

240-403-1901
ffcmh@ffcmh.org
www.ffcmh.org

The National family run organization is dedicated exclusively to helping children with mental health needs and their families achieve a better quality of life.

Lynda Gargan, PhD, Executive Director

2211 **National Multiple Sclerosis Society**
733 Third Avenue, 3rd Floor
New York, NY 10017

www.nationalmssociety.org

The National MS Society is a collective of passionate individuals who want to do something about MS now - to move together toward a world free of multiple sclerosis. MS stops people from moving.

Cyndi Zagieboylo, President & CEO
Tami Caesar, Chief Operating Officer

2212 **National Network of Depression Centers**
2350 Green Road, Suite 191
Ann Arbor, MI 48105

www.nndc.org

There goal is to show the many, many people affected by depression, bipolar and other related mood illnesses. Some are people who live with depression, others are family members, co-workers, neighbors of those who do. People of all ages, races, genders, education levels, income levels, jobs, geography, etc.

Dane Larsen, Executive Director
Sagar Parikh, MD, Medical Director
Brad Hovermale, Operations Manager

2213 **Postpartum Support International**
6706 SW 54th Avenue
Portland, OR 97219

503-894-9453
800-944-4PPD
Fax: 503-894-9452
www.postpartum.net

The purpose of the organization is to increase awareness among public and professional communities about the emotional changes that women experience during pregnancy and postpartum.

Wendy N. Davis, PhD, Executive Director

2214 **Suicide Awareness Voices of Education**
7900 Xerxes Avenue S, Suite 810
Bloomington, MN 55431

952-946-7998
www.save.org

The mission of SAVE is to prevent suicide through public awareness and education, reduce stigma and serve as a resource to those touched by suicide.

Pete Theisen, Chief Executive Officer
Daniel J. Reidenberg, Executive Director
Terriann Thommes, Engagement & Events Director

2215 **Suicide Prevention Resource Center**
1000 NE 13th Street, Nicholson Tower, Suite 4900
Oklahoma City, OK 73104

www.sprc.org

SPRC is the a federally supported resource center devoted to advancing the National Strategy for Suicide Prevention. They provide technical assistance, training, and materials to increase the knowledge and expertise of suicide prevention practitioners and other professionals serving people at risk for suicide. They also promote collaboration among a variety of organizations that play a role in developing the field of suicide prevention.

Shelby Rowe, Executive Director

2216 **The Stanley Medical Research Institute**
9800 Medical Center, Suite C-050
Rockville, MD 20850

301-571-0760
Fax: 301-571-0769
info@stanleyresearch.org
www.stanleyresearch.org

The Stanley Medical Research Institute (SMRI) is a nonprofit organization supporting research on the causes of, and treatments for, schizophrenia and bipolar disorder. Since it began in 1989, SMRI has supported more than $550 million in research in over 30 countries.

Maree J. Webster, Ph.D., Executive Director
Wendy Simmons, Research Assistant
Jana Bowcut, M.P.H., Treatment Trials Administrator

State Agencies & Support Groups

2217 **Depressive and Manic-Depressive Assocation of Mount Sinai**
100 LaSalle Street, Suite 5A
New York, NY 10027

917-445-2399
jgg17@columbia.edu
www.columbia.edu

The NYC Depressive and Manic-Depressive Group is a support group for persons with mood disorders, depression and bipolar disorder, as well as their family members and friends.

Research Centers

2218 **University of Pennsylvania, Depression Research Unit**
School of Medicine, Department of Psychiatry
3600 Spruce Street
Philadelphia, PA 19104

215-349-5979
Fax: 215-662-6443
www.med.upenn.edu

The mission of the Depression Research Unit (DRU) at Penn is to foster a greater understanding and knowledge of the causes, diagnosis, and treatment of mood disorders.

Adam I Rubin, Director

Depression / Conferences

2219 University of Texas, Mental Health Clinical Research Center
5323 Harry Hines Boulevard
Dallas, TX 75235
214-648-2951

UT Southwestern Medical Center is home to one of the premier centers in the world for the study, diagnosis and treatment of mental health and addictive disorders.

A John Rush, MD, Director

2220 Yale University, Behavioral Medicine Clinic
Yale School of Medicine
333 Cedar Street
New Haven, CT 06510
203-785-4231

Focuses on mental disorders including schizophrenia and depression.

Henry M Rinder, Director

2221 Yale University, Ribicoff Research Facilities
CT Medical Health Center
34 Park Street
New Haven, CT 06519
203-764-9765
Fax: 203-688-2491

Clinical research in the areas of schizophrenia, depression and mental disorders.

George Heninger, MD, Director

Conferences

2222 ADAA Annual Conference
Anxiety Disorders Association of America
8701 Georgia Avenue, Suite 412
Silver Spring, MD 20910
240-485-1018
information@adaa.org
www.adaa.org

Focusing exclusively on advancing science and treatment of anxiety and related disorders in children and adults.

April

Susan K Gurley, Executive Director

2223 American School Counselor Association Annual Conference
1101 King Street, Suite 310
Alexandria, VA 22314
703-683-2722
800-306-4722
Fax: 703-997-7572
asca@schoolcounselor.org
www.schoolcounselor.org

The mission of ASCA is to represent professional school counselors and to promote professionalism and ethical practices.

3,000 Attendees

Richard Wong, Executive Director
Jennifer Walsh, Director, Education & Training
Kathleen M Rakestraw, Director of Communications

2224 FFCMH Annual Conference
National Federation of Families
15800 Crabbs Branch Way, Suite 300
Rockville, MD 20855
240-403-1901
ffcmh@ffcmh.org
www.ffcmh.org

The only national conference dedicated solely to supporting families whose children - of any age - experience mental health and/or substance use challenges during their lifetime.

November

Lynda Gargan, PhD, Executive Director

2225 NADD Annual Conference & Exhibit Show
National Association for the Dually Diagnosed
12 Hurley Avenue
Kingston, NY 12401
845-331-4336
800-331-5362
Fax: 845-331-4569
info@thenadd.org
www.thenadd.org

Fall

Jeanne Farr, CEO
Michelle Jordan, Office Manager
Edward Seliger, Project Coordinator

2226 NAMI Convention
National Alliance on Mental Illness
3803 N. Fairfax Dr.Suite 100
Arlington, VA 22203
703-524-7600
800-950-6264
Fax: 703-524-9094
TDD: 703-516-7227
info@nami.org
www.nami.org

The NAMI Convention is packed with information, chances to network, leadership development opportunities, and lots more

Summer

Richele Keas, Senior Mgr, Media Relations

Audio Video

2227 Coping with Depression
New Harbinger Publications
5674 Shattuck Avenue
Oakland, CA 94609
510-652-2002
800-748-6273
Fax: 510-652-1613
customerservice@newharbinger.com
newharbinger.com

60 minute videotape that offers a powerful message of hope for anyone struggling with depression.

ISBN: 1-879237-62-8

2228 Cry for Help - How to Help a Friend Who is Depressed or Suicidal
Aquarius Health Care Videos
36 Southern Eagle Cartway
Brewster, MA 2631
508-255-4685
800-451-5006
Fax: 508-255-5705
customerservice@paracletepress.com
www.paracletepress.com

Most suicidal young people don't really want to die; they just want their pain to end. Teen sucide is often preventable if young people know the signs to look for and the steps to take when they suspect a friend is suicidal. This video teaches young people to recognize the warning signs and to take specific actions to help a friend.

22 Minutes

Donna Kaufman

2229 Day for Night: Recognizing Teenage Depression
DRADA-Depression and Related Affective Disorders
600 N Wolfe Street
Baltimore, MD 21287
410-955-4647
Fax: 410-614-3241

2230 Living with Depression and Manic Depression
New Harbinger Publications
5674 Shattuck Avenue
Oakland, CA 94609
510-652-2002
800-748-6273
Fax: 510-652-1613
customerservice@newharbinger.com
newharbinger.com

Describes a program based on years of research and hundreds of interviews with depressed persons. Warm, helpful, and engaging, this tape validates the feelings of people with depression while it encourages positive change.

Depression / Government Agencies

ISBN: 1-879237-63-6

2231 Why Isn't My Child Happy? A Video Guide About Childhood Depression
ADD WareHouse
300 Northwest 70th Avenue, Suite 102
Plantation, FL 33317
954-792-8100
800-233-9273
Fax: 954-792-8545
websales@addwarehouse.com
addwarehouse.com

The first of its kind, this new video deals with childhood depression. Informative and frank about this common problem, this book offers helpful guidance for parents and professionals trying to better understand childhood depression. 110 minutes.

Web Sites

2232 American Academy of Child and Adolescent Psychiatry
3615 Wisconsin Avenue NW
Washington, DC 20016
202-966-7300
Fax: 202-464-0131
www.aacap.org

The AACAP (American Academy of Child and Adolescent Psychiatry) is the leading national professional medical association dedicated to the promotion of healthy development for children, adolescents, and families.

Heidi B. Fordi, Executive Director

2233 Anxiety Disorders Association of America

NOP-ONE-

Offers resources and information for persons with anxiety and stress-related disorders.

2234 Dr. Ivan's Depression Central
www.psycom.net/depression.central.html

www.psycom.net/depression.central.html

This site is the Internet's central clearinghouse for information on all types of depressive disorders and on the most effective treatments for individuals suffering from Major Depression, Manic Depression (Bipolar Disorder), Cyclothymia, Dysthymia and other mood disorders.

Ivan Goldberg, MD, Founder
Satish Reddy, M.D., Editor

2235 Internet Mental Health
www.mentalhealth.com/

internetmentalhealth@shaw.ca
www.mentalhealth.com/

Our goal is to improve understanding, diagnosis, and teatment of meantal illness throughout the world.

Phillip W. Long, M.D., Psychiatrist

2236 Mental Health Net
Po Box 20709
Columbus, OH 43220
614-448-4055
info@centersite.net, editor@centersite.n
www.mentalhelp.net

We wish to provide the following: to discuss, develop and debate in an open forum the future of the mental health field in America and throughout the world. To help coordinate various components of the mental health field so as to bring about greater communication between them. To educate the public about mental health issues, to promote active collaboration between professionals in all segments of mental health development, implementation and policy.

2237 NADD: National Association for the Dually Diagnosed
12 Hurley Avenue
Kingston, NY 12401
845-331-4336
800-331-5362
Fax: 845-331-4569
info@thenadd.org
www.thenadd.org

Nonprofit organization designed to promote the interests of professional and care providers for individuals who have the coexistence of mental illness and intellectual disabilities. NADD provides conferences, educational services and training materials to professionals, parents, concerned citizens and service organizations.

Jeanne Farr, CEO
Michelle Jordan, Office Manager
Edward Seliger, Project Coordinator

2238 Online Mendelian Inheritance in Man
McKusick-Nathans Institue of Genetic Medicine-JHU
Baltimore, MD 21205
www.omim.org

This database is a catalog of human genes and genetic disorders.

Ada Hamosh, MD, Scientific Director

2239 Seasonal Affective Disorder
www.alt.support.depression.seasonal

www.alt.support.depression.seasonal

The SAD Association is a voluntary organization and registered charity which informs the public and health professions about SAD and supports and advises sufferers of the illness.

2240 Understanding and Treating Depression
www.couns.uiuc.edu/depression.htm

www.couns.uiuc.edu/depression.htm

Offers an understanding of depression, causes, how to help yourself, things to do, what to avoid while in the depression state, and treatments of the depression.

2241 Wing of Madness: A Depression Guide
www.wingofmadness.com

www.wingofmadness.com

Is a nonprofit organization dedicated to disseminating information about depression to consumers.

Book Publishers

2242 Anxiety & Depression In Adults & Children
Sage Publications
2455 Teller Road
Newbury Park, CA 91320
805-499-0721

1994 304 pages Softcover
ISBN: 0-803970-21-8

2243 Ask the Doctor: Depression
Andrews McMeel Publishing
PO Box 419150
Kansas City, MO 64141
816-932-6700
800-233-2336
Fax: 212-698-7336

A look at depression, its symptoms, what causes it, and what you can do about it. Learn the difference between mood problems and genuine depression, and how to read warning signs such as sleep abnormalities, nervousness, and suicidal thoughts. Information on chemicals, genetics, and medical solutions.

128 pages Softcover
ISBN: 0-836227-11-5

2244 Coping with Depression
Rosen Publishing Group
29 E 21st Street
New York, NY 10010
800-237-9932
Fax: 888-436-4643
rosenpub@tribeca.ios.com
www.rosenpublishing.com

With an emphasis on life's myriad difficulties, the authors help teens find practical ways to cope with depression.

Depression / Book Publishers

ISBN: 0-823919-51-0

2245 Dealing with Depression: Five Ways to Help
Haworth Press
10 Alice Street
Binghamton, NY 13904
607-722-8277
Fax: 607-722-1424

1995
ISBN: 1-560249-33-1

2246 Depression and Its Treatment
Warner Books
1271 Avenue of the Americas
New York, NY 10020
212-522-7200

A layman's guide to help one understand and cope with America's number one mental health problem.

157 pages

2247 Depression, the Mood Disease
Johns Hopkins University Press
2715 N Charles Street
Baltimore, MD 21218
410-516-6900
800-537-5487
Fax: 410-516-6998
www.highbeam.com/doc/1G1-159331264.html

This book explores the many faces of an illness that will affect as many as 36 million Americans at some point in their lives. Updated to reflect state-of-the-art treatment.

1993 240 pages
ISBN: 0-801851-84-X

2248 Depressive Illnesses: Treatments Bring New Hope
Superintendent of Documents
PO Box 371954
Pittsburgh, PA 15250
202-512-2250

Offers the general public an overview of the various depressive illnesses. Topics include causes, symptoms and types of depression, clinical evaluation and treatment, helpful suggestions for family and friends, and other sources of information.

28 pages

2249 Encyclopedia of Depression
Facts on File
Department M274, 11 Penn Plaza
New York, NY 10001
212-290-8090
800-322-8755
Fax: 212-678-3633

This volume defines and explains all terms and topics relating to depression.

170 pages Hardbound

2250 Essential Guide to Psychiatric Drugs
Saint Martin's Press
175 5th Avenue
New York, NY 10010
212-674-5151
800-221-7945
Fax: 212-420-9314

Basic information on 123 drugs used for depression, anxiety and bipolar illness.

2251 Everything You Need To Know About Depression
Rosen Publishing Group
29 E 21st Street
New York, NY 10010
212-777-3017
800-237-9932
Fax: 212-436-4643
rosenpub@tribeca.ios.com
www.rosenpublishing.com

An important resource for teens who are looking for help with depression.

Grades 7-12
ISBN: 0-823926-06-0

2252 Handbook of School-Based Interventions
Courage to Change
PO Box 1268
Newburgh, NY 12551
800-440-4003
Fax: 800-772-6499

Comprehensive volume that describes interventions for virtually every major problem behavior students may exhibit from K-12. All interventions are research-based and guidance is given for practical application of the techniques. Topics range from dishonesty, academic performance, procrastination and low self-esteem to obsessive-compulsive behavior, substance abuse, AIDS and depression.

512 pages Hardcover

2253 Help Me, I'm Sad
Penguin Putnam
PO Box 999
Bergenfield, NJ 07621
800-526-0275
Fax: 800-227-9604

Helping and understanding a child with depression.

2254 Helping Your Child Cope with Depression and Suicidal Thoughts
Jossey-Bass
111 River Street
Hoboken, NJ 07030
201-748-6000
800-956-7739
Fax: 201-748-6088
www.josseybass.com

Shows parents how to learn to talk, listen, and communicate effectively with a depressed child; signs to watch for and situations which may cause a wish to commit suicide.

192 pages
ISBN: 0-787908-44-4

2255 Helping Your Depressed Child
Prima Publishing
PO Box 1260
Rocklin, CA 95677
916-624-5718

Reassuring guide to the causes and treatment of childhood and adolescent depression.

284 pages

2256 Mood Apart
Basic Books
10 E 53rd Street
New York, NY 10022
212-207-7057

An overview of depression and manic depression and the available treatments for them.

363 pages

2257 Overcoming Depression
Harper & Row
10 E 53rd Street
New York, NY 10022
212-207-7000

1987 318 pages Softcover

2258 Panic Disorder in the Medical Setting
Superintendent of Documents
PO Box 371954
Pittsburgh, PA 15250
202-512-2250

This book serves the primary care physicians as a helpful guide in recognizing and treating panic disorder in patients and in identifying those who need psychiatric consultation or referrals.

1993 135 pages

2259 Prozac Nation: Young & Depressed in America, A Memoir
Houghton Mifflin Company
222 Berkeley Street
Boston, MA 02116
617-351-3698
800-225-3362

Struck with depression at 11, now 27, Wurtzel chronicles her struggle with the illness. Witty, terrifying and sometimes funny, it tells the story of a young life almost destroyed by depression.

317 pages

2260 Psychotherapy of Severe and Mild Depression
Jason Aronson
400 Keystone Industrial Park
Dunmore, PA 18521
800-782-0015
Fax: 201-840-7242
www.aronson.com

464 pages Softcover
ISBN: 1-568211-46-5

2261 Report of the Secretary's Task Force on Youth Suicide
Superintendent of Documents
PO Box 371954
Pittsburgh, PA 15250
202-512-2250

A comprehensive review of information about youth suicide. The task force recommendations are presented in Volume 1.

110 pages

2262 Sad Days, Glad Days
National Alliance for the Mentally Ill
PO Box 753
Waldorf, MD 20604
703-524-7600
www.NIMF.org

Helps five to nine-year-olds understand a parent's depression.
1995

2263 Suicide, Why?
National Alliance for the Mentally Ill
PO Box 753
Waldorf, MD 20604
703-524-7600
www.NAMI.org

An authoritative book, noting that suicide is usually caused by brain disorders.
1989

2264 Surprising Truth About Depression: Medical Breakthroughs That Can Work
Zondervan
5300 Patterson SE
Grand Rapids, MI 49530
616-698-6900
Fax: 616-698-3439
www.zondervan.com

1994 224 pages Softcover
ISBN: 0-310401-01-1

2265 Treating Depressed Children
New Harbinger Publications
5674 Shattuck Avenue
Oakland, CA 94609
800-748-6273
Fax: 510-652-5472
customerservice@newharbinger.com
www.newharbinger.com

This book explains a 12-session treatment program to help children change their negative thoughts, gain confidence and recognize their emotions. These actions are achieved with the help of cartoons and role-playing games.

160 pages Hardcover
ISBN: 1-572240-61-X

Laseu Pfaff, Publicist

2266 Treating Depression
Jossey-Bass
111 River Street
Hoboken, NJ 07030
201-748-6000
800-956-7739
Fax: 201-748-6088
www.josseybass.com

Offers guidelines and specific models for intervention in the treatment of numerous types and subtypes of depression. Also will assist you in deciding if it is appropriate to prescribe medication, if psychotherapy is the proper course of action, or if it is best to use a combination of medication and psychotherapy.

1997 223 pages
ISBN: 0-787915-85-8

2267 Understanding Depression
University Press of Mississippi
3825 Ridgewood Road
Jackson, MS 39211
601-432-6205
800-737-7788
Fax: 601-432-6217
press@ihl.state.ms.us
www.upress.state.ms.us

A clear explanation for those who know the illness personally and for those who want to understand them.

120 pages Hardcover/Ppbck
ISBN: 1-578061-68-7

2268 Understanding Your Teenager's Depression
Berkley Books
200 Madison Avenue
New York, NY 10016
212-951-8800

1994 352 pages Softcover
ISBN: 0-399518-56-8

2269 When Nothing Matters Anymore: A Survival Guide for Depressed Teens
Free Spirit Publishing
217 5th Avenue N
Minneapolis, MN 55401
612-338-2068
800-735-7323
Fax: 612-337-5050
help4kids@freespirit.com
www.freespirit.com

Written for teens with depression and those who feel despondent, dejected or alone. This powerful book offers help, hope, and potentially lifesaving facts and advice.

176 pages
ISBN: 1-575420-36-8

Penne Post, Tradesales Associate

2270 Working with Children and Adolescents in Groups
Courage to Change
PO Box 1268
Newburgh, NY 12551
800-440-4003
Fax: 800-772-6499

Step-by-step guide that discusses how to effectively treat problem behavior in children and adolescents using small groups. Based on empirical research and their own work with groups, the authors show how a variety of approaches can be effectively combined to help resolve such problem behaviors as fighting and low self-esteem.

384 pages Hard Cover

2271 Yesterday's Tomorrow
Hazelden
15251 Pleasant Valley Road
Center City, MN 55012
612-257-4010
800-328-9000
Fax: 917-339-0325
www.hazelden.org

A meditation book that shows why and how recovery works, from the author's own experiences.

Depression / Magazines

432 pages Softcover
ISBN: 1-568381-60-3

Magazines

2272 EA Message
Emotions Anonymous
PO Box 4245
Saint Paul, MN 55104
651-647-9712
Fax: 651-647-1593
info@emotionsanonymous.org
www.emotionsanonymous.org

Quarterly magazine.
Electronic
Karen Mead, Executive Director

Newsletters

2273 National Foundation for Depressive Illness
PO Box 2257
New York, NY 10116
212-268-4260
800-248-4344
Fax: 212-268-4434
www.depression.org

Information on the myths and misconceptions surrounding the illness. Informs the public, health care providers, healthcare professionals and corporations about depression and manic depression, and provides the information about correct diagnosis and treatment and the availability of qualified doctors and support groups.

4 pages Quarterly
Amy C Russell, Editor

Pamphlets

2274 Depression Is a Treatable Illness: A Patients Guide
Department of Health & Human Services
2101 E Jefferson Street, Suite 501
Rockville, MD 20852
301-217-1245

Tells about major depressive disorder, which is only one form of depressive illness. This booklet answers important questions regarding this disorder and gives information on where to go for more help.

2275 Depression in Children and Adolescents: A Fact Sheet for Physicians
National Institute of Mental Health
6001 Executive Boulevard, Room 6200, MSC 9663
Bethesda, MD 20892
301-443-4536
866-615-6464
Fax: 301-443-4279
TTY: 301-443-8431
nimhinfo@nih.gov
www.nimh.nih.gov

Discusses the scope of the problem and the screening tools used in evaluating children with depression.

8 pages
Dr. Francis S. Collins, Director

2276 Let's Talk About Depression
Superintendent of Documents
PO Box 371954
Pittsburgh, PA 15250
202-512-2250

Targeted especially for inner-city youth. The colorful design will capture attention and focus on depression in a way that young people will understand and identify with.

2277 Let's Talk Facts About Childhood Disorders
American Psychiatric Association
1400 K Street NW
Washington, DC 20005
202-682-6220

Offers information on depression and depressive disorders including the causes, symptoms, treatments, anxiety, and various other phobias.

2278 Living Without Depression & Manic Depression: A Workbook
National Alliance for the Mentally Ill
3803 N. Fairfax Drive, Suite 100
Arlington, VA 22203
703-524-7600
800-950-6264
Fax: 703-524-9094
www.NAMI.org

Workbook offering checklists and helpful advice targeted for individuals whose depressive illness is stabilized.
1994
Jim Payne, J.D., President
Ralph E. Nelson, Jr., M.D., First Vice President
Marilyn Ricci, M.S., R.D., Second Vice President

2279 Major Depression in Children and Adolescents
Center for Mental Health Services
PO Box 42490
Washington, DC 20015
800-789-2647
Fax: 301-984-8796
ken@mentalhealth.org
mentalhealth.org

This fact sheet defines depression and its signs, identifies types of help available, and suggests what parents or other caregivers can do.
2 pages

2280 Now We Can Successfully Treat the Illness Called Depression
National Foundation for Depressive Illness (NAFDI)
PO Box 2257
New York, NY 10116
212-268-4260
800-248-4344
Fax: 212-268-4434
www.depression.org

Basic information on depression and manic depression, gives symptoms, encourages persons who have symptoms to seek medical treatment. Tips on managing depressive illness.
Amy C Russell, Editor

2281 Panic Disorder
National Institutes of Health
5600 Fishers Lane, Room 7C-02
Rockville, MD 20857
301-443-4707
Fax: 301-443-6000

Written for the lay public, this pamphlet contains a description of panic disorder, gives the symptoms, describes treatment methods, and encourages the person who has the symptoms to seek treatment.

2282 Plain Talk About Depression
Superintendent of Documents
PO Box 371954
Pittsburgh, PA 15250
202-512-2250

A flyer discussing types of depression, major depression; symptoms and causes.

2283 Understanding Panic Disorder
National Institutes of Health
5600 Fishers Lane, Room 7C-02
Rockville, MD 20857
301-443-4707
Fax: 301-443-6000

Offers information on what panic disorder is, symptoms, causes, treatment, medications and therapy.

2284 Useful Information on Phobias and Panic
Superintendent of Documents
PO Box 371954
Pittsburgh, PA 15250
202-512-2250

This booklet provides information on both phobias and panic. Symptoms, causes and treatments of these disorders are referred to. If you know someone who is excessively fearful, this booklet will be of great help to them in understanding their problem.

40 pages 50 copies

2285 What to Do When a Friend Is Depressed: Guide for Students
Superintendent of Documents
PO Box 371954
Pittsburgh, PA 15250   202-512-2250

Offers information on depression and its symptoms and suggests things a young person can do to guide a depressed friend in finding help.

Diabetes Mellitus / Description

Description

2286 DIABETES MELLITUS
Involves the following Biologic System(s):
Endocrinologic Disorders

Diabetes mellitis refers to an inability of the body to utilize glucose. There are two types of DM: Insulin-dependent diabetes mellitus, referred to as Type I diabetes, is a disorder in which insufficient production of insulin by the pancreas results in abnormally high levels of the sugar glucose in the blood. Insulin is a hormone that regulates and stabilizes blood glucose levels by promoting the movement of energy-rich glucose into body cells for energy production or into the liver and fat cells for storage. Type I diabetes may also cause impaired fat metabolism and long-term complications affecting certain large and small blood vessels (angiopathy), the nerve-rich membranes at the back of the eyes (retinas), skin, kidneys, nerves, or other tissues of the body. The exact cause of Type I diabetes is unknown. However, researchers speculate that certain environmental factors, such as a viral infection, may inappropriately trigger the immune system to destroy insulin-producing cells within the pancreas (beta cells), resulting in severe insulin deficiency. Genetic factors are also thought to play some role in causing a predisposition for the disorder.

Type I diabetes is the major form of diabetes affecting children. It affects 1 million patients in the United States, most often in young people, 10-14 years of age. The other major type of diabetes, Type II diabetes, may be characterized by a resistance to the effects of insulin. Although this type of diabetes may occur at any age, it most commonly becomes apparent in middle-aged or older people, but is increasingly common during childhood and adolescence. It is most common in obese patients. In some children, various forms of diabetes may occur secondary to certain genetic multisystemic disorders that affect the pancreas, such as cystic fibrosis; other endocrine disorders, such as Cushing's syndrome; the administration of particular drugs; or exposure to certain poisons.

In most children with Type I diabetes, associated symptoms and findings may appear to occur suddenly and may include excessive urine production by the kidneys, causing increased urination (polyuria) and excessive thirst (polydipsia); weight loss; and abnormally increased hunger (polyphagia). Additional abnormalities may include exhaustion, blurred vision, abnormal sensations (paresthesias) in the hands and feet, and increased irritability. Without prompt diagnosis and treatment, symptoms may rapidly progress to a metabolic condition known as ketoacidosis. Because of deficient insulin production, the body's cells begin to rely on sources of energy other than glucose, causing an excessive breakdown of fats and an abnormal accumulation of certain chemical compounds (ketones) in body tissues and fluids. Early symptoms associated with ketoacidosis may be relatively mild, including increased urination, vomiting and dehydration but, without appropriate treatment, coma and potentially life-threatening complications may occur. The treatment of ketoacidosis may include the immediate administration of intravenous fluids; replacement of electrolytes, such as sodium and potassium; initiation of intravenous insulin therapy; measures to prevent or appropriately treat increased fluid pressure within the brain; and other therapies as required.

Patients with either Type I or Type II diabetes may eventually develop certain long-term complications associated with the disease. Complications may include thickening and leaking of the walls of certain small blood vessels, narrowing of medium and large-size arteries due to plaque development (atherosclerosis), abnormally high blood pressure (hypertension), poor blood circulation, and problems affecting the eyes, kidneys, nerves, and skin. For example, kidney damage may result in impaired kidney function and kidney failure; damage to blood vessels within the nerve-rich membranes at the back of the eyes (diabetic retinopathy) may lead to visual impairment; and nerve damage may cause weakness or the loss of certain sensations, such as changes in temperature or pressure, increasing the risk of injury. In addition, impaired blood supply to certain skin areas may increase the risk of developing skin sores (ulcers). Poor wound healing and susceptibility to infected foot ulcers may lead to localized loss of tissue (necrosis), potentially requiring amputation. Diet is central to management of diabetes and must be individualized according to the patient's activity level, food preferences, and need to attain and maintain ideal weight. Regular exercise is also correlated with better glucose control. Individuals with Type I diabetes take insulin, delivered either by injection or by insulin pump. Type II diabetics can take oral blood-sugar lowering (hypoglycemic) drugs that potentiate insulin secretion. Other drugs help regulate glucose storage or release.

National Associations & Support Groups

2287 American Academy of Pediatrics
345 Park Blvd
Itasca, IL 60143
800-433-9016
Fax: 847-434-8000
mcc@aap.org
www.aap.org

The American Academy of Pediatrics and its member pediatricians are committed to the attainment of optimal physical, mental and social health and well-being for all infants, children, adolescents, and young adults.

Lynn Olson, PhD, President
Mark Del Monte, JD, CEO/Executive VP
Vera Tait, MD, FAAP, Chief Medical Officer

2288 American Association of Diabetes Educators
125 S Wacker Drive, Suite 600
Chicago, IL 60606
800-338-3633
www.diabeteseducator.org

Founded in 1973, AADE is a multidisciplinary association of healthcare professionals dedicated to integrating self-management as a key outcome in the care of people with diabetes and related chronic conditions.

Matthew Hornberger, Chief Executive Officer
Leslie Kolb, Chief Operating Officer
Jackie Bellan, Director of Meetings

2289 American Autoimmune Related Diseases Association
19176 Hall Road, Suite 130
Clinton, MI 48038
586-776-3900
aarda@aarda.org
www.aarda.org

The American Autoimmune Related Diseases Association is dedicated to the eradication of autoimmune diseases and the alleviation of suffering and the socioeconomic impact of autoimmunity through fostering and facilitating collaboration in the areas of education, public awareness, research, and patient services in an effective, ethical and efficient manner.

Lilly Stairs, Interim President/CEO
Laura Simpson, COO

2290 American Diabetes Association
2451 Crystal Drive, Ste 900
Arlington, VA 22202
703-549-1500
800-342-2383
Fax: 703-836-7439
askada@diabetes.org
www.diabetes.org

The nation's leading voluntary organization concerned with diabetes and its complications. The mission of the organization is to prevent and cure diabetes and to improve the lives of persons with diabetes. Offers a network of 52 affiliates with over 1 million volunteers, including a professional membership of more than 14,000 physicians, social workers, nutritionists, educators and nurses.

Tracey D. Brown, CEO

2291 Center for Disabilities and Development
University of Iowa Stead Family Children's Hospita
100 Hawkins Drive
Iowa City, IA 52242
319-353-6900
877-686-0031
Fax: 319-356-7700
cdd-webmaster@uiowa.edu
www.uiowa.edu

A trusted resource for healthcare, training, research and information for people with disabilities that include: behavior disorders, brain injury, cerebral palsy, diabetes, down syndrome, learning disabilities, sleep disorders and spina bifida.

Dianne McBrien, MD, Medical Director

2292 Child Neurology Foundation
601 W Short Street
Lexington, KY 40508
888-417-3435
info@childneurologyfoundation.org
childneurologyfoundation.org

The Child Neurology Foundation connects partners from all areas of the child neurology community so those navigating the journey of disease diagnosis, management, and care have the ongoing support from those dedicated to treatments and cures.

Amy Brin, Executive Director
Katie Hentges, Director, Programs
Brea McCormley, Director, Development

2293 Juvenile Diabetes Foundation International
200 Vesey Street, 28th Floor
New York, NY 10281
800-533-2873
Fax: 212-785-9595
info@jdrf.org
www.jdrf.org

Focuses energies on fund-raising, referrals, educational materials and information pertaining to juvenile diabetes.

Aaron J. Kowalski, PhD, Chief Executive Officer
Rob King, Chief Financial/Admin Officer
Sanjoy Dutta, PhD, Chief Scientific Officer

Libraries & Resource Centers

2294 National Diabetes Information Clearinghouse
1 Information Way
Bethesda, MD 20892
301-654-3327
800-860-8747
Fax: 703-738-4929
TTY: 866-569-1162
healthinfo@niddk.nih.gov
www.niddk.nih.gov/health-information/

Offers various materials, resources, books, pamphlets and more for persons and families in the area of diabetes.

Research Centers

2295 Center for the Partially Sighted
6101 W Centinela Ave, Suite 150
Culver City, CA 90230
310-988-1970
Fax: 310-458-8179
info@low-vision.org
www.low-vision.org

Provides professional, comprehensive vision rehabilitation services to visually impaired people of all ages. For those whose sight is severely limited due to macular degeneration, diabetic retinopathy, glaucoma, retinal detachment, stroke or other conditions not correctable medically or surgically.

Sidney Machtinger, Chairman
Linnae M Anderson, Secretary

2296 Joslin Diabetes Center
One Joslin Place
Boston, MA 02215
617-309-2400
800-567-5461
diabetes@joslin.harvard.edu
www.joslin.org

Joslin Diabetes Center, a teaching a research affiliate of Harvard Medical School, is a one-of-a-kind institution on the front lines of the world epidemic of diabetes - leading the battle to conquer diabetes in all of its forms through cutting-edge research and innovative approaces to clinical care and education.

John L Brooks III, President & CEO
Martin J Abrahamson, MD, Senior Vice President, Director
George L King, MD, SVP & Research Director

Audio Video

2297 Not So Sweet: Living With Diabetes
Fanlight Productions
32 Court Street, 21st Floor
Brooklyn, NY 11201
718-488-8900
800-876-1710
Fax: 718-488-8642
info@fanlight.com, orders@fanlight.com
www.fanlight.com

Exciting new approaches to the prevention and control of diabetes, and a look at its prevalence in Native American communities in particular.

47 minutes VHS

Web Sites

2298 Mediconsult
A13/5/5 One Ampang Business Avenue, Jalan Ampang U
Selangor, Ma
6- 3 -253
Fax: 6- 3 -253
info@mediconsult.com.my
www.mediconsult.com.my

We are committed to provide excellent and professional services to our business partners. Through a team approach we will develop, provide and continuously improve our knowledge and competency. We work towards the betterment of healthcare delivery systems for the community.

Sharif Lough Abdullah, Director
Dieter Nassler, Director
Nguyen Thi Dung, Director

2299 National Diabetes Information Clearinghouse
1 Information Way
Bethesda, MD 20892
800-860-8747
Fax: 703-738-4929
healthinfo@niddk.nih.gov
www.niddk.nih.gov/health-information/

The Information Clearinghouse is an information dissemination service of the National Institute of Diabetes and Digestive and Kidney Diseases.

Book Publishers

2300 Diabetes 101
Wiley
1 Wiley Drive
Somerset, NJ 08875
732-469-4400
800-225-5945
Fax: 732-302-2300
bookinfo@wiley.com
www.wiley.com

Revised and expanded second edition. A layman's guide to everything you need to know to live healthfully with diabetes.

Diabetes Mellitus / Book Publishers

175 pages
ISBN: 1-565610-24-5

2301 Diabetes Dictionary
National Diabetes Information Clearinghouse
2 Information Way
Bethesda, MD 20892
301-654-3810
Fax: 301-907-8906
nddic@info.niddk.nih.gov
www.niddk.nih.gov

Illustrated glossary of more than 300 diabetes-related terms.

2302 Diabetes Medical Nutition Therapy
American Diabetes Association
1701 North Beauregard Street
Alexandria, VA 22311
800-232-3472
Fax: 703-549-6995
www.diabetes.org

A professional guide to management and nutrition education resources. Provides in-depth coverage of nutrition assessment, goal setting, intervention, and outcome evaluation. Information is provided on specific resources and case studies are cited for practical examples.

2303 Diabetes Teaching Guide for People Who Use Insulin
Joslin Diabetes Center
1 Joslin Place
Boston, MA 02215
617-732-2400

Discusses the causes of diabetes, the role of diet and exercise, meal planning and complications. Also provides information on drawing blood, mixing and injecting insulin.

2304 Endocrine & Metabolic Disorders Sourcebook 3rd Edition
Keith Jones, author

Omnigraphics
615 Griswold Street, Ste 520
Detroit, MI 48226
610-461-3548
800-234-1340
Fax: 800-875-1340
contact@omnigraphics.com
www.omnigraphics.com

Basic information for the lay person about pancreatic and insulin-related disorders such as pancreatitis, diabetes and hypoglycemia; adrenal gland disorders such as Cushing's syndrome, Addison's disease and congenital adrenal hyperplasia; pituitary gland disorders such as growth hormone deficiency, acromegaly and pituitary tumors; and thyroid disorders such as hypothyroidism, Grave's disease, Hashimoto's disease and goiter.

560 pages
ISBN: 0-780815-43-8

2305 Even Little Kids Get Diabetes
Albert Whitman & Company
6340 Oakton Street
Morton Grove, IL 60053
847-531-0033
800-255-7675
Fax: 847-531-0039
www.albertwhitman.com

A preschooler tells how when she was only two, that she was diagnosed with this common disease and describes her daily treatment and the precautions her family must observe.

ISBN: 0-807521-58-2

Joseph Boyd, President
Joe Campbell, Customer Service

2306 Everyone Likes to Eat
Wiley
1 Wiley Drive
Somerset, NJ 08875
732-469-4400
800-225-5945
Fax: 732-302-2300
custserv@wiley.com
www.wiley.com

Revised and up-to-date second edition. How children can eat most of the foods they enjoy and still take care of their diabetes. Intended for elementary-school-age children, this guide is filled with activities, puzzles, and problem-solving exercises.

ISBN: 1-565610-26-1

2307 Grilled Cheese
American Diabetes Association
1701 North Beauregard Street
Alexandria, VA 22311
800-232-3472
Fax: 703-549-6995
www.diabetes.org

Story designed to ease children's fears and frustrations of having diabetes.

2308 If Your Child Has Diabetes: An Answer Book for Parents
Putnam Publishing Group
200 Madison Avenue
New York, NY 10016
212-951-8400

Provides information and recommendations for parents of children with diabetes on subjects such as school, recreation, medical and life insurance and employment as well as general information about diabetes.

2309 In Control: Guide for Teens with Diabetes
Wiley
1 Wiley Drive
Somerset, NJ 08875
732-469-4400
800-225-5945
Fax: 732-302-2300
custserv@wiley.com
www.wiley.com

Dispels myths and tackles the real issues that teens with diabetes face. Teaches how to care for their diabetes without letting it get in the way of their lives.

ISBN: 1-565610-61-X

Mari Baker, Former Chief Executive Officer
Jean-Lou Chameau, President

2310 Kiss the Candy Days Good-Bye
Delacorte Press
1540 Broadway
New York, NY 10036
212-354-6500

This book focuses on Jimmy who is surprised to learn he has diabetes after seeming so healthy and fit. The story contains information on symptoms and the dangers of untreated diabetes.

2311 Let's Talk About Diabetes
Rosen Publishing Group's PowerKids Press
29 E 21st Street
New York, NY 10010
212-777-3017
800-237-9932
Fax: 888-436-4643
rosenpub@tribeca.ios.com
www.powerkidspress.com

Defines diabetes and shows how a child can live a very normal life with the disease. Grades K-5.

24 pages
ISBN: 0-823951-96-0

2312 Life with Diabetes: A Series of Teaching Outlines
American Diabetes Association
1701 North Beauregard Street
Alexandria, VA 22311
800-342-2383
Fax: 703-549-6995
www.diabetes.org

Presents a comprehensive curriculum for diabetes education. Each outline includes a statement of purpose, pre-requisites for attending the session, materials needed for teaching the session, recommended teaching method, a content outline, instructor notes, and evaluation and documentation plan, and suggested readings related to each topic.

Larry Hausner, Chief Executive Officer
Shereen Arent, Executive Vice President

2313 Raising a Child with Diabetes: A Guide for Parents
American Diabetes Association
1701 North Beauregard Street
Alexandria, VA 22311
800-342-2383
Fax: 703-549-6995
www.diabetes.org

You'll learn how to help your child adjust to insulin, to allow for favorite foods, have a busy schedule and still feel healthy and strong, negotiate the twists and turns of being different, and much more.

Larry Hausner, Chief Executive Officer
Shereen Arent, Executive Vice President

Magazines

2314 Countdown
Juvenile Diabetes Foundation International
432 Park Avenue S
New York, NY 10016
212-889-7575
Fax: 212-532-7891

Offers the latest news and information in diabetes research and treatment to everyone from an international arena of diabetes investigators to parents of small children with diabetes, from physicians to school teachers, from pharmacists to corporate executives.

Sandy Dylak, Editor

2315 Diabetes Forecast
American Diabetes Association
1701 North Beauregard Street
Alexandria, VA 22311
800-342-2383
Fax: 703-549-6995
www.diabetes.org

The monthly lifestyle magazine for people with diabetes, featuring complete, in-depth coverage of all aspects of living with diabetes.

Janel Wright, JD, Chair, Anchorage, AK
David G. Marrero, PhD, President, Health Care
Suzanne Berry, MBA, CAE, Interim CEO

2316 Voice of the Diabetic
National Federation of the Blind
200 East Wells Street at Jernigan Place
Baltimore, MD 21230
410-659-9314
Fax: 410-685-5653
nfb@nfb.org
nfb.org/voice-diabetic

The leading publication in the diabetes field. Each issue addresses the problems and concerns of diabetes, with a special emphasis for those who have lost vision due to diabetes. Available in print and on cassette.

Journals

2317 Diabetes
American Diabetes Association
1701 North Beauregard Street
Alexandria, VA 22311
800-342-2383
Fax: 703-549-6995
www.diabetes.org

A peer-reviewed journal focusing on laboratory research.

Janel Wright, JD, Chair, Anchorage, AK
David G. Marrero, PhD, President, Health Care
Suzanne Berry, MBA, CAE, Interim CEO

2318 Diabetes Care
American Diabetes Association
1701 North Beauregard Street
Alexandria, VA 22311
800-342-2383
Fax: 703-549-6995
www.diabetes.org

A peer-reviewed journal emphasizing reviews, documentaries and original research on topics of interest to clinicians.

Janel Wright, JD, Chair, Anchorage, AK
David G. Marrero, PhD, President, Health Care
Suzanne Berry, MBA, CAE, Interim CEO

2319 Diabetes Spectrum: From Research to Practice
American Diabetes Association
1701 North Beauregard Street
Alexandria, VA 22311
800-342-2383
Fax: 703-549-6995
www.diabetes.org

A journal translating research into practice and focusing on diabetes education and counseling.

Janel Wright, JD, Chair, Anchorage, AK
David G. Marrero, PhD, President, Health Care
Suzanne Berry, MBA, CAE, Interim CEO

Newsletters

2320 Clinical Diabetes
American Diabetes Association
1701 North Beauregard Street
Alexandria, VA 22311
800-342-2383
Fax: 703-549-6995
www.diabetes.org

A bimonthly newsletter providing practical treatment information for primary care physicians.

Janel Wright, JD, Chair, Anchorage, AK
David G. Marrero, PhD, President, Health Care
Suzanne Berry, MBA, CAE, Interim CEO

2321 Diabetes Advisor
American Diabetes Association
1701 North Beauregard Street
Alexandria, VA 22311
800-342-2383
Fax: 703-549-6995
www.diabetes.org

Offers informative articles and research in the area of diabetes for professionals and patients. Offers facts and research on diagnosis, symptoms, technology and the newest devices for persons with diabetes, as well as referral and hotline numbers.

Janel Wright, JD, Chair, Anchorage, AK
David G. Marrero, PhD, President, Health Care
Suzanne Berry, MBA, CAE, Interim CEO

2322 Diabetes Dateline
National Diabetes Information Clearinghouse
9000 Rockville Pike
Bethesda, MD 20892
301-496-3583
Fax: 301-907-8906
nddic@info.niddk.nih.gov
www.niddk.nih.gov

Griffin P. Rodgers, MD, MACP, Director
Dr. Gregory Germino, Deputy Director
Kevin Abbott, Program Director

2323 Diabetes Educator
American Association of Diabetes Educators
444 N Michigan Avenue, Suite 1240
Chicago, IL 60611
312-424-2426
800-338-3633
Fax: 312-424-2427
www.aadenet.org

Offers information to health professionals working with persons with diabetes.

James J Balija, Executive Director

2324 Kid's Corner
American Diabetes Association
1701 North Beauregard Street
Alexandria, VA 22311
800-342-2383
Fax: 703-549-6995
www.diabetes.org

A mini-magazine for kids that offers word searches, puzzles and jokes-plus an encouraging story in each issue about kids with diabetes.

Janel Wright, JD, Chair, Anchorage, AK
David G. Marrero, PhD, President, Health Care
Suzanne Berry, MBA, CAE, Interim CEO

Diabetes Mellitus / Pamphlets

Pamphlets

2325 Children with Diabetes
9000 Rockville Pike
Bethesda, MD 20892
301-496-3583
Fax: 301-907-8906
nddic@info.niddk.nih.gov
www.niddk.nih.gov

Griffin P. Rodgers, MD, MACP, Director
Dr. Gregory Germino, Deputy Director
Kevin Abbott, Program Director

2326 Complementary and Alternative Therapies for Diabetes Treatment
9000 Rockville Pike
Bethesda, MD 20892
301-496-3583
Fax: 301-907-8906
nddic@info.niddk.nih.gov
www.niddk.nih.gov

Griffin P. Rodgers, MD, MACP, Director
Dr. Gregory Germino, Deputy Director
Kevin Abbott, Program Director

2327 Diabetes Insipidus
9000 Rockville Pike
Bethesda, MD 20892
301-496-3583
Fax: 301-907-8906
nddic@info.niddk.nih.gov
www.niddk.nih.gov

Griffin P. Rodgers, MD, MACP, Director
Dr. Gregory Germino, Deputy Director
Kevin Abbott, Program Director

2328 Diabetes Overview
9000 Rockville Pike
Bethesda, MD 20892
301-496-3583
Fax: 301-907-8906
nddic@info.niddk.nih.gov
www.niddk.nih.gov

Griffin P. Rodgers, MD, MACP, Director
Dr. Gregory Germino, Deputy Director
Kevin Abbott, Program Director

2329 Diabetes in African Americans
9000 Rockville Pike
Bethesda, MD 20892
301-496-3583
Fax: 301-907-8906
nddic@info.niddk.nih.gov
www.niddk.nih.gov

Griffin P. Rodgers, MD, MACP, Director
Dr. Gregory Germino, Deputy Director
Kevin Abbott, Program Director

2330 Diabetes in Hispanic Americans
9000 Rockville Pike
Bethesda, MD 20892
301-496-3583
Fax: 301-907-8906
nddic@info.niddk.nih.gov
www.niddk.nih.gov

Griffin P. Rodgers, MD, MACP, Director
Dr. Gregory Germino, Deputy Director
Kevin Abbott, Program Director

2331 Diabetic Neuropathy: the Nerve Damage of Diabetes
9000 Rockville Pike
Bethesda, MD 20892
301-496-3583
Fax: 301-907-8906
nddic@info.niddk.nih.gov
www.niddk.nih.gov

Griffin P. Rodgers, MD, MACP, Director
Dr. Gregory Germino, Deputy Director
Kevin Abbott, Program Director

2332 Diabetics Control and Complications Trial
9000 Rockville Pike
Bethesda, MD 20892
301-496-3583
Fax: 301-907-8906
nddic@info.niddk.nih.gov
www.niddk.nih.gov

Griffin P. Rodgers, MD, MACP, Director
Dr. Gregory Germino, Deputy Director
Kevin Abbott, Program Director

2333 Financial Help for Diabetics Care
Information Clearinghouse
9000 Rockville Pike
Bethesda, MD 20892
301-496-3583
Fax: 301-907-8906
nddic@info.niddk.nih.gov
www.niddk.nih.gov

Griffin P. Rodgers, MD, MACP, Director
Dr. Gregory Germino, Deputy Director
Kevin Abbott, Program Director

2334 Gastoparesis in Diabetes
Information Clearinghouse
9000 Rockville Pike
Bethesda, MD 20892
301-496-3583
Fax: 301-907-8906
nddic@info.niddk.nih.gov
www.niddk.nih.gov

Griffin P. Rodgers, MD, MACP, Director
Dr. Gregory Germino, Deputy Director
Kevin Abbott, Program Director

2335 I Have Diabetes: How Much Should I Eat?
9000 Rockville Pike
Bethesda, MD 20892
301-496-3583
Fax: 301-907-8906
nddic@info.niddk.nih.gov
www.niddk.nih.gov

Griffin P. Rodgers, MD, MACP, Director
Dr. Gregory Germino, Deputy Director
Kevin Abbott, Program Director

2336 I Have Diabetes: What Should I Eat?
9000 Rockville Pike
Bethesda, MD 20892
301-496-3583
Fax: 301-907-8906
nddic@info.niddk.nih.gov
www.niddk.nih.gov

Griffin P. Rodgers, MD, MACP, Director
Dr. Gregory Germino, Deputy Director
Kevin Abbott, Program Director

2337 I Have Diabetes: When Should I Eat?
9000 Rockville Pike
Bethesda, MD 20892
301-496-3583
Fax: 301-907-8906
nddic@info.niddk.nih.gov
www.niddk.nih.gov

Griffin P. Rodgers, MD, MACP, Director
Dr. Gregory Germino, Deputy Director
Kevin Abbott, Program Director

2338 Kidney Disease of Diabetes
Information Clearinghouse
9000 Rockville Pike
Bethesda, MD 20892
301-496-3583
Fax: 301-907-8906
ndoc@info.niddk.nih.gov
www.niddk.nih.gov

Griffin P. Rodgers, MD, MACP, Director
Dr. Gregory Germino, Deputy Director
Kevin Abbott, Program Director

Camps

2339 American Diabetes Association
2451 Crystal Drive, Ste 900
Arlington, VA 22202
800-342-2383
askada@diabetes.org
www.diabetes.org

The American Diabetes Association provides research, and provides information and advocacy for people with diabetes and their families. The Asssociation also provides seminars for health care professionals.

Tracey D. Brown, CEO

Diabetes Mellitus / Camps

2340 Camp Discovery American Diabetes Association
1168 K-157 Highway
Junction City, KS 66441
316-684-6091
Fax: 316-941-5699
lgiles@diabetes.org
www.diabetes.org

Offers young people with diabetes a week of fun at rock springs 4-H Center. Special attention to diabetes makes Camp Discovery a safe environment for active youth while providing valuable diabetes management education. Call the American Diabetes Association-Kansas area office for more information.

Lindsay Giles, District Manager

2341 Camp Hodia
1701 N 12th St
Boise, ID 83702
208-891-1023
Fax: 208-454-2841
www.hodia.org

Camp for children with Type 1 Diabetes. Campers learn self care, good nutrition and blood-sugar control.

Don Scott, Director

2342 Camp Joslin
The Barton Center for Diabetes Education, Inc.
150 Richardson Corner Road
Charlton, MA 01507
507-987-2056
Fax: 508-987-2002
info@bartoncenter.org
www.joslin.org

Camp Joslin's programs combine camping, sports and fun with diabetes education and support to give children with diabetes, and their families, the tools they need to live happy, healthy, balanced lives.

Michael Kasparian, Camp Director
Sarah Gorman, Camp Coordinator

2343 Camp Kudzu
5885 Glenridge Drive, Suite 160
Atlanta, GA 30328
404-250-1811
Fax: 404-250-1812
info@campkudzu.org
www.campkudzu.org

Provides education, recreation and peer-networking for Georgia's children with Type 1 Diabetes.

2344 Camp Kushtaka
801 W. Fireweed Lane, Suite 103
Anchorage, AK 99503
907-272-1428
888-342-2383
skamahele@diabetes.org
http://www.childrenwithdiabetes.com/camps/

Camp for children with diabetes and, space permitting, their siblings.

2345 Camp de los Ninos - Diabetes Society
1165 Lincoln Avenue, Ste 300
San Jose, CA 95125
408-287-3785
800-800-989
Fax: 408-287-2701
campt@diabetessociety.org
www.childrenwithdiabetes.com/camps

Since 1974, the Diabetes Society of Santa Clara Valley has sponsored Camp de los Ninos, a resident camp for children 6 through 14. This camp provides an opportunity for children with diabetes to go to camp, meet other children and gain a better understanding of their diabetes. The total experience can help campers develop more confidence in their abilities to control their diabetes effectively while enjoying the traditional camp experience.

Sharon Ogbor, Executive Director

2346 Clara Barton Camp
PO Box 356
North Oxford, MA
508-987-2056
Fax: 508-987-2002
bcdecamp@aol.com
www.bartoncenter.org

Girls, ages 6-17, with diabetes participate in a well-rounded camp program with special education in diabetes, health and safety. Activities include swimming, boating, sports, dance, music and arts and crafts. Two week adventure camp for high school girls offering camping, hiking, canoeing, etc. Also a minicamp (one week) for girls 6-12. Day camps are offered in Worcester, Boston and New York City.

Brooke Beverly, Resident Camp Director
Kerry Packard, Day Camp Director
Beth Sayers, Adventure Camp Director

2347 Des Moines YMCA Camp
1192 166th Drive
Boone, IA 50036
515-432-7558
Fax: 515-432-5414
ycamp@dmymca.org
www.y-camp.org

For boys and girls with cancer, diabetes, asthma, cystic fibrosis, hearing impaired and other disabilities.

David Sherry, Executive Director

2348 EDI
1020 Madison 9570
Fredericktown, MO 63645
chartmann@diabetes.org
www.diabetes.org

Youngsters with diabetes learn how to care for themselves while participating in a wide variety of outdoor activities and trips. The camp, managed and financed by the American Diabetes Association Greater St. Louis Affiliate, offers camperships to children from the Greater St. Louis area, ages 7-16, but nonresidents may also apply.

Fred Schaljo

2349 Easter Seal Kysoc
9810 Bluegrass Pkwy
Louisville, KY 40299
502-584-9781
Fax: 502-732-0783
ek1@cardinalhill.org
www.cardinalhill.org

Designed for the fullest camping experience for children or adults with physical disabilities, blind, deaf, behavior disorders, diabetes and multiple handicaps, ages 7 and up.

Heide Miller, CCD, CTRS, Director

2350 Florida Camp for Children and Youth
1701 SW 16th Ave
Gainesville, FL 32608
352-334-1321
Fax: 352-334-1326

An adventure camp for children and youth with diabetes.

Rhonda Rogers

2351 Floyd Rogers
PO Box 31536
Omaha, NE 68131
402-341-0866
www.campfloydrogers.com

A camp for diabetic children, ages 8 to 18

Sherman Poska

2352 Hickory Hill
PO Box 1942
Columbia, MO 65205
573-698-2510
camphickoryhill@gmail.com
www.camphicoryhill.com

Educates diabetic children concerning diabetes and its care. In addition to daily educational sessions on some aspects of diabetes, campers participate in swimming, sailing, arts and crafts and overnight camping.

William Mees

2353 John Warvel
American Diabetes Association
Camp Crosley YMCA, 165 EMS T2 Land
North Webster, IN 46555
317-352-9226
Fax: 317-913-1592
bookorders@diabetes.org

Diabetes Mellitus / Camps

Provides an enjoyable, safe and educational out-of-doors experience for children with insulin-dependent diabetes. A unique learning atmosphere for children to acquire new skills in caring for their disease. The camp experience instills confidence for the child's self-management of diabetes. Offers one-week sessions and can accommodate 200 campers.

Carol Helming, Executive Director

2354 Makemie Woods Camp Conference Center
PO Box 39
Barhamsville, VA 23011
757-566-1496
800-566-1496
Fax: 757-566-8003
www.makwoods.org

Counselors serve as teachers, friends and activity leaders. The individual is important within the small group. No camper is lost in the crowd, but is an integral partner in the group process. Residential Christian Camp and conference center. Summer camp for children 8-18 special camp for children with diabetes.

Michelle Burcher, Director

2355 Sweeney
PO Box 918
Gainesville, TX 76241
940-665-2011
Fax: 940-665-9467
info@campsweeney.org
www.campsweeney.org

Teaches self-care and self-reliance to children with diabetes. Campers participate in such activities as swimming, fishing, horseback riding, arts and crafts while learning about diabetes and how to cope with it.

T. Milton Dickson, Jr. DDS, Chairman
Robert D. Vandermeer, MD, Vice Chairman
Ernie M. Fernandez, MD, Secretary

Description

2356 DIGEORGE SYNDROME

Synonyms: DiGeorge sequence, Thymic agenesis immunodeficiency

Involves the following Biologic System(s):
Genetic/Chromosomal/Syndrome/Metabolic Disorders, Immunologic and Rheumatologic Disorders

DiGeorge syndrome is a disorder present at birth (congenital) that is characterized by some combination of absence (aplasia) or underdevelopment (hypoplasia) of the thymus gland and the parathyroid glands, malformations of the heart and its major blood vessels (cardiovascular abnormalities), and characteristic malformations of the head and facial (craniofacial) area. Due to absence or underdevelopment of the thymus gland, affected children may have abnormalities of the immune system, causing impaired resistance to certain infections. DiGeorge syndrome occurs as the result of abnormal development of certain embryonic structures (third and fourth pharyngeal pouches) that later develop into the thymus and parathyroid glands. In some cases, other embryonic structures that are forming during the same approximate period may also be affected, resulting in certain cardiovascular, craniofacial, or other malformations. The thymus, a lymphoid tissue organ located in the upper portion of the chest, plays an essential role in the immune system beginning at approximately the 12th week of fetal development and lasts until puberty. It serves as a source of certain white blood cells (lymphocytes) before birth and then promotes the development of certain specialized lymphocytes, known as T lymphocytes, through secretion of particular hormones (e.g., thymosin). The actions of the T lymphocytes help to defend the body against certain microorganisms (i.e., cell-mediated immunity). The parathyroid glands, which are two pairs of small glands on the sides of the thyroid gland, produce parathyroid hormone, which helps to maintain normal levels of calcium in the blood.

DiGeorge syndrome usually occurs randomly and is caused by spontaneous, minute deletions of material from the long arm of chromosome 22 (22q11.2). DiGeorge syndrome may also occur in association with certain chromosomal abnormalities (e.g., chromosome 10, monosomy 10p; chromosome 22, monosomy 22q). In addition, there have been some cases in which DiGeorge syndrome affected individuals within certain families (kindreds) yet did not appear to result from known chromosome syndromes. In some familial cases, DiGeorge syndrome may have autosomal dominant inheritance. The disorder is thought to affect approximately one in 20,000 newborns.

In infants and children with DiGeorge syndrome, associated symptoms and findings may be extremely variable. Patients who have absence or severe underdevelopment of the thymus gland are prone to frequent infections from fungi, viruses, and certain bacteria (such as Pneumocystis jiroveci, previously knowns as Pneumocystis carinii). These patients often experience chronic inflammation of the mucous membranes of the nose (rhinitis), recurrent inflammation of the lungs (pneumonia), fungal infection of the mucous membranes of the mouth (oral candidiasis), recurrent diarrhea, or systemic infections in which invading microorganisms or their toxins are present inthe blood circulation (septicemia). In some cases of serious infection, life-threatening complications may result. Infants and children with mild underdevelopment (hypoplasia) of the thymus are said to have partial DiGeorge syndrome and may have little difficulty with recurring infections. Because of absence or underdevelopment of the parathyroid glands (hypoparathyroidism), many affected infants experience certain symptoms and findings during the first days of life, including abnormally low calcium levels in the blood (hypocalcemia) and muscle twitching, tremors and cramps, (neonatal tetany) and even seizures. Such symptoms and findings can be treated with calcium supplementation and are usually temporary but may recur later in life.

Some newborns with DiGeorge syndrome may also have defects of the heart and its great arteries. Some of these may be simple defects while others may be more complex, such as interrupted aortic arch, ventricular septal defects, and tetralogy of Fallot.

Infants with DiGeorge syndrome may have an unusually narrow or blind-ending esophagus (esophageal atresia) that does not form a passageway into the stomach. In addition, affected newborns may have characteristic malformations of the head and facial (craniofacial) area, such as widely spaced eyes (ocular hypertelorism); downwardly slanting eyelid folds (palpebral fissures); a small mouth; an unusually short, vertical groove in the center of the upper lip (philtrum); and low-set, notched ears. Some patients may also have mild to moderate intellectual disabilities.

The treatment of infants and children with DiGeorge syndrome is symptomatic and supportive. Treatment measures may include the administration of calcium in those with hypoparathyroidism and hypocalcemia, therapies to help prevent and aggressively treat infections (e.g., antiviral, antifungal, and antibiotic agents) in patients with immunodeficiency, medical and surgical measures for cardiovascular malformations, or other measures as required. If patients with immunodeficiency require blood transfusions, donor blood must be exposed to high levels of radiation (irradiated) to kill the donor lymphocytes and thus prevent the occurrence of graft-versus-host disease, a serious disease caused by an immune response of donor cells against the recipient's tissues.

National Associations & Support Groups

2357 22Q and You Center
34th Street and Civic Center Boulevard
Philadelphia, PA 19104   215-590-2920
www.chop.edu/service/22q-and-you-center/home.html

Services offered by the Department of Clinical Genetics in the Children's Hospital of Philadelphia, include literature, support groups and referrals.

Daniel J. Rader, MD, Chief, Human Genetics

2358 American Academy of Pediatrics
345 Park Blvd
Itasca, IL 60143   800-433-9016
          Fax: 847-434-8000
          mcc@aap.org
          www.aap.org

The American Academy of Pediatrics and its member pediatricians are committed to the attainment of optimal physical, mental and social health and well-being for all infants, children, adolescents, and young adults.

Lynn Olson, PhD, VP, Research
Mark Del Monte, JD, CEO/Executive VP
Vera Tait, MD, FAAP, Chief Medical Officer

2359 Genetic Alliance
426400 Woodfield Road, Ste 189
Damascus, MD 20872   202-966-5557
          Fax: 202-966-8553
          info@geneticalliance.org
          www.geneticalliance.org

DiGeorge Syndrome / Conferences

World's leading nonprofit health advocacy organization committed to transforming health through genetics and promoting an environment of openness centered on the health of individuals, families, and communities.

Sharon Terry, CEO
Ruth Child, CFO
Natasha Bonhomme, Chief Strategy Officer

2360 Immune Deficiency Foundation
7550 Teague Road, Suite 220
Hanover, MD 21076
410-321-6647
Fax: 410-321-9165
www.primaryimmune.org

The only national charitable organization aimed at fighting the primary immune deficiency diseases. The founders included parents of children with primary immune deficiency, immunologists who treat immune deficient patients and other individuals with an interest in helping others. The Foundation's main goal is to improve the care and treatment of adults and children with primary immune deficiency diseases and to promote public education and awareness about the diseases.

Jorey Berry, President & CEO

2361 March of Dimes Foundation
1550 Crystal Drive, Ste 1300
Arlington, VA 22202
888-663-4637
www.marchofdimes.org

March of Dimes help moms have full-term pregnancies and research the problems that threaten the health of babies. The March of Dimes also acts globally: sharing best practices in perinatal health and helping improve birth outcomes where the needs are the most urgent.

Stacey D. Stewart, President
Alan Brogdon, SVP/COO/Board Officer
Rahul Gupta, MD, SVP & Chief Medical/Health Officer

Conferences

2362 Immune Deficiency Foundation National Conference
7550 Teague Road, Suite 220
Hanover, MD 21076
410-321-6647
Fax: 410-321-9165
www.primaryimmune.org

Annual conference hosted by an organization aimed at fighting the primary immune deficiency diseases. The founders included parents of children with primary immune deficiency, immunologists who treat immune deficient patients and other individuals with an interest in helping others. The Foundation's main goal is to improve the care and treatment of adults and children with primary immune deficiency diseases and to promote public education and awareness about the diseases.

June

Jorey Berry, President & CEO

Web Sites

2363 International Patient Organization for Primary Immunodeficiencies
Av. Aida, Bloco 8, escritòrio 821
Estoril, 2765-
35- 21-407
info@ipopi.org
ipopi.org

IPOPI is an international organization whose members are national patient organizations for the primary immunodeficiencies (PID's). It was formed to benefit and serve its members and patients with expertise and resources and influence of members in order to achieve worlwide improvement in the care and treatment of patients with PID's.

Jose Drabwell, Chairman
Martine Pergent, Vice Chairman
Johan Prevot, Executive Director

2364 Jeffrey Modell Foundation
www.jmfworld.com

www.jmfworld.com

The foundation is dedicated to the early and precise diagnosis, meaningful treatment, and ultimate cure of Primary Immunodeficiencies.

2365 Kansas University Medical Center
www.kumc.edu/gec/support/velo.html

dcollins@kumc.edu
www.kumc.edu/gec/support/velo.html

Offers information for genetic professionals, information on genetic conditions and support groups, and genetic educational information.

Debra Collins, MS, CGC, Genetic Counselor

2366 National Center for Biotechnology Information
National Library of Medicine, 8600 Rockville Pike
Bethesda, MD 20894
888-346-3656
info@ncbi.nlm.nih.gov
www.ncbi.nlm.nih.gov

NCBI's mission is to develop new information technologoes to aid in the understanding of fundamental molecular and genetic processes that control health and disease.

Patricia Flatley Brennan, RN, PhD, Director
James Ostell, PhD, Executive Secretary

2367 Online Mendelian Inheritance in Man
McKusick-Nathans Instiute of Genetic Medicine-JHU
Baltimore, MD 21205
www.omim.org

This database is a catalog of human genes and genetic disorders.

Ada Hamosh, MD, Scientific Director

Book Publishers

2368 Let's Talk About Going to the Hospital
Rosen Publishing Group's PowerKids Press
29 E 21st Street
New York, NY 10010
212-777-3017
800-237-9932
Fax: 888-436-4643
rosenpub@tribeca.ios.com
www.rosenpublishing.com

If a child has to check into the hospital, chances are he or she is already upset about being ill. Knowing how a hospital functions and what the procedures are, such as when family members can visit, will help in what is already a stressful situation. Grades K-5.

24 pages
ISBN: 0-823950-36-0

Roger Rosen, President

Description

2369 DOWN SYNDROME

Synonyms: Chromosome 21, trisomy 21, Trisomy 21 syndrome

Covers these related disorders: Trisomy 21 mosaicism, Trisomy 21 translocation

Involves the following Biologic System(s):

Genetic/Chromosomal/Syndrome/Metabolic Disorders

Down syndrome, also known as trisomy 21, is a chromosomal disorder that affects approximately one in 660 newborns, making it the most common genetic syndrome. Cells of the body (with the exception of reproductive cells) typically contain 23 pairs of chromosomes that are numbered from 1 to 22. The 23rd pair consists of one X chromosome from the mother and an X or Y chromosome from the father. However, in infants with Down syndrome, all or a portion of chromosome 21 is present three times rather than twice in cells of the body (trisomy). In rare cases, a certain percentage of cells contain the extra chromosome 21, whereas other cells have the normal two. This finding is known as chromosomal mosaicism.

The symptoms and physical findings associated with Down syndrome vary in range and severity and depend in part on the exact location and the percentage of body cells containing the extra chromosome 21.

Down syndrome is usually the result of errors during the division of a parent's reproductive cells. Increased maternal age (over 35) presents additional risk. The disorder may also result due to a chromosome 21 translocation that is transmitted by a parent or occurs sporadically. Translocations are chromosomal abnormalities in which pieces of two or more chromosomes break off and are rearranged, resulting in an altered set of chromosomes.

Many infants with Down syndrome have abnormally diminished muscle tone (hypotonia), a tendency to keep the mouth open, protrusion of the tongue, excessive mobility of the joints, absence of certain reflexes, and excessive skin on the back of the neck. Other abnormalities may include a small, short head, flattened facial features, upwardly slanting eyelid folds, vertical skin folds over the eyes' inner corners, a highly arched roof of the mouth, a small nose and depressed nasal bridge, and small, misshapen ears. Abnormalities of the limbs may also be present, including unusually short arms and legs; short, broad hands; improper positioning of the fifth fingers (clinodactyly); abnormal skin ridge patterns on the fingers, hands, toes, and feet (dermatoglyphics); and a wide gap between the first and second toes. Infants with Down syndrome have an increased frequency of intestinal narrowing or obstruction (atresia) at birth. Patients also tend to have relatively short stature, progressive delays in the acquisition of skills requiring the coordination of physical and mental activities (psychomotor delays), poor coordination, an awkward manner of walking (gait), and varying levels of intellectual disabilities.

Approximately 40 percent of infants with Down syndrome have heart defects at birth (congenital heart defects). In some patients, such heart defects may require surgical repair. In addition, some individuals with Down syndrome are prone to recurrent respiratory infections and chronic inflammation of the membranes that line the eyes and eyelids (conjunctivitis) or the nasal cavity (rhinitis). Treatment of individuals with Down syndrome includes symptomatic and supportive measures, such as possible surgical correction of congenital heart defects, and special education.

Government Agencies

2370 NIH/ Eunice Kennedy Shriver National Institute of Child Health & Human Development
P.O. Box 3006
Rockville, MD 20847

800-370-2943
Fax: 866-760-5947
www.nichd.nih.gov

Conducts and supports research on topics related to the health of children, adults, families and populations. Some of these topics include: developmental disabilities, growth and development, infant death, reproductive health and birth defects.

Diana W. Bianchi, Director
Alison Cernich, PhD, Deputy Director

National Associations & Support Groups

2371 American Academy of Pediatrics
345 Park Blvd
Itasca, IL 60143

800-433-9016
Fax: 847-434-8000
mcc@aap.org
www.aap.org

The American Academy of Pediatrics and its member pediatricians are committed to the attainment of optimal physical, mental and social health and well-being for all infants, children, adolescents, and young adults.

Lynn Olson, PhD, VP, Research
Mark Del Monte, JD, CEO/Executive VP
Vera Tait, MD, FAAP, Chief Medical Officer

2372 American Association for Pediatric Opthalmology and Strabismus
1935 Country Road B2 W, Suite 165
Roseville, MN 55113

952-646-2045
Fax: 415-561-8531
info@aapos.org
www.aapos.org

AAPOS is the American Association for Pediatric Ophthalmology and Strabismus. The organization's goals are to advance the quality of children's eye care, support the training of pediatric ophthalmologists, support research activities in pediatric ophthalmology, and advance the care of adults with strabismus.

Danielle Bogert McKay, Executive Director
Christina Scott, Membership & Communication Manager
Ashley Crunstedt, CMP, Meetings & Marketing Manager

2373 American School Counselor Association
1101 King Street, Ste 310
Alexandria, VA 22314

703-683-2722
asca@schoolcounselor.org
www.schoolcounselor.org

The mission of ASCA is to represent professional school counselors and to promote professionalism and ethical practices.

Jill Cook, Executive Director
Amanda Fitzgerald, Assistant Deputy Executive Director
Kathleen M Rakestraw, Director of Communications

2374 Arc of Montgomery County
7362 Calhound Place
Rockville, MD 20855

301-984-5777
thearcmontgomerycounty.org

Aims to provide support, advocacy and choices for people who have developmental disabilities and their families.

Daria Cervantes, Chief Executive Officer
James Gipson, Chief Operating Officer

2375 Arc of the United States
1825 K Street NW, Ste 1200
Washington, DC 20006

202-534-3700
800-433-5255
Fax: 202-534-3731
info@thearc.org
www.thearc.org

Down Syndrome / National Associations & Support Groups

The Arc of the United States advocates for the rights and full participation of all children and adults with intellectual and developmental disabilities. Together with a network of members and affiliated chapters, they improve systems of support and services; connect families; inspire communities and influence public policy.

Peter V. Berns, CEO

2376 Association for Children with Down Syndrome
4 Fern Place
Plainview, NY 11803
516-933-4700
info@acds.org
www.acds.org

Dedicated to providing lifetime resources of exceptional quality, innovation and inclusion for individuals with Down syndrome and other developmental disabilities and their families.

Michael Smith, Executive Director
Jennifer Mosera, Director of Finance
Megan Lombardo, Director of Development

2377 Birth Defect Research for Children
976 Lake Baldwin Lane, Suite 104
Orlando, FL 32814
407-895-0802
staff@birthdefects.org
www.birthdefects.org

Birth Defect Research for Children is a non-profit organization that provides parents and expectant parents with information about birth defects and support services for their children.

Betty Mekdeci, Executive Director

2378 Center for Disabilities and Development
University of Iowa Stead Family Children's Hospital
100 Hawkins Drive
Iowa City, IA 52242
319-353-6900
888-573-5437
Fax: 319-356-7700
cdd-webmaster@uiowa.edu
www.uichildrens.org

A trusted resource for healthcare, training, research and information for people with disabilities that include: behavior disorders, brain injury, cerebral palsy, diabetes, down syndrome, learning disabilities, sleep disorders and spina bifida.

Dianne McBrien, MD, Medical Director

2379 Center for Parent Information and Resources (CPIR)
c/o SPAN, 35 Halsey Street, 4th Floor
Newark, NJ 07102
973-642-8100
malizo@spanadvocacy.org
www.parentcenterhub.org

Family-friendly information and research-based materials on key topics for Parent Centers. Private workspaces for Parent Centers to exchange resources, discuss high-priority topics, and solve mutual challenges. Coordination of parent training efforts throughout the network.

Myriam Alizo, Project Assistant

2380 Child Neurology Foundation
601 W Short Street
Lexington, KY 40508
888-417-3435
info@childneurologyfoundation.org
childneurologyfoundation.org

The Child Neurology Foundation connects partners from all areas of the child neurology community so those navigating the journey of disease diagnosis, management, and care have the ongoing support from those dedicated to treatments and cures.

Amy Brin, Executive Director
Katie Hentges, Director, Programs
Brea McCormley, Director, Development

2381 Down Syndrome Affiliates in Action
PO Box 7192
Missoula, MT 59807
701-354-7255
info@dsaia.org
www.dsaia.org

To support and advance the growth and service capabilities of the local and regional Down syndrome organizations we serve, to be the conduit of value-driven training, programs, best practices and support for our members.

Sarah Mulligan, Executive Director

2382 Down Syndrome Information Alliance
5098 Foothills Boulevard, Suite 3, Suite 464
Roseville, CA 95747
916-658-1686
info@downsyndromeinfo.org
downsyndromeinfo.org

The Down Syndrome Information Alliance provides support and resources to empower individuals with Down syndrome, their families, and our community.

Allison Olson, Executive Director

2383 Down Syndrome Innovations
5916 Dearborn Street
Mission, KS 66202
913-384-4848
kcdsi.org

Down Syndrome Innovations, formerly Down Syndrome Guild of Greater Kansas City (DSG), was founded in 1984 by a group of parents who shared a vision to support families experiencing the birth of a child with Down syndrome. Like all loving parents, they wanted their kids to thrive and wanted support and community. They wanted their children to grow up happy, healthy, encouraged, and empowered.

Jason Drummond, EdD, President & CEO

2384 Genetic Alliance
426400 Woodfield Road, Ste 189
Damascus, MD 20872
202-966-5557
Fax: 202-966-8553
info@geneticalliance.org
www.geneticalliance.org

World's leading nonprofit health advocacy organization committed to transforming health through genetics and promoting an environment of openness centered on the health of individuals, families, and communities.

Sharon Terry, CEO
Ruth Child, CFO
Natasha Bonhomme, Chief Strategy Officer

2385 Global Down Syndrome Foundation
3239 E 2nd Avenue
Denver, CO 80206
303-321-6277
info@globaldownsyndrome.org
www.globaldownsyndrome.org

The Global Down Syndrome Foundation is dedicated to significantly improving the lives of people with Down syndrome through Research, Medical Care, Education and Advocacy.

Michelle Sie Whitten, President & CEO
Tamara Pursley, Events Senior Director
Kayla Albrechtson, Senior Database Coordinator

2386 International Mosaic Down Syndrome Association
PO Box 321
Grand Haven, MI 49417
855-IMD-SA21
www.imdsa.org

IMDSA is designed to support any family or individual whose life has been touched by mosaic Down syndrome by continuously pursuing research opportunities and increasing awareness in the medical, educational and public communities throughout the world

2387 March of Dimes Foundation
1550 Crystal Drive, Ste 1300
Arlington, VA 22202
888-663-4637
www.marchofdimes.org

March of Dimes help moms have full-term pregnancies and research the problems that threaten the health of babies. The March of Dimes also acts globally: sharing best practices in perinatal health and helping improve birth outcomes where the needs are the most urgent.

Stacey D. Stewart, President
Alan Brogdon, SVP/COO/Board Officer
Rahul Gupta, MD, SVP & Chief Medical/Health Officer

2388 National Association for Down Syndrome (NADS)
1460 Renaissance Drive, Suite 102
Park Ridge, IL 60068
630-325-9112
Fax: 847-376-8908
info@nads.org
www.nads.org

Established by parents of children with Down syndrome who felt a need to create a better environment and bring about understanding and acceptance of people with Down syndrome.

Linda Smarto, Executive Director

2389 **National Down Syndrome Adoption Network**
www.ndsan.org

The mission of the NDSAN is to ensure that every child with Down syndrome has the opportunity to grow up in a loving family.

Stephanie Thompson, Director

2390 **National Down Syndrome Coalition**
PO Box 725
Roseville, CA 95661

916-532-4773
heather@ndscoalition.org
ndscoalition.org

The mission is to demonstrate to society the positive impacts of Down syndrome with various forms of media, parent support groups, parent counseling, provision of resources, community outreach, and with the education and training of parents and professionals.

Heather M. Haskin, President & CEO

2391 **National Down Syndrome Congress**
30 Mansell Court, Suite 108
Roswell, GA 30076

770-604-9500
800-232-6372
Fax: 770-604-9898
info@ndsccenter.org
www.ndsccenter.org

It is the mission of the National Down Syndrome Congress to be the national advocacy organization for Down syndrome and to provide leadership in all areas of concern related to persons with Down syndrome. In that capacity, NDSC will function as a major source of support and empowerment to persons with down syndrome and their families.

Jordan Kough, Executive Director
Rhonda Rice, Engagement Director
Erin Schmitz, Convention Director

2392 **National Down Syndrome Society**
1155 - 15th Street NW, Suite 540
Washington, DC 20005

800-221-4602
info@ndss.org
www.ndss.org

The mission is to be the national advocate for the value, acceptance and inclusion of people with Down Syndrome. The NDSS envisions a world in which people with Down Syndrome have the opportunity to enhance their quality of life, realize their life aspirations, and become valued members of welcoming communities.

Kandi Pickard, President & CEO

2393 **National Early Childhood Technical Assistance Center**
517 S Greensboro Street
Carrboro, NC 27510

ectacenter.org

Supports the national implementation of the early childhood provisions of the Individuals with Disabilities Education Act (IDEA). The mission is to strengthen systems at all levels to ensure that children (birth through five) with disabilities and their families receive and benefit from high quality, culturally appropriate and family centered supports and services.

Christina Kasprzak, Co-Director
Megan Vinh, Co-Director

State Agencies & Support Groups

California

2394 **Down Syndrome Association of Los Angeles**
16461 Sherman Way, Suite 180
Van Nuys, CA 91406

818-786-0001
Fax: 818-786-0004
info@dsala.org
www.dsala.org

Offers information on Down syndrome, counseling, resources, facts, laws and other forms of information.

Gail Williamson, Executive Director
Jim Hodgson, Senior Director

Colorado

2395 **Mile High Down Syndrome Association**
3515 South Tamarac Drive, Suite 320
Denver, CO 80237

303-756-6144
Fax: 303-756-6144
info@mhdsa.org
www.mhdsa.org

Serves families of children and adults with Down syndrome, and interested professionals in the Mountain States region. Provides education, resources and support in partnership with individuals, families, professionals, and the community.

Mac Macsovits, Executive Director
Laurie Herrera, Family/Outreach Programs Director

Connecticut

2396 **Connecticut Down Syndrome Congress**
C/O: A.J. Pappanikou, University of Connecticut
200 Research Parkway
Meriden, CT 06450

860-563-9114
888-486-8537
manager@ctdownsyndrome.org
www.ctdownsyndrome.org/

Established as a special interest group to advocate for persons with Down syndrome in the State of Connecticut. The mission is to advocate for the realization and enhancement of the full spectrum of human and civil rights for persons with Down syndrome, gather and disseminate accurate information regarding Down syndrome, provide support to families of children with Down syndrome, and to encourage quality services for persons with Down syndrome.

Walter Glomb, President
Karen Zbierski, Executive VP
Chris McAuliffe, Secretary/Director

Florida

2397 **Gold Coast Down Syndrome Organization**
2255 Glades Road, 342W
Boca Raton, FL 33431

561-912-1231
Fax: 561-912-1232
gcdso@bellsouth.net
www.goldcoastdownsyndrome.org

Gold Coast Down Syndrome Organization is a private, nonprofit corporation dedicated to making the future brighter for people with Down syndrome in Palm Beach County, Florida.

Terri Harmon, Executive Director

2398 **Goodwill Industries-Suncoast**
10596 Gandy Boulevard
St. Petersburg, FL 33702

727-523-1512
888-279-1988
Fax: 727-563-9300
TDD: 727-579-1068
gw.marketing@goodwill-suncoast.com
www.goodwill-suncoast.org

Nonprofit organization that helps people achieve their full potential through the dignity and power of work. The agency offers a variety of employment and training services to promote self-sufficiency, and contribute to community conservation through recycling.

Lee Waits, President
R Lee Waits, President/CEO

Down Syndrome / State Agencies & Support Groups

Georgia

2399 Down Syndrome Association of Atlanta
2221 Peachtree Road NE, Ste 226
Atlanta, GA 30339
404-320-3233
Fax: 404-228-7475
www.atlantadsaa.org

A source of information and support to families, as well as working to promote public awareness and encouraging a better understanding of Down syndrome and individuals with Down syndrome.

Michelle Norweck, Executive Director

Hawaii

2400 Hawaii Down Syndrome Congress
419 Keoniana Street, Suite 804
Honolulu, HI 96815
808-949-1999
Conkay@AOL.com
www.hawaiidownsyndrome.com

An organization of families and professionals concerned with all aspects of Down Syndrome. We provide outreach to parents of newborns to foster fellowship and social interaction, educational opportunities and resources, public relation activities to inform the general public about Down syndrome, monthly meetings that provide emotional and psychological support, and serve as activists and advocates on behalf of children with special needs.

Connie Smith, President

Indiana

2401 Down Syndrome Association of NWI
2927 Jewett Avenue
Highland, IN 46322
219-838-3656
Fax: 219-838-6959
dsa@dsaofnwi.org
www.dsaofnwi.org

Provides informational and emotional support to parents who have a child, adolescent, or adult family member with special needs. Program offers an important connection for a parent who is seeking support for a special disability issue, by matching him or her with a trained veteran parent.

Christine Gill, President
Randy Sassano, Vice President
Dawn Weiler, Treasurer

2402 Down Syndrome Support Association of Southern Indiana (DSSASI)
1939 State Street
New Albany, IN 47150
812-725-1416
www.dssasi.org

Provides informational and emotional support to parents who have a child, adolescent, or adult family member with special needs. Program offers an important connection for a parent who is seeking support for a special disability issue, by matching him or her with a trained veteran parent.

Kelley Jacquay, President
Michelle Engle, Vice President
Gina DeWilde, Treasurer

Maryland

2403 Parents of Children with Down Syndrome Arc of Montgomery County
PO Box 10416
Rockville, MD 20849
301-916-4985
Fax: 301-816-2429
firemom31@yahoo.com
www.downsyndromehelp.boomja.com

Aims to provide support, advocacy and choices for people who have developmental disabilities and their families.

Peter Holden, Executive Director
John Slavcoff, President

Massachusetts

2404 Massachusetts Down Syndrome Congress (MDSC)
20 Burlington Mall Road, Ste 261
Burlington, MA 01803
781-221-0024
800-664-6372
Fax: 781-221-0011
mdsc@mdsc.org
www.mdsc.org

An all-volunteer, non-profit organization made up of parents, professionals and anyone interested in gaining a better understanding of Down syndrome. The mission is to enhance on a continuous basis the lives of individuals with Down syndrome through the education and support of people with Down syndrome, their families, their friends, their teachers, and the community as a whole. To ensure individuals are valued, included, and live fulfilling lives in the community.

Suzanne Boudrot Shea, President
Jonathan Fee, Vice President
Leo Hogan, Secretary

Minnesota

2405 Down Syndrome Association of Minnesota
656 Transfer Road
St. Paul, MN 55114
651-603-0720
800-511-3696
www.dsamn.org

A nonprofit organization composed of some 3,000 members; more than 900 people with Down syndrome, their families and friends, plus health-care, education and developmental professionals. We are the only organization in our region devoted exclusively to the needs of people with Down syndrome and their families.

Kathleen Forney, Executive Director
Connie Gunderson Warner, Program Coordinator
Jim Belka, Resource Coordinator

New York

2406 Center for Family Support
2811 Zulette Avenue
Bronx, NY 10461
718-518-1500
Fax: 718-518-8200
www.cfsny.org

The Center for Family Support (CFS) is a not-for-profit human service agency providing support and assistance to individuals with developmental disabilities and traumatic brain injuries throughout New York City, Long Island, the lower Hudson Valley region and New Jersey.

Steven Vernikoff, Executive Director

Ohio

2407 Miami Valley Downs Syndrome Association
1133 Edwin C Moses Boulevard, Suite 190
Dayton, OH 45408
937-222-0744
Fax: 937-222-0396
www.mvdsa.org

Informational and emotional support to parents who have a child, adolescent, or adult family member with special needs.

Tennessee

2408 Down Syndrome Association of Middle Tennessee
111 N Wilson Boulevard
Nashville, TN 37205
615-386-9002
Fax: 615-386-9754
dsamt@bellsouth.net
www.dsamt.org

Down Syndrome / Research Centers

A nonprofit organization that is affiliated with the National Down Syndrome Society and the National Down Syndrome Congress. DSAMT works closely with The Arc of Tennessee and other disability organizations locally and throughout the state to provide support for individuals with Down syndrome.

Sheila Moore, Executive Director

Texas

2409 AAIDD Texas Chapter
PO Box 28076
Austin, TX 78755
512-349-7470
Fax: 512-349-2117
patholder@austin.rr.com
www.aaiddtx.org

An organization made up of professionals, parents, consumers and advocates. The goal is to create an accessible system of services and resources which support personal choice and promotes lives of dignity and self-determination. An Annual Convention is a forum for sharing ideas and research, offering opportunities for exchanging information, and developing an understanding for other perspectives.

Pat Holder, Executive Director

2410 Down Syndrome Guild of Dallas
701 N Central Expressway, Building I
Richardson, TX 75080
214-267-1374
dsged@sbcglobal.net
www.downsyndromedallas.org

Aims to impact the community so that everyone will acknowledge the inherent dignity and abilities of people with Down syndrome with full participation in society.

Becky Slakman, Executive Director
Kelly Drablos, Vice President
Minnie Blackwell, Membership Committee Chairperson

Research Centers

Alabama

2411 Down Syndrome Clinic, Children's Hospital of Alabama
1600 7th Avenue S
Birmingham, AL 35233
205-368-9585
Fax: 205-975-6330
www.childrensal.org

Dr. Diane K Donley

California

2412 Children's Hospital & Research Center of Oakland
747 52nd Street
Oakland, CA 94609
510-428-3259
www.childrenshospitaloakland.org

Scientific research is an important part of the work that goes on at Children's Hospital & Research Center Oakland. Researchers are making significant progress in such areas as diagnosing and treating pediatric cancers, sickle cell disease, AIDS and HIV, hemophilia, cystic fibrosis, developing prenatal techniques for diagnosing intellectual disabilities and birth defects, and improving infant nutrition.

Kevan McCarten-Gibbs, Senior VP/Chief Medical Officer
Nancy Shibata, RN, Nursing VP
Donald Livsey, VP/Chief Information Officer

2413 Pediatric Disabilities Clinic, Down Syndrome Clinic
University of California Medical Center
400 Parnassus, Box 0374
San Francisco, CA 94143
415-476-3276
www.ucsfhealth.org

Dorothy Pang

Georgia

2414 Pediatric Neurodevelopmental Center at Marcus Institute
Marcus Institute
1920 Briarcliff Road
Atlanta, GA 30329
404-419-5300
Fax: 404-419-5410
ccoles@emory.edu
www.marcus.org

Provides an array of evaluation and treatment services for individuals from infancy through adolescence. As well as providing individual evaluations, we feature a number of unique multispecialty programs. Once a child is evaluated, the proper course of treatment and/or therapy can be determined. The evaluation may result in a recommendation for further treatment at the Marcus Institute, or may involve other programs and services in the child's community.

Howard S Schub, MD, Medical Director

Illinois

2415 Adult Down Syndrome Center of Lutheran General Hospital
1999 Dempster Street
Park Ridge, IL 60068
847-318-2303
Fax: 847-318-2377
www.advocatehealth.com

A comprehensive medical resource providing multidisciplinary medical and psychosocial care for adults with Down syndrome, with an emphasis on health promotion.

Brian Chicoine, MD, Medical Director
Jenny Lobough-Howard, Outreach Specialist
Ann Jonaitis, Resource Coordinator

2416 Advocate Lutheran General Children's Hospital, Pediatric Research
1775 Dempster Street
Park Ridge, IL 60068
847-318-9330
denise.angst@advocatehealth.com
www.advocatehealth.com

An organization of physicians and health care professionals dedicated to serving the health needs of individuals, families and communities in Northern Illinois. Ongoing research on Pediatric disorders are being conducted and finding new procedures and medicines.

Marissa Lowenthal, Medical Director
Denise B Angst, DNSc, Research Director
Sandy Maki, MAT; CCRP, Research Operations Manager

2417 LaRabida Children's Hospital, Down Syndrome Clinic
E 65th Street @ Lake Michigan
Chicago, IL 60649
773-753-8646
Fax: 773-363-7160
info@larabida.org
www.larabida.org

Recognized as a leader in the diagnosis and treatment of children with developmental disabilities and delays. La Rabida provides comprehensive care and services for children with Down syndrome. The Down syndrome program at La Rabida is designed to provide medical and developmental evaluations and be a resource for both parents and pediatricians caring for children with this chronic condition.

Paula Jaudas, Executive Director

Indiana

2418 Ann Whitehill Down Syndrome Program
Riley Hospital for Children
702 Barnhill Drive
Indianapolis, IN 46202
317-274-4846
Fax: 317-274-4471
www.rileychildrenshospital.com

Down Syndrome / Research Centers

Brings together specialists from many areas to address the medical and psychosocial needs of children with Down Syndrome. A developmental pediatrician, pediatric nurse practitioner, pediatric social worker, pediatric occupational therapist, physical therapist and certified speech pathologist work closely with the primary care physician to help each child achieve his or her optimal potential. We also refer the family to local resources for therapy and developmental programs.

Marilyn Bell, MD

Maryland

2419 Behavioral and Developmental Pediatrics Division, University of Maryland
22 S Greene Street
Baltimore, MD 21201
410-328-2214
800-492-5538
Fax: 410-328-3981
www.umm.edu

Offers comprehensive consultation, evaluation and treatment for children, birth to age 21, with developmental and behavioral problems.

Linda Grossman, MD, Associate Professor

2420 Kennedy Krieger Institute, Down Syndrome Clinic
1750 E Fairmount Avenue
Baltimore, MD 21231
443-923-9140
Fax: 410-550-9292
koller@kennedykrieger.org
www.kennedykrieger.org/

Develop and conduct clinical research studies into the neurobiologic basis of cognitive impairment and co-morbid psychiatric disorders in Down syndrome; to study potential therapies for safety and efficacy; and to investigate genetic and environmental factors relevant to AV Canal defect.

George Capone, Director
Char Koller, Research Contact

Massachusetts

2421 Down Syndrome Program, Children's Hospital Boston
300 Longwood Avenue
Boston, MA 02115
617-355-6000
Fax: 617-735-7429
TTY: 617-730-0152
CROCKER_A@A1.TCH.Harvard.edu
www.childrenshospital.org/

Medical and developmental monitoring for children from birth to 3 years of age. Evaluations are provided every 4 to 6 months by an interdisciplinary team comprised of a developmental pediatrician, physical therapist, nutritionist, audiologist, speech pathologist, and social worker. Individual support is available for families, along with information, referral, and case management assistance.

Dr. Allen Crocker, Director

Minnesota

2422 Down Syndrome Clinic of Minneapolis Children's Medical Center
2525 Chicago Avenue
Minneapolis, MN 55404
612-813-7800
Fax: 612-813-6100
dmcconn606@aol.com

Mission of the clinic is to improve the quality of life for children and adolescents with Down syndrome and to help them reach their full potentials. A multi-disciplinary team of professionals provide care to the children and adolescents who come to the clinic. Because of the full spectrum of services available, the program can provide consultation for specific medical and developmental problems, developmental assessments, management of behavioral difficulties, and family support.

Dr. Kim McConnell, Director
Mary Bergs, Social Worker

Missouri

2423 Children's Mercy Hospital, Down Syndrome Clinic
2401 Gillham Road
Kansas City, MO 64108
816-234-3041
Fax: 816-842-6107
www.childrens-mercy.org

Medical staff of nearly 600 pediatric specialists with a comprehensive range of programs and services, representing more than 40 pediatric specialities.

Erica Molitor-Kirsch, Executive Medical Director/SVP
Barbara Mueth, Community Relations VP
Davoren Tempel, Resource Development VP

2424 Down's Syndrome Medical Clinic
Washington University Medical Center
400 S Kingshighway Boulevard
Saint Louis, MO 63110
314-454-5437
800-678-5437
www.stlouischildrens.org

Dr. Arnold Strauss

New Hampshire

2425 Medical Genetics Clinic
Dartmouth-Hitchcock Medical Center
1 Medical Center Drive
Lebanon, NH 03756
603-653-6044
Fax: 603-650-8268
www.dhmc.org

Provides specialty consultations for diagnosis and treatment of suspected inherited conditions or syndromes.

John Moeschler, MD, Program Director
Mary Beth Dinulos, MD, Medical Geneticist
Susan Berg, MS, Genetic Counselor

New York

2426 Child Development Clinical Services
Westchester Institute for Human Development
Cedarwood Hallÿ
Valhalla, NY 10595
914-285-8178
Fax: 914-285-1973
info@WIHD.org
www.wihd.org

Diagnostic evaluation and treatment services are provided for children with developmental concerns, communication disorders, attention deficit disorders (including ADHD) and learning disabilities, as well as cerebral palsy and other neuromotor disorders, spina bifida, intellectual disabilities, and autism.

Mark Bertin, MD, Director
Karen Edwards, MD, Pediatrics Director

North Dakota

2427 Children's Hospital Merit Care Down Syndrome Service
737 Broadway
Fargo, ND 58102
701-234-2568
Fax: 701-234-6965

Dr. Guy Carter

Ohio

2428 Down Syndrome Clinic, Rainbow Babies and Children's Hospital
11100 Euclid Avenue
Cleveland, OH 44106
216-844-8447
888-844-844
Fax: 216-844-8444
www.uhhospitals.org/rainbow

Dr. Joanne Mortimer

Down Syndrome / Research Centers

2429 Jane and Richard Thomas Center for Down Syndrome
Cincinnati Children's Hospital Medical Center
3430 Burnet Avenue
Cincinnati, OH 45229
513-636-4561
800-344-2462
Fax: 513-636-7173
development@cchmc.org
www.cincinnatichildrens.org

Conducts research and offers interdisciplinary evaluations and intervention for infants, children, adolescents and young adults with Down syndrome. By providing a range of comprehensive services within one center, families can now spend less time pursuing services through multiple agencies and professionals.

Susan E. Wiley, MD, Co-Director

2430 Pediatric Clinical Trials International
10 Winthrop Square, Fifth Floor
Boston, MA 02110
617-948-5100
866-219-3440
Fax: 617-948-5101
marketing@centerwatch.com
www.centerwatch.com/

Consists of inpatient and outpatient capabilities. The inpatient facility includes research beds, a psychophysiological recording and observation/recording center. The latter, located on the neuromonitoring unit, consists of a subject testing room equipped with video cameras and psychological recording systems, and the second is the monitoring room equipped with computer programming and audio-video monitoring, etc.

Daniel R Boue, Medical Director
John P Niles, CEO
Karen Miller, RN, Affiliate Operations Manager

Pennsylvania

2431 Children's Hospital of Pittsburgh General Clinical Research Center
401 Penn Avenue
Pittsburgh, PA 15224
412-692-6438
Fax: 412-692-5723
linda.cherok@chp.edu
www.chp.edu/research

Established to increase medical knowledge about childhood diseases and to improve the management and treatment of these diseases. Participation is of great importance and value to medical research. We have a dedicated staff of physicians, nurses and health care professionals experienced in health care delivery and research who will ensure your comfort and safety as you participate in medical studies.

Pamela Murray, Program Director
Diane E Cline, Administrative Manager

2432 Children's Seashore House
Children's Hospital in Philadelphia
3405 Civic Center Boulevard
Philadelphia, PA 19104
215-590-1734
rac@email.chop.edu
www.chop.edu

Leading research institution quickly bringing scientific discoveries into the clinical setting and community to improve care. Some current research studies include: cognitive studies of the development of mathematical competence in normal children and in those with congenital defects, studies of language development in children with inherited syndromes, and development of novel strategies to prevent violence in the school setting.

Marc Yudkoff, MD, Division Chief
Nathan Blum, MD, Behavioral Pediatrics

2433 Dr. Gertrude A. Barber National Institute
100 Barber Place
Erie, PA 16507
814-45-766
Fax: 814-455-1132
BNIerie@barberinstitute.org
www.barbercenter.org

Committed to remaining on the cutting-edge of breakthrough technologies and practices. We seek out research opportunities that will enhance our services and will provide the most current proven information to present to the public.

John J Barber, President
Maureen Barber-Carey, Executive VP
Karen Hahn Berry, RN, Health Services Director

2434 International Foundation for Genetic Research/Michael Fund
4371 Northern Pike
Pittsburgh, PA 15146
412-374-0111
www.michaelfund.org

Research is directed toward preventing and treating the harmful consequences of the extra chromosome in Down's Syndrome. Also; dedicated to reversing this destructive universal trend by opening up new doors of therapy in the field of intellectual disabilities associated with chromomal disorders such as Down Syndrome and continuing the curative research program.

Dr. Paddy Jim Baggot, Executive Director

Rhode Island

2435 Children's Neurodevelopment Center at Hasbro Children's Hospital
Rhode Island Hospital
593 Eddy Street
Providence, RI 02903
401-444-4000
Fax: 401-444-6115
sigpueschel@aol.com
www.lifespan.org/hch/services/

A site for the evaluation and treatment of children with neurological, genetic, developmental, metabolic and behavioral disorders.

Lee V Wesner, Director

Texas

2436 Down Syndrome Specialty Clinic
Children's Medical Center
1935 Medical District Dr.
Dallas, TX 75235
214-456-6388
Fax: 214-456-2567
www.childrens.com

Comprehensive care for children with Down syndrome and their families including; medical management, genetic counseling, speech and oral motor developmental evaluation and recommendations, psychosocial support, screening and referral for behavioral or psychiatric problems, and referrals to community agencies for educational intervention or therapies.

Mary Esther Carlin MD, Clinical Medical Doctor
Joanna Spahis, RN, Clinical Nurse Specialist

Washington

2437 University of Washington: Experimental Education Unit
University of Washington
Columbia Road, Gate #6
Seattle, WA 98195
206-543-2100
www.depts.washington.edu/

Provide clinical services to children and their families, and conduct interdisciplinary research.

Rick Neel, Director
Kate Ahern, Admissions Coordinator

Wisconsin

2438 Center for the Study of Bioethics
Medical College of Wisconsin
8701 Watertown Plank Road
Milwaukee, WI 53226
414-527-8191
centerbioethics@mcw.edu
www.mcw.edu/bioethics

Down Syndrome / Conferences

Center for the Study of Bioethics is a leader in the field of bioethics. The Center has conscientiously served the functions of a typical institution of higher learning; research, education, and service.

Robyn S Shapiro, Director
Kristen Tym, Assistant Director

Conferences

2439 American School Counselor Association Annual Conference
1101 King Street, Suite 310
Alexandria, VA 22314
703-683-2722
800-306-4722
Fax: 703-997-7572
asca@schoolcounselor.org
www.schoolcounselor.org

The mission of ASCA is to represent professional school counselors and to promote professionalism and ethical practices.

3,000 Attendees

Richard Wong, Executive Director
Jennifer Walsh, Director, Education & Training
Kathleen M Rakestraw, Director of Communications

2440 Arc Annual National Convention
Arc of the United States
1825 K Street NW, Ste 1200
Washington, DC 20006
202-534-3700
800-433-5255
Fax: 202-534-3731
mckiernan@thearc.org
www.thearc.org

Held in cities throughout the U.S. each fall which attracts nearly 1000 people for educational sessions, business meetings and social events.

Peter V. Berns, CEO
Kristen McKiernan, Sr Exec. Offcr, Comms & Marketing
Liz Mahar, Director, Family/Sibling Initiative

2441 NDSC Annual Convention
National Down Syndrome Congress
30 Mansell Court, Suite 108
Roswell, GA 30076
770-604-9500
800-232-6372
Fax: 770-604-9898
info@ndsccenter.org
www.ndsccenter.org

Offers parents and professionals an opportunity to learn from the best speakers from around the world and share experiences with one another.

August

Jordan Kough, Executive Director
Rhonda Rice, Engagement Director
Erin Schmitz, Convention Director

2442 National Down Syndrome Society Annual National Conference
1155 - 15th Street Nw, Suite 540
Washington, DC 20005
800-221-4602
jnfo@ndss.org
www.ndss.org

The focus is on working together to improve the lives of individuals with Down syndrome, enabling them to enjoy the benefits of, and contribute to, their communities.

Kandi Pickard, President & CEO

Audio Video

2443 A Special Love
Association for Children with Down Syndrome
2616 Martin Avenue
Bellmore, NY 11710
516-221-4700
Fax: 516-221-4311

A candid video of a ten-year-old brother playing with his six-year-old sister with Down Syndrome. The brother describes his perceptions of intellectual disability and his feelings towards his sister.

4 minutes, b/w

DB Shalom, Editor

2444 Boy in the World
Fanlight Productions
32 Court Street, 21st Floor
Brooklyn, NY 11201
718-488-8900
800-876-1710
Fax: 718-488-8642
info@fanlight.com, orders@fanlight.com
www.fanlight.com

Following four-year-old Ronen, a young boy with down syndrome, this intimate documentary concretely demonstrates that inclusive preschool classrooms benefit both children with special needs and their typical peers. It examines the nuts and bolts of successful inclusion as well as the challenges of educationsl practices that help all children to learn - and find their place in the world. ISBN: DVD: 1-57295-944-4; VHS: 1-57295-488-4

44 minutes DVD of VHS

2445 Congratulations? An Introduction to Down Syndrome for Parents/Family/Friends
New Challenges
96 Ogden Avenue
White Plains, NY 10605
914-287-0723

A film for parents which addresses some of the most commonly asked questions about raising a child with Down syndrome.

57 mins.

2446 Daddy's Girl
Carle Media
110 W Main Street
Urbana, IL 61801
217-384-4838

Dina Lev, a 12-year-old actress with Down syndrome, portrays Nancy, a girl trying to deal with her divorced father's inability to accept the fact that his daughter has Down syndrome.

28 mins.

Bruce Postman, Producer
Regina Conroy, Writer/Director

2447 Educating Peter
State of the Art Production
2470 Fox Hill Road
State College, PA 16803
814-355-8004
800-458-3401
Fax: 814-355-2714
www.resistor.com

Thought-provoking film follows a child with Down syndrome through a year of inclusion in a public school in Mrs. Stallings' third grade class. The film raises many questions about inclusion by honestly presenting the reactions to, and methods of, dealing with Peter's behavior problems.

30 Minutes

Thomas C Goodwin, Producer/Director
Gerardine Wurzburg, Producer/Director

2448 Infant Motor Development: A Look at the Phases
Therapy Skill Builders
San Antonio, TX 78283
732-441-0404

Shows normal infant motor development from birth to 12 months. Identifies components of movement and specific skills that are acquired during 4 phases of motor development: infantile, preparation, modification, and refinement. Transitional movement patte rns and their relationship to skill acquisition are also described.

20 Minutes

Kerry Goudy, Producer
Joan Winger, Producer

2449 New Expectations
Altschul Group Corporation
1560 Sherman Avenue, Suite 100
Evanston, IL 60201
800-421-2363

Focuses on the emotional and technical aspects of Down syndrome. Highlights four persons at various life stages from infancy to adulthood in the areas of education and employment.

Web Sites

2450 Arc of the United States
1825 K Street NW, Ste 1200
Washington, DC 20006
202-534-3700
800-433-5255
Fax: 202-534-3731
info@thearc.org
www.thearc.org

The Arc of the United States advocates for the rights and full participation of all children and adults with intellectual and developmental disabilities. Together with a network of members and affiliated chapters, they improve systems of support and services; connect families; inspire communities and influence public policy.

Peter V. Berns, CEO

2451 Association for Children with Down Syndrome
4 Fern Place
Plainview, NY 11803
516-933-4700
info@acds.org
www.acds.org

Dedicated to providing lifetime resources of exceptional quality, innovation and inclusion for individuals with Down syndrome and other developmental disabilities and their families.

Michael Smith, Executive Director
Jennifer Mosera, Director of Finance
Megan Lombardo, Director of Development

2452 Birth Defect Research for Children
976 Lake Baldwin Lane, Suite 104
Orlando, FL 32814
407-895-0802
staff@birthdefects.org
www.birthdefects.org

Birth Defect Research for Children is a non-profit organization that provides parents and expectant parents with information about birth defects and support services for their children.

Betty Mekdeci, Executive Director

2453 Down Syndrome Guild
www.downsyndromedallas.com

www.downsyndromedallas.com

Provides new baby/parent hospital visits, monthly newsletter, support and encouragement for individuals with Down Syndrome and their families. Bi-lingual group. Job coaching scholarships.

2454 Health Answers Education Sudler-WPP Health Practice
700 Dresher Road
Horsham, PA 19044
215-442-9010
www.healthanswers.com

HealthAnswers offers a breadth of services in medical education, sales force training, patient support, solutions, professional promotion and consumer solutions.

Mike Hudnall, CEO

2455 National Association for Down Syndrome (NADS)
1460 Renaissance Drive, Suite 102
Park Ridge, IL 60068
630-325-9112
Fax: 847-376-8908
info@nads.org
www.nads.org

Established by parents of children with Down syndrome who felt a need to create a better environment and bring about understanding and acceptance of people with Down syndrome.

Linda Smarto, Executive Director

2456 National Down Syndrome Congress
30 Mansell Court, Suite 108
Roswell, GA 30076
770-604-9500
800-232-6372
Fax: 770-604-9898
info@ndsccenter.org
www.ndsccenter.org

It is the mission of the National Down Syndrome Congress to be the national advocacy organization for Down syndrome and to provide leadership in all areas of concern related to persons with Down syndrome. In that capacity, NDSC will function as a major source of support and empowerment to persons with down syndrome and their families.

Jordan Kough, Executive Director
Rhonda Rice, Engagement Director
Erin Schmitz, Convention Director

2457 National Down Syndrome Society
1155 - 15th Street Nw, Suite 540
Washington, DC 20005
800-221-4602
info@ndss.org
www.ndss.org

The mission is to be the national advocate for the value, acceptance and inclusion of people with Down Syndrome. The NDSS envisions a world in which people with Down Syndrome have the opportunity to enhance their quality of life, realize their life aspirations, and become valued members of welcoming communities.

Kandi Pickard, President & CEO

2458 Online Mendelian Inheritance in Man
McKusick-Nathans Institue of Genetic Medicine-JHU
Baltimore, MD 21205
www.omim.org

This database is a catalog of human genes and genetic disorders.

Ada Hamosh, MD, Scientific Director

Book Publishers

2459 Adolescents with Down Syndrome
University of Victoria
3800 Finnerty Road
Victoria, BC, V8P
Canada
250-721-7211
www.uvic.ca

Adolescents with Down syndrome: International perspectives on research and programme development: Implications for parents, researchers, and practitioners.

165 pages
ISBN: 0-919955-16-9

Carey Denholm, Editor

2460 Babies with Down Syndrome
Woodbine House
6510 Bells Mill Road
Bethesda, MD 20817
301-897-3570
800-843-7323
Fax: 301-897-5838

Praised as the finest book ever written for new parents, this book covers everything they need to know about rearing these beautiful and special children in a loving environment.

340 pages Paperback
ISBN: 0-933149-64-6

Karen Stray-Gundersen, Editor

2461 Biomedical Concerns in Persons with Down's Syndrome
Brookes Publishing Company
PO Box 10624
Baltimore, MD 21285
410-337-9580
800-638-3775
Fax: 410-337-8539
www.brookespublishing.com

Written by leading authorities and spanning many disciplines and specialties, this comprehensive resource provides vital information on biomedical issues concerning individuals with Down's syndrome.

336 pages Hardcover
ISBN: 1-557660-89-1

Siegfried M Pueschel, Editor
Jeanette K Pueschel, Editor

Down Syndrome / Book Publishers

2462 Communication Skills in Children with Down Syndrome: A Guide for Parents
Woodbine House
6510 Bells Mill Road
Bethesda, MD 20817
301-468-8800
800-843-7323
Fax: 301-897-5838
info@woodbinehouse.com
www.woodbinehouse.com

Offers parents a chance to learn what to expect as communication skills progress from infancy through early teenage years. Discussions are included on speech and language therapy, hearing problems, school performance and intelligibility issues.

241 pages Paperback
ISBN: 0-933149-53-0

Libby Kumin, Editor

2463 Count Us In: Growing up with Down Syndrome
Harvest Book Company
185 Commerce Drive
Fort Washington, PA 19034
215-619-0307
877-512-3022
webservice@Harvestbooks.com
www.harvestbooks.com/

Mitchell Levitz and Jason Kingsley share their innermost thoughts, feelings, hopes and dreams, their lifelong friendship and their experiences of growing up with Down Syndrome.

1994 208 pages Paperback
ISBN: 0-156226-60-X

Jason Kingsley, Editor
Mitchell Levitz, Editor

2464 Current Approaches to Down's Syndrome
Greenwood Publishing Group
88 Post Road W, Suite 5007
Westport, CT 06880
203-226-3571
www.greenwood.com

An exploration of current initiatives relating to Down syndrome in the medical, educational and social fields.

447 pages Hardcover
ISBN: 0-275902-12-9

David Lane, Editor
Brian Stratford, Editor

2465 Down Sydrome: Living and Learning in the Community
Wiley & Sonecial Children
10475 Crosspoint Boulevard
Indianapolis, IN 46256
877-762-2974
Fax: 800-597-3299
www.wiley.com

Four parents' personal observations. Challenges of people with DS as they become integrated into community, family role, cognitive development and acquisition of language, education, health care, independent living arrangement.

1995 312 pages Hardcover
ISBN: 0-471022-01-2

Lynn Nadel, Editor
Donna Rosenthal, Editor

2466 Down Syndrome: Birth to Adulthood: Giving Families an Edge
Love Publishing Company
9101 E Kenyon Evenue
Denver, CO 80237
303-221-7333
Fax: 303-221-7444
lpc@lovepublishing.com
www.lovepublishing.com

Provides a collection of longitudinal perspectives on experiences of individuals with Down Syndrome, from birth to adulthood.

1995 356 pages Paperback
ISBN: 0-891082-36-0

John R Rynders, Editor

2467 Down Syndrome: The Facts
Oxford University Press
2001 Evans Road
Cary, NC 27513
212-726-6000
800-451-7556
Fax: 919-677-1303
www.oup-usa.org

A book for parents who have a child with Down Syndrome, written by a pediatrician who works with Down syndrome children.

208 pages Paperback
ISBN: 0-192626-62-0

Mark Selikowitz, Editor

2468 Let's Talk About Down Syndrome
Rosen Publishing Group's PowerKids Press
29 E 21st Street
New York, NY 10010
212-777-3017
800-237-9932
Fax: 888-436-4643
rosenpub@tribeca.ios.com
www.rosenpublishing.com

By stressing that children with Down syndrome are wonderful, viable members of society, this book lessens the stigma attached to this rather common genetic condition.

Ages: 4-8 24 pages Library Binding
ISBN: 0-823951-97-9

Melanie Apel Gordon, Editor

2469 Medical and Surgical Care for Children with Down Syndrome
Woodbine House
6510 Bells Mill Road
Bethesda, MD 20817
301-897-3570
800-843-7323
Fax: 301-897-5838
info@woodbinehouse.com
www.woodbinehouse.com

Provides detailed and easy-to-understand information for parents on a wide range of medical conditions and treatments including: heart disease, recurrent infections, thyroid problems, eye problems, skin conditions, ear, nose and throat problems, orthopedic conditions, leukemia, facial and dental concerns and neurological problems.

395 pages Paperback
ISBN: 0-933149-54-9

Philip Matheis, MD, Editor
Don Van Dyke, MD, Editor

2470 Our Brother Has Down's Syndrome: An Introduction for Children
Annick Press
15 Patricia Avenue
Toronto, ON, M2M
Canada
416-221-4802
Fax: 416-221-8400
www.annickpress.com

Two young sisters tell about their little brother Jai, who has Down's Syndrome. The text stresses the ways in which he is like all children, although he needs extra help to walk, use a spoon, stack blocks, etc. The color photographs show an engaging little boy going about his daily activities, often with other family members.

24 pages Paperback
ISBN: 0-920303-31-5

Shelly Cairo, Editor
Jasmine Cairo, Editor
Irene McNeil, Editor

2471 Parent's Guide to Down Syndrome: Toward a Brighter Future
Brookes Publishing Company
PO Box 10624
Baltimore, MD 21285
410-337-9580
800-638-3775
Fax: 410-337-8539
custserv@brookespublishing.com
www.brookespublishing.com

A comprehensive reference book especially for new parents, but useful and informative to seasoned parents as well. Range of topics include a history of Down syndrome, physical characteristics, developmental expectations, early intervention, feeding the young child and the school years.

352 pages Paperback
ISBN: 1-557664-52-8

Siegfried M Pueschel, Editor

2472 Perceptual-Motor Behavior in Down Syndrome
Human Kinetics Publishing
1607 N Market Street
Champaign, IL 61825
217-351-5076
800-747-4457
Fax: 217-351-2674
www.humankinetics.com

A comprehensive collection of contemporary research and provides readers a window into the life of someone with Down Syndrome.

365 pages Hardcover
ISBN: 0-880119-75-6

Daniel J Weeks, Editor
Romeo Chua, Editor
Dibgy Elliott, Editor

2473 Screening for Down Syndrome
Cambridge University Press
32 Avenue of the Americas
New York, NY 10013
212-337-5000
Fax: 212-691-3239
newyork@cambridge.org
www.cambridge.org

Summarises the recent exciting advances in screening for Down's syndrome. It addresses important clinical questions such as; risk assessment, whom to screen, when to screen, which techniques to use and the organisation of screening programmes nationally and internationally.

1995 358 pages Hardcover
ISBN: 0-521452-71-6

J G Grudzinskas, Editor
T Chard, Editor
M Chapman, Editor

2474 Shattered Dreams - Lonely Choices: Birth Parents of Babies with Disabilities
Bergin & Garvey/Greenwood Publishing
88 Post Road W, PO Box 5007
Westport, CT 06880
203-226-3571
800-225-5800
Fax: 203-222-1502
www.greenwood.com

Joanne Finnegan shares her personal experience and that of several families she interviewed who, like herself, explored options other than raising their child with a disability. Parents express with candor the overwhelming pain they felt when receiving the news, the frustration when searching for options, the no-win feeling of decision making, the resolve with a final decision, and finally, life after the decision.

208 pages Hardcover
ISBN: 0-897892-86-0

Joanne Finnegan, Editor

2475 Show Me No Mercy: Compelling Story of Remarkable Courage
Abingdon Press
201 8th Avenue South, P.O. Box 801
Nashville, TN 37202
800-251-3320
orders@abingdonpress.com
www.abingdonpress.com

A father of a young adult man with Down syndrome relates the experience of his attempt to be reunited with his son after a family tragedy separates them.

144 pages Paperback
ISBN: 0-687384-35-4

Robert Perske, Editor

2476 Since Owen
Johns Hopkins University Press
2715 N Charles Street
Baltimore, MD 21218
410-516-6900
800-537-5487
Fax: 410-516-6968
webmaster@jhupress.jhu.edu
www.press.jhu.edu

A well written book displaying understanding from a veteran parent communicating with other parents of children with disabilities.

488 pages Paperback
ISBN: 0-801839-64-5

Charles R Callanan, Editor
Alfred R. Berkeley, Chairman

2477 To Give An Edge: A Guide for New Parents of Children with Down's Syndrome
Colwell Systems
1031 Mendola Heights Road
St. Paul, MN 55120
651-232-7800

A guide for new parents designed to provide information about the disorder and how other parents of children with Down syndrome have coped.

Paperback
ISBN: 9-993370-55-X

JM Horrobin, Editor

2478 Understanding Down Syndrome
Brookline Books
8 Trumbull Rd, Suite B-001
Northampton, MA 01060
413-584-0184
800-666-2665
Fax: 413-584-6184
brbooks@yahoo.com
www.brooklinebooks.com

The author provides answers and explanations to the countless questions directed to him during his twenty years' involvement with Down syndrome individuals and their families.

243 pages Paperback
ISBN: 1-571290-09-5

Cliff Cunningham, Editor

2479 Where's Chimpy?
Albert Whitman & Company
250 South Northwest Highway, Suite 320
Park Ridge, IL 60068
847-581-0033
800-255-7675
Fax: 847-581-0039
mail@albertwhitman.com
www.albertwhitman.com

Text and photographs show Misty, a little girl with Down syndrome and her father reviewing her day's activities in their search for her stuffed monkey.

32 pages Paperback
ISBN: 0-807589-27-6

Berniece Rabe, Editor
Diane Schmidt, Illustrator

Newsletters

2480 Communicating Together
PO Box 6395
Columbia, MD 21045
408-253-0246
Fax: 408-253-7391
karen@kidsource.com
www.kidsource.com

An excellent resource for parents and professionals. Each issue includes a feature article, a question and answer section and home activities.

6x/year

Dr. Libby Kumin, Editor
Karen Dillon, Media Inquiries

Down Syndrome / Camps

Camps

2481 Camp Friendship
Friendship Ventures
10509 108th Street NW
Annandale, MN 55302

952-852-0101
800-450-8376
Fax: 952-852-0123
info@friendshipventures.org
www.friendshipventures.org

Camp Friendship offers kids, teens, and adults the chance to have the time of their lives. The program focuses on building self-esteem and independence, and practicing social skills; and we nurture each person's strengths and abilities and encourage participation in activies at their own pace. Specially designed for persons with developmental, physical or multiple disabilities, special medical conditions, Down syndrome, autism or other conditions. Weekend camps and longer available.

Georgann Rumsey, Vice President, Programs
Laurie Tschetter, Program Director

2482 Camp Hawkins
800 Rudeseal Road
Mt. Airy, GA 30563

706-894-1678
ksewell@gbchfm.org
www.gbchfm.org

Summer residential camp for children ages 8 to 21 with varying disabilities such as Cerebral Palsy, Down Syndrome, brain injuries and/or developmental delays.

Chris Hobbs, VP of Communications
Alice Bagley, Public Relations
Kendra Sewell, Director

2483 Camp Huntington
56 Bruceville Road
High Falls, NY 12440

845-687-7840
855-707-2267
Fax: 845-213-4313
www.camphuntington.com

Summer activities include recreational, academic and vocational programs for the learning disabled and neurologically impaired. An Olympic pool, horse riding and a special work training program are featured. Programs are tailored to meet individual needs, ages 6-21, and campers may enroll for 4 to 8 weeks.

Michael Bednarz, Executive Director, MS, MBA
Alex Mellor, Program Director, MA
Dr. Bruria Bodek, Consultant, Executive Director

2484 Camp Merrimack
3320 Triana Boulevard
Huntsville, AL 35805

256-534-6455
ksimari@merrimackhall.com
www.merrimackhall.com

A unique arts half-day camp for children ages 3 through 12; open to children with special needs including Cerebral Palsy, Down Syndrome, autism and others.

Ashley Dinges, Executive Director
Kim Simari, Managing Director

2485 Camp New Hope
Friendship Ventures
53035 Lake Avenue
McGregor, MN 55760

952-852-0101
800-450-8376
Fax: 952-852-0123
fv@friendshipventures.org
www.friendshipventures.org

Camp New Hope is a great place for children, teens, and adults to have the time of their lives. The program provides a unique opportunity for having fun, learning skills, boosting confidence, and making friends. Services are specifically designed for persons with developmental, phyisical or multiple disabilities, special medical needs, Down syndrome, autism, or other conditions. Weekend camps and longer available. Other services available throughout the year.

Georgann Rumsey, Vice President, Programs
Laurie Tschetter, Program Director

2486 Camp PALS
4368 Farmington Circle
Allentown, PA 18104

215-501-7157
jenni@palsprograms.org
www.camppals.org

One-week summer camp for young adults with Down syndrome held at Cabrini College in PA.

Jason Toff, Board Chair
Jenni Newbury Ross, Executive Director
Sarah Barnes, Program Coordinator

2487 Eden Wood Center
Friendship Ventures
16165 Hillcrest Lane
Eden Prairie, MN 44346

952-852-0101
Fax: 952-934-5656
fbiw.info@gmail.com
fbiw.net/old_site/JoinIn/meetings.htm

Offers resident camp programs for children, teenagers and adults with developmental, physical or multiple disabilities, Down Syndrome, special medical conditions, Williams Syndrome, autism and/or other conditions. Fishing, creative arts, golf, sports and other activities are available. Creative Options Respite Care offers weekend camps year round for children, teenagers and adults. Ventures Travel offers guided vacations for teens and adults with developmental disabilities or other unique needs.

Vicky Miller, President
Roger Person, Vice President
Marcus Johnson, Director

Description

2488 DYSLEXIA

Involves the following Biologic System(s):

Neurologic Disorders

Dyslexia refers to a specific learning disability characterized by the impaired ability to process written symbols. Although individuals with dyslexia are able to see and recognize letters, this disorder impairs their ability to read, write, and spell. Affected individuals typically have no problems with the correct recognition of pictures and objects.

No definition of dyslexia is universally accepted, thus incidence is difficult to determine. An estimated 15% of public school children receive special education for reading problems of whom 3 to 5% are probably dyslexic. Young children with dyslexia may have difficulty remembering the correct names of letters and numbers. Articulating proper speech may be difficult. Some children of school age may reverse letters and words when writing. For example, affected children may substitute the letter p for q or the word was for saw, while transposing letters so that bets may become best. Children with dyslexia may also have difficulty reading due to an impaired ability to determine the sequence of letters within words and to distinguish right from left. The hallmark of this learning disability is the fact that, despite the difficulties associated with dyslexia, affected children are of average or above average intelligence as evidenced by I.Q. testing as well as their success in other scholastic achievements.

Early diagnosis of dyslexia is an important factor in treating this learning disability. Children nearing the end of first grade who exhibit difficulties with word skills or any children whose reading and writing ability is not commensurate with that of their other scholastic abilities may be tested for dyslexia. Although dyslexia is not related to eye defects, an ophthalmologic evaluation is beneficial in determining if ocular abnormalities may be eliminated as a cause of symptoms. Also, eye irregularities may be present in addition to dyslexia and, therefore, may be diagnosed and corrected at that time. Treatment for dyslexia is geared toward remedial teaching techniques specific to this disability.

Dyslexia is thought to be a familial disorder that may be inherited through an autosomal dominant trait. Boys are more frequently affected than girls.

Government Agencies

2489 NIH/ Eunice Kennedy Shriver National Institute of Child Health & Human Development
P.O. Box 3006
Rockville, MD 20847
800-370-2943
Fax: 866-760-5947
www.nichd.nih.gov

Conducts and supports research on topics related to the health of children, adults, families and populations. Some of these topics include: developmental disabilities, growth and development, infant death, reproductive health and birth defects.

Diana W. Bianchi, Director
Alison Cernich, PhD, Deputy Director

National Associations & Support Groups

2490 American Academy of Pediatrics
345 Park Blvd
Itasca, IL 60143
800-433-9016
Fax: 847-434-8000
mcc@aap.org
www.aap.org

The American Academy of Pediatrics and its member pediatricians are committed to the attainment of optimal physical, mental and social health and well-being for all infants, children, adolescents, and young adults.

Lynn Olson, PhD, VP, Research
Mark Del Monte, JD, CEO/Executive VP
Vera Tait, MD, FAAP, Chief Medical Officer

2491 American School Counselor Association
1101 King Street, Ste 310
Alexandria, VA 22314
703-683-2722
asca@schoolcounselor.org
www.schoolcounselor.org

The mission of ASCA is to represent professional school counselors and to promote professionalism and ethical practices.

Jill Cook, Executive Director
Amanda Fitzgerald, Assistant Deputy Executive Director
Kathleen M Rakestraw, Director of Communications

2492 American Speech Language Hearing Association (ASHA)
2200 Research Blvd
Rockville, MD 20852
301-296-5700
800-638-8255
Fax: 301-296-8580
productsales@asha.org
www.asha.org

The mission of the American Speech-Language-Hearing Association is to promote the interests of and provide the highest quality services for professionals in audiology, speech-language pathology, speech and hearing science, and to advocate for people with communication disabilities.

Shari B. Robertson, President
Theresa H. Rodgers, President-Elect

2493 Center for Disabilities and Development
University of Iowa Stead Family Children's Hospita
100 Hawkins Drive
Iowa City, IA 52242
319-353-6900
877-686-0031
Fax: 319-356-7700
cdd-webmaster@uiowa.edu
www.uiowa.edu

A trusted resource for healthcare, training, research and information for people with disabilities that include: behavior disorders, brain injury, cerebral palsy, diabetes, down syndrome, learning disabilities, sleep disorders and spina bifida.

Dianne McBrien, MD, Medical Director

2494 Davis Dyslexia Association International
1601 Bayshore Highway, Suite 260
Burlingame, CA 94010
650-692-7141
888-805-7216
www.davislearn.com

Offers books, materials, workshops and certification in the Davis Dyslexia Correction method.

2495 Genetic Alliance
426400 Woodfield Road, Ste 189
Damascus, MD 20872
202-966-5557
Fax: 202-966-8553
info@geneticalliance.org
www.geneticalliance.org

World's leading nonprofit health advocacy organization committed to transforming health through genetics and promoting an environment of openness centered on the health of individuals, families, and communities.

Dyslexia / Conferences

Sharon Terry, CEO
Ruth Child, CFO
Natasha Bonhomme, Chief Strategy Officer

2496 **International Dyslexia Association**
1829 Reisterstown Rd., Suite 350
Pikesville, MD 21208
410-296-0232
Fax: 410-321-5069
info@dyslexiaida.org
dyslexiaida.org

Our mission is to pursue and provide the most comprehensive range of information and services that address the full scope of dyslexia and related difficulties in learning to read and write.

Sonja Banks, Chief Executive Officer
Gina Schuh, Chief Operating Officer
Dana Nwoye, Partner Relations & Outreach

2497 **Learning Disabilities Association of America**
PO Box 10369, 4156 Library Road
Pittsburgh, PA 15234
412-341-1515
888-300-6710
Fax: 412-344-0224
info@LDAAmerica.org
www.ldaamerica.org

Helps families of the affected individual through information and referral to professionals in their area. A membership organization with affiliates across the country.

Stephanie Fedro-Byrom, Operations Manager
Maureen Swanson, Director, Healthy Children Project
Ericka Pardun, Communications Coordinator

2498 **March of Dimes Foundation**
1550 Crystal Drive, Ste 1300
Arlington, VA 22202
888-663-4637
www.marchofdimes.org

March of Dimes help moms have full-term pregnancies and research the problems that threaten the health of babies. The March of Dimes also acts globally: sharing best practices in perinatal health and helping improve birth outcomes where the needs are the most urgent.

Stacey D. Stewart, President
Alan Brogdon, SVP/COO/Board Officer
Rahul Gupta, MD, SVP & Chief Medical/Health Officer

2499 **Option Institute: Son Rise Program**
Autism Treatment Center of America
2080 S Undermountain Road
Sheffield, MA 01257
877-766-7473
www.son-rise.org

Describes an effective, loving and respectful method for treating children with autism. It teaches parents and healing professionals how to set up a home based program using the child's motivation to reach their special child.

Barry Neil Kaufman, Co-Founder/Co-Creator
Samahria Lyte Kaufman, Co-Founder/Co-Creator

Conferences

2500 **ASHA Convention**
American Speech-Language-Hearing Association
2200 Research Blvd
Rockville, MD 20850
301-296-5700
800-638-8255
Fax: 301-296-5650
exhibits@asha.org
convention.asha.org

The premier annual professional education event for speech-language pathologists, audiologists, and speech, language, and hearing scientists. Bringing together nearly 15,000 attendees, the Convention provides unparalleled opportunities to hear the latest evidence-based research and gain new skills and resources to advance your career.

November

Nancye Berman, Manager, Exhibits

2501 **American School Counselor Association Annual Conference**
1101 King Street, Suite 310
Alexandria, VA 22314
703-683-2722
800-306-4722
Fax: 703-997-7572
asca@schoolcounselor.org
www.schoolcounselor.org

The mission of ASCA is to represent professional school counselors and to promote professionalism and ethical practices.

3,000 Attendees

Richard Wong, Executive Director
Jennifer Walsh, Director, Education & Training
Kathleen M Rakestraw, Director of Communications

2502 **International Dyslexia Association Conference**
1829 Reisterstown Rd., Suite 350
Pikesville, MD 21208
410-296-0232
Fax: 410-321-5069
info@dyslexiada.org
dyslexiada.org

Focuses on the latest advances in dyslexia, related language difficulties and related fields. Individual sessions are geared towards educators and educational administrators, educational diagnosticians and therapists, parents, speech and language pathologists and of course, individuals with dyslexia and their families.

Sonja Banks, Chief Executive Officer
Gina Schuh, Chief Operating Officer
Dana Nwoye, Partner Relations & Outreach

2503 **LDA Annual Conference**
Learning Disabilities Association of America
PO Box 10369, 4156 Library Road
Pittsburgh, PA 15234
412-341-1515
888-300-6710
Fax: 412-344-0224
info@LDAAmerica.org
www.ldaamerica.org

Meeting on learning disabilities, featuring over 200 workshops and exhibits.

February

Stephanie Fedro-Byrom, Operations Manager

Audio Video

2504 **Dyslexia**
Fanlight Productions
32 Court Street, 21st Floor
Brooklyn, NY 11201
718-488-8900
800-876-1710
Fax: 718-488-8642
info@fanlight.com, orders@fanlight.com
www.fanlight.com

Looks at the experiences of people with these learning disabilities as well as the potential value to society of their alternative ways of learning. Dartmouth Hitchcock Medical Center Series, The Doctor is In...

28 minutes VHS

Nicole Johnson, Publicity Coordinator

Web Sites

2505 **American Speech Language Hearing Association (ASHA)**
2200 Research Blvd
Rockville, MD 20852
301-296-5700
800-638-8255
Fax: 301-296-8580
TTY: 301-296-5650
nsslha@asha.org
www.asha.org

An organization working to promote a better quality of life for children and adults with communication disorders. Our mission is to advance knowledge about the causes and treatment of hearing, speech, and language problems.

Dyslexia / Book Publishers

Shari B. Robertson, President
Theresa H. Rodgers, President-Elect

2506 **British Dyslexia Association**
Unit 8 Bracknell Beeches, Old Bracknell Lane
Bracknell, RG12
033- 40- 455
www.bdadyslexia.org.uk

The BDA offers a range of practical help for dyslexic children, dyslexic adults, parents and professionals in education.

Margaret Malpas, Chair of Trustees
Diana Baring, Vice President
Kevin Morley, Vice President

2507 **Davis Dyslexia Association International Dyslexia: The Gift**
1601 Bayshore Highway 260
Burlingame, CA 94010
650-692-7141
888-999-3324
Fax: 650-692-7075
www.dyslexia.com

Offers information and training in methods for overcoming learning problems developed by Ron Davis, author of 'The Gift of Dyslexia,' listings of Davis Dyslexia Correction providers worldwide, a forum for networking and articles and reports on learning styles and educational approaches.

2508 **International Dyslexia Association**
1829 Reisterstown Rd., Suite 350
Pikesville, MD 21208
410-296-0232
Fax: 410-321-5069
info@dyslexiada.org
dyslexiada.org

Our mission is to pursue and provide the most comprehensive range of information and services that address the full scope of dyslexia and related difficulties in learning to read and write.

Sonja Banks, Chief Executive Officer
Gina Schuh, Chief Operating Officer
Dana Nwoye, Partner Relations & Outreach

2509 **Learning Disabilities Association of America**
PO Box 10369, 4156 Library Road
Pittsburgh, PA 15234
412-341-1515
888-300-6710
Fax: 412-344-0224
info@LDAAmerica.org
www.ldaamerica.org

Helps families of the affected individual through information and referral to professionals in their area. A membership organization with affiliates across the country.

Stephanie Fedro-Byrom, Operations Manager
Maureen Swanson, Director, Healthy Children Project
Ericka Pardun, Communications Coordinator

2510 **Mental Health Net**
P.O. Box 20709
Columbus, OH 43220
614-448-4055
800-232-TALK
info@centersite.net, editor@centersite.n
www.mentalhelp.net

We wish to provide the following: to discuss, develop and debate in an open forum the future of the mental health field in America and throughout the world. To help coordinate various components of the mental health field so as to bring about greater communication between them.

2511 **NIH/ Eunice Kennedy Shriver National Institute of Child Health & Human Development**
P.O. Box 3006
Rockville, MD 20847
800-370-2943
Fax: 866-760-5947
www.nichd.nih.gov

Conducts and supports research on all stages of human development to better understand the health of children, adults, families and communities. Topics of research include: birth defects, developmental disabilities, reproductive health, growth and development, and infant death.

Diana W. Bianchi, Director
Alison Cernich, PhD, Deputy Director

2512 **Option Institute: Son Rise Program**
www.son-rise.org

www.son-rise.org

Describes an effective, loving and respectful method for treating children with autism. It teaches parents and healing professionals how to set up a home based program using the child's motivation to reach their special child.

Barry Neil Kaufman, Co-Founder

Book Publishers

2513 **Let's Talk About Dyslexia**
Melanie Apel Gordon, author

Rosen Publishing Group's PowerKids Press
29 E 21st Street
New York, NY 10010
212-777-3017
800-237-9932
Fax: 888-436-4643
rosenpub@tribeca.ios.com
www.powerkidspress.com

Children will learn what dyslexia is and how to tell if they have it. This book stresses that children with dyslexia are just as smart as their classmates. Tells about Albert Einstein and other well known people who were dyslexic. Grades K-5.

24 pages
ISBN: 0-823951-99-5

2514 **Misunderstood Child**
Larry B Silver, MD, author

Active Parenting Publishers
1220 Kennestone Circle, Suite 130
Marietta, GA 30066
770-429-0565
800-825-0060
Fax: 770-429-0334
cservice@activeparenting.com
www.activeparenting.com

The fully revised and updated must-have resource to help you become a supportive and assertive advocate for your child. The Misunderstood Child, Fourth Edition has become the go-to reference guide for families of children with learning disorders. Item #8825.

432 pages

2515 **Overcoming Dyslexia in Children, Adolescents, and Adults**
Dale R Jordan, author

Pro-Ed
8700 Shoal Creek Boulevard
Austin, TX 78757
512-451-3246
800-897-3202
Fax: 800-397-7633
www.proedinc.com

The third edition summarizes what science knows today about what causes the forms of dyslexia that are related to left-brain language processing. This book also discusses in detail nonverbal types of learning disabilities (LD) and social and emotional types of LD. All forms of dyslexia are described in detail with graphic illustrations of how dyslexia impacts classroom learning, social behavior, emotional maturity and development.

432 pages Softcover
ISBN: 0-890796-42-4

2516 **Straight Talk about Psychological Testing for Kids**
Ellen Braaten PhD, Gretcen Felopulos PhD, author

Active Parenting Publishers
1220 Kennestone Circle, Suite 130
Marietta, GA 30066
770-429-0565
800-825-0060
Fax: 770-429-0334
cservice@activeparenting.com
www.activeparenting.com

This authoritative guide gives parents the inside scoop on how psychological testing works and how to use testing to get the best help for their children. Item #8670.

260 pages Softcover

Camps

2517 Camp Dunnabeck at Kildonan
425 Morse Hill Road
Amenia, NY 12501

845-373-8111
Fax: 845-373-2004
www.kildonan.org

Specializes in helping intelligent children with specific reading, writing and spelling disablities. Provides Orton-Gillingham tutoring with camp activities, including swimming, sailing, waterskiing, horseback riding, ceramics, tennis and woodworking.

Ages 9-15

Christina Lang, Chair
Richard S. Berg, Vice Chair
Kevin F. Pendergast, Headmaster

2518 Landmark School
429 Hale Street, PO Box 227
Prides Crossing, MA 1965

978-236-3010
Fax: 978-927-7268
admission@landmarkschool.org
www.landmarkschool.org

Offers academic skill development and exciting activities for boys and girls in grades 1-12, who have been diagnosed with a language-based learning disability.

Moira M. James, Chair
Martin P. Slark, Vice Chair
Robert J. Broudo, President & Headmaster

2519 Marvelwood Summer
Marvelwood School
476 Skiff Mountain Road, PO Box 3001
Kent, CT 6757

860-927-0047
800-440-9107
Fax: 860-927-5325
www.themarvelwoodschool.com

The emphasis in this summer program is on diagnosis and remediation of individual reading, spelling, writing, mathematics and study problems. Participants are boys and girls entering grades 6-10.

Scott E Pottbecker, Head of School
Katherine Almquist, Summer Admissions

Description

2520 DYSTONIA

Covers these related disorders: Dopa-responsive dystonia (DRD) or Segawa syndrome, Drug-induced dystonia, Dystonia musculorum deformans (DMD) or torsion, Focal dystonia

Involves the following Biologic System(s):
Neurologic Disorders, Orthopedic and Muscle Disorders

Dystonia is a neurologic movement disorder characterized by relatively slow, involuntary, writhing motions that may result in twisting or distorted posturing of affected muscles. The abnormal motions associated with dystonia result from unusually increased muscle rigidity due to simultaneous contractions of certain muscles termed agonists and antagonists. In unaffected individuals, when voluntary movements occur, there are usually coordinated contractions and simultaneous relaxations of several muscles. Muscles known as agonists are primarily responsible for producing a particular movement, and other muscles, called synergists, contract to assist the agonist muscles. While these muscles contract, other muscles known as antagonists normally simultaneously relax, helping to ensure smooth rather than jerky, uncoordinated motions. However, in patients with dystonia, agonist and antagonist muscles simultaneously contract, resulting in abnormally distorted movements. Depending upon the form of dystonia present, abnormal motions may vary greatly in severity and may be limited to one muscle group or may affect many muscles of the body, causing severely distorted postures and significantly interfering with activities of daily living.

Dystonias that are limited to certain specific muscle groups may be referred to as focal dystonias. Focal dystonias may be confined to muscles of the neck (cervical dystonia or spasmodic torticollis); the eyelids, causing near or complete closure of the eyelids (blepharospasm) and functional blindness; the mouth and jaw (buccomandibular dystonia); the hand (writer's cramp); or certain other areas of the body. Although such conditions are considered the most prevalent forms of dystonia, they occur much more commonly in adults than children. The main causes of dystonia during childhood include certain genetic disorders, such as dystonia musculorum deformans, dopa-responsive dystonia, Wilson disease, or Hallervorden-Spatz disease; lack of oxygen during labor, delivery, or immediately after birth (perinatal asphyxia), causing brain damage (hypoxicischemic encephalopathy); or exposure to particular medications.

The most pronounced form of dystonia is observed in a group of genetic disorders known as dystonia musculorum deformans (DMD) or torsion dystonia. One form of the disorder is thought to most commonly affect individuals of Eastern European Ashkenazi Jewish descent. Symptoms typically become apparent between the ages of six to 14 years and initially include involuntary movement or posturing of one area of the body, particularly the foot. Most patients first experience abnormal periodic bending of one foot with the toes downward (plantar flexion), potentially causing tip-toe walking. Such posturing of the foot gradually becomes constant, and muscles in other areas of the body, such as the shoulders, pelvis, and spine, begin to develop periodic, involuntary, spasmodic, twisting movements. With disease progression, spasms become frequent and, eventually, are ongoing, causing contortion and severely distorted posturing of affected muscles. Although dystonic movements may initially subside during sleep, they may eventually be present at all times, severely restricting activities of daily living and causing a high level of functional disability. Treatment may include administration of the drug trihexyphenidyl or certain other medications, such as carbamazepine, bromocriptine, levodopa, or diazepam.

Dopa-responsive dystonia (DRD), also known as Segawa syndrome, is a genetic disorder that is thought to be transmitted as an autosomal dominant trait. The disorder more commonly affects females and usually becomes apparent between four to eight years of age. Initial symptoms often include periodic, involuntary stiffening and abnormal posturing of the foot. As the disease progresses, dystonia may also eventually affect muscles of the arms, torso, and, in some patients, the neck. Within about four to five years, all areas of the body are usually affected. Some patients may also have unusually slow movements (bradykinesia) and involuntary, rhythmic movements (tremors) of certain muscles while at rest. Symptoms usually subside with sleep and gradually worsen during the day. Administration of the medication levodopa, a biological forerunner or precursor of the neurotransmitter dopamine, typically causes a dramatic improvement of symptoms.

Wilson disease is an autosomal recessive disorder in which copper metabolism causes an abnormal accumulation of copper in the liver, brain, kidneys, corneas, and other tissues of the body. The disorder is often characterized by progressive liver disease, degenerative changes of the brain, kidney failure, and the presence of characteristic grayish-green or reddish-gold rings at the outer margins of the corneas (Kayser-Fleischer rings). Neurologic symptoms, which rarely become apparent before age 10, are thought to result from progressive involvement of a region of the brain that assists in regulating muscular movements (basal ganglia). Such symptoms usually initially include progressive dystonia that is characterized by abnormalities of muscle tone, muscle stiffness and rigidity, muscle spasms, and abnormal movement patterns and fixed postures, such as a fixed smile due to drawing back of the upper lip. Patients also experience involuntary, rhythmic, quivering movements of the extremities on one side of the body (unilateral) that eventually become generalized and disabling. The treatment of patients with Wilson disease often consists of administration of penicillamine, a medication that binds with copper and enables it to be excreted from the body; supplementation of vitamin B6; and a diet that is low in copper intake (less than one mg/day).

Hallervorden-Spatz disease is a rare autosomal recessive disorder characterized by an abnormal accumulation of iron pigment in certain areas of the brain. Symptoms usually develop during childhood and may include progressive dystonia characterized by muscle stiffness, rigidity, and relatively slow, involuntary, twisting and distorted posturing of affected muscles. By adolescence, patients may have restricted movements of certain muscles due to increased muscle rigidity (spasticity); an inability to coordinate voluntary movements (ataxia); difficulty speaking (dysarthria); and progressive confusion, disorientation, and deterioration of intellectual abilities (dementia). The treatment of patients with Hallervorden-Spatz disease is symptomatic and supportive.

In some children, the administration of certain drugs may cause a sudden (acute) development of dystonia, such as certain antiseizure (anticonvulsant) medications or antipsychotic drugs (phenothiazines). In addition, particular medications may cause acute or chronic progressive dystonia, such as the antiseizure medications phenytoin or carbamazepine, or the antipsychotic drug haloperidol. Treatment may include the withdrawal of the offending drug and intravenous administration of the medication, diphenhydramine.

Dystonia / Government Agencies

Depending upon its underlying cause or specific form, treatment measures for chronic dystonia may include the administration of certain medications (anticholinergic agents), such as trihexyphenidyl or ethopropazine. These drugs inhibit the transmission of particular nerve impulses to muscles.|In addition, focal dystonias such as dystonia limited to muscles of the neck (cervical dystiodic torticollis), are often treated with periodic injections of botulin (botulinum toxin) into affected muscles. Botulin is a bacterial toxin that blocks the release of a particular neurotransmitter (acetylcholine), resulting in temporary paralysis and thus relief from discomfort and disability associated with muscle rigidity.

Government Agencies

2521 NIH/National Institute of Neurological Disorders and Stroke (NINDS)
PO Box 5801
Bethesda, MD 20824
800-352-9424
www.ninds.nih.gov

Works to reduce the burden of neurological disease by conducting, fostering, coordinating and guiding research on the causes, prevention, diagnosis and treatment of neurological disorders and stroke, while supporting basic research in related scientific areas.

Walter J. Koroshetz, MD, Director

National Associations & Support Groups

2522 American Academy of Pediatrics
345 Park Blvd
Itasca, IL 60143
800-433-9016
Fax: 847-434-8000
mcc@aap.org
www.aap.org

The American Academy of Pediatrics and its member pediatricians are committed to the attainment of optimal physical, mental and social health and well-being for all infants, children, adolescents, and young adults.

Lynn Olson, PhD, VP, Research
Mark Del Monte, JD, CEO/Executive VP
Vera Tait, MD, FAAP, Chief Medical Officer

2523 American Speech Language Hearing Association (ASHA)
2200 Research Blvd
Rockville, MD 20852
301-296-5700
800-638-8255
Fax: 301-296-8580
pr@asha.org
www.asha.org

Works to promote a better quality of life for children and adults with communication disorders. Part of their mission is to advance knowledge about the causes and treatment of hearing, speech, and language problems.

Shari B. Robertson, President
Theresa H. Rodgers, President-Elect

2524 Child Neurology Foundation
601 W Short Street
Lexington, KY 40508
888-417-3435
info@childneurologyfoundation.org
childneurologyfoundation.org

The Child Neurology Foundation connects partners from all areas of the child neurology community so those navigating the journey of disease diagnosis, management, and care have the ongoing support from those dedicated to treatments and cures.

Amy Brin, Executive Director
Katie Hentges, Director, Programs
Brea McCormley, Director, Development

2525 Dystonia Medical Research Foundation
One E Wacker Drive, Suite 1730
Chicago, IL 60601
312-755-0198
800-377-3978
Fax: 312-803-0138
dystonia@dystonia-foundation.org
www.dystonia-foundation.org

The mission of the Dystonia Medical Research Foundation is to advance research for more treatments and ultimately a cure; to promote awareness and education; and to support the needs and well being of affected individuals and families.

Janet Hieshetter, Executive Director
Joel S. Perlmutter, MD, Scientific Director

2526 Genetic Alliance
426400 Woodfield Road, Ste 189
Damascus, MD 20872
202-966-5557
Fax: 202-966-8553
info@geneticalliance.org
www.geneticalliance.org

World's leading nonprofit health advocacy organization committed to transforming health through genetics and promoting an environment of openness centered on the health of individuals, families, and communities.

Sharon Terry, CEO
Ruth Child, CFO
Natasha Bonhomme, Chief Strategy Officer

2527 March of Dimes Foundation
1550 Crystal Drive, Ste 1300
Arlington, VA 22202
888-663-4637
www.marchofdimes.org

March of Dimes help moms have full-term pregnancies and research the problems that threaten the health of babies. The March of Dimes also acts globally: sharing best practices in perinatal health and helping improve birth outcomes where the needs are the most urgent.

Stacey D. Stewart, President
Alan Brogdon, SVP/COO/Board Officer
Rahul Gupta, MD, SVP & Chief Medical/Health Officer

2528 Muscular Dystrophy Association
16 N Clark, Ste 3550
Chicago, IL 60601
646-992-2908
800-572-1717
resourcecenter@mda.org
www.mda.org

Voluntary health agency aimed at conquering neuromuscular diseases. The diseases in MDA's program include muscular dystrophy, ALS and numerous related muscle-debilitating diseases. With almost 100 field offices and over 150 affiliated MDA Care Centers nationwide, MDA conducts research, provides medical and community services, clinics, support groups, summer camps for youngsters and much more.

R. Rodney Howell, MD, Chairman
Lynn O'Connor Vos, President & CEO
Mary Fiance, Director, PR & Communications

2529 National Spasmodic Torticollis Association
17151 Newhope Street, Suite 208
Fountain Valley, CA 92708
657-554-0661
info@cdtorticollis.org
www.cdtorticollis.org

Nonprofit organization, providing support, referrals and information for ST patients and family members.

Justin Aqunies, Executive Director

2530 WE MOVE (Worldwide Education and Awareness ofement Disorders)
204 West 84th Street
New York, NY 10024
wemove@wemove.org

WE MOVE provides movement disorder information and educational materials to physicians, patients, the media, and the public via its comprehensive Web sites training courses, and more. It's goal is to make early diagnosis, up-to-date treatment and patient support a reality for all people living with movement disorders.

Susan Bressman, MD, President

Dystonia / Web Sites

Research Centers

2531 Benign Essential Blepharospasm Research Foundation
637 N 7th Street, Suite 102, PO Box 12468
Beaumont, TX 77726
409-832-0788
Fax: 409-832-0890
www.blepharospasm.org

The purpose of BEBRF is to undertake, promote, develop and carry on the search for the cause and a cure for benign essential blepharospace and other related disorders and infirmities of the facial musculature.

Mary Lou Thompson, President
Glynda Lucas, First Vice President

2532 Dystonia Medical Research Foundation
One E Wacker Drive, Suite 1730
Chicago, IL 60601
312-755-0198
800-377-3978
Fax: 312-803-0138
www.dystonia-foundation.org

The mission of the Dystonia Medical Research Foundation is to advance research for more treatments and ultimately a cure; to promote awareness and education; and to support the needs and well being of affected individuals and families.

Janet Hieshetter, Executive Director
Joel S. Perlmutter, MD, Scientific Director

Conferences

2533 ASHA Convention
American Speech-Language-Hearing Association
2200 Research Blvd
Rockville, MD 20850
301-296-5700
800-638-8255
Fax: 301-296-5650
exhibits@asha.org
convention.asha.org

The premier annual professional education event for speech-language pathologists, audiologists, and speech, language, and hearing scientists. Bringing together nearly 15,000 attendees, the Convention provides unparalleled opportunities to hear the latest evidence-based research and gain new skills and resources to advance your career.

November

Nancye Berman, Manager, Exhibits

2534 Jake's Ride for Dystonia Research
The Bachmann-Strauss Dystonia Parkinson Foundation
PO Box 38016
Albany, NY 12203
212-509-0995
www.dystonia-parkinsons.org

Jake's Ride for Dystonia Research began in 2007, when a young boy named Jake Silverman was diagnosed with early onset childhood dystonia. After hearing Jake's story, a neighbor and father of one of Jake's classmates, David Gardner, came up with the idea to create a bike ride that would raise awareness and needed funds for this disorder.

Web Sites

2535 American Speech Language Hearing Association (ASHA)
2200 Research Blvd
Rockville, MD 20852
301-296-5700
800-638-8255
Fax: 301-296-8580
TTY: 301-296-5650
nsslha@asha.org
www.asha.org

An organization working to promote a better quality of life for children and adults with communication disorders. Our mission is to advance knowledge about the causes and treatments of hearing, speech, and language problems.

Shari B. Robertson, President
Theresa H. Rodgers, President-Elect

2536 Dystonia Medical Research Foundation
One East Wacker Drive, Suite 1730
Chicago, IL 60601
312-755-0198
800-377-3978
Fax: 312-803-0138
dystonia@dystonia-foundation.org
www.dystonia-foundation.org

Dedicated to serving people with dystonia, a neurological disorder. The goals of the the Foundation is to advance research into the causes of and treatments for dystonia; to build awareness of dystonia in both the medical and lay communities; and to sponsor patient and family support groups and programs.

Janet Hieshetter, Executive Director
Joel S. Perlmutter, MD, Scientific Director

2537 Muscular Dystrophy Association
16 N Clark, Ste 3550
Chicago, IL 60601
800-572-1717
resourcecenter@mda.org
www.mda.org

Voluntary health agency aimed at conquering neuromuscular disease that affect more than 1 million Americans.

R. Rodney Howell, MD, Chairman
Lynn O'Connor Vos, President & CEO
Mary Fiance, Director, PR & Communications

2538 NIH/National Institute of Neurological Disorders and Stroke (NINDS)
www.ninds.nih.gov

www.ninds.nih.gov

Supports and conducts research and research training on the normal structure and function of the nervous system and on the causes, prevention, diagnosis and treatment of nervous system disorders including stroke, epilepsy, multiple sclerosis, Parkinson's disease, head and spinal cord injury, Alzheimer's disease and brain tumors.

Walter J. Koroshetz, MD, Director

2539 National Spasmodic Torticollis Association
9920 Talbert Avenue
Fountain Valley, CA 92708
714-378-9837
800-487-8385
NSTAmail@aol.com
www.torticollis.org

Nonprofit organization, providing support, referrals and information for ST patients and family members.

Ken Price, President/ Treasurer
Diane Truong, Vice President
Justin G. Aquines, Executive Director

2540 Online Mendelian Inheritance in Man
McKusick-Nathans Institue of Genetic Medicine-JHU
Baltimore, MD 21205
www.omim.org

This database is a catalog of human genes and genetic disorders.

Ada Hamosh, MD, Scientific Director

2541 WE MOVE (Worldwide Education and Awareness ofement Disorders)
204 West 84th Street
New York, NY 10024
NOP-ONE-

WE MOVE provides movement disorder information and educational materials to physicians, patients, the media, and the public via its comprehensive Web sites training courses, and more. It's goal is to make early diagnosis, up-to-date treatment and patient support a reality for all people living with movement disorders.

Newsletters

2542 **Benign Essential Blepharospasm Research Foundation Newsletter**
PO Box 12468
Beaumont, TX 77726
409-832-0788
Fax: 409-832-0890
bebrf@blepharospasm.org
www.blepharospasm.org

BEBRF Focus for 2006: Twenty-five years of hope, and progress.

12 pages Bimonthly

Mary Lou Thompson, President
Glynda Lucas, First Vice President

Pamphlets

2543 **DMRF/NINDS Dystonia Workshop: From Gene to Function in Dystonia**
National Inst. of Neurological Disorders/Stroke
PO Box 5801
Bethesda, MD 20824
301-496-5751
800-352-9424
www.ninds.nih.gov

Health Disparities: Working Group-Cognitive and Emotional Health in Minority Children Workshop.

Dr. Story Landis, Director
Alan L. Wlliard, PhD, Deputy Director
Caroline Lewis, Executive Officer

2544 **Dytonias: Fact Sheet**
National Inst. of Neurological Disorders/Stroke
PO Box 5801
Bethesda, MD 20824
301-496-5751
800-352-9424
www.ninds.nih.gov

Fact Sheet listing the following contents: What are the Dystonias, What are the symptoms, How are the Dystonias classified, What do scientists know about the Dystonias, When do symptoms occur, Are their any treatments, What research is being done, Where can I get more information.

Dr. Story Landis, Director
Alan L. Wlliard, PhD, Deputy Director
Caroline Lewis, Executive Officer

2545 **NINDS Seeks Patients with Generalized Dystonia**
National Inst. of Neurological Disorders/Stroke
PO Box 5801
Bethesda, MD 20824
301-496-5751
800-352-9424
www.ninds.nih.gov

NINDS program announcements, requests for applications and clinical studies seeking patients.

Dr. Story Landis, Director
Alan L. Wlliard, PhD, Deputy Director
Caroline Lewis, Executive Officer

2546 **Patients with Cervical or Focal Hand Dystonia Sought**
National Inst. of Neurological Disorders/Stroke
PO Box 5801
Bethesda, MD 20824
301-496-5751
800-352-9424
karpb@ninds.nih.gov
www.ninds.nih.gov

NINDS program announcements, requests for applications and clinical studies seeking patients.

Dr. Story Landis, Director
Alan L. Wlliard, PhD, Deputy Director
Caroline Lewis, Executive Officer

Description

2547 EATING DISORDERS

Synonyms: Anorexia Nervosa, Bulimia Nervosa, Binge Eating Disorder

Involves the following Biologic System(s):
Developmental/Behavioral/Psychiatric Disorders

There are two major types of eating disorders — Anorexia Nervosa and Bulimia Nervosa. A third category, according to the American Psychiatric Association (APA), is termed Eating Disorders Not Otherwise Specified (EDNOS) and includes Binge Eating Disorder. Although different in the symptoms they manifest, the three disorders are quite similar in their underlying pathology: disturbed eating patterns and dysfunctional attitudes toward food, eating, and body shape. Primary features of eating disorders are compulsive behavior, loss of control, and continuing behavior despite negative consequences. Genetic and environmental factors appear to be at the root of eating disorders, although exact mechanisms remain unknown. Eating disorders occur more frequently in females; males are also affected, but are less likely than females to be daignosed with an eating disorder. The median age range for the onset of eating disorders is between ages 8 and 21, although they can begin earlier or later in life.

There are numerous psychosocial consequences of eating disorders (e.g. problems with family, friends, school, or work; lowered perceived happiness). Eating disorders may cause grave physical damage, so treatment first involves restoring patients to a safe and healthy body weight. Once out of physical danger, patients undergo a long-term process that includes medication and psychotherapy. Fortunately, most people who undergo appropriate treatment do recover from eating disorders.

An orexia Nervosa is diagnosed when a person refuses to maintain a body weight at or above 85 percent of their normal weight. Patients have an intense fear of gaining weight or becoming fat, despite being underweight. They are disturbed by the way their body weight or shape is experienced, give it undo influence, and deny the seriousness of low body weight. Patients with anorexia nervosa may be severely depressed and may experience insomnia and irritability. In menstruating females, anorexia may disrupt normal menstrual cycles. More than 10 percent of those diagnosed with the disorder die from it. Death typically is caused by starvation, suicide, or electrolyte imbalance.

Individuals with Bulimia Nervosa eat large amounts of food in a short time. Guilt and fear then cause them to get rid of the food by vomiting (purge) or by other means, including periods of fasting, misuse of laxatives and diuretics, use of enemas, and excessive exercise. Individuals with bulimia nervosa typically are of normal or higher than normal weight. Medical consequences of bulimia nervosa include potentially dangerous fluid and electrolyte imbalances, nutritional deficiencies, menstrual and other reproductive system irregularities. Rare but potentially fatal complications include esophageal tears, gastric rupture from purging, cardiac arrhythmia, tooth decay (due to stomach acid), swollen face and throat, dizziness, blackouts, constant upset stomach, constipation, sore throat and damage to vital organs such as the liver and kidneys.

Binge Eating Disorder causes a loss of control of eating. Unlike bulimia nervosa, periods of binge eating are not followed by purging, excessive exercise, or fasting. Those affected do experience guilt, shame, and distress about their binge eating, which can lead to more binge eating. As a result, people with binge eating disorder often are over-weight or obese and are at a higher risk for developing type 2 diabetes, high blood pressure, high cholesterol, stroke, certain cancers, osteoarthritis, liver and gallbladder disease, abnormal menstrual cycles and infertility.

Related disorders include dieting and restrictive eating, which are characterized by a preoccupation with the need to lose weight. Children with these issues weigh themselves frequently, engage in fad diets, and are unreasonably restrictive about food intake. This behavior pattern is unrelated to the affected child's body weight. Being on a diet is the common denominator for those suffering from disordered eating, which, taken to the extreme, can lead to serious health problems.

The restrictive eating child is often called a picky eater, cutting out certain foods or food groups (i.e. meat). Since these children have normal appetites, their eating behavior is often considered a way of exerting control over the adults in their lives, which frequently leads to emotional struggles. Because of social pressure to be thin, parents and other adults sometimes succumb tochildren's controlling eating behavior.

Orthorexia is an unhealthy fixation on eating only healthy or pure foods. Like anorexia nervosa, orthorexia is rooted in food restriction. Orthorexics focus on the quality of food, while anorexics focus on the quantity. Orthorexics typically do not fear gaining weight in the way anorexics would, but the obsessive and progressive nature of the disorder is similar. Typical behavior is avoidance of anything processed, like white flour and sugar, food considered unpure, or food that someone else has prepared. This constant preoccupation causes an extreme amount of anxiety. Individuals suffering from orthorexia may eliminate entire groups of food from their diets in the quest for a perfectly clean, healthy diet. In severe cases, orthorexia may lead to malnourishment.

Eating disorders are a pervasive problem in our communities, states, country and around the world. They cross gender, racial, and socioeconomic barriers and the problem is worsening. In the United States approximately 10 percent of girls and women (numbering up to 10 million) and 1 million boys and men are struggling with eating disorders. According to the Journal of the American Dietetic Association, 81 percent of 10 year olds are afraid of being fat, 51 percent of 9 and 10 year old girls feel better about themselves if they are on a diet, and 35 percent of normal dieters progress to unhealthy dieting. At least 50,000 individuals will die each year as a direct resultof an eating disorder.

Prevalence studies in adolescent females show rates of 0.5 to one percent for anorexia nervosa, and one to three percent for bulimia nervosa. Binge eating disorder affects far more boys than either anorexia or bulimia; more than one-third of compulsive over eaters are men. Patients rarely seek treatment, and family members will often intervene. A multidisciplinary approach to treatment is essential. Medications, especially SSRIs (Selective Serotonin Reuptake Inhibitors), which were originally developed as antidepressants have been found to be very effective in the treatment of eating disorders. They can help restore and build self-esteem, and thereby help the patient maintain a positive attitude as well as a safe and healthy body image and body weight. Because of the physical damage that eating disorders can create, nutritional counseling and monitoring is often vital to restore and maintain proper body weight. Hospitalization is often indicated in anorexia, especially if the patient is more than 20 percent below normal body weight.

Eating Disorders / Government Agencies

Restoration of fluids and chemicals in the blood (electrolytes) is critical. Outpatient management for anorxia also includes a supervised weight-gain program. The prognosis for patients with bulimia is better than that for patients with anorexia and they are more likely to seek treatment. Eating disorders are extremely complex, and patients often have conflicting psychological issues that trigger the compulsion to binge, and the morbid fear of gaining weight. Psychotherapy and cognitive behavior therapy may be required for a number of years.

Government Agencies

2548 NIH/National Institute of Mental Health Eating Disorders Program
6001 Executive Blvd, Room 6200, MSC 9663
Bethesda, MD 20892
866-615-6464
Fax: 301-443-4279
TTY: 301-443-8431
nimhinfo@nih.gov
www.nimh.nih.gov

The mission of NIMH is to transform the understanding and treatment of mental illnesses through basic and clinical research, paving the way for prevention, recovery, and cure.

Joshua A. Gordon, MD, PhD, Director
Shelli Avenevoli, PhD, Deputy Director

2549 Substance Abuse and Mental Health Services Administration
5600 Fishers Lane
Rockville, MD 20857
877-726-4727
www.samhsa.gov

SAMHSA leads public health efforts to advance the behavioral health of the nation and to improve the lives of individuals living with mental and substance use disorders, and their families.

Neeraj Gandotra, MD, Chief Medical Officer

2550 The National Women's Health Information Center
200 Independence Avenue SW
Washington, DC 20201
202-690-7650
800-994-9662
Fax: 202-205-2631
www.womenshealth.gov

The Office on Women's Health provides national leadership and coordination to improve the health of women and girls through policy, education and model programs.

Richelle West Marshall, Deputy Director of Operations

National Associations & Support Groups

2551 Academy of Nutrition and Dietetics
120 South Riverside Plaza, Suite 2190
Chicago, IL 60606
312-899-0040
foundation@eatright.org
www.eatright.org

The Academy of Nutrition and Dietetics is the worlds's largest organization of food and nutrition professionals. The academy is committed to improving the nation's health and advancing the profession of dietetics through research, education and advocacy.

2552 American Academy of Pediatrics
345 Park Blvd
Itasca, IL 60143
800-433-9016
Fax: 847-434-8000
mcc@aap.org
www.aap.org

The American Academy of Pediatrics and its member pediatricians are committed to the attainment of optimal physical, mental and social health and well-being for all infants, children, adolescents, and young adults.

Lynn Olson, PhD, VP, Research
Mark Del Monte, JD, CEO/Executive VP
Vera Tait, MD, FAAP, Chief Medical Officer

2553 American Psychiatric Association
800 Maine Avenue SW, Suite 900
Washington, DC 20024
202-559-3900
apa@psych.org
www.psychiatry.org

It is a medical specialty society representing growing membership of more than 36,000 psychiatrists.

Saul Levin, MD, CEO & Medical Director

2554 American Psychological Association
750 First St. NE
Washington, DC 20002
202-336-5500
800-374-2721
TTY: 202-336-6123
www.apa.org

The mission is to advance the creation, communication and application of psychological knowledge to benefit society and improve people's lives.

Arthur C. Evans Jr, PhD, CEO/EVP

2555 American Public Health Association
800 I Street, NW
Washington, DC 20001
202-777-2742
Fax: 202-777-2534
TTY: 202-777-2500
www.apha.org

APHA champions the health of all people and all communities. They aim to strengthen the public health profession and speak out for public health issues and policies backed by science.

Georges C. Benjamin, MD, Executive Director
Kemi Oluwafemi, MBA, CPA, Chief Financial Officer
Susan Polan, PhD, Associate Executive Director

2556 American School Counselor Association
1101 King Street, Ste 310
Alexandria, VA 22314
703-683-2722
asca@schoolcounselor.org
www.schoolcounselor.org

The mission of ASCA is to represent professional school counselors and to promote professionalism and ethical practices.

Jill Cook, Executive Director
Amanda Fitzgerald, Assistant Deputy Executive Director
Kathleen M Rakestraw, Director of Communications

2557 Association for Size Diversity and Health
www.sizediversityandhealth.org

The mission of the Association for Size Diversity and Health (ASDAH) is to promote education, research, and the provision of services which enhance health and well-being, and which are free from weight-based assumptions and weight discrimination.

2558 BeyondHunger
PO Box 151148
San Rafael, CA 94915
415-459-2270
beyondhunger.org

Beyond Hunger is a non-profit organization dedicated to helping individuals overcome the obsession with food and weight and find a natural, loving and peaceful relationship with their food, weight, and selves.

Laurelee Roark, Co-Founder

2559 Community Outreach for Prevention of Eating Disorders
PO BOX 128
Flagler Beach, FL 32136
www.cope-ecf.org

The mission is to eliminate eating disorders, promote widespread positive body image, and raise public awareness of how to influence both.

2560 Compulsive Eaters Anonymous
3371 Glendale Boulevard, Suite 104
Los Angeles, CA 90039
323-660-4333
Fax: 323-660-4334
gso@ceahow.org
www.ceahow.org

Purpose is to stop eating compulsively and carry the message to those that still suffer.

Eating Disorders / National Associations & Support Groups

2561 Council on Size and Weight Discrimination (CSWD)
PO Box 305
Mount Marion, NY 12456
845-750-7710
Fax: 845-802-0000
info@cswd.org
www.cswd.org

Works to influence public policy and opinion in an effort to eliminate oppression and discrimination based on body size, shape, or weight standards. Projects include International No Diet Coalition. Publications: Annotated Bibliography on Size Acceptance, Anti-Dieting, Eating Disorders and Related Issues, book. International No Diet Coalition Directory of Resources, books.

Miriam Berg, President
Lynn McAfee, Medical Advocacy Director

2562 Eating Disorder Anonymous EDA, Inc.
PO Box 5243
Chico, CA 95927
info@eatingdisordersanonymous.org
www.eatingdisordersanonymous.org

Eating Disorders Anonymous is a fellowship of individuals who share their experience, strength and hope that with each other, they may solve their common problems and help others to recover from their eating disorders.

2563 Eating Disorder Hope
www.eatingdisorderhope.com
800-273-8255
TTY: 800-799-4889
www.eatingdisorderhope.com

The mission is to offer hope, information and resources to individual eating disorder sufferers, their family members and treatment providers.

Jacquelyn Ekern, Founder & President
Baxter Ekern, Chief Executive Officer

2564 Eating Disorder Recovery Support
911 Lakeville Street, Suite 217
Petaluma, CA 94952
info@edrecoverysupport.org
edrecoverysupport.org

A nonprofit committed promoting recovery and wellness for those impacted by eating disorders by providing support, information, and education to individuals, families, professionals and the community at large regarding eating disorders and recovery resources.

Corinne Dobbas, President
Emily Behrs, Vice President
Theresa Carpinito Kira, Treasurer

2565 Eating Disorders Coalition
PO Box 96503-98807
Washington, DC 20090
202-543-9570
eatingdisorderscoalition.org

The Eating Disorders Coalition is the advocacy organization for eating disorders. We advance the recognition of eating disorders as a public health priority at the federal and state level.

2566 Eating Disorders Information Network
4780 Ashford Dunwoody Road, Suite 375
Atlanta, GA 30338
inquiries@myedin.org
www.myedin.org

The mission is to make it easier for people with eating disorders to find help. EDIN's mission was also to reduce the stigma of eating disorders and offer hope to sufferers through stories of recovery in a monthly newsletter.

2567 Eating Disorders Research Society
2111 Chestnut Avenue, Suite 145
Glenview, IL 60025
847-666-5920
Fax: 312-896-5614
info@edresearchsociety.org
www.edresearchsociety.org

The purpose of the organization is to hold an annual scientific meeting during which the most recent research in the field can be presented and discussed.

2568 Food Addicts Anonymous
World Service Office
529 N W Prima Vista Blvd., Suite 301 A
Port St. Lucie, FL 34983
772-878-9657
faawso@faacanhelp.org
faacanhelp.org

A 12-step fellowship of men and women who are willing to recover from the disease of food adiction. Primary purpose is to maintain abstinence from sugar, flour, and wheat. Information and referral, pen pals, online contacts, conferences. Assistance in starting groups.

2569 International Association of Eating Disorders Professionals
PO Box 1295
Pekin, IL 61555
800-800-8126
iaedpmembers@earthlink.net
www.iaedp.com

The International Association of Eating Disorders Professionals provides first-quality education and high-level training standards to an international multidisciplinary group of various healthcare treatment providers and helping professions, who treat the full spectrum of eating disorder problems.

Bonnie Harken, Executive Director
Blanche Williams, Director, International Affairs
Marie Grover, Director, Events Manager

2570 Klaman Eating Disorders Center at McLean Hospital
McClean Hospital
115 Mill Street
Belmont, MA 02478
877-781-5513
mcleanklarman@partners.org
www.mcleanhospital.org/treatment/klarman

Founded with the generous support of the Klarman Family Foundation, the Klarman Eating Disorders Center at Harvard-affiliated McLean Hospital provides state-of-the-art treatment for eating disorders in girls and young women ages 13 to 23. Housed in its own newly renovated building on the grounds of McLean, the Center provides a unique therapeutic environment that is conducive to recovery.

Esther Dechant, MD, Medical Director
David J. Alperovitz, PsyD, Program Director

2571 McCallum Place
231 W. Lockwood Avenue, Suite 202
St. Louis, MO 63119
888-350-1884
www.mccallumplace.com

McCallum Place provides comprehensive medical and psychiatric care, specialized psychotherapies and nutritional support for patients with eating disorders. Our state-of-the-art treatment and programs, which integrate the latest findings from eating disorders research with experienced clinical practice, are designed to create an environment of structure and support.

Kimberli McCallum, MD, Founder
Monica Bishop, MD, Medical Director
John Rapp, LCSW, Clinical Director

2572 Mental Fitness, Inc.
mentalfitness5.godaddysites.com
rfarrell@sharpenminds.com
mentalfitness5.godaddysites.com

The mission of Mental Fitness Inc. is to build mental fitness in all youth through arts-based awareness and prevention programs.

Robyn Hussa Farrell, Founder & CEO

2573 National Alliance for Eating Disorders
4400 North Congress Avenue, Suite 100
West Palm Beach, FL 33407
866-662-1235
info@allianceforeatingdisorders.com
www.allianceforeatingdisorders.com

The Alliance is dedicated to providing programs and activities aimed at outreach and education related to health promotion, including all eating disorders, obesity, positive body image, and self-esteem.

Johanna Kandel, Founder & CEO

Eating Disorders / State Agencies & Support Groups

2574 **National Association of Addiction Treatmemt Providers**
PO Box 271686
Lousville, MO 80027
888-574-1008
info@naatp.org
www.naatp.org

The mission is to provide leadership, advocacy, training and other member support services to assure the continued availability and highest quality of addiction treatment.

Marvin Ventrell, MD, Chief Executive Officer
Katie Strand, MS, CMP, Chief Operating Officer
Annie Peters, PhD, LP, Director, Research & Education

2575 **National Association of Anorexia Nervosa and Associated Disorders (ANAD)**
PO Box 409047
Chicago, IL 60640
888-375-7767
hello@anad.org
www.anad.org

Sponsors national and local programs to prevent eating disorders and assist people with eating disorders and their families. Provides a national clearinghouse of information and is a grassroots association for laypeople and professionals. It operates a national network of free support groups for people with eating disorders and their families, and provides prevention information and education to students and lecturers.

2576 **National Association to Advance Fat Acceptance (NAAFA)**
P.O. Box 4662
Foster City, CA 94404
916-558-6880
800-442-1214
Fax: 415-863-8596
naafa@naafa.org
naafa.org

Nonprofit organization dedicated to improving the quality of life for fat people. Opposes discrimination against fat people including discrimination in advertising, employment, fashion, medicine, insurance, social acceptance, the media, schooling and public accommodations. Monitors legislative activity and litigation affecting fat people. Publications: NAAFA Newsletter, bimonthly. Annual conference and symposium, always mid-August.

Darliene Howell, Board Chair
Peggy Howell, Vice Chair & Public Relations Dir.
Tigress Osborn, Director of Community Outreach

2577 **National Eating Disorders Association (NED A)**
333 Mamaroneck Avenue, Suite 214
White Plains, NY 10605
212-575-6200
info@NationalEatingDisorders.org
www.nationaleatingdisorders.org

The National Eating Disorders Association (NEDA) is the largest not-for-profit organization in the United States working to prevent eating disorders and provide treatment referrals to those suffering from anorexia, bulimia and binge eating disorder and those concerned with body image and weight issues.

Elizabeth Thompson, Chief Executive Officer
Sarah Chase, VP, Communications & Marketing
Lauren Smolar, VP, Mission & Education

2578 **Overeaters Anonymous, World Service Office**
PO Box 44727
Rio Rancho, NM 87174
505-891-2664
www.oa.org

Overeaters Anonymous is a 12-step program dealing with food and compulsive overeating. There are no fees or dues. The only requirement for membership is the desire to stop eating compulsively. Call the World Service Office for a location near you.

2579 **TOPS Club**
4575 South 5th Street
Milwaukee, WI 53207
414-482-4620
www.tops.org

Weight control self-help association using group dynamics, competition and recognition to help members lose weight. TOPS is medically oriented requiring physician-approved individual diet programs and physician-set weight goals. Publications: TOPS News, monthly, a magazine that contains member news, success stories, inspirational materials and features on diet-related subjects, chapter news, medical questions and answers. Annual International Recognition Days.

2580 **The Body Positive**
PO Box 7801
Berkeley, CA 94707
info@thebodypositive.org
www.thebodypositive.org

The Body Positive is a nonprofit organization that teaches people to listen to their bodies, learn and thrive. The ultimate goal is to end the harmful consequences of negative body image: eating disorders, depression, anxiety, cutting, suicide, substance abuse, and relationship violence. Offers online training courses.

Connie Sobczak, Founder & Executive Director
Elizabeth Scott, Co-Founder & Training Director

State Agencies & Support Groups

Connecticut

2581 **Renfrew Center of Connecticut**
475 Spring Lane
Philadelphia,, PA 19128
203-834-1635
877-367-3383
Fax: 215-482-2695
info@renfrewcenter.com
www.renfrewcenter.com

The Renfrew Center of Connecticut provides an Eating Disorders Group led by experienced therapists the sessions of which provide a safe, sympathetic atmosphere where group members explore what triggers their eating disorders as well as issues concerning body image, relationships, school, work and home. A therapeutic approach that allows women to recognize and confront negative thoughts and feelings about their bodies and to replace them with realistic and healthy views about themselves is used.

Douglas W Bunnell, Executive Director
Gayle Brooks, Ph.D, Clinical Director

Florida

2582 **Coconut Creek Eating Disorders Support Group**
Renfrew Center
7700 Renfrew Lane
Coconut Creek, FL 33073
954-698-9222
800-736-3739
Fax: 954-698-9007
info@renfrewcenter.org
www.renfrewcenter.com/locations/coconut-creek.asp

The Coconut Creek Eating Disorders Support Group at the Renfrew Center is led by experienced therapists where the sessions provide a safe, sympathetic atmosphere in which group members explore what triggers their eating disorders as well as issues concerning body image, relationships, school, work and home.

Jane Fleming, Executive Director
Gayle Brooks, Ph.D, Clinical Director

2583 **Renfrew Center of Miami**
151 Majorca Avenue
Coral Gables, FL 33134
800-736-3739
Fax: 605-445-2779
info@renfrewcenter.org
www.renfrewcenter.com/locations/coral-gables.asp

The Renfrew Center of Miami provides an Eating Disorders Group led by experienced therapists the sessions of which provide a safe, sympathetic atmosphere where group members explore what triggers their eating disorders as well as issues concerning body image, relationships, school, work and home.

Jane Fleming, Executive Director
Gayle Brooks, Ph.D, Clinical Director

Eating Disorders / State Agencies & Support Groups

Illinois

2584 Academy for Eating Disorders (AED)
Ste 100
Deerfield, IL 60015
847-498-4274
Fax: 847-480-9282
info@aedweb.org
www.aedweb.org/index.cfm

The Academy for Eating Disorders is an international transdisciplinary professional organization that promotes excellence in research, treatment and prevention of eating disorders. The AED provides education, training and a forum for collaboration and professional dialogue.

Sally Finney, Executive Director
Eric Van Furth, Ph.D, President/Officers Board
Judith Banker, Treasurer

Maryland

2585 Center for Eating Disorders
Saint Josephs Medical Center
Physicians Pavilion North, Ste 300
Baltimore, MD 21204
410-938-5252
Fax: 410-938-5250
EatingDisorderInfo@sheppardpratt.org
www.eatingdisorder.org

At the Center for Eating Disorders, the staff focuses on each patient's personal needs and works with him or her to gain new confidence and coping skills. The center offers a full spectrum of services in a supportive environment.

Harry A Brandt, MD, Executive Director
Steven Crawford, MD, Associate Director
David Roth, Ph.D, Program Coordinator

Massachusetts

2586 Massachusetts Eating Disorder Association (MEDA)
92 Pearl Street
Newton, MA 02458
617-558-1881
Fax: 617-558-1771
www.medainc.org

MEDA is a non-profit organization dedicated to the prevention and treatment of eating disorders and disordered eating. MEDA's mission is to prevent the continuing spread of eating disorders through educational awareness and early detection. MEDA serves as a support network and resource for clients, loved ones, clinicians, educators and the general public.

100+ Members

Beth Mayer, Executive Director
Aiden Winslow, Assistant Director
Kristin Fabbri, Education/Outreach Director

New Jersey

2587 Eating Disorders Association of New Jersey
10 Sation Place, Suite 15
Metuchen, NJ 08840
732-549-6886
800-522-2230
Fax: 609-688-1544

Eating Disorders Association of New Jersey is dedicated to the study, prevention and treatment of eating disorders: anorexia nervosa, bulimia nervosa and binge eating disorder. We are a non-profit organization that provides education and support services in New Jersey to individuals affected by eating disorders, including sufferers, family members, friends, educators, and therapists.

Leigh Garfield, LCSW, President
Maureen Kritzer Lange, LCSW, Support Group Coordinator

2588 Renfrew Center of Northern New Jersey
174 Union Street
Ridgewood, NJ 07450
201-652-5114
Fax: 201-652-6253
info@renfrewcenter.org
www.renfrewcenter.com

A weekly group that helps women overcome compulsive overeating and make positive lifestyle changes. The group focuses on the needs of the participants and may include looking deeper at culture, family and self within a sympathetic and safe atmosphere.

Jane Fleming, Executive Director
Gayle Brooks, Ph.D, Clinical Director

New York

2589 Metro Intergroup of Overeaters Anonymous
PO Box 1235
New York, NY 10159
212-946-4599
NYOAMetroOffiice@yahoo.com
www.oanyc.org/oanyc/

Overeaters Anonymous offers a program of recovery from compulsive overeating using the Twelve Steps and Twelve Traditions of OA. Worldwide meetings and other tools provide a fellowship of experience, strength and hope where members respect one another's anonymity. OA charges no dues or fees; it is self-supporting through member contributions.

Naomi Lippel, Managing Director
Sarah Armstrong, Associate Director
Joi Young, Web Coordinator

2590 National Eating Disorders Association-Long Island (NEDA-LI)
50 Charles Lindbergh Blvd
Uniondale, NY 11553
516-237-6200

NEDA LI is a non-profit organization devoted to prevention, education and support: prevention of eating disorders, education about eating disorders and support to sufferers of eating disorders, their families and their friends. The organization is comprised of professionals who specialize in eating disorders including psychiatrists, psychologists, social workers, counselors and nutritionists.

Sondra Kronberg, MS/RD/CDN, Executive Director
Vivian Delman, MS/RD/CDN, Board-Directors President
Irene Schlagman, CEDA, Board-Directors Secretary

2591 Overeaters Anonymous Support Group
Holliswood Hospital
87-37 Palermo Street
Holliswood, NY 11423
718-776-8181
800-486-3005
Fax: 718-716-8572
HolliswoodInfo@libertymgt.com
www.holliswoodhospital.com/

The Holliswood Hospital, a 110-bed private psychiatric hospital located in a quiet residential Queens community, is a leader in providing quality, acute inpatient mental health care for adult, adolescent, geriatric and dually diagnosed patients. Services include an Overeaters Anonymous Support Group.

Alan Eskenazi, CEO
Dr. Douglas ÿ Munsey, Medical Director
Dr. John Udarbe, Adult Unit Chief

2592 Renfrew Center of New York City
11 East 36th Street
New York, NY 10016
212-685-6856
800-736-3739
Fax: 212-686-1865
info@renfrewcenter.org
www.renfrewcenter.com

Women struggling to overcome anorexia, bulimia or other disordered eating patterns involving binge eating or restricting can benefit from these weekly groups. Led by experienced therapists, the sessions provide a safe, sympathetic atmosphere where group members explore what triggers their eating disorders as well as issues concerning body image, relationships, school, work and home.

Gail Purvis, Manager
Gayle Brooks, Clinical Director

Eating Disorders / Libraries & Resource Centers

2593 Westchester Center for Eating Disorders
14 Rolling Way
New Rochelle, NY 10804
914-633-7654
Fax: 914-633-7349

Program and support group for individuals struggling with eating disorders.

Ann L Rothstein, Manager

Oregon

2594 Rainrock Treatment Center
1863 Pioneer Parkway, Suite 304 (Mailing Only)
Springfield, OR 97477
541-896-9300
Fax: 541-896-9320
mntc@montenido.com
www.montenido.com/rainrock/

Rainrock is a private residential treatment center designed and created by Annie Laughlin and Carolyn Costin to heal women suffering from anorexia, bulimia, and exercise addiction. RainRock, an affiliate of the Monte Nido Treatment Center in Malibu, California, opened in Summer 2006. It is located on four beautifully maintained acres along the McKenzie River just outside Eugene, Oregon with an ideal therapeutic environment for self-reflection, personal growth, and healing.

Carolyn Costin, LMFT, Founder/Executive Director
Annie Lauglin, Founder/Program Coordinator
Anthony Laughlin, Founder/Program Administrator

Pennsylvania

2595 Pennsylvania Chapter of the American Anorexia Bulimia Association
4200 Monument Avenue, PO Box 1287
Philadelphia, PA 19105
215-221-1864
mail.aabaphila@yahoo.com
www.aabaphila.org/

The American Anorexia / Bulimia Association of Philadelphia (American Anorexia and Bulimia (AABAP), is non-profit, providing services and programs for anyone interested in or affected by, Anorexia, Bulimia and/or related disorders. Its purpose is to aid in the education and prevention of these life threatening disorders. AABAP is a member organization of the Eating Disorders Coalition.

Samuel A Menaged, Board-Directors President EDC

2596 Pennsylvania Educational Network for Eating Disorders (PENED)
801 McKnight Rd., RM 205
Pittsburgh, PA 15237
412-215-7967
Fax: 412-487-6850
pened1@aol.com
www.pened.org/

PENED is a non-profit organization providing educational, supportive and referral services to the general and professional public on the causes, treatment, and prevention of eating disorders and related issues.

Anita Sinicrope-Maier, MSW, Executive Director

2597 Renfrew Center of Bryn Mawr
735 Old Lancaster Road
Bryn Mawr, PA 19010
800-736-3739
Fax: 610-527-9361
info@renfrewcenter.org
www.renfrewcenter.com/locations/bryn-mawr.asp

Support group for women to overcome compulsive overeating and make positive lifestyle changes. Focuses on the needs of the participants and may include looking deeper at culture, family and self within a sympathetic and safe atmosphere. Led by experienced therapists, sessions provide safe, sympathetic atmosphere where women in midlife faced with new stresses such as divorce, empty-nest syndrome,'chronic illness or career changes come together to explore what triggers their eating disorders.

Jane Fleming, Executive Director
Gayle Brooks, Clinical Director

2598 Renfrew Center of Philadelphia
475 Spring Lane
Philadelphia, PA 19128
215-482-5353
800-736-3739
Fax: 215-482-7390
www.renfrewcenter.com/locations/location.asp?id=2

Women struggling to overcome anorexia, bulimia or other disordered eating patterns involving binge eating or restricting can benefit from this weekly group. Led by experienced therapists, the sessions provide a safe, sympathetic atmosphere where group members explore what triggers their eating disorders as well as issues concerning body image, relationships, school, work and home.

Sam Menaged, President
Gayle Brooks, Clinical Director

2599 University of Pennsylvania Weight and Education Program
3535 Market Street, Suite 3108
Philadelphia, PA 19104
215-898-7314
Fax: 215-898-2878
www.med.upenn.edu/weight/

The Center for Weight and Eating Disorders was founded by Albert J. Stunkard, M.D., over 45 years ago to better understand the causes of weight and weight-related disorders. The Center continues to conduct a wide variety of studies on the causes and treatment of weight-related disorders. More recently, the Center for Weight and Eating Disorders has begun to offer professional services to the general public rather than only to participants in research studies.

Dr. Albert Stunkard, Founder
Thomas A Wadden, Ph.D, Director

Libraries & Resource Centers

2600 Association of Gastrointestinal Motility Disorders
140 Pleasant Street
Lexington, MA 02421
781-275-1300
info@agmdhope.org
agmdhope.org

AGMD is a non-profit organizations in existence with a focus on digestive motility diseases and disorders.

2601 Families Empowered and Supporting Treatmen t of Eating Disorders
PO Box 331
Warrenton, VA 20188
540-227-8518
info@feast-ed.org
www.feast-ed.org

F.E.A.S.T. is an international organization of and for parents and caregivers to help loved ones recover from eating disorders by providing information and mutual support, promoting evidence-based treatment, and advocating for research and education to reduce the suffering associated with eating disorders.

2602 National Eating Disorder Association of Lo ng Island (NEDA-LI)
50 Charles Lindbergh Blvd, Suite 400
Uniondale, NY 11553
516-222-4990
Fax: 516-414-6322
www.edap.org/p.asp?WebPage_ID=717

The National Eating Disorders Association (NEDA) was formed in 2001, when Eating Disorders Awareness & Prevention (EDAP) joined forces with the American Anorexia Bulimia Association (AABA). NEDA LI is a non-profit organization devoted to prevention, education and support: prevention of eating disorders, education about eating disorders and support to sufferers of eating disorders, their families and their friends.

John Marrah, Ceo
Susan Morin, NPP, Board-Directors Vice President
Sondra Kronberg, MS/RD/CDN, Executive Director

Eating Disorders / Audio Video

Research Centers

2603 Center for the Research and Treatment of Anorexia Nervosa
UCLA Neuropsychiatric Institute
760 Westwood Plaza
Los Angeles, CA 90024
310-825-9822
800-825-1192
research.ucla@yahoo.com
www.wpic.pitt.edu/research/angenetics/contact.html

Appointed to the faculty of the department of psychiatry at the UCLA School of Medicine in 1975, Michael Strober, Ph.D., now holds the rank of full professor, and is director of the eating disorders program and the adolescent mood disorders program at the UCLA Neuropsychiatric Institute and Hospital. Dr. Strober's primary research activities center on the long-term course and outcome, psychopathology and genetics of eating disorders.

Michael Strober, Ph.D, Program Director

2604 Center for the Study of Anorexia and Bulimia
1841 Broadway @ 60th Street, 4th Floor
New York, NY 10023
212-333-3444
Fax: 212-333-5444
Info@csabnyc.org
www.csabnyc.org/

The Center for the Study of Anorexia and Bulimia was established as a division of the Institute for Contemporary Psychotherapy in 1979 and is the oldest non-profit eating disorders clinic in New York City. Using an eclectic approach, the professional staff and affiliates are on the cutting edge of treatment in their field. The treatment staff includes social workers, psychologists, registered nurses and nutritionists, all with special training in the treatment of eating disorders.

Jill M Pollack, LCSW/BCD, Executive Director

2605 Eating Disorders Research and Treatment Program
Michael Reese Hospital and Medical Center
4510 Executive Drive, Suite 315
San Diego,, CA 92121
858-534-8019
Fax: 858-534-6727
edresearch@ucsd.edu
www.eatingdisorders.ucsd.edu/

Michael Reese Hospital maintains a full spectrum psychiatric care for children, adolescents and adults including inpatient hospitalization for acute psychiatric cases as well as an intensive outpatient program for individuals in need of ongoing support, including that of eating disorders.

Regina Casper, Director
Enrique Beckman, MD, Chairman/CEO

2606 New York Obesity Research Center
Saint Luke's-Roosevelt Hospital
1090 Amsterdam Avenue, 14th Floor
New York, NY 10025
212-523-3622
Fax: 212-523-3571
katmarquez@chpnet.org
www.nyorc.org/

The mission of the New York Obesity Research Center is to help reduce the incidence of obesity and related diseases through leadership in basic research, clinical research, epidemiology and public health, patient care, and public education.

Dr. Xavier Pi-Sunyer, MD/MPH, Director
Richard Weil, M.Ed/CDE, Exercise Physiologist
Betty Kovac, MS/RD, Dietitian

Conferences

2607 American School Counselor Association Annual Conference
1101 King Street, Suite 310
Alexandria, VA 22314
703-683-2722
800-306-4722
Fax: 703-997-7572
asca@schoolcounselor.org
www.schoolcounselor.org

The mission of ASCA is to represent professional school counselors and to promote professionalism and ethical practices.

3,000 Attendees
Richard Wong, Executive Director
Jennifer Walsh, Director, Education & Training
Kathleen M Rakestraw, Director of Communications

2608 CEA-HOW Annual Global Convention
Compulsive Eaters Anonymous
3371 Glendale Boulevard,Suite 104
Los Angeles, CA 90039
323-660-4333
Fax: 323-660-4334
gso@ceahow.org
www.ceahow.org

July

2609 FAA World Convention
Food Addicts Anonymous
529 N W Prima Vista Blvd. Suite 301 A
Port St. Lucie, FL 34983
561-967-3871
Fax: 561-967-9815
faawso@bellsouth.net
www.foodaddictsanonymous.org

September
Linda Closy, Manager

2610 IAEDP Symposium
Internat. Assn. of Eating Disorder Professionals
PO Box 1295
Pekin, IL 61555
800-800-8126
symposium@iaedp.com
www.iaedp.com

Draws attendees from all corners of the globe. Geared to the needs and problems of those who work with patients in a therapeutic environment.

March
Bonnie Harken, Executive Director
Marie Grover, Director, Events Manager

2611 NAAFA Annual Convention
National Association to Advance Fat Acceptance
PO Box 4662
Foster City, CA 94404
916-558-6880
800-442-1214
Fax: 415-863-8596
www.naafa.org

August
Darliene Howell, Board Chair
Peggy Howell, Vice Chair & Public Relations Dir.
Tigress Osborn, Director of Community Outreach

2612 NEDA Annual Conference
National Eating Disorders Association (NEDA)
333 Mamaroneck Avenue, Suite 214
White Plains, NY 10605
212-575-6200
info@NationalEatingDisorders.org
www.nationaleatingdisorders.org

Brings together people in recovery, their families and professionals.

October
Elizabeth Thompson, Chief Executive Officer
Sarah Chase, VP, Communications & Marketing
Lauren Smolar, VP, Mission & Education

Audio Video

2613 Bulimia
Baxley Media Group
510 West Main Street
Urbana, IL 61801
217-384-4838
Fax: 217-384-8280
baxley@baxleymedia.com
www.baxleymedia.com/

Award-winning video presentation explores the causes and effects of bulimia. Addresses the fact that many high school and college women view this type of behavior as routine aspect of their everyday lives.

Eating Disorders / Web Sites

Videotape
Carolyn Baxley, President

2614 Eating Disorder Video
Library Video
PO Box 580
Wynnewood, PA 19096
610-645-4000
800-843-3620
Fax: 610-645-4040
comments@libraryvideo.com
www.libraryvideo.com

Features compelling interviews with several young people who have suffered from anorexia nervosa, bulimia and compulsive eating. Discusses the treatments, causes, and techniques for prevention with field experts.

2615 Inside Out: Stories of Bulimia
Fanlight Productions
32 Court Street, 21st Floor
Brooklyn, NY 11201
718-488-8900
800-876-1710
Fax: 718-488-8642
info@fanlight.com, orders@fanlight.com
www.fanlight.com

Bulimia can affect women and men from all walks of life, and it kills nearly 20 percent of its victims every year. This moving documentary profilesindividuals and families affected by this eating disorder. ISBN: DVD: 1-57295-856-1; VHS: 1-57295-366-7

56 minutes DVD or VHS

Ben Achtenberg, President
Sandy St. Louis, Marketing Director
Nicole Johnson, Publicity Coordinator

2616 It Only Takes One Bite: Food Allergy and Anaphylaxis
Food Allergy Network
7925 Jones Branch Dr., Suite 1100
McLean, VA 22102
703-691-3179
Fax: 703-691-2713
www.foodallergy.org

Nonprofit organization dedicated to bringing about a clearer understanding of the issues surrounding food allergies and providing helpful resources. Explains food induced anaphylaxis and how to live with it. An excellent resource for training parents, teachers, caregivers and patients.

18 mins.

Janet Atwater, Chair
Robert Nichols, Vice Chair
James R. Baker, Jr., MD, CEO & Chief Medical Officer

Web Sites

2617 Eating Disorders Online.com: 15 Styles of Distorted Thinking
www.eatingdisordersonline.com/specific/disthink.php

www.eatingdisordersonline.com/specific/disthink.php

Reference useful for cognitive therapy.

2618 Food Allergy Research & Education
7901 Jones Branch Dr., Suite 240
McLean, VA 22102
703-691-3179
Fax: 703-691-2713
www.foodallergy.org

FARE works on behalf of the 15 million Americans with food allergies, including all those at risk for life-threatening anaphylaxis.

Sung Poblete, PhD, NR, President

2619 Gurze Bookstore
www.bulimia.com
888-920-1501
www.bulimia.com

Specializes in information about eating disorders including anorexia nervosa, bulimia nervosa, and binge eating, plus related topics such as body image and obesity. We offer books at discounted prices, many free articles about eating disorders, newsletters, links to treatment facilities, organizations, other websites and much more.

2620 Health Answers Education Sudler-WPP Health Practice
700 Dresher Road
Horsham, PA 19044
215-442-9010
www.healthanswers.com

HealthAnswers offers a breadth of services in medical education, sales force training, patient support, solutions, professional promotion and consumer solutions.

Mike Hudnall, CEO

2621 Mental Help Net- Eating Disorders
P.O. Box 20709
Columbus, OH 43220
614-448-4055
800-232-TALK
info@centersite.net, editor@centersite.n
www.mentalhelp.net/guide/eating.htm

We wish to provide the following: to discuss, develop and debate in an open forum the future of the mental health field in America and throughout the world. To help coordinate various components of the mental health field, so as to bring about greater communication between them and to educate the public about mental health issues.

2622 Mirror, Mirror
www.mirror-mirror.org/eatdis.htm

www.mirror-mirror.org/eatdis.htm

Helps with eating disorders, like how to get help, myths and realities, other websites, and about recovery.

Scott Mogul, Director
Dr. Lauren Muhlheim, Clinical Director
Dr. Elisha Carcieri, Editor

2623 National Association for Anorexia Nervosa and Associated Disorders (ANAD)
750 E Diehl Road #127
Naperville, IL 60563
630-577-1330
anadhelp@anad.org
www.anad.org

We provide hotline counseling, a national network of free support groups, referrals to healh care professionals, and education and prevention programs to promote self-acceptance and health lifesyles. All of our services are free of charge. ANAD also lobbies for state and national health insurance parity, undertakes and encourages advocacy campaigns to protect potential victims of eating disorders. ANAD stands with individuals and families and helps them win.

Patricia Santucci, MD, President
Kimberly Dennis, MD, Member, Scientific & Medical Board
Nomi Fredricks, MD, Member, Scientific & Medical Board

2624 Something Fishy
www.something-fishy.org

www.something-fishy.org

Dedicated to raising awareness, emphasizing always that Eating Disorders are NOT about food and weight, they are just the symptoms of something deeper going on, inside. We are determined to remind each and every sufferer that they are not alone, and that complete recovery is possible.

Book Publishers

2625 Anorexia Nervosa & Recovery: A Hunger for Meaning
The Haworth Press
10 Alice Street
Binghamton, NY 13904
607-771-0012
800-895-0582
getinfo@haworthpress.com
www.haworthpress.com/

Eating Disorders / Book Publishers

Anorexia Nervosa and Recovery lets the reader hear the personal struggles of women who have fought this powerful disease. They describe how anorexia controlled their lives and how, once they overcame their obsessions with food, weight, and thinness, they were able to lead fulfilling lives.

1993 142 pages Paperback
ISBN: 0-918393-95-7

William Cohen, President/Publisher
Al Horowitz, Chief Financial Officer
Sandra Jones Sickels, VP Marketing

2626 Body Betrayed
Gurze Books
5145 B Avenida Encinas, PO Box 2238
Carlsbad, CA 92008
760-434-7533
800-756-7533
Fax: 760-434-5476
leigh@gurze.net
www.gurze.com

Covers the most important aspects of diagnosis and treatment for eating disorders. Particularly appropriate for parents and loved ones who want a deeper, more thorough understanding of eating disorders.

447 pages Paperback

Kathryn J Zerbe, Author
Leigh Cohn, Publisher
Lindsey Hall Cohn, Editor in Chief

2627 Bulimia Nervosa & Binge Eating: A Guide to Recovery
New York University Press
838 Broadway, Third Floor
New York, NY 10003
212-998-2575
800-996-6987
Fax: 212-995-3833
www.nyupress.nyu.edu

Book offers guidance and advice for the understanding of the eating disorder bulimia and inspiring hope for change and regaining control of one's life.

1995 170 pages
ISBN: 0-814715-23-0

Steve Maikowski, Director
Ilene Kalish, Executive Editor
Eric Zinner, Editor-in-Chief

2628 Bulimia: A Guide to Recovery
Gurze Books
5145 B Avenida Encinas, PO Box 2238
Carlsbad, CA 92008
760-434-7533
800-756-7533
Fax: 760-434-5476
leigh@gurze.net
www.gurze.com

This intimate guidebook offers a complete understanding of bulimia and a plan for recovery. Contains updated information from previous editions, and has added material on men and bulimia, sexual trauma, body image, relationships and much more.

285 pages Paperback

Lindsey Hall, Author
Leigh Cohn, Author

2629 Conversation with Anorexics: A Compassionate & Hopeful Journey
Rowman & Littlefield Publisher
4501 Forbes Blvd, Suite 200
Lanham, MD 20706
301-459-3366
Fax: 301-429-5748
custserv@rowman.com
www.rowmanlittlefield.com/aronsonp/

Book is a collection of case studies on anorexia more aptly geared toward the professional as it does not provide guidance but more of an overview on the treatment of the eating disorder.

1994 238 pages Paperback
ISBN: 1-568212-61-5

Jonathan Sisk, Publisher
Christopher Anzalone, Washington Editor
Jack Meinhardt, Acquisitions Editor

2630 Coping with Eating Disorders
Rosen Publishing Group
29 East 21st Street
New York, NY 10010
212-777-3017
800-237-9932
Fax: 888-436-4643
rosenpub@tribeca.ios.com
www.rosenpublishing.com/

This book offers practical suggestions on coping with eating disorders, explaining how to set positive goals, and briefly discusses where to go for additional help.

ISBN: 0-823929-74-4

Miriam Gilbert, Sales and Marketing Director

2631 Cult of Thinness
Oxford University Press
198 Madison Avenue
New York, NY 10016
212-726-6000
800-445-9714
Fax: 919-677-1303
custserv.us@oup.com
www.oup.com/usa

Examining the testimonies of young women concerning the practice of body rituals, the author Hesse-Biber observes the extent to which these women sacrifice their bodies and minds to the pursuit of the ultra-slender ideal. Hesse-Biber provides new frameworks for envisioning femininity and personal power, overcoming body insecurity, strengthening the inner self, and changing the cultural environment itself.

1996 256 pages
ISBN: 0-195178-78-5

Joan Bossert, Psych/Behavioral Sciences Editor
Catharine Carlin, Health Psychology Editor

2632 Deadly Diet: Recovering From Anorexia and Bulimia
New Harbinger Publications
5674 Shattuck Avenue
Oakland, CA 94609
510-652-0215
800-748-6273
Fax: 800-652-1613
customerservice@newharbinger.com
www.newharbinger.com

This book provides the reader with a great discussion of the use of cognitive-behavioral therapy in the treatment of eating disorders. The author also provides the reader with a step-by-step guide to implementing this approach in his or her own life during recovery from an eating disorder.

1993 248 pages Paperback
ISBN: 1-879237-42-3

Matthew McKay, Ph.D, Publisher
Earlita Chenault, Publicist

2633 Do I Look Fat in This?: Life Doesn't Begin Five Pounds From Now
Simon & Schuster Free Press
866 3rd Avenue
New York, NY 10022
877-989-0009
Fax: 800-943-9831
www.simonsays.com

For any woman who has bonded with a stranger by complaining about how fat she feels, here is a thoughtful and inspiring guide to breaking the cycle of body criticism and creating a powerful and healthy self-image.

2006 200 pages
ISBN: 1-416913-57-2

Jack Romanos, President/CEO
David England, SVP/Chief Financial Officer
Anne Lloyd Davies, SVP/Chief Information Officer

2634 Eating Disorder Sourcebook
Gurze Books
5145 B Avenida Encinas, PO Box 2238
Carlsbad, CA 92008
760-434-7533
800-756-7533
Fax: 760-434-5476
leigh@gurze.net
www.gurze.com

Eating Disorders / Book Publishers

This third edition is a welcomed revision and update of this popular reference guide for both the lay public and professionals.

328 pages Paperback

Carolyn Costin, Author

2635 Eating Disorders
Thomson Gale
PO Box 95501
Chicago, IL 60694
800-877-4253
Fax: 800-414-5043
gale.galeord@cengage.com
www.gale.com/lucent/index.htm

This book examines how eating disorders can be identified, who is affected by them, and how they can be treated.

1991
ISBN: 1-560061-29-4

Andrew Becker, Director
John Barnes, EVP Strategic Business Development

2636 Eating Disorders & Obesity, 2nd Ed.
Guilford Press
72 Spring Street
New York, NY 10012
212-431-9800
800-365-7006
Fax: 212-966-6708
info@guilford.com
www.guilford.com

Presents and integrates virtually all that is currently known about eating disorders and obesity in one authorative, accessible, and eminently practical volume. A comprehensive handbook for medical and social service professionals. Hard- or paperback.

2005 633 pages Paperback
ISBN: 1-593852-36-8

Robert Matloff, President
Seymoure Weingarten, Editor-in-Chief
Marian Robinson, Marketing Director

2637 Eating Disorders Resource Catalogue
Gurze Books
5145 B Avenida Encinas, PO Box 2238
Carlsbad, CA 92008
760-434-7533
800-756-7533
Fax: 760-434-5476
leigh@gurze.net
www.gurze.com/

This catalogue of resources contains over 140 books, videos, and audiotapes, lists of national organizations and treatment facilities, and basic facts about eating disorders. It is widely distributed by individuals who are suffering, their loved-ones, the health care professionals who treat them, and educators who are working towards prevention.

24 pages Annually

Lindsey Hall, Editor in Chief
Leigh Cohn, Publisher

2638 Eating Disorders: When Food Turns Against You
Franklin Watts c/o Grolier
90 Old Sherman Turnpike
Danbury, CT 06816
203-797-3500
Fax: 203-797-3197
www.grolier.com

Anorexia nervosa and bulimia are specifically examined, including a listing of the danger signals of each. A final chapter suggests places to secure help.

1993 96 pages
ISBN: 0-531111-75-0

Richard Robinson, President/Chairman/CEO
Mary Winston, EVP/Chief Financial Officer
Jeffrey Mathews, VP/Investor Relations

2639 Encyclopedia of Obesity and Eating Disorders
Facts on File
132 West 31st Street, 17th Floor
New York, NY 10001
212-967-8800
800-322-8755
Fax: 800-678-3633
custserv@factsonfile.com
www.factsonfile.com/

This revised and expanded edition includes more than 450 entries, more than 140 of them new. Complete with a history of obesity and eating disorders; chronology of key events, research, and breakthroughs; tables listing key facts and statistics; and a directory of resources and Web sites, this single-volume reference is the first stop in any serious research of these troubling health afflictions.

2006 384 pages Hardcover
ISBN: 0-816061-97-1

Laurie Katz, Publicity Director
Coreena Schultz, Library Sales Director
T J Mancini, Production Director

2640 Endorphins: Eating Disorders & Other Addictive Behavior
WW Norton & Company
500 5th Avenue
New York, NY 10110
212-354-5500
Fax: 212-869-0856
www.wwnorton.com

Dr. Huebner discusses anorexia nervosa and bulimia as addictions to endorphins, and presents a treatment model involving education about the addictive process, cognitive/behavioral strategies, and psychotherapy. He then reveals the role of endorphin addiction in other compulsive behaviors such as obsessive exercise, religious fanaticism, and cult involvement.

1993 320 pages
ISBN: 0-393701-56-5

William Drake McFeely, President

2641 Fear of Being Fat
Rowman & Littlefield Publishers
4501 Forbes Blvd, Suite 200
Lanham, MD 20706
301-459-3366
Fax: 301-429-5748
www.rowmanlittlefield.com/aronsonj/

This book, which presents one psychoanalytic approach to the treatment of anorexia nervosa, has been written by a number of authors, all members of the Psychosomatic Study Group of the Psychoanalytic Association of New York. The theoretical positions and therapeutic approaches are, consequently, conclusions based on extensive clinical experience acquired over many years. Geared more for the professional.

366 pages
ISBN: 0-876688-99-7

Thomas Koerner, Ph.D, VP/Editorial Director
Wanda Mathews, Marketing Manager

2642 Food for Recovery
Crown Publishing Group/Random House
280 Park Avenue
New York, NY 10017
212-572-6117
Fax: 212-940-7868
crownpublicity@randomhouse.com
www.randomhouse.com/

Written for those in recovery from alcohol and drug abuse and eating disorders, this is an excellent basic book on nutrition. Beasley, director of a clinic that focuses on addictive diseases and nutritional medicine, and Knightly, a faculty member of Manhattan's Natural Gourmet Cooking School, discuss nutrition basics and explain how to select wholesome, unprocessed food.

1994 374 pages
ISBN: 0-517586-94-0

Jenny Frost, President/Publisher
Tina Constable, VP/Publicity Executive Director

Eating Disorders / Book Publishers

2643 Getting Better Bit(e) by Bit(e)
Gurze Books
5145 B Avenida Encinas, PO Box 2238
Carlsbad, CA 92008
760-434-7533
800-756-7533
Fax: 760-434-5476
leigh@gurze.net
www.gurze.com

Written by specialists from London, the author's addresses the day-to-day problems faced by bulimia and binge eating sufferers and key behavior changes for progress.

143 pages Paperback

Ulrike Schmidt, Author
Janet Treasure, Author

2644 Group Psychotherapy for Eating Disorders
American Psychiatric Press
1000 Wilson Boulevard, Suite 1825
Arlington, VA 22209
703-907-7322
800-368-5777
Fax: 703-907-1091
appi@psych.org
www.appi.org/

The first book to fully explore the use of group therapy in the treatment of eating disorders.

353 pages Hardcover
ISBN: 0-880484-19-5

Robert E Hales, MD, Editor-in-Chief
Ron McMillen, Chief Executive Officer
John McDuffie, Editorial Director

2645 Hope and Recovery: A Mother-Daughter Story About Anorexia Nervosa & Bulimia
Franklin Watts
90 Old Sherman Turnpike
Danbury, CT 06816
800-621-1115
custserv@scholastic.com
www.scholastic.com/aboutscholastic/

Mother and daughter tell a story of a young woman's recovery from the horror of an eating disorder. This compelling account shows how anorexia and bulimia can affect an entire family.

192 pages
ISBN: 0-531111-40-7

Richard Robinson, Chairman/President/CEO
Mary A Winston, EVP/Chief Financial Officer
Lisa Holton, EVP/Book Fairs and Trade Shows

2646 How to get Your Kid to Eat...
Bull Publishing
PO Box 1377
Boulder, CO 80306
800-676-2855
Fax: 303-545-6354
bullpublishing@msn.com
www.bullpub.com

Touches on the various reasons for a child not wanting to eat, as well as continuos snacking, and not eating vegetables.

408 pages
ISBN: 0-915950-83-9

Jim Bull, Publisher

2647 I Was a Fifteen-Year-Old Blimp
Harper & Row
10 East 53rd Street
New York, NY 10022
212-207-7000
www.harpercollins.com/

This story focuses on Gabby, a teenage girl who overhears others discuss her weight and takes radical steps to become popular.

Grades 6-9

Jane Friedman, President/CEO
Lisa Herling, SVP/Corporate Communications
Brian Murray, Group President

2648 Insights in the Dynamic Psychotherapy of Anorexia And Bulimia
Rowman & Littlefield Publishers
4501 Forbes Blvd, Suite 200
Lanham, MD 20706
301-459-3366
Fax: 301-429-5748
www.rowmanlittlefield.com/

Discusses the eating disorders of anorexia and bulimia providing an overview of the dynamics in diagnosing the disease in addition to developmental and sociocultural issues, therapy and hospitalization.

320 pages Hardcover
ISBN: 0-876685-68-8

Shiela Burnett, Vice President/Marketing Director
Christopher Anzalone, Washington Editor/Director
Jack Meinhardt, Acquisitions Editor

2649 Life Beyond Your Eating Disorder
Johana S. Kandel, author

Harlequin
PO Box 5190
Buffalo, NY 14240
888-432-4879
cutomerservice@harlequin.com
www.harlequin.com

With the collaboration of professionals in the field of eating disorders, the author developed a set of practical tools to address the everyday challenges of recovery.

ISBN: 0-373892-26-6

2650 Making Peace with Food
Gurze Books
5145 B Avenida Encinas, PO Box 2238
Carlsbad, CA 92008
760-434-7533
800-756-7533
Fax: 760-434-5476
leigh@gurze.net
www.gurze.com

Filled with ideas, workbook pages, exercises, and resources, Kano's book is an excellent aid to clarifying and overcoming your personal diet/weight struggle.

224 pages Paperback

Susan Kano, Author

2651 Management of Eating Disorders and Obesity
Humana Press Scientific and Medical Publishers
999 Riverview Drive, Suite 208
Totowa, NJ 07512
973-256-1699
Fax: 973-256-8341
www.humanapress.com/

Stressing human physiology, treatment, and disease prevention, the authors take advantage of the new molecular understanding of the biological regulation of energy. Updated chapters review specific evidence-based and future treatment modalities, present an objective evaluation of the treatment, and identify the positives and negatives that have been seen during clinical studies, as well as cumulative data derived from clinical practice.

2004 448 pages Hardcover
ISBN: 1-588293-41-6

Paul Dolgert, Editorial Director
Ellie Shaw, Developmental Editor
Robin Weisberg, Director Editorial Services

2652 Meals Without Squeals Sense
Bull Publishing
PO Box 1377
Boulder, CO 80306
800-676-2855
Fax: 303-545-6354
bullpublishing@msn.com
www.bullpub.com

Straightforward information on childrens, growth accompanies age-specific, child-tested recipes. Explained is how common feeding problems can be solved and show ways to offer children positive experiences with food.

Eating Disorders / Journals

288 pages
ISBN: 0-923521-39-9
Jim Bull, Publisher/President

2653 Practice Guidelines for Eating Disorders
American Psychiatric Publishing
1000 Wilson Boulevard, Suite 1825
Arlington, VA 22209
703-907-7322
800-368-5777
Fax: 703-907-1091
appi@psych.org
www.appi.org/books.cfx

Designed for health care professionals, this guideline includes information on all aspects of anorexia nervosa and bulimia nervosa, including self-induced vomiting, use of laxatives and vigorous exercise to prevent weight gain.

38 pages Paperback
ISBN: 0-890423-00-8
Robert S Pursell, Marketing
John McDuffie, Product Information
Aimee Aponte, Technology/Webmaster

2654 Self-Starvation: from Individual to Family Therapy in the Treatment of Anorexia Ne
rvosa, author
Rowman & Littlefield Publishers
4501 Forbes Blvd, Suite 200
Lanham, MD 20706
301-459-3366
Fax: 301-429-5748
custserv@rowman.com
www.rowmanlittlefield.com/

Discusses the eating disorder anorexia nervosa and how it affects both the individual and family members alike, including information on possible treatment options.

1978 296 pages Hardcover
ISBN: 0-876683-10-3
Sheila Burnett, Marketing
Jack Meinhardt, Acquisitions Editor
Christopher Anzalone, Washington Editor/Director

2655 Starving to Death in a Sea of Objects
Rowman & Littlefield Publishers
4501 Forbes Blvd, Suite 200
Lanham, MD 20706
301-459-3366
Fax: 301-429-5748
www.rowmanlittlefield.com

How emanciation becomes security for anorexics.

464 pages Softcover
ISBN: 0-876684-35-5
Sheila Burnett, Marketing
Jack Meinhardt, Acquisitions Editor
Christopher Anzalone, Washington Editor/Director

2656 Surviving an Eating Disorder
Gurze Books
5145 B Avenida Encinas, PO Box 2238
Carlsbad, CA 92008
760-434-7533
800-756-7533
Fax: 760-434-5476
leigh@gurze.net
www.gurze.com

Discusses the psychological and behavioral aspects of eating disorders, pharmacology, and family therapy, with an emphasis on bringing eating disorders out in the open, seeking help, coping with anger and denial, developing a healthier relationship, and guidance for making the situation better - now.

222 pages Paperback
Michelle Siegel PhD, Author
Judith Brisman PhD, Author
Margot Weinshel PhD, Author

2657 Treating Bulimia: A Psychoeducational Approach
American Anorexia/Bulimia Association
4200 Monument Avenue
Philadelpha, PA 19131
215-877-2000
jbsmje@epix.net
www.aabaphila.org/

Book discusses the eating disorder bulimia focusing on utlizing the multifaceted treatment approach through the incorporation of education, self-monitoring, goal setting, assertion training, relaxation, and cognitive restructuring.

ISBN: 0-080323-99-5
Randi E Wirth, Ph.D, Executive Director

2658 When Food is Love
Gurze Books
5145 B Avenida Encinas, PO Box 2238
Carlsbad, CA 92008
760-434-7533
800-756-7533
Fax: 760-434-5476
leigh@gurze.net
www.gurze.com

Roth's personal sharing in this book is both courageous and unforgettable. Explores similarities between eating and loving by exploring topics such as fantasizing, wanting the forbidden, creating drama, control issues, being strong in the broken places, and relationships.

205 pages Paperback
Geneen Roth, Author

2659 Withering Child
University of Georgia Press
320 South Jackson Street
Athens, GA 30602
404-542-2830
Fax: 706-542-6770
www.uga.edu/ugapress

Non-fiction book of a parents' struggle with their son and his diagnosis of borderline attention deficit disorder, therapy and his eventual return to school.

1993 288 pages
ISBN: 0-820315-60-5
Nicole Mitchell, Administrative Director
Lane Stewart, Development Director
John McLeod, Marketing Director

Journals

2660 BASH Magazine
Bulimia Anorexia Self-Help/Behavior Adaptation
6125 Clayton Avenue, Suite 215
Saint Louis, MO 63139
314-567-4080
800-227-4785
www.caringonline.com/eatdis/treatment.htm

A journal of eating and mood disorders.

Monthly

2661 Internal Journal of Eating Disorders
Wiley
350 Main Street
Malden, MA 02148
781-388-8598
800-835-6770
cs-journals@wiley.com
www.onlinelibrary.wiley.com

In an effort to advance the scientific knowledge needed for understanding, treating and preventing eating disorders, the IJED publishes rigorously evaluated, high-quality manuscripts for distribution through print and electronic platforms.

2662 Journal of the American Dietetic Associati On
Elsevier Inc.
1600 John F. Kennedy Blvd. - Suite 1800
Philadelphia, PA 19103
215-239-3362
800-654-2452
Fax: 314-447-8029
journalcustomerservice-usa@elsevier.com
www.adajournal.org

Eating Disorders / Pamphlets

The American Dietetic Association is a source for accurate, credible and timely food and nutrition information.

Dan McCormick, CEO
David Kitchen, MBA, CFO
Matt McDowell, BS, Director, Marketing

Newsletters

2663 AABA Newsletter
American Anorexic and Bulimia Association
PO Box 27156
Philadelphia, PA 19118
215-221-1864
mail.aabaphila@yahoo.com
www.aabaphila.org/

The American Anorexia Bulimia Association is a national, non-profit organization dedicated to the prevention and treatment of eating disorders. Publishes a monthly newsletter.

Randi E Wirth, Ph.D, Executive Director

2664 Eating Disorders Review
Gurze Books
PO Box 2238
Carlsbad, CA 92018
760-434-7533
800-756-7533
Fax: 760-434-5476
leigh@gurze.net
www.gurze.com

Presents current clinical information for the professional treating eating disorders. Review features summaries of relevant research of journals and unpublished studies

8 pages Bimonthly

Joel Yager MD, Editor-in-Chief
Leigh Hall, Co Founder
Leigh Cohn, Co Founder

2665 Working Together
Anorexia Nervosa and Associated Disorders
750 E Diehl Road #127
Naperville, IL 60563
630-577-1330
Fax: 847-433-4632
anadhelp@anad.org
www.anad.org

Designed for individuals, families, group leaders and professionals concerned with eating disorders. Provides updates on treatments, resources, conferences, programs, articles by therapists, recovered victims, group members and leaders.

Quarterly

Patricia Santucci, MD, President
Kimberly Dennis, MD, Member, Scientific & Medical Board
Nomi Fredricks, MD, Member, Scientific & Medical Board

Pamphlets

2666 Applying New Attitudes & Directions
Anorexia Nervosa and Associated Disorders
750 E Diehl Road #127
Naperville, IL 60563
630-577-1330
Fax: 847-433-4632
anadhelp@anad.org
www.anad.org

Self-help booklet offering an eight-step program to recovery with suggestions, information and recovery stories.

Patricia Santucci, MD, President
Kimberly Dennis, MD, Member, Scientific & Medical Board
Nomi Fredricks, MD, Member, Scientific & Medical Board

2667 Body Image
ETR Associates
100 Enterprise Way, Suite G300
Scotts Valley, CA 95066
800-620-8884
Fax: 831-438-4284
customerservice@etr.org
www.etr.org

Discusses the difference between healthy and distorted body image; the link between poor body image and low self esteem; five point list to help people check out their own body image.

Ectodermal Dysplasias / Description

Description

2668 ECTODERMAL DYSPLASIAS
Synonyms: Christ-Siemens-Touraine Syndrome, Clouston Syndrome
Involves the following Biologic System(s):
Dental Disorders, Dermatologic Disorders

Ectodermal dysplasia is the term used to describe a large group of hereditary disorders in which there are defects in two or more body structures or organs derived from the body's outermost later of cells, known as the ectoderm. These body structures include the central nervous system, consisting of the brain and spinal cord, and the eyes, ears, lips, teeth, hair, sweat glands of the skin (sebaceous glands), nails, and mucous membranes that line the mouth and nose.

There are more than 150 different kinds of ectodermal dysplasia, all of which stem from aberrations or mutations in genes. Because they originate in genes, the conditions included by the term ectodermal dysplasia are typically transmitted from parents to their offspring, and inherited. However, they may also arise directly, from gene mutations occurring prenatally in an individual's own cells. Each of the various kinds of ectodermal dysplasia is present at birth, and although their effects are not usually seen in newborn infants, and may not become apparent until later in infancy or childhood, none of the different kinds of ectodermal dysplasia progresses or becomes more severe with growth. Ectodermal dysplasia may also occur as an integral part of syndromes in which it is accompanied by other disorders.

The manifestations and symptoms of a particular kinds of ectodermal dysplasia depend on the body structures it affects and the degree to which it affects them. Diminished tear flow (xerophthalmia) and conjunctivitis, diminished salivation (xerostomia), irritation and soreness of the nose and throat from deficient production of mucus, high body temperatures and fever from deficient sweat loss, cleft palate or cleft lip, missing fingers or toes, and webbings of skin between fingers and toes are among the effects of various ectodermal dysplasias and of syndromes of which these dysplasias are a part.

The two most common types of ectodermal dysplasia are X-linked recessive anhydrotic or hypohidrotic ectodermal dysplasia (Christ-Siemens-Touraine syndrome) and hidrotic ectodermal dysplasia (Clouston syndrome). The first of these syndromes is usually inherited as an X-linked recessive trait that is transmitted along with the X or female sex chromosome and is fully expressed in boys; however, some children may inherit anhidrotic or hypohidrotic ectodermal dysplasia as an autosomal recessive trait that affects boys and girls in equal numbers. This type of ectodermal dysplasia is characterized by absent (aplastic) or underdeveloped (hypoplastic) sweat glands, dental irregularities such as absent or widely-spaced, cone-shaped teeth, and sparse, light-colored hair (hypotrichosis). Facial features of this condition may include a large chin; thick lips; bulging forehead (frontal bossing); flat nasal bridge; prominent, low-set ears; and wrinkled, dark skin around the eyes. Children with this form of ectodermal dysplasia may be at increased risk for gastrointestinal infections as well as potentially life-threatening respiratory infections.

The second most common form of ectodermal dysplasia, hidrotic ectodermal dysplasia, also known as Clouston's syndrome, is inherited as an autosomal dominant trait, and is characterized by defective or absent nails, thickening of the skin on the palms of the hands and soles of the feet (palmar/plantar hyperkeratosis), and sparse hair. Other findings may include abnormally increased coloration of the skin over major joints and the development of unusually small teeth that are prone to decay. Treatment is symptomatic and supportive.

Prominent among syndromes of which ectodermal dysplasia is a part is EEC (ectrodactyly-ectodermal dysplasia-clefting) syndrome (EEC), which is inherited as an autosomal dominant trait. Symptoms and physical findings associated with this disorder are variable and may include lightly-pigmented skin, sparse hair and eyebrows, absent eyelashes, a split or opening (cleft) in the lip and palate, defective nails, tear duct irregularities, and absence of all or part of one or more fingers or toes (ectrodactyly). Other findings may include deafness and irregularities of the teeth, eyes, and urinary tract.

The treatment of ecotdermal dysplasia is focused on the structures its affects. Parents and caregivers are counseled to protect children from high environmental temperatures to avoid excessive loss of body water. Consumption of fluids and air conditioning are useful to patients who do not sweat or have deficient sweating. Artificial tears and nasal sprays may be used to ease drying of the membranes of the eyes and nose. Ointments and creams may be useful for relieving drying or scaling of the skin or scalp, as may antibiotic ointments to prevent or treat infection. Dentures and dental implants may be used to replace teeth affected by ectodermal dysplasia, and surgery may be done to correct cleft palate and deformities of the feet and hands. Genetic counseling is recommended for advising the parents of children with ectodermal dysplasia about the chance of the condition recurring in subsequent children.

Government Agencies

2669 NIH/National Institute of Arthritis and Musculoskeletal and Skin Diseases
1 AMS Circle
Bethesda, MD 20892
301-495-4484
877-226-4267
Fax: 301-718-6366
TTY: 301-565-2966
niamsinfo@mail.nih.gov
www.niams.nih.gov

The mission of the NIAMS, a part of the NIH, is to support research into the causes, treatment and prevention of arthritis and musculoskeletal and skin diseases, the training of basic and clinical scientists to carry out this research, and the dissemination of information on research progress in these diseases.

Lindsey A. Criswell, MD, Director
Rick Phillips, Executive Officer

2670 NIH/National Institute of Dental and Craniofacial Research (NIDCR)
National Institutes of Health
Bldg 31, Rm 2C39, 31 Center Drive, MSC 2560
Bethesda, MD 20892
866-232-4528
nidcrinfo@mail.nih.gov
www.nidcr.nih.gov

The Institute promotes the general health of the American people by improving their oral, dental and craniofacial health. The NIDCR aims to promote health, to prevent diseases and conditions, and to develop new diagnostics and therapeutics.

Rena D'Souza, DDS, PhD, Director
Jonathan Horsford, PhD, Acting Deputy Director

Ectodermal Dysplasias / Journals

National Associations & Support Groups

2671 American Academy of Pediatrics
345 Park Blvd
Itasca, IL 60143
800-433-9016
Fax: 847-434-8000
mcc@aap.org
www.aap.org

The American Academy of Pediatrics and its member pediatricians are committed to the attainment of optimal physical, mental and social health and well-being for all infants, children, adolescents, and young adults.

Lynn Olson, PhD, VP, Research
Mark Del Monte, JD, CEO/Executive VP
Vera Tait, MD, FAAP, Chief Medical Officer

2672 American Dental Association
211 E Chicago Avenue
Chicago, IL 60610
312-440-2500
msc@ada.org
www.ada.org

Founded in 1859, the American Dental Association is the oldest and largest national dental society in the world. Since then, the ADA has grown to become the leading source of oral health related information for dentists and their patients.

Raymond A. Cohlmia, Executive Director

2673 Genetic Alliance
426400 Woodfield Road, Ste 189
Damascus, MD 20872
202-966-5557
Fax: 202-966-8553
info@geneticalliance.org
www.geneticalliance.org

World's leading nonprofit health advocacy organization committed to transforming health through genetics and promoting an environment of openness centered on the health of individuals, families, and communities.

Sharon Terry, CEO
Ruth Child, CFO
Natasha Bonhomme, Chief Strategy Officer

2674 March of Dimes Foundation
1550 Crystal Drive, Ste 1300
Arlington, VA 22202
888-663-4637
www.marchofdimes.org

March of Dimes help moms have full-term pregnancies and research the problems that threaten the health of babies. The March of Dimes also acts globally: sharing best practices in perinatal health and helping improve birth outcomes where the needs are the most urgent.

Stacey D. Stewart, President
Alan Brogdon, SVP/COO/Board Officer
Rahul Gupta, MD, SVP & Chief Medical/Health Officer

2675 National Foundation for Ectodermal Dysplasias
6 Executive Drive, Suite 2
Fairview Heights, IL 62208
618-566-2020
info@nfed.org
www.nfed.org

Seeks to enrich the lives of individuals affected by all forms of the ectodermal dysplasia syndromes.

Mary Fete, MSN, RN, CCM, Executive Director
Kelly Atchison, Director, Community Programs
Becky Abbott, MPH, Director, Research Advocacy

2676 Society for Pediatric Dermatology
8365 Keystone Crossing, Ste 107
Indianapolis, IN 46240
317-202-0224
Fax: 317-205-9481
info@pedsderm.net
www.pedsderm.net

The objective of the Society is to promote, develop and advance education, research and care of skin disease in all pediatric age groups.

Kent Lindeman, Executive Director

Libraries & Resource Centers

2677 International Center for Skeletal Dysplasia Registry
St. Joseph Hospital
7620 York Road
Townson, MD 21204
310-423-9915
Fax: 310-423-9939

Provides patient services for those with skeletal dysplasia; does s research in dwarfism.

Dr. Steven Kopitis, Director

Conferences

2678 Society for Pediatric Dermatology Annual Meeting
Society for Pediatric Dermatology
8365 Keystone Crossing, Suite 107
Indianapolis, IN 46240
317-202-0224
Fax: 317-205-9481
info@pedsderm.net
www.pedsderm.net

July

Kent Lindeman, Executive Director
Stephanie Garwood, Meetings Manager

Web Sites

2679 American Dental Association
211 E Chicago Avenue
Chicago, IL 60610
312-440-2500
msc@ada.org
www.ada.org

Founded in 1859, the American Dental Association is the oldest and largest national dental society in the world. Since then, the ADA has grown to become the leading source of oral health related information for dentists and their patients.

Raymond A. Cohlmia, Executive Director

2680 Dental Resources on the Web
www.dental-resources.com

www.dental-resources.com

Dental sites for education, practices, laboratories, office supplies, dental care and associations.

2681 National Center for Biotechnology Information
National Library of Medicine, 8600 Rockville Pike
Bethesda, MD 20894
888-346-3656
info@ncbi.nlm.nih.gov
www.ncbi.nlm.nih.gov

NCBI's mission is to develop new information technologoes to aid in the understanding of fundamental molecular and genetic processes that control health and disease.

Patricia Flatley Brennan, RN, PhD, Director
James Ostell, PhD, Executive Secretary

2682 Online Mendelian Inheritance in Man
McKusick-Nathans Institue of Genetic Medicine-JHU
Baltimore, MD 21205
www.omim.org

This database is a catalog of human genes and genetic disorders.

Ada Hamosh, MD, Scientific Director

Journals

2683 Pediatric Dermatology Journal
Society for Pediatric Dermatology
8365 Keystone Crossing, Suite 107
Indianapolis, IN 46240
317-202-0224
Fax: 317-205-9481
info@pedsderm.net
www.pedsderm.net

Answers the need for new ideas and strategies for today's pediatrician or dermatologist.

6 issues/yr

Kent Lindeman, Executive Director

Description

2684 ECZEMA

Synonym: Eczematous dermatitis

Covers these related disorders: Allergic contact dermatitis, Atopic dermatitis, Dyshidrosis, Irritant contact dermatitis, Seborrheic dermatitis

Involves the following Biologic System(s):

Dermatologic Disorders

Eczema is a common inflammatory condition of the skin (dermatitis) characterized by redness, itching, blistering, and oozing of affected areas. As the condition progresses, the skin often becomes abnormally dry and may scale, crust over, thicken, or develop increased or decreased areas of coloration. There are several different types of eczema that may be caused by various internal or external factors. Children are mainly affected by certain forms of the condition, including atopic dermatitis, irritant and allergic contact dermatitis, seborrheic dermatitis, or dyshidrosis.

Approximately 2-8% of children develop atopic dermatitis, which is the most common form of childhood eczema. Also known as infantile eczema when it occurs during childhood, this form of eczema is characterized by an excessive immune response to particular substances (sensitizing antigens) that the body perceives as foreign. This excessive response, known as an allergic or hypersensitivity reaction, occurs upon exposure to previously encountered, usually environmental substances (allergens). Patients with atopic dermatitis are thought to have an inherited tendency toward allergy. This may be supported by the finding that many infants and children with this type of dermatitis later develop additional conditions caused by exposure to certain allergens. These additional conditions particularly include inflammation of the mucous membranes of the nose (allergic rhinitis) and inflammation and narrowing of the airways (asthma).

Atopic dermatitis usually begins during the first year of life, and up to 90% of affected patients have symptoms by five years of age. The disorder often occurs with the introduction of particular foods into a child's diet, such as wheat, cow's milk, soy, eggs, or peanuts. Although atopic dermatitis tends to subside with advancing age, the condition may recur over a period of many years before completely disappearing. Atopic dermatitis is characterized by the development of reddish, inflamed, intensely itchy (pruritic) patches that rapidly begin to ooze and crust over. During infancy, the condition usually initially affects the skin of the cheeks and gradually extends to involve the rest of the face; the neck, abdomen, wrists, and hands; the insides of the elbows; the areas behind the knees; or other areas. In response to intense itching, infants with atopic dermatitis may rub affected areas against their cribs, clothes, or other surfaces in an attempt to obtain relief. The repeated rubbing or scratching of affected areas may lead to their infection by bacteria on the skin, on clothing, or from other sources. With the passage of time, skin areas affected by atopic dermatitis may become dry and scaly and develop changes in color. In addition, the skin may thicken, accentuating skin lines and causing an unusual, "bark-like" skin appearance (lichenification).

The treatment of atopic dermatitis may include measures to eliminate or avoid certain factors that might worsen the condition, such as certain foods, extremes of humidity and temperature, detergents or soaps, or potentially abrasive textures, such as wool. Affected children should be dressed in garments with smooth textures, such as cotton; their fingernails should be kept as short as possible to discourage scratching; and excessive bathing should be avoided. Adding bath oil to bath water and applying moisturizing lotions and creams to damp skin after bathing may help to ease some symptoms of atopic dermatitis. At locations where inflammation is severe, the application of wet dressings may reduce inflammation and associated itching. Treatment may also include the direct (topical) application of medicated skin creams and ointments, such as corticosteroid preparations, as well as medications such as oral antihistamines to help reduce itching. Bacterial infections of skin affected by atopic dermatitis are treated with appropriate antibiotics.

Contact dermatitis, another common form of eczema, is a skin inflammation that is typically confined to a particular area and may have clearly defined boundaries. This disorder is often subdivided into irritant and allergic contact dermatitis. Irritant contact dermatitis is a skin inflammation caused by repetitive or prolonged exposure to certain substances that damage the skin. Allergic contact dermatitis is an inflammatory response of the skin caused by subsequent exposure to an allergen to which the skin has previously become sensitized.

Irritant contact dermatitis may be caused by repetitive or prolonged exposure to certain soaps or detergents, citrus juices, bubble bath preparations, or other substances. In many infants, saliva from drooling may cause inflammation of the skin of the face and neck folds. Diaper dermatitis is another common form of irritant contact dermatitis. Affected infants may develop a reddish, scaling, blistering skin inflammation and secondary bacterial infections from prolonged contact with waste materials, diaper soaps, and topical skin lotions. The treatment of irritant contact dermatitis includes removal or avoidance of the responsible irritants and topical application of corticosteroid creams or ointments. Affected areas of skin should also be carefully and regularly washed with warm water and a mild soap. To help prevent diaper dermatitis, physicians may recommend frequent changing of diapers; gentle, thorough cleansing of genitals with warm water and mild soaps, and application of mild protective topical preparations during the diaper changes; or the use of disposable diapers made with absorbent materials.

Allergic contact dermatitis is characterized by a hypersensitive or allergic response to previously encountered allergens. Common causes of this form of dermatitis include metal compounds in jewelry; particular plants, such as poison ivy, poison oak, or poison sumac; medications in skin creams, such as certain antibiotic- or antihistamine-containing creams; shoes; or clothing. Patients with allergic contact dermatitis may experience intensely itchy, reddish, blistering skin inflammations, with the affected areas of skin later developing scaling, cracking, (fissuring), changes in color, or an abnormal, thickened, bark-like appearance. Treatment includes the removal or avoidance of allergens responsible for the condition and the application of cool compresses, corticosteroid ointments or oral medications, antihistamine medications, and antibiotic therapy for secondary bacterial infections.

Seborrheic dermatitis is a chronic inflammatory disorder of unknown cause that may occur at any age and may appear to follow the distribution of sebaceous glands in skin tissue. These relatively small glands, which open into hair follicles, produce an oily secretion known as sebum that helps to lubricate the hair and skin and protect the skin from drying. In children, seborrheic dermatitis most commonly occurs during infancy. Affected infants may initially develop localized or widespread crusting and scaling of the scalp, known as cradle cap. In some patients, this may be the only effect of this form of dermatitis. Other infants may develop reddish, greasy, scaling patches that may be localized or may spread

Eczema / Government Agencies

to affect most of the body. Affected areas often include the face, the regions behind the ears, the neck, the diaper region, or the armpits and underarm areas. Patients with seborrheic dermatitis may experience associated itching hair loss, or changes in skin color. Treatment may include the use of special anti-seborrheic shampoos or the application of wet compresses or topical corticosteroid creams or ointments.

Dyshidrotic eczema, also known as dyshidrosis or pompholyx, is another form of eczema that may occur during childhood. It is a recurrent, potentially seasonal blistering condition that affects the palms of the hands and soles of the feet. The condition is initially characterized by recurrent crops of severely itchy blisters. Affected skin areas gradually become abnormally thickened and may have cracking or fissuring. Many patients with dyshidrotic eczema also experience excessive sweating (hyperhidrosis) in affected areas, and may develop secondary bacterial infections from scratching of such areas. Because dyshidrotic eczema is typically a recurrent condition, appropriate measures should be taken to protect the hands and feet of infants and children with this condition from harsh soaps, chemicals, the effects of excessive sweating or adverse weather, or other factors that may trigger the condition. Treatment of dyshidrotic eczema may include the application of wet dressings, topical corticosteroid ointments or creams, or mild topical preparations that promote skin softening and peeling (keratolytic agents), and the administration of antibiotics to treat secondary bacterial infections.

Government Agencies

2685 **NIH/National Institute of Allergy and Infectious Diseases**
5601 Fishers Lane, MSC 9806
Bethesda, MD 20892
301-496-5717
866-284-4107
Fax: 301-402-3573
TDD: 800-877-8339
ocpostoffice@niaid.nih.gov
www.niaid.nih.gov

The principal advisory board of the NIAID. The council is composed of physicians, scientists and representatives of the public and advises on the conduct and support or research, training and dissemination of health information regarding allergies and infectious diseases.

Anthony S. Fauci, MD, Director

2686 **NIH/National Institute of Arthritis and Musculoskeletal and Skin Diseases**
1 AMS Circle
Bethesda, MD 20892
301-495-4484
877-226-4267
Fax: 301-718-6366
TTY: 301-565-2966
niamsinfo@mail.nih.gov
www.niams.nih.gov

The mission of the NIAMS, a part of the NIH, is to support research into the causes, treatment and prevention of arthritis and musculosketal and skin diseases, the training of basic and clinical scientists to carry out this research, and the dissemination of information on research progress in these diseases.

Lindsey A. Criswell, MD, Director
Rick Phillips, Executive Officer

National Associations & Support Groups

2687 **American Academy of Pediatrics**
345 Park Blvd
Itasca, IL 60143
800-433-9016
Fax: 847-434-8000
mcc@aap.org
www.aap.org

The American Academy of Pediatrics and its member pediatricians are committed to the attainment of optimal physical, mental and social health and well-being for all infants, children, adolescents, and young adults.

Lynn Olson, PhD, VP, Research
Mark Del Monte, JD, CEO/Executive VP
Vera Tait, MD, FAAP, Chief Medical Officer

2688 **American Dermatological Association**
531 N Ocean Boulevard, Suite 1907
Pompano Beach, FL 33062
305-804-1150
Fax: 954-252-2093
ameriderm1930@gmail.com
ada1.org

Professional society of physicians specializing in dermatology. Promotes teaching, practice, public education and research into dermatology.

2689 **National Eczema Association**
505 San Marin Drive, Suite B300
Novato, CA 94945
415-499-3474
800-818-7546
www.nationaleczema.org

Works to improve the health and the quality of life of persons living with atopic dermatitis/eczema, including those who have the disease as well as their loved ones.

Julie Block, President & CEO

2690 **Society for Pediatric Dermatology**
8365 Keystone Crossing, Ste 107
Indianapolis, IN 46240
317-202-0224
Fax: 317-205-9481
info@pedsderm.net
www.pedsderm.net

The objective of the Society is to promote, develop and advance education, research and care of skin disease in all pediatric age groups.

Kent Lindeman, Executive Director

Libraries & Resource Centers

California

2691 **University of California, San Francisco Dermatology Drug Research**
515 Spruce
San Francisco, CA 94143
415-476-2001
Fax: 415-476-6014
cc.ucsf.edu/people

Conducts clinical testing of new or existing pharmalogic agents used in the treatment of skin disorders.

John Koo, MD, Director

Illinois

2692 **Dermatology Information Network (DERMINFONET)**
American Academy of Dermatology
9500 W. Bryn Mawr Avenue, Ste 500
Rosemont, IL 60018
847-240-1737
888-462-3376
Fax: 847-240-1859
info@aad.org
www.meddermsociety.org/Resource_Links.asp

Consists of a collection of dermatologic databases that are available to members on a subscription and/or purchase basis. These databases are designed to run on a wide variety of personal computers.

Irvin Bomberger, Interim Executive Director

Eczema / Newsletters

2693 National Library of Dermatologic Teaching Slides
American Academy of Dermatology
9500 W. Bryn Mawr Avenue, Ste 500
Rosemont, IL 60018
847-240-1737
888-462-3376
Fax: 847-240-1859
info@aad.org
www.aad.org

A collection of dermatologic teaching slides offering the most comprehensive series ever assembled. Each set offers a realistic presentation of classic clinical skin conditions encountered by the dermatologist.

Irvin Bomberger, Interim Executive Director

New York

2694 Laboratory of Dermatology Research
Memorial Sloan-Kettering Cancer Center
1275 York Avenue
New York, NY 10065
212-639-2000
Fax: 212-639-3576
www.mskcc.org

Specific studies on the identification of skin disorders and dermatology.

Biijan Safai, MD, Head

2695 Rockefeller University Laboratory for Investigative Dermatology
1230 York Avenue
New York, NY 10065
212-327-8000
Fax: 212-327-7459
www.rockefeller.edu/research/faculty/labheads/JamesK

Research into skin disorders and the whole specialty of dermatology in general.

Barry Coller, Head

Research Centers

2696 University of California, San Francisco Dermatology Drug Research
515 Spruce
San Francisco, CA 94143
415-476-2001
Fax: 415-221-4751

Conducts clinical testing of new or existing pharmacologic agents used in the treatment of skin disorders.

John Koo, MD, Director

Conferences

2697 Society for Pediatric Dermatology Annual Meeting
Society for Pediatric Dermatology
8365 Keystone Crossing, Suite 107
Indianapolis, IN 46240
317-202-0224
Fax: 317-205-9481
info@pedsderm.net
www.pedsderm.net

July

Kent Lindeman, Executive Director
Stephanie Garwood, Meetings Manager

Audio Video

2698 National Library of Dermatologic Teaching Slides
American Academy Of Dermatology
PO Box 94020
Palatine, IL 60094
847-330-0230
Fax: 847-330-0050

A collection of dermatologic teaching slides offering the most comprehensive series ever assembled. Each set offers a realistic presentation of classic clinical skin conditions encountered by the dermatologist.

Magazines

2699 International Journal of Dermatology
International Society of Dermatology
138 Palm Coast Parkway, NE No 333
Palm Coast, FL 32137
386-437-4405
Fax: 386-437-4427
info@intsocdermatol.org
www.intsocderm.org

Focuses on information for dermatologists and the whole specialty of dermatology research and education.

10 times a year

2700 Journal of Dermatologic Surgery and Oncology
International Society for Dermatologic Surgery
930 N Meachan Road
Schaumburg, IL 60173
847-330-9830
Fax: 847-330-1135
onlinelibrary.wiley.com/journal/10.1111/(ISSN)1524-4

Focuses on medical updates and information on dermatology.

Monthly

Journals

2701 Pediatric Dermatology Journal
Society for Pediatric Dermatology
8365 Keystone Crossing, Suite 107
Indianapolis, IN 46240
317-202-0224
Fax: 317-205-9481
info@pedsderm.net
www.pedsderm.net

Answers the need for new ideas and strategies for today's pediatrician or dermatologist.

6 issues/yr

Kent Lindeman, Executive Director

Newsletters

2702 DVH Quarterly
University of Arkansas at Little Rock
2801 S University Avenue
Little Rock, AR 72204
Fax: 501-663-3536

Offers information on upcoming events, conferences and workshops on and for visual disabilities. Book reviews, information on the newest resources and technology, educational programs, want ads and more.

Quarterly

Bob Brasher, Editor

2703 Dermatology Focus
Dermatology Foundation
1560 Sherman Avenue, Suite 870
Evanston, IL 60201
847-328-2256
Fax: 847-328-0509
dermatologyfoundation.org

Includes membership activities, research articles and lists recipients of foundation awards.

Quarterly

Bruce U. Wintroub, MD, Chair
Michael D. Tharp, MD, President
Stuart R. Lessin, MD, Vice President

2704 Dermatology World
American Academy of Dermatology
9500 W. Bryn Mawr Avenue, Ste 500
Rosemont, IL 60018
847-240-1737
888-462-3376
Fax: 847-240-1859
info@aad.org

Eczema / Pamphlets

Offers Academy members information outside the clinical realm. It carries news of government actions, reports of socioeconomic issues, societal trends and other events which impinge on the practice of dermatology.

Monthly

Irvin Bomberger, Interim Executive Director

2705 Progress in Dermatology
Dermatology Foundation
1560 Sherman Avenue, Suite 870
Evanston, IL 60201

847-328-2256
Fax: 847-328-0509
dermatologyfoundation.org

Bulletin offering information on research reports and clinical trials.

Quarterly

Bruce U. Wintroub, MD, Chair
Michael D. Tharp, MD, President
Stuart R. Lessin, MD, Vice President

Pamphlets

2706 Eczema/Atopic Dermatitis
American Academy of Dermatology
9500 W. Bryn Mawr Avenue, Ste 500
Rosemont, IL 60018

847-240-1737
888-462-3376
Fax: 847-240-1859
info@aad.org
www.aad.org

Explains how to recognize and treat dermatitis.

1995

Irvin Bomberger, Interim Executive Director

2707 Hand Eczema
American Academy of Dermatology
9500 W. Bryn Mawr Avenue, Ste 500
Rosemont, IL 60018

847-240-1737
888-462-3376
Fax: 847-240-1859
info@aad.org
www.aad.org

Shows examples of hand rashes, explains causes, lists protective measures and treatments.

1993

Irvin Bomberger, Interim Executive Director

Camps

2708 Camp Discovery
American Academy of Dermatology
9500 W. Bryn Mawr Avenue, Ste 500
Rosemont, IL 60018

847-240-1737
Fax: 847-240-1859
jmueller@aad.org
www.campdiscovery.org

A camp for young people with chronic skin conditions. There is no fee and transportation is provided. Five locations: Camp Victory in Millville, PA, Camp Knutson in Crosslake, MN, Camp For All in Burton, TX, Channel 3 Kids Camp in Andover, CT, and Camp Seymour in Gig harbor, WA.

J Mueller, Camp Contact
Irvin Bomberger, Interim Executive Director

Description

2709 EHLERS-DANLOS SYNDROME
Involves the following Biologic System(s):
Connective Tissue Disorders

Ehlers-Danlos syndrome is a group of hereditary connective tissue disorders characterized by abnormalities of collagen, the major structural protein in the body. At least 10 forms of the disorder have been identified based upon underlying biochemical and genetic abnormalities and associated symptoms and findings. Although such subtypes were previously indentified by Roman numerals (e.g., I to X), different classification systems have since been proposed. Most forms of Ehlers-Danlos syndrome are thought to have autosomal dominant inheritance. However, other subtypes have been identified that may be inherited as an autosomal recessive or an X-linked recessive trait. Although certain symptoms and findings are commonly associated with Ehlers-Danlos syndrome, other abnormalities may be variable in range and severity, depending upon the form of the disorder present.

Although infants with Ehlers-Danlos syndrome often appear normal at birth, associated symptoms and findings soon become apparent. The main symptoms associated with the disorder may include abnormally thin, elastic skin that is excessively fragile and unusually loose, flexible (hyperextensible) joints that may be prone to recurrent dislocation. Due to abnormal fragility of the skin, blood vessels, and other tissues, patients may be prone to tearing or splitting of the skin, be susceptible to easy bruising and bleeding, and tend to heal slowly. Healing of skin wounds may leave distinctive, cigarette paper-like scars, such as over the knees, shins, elbows, and forehead. In addition, due to abnormal accumulations of scar tissue, patients may develop small, rounded skin growths that resemble tumors (molluscoid pseudotumors). In some cases, small, round, hard lumps (calcified spheroids) may also develop under the skin.

Depending upon the form of the disorder present, affected children may have additional, variable symptoms, such as certain skeletal, blood vessel, or eye (ocular) abnormalities. Associated skeletal malformations may include front-to-back and sideways curvature of the spine (kyphoscoliosis); short, wide collarbones (clavicles); bowing of bones of the arms and legs; bone fragility; short stature; or other abnormalities. Fragility of certain blood vessels may lead to ballooning of the wall of the major artery in the body (aortic aneurysm) or spontaneous rupture of certain intermediate- or large-sized arteries, potentially causing life-threatening complications. In addition, in some patients, ocular abnormalities may include fragility of the front, transparent region of the eye (cornea); noninflammatory protrusion of the cornea (keratoconus); rupture of the cornea or the tough, fibrous, outer coating of the eye (sclera); or detachment of the nerve-rich membrane at the back of the eye (retina). Additional symptoms and findings may include diminished muscle tone (hypotonia); abnormal prominence of blood vessels under the skin; protrusion of one of the heart valves back into the left upper chamber (atrium) of the heart during contraction of the left lower heart chamber (mitral valve prolapse); severe inflammation of the tissues that surround and support the teeth (periodontitis), leading to premature tooth loss; rupture of the intestine; or other abnormalities.

The treatment of children with Ehlers-Danlos syndrome is symptomatic and supportive. Appropriate measures must be taken to avoid trauma and injuries, such as those that may occur in contact sports. Wearing protective clothing and padding may be beneficial. In addition, appropriate precautions must be taken during dental or surgical procedures.

Government Agencies

2710 NIH/National Institute of Arthritis and Musculoskeletal and Skin Diseases
1 AMS Circle
Bethesda, MD 20892
301-495-4484
877-226-4267
Fax: 301-718-6366
TTY: 301-565-2966
niamsinfo@mail.nih.gov
www.niams.nih.gov

The mission of the NIAMS, a part of the NIH, is to support research into the causes, treatment and prevention of arthritis and musculoskeletal and skin diseases, the training of basic and clinical scientists to carry out this research, and the dissemination of information on research progress in these diseases.

Lindsey A. Criswell, MD, Director
Rick Phillips, Executive Officer

National Associations & Support Groups

2711 American Academy of Pediatrics
345 Park Blvd
Itasca, IL 60143
800-433-9016
Fax: 847-434-8000
mcc@aap.org
www.aap.org

The American Academy of Pediatrics and its member pediatricians are committed to the attainment of optimal physical, mental and social health and well-being for all infants, children, adolescents, and young adults.

Lynn Olson, PhD, VP, Research
Mark Del Monte, JD, CEO/Executive VP
Vera Tait, MD, FAAP, Chief Medical Officer

2712 Genetic Alliance
426400 Woodfield Road, Ste 189
Damascus, MD 20872
202-966-5557
Fax: 202-966-8553
info@geneticalliance.org
www.geneticalliance.org

World's leading nonprofit health advocacy organization committed to transforming health through genetics and promoting an environment of openness centered on the health of individuals, families, and communities.

Sharon Terry, CEO
Ruth Child, CFO
Natasha Bonhomme, Chief Strategy Officer

2713 March of Dimes Foundation
1550 Crystal Drive, Ste 1300
Arlington, VA 22202
888-663-4637
www.marchofdimes.org

March of Dimes help moms have full-term pregnancies and research the problems that threaten the health of babies. The March of Dimes also acts globally: sharing best practices in perinatal health and helping improve birth outcomes where the needs are the most urgent.

Stacey D. Stewart, President
Alan Brogdon, SVP/COO/Board Officer
Rahul Gupta, MD, SVP & Chief Medical/Health Officer

2714 The Ehlers-Danlos Society
447 Broadway, 2nd Floor, Suite 670
New York, NY 10013
410-670-7577
www.ehlers-danlos.com

The Ehlers-Danlos Society is dedicated to advancing and accelerating research and education in Ehlers-Danlos syndromes (EDS) and hypermobility spectrum disorders (HSD). We support the development of effective and equitable EDS and HSD therapies and work collaboratively to improve the lives of individuals affected by EDS and HSD.

Lara Bloom, President & CEO

Ehlers-Danlos Syndrome / Web Sites

Web Sites

2715 Wheeless' Textbook of Orthopaedics
www.wheelessonline.com

www.wheelessonline.com

Derives from a variety of sources, including journals, articles, national meetings lectures and other textbooks.

Clifford R. Wheeless III, MD, Editor-in-Chief
James A. Nunley, II, Managing Editor
James R. Urbaniak, MD, Managing Editor

Description

2716 ENCEPHALOCELE

Involves the following Biologic System(s):

Neurologic Disorders

Encephalocele is an abnormality that is present at birth (congenital) and belongs to a group of birth defects known as neural tube defects. These defects develop during the early stages of pregnancy at which time a specialized layer of tissue forms and extends along the back portion of the developing embryo. As the embryo grows, this tissue, known as the neural plate, forms a groove that is bordered by folds. This groove eventually deepens and closes to form the neural tube. Later in development, the neural tube gives rise to tissue that later forms the brain and spinal cord. The neural tube is surrounded and protected by the bones of the back (vertebrae). Failure in this sequence of developmental events results in a neural tube defect.

In newborns with encephalocele, a portion of the brain protrudes through a defect in the skull. This defect may be located at the back of the head (occipital region), the forehead (frontal region), or the area of the forehead and nose (nasofrontal region). Affected children may experience visual abnormalities, intellectual disabilities, an abnormally small head (microcephaly), and seizures. Affected newborns may also have an increase in the volume of fluid surrounding the brain (hydrocephalus), possibly resulting in increased pressure within the skull, enlargement of the head, and convulsions.

Encephalocele may occur as the result of different genetic and environmental factors (multifactorial), alone or in combination. Such factors may include vitamin deficiencies or toxic factors. Genetic transmission in some children is supported by the fact that multiple cases of this neural tube defect have been reported in some families. In addition, encephalocele may sometimes be associated with other disorders. For example, physical characteristics of Meckel-Gruber syndrome, a rare, life-threatening disorder inherited as an autosomal recessive trait, include encephalocele in the back of the head; an abnormal ridge (cleft) or opening in the lip or palate; a sloping forehead, extra fingers or toes (polydactyly); and enlarged kidneys that contain multiple cysts (polycystic kidneys).

Treatment of encephalocele may often involve a team of medical specialists working together to determine the best course of therapy or management. Such treatment may include surgery, medication, or the insertion of a tube known as a shunt into the brain. This shunt diverts fluid away from the brain into the abdominal cavity where it is harmlessly absorbed into the systemic circulation.

The risk of neural tube defects is significantly reduced when supplemental folic acid is consumed in addition to a healthful diet prior to and during the first month following conception. Women who could become pregnant, especially those at risk who may have previously delivered a child with a neural tube defect, are advised to eat foods fortified with folic acid or take a folic acid supplement in addition to eating folate-rich foods to reduce the risk of some serious birth defects.

Government Agencies

2717 NIH/ Eunice Kennedy Shriver National Institute of Child Health & Human Development
P.O. Box 3006
Rockville, MD 20847
800-370-2943
Fax: 866-760-5947
www.nichd.nih.gov

Conducts and supports research on topics related to the health of children, adults, families and populations. Some of these topics include: developmental disabilities, growth and development, infant death, reproductive health and birth defects.

Diana W. Bianchi, Director
Alison Cernich, PhD, Deputy Director

National Associations & Support Groups

2718 AmeriFace
PO Box 751112
Las Vegas, NV 89130
702-341-5351
888-486-1209
Fax: 702-341-5351
info@ameriface.org
www.ameriface.org

Provides information, services, emotional support and educational programs for and on behalf of individuals with facial differences and their families. Working to increase understanding through public awareness and education.

3M members

Debbie Oliver, Executive Director

2719 American Academy of Pediatrics
345 Park Blvd
Itasca, IL 60143
800-433-9016
Fax: 847-434-8000
mcc@aap.org
www.aap.org

The American Academy of Pediatrics and its member pediatricians are committed to the attainment of optimal physical, mental and social health and well-being for all infants, children, adolescents, and young adults.

Lynn Olson, PhD, VP, Research
Mark Del Monte, JD, CEO/Executive VP
Vera Tait, MD, FAAP, Chief Medical Officer

2720 Birth Defect Research for Children
976 Lake Baldwin Lane, Suite 104
Orlando, FL 32814
407-895-0802
staff@birthdefects.org
www.birthdefects.org

Birth Defect Research for Children is a non-profit organization that provides parents and expectant parents with information about birth defects and support services for their children.

Betty Mekdeci, Executive Director

2721 Children's Craniofacial Association
13140 Coit Road, Suite 517
Dallas, TX 75240
214-570-9099
800-535-3643
contactCCA@ccakids.com
www.ccakids.com

A national, nonprofit organization dedicated to improving the quality of life for people with facial differences and their families. CCA's mission is to empower and give hope to facially disfigured children and their families.

Erica Klauber, Executive Director
Annie Reeves, Program Director
Khadija Z. Moten, Outreach Director

2722 FACES: National Craniofacial Association
PO Box 11082
Chattanooga, TN 37401
800-332-2373
faces@faces-cranio.org
www.faces-cranio.org

Provides information to affected individuals; families of affected individuals; the public or media and professionals. We also provide peer support; professional counseling; medical referrals; referrals for non-medical services and to local chapters or groups.

Lynne Mayfield, Director

2723 Hydrocephalus Association
4340 East West Highway, Suite 905
Bethesda, MD 20814

301-202-3811
888-598-3789
Fax: 301-202-3813
info@hydroassoc.org
www.hydroassoc.org

A national nonprofit organization devoted exclusively to hydrocepahalus. We provide support, education and an extensive range of resources to families and professionals dealing with the complex issues of hydrocephalus, the abnormal accumulation of cerebrospinal fluid within the brain. Our resources cover all age groups, from prenatal to adults with normal pressure hydrocepahalus.

Diana Gray, President & CEO
Amanda Garzon, Chief Operations Officer
Brian Saphier, Chief Financial Officer

2724 March of Dimes Foundation
1550 Crystal Drive, Ste 1300
Arlington, VA 22202

888-663-4637
www.marchofdimes.org

March of Dimes help moms have full-term pregnancies and research the problems that threaten the health of babies. The March of Dimes also acts globally: sharing best practices in perinatal health and helping improve birth outcomes where the needs are the most urgent.

Stacey D. Stewart, President
Alan Brogdon, SVP/COO/Board Officer
Rahul Gupta, MD, SVP & Chief Medical/Health Officer

2725 National Hydrocephalus Foundation
12413 Centralia Road
Lakewood, CA 90715

562-924-6666
info@nhfonline.org
www.nhfonline.org

Promotes information and educational assistance. Establishes and facilitates a communication network and works to increase public awareness. Promote and support research.

Debbi Fields, Executive Director

Web Sites

2726 Clinical Genetic Services-Department of Pediatrics
Hassenfeld Children's Hospital at NYU Langone
424 East 34th Street
New York, NY 10016

212-263-7300
Fax: 646-754-2250
nyulangone.org

Offers evaluations, genetic counseling and testing. Clinical services include carrier testing, prenatal counseling, and complete genetic evaluations for children and adults.

John G. Pappas, MD, Pediatric Genetic Associate
Naomi Yachelevich, MD, Pediatric Genetic Associate

2727 National Hydrocephalus Foundation
www.nhfonline.org

562-924-6666
info@nhfonline.org
www.nhfonline.org

Promotes information and educational assistance. Establishes and facilitates a communication network and works to increase public awareness. Promote and support research.

Book Publishers

2728 Congenital Disorders Sourcebook
Greg Mullin, author

Omnigraphics
615 Griswold Street, Ste 520
Detroit, MI 48226

610-461-3548
800-234-1340
Fax: 800-875-1340
contact@omnigraphics.com
www.omnigraphics.com

Basic consumer health information on disorders aquired during gestation, including spina bifida, hydrocephalus, cerebral palsy, heart defects, craniofacial abnormalities and fetal alcohol syndrome.

664 pages
ISBN: 0-780816-13-8

Encopresis / Government Agencies

Description

2729 ENCOPRESIS

Involves the following Biologic System(s):

Developmental/Behavioral/Psychiatric Disorders, Gastrointestinal Disorders

Encopresis refers to the passage of feces in inappropriate or unacceptable places by children who have no detectable disorder or organic abnormality and who are past the age when toilet training is typically completed. This type of soiling may be considered primary encopresis, in which fecal incontinence persists from birth, or secondary encopresis, a regressive form of this disorder in which fecal incontinence occurs in children who were previously toilet trained. Children with this disorder may refuse to use a commode, may soil their clothing, or may defecate in secret places. Other associated findings may include chronic constipation leading to the presence of large, hardened fecal masses in the colon or rectum (fecal impaction) that, in turn, may result in an abnormally enlarged or dilated colon (megacolon). Encopresis occurs in approximately one percent of school children and is much more common in boys than it is in girls.

The causes of encopresis may sometimes be linked to anger, defiance, resistance, or fear of toilet training and, as such, may indicate the need for psychotherapeutic intervention that includes parents or caregivers, as well as the affected child. Treatment is often supportive. For example, a reward system may be established so that the child has an incentive to cooperate. In addition, the affected child may be encouraged to use the bathroom at specific times (e.g., after meals) and for specified periods of time. Parents are advised to remain nonjudgmental and nonretaliatory, so that consequences for noncompliance are minor. Additional treatment for primary encopresis may initially include the carefully monitored, short-term use of laxatives and enemas to relieve constipation and subsequent complications. Affected children may sometimes benefit from biofeedback, during which individuals learn how to control certain involuntary physiologic functions such as, in this case, the anal sphincter muscle. In addition, the careful administration of mineral oil, together with a high fiber diet, may be effective in relieving constipation and associated complications in children with secondary encopresis. Other treatment is symptomatic and supportive.

Government Agencies

2730 NIH/ Eunice Kennedy Shriver National Institute of Child Health & Human Development
P.O. Box 3006
Rockville, MD 20847

800-370-2943
Fax: 866-760-5947
www.nichd.nih.gov

Conducts and supports research on topics related to the health of children, adults, families and populations. Some of these topics include: developmental disabilities, growth and development, infant death, reproductive health and birth defects.

Diana W. Bianchi, Director
Alison Cernich, PhD, Deputy Director

National Associations & Support Groups

2731 American Academy of Pediatrics
345 Park Blvd
Itasca, IL 60143

800-433-9016
Fax: 847-434-8000
mcc@aap.org
www.aap.org

The American Academy of Pediatrics and its member pediatricians are committed to the attainment of optimal physical, mental and social health and well-being for all infants, children, adolescents, and young adults.

Lynn Olson, PhD, VP, Research
Mark Del Monte, JD, CEO/Executive VP
Vera Tait, MD, FAAP, Chief Medical Officer

2732 International Foundation for Functional Gastrointestinal Disorders (IFFGD)
3015 Dunes W Boulevard, Suite 512
Mount Pleasant, SC 29466

414-964-1799
www.iffgd.org

The organization offers responses to those commonly asked questions for families and individuals whose lives have been touched with the disorder.

Nancy J. Norton, Founder
Ceciel T. Rooker, President

2733 March of Dimes Foundation
1550 Crystal Drive, Ste 1300
Arlington, VA 22202

888-663-4637
www.marchofdimes.org

March of Dimes help moms have full-term pregnancies and research the problems that threaten the health of babies. The March of Dimes also acts globally: sharing best practices in perinatal health and helping improve birth outcomes where the needs are the most urgent.

Stacey D. Stewart, President
Alan Brogdon, SVP/COO/Board Officer
Rahul Gupta, MD, SVP & Chief Medical/Health Officer

Conferences

2734 IFFGD Professional Symposia
3015 Dunes W Boulevard, Suite 512
Mount Pleasant, SC 29466

414-964-1799
www.iffgd.org

Aimed at promoting education and awareness among professionals from multiple disciplines who treat gastrointestinal disorders and incontinence.

April

Nancy J. Norton, Founder
Ceciel T. Rooker, President

Web Sites

2735 Mental Help Net
P.O. Box 20709
Columbus, OH 43220

614-448-4055
800-232-TALK
info@centersite.net, editor@centersite.n
mentalhelp.net

We wish to provide the following: to develop and debate in an open forum the future of the mental health field in America and throughout the world; to help coordinate various components of the mental health field, so as to bring about greater communication between them; also to educate the public about mental health issues.

Encopresis / Book Publishers

Book Publishers

2736 What I Need to Know About Constipation
Nat'l Digestive Diseases Information Clearinghouse
31 Center Drive
Bethesda, MD 20892
301-496-3583
Fax: 301-907-8906
nddic@info.niddk.nih.gov
www.niddk.nih.gov

Defines constipation and includes a list of steps for prevention, as well as a list of additional resources

Pamphlets

2737 Constipation
NDDIC
9000 Rockville Pike
Bethesda, MD 20892
301-496-3583
800-891-5389
Fax: 301-907-8906
nddic@info.niddk.nih.gov
www.niddk.nih.gov

Includes a definition of constipation and information on how it develops, how it is diagnosed, and how it can be treated. Also provides details on misconceptions about constipation.

8 pages

Griffin P. Rodgers, MD, MACP, Director
Dr. Gregory Germino, Deputy Director
Kevin Abbott, Program Director

2738 Constipation in Children
Nat'l Digestive Diseases Information Clearinghouse
9000 Rockville Pike
Bethesda, MD 20892
301-496-3583
Fax: 301-907-8906
nddic@info.niddk.nih.gov
www.niddk.nih.gov

Griffin P. Rodgers, MD, MACP, Director
Dr. Gregory Germino, Deputy Director
Kevin Abbott, Program Director

2739 Fecal Incontinence
NDDIC
9000 Rockville Pike
Bethesda, MD 20892
301-496-3583
800-891-5389
Fax: 301-907-8906
nddic@info.niddk.nih.gov
www.niddk.nih.gov

8 pages

Griffin P. Rodgers, MD, MACP, Director
Dr. Gregory Germino, Deputy Director
Kevin Abbott, Program Director

Description

2740 EPIDERMOLYSIS BULLOSA
Covers these related disorders: Epidermolysis bullosa dystrophica, Epidermolysis bullosa simplex, Junctional epidermolysis bullosa
Involves the following Biologic System(s):
Dermatologic Disorders

Epidermolysis bullosa is a group of inherited diseases that are often apparent at birth (congenital) and characterized by blistering of the skin after minor injury or trauma. In addition, blistering tends to worsen in warm temperatures. These disorders vary in severity, specific features, and mode of inheritance, and are classified under one of three groupings.

Epidermolysis bullosa simplex is a relatively mild, non-scarring form of this disorder that is inherited as an autosomal dominant trait. Epidermolysis bullosa simplex is further categorized as generalized or localized. The generalized type is usually apparent at birth or soon thereafter. The blisters, also known as bullae, are usually located on areas of the body that are prone to injury such as the hands, feet, elbows, knees, etc. Blistering tendencies usually lessen with advancing age with no long-term effects or scarring. The localized form of this disorder, known as Weber-Cockayne syndrome, affects the hands and feet and may not become apparent until walking commences or, in some cases, adolescence or adulthood. Blistering may be mild, but may severely worsen with such activities as extended walking. Treatment is symptomatic and supportive and may be directed toward prevention and treatment of secondary infections.

Junctional epidermolysis bullosa is inherited as an autosomal recessive trait and is also apparent at birth or soon thereafter. Characteristic findings and symptoms associated with this potentially life-threatening form of the disorder may include severe blistering around the mouth and on the scalp, trunk, diaper area, and legs. In addition, slow-healing lesions may develop in the mucous membranes of the respiratory, gastrointestinal, and genitourinary tracts. Affected infants are also at increased risk for infections such as septicemia, a life-threatening condition in which harmful bacteria multiply in the bloodstream. In addition, the nails may appear defective and teeth may decay easily. Other findings may include stunted growth and abnormally low levels of circulating red blood cells (anemia). Treatment for junctional epidermolysis bullosa may include the administration of antibiotics to treat infections and blood transfusions to treat anemia. In addition, nutritional supplementation may be beneficial. Other treatment is symptomatic and supportive.

Epidermolysis bullosa dystrophica may be inherited as an autosomal dominant trait, an autosomal recessive trait, or it may appear sporadically. Findings associated with autosomal dominant inheritance are less severe than those of autosomal recessive transmission. This form of epidermolysis bullosa may be further categorized as the albopapuloid Pasini variant and the Cockayne-Touraine variant. The albopapuloid Pasini variant may first appear as early as infancy or as late as adolescence and is characterized by extensive, scarring-type blistering of the skin on the joints, arms, and legs; the appearance during adolescence of flesh-colored (albopapuloid) lesions on the trunk; and involvement of certain mucuous memberanes. The Cockayne-Touraine variant of this disorder develops during infancy or early childhood and is characterized by blisters that most commonly appear on the arms and legs. Epidermolysis bullosa dystrophica that is inherited as an autosomal recessive trait is a severe form of this disorder that may be characterized at birth by extensive blistering and erosions of the body surfaces and mucous membranes. As the lesions heal, scarring may result in deformity and limited mobility. In addition, healing of the mucous membranes of the esophagus may cause narrowing of this structure, leading to difficulties in feeding and eating. Treatment may include the implementation of a special diet or use of special feeding devices necessitated by scarring or narrowing of the esophagus. Additional treatment may be directed toward the prevention or care of associated secondary infections. Other treatment is symptomatic and supportive.

Government Agencies

2741 NIH/National Institute of Arthritis and Musculoskeletal and Skin Diseases
1 AMS Circle
Bethesda, MD 20892
301-495-4484
877-226-4267
Fax: 301-718-6366
TTY: 301-565-2966
niamsinfo@mail.nih.gov
www.niams.nih.gov

The mission of the NIAMS, a part of the NIH, is to support research into the causes, treatment and prevention of arthritis and musculoskeletal and skin diseases, the training of basic and clinical scientists to carry out this research, and the dissemination of information on research progress in these diseases.
Lindsey A. Criswell, MD, Director
Rick Phillips, Executive Officer

National Associations & Support Groups

2742 American Academy of Pediatrics
345 Park Blvd
Itasca, IL 60143
800-433-9016
Fax: 847-434-8000
mcc@aap.org
www.aap.org

The American Academy of Pediatrics and its member pediatricians are committed to the attainment of optimal physical, mental and social health and well-being for all infants, children, adolescents, and young adults.
Lynn Olson, PhD, VP, Research
Mark Del Monte, JD, CEO/Executive VP
Vera Tait, MD, FAAP, Chief Medical Officer

2743 DebRA: Dystrophic Epidermolysis Bullosa Research Association of America
75 Broad Street, Suite 300
New York, NY 10004
866-332-7276
Fax: 212-868-9296
staff@debra.org
www.debra.org

Committed to providing referrals, patient advocacy and lobbying, offers networking services, and engages in patient and professional education.
Brett Kopelan, Executive Director
Jeanette Gissen, Programs Director
Jenna Kubeck, Special Events Director

2744 Genetic Alliance
426400 Woodfield Road, Ste 189
Damascus, MD 20872
202-966-5557
Fax: 202-966-8553
info@geneticalliance.org
www.geneticalliance.org

World's leading nonprofit health advocacy organization committed to transforming health through genetics and promoting an environment of openness centered on the health of individuals, families, and communities.

Sharon Terry, CEO
Ruth Child, CFO
Natasha Bonhomme, Chief Strategy Officer

2745 March of Dimes Foundation
1550 Crystal Drive, Ste 1300
Arlington, VA 22202   888-663-4637
www.marchofdimes.org

March of Dimes help moms have full-term pregnancies and research the problems that threaten the health of babies. The March of Dimes also acts globally: sharing best practices in perinatal health and helping improve birth outcomes where the needs are the most urgent.

Stacey D. Stewart, President
Alan Brogdon, SVP/COO/Board Officer
Rahul Gupta, MD, SVP & Chief Medical/Health Officer

Web Sites

2746 EB Medical Research Foundation
2757 Anchor Ave
Los Angeles, CA 90064   www.ebkids.org

The EBMRF is a nonprofit, whose sole purpose is dedicated to the support of medical research of epidermolysis bullosa — its causes, its cure, and the development of successful treatments.

Jerry J. Joseph, Chair
Lynn Anderson, President & Founder
Paul J. Joseph, CFO

2747 Online Mendelian Inheritance in Man
McKusick-Nathans Institue of Genetic Medicine-JHU
Baltimore, MD 21205   www.omim.org

This database is a catalog of human genes and genetic disorders.

Ada Hamosh, MD, Scientific Director

Description

2748 ERB'S PALSY

Synonym: Erb-Duchenne paralysis

Involves the following Biologic System(s):

Neurologic Disorders

Erb's palsy is a form of paralysis in newborns resulting from injury to certain nerves (i.e., fifth and sixth cervical nerves of upper brachial plexus) that supply specific muscles of the shoulder and arm. Nerve injury may be the result of a difficult delivery (e.g., breech presentation, delivery of an unusually large newborn, etc.). During delivery, lateral traction of the head and neck may occur and lead to stretching of these nerves, potentially resulting in such injury.

Newborns with Erb's palsy typically experience swelling and inflammation of the affected nerves and paralysis of the affected shoulder and arm muscles (e.g., deltoid, biceps, brachialis). This causes the arm to hang loosely with the elbow extended and inwardly rotated. Newborns with the condition are unable to move the affected arm away from the shoulder or rotate the arm away from the body. In addition, although they may extend the forearm, affected newborns lack a startle reflex known as Moro's reflex on the affected side. Moro's reflex, which is usually present at birth, involves stretching of the arms and legs forward and out and extension of the fingers when startled. In some severe cases, paralysis and associated loss of the muscle mass (atrophy) in the shoulder area (deltoid muscle) may cause drop shoulder, which is characterized by depression of the affected shoulder below the level of the other. Some infants may experience impairment of sensation in affected areas. Movements of the hand are typically not affected.

The effectiveness of certain treatments for Erb's palsy may vary, depending upon whether affected nerves (i.e., fifth and sixth cervical nerves) were torn or injured in a manner that allows a return of function within a few months. Treatment measures may include initial immobilization of the affected arm and shoulder with braces or splints and physical therapy including range of motion exercises, massage, and active and passive corrective exercises. Such therapy may help to improve muscle function and prevent permanent bending of affected joints in a fixed posture (flexion contractures). If paralysis continues at three to six months of age, surgical measures may be considered in some cases.

National Associations & Support Groups

2749 American Academy of Pediatrics
345 Park Blvd
Itasca, IL 60143

800-433-9016
Fax: 847-434-8000
mcc@aap.org
www.aap.org

The American Academy of Pediatrics and its member pediatricians are committed to the attainment of optimal physical, mental and social health and well-being for all infants, children, adolescents, and young adults.

Lynn Olson, PhD, VP, Research
Mark Del Monte, JD, CEO/Executive VP
Vera Tait, MD, FAAP, Chief Medical Officer

2750 March of Dimes Foundation
1550 Crystal Drive, Ste 1300
Arlington, VA 22202

888-663-4637
www.marchofdimes.org

March of Dimes help moms have full-term pregnancies and research the problems that threaten the health of babies. The March of Dimes also acts globally: sharing best practices in perinatal health and helping improve birth outcomes where the needs are the most urgent.

Stacey D. Stewart, President
Alan Brogdon, SVP/COO/Board Officer
Rahul Gupta, MD, SVP & Chief Medical/Health Officer

2751 United Brachial Plexus Network
32 William Road
Reading, MA 01867

781-315-6161
info@ubpn.org
www.ubpn.org

A registered non-profit organization devoted to providing information, support, and leadership for families and those concerned with brachial plexus injuries worldwide. Also provided is an online registry, various outreach and awareness programs and publications.

Libraries & Resource Centers

2752 National Rehabilitation Information Center
8400 Corporate Drive, Suite 500
Landover, MD 20785

800-346-2742
Fax: 301-459-4263
TTY: 301-459-5984
naricinfo@heitechservices.com
www.naric.com

Committed to providing direct, personal and information services to anyone interested in disability rehabilitation issues; Committed to serving consumers, researchers, family members, health professionals, educators, counselors, students, librarians and the administrators.

Mark X. Odum, Project Director
Jessica H. Chaiken, Media/Information Services Manager
Natalie J. Collier, Library and Acquisitions Manager

Web Sites

2753 Texas Children's Hospital
6621 Fannin Street
Houston, TX 77030

832-824-1000
www.texaschildrenshospital.org

Is an internationally recognized full-care pediatric hospital located in the Texas Medical Center in Houston. The largest pediatric hospital in the United States, Texas Children's is nationaly ranked in the top 5 among children's hospitals.

Mark A. Wallace, President & CEO
Dr. Mark Kline, Physician-in-Chief
Dr. Charles D. Fraser, Jr., Surgeon-in-Chief

Erythema Infectiosum / Description

Description

2754 ERYTHEMA INFECTIOSUM

Synonyms: EI, Fifth disease, Sticker's disease, Parvovirus, Slapped Cheek

Involves the following Biologic System(s):

Infectious Disorders

Erythema infectiosum, or Fifth disease, is a contagious infection caused by the human parvovirus B19. It is characterized by a three-stage rash. First, there is the sudden appearance of a red rash on the face that may look as if the cheeks had been slapped. Then the rash progresses to a reddish, raised-spot, blotchy eruption that spreads to the trunk, buttocks, arms, and legs. When it begins to fade, the rash takes on a lacy-type appearance. The rash usually subsides within five to 10 days, but may reappear within a month's time, especially after exercise, stress, skin irritation, or exposure to sunlight. Transmission of this virus is through inhalation of droplets exhaled or coughed into the air by infected individuals. The incubation period for erythema infectiosum is approximately four to 14 days.

Erythema infectiosum occurs most commonly in preschool and young school-age children. The first symptoms may be low-grade fever and headache. Once the rash appears or shortly thereafter, fever and other signs of illness may be absent. However, some older children and adults may develop mild itching (pruritus), joint pain (arthralgia), and inflammation of the joints (arthritis). In addition, under certain circumstances, exposure to human parvovirus B19 may result in more severe complications. For example, individuals with certain blood disorders such as thalessemia or sickle cell anemia may develop a temporary inability to produce red blood cells, resulting in a decrease in the body's capacity to supply oxygen to the tissues of the body (anemia). Symptoms associated with severe anemia may include weakness, discomfort, pale skin (pallor), rapid breathing (tachypnea), and rapid heartbeat (tachycardia). In addition, those who have impaired immune function may experience severe consequences upon exposure to human parvovirus B19. For example, individuals undergoing certain types of chemotherapy, those with acquired immunodeficiency syndrome (AIDS), or those with certain types of primary, inherited immune defects may experience recurrent or prolonged infections, anemia, or other blood abnormalities.

Pregnant women infected with parvovirus B19 may transmit it to their unborn children, resulting, in rare cases, in miscarriage or stillbirth; however, most of those exposed in utero are born with no apparent consequences. Other viral-exposed infants may have abnormal accumulations of fluid in the tissues or cavities of the body (hydrops). If this condition is diagnosed before birth, special blood transfusions delivered by way of the umbilical vein may be of benefit to the affected fetus. Treatment for this viral infection is symptomatic.

Government Agencies

2755 NIH/National Institute of Allergy and Infectious Diseases
5601 Fishers Lane, MSC 9806
Bethesda, MD 20892

301-496-5717
866-284-4107
Fax: 301-402-3573
TDD: 800-877-8339
ocpostoffice@niaid.nih.gov
www.niaid.nih.gov

The principal advisory board of the NIAID. The council is composed of physicians, scientists and representatives of the public and advises on the conduct and support or research, training and dissemination of health information regarding allergies and infectious diseases.

Anthony S. Fauci, MD, Director

National Associations & Support Groups

2756 American Academy of Pediatrics
345 Park Blvd
Itasca, IL 60143

800-433-9016
Fax: 847-434-8000
mcc@aap.org
www.aap.org

The American Academy of Pediatrics and its member pediatricians are committed to the attainment of optimal physical, mental and social health and well-being for all infants, children, adolescents, and young adults.

Lynn Olson, PhD, VP, Research
Mark Del Monte, JD, CEO/Executive VP
Vera Tait, MD, FAAP, Chief Medical Officer

2757 March of Dimes Foundation
1550 Crystal Drive, Ste 1300
Arlington, VA 22202

888-663-4637
www.marchofdimes.org

March of Dimes help moms have full-term pregnancies and research the problems that threaten the health of babies. The March of Dimes also acts globally: sharing best practices in perinatal health and helping improve birth outcomes where the needs are the most urgent.

Stacey D. Stewart, President
Alan Brogdon, SVP/COO/Board Officer
Rahul Gupta, MD, SVP & Chief Medical/Health Officer

2758 World Health Organization
Avenue Appia 20
1202 Geneva,
Switzerland

www.who.int

WHO is the directing and coordinating authority for health within the United Nations system. WHO operates in more than 150 countries around the world.

Dr. Tedros Adhanom Ghebreyesus, Director General
Dr. Zsuzsanna Jakab, Deputy Director General
Stewart Simonson, Asst Director General, UN NYC

Web Sites

2759 Kid's Health
kidshealth.org

kidshealth.org

KidsHealth provides doctor-approved health information about children from before birth through adolescence. Kids health provides families with accurate, up to date and jargon free health information they can use.

Neil Izenberg, MD, Editor-in-Chief & Founder

2760 Med Help International
www.medhelp.org

800-522-5006
www.medhelp.org

Is dedicated to helping patients find the highest quality medical information in the world today. We offer patients the tools necessary to make informed treatment decisions within the short time lines dedicated by their illness or disease.

2761 New York State Department of Health
www.medhelp.org/lib/fifth.htm

800-522-5006
www.medhelp.org/lib/fifth.htm

Information on erythema infectiosum, like how does anyone get it, what is the treatment, and what can be done to prevent this disease from occuring.

Esophageal Atresia / Description

Description

2762 ESOPHAGEAL ATRESIA

Synonyms: Tracheo-esophageal fistula, Vacterl, Vater

Involves the following Biologic System(s):

Gastrointestinal Disorders

Esophageal atresia is a defect that is present at birth (congenital). The esophagus, which is a muscular tube, is that portion of the digestive system that connects the throat and the stomach. In infants with esophageal atresia, the channel (lumen) within the tubular esophagus fails to develop properly, resulting in an esophagus that ends in a blind pouch, failing to provide a continuous passage to the stomach. In some infants, the upper section of the esophagus may be dramatically narrowed or it may be closed at its lower end. In others, the closed-end lower portion extends upward from the stomach and there is no through connection between the two. Most affected infants also have an abnormal tube-like connection or opening between the windpipe (trachea) and either the upper or lower portion of the esophagus. This is known as a tracheoesophageal fistula. In some children, there is a double connection in which there is an abnormal passage between the trachea and part of the esophagus, as well as between the trachea and a lower region of the esophagus.

Infants with esophageal atresia cannot swallow at all and therefore salivate and regurgitate excessively. If a tracheoesophageal fistula exists between the windpipe and upper portion of the esophagus, fluid may enter the lungs, resulting in coughing, choking, a bluish discoloration (cyanosis) of the nail beds, lips, and mucous membranes, and possibly pneumonia. The presence of an abnormal passage between the trachea and the lower section of the esophagus may allow air to enter the abdomen, resulting in excessive abdominal swelling (distension) that may interfere with normal breathing. In addition, contents of the abdomen may enter the lungs and severe inflammation may occur. If esophageal atresia is present without a fistula, characteristic findings may include a boat-shaped abdomen that is devoid of air.

Treatment includes surgery to join or connect the two sections of the esophagus. This procedure is known as an esophageal anastomosis. Tracheoesophageal fistulas may be surgically corrected by ligation, a procedure in which the passageway is tied off. Before surgery, special care is taken to ensure the infants do not draw fluid (aspirate) into their lungs through the esophagus.

As many as 50 percent of infants with esophageal atresia have associated structural malformations of other organs. For example, if a tracheoesophageal fistula is present, other abnormalities of the trachea may also be apparent. In addition, approximately half of all affected infants have a complex of congenital anomalies (VACTERL syndrome) characterized by additional malformations involving the heart, skeleton, kidneys, and urinary and genital systems. Treatment for esophageal atresia includes management or correction of associated anomalies. Esophageal atresia occurs in approximately one in 3,500 births in the United States. About 33 percent of these infants are born prematurely.

National Associations & Support Groups

2763 American Academy of Pediatrics
345 Park Blvd
Itasca, IL 60143

800-433-9016
Fax: 847-434-8000
mcc@aap.org
www.aap.org

The American Academy of Pediatrics and its member pediatricians are committed to the attainment of optimal physical, mental and social health and well-being for all infants, children, adolescents, and young adults.

Lynn Olson, PhD, VP, Research
Mark Del Monte, JD, CEO/Executive VP
Vera Tait, MD, FAAP, Chief Medical Officer

2764 American College of Gastroenterology
6400 Goldsboro Road
Bethesda, MD 20817

301-263-9000
www.gi.org

The American College of Gastroenterology was founded in 1932 to advance the scientific study and medical practice of diseases of the GI tract.

13,000 members

2765 Digestive Disease National Coalition
507 Capitol Court NE, Suite 200
Washington, DC 20002

202-544-7497
Fax: 202-546-7105
www.ddnc.org

Advocacy organization comprised of over 30 voluntary and professional societies concerned with the many diseases of the digestive tract and liver.

Ceciel Rooker, Chairperson
Bryan Green, MD, President
Cathy Griffith, Vice Chairperson

2766 International Foundation for Functional Gastrointestinal Disorders (IFFGD)
3015 Dunes W Boulevard, Suite 512
Mount Pleasant, SC 29466

414-964-1799
www.iffgd.org

The organization offers responses to those commonly asked questions for families and individuals whose lives have been touched by gastrointestinal disorders.

Nancy J. Norton, Founder
Ceciel T. Rooker, President

2767 North American Society for Pediatric Gastroenterology/Hepatology/Nutrition
714 N Bethlehem Pike, Suite 300
Ambler, PA 19002

215-641-9800
Fax: 215-641-1995
www.naspghan.org

Strives to improve the care of infants, children and adolescents with digestive disorders by promoting advances in clinical care of children with chronic abdominal pain, diarrhea, constipation, vomiting, bleeding from the GI tract, inflammatory bowel disease, liver diseases, diseases of the pancreas, poor weight gain and nutritional problems.

Margaret K Stallings, Executive Director
Kim Rose, Associate Director
Gina Brown, Membership

Libraries & Resource Centers

2768 National Digestive Diseases Information Clearinghouse (NDDIC)
NIH
2 Information Way
Bethesda, MD 20892

301-654-3810
800-891-5389
Fax: 301-907-8906
nddic@info.niddk.nih.gov
www.digestive.niddk.nih.gov

The National Institute of Diabetes and Digestive and Kidney Diseases conducts and supports research on many of the most serious diseases affecting public health. The Institute supports much of the clinical research on the diseases of internal medicine and related subspecialty fields as well as many basic science disciplines.

Griffin P. Rodgers, MD, Director
Gregory G. Germino, MD, Deputy Director
Kathy Kranzfelder, Communications Director

Conferences

2769 IFFGD Professional Symposia
3015 Dunes W Boulevard, Suite 512
Mount Pleasant, SC 29466
414-964-1799
www.iffgd.org

Aimed at promoting education and awareness among professionals from multiple disciplines who treat gastrointestinal disorders and incontinence.

April

Nancy J. Norton, Founder
Ceciel T. Rooker, President

2770 NASPGHAN Annual Meeting
NASPGHAN
714 N. Bethlehem Pike, Ste 300
Ambler, PA 19002
215-641-9800
Fax: 215-641-1995
www.naspghan.org

Strives to improve the care of infants, children and adolescents with digestive disorders by promoting advances in clinical care of children with chronic abdominal pain, diarrhea, constipation, vomiting, bleeding from the GI tract, inflammatory bowel disease, liver diseases, diseases of the pancreas, poor weight gain and nutritional problems.

Fall

Margaret K Stallings, Executive Director
Kim Rose, Associate Director
Gina Brown, Membership

Web Sites

2771 National Digestive Diseases Information Clearinghouse (NDDIC)
NIH
2 Information Way
Bethesda, MD 20892
301-654-3810
800-891-5389
Fax: 301-907-8906
nddic@info.niddk.nih.gov
www.digestive.niddk.nih.gov

The National Institute of Diabetes and Digestive and Kidney Diseases conducts and supports research on many of the most serious diseases affecting public health. The Institute supports much of the clinical research on the diseases of internal medicine and related subspecialty fields as well as many basic science disciplines.

Griffin P. Rodgers, MD, Director
Gregory G. Germino, MD, Deputy Director
Kathy Kranzfelder, Communications Director

Journals

2772 Journal of Pediatric Gastroenterology and Nutrition
NASPGHAN, author

Lippincott Williams & Wilkins
530 Walnut Street
Philadelphia, PA 19106
215-521-8300
Fax: 215-521-8902
www.lww.com

Publication of the North American Society for Pediatric Gastroenterolgy, Hepatology and Nutrition, which strives to improve the care of infants, children and adolescents with digestive disorders by promoting advances in clinical care of children with chronic abdominal pain, diarrhea, constipation, vomiting, bleeding from the GI tract, inflammatory bowel disease, liver diseases, diseases of the pancreas, poor weight gain and nutritional problems.

Newsletters

2773 NASPGHAN News
714 N. Bethlehem Pike, Ste 300
Ambler, PA 19002
215-641-9800
Fax: 215-641-1995
www.naspghan.org

Publication of the North American Society for Pediatric Gastroenterolgy, Hepatology and Nutrition, which strives to improve the care of infants, children and adolescents with digestive disorders by promoting advances in clinical care of children with chronic abdominal pain, diarrhea, constipation, vomiting, bleeding from the GI tract, inflammatory bowel disease, liver diseases, diseases of the pancreas, poor weight gain and nutritional problems.

Margaret K Stallings, Executive Director
Kim Rose, Associate Director
Gina Brown, Membership

2774 TEF/VATER International Support Network
9005 N Van Houten
Portland, OR 97203
301-535-7185
Fax: 301-952-9152
www.tefvater.org

Provides support to children and adults born with esophageal atresia.

Ewing's Sarcoma / Description

Description

2775 **EWING'S SARCOMA**

Synonym: Ewing's tumor

Involves the following Biologic System(s):

Hematologic and Oncologic Disorders, Orthopedic and Muscle Disorders

Ewing's sarcoma is a malignant tumor that typically occurs in individuals under the age of 20 years. The tumor most often arises in the long bones of the shin (tibia), thigh (femur), or upper arm (humerus) or the flat bones of the pelvis, vertebrae, or chest wall. Ewing's sarcoma often invades surrounding soft tissues and tends to spread (metastasize) to other bones, the lungs, and, less frequently, to the bone marrow or other organs. In some cases, the primary tumor may develop in soft tissue. Approximately 75 percent of these tumors occur in the legs or arms as well as the bones of the shoulders.

The most common symptoms of Ewing's sarcoma include fever, as well as pain, tenderness, and swelling in the area of the tumor. Some children may also experience weight loss, low levels of circulating red blood cells (anemia), and elevated levels of circulating white blood cells (leukocytosis). In addition, the tumor may weaken the surrounding bone and thus increase vulnerability to bone fracture. The diagnosis of Ewing's tumor is established through the use of x-rays along with examination of tissue samples obtained through biopsy. In addition, other procedures such as bone scanning, computed tomography (CT), and magnetic resonance imaging (MRI) may be used to confirm the presence of lung, bone, or other metastases.

Ewing's sarcoma develops most frequently between the ages of 10 and 20 years of age and affects boys more often than girls by a ratio of two to one. These tumors rarely occur in black children. Treatment of Ewing's sarcoma may include the use of chemotherapy and radiation. Patients are also evaluated for possible surgical removal of the tumor. Other treatment is symptomatic and supportive. Outcome (prognosis) for children with Ewing's sarcoma depends on several factors that include the extent of the disease, the size and location of the tumor, presence or absence of metastases, the tumor's response to therapy, and the age and overall health of the child. Prompt medical attention and aggressive therapy are important for the best prognosis.

Government Agencies

2776 **NIH/National Cancer Institute**
Bethesda, MD 20892

800-422-6237
NCIinfo@nih.gov
www.cancer.gov

The National Cancer Institute coordinates the National Cancer Program, which conducts and supports research, training, health information dissemination, and other programs with respect to the cause, diagnosis, prevention, and treatment of cancer, rehabilitation from cancer, and the continuing care of cancer patients and the families of cancer patients.

Norman E. Sharpless, MD, Director
Douglas R. Lowy, MD, Principal Deputy Director

National Associations & Support Groups

2777 **American Academy of Pediatrics**
345 Park Blvd
Itasca, IL 60143

800-433-9016
Fax: 847-434-8000
mcc@aap.org
www.aap.org

The American Academy of Pediatrics and its member pediatricians are committed to the attainment of optimal physical, mental and social health and well-being for all infants, children, adolescents, and young adults.

Lynn Olson, PhD, VP, Research
Mark Del Monte, JD, CEO/Executive VP
Vera Tait, MD, FAAP, Chief Medical Officer

2778 **American Cancer Society**
3380 Chastain Meadows Parkway NW, Suite 200
Kennesaw, GA 30144

800-227-2345
www.cancer.org

The American Cancer Society is the leading cancer-fighting organization with a vision of ending cancer as we know it, for everyone. We are the only organization working to improve the lives of people with cancer and their families through advocacy, research, and patient support, to ensure everyone has an opportunity to prevent, detect, treat, and survive cancer.

Karen E Knudsen, Chief Executive Officer
William L Dahut, MD, Chief Scientific Officer
Kymm Martinez, Chief Marketing Officer

2779 **American Childhood Cancer Organization**
P.O. Box 498
Kensington, MD 20895

301-962-3520
800-366-2223
Fax: 310-962-3521
staff@acco.org
www.acco.org

The American Childhood Cancer Organization (ACCO) was founded in 1970 by a group of parents whose children had been diagnosed with cancer. Today ACCO is one of the largest grassroots, national organizations dedicated to improving the lives of children and adolescents with cancer and their families.

Ruth I. Hoffman, MPH, CEO
Krista Novak, Programs Manager
Blair Scroggs, Public Relations Coordinator

2780 **B.A.S.E. Camp Children's Cancer Foundation**
650 North Wymore Rd, #103
Winter Park, FL 32789

407-673-5060
Fax: 407-673-5095
info@basecamp.org
www.basecamp.org

Provides a year round base of support for children and families facing the challenge of living with cancer, hemophilia and other blood related illnesses.

Terri Jones, President
Cindy Whitaker, Program Coordinator
Rachel Perez, Office Administrator

2781 **Believe In Tomorrow Children's Foundation**
6601 Fredrick Road
Baltimore, MD 21228

410-744-1032
Fax: 410-744-1984
www.believeintomorrow.org

Provides housing services and a variety of special services and programs (such as beach and mountain retreats or attending Orioles games) to any child up to 18 years of age who is being treated for cancer. Services are provided free of charge and are available on an ongoing basis throughout treatment.

Brian Morrison, Founder & CEO
Richard E. McCready, Chairman
David Reymann, Vice Chairman

Ewing's Sarcoma / Book Publishers

2782 **CancerCare**
275 7th Avenue
New York, NY 10001
212-712-8400
800-813-4673
Fax: 212-712-8495
info@cancercare.org
www.cancercare.org

Dedicated to providing emotional support, information, and practical help to people with cancer and their loved ones. CancerCare is the oldest, largest, nonprofit agency devoted to offering professional services.

Patricia J Goldsmith, CEO
Christine Verini, RPh, COO

2783 **CureSearch for Children's Cancer**
P.O. Box 45781
Baltimore, MD 21297
800-458-6223
Fax: 301-718-0047
info@curesearch.org
www.curesearch.org

CureSearch for Children's Cancer is a national non-profit foundation that accelerates the cure for children's cancer by driving innovation, eliminating research barriers and solving the field's most challenging problems.

Kay Koehler, CEO
Katharine A. Burke, COO & VP, Financing
Caitlyn W. Barrett, National Director, Research & Prgms

2784 **HairClub**
www.hairclub.com
800-290-5511
www.hairclub.com

Since 1992, HairClub has offered free hair restoration services to children who suffer from diseases that lead to hair loss or alopecia. HairClub is a non-profit program that's available at no charge to children ages 6-17.

Sy Sperling, Founder

2785 **Just In Time**
1737 Chestnut Street, #600
Philadelphia, PA 19103
215-977-7777
Fax: 215-247-0956
tome@softhats.com
www.softhats.com

100% cotton hat, turbans and caps designed for women with hair loss due to cancer, chemotherapy, alopecia or trichotillomania.

Verley Platt, President

2786 **National Coalition for Cancer Survivorship**
8455 Colesville Road, Ste 930
Silver Spring, MD 20910
877-622-7937
info@canceradvocacy.org
www.canceradvocacy.org

NCCS advocates for quality cancer care for all people touched by cancer and provides tools that empower people to advocate for themselves. Founded by and for cancer survivors, NCCS created the widely accepted definition of survivorship and defines someone as a cancer survivor from the time of diagnosis and for the balance of life.

Samira K. Beckwith, Acting Chair
Shelley Fuld Nasso, CEO
Elena Jeannotte, VP, External Affairs

Web Sites

2787 **CancerCare**
275 7th Avenue
New York, NY 10001
212-712-8400
800-813-4673
Fax: 212-712-8495
info@cancercare.org
www.cancercare.org

Dedicated to providing emotional support, information, and practical help to people with cancer and their loved ones. CancerCare is the oldest, largest, nonprofit agency devoted to offering professional services.

Patricia J Goldsmith, CEO
Christine Verini, RPh, COO

2788 **Children's Cancer Web**
www.cancerindex.org/ccw

www.cancerindex.org/ccw

An independent nonprofit site, established to provide a directory of childhood cancer resources.

2789 **Ewing's Sarcoma Support Group Resources Page**
www.cureourchildren.org
310-355-6046
Fax: 310-454-9592
www.cureourchildren.org

2790 **OncoLink: The University of Pennslyvania Cancer Center Resource**
www.oncolink.upenn.edu

www.oncolink.upenn.edu

Book Publishers

2791 **Cancer Information for Teens, 4th Edition**
Omnigraphics
615 Griswold Street, Ste 520
Detroit, MI 48226
610-461-3548
800-234-1340
Fax: 800-875-1340
contact@omnigraphics.com
www.omnigraphics.com

Updated information and facts about cancer causes, diagnosis, prevention and treatment especially for teens.

480 pages
ISBN: 0-780816-15-2

2792 **Cancer Sourcebook**
Angela L. Williams, author

Omnigraphics
615 Griswold Street, Ste 520
Detroit, MI 48226
610-461-3548
800-234-1340
Fax: 800-875-1340
contact@omnigraphics.com
www.omnigraphics.com

Updated information and facts about cancer causes, diagnosis, prevention and treatment. Nearly 1.5 million people in the US are diagnosed with cancer every year.

1224 pages 8th Edition
ISBN: 0-780816-22-0

2793 **Childhood Diseases and Disorders Sourcebook, 4th Edition**
Omnigraphics
615 Griswold Street, Ste 520
Detroit, MI 48226
610-461-3548
800-234-1340
Fax: 800-875-1340
contact@omnigraphics.com
www.omnigraphics.com

Basic and up to date consumer health information about common disorders that affect the physical, mental, and developmental health of school-age children.

792 pages
ISBN: 0-780815-38-4

2794 **Let's Talk About Going to the Hospital**
Rosen Publishing Group's PowerKids Press
29 E 21st Street
New York, NY 10010
212-777-3017
800-237-9932
Fax: 888-436-4643
rosenpub@tribeca.ios.com
www.rosenpublishing.com

If a child has to check into the hospital, chances are he or she is already upset about being ill. Knowing how a hospital functions and what the procedures are, such as when family members can visit, will help in what is already a stressful situation. Grades K-5.

24 pages
ISBN: 0-823950-36-0

Roger Rosen, President

2795 Let's Talk About When Kids Have Cancer
Rosen Publishing Group's PowerKids Press
29 E 21st Street
New York, NY 10010
212-777-3017
800-237-9932
Fax: 888-436-4643
customerservice@rosenpub.com
www.rosenpublishing.com

In a straightforward yet comforting way, this book explains what cancer is, what kinds of treatments surround the disease and how to cope if a child or the friend of a child has cancer. K-5.

24 pages Paperback
ISBN: 0-823951-95-6

Camps

2796 Arizona Camp Sunrise & Sidekicks
PO Box 27872
Tempe, AZ 85285
480-382-8564
928-478-4564
melissa@azcampsunrise.org
www.azcampsunrise.org

The camp is dedicated to provide an exciting, medically safe camp program for children whose families have been affected by cancer.

Melissa Lee, Camp Director

2797 Camp Catch-A-Rainbow
American Cancer Society
1205 E Saginaw Street
Lansing, MI 48906
248-302-8985
kwilson@ymcastorercamps.org
www.ymcastorercamps.org/ccar/camp-catch-a-rainbow/

Open to any child, ages 7 thru 15, who has, or has had, cancer.

Katie Wilson, Coordinator

2798 Camp Sunshine Dreams
PO Box 28232
Fresno, CA 93729
contact@campsunshinedreams.com
www.campsunshinedreams.com

Summer camp for children with cancer.

Anthony Aiello, Board Member

2799 Okizu Foundation Camps
16 Digital Drive, Suite 130
Novato, CA 94949
415-382-9083
Fax: 415-382-8384
info@okizu.org
www.okizu.org

This foundation runs family camp programs for children who have cancer and their families, and for children who have or had a parent with cancer.

Lori Sparrow, Executive Director
Heather Ferrier, Camp Director of Operations

Description

2800 FAMILIAL DYSAUTONOMIA

Synonyms: FD, HSAN-III, Riley-Day syndrome

Involves the following Biologic System(s):

Genetic/Chromosomal/Syndrome/Metabolic Disorders, Neurologic Disorders

Familial dysautonomia (FD) is a rare inherited disorder of that part of the nervous system responsible for regulating various essential involuntary functions (autonomic nervous system). This disorder is characterized in infants by feeding difficulties, including excessive salivation and poor swallowing and sucking reflexes. The breathing in of liquid or other substances into the lungs (aspiration) may lead to repeated episodes of bronchial pneumonia. Other associated symptoms and findings include skin blotching, sweating, fluctuating extremes in body temperature, and defective tear secretion (lacrimation). Affected children develop an reduced sensitivity to temperature and pain. This may lead to frequent injuries such as irritation of the corneas of the eyes. Corneal injury may also occur as the result of decreased tear production. In addition, slurred speech and drooling may become evident. Children with familial dysautonomia typically have weak reflex responses (hyporeflexia) and experience delays in walking accompanied by the inability to coordinate voluntary movements (motor incoordination). After three years of age, affected children often develop severe vomiting episodes (hyperemesis) that may occur three or four times an hour and, in some cases, may last for three days or more. These episodes may sometimes be accompanied by elevated blood pressure (hypertension), abdominal pain and swelling, increased irritability, or breathing difficulties (dyspnea). As children with this disorder reach adolescence, a sideward curvature of the spine (scoliosis) may become evident along with leg cramping and weakness. In addition, some children may experience a delay in the onset of puberty. Older children may develop emotional and behavioral changes, such as irritability and depression. Intolerance for anesthetics is a common finding among children with FD.

Treatment for familial dysautonomia is symptomatic and supportive. Artificial tears, drops, or ointments may be placed in the eyes to prevent injury to corneas. Certain medications known as antiemetics may be prescribed to help control episodes of vomiting. In addition, replacement fluids and electrolytes may be administered to prevent excessive fluid loss (dehydration) resulting from vomiting episodes. Other treatment may include surgery or the use of orthopedic aids to correct scoliosis.

Familial dysautonomia is inherited as an autosomal recessive trait and occurs most commonly among certain individuals of eastern European descent, particularly Ashkenazi Jews at a rate of one out of 10,000 to 20,000 births. The disease gene for this disorder is located on the long arm of chromosome 9 (9c31-33).

National Associations & Support Groups

2801 American Academy of Pediatrics
345 Park Blvd
Itasca, IL 60143
800-433-9016
Fax: 847-434-8000
mcc@aap.org
www.aap.org

The American Academy of Pediatrics and its member pediatricians are committed to the attainment of optimal physical, mental and social health and well-being for all infants, children, adolescents, and young adults.

Lynn Olson, PhD, VP, Research
Mark Del Monte, JD, CEO/Executive VP
Vera Tait, MD, FAAP, Chief Medical Officer

2802 Familial Dysautonomia Foundation
315 West 39th Street, Suite 701
New York, NY 10018
212-279-1066
Fax: 212-279-2066
info@famdys.org
www.familialdysautonomia.org

Provides parents the knowledge regarding both national and international facilities that specialize in the treatment of the disorder.

Lanie Etkind, Executive Director
Albulena Prelvukaj, Manager, Fundraising/Communication
Julia Winter, Development Operations Associate

2803 Genetic Alliance
426400 Woodfield Road, Ste 189
Damascus, MD 20872
202-966-5557
Fax: 202-966-8553
info@geneticalliance.org
www.geneticalliance.org

World's leading nonprofit health advocacy organization committed to transforming health through genetics and promoting an environment of openness centered on the health of individuals, families, and communities.

Sharon Terry, CEO
Ruth Child, CFO
Natasha Bonhomme, Chief Strategy Officer

2804 March of Dimes Foundation
1550 Crystal Drive, Ste 1300
Arlington, VA 22202
888-663-4637
www.marchofdimes.org

March of Dimes help moms have full-term pregnancies and research the problems that threaten the health of babies. The March of Dimes also acts globally: sharing best practices in perinatal health and helping improve birth outcomes where the needs are the most urgent.

Stacey D. Stewart, President
Alan Brogdon, SVP/COO/Board Officer
Rahul Gupta, MD, SVP & Chief Medical/Health Officer

Web Sites

2805 NYU
530 First Avenue
New York, 10016
212-263-7225
www.med.nyu.edu/fd/fdcenter.html

Offers information about Familial Dysautonomia.

Horacio Kaufman, MD, FAAN, Director
Felicia Axelrod, MD, FAAP, Co Director
Jose Martinez, MA, Research Faculty

2806 Online Mendelian Inheritance in Man
McKusick-Nathans Institue of Genetic Medicine-JHU
Baltimore, MD 21205
www.omim.org

This database is a catalog of human genes and genetic disorders.

Ada Hamosh, MD, Scientific Director

Fetal Alcohol Syndrome / Description

Description

2807 FETAL ALCOHOL SYNDROME

Synonyms: FAS, Fetal alcohol effect (FAE), Alcohol-related neurodevelopmental, Alcolol-related birth defects

Involves the following Biologic System(s):

Genetic/Chromosomal/Syndrome/Metabolic Disorders

Fetal alcohol syndrome, or FAS, is a condition that is present at birth and the result of persistent maternal alcohol consumption during pregnancy. This condition is characterized by various birth defects such as low birth weight, short birth length, and an unusually small head (microcephaly) that may be associated with slowed development of the brain. Infants with FAS may also have several abnormalities of the face and skull including an unusually short opening between the margins of the upper and lower eyelids (palpebral fissures), vertical folds of skin that extend from the inner corners of the upper eyelids to the sides of the nose (epicanthal folds), an abnormally small lower jaw (micrognathia), or a poorly developed upper jaw (maxillary hypoplasia). Additional unusual features may include an abnormal opening in the roof of the mouth (cleft palate), a prominent forehead (frontal bossing), a flattened nasal bridge, and a thin, smooth upper lip. Other characteristic findings may include heart defects, abnormalities of the limbs and joints (e.g., dislocated hip, etc.), and irregular skin crease patterns on the palms of the hands. Within the first day of life, affected newborns may also exhibit characteristic symptoms of alcohol withdrawal such as tremor, increased irritability, muscle spasms, vomiting, or other problems. The development of the brain may also be impaired resulting in moderate to severe intellectual disabilities. Approximately 20 percent of newborns with fetal alcohol syndrome risk life-threatening symptoms and complications within the first few weeks of life.

Alcohol consumption during pregnancy affects the growth and development of the fetus within the uterus and may result not only in birth defects but, in some cases, miscarriage or stillbirth. Although it is believed that fetal alcohol syndrome results from persistent moderate or heavy drinking, no safe levels of alcohol intake during pregnancy have been established; therefore, pregnant women are counseled to avoid alcohol consumption. It has, however, been determined that the more alcohol consumed, the greater the chances of giving birth to children with associated abnormalities. Therefore, treatment is directed toward identification, counseling, and education of women at risk. Other treatment is symptomatic and supportive.

Government Agencies

2808 NIH/ Eunice Kennedy Shriver National Insti tute of Child Health & Human Development
P.O. Box 3006
Rockville, MD 20847

800-370-2943
Fax: 866-760-5947
www.nichd.nih.gov

Conducts and supports research on topics related to the health of children, adults, families and populations. Some of these topics include: developmental disabilities, growth and development, infant death, reproductive health and birth defects.

Diana W. Bianchi, Director
Alison Cernich, PhD, Deputy Director

2809 NIH/National Institute of Mental Health
6001 Executive Blvd, Rm 6200, MSC 9663
Bethesda, MD 20892

866-615-6464
Fax: 301-443-4279
TTY: 301-443-8431
nimhinfo@nih.gov
www.nimh.nih.gov

The mission of NIMH is to transform the understanding and treatment of mental illnesses through basic and clinical research, paving the way for prevention, recovery, and cure.

Joshua A. Gordon, MD, PhD, Director
Shelli Avenevoli, PhD, Deputy Director

2810 NIH/National Institute on Alcohol Abuse an d Alcoholism (NIAAA)
5600 Fishers Lane
Bethesda, MD 20892

301-443-3860
877-266-4267
niaaaweb-r@exchange.nih.gov
www.niaaa.nih.gov

Established in 1970, NIAAA conducts research focused on improving the treatment and prevention of alcoholism and alcohol-related problems to reduce the enormous health, social, and econmic consequences of this disease.

George F. Koob, PhD, Director

National Associations & Support Groups

2811 American Academy of Pediatrics
345 Park Blvd
Itasca, IL 60143

800-433-9016
Fax: 847-434-8000
mcc@aap.org
www.aap.org

The American Academy of Pediatrics and its member pediatricians are committed to the attainment of optimal physical, mental and social health and well-being for all infants, children, adolescents, and young adults.

Lynn Olson, PhD, VP, Research
Mark Del Monte, JD, CEO/Executive VP
Vera Tait, MD, FAAP, Chief Medical Officer

2812 American Association for Pediatric Opthalmology and Strabismus
1935 Country Road B2 W, Suite 165
Roseville, MN 55113

952-646-2045
Fax: 415-561-8531
info@aapos.org
www.aapos.org

AAPOS is the American Association for Pediatric Ophthalmology and Strabismus. The organization's goals are to advance the quality of children's eye care, support the training of pediatric ophthalmologists, support research activities in pediatric ophthalmology, and advance the care of adults with strabismus.

Danielle Bogert McKay, Executive Director
Christina Scott, Membership & Communication Manager
Ashley Crunstedt, CMP, Meetings & Marketing Manager

2813 American Pregnancy Association
3007 Skyway Circle N., Ste 800
Irving, TX 75038

800-672-2296
info@americanpregnancy.org
americanpregnancy.org

The American Pregnancy Association is a 501(c)(3) nonprofit organization committed to promoting pregnancy wellness through education, advocacy and community awareness.

2814 Arc of the United States
1825 K Street NW, Ste 1200
Washington, DC 20006

202-534-3700
800-433-5255
Fax: 202-534-3731
info@thearc.org
www.thearc.org

Fetal Alcohol Syndrome / Pamphlets

The Arc of the United States advocates for the rights and full participation of all children and adults with intellectual and developmental disabilities. Together with a network of members and affiliated chapters, they improve systems of support and services; connect families; inspire communities and influence public policy.

Peter V. Berns, CEO

2815 March of Dimes Foundation
1550 Crystal Drive, Ste 1300
Arlington, VA 22202
888-663-4637
www.marchofdimes.org

March of Dimes help moms have full-term pregnancies and research the problems that threaten the health of babies. The March of Dimes also acts globally: sharing best practices in perinatal health and helping improve birth outcomes where the needs are the most urgent.

Stacey D. Stewart, President
Alan Brogdon, SVP/COO/Board Officer
Rahul Gupta, MD, SVP & Chief Medical/Health Officer

2816 Mental Health America
500 Montgomery Street, Ste 820
Alexandria, VA 22314
703-684-7722
800-969-6642
Fax: 703-684-5968
www.mentalhealthamerica.net

MHA, the leading advocacy organization addressing the full spectrum of mental and substance use conditions and their effects nationwide, works to inform, advocate and enable access to quality behavioral health services for all Americans.

Paul Gionfriddo, President/CEO
Whitney Ball, Assoc. Dir., Marketing/Outreach
Sachin Doshi, Sr. Dir, Finance/Operations

2817 National Alliance on Mental Illness (NAMI)
4301 Wilson Blvd., Suite 300
Arlington, VA 22203
703-524-7600
800-999-6264
info@nami.org
www.nami.org

NAMI provides advocacy, education, support and public awareness so that all individuals and families affected by mental illness can build better lives.

Daniel H. Gillison, CEO
David Levy, CFO
Ken Duckworth, Chief Medical Officer

2818 National Mental Health Consumers' Self-Help Clearinghouse
1211 Chestnut Street, Suite 1207
Philadelphia, PA 19107
215-751-1810
800-553-4539
Fax: 215-636-6312
selfhelpclearinghouse@gmail.com
www.mhselfhelp.org

Offers information, support and appropriate referrals; and promotes public and professional education. Provides networking for those with special interests related to albinism. Promotes and supports research and funding that will improve diagnosis and management of albinism and hypopigmentation.

Joseph Rogers, Founder/Executive Director
Susan Rogers, Director

Conferences

2819 Arc Annual National Convention
Arc of the United States
1825 K Street NW, Ste 1200
Washington, DC 20006
202-534-3700
800-433-5255
Fax: 202-534-3731
mckiernan@thearc.org
www.thearc.org

Each year hundreds of members, staff, volunteers, professionals, experts, self advocates and their families gather for a dynamic convention to meet each other, learn from each other, and tackle the tough issues facing the intellectual and developmental disability (I/DD) community together.

Peter V. Berns, CEO
Kristen McKiernan, Sr Exec. Offcr, Comms & Marketing
Liz Mahar, Director, Family/Sibling Initiative

Book Publishers

2820 Alcohol, Tobacco and Other Drugs May Harm the Unborn
National Clearinghouse for Alcohol and Drug Info.
PO Box 2345
Rockville, MD 20847
800-729-6686

Presents the most recent findings of basic research and clinical studies conducted on the effects of alcohol, drugs and tobacco on the unborn.

2821 Congenital Disorders Sourcebook
Greg Mullin, author

Omnigraphics
615 Griswold Street, Ste 520
Detroit, MI 48226
610-461-3548
800-234-1340
Fax: 800-875-1340
contact@omnigraphics.com
www.omnigraphics.com

Basic consumer health information on disorders aquired during gestation, including spina bifida, hydrocephalus, cerebral palsy, heart defects, craniofacial abnormalities and fetal alcohol syndrome.
664 pages
ISBN: 0-780816-13-8

2822 Drugs and Pregnancy: It's Not Worth The Risk
American Council On Drug Education
204 Monroe Street, Suite 110
Rockville, MD 20850
800-488-3784

A scientific monograph for health care providers which teaches them to identify alcohol and drug problems in their patients.
48 pages

2823 Pregnancy and Exposure to Alcohol and Other Drug Use
National Clearinghouse for Alcohol and Drug Info.
PO Box 2345
Rockville, MD 20849
800-729-6686
www.health.org

This report is for health care professionals presenting state-of-the-art information about preventing alcohol use among women of childbearing age.

2824 Prevention Resource Guide: Pregnant, Postpartum Women and Their Infants
National Clearinghouse for Alcohol and Drug Info.
PO Box 2345
Rockville, MD 20849
800-729-6686
www.health.org

This resource guide targets health care providers, prevention program planners and counselors of pregnant and postpartum women between the ages of 15 and 44.
30 pages

Pamphlets

2825 Effects of Alcohol on Pregnancy National Clearinghouse for Alcohol Information
PO Box 2345
Rockville, MD 20847
301-468-2600

Free publications are available that discuss the effects of alcohol on pregnancy: Fetal Alcohol Syndrome; and The Fact Is Alcohol and Other Drugs Can Harm an Unborn Baby.

Fetal Alcohol Syndrome / Pamphlets

2826 Fetal Alcohol Syndrome
Hazelden
PO Box 11
Center City, MN 55012
651-213-4200
800-257-7810
Fax: 612-257-1331
info@hazeldenbettyford.org
www.hazelden.org

A source of information about the effects of drinking while pregnant.

Mark Mishek, President & CEO
Sharon Birnbaum, Director of Human Resources
Jim Blaha, VP, CFO & CAO

2827 Fight Drug Abuse at Home, Work, School and in the Community
American Council for Drug Education
204 Monroe Street, Suite 110
Rockville, MD 20850
800-488-3784

A catalog of print and video materials pertaining to substance abuse, alcoholism and drugs.

2828 Foods to Avoid or Limit During Pregnancy
March of Dimes Foundation
1550 Crystal Drive, Ste 1300
Arlington, VA 22202
914-997-4488
Fax: 914-997-4763
answers@marchofdimes.org
www.marchofdimes.org/pregnancy/

Information about the effects of certain drugs, stress, pets, abuse, and hazardous materials. Each topic is an online article available under the link: During Your Pregnancy.

2014

2829 How to Take Care of Your Baby Before Birth
National Clearinghouse for Alcohol and Drug Info.
PO Box 2345
Rockville, MD 20849
800-729-6686
www.health.org

A low-literacy brochure aimed at pregnant women that describes what they should and should not do during pregnancy.

Description

2830 FETAL RETINOID SYNDROME
Covers these related disorders: Etretinate embryopathy, Isotretinoin embryopathy, Retinol embryopathy
Involves the following Biologic System(s):
Neonatal and Infant Disorders

Fetal retinoid syndrome is a characteristic pattern of birth defects caused by exposure to vitamin A (retinol) or its derivatives during early pregnancy. The term retinoid refers to retinol or any natural or artificially created derivative of vitamin A. In newborns with fetal retinoid syndrome, characteristic symptoms and findings include small, low-set ears or complete absence of the outer ears and external ear canals (microtia); an abnormally small head (microcephaly); enlargement of the cavities (ventricles) within the brain; and underdevelopment (hypoplasia) of the thymus, a small gland in the upper portion of the chest that functions as an essential part of the immune system during infancy and childhood.

Several studies have reported fetal retinoid syndrome in newborns as a result of maternal use of vitamin A derivatives such as isotretinoin during early pregnancy. In addition, an increasing number of studies reveal the occurrence of such birth defects due to maternal use of other vitamin A derivatives, particularly the medication etretinate, or large doses of vitamin A (e.g., greater than 15,000 units daily) during early embryonic development. Although the frequency of fetal retinoid syndrome is unknown, reported cases represent only a small percentage of actual occurrences of the syndrome. Moreover, there is ongoing concern that increasing use of high dose vitamin A preparations and of vitamin A derivatives to treat certain common skin conditions, such as cystic acne or psoriasis, may result in additional cases of fetal retinoid syndrome. The most well known retinoid is isotretinoin. Because it can cause severe birth defects, including intellectual disabilities and physical malformations, a woman must not become pregnant while taking it. If a woman of childbearing age requests isotretinoin, her doctor will ask her to sign a detailed consent form before presribing it. If a woman accidentally becomes pregnant while taking the medication, she should immediately consult her doctor. Dosage levels and the stage of embryonic development during which retinoid exposure occurs are thought to be the major factors influencing the occurrence of fetal retinoid syndrome. The period of greatest risk may occur between approximately two to five weeks after conception. The specific underlying abnormality that causes fetal retinoid syndrome is not known. Studies indicate that retinoid exposure may cause disrupted development in the embryonic region that later becomes the brain and spinal cord (neural crest). The role that genetic influences or other environmental factors may have in contributing to fetal retinoid syndrome is unknown.

Although the symptoms and findings associated with fetal retinoid syndrome vary somewhat from case to case, affected newborns typically have a characteristic pattern of malformations. Affected newborns may have abnormalities of the head and face, including premature closure of the fibrous joint between the bones forming the forehead (metopic craniosynostosis); downslanting eyelid folds (palpebral fissures); widely spaced eyes (ocular hypertelorism) that may be abnormally small (microphthalmia); a short or broad nose; a small jaw (micrognathia); or incomplete closure of the roof of the mouth (cleft palate) and a groove in the upper lip (cleft lip). Abnormalities of the brain and spinal cord (central nervous system) are also common and include obstruction of the flow of cerebrospinal fluid around the brain, causing the fluid to accumulate under increasing pressure within the cavities of the brain (hydrocephalus); loss of vision; or other abnormalities (e.g., holoprosencephaly [failure of the forebrain (prosencephalon) to grow as two separate hemispheres in the first few weeks of fetal life], posterior fossa cyst). Additional neurologic problems may include paralysis of the nerves that supply muscles responsible for eye movements (oculomotor paralysis) or weakness or paralysis of the nerve that supplies the forehead, scalp, eyelids, cheeks, jaws, and muscles of facial expression (facial nerve palsy).

Newborns with fetal retinoid syndrome may also have clouding of the lenses of the eyes (congenital cataracts); malformations of the heart and its major blood vessels (e.g., ventricular septal defects, hypoplastic aortic arch, transposition of the great arteries); underdevelopment (hypoplasia) of the kidneys and tubes (ureters) that carry urine from the kidneys into the bladder; and ab normalities of the liver. Many affected newborns may also have malformations of the arms, legs, hands, and feet, such as webbing or fusion of the fingers and toes (syndactyly); malformations of the bone on the thumb side of the forearm (radial defects); a defect in which the foot is twisted out of shape or position (clubfoot or talipes); or fusion of the lower legs and absence of the feet (sirenomelia). In some patients, life-threatening complications may occur soon after birth. Treatment of newborns with fetal retinoid syndrome includes symptomatic a|nd supportive measures.

Government Agencies

2831 NIH/ Eunice Kennedy Shriver National Institute of Child Health & Human Development
P.O. Box 3006
Rockville, MD 20847

800-370-2943
Fax: 866-760-5947
www.nichd.nih.gov

Conducts and supports research on topics related to the health of children, adults, families and populations. Some of these topics include: developmental disabilities, growth and development, infant death, reproductive health and birth defects.
Diana W. Bianchi, Director
Alison Cernich, PhD, Deputy Director

National Associations & Support Groups

2832 American Academy of Pediatrics
345 Park Blvd
Itasca, IL 60143

800-433-9016
Fax: 847-434-8000
mcc@aap.org
www.aap.org

The American Academy of Pediatrics and its member pediatricians are committed to the attainment of optimal physical, mental and social health and well-being for all infants, children, adolescents, and young adults.
Lynn Olson, PhD, VP, Research
Mark Del Monte, JD, CEO/Executive VP
Vera Tait, MD, FAAP, Chief Medical Officer

2833 Association of Children's Prosthetic/ Orthotic Clinics
403 W St. Charles Road, Suite 403B
Lombard, IL 60148

acpoc@affinity-strategies.com
www.acpoc.org

The Association of Children's Prosthetic-Orthotic Clinics (ACPOC) provides a comprehensive resource of treatment options provided by professionals who serve children, adolescents, and young adults with various musculoskeletal differences.

329

2834 **March of Dimes Foundation**
1550 Crystal Drive, Ste 1300
Arlington, VA 22202
888-663-4637
www.marchofdimes.org

March of Dimes help moms have full-term pregnancies and research the problems that threaten the health of babies. The March of Dimes also acts globally: sharing best practices in perinatal health and helping improve birth outcomes where the needs are the most urgent.

Stacey D. Stewart, President
Alan Brogdon, SVP/COO/Board Officer
Rahul Gupta, MD, SVP & Chief Medical/Health Officer

2835 **National Rehabilitation Information Center**
8400 Corporate Drive, Suite 500
Landover, MD 20785
800-364-2742
Fax: 301-459-4263
TTY: 301-459-5984
naricinfo@heitechservices.com
www.naric.com

Committed to providing direct, personal and information services to anyone interested in disability rehabilitation issues; Committed to serving consumers, researchers, family members, health professionals, educators, counselors, students, librarians and the administrators.

Mark X. Odum, Project Director
Jessica H. Chaiken, Media/Information Services Manager
Natalie J. Collier, Library and Acquisitions Manager

Web Sites

2836 **Association of Children's Prosthetic/ Orthotic Clinics**
403 W St. Charles Road, Suite 403B
Lombard, IL 60148
acpoc@affinity-strategies.com
www.acpoc.org

The Association of Children's Prosthetic-Orthotic Clinics (ACPOC) provides a comprehensive resource of treatment options provided by professionals who serve children, adolescents, and young adults with various musculoskeletal differences.

2837 **March of Dimes Foundation**
www.marchofdimes.com

www.marchofdimes.com

Partnership of volunteers and professionals dedicated to improving the health of babies by preventing birth defects and infant mortality. Over 100 chapters are located across the country and can be located through the National Office.

2838 **National Rehabilitation Information Center**
8400 Corporate Drive, Suite 500
Landover, MD 20785
800-346-2742
Fax: 301-459-4263
TTY: 301-459-5984
naricinfo@heitechservices.com
www.naric.com

Committed to providing direct, personal and information services to anyone interested in disability rehabilitation issues; Committed to serving consumers, researchers, family members, health professionals, educators, counselors, students, librarians and the administrators.

Mark X. Odum, Project Director
Jessica H. Chaiken, Media/Information Services Manager
Natalie J. Collier, Library and Acquisitions Manager

Fragile X Syndrome / National Associations & Support Groups

Description

2839 FRAGILE X SYNDROME
Synonyms: Marker X Syndrome, Martin-Bell Syndrome
Involves the following Biologic System(s):
Genetic/Chromosomal/Syndrome/Metabolic Disorders

Fragile X Syndrome, a disorder that results from an inherited defect of the X chromosome, is the most common cause of intellectual disabilities in males. The disorder is thought to affect approximately one in 2,000 to 4,000 males and to be slightly less frequent in females. Although symptoms may be variable, the most common feature associated with fragile X syndrome is intellectual disabilities.

Most males with fragile X syndrome have mild to profound intellectual disabilities (e.g., an intelligence quotient or I.Q. ranging from approximately 30 to 55.) However, some may have an I.Q. that is considered borderline normal. Affected males with mild intellectual disabilities may have a distinctive speech pattern characterized by rapid speech with a variable rhythm (cluttering). Those with more severe intellectual disabilities typically communicate in bursts of repetitive speech. Affected males with severe or profound intellectual disabilities may lack the ability to speak. In addition, most males with fragile X syndrome may have poor eye contact or experience emotional difficulties. Some may have poor concentration associated with hyperactivity or engage in autistic-like behaviors, such as hand biting or hand flapping.

In many cases, affected males may also have physical abnormalities. For example, many males with fragile X syndrome may have unusually large testes (macroorchidism), a finding that is most apparent after puberty; however, testicular function is normal. Affected males may also typically have characteristic facial features, such as a large head (macrocephaly) and forehead, a relatively long face and prominent jaw, thick lips, and prominent ears. Other findings may include crowding of the teeth, excessive flexibility of the finger joints, or flat feet (pes planus). In addition, approximately 50 percent of affected females have varying degrees of intellectual disabilities or learning difficulties. In some cases, females with fragile X syndrome may also have physical abnormalities, such as irregular teeth or unusually flexible finger joints. The treatment of children with fragile X syndrome includes symptomatic and supportive measures, such as special education, speech therapy, and, in some cases, multidisciplinary techniques such as behavioral therapies to help manage hyperactivity or autistic-like behaviors.

Individuals with fragile X syndrome inherit a fragile area or site on the long arm (q) of the X chromosome (Xq27.3). Chromosomal analysis reveals that the genetic material on the end of this arm appears to be broken off. In reality, this genetic material is actually dangling from the end of the long arm. The diseased gene within this area is known as the FRAXA gene. This region (locus) of the X chromosome contains abnormally long repeats (e.g., over 200 repeats) of coded DNA instructions (CGG trinucleotide repeat expansion). Males have only one X chromosome; therefore, if they inherit a fragile X locus containing more than 200 CGG repeats, they generally express the symptoms associated with this syndrome and are typically more severely affected than females. However, because females have two X chromosomes, certain disease traits may be masked by the presence of a normal gene on the other X chromosome, resulting in lower frequency and decreased severity of the disease among females.

Government Agencies

2840 NIH/ Eunice Kennedy Shriver National Institute of Child Health & Human Development
P.O. Box 3006
Rockville, MD 20847

800-370-2943
Fax: 866-760-5947
www.nichd.nih.gov

Conducts and supports research on topics related to the health of children, adults, families and populations. Some of these topics include: developmental disabilities, growth and development, infant death, reproductive health and birth defects.

Diana W. Bianchi, Director
Alison Cernich, PhD, Deputy Director

National Associations & Support Groups

2841 American Academy of Pediatrics
345 Park Blvd
Itasca, IL 60143

800-433-9016
Fax: 847-434-8000
mcc@aap.org
www.aap.org

The American Academy of Pediatrics and its member pediatricians are committed to the attainment of optimal physical, mental and social health and well-being for all infants, children, adolescents, and young adults.

Lynn Olson, PhD, VP, Research
Mark Del Monte, JD, CEO/Executive VP
Vera Tait, MD, FAAP, Chief Medical Officer

2842 Arc of the United States
1825 K Street NW, Ste 1200
Washington, DC 20006

202-534-3700
800-433-5255
Fax: 202-534-3731
info@thearc.org
www.thearc.org

The Arc of the United States advocates for the rights and full participation of all children and adults with intellectual and developmental disabilities. Together with a network of members and affiliated chapters, they improve systems of support and services; connect families; inspire communities and influence public policy.

Peter V. Berns, CEO

2843 FRAXA Research Foundation
10 Prince Place, Suite 203
Newburyport, MA 01950

978-462-1866
info@fraxa.org
www.fraxa.org

FRAXA supports research on fragile X syndrome, a genetic disorder which is the most common inherited cause of intellectual disabilities.

2,500 members

Katie Clapp, Co-Founder & President
Michael Tranfaglia, MD, Co-Founder & Medical Director
Holly Roos, Community Services Director

2844 Genetic Alliance
426400 Woodfield Road, Ste 189
Damascus, MD 20872

202-966-5557
Fax: 202-966-8553
info@geneticalliance.org
www.geneticalliance.org

World's leading nonprofit health advocacy organization committed to transforming health through genetics and promoting an environment of openness centered on the health of individuals, families, and communities.

Sharon Terry, CEO
Ruth Child, CFO
Natasha Bonhomme, Chief Strategy Officer

Fragile X Syndrome / State Agencies & Support Groups

2845 **National Fragile X Foundation**
1012 - 14th Street NW, Suite 500
Washington, DC 20005
202-594-8376
800-688-8765
contact@fragilex.org
www.fragilex.org

Unites the Fragile X community with support, education, awareness, research and advocacy.

Hilary Rosselot, Executive Director
Jayne Dixon Weber, Director, Community Education
Robby Miller, Director, Clinic Relations

State Agencies & Support Groups

California

2846 **Fragile X Association of Southern California**
PO Box 6924
Burbank, CA 91510
818-754-4227
Fax: 310-276-9251
info@fraxsocal.org
www.fraxsocal.org

Promotes awareness of Fragile X syndrome with special emphasis on educators and health professionals; provides a forum for families of children with fragile X to meet and share their ideas, concerns and problems; and supports scientific research on fragile X syndrome.

Naomi Star, President
Diane Bateman, Vice President

2847 **Fragile X Center of San Diego**
4653 Carmel Mountain Rd, Ste 308-515
San Diego, CA 92130
760-434-6290
877-300-7143
www.fragilexsandiego.org

Provides information for families and professionals. Activities include: family support, improving awareness of fragile X syndrome, increasing the identification for affected families, promoting research into fragile X syndrome.

Nicole Schweizer, Secretary

Ohio

2848 **Fragile X Alliance of Ohio**
6790 Ridgecliff Drive
Solon, OH 44139
440-519-1517
Fax: 440-519-1518
www.fragilexohio.org

Promotes awareness of Fragile X syndrome with special emphasis on educators and health professionals; provides a forum for families of children with fragile X to meet and share their ideas, concerns and problems; and supports scientific research on fragile X syndrome.

Leslie A. Bagdasarian, President

Conferences

2849 **Arc Annual National Convention**
Arc of the United States
1825 K Street NW, Ste 1200
Washington, DC 20006
202-534-3700
800-433-5255
Fax: 202-534-3731
mckiernan@thearc.org
www.thearc.org

Held in cities throughout the U.S. each fall which attracts nearly 1000 people for educational sessions, business meetings and social events.

Peter V. Berns, CEO
Kristen McKiernan, Sr Exec. Offcr, Comms & Marketing
Liz Mahar, Director, Family/Sibling Initiative

Web Sites

2850 **American College of Medical Genetics**
7220 Wisconsin Ave., Suite 300
Bethesda, MD 20814
301-718-9603
Fax: 301-718-9604
acmg@acmg.net
www.acmg.net

Offers information about fragile X syndrome.

2851 **Arc of the United States**
1825 K Street NW, Ste 1200
Washington, DC 20006
202-534-3700
800-433-5255
Fax: 202-534-3731
info@thearc.org
www.thearc.org

The Arc of the United States advocates for the rights and full participation of all children and adults with intellectual and developmental disabilities. Together with a network of members and affiliated chapters, they improve systems of support and services; connect families; inspire communities and influence public policy.

Peter V. Berns, CEO
Kristen McKiernan, Sr Exec. Offcr, Comms & Marketing
Liz Mahar, Director, Family/Sibling Initiative

2852 **FRAXA Research Foundation**
10 Prince Place, Suite 203
Newburyport, MA 01950
978-462-1866
info@fraxa.org
www.fraxa.org

FRAXA supports research on fragile X syndrome, a genetic disorder which is the most common inherited cause of intellectual disabilities.

Katie Clapp, Co-Founder & President
Michael Tranfaglia, MD, Co-Founder & Medical Director
Holly Roos, Community Services Director

2853 **National Fragile X Foundation**
1012 - 14th Street NW, Suite 500
Washington, DC 20005
202-594-8376
800-688-8765
contact@fragilex.org
www.fragilex.org

Unites the Fragile X community with support, education, awareness, research, and advocacy.

Hilary Rosselot, Executive Director
Jayne Dixon Weber, Director, Community Education
Robby Miller, Director, Clinic Relations

Book Publishers

2854 **Children With Fragile X Syndrome**
Jayne Dixon Weber, author

Peytral Publications
PO Box 1162
Minnetonka, MN 55345
952-949-8707
877-739-8725
Fax: 952-906-9777
www.peytral.com

A complete, sensitive introduction to Fragile X Syndrome, covering diagnosis, parental emotions, therapies and medications, early intervention, education, daily care, legal rights and more. Item #WP-307X.

472 pages

Galactosemia / National Associations & Support Groups

Description

2855 GALACTOSEMIA

Covers these related disorders: Classic galactosemia, Galactokinase deficiency, Deficiency of uridyl diphosphogalactose-4-epimerase

Involves the following Biologic System(s):
Gastrointestinal Disorders,
Genetic/Chromosomal/Syndrome/Metabolic Disorders

Galactosemia is a disorder in which the body cannot use the sugar known as galactose, which is an important component of the sugar in milk (lactose) and an important source of nutrition for infants and children. Because of this inability, this sugar accumulates in the blood, and substances produced by the partial breakdown of galactose build up in the body, where they can damage the kidneys, liver, brain, and eyes.

Galactosemia is a hereditary genetic disorder, caused by mutations in genes that carry the structural codes for three enzymes that normally break down or digest galactose. As a result, there are three forms of galactosemia, each stemming from a deficiency of one of the three galactose-digesting enzymes. The most frequent and severe form of galactosemia, named classic galatosemia, results from deficiency of galactose-1 phosphate uridyl transferase. A second form of galactosemia stems from deficiency of galactose kinase, and the third form comes from deficiency of galactose epimerase. All three forms of galactosemia are transmitted in an autosomal recessive manner, meaning that each parent of an affected child must carry a copy of the gene responsible for the same form of galactosemia.

Symptoms of galactosemia may include a yellowish discoloration of the skin, eyes, and mucous membranes (jaundice); opacity of the lenses of the eyes (cataracts); vomiting; convulsions; increased irritability; sluggishness; difficulty in feeding; and failure to gain weight. Characteristic findings may include enlargement of the liver and spleen (hepatosplenomegaly), low blood sugar (hypoglycemia), the presence of amino acids in the urine (aminoaciduria), an abnormal accumulation of fluid in the abdomen (ascites), the formation of scar tissue in the liver (cirrhosis), and intellectual disabilities.

If infants with classic galactosemia are not treated promptly with a low-galactose diet, life-threatening complications appear within a few days after birth. Affected infants typically develop feeding difficulties, a lack of energy (lethargy), a failure to gain weight and grow (failure to thrive), yellowing of the skin and whites of the eyes (jaundice), liver damage, and bleeding. Affected children are also at increased risk of delayed development, clouding of the lens of the eye (cataract), speech difficulties, and intellectual disability. Complications of galactosemia can include severe infection and shock. Women with classic galactosemia, caused by deficiency of the enzyme galactose-1 phosphate uridyl transferase, may have disorders of the reproductive system.

The most effective treatment for galactosemia is the complete elimination of milk and milk products from the diet. Women who carry any of the three genes responsible for galactosemia should avoid lactose-containing foods during pregnancy, to prevent galactose from crossing the placenta and causing disease in the fetus. Although a completely lactose-free diet may prevent the complications of galactosemia, some affected children and adults may experience delays in growth and development, speech irregularities, and difficulties with motor function.

National Associations & Support Groups

2856 American Academy of Pediatrics
345 Park Blvd
Itasca, IL 60143
800-433-9016
Fax: 847-434-8000
mcc@aap.org
www.aap.org

The American Academy of Pediatrics and its member pediatricians are committed to the attainment of optimal physical, mental and social health and well-being for all infants, children, adolescents, and young adults.

Lynn Olson, PhD, VP, Research
Mark Del Monte, JD, CEO/Executive VP
Vera Tait, MD, FAAP, Chief Medical Officer

2857 American Liver Foundation
P.O. Box 299
West Orange, NJ 07052
800-465-4837
www.liverfoundation.org

The American Liver Foundation is the nationleading nonprofit organization promoting liver health and disease prevention. ALF provides research, education and advocacy for those affected by liver-related diseases, including hepatitis.

Lorraine Stiehl, CEO
David Ticker, Executive VP & CFO

2858 Galactosemia Foundation
350 Northern Boulevard, Suite 324-1079
Albany, NY 12204
www.galactosemia.org

Galactosemia Foundation Inc. is a non-profit charitable organization that advocates for people with galactosemia and their families. Founded in February 1985, Galactosemia Foundation helps provide families information about Galactosemia and facilitates networkings between families, clinicians and researchers.

Nicole Casale, President
Scott Saylor, Treasurer
Jodie Solari, Communications Lead

2859 Genetic Alliance
426400 Woodfield Road, Ste 189
Damascus, MD 20872
202-966-5557
Fax: 202-966-8553
info@geneticalliance.org
www.geneticalliance.org

World's leading nonprofit health advocacy organization committed to transforming health through genetics and promoting an environment of openness centered on the health of individuals, families, and communities.

Sharon Terry, CEO
Ruth Child, CFO
Natasha Bonhomme, Chief Strategy Officer

2860 March of Dimes Foundation
1550 Crystal Drive, Ste 1300
Arlington, VA 22202
888-663-4637
www.marchofdimes.org

March of Dimes help moms have full-term pregnancies and research the problems that threaten the health of babies. The March of Dimes also acts globally: sharing best practices in perinatal health and helping improve birth outcomes where the needs are the most urgent.

Stacey D. Stewart, President
Alan Brogdon, SVP/COO/Board Officer
Rahul Gupta, MD, SVP & Chief Medical/Health Officer

Galactosemia / Libraries & Resource Centers

Libraries & Resource Centers

2861 National Digestive Diseases Information Clearinghouse (NDDIC)
NIH
2 Information Way
Bethesda, MD 20892
301-654-3810
800-891-5389
Fax: 301-907-8906
nddic@info.niddk.nih.gov
www.digestive.niddk.nih.gov

The National Institute of Diabetes and Digestive and Kidney Diseases conducts and supports research on many of the most serious diseases affecting public health. The Institute supports much of the clinical research on the diseases of internal medicine and related subspecialty fields as well as many basic science disciplines.

Griffin P. Rodgers, MD, Director
Gregory G. Germino, MD, Deputy Director
Kathy Kranzfelder, Communications Director

Web Sites

2862 American Liver Foundation
P.O. Box 299
West Orange, NJ 07052
800-465-4837
www.liverfoundation.org

The American Liver Foundation is the nation leading nonprofit organization promoting liver health and disease prevention. ALF provides research, education and advocacy for those affected by liver-related diseases, including hepatitis.

Lorraine Stiehl, CEO
David Ticker, Executive VP & CFO

2863 Clinical Genetic Services-Department of Pediatrics
Hassenfeld Children's Hospital at NYU Langone
424 East 34th Street
New York, NY 10016
212-263-7300
Fax: 646-754-2250
nyulangone.org

Offers evaluations, genetic counseling and testing. Clinical services include carrier testing, prenatal counseling, and complete genetic evaluations for children and adults.

John G. Pappas, MD, Pediatric Genetic Associate
Naomi Yachelevich, MD, Pediatric Genetic Associate

2864 Disability Information and Resource Center
www.dircsa.org.au/pub/docs/galac.txt

www.dircsa.org.au/pub/docs/galac.txt

DIRC provides a professional and friendly information and referral service to the people of South Australia.

2865 Galactosemia Resources and Information
PO Box 1512
Deerfield Beach, FL 33443
866-900-7421
www.galactosemia.com

Information about galactosemia.

Scott Shepard, President
Scott Saylor, Vice President
Paul Fowler, Treasurer

2866 Online Mendelian Inheritance in Man
McKusick-Nathans Institue of Genetic Medicine-JHU
Baltimore, MD 21205
www.omim.org

This database is a catalog of human genes and genetic disorders.

Ada Hamosh, MD, Scientific Director

2867 Parents of Galactosemic Children
www.galactosemia.com

www.galactosemia.com

National nonprofit, volunteer organization whose mission is to provide information, support and networking opportunities to families affected by galactosemia.

Scott Shepard, President
Scott Saylor, Vice President
Paul Fowler, Treasurer

2868 Save Babies Through Screening Foundation
PO Box 2313
Palm Harbor, FL 34682
888-454-3383
email@savebabies.org
www.savebabies.org

Is a national, nonprofit, public charity run by volunteers. Its mission is to improve the lives of babies by working to prevent disabilities and early death resulting from disorders detectable through newborn screening.

Jill Levy-Fisch, President
Sarah Wilkerson, Vice President
Anne Rugari, Treasurer

Description

2869 GAUCHER'S DISEASE
Synonyms: Gaucher disease, Glucosylceramide lipidosis, Glucosyl cerebroside lipidosis
Covers these related disorders: Chronic Gaucher's disease (Adult or Classic Gaucher's disease), Infantile Gaucher's disease, Juvenile Gaucher's disease
Involves the following Biologic System(s):
Genetic/Chromosomal/Syndrome/Metabolic Disorders

Gaucher's disease is an inherited metabolic disorder characterized by a deficiency of the enzyme glucocerebrosidase (glucosylceramidase), which assists in the metabolism of certain fats (lipidosis). This deficiency results in the accumulation of certain fatty substances (glucocerebroside or glucosylceramide) throughout the body. Although uncommon, Gaucher's disease is the lipidosis seen most often by physicians. Gaucher's disease is subdivided into three main types. The first, known as chronic, adult, or classic Gaucher's disease, may develop at any age from birth to 80 years old. This form of the disease is common among eastern European Jews, with an incidence rate of as many as one in 500 births. Findings associated with chronic Gaucher's disease include enlargement of the spleen (splenomegaly) or liver (hepatomegaly), or both (hepatosplenomegaly); a decrease in levels of hemoglobin in the blood (anemia); decreased numbers of circulating white blood cells (leukopenia); and abnormally low levels of circulating platelets (thrombocytopenia), which may lead to easy bruising or bleeding. Symptoms may include a brownish-pigmented skin; yellow spots in the eyes resulting from accumulation of fatty substances; and bone pain resulting from accumulations in the bone marrow. Treatment for chronic Gaucher's disease includes enzyme replacement therapy.

Infantile Gaucher's disease, a life-threatening form of this disorder, affects the central nervous system of the newborn. Symptoms and findings may include enlargement of the spleen, crossed eyes (strabismus); muscle spasms in the jaw (trismus or lockjaw); seizures; backward bending of the head; or a rigid, arched back. Additional abnormalities of the central nervous system may become apparent.

Juvenile Gaucher's disease may appear at any time during childhood. Characteristic findings may include enlargement of the liver and spleen (hepatosplenomegaly), bone abnormalities resulting in pain and swelling of the joints, anemia, and abnormally low levels of circulating white blood cells and platelets. Affected children may be pale, weak, and particularly susceptible to bleeding and recurring infection. Symptoms related to nervous system involvement include lack of motor coordination and loss of balance, inflammation of the nerves in the arms and legs accompanied by abnormal sensations and discomfort, muscle spasms, paralysis of the nerves of the eye (ophthalmoplegia), and impairment of mental function.

Enzyme replacement therapy is usually not effective in the treatment of the infantile and juvenile forms of Gaucher's disease. Alternative treatment may include removal of the spleen (splenectomy). Other treatment is symptomatic and supportive.

Gaucher's disease is inherited as an autosomal recessive trait. The gene responsible for the regulation of the enzyme glucocerebrosidase is located on the long arm of chromosome 1 (1q21-q31).

National Associations & Support Groups

2870 American Academy of Pediatrics
345 Park Blvd
Itasca, IL 60143
800-433-9016
Fax: 847-434-8000
mcc@aap.org
www.aap.org

The American Academy of Pediatrics and its member pediatricians are committed to the attainment of optimal physical, mental and social health and well-being for all infants, children, adolescents, and young adults.
Lynn Olson, PhD, VP, Research
Mark Del Monte, JD, CEO/Executive VP
Vera Tait, MD, FAAP, Chief Medical Officer

2871 Arc of the United States
1825 K Street NW, Ste 1200
Washington, DC 20006
202-534-3700
800-433-5255
Fax: 202-534-3731
info@thearc.org
www.thearc.org

The Arc of the United States advocates for the rights and full participation of all children and adults with intellectual and developmental disabilities. Together with a network of members and affiliated chapters, they improve systems of support and services; connect families; inspire communities and influence public policy.
Peter V. Berns, CEO

2872 Genetic Alliance
426400 Woodfield Road, Ste 189
Damascus, MD 20872
202-966-5557
Fax: 202-966-8553
info@geneticalliance.org
www.geneticalliance.org

World's leading nonprofit health advocacy organization committed to transforming health through genetics and promoting an environment of openness centered on the health of individuals, families, and communities.
Sharon Terry, CEO
Ruth Child, CFO
Natasha Bonhomme, Chief Strategy Officer

2873 National Gaucher Foundation
5410 Edson Lane, Suite 220
Rockville, MD 20852
800-504-3189
www.gaucherdisease.org

A nonprofit organization whose primary objective is to assist in perfecting a treatment program and discovering a cure for Gaucher disease. The Foundation supports medical research and clinical programs which enhance the current understanding of Gaucher disease.
Brian Berman, President & CEO
Robin Ely, Clinical Director
Noreen Layne, Program Manager

2874 National Tay-Sachs and Allied Diseases Association
2001 Beacon Street, Suite 204
Boston, MA 02135
617-277-4463
info@ntsad.org
www.ntsad.org

Direct, fund and promote research to develop treatments and cures; provides comprehensive support services to affected families and individuals; guides prevention, education, awareness and screening through effective grassroots collaborations with chapters and affiliates; lead advocacy efforts as the recognized authority for this family of genetic diseases.
Kathleen Flynn, Chief Executive Officer
Valerie Greger, PhD, Director of Research
Diana Jussila, Director of Family Services

Gaucher's Disease / Web Sites

Web Sites

2875 Arc of the United States
1825 K Street NW, Ste 1200
Washington, DC 20006
202-534-3700
800-433-5255
Fax: 202-534-3731
info@thearc.org
www.thearc.org

The Arc of the United States advocates for the rights and full participation of all children and adults with intellectual and developmental disabilities. Together with a network of members and affiliated chapters, they improve systems of support and services; connect families; inspire communities and influence public policy.

Peter V. Berns, CEO
Kristen McKiernan, Sr Exec. Offcr, Comms & Marketing
Liz Mahar, Director, Family/Sibling Initiative

2876 Children's Gaucher Research Fund
8110 Warren Court
Granite Bay, CA 95746
916-797-3700
Fax: 916-797-3707
research@childrensgaucher.org
www.childrensgaucher.org

We are a nonprofit organization, that raises funds to coordinate and support research to find a cure for type 2 and type 3 Gaucher disease.

Roscoe Brady, MD, Member, Scientific Advisory Board
Gregory Grabowski, MD, Member, Scientific Advisory Board
Kondi Wong, MD, USAF, MC, Member, Scientific Advisory Board

2877 Clinical Genetic Services-Department of Pediatrics
Hassenfeld Children's Hospital at NYU Langone
424 East 34th Street
New York, NY 10016
212-263-7300
Fax: 646-754-2250
nyulangone.org

Offers evaluations, genetic counseling and testing. Clinical services include carrier testing, prenatal counseling, and complete genetic evaluations for children and adults.

John G. Pappas, MD, Pediatric Genetic Associate
Naomi Yachelevich, MD, Pediatric Genetic Associate

2878 Gaucher Registry
Genzyme Corporation, 500 Kendall Street
Cambridge, MA 2142
617-591-5500
800-745-4447
www.registrynxt.com

Our goal is to significantly contribute to the medical understanding of Gaucher disease and to improve the quality of care for Gaucher patients worldwide through active publication of Registry findings and disease management approaches.

2879 Health Answers Education Sudler-WPP Health Practice
700 Dresher Road
Horsham, PA 19044
215-442-9010
www.healthanswers.com

HealthAnswers offers a breadth of services in medical education, sales force training, patient support, solutions, professional promotion and consumer solutions.

Mike Hudnall, CEO

2880 National Gaucher Foundation
5410 Edson Lane, Suite 220
Rockville, MD 20852
800-504-3189
www.gaucherdisease.org

A non-profit organization whose primary objective is to assist in perfecting a treatment program and discovering a cure for Gaucher disease. The Foundation supports medical research and clinical programs which enhance the current understanding of Gaucher disease.

Brian Berman, President & CEO
Robin Ely, Clinical Director
Noreen Layne, Program Manager

Description

2881 GROWTH HORMONE DEFICIENCY
Synonym: GH deficiency
Involves the following Biologic System(s):
Endocrinologic Disorders

Growth hormone deficiency is a condition characterized by deficient production or an impaired response to growth hormone (GH), resulting in growth impairment and short stature with normal proportions of the head, limbs, hands, and feet (pituitary dwarfism). Secreted by the pituitary gland in the brain. GH, also known as somatotropin, stimulates body growth and development by promoting the production of protein in cells, releasing energy through the breakdown of fats, and performing other vital functions. Also known as the master gland, the pituitary gland is connected, through a bundle of nerve fibers known as the pituitary stalk, to a region of the brain known as the hypothalamus, which controls the functioning of the pituitary gland through direct stimulation by nerves as well as through the actions of proteins known as hormone-releasing and hormone-inhibiting factors that the hypothalamus releases into the bloodstream for transport to the pituitary gland. The forward or anterior region of the pituitary gland secretes GH in response to the particular hormone-releasing factor known as growth hormone releasing factor (GHRF), which is carried by the blood from the hypothalamus to the pituitary gland.

Depending upon the underlying cause of GH deficiency, some patients with this condition may also have deficiencies of other hormones produced by the anterior pituitary gland, such as thyroid-stimulating hormone (TSH), which stimulates the production of thyroid hormones, or adrenocorticotropic hormone (ACTH), which promotes the growth and production of hormones by cells in the outer region (cortex) of the adrenal gland. Inadequate functioning of the pituitary gland is known as hypopituitarism.

GH deficiency may have many different causes, including absence, underdevelopment, or malformation of the pituitary gland or hypothalamus at birth; tumors of the anterior pituitary gland, pituitary stalk, or hypothalamus, particularly the type of pituitary tumors known as craniopharyngiomas; or radiation given for the treatment of certain cancers of the brain or other organs in the head. GH deficiency may also result from trauma affecting the pituitary gland or hypothalamus, such as injury during birth or interruption of the oxygen supplied to the brain (anoxia) by the lungs and red cells of the blood. Other causes of GH deficiency include some abnormalities affecting the genes or chromosomes that carry the structural plans for GH and the body's other substances, and some conditions that occur randomly for unknown reasons (idiopathic hypopituitarism). Moreover, some genetically caused types of hypopituitarism may result in GH deficiency alone or accompanied by deficiencies of other hormones produced by the anterior pituitary gland.

There are several genetic subtypes of isolated growth hormone deficiency (IGHD), including those that may be inherited as an autosomal recessive, autosomal dominant, or X-linked trait. Autosomal recessive IGHD may be caused by the complete absence of a gene known as the GH1 gene, located on chromosome 17. This form of IGHD is typically characterized by marked growth delays after birth and severe shortness of stature. Other types of autosomal recessive IGHD are caused by various other abnormalities (mutations) of the GH1 gene, causing varying degrees of growth failure and short stature. Some patients with autosomal dominant IGHD may also have mutations of the GH1 gene. The gene responsible for X-linked IGHD, so named because this gene is located on the X chromosome, has not yet been identified. The genetic form of growth impairment known as Laron syndrome is caused by deficient function of the pituitary gland, (hypopituitarism) and is thought to result from an impaired response to GH. This condition is characterized by abnormally increased levels of GH in the blood.

Most children with GH deficiency are of normal weight and length at birth. By the first year of life, children with severe GH deficiency or Laron syndrome may be significantly shorter than would be expected for their age and sex. Patients with less severe GH deficiency experience regular growth spurts that alternate with periods during which no growth occurs. Patients with GH deficiency may continue to experience growth beyond the age when most individuals attain their adult height. This is due to abnormal delays in the fusion of the growing ends (epiphyseal plates) and shafts of the long bones of the legs and arms. If children with GH deficiency do not receive treatment, their adult height may range from moderately to severely below the average height for a mature adult.

Children with GH deficiency typically have normally proportioned arms and legs, but they may have relatively small hands and feet. Many also have a characteristic facial appearance, including a short, broad face and relatively round head; an undeveloped upper and lower jaw; a small, saddle-shaped nose with a depressed nasal bridge; a small neck; delayed eruption and crowding of the teeth; and fine, sparse scalp hair. Because of abnormal smallness of the voice box (larynx), many patients with GH deficiency have a high-pitched voice. Other findings may include underdeveloped genitals, delayed or absent sexual development, and abnormally low concentrations of the sugar known as glucose (hypoglycemia).

Children with GH deficiency caused by tumors of the pituitary gland or hypothalamus may experience effects beyond growth deficiency, depending upon the location, nature, and growth of the tumor. In some patients, invasion and destruction of the pituitary gland cause degeneration (atrophy) of the thyroid gland, sex glands (gonads), and outer regions of the adrenal glands (adrenal cortex). Associated findings may include absence of sweating, weight loss, abnormal sensitivity to cold, delayed or absent sexual maturation, lack of response to certain stimuli (torpor), or other abnormalities. Tumors in the pituitary gland or hypothalamus may also cause total growth failure, abnormally increased urination (polyuria), vomiting, headaches, visual disturbances, episodes of abnormally increased electrical activity in the brain (seizures), and other abnormalities.

The treatment of GH deficiency depends on its underlying cause and nature. If GH deficiency is caused by a tumor, its treatment may include surgery, radiation therapy, or other appropriate measures to eliminate the tumor. Pituitary function should be carefully evaluated after such measures, in order to determine the appropriate treatment for pituitary abnormalities caused by the tumor or its treatment. The treatment of children with IGHD includes early replacement therapy with synthetic GH, which is continued until there is no further growth in response to the treatment. The maximum response usually occurs during the first year of treatment, with further treatment producing slower growth. Because such therapy may cause abnormally decreased activity of the thyroid gland (hypothyroidism), thyroid function should be regularly evaluated. Children with deficiencies of other anterior pituitary hormones in association with GH deficiency may receive additional hormone replacement therapies as required. Other treatment for GH deficiency is symptomatic and supportive.

Growth Hormone Deficiency / Government Agencies

Government Agencies

2882 NIH/ Eunice Kennedy Shriver National Institute of Child Health & Human Development
P.O. Box 3006
Rockville, MD 20847

800-370-2943
Fax: 866-760-5947
www.nichd.nih.gov

Conducts and supports research on topics related to the health of children, adults, families and populations. Some of these topics include: developmental disabilities, growth and development, infant death, reproductive health and birth defects.

Diana W. Bianchi, Director
Alison Cernich, PhD, Deputy Director

National Associations & Support Groups

2883 American Academy of Pediatrics
345 Park Blvd
Itasca, IL 60143

800-433-9016
Fax: 847-434-8000
mcc@aap.org
www.aap.org

The American Academy of Pediatrics and its member pediatricians are committed to the attainment of optimal physical, mental and social health and well-being for all infants, children, adolescents, and young adults.

Lynn Olson, PhD, VP, Research
Mark Del Monte, JD, CEO/Executive VP
Vera Tait, MD, FAAP, Chief Medical Officer

2884 Genetic Alliance
426400 Woodfield Road, Ste 189
Damascus, MD 20872

202-966-5557
Fax: 202-966-8553
info@geneticalliance.org
www.geneticalliance.org

World's leading nonprofit health advocacy organization committed to transforming health through genetics and promoting an environment of openness centered on the health of individuals, families, and communities.

Sharon Terry, CEO
Ruth Child, CFO
Natasha Bonhomme, Chief Strategy Officer

2885 Human Growth Foundation
997 Glen Cove Avenue, Suite 5
Glen Head, NY 11545

800-451-6434
Fax: 516-671-4055
hgfl@hgfound.org
www.hgfound.org

A voluntary, nonprofit organization whose mission is to help children and adults with disorders of growth and growth hormones through research, education, support and advocacy. The foundation is dedicated to helping medical science to better understand the process of growth. It is composed of concerned parents and friends of children and adults with growth problems; and interested health professionals.

Joel Steelman, MD, President
Emily Germain-Lee, MD, Vice President

2886 Little People of America
617 Broadway #518
Sonoma, CA 95476

714-368-3689
888-572-2001
Fax: 707-721-1896
info@lpaonline.org
www.lpaonline.org

A nonprofit organization that provides support and information to people of short stature and their families.

Deb Himsel, Executive Director
Mark Povinelli, President

2887 MAGIC Foundation: Major Aspects of Growth in Children
4200 Cantera Drive, #106
Warrenville, IL 60555

630-836-8200
800-362-4423
Fax: 630-836-8181
contactus@magicfoundation.org
www.magicfoundation.org

A national nonprofit organization providing support and education regarding growth disorders in children and related adult disorders. Provides educational information, networking, a national conference, a kids' program and an extensive medical library.

10,000 members

Dianne Kremidas, Executive Director
Mary Andrews, CEO
Teresa Tucker, Patient Advocacy

2888 March of Dimes Foundation
1550 Crystal Drive, Ste 1300
Arlington, VA 22202

888-663-4637
www.marchofdimes.org

March of Dimes help moms have full-term pregnancies and research the problems that threaten the health of babies. The March of Dimes also acts globally: sharing best practices in perinatal health and helping improve birth outcomes where the needs are the most urgent.

Stacey D. Stewart, President
Alan Brogdon, SVP/COO/Board Officer
Rahul Gupta, MD, SVP & Chief Medical/Health Officer

State Agencies & Support Groups

Arkansas

2889 Little People of America - District 7
National Headquarters
617 Broadway #518
Sonoma, CA 95476

714-368-3689
888-572-2001
Fax: 707-721-1896
info@lpaonline.org
www.lpaonline.org

District 7 of the Little People of America represents short stature individuals from the states of Arkansas, Kansas, Missouri and Oklahoma.

Deb Himsel, Executive Director
Mark Povinelli, President
Cuquis Robledo, Public Relations Director

California

2890 Little People of America - San Francisco Bay Area Chapter
National Headquarters
617 Broadway #518
Sonoma, CA 95476

714-368-3689
888-572-2001
Fax: 707-721-1896
info@lpaonline.org
www.lpaonline.org

A nonprofit organization that provides support and information to people of short stature and their families.

Deb Himsel, Executive Director
Mark Povinelli, President
Cuquis Robledo, Public Relations Director

Kansas

2891 Little People of America - District 7
National Headquarters
617 Broadway #518
Sonoma, CA 95476

714-368-3689
888-572-2001
Fax: 707-721-1896
info@lpaonline.org
www.lpaonline.org

Growth Hormone Deficiency / Research Centers

District 7 of the Little People of America represents short stature individuals from the states of Arkansas, Kansas, Missouri and Oklahoma.

Deb Himsel, Executive Director
Mark Povinelli, President
Cuquis Robledo, Public Relations Director

Missouri

2892 Little People of America - District 7
National Headquarters
617 Broadway #518
Sonoma, CA 95476
714-368-3689
888-572-2001
Fax: 707-721-1896
info@lpaonline.org
www.lpaonline.org

District 7 of the Little People of America represents short stature individuals from the states of Arkansas, Kansas, Missouri and Oklahoma.

Deb Himsel, Executive Director
Mark Povinelli, President
Cuquis Robledo, Public Relations Director

New Jersey

2893 Little People of America - District 2
National Headquarters
617 Broadway #518
Sonoma, CA 95476
714-368-3689
888-572-2001
Fax: 707-721-1896
info@lpaonline.org
www.lpaonline.org

A nonprofit organization that provides support and information to people of short stature and their families.

Deb Himsel, Executive Director
Mark Povinelli, President
Cuquis Robledo, Public Relations Director

New York

2894 Little People of America - District 2
National Headquarters
617 Broadway #518
Sonoma, CA 95476
714-368-3689
888-572-2001
Fax: 707-721-1896
info@lpaonline.org
www.lpaonline.org

A nonprofit organization that provides support and information to people of short stature and their families.

Deb Himsel, Executive Director
Mark Povinelli, President
Cuquis Robledo, Public Relations Director

Oklahoma

2895 Little People of America - District 7
National Headquarters
617 Broadway #518
Sonoma, CA 95476
714-368-3689
888-572-2001
Fax: 707-721-1896
info@lpaonline.org
www.lpaonline.org

District 7 of the Little People of America represents short stature individuals from the states of Arkansas, Kansas, Missouri and Oklahoma.

Deb Himsel, Executive Director
Mark Povinelli, President
Cuquis Robledo, Public Relations Director

Pennsylvania

2896 Little People of America - District 2
National Headquarters
617 Broadway #518
Sonoma, CA 95476
714-368-3689
888-572-2001
Fax: 707-721-1896
info@lpaonline.org
www.lpaonline.org

A nonprofit organization that provides support and information to people of short stature and their families.

Deb Himsel, Executive Director
Mark Povinelli, President
Cuquis Robledo, Public Relations Director

Utah

2897 Little People of America - Utah Seagulls
National Headquarters
250 El Camino Real, Suite 218
Tustin, CA 92780
714-368-3689
888-572-2001
Fax: 714-368-3367
info@lpaonline.org
www.utahlittlepeople.org

A nonprofit organization that provides support and information to people of short stature and their families.

Steve Hatch, President

Research Centers

2898 Case Western Research University, Bolton Brush Growth Study Center
10900 Euclid Ave.
Cleveland, OH 44106
216-368-0592
Fax: 216-368-3204
mgh4@cwru.edu
www.case.edu

Investigations and research into the growth and development of the human body.

Kate Chapman, Manager

2899 Jackson Laboratory
600 Main Streeet
Bar Harbor, ME 04609
207-288-6000
800-474-9880
Fax: 207-288-6079
www.jax.org

Studies focusing on growth disorders and human genetics.

Rick Woychik, Executive Director

2900 New Jersey Institute of Technology Center for Biomedical Engineering
323 Martin Luther King Jr Boulevard
Fenster Hall, Sixth Floor, University Heights
Newark, NJ 07102
973-596-5268
Fax: 973-596-5222
www.njit.edu

Offers research into facial and bone disorders.

Richard Foulds, Director, Masters Program
Judith D. Redling, Coordinator, Undergraduate Program

2901 W.M. Krogman Center for Research In Child Growth and Development
University of Pennsylvania
3451 Walnut Street
Philadelphia, PA 19104
215-898-1470

Focuses research and studies on growth disorders and birth defects.

Solomon Katz, MA, PhD, Director

Growth Hormone Deficiency / Conferences

Conferences

2902 **LPA National Conference**
Little People of America
617 Broadway #518
Sonoma, CA 95476
714-368-3689
888-572-2001
Fax: 707-721-1896
info@lpaonline.org
www.lpaonline.org

July

Deb Himsel, Executive Director
Mark Povinelli, President
Cuquis Robledo, Public Relations Director

Web Sites

2903 **Alliance of Genetic Support Groups**
4301 Conneticut Ave. NW, Suite 404
Washington, DC 20008
202-966-5557
Fax: 202-966-8553
www.geneticalliance.org

Is an international coalition comprised of millions of individuals with genetic conditions and more than 600 advocacy, research and health care orgainizations that represent their interests. As a broad-based coalition of key stakeholders, the Alliance builds partnerships to promote healthy lives for all those living with genetic condtions.

2904 **Health Answers Education Sudler-WPP Health Practice**
700 Dresher Road
Horsham, PA 19044
215-442-9010
www.healthanswers.com

HealthAnswers offers a breadth of services in medical education, sales force training, patient support solutions, professional promotion and consumer solutions.

Mike Hudnall, CEO

2905 **Human Growth Foundation**
www.hgfound.org

www.hgfound.org

A voluntary, nonprofit organization whose mission is to help children and adults with disorders of growth and growth hormones through research, education, support and advocacy. The foundation is dedicated to helping medical science to better understand the process of growth. It is composed of concerned parents and friends of children and adults with growth problems; and interested health professionals.

2906 **Little People of America**
617 Broadway #518
Sonoma, CA 95476
714-368-3689
888-572-2001
Fax: 707-721-1896
info@lpaonline.org
www.lpaonline.org

A nonprofit organization that provides support and information to people of short stature and their families.

Deb Himsel, Executive Director
Mark Povinelli, President

2907 **National Center for Biotechnology Information**
National Library of Medicine, 8600 Rockville Pike
Bethesda, MD 20894
888-346-3656
info@ncbi.nlm.nih.gov
www.ncbi.nlm.nih.gov

NCBI's mission is to develop new information technologoes to aid in the understanding of fundamental molecular and genetic processes that control health and disease.

Patricia Flatley Brennan, RN, PhD, Director
James Ostell, PhD, Executive Secretary

2908 **OHSU Homepage Search**
www.ohsu.edu

www.ohsu.edu

Educates health and high-technology professionals, scientists and enviromental engineers, and it undertakes the indispendible functions of patient care, community service and biomedical research.

2909 **Online Mendelian Inheritance in Man**
McKusick-Nathans Institue of Genetic Medicine-JHU
Baltimore, MD 21205
www.omim.org

This database is a catalog of human genes and genetic disorders.

Ada Hamosh, MD, Scientific Director

2910 **Society for Endocrinology**
22 Apex Court, Woodlands, Bradley Stoke
Bristol, UK BS32
145-464-2200
TTY: 145-464-2210
www.endocrinology.org

Aims to advance education and research in endocrinology for the public benefit.

G R Williams, Chair, Finance Committee
C J McCabe, Chair, Program Committee
D W Ray, Chair, Publications Committee

Book Publishers

2911 **Endocrine & Metabolic Disorders Sourcebook 3rd Edition**
Keith Jones, author

Omnigraphics
615 Griswold Street, Ste 520
Detroit, MI 48226
610-461-3548
800-234-1340
Fax: 800-875-1340
contact@omnigraphics.com
www.omnigraphics.com

Basic information for the lay person about pancreatic and insulin-related disorders such as pancreatitis, diabetes and hypoglycemia; adrenal gland disorders such as Cushing's syndrome, Addison's disease and congenital adrenal hyperplasia; pituitary gland disorders such as growth hormone deficiency, acromegaly and pituitary tumors; and thyroid disorders such as hypothyroidism, Grave's disease, Hashimoto's disease and goiter.

560 pages Hardcover
ISBN: 0-780815-43-8

2912 **Growing Children: A Parent's Guide**
Human Growth Foundation
977 Glen Cove Avenue, Suite 5
Glen Head, NY 11545
516-671-4041
800-451-6434
Fax: 516-671-4055
hgfl@hgfound.org
www.hgfound.org

Offers parents information on the normal pattern of their child's growth, growth charts, recognition of growth problems, evaluation of growth problems and resources for more information. Available to members.

Frank Diamond, MD, President
Emily Germain-Lee, MD, Vice President
Patricia D. Costa, Executive Director

2913 **Short and OK**
Patricia Rieser, Heino FL Mayer-Bahlbug, author

Human Growth Foundation
977 Glen Cove Avenue, Suite 5
Glen Head, NY 11545
516-671-4041
800-451-6434
www.hgfound.org

This is a guide for parents of short children offering information on behavior issues, medical issues and psychological warning signs.

Growth Hormone Deficiency / Pamphlets

54 pages

Newsletters

2914 MAGIC Foundation: Major Aspects of Growth in Children
4200 Cantera Drive, #106
Warrenville, IL 60555
630-836-8200
800-362-4423
Fax: 630-836-8181
TTY: 123-019-99
contactus@magicfoundation.org
www.magicfoundation.org

A national nonprofit organization providing support and education regarding growth disorders in children and related adult disorders. Provides educational information, networking, a national conference, a kids' program and an extensive medical library.

36 pages Quarterly

Dianne Kremidas, Executive Director
Mary Andrews, Chief Executive Officer
Teresa Tucker, Patient Advocacy

2915 Orphan Disease Update
National Organization for Rare Disorders
55 Kenosia Avenue
Danbry, CT 6810
203-744-0100
800-999-6673
Fax: 203-798-2291
orphan@rarediseases.org
www.rarediseases.org

It provides updates on research, advocacy, and special events, as well as advice and sources of help for caregivers, Web sites of interest, current clinical trials, and funding opportunities.

16 pages 3/year

Sheldon M. Schuster, Chair
Peter L Saltonstall, President & CEO
Pamela Gavin, COO

Pamphlets

2916 Dental Problems with Growth Hormone Deficiency
Human Growth Foundation
997 Glen Cove Avenue, Suite 5
Glen Head, NY 11545
516-671-4041
800-451-6434
Fax: 516-671-4055
hgfl@hgfound.org
www.hgfound.org

Growth hormone has a strong effect on bone growth, including the bones of the upper and lower jaws.

Pisit (Duke) Pitukcheewanont, MD, President
Emily Germain-Lee, MD, Vice President
Patricia (Patti) D. Costa, Executive Director

2917 Growth Hormone Deficiency
Human Growth Foundation
997 Glen Cove Avenue, Suite 5
Glen Head, NY 11545
516-671-4041
800-451-6434
Fax: 516-671-4055
hgfl@hgfound.org
www.hgfound.org

Causes and control of growth hormone deficiency.

Pisit (Duke) Pitukcheewanont, MD, President
Emily Germain-Lee, MD, Vice President
Patricia (Patti) D. Costa, Executive Director

2918 Growth Hormone Testing
Human Growth Foundation
997 Glen Cove Avenue, Suite 5
Glen Head, NY 11545
516-671-4041
800-454-6434
Fax: 516-671-4055
hgfl@hgfound.org
www.hgfound.org

Describes how growth hormone testing is used, when growth hormone test is ordered, and what growth hormone test results might mean.

Pisit (Duke) Pitukcheewanont, MD, President
Emily Germain-Lee, MD, Vice President
Patricia (Patti) D. Costa, Executive Director

2919 Intrauterine Growth Restriction
Human Growth Foundation
977 Glen Cove Avenue, Suite 5
Glen Head, NY 11545
516-671-4041
800-451-6434
Fax: 516-761-4055
hgfound.org

Offers information on how to understand this growth disorder and how to cope with it.

Pisit (Duke) Pitukcheewanont, MD, President
Emily Germain-Lee, MD, Vice President
Patricia (Patti) D. Costa, Executive Director

2920 Most Frequently Asked Questions with Growth Hormone Deficiency
Human Growth Foundation
977 Glen Cove Avenue, Suite 5
Glen Head, NY 11545
516-671-4041
800-451-6434
Fax: 516-671-4055
hgfl@hgfound.org
www.hgfound.org

Discusses the consequences of growth hormone deficiency in chidlren and adults.

Pisit (Duke) Pitukcheewanont, MD, President
Emily Germain-Lee, MD, Vice President
Patricia (Patti) D. Costa, Executive Director

Guillain-Barre Syndrome / Description

Description

2921 GUILLAIN-BARRE SYNDROME

Synonyms: Acute ascending polyneuritis, Acute febrile polyneuritis, Acute idiopathic polyneuritis, Acute postinfectious polyneuropathy, GBS, Landry's paralysis

Involves the following Biologic System(s):

Neurologic Disorders

Guillain-Barre syndrome (GBS) (pronounced gE-Ian-ba-rA) is a progressive neurologic disorder that affects many nerves (polyneuropathy) and is characterized by unusual sensations (paresthesias) in the arms, legs, or both. GBS generally causes progressive muscle weakness over days and, in some cases, paralysis accompanied by lack of muscle tone. Guillain-Barre syndrome is thought to be an autoimmune disorder and may occur as a reaction to a previous viral infection, immunization, or bacterial infection (e.g., Lyme disease). Autoimmune disorders involve the body's inappropriate immune response to its own healthy tissues.e symptoms of GBS typically begin approximately one to three weeks following the triggering event.

Symptoms associated with Guillain-Barre syndrome range from mild to severe and may include numbness, tingling, muscle weakness, and sometimes paralysis that begins in the legs and then usually spreads upward toward the trunk, arms, muscles of the chest, and sometimes the face (ascending paralysis). Affected children may become irritable and unable or unwilling to walk. As weakness spreads to the chest and facial areas, muscles required for speech, breathing, and eating may become affected. In addition, if the nerves of the autonomic nervous system which control vital involuntary functions are affected, individuals with GBS may develop fluctuations in blood pressure and heart rate as well as other heart irregularities. A rare form of Guillain-Barreyndrome called the Miller-Fisher syndrome is characterized by paralysis of the nerves and muscles of the eyes (ophthalmoplegia), an absence of normal reflexes (areflexia), and an inability to coordinate voluntary movement (ataxia).

Most children with Guillain-Barre syndrome recover completely within two to three weeks. Some may experience ongoing muscular weakness. In addition, in rare cases, affected individuals may experience prolonged or recurring episodes of GBS that may last for months or years. These uncommon manifestations are referred to as chronic unremitting polyradiculoneuropathy and chronic relapsing polyradiculoneuropathy.

Guillain-Barre syndrome may be diagnosed through specialized tests of the fluid that surrounds the brain and spinal cord (cerebrospinal fluid) and other clinical findings. Early diagnosis and hospitalization allow for observation and monitoring of affected individuals. If the progression of muscle weakness or paralysis is very slow and limited, treatment may include observation and supportive care until recovery is complete. If, however, paralysis progresses to involve breathing and swallowing, appropriate support is necessary. Other treatment may include plasma exchange (plasmapheresis), a procedure during which blood is withdrawn and the liquid portion (plasma) removed in order to filter out harmful substances. A plasma substitute is then mixed with the blood, and the reconstituted blood is then returned to the body. Alternative treatment may include the intravenous administration of immunoglobulin (IVIG). In some cases, certain immunosuppressive drugs or corticosteroids may be effective.

Physical therapy may aid in the maintenance of joint and muscle function. Other treatment is symptomatic and supportive.

National Associations & Support Groups

2922 American Academy of Pediatrics
345 Park Blvd
Itasca, IL 60143
800-433-9016
Fax: 847-434-8000
mcc@aap.org
www.aap.org

The American Academy of Pediatrics and its member pediatricians are committed to the attainment of optimal physical, mental and social health and well-being for all infants, children, adolescents, and young adults.

Lynn Olson, PhD, VP, Research
Mark Del Monte, JD, CEO/Executive VP
Vera Tait, MD, FAAP, Chief Medical Officer

2923 American Autoimmune Related Diseases Association
19176 Hall Road, Suite 130
Clinton, MI 48038
586-776-3900
aarda@aarda.org
www.aarda.org

The American Autoimmune Related Diseases Association is dedicated to the eradication of autoimmune diseases and the alleviation of suffering and the socioeconomic impact of autoimmunity through fostering and facilitating collaboration in the areas of education, public awareness, research, and patient services in an effective, ethical and efficient manner.

Lilly Stairs, Interim President/CEO
Laura Simpson, COO

2924 GBS/CIDP Foundation International
375 E Elm Street, Suite 101
Conshohocken, PA 19428
866-224-3301
www.gbs-cidp.org

Provides emotional support and assistance to people affected by this rare disease. Arranges personal visits to affected individuals in hospitals and rehabilitation centers. Fosters research into the cause, treatment, and other aspects of the disorder and directs affected individuals with long-term disabilities to resources for vocational, financial, and other aspects of the disorder.

Lisa Butler, Executive Director
Laura Blair, Chief Financial Officer
Estelle Benson, Founder

Web Sites

2925 American Autoimmune Related Diseases Association
www.aarda.org
586-776-3900
aarda@aarda.org
www.aarda.org

The American Autoimmune Related Diseases Association is dedicated to the eradication of autoimmune diseases and the alleviation of suffering and the socioeconomic impact of autoimmunity through fostering and facilitating collaboration in the areas of education, public awareness, research, and patient services in an effective, ethical and efficient manner.

2926 GBS Support Group of the UK
Woodholme House, Heckingt, Li NG34
152-946-9910
080-037-4803
Fax: 152-946-9915
www.gbs.org.uk/

Objectives are to: provide emotional support to patients, families and friends; provide, when possible, personal visits by former patients to those currently in hospitals and rehabilitation centres and those recovering; supply a comprehensive short guide for patients, relatives and friends, and other literature, so that patients and their families can learn what to expect during the illness; and to educate the public and medical community about the Support Group.

Caroline Morrice, Director
Lesley Dimmick, Charity Officer
Chris Fuller, Trustee

Book Publishers

2927 **Immune System Disorders Sourcebook 3rd Edition**
Keith Jones, author

Omnigraphics
615 Griswold Street, Ste 520
Detroit, MI 48226

610-461-3548
800-234-1340
Fax: 800-875-1340
contact@omnigraphics.com
www.omnigraphics.com

Basic information about lupus, multiple sclerosis, guillain-barre syndrome and more.

624 pages Hardcover
ISBN: 0-780807-48-0

Pamphlets

2928 **Fact Sheet: Guillain-Barre Syndrome**
National Inst. of Neurological Disorders/Stroke
PO Box 5801
Bethesda, MD 20824

301-496-5751
800-352-9424

Information about Guillain-Barren Syndrome, what causes Guillain-Barren Syndrome, how is it diagnosed and treated, etc. Also available in Spanish.

HIV Infection / Description

Description

2929 HIV INFECTION
Synonyms: Fetal AIDS, Acquired Immune Deficiency Syndrome
Involves the following Biologic System(s):
Immunologic and Rheumatologic Disorders, Infectious Disorders

HIV Infection destroys the body's ability to fight infections, resulting in Acquired Immune Deficiency, or AIDS. T-cells, which are responsible for responding to infections, are destroyed by the virus. The process is slow and silent, which means that HIV can be contracted unwittingly years before any symptoms appear. As the T-cells are destroyed, organisms that are usually defeated by a normal immune system, infect the body. Patients suffer from one infection after another. HIV is usually spread from an infected person to a non-infected person by unprotected sexual intercourse, or by sharing needles. Most young children with AIDS contract the disease through in utero transmission; however, infants may occasionally acquire the infection through mother's milk. In addition, children with hemophilia and others who may have received transfusions of blood or blood products before HIV blood-screening became standard in 1985 may have become infected by contaminated blood.

Some children with HIV infection develop symptoms in the first or second year of life, while the majority may not show signs of infection for several years. AIDS is diagnosed in about 50 percent of HIV-infected children by three years of age. Early signs may include chronic or recurrent fevers and diarrhea, rashes, swollen lymph glands (lymphadenopathy), enlarged liver and spleen (hepatosplenomegaly), and delays in growth and nervous system development. Some infants and young children are anemic, experience weight and appetite loss, decreased energy, and irregularities of the heart and kidneys. Early symptoms may include chronic or recurrent bacterial infections and uncommon viral, fungal, and other types of infections caused by microorganisms that do not ordinarily cause disease or infections. As the immune system continues to weaken, children may develop lung inflammations and potentially life-threatening pneumocystis pneumonia. Children with AIDS are also at increased risk for certain types of malignant diseases such as non-Hodgkin's lymphoma.

Most infants born to mothers with HIV show antibodies in their blood for approximately 12 to 14 months. In infants who are not infected with the virus, these passive antibodies disappear. For this reason, standardized HIV testing is not conclusive in children younger than 18 months. However, HIV infection in these children may often be detected through the use of virus cultures and a specialized DNA-copying technique called polymerase chain reaction or| PCR.

Prevention of HIV and subsequent AIDS infection in infants may be directed toward counseling of at-risk women of child-bearing age who may be advised to avoid becoming pregnant. The strictly prescribed administration of the drug AZT during the last six months of pregnancy, as well as during labor and delivery, has been shown to greatly improve the chances of an HIV-infected mother delivering an infant who is not infected with HIV. In fact, congenitally acquired HIV has been reduced dramatically in recent years. Delivery by Cesarean section may also reduce risk of transmission to the newborn. In addition, mothers with HIV should refrain from breast-feeding their infants, as there is some evidence of HIV transmission from mother to child in women who may have contracted the virus after pregnancy.

Infants and children with HIV may be treated with antibiotics to prevent pneumocystis pneumonia. Intravenous gamma globulin therapy may be used to maintain or increase the ability of the immune system to fight the effects of secondary infections. In addition, certain steroidal drugs may be administered to treat lymphoid interstitial pneumonitis, while AZT, alone or in combination, is often used to treat children and has been found to be particularly effectiv|e against neurologic irregularities. Additional therapies are also being tested in children. Other treatment is symptomatic and supportive.

Government Agencies

2930 NIH/National Institute of Allergy and Infectious Diseases
5601 Fishers Lane, MSC 9806
Bethesda, MD 20892
301-496-5717
866-284-4107
Fax: 301-402-3573
TDD: 800-877-8339
ocpostoffice@niaid.nih.gov
www.niaid.nih.gov

The principal advisory board of the NIAID. The council is composed of physicians, scientists and representatives of the public and advises on the conduct and support or research, training and dissemination of health information regarding allergies and infectious diseases.

Anthony S. Fauci, MD, Director

National Associations & Support Groups

2931 AIDS Healthcare Foundation
6255 Sunset Boulevard, 21st Floor
Los Angeles, CA 90028
323-860-5200
info@aidshealth.org
www.aidshealth.org

AIDS Healthcare Foundation (AHF) is a global organization providing cutting-edge medicine and advocacy to over 1 million patients in 43 countries worldwide in the US, Africa, Latin America/Caribbean, the Asia/Pacific Region and Eastern Europe.

Michael Weinstein, President
Peter Reis, Senior Vice President
Lyle Honig Mojica, Chief Financial Officer

2932 AIDS United
1634 Eye Street NW, Suite 1100
Washington, DC 20006
202-408-4848
Fax: 202-408-1818
www.aidsunited.org

AIDS United's mission is to end the HIV epidemic in the United States.

Jesse Milan, Jr., President & CEO
Bradley Kiley, VP & Chief Operating Officer
Athena Cross, VP & Chief Programs Officer

2933 American Academy of HIV Medicine
1600 K Street NW, Suite 350
Washington, DC 20006
202-659-0699
Fax: 202-659-0976
www.aahivm.org

The American Academy of HIV Medicine is the nation's leading independent organization of healthcare professionals dedicated to providing excellence in HIV care and prevention. Our membership of practitioners and credentialed clinicians manage the health of the majority of people with and at risk for HIV in the United States.

Bruce J. Packett II, Executive Director
Scott Brawley, Director, Policy & Programs
Aaron Austin, Director, Membership Services

2934 American Academy of Pediatrics
345 Park Blvd
Itasca, IL 60143
800-433-9016
Fax: 847-434-8000
mcc@aap.org
www.aap.org

The American Academy of Pediatrics and its member pediatricians are committed to the attainment of optimal physical, mental and social health and well-being for all infants, children, adolescents, and young adults.

Lynn Olson, PhD, VP, Research
Mark Del Monte, JD, CEO/Executive VP
Vera Tait, MD, FAAP, Chief Medical Officer

2935 American College of Preventive Medicine
1200 First Street NE, Suite 315
Washington, DC 20002
202-466-2044
info@acpm.org
www.acpm.org

The mission is to improve the health of individuals and populations through evidence-based health promotion, disease prevention, and systems-based approaches to improving health and health care.

Donna Grande, Chief Executive Officer
Anita Balan, Project Director
Melissa Ferrari, VP, Memberships & Operations

2936 American Foundation for Children with AIDS
1520 Greening Lane
Harrisburg, PA 17110
888-683-8323
info@afcaids.org
www.afcaids.org

A non-profit organization providing critical support to infected and affected HIV and children and their caregivers.

Tanya Weaver, Executive Director
Michelle Miller, Executive Assistant
Betsy Dorsey, Warehouse Manager

2937 American Nurses Association
8515 Georgia Avenue, Suite 400
Silver Spring, MD 20910
800-284-2378
customerservice@ana.org
www.nursingworld.org

The American Nurses Association (ANA) is the only full-service professional organization representing the interests of the nation's 3.1 million registered nurses through its constituent and state nurses associations and its organizational affiliates.

Loressa Cole, Chief Executive Officer

2938 American Psychiatric Association
800 Maine Avenue SW, Suite 900
Washington, DC 20024
202-559-3900
apa@psych.org
www.psychiatry.org

It is a medical specialty society representing growing membership of more than 36,000 psychiatrists.

Saul Levin, MD, CEO & Medical Director

2939 American Psychological Association
750 First St. NE
Washington, DC 20002
202-336-5500
800-374-2721
TTY: 202-336-6123
www.apa.org

The mission is to advance the creation, communication and application of psychological knowledge to benefit society and improve people's lives.

Arthur C. Evans Jr, PhD, CEO/EVP

2940 American Public Health Association
800 I Street, NW
Washington, DC 20001
202-777-2742
Fax: 202-777-2534
TTY: 202-777-2500
www.apha.org

APHA champions the health of all people and all communities. They aim to strengthen the public health profession and speak out for public health issues and policies backed by science.

Georges C. Benjamin, MD, Executive Director
Kemi Oluwafemi, MBA, CPA, Chief Financial Officer
Susan Polan, PhD, Associate Executive Director

2941 American Sexual Health Association
PO Box 13827
Research Triangle Park, NC 27709
919-361-8400
Fax: 919-361-8425
info@ashasexualhealth.org
www.ashasexualhealth.org

The American Sexual Health Association (ASHA) empowers individuals, families, and communities to achieve sexually healthy lives through education and advocacy. ASHA is an award-winning non-profit organization that has advocated on behalf of those at risk for sexually transmitted infections (STIs) since 1914.

Lynn Barclay, President & CEO
Deborah Arrindell, Vice President, Health Policy

2942 American Society for Microbiology
1752 N Street NW
Washington, DC 20036
202-737-3600
service@asmusa.org
www.asm.org

The American Society for Microbiology is a life science membership organization. Members represent 26 disciplines of microbiological specialization plus a division for microbiology educators.

Jonathan Stevens-Garcia, Chief Operations Officer
Chris DeCesaris, Chief Financial Officer
Catherine Ort-Mabry, Chief Marketing/Comm. Officer

2943 American Society of Clinical Oncology
2318 Mill Road, Suite 800
Alexandria, VA 22314
703-299-0158
888-282-2552
Fax: 703-299-0255
customerservice@asco.org
www.asco.org

Founded in 1964, the American Society of Clinical Oncology is the world's leading professional organization for physicians and oncology professionals caring for people with cancer.

2944 Association of Nurses in AIDS Care
11230 Cleveland Ave. NW, Suite 986
Uniontown, OH 44685
330-670-0101
800-260-6780
Fax: 330-670-0109
anac@anacnet.org
www.nursesinaidscare.org

The mission of the Association is to promote the individual and collective professional development of nurses involved in the delivery of health care to persons infected or affected by the Human Immunodeficiency Virus (HIV) and to promote the health and welfare of infected persons.

Carole Treston, Executive Director
Nakera Dumas, Membership Manager
Bernadette Githiora, Global Coordinator

2945 Association of State and Territorial Health Officials
2231 Crystal Drive, Suite 450
Arlington, VA 22202
202-371-9090
Fax: 571-527-3189
info@astho.org
www.astho.org

The mission is to transform public health within states and territories to help members dramatically improve health and wellness.

Michael R. Fraser, Chief Executive Officer

2946 Black AIDS Institute
3894 Crenshaw Boulevard, Suite 56858
Los Angeles, CA 90056
213-353-3610
www.blackaids.org

It is the only national HIV/AIDS think tank focused exclusively on Black people. The Institute's Mission is to stop the AIDS pandemic in Black communities by engaging and mobilizing Black institutions and individuals in efforts to confront HIV.

Michelle Reese, Chief Program Officer
Wendell Miller, Senior Manager, Operations
Deja Abdul-Haqq, Director, Communications

HIV Infection / National Associations & Support Groups

2947 Elizabeth Glazer Pediatric AIDS Foundation
150 Eye Street NW, Suite 400
Washington, DC 20005
202-296-9165
888-499-4673
Fax: 202-296-9185
info@pedsaids.org
www.pedsaids.org

A national nonprofit organization dealing with medical problems unique to children infected with HIV/AIDS. The foundation is focused specifically on creating a future that will offer hope, finding effective therapies and issues of pregnancy and HIV. The foundation encourages students to enter the world of pediatric AIDS through a student intern program and more.

Charles Lyons, President & CEO

2948 Global Advocacy for HIV Prevention
New York, NY
212-796-6423
Fax: 646-365-3452
www.avac.org

AVAC works to accelerate the ethical development and global delivery of HIV prevention options as part of a comprehensive and integrated response to the epidemic. AVAC's work through education, policy analysis, advocacy and a network of global collaborations aims to deliver proven HIV prevention tools for immediate impact and develop long-term solutions needed to end the epidemic.

Mitchell Warren, Executive Director
Erin Kiernon, Chief Operations Officer
Abigail Smith, Chief Financial Officer

2949 HIV Medicine Association
4040 Wilson Boulevard, ÿSuite 300
Arlington, VA 22203
703-299-0200
Fax: 703-299-0204
info@hivma.org
www.hivma.org

The HIV Medicine Association is an organization of medical professionals who practice HIV medicine.

Andrea Weddle, MSW, Executive Director

2950 Hemophilia Federation of America
999 N Capital Street NE, Suite 301
Washington, DC 20002
202-675-6984
www.hemophiliafed.org

Hemophilia Federation of America (HFA) is a community based organization that serves people with bleeding disorders and their families in the USA. With a broad mission to assist and advocate, HFA provides programs, services and policy education and support through its Member Organization affiliations as well as direct to consumers.

Barbra Kavanaugh, Interim CEO
Heather E. Case, Vice President, Education
Pat Brown, Vice President, Meetings & Services

2951 Immune Deficiency Foundation
7550 Teague Road, Suite 220
Hanover, MD 21076
410-321-6647
Fax: 410-321-9165
www.primaryimmune.org

The only national charitable organization aimed at fighting the primary immune deficiency diseases. The founders included parents of children with primary immune deficiency, immunologists who treat immune deficient patients and other individuals with an interest in helping others. The Foundation's main goal is to improve the care and treatment of adults and children with primary immune deficiency diseases and to promote public education and awareness about the diseases.

Jorey Berry, President & CEO

2952 Infectious Diseases Society of America
4040 Wilson Blvd, Suite 300
Arlington, VA 22203
703-299-0200
www.idsociety.org

The Infectious Diseases Society of America (IDSA) represents physicians, scientists and other health care professionals who specialize in infectious diseases. IDSA's purpose is to improve the health of individuals, communities, and society by promoting excellence in patient care, education, research, public health, and prevention relating to infectious diseases.

Carlos del Rio, President
Jeff Duchin, Secretary
Jeanne Marrazzo, Treasurer

2953 International Antiviral Society-USA
131 Steuart Street, Suite 500
San Francisco, CA 94105
415-544-9400
info@iasusa.org
www.iasusa.org

TheÿIAS-USAÿis a not-for-profit professional education organization that has been sponsoring continuing medical education (CME) programs for physicians since 1992 and is accredited by the Accreditation Council for Continuing Medical Education (ACCME).

Donna M. Jacobsen, Executive Director
Jay Batley, Director of Operations
Kevin Bowen, Scientific Program Director

2954 International Association of Providers of AIDS Care
1701 Pennsylvania Avenue NW, Suite 200
Washington, DC 20006
202-507-5899
Fax: 202-315-3651
iapac@iapac.org
www.iapac.org

IAPAC envisions a world in which people at risk for and those living with HIV/AIDS may access the best prevention, care, and treatment services delivered by clinicians and allied health workers armed with cutting-edge knowledge and expertise.

Jos, M. Zuniga, President & CEO
Chris Duncombe, VP & Chief Medical Officer
Sindhu Ravishankar, VP, Program & Research

2955 NMAC
1000 Vermont Avenue NW, Suite 200
Washington, DC 20005
202-744-6517
communications@nmac.org
nmac.org

Formerly known as National Minority AIDS Council, NMAC leads with race to urgently fight for health equity and racial justice to end the HIV epidemic in America.

Paul Kawata, Executive Director
Kim Ferrell, Deputy Director of Operations
Tara Barnes-Darby, Director of Conferences

2956 National Alliance of State & Territorial AIDS Directors
444 N Capitol Street NW, Suite 339
Washington, DC 20001
202-434-8090
Fax: 202-434-8092
communications@NASTAD.org
www.nastad.org

NASTAD is a leading non-partisan non-profit association that represents public health officials who administer HIV and hepatitis programs in the U.S. We work to advance the health and dignity of people living with and impacted by HIV/AIDS, viral hepatitis, and intersecting epidemics by strengthening governmental public health through advocacy, capacity building, and social justice.

Stephen Lee, Executive Director

2957 National Association of Community Health Centers
7501 Wisconsin Ave, Suite 1100W
Bethesda, MD 20814
301-347-0400
www.nachc.org

The National Association of Community Health Centers (NACHC) was founded in 1971 to promote efficient, high-quality, comprehensive health care that is accessible, culturally and linguistically competent, community directed, and patient centered for all. Provides training, leadership development and technical assistance to health center staff and boards to support and strengthen health center operations and governance.

Ron Yee, Chief Medical Officer
Mary Hawbecker, SVP, COO & CFO

2958 National Black Leadership Commission on Health, Inc.
215 W. 125th Street, 2ndÿFloor
New York, NY 10027
212-614-0023
Fax: 212-614-0508
info@nblch.org
nblch.org

The National Black Leadership Commission on Health, Inc. is a non-profit organization in the United States. There mission is to educate, mobilize, and empower black leaders to meet the challenge of fighting HIV/AIDS epidemic, addressing Hepatitis C while expanding to include cardiovascular disease, breast cancer, prostate cancer, sickle cell, diabetes, and mental health.

C. Virginia Fields, President and CEO
Melissa Baker, Chief Operating Officer
Evelyn Botwe, Director of Programs

2959 National Medical Association
8403 Colesville Road, Suite 820
Silver Spring, MD 20910
202-347-1895
www.nmanet.org

The National Medical Association (NMA) is the collective voice of African American physicians and the leading force for parity and justice in medicine and the elimination of disparities in health.

Martin Hamlette, JD, MHA, Executive Director

2960 Physician's Research Network
545 W 45th Street, 9th Floor
New York, NY 10036
212-924-0857
Fax: 212-924-0759
www.prn.org

The Physicians' Research Network (PRN) is a not-for-profit, peer-support and educational organization serving clinicians working in the fight against HIV/AIDS and viral hepatitis.

James F. Braun, DO, President
Edward Vladich, Office Manager

2961 World Health Organization
Avenue Appia 20
1202 Geneva,
Switzerland
www.who.int

WHO is the directing and coordinating authority for health within the United Nations system. WHO operates in more than 150 countries around the world.

Dr. Tedros Adhanom Ghebreyesus, Director General
Dr. Zsuzsanna Jakab, Deputy Director General
Stewart Simonson, Asst Director General, UN NYC

2962 anfAR
120 Wall Street, 13th Floor
New York, NY 10005
212-806-1600
Fax: 212-806-1601
information@amfar.org
www.amfar.org

amfAR, The Foundation for AIDS Research, is one of the world's leading nonprofit organizations dedicated to the support of AIDS research, HIV prevention, treatment education, and advocacy. Since 1985, amfAR has invested nearly $617 million in its programs and has awarded more than 3,500 grants to research teams worldwide.

Kevin R. Frost, Chief Executive Officer
Bradley Jensen, Chief Financial Officer
Kyle Clifford, Chief Development Officer

Research Centers

2963 Children's Clinical Research Center
New York Hospital, Cornell Medical Center
525 E 68th Street, Box 149
New York, NY 10065
212-746-4745
Fax: 212-746-8922
www.ccrc.med.cornell.edu

Offers research into the study of pediatric AIDS and other disorders.

Julianne Imperato-McGinley, MD, Program Director
Patricia Giardina, MD, Associate Program Director

2964 Developmental Medicine Center
Children's Hospital
300 Longwood Avenue
Boston, MA 02115
617-355-6000
800-355-7944
Fax: 617-735-7429
TTY: 617-730-0152
webteam@tch.harvard.edu
www.childrenshospital.org

The Developmental Medicine Center (DMC) at Children's Hospital Boston provides developmental evaluation and treatment services for children aged birth to adolescence with a wide range of developmental, behavioral and learning difficulties. The Center was founded for the purpose of enhancing the coordination of services for children and families with special needs.,

Leonard A. Rappaport MD, MS, Program Director

Conferences

2965 Immune Deficiency Foundation National Conference
7550 Teague Road, Suite 220
Hanover, MD 21076
410-321-6647
Fax: 410-321-9165
www.primaryimmune.org

Annual conference hosted by an organization aimed at fighting the primary immune deficiency diseases. The founders included parents of children with primary immune deficiency, immunologists who treat immune deficient patients and other individuals with an interest in helping others. The Foundation's main goal is to improve the care and treatment of adults and children with primary immune deficiency diseases and to promote public education and awareness about the diseases.

June

Jorey Berry, President & CEO

Web Sites

2966 AEGIS
10866 Washington Blvd., #309
Culver City, CA 90232
310-838-2787
info@aegis.com
www.aegis.com/

Web based reference for HIV/AIDS-related information.

Jeff Zisner, President & CEO

2967 AIDS Knowledge Base
hivinsite.ucsf.edu/InSite
415-476-9000
webdev@pubaff.ucsf.edu
hivinsite.ucsf.edu/InSite

A comprehensive, on-line textbook of HIV disease from the University of California San Francisco and San Francisco Hospital.

Sam Hawgood, MBBS, Chancellor
Daniel Lowenstein, MD, Executive Vice Chancellor & Provost
Bruce Wintroub, Interim Dean, School of Medicine

2968 American Sexual Health Association
www.ashasexualhealth.org
919-361-8400
infoashasexualhealth.org
www.ashasexualhealth.org

The American Sexual Health Association (ASHA) empowers individuals, families, and communities to achieve sexually healthy lives through education and advocacy. ASHA is an award-winning non-profit organization that has advocated on behalf of those at risk for sexually transmitted infections (STIs) since 1914.

2969 Children with AIDS Project
PO Box 23778
Tempe, AZ 85285
480-774-9718
www.aidskids.org/

HIV Infection / Book Publishers

The mission is to transform the silent that surrounds HIV infected, children and AIDS orphans into an audible sound. This sound must be amplified until the needs are met for all children in the nation and globally affected by the AIDS epidemic.

2970 Elizabeth Glazer Pediatric AIDS Foundation
150 Eye Street NW, Suite 400
Washington, DC 20005
202-296-9165
888-499-4673
Fax: 202-296-9185
info@pedaids.org
pedaids.org

A national non-profit organization dealing with medical problems unique to children infected with HIV/AIDS. The foundation is focused specifically on creating a future that will offer hope, finding effective therapies and issues of pregnancy and HIV. The foundation encourages students to enter the world of pediatric AIDS through a student intern program and more.

Charles Lyons, President & CEO

2971 Food and Drug Administration
10903 New Hampshire Avenue
Silver Spring, MD 20903
301-796-8240
888-463-6332
webmail@oc.fda.gov
www.fda.gov

The FDA is responsible for protecting the public health by assuring the safety, efficacy, and security of human and veterinary drugs, biological products, medical devices, our nation's food supply, cosmetics, and products that emit radiation. The FDA is also responsible for advancing the public health by helping to speed innovations that make medicines and foods more effective, safer, and more affordable and helping the public get accurate, science-based information they need to improve health.

Margaret A. Hamburg, Commissioner
Walter S. Harris, MBA, PMP, Deputy Commissioner
James Tyler, CFO

2972 Immune Deficiency Foundation
7550 Teague Road, Suite 220
Hanover, MD 21076
410-321-6647
Fax: 410-321-9165
www.primaryimmune.org

The only national charitable organization aimed at fighting the primary immune deficiency diseases. The founders included parents of children with primary immune deficiency, immunologists who treat immune deficient patients and other individuals with an interest in helping others.

Jorey Berry, President & CEO

2973 National Pediatric & Family HIV Resource Center
www.womenchildrenhiv.org

www.womenchildrenhiv.org

The goal of this site is to contribute to an improvement in the scale and quality of international HIV/AIDS prevention care and treatment programs for women and children by increasing access to authoritative HIV/AIDS information.

Arthur Ammann, MD, President
Heather Dron, MPH, Project Manager
Robert Grey, Programmer

2974 National Pediatric AIDS Network
PO Box 1507
Nevada City, CA 95959
gary@npan.org
www.npan.org/

Is a nonprofit organization, that works collaboratively with a number of other HIV/AIDS information providers.

Gary Gale, Director

2975 Parents Helping Parents
1400 Parkmoor Avenue, Suite 100
San Jose, CA 95126
408-727-5775
855-727-5775
Fax: 408-286-1116
info@php.com
www.php.com

Parents Helping Parents supports, educates, and inspires families and the community to build bright futures for youth and adults with special needs.

Maria Daane, Executive Director
Janet Nunez, Director, Programs
Virginia Hildebrand, Director, Finance

2976 Pediatric AIDS Clinical Trials Group
pactg.s-3.com

pactg.s-3.com

Goals are: to optimize strategies to maintain or improve mother to infant transmission at less than 2% without long termn toxicity to exposed infants or treated pregnant women in the United States; and to enable more than 90% of children perinatally infected with HIV to achieve normal growth and development, and more than 20 years survival in the United States.

2977 Sunshine for HIV Kids
www.sunshinesite.com

www.sunshinesite.com

Is a nonprofit tax exempt organization that identifies and raises funds for charities who directly deliver care to children afflicted with HIV/AIDS and their families.

2978 Wayne State University
42. West Warren Ave.
Detroit, MI 48202
315-577-2424
www.research.wayne.edu

Advances in therapy to prevent HIV transmission from mothers to infants have brought hope to thousands, but transmission of HIV continues to increase in developing countries. We must identify effective intervention strategies usable by all nations if we are to reduce the incidence of mother to infant HIV transmission worldwide.

Debbie Dingell, Chair
Gary S. Pollard, Vice Chair
M. Roy Wilson, President

Book Publishers

2979 AIDS Awareness Library

Anna Forbes, MSS, author

Rosen Publishing Group
29 E 21st Street
New York, NY 10010
212-777-3017
800-237-9932
Fax: 888-436-4643
info@rosenpub.com
www.rosenpublishing.com

This series of eight 24-page books for grades K-5, speaks to children in nonthreatening langauge that provides vital information without graphic detail. This series is meant to be a gentle introduction to this frightening epidemic. Titles in series: Heroes Against AIDS, Kids with AIDS, Living in a World with AIDS, Myths and Facts About AIDS, What is AIDS?, What You Can Do About AIDS, When Someone You Know Has AIDS, Where Did AIDS Come From?.

24 pages
ISBN: 0-823974-06-5

2980 AIDS and the Education of Our Children
Consumer Information Center
US Department of Education
Pueblo, CO 81009
719-948-3334
888-878-3256
www.pueblo.gsa.gov

A guide for parents and teachers offering helpful information on the topic of AIDS education.

28 pages

2981 Heroes Against AIDS
Anna Forbes, MSS, author
Rosen Publishing Group
29 E 21st Street
New York, NY 10010
212-777-3017
800-237-9932
Fax: 888-436-4643
info@rosenpub.com
www.rosenpublishing.com

Ryan White and Magic Johnson are just two of the heroes in this book who demonstrate through their courage and kindness their strength in adversity.

K-5 24 pages
ISBN: 0-823923-71-1

2982 Kids with AIDS
Anna Forbes, MSS, author
Rosen Publishing Group
29 E 21st Street
New York, NY 10010
212-777-3017
800-237-9932
Fax: 888-436-4643
info@rosenpub.com
www.rosenpublishing.com

This book is written so as not to scare kids but teach compassion for their peers who might have AIDS. It stresses the importance of eliminating blame from this disease.

K-5 24 pages
ISBN: 0-823923-72-X

2983 Let's Talk About Going to the Hospital
Rosen Publishing Group's PowerKids Press
29 E 21st Street
New York, NY 10010
212-777-3017
800-237-9932
Fax: 888-436-4643
rosenpub@tribeca.ios.com
www.rosenpublishing.com

If a child has to check into the hospital, chances are he or she is already upset about being ill. Knowing how a hospital functions and what the procedures are, such as when family members can visit, will help in what is already a stressful situation. Grades K-5.

24 pages
ISBN: 0-823950-36-0

Roger Rosen, President

2984 Living in a World with AIDS
Anna Forbes, MSS, author
Rosen Publishing Group
29 E 21st Street
New York, NY 10010
212-777-3017
800-237-9932
Fax: 888-436-4643
info@rosenpub.com
www.rosenpublishing.com

AIDS is a reality. Kids hear about it on TV, at school, and on the streets. This introductory volume reassures kids about their basic safety and provides gentle preventative advice that is age appropriate.

K-5 24 pages
ISBN: 0-823923-67-3

2985 Myths and Facts About AIDS
Rosen Publishing Group's PowerKids Press
29 E 21st Street
New York, NY 10010
212-777-3017
800-237-9932
Fax: 888-436-4643
rosenpub@tribeca.ios.com
www.powerkidspress.com

In a simple and reassuring manner, the author demystifies this disease and puts to rest many misconceptions. Grades K-5.

K-5 24 pages
ISBN: 0-823923-66-5

2986 What Is AIDS?
Rosen Publishing Group's PowerKids Press
29 E 21st Street
New York, NY 10010
212-777-3017
800-237-9932
Fax: 888-436-4643
rosenpub@tribeca.ios.com
www.powerkidspress.com

Accessible scientific look at AIDS puts it in the context of other diseases, teaching about the human organism in an age-appropriate manner. Grades K-5.

K-5 24 pages
ISBN: 0-823923-68-1

2987 What You Can Do About AIDS
Anna Forbes, MSS, author
Rosen Publishing Group
29 E 21st Street
New York, NY 10010
212-777-3017
800-237-9932
Fax: 888-436-4643
info@rosenpub.com
www.rosenpublishing.com

It's never too early to teach kids about social responsibility. This book emphasizes community participation.

K-5 24 pages
ISBN: 0-823923-70-3

2988 When Someone You Know Has AIDS
Anna Forbes, MSS, author
Rosen Publishing Group
29 E 21st Street
New York, NY 10010
212-777-3017
800-237-9932
Fax: 888-436-4643
info@rosenpub.com
www.rosenpublishing.com

This unique volume helps kids who might know someone with AIDS to approach that person with love and compassion as one would any sick person.

K-5 24 pages
ISBN: 0-823923-69-X

2989 Where Did AIDS Come From?
Anna Forbes, MSS, author
Rosen Publishing Group
29 E 21st Street
New York, NY 10010
212-777-3017
800-237-9932
Fax: 888-436-4643
info@rosenpub.com
www.rosenpublishing.com

AIDS is frightening, especially to young children who sense the secrecy around it. This is a gentle introduction to the topic. It treats AIDS like any other epidemic.

K-5 24 pages
ISBN: 0-823923-65-7

Pamphlets

2990 Hope for Children with AIDS
Elizabeth Glazer Pediatric AIDS Foundation
1140 Connecticut Avenue NW, Suite 200
Washington, DC 20036
202-296-9165
888-499-4693
Fax: 202-296-9185
www.pedaids.org

HIV Infection / Camps

The Elizabeth Glaser Pediatric AIDS Foundation creates a future of hope for children and families worldwide by eradicating pediatric AIDS, providing care and treatment to people with HIV/AIDS, and accelerating the discovery of new treatments for other serious and life-threatening pediatric illnesses. In working toward our mission the foundation is committed to ensuring that the vast majority of every dollar raised goes directly into our research education and outreach program.

Russ Hagey, Chair
Charles Lyons, President & CEO
Brad Kiley, COO

Camps

2991 Camp Heartland
1845 N Farwell Avenue, Suite 310
Millwaukee, WI 53202
414-272-1118
800-724-4673
Fax: 414-272-9916
webmaster@campheartland.org
www.campheartland.org

Set up to provide children impacted by HIV/AIDS with the best week of their lives. Provides children forever affected by the isolation and tragedy of the disease the opportunity to experience - sometimes for the first time - the pure joys of being a kid.

Neil Willenson, Founder/CEO
Jeffrey Maiken, President
Patrick Kindler, Program Manager

2992 Camp Kindle
PO Box 81147
Lincoln, NE 81147
661-257-1901
877-800-2267
Fax: 702-995-9186
info@projectkindle.org
www.campkindle.org

Camp with the purpose to enhance the overall well-being of children and young people infected with or affected by HIV and AIDS.

Eva Payne, Founder & Executive Director
Mandy Nickolite, VP & Psychosocial lead
Erin Fitzgerald, Program Coordinator

2993 Camp Kindle- Project Kindle
28245 Ave Crocker, Ste 104
Santa Clarita, CA 91355
661-257-1901
877-800-2267
Fax: 702-995-9186
www.campkindle.org

Camp for youth ages 7-18 who are infected with or affected by HIV and AIDS.

Eva Payne, Founder & Executive Director
Alison Boring, Co-Camp Director

2994 Hole in the Wall Gang Camp
565 Ashford Center Road
Ashford, CT 6278
860-429-3444
Fax: 860-429-7295
ashford@holeinthewallgang.org
www.holeinthewallgang.org

Nonprofit organization that provides a recreational camp experience for children ages 7-15 with cancer, genetic blood diseases and HIV/AIDS.

Raymond Lamontagne, Chair
James Canton, CEO
Kevin Magee, CFO

Description

2995 HEAD INJURIES

Synonyms: Closed head injury, Concussion, Traumatic brain injury

Involves the following Biologic System(s):
Neurologic Disorders

Head injuries describe trauma to the head that results in damage to the scalp, skull, or brain and associated membranes, nerves, or blood vessels. Every year in the United States, approximately 100,000 children require hospitalization because of head injuries. Many of these injuries are the result of motor vehicle and bicycle accidents. The risk of sustaining head or brain injury during a vehicular or bicycle accident is reduced by the proper use of restraint systems such as approved car seats, seat belts, or helmets. There are different types of head injuries, some of which are minor and, after healing, of no further significance; however, certain injuries that impact upon the brain may have severe complications and be potentially life-threatening. These include skull fractures, concussions, brain contusions and lacerations, and bleeding in the brain (e.g., subdural or epidural hematomas). Brain injury may result in mild, moderate, or severe functional disabilities, depending upon the particular area of brain tissue that is damaged or destroyed. Disabilities may affect physical, emotional, or intellectual development and include impairment in the comprehension or production of speech and language (aphasia); the inability to remember or perform certain familiar tasks requiring sequential movements (apraxia); the failure to remember past events or experiences (amnesia); the lack of ability to recognize familiar persons or objects (agnosia); and the development of episodes of uncontrolled electrical activity in the brain (posttraumatic epilepsy), usually within two years of the initial head injury.

In children with skull fractures or an open-head injury, there is an actual break in the skull bone (cranium). Many skull fractures do not interfere with normal brain function and will heal with no complications. However, in some patients, fractures may damage blood vessels or the membranes surrounding the brain (meninges), resulting in leakage of the fluid that surrounds the brain and spinal cord (cerebrospinal fluid). The break in the skull may also serve as an entry point for bacteria that may subsequently cause serious infection. A thorough evaluation is necessary to determine the extent of the injury. Surgical intervention may sometimes be necessary.

Concussions are closed-head injuries that occur as a result of a jarring of the brain within the skull. Symptoms and findings associated with this type of injury in children may include a temporary loss of consciousness, lack of muscle tone, poor or absent reflexes (areflexia), dilated pupils, blurred vision, irritability, or restlessness. These signs of concussion may be followed by rapid heartbeat (tachycardia), vomiting, listlessness, drowsiness, apathy, a pale skin color, or confusion. Treatment for concussion always involves observation. Although most children recover completely, hospitalization may be required for those whose level of consciousness continues to drop or those who appear listless, drowsy, or confused. Those who vomit excessively or experience seizures or other neurological symptoms may also require hospitalization.

Other closed-head injuries may include contusions, characterized by bruises on the brain; lacerations, characterized by tears in the brain tissue; subdural hematomas, characterized by accumulations of blood under the outermost membrane layer surrounding the brain (dura mater); and epidural hematomas, characterized by blood between the dura mater and the skull. Hematomas may result from ruptures or lacerations in certain blood vessels. Contusions and hematomas may cause the brain to swell with an accompanying buildup of fluid (edema). Increasing pressure within the skull may result in brain damage. Symptoms and findings may include headache; seizures; altered levels of consciousness sometimes leading to coma; loss of strength; numbness; paralysis; confusion; amnesia; or life-threatening complications such as respiratory distress and heart irregularities. Treatment is aimed at the maintenance of respiratory and cardiovascular function in order to prevent further injury. If necessary, the upper spine (cervical spine) is stabilized. The monitoring and management of brain swelling and fluid accumulation may include the careful administration of intravenous fluids and medications, bed elevation, and the use of supplemental oxygen. In addition, surgical intervention may be required to relieve intracranial pressure, remove blood clots, or control bleeding around the brain. Further treatment may include medication for the control of seizures. Recovery from major head or brain trauma may be a very slow, progressive process and, as such, may require the assistance of a team of specialists who will work with the family or caregivers of the child to coordinate symptomatic and supportive care.

Government Agencies

2996 NIH/National Institute of Neurological Disorders and Stroke (NINDS)
PO Box 5801
Bethesda, MD 20824
800-352-9424
www.ninds.nih.gov

Works to reduce the burden of neurological disease by conducting, fostering, coordinating and guiding research on the causes, prevention, diagnosis and treatment of neurological disorders and stroke, while supporting basic research in related scientific areas.

Walter J. Koroshetz, MD, Director

National Associations & Support Groups

2997 Acoustic Neuroma Association
600 Peachtree Parkway, Suite 108
Cumming, GA 30041
770-205-8211
info@anausa.org
www.anausa.org

The Acoustic Neuroma Association provides information and support to patients who have been diagnosed with or experienced an acoustic neuroma or other benign problem affecting the cranial nerves. The ANA is an incorporated, nonprofit organization, and is supported by contributions from its members. The association also furnishes information on patient rehabilitation to physicians and health care personnel, promotes research on acoustic neuroma, and educates the public.

Jim Shea, Chief Executive Officer
Matthew Balte, Manager, Membership & Development
Melanie Hutchins, Manager, Volunteer Programs

2998 American Academy of Pediatrics
345 Park Blvd
Itasca, IL 60143
800-433-9016
Fax: 847-434-8000
mcc@aap.org
www.aap.org

The American Academy of Pediatrics and its member pediatricians are committed to the attainment of optimal physical, mental and social health and well-being for all infants, children, adolescents, and young adults.

Lynn Olson, PhD, VP, Research
Mark Del Monte, JD, CEO/Executive VP
Vera Tait, MD, FAAP, Chief Medical Officer

Head Injuries / State Agencies & Support Groups

2999 **Brain Injury Association of America**
3057 Nutley Street, Suite 805
Fairfax, VA 22031
703-761-0750
800-444-6443
Fax: 703-761-0755
info@biausa.org
www.biausa.org

The mission of the Brain Injury Association is to create a better future through brain injury prevention, research, education and advocacy.

Rick Willis, President & CEO
Mary S Reitter, CAE, Executive Vice President & COO

3000 **Brain Trauma Foundation**
228 Hamilton Avenue, 3rd Floor
Palo Alto, CA 94301
www.braintrauma.org

The Brain Trauma Foundation mission is to improve the outcome of Traumatic Brain Injury (TBI) patients nationwide.

Jamshid Ghajar, President
Alan Quasha, Chairman
Pamela J. Newman, Executive Director

3001 **Center for Disabilities and Development**
University of Iowa Stead Family Children's Hospita
100 Hawkins Drive
Iowa City, IA 52242
319-353-6900
877-686-0031
Fax: 319-356-7700
cdd-scheduling@uiowa.edu
www.uichildrens.org/cdd

A trusted resource for healthcare, training, research and information for people with disabilities that include: behavior disorders, brain injury, cerebral palsy, diabetes, down syndrome, learning disabilities, sleep disorders and spina bifida.

Dianne McBrien, MD, Medical Director

3002 **Child Neurology Foundation**
601 W Short Street
Lexington, KY 40508
888-417-3435
info@childneurologyfoundation.org
childneurologyfoundation.org

The Child Neurology Foundation connects partners from all areas of the child neurology community so those navigating the journey of disease diagnosis, management, and care have the ongoing support from those dedicated to treatments and cures.

Amy Brin, Executive Director
Katie Hentges, Director, Programs
Brea McCormley, Director, Development

3003 **Children's Hemiplegia & Stroke Association**
4101 W Green Oaks, Suite 305-149
Arlington, TX 76016
chasa.org

The Children's Hemiplegia and Stroke Association, CHASA, is a non-profit organization founded by parents of children with hemiplegia in 1996 to provide information and support to families of children who have hemiplegia, hemiparesis, or hemiplegic cerebral palsy. These conditions are often caused by stroke in an infant and may also be the result of a number of different conditions.

State Agencies & Support Groups

Alabama

3004 **Alabama Head Injury Foundation**
3100 Lorna Road, Suite 200
Hoover, AL 35216
205-823-3818
800-433-8002
Fax: 205-823-4544
ahif1@bellsouth.net
www.ahif.org

Our mission is to improve the quality of life for survivors of traumatic brain injury and for their families and to increase public awareness of (TBI).

Keith T. Belt, Jr., President
Kim F. Hooks, VP
Charles D Priest, Executive Director

Arizona

3005 **Brain Injury Association of Arizona**
5025 E Washington St., Suite 108
Phoenix, AZ 85034
602-508-8024
888-500-9165
Fax: 602-508-8285
info@biaaz.org
www.biaaz.org

A non-profit membership organiation of people with brain injuries, their families, friends and service providers working together since 1983 to provide information and referrals, education, advocacy and support for those affected by brain injury.

Lisa Counters, President
Rebecca Armendariz, VP
Mattie Cummins, Executive Director

Arkansas

3006 **Brain Injury Association of Arkansas**
PO Box 26236
Little Rock, AR 72221
501-374-3585
866-610-4841
Fax: 501-918-6595
www.brainassociation.org

Creating a better future through brain injury prevention, research, education and advocacy.

Dana Austen, President
Kortney E Gold, VP
Tessa Davis, Secretary

California

3007 **California Brain Injury Association**
1800 30th St., Suite 250
Bakersfield, CA 93301
661-872-4903
888-662-4222
Fax: 661-873-2508
calbiainfo@yahoo.com
www.biacal.org

Our mission is to serve and empower the community of many thousands of persons living in California with brain injuries and to enable them to live with dignity and to access all therapy, hospitalization, long term care, and all possible means for recovery and rehabilitation and to support their families.

Paula Daoutis, Administrative Director
Ursula Pesta, Project Coordinator
Elaine Solan, Community Liaison

3008 **Jodi House**
1235 C Veronica Springs Road
Santa Barbara, CA 93105
805-563-2882
Fax: 805-593-3982
info@jodihouse.org

The mission of Jodi House is to create a nurturing place of order, caring, acceptance and motivation for people with acquired brain injury,and to provide opportunities for each person to discover new paths to regain responsible independence and effective interdependence to the best of our ability, in order to achieve worthwhile purposes in our community.

Jim Cook, President
Andrew Chung, VP
Tracy Cohn, Treasurer

Head Injuries / State Agencies & Support Groups

Colorado

3009 Brain Injury Association of Colorado
1385 South Colorado Boulevard, Ste 606, Building A
Denver, CO 80204
303-355-9969
800-955-2443
Fax: 303-355-9968
www.biacolorado.org

The Brain Injury Association of Colorado began in April 1980. BIAC was formed by a group of family members and professionals in Denver and Colorado Springs who were concerned with the lack of support services for survivors and family members affected by head injury. The mission is to improve the quality of life for survivors of brain injury and their families, and to support programs that prevent brain injury.

Dannis Schanel, President
Helen Kellogg, Executive Director
Peggy Spaulding, Executive Director

Connecticut

3010 Brain Injury Association of Connecticut
200 Day Hill Road, Suite 250
Windsor, CT 06095
860-219-0291
800-278-8242
Fax: 860-219-0568
general@biact.org
www.biact.homestead.com

Supports persons with brain injuries and their families by promoting services to facilitate full inclusion within their local community, and to increase awareness and understanding of brain injury and its prevention through community education.

500 Members

Paul A. Slager, Esq., President
Dr. Johnny Magwood, BSME, MBA, DBA, Vice President
Julie Peters, Executive Director

3011 TBI Support Group for Families & Survivors
Gaylord Hospital Conference Room
Wallingford, CT 06492
203-284-2800
TDD: 203-284-2700

Our mission is to preserve and enhance a person's health and function. We offer people a comprehensive continuum of care ranging from our Medically Complex Program and inpatient rehabilitation programs to outpatient services and sleep services.

District of Columbia

3012 Brain Injury Association of Washington DC
1232 17th St, N.W.
Washington, DC 20036
202-659-0122
Fax: 202-291-5366
info@biadc.org
www.biadc.org

Provide support to survivors of brain injury and their families, education to those who are being effected by brain injury, including the general public, and advocacy, to give the many suffering from this silent epidemic a public voice.

Joseph Cammarata, President/Treasurer
Ira Sherman, VP
Michael Yochelson, M.D., Board of Director

Florida

3013 Brain Injury Association of Florida
1637 Metropolitan Blvd, Suite B
Tallahassee, FL 32308
850-410-0103
800-992-3442
Fax: 954-786-2437
admin@biaf.org
www.biaf.org

A non profit organization founded in 1985, with the mission to improve the quality of life for persons with brain injury and their families by creating a better future through brain injury prevention, research, education, suport services and advocacy.

Mark Todd, PhD, President
Elynor Kazuk, Executive Director
Marilyn Ronshausen, Admin Secretary

3014 Family/Community Support Group of the Brain Injury Association of Florida
North Broward Medical Center
201 E Sample Road
Pompano Beach, FL 33064
954-786-2400
800-992-3442
www.biaf.org

Helping individuals with traumatic brain injuries and their families find practical solutions to the difficult problems faced when living with the long-term consequences of a traumatic brain injury (TBI).

Gary Clarke, Chairman
Johny Jallad, Chair-Elect
Larry Baxter, Secretary

3015 Goodwill Industries-Suncoast: Choices for Work Program
Goodwill Industries-Suncoast
10596 Gandy Boulevard
St. Petersburg, FL 33702
727-523-1512
888-297-1988
Fax: 727-579-1068
www.goodwill-suncoast.org

Provides short-term, light-duty work options for individuals recovering from on-the-job injuries. Participants are sponsored by a referring insurance company. This service is available in Hillsborough, Pinellas, Pasco and Polk counties through Suncoast Business Solutions.

Deborah A. Passerini, President
Oscar J. Horton, Chair
Martin W. Gladysz, Vice Chair

Georgia

3016 Brain Injury Resource Foundation
1841 Montreal Road, Suite 220
Tucker, GA 30084
678-937-1555
888-334-2424
Fax: 678-937-1557
www.birf.info/index.shtml

A nonprofit charitable orginazation working together with families and professionals since 1982 to provide education, advocacy and support for those effected by brain injury. Our mission is to empower individuals with brain injury by making available resources that may improve the quality of their lives.

Karen Parsley, Executive Director

Hawaii

3017 Special Education Center of Hawaii
708 Palekaua Street
Honolulu, HI 96816
808-734-0233
Fax: 808-734-0391
info@secoh.org
www.secoh.org

Committed to providing individual and family supports that promote successful community living in the lifestyle of choice. Services and supports are provided to people with developmental disabilities, or acquired disabilities due to aging or head injury. Services include day care, respite care, and supported employment.

Jon McKenna, President
Douglas Inouye, VP
Debbie Hiraoka, Treasurer

Head Injuries / State Agencies & Support Groups

Idaho

3018 Brain Injury Association of Idaho
1055 North Curtis Road, PO Box 414
Boise, ID 83706
208-367-2747
800-444-6443
Fax: 208-333-0026
info@biaid.org
www.biaid.org

A non-profit organization helping persons with brain injury and their familiy members.

Michelle Featherson, President

Illinois

3019 Brain Injury Association of Illinois
PO Box 64420
Chicago, IL 60664
312-726-5699
800-699-6443
Fax: 312-630-4011
info@biail.org
www.biail.org

A not-for-profit statewide membership organization comprised of people with brain injuries, family members, friends and professionals, with the mission to create a better future through brain injury awareness, prevention, education and advocacy.

Ginny Lazzara, President
Philicia Deckard, Executive Director
Irene Pedersen, Founder

Indiana

3020 Brain Injury Association of Indiana
9531 Valparaiso Court, Suite A
Indianapolis, IN 46268
317-356-7722
866-854-4246
Fax: 317-808-7770
www.biai.org

A nonprofit service organization comprised of people with brain injury, their families, and concerned stakeholders who are dedicated to creating a better future by reducing the incidence and effects of brain injury through public and professional education, advocacy, support, and by facilitating inter-agency commitment and collaboration.

Nancy Ritter, Chairman
Tom John, VP
Scott Branam, Secretary

Iowa

3021 Brain Injury Association of Iowa
7025 Hickman Road, Suite 7
Urbandale, IA 50322
319-233-3235
855-444-6443
Fax: 319-272-2109
info@biai.org
www.biaia.org

Founded in 1980, exists to support, assist, and advocate for persons with acquired brain damage and for their families; advocates for and with people with brain injury and family members by responding to their challenges and representing their concerns through legislative efforts and active support of programs created for their needs.

Jackie Preston, Manager
Geoffrey Lauer, MA, LOC, Executive Director
Natasha Retz, BS, CBIS, Director of Programs and Services

Kansas

3022 Brain Injury Association of Kansas & Greater Kansas City
6701 W. 64th St., Suite 120
Overland Park, KS 66202
913-754-8883
800-783-1356
Fax: 816-842-1531
Lliggett@biaks.org
www.biaks.org

Offers support services to individuals and their families in the greater Kansas City area and throughout the state of Kansas who are recovering from traumatic brain injury.

Terrie Price, President
Whitney Sunderland, VP
Bonnie Stephens, Secretary

Kentucky

3023 Brain Injury Association of Kentucky
7321 New LaGrange Road, Suite 100
Louisville, KY 40222
502-493-0609
800-592-1117
Fax: 502-426-2993
www.biak.us

Serves those affected by brain injury through advocacy, education, injury prevention, research, service and support.

Andrew Horne, President
Eileen Edlin, Treasurer
Ben Ruiz, Secretary

Louisiana

3024 Brain Injury Association of Louisiana
8325 Oak Street, PO Box 57527
New Orleans, LA 70118
504-982-0685
800-500-2026
www.biala.org

A non-profit organization that serves the needs of persons with brain injury, their families, and care providers. The focus is to create a better future for individuals who have survived brain injury through brain injury prevention awareness, promotion of research, public education, and advocacy.

Janet Clark, Chairman
Paul Genco, Vice Chairman
William E Moak, President/Executive Director

Maine

3025 Brain Injury Association of Maine
109 North State Street, Suite 2
Concord, NH 03301
603-225-8400
800-773-8400
Fax: 603-228-6749
www.biame.org

A nonprofit organization that looks to create a better future for the people of Maine, through brain injury awareness, prevention, education and advocacy.

Bev Bryant, President
John Bott, Executive Director

Maryland

3026 Brain Injury Association of Maryland
2200 Kernan Drive
Baltimore, MD 21207
410-448-2924
800-221-6443
Fax: 410-448-3541
info@biamd.org
www.biamd.org

Our mission is to create a better future through brain injury prevention, research, education and advocacy.

Head Injuries / State Agencies & Support Groups

Diane Triplett, Executive Director
Diane Triplett, Executive Director

Massachusetts

3027 Brain Injury Association of Massachusetts
30 Lyman Street
Westborough, MA 01581
508-475-0032
800-242-0030
Fax: 508-475-0040
biama@biama.org
www.biama.org

Our mission is to serve as an information and resource center for persons with brain injury, their families and friends, and providers and professionals in the field of brain injury treatment and rehabilitation.

Teresa Hayes, President
Harold Wilkinson, Secretary
Matthew Martino, Executive Board Member

Michigan

3028 Rehabilitation Institute of Michigan
261 Mack Avenue
Detroit, MI 48201
313-745-1203
Fax: 313-745-9863
www.rimrehab.org

Providing quality patient care, academic excellence and cutting-edge research in physical medicine and rehabilitation.

Mildred Matlock, Ceo
William H. Restum, PhD, President

Minnesota

3029 Brain Injury Association of Minnesota
34 13th Avenue NE, Suite B001
Minneapolis, MN 55413
612-378-2742
800-669-6442
Fax: 612-378-2789
info@braininjurymn.org
www.braininjurymn.org

The only non-profit organization in the state devoted solely to serving the needs of the 100,000 Minnesotans who live with a disability due to brain injury. Providing hope, help and a voice for brain injured persons for over 20 years.

quaterly 20-24 pages

Ardis Sandstrom, Executive Director
Ardis Sandstrom, Executive Director

Mississippi

3030 Brain Injury Association of Mississippi
2727 Old Canton Road, Suite 191
Jackson, MS 39216
601-981-1021
800-444-6443
Fax: 601-981-1039
biaofms@aol.com
www.msbia.org

Enhances the quality of life for Traumatic Brain Injury survivors and their families, and to develop and support programs that prevent brain injury.

Lee Jenkins, Executive Director
Paul Gospodarski, EdD, Executive Director
Dana C. Pierce, Associate Director

Missouri

3031 Brain Injury Association of Missouri
2265 Schuetz Road
Saint Louis, MO 63146
314-426-4024
800-444-6443
Fax: 314-426-3290
info@biamo.org
www.biamo.org

Founded in 1982, a community based organization serving persons with brain injury, their families, caregivers, physicians, therapists, case managers, and others throught the state of Missouri.

Eric Hart, President
Scott Gee, Executive Director
Scott Gee, Executive Director

Montana

3032 Brain Injury Association of Montana
1280 S 3rd West, Suite 4
Missoula, MT 59801
406-541-6442
800-241-6442
Fax: 406-541-4360
www.biamt.org

To create a better future through brain injury prevention, research, education and advocacy.

Kristen Morgan, Program Director
Christien Morgan, Manager
Stacy Rye, Executive Director

New Hampshire

3033 Brain Injury Association of New Hampshire
109 N State Street, Suite 2
Concord, NH 03301
800-773-8400
800-444-8400
Fax: 603-228-6749
mail@bianh.org
www.bianh.org

Founded in 1983, a private, non-profit family and consumer run organization representing over 5000 New Hamphire residents with acquired brain disorders and stroke.

Steven D. Wade, Executive Director
Laura Flashman, Ph.D, President
Amy Messer, Vice-President

New Jersey

3034 Brain Injury Association of New Jersey
825 Georges Road, Second Floor
North Brunswick, NJ 08902
732-745-0200
732-745-0211
Fax: 732-738-1132
info@bianj.org
www.bianj.org

A nonprofit organization that brings together people with brain injury, their families and friends, and concerned allied health professionals to improve the quality of life people experience after brain injury.

Edward Kim, Chairperson
Anthony G. Cuzzola, Vice-Chairperson
Michael H. Greenwald, Secretary

New Mexico

3035 Brain Injury Association of New Mexico
3232 Candelaria NE
Albuquerque, NM 87107
505-292-7414
888-292-7415
Fax: 505-271-8983
www.braininjurynm.org

Head Injuries / State Agencies & Support Groups

Actively supports progressive public policy for persons with traumatic brain injury on both state and federal levels.

John Tiwald, Board President
Clara Holguin, Executive Director

New York

3036 Brain Injury Association of New York State
10 Colvin Avenue
Albany, NY 12206
518-459-7911
800-228-8201
Fax: 518-482-5285
info@bianys.org
www.bianys.org

A statewide non-profit membership organization that advocates on behalf of individuals with brain injury and their families, and promotes prevention. Established in 1982, provides education, advocacy, and community support services that lead to improved outcomes for children and adults with brain injuries and their families.

Debbie Berenda, Manager
Judy Avner, Executive Director
Jutith Sandman, Director Membership/Development

3037 Hy Feinstein Clubhouse
Long Island Head Injury Association
300 Kennedy Drive
Hauppauge, NY 11788
631-543-2245
Fax: 631-543-2261
club@lihia.org
www.lihia.org

A non-profit organization whose primary mission is to provide a place for people with head injuries to participate in meaningful work; to have the opportunity to meet and build friendships; and ulimately seek employment within the community.

3038 Mount Sinai Traumatic Brain Injury
Mt Sinai Medical Center
5 E. 98th Street, B-15
New York, NY 10029
212-241-7911
888-241-5152
margaret.brown@mssm.edu
www.icahn.mssm.edu

Specializing not only in helping patients regain mastery over their physical environment, but also in addressing the cognitive and emotional aftermaths, including anxiety and depression, which are frequently triggered by such injuries. The program contains different treatment levels to address the very specific needs of this population.

David Vandergoot, President
Wayne A. Gordon, Director
Joshua Cantor, Co-Director

North Carolina

3039 Brain Injury Association of North Carolina
2113 Cameron Street, Bryan Bldg, Suite 242, PO Box
Raleigh, NC 27605
919-833-9634
800-377-1464
Fax: 919-833-5415
bianc@bianc.net
www.bianc.net

Founded in 1982 by families and concerned professionals. The Association is an affiliate of the Brain Injury Association of America. Today, the Association has Family and Community Support Centers in Raleigh, Greenville, and Charlotte and 29 local chapters and support groups across the state.

Marylin Lash, President
Pam Gutherie, Vice President
Karen L. McCulloch, Co-Chair Elect

North Dakota

3040 Brain Injury Association of North Dakota
Open Door Center
1225 South 12th Street
Bismarck, ND 58504
701-845-1124
877-525-2724
Fax: 701-845-1175
www.braininjurynd.com

Mary Simonson, President
Richard Ott, Executive Director
Rebecca Quinn

Ohio

3041 Brain Injury Association of Ohio
855 Grandview Avenue, Suite 225
Columbus, OH 43215
614-481-7100
800-444-6443
Fax: 614-481-7103
help@biaoh.org
www.biaoh.org

The Brain Injury Association of Ohio aims to improve community services, supports, and awareness for the life-long challenges presented by brain injury and to increase the independence of those coping with its impact. There are five core services designed to achieve this: information & resource coordination; education & training for professionals; support groups for Ohio residents; prevention initiatives; advocacy for policies and funding that address service system gaps.

Stephanie Ramsey, President
Anthon Brooks, Vice President
Julie Robbins, Vice President

Oklahoma

3042 Brain Injury Association of Oklahoma
3015 E Skelly Dr.
Tulsa, OK 74105
918-789-0406
800-765-6809
Fax: 918-712-9019
braininjuryoklahoma@gmail.com
www.braininjuryoklahoma.org

Adam Sherman, President
Mary Dobbs, Vice President
Joan Gass, Treasurer

Oregon

3043 Brain Injury Association of Oregon
Po Box 549
Molalla, OR 97038
503-413-7707
800-544-5243
Fax: 503-961-8730
biaor@biaoregon.org
www.biaoregon.org

To improve the quality of life of persons with brain injury and their families; and to prevent brain injury.

Ralph Wiser, President
Chuck McGilvrary, Vice President
Carol Altman, Treasurer

3044 Oregon Brain Injury Resource Network
345 N Monmouth Avenue, PO Box 1329
Monmouth, OR 97361
541-346-0593
877-872-7246
Fax: 541-346-0599
tbi@wou.edu
www.tr.wou.edu/tbi/

Aims to improve access to information and services for individuals with brain injuries, their families, and the professionals who serve them. The Resource Network houses information on all aspects of brain injury, from the point of initial injury throughout the life span of the individual.

Head Injuries / State Agencies & Support Groups

Pennsylvania

3045 Pittsburgh Area Brain Injury Alliance
630 Bascom Avenue
Pittsburgh, PA 15212
412-481-0443
www.pabia.org

Dedicated to the people recovering from Brain Injury and who live with the consequences of Traumatic Brain Injury. The purpose is to provide a forum for peer-to-peer support and to assist in the development of peer-to-peer support groups in Western Pennsylvania.

Ed Crinnion, President

Tennessee

3046 Brain Injury Association of Tennessee
955 Woodland St
Nashville, TN 37206
615-248-2541
800-444-6443
Fax: 615-383-1176
biaoftn@yahoo.com
www.braininjurytn.com

The mission is to improve the quality of life for persons with brain injuries and their families and to reduce the incidence of brain injury.

Guynn Edwards, President
Pam Bryan, Executive Director
Brian Webb, Treasurer

Texas

3047 Brain Injury Association of Texas
316 W 12th Street, Suite 405
Austin, TX 78701
512-326-1212
800-392-0040
Fax: 512-478-3370
www.texasbia.org

A non-profit public service organization, strives to meet the urgent need to develop programs for public awareness and education, to support research and rehabilitation and to provide family guidance.

San Marcos, President
Amy Santus, Vice President
Erin Garrison, Admin Director

Utah

3048 Brain Injury Association of Utah
5280 Commerce Dr., Suite E-190
Murray, UT 84107
801-716-4993
800-281-8442
Fax: 801-716-4995
info@biau.org
www.biau.org

Created in 1984, the only non-profit organization dedicated exclusively to education and support for the issues of prevention and recovery of brain injury in the state of Utah. The mission of the Brain Injury Association of Utah is to create a better future through brain injury prevention, research, education and advocacy.

Antonietta Anna Rosso, President
Pauline Fontaine, Treasurer
Ron S. Roskos, Executive Director

Vermont

3049 Brain Injury Association of Vermont
92 South Main Street, PO Box 482
Waterbury, VT 05676
802-244-6850
877-856-1772
Fax: 802-244-4005
support1@biavt.org
www.biavt.org

To create a better future through brain injury, prevention, research, education, and advocacy.

Trevor Squirrell, Executive Director
Barb Winters, Program Manager
Christy Opuszynski, Office Administrator

Virginia

3050 Brain Injury Association of Virginia
1506 Willow Lawn Dr., Suite 212
Richmond, VA 23230
804-355-5748
800-444-6443
Fax: 804-355-6381
www.biav.net

Nonprofit organization Creating a better future through brain injury education, awareness, advocacy, and support.

Irv Cantor, President
Anne McDonnell, Executive Director
Theresa Alonso, Data Coordinator

Washington

3051 Brain Injury Association of Washington
PO Box 3044
Seattle, WA 98114
206-388-0900
877-982-4292
Fax: 206-388-0901
admin@braininjurywa.org
www.braininjurywa.org

The mission, which begins with prevention, is to provide support to survivors of brain injury and their families, education to those who are being effected by brain injury, including the general public, and advocacy, to give the many suffering from this silent epidemic a public voice.

Mark T. Long, President
David A. Butters, Chair
Patrice Roney, Co-Chair Elect

West Virginia

3052 Brain Injury Association of West Virginia
PO Box 574
Institute, WV 25112
304-400-4506
800-356-6443
Fax: 304-205-7915
biawv@aol.com
www.biawestvirginia.org

A nonprofit agency dedicated to providing support, advocacy, education and training on behalf of survivors of brain injuries, their families and those who provide services or care for them.

Michael W Davis, President
Sharon McKenny Lord
Jennifer Rhule Stockton

Wisconsin

3053 Brain Injury Association of Wisconsin
N63 W23583 Main Street, Suite A
Sussex, WI 53089
262-790-9660
800-882-9282
Fax: 262-790-9670
lschultz@biaw.org
www.biaw.org

Established in 1980 by a group of individuals with brain injury, their families, friends, and professionals. BIAW is a chartered member affiliate of the national Brain Injury Association, Inc. BIAW provides services in these 5 core areas: information and resources, education, prevention, advocacy, and support services

Audrey Nelson, President
Lori Schultz, Executive Director
Patricia David, Operations Director

Head Injuries / Libraries & Resource Centers

Wyoming

3054 **Brain Injury Association of Wyoming**
111 W 2nd Street, Suite 106
Casper, WY 82601
307-473-1767
800-643-6457
Fax: 307-237-5222
director@wybia.org
www.wybia.org

The mission is to create a better future through brain injury prevention, research, education, and advocacy.
Dorothy Cronin, Executive Director
Dorothy Cronin, Executive Director

Libraries & Resource Centers

3055 **University of Illinois at Chicago, Craniofacial Center**
College of Medicine
808 S Wood Street
Chicago, IL 60612
312-996-7870
Fax: 312-413-1526
www.medicine.uic.edu

Richard M Novak, Director

Research Centers

California

3056 **Brain Imaging Center at the University of California, Irvine**
University of California, Irvine
Irvine, CA 92697
949-824-7872
Fax: 949-824-7873
bic@msx.hsis.uci.edu
www.bic.uci.edu

Performs clinical assessment of regional brainmetabolism for Parkinson's disease, epilepsy, brain tumor evaluation, Alzheimer'sdisease, and head injury. Other neuropsychiatric illnesses that are assessed with PETscans at UCI include stroke, psychotic disorders, and movement disorders.
Steven L Small, Director
David B. Keator, Technical Director
Jill Upton, Research Coordinator

3057 **Brain Research Institute**
Brain Research Institute UCLA
1506 Gonda, PO Box 951761
Los Angeles, CA 90095
310-825-5061
Fax: 310-206-5855
www.bri.ucla.edu

An organization research unit within the School of Medicine at the University of California, Los Angeles.
Christopher J. Evans, Director
J David Jentsch, Associate Director for Research
Michael S Levine, PhD, Associate Director for Education

3058 **Brain and Spinal Injury Center (BASIC) Research at University of California**
UCSF Department of Neurological
505 Parnassus Avenue, Room 779 M, PO Box 0112
San Francisco, CA 94143
415-353-7500
Fax: 415-353-2889
www.neurosurgery.medschool.ucsf.edu

Established to promote collaborative basic, translational, and clinical studies on injuries to the brain and spinal cord. BASIC is a joint effort between the Departments of Neurological Surgery and Neurology. Both departments bring their particular areas of expertise to a multidisciplinary effort centered on translational research.
Mitchel S. Berger, Managing Director
Manish Aghi, Managing Director
Christopher P. Ames, Managing Director

Louisiana

3059 **Tulane University, US-Japan Biomedical Research Laboratories**
Herbert Research Center
6823 St. Charles Avenue
New Orleans, LA 70118
504-862-8000
Fax: 504-394-7169
pr@tulane.edu
www.tulane.edu

Focuses research efforts on neuroendocrinology and neurosciences.
Yvette M. Jones, Vice President
Michael A. Bernstein, Provost/Vice President
Benjamin P. Sachs, Senior Vice President/Dean

Massachusetts

3060 **Harold Goodglass Aphasia Research Center**
150 S Huntington Avenue (12A), PO Box 4817
Boston, MA 02130
617-232-9500
857-364-4774
Fax: 617-739-8926
aphasia@bu.edu
www.bu.edu/aphasia

Research done into cognitive and language impairment following brain damage and closely related topics.
Harold Goodglass, MD, Director
Martin L. Albert, Managing Director
Lena Maskowich, Managing Director

Michigan

3061 **Bioengineering Center of Wayne State University**
Wayne State University
818 W Hancock
Detroit, MI 48201
313-577-1345
Fax: 313-577-8333
bmeinfo@eng.wayne.edu
www.engineering.wayne.edu

A leading laboratory doing research work in the areas of impact trauma, low back pain and orthopedic biomechanics. Current projects in impact trauma include research on side impact, rear end collisions, head injury and lower extremity injuries.
Albert I King, Director
Farshad Fotouhi, Dean of Engineering
Michael A. Anderson, Research Support Officer

3062 **Rehabilitation Institute of Michigan**
Detroit Medical Center/Wayne State University
261 Mack Avenue
Detroit, MI 48201
313-745-1203
Fax: 313-745-9863
www.rimrehab.org

Our dedicated group of board certified physicians are committed to improving the lives of their patients by providing quality, compassionate medical care and contributing to the science of rehabilitation medicine.
Mildred Matlock, Ceo
William H. Restum, PhD, President

New York

3063 **Brady Institute for Traumatic Brain Injury**
Jamaica Hospital Medical Center
8900 Van Wyck Expressway
Jamaica, NY 11418
718-206-6000
hr@jhmc.org
www.jamaicahospital.org

Provides general medical, pediatric,and psychiatric emergency services, ambulatory care, on and off campus ambulatory surgery, a broad spectrum of diagnostic and treatment services, and home health services.

3064 **Dana Alliance for Brain Initiatives**
505 5th Avenue, 6th Floor
New York, NY 10017
212-223-4040
Fax: 212-317-8721
dabiinfo@dana.org
www.dana.org

A nonprofit organization of more than 250 pre-eminent scientists dedicated to advancing education about the progress and promise of brain research.

Edward F Rover, President
Barbara E. Gill, Vice President
Burton M. Mirsky, Vice President-Finance

3065 **Rehabilitation Research and Training Center on Traumatic Brain Injury**
Mt. Sinai School of Medicine, Dept. Rehabilitation
155 Washington Ave, Suite 410, PO Box 2332
New York, NY 12210
518-449-2976
Fax: 518-426-4329
TDD: 518-449-2993
wayne.gordon@mssm.edu
www.rrti.org

Research to improve mood in people with TBI; analyze the content and quality of recently published post-TBI intervention studies; development of new measures of rehabilitation outcomes that incorporates both objective and subjective perspectives on participation in home and community activities; and a capacity building program to better educate professionals in identifying, assessing and providing appropriate interventions, treatments and accommodations for people with TBI.

Jacqueline A. Negri, Interim CEO
Stacie Muscolino-Benfer, Directors of Event & Administration
Lisa Zimmermann, HRSA Program Assisstant

3066 **Stroke Rehabilitation & Traumatic Brain Injury Research**
Ruft Institute at NYU Medical Center
400 E 34th Street
New York, NY 10016
212-263-6519
Fax: 212-263-8510
yehuda.ben-yishay@med.nyu.edu
www.med.nyu.edu/rusk/research

Ways of improving problem-solving behavior in individual with acquired brain damage are being investigated and instruments measuring problem solving in interpersonal situations are being developed.

Joan T Gold, Medical Director

Ohio

3067 **Ohio State University Laboratory of Psychobiology**
225 Psychology Bldg., 1835 Neil Avenue
Columbus, OH 43210
614-292-8185
Fax: 614-292-4537
www.psy.ohio-state.edu

Studies done on recovery of function after brain damage.

Karissa Basey, Fiscal/HR Associate
Stephanie Fowler, CCBBI Business Manager
Blanche Hollingshead, Fiscal/HR Associate

Pennsylvania

3068 **Institutes for Achievement of Human Potential**
8801 Stenton Avenue
Wyndmoor, PA 19038
215-233-2050
800-344-8322
Fax: 215-233-9312
institutes@iahp.org
www.iahp.org

A teaching institute that focuses on home-based neurological training for brain-injured children. Commited to the significant increases of the ability of all children to perform in the physical, intellectual and social realms. Our work has led to powerful insights about the brain and, especially, about its development in the neonate and very young children. We have developed exciting concepts and practices applied by parents at home, to mulitply the intelligence of tiny children.

500 members
Janet Doman, President
Glenn Doman, Founder
Dr. Ralph Pelligra, Chairman

3069 **Thomas Jefferson University Brain Injury Rehabilitation Program**
Thomas Jefferson University Hospital
111 South 11th Street
Philadelphia, PA 19107
215-955-6000
www.jeffersonhealth.org

Provides coordinated, multidisciplinary acute medical and surgical care for all levels of brain injury. The program delivers care for the acute phases of injury at Jefferson and shifts follow-up care to Magee Rehabilitation Hospital.

Thomas J Lewis, Ceo

Tennessee

3070 **University of Memphis Neuropsychology Lab**
Department of Psychology
202 Psychology Building, Room 126
Memphis, TN 38152
901-678-2000
Fax: 901-678-2579
www.memphis.edu

Evaluation and development of assessment and treatment procedures for neurologically impaired persons.

Shirley C. Raines, President
Rosie Phillips Bingham, Vice President for Student Affairs
Linda Bonnin, Vice President for Communications,

Texas

3071 **Brain Injury Research Center of the Institute for Rehabilitation & Research**
1333 Moursund Avenue
Houston, TX 77030
713-799-5000
www.tirr.memorialhermann.org

Brings together world-renowned researchers to study the many complicated facets of recovery from brain injury. BIRC has been able to leverage resources from the US Department of Education's National Institute for Rehabilitation and Research (NIDRR) and from NIH to conduct its research in a manner that facilitates the greatest progress in identifying effective treatments.

Carl Josehart, CEO
Gerard E. Francisco, MD/Chief Medical Officer
Mary Ann Euliarte, CNO/COO

Virginia

3072 **Virginia Commonwealth University Department of Neurosurgery Research**
417 North 11th Street, 6th Floor, PO Box 980631
Richmond, VA 23298
804-828-9165
Fax: 804-828-0374
www.neurosurgery.vcu.edu

Studies include work on cerebral blood flow, subarachnoid hemorrhage, vasospasm, ischemia, metabolism, cerebral edema, elevated intracranial pressure, trauma, secondary neural insults, CNS tumor biology, clinical trials for new brain tumor therapies, spinal biomechanics, computer imaging on the CNS and immunology of the nervous system.

Stuart P Adler, Research Director
Paul Dent, Vice Chair/Professor
Andrey Budanov, Asst. Professor

Head Injuries / Audio Video

Audio Video

3073 **Face First**
Fanlight Productions
32 Court Street, 21st Floor
Brooklyn, NY 11201
718-488-8900
800-876-1710
Fax: 718-488-8642
www.fanlight.com

Profiles of several people born with facial deformities; they chronicle both physical pain and the pain of rejection, as well as the strengths that have enabled them to achieve successful adult lives. ISBN: DVD: 1-57295-886-3; VHS: 1-572952-59-8

29 minutes DVD or VHS

Nicole Johnson, Publicity Coordinator

3074 **Surviving Coma: the Journey Back**
Brain Injury Association of Mississippi
2727 Old Canton Road
Jackson, MS 39296
601-981-1021
Fax: 601-981-1039
biaofms@aol.com

A realistic presentation about coma survival and the problems encountered during the long journey through rehabilitation.

19 Minutes

Paul Gospodarski, Ed.D, Executive Director

Web Sites

3075 **Brain Injury Association**
www.biausa.org
703-761-0750
800-444-6443
Fax: 703-761-0755
info@biausa.org
www.biausa.org

The mission of the Brain Injury Association is to create a better future through brain injury prevent, research, education and advocacy.

3076 **Brain Research Institute (BRI) School of Medicine University of California LA**
PO Box 951761
Los Angeles, CA 90095
310-825-5061
Fax: 310-206-5855
bri@mednet.ucla.edu
www.bri.ucla.edu

BRI's mission is to increase understanding of how the brain works, how it dvelops, and how it responds to experience, injury and disease, and to help make UCLA the preeminent center for translating basic knowledge into medical interventions and new technologies.

Dr. Christopher Evans, Director
Rafael Romero, Asst Director for Outreach
Baljit Khakh, Assoc. Dir. For Research

3077 **Centre for Neuro Skills**
5215 Ashe Rd.
Bakersfield, CA 93313
661-872-3408
800-922-4994
Fax: 661-872-5150
www.neuroskills.com

The TBI Resource Guide is the internet's central source of information, services, and products relating to traumatic brain injury, brain injury recovery, and post-acute rehabilitation.

Mark J. Ashley, ScD, CCM, President & CEO/ Co Founder

3078 **Dana Alliance for Brain Initiatives**
505 Fifth Ave., 6th Floor
New York, NY 10017
212-223-4040
Fax: 212-317-8721
www.dana.org/brainweb

Is a nonprofit organization of more then 200 neuroscientists, formed to help provide information about the personal and public benefits of brain research. Today one out of five Americans suffers from a brain-related disease or disorder, ranging from cocain addiction to learning diabilities from Alzheimer's disease to spinal cord injuries.

Edward F. Rover, Chair & President
Burton M. Mirsky, EVP, Finance
Barbara E. Gill, EVP, Public Affairs, Executive Dir.

3079 **NIH/National Institute of Neurological Disorders and Stroke (NINDS)**
PO Box 5801
Bethesda, MD 20824
301-496-5751
800-352-9424
www.ninds.nih.gov

The mission of NINDS is to reduce the burden of neurological disease, a burden borne by every age group, by every segment of society, by people all over the world.

Walter J. Koroshetz, MD, Director

3080 **Northeast Rehabilitation Health Network**
70 Butler Street
Salem, NH 3079
603-893-2900
800-439-0183
TTY: 800-439-2370
webmaster@northeastrehab.com
www.northeastrehab.com

We provide services within a continuum of care to individuals and families whos lives have been impcated by illness or injury in order to restore stability and maximize their potential for independence, functional abilites, and quality of life. In addition, we provide services that encourage well being. Our customers include: patients, families, physicians, referrers, payers, employees and the community.

John Prochilo, CEO & Administrator

3081 **Traumatic Brain Injury Model Systems Natio nal Data and Statistical Center**
www.tbindc.org

www.tbindc.org

The TBIMS program seeks to improve the lives of persons who experience traumatic brain injury, their families and their communities by creating and disseminating new knowledge about the course, treatment and outcomes relating to their condtion.

Book Publishers

3082 **Brain Disorders Sourcebook**
John Tilly, author

Omnigraphics
615 Griswold Street, Ste 520
Detroit, MI 48226
610-461-3548
800-234-1340
Fax: 800-875-1340
contact@omnigraphics.com
www.omnigraphics.com

Basic consumer information for the layperson about open-head and closed-head injuries, treatment advances, recovery and rehabilitation.

672 pages 5th Ed.
ISBN: 0-780816-20-6

3083 **Children with Traumatic Brain Injury**
Peytral Publications
PO Box 1162
Minnetonka, MN 55345
952-949-8707
877-739-8725
Fax: 952-949-8707
www.peytral.com

Comprehensive, must-have reference that provides parent with the support and information needed to help their child recover from a closed-head injury. Written by a team of medical specialists, therapists, educators and an attorney this publications covers medical concerns, rehabilitation, treatment, adjustment, effects on learning, thinking, language behavior and more.

482 pages
Lisa Schoenbrodt, EdD, Editor

3084 Cognitive Effects of Early Brain Injury
John's Hopkins University Press
2715 N Charles Street
Baltimore, MD 21218
410-516-6900
800-537-5487
Fax: 410-516-6968
webmaster@jhupress.jhu.edu
www.press.jhu.edu

This book offers a detailed overview of the effects of genetic, prenatal, and perinatal brain disorders on cognitive development and learning in children. Summarizing the available data as well as presenting previously unpublished research, the book provides clinicians with practical information that will aid their diagnostic and therapeutic work with children who have sustained early brain injury.

1994 336 pages Hardcover
ISBN: 0-801848-56-3

Kathleen Keane, Director
Erik A Smist, Director
Timothy D Fuller, Chief Information Officer

3085 Cognitive Rehabilitation for Persons with Traumatic Brain Injury
Paul H Brookes Publishing/Brookes
PO Box 10624
Baltimore, MD 21285
410-337-9580
800-638-3775
Fax: 410-337-8539
custserv@brookespublishing.com
www.brookespublishing.com

Virtually all persons with brain injury retain ability to learn. Cognitive rehab is a set of stategies to improve problems. Reports on theory, practices, research, consequences of brain trauma and assessment & intervention. Case studies.

1991 299 pages Hardcover
ISBN: 1-557660-71-9

Jeffrey S Kreutzer, Editor
Paul H Wehman, Editor

3086 Handbook of Head Truma: Acute Care to Recovery
Springer Publishing Company
11 W 42nd Street, 15th Floor
New York, NY 10036
877-687-7476
Fax: 212-941-7842
www.springerpub.com

Providing a thorough collection of information regarding clinical aspects of head injury from acute care to recovery, this treatise interrelates a variety of neural specialties and broadens the rehabilitation process to include the family

1992 472 pages
ISBN: 0-306439-47-6

Charles Long, Editor
Leslie Ross, Editor

3087 Head Injury in Children and Adolescents: A Resource and Review for School
John Wiley & Sons
10475 Crosspoint Boulevard
Indianapolis, IN 46256
877-762-2974
Fax: 800-597-3299
consumers@wiley.com
www.wiley.com

Complex nature of traumatic brain injury and its implications are examined carefully from medical, neuropsychological, rehabilitative and educational perspectives. Contents are arranged in a spiraling manner to provide the reader with a progressive and practical appreciation of traumatic brain injury and its neurobehavioral effects.

260 pages Hardcover
ISBN: 0-884220-98-2

Vivian Begali, Editor

3088 Let's Talk About Going to the Hospital
Rosen Publishing Group's PowerKids Press
29 E 21st Street
New York, NY 10010
212-777-3017
800-237-9932
Fax: 888-436-4643
rosenpub@tribeca.ios.com
www.rosenpublishing.com

If a child has to check into the hospital, chances are he or she is already upset about being ill. Knowing how a hospital functions and what the procedures are, such as when family members can visit, will help in what is already a stressful situation. Grades K-5.

24 pages
ISBN: 0-823950-36-0

Roger Rosen, President

3089 What To Do About Your Brain Injured Child
National Book Network
8801 Stenton Avenue
Wyndmoor, PA 19038
215-233-2050
800-344-8322
Fax: 215-233-3940
institutes@iahp.org
www.iahp.org

The author reveals life saving techniques to measure mobility, language, and manual, visual, auditory and tactile development.

318 pages
ISBN: 1-591170-23-0

Glen Doman, Editor

Journals

3090 Journal of Head Trauma Rehabilitation
Aspen Publishers
7201 McKinney Circle
Frederick, MD 21704
301-698-7100
800-234-1660
Fax: 800-901-9075
customer.service@wolterskluwer.com
www.wklawbusiness.com

A leading, peer-reviewed resource that provides up-to-date information on the clinical management and rehabilitation of persons with traumatic brain injuries. The journal is comprised of feature articles, brief reports, pharmacological updates, legislative and public policy updates, columns on ethics, book reviews, abstracts of selected literature, and more.

Mitchell Rosenthal, MD, Editor

Newsletters

3091 Headlines
Brain Injury Association of Minnesota
2277 Highway 36 West, Suite 200
Roseville, MN 55113
612-378-2742
800-669-6442
Fax: 612-378-2789
info@braininjurymn.org
www.braininjurymn.org

Published for the families and professionals who are involved with brain injuries. We also have an e-mail newsletter that reaches several hundred.

Quarterly

Ardis Sandstrom, Executive Director
Brad Donaldson, Associate Director of Operations
Richard Bloom, Board Treasurer

3092 Headway
Brain Injury Association of Virginia
1506 Willow Lawn Dr., Suite 212
Richmond, VA 23230
804-355-5748
800-444-6443
Fax: 804-355-6381
www.biav.net

Head Injuries / Pamphlets

Information and resources for individuals with brain injury, their family members and professionals dealing with brain injury.

16 pages Quarterly

Michelle Ward, Editor
Stephen Smith, President
Steve Hicks, Director of Development

3093 The Headliner
Brain Injury Association of Oregon
2145 NW Overton Street
Portland, OR 97210

503-413-7707
800-544-5243
Fax: 503-413-6849
biaor@biaoregon.org
www.biaoregon.org

To improve the quality of life of persons with brain injury and their families; and to prevent brain injury.

16 pages Quarterly

Craig Nichols, JD, President
Chuck McGilvrary, Vice President
Sherry Stock, Executive Director

Pamphlets

3094 Brain Injury Glossary
HDI Publishers
2407 Waugh Drive, PO Box 131401
Houston, TX 77219

713-526-6900
800-321-7037
Fax: 713-526-7787
sales@braininjurybooks.com
www.braininjurybooks.com

Contains special sections on terms relating to insurance, definitions relating to The Americans with Disabilities Act and descriptions of commonly prescribed medications. The Brain Injury Glossary is a must for all persons working or involved in brain injury rehabilitation.

1993 46 pages

L Don Lehmkuhl, Editor

3095 Brain Injury Update
HDI Publishers
2407 Waugh Drive, PO Box 131401
Houston, TX 77219

713-526-6900
800-321-7037
Fax: 713-526-7787
www.braininjurybooks.com

Monthly digest of news and information from the brain injury research and rehabilitation fields. Expanded summaries of journal articles, research papers, news releases and government reports are provided in a concise, time saving format. Brain Injury Update also provides information on grant opportunities, pharmacological intervention, calls for papers, people in the news, listings of upcoming conferences and symposia, legal and legislative developments and advances in prevention.

1991 Annual

Dr. Linda Thoi, Editor-in-Chief
Nathan D Zasler, MD, Contributing Editor

Camps

3096 Camp Hickory Wood
Traumatic Brain Injury Program
425 5th Avenue N, Cordell Hull Building
Nashville, TN 37243

800-882-0611
health.state.tn.us/TBI/index.htm

Each year the TBI Program in collaboration with Easter Seals Tennessee Inc. sponsors a weekend and a weeklong camp for adult and youth survivors of brain injury. These camps focus on providing a unique social and recreational opportunity to persons with brain injury. Nestled between the banks of Old Hickory Lake and surrounded by protective woods, camp offers great outdoor fun.

3097 Crotched Mountain School & Rehabilitation Center
1 Verney Drive
Greenfield, NH 3047

603-547-3311
800-800-966
Fax: 603-547-3232
info@crotchedmountain.org
www.cmf.org

Currently serves children ages 6-22 with multiple-handicaps including: Cerebral Palsy, Spina Bifida, visual and hearing impairments and neurological disabilities, developmental disorders, autism, behavioral and emotional disorders, seizure disorders, spinal cord and head injuries. Member of the National Association of Independent Schools and accredited with the NE Association of Schools and Colleges, Independent Schools of Northern NE.

Kathleen C. Brittan, Vice President of Development
William Cossaboon, MS, Director of Education
W. Carl Cooley, MD, Chief Medical Officer

3098 Oklahoma Brain Injury Camp
Oklahoma Brain Injury Association
3015 E. Skelly Dr.
Tulsa, OK 74105

405-928-1647
Fax: 918-712-9019
braininjuryoklahoma@gmail.com
www.braininjuryoklahoma.org

An annual camp for brain injury survivors sponsored by the Brain Injury Association of Oklahoma. Great fun had by all with music, games, crafts, a hayride, cookout, bingo, fishing, and paddle boat rides.

Cathe Fox, Camp Director
Adam Sherman, Ph.D, President
Mary Dobbs, BSN, RN, CRRN, Vice President

Description

3099 HEARING IMPAIRMENT/DEAFNESS
Covers these related disorders: Conductive deafness or hearing loss, Mixed hearing loss, Sensorineural deafness or hearing loss, Noise Induced Hearing Loss
Involves the following Biologic System(s):
Neurologic Disorders

Hearing impairment may be defined as a loss of the ability to hear that is sufficient enough to impede the ability to communicate. Deafness refers to severe or profound hearing loss. Hearing loss or deafness may occur as the result of hereditary factors or birth defects. Hearing loss may also be acquired and occur after birth (e.g., from disease or physical damage to the hearing mechanism). However, genetic factors are thought to be responsible for moderate to severe hearing loss in about half of affected children. Hearing loss may be further categorized into three types: conductive, sensorineural, or mixed.

Conductive hearing loss occurs as a result of the faulty transmission of sound through the external or middle ear to the inner ear. This transmission problem may be due to infections of the middle ear (otitis media), damage to the eardrum or bones of the middle ear, the absence or the narrowing of the ear canal, impacted earwax (cerumen), foreign bodies in the ear canal, or other physical causes. In addition, conductive hearing loss is sometimes inherited as a feature of certain syndromes such as Klippel-Feil syndrome, Crouzon syndrome, osteogenesis imperfecta, and others. In children with sensorineural hearing loss, sounds are conducted to the inner ear through the external and middle ear, but are not transmitted from there to the brain. This occurs as the result of a defect in the structure of the inner ear or problems with the nerve that conveys impulses from the inner ear to the brain (auditory nerve; acoustic nerve; eighth cranial nerve). Sensorineural hearing loss that results from defects of inner ear structures is considered sensory and includes: the absence or underdevelopment of the snail shell-type tubular structure of the inner ear (cochlea); damage to hair cells or other inner ear structures from prolonged exposure to loud noise, certain drugs; viral infections or other diseases; and other irregularities.

Noise Induced Hearing Loss (NIHL) results from exposure to harmful noise levels that trigger the formation of molecules inside the ear that damage hair cells. The hair cells are small sensory cells that convert sound energy into electrical signals that travel to the brain. Damaged hair cells cannot grow back. These destructive molecules play an important role in hearing loss in children and adults who are exposed to loud noise for extended periods. Individuals of all ages, including children, can develop NIHL.

Sensorineural hearing loss that results from damage to the auditory nerve pathway is considered neural and may be due to brain lesions or tumors; childhood disorders such as German measles, mumps, inner ear infections, etc.; certain hereditary disorders (e.g., Waardenburg syndrome, Usher syndrome, etc.); diseases that affect the myelin sheath, which is the fatty, protective, insulating covering on certain nerve fibers (demyelinating diseases); or seizures. Mixed hearing loss refers to a combination of both conductive and sensorineural hearing loss.

Early screening for hearing loss is important in order to provide early intervention that will allow the best outcome for educational and social development. Treatment may require the cooperation of parents, caregivers, pediatricians, speech and language pathologists, and specialists in hearing loss (audiologists) who assess the extent of hearing loss through the use of specialized tests. Infant screening by specialists may include tests that gauge behavioral responses to noise through observation, such as a startle response to a sudden hand clap. Other tests may electronically assess hearing loss (audiometry); measure the head-turning response of an infant or toddler using animated aids in conjunction with sounds emitted through a loudspeaker (visual reinforcement audiometry or VRA); measure the lowest intensity at which certain words are heard or understood (speech recognition threshold or SRT); measure the ability of the middle ear to impede or resist sound energy (tympanometry); differentiate between sensory and neural hearing loss (auditory brain stem response); measure the integrity of the cochlea (otoacoustic emissions or OAEs).

According to the National Institute on Deafness and Other Communication Disorders, males are more likely to experience hearing loss than females. Two to three of every 1,000 children who are born deaf have hearing parents.

Treatment for conductive hearing loss may include the removal of fluid, earwax, or foreign bodies through drainage or other means. Surgical intervention may be indicated for the correction of structural abnormalities. Children as well as infants with hearing loss may benefit from the use of certain types of hearing aids; however, repeat testing is necessary to provide more exact hearing aid specification.

In the United States, roughly 41,500 adults and 25,500 children receive cochlear implants per year. Hearing loss affects only one ear in nine out of 10 people who experience sudden deafness. Approximately 26 million Americans have Noise Induced Hearing Loss (NIHL). Recreational activities that can put someone at risk for NIHL include target shooting and hunting, snowmobile riding, woodworking and other hobbies, playing in a band, and attending rock concerts. Harmful noises at home may come from lawnmowers, leaf blowers, and shop tools.

In addition, cochlear implants are available to children with severe or profound hearing loss. Other treatment is directed toward the teaching of communication skills such as lip-reading, sign language, and speech. Cooperation and support of family, medical specialists, and educators is important in determining the best approach for the education and social development of the individual child.

Government Agencies

3100 NIH/National Institute on Deafness and Other Communication Disorders (NIDCD)
31 Center Drive, MSC 2320
Bethesda, MD 20892
800-241-1044
TTY: 800-241-1055
nidcdinfo@nidcd.nih.gov
www.nidcd.nih.gov

Conducts and supports biomedical research and research training on normal mechanisms, as well as diseases and disorders of hearing, balance, smell, taste, voice, speech and language.
Debara L. Tucci, MD, Director
Judith A. Cooper, PhD, Deputy Director
Timothy J. Wheeles, Executive Officer

3101 Office of Special Education and Rehabilitation Services
400 Maryland Avenue SW
Washington, DC 20202
202-245-7468
www.ed.gov

Hearing Impairment/Deafness / National Associations & Support Groups

Information and advocacy resources for families and professionals. Includes listings of organizations providing general information and organizations focusing on more specific areas of concern to families and young adults who have disabilities.

David Cantrell, Assistant Secretary
Paul Steenen, Director, Communications

National Associations & Support Groups

3102 ASHFoundation
2200 Research Blvd.
Rockville, MD 20850
301-296-8700
foundationprograms@asha.org
www.ashfoundation.org

An organization which promotes a better quality of life for children and adults with communication disorders.

Sharon Moss, Executive Director
Allison Oakes, Programs Administrator

3103 Academy of Rehabilitative Audiology
www.audrehab.org

ara@audrehab.org
www.audrehab.org

The primary purpose of ARA is to promote excellence in hearing care through the provision of comprehensive rehabilitative and habilitative services.

Carole E. Johnson, President
Brittney Carlson, Treasurer
Laura Gaeta, Secretary

3104 Acoustical Society of America
1305 Walt Whitman Road, Suite 110
Melville, NY 11747
516-576-2360
Fax: 631-923-2875
asa@acousticalsociety.org
www.acousticalsociety.org

The ASA specializes in acoustics. They are dedicated to diffusing and increasing the knowledge of acoustics and its practical application.

3105 Alexander Graham Bell Association for the Deaf and Hearing Impaired
3417 Volta Place NW
Washington, DC 20007
202-337-5220
Fax: 202-337-8314
TTY: 202-337-5221
info@agbell.org
www.agbell.org

The Alexander Graham Bell Association for the Deaf and Hard of Hearing (AG Bell) is a lifelong resource, support network and advocate for listening, learning, talking, and living independently with hearing loss. Through publications, advocacy, training, scholarships, and financial aid, AG Bell promotes the use of spoken language and hearing technology.

Emilio Alonso-Mendoza, Chief Executive Officer
Lisa Chutjian, Chief Development Officer
Trenita Dickey, Manager, Membership/Donor Relations

3106 American Academy of Audiology
11480 Commerce Park Drive, Suite 220
Reston, VA 20191
703-790-8466
Fax: 703-790-8631
info@audiology.org
www.audiology.org

A professional organization dedicated to providing high quality and balanced hearing care to the public. Provides professional development, education and research and provides increased public awareness of hearing disorders and audiologic services.

Patrick E. Gallagher, Executive Director
Anne Poodiak, VP, Meetings & Educations
Glenn Feder, Senior Director, Sales

3107 American Academy of Pediatrics
345 Park Blvd
Itasca, IL 60143
800-433-9016
Fax: 847-434-8000
mcc@aap.org
www.aap.org

The American Academy of Pediatrics and its member pediatricians are committed to the attainment of optimal physical, mental and social health and well-being for all infants, children, adolescents, and young adults.

Lynn Olson, PhD, VP, Research
Mark Del Monte, JD, CEO/Executive VP
Vera Tait, MD, FAAP, Chief Medical Officer

3108 American Cochlear Implant Alliance
PO Box 103
McLean, VA 22101
703-534-6146
info@acialliance.org
www.acialliance.org

TheÿAmerican Cochlear Implant Allianceÿis a not-for-profit membership organization created with the purpose of eliminating barriers to cochlear implantation by sponsoring research, driving heightened awareness and advocating for improved access to cochlear implants for patients of all ages across the US.

Donna L. Sorkin, Executive Director
Laura Odato, Director, Operations & Marketing
Jessica Houk, Manager, Membership Services

3109 American Deafness and Rehabilitation Assoc iation (ADARA)
PO Box 675
Lakeville, MN 55044
office@adara.org
www.adara.org

The mission of the ADARA is to facilitate excellence in human service delivery with individuals who are Deaf or Hard of Hearing. This mission is accomplished by enhancing the professional competencies of the membership, expanding opportunities for networking among ADARA colleagues and supporting positive public policies for individuals who are Deaf or Hard of Hearing.

3110 American Hearing Impaired Hockey Association
ahiha.org

kdelaney@ahiha.org
ahiha.org

TheÿAmerican Hearing Impaired Hockey Associationÿprovides deaf and hard of hearing hockey players the opportunity to learn about and improve their hockey skills through our program. We offer these hockey players the opportunity to be coached by a coaching staff with college, national and international experience.

3111 American Hearing Research Foundation
154 W Park Avenue, Suite 586
Elmhurst, IL 60126
630-617-5079
ahrf@american-hearing.org
www.american-hearing.org

Funds medical research and education into the causes, prevention, and cures of hearing losses, and balance disorders. Also keeps physicians and the public informed of the latest developments in hearing research and education.

Richard G. Muench, Chair
Alan G. Micco, President
David J. Wuertz, Treasurer

3112 American Society for Deaf Children
PO Box 23
Woodbine, MD 21797
800-942-2732
info@deafchildren.org
deafchildren.org

A nonprofit parent-helping-parent organization promoting a positive attitude toward signing and deaf culture. Also provides support, encouragement, and current information about deafness to families with deaf and hard-of-hearing children.

Hearing Impairment/Deafness / National Associations & Support Groups

3113 **American Speech Language Hearing Association (ASHA)**
2200 Research Blvd
Rockville, MD 20852
301-296-5700
800-638-8255
Fax: 301-296-8580
TTY: 301-296-5650
actioncenter@asha.org
www.asha.org

ASHA is the professional, scientific and credentialling association for more than 123,000 members and affiliates who are speech-language pathologists, audiologists, and speech, language, and hearing scientitsts. Their mission is to promote the interests of and provide the highest quality services for proesstionals, and to advocate for people with communication disabilities.

Shari B. Robertson, President
Theresa H. Rodgers, President-Elect

3114 **American Tinnitus Association**
PO Box 424049
Washington, DC 20042
800-634-8978
www.ata.org

The American Tinnitus Association exists to cure tinnitus through the development of resources that advance tinnitus research.

Torryn Brazell, Executive Director

3115 **Better Hearing Industries Association**
1301 K Street NW, Suite 300W
Washington, DC 20005
202-975-0905
betterhearing.org

The Hearing Industries Association (HIA) was formed in 1955 and serves as a forum for hearing aid manufacturers, suppliers, distributors, and hearing health professionals. Our members are responsible for the majority of the over 4 million hearing aids that are purchased in the United States on an annual basis. Today, HIA remains the only association in America to represent hearing aid technology.

Kate Carr, President
Lindsay Robinson, Program Coordinator
Bridget Dobyan, Director, Public Policy & Advocacy

3116 **Center for Early Intervention of Deafness (CEID)**
1035 Grayson Street
Berkeley, CA 94710
510-848-4800
info@ceid.org
www.ceid.org

A non-profit organization dedicated to providing a program of intensive and comprehensive early intervention services to young children up to five years old who have hearing losses or severe speech/language delays and their families. CEID uses 'Total Communication', which includes the simultaneous use of spoken English, audition, and literal representation of sign language (SEE signing), in a play based curriculum incorporating thematic active learning strategies and total family involvement.

Cindy Dickeson, President & CEO
Kate Glass, Development Director
Anna Philips, Operations Director

3117 **Coalition for Global Hearing Health**
www.coalitionforglobalhearinghealth.org

Works with the mission to promote and enhance hearing health services in low-resourced communities.

3118 **Cochlear Implant Awareness Foundation**
830 South Grand Avenue W
Springfield, IL 62704
217-679-4643
info@ciafonline.org
www.ciafonline.org

The mission of CIAF is to raise awareness of how cochlear implants restore sound to the hearing impaired and to provide cochlear implant equipment to qualified applicants in need.

Michelle Tjelmeland, Founder & Chair
Sheryl Klemm, Director
Max Klemm, Director

3119 **Council of the American Instructors of the Deaf**
www.caid.org

The organization for all teachers, administrators, educational interpreters, residential personnel, and other concerned professionals involved in education of the deaf.

Stephanie Kessen, President
Natasha Kraft, Treasurer

3120 **Council on Education of the Deaf**
7703 Floyd Curl Drive
San Antonio, TX 78229
executivedirector@councilondeafed.org
councilondeafed.org

The Council on Education of the Deaf (CED) is an organization sponsored by eight major national organizations dedicated to quality education for all deaf and hard of hearing students.

Sarah Ammerman, Co-Executive Director
Blane Trautwein, Co-Executive Director

3121 **Deaf Counseling, Advocacy & Referral Agency**
14895 E. 14th Street, Suite 200
San Leandro, CA 94578
510-343-6670
info@dcara.org
www.dcara.org

Deaf, Counseling, Advocacy & Referral Agency (DCARA), is a non-profit, community-based social service agency serving the Deaf, Hard of Hearing, Late-Deafened and Deaf-blind (D/HH/LD/DB) community.

3122 **Deaf REACH**
3722 - 12th Street NE
Washington, DC 20017
202-832-6681
www.deaf-reach.org

Nonprofit organization: our mission is to maximize the self-sufficiency of deaf adults needing special services by providing referral, education, advocacy, counseling, and housing.

Michele May, Executive Director

3123 **Educational Audiology Association**
24123 Peachland Boulevard, Suite C4 #349
Port Charlotte, FL 33954
800-460-7322
admin@edaud.org
edaud.org

The Educational Audiology Association is an international organization of audiologists and related professionals who deliver a full spectrum of hearing services to all children, particularly those in educational settings.

Krista Yuskow, AuD, President
Cassie Thomas, AuD, F-AAA, Vice President of Publications
Kathleen Riley, AuD, CCC-A, F-AAA, Vice President of Advocacy

3124 **Episcopal Conference of the Deaf**
9373 Garber Road
Crestwood, MO 63126
info@ecdeaf.org
www.ecdeaf.org

The ECD is a central clearing house concerning all aspects of work among Deaf people in the Episcopal Church. Episcopal Conference of the Deaf spreads the Gospel of Christ among Deaf people.

Rev. Dr. Cathy Deats, Chaplain
Robert Hartzog, Membership Secretary
Jason D. Boyd, Communications Coordinator

3125 **Hands & Voices National**
PO Box 3093
Boulder, CO 80307
303-492-6283
parentaladvocate@handsandvoices.org
www.handsandvoices.org

A nationwide non-profit organization dedicated to supporting families and their children who are deaf or hard-of-hearing as well as the professionals who serve them.

Janet DesGeorges, Executive Director
Lisa Kovacs, Director of Programs
Helen Cotton Leiser, Director of Fundraising

3126 **Hearing Health Foundation**
PO Box 1397
New York, NY 10018
212-257-6140
info@hhf.org
hearinghealthfoundation.org

Hearing Impairment/Deafness / National Associations & Support Groups

Hearing Health Foundation (HHF) is the largest private funder of hearing research, with a mission to prevent and cure hearing loss and tinnitus through groundbreaking research.

Timothy Higdon, President & CEO
Noemi Disla, Director, Finance/Operations/Admin
Christopher Geissler, Director, Programs/Research Support

3127 Hearing Loss Association of America
6116 Executive Boulevard, Suite 230
Rockville, MD 20852
301-657-2248
Fax: 301-913-9413
www.hearingloss.org

HLAA provides assistance and resources for people with hearing loss and their families to learn how to adjust to living with hearing loss. HLAA is working to eradicate the stigma associated with hearing loss and raise public awareness about the need for prevention, treatment, and regular hearing screenings throughout life.

Barbara Kelley, Executive Director
Lise Hamlin, Director of Public Policy
Rini Indrawati, Director of Finance & Operations

3128 Hearts and Homes For Youth
3919 National Drive, Suite 400
Burtonsville, MD 20866
301-589-8444
Fax: 301-495-0923
hhyinfo@heartsandhomes.org
heartsandhomes.org

Hearts & Homes for Youth is a nonprofit organization dedicated to empowering youth who have experienced abuse, neglect, mental health issues, homelessness, and other trauma, to make positive life choices and build brighter futures. Offers assistance through group homes, therapeutic group homes, foster care, independent living, a program for pregnant and parenting teen mothers, and a workforce readiness program.

Chloe Bernardi, President & CEO

3129 International Deaf Education Association
P.O. Box 20715
Billings, MT 59104
406-272-3240
info@ideadeaf.org
www.ideadeaf.org

IDEA is a USA non-profit foundation that is working to educate impoverished and neglected deaf children in the Philippines.

3130 International Hearing Society
16880 Middlebelt Road, Suite 4
Livonia, MI 48154
734-522-7200
Fax: 734-522-0200
www.ihsinfo.org

The International Hearing Society (IHS) is a membership association that represents hearing healthcare professionals worldwide. IHS members are engaged in the practice of testing human hearing and selecting, fitting and dispensing hearing instruments and counseling patients. Founded in 1951, the Society continues to recognize the need for promoting and maintaining the highest possible standards for its members in the best interests of the hearing impaired it serves.

3000 members

Alissa Parady, Executive Director
Kelsey Burch, Manager of Operations
Katie Chuba, Director of Membership

3131 John Tracy Clinic
2160 W Adams Boulevard
Los Angeles, CA 90018
213-748-5481
web@jtc.org
www.jtc.org

A private, non-profit education center whose mission is to offer hope, guidance and encouragement to families of infants and preschool children with hearing loss by providing free, parent-centered services worldwide. The center has over 60 years of expertise in the spoken language option.

Cathleen Mathes, President & CEO
Cecilia Vanin, Chief Operating Officer
Kevin Matthews, Chief Financial Officer

3132 Junior National Association of the Deaf
8630 Fenton Street, Suite 820
Silver Spring, MD 20910
301-587-1788
TTY: 301-810-3182
nad.info@nad.org
youth.nad.org/junior-nad

The Jr. NAD, a program of the NAD, offers deaf and hard of hearing students in 7th through 12th grade opportunities to develop leadership skills, learn and demonstrate citizenship, and meet and interact with students from other schools and states. Students can participate in the Jr. NAD by joining chapters established by their schools. Jr. NAD chapters focus on advocacy, attitude, awareness, commitment, cooperation, friendship, information exchange, involvement and leadership skills.

3133 NC BEGINNINGS
156-A Wind Chime Court
Raleigh, NC 27615
919-715-4092
Fax: 919-715-4093
ncbegin.org

BEGINNINGS provides emotional support and access to as a central resource for families with deaf or hard of hearing children, age birth through 21. These services are also available to deaf parents who have hearing children. Their mission is to help parents to be informed, empowered and supported as they make decisions about their child. In addition, they are committed to providing technical assistance to professionals who work with these families.

Diane E. Doak, Executive Director
Joanna D. Chantemerle, Director of Programs
Ellen Fort, Director of Delevement & Marketing

3134 National Association for Hearing and Speech Action
American Speech Language Hearing Association
2200 Research Blvd., PO Box 3289
Rockville, MD 20850
301-296-5700
800-478-2071
Fax: 301-296-5777
TDD: 301-296-5650
nasha@asha.org
www.asha.org

Provides general information on speech, language and hearing disorders to members and the public. Provides referrals to speech/language pathologists and audiologists.

77,346 members

Arlene A. Pietranton, PhD, President

3135 National Association of School Psychologists
4340 East West Highway, Suite 402
Bethesda, MD 20814
301-657-0270
866-331-NASP
Fax: 301-657-0275
www.nasponline.org

NASP empowers school psychologists by advancing effective practices to improve students' learning, behavior, and mental health.

Kathleen Minke, Executive Director
Pavel Obgolz, Chief Operating Officer

3136 National Association of the Deaf (NAD)
8630 Fenton Street, Suite 820
Silver Spring, MD 20910
301-587-1788
Fax: 301-587-1791
TTY: 301-587-1791
nad.info@nad.org
www.nad.org

Established in 1880, the vision of NAD is that the language, culture, and heritage of hard of hearing Americans will be acknowledged and respected in pursuit of life, liberty and equality. There efforts to realize the vision have been in preserving, protecting, and promoting civil, human and liguitis rights of deaf and hard of hearing persons in America.

Howard Rosenblum, Chief Executive Officer
Tom Well, Director of Finance
Angela Ellman, Conference Coordinator

3137 National Black Deaf Advocates
1500 Chestnut Street, Suite 2224
Philadelphia, PA 19102
info@nbda.org
www.nbda.org

Hearing Impairment/Deafness / Libraries & Resource Centers

The National Black Deaf Advocates (NBDA) is the official advocacy organization for thousands of Black Deaf and hard of hearing people in the United States.ÿ

3138 National Captioning Institute
14801 Murdock Street, Suite 210
Chantilly, VA 20151
703-917-7600
TTY: 703-917-7600
www.ncicap.org

NCI was established in 1979 as a non-profit corporation with the mission of ensuring that deaf and hard of hearing people, as well as others who can benefit from the same service, have access to television's entertainment and news through the technology of closed captioning.

Gene Chao, Chair & CEO
Beth Nubbe, SVP, Finance
Meredith Patterson, SVP, Operations & COO

3139 National Catholic Office for the Deaf
7202 Buchanan Street
Landover Hills, MD 20784
301-577-1684
info@ncod.org
www.ncod.org

The National Catholic Office for the Deaf is a non-profit membership organization dedicated to pastoral ministry with deaf and hard of hearing persons. NCOD serves 5.7 million deaf and hard of hearing Catholics through its pastoral ministry and through its special advocacy to bishops, pastors and families with children who are deaf and hard of hearing.

3140 National Center On Deaf-Blindness
Helen Keller National Center
141 Middle Neck Road
Sands Point, NY 11050
516-366-0047
support@nationaldb.org
nationaldb.org

NCDB works to improve the quality of life for children who are deaf-blind and their families.

Sam Morgan, Project Co-Director
Julie Durando, Project Co-Director

3141 National Cued Speech Association
PO Box 2733
Fairfax, VA 22031
800-459-3529
info@cuedspeech.org
www.cuedspeech.org

A non-profit membership organization founded in 1982 to promote and support the effective use of Cued Speech. They raise awareness of Cued Speech and its applications, provide educational services, assist local affiliate chapters, establish standards for Cued Speech and certify Cued Speech instructors and transliterators. Their mission and goals are to promote and support the effectuve use of Cued Speech for communication, language acquistion and literacy.

3142 National Family Association for Deaf-Blind
PO Box 1667
Sands Point, NY 11050
800-255-0411
Fax: 516-883-9060
info@nfadb.org
www.nfadb.org

A nonprofit, volunteer based, family association that believes individuals who are deaf-blind are valued members of society and are entitled to the same opportunity and choices as other members of the community

Patti McGowan, President
Brandi Hitzelberger, Treasurer
Katrina Michel, Secretary

3143 National Rehabilitation Information Center
8400 Corporate Drive, Suite 500
Landover, MD 20785
800-346-2742
Fax: 301-459-4263
TTY: 301-459-5984
www.naric.com

Committed to providing direct, personal and information services to anyone interested in disability rehabilitation issues; Committed to serving consumers, researchers, family members, health professionals, educators, counselors, students, librarians and the administrators.

Mark X. Odum, Project Director
Jessica H. Chaiken, Media/Information Services Manager
Natalie J. Collier, Library and Aquisitions Manager

3144 National Technical Institute for the Deaf
Rochester Institute of Technology
52 Lomb Memorial Drive
Rochester, NY 14623
585-475-6400
TTY: 585-475-6400
ntidmc@rit.edu
www.rit.edu/ntid

Technical college for students who are deaf or hard of hearing. Its mission is to provide these students with outstanding state-of-the-art technical and professional programs, complemented by a strong liberal arts and sciences curriculum, that prepare them to live and work in the mainstream of a rapidly changing global community and enhances their lifelong learning.

Gerard Buckley, President

3145 Telecommunications for the Deaf and Hard of Hearing
www.tdiforaccess.org

TDI monitors and comments on federal policies and rules involving access to information and communication technologies. To best represent the diverse DHH community, TDI engages, interacts, and networks with many DHH stakeholders through a variety of programs: online DHH directory, a biennial conference coined TDIConf, an on-demand video learning resource, and a digital publication.

Genelle Sanders, Director of Programming

3146 The House Institute Foundation
1127 Wilshire Boulevard, Suite 1620
Los Angeles, CA 90017
213-770-2187
hello@hifla.org
hifla.org

The House Institute Foundation provides hearing health information to the public and education programs for medical professionals. The foundation's search focuses on defining causes of hearing and balance disorders and developing the solutions necessary to aid the deaf and hard-of-hearing. The foundation's global mission is to further access to treatments, technology, and training in high-need communities locally and worldwide.

Catherine D. Meyer, Chair
David Z. D'Argenio, Vice Chair
William B. Witte, Treasurer

Libraries & Resource Centers

3147 AbleData
8630 Fenton Street - Suite 300 B
Lexington, KY 40513
301-608-8998
800-227-0216
Fax: 301-608-8958
TTY: 301-608-8912
abledata@macrointernational.com
www.abledata.com

AbleData provides information on assistive technology and rehabilitation equipment available from international and domestic sources to consumers, professionals, organizations, and caregivers within the United States.

3148 Center for Hearing and Communication
50 Broadway - 6th Fl
New York, NY 10004
917-305-7700
Fax: 917-305-7888
TTY: 917-305-7999
www.chchearing.org

This organization provides hearing health services to people of all ages who have a hearing loss.

3149 Communication Service for the Deaf, Inc.
102 North Krohn Place
Sioux Falls, SD 57103
800-642-6410
TTY: 866-273-3323
inquiry@c-s-d.org
www.ceasd.org

Hearing Impairment/Deafness / Libraries & Resource Centers

CSD Relay is a telephone service which allows persons with hearing or speech disabilities to place and receive telephone calls.

3150 Dangerous Decibels Oregon Health & Science University
3181 SW Sam Jackson Park Road - NRC-04
Portland, OR 97239
503-494-0670
Fax: 503-494-0670
dd@ohsu.edu
www.dangerousdecibels.com

Through the creation of exhibits, education and research this organization helps to reduce the incidence and prevalence of Noise Induced Hearing Loss (NIHL) and tinnitus (ringing in the ear) by changing knowledge, attitudes, and behaviours of school-aged children.

3151 Hard of Hearing Advocates
245 Prospect St, PO Box 1184
Upton, MA 01701
hoha@charter.net
www.hohadvocates.org

This organization helps hard-of-hearing (HOH) people by creating and implementing programs and solutions where HOH people have undue problems.

3152 Hearing Education & Awareness for Rockers
PO Box 460847
San Francisco, CA 94146
415-409-3277
hear@hearnet.com
www.hearnet.com

H.E.A.R. is a hearing information source for musicians and music lovers.

Alabama

3153 Alabama Institute for the Deaf & Blind
PO Box 698
Talladega, AL 35161
256-761-3331
Fax: 256-761-3344
www.aidb.org

Services include central directory, representatives of agencies, service providers, families, and coordinators of infant, toddler, and preschool special education programs.

Terry Graham, President

3154 University of Alabama Speech and Hearing Center
Deparment of Communicative Disorders
166 Rose Administration Building Box 870144
Tuscaloosa, AL 35487
205-348-5320
Fax: 205-348-8320
www.universityrelations.ua.edu

Enhancing the educational mission of the Department, the Speech and Hearing Center is further dedicated to reducing the impact of communicative disorders affecting diverse populations across a life-span.

Carl E Ferguson, Executive Director
Austin Dare, Director,Office of Design/Productio

California

3155 American Action Fund for Blind Children and Adults
18440 Oxnard Street
Tarzana, CA 91356
818-343-2022
Fax: 818-343-3219
lucyabba@aol.com
www.actinfund.org

A lending library for the visually impaired. We send out a weekly Braille newspaper for the deaf-blind (worldwide), we also send out pocket-sized Braille calendars. Our lending library is for pre-school thru high school. All of our services are free.

Lucille Abbazia, Manager

3156 Hear Center
301 E Del Mar Boulevard
Pasadena, CA 91101
626-796-2016
Fax: 626-796-2320
www.hearcenter.org

The Hear Center's mission is to help individuals with hearing loss or speech and language impairments integrate into the mainstream of the community by providing them with the means for developing auditory and oral communication skills.

Ellen Simon, Executive Director

District of Columbia

3157 Center for Auditory and Speech Sciences-Gallaudet University
800 Florida Avenue NE
Washington, DC 20002
202-651-5000
Fax: 202-651-5295
clerc.center@gallaudet.edu
www.gallaudet.edu

The Hearing and Speech Center provides comprehensive speech, language, and audiology services to Gallaudet students, faculty, staff and to clients in the Washington, D.C. area. These services include hearing and hearing aid evaluations, hearing aid dispensing, assistive devices evaluations, speech-language evaluations and therapy, communication therapy, and speech reading classes.

I King Jordon, President
Jane K Fernandes, Provost
Paul Kelly, VP Administration and Finance

3158 District of Columbia Public Library/ Librarian for the Deaf Community
901 G Street NW, Room 215
Washington, DC 20001
202-727-2142
Fax: 202-727-1129
lbphb_2000@yahoo.com
www.dclibrary.org

Offers reference services through TDD, portable TDD for public use at pay phones, signers for library programs, sign language classes, information about deafness, print and nonprint materials for persons who are deaf.

Vaneisha Denson, Manager

3159 Laurent Clerc National Deaf Education Center-Gallaudet Universty
800 Florida Avenue NE
Washington, DC 20002
202-651-5300
Fax: 202-651-5477
TTY: 202-651-5300
www.gallaudet.edu

Gallaudet University's Laurent Clerc National Deaf Education Center provides deaf and hard of hearing children through the Model Secondary School for the Deaf and the Kendall Demonstration Elementary School and also collects, evaluates and disseminates best practices in deaf education.

I King Jordan, President
Katherine Jankowski, Dean
Paul Kelly, VP Administration/Finance

3160 Volta Bureau Library
Alexander Graham Bell Association for the Deaf
3417 Volta Place NW
Washington, DC 20007
202-337-5220
866-337-5220
Fax: 202-337-8314
TTY: 202-337-5221
agbell2@aol.com
www.agbell.org

Contains one of the world's largest historical collections of publications, documents and information on deafness. In addition to the main collection, which includes books, periodicals and indexed clipping files dating from the turn of the century, the library also houses a significant archival collection dealing with the history of deafness since the 16th century. Membership dues for professionals are $50.00.

4500 members

Rebecca Parlakian, Director Member Services

Hearing Impairment/Deafness / Research Centers

Illinois

3161 Loyola University of Children, Parmly Hearing Institute
6525 N Sheridan Road
Chicago, IL 60626
773-508-2766
Fax: 773-508-2719

The Parmly Hearing Institute is part of Loyola University Chicago.

Stanley Edward Sheft PhD, Director

Maine

3162 University of Maine, Conley Speech and Hearing Center
5724 Dunn Hall, Room 336
Orono, ME 04469
207-581-2006

The Madelyn E and Albert D Conley Speech, Language and Hearing Center is a center for clinical education and research as well as a facility for comprehensive state-of-the-art speech, language and hearing services. Both the Audiology Clinic and the Speech-Language Clinic provide services for individuals across the lifespan. The Speech-Language Clinic includes a Diagnostic Clinic, a Family-Based Treatment Clinic, and a Stuttering Clinic.

Susan K Riley MS, Clinic Director

Massachusetts

3163 Eaton-Peabody Laboratory of Auditory Physiology
Massachusetts Eye & Ear Institute
243 Charles Street
Boston, MA 02114
617-573-7900
Fax: 617-720-4408
TDD: 617-523-5498
www.meei.harvard.edu

A consortium between the Massachusetts Eye and Ear Infirmary, the Harvard Medical School, the Research Laboratory of Electronics at Massachusetts Institute of Technology, and the Massachusetts General Hospital. Research interests span the auditory system from peripheral to central, from normal to abnormal function, from neurophysiology to behavior, and from the molecular and genetic bases of deafness, to its treatment via hearing aids and cochlear implants.

Nelson YS Kiang, PhD, Director

Nebraska

3164 University of Nebraska, Lincoln Barkley Memorial Center
Barkley Center 301
Lincoln, NE 68583
402-472-2145
Fax: 402-472-7697
www.unl.edu.barkley/index.shtml

The University of Nebraska-Lincoln Barkley Memorial Center and Boys Town National Research Hospital have joined forces to offer an exciting future in the audiology profession.

John E Bernthal, Director

New York

3165 Wallace Memorial Library
Rochester Institute of Technology
90 Lomb Memorial Drive
Rochester, NY 14623
585-475-2562
www.library.rit.edu/collections/wallace.html

A multimedia resource center with a collection of more than 750,000 items. Resource materials include more than 350,000 books; 2900 print journals subscriptions; 380,000 microforms; 3,100 audio cassettes and recordings; 6,700 film and video titles. They have an extensive web-based online collection which features over 150 research databases, 7,000+ eBooks, 16,000 electronic journal subscriptions and thousands of digital images in various collections.

Melanie Norton, Reference Librarian

Oregon

3166 Regional Resource Center on Deafness
Western Oregon State University
345 N Monmouth Avenue
Monmouth, OR 97361
503-838-8444
877-877-1593
Fax: 503-838-8228
webmaster@wou.edu
www.wou.edu

Prepares professionals in the Northwest to be qualified to serve the unique communication, rehabilitation, and educational needs of deaf and hard of hearing individuals. The Center offers graduate and undergraduate degree programs for professionals entering fields that serve people who are deaf or hard of hearing, continuing education opportunities for currently practicing professionals, and consultation and community service activities designed to enhance the quality of life for all affected.

Cheryl Davis, Director
Hilda Rosselli PhD, Dean

South Carolina

3167 Described and Captioned Media Program
National Association of the Deaf
1447 E Main Street
Spartanburg, SC 29307
864-585-1778
800-237-6213
Fax: 864-585-2611
TTY: 864-585-2617
www.cfv.org

Renamed the Described and Captioned Media Program, CMP continues to provide all persons who are deaf or hard of hearing awareness of and equal access to communication and learning through the use of captioned educational media and supportive collateral materials. They also act as a captioning information and training center. Their ultimate goal is to permit media to be an integral part in the lifelong learning process for all stakeholders in the deaf and hard of hearing community.

Bill Stark, Manager

Research Centers

3168 Boston Children's Hospital Dept. of Otolaryngology & Communication
300 Longwood Ave
Boston, MA 02115
617-355-6000
TTY: 617-730-0152
www.childrenshospital.com

Provides diagnosis and surgical treatment for disorders of the head and neck.

Arkansas

3169 Arkansas Rehabilitation Research and Training Center for Deaf Persons
University of Arkansas
4601 W Markham Street
Little Rock, AR 72205
501-686-9691
Fax: 501-686-9698
TTY: 501-686-9698

The center focuses on issues affecting the employability of deaf and hard-of-hearing rehabilitation clients.

Douglas Watson, PhD, Director

Hearing Impairment/Deafness / Research Centers

Massachusetts

3170 National Temporal Bone, Hearing and Balance Pathology Resource Registry
Massachusetts Eye & Ear Infirmary
243 Charles Street, PO Box 3096
Boston, MA 02114
617-573-3711
800-822-1327
Fax: 617-573-3838
TTY: 800-439-0183
tbregistry@meei.harvard.edu
www.tbregistry.org

The Registry, established by the National Institute on Deafness and Other Communication Disorders, maintains a database of human temporal bone collections, responds to inquiries from the public and researchers interested in temporal bone donation or research, disseminates information about temporal bone collection and its importance, implements professional educational activities in the field of temporal bone and auditory brain cell stem study and implements a national acquistion network.

Nicole Pelletier, Coordinator

Michigan

3171 University of Michigan, Kresge Hearing Research Institute
1301 E Ann Street, Room 5032
Ann Arbor, MI 48109
734-763-9600
Fax: 734-764-0014
TTY: 734-764-8110

Research programs include multi-disciplinary projects in behavior, morphology, physiology, molecular biology and genetics, bioengineering, pharmacology and biochemistry. They include: the genetics of hearing and deafness, mechanisms of auditory processing, molecular otology, cochlear prosthesis and tissue bioengineering, and training.

Jochen Schacht PhD, Scientific Director
Diana Gilham, Finance
Gary Dootz, Grant Administrator

Missouri

3172 Central Institute for the Deaf
825 S Taylor Ave
Saint Louis, MO 63110
314-977-0000
888-444-4565
Fax: 314-977-0223
TTY: 314-997-0001
TDD: 314-977-0037
www.cid.wustl.edu

Central Institute for the Deaf is a private, nonprofit institute composed of research laboratories in which scientists study the normal aspects as well as the disorders of hearing, language, and speech; a school for children who have hearing impairments; speech, language, and hearing clinics; and professionals with hearing impairment, and communication sciences.

Robin Feder, Ceo

Nebraska

3173 Lied Learning and Technology Center for Childhood Deafness and Vision Disorders
Boys Town National Research Hospital
555 North 30th Street
Omaha, NE 68131
402-498-6511
800-448-3000
Fax: 402-498-1348
TTY: 402-498-6543
www.boystown.org/chlc

A not-for-profit corporation closely affiliated with the Boys Town National Research Hospital. The center houses Model Childhood Education Classrooms, a Cochlear Implant Clinic and Research Center, Educational Media Production Studios, Distance Learning and Family Outreach Center, Hearing and Vision Laboratories, Bio-informatics and Computer Center and a Communication Technology Development Center.

Patrick E Brookhouser MD, President
John K. Arch, Executive VP
Edward M. Kolb, Medical Director

New York

3174 Montifiore Medical Center
2475 St. Raymonds Avenue
Bronx, NY 10461
718-430-7300
800-636-6683
Fax: 718-741-2033
www.montefiore.org

Provides diagnosis, treatment and research of diseases of the ear, nose and throat.

Steven M. Safyer, MD, President/Chief Executive Officer
Philip O. Ozuah, MD, PhD, Executive Vice President/Chief Oper
Joel A. Perlman, Executive Vice President/Chief Fina

3175 State University College at Plattsburgh Auditory Research Laboratory
101 Broad Street
Plattsburgh, NY 12901
518-564-2040
888-673-0012
Fax: 518-564-2045
hamernrp@plattsburgh.edu
www.plattsburgh.edu

The Auditory Research Laboratory (ARL) is home to several laboratories, including acoustics lab, anatomy lab, auditory evoked potential lab, and otoacoustic emissions lab. Facilities include: acoustics and vibrations laboratory, otoacoustic emmissions laboratory, middle ear analysis laboratory, auditory evoked potential laboratory, and cochlear anatomy laborator.

Roger Hamernik, MD, Director

3176 Syracuse University, Institute for Sensory Research
621 Skytop Road, PO Box 5290
Syracuse, NY 13244
315-443-4164
Fax: 315-443-1184
rlsmith@syr.edu
www.isr.syr.edu

Research center dedicated to the discovery and application of knowledge of the sensory systems. Integration of engineering, life, and physical sciences, combining rigorous experimental methodology with mathematical analysis is stressed.

Robert Smith, MD, Director

Oregon

3177 Oregon Health Sciences University Research Center
3181 SW Sam Jackson Park Road, PO Box 3098
Portland, OR 97239
503-494-8311
Fax: 503-494-5656
www.ohsuhealth.com

OSHU blends education, research, patient care and community outreach into one shared mission: to improve the well-being of people in Oregon and beyond. They incorporate the latest medical research, technology and innovation.

Michael Heinrich

Pennsylvania

3178 Temple University, Section of Auditory Research
1801 N. Broad Street
Philadelphia, PA 19122
215-707-3663
Fax: 215-707-7523
www.temple.edu

The Auditory Research Section includes the Garfied Auditory Research Laboratory, the Hearing Science Research Program and the Electrophysiology Progject.

Anita Cilea, Departmental Administrator
Kate Haney, Financial Administrator
Neil D. Theobald, President

Tennessee

3179 Bill Wilkerson Center
1211 Medical Center Drive
Nashville, TN 37232
615-322-5000
Fax: 615-936-5013
kate.carney@vanderbilt.edu
www.mc.vanderbilt.edu

The Vanderbilt Bill Wilkerson Center for Otolaryngology and Communication Sciences is dedicated to serving persons with diseases of the ear, nose, throat, head and neck, and hearing, speech, language and related disorders.

Robert H Ossoff DMD MD, Director
Fred H Bess PhD, Associate Director

Texas

3180 Houston Ear Research Foundation
7737 SW Freeway, Suite 630
Houston, TX 77074
713-771-9966
800-843-0807
Fax: 713-771-0546
TTY: 800-843-0807
www.houstoncochlear.org

The Foundation was incorporated in August, 1983 as a center to provide excellence in service dedicated to the cochlear implant.

Jan Gilden, Executive Director

Conferences

3181 AG Bell Biennial Convention
Alexander Graham Bell Association for the Deaf
3417 Volta Place NW
Washington, DC 20007
202-337-5220
800-432-7543
Fax: 202-337-8314
TTY: 202-337-5221
info@agbell.org
www.agbell.org

June

Alexander T Graham, Executive Director

3182 ASCD Biennial Conference
American Society for Deaf Children
800 Florida Ave NE, Suite 2047
Washington, DC 20002
800-942-2732
Fax: 410-795-0965
asdc@deafchildren.org
www.deafchildren.org

Provides families with five days of information and fun. Daytime workshops captivates parents while children participate in educational and recreational activities. Evening events bring families together, providing the opportunity to form new friendships and peer support.

June

Beth S Benedict, President

3183 ASHA Convention
American Speech-Language-Hearing Association
2200 Research Blvd
Rockville, MD 20850
301-296-5700
800-638-8255
Fax: 301-296-5650
TTY: 301-296-5700
exhibits@asha.org
convention.asha.org

Professional education event for speech-language pathologists, audiologists, and speech, language, and hearing scientists. Provides unparalleled opportunities to hear the latest evidence-based research and gain new skills and resources to advance your career.

12,000 November

Nancye Berman, Manager, Exhibits

3184 NAD Biennial Conference
National Association of the Deaf
8630 Fention Street, Suite 820
Silver Spring, MD 20910
301-587-1788
Fax: 301-587-1791
TTY: 301-587-1791
nad.info@nad.org
www.nad.org

Held in the even numbered years, brings together deaf,hard of hearing, late-deafened, deaf-blind and hearing consumers, parents, youth, professionals, educators, organizational and corporate representatives for professional development, enrichment, training, networking, governance meetings, exhibits, receptions, and related evening.

2,000 July

Howard Rosenblum, Chief Executive Officer
Tom Well, Director of Finance
Angela Ellman, Conference Coordinator

Audio Video

3185 50th Anniversary Collection
Harris Communications
15155 Technology Drive
Eden Prairie, MN 55344
952-906-1180
800-825-6758
Fax: 952-906-1099
TTY: 800-825-9187
info@harriscomm.com
www.harriscomm.com

Stories: A picture for Harold's Room; Corduroy; Danny and the Dinosaur; Harry the Dirty Dog; Click, clack moo, Cows that type. DVD-R, voiced; signed in ASL, no captions.

3186 A Few Errands
Modern Sign Press
10443 Los Alamitos Boulevard, PO Box 1181
Los Alamitos, CA 90720
562-596-8548
800-572-7332
Fax: 562-795-6614
TTY: 562-493-4168
modsigns@modernsignspress.com
www.modernsignspress.com

Basic level videotape of signed story for Expressive and Receptive practice. Story is repeated three times for ease of use. Watch how the visual features are incorporated. Turn the sound off for receptive practice. Written script and tape use suggestions included. VHS

Esther Zawolkow, President

3187 A Lesson With Heart
American Sign Language Productions
4450 La Crosse Ave
San Diego, CA 92117
952-906-1180
800-767-4461
Fax: 952-906-1099
TTY: 952-906-1198
SignEnhancers@iCloud.com
www.signenhancers.com

A skilled 4th grade teacher presents a lesson on Anatomy including the respiratory system, digestive system, and the heart that will increase your familiarity with this vocabulary and content. Improve your interpreting skills for this subject matter and grade level by accepting this assignment. You won't be alone...we provide two interpreters to demonstrate it for your. 55 minutes. DVD - $59.95; VHS - 49.95

Hearing Impairment/Deafness / Audio Video

3188 A Mother's Persepctive on the IEP Process
American Sign Language Productions
4450 La Crosse Ave
San Diego, CA 92117
952-906-1180
800-767-4461
Fax: 952-906-1099
TTY: 952-906-1198
SignEnhancers@iCloud.com
www.signenhancers.com

Maxine Camvel is a parent of a Deaf daughter wanting to make it easier for other parents. She gives valuable insight into how to advocate for your children by maximizing parent input to the Individualized Education Plan (IEP) process. This program also provides an opportunity to interpret vocabulary and emotional content commonly expressed by parents. Your two team interpreters demonstrate how to interpret this sample. 1 hour. DVD - $59.95; VHS - $49.95

3189 A is for Access: Creating Full & Interactive Access for Students
Hands and Voices
PO Box 3093
Boulder, CO 80307
303-492-6283
866-422-0422
parentadvocate@handsandvoices.org
www.handsandvoices.org

This video is a source to generate greater awareness of communication access issues for students who are deaf or hard of hearing. DVD or VHS, captioned.

3190 ABC Stories DVD
Sign Media
4020 Blackburn Lane
Burtonsville, MD 20866
301-421-0268
800-475-4756
Fax: 301-421-0270
info@signmedia.com
www.signmedia.com

You will marvel at the skill of these Deaf performers as they use every letter of the manual alphabet, in sequence, to tell a story. To capture the creativity and genius of the stories, the videotape uses slow motion and graphic displays. 1 hour

3191 ABCs of AVT: Analyzing Auditory-Verbal Therapy
Alexander Graham Bell Association for the Deaf
3417 Volta Place NW
Washington, DC 20007
202-337-5220
800-432-7543
Fax: 202-337-8314
TTY: 202-337-5221
info@agbell.org
listeningandspokenlanguage.org

An Educational Tool for Professionals. Developed for use in university classrooms and training environments; provides an overview of Auditory-Verbal techniques and guidance on appropriate intervention for children experiencing difficulties with language development.

2005 104 pages 46 Minute video

Warren Estabrooks MEd, Author
Rhonda Schwartz MA, Co-Author
Lisa Chutjian, Chief Development Officer

3192 ASL Stories: Christmas Stories
Harris Communications
15155 Technology Drive
Eden Prairie, MN 55344
952-906-1180
800-825-6758
Fax: 952-906-1099
TTY: 800-825-9187
info@harriscomm.com
www.harriscomm.com

This video is one in a collection of videotapes featuring classic fairy tales signed by Deaf storytellers, and is a wonderful way to get into the spirit of Christmas. This video also makes a welcome gift. Stories include: The Night Before Christmas, A Christmas Carol, The First Christmas Tree, The Birth of Christ, In the Great Walled City, and The Little Match Girl. For ages 10 and over. VHS: 80 minutes; signed in ASL; no captions; voice over.

3193 ASL Stories: Fairy Tales I
Harris Communications
15155 Technology Drive
Eden Prairie, MN 55344
952-906-1180
800-825-6758
Fax: 952-906-1099
TTY: 800-825-9187
info@harriscomm.com
www.harriscomm.com

This video is one of a collection of videotapes featuring classic fairy tales signed by Deaf storytellers. Stories include Rapunzel, Snow White and Rose Red, The Frog Prince, Hansel and Gretel, and The Brave Little Tailor. For ages 10 and over. VHS: 114 minutes; signed in ASL; no captions; voice-over.

3194 ASL Stories: Fairy Tales II
Harris Communications
15155 Technology Drive
Eden Prairie, MN 55344
952-906-1180
800-825-6758
Fax: 952-906-1099
TTY: 800-825-9187
info@harriscomm.com
www.harriscomm.com

This video is one of a collection of videotapes featuring classic fairy tales signed by Deaf storytellers. Stories include Sleeping Beauty, The Golden Goose, Little Red Riding Hood, The Princess and the Pea, and The Tinder Box. For ages 10 and over. VHS: 83 minutes; signed in ASL; no captions; voice-over.

3195 Acoustics, Audition and Speech Reception
Daniel Lind OC, PhD, author

Alexander Graham Bell Association for the Deaf
3417 Volta Place NW
Washington, DC 20007
202-337-5220
202-337-8314
Fax: 202-337-8314
TTY: 203-337-5221
info@agbell.org
listeningandspokenlanguage.org

This videotape of four professionals provides viewers with an overview of the properties of speech and the ways children can get the most from their hearing aids or cochlear implants. The tape is a practical how-to guide in which team members demonstrate how speech sounds are created in the vocal tract, how distance affects the intensity of spoken language and how patterns are distorted by profound hearing loss.

Lisa Chutjian, Chief Development Officer
Emilio Alonso-Mendoza, Chief Executive Officer
Judy Harrison, Director of Programs

3196 American Sign Language Handshape Dictionary DVD
Gallaudet University Press
800 Florida Avenue NE
Washington, DC 20002
202-651-5448
Fax: 202-651-5489
TTY: 202-651-5444
gupress@gallaudet.edu
gupress.gallaudet.edu

A perfect complement to the dictionary, this new DVD features a diverse cast of native signers forming more than 1,400 ASL signs organized by 40 basic handshapes, with a complete list of English glosses and synonyms for each sign.

Richard Tennant, Co-Producer
Marianne Gluszak Brown, Co-Producer

3197 American Sign Language Video Series
DeBee Communications/TJ Publishers
P.O. Box 702701
Dallas, TX 75370
972-416-0800
800-999-1168
Fax: 972-416-0944
TTY: 972-416-0933
customerservice@tjpublishers.com
https://www388.safesecureweb.com/tjpublishers/store/

Learning ASL with the Deaf Robinson family. The family acts out scenes that occur in everyday life in this videotape series. Each situation is reviewed in an ASL classroom with a deaf teacher. This series also includes sections on Deaf culture and grammar, rounding off a complete and effective instructional tool. Work Day-VHS-90 minutes, School Day-VHS-90 minutes, Shopping-VHS-90 minutes, Softball Game-VHS-90 minutes. $39.95 each

3198 American Sign Language: Green Books Text a nd Tapes
Sign Media
4020 Blackburn Lane
Burtonsville, MD 20866
301-421-0268
800-475-4756
Fax: 301-421-0270
info@signmedia.com
www.signmedia.com

The classic ASL series. This unique set of texts, written by Dennis Cokely and Charlotte Baker-Shenk, is complimented by DVDs. The DVDs explain difficult concepts and offer practice situations to improve your sign language skills. The series may be ordered as a complete set of books and DVDs, a complete set of DVDs only, individual books and DVDs, or a specific DVD and book combination set. Individual DVD $44.95, DVD set & books $379.95, DVD set $233.95

3199 Ancient Greece
American Sign Language Productions
4450 La Crosse Ave
San Diego, CA 92117
952-906-1180
800-767-4461
Fax: 952-906-1099
TTY: 952-906-1198
SignEnhancers@iCloud.com
www.signenhancers.com

We often think about interpreting for Deaf children, but often need to understand the speech and thought patterns of their hearing classmates. Krisjana is a hearing child presenting a report on Ancient Greece. A great way to practice with vocabulary from the classroom before you have to sit in the hot seat. Is it all Greek to you? No need to worry. Two interpreters will show you how. 30 minutes. DVD - $59.95; VHS - $49.95

3200 Animals, Insects, School, Colors Spanish/E nglish Videos
Modern Signs Press
10443 Los Alamitos Boulevard, PO Box 1181
Los Alamitos, CA 90720
562-596-8548
800-572-7332
Fax: 562-795-6614
TTY: 562-493-4168
modsigns@modernsignspress.com
www.modernsignspress.com

Entertaining sign language instructional videos in Spanish and English. Great tool to help bridge the gap between Spanish, English and Sign Language. The videos have a split screen - Connie and Merced teach you the sign and say the word in both Spanish and English. Vocabulary words are used in sentences to reinforce the signs. There are graphics showing the vocabulary they are reviewing. 10 titles available, either alone or in a complete package.

Esther Zawolkow, President

3201 Art Show
Modern Sign Press
10443 Los Alamitos Boulevard, PO Box 1181
Los Alamitos, CA 90720
562-596-8548
800-572-7332
Fax: 562-795-6614
TTY: 562-493-4168
modsigns@modernsignspress.com
www.modernsignspress.com

Basic level videotape of signed story for Expressive and Receptive practice. Story is repeated three times for ease of use. Watch how the visual features are incorporated. Turn the sound off for receptive practice. Written script and tape use suggestions included. VHS

Esther Zawolkow, President

3202 Baby See 'n Sign
Harris Communications
15155 Technology Drive
Eden Prairie, MN 55344
952-906-1180
800-825-6758
Fax: 952-906-1099
TTY: 800-825-9187
info@harriscomm.com
www.harriscomm.com

Features American Sign Language signs and real-life images in full color. They may be used as an educational tool for effectively promoting communication with people who are autistic, have Down Syndrome, or are ESL. For parents who have decided to sign to their children, this is a great video. Over 60 basic American Sign Language signs and real-life images are presented in full-color, making it enjoyable for parents and children to watch. A parental question and answer guide is included.

6 months + DVD 45 minutes

3203 Baby See 'n Sign II
Harris Communications
15155 Technology Drive
Eden Prairie, MN 55344
952-906-1180
800-825-6758
Fax: 952-906-1099
TTY: 800-825-9187
info@harriscomm.com
www.harriscomm.com

This DVD shows over 100 real-life images that relate to your child's daily life, including animals, foods, toys and activities. Volume II has beginning abstract concepts and continues with object-word association. It is never too late to begin signing. Ages 6 months and up. DVD: 50 minutes.

3204 Baby Signing Time
Harris Communications
15155 Technology Drive
Eden Prairie, MN 55344
952-906-1180
800-825-6758
Fax: 952-906-1099
TTY: 800-825-9187
info@harriscomm.com
www.harriscomm.com

Designed specifically for babies 3-36 months old, the DVD combines sign-along songs, playful animation and the positive reinforcement of signing babies - who are all ages 2 and under - to teach you and your baby to sign the easy way. Baby Signing Time sets your baby's day to music as you learn sign and sogns for everyday events in baby's life - eating, family, pets and more.

3205 Baby Signing Time DVD 2
Harris Communications
15155 Technology Drive
Eden Prairie, MN 55344
952-906-1180
800-825-6758
Fax: 952-906-1099
TTY: 800-825-9187
info@harriscomm.com
www.harriscomm.com

This video sets your baby's day to music as you learn signs and sogns for everyday events in baby's life - eating, family, pets and more. Designed specifically for babies 3-36 months old, this DVD combines sign-along songs, playful animation and the positive reinforcement of signing babies - who are all ages 2 and under - to teach you and your baby to sign the easy way.

3206 Bachelor Father
Modern Sign Press
10443 Los Alamitos Boulevard, PO Box 1181
Los Alamitos, CA 90720
562-596-8548
800-572-7332
Fax: 562-795-6614
TTY: 562-493-4168
modsigns@modernsignspress.com
www.modernsignspress.com

Hearing Impairment/Deafness / Audio Video

Basic level videotape of signed story for Expressive and Receptive practice. Story is repeated three times for ease of use. Watch how the visual features are incorporated. Turn the sound off for receptive practice. Written script and tape use suggestions included. VHS

Esther Zawolkow, President

3207 Basic Course in American Sign Language Videotape Package
TJ Publishers
P.O. Box 702701
Dallas, TX 75370
800-999-1168
Fax: 972-416-0944
TTY: 972-416-0933
customerservice@tjpublishers.com
https://www388.safesecureweb.com/tjpublishers/store/

This videotape features four Deaf models signing each vocabulary word contained in all 22 lessons of the text plus the alphabet and numbers. The tape has captions and voice which can be turned off to sharpen visual acuity. It is ideal for classroom reinforcement and independent home study. Available on VHS or DVD

Video

Angela K Thames, President

3208 Beginning Level Curriculum Tapes Complete Set
Modern Signs Press
10443 Los Alamitos Boulevard, PO Box 1181
Los Alamitos, CA 90720
562-596-8548
800-572-7332
Fax: 562-795-6614
TTY: 562-493-4168
modsigns@modernsignspress.com
www.modernsignspress.com

A good way to learn the beginning lessons of Signing Exact English with Dr. Gerilee Gustason, co-author of SEE. The full set of tapes introduce more than 700 words and signs. There are 14 lessons with approximately 50 vocabulary items and practice sentences in each lesson. Words and sentences are presented twice allowing time for observation and ability to imitate presenter. Words are also shown in text form for both the individual vocabulary words and sentences to help with clarity.

VHS and DVD

Esther Zawolkow, President

3209 Beginning Reading and Sign Language Video
TJ Publishers
P.O. Box 702701
Dallas, TX 75370
972-416-0800
800-999-1168
Fax: 972-416-0944
TTY: 972-416-0933
https://www388.safesecureweb.com/tjpublishers/store/

Great for kids from 2 to 12, this video picture book feature Deaf actress Susan Bressler signing over a hundred words at the zoos, at home and around the community. Don't tell your kids that learning Sign language improves reading, motor skills and visual perception and increases language acquisition abilities. English captions give reading practice, too. Great for hearing and Deaf children. VHS 30 minutes.

Video
ISBN: 0-932314-00-7

Angela K Thames, President

3210 Blue's Clues: All Kinds of Signs
Harris Communications
15155 Technology Drive
Eden Prairie, MN 55344
952-906-1180
800-825-6758
Fax: 952-906-1099
TTY: 800-825-9187
info@harriscomm.com
www.harriscomm.com

Preschoolers play along with Steve and Blue with the two episodes in this video. The video uses different kinds of signs - from directional signs to American Sign Language - to figure out where Blue wants to eat in Where does Blue want to have her snack?, and where she would like to go in Where does Blue want to go? Guest appearance by Marlee Matline. Approximately 50 minutes. Closed captioned. VHS.

3211 Bold as Brianna
American Sign Language Productions
15155 Technology Drive
Eden Prairie, MN 55344
952-906-1180
800-825-6758
Fax: 952-906-1099
TTY: 800-825-9187
info@harriscomm.com
www.harriscomm.com

Elementary: 7-Year-Old Deaf Child. A Confident, articulate seven-year-old willing and able to give you an eye-full. Precious and precocious, Briana will entertain you as you improve your receptivity and sign-to-voice interpreting skills. Two certified interpreters provide interpretations for your to compare and contrast to each other and your own work. 33 minutes. DVD - $59.95; VHS - $49.95

3212 Building Cue Reading
Melanie Metzger, PhD and Earl Fleetwood, MA, author

Alexander Graham Bell Association for the Deaf
3417 Volta Place NW
Washington, DC 20007
202-337-5220
202-337-8314
Fax: 202-337-8314
TTY: 203-337-5221
info@agbell.org
listeningandspokenlanguage.org

Designed for hearing individuals who already cue expressively, this two videotape set offers lessons to develop receptive Cued English skills. The videos comprise 15 lessons with drills and practice exercises.

Lisa Chutjian, Chief Development Officer
Emilio Alonso-Mendoza, Chief Executive Officer
Judy Harrison, Director of Programs

3213 Deaf Children Signers
Harris Communications
15155 Technology Drive
Eden Prairie, MN 55344
952-906-1180
800-825-6758
Fax: 952-906-1099
TTY: 800-825-9187
info@harriscomm.com
www.harriscomm.com

This five-part collection of children signers is great for children, teachers, parents and interpreters. Available in VHS and DVD

Bill Williams, National Sales Manager

3214 Delightful as Derek
American Sign Language Productions
4450 La Crosse Ave
San Diego, CA 92117
952-906-1180
800-767-4461
Fax: 952-906-1099
TTY: 952-906-1198
SignEnhancers@iCloud.com
www.signenhancers.com

Join Derek, a bright and linguistically advanced 10-year-old, as he shares his passion for creative projects and home schooling. His use of ASL will delight and assist you to enhance you own signing and voicing skills. Benefit from two certified interpreters demonstrating how to interpret for Derek. 40 minutes. DVD - $59.95; VHS - $49.95

3215 Discovering Cued Speech
Pamela H. Beck, author

Alexander Graham Bell Association for the Deaf
3417 Volta Place NW
Washington, DC 20007
202-337-5220
202-337-8314
Fax: 202-337-8314
TTY: 203-337-5221
info@agbell.org
listeningandspokenlanguage.org

Two-volume video and personal workbook are used in conjunction to make the learning and practice of Cued Speech interesting and effective. A Quick Review at the beginning of each workbook lesson lists the specific goals of that lesson. Participants will read through the lesson in the workbook, use the video instruction to learn, return to the workbook to practice, then return to the video as needed.

78 pages VHS 2:52 min

Lisa Chutjian, Chief Development Officer
Emilio Alonso-Mendoza, Chief Executive Officer
Judy Harrison, Director of Programs

3216 Economic Glitch
Modern Sign Press
10443 Los Alamitos Boulevard, PO Box 1181
Los Alamitos, CA 90720   562-596-8548
800-572-7332
Fax: 562-795-6614
TTY: 562-493-4168
modsigns@modernsignspress.com
www.modernsignspress.com

Basic level videotape of signed story for Expressive and Receptive practice. Story is repeated three times for ease of use. Watch how the visual features are incorporated. Turn the sound off for receptive practice. Written script and tape use suggestions included. VHS

Esther Zawolkow, President

3217 Family Traditions
Modern Sign Press
10443 Los Alamitos Boulevard, PO Box 1181
Los Alamitos, CA 90720   562-596-8548
800-572-7332
Fax: 562-795-6614
TTY: 562-493-4168
modsigns@modernsignspress.com
www.modernsignspress.com

Basic level videotape of signed story for Expressive and Receptive practice. Story is repeated three times for ease of use. Watch how the visual features are incorporated. Turn the sound off for receptive practice. Written script and tape use suggestions included. VHS

Esther Zawolkow, President

3218 Fantastic Videos: Colonial Times, Chocolate, and Cars
Gallaudet University Press
800 Florida Avenue NE
Washington, DC 20002   202-651-5488
Fax: 202-651-5489
TTY: 202-651-5444
gupress@gallaudet.edu
gupress.gallaudet.edu

Young viewers visit Colonial Williamsburg in Virginia to see various crafts. Other parts show chocolate being made, and films of old cars. VHS, color, voice-over, captions.

VHS 28 minutes
ISBN: 1-563680-06-8

3219 Fantastic Videos: Dogs at Work and Play
Gallaudet University Press
800 Florida Avenue NE
Washington, DC 20002   202-651-5488
Fax: 202-651-5489
TTY: 202-651-5444
gupress@gallaudet.edu
gupress.gallaudet.edu

See how dogs are trained, including Fantastic's own hearing-ear dog, police dogs, plus puppies and dogs in space? VHS, color, voice-over, captions.

VHS 28 minutes
ISBN: 1-563680-03-3

3220 Fantastic Videos: Exciting People, Places and Things!
Gallaudet University Press
800 Florida Avenue NE
Washington, DC 20002   202-651-5488
Fax: 202-651-5489
TTY: 202-651-5444
gupress@gallaudet.edu
gupress.gallaudet.edu

In this program, Rita Corey welcomes young viewers for a trip to a crayon factory, a jump rope tournament, and mime by actor Bernard Bragg. VHS, color, voice-over captions.

VHS 28 minutes
ISBN: 1-563680-01-7

3221 Fantastic Videos: From Post Offices to Dairy Goats!
Gallaudet University Press
800 Florida Avenue NE
Washington, DC 20002   202-651-5488
Fax: 202-651-5489
TTY: 202-651-5444
gupress@gallaudet.edu
gupress.gallaudet.edu

In this program, children follow the route of a letter from mailbox through the post office to its final destination. Also, they visit dairy goats and other animals. VHS, color, voice-over, captions

VHS 28 minutes
ISBN: 1-563680-05-X

3222 Fantastic Videos: Imagination, Actors, and 'Deaf Way!'
Gallaudet University Press
800 Florida Avenue NE
Washington, DC 20002   202-651-5488
Fax: 202-651-5489
TTY: 202-651-5444
gupress@gallaudet.edu
gupress.gallaudet.edu

Deaf clowns, mimes and actors display the wonders of imaginagion, along with performances at the international cultural celebration 'Deaf Way.' VHS, color, voice-over, captions.

VHS 28 minutes
ISBN: 1-563680-04-1

3223 Fantastic Videos: Roller Coasters, Maps, and Ice Cream!
Gallaudet University Press
800 Florida Avenue NE
Washington, DC 20002   202-651-5488
Fax: 202-651-5489
TTY: 202-651-5444
gupress@gallaudet.edu
gupress.gallaudet.edu

Mike Montangino leads the way on rides at Kings Dominion, and also to see how maps are drawn and how ice cream is made. VHS, color, voice-over, captions.

VHS 28 minutes
ISBN: 1-563680-07-6

3224 Fantastic Videos: Skiing, Factories, and Race Horses
Gallaudet University Press
800 Florida Avenue NE
Washington, DC 20002   202-651-5488
Fax: 202-651-5489
TTY: 202-651-5444
gupress@gallaudet.edu
gupress.gallaudet.edu

Snow Skiing starts this program, which continues in a factory where 'who-knows-what' is made. Also, young viewers learn about horse care, and also the making of Oreos. VHS, color, voice-over, captions.

VHS 28 minutes
ISBN: 1-563680-08-4

3225 Fantastic Videos: The Wonderful Worlds of Sports and Travel
Gallaudet University Press
800 Florida Avenue NE
Washington, DC 20002   202-651-5488
Fax: 202-651-5489
TTY: 202-651-5444
gupress@gallaudet.edu
gupress.gallaudet.edu

In this program, young viewers ride on a train, watch deaf athletes compete, and see actor Bernard Bragg perform The Lion and the Mouse. VHS, color, voice-over, captions.

Hearing Impairment/Deafness / Audio Video

VHS 28 minutes
ISBN: 1-563680-02-5

3226 Fingerspelling: Expressive and Receptive Fluency
DawnSign Press
6130 Nancy Ridge Drive
San Diego, CA 92121
858-625-0600
800-549-5350
Fax: 858-625-2336
info@dawnsign.com
www.dawnsign.com

This videotape makes the elements of fingerspelling understandable to ASL students. Based on her highly successful and popular workshopes, Joyce Lindene Groode presents a variety of strategies for building and improving the skills for producing fingerspelled words. VHS.

120 minutes
ISBN: 0-915035-13-8

Joyce Linden Groode

3227 Four for You! Fables and Fairy Tales Serie s
Sign Media
4020 Blackburn Lane
Burtonsville, MD 20866
301-421-0268
800-475-4756
Fax: 301-421-0270
info@signmedia.com
www.signmedia.com

Aesop's fables and classic fairy tales performed in ASL. Stars four Sign Language performers and storytellers. Each volume contains four Aesop's fables and two classic fairy tales. The fables are presented twice - first as a straightforward rendition of the story: the second as a dramatized version using minimal sets and props. Voice-over is provided. Activity Packets include printed text of each story in the volume, crossword puzzles, word find challenges, secret message decoding and more.

5 tapes/packets

3228 From Mime to Sign
TJ Publishers
P.O. Box 702701
Dallas, TX 75370
972-416-0800
800-999-1168
Fax: 972-416-0944
TTY: 972-416-0933
customerservice@tjpublishers.com
https://www388.safesecureweb.com/tjpublishers/store/

More than 1,000 photographs illustrate how natural gestures, mime and facial expressions used every day can become the basis for learning sign language. Three videotapes accompany and enhance the text, demonstrating techniques chapter by chapter. Learn to synthesize gesture, mime, facial expression and American Sign Language to truly open the door to visual thinking. VHS or DVD.

1989

Gilbert G Eastman

3229 Generating Business
Modern Sign Press
10443 Los Alamitos Boulevard, PO Box 1181
Los Alamitos, CA 90720
562-596-8548
800-572-7332
Fax: 562-795-6614
TTY: 562-493-4168
modsigns@modernsignspress.com
www.modernsignspress.com

Basic level videotape of signed story for Expressive and Receptive practice. Story is repeated three times for ease of use. Watch how the visual features are incorporated. Turn the sound off for receptive practice. Written script and tape use suggestions included. VHS

Esther Zawolkow, President

3230 Getting Ready for the Big Date
Modern Sign Press
10443 Los Alamitos Boulevard, PO Box 1181
Los Alamitos, CA 90720
562-596-8548
800-572-7332
Fax: 562-795-6614
TTY: 562-493-4168
modsigns@modernsignspress.com
www.modernsignspress.com

Basic level videotape of signed story for Expressive and Receptive practice. Story is repeated three times for ease of use. Watch how the visual features are incorporated. Turn the sound off for receptive practice. Written script and tape use suggestions included. VHS

Esther Zawolkow, President

3231 Ghost Investigation
Modern Sign Press
10443 Los Alamitos Boulevard, PO Box 1181
Los Alamitos, CA 90720
562-596-8548
800-572-7332
Fax: 562-795-6614
TTY: 562-493-4168
modsigns@modernsignspress.com
www.modernsignspress.com

Basic level videotape of signed story for Expressive and Receptive practice. Story is repeated three times for ease of use. Watch how the visual features are incorporated. Turn the sound off for receptive practice. Written script and tape use suggestions included. VHS

Esther Zawolkow, President

3232 Governor's Campaign
Modern Sign Press
10443 Los Alamitos Boulevard, PO Box 1181
Los Alamitos, CA 90720
562-596-8548
800-572-7332
Fax: 562-795-6614
TTY: 562-493-4168
modsigns@modernsignspress.com
www.modernsignspress.com

Basic level videotape of signed story for Expressive and Receptive practice. Story is repeated three times for ease of use. Watch how the visual features are incorporated. Turn the sound off for receptive practice. Written script and tape use suggestions included. VHS

Esther Zawolkow, President

3233 Graduate School
Modern Sign Press
10443 Los Alamitos Boulevard, PO Box 1181
Los Alamitos, CA 90720
562-596-8548
800-572-7332
Fax: 562-795-6614
TTY: 562-493-4168
modsigns@modernsignspress.com
www.modernsignspress.com

Basic level videotape of signed story for Expressive and Receptive practice. Story is repeated three times for ease of use. Watch how the visual features are incorporated. Turn the sound off for receptive practice. Written script and tape use suggestions included. VHS

Esther Zawolkow, President

3234 High Five! Fables and Fairy Tales
Sign Media
4020 Blackburn Lane
Burtonsville, MD 20866
301-421-0268
800-475-4756
Fax: 301-421-0270
info@signmedia.com
www.signmedia.com

The cast of Four for You retuns with the addition of one new member for even more enjoyment. The same format is used here. Each tape includes five fables and two fairy tales. As an added bonus, two fables and one fairy tale are told twice. The first version is the traditional story, the second is how Deaf people would tell each tale. Each tape has a translated voice-over. Set of five 90 minute tapes.

Hearing Impairment/Deafness / Audio Video

3235 **House Guests**
Modern Sign Press
10443 Los Alamitos Boulevard, PO Box 1181
Los Alamitos, CA 90720
562-596-8548
800-572-7332
Fax: 562-795-6614
TTY: 562-493-4168
modsigns@modernsignspress.com
www.modernsignspress.com

Basic level videotape of signed story for Expressive and Receptive practice. Story is repeated three times for ease of use. Watch how the visual features are incorporated. Turn the sound off for receptive practice. Written script and tape use suggestions included. VHS

Esther Zawolkow, President

3236 **Hungry Caterpillar and Goodnight Moon**
Modern Signs Press
10443 Los Alamitos Boulevard, PO Box 1181
Los Alamitos, CA 90720
562-596-8548
800-572-7332
Fax: 562-795-6614
TTY: 562-493-4168
modsigns@modernsignspress.com
www.modernsignspress.com

Two favorite stories beautifully animated and signed using Signing Exact English. VHS

Esther Zawolkow, President

3237 **I Remember it Well**
Modern Sign Press
10443 Los Alamitos Boulevard, PO Box 1181
Los Alamitos, CA 90720
562-596-8548
800-572-7332
Fax: 562-795-6614
TTY: 562-493-4168
modsigns@modernsignspress.com
www.modernsignspress.com

Basic level videotape of signed story for Expressive and Receptive practice. Story is repeated three times for ease of use. Watch how the visual features are incorporated. Turn the sound off for receptive practice. Written script and tape use suggestions included. VHS

Esther Zawolkow, President

3238 **Kudos to Kuualoha**
American Sign Language Productions
4450 La Crosse Ave
San Diego, CA 92117
952-906-1180
800-767-4461
Fax: 952-906-1099
TTY: 952-906-1198
SignEnhancers@iCloud.com
www.signenhancers.com

From Hawaii, Kuuolaha, a beautiful, doe eyed child provides commentary on a number of subjects, along with the opportunity to practice reading a child's signs. Prepares you for interpreting in the middle school environment. Two certified interpreters demonstrate for you to compare, contrast and incorporate what you learn to your own skills. 30 minutes. DVD - $59.95; VHS - $49.95

3239 **Let's Eat**
Modern Sign Press
10443 Los Alamitos Boulevard, PO Box 1181
Los Alamitos, CA 90720
562-596-8548
800-572-7332
Fax: 562-795-6614
TTY: 562-493-4168
modsigns@modernsignspress.com
www.modernsignspress.com

Basic level videotape of signed story for Expressive and Receptive practice. Story is repeated three times for ease of use. Watch how the visual features are incorporated. Turn the sound off for receptive practice. Written script and tape use suggestions included. VHS

Esther Zawolkow, President

3240 **Life in the Country**
Modern Sign Press
10443 Los Alamitos Boulevard, PO Box 1181
Los Alamitos, CA 90720
562-596-8548
800-572-7332
Fax: 562-795-6614
TTY: 562-493-4168
modsigns@modernsignspress.com
www.modernsignspress.com

Basic level videotape of signed story for Expressive and Receptive practice. Story is repeated three times for ease of use. Watch how the visual features are incorporated. Turn the sound off for receptive practice. Written script and tape use suggestions included. VHS

Esther Zawolkow, President

3241 **Listen Learn and Talk**
Alexander Graham Bell Association for the Deaf
3417 Volta Place NW
Washington, DC 20007
202-337-5220
202-337-8314
Fax: 202-337-8314
TTY: 203-337-5221
info@agbell.org
listeningandspokenlanguage.org

Three-volume videotape and guidebook set provides general guiding theory, support materials and age-appropriate strategies for parents, families, and early interventionists who practice listening skills with young children. Videos are age specific and include the following developmental categories: 0-15 months, 16-30 months, and 31 months to school age. Softcover, spiral binding manual and three tape VHS set, 1:20 minutes.

Lisa Chutjian, Chief Development Officer
Emilio Alonso-Mendoza, Chief Executive Officer
Judy Harrison, Director of Programs

3242 **Listen to This, Volume One**
Warren Eastabrooks, Karen MacIver Lux, Lisa Katz, author

Alexander Graham Bell Association for the Deaf
3417 Volta Place NW
Washington, DC 20007
202-337-5220
202-337-8314
Fax: 202-337-8314
TTY: 203-337-5221
info@agbell.org
listeningandspokenlanguage.org

An Auditory-Verbal Therapy Videotape and Guidebook for Professionals and Parents designed for professionals in the fields of Auditory-Verbal therapy, auditory learning and professional education who want to enhance their service delivery of Auditory-Verbal therapy and auditory based learning and for parents of children who are participating in Auditory-Verbal therapy. Workbook - 76 pp., VHS - 47:14 minutes.

Lisa Chutjian, Chief Development Officer
Emilio Alonso-Mendoza, Chief Executive Officer
Judy Harrison, Director of Programs

3243 **Listen to This, Volume Two**
Warren Eastabrooks, Karen MacIver Lux, Lisa Katz, author

Alexander Graham Bell Association for the Deaf
3417 Volta Place NW
Washington, DC 20007
202-337-5220
202-337-8314
Fax: 202-337-8314
TTY: 203-337-5221
info@agbell.org
listeningandspokenlanguage.org

For health professional and parents of children with hearing loss, this interactive training resource builds upon the Auditory-Verbal therapy skills introduced in Volume 1 and chronicles the journey of Annie, a young girl who lost her hearing as an infant to meningitis. The DVD and step-by-step guidebook models more advance Auditory-Verbal therapy techniques and strategies and features the parent-professional partnership critical to guiding children with hearing loss along the path to listening.

Hearing Impairment/Deafness / Audio Video

DVD

Lisa Chutjian, Chief Development Officer
Emilio Alonso-Mendoza, Chief Executive Officer
Judy Harrison, Director of Programs

3244 Literacy, Classroom Amplification and the Brain DVD

Carol Flexer, PhD, author

Alexander Graham Bell Association for the Deaf
3417 Volta Place NW
Washington, DC 20007 202-337-5220
 202-337-8314
 Fax: 202-337-8314
 TTY: 203-337-5221
 info@agbell.org
 listeningandspokenlanguage.org

This intermediate level program focuses on the essential components for enhancing classrooms to optimize the listening environment for school-age children. This video will provide educational information about sound field technology and how to create a favorable listening environment for enhanced development of learning, language and literacy.

DVD

Lisa Chutjian, Chief Development Officer
Emilio Alonso-Mendoza, Chief Executive Officer
Judy Harrison, Director of Programs

3245 Literacy, Classroom Amplification and the Brain

Carol Flexer, PhD, author

Alexander Graham Bell Association for the Deaf
3417 Volta Place NW
Washington, DC 20007 202-337-5220
 202-337-8314
 Fax: 202-337-8314
 TTY: 203-337-5221
 info@agbell.org
 listeningandspokenlanguage.org

This intermediate level program focuses on the essential components for enhancing classrooms to optimize the listening environment for school-age children. This video will provide educational information about sound field technology and how to create a favorable listening environment for enhanced development of learning, language and literacy.

VHS

Lisa Chutjian, Chief Development Officer
Emilio Alonso-Mendoza, Chief Executive Officer
Judy Harrison, Director of Programs

3246 Loss & Found Hands & Voices

PO Box 3093
Boulder, CO 80307 303-492-6283
 866-422-0422
 parentadvocate@handsandvoices.org
 www.handsandvoices.org

Advice on what to do if your baby did not pass the newborn hearing screening. DVD, voiced, captioned.

3247 Lydia's Lessons

American Sign Language Productions
4450 La Crosse Ave
San Diego, CA 92117 952-906-1180
 800-767-4461
 Fax: 952-906-1099
 TTY: 952-906-1198
 www.signenhancers.com

Lydia shares her school and camp experiences along with a rare opportunity to practice receptive skills and interpreting with a 12-year-old client. Here's your stress-free chance to hone your skills for middle school interpreting. Remember, you have two team interpreters to demonstrate how to interpret for Lydia. 40 minutes. DVD - $59.95; VHS - $49.95

3248 Mercer Mayer Frog Stories

Harris Communications
15155 Technology Drive
Eden Prairie, MN 55344 952-906-1180
 800-825-6758
 Fax: 952-906-1099
 TTY: 800-825-9187
 info@harriscomm.com
 www.harriscomm.com

Three classic Mercer Mayer stories on DVD-R; voiced; signed in ASL; no captions. Features: A Boy, a Dog and a Frog; Frog on His Own; and Frog, Where are You?

3249 My Baby Can Talk: First Signs

Harris Communications
15155 Technology Drive
Eden Prairie, MN 55344 952-906-1180
 800-825-6758
 Fax: 952-906-1099
 TTY: 800-825-9187
 info@harriscomm.com
 www.harriscomm.com

This is the only baby sign language video that features a young baby signing all the words presented and is considered engaging for young babies. Brightly colored toys, beautiful live footage, engaging images and a young baby signing captivate your baby and as a result your baby learns to sign. This DVD was specifically developed to respect the developmental stage, attention span and intellect of babies from 10 to 24 months. Teaches elementary signs based upon ASL. Ages 10 months and up.

2004 DVD 45 minutes

3250 My Surprise

Modern Sign Press
10443 Los Alamitos Boulevard, PO Box 1181
Los Alamitos, CA 90720 562-596-8548
 800-572-7332
 Fax: 562-795-6614
 TTY: 562-493-4168
 modsigns@modernsignspress.com
 www.modernsignspress.com

Basic level videotape of signed story for Expressive and Receptive practice. Story is repeated three times for ease of use. Watch how the visual features are incorporated. Turn the sound off for receptive practice. Written script and tape use suggestions included. VHS

Esther Zawolkow, President

3251 New Neighbors

Modern Sign Press
10443 Los Alamitos Boulevard, PO Box 1181
Los Alamitos, CA 90720 562-596-8548
 800-572-7332
 Fax: 562-795-6614
 TTY: 562-493-4168
 modsigns@modernsignspress.com
 www.modernsignspress.com

Basic level videotape of signed story for Expressive and Receptive practice. Story is repeated three times for ease of use. Watch how the visual features are incorporated. Turn the sound off for receptive practice. Written script and tape use suggestions included. VHS

Esther Zawolkow, President

3252 Number Signs for Everyone: Numbering in American Sign Language

DawnSign Press
6130 Nancy Ridge Drive
San Diego, CA 92121 858-625-0600
 800-549-5350
 Fax: 858-625-2336
 info@dawnsign.com
 www.dawnsign.com

Presenter Cinnie MacDougall shows you all the different rules and handshapes for clearly and accurately communicating numbers within ASL sentences in proper context. VHS.

90 minutes
ISBN: 0-915035-32-4

Cinnie MacDougall, Presenter

Hearing Impairment/Deafness / Audio Video

3253 Opinion Section
Modern Sign Press
10443 Los Alamitos Boulevard, PO Box 1181
Los Alamitos, CA 90720
562-596-8548
800-572-7332
Fax: 562-795-6614
TTY: 562-493-4168
modsigns@modernsignspress.com
www.modernsignspress.com

Basic level videotape of signed story for Expressive and Receptive practice. Story is repeated three times for ease of use. Watch how the visual features are incorporated. Turn the sound off for receptive practice. Written script and tape use suggestions included. VHS

Esther Zawolkow, President

3254 Parent Sign Series
Sign Media
4020 Blackburn Lane
Burtonsville, MD 20866
301-421-0268
900-475-4756
Fax: 301-421-0270
info@signmedia.com
www.signmedia.com

Learn sign language within the situations that you face everyday. Rather than wasting time learning vocabulary that doesn't fit your needs, learn the signs that help you communicate quickly with your deaf child. Each tape shows conversations and interactions within a family followed by review sentences and vocabulary items. Perfect for parents to use at home or for sign language programs that offer instruction to parents and beginning signers. Comes in ten one-hour tapes.

VHS

3255 Rainbow's End
Sign Media
4020 Blackburn Lane
Burtonsville, MD 20866
301-421-0268
800-475-4756
Fax: 301-421-0270
info@signmedia.com
www.signmedia.com

It's like Sesame Street but with Deaf characters who use ASL. Designed to enhance the self-image of Deaf children, these five videotapes teach while they entertain. They encourage and lead children to acquisition of English language and reading skills. The Pot of Gold Resource Workbook containes activities and exercises and is fully reproducible. Set includes five 30 minute tapes and workbook.

3256 Rather Strange Stories
Modern Sign Press
10443 Los Alamitos Boulevard, PO Box 1181
Los Alamitos, CA 90720
562-596-8548
800-572-7332
Fax: 562-795-6614
TTY: 562-493-4168
modsigns@modernsignspress.com
www.modernsignspress.com

Created to provide practice in word groups at the intermediate level in Signing Exact English. The word groups were established by topic, and the stories created to use all the words in a given group in the shortest story possible...which is why they are Rather Strange Stories at time. 14 titles: Math/Science, Words Around the House, Prepositions, Words for People, Education/English, Body & Health, Nature, Picnic, Playacting, Sports, Grand Ball, Rabbit/Beaver, Transportation and Religion.

$15 each tape

Esther Zawolkow, President

3257 Russian Soldier
Modern Sign Press
10443 Los Alamitos Boulevard, PO Box 1181
Los Alamitos, CA 90720
562-596-8548
800-572-7332
Fax: 562-795-6614
TTY: 562-493-4168
modsigns@modernsignspress.com
www.modernsignspress.com

Basic level videotape of signed story for Expressive and Receptive practice. Story is repeated three times for ease of use. Watch how the visual features are incorporated. Turn the sound off for receptive practice. Written script and tape use suggestions included. VHS

Esther Zawolkow, President

3258 Science, Math
Modern Sign Press
10443 Los Alamitos Boulevard, PO Box 1181
Los Alamitos, CA 90720
562-596-8548
800-572-7332
Fax: 562-795-6614
TTY: 562-493-4168
modsigns@modernsignspress.com
www.modernsignspress.com

Basic level videotape of signed story for Expressive and Receptive practice. Story is repeated three times for ease of use. Watch how the visual features are incorporated. Turn the sound off for receptive practice. Written script and tape use suggestions included. VHS

Esther Zawolkow, President

3259 Sign Songs: Fun Songs to Sign and Sing
Aylmer Press/TJ Publishers
P.O. Box 702701
Dallas, TX 75370
972-416-0800
800-999-1168
Fax: 972-416-0944
TTY: 972-416-0933
customerservice@tjpublishers.com
https://www388.safesecureweb.com/tjpublishers/store/

Features performers John Kinstler, formerly with the National Theatre of the Deaf, signing along to the lyrics of the eleven kids' songs written and performed by guitarist/singer Ken Lonnquist. Songs include 'Alligator Rag,' 'One Speed Bike,' 'Nattie of the Jungle' plus eight more delightful and fun songs. Lyrics included. VHS.

29 minutes
ISBN: 0-932314-45-7

3260 Sign With Your Baby-Complete Learning Kit
Modern Sign Press
10443 Los Alamitos Boulevard, PO Box 1181
Los Alamitos, CA 90720
562-596-8548
800-572-7332
Fax: 562-795-6614
TTY: 562-493-4168
modsigns@modernsignspress.com
www.modernsignspress.com

Includes video, book and quick reference guide. The video makes learning easy with instruction, demonstrations and tips from the author and Speech-Language Pathologist. Interviews with parents and grandparents who share their experiences and footage of signing babies offers inspirational vision of the power of the system. The book is filled with anecdotes, practical guidelines and humor and offers an effective way to teach parents and infants how to communicate through sign.

VHS and DVD

Joseph Garcia, Author
Alice Stroutsos, Speech-Language Pathologist
Esther Zawolkow, President

3261 Signing Naturally
TJ Publishers
P.O. Box 702701
Dallas, TX 75370
972-416-0800
800-999-1168
Fax: 972-416-0944
TTY: 972-416-0933
customerservice@tjpublishers.com
https://www388.safesecureweb.com/tjpublishers/store/

This series is based on the functional-notional approach to teaching sign language developed at Vista Community College at Berkeley. Signing Naturally organizes language lessons around everyday interaction. Exercises in the student workbooks coincide with exercises on the videotapes. VHS and DVD

Cheri Smith, Producer
Ella Mae Lentz, Producer
Ken Mikos, Producer

Hearing Impairment/Deafness / Audio Video

3262 Sleeping Beauty
Gallaudet University Press
800 Florida Avenue NE
Washington, DC 20002
202-651-5488
Fax: 202-651-5489
TTY: 202-651-5444
gupress@gallaudet.edu
gupress.gallaudet.edu

The Sleeping Beauty videotape features the full story in ASL and includes vocabulary and sentence structure focusing on adjectives, with a voice-over throughout. Color, 30 minutes

VHS
ISBN: 0-930323-98-X

3263 Sound & Fury
Aquarius Health Care Videos
18 N Main Street, PO Box 1159
Sherborn, MA 1770
508-650-1616
888-440-2963
Fax: 508-650-1665
info@aquariusproductions.com
www.aquariusproductions.com

This film takes viewers inside the seldom seen world of the deaf to witness a painful family struggle over a controversial medical technology called the cochlear implant. Illuminates the ongoing struggle for identity among deaf people today. Available in VHS and DVD

55 Minutes

Leslie Kusman, President/Producer

3264 Sound and Fury: Six Years Later
Aquarius Health Care Media
18 North Main Street, PO Box 1159
Sherborn, MA 1770
888-440-2963
Fax: 508-650-1665
www.aquariousproductions.com

In 2000, the first Sound & Fury captured audiences around the world and an Academy Award nomination through the riveting story of the Artinian family of Long Island. This sequel gives a new look at the family as it follows them in the next six years of their life. An excellent film for anyone dealing with issues of hearing loss. A must for both professionals and families to see. 2006 - 29 minutes, DVD

3265 Stories About Growing Up
Harris Communciations
15155 Technology Drive
Eden Prairie, MN 55344
952-906-1180
800-825-6758
Fax: 952-906-1099
TTY: 800-825-9187
info@harriscomm.com
www.harriscomm.com

DVD-R - voiced; signed in ASL; no captions. Three Scholastic stories: Leo the Late Bloomer by Robert Kraus (One day, in his own good time, Leo shows everyone how glorious it is to finally bloom); A Weekend with Wendell by Kevin Henkes (Three cheers for compromise as quiet-as-a-mouse Sophie learns to assert herself with big-mouthed Wendell), and Joey Runs Away by Jack Kent (Joey looks for another home when he doesn't like cleaning his room).

3266 The Big Test
Modern Sign Press
10443 Los Alamitos Boulevard, PO Box 1181
Los Alamitos, CA 90720
562-596-8548
800-572-7332
Fax: 562-795-6614
TTY: 562-493-4168
modsigns@modernsignspress.com
www.modernsignspress.com

Basic level videotape of signed story for Expressive and Receptive practice. Story is repeated three times for ease of use. Watch how the visual features are incorporated. Turn the sound off for receptive practice. Written script and tape use suggestions included. VHS

Esther Zawolkow, President

3267 The Driving Test
Modern Sign Press
10443 Los Alamitos Boulevard, PO Box 1181
Los Alamitos, CA 90720
562-596-8548
800-572-7332
Fax: 562-795-6614
TTY: 562-493-4168
modsigns@modernsignspress.com
www.modernsignspress.com

Basic level videotape of signed story for Expressive and Receptive practice. Story is repeated three times for ease of use. Watch how the visual features are incorporated. Turn the sound off for receptive practice. Written script and tape use suggestions included. VHS

Esther Zawolkow, President

3268 The Gossip
Modern Sign Press
10443 Los Alamitos Boulevard, PO Box 1181
Los Alamitos, CA 90720
562-596-8548
800-572-7332
Fax: 562-795-6614
TTY: 562-493-4168
modsigns@modernsignspress.com
www.modernsignspress.com

Basic level videotape of signed story for Expressive and Receptive practice. Story is repeated three times for ease of use. Watch how the visual features are incorporated. Turn the sound off for receptive practice. Written script and tape use suggestions included. VHS

Esther Zawolkow, President

3269 The Grocer and the Cook
Modern Sign Press
10443 Los Alamitos Boulevard, PO Box 1181
Los Alamitos, CA 90720
562-596-8548
800-572-7332
Fax: 562-795-6614
TTY: 562-493-4168
modsigns@modernsignspress.com
www.modernsignspress.com

Basic level videotape of signed story for Expressive and Receptive practice. Story is repeated three times for ease of use. Watch how the visual features are incorporated. Turn the sound off for receptive practice. Written script and tape use suggestions included. VHS

Esther Zawolkow, President

3270 The Memo
Modern Sign Press
10443 Los Alamitos Boulevard, PO Box 1181
Los Alamitos, CA 90720
562-596-8548
800-572-7332
Fax: 562-795-6614
TTY: 562-493-4168
modsigns@modernsignspress.com
www.modernsignspress.com

Basic level videotape of signed story for Expressive and Receptive practice. Story is repeated three times for ease of use. Watch how the visual features are incorporated. Turn the sound off for receptive practice. Written script and tape use suggestions included. VHS

Esther Zawolkow, President

3271 The Pet Show
Modern Sign Press
10443 Los Alamitos Boulevard, PO Box 1181
Los Alamitos, CA 90720
562-596-8548
800-572-7332
Fax: 562-795-6614
TTY: 562-493-4168
modsigns@modernsignspress.com
www.modernsignspress.com

Basic level videotape of signed story for Expressive and Receptive practice. Story is repeated three times for ease of use. Watch how the visual features are incorporated. Turn the sound off for receptive practice. Written script and tape use suggestions included. VHS

Esther Zawolkow, President

Hearing Impairment/Deafness / Computer Software

3272 The Race
Modern Sign Press
10443 Los Alamitos Boulevard, PO Box 1181
Los Alamitos, CA 90720
562-596-8548
800-572-7332
Fax: 562-795-6614
TTY: 562-493-4168
modsigns@modernsignspress.com
www.modernsignspress.com

Basic level videotape of signed story for Expressive and Receptive practice. Story is repeated three times for ease of use. Watch how the visual features are incorporated. Turn the sound off for receptive practice. Written script and tape use suggestions included. VHS

Esther Zawolkow, President

3273 The Snowman
HEAR-MORE
42 Executive Boulevard
Farmingdale, NY 11735
800-881-4327
Fax: 631-752-0689
TTY: 800-281-4327
www.hearmore.com

This delightful animation weaves a spell of magic enchantment as a young boy's snowman comes to life and escorts him on a fantasy dream visit to the North Pole.

3274 The Treasure Chest
Drs Michelle Anthony and Reyna Lindert, author
HEAR-MORE
42 Executive Boulevard
Farmingdale, NY 11735
800-881-4327
Fax: 631-752-0689
TTY: 800-281-4327
www.hearmore.com

Children of all ages will be delighted by this magical journey of discovery. Join us as we lead you and your child to a treasure trove of toys, plays, songs, and signs. The visually engaging images in the video present families with endless opportunities to make meaningful connections with their little ones. Designed for children agest 0-36 months. Running time is approximately 30 minutes. Includes more than 35 ASL signs.

DVD

3275 The World According to Pat: Reflections of Residential School Days
TJ Publishers
P.O. Box 702701
Dallas, TX 75370
972-416-0800
800-999-1168
Fax: 972-416-0944
TTY: 972-416-0933
customerservice@tjpublishers.com
https://www388.safesecureweb.com/tjpublishers/store/

Pat Graybill's one-man show offers humerous and touching insights into life in a residential school dormitory. Includes appearances by others who provide their own recollections of residential school days.
VHS

90 minutes

3276 University Professor
Modern Sign Press
10443 Los Alamitos Boulevard, PO Box 1181
Los Alamitos, CA 90720
562-596-8548
800-572-7332
Fax: 562-795-6614
TTY: 562-493-4168
modsigns@modernsignspress.com
www.modernsignspress.com

Basic level videotape of signed story for Expressive and Receptive practice. Story is repeated three times for ease of use. Watch how the visual features are incorporated. Turn the sound off for receptive practice. Written script and tape use suggestions included. VHS

Esther Zawolkow, President

3277 Why We Can Hear And Speak
Alexander Graham Bell Association for the Deaf
3417 Volta Place NW
Washington, DC 20007
202-337-5220
202-337-8314
Fax: 202-337-8314
TTY: 203-337-5221
info@agbell.org
listeningandspokenlanguage.org

This documentary was developed to show the children of Natural Communication, Inc. at different stages of language development. Each vignette inclueds an introductory biography that briefly describes the child's diagnosis, current age, therapy history and amplification technology. The principles of Auditory-Verbal philosophy are described throughout the tape. All children featured use the Auditory-Verbal approach.

VHS 23 minutes

Lisa Chutjian, Chief Development Officer
Emilio Alonso-Mendoza, Chief Executive Officer
Judy Harrison, Director of Programs

Computer Software

3278 ASL Clip and Create Version 3
HEAR-MORE
42 Executive Boulevard
Farmingdale, NY 11735
800-881-4327
Fax: 631-752-0689
TTY: 800-281-3555
www.hearmore.com

Design learning materials, posters, cards, labels, postcards, and banners using over 3,500 American Sign Language pictures. Four sign-skill enhancing games. Six different templates to customize. Custom design & printing capabilities. Suggestions for learning activities and games. Minimum requirements: Windows 98 SE, Pentium II or equivalent, 64 Mb memory.

3279 ASL Songs for Kids
HEAR-MORE
42 Executive Boulevard
Farmingdale, NY 11735
800-881-4327
Fax: 631-752-0689
TTY: 800-281-3555
www.hearmore.com

This CD-Rom presents six songs typically learned by young children-sung and signed. The CD contains two short songs-Twinkle, Twinkle Little Star & Happy Birthday, and four songs that have multiple verses-The Ants Go Marching, Old McDonald, The Wheels on the Bus and The Greeen Grass Grows All Around. 'As the songs are sung, Paws the dog sings, and graphics convey the lyrics, as well as information about the notes and volume. The songs can be viewed with signs in English word order or in ASL.

3280 ASL Tales and Games for Kids
HEAR-MORE
42 Executive Boulevard
Farmingdale, NY 11735
800-881-4327
Fax: 631-752-0689
TTY: 800-281-3555
www.hearmore.com

This CD series follows Paws, the signing dog, and his friends as they explore their neighborhood. This program contains 3 community-focused stories and 10 games. The neighborhood children are deaf or hard of hearing and represent different ethnic groups. Minimum system requirements: Windows (95,98,NT,ME,2000), 166 MHz Pentium, 4x CD-ROM Drive

3281 ASL Tales and Games for Kids 2
HEAR-MORE
42 Executive Boulevard
Farmingdale, NY 11735
800-881-4327
Fax: 631-752-0689
TTY: 800-281-3555
www.hearmore.com

Hearing Impairment/Deafness / Computer Software

In this CD-ROM, Biscuit Boulevard focuses on events that take place on one street in Pawstown, Biscuit Boulevard. The stories are original and written to promote good English literacy, while simultaneously teaching important aspects of ASL. Each story can be viewed continuously, without the child needing to manipulate the mouse, or the child can control the story himself.

3282 ASL Tales and Songs for Kids CD-1
Harris Communications
15155 Technology Drive
Eden Prairie, MN 55344
952-906-1180
800-825-6758
Fax: 952-906-1099
TTY: 800-825-9187
info@harriscomm.com
www.harriscomm.com

In 'Woof, Woof Way' Paws the Dog helps children build their skills with colorful graphics. Paws, the signing dog, and the Pawstown neighborhood kids on adventures in their own community. System requirements: Windows 95, 98, NT, ME, 2000; Pentium 166MHz; 4X or more CD-ROM drive; works with most popular monochrome and color printers supported by Windows.

CD-ROM

3283 ASL Tales and Songs for Kids CD-2
Harris Communications
15155 Technology Drive
Eden Prairie, MN 55344
952-906-1180
800-825-6758
Fax: 952-906-1099
TTY: 800-825-9187
info@harriscomm.com
www.harriscomm.com

Paws, the signing dog, and the Pawstown neighborhood kids on adventures in their own community. In CD-2, 'Biscuit Boulevard,' Paws the Dog helps children build their skills with colorful graphics. System requirements: Windows 95, 98, NT, ME, 2000; Pentium 166MHz; 4X or more CD-ROM drive; works with most popular monochrome and color printers supported by Windows.

CD-ROM

3284 American Sign Language V2.0
HEAR-MORE
42 Executive Boulevard
Farmingdale, NY 11735
800-881-4327
Fax: 631-752-0689
TTY: 800-281-3555
www.hearmore.com

This updated version comes as a 5 CD-ROM set. Customize signing pace with the speed control feature. Takes you from beginner to advanced intermediate levels. Set includes SigningAvatar, HyperSign Jr, Ready! Set! Sign! Starter version, ASL Condensed Dictionary, and ASL introduction which aids children in developing essential analytical skills. System requirements: 500 MHz or faster, Windows 98/ME/XP, 128 MB RAM, 100 MB hard drive.

3285 American Sign Language Vocabulary
HEAR-MORE
42 Executive Boulevard
Farmingdale, NY 11735
800-881-4327
Fax: 631-752-0689
TTY: 800-281-3555
www.hearmore.com

PC requirements: Pentium 120 MHz or faster, Win 95, 98, NT4, 2000, 64 MB RAM, active movie 1.0 or higher, DirectShow 6.0 recommended, Active X Network libraries. Macintosh Requirements: PowerPC or later, 120 MHz or faster, MacOS 7+, 64 MB RAM, Quicktime 3 or higher, Quicktime mpeg extension v1.1.1 or higher.

3286 Baby's First Book of Signs: An ASL Word Book (Volume 1-3)
HEAR-MORE
42 Executive Boulevard
Farmingdale, NY 11735
800-881-4327
Fax: 631-752-0689
TTY: 800-281-3555
www.hearmore.com

Three sweet little electronic books depict the signs for basic words. Signs are shown in video and pictures. English equivalents, as well as concept graphics, are included. Easy to use-just click to turn each page. Volume 1 includes: Animals, Clothes, Colors, Food and Toys. Volume 2 includes: Actions, Descriptions, Feelings, When and Where. Volume 3 includes: Alphabet, Numbers, Home, Outside and People. CD-ROM

3287 Baby's First Book of Signs: Volumes I-III
Harris Communications
15155 Technology Drive
Eden Prairie, MN 55344
952-906-1180
800-825-6758
Fax: 952-906-1099
TTY: 800-825-9187
info@harriscomm.com
www.harriscomm.com

An ASL Word Book with Video and Audio Clips. Each CD-ROM contains an electronic flip book for basic words in video and pictures. English equivalents (in print and audio), as well as concept graphics, are included. In these three CD-ROMs, you can learn 390 words in sign language. Minimum PC requirements: Windows 98, ME, 2000, XP; 64 MB RAM, 800x600 pixels screen area; Pentium II'300 MHz; 16-bit color display; CD-ROM drive.

3288 Cochlear Impant Auditory Training Guide
David Sindrey, Cert. AVT, author

Alexander Graham Bell Association for the Deaf
3417 Volta Place NW
Washington, DC 20007
202-337-5220
202-337-8314
Fax: 202-337-8314
TTY: 203-337-5221
info@agbell.org
listeningandspokenlanguage.org

This second edition comes with games pieces, peg boards, and two print CDs. The manual presents easy to follow hierarchy and the CDs include a placement test, lesson plan forms, acoustic screens, and hundreds of discrimination cards and activities for single word, multiple element and broader language listening at all levels. The Wordplay product Vattier Boards has now been incorporated into this package.

Lisa Chutjian, Chief Development Officer
Emilio Alonso-Mendoza, Chief Executive Officer
Judy Harrison, Director of Programs

3289 Elf on a Shelf for Minimal Pairs: Giant CD Print Program
David Sindrey, Cert. AVT, author

Alexander Graham Bell Association for the Deaf
3417 Volta Place NW
Washington, DC 20007
202-337-5220
202-337-8314
Fax: 202-337-8314
TTY: 203-337-5221
info@agbell.org
listeningandspokenlanguage.org

Print more than 1100 English words. This program organizes effective word-pair practice into the following formats: Lotto games, Dixie Cup games, Matrix games, Fiv. Operates on any PC or MAC system.

Lisa Chutjian, Chief Development Officer
Emilio Alonso-Mendoza, Chief Executive Officer
Judy Harrison, Director of Programs

3290 Hear & Listen! Talk & Sing!
Warren Estabrooks MEd, Lois Birkenshaw-Fleming BA, author

Alexander Graham Bell Association for the Deaf
3417 Volta Place NW
Washington, DC 20007
202-337-5220
202-337-8314
Fax: 202-337-8314
TTY: 203-337-5221
info@agbell.org
listeningandspokenlanguage.org

This music book and CD integrates songs with speech sounds to enable young children with hearing loss to develop melodic, natural-sounding voices and enhance linguistic skills. Songs include sounds that are acoustically relevant to children with severe or profound hearing loss ages 18 months to 7 years. Songs are grouped in categories such as animals, weather and holidays and vary in difficulty

Lisa Chutjian, Chief Development Officer
Emilio Alonso-Mendoza, Chief Executive Officer
Judy Harrison, Director of Programs

3291 Hearing is Believing, Volume One
Dimity Dornan, BA, author

Alexander Graham Bell Association for the Deaf
3417 Volta Place NW
Washington, DC 20007
202-337-5220
202-337-8314
Fax: 202-337-8314
TTY: 202-337-5221
info@agbell.org
listeningandspokenlanguage.org

The first volume of the Hearing is Believing distance education series on CD-ROM offers self-directed learning through four hours of lectures on the following Auditory-Verbal topics: Current Auditory-Verbal PRactice and Research, Auditory Learning, Listening for Older Children, Integration into the Mainstream School. Includes lectures within the framework of the Auditory-Verbal Curriculum, accompanying PowerPoint slides, video excerpts of Auditory-Verbal therapy sessions and transcripts.

Lisa Chutjian, Chief Development Officer
Emilio Alonso-Mendoza, Chief Executive Officer
Judy Harrison, Director of Programs

3292 Hearing is Believing, Volume Three
Dimity Dornan, BA, author

Alexander Graham Bell Association for the Deaf
3417 Volta Place NW
Washington, DC 20007
202-337-5220
202-337-8314
Fax: 202-337-8314
TTY: 202-337-5221
info@agbell.org
listeningandspokenlanguage.org

This third volume in the Hearing is Believing series provides four hours of self-directed learning on the following Auditory-Verbal topics: Teaching Spoken Language, Speech Development, Working with Parents and Infants. Includes lectures within the framework of the Auditory-Verbal curriculum, accompanying PowerPoint slides, video excerpts of Audio-Verbal therapy sessions and transcripts. A note-taking feature allows you to jot down ideas and questions as you learn.

Lisa Chutjian, Chief Development Officer
Emilio Alonso-Mendoza, Chief Executive Officer
Judy Harrison, Director of Programs

3293 Hearing is Believing, Volume Two
Judith A Marlow, PhD, author

Alexander Graham Bell Association for the Deaf
3417 Volta Place NW
Washington, DC 20007
202-337-5220
202-337-8314
Fax: 202-337-8314
TTY: 202-337-5221
info@agbell.org
listeningandspokenlanguage.org

This interactive CD-ROM, the second volume in the Hearing is Believing distance eduction series includes two hours of lectures on early detection and intervention: The Rationale for Early Detection and Current Status, Achieving Timely Evaluation and Intervention, Shifting Paradigms. Includes lectures within the framework of the Auditory-Verbal curriculum, accompanying PowerPoint slides, video excerpts of Auditory-Verbal therapy sessions and transcripts.

Lisa Chutjian, Chief Development Officer
Emilio Alonso-Mendoza, Chief Executive Officer
Judy Harrison, Director of Programs

3294 Holidays CD-ROM
Harris Communications
15155 Technology Drive
Eden Prairie, MN 55344
952-906-1180
800-825-6758
Fax: 952-906-1099
TTY: 800-825-9187
info@harriscomm.com
www.harriscomm.com

This electronic book teaches 303 basic signs for 13 holidays: New Year, Valentine's Day, Patriotic Days, St. Patrick's Day, Easter, Graduation, Jewish Holidays, Parents' Days, Halloween, Christmas, Birthdays, Weddings and Thanksgiving. Minimum PC requirements: Windows 98, ME, 2000, XP; Pentium II 300MHz; 64 MB RAM; 16-bit color display; 800x600 pixels screen area; CD-ROM drive.

3295 Holidays: An ASL Word Book
HEAR-MORE
42 Executive Boulevard
Farmingdale, NY 11735
800-881-4327
Fax: 631-752-0689
TTY: 800-281-3555
www.hearmore.com

This electronic book teaches all of the basic signs for 13 holidays. Signs are shown in video and pictures. English equivalents, as well as concept graphics, are included. Holidays covered include: New Year, Valentine's Day, Patriotic Days, St. Patrick's Day, Easter, Christmas, Jewish Holidays, Thanksgiving, Graduation, Weddings/Anniversaries, Hallowwen, Birthday, and Parents' Days. Easy to use-just click to turn each page. Windows 98/ME/2000/XP, Pentium 2 300 MHz, 64 MB Ram, CD drive

3296 I Cue, U Cue
HEAR-MORE
42 Executive Boulevard
Farmingdale, NY 11735
800-881-4327
Fax: 631-752-0689
TTY: 800-281-3555
www.hearmore.com

This software provides information about Cued Speech. Cued Speech combines hand-shapes and placements with mouth movements to represent the consonants and vowels of a language. The complete American English system is taught through 14 classes, with an additional class providing extra practice. Includes guide. Windows 98SE, ME, 2000, XP; CD-ROM drive, 16X; Pentium III, 600 MHz or eqivalent; 190 MD hard drive space.

3297 Illustrated Dictionary - 3D ASL
HEAR-MORE
42 Executive Boulevard
Farmingdale, NY 11735
800-881-4327
Fax: 631-752-0689
TTY: 800-281-3555
www.hearmore.com

This CD-ROM Dictionary is designed for everyone who wants to learn American Sign Language. Choose one of nine characters with different personalities and ethnic backgrounds. Characters fidget while waiting and show emotions, like impatience or happiness. Every word in the dictionary is represented by a picture, used in a sentence and signed by your selected character. System requirements: 300 MHz PC, Windows 98/ME/NT/2000/XP, Internet Explorer 4+, CD-ROM, 1024X768 monitor, 100MB hard drive space

3298 Johnny Rock's Christmas
HEAR-MORE
42 Executive Boulevard
Farmingdale, NY 11735
800-881-4327
Fax: 631-752-0689
TTY: 800-281-3555
www.hearmore.com

This software is specially designed to enhance vocabulary development for deaf and hard of hearing students and elementary aged students with similar language needs. Teachers and Parents will love it as much as the kids will. Delightful graphics. Easy installation. Non-auditory. On-line technical support. Two 3.5 diskettes. Runs on Windows/Win95/Win98.

Hearing Impairment/Deafness / Computer Software

3299 Ling Series
Daniel Ling, PhD, author

Alexander Graham Bell Association for the Deaf
3417 Volta Place NW
Washington, DC 20007
 202-337-5220
 202-337-8314
 Fax: 202-337-8314
 TTY: 202-337-5221
 info@agbell.org
 listeningandspokenlanguage.org

Learn at your own pace with this CD-ROM distance education program featuring lectures from the University of Ottawa seminar in Auditory-Verbal practices. Topics include: Assessment of Spoken Language, Phonological Processes, Remediation of Deviant Speech. The CD includes the lecture, accompanying PowerPoint slides, clips of Ling's students, full lecture transcripts and a note-taking feature that allows you to jot down ideas and questions as you learn.

Lisa Chutjian, Chief Development Officer
Emilio Alonso-Mendoza, Chief Executive Officer
Judy Harrison, Director of Programs

3300 Marvin Teaches Fingerspelling
HEAR-MORE
42 Executive Boulevard
Farmingdale, NY 11735
 800-881-4327
 Fax: 631-752-0689
 TTY: 800-281-3555
 www.hearmore.com

This CD is the coolest way yet to improve your receptive fingerspelling skills. Beginners can learn to recognize the different handshapes that make up the letters of the alphabet. Signers of every ability level can practice reading many fingerspelled words at speeds varying from novice to expert. Minimum system requirements: Pentium I, Windows 95, CD drive.

3301 MyTTY Phone Messenger Software for Windows
HEAR-MORE
42 Executive Boulevard
Farmingdale, NY 11735
 800-881-4327
 Fax: 631-752-0689
 TTY: 800-281-3555
 www.hearmore.com

myTTY Phone Messenger is out-dialing software. It allows you to send pre-recorded TTY text and/or voice message to each telephone number on a customizable list. It can be used for such purposes as emergency, informational, meeting, and advertising notifications. Requires Windows 2000 or XP; 32 MB memory, Pentium Processor or compatible, CD-Rom dirve; TAPI-complieant voice modem.

3302 MyTTY for Windows 95, 98, ME, 2000, XP
HEAR-MORE
42 Executive Boulevard
Farmingdale, NY 11735
 800-881-4327
 Fax: 631-752-0689
 TTY: 800-281-3555
 www.hearmore.com

Now you can use your PC as a TTY too. myTTY is a computer program that runs under the Microsoft Windows operating system. If the computer is equipped with a voice modem, myTTY will make the computer perform like a TTY. The program allows your computer to communicate with any Baudot TTY over a telephone line. Requirements: Windows 98, SE or later (XP compatible) with Internet Explorer 4.0 or later, a Pentium processor or equivalent, CD drive, TAP compliant modem and 32 MB of memory.

3303 Paws Sign Stories
Harris Communications
15155 Technology Drive
Eden Prairie, MN 55344
 952-906-1180
 800-825-6758
 Fax: 952-906-1099
 TTY: 800-825-9187
 info@harriscomm.com
 www.harriscomm.com

An educational and entertaining program designed for deaf and hard of hearing children who want to learn American Sign Language. Includes 5 stories and 15 games. Click on individual words or whole sentences to have them signs and voiced. Includes video clips of a person dressed as Paws, using ASL so all information is accessible to deaf and hard of hearing children. Ages 3-7.

CD-ROM

3304 Ready! Set! Sign!
HEAR-MORE
42 Executive Boulevard
Farmingdale, NY 11735
 800-881-4327
 Fax: 631-752-0689
 TTY: 800-281-3555
 www.hearmore.com

Begin with 100 signs you already know. Then continue learning over 1,000 more using video clips, photos, animations and graphics as visual aids for learning and remembering signs. Afterwards study the topics that interest you: fingerspelling, numbers, grammar concepts, and more. Learn the vocabulary you want, when you want it. Test your current sign language knowledge by reading over 1,750 signed practice sentences, phrases, words and numbers. View one or more of twenty-three Cultural Moments.

3305 School Days
Harris Communications
15155 Technology Drive
Eden Prairie, MN 55344
 952-906-1180
 800-825-6758
 Fax: 952-906-1099
 TTY: 800-825-9187
 info@harriscomm.com
 www.harriscomm.com

An ASL Word Book with Video and Audio Clips. Prepare your child for school with this fun electronic book of 76 basic school vocabulary words. Each page shows the sign in both video and a picture. English equivalents in print and audio, plus concept graphics are included. Minimum system requirements: Windows 98, ME, 2000, XP; Pentium II 300MHz; 64MB RAM; 16-bit color display; 800x600 pixels screen area; CD-ROM drive.

CD-ROM

3306 School Days: An ASL Word Book
HEAR-MORE
42 Executive Boulevard
Farmingdale, NY 11735
 800-881-4327
 Fax: 631-752-0689
 TTY: 800-281-3555
 www.hearmore.com

Prepare your child for school with this fun little electronic book of basic school signs. Each page shows the sign in both video and a picture. English equivalents (in print and audio), as well as concept graphics, are included. 76 signs in all. Easy to use-just click to turn each page. Minimum system requirements: Windows 98/ME/2000/XP, Pentium 2 300 MHz, 64 MB Ram, 16-bit color display, 800x600 pixels screen area, CD drive.

3307 Sign Fine - Vacations
HEAR-MORE
42 Executive Boulevard
Farmingdale, NY 11735
 800-881-4327
 Fax: 631-752-0689
 TTY: 800-281-3555
 www.hearmore.com

Join Paws, the signing dog, as he goes to 14 different travel destinations. Just click on any of the items in the picture to see a video of Paws signing the vocabulary word and an English word equivalent. This CD-Rom software for Windows has over 550 American Sign Language videos that illustrate signs and three fun games to play. Requires Windows 98, ME, 200, XP, Pentium III, 600 MHZ or equivalent, CD-Rom drive and 90 MB of hard drive space.

Hearing Impairment/Deafness / Book Publishers

3308 Simser Series

Judith Simser, author

Alexander Graham Bell Association for the Deaf
3417 Volta Place NW
Washington, DC 20007
202-337-5220
202-337-8314
Fax: 202-337-8314
TTY: 202-337-5221
info@agbell.org
listeningandspokenlanguage.org

Enhance your knowledge with this interactive CD-ROM distance education program featuring lectures from the University of Ottowa seminar in Auditory-Verbal practices. Topics include: Auditory-Verbal Techniques and Hierarchies, Ongoing Assessment, The Why and How of Toys and Games, Goals for the Cochlear Implant User. The CD includes the lectures, accompanying PowerPoint slides, demonstrations of an Auditory-Verbal therapy session, audio clips of students, and full lecture transcripts.

Lisa Chutjian, Chief Development Officer
Emilio Alonso-Mendoza, Chief Executive Officer
Judy Harrison, Director of Programs

3309 Smile

Enid G Wolf-Schein, EdD, CCC-SLP, author

Alexander Graham Bell Association for the Deaf
3417 Volta Place NW
Washington, DC 20007
202-337-5220
202-337-8314
Fax: 202-337-8314
TTY: 203-337-5221
info@agbell.org
listeningandspokenlanguage.org

SMILE is a multisensory program that teaches speech, reading, and writing to children with severe language and communication delays, including those with hearing loss, dyslexia, or autism. Unique in its engaging yet simple focus, SMILE uses expressive and receptive modalities to improve the reading skills of target and general populations. Softcover manual 138 pp. CD and five-Teacher's Guide set.

Lisa Chutjian, Chief Development Officer
Emilio Alonso-Mendoza, Chief Executive Officer
Judy Harrison, Director of Programs

3310 Snap! Kids American Sign Language

HEAR-MORE
42 Executive Boulevard
Farmingdale, NY 11735
800-881-4327
Fax: 631-752-0689
TTY: 800-281-3555
www.hearmore.com

This CD-ROM focuses on ASL basics. Especially for young readers, this disc is full of interactive games and animated vocabulary allowing kids to master new signs while having fun. 26 vocabulary 'books' covering subjects from Action words to Animals; Transportation to Telling Time. Instructional Demos featuring Live-action video signing. ASL Games including Tic Tac Toe and Multiple Choice. System Requirements: Processor 386 DX/33 MHz or faster, Win 3.1, 8 MB RAM, 6 MB HD, 2X CD-ROM, Sound card

3311 Songs for Listening! Songs for Life!

Warren Estabrooks MEd, Lois Birkenshaw-Fleming BA, author

Alexander Graham Bell Association for the Deaf
3417 Volta Place NW
Washington, DC 20007
202-337-5220
202-337-8314
Fax: 202-337-8314
TTY: 203-337-5221
info@agbell.org
listeningandspokenlanguage.org

A song book/CD set and therapy guide. Designed to teach children with hearing loss how to listen and talk through the use of singing and music. It includes early intervention activities as well as resources for parents and professionals who work to develop audition and spoken language in children with hearing loss and/or other communicative disorders. This publication incorporates current language-learning therapy, is presented in an easy-to-read format, and includes technical references.

Lisa Chutjian, Chief Development Officer
Emilio Alonso-Mendoza, Chief Executive Officer
Judy Harrison, Director of Programs

3312 The Ultimate ASL Dictionary

HEAR-MORE
42 Executive Boulevard
Farmingdale, NY 11735
800-881-4327
Fax: 631-752-0689
TTY: 800-281-3555
www.hearmore.com

Over 2400 signs included. Identify words through ASL or English, Words and definitions in video clips, graphics, text and audio, variations of English words that relate to a single sign, spell-check and parameter check.

3313 Troll In A Bowl: Games and Card Print Factory

David Sindrey, Cert. AVT, author

Alexander Graham Bell Association for the Deaf
3417 Volta Place NW
Washington, DC 20007
202-337-5220
202-337-8314
Fax: 202-337-8314
TTY: 203-337-5221
info@agbell.org
listeningandspokenlanguage.org

Features over 2000 articulation, minimal pair, and vocabulary cards organized by a Speech-Language Pathologist. Operates on any PC or MAC system. Includes 54 page soft-cover spiral-binding workbook, game piece and CD

Lisa Chutjian, Chief Development Officer
Emilio Alonso-Mendoza, Chief Executive Officer
Judy Harrison, Director of Programs

Book Publishers

3314 50 Freqeuntly Asked Questions About Auditory-Verbal Therapy

Warren Estabrooks, MEd, author

Alexander Graham Bell Association for the Deaf
3417 Volta Place NW
Washington, DC 20007
202-337-5220
Fax: 202-337-8314
TTY: 202-337-5221
info@agbell.org
www.agbell.org

A prolific collection of responses to most frequently asked questions about auditory-verbal therapy and its application for children who are deaf and hard of hearing. Parents, professionals and everyone concerned with deafness will welcome the guidance, encouragement and knowledge found within this collaboration of professionals who have joined both hearts and minds to provide an extraordinary, informative and invaluable worldwide resource.

213 pages Softcover

3315 A Basic Course in American Sign Lanugage, Second Edition

Tom Humphries, Carol Padden, Terrenc J O'Rourke, author

TJ Publishers
P.O Box 702701
Dallas, TX 75370
972-416-0800
800-999-1168
Fax: 972-416-0944
TTY: 972-416-0933
customerservice@tjpublishers.com
www.tjpublishers.com

Features a new introduction, which includes a section on Deaf Culture and Community, expanded dialogue introductions that incorporate cultural information, revised grammar notes and an updated bibliography.

Hearing Impairment/Deafness / Book Publishers

288 pages Spiral bound
ISBN: 0-932666-42-6

3316 A Basic Vocabulary: American Sign Language for Parents and Children

Terrence J O'Rourke, author

TJ Publishers
P.O Box 702701
Dallas, TX 75370

972-416-0800
800-999-1168
Fax: 972-416-0944
TTY: 972-416-0933
customerservice@tjpublishers.com
www.tjpublishers.com

Carefully selected words and signs include those families use every day. Alphabetically organized vocabulary incorporates developmental lists helpful to both Deaf and hearing children and over 1000 clear sign language illustrations.

240 pages Softcover
ISBN: 0-932666-00-0

3317 A Book of Colors: Baby's First Sign Book

Kim Votry and Curt Waller, author

Gallaudet University Press
800 Florida Avenue NE
Washington, DC 20002

202-651-5488
Fax: 202-651-5489
gupress@gallaudet.edu
www.gupress.gallaudet.edu

Depicts the charming character with the favorite hat signing all of the primary and secondary colors - red, yellow, blue, orange green and purple - in interesting settings. The other pages display a wide variety of appealing colors, too, including pink, white, black, gray, brown, and tan, topped off with a richly rendered illustration of a rainbow.

16 pages Board book
ISBN: 1-563681-47-1

3318 A Season of Change

Lois L Hodge, author

Gallaudet University Press
800 Florida Avenue NE
Washington, DC 20002

202-651-5488
Fax: 202-651-5489
gupress@gallaudet.edu
www.gupress.gallaudet.edu

Okay, so she can't hear as well as other people, but do they believe she can't think as well? Everyone, it seems, in 13-going-on-14-year-old Biney Richmond's life treats her as though she should be wrapped in cotton and set on a shelf. Her parents act as though she can't do things for herself. The only one who seems to have any confidence in her is her best friend, Pat. When Pat's older brother, Gene-who secretly wants to date Biney-gets in trouble, Biney proves to everyone how grown up she is.

108 pages Softcover
ISBN: 0-930323-27-0

3319 ABC's of Finger Spelling

Modern Signs Press
PO Box 1181
Los Alamitos, CA 90720

562-596-8548
800-572-7332
Fax: 562-795-6614
TTY: 562-493-4168
modsigns@modernsignspress.com
www.modernsignspress.com

Helps teach upper and lower case letters of the alphabet. Includes printed letters and easy-to-follow drawings of the hand shapes.

1984 60 pages paperback

3320 ABCs of AVT: Analyzing Auditory-Verbal Therapy

Warren Estabrooks, MEd and Rhonda Schwartz, MA, author

Alexander Graham Bell Association for the Deaf
3417 Volta Place NW
Washington, DC 20007

202-337-5220
Fax: 202-337-8314
TTY: 202-337-5221
info@agbell.org
www.agbell.org

Provides an overview of Auditory-Verbal techniques and guidance on appropriate intervention for children experiencing difficulties with language development. Task analysis exercises outlined in the manual and demonstrated in the video, which contains excerpts of therapy sessions and longitudinal studies, are designed to help students and professionals of all levels of experience hone their clinical skills. Softcover/Spiral binding/manual and VHS set/Open-Captioned 46:04

104 pages Softcover

3321 ASL Babies: First Signs

Tina Jo Breindel and Michael Carter, author

Harris Communications
15155 Technology Drive
Eden Prairie, MN 55344

952-906-1180
800-825-6758
Fax: 952-906-1099
TTY: 800-825-9187
info@harriscomm.com
www.harriscomm.com

A toddler signs 14 words that first appear in a child's vocabulary: airplane, baby, bath, bed, dad, help, hot, hurt, mom, more, please, thank you, tired and toilet.

16 pages Board book

3322 ASL Babies: Let's Eat

Tina Jo Breindel and Michael Carter, author

Harris Communications
15155 Technology Drive
Eden Prairie, MN 55344

952-906-1180
800-825-6758
Fax: 952-906-1099
TTY: 800-825-9187
info@harriscomm.com
www.harriscomm.com

Food-related vocabulary words in English and American Sign Language are beautifully illustrated in this board book.

16 pages Board book

3323 AUSPLAN Auditory Speech and Language

Adeline McClatchie, LCST and MaryKay Therres, MS, author

Alexander Graham Bell Association for the Deaf
3417 Volta Place NW
Washington, DC 20007

202-337-5220
Fax: 202-337-8314
TTY: 202-337-5221
info@agbell.org
www.agbell.org

AuSpLan is a communication therapy manual for children using choclear implants or hearing aids. It addresses auditory, speech/articulation, and language skills of children between the ages of 18 months and 5 years.

212 pages Softcover

3324 Alandra's Lilacs

Tressa Bowers, author

Gallaudet University Press
800 Florida Avenue NE
Washington, DC 20002

202-651-5488
Fax: 202-651-5489
gupress@gallaudet.edu
www.gupress.gallaudet.edu

When, in 1968, 19-year-old Tressa Bowers took her baby daughter to an expert on deaf children, he pronounced that Alandra was 'stone deaf,' she most likely would never be able to talk, and she probably would not get much of an education because of her communication limitations. Tressa refused to accept this stark assessment of Alandra's prospects. Instead, she began the arduous process of starting her daughter's education.

158 pages Softcover
ISBN: 1-563680-82-3

3325 All of Us Together

Jeri Banks, author

Gallaudet University Press
800 Florida Avenue NE
Washington, DC 20002
202-651-5488
Fax: 202-651-5489
gupress@gallaudet.edu
www.gupress.gallaudet.edu

John H. Kinzie Elementary School, in Chicago, for decades was the pride of its neighborhood until changing demographics, racial conflict, and desegregation mandates threatened its existance. Then, its new principal, James Burke, welcomed 15 classes of deaf and hard of hearing children. This is the story of the Kinzie School from 1982, when hearing and nonhearing populations were kept in separate parts of the school, to the present in which all students intermingle freely and achieve together.

212 pages Hardcover
ISBN: 1-563680-28-9

3326 Alone in the Mainstream: A Deaf Women Remembers Public School

Gina A Oliva, author

Gallaudet University Press
800 Florida Avenue NE
Washington, DC 20002
202-651-5488
Fax: 202-651-5489
gupress@gallaudet.edu
www.gupress.gallaudet.edu

When Gina Oliva first went to school in 1955, she didn't know that she was 'different.' If the kindergarten teacher played a tune on the piano to signal the next exercise, Olivia didn't react because she couldn't hear the music. So began her journey as a 'solitary,' her term for being the only deaf child in the entire school. Gina felt alone because she couldn't communicate easily with her classmates, but also because none of them had a hearing loss like hers.

224 pages Softcover
ISBN: 1-563683-00-8

3327 Alphabet of Animal Signs

HEAR-MORE
42 Executive Boulevard
Farmingdale, NY 11735
800-881-4327
Fax: 631-752-0689
TTY: 800-281-3555
www.hearmore.com

This book includes animal illustrations and associated signs for each letter of the alphabet.

3328 American Deaf Culture: An Anthology

Sign Media
4020 Blackburn Lane
Burtonsville, MD 20866
301-421-0268
800-475-4756
Fax: 301-421-0270
TDD: 301-421-4460
signmedia@aol.com
www.signmedia.com

Features deaf and hearing authors offering their experience and perspectives on cultural values, ASL, social interaction in the deaf community, education, folklore and more.

202 pages Paperback
ISBN: 0-932130-09-7

Barbara Olmert, Director Marketing

3329 American Sign Language Dictionary Third Edition

Martin L A Stemberg, author

TJ Publishers
P.O Box 702701
Dallas, TX 75370
972-416-0800
800-999-1168
Fax: 972-416-0944
TTY: 972-416-0933
customerservice@tjpublishers.com
www.tjpublishers.com

Completely updated and revised, this easy to use abridged version of the American Sign Language: A Comprehensive Dictionary has more than 500 new signs and 1500 new illustrations. It contains more than 5000 of the most widely used words, phrases, and idioms, accompanied by 8000 easy-to-follow illustrations of the hand, arm and facial movements that express each one.

772 pages Softcover
ISBN: 0-062736-34-5

3330 American Sign Language: A Student Text; Units 10-18

Sign Media
4020 Blackburn Lane
Burtonsville, MD 20866
800-475-4756
Fax: 301-421-0270
www.signmedia.com

These texts were designed to help students acquire conversational abilities in American Sign Language. Each unit targets a specific grammatical feature of ASL and presents a dialogue focusing on that grammatical feature. Dialogues are presented three times - the first is a shot of both conversational participants, the second and third presentations each focus on one of the participants. Following the dialogues are anecdotes, stories and poems.

ISBN: 0-930323-87-4

3331 American Sign Language: A Student Text; Units 1-9

Sign Media
4020 Blackburn Lane
Burtonsville, MD 20866
800-475-4756
Fax: 301-421-0270
www.signmedia.com

These texts were designed to help students acquire conversational abilities in American Sign Language. Each unit targets a specific grammatical feature of ASL and presents a dialogue focusing on that grammatical feature. Dialogues are presented three times - the first is a shot of both conversational participants, the second and third presentations each focus on one of the participants. Following the dialogues are anecdotes, stories and poems.

ISBN: 0-930323-86-6

3332 American Sign Language: A Student Text; Units 19-27

Sign Media
4020 Blackburn Lane
Burtonsville, MD 20866
800-475-4756
Fax: 301-421-0270
www.signmedia.com

These texts were designed to help students acquire conversational abilities in American Sign Language. Each unit targets a specific grammatical feature of ASL and presents a dialogue focusing on that grammatical feature. Dialogues are presented three times - the first is a shot of both conversational participants, the second and third presentations each focus on one of the participants. Following the dialogues are anecdotes, stories and poems.

ISBN: 0-930323-88-2

3333 Animal Signs: A First Book of Sign Language

Debbie Slier, author

Gallaudet University Press
800 Florida Avenue NE
Washington, DC 20002
202-651-5488
Fax: 202-651-5489
gupress@gallaudet.edu
www.gupress.gallaudet.edu

Charming, full-color photographs of basic animals plus illustrations of their corresponding signs offer children ages 1 to 4 a fun way to learn their first signs and vocabulary words.

Hearing Impairment/Deafness / Book Publishers

16 pages Board Book
ISBN: 1-563680-49-1

3334 Approaching Equality
TJ Publishers
P.O Box 702701
Dallas, TX 75370

972-416-0800
800-999-1168
Fax: 972-416-0944
TTY: 972-416-0933
customerservice@tjpublishers.com
www.tjpublsihers.com

Public education laws guarantee special education programs for all Deaf children, but many find the special education system confusing, or are unsure of their rights under the current law. Those with an interest in education, advocacy and the Deaf community will find this review of dramatic developments in the education of Deaf children, youth and adults most informative. Written by the former chair of the Commission on the Education of the Deaf.

1991 112 pages Softcover
ISBN: 0-932666-39-6

Frank Bowe, Author

3335 Auditory-Verbal Therapy and Practice
Alexander Graham Bell Association for the Deaf
3417 Volta Place NW
Washington, DC 20007

202-337-5220
800-432-7543
Fax: 202-337-8314
TTY: 202-337-5221
info@agbell.org
www.agbell.org

A comprehensive book introducing auditory-verbal therapy and its impact on children with hearing impairments and their families.

Warren Estabrooks MEd, Editor

3336 Baby Sign Language Basics
Monta Z Briant, author

Harris Communications
15155 Technology Drive
Eden Prairie, MN 55344

952-906-1180
800-825-6758
Fax: 952-906-1099
TTY: 800-825-9187
info@harriscomm.com
www.harriscomm.com

This is the perfect book for new parents - now, they can understand what their baby is trying to tell them. This books makes learning fun and easy, and it is small enough to take anywhere. It includes 60 baby-friendly American Sign Language signs like bird, happy, baby, and mommy, just to name a few. There are also baby-specific signing techniques, black and white photographs, songs and games.

329 pages Softcover

3337 Baby's First Signs
Kim Voltry and Curt Waller, author

Gallaudet University Press
800 Florida Avenue NE
Washington, DC 20002

202-651-5488
Fax: 202-651-5489
gupress@gallaudet.edu
www.gupress.gallaudet.edu

A durable board book, lavishly colored in bright reds, blues, greens, and yellows sure to please your child's eye. Each page features an illustration of a toddler signing a word as well as demonstrating what the sign is about. For example, on the baby page, a toddler makes the sign for baby by mimicking the cradling of a child in his arms while also smiling at his baby sister sitting beside him. The illustrations include both a diagram box that depicts how to berform the sign and English word.

16 pages Board Book
ISBN: 1-563681-14-5

3338 Be Careful
HEAR-MORE
42 Executive Boulevard
Farmingdale, NY 11735

800-881-4327
Fax: 631-752-0689
TTY: 800-281-3555
www.hearmore.com

A What-Will-Happen-Next Book of Safety, a book of cautions. It shows the child, in an amusing and dramatic manner, just what can happen to a careless or thoughtless child. Read the story aloud and sign to the child while looking at the pictures together. Let the child see your lips when you read and sign.

3339 Be Happy Not Sad
Modern Signs Press
PO Box 1181
Los Alamitos, CA 90720

562-596-8548
800-572-7332
Fax: 562-795-6614
TTY: 562-493-4168
www.modernsignspress.com

These books help children understand hard to explain emotions through signing. Includes Be Happy Not Sad coloring workbook.

1988 2 Book Set
ISBN: 0-916708-19-5

3340 Belonging
Virginia M Scott, author

Gallaudet University Press
800 Florida Avenue NE
Washington, DC 20002

202-651-5488
Fax: 202-651-5489
gupress@gallaudet.edu
www.gupress.gallaudet.edu

Gustie is 15 when she contracts meningitis during which she loses the small amount of residual hearing she had seemed to retain, Gustie tires to pick up the pieces of her life. Her parents are unrealistic and over protective; her best friend rejects her; her teachers run the gamut from being convinced Gustie cannot function in the mainstream to being supportive...through a new boyfriend who has a deaf brother and sister-in-law, and through visits with an understanding special education teacher

176 pages Softcover
ISBN: 0-903233-35-5

3341 Children with Hearing Difficulties
Scholars International Corporation
2630 W Barry Avenue
Chicago, IL 60618

410-337-3775
800-638-3775
Fax: 410-337-8539
scholars@ameritech.net

Based on ten years of research into hearing and hearing-impaired children, this book looks at the impact of deafness on all aspects of the development and education of young children.

192 pages Softcover
ISBN: 0-304317-24-1

David Wood, Co-Author
Alec Webster, Co-Author

3342 Chris Gets Ear Tubes
Gallaudet University Press
800 Florida Avenue NE
Washington, DC 20002

202-651-5488
800-621-2736
Fax: 202-651-5489
TTY: 202-651-5488
gupress@gallaudet.edu
www.gupress.gallaudet.edu

A helpful book for parents and children to share concerning ear tubes and hospitals.

48 pages paperback
ISBN: 0-930323-36-x

3343 Chris Gets Ear Tubes: Spanish Edition

Betty Pace, author

Gallaudet University Press
800 Florida Avenue NE
Washington, DC 20002
202-651-5488
Fax: 202-651-5489
gupress@gallaudet.edu
www.gupress.gallaudet.edu

Chris Get Ear Tubes describes what happens, before, during, and after the surgery in a language a child understands. It takes away the child's natural fear of the unknown. Also available in English

48 pages Softcover
ISBN: 1-563680-93-9

3344 Classroom GOALS

Jill B Firszt, MA and Ruth M Reeder, MA, author

Alexander Graham Bell Association for the Deaf
3417 Volta Place NW
Washington, DC 20007
202-337-5220
Fax: 202-337-8314
TTY: 202-337-5221
info@agbell.org
www.agbell.org

Classroom GOALS was designed to help teachers incorporate auditory goals into academic lessons after those specific goals have been identified. Objectives accommodate students with hearing loss regardless of the degree of loss, sensory devise, grade level, mode of communication or school placement.

199 pages Softcover

3345 Classroom Notetaker

Jimmie Joan Wilson, author

Alexander Graham Bell Association for the Deaf
3417 Volta Place NW
Washington, DC 20007
202-337-5220
Fax: 202-337-8314
TTY: 202-337-5221
info@agbell.org
www.agbell.org

How to organize a program serving students with hearing impairments. Designed to help teachers incorporate auditory goals into academic lessons, after those specific goals have been identified. Objectives accommodate students with hearing loss regardless of the degree of loss, sensory device, grade level, mode of communication or school placement. This guide describes practical ways for teachers to create situations during academic instruction that encourage the use of residual hearing.

127 pages Softcover

3346 Cochlear Implant Auditory Training Guidebook

Alexander Graham Bell Association for the Deaf
3417 Volta Place NW
Washington, DC 20007
202-337-5220
800-432-7543
Fax: 202-337-8314
TTY: 202-337-5221
publications@agbell.org
www.agbell.org

Designed for parents and professionals working with children ages four and up who have cochlear implants. It includes an easy to follow hierarchy for listening goals and a quick placement test to help you find where to start. Comes with CD

236 pages
David Sindrey

3347 Cochlear Implants for Kids

Warren Estabrooks, MEd, author

Alexander Graham Bell Association for the Deaf
3417 Volta Place NW
Washington, DC 20007
202-337-5220
Fax: 202-337-8314
TTY: 202-337-5221
info@agbell.org
www.agbell.org

Written to educate parents and the professional community about cochlear implants for the pediatric population. Sections include: History and ethical issues, Surgery and programming, Habilitation, Family stories from around the world. Its accessible language and photography make this text a perfect resource for anyone interested in therapy for pre and post cochlear implantation and in the entire family experience.

404 pages Softcover

3348 Cochlear Implants in Children

John B Christiansen and Irene W Leigh, author

Alexander Graham Bell Association for the Deaf
3417 Volta Place NW
Washington, DC 20007
202-337-5220
Fax: 202-337-8314
TTY: 202-337-5221
info@agbell.org
www.agbell.org

Based on a survey of 439 parents of children who have cochlear implants, this book addresses every facet of the controversy over early implantation.

360 pages Hardcover

3349 Cochlear Implants in Children: Ethics and Choices

John B Christiansen and Irene W Leigh, author

Gallaudet University Press
800 Florida Avenue NE
Washington, DC 20002
202-651-5488
Fax: 202-651-5489
gupress@gallaudet.edu
www.gupress.gallaudet.edu

Addresses every facet of the ongoing controversy about implanting cochlear hearing devices in children as young as 12 months old and in some cases, younger. The authors analyzed the sensitive issues connected witht he procedure by reviewing 439 responses to a survey of parents with children who have cochlear implants. They followed up with interviews of the parents of children who have had a year's experience using the implants, and also the children themselves.

340 pages Hardcover
ISBN: 1-563681-16-1

3350 Cognition, Eduction, and Deafness: Directi ons for Research and Instruction

David S Martin, Editor, author

Gallaudet University Press
800 Florida Avenue NE
Washington, DC 20002
202-651-5488
Fax: 202-651-5489
gupress@gallaudet.edu
www.gupress.gallaudet.edu

This book integrates the work of 54 contributors to the 1984 symposium on cognition, education and deafness. It focuses on cognition and deaf students' growth and development, problem-solving strategies, thinking processes, language development, reading methodology, measurement of potential, and intervention programs. A synthesis of these discoveries establishes directions for new research and outlines implications for all professionals working with hearing-impaired learners.

Hearing Impairment/Deafness / Book Publishers

248 pages Softcover
ISBN: 1-563681-49-8

3351 Colors

HEAR-MORE
42 Executive Boulevard
Farmingdale, NY 11735

800-881-4327
Fax: 631-752-0689
TTY: 800-281-3555
www.hearmore.com

The Early Sign Language Series: A fascinating and enjoyable way for children and adults to learn sign language. Colors presents the early concepts of color recognition. It fosters both receptive and expressive language through signs and pictures, and it is perfect for young children whether hearing impaired, hearing, pre-verbal or verbal. Reviews ten colors in bright cheery illustrations.

3352 Come Sign With Us: Sign Language Activities for Children

David S Martin, Editor, author

Gallaudet University Press
800 Florida Avenue NE
Washington, DC 20002

202-651-5488
Fax: 202-651-5489
gupress@gallaudet.edu
www.gupress.gallaudet.edu

Completely revised, this book now offers more follow-up activities, including many in context, to teach children sign language. The second edition of this fun, fully illustrated activities manual features more than 300 line drawings of both adults and children signing familiar words, phrases, and sentences using American Sign Language signs in English word order. Twenty lively lessons each introduce ten selected target vocabulary words in a format familiar and exciting to children.

160 pages Softcover
ISBN: 1-563680-51-3

3353 Come Sign with Us Sign Language Activities for Children

Gallaudet University Press
800 Florida Avenue NE
Washington, DC 20002

202-651-5488
800-621-2736
Fax: 202-651-5489
TTY: 202-651-5488
gupress@gallaudet.edu
www.gupress.gallaudet.edu

Revised version, offering more follow-up activities, including many in context, to teach children sign language. Features more than 300 line drawings of both adults and children signing familiar words, phrases, and sentences using ASL. Shows how to form each sign exactly and also presents the origins of ASL, facts about deafness, and the deaf community.

2002 160 pages Softcover
ISBN: 1-563680-51-3

3354 Cosmo Gets An Ear

Gary Clementine, author

Modern Signs Press
PO Box 1181
Los Alamitos, CA 90720

562-596-8548
800-572-7332
Fax: 562-795-6614
TTY: 562-493-4168
modsigns@modernsignspress.com
www.modernsignspress.com

Welcome to the world of 'Cosmo'. Once you get past the normal turmoil of his impossible room, you find a boy who needs to have the TV loud and his mother shouting at him to respond. Cosmo has a hearing problem. This story was written by a man who is hearing impaired and regretfully did not use an aid until much later in life. It is colorfully and humorously illustrated by an artist who captures the exuberance and fears of the youngster. An excellent way to help others understand what it is like.

48 pages

3355 Cued Speech Resource Book

Orin Cornett and Mary Elsie Daisey, author

Alexander Graham Bell Association for the Deaf
3417 Volta Place NW
Washington, DC 20007

202-337-5220
Fax: 202-337-8314
TTY: 202-337-5221
info@agbell.org
www.agbell.org

A fact book for parents and professionals who want to use this system of hand cues with speech to help children affected by hearing loss or auditory neuropathy learn spoken languages. Explains Cued Speech and how to use it and includes personal accounts, practice materials, and guidance. Second edition revisions describe legal rights and the mechanics of cueing. This classic text explains: Initiating communication, Language development, Reading, Speech Production, Multiple Disabilities and more.

832 pages Hardcover

3356 Dad and Me in the Morning

Patricia Lakin and Robert G steele, author

Harris Communications
15155 Technology Drive
Eden Prairie, MN 55344

952-906-1180
800-825-6758
Fax: 952-906-1099
TTY: 800-825-9187
info@harriscomm.com
www.harriscomm.com

Warm and fuzzy and beautifully illustrated! This delightful book will provide enjoyable reading and superb pictures for a cozy, shared reading adventure for parent and a hard of hearing child.

3357 Deaf Children in China

Alison Callaway, author

Gallaudet University Press
800 Florida Avenue NE
Washington, DC 20002

202-651-5488
Fax: 202-651-5489
gupress@gallaudet.edu
www.gupress.gallaudet.edu

Provides a striking profile of the views and attitudes of well-educated Chinese parents with preschool-age deaf children. The author's inclusion of a survey of 122 English mothers of deaf children reveals the differences between Western and Chinese parents, who rely upon grandparents to help them and who frequently search for medical cures. She also discovered that many issues cross cultures and contexts, especially the problems of achieving early diagnosis and intervention for all deaf children

256 pages Hardcover
ISBN: 1-563680-85-8

3358 Deaf Children in Public Schools: Placement, Context, and Consequences

Claire L Ramsey, author

Gallaudet University Press
800 Florida Avenue NE
Washington, DC 20002

202-651-5488
Fax: 202-651-5489
gupress@gallaudet.edu
www.gupress.gallaudet.edu

Assesses the progress of three second-grade deaf students to demonstrate the importance of placement, context, and language in their development. The autor points out that these deaf children were placed in two different environments, with the general population of hearing students, and separately with other deaf and hard of hearing children. The answers found in this cohesive book offer educators and parents a remarkable stage for assessing and enhancing the education context for deaf children.

142 pages Hardcover
ISBN: 1-563680-62-9

3359 Deaf Daughter, Hearing Fahter
Richard Medugno, author
Gallaudet University Press
800 Florida Avenue NE
Washington, DC 20002
202-651-5488
Fax: 202-651-5489
gupress@gallaudet.edu
www.gupress.gallaudet.edu

A father shares practical information on many of the common challenges faced by hearing parents. e provides a list of games that hearing and deaf children can play together, a consideration for many families. His enthusiasm for all possibilities, from exploring the potential of video phones to helping stage CSD musicals, reveals his abiding devotion to Miranda. This has enabled her to feel proud, confident and happy in her pursuits. Medugno realizes that the rewards of having a deaf daughter

184 pages Softcover
ISBN: 1-563681-77-X

3360 Deaf Side Story: Deaf Sharks, Hearing Jets, and a Classic American Musical
Mark Rigney, author
Gallaudet University Press
800 Florida Avenue NE
Washington, DC 20002
202-651-5488
Fax: 202-651-5489
gupress@gallaudet.edu
www.gupress.gallaudet.edu

The 1957 classic American Musical West Side Story has been staged by many community and school theater groups. At a small school in Jacksonville, IL, the new drama head, determined to add an extra element to the usual demands of putting on a show by having deaf students perform half of the parts. The author portrays the progress of the production, including the frustrations and triumphs of the leads, the campus and community politics, and the clashes between the deaf cast members and hearing.

232 pages Softcover
ISBN: 1-563681-45-5

3361 Deaf Students Can Be Great Readers
Modern Signs Press
PO Box 1181
Los Alamitos, CA 90720
562-596-8548
800-572-7332
Fax: 562-795-6614
TTY: 562-493-4168
modsigns@modernsignspress.com
www.modernsignspress.com

Detailed analytical review of a case study of one deaf child. Also, information about the place on phonological awareness in developing reading capability. Includes a comprehensive annotated bibliography related to education of deaf and hard of hearing children.

3362 Educating Deaf Students: Global Perspectives
Des Power and Greg Leigh, Editors, author
Gallaudet University Press
800 Florida Avenue NE
Washington, DC 20002
202-651-5488
Fax: 202-651-5489
gupress@gallaudet.edu
www.gupress.gallaudet.edu

The 19 chapters of this book present a select cross-section of the issues addressed at the 19th International Congress of Education of the Deaf. Divided into four distinct parts - Contemporary Issus for all Learners, The Eary Years, The School Years, and Contemporary Issues in Postsecondary Education - the themes considered here span the entire student age range. Authored by 27 different researchers and practitioners from six different countries.

248 pages Hardcover
ISBN: 1-563683-08-3

3363 Educational Audiology for the Limited-Hear ing Infant and Preschooler
Charles C Thomas Publishers
2600 South First Street
Springfield, IL 62704
217-789-8980
800-258-8980
books@ccthomas.com
www.ccthomas.com

The third edition of this book brings up to date the material that so many readers found helpful in the previous editions. The entire text has been rewritten and reorganized with revised chapters focusing on current concepts and practices in audiologic screening and evaluation, development of language, the role of parents, parent education, mainstreaming of the limited-hearing child, and program modifications for the severely learning disabled child. Includes 18 tables.

430 pages Softcover

3364 Educational Interpreting: How It Can Succe ed
Elizabeth A Winston, Editor, author
Gallaudet University Press
800 Florida Avenue NE
Washington, DC 20002
202-651-5488
Fax: 202-651-5489
gupress@gallaudet.edu
www.gupress.gallaudet.edu

This book explores the current state of educational interpreting and how it is failing deaf students. The contributors, all experts in their field, include former educational interpreters, teachers of deaf students, interpreter trainers, and deaf recipients of interpreted educations. It presents the salient issues in three distinct sections. Part 1 focuses on deaf students. Part 2 raises the questions about the support and training intrepreters receive. Part 3 presents possible suggestions.

224 pages Hardcover
ISBN: 1-563683-09-1

3365 Educational and Development Aspects of Deafness
Gallaudet University Press
800 Florida Avenue NE
Washington, DC 20002
202-651-5488
Fax: 202-651-5489
TTY: 202-651-5488
gupress@gallaudet.edu
www.gupress.gallaudet.edu

Book detailing the ongoing revolution in the education of deaf children.

415 pages
Donald F Moores, Editor
Kathryn P Meadow-Orlans, Editor

3366 Educational and Developmental Aspects of D eafness
Donald Moores and Kathryn Meadow-Orlans, Editors, author
Gallaudet University Press
800 Florida Avenue NE
Washington, DC 20002
202-651-5488
Fax: 202-651-5489
gupress@gallaudet.edu
www.gupress.gallaudet.edu

Details the ongoing revolution in the eduction of deaf children. More than 20 researchers contributed their discoveries in anthropology, education, linguistics, psychology, sociology, and other major disciplines, with special concentration upon the education of deaf children. Divided into two parts on education at home and in school, this book documents breakthroughs such as the public's interest in sign language, the increasing availability of interpreters, and other positive trends.

451 pages Hardcover
ISBN: 0-930323-52-1

3367 Fire Fighter Brown
HEAR-MORE
42 Executive Boulevard
Farmingdale, NY 11735
800-881-4327
Fax: 631-752-0689
TTY: 800-281-3555
www.hearmore.com

The Fire Fighter Brown book tells about the Fire Fighter Brown's work, the clothes he wears, and the equipment he uses in rescuing a little boy from a burning building. Use the signs when reading the book to your child, and let the child see your lips as you read and sign. This will help your child learn to associate the signs with sounds and lip shapes.

3368 First Signs at Home
HEAR-MORE
42 Executive Boulevard
Farmingdale, NY 11735
800-881-4327
Fax: 631-752-0689
TTY: 800-281-3555
www.hearmore.com

The Early Sign Language Series: A fascinating and enjoyable way for children and adults to learn sign language. First Signs present some of the very first words for parents and children.

3369 First Signs at Play
HEAR-MORE
42 Executive Boulevard
Farmingdale, NY 11735
800-881-4327
Fax: 631-752-0689
TTY: 800-281-3555
www.hearmore.com

The Early Sign Language Series: A fascinating and enjoyable way for children and adults to learn sign language. First Signs present some of the very first words for parents and children.

3370 Foundations of Spoken Language for Hearing -Impaired Children
Daniel Ling, PhD, author

Alexander Graham Bell Association for the Deaf
3417 Volta Place NW
Washington, DC 20007
202-337-5220
Fax: 202-337-8314
TTY: 202-337-5221
info@agbell.org
www.agbell.org

Emphasizes the perception of speech through residual hearing, either through the use of modern hearing aids or cochlear implants. A feature of the book is the presentation of the aspects of speech that appear in the octave bands centered on frequencies depicted in audiograms. This knowledge, in conjunction with the Six-Sound Test, allows teachers and clinicians to determine whether the frequency response characteristics of hearing aids are adjusted to provide optimal levels of hearing.

447 pages Softcover

3371 Free Hand: Enfranchising the Education of Deaf Children
TJ Publishers
P.O Box 702701
Dallas, TX 75370
972-416-0800
800-999-1186
Fax: 972-416-0944
TTY: 972-416-0933
customerservice@tjpublishers.com
www.tjpublishers.com

Based on the proceedings of a 1990 symposium on the educational uses of ASL, A Free Hand presents papers by prominent educators, researchers and linguists in the changing role of American Sign Language in the classroom.

1992 204 pages Softcover
ISBN: 0-932666-40-X

Angela K Thames, President
Jerald Murphy, Vice President

3372 From Gesture to Language in Hearing and De af Children
Virginia Volterra and Carol J Ertling, Editors, author

Gallaudet University Press
800 Florida Avenue NE
Washington, DC 20002
202-651-5488
Fax: 202-651-5489
gupress@gallaudet.edu
www.gupress.gallaudet.edu

In 21 essays on communicative gesturing in the first two years of life, this collection demonstrates the importance of gesture in a child's transition to a linguistic system. Introductions preceding each section emphasize the parallels between the findings in these studies and the general body of scholarship devoted to the process of spoken language acquisition. Scholars contributing to this volume include Ursula Bellugi, Judy Snitzer Reilly, Susan Goldwin-Meadow, Andrew Lock, and many others.

358 pages Softcover
ISBN: 1-563680-78-5

3373 Genetics, Disability and Deafness
John Vickrey Van Cleve, Editory, author

Gallaudet University Press
800 Florida Avenue NE
Washington, DC 20002
202-651-5488
Fax: 202-651-5489
gupress@gallaudet.edu
www.gupress.gallaudet.edu

This volume brings together 13 essays from science, history, and the humanities, history and the present, to show the many ways that disability, deafness and the new genetics interact and what that interaction means for society. Prize-winning author Louis Menand begins this volume by expressing the position shared by most authors in this wide-ranging forum—the belief in the value of human diversity and skepticism of actions that could eliminate it through modification of the human genome.

240 pages Hardcover
ISBN: 1-563683-07-5

3374 Go Togethers
HEAR-MORE
42 Executive Boulevard
Farmingdale, NY 11735
800-881-4327
Fax: 631-752-0689
TTY: 800-281-3555
www.hearmore.com

The Early Sign Language Series: A fascinating and enjoyable way for children and adults to learn sign language. Go-Togethers presents early objects and concepts that are complimentary. It fosters both receptive and expressive language through signs and pictures, and it is perfect for young children whether hearing impaired, hearing, pre-verbal or verbal. Learn 10 go-together items (20 in total).

3375 Goldilocks and the Three Bears Told in Sig ned English
Harry Bornstein and Karen L Saulnier, author

Gallaudet University Press
800 Florida Avenue NE
Washington, DC 20002
202-651-5488
Fax: 202-651-5489
gupress@gallaudet.edu
www.gupress.gallaudet.edu

Offers children ages 3-8 all of the fun their parents had when they first read about the little girl with the golden curls who turned the Bears' house upside down. In this exciting new edition, children can learn new words and the matching signs, which will help them to remember both.

48 pages
ISBN: 1-563680-57-2

3376 Good Morning Me! Hand and Voices
PO Box 3093
Boulder, CO 80307
303-492-6283
866-422-0422
parentadvocate@handsandvoices.org
www.handsandvoices.org

This book teaches your child to initial vowel/consonant combinations through fun repetition.

3377 Grandfather Moose!

Harley Hamilton, author

Modern Signs Press
PO Box 1181
Los Alamitos, CA 90720
562-596-8548
800-572-7332
Fax: 562-795-6614
TTY: 562-493-4168
modsigns@modernsignspress.com
www.modernsignspress.com

Move over 'Mother Goose'...here comes 'Grandfather Moose'! Exciting and beautifully illustrated book of rhythms, games, and chants in sign language. Hearing children enjoy the sound of rhyming words. Deaf and hard of hearing children will delight in the rythmic quality of these signing tales. Rhymes are made up of words whose signs have similar hand shapes. Games and chants provide group sign language activities for home and school.

32 pages

3378 How Children Learn Language

James McLean, PhD And Lee Snyder-McLean, PhD, author

Alexander Graham Bell Association for the Deaf
3417 Volta Place NW
Washington, DC 20007
202-337-5220
Fax: 202-337-8314
TTY: 202-337-5221
info@agbell.org
www.agbell.org

This introductory text guides professionals in nonlanguage fields and students in education/special education courses through the miracle of typical child's language development.

227 pages Softcover

3379 I Can Sign my ABCs

Susan Gibbons Chaplin, author

Harris Communications
15155 Technology Drive
Eden Prairie, MN 55344
952-906-1180
800-825-6758
Fax: 952-906-1099
TTY: 800-825-9187
info@harriscomm.com
www.harriscomm.com

In this full-color picture book, each letter's manual alphabet handshape is followed by the picture, name, and sign of an object beginning with that letter. Ideal for teaching children the English and the American Manual alphabets.

52 pages Hardcover

3380 I Can't Hear You in the Dark: How to Learn and Teach Lipreading

Betty Woerner Carter, author

Charles C Thomas Publishers
2600 South First Street
Springfield, IL 62704
217-789-8980
800-258-8980
books@ccthomas.com
www.ccthomas.com

I can't hear you in the dark, but I can lipread you in the light.' Lipreading is one of the ways that hearing-impaired people can communicate and strengthen relationships with others. Written for the beginning lipreader and the experienced, this book shows how lipreading can be taught by supplying ready-to-use lessons.

226 pages Softcover
ISBN: 0-393067-89-9

3381 I Love You Story

Walter Paul Kelly, author

Harris Communications
15155 Technology Drive
Eden Prairie, MN 55344
952-906-1180
800-825-6758
Fax: 952-906-1099
TTY: 800-825-9187
info@harriscomm.com
www.harriscomm.com

A black and white illustrated story on how love and eventually the ILY handsign in American Sign Language got started.
Hardcover

3382 I'M Deaf and It's Okay

Lorraine Aseltine, Evelyn Mueller, Nancy Tate, author

Harris Communications
15155 Technology Drive
Eden Prairie, MN 55344
952-906-1180
800-825-6758
Fax: 952-906-1099
TTY: 800-825-9187
info@harriscomm.com
www.harriscomm.com

A young boy explains how lonely and frustrated he feels because he can't hear. He dislikes the hearing aids he wears and is angered because he will never be rid of them. His feelings begin to change when he is befriended by a teenage boy who also wears hearing aids. This book is well-illustrated with sensitive line drawings done by Helen Cogancherry.

36 pages Hardcover

3383 In Our House

Carolyn Norris, author

Modern Signs Press
PO Box 1181
Los Alamitos, CA 90720
562-596-8548
800-572-7332
Fax: 562-795-6614
TTY: 562-493-4168
modsigns@modernsignspress.com
www.modernsignspress.com

This colorful picture book tells the story of Joy and Jason helping Mom and Dad around the house. Demonstrates cooking, cleaning, gardening, etc. Has a 140 word vocabulary listed in an alphabetical glossary and the manual alphabet.

3384 In Silence: Growing Up Hearing in a Deaf World

Ruth Sidransky, author

Gallaudet University Press
800 Florida Avenue NE
Washington, DC 20002
202-651-5488
Fax: 202-651-5489
gupress@gallaudet.edu
www.gupress.gallaudet.edu

This is an account of growing up as the hearing daughter of deaf Jewish parents in the Bronx and Brooklyn during the 1930s and 1940s. It reveals the challenges deaf people faced during the Depression and afterward. The author portrays her family with deep affection and honesty, and her frank account provides a living narrative of the Deaf experience in pre- and post-World War II America.

Hearing Impairment/Deafness / Book Publishers

352 pages Softcover
ISBN: 1-563682-87-7

3385 Inner Lives of Deaf Children: Interviews and Analysis

Martha Sheridan, author

Gallaudet University Press
800 Florida Avenue NE
Washington, DC 20002
202-651-5488
Fax: 202-651-5489
gupress@gallaudet.edu
www.gupress.gallaudet.edu

Conducting interviews with seven deaf children between the ages of 7 and 10, the author offers a fresh look at the private thoughts and feels of deaf children. 'What does it mean to be a child who is deaf or hard of hearing?' Sheridan asks in the beginning of her study. She turns to Danny, Angie, Joe, Alex, Lisa, Mary and Pat for the answer. Footnotes, bibliography, index.

256 pages Softcover
ISBN: 1-563682-89-3

3386 Kid-Friendly Parenting with Deaf and Hard of Hearing Children

Gallaudet University Press
800 Florida Avenue NE
Washington, DC 20002
202-651-5488
Fax: 202-651-5489
TTY: 202-651-5488
gupress@gallaudet.edu
www.gupress.gallaudet.edu

A step-by-step guide offering parents hundreds of ideas and play activities for children ages three to 12.

320 pages

3387 King Midas

Robert Newby, author

Gallaudet University Press
800 Florida Avenue NE
Washington, DC 20002
202-651-5488
Fax: 202-651-5489
gupress@gallaudet.edu
www.gupress.gallaudet.edu

Now the tale of King Midas and his golden touch is retold with full-color illustrations, and key sentences shown in American Sign Language. The line drawings of the story teller (who appears in both the book and videotape) recreate 44 sentences, making this ideal for helping both hearing and deaf children to learn reading skills. The videotape shows the entire classic story performed in ASL by the storyteller accompanied by a voiceover. A perfect complement to the book. VHS, color, 30 minutes.

VHS-$39.95 72 pages Hardcover book
ISBN: 0-930323-75-0

3388 Learning Ladder: Assessing and Teaching Text Comprehension

Elisabeth H Wiig, PhD and Carolyn C Wilson, MS, author

Alexander Graham Bell Association for the Deaf
3417 Volta Place NW
Washington, DC 20007
202-337-5220
Fax: 202-337-8314
TTY: 202-337-5221
info@agbell.org
www.agbell.org

A general education program developed for students, aged 7 to 12 years, with reading comprehension difficulties. Major sections of the text include two components: assessment and interventions. The assessment component describes typical home and school social interactions. The intervention component introduces intervention options including grade-level activities, resources, and graphic organizers. The intervention component also responds to the Least Restrictive Environment provision of IDEA.

269 pages Softcover/CD

3389 Learning to See: American Sign Language as a Second Language

Gallaudet University Press
800 Florida Avenue NE
Washington, DC 20002
202-651-5488
Fax: 202-651-5489
TTY: 202-561-5488
gupress@gallaudet.edu
www.gupress.gallaudet.edu

Provides a comprehensive introduction to the history and structure of ASL to the deaf community.

160 pages
ISBN: 1-563680-59-9

3390 Legal Rights: The Guide for Deaf and Hard of Hearing People - Fifth Edition

Gallaudet University Press
800 Florida Avenue NE
Washington, DC 20002
202-651-5488
Fax: 202-651-5489
TTY: 202-651-5488
gupress@gallaudet.edu
www.gupress.gallaudet.edu

Includes updated interpretations of legislation affecting hearing-impaired people, including chapters dealing with the ADA.

3391 Listen Little Star

Dimity Dornan, BA, author

Alexander Graham Bell Association for the Deaf
3417 Volta Place NW
Washington, DC 20007
202-337-5220
Fax: 202-337-8314
TTY: 202-337-5221
info@agbell.org
www.agbell.org

Maximize your child's auditory potential with this series of parent-child activities designed to help your baby develop listening and speaking skills using techniques based on the Auditory-Verbal approach. Designed to take approximately four-to-six months to complete. Includes: 12 parent-child activities that build auditory skills, a caregiver workbook to guide you through each exercise, a note-taking section to document your child's progress, a reminder checklist, and a plush toy star.

3392 Literacy and Your Deaf Child: What Every Parent Should Know

David A Steward and Bryan R Clarke, author

Gallaudet University Press
800 Florida Avenue NE
Washington, DC 20002
202-651-5488
Fax: 202-651-5489
gupress@gallaudet.edu
www.gupress.gallaudet.edu

This book begins by introducing some common concepts, among them the importance of parental involvement in a deaf child's education. It outlines how children acquire language and describes the auditory and visual links to literacy. With this information, parents can make informed decisions regarding hearing aids, cochlear implants, speechreading, and sign communication all of which can have a marked influence on their child's language development.

240 pages Softcover
ISBN: 1-563681-36-6

3393 Little Read Riding Hood: Told in Signed Enlish

Harry Bornstein and Karen Luczak Saulnier, author

Gallaudet University Press
800 Florida Avenue NE
Washington, DC 20002
202-651-5488
Fax: 202-651-5489
gupress@gallaudet.edu
www.gupress.gallaudet.edu

Now one of the most beloved of all folktales, Little Red Riding Hood in a new Signed Enlish edition illustrated in full color. It presents a vivacious version of this favorite story that will intrigue and delight children. Along with the story illustrations, line drawings showing the characters and a narrator signing the story in Signed English, a system that uses American Sign Language in English grammatical order.

48 pages Hardcover
ISBN: 0-930323-63-7

3394 Living with Hearing Loss

Marcia B Dugan, author

Gallaudet University Press
800 Florida Avenue NE
Washington, DC 20002
202-651-5488
Fax: 202-651-5489
TTY: 888-630-9347
gupress@gallaudet.edu
www.gupress.gallaudet.edu

192 pages
ISBN: 1-563681-34-0

3395 Mandy

Barbara D Booth, author

Harris Communications
15155 Technology Drive
Eden Prairie, MN 55344
952-906-1180
800-825-6758
Fax: 952-906-1099
TTY: 800-825-9187
info@harriscomm.com
www.harriscomm.com

Mandy is a young deaf girl who goes searching in the woods for her grandmother's silver pin as a thunderstorm approaches. She will touch readers with her peceptions of the world and her wonder of what sound is.

32 pages Hardcover

3396 Medical Sign Language: Easily Understood Definitions of Commonly Used Medical Term

W Joseph Garcia, author

Charles C Thomas Publishers
2600 South First Street
Springfield, IL 62704
217-789-8980
800-258-8980
books@ccthomas.com
www.ccthomas.com

In this glossary, a multitude of medical and dental terms are accurately defined and precisely translated, through description and illustration, into American Sign Language. The book easily lends itself to use at both ends of the chain of communication that links health care professionals with their deaf patients. Includes bibliography. Comes in both hardcover and softcover

726 pages

3397 Messy Monsters Jungle Joggers and Bubble Baths

Nehama Pluznik and Rochelle Sobel, author

Alexander Graham Bell Association for the Deaf
3417 Volta Place NW
Washington, DC 20007
202-337-5220
Fax: 202-337-8314
TTY: 202-337-5221
info@agbell.org
www.agbell.org

An illustrated book of poetry for children with hearing loss. Poems are organized according to the accepted group of speechreading phonemes which are classified by their appearance on the lips. Each poem emphasizes a particular phoneme which appears in the initial, medial, or final position of the word. Four worksheets accompany each poem: About the poem, Tell me more, Speech practice, and Language activities.

97 pages Softcover

3398 Nursery Rhymes from Mother Goose: Told in Signed English

Harry Bornstein and Karen L Saulnier, author

Gallaudet University Press
800 Florida Avenue NE
Washington, DC 20002
202-651-5488
Fax: 202-651-5489
gupress@gallaudet.edu
www.gupress.gallaudet.edu

More than a dozen favorite nursery rhymes are presented in this unique edition of Mother Goose. All of the rhymes are illustrated with full-color paintings accompanied by more than 389 drawings showing the verses in Signed English. Young readers, both hearing and deaf, will learn the special charm of rhyme while also discovering new vocabulary and new ways to experience English through signing. As they learn and memorize their favorite verses, children will also strengthen their language skills.

64 pages Hardcover
ISBN: 0-930323-99-8

3399 Opposites

HEAR-MORE
42 Executive Boulevard
Farmingdale, NY 11735
800-881-4327
Fax: 631-752-0689
TTY: 800-281-4327
www.hearmore.com

The Early Sign Language Series: A fascinating and enjoyable way for children and adults to learn sign language. Opposites presents the early concepts of opposite relationships. It fosters both recptive and expressive language through signs and pictures, and it is perfect for young children whether hearing impaired, hearing, pre-verbal or verbal. Reviews 10 opposite items (20 in total).

3400 Out for a Walk: Baby's First Sign Book

Kim Votry and Curt Waller, author

Gallaudet University Press
800 Florida Avenue NE
Washington, DC 20002
202-651-5488
Fax: 202-651-5489
gupress@gallaudet.edu
www.gupress.gallaudet.edu

Offers toddlers their first look at signs for the world around them. As they follow our distinctively hatted youngster on a stroll, they encounter familiar animals and insect, among them a dog, cat, butterfly, and squirrel, and learn which ones can be pets. They'll enjoy imaginative images of senses, too - sight, smell, hearing, taste, and touch.

16 pages Board Book
ISBN: 1-563681-46-3

3401 Parent's Guide to Chochlear Implants

Patricia M Chute and Mary Ellen Nevins, author

Gallaudet University Press
800 Florida Avenue NE
Washington, DC 20002
202-651-5488
Fax: 202-651-5489
gupress@gallaudet.edu
www.gupress.gallaudet.edu

Now, parents of deaf children have at hand a complete guide to the process of cochlear implantation. It explains in a friendly easy-to-follow style each stage of the process. Parents will discover how to have their child evaluated to determine his or her suitability for an implant. They'll learn about implant device options, how to choose an implant center, and every detail of the surgical procedure. The initial 'switch-on' is described along with counseling about device maintainance.

Hearing Impairment/Deafness / Book Publishers

208 pages Softcover
ISBN: 1-563681-29-3

3402 Parents and Their Deaf Children: The Early Years
Gallaudet University Press
800 Florida Avenue NE
Washington, DC 20002
202-651-5488
Fax: 202-651-5489
gupress@gallaudet.edu
http://gupress.gallaudet.edu

This book stems from a nationwide survey of parents with 6-7 year old deaf or hard of hearing children, followed up by interviews with 80 parents. The authors not only discuss the parents' communication choices for their children, but also provide how parents' experiences differ, especially for those whose children are hard of hearing, have additional conditions, or have cochlear implants. One chapter is devoted to minority cultures. Includes tables, figures, references and index.

272 pages Hardcover
ISBN: 1-563681-37-4

Kathryn P Meadow-Orlans, Co-Author
Donna M Mertens, Co-Author
Marilyn S Sass-Lehrer, Co-Author

3403 Police Officer Jones
HEAR-MORE
42 Executive Boulevard
Farmingdale, NY 11735
800-881-4327
Fax: 631-752-0689
TTY: 800-281-4327
www.hearmore.com

This beginning book describes a police officer and his exciting job. Use the signs when reading the book to your child and speak when you sign so the child will learn to associate the sign with sound and lip shape.

3404 Religious Signing: A Comprehensive Guide for All Faiths
Elaine Costello, author

TJ Publishers
P.O Box 702701
Dallas, TX 75370
972-416-0800
800-999-1168
Fax: 972-416-0944
TTY: 972-416-0933
customerservice@tjpublishers.com
www.tjpublishers.com

Contains over 500 religious signs and their meanings for all denominations. Clearly demonstrated and defined through illustrations that show movement of hands, body and face. Includes a special section on favorite verses, prayers and blessings.

219 pages Softcover
ISBN: 0-553342-44-4

3405 Rhode Island Test of Language Structure RITLS
Pro Ed
8700 Shoal Creed Boulevard
Austin, TX 78757
512-451-3246
800-897-3202
Fax: 800-397-7633
info@proedinc.com
www.proedinc.com

The Rhode Island Test of Language Structure (RITLS) provides a measure of English language development and assessment data. It is designed primarily for use with children who are hearing impaired, but also useful in other areas where level of language development is of concern, including intellectual disability, learning disability, and bilingual programs. The RITLS focuses on syntax, unlike other tests compared with other reading, language, intelligence, and achievement tests frequently used.

1983

3406 Schedules of Development for Hearing Impaired Infants and Their Parents
Alexander Graham Bell Association for the Deaf
3417 Volta Place NW
Washington, DC 20007
202-337-5220
Fax: 202-337-8314
TTY: 202-337-5221
info@agbell.org
www.agbell.org

Written for parents and teachers, this assessment record of verbal learning will help to evaluate each child's language development.

1977 14 pages

Agnes Ling Philips PhD, Author

3407 Screening for Hearing Loss and Otitis Media in Children
Jackson Roush PhD, author

Alexander Graham Bell Association for the Deaf
3417 Volta Place NW
Washington, DC 20007
202-337-5220
Fax: 202-337-8314
TTY: 202-337-5221
info@agbell.org
www.agbell.org

Provides a concise yet comprehensive guide to hearing and middle ear screening in children. From acoustic emissions and automated ABR in newborns to hearing screening of school-age children.

245 pages Softcover

3408 Sign Language for Babies
Walter Paul Kelly, author

Harris Communications
15155 Technology Drive
Eden Prairie, MN 55344
952-906-1180
800-825-6758
Fax: 952-906-1099
TTY: 800-825-9187
info@harriscomm.com
www.harriscomm.com

A black and white illustrated story on how love and eventually the ILY handsign in American Sign Language got started.

Hardcover

3409 Sign Numbers
Nancy Bartusch, author

Modern Signs Press
PO Box 1181
Los Alamitos, CA 90720
562-596-8548
800-572-7332
Fax: 562-795-6614
TTY: 562-493-4168
modsigns@modernsignspress.com
www.modernsignspress.com

Mandy helps Handy teach manual and written numbers. Includes printed numbers and easy-to-follow drawings of the number hand shapes. Also shows words and signs for the objects counted in a picture on each page. Black and white drawings make this a coloring book, too.

60 pages

3410 Sign With Kids Supplement
Modern Signs Press
PO Box 1181
Los Alamitos, CA 90720
562-596-8548
800-572-7332
Fax: 562-795-6614
TTY: 562-493-4168
modsigns@modernsignspress.com
www.modernsignspress.com

The supplement contains easy to use illustrations for all the signs in every lesson of Sign With Kids. Both volumes together provide a comprehensive program for teaching sign language to hearing kids.

Hearing Impairment/Deafness / Book Publishers

3411 Sign-Me-Fine

Gallaudet University Press
800 Florida Avenue NE
Washington, DC 20002

202-651-5488
Fax: 202-651-5489
TTY: 202-651-5488
gupress@gallaudet.edu
www.gupress.gallaudet.edu

Written for young adults, this book introduces American Sign Language and how it differs from English.

1997 120 pages paperback
ISBN: 0-930323-76-9

3412 Signing Exact English Using Affixes

Modern Signs Press
PO Box 1181
Los Alamitos, CA 90720

562-596-8548
800-572-7332
Fax: 562-795-6614
TTY: 562-493-4168
modsigns@modernsignspress.com
www.modernsignspress.com

A catalog of signed vocabulary extended by prefixes, suffixes, contractions and tenses.

3413 Signing Family: What Every Parent Should Know About Sign Communication

David A Stewart and Barbara Leutke-Stahlman, author

Gallaudet University Press
800 Florida Avenue NE
Washington, DC 20002

202-651-5488
Fax: 202-651-5489
gupress@gallaudet.edu
www.gupress.gallaudet.edu

Parents of deaf children concerned with finding the best means of communication for their family will welcome the straightforward, reader-friendly information in this book. In a style both positive and pragmatic, the authors employ common-sense reasoning to establish the importance of teach deaf children language fundamentals as early as possible. This essential book for parents continues by explaining why the visual-gestural nature of signing is generally the best languge mode for deaf children

192 pages Softcover
ISBN: 1-563680-69-6

3414 Signing Fun: American Sign Language Vocabulary, Phrases, Games and Activities

Penny Warner and Paula Gray, author

Gallaudet University Press
800 Florida Avenue NE
Washington, DC 20002

202-651-5488
Fax: 202-651-5489
gupress@gallaudet.edu
www.gupress.gallaudet.edu

For young adults age 11 and up. Signing is visual, easy to learn, and fun to use. Offers 441 useful signs on a variety of favorite topics: activities, animals, fashion, food, holidays, home, outdoors, parties, people, places, play, emotions, school, shopping, travel, plus extra fun signs for especially popular words. Each chapter includes practice sentences using everyday phrases to help new signers learn in a fun way. Provides dozens of entertaining games and activities.

192 pages Softcover
ISBN: 1-563629-23-6

3415 Signing: How to Speak With Your Hands, Second Edition

Elaine Costello, author

TJ Publishers
P.O Box 702701
Dallas, TX 75370

972-416-0800
800-999-1168
Fax: 972-416-0944
TTY: 972-416-0933
customerservice@tjpublishers.com
www.tjpublishers.com

This book presents more than 1300 signs and their descriptions. Linguistic principles are described at the beginning of each chapter giving insight into the rules which govern American Sign Language.

248 pages Softcover
ISBN: 0-553375-39-3

3416 Signs for Me

Ben Bahan and Joe Dannis, author

Harris Communications
15155 Technology Drive
Eden Prairie, MN 55344

952-906-1180
800-825-6758
Fax: 952-906-1099
TTY: 800-825-9187
info@harriscomm.com
www.harriscomm.com

Ideal for youngsters and other sign language beginners, a unique illustrated approach to presenting basic vocabulary. While the book provides a multidimentional sign vocabulary for pre-school and elementary school children, its appealing format makes it suitable for signers of all ages.

111 pages Softcover

3417 Signs for Me: Basic Sign Vocabulary for Children, Parents and Teachers

Ben Bahan and Joe Dannis, author

TJ Publishers
P.O Box 702701
Dallas, TX 75370

972-416-0800
800-999-1168
Fax: 972-416-0944
TTY: 972-416-0933
customerservice@tjpublishers.com
www.tjpublishers.com

Sign language vocabulary for preschool and elementary school children introduces household items, animals, family members, actions, emotions, safety concerns and other concepts. Over 300 vocabulary words, pictures and sign illustrations.

112 pages Softcover
ISBN: 0-915035-27-8

3418 Signs of Sharing: An Elementary Sign Language and Deaf Awareness Curriculum

Charles C Thomas Publisher
2600 S 1st Street
Springfield, IL 62704

217-789-8980
800-258-8980
Fax: 217-789-9130
books@ccthomas.com
www.ccthomas.com

A unique set of materials that provides educators whose responsibilities include the integration of hearing-impaired children, with a multifaceted tool to teach sign language and deaf awareness.

1993 380 pages
ISBN: 0-398058-51-2

Sue F V Rakow, Co-Author
Carol B Carpenter, Co-Author

3419 Silent Garden

Paul W Ogden, author

Gallaudet University Press
800 Florida Avenue NE
Washington, DC 20002

202-651-5488
Fax: 202-651-5489
gupress@gallaudet.edu
www.gupress.gallaudet.edu

This completely rewritten edition presents parents of deaf children with more crucial information enhanced by the advances made in the general understanding of what it means to be deaf and the greater possibilities afforded deaf children today. Provides parents with a firm foundation for making the difficult decisions necessary to begin their child on the road to realizing his or her full potential.

Hearing Impairment/Deafness / Book Publishers

304 pages Softcover
ISBN: 1-563680-58-0

3420 Silent Observer

Christy MacKinnon, author

Gallaudet University Press
800 Florida Avenue NE
Washington, DC 20002
202-651-5488
Fax: 202-651-5489
gupress@gallaudet.edu
www.gupress.gallaudet.edu

An affectionage, poignant memoir of childhood as seen through the eyes of a vivacious young girl. Teachers, parents, and children will share in their enjoyment of this beautiful, sensitive story of a harder but wonderful time that has passed.

48 pages Hardcover
ISBN: 1-563680-22-X

3421 Simple Signs

Cindy Wheeler, author

Harris Communications
15155 Technology Drive
Eden Prairie, MN 55344
952-906-1180
800-825-6758
Fax: 952-906-1099
TTY: 800-825-9187
info@harriscomm.com
www.harriscomm.com

Children have a lot to say, whether through gestures, movement, pictures or words. American Sign Language incorporates all these natural skills. With pictures, clear diagrams, and hints, learn from these 28 signs. Ages 3-6 years.

30 pages Softcover

3422 Six-Sound Song

Warren Estabrooks MEd, author

Alexander Graham Bell Association for the Deaf
3417 Volta Place NW
Washington, DC 20007
202-337-5220
Fax: 202-337-8314
TTY: 202-337-5221
info@agbell.org
www.agbell.org

Based on the Six-Sound Tests developed by the late Daniel Ling, PhD. Used for both individual and group therapy sessions in auditory and oral environments. Children will enjoy the illustrations created by seven-year-old Hunter Jackson who received his cochlear implant while the Auditory-Verbal Centre of the Learning to Listen Foundation. Hardcover Book and CD set

3423 Songs in Sign

S Harold Collins, author

TJ Publishers
P.O Box 702701
Dallas, TX 75370
972-416-0800
800-999-1168
Fax: 972-416-0944
TTY: 972-416-0933
customerservice@tjpublishers.com
www.tjpublishers.com

Presents six songs in Signed English. The easy-to-follow illustrations enable you to sign: Twinkle, Twinkle Litt Star; The Mulberry Bush; Row, Row, Row Your Boat; If You're Happy; Bingo and The Muffin Man.

16 pages Softcover
ISBN: 0-931993-71-7

3424 Speak to Me (Second Edition)

Marcia Calhoun Forecki, author

Gallaudet University Press
800 Florida Avenue NE
Washington, DC 20002
202-651-5488
Fax: 202-651-5489
gupress@gallaudet.edu
www.gupress.gallaudet.edu

An engrossing, personal account of life with Charlie, an adorable, active, deaf seven-year-old. The story of an ordinary person confronted with an overwhelming reality - the fact that her son is deaf. Forecki's struggle as a single parent to care for her child, to find the right schools, and to establish communication with her son will strike a familiar chord in all hearing parents of deaf children. All readers will be touched by the mixture of pathos and humor in this account.

154 pages Softcover
ISBN: 0-930323-68-8

3425 Speech and the Hearing Impaired Child (Second Edition)

Daniel Ling, PhD, author

Alexander Graham Bell Association for the Deaf
3417 Volta Place NW
Washington, DC 20007
202-337-5220
Fax: 202-337-8314
TTY: 202-337-5221
info@agbell.org
www.agbell.org

An extension of the original text published by the late Daniel Ling in 1976. It looks much more closely at the development of speech in the context of spoken language. It incorporates informal strategies for promoting spoken language development that are appropriate for use with modern technology such as digital hearing aids and cochlear implants. Considerable emphasis is placed on the ongoing evaluation of speech in the context of spoken language.

440 pages Softcover

3426 Speechreading: A Way to Improve Understanding

Gallaudet University Press
800 Florida Avenue NE
Washington, DC 20002
202-651-5488
Fax: 202-651-5489
TTY: 202-651-5488
gupress@gallaudet.edu
www.gupress.gallaudet.edu

This useful guide for teachers and therapists approaches speechreading instruction with the help of context cues.

160 pages

3427 Student Study Guide to A Basic Course in American Sign Language

Frances DeCapite, author

TJ Publishers
P.O Box 702701
Dallas, TX 75370
972-416-0800
800-999-1168
Fax: 972-416-0944
TTY: 972-416-0933
customerservice@tjpublishers.com
www.tjpublishers.com

Designed to supplement the text of A Basic Course in American Sign Language, the guide provides a wide array of supplemental practice materials for student and teacher. Exercises and practice sentences allow students to practice receptive and expressive skills.

197 pages Spiral bound
ISBN: 0-932666-33-7

3428 Talking Finger Series - At Grandma's House
Modern Signs Press
PO Box 1181
Los Alamitos, CA 90720
562-596-8548
800-572-7332
Fax: 562-795-6614
TTY: 562-493-4168
modsigns@modernsignspress.com
www.modernsignspress.com

Pictures, signs and printed words tell the tale of April, a cuddly little rabbit who loves to play with her beloved Grandma. Uses 27-word vocabulary, includes manual alphabet and glossary of signs.

3429 Talking Finger Series - Little Green Monster
Modern Signs Press
PO Box 1181
Los Alamitos, CA 90720
562-596-8548
800-572-7332
Fax: 562-795-6614
TTY: 562-493-4168
modsigns@modernsignspress.com
www.modernsignspress.com

This storybook features Becky and Barry, two playful little bears who keep you in suspense. The 45-word vocabulary in signs and printed words introduces concept of directionality (here, there, behind, etc.). Includes manual alphabet and glossary of signs.

36 pages

3430 Teach Your Tot to Sign
Stacy A Thompson and Valerie Nelson-Metlay, author

Gallaudet University Press
800 Florida Avenue NE
Washington, DC 20002
202-651-5488
Fax: 202-651-5489
gupress@gallaudet.edu
www.gupress.gallaudet.edu

This book provides parents and teachers the opportunity to teach more than 500 basic American Sign Language signs to their infants, toddlers, and young children. It features fundamental signs of great appeal to young children and concise instructions on how to sign, including the critical importance of facial expression. Anticipates all of the common desires and interests of young children - food, pets, planes, trains, cars and boats, games, holidays, vegetables, family - nearly everything.

232 pages Softcover
ISBN: 1-563683-11-3

3431 The Book of Choice
Hands and Voices
PO Box 3093
Boulder, CO 80307
303-492-6283
866-422-0422
parentadvocate@handsandvoices.org
www.handsandvoices.org

Support for parents of a child who is deaf or hard of hearing. Also available in Spanish.

3432 The Development of Deaf Children: Academic Achievement Levels and Social Processes
Kerstin Heiling, author

Gallaudet University Press
800 Florida Avenue NE
Washington, DC 20002
202-651-5488
Fax: 202-651-5489
gupress@gallaudet.edu
www.gupress.gallaudet.edu

This revealing volume presents the research from a videotape study of the behavior of 20 deaf children for 14 years, and a comprehensive test at age 15 to assess their development.

280 pages Hardcover
ISBN: 3-927731-58-7

3433 The Handbook of Pediatric Audiology
Sanford E Gerber, Editor, author

Gallaudet University Press
800 Florida Avenue NE
Washington, DC 20002
202-651-5488
Fax: 202-651-5489
gupress@gallaudet.edu
www.gupress.gallaudet.edu

Presents 14 comprehensive chapters written by expert in each discipline. Clinicians and students now can refer to specific subjects in pediatric audiology for treating children from infancy through their elementary school years. Contributors include: Yash Pal Kapur, Franklin A. Katz, Robert J. Ruben, Allen O. Diefendorf, Judith S. Gravel, Jane R. Madell, Shlomo Silman, Carol A. Silverman, Herbert Jay Gold, and Maurice Mendel. Tables, figures, references, bibliography, author and subject index

478 pages Softcover
ISBN: 1-563680-99-7

3434 The Hearing Aid Handbook: Clinician's Guide to Client Orientation
Donna S Wayner, author

Gallaudet University Press
800 Florida Avenue NE
Washington, DC 20002
202-651-5488
Fax: 202-651-5489
gupress@gallaudet.edu
www.gupress.gallaudet.edu

This handbook consists of three volumes for audiologists and other clinicians to help clients learn to use hearing aids. Planned for three classes, the guide explains exactly how to conduct the initial visit, fit ear molds, clean and maintain hearing aids and adjust amplification. Clinicians will also learn to encourage the use of visual cues, speechreading, and contextual clues to ensure a high rate of success for their clients. Users Guides feature information and worksheets.

172 pages Softcover
ISBN: 0-930323-56-4

3435 The Joy of Signing Second Edition
Lottie L Riekehof, author

TJ Publishers
P.O Box 702701
Dallas, TX 75370
972-416-0800
800-999-1168
Fax: 972-416-0944
TTY: 972-416-0933
customerservice@tjpublishers.com
www.tjpublishers.com

This popular dictionary of approximately 1500 known signs makes them easier to remember. Sentences present signs in proper context. Appendix gives information about the most effective way to add signs to spoken English.

352 pages Hardcover
ISBN: 0-882435-20-5

3436 The Listener
Warren Estabrooks, MEd, author

Alexander Graham Bell Association for the Deaf
3417 Volta Place NW
Washington, DC 20007
202-337-5220
Fax: 202-337-8314
TTY: 202-337-5221
info@agbell.org
www.agbell.org

Subject material is centered around listening, speech, language, spoken communication, and cognitive, social and psychological development of children who are deaf or hard of hearing and their families. Articles address: Making sense of complex skills lesson planning, Morphosyntax: evidence-based AVT, Your young child's newly diagnosed hearing loss: knowing how to cope, What is Auditory-Verbal Therapy?, Teachers' perceptions of the integration of children with hearing loss.

Hearing Impairment/Deafness / Book Publishers

64 pages Softcover

3437 The Night Before Christmas told in Signed english

Adapted By Harry Bornstein and Karen L Saulnier, author

Gallaudet University Press
800 Florida Avenue NE
Washington, DC 20002
202-651-5488
Fax: 202-651-5489
gupress@gallaudet.edu
www.gupress.gallaudet.edu

Now this wonderful, seasonal poem can be enjoyed in a new way by both hearing and deaf children. Accompanying the complete verses and full-color illustrations, line drawings show this holiday favorite in Signed English, the system that uses American Sign Language signs in English word order. Uses both rhyme and signing to help children practice their vocabulary and learn English grammar. Entertains at the same time that it teaches.

64 pages Hardcover
ISBN: 1-563680-20-3

Clement C Moore, Original Author

3438 The Rising of Lotus Flowers: Self-Educating Deaf Children in Thai Boarding Schools

Charles B Reilly and Nipapon Reilly, author

Gallaudet University Press
800 Florida Avenue NE
Washington, DC 20002
202-651-5488
Fax: 202-651-5489
gupress@gallaudet.edu
www.gupress.gallaudet.edu

In developed nations around the world, residential schools for deaf students are giving way to the trend of inclusion in regular classrooms. Nonetheless, deaf education continues to lag as students struggle to communicate. In the Bua School in Thialand, however, 400 residential deaf students ranging in age from 6 to 19 have met with great success in teaching each other Thai Sign Language and a world of knowledge once thought to be lost to them.

272 pages Hardcover
ISBN: 1-563682-75-3

3439 The Young Deaf Child

David Luterman, PhD, author

Alexander Graham Bell Association for the Deaf
3417 Volta Place NW
Washington, DC 20007
202-337-5220
Fax: 202-337-8314
TTY: 202-337-5221
info@agbell.org
www.agbell.org

A valuable resource for audiologists, early interventionists and special educators who provide diagnostic or therapeutic services to parents of newborns and children with hearing loss. Discusses the history of deaf education in the United States and offers valuable information on the pros and cons of screening, elements essential to effective programming and therapy, a model for intervention centered on the parent-child connection, assistive hearing technologies and counseling techniques.

3440 Un Curso Basico de Lenguaje Americano de S enas
TJ Publishers
P.O Box 702701
Dallas, TX 75370
972-416-0800
800-999-1168
Fax: 972-416-0944
TTY: 972-416-0933
customerservice@tjpublishers.com
www.tjpublishers.com

Features English and Spanish translations side by side. It is designed for teachers, parents and students working with Deaf Hispanic American children and adults learning English and American Sign Language.

356 pages Spiral bound
ISBN: 0-932666-35-3

3441 We Can Hear and Speak
Alexander Graham Bell Association for the Deaf
3417 Volta Place NW
Washington, DC 20007
202-337-5220
Fax: 202-337-8314
TTY: 202-337-5221
info@agbell.org
www.agbell.org

Written by parents for families of children who are deaf or hard-of-hearing, this work describes auditory-verbal terminology and approaches and contains personal narratives written by parents and their children who are deaf or hard-of-hearing.

1998 184 pages Softcover

Carol Flexer PhD, Contributor
Catherine Richards, Contributor

3442 Winnie-the-Pooh's ABCs
HEAR-MORE
42 Executive Boulevard
Farmingdale, NY 11735
800-881-4327
Fax: 631-752-0689
TTY: 800-281-4327
www.hearmore.com

In this special edition of Winnie-the-Pooh's ABC, both hearing and deaf children are introduced to the written and ASL alphabets, Hundred Acre Wood-Style. Inspired by A.A. Milne

32 pages

3443 Word Signs: A First Book of Sign Language

Debbie Slier, author

Gallaudet University Press
800 Florida Avenue NE
Washington, DC 20002
202-651-5488
Fax: 202-651-5489
gupress@gallaudet.edu
www.gupress.gallaudet.edu

Charming, full-cover photographs of basic animals plus illustrations of their corresponding signs offer children ages 1 to 4 a fun way to learn their first signs and vocabulary words.

164 pages Board book
ISBN: 1-563680-48-3

3444 You and Your Deaf Child
Gallaudet University Press
800 Florida Avenue NE
Washington, DC 20002
202-651-5488
Fax: 202-651-5489
TTY: 202-651-5489
gupress@gallaudet.edu
www.gupress.gallaudet.edu

This guide for parents explores how families interact to deal with the special impact of a child who is hearing impaired.

1997 224 pages softcover
ISBN: 0-563680-60-2

3445 You and Your Deaf Child: A Self-Help Guide for Parents of Deaf and Hard of Hearing

John W Adams, author

Gallaudet University Press
800 Florida Avenue NE
Washington, DC 20002
202-651-5488
Fax: 202-651-5489
gupress@gallaudet.edu
www.gupress.gallaudet.edu

A guide for parents of deaf or hard of hearing children that explores how parents and their children interact. It examines the special impact of having a deaf child in the family. Eleven chapters focus on such topics as feelings about hearing loss, the importance of communication in the family, and effective behavior management. Many chapters contain practice activities and check their grasp of the material.

224 pages Softcover
ISBN: 1-563680-60-2

3446 **Young Deaf Child**
Alexander Graham Bell Association for the Deaf
3417 Volta Place NW
Washington, DC 20007
202-337-5220
Fax: 202-337-8314
TTY: 202-337-5221
info@agbell.org
www.agbell.org

With a foreword by Mark Ross, Ph.D., this book is based on experience by the three authors and outlines the best approach for the child, early intervention, maximization of technology and strong family involvement.

1999 235 pages

David Luterman PhD, Author

Magazines

3447 **Auditory - Verbal International**
2121 Eisenhower Avenue, Suite 402
Alexandria, VA 22314
703-739-1049
Fax: 703-739-0395
TTY: 703-739-0874
audiverb@aol.com

Magazine of the organization dedicated to helping children who have hearing losses learn to listen and speak. Promotes the Auditory-Verbal Therapy approach, which is based on the belief that the overwhelming majority of these children can hear and talk by using their residual hearing and hearing aids. Membership dues for Canada are $55, International, $60, US, $50, and students are charged $30.

Quarterly

Sara Lake, Executive Director/CEO
Mary Benson, Executive Assistant

3448 **Deaf Life**
c/o MSM Productions, LTD
1095 Meigs Street
Rochester, NY 14620
716-442-6370
Fax: 716-442-6371
TTY: 716-442-6370
deaflife@deaflife.com
www.deaflife.com

This magazine focuses on profiles, news, controversial issues, cultural topics and more relating to the deaf community, first published in 1988.

64 pages Monthly
ISSN: 0898-719x

Matthew Moore, Publisher

3449 **Deaf USA**
Eye Festival Communications
6917B Woodley Avenue
Van Nuys, CA 91406
Fax: 818-902-9840

Provides news coverage on all activities and issues of interest to deaf and hard-of-hearing readers as well as professionals and associates within this specialized market.

Monthly

David Rosenbaum, Editor

3450 **Perspectives in Education and Deafness**
Gallaudet University Press
800 Florida Avenue NE
Washington, DC 20002
202-651-5488
800-621-2736
Fax: 800-621-8476
TTY: 202-651-5444
gupress@gallaudet.edu
gupress.gallaudet.edu

A practical, reader-friendly magazine, offering help and advice in and beyond the classroom, tuned to the needs of today's students, teachers and families.

5 times a year

Mary Abrams Perica, Editor

3451 **Volta Voices**
Alexander Graham Bell Association for the Deaf
3417 Volta Place NW
Washington, DC 20007
202-337-5220
800-432-7543
Fax: 202-337-8314
TTY: 203-337-5221
info@agbell.org
listeningandspokenlanguage.org

A magazine highlighting inspirational stories from parents of children who are deaf, legislative news, technology update, and stories pertaining to speech, speech-reading, and the use of residual hearing.

Bimonthly

Brooke Rigler, Editor
Lisa Chutjian, Chief Development Officer
Emilio Alonso-Mendoza, Chief Executive Officer

Journals

3452 **American Annals of the Deaf**
Convention of American Instructors of the Deaf
800 Florida Avenue NE, Fowler Hall 409
Washington, DC 20002
202-651-5488
Fax: 202-651-5708
TTY: 202-651-5444
gupress@gallaudet.edu
gupress.gallaudet.edu

Scholarly journal at the forefront of research related to the education of deaf people. Annual reference Issue identifies programs and services for deaf people nationwide.

5 times a year

Donald F Moores, Editor
Mary Ellen Carew, Managing Editor

3453 **Journal of Speech, Language, and Hearing Research**
American Speech Language Hearing Association
2200 Research Blvd
Rockville, MD 20850
301-296-5700
800-478-2071
Fax: 301-296-8580
TTY: 301-296-5650
TDD: 301-296-5650
productsales@asha.org
www.asha.org

Pertains broadly to studies of the processes and disorders of hearing, language, and speech and to the diagnosis and treatment of such disorders.

Bi-monthly

Bharath Chandrasekaran, Editor in Chief, Speech
Sean Richmond, Editor in Chief, Language
Frederick Gallun, Editor in Chief, Hearing

3454 **Language, Speech, and Hearing in Schools**
American Speech Language Hearing Association
2200 Research Blvd
Rockville, MD 20850
301-296-5700
800-478-2071
Fax: 301-296-8580
TTY: 301-296-5650
TDD: 301-296-5650
productsales@asha.org
www.asha.org

An archival journal for research and practice in educational settings. Publishes studies and articles that pertain to speech, language, and hearing disorders and differences in children and adolescents, as well as to professional issues affecting service delivery in educational setting.

Quarterly

Dr Kenn Apel, Editor
Judith L. Page, PhD, CCC-SLP, President
Margot L. Beckerman, AuD, CCC-A, Chair

Hearing Impairment/Deafness / Newsletters

Newsletters

3455 Endeavor
American Society for Deaf Children
PO Box 3355
Gettysburg, PA 17325
717-334-7922
800-942-2732
Fax: 717-334-8808

Newsletter for parents of deaf children.

Quarterly

Barbara Aschembrenner, Editor

3456 Gallaudet Today
Gallaudet University Press
800 Florida Avenue NE
Washington, DC 20002
202-651-5488
800-621-2736
Fax: 800-621-8476
TTY: 202-651-5444
gupress@gallaudet.edu
gupress.gallaudet.edu

A university alumni publication with both general and special issues on deafness-related topics.

44 pages Quarterly

Roz Prickett, Publications Manager

3457 Hear
Deafness Research Foundation
15 W 39th Street
New York, NY 10018
212-768-1181

Offers information on the Foundation's activities and events, technical updates on assistive devices, legislative and medical information on the latest breakthroughs and laws for the hearing impaired, book reviews and resources.

Monte H Jacoby, Executive Director

3458 Newsline
Sertoma Foundation
1912 E Meyer Boulevard
Kansas City, MO 64132
816-333-8300
infosertoma@sertomahq.org
www.sertoma.org

Reports on activities of the Sertoma Foundation in the field of speech and hearing impairments.

David Johnson, President
Don Bartelmay, Senior Vice President
Cheryl Cherny, Junior Vice President

3459 Signs for Me: Basic Sign Vocabulary for Children, Parents, & Teachers
TJ Publishers
817 Silver Spring Avenue, Suite 206
Silver Spring, MD 20910
301-585-4440
800-999-1168
Fax: 301-585-5930
TTY: 301-585-4440
TDD: 301-585-4441
TJPubinc@aol.com

Sign language vocabulary for preschool and elementary school children introduces household items, animals, family members, actions, emotions, safety concerns and other concepts.

112 pages Softcover

3460 Speech and Deafness Newsletter
Hearing, Speech
1620 18th Avenue
Seattle, WA 98122
206-323-5770

Agency newsletter for membership and community.

8 pages

Patty Tumberg, Editor

3461 Volta Review
Alexander Graham Bell Association for the Deaf
3417 Volta Place NW
Washington, DC 20007
202-337-5220
800-432-7543
Fax: 202-337-8314
TTY: 203-337-5221
info@agbell.org
listeningandspokenlanguage.org

Offers the latest theory, research, current perspectives and practical guidance from noted specialists in education, audiology, speech and language sciences and psychology. Each issue contains a Special Focus-a group of chapters exploring a specific topic in detail.

Quarterly

Lisa Chutjian, Chief Development Officer
Emilio Alonso-Mendoza, Chief Executive Officer
Judy Harrison, Director of Programs

Pamphlets

3462 25 Ways to Promote Spoken Language in Your Child with a Hearing Loss
Alexander Graham Bell Association for the Deaf
3417 Volta Place NW
Washington, DC 20007
202-337-5220
800-432-7543
Fax: 202-337-8314
TTY: 203-337-5221
info@agbell.org
listeningandspokenlanguage.org

This pamphlet teaches twenty-five golden rules about preparing your child to listen and to speak.

1995 62 pages

Lisa Chutjian, Chief Development Officer
Emilio Alonso-Mendoza, Chief Executive Officer
Judy Harrison, Director of Programs

3463 Books for Parents of Deaf and Hard-of- Hearing Children
National Information Center on Deafness
800 Florida Avenue NE
Washington, DC 20002
202-651-5488
Fax: 202-651-5054
TTY: 202-651-5444
gupress@gallaudet.edu
gupress.gallaudet.edu

Identifies books written for parents and everday experiences of deaf and hard-of-hearing children.

3464 Can Your Baby Hear?
Alexander Graham Bell Association for the Deaf
3417 Volta Place NW
Washington, DC 20007
202-337-5220
800-432-7543
Fax: 202-337-8314
TTY: 203-337-5221
info@agbell.org
listeningandspokenlanguage.org

This simple card for parents lists risk indicators and warning signs of hearing loss in babies.

Lisa Chutjian, Chief Development Officer
Emilio Alonso-Mendoza, Chief Executive Officer
Judy Harrison, Director of Programs

3465 Communicating with People who Have a Hearing Loss
Alexander Graham Bell Association for the Deaf
3417 Volta Place NW
Washington, DC 20007
202-337-5220
800-432-7543
Fax: 202-337-8314
TTY: 203-337-5221
info@agbell.org
listeningandspokenlanguage.org

This brochure describes ways to communicate more effectively with people who have hearing losses.

Hearing Impairment/Deafness / Pamphlets

1994
Lisa Chutjian, Chief Development Officer
Emilio Alonso-Mendoza, Chief Executive Officer
Judy Harrison, Director of Programs

3466 Deafness: A Fact Sheet
National Information Center On Deafness
800 Florida Avenue NE
Washington, DC 20002
202-651-5488
Fax: 202-651-5054
TTY: 202-651-5444
gupress@gallaudet.edu
gupress.gallaudet.edu

3467 Developing Cognition in Young Children Who are Deaf
Hope
55 E 100 N
Logan, UT 84321
435-752-9533
Fax: 435-752-9533

Presents interesting, updated information on the importance of early cognition development in young children who are deaf. Contains many ideas for ways to promote early thinking skills, especially those that promote and enhance early communication and language development.

3468 Educating Deaf Children: An Introduction
National Information Center on Deafness
800 Florida Avenue NE
Washington, DC 20002
202-651-5488
Fax: 202-651-5054
TTY: 202-651-5444
gupress@gallaudet.edu
gupress.gallaudet.edu

Describes the different settings in which deaf children are currently educated.

3469 Hearing Alert Informational Brochures
Alexander Graham Bell Association for the Deaf
3417 Volta Place NW
Washington, DC 20007
202-337-5220
800-432-7543
Fax: 202-337-8314
TTY: 203-337-5221
info@agbell.org
listeningandspokenlanguage.org

These brochures encourage early detection of hearing loss in young children; for medical facilities, speech and hearing clinics, and schools.

Lisa Chutjian, Chief Development Officer
Emilio Alonso-Mendoza, Chief Executive Officer
Judy Harrison, Director of Programs

3470 Helping Your Hard-of-Hearing Child Succeed
Alexander Graham Bell Association for the Deaf
3417 Volta Place NW
Washington, DC 20007
202-337-5220
800-432-7543
Fax: 202-337-8314
TTY: 203-337-5221
info@agbell.org
listeningandspokenlanguage.org

Offers information on how to help children succeed in school with speech and language development.

Lisa Chutjian, Chief Development Officer
Emilio Alonso-Mendoza, Chief Executive Officer
Judy Harrison, Director of Programs

3471 How Does Your Child Hear and Talk?
American Speech Language Hearing Association
2200 Research Blvd
Rockville, MD 20850
301-296-5700
800-478-2071
Fax: 301-296-8580
TTY: 301-296-5650
TDD: 301-296-5650
productsales@asha.org
www.asha.org

Offers a chart to parents on children's growth pertaining to their hearing and speech.

Judith L. Page, PhD, CCC-SLP, President
Margot L. Beckerman, AuD, CCC-A, Chair
Barbara K. Cone, PhD, CCC-A, VP, Academic Affairs in Audiology

3472 Leading National Publications of and for Deaf People
National Information Center On Deafness
800 Florida Avenue NE
Washington, DC 20002
202-651-5488
Fax: 202-651-5054
TTY: 202-651-5444
gupress@gallaudet.edu
gupress.gallaudet.edu

Identifies publications with national circulations to deaf audiences.

3473 Listen - Hear for Parents of Hearing Impaired Children
Alexander Graham Bell Association for the Deaf
3417 Volta Place NW
Washington, DC 20007
202-337-5220
800-432-7543
Fax: 202-337-8314
TTY: 203-337-5221
info@agbell.org
listeningandspokenlanguage.org

Offers information that parents of deaf and hard-of-hearing children need to be aware of. Also includes information on hearing aids, hearing loss and the association in general.

Lisa Chutjian, Chief Development Officer
Emilio Alonso-Mendoza, Chief Executive Officer
Judy Harrison, Director of Programs

3474 Parent Packets
Alexander Graham Bell Association for the Deaf
3417 Volta Place NW
Washington, DC 20007
202-337-5220
800-432-7543
Fax: 202-337-8314
TTY: 203-337-5221
info@agbell.org
listeningandspokenlanguage.org

These educational packets for parents are specifically designed to address important age-related topics about your child with a hearing impairment.

Packet

Lisa Chutjian, Chief Development Officer
Emilio Alonso-Mendoza, Chief Executive Officer
Judy Harrison, Director of Programs

3475 Perspectives Folio: Parent-Child
Gallaudet University Press
800 Florida Avenue NE
Washington, DC 20002
202-651-5488
800-621-2736
Fax: 800-621-8476
TTY: 202-651-5444
gupress@gallaudet.edu
gupress.gallaudet.edu

Seven articles emphasizing family communication while providing important information for parents about deafness and the deaf culture.

29 pages

3476 Publications From the National Information Center on Deafness
National Information Center on Deafness
800 Florida Avenue NE
Washington, DC 20002
202-651-5488
Fax: 202-651-5054
TTY: 202-651-5444
gupress@gallaudet.edu
gupress.gallaudet.edu

Order form and explanations of NICD publications.

Hearing Impairment/Deafness / Camps

3477 Signs for Me: Basic Sign Vocabulary for Children, Parents, & Teachers
DawnSignPress
6130 Nancy Ridge Drive
San Diego, CA 92121

858-625-0600
800-549-5350
Fax: 858-625-2336
info@dawnsign.com
www.dawnsign.com

ASL/English vocabulary primer. Young readers will associate a sign and picture with the English form of a word. Introduces more than 300 primary words arranged in thematic groupings. Captures students' interest through clearly illustrated signs and actions; includes an illustrated look at the English word for effective bilingual learning.

128 pages paperback
ISBN: 0-915035-27-8

Ben Bahan, Co-Author
Joe Dannis, Co-Author

3478 Statewide Services for Deaf and Hard of Hearing People
National Information Center on Deafness
800 Florida Avenue NE
Washington, DC 20002

202-651-5488
Fax: 202-651-5054
TTY: 202-651-5444
gupress@gallaudet.edu
gupress.gallaudet.edu

A resource list of states that have established commissions and other offices to serve deaf people.

3479 World of Sound
International Hearing Society
16880 Middlebelt Road, Suite 4
Livonia, MI 48154

734-522-7200
Fax: 734-522-0200
www.hearingihs.org

The purpose of this booklet is to provide basic information for those with questions about hearing loss, hearing aids and hearing instrument specialists.

Camps

3480 Camp Civitan
12635 North 42nd Street
Phoenix, AZ 85032

602-953-2944
Fax: 602-953-2946
info@campcivitan.org
www.campcivitan.org

A 501c3 non-profit organization, that has been providing multiple ever-changing programs to meet the needs of children and adults who are developmentally disabled.

Rob Adams, Camp Director
Charlie Riggs, Camp Maintenance
Mary Kellogg, Operations

3481 Camp Emanuel
PO Box 752343
Dayton, OH 45475

973-477-5504
ginter.7@wright.edu
campemanuel.weebly.com

Camp Emanuel is a camp for children with and without disabilities. It is the only camp of its kind in southwestern Ohio. The camp is designed to promote decision-making, team building skills, self-esteem, and an understanding of acceptance between all children.

Stephanie Ackner, President
Brian Demarke, Vice President
Mary Foreman, Secretary

3482 Camp Grizzly
4708 Roseville Road, Suite 112
North Highlands, CA 95660

916-349-7500
Fax: 916-993-3048
TTY: 916-349-7500
sfarinha@norcalcenter.org
www.norcalcenter.org

A one-week residential camp program for deaf and hard of hearing youth age 7 to 17.

Sheri Farinha, CEO
Cheryl Bella, Chair
Michael D. Wilson, Vice Chair

3483 Camp Juliena
4151 Memorial Dr, Suite 103-B
Decatur, GA 30032

404-292-5312
800-541-0710
Fax: 404-299-3642
campjuliena@gmail.com
www.gachi.org

A weeklong residential summer camp for youths and teens who are deaf or hard of hearing. Through challenging, team-oriented activities, campers form lasting friendships and acquire valuable leadership, social and communication skills.

Pat Ford, President
Jeanette Lorch, Vice President
Martha Timms, Secretary

3484 Camp Shocco for the Deaf
PO Box 6569
Talladega, AL 35161

256-761-1100
campshocco@albcdeaf.org
www.campshocco.org

Camp for deaf and hard of hearing students age 8 through high school. The campers will learn about Bible stories, teamwork, and have plenty of fun with various activities during recreation time.

Chad Fleming, Camp Director
Matthew Dixon, Co-Director
Linnea Elliott, Assistant Director

3485 Central Michigan University Summer Clinics
444 Moore
Mount Pleasant, MI

517-774-3803

Designed for children, ages 6 and up, with speech, language and hearing disorders who can benefit from intensive clinical work. A wide range of recreational and social activities form part of the clinical program and promote the social use of skills learned in class.

3486 Children's Beach House
100 W, 10th Street, Suite 411
Wilmington, DE 19801

302-655-4288
Fax: 302-655-4216
www.cbhinc.org

Summer camp for children from Delaware of normal mental level, with speech, language and hearing disorders are accepted, ages 6-13. Activities include aquatics, art, music, nature and dramatics. Speech and language therapy are provided. Also school-year environmental education for Delaware students of all exceptionalities.

Richard T. Garrett, Executive Director
Jennifer A. Clement, Director
Nicholas Imhoff, Business Manager

3487 Des Moines YMCA Camp
1192 166th Drive
Boone, IA 50036

515-432-7558
Fax: 515-432-5414
ycamp@dmymca.org
www.y-camp.org

For boys and girls with cancer, diabetes, asthma, cystic fibrosis, hearing impaired and other disabilities.

David Sherry, Executive Director
Mike Havlik, Program Director
Alex Kretzinger, Program Director- Summer Camp

3488 Easter Seal Kysoc
2050 Versailles Road
Lexington, KY 40504

859-254-5701
800-800-888
Fax: 502-732-0783
ek1@cardinalhill.org
www.cardinalhill.org

Designed for the fullest camping experience for children or adults with physical disabilities, blind, deaf, behavior disorders, diabetes and multiple handicaps, ages 7 and up.

Hearing Impairment/Deafness / Camps

Heide Miller, CCD, CTRS, Director
Gary Payne, President/CEO

3489 Enchanted Hills Camp
Lighthouse
214 Van Ness Avenue
San Francisco, CA 94102
415-431-1481
Fax: 415-863-7568
TTY: 415-431-4572
info@lighthouse-sf.org
lighthouse-sf.org

For blind, deaf/blind children and adults, ages 5 and up. This program offers a basic camping experience. Activities include music, art, dance, hiking and riding. Camperships are available to California residents.

Joshua A. Miele, Ph.D., President
Chris Downey, 1st Vice President
Kathleen Knox, 2nd Vice President

3490 Florida School-Deaf and Blind Summer Camp
207 N. San Marco Avenue
Saint Augustine, FL 32084
904-827-2200
800-800-344
info@fsdb.k12.fl.us
www.fsdb.k12.fl.us

The Florida School for the Deaf and the Blind hosts summer campers from all over teh state of Florida for a week of fun and adventure. FSDB's 80 acre campus is where campers participate in a variety of activities including rock climbing, archery, swimming, kayaking, team games, arts and crafts, dance music, and much more.

Jeanne Glidden Prickett, President
Nancy Bloch, Executive Director, Comm & PR
Tanya Rhodes, Executive Director, Advancement

3491 Indiana Deaf Camp
100 West 86th Street
Indianapolis, IN 46260
317-846-3404
Fax: 317-844-1034
deafcamp@hotmail.com
www.indeafcamps.org

Camp dedicated to promoting the educational, social, spiritual, physical and personal development of individuals with a hearing loss, or who are related to individuals with a hearing loss.

Nunery, President

3492 Meadowood Springs Speech and Hearing Camp
PO Box 1025
Pendleton, OR 97801
541-276-2752
Fax: 541-276-7227
info@meadowoodsprings.org
www.meadowoodsprings.org

On 143 acres in the Blue Mountains of Eastern Oregon, this camp is designed to help young people who have diagnosed clinical disorders of speech, hearing or language. A full range of activities in recreational and clinical areas is available. For cabin reservations 541-566-2191.

Rosemarie Atfield, Executive Director
Marie Story, Camp Manager
Cliff Story, Camp Manager

3493 NAD Youth Leadership Camp
National Association of the Deaf
8630 Fenton Street, Suite 820
Silver Spring, MD 20910
301-587-1788
Fax: 301-587-1791
TTY: 301-587-1791
nad.info@nad.org
www.nad.org

An annual 4-week summer program designed to foster leadership and teamwork skills in deaf and hard of hearing high school students. Campers have the opportunity to build and develop their knowledge, social interaction, and leadership skills through hands-on activities focusing on literacy, and often make life-long friends here.

Howard Rosenblum, Chief Executive Officer
Tom Well, Director of Finance
Angela Ellman, Conference Coordinator

3494 Texas Lions Camp
Lions Clubs of Texas
PO Box 290247
Kerrville, TX 78029
830-896-8500
830-896-8500
Fax: 830-896-3666
tlc@ktc.com
www.lionscamp.com

The primary purpose of Texas Lions camp is to provide, without charge, a camp for physically disabled, hearing/vision impaired and diabetic children from the State of Texas, regardless of race, religion, or national origin. Our goal is to create an atmosphere wherein campers will learn the can do philosophy and be allowed to achieve maximum personal growth and self esteem. The camp welcomes boys and girls ages 7-16.

Stephen Mabry, CEO
Doug Parker, Business Manager
Steven King, Program/Client Service Director

3495 University of Iowa - Wendell Johnson Speech and Hearing Clinic
Wendell Johnson Speech And Hearing Center
Iowa City, IA 52242
319-335-1845
Fax: 319-335-8851
www.uiowa.edu

The clinic offers assessment and remediation for disordered communication in adults and children. The clinic also offers an Intensive Summer Residential Clinic for school age children needing intervention services because of speech, language, hearing and/or reading problems.

Richard Hurtig, Professor/Chair
Ann L Michael, Clinic Director

3496 Windsor Mountain Camp
One World Way
Windsor, NH 3244
603-478-3166
jake@windsormountain.org
www.windsormountain.org

Summer camp for deaf and hard of hearing students and for hearing campers who want to learn ASL.

Jake Labovitz, Director
Dianna Hahn, Student Travel Programs
Pam Butler, Administrative Assistant

3497 Wisconsin Lions Camp
3834 County Road A
Rosholt, WI 54473
715-677-4969
Fax: 715-677-3297
TTY: 715-677-6999
wlf@wlf.info
www.wisconsinlionscamp.com

Serves children who have either a visual, hearing or mild cognitive disability. Many of the children also have multiple disabilities or medical conditions. Program activities include sailing, ropes course, bike and canoe trips, environmental education, swimming, camping, canoeing, outdoor living skills and handicrafts. ACA accredited, located in central Wisconsin, near Stevens Point.

Evett J. Hartvig, Executive Director
Dale Schroeder, Facility Director
Elizabeth Shelley, Administrative Assistant

Hemangiomas and Lymphangiomas / Description

Description

3498 HEMANGIOMAS AND LYMPHANGIOMAS

Covers these related disorders: Capillary hemangiomas, Cavernous hemangiomas, Cystic hygromas, Disseminated hemangiomatosis, Mixed hemangiomas, Port-wine stains (or salmon patches), Kasabach-merritt syndrome

Involves the following Biologic System(s):
Dermatologic Disorders

Hemangiomas are the most common benign tumors in infants. In addition, during childhood, lymphangiomas, also known as lymphatic malformations, are the second most common benign tumor affecting vessels of the body. Hemangiomas consist of an abnormal distribution of relatively small blood vessels (e.g., capillaries) due to malformation of developing fetal tissue from which the vessels arise. Lymphangiomas consist of masses of abnormally enlarged (dilated), newly formed lymph vessels, which are the channels that transport lymphatic fluid throughout the body. Lymph, a thin bodily fluid that consists of proteins, fats, and certain white blood cells (lymphocytes), accumulates in spaces between tissue cells and flows back into the bloodstream via lymph vessels.

Hemangiomas usually affect blood vessels of the skin (cutaneous hemangiomas). They most commonly develop in the head and neck regions and are rarely fully formed at birth. These tumors, which occur more frequently in females than males, are usually single growths that occur randomly for unknown reasons. However, some multigenerational families (kindreds) have been reported in which several individuals developed isolated hemangiomas. In such cases, the condition may be transmitted as an autosomal dominant trait. In addition, in rare cases, certain forms of hemangiomas may occur in association with particular underlying syndromes.

Cutaneous hemangiomas may be superficial (capillary hemangiomas), deep (cavernous hemangiomas), or both (mixed hemangiomas). Capillary hemangiomas are considered the most common type of hemangioma, affecting approximately 60 percent of patients. These hemangiomas include port-wine stains (a form of nevus flammeus) and strawberry hemangiomas (strawberry nevi). Port-wine stains are present at birth (congenital) and are typically permanent defects. These lesions consist of mature, abnormally widened capillaries; are flat (macular) with sharply defined borders; and are usually reddish purple in color. They may vary greatly in size and typically develop on the head, face, and neck areas. As patients reach adulthood, port-wine stains may darken and form elevated (papular) areas that may occasionally bleed. Port-wine stains must be differentiated from salmon patches, which are flat, salmon-colored lesions that are typically present during infancy on certain facial areas, such as over the eyelids, on the middle of the forehead, or between the eyes. Salmon patches typically fade completely over time. Port-wine stains may be an isolated condition or may occur in association with several rare underlying syndromes (e.g., Klippel-Trenaunay-Weber syndrome, Sturge-Weber syndrome, etc.). Treatment may include a variety of measures, such as laser therapy, destruction of affected tissue through the use of extreme cold (cryosurgery), surgical removal (excision), transplantation of skin tissues (grafting), or masking with cosmetics.

Strawberry hemangiomas are dull or bright red and elevated, have clearly defined borders, and consist of immature capillaries. The lesions, which may develop as single or multiple growths, may affect any area of the body; however, they are most common on the scalp, face, chest, or back. Strawberry hemangiomas usually appear within approximately two months after birth. In most patients, the hemangiomas initially grow rapidly, cease such growth (stationary phase), and then gradually begin to regress in size (involution). After the lesions have reduced in size, approximately 10 percent of patients have residual discoloration or puckering of affected skin. In rare cases, complications associated with strawberry hemangiomas may include infection; destruction of the skin's surface, resulting in open sores and inflammation (ulceration); bleeding (hemorrhaging); or extensive growth that interferes with necessary functions, such as breathing difficulties due to tumor growth affecting the airways. Because most strawberry hemangiomas spontaneously regress, treatment typically consists of careful, ongoing observation. However, if hemangiomas rapidly grow, potentially causing tissue destruction, removal, using elastic bandages or other measures, may be recommended in selected patients. If there is rapid growth that may ultimately cause life-threatening complications, treatment may include the administration of corticosteroids by injection or mouth or therapy with an artificial (synthetic) form of interferon (interferon alpha-2a). Interferons are natural proteins that are produced by the body's immune system in response to certain invading viruses or other stimuli. In the most severe cases, radiation therapy may be necessary. Other treatment is symptomatic and supportive.

Cavernous hemangiomas may be firm or form cysts. The skin overlying such hemangiomas is often bluish in color. However, if physicians suspect that underlying structures may be affected, specialized imaging techniques, such as CT scanning or ultrasonography, are conducted to detect and characterize such involvement. Rarely, some patients develop multiple hemangiomas. In such cases, affected children may have numerous small, red or purplish, raised hemangiomas on the skin. In addition, internal hemangiomas may be present involving certain organs, particularly the liver, lungs, brain and spinal cord, and organs of the gastrointestinal tract. In such cases, affected children are said to have disseminated hemangiomatosis. Life-threatening complications may potentially arise due to hemorrhage, tissue compression (e.g., neural tissue compression), obstruction of the airways, or an inability of the heart to effectively pump blood to the lungs and throughout the body (heart failure). In some cases, multiple internal and cutaneous hemangiomas occur in association with certain rare, underlying syndromes (e.g., macrocephaly with pseudopapilledema).

Lymphangiomas may be localized or widely distributed growths that, in some cases, may have hemangioma-like components. In almost all affected children, lymphangiomas are apparent by approximately age three. Lymphangiomas most commonly develop in the neck and facial regions, in the chest area (thorax), or under the arms (axillae). For example, some affected children may have an abnormal cystic growth consisting of dilated lymph vessels beneath the skin in the neck area (cystic hygroma). Lymphangiomas, such as cystic hygroma, may occur as isolated findings or in association with certain underlying syndromes (e.g., Noonan syndrome). Unlike hemangiomas, lymphangiomas rarely spontaneously regress. In some patients, they may expand in size and may obstruct the gastrointestinal tract or the airways, potentially causing life-threatening complications without appropriate treatment. Because most lymphangiomas are relatively widely distributed (diffuse), treatment often includes removal of the growths in several stages (staged surgical resection). Additional treatment includes symptomatic and supportive measures.

Government Agencies

3499 **NIH/National Institute of Arthritis and Musculoskeletal and Skin Diseases**
1 AMS Circle
Bethesda, MD 20892
301-495-4484
877-226-4267
Fax: 301-718-6366
TTY: 301-565-2966
niamsinfo@mail.nih.gov
www.niams.nih.gov

The mission of the NIAMS, a part of the NIH, is to support research into the causes, treatment and prevention of arthritis and musculoskeletal and skin diseases, the training of basic and clinical scientists to carry out this research, and the dissemination of information on research progress in these diseases.

Lindsey A. Criswell, MD, Director
Rick Phillips, Executive Officer

National Associations & Support Groups

3500 **American Academy of Dermatology**
P.O. Box 1968
Des Plaines, IL 60017
847-240-1280
888-462-3376
mrc@aad.org
www.aad.org

To promote and advance the art of medicine and surgery of the skin; promote the highest possible standards in clinical practice, education and research in dermatology and related disciplines.

3501 **American Academy of Pediatrics**
345 Park Blvd
Itasca, IL 60143
800-433-9016
Fax: 847-434-8000
mcc@aap.org
www.aap.org

The American Academy of Pediatrics and its member pediatricians are committed to the attainment of optimal physical, mental and social health and well-being for all infants, children, adolescents, and young adults.

Lynn Olson, PhD, VP, Research
Mark Del Monte, JD, CEO/Executive VP
Vera Tait, MD, FAAP, Chief Medical Officer

3502 **American Skin Association**
335 Madison Avenue, 22nd Floor
New York, NY 10017
212-889-4858
info@americanskin.org
www.americanskin.org

The American Skin Association is the only volunteer led health organization dedicated through research, education and advocacy to saving lives and alleviating human suffering caused by the full spectrum of skin disorders.

Kathleen Reichert, Executive Vice President
Kristin Ludl, Operations Manager

3503 **Society for Pediatric Dermatology**
8365 Keystone Crossing, Ste 107
Indianapolis, IN 46240
317-202-0224
Fax: 317-205-9481
info@pedsderm.net
www.pedsderm.net

The objective of the Society is to promote, develop and advance education, research and care of skin disease in all pediatric age groups.

Kent Lindeman, Executive Director

3504 **Vascular Birthmarks Foundation**
PO Box 106
Latham, NY 12110
877-823-4646
vbfpresident@gmail.com
www.birthmark.org

A non-profit organization that provides support and informational resources for individuals affected by hemangiomas, port wine stains, and other vascular birthmarks and tumors.

Linda Rozell-Shannon, President & Founder

Libraries & Resource Centers

3505 **Children's Center for Cancer and Blood Disorders**
University of South Carolina School of Medicine
5 Richland Memorial Park
Columbia, SC 29203
803-434-3533

Joint clinical and basic research of juvenile cancer and blood disorders.

Fauni Lowe, Manager

Web Sites

3506 **Vascular Anomalies Center**
www.hemangioma.org/

www.hemangioma.org/

Provide the most up-to-date information to parents and patients as well as give the resources to help understand vascular anomaly.

Book Publishers

3507 **Sturge-Weber Syndrome: A Resource Guide for a Reason, a Season and a Lifetime**
Sturge-Weber Foundation
PO Box 418
Mt. Freedom, NJ 07970
973-895-4445
800-627-5482
Fax: 973-895-4846
www.sturge-weber.com

Covers most of the issues and concerns of parents and individuals with SWS, PWS and KT in short essays and chapters that provide practical and helpful advice

95 pages Paperback
ISBN: 0-967048-40-0

Carol Buck, Patient/Family Services Director
Lauris Partizian, Information Services Manager

Journals

3508 **Pediatric Dermatology Journal**
Society for Pediatric Dermatology
8365 Keystone Crossing, Suite 107
Indianapolis, IN 46240
317-202-0224
Fax: 317-205-9481
info@pedsderm.net
www.pedsderm.net

Answers the need for new ideas and strategies for today's pediatrician or dermatologist.

6 issues/yr

Kent Lindeman, Executive Director

Hemolytic Disease of the Newborn / Description

Description

3509 HEMOLYTIC DISEASE OF THE NEWBORN
Synonyms: Erythroblastosis fetalis, Erythroblastosis neonatorum
Involves the following Biologic System(s):
Hematologic and Oncologic Disorders, Neonatal and Infant Disorders

Hemolytic disease of the newborn, also known as erythroblastosis neonatorum or erythroblastosis fetalis, is characterized by destruction of a newborn's red blood cells by antibodies that crossed the placenta from the mother's bloodstream during pregnancy. Antibodies are produced by certain white blood cells in response to foreign proteins (antigens) that are present in some cells and invading microorganisms. In hemolytic disease of the newborn the mother's immune system treats the baby's blood cells as foreign and makes antibodies against them. In most cases, the condition occurs when a developing fetus has Rh-positive blood (i.e., inherited from the father), but the mother has Rh-negative blood.

In approximately 85 percent of individuals, red blood cells contain an antigen called the Rh factor. Those with this antigen are said to have Rh-positive blood, whereas those without the antigen have Rh-negative blood. The blood plasma does not naturally contain antibodies to inactivate or destroy the Rh antigen (anti-Rh antibodies). However, if a fetus has Rh-positive blood and the mother is Rh negative, the presence of the Rh factor in the fetus' red blood cells causes the mother's body to produce anti-Rh antibodies. If the woman becomes pregnant again and the developing fetus has Rh-positive blood, the mother's antibodies may react with the fetus' Rh-positive cells, resulting in hemolysis (breakdown of red blood cells). In many cases, mothers who are known to have Rh-negative blood may be treated with a protein to help prevent them from producing anti-Rh antibodies (e.g., injection of human anti-D globulin), thereby lowering the risk of erythroblastosis fetalis during future pregnancies.

In infants affected by hemolytic disease of the newborn, associated symptoms and findings may vary. These may range from a mild breakdown of red blood cells to severely low levels of circulating red blood cells (anemia); paleness of the skin (pallor); tiny reddish, purplish spots on the skin (petechiae) due to abnormal bleeding under the skin's surface; enlargement of the liver and spleen (hepatosplenomegaly); or development of abnormal yellowish coloring of the mucous membranes, whites of the eyes, and skin (jaundice). In extremely severe cases, affected newborns may experience low levels of oxygen supply (hypoxia), difficulty breathing (respiratory distress), heart (cardiac) failure, severe abnormal accumulations of fluid in body tissues and cavities (hydrops), and potentially life-threatening complications. Depending upon the severity of the condition, treatment may include transfusions (e.g., partial or full exchange transfusions with Rh-negative blood) and supportive measures, such as ventilation assistance.

Hemolytic disease of the newborn may also result due to other blood type incompatibilities, primarily if the mother is type O and the developing fetus is type A or B. However, the condition develops in only about 10 percent of such cases of ABO incompatibility. In addition, the condition is typically less severe than that associated with Rh incompatibility. In cases of ABO blood type incompatibility, the development of jaundice approximately a day after birth may be the only associated symptom.

Government Agencies

3510 NIH/ Eunice Kennedy Shriver National Institute of Child Health & Human Development
P.O. Box 3006
Rockville, MD 20847
800-370-2943
Fax: 866-760-5947
www.nichd.nih.gov

Conducts and supports research on topics related to the health of children, adults, families and populations. Some of these topics include: developmental disabilities, growth and development, infant death, reproductive health and birth defects.

Diana W. Bianchi, Director
Alison Cernich, PhD, Deputy Director

3511 NIH/National Heart, Lung and Blood Institute
31 Center Drive, Bldg 31
Bethesda, MD 20824
877-645-2448
www.nhlbi.nih.gov

Primary responsibility of this organization is the scientific investigation of heart, blood vessel, lung and blood disorders. Oversees research, demonstration, prevention, education, control and training activities in these fields and emphasizes the prevention and control of heart diseases.

Gary H. Gibbons, MD, Director
Kate O'Sullivan, Executive Officer

National Associations & Support Groups

3512 American Academy of Pediatrics
345 Park Blvd
Itasca, IL 60143
800-433-9016
Fax: 847-434-8000
mcc@aap.org
www.aap.org

The American Academy of Pediatrics and its member pediatricians are committed to the attainment of optimal physical, mental and social health and well-being for all infants, children, adolescents, and young adults.

Lynn Olson, PhD, VP, Research
Mark Del Monte, JD, CEO/Executive VP
Vera Tait, MD, FAAP, Chief Medical Officer

3513 American Autoimmune Related Diseases Association
19176 Hall Road, Suite 130
Clinton, MI 48038
586-776-3900
aarda@aarda.org
www.aarda.org

The American Autoimmune Related Diseases Association is dedicated to the eradication of autoimmune diseases and the alleviation of suffering and the socioeconomic impact of autoimmunity through fostering and facilitating collaboration in the areas of education, public awareness, research, and patient services in an effective, ethical and efficient manner.

Lilly Stairs, Interim President/CEO
Laura Simpson, COO

Web Sites

3514 American Autoimmune Related Diseases Association
www.aarda.org

586-776-3900
aarda@aarda.org
www.aarda.org

The American Autoimmune Related Diseases Association is dedicated to the eradication of autoimmune diseases and the alleviation of suffering and the socioeconomic impact of autoimmunity through fostering and facilitating collaboration in the areas of education, public awareness, research, and patient services in an effective, ethical and efficient manner.

3515 NIH/National Institutes of Health-Genetic & Rare Diseases Information Ctr (GARD)
PO Box 8126
Gaithersburg, MD 20898
301-251-4925
888-205-2311
Fax: 301-251-4911
anne.pariser@nih.gov
rarediseases.info.nih.gov/

Provides the public with information that is current, reliable and easy to understand about rare and genetic diseases in both English and Spanish.

Anne Pariser, MD, Director

3516 Online Mendelian Inheritance in Man
McKusick-Nathans Institue of Genetic Medicine-JHU
Baltimore, MD 21205
www.omim.org

This database is a catalog of human genes and genetic disorders.

Ada Hamosh, MD, Scientific Director

Hemophilia / Description

Description

3517 HEMOPHILIA

Synonyms: AHF, Antihemophilic factor deficiency, Classic hemophilia, Factor VIII deficiency, Hemophilia A

Covers these related disorders: Hemophilia A, Hemophilia B (Christmas disease; Factor IX deficiency), Von Willebrand's disease (Factor VIIIR deficiency)

Involves the following Biologic System(s):

Hematologic and Oncologic Disorders

The term hemophilia refers to a group of bleeding disorders including hemophilia A, hemophilia B, and von Willebrand's disease. Each of these diseases is characterized by the deficiency of a specific blood-clotting protein (factor). Hemophilia A, the most common form of the disease, affects approximately 80 percent of people with hemophilia and is caused by a deficiency of factor VIII. Hemophilia B, accounting for approximately 12 to 15 percent of all cases, results from a deficiency in clotting factor IX. In both forms of hemophilia, the severity of the disease and associated symptoms depend upon the level of coagulating activity of the individual clotting factors; the lower the activity of these factors, the more severe the disease. The most common symptoms, usually appearing at about 18 months when the child becomes more physically active, include easy bruising and bleeding into the joints (hemarthrosis) and muscles. Pain and swelling in the ankles, knees, and elbows may follow and eventually lead to degenerative changes and limited range of motion. Bleeding episodes may occur after injury, trauma, minor surgery, and, in some cases, for no apparent reason (spontaneously). Von Willebrand's disease involves a deficiency of factor VIIIR and is characterized by easy bruising, nose bleeds and bleeding into the gastrointestinal tract. In affected females, excessive uterine bleeding may occur during menstruation or childbirth. In some patients, blood may be present in the urine (hematuria). Unlike hemophilia A or B, bleeding into the joints is rare and the disorder seems to improve with advancing age.

Treatment of hemophilia A and B includes transfusions of appropriate clotting factor when a bleeding episode occurs. These concentrates may also be regularly self-administered to prevent bleeds. Other preventive measures may include the administration of certain clot-aiding drugs before surgery, the avoidance of certain drugs that may exacerbate bleeding problems, and avoidance of participation in contact sports or other similar activities that could provoke a bleeding episode. The treatment of von Willebrand's disease may include the infusion of DDAVP or VW protein prior to surgery or childbirth.

Hemophilia A and hemophilia B are transmitted as x-linked recessive traits and affect males almost exclusively. Approximately 10 males out of every 100,000 are born with hemophilia A, while the rate of occurrence of hemophilia B is about two males out of every 100,000. For the most part, von Willebrand's disease is inherited as an autosomal dominant disorder. In rare instances, the disease may be inherited as a recessive gene. Children with hemophilia who may have received transfusions of blood or blood products before HIV blood-screening became standard in 1985 may have unwittingly become infected by receiving contaminated blood.

National Associations & Support Groups

3518 American Academy of Pediatrics
345 Park Blvd
Itasca, IL 60143

800-433-9016
Fax: 847-434-8000
mcc@aap.org
www.aap.org

The American Academy of Pediatrics and its member pediatricians are committed to the attainment of optimal physical, mental and social health and well-being for all infants, children, adolescents, and young adults.

Lynn Olson, PhD, VP, Research
Mark Del Monte, JD, CEO/Executive VP
Vera Tait, MD, FAAP, Chief Medical Officer

3519 Baxter Healthcare Hyland Division
One Baxter Parkway
Deerfield, IL 60015

www.baxter.com

Government affairs office that monitors and selectively lobbies on issues relating to Medicare, Medicaid, orphan drugs and other subjects relating to hemophilia.

3520 Children's Cancer & Blood Foundation
466 Lexington Avenue, 16th Floor
New York, NY 10017

info@childrenscbf.org
www.childrenscbf.org

The foundation's major emphasis is on blood diseases affecting children: leukemia, thalassemia, hemophilia, sickle cell anemia, platelet disorders. retinoblastoma and AIDS.

Les J. Lieberman, Co-Chairman & Co-President
Ronald J. Iervolino, Co-Chairman & Co-President

3521 National Hemophilia Foundation
7 Penn Plaza, Suite 1204
New York, NY 10001

212-328-3700
888-463-6643
Fax: 212-328-3777
info@hemophilia.org
www.hemophilia.org

Since 1948, NHF has supported people with inherited blood disorders through research, education, and advocacy.

Leonard Valentino, MD, Presient & CEO
Dawn Rotellini, Chief Operating Officer
Peter Harvey, Chief Business Officer

State Agencies & Support Groups

Arkansas

3522 Hemophilia Center of Arkansas
Arkansas Children's Hospital
1 Children's Way, PO Box 3591
Little Rock, AR 72202

501-364-1100
TDD: 501-364-1184
www.archildrens.org

Patients with coagulation disorders can be diagnosed and evaluated by a group of physicians, physical therapists, dentists, psychologists and geneticists to provide education, prevention and continuity of care. The Hemophilia Center of Arkansas offers the latest diagnosis, prevention and treatment modalities for children and adults.

David Becton, MD, Medical Director

California

3523 Hemophilia Association of San Diego County
3550 Camino Del Rio N, Suite 105
San Diego, CA 92108

619-325-3570
Fax: 619-325-4350
info@hasdc.org
www.hasdc.org

Hemophilia / State Agencies & Support Groups

An organization devoted to improving the quality of life for persons affected with bleeding disorders and their complications. This is accomplished through outreach development, educational programs, informational literature, support services and patient referrals.

Michael Brown, Esq., President
Heather Masserly, Director at Large
Judy Faitek, Director at Large

3524 Hemophilia Foundation of Northern California
6400 Hollis St Suite 6
Emeryville, CA 94608
ÿ51-65-332
888-749-4362
Fax: 510-658-3384
execadmin@hfnconline.org
www.hemofoundation.org

An organization devoted to improving the quality of life for persons affected with bleeding disorders and their complications. This is accomplished through outreach development, educational programs, informational literature, support services and patient referrals.

Bethane Deuel, President
Ben Martin, Secretary
Hari Young, Treasurer

3525 Hemophilia Foundation of Southern California
6720 Melrose Avenue
Hollywood, CA 90038
323-525-0440
800-371-4123
Fax: 323-525-0445
hfsc@hemosocal.org
www.hemosocal.org

An organization devoted to improving the quality of life for persons affected with bleeding disorders and their complications. This is accomplished through outreach development, educational programs, informational literature, support services and patient referrals.

Tamara Kato, President
Judy Mangione, Secretary
Michael Franzen, Treasurer

Colorado

3526 Hemophilia Society of Colorado
2465 Sheridan Blvd.
Edgewater, CO 80214
720-626-1263
888-687-2568
Fax: 303-629-7035
info@cohemo.org
www.cohemo.org

An organization devoted to improving the quality of life for persons affected with bleeding disorders and their complications. This is accomplished through outreach development, educational programs, informational literature, support services and patient referrals.

Larry Hoyle, Manager
Daniel Reilly, President
Sean Perkins, Development Coordinator

Florida

3527 Hemophilia Foundation of Greater Florida
1350 N Orange Avenue, Suite 227
Winter Park, FL 32789
407-629-0000
800-293-6527
Fax: 407-629-9600
www.hemophiliaflorida.org

An organization devoted to improving the quality of life for persons affected with bleeding disorders and their complications. This is accomplished through outreach development, educational programs, informational literature, support services and patient referrals.

Alan Apte, VP
Ron Sachs, President
Mike Berkman, Secretary

Georgia

3528 Hemophilia Foundation of Georgia
8800 Roswell Road, Suite 170, PO Box 1844
Atlanta, GA 30350
770-518-8272
800-866-4366
Fax: 770-518-3310
mail@hog.org
www.hog.org

An organization devoted to improving the quality of life for persons affected with bleeding disorders and their complications. This is accomplished through outreach development, educational programs, informational literature, support services and patient referrals.

Andrew Maurer, Chief Governance Officer
Nick Blackmon, Vice CGO
Jonathan Lawrie, Secretary

Hawaii

3529 Hemophilia Foundation of Hawaii
1164 Bishop Street, Suite 1501
Honolulu, HI 96813
281-379-4600
Fax: 281-379-1450
www.bleedingdisorders.org

An organization devoted to improving the quality of life for persons affected with bleeding disorders and their complications. This is accomplished through outreach development, educational programs, informational literature, support services and patient referrals.

Rita Gonzales, President

Idaho

3530 Hemophilia Foundation of Idaho
4696 Overland Road, Suite 234
Boise, ID 83705
208-344-4476
866-453-4476
Fax: 208-344-4476
www.idahoblood.org

An organization devoted to improving the quality of life for persons affected with bleeding disorders and their complications. This is accomplished through outreach development, educational programs, informational literature, support services and patient referrals.

Shane Bell, President
Ryan Hein, VP
Taryn Magrini, Executive Director

Illinois

3531 Hemophilia Foundation of Illinois
210 S. DesPlaines St, PO Box 5500
Chicago, IL 60661
312-427-1495
Fax: 312-427-1602
info@bdai.org
www.hemophiliaillinois.org

An organization devoted to improving the quality of life for persons affected with bleeding disorders and their complications. This is accomplished through outreach development, educational programs, informational literature, support services and patient referrals.

Bill Eftax, President
Eric Sary, VP
Robert Stewart, Treasurer

Indiana

3532 Hemophilia Foundation of Indiana
5172 E. 65th Street, Suite 105
Indianapolis, IN 46220
317-570-0039
800-241-2873
Fax: 317-396-0058
www.hemophiliaofindiana.org

Hemophilia / State Agencies & Support Groups

An organization devoted to improving the quality of life for persons affected with bleeding disorders and their complications. This is accomplished through outreach development, educational programs, informational literature, support services and patient referrals.

Kasey Shade, President
Joseph McKamey, VP
Melissa Breedlove, Secretary

Kentucky

3533 Kentucky Hemophilia Foundation
1850 Taylor Avenue, Suite 2
Louisville, KY 40213
502-456-3233
800-582-2873
Fax: 502-456-3234
info@kyhemo.org
www.kyhemo.org

An organization devoted to improving the quality of life for persons affected with bleeding disorders and their complications. This is accomplished through outreach development, educational programs, informational literature, support services and patient referrals.

Ursela Lacer, Executive Director

Maryland

3534 Hemophilia Foundation of Maryland
13 Class Court
Parkville, MD 21234
410-661-2307
800-964-3131
Fax: 410-661-2308
Miller8043@comcast.net
www.hfmonline.org

An organization devoted to improving the quality of life for persons affected with bleeding disorders and their complications. This is accomplished through outreach development, educational programs, informational literature, support services and patient referrals.

Harvey Gates, President
Ryan Melton, VP
Annette Maurits, Secretary

Michigan

3535 Hemophilia Foundation of Michigan
1921 W Michigan Avenue
Ypsilanti, MI 48197
734-544-0015
800-482-3041
Fax: 734-544-0095
harner@hfmich.org
www.hfmich.org

An organization devoted to improving the quality of life for persons affected with bleeding disorders and their complications. This is accomplished through outreach development, educational programs, informational literature, support services and patient referrals.

Ivan Harner, Executive Director
Calvin DeKuiper, President
Amy Denton, VP

Minnesota

3536 Hemophilia Foundation of Minnesota and the Dakotas
750 S Plaza Drive, Suite 207
Mendota Heights, MN 55120
651-406-8655
800-994-4363
Fax: 651-406-8656
hemophiliafoundation@visi.com
www.hfmd.org

An organization devoted to improving the quality of life for persons affected with bleeding disorders and their complications. This is accomplished through outreach development, educational programs, informational literature, support services and patient referrals.

John Schulte, President
Mike Neubert, VP
Elizabeth Myers, Secretary

Mississippi

3537 Mississippi Hemophilia Foundation
36 Avery Circle, PO Box 13608
Jackson, MS 39236
601-957-2706
patty8501@aol.com
www.mshemophilia.com

An organization devoted to improving the quality of life for persons affected with bleeding disorders and their complications. This is accomplished through outreach development, educational programs, informational literature, support services and patient referrals.

Haley Jones, President
Leslee Londen, VP
Patty Lyons, Treasurer

Nebraska

3538 Nebraska Chapter of the National Hemophilia Foundation
215 Centennial Mail South, Suite 512
Lincoln, NE 68508
402-742-5663
Fax: 402-742-5677
office@nebraskanhf.org
www.nebraskanhf.org

An organization devoted to improving the quality of life for persons affected with bleeding disorders and their complications. This is accomplished through outreach development, educational programs, informational literature, support services and patient referrals.

Jason Everts, President
Karie Quintana, VP
Mollie Lovell, Secretary

New York

3539 Bleeding Disorders Association of Northeastern New York
BDANENY, PO Box 947
Rensselaer, NY 12144
518-782-9787
Fax: 518-356-5612
bdaneny@bdaneny.org
www.bdaneny.org

Formerly known as the Upper Hudson Valley Chapter of the National Hemophilia Foundation. The Association endeavors to meet the diverse needs of a geographically dispersed community through a variety of programs, including; emergency financial support, scholarships, Camp High Hopes, Double Hole in the Woods Ranch, HIV/AIDS education, outreach and support, and recreational community activities.

Deborah Huskie, Co-Executive Director
Kevin Pelletier, Co-Executive Director
David Huskie, President

3540 Hemophilia Center of Western New York
936 Delaware Avenue, Suite 300
Buffalo, NY 14209
716-896-2470
866-434-6551
Fax: 716-218-4010
www.hemophiliawny.com

A nonprofit, licensed diagnostic and treatment center. It offers a variety of services for persons with hemophilia and other herditary blood disorders ensuring that the patient is cared for at all times whether at the hospital, at home, at the center at school or on the job.

Robert Long, Chairman
Marcia Gellin, VP
Mary Haggerty, VP

3541 Mary M Gooley Hemophilia Center of the National Hemophilia Foundation
1415 Portland Avenue, Suite 500
Rochester, NY 14621
585-922-5700
Fax: 585-922-5775
Robert.Fox@viahealth.org
www.hemocenter.org

Specialized diagnostic testing, expert medical evaluation and diagnosis, personal counseling and support groups, home care treatment training, routine and urgent care, education of school and daycare personnel, research to advance knowledge, improve treatment and enhance quality of life for patients and families.

Robert Fox, President
Linda Magliocco, Sr. VP
Jennifer LaFranco, VP

North Carolina

3542 **Hemophila Foundation of North Carolina**
260 Town Hall Dr., Suite A
Morrisville, NC 27560

336-289-4446
880-990-5557
Fax: 336-725-4873
www.hemophilia-nc.org

An organization devoted to improving the quality of life for persons affected with bleeding disorders and their complications. This is accomplished through outreach development, educational programs, informational literature, support services and patient referrals.

Steven Peretti, President
Leonard Poe, VP
Kathy Register, Treasurer

Ohio

3543 **Central Ohio Chapter of the National Hemophilia Foundation**
PO Box 345
Worthington, OH 43085

614-457-0027
800-847-0345
steje08@aol.com
www.nhfcentralohio.org

An organization devoted to improving the quality of life for persons affected with bleeding disorders and their complications. This is accomplished through outreach development, educational programs, informational literature, support services and patient referrals.

Jeff Stewart, President
Tracy Kauffman, Treasurer
Anish Mistry, Secretary

3544 **Northern Ohio Chapter of the National Hemophilia Foundation**
One Independence Place
5000 Rockside Road, Suite 230
Independence, OH 44131

216-834-0051
800-554-4366
Fax: 216-834-0055
www.nohf.org

The mission is to enhance the quality of life for people with genetic bleeding disorders and their families, through advocacy, education, research and other constituency services.

Marlene Piatak, President
Michelle Zawadski, VP
Katey Vanderwyst, Treasurer

3545 **Southwestern Ohio Chapter of the National Hemophilia Foundation**
82 Elva Court, Suite B
Dayton, OH 45377

937-415-0644
Fax: 937-415-0604
SWOF@aol.com

Serving people with hemophilia and blood clotting disorders in an 11 county area. Dedicated to offering people and their families; educational opportunities about the physical, psychological and social aspects of these disorders. Workshops and seminars are regularly offered to address these issues. Offers support groups, volunteer services, telephone and walk-in education, information, counseling and referrals.

Dena M Shephard, President

3546 **Tri-State Bleeding Disorders Chapter of the National Hemophilia Foundation**
635 W 7th Street, Suite 407
Cincinnati, OH 45203

513-961-4366
Fax: 513-961-1740
hemophilia@fuse.net
www.tsbdf.com

Formerly known as the Greater Cincinnati/Northern Kentucky Chapter of the National Hemophilia Foundation. An organization devoted to improve the quality of life for persons affected with bleeding disorders and their complications. This is accomplished through outreach development, educational programs, informational literature, support services and patient referrals.

Lisa Raterman, Executive Director
Jeff Reichert, President
Andy Proeschel, Secretary

Oregon

3547 **Hemophilia Foundation of Oregon**
10940 SW Barnes Rd #129
Portland, OR 97225

503-297-7207
Fax: 503-297-0127
info@hemophiliaoregon.org
www.hemophiliaoregon.org

An organization devoted to improving the quality of life for persons affected with bleeding disorders and their complications. This is accomplished through outreach development, educational programs, informational literature, support services and patient referrals.

Linda Charles, President
Dave Worthington, Vice President

Pennsylvania

3548 **Delaware Valley Chapter of the National Hemophilia Foundation**
14 E. 6th St. First Floor
Lansdale, PA 19446

215-393-3611
Fax: 215-393-9419
hemophilia@navpoint.com
www.hemophiliasupport.org

An organization devoted to improving the quality of life for persons affected with bleeding disorders and their complications. This is accomplished through outreach development, educational programs, informational literature, support services and patient referrals.

Thomas Galvin, President
William Widerman, Vice President
Jon Worthington, Treasurer

3549 **Western Pennsylvania Chapter of The National Hemophilia Foundation**
532 S Aiken Avenue, Suite 102
Pittsburgh, PA 15232

412-683-2231
Fax: 412-683-2568

Brings together and serves as a focal point for those segments of the community most concerned with hemophilia. They include medical and social service providers, people with hemophilia and their families, educators and the general public. This chapter combines service, education and advocacy programs.

Kerry Fatula, Executive Director
Ida McFarren, President

South Carolina

3550 **Hemophilia Association of South Carolina**
PO Box 3874
Sumter, SC 29151

864-350-9941
888-829-4849
Fax: 888-829-4849
www.hemophiliaofsouthcarolina.net

Hemophilia / Libraries & Resource Centers

An organization devoted to improving the quality of life for persons affected with bleeding disorders and their complications. This is accomplished through outreach development, educational programs, informational literature, support services and patient referrals.

Mark Eichelberger, President
Brandy Stewart, Vice President

Tennessee

3551 Tennesse Hemophilia & Bleeding Disorders Foundation
1819 Ward Drive, Suite 102
Murfreesboro, TN 37129
615-900-1486
888-703-3269
Fax: 615-900-1487
mail@thbdf.org
www.thbdf.org

Offers a hemophilia clinic, social workers and consultants, a state hemophilia program, blood donor programs, counseling programs, genetic counseling, literature and resources, summer camp, grants and more for the hemophilia and HIV/AIDS community.

Kent Russ, President
John Snook, West-TN VP
Jerry Duntop, East-TN VP

Texas

3552 Texas Central Chapter of the National Hemophilia Foundation
12700 Hillcrest Road, Suite 191
Dallas, TX 75230
972-386-3865
Fax: 214-654-9954
mail@texcen.org
www.texcen.org

A group of volunteers seeking solutions to the various aspects of the hemophilia problem. Supports blood drives, sponsors a summer camp for hemophiliac children, conducts educational member meetings, arranges for genetic counseling and sponsors group support meetings.

Shannon Brush, President
Jacob Banker, Vice President
David Simmons, Treasurer

Utah

3553 Utah Chapter of the National Hemophilia Foundation
772 East 3300 South, Suite 210
Salt Lake City, UT 84106
801-484-0325
877-INF- VWD
Fax: 801-484-2488
smuir@hemophiliautah.org
www.hemophiliautah.org

Offers educational information, pamphlets, fundraising events and more for persons and families affected by hemophilia.

Scott Muir, Executive Director
Reg Ecker, President
Lynn Barker, VP

Virginia

3554 Hemophilia Association of the Capital Area
10560 Main Street, Suite 419
Fairfax, VA 22030
703-267-6502
Fax: 703-352-2145
admin@hacacares.org
www.hacacares.org

A nonprofit organization serving persons with bleeding disorders and their families in northern Virginia, Washington, DC and Montgomery and Prince George's Counties in Maryland. The mission is to improve the quality of life for persons with hemophilia and Von Willebrand's disease and their families, to educate, to act as an advocate, to provide member services and to raise money to fulfill all these purposes.

Sandi Qualley, Executive Director
Miriam Goldstein, President
Paul Brayshaw, VP

Washington

3555 Bleeding Disorders Foundation of Washington
9639 Firdale Ave, Ste A
Edmunds, WA 98020
206-533-1660
Fax: 206-533-1686
general@bdfwa.org
www.bdfwa.org

An organization devoted to improving the quality of life for persons affected with bleeding disorders and their complications. This is accomplished through outreach development, educational programs, informational literature, support services and patient referrals.

Regina Timmons, Executive Director
Reid Morgan, President
Caprice Sauter, Board President

3556 Hemophilia Foundation of Washington
PO Box 4565
West Richland, WA 99353
509-967-0203
iebd4u@verizon.net

The Foundation's mission is to provide a conduit for education and information, advocate for excellent medical care, and support affected individuals and their families via peer outreach programs and special events

Jill McCary, President
Debbie Campeau, Executive Director

Wisconsin

3557 Great Lakes Hemophilia Foundation
638 N 18th Street, Suite 108
Milwaukee, WI 53233
414-257-0200
888-797-4543
Fax: 414-257-1225
info@glhf.org
www.glfh.org

The only Wisconsin organization that addresses the physical, emotional, social and financial needs of individuals affected by hemophilia. This chapter supports high-quality, cost-effective programs for patient care, education, research and public awareness.

Bill Finn, President
Jeff Koopmeiners, VP
David Osswald, Secretary

Libraries & Resource Centers

Alabama

3558 Alabama Department of Rehabilitation Services
602 S Lawrence St.
Montgomery, AL 36104
334-293-7500
800-441-7607
Fax: 334-293-7383
www.rehab.state.al.us

Mission is to enable children and adolescents with special health needs and adults with hemophilia to achieve their maximum potential within a community-based, family-centered, comprehensive, culturally sensitive and coordinated system of services.

Cary Boswell, Ed.D, Director

Indiana

3559 Riley Hemophilia and Thrombophilia Center
702 Barnhill Drive, ROC 4270
Indianapolis, IN 46202
317-274-2153
800-769-2848
Fax: 317-278-3751
anholcom@iupui.edu
www.rileypeds.org

Hemophilia / Research Centers

We strive to improve the health and health care of children by developing and applying best scientific evidence and methods in health services research and informatics.

Richard Schreiner, MD, Chairman of Pediatrics
Anna Holcomb, Executive Director

Wisconsin

3560 Hemophilia Outreach Center
2060 Bellevue St
Green Bay, WI 54311
920-965-0606
800-992-6026
Fax: 920-965-0607
info@hemophiliaoutreach.org
www.hemophiliaoutreach.org

A comprehensive treatment center serving individuals and families with bleeding disorders. A facility maintained and administered through the collaboration of lay people, professionals, medical providers, consumers and families. Offering a variety of programs and services in a family-oriented, safe environment directed toward a holistic approach to wellness and to living a full life, including coordinating comprehensive care, consumer advocacy and financial and emotional support.

Katie Kralovetz, Executive Director

Research Centers

3561 Albany New York Regional Comprehensive Hemophilia Treatment Center
Albany Medical College
43 New Scotland Avenue
Albany, NY 12208
518-262-3125
800-773-7080
Fax: 518-262-6320
ALBANYHTC@mail.amc.edu
www.amc.edu/patient/services/hemophilia

Providing comprehensive health care for patients with mild to severe hemophilia A, hemophilia B, von Willebrand's disease and thrombophilia in the Albany, New York region.

Barbara Leckerling, Administrator
Joanne Porter, MD, Director

3562 Blood Research Institute of Saint Michael's Medical Center
Cathedral Healthcare System
111 Central Avenue
Newark, NJ 07102
973-877-5000
Fax: 973-877-5466
www.smmcnj.org

Dedicated to research and the treatment of blood-related disorders and cancers, the Blood Research Institute is a multi-disciplinary unit of the hematology/oncology departments.

Yale S Arkel, MD

3563 Boston Hemophilia Center
Children's Hospital Boston
300 Longwood Avenue, Fegan 7
Boston, MA 02115
617-355-4977
Fax: 617-730-0641
www.childrenshosptial.org

A federally funded hemophilia treatment center, the program offers comprehensive care to people with hemophilia and their families. Services range from medical treatment, counseling and support to discounts on clotting-factor replacement and other products that people with hemophilia require.

Haroon Patel

3564 Cancer & Blood Diseases Institute
Cincinnati Children's Hospital Medical Center
3333 Burnet Avenue, PO Box 3026
Cincinnati, OH 45229
513-636-4200
800-344-2462
Fax: 513-636-4900
blood@cchmc.org
www.cincinnatichildrens.org

Aim is to improve the lives of children and adolescents with hemophilia and thrombophilia. This is achieved by offering compassionate, state-of-the-art clinical care to patients and their families, advancing our understanding of the disorder through research and educating future health care providers and leaders in the field.

Russell E. Ware, MD, PhD, Director, Divion of Hematology
John P. Perentesis, MD, Director, Division of Oncology

3565 Cardeza Foundation Hemophilia Center
Thomas Jefferson University Hospital
705 Curtis Building, 1015 Walnut Street
Philadelphia, PA 19107
215-955-8544
www.jefferson.edu

Devoted to research into the causes of a wide variety of diseases of the blood and to the diagnosis and care of patients with blood and lvmphatic diseases. Our members have competence in all areas of hematology, with particularly well recognized depth and experience in diseases affecting blood platelets, hemorrhagic (bleeding) and thrombotic (clotting) disorders, hematologic malignancies (leukemia, lymphoma and multiple myeloma) and other bone marrow disorders.

Jamie Siegel, MD, Director
Pamela Scruci, Admin Asst.
David Boligitz, Interim Business Manager

3566 Center for Cancer and Blood Disorders at Children's Medical Center in Dallas
1935 Medical District Drive
Dallas, TX 75235
214-456-7000
Fax: 214-456-6133
CCBDinfo@childrens.com
www.childrens.com/ccbd

Comprehensive diagnostic and treatment program for patients with disorders of blood coagulation which results in increased risk of bleeding or clotting.

George Buchanan, MD, Director

3567 Children's Center for Cancer and Blood Disorders of Palmetto Health Richland
7 Richland Medical Park Drive
Columbia, SC 29203
803-434-3533
800-775-2287
Fax: 803-434-4598
www.palmettohealth.org

Diagnosis and treatment of cancer and blood disorders. The staff includes a nurse practitioner and a patient and family educator who provide complex nursing management, treatment and navigation through the healthcare system. The multidisciplinary team also includes skilled social workers, therapists, nutritionists and child-life specialists, all of whom play an active role in each child's care.

Fauni Lowe, Manager
Beth Blackmon, Public Relations Director

3568 Children's Hospital of Philadelphia Hemophilia Program
34th Street & Civic Center Boulevard
Philadelphia, PA 19104
215-590-1000
800-879-2467
Fax: 215-426-5480
www.chop.edu

Provides multidisciplinary comprehensive care for children and adolescents with inherited bleeding disorders. Services include diagnosis, acute and chronic medical management of hemophilia and its complications, genetic counseling, physical therapy, HIV care and counseling and coordination with other services.

A Michael Broennle, Program Director
Regina B Bulter, RN, Program Nurse Coordinator

3569 Comprehensive Bleeding Disorder Center
Children's Hospital of Illinois
4727 N. Sheridan Rd.
Peoria, IL 61614
309-655-7171
Fax: 309-688-0917
www.compbleed.com

Hemophilia / Research Centers

Provides and facilitates state-of-the-art treatment for children and adults with hemophilia and related bleeding and thrombatic disorders. The staff includes a board-certified physician in pediatrics and pediatric hematology/oncology, nurses, social worker, rural outreach coordinator, reimbursement specialist/patient advocate, physical therapist and dentist.

Edward Hui, Executive Director
Sara Dill, Administration Director
John Redington, Executive Director

3570 Comprehensive Pediatric Hemophilia Treatment Center
University of Miami
1150 NW 14th Street
Miami, FL 33136
305-243-7570
www.pediatrics.med.miami.edu

Provided excellent medical and psychological care and emotional support for patients with bleeding disorders and their families since 1987. The HTC participates in national and regional research protocols dealing with various aspects of coagulation disorders. Orthopaedic and physical therapy are also offered at the monthly comprehensive clinic.

Maria Santaella, RN, Director
Steve E Lipshultz, MD, Chairman

3571 East Tennessee Comprehensive Hemophilia Center
University of Tennessee Medical Center
1924 Alcoa Highway 4 NW, Suite 180, Building E
Knoxville, TN 37920
865-454-9170
Fax: 865-544-9876
www.utmedicalcenter.org/hemophilia_services

Provides multidisciplinary comprehensive care to persons with bleeding disorders, including information, education and counseling to families affected by these disorders. The center's professional staff and consultants serve patients with hereditary bleeding disorders in Knoxville and surrounding counties.

William Rukeyser, Chairman
Renda Burkhart, Vice Chair
Bernard Bernstein, Secretary/Treasurer

3572 Eastern Michigan Hemophilia Center
Hurley Medical Center
1921 W. Michigan Avenue
Ypsilanti, MI 48197
734-544-0015
800-482-3041
Fax: 734-544-0095
www.hfmich.org/medical_resources

Provide and coordinate a broad range of treatment and prevention services provided by physicians who specialize in hematology and other relevant specialties such as orthopedics, social work, psychologists, nurses with extensive training and experience with hemophilia, genetic counselors, dentists, dental hygienists, and dieticians.

Calvin DeKuiper, President
Amy Denton, VP
Peter Deininger, Treasurer

3573 Federal Hemophilia Treatment Center Program of Los Angeles
Children's Hospital of LA
4650 Sunset Boulevard
Los Angeles, CA 90027
323-660-2450
Fax: 323-660-7128
www.chla.org

Provides continuing and comprehensive care to children and young adults with inherited bleeding disorders (in particular, hemophilia). The hemophilia treatment program is a federally funded resource which focuses on multidisciplinary management of bleeding disorders and collaborates with other programs in the United States to provide comprehensive care and teaching for patients and health care providers.

Wing-Yen Wong, MD, Director
Robert Miller, Coordinator

3574 Federal Hemophilia Treatment Center of Hawaii
Kapiolani Medical Center for Women and Children
1319 Punchou Street Pau
Honolulu, HI 96826
808-983-8551
Fax: 808-983-6000
martha.smith@kapiolani.org
www.kapiolani.org

Part of a nation-wide network established to promote comprehensive hemophilia care and to prevent hemophilia complications.

Desiree Medeiros, MD, Director
Dee Ann Omatsu, RN, Coordinator

3575 First Regional Hemophilia Center
James H Quillen College of Medicine
400 N State of Franklin Road, 1st Floor
Johnson City, TN 37604
423-433-6206
Fax: 423-433-6220

Helping patients and families to manage every aspect of living with hemophilia, from providing information about the latest medical developments to organizing support groups for parents and teens.

Sheri Miller, RN

3576 Hemophilia & Thrombosis Program at Children's National Health System
Center for Cancer & Blood Disorders
111 Michigan Avenue NW
Washington, DC 20010
202-476-7060
www.childrensnational.org

The program offers high quality, comprehensive care for children with hemophilia and thrombosis. Children's is the only program in the Metropolitan DC are that is supported by the National Institutes of Health. More than 240 children and teens are treated here annually.

Michael Guerrera, Director
Jay Greenberg, Hematologist Oncologist
Christine Guelcher, Nurse Coordinator

3577 Hemophilia Center of Arkansas
Arkansas Children's Hospital
1 Children's Way, PO Box 3591
Little Rock, AR 72202
501-364-1100
Fax: 501-364-4332
TDD: 501-364-1184
www.archildrens.org/

Patients with coagulation disorders can be diagnosed and evaluated by a group of physicians, physical therapists, dentists, psychologists and geneticists to provide education, prevention and continuity of care. The Hemophilia Center of Arkansas offers the latest diagnosis, prevention and treatment modalities for children and adults.

Nikki Shock

3578 Hemophilia Center of Western New York
936 Delaware Avenue, Suite 300
Buffalo, NY 14209
716-896-2470
866-434-6551
Fax: 716-218-4010
hemoctr@pce.net
www.hemophiliawny.com

The center provides a variety of services to the hemophilia and HIV/AIDS community. Included among these services are diagnostics, registration, outpatient treatment, home care programs, home visits, school visits, dental services and counseling services. Offers an adult unit and a pediatric unit.

Thomas Long, President
Marcia Gellin, VP
Mary Haggerty, VP

3579 Hemophilia Center of Western Pennsylvania
3636 Boulevard of the Allies
Pittsburgh, PA 15213
412-209-7280
Fax: 412-683-4029
www.hcwp.net

Comprehensive care to all individuals who are diagnosed with Hemophilia residing in Western Pennsylvania.

Karen Saban, Manager
A. Kim Ritchey, MD, Vice Chair
Kim Goldby-Reffner, Co-Ordinator

3580 Hemophilia Center of the New England Medical Center
UMass Memorial Medical Center; Memorial Campus
119 Belmont Street
Worcester, MA 01605
508-334-1000
www.umassmemorial.org

Hemophilia / Research Centers

Family-oriented, state-of-the-art medical and psychosocial services, education and research. Provides diagnostic and treatment services for individuals with bleeding disorders using a community-based, family centered and culturally sensitive approach. A hematologist is available 24 hours a day.

Doreen Brettler, MD, Director
Ann Forsberg, Program Administrator

3581 Hemophilia Treatment Center at the University of Iowa
UI Health Care Department of Pediatrics
200 Hawkins Drive
Iowa City, IA 52242
319-356-1616
Fax: 319-356-3862
melinda-schultz@uiowa.edu
www.uihealthcare.com

Committed to provide the best care for individuals with bleeding disorders. To accomplish this mission we offer state of the art comprehensive clinical care, education to patients and their families and accessibility to clinical research projects that are oriented to improve the lives of people with these type of disorders.

Donna Katen-Bahensky, Ceo
Donald E McFarlane, MD, Co-Director
Mindy Schultz, Secretary

3582 Hemophilia and Coagulation Programs
Norris Cotton Cancer Center
1 Medical Center Drive
Lebanon, NH 03756
603-650-5000
Fax: 603-650-7791
www.cancer.dartmouth.edu/services/hemophilia

Provides complete clinical and laboratory diagnostic facilities for evaluation and treatment of patients with cogenital bleeding disorders and disorders of thrombosis and hemostasis.

Sophia Ouhilal, Program Director

3583 Hemophilia and Thrombosis Center at the University of Minnesota Medical Center
Phillips-Wangensteen Building, Sixth Floor, Clinic
Minneapolis, MN 55455
612-626-6455
800-688-5252
Fax: 612-625-4955
htc@fairview.org
www.uofmmedicalcenter.org

Offers a wide range of services for patients with inherited bleeding and clotting disorders. We care for patients of all ages using a team approach. Hematologists and nurse clinicians are involved and provide services including diagnostic evaluations, treatment, education, research and care coordination.

Beverly Christie, Manager
Margaret Heisel Kurth, MD, Co-Director
Shannon Fabick, Administrative Secretary

3584 Hemophilia and Thrombosis Center of Nevada
2020 W Palomino Lane, Suite 110
Las Vegas, NV 89106
702-385-2702
Fax: 702-322-0158
www.htcnevada.org

Offers diagnosis and management for persons with inherited or acquired bleeding disorders including hemophilia, von Willebrand's Disease, and platelet disorders. Comprehensive care is administered using a team approach with input from social services, physical therapy, orthopedic specialists, dentist, nursing, laboratory support, and medical services.

Nancy Sewell, Manager

3585 Indiana Hemophilia and Thrombosis Center
8402 Harcourt Road, Suite 420
Indianapolis, IN 46260
317-871-0000
888-256-8837
Fax: 317-871-0010
info@ihtc.org
www.ihtc.org

Multidisciplinary evaluation and treatment facility serving the people of Indiana who have bleeding disorders or thrombotic disease (known collectively as disorders of coagulation). The center aids local medical providers in the care of individuals of all ages with blood disorders and their families.

Phillip E. Himelstein, Founder
Ike G. Batalis, President
Edward R. Schmidt, President

3586 Kalamazoo Comprehensive Hemophilia Treatment Center
Michigan State University
1000 Oakland Drive, PO Box 8000
Kalamazoo, MI 49008
269-337-4400
webmaster@med.wmich.edu
www.kcms.msu.edu

Offers diagnosis, management, and genetic counseling for these patients, as well.

Frank J. Sardone, President/CEO
John M. Dunn, Chairman of the Board
Hal B. Jenson, Dean

3587 Louisiana Comprehensive Hemophilia Care Center
Tulane University School of Medicine
6823 St. Charles Avenue
New Orleans, LA 70118
504-865-5000
Fax: 504-988-6808
website@tulane.edu
www.tulane.edu

Provides diagnostic, evaluation and treatment services for individuals with hemophilia, von Willebrand disease and other coagulopathies throughout Louisiana and the Mississippi gulf coast. The Center provides comprehensive medical and psychosocial evaluations through a multi-disciplinary team of adult and pediatric hematologists, orthopedists, nurses, social workers, physical therapists and dentists.

Anthony Lorino, Senior Vice President for Operation
Frances Vickers, Executive Assistant to the Senior V

3588 Maine Hemophilia and Thrombosis Center
Maine Medical Center
22 Bramhall Street, PO Box 3175
Portland, ME 04102
207-662-0111
877-339-3107
Fax: 207-885-7687
TTY: 207-662-4900
www.mmc.org

Offers a wide range of services for patients with inherited bleeding and clotting disorders. We care for patients of all ages using a team approach. Hematologists and nurse clinicians are involved and provide services including diagnostic evaluations, treatment, education, research and care coordination. Also, a full-time social worker provides psychosocial assessment, counseling and resource information.

Glen Roy, RN, Contact

3589 Mayo Comprehensive Hemophilia Center
13400 E. Shea Blvd.
Scottsdale, AZ 85259
480-301-8000
800-446-2279
Fax: 507-284-0161
www.mayoclinic.org

Specializes in treating people with hemophilia and other bleeding disorders. The Center provides evaluation and care to approximately 200 patients per year. It also assists in the management and care of another 100 patients annually who come to Mayo Clinic for initial evaluation or consultation.

Denis Cortese, MD, CEO

3590 Miami Comprehensive Hemophilia Center
University of Miami, Department of Pediatrics
1601 N.W. 12th Ave
Miami, FL 33136
305-270-3400
Fax: 305-325-8387
pedsinformation@med.miami.edu
www.pediatrics.med.miami.edu

The Comprehensive Pediatric Hemophilia Treatment Center has provided excellent medical and psychological care and emotional support for patients with bleeding disorders and their families since 1987. HTC participates in national and regional research protocols dealing with various aspects of coagulation disorders. The major goal of the HTC medical team is to improve the quality of life for patients and their families coping with the stress and discomfort of living with a chronic illness.

Luis Caldera-Nieves, Medical Director

Hemophilia / Research Centers

3591 Michigan State University Comprehensive Center for Bleeding Disorders
138 Service Road, Suite A-225
East Lansing, MI 48824
517-353-4920
800-759-5595
Fax: 517-353-9421
www.healthteam.msu.edu/

Offering education and information to individuals and families affected by blood clots and blood clotting disorders, and to assist with research efforts relating to all aspects of thrombosis and thrombophilia.

Gerald R Aben, Director
Roshni Kulkarni, MD, Coordinator

3592 Nebraska Regional Hemophilia Center
Nebraska Medical Center
42nd and Emile
Omaha, NE 68198
402-559-4000
800-922-0000
Fax: 402-552-2410
nmamdani@nebraskamed.com
www.unmc.edu/

Medical and educational support for those dealing with hemophilia, and their families.

Nizar Mamdani, Executive Director

3593 North Dakota Comprehensive Hemophilia and Thrombosis Treatment Center
Roger Maris Cancer Center/MeritCare Health System
820 4th Street N
Fargo, ND 58122
701-234-7544
800-437-4010
Fax: 701-234-7577
www.meritcare.com/specialties/more/hemophilia

Provides comprehensive care for people who have hemophilia, von Willebrand's disease and many other types of bleeding and clotting disorders. Using a team approach, professionals work together to provide evaluations, recommendations, treatment plans and follow-up care. They also offer a variety of services including assistance with clotting factors and home therapy.

Dr. Nathan Kobrinsky, MD, Director

3594 Northern Regional Bleeding Disorder Center
1105 6th Street
Traverse City, MI 49684
231-935-7227
800-468-6766
Fax: 231-935-6582
contact@mhc.net
www.munsonhealthcare.org

A program which cares for patients with all types of bleeding disorders from 26 northern Michigan counties. Provides specialty treatment to patients with hemophilia with the goal of minimizing complications from bleeding episodes.

Dan Wolf, Chairman
John Pelizzari, Vice Chairman
Bob Sprunk, Secretary

3595 Northwest Ohio Hemophilia Treatment Center
Toledo Childrens Hospital
2142 N Cove Boulevard
Toledo, OH 43606
419-291-5437
888-291-5437
Fax: 419-479-3258
www.promedica.org

A full range of inpatient and outpatient services is provided for children and adolescents with blood conditions and cancer. The patient care program also offers support for the psychosocial needs of patients and their families.

Ann Gilbert, RN, Director

3596 Orthopaedic Hospital's Hemophilia Treatment Center
2400 S Flower Street
Los Angeles, CA 90007
213-742-1000
Fax: 213-741-8338
www.orthohospital.org

Objective of the Center is the diagnosis and optimal management of bleeding disorders and their complications. Disorders treated include hemophilia A and B, von Willebrand's disease, and other inborn deficiencies of plasma clotting factors and platelets. Adolescents and adults who have acquired blood-borne infections, including chronic hepatitis and HIV infection, through prior treatment with blood products, are also treated at the Center.

Joseph Mirra, Director
Carol K Kasper, MD, Emeritus Director
James V Luck, Jr.; MD, Center's Surgeon

3597 Pediatric Hemophilia Program of Pennsylvania
Children's Hospital of Pittsburgh
4401 Penn Ave
Pittsburgh, PA 15224
412-692-5325
www.chp.edu

Provides high quality, comprehensive care for children with hemophilia and thrombophilia through research and clinical programs.

Vincent Deeney, Director
Kim Ritchey, MD, Pediatric Program Director
Melanie Finnigan, Public Affairs Director

3598 Phoenix Center for Cancer and Blood Disorders
Phoenix Children's Hospital
1919 E Thomas Road
Phoenix, AZ 85016
602-546-1000
888-908-5437
www.phoenixchildrens.com

Largest program of its kind in Arizona and is making significant difference in the quality of life for pediatric and adult hemophilia patients. It is one of only two federally funded hemophilia treatment programs in the state. The Center treats children with sickle cell disease, hemophilia and other hematologic disorders, and it is a designated center for the treatment and study of Gaucher's disease, an inherited metabolic disorder that can cause multiple medical problems.

Mark Bonsall, Chairman of the Board
Jon Hulburd, Vice Chairman
Robert L Meyer, President/CEO

3599 Puget Sound Blood Center
921 Terry Avenue
Seattle, WA 98104
206-292-6500
HumanResources@psbc.org
www.psbc.org

Puget provides all the blood and tissue services that people in our region need. It is this longstanding pledge to the community that has guided the Blood Center to more than sixty years of unparalleled success and to a leadership position in healthcare. In addition, our work in medical research is advancing medical care and making cures possible for patients around the world.

Jmaes P. AuBuchon, President/CEO
A. Kent Fisher, VP
Frederick R. Appelbaum, Executive Director

3600 Regional Hemophilia Program
Children's Hospital of Michigan
3901 Beaubien Street
Detroit, MI 48201
313-745-5437
888-362-2500
www.chmkids.org/

Clinical evaluations and recommendations by a team of experts, home treatment, training and educational programs, HIV/AIDS counceling and management, carrier detection and genetic counceling. Clinical trials provide our patients with the latest treatment modalities and in-depth surveillence of complications.

Lynne Thomas Gordon, COO
Herman Gray, MD, President

3601 Research at BloodCenter of Wisconsin
638 North 18th Street
Milwaukee, WI 53233
414-257-2424
877-232-4376
Fax: 414-937-6580
jeanne.mccabe@bcw.edu
www.bcw.edu

Hemophilia / Research Centers

Through basic, clinical and applied research programs, the center's scientists are enable to continue discoveries that enables to extend continuum of care.

Jeanne McCabe, Research Administration Director

3602 Rhode Island Hemostasis and Thrombosis Center
Rhode Island Hospital
593 Eddy Street, Hasbro Lower Level
Providence, RI 02903
401-444-7731
Fax: 401-444-6104
www.rhodeislandhospital.org

Formerly known as the Rhode Island Hemophilia Treatment Center, we have expanded our services to offer to persons with clotting disorders the same cutting edge, comprehensive program that has been extremely successful for our bleeding disorders community

Timothy J. Babineau, President/CEO
Cathy Duquette, Executive Vice President
Mamie Wakefield, Executive VP/CFO

3603 SUNY Upstate Medical University Research Development
750 E Adams Street, PO Box 2375
Syracuse, NY 13210
315-464-5540
Fax: 315-464-4318
www.upstate.edu/research

In collaboration with Upstate faculty, the Center conducts research and executes data analyses designed to guide the improvement of patient care and associated patient outcomes.

William J Hardoby, Research VP

3604 South Dakota Center For Bleeding Disorders
Sioux Valley Hospital
1600 W. 22nd St
Sioux Falls, SD 57117
605-312-1000
www.glhf.org

Provides comprehensive care based on family centered/community based health care. Hemophilia specialists are available 24 hours a day.

Bill Finn, President
Jeff Koopmeiners, VP
David Osswald, Secretary

3605 South Texas Comprehensive Hemophilia and Thrombophilia Treatment Center
University of Texas Medicine
7703 Floyd Curl Drive
San Antonio, TX 78229
210-567-5200
Fax: 210-567-6921
NAVAE@UTHSCSA.EDU
www.pediatrics.uthscsa.edu

A federally funded program focusing on the evaluation, treatment, and prevention of complications from Hemophilia, Von Willebrand's disease, thrombophilia, and menorrhagia in adolescents and women.

Thomas C. Mayes, M.D., MBA, Chairman
Steven R. Neish, MD, SM, Vice Chairman
Dennis A. Conrad, MD, Associate Chairman for Continuing M

3606 Spectrum Health Research
DeVos Hospital/Spectrum Health
100 Michigan Street NE
Grand Rapids, MI 49503
616-391-9000
866-989-7999
research.department@spectrum-health.org
www.helendevoschildrens.org

Formerly known as the Cook Institute for Research and the Cook Research Department. The Spectrum Health research department has a reputation for selectively participating in clinical research that brings cutting-edge treatments to the people of West Michigan. Many of the diseases under study currently have limited or no treatment options.

David T Lock, President
Dominic Sanfilippo, MD, Executive Medical Director

3607 Steele Children's Research Center
University of Arizona College of Medicine
1501 N Campbell Avenue, Suite 3301, PO Box 245073
Tucson, AZ 85724
520-626-2221
Fax: 520-626-7176
www.steelecenter.arizona.edu

At the University of Arizona College of Medicine, internationally known physicians and scientists, who also are professors in the UA Department of Pediatrics, work together to research causes and develop cures for childhood illnesses and diseases. Our goal is to advance medical knowledge to help improve the health of Arizona's children and children throughout the world.

Fayez Ghishan, MD, Director
Lori Stratton, MPH, Director of Development
Darci Slaten, MA, Director of Communications and Mark

3608 Ted R. Montoya Hemophilia Program
University of New Mexico Health Sciences Center
2211 Lomas Blvd NE
Albuquerque, NM 87131
505-272-2111
Fax: 505-272-6845
www.hospitals.unm.edu/outpt/trmhp/

Division program provides comprehensive care to the individual (child and adult) with hemophilia and other hereditary bleeding disorders.

Steve Mckernan, Chief Operations Officer
Carolyn Voss, Chief Operations Officer
David Pitcher, Chief Medical Officer

3609 UCD Hemophilia Treatment Center
2315 Stockton Boulevard
Sacramento, CA 95817
916-734-2011
800-2 U- DAV
TDD: 916-734-9230
www.ucdmc.ucdavis.edu

Offers a variety of medical, educational and social services to people with hemophilia or other inherited bleeding disorders and their families across Northern California.

John Meyer, Vice Chancellor
Linda P.B. Katehi, Chancellor
Ralph Hexter, Provost and Executive Vice Chancell

3610 UCSD Hemophilia Treatment Center
Div of Hematology-Oncology, UCSD Med Ctr Hillcrest
9500 Gilman Dr., La Jolla
San Diego, CA 92093
858-534-2230
Fax: 858-822-6288
kdherbst@ucsd.edu
www.ucsd.edu

Part of the federal network of over 140+ specialty centers for bleeding disorder diagnosis and management. These two HTCs are funded, in part, by grants from the Maternal and Child Health Bureau and Centers for Disease Control and Prevention. The purpose of the grants is to support a multidisciplinary team which can provide comprehensive care and conduct research to prevent hemophilia complications.

Amy Lovejoy, MD, Director
Catherine Glass, RN, Nurse Coordinator

3611 UT Southwestern Medical Center at Dallas: Hematology-Oncology Research
5323 Harry Hines Boulevard
Dallas, TX 75390
214-648-3111
Fax: 214-645-7999
www.utsouthwestern.edu

Basic science research is enhanced by the world class investigative environment at UT Southwestern that includes 4 Nobel Prize winners and other internationally known scientists with whom hematology-oncology faculty regular collaborate. Cutting edge clinical research in hemophilia/thrombophilia and ITP are also major commitments.

Daniel K. Podolsky, President
Robin M. Jacoby, VP/Chief of Staff

3612 United Health Services Blood Disorder Center
Wilson Regional Medical Center
33-57 Harrison Street
Johnson City, NY 13790
607-763-6000
Fax: 607-763-5514
www.uhs.net/

Hemophilia / Web Sites

Provides comprehensive care for those with blood disorders from diagnosis to treatment to home care and support services. Physicians, nurse specialists, dentists, orthopedists, physical therapists, and social workers treat people diagnosed with hemophilia and vWD at a dedicated site at Wilson Memorial Regional Medical Center. They also assist family physicians throughout the region in caring for persons with blood disorders.

Rajesh J Dave', President/CEO
Peter LoFaso, Chair
Roger Scott, Managing Director

3613 University of Cincinnati Adult Hemophilia Program
Division of Hematology & Oncology
Mail Location 11009, 3333 Burnet Avenue
Cincinnati, OH 45229
513-636-4269
Fax: 513-636-5599
palascje@ucmail.uc.edu
www.hemophilia-information.com

Patient care, teaching, and research in the area of hematology/oncology. Rapidly growing in all research, clinical, and educational components. The division participates in investigator-initiated protocols, pharmaceutical or industry-sponsored studies, as well as cooperative groups, such as the Southwest Oncology Group and Radiotherapy Oncology Group.

Joseph Palascak, MD, Director
Albert Muhleman, MD, Division Director
Madeline Heffner, RN, Nurse Coordinator

3614 University of Michigan Adult Hemophilia and Cougulation Disorders Program
1500 E Medical Center Drive, Floor B1
Ann Arbor, MI 48109
734-936-6641
800-211-8181
Fax: 734-936-6666
www2.med.umich.edu/healthcenters

Provides comprehensive, coordinated assessments and management services for individuals with blood disorders. Disorders may include disorders of blood coagulation (abnormal bleeding and clotting), hematology, hematopoietic malignancies, coagulation disorders, Von Willebrand's disease, lupus anticoagulant and thrombosis, and hemophilia.

Christine L Holland, Director

3615 University of Tennessee Hemophilia Clinic
UT Health Science Center
920 Madison Avenue, Suite 822
Memphis, TN 38163
901-448-1751
Fax: 901-448-7929
TDD: 901-448-7382
www.uthsc.edu

Diagnosis, evaluation, management, and treatment. The Hemophilia Center uses a comprehensive model to deliver effective care coordinated in the community. Emphasis is on educating providers, educators, patients, and their families for successful management. The center also manages a hemophilia factor concentrate program.

Dr. Marion Dugdale, Director
Steve J. Schwab, CEO/MD

3616 University of Texas Department of Hematology Research
University of Texas Medical School at Houston
7000 Fannin, Suite 1200
Houston, TX 77030
713-500-4HSC
Fax: 713-500-3026
www.uthouston.edu

Major research activities include a multidisciplinary center for vascular and thrombosis research and diversified hematologic and oncologic research projects covering a wide scope of disciplines from molecular biology to clinical trials.

Giuseppe N. Colasurdo, President
Kevin Dillon, Sr. VP
George M. Stancel, VP

3617 Vanderbilt Hemostasis-Thrombosis Clinic
Vanderbilt University Medical Center
2200 Children's Way, 6105 DOT, PO box 9830
Nashville, TN 37232
615-936-1765
866-372-5663
Fax: 615-936-8400
VHTCClinic@vanderbilt.edu
www.vanderbiltchildrens.com

Comprehensive health promotion; preventive medical and dental services; diagnostic testing; genetic testing and counseling; individual case management; specific and prompt treatments as needed; education and training; options for home treatment; and referrals, when necessary.

Anderson B Collier III, MD, Director
Mary G Hudson, RN, Nursing Coordinator
Kim Blittle, Administrative Assistant

3618 Vermont Regional Hemophilia Center
Fletcher Allen Health Care
UHC Campus, Old Hall Room 2106A, 1 South Prospect
Burlington, VT 05401
802-847-8041
Fax: 802-847-8041
www.hemophilia-information.com

Miriam Grant, RN
Alan Homans, MD

3619 West Central Ohio Hemophilia Center
Children's Medical Center of Dayton
1 Childrens Plaza, PO Box 1815
Dayton, OH 45404
937-641-5877
Fax: 937-641-5878
www.hemophilia-information.com

The center provides complete care for individuals and families with hemophilia and related bleeding disorders. Some of the services offered include a comprehensive clinic, emergency treatment network, consultations, diagnostic coagulation laboratory, home infusion programs, HIV/AIDS education and counseling and more.

James French III, MD, Medical Director

3620 Yale Pediatric Hematology/Oncology Research Center
Yale School of Medicine
333 Cedar Street
New Haven, CT 06510
203-785-4640
Fax: 203-737-2228
diana.beardsley@yale.edu
www.medicine.yale.edu

Oriented toward improving the lives of children with blood disorders and childhood cancer, while working toward future improved treatments and outcomes.

Diana S Beardsley, MD; PhD, Research Director
Robert J. Alpern, MD
James E. Rothman, Chairman

Web Sites

3621 Health Answers Education Sudler-WPP Health Practice
700 Dresher Road
Horsham, PA 19044
215-442-9010
www.healthanswers.com

HealthAnswers offers a breadth of services in medical education, sales force training, patient support solutions, professional promotion and customer solutions.

Mike Hudnall, CEO

3622 National Hemophilia Foundation
7 Penn Plaza, Suite 1204
New York, NY 10001
212-328-3700
888-463-6643
Fax: 212-328-3777
info@hemophilia.org
www.hemophilia.org

Since 1948, NHF has supported people with inherited blood disorders through research, education, and advocacy.

Leonard Valentino, MD, President & CEO
Dawn Rotellini, Chief Operating Officer
Peter Harvey, Chief Business Officer

3623 Online Mendelian Inheritance in Man
McKusick-Nathans Institue of Genetic Medicine-JHU
Baltimore, MD 21205

www.omim.org

This database is a catalog of human genes and genetic disorders.

Ada Hamosh, MD, Scientific Director

Book Publishers

3624 Adventures of Maxx
Nova Factor
1620 Century Centery Parkway, Suite 109
Memphis, TN 38137

901-385-3600
800-235-8498
Fax: 901-385-3778

An activity book for children with hemophilia, this publication is intended to be both educational and entertaining.

1991 15 pages

3625 Genetics Coloring Book
Medical College of Virginia
P.O Box 980565
Richmond, VA 23298

804-828-9793
Fax: 804-828-5115
www.medschool.vcu.edu/

Adventures of Gene coloring book for children ages 5-9. Two coloring books, one dealing with cystic fibrosis and one with hemophilia.

1994-1995 Comic/Coloring

3626 Guide to Insurance Coverage for People With Hemophilia
Armour Pharmaceutical Company
500 Arcola Road
Collegeville, PA 19426

215-454-3720

An educational guide designed to assist with health insurance concerns.

3627 Harold Talks About How He Inherited Hemophilia
Hemophilia Foundation
1850 Taylor Avenue, Suite 2
Louisville, KY 40213

502-456-3233
800-582-2873
Fax: 502-456-3234
info@kyhemo.org
www.kyhemo.org

Children's brochure explaining hemophilia causes, symptoms and living a regular life.

3628 Harold's Secret: A Boy with Hemophilia
Bayer
400 Morgan Lane
West Haven, CT 06516

203-937-2765

A comic book for youngsters pertaining to children with hemophilia and understanding of the illness among school friends.

16 pages

3629 Hemophilia Diseases and People
Enslow Publishers
40 Industrial Road
Berkeley Heights, NJ 07922

908-771-9400
800-398-2504
Fax: 908-771-0925
CustomerService@enslow.com
www.enslow.com

An excellent resource for basic research for personal or academic use. The disease is carefully described, with effective black-and-white graphics, charts, and photos, showing blood biology and the circulatory system and the various levels of severity (depending on what clotting factors the individual is missing).

Ages: 9-12 128 pages Library Binding
ISBN: 0-766016-84-6

Edward Willet, Editor

3630 Hemophilia Handbook
Hemophilia of Georgia
8800 Roswell Road, Suite 170
Atlanta, GA 30350

770-518-8272
Fax: 770-518-3310
mail@hog.org
www.hog.org

A comprehensive, easy-to-read resource for people with hemophilia and their families. The fourth edition of this handbook, contains up-to-date information on all important topics.

1988 348 pages

Hikie Allen, Director
Arthur Herman, Director

3631 Let's Talk About Going to the Hospital
Rosen Publishing Group's PowerKids Press
29 E 21st Street
New York, NY 10010

212-777-3017
800-237-9932
Fax: 888-436-4643
rosenpub@tribeca.ios.com
www.rosenpublishing.com

If a child has to check into the hospital, chances are he or she is already upset about being ill. Knowing how a hospital functions and what the procedures are, such as when family members can visit, will help in what is already a stressful situation. Grades K-5.

24 pages
ISBN: 0-823950-36-0

Roger Rosen, President

3632 Passport: Global Treatment Centre Directory
World Federation of Hemophilia
1425 Rene Levesque Boulevard W, Suite 1010
Montreal, Quebec, H3G
Canada

514-875-7944
Fax: 514-875-8916
wfh@wfh.org
www.wfh.org

Lists over 900 hemophilia treatment centres and national hemophilia organizations in more than 100 countries, including contact names, telephone and fax numbers, as well as e-mail and web site addresses. It is very useful for people with hemophilia who are travelling to other countries and as a directory of hemophilia treaters around the world.

1990 188 pages Members: $6

Magazines

3633 Bloodstone Magazine
Hemophilia Health Services
1640 Century Center Parkway
Memphis, TN 38134

877-222-7336
info@hemophiliahealth.com
www.hemophiliahealth.com

A premier magazine of the bleeding disorders community. Features of community news, The Adventures of Welligan Hugsley, ProToCall, and human interest stories. A must read for anyone interested in the latest hemophilia related information.

Quarterly

Kyle J Callahan, Publisher/President
Lydia Dixon Harden, Editor-in-Chief

3634 HEMALOG
Materia Medica
208 E 51st Street, Box 234
New York, NY 10022

212-725-5151
Fax: 212-725-2794
www.mmca.com

The purpose of Hemalog is to serve as a national forum for the hemophilia community, providing current news, information, opinion, and contact with others in the community. The material contained in this journal reflects the experience and opinion of a wide range of people connected with hemophilia, and encourages story and art contributions.

Hemophilia / Newsletters

Quarterly
Barbara Robin Slonevsky, Publisher
Janet Spencer-King

Newsletters

3635 Artery
Hemophilia Foundation of Michigan
1921 W Michigan Avenue
Ypsilanti, MI 48197
734-544-0015
800-482-3041
Fax: 734-544-0095
www.hfmich.orgs

Features articles on people in the bleeding disorders community, information and reviews on programs and services, memorials and donors.
Quarterly
Susan Lerch, Executive Director
Ann LeWalk, MA, Associate Director
Carrie McCulloch, Office Manager

3636 Big Red Factor
National Hemophilia Foundation of Nebraska
215 Centennial Mall South, Suite 512
Lincoln, NE 68508
402-742-5663
Fax: 402-742-5677
www.nebraskanhf.org

Chapter newsletter offering legislative and medical updates, technology, resources, assistive devices and more for persons affected by hemophilia and other blood disorders.
Karie Quintana, President
Mollie Lovell, Vice President
Dale Gibbs, Secretary

3637 Bloodlines
Hemophilia Association of San Diego County
3570 Camoni Del Rio N, Suite 108
San Diego, CA 92108
619-325-3570
Fax: 619-325-4350
info@hasdc.org
www.hasdc.org

Updates membership on the newest techniques and technologies on the treatment of hemophilia.
Quarterly
Teresa Ramirez, Executive Director

3638 COTT Washington Update
Committee of Ten Thousand
236 Massachusetts Avenue NE, Suite 609
Washington, DC 20002
202-543-0988
800-488-2688
Fax: 202-543-6720
www.cott1.org

Reports monthly (when possible) on Congress, Federal policy, agencies like FDA and CDL, with regard to blood safety, hemophilia.
Quarterly
Corey Dubin, President
Mary Lou Murphy, Co-Vice President
Terry MacNeill, Co-Vice President

3639 Factor Nine News
Coalition for Hemophilia B
825 Third Avenue Suite 226
New York, NY 10022
212-520-8272
Fax: 212-554-6900
info@coalitionforhemophiliab.org
www.coalitionforhemophiliab.org

Offers information on FDA approvals, annual meetings and the latest in technology and information regarding hemophilia.
Quaterly
Kimberly Phelan, Executive Director

3640 Headline News
Great Lakes Hemophilia Foundation
638 N 18th Street, PO Box 108
Milwaukee, WI 53233
414-257-0200
Fax: 414-257-1225
info@glhf.org
www.glhf.org

Provides information on research, new treatments and support groups.
Danielle Leitner Baxter, Executive Director
Adam Haggerty, Public Ally Program Assistant
Jayne Holmes, Administrative Assistant

3641 Hemophilia Headlines
Hemophilia Foundation of Oregon
5319 SW Westgate Drive, Suite 126
Portland, OR 97204
503-297-7207
Fax: 503-297-0127
www.hfo.info

Contains local, national and international news regarding bleeding disorders. It educates its readers with legislative and medical updates, as well as a current events calendar.
Quarterly
Jamie Dessellier, Editor
Dave Worthington, Vice President

3642 Infusions
Northern California Chapter of the NHF
7700 Edgewater Drive, Suite 710
Oakland, CA 94621
650-568-6243
888-749-4362
Fax: 510-568-6111

Informs members of medical, dental and orthopedic treatment advances and the latest research in the field. Helps to keep people with hemophilia and their families aware of relevant local and national meetings and includes important updates regarding research and treatment.
Bimonthly

3643 Initiatives
Philanthropic Initiative
420 Boylston Street, Floor 4
Boston, MA 2116
60
617-338-2590
Fax: 617-338-2591
www.tpi.org

Aimed at keeping patients and other interested individuals informed on important economic trends, legislation and medical issues.
Quarterly
Jane Maddox, Senior Editor
Joe Breiteneicher, President/CEO

3644 Linking Factor
Utah Hemophilia Foundation
772 East 3300 South, Suite 210
Salt Lake City, UT 84106
801-484-0325
877-463-6893
Fax: 801-746-2488
info@hemophiliautah.org
www.hemophiliautah.org

Features news pertinent to the bleeding disorders community.
Quarterly
Reg Ecker, President
Erik Rolstad, Vice President
Emmie Gardner, Secretary

3645 Newsline Eight & Nine
National Hemophilia Foundation, Florida Chapter
2176 Bent Oak Drive
Apopka, FL 32712
407-880-8330
Fax: 407-886-7649

State association news and information.

Quarterly

Pamphlets

3646 Child With A Bleeding Disorder: First Aid For School Personnel
National Hemophilia Foundation
116 W 32nd Street, 11th Floor
New York, NY 10001
212-328-3700
800-424-2634
Fax: 212-328-3799
handi@hemophilia.org
www.hemophilia.org

Aimed at school nurses and teachers who have a student with a bleeding disorder. Descriptions of typical injuries and other incidences when bleeding occurs are discussed with proper steps that need to be followed as well as standard precautions and medications.

Val Bias, CEO
John Indence, VP, Marketing & Communications
Mary Ann Ludwig, Vice President for Development

3647 Hemophilia and Mild Hemophilia What To Expect
American Home Federation
PO Box 985
Enfield, CT 6083
800-243-4621
Fax: 860-763-7022
www.ahfinfo.com

Written in clear and easy to understand language, to provide information to those living with bleeding disorders, those who serve our children in school, and those who provide our medical care. A child or adult with mild hemophilia can live a healthy and long life. Physical activity is good and will help build strong muscles. Children and adults with mild hemophilia can do most things others can do.

1991 13 pages

3648 Hemophilia, Sports, and Exercise
National Hemophilia Foundation
116 W 32nd Street, 11th Floor
New York, NY 10001
212-328-3700
800-424-2634
Fax: 212-328-3777
handi@hemophilia.org
www.hemophilia.org

This fully revised guide presents valuable information for the person with a bleeding disorder or his/her parents considering participation in sports activities. Topics covered include conditioning, stretching and flexibility, strength, weight training, prophylaxis, and physical activities for infants, toddlers, preschoolers, and school-age children.

1996 30 pages Free to Members

Val Bias, CEO
John Indence, VP, Marketing & Communications
Mary Ann Ludwig, Vice President for Development

3649 Hemophilia: Current Medical Management
National Hemophilia Foundation
116 W 32nd Street, 11th Floor
New York, NY 10001
212-328-3700
800-424-2634
Fax: 212-328-3777
handi@hemophilia.org
www.hemophilia.org

Provides an overview of all aspects of hemophilia treatment, including prophylaxis, home therapy, inhibitors, orthopedic solutions, surgery, and dental care.

1994 30 pages

Jonathan C Goldsmith, Author
Val Bias, CEO
John Indence, VP, Marketing & Communications

3650 Inheritance of Hemophilia
National Hemophilia Foundation
116 W 32nd Street, 11th Floor
New York, NY 10001
212-328-3700
800-424-2634
Fax: 212-328-3777
handi@hemophilia.org
www.hemophilia.org

Booklet provides a sophisticated explanation of the genetic transmission of hemophilia. It also describes tests used to find out if the hemophilia gene is present, particularly in women who may carry the gene but show no signs of excessive bleeding. Reproductive choices for men and women with the hemophilia gene are reviewed.

1998 15 pages

Val Bias, CEO
John Indence, VP, Marketing & Communications
Mary Ann Ludwig, Vice President for Development

3651 Living with HIV: Talking With Your Child
National Hemophilia Foundation
116 W 32nd Street, 11th Floor
New York, NY 10001
212-328-3700
800-424-2634
Fax: 212-328-3777
handi@hemophilia.org
www.hemophilia.org

A pamphlet directed at caregivers of young children living with hemophilia and HIV disease.

1990 8 pages

Val Bias, CEO
John Indence, VP, Marketing & Communications
Mary Ann Ludwig, Vice President for Development

3652 What Is Hemophilia?
American Federation Home (AFH)
PO Box 985
Enfield, CT 6083
800-243-4621
Fax: 860-763-7022
info@ahfinfo.com
www.ahfinfo.com

Offers information on what hemophilia is, common factors in hemophilia, the cost and treatments offered to hemophiliacs and more.

3653 What You Should Know About Bleeding Disorders
National Hemophilia Foundation
116 W 32nd Street, 11th Floor
New York, NY 10001
212-328-3700
800-424-2634
Fax: 212-328-3777
handi@hemophilia.org
www.hemophilia.org

Explains hemophilia, von Willebrand disease, blood safety issues, joint problems, HIV infection, hepatitis, special bleeding problems in women, prophylaxis, recombinant therapy, the cost of care, comprehensive care and other issues of concern to the bleeding disorders community.

1997 23 pages

Val Bias, CEO
John Indence, VP, Marketing & Communications
Mary Ann Ludwig, Vice President for Development

Camps

3654 Hole in the Wall Gang Camp
565 Ashford Center Road
Ashford, CT 6278
860-429-3444
Fax: 860-429-7295
ashford@holeinthewallgang.org
www.holeinthewallgang.org

Nonprofit organization that provides a recreational camp experience for children ages 7-15 with cancer, genetic blood diseases and HIV/AIDS.

James Canton, CEO
Kevin M. Magee, Chief Financial Officer
Padraig Barry, Chief Program Officer

Hepatitis / Description

Description

3655 HEPATITIS
Covers these related disorders: Hepatitis A, Hepatitis B, Hepatitis C, Hepatitis D, Hepatitis E
Involves the following Biologic System(s):
Gastrointestinal Disorders, Infectious Disorders

Hepatitis refers to an inflammatory condition of the liver that may result from viral, bacterial, or parasitic infection; certain blood disorders; or exposure to certain drugs, toxins, or alcohol. However, viral infection is most frequently the cause of hepatitis. Liver inflammation may develop in association with certain viral infections such as German measles (rubella), chickenpox (varicella), or HIV. In addition, there are at least five infectious agents known as hepatotropic viruses that specifically target the liver.

Hepatitis A virus is thought to be the most common cause of hepatitis in children, with an extremely high prevalence rate in underdeveloped countries. In addition, approximately 30 percent of adults in the United States show evidence of a previous infection with hepatitis A. This form of hepatitis is usually spread by fecal-oral contamination through drinking water, food, or direct contact. Children under five years of age often have no symptoms, but still acquire immunity to future hepatitis A infection. When symptoms become evident in children, they are often mild and may include fever, weakness, general discomfort (malaise), loss of appetite (anorexia), nausea and vomiting, diarrhea, and abdominal distress. Occasionally, some children develop a very slight yellowing of the eyes (scleral icterus), skin, and mucous membranes (jaundice). Hepatitis A is an acute, self-limited form of this disease, with a return to general health typically within one month, although relapses may occur. Life-threatening complications associated with this type of hepatitis are extremely rare. Prevention of hepatitis A transmission is directed toward the teaching of good hygiene (e.g., frequent hand washing) in hospitals, child-care facilities, etc. In addition, the administration of recently developed vaccines or immunoglobulin is recommended for children and adults who plan to travel to countries with a high incidence of hepatitis A. Young children are at risk for becoming carriers of this disease while older travelers may be at risk for more significant disease involvement. Early administration of immunoglobulin is also recommended for children and adults who may have been exposed to the virus. Other treatment is symptomatic and supportive.

Hepatitis B infection in children and adolescents may be transmitted through intravenous injection of blood, blood products, or drugs; sharing of needles or razors; ear piercing with contaminated equipment; and other carrier-contact modes of transmission. For example, the hepatitis B virus may be spread by apparently healthy people who are chronic carriers. Symptoms usually develop six to seven weeks after exposure, persist for six to eight weeks, and are similar to those of hepatitis A, but are often more severe. Additional manifestations may include tenderness and enlargement of the liver (hepatomegaly), enlargement of the spleen (splenomegaly), swollen lymph glands (lymphadenopathy), accumulation of fluid within the abdomen (ascites), skin lesions, or joint pain (arthralgia). Newborns of infected mothers are at high risk for infection during delivery, possibly through infected amniotic fluid, blood, or fecal material. Although infected newborns usually do not manifest symptoms, if left untreated, most develop a chronic form of hepatitis that may result in potentially life-threatening liver disease during adulthood. Prevention of hepatitis B infection in newborns is first directed toward testing for infection in pregnant women. If a mother is positive for infection, her newborn is given a hepatitis B immune globulin injection within the first day of life, followed by immunization with hepatitis B vaccine. Immunizations are also recommended to anyone who may have been exposed to hepatitis B. Treatment is symptomatic and supportive.

Hepatitis C may be transmitted among the general population through intravenous drug use, transfusions of blood or blood products, sexual contact, and other, unknown causes. Although transmission from an infected mother to her infant is possible, it is rare except in instances where the mother also has HIV or other contributing factors. The onset of disease is approximately seven to nine weeks after exposure and symptoms are similar to those of other types of viral hepatitis. Hepatitis C is the most likely of all the hepatotropic viruses to cause chronic hepatitis, a condition associated with prolonged inflammation of the liver that persists for six months or longer. Complications may also include cirrhosis and cancer of the liver, and rarely fulminant (very severe) hepatitis. Because infection with the hepatitis C virus may occur more than once in the same person, a preventive vaccine is not effective. Treatment is symptomatic and supportive.

The hepatitis D virus cannot replicate itself without the help of the hepatitis B virus; therefore, hepatitis D only occurs in people with prior or simultaneous infection with hepatitis B. The most common mode of transmission in the United States is through intimate contact and needle sharing; therefore, this form of hepatitis is relatively rare in children in this country. Symptoms and findings may be similar to but more severe than those of hepatitis B infection. There is no vaccine for hepatitis D; therefore, prevention is directed toward prevention of hepatitis B infection. Treatment is symptomatic and supportive.

Hepatitis E is the cause of epidemic-associated infection and is spread by fecal-oral transmission, usually through contaminated water or food. The symptoms and findings of this form of disease are similar to but more severe than those associated with hepatitis A. However, this acute, self-limited infection may pose a life-threatening risk to pregnant women. Hepatitis E is extremely rare in the United States, thus far occurring only in people who have traveled to or emigrated from indigenous countries. No vaccine is available. Treatment is symptomatic and supportive. There are some reports about the use of interferon, either alone or in combination with ribavirin, another antiviral drug, in the treatment of children with Hepatitis C. However, only a partial antiviral response response occurred.

Government Agencies

3656 NIH/National Institute of Allergy and Infectious Diseases
5601 Fishers Lane, MSC 9806
Bethesda, MD 20892
301-496-5717
866-284-4107
Fax: 301-402-3573
TDD: 800-877-8339
ocpostoffice@niaid.nih.gov
www.niaid.nih.gov

The principal advisory board of the NIAID. The council is composed of physicians, scientists and representatives of the public and advises on the conduct and support or research, training and dissemination of health information regarding allergies and infectious diseases.

Anthony S. Fauci, MD, Director

Hepatitis / Book Publishers

National Associations & Support Groups

3657 **American Academy of Pediatrics**
345 Park Blvd
Itasca, IL 60143
800-433-9016
Fax: 847-434-8000
mcc@aap.org
www.aap.org

The American Academy of Pediatrics and its member pediatricians are committed to the attainment of optimal physical, mental and social health and well-being for all infants, children, adolescents, and young adults.

Lynn Olson, PhD, VP, Research
Mark Del Monte, JD, CEO/Executive VP
Vera Tait, MD, FAAP, Chief Medical Officer

3658 **American Liver Foundation**
P.O. Box 299
West Orange, NJ 07052
800-465-4837
www.liverfoundation.org

The American Liver Foundation is the nationleading nonprofit organization promoting liver health and disease prevention. ALF provides research, education and advocacy for those affected by liver-related diseases, including hepatitis.

Lorraine Stiehl, CEO
David Ticker, Executive VP & CFO

3659 **Hepatitis B Foundation**
3805 Old Easton Road
Doylestown, PA 18902
215-489-4900
info@hepb.org
www.hepb.org

Dedicated to finding a cure and improving the quality of life for those affected by hepatitis B worldwide. Our commitment includes funding focused research, promoting disease awareness, supporting immunization and treatment initatives and serving as the primary source of information for patients and their families, the medical and scientific community, and the general public.

3660 **Hepatitis Education Project**
1621 S. Jackson Street, Suite 201
Seattle, WA 98144
206-732-0311
Fax: 206-299-0855
www.hepeducation.org

The mission of the Hepatitis Education Project is to help raise awareness among patients, medical personnel and the public of the facts concerning hepatitis patients and the resources available to help those who live with the disease.

3661 **March of Dimes Foundation**
1550 Crystal Drive, Ste 1300
Arlington, VA 22202
888-663-4637
www.marchofdimes.org

March of Dimes help moms have full-term pregnancies and research the problems that threaten the health of babies. The March of Dimes also acts globally: sharing best practices in perinatal health and helping improve birth outcomes where the needs are the most urgent.

Stacey D. Stewart, President
Alan Brogdon, SVP/COO/Board Officer
Rahul Gupta, MD, SVP & Chief Medical/Health Officer

3662 **World Health Organization**
Avenue Appia 20
1202 Geneva,
Switzerland
www.who.int

WHO is the directing and coordinating authority for health within the United Nations system. WHO operates in more than 150 countries around the world.

Dr. Tedros Adhanom Ghebreyesus, Director General
Dr. Zsuzsanna Jakab, Deputy Director General
Stewart Simonson, Asst Director General, UN NYC

Web Sites

3663 **American Liver Foundation**
P.O. Box 299
West Orange, NJ 07052
800-465-4837
www.liverfoundation.org

The American Liver Foundation is the nationleading nonprofit organization promoting liver health and disease prevention. ALF provides research, education and advocacy for those affected by liver-related diseases, including hepatitis.

Lorraine Stiehl, CEO
David Ticker, Executive VP & CFO

3664 **Centers for Disease Control and Prevention**
1600 Clifton Road
Atlanta, GA 30329
800-232-4636
TTY: 888-232-6348
www.cdc.gov

Federal agency that promotes America's health and safety, providing information to guide health decisions, and building strong partnerships to promote health and prevent disease.

Rochelle P. Walensky, MD, Director
Anne Schuchat, MD, Principal Deputy Director
Abbigail Tumpey, MPH, Associate Director, Communication

3665 **Hepatitis B Foundation**
3805 Old Easton Road
Doylestown, PA 18902
215-489-4900
info@hepb.org
www.hepb.org

Dedicated to finding a cure and improving the quality of life for those affected by hepatitis B worldwide. Our commitment includes funding focused research, promoting disease awareness, supporting immunization and treatment initatives and serving as the primary source of information for patients and their families, the medical and scientific community, and the general public.

3666 **Hepatitis Education Project**
The Maritime Building, 911 Western Ave #302
Seattle, WA 98104
206-732-0311
800-218-6932
www.hepeducation.org

The mission of the Hepatitis Education Project is to help raise awareness amoung patients, medical personnel and the public of the facts concerning hepatitis patients and the resources available to help those who live with the disease.

Steve Graham, President
Anne Croghan, MN ARNP, Vice President
Jeffrey R. King, CPA, Treasurer

3667 **Hepatitis International Foundation**
8121 Georgia Avenue, Suite 350
Silver Spring, MD 20910
301-565-9410
800-891-0707
www.hepfi.org

Our mission is to teach the public and hepatitis patients how to prevent, diagnose and treat viral hepatitus; prevent viral hepatitis by promoting liver wellness and healthful lifestyles; serve as advocates for hepatitis patients and the related medical community worldwide; support research into prevention, treatment and cures for viral hepatitis.

Karen Wirth, Chair
Dane R. Christiansen, BA, Vice Chair
Ivonne Perlaza Fuller, Secretary, CEO

Book Publishers

3668 **Hepatitis B Prevention: A Resource Guide**
National Digestive Diseases Info. Clearinghouse
2 Information Way
Bethesda, MD 20892
800-891-5389
Fax: 703-735-4929
TTY: 866-569-1162
nddic@info.niddk.nih.gov
www.digestive.niddk.nih.gov

Designed to assist health care and other professionals who work in planning or administering hepatitis B prevention programs.

Hepatitis / Newsletters

252 pages
Kathy Kranzfelder, Director

3669 Hepatitis C: An Information Resource
American Liver Foundation
39 Broadway, Suite 2700
New York, NY 10006
212-668-1000
800-223-0179
Fax: 212-483-8179
info@liverfoundation.org
www.liverfoundation.org

Explains viral hepatitis, transmission, symptoms, testing and acute chronic hepatitis.

Alan P Brownstein, President/CEO
Paul D Berk, Chair

3670 Let's Talk About Going to the Hospital
Rosen Publishing Group's PowerKids Press
29 E 21st Street
New York, NY 10010
212-777-3017
800-237-9932
Fax: 888-436-4643
rosenpub@tribeca.ios.com
www.rosenpublishing.com

If a child has to check into the hospital, chances are he or she is already upset about being ill. Knowing how a hospital functions and what the procedures are, such as when family members can visit, will help in what is already a stressful situation. Grades K-5.

24 pages
ISBN: 0-823950-36-0

Roger Rosen, President

3671 Liver Disease in Children
Lippincott Williams & Wilkins
530 Walnut Street
Philadelphia, PA 19106
215-521-8300
Fax: 215-521-8902
www.lww.com

A difinitive book on pediatric liver disease, providing extensive, well-edited information that is not easily accessible or available in other textbooks.

2000 1008 pages
ISBN: 1-556443-77-2

Newsletters

3672 American Liver Foundation
39 Broadway, Suite 2700
New York, NY 10006
212-668-1000
800-465-4837
Fax: 212-483-8179
info@liverfoundation.org
www.liverfoundation.org

Newsletter of the preeminent voluntary organization dedicated to promoting liver wellness and eradicating liver disease.

Quarterly

Tom Nealon III, President & CEO
Lynn Gardiner Seim, Executive VP & COO

Pamphlets

3673 Chronic Viral Hepatitis Backgrounder
Centers for Disease Control
1600 Clifton Road NE
Atlanta, GA 30329
404-639-3311
800-232-4636
TTY: 888-232-6348
cdcinfo@cdc.gov
www.cdc.gov

Offers information and statistics on viral hepatitis.

Tom Frieden, Director
Ileana Arias, PhD, Principal Deputy Director
John Auerbach, Associate Director for Policy

3674 Hepatitis
National Institute of Allergy & Infectious Disease
National Institutes of Health
Bethesda, MD 20892
301-496-4000
Fax: 301-402-3573
TDD: 800-877-8339
www.3.niaid.nih.gov

A pamphlet discussing the cause, symptoms, transmission, diagnosis, tests, prevention and the latest research on hepatitis.

Anthony S. Fauci MD, Director

3675 Hepatitis B: Your Child at Risk
American Liver Foundation
1425 Pompton Avenue
Cedar Grove, NJ 7009
973-857-2626
800-223-0179

3676 Hepatitis Fact Sheet
Centers for Disease Control
1600 Clifton Road NE
Atlanta, GA 30329
404-639-3311
800-232-4636
TTY: 888-232-6348
cdcinfo@cdc.gov
www.cdc.gov

Offers information on the causes, symptoms, prevention and treatments for hepatitis.

Tom Frieden, Director
Ileana Arias, PhD, Principal Deputy Director
John Auerbach, Associate Director for Policy

3677 How Many Times a Day Do You Risk Being Infected with Hepatitis B?
American Liver Foundation
39 Broadway, Suite 2700
New York, NY 10006
212-668-1000
800-465-4837
Fax: 212-483-8179
info@liverfoundation.org
www.liverfoundation.org

A flyer emphasizing the importance of vaccination against hepatitis B.

Hamilton Baiden, President
Jodi Bohr, Director
Jill Evans, R.N., M.S, Director

3678 Q and A: Hepatitis B Prevention
SmithKline Beecham Pharmaceuticals
1 Franklin Plaza, 200 N 16th Street
Philadelphia, PA 19010
215-751-4000
Fax: 215-751-3400
www.gsk.com

Informational booklet written for healthcare personnel by the manufacturer of Engerix-B vaccine, reviews hepatitis B prevention.

Jean-Pierre Garnier PhD, Chief Executive Officer

3679 Viral Hepatitis: Everybody's Problem?
American Liver Foundation
39 Broadway, Suite 2700
New York, NY 10006
212-668-1000
800-465-4837
Fax: 212-483-8179
www.liverfoundation.org

Covering a broad range of topics including: a definition of the disease, descriptions of types of infections, transmission, symptoms, treatment options and prevention.

Hamilton Baiden, President
Jodi Bohr, Director
Jill Evans, R.N., M.S, Director

3680 What Health Care Workers Should Know About Hepatitis B
Channing L Bete Company
One Community Place
South Deerfield, MA 1373-   800-477-4776
                              Fax: 800-499-6464
                         custsvcs@channing-bete.com
                          www.channing-bete.com

Presents information in easy-to-read, simple English for health care workers about hepatitis B.

16 pages

Mike Bete, President/CEO

Hereditary Fructose Intolerance / Description

Description

3681 HEREDITARY FRUCTOSE INTOLERANCE
Synonym: Deficiency of phosphofructaldolase
Involves the following Biologic System(s):
Genetic/Chromosomal/Syndrome/Metabolic Disorders

Hereditary fructose intolerance is a metabolic disorder characterized by a deficiency of the enzyme phosphofructaldolase (fructose-1,6-bisphosphate aldolase), resulting in the body's inability to process or metabolize fructose, a simple sugar (monosaccharide). Fructose is found in honey, certain sweet fruits, baby food and baby formula sweeteners. In combination with more complex sugars (disaccharides and polysaccharides), it is converted in the liver into glucose and is either distributed immediately for use as energy or converted into glycogen and stored in the liver, muscle, or fat for later energy use. The deficiency of the enzyme phosphofructaldolase results in the accumulation in the body of fructose-1-phosphate, a compound in the chain of fructose metabolism. This accumulation inhibits glucose production as well as the glycogen processing into energy-producing glucose.

Ingestion of fructose by affected infants may result in extremely low blood sugar (hypoglycemia), yellowing of the skin, eyes, and mucous membranes (jaundice), enlargement of the liver (hepatomegaly), bleeding from within the digestive tract, kidney involvement (i.e., proximal tubular dysfunction), vomiting, sluggishness, sweating, tremors, irritability, and seizures. Affected children have an aversion to sweets and fruits and typically do not have dental cavities (caries). However, physical findings and symptoms may be variable in their severity and manifestation.

Treatment for hereditary fructose intolerance includes total elimination of fructose from the diet. Vigilance is extremely important in that fructose is present in many foods and medicines as an additive. Other treatment may include administration of supplemental glucose to counteract the effects of hypoglycemia.

Hereditary fructose intolerance is transmitted as an autosomal recessive trait. The defective gene for this disorder is located on the long arm of chromosome 9 (9q22). Approximately one of every 40,000 is affected with this disorder.

National Associations & Support Groups

3682 American Academy of Pediatrics
345 Park Blvd
Itasca, IL 60143
800-433-9016
Fax: 847-434-8000
mcc@aap.org
www.aap.org

The American Academy of Pediatrics and its member pediatricians are committed to the attainment of optimal physical, mental and social health and well-being for all infants, children, adolescents, and young adults.

Lynn Olson, PhD, VP, Research
Mark Del Monte, JD, CEO/Executive VP
Vera Tait, MD, FAAP, Chief Medical Officer

3683 American College of Gastroenterology
6400 Goldsboro Road
Bethesda, MD 20817
301-263-9000
www.gi.org

The American College of Gastroenterology was founded in 1932 to advance the scientific study and medical practice of diseases of the GI tract.

13,000 members

3684 Genetic Alliance
426400 Woodfield Road, Ste 189
Damascus, MD 20872
202-966-5557
Fax: 202-966-8553
info@geneticalliance.org
www.geneticalliance.org

World's leading nonprofit health advocacy organization committed to transforming health through genetics and promoting an environment of openness centered on the health of individuals, families, and communities.

Sharon Terry, CEO
Ruth Child, CFO
Natasha Bonhomme, Chief Strategy Officer

3685 March of Dimes Foundation
1550 Crystal Drive, Ste 1300
Arlington, VA 22202
888-663-4637
www.marchofdimes.org

March of Dimes help moms have full-term pregnancies and research the problems that threaten the health of babies. The March of Dimes also acts globally: sharing best practices in perinatal health and helping improve birth outcomes where the needs are the most urgent.

Stacey D. Stewart, President
Alan Brogdon, SVP/COO/Board Officer
Rahul Gupta, MD, SVP & Chief Medical/Health Officer

3686 North American Society for Pediatric Gastroenterology/Hepatology/Nutrition
714 N Bethlehem Pike, Suite 300
Ambler, PA 19002
215-641-9800
Fax: 215-641-1995
www.naspghan.org

Strives to improve the care of infants, children and adolescents with digestive disorders by promoting advances in clinical care of children with chronic abdominal pain, diarrhea, constipation, vomiting, bleeding from the GI tract, inflammatory bowel disease, liver diseases, diseases of the pancreas, poor weight gain and nutritional problems.

Margaret K Stallings, Executive Director
Kim Rose, Associate Director
Gina Brown, Membership

Libraries & Resource Centers

3687 National Digestive Diseases Information Clearinghouse (NDDIC)
NIH
2 Information Way
Bethesda, MD 20892
301-654-3810
800-891-5389
Fax: 301-907-8906
nddic@info.niddk.nih.gov
www.digestive.niddk.nih.gov

The National Institute of Diabetes and Digestive and Kidney Diseases conducts and supports research on many of the most serious diseases affecting public health. The Institute supports much of the clinical research on the diseases of internal medicine and related subspecialty fields as well as many basic science disciplines.

Griffin P. Rodgers, MD, Director
Gregory G. Germino, MD, Deputy Director
Kathy Kranzfelder, Communications Director

Conferences

3688 NASPGHAN Annual Meeting
NASPGHAN
714 N. Bethlehem Pike, Ste 300
Ambler, PA 19002
215-641-9800
Fax: 215-641-1995
www.naspghan.org

Strives to improve the care of infants, children and adolescents with digestive disorders by promoting advances in clinical care of children with chronic abdominal pain, diarrhea, constipation, vomiting, bleeding from the GI tract, inflammatory bowel disease, liver diseases, diseases of the pancreas, poor weight gain and nutritional problems.

Fall

Margaret K Stallings, Executive Director
Kim Rose, Associate Director
Gina Brown, Membership

Web Sites

3689 **American College of Gastroenterology**
6400 Goldsboro Road
Bethesda, MD 20817
301-263-9000
www.gi.org

The American College of Gastroenterology was founded in 1932 to advance the scientific study and medical practice of diseases of the GI tract.

13,000 members

3690 **Clinical Genetic Services-Department of Pediatrics**
Hassenfeld Children's Hospital at NYU Langone
424 East 34th Street
New York, NY 10016
212-263-7300
Fax: 646-754-2250
nyulangone.org

Offers evaluations, genetic counseling and testing. Clinical services include carrier testing, prenatal counseling, and complete genetic evaluations for children and adults.

John G. Pappas, MD, Pediatric Genetic Associate
Naomi Yachelevich, MD, Pediatric Genetic Associate

3691 **National Digestive Diseases Information Clearinghouse (NDDIC)**
NIH
2 Information Way
Bethesda, MD 20892
301-654-3810
800-891-5389
Fax: 301-402-2125
nddic@info.niddk.nih.gov
www.digestive.niddk.nih.gov

The National Institute of Diabetes and Digestive and Kidney Diseases conducts and supports research on many of the most serious diseases affecting public health. The Institute supports much of the clinical research on the diseases of internal medicine and related subspecialty fields as well as many basic science disciplines.

Griffin P. Rodgers, MD, Director
Gregory G. Germino, MD, Deputy Director
Kathy Kranzfelder, Communications Director

3692 **North American Society for Pediatric Gastroenterology/Hepatology/Nutrition**
www.naspghan.org

www.naspghan.org

Strives to improve the care of infants, children and adolescents with digestive disorders by promoting advances in clinical care of children with chronic abdominal pain, diarrhea, constipation, vomiting, bleeding from the GI tract, inflammatory bowel disease, liver diseases, diseases of the pancreas, poor weight gain and nutritional problems.

3693 **Online Mendelian Inheritance in Man**
McKusick-Nathans Institue of Genetic Medicine-JHU
Baltimore, MD 21205
www.omim.org

This database is a catalog of human genes and genetic disorders.

Ada Hamosh, MD, Scientific Director

Journals

3694 **Journal of Pediatric Gastroenterology and Nutrition**
NASPGHAN, author

Lippincott Williams & Wilkins
Two Commerce Square, 2001 Market Street
Philadelphia, PA 19103
215-521-8300
Fax: 215-521-8902
orders@lww.com
www.lww.com

Publication of the North American Society for Pediatric Gastroenterolgy, Hepatology and Nutrition, which strives to improve the care of infants, children and adolescents with digestive disorders by promoting advances in clinical care of children with chronic abdominal pain, diarrhea, constipation, bleeding from the GI tract, inflammatory bowel disease, liver diseases, diseases of the pancreas, poor weight gain and nutritional problems.

Newsletters

3695 **NASPGHAN News**
714 N. Bethlehem Pike, Ste 300
Ambler, PA 19002
215-641-9800
Fax: 215-641-1995
www.naspghan.org

Publication of the North American Society for Pediatric Gastroenterolgy, Hepatology and Nutrition, which strives to improve the care of infants, children and adolescents with digestive disorders by promoting advances in clinical care of children with chronic abdominal pain, diarrhea, constipation, bleeding from the GI tract, inflammatory bowel disease, liver diseases, diseases of the pancreas, poor weight gain and nutritional problems.

Margaret K Stallings, Executive Director
Kim Rose, Associate Director
Gina Brown, Membership

Herpes Simplex / Description

Description

3696 HERPES SIMPLEX

Covers these related disorders: Herpes simplex virus type 1 (HSV-1), Herpes simplex virus type 2 (HSV-2)

Involves the following Biologic System(s):

Infectious Disorders

Herpes simplex refers to a contagious infection caused by the herpes simplex virus. This infection is characterized by the formation of small, sometimes painful, fluid-filled, blister-like lesions (vesicles) on the skin and various mucous membranes. There are two strains of herpes simplex virus: type 1 (HSV-1) and type 2 (HSV-2). More than 85% of the U.S. population has evidence of infection with HSV-1, while 25% is infected with HSV-2. Although there is some overlap, HSV-1 is usually responsible for lesions of the lips such as cold sores (herpes labialis), the mouth (herpetic gingivostomatitis), and the eyes (e.g., corneal lesions, conjunctivitis, etc.). HSV-2 usually produces genital herpes and herpes associated with infections of the newborn that occur before or during birth (congenital herpes). HSV-1 is transmitted by direct contact through the saliva, while HSV-2 is generally transmitted through direct sexual contact. In addition, HSV-2 may be acquired by the fetus of an infected mother through the placenta or by direct contact during the birthing process.

Symptoms and findings associated with an initial or primary infection with herpes simplex virus usually appear in one to two weeks after contact and may range from no significant illness to the appearance of flu-like symptoms, sometimes in conjunction with blister-like lesions that usually scab and heal in a week to 10 days. Initial infection has a higher rate and longer duration of symptoms. Lesions associated with the first outbreak can be exceedingly painful. Newborns, malnourished infants, and individuals with compromised immune function may develop severe infection involving the entire body (systemic infection). After the primary infection, HSV becomes inactive but travels through the nerves that gave sensation to the affected area. Once it enters the roots of these nerves, it remains there for life. Recurrent episodes may be triggered by such factors as sun exposure, fever, physical and emotional stress, suppression of the immune system, the ingestion of certain medications or specific foods, and other factors. Such episodes may begin with mild irritation, itching, burning, tingling, or sometimes severe pain in the affected area followed a few hours or days later by the formation vesicles that often merge to form one large lesion. Associated symptoms and findings may include itching or discomfort in the affected area, fever, and swollen lymph nodes in the neck. The lesions sometimes become infected, especially in children. Typically, however, the lesions ulcerate and form a yellowish crust within a few days, with healing completed in about three weeks.

Symptoms associated with primary oral herpes infection (herpetic gingivostomatitis) usually appear suddenly and include pain, fever, excessive salivation, bad breath, and difficulty eating. Lesions may appear anywhere in the mouth, although the tongue and inside the cheeks are most frequently involved. In addition, the gums are usually inflamed and nearby lymph nodes may become enlarged. Primary episodes typically persist for about five to nine days. Lesions associated with recurrent oral herpes infection are often accompanied by itching, pain, or tingling that usually subsides within a week. Recurrent cold sore lesions sometimes precede oral herpes infections. Eye lesions may result from both primary and recurrent infections and include inflammation of the delicate mucous membranes that line the inside of the eyelids and the whites of the eyes (conjunctivitis) or inflammation and dryness involving the corneas as well as the conjunctiva.

Genital herpes most often affects adolescents and adults and is usually caused by HSV-2; however, approximately 10 to 25 percent of primary genital herpes infection results from HSV-1 through such factors as oral-genital transmission. This type of infection may be characterized by fever, painful urination, and swollen glands in the genital area. Females may develop herpetic lesions on the cervix and, less commonly, in the vagina and on the external genitalia while males typically develop lesions on the penis. Many patients exhibit few or no symptoms during asecondary episodes. However, infected individuals may unknowingly transmit the virus during this time through sexual activity or from a mother to her newborn.

Additional findings and complications associated with herpes simplex include a condition called herpetic whitlow, which is an infection of the finger resulting from transmission of HSV through a skin break. Whitlow is characterized by painful blistering and swelling at the fingertip. Eczema herpeticum is a severe condition in which patients with certain preexisting inflammatory skin conditions are infected with HSV and develop widespread blistering. Potentially life-threatening associated findings include high fever; excessive fluid loss (dehydration); decreases in the levels of essential elements known as electrolytes in the fluid portion of the blood (e.g., calcium, potassium, and sodium); spread of HSV to the brain and other organs; and bacterial infection. In addition, patients with suppressed immune systems are at risk for potentially life-threatening complications resulting from spread of disease to the liver, lungs, central nervous system, and other organs.

Treatment for herpes simplex is dependent upon the site affected as well as the severity and type of infection. For example, keeping affected areas dry is an important aspect of treatment as moisture tends to promote bacterial infection. Therefore, mild infections such as those associated with herpes of the lip may be treated by cleansing of the affected area with soap and water followed by careful drying of the lesion. Secondary bacterial infections may be treated with antibiotics. In addition, antiviral drugs such as acyclovir are often effective in treating various types of infection as well as preventing recurrences if administered during high-risk periods. Adolescents and young adults should receive counseling or training in order to reduce the risk of transmission. Other treatment is symptomatic and supportive. Patients with frequent outbreaks may benefit from suppressive therapy.

Government Agencies

3697 NIH/National Institute of Allergy and Infectious Diseases
5601 Fishers Lane, MSC 9806
Bethesda, MD 20892
301-496-5717
866-284-4107
Fax: 301-402-3573
TDD: 800-877-8339
ocpostoffice@niaid.nih.gov
www.niaid.nih.gov

The principal advisory board of the NIAID. The council is composed of physicians, scientists and representatives of the public and advises on the conduct and support or research, training and dissemination of health information regarding allergies and infectious diseases.

Anthony S. Fauci, MD, Director

National Associations & Support Groups

3698 **American Academy of Pediatrics**
345 Park Blvd
Itasca, IL 60143
800-433-9016
Fax: 847-434-8000
mcc@aap.org
www.aap.org

The American Academy of Pediatrics and its member pediatricians are committed to the attainment of optimal physical, mental and social health and well-being for all infants, children, adolescents, and young adults.

Lynn Olson, PhD, VP, Research
Mark Del Monte, JD, CEO/Executive VP
Vera Tait, MD, FAAP, Chief Medical Officer

3699 **American Social Health Association**
PO Box 13827
Research Triangle Park, NC 27709
919-361-8400
Fax: 919-361-8425
info@ashasexualhealth.org
www.ashasexualhealth.org

The American Sexual Health Association (ASHA) empowers individuals, families, and communities to achieve sexually healthy lives through education and advocacy. ASHA is an award-winning non-profit organization that has advocated on behalf of those at risk for sexually transmitted infections (STIs) since 1914.

Lynn Barclay, President & CEO
Deborah Arrindell, Vice President, Health Policy

3700 **March of Dimes Foundation**
1550 Crystal Drive, Ste 1300
Arlington, VA 22202
888-663-4637
www.marchofdimes.org

March of Dimes help moms have full-term pregnancies and research the problems that threaten the health of babies. The March of Dimes also acts globally: sharing best practices in perinatal health and helping improve birth outcomes where the needs are the most urgent.

Stacey D. Stewart, President
Alan Brogdon, SVP/COO/Board Officer
Rahul Gupta, MD, SVP & Chief Medical/Health Officer

3701 **World Health Organization**
Avenue Appia 20
1202 Geneva,
Switzerland
www.who.int

WHO is the directing and coordinating authority for health within the United Nations system. WHO operates in more than 150 countries around the world.

Dr. Tedros Adhanom Ghebreyesus, Director General
Dr. Zsuzsanna Jakab, Deputy Director General
Stewart Simonson, Asst Director General, UN NYC

Web Sites

3702 **American Sexual Health Association**
www.ashasexualhealth.org
919-361-8400
Fax: 919-361-8425
info@ashasexualhealth.org
www.ashasexualhealth.org

The American Sexual Health Association (ASHA) empowers individuals, families, and communities to achieve sexually healthy lives through education and advocacy. ASHA is an award-winning non-profit organization that has advocated on behalf of those at risk for sexually transmitted infections (STIs) since 1914.

3703 **Health Research Program (HaRP)**
www.harpnet.org

www.harpnet.org

A program by USAID, the project strives to improve the health status of infants, children, mothers and families through the development and research of new tools, technologies, policies and approaches.

3704 **HerpeSite**
www.herpesite.org

www.herpesite.org

Information outlining aspects and issues relating to herpes simplex virus (HSV).

3705 **Herpes.com**
www.herpes.com

www.herpes.com

Purpose of this website is to fill the desperate need for herpes education, make it easier to manage herpes, inform people of ways to limit herpes reaccurrences, to inform people of the beneficial products for herpes sufferers, to show the relationship between good health and herpes, to provide an opportunity for herpes sufferers to share their personal experiences and to provide communication via our live chat.

3706 **International Herpes Management Forum**
www.ihmf.org

www.ihmf.org

Established to improve the awareness and understanding of herpes virus, and the counselling and management of people with these infections.

3707 **Slack**
6900 Grove Road
Thorofare, NJ 8086
856-848-1000
Fax: 856-848-6091
email@slackinc.com
www.slackinc.com

Is a leading provider of healthcare information, educational programs, and meeting and exhibit management services worldwide.

3708 **Virtual Pediatric Hospital**
www.virtualpediatrichospital.org

www.virtualpediatrichospital.org

A digital library of pediatric information including resources for patients and health care professionals.

Book Publishers

3709 **Understanding Herpes**

Lawrence R. Stanberry MD, PhD, author

University Press of Mississippi
3825 Ridgewood Road
Jackson, MS 39211
601-432-6205
800-737-7788
Fax: 601-432-6217
press@ihl.state.ms.us
www.upress.state.ms.us

A most informative overview of herpes written for the general reader.

120 pages Hardcover/Ppbck
ISBN: 1-578060-40-0

Hirschsprung Disease / Description

Description

3710 HIRSCHSPRUNG DISEASE

Synonyms: Aganglionic megacolon, Congenital aganglionic megacolon

Involves the following Biologic System(s):

Gastrointestinal Disorders

Hirschsprung disease is a gastrointestinal disorder that is usually apparent within the first few days after birth. However, in some affected infants, symptoms may not become apparent until the first weeks of life. Hirschsprung disease is characterized by absence of groups of certain nerve cell bodies (ganglia) in the smooth muscle wall of the large intestine. In most affected infants, the affected segment begins at the ring-shaped involuntary muscle of the anus (internal anal sphincter) and extends to the lowest region of the colon (sigmoid colon). However, in other cases, this segment may extend to involve the entire colon.

In infants with Hirschsprung disease, absence of these nerve groups results in impairment or absence of rhythmic contractions that propel food through the digestive system (peristalsis). Due to impaired peristalsis, most affected newborns have inadequate or delayed passage of meconium, the thick, sticky, darkish green material that accumulates in the fetal intestines and forms a newborn's first stools. Although some affected newborns may pass meconium normally, they may subsequently experience chronic constipation. In infants with Hirschsprung disease, failure to properly pass stools results in widening of the colon (megacolon) above the affected segment and severe abdominal bloating (abdominal distension). Additional symptoms and findings may include episodes of diarrhea, nausea and vomiting, dehydration, loss of appetite (anorexia) and malnutrition, failure to grow and gain weight at the expected rate (failure to thrive), listlessness (lethargy), and other abnormalities. In addition, widening of the colon may result in deterioration of the colon's mucous membranes (mucosal barrier), potentially allowing increased reproduction of certain bacteria and associated inflammation of the colon (i.e., enterocolitis). In severe cases, severe diarrhea and potentially life-threatening complications may result.

In infants with Hirschsprung disease, treatment includes surgical removal of the affected area of the colon and rejoining of healthy areas of the colon and rectum. In some patients, before surgical correction, a temporary colostomy may be required. Colostomy is a procedure in which the lower end of the healthy region of the colon is connected to a surgically created opening in the abdominal wall.

Hirschsprung disease affects approximately one in 5,000 newborns and is considered the most common cause of lower intestinal obstruction in infants during the first month of life. The condition is about four times as common in males as females. Hirschsprung disease may occur in association with other disorders or conditions that are apparent at birth (congenital disorders) or as an isolated finding for unknown reasons (sporadic occurrence). In addition, there have been many reports of Hirschsprung disease in infants within certain families (kindreds). Researchers suggest that sporadic and familial cases may result from abnormal changes or mutations of one of several different genes expressed either alone or together (polygenic). Depending upon the specific disease gene or genes, the condition may have autosomal dominant, autosomal recessive, or polygenic inheritance.

National Associations & Support Groups

3711 American Academy of Pediatrics
345 Park Blvd
Itasca, IL 60143
800-433-9016
Fax: 847-434-8000
mcc@aap.org
www.aap.org

The American Academy of Pediatrics and its member pediatricians are committed to the attainment of optimal physical, mental and social health and well-being for all infants, children, adolescents, and young adults.

Lynn Olson, PhD, VP, Research
Mark Del Monte, JD, CEO/Executive VP
Vera Tait, MD, FAAP, Chief Medical Officer

3712 Genetic Alliance
426400 Woodfield Road, Ste 189
Damascus, MD 20872
202-966-5557
Fax: 202-966-8553
info@geneticalliance.org
www.geneticalliance.org

World's leading nonprofit health advocacy organization committed to transforming health through genetics and promoting an environment of openness centered on the health of individuals, families, and communities.

Sharon Terry, CEO
Ruth Child, CFO
Natasha Bonhomme, Chief Strategy Officer

3713 March of Dimes Foundation
1550 Crystal Drive, Ste 1300
Arlington, VA 22202
888-663-4637
www.marchofdimes.org

March of Dimes help moms have full-term pregnancies and research the problems that threaten the health of babies. The March of Dimes also acts globally: sharing best practices in perinatal health and helping improve birth outcomes where the needs are the most urgent.

Stacey D. Stewart, President
Alan Brogdon, SVP/COO/Board Officer
Rahul Gupta, MD, SVP & Chief Medical/Health Officer

3714 PullThrough
2312 Savoy Street
Hoover, AL 35226
205-978-2930
info@pullthrough.org
www.pullthrough.org

A chapter of the United Ostomy Association dedicated to the support and information needs of the families of children born with imperforate anus, cloaca, cloaca exstrophy, bladder exstrophy, VATER Syndrome, Hirschsprung's Disease and other related birth anomalies.

Bonnie McElroy, President

3715 United Ostomy Association
PO Box 525
Kennebunk, ME 04043
800-826-0826
www.uoaa.org

An association of affiliated, non-profit, support groups committed to improving the quality of life of people who have, or will have, an intestinal or urinary diversion.

Christine Ryan, Executive Director

Libraries & Resource Centers

3716 National Digestive Diseases Information Clearinghouse (NDDIC)
NIH
2 Information Way
Bethesda, MD 20892
301-654-3810
800-891-5389
Fax: 301-907-8906
nddic@info.niddk.nih.gov
www.digestive.niddk.nih.gov

The National Institute of Diabetes and Digestive and Kidney Diseases conducts and supports research on many of the most serious diseases affecting public health. The Institute supports much of the clinical research on the diseases of internal medicine and related subspecialty fields as well as many basic science disciplines.

Griffin P. Rodgers, MD, Director
Gregory G. Germino, MD, Deputy Director
Kathy Kranzfelder, Communications Director

Web Sites

3717 NIH News Advisory
9000 Rockville Pike
Bethesda, MD 20892
301-496-4000
TTY: 301-402-9612
NIHinfo@od.nih.gov
www.nih.gov

The National Institute of Health is the steward of medical and behavioral research for the nation.

Francis S. Collins, M.D., Ph.D., Director

3718 Online Mendelian Inheritance in Man
McKusick-Nathans Institue of Genetic Medicine-JHU
Baltimore, MD 21205
www.omim.org

This database is a catalog of human genes and genetic disorders.

Ada Hamosh, MD, Scientific Director

3719 Pull-Thru Network
Normal, IL 61761
pullthrunetwork@gmail.com
www.pullthrunetwork.org

Pull-thru Network (PTN) is one of the largest organizations in the world dedicated to the needs of those born with an anorectal malformation or colon disease and any of the associated diagnoses.

Lori Parker, Executive Director
Hollie Filce, Associate Director
Carmell Burns, Director

Book Publishers

3720 Online Pediatric Surgery Handbook
PO Box 10426, Caparra Heights Station
San Juan, PR 00922
787-786-3496
Fax: 787-720-6103
titolugo@coqul.net
www.home.coqui.net/titolugo/handbook.htm#IIIF

An online handbook about many different diseases and disabilities.

Newsletters

3721 PTN News
Normal, IL 61761
pullthrunetwork@gmail.com
www.pullthrunetwork.org

Newsletter of the Pull-thru Network, one of the largest organizations in the world dedicated to the needs of those born with an anorectal malformation or colon disease and any of the associated diagnoses.

Lori Parker, Executive Director
Hollie Filce, Associate Director
Carmell Burns, Director

3722 Pediatric Surgery Update
PO Box 10426, Caparra Heights Station
San Juan, PR 922
787-786-3496
Fax: 787-720-6103
home.coqui.net/titolugo/handbook.htm#IIIF

Periodical electronic newsletter of interest to Primary Physicians, Pediatricians, Surgeons, Residents, Medical Students, Nurses and Health-related professionals dealing with evidence-based medicine and reviews in the practice of pediatric surgery.

Humberto Lugo-Vicente MD, FACS, Editor-in-Chief

Pamphlets

3723 Hirschsprung Disease
Nat'l Digestive Diseases Information Clearinghouse
The National Institute of Diabetes and Digestive a
Bethesda, MD 20892
301-496-3583
Fax: 301-402-2125
germinogg@mail.nih.gov
www.niddk.nih.gov

Defines and explains the causes, symptoms, and treatment of Hirschsprung's Disease. Includes a glossary of terms associated with the condition.

Griffin P. Rodgers, M.D., M.A.C.P., Director
Dr. Gregory Germino, Deputy Director

Histiocytosis / Description

Description

3724 HISTIOCYTOSIS

Synonyms: Class I histiocytosis, Langerhans cell histiocytosis, LCH

Involves the following Biologic System(s):
Hematologic and Oncologic Disorders

Histiocytosis X, also known as Langerhans cell histiocytosis, LCH, or Class I histiocytosis, refers to a group of three similar disorders called eosinophilic granuloma, Hand-Schuller-Christian disease, and Letterer-Siwe disease. These disorders are all characterized by the excessive production and accumulation of certain types of tissue cells known as histiocytes, resulting in benign growth or scar formation. Characteristic findings and symptoms are variable and depend upon the organ or organ system affected; however, approximately 80 percent of individuals with LCH have skeletal involvement. Associated bone lesions may appear in isolation or in many parts of the body. These lesions occur most often in the skull, although their appearance in other areas of the skeleton is not uncommon. Some individuals may experience complications resulting from bone involvement. For example, involvement of a certain bone near the ear (mastoid) may result in chronic ear infections and persistent drainage. Involvement of certain weight-bearing bones may result in fractures.

Letterer-Siwe disease occurs during early childhood, usually before three years of age. This disease is characterized by skin eruptions, enlargement of the liver and spleen (hepatosplenomegaly) and certain lymph nodes (lymphadenopathy), and abnormally low levels of circulating red blood cells resulting in anemia. In addition, some children may experience involvement of the lungs, sometimes resulting in lung collapse (pneumothorax). Hand-Schuller-Christian disease often appears during early childhood and is characterized by bulging of the eyeballs (exophthalmos); excessive urinary excretion (polyuria), a decrease in body fluid volume (dehydration), and excessive thirst (polydipsia); elevated cholesterol levels (hypercholesterolemia); and involvement of soft tissues and bone. Eosinophilic granulomas most often occur during the second to fourth decade of life; however, they may develop during childhood, especially between the ages of five to 10 years. Benign growths may develop in the skull, jaw, and the long bones of the arms and legs, sometimes resulting in pain and fractures. In addition, lung involvement may result in respiratory symptoms such as coughing and shortness of breath, fever, and lung collapse.

Other findings and symptoms sometimes associated with Class I histiocytoses may include stunted growth, thyroid deficiency, and other abnormalities resulting from disruption in pituitary gland function or involvement of another gland in the brain known as the hypothalamus; difficulty walking and other neurologic symptoms resulting from involvement of the central nervous system; and additional irregularities of the blood resulting from involvement of the bone marrow.

Although the exact cause of each of the disorders that comprise Class I histiocytoses is unknown, it is believed that Letterer-Siwe disease may be inherited as an autosomal recessive trait and that the diseases develop as a result of disturbanc|es within the immune system. Treatment for LCH depends upon the extent and severity of involvement. For example, if only one organ or organ system (e.g., skeletal or skin, etc.) is affected, the disease is often self-limited; therefore, treatment may be directed toward control and resolution of specific lesions through low-dose radiation therapy or removal by means of a scraping procedure (curettage). If more than one system of the body is affected, treatment may involve a chemotherapy regimen that includes the use of one or two specific drugs (i.e., etoposide and vinblastine). More resistant disease may necessitate the use of other immunosuppressive drugs, bone marrow transplantation, or experimental treatments. Other treatment is symptomatic and supportive.

Government Agencies

3725 NIH/National Cancer Institute
Bethesda, MD 20892

800-422-6237
NCIinfo@nih.gov
www.cancer.gov

The National Cancer Institute coordinates the National Cancer Program, which conducts and supports research, training, health information dissemination, and other programs with respect to the cause, diagnosis, prevention, and treatment of cancer, rehabilitation from cancer, and the continuing care of cancer patients and the families of cancer patients.

Norman E. Sharpless, MD, Director
Douglas R. Lowy, MD, Principal Deputy Director

National Associations & Support Groups

3726 American Academy of Pediatrics
345 Park Blvd
Itasca, IL 60143

800-433-9016
Fax: 847-434-8000
mcc@aap.org
www.aap.org

The American Academy of Pediatrics and its member pediatricians are committed to the attainment of optimal physical, mental and social health and well-being for all infants, children, adolescents, and young adults.

Lynn Olson, PhD, VP, Research
Mark Del Monte, JD, CEO/Executive VP
Vera Tait, MD, FAAP, Chief Medical Officer

3727 Genetic Alliance
426400 Woodfield Road, Ste 189
Damascus, MD 20872

202-966-5557
Fax: 202-966-8553
info@geneticalliance.org
www.geneticalliance.org

World's leading nonprofit health advocacy organization committed to transforming health through genetics and promoting an environment of openness centered on the health of individuals, families, and communities.

Sharon Terry, CEO
Ruth Child, CFO
Natasha Bonhomme, Chief Strategy Officer

3728 Histiocytosis Association
332 North Broadway
Pitman, NJ 08071

856-589-6606
Fax: 856-589-6614
info@histio.org
www.histio.org

The Histiocytosis Association Inc. is a global, nonprofit organization dedicated to supporting, educating, and connecting those who are fighting histiocytic disorders, and ultimately, finding a cure. It is the only organization of its kind-bringing together the patient and medical communities to grow and share knowledge; providing critical support and education to patients and families; and identifying and funding key research initiatives that will lead to a world free of these disorders.

Deanna Fournier, Executive Director

3729 March of Dimes Foundation
1550 Crystal Drive, Ste 1300
Arlington, VA 22202

888-663-4637
www.marchofdimes.org

March of Dimes help moms have full-term pregnancies and research the problems that threaten the health of babies. The March of Dimes also acts globally: sharing best practices in perinatal health and helping improve birth outcomes where the needs are the most urgent.

Stacey D. Stewart, President
Alan Brogdon, SVP/COO/Board Officer
Rahul Gupta, MD, SVP & Chief Medical/Health Officer

Web Sites

3730 Histicytosis Association
332 North Broadway
Pitman, NJ 08071
856-589-6606
Fax: 856-589-6614
info@histio.org
www.histio.org/

The Histiocytosis Association Inc. is a global, nonprofit organization dedicated to supporting, educating, and connecting those who are fighting histiocytic disorders, and ultimately, finding a cure. It is the only organization of its kind-bringing together the patient and medical communities to grow and share knowledge; providing critical support and education to patients and families; and identifying and funding key research initiatives that will lead to a world free of these disorders..

Deanna Fournier, Executive Director

3731 Online Mendelian Inheritance in Man
McKusick-Nathans Institue of Genetic Medicine-JHU
Baltimore, MD 21205
www.omim.org

This database is a catalog of human genes and genetic disorders.

Ada Hamosh, MD, Scientific Director

3732 Texas Children's Cancer Center
P.O. Box 2659
Austin, TX 78768
512-474-1798
www.txcc.org

Offers innovative therapies for all forms of childhood cancer and blood disorders. The Cancer Center is working to improve the outcome for all patients afflicted with these diseases and to develop and perfect new treatment approaches that are born from only the most extraordinary scientific insights.

Geanie Morrison, President
James Frank, Vice President
Jodie Laubenberg, Secretary

Book Publishers

3733 Let's Talk About Going to the Hospital
Rosen Publishing Group's PowerKids Press
29 E 21st Street
New York, NY 10010
212-777-3017
800-237-9932
Fax: 888-436-4643
rosenpub@tribeca.ios.com
www.rosenpublishing.com

If a child has to check into the hospital, chances are he or she is already upset about being ill. Knowing how a hospital functions and what the procedures are, such as when family members can visit, will help in what is already a stressful situation. Grades K-5.

24 pages
ISBN: 0-823950-36-0

Roger Rosen, President

Hodgkin's Disease / Description

Description

3734 HODGKIN'S DISEASE

Synonym: Hodgkin's lymphoma

Covers these related disorders: Hodgkin's disease—lymphocyte depletion type, Hodgkin's disease—lymphocyte predominance type, Hodgkin's disease—mixed cellularity type, Hodgkin's disease—nodular sclerosing type

Involves the following Biologic System(s):

Hematologic and Oncologic Disorders

Hodgkin's disease is a malignant disorder (cancer) characterized by painless, progressive enlargement of the lymph nodes, spleen, and other lymphoid tissues (lymphoma). The lymphatic system includes a network of vessels that collect a fluid known as lymph from different areas of the body and drain this fluid into the bloodstream. As lymph moves through the lymphatic system, it is filtered by a network of lymph nodes, which are small structures located along the course of the lymphatic vessels. Most lymph nodes that can be felt (palpable) are located in the neck, mouth, and groin and under the arms (axillae). Lymph nodes store certain white blood cells and are thought to play a role in producing antibodies, thus functioning as part of the body's immune system.

Malignancies of lymph tissue, known as lymphomas, are the third most common form of cancer affecting children in the United States. Approximately 13 per one million children are affected by lymphoma in the U.S. each year. There are two main categories of lymphoma, including Hodgkin's disease and non-Hodgkin's lymphoma. Although Hodgkin's disease may affect individuals of any age, it usually occurs between the ages of 15 and 35 or after age 50. In children, the disease is most common during late childhood or early adolescence and rarely affects those younger than five years of age. About 6,000 to 7,000 cases of the disease occur in the U.S. annually. Epstein-Barr virus, a member of the herpesvirus family that causes mononucleosis 35-50 percent of the time, may play some role in the disease. In addition, some familial cases have been reported, suggesting possible genetic mechanisms.

Hodgkin's disease is characterized by the presence of relatively large, abnormal white blood cells that have more than one nucleus and a distinctive appearance under a microscope. These cancerous cells, known as Reed-Sternberg cells, may be seen during the microscopic examination of small tissue samples removed from affected lymph nodes or other lymphoid tissues. Hodgkin's disease is categorized into four main subtypes based upon the number and relative proportion of such cells as well as the proportions of certain other white blood cells (e.g., plasma cells, eosinophils, macrophages, etc.). The frequency of the different subtypes varies with age. For example, nodular sclerosing type is the most common form of the disease and affects approximately 50 percent of children and up to 70 percent of adolescents with Hodgkin's disease. Another subtype, known as the mixed cellularity type, affects about 40 to 50 percent of patients, and the lymphocyte predominance type of the disease primarily occurs in males and younger patients. The fourth subtype, called lymphocyte depletion type, is the rarest and most aggressive form of the disorder and occurs in fewer than 10 percent of patients.

Hodgkin's disease usually originates in the lymphatic vessels. As the disease progresses, the malignancy may spread from lymph nodes and infiltrate certain organs, particularly the spleen, lungs, liver, and bone marrow. Most patients initially experience painless swelling of lymph nodes in the neck or, in some cases, under the arm or in the groin area. Some may gradually develop generalized symptoms including fever, night sweats, fatigue, listlessness (lethargy), generalized itching (pruritus), loss of appetite (anorexia), and weight loss. Involvement of other organs or tissues may cause varying symptoms. For example, if the lungs are affected, patients may experience coughing and shortness of breath (dyspnea). Advanced involvement of the bone marrow may result in abnormally low levels of circulating red blood cells (anemia), platelets (thrombocytopenia), or certain white blood cells (neutropenia). Advanced disease may cause progressive impairment of the body's immune system, resulting in an increased susceptibility to certain infections. In patients with severe disease progression, infection with certain microorganisms that typically cause no or only minor symptoms in healthy individuals may result in severe or potentially life-threatening complications.

Treatment of patients with the disease varies, depending on the stage of the disease and other factors. For patients in early stages who have localized disease and have obtained full growth, radiation therapy alone may be effective; the 10-year survival rate exceeds 80 percent. However, up to 15 percent of such patients may experience recurrences, requiring therapy with certain anticancer drugs (combination chemotherapy). However, combination therapy cures more than 50 percent of patients, even those with advanced-stage disease. Combination chemotherapy may include the drugs doxorubicin (Adriamycin), bleomycin, vinblastine, and dacarbazine (known as ABVD) or a combination of mechlorethamine, vincristine (Oncovin), procarbazine, and prednisone (called MOPP). Physicians who specialize in the treatment of childhood cancers (pediatric oncologists) often select alternating therapy with MOPP and ABVD in combination with low-dose radiation therapy due to this treatment's high success and a reduction in certain long-term effects potentially associated with treatment for Hodgkin's disease. For example, such combination chemotherapy/radiation therapy may help reduce the risk of potential growth defects in affected children, damage to heart and lung tissue, infertility, or the development of certain secondary malignancies later in life, such as acute myeloid leukemia (AML) or certain solid tumors. Patients should receive ongoing monitoring throughout life to ensure prompt detection and treatment of possible recurrences or secondary malignancies.

Government Agencies

3735 NIH/National Cancer Institute
Bethesda, MD 20892

800-422-6237
NCIinfo@nih.gov
www.cancer.gov

The National Cancer Institute coordinates the National Cancer Program, which conducts and supports research, training, health information dissemination, and other programs with respect to the cause, diagnosis, prevention, and treatment of cancer, rehabilitation from cancer, and the continuing care of cancer patients and the families of cancer patients.

Norman E. Sharpless, MD, Director
Douglas R. Lowy, MD, Principal Deputy Director

National Associations & Support Groups

3736 American Academy of Pediatrics
345 Park Blvd
Itasca, IL 60143

800-433-9016
Fax: 847-434-8000
mcc@aap.org
www.aap.org

The American Academy of Pediatrics and its member pediatricians are committed to the attainment of optimal physical, mental and social health and well-being for all infants, children, adolescents, and young adults.

Lynn Olson, PhD, VP, Research
Mark Del Monte, JD, CEO/Executive VP
Vera Tait, MD, FAAP, Chief Medical Officer

3737 American Childhood Cancer Organization
P.O. Box 498
Kensington, MD 20895
301-962-3520
855-858-2226
Fax: 310-962-3521
staff@acco.org
www.acco.org

The American Childhood Cancer Organization (ACCO) was founded in 1970 by a group of parents whose children had been diagnosed with cancer. Today ACCO is one of the largest grassroots, national organizations dedicated to improving the lives of children and adolescents with cancer and their families.

Ruth I. Hoffman, MPH, CEO
Krista Novak, Programs Manager
Blair Scroggs, Public Relations Coordinator

3738 Childhood Leukemia Foundation
807 Mantoloking Road
Brick, NJ 08723
732-920-8860
888-253-7109
www.clf4kids.org

Childhood Leukemia Foundation proudly promotes patient education, advocacy and self-esteem.

3739 CureSearch for Children's Cancer
P.O. Box 45781
Baltimore, MD 21297
800-458-6223
Fax: 301-718-0047
info@curesearch.org
www.curesearch.org

CureSearch for Children's Cancer is a national non-profit foundation that accelerates the cure for children's cancer by driving innovation, eliminating research barriers and solving the field's most challenging problems.

Kay Koehler, CEO
Katharine A. Burke, COO & VP, Financing
Caitlyn W. Barrett, National Director, Research & Prgms

3740 Leukemia & Lymphoma Society
3 International Drive, Ste 200
Rye Brook, NY 10573
888-557-7177
www.lls.org

Large voluntary health organization dedicated to funding blood cancer research, education and patient services.

Louis J. DeGennaro, PhD, President & CEO
Troy Dunmire, COO
Gwen Nichols, MD, Chief Medical Officer

3741 Lymphoma Research Foundation
88 Pine Street, Suite 2400
New York, NY 10005
212-349-2910
800-500-9976
helpline@lymphoma.org
lymphoma.org

National nonprofit organization dedicated to eradicating lymphoma and serving those touched by this disease. LRF funds research to develop safer, more effective treatments and ultimately, a cure for lymphoma. LRF delivers a comprehensive slate of educational and support programs, services, and publications for lymphoma patients and their loved ones.

Meghan Gutierrez, Chief Executive Officer
Kyle Haines, Chief Information Officer
Sarah Quinlan, Chief Program Officer

3742 National Foundation for Cancer Research
5515 Security Lane, Suite 1105
Rockville, MD 20852
800-321-2873
info@nfcr.org
www.nfcr.org

The National Foundation for Cancer Research (NFCR) was founded in 1973 to support cancer research and public education relating to the prevention, early diagnosis, better treatments and ultimately, a cure for cancer. NFCR promotes and facilitates collaboration among scientists to accelerate the pace of discovery from bench to bedside.

Sujuan Ba, President & CEO
Kwok Leung, Chief Financial Officer & Secretary
Brian Wachtel, Executive Director

Web Sites

3743 Children's Cancer Web
www.cancerindex.org/ccw

www.cancerindex.org/ccw

An independent nonprofit site, established to provide a directory of childhood cancer resources.

Book Publishers

3744 Let's Talk About Going to the Hospital
Rosen Publishing Group's PowerKids Press
29 E 21st Street
New York, NY 10010
212-777-3017
800-237-9932
Fax: 888-436-4643
rosenpub@tribeca.ios.com
www.rosenpublishing.com

If a child has to check into the hospital, chances are he or she is already upset about being ill. Knowing how a hospital functions and what the procedures are, such as when family members can visit, will help in what is already a stressful situation. Grades K-5.

24 pages
ISBN: 0-823950-36-0

Roger Rosen, President

3745 Let's Talk About When Kids Have Cancer
Rosen Publishing Group's PowerKids Press
29 E 21st Street
New York, NY 10010
212-777-3017
800-237-9932
Fax: 888-436-4643
rosenpub@tribeca.ios.com
www.rosenpublishing.com

In a straightforward yet comforting way, this book explains what cancer is, what kinds of treatments surround the disease and how to cope if a child has cancer. K-5.

24 pages Paperback
ISBN: 0-823951-95-6

3746 Living with Childhood Cancer: A Practical Guide to Help Families Cope

Leigh A. Woznick, Carol D. Goodheart EdD, author

American Psychological Association
750 1st Street
Washington, DC 20002
202-336-5500
800-374-2721
TTY: 202-336-6123
www.apa.org

This book offers information for families faced with the shattering experience of having a child with cancer.

2001 359 pages Hardcover
ISBN: 1-557988-72-2

Donald N. Bersoff, PhD, JD, President
Norman B. Anderson, PhD, Chief Executive Officer & Executive
Bonnie Markham, PhD, Treasurer

Hodgkin's Disease / Pamphlets

3747 Surviving Childhood Cancer: A Guide for Families
New Harbinger Publications
5674 Shattuck Avenue
Oakland, CA 94609

510-652-0215
800-748-6273
Fax: 800-652-1613
customerservice@newharbinger.com
www.newharbinger.com

Cancer in a child is an overwhelming experience for a family. This book explains common medical procedures and offers readers practical advice about how to cope with emotions and stress during this time.

1998 215 pages
ISBN: 1-572241-02-0

Pamphlets

3748 Hodgkin's Disease and Non-Hodgkin's Lymphomas
Leukemia and Lymphoma Society
3 International Drive, Ste 200
Rye Brook, NY 10573

914-949-5213
800-955-4572
Fax: 914-949-6691
infocenter@lls.org
www.lls.org

Explanation of the disease, its symptoms, diagnosis, prognosis and treatment, psychological responses to a confirmed diagnosis and current research.

36 pages

Louis J. DeGennaro, Ph.D., President & CEO

Description

3749 HOMOCYSTINURIA

Covers these related disorders: Homocystinuria Type I (Classic homocystinuria), Homocystinuria Type II, Homocystinuria Type III

Involves the following Biologic System(s):
Genetic/Chromosomal/Syndrome/Metabolic Disorders

Homocystinuria is a metabolic disorder characterized by an inborn error in the metabolism of the amino acid methionine. There are three types of homocystinuria, each resulting from a deficiency or defect of a specific enzyme or compound that is essential in the processing of methionine.

Homocystinuria Type I (Classic homocystinuria) is caused by a deficiency of the enzyme cystathionine synthase Although symptoms and physical findings are not apparent at birth, early symptoms may include delays in development and failure to thrive. Characteristic findings, which are often not apparent until after the age of three years, may include eye abnormalities such as dislocation of the lens of the eyes (ectopia lentis), followed by nearsightedness (myopia) and tremors of the iris (iridodonesis). Other physical findings may include skeletal abnormalities such as osteoporosis, sideways curvature of the spine (scoliosis), either a sunken or prominent chest (pectus deformity), and a condition known as genu valgum in which the legs curve inward causing the knees to touch (knock-knee) and the space between the feet to increase. Affected children often have a fair complexion, blue eyes, sparse blonde hair, and a characteristic flushed face (malar flush). In addition, there is a tendency to develop blood clots (thromboemboli) in the veins and arteries.These clots may occur at any time, and if they lodge in the brain can result in paralysis and seizures heart problems and high blood pressure may also occur. Laboratory findings may include elevated levels of both methionine and the sulfur compound homocystine in body fluids. intellectual disabilities is apparent in approximately 65 percent of affected people. It is estimated that about 50 percent of patients experience some form of psychiatric disorder.

Treatment for classic homocystinuria includes aggressive vitamin B6 supplementation. In addition, restriction of foods that contain methionine is recommended in conjunction with supplementation of cysteine, also a sulfur-containing amino acid. In some affected individuals who do not respond to vitamin B6 treatment, administration of betaine may be effective. Classic homocystinuria is inherited as an autosomal recessive trait and occurs in approximately one in 200,000 live births. The gene for cystathionine synthase is located on the long arm of chromosome 21 (21q22.3).

Homocystinuria Type II is transmitted as an autosomal recessive trait and results from a defect in the formation of methylcobalamin. Characteristic symptoms and findings depend on the particular underlying defect. Some children with homocystinuria type II may also have a condition called methylmalonic aciduria characterized by excessive methylmalonic acid in the urine. Symptoms usually develop in the early months of life and may include difficulty in feeding, listlessness, vomiting, diminished muscle tone (hypotonia), and delays in development. Treatment for this form of homo stinuria includes vitamin B12 supplementation (cobalamin).

Homocystinuria Type III, a very rare form of the disorder, results from a deficiency of the enzyme methylenetetrahydrofolate reductase (MTHFR), also essential to the maintenance of methionine. Symptoms and physical findings are extremely variable and depend upon the extent of the deficiency. Complete absence of this enzyme may result in life-threatening episodes of respiratory distress as well as seizure-like muscle contractions (myoclonus). A partial enzyme deficiency may cause convulsions, an abnormally small head (microcephaly), intellectual disabilities, and muscular irregularities. Occasional findings may include psychiatric disturbances, abnormalities of certain blood vessels, and inflammation or degenerative changes of specific nerves. In addition, blood clot activity may be apparent in some affected individuals.

Treatment for homocystinuria type III may include supplementation with folic acid, vitamin B6 (pyridoxine), vitamin B12, methionine, and betaine (also known as trimethylglycine). Early intervention with betaine has a particularly effective outcome. Homocystinuria Type III is transmitted as an autosomal recessive trait. The gene for methylenetetrahydrofolate reductase is located on the short arm of chromosome 1 (1p36.3).

National Associations & Support Groups

3750 American Academy of Pediatrics
345 Park Blvd
Itasca, IL 60143
800-433-9016
Fax: 847-434-8000
mcc@aap.org
www.aap.org

The American Academy of Pediatrics and its member pediatricians are committed to the attainment of optimal physical, mental and social health and well-being for all infants, children, adolescents, and young adults.

Lynn Olson, PhD, VP, Research
Mark Del Monte, JD, CEO/Executive VP
Vera Tait, MD, FAAP, Chief Medical Officer

3751 Arc of the United States
1825 K Street NW, Ste 1200
Washington, DC 20006
202-534-3700
800-433-5255
Fax: 202-534-3731
info@thearc.org
www.thearc.org

The Arc of the United States advocates for the rights and full participation of all children and adults with intellectual and developmental disabilities. Together with a network of members and affiliated chapters, they improve systems of support and services; connect families; inspire communities and influence public policy.

Peter V. Berns, CEO

3752 Genetic Alliance
426400 Woodfield Road, Ste 189
Damascus, MD 20872
202-966-5557
Fax: 202-966-8553
info@geneticalliance.org
www.geneticalliance.org

World's leading nonprofit health advocacy organization committed to transforming health through genetics and promoting an environment of openness centered on the health of individuals, families, and communities.

Sharon Terry, CEO
Ruth Child, CFO
Natasha Bonhomme, Chief Strategy Officer

3753 March of Dimes Foundation
1550 Crystal Drive, Ste 1300
Arlington, VA 22202
888-663-4637
www.marchofdimes.org

March of Dimes help moms have full-term pregnancies and research the problems that threaten the health of babies. The March of Dimes also acts globally: sharing best practices in perinatal health and helping improve birth outcomes where the needs are the most urgent.

Stacey D. Stewart, President
Alan Brogdon, SVP/COO/Board Officer
Rahul Gupta, MD, SVP & Chief Medical/Health Officer

Conferences

3754 **Arc Annual National Convention**
Arc of the United States
1825 K Street NW, Ste 1200
Washington, DC 20006

202-534-3700
800-433-5255
Fax: 202-534-3731
mckiernan@thearc.org
www.thearc.org

Held in cities throughout the U.S. each fall which attracts nearly 1000 people for educational sessions, business meetings and social events.

Peter V. Berns, CEO
Kristen McKiernan, Sr Exec. Offcr, Comms & Marketing
Liz Mahar, Director, Family/Sibling Initiative

Web Sites

3755 **Arc of the United States**
1825 K Street NW, Ste 1200
Washington, DC 20006

202-534-3700
800-433-5255
Fax: 202-534-3731
info@thearc.org
www.thearc.org

The Arc of the United States advocates for the rights and full participation of all children and adults with intellectual and developmental disabilities. Together with a network of members and affiliated chapters, they improve systems of support and services; connect families; inspire communities and influence public policy.

Peter V. Berns, CEO

3756 **CLIMB: Children Living with Inherited Metabolic Disorders**
www.climb.org.uk

800-652-3181
www.climb.org.uk

Official website for the organization, committed to fighting metabolic diseases through research, awareness and support, providing advice, information and support on all metabolic diseases to children, young adults, families, carers and professionals. Includes links to other sites.

3757 **Clinical Genetic Services-Department of Pediatrics**
Hassenfeld Children's Hospital at NYU Langone
424 East 34th Street
New York, NY 10016

212-263-7300
Fax: 646-754-2250
nyulangone.org

Offers evaluations, genetic counseling and testing. Clinical services include carrier testing, prenatal counseling, and complete genetic evaluations for children and adults.

John G. Pappas, MD, Pediatric Genetic Associate
Naomi Yachelevich, MD, Pediatric Genetic Associate

3758 **Genetic Alliance**
4301 Connecticut Avenue NW, Suite 404
Washington, DC 20008

202-966-5557
www.geneticalliance.org

A nonprofit tax exempt organization founded in 1986 as a national coalition of consumers, professionals and genetic support groups to voice the common concerns of children and adults and families living with, and at risk of, genetic conditions. The Alliance builds partnerships among consumers and professionals and the private and public sectors to promote optimum healthcare and enhanced quality of life for individuals identified with genetic conditions.

Sharon Terry, President/CEO
Tetyana Murza, Managing Director
Natasha Bonhomme, Chief Strategy Officer

3759 **March of Dimes Foundation**
1550 Crystal Drive, Ste 1300
Arlington, VA 22202

888-663-4637
www.marchofdimes.org

March of Dimes help moms have full-term pregnancies and research the problems that threaten the health of babies. The March of Dimes also acts globally: sharing best practices in perinatal health and helping improve birth outcomes where the needs are the most urgent.

Stacey D. Stewart, President
Alan Brogdon, SVP/COO/Board Officer
Rahul Gupta, MD, SVP & Chief Medical/Health Officer

3760 **Maryland Department of Health**
201 W. Preston Street
Baltimore, MD 21201

410-767-6500
877-463-3464
dhmh.healthmd@maryland.gov
dhmh.maryland.gov

Our mission is to protect, promote and improve the health and well-being of all Maryland citizens in a fiscally responsible way.

3761 **National Center for Biotechnology Information**
National Library of Medicine, 8600 Rockville Pike
Bethesda, MD 20894

888-346-3656
info@ncbi.nlm.nih.gov
www.ncbi.nlm.nih.gov

NCBI's mission is to develop new information technologoes to aid in the understanding of fundamental molecular and genetic processes that control health and disease.

Patricia Flatley Brennan, RN, PhD, Director
James Ostell, PhD, Executive Secretary

3762 **Online Mendelian Inheritance in Man**
McKusick-Nathans Institue of Genetic Medicine-JHU
Baltimore, MD 21205
www.omim.org

This database is a catalog of human genes and genetic disorders.

Ada Hamosh, MD, Scientific Director

3763 **Save Babies Through Screening Foundation**
PO Box 2313
Palm Harbor, FL 34682

888-454-3383
email@savebabies.org
www.savebabies.org

Is a national nonprofit public charity run by volunteers. Its mission is to improve the lives of babies by working to prevent disabilities and early death resulting from disorders detectable through newborn screening.

Jill Levy-Fisch, President
Sarah Wilkerson, Vice President
Anne Rugari, Treasurer

Description

3764 HYDROCEPHALUS

Synonym: Hydrocephaly

Covers these related disorders: Acute hydrocephalus, Occult tension hydrocephalus, Overt tension hydrocephalus, Communicating hydrocephalus, Non-communicating hydrocephalus, Obstructive hydrocephalus, Non-obstructive hydrocephalus

Involves the following Biologic System(s):

Neurologic Disorders

Hydrocephalus is a general term used to describe a group of conditions characterized by the accumulation of cerebrospinal fluid (CSF) around the brain. This fluid, which acts as a protective shock absorber for the brain and spinal cord, flows through the four cavities in the brain (ventricles); through the cavity containing the spinal fluid (spinal canal); and between layers of the membrane that surrounds the brain and spinal cord (subarachnoid space). Obstructed flow or impaired absorption of the CSF results in increasing fluid pressure within the brain. Hydrocephalus is thought to affect approximately one in 500 to 1,500 births. The condition may occur as a result of certain malformations that are present at birth, such as Arnold-Chiari malformation or Dandy-Walker syndrome, certain infectious diseases, head injuries, bleeding within the brain, or certain tumors.

Symptoms associated with hydrocephalus may vary, depending upon the nature of the underlying abnormality, the age of onset, and the rate and duration of increasing pressure within the brain. Hydrocephalus may be apparent at birth (congenital) or develop during the first few months or years of life. Because the fibrous joints of the skull (fontanels) have not fused or completely closed, rapid enlargement of the head may occur. The forehead appears abnormally prominent; the skin over the skull is thin with obvious scalp veins; and the face may appear relatively small. Additional symptoms and findings many include difficulties feeding, irritability, sluggishness, lack of interest in surroundings, lack of normal reflex responses, and downward turning of the eyes. Progression of the condition without treatment may result in extreme drowsiness, episodes of uncontrolled electrical disturbances in the brain (seizures), and potentially life-threatening complications.

In other children, hydrocephalus becomes apparent after the bones of the skull are fused (i.e., after two years of age). Some children may have no apparent symptoms, whereas others may have mild, intermittent, or progressive symptoms. These symptoms may include headaches, easy distractibility, poor memory, and progressively impaired walking and balance. Others may experience an acute form of hydrocephalus in which there is rapidly increasing intracranial pressure, causing severe headache, vomiting, visual disturbances, increasing drowsiness over the period of minutes or hours, potential coma, and possibly life-threatening complications.

Treatment of infants and children with hydrocephalus depends upon the underlying cause of the condition. Therapeutic measures may include use of certain medications, such as acetazolamide and furosemide, which are diuretics ("water pills") that help to reduce the build up of cerebrospinal fluid. Other treatment options may include surgical removal of any obstruction or surgical implantation of a specialized device known as a shunt. Shunts allow excess fluid to drain away from the brain to another part of the body for absorption into the bloodstream. After treatment, many affected children may continue to have associated impairment, such as intellectual deficits, impaired memory, and visual abnormalities. Physicians may regularly monitor affected children and suggest a variety of multidisciplinary measures.

National Associations & Support Groups

3765 American Academy of Pediatrics
345 Park Blvd
Itasca, IL 60143

800-433-9016
Fax: 847-434-8000
mcc@aap.org
www.aap.org

The American Academy of Pediatrics and its member pediatricians are committed to the attainment of optimal physical, mental and social health and well-being for all infants, children, adolescents, and young adults.

Lynn Olson, PhD, VP, Research
Mark Del Monte, JD, CEO/Executive VP
Vera Tait, MD, FAAP, Chief Medical Officer

3766 Birth Defect Research for Children
976 Lake Baldwin Lane, Suite 104
Orlando, FL 32814

407-895-0802
staff@birthdefects.org
www.birthdefects.org

Birth Defect Research for Children is a non-profit organization that provides parents and expectant parents with information about birth defects and support services for their children.

Betty Mekdeci, Executive Director

3767 Child Neurology Foundation
601 W Short Street
Lexington, KY 40508

888-417-3435
info@childneurologyfoundation.org
childneurologyfoundation.org

The Child Neurology Foundation connects partners from all areas of the child neurology community so those navigating the journey of disease diagnosis, management, and care have the ongoing support from those dedicated to treatments and cures.

Amy Brin, Executive Director
Katie Hentges, Director, Programs
Brea McCormley, Director, Development

3768 Genetic Alliance
426400 Woodfield Road, Ste 189
Damascus, MD 20872

202-966-5557
Fax: 202-966-8553
info@geneticalliance.org
www.geneticalliance.org

World's leading nonprofit health advocacy organization committed to transforming health through genetics and promoting an environment of openness centered on the health of individuals, families, and communities.

Sharon Terry, CEO
Ruth Child, CFO
Natasha Bonhomme, Chief Strategy Officer

3769 Hydrocephalus Association
4340 East West Highway, Suite 905
Bethesda, MD 20814

301-202-3811
888-598-3789
Fax: 301-202-3813
info@hydroassoc.org
www.hydroassoc.org

A national nonprofit organization devoted exclusively to hydrocepahlus. We provide support, education and an extensive range of resources to families and professionals dealing with the complex issues of hydrocephalus, the abnormal accumulation of cerebrospinal fluid within the brain. Our resources cover all ages, from prenatal to adult normal pressure hydrocephalus.

Diana Gray, President & CEO
Amanda Garzon, Chief Operations Officer
Brian Saphier, Chief Financial Officer

Hydrocephalus / State Agencies & Support Groups

3770 **March of Dimes Foundation**
1550 Crystal Drive, Ste 1300
Arlington, VA 22202
888-663-4637
www.marchofdimes.org

March of Dimes help moms have full-term pregnancies and research the problems that threaten the health of babies. The March of Dimes also acts globally: sharing best practices in perinatal health and helping improve birth outcomes where the needs are the most urgent.

Stacey D. Stewart, President
Alan Brogdon, SVP/COO/Board Officer
Rahul Gupta, MD, SVP & Chief Medical/Health Officer

3771 **MyFace**
333 East 30th Street, Lobby Unit
New York, NY 10016
917-720-4701
info@myface.org
myface.org

MyFace is a non-profit organization dedicated to changing the faces and transforming the lives of children and adults with facial differences.

Stephanie Paul, Executive Director
Dina Zuckerberg, Director of Family Programs
Katie Bazyluk, Communications Manager

3772 **National Hydrocephalus Foundation**
12413 Centralia Road
Lakewood, CA 90715
562-924-6666
info@nhfonline.org
www.nhfonline.org

Promotes information and educational assistance. Establishes and facilitates a communication network and works to increase public awareness. Promote and support research.

Debbi Fields, Executive Director

State Agencies & Support Groups

Arizona

3773 **Injury Prevention Center**
Phoenix Children's Hospital
1919 E Thomas Road
Phoenix, AZ 85016
602-933-1000
888-908-5437
nquay@phxchildrens.com
www.phoenixchildrens.com

Their mission is to promote family-directed care through education and support of children and families with hydrocephalus. Biannual newsletter published, yearly educational conference.

Mark Bonsall, Chairman
Robert Meyer, President/CEO
Jon Hulburd, VP

Florida

3774 **Hydrocephalus Family Support Group of Central Florida**
22 Lake Beauty Drive, Suite 204, PO Box 2010
Orlando, FL 32806
407-649-7686
Fax: 407-649-7692
mrssm1000@aol.com
www.oreilly.com

Their mission is to nurture understanding and increase awareness of hydrocephalus in their community.

Jogi V Pattisapu MD
Tim O'Reilly, Founder/CEO

Michigan

3775 **SW Michican Spina Bifida & Hydrocephalus Association**
PO Box 212
Mattawan, MI 49071
269-385-3959
Fax: 269-342-9765

Provides support, education, and advocacy for families with spina bifida and/or hydrocephalus.

Richard Benthin, President

New Jersey

3776 **Hydrocephalus Group - Children's Hospital of New Jersey**
Children's Hospital of New Jersey
201 Lyons Avenue at Osborne Terrace
Newark, NJ 07112
973-926-7000
Fax: 973-325-2078
www.sbhcs.com

Serves parents of infants and children in the local community and around the state.

Timothy S Yeh MD, FAAP, FAACM, Physician-in-Chief

New York

3777 **New York University Langone Medical Center Auxillary of Tisch Hospital**
530 1st Avenue
New York, NY 10016
212-263-8122
auxiliary.med.nyu.edu

Conducts national symposiums on hydrocephalus.

North Carolina

3778 **Lipomyelomeningocele Family Support**
415 Webster Street
Cary, NC 27511
919-844-2043
Fax: 919-844-2044
www.lfsn.org

Providing support services to families and individuals affected by Occult Spinal Dysraphisms.

Bonnie Borchert, Director

Ohio

3779 **Cleveland Clinic**
9500 Euclid Avenue
Cleveland, OH 44195
216-444-4508
800-223-2273
Fax: 216-444-9050
www.clevelandclinic.org

Provides education about hydrocephalus using speakers and parent-to-parent information.

Gene Altus, Executive Director

Rhode Island

3780 **Hydrocephalus Association of Rhode Island**
PO Box 343
Valley Falls, RI 02864
401-723-6065

The mission of this Association is to provide information, support and advocacy for individuals with hydrocephalus and for friends and family members.

Gabriella Halmi, Director

Texas

3781 **Hydrocephalus Association of N Texas**
PO Box 670552
Dallas, TX 75367
214-528-2877
Fax: 214-528-8097

The mission is to provide information and support to parents of children with hydrocephalus in the state of Texas and neighboring states.

Jana Dransfield, Director

Research Centers

3782 **New York University Medical Center Auxillary of Tisch Hospital**
560 1st Avenue
New York, NY 10016
212-263-5800
Stevenb.Abramson@nyumc.org
www.med.nyu.edu

Conducts national symposiums on hydrocephalus.

Steven B. Abramson, Sr. VP
Dianna Jacob, VP
Ramona Batra, Business Operations Manager

3783 **Seeking Techniques Advancing Research in Shunts (STARS)**
33006 Seven Mile Road, Suite 113
Livonia, MI 48152
313-384-3232
www.stars-kids.org

Offers support to patients with hydrocephalus and their families.

Judy Brady, President

Audio Video

3784 **Hydrocephalus, a Neglected Disease**
Guardians of Hydrocephalus Research Foundation
2618 Avenue Z
Brooklyn, NY 11235
718-748-4473
Fax: 718-743-1171
ghrf2618@aol.com
www.ghrf.homestead.com/ghrf

Information on Hydrocephalus.

Michael Fischette, Founder
Katherine Soriano, National Vice President

Web Sites

3785 **Beth Israel Medical Center-Hydrocephalus**
330 Brookline Avenue
Boston, MA 2215
617-667-7000
800-667-5356
TDD: 800-439-0183
custserv@bidmc.harvard.edu
www.bidmc.org

Is a full tertiary teaching hospital that was originally dedicated to serving a vulnerable population in that community.

Daniel J. Jick, Chair
Edward H. Ladd, Vice Chair
Margaret A. McKenna, Vice Chair

3786 **Birth Defect Research for Children**
976 Lake Baldwin Lane, Suite 104
Orlando, FL 32814
407-895-0802
staff@birthdefects.org
www.birthdefects.org

Birth Defect Research for Children is a non-profit organization that provides parents and expectant parents with information about birth defects and support services for their children.

Betty Mekdeci, Executive Director

3787 **Clinical Genetic Services-Department of Pediatrics**
Hassenfeld Children's Hospital at NYU Langone
424 East 34th Street
New York, NY 10016
212-263-7300
Fax: 646-754-2250
nyulangone.org

Offers evaluations, genetic counseling and testing. Clinical services include carrier testing, prenatal counseling, and complete genetic evaluations for children and adults.

John G. Pappas, MD, Pediatric Genetic Associate
Naomi Yachelevich, MD, Pediatric Genetic Associate

3788 **Guardians of Hydrocephalus Research Foundation**
1101 Wootton Parkway, Suite LL100
Rockville, MD 20852
240-453-8282
odphpinfo@hhs.gov
www.health.gov

Nonprofit group dedicated to research into the cause and treatment of hydrocephalus. Guardians operate a laboratory in the Department of Neurology at New York University Medical Center, in which information from clinical and research facilities is integrated to provide for better diagnosis and treatment of hydrocephalus, a frequently occuring congenital disorder that can also occur shortly after birth. Hydrocephalus accounts for a large portion of adult patients with a diagnosis of dementia.

3789 **HYCEPH-L**
www.geocities.com/HotSprings/Villa/2020/

www.geocities.com/HotSprings/Villa/2020/

The purpose of the list is to share information and support in dealing with hydrocephalus.

3790 **Hydrohaven Chat Room**
www.geocities.com/HotSprings/Villa/2020/hydrohav

www.geocities.com/HotSprings/Villa/2020/hydrohav

Hydrocephalus support group for patients, family and friends.

3791 **National Hydrocephalus Foundation**
www.nhfonline.org
562-924-6666
info@nhfonline.org
www.nhfonline.org

Promotes information and educational assistance. Establishes and facilitates a communication network and works to increase public awareness. Promote and support research.

3792 **Online Mendelian Inheritance in Man**
McKusick-Nathans Institue of Genetic Medicine-JHU
Baltimore, MD 21205
www.omim.org

This database is a catalog of human genes and genetic disorders.

Ada Hamosh, MD, Scientific Director

3793 **Pediatric Neurosurgery-Hydrocephalus**
710 West 168 Street
New York, NY 10032
212-305-4118
Fax: 212-305-2026
www.columbianeurosurgery.org

This site is dedicated to providing families regarding various aspects of the field of pediatric neurosurgery.

Book Publishers

3794 **Congenital Disorders Sourcebook**

Greg Mullin, author

Omnigraphics
615 Griswold Street, Ste 520
Detroit, MI 48226
610-461-3548
800-234-1340
Fax: 800-875-1340
contact@omnigraphics.com
www.omnigraphics.com

Basic consumer health information on disorders aquired during gestation, including spina bifida, hydrocephalus, cerebral palsy, heart defects, craniofacial abnormalities and fetal alcohol syndrome.

Hydrocephalus / Newsletters

664 pages
ISBN: 0-780816-13-8

3795 Hydrocephalus: A Guide for Patients, Families, and Friends
Chuck Toporek, Kellie Robinson, author

O'Reilly & Associates
1005 Gravenstein Highway N
Sebastopol, CA 95472
707-827-7019
800-889-8969
Fax: 707-824-8268
www.oreilly.com

This book educates families so they can select a skilled neurosurgeon, understand treatments, participate in care and know what symptoms need attention, keep records needed for follow-up treatments and make wise lifestyle choices.

1999 377 pages Softcover
ISBN: 1-565924-10-X

Tim O'Reilly, Founder & CEO

Newsletters

3796 G. Advocacy
Genetic Alliance
4301 Connecticut Avenue NW, Suite 404
Washington, DC 20008
202-966-5557
800-336-4363
Fax: 202-966-8553
info@geneticalliance.org
www.geneticalliance.org

Our e-newsletter features news about upcoming events, spotlights member organizations, and keeps you informed about legislation before Congress. We welcome your feedback on articles and suggestions on future topics.

Sharon F. Terry MA, President/CEO
Natasha Bonhomme, VP, Strategic Development
Ruth Evans, Director of Accounting

3797 LINK
Hydrocephalus Association
4340 East West Highway, Suite 905
Bethesda, MD 20814   NOP-ONE-

Provides members with direct access to other families and individuals coping with the complexities of hydrocephalus with the goal being to develop a nationwide network of individuals supporting one another, sharing information and strategies which enable them to become educated and empowered advocates.

12 pages Quarterly

3798 Update
Spina Bifida and Hydrocephalus Association/Canada
Suite 647-167 av. Lombard Avenue
Winnipeg, MB R3B 0
Canada
204-925-3650
800-565-9488
Fax: 204-925-3654
info@sbhac.ca
www.sbhac.ca

Newsletter dedicated to improving the quality of life of individuals with spina bifida and/or hydrocephalus and their families.

4 pages Quarterly

Colleen Talbot, President
Linda Randall, Vice President
Sarah Williams, Secretary

Pamphlets

3799 About Hydrocephalus - Book for Families
Hydrocephalus Association
4340 East West Highway, Suite 905
Bethesda, MD 20814   NOP-ONE-

Booklet in either English or Spanish, detailing all aspects of hydrocephalus from diagnosis and treatment to complications and follow-up care.

36 pages Paperback

3800 Cephalic Disorders Fact Sheet
National Inst. of Neurological Disorders/Stroke
PO Box 5801
Bethesda, MD 20824
301-496-5751
800-352-9424
www.ninds.nih.gov

Fact sheet indexing the following: What are Cephalic Disorders?, What are the Different Kinds of Cephalic Disorders?, What are Other Less Common Cephalics?, What Research is Being Done?, Where Can I Get More Information?.

Walter J. Koroshetz, M.D., Acting Director
Audrey S. Penn MD, Special Advisor to the Director
Caroline Lewis, Executive Officer

3801 Cerebrospinal Fluid Shunt Systems for the Management of Hydrocephalus
Hydrocephalus Association
4340 East West Highway, Suite 905
Bethesda, MD 20814   NOP-ONE-

Our resources cover hydrocephalus in all age groups from prenatal diagnosis to adult normal pressure hydrocephalus. Our office is staffed daily from 10 AM to 4 PM Pacific time. We invite your inquiries.

3802 Directory of Pediatric Neurosurgeons
Hydrocephalus Association
4340 East West Highway, Suite 905
Bethesda, MD 20814   NOP-ONE-

Names and addresses of more than 200 neurosurgeons who specialize in pediatrics, listed alphabetically and geographically.

3803 Durable Power of Attorney for Health Care Decisions
Hydrocephalus Association
4340 East West Highway, Suite 905
Bethesda, MD 20814   NOP-ONE-

Provided by The Hydrocephalus Association. Our resources cover hydrocephalus in all age groups from prenatal diagnosis to adult normal pressure hydrocepahlus. Our office is staffed daily from 10 AM to 4 PM Pacific time. We invite your inquiries.

3804 Endoscopic Third Ventriculoscopy
Hydrocephalus Association
4340 East West Highway, Suite 905
Bethesda, MD 20814   NOP-ONE-

Provided by the Hydrocephalus Association. Our resources cover all age groups from prenatal diagnosis through normal pressure hydrocephalus in older adults. Our office is staffed daily from 10 AM to 4 PM Pacific time. We invite your inquiries.

3805 Eye Problems Associated with Hydrocephalus in Children
Hydrocephalus Association
4340 East West Highway, Suite 905
Bethesda, MD 20814   NOP-ONE-

Provided by the Hydrocephalus Association. Our resources cover all age groups from prenatal diagnosis to normal pressure hydrocephalus in older adults. Our office is staffed daily from 10 AM to 4 PM Pacific time. We invite your inquiries.

3806 Fact Sheet: Hydrocephalus
Hydrocephalus Association
4340 East West Highway, Suite 905
Bethesda, MD 20814   NOP-ONE-

Also available in Spanish, provided by the Hydrocephalus Association. Our resources cover all age groups from prenatal diagnosis to normal pressure hydrocephalus in older adults. Our office is staffed daily from 10 AM to 4 PM Pacific time. We invite your inquiries.

Hydrocephalus / Pamphlets

3807 Fact Sheet: Syringomyelia
National Inst. of Neurological Disorders/Stroke
PO Box 5801
Bethesda, MD 20892
301-496-5751
800-352-9424
www.ninds.nih.gov

Provided by the Hydrocephalus Association. Our resources cover all age groups, from prenatal diagnosis to normal pressure hydrocephalus in older adults. We welcome your inquiries.

Walter J. Koroshetz, M.D., Acting Director
Audrey S. Penn MD, Special Advisor to the Director
Caroline Lewis, Executive Officer

3808 Headaches and Hydrocephalus
Hydrocephalus Association
4340 East West Highway, Suite 905
Bethesda, MD 20814
NOP-ONE-

Causes and tips for headache relief unique to hydrocephalus.

3809 Hospitalization Tips
Hydrocephalus Association
4340 East West Highway, Suite 905
Bethesda, MD 20814
NOP-ONE-

Provided by the Hydrocephalus Association. Our resources cover all age groups, from prenatal diagnosis, to normal pressure hydrocephalus in older adults. Our office is staffed daily from 10 AM to 4 PM, Pacific time. We welcome your inquiries.

1997

3810 How to be an Assertive Member of the Treatment Team
Hydrocephalus Association
4340 East West Highway, Suite 905
Bethesda, MD 20814
NOP-ONE-

Hydrocephalus information to ask involved treatment questions.

3811 Hydrocephalus: Fact Sheet
National Inst. of Neurological Disorders/Stroke
PO Box 5801
Bethesda, MD 20824
301-496-5751
800-352-9424
www.ninds.nih.gov

Our fact sheet covers all age groups, from prenatal diagnosis to normal pressure hydrocephalus in older adults. Also available in Spanish.

Walter J. Koroshetz, M.D., Acting Director
Audrey S. Penn MD, Special Advisor to the Director
Caroline Lewis, Executive Officer

3812 ID Card for Third Ventriculostomy Patients
Hydrocephalus Association
4340 East West Highway Suite 905
Bethesda, MD 20814
NOP-ONE-

Patients with hydrocephalus managed by an ETV may request a free patient ID card from the Hydrocephaus Association. This card idenifies them as patients with hydrocephalus being managed by this procedure.

3813 Individualized Education Program (IEP) - Communication Skills for Parents
Hydrocephalus Association
4340 East West Highway Suite 905
Bethesda, MD 20814
NOP-ONE-

Is a written education plan that describes the special education and related services a student will receive.

3814 LINK Directory Information
Hydrocephalus Association
4340 East West Highway Suite 905
Bethesda, MD 20814
NOP-ONE-

A nationwide network of individuals listed in Directory format giving members direct access to others in similar circumstances.

3815 Learning Disabilities in Children with Hydrocephalus
Hydrocephalus Association
4340 East West Highway Suite 905
Bethesda, MD 20814
NOP-ONE-

Also available in Spanish and English. Our offices are staffed daily from 10 AM to 4 PM, Pacific time. We welcome your inquiries.

3816 National Directory of Hydrocephalus Support Groups
Hydrocephalus Association
4340 East West Highway Suite 905
Bethesda, MD 20814
NOP-ONE-

The Directory lists information on 16 hydrocephalus groups nationwide.

3817 Nonverbal Learning Disorder Syndrome
Hydrocephalus Association
4340 East West Highway Suite 905
Bethesda, MD 20814
NOP-ONE-

Is a specific type of learning disability that affect's children's academic progress as well as their social and emotional development. This specific type of learning disability has been identified in some children with Hydrocephalus.

3818 Prenatal Hydrocephalus-Book for Parents
Hydrocephalus Association
4340 East West Highway Suite 905
Bethesda, MD 20814
NOP-ONE-

Provides information about the diagnosis of prenatal-onset hydrocephalus.

16 pages

3819 Primary Care Needs of Children with Hydrocephalus
Hydrocephalus Association
4340 East West Highway Suite 905
Bethesda, MD 20814
NOP-ONE-

Our office is staffed daily from 10 AM to 4 PM Pacific time. We welcome your inquiries.

28 pages

3820 Resource Guide
Hydrocephalus Association
4340 East West Highway Suite 905
Bethesda, MD 20814
NOP-ONE-

A comprehensive listing of 450 articles on all aspects of hydrocephalus. Articles may be ordered from the Association for a small fee.

3821 Social Skills Development in Children with Hydrocephalus
Hydrocephalus Association
4340 East West Highway Suite 905
Bethesda, MD 20814
NOP-ONE-

3822 Survival Skills for the Family Unit
Hydrocephalus Association
4340 East West Highway Suite 905
Bethesda, MD 20814
NOP-ONE-

Our resources cover hydrocepahlus in all age groups from prenatal diagnosis through normal pressure hydrocephalus in older adults.

3823 Understanding Your Child's Education Needs /Individualized Education Program Packet
Hydrocephalus Association
4340 East West Highway Suite 905
Bethesda, MD 20814
NOP-ONE-

From the Hydrocephalus Association the nations largest nonprofit group devoted exclusively to this disorder. Our offices are staffed daily from 10 AM to 4 PM, Pacific time. We welcome your inquiries.

Hypertrophic Cardiomyopathy / Description

Description

3824 HYPERTROPHIC CARDIOMYOPATHY
Involves the following Biologic System(s):
Cardiovascular Disorders

Hypertrophic cardiomyopathy is a genetic disease that occurs because of mutations in the contraction mechanisms in the muscles of the heart. Because of this genetic abnormality, the heart muscle fibers are arranged in a disorganized fashion. This leads to enlargement of the left ventricular muscle (hypertrophy). This hypertrophic muscle may lead to variable amounts of obstruction of blood flow out of the heart into the general circulation and a spectrum of clinical manifestations. There have been several genes that have been found to be abnormal in patients with hypertrophic cardiomyopathy. Depending on the different genetic abnormality there may be different clinical findings ranging from no symptomatology to severe disease.

Hypertrophic cardiomyopathy is most commonly inherited in an autosomal dominant pattern, meaning that a child inherits a copy of the gene from one of his or her parents.aAs a result, the majority of children and adolescents who are diagnosed with the disease have a parent who also suffers from the entity. Sporadic cases are also well documented where neither parent has the disease but the child has the disease. It is presumed that in these cases, there has been a spontaneous mutation in the gene in the earliest stages of embryonic development.

Hypertrophic cardiomyopathy may become clinically evident at any time during the first two decades of life, though typically it is not diagnosed until the adolescent years. It is important to note that the hypertrophic changes that are the hallmark of the disease may not develop until as late as the teens or early twenties. As a result, in families where a parent has the disease, children should undergo repeated interval examination by a pediatric cardiologist through their adolescence.

The diagnosis is hypertrophic cardiomyopathy relies heavily on good history taking from the primary care provider. There are several important questions to ask in order to assess for risk. A family history should be taken, asking about unexplained deaths, family members with frequent episodes of fainting, or cardiac arrhythmia (abnormal heart rhythm). Patients should be questioned about episodes of shortness of breath (dyspnea) and chest pain. Any recent change in exercise tolerance should be evaluated closely. Additionally, a known history of family members with documented hypertrophic cardiomyopathy should raise the concern of disease in other family members.

There are many patients with hypertrophic cardiomyopathy who are largely asymptomatic. When patients are symptomatic they usually exhibit a slow decline in function. Often, patients may not experience symptoms until they exert themselves. Symptoms may consist of shortness of breath with exertion or when lying down, chest pain, fainting (syncope) or lightheadedness, palpitations (racing heart), and fatigue. Although it is agreed that the thickened left ventricular muscle may cause some obstruction to blood flow out of the aora (the main blood vessel leading from the left side of the heart to the general circulation), this is not the only mechanism causing symptoms. In fact, there are some patients with a great deal of obstruction who have minimal symptoms, while other patients with minimal obstruction may have severe symptoms. Patients may also experience some of the above symptoms from decreased functioning of the heart muscle itself, or arrhythmia.

Hypertrophic cardiomyopathy is the most common cause of sudden death in young athletes who die during sports; clearly those individuals with HCM should be restricted from participating in sports.

The physical exam of patients with hypertrophic cardiomyopathy may be normal if there is no significant obstruction to blood flow. In some patients, findings may include a fourth heart sound or a systolic murmur heard best at the left lower sternal border. This murmur is often heard more easily during maneuvers that increase the amount of resistance in the body's tissues from muscular contraction, for example, when patients stand up after a sitting or squatting position, or when patients bear down (Valsalva maneuver). Additional findings may include increased carotid pulses, increased force of the heart beat felt near the left lower sternum or axilla (parasternal lift).

Patients with suspected hypertrophic cardiomyopathy should be referred to a pediatric cardiologist for further testing, which may consist of an echocardiogram (ultrasound imaging of the heart), electrocardiogram and perhaps an exercise stress test.

Treatment options are varied. Medical management may be difficult and surgical or catheter interventions may be recommended to decrease the amount of obstructing tissue in the heart. Mainstays of medical treatment include calcium channel blockers, beta blockers, and anti-arrhythmics. Most recently, the use of implantable defribrillators (small pacemaker-like devices that correct severe heart arrhythmias) have become common. It is critical that patients with confirmed hypertrophic cardiomyopathy be restricted from playing competitive sports. Additionally, patients should receive prophylactic antibiotics for prevention of endocarditis before dental or invasive procedures.

National Associations & Support Groups

3825 American Academy of Pediatrics
345 Park Blvd
Itasca, IL 60143
800-433-9016
Fax: 847-434-8000
mcc@aap.org
www.aap.org

The American Academy of Pediatrics and its member pediatricians are committed to the attainment of optimal physical, mental and social health and well-being for all infants, children, adolescents, and young adults.

Lynn Olson, PhD, VP, Research
Mark Del Monte, JD, CEO/Executive VP
Vera Tait, MD, FAAP, Chief Medical Officer

3826 American Heart Association
7272 Greenville Avenue
Dallas, TX 75231
214-570-5978
800-242-8721
www.heart.org

The mission of the American Heart Associate is to build healthier lives, free of cardiovascular diseases and stroke.

Nancy Brown, CEO
Mitchell S.V. Elkind, President
Suzie Upton, Chief Operating Officer

3827 Hypertrophic Cardiomyopathy Association
66 Ford Road, Suite 213B
Denville, NJ 07834
973-983-7429
support@4hcm.us
www.4hcm.org

A not-for-profit organization that provides information, support and advocacy to patients, their families and medical providers.

Lisa Salberg, Founder & President

3828 **March of Dimes Foundation**
1550 Crystal Drive, Ste 1300
Arlington, VA 22202
888-663-4637
www.marchofdimes.org

March of Dimes help moms have full-term pregnancies and research the problems that threaten the health of babies. The March of Dimes also acts globally: sharing best practices in perinatal health and helping improve birth outcomes where the needs are the most urgent.

Stacey D. Stewart, President
Alan Brogdon, SVP/COO/Board Officer
Rahul Gupta, MD, SVP & Chief Medical/Health Officer

Research Centers

3829 **Hypertrophic Cardiomyopathy Program at St. Luke's-Roosevelt Hospital Center**
University Medical Practice Associates
425 W 59th Street, Suite 9C
New York, NY 10019
212-492-5550
Fax: 212-492-5555
www.hcmny.org

We offer comprehensive diagnostic evaluation, a range of treatments and screening for relatives of affected patients.

Mark V Sherrid MD FACC FASE, Director

Web Sites

3830 **American Heart Association**
7272 Greenville Avenue
Dallas, TX 75231
214-570-5978
800-242-8721
www.heart.org

The mission of the American Heart Associate is to build healthier lives, free of cardiovascular diseases and stroke.

Nancy Brown, CEO
Mitchell S.V. Elkind, President
Suzie Upton, Chief Operating Officer

3831 **Hypertrophic Cardiomyopathy Association**
66 Ford Road, Suite 213B
Denville, NJ 07834
973-983-7429
support@4hcm.org
www.4hcm.org

A not-for-profit organization that provides information, support and advocacy to patients, their families and medical providers.

3832 **Hypertrophic Cardiomyopathy: Heart Center Online for Patients**
www.heartcenteronline.com

www.heartcenteronline.com

The mission of the HeartCenterOnline is to give our premier cardiovascular patients, their families and other site visiors with the tools they need to better understand the complex nature of heart-related conditions, treatments and preventive care, and to provide services and applications that deliver value to cardiovascular practices.

3833 **Implantable Defibrillators in Preventing Sudden Death**
www.findarticles.com

www.findarticles.com

Article from American Family Physician magazine. Search by article name.

3834 **MEDLINEplus**
8600 Rockville Pike
Bethesda, MD 20894
nlm.nih.gov/medlineplus/ency/article/000192.htm

MedlinePlus has extensive information from the National Institutes of Health and other trusted sources on over 650 diseases and conditions. There are also lists of hospitals and physicians, a medical encyclopedia and a medical dictionary, health information in Spanish, extensive information on perscription and nonperscription drugs, health information from the media and links to thousands of clinical trials.

Dr. Donald A.B. Lindberg, Director

3835 **March of Dimes Foundation**
1550 Crystal Drive, Ste 1300
Arlington, VA 22202
888-663-4637
www.marchofdimes.org

March of Dimes help moms have full-term pregnancies and research the problems that threaten the health of babies. The March of Dimes also acts globally: sharing best practices in perinatal health and helping improve birth outcomes where the needs are the most urgent.

Stacey D. Stewart, President
Alan Brogdon, SVP/COO/Board Officer
Rahul Gupta, MD, SVP & Chief Medical/Health Officer

3836 **Sudden Death of Young Athletes Can Be Prevented (Hypertrophic Cardiomyopathy)**
www.findarticles.com

www.findarticles.com

Article from USA Today. Search by article name.

Book Publishers

3837 **Let's Talk About Going to the Hospital**
Rosen Publishing Group's PowerKids Press
29 E 21st Street
New York, NY 10010
212-777-3017
800-237-9932
Fax: 888-436-4643
rosenpub@tribeca.ios.com
www.rosenpublishing.com

If a child has to check into the hospital, chances are he or she is already upset about being ill. Knowing how a hospital functions and what the procedures are, such as when family members can visit, will help in what is already a stressful situation. Grades K-5.

24 pages
ISBN: 0-823950-36-0

Roger Rosen, President

Hypoplastic Left Heart Syndrome / Description

Description

3838 HYPOPLASTIC LEFT HEART SYNDROME
Synonym: HLHS
Involves the following Biologic System(s):
Cardiovascular Disorders

Hypoplastic Left Heart Syndrome, also referred to as HLHS, is a severe and complex form of congenital heart disease, wherein the entire left side of the heart is underdeveloped and unable to pump blood to the body. Classically, this involves underdevelopment (hypoplasia) of the: 1) mitral valve, which connects the left atrium to the left ventricle, 2) left ventricle, which is the pumping chamber that delivers oxygenated blood to the body and 3) aortic valve and aorta, the valve and blood vessel, respectively, which carry oxygenated blood from the left ventricle to the organs and the tissues of the body.

Hypoplastic Left Heart Syndrome is the 4th most common congenital heart disorder diagnosed in the first year of life and almost always in the first few days of life. Typically, infants with HLHS are full term and tend to have normal birth weights and few non-cardiac defects. In those born with the disorder, males out number female. The cause of this HLHS remains unclear, but like many of the congenital heart diseases, it likely develops in most pregnancies early in the first trimester and may very well have a genetic component.

Because of the underdevelopment of the left side of the heart, infants born with Hypoplastic Left Heart Syndrome become gravely ill soon after birth. In the fetus, a specialized blood vessel, known as the ductus arteriosus, connects the aorta and the pulmonary artery. In normal fetal heart structure, the ductus arteriosus allows the deoxy genated (blue) blood pumped by the right ventricle to the pulmonary artery to avoid going to the lungs (which in the fetus are non-functioning and filled with fluid), delivering it to the placenta for oxygenation. After birth the lungs are inflated with air and the ductus arteriosus, which is no longer necessary, begins to undergo a natural closure process. In the infant with Hypoplastic Left Heart Syndrome, the ductus arteriosus is the only source of blood flow into the aorta, as the left heart is unable to pump adequate (if any) blood forward and, therefore, crucial to the survival of the infant; without it, inadequate blood flow to the organs and tissues leads to shock. Prior to the advent of specialized medications, such as prostaglandins, that prevent the closing process of the ductus arteriosus, patients with Hypoplastic Left Heart Syndrome would not be able to survive when the ductus underwent its natural closure.

Over the last two decades, congenital heart surgery techniques have been developed to surgically alter the path of blood leaving the right heart. Surgery for Hypoplastic Left Heart Syndrome typically involves three separate operations, the first being the most difficult and complicated, occurring in the first week or two of life. The second operation usually occurs between 4 and 6 months of life and the third may be undertaken between 18 and 36 months. Alternatively, some pediatric cardiac centers have promoted heart transplant for the patient with Hypoplastic Left Heart Syndrome. Children with Hypoplastic Left Heart Syndrome require lifelong follow-up by a cardiologist for repeated checks of how their heart is working. Virtually all the children will require heart medicines. They also risk infection on the heart's valves (endocarditis) and will need antibiotics, such as amoxicillin, before dental work and certain surgeries to help prevent endocarditis.

National Associations & Support Groups

3839 American Academy of Pediatrics
345 Park Blvd
Itasca, IL 60143

800-433-9016
Fax: 847-434-8000
mcc@aap.org
www.aap.org

The American Academy of Pediatrics and its member pediatricians are committed to the attainment of optimal physical, mental and social health and well-being for all infants, children, adolescents, and young adults.

Lynn Olson, PhD, VP, Research
Mark Del Monte, JD, CEO/Executive VP
Vera Tait, MD, FAAP, Chief Medical Officer

3840 The Heart Institute
Cincinnati Children's Hospital Medical Center
3333 Burnet Avenue, MLC 7020
Cincinnati, OH 45229

513-636-7058
800-344-2462
Fax: 513-636-5958
TTY: 513-636-4900
www.cincinnatichildrens.org

Cincinnati Children's Heart Center is dedicated to serving the cardiac care needs of patients, fetus through young adult, and their families in a convenient, compassionate and high quality manner. The Heart Center is committed to providing research and teaching programs in an enviroment characterized by intergrity, innovation, excellence, and respect.

Andrew Redington, MD, Exec. Co-Dir/Pediatric Cardiology
Jeffrey Robbins, PhD, Executive Co-Director
James Tweddell, MD, Executive Co-Director

State Agencies & Support Groups

Arizona

3841 Arizona HeartLight
University Medical Center
PO Box 286
Hallsville, TX 75650

903-668-2173
Fax: 903-668-3453
www.heartlightministries.org

Joe Crawford, Chairman
Jana Crawford, Chairman

Colorado

3842 Cardiac Kids/Association of Volunteers
13123 E. 16th Avenue, PO Box 465
Aurora, CO 80045

303-861-6259
www.childrenscolorado.org

Mark Erickson

Florida

3843 Pediatric Heart Foundation
PO Box 540354
Lake Worth, FL 33454

561-738-4554
phfheart@aol.com
www.pediatricheartfoundation.org

Urquisa Fernandez, President
Reese Robinson
Laurie Bernat, Contact

Hypoplastic Left Heart Syndrome / State Agencies & Support Groups

Georgia

3844 **Heart to Heart**
401 S. Clairborne Rd., Suite 302
Olathe, KS 66062
913-764-5200
Fax: 913-764-0809
info@hearttoheart.org
www.hearttoheart.org

Gary Morsch, Founder/President
Jim Kerr, Board Chair
Krystal Barr, Interim CEO

Hawaii

3845 **Kardiac Kids**
C/O Kapi'olani Medical Center for Women & Children
1319 Punahou Street
Honolulu, HI 96826
808-983-8166
www.thekardiackids.com

Lisa Rohr RN, Contact

Illinois

3846 **Chilren's Heart Services**
PO Box 8275
Bartlett, IL 60103
630-415-0282
CHILDHRTSVC@aol.com

3847 **Heart of the Matter**
4760 Highland Drive, Suite 515
Salt Lake City, UT 84117
815-469-9146
888-868-4686
CT875@aol.com
www.hotm.tv

Indiana

3848 **Our Hearts**
1738 N Shortridge Road
Indianapolis, IN 46219
317-322-1017
ourhearts@iquest.net

Massachusetts

3849 **Heart to Heart Fund**
750 Washington Street, Suite 313
Boston, MA 02111
617-636-8101
info@heart2heartfund.org

Michigan

3850 **Families at Heart**
100 Michigan Ave, MC117
Grand Rapids, MI 49503
616-391-4327

Rick Breon, Ceo

Minnesota

3851 **Parents For Heart of Minnesota**
Attention: 32-P190
2525 Chicgo Avenue S
Minneapolis, MN 55404
mailinglist@parentsforheart.org
www.parentsforheart.org

Celeste Gebauer, Contact

Missouri

3852 **Heart to Heart - St. Louis**
St Louis Children's Hospital
One Children's Place
St Louis, MO 63110
314-454-6000
www.heart2heartstl.com

Elaine Wear, Contact
Nan Winters, Contact

New Hampshire

3853 **Families with Heart**
824 High Street
Candia, NH 03034
603-483-3025

Laura Briggs, Contact

New Jersey

3854 **Young Hearts**
791 Fredrick Court
Wyckoff, NJ 07481
201-848-9608

Barbara Mcfadden, Contact

New York

3855 **Big Hearts for Little Hearts**
34 Sintsink Drive West
Port Washington, NY 11050
516-883-4080

Ruth Maszrik, Contact

3856 **Cardiac Kids**
PO Box 154
Fishkill, NY 12524
845-896-7321

Cindy-Jean Dennis, Contact

3857 **Helping Hearts**
601 Elmwood Avenue, PO Box 631
Rochester, NY 14642
716-275-6108

Ohio

3858 **Healing Hearts**
PO Box 7890
Bonney Lake, WA 98391
253-268-0348
866-230-3463
Fax: 330-543-3084
flemings249@aol.com
www.healinghearts.org

Provides participants with an opportunity to share their emotions and concerns.

Sue Liljenberg, Founder/President
Judy Hansen, Secretary
Dan Morton, Member

Pennsylvania

3859 **Fontan Friends**
482 Reginald Lane
Collegeville, PA 19426
610-831-9878

Barbara Lewis, Contact

South Dakota

3860 **Thumpers**
HC 58, Box 26
Fairburn, SD 57738
605-255-4377
clsogge@cs.com

Tammy Sogge, Contact

Hypoplastic Left Heart Syndrome / Web Sites

Tennessee

3861 Tennessee Saving Little Hearts
5629 Barineau Lane, PO Box 52285
Knoxville, TN 37950

865-748-4605
info@savinglittlehearts.com
www.savinglittlehearts.com

Provides emotional assistance, educational information, and fun experiences for children that will help them build friendship and confidence.

Karen Coulter, President
Brad Coulter, Vice President

Texas

3862 Heart to Heart
401 S. Clairborne Rd., Suite 302
Olathe, KS 66062

913-764-5200
Fax: 913-764-0809
info@hearttoheart.org
www.hearttoheart.org

Gary Morsch, Founder/President
Jim Kerr, Board Chair
Krystal Barr, Interim CEO

3863 Texas Heart to Heart
Po Box 720072
Dallas, TX 75372

888-475-2787
www.heart-to-heart-tx.org

Offering hope, education, and support to families.

Sally Pearson, Contact

Vermont

3864 Heart to Heart
401 S. Clairborne Rd., Suite 302
Olathe, KS 66062

913-764-5200
Fax: 913-764-0809
info@hearttoheart.org
www.hearttoheart.org

Gary Morsch, Founder/President
Jim Kerr, Board Chair
Krystal Barr, Interim CEO

Virginia

3865 Precious Hearts
144 Locust Avenue
Winchester, VA 22601

540-678-0654
hurlbutK@aol.com

Washington

3866 Heart to Heart
401 S. Clairborne Rd., Suite 302
Olathe, KS 66062

913-764-5200
Fax: 913-764-0809
info@hearttoheart.org
www.hearttoheart.org

Gary Morsch, Founder/President
Jim Kerr, Board Chair
Krystal Barr, Interim CEO

Wisconsin

3867 Kids With Heart
1578 Careful Drive
Green Bay, WI 54304

920-498-0058
800-538-5390
www.kidswithheart.org

Michelle Rintamaki, President
Dean Rintamaki, VP
Melody Burkard, Secretary/Treasurer

3868 Left Hearts
250 N 6th Street
DePere, WI 54115
Dyan Larmay, Contact

920-403-1154

Web Sites

3869 Children's Heart Society
www.childrensheart.org

www.childrensheart.org

Reliable information and resources to families of children with congenital heart defects and acquired heart disease.

3870 Cincinnati Children's Hospital Medical Center
3333 Burnet Avenue
Cincinnati, OH 45229

513-636-4200
800-344-2462
TTY: 513-636-4900
www.cincinnatichildrens.org

Cincinnati Children's Hospital is dedicated to serving the cardiac care needs of patiens, fetus through young adult, and is committed to providing research and teaching programs.

3871 Yale University School of Medicine
330 Cedar St, Boardman 110. P.O. Box 208056
New Haven, CT 06520

medicine.yale.edu/intmed/cardio/

Information on congenital heart conditions, including Hypoplastic Left Heart Syndrome symptoms, treatments and support.

Henry Scott Cabin, Professor of Medicine
Joseph Akar, Associate Professor of Medicine
Henry Cabin, Acting Section Chief

Book Publishers

3872 Parent's Guide to Children's Congenital Heart Defects
Random House
280 Park Avenue (11-3)
New York, NY 10017

800-733-3000
Fax: 212-940-7381
www.crownpublishing.com

A practical and useful resource for families coping with a child who has CHD. An easy to read book uses personal stories and a question and answer format on a wide range of medical and daily living issues.

ISBN: 0-609807-75-7

3873 Young People and Chronic Illness: True Stories, Help and Hope
Congenital Heart Information Network
P.O. Box 3397
Margate City, NJ 08402

609-823-4507
mb@tchin.org
www.tchin.org

Presents inspirational chapters based upon interviews of young people growing up with various chronic illnesses, including a chapter on Congenital Heart Disease.

ISBN: 1-575420-41-4

Mona Barmash, President

Description

3874 HYPOTHYROIDISM
Covers these related disorders: Acquired hypothyroidism, Congenital hypothyroidism, Hoishimoto's disease
Involves the following Biologic System(s):
Endocrinologic Disorders

Hypothyroidism is a condition characterized by decreased activity of the thyroid gland, an endocrine gland that consists of two lobes on either side of the windpipe (trachea). Certain specialized cells within the thyroid gland secrete the thyroid hormones thyroxine (T-4) and triiodothyronine (T-3), which assist in regulating the rate of metabolism. Metabolism refers to the chemical activities within cells that release energy from nutrients or consume energy to create certain substances. The thyroid hormones also play a vital role in the normal mental and physical development and growth of infants and children. Other specialized cells in the thyroid gland secrete the hormone calcitonin, which helps to regulate concentrations of calcium in the body by inhibiting the loss of bone.

Hypothyroidism may result from an underlying defect that is present at birth (congenital). In children with congenital hypothyroidism, associated symptoms may begin at birth or be delayed until later during childhood, depending upon the nature of the underlying abnormality. Congenital hypothyroidism may result from several underlying causes, such as abnormal development (dysplasia) or absence (aplasia) of the thyroid gland; abnormalities in the production of certain hormones due to particular biochemical defects; or fetal exposure to particular medications or therapies (e.g., radioiodine therapy) during pregnancy. In children with malformation of the thyroid gland or abnormalities in hormonal production, the condition may appear to occur randomly for unknown reasons (sporadically) or may be familial. Congenital hypothyroidism affects approximately one in 4,000 infants worldwide and is about twice as common in females as in males.

Hypothyroidism may also occur later during childhood (acquired hypothyroidism) due to an autoimmune disorder in which the immune system develops antibodies against cells of the thyroid gland (Hashimoto's disease) or in association with other underlying disorders (e.g., nephropathic cystinosis, histiocytosis). Acquired hypothyroidism may also develop due to the use of particular medications or surgical removal of all or a portion of the thyroid gland as a treatment for certain diseases or conditions (e.g., thyroid cancer, thyrotoxicosis).

In newborns and infants with congenital hypothyroidism, associated symptoms may vary in range, severity, and rate of progression, depending upon the degree of thyroid hormone deficiency. Some patients may have an abnormally enlarged thyroid gland (goiter), causing swelling in front of the neck. In addition, early symptoms may include yellowish discoloration of the skin, mucous membranes, and whites of the eyes (jaundice); sluggishness; and feeding difficulties, including choking episodes during nursing. Many patients also have a large abdomen; a weakening of the abdominal wall muscles through which an abdominal organ or fatty tissue may protrude (umbilical hernia); constipation; widely open soft spots (fontanels) under the front and back of the scalp; and respiratory difficulties, including episodes in which there is a temporary cessation of spontaneous breathing (apnea). Some patients may have progressive mental and physical disabilities that become increasingly severe without early diagnosis and prompt treatment. Patients may experience delays in obtaining certain developmental milestones, such as sitting up and standing; may not learn to speak; and may be increasingly lethargic. Additional physical findings associated with severe hypothyroidism include delayed skeletal maturation; a short, thick neck; short fingers and broad hands; a thick, protruding tongue; delayed eruption of the teeth (dentition); dry, scaly skin; coarse, scanty hair; and an abnormal, progressive accumulation of fluid within body tissues and associated swelling, particularly in the genital area, eyelids, and backs of the hands (myxedema).

The symptoms and findings associated with acquired hypothyroidism may also vary, depending upon the underlying cause, the age at onset, and the degree of thyroid hormone deficiency. Children with acquired hypothyroidism may experience an abnormally decreased rate of growth, decreased energy, puffiness of the skin (myxedematous changes), constipation, cold intolerance, headaches, visual problems, or other abnormalities.

In the United States, thyroid hormone levels in the blood are routinely tested in all newborns shortly after birth. Early diagnosis and prompt treatment of congenital hypothyroidism are essential for normal brain development during infancy. Such treatment includes thyroid hormone replacement therapy (e.g., sodium-L-thyroxine by mouth). The treatment of children with acquired hypothyroidism also includes thyroid hormone replacement therapy. Additional treatment is symptomatic and supportive.

National Associations & Support Groups

3875 American Academy of Pediatrics
345 Park Blvd
Itasca, IL 60143
800-433-9016
Fax: 847-434-8000
mcc@aap.org
www.aap.org

The American Academy of Pediatrics and its member pediatricians are committed to the attainment of optimal physical, mental and social health and well-being for all infants, children, adolescents, and young adults.

Lynn Olson, PhD, VP, Research
Mark Del Monte, JD, CEO/Executive VP
Vera Tait, MD, FAAP, Chief Medical Officer

3876 American Association of Clinical Endocrinologists
245 Riverside Avenue, Suite 200
Jacksonville, FL 32202
904-353-7878
www.aace.com

A professional medical organization aimed at promoting the quality of clinical endocrinology research and improving the knowledge base for the diagnosis, prognosis, prevention and treatment of health conditions through the advancement and application of innovative methods.

3877 American Thyroid Association
2000 Duke Street, Suite 300
Alexandria, VA 22314
www.thyroid.org

ATA provides researchers and clinicians with networking opportunities and resources that will help them grow their careers and stay current on leading-edge research and advances in clinical care. Additionally, ATA is committed to providing patients and their families with reliable information and tools to help them learn more about and manage their thyroid disease and thyroid cancer.

Amanda Perl, Executive Director
Sharleene E. Cano, Director, Publications & Membership
Kelly C. Hoff, Director, Development & Technology

Hypothyroidism / Libraries & Resource Centers

3878 **Genetic Alliance**
426400 Woodfield Road, Ste 189
Damascus, MD 20872
202-966-5557
Fax: 202-966-8553
info@geneticalliance.org
www.geneticalliance.org

World's leading nonprofit health advocacy organization committed to transforming health through genetics and promoting an environment of openness centered on the health of individuals, families, and communities.

Sharon Terry, CEO
Ruth Child, CFO
Natasha Bonhomme, Chief Strategy Officer

3879 **March of Dimes Foundation**
1550 Crystal Drive, Ste 1300
Arlington, VA 22202
888-663-4637
www.marchofdimes.org

March of Dimes help moms have full-term pregnancies and research the problems that threaten the health of babies. The March of Dimes also acts globally: sharing best practices in perinatal health and helping improve birth outcomes where the needs are the most urgent.

Stacey D. Stewart, President
Alan Brogdon, SVP/COO/Board Officer
Rahul Gupta, MD, SVP & Chief Medical/Health Officer

Libraries & Resource Centers

3880 **National Digestive Diseases Information Clearinghouse (NDDIC)**
NIH
2 Information Way
Bethesda, MD 20892
301-654-3810
800-891-5389
Fax: 301-907-8906
nddic@info.niddk.nih.gov
www.digestive.niddk.nih.gov

The National Institute of Diabetes and Digestive and Kidney Diseases conducts and supports research on many of the most serious diseases affecting public health. The Institute supports much of the clinical research on the diseases of internal medicine and related subspecialty fields as well as many basic science disciplines.

Griffin P. Rodgers, MD, Director
Gregory G. Germino, MD, Deputy Director
Kathy Kranzfelder, Communications Director

Web Sites

3881 **American Association of Clinical Endocrinologists**
245 Riverside Avenue, Suite 200
Jacksonville, FL 32202
904-353-7878
www.aace.com

A professional medical organization aimed at promoting the quality of clinical endocrinology research and improving the knowledge base for the diagnosis, prognosis, prevention and treatment of health conditions through the advancement and application of innovative methods.

3882 **Online Mendelian Inheritance in Man**
McKusick-Nathans Institue of Genetic Medicine-JHU
Baltimore, MD 21205
www.omim.org

This database is a catalog of human genes and genetic disorders.

Ada Hamosh, MD, Scientific Director

3883 **Thyroid Federation International**
P.O. Box 471
Bath, ON K0H 1
webmaster@thyroid-fed.org
www.thyroid-fed.org/

The Thyroid Federation International aims to work for the benefit of those affected by thyroid disorders throughout the world. Its objectives are to encourage and assist the formation of patient oriented thyroid organizations, to work closely with the medical professions to promote awareness and understanding of thyroid disorders and their complications, to provide through member organizations, information and moral support to those affected by thyroid disorders and to promote education.

Ashok Bhaseen, President
Beate BartSs, Secretary
Asta Tirronen, Treasurer

Book Publishers

3884 **Endocrine & Metabolic Disorders Sourcebook 3rd Edition**
Keith Jones, author

Omnigraphics
615 Griswold Street, Ste 520
Detroit, MI 48226
610-461-3548
800-234-1340
Fax: 800-875-1340
contact@omnigraphics.com
www.omnigraphics.com

Basic information for the lay person about pancreatic and insulin-related disorders such as pancreatitis, diabetes and hypoglycemia; adrenal gland disorders such as Cushing's syndrome, Addison's disease and congenital adrenal hyperplasia; pituitary gland disorders such as growth hormone deficiency, acromegaly and pituitary tumors; and thyroid disorders such as hypothyroidism, Grave's disease, Hashimoto's disease and goiter.

560 pages
ISBN: 0-780815-43-8

Description

3885 ICHTHYOSIS

Covers these related disorders: Collodion baby, Congenital ichthyosiform erythroderma, Epidermolytic hyperkeratosis, Harlequin fetus, Ichthyosis vulgaris, X-linked ichthyosis

Involves the following Biologic System(s):
Dermatologic Disorders

Ichthyosis, literally meaning "fish skin," is a group of disorders characterized by abnormal thickening, dryness, and scaling of the skin due to abnormalities in the production of keratin, a protein that is the primary component of the skin, hair, and nails. Most forms of ichthyosis are genetic disorders that are usually apparent at birth (congenital) or during the first months of life. The genes that cause some congenital forms of ichthyosis have been mapped to particular chromosomes. Ichthyosis may also be due to other underlying genetic syndromes or may be an acquired condition due to certain nutritional deficiencies, the administration of particular drugs, or certain conditions, such as abnormally decreased activity of the thyroid gland (hypothyroidism) or Hodgkin's disease, a malignancy of the lymphatic system.

One congenital form of ichthyosis is known as harlequin fetus and may result from several different genetic abnormalities, most of which are thought to be transmitted as an autosomal recessive trait. Affected newborns may be covered with thickened, ridged, armor-like plates that confine the fingers and toes, restrict movements of the joints, and flatten the nose and ears. Additional features may include eyelids that are turned outward (ectropion), causing eyes to be indistinct; gaping lips; and absent hair and nails. Newborns with the condition may experience difficulties breathing, be susceptible to repeated skin infections, and develop life-threatening complications during the first days or weeks of life.

Another congenital form of ichthyosis, known as collodion baby, may also result from many different genetic abnormalities. Affected newborns are covered by a thick membrane that resembles an oiled parchment (collodion membrane), causing flattening of the nose and ears, abnormalities of the eyelids (ectropion), gaping of the lips, or other abnormalities. The membrane begins to crack as patients breathe and is gradually shed in large sheets. This condition is usually an early manifestation of specific genetic forms of ichthyosis (e.g., lamellar ichthyosis or congenital ichthyosiform erythroderma). Patients may develop potentially life-threatening symptoms due to skin infection, inflammation of the lungs (pneumonia), excessive loss of bodily fluids (dehydration), or other abnormalities.

Congenital ichthyosiform erythroderma is an autosomal recessive disorder that typically becomes apparent shortly after birth and may often present as collodion baby, the name given to a baby who is born encased in a skin that resembles a yellow, tight and shiny film or dried collodion (sausage skin) This form of ichthyosis is characterized by abnormal redness of the skin (erythroderma); generalized, fine, white scaling of the skin; and potentially severe itching (pruritus). Many children also have abnormally thickened skin (hyperkeratosis) on the palms of the hands and soles of the feet as well as around the knees, ankles, and elbo. Additional findings may include unusually sparse hair and abnormalities of the nails. Another form of the disorder, known as lamellar ichthyosis or nonbullous congenital ichthyosiform erythroderma, is usually inherited as an autosomal recessive trait. This form of ichthyosis becomes apparent shortly after birth and may also present as a collodion baby. After the collodion membrane is shed, the skin becomes covered with relatively large, coarse scales. Scaling often affects all surfaces of the body and may be associated with pruritus. Patients may also have thickened skin on the palms and soles, usually small ears, ectropion, and abnormally sparse, fine hair.

Another form of the disorder, known as X-linked ichthyosis, is often apparent at birth or during early infancy. Although males are primarily affected, some females who carry a single copy of the disease gene may also experience some symptoms. Patients develop prominent darkened scales on the scalp, ears, neck, arms and legs, torso, or other areas. Scaling may gradually worsen in severity and progress to affect other areas of the skin. By late childhood or adolescence, many patients develop clouding of the corneas (corneal opacities) that does not interfere with vision.

The most common form of the disorder is ichthyosis vulgaris, also known as ichthyosis simplex, an autosomal dominant disorder that affects about one in 250 to 300 children. Symptoms, which typically become apparent by the age of six months, may include slight roughness and scaling of the skin, particularly of the back and the legs. Scaling may worsen upon exposure to cold temperatures and may subside during warm months of the year. There may also be overgrowth of hair follicles (keratosis pilaris), particularly those of the thighs and upper arms, as well as abnormal thickening of the skin of the palms and soles. The condition may gradually improve or subside with age.

Another form of ichthyosis, known as epidermolytic hyperkeratosis or bullous congenital ichthyosiform erythroderma, may occur randomly for unknown reasons or be inherited as an autosomal dominant trait. This form of ichthyosis typically becomes apparent shortly after birth and is characterized by erythroderma, hyperkeratosis in certain areas, and small, rough, wart-like scales over body surfaces. Skin overgrowth may be most apparent on the neck and hips, under the arms, or at the elbows or knees and may affect the skin of the palms and soles. Recurrent blistering (bullae) may also develop, particularly on the lower legs, knees, or elbows.

The methods used to treat ichthyosis depend upon the specific disorder type as well as the severity and extent of associated symptoms. In severe neonatal forms, such as collodion baby and harlequin fetus, supportive measures may include administration of fluids to prevent dehydration; use of specialized support equipment such as an incubator that provides a heated, appropriately moisturized (hum idified) environment; and use of measures to help prevent or aggressively treat infections. Treatment may also include the administration of certain vitamin A derivatives (retinoids) or emulsifying ointments or lubricants. Bathing with oils may help to moisten the skin, and the application of certain emulsifying ointments and lubricants that soften the skin may alleviate dryness and scaling. In addition, applying topical agents that promote skin softening and peeling (keratolytic agents) may facilitate the removal of scales. In some patients, the use of air conditioning in warmer months and exposure to a high-humidity environment during the colder months may also be beneficial. Additional treatment is symptomatic and supportive.

Ichthyosis / Government Agencies

Government Agencies

3886 **NIH/ Eunice Kennedy Shriver National Institute of Child Health & Human Development**
P.O. Box 3006
Rockville, MD 20847

800-370-2943
Fax: 866-760-5947
www.nichd.nih.gov

Conducts and supports research on topics related to the health of children, adults, families and populations. Some of these topics include: developmental disabilities, growth and development, infant death, reproductive health and birth defects.

Diana W. Bianchi, Director
Alison Cernich, PhD, Deputy Director

3887 **NIH/National Institute of Allergy and Infectious Diseases**
5601 Fishers Lane, MSC 9806
Bethesda, MD 20892

301-496-5717
866-284-4107
Fax: 301-402-3573
TDD: 800-877-8339
ocpostoffice@niaid.nih.gov
www.niaid.nih.gov

The principal advisory board of the NIAID. The council is composed of physicians, scientists and representatives of the public and advises on the conduct and support or research, training and dissemination of health information regarding allergies and infectious diseases.

Anthony S. Fauci, MD, Director

3888 **NIH/National Institute of Arthritis and Musculoskeletal and Skin Diseases**
1 AMS Circle
Bethesda, MD 20892

301-495-4484
877-226-4267
Fax: 301-718-6366
TTY: 301-565-2966
niamsinfo@mail.nih.gov
www.niams.nih.gov

The mission of the NIAMS, a part of the NIH, is to support research into the causes, treatment and prevention of arthritis and musculoskeletal and skin diseases, the training of basic and clinical scientists to carry out this research, and the dissemination of information on research progress in these diseases.

Lindsey A. Criswell, MD, Director
Rick Phillips, Executive Officer

National Associations & Support Groups

3889 **American Academy of Pediatrics**
345 Park Blvd
Itasca, IL 60143

800-433-9016
Fax: 847-434-8000
mcc@aap.org
www.aap.org

The American Academy of Pediatrics and its member pediatricians are committed to the attainment of optimal physical, mental and social health and well-being for all infants, children, adolescents, and young adults.

Lynn Olson, PhD, VP, Research
Mark Del Monte, JD, CEO/Executive VP
Vera Tait, MD, FAAP, Chief Medical Officer

3890 **FIRST: Foundation for Ichthyosis and Related Skin Types**
PO Box 1067
Lansdale, PA 19446

215-997-9400
800-545-3286
www.firstskinfoundation.org

Dedicated to helping individuals and families affected by the inherited skin diseases collectively called the Ichthyoses. Provides support, information, education, and advocacy for individuals and families affected by ichthyosis.

Christopher Boynton, Chief Executive Officer
Lisa Breuning, Director of Operations
Denise Gass, Director of Development

3891 **Genetic Alliance**
426400 Woodfield Road, Ste 189
Damascus, MD 20872

202-966-5557
Fax: 202-966-8553
info@geneticalliance.org
www.geneticalliance.org

World's leading nonprofit health advocacy organization committed to transforming health through genetics and promoting an environment of openness centered on the health of individuals, families, and communities.

Sharon Terry, CEO
Ruth Child, CFO
Natasha Bonhomme, Chief Strategy Officer

3892 **March of Dimes Foundation**
1550 Crystal Drive, Ste 1300
Arlington, VA 22202

888-663-4637
www.marchofdimes.org

March of Dimes help moms have full-term pregnancies and research the problems that threaten the health of babies. The March of Dimes also acts globally: sharing best practices in perinatal health and helping improve birth outcomes where the needs are the most urgent.

Stacey D. Stewart, President
Alan Brogdon, SVP/COO/Board Officer
Rahul Gupta, MD, SVP & Chief Medical/Health Officer

3893 **Society for Pediatric Dermatology**
8365 Keystone Crossing, Ste 107
Indianapolis, IN 46240

317-202-0224
Fax: 317-205-9481
info@pedsderm.net
www.pedsderm.net

The objective of the Society is to promote, develop and advance education, research and care of skin disease in all pediatric age groups.

Kent Lindeman, Executive Director

Web Sites

3894 **Ichthyosis Information**
www.ichthyosis.com/

chris@ichthyosis.com
www.ichthyosis.com/

This website is to furnish users with general information.

Journals

3895 **Pediatric Dermatology Journal**
Society for Pediatric Dermatology
8365 Keystone Crossing, Suite 107
Indianapolis, IN 46240

317-202-0224
Fax: 317-205-9481
info@pedsderm.net
www.pedsderm.net

Answers the need for new ideas and strategies for today's pediatrician or dermatologist.

6 issues/yr

Kent Lindeman, Executive Director

Description

3896 INTELLECTUAL DISABILITIES
Synonym: Intellectual Disabilities
Involves the following Biologic System(s):
Developmental/Behavioral/Psychiatric Disorders, Neurologic Disorders

Intellectual disabilities are characterized by impaired or below average intellectual functioning that results in deficits in learning ability and adaptive behaviors. The disorder is thought to affect approximately three percent of the general population. About 80 to 90 percent of patients have mild intellectual disabilities, whereas 10 to 20 percent are affected by moderate to profound degrees of impairment.

The causes of intellectual disabilities may be biological as well as psychosocial or sociocultural in nature. In other words, the disorder may be due to a combination of several factors and influenced both by biological abnormalities of the brain as well as the nature of a child's life experiences, such as those resulting from parent-child interactions and overall family dynamics. Biological causes of intellectual disabilities may include fetal exposure to certain drugs, maternal infections, or radiation therapy; premature birth; or certain underlying disorders, such as inborn errors of metabolism, chromosomal abnormalities including Down syndrome and fragile X syndrome, or other genetic disorders. Intellectual disabilities may also result from head injuries or low levels of oxygen to the brain during delivery, childhood exposure to lead, or certain infections during infancy or early childhood, such as inflammation of the protective membranes surrounding the brain and spinal cord (meningitis). Some underlying causes may be correctable before intellectual before intellectual disabilities occurs, such as phenylketonuria (PKU), which is a metabolic disorder, or hypothyroidism, a condition characterized by decreased activity of the thyroid gland. Additional contributing factors may include malnutrition; dysfunctional interactions between caregivers and infants; or other psychosocial or sociocultural factors. In many children with intellectual disabilities, the specific causes remain unknown. The condition may occur as the result of the interactions of several genes (polygenic inheritance), possibly in association with certain environmental influences (multifactorial).

During normal development, infants and children acquire mental, physical, and behavioral skills in certain stages known as developmental milestones. Although the particular rate of development is variable, most children acquire such skills at certain ages. However, infants and children with intellectual disabilities typically experience delays in achieving certain developmental milestones. For example, in severe cases, patients may initially have delays in the acquisition of certain motor skills. In more moderate cases, children may achieve early motor milestones yet be delayed in acquiring certain skills that require the coordination of physical and mental abilities (psychomotor delays), such as delayed speech and language skills. In children with mild or borderline impairment, below average intellectual functioning may not be suspected until the early school years. Varying degrees of intellectual disabilities are based upon the different levels of support that may be required for daily functioning as well as intelligence quotient (I.Q.), which is a standardized, age-related measure of intelligence. Intellectual disabilities may be defined as having an I.Q. below 70 and is often subdivided into mild, moderate, severe, and profound intellectual disabilities. Most individuals in the general population have an I.Q. between 80 and 120.

Children with what is known as borderline intellectual functioning have very mild intellectual deficits (e.g., I.Q. between 70 to 85) and minor impairments in adaptive behaviors. These behaviors include certain adaptive skills, such as social, self-care, communication, and vocational skills. Patients with mild impairment (I.Q. between 50 and 70) may develop academic skills up to the sixth grade level. In addition, with appropriate support, they may achieve social skills that enable them to function relatively independently during adulthood. Patients with moderate impairment (I.Q. between 35 and 50) may learn to communicate and tend to have only fair motor development. Although these patients rarely develop academic skills up to the second grade level, they may benefit from vocational training and achieve limited independence with appropriate supervision. Children with severe intellectual disabilities (I.Q. between 20 and 35) typically have poor motor development and little speech or communication skills. With appropriate education and support, they may develop speech by late adolescence. In addition, with close supervision, they may learn basic hygienic skills and simple tasks by adulthood. Although children with profound impairment (I.Q. under 20) may learn some basic hygienic skills, they typically have limited psychomotor development and require close, ongoing supervision.

In infants with suspected intellectual disabilities, a number of specialized laboratory tests may be conducted to rule out certain underlying disorders, such as fragile X syndrome or other chromosomal or genetic syndromes. The management of intellectual disabilities is individualized for each child and may include therapeutic and special educational services as well as special social support and counseling services. Early diagnosis and the prompt development of an individualized, comprehensive intervention program is essential in helping affected children reach their potential. Prenatal screening for genetic defects, and genetic counseling for families at risk for known heritable disorders can decrease the incidence of genetically caused intellectual disabilities. Primary care pediatricians lay an important role in consulting with specialists and other health care providers as required and developing an appropriate intervention program. As patients with mild to moderate impairment reach adolescence, specialized services may include a focus on vocational training and community living.

National Associations & Support Groups

3897 AHRC New York City
83 Maiden Lane
New York, NY 10038
212-780-2500
www.ahrcnyc.org

Developmentally disabled children and adults, their families, and interested individuals. Provides support services, training programs, clinics, schools and residential facilities to the developmentally disabled.

Marco Damiani, Chief Executive Officer
Amy West, EVP & CFO
Elizabeth Lynam, EVP & Chief Program Officer

3898 American Academy of Pediatrics
345 Park Blvd
Itasca, IL 60143
847-434-4000
800-433-9016
Fax: 847-434-8000
csc@aap.org
www.aap.org

The American Academy of Pediatrics and its member pediatricians are committed to the attainment of optimal physical, mental and social health and well-being for all infants, children, adolescents, and young adults.

Intellectual Disabilities / National Associations & Support Groups

Kyle E. Yasuda, MD, FAAP, President
Mark Del Monte, JD, CEO/Executive VP
Vera Tait, MD, FAAP, Chief Medical Officer

3899 American Association of People with Disabilities
2020 Pensylvania Avenue, PO Box 263
Washington, DC 20006
202-521-4316
800-840-8844
www.aapd.com

As a national cross-disability rights organization, AAPD advocates for full civil rights for the over 60 million Americans with disabilities by promoting equal opportunity, economic power, independent living, and political participation.

Maria Town, President & CEO
Jasmin Bailey, Operations Director
Christine Liao, Programs Director

3900 American Association on Health and Disabilities
110 N. Washington Street, Suite 407
Rockville, MD 20850
301-545-6140
Fax: 301-545-6144
contact@aahd.us
www.aahd.us

It is dedicated to improve overall health and reduce health disparities for people with disabilities through health promotion and wellness.

Roberta Carlin, Executive Director
Karl Cooper, Director, Public Health Programs

3901 American Mental Health Foundation (AMHF)
PO Box 3
Riverdale, NY 10471
USA
212-737-9027
elomke@americanmentalhealthfoundation.or
www.americanmentalhealthfoundation.org

Dedicated to the extensive and intensive research in the theories and techniques of treatment of emotional illness and to the implementation of reforms in the mental health system. Efforts have resulted in development of better and less expensive treatment methods. Findings are disseminated in English and other major languages.

Sister Joan Curtin, Director
John P. Fowler, Treasurer
Eugene Gollogly, VP

3902 American Network of Community Options & Resources
www.ancor.org

It is the advocate and resource for private community providers of services to people with disabilities.

Barbara Merrill, Chief Executive Officer
Gabrielle Sedor, Chief Operations Officer
Cindy Ramos, Chief Financial Officer

3903 American Occupational Therapy Association
6116 Executive Boulevard, Suite 200
Bethesda, MD 20852
301-652-6611
800-729-2682
customerservice@aota.org
www.aota.org

AOTA represents more than 230,000 occupational therapists, occupational therapy assistants, and occupational therapy students in the United States and beyond, to advance occupational therapy practice, education, and research.

Sherry Keramidas, Executive Director
Tricia Hopkins, Chief Financial Officer
Neil Harvison, Chief Officer, Knowledge Division

3904 American Public Health Association
800 I Street, NW
Washington, DC 20001
202-777-2742
Fax: 202-777-2534
TTY: 202-777-2500
www.apha.org

APHA champions the health of all people and all communities. They aim to strengthen the public health profession and speak out for public health issues and policies backed by science.

Georges C. Benjamin, MD, Executive Director
Kemi Oluwafemi, MBA, CPA, Chief Financial Officer
Susan Polan, PhD, Associate Executive Director

3905 Arc of the United States
1825 K Street NW, Ste 1200
Washington, DC 20006
202-534-3700
800-433-5255
Fax: 202-534-3731
info@thearc.org
www.thearc.org

The Arc of the United States advocates for the rights and full participation of all children and adults with intellectual and developmental disabilities. Together with a network of members and affiliated chapters, they improve systems of support and services; connect families; inspire communities and influence public policy.

Peter V. Berns, CEO

3906 Association of Developmental Disabilities
1671 Worcester Road, Suite 201
Framingham, MA 01701
508-405-8000
Fax: 508-405-8001
www.addp.org

The mission is to promote and ensure the strength of the community-based provider community and its members so that our members can be successful in improving the quality, access and value of community based services.

3907 Association of Professional Developmental Disabilities Administrators
www.apdda.org
info@apdda.org
www.apdda.org

The mission is to supports the continuous improvement of a comprehensive array of individual and accessible services designed to enhance the quality of life for persons with intellectual disabilities and other developmental disabilities.

Robert D. Shrewsberry, Administrative Director
Ted Williams, Publications Coordinator

3908 Association of University Centers on Disabilities
1100 Wayne Ave., Suite 1000
Silver Spring, MD 20910
301-588-8252
Fax: 301-588-2842
aucdinfo@aucd.org
www.aucd.org

The Association of University Centers on Disabilities (AUCD) is a membership organization that supports and promotes a national network of university-based interdisciplinary programs.

John Tschida, Executive Director
Jeannette Cordova, Program Manager
Chevelle Glymph, Senior Director of Public Health

3909 Center for Disabilities and Development
University of Iowa Stead Family Children's Hospita
100 Hawkins Drive
Iowa City, IA 52242
319-353-6900
877-686-0031
Fax: 319-356-7700
cdd-webmaster@uiowa.edu
www.medicine.uiowa.edu

A trusted resource for healthcare, training, research and information for people with disabilities that include: behavior disorders, brain injury, cerebral palsy, diabetes, down syndrome, learning disabilities, sleep disorders and spina bifida.

Dianne McBrien, MD, Medical Director

3910 Council on Quality and Leadership
100 West Road, Suite 300
Towson, MD 21204
410-275-0488
www.c-q-l.org

CQL offers training, accreditation, consultation and certification services to organizations and systems that share our vision of dignity, opportunity and community for all people.

Mary Kay Rizzolo, President & CEO
Trina Meeth, VP, Finance & Administration
Rebecca Kasey, Director, Special Projects

Intellectual Disabilities / National Associations & Support Groups

3911 Developmental Disabilities Nurses Association
1501 South Loop 288, Suite 104 - 381
Denton, TX 76205
800-888-6733
Fax: 844-336-2329
ddna.org

Developmental Disabilities Nurses Association (DDNA) is a 501(c)(3) not-for-profit nursing specialty organization that is committed to advocacy, education, and support for nurses who provide services to persons with intellectual and developmental disabilities (IDD).

S. Diane Moore, Executive Director

3912 Institute on Community Integration
University of Minnesota
2025 East River Parkway
Minneapolis, MN 55414
612-624-6300
Fax: 612-624-9344
ici@umn.edu
ici.umn.edu

The Community Living and Employment area of the Institute on Community Integration works to ensure that public policy and services are helping people with disabilities live their best lives in inclusive communities. Through applied research, policy advocacy, and training, we engage with individuals with disabilities, families, providers, policymakers, and community members to influence local, state, and federal policies and support individuals with disabilities.

Debbie Hansen, Executive Officer

3913 Judge David L. Bazelon Center for Mental Health
1090 Vermont Avenue NW, Suite 220
Washington, DC 20005
202-467-5730
communications@bazelon.org
www.bazelon.org

The mission of the Judge David L. Bazelon Center for Mental Health Law is to protect and advance the rights of adults and children who have mental disabilities.

Holly O'Donnell, Chief Executive Officer
Ira Burnim, Director, Legal
Jalyn Radziminski, Director of Engagement

3914 Mosaic
4980 S. 118th Street
Omaha, NE 68137
877-366-7242
Fax: 402-896-1511
info@mosaicinfo.org
www.mosaicinfo.org

Mosaic serves nearly 4,900 people in more than 700 communities. Services are tailored to meet individual needs and goals, allowing people to be as independent as possible. Services are designed for people with disabilities, mental and behavioral health needs and autism, as well as aging adults.

Linda Timmons, President & CEO
Jennifer LeDoux, Senior Vice President, Operations
Scott Hoffman, Senior Vice President, Finance

3915 NADD: National Association for the Dually Diagnosed
12 Hurley Avenue
Kingston, NY 12401
845-331-4336
800-331-5362
Fax: 845-331-4569
info@thenadd.org
www.thenadd.org

Nonprofit organization designed to promote the interests of professional and parent development with resources for individuals who have the coexistence of mental illness and intellectual disabilities. Provides conferences, educational services and training materials to professionals, parents, concerned citizens and service organizations. Formerly known as the National Association for the Dually Diagnosed.

Jeanne Farr, CEO
Michelle Jordan, Office Manager
Edward Seliger, Project Coordinator

3916 NAQ
101 Hempstead Place, Suite 1B
Joliet, IL 60433
815-320-7301
admin@n-a-q.org
www.n-a-q.org

Founded in 1996, NAQ began its commitment to supporting people with Intellectual and Developmental Disabilities (I/DD) to live their best possible life by strengthening the learning, training, and personal growth of professionals working within the field of I/DD. Today, NAQ focuses on coaching and inspiring these dedicated professionals by conducting webinars, hosting a certification program, and an annual conference.

Amy Tabor, Executive Director
Beth Dyer, Director of Operations

3917 National Alliance on Mental Illness (NAMI)
4301 Wilson Blvd., Suite 300
Arlington, VA 22203
703-524-7600
800-999-6264
info@nami.org
www.nami.org

NAMI provides advocacy, education, support and public awareness so that all individuals and families affected by mental illness can build better lives.

Daniel H. Gillison, CEO
David Levy, CFO
Ken Duckworth, Chief Medical Officer

3918 National Association of Councils on Developmental Disabilities
1825 K Street NW, Suite 1250
Washington, DC 20006
202-506-5813
info@nacdd.org
www.nacdd.org

The National Association of Councils on Developmental Disabilities (NACDD) is a national membership organization representing the 56 State and Territorial Councils on Developmental Disabilities.

Donna A. Meltzer, Chief Executive Officer
Robin Troutman, Deputy Director
Rafael Rolon-Muniz, Programs Coordinator

3919 National Association of State Directors of Developmental Disabilities Services
PO Box 26128
Alexandria, VA 22313
703-683-4202
cmcgraw@nasddds.org
www.nasddds.org

The NASDDDS mission is to assist member state agencies in building person-centered systems of services and supports for people with intellectual and developmental disabilities and their families.

Mary P. Sowers, Executive Director
Carrie M. McGraw, Director of Communications
Dan Berland, Director of Federal Policy

3920 National Association of State Mental Health Program Directors
675 N Washington Street, Suite 470
Alexandria, VA 22314
703-739-9333
www.nasmhpd.org

Founded in 1959 and based in Alexandria, VA, the National Association of State Mental Health Program Directors (NASMHPD) represents the $37.6 billion public mental health service delivery system serving 7.1 million people annually in all 50 states, 4 territories, and the District of Columbia.

Jay Meek, CPA, MBA, Chief Financial Officer
Robert W. Glover, PhD, Executive Director
David Miller, MPAff, Project Director

3921 National Disability Rights Network
820 1st Street NE, Suite 740
Washington, DC 20002
202-408-9514
Fax: 202-408-9520
TTY: 220-408-9521
www.ndrn.org

The National Disability Rights Network (NDRN) works to improve the lives of people with disabilities by guarding against abuse; advocating for basic rights; and ensuring accountability in health care, education, employment, housing, transportation, and within the juvenile and criminal justice systems.

Marlene Sallo, Executive Director
Marcia Baldwin, Deputy Director, Traning/Operations
Eric Buehlmann, Deputy Director, Public Policy

Intellectual Disabilities / State Agencies & Support Groups

3922 **VOR**
836 S. Arlington Heights Rd., #351
Elk Grove Village, IL 60007

877-399-4867
Fax: 877-866-8377
info@vor.net
www.vor.net

Founded 40 years ago in 1983, VOR is a national nonprofit that advocates for a full range of quality residential options and services, including own home, family home, community-based service options, and licensed facilities. We support the expansion of quality community-based service options; we oppose the elimination of specialized facility-based (institutional) option.

Hugo Dwyer, Executive Director

State Agencies & Support Groups

3923 **Arc of New York**
29 British American Blvd, 2nd Floor
Latham, NY 12110

518-439-8311
Fax: 518-439-1893
info@thearcny.org
www.thearcny.org

The Arc of New York's mission is to advocate for persons with intellectual and other developmental disabilities in every manner possible. In its advocacy role, NYSARC is committed to a full quality of life for every person, as it recognizes the challenges of the present and has a clear vision for the future.

Mark van Voorst, Executive Director
Cyndi Borozny, Deputy Executive Director
Kate Geurin, Assoc. Exec. Dir., Communications

3924 **Center for Family Support**
333 7th Avenue, #901
New York, NY 10001

212-629-7939
Fax: 212-239-2211
www.cfsny.org

The Center for Family Support (CFS) is a not-for-profit human service agency providing support and assistance to individuals with developmental disabilities and traumatic brain injuries throughout New York City, Long Island, the lower Hudson Valley region and New Jersey.

Steven Vernikoff, Executive Director
Linda Schellenberg, Director, Community Service
Barbara Greenwald, Associate Executive Director

3925 **KenCrest Services**
502 W Germantown Pike Suite 200
Plymouth Meeting, PA 19462

610-825-9360
Fax: 610-825-4127
www.kencrest.org

Multi-service organization with programs specifically designed for children and youth with developmental disabilities and autism, throughout Pennsylvania, Delaware, & Connecticut.

Bill Nolan, Executive Director
Jim McFalls, Executive Director
Toni McNeal, CFO

California

3926 **People First of California**
PO Box 2223
Elk Grove, CA 95759

916-552-6625
Fax: 916-387-2398
info@peoplefirstca.org
www.peoplefirstca.org

Developmentally disabled people joining together to learn how to speak for themselves. Offers support, information, assistance and advocacy.

Ron Peterson, President

Missouri

3927 **People First of Missouri**
PO Box 30142
Kansas City, MO 64112

800-558-8652
missouripeoplefirst@gmail.com
www.missouripeoplefirst.org

Developmentally disabled people joining together to learn how to speak for themselves. Offers support, information, assistance and advocacy.

Cathy Enfield, President

Ohio

3928 **People First of Ohio**
1335 Dublin Road, Ste 100-A
Columbus, OH 43215

614-487-4720
peoplefirstohio@gmail.com
www.peoplefirstofohio.org

Developmentally disabled people joining together to learn how to speak for themselves. Offers support, information, assistance and advocacy.

John Hannah, President

West Virginia

3929 **People First-West Virginia**
912 Market Street
Parkersburg, WV 26101

304-422-3151
Fax: 304-865-2072
info@peoplefirstwv.org
peoplefirstwv.org

Developmentally disabled people joining together to learn how to speak for themselves. Offers support, information, assistance and advocacy.

Liz Ford, Executive Director
Melissa Southall, Self Advocate Coordinator
Doug Hess, State Advisor

Web Sites

3930 **American Association on Intellectual and Developmental Disabilities**
8403 Colesville Road, Ste 900
Silver Spring, MD 20910

202-387-1968
Fax: 202-387-2193
maria@aaidd.org
www.aamr.org

Promotes progressive policies, sound research, effective practices, and universal human rights for people with intellectual disabilites.

Margaret A. Nygren, Executive Director & CEO
Maria Alfaro, Manager, Meetings & Website
Laura Thorn, Manager, Membership/Communications

3931 **NADD: National Association for the Dually Diagnosed**
12 Hurley Avenue
Kingston, NY 12401

845-331-4336
info@thenadd.org
www.thenadd.org

Nonprofit organization designed to promote the interests of professional and care providers for individuals who have the coexistence of mental illness and intellectual disabilities. NADD provides conferences, educational services and training materials to professionals, parents, concerned citizens and service organizations.

Jeanne Farr, CEO
Michelle Jordan, Office Manager
Edward Seliger, Project Coordinator

3932 **People First International**
PO Box 12642
Salem, OR 97309

503-362-0336
Fax: 503-585-0287
www.people1.org

Developmentally disabled people joining together to learn how to speak for themselves. Offers support, information, assistance and advocacy.

Dennis L Heath, Manager

Magazines

3933 **American Journal on Intellectual Disabilities**
AAIDD
8043 Colesville Road, Ste 900
Silver Spring, MD 20910

202-387-1968
Fax: 202-387-2193
symon007@umn.edu
aaidd.org

The flagship journal of AAIDD, offering critical research in behavioral, biological, and educational sciences.

Margaret A. Nygren, Executive Director & CEO
Frank Symons, Editor
Kathleen McLane, Director, Publications Program

3934 **Intellectual Disability**
AAIDD
8403 Colesville Road, Ste 900
Silver Spring, MD 20910

202-387-1968
Fax: 202-387-2193
www.aamr.org

Provides information on the latest program advances, current research, and information on products and services in the developmental disabilities field.

Bimonthly

Newsletters

3935 **NADD Bulletin**
132 Fair Street
Kingston, NY 12401

845-331-4336
800-331-5362
Fax: 845-331-4569
info@thenadd.org
www.thenadd.org

Official publication of the National Association for the Dually Diagnosed. It features articles that address clinical, programmatic, research or family oriented issues concerning mental health aspects in persons with disabilities.

20 pages Bimonthly

Jeanne Farr, CEO
Lucy Esralew, Co Editor
Bob Klaehn, Co Editor

Camps

3936 **Camp Huntington**
56 Bruceville Road
High Falls, NY 12440

845-687-7840
855-707-2267
Fax: 845-687-7211
camohtgtn@aol.com
www.camphuntington.com

Summer activities include recreational, academic and vocational programs for the learning disabled and neurologically impaired. An Olympic pool, horse riding and a special work training program are featured. Programs are tailored to meet individual needs, ages 6-21, and campers may enroll for 4 to 8 weeks.

Dr. Bruria Falik, Director
Michael Bednarz, Executive Director
Alex Mellor, Program Director

3937 **Crotched Mountain School & Rehabilitation Center**
1 Verney Drive
Greenfield, NH 3047

603-547-3311
800-800-966
Fax: 603-547-3232
info@crotchedmountain.org
www.cmf.org

Currently serves children ages 6-22 with multiple-handicaps including: Cerebral Palsy, Spina Bifida, visual and hearing impairments and neurological disabilities, developmental disorders, autism, behavioral and emotional disorders, seizure disorders, spinal cord and head injuries. Member of the National Association of Independent Schools and accredited with the NE Association of Schools and Colleges, Independent Schools of Northern NE.

Donald L Shumway, President & CEO
Tom Zubricki, Chief Financial Officer
Michael Redmond, Senior Vice President

3938 **Easter Seal Kysoc**
2050 Versailles Road
Lexington, KY 40504

859-254-5701
800-233-3260
Fax: 502-732-0783
ek1@cardinalhill.org
www.cardinalhill.org

Designed for the fullest camping experience for children or adults with physical disabilities, blind, deaf, behavior disorders, diabetes and multiple handicaps, ages 7 and up.

Gary Payne, President & CEO
Heide Miller, CCD, CTRS, Director

3939 **New Jersey Camp Jaycee**
985 Livingston Avenue
North Brunswick, NJ 8902

732-246-2525
Fax: 732-214-1834
www.campjaycee.org

This camp is for children and adults with intellectual disabilities and is sponsored jointly by the New Jersey Jaycees and the ARC of New Jersey. Activities at the 185-acre Pocono Mountain camp include arts and crafts, games and sports, music, nature, swimming, boating, horseback riding and self-help skills.

Frank Pirrello, President
John O'Brien, Vice President
Patricia Rhein, Secretary

3940 **Raven Rock Lutheran Camp**
17912 Harbaugh Valley Road
Sabillasville, MD

717-794-2667

Christ-centered program for youth and intellectually disabled adults.

Lee Sodowsky

3941 **Thorpe Camp**
680 Capen Hill Road
Goshen, VT 5733

802-247-6611
info@campthorpe.org
www.campthorpe.com

Summer camp for children and adults with special needs.

Intraventricular Hemorrhage / Description

Description

3942 INTRAVENTRICULAR HEMORRHAGE

Synonyms: IVH, germinal matrix hemorrhage, GMH, Periventricular hemorrhage, PVH

Involves the following Biologic System(s):

Neonatal and Infant Disorders, Neurologic Disorders

Intraventricular Hemorrhage (IVH) is a disease of premature infants in which there is bleeding inside or around the ventricles, the spaces in the brain that contain the cerebrospinal fluid (CSF). Bleeding in the brain can put pressure on the nerve cells and damage them. Severe damage to cells can lead to brain injury. Intraventricular hemorrhage is most common in premature babies, especially very low birthweight babies. The younger the gestational age, the higher the incidence of IVH. It is not clear why IVH occurs. Bleeding can occur because blood vessels in a premature baby's brain are very fragile and immature and easily rupture. The risk of rupture is greatest in the first 4-5 days after birth. Abrupt changes in cerebral blood flow are thought to be one of the causes of IVH. Symptoms of IVH include apnea (stopped breathing), bradycardia (slow heart rate), pale or blue coloring (cyanosis), weak suck, high-pitched cry, and seizures.

IVH is diagnosed by cranial ultrasound and graded I through IV (IV being most severe). Infants with IVH are at higher risk for neurological disease including seizures, developmental delay, and hydrocephalus. Infants with IVH also have a higher incidence of death. With higher grades of IVH, the risk of future morbidity and mortality increases.

The treatment of IVH is supportive care. The best prevention of IVH is to prevent premature birth. When this is unavoidable, the use of anti-inflammatory medication (indomethacin) in the first 48 hours of life has been shown to decrease the incidence of IVH.

National Associations & Support Groups

3943 American Academy of Pediatrics
345 Park Blvd
Itasca, IL 60143

800-433-9016
Fax: 847-434-8000
mcc@aap.org
www.aap.org

The American Academy of Pediatrics and its member pediatricians are committed to the attainment of optimal physical, mental and social health and well-being for all infants, children, adolescents, and young adults.

Lynn Olson, PhD, VP, Research
Mark Del Monte, JD, CEO/Executive VP
Vera Tait, MD, FAAP, Chief Medical Officer

3944 Children's Hospital at Montefiore
3415 Bainbridge Avenue
Bronx, NY 10467

718-741-2426
www.cham.org

The Children's Hospital at Montefiore is one of the most technologically advanced hospitals for children in the world. Staffed by the nationally renowned faculty of the Albert Einstein College of Medicine, our pediatric specialists and caregivers are ranked among the best in the nation.

Michael D. Cabana, Physician-in-Chief
Patricia Hametz, Senior Medical Director

3945 Lucile Packard Children's Hospital
Stanford Medicine Children's Health
725 Welch Road
Palo Alto, CA 94304

650-497-8000
www.stanfordchildrens.org

Devoted entirely to the care of babies, children, adolescents and expectant mothers. To best serve our communitites we advocate on behalf of the children and expectant mothers, advance family centered care, foster innovation, and educate health care providers and leaders.

Paul A. King, President & CEO
Dana Haering, EVP & CFO
Grace Lee, Chief Quality Officer

3946 New York Presbyterian Morgan Stanley Children's Hospital
3959 Broadway (165th Street and Broadway)
New York, NY 10032

212-305-5437
800-245-5437
www.nyp.org/morganstanley

NewYork-Presbyterian Morgan Stanley Children's Hospital can trace its roots to Babies Hospital, which was founded in 1887 as the first dedicated hospital for children in New York City. Today, NewYork-Presbyterian Morgan Stanley Children's Hospital is affiliated with the Department of Pediatrics at Columbia University Vagelos College of Physicians and Surgeons.

Web Sites

3947 Children's Hospital at Montefiore
3415 Bainbridge Avenue
Bronx, NY 10467

718-741-2426
www.cham.org

The Children's Hospital at Montefiore is one of the most technologically advanced hospitals for children in the world. Staffed by the nationally renowned faculty of the Albert Einstein College of Medicine, our pediatric specialists and caregivers are ranked among the best in the nation.

Michael D. Cabana, Physician-in-Chief
Patricia Hametz, Senior Medical Director

3948 Children's Hospital of New York Presbyterian
nyp.org/kids/index.html

nyp.org/kids/index.html

Provides comprehensive information for children with serious disearse, associated with Children's Hospital of New York Presbyterian.

3949 Yale University School of Medicine
330 Cedar St, Boardman 110, P.O. Box 208056
New Haven, CT 06520

medicine.yale.edu/intmed/cardio/

Information on heart conditions, including Intraventricular Hemorrhage — symptoms, treatments and support.

Henry Scott Cabin, Professor of Medicine
Joseph Akar, Associate Professor of Medicine
Henry Cabin, Acting Section Chief

Description

3950 JUVENILE RHEUMATOID ARTHRITIS

Synonym: JRA

Covers these related disorders: Pauciarticular juvenile arthritis, Systemic-onset juvenile arthritis (Still's disease), Type I polyarticular juvenile arthritis, Type II polyarticular juvenile arthritis

Involves the following Biologic System(s):
Immunologic and Rheumatologic Disorders

Juvenile rheumatoid arthritis (JRA) is a group of disorders of childhood characterized by inflammation (arthritis), tenderness, pain, and swelling of one or more joints, potentially causing impaired development, limited movements, and permanent bending or extension of affected joints in various fixed postures (contractures). The symptoms and findings associated with JRA occur as the result of inflammation of the synovial membrane of affected joints (synovitis). Synovial membranes are connective tissue membranes that line the spaces between joints and bones and secrete a thick fluid to lubricate the joints. Although the cause of JRA is unknown, researchers speculate that the disorder may be the result of infection by an unidentified microorganism, an excessive immune response to a substance that the body perceives as foreign (hypersensitivity response), or abnormal immune responses against the body's own cells or tissues (autoimmune response). Certain antibodies often present in the blood of adults with rheumatoid arthritis (e.g., rheumatoid factors) are only rarely present in children with JRA. In such cases, researchers indicate that affected children may have some genetic predisposition for certain forms of JRA. Approximately 250,000 children are thought to be affected by JRA in the United States. Females are more commonly affected than males.

There are three major categories of JRA: polyarticular (30 percent), pauciarticular (50 percent), and systemic-onset juvenile arthritis (20 percent). Polyarticular juvenile arthritis typically involves several joints. Associated symptoms and findings include inflammation, swelling, abnormal warmth, tenderness, and pain of affected joints. This form of JRA often affects joints of the elbows, wrists, fingers, knees, feet, and ankles. In addition, patients may have involvement of joints of the jaw (temporomandibular joints), causing limited opening of the mouth; the neck (cervical spine), resulting in neck pain and stiffness; and the hips, causing pain, stiffness, and limited movements. Normal growth may be delayed during periods of active disease, causing such abnormalities as unusually short fingers, small feet, or underdevelopment of the jaw (micrognathia). Some children with polyarticular juvenile arthritis may also experience more generalized symptoms, such as low-grade fever, lack of appetite (anorexia), increased irritability, a mild decrease in the level of circulating red blood cells (anemia), swelling of certain lymph nodes (lymphadenopathy), or mild enlargement of the liver and spleen (hepatosplenomegaly).

Pauciarticular juvenile arthritis is characterized by involvement of larger joints, usually four or fewer for six consecutive weeks. Type I pauciarticular juvenile arthritis primarily affects females andhas an early onset. Affected joints typically include the elbows, knees, and ankles. In addition, other joints may sometimes be affected, such as those of a single finger or toe, the wrists, the neck, or the jaw. Patients are also at risk (girls more than boys) for chronic inflammation of the colored region of the eye (iris) and its muscle (iridocyclitis). One or both eyes may be affected. Some patients may experience associated redness, sensitivity to light (photophobia), pain, or decreased clearness of vision (visual acuity). Without appropriate treatment, visual impairment or, in severe cases, blindness may result. Boys are at higher risk of arthritis of the spine. Symptoms may include a general feeling of ill health (malaise), low-grade fever, mild hepatosplenomegaly, and mild anemia. Type II pauciarticular juvenile arthritisis most common in males older than age eight. Affected joints usually include those of the hips, knees, toes, and heels. In some patients, joints of the elbows, fingers, wrists, or jaw may also be affected. In patients with this form of JRA, associated foot and hip pain may sometimes be disabling. In addition, chronic, progressive, inflammatory disease of joints of the spine (spondyloarthropathy) may develop. Symptoms may include pain, stiffness, and loss of mobility of joints of the upper and lower back (ankylosing spondylitis). In addition, some affected children may experience sudden (acute) episodes of iridocyclitis.

Systemic-onset juvenile arthritis appears to affect females and males equally. This form of JRA usually begins with generalized symptoms, such as a high, intermittent fever that rapidly returns to normal; a characteristic rash; anemia; hepatosplenomegaly; lymphadenopathy; mild liver dysfunction (hepatitis); and, in about one third of patients, inflammation of the membranous sac surrounding the heart (pericarditis) or the membrane lining the lungs and chest cavity (pleuritis). The fever associated with systemic JRA tends to rise in the evenings, although it may also be elevated in the mornings, and is often associated with shaking chills. During fever episodes, a temporary, salmon-colored rash often appears on the trunk or arms or legs (extremities), although it may appear anywhere on the body. Such a rash may also temporarily appear in association with heat exposure or stress. In patients with systemic disease, joint inflammation, swelling, stiffness, and pain may occur at disease onset or months later. Joint involvement is usually similar to that seen in patients with polyarticular juvenile arthritis. Systemic symptoms and findings typically have a self-limited course that lasts for several months. However, such findings may recur in some patients.

In approximately 75 percent of affected children, symptoms associated with JRA completely disappear with little loss of function or deformity. However, other patients, particularly those with multiple joint involvement or rheumatoid factor, may experience repeated or chronic joint inflammation and permanent stiffness, limited movement, and deformity of certain affected joints. In addition, some patients with pauciarticular juvenile arthritis may later experience additionaljoint involvement (polyarthritis) or ongoing symptoms due to progressive, inflammatory disease of joints of the spine (spondyloarthropathy).

Children with JRA should receive regular eye (e.g., slit-lamp) examinations to ensure early detection and treatment of iridocyclitis. Treatment of iridocyclitis includes the use of corticosteroid eyedrops and drugs that widen (dilate) the pupil. Joint inflammation, pain, and stiffness may be alleviated with aspirin, nonsteroidal anti-inflammatory drugs (NSAIDs), medications such as methotrexate or hydroxychloroquine, or, in extremely severe cases, corticosteroids administered by mouth (orally). Due to the potential association of aspirin and the occurrence of Reye's syndrome, NSAIDs (e.g., tolmetin, naproxen, etc.) are currently being prescribed more frequently than aspirin as a treatment for JRA. Children with JRA who do not respond to NSAIDs therapy may be treated with low-dose methotrexate. If JRA is severe and systemic or, in patients in whom iridocyclitis is uncontrolled by corticosteroid eyedrops, oral corticosteroid therapy may be prescribed. However, oral corticosteroid therapy is usually avoided in children, if possible, since such therapy may slow the growth rate and is associated with other negative side effects. Children who don't respond well to methotrexate can be offered similar medications, sometimes referred to as disease-modifying antirheumatic drugs (DMARDs). Agents being tried in therapy of JRA include sulfasalazine, intravenous immunoglobulin, and cyclosporine. Splints may be used during the day to help rest inflamed joints and at night to minimize the risk of contracture development and associated deformity. Special exercises may also be recommended to help reduce possible muscle wasting and contractures. In some patients, surgery may be required to help correct contractures. Children should also be monitored for growth abnormalities, nutritional deficiencies, and school/social impairment.

Government Agencies

3951 NIH/National Institute of Arthritis and Musculoskeletal and Skin Diseases
1 AMS Circle
Bethesda, MD 20892
301-495-4484
877-226-4267
Fax: 301-718-6366
TTY: 301-565-2966
niamsinfo@mail.nih.gov
www.niams.nih.gov

The mission of the NIAMS, a part of the NIH, is to support research into the causes, treatment and prevention of arthritis and musculosketal and skin diseases, the training of basic and clinical scientists to carry out this research, and the dissemination of information on research progress in these diseases.

Lindsey A. Criswell, MD, Director
Rick Phillips, Executive Officer

National Associations & Support Groups

3952 American Academy of Pediatrics
345 Park Blvd
Itasca, IL 60143
800-433-9016
Fax: 847-434-8000
mcc@aap.org
www.aap.org

The American Academy of Pediatrics and its member pediatricians are committed to the attainment of optimal physical, mental and social health and well-being for all infants, children, adolescents, and young adults.

Lynn Olson, PhD, VP, Research
Mark Del Monte, JD, CEO/Executive VP
Vera Tait, MD, FAAP, Chief Medical Officer

3953 Arthritis Foundation
1335 Peachtree Street NE, Suite 600
Atlanta, GA 30309
800-283-7800
www.arthritis.org

The Arthritis Foundation is committed to raising awareness and reducing the unacceptable impact of arthritis, a disease which must be taken as seriously as other chronic diseases because of its devastating consequences.

Ann M. Palmer, President & CEO
Sabrina Sexton, SVP, Marketing & Communications
Robin Kindard, SVP, Operations

3954 Genetic Alliance
426400 Woodfield Road, Ste 189
Damascus, MD 20872
202-966-5557
Fax: 202-966-8553
info@geneticalliance.org
www.geneticalliance.org

World's leading nonprofit health advocacy organization committed to transforming health through genetics and promoting an environment of openness centered on the health of individuals, families, and communities.

Sharon Terry, CEO
Ruth Child, CFO
Natasha Bonhomme, Chief Strategy Officer

Research Centers

3955 John Hopkins Arthritis Center
5200 Eastern Avenue, Suite 4100
Baltimore, MD 21224
410-550-0545
Fax: 410-550-2090
arthritis@jhmi.edu
www.hopkins-arthritis.org

The Johns Hopkins Arthritis Center has assembled a team of some of the world's leading experts and specializes in the care of inflammatory arthritis. This includes, most notably, osteoarthritis and rheumatoid arthritis.

Penny Athanasiou, Clinic Coordinator

3956 Pediatric Rheumatoid Clinic
Duke Medical Center
Box 3212
Durham, NC 27710
919-684-6575

Clinical and laboratory pediatric rheumatoid studies.

Dr. Deborah Kredich, Chairman
Stacy Ardman

Web Sites

3957 Online Mendelian Inheritance in Man
McKusick-Nathans Institue of Genetic Medicine-JHU
Baltimore, MD 21205
www.omim.org

This database is a catalog of human genes and genetic disorders.

Ada Hamosh, MD, Scientific Director

Book Publishers

3958 Arthritis
Franklin Watts
90 Old Sherman Turnpike
Danbury, CT 06816
203-797-3500
800-724-6527
Fax: 203-797-3197
www.scholastic.com

This book offers a clear explanation of the various forms and effects of the disease of arthritis and what treatments are available.

96 pages Grades 7-12
ISBN: 0-531108-01-5

Dick Robinson, President & CEO

3959 Arthritis Sourcebook 5th Edition
Omnigraphics
615 Griswold Street, Ste 520
Detroit, MI 48226
610-461-3548
800-234-1340
Fax: 800-875-1340
contact@omnigraphics.com
www.omnigraphics.com

Basic consumer health information on specific forms of arthritis and related disorders.

568 pages Hardcover
ISBN: 0-780816-26-8

3960 Educational Rights for Children With Arthritis: Parents Manual
AJAO
1335 Peachtree Street NE, Suite 600
Atlanta, GA 30309
404-872-7100
800-283-7800
help@arthritis.org
www.arthritis.org

A self-instructional manual helping parents to identify and obtain school services needed by their child with arthritis. Covers laws and special services, explores strategies for working with school personnel and stresses good communication and advocacy techniques.

Ann M. Palmer, President & CEO
Melissa Honabach, SVP, Marketing & Communications
David McLoughlin, COO

3961 **JRA and Me**
American Juvenile Arthritis Organization
PO Box 19000
Atlanta, GA 30326
800-283-7800

A workbook for school-aged children who have juvenile arthritis. This book offers a variety of educational games, puzzles and worksheets to teach children about their illness and how to take care of themselves.

57 pages

3962 **Living with Arthritis**
Franklin Watts
90 Old Sherman Turnpike
Danbury, CT 06816
203-797-3500
800-621-1115
Fax: 203-797-3197
www.scholastic.com

Shows how people with arthritis can overcome their pain and lead productive, full lives.

32 pages Grades 5-7

Dick Robinson, President & CEO

3963 **Raising a Child With Arthritis**
American Juvenile Arthritis Organization
1335 Peachtree Street NE, Suite 600
Atlanta, GA 30309
404-872-7100
800-283-7800
help@arthritis.org
www.arthritis.org

372 pages

Ann M. Palmer, President & CEO
Melissa Honabach, SVP, Marketing & Communications
David McLoughlin, COO

3964 **Understanding Juvenile Rheumatoid Arthritis**
American Juvenile Arthritis Organization
1335 Peachtree Street NE, Suite 600
Atlanta, GA 30309
404-872-7100
800-283-7800
help@arthritis.org
www.arthritis.org

A manual for health professionals to use in teaching children with JRA and their families about disease management and self-care.

372 pages

Ann M. Palmer, President & CEO
Melissa Honabach, SVP, Marketing & Communications
David McLoughlin, COO

3965 **We Can: Guide for Parents of Children with Arthritis**
American Juvenile Arthritis Association
1335 Peachtree Street NE, Suite 600
Atlanta, GA 30309
404-872-7100
800-283-7800
help@arthritis.org
www.arthritis.org

Offers parents tips for daily living and practical points for helping their child toward independent adulthood.

Ann M. Palmer, President & CEO
Melissa Honabach, SVP, Marketing & Communications
David McLoughlin, COO

3966 **Yard Sale Coloring Book**
American Juvenile Arthritis Organization
PO Box 19000
Atlanta, GA 30326
800-283-7800

A coloring/activity book based on a Kids on the Block script, written for third and fourth grade students. It can be used with Kids on the Block performances, as a stand-alone piece or with a free lesson plan packet.

Newsletters

3967 **AJAO Newsletter**
American Juvenile Arthritis Organization
1335 Peachtree Street NE, Suite 600
Atlanta, GA 30309
404-872-7100
800-283-7800
kgatmail@arthritis.org
www.arthritis.org

This reliable and comprehensive newsletter for families coping with childhood arthritis and related conditions contains the latest research findings, responsible advice from pediatric specialists, practical methods to help improve quality of life, and informative updates about medications and how they affect children. Articles are written in clear understandable language. Timely medical insights and life enhancing information that provides solutions to everyday problems.

Quarterly

Ann M. Palmer, President & CEO
Melissa Honabach, SVP, Marketing & Communications
David McLoughlin, COO

Pamphlets

3968 **Arthritis in Children and La Artritis Infantojuvenil**
American Juvenile Arthritis Organization
PO Box 7669
Atlanta, GA 30357
404-872-7100
800-568-4045

A medical information booklet about juvenile rheumatoid arthritis. This booklet is written for parents or other adults and includes details about different forms of JRA, medications, therapies and coping issues.

3969 **Arthritis in Children: Resources for Children, Parents and Teachers**
National Arthritis and Skin Diseases Clearinghouse
9000 Rockville Pike
Bethesda, MD 20892
301-495-4484
www.niams.nih.gov/health_info

A resource offering information on juvenile arthritis, causes, treatments and prevention.

38 pages

3970 **Juvenile Arthritis**
Arthritis Foundation
1335 Peachtree Street NE, Suite 600
Atlanta, GA 30309
404-872-7100
800-283-7800
www.arthritis.org

Ann M. Palmer, President & CEO
Melissa Honabach, SVP, Marketing & Communications
David McLoughlin, COO

3971 **Juvenile Arthritis: A Teacher's Guide**
Arthritis Foundation
1335 Peachtree Street NE, Suite 600
Atlanta, GA 30309
404-872-7100
800-283-7800
www.arthritis.org

A medical information booklet written for teachers or other adults who have arthritis. The booklet describes different forms of juvenile arthritis, how arthritis might affect the child at school, and how to help the child work around these problems.

Ann M. Palmer, President & CEO
Melissa Honabach, SVP, Marketing & Communications
David McLoughlin, COO

3972 Rheumatoid Arthritis
NAMSIC, National Institutes of Health
1 AMS Circle
Bethesda, MD 20892

301-495-4484
877-226-4267
Fax: 301-718-6366
TTY: 301-565-2966
NIAMSinfo@mail.nih.gov
www.nih.gov/niams/

Offers an introduction and definition of rheumatoid arthritis, treatments, causes, objectives, daily living, resources and medical information.

Robert H. Carter, MD, Acting Director

Description

3973 KAWASAKI DISEASE

Synonyms: MLNS, Mucocutaneous lymph node syndrome

Involves the following Biologic System(s):

Cardiovascular Disorders, Immunologic and Rheumatologic Disorders

Kawasaki disease is a syndrome of unknown origin that primarily affects infants and young children. The disease was initially observed in Japanese children after World War II. Kawasaki disease is becoming increasingly frequent in the United States, has been reported worldwide, and is currently considered the leading cause of acquired heart disease in children in the U.S. Although Kawasaki disease has been reported in people in all racial groups, individuals of Japanese descent appear to be most commonly affected. The disease may occur commonly in a random or an isolated manner (sporadic form) or, rarely, may suddenly affect large numbers of individuals (epidemic form). Although the cause of Kawasaki disease is unknown, researchers suspect that toxic substances produced by certain bacteria (e.g., staphylococcal toxins) may play some role. There is no evidence of transmission of the disease from one affected individual to another (person-to-person transmission).

Kawasaki disease most commonly affects children who are five years of age or younger. Affected children typically develop a sudden, sustained, high fever that is often greater than 104 degrees and unresponsive to therapy with fever-reducing (antipyretic) medications. Most patients also have inflammation of the whites of both eyes and the lining inside the eyelids (bilateral conjunctivitis), causing redness but no associated discharge; dry, red (erythematous), cracked (fissured) lips; a strawberry-red tongue; and swelling of one or several lymph nodes, particularly those of the neck (cervical lymphadenopathy). Patients also typically develop a reddish skin rash that may consist of flat, discolored spots and small, raised areas (maculopapular) or appear similar to that seen in measles (morbilliform). The trunk, the hands and feet, and the face may be affected. Patients usually experience subsequent swelling and associated pain of the hands and feet. By approximately the second to third week, affected skin may begin to peel (desquamate) from the palms of the hands, the soles of the feet, and the tips of the fingers and toes. Such peeling may also involve other affected areas, such as the trunk. In addition, children with Kawasaki disease are usually irritable and may develop joint swelling and pain (arthritis), abdominal pain, diarrhea, vomiting, coughing, inflammation of the gall bladder, or enlargement of the liver and spleen (hepatosplenomegaly). Additional symptoms and findings may include inflammation of certain muscles (myositis), nasal discharge of a thin fluid (rhinorrhea), episodes of increased electrical activity in the brain (seizures), mild inflammation of the protective membrane surrounding the brain (aseptic meningitis), or other abnormalities.

The most serious complication potentially associated with Kawasaki disease is involvement of the heart. Within the first few weeks after disease onset, approximately 25 percent of untreated patients develop inflammation of arteries that carry blood to the heart muscle (coronary arteritis) and associated widening or bulging (aneurysms) of the walls of these arteries. In rare cases, affected children, particularly those under the age of one year, may experience few early symptoms associated with the disease, yet later develop coronary arteritis. Patients with cardiac involvement may develop inflammation of heart muscle (myocarditis); deficient blood supply to heart muscle (myocardial ischemia), resulting in localized loss of tissue (infarction); and inflammation of the membranous sac surrounding the heart (pericarditis). Additional findings may include inflammation of the membrane lining the internal surfaces of the cavities of the heart (endocarditis), an inability of the heart to sufficiently pump blood to the lungs and the rest of the body (heart failure), or abnormalities of the rhythm or rate of the heartbeat (arrythmias). In some cases, without appropriate treatment, patients with severe cardiac involvement may experience potentially life-threatening complications.

All patients with diagnosed or suspected Kawasaki disease should undergo specialized diagnostic tests, such as chest x-rays, electrocardiograms, and echocardiograms. Additional testing (e.g., two-dimensional echocardiogram) may also be conducted during the first two weeks of disease. The treatment of children with Kawasaki disease should include intravenous (IV) infusion with a preparation of antibodies (immunoglobulins) obtained from plasma, the liquid portion of the blood (intravenous gammaglobulin), and therapy with high-dose aspirin (salicylate therapy). Early (within 10 days of fever onset) intravenous gammaglobulin therapy helps to alleviate fever and other associated symptoms; in addition, controlled studies have demonstrated that such therapy decreases heart involvement to some patients. Once the fever has subsided, patients may receive therapy with lower doses of aspirin. Such therapy typically continues until coronary arteritis resolves. In the rare patient with large or multiple coronary artery aneurysms, treatment may include therapy with anticlotting medications, such as warfarin or heparin. Other treatment is symptomatic and supportive. All children diagnosed with Kawasaki disease receive outpatient follow-up with a pediatric cardiologist.

Government Agencies

3974 NIH/ Eunice Kennedy Shriver National Institute of Child Health & Human Development
P.O. Box 3006
Rockville, MD 20847
800-370-2943
Fax: 866-760-5947
www.nichd.nih.gov

Conducts and supports research on topics related to the health of children, adults, families and populations. Some of these topics include: developmental disabilities, growth and development, infant death, reproductive health and birth defects.

Diana W. Bianchi, Director
Alison Cernich, PhD, Deputy Director

3975 NIH/National Heart, Lung and Blood Institute
31 Center Drive, Bldg 31
Bethesda, MD 20892
877-645-2448
www.nhlbi.nih.gov

Primary responsibility of this organization is the scientific investigation of heart, blood vessel, lung and blood disorders. Oversees research, demonstration, prevention, education, control and training activities in these fields and emphasizes the prevention and control of heart diseases.

Gary H. Gibbons, MD, Director
Kate O'Sullivan, Executive Officer

3976 NIH/National Institute of Allergy and Infectious Diseases
5601 Fishers Lane, MSC 9806
Bethesda, MD 20892
301-496-5717
866-284-4107
Fax: 301-402-3573
TDD: 800-877-8339
ocpostoffice@niaid.nih.gov
www.niaid.nih.gov

The principal advisory board of the NIAID. The council is composed of physicians, scientists and representatives of the public and advises on the conduct and support or research, training and dissemination of health information regarding allergies and infectious diseases.

Anthony S. Fauci, MD, Director

National Associations & Support Groups

3977 American Academy of Pediatrics
345 Park Blvd
Itasca, IL 60143

800-433-9016
Fax: 847-434-8000
mcc@aap.org
www.aap.org

The American Academy of Pediatrics and its member pediatricians are committed to the attainment of optimal physical, mental and social health and well-being for all infants, children, adolescents, and young adults.

Lynn Olson, PhD, VP, Research
Mark Del Monte, JD, CEO/Executive VP
Vera Tait, MD, FAAP, Chief Medical Officer

3978 Kawasaki Disease Foundation
11 Walley Street, Unit 401
Boston, MA 02128

kdfoundation.org

Raising awareness among the medical community, childcare providers, and the general public is critical to early diagnosis and treatment. Facilitating support among families is essential to helping families cope with this uncommon illness and the potentially devastating effects of heart damage. Increasing funding for research is necessary to advance diagnostic guidelines, enhance the existing treatment, improve short-term and long-term follow-up care and find a cause.

Gregory Chin, Founder & Treasurer
Vanessa Gutierrez, President
Kate Davila, Vice President

3979 Kawasaki Kids Foundation
www.kawasakikidsfoundation.org

Building a friendly and knowledgeable community to help save kids hearts and cure Kawasaki Disease by increasing awareness. Creating national awareness of Kawasaki Disease, find a cure of through research, support families by creating a supportive network, and educate families, communities, and health care professionals.

Shawn Logan, Executive Director
Ashley Brown, President
Pei-Ni Jone, Vice President

Description

3980 KELOIDS

Synonym: Cheloids

Involves the following Biologic System(s):
Dermatologic Disorders

Keloids are firm, nodule-like overgrowths of scar tissue that occur at the sites of surgery, injury, or trauma to the skin. These overgrowths result from the formation, during the healing process, of excessive amounts of the fibrous protein collagen, which is a major structural component of connective tissue. Doctors do not understand exactly why keloids form in certain people or situations and not in others. Changes in the signals sent out by cells that control growth and proliferation may be related to the process of keloid formation, but these changes have not yet been scientifically proven. Keloids may be itchy and are usually pink in color, shiny, smooth, irregularly shaped, firm, and rubbery. Some keloids may be tender or painful. Although keloids may appear on the face, neck, earlobes, legs, or other areas, they most often occur over the breastbone (sternum) and the shoulders.

Keloid development may sometimes result following surgery, body piercing, and other types of trauma to the skin such as burns or scalds. In addition, keloids may develop in association with severe acne and occasionally with certain connective tissue disorders such as Ehlers-Danlos syndrome or skin disorders such as Touraine-Solente-Gole syndrome. In some cases, keloid development may be inherited as an autosomal recessive or autosomal dominant trait. In addition, keloids are more common in black individuals.

Without treatment, keloids tend to flatten out and become less obvious within a period of months or years. However, monthly injections of certain corticosteroid drugs directly into the lesions (intralesional) may successfully decrease their size and reduce itching, but treatment should be initiated early in their development. Treatment of large keloids may include surgical removal followed by corticosteroid injections into the lesions. Surgery alone most often results in a recurrence of the keloid. Other treatment may include laser therapy that reduces the redness of the keloid; freezing keloids (cryotherapy) may also flatten them. The direct application of silicone patches or sheeting may promote shrinkage.

Government Agencies

3981 NIH/National Institute of Arthritis and Musculoskeletal and Skin Diseases
1 AMS Circle
Bethesda, MD 20892
301-495-4484
877-226-4267
Fax: 301-718-6366
TTY: 301-565-2966
niamsinfo@mail.nih.gov
www.niams.nih.gov

The mission of the NIAMS, a part of the NIH, is to support research into the causes, treatment and prevention of arthritis and musculosketal and skin diseases, the training of basic and clinical scientists to carry out this research, and the dissemination of information on research progress in these diseases.

Lindsey A. Criswell, MD, Director
Rick Phillips, Executive Officer

National Associations & Support Groups

3982 American Academy of Dermatology
P.O. Box 1968
Des Plaines, IL 60017
847-240-1280
888-462-3376
mrc@aad.org
www.aad.org

To promote and advance the art of medicine and surgery of the skin; promote the highest possible standards in clinical practice, education and research in dermatology and related disciplines.

3983 American Academy of Pediatrics
345 Park Blvd
Itasca, IL 60143
800-433-9016
Fax: 847-434-8000
mcc@aap.org
www.aap.org

The American Academy of Pediatrics and its member pediatricians are committed to the attainment of optimal physical, mental and social health and well-being for all infants, children, adolescents, and young adults.

Lynn Olson, PhD, VP, Research
Mark Del Monte, JD, CEO/Executive VP
Vera Tait, MD, FAAP, Chief Medical Officer

3984 American Osteopathic College of Dermatology
1501 E Illinois Street, PO Box 7525
Kirksville, MO 63501
660-665-2184
Fax: 660-627-2623
info@aocd.org
www.aocd.org

Strives to improve the standards of the practice of dermatology, to stimulate the study and extend knowledge in the field of dermatology, and to promote a more general understanding of the nature and scope of services rendered by osteopathic dermatologists to other divisions of practice, hospitals, clinics and the public.

Marsha Wise, Executive Director
John Wise, Director of Events
John C. Crogan, Member Services Coordinator

3985 American Skin Association
335 Madison Avenue, 22nd Floor
New York, NY 10017
212-889-4858
info@americanskin.org
www.americanskin.org

The American Skin Association is the only volunteer led health organization dedicated through research, education and advocacy to saving lives and alleviating human suffering caused by the full spectrum of skin disorders.

Kathleen Reichert, Executive Vice President
Kristin Ludl, Operations Manager

3986 Society for Pediatric Dermatology
8365 Keystone Crossing, Ste 107
Indianapolis, IN 46240
317-202-0224
Fax: 317-205-9481
info@pedsderm.net
www.pedsderm.net

The objective of the Society is to promote, develop and advance education, research and care of skin disease in all pediatric age groups.

Kent Lindeman, Executive Director

Journals

3987 Pediatric Dermatology Journal
Society for Pediatric Dermatology
8365 Keystone Crossing, Suite 107
Indianapolis, IN 46240
317-202-0224
Fax: 317-205-9481
info@pedsderm.net
www.pedsderm.net

Answers the need for new ideas and strategies for today's pediatrician or dermatologist.

Keloids / Journals

6 issues/yr
Kent Lindeman, Executive Director

Description

3988 KERNICTERUS
Synonym: Bilirubin encephalopathy
Involves the following Biologic System(s):
Neonatal and Infant Disorders

Kernicterus refers to a rare neurologic condition in which excessive amounts of bilirubin accumulate in the brain of affected newborns, resulting in damage to the central nervous system. Bilirubin, a reddish-yellow pigment present in bile, is derived from the breakdown of the protein in red blood cells that carries oxygen (hemoglobin). Premature infants and newborns with certain congenital disorders (e.g., erythroblastosis fetalis and Crigler-Najjar syndrome) are at risk for this life-threatening condition. In premature infants, the processes needed for bilirubin excretion may not be fully developed. Factors that put extra strain on this immature metabolic process may result in increased levels of bilirubin in the blood (hyperbilirubinemia). If these levels become excessive and are left untreated, bilirubin may be deposited in the brain. For example, in infants with erythroblastosis fetalis, antibodies from the mother's blood cross the placental barrier and destroy red blood cells of the fetus, resulting in release of excessive amounts of bilirubin. In some cases, bilirubin builds up faster than the liver is able to eliminate it, resulting in hyperbilirubinemia. Signs of this condition include a yellowing of the eyes, skin, and mucous membranes (jaundice).

Crigler-Najjar syndrome results from the deficiency of an enzyme that is required to convert bilirubin to a form that may be excreted from the body, thus causing hyperbilirubinemia. Other conditions or disorders that cause hyperbilirubinemia place the newborn, especially those who are born prematurely, at risk for kernicterus.

Symptoms of kernicterus usually become apparent within the first week of life. However, hyperbilirubinemia that occurs anytime within the first month of life may result in kernicterus. Symptoms and characteristic findings may include difficulty in feeding; vomiting; lethargy; and lack of a normal response to sudden, loud noises (Moro or startle reflex). Further signs of this condition may include breathing difficulties; severe muscle spasms resulting in a backward arching of the back and neck (opisthotonos); twitching of the arms, legs, and face; a high-pitched cry, and convulsions. In some affected infants, severe involvement of the central nervous system may cause life-threatening complications. In others, findings associated with permanent disability may be observed periodically until the third year of life when the complete neurologic picture emerges. Symptoms may include involuntary spasms of the muscles, hearing loss, eye movement irregularities, deficiencies in motor development, difficulties in speech, seizures, and intellectual disabilities. Some infants who experience only slight kernicterus may experience mild irregularities in neuromuscular coordination, moderate deafness, and slight intellectual disabilities.

Treatment of kernicterus is directed toward prevention involving the correction of hyperbilirubinemia and jaundice before kernicterus can develop. Treatment may include phototherapy in which, under careful monitoring, the infant's skin is exposed to high-intensity fluorescent light. Although phototherapy is often effective in reducing levels of bilirubin, the underlying cause of hyperbilirubinemia and jaundice must be identified and treated as well. Some infants, especially those at higher risk for kernicterus, may be effectively treated with exchange blood transfusions in which small amounts of the infant's circulating blood are repeatedly withdrawn and replaced with equal amounts of whole blood from a donor until about 80 percent of the newborn's blood has been replaced. Other treatment is symptomatic and supportive.

Government Agencies

3989 NIH/ Eunice Kennedy Shriver National Institute of Child Health & Human Development
P.O. Box 3006
Rockville, MD 20847
800-370-2943
Fax: 866-760-5947
www.nichd.nih.gov

Conducts and supports research on topics related to the health of children, adults, families and populations. Some of these topics include: developmental disabilities, growth and development, infant death, reproductive health and birth defects.

Diana W. Bianchi, Director
Alison Cernich, PhD, Deputy Director

National Associations & Support Groups

3990 American Academy of Pediatrics
345 Park Blvd
Itasca, IL 60143
800-433-9016
Fax: 847-434-8000
mcc@aap.org
www.aap.org

The American Academy of Pediatrics and its member pediatricians are committed to the attainment of optimal physical, mental and social health and well-being for all infants, children, adolescents, and young adults.

Lynn Olson, PhD, VP, Research
Mark Del Monte, JD, CEO/Executive VP
Vera Tait, MD, FAAP, Chief Medical Officer

3991 American Liver Foundation
P.O. Box 299
West Orange, NJ 07052
800-465-4837
www.liverfoundation.org

The American Liver Foundation is the nation leading nonprofit organization promoting liver health and disease prevention. ALF provides research, education and advocacy for those affected by liver-related diseases, including hepatitis.

Lorraine Stiehl, CEO
David Ticker, Executive VP & CFO

3992 Genetic Alliance
426400 Woodfield Road, Ste 189
Damascus, MD 20872
202-966-5557
Fax: 202-966-8553
info@geneticalliance.org
www.geneticalliance.org

World's leading nonprofit health advocacy organization committed to transforming health through genetics and promoting an environment of openness centered on the health of individuals, families, and communities.

Sharon Terry, CEO
Ruth Child, CFO
Natasha Bonhomme, Chief Strategy Officer

3993 March of Dimes Foundation
1550 Crystal Drive, Ste 1300
Arlington, VA 22202
888-663-4637
www.marchofdimes.org

March of Dimes help moms have full-term pregnancies and research the problems that threaten the health of babies. The March of Dimes also acts globally: sharing best practices in perinatal health and helping improve birth outcomes where the needs are the most urgent.

Stacey D. Stewart, President
Alan Brogdon, SVP/COO/Board Officer
Rahul Gupta, MD, SVP & Chief Medical/Health Officer

Libraries & Resource Centers

3994 **National Digestive Diseases Information Clearinghouse (NDDIC)**
NIH
2 Information Way
Bethesda, MD 20892

301-654-3810
800-891-5389
Fax: 301-907-8906
nddic@info.niddk.nih.gov
www.digestive.niddk.nih.gov

The National Institute of Diabetes and Digestive and Kidney Diseases conducts and supports research on many of the most serious diseases affecting public health. The Institute supports much of the clinical research on the diseases of internal medicine and related subspecialty fields as well as many basic science disciplines.

Griffin P. Rodgers, MD, Director
Gregory G. Germino, MD, Deputy Director
Kathy Kranzfelder, Communications Director

Web Sites

3995 **Clinical Genetic Services-Department of Pediatrics**
Hassenfeld Children's Hospital at NYU Langone
424 East 34th Street
New York, NY 10016

212-263-7300
Fax: 646-754-2250
nyulangone.org

Offers evaluations, genetic counseling and testing. Clinical services include carrier testing, prenatal counseling, and complete genetic evaluations for children and adults.

John G. Pappas, MD, Pediatric Genetic Associate
Naomi Yachelevich, MD, Pediatric Genetic Associate

3996 **Online Mendelian Inheritance in Man**
McKusick-Nathans Institue of Genetic Medicine-JHU
Baltimore, MD 21205

www.omim.org

This database is a catalog of human genes and genetic disorders.

Ada Hamosh, MD, Scientific Director

3997 **Parents of Infants and Children with Kernicterus**
www.pickonline.org

www.pickonline.org

Provides information and support to families of children with kernicterus.

3998 **Save Babies Through Screening Foundation**
PO Box 2313
Palm Harbor, FL 34682

888-454-3383
email@savebabies.org
www.savebabies.org

Is a national nonprofit public charity run by volunteers. Its mission is to improve the lives of babies by working to prevent disabilities and early death resulting from disorders detectable through newborn screening.

Jill Levy-Fisch, President
Sarah Wilkerson, Vice President
Anne Rugari, Treasurer

Description

3999 KLINEFELTER SYNDROME

Synonyms: Chromosome XXY, XXY syndrome

Covers these related disorders: 45,X/46,XY/47,XXY mosaicism, 46,XY/47,XXY mosaicism, 46,XY/48,XXYY mosaicism, 46,XX/47,XXY mosaicism, 48,XXXY, 49,XXXYY

Involves the following Biologic System(s):

Genetic/Chromosomal/Syndrome/Metabolic Disorders

Klinefelter syndrome is a chromosomal disorder that appears to affect approximately one in 1,000 males. Males usually have one X and one Y chromosome; however, those with Klinefelter syndrome have an extra X chromosome in cells of the body. In some patients, only a certain percentage of cells contain the XXY chromosomal abnormality. This finding is known as chromosomal mosaicism. Other cells may have the normal XY chromosomal pair or other sex chromosome abnormalities (e.g., XX, XXYY, etc.). Some males may have Klinefelter variants in which some or all cells contain more than two X chromosomes.

Because only a few or subtle symptoms may be associated with Klinefelter syndrome, the disorder is rarely diagnosed before puberty. Males with the disorder may have extremely variable I.Q.s (intelligence quotients), ranging from well above to far below average; however, most affected males have an I.Q. within average limits (mean of 85 to 90). Some children with Klinefelter syndrome may have learning problems, such as difficulties with verbal expression, reading, and spelling, potentially requiring special assistance or full-time special education classes. Children with the disorder also tend to have behavioral problems, such as immaturity, excessive shyness, anxiety, poor judgment, aggressive activity, and poor social skills. Such behavioral difficulties tend to begin when affected children begin school.

Many children with Klinefelter syndrome have slim, tall stature; long legs; and small testes and a relatively small penis (hypogenitalism). As affected males enter puberty, they may experience partial, inadequate development of secondary sexual characteristics (impaired virilization). For example, facial hair tends to be unusually sparse, the testes remain unusually small, and, in many cases, there is abnormal enlargement of the breasts (gynecomastia). In addition, many affected males experience inadequate production of the male hormone testosterone and deficient production of male reproductive cells (azoospermia), resulting in infertility. In males with deficient testosterone production, treatment may include testosterone replacement therapy beginning at approximately 11 to 12 years of age. In most cases, Klinefelter syndrome results from errors during the division of a parent's reproductive cells (meiosis). In rare cases, the disorder may result from errors during cellular division after fertilization (mitosis).

In males with XY/XXY mosaicism (i.e., a percentage of cells containing the normal XY chromosomal pair), the range and severity of associated symptoms and findings may be less severe, and there may be an increased likelihood of fertility and improved psychosocial adjustment. Affected males with Klinefelter variants (i.e., in which cells contain more than two X chromosomes) may have more severe symptoms and findings, such as a greater risk of intellectual disabilities and impaired virilization and fertility as well as additional physical abnormalities, including malformations of the head and facial (craniofacial) areas and other skeletal abnormalities.

Government Agencies

4000 NIH/ Eunice Kennedy Shriver National Institute of Child Health & Human Development
P.O. Box 3006
Rockville, MD 20847

800-370-2943
Fax: 866-760-5947
www.nichd.nih.gov

Conducts and supports research on topics related to the health of children, adults, families and populations. Some of these topics include: developmental disabilities, growth and development, infant death, reproductive health and birth defects.

Diana W. Bianchi, Director
Alison Cernich, PhD, Deputy Director

National Associations & Support Groups

4001 American Academy of Pediatrics
345 Park Blvd
Itasca, IL 60143

800-433-9016
Fax: 847-434-8000
mcc@aap.org
www.aap.org

The American Academy of Pediatrics and its member pediatricians are committed to the attainment of optimal physical, mental and social health and well-being for all infants, children, adolescents, and young adults.

Lynn Olson, PhD, VP, Research
Mark Del Monte, JD, CEO/Executive VP
Vera Tait, MD, FAAP, Chief Medical Officer

4002 American Association for Klinefelter Syndrome Information & Support (AAKSIS)
3796 Ogden Lane
Mundelein, IL 60060

847-566-5992
KSinfo@aaksis.org
www.aaksis.org

The American Association for Klinefelter Syndrome Information and Support (AAKSIS) is a national volunteer association with the mission of education, support, research, and understanding of 47,XXY and its variants, collectively known as Klinefelter syndrome.

4003 Association For X And Y Chromosome Variations (AXYS)
PO Box 659
Paoli, PA 19301

267-338-4262
info@genetic.org
genetic.org

The Association for X and Y Chromosome Variations (AXYS) is dedicated to addressing the needs of those affected by one or more extra X and/or Y chromosomes. We are focused on sharing knowledge, offering support, and initiating action to help improve lives of individuals and families.

Carol Meerschaert, Executive Director

4004 Genetic Alliance
426400 Woodfield Road, Ste 189
Damascus, MD 20872

202-966-5557
Fax: 202-966-8553
info@geneticalliance.org
www.geneticalliance.org

World's leading nonprofit health advocacy organization committed to transforming health through genetics and promoting an environment of openness centered on the health of individuals, families, and communities.

Sharon Terry, CEO
Ruth Child, CFO
Natasha Bonhomme, Chief Strategy Officer

Web Sites

4005 Klinefelter Syndrome Support Group
www.klinefeltersyndrome.org/

www.klinefeltersyndrome.org/

An online support group which offers information about the group, organizations, online pharmacies, other web sites, and current research studies.

4006 NIH/National Institute of Mental Health
6001 Executive Blvd, Rm 6200, MSC 9663
Bethesda, MD 20892

301-443-4536
866-615-6464
Fax: 301-443-4279
TTY: 301-443-8431
nimhinfo@nih.gov
www.nimh.nih.gov

The mission is to reduce the burden of mental illness and behavioral disorders through research on mind, brain, and behavior. This public health mandate demands that we harness powerful scientific tools to achieve better understanding, treatment, and eventually prevention of these disabling conditions that affect millions of Americans.

Joshua A. Gordon, MD, PhD, Director
Shelli Avenevoli, PhD, Deputy Director

Description

4007 KLIPPEL-FEIL SYNDROME
Synonym: KFS
Covers these related disorders: Klippel-Feil syndrome Type I, Klippel-Feil syndrome Type II, Klippel-Feil syndrome Type III
Involves the following Biologic System(s):
Genetic/Chromosomal/Syndrome/Metabolic Disorders

Klippel-Feil syndrome (KFS) is a congenital malformation characterized by the fusion of two or more vertebrae, especially in the neck or cervical region (congenital synostosis) or by the absence of one or more cervical vertebrae. Klippel-Feil syndrome Type I involves extensive fusion of several cervical vertebrae and thoracic vertebrae located in the upper back. Type II involves fusion of a limited number of incompletely developed vertebrae (hemivertebrae) and vertebrae, fusion of the uppermost cervical vertebra with the bone at the back of the skull (occipital bone), and other irregularities. Klippel-Feil syndrome Type III is characterized by fusion of the cervical, lower thoracic, or lumbar vertebrae. Physical findings associated with Klippel-Feil syndrome may include a short neck with limited range of motion, a low hairline, and irregularities of the urinary tract and reproductive, cardiovascular, pulmonary, and nervous systems. Additional abnormalities may include curvatures of the spine (scoliosis or kyphosis), an inclination of the neck to one side (torticollis), webbing of the neck (pterygium colli) and fingers (syndactyly), and other irregularities of the bones and muscles.

Treatment of Klippel-Feil syndrome may be directed toward the particular physical findings and symptoms associated with this disorder. Such treatment may include measures to correct or halt the progression of various spinal irregularities and to correct other abnormalities as warranted. Other treatment is supportive.

In some children, Klippel-Feil syndrome is transmitted as an autosomal dominant trait, while transmission by autosomal recessive inheritance is possible in others. In addition, some affected children have no recognizable pattern of genetic transmission.

Government Agencies

4008 NIH/ Eunice Kennedy Shriver National Institute of Child Health & Human Development
P.O. Box 3006
Rockville, MD 20847
800-370-2943
Fax: 866-760-5947
www.nichd.nih.gov

Conducts and supports laboratory research, clinical trials, and epidemiological studies that explore health processes; examines the impact of disabilities, diseases, and variations on the lives of individuals; and sponsors training programs for scientists, health care providers, and researchers to ensure that NICHD research can continue.

Diana W. Bianchi, Director
Alison Cernich, PhD, Deputy Director

4009 NIH/National Institute of Arthritis and Musculoskeletal and Skin Diseases
1 AMS Circle
Bethesda, MD 20892
301-495-4484
877-226-4267
Fax: 301-718-6366
TTY: 301-565-2966
niamsinfo@mail.nih.gov
www.niams.nih.gov

The mission of the NIAMS, a part of the NIH, is to support research into the causes, treatment and prevention of arthritis and musculoskeletal and skin diseases, the training of basic and clinical scientists to carry out this research, and the dissemination of information on research progress in these diseases.

Lindsey A. Criswell, MD, Director
Rick Phillips, Executive Officer

4010 NIH/Osteoporosis and Related Bone Diseases National Resource Center
2 AMS Circle
Bethesda, MD 20892
202-223-0344
800-624-2663
Fax: 202-293-2356
TTY: 202-466-4315
NIHBoneInfo@mail.nih.gov
www.bones.nih.gov

The National Resource Center is an information service that provides general information on metabolic bone conditions.

National Associations & Support Groups

4011 American Academy of Pediatrics
345 Park Blvd
Itasca, IL 60143
800-433-9016
Fax: 847-434-8000
mcc@aap.org
www.aap.org

The American Academy of Pediatrics and its member pediatricians are committed to the attainment of optimal physical, mental and social health and well-being for all infants, children, adolescents, and young adults.

Lynn Olson, PhD, VP, Research
Mark Del Monte, JD, CEO/Executive VP
Vera Tait, MD, FAAP, Chief Medical Officer

4012 March of Dimes Foundation
1550 Crystal Drive, Ste 1300
Arlington, VA 22202
888-663-4637
www.marchofdimes.org

March of Dimes help moms have full-term pregnancies and research the problems that threaten the health of babies. The March of Dimes also acts globally: sharing best practices in perinatal health and helping improve birth outcomes where the needs are the most urgent.

Stacey D. Stewart, President
Alan Brogdon, SVP/COO/Board Officer
Rahul Gupta, MD, SVP & Chief Medical/Health Officer

Web Sites

4013 Clinical Genetic Services-Department of Pediatrics
Hassenfeld Children's Hospital at NYU Langone
424 East 34th Street
New York, NY 10016
212-263-7300
Fax: 646-754-2250
nyulangone.org

Offers evaluations, genetic counseling and testing. Clinical services include carrier testing, prenatal counseling, and complete genetic evaluations for children and adults.

John G. Pappas, MD, Pediatric Genetic Associate
Naomi Yachelevich, MD, Pediatric Genetic Associate

4014 Online Mendelian Inheritance in Man
McKusick-Nathans Institue of Genetic Medicine-JHU
Baltimore, MD 21205
www.omim.org

This database is a catalog of human genes and genetic disorders.

Ada Hamosh, MD, Scientific Director

4015 Wheeless' Textbook of Orthopaedics
www.wheelessonline.com

410-494-4994
www.wheelessonline.com

Klippel-Feil Syndrome / Web Sites

Derives from a variety of sources, including journals, articles, national meetings lectures and other textbooks.

Clifford R. Wheeless, Editor in chief
James A Nunley, Managing Editor
James R. Urbaniak, Managing Editor

Lazy Eye / Libraries & Resource Centers

Description

4016 LAZY EYE

Synonym: Amblyopia

Covers these related disorders: Anisometropic Amblyopia

Involves the following Biologic System(s):

Ophthalmologic Disorders

Lazy eye, also known as amblyopia, is a condition in which the vision in one eye is impaired because the images of objects seen by the affected eye are not clearly transmitted to the brain. This visual impairment results from interference with the vision in the affected eye, such as from a cataract, or from an eye-muscle weakness. This impairment prevents the affected eye from turning normally and focusing clearly on objects.

Typically, lazy eye affects only one eye, and develops in 1 to 5% of children, usually before the age of 6 years. Its existence is not always apparent, but its symptoms may include favoring the use of one eye over another, or a tendency to miss objects in the periphery of vision, causing patients to bump into objects on the side of the affected eye. However, symptoms of this condition are not always obvious either to the patient or to others, since it neither reduces the amount of light entering the affected eye nor interferes with the vision in the unaffected eye. Thus, any adjustments made by patients seem normal to them. In many cases, persons with lazy eye discover it only through an eye examination.

If not corrected early in life, lazy eye may prevent the affected eye from ever developing clear and effective vision. Because of this, it is recommended that infants have an eye examination at the age of 6 months, and that examinations are repeated regularly and at frequent intervals, up until 6 years of age.

Treatment of lazy eye may involve forcing the use of the amblyopic eye by applying a patch over its neighboring (good) eye, for periods ranging from weeks to months. This has been shown to strengthen the vision in the weakened eye. Eyeglasses may be prescribed to improve the visual acuity in the affected eye. In some cases surgery can repair muscles of the affected eye, thus improving its coordination with the non-affected eye in looking at and focusing on objects. Eye exercises, to strengthen the affected eye, are often used by themselves or in conjunction with surgery.

Government Agencies

4017 NIH/National Eye Institute
31 Center Drive MSC 2510
Bethesda, MD 20892

301-496-5248
2020@nei.nih.gov
www.nei.nih.gov

Conducts and supports research that helps prevent and treat eye diseases and other disorders of vision. This research leads to sight-saving treatments, reduces visual impairment and blindness, and improves the quality of life for people of all ages. NEI-supported research has advanced our knowledge of how the eye functions in health and disease.

Michael F. Chiang, MD, Director
Santa Tumminia, Deputy Director

National Associations & Support Groups

4018 American Academy of Pediatrics
345 Park Blvd
Itasca, IL 60143

800-433-9016
Fax: 847-434-8000
mcc@aap.org
www.aap.org

The American Academy of Pediatrics and its member pediatricians are committed to the attainment of optimal physical, mental and social health and well-being for all infants, children, adolescents, and young adults.

Lynn Olson, PhD, VP, Research
Mark Del Monte, JD, CEO/Executive VP
Vera Tait, MD, FAAP, Chief Medical Officer

4019 American Foundation for the Blind
1401 South Clark Street, Ste 730
Arlington, VA 22202

212-502-7600
info@afb.net
www.afb.org

The American Foundation of the Blind, has been eliminating barriers the prevent people who are blind or visually impaired from reaching their potential. AFB is dedicated to addressing the most critical issues of facing this growing population: independent living, literacy, employment, and technology.

Kirk Adams, President & CEO
Elizabeth Neal, Director, Communications
Adrianna Montague, Chief Community Engagement Officer

4020 Lighthouse Guild
250 West 64th Street
New York, NY 10023

800-284-4422
info@lighthouseguild.org
www.lighthouseguild.org

Lighthouse Guild is dedicated to providing exceptional services that inspire people who are visually impaired to attain their goals.

James M. Dubin, Chair
Calvin W. Roberts, President & CEO
Maura J. Sweeney, SVP, Programs & Services

4021 National Organization of Parents of Blind Children
National Federation of the Blind
200 East Wells Street
Baltimore, MD 21230

816-787-0140
PresidentofNOPBC@gmail.com
nopbc.org

Enables parents to find resources and information for their children who are visually impaired, blind or have additional disabilities. NAPVI provides support, leadership, and training.

Carla Keirns, President
Carol Castellano, Secretary
Sandra Oliver, Treasurer

4022 Vision Service Plan
3333 Quality Drive
Rancho Cordova, CA 95670

800-852-7600
www.vspvision.com

As the first and only not-for-profit eye health company, VSP offers integrated portfolio of eye care services, eyewear solutions, and practice solutions.

Michael Guyette, President & CEO

Libraries & Resource Centers

4023 Talking Books - National Library Service
NLS for the Blind & Physically Handicapped
Library of Congress
Washington, DC 20542

202-707-5100
888-657-7323
Fax: 202-707-0712
TDD: 202-707-0744
nls@loc.gov
www.loc.gov/nls

Lazy Eye / Research Centers

Administers a free library program of audio materials through a network of cooperating libraries to eligible borrowers in the U.S.

Karen Keninger, Director
Jane Caulton, Head, Publications & Media
Marsha Jackson, Head, Administrative Section

Research Centers

4024 **Visual Systems Research Group**
Cincinnati Children's Research Foundation
3333 Burnet Avenue, PO Box 3026
Cincinnati, OH 45229
513-803-2230
800-344-2462
Fax: 513-636-4317
TTY: 513-636-4900
cincinnatichildrens.org/research/divisions/

A collaboration between the Developmental Biology and Pediatric Ophthalmology divisions, the program is designed to bring basic research to Ophthalmology and to foster research efforts of the clinical faculty.

Richard Lang, PhD, Director

Web Sites

4025 **3D Vision**
www.vision3d.org

www.vision3d.org

Learn about binocular or stereoscopic vision in a fun way.

4026 **All About Amblyopia (Lazy Eye)**
58 Mohonk Road
High Falls, NY 12440
www.lazyeye.org

Research and information from the National Eye Institute (part of the National Institutes of Health, NIH).

4027 **All About Vision**
1010 Turquoise Street, Suite 275
San Diego, CA 92109
858-454-2145
www.allaboutvision.org

Lists humanitarian eye care organizations that serve the needs of those with vision challenges.

Joseph T. Barr, Advisory Board
Brian S. Boxer Wachler, Advisory Board
Michael DePaolis, Advisory Board

4028 **All About Vision.Com**
1010 Turquoise Street, Suite 275
San Diego, CA 92109
858-454-2145
www.allaboutvision.com

Provides consumers with information resources on eye health and vision correction options.

Joseph T. Barr, Advisory Board
Brian S. Boxer Wachler, Advisory Board
Michael DePaolis, Advisory Board

4029 **Attention Disorders and Eyesight**
58 Mohonk Road
High Falls, NY 12440
212-923-0496
www.optometrists.org

Provides information on the link between vision problems and ADD/ADHD. Articles by third-party professionals are added/updated each year.

4030 **Children Special Needs-Pediatric Eye Care**
58 Mohonk Road
High Falls, NY 12440
212-923-0496
www.optometrists.org

Provides information on visual health including: pediatric eye doctor search; tools for parents (glossary, checklists, book list); and descriptions of vision impairments.

4031 **Convergence Insufficiency**
58 Mohonk Road
High Falls, NY 12440
212-923-0496
www.optometrists.org

Contains an in-depth review of Convergence Insufficiency (CI) including what it is; the symptoms; how common it is; detection and diagnosis; and treatment.

4032 **FamilyConnect**
www.familyconnect.org

800-232-5463
connectcenter@aph.org
www.familyconnect.org

An online, multimedia community resource for parents and guardians of children with visual impairments. 24-hour support and access to message boards, real life videos, parent blogs, and parenting articles.

4033 **Lazy Eye Discussion Group**
health.groups.yahoo.com/group/LazyEye/

health.groups.yahoo.com/group/LazyEye/

An email list (955 members) for parents of children with amblyopia, strabismus or other conditions associated with the disorder.

4034 **Optometrists Network**
58 Mohonk Road
High Falls, NY 12440
212-923-0496
www.optometrists.org

Twelve education websites for patients that are free of advertisements and require no registraion. There is also a free eye doctor referral directory.

4035 **Strabismus**
58 Mohonk Road
High Falls, NY 12440
212-923-0496
www.strabismus.org

All about strabismus: what is it? who does it affect? what types exist? and how can it be treated?

4036 **Vision Therapy**
58 Mohonk Road
High Falls, NY 12440
212-923-0496
www.visiontherapy.org

The site provides an interview of frequently asked questions with an eye doctor who is an expert in the field of vision therapy. The effectiveness of therapy and what it involves is addressed.

4037 **Vision Therapy Success Stories**
58 Mohonk Road
High Falls, NY 12440
212-923-0496
www.visiontherapystories.org

Children and adult vision therapy patients express their own success stories. There are over 525 stories covering many topics.

Book Publishers

4038 **All Children Have Different Eyes**
Edie Glaser / Dr. Maria Burgio, author

Vidi Press
11721 Whittier Blvd, #203
Whittier, CA 90601
800-409-7170
www.lowvisionkids.com

An illustrated book for children that models for children with visual impairment how to play and make friends competently and with confidence.

48 pages

4039 Blueberry Eyes

Monica Driscoll Beatty, author

Health Press
2920 Carlisle Blvd, NE
Albuquerque, NM 87110

505-888-1394
877-411-0707
www.healthpress.com

Children's book that addresses the different aspects of eye treatment including eye patches, eye muscle surgery, and wearing glasses. Reading level: ages 4 thru 8.

32 pages
ISBN: 0-929173-24-4

4040 My Travelin' Eye

Jenny Sue Kostecki-Shaw, author

Henry Holt & Company, Inc.
175 Fifth Avenue
New York, NY 10010

646-307-5151
Fax: 212-633-0748
customerservice@mpsvirginia.com
us.macmillan.com

Audience: pre-school- grade 3. Jenny has an eye that wanders sometimes. Although this makes her different, she is also able to see the world in a special way.

40 pages Hardcover
ISBN: 0-805081-69-0

Stefan von Holtzbrinck, Chairman, Executive Board
Klaus-Dieter Lehmann, Chairman, Supervisory Board
Sandra Dittert, Senior Vice President

4041 The Patch

Justina Chen Headley, author

Charlesbridge Publishing
85 Main Street
Watertown, MA 02472

617-926-0329
800-225-3214
Fax: 800-926-5775
books@charlesbridge.com
www.charlesbridge.com

Becca wears glasses and an eye patch. She leads the kids in her class on an imaginative adventure to explain her new fashion accessories.

32 pages
ISBN: 1-580890-49-0

Brian Walker, VP Production
Mary Ann Sabia, VP Marketing and Sales and Associat
Bob Sammartino, Sammartino

Magazines

4042 Eye on NEI

31 Center Dr, MSC 2510
Bethesda, MD 20892

301-496-5248
2020@nei.nih.gov
www.nei.nih.gov

The National Eye Institute's online news magazine is published two times a month. It features articles on vision research projects, answers to eye questions, interviews with scientists, and provides a general look into the vision research process.

Dr. Paul A. Sieving, Director
Dr. Belinda Seto, Deputy Director
Allyson T. Collins, Editor

4043 EyeWorld

American Society Cataract/Refractive Surgery-ASCRS
4000 Legato Road, Suite 700
Fairfax, VA 22033

703-591-2220
Fax: 703-591-0614
dlong@eyeworld.org
www.eyeworld.org

The monthly news magazine for the American Society of Cataract & Refractive Surgery (ASCRS).

David F. Chang, Chief Medical Editor
John A. Vukich, International Editor
Bonnie An Henderson, Cataract Editor

Newsletters

4044 Awareness

NAPVI
PO Box 317
Watertown, MA 2471

800-562-6265
www.spedex.com

Quarterly newsletter of the National Association for Parents of Children with Visual Impairments. It contains regional news and announcements, notices of events and conferences, legislative updates and articles.

32 pages

Pamphlets

4045 Amblyopia

National Eye Institute (NIH)
Information Office, 31 Center Dr, MSC 2510
Bethesda, MD 20892

301-496-5248
nei.nih.gov/health/amblyopia

Provides a description of the causes, symptoms, diagnosis and treatment for the disorder. The information is also available in Spanish.

5 pages Pub # EY-145

Description

4046 LEAD POISONING

Involves the following Biologic System(s):

Developmental/Behavioral/Psychiatric Disorders, Neurologic Disorders

Children and adults exposed to lead chronically over time can develop toxic levels in their blood. Traditionally, the lead level that raises concern is 10mcg/dl or above. Lead is much more harmful to children than adults because it can affect children's developing nerves and brains. The younger the child, the more harmful lead can be. Unborn children are the most vulnerable. However, many children with these levels may be asymptomatic. There are a number of sources for lead exposure. Although paint is a common source of lead, other products that may contain lead include ceramics, crystal, gasoline, batteries, and cosmetics. In the United States, the primary sources for lead exposure include household plumbing, paint made prior to 1977, and gasoline with tetraethyl lead as an additive. Although there has been a growing movement in the US to restrict the use of lead in these products, its prior use in many products continues to pose a hazard to the general population, especially young children. Lead may be inadvertently ingested, inhaled, or absorbed through the skin. One of the most common ways small children become exposed to lead is through the ingestion of fine dust from lead based paints, by licking their hands that are coated with lead dust, or by inhaling lead dust that is then swallowed. Lead makes things taste sweet, so children are attracted to the taste of lead paint chips and especially to lead dust. Lead that enters the body gets absorbed into the blood stream. It is then deposited in soft tissue and organs, or excreted through the kidney. Most of the lead that remains in the body, though, is deposited in bones. Lead toxicity primarily involves the central nervous system and the gastrointestinal system. Although many children with lead ingestion will have asymptomatic disease, they may show increased behavioral problems, poor school performance, decreased height, and decreased cognitive function. Children with more severe lead exposure may complain of anorexia, nausea, vomiting, abdominal pain and constipation. These symptons have been reported at lead levels as low as 20 mcg/dl but more commonly seen at lead levels greater than 50 mcg/dl. Neurological symptoms may include ataxia (staggering gait), seizures, coma, and encephalopathy. Screening for lead exposure should be performed in all children under 5. A thorough history should be taken, focusing on age of the patient's home, behavioral changes, exposure to battery factories or ceramics, recent home renovations (in homes pre-1978), and history of lead poisoning in a sibling. The frequency of the blood test screening will increase based on the patient's environmental exposure. A lead level of 10 mcg/dl or greater is considered a significant exposure and warrants further evaluation. An assessment of the home should be undertaken and the patient should have repeat blood lead levels tested no later than 3 months of age. The American Academy of Pediatrics recommends repeating a lead level by 3 months. Lead exposure may in some cases also be confirmed by x-ray, studies in the abdomen and in bones (lead lines). Therapy for lead exposure/toxicity generally focuses on removing the lead from the patient's environment, diminishing hand to mouth behaviors, improving nutrition in exposed patients and removing the lead from the patient's body. Homes may be cleaned properly by professionals and old paint must be removed from environment or sealed in a fashion that will eliminate the family's exposure to paint dust and chips. Some children will need to be moved to a lead-free safehouse while this is occurring. Frequent washing of hands and toys will cut down on exposure from hand to mouth behavior exhibited by young children. Lead levels greater than 44mcg/dl are considered significant enough to warrant chelation therapy and levels greater than 70 mcg/dl should prompt referral for chelation and hospitalization. Chelation therapy involves giving patients chelating, or binding, agents which bind to the lead and make it easier to excrete from the body. This type of therapy should begin only after the source of lead in the environment has been eliminated.

National Associations & Support Groups

4047 American Academy of Pediatrics
345 Park Blvd
Itasca, IL 60143

800-433-9016
Fax: 847-434-8000
mcc@aap.org
www.aap.org

The American Academy of Pediatrics and its member pediatricians are committed to the attainment of optimal physical, mental and social health and well-being for all infants, children, adolescents, and young adults.

Lynn Olson, PhD, VP, Research
Mark Del Monte, JD, CEO/Executive VP
Vera Tait, MD, FAAP, Chief Medical Officer

State Agencies & Support Groups

4048 Connecticut Lead Poisoning Prevention Program
410 Capitol Avenue, Ms#51LED P.O. Box 340308
Hartford, CT 06134

860-509-7299
Fax: 860-509-7295

Workshops and literature on how to diagnose and prevent lead poisoning.

Web Sites

4049 Consumer Product Safety Commission Hotline
4330 East West Highway
Bethesda, MD 20814

301-504-7923
Fax: 301-504-0124
www.cpsc.gov

CPSC is an Independent Federal Regulatory Agency that works to save lives and keep families safe by reducing the risk of injuries and deaths associated with consumer products.

Elliot F. Kaye, Chairman

4050 National Conference of State Legislatures
444 North Capitol Street, N.W., Suite 515
Washington, D. 20001

202-624-5400
Fax: 202-737-1069
www.ncsl.org

The National Conference of State Legislatures is a bipartisan organization that serves the legislators and staffs of the nation's 50 states, its commonwealths and territories. NCSL provides research, technical assistance and opportunities for policymakers to exchange ideas on the most pressing state issues. NCSL is an effective and respected advocate for the interests of state governments before Congress and federal agencies.

Senator Pamela, President
Jean Cantrel, Vice President
Tom Wright, Secretary/Treasurer

4051 Safe Drinking Water Hotline
www.epa.org/safewater/

www.epa.org/safewater/

Together with the states, tribes, and its many partners, protects public health by ensuring safe drinking water and protecting ground water. Along with EPS's ten regional drinking water programs, oversees implementation of the SAFE DRINKING WATER ACT, which is the national law safeguarding tap water in America.

Learning Disability/Reading Dyslexia / National Associations & Support Groups

Description

4052 LEARNING DISABILITY/READING DYSLEXIA

Synonyms: Learning Disorders, LDD

Covers these related disorders: Dyscalculia, Dyslexia, Dysgraphia

Involves the following Biologic System(s):

Developmental/Behavioral/Psychiatric Disorders

Learning Disability (LD) is a general term that refers to a group of disorders characterized by problems with learning, processing, or expressing information. When LD involves speech and language, it can affect how a person hears words (receptive language disorder), how they put thoughts into words (expressive language disorder), or how words are put together when spoken (articulation disorder).

LD can also affect academic skills. Dyscalculia is a learning disability characterized by difficulty in using mathematical symbols and understanding mathematical concepts. Dysgraphia is the difficulty in the physical process of writing letters and words. A person with dyspraxia can understand sentences in a normal way, but has difficulty putting words together into a coherent sentence. Dyslexia is characterized by the impairment in the ability to process written symbols.

Young children with dyslexia may have difficulty remembering the correct names of letters and numbers. Some school aged children may reverse letters and words when writing. For example, affected children may substitute the letter P for Q, reverse the word WAS to become SAW, or transpose letters so that BETS becomes BEST. Children with dyslexia may also have difficulty reading due to an impaired ability to determine the sequence of letters within words and to distinguish right from left. The hallmark of this learning disability is the fact that despite their difficulties, affected children are of average or above average intelligence by IQ testing and scholastic achievement.

Although learning disabilities occur in very young children, the disorders are usually not recognized until the child reaches school age. Early diagnosis of LD is an important factor in treatment. Children nearing the end of first grade who exhibit difficulties with word skills, or any children whose reading, writing, or mathematical skills are not commensurate with that of their other scholastic abilities should be tested for LD. Although LD is not related to eye defects, an ophthalmologic evaluation is beneficial in eliminating vision problems as a cause for symptoms. Treatment for LD is geared towards remedial teaching techniques specific to the disability.

LD is thought to be a familial disorder and may be inherited in an autosomal dominant fashion.

National Associations & Support Groups

4053 American Academy of Pediatrics
345 Park Blvd
Itasca, IL 60143
800-433-9016
Fax: 847-434-8000
mcc@aap.org
www.aap.org

The American Academy of Pediatrics and its member pediatricians are committed to the attainment of optimal physical, mental and social health and well-being for all infants, children, adolescents, and young adults.

Lynn Olson, PhD, VP, Research
Mark Del Monte, JD, CEO/Executive VP
Vera Tait, MD, FAAP, Chief Medical Officer

4054 American School Counselor Association
1101 King Street, Ste 310
Alexandria, VA 22314
703-683-2722
asca@schoolcounselor.org
www.schoolcounselor.org

The mission of ASCA is to represent professional school counselors and to promote professionalism and ethical practices.

Jill Cook, Executive Director
Amanda Fitzgerald, Assistant Deputy Executive Director
Kathleen M Rakestraw, Director of Communications

4055 American Speech Language Hearing Association (ASHA)
2200 Research Blvd
Rockville, MD 20852
301-296-5700
800-638-8255
Fax: 301-296-8580
TTY: 301-296-5650
nsslha@asha.org
www.asha.org

A certifying body of 123,000 professionals providing speech, language and hearing services to the public. It is an accrediting agency for college and university graduate school programs in speech-language pathology and audiology.

Shari B. Robertson, President
Theresa H. Rodgers, President-Elect

4056 Center for Parent Information and Resources (CPIR)
c/o SPAN, 35 Halsey Street, 4th Floor
Newark, NJ 07102
973-642-8100
malizo@spanadvocacy.org
www.parentcenterhub.org

Family-friendly information and research-based materials on key topics for Parent Centers. Private workspaces for Parent Centers to exchange resources, discuss high-priority topics, and solve mutual challenges. Coordination of parent training efforts throughout the network.

Myriam Alizo, Project Assistant

4057 Council for Learning Disabilities
11184 Antioch Road Box 405
Overland Park, KS 66210
913-491-1011
Fax: 913-491-1011
www.cldinternational.org

An international organization that promotes effective teaching and research. CDL is composed of professionals who represent diverse disciplines and who are committed to enhancing the education and life span development of individuals with learning disabilities.

Julie Cordell, Executive Director

4058 Division for Learning Disabilities
www.teachingld.org

The Division for Learning Disabilities is a national professional organization consisting of teacher, higher education professionals, administrators, and parents. The major purpose of DLD is to promote the education and general welfare of persons with learning disabilities, provide a forum for discussion of issues facing the field of learning disabilities, and to encourage interaction among the many groups whose research and service efforts impact persons with learning disabilities.

Miriam Ortiz, Executive Director

4059 Dyslexia Research Institute
5746 Centerville Road
Tallahassee, FL 32309
850-893-2216
Fax: 850-893-2440
www.dyslexia-add.org

Addresses academic, social and self-concept issues for dyslexic and ADD children and adults. College prep courses, study skills, advocacy, diagnostic testing, seminars, teachers training, day school, tutoring and adult literacy and life skills programs are available using an accredited MSLE approach.

Learning Disability/Reading Dyslexia / Libraries & Resource Centers

4060 Federation for Children with Special Needs
529 Main Street, Suite 1M3
Boston, MA 02129
617-236-7210
800-331-0688
Fax: 617-241-0330
info@fcsn.org
www.fcsn.org

The mission of the Federation for Children with Special Needs provides information, support, and assistance to parents of children with disabilities, and encouraging full participation in community life by all people, especially those with disabilities.

Pam Nourse, Executive Director

4061 International Dyslexia Association
1829 Reisterstown Rd., Suite 350
Pikesville, MD 21208
410-296-0232
Fax: 410-321-5069
info@dyslexiada.org
dyslexiada.org

Our mission is to pursue and provide the most comprehensive range of information and services that address the full scope of dyslexia and related difficulties in learning to read and write.

Sonja Banks, Chief Executive Director
Gina Schuh, Chief Operating Officer
Dana Nwoye, Partner Relations & Outreach

4062 Learning Disabilities Association of America
PO Box 10369, 4156 Library Road
Pittsburgh, PA 15234
412-341-1515
888-300-6710
Fax: 412-344-0224
info@LDAAmerica.org
www.ldaamerica.org

Helps families of the affected individual through information and referral to professionals in their area. A membership organization with affiliates across the country.

Stephanie Fedro-Byrom, Operations Manager
Maureen Swanson, Director, Healthy Children Project
Ericka Pardun, Communications Coordinator

4063 National Center for Learning Disabilities
1 Thomas Circle NW, #700
Washington, DC 20005
212-545-7510
888-575-7373
Fax: 212-545-9665
www.ncld.org

The mission is to increase opportunities for all individuals with learning disabilities to achieve their potential.NCLD accomplishes this mission by increasing public awareness and understanding of learning disabilities, conducting educational programs and services that promote research-based knowledge, and providing national leadership in shaping public policy.

Lindsay E. Jones, Esq., CEO
Quinn Bradlee, Youth Engagement Associate
Meghan Whittaker, Esq., Director of Policy

4064 New England Center for Children
33 Turnpike Road
Southborough, MA 01772
508-481-1015
Fax: 508-485-3421
www.necc.org

Serving students between the ages of 3 and 22 diagnosed with autism, learning disabilities, language delays, behavior disorders and related disabilities; educational curriculum encompasses both the teaching of functional life skills and traditional academics; communication skills are taught throughout all activities in the school, residence, and community. Tuition and fees are set by the state. Consulting services also available.

Vicent Strully, Jr, President & CEO
Michael S Downey, EVP & CFO
Susan Langer, Chief Program Officer

4065 Parents Helping Parents
1400 Parkmoor Avenue, Suite 100
San Jose, CA 95126
408-727-5775
855-727-5775
Fax: 408-286-1116
info@php.com
www.php.com

Parents Helping Parents supports, educates, and inspires families and the community to build bright futures for youth and adults with special needs.

Maria Daane, Executive Director
Janet Nunez, Director, Programs
Virginia Hildebrand, Director, Finance

Libraries & Resource Centers

4066 Berkshire Center
18 Park Street #160
Lee, MA 01238
413-243-2576

A postsecondary program for young adults with learning disabilities ages eighteen-twenty-six. Half the students attend Berkshire Community College part-time while others go directly into the working world. Services include vocational/adacademic preparation, tutoring, college liason, life skills instruction, driver's education, money management, psychotherapy, and more. The program is year-round with an average stay of two years.

4067 Carroll Center for the Blind
770 Centre Street
Newton, MA 02458
617-969-6200
800-852-3131
Fax: 617-969-6204
www.carroll.org

Assists blind and visually impaired adults and adolescents to adjust to loss of vision. The goal of this dynamic program is to help the person become more independent, to restore self-confidence, prepare for employment and improve the quality of life. Programs of individual counseling are offered as part of the program.

Rachel Rosenbaum, President

4068 University of Kansas Center for Research on Learning
1122 West Campus Road, Room 521
Lawrence, KS 66045
785-864-4780
Fax: 785-864-5728
crl@ku.edu
www.kucrl.org

A research center working to improve learning and performance of adolescents and adults considered to be at risk for failure in today's schools, work places, and communities. Develops products and procedures that can be used to more effectively teach these individuals. Provides support and research-validated instructional materials to an international training network that promotes system change in our schools and institutions. Newsletter for teachers containing tips and advice used in class.

Don Deshler, Director
Mike Hock, Associate Director
Julie Tollefson, Director of Communications

Conferences

4069 American School Counselor Association Annual Conference
1101 King Street, Suite 310
Alexandria, VA 22314
703-683-2722
800-306-4722
Fax: 703-997-7572
asca@schoolcounselor.org
www.schoolcounselor.org

The mission of ASCA is to represent professional school counselors and to promote professionalism and ethical practices.

3,000 Attendees

Richard Wong, Executive Director
Jennifer Walsh, Director, Education & Training
Kathleen M Rakestraw, Director of Communications

Learning Disability/Reading Dyslexia / Magazines

Audio Video

4070 How to Help Your Child Succeed in School
Sandra Rief, author

Peytral Publications
PO Box 1162
Minnetonka, MN 55345
952-949-8707
877-739-8725
Fax: 952-906-9777
help@peytral.com
www.peytral.com

Essential information needed by parents and educators. Topics include developiong reading, writing and math skills, building organization and study skills, surviving daily homework assignments and coping with learning disabilities.

56 minutes

Web Sites

4071 Center for Parent Information and Resources (CPIR)
c/o SPAN, 35 Halsey Street, 4th Floor
Newark, NJ 07102
973-642-8100
malizo@spanadvocacy.org
www.parentcenterhub.org

Family-friendly information and research-based materials on key topics for Parent Centers. Private workspaces for Parent Centers to exchange resources, discuss high-priority topics, and solve mutual challenges. Coordination of parent training efforts throughout the network.

Myriam Alizo, Project Assistant

4072 Children's Hospital of New York Presbyterian
nyp.org/kids/index.html

nyp.org/kids/index.html

A high quality, world class center that improves the health status of children.

4073 Division for Learning Disabilities
www.teachingld.org

Promotes the education and general welfare of persons with learning disabilities.

Miriam Ortiz, Executive Director

4074 Learning Disabilities Association of America
PO Box 10369, 4156 Library Road
Pittsburgh, PA 15234
412-341-1515
888-300-6710
Fax: 412-344-0224
info@LDAAmerica.org
www.ldaamerica.org

Helps families of the affected individual through information and referral to professionals in their area. A membership organization with affiliates across the country.

Stephanie Fedro-Byrom, Operations Manager
Maureen Swanson, Director, Healthy Children Project
Ericka Pardun, Communications Coordinator

4075 The Parent Educational Advocacy Training Center
100 N Washington St, Suite 234
Falls Church, VA 22046
703-923-0010
800-869-6782
Fax: 800-693-3514
TTY: 703-923-0010
partners@peatc.org
www.peatc.org

Provides general research about special education and learning disabilities.

Michael Jefferson, President
Betsy McGuire, Vice President
Linda Feldstein, Secretary

Book Publishers

4076 Learning Disabilities and Challenging Behaviors
Nancy Mather PhD, Sam Goldstein PhD, author

Brooks Publishing
PO Box 10624
Baltimore, MD 21285
410-337-9850
800-638-3775
Fax: 410-337-8539
webmaster@brookespublishing.com
www.brookespublishing.com

A working manual for educators and others who teach children with learning disabilities. Helps readers to understand how specific developmental, behaviour, and academic problems influence school success.

416 pages

Paul H. Brookes, Chairman
Jeff Brookes, President
Melissa A. Behm, Executive Vice President

Magazines

4077 Get Ready to Read!
National Center for Learning Disabilities
32 Laight Street, Second Floor
New York, NY 10013
212-545-7510
888-575-7373
Fax: 212-545-9665
hlp@ncld.org
www.getreadytoread.org; www.ncld.org

Quartely

Quinn Bradlee, Youth Engagement Associate

4078 LD Advocate
National Center for Learning Disabilities
32 Laight Street, Second Floor
New York, NY 10013
212-545-7510
888-575-7373
Fax: 212-545-9665
help@ncld.org
www.ld.org

Quartely

Frederic M Poses, Chairman
Mary Kalikow, Vice Chairman
William Haney, Secretary

4079 LD News
National Center for Learning Disabilities
32 Laight Street, Second Floor
New York, NY 10013
212-545-7510
888-575-7373
Fax: 212-545-9665
hlp@ncld.org
www.ncld.org

Quartely

Frederic M Poses, Chairman
Mary Kalikow, Vice Chairman
William Haney, Secretary

4080 Our World
National Center for Learning Disabilities
32 Laight Street, Second Floor
New York, NY 10013
212-545-7510
888-575-7373
Fax: 212-545-9665
hlp@ncld.org
www.getreadytoread.org; www.ncld.org

Quartely

Quinn Bradlee, Youth Engagement Associate

Learning Disability/Reading Dyslexia / Journals

Journals

4081 **Journal of Learning Disabilities**
Hammill Institute on Disabilities/Sage Publication
2455 Teller Road
Thousand Oaks, CA 91230
800-818-7243
Fax: 800-583-2665
journals@sagepub.com
www.sagepub.com

JLD is internationally recognized as the oldest and most authoritative journal in the area of learning disabilities. The editorial board reflects the international, multidisciplinary nature of JLD, comprising researchers and practitioners in numerous fields, including education, psychology, neurology, medicine, law and counseling. ISSN: Print: 0022-2194; Electronic: 1538-4780. Avaiable: Institutional - Print: $218, Institutional - Print & E-access $222, Individual - Print & E-access $71.

Bi-monthly

H Lee Swanson PhD, Editor

Newsletters

4082 **Perspectives on Language and Literacy**
IDA
40 York Road Suite 400
Baltimore, MD 21204
410-296-0232
800-223-3123
Fax: 410-321-5069
info@interdys.org
www.interdys.org

Features practical articles for educators and other professionals dedicated to the identification and intervention of dyslexia and other reading problems.

50-56 pages quarterly

Hal Malchow, President
Ben Shifrin, Vice President
Suzanne Carreker, Secretary

Camps

4083 **Beech Brook**
3737 Lander Road
Cleveland, OH
216-831-2255
877-546-1225
Fax: 216-831-0436
www.beechbrook.org

A year-round residential and day treatment center, accepts summer residents when there are openings in the regular enrollment. The program is designed for emotionally disturbed, learning disabled and autistic children, providing therapeutically oriented teaching and programming techniques in a camp setting.

Philip M. Dawson, Chair
Thomas A. Seifert, Vice Chair
Brandon R. Miller, Vice Chair

4084 **Camp Buckskin**
4124 Quebec Ave. N, Suite 300
Minneapolis, MN 55427
763-432- 917
Fax: 952-938-6996
info@campbuckskin.com
www.campbuckskin.com

LD and ADD/ADHD youth have often experienced frustration and a lack of success. Buckskin assists these individuals to realize and develop the potentials and abilities which they possess. Teaches a combination of academic and camp activities, so the campers experience success in many areas. By necessity fairly structured, the 1:3 staff ratio ensures the program is individualized to meet each camper's needs. Parents report that their children benefit from the experience in many ways.

Thomas R Bauer, CCD, Camp Director

4085 **Camp Huntington**
56 Bruceville Road
High Falls, NY 12440
845-687-7840
855-707-2267
Fax: 845-687-7211
camohtgtn@aol.com
www.camphuntington.com

Summer activities include recreational, academic and vocational programs for the learning disabled and neurologically impaired. An Olympic pool, horse riding and a special work training program are featured. Programs are tailored to meet individual needs, ages 6-21, and campers may enroll for 4 to 8 weeks.

Dr. Bruria Falik, Director
Michael Bednarz, Executive Director
Alex Mellor, Program Director

4086 **Camp Nuhop**
404 Hillcrest Drive
Ashland, OH
419-289-2227
Fax: 419-289-2227
www.nuhop.org

A summer residential program for any youngster from 6 to 18 with a learning disability, behavior disorder or Attention Deficit Disorder. Sixty two campers and 35 staff members live on site in groups of 7 campers to every 3 counselors. Activities focus on positive self-concept and behaviors and teach children to learn how to find their strengths, abilities and talents from a positive, yet realistic viewpoint.

Trevor Dunlap, Executive Director
Chris Clyde, Associate Director
Jerry Dunlap, Director

4087 **Camp O' Fair Winds**
2300 Austins Parkway
Flint, MI 48507
810-230-0244
800-482-6734
Fax: 810-230-0955
www.gsfwc.org/camps.htm

Outdoor program for all girls, ages 7-11. Our goal is to build confidence by giving girls a chance to voice their opinions and make their own decisions. We are able to accommodate girls with diabetes, ADHD, and learning disabilities. We are willing to make special accommodations - including hiring individual assistants for girls with hearing impairments and physical disabilities.

Therese Plotz, Camp Director
Olga Recio, Camp Secretary

4088 **Dallas Academy**
950 Tiffany Way
Dallas, TX
214-324-1481
Fax: 214-327-8537
mail@dallas-academy.com
www.dallas-academy.com

7-week summer session for students who are having difficulty in regular school classes.

Troy Sturrock, Chair
Terrence S Welch, Vice Chair
Dallas Cothrum, Secretary

4089 **Developmental Center**
6710 86th Avenue N
Pinellas Park, FL
727-541-5716
Fax: 727-544-8186
NickiMaddalena@centeracademy.com
centeracademy.com

Specifically designed for the learning disabled child and other children with difficulties in concentration, strategy, social skills, impulsivity, distractibility and study strategies. Programs offered include: attention training, visual-motor remediation, socialization skills training, relaxation training, horseback riding and more. The day camp meets weekdays from 9-3 for 3,4 or 5 week sessions.

Mack R. Hicks, Chairman
Eric V. Larson, President
Andrew P. Hicks, Chief Executive Officer

Learning Disability/Reading Dyslexia / Camps

4090 Eagle Hill School - Summer Program
242 Old Petersham Road
Hardwick, MA 1037
413-477-6000
Fax: 413-477-6837
admission@eaglehillschool.com
www.ehs1.org

For the child, age 9-19, with a specific learning disability or Attention Deficit Disorder, this summer program offers a structured curriculum designed to build a basic foundation of academic competence. Extra-curricular and outdoor activities complement the educational program.

Jim Richardson, Chairman
Marilyn Waller, President
Alden Bianchi, Vice President

4091 Groves Academy
3200 Highway 100 South
Saint Louis Park, MN 55416
952-920-6377
Fax: 952-920-2068
www.grovesacademy.org

A nonprofit day school in Minnesota designed especially for children with learning differences. The Center has a full day academic program from September through June, as well as an 8 week summer program. Groves also offers community services such as: psychoeducational testing for children and adults, consulting services, workshops on learning disabilities and other special learning needs, and afternoon/evening tutorial services for children and adults.

Karen Sanger, Chair
Thomas Schnack, Vice Chair
Tom Sass, Secretary

4092 Hill School of Fort Worth
4817 Odessa Avenue
Fort Worth, TX 76133
817-923-9482
Fax: 817-923-4894
hillschool@hillschool.org
www.hillschool.org

Provides an alternative learning environment for students having average or above-average intelligence with learning differences. Hill school is an established leader in North Texas with a 25 year history of effectively serving LD children. Beginning in 1961 as a tutorial service, Hill became a formal school in 1973. Our mission is to help those who learn differently develop skills and strategies to succeed. We do this by developing academic/study skills, and self-discipline.

John W. Wright, Chairman
Randall Canedy, Vice Chairman
Ralph Torres, Secretary

4093 Lab School of Washington Summer Program
4759 Reservoir Road NW
Washington, DC 20007
202-965-6600
Fax: 202-965-5106
alexandra.freeman@labschool.org
www.labschool.org

The Lab School 5-week summer session includes individualized reading, spelling, writing, study skills, and math programs. A multisensory approach addresses the needs of bright learning disabled children. Related services such as speech/language therapy and occupational therapy are integrated into the curriculum. Elementary/Intermediate; Junior High/High School.

Sally Smith, Founder
Susan Feeley, Admissions Director

4094 Maplebrook School
5142 Route 22
Amenia, NY 12501
845-373-9511
Fax: 845-373-7029
mbsecho@aol.com
www.maplebrookschool.org

A coeducational boarding school for students with learning differences and ADD. A New York State registered high school servicing ages 11-18. Post secondary options offered to 18-21.

Mark J. Metzger, Chairman
Robert Audia, Vice Chairman
Charles F. Chiusano, Secretary

4095 Oakland School & Camp
128 Oakland Farm Way
Troy, VA 22974
434-293-9059
Fax: 434-296-8930
information@oaklandschool.net
www.oaklandschool.net

A highly individualized program stresses improving reading ability. Subjects taught are reading, English composition, math and word analysis. Recreational activities include horseback riding, sports, swimming, tennis, crafts, archery and camping. For girls and boys, ages 8-14.

Carol Williams, Head of School
Jamie Cato, Admissions Director

4096 Phelps School
583 Sugartown Road
Malvern, PA 19355
610-644-1754
Fax: 610-644-6679
admis@thephelpsschool.org
www.thephelpsschool.org

Phelps School is dedicated to a personalized education for the boy who seeks success academically, personally, and socially. This philosophy is accentuated by the disciplined atmosphere, small classes, and daily tutorial support. The idea which inspired Norman T. Phelps, Sr. to begin a school dedicated to the individual boy has never been more relevant that it is today. The model of educating boys according to thier interests and abilities is designed to generate success & improve self-esteem.

Norman T. Phelps, Chairman
Stephany Phelps Fahey, President
Andrew Wilmerding, Secretary

4097 Ramapo Anchorage Camp
PO Box 266, Rt. 52/Salisbury Turnpike
Rhinebeck, NY 12572
845-876-8403
Fax: 845-876-8414
www.ramapoforchildren.org

Residential program which serves children, ages 4-16, with a wide range of emotional, behavoral, and learning problems. A one-to-one ratio of counselors-to-campers enables children to build healthy relationships, increase self-esteem and improve learning skills. Character values such as honesty, concern for others, responsibility, and the courage to do one's best are encouraged. Campers demonstrate significant gains in their ability to maintain relationships, control impulses and adjust.

Teri Goldberg Horowitz, President
David Ross, Vice President
Adam Weiss, Chief Executive Officer

4098 Round Lake Camp
570 Sawkill Road
Milford, PA 18337
570-296-8596
Fax: 570-296-6381
rlc@njycamps.org
www.njycamps.org

For ages 7-18, this camp provides individualized academics in reading, language development and math for children with mild learning disabilities, Round Lake also offers therapeutic recreation and Jewish cultural values to its participants.

Sheira Director, Asst. Director

4099 Squirrel Hollow
5665 Milam Road
Fairburn, GA 30213
770-774-8001
Fax: 770-774-8005
bbox@thebedfordschool.org
www.thebedfordschool.org

A remedial summer program of The Bedford School; serves children with academic needs due to learning difficulties. For students ages 6-16 and held on the campus of The Bedford School in Fairburn, GA. Campers participate in an individualized academic program as well as recreational activities. Students receive the proper academic remediation as well as specific remedial help with physical skills, peer interaction and self-esteem.

Michael Vigil, Chairman
Betsy E Box, Director
Jeff James, Assistant Director

Learning Disability/Reading Dyslexia / Camps

4100 Summer Experience
Vanguard School
PO Box 730
Paoli, PA
610-296-6700

For students who are experiencing learning difficulties due to neurological impairment, social/emotional disturbance and/or autism/pervasive developmental disorder.

Susan Snyder, Admissions Director
John D Wilson, Education Director

4101 Wesley Woods
1001 Fiddlersgreen Road
Grand Valley, PA 16420
814-430-7802
Fax: 814-436-7669
info@wesleywoods.com
www.wesleywoods.com

Exceptional children's camp for children with emotional and intellectual handicaps.

Herb West

4102 Worthmore Academy
3535 Kessler Boulevard East Drive
Indianapolis, IN 46220
317-253-5367
877-700-6516
Fax: 317-251-6516
bjackson@worthmoreacademy.org
www.worthmoreacademy.org

A center for learning disabilities providing educational assessments, alternative educational programs, academic guidance and public awareness services available as follows: full-time day school, K-8th, 1 to 1 teacher student ratio; six week summer school, K-12th, 1 to 1 teacher student ratio; after school tutoring; adult tutoring, educational assessments, counseling and educational seminars.

Brenda J Jackson, Director
Diana Buser, Assistant

Description

4103 LEGG-CALVE-PERTHES DISEASE
Synonyms: LCPD, Perthes disease, Avascular necrosis of femoral head
Involves the following Biologic System(s):
Orthopedic and Muscle Disorders

Legg-Calve-Perthes disease (LCPD) belongs to a group of disorders in which abnormalities of the growth centers of certain bones result in degeneration and gradual regeneration of the affected bone. This group of disorders is known as the osteochondroses. LCPD affects the growing end of the head of the thigh bone (femoral capital epiphysis). In most affected children, the thigh bone (femur) on one side of the body is affected (unilateral); however, in approximately 20 percent of patients, the disorder may eventually involve the other femur (bilateral). The age of onset and the severity and duration of the disease are variable. Legg-Calve-Perthes disease typically becomes apparent between the ages of two to 12 years, with the average age of onset approximately seven years of age. Males are affected four to five times as often as females; however, females may tend to have more severe symptoms. LCPD is thought to affect approximately one in 1,000 to 5,000 children.

Degeneration of the head of the femur is thought to occur due to insufficient blood supply (ischemia) to this area of bone, resulting in the localized loss of bone and cartilage as well as the loss of bone mass. The onset of symptoms associated with LCPD is typically slow and progressive. Many affected children initially experience muscle spasms, a limp, or mild or periodic pain that may affect the thigh, hip, knee, or groin area. As the disorder progresses, additional symptoms and findings often include delayed maturation of the thigh bone (delayed bone age); mild restriction of movements of the affected hip; potential degeneration of the front thigh muscles; abnormal positioning of the hip and thigh toward the body (internal rotation); and, in some patients, mild short stature. LCPD is considered a self-limiting disorder because, even without medical intervention, new blood supplies are eventually spontaneously reestablished (revascularization) to the femoral head, causing the formation of new bone tissue in the affected area. This may occur approximately two to four years after the onset of symptoms. In some affected children, new bony growth may be misshapen, potentially causing the affected leg to be relatively shorter than the unaffected leg, an associated limp, and an increased risk for degenerative changes of the hips, resulting in swelling, pain or tenderness, and stiffness (osteoarthritis).

Because Legg-Calve-Perthes disease is a self-limiting disorder, treatment usually is directed toward preventing deformity of the femoral head and secondary osteoarthritis. Such measures may include ongoing clinical assessment and specialized x-ray tests to monitor the progress of the disease; bed rest or special stretching exercises; the use of braces or casts; or surgery.

There is no specific cause known for LCPD and, in most cases, it is though to occur randomly for unknown reasons. However, there are some risk factors including possible links to children who are small for their age and are extremely active. Interestingly, exposure to secondhand smoke is correlated with LCPD. There have also been reports of several affected individuals within certain families (kindreds) that suggest autosomal dominant inheritance. Some researchers suspect that LCPD may be caused by the interaction of several different genes, possibly in association with the involvement of certain environmental factors (multifactorial disorder). Although Legg-Calvé-Perthes disease cannot be prevented, much has been accomplished toward minimizing its effects.

Government Agencies

4104 NIH/ Eunice Kennedy Shriver National Institute of Child Health & Human Development
P.O. Box 3006
Rockville, MD 20847

800-370-2943
Fax: 866-760-5947
www.nichd.nih.gov

Conducts and supports research on topics related to the health of children, adults, families and populations. Some of these topics include: developmental disabilities, growth and development, infant death, reproductive health and birth defects.

Diana W. Bianchi, Director
Alison Cernich, PhD, Deputy Director

4105 NIH/National Institute of Arthritis and Musculoskeletal and Skin Diseases
1 AMS Circle
Bethesda, MD 20892

301-495-4484
877-226-4267
Fax: 301-718-6366
TTY: 301-565-2966
niamsinfo@mail.nih.gov
www.niams.nih.gov

The mission of the NIAMS, a part of the NIH, is to support research into the causes, treatment and prevention of arthritis and musculoskeletal and skin diseases, the training of basic and clinical scientists to carry out this research, and the dissemination of information on research progress in these diseases.

Lindsey A. Criswell, MD, Director
Rick Phillips, Executive Officer

National Associations & Support Groups

4106 American Academy of Pediatrics
345 Park Blvd
Itasca, IL 60143

800-433-9016
Fax: 847-434-8000
mcc@aap.org
www.aap.org

The American Academy of Pediatrics and its member pediatricians are committed to the attainment of optimal physical, mental and social health and well-being for all infants, children, adolescents, and young adults.

Lynn Olson, PhD, VP, Research
Mark Del Monte, JD, CEO/Executive VP
Vera Tait, MD, FAAP, Chief Medical Officer

4107 March of Dimes Foundation
1550 Crystal Drive, Ste 1300
Arlington, VA 22202

888-663-4637
www.marchofdimes.org

March of Dimes help moms have full-term pregnancies and research the problems that threaten the health of babies. The March of Dimes also acts globally: sharing best practices in perinatal health and helping improve birth outcomes where the needs are the most urgent.

Stacey D. Stewart, President
Alan Brogdon, SVP/COO/Board Officer
Rahul Gupta, MD, SVP & Chief Medical/Health Officer

4108 National Deaf Center
University of Texas at Austin
1912 Speedway, Stop D4900
Austin, TX 78712

512-436-0144
nationaldeafcenter.org

The National Deaf Center is a technical assistance and dissemination center funded by the U.S. Department of Education's Office of Special Education Programs (OSEP). The Center offers online courses, online gaming tools for youth, data reports, research summaries, evidence-based resources, webinars, and provides individualized consultation, training, and resources that help community members, organizations, and schools improve outcomes for deaf people in continuing education and training.

Carrie Lou Bloom, Co-Director
Tia Ivanko, Co-Director

Web Sites

4109 Articles on Legg-Calve-Perthes
www.orthoseek.com/articles/perthes.html

admin@orthoseek.com
www.orthoseek.com/articles/perthes.html

A source of authoritative information on pediatric orthopedics and pediatric information regarding your child's orthopedic condition or sports injury, and you can find useful articles that you can reproduce for yourself or others.

4110 Online Support Group
www.maxpages.com/lpsupportgroup

www.maxpages.com/lpsupportgroup

Provides support groups for families with children diagnosed with Legg-Perthes disease.

4111 Wheeless' Textbook of Orthopaedics
www.wheelessonline.com

410-494-4994
www.wheelessonline.com

Derives from a variety of sources, including journals, articles, national meetings lectures and other textbooks.

Clifford R. Wheeless, Editor in chief
James A Nunley, Managing Editor
James R. Urbaniak, Managing Editor

Description

4112 LEUKODYSTROPHIES
Covers these related disorders: Adrenoleukodystrophy, ALD, Adrenomyeloneuropathy, Krabbe disease, Methachromatic leukodystrophy, Pelizaeus-Merzbacher disease
Involves the following Biologic System(s):
Genetic/Chromosomal/Syndrome/Metabolic Disorders

The leukodystrophies are a group of inherited neurodegenerative diseases that affect the white (leuko) matter of the brain and are characterized by the destruction of the fatty, protective covering around the nerve fibers (myelin sheaths). The symptoms of some forms of these diseases become obvious during childhood. These diseases include adrenoleukodystrophy (ALD), adrenomyeloneuropathy, Krabbe disease, metachromatic leukodystrophy, and Pelizaeus-Merzbacher disease.

Classic adrenoleukodystrophy, or ALD, is a metabolic disorder transmitted as an X-linked recessive trait that is fully expressed in boys. This type of adrenoleukodystrophy becomes apparent between the ages of five and 15 years and is characterized by behavioral disturbances, mental deterioration, seizures, lack of coordination, and motor weakness or partial paralysis with increased muscle tone in the arms and legs accompanied by exaggerated reflex responses (spasticity). In addition, boys with ALD may have difficulty with swallowing, language development, and speech. Vision may be impaired. Other findings include insufficient adrenal gland function characterized by a darkening or tanning of the skin. Experimental treatments include bone marrow transplantation and dietary considerations. Other treatment is symptomatic and supportive. The gene for classic ALD is located on the long arm of the X chromosome (Xq28). Adrenomyeloneuropathy is considered a milder, adult form of adrenoleukodystrophy, although its onset may occur as early as late adolescence.

Neonatal adrenoleukodystrophy is inherited as an autosomal recessive trait and is characterized by seizures, severe delays in skills that involve the coordination of mental and muscular activities (psychomotor coordination), and insufficiency of the adrenal glands. Treatment is symptomatic and supportive.

Krabbe disease, sometimes called globoid cell leukodystrophy, is a rare neurodegenerative disorder that is inherited as an autosomal recessive trait. This life-threatening, progressive disease results from a deficiency of the enzyme galactocerebrosidase and is characterized during early infancy by irritability, vomiting, extremely high fevers, difficulty feeding, and failure to thrive. Seizures may develop followed by muscular rigidity, convulsions, paralysis, , loss of vision and hearing, mental deterioration, or other irregularities. Krabbe disease may sometimes have a later onset with symptoms and findings developing during childhood or adolescence. Treatment is symptomatic and supportive. The gene for Krabbe disease is located on the long arm of chromosome 14 (14q21-q31).

Metachromatic leukodystrophy (MLD) is inherited in an autosomal recessive pattern and occurs as the result of a deficiency of the enzyme sulfatase A. Late infantile MLD usually occurs in the first or second year of life and is characterized by progressive irregularities in the manner of walking (gait), frequent falling, developmental delays, seizures, diminished muscle tone in the arms and legs, and diminished deep tendon reflexes. As the disease progresses, children may be unable to stand and signs of intellectual degeneration become apparent. Additional findings include impaired speech and deteriorating visual activity or blindness. Approximately one year after symptom onset, most children are unable to sit without support and may experience swallowing and eating difficulties. Life-threatening complications such as pneumonia may develop. Juvenile MLD occurs from the ages of four to 12 years and is characterized by behavioral and intellectual deterioration followed by walking and speech difficulties, urinary incontinence, lack of coordination, impaired muscle tone, and convulsions. This form of MLD has a slower progression than that of late infantile MLD. One variant of juvenile MLD results from a deficiency of a protein that aids in the activation of cerebroside sulfatase. The gene for metachromatic leukodystrophy is located on the long arm of chromosome 22 (22q13.31-qter).

Pelizaeus-Merzbacher disease is inherited as an X-linked recessive trait. This disorder occurs during infancy or early childhood and progresses slowly into adolescence or adulthood. This life-threatening form of leukodystrophy is characterized in infancy by head-nodding and eye irregularities such as involuntary, rhythmic movement of the eyes (nystagmus). Boys with this disorder experience developmental delays followed by tremors; well-coordinated but involuntary jerky, writhing movements; a mask-like, frozen expression (parkinsonian facies); difficulty with speech; and deterioration of mental function. Treatment is symptomatic and supportive. The gene for Pelizaeus-Merzbacher disease is located on the long arm of the X chromosome (Xq22). Bone marrow transplantation is showing promise for a few of the leukodystrophies.

National Associations & Support Groups

4113 American Academy of Pediatrics
345 Park Blvd
Itasca, IL 60143
800-433-9016
Fax: 847-434-8000
mcc@aap.org
www.aap.org

The American Academy of Pediatrics and its member pediatricians are committed to the attainment of optimal physical, mental and social health and well-being for all infants, children, adolescents, and young adults.

Lynn Olson, PhD, VP, Research
Mark Del Monte, JD, CEO/Executive VP
Vera Tait, MD, FAAP, Chief Medical Officer

4114 Genetic Alliance
426400 Woodfield Road, Ste 189
Damascus, MD 20872
202-966-5557
Fax: 202-966-8553
info@geneticalliance.org
www.geneticalliance.org

World's leading nonprofit health advocacy organization committed to transforming health through genetics and promoting an environment of openness centered on the health of individuals, families, and communities.

Sharon Terry, CEO
Ruth Child, CFO
Natasha Bonhomme, Chief Strategy Officer

4115 March of Dimes Foundation
1550 Crystal Drive, Ste 1300
Arlington, VA 22202
888-663-4637
www.marchofdimes.org

March of Dimes help moms have full-term pregnancies and research the problems that threaten the health of babies. The March of Dimes also acts globally: sharing best practices in perinatal health and helping improve birth outcomes where the needs are the most urgent.

Stacey D. Stewart, President
Alan Brogdon, SVP/COO/Board Officer
Rahul Gupta, MD, SVP & Chief Medical/Health Officer

4116 National Tay-Sachs and Allied Diseases Association
2001 Beacon Street, Suite 204
Boston, MA 02135
617-277-4463
info@ntsad.org
www.ntsad.org

Direct, fund and promote research treatments and cures; provides comprehensive support services to affected families and individuals; guides prevention, education, awareness and screening through effective grassroots collaborations with chapters and affiliates; leads advocacy efforts as the recognized authority for this family of genetic diseases

Kathleen Flynn, Chief Executive Officer
Valerie Greger, PhD, Director of Research
Diana Jussila, Director of Family Services

4117 United Leukodystrophy Foundation
224 North Second Street, Suite 2
DeKalb, IL 60115
815-748-3211
800-728-5483
office@ulf.org
www.ulf.org

Organization that aids those with leukodystrophy and those who care for them.

Susannah Erler, Interim Executive Director
Keely Mata, Director of Operations
Tara Nunez, Financial & Operations Coordinator

Web Sites

4118 Medical College of Wisconsin
8701 Watertown Plank Road
Milwaukee, WI 53226
414-456-8296
webmaster@mcw.edu
www.mcw.edu

Mary Ellen Stanek, Chair
Stephen Roell, Vice Chairman
Jay B Williams, President

4119 NYU
550 First Avenue
New York, NY 10016
212-263-7300
www.med.nyu.edu

Robert I. Grossman, MD
Steven B Abramson, Senior Vice President
Andrew W Brotman, Senior Vice President

4120 Online Mendelian Inheritance in Man
McKusick-Nathans Institue of Genetic Medicine-JHU
Baltimore, MD 21205
www.omim.org

This database is a catalog of human genes and genetic disorders.

Ada Hamosh, MD, Scientific Director

4121 Virtual Pediatric Hospital
www.virtualpediatrichospital.org

www.virtualpediatrichospital.org

A digital library of pediatric information including resources for patients and health care professionals.

Book Publishers

4122 Let's Talk About Going to the Hospital
Rosen Publishing Group's PowerKids Press
29 E 21st Street
New York, NY 10010
212-777-3017
800-237-9932
Fax: 888-436-4643
rosenpub@tribeca.ios.com
www.rosenpublishing.com

If a child has to check into the hospital, chances are he or she is already upset about being ill. Knowing how a hospital functions and what the procedures are, such as when family members can visit, will help in what is already a stressful situation. Grades K-5.

24 pages
ISBN: 0-823950-36-0

Roger Rosen, President

Description

4123 LISSENCEPHALY

Synonym: Agyria

Covers these related disorders: Isolated lissencephaly sequence, Miller-Dieker lissencephaly syndrome, Norman-Roberts lissencephaly syndrome, Walker-Warburg syndrome, X-linked lissencephaly

Involves the following Biologic System(s):

Neurologic Disorders

Lissencephaly is a developmental abnormality in which the brain's surface is relatively smooth, resulting from incomplete formation of the folds or convolutions (gyri) of its surface (cerebral cortex). In most patients, the folds may be partially developed or altogether absent. Although lissencephaly was once thought to be a rare malformation, it is now considered more common, largely because of an increase in the number of diagnosed cases resulting from the use of advanced imaging techniques.

Lissencephaly has multiple causes and may occur in isolation, or in association with several underlying syndromes. Newborns with lissencephaly typically have a small head (microcephaly); episodes of uncontrolled electrical disturbances within the brain (seizures); difficulty in swallowing; muscle spasms; deformities of the hands, fingers, or toes; and intellectual disabilities. When an underlying syndrome is present, lissencephaly may be accompanied by additional physical abnormalities. In some patients, lissencephaly can produce life-threatening complications during infancy or childhood. Isolated lissencephaly, which is an autosomal dominant trait, is caused by mutations of a gene known as the LIS 1 gene, which is located on chromosome 17. There have also been reports of numerous cases of lissencephaly in multigenerational families caused by mutations on chromosome X, which determines the female sex when paired with another X chromosome and male sex when paired with a Y chromosome. In male infants, this condition may include seizures that do not respond to treatment (intractable), growth failure, intellectual disabilities, absence of the thick band of nerve fibers (corpus callosum) that connects the left and right halves or hemispheres of the brain, an abnormally small penis (microphallus), and life-threatening complications shortly after birth. In affected females who inherit only a single copy of the aberrant gene (heterozygotes), abnormalities are milder, including an unusual band of brain tissue under the cerebral cortex (subcortical heterotopia) and mild intellectual disabilities and seizures.

Lissencephaly may also occur in association with several syndromes, including Miller-Dieker syndrome and Walker-Warburg syndrome. In a third syndrome, known as Norman-Roberts syndrome, lissencephaly is inherited in an autosomal recessive manner.

Treatment of lissencephaly most often only includes symptomatic and supportive measures. The effects of lissencephaly on the structure and function of the brain are largely untreatable, depending on the severity of this malformation. Many infants with lissencephaly die before the age of 2, often from respiratory infection or other respiratory disease, while others may survive but not develop beyond 3 to 5 months of age. In some cases, infants with lissencephaly survive and experience varying limitations in development, extending to nearly normal function and growth.

Government Agencies

4124 NIH/ Eunice Kennedy Shriver National Institute of Child Health & Human Development
P.O. Box 3006
Rockville, MD 20847

800-370-2943
Fax: 866-760-5947
www.nichd.nih.gov

Conducts and supports research on topics related to the health of children, adults, families and populations. Some of these topics include: developmental disabilities, growth and development, infant death, reproductive health and birth defects.

Diana W. Bianchi, Director
Alison Cernich, PhD, Deputy Director

National Associations & Support Groups

4125 AmeriFace
PO Box 751112
Las Vegas, NV 89136

702-341-5351
888-486-1209
Fax: 702-341-5351
info@ameriface.org
www.ameriface.org

To provide information, services, emotional support and educational programs for and on behalf of individuals with facial difference and their families. Working to increase understanding through public awareness and education.

Debbie Oliver, Executive Director
Robin Remele, Program Director
Joyce Bentz, National Action Team Coordinator

4126 American Academy of Pediatrics
345 Park Blvd
Itasca, IL 60143

800-433-9016
Fax: 847-434-8000
mcc@aap.org
www.aap.org

The American Academy of Pediatrics and its member pediatricians are committed to the attainment of optimal physical, mental and social health and well-being for all infants, children, adolescents, and young adults.

Lynn Olson, PhD, VP, Research
Mark Del Monte, JD, CEO/Executive VP
Vera Tait, MD, FAAP, Chief Medical Officer

4127 Birth Defect Research for Children
976 Lake Baldwin Lane, Suite 104
Orlando, FL 32814

407-895-0802
staff@birthdefects.org
www.birthdefects.org

Birth Defect Research for Children is a non-profit organization that provides parents and expectant parents with information about birth defects and support services for their children.

Betty Mekdeci, Executive Director

4128 Center for Parent Information and Resources (CPIR)
c/o SPAN, 35 Halsey Street, 4th Floor
Newark, NJ 07102

973-642-8100
malizo@spanadvocacy.org
www.parentcenterhub.org

Family-friendly information and research-based materials on key topics for Parent Centers. Private workspaces for Parent Centers to exchange resources, discuss high-priority topics, and solve mutual challenges. Coordination of parent training efforts throughout the network.

Myriam Alizo, Project Assistant

4129 Children's Craniofacial Association
13140 Coit Road, Suite 517
Dallas, TX 75240

214-570-9099
800-535-3643
contactCCA@ccakids.com
www.ccakids.com

A national, nonprofit organization dedicated to improving the quality of life for people with facial differences and their families. CCA's mission is to empower and give hope to facially disfigured children and their families.

Erica Klauber, Executive Director
Annie Reeves, Program Director
Khadija Z. Moten, Outreach Director

4130 FACES: National Craniofacial Association
PO Box 11082
Chattanooga, TN 37401
423-266-1632
800-332-2373
info@faces-cranio.org
www.faces-cranio.org

Assists individuals with facial disfigurations and their families They maintain a registry of centers offering corrective surgery for craniofacial deformities and financial assistance to qualified applicants.

Kim Teems Fox, President
Emily McKay, Communications Director
Ashley Rhodes, FACES Camp Director

4131 March of Dimes Foundation
1550 Crystal Drive, Ste 1300
Arlington, VA 22202
888-663-4637
www.marchofdimes.org

March of Dimes help moms have full-term pregnancies and research the problems that threaten the health of babies. The March of Dimes also acts globally: sharing best practices in perinatal health and helping improve birth outcomes where the needs are the most urgent.

Stacey D. Stewart, President
Alan Brogdon, SVP/COO/Board Officer
Rahul Gupta, MD, SVP & Chief Medical/Health Officer

4132 National Hydrocephalus Foundation
12413 Centrailia Road
Lakewood, CA 90715
562-924-6666
info@nhfonline.org
www.nhfonline.org

Promotes information and educational assistance. Establishes and facilitates a communication network and works to increase public awareness.

Debbi Fields, Executive Director

4133 World Craniofacial Foundation
7777 Forest Lane, Suite C-616
Dallas, TX 75230
972-566-6669
800-533-3315
info@worldcf.org
www.worldcf.org

The World Craniofacial Foundation is a nonprofit corporation, dedicated to helping children obtain the life-changing craniofacial surgery they deserve.

Web Sites

4134 Clinical Genetic Services-Department of Pediatrics
Hassenfeld Children's Hospital at NYU Langone
424 East 34th Street
New York, NY 10016
212-263-7300
Fax: 646-754-2250
nyulangone.org

Offers evaluations, genetic counseling and testing. Clinical services include carrier testing, prenatal counseling, and complete genetic evaluations for children and adults.

John G. Pappas, MD, Pediatric Genetic Associate
Naomi Yachelevich, MD, Pediatric Genetic Associate

4135 Independent Holoprosencephaly Support Site
hpe.home.att.net

hpe.home.att.net

This site is home to an online support group for parents of children with HPE, or anyone who cares for a child with HPE.

4136 National Hydrocephalus Foundation
www.nhfonline.org
562-924-6666
info@nhfonline.org
www.nhfonline.org

Promotes information and educational assistance. Establishes and facilitates a communication network and works to increase public awareness. Promote and support research.

4137 Online Mendelian Inheritance in Man
McKusick-Nathans Institue of Genetic Medicine-JHU
Baltimore, MD 21205
www.omim.org

This database is a catalog of human genes and genetic disorders.

Ada Hamosh, MD, Scientific Director

Book Publishers

4138 Congenital Disorders Sourcebook 2nd Edit.
Greg Mullin, author

Omnigraphics
615 Griswold Street, Ste 520
Detroit, MI 48226
610-461-3548
800-234-1340
Fax: 800-875-1340
contact@omnigraphics.com
www.omnigraphics.com

Basic consumer health information on disorders aquired during gestation, including spina bifida, hydrocephalus, cerebral palsy, heart defects, craniofacial abnormalities and fetal alcohol syndrome.

664 pages
ISBN: 0-780816-13-8

4139 Let's Talk About Going to the Hospital
Rosen Publishing Group's PowerKids Press
29 E 21st Street
New York, NY 10010
212-777-3017
800-237-9932
Fax: 888-436-4643
rosenpub@tribeca.ios.com
www.rosenpublishing.com

If a child has to check into the hospital, chances are he or she is already upset about being ill. Knowing how a hospital functions and what the procedures are, such as when family members can visit, will help in what is already a stressful situation. Grades K-5.

24 pages
ISBN: 0-823950-36-0

Roger Rosen, President

Description

4140 LYME DISEASE

Synonym: Deer tick disease

Covers these related disorders: Bell's palsy

Involves the following Biologic System(s):

Infectious Disorders

Lyme disease is a bacterial (Borrelia burgdorferi) infection that is transmitted by being bitten by the nymph stage of the deer tick Ixodides. It is not contagious, that is, it is not spread by contact with people or animals with Lyme disease. Lyme disease has been found in the Northeast from Maine to Virginia, the upper Midwest and on the West Coast. The most common first sign of Lyme disease is a rash at the site of the tick bite. It is a red circular rash, often with an area of central clearing (target lesion) and is called erythema migrans.

Lyme disease has three stages, early localized, early disseminated and late disease. Early localized disease is marked by the typical rash and may also include flu-like symptoms. It occurs between 7 and 10 days after the tick bite. The most common symptom of early disseminated disease is multiple erythema migrans, but patients can develop cranial nerve palsies (including Bell's palsy), meningitis, or carditis leading to heartblock on seen on an electrocardiogram (ECG). Systemic symptoms can include muscle and joint aches, fatigue and headaches. Symptoms of early disseminated disease develop from days to weeks in the untreated patient. Late Lyme disease happens weeks to months after the tick bite and is marked by arthritis of one or more large joints.

Diagnosis of Lyme disease is primarily made based on history and physical findings. Serologic testing (i.e. blood test) can be useful for diagnosis in some cases, but interpreting the immunologic tests can be difficult and it is important to utilize a high quality lab for testing. The serologic testing can not be used to assess treatment success.

Antibiotics are used to treat all stages of Lyme disease. The stage and specific symptoms determine how long treatment needs to be and whether or not the therapy can be oral or intravenous. Doxycycline is the drug of choice in patients with erythema migrans or a suspicion of Lyme disease based on clinical findings. There is no evidence supporting chronic or multiple courses of antibiotics for Lyme disease. Patients who continue to have symptoms more than six months after treatment should be evaluated for other inflammatory diseases. Prevention is important. Tick bites can be prevented by taking precautions when spending time outdoors, for instance, wearing loose fitting long sleeves and long pants; applying tick repellant; and decreasing environmental contacts with deer. A thorough search for ticks after outdoor exposure is essential. The LYMErix vaccine is no longer being manufactured, owing to its pain and at times debilitatin side effects.

National Associations & Support Groups

4141 American Academy of Pediatrics
345 Park Blvd
Itasca, IL 60143

800-433-9016
Fax: 847-434-8000
mcc@aap.org
www.aap.org

The American Academy of Pediatrics and its member pediatricians are committed to the attainment of optimal physical, mental and social health and well-being for all infants, children, adolescents, and young adults.

Lynn Olson, PhD, VP, Research
Mark Del Monte, JD, CEO/Executive VP
Vera Tait, MD, FAAP, Chief Medical Officer

4142 American Camp Association
5000 State Road 67 North
Martinsville, IN 46151

765-342-8456
800-428-2267
www.acacamps.org

The American Camp Association is a community of camp professionals who, for over 100 years, have joined together to share our knowledge and experience and to ensure the quality of camp programs.

Tom Rosenberg, President & CEO

4143 American Lyme Disease Foundation
157 Church Street, 19th Floor
New Haven, CT 06510

questions@aldf.com
www.aldf.com

Supports research and plays a key role in providing reliable and scientifically accurate information to the public, health care provider, and government agencies about tick-borne diseases and their potentially serious effects on our health and quality of life.

Andrea C. Love, Executive Director

4144 Center for Peripheral Neuropathy
University of Chicago
5841 South Maryland Avenue, Suite MC2030
Chicago, IL 60637

773-702-6222
peripheralneuropathycenter.uchicago.edu

The Center for Peripheral Neuropathy are committed to educating the public and healthcare providers about this disease, providing state-of-the-art care to patients affected by peripheral neuropathy, and contributing to basic and clinical research in an effort to identify the causes and potential cures for these disorders.

4145 Child Neurology Foundation
601 W Short Street
Lexington, KY 40508

888-417-3435
info@childneurologyfoundation.org
childneurologyfoundation.org

The Child Neurology Foundation connects partners from all areas of the child neurology community so those navigating the journey of disease diagnosis, management, and care have the ongoing support from those dedicated to treatments and cures.

Amy Brin, Executive Director
Katie Hentges, Director, Programs
Brea McCormley, Director, Development

4146 Children's Lyme Disease Network
76 Kettles Way, Suite 150
Queensbury, NY 12804

info@childrenslymenetwork.org
www.childrenslymenetwork.org

Children's Lyme Disease Network is an all-volunteer organization consisting of parents, caregivers and family members who have seen first-hand the struggles a child can face once infected with Lyme Disease.

4147 Global Lyme Alliance
1290 East Main Street, 3rd Floor
Stamford, CT 06902

203-969-1333
info@gla.org
globallymealliance.org

Global Lyme Alliance is the leading 501(c)(3) whose mission is to cure Lyme and other tick-borne diseases through innovation research, awareness, and empowering the patient voice.

Laura MacNeill, Chief Executive Officer
Timothy J. Sellati, Chief Scientific Officer
Paul Ross, Chair

Lyme Disease / Research Centers

4148 Lyme Disease Association, Inc. (LDA)
PO Box 1438
Jackson, NJ 08527
Fax: 732-938-7215
www.lymediseaseassociation.org

A national organization dedicated to raising funds for Lyme and tick-borne diseases education, prevention, research and patient support. LDA has funded dozens of research projects nationally, helped endow a research center for chronic Lyme and Columbia.

4149 Lyme Disease Foundation
384 Merrow Road
Tolland, CT 06084
860-454-8909
lymediseasefoundation@gmail.com
www.lyme.org

Nonprofit organization dedicated to finding solutions for tick-borne disorders. Offers support to the public and medical communities.

Karen Vanderhoof-Forschner, President
Christy Vanderhoof-Forschner, Digital Director

4150 Lyme Disease Research Foundation
2360 W. Joppa Road, Suite 320
Lutherville, MD 21093
www.lymemd.org

LymeMD, a non-profit organization, was created in 2007 by Dr. John Aucott, an infectious disease specialist, in response to the devastating toll that Lyme disease takes on previously healthy, energetic individuals. LymeMD has become a nationally recognized program attracting top collaborators around the country.

Alex Mason, President
Joseph Hardiman, Vice-President
Lawrence Macks, Vice-President

4151 NIH/National Institute of Arthritis and Musculoskeletal and Skin Diseases
1 AMS Circle
Bethesda, MD 20892
301-495-4484
877-226-4267
Fax: 301-718-6366
TTY: 301-565-2966
NIAMSinfo@mail.nih.gov
www.niams.nih.gov

The mission of the NIAMS, a part of the NIH, is to support research into the causes, treatment and prevention of arthritis and musculoskeletal and skin diseases, the training of basic and clinical scientists to carry out this research, and the dissemination of information on research progress in these diseases.

Lindsey A. Criswell, MD, Director
Rick Phillips, Executive Officer

4152 National Capital Lyme Disease Association
PO Box 8211
McLean, VA 22106
703-821-8833
natcaplyme@natcaplyme.org
www.natcaplyme.org

The National Capital Lyme Disease Association is an all volunteer not-for-profit organization that is committed to helping patients diagnosed with tick-borne illnesses.

Monte Skall, Executive Director

Research Centers

4153 John Hopkins Arthritis Center
5200 Eastern Avenue, Suite 4100
Baltimore, MD 21224
410-550-0545
Fax: 410-550-2090
arthritis@jhmi.edu
www.hopkins-arthritis.org

The Johns Hopkins Arthritis Center has assembled a team of some of the world's leading experts and specializes in the care of inflammatory arthritis. This includes, most notably, osteoarthritis and rheumatoid arthritis.

Penny Athanasiou, Clinic Coordinator

Web Sites

4154 American Lyme Disease Foundation
157 Church Street, 19th Floor
New Haven, CT 06510
questions@aldf.com
www.aldf.com

Provides reliable and scientifically accurate information to the public about tick borne diseases and their potentially serious effects on our life.

Andrea C. Love, Executive Director

4155 Lyme Disease Association, Inc. (LDA)
PO Box 1438
Jackson, NJ 08527
Fax: 732-938-7215
www.lymediseaseassociation.org

A national organization dedicated to raising funds for Lyme and tick-borne diseases education, prevention, research and patient support. LDA has funded dozens of research projects nationally, helped endow a research center for chronic Lyme and Columbia.

4156 Lyme Disease Foundation
384 Merrow Road
Tolland, CT 06084
860-454-8909
lymediseasefoundation@gmail.com
www.lyme.org

Nonprofit organization dedicated to finding solutions for tick-borne disorders. Offers support to the public and medical communities.

Book Publishers

4157 Aspects of Lyme Borreliosis
Springer-Verlag
11 West 42nd Street 15th Floor
New York, NY 10036
212-431-4370
877-687-7476
Fax: 212-941-7842
cs@springerpub.com
www.springerpub.com

1992 384 pages hardcover
ISBN: 0-387556-28-1

Theodore C. Nardin, CEO

4158 Ecology and Enviromental Management of Lyme Disease
Rutgers University Press
100 Joyce Kilmer Avenue
Piscataway, NJ 8854
732-445-7762
800-446-9323
Fax: 732-445-7039
bksales@rci.rutgers.edu

1993 hardcover
ISBN: 0-813519-28-4

Marlie Wasserman, Director
Christina Brianik, Assistant to the Director
Molly Venezia, Director of Finance

4159 Let's Talk About Having Lyme Disease
Rosen Publishing Group
29 E 21st Street
New York, NY 10010
800-237-9932
Fax: 888-436-4643
customerservice@rosenpub.com
www.rosenpublishing.com

Discusses what Lyme disease is, how one gets it, and what to do about it.

2003 24 pages hardcover
ISBN: 0-823950-29-8

Roger Rosen, President

4160 Lyme Disease
Enslow Publishers
Box 398 40 Industrial Road,
Berkeley Heights, NJ 07922

908-771-9400
800-398-2504
Fax: 908-771-0925
customerService@enslow.com

Outlines Lyme Disease, from its discovery to current trends. The transmission of the disease from the deer tick, and its course of infection in the body are clearly discribed. Methods for protection from the disease are mixed with real life stories of patients who have contracted Lyme disease. The symptoms, diagnosis, treatment, and prevention are also covered.

104 pages hardcover
ISBN: 0-766010-52-x

Mark Enslow, President
Brian Enslow, Vice President/Publisher

4161 Lyme Disease (Deadly Diseases and Epidemics)
Chelsea House Publishing
2080 Cabot Boulevard W, Suite 201
Langhorne, PA 19047

800-848-2665
Fax: 877-780-7300

110 pages

Journals

4162 Journal of Spirochetal and Tick-borne Diseases
1 Financial Plaza
Hartford, CT 6103

860-525-2000
Fax: 860-525-8425
lymefnd@aol.com
www.jstd.org

Reviews all aspects of spirochetal or tick-borne disorders. Clinical topics may involve all medical disciplines, nursing, and pharmacy, as well as the social, ethnical and biological features of such disorders.

Quaterly

Ronald Schell PHD, Editor in Chief
Willy Burgdorfer PHD, Deputy Editor
Sam Donta, Consulting Editor

Newsletters

4163 Journal of the American Medical Association
PO Box 10946
Chicago, IL 60610

312-670-7827
800-262-2350
subscriptions@jamanetwork.com
jama.ama-assn.org

To promote the science and art of medicine and the betterment of the public health.

Macrocephaly / Description

Description

4164 MACROCEPHALY

Synonyms: Macrocephalia, Megalocephaly

Covers these related disorders: Benign familial macrocephaly, Megalencephaly

Involves the following Biologic System(s):

Neurologic Disorders

Macrocephaly (macro = long; cephaly = head) is a term that is used to describe an isolated or primary condition in which an infant's or a child's head circumference is more than two standard deviations above the mean for age and sex. As a rule of thumb, a newborn's head is usually about 2 centimeters larger than the chest size. Between 6 months and 2 years, both measurements are about equal. After 2 years, the chest size becomes larger than the head.

Primary macrocephaly may be apparent at birth or during early infancy. In some affected infants and children, overgrowth of the brain results in varying degrees of intellectual disabilities. Associated symptoms and findings may include episodes of uncontrolled electrical disturbances in the brain (seizures); unusually large or small stature; and motor abnormalities ranging from diminished muscle tone (hypotonia) to muscle rigidity and associated restrictions of movement (spasticity). Patients with overgrowth of the brain (megalencephaly) have normally sized or slightly enlarged cavities of the brain (ventricles) and no evidence of underlying conditions, such as certain metabolic disorders (metabolic megalencephaly). Although infants and children with macrocephaly may have abnormal delays in the acquisition of skills requiring the coordination of physical and mental activities (psychomotor delays), they do not experience regression of such skills, a finding that is typically associated with infantile metabolic megalencephaly or certain other underlying conditions.

Some infants and children with primary macrocephaly experience no associated intellectual disabilities or other neurologic deficits. Several such cases have been reported in individuals within certain multigenerational families. This form of benign or nonsyndromic macrocephaly, known as benign familial macrocephaly, is thought to have autosomal dominant inheritance.

Although infants with primary macrocephaly experience increasing head size, they typically do not have symptoms and findings associated with increased cerebrospinal fluid (CSF) pressure within the brain (intracranial pressure). This is in contrast to hydrocephalus, a condition in which the brain swells due to an abnormal accumulation of CSF under increasing pressure within the brain's ventricles. However, some infants with primary macrocephaly may have a slight separation of the fibrous joints (cranial sutures) between certain bones in the skull.

Although the specific underlying cause of primary macrocephaly is not understood, overgrowth of the brain is due to the presence of abnormally large or an unusually increased number of brain cells. The outer region of the brain (cerebral cortex) appears normal in some cases; however, others have structural abnormalities.

As mentioned above, overgrowth of the brain may occur as a secondary finding associated with certain progressive infantile metabolic diseases, such as Tay-Sachs disease, or other underlying geneticdisorders, such as neurofibromatosis. The condition may also occur as a result of certain structural abnormalities of the brain, such as absence of the band of nerve fibers that joins the two cerebral hemispheres (agenesis of corpus callosum), or due to a localized accumulation of blood between the outer and middle layers of the membrane that surrounds and protects the brain and spinal cord (subdural hematoma). Infants and children with macrocephaly who experience psychomotor regression should receive thorough clinical, neurologic, metabolic, and other appropriate evaluations to rule out or confirm the presence of certain underlying disorders or conditions.

The treatment of infants and children with isolated or primary macrocephaly includes symptomatic and supportive measures. These may include the prescription of certain medications to help treat or control seizures (e.g., anticonvulsants) and physical therapy, special education, and other multidisciplinary measures to ensure that patients with motor impairments and intellectual disabilities reach their potential. In infants and children with secondary macrocephaly, treatment includes appropriate therapies for any diagnosed, underlying causes of the condition.

Government Agencies

4165 NIH/ Eunice Kennedy Shriver National Institute of Child Health & Human Development
P.O. Box 3006
Rockville, MD 20847

800-370-2943
Fax: 866-760-5947
www.nichd.nih.gov

Conducts and supports research on topics related to the health of children, adults, families and populations. Some of these topics include: developmental disabilities, growth and development, infant death, reproductive health and birth defects.

Diana W. Bianchi, Director
Alison Cernich, PhD, Deputy Director

National Associations & Support Groups

4166 American Academy of Pediatrics
345 Park Blvd
Itasca, IL 60143

800-433-9016
Fax: 847-434-8000
mcc@aap.org
www.aap.org

The American Academy of Pediatrics and its member pediatricians are committed to the attainment of optimal physical, mental and social health and well-being for all infants, children, adolescents, and young adults.

Lynn Olson, PhD, VP, Research
Mark Del Monte, JD, CEO/Executive VP
Vera Tait, MD, FAAP, Chief Medical Officer

4167 Arc of the United States
1825 K Street NW, Ste 1200
Washington, DC 20006

202-534-3700
800-433-5255
Fax: 202-534-3731
info@thearc.org
www.thearc.org

The Arc of the United States advocates for the rights and full participation of all children and adults with intellectual and developmental disabilities. Together with a network of members and affiliated chapters, they improve systems of support and services; connect families; inspire communities and influence public policy.

Peter V. Berns, CEO

4168 Birth Defect Research for Children
976 Lake Baldwin Lane, Suite 104
Orlando, FL 32814

407-895-0802
staff@birthdefects.org
www.birthdefects.org

Birth Defect Research for Children is a non-profit organization that provides parents and expectant parents with information about birth defects and support services for their children.

Betty Mekdeci, Executive Director

4169 Center for Parent Information and Resources (CPIR)
c/o SPAN, 35 Halsey Street, 4th Floor
Newark, NJ 07102
973-642-8100
malizo@spanadvocacy.org
www.parentcenterhub.org

Family-friendly information and research-based materials on key topics for Parent Centers. Private workspaces for Parent Centers to exchange resources, discuss high-priority topics, and solve mutual challenges. Coordination of parent training efforts throughout the network.

Myriam Alizo, Project Assistant

4170 Genetic Alliance
426400 Woodfield Road, Ste 189
Damascus, MD 20872
202-966-5557
Fax: 202-966-8553
info@geneticalliance.org
www.geneticalliance.org

World's leading nonprofit health advocacy organization committed to transforming health through genetics and promoting an environment of openness centered on the health of individuals, families, and communities.

Sharon Terry, CEO
Ruth Child, CFO
Natasha Bonhomme, Chief Strategy Officer

Web Sites

4171 Online Mendelian Inheritance in Man
McKusick-Nathans Institue of Genetic Medicine-JHU
Baltimore, MD 21205
www.omim.org

This database is a catalog of human genes and genetic disorders.

Ada Hamosh, MD, Scientific Director

Maple Syrup Urine Disease / Description

Description

4172 MAPLE SYRUP URINE DISEASE

Synonyms: Branched chain ketoaciduria, MSUD

Covers these related disorders: Classic MSUD, Mild (intermediate) MSUD, Intermittent MSUD, Thiamine-responsive MSUD

Involves the following Biologic System(s):

Genetic/Chromosomal/Syndrome/Metabolic Disorders

Maple syrup urine disease (MSUD) is a metabolic disorder characterized by the deficiency of certain enzymes of the branched-chain alpha-ketoacid dehydrogenase complex that break down (catabolize) three essential organic compounds. These compounds are known as amino acids and are the building blocks of protein. These amino acids include leucine, isoleucine, and valine. A deficiency of any enzyme within this complex results in the symptoms of MSUD and leads to encephalopathy, a condition characterized by altered brain function. There are four basic types of maple syrup urine disease.

Classic MSUD, the most severe form of this disorder, becomes apparent within the first week of life and is recognizable by a characteristic maple syrup odor of the urine and on the body. Symptoms and physical findings associated with this life-threatening form of MSUD include listlessness, drowsiness, exaggerated muscular tension (hypertonicity) and rigidity with periods of loss of muscle tone (flaccidity), severe muscle spasms resulting in a backward arching of the back and neck (opisthotonus), convulsions, and coma. Additional findings include low blood sugar (hypoglycemia) and higher-than-normal acidic levels in the blood as well as abnormally low bicarbonate levels (metabolic acidosis). In addition, severe life-threatening complications may occur following infection, surgery, or other stressful events. Such complications include an excessive accumulation of fluid around the brain (cerebral edema) and acidosis accompanied by excessive levels of certain organic compounds in the tissues and body fluids (ketosis). Many affected children experience neurologic and mental deficiencies.

Treatment for classic MSUD includes the removal of leucine, isoleucine, valine, and certain other related elements from the blood by a procedure known as peritoneal dialysis. Subsequent therapy includes a diet low in leucine, isoleucine, and valine.

Intermittent MSUD develops suddenly in children who had previously exhibited no signs of the disease. Though this form of the disease is intermittent, the characteristic findings, symptoms, severity of complications, and treatment are similar to those of classic MSUD. In addition, children with this form of the disorder may exhibit more activity of certain enzymes than those with the classic form.

Mild or intermediate MSUD is a less severe form of this disorder that usually affects children after the first month of life. Affected infants may have mild intellectual disabilities and usually emit the characteristic maple syrup odor in their urine, sweat, and earwax (cerumen).

Characteristic findings and symptoms associated with thiamine-responsive MSUD are similar to those of intermittent or intermediate disease. The distinguishing feature is that treatment with high doses of vitamin B1 (thiamine) often results in a favorable response. Early diagnosis and dietary intervention prevent complications and may allow for normal intellectual development.

Consequently, MSUD has been added to many newborn screening programs, and preliminary results indicate that asymptomatic newborns with MSUD have a better outcome compared with infants who are diagnosed after they become symptomatic.

Maple syrup urine disease is inherited as an autosomal recessive trait. Approximately one in 200,000 people in the United States is affected by this disorder.

National Associations & Support Groups

4173 American Academy of Pediatrics
345 Park Blvd
Itasca, IL 60143

800-433-9016
Fax: 847-434-8000
mcc@aap.org
www.aap.org

The American Academy of Pediatrics and its member pediatricians are committed to the attainment of optimal physical, mental and social health and well-being for all infants, children, adolescents, and young adults.

Lynn Olson, PhD, VP, Research
Mark Del Monte, JD, CEO/Executive VP
Vera Tait, MD, FAAP, Chief Medical Officer

4174 Arc of the United States
1825 K Street NW, Ste 1200
Washington, DC 20006

202-534-3700
800-433-5255
Fax: 202-534-3731
info@thearc.org
www.thearc.org

The Arc of the United States advocates for the rights and full participation of all children and adults with intellectual and developmental disabilities. Together with a network of members and affiliated chapters, they improve systems of support and services; connect families; inspire communities and influence public policy.

Peter V. Berns, CEO

4175 Genetic Alliance
426400 Woodfield Road, Ste 189
Damascus, MD 20872

202-966-5557
Fax: 202-966-8553
info@geneticalliance.org
www.geneticalliance.org

World's leading nonprofit health advocacy organization committed to transforming health through genetics and promoting an environment of openness centered on the health of individuals, families, and communities.

Sharon Terry, CEO
Ruth Child, CFO
Natasha Bonhomme, Chief Strategy Officer

4176 MSUD:(Maple Syrup Urine Disease) Family Support Group
4656 Winding Oak Drive
Delaware, OH 43015

740-972-5618
www.msud-support.org

MSUD is a nonprofit (501)(c)(3) organization for parents of children with MSUD, adults with MSUD, health-care professionals and others interested in MSUD. Dedicated to providing opportunities for support and personal contact for those with MSUD and their families, distributing information and raising public awareness of MSUD, strengthening the liaison between families and professionals and encouraging newborn screening programs and research for MSUD.

Sandy Bulcher, President
Dave Bulcher, Treasurer
Jordann Coleman, Advocacy Chair

4177 March of Dimes Foundation
1550 Crystal Drive, Ste 1300
Arlington, VA 22202

888-663-4637
www.marchofdimes.org

March of Dimes help moms have full-term pregnancies and research the problems that threaten the health of babies. The March of Dimes also acts globally: sharing best practices in perinatal health and helping improve birth outcomes where the needs are the most urgent.

Stacey D. Stewart, President
Alan Brogdon, SVP/COO/Board Officer
Rahul Gupta, MD, SVP & Chief Medical/Health Officer

Libraries & Resource Centers

4178 National Digestive Diseases Information Clearinghouse (NDDIC)
NIH
2 Information Way
Bethesda, MD 20892
301-654-3810
800-891-5389
Fax: 301-907-8906
nddic@info.niddk.nih.gov
www.digestive.niddk.nih.gov

The National Institute of Diabetes and Digestive and Kidney Diseases conducts and supports research on many of the most serious diseases affecting public health. The Institute supports much of the clinical research on the diseases of internal medicine and related subspecialty fields as well as many basic science disciplines.

Griffin P. Rodgers, MD, Director
Gregory G. Germino, MD, Deputy Director
Kathy Kranzfelder, Communications Director

Book Publishers

4179 Let's Talk About Going to the Hospital
Rosen Publishing Group's PowerKids Press
29 E 21st Street
New York, NY 10010
212-777-3017
800-237-9932
Fax: 888-436-4643
rosenpub@tribeca.ios.com
www.rosenpublishing.com

If a child has to check into the hospital, chances are he or she is already upset about being ill. Knowing how a hospital functions and what the procedures are, such as when family members can visit, will help in what is already a stressful situation. Grades K-5.

24 pages
ISBN: 0-823950-36-0

Roger Rosen, President

Newsletters

4180 MSUD Newsletter
MSUD Family Support Group
4656 Winding Oak Drive
Delaware, OH 43015
740-972-5618
www.msud-support.org

Provides the latest information on the treatment of the disorder, reports on the latest research, current diet information, family news and related topics.

16 pages

Sandy Bulcher, President
Amber Raye, Co-Editor
Susan Needleman, Co-Editor

Description

4181 MARFAN SYNDROME
Synonym: MFS
Covers these related disorders: Neonatal or infantile Marfan syndrome
Involves the following Biologic System(s):
Cardiovascular Disorders,
Genetic/Chromosomal/Syndrome/Metabolic Disorders, Orthopedic and Muscle Disorders

Marfan syndrome is a connective tissue disorder that may result in heart (cardiac), blood vessel, skeletal, and eye (ocular) abnormalities. Children with Marfan syndrome tend to be unusually tall and slim; in some cases, this may be apparent at birth. Many affected infants also have deficiency of the layer of fat under the skin and abnormally diminished muscle tone (hypotonia) that may contribute to motor delays. In addition, in some infants with Marfan syndrome, several additional characteristic symptoms and findings may be apparent during later childhood. Neonatal or infantile Marfan syndrome is characterized by abnormal flexions (contractures), dislocations, and limited ranges of movement; an abnormally long head and face (dolichocephaly); a highly arched roof of the mouth (palate); unusually large corneas of the eyes (megalocornea); abnormal quivering movements of the colored portions of the eyes (irides); and heart defects (e.g., aortic root dilatation, mitral valve prolapse).

Older children with Marfan syndrome also tend to have an unusually long, narrow face as well as a narrow, highly arched palate and abnormal crowding of the teeth. Affected children and adults also have unusually long, thin arms and legs; a wide arm span; and long, thin fingers (arachnodactyly) with abnormally increased extension (hyperflexibility). Additional skeletal abnormalities are often present, such as unusually thin, fragile ribs; abnormal protrusion or depression of the breastbone (pectus carinatum or excavatum); and, in older children and adolescents, progressive abnormal sideways curvature (scoliosis) or front-to-back curvature (kyphosis) of the spine.

In many cases, affected children also have additional ocular abnormalities, such as dislocation (subluxation) of the lenses of the eyes (ectopia lentis); abnormal bluish coloration of the tough, outer membrane of the eyes; and severe nearsightedness (myopia). In addition, in some cases, the nerve-rich membrane at the back of the eyes (retina) may become detached.

Most individuals with Marfan syndrome also experience abnormalities of the heart and certain blood vessels (cardiovascular defects) that may be life-threatening. These may include progressive widening of the major artery of the body (aorta), causing leakage of blood through the valve between the left ventricle and the aorta (aortic regurgitation). In addition, the valve between the left ventricle and the left upper chamber (atrium) of the heart may bulge backward (prolapse) into the atrium, causing leakage of blood into the atrium.

The treatment of Marfan syndrome is directed toward preventing potential complications associated with progression of the disease. Affected children should receive regular evaluations to detect ocular defects, abnormal spinal curvatures, or cardiovascular defects. Treatment includes symptomatic and supportive measures, such as orthopedic techniques to help prevent or treat scoliosis or kyphosis; therapy with certain medications (beta-adrenergic blocking agents, e.g., propranolol) that may help to prevent or reduce the progression of certain cardiovascular abnormalities (e.g., aortic dilatation and associated complications); or surgical correction of cardiovascular defects as required. At one time, affected individuals were provided with antibiotic medications before dental visits and surgical procedures to reduce the incidence of endocarditis (an infection of the heart wall or heart valve when bacteria enter the bloodstream). The American Heart Association no longer recommends taking routine antibiotics before certain dental procedures except for people at highest risk for bad outcomes if they develop endocarditis. Individuals with Marfan syndrome do not fall into this high-risk category.

Marfan syndrome results from abnormal changes (mutations) in a gene (fibrillin gene) located on the long arm of chromosome 15 (15q21.1). Such mutations may occur spontaneously (sporadically) for unknown reasons or may be inherited as an autosomal dominant trait. In individuals with the disease gene, the range and severity of associated symptoms and findings may vary from case to case (variable expressivity). Marfan syndrome is thought to affect about one in 10,000 individuals.

Government Agencies

4182 NIH/National Institute of Arthritis and Musculoskeletal and Skin Diseases
1 AMS Circle
Bethesda, MD 20892
301-495-4484
877-226-4267
Fax: 301-718-6366
TTY: 301-565-2966
niamsinfo@mail.nih.gov
www.niams.nih.gov

The mission of the NIAMS, a part of the NIH, is to support research into the causes, treatment and prevention of arthritis and musculosketal and skin diseases, the training of basic and clinical scientists to carry out this research, and the dissemination of information on research progress in these diseases.

Lindsey A. Criswell, MD, Director
Rick Phillips, Executive Officer

National Associations & Support Groups

4183 American Academy of Pediatrics
345 Park Blvd
Itasca, IL 60143
800-433-9016
Fax: 847-434-8000
mcc@aap.org
www.aap.org

The American Academy of Pediatrics and its member pediatricians are committed to the attainment of optimal physical, mental and social health and well-being for all infants, children, adolescents, and young adults.

Lynn Olson PhD, VP, Research
Mark Del Monte, JD, CEO/Executive VP
Vera Tait, MD, FAAP, Chief Medical Officer

4184 Genetic Alliance
426400 Woodfield Road, Ste 189
Damascus, MD 20872
202-966-5557
Fax: 202-966-8553
info@geneticalliance.org
www.geneticalliance.org

World's leading nonprofit health advocacy organization committed to transforming health through genetics and promoting an environment of openness centered on the health of individuals, families, and communities.

Sharon Terry, CEO
Ruth Child, CFO
Natasha Bonhomme, Chief Strategy Officer

Marfan Syndrome / Pamphlets

4185 **March of Dimes Foundation**
1550 Crystal Drive, Ste 1300
Arlington, VA 22202
888-663-4637
www.marchofdimes.org

March of Dimes help moms have full-term pregnancies and research the problems that threaten the health of babies. The March of Dimes also acts globally: sharing best practices in perinatal health and helping improve birth outcomes where the needs are the most urgent.

Stacey D. Stewart, President
Alan Brogdon, SVP/COO/Board Officer
Rahul Gupta, MD, SVP & Chief Medical/Health Officer

4186 **National Marfan Foundation**
22 Manhasset Avenue
Port Washington, NY 11050
516-883-8712
800-862-7326
www.marfan.org

A nonprofit voluntary health organization dedicated to saving lives and improving the quality of life for individuals and families affected by the Marfan Syndrome and related disorders.

Michael Weamer, President & CEO
Judy Gibaldi, Chief Operating Officer
Josephine Grima, Chief Scientific Officer

Web Sites

4187 **National Marfan Foundation**
22 Manhasset Avenue
Port Washington, NY 11050
516-883-8712
800-862-7326
www.marfan.org

A nonprofit voluntary health organization dedicated to saving lives and improving the quality of life for individuals and families affected by the Marfan Syndrome and related disorders.

Michael Weamer, President & CEO
Judy Gibaldi, Chief Operating Officer
Josephine Grima, Chief Scientific Officer

4188 **Wheeless' Textbook of Orthopaedics**
www.wheelessonline.com
410-494-4994
www.wheelessonline.com

Derives from a variety of sources, including journals, articles, national meetings lectures and other textbooks.

Clifford R. Wheeless, Editor in chief
James A Nunley, Managing Editor
James R. Urbaniak, Managing Editor

Book Publishers

4189 **Let's Talk About Going to the Hospital**
Rosen Publishing Group's PowerKids Press
29 E 21st Street
New York, NY 10010
212-777-3017
800-237-9932
Fax: 888-436-4643
rosenpub@tribeca.ios.com
www.rosenpublishing.com

If a child has to check into the hospital, chances are he or she is already upset about being ill. Knowing how a hospital functions and what the procedures are, such as when family members can visit, will help in what is already a stressful situation. Grades K-5.

24 pages
ISBN: 0-823950-36-0

Roger Rosen, President

Pamphlets

4190 **Marfan Syndrome**
March of Dimes Foundation
1550 Crystal Drive, Ste 1300
Arlington, VA 22202
914-977-4488
888-663-4637
Fax: 914-997-4763
answers@marchofdimes.org
www.marchofdimes.org

A series of fact sheets each discussing an aspect of Marfan, inlcuding prevention, research, causes, treamtents, diagnosis, affects, eye problems, heart problems, and skeletal problems.

McCune-Albright Syndrome / Description

Description

4191 MCCUNE-ALBRIGHT SYNDROME
Synonyms: Albright syndrome, MAS, PFD, POFD, Polyostotic fibrous dysplasia, Precocious puberty with polyostotic
Involves the following Biologic System(s):
Endocrinologic Disorders,
Genetic/Chromosomal/Syndrome/Metabolic Disorders

McCune-Albright syndrome is a genetic disorder characterized by multiple areas of abnormal, fiber-like tissue growths (bone lesions) that replace normal bone tissue (polyostotic fibrous dysplasia); irregular, patchy areas of light brown pigmentation on the skin (cafe-au-lait spots); and abnormalities of certain hormone-producing glands that assist in regulating the body's growth, controlling the rate of metabolism, and promoting the development of secondary sexual characteristics. Although bone lesions are most common in the pelvis and the long bones of the arms and legs, other bones may be affected, including the ribs, skull and facial bones, and bones of the spinal column (vertebrae). These bone lesions may cause abnormal thickness and deformity of affected bones, susceptibility to fractures, and bone pain. In addition, lesions may cause corresponding bones to develop unevenly. For example, one leg may appear unusually short, or one side of the face may appear different from the other (facial asymmetry). Bone lesions of the skull and face may eventually result in hearing loss and visual impairment.

Many girls with McCune-Albright syndrome undergo early development of secondary sexual characteristics (precocious puberty), including early breast development and onset of menstrual cycles (menstruation). Some boys with the disorder may also experience precocious puberty, including genital development and unusually accelerated growth. In many patients, additional endocrine abnormalities may be present. For example, some affected children may produce excessive amounts of the hormone cortisol, resulting in Cushing's syndrome. This disorder is characterized by excessive weight gain in the chest and abdominal area; a moon-shaped, rounded face; abnormal pads of fat in certain areas of the body; high blood pressure (hypertension); weakening of bones, causing increased susceptibility to fractures; thin, and fragile skin.

Some children with McCune-Albright syndrome may also produce excessive amounts of thyroid hormones (hyperthyroidism), potentially leading to heart palpitations, anxiety, heat intolerance, excessive sweating, muscle weakness, or weight loss. In addition, some affected children may be prone to developing tumors of the pituitary gland, resulting in increased secretion of growth hormone, which stimulates body growth and development. Affected children may experience enlargement of bones and soft tissues of the hands, feet, and face (acromegaly); lengthening and coarsening of the face; and enlargement of certain organs (e.g., heart). In some patients, excessive growth during childhood (gigantism) and tall stature may occur.

McCune-Albright syndrome may be obvious at birth because of unusual skin pigmentation. Alternatively, it may not be apparent until late infancy or early childhood when precocious puberty or bone lesions become apparent. The disorder is caused by spontaneous (sporadic) changes (mutations) of a gene known as the GNAS1 gene. The disease gene is located on the long arm (q) of chromosome 20 (20q13.2). Because the gene mutation is present in only some cells of the body (mosaicism), symptoms and findings may vary among affected individuals, depending upon the specific body cells affected. Treatment of McCune-Albright syndrome includes symptomatic and supportive measures. These may include drug therapy to help prevent or treat precocious puberty, surgical removal of pituitary tumors or the thyroid gland, and appropriate treatment of bone lesions and associated abnormalities.

Government Agencies

4192 NIH/ Eunice Kennedy Shriver National Institute of Child Health & Human Development
P.O. Box 3006
Rockville, MD 20847
800-370-2943
Fax: 866-760-5947
www.nichd.nih.gov

Conducts and supports research on topics related to the health of children, adults, families and populations. Some of these topics include: developmental disabilities, growth and development, infant death, reproductive health and birth defects.

Diana W. Bianchi, Director
Alison Cernich, PhD, Deputy Director

4193 NIH/National Institute of Arthritis and Musculoskeletal and Skin Diseases
1 AMS Circle
Bethesda, MD 20892
301-495-4484
877-226-4267
Fax: 301-718-6366
TTY: 301-565-2966
niamsinfo@mail.nih.gov
www.niams.nih.gov

The mission of the NIAMS, a part of the NIH, is to support research into the causes, treatment and prevention of arthritis and musculoskeletal and skin diseases, the training of basic and clinical scientists to carry out this research, and the dissemination of information on research progress in these diseases.

Lindsey A. Criswell, MD, Director
Rick Phillips, Executive Officer

National Associations & Support Groups

4194 American Academy of Pediatrics
345 Park Blvd
Itasca, IL 60143
800-433-9016
Fax: 847-434-8000
mcc@aap.org
www.aap.org

The American Academy of Pediatrics and its member pediatricians are committed to the attainment of optimal physical, mental and social health and well-being for all infants, children, adolescents, and young adults.

Lynn Olson, PhD, VP, Research
Mark Del Monte, JD, CEO/Executive VP
Vera Tait, MD, FAAP, Chief Medical Officer

4195 Genetic Alliance
426400 Woodfield Road, Ste 189
Damascus, MD 20872
202-966-5557
Fax: 202-966-8553
info@geneticalliance.org
www.geneticalliance.org

World's leading nonprofit health advocacy organization committed to transforming health through genetics and promoting an environment of openness centered on the health of individuals, families, and communities.

Sharon Terry, CEO
Ruth Child, CFO
Natasha Bonhomme, Chief Strategy Officer

4196 International Skeletal Dysplasia Registry
UCLA Health
Los Angeles, CA
isdr@mednet.ucla.edu
www.uclahealth.org/departments/ortho/isdr

The International Skeletal Dysplasia Registry (ISDR), which has moved from Cedars-Sinai to UCLA, is a long-term research project that was established in 1970 to assist in the diagnosis, management, and etiology of the skeletal dysplasias.

Daniel Cohn, Co-Director
Deborah Krakow, Co-Director
Ralph Lachman, Co-Director

4197 MAGIC Foundation: Major Aspects of Growth in Children
4200 Cantera Drive, #106
Warrenville, IL 60555

630-836-8200
800-362-4423
Fax: 630-836-8181
contactus@magicfoundation.org
www.magicfoundation.org

A national nonprofit organization providing support and education regarding growth disorders in children and related adult disorders. Provides educational information, networking, a national conference, a kids' program and an extensive medical library.

10,000 members

Dianne Kremidas, Executive Director
Mary Andrews, CEO
Teresa Tucker, Patient Advocacy

4198 March of Dimes Foundation
1550 Crystal Drive, Ste 1300
Arlington, VA 22202

888-663-4637
www.marchofdimes.org

March of Dimes help moms have full-term pregnancies and research the problems that threaten the health of babies. The March of Dimes also acts globally: sharing best practices in perinatal health and helping improve birth outcomes where the needs are the most urgent.

Stacey D. Stewart, President
Alan Brogdon, SVP/COO/Board Officer
Rahul Gupta, MD, SVP & Chief Medical/Health Officer

Web Sites

4199 Human Growth Foundation
997 Glen Cove Avenue, Suite 5
Glen Head, NY 11545

800-451-6434
Fax: 516-671-4055
hgf1@hgfound.org
www.hgfound.org

A voluntary, nonprofit organization whose mission is to help children and adults with disorders of growth and growth hormones through research, education, support and advocacy. The foundation is dedicated to helping medical science to better understand the process of growth. It is composed of concerned parents and friends of children and adults with growth problems; and interested health professionals.

Joel Steelman, MD, President
Emily Germain-Lee, MD, Vice President

4200 University Alabama Birmingham
1720 2nd Ave South
Birmingham, AL 35294

205-934-4011
TDD: 205-934-4642
www.uab.edu/home

Dr. Margaret A. Purcell, Executive Director
Michael A Bownes, Secretary
Linda Beasley, Assistant to Secretary

Book Publishers

4201 Let's Talk About Going to the Hospital
Rosen Publishing Group's PowerKids Press
29 E 21st Street
New York, NY 10010

212-777-3017
800-237-9932
Fax: 888-436-4643
rosenpub@tribeca.ios.com
www.rosenpublishing.com

If a child has to check into the hospital, chances are he or she is already upset about being ill. Knowing how a hospital functions and what the procedures are, such as when family members can visit, will help in what is already a stressful situation. Grades K-5.

24 pages
ISBN: 0-823950-36-0

Roger Rosen, President

Meningitis / Description

Description

4202 MENINGITIS

Covers these related disorders: Bacterial meningitis, Chronic meningitis, Neonatal meningitis, Viral meningitis

Involves the following Biologic System(s):
Infectious Disorders, Neurologic Disorders

Meningitis is an inflammation of the protective membranes that cover the brain and spinal cord (meninges). It most often occurs from infancy to young adulthood, but can develop in persons of any age, and is most commonly caused by a viral (viral meningitis) or bacterial infection (bacterial meningitis) that reaches the meninges by way of the blood and through the cerebrospinal fluid (CSF) that surrounds the brain and spinal cord. Meningitis may also be caused by fungi and other kinds of microorganisms, by noninfectious disease, head injury, medications, and exposure to chemical substances. Cases of meningitis in which no causative infecting organism can be identified are sometimes called aseptic meningitis. However, specialized testing often reveals specific kinds of bacteria or viruses as the cause of such disease.

All types of meningitis are serious and require prompt medical attention to prevent injury to the brain, and death, but bacterial meningitis is typically more serious than viral meningitis. Bacterial meningitis most commonly affects children from 1 month to 5 years old. In children aged approximately 2 months to 12 years, bacterial meningitis is most commonly caused by two species of bacteria: *Neisseria meningitidis* (meningococcus), and *Streptococcus pneumoniae*. These bacteria are spread by the inhalation of airborne cough or sneeze droplets from infected persons, or through contact with feces or other infected body products. Viral meningitis is more common and typically less severe than bacterial meningitis, but is spread in the same way, through saliva, mucus, fecal matter, and other infected body materials.

Symptoms of meningitis include headache and stiff neck, nausea and vomiting, fever, sensitivity to light (photophobia), unnatural sleepiness, confusion, and seizures. Symptoms of meningitis in infants and young children may include irritability and loss of appetite. Meningitis that occurs within the first month of life, known as neonatal meningitis, may produce a different pattern of symptoms than that seen in older infants and children. Such meningitis affects approximately 0.2 to 0.4 in every 1,000 newborns, and is more frequent among infants born prematurely (before 37 weeks). As a result of increased fluid pressure, meningitis in newborns may cause bulging of the skull in the fontanels at the forward sides of the head, where bones of the skull have not fully fused, and enlargement of the head (hydrocephalus). Other symptoms of meningitis in children include coughing and difficulty in breathing. Without prompt treatment, these effects of meningitis can progress to coma and death.

The diagnosis of meningitis, and the type microorganism causing a particular case of infectious meningitis, is made by testing a sample of CSF from the lower back. As the treatment of meningitis proceeds, lumbar puncture and analysis of the CSF are repeated to assess the patient's response to treatment..

Prompt diagnosis and immediate treatment of bacterial meningitis are essential to help prevent brain damage and potentially life-threatening complications. Treatment requires immediate hospitalization and the intravenous administration of antibiotics, as well as careful, close monitoring and measures for reducing the increased pressure on the brain caused by fluid that passes through the inflamed meninges. Antibiotic treatment for bacterial meningitis usually lasts for a couple of weeks, but may continue after a patient is discharged from the hospital. Additional treatment of bacterial meningitis is symptomatic and supportive. Preventive antibiotic therapy may be recommended for persons who have had close contact with children or other persons who have bacterial meningitis. Currently, routine childhood immunization plays an essential role in preventing meningitis caused by the species of bacteria known as Haemophilus influenzae type b (Hib), which used to be one of the most common causes of childhood bacterial meningitis. Vaccines that can protect against some other types of meningitis are also available, such as that caused by *Streptococcus pneumoniae*.

Like bacterial meningitis, viral meningitis requires prompt medical attention, but usually disappears gradually of its own accord within a period of 2 weeks. Because they do not affect viruses, antibiotic drugs are not useful for treating this type of meningitis. Instead, treatment of viral meningitis is usually focused on relieving fever and its other symptoms, and on supporting the patient's respiration, nutrition, and movement. In more severe cases, however medications specifically directed at viruses, known as antiviral drugs, may be given to patients with viral meningitis.

Some patients with meningitis may develop fever, headache, a stiff neck, back pain, vomiting, and other symptoms that last for a month or longer. This condition, known as chronic meningitis, may result from certain bacterial, viral, or other infections, or may be due to noninfectious disorders that can affect the brain, such as sarcoidosis or multiple sclerosis; certain medications, such as some anticancer drugs; or other factors. Individuals whose immune systems have been impaired by disease or by surgical or medical treatment for disease may also be more susceptible to chronic meningitis. The treatment of chronic meningitis is based on the underlying cause of the condition.

For more information on a meningitis vaccine, see chapter on Preventable Childhood Infections.

Government Agencies

4203 NIH/National Institute of Allergy and Infectious Diseases
5601 Fishers Lane, MSC 9806
Bethesda, MD 20892
                                    301-496-5717
                                    866-284-4107
                              Fax: 301-402-3573
                              TDD: 800-877-8339
                        ocpostoffice@niaid.nih.gov
                                www.niaid.nih.gov

The principal advisory board of the NIAID. The council is composed of physicians, scientists and representatives of the public and advises on the conduct and support or research, training and dissemination of health information regarding allergies and infectious diseases.
Anthony S. Fauci, MD, Director

National Associations & Support Groups

4204 American Academy of Pediatrics
345 Park Blvd
Itasca, IL 60143
                                    847-434-4000
                                    800-433-9016
                              Fax: 847-434-8000
                                    csc@aap.org
                                    www.aap.org

The American Academy of Pediatrics and its member pediatricians are committed to the attainment of optimal physical, mental and social health and well-being for all infants, children, adolescents, and young adults.

Kyle E. Yasuda, MD, FAAP, President
Mark Del Monte, JD, CEO/Executive VP
Vera Tait, MD, FAAP, Chief Medical Officer

4205 March of Dimes Foundation
1550 Crystal Drive, Ste 1300
Arlington, VA 22202
888-663-4637
www.marchofdimes.org

March of Dimes help moms have full-term pregnancies and research the problems that threaten the health of babies. The March of Dimes also acts globally: sharing best practices in perinatal health and helping improve birth outcomes where the needs are the most urgent.

Stacey D. Stewart, President
Alan Brogdon, SVP/COO/Board Officer
Rahul Gupta, MD, SVP & Chief Medical/Health Officer

4206 Meningitis Foundation of America
www.musa.org

Goals and objectives are: help support sufferers of Spinal Meningitis and their families; provide information to educate the public and medical professionals about meningitis so that its early diagnosis and treatment will save lives; and support development of vaccines and other preventions.

Web Sites

4207 Maryland Department of Health
www.dhml.state.md.us

www.dhml.state.md.us

Book Publishers

4208 Let's Talk About Going to the Hospital
Rosen Publishing Group's PowerKids Press
29 E 21st Street
New York, NY 10010
212-777-3017
800-237-9932
Fax: 888-436-4643
rosenpub@tribeca.ios.com
www.rosenpublishing.com

If a child has to check into the hospital, chances are he or she is already upset about being ill. Knowing how a hospital functions and what the procedures are, such as when family members can visit, will help in what is already a stressful situation. Grades K-5.

24 pages
ISBN: 0-823950-36-0

Roger Rosen, President

Microcephaly / Description

Description

4209 MICROCEPHALY

Synonyms: Microcephalia, Microcephalism, Microencephaly

Involves the following Biologic System(s):

Neurologic Disorders

Microcephaly is a developmental abnormality in which an infant's or child's head circumference is smaller than would be expected for his or her age and sex (i.e., two or three standard deviations below the mean). In most affected infants and children, underdevelopment of the brain (microencephaly) may result in varying degrees of intellectual disabilities. Microcephaly is considered a relatively common condition, particularly among individuals affected by intellectual disabilities.

In some affected infants and children, microcephaly occurs as an isolated genetic condition. Familial cases of isolated microcephaly have been reported that appear to have autosomal recessive or dominant inheritance. Autosomal recessive microcephaly is characterized by a narrow, sloping forehead; a flat back portion of the head (occiput); varying levels of intellectual disabilities (although severe intellectual disabilities are most common); and, in some cases, episodes of uncontrolled electrical disturbances in the brain (seizures). Autosomal dominant microcephaly may be characterized by mild slanting of the forehead, upslanting eyelid folds (palpebral fissures), prominent ears, short stature, and borderline or mild intellectual disabilities. In others, the condition occurs in association with certain underlying genetic disorders, such as Cornelia de Lange syndrome. It may also be part of chromosomal malformation syndromes, such as trisomy 13 and trisomy 18 syndromes.

Microcephaly may also occur secondary to particular environmental factors, such as exposure before birth to radiation, certain chemical agents (e.g., alcohol), or certain maternal infections (e.g., rubella). In addition, the condition may result from particular conditions (e.g., meningitis, hyperthermia, etc.) during periods of rapid brain development after birth, particularly during the first two years of life.

When infants and children have a very small head circumference, the underlying abnormality may have begun during early embryonic or fetal development. Although the exact cause is not understood, the condition is thought to result from abnormal development of the outer region of the brain (cerebral cortex).

When infants or children are diagnosed with microcephaly, physicians typically take thorough family histories to determine whether other family members are affected or other disorders or syndromes may be present that are associated with microcephaly. The head circumference is measured periodically for a direct comparison to measurements at birth. Head circumference measurements may also be taken of both parents and any siblings. Additional testing may be undertaken to rule out potential underlying disorders or associated conditions. These tests may include advanced imaging techniques (e.g., CT scanning, MRI) of the brain, chromosomal testing (karyotyping), or certain laboratory tests to detect antibodies against certain infectious agents (e.g., rubella titers) in the child's and mother's bloodstream. Treatment of infants and children with microcephaly includes symptomatic and supportive measures, such as the prescription of certain medications to help treat or control seizures (e.g., anticonvulsants) and special education and other multidisciplinary measures to help ensure that affected children with intellectual disabilities reach their potential. Prenatal screening for genetic defects, and genetic counseling for families at risk for known heritable disorders can decrease the incidence of genetically caused intellectual disabilities. Primary care pediatricians lay an important role in consulting with specialists.

Government Agencies

4210 Arc of the United States
1825 K Street NW, Ste 1200
Washington, DC 20006

202-534-3700
800-433-5255
Fax: 202-534-3731
info@thearc.org
www.thearc.org

The Arc of the United States advocates for the rights and full participation of all children and adults with intellectual and developmental disabilities. Together with a network of members and affiliated chapters, they improve systems of support and services; connect families; inspire communities and influence public policy.

Peter V. Berns, CEO

4211 NIH/ Eunice Kennedy Shriver National Institute of Child Health & Human Development
P.O. Box 3006
Rockville, MD 20847

800-370-2943
Fax: 866-760-5947
www.nichd.nih.gov

Conducts and supports research on topics related to the health of children, adults, families and populations. These topics include: developmental disabilities, growth and development, infant death, reproductive health, and rehabilitation.

Diana W. Bianchi, Director
Alison Cernich, PhD, Deputy Director

National Associations & Support Groups

4212 American Academy of Pediatrics
345 Park Blvd
Itasca, IL 60143

847-434-4000
800-433-9016
Fax: 847-434-8000
csc@aap.org
www.aap.org

The American Academy of Pediatrics and its member pediatricians are committed to the attainment of optimal physical, mental and social health and well-being for all infants, children, adolescents, and young adults.

Kyle E. Yasuda, MD, FAAP, President
Mark Del Monte, JD, CEO/Executive VP
Vera Tait, MD, FAAP, Chief Medical Officer

4213 Birth Defect Research for Children
976 Lake Baldwin Lane, Suite 104
Orlando, FL 32814

407-895-0802
staff@birthdefects.org
www.birthdefects.org

Birth Defect Research for Children is a non-profit organization that provides parents and expectant parents with information about birth defects and support services for their children.

Betty Mekdeci, Executive Director

4214 Center for Parent Information and Resources (CPIR)
c/o SPAN, 35 Halsey Street, 4th Floor
Newark, NJ 07102

973-642-8100
malizo@spanadvocacy.org
www.parentcenterhub.org

Family-friendly information and research-based materials on key topics for Parent Centers. Private workspaces for Parent Centers to exchange resources, discuss high-priority topics, and solve mutual challenges. Coordination of parent training efforts throughout the network.

Myriam Alizo, Project Assistant

4215 Genetic Alliance
426400 Woodfield Road, Ste 189
Damascus, MD 20872
202-966-5557
Fax: 202-966-8553
info@geneticalliance.org
www.geneticalliance.org

World's leading nonprofit health advocacy organization committed to transforming health through genetics and promoting an environment of openness centered on the health of individuals, families, and communities.

Sharon Terry, CEO
Ruth Child, CFO
Natasha Bonhomme, Chief Strategy Officer

4216 March of Dimes Foundation
1550 Crystal Drive, Ste 1300
Arlington, VA 22202
888-663-4637
www.marchofdimes.org

March of Dimes help moms have full-term pregnancies and research the problems that threaten the health of babies. The March of Dimes also acts globally: sharing best practices in perinatal health and helping improve birth outcomes where the needs are the most urgent.

Stacey D. Stewart, President
Alan Brogdon, SVP/COO/Board Officer
Rahul Gupta, MD, SVP & Chief Medical/Health Officer

Web Sites

4217 Online Mendelian Inheritance in Man
McKusick-Nathans Institue of Genetic Medicine-JHU
Baltimore, MD 21205
www.omim.org

This database is a catalog of human genes and genetic disorders.

Ada Hamosh, MD, Scientific Director

Microdontia / Description

Description

4218 MICRODONTIA

Synonym: Microdontism

Involves the following Biologic System(s):
Dental Disorders

Microdontia is a term that refers to a developmental dental irregularity in which one or more teeth are abnormally small. This tooth abnormality often occurs in association with certain disorders, conditions, and syndromes and usually affects a single tooth or specific groups of teeth, namely the second or lateral incisors and the molars of the upper jaw. However, in rare instances, microdontia occurs in association with certain other disorders and may affect all or most of the teeth. These other disorders may include pituitary dwarfism, Down's syndrome, and certain forms of congenital heart disease.

Children with certain abnormalities of the face or skull (craniofacial defects) may often exhibit some form of microdontia. These disorders include Turner syndrome, a chromosomal disorder affecting females and characterized by various symptoms including a narrow palate and a small jaw (micrognathia); Crouzon's disease, an autosomal dominant disorder characterized by underdevelopment of the upper jaw and protrusion of the lower jaw (prognathism), a beaked nose, and other symptoms; and cleft lip, a congenital defect in which there is a split or fissure (cleft) in the upper lip. Microdontia is also manifested in several other disorders (e.g., focal dermal hypoplasia, progeria, oculomandibulodyscephaly, oculo-auriculo-vertebral anomaly, and others). Small teeth with a characteristic cone shape are often present in conjunction with missing teeth (anodontia) in certain syndromes known as ectodermal dysplasias, in which there is abnormal development of embryonic tissues that give rise to tooth enamel, hair, nails, skin glands, the outermost layer of the skin (epidermis), the nervous system, the ears and eyes, and mucous membranes of the anus and mouth. Other syndromes that involve microdontia include Williams syndrome, in which the second primary molar of the upper jaw is abnormally small. Aglossia-adactylia syndrome is characterized by partial or total absence of the tongue and missing or abnormally small incisors in the lower jaw.

Microdontia is thought to be genetically transmitted and results from an unknown factor or factors that affect the normal development of the main component of teeth (dentin) and their outermost covering (enamel). This condition is slightly more prevalent in females than males. Treatment may include oral surgery, orthodontic procedures, tooth restoration, and the use of implants or other dental appliances.

Government Agencies

4219 NIH/ Eunice Kennedy Shriver National Institute of Child Health & Human Development
P.O.Box 3006
Rockville, MD 20847
800-370-2943
Fax: 866-760-5947
www.nichd.nih.gov

Conducts and supports research on topics related to the health of children, adults, families and populations. Some of these topics include: developmental disabilities, growth and development, infant death, reproductive health and birth defects.

Diana W. Bianchi, Director
Alison Cernich, PhD, Deputy Director

4220 NIH/National Institute of Dental and Craniofacial Research (NIDCR)
National Institutes of Health
Bldg 31, Rm 2C39, 31 Center Drive, MSC 2560
Bethesda, MD 20892
866-232-4528
nidcrinfo@mail.nih.gov
www.nidcr.nih.gov

The Institute promotes the general health of the American people by improving their oral, dental and craniofacial health. The NIDCR aims to promote health, to prevent diseases and conditions, and to develop new diagnostics and therapeutics.

Rena D'Souza, DDS, PhD, Director
Jonathan Horsford, PhD, Acting Deputy Director

National Associations & Support Groups

4221 American Academy of Pediatrics
345 Park Blvd
Itasca, IL 60143
847-434-4000
800-433-9016
Fax: 847-434-8000
csc@aap.org
www.aap.org

The American Academy of Pediatrics and its member pediatricians are committed to the attainment of optimal physical, mental and social health and well-being for all infants, children, adolescents, and young adults.

Kyle E. Yasuda, MD, FAAP, President
Mark Del Monte, JD, CEO/Executive VP
Vera Tait, MD, FAAP, Chief Medical Officer

4222 American Dental Association
211 E Chicago Avenue
Chicago, IL 60610
312-440-2500
msc@ada.org
www.ada.org

Founded in 1859, the American Dental Association is the oldest and largest national dental society in the world. Since then, the ADA has grown to become the leading source of oral health related information for dentists and their patients.

Raymond A. Cohlmia, Executive Director

Web Sites

4223 American Dental Association
211 E Chicago Avenue
Chicago, IL 60610
312-440-2500
msc@ada.org
www.ada.org

Founded in 1859, the American Dental Association is the oldest and largest national dental society in the world. Since then, the ADA has grown to become the leading source of oral health related information for dentists and their patients.

Raymond A. Cohlmia, Executive Director

4224 Dental Consumer Advisory
toothinfo.com/

toothinfo.com/

Purpose is to provide useful and practical information for the public concerning issues of dental care.

4225 Dental Resources on the Web
dental-resources.com/

dental-resources.com/

Dental sites for education, practices, laboratories, office supplies, dental care and associations.

Description

4226 MIGRAINE HEADACHES

Covers these related disorders: Common migraine (Migraine without aura), Classic migraine (Migraine with aura)

Involves the following Biologic System(s):
Developmental/Behavioral/Psychiatric Disorders

The term migraine refers to a headache that is recurring and accompanied by three or more symptoms or findings that include the presence of certain visual, motor, or other sensations (aura or prodrome) preceding onset; head throbbing; pain on one side of the head (unilateral); nausea; vomiting; and abdominal pain. Additional associated findings include cessation of pain following sleep and a history of migraines in other family members. Migraines are the most common type of recurrent headaches that occur among children. In children younger than 10 years of age, boys are slightly more apt to develop migraines, while adolescent girls and adult females are more prone to migraines than are adolescent boys or adult men. Migraines may be caused by several different factors, alone or in combination. Such factors include genetic influences; stress-related factors; certain foods such as chocolate, citrus fruit, cheese, monosodium glutamate, etc.; red wine; stimuli such as bright lights, loud noises, etc.; medications such as birth control pills; menstruation; and other factors. Pain associated with migraines results from the narrowing and subsequent widening of the arteries that lead to the brain. This action triggers the pain receptors in that region, thus producing the characteristic pain of migraine headaches. More recent theories relate to the role played by the nervous system in the development of migraine headaches. It has been found that nerve cells in blood vessels of the migraine patient release a compound called "substance P." Substance P triggers pain and its release into the arteries is associated with the dilation of blood vessels and the release of histamine and other allergic compounds.

Migraine without aura (formerly called common migraine), is the type of migraine most likely to occur in children. Common migraine is characterized by a pounding or throbbing pain in the front or side(s) of the head. This headache may or may not be one-sided, may persist from one to 24 hours, and is usually accompanied by nausea, vomiting, and abdominal pain. Other associated symptoms may include fever, an unusual sensitivity to light (photophobia), numbness or tingling of the hands and feet, and dizziness or lightheadedness.

Migraine with aura (formerly called classic migraine), is characterized by similar symptoms and findings to those associated with common migraine; however, classic migraine is always preceded by an aura that occurs from 10 to 30 minutes before onset of the headache. This phenomenon may be characterized by visual, motor, or other sensations such as the appearance of shimmering or flashing lights (photopsia) as well as distorted images, loss of vision in part of the visual field (blind spot or scotoma), dizziness, tingling or weakness in an arm or leg, prickling or burning sensation around the mouth, and other irregularities.

In addition to the two primary types of migraine headaches, some children may develop unusual migraine headaches, called migraine variants, that may be characterized by vomiting that recurs at irregular intervals, sudden attacks of dizziness, and confusion. Children with this type of migraine, especially infants, may experience monthly episodes of severe vomiting resulting in excessive fluid loss (dehydration); the loss of essential compounds, known as electrolytes, in the fluid portion of the blood (i.e., sodium, calcium, and potassium); and associated fever, abdominal pain, and diarrhea. Children with migraine variants may at times appear disoriented, hyperactive, and nonresponsive. Other types of migraine include complicated migraine and cluster headaches. Complicated migraines refer to migraine headaches accompanied by neurologic findings that persist beyond the headache and may be further categorized as basilar migraine, ophthalmoplegic migraine, and hemiplegic migraine. These types of headaches may sometimes indicate the presence of an underlying lesion. Basilar migraine is characterized by problems with equilibrium, double or blurred vision, loss of vision in part of the visual field, lack of muscular coordination (ataxia), seizures, or other irregularities. Ophthalmoplegic migraine, which is characterized by paralysis of the eye muscles on the same side as the migraine, does not commonly occur in children. Amaurosis fugax, a variant of complicated migraine, is characterized by reversible blindness or partial blindness in one eye. Hemiplegic migraine is characterized by numbness and muscular weakness or paralysis affecting only one side of the body. It is rare for children to experience more than one hemiplegic migraine episode. Cluster headaches do not commonly occur in children.

Treatment for migraine headaches may first be directed toward prevention by identifying and removing or avoiding stimulating influences such as certain foods, medications, or underlying stress factors. Many children may benefit from simply resting in a quiet, darkened room. Treatment for pain and vomiting associated with migraine headaches may include administration of pain relievers such as acetaminophen or ibuprofen along with drugs to reduce vomiting (antiemetics). These drugs are often administered rectally in suppository form. In more severe episodes, older children and adolescents may require the administration of a preparation called ergotamine, which is most effective if taken during the early stages of the migraine episode. Ergotamine should not be administered to children with hemiplegic migraines. Some children and adolescents may benefit from behavior management therapy. Other treatment is symptomatic and supportive.

Government Agencies

4227 NIH/National Eye Institute
31 Center Drive MSC 2510
Bethesda, MD 20892
301-496-5248
2020@nei.nih.gov
www.nei.nih.gov

Conducts and supports research that helps prevent and treat eye diseases and other disorders of vision. This research leads to sight-saving treatments, reduces visual impairment and blindness, and improves the quality of life for people of all ages. NEI-supported research has advanced our knowledge of how the eye functions in health and disease.

Michael F. Chiang, MD, Director
Santa Tumminia, Deputy Director

National Associations & Support Groups

4228 American Academy of Neurology
201 Chicago Avenue
Minneapolis, MN 55415
612-928-6000
800-879-1960
Fax: 612-454-2746
memberservices@aan.com
www.aan.com

Migraine Headaches / Research Centers

Medical society established to advance the art and science of neurology, and thereby promote the best possible care for patients with neurological disorders by: ensuring appropriate access to neurological care, supporting and advocating for an environment which ensures ethical, high quality neurological care and supporting clinical and basic research in the neurosciences and related fields.

19,000 members

Mary E. Post, Chief Executive Officer
Kelly Ricker, Chief Learning Officer
Kevin C. Myren, Chief Financial Officer

4229 American Academy of Pediatrics
345 Park Blvd
Itasca, IL 60143

847-434-4000
800-433-9016
Fax: 847-434-8000
csc@aap.org
www.aap.org

The American Academy of Pediatrics and its member pediatricians are committed to the attainment of optimal physical, mental and social health and well-being for all infants, children, adolescents, and young adults.

Kyle E. Yasuda, MD, FAAP, President
Mark Del Monte, JD, CEO/Executive VP
Vera Tait, MD, FAAP, Chief Medical Officer

4230 American Headache Society
19 Mantua Road
Mount Royal, NJ 08061

856-423-0043
Fax: 856-423-0082
ahshq@talley.com
www.americanheadachesociety.org

A professional society of health care providers dedicated to the study and treatment of headache and face pain. It was founded in 1959 and sponsors the American Council for Headache Education (ACHE), which will soon become a committee of the AHS.

4231 Child Neurology Foundation
601 W Short Street
Lexington, KY 40508

888-417-3435
info@childneurologyfoundation.org
childneurologyfoundation.org

The Child Neurology Foundation connects partners from all areas of the child neurology community so those navigating the journey of disease diagnosis, management, and care have the ongoing support from those dedicated to treatments and cures.

Amy Brin, Executive Director
Katie Hentges, Director, Programs
Brea McCormley, Director, Development

4232 National Headache Foundation
820 N Orleans, Suite 201
Chicago, IL 60610

312-274-2650
888-643-5552
info@headaches.org
www.headaches.org

Nonprofit organization dedicated to the education of headache sufferers and health care professionals about the causes and treatment of headaches.

Thomas Dabertin, Executive Director

Research Centers

4233 Kennedy Krieger Institute
Pediatric Headache Program
707 N Broadway
Baltimore, MD 21205

443-923-9200
800-873-3377
webmaster@kennedykrieger.org
www.kennedykrieger.org

The Pediatric Headache Program was started in 2005 in order to facilitate the diagnosis, treatment and management of children and adolescents who suffer from persistent headaches, including migraine, tension and chronic daily.

John J Laterra, Program Clinical Coordinator
Terri Holbrook, Neurology/Nursing Staff Coordinator

Web Sites

4234 American Academy of Neurology
201 Chicago Avenue
Minneapolis, MN 55415

612-928-6000
800-879-1960
Fax: 612-454-2746
memberservices@aan.com
www.aan.com

Medical society established to advance the art and science of neurology, and thereby promote the best possible care for patients with neurological disorders by: ensuring appropriate access to neurological care, supporting, and advocating for an environment which ensures ethical, high quality neurological care and supporting clinical and basic research in the neurosciences and related fields.

4235 National Headache Foundation
820 N Orleans, Suite 411
Chicago, IL 60610

312-274-3650
888-643-5552
info@headches.com
www.headaches.org

A nonprofit organization dedicated to educating headache sufferers and healthcare professionals about headache causes and treatments.

Thomas Dabertin, Executive Director

Book Publishers

4236 Freedom From Headaches

Joel Saper, author

Simon & Schuster
100 Front Street
Riverside, NJ 8075

856-461-6500
800-223-2336
Fax: 212-698-7099
www.simonandschuster.com

236 pages paperback
ISBN: 0-671254-04-9

Carolyn Reidy, President and Chief Executive Offic
Liz Perl, Senior Vice President, Marketing
Dennis Eulau, Executive Vice President, Operation

4237 Handbook of Headache

Lippincott Williams & Wilkins
351 W Camden Street
Baltimore, MD 21201

410-528-4000
800-638-3030
www.lww.com

2004 400 pages softbound
ISBN: 0-781752-23-0

Edward B. Hutton Jr., Chief Executive Officer, President
E. Passano Jr., Vice Chairman of the Board and Secr

4238 Headache Book: Prevention & Treatment for All Types of Headaches

Frank B. Minirth, author

Thomas Nelson Publishers
1 Gateway Plaza
Port Chester, NY 10573

914-937-2320
Fax: 914-937-3183
www.fsw.org

1994
ISBN: 0-785282-56-4

Susan B. Wayne, President/CEO
Geoffrey Barsky, CFO
Polly Kerrigan, Senior Vice President Program Opera

4239 **Management of Headache & Headache Medications**
Lawrence D. Robbins, author

Spring-Verlag
175 5th Avenue
New York, NY 10010
646-307-5151
Fax: 212-633-0748
www.us.macmillan.com

1994 294 pages
ISBN: 0-387989-44-7

Stefan von Holtzbrinck, Chairman, Executive Board
Klaus-Dieter Lehmann, Chairman, Supervisory Board
Sandra Dittert, Senior Vice President

4240 **Migraine and Other Headaches: Vascular Mechanisms**
Raven Press
19710 Ventura Blvd., Ste 108
Woodland Hills, CA 91364
818-888-3388
Fax: 818-888-1881
www.raven.com

Leading international experts present new concepts on the mechanisms of migraine and other vascular headaches and detail the latest strategies for diagnosis and treatment of migraine with and without aura, tension-type headaches, cluster headaches and other vascular disorders.

368 pages
ISBN: 0-881677-95-7

4241 **Overcoming Headaches & Migraines**
Longmeadow Press
PO Box 10218
Stamford, CT 06904
203-352-2110

1993 128 pages Paperback
ISBN: 0-681417-92-7

4242 **Treating the Headache Patient**
Roger K. Cady, author

Marcell Dekker, Inc.
270 Madison Avenue
New York, NY 10016
212-696-9000
Fax: 800-228-1160

1994 366 pages
ISBN: 0-824791-09-6

4243 **Wolff's Headaches & Other Head Pain**
Stephen D. Silberstein, author

Oxford University Press
198 Madison Avenue
New York, NY 10016
212-726-6000
800-445-9714
Fax: 919-677-1303
custserv.us@oup.com
www.us.oup.com/us

1993
ISBN: 0-195082-50-8

Newsletters

4244 **Headache**
American Council for Headache Education
19 Mantua Road
Mount Royal, NJ 8061
856-423-0043
Fax: 856-423-0082
achehq@talley.com
www.achenet.org

Provides valuable and current information on new treatments, as well as time-proven headache management strategies. All articles are written or reviewed by headache experts from the American Headache Society (AHS). Recent issues have included articles by headache experts on drug and nondrug treatment options and information on new treatments and research is regularly included.

12 pages Quarterly
Paul Winner, Chair
Arthur H. Elkind MD, President
Vincent Martin MD, Vice President

Pamphlets

4245 **Headache Facts-What Everyone Should Know**
American Council for Headache Education
19 Mantua Road
Mount Royal, NJ 8061
856-423-0043
Fax: 856-423-0082
achehq@talley.com
www.achenet.org

Paul Winner, DO, Chair
Barry Baumel, Chair Of Funding Committee
John Rothrock, Journal Editor

4246 **Impact of Migraine-A Disabling and Costly Condition**
American Council for Headache Education
19 Mantua Road
Mount Royal, NJ 8061
856-423-0043
Fax: 856-423-0082
achehq@talley.com
www.achenet.org

Paul Winner, DO, Chair
Barry Baumel, Chair Of Funding Committee
John Rothrock, Journal Editor

4247 **Migraine and Coexisting Conditions-Other Illnesses That May Affect Migraine**
American Council for Headache Education
19 Mantua Road
Mount Royal, NJ 8061
856-423-0043
Fax: 856-423-0082
achehq@talley.com
www.achenet.org

Paul Winner, DO, Chair
Barry Baumel, Chair Of Funding Committee
John Rothrock, Journal Editor

4248 **What's the Best Medicine for My Headaches?**
American Council for Headache Education
19 Mantua Road
Mount Royal, NJ 8061
856-423-0043
Fax: 856-423-0082
achehq@talley.com
www.achenet.org

Paul Winner, DO, Chair
Barry Baumel, Chair Of Funding Committee
John Rothrock, Journal Editor

4249 **When Are Opioid (Narcotic) Drugs Appropriate for Headache?**
American Council for Headache Education
19 Mantua Road
Mount Royal, NJ 8061
856-423-0043
Fax: 856-423-0082
achehq@talley.com
www.achenet.org

Paul Winner, DO, Chair

4250 **Women and Headache**
American Council for Headache Education
19 Mantua Road
Mount Royal, NJ 8061
856-423-0043
Fax: 856-423-0082
achehq@talley.com
www.achenet.org

Paul Winner, DO, Chair

Milk Protein Allergy/Lactose Intolerance / Description

Description

4251 MILK PROTEIN ALLERGY/LACTOSE INTOLERANCE
Involves the following Biologic System(s):
Gastrointestinal Disorders

Milk protein allergy is an allergic reaction to the proteins found in cow's milk and is the most common food allergy in children. Cow's milk is a large source of nutrition for infants and children. Infant formulas are primarily composed of cow's milk proteins, and milk products are often a major source of calories, protein, vitamins, and minerals in a child's diet. Cow's milk contains proteins, sugars (carbohydrates), as well as fats. Breastmilk can also contain these proteins from the mother's diet. There are several distinct diseases entities that would fall under the category of milk allergy or intolerance.

Most infants show symptoms of cow's milk protein allergy within the first three to six months of exposure. The immune system of the infant recognizes the milk protein as foreign and reacts by making immune proteins (antibodies also known as immunoglobulins) to defend the body against the foreign protein. Milk protein allergy can be either an immediate-onset or delayed-onset allergic reaction. Immediate-onset reactions can manifest acutely with gastrointestinal (diarrhea, vomiting, abdominal pain), respiratory (asthma, wheezing), or dermatologic (eczema, hives) symptoms. Delayed-onset reactions usually manifest with chronic diarrhea that may be bloody (hematochezia). More severe disease leads to small bowel damage and poor weight gain (failure to thrive).

The diagnosis of milk protein allergy can be made by history and physical exam. Stool, blood, skin and/or milk challenge tests may also be used to aid in diagnosis. Milk protein allergy is reported in up to 4% of infants, and usually resolves by age three. Until that time, infants on formula are fed special formulas (hydrolysate formula) and breastfeeding mothers should avoid milk and milk products. Infants with cow's milk protein allergy have a higher chance of having soy milk protein allergy and therefore soy formulas are not recommended. As children get older, milk is slowly reintroduced. Fortunately, most babies outgrow their milk allergies by their second or third year.

Lactose intolerance is not an allergic reaction, but an inability to digest the primary sugar found in milk (lactose). In the small intestine there is an enzyme (lactase) that breaks lactose down into smaller sugars to be used by the body. Symptoms of lactose intolerance include abdominal cramping, bloating, diarrhea, and flatulence. There are large racial differences in the incidence of lactose intolerance; persons of Asian and African descent have a higher incidence in comparison to Caucasians.

Symptoms of lactose intolerance can occur any time after age 5 because lactase enzyme activity peaks in infancy and early childhood. One exception is congenital lactase deficiency. In this genetic disorder, infants are born without the enzyme lactase and symptoms, such as abdominal bloating and diarrhea, occur in the first week of life.

The treatment for lactose intolerance is avoidance of milk or lactase enzyme supplementation (available in pill form or added to milk products).

National Associations & Support Groups

4252 American Academy of Pediatrics
345 Park Blvd
Itasca, IL 60143
847-434-4000
800-433-9016
Fax: 847-434-8000
csc@aap.org
www.aap.org

The American Academy of Pediatrics and its member pediatricians are committed to the attainment of optimal physical, mental and social health and well-being for all infants, children, adolescents, and young adults.

Kyle E. Yasuda, MD, FAAP, President
Mark Del Monte, JD, CEO/Executive VP
Vera Tait, MD, FAAP, Chief Medical Officer

4253 Galactosemia Foundation
350 Northern Boulevard, Suite 324-1079
Albany, NY 12204
www.galactosemia.org

Galactosemia Foundation Inc. is a non-profit charitable organization that advocates for people with galactosemia and their families. Founded in February 1985, Galactosemia Foundation helps provide families information about Galactosemia and facilitates networkings between families, clinicians and researchers.

Nicole Casale, President
Scott Saylor, Treasurer
Jodie Solari, Communications Lead

4254 International Foundation for Functional Gastrointestinal Disorders (IFFGD)
3015 Dunes W Boulevard, Suite 512
Mount Pleasant, SC 29466
414-964-1799
www.iffgd.org

The organization offers responses to those commonly asked questions for families and individuals whose lives have been touched by gastrointestinal disorders.

Nancy J. Norton, Founder
Ceciel T. Rooker, President

4255 North American Society for Pediatric Gastroenterology/Hepatology/Nutrition
714 N Bethlehem Pike, Suite 300
Ambler, PA 19002
215-641-9800
Fax: 215-641-1995
www.naspghan.org

Strives to improve the care of infants, children and adolescents with digestive disorders by promoting advances in clinical care of children with chronic abdominal pain, diarrhea, constipation, vomiting, bleeding from the GI tract, inflammatory bowel disease, liver diseases, diseases of the pancreas, poor weight gain and nutritional problems.

Margaret K Stallings, Executive Director
Kim Rose, Associate Director
Gina Brown, Membership

Web Sites

4256 Galactosemia Foundation
350 Northern Boulevard, Suite 324-1079
Albany, NY 12201
www.galactosemia.org

Galactosemia Foundation Inc. is a non-profit charitable organization that advocates for people with galactosemia and their families. Founded in February 1985, Galactosemia Foundation helps provide families information about Galactosemia and facilitates networkings between families, clinicians and researchers.

Nicole Casale, President
Scott Saylor, Treasurer
Jodie Solari, Communications Lead

4257 International Foundation for Functional Gastrointestinal Disorders (IFFGD)
www.iffgd.org

414-964-1799
www.iffgd.org

Milk Protein Allergy/Lactose Intolerance / Pamphlets

The organization offers responses to those commonly asked questions for families and individuals whose lives have been touched by gastrointestinal disorders.

Nancy J. Norton, Founder
Ceciel T. Rooker, President

4258 NASPGHAN
714 N. Bethlehem Pike, Ste 300
Ambler, PA 19002
215-641-9800
Fax: 215-641-1995
www.naspghan.org

Strives to improve the care of infants, children and digestive disorders by promoting advances in clinical care of children with chronic abdominal pain, diarrhea, constipation, vomiting, bleeding from the GI tract, inflammatory bowel disease, liver diseases, diseases of the pancreas, poor weight gain and nutritional problems.

Margaret K Stallings, Executive Director
Kim Rose, Associate Director
Gina Brown, Membership

Book Publishers

4259 Raising Your Child Without Milk: Reassuring Advice and Recipes For Parent
Simon & Simon
100 Front Street
Riverside, NJ 08075
856-461-6500
800-488-4308
Fax: 800-943-9831
info@simonsays.com
www.simonandschuster.com

This book offers parents of milk-allergic or lactose intolerant children and the most up-to-date medical and nutritional information. It contains 125 dairy free recipes, and answers questions sent in from parents across the country.

384 pages Paperback

Carolyn Reidy, President/CEO
Liz Perl, Senior Vice President, Marketing
Dennis Eulau, Executive Vice President, Operation

4260 What You Need To Know About Lactose Intolerance
NIDDK Health Information Center
1 Information Way
Bethesda, MD 20892
800-860-8747
TTY: 866-569-1162
healthinfo@niddk.nih.gov
catalog.niddk.nih.gov

Defines lactose intolerance and provides information on symptoms, diagnosis and treatment.

16 pages Spanish

Griffin P. Rodgers, M.D, Director

Journals

4261 Managing Food Allergy and Intolerance
Janice Vickerstaff Joneja, PhD, author

J A Hall Publications
2401-9304 Salish Court
Burnaby, BC
Canada
604-738-9688
888-993-6133
Fax: 604-738-9425
www.hallpublications.com

This is a fully-referenced, extensively researched and indexed manual for health care professionals counseling those with food allergy or intolerance.

581 pages
ISBN: 0-968209-80-7

Newsletters

4262 NASPGHAN News
714 N. Bethlehem Pike, Ste 300
Ambler, PA 19002
215-641-9800
Fax: 215-641-1995
www.naspghan.org

Publication of the North American Society for Pediatric Gastroenterolgy, Hepatology and Nutrition, which strives to improve the care of infants, children and adolescents with digestive disorders by promoting advances in clinical care of children with chronic abdominal pain, diarrhea, constipation, vomiting, bleeding from the GI tract, inflammatory bowel disease, liver diseases, diseases of the pancreas, poor weight gain and nutritional problems.

Margaret K Stallings, Executive Director
Kim Rose, Associate Director
Gina Brown, Membership

Pamphlets

4263 Lactose Intolerance
NDDIC
2 Information Way
Bethesda, MD 20892
301-496-3583
800-891-5389
Fax: 703-738-4929
nddic@info.niddk.nih.gov
www.niddk.nih.gov

8 pages

Griffin P. Rodgers, M.D., Director
Dr. Gregory Germino, Deputy Director
Kevin Abbott, Program Director

Mucolipidoses / Description

Description

4264 MUCOLIPIDOSES

Synonym: ML

Involves the following Biologic System(s):

Genetic/Chromosomal/Syndrome/Metabolic Disorders

The mucolipidoses (ML) are inborn errors of metabolism that belong to a group of diseases known as lysosomal storage disorders. Lysosomes are the major digestive structures within cells. Certain proteins known as enzymes break down or digest nutrients, such as particular fats or carbohydrates. The mucolipidoses are characterized by a deficiency or the abnormal functioning of certain lysosomal enzymes, causing the abnormal accumulation of complex carbohydrates (glycosaminoglycans) and fats (lipids) in cells within particular tissues. Such tissues may include those of the brain and spinal cord (central nervous system), skeleton, joints, heart, liver, spleen, or eyes. The mucolipidoses are thought to be inherited as an autosomal recessive trait.

Specific names as well as Roman numerals are used to classify the different forms of ML. Different types of mucolipidosis include I-Cell disease (ML II), pseudo-Hurler polydystrophy (ML III), and Berman syndrome (ML IV). Some forms of ML are further divided into different subtypes, such as sialidosis (ML I) types I and II, based on age of onset, associated symptoms, or other factors.

In children with mucolipidosis, associated symptoms and findings may be variable, depending upon the specific form of ML that is present. However, certain abnormalities occur in association with most forms of ML. Such findings include mild to severe coarsening of facial features, characteristic skeletal abnormalities (known as dysostosismultiplex), changes of the joints, and varying levels of intellectual disabilities. In children with ML, skeletal malformations may include short stature; abnormal front-to-back or sideways curvature of the spine (kyphosis or scoliosis) or both; improper development of the hips (hip dysplasia); abnormally short neck; or premature fusion of the fibrous joints (sutures) between certain bones of the skull. Many affected children may develop joint stiffness and abnormal bending of certain joints in a fixed position (contractures). In addition, in some patients, neuromuscular abnormalities may be present, such as unusually decreased muscle tone (hypotonia) followed by abnormally exaggerated reflexes (hyperreflexia); shock-like contractions of certain muscles or muscle groups (myoclonus); or involuntary, rapid or writhing movements of the arms and legs (choreoathetoid movements).

Some forms of ML may also be associated with distinctive eye abnormalities, such as clouding of the corneas (corneal opacities), the development of abnormal red circular areas of the middle layer of the eyes (cherry-red spots), or other defects, causing visual impairment. Additional physical abnormalities associated with ML may include bulging of part of the intestine through a weak area in the abdominal wall (hernias), enlargement of the liver or spleen, enlargement of the heart or other heart defects, or increased susceptibility to repeated respiratory infections. Some children with these disorders may also experience delays in the acquisition of skills that require the coordination of physical and mental activities and may develop progressively severe intellectual disabilities. Other patients may experience mild, nonprogressive intellectual disabilities. Some of the mucolipidoses may result in potentially life-threatening complications during childhood, adolescence, or young adulthood.

The treatment of children with mucolipidosis is symptomatic and supportive. Such measures may include therapies to help prevent or aggressively treat respiratory infections; surgical correction of joint contractures, heart abnormalities, hernias, or other defects; physical therapy; special education; or other measures as required.

National Associations & Support Groups

4265 American Academy of Pediatrics
345 Park Blvd
Itasca, IL 60143

847-434-4000
800-433-9016
Fax: 847-434-8000
csc@aap.org
www.aap.org

The American Academy of Pediatrics and its member pediatricians are committed to the attainment of optimal physical, mental and social health and well-being for all infants, children, adolescents, and young adults.

Kyle E. Yasuda, MD, FAAP, President
Mark Del Monte, JD, CEO/Executive VP
Vera Tait, MD, FAAP, Chief Medical Officer

4266 March of Dimes Foundation
1550 Crystal Drive, Ste 1300
Arlington, VA 22202

888-663-4637
www.marchofdimes.org

March of Dimes help moms have full-term pregnancies and research the problems that threaten the health of babies. The March of Dimes also acts globally: sharing best practices in perinatal health and helping improve birth outcomes where the needs are the most urgent.

Stacey D. Stewart, President
Alan Brogdon, SVP/COO/Board Officer
Rahul Gupta, MD, SVP & Chief Medical/Health Officer

4267 Mucolipidosis IV Foundation
1440 Spring Street NW
Atlanta, GA 30309

877-654-5459
info@ml4.org
ml4.org

The ML4 Foundation, originally known as CHARM (Children's Association for Research on Mucolipidosis), was founded in 1982 to promote research as well as to reach out to other families affected by this debilitating disease.

Rebecca Oberman, Executive Director

4268 National MPS Society
PO Box 14686
Durham, NC 27709

919-806-0101
877-MPS-1001
www.mpssociety.org

Organization that serves as a support group for those affected by mucopolysaccharidoses and related disorders. Raises funds to promote research and increases awareness of the disorder.

Terri Klein, President & CEO
Matthew Ellinwood, Chief Scientific Officer
Tracy Kirby, Director of Development

Web Sites

4269 Healthfinder
1101 Wootton Parkway
Rockville, MD 20852

healthfinder@hhs.gov
www.healthfinder.gov

Links to carefully selected information and Web sites from over 1,500 health-related organizations.

4270 Mucolipidosis IV Foundation
1440 Spring Street NW
Atlanta, GA 30309

877-654-5459
info@ml4.org
ml4.org

The ML4 Foundation, originally known as CHARM (Children's Association for Research on Mucolipidosis), was founded in 1982 to promote research as well as to reach out to other families affected by this debilitating disease.

Rebecca Oberman, Executive Director

4271 National MPS Society
PO Box 14686
Durham, NC 27709

919-806-0101
877-MPS-1001
www.mpssociety.org

Shares information on the care and management of the children with Mucopolysaccharide diseases. The conference also brings in Medical Researchers reporting on advances in research related to these diseases.

4272 Online Mendelian Inheritance in Man
McKusick-Nathans Institue of Genetic Medicine-JHU
Baltimore, MD 21205   www.omim.org

This database is a catalog of human genes and genetic disorders.

Ada Hamosh, MD, Scientific Director

Book Publishers

4273 Let's Talk About Going to the Hospital
Rosen Publishing Group's PowerKids Press
29 E 21st Street
New York, NY 10010

212-777-3017
800-237-9932
Fax: 888-436-4643
rosenpub@tribeca.ios.com
www.rosenpublishing.com

If a child has to check into the hospital, chances are he or she is already upset about being ill. Knowing how a hospital functions and what the procedures are, such as when family members can visit, will help in what is already a stressful situation. Grades K-5.

24 pages
ISBN: 0-823950-36-0

Roger Rosen, President

Mucopolysaccharidoses / Description

Description

4274 MUCOPOLYSACCHARIDOSES
Synonym: MPS
Involves the following Biologic System(s):
Genetic/Chromosomal/Syndrome/Metabolic Disorders

The mucopolysaccharidoses (MPS) are hereditary metabolic disorders that belong to a group of diseases known as lysosomal storage disorders. Lysosomes are the major digestive units within cells. Enzymes within lysosomes break down nutrients, such as certain fats and carbohydrates. The mucopolysaccharidoses are characterized by deficiency of certain lysosomal enzymes, causing the abnormal accumulation of complex carbohydrates in cells within particular tissues of the body. Affected tissues and organs typically include the skeleton, joints, brain and spinal cord (central nervous system), heart, liver, spleen, and eyes. The genes that encode most of these enzymes have been mapped to particular chromosomes. All of the mucopolysaccharidoses are inherited as an autosomal recessive trait, with the exception of Hunter syndrome, which has X-linked recessive inheritance. Collectively, these disorders are thought to affect approximately one in 10,000 newborns.

The various forms of MPS are typically designated by a Roman numeral and a specific name, such as Hunter syndrome (MPS II) or Sanfilippo syndrome (MPS III). In addition, some forms of MPS are divided into different subtypes, such as Hurler syndrome (MPS I H) and Hurler-Scheie syndrome (MPS I H/S), based on different changes (mutations) of the disease gene, age of onset, clinical course, or other factors. The range and severity of associated symptoms and findings may vary, depending upon the specific form of MPS that is present. However, certain findings are common to most forms of MPS, such as characteristic skeletal abnormalities (known as dysostosis multiplex), changes of the joints, growth delays, a characteristic facial appearance, and progressive intellectual disabilities. For example, beginning in the first year of life or during later childhood, many patients develop progressively coarse facial features. Many children with MPS also experience delays in the acquisition of skills requiring the coordination of physical and mental activities, a gradual loss of previously acquired skills (developmental regression), and progressively severe intellectual disabilities. However, in a few forms of MPS, children may have average intelligence.

Many children with MPS also have short stature; sideways or front-to-back curvature of the spine (scoliosis or kyphosis) or both; other bone abnormalities; joint stiffness; and abnormal bending of certain joints in a fixed position (contractures). Other common findings include clouding of the corneas of the eyes and associated visual impairment, abnormal bulging of part of the intes|tine through a weak area in the abdominal wall (hernias), and enlargement of the liver and spleen (hepatosplenomegaly). Some patients also have associated abnormalities of the heart and its major blood vessels (cardiovascular defects), such as narrowing of the arteries supplying the heart; improper closure of one of the heart valves, allowing blood to leak back into the left upper chamber of the heart (mitral insufficiency); or other cardiac defects. Many of these disorders may result in potentially life-threatening complications during childhood or adolescence.

The treatment of children with MPS includes symptomatic and supportive measures, such as surgical correction of hernias, cardiovascular defects, joint contractures, or other abnormalities as required; physical therapy; or special education. In patients with some forms of MPS, enzyme replacement therapy has been shown to provide some temporary benefit. In addition, bone marrow transplantation may be effective in some patients with certain forms of mucopolysaccharidosis (e.g., Hurler syndrome).

National Associations & Support Groups

4275 American Academy of Pediatrics
345 Park Blvd
Itasca, IL 60143
847-434-4000
800-433-9016
Fax: 847-434-8000
csc@aap.org
www.aap.org

The American Academy of Pediatrics and its member pediatricians are committed to the attainment of optimal physical, mental and social health and well-being for all infants, children, adolescents, and young adults.

Kyle E. Yasuda, MD, FAAP, President
Mark Del Monte, JD, CEO/Executive VP
Vera Tait, MD, FAAP, Chief Medical Officer

4276 March of Dimes Foundation
1550 Crystal Drive, Ste 1300
Arlington, VA 22202
888-663-4637
www.marchofdimes.org

March of Dimes help moms have full-term pregnancies and research the problems that threaten the health of babies. The March of Dimes also acts globally: sharing best practices in perinatal health and helping improve birth outcomes where the needs are the most urgent.

Stacey D. Stewart, President
Alan Brogdon, SVP/COO/Board Officer
Rahul Gupta, MD, SVP & Chief Medical/Health Officer

4277 National MPS Society
PO Box 14686
Durham, NC 27709
919-806-0101
877-MPS-1001
www.mpssociety.org

Organization that serves as a support group for those affected by mucopolysaccharidoses and related disorders. Raises funds to promote research and increases awareness of the disorder.

Terri Klein, President & CEO
Matthew Ellinwood, Chief Scientific Officer
Tracy Kirby, Director of Development

Web Sites

4278 Canadian Society for Mucopolysaccharide & Related Diseases Inc
218-2055 Commercial Drive
Vancouver, BC
Canada
604-924-5130
info@mpssociety.ca
www.mpssociety.ca

The Canadian Society for Mucopolysaccharide and Related Diseases Inc. (The Canadian MPS Society), founded in 1984, serves all Canadians affected by MPS and related diseases through support, education, advocacy and by advancing research.

Kim Angel, Executive Director

4279 Healthfinder
1101 Wootton Parkway
Rockville, MD 20852
healthfinder@hhs.gov
www.healthfinder.gov

Links to carefully selected information and Web sites from over 1,500 health-related organizations.

4280 National MPS Society
PO Box 14686
Durham, NC 27709
919-806-0101
877-MPS-1001
www.mpssociety.org

Shares information on the care and management of the children with Mucopolysaccharide diseases. The conference also brings in Medical Researchers reporting on advances in research related to these diseases.

4281 Online Mendelian Inheritance in Man
McKusick-Nathans Institue of Genetic Medicine-JHU
Baltimore, MD 21205
www.omim.org

This database is a catalog of human genes and genetic disorders.

Ada Hamosh, MD, Scientific Director

4282 Society for Mucopolysaccharide Diseases
MPS House, Repton Place, White Lion Road
Amersham, Bu HP7 9
345-389-9901
Fax: 345-389-9902
mps@mpssociety.org.uk
www.mpssociety.co.uk

A voluntary support group that represents from throughout the UK over 1200 children and adults suffering from mucopolysaccharide and related diseases, their families, caregivers and professionals. It is a registered charity entirely supported by voluntary donations and fundraising. It is managed by the members themselves.

Book Publishers

4283 Let's Talk About Going to the Hospital
Rosen Publishing Group's PowerKids Press
29 E 21st Street
New York, NY 10010
212-777-3017
800-237-9932
Fax: 888-436-4643
rosenpub@tribeca.ios.com
www.rosenpublishing.com

If a child has to check into the hospital, chances are he or she is already upset about being ill. Knowing how a hospital functions and what the procedures are, such as when family members can visit, will help in what is already a stressful situation. Grades K-5.

24 pages
ISBN: 0-823950-36-0

Roger Rosen, President

Description

4284 MUSCULAR DYSTROPHIES

Synonyms: Duchenne muscular dystrophy, Becker muscular dystrophy, Landouzy-Dejerine disease

Involves the following Biologic System(s):
Neurologic Disorders, Orthopedic and Muscle Disorders

Muscular dystrophies are a group of inherited neuromuscular disorders characterized by the progressive weakness and degeneration of muscles without accompanying nerve tissue involvement. Each of these disorders is different from the others with respect to its age of onset, clinical manifestations, severity, course, and underlying genetic defect.

Duchenne muscular dystrophy, the most common of these disorders, is transmitted as an X-linked recessive trait and, as such, is fully expressed in boys; however, on rare occasions, girls who are carriers of the disease gene may exhibit mild symptoms. The incidence rate for this disorder is about one out of every 3,600 newborn boys. Although some affected infants may exhibit signs of diminished muscle tone such as poor head control, most boys do not develop symptoms until three to seven years of age. Early symptoms may include weakness in the pelvic girdle area that may be manifested by an unusual method of moving from the supine position to the standing position (Gowers' sign). In addition, boys with this disorder may develop a waddling manner of walking (Trendelenburg gait), be prone to stumbling and falling, or having difficulty climbing stairs and standing up from a sitting position. As the disease progresses, muscles around the joints may contract resulting in the inability to fully extend the knees and elbows. In addition, the spine may develop a side-to-side curve (scoliosis) and muscles, especially of the calves, become bulky due to the enlargement (hypertrophy) of the muscle fibers, the infiltration of fat into the muscles, and the increase of connective tissue protein (collagen) in the muscles. Other findings include involvement of the heart muscle (cardiomyopathy) and intellectual impairment ranging from learning disabilities to intellectual disabilities. Most boys with Duchenne muscular dystrophy are able to walk until the age of 10 or 12 years, at which time they may be confined to a wheelchair. Life-threatening complications such as pneumonia, respiratory failure, and congestive heart failure often occur during late adolescence or early adulthood. This disorder is believed to result from the deficiency of the essential muscle protein dystrophin. The gene for Duchenne muscular dystrophy is located on the short arm of the X chromosome (Xp21).

Duchenne muscular dystrophy is initially diagnosed through evaluation of physical findings and through tests that show increased blood levels of the enzyme creatinine kinase. Additional diagnostic screening may include the use of an electrical muscle function test called electromyography or EMG. Confirmation, however, must be determined through microscopic examination of a muscle tissue sample (biopsy). Treatment is symptomatic and supportive. For example, nutritional vigilance and immunizations against flu and other childhood diseases may help to avoid or postpone complications. The administration of digitalis medications may help to alleviate certain heart-related complications. Some children may benefit from physical therapy, exercise, or surgical intervention to aid in walking.

Becker muscular dystrophy results in symptoms similar to those of Duchenne muscular dystrophy; however, these symptoms are usually less severe, do not appear until about the age of 10 years, and follow a long course. Patients usually remain ambulatory, and most survive into their 30s and 40s. The gene for Becker muscular dystrophy is also located on the short arm of the X chromosome (Xp21); however, the essential muscle protein dystrophin is defective and dysfunctional rather than deficient.

Less common forms of muscular dystrophy include facioscapulohumeral muscular dystrophy (Landouzy-Dejerine disease), limb-girdle muscular dystrophy, and others. Facioscapulohumeral muscular dystrophy, which is an autosomal dominant disorder occurring in both males and females, is characterized by facial and shoulder muscle weakness and sometimes weakness in the lower legs. This is a relatively mild disease that usually occurs between seven years of age and early or mid-adulthood. The gene for this disorder is located on the long arm of chromosome 4 (4q35). Limb-girdle muscular dystrophy is usually transmitted as an autosomal recessive trait, although autosomal dominant inheritance has also been documented. This disorder usually occurs in late childhood or early adulthood and is characterized by the progressive weakness and degeneration of the muscles of the hips and shoulders. Treatment for these types of muscular dystrophy is symptomatic and supportive.

National Associations & Support Groups

4285 American Academy of Pediatrics
345 Park Blvd
Itasca, IL 60143

847-434-4000
800-433-9016
Fax: 847-434-8000
csc@aap.org
www.aap.org

The American Academy of Pediatrics and its member pediatricians are committed to the attainment of optimal physical, mental and social health and well-being for all infants, children, adolescents, and young adults.

Kyle E. Yasuda, MD, FAAP, President
Mark Del Monte, JD, CEO/Executive VP
Vera Tait, MD, FAAP, Chief Medical Officer

4286 Child Neurology Foundation
601 W Short Street
Lexington, KY 40508

888-417-3435
info@childneurologyfoundation.org
childneurologyfoundation.org

The Child Neurology Foundation connects partners from all areas of the child neurology community so those navigating the journey of disease diagnosis, management, and care have the ongoing support from those dedicated to treatments and cures.

Amy Brin, Executive Director
Katie Hentges, Director, Programs
Brea McCormley, Director, Development

4287 Facioscapulohumeral Dystrophy Society
75 North Main Street, Suite 1073
Randolph, MA 02368

781-301-6060
www.fshsociety.org

The FSHD Society is the world's largest research-focused patient organization for facioscapulohumeral muscular dystrophy (FSHD), one of the most prevalent forms of muscular dystrophy. The Society works to advance and accelerate the development of treatments and a cure to end the pain, disability, and suffering

Mark A. Stone, Chief Executive Director
Jamshid Arjomand, Chief Science Officer
Jess Carter, Operations

4288 Muscular Dystrophy Association
16 N Clark, Ste 3550
Chicago, IL 60601

646-992-2908
800-572-1717
resourcecenter@mda.org
www.mda.org

Muscular Dystrophies / Research Centers

Voluntary health agency aimed at conquering neuromuscular diseases. The diseases in MDA's program include muscular dystrophy, ALS and numerous related muscle-debilitating diseases. With almost 100 field offices and over 150 affiliated MDA Care Centers nationwide, MDA conducts research, provides medical and community services, clinics, support groups, summer camps for youngsters and much more.

R. Rodney Howell, MD, Chairman
Lynn O'Connor Vos, President & CEO
Mary Fiance, Director, PR & Communications

4289 Muscular Dystrophy Family Foundation
PO Box 776
Carmel, IN 46032
317-615-9140
www.mdff.org

Provides adaptive equipment and emotional support to individuals and families affected by one of the over forty neuromuscular diseases. Established in 1958, some of the equipment provided includes: hospital beds, wheelchairs, ramps, communication devices, and lifts.

Hannah Oosterlinck, Executive Director
Kara Hanley, Administrative & Events Coordinator

4290 Parent Project for Muscular Dystrophy
1012 - 14th Street NW, Suite 500
Washington, DC 20005
201-250-8440
800-714-5437
Fax: 201-250-8435
info@parentprojectmd.org
www.parentprojectmd.org

Parent Project Muscular Dystrophy is a not-for-profit organization founded in 1994 by parents of children with Duchenne and Becker muscular dystrophy. Today, the focus is on areas such as; seeking to ensure that all families, caregivers, health care professionals and others have access to state-of-the-art information about treatment and care options for children with Duchenne and Becker MD, and to ensure that the voices of people with and affected by Duchenne and Becker are heard.

Pat Furlong, Founding President & CEO
Kaylan Moitoso, Chief Business Officer
Brian Denger, Community Engagement Coordinator

4291 Reflex Sympathetic Dystrophy Syndrome Association
99 Cherry Street
Milford, CT 06460
203-877-3790
877-662-7737
Fax: 203-882-8362
info@rsds.org
www.rsds.org

The Reflex Sympathetic Dystrophy Syndrome Association was founded in 1984 to promote public and professional awareness of Reflex Sympathetic Dystrophy Syndrome, also known as Complex Regional Pain Syndrome. Educates those afflicted with this syndrome, their family, friends, insurance and healthcare providers, on the disabling pain the syndrome causes.

Jim Broatch, EVP & Director
Jeri Krassner, Special Events Coordinator

Research Centers

4292 Rusk Institute of Rehabilitation Medicine
NYU Langone Medical Center
400 E 34th Street
New York, NY 10016
212-263-6034
Fax: 212-263-8510
www.rusk.med.nyu.edu

The world's first university-affiliated facility devoted entirely to rehabilitation medicine, Rusk is among the most renowned center of its kind for the treatment of adults and children with disabilities-home to innovations and advances that have set the standard in rehabilitation care for every stage of life and for every stage of recovery.

Dr. Steven Flanagan, Professor & Chairman
Marilyn Shoo, Pediatrics Director

Minnesota

4293 Mayo Clinic and Foundation
200 First Street S.W.
Rochester, MN 55905
507-284-2511
800-660-4582
Fax: 507-284-0161
www.mayo.edu

Neuromuscular clinical research center with a primary research interest in neuropathies.

Julie E Hammack, CEO

New York

4294 Columbia Presbyterian Medical Center
Neurology Institute of NY/Research Center
630 W 168th Street
New York, NY 10032
212-305-3880
alscenter@columbia.edu
www.nyp.org

Neuromuscular clinical research center.

Steven J. Corwin, CEO
Robert E. Kelly, President

4295 NYU Rusk Institute
301 East 17th Street, Second Avenue
New York, NY 10003
212-263-6034
Fax: 212-263-8510
www.rusk.med.nyu.edu

Focuses on Muscular Dystrophy and related bone disorders.

Jeffrey Cohen MD, Director
Marilyn Shoo, Pediatrics Director

Ohio

4296 Parent Project for Muscular Dystrophy
1012 - 14th Street NW, Suite 500
Washington, DC 20005
201-250-8440
800-714-5437
Fax: 201-250-8435
info@parentprojectmd.org
www.parentprojectmd.org

Parent Project Muscular Dystrophy is a not-for-profit organization founded in 1994 by parents of children with Duchenne and Becker muscular dystrophy. Today, the focus is on areas such as; seeking to ensure that all families, caregivers, health care professionals and others have access to state-of-the-art information about treatment and care options for children with Duchenne and Becker MD, and to ensure that the voices of people with and affected by Duchenne and Becker are heard.

Pat Furlong, Founding President & CEO
Kaylan Moitoso, Chief Business Officer
Brian Denger, Community Engagement Coordinator

Pennsylvania

4297 Penn Neurological Institute
Hospital of the University of Pennsylvania
3417 Spruce Street
Philadelphia, PA 19104
215-662-3396
800-789-7366
www.pennmedicine.org

Research program centering its efforts on finding better ways to prevent and treat neuromuscular disorders.

Michael E Selzer, Director Neuromuscular Diseases

Muscular Dystrophies / Audio Video

Texas

4298 **Baylor College of Medicine**
Neuromuscular Disease Research
1 Baylor Plaza
Houston, TX 77030
713-798-4951
neurons@bcm.tmc.edu
www.bcm.edu

Offers research into biochemistry, molecular genetics and neuromuscular disorders.

Laura J Morrison, Professor And Chair
Michael Vincent Abene M.D., Assistant Professor
Farah F. Atassi, Instructor

Utah

4299 **University of Utah**
Eccles Institute of Human Genetics
15 N 2030 E, Room 2100
Salt Lake City, UT 84112
801-581-4422
Fax: 801-581-7796
www.genetics.utah.edu

John F Atkins PhD, Research Professor
Mario R. Capecchi Ph.D, Distinguished Professor & Co-Chair
Richard M. Cawthon, M.D. Ph.D., Research Associate Professor

Audio Video

4300 **Muscular Dystrophy**
Films for Humanities/Films Media Group
132 West 31st Street, 17th Floor
New York, NY 10001
800-322-8755
Fax: 609-671-0266
www.films.com

Muscular Dystrophy attacks muscles, so that people lose the ability to walk, talk, and in some cases, to breath. About two thirds of those affected are children, but symptoms can appear any time between birth and adolescence. This video looks at how people deal with a disease that has no cure. A young boy, a six year old girl, and a young mother are managing their disease and show us the medical interventions used to help them live more fully.

1990 VHS/DVD
ISBN: 1-421336-46-4

Web Sites

4301 **Muscular Dystrophy Association**
16 N Clark, Ste 3550
Chicago, IL 60601
646-992-2908
800-572-1717
resourcecenter@mda.org
www.mda.org

Voluntary health agency aimed at conquering neuromuscular diseases.

R. Rodney Howell, MD, Chairman
Lynn O'Connor Vos, President & CEO
Mary Fiance, Director, PR & Communications

4302 **Muscular Dystrophy Family Foundation**
PO Box 776
Carmel, IN 46082
317-615-9140
www.mdff.org

Provides adaptive equipment and emotional support to individuals and families affected by one of the over forty neuromuscular diseases. Established in 1958, some of the equipment provided includes: hospital beds, wheelchairs, ramps, communication devices, and lifts.

Hannah Oosterlinck, Executive Director
Kara Hanley, Administrative & Events Coordinator

4303 **Parent Project for Muscular Dystrophy**
1012 - 14th Street NW, Suite 500
Washington, DC 20005
201-250-8440
800-714-5437
Fax: 201-250-8435
info@parentprojectmd.org
www.parentprojectmd.org

Parent Project Muscular Dystrophy is a not-for-profit organization founded in 1994 by parents of children with Duchenne and Becker muscular dystrophy. Today, the focus is on areas such as; seeking to ensure that all families, caregivers, health care professionals and others have access to state-of-the-art information about treatment and care options for children with Duchenne and Becker MD, and to ensure that the voices of people with and affected by Duchenne and Becker are heard.

Pat Furlong, Founding President & CEO
Kaylan Moitoso, Chief Business Officer
Brian Denger, Community Engagement Coordinator

Book Publishers

4304 **Journey of Love: Parent's Guide to Duchenne Muscular Dystrophy**
Muscular Dystrophy Association
222 S. Riverside Plaza, Ste 1500
Chicago, IL 60606
520-529-2000
800-572-1717
Fax: 520-529-5300
mda@mdausa.org
www.mda.org/publications/journey/misc.html

Complete guide for parents with children diagnosed with DMD. Information includes explanation of the disease, treatments, research, services provided by MDA, guides to finding assistance and more. Available in paperback and online; free from a local MDA office to families with a member affected by DMD or BMD who is registered with the MDA.

1988 170 pages

Kristine Welker, Interim President/CEO
Valerie A. Cwik, MD, EVP, Chief Medical & Scientific
Julie Faber, EVP, CFO

4305 **Let's Talk About Going to the Hospital**
Rosen Publishing Group's PowerKids Press
29 E 21st Street
New York, NY 10010
212-777-3017
800-237-9932
Fax: 888-436-4643
rosenpub@tribeca.ios.com
www.rosenpublishing.com

If a child has to check into the hospital, chances are he or she is already upset about being ill. Knowing how a hospital functions and what the procedures are, such as when family members can visit, will help in what is already a stressful situation. Grades K-5.

24 pages
ISBN: 0-823950-36-0

Roger Rosen, President

4306 **Medifocus Guidebook On Reflex Sympathetic Dystrophy**
Medifocus.Com
11529 Daffodil Lane, Suite 200
Silver Spring, MD 20902
301-649-9300
800-965-3002
info@medifocus.com
www.medifocus.com

A patient's comprehensive guide to treatment options and the latest medical advances for RSD. The book provides information about the signs and symptoms of RSD, the treatment options including drug therapy, sympathetic nerve blocks, chemical and surgical sympathectomy, physical therapy, and other methods used for controlling pain and improving quality of life. Updated regularly, purchase includes free updates for 1 year. Available online or in print; see website for details of print vs. online.

April 2009 130 pages Print

4307 Muscular Dystrophy and Allied Diseases: Impacts on Patients, Family, and Staff
Leon I Charash, author
Center for Thanatology Research & Education
391 Atlantic Avenue
Brooklyn, NY 11217
718-858-3026
Fax: 718-852-1846
thanatology@pipeline.com
www.thanatology.org

An Internet best-seller, it covers Duchenne Muscular Dystrophy, psychosocial aspects, anticipatory grief of parents, education issues, etc.

1988 90 pages Paper
ISBN: 0-930194-38-1

Roberta Halporn, Director

4308 Muscular Dystrophy and Other Neuromuscular Diseases
Haworth Press
711 Third Avenue
New York, NY 10017
212-216-7800
800-429-6784
Fax: 212-244-1563
getinfo@haworthpress.com
www.tandf.co.uk

A thoughtful book from professionals who assist persons afflicted with neuromuscular disorders to help them and their families adapt to lifestyle changes accompanying the onset of these disorders.

1991 250 pages Hardcover
ISBN: 1-560240-77-6

4309 Realities in Coping with Progressive Neuromuscular Diseases
Charles C. Thomas
2037 Chestnut Street, PO Box 15715
Philadelphia, PA 19103
215-561-2786
Fax: 215-600-1248
mailbox@charlespresspub.com
www.charlespresspub.com

248 pages Hardcover
ISBN: 0-914783-20-3

4310 Travis:I Got Lots of Neat Stuff Children Living with Muscular Dystrophy
Kathy L Gordon, author
Muscular Dystrophy Association
222 S. Riverside Plaza, Ste 1500
Chicago, IL 60606
800-572-1717
publications@mdausa.org
www.mda.org/publications/travis/

Travis' mother shares his story with other children, helping them to accept their muscular dystrophy and see the world of possibilities before them.

Online

Kristine Welker, Interim President/CEO
Valerie A. Cwik, MD, EVP, Chief Medical & Scientific
Julie Faber, EVP, CFO

Magazines

4311 MDA/ALS Newsmagazine
Muscular Dystrophy Association
222 S. Riverside Plaza, Suite 1500
Chicago, IL 60606
520-529-2000
800-322-8755
Fax: 520-529-5300
publications@mdausa.org
www.mda.org

A national magazine that goes out to everyone registered with MDA, MDA clinics, reseacgers and subscribers. It presents news related to ALS including research, personal profiles, fund raising activities, patient services, and lifestyle information including products and trends.

125,000 circ Bimonthly

Kristine Welker, Interim President/CEO
Valerie A. Cwik, MD, EVP, Chief Medical & Scientific
Julie Faber, EVP, CFO

4312 Quest Magazine
MDA Publications
222 S. Riverside Plaza, Suite 1500
Chicago, IL 60606
520-529-2000
800-322-8755
Fax: 520-529-5300
publications@mdausa.org
www.mda.org

A national magazine that goes out to everyone registered with MDA, MDA clinics, researchers and subscribers. It presents news related to muscular dystrophy and other neuromuscular diseases including research, personal profiles, fund raising activities, patient services, and lifestyle information including products and trends.

Bimonthly

Steven M. Derks, President and CEO
Valerie A. Cwik, M.D., EVP, Chief Medical & Scientific
Julie Faber, EVP, CFO

Pamphlets

4313 Breathe Easy: Respiratory Care in Neuromuscular Disorders
Muscular Dystrophy Association
222 S. Riverside Plaza, Suite 1500
Chicago, IL 60606
520-529-2000
800-322-8755
Fax: 520-529-5300
publications@mdausa.org
www.mda.org/publications/breathe/

Respiratory health is a vital issue for children and adults with NMDs, which progressively weaken muscles, sometimes including those we need to breathe. A guide to respiratory care for children with muscular dystrophy. This guide is the result of efforts by a number of highly respected experts in the fileds of NMDs and children's medicine. Also available in Spanish and online.

2006

Kristine Welker, Interim President/CEO
Valerie A. Cwik, MD, EVP, Chief Medical & Scientific
Julie Faber, EVP, CFO

4314 Conference on the Cause and Treatment of Facioscapulohumeral Muscular Dystrophy
National Inst. of Neurological Disorders/Stroke
P.O. Box 5801
Bethesda, MD 20824
301-496-5751
800-352-9424
www.ninds.nih.gov

4315 Congressional Testimony on Muscular Dystrophy
National Inst. of Neurological Disorders/Stroke
P.O. Box 5801
Bethesda, MD 20824
301-496-5751
800-352-9424
www.ninds.nih.gov

Testimony by Dr. Audrey Penn, Acting Director, NINDS, from February, 2001.

4316 Everybody's Different, Nobody's Perfect
Muscular Dystrophy Association
222 S. Riverside Plaza, Suite 1500
Chicago, IL 60606
520-529-2000
800-572-1717
Fax: 520-529-5300
mda@mdausa.org
www.mda.org/publications/nobody/

Explains how muscular dystrophy affects children and describes how people are different from each other in many ways. Emphasizing fun, friendship, and caring, this booklet is ideal for heightening awareness and encouraging understanding of persons with disabilities. Pre-school edition also available; and in Spanish and online.

Muscular Dystrophies / Pamphlets

1999 11 pages
Kristine Welker, Interim President/CEO
Valerie A. Cwik, MD, EVP, Chief Medical & Scientific
Julie Faber, EVP, CFO

4317 Facts About Duchenne and Becker Muscular Dystrophies
Muscular Dystrophy Association
222 S. Riverside Plaza, Suite 1500
Chicago, IL 60606
520-529-2000
800-322-8755
Fax: 520-529-5300
publications@mdausa.org
www.mda.org/publications/

Describes in layman's terms Duchenne and Becker Muscular Dystrophies and addresses the most currently asked questions about these diseases, research, inheritance and treatments. Also available in Spanish or online.

2009
Kristine Welker, Interim President/CEO
Valerie A. Cwik, MD, EVP, Chief Medical & Scientific
Julie Faber, EVP, CFO

4318 Facts About Facioscapulohumeral Muscular Dystrophy
Muscular Dystrophy Association
222 S. Riverside Plaza, Suite 1500
Chicago, IL 60606
520-529-2000
800-322-8755
Fax: 520-529-5300
publications@mdausa.org
www.mda.org/publications/

Explains facioscapulohumeral muscular dystrophy (FHSD) in layman's terms and answers commonly asked questions. Also available in Spanish.

2009 20 pages Paperback
Kristine Welker, Interim President/CEO
Valerie A. Cwik, MD, EVP, Chief Medical & Scientific
Julie Faber, EVP, CFO

4319 Facts About Inflammatory Myopathies-DM, PM and IBM
Muscular Dystrophy Association
222 S. Riverside Plaza, Suite 1500
Chicago, IL 60606
520-529-2000
800-322-8755
Fax: 520-529-5300
publications@mdausa.org
www.mda.org/publications/fa-myosi.html

Outlines these forms of inflammatory myopathy. Current approaches to treatment and MDA's efforts in continued research are described. Also available in Spanish and online.

Kristine Welker, Interim President/CEO
Valerie A. Cwik, MD, EVP, Chief Medical & Scientific
Julie Faber, EVP, CFO

4320 Facts About Limb-Girdle Muscular Dystrophy
Muscular Dystrophy Association
222 S. Riverside Plaza, Suite 1500
Chicago, IL 60606
520-529-2000
800-322-8755
Fax: 520-529-5300
publications@mdausa.org
www.mda.org/publications/fa-lgmd.html

Overview of the various forms of LGMD encompassed by MDA's program. Addresses commonly asked questions and highlights MDA's research efforts aimed at finding the causes of and effective treatments for these disorders. Also available in Spanish and online.

2007 19 pages
Kristine Welker, Interim President/CEO
Valerie A. Cwik, MD, EVP, Chief Medical & Scientific
Julie Faber, EVP, CFO

4321 Facts About Metabolic Diseases of Muscle
Muscular Dystrophy Association
222 S. Riverside Plaza, Suite 1500
Chicago, IL 60606
520-529-2000
800-322-8755
Fax: 520-529-5300
www.mda.org/publications/fa-metab.html

Provides an overview of the 10 heritable metabolic diseases of muscle encompassed by MDA's program. Addresses commonly asked questions and highlights MDA's research efforts aimed at finding the causes of and effective treatments for these disorders. Also online and in Spanish.

Kristine Welker, Interim President/CEO
Valerie A. Cwik, MD, EVP, Chief Medical & Scientific
Julie Faber, EVP, CFO

4322 Facts About Mitochondrial Myopathies
Muscular Dystrophy Association
222 S. Riverside Plaza, Suite 1500
Chicago, IL 60606
520-529-2000
800-572-1717
Fax: 520-529-5300
publications@mdausa.org
www.mda.org/publications/mitchondrial_myopathies.htm

Explains Mitochondrial myopathies in layman's terms and answers the most frequently asked questions about this disease. Also available in Spanish and online.

2008 24 pages
Kristine Welker, Interim President/CEO
Valerie A. Cwik, MD, EVP, Chief Medical & Scientific
Julie Faber, EVP, CFO

4323 Facts About Muscular Dystrophy
Muscular Dystrophy Association
222 S. Riverside Plaza, Suite 1500
Chicago, IL 60606
520-529-2000
800-322-8755
Fax: 520-529-5300
www.mda.org/publications/fa-md-help.html

Answers many questions commonly asked about the forty-plus forms of the disease encompassed by MDA's program.

Kristine Welker, Interim President/CEO
Valerie A. Cwik, MD, EVP, Chief Medical & Scientific
Julie Faber, EVP, CFO

4324 Facts About Myasthenia Gravis (MG, LEMS, & CMS)
Muscular Dystrophy Association
222 S. Riverside Plaza, Suite 1500
Chicago, IL 60606
520-529-2000
800-322-8755
Fax: 520-529-5300
publications@mdausa.org
www.mda.org/publications/fa-mg.html

Explains myasthenia gravis and Lambert-Eaton syndrome in layman's terms and answers the most frequently asked questions about these diseases. Also available in Spanish and online.

2001 19 pages
Kristine Welker, Interim President/CEO
Valerie A. Cwik, MD, EVP, Chief Medical & Scientific
Julie Faber, EVP, CFO

4325 Facts About Myopathies
Muscular Dystrophy Association
222 S. Riverside Plaza, Suite 1500
Chicago, IL 60606
520-529-2000
800-322-8755
Fax: 520-529-5300
www.mda.org/publications/fa-myop.html

Describes the six inheritable myopathies encompassed by MDA's program, as well as current methods for diagnosing and managing these disorders. Also online and in Spanish.

2003
Kristine Welker, Interim President/CEO
Valerie A. Cwik, MD, EVP, Chief Medical & Scientific
Julie Faber, EVP, CFO

4326 Facts About Myotonic Muscular Dystrophy
Muscular Dystrophy Association
222 S. Riverside Plaza, Suite 1500
Chicago, IL 60606
520-529-2000
800-322-8755
Fax: 520-529-5300
publications@mdausa.org
www.mda.org/publications/fa-mmd.html

Muscular Dystrophies / Government Agencies

Basic knowledge about Myotonic Muscular Dystrophy, precautions, treatments, research and answers to most commonly asked questions. Also available in Spanish and online.

2009 23 pages

Kristine Welker, Interim President/CEO
Valerie A. Cwik, MD, EVP, Chief Medical & Scientific
Julie Faber, EVP, CFO

4327 Facts About Plasmapheresis
Muscular Dystrophy Association
222 S. Riverside Plaza, Suite 1500
Chicago, IL 60606
520-529-2000
800-322-8755
Fax: 520-529-5300
publications@mdausa.org
www.mda.org/publications/fa-plasmaph.html

Describes plasmapheresis, a plasma exchange procedure often utilized as a treatment for autoimmune diseases such as myasthenia gravis and Lambert-Eaton syndrome. Available in paperback or online.

2005

Kristine Welker, Interim President/CEO
Valerie A. Cwik, MD, EVP, Chief Medical & Scientific
Julie Faber, EVP, CFO

4328 Facts About Rare Muscular Dystrophies
Muscular Dystrophy Association
222 S. Riverside Plaza, Suite 1500
Chicago, IL 60606
520-529-2000
800-322-8755
Fax: 520-529-5300
publications@mdausa.org
www.mda.org

This brochure gives basic facts about four forms of muscular dystrophy (congenital, distal, Emery-Dreifuss and oculopharyngeal) and addresses commonly asked questions. Also available in Spanish.

28 pages

Kristine Welker, Interim President/CEO
Valerie A. Cwik, MD, EVP, Chief Medical & Scientific
Julie Faber, EVP, CFO

4329 Genetics and Neuromuscular Diseases
Muscular Dystrophy Association
222 S. Riverside Plaza, Suite 1500
Chicago, IL 60606
520-529-2000
800-322-8755
Fax: 520-529-5300
publications@mdausa.org
www.mda.org

An up-to-date review of genetics information relating to neuromatic diseases, specifically describing what a genetic disorder is, genetic testing and counseling and inheritance patterns. Also available in Spanish and online.

19 pages

Kristine Welker, Interim President/CEO
Valerie A. Cwik, MD, EVP, Chief Medical & Scientific
Julie Faber, EVP, CFO

4330 Hey! I'm Here, Too!
Irwin M Siegel, MD, author

Muscular Dystrophy Association
222 S. Riverside Plaza, Suite 1500
Chicago, IL 60606
520-529-2000
800-322-8755
Fax: 520-529-5300
publications@mdausa.org
www.mda.org/publications/hey/

Help for siblings of boys with Duchenne muscular dystrophy. Explores how they feel about themselves, their brothers, and their families. Also provides specific answers to some questions that siblings may wonder about. Has the option for an introduction for parents or for children. Available online and in Spanish.

1989

Kristine Welker, Interim President/CEO
Valerie A. Cwik, MD, EVP, Chief Medical & Scientific
Julie Faber, EVP, CFO

4331 Learning to Live with Neuromuscular Disease: A Message for Parents
Muscular Dystrophy Association
222 S. Riverside Plaza, Suite 1500
Chicago, IL 60606
520-529-2000
800-322-8755
Fax: 520-529-5300
publications@mdausa.org
www.mda.org/publications/learning/

Intended to help parents and families cope with the knowledge that their child has a neuromuscular disease and with the impact the disease will have on everyday life. Online and in Spanish.

2006

Kristine Welker, Interim President/CEO
Valerie A. Cwik, MD, EVP, Chief Medical & Scientific
Julie Faber, EVP, CFO

4332 MDA Fact Sheet
Muscular Dystrophy Association
222 S. Riverside Plaza, Suite 1500
Chicago, IL 60606
520-529-2000
800-572-1717
Fax: 520-529-5300
publications@mdausa.org
www.mda.org/publications/

Outlines the history of MDA, the diseases included in MDA's program, and the services available through the Association.

Kristine Welker, Interim President/CEO
Valerie A. Cwik, MD, EVP, Chief Medical & Scientific
Julie Faber, EVP, CFO

4333 MDA Services for the Individual, Family and Community
Muscular Dystrophy Association
222 S. Riverside Plaza, Suite 1500
Chicago, IL 60606
520-529-2000
800-322-8755
Fax: 520-529-5300
publications@mdausa.org
www.mda.org/publications/mdasvcs/

Contains a list of the diseases covered by MDA as well as eligibility criteria for MDA's services program, a list of MDA-sponsored clinics nationwide, and the services available through these clinics. Also in Spanish and online.

2009

Kristine Welker, Interim President/CEO
Valerie A. Cwik, MD, EVP, Chief Medical & Scientific
Julie Faber, EVP, CFO

4334 MDA Summer Camp Brochure
Muscular Dystrophy Association
222 S. Riverside Plaza, Suite 1500
Chicago, IL 60606
520-529-2000
800-322-8755
Fax: 520-529-5300
www.mda.org/clinics/camp

Highlights the activities of MDA summer camps for youngsters diagnosed with one of the more than 40 diseases in MDA's program. Shares camper and volunteer reactions. Also available in Spanish and online.

Kristine Welker, Interim President/CEO
Valerie A. Cwik, MD, EVP, Chief Medical & Scientific
Julie Faber, EVP, CFO

4335 Neuromuscular Disease Guidebooks & Pamphlets
222 S. Riverside Plaza, Suite 1500
Chicago, IL 60606
520-529-2000
800-572-1717
Fax: 520-529-5300
publications@mdausa.org
www.mda.org/services/guidebooks-and-pamphlets

Guides to everyday living with NMD's.

Kristine Welker, Interim President/CEO
Valerie A. Cwik, M.D., EVP, Chief Medical & Scientific
Julie Faber, EVP, CFO

Muscular Dystrophies / Camps

4336 Teacher's Guide to Neuromuscular Disease
Muscular Dystrophy Association
222 S. Riverside Plaza, Suite 1500
Chicago, IL 60606

520-529-2000
800-322-8755
Fax: 520-529-5300
publications@mdausa.org
www.mda.org/publications/tchrdmd/

A source of guidance and information to educators detailing neuromuscular disease, how it affects school participation, and ways that teachers can help meet the academic and social needs of students affected by the disorder. Online and in Spanish.

2005

Kristine Welker, Interim President/CEO
Valerie A. Cwik, MD, EVP, Chief Medical & Scientific
Julie Faber, EVP, CFO

4337 Workshop on Therapeutic Approaches for Duchenne Muscular Dystrophy
National Inst. of Neurological Disorders/Stroke
PO Box 5801
Bethesda, MD 20824

301-496-5751
800-352-9424
www.ninds.nih.gov/news_and_events/proceedings/

Camps

4338 MDA Summer Camp
Muscular Dystrophy Association
222 S. Riverside Plaza, Suite 1500
Chicago, IL 60606

520-529-2000
800-322-8755
Fax: 520-529-5300
mda@mdausa.org
www.mda.org/clinics/camp

With over 90 camps across the country MDA camp is a magical place where year-round skills are developed and where a child with a disability can just be a kid. In addition to camp and medical staff, most campers have their own 1-on-1 volunteer to help with fun and personal care. Activites are designed for young people with limited mobility or wheelchairs, and include swimming, boating, baseball, football, horseback riding, arts, crafts and talent shows. Free for families registered with MDA.

Kristine Welker, Interim President/CEO
Valerie A. Cwik, MD, EVP, Chief Medical & Scientific
Julie Faber, EVP, CFO

Description

4339 NARCOLEPSY

Synonyms: Gelineau's syndrome, Hypnolepsy, Paroxysmal sleep

Involves the following Biologic System(s):

Neurologic Disorders

Narcolepsy refers to a sleep disorder characterized by profound drowsiness during the day and sudden daytime attacks of sleep that may last from a few seconds to one or more hours. These episodes are sometimes accompanied by sudden loss of muscle tone (hypotonia) in response to emotional stimuli such as anger, fear, joy, or surprise (cataplexy). During a cataplectic episode, the patient remains conscious but is not able to speak or move. Some patients experience sleep paralysis and are unable to move at the onset of sleep or immediately upon waking. Hypnagogic hallucinations are disquieting occurrences that take place at onset of sleep or, less commonly, upon awakening. During these hallucinations, patients may see or hear things that are not grounded in reality. In most cases, narcolepsy begins during adolescence or early adulthood and persists throughout the life of the affected individual. Sleep attacks associated with narcolepsy may occur at any time and may take place many times during the day; however, most individuals may be easily awakened.

Very few people with narcolepsy exhibit all the symptoms associated with this disorder and, occasionally, children and adults who do not have this disorder may experience similar signs and symptoms. For this reason, diagnosis of narcolepsy may necessitate confirmation by a sleep study which uses a procedure called electroencephalography (EEG), during which electrical brain-wave activity is recorded. An EEG may demonstrate an abnormal sleep pattern in which rapid eye movement or REM-type sleep occurs at the onset of sleep. There are no pathologic changes that occur in the brain. In individuals who do not have narcolepsy, REM sleep or periods of deep sleep normally follow nonrapid eye movement sleep (NREM). The cause of narcolepsy is unknown, but researchers think that, in some cases, it may be related to genetic influences as evidenced by the tendency of this disorder to occur within families. Approximately 200,000 people in the United States are affected by narcolepsy.

Treatment for narcolepsy may include regular napping and the administration of stimulant medications to control attacks of drowsiness and sleep, while antidepressant medications may help control episodes of cataplexy. Because this disorder may increase the risk of accidents, appropriate care and caution is advised in the performance of certain tasks or jobs. Other treatment is symptomatic and supportive.

Government Agencies

4340 NIH/National Institute of Neurological Disorders and Stroke (NINDS)
PO Box 5801
Bethesda, MD 20824

800-352-9424
www.ninds.nih.gov

Works to reduce the burden of neurological disease by conducting, fostering, coordinating and guiding research on the causes, prevention, diagnosis and treatment of neurological disorders and stroke, while supporting basic research in related scientific areas.

Walter J. Koroshetz, MD, Director

National Associations & Support Groups

4341 American Academy of Pediatrics
345 Park Blvd
Itasca, IL 60143

847-434-4000
800-433-9016
Fax: 847-434-8000
csc@aap.org
www.aap.org

The American Academy of Pediatrics and its member pediatricians are committed to the attainment of optimal physical, mental and social health and well-being for all infants, children, adolescents, and young adults.

Kyle E. Yasuda, MD, FAAP, President
Mark Del Monte, JD, CEO/Executive VP
Vera Tait, MD, FAAP, Chief Medical Officer

4342 American Academy of Sleep Medicine
2510 N Frontage Road
Darien, IL 60561

630-737-9700
Fax: 630-737-9790
contact@aasm.org
aasm.org

As the leading voice in the sleep field, the AASM sets standards and promotes excellence in sleep medicine health care, education, and research. The AASM has a combined membership of 11,000 accredited member sleep centers and individual members, including physicians, scientists, and other health care professionals.

Steve Van Hout, Executive Director

4343 Child Neurology Foundation
601 W Short Street
Lexington, KY 40508

888-417-3435
info@childneurologyfoundation.org
childneurologyfoundation.org

The Child Neurology Foundation connects partners from all areas of the child neurology community so those navigating the journey of disease diagnosis, management, and care have the ongoing support from those dedicated to treatments and cures.

Amy Brin, Executive Director
Katie Hentges, Director, Programs
Brea McCormley, Director, Development

4344 Genetic Alliance
426400 Woodfield Road, Ste 189
Damascus, MD 20872

202-966-5557
Fax: 202-966-8553
info@geneticalliance.org
www.geneticalliance.org

World's leading nonprofit health advocacy organization committed to transforming health through genetics and promoting an environment of openness centered on the health of individuals, families, and communities.

Sharon Terry, CEO
Ruth Child, CFO
Natasha Bonhomme, Chief Strategy Officer

4345 NIH/National Institute of Neurological Disorders and Stroke (NINDS)
PO Box 5801
Bethesda, MD 20824

800-352-9424
www.ninds.nih.gov

Works to reduce the burden of neurological disease by conducting, fostering, coordinating and guiding research on the causes, prevention, diagnosis and treatment of neurological disorders and stroke, while supporting basic research in related scientific areas.

Walter J. Koroshetz, MD, Director

4346 Narcolepsy Network
3242 NE 3rd Avenue, Suite 1101
Camas, WA 98607

401-667-2523
888-292-6522
info@narcolepsynetwork.org
www.narcolepsynetwork.org

Narcolepsy / State Agencies & Support Groups

Nonprofit organization that serves as a resource center, to assist support groups, to educate the public, to facilitate early diagnosis, to protect the rights of those with narcolepsy, and to encourage on-going scientific research in sleep medicine.

Amy Kant, Transition Director
Christine Hackenbruck, Operations & Program Manager

4347 **National Sleep Foundation**
1414 NE 42nd St, Ste 400
Seattle, WA 98105

contact@sleepfoundation.org
www.sleepfoundation.org

Works to improve the quality of life for millions of Americans who suffer from sleep disorders, and to prevent the catastrophic accidents that are related to poor or disordered sleep through research, education and the dissemination of information towards the cause of the Narcolepsy Project. Seeks patients to aid new research project targeting the cause of the disorder.

Bill Fish, General Manager

State Agencies & Support Groups

Arizona

4348 **Arizona Sleep Disorders Center**
University of Arizona, College of Medicine
1501 N Campbell Avenue, PO Box 245017
Tucson, AZ 85724

520-626-4555
Fax: 520-626-6623
www.medicine.arizona.edu/centers/index.cfm

The newest addition to the University of Arizona's College of Medicine. Program and website under development at time of publication.

Steven Goldschmid, Dean
Judith DiMarco, Associate Dean

California

4349 **Loma Linda University Sleep Disorders Cent er**
11139 Anderson St.
Loma Linda, CA 92350

909-558-6344
Fax: 909-558-6343
www.llu.edu

Richard H Hart, CEO
Philip M. Gold, Medical Director
Richard E. Chinnock, MD, Medical Director

4350 **Stanford University Center for Narcolepsy**
450 Broadway Street, Pav B, 2nd Floor
Redwood City, CA 94063

650-721-7550
Fax: 650-721-3466
www.med.stanford.edu/school/psychiatry/narcolepsy/

Theodore Chen, Director

Connecticut

4351 **Gaylord Hospital Sleep Medicine**
Gaylord Farm Road, PO Box 400
Wallingford, CT 06492

203-284-2800
866-429-5673
TTY: 203-284-2700
TDD: 203-284-2700
lcrispino@gaylord.org
www.gaylord.org

Nadine Cartwright

District of Columbia

4352 **Georgetown University Sleep Disorders Center**
3800 Reservoir Road NW
Washington, DC 20007

202-444-2000
Fax: 202-444-2336
pme2@gunet.georgetown.edu
www.georgetownuniversityhospital.org

Anne O'Donnel, Chair
Raoul L Wientzen, President

Indiana

4353 **Methodist Hospital Sleep Disorders Center**
Rehab Centers
8701 Broadway
Merrillville, IN 46410

219-738-5500
800-909-3627
Fax: 219-738-6624
www.methodisthospitals.org

Ian E. McFadden, President/CEO
Robin Logsdon, Manager

4354 **MidWest Medical Center - Sleep Disorders Center**
3232 N Meridian Street
Indianapolis, IN 46208

317-927-2100

Kenneth Wiesert, MD

4355 **Sleep Disorder Center, St Elizabeth Medica l Center**
1501 Hartford Street, PO Box 7501
Lafayette, IN 47903

766-423-6518
800-371-6011
Fax: 765-423-6525
www.glhsi.org

Dr Shahid M Ahsan, Medical Director

4356 **Sleep Disorders Center-Good Samaritan Hospital**
520 S 7th Street
Vincenne, IN 47591

812-885-3988
812-882-5220
gsh@gshvin.org
www.gshvin.org/goodsamaritan/

4357 **Sleep/Wake Disorders Center-Community Heal th Network**
1500 N Ritter Avenue, Suite 451
Indianapolis, IN 46219

317-355-1411
Fax: 317-351-2785
sleepcenter@ecommunity.com
www.ecommunity.com/sleep/

Marvin E Vollmer, MD, Co-Director

Maryland

4358 **Johns Hopkins University Sleep Disorders Center**
Francis Scott Key Medical Center
301 Bayview Boulevard
Baltimore, MD 21224

410-550-0571
Fax: 410-550-3374
nschube1@jhmi.edu

Alan Schwartz, MD, Medical Director

Massachusetts

4359 **Sleep Disorders Unit, Beth Israel Hospital**
330 Brookline Avenue
Boston, MA 02215

617-667-7000
800-439-0183
Fax: 617-975-5506
patsite@bidmc.harvard.edu
www.bidmc.org

Stephan B. Kay, Chair
Daniel Jick, First Vice Chair
Carol Anderson, Vice Chairperson

Michigan

4360 **Center for Sleep Science at University of Michigan**
University of Michigan Health System
2799 West Grand Boulevard Cfp3
Detroit, MI 48202

313-916-5176
Fax: 313-916-5150
dhudgel1@hfhs.org
www.med.umich.edu/umsleepscience/

The center's main goal is to advance knowledge and understanding in these three areas: the physiology of normal sleep; the diagnosis of sleep disorders; and the treatment of sleep problems.

Ronald D Chervin MD, Director
Barbara T Felts MD, Pediatrics

Minnesota

4361 Center for Sleep Diagnostics
1455 St. Frances Ave.
Shakopee, MN 55379
952-428-3000
askstfrancis@allina.com
www.st-francis-shakopee.com

Is dedicated to providing information, education, and support for all your sleep needs. Our goal is to be the center of sleep information and discussion on the internet.

David Zelinsky, Chair
Kelly J. DiGrado, Vice Chairman
Lee Shimek, Secretary

New Hampshire

4362 Dartmouth-Hitchcock Sleep Disorders Center Dartmouth Medical Center
One Medical Center Drive
Lebanon, NH 03756
603-650-7534
Fax: 603-650-7820
www.dartmouth-hitchcock.org

Rocco R Addante, Director
Glen Greenough MD, Fellowship Director
Joanne MacQuarrie, BS,RPSGT,RRT, Administrator

4363 Sleep/Wake Disorders Center, Hampstead Hospital
218 East Road
Hampstead, NH 03841
603-329-5311
Fax: 603-329-4746
www.hampsteadhospital.com

Philip Kubaik, CEO
Cynthia Gove, COO
Scott Ranks, Director support Services

New Jersey

4364 Newark Sleep Disorders Center
Newark Beth Israel Medical Center
201 Lyons Avenue
Newark, NJ 07112
973-926-7163
Fax: 973-926-6672
www.njsleephelp.com

Dr Monroe S Karetzky, Director

New York

4365 Capital Regional Sleep-Wake Disorders Center
Saint Peter's Hospital & Albany Medical Center
1220 New Scotland Road
Slingerlands, NY 12159
518-439-4326
Fax: 518-439-6143
bwenzel@stpetershealthcare.org
www.capitalregionspecialsurgery.com/sleep-wake/

William Wenzel, Manager

4366 Center for Sleep Medicine of the Mount Sinai Medical Center
Box 1232, One Gustave L Levy Place
New York, NY 10029
212-241-6500
800-637-4624
Fax: 212-987-5584
www.mountsinai.org

Kenneth L. Davis, President/CEO
Dennis S. Charney, Executive VP
Douglas Jabs, CEO

4367 Columbia Presbyterian Medical Center Sleep Disorders Center
630 West 168th St
New York, NY 10032
212-305-5371
Fax: 212-305-5496
www.nyp.org

Ronald E Drusin

4368 Saint Joseph's Hospital Health Center Sleep Laboratory
301 Prospect Ave.
Syracuse, NY 13203
315-448-5111
888-785-6371
www.sjhsyr.org

George Deptula, Chairperson
Kathryn H. Ruscitto, President
Sister Mary Obrist, Secretary

4369 Sleep Center, Community General Hospital
4900 Broad Road
Syracuse, NY 13215
315-492-5877
www.chg.org

Robert Westlake, MD

4370 Sleep Disorders Center of Western New York Millard Fillmore Hospital
3 Gates Circle
Buffalo, NY 14209
716-887-5337
Fax: 716-887-5332
drifkin@kaleidahealth.org
www.sleepcenterwny.com

Daniel Rifkin MD, Medical Director

4371 Sleep Disorders Center, University Hospital
101 Nicolls Road
Stony Brook, NY 11794
631-444-4000
Fax: 631-444-8821
craig.lehmann@stonybrook.edu
www.healthtechnology.stonybrookmedicine.edu

Craig A. Lehmann, Dean
Richard W. Johnson, Associate Dean
Carol Vidal, Associate Dean for community Engage

4372 Sleep-Wake Disorders Center, Montefiore Sleep Disorders Center
111 E 210th Street
Bronx, NY 10467
718-920-4841
Fax: 718-798-4352
www.cloud9.net/~thorpy/mmc

Center that provides diagnostic and treatment services for children with sleep disorders, such as sleep apnea, narcolepsy, insomnia, daytime sleepiness, sleepwalking, or night terrors.

Michael J Thorpy, MD, Medical Director
Karen Balaban-Gil, MD

4373 Sleep-Wake Disorders Center, New York Presbyterian Hospital
Cornell Medical Center
21 Bloomingdale Road
White Plains, NY 10605
914-997-5751
800-694-7533
Fax: 914-682-6911
www.cornellphysicians.com/sleepWake/

Provides outpatient diagnostic evaluation and treatment for adults and children with problems associated with sleeping and waking. More common pediatric sleep problems include complaints of difficulty falling asleep and staying asleep, snoring, sleep apnea, sleepwalking, sleep terrors, nightmares, excessive difficulty waking up, bedwetting, and narcolepsy. Many can be successfully treated in one or several visits although some may require an overnight or daytime sleep study.

Margaret Moline, PHD, Director

4374 Unity Sleep Disorders Clinic Unity Health System
89 Genesee Street
Rochester, NY 14611
585-723-7000
Fax: 585-442-6259
www.unityhealth.org

Narcolepsy / State Agencies & Support Groups

Warren Hern, President/CEO
Annette Leahy, President
Tom Crilly, Executive VP/CFO

4375 Winthrop-University Hospital Sleep Disorders Center
1300 Franklin Avenue, Suite UL-5
Garden City, NY 11530
516-663-3907
Fax: 516-663-4788
www.winthrop.org/departments/specialtycenters/?id=31
Charles M. Strain, Chairman
John F. Collins, President/CEO
Michael Weinstein, Medical Director

Ohio

4376 Bethesda Oak Hospital, Sleep Disorders Center
619 Oak St.
Cincinnati, OH 45206
513-569-5400
Fax: 513-745-1691
michael_fletcher@trihealth.com
www.trihealth.com

Anthony P Borzotta

4377 Center for Sleep & Wake Disorders, Miami Valley Hospital
One Wyoming Street
Dayton, OH 45409
937-208-8000
Fax: 937-208-2006
www.miamivalleyhospital.com

M Dallal, Manager

4378 Cleveland Clinic Foundation, Sleep Disorders Center
9500 Euclid Avenue FA20
Cleveland, OH 44195
216-444-4508
800-223-2273
Fax: 216-445-6205
foldvan@ccf.org
my.clevelandclinic.org

Petra Podmore, Manager

4379 Kettering Medical Center, Sleep Disorders Center
3095 Dayton-Xenia Rd
Beavercreek, OH 45439
937-458-4010
www.ketteringhealth.org

George G. Burton MD, Medical Director

4380 NW Ohio Sleep Disorders Center
Toledo Hospital
2121 Hughes Drive Harris-McIntosh Tower 2nd Floor
Toledo, OH 43606
419-291-5629
Fax: 419-479-6954
pam.lang@promedica.org
www.nwosemsleep.org

Navin K. Jain, President
Michael Neeb, VP
James Kusina, Secretary

4381 Ohio Sleep Medicine Institute
4975 Bradenton Avenue
Dublin, OH 43017
614-766-0773
Fax: 614-766-2599
info@sleepmedicine.com
www.sleepmedicine.com

Dr. Markus Schmidt, MD, President
Dr. Asim Roy, Clinic Associate

4382 Ohio State University Hospitals, Sleep Disorders Center
410 W 10th Avenue
Columbus, OH 43210
614-293-8652
Fax: 614-257-2551
www.medicalcenter.osu.edu

Larry Anstine, CEO

4383 Saint Vincent Medical Center, Sleep Disorders Center
3829 Woodley Road Suite 1
Toledo, OH 43606
419-250-5702
Fax: 419-251-0574
www.stvincent.org

Joseph Schaffer, PhD, Director
Gary Fammartino, Site Admin

Pennsylvania

4384 Community Medical Center, Sleep Disorders Clinic
1800 Mulberry Street
Scranton, PA 18510
570-969-8000
www.cmchealthsys.org

Michael Aronica, Director

4385 Crozer-Chester Medical Center
Sleep Disorders Center
Department of Neurology
Upland-Chester, PA 19013
610-447-2689
800-254-3258
CKHSInfo@crozer.org
www.crozerkeystone.org

Joan Richards, President/CEO
Calvin Stafford, MD, Director

4386 Geisinger Wyoming Valley Medical Center, Sleep Disorders Center
1000 E. Mountain Blvd.
Wilkes-Barre, PA 18711
570-808-7300
800-275-6401
Fax: 570-826-7650
lvender@geisinger.edu
www.geisinger.org

John W. McBurney, MD, Medical Director

4387 Lankenau Hospital, Sleep Disorders Center
100 Lancaster Avenue
Wynnewood, PA 19096
484-476-2000
866-CAL- MLH
Fax: 610-645-2291
pressmanm@mlhs.org
www.mainlinehealth.org

Sandra V Abramson, Director

4388 Medical College of Pennsylvania, Sleep Disorders Center
3300 Henry Avenue
Philadelphia, PA 19129
215-842-6000

Farhana Bashar, Director

4389 Mercy Hospital of Johnstown, Sleep Disorders Center
1086 Franklin Street
Johnstown, PA 15905
814-534-9000

William F Pruchnic, Director

4390 Penn Center for Sleep Disorders, Hospital of the University of Pennsylvania
3624 Market Street, Suite 201
Philadelphia, PA 19104
215-590-3703
800-789-PENN
Fax: 215-590-2632

Indira Gurubhagavatula, MD, Director

4391 Presbyterian-University Hospital, Pulmonary Sleep Evaluation Center
200 Lothrop Street
Pittsburgh, PA 15213
412-647-2345
www.upmc.com

Mark Sanders, MD, Director

4392 Thomas Jefferson University Sleep Disorders Center
Jefferson Medical College
Suite 500, 211 S 9th St
Philadelphia, PA 19107
215-955-6175
Fax: 215-923-8219
www.jeffersonhospital.org

Karl Doghramji, MD, Director

4393 Western Psychiatric Institute & Clinic, Sleep Evaluation Center
3811 O'Hara Street
Pittsburgh, PA 15213
412-624-3934
Fax: 412-246-5300

David Alan Lewis, Director

Narcolepsy / Research Centers

Rhode Island

4394 Sleep Disorders Center of Lifespan Hospitals
Rhode Island Hospital
167 Point Street
Providence, RI 02903
401-444-3500
Fax: 404-431-5429
www.lifespan.org

Timothy J. Babineau, President/CEO
Kenneth E. Arnold, Senior Vice-President
August Cordeiro, President

Texas

4395 Sleep Disorders Center for Children
Children's Medical Center of Dallas
1935 Medical District Dr
Dallas, TX 75235
214-456-7000
Fax: 214-456-8740
larry.brewer@childrens.com
www.childrens.com

Dr S K Naqvi, Medical Director
Dr John Herman PhD, Contact for Children

4396 Sleep Medicine Associates of Texas
5477 Glen Lakes Drive, Suite 100
Dallas, TX 75231
214-750-7776
Fax: 214-750-4621
www.sleepmed.com

Philip M Becker, President

4397 University of Texas Sleep/Wake Disorders Center
Southwestern Medical Center
5323 Harry Hines Boulevard
Dallas, TX 75235
214-648-3111
Fax: 214-648-3112

Studies sleep/wake disorders including insomnia, apnea and narcolepsy.

Howard Roffwrag, MD, Director

Research Centers

Illinois

4398 Center for Narcolepsy Research at the University of Illinois at Chicago
College of Nursing M/C 802
845 S Damen Avenue
Chicago, IL 60612
312-996-5176
Fax: 312-996-7008
CNSHR@listserv.uic.edu
www.uic.edu

David W. Carley, PhD, Director
Mary Kapella, Associate Director
Julie Law, Center Administration

Iowa

4399 Mercy Sleep Laboratory
Mercy Medical Center
1111 6th Avenue
Des Moines, IA 50314
515-358-9600
Fax: 515-643-8905
cmann@mercydesmoines.org
www.mercydesmoines.org

Sleep is an integral part of life, but it's not always a welcome or peaceful close to a busy day. Some people suffer almost unbearable torture as they toss and turn. Others find sleepiness an uncontrollable intruder. It's been estimated that 30 to 40 percent of the population suffers from a sleeping problem at some time in their lives. Mercy's Sleep Center helps patients with sleep problems.

Donald L. Burrows, MD, Medical Director

Maine

4400 Sleep Laboratory, Maine Medical Center
930 Congress Street
Portland, ME 04102
207-662-4535
Fax: 207-662-6005
www.mmc.org

Christopher W. Emmons, Chairman
Frank H. Frye, Vice-Chairman
Richard W. Peterson, President

Maryland

4401 University of Maryland Medical Center
Pediatric Sleep Disorders Center
22 S Greene Street
Baltimore, MD 21201
866-408-6885
800-492-5538
TDD: 800-735-2258
www.umm.edu

Carol J Blaisdell MD, Director

Ohio

4402 Tri-State Sleep Disorders Center Center for Research in Sleep Disorders
1275 E Kemper Road
Cincinnati, OH 45246
513-671-3101
800-838-4322
Fax: 513-671-4159
www.tristatesleep.com

Provides diagnostics and treatment services to thousands of people in Cincinnati and throughout the country at our state-of-the-art sleep clinic through cutting edge research efforts.

Martin B Scharf, Executive Director
Dr. David Berkowitz
Cara Zurmehly PA-C

Texas

4403 Baylor Sleep Wellness Center
Baylor Clinic
6620 Main Street
Houston, TX 77030
713-798-1000
800-229-5671
www.baylorclinic.com

A comprehensive program with a multidisciplinary approach to sleep disorders.

Sr Shyam Subramanian, Director, Sigworth
VP Rose, Clinical Psychologist

4404 University of Texas Medical Branch at Galveston, Clinical Research Center
301 University Boulevard
Galveston, TX 77555
409-772-2222
800-917-8906
Fax: 409-772-6216
public.affairs@utmb.edu
www.utmb.edu

Research focusing on sleep disorders including apnea and narcolepsy.

David L. Callender, President
Cary W. Cooper, VP/Dean
William R. Elger, Executive VP

Narcolepsy / Audio Video

Audio Video

4405 Narcolepsy
Fanlight Productions
32 Court Street
Brooklyn, NY 11201
718-488-8900
800-876-1710
Fax: 718-488-8642
info@fanlight.com
www.fanlight.com

Presents the experiences of three individuals whose lives and relationships have been disrupted by narcolepsy, while offering solid, comprehensive scientific information about the disorder. ISBN: DVD: 1-57295-974-6; VHS: 1-572953-23-2

25 minutes DVD or VHS

Ben Achtenberg, President
Anthony Sweeney, Marketing Director
Nicole Johnson, Publicity Coordinator

4406 Narcolepsy: Evaluation and Treatment
American Academy of Sleep Medicine
2510 North Frontage Road
Darien, IL 60561
630-737-9700
Fax: 630-737-9790
www.aasmnet.org

A 97 slide presentation designed as a foundation for a teaching curriculum on the recognition and traetment of narcolepsy.

Timothy I. Morgenthaker, MD, President
Nathaniel F. Watson, MD, President-Elect
Ronald D. Chervin, MD, MS, Secretary/Treasurer

Web Sites

4407 National Center for Biotechnology Information
National Library of Medicine, 8600 Rockville Pike
Bethesda, MD 20894
888-346-3656
info@ncbi.nlm.nih.gov
www.ncbi.nlm.nih.gov

NCBI's mission is to develop new information technologoes to aid in the understanding of fundamental molecular and genetic processes that control health and disease.

Patricia Flatley Brennan, RN, PhD, Director
James Ostell, PhD, Executive Secretary

4408 Online Mendelian Inheritance in Man
McKusick-Nathans Institue of Genetic Medicine-JHU
Baltimore, MD 21205
www.omim.org

This database is a catalog of human genes and genetic disorders.

Ada Hamosh, MD, Scientific Director

4409 Sleep Disorders
http://talhost.net/sleep/narcolepsy.htm

http://talhost.net/sleep/narcolepsy.htm

Descriptions of certain sleep disorders and useful links.

4410 Talk About Sleep
www.talkaboutsleep.com

www.talkaboutsleep.com

Sleep disorder information and resources.

Book Publishers

4411 Narcolepsy Primer
Montefiore Medical Center
111 E 210th Street
Bronx, NY 10467
718-920-4321
info@montefiore.org
www.montefiore.org

A guide for physicians, patients and their families on the affects, causes and prevention of narcolepsy.

Steven M. Safyer, MD, President/CEO
Philip O. Ozuah, Chief Operating Officer
Joel A. Perlman, Chief Financial Officer

4412 Psychosocial Aspects of Narcolepsy
Meeta Goswami, author

Haworth Press
PO BOX 8002
Aston, PA 19014
800-234-1340
Fax: 800-875-1340
info@omnigraphics.com
www.omnigraphics.com

Addresses the diagnosis, treatment and management of narcolepsy with particular emphasis on psychological and social aspects of care.

567 pages Hardcover
ISBN: 1-560242-22-1

Peter Ruffner, Publisher

4413 Sleep Disorders Sourcebook
Omnigraphics
615 Griswold Street, Ste 520
Detroit, MI 48226
610-461-3548
800-234-1340
Fax: 800-875-1340
contact@omnigraphics.com
www.omnigraphics.com

Basic consumer health information about sleep and its disorders, including narcolepsy, insomnia, sleepwalking, sleep apnea, and restless leg syndrome.

504 pages 4th Ed.
ISBN: 0-780814-74-5

4414 Sleep Disorders and Psychiatry
Daniel J Buysse MD, author

American Psychiatric Publishing
1000 Wilson Boulevard, Ste 1825
Arlington, VA 22209
703-907-7322
800-368-5777
Fax: 703-907-1091
appi@psych.org
www.appi.org

Summarizes the major categories of sleep disorders including parasomnias and narcolepsy.

2005 256 pages Paperback
ISBN: 1-585622-29-0

Robert E. Hales, M.D., Editor-in-Chief
Rebecca D. Rinehart, Publisher
John McDuffie, Editorial Director

Pamphlets

4415 Living with Narcolepsy
National Sleep Foundation
1010 N. Glebe Road, Suite 310
Arlington, VA 22201
703-243-1697
Fax: 202-347-3472
www.sleepfoundation.org

For people with narcolepsy and their families; defines and describes narcolepsy, as well as the effects on education, social and family life.

packet of 25

Charles A. Czeisler, PhD, MD, Chairman
Max Hirshkowitz, PhD, Vice Chairman
Joseph Ojile, MD, Secretary

4416 Narcolepsy
American Academy of Sleep Medicine
2510 North Frontage Road
Darien, IL 60561
630-737-9700
Fax: 630-737-9790
www.aasmnet.org

Describes the causes, symptoms and treatments of a disorder characterized by excessive sleepiness.

Lot of 50

Timothy I. Morgenthaker, MD, President
Nathaniel F. Watson, MD, President-Elect
Ronald D. Chervin, MD, MS, Secretary/Treasurer

Neonatal Herpes Simplex / Description

Description

4417 NEONATAL HERPES SIMPLEX

Synonym: Congenital herpes

Involves the following Biologic System(s):

Infectious Disorders, Neonatal and Infant Disorders

Neonatal herpes simplex refers to an infection of the newborn caused by the herpes simplex virus (HSV) that is transmitted before birth from mother to fetus through the placenta, or more commonly, during birth as the baby passes through the birth canal. There are two strains of herpes simplex virus known as HSV-1 and HSV-2. Herpes simplex virus type 1 commonly causes infections of the skin and mucous membranes of the lips, mouth, and eyes, while type 2 typically causes genital herpes as well as approximately 75 percent of all neonatal herpes simplex infections.

Herpes simplex may be categorized as an initial (primary) infection or a recurrent infection. After an initial infection, the virus becomes inactive or latent; however, the virus may be reactivated by many different factors including stress, sun exposure, suppression of the immune system, and certain foods or drugs. Mothers with a primary genital herpes simplex virus infection have an approximately 45 percent chance of transmitting HSV-2 to their infants, while risk of transmission from a recurrent infection is less than five percent. In addition, newborns are at risk for HSV-1 transmission through such direct contact as kissing near the eyes or mouth by someone with a cold sore.

Symptoms of HSV infection transmitted through contact with infectious secretions during the birthing process may occur anywhere from one to four weeks after birth and may sometimes commence with the appearance of small, fluid-filled blisters (vesicles) on the skin or inflammation of the front part of the eyeball (cornea) and the delicate mucous membranes (conjunctiva) that line the inside of the eyelids and the whites of the eyes (keratoconjunctivitis). Other findings may include fever, drowsiness, loss of muscle tone, irritability, seizures, and inflammation of the liver (hepatitis) and brain (encephalitis), as well as other severe irregularities. If left untreated, HSV infection may cause potentially life-threatening complications. Some infants may have no skin involvement but manifest such symptoms as fluctuating temperature, listlessness, poor sucking, chills, shaking, nausea, vomiting, and diarrhea.

Transmission of the herpes simplex virus through the placenta is a rare but potentially life-threatening occurrence. This type of infection usually affects the skin, eyes, and central nervous system and is characterized by blister-type rashes and scarring, abnormally small eyes (microphthalmia) and other eye abnormalities, an abnormally small head (microcephaly), and brain and spinal cord irregularities. Some infants may also have hepatitis or lung involvement.

Prevention of neonatal herpes simplex infection may include delivery by Cesarean section, especially if the mother has a primary genital herpes infection. Treatment is directed toward early diagnosis and intervention. Such therapy may include the intravenous administration of antiviral drugs such as acyclovir in conjunction with regular testing to preclude possible associated toxic side effects related to kidney dysfunction. Eye involvement may indicate the application of antiviral ointments or drops directly into the eyes. Other treatment is symptomatic and supportive.

Government Agencies

4418 NIH/National Institute of Allergy and Infectious Diseases
5601 Fishers Lane, MSC 9806
Bethesda, MD 20892

301-496-5717
866-284-4107
Fax: 301-402-3573
TDD: 800-877-8339
ocpostoffice@niaid.nih.gov
www.niaid.nih.gov

The principal advisory board of the NIAID. The council is composed of physicians, scientists and representatives of the public and advises on the conduct and support or research, training and dissemination of health information regarding allergies and infectious diseases.

Anthony S. Fauci, MD, Director

National Associations & Support Groups

4419 American Academy of Pediatrics
345 Park Blvd
Itasca, IL 60143

847-434-4000
800-433-9016
Fax: 847-434-8000
csc@aap.org
www.aap.org

The American Academy of Pediatrics and its member pediatricians are committed to the attainment of optimal physical, mental and social health and well-being for all infants, children, adolescents, and young adults.

Kyle E. Yasuda, MD, FAAP, President
Mark Del Monte, JD, CEO/Executive VP
Vera Tait, MD, FAAP, Chief Medical Officer

4420 American Sexual Health Association
PO Box 13827
Research Triangle Park, NC 27709

919-361-8400
Fax: 919-361-8425
info@ashasexualhealth.org
www.ashasexualhealth.org

The American Sexual Health Association (ASHA) empowers individuals, families, and communities to achieve sexually healthy lives through education and advocacy. ASHA is an award-winning non-profit organization that has advocated on behalf of those at risk for sexually transmitted infections (STIs) since 1914.

Lynn Barclay, President & CEO
Deborah Arrindell, Vice President, Health Policy

Web Sites

4421 American Sexual Health Association
www.ashasexualhealth.org

919-361-8400
Fax: 919-361-8425
info@ashasexualhealth.org
www.ashasexualhealth.org

The American Sexual Health Association (ASHA) empowers individuals, families, and communities to achieve sexually healthy lives through education and advocacy. ASHA is an award-winning non-profit organization that has advocated on behalf of those at risk for sexually transmitted infections (STIs) since 1914.

4422 Health Research Program (HaRP)
www.harpnet.org

www.harpnet.org

A program by USAID, the project strives to improve the health status of infants, children, mothers and families through the development and research of new tools, technologies, policies and approaches.

4423 HerpeSite
www.herpesite.org

800-273-8255
TTY: 800-799-4889
www.herpesite.org

Provides online personal empowerment and support; a compendium of information outlining aspects and issues relating to Herpes Simplex Virus.

4424 Herpes.com
www.herpes.com

www.herpes.com

Purpose of this website is to fill the desperate need for herpes education, make it easier to manage herpes, inform people of ways to limit herpes reoccurrences, to inform people of the beneficial products for herpes sufferers, to show the relationship between good health and herpes, to provide an opportunity for herpes sufferers to share their personal experiences and to provide communication via our live chat.

4425 Infectious Diseases in Children
6900 Grove Road
Thorofare, NJ 8086

856-848-1000
editor@healio.com
http://idinchildren.com

A leading provider of healthcare information, educational programs, and meeting and exhibit management services worldwide.

4426 International Herpes Alliance
www.herpesalliance.org

www.herpesalliance.org

4427 Virtual Pediatric Hospital
www.virtualpediatrichospital.org

www.virtualpediatrichospital.org

A digital library of pediatric informaion dedicated to helping patients find the highest quality medical information in the world today. Offers patients the tools necessary to make informed treatment decisions within the short time lines dictated by their illness or disease.

Book Publishers

4428 Understanding Herpes

Dr Lawrence R Stanberg, author

University Press of Mississippi
3825 Ridgewood Road
Jackson, MS 39211

601-432-6205
800-737-7788
Fax: 601-432-6217
press@ihl.state.ms.us
www.upress.state.ms.us

A most informative overview of herpes written for the general reader.

120 pages Cloth
ISBN: 1-578060-40-0

Leila W. Salisbury, Director
Cynthia Foster, Administrative Assistant
Tracey Curtis, Assistant For Development

Neonatal Jaundice / Description

Description

4429 NEONATAL JAUNDICE
Synonym: Icterus neonatorum
Involves the following Biologic System(s):
Neonatal and Infant Disorders

Neonatal jaundice refers to a condition of the newborn in which high blood levels of the reddish-orange bile pigment bilirubin cause a yellowing of the skin, eyes, and mucous membranes. Bilirubin is derived from the breakdown of the protein, hemoglobin, in red blood cells. Neonatal jaundice may be the result of many different factors including metabolic disturbances or deficiencies; certain genetic disorders; conditions associated with an increased rate of red blood cell destruction (hemolysis); conditions that affect liver function; and certain types of infections.

Blood levels of bilirubin may be somewhat elevated after the first day of life, usually peak by the fourth day, and fall to normal levels by the end of the first week. This temporary rise, frequently accompanied by jaundice, results from the increased destruction of fetal red blood cells and the inability of a still-developing metabolic mechanism to efficiently eliminate bile from the body. In addition, an enzyme present in the intestines of newborns may convert bilirubin to a form that allows it to be reabsorbed into the blood, resulting in even higher bilirubin blood levels. Premature infants are particularly at risk for jaundice. If no other underlying cause is responsible, jaundice typically resolves spontaneously along with bilirubin level stabilization.

The appearance of jaundice in a newborn is carefully evaluated for underlying causes. Factors that may indicate the presence of an underlying disorder may include jaundice within the first 24 hours of life; a higher and faster-than-expected rise in bilirubin levels; birth defects, especially those that affect the liver such as biliary atresia; a family history of diseases that cause the early destruction of red blood cells such as hemolytic disease of the newborn; or rare disorders associated with hyperbilirubinemia (e.g., Crigler-Najjar syndrome, transient familial neonatal hyperbilirubinemia, etc.). Other suspect findings may include an enlarged liver (hepatomegaly), enlarged spleen (splenomegaly), lethargy, unusual paleness, difficulty in feeding, vomiting, or excessive weight loss.

Treatment of neonatal jaundice depends upon the underlying cause. Some infants with jaundice associated with breast-feeding may benefit from phototherapy. During this treatment, which is carefully monitored, the infant's bare skin is exposed to high intensity fluorescent lights that speed up the excretion and elimination of bilirubin in the skin. Other treatment is symptomatic and supportive.

Government Agencies

4430 NIH/ Eunice Kennedy Shriver National Institute of Child Health & Human Development
P.O. Box 3006
Rockville, MD 20847
800-370-2943
Fax: 866-760-5947
www.nichd.nih.gov

Conducts and supports research on topics related to the health of children, adults, families and populations. Some of these topics include: developmental disabilities, growth and development, infant death, reproductive health and birth defects.

Diana W. Bianchi, Director
Alison Cernich, PhD, Deputy Director

National Associations & Support Groups

4431 American Academy of Pediatrics
345 Park Blvd
Itasca, IL 60143
847-434-4000
800-433-9016
Fax: 847-434-8000
csc@aap.org
www.aap.org

The American Academy of Pediatrics and its member pediatricians are committed to the attainment of optimal physical, mental and social health and well-being for all infants, children, adolescents, and young adults.

Kyle E. Yasuda, MD, FAAP, President
Mark Del Monte, JD, CEO/Executive VP
Vera Tait, MD, FAAP, Chief Medical Officer

4432 American College of Gastroenterology
6400 Goldsboro Road
Bethesda, MD 20817
301-263-9000
www.gi.org

The American College of Gastroenterology was founded in 1932 to advance the scientific study and medical practice of diseases of the GI tract.

13,000 members

4433 American Liver Foundation
P.O. Box 299
West Orange, NJ 07052
800-465-4837
www.liverfoundation.org

The American Liver Foundation is the nationleading nonprofit organization promoting liver health and disease prevention. ALF provides research, education and advocacy for those affected by liver-related diseases, including hepatitis.

Lorraine Stiehl, CEO
David Ticker, Executive VP & CFO

4434 Digestive Disease National Coalition
507 Capitol Court NE, Suite 200
Washington, DC 20002
202-544-7497
Fax: 202-546-7105
www.ddnc.org

Advocacy organization comprised of over 30 voluntary and professional societies concerned with the many diseases of the digestive tract and liver.

Ceciel Rooker, Chairperson
Bryan Green, MD, President
Cathy Griffith, Vice Chairperson

4435 International Foundation for Functional Gastrointestinal Disorders (IFFGD)
3015 Dunes W Boulevard, Suite 512
Mount Pleasant, SC 29466
414-964-1799
www.iffgd.org

The organization offers responses to those commonly asked questions for families and individuals whose lives have been touched by gastrointestinal disorders.

Nancy J. Norton, Founder
Ceciel T. Rooker, President

4436 March of Dimes Foundation
1550 Crystal Drive, Ste 1300
Arlington, VA 22202
888-663-4637
www.marchofdimes.org

March of Dimes help moms have full-term pregnancies and research the problems that threaten the health of babies. The March of Dimes also acts globally: sharing best practices in perinatal health and helping improve birth outcomes where the needs are the most urgent.

Stacey D. Stewart, President
Alan Brogdon, SVP/COO/Board Officer
Rahul Gupta, MD, SVP & Chief Medical/Health Officer

Neonatal Jaundice / Newsletters

4437 North American Society for Pediatric Gastroenterology/Hepatology/Nutrition
714 N Bethlehem Pike, Suite 300
Ambler, PA 19002
215-641-9800
Fax: 215-641-1995
www.naspghan.org

Strives to improve the care of infants, children and adolescents with digestive disorders by promoting advances in clinical care of children with chronic abdominal pain, diarrhea, constipation, vomiting, bleeding from the GI tract, inflammatory bowel disease, liver diseases, diseases of the pancreas, poor weight gain and nutritional problems.

Margaret K Stallings, Executive Director
Kim Rose, Associate Director
Gina Brown, Membership

Libraries & Resource Centers

4438 National Digestive Diseases Information Clearinghouse (NDDIC)
NIH
2 Information Way
Bethesda, MD 20892
301-654-3810
800-891-5389
Fax: 301-907-8906
nddic@info.niddk.nih.gov
www.digestive.niddk.nih.gov

The National Institute of Diabetes and Digestive and Kidney Diseases conducts and supports research on many of the most serious diseases affecting public health. The Institute supports much of the clinical research on the diseases of internal medicine and related subspecialty fields as well as many basic science disciplines.

Griffin P. Rodgers, MD, Director
Gregory G. Germino, MD, Deputy Director
Kathy Kranzfelder, Communications Director

Web Sites

4439 American Liver Foundation
P.O. Box 299
West Orange, NJ 07052
800-465-4837
www.liverfoundation.org

The American Liver Foundation is the nationleading nonprofit organization promoting liver health and disease prevention. ALF provides research, education and advocacy for those affected by liver-related diseases, including hepatitis.

Lorraine Stiehl, CEO
David Ticker, Executive VP & CFO

4440 National Digestive Diseases Information Clearinghouse (NDDIC)
2 Information Way
301-654-3810
800-891-5389
nddic@info.niddk.nih.gov
www.digestive.niddk.nih.gov

The National Institute of Diabetes and Digestive and Kidney Diseases conducts and supports research on many of the most serious diseases affecting public health. The Institute supports much of the clinical research on the diseases of internal medicine and related subspecialty fields as well as many basic science disciplines.

4441 Online Mendelian Inheritance in Man
McKusick-Nathans Institue of Genetic Medicine-JHU
Baltimore, MD 21205
www.omim.org

This database is a catalog of human genes and genetic disorders.

Ada Hamosh, MD, Scientific Director

Journals

4442 Journal of Pediatric Gastroenterology and Nutrition
NASPGHAN, author

Lippincott Williams & Wilkins
2001 Market Street
Philadelphia, PA 19103
215-521-8300
Fax: 215-521-8902
www.lww.com

Publication of the North American Society for Pediatric Gastroenterolgy, Hepatology and Nutrition, which strives to improve the care of infants, children and adolescents with digestive disorders by promoting advances in clinical care of children with chronic abdominal pain, diarrhea, constipation, vomiting, bleeding from the GI tract, inflammatory bowel disease, liver diseases, diseases of the pancreas, poor weight gain and nutritional problems.

Newsletters

4443 NASPGHAN News
714 N. Bethlehem Pike, Ste 300
Ambler, PA 19002
215-641-9800
Fax: 215-641-1995
www.naspghan.org

Publication of the North American Society for Pediatric Gastroenterolgy, Hepatology and Nutrition, which strives to improve the care of infants, children and adolescents with digestive disorders by promoting advances in clinical care of children with chronic abdominal pain, diarrhea, constipation, vomiting, bleeding from the GI tract, inflammatory bowel disease, liver diseases, diseases of the pancreas, poor weight gain and nutritional problems.

Margaret K Stallings, Executive Director
Kim Rose, Associate Director
Gina Brown, Membership

Description

4444 NEPHROTIC SYNDROME

Synonyms: Minimal change nephrotic syndrome, MCNS

Covers these related disorders: Infantile nephrotic syndrome, Primary nephrotic syndrome, Secondary nephrotic syndrome

Involves the following Biologic System(s):

Renal and Urologic Disorders

Nephrotic syndrome is characterized by an abnormality of the kidney that allows proteins to leak out of the blood and into the urine. The loss of these proteins leads to proteinuria (protein in the urine), edema (swelling) of the body, hypoproteinemia (low blood levels of protein), hyperlipidemia (high fat levels in the blood) and lipiduria (fat in the urine). Clinical examination of a patient with nephrotic syndrome will reveal swelling of the eyelids and skin around the eyes (periorbital edema), swelling of the extremities, especially feet and lower legs, and fluid in the abdomen (ascites). Laboratory examination will show large amounts of urinary protein, low serum albumin and high cholesterol.

There are three categories of nephrotic syndrome: infantile; primary; and secondary:

Infantile nephrotic syndrome is usually the result of an inherited form and symptoms occur in the first few months of life. Secondary nephrotic syndrome is nephrotic syndrome associated with another disease process. These can include infection, connective tissue disorders such as lupus erythematosus, allergen exposure and medications.

Primary nephrotic syndrome results from disease in the kidney alone. The most common form is minimal change nephrotic syndrome (MCNS), or minimal change disease. It is called minimal change because little change is seen in the kidneys when a biopsy of the kidney is examined. Minimal change nephrotic syndrome almost always responds to steroids. Although relapses are not uncommon the long-term prognosis is excellent. Other causes of primary nephrotic syndrome, such as focal segmental glomerulosclerosis, mesangial proliferative glomeruloephritis, and membranous nephropathy, may or may not improve with the steroids and generally have a worse prognosis than MCNS. These patients can be treated with immunosuppressive therapy but may progress to end-stage renal disease requiring dialysis or kidney transplant.

Children with nephrotic syndrome are at risk for several complications. These include increased risk of infection, blood clots and cardiovascular disease. Dietary management includes restriction of sodium and fluid intake. Excessive sunlight should be avoided, because sensitivity to light (photosensitivity) is common.

National Associations & Support Groups

4445 American Academy of Pediatrics
345 Park Blvd
Itasca, IL 60143
847-434-4000
800-433-9016
Fax: 847-434-8000
csc@aap.org
www.aap.org

The American Academy of Pediatrics and its member pediatricians are committed to the attainment of optimal physical, mental and social health and well-being for all infants, children, adolescents, and young adults.

Kyle E. Yasuda, MD, FAAP, President
Mark Del Monte, JD, CEO/Executive VP
Vera Tait, MD, FAAP, Chief Medical Officer

4446 American Kidney Fund
11921 Rockville Pike, Suite 300
Rockville, MD 20852
800-638-8299
www.akfinc.org

The American Kidney Fund is the nation's leading voluntary health organization serving people with and at risk for kidney disease through direct financial assistance, comprehensive education, clinical research and community service programs.

LaVarne A. Burton, President & CEO
Tara Bunch, EVP & COO
Tamara Ruggiero, VP & CMO

4447 National Kidney Foundation
30 E 33rd Street
New York, NY 10016
800-622-9010
Fax: 212-689-9261
info@kidney.org
www.kidney.org

A major voluntary health organization, seeking to prevent kidney and urinary tract diseases, improve the health and well-being of individuals and families affected by these diseases, and increases the availability of all organs for transplant.

Kevin Longino, Chief Executive Officer
Joseph A. Vassalotti, Chief Medical Officer
Kerry Willis, Chief Scientific Officer

4448 NephCure Foundation
150 S. Warner Road, Suite 402
King of Prussia, PA 19406
866-637-4287
info@nephcure.org
www.nephcure.org

The only organization committed exclusively to support research seeking the cuses of the potentially debilitating kidney diseases, Nephrotic Syndrome and Focal Segmental Glomerulosclerosis (FSGS), improve treatment and find a cure.

Joshua M. Tarnoff, Chief Executive Officer
Rebecca Cook, Director, Program Operations
Kylie Karley, Director, Marketing/Communications

Web Sites

4449 American Kidney Fund
11921 Rockville Pike, Suite 300
Rockville, MD 20852
800-638-8299
www.akfinc.org

The American Kidney Fund is the nation's leading voluntary health organization serving people with and at risk for kidney disease through direct financial assistance, comprehensive education, clinical research and community service programs.

LaVarne A. Burton, President & CEO
Tara Bunch, EVP & COO
Tamara Ruggiero, VP & CMO

4450 National Kidney Foundation
30 E 33rd Street
New York, NY 10016
800-622-9010
Fax: 212-689-9261
info@kidney.org
www.kidney.org

A site that offers information to prevent kidney and urinary tract diseases, improve the health and well-being of individuals and families affected by these diseases, and increases the availability of all organs for transplant.

Kevin Longino, Chief Executive Officer
Joseph Vassalotti, Chief Medical Officer
Kerry Willis, Chief Scientific Officer

4451 NephCure Foundation
150 S. Warner Road, Suite 402
King of Prussia, PA 19406
866-637-4287
info@nephcure.org
nephcure.org

The only organization committed exclusively to support research seeking the cuses of the potentially debilitating kidney diseases, Nephrotic Syndrome and Focal Segmental Glomerulosclerosis (FSGS), improve treatment and find a cure.

Joshua M. Tarnoff, Chief Executive Officer
Rebecca Cook, Director, Program Operations
Kylie Karley, Director, Marketing/Communications

Book Publishers

4452 The Official Parent's Sourcebook on Childhood Nephrotic Syndrome

James N. Parker, author

Icon Group International
9606 Tierra Grande St., Suite 205
San Diego, CA 92126

Fax: 858-635-9414
orders@icongroupbooks.com
www.icongrouponline.com

A comprehensive manual for anyone interested in self-directed research on childhood Nephrotic Syndrome. Fully referenced with ample internet listings and glossary.

2002 136 pages Paperback
ISBN: 0-597832-16-1

Newsletters

4453 NephCure Now

NephCure Foundation
150 S. Warner Road, Suite 402
King of Prussia, PA 19406

866-637-4287
info@nephcure.org
www.nephcure.org

The NephCure Foundation's newsletter that contains news and information on a variety of topics including the latest research updates, NephCure events and fundraisers and much more.

Joshua M. Tarnoff, Chief Executive Officer
Rebecca Cook, Director, Program Operations
Kylie Karley, Director, Marketing/Communications

Pamphlets

4454 Childhood Nephrotic Syndrome

Information Clearinghouse
2 Information Way
Bethesda, MD 20892

301-496-3583
Fax: 301-907-8906
nddic@info.niddk.nih.gov
www.niddk.nih.gov

4455 Financial Assistance and Insurance for People with Kidney Disease

Information Clearinghouse
2 Information Way
Bethesda, MD 20892

301-496-3583
Fax: 301-907-8906
nddic@info.niddk.nih.gov
www.niddk.nih.gov

4456 Kidney Disease of Diabetes

Information Clearinghouse
1 Information Way
Bethesda, MD 20892

301-496-3583
Fax: 301-907-8906
ndoc@info.niddk.nih.gov
www.niddk.nih.gov

Description

4457 NEUROFIBROMATOSIS
Synonym: NF
Covers these related disorders: Neurofibromatosis type I (von Recklinghausen disease) (NF1), Neurofibromatosis type II (NF2)
Involves the following Biologic System(s):
Dermatologic Disorders, Orthopedic and Muscle Disorders

The term neurofibromatosis is often used to refer to neurofibromatosis type I (NF1), an autosomal dominant disorder that affects approximately one in 3,500 to 4,000 individuals. Neurofibromatosis type I, also known as von Recklinghausen disease, is characterized by the appearance of pale tan or light brown discolorations (macules) on the skin (cafe-au-lait spots) and multiple benign, fibrous tumors of nerves and skin (neurofibromas). A second, distinctive form of neurofibromatosis (NF), known as neurofibromatosis type II (NF2), accounts for about 10 percent of all cases of NF. Neurofibromatosis type II, also an autosomal dominant disorder, is characterized by the development of benign tumors on both acoustic nerves (bilateral acoustic neuromas), resulting in progressive hearing impairment.

In most children with neurofibromatosis type I, skin discoloration may develop by the age of one year. Such skin lesions typically increase in number and size over time, and most affected individuals have six or more spots measuring 1.5 centimeters or more in diameter after the onset of puberty. Although these cafe-au-lait spots are often distributed in various areas of the body, they are most commonly present on the trunk. In addition, after three years of age, areas of freckling, particularly under the arms (axillary) and in the groin (inguinal) area, may also be present.

In approximately 95 percent of children with NF1 over six years of age, two or more benign, tumor-like nodules, known as Lisch nodules, are present on the pigmented areas of the eyes. Benign, fibrous tumors of the skin (cutaneous neurofibromas) tend to develop during the second decade of life, typically appearing as small, soft, raised, and slightly purplish discolorations of the overlying skin. These tumors, which rarely develop before six years of age, may increase in number and size during puberty. In addition, large benign tumors composed of bundles of nerves (plexiform neurofibromas) may be apparent at birth or during early childhood. Approximately two to four percent of individuals with NF1 may develop malignant tumors (e.g., neurofibrosarcomas). Physical findings that may be associated with malignant transformation include increasing tumor size, associated pain, or various neurologic symptoms due to tumor growth. Approximately 15 percent of affected individuals may also develop tumors of the optic nerve (optic glioma), which is the cranial nerve that carries visual impulses from the back of the eye (retina) to the brain. These tumors are usually considered relatively benign and may cause no associated symptoms (asymptomatic). However, in some cases, depending upon their specific location, growth, and nature, such tumors may affect vision. In these patients, associated findings may include visual impairment; degeneration (atrophy) of the optic nerve; abnormal deviation of the eye (strabismus); or involuntary, rhythmic eye movements (nystagmus). In addition, some affected individuals may have an increased risk of developing tumors of the brain and spinal cord (e.g., astrocytomas, meningiomas, neurilemmomas, etc.).

Some individuals with NF1 may also experience associated skeletal abnormalities, such as bowing of the lower legs; improper development of a bone at the base of the skull (sphenoid wing dysplasia), potentially causing pronounced bulging of the eyes (exophthalmos); and progressive sideways curvature of the spine (scoliosis). Additional abnormalities may be present, such as mild short stature, abnormal largeness of the head (macrocephaly), and episodes of uncontrolled electrical activity in the brain (seizures). In addition, many affected children may have learning disabilities and speech abnormalities. Neurofibromatosis type I is caused by abnormal changes (mutations) of a gene located on the long arm of chromosome 17 (17q11.2). In approximately 50 percent of patients, the disease gene is inherited an an autosomal dominant trait; the remaining cases result from new (sporadic) mutations of the gene that occur for unknown reasons.

Neurofibromatosis type II (NF2) is also characterized by bilateral acoustic neuromas that are responsible for carrying sound impulses from the inner ear to the brain. Symptoms may become apparent during childhood or the second or third decades of life. These may include a facial numbness or weakness, headache, dizziness, unsteadiness, and progressive hearing loss. Individuals with NF2 may also develop clouding of the lenses of the eyes (i.e., posterior subcapsular opacities), have an increased risk of developing tumors of the brain and spinal cord (e.g., gliomas, meningiomas, schwannomas, etc.), or experience progressive visual impairment. NF2 is caused by a disease gene located on the long arm of chromosome 22 (22q12.2).

The treatment of neurofibromatosis is directed toward ensuring early detection and prompt, appropriate management of potentially associated findings or complications. Affected individuals are typically regularly monitored with complete neurologic evaluations (e.g., including visual and auditory screening) and thorough examinations to detect potential complications associated with NF. In most cases, symptoms of NF1 are mild, and patients live normal and productive lives. In some cases, however, NF1 can be severely debilitating. In some cases of NF2, the damage to nearby vital structures, such as other cranial nerves, can be life-threatening. Some tumors may be surgically removed or treated using other appropriate methods (e.g., radiation or chemotherapy for certain malignancies). Other treatment is symptomatic and supportive.

National Associations & Support Groups

4458 American Academy of Pediatrics
345 Park Blvd
Itasca, IL 60143

847-434-4000
800-433-9016
Fax: 847-434-8000
csc@aap.org
www.aap.org

The American Academy of Pediatrics and its member pediatricians are committed to the attainment of optimal physical, mental and social health and well-being for all infants, children, adolescents, and young adults.

Kyle E. Yasuda, MD, FAAP, President
Mark Del Monte, JD, CEO/Executive VP
Vera Tait, MD, FAAP, Chief Medical Officer

4459 Child Neurology Foundation
601 W Short Street
Lexington, KY 40508

888-417-3435
info@childneurologyfoundation.org
childneurologyfoundation.org

The Child Neurology Foundation connects partners from all areas of the child neurology community so those navigating the journey of disease diagnosis, management, and care have the ongoing support from those dedicated to treatments and cures.

Neurofibromatosis / State Agencies & Support Groups

Amy Brin, Executive Director
Katie Hentges, Director, Programs
Brea McCormley, Director, Development

4460 Children's Tumor Foundation
697 Third Avenue, Suite 418
New York, NY 10017
212-344-6633
800-323-7938
Fax: 212-747-0004
info@ctf.org
www.ctf.org

The Children's Tumor Foundation funds research, patient support, and public awareness of the neurofibromatoses (NF1, NF2 & Schwannomatosis) genetic disorders that cause random tumor growth throughout the body.

Annette Bakker, President
Salvatore La Rosa, Chief Scientific Officer
Sarah Bourne, SVP, Finance & Operations

4461 Genetic Alliance
426400 Woodfield Road, Ste 189
Damascus, MD 20872
202-966-5557
Fax: 202-966-8553
info@geneticalliance.org
www.geneticalliance.org

World's leading nonprofit health advocacy organization committed to transforming health through genetics and promoting an environment of openness centered on the health of individuals, families, and communities.

Sharon Terry, CEO
Ruth Child, CFO
Natasha Bonhomme, Chief Strategy Officer

4462 March of Dimes Foundation
1550 Crystal Drive, Ste 1300
Arlington, VA 22202
888-663-4637
www.marchofdimes.org

March of Dimes help moms have full-term pregnancies and research the problems that threaten the health of babies. The March of Dimes also acts globally: sharing best practices in perinatal health and helping improve birth outcomes where the needs are the most urgent.

Stacey D. Stewart, President
Alan Brogdon, SVP/COO/Board Officer
Rahul Gupta, MD, SVP & Chief Medical/Health Officer

4463 Neurofibromatosis, Inc
PO Box 1530
Wheaton, IL 60187
630-510-1115
800-942-6825
Fax: 630-510-8508
admin@nfnetwork.org
www.nfnetwork.org

An organization of independent state and regional chapters that provides support and services to families coping with neurofibromatosis. Works closely with clinical and research professionals who specialize in the treatment of NF. Has a newsletter and other printed materials.

Kim Bischoff, Executive Director
Deb Potter, Member Services Coordinator
Ashley Sola, Marketing & Events Coordinator

State Agencies & Support Groups

Arizona

4464 Neurofibromatosis, Inc - Arizona Chapter
PO Box 2718
Chandler, AZ 85244
480-945-9650
www.nfarizona.org

Arkansas

4465 Children's Tumor Foundation-Arkansas Infor www.php.com
PO Box 7262
Little Rock, AR 72217
501-920-5588
loslica@gmail.com
www.ctfarkansas.com

Lesley Oslica, Contact

California

4466 Neurofibromatosis, Inc - California Chapter
PO Box 1234
Vacaville, CA 95696
707-469-0467
Fax: 866-571-2366
info@nfcalifornia.org
www.nfcalifornia.org

Debbie Bell, President
Dana Inigues, VP
Katie Sperring, Secretary

Illinois

4467 Neurofibromatosis, Inc - Illinois/Midwest
473 Dunham Rd, Suite 3
St. Charles, IL 60174
630-945-3562
800-322-6363
Fax: 630-932-8119
Diana@nfmidwest.org
www.nfmidwest.org

Diana Haberkamp, Executive Director
Jenny Perkins, Development Director
Liz Campana, Administrative Assistant

Indiana

4468 Children's Tumor Foundation - Indiana Affiliate
Suite 4700, 355 W, 16th Street
Indiannapolis, IN 46202
317-948-5450
Fax: 317-963-7533
kym1577@sbcglobal.net
www.indiananf.com

Kim Bebley, Affiliate Representative

Kansas

4469 Neurofibromatosis, Inc - Kansas & Central Plains
9218 Metcalf, Ste. 335
Overland Park, KS 66212
316-669-8453
800-942-6825
www.nfcentralplains.org

Nichole Servos, President
Mike Montgomery, VP
Sharon Loftspring, Secretary

Maryland

4470 Neurofibromatosis, Inc - MidAtlantic
2 Village Square., Suite #213, 5100 Falls Road
Baltimore, MD 21210
443-423-0535
Fax: 410-889-0400
www.nfmidatlantic.org

Diana Bark, President
Lee Herman, Board of Directors
Aaron Jumani, VP

Neurofibromatosis / Research Centers

Oregon

4471 **Legacy Good Samaritan Hospital & Medical Center**
Neurofibromatosis Support Group
1015 NW 22nd Avenue, N-300
Portland, OR 97210
503-413-7711
800-733-9959
www.legacyhealth.org

Amy Marr, Coordinator

Research Centers

4472 **NF Clinic - University of Pittsburgh Children's Hospital**
5501 Old York Road
Philadelphia, PA 19141
215-456-8722
Fax: 215-456-2356
scheida@einstein.edu
www.nfmidatlantic.org

Jennifer Berkowitz, Contact

4473 **Neurofibromatosis Center at North Broward Medical Center**
303 SE 17th Street
Fort Lauderdale, FL 33316
954-784-1521
www.browardhealth.org

Frank Nask, President

4474 **Neuroscience Institute at Mercy Hospital**
4120 W Memorial Road
Oklahoma City, OK 73120
405-302-2661
Fax: 405-302-2670
www.mercy..net

Gary Brown PhD, Contact

Web Sites

4475 **Children's Tumor Foundation**
697 Third Avenue, Suite 412
New York, NY 10017
212-344-6633
800-323-7938
Fax: 212-747-0004
info@ctf.org
www.ctf.org

The Children's Tumor Foundation funds research, patient support and public awareness of the neurofibromatoses (NF1, NF2 and Schwannomatosis) genetic disorders that cause random tumor growth throughout the body.

Annette Bakker, President
Salvatore La Rosa, Chief Scientific Officer
Sarah Bourne, SVP, Finance & Operations

4476 **Neurofibromatosis, Inc**
213 S. Wheaton Ave.
Wheaton, IL 60187
630-510-1115
800-942-6825
Fax: 630-510-8508
admin@nfnetwork.org
www.nfinc.org

An organization made up of independent state and regional chapters, providing support and services to NF families. In addition to assisting individuals and families, NF, Inc. works closely with clinical and research professionals who specialize in the treatment of NF.

Cheri Stewart, President
Nicole Hicks, Secretary
Mike Montgomery, Treasurer

4477 **Online Mendelian Inheritance in Man**
McKusick-Nathans Institue of Genetic Medicine-JHU
Baltimore, MD 21205
www.omim.org

This database is a catalog of human genes and genetic disorders.

Ada Hamosh, MD, Scientific Director

Book Publishers

4478 **Let's Talk About Going to the Hospital**
Rosen Publishing Group's PowerKids Press
29 E 21st Street
New York, NY 10010
212-777-3017
800-237-9932
Fax: 888-436-4643
rosenpub@tribeca.ios.com
www.rosenpublishing.com

If a child has to check into the hospital, chances are he or she is already upset about being ill. Knowing how a hospital functions and what the procedures are, such as when family members can visit, will help in what is already a stressful situation. Grades K-5.

24 pages
ISBN: 0-823950-36-0

Roger Rosen, President

Newsletters

4479 **Neurofibromatosis Ink**
Neurofibromatosis, Inc
213 S. Wheaton Ave.
Wheaton, IL 60187
630-510-1115
800-942-6825
Fax: 630-510-8508
admin@nfnetwork.org
www.nfinc.org

Cheri Stewart, President
Nicole Hicks, Secretary
Mike Montgomery, Treasurer

Camps

4480 **Camp New Friends**
Neurofibromatosis, Inc
213 S. Wheaton Ave.
Wheaton, IL 60187
630-510-1115
800-942-6825
Fax: 630-510-8508
admin@nfnetwork.org
www.nfinc.org

A summer camp for those affected with NF1 or NF2, between the ages of 7 and 15. Those aged 18 and over may apply as counselors or counselors-in-training. The camp is held in collaboration with Children's National Medical Center.

Cheri Stewart, President
Nicole Hicks, Secretary
Mike Montgomery, Treasurer

Description

4481 NEUROBLASTOMA
Synonym: NB
Involves the following Biologic System(s):
Hematologic and Oncologic Disorders

Neuroblastomas are malignant tumors that account for approximately eight to 10 percent of childhood cancers. They are the most common solid tumors that develop outside the skull in children. About 500 to 600 new cases are reported each year in the United States, with males affected slightly more frequently than females. In approximately 90 percent of affected infants and children, neuroblastoma is diagnosed before age five. Neuroblastoma sometimes occurs in members of certain families (kindreds), although the specific underlying cause is unknown.

Neuroblastomas may originate in any part of the sympathetic nervous system but most commonly develop in the inner region of the adrenal gland (adrenal medulla). In other patients, neuroblastomas may arise in the chest. The sympathetic nervous system controls certain involuntary activities during times of stress, such as raising blood pressure and increasing the heart rate. The adrenal glands, two relatively small organs that curve over the top of each kidney, secrete certain hormones directly into the bloodstream.

A neuroblastoma often invades surrounding tissues and spreads to small, node-like structures located along the course of the lymphatic vessels (lymph nodes). The tumor may then spread to other parts of the body (metastasize), particularly the liver, skeleton, and bone marrow. Rarely, neuroblastomas spread to the lungs or the brain. Associated symptoms and findings are highly variable and depend upon the specific location of the tumor and the extent to which it may have spread. Many infants and children may have a hard, solid, painless lump or mass in the neck or a large mass that may be felt in the abdomen or on the back. Patients often have a general feeling of ill health (malaise) and appear pale (pallor). Those with skeletal involvement typically experience tumor-associated bone pain. In addition, because the bone marrow is a blood-producing tissue, tumor infiltration of the bone marrow may result in abnormally decreased levels of the different blood cells, including circulating red blood cells (anemia), platelets (thrombocytopenia), and certain white blood cells, (neutropenia). Due to low levels of platelets, patients may experience abnormal bleeding and easy bruising. Decreased levels of white blood cells may cause an increased susceptibility to certain infections.

Depending upon the location and potential spread of the tumor, additional symptoms and findings may occur. If a neuroblastoma spreads to the bony cavities surrounding the eyes, associated symptoms may include abnormal protrusion of the eyes (proptosis) and the appearance of bluish-purple patches (ecchymosis) around the eyes. Tumor development near the spinal cord may result in weakness or paralysis of the legs (paresis). In addition, involvement of the liver typically causes abnormal liver enlargement (hepatomegaly). Tumor growth within the adrenal glands may cause excessive secretion of the hormones epinephrine and norepinephrine, resulting in increased irritability, high blood pressure (hypertension), increased heart rate (tachycardia), flushing of the skin, severe diarrhea, and other symptoms.

Some patients may also develop Horner's syndrome, which is characterized by ptosis, absence of sweating (anhidrosis), and narrowing of the pupil of the eye (miosis). Skin abnormalities may also be present, including firm, bluish nodules under the skin or skin lesions on the scalp. Approximately four percent of patients experience a sudden onset of neuromuscular symptoms due to abnormal functioning of the cerebellum (acute cerebellar encephalopathy). The cerebellum is a region of the brain that plays an essential role in maintaining normal postures, sustaining balance, and producing coordinated movements. Neuroblastoma symptoms may include an impaired ability to coordinate voluntary movements (cerebellar ataxia); random, rapid, uncontrolled eye movements (opsoclonus); and shock-like contractions of certain muscles or muscle groups (myoclonic jerks).

In infants and children with neuroblastoma, treatment may depend upon the location of the tumor, whether it has spread, the patient's age, or other factors. If the tumor is contained and has not spread, treatment may consist of surgical removal of the tumor. When the tumor may not be removed surgically or has spread to other parts of the body, treatment measures may include the use of certain drugs (chemotherapy) or radiation therapy. Additional treatments for advanced disease may be considered.

Government Agencies

4482 NIH/National Cancer Institute
Bethesda, MD 20892

800-422-6237
NCIinfo@nih.gov
www.cancer.gov

The National Cancer Institute coordinates the National Cancer Program, which conducts and supports research, training, health information dissemination, and other programs with respect to the cause, diagnosis, prevention, and treatment of cancer, rehabilitation from cancer, and the continuing care of cancer patients and the families of cancer patients.

Norman E. Sharpless, MD, Director
Douglas R. Lowy, MD, Principal Deputy Director

National Associations & Support Groups

4483 American Academy of Pediatrics
345 Park Blvd
Itasca, IL 60143

847-434-4000
800-433-9016
Fax: 847-434-8000
csc@aap.org
www.aap.org

The American Academy of Pediatrics and its member pediatricians are committed to the attainment of optimal physical, mental and social health and well-being for all infants, children, adolescents, and young adults.

Kyle E. Yasuda, MD, FAAP, President
Mark Del Monte, JD, CEO/Executive VP
Vera Tait, MD, FAAP, Chief Medical Officer

4484 American Childhood Cancer Organization
P.O. Box 498
Kensington, MD 20895

301-962-3520
800-366-2223
Fax: 310-962-3521
staff@acco.org
www.acco.org

The American Childhood Cancer Organization (ACCO) was founded in 1970 by a group of parents whose children had been diagnosed with cancer. Today ACCO is one of the largest grassroots, national organizations dedicated to improving the lives of children and adolescents with cancer and their families.

Ruth I. Hoffman, MPH, CEO
Krista Novak, Programs Manager
Blair Scroggs, Public Relations Coordinator

Neuroblastoma / Web Sites

4485 CancerCare
275 7th Avenue
New York, NY 10001
212-712-8400
800-813-4673
Fax: 212-712-8495
info@cancercare.org
www.cancercare.org

Dedicated to providing emotional support, information, and practical help to people with cancer and their loved ones. CancerCare is the oldest, largest, nonprofit agency devoted to offering professional services.

Patricia J Goldsmith, CEO
Christine Verini, RPh, COO

4486 Child Neurology Foundation
601 W Short Street
Lexington, KY 40508
888-417-3435
info@childneurologyfoundation.org
childneurologyfoundation.org

The Child Neurology Foundation connects partners from all areas of the child neurology community so those navigating the journey of disease diagnosis, management, and care have the ongoing support from those dedicated to treatments and cures.

Amy Brin, Executive Director
Katie Hentges, Director, Programs
Brea McCormley, Director, Development

4487 Children's Wish Foundation International
8615 Roswell Road
Atlanta, GA 30350
800-323-9474
info@childrenswish.org
www.childrenswish.org

Children's Wish Foundation International is dedicated to bringing joy and hope to seriously ill children and their families world wide by involving the public in putting children first with opportunities to experience the enhanced value and quality of life through the magic of a fulfilled wish.

Linda Dozoretz, Founder

4488 Genetic Alliance
426400 Woodfield Road, Ste 189
Damascus, MD 20872
202-966-5557
Fax: 202-966-8553
info@geneticalliance.org
www.geneticalliance.org

World's leading nonprofit health advocacy organization committed to transforming health through genetics and promoting an environment of openness centered on the health of individuals, families, and communities.

Sharon Terry, CEO
Ruth Child, CFO
Natasha Bonhomme, Chief Strategy Officer

4489 Neuroblastoma Children's Cancer Society
PO Box 957672
Hoffman Estates, IL 60169 neuroblastomachildrenscancersociety.org

The Neuroblastoma Children's Cancer Society is a group made up of volunteers, many of whom have children or relatives who are victims or survivors of this disease. The organization is an advocate for the children who suffer from neuroblastoma and is dedicated to serving as a support center for their families.

James F. Sexton, Co-Founder & Chair
Dori Sexton, Co-Founder

Web Sites

4490 CancerCare
275 7th Avenue
New York, NY 10001
212-712-8400
800-813-4673
Fax: 212-712-8495
www.cancercare.org

Dedicated to providing emotional support, information, and practical help to people with cancer and their loved ones. CancerCare is the oldest, largest, nonprofit agency devoted to offering professional services.

Patricia J Goldsmith, CEO
Christine Verini, RPh, COO

4491 Children's Cancer Web
www.cancerindex.org/ccw

www.cancerindex.org/ccw

An independent nonprofit site, established to provide a directory of childhood cancer resources.

4492 Online Mendelian Inheritance in Man
McKusick-Nathans Institue of Genetic Medicine-JHU
Baltimore, MD 21205
www.omim.org

This database is a catalog of human genes and genetic disorders.

Ada Hamosh, MD, Scientific Director

Book Publishers

4493 Cancer Information for Teens, 4th Edition
Omnigraphics
615 Griswold Street, Ste 520
Detroit, MI 48226
610-461-3548
800-234-1340
Fax: 800-875-1340
contact@omnigraphics.com
www.omnigraphics.com

Updated information and facts about cancer causes, diagnosis, prevention and treatment especially for teens.

480 pages
ISBN: 0-780816-15-2

4494 Cancer Sourcebook
Angela L. Williams, author

Omnigraphics
615 Griswold Street, Ste 520
Detroit, MI 48226
610-461-3548
800-234-1340
Fax: 800-875-1340
contact@omnigraphics.com
www.omnigraphics.com

Updated information and facts about cancer causes, diagnosis, prevention and treatment. Nearly 1.5 million people in the US are diagnosed with cancer every year.

1224 pages 8th Edition
ISBN: 0-780816-22-0

4495 Childhood Diseases and Disorders Sourcebook, 4th Edition
Omnigraphics
615 Griswold Street, Ste 520
Detroit, MI 48226
610-461-3548
800-234-1340
Fax: 800-875-1340
contact@omnigraphics.com
www.omnigraphics.com

Basic and up to date consumer health information about common disorders that affect the physical, mental, and developmental health of school-age children.

792 pages
ISBN: 0-780815-38-4

4496 Let's Talk About Going to the Hospital
Rosen Publishing Group's PowerKids Press
29 E 21st Street
New York, NY 10010
212-777-3017
800-237-9932
Fax: 888-436-4643
rosenpub@tribeca.ios.com
www.rosenpublishing.com

If a child has to check into the hospital, chances are he or she is already upset about being ill. Knowing how a hospital functions and what the procedures are, such as when family members can visit, will help in what is already a stressful situation. Grades K-5.

24 pages
ISBN: 0-823950-36-0
Roger Rosen, President

4497 Let's Talk About When Kids Have Cancer
Melanie Apel Gordon, author

Rosen Publishing Group's PowerKids Press
29 E 21st Street
New York, NY 10010   212-777-3017
                                            800-237-9932
                                       Fax: 888-436-4643
                           customerservice@rosenpub.com
                                   www.rosenpublishing.com

In a straightforward yet comforting way, this book explains what cancer is, what kinds of treatments surround the disease and how to cope if a child or the friend of a child has cancer. K-5.

24 pages Paperback
ISBN: 0-823951-95-6
Roger Rosen, President

4498 Resource Survival Handbook
Neuroblastoma Children's Cancer Society
PO Box 957672
Hoffman Estates, IL 60195   847-605-0705
                                            800-532-5162
                                       Fax: 847-605-0705
                              www.neuroblastomacancer.org

An accumulation of resource information of facts about neuroblastoma and related treatments, national and local resources for families and patients, health claim forms, pamphlets, and other relevant forms.

Online

Jim Sexton, Chairman

4499 Surviving Childhood Cancer: A Guide for Families
New Harbinger Publications
5674 Shattuck Avenue
Oakland, CA 94609   510-652-0215
                                            800-748-6273
                                       Fax: 800-652-1613
                        customerservice@newharbinger.com
                                   www.newharbinger.com

Cancer in a child is an overwhelming experience for a family. This book explains common medical procedures and offers readers practical advice about how to cope with emotions and stress during this time.

215 pages Paperback
ISBN: 1-572241-02-0

Journals

4500 American Childhood Cancer Organization
P.O. Box 498
Kensington, MD 20895   301-962-3520
                                            855-858-2226
                                       Fax: 310-962-3521
                                         staff@acco.org
                                           www.acco.org

The American Childhood Cancer Organization (ACCO) was founded in 1970 by a group of parents whose children had been diagnosed with cancer. Today ACCO is one of the largest grassroots, national organizations dedicated to improving the lives of children and adolescents with cancer and their families.

Quarterly

Ruth I. Hoffman, MPH, CEO
Krista Novak, Programs Manager
Blair Scroggs, Public Relations Coordinator

Neutropenia / Description

Description

4501 NEUTROPENIA

Covers these related disorders: Chronic neutropenia, Transient neutropenia

Involves the following Biologic System(s):
Hematologic and Oncologic Disorders

Neutropenia is a blood condition characterized by decreased numbers of circulating white blood cells known as neutrophils. These white blood cells play an essential role in fighting bacterial infections by detecting, engulfing, and digesting invading bacteria (phagocytosis). Neutrophils mature in the bone marrow and are then released into the bloodstream, where they may circulate for approximately six to eight hours. When responding to invading microorganisms or inflammation, neutrophils may leave the blood circulation, move into affected tissues, and digest microbes or other invaders as required.

Neutropenia is specifically defined as the presence of fewer than 1,500 neutrophils per microliter of blood. The condition may result from deficient production of neutrophils by the bone marrow or abnormally increased loss of neutrophils from the blood circulation. Depending upon the nature of the condition, its underlying cause, and other factors, neutropenia may occur for only days or weeks (transient neutropenia) or be present for months or a patient's lifetime (chronic neutropenia). In addition, the findings potentially associated with neutropenia are extremely variable and may include no apparent symptoms (asymptomatic), mild infections of the mucous membranes and the skin, or, in severe cases, potentially life-threatening complications.

In children, transient neutropenia may be caused by certain viral or bacterial infections; a deficiency of folic acid or vitamin B12; or the administration of certain medications, such as a class of antipsychotic drugs (phenothiazines), penicillin preparations, nonsteroidal anti-inflammatory agents, or anticancer drugs that may suppress bone marrow production. Chronic neutropenia also has several different causes and occurs in many different forms. Benign chronic neutropenia is a condition of childhood in which patients have chronically low levels of circulating neutrophils in the blood. This may result in increased susceptibility to recurrent infections of the skin, the mouth, or other areas. The condition typically resolves on its own by age four. Patients with immune deficiency disorders that are present at birth (primary inherited immunodeficiencies) or acquired (such as acquired immune deficiency syndrome, AIDS) often develop chronic neutropenia during infancy or early childhood. These children often fail to grow and gain weight at the expected rate (failure to thrive) and may experience recurrent bacterial infections, enlargement of the liver and spleen (hepatosplenomegaly), and potentially life-threatening complications.

Other uncommon forms of childhood neutropenia include cyclic neutropenia and Kostmann's disease. In patients with cyclic neutropenia, neutropenia recurs in regular cycles (e.g., every 18 to 21 days). When circulating neutrophils are abnormally decreased, these patients may experience fever, a general feeling of ill health (malaise), and susceptibility to mouth ulcers and infections of the skin, mucous membranes, and tissues that surround and support the teeth. Cyclic neutropenia typically becomes apparent during childhood and often runs in certain families. Kostmann's disease, also known as genetic infantile agranulocytosis, is a rare, autosomal recessive disorder characterized by persistent, extremely low levels of circulating neutrophils (fewer than 200 per microliter), frequent bacterial infections, and potentially life-threatening complications by approximately age three.

Neutropenia may also occur as a component of certain genetic, multisystemic diseases, such as Shwachman syndrome and metaphyseal chondrodysplasia, or in association with certain cancers, including leukemia and lymphoma.

The treatment of children with neutropenia depends upon the condition's severity and its underlying cause. In those with mild neutropenia, treatment may not be required. If a particular medication is responsible for the condition, such drug therapy is discontinued if possible. In patients with chronic neutropenia, physicians may recommend steps to help prevent bacterial infection and institute immediate antibiotic therapy should infections occur. In severe cases of bacterial infection, hospitalization may be required. In addition, in some patients with severe neutropenia, therapies may be administered to help stimulate the bone marrow's production of neutrophils (granulocyte colony-stimulating factor [G-CSF]). In some cases, bone marrow transplantation is an option, a procedure in which healthy bone marrow is given to replace defective bone marrow.

Government Agencies

4502 NIH/ Eunice Kennedy Shriver National Institute of Child Health & Human Development
P.O. Box 3006
Rockville, MD 20847

800-370-2943
Fax: 866-760-5947
www.nichd.nih.gov

Conducts and supports research on topics related to the health of children, adults, families and populations. Some of these topics include: developmental disabilities, growth and development, infant death, reproductive health and birth defects.

Diana W. Bianchi, Director
Alison Cernich, PhD, Deputy Director

4503 NIH/National Heart, Lung and Blood Institute
31 Center Drive, Bldg 31
Bethesda, MD 20824

877-645-2448
www.nhlbi.nih.gov

Primary responsibility of this organization is the scientific investigation of heart, blood vessel, lung and blood disorders. Oversees research, demonstration, prevention, education, control and training activities in these fields and emphasizes the prevention and control of heart diseases.

Gary H. Gibbons, MD, Director
Kate O'Sullivan, Executive Officer

National Associations & Support Groups

4504 American Academy of Pediatrics
345 Park Blvd
Itasca, IL 60143

847-434-4000
800-433-9016
Fax: 847-434-8000
csc@aap.org
www.aap.org

The American Academy of Pediatrics and its member pediatricians are committed to the attainment of optimal physical, mental and social health and well-being for all infants, children, adolescents, and young adults.

Kyle E. Yasuda, MD, FAAP, President
Mark Del Monte, JD, CEO/Executive VP
Vera Tait, MD, FAAP, Chief Medical Officer

4505 American Autoimmune Related Diseases Association
19176 Hall Road, Suite 130
Clinton, MI 48038
586-776-3900
aarda@aarda.org
www.aarda.org

The American Autoimmune Related Diseases Association is dedicated to the eradication of autoimmune diseases and the alleviation of suffering and the socioeconomic impact of autoimmunity through fostering and facilitating collaboration in the areas of education, public awareness, research, and patient services in an effective, ethical and efficient manner.

Lilly Stairs, Interim President/CEO
Laura Simpson, COO

4506 Genetic Alliance
426400 Woodfield Road, Ste 189
Damascus, MD 20872
202-966-5557
Fax: 202-966-8553
info@geneticalliance.org
www.geneticalliance.org

World's leading nonprofit health advocacy organization committed to transforming health through genetics and promoting an environment of openness centered on the health of individuals, families, and communities.

Sharon Terry, CEO
Ruth Child, CFO
Natasha Bonhomme, Chief Strategy Officer

4507 March of Dimes Foundation
1550 Crystal Drive, Ste 1300
Arlington, VA 22202
888-663-4637
www.marchofdimes.org

March of Dimes help moms have full-term pregnancies and research the problems that threaten the health of babies. The March of Dimes also acts globally: sharing best practices in perinatal health and helping improve birth outcomes where the needs are the most urgent.

Stacey D. Stewart, President
Alan Brogdon, SVP/COO/Board Officer
Rahul Gupta, MD, SVP & Chief Medical/Health Officer

4508 Severe Chronic Neutropenia International Registry (SCNIR)
1959 NE Pacific Street, Box 356422
Seattle, WA 98195
206-543-7218
Fax: 206-685-8055
registry@uw.edu
www.depts.washington.edu/registry

The SCNIR was established in the United States, Australia, Canada, and the European Community. The SCNIR is directed by a scientific advisory board of physicians from around the world who care for SCN patients. Our mission is to established a world-wide database of treatment and disease-related outcomes for persons diagnosed with SCN. Collection of this information will lead to improved medical care and is used for research to determine the causes of neutropenia.

David C. Dale, Clinical Manager

Web Sites

4509 American Autoimmune Related Diseases Association
www.aarda.org
586-776-3900
aarda@aarda.org
www.aarda.org

The American Autoimmune Related Diseases Association is dedicated to the eradication of autoimmune diseases and the alleviation of suffering and the socioeconomic impact of autoimmunity through fostering and facilitating collaboration in the areas of education, public awareness, research, and patient services in an effective, ethical and efficient manner.

4510 National Neutropenia Network
www.neutropenianet.org

www.neutropenianet.org

Supports general and clinical research and provides information to the families, the medical community and the general public. Also committed to helping affected families and individuals work with hospitals, physicians, nurses, and other health care professionals.

4511 Online Mendelian Inheritance in Man
McKusick-Nathans Institue of Genetic Medicine-JHU
Baltimore, MD 21205
www.omim.org

This database is a catalog of human genes and genetic disorders.

Ada Hamosh, MD, Scientific Director

Book Publishers

4512 Let's Talk About Going to the Hospital
Rosen Publishing Group's PowerKids Press
29 E 21st Street
New York, NY 10010
212-777-3017
800-237-9932
Fax: 888-436-4643
rosenpub@tribeca.ios.com
www.rosenpublishing.com

If a child has to check into the hospital, chances are he or she is already upset about being ill. Knowing how a hospital functions and what the procedures are, such as when family members can visit, will help in what is already a stressful situation. Grades K-5.

24 pages
ISBN: 0-823950-36-0

Roger Rosen, President

Nightmares / Description

Description

4513 NIGHTMARES

Involves the following Biologic System(s):

Developmental/Behavioral/Psychiatric Disorders

Nightmares are a type of sleep disturbance that occurs during the rapid eye movement (REM) phase of sleep, or deep sleep stage. Vivid, disturbing dreams often evoke feelings of extreme and inescapable fear, terror, anxiety, and distress. Nightmares are often so intense that they awaken the sleeping individual, who is then usually able to recall all or most details of the dream.

Nightmares are quite common in children, particularly in the eight to 10 year old age group. Girls are more prone to this type of sleep disturbance than boys. Precipitating factors vary and may include breathing irregularities caused by the common cold or other illnesses; violent movies or television programs, especially in younger children; separation anxiety; and other traumatic experiences or events. In addition, children with certain types of psychological disturbances (e.g., affective, mood, or anxiety disorders) may experience repeated episodes of nightmares.

It is common for most children to experience occasional nightmares and, until the anxiety or fear of the experience passes, understanding and comfort by parents or caregivers is usually helpful. However, children who experience frequent nightmares may require a careful evaluation to determine if these episodes are a manifestation of an underlying psychologic disorder or other irregularity. If this is the case, treatment may be directed toward the underlying condition. Other treatment is supportive. For example, parents and caregivers are encouraged to be reassuring, understanding, and firm but nonthreatening. Reading or other quiet or soothing activities or rituals before bedtime may also be beneficial. In addition, night lights or other reasonable accommodations may be provided to reassure or comfort affected children.

Government Agencies

4514 Center for Mental Health Services
5600 Fishers Lane
Rockville, MD 20857
240-276-1310
www.samhsa.gov

Encourages a range of programs such as systems of care to respond to the increasing number of mental, emotional, and behavioral problems among children. Supports outreach and case management programs for the thousands of Americans who are homeless and the improvement of these services.

Anita Everett, MD, Director

4515 NIH/National Institute of Mental Health
6001 Executive Blvd, Rm 6200, MSC 9663
Bethesda, MD 20892
866-615-6464
Fax: 301-443-4279
TTY: 301-443-8431
nimhinfo@nih.govh.gov
www.nimh.nih.gov

The mission of NIMH is to transform the understanding and treatment of mental illnesses through basic and clinical research, paving the way for prevention, recovery, and cure.

Joshua A. Gordon, MD, PhD, Director
Shelli Avenevoli, PhD, Deputy Director

National Associations & Support Groups

4516 American Academy of Pediatrics
345 Park Blvd
Itasca, IL 60143
847-434-4000
800-433-9016
Fax: 847-434-8000
csc@aap.org
www.aap.org

The American Academy of Pediatrics and its member pediatricians are committed to the attainment of optimal physical, mental and social health and well-being for all infants, children, adolescents, and young adults.

Kyle E. Yasuda, MD, FAAP, President
Mark Del Monte, JD, CEO/Executive VP
Vera Tait, MD, FAAP, Chief Medical Officer

4517 American Academy of Sleep Medicine
2510 N Frontage Road
Darien, IL 60561
630-737-9700
Fax: 630-737-9790
contact@aasm.org
aasm.org

As the leading voice in the sleep field, the AASM sets standards and promotes excellence in sleep medicine health care, education, and research. The AASM has a combined membership of 11,000 accredited member sleep centers and individual members, including physicians, scientists, and other health care professionals.

Steve Van Hout, Executive Director

4518 American Association of Sleep Technologists
330 N Wabash Avenue, Suite 2000
Chicago, IL 60611
312-321-5191
info@aastweb.org
www.aastweb.org

The American Association of Sleep Technologists is the leading advocate for the sleep technologist profession. Our mission is to promote and advance the profession through the continued development of educational, technical and clinical excellence in sleep disorders.

Heather Rich, Executive Director
Leah Laskowski, Operations Senior Coordinator

4519 American Board of Sleep Medicine
2510 North Frontage Road
Darien, IL 60561
630-737-9701
Fax: 630-737-9790
www.absm.org

The American Board of Sleep Medicine (ABSM) is an independent, nonprofit organization whose certificates are recognized throughout the world as a credential signifying a high level of competence for sleep medicine physicians, PhDs, behavioral sleep medicine specialists and sleep technologists.

Steve Van Hout, Executive Director

4520 American Mental Health Foundation (AMHF)
P.O. Box 3
Riverdale, NY 10471
USA
212-737-9027
elomke@americanmentalhealthfoundation.or
www.americanmentalhealthfoundation.org

Dedicated to the extensive and intensive research in the theories and techniques of treatment of emotional illness and to the implementation of reforms in the mental health system. Efforts have resulted in development of better and less expensive treatment methods. Findings are disseminated in English and other major languages.

Sister Joan Curtin, Director
John P. Fowler, Treasurer
Eugene Gollogly, VP

4521 American Sleep Medicine Foundation
2510 North Frontage Road
Darien, IL 60561
630-737-9724
Fax: 630-737-9700
foundation@aasm.org
foundation.aasm.org

Founded in 1998, the American Academy of Sleep Medicine Foundation (AASM Foundation) is a not-for-profit 501(c)(3) charitable and scientific organization that was established by the AASM. Formerly the American Sleep Medicine Foundation (ASMF), the AASM Foundation has invested in the future of sleep medicine by supporting more than 311 grants totaling over $23.6 million in funding. Our portfolio includes research grants for all career stages, community grants and training grants.

4522 Mental Health America
500 Montgomery Street, Ste 820
Alexandria, VA 22314

703-684-7722
800-969-6642
Fax: 703-684-5968
www.mentalhealthamerica.net

MHA, the leading advocacy organization addressing the full spectrum of mental and substance use conditions and their effects nationwide, works to inform, advocate and enable access to quality behavioral health services for all Americans.

Paul Gionfriddo, President/CEO
Whitney Ball, Assoc. Dir., Marketing/Outreach
Sachin Doshi, Sr. Dir, Finance/Operations

4523 NADD: National Association for the Dually Diagnosed
12 Hurley Avenue
Kingston, NY 12401

845-331-4336
800-331-5362
Fax: 845-331-4569
info@thenadd.org
www.thenadd.org

Nonprofit organization designed to promote the interests of professional and parent development with resources for individuals who have the coexistence of mental illness and intellectual disabilities. Provides conferences, educational services and training materials to professionals, parents, concerned citizens and service organizations.

Jeanne Farr, CEO
Michelle Jordan, Office Manager
Edward Seliger, Project Coordinator

4524 National Alliance on Mental Illness (NAMI)
4301 Wilson Blvd., Suite 300
Arlington, VA 22203

703-524-7600
888-999-6264
info@nami.org
www.nami.org

NAMI provides advocacy, education, support and public awareness so that all individuals and families affected by mental illness can build better lives.

Daniel H. Gillison, CEO
David Levy, CFO
Ken Duckworth, Chief Medical Officer

4525 National Federation of Families
15800 Crabbs Branch Way, Suite 300
Rockville, MD 20855

240-403-1901
ffcmh@ffcmh.org
www.ffcmh.org

The National family run organization is dedicated exclusively to helping children with mental health needs and their families achieve a better quality of life.

Lynda Gargan, PhD, Executive Director

4526 National Mental Health Consumers' Self-Help Clearinghouse
1211 Chestnut Street, Suite 1207
Philadelphia, PA 19107

267-507-3810
800-553-4539
Fax: 215-636-6312
selfhelpclearinghouse@gmail.com
www.mhselfhelp.org

Offers information, support and appropriate referrals; and promotes public and professional education. Provides networking for those with special interests related to albinism. Promotes and supports research and funding that will improve diagnosis and management of albinism and hypopigmentation.

Joseph Rogers, Founder/Executive Director
Susan Rogers, Director

4527 National Sleep Foundation
1414 NE 42nd St, Ste 400
Seattle, WA 98105

contact@sleepfoundation.org
www.sleepfoundation.org

Works to improve the quality of life for millions of Americans who suffer from sleep disorders, and to prevent the catastrophic accidents that are related to poor or disordered sleep through research, education and the dissemination of information towards the cause of the Narcolepsy Project. Seeks patients to aid new research project targeting the cause of the disorder.

Bill Fish, General Manager

4528 Sleep Research Society
2510 North Frontage Road
Darien, IL 60561

630-737-9702
coordinator@srsnet.org
www.sleepresearchsociety.org

The Sleep Research Society (SRS) is organization for scientific investigators who educate and research sleep and sleep disorders. The SRS serves its members and the field of sleep research through training and education, and by providing forums for the collaboration and the exchange of ideas.

John A. Noel, Executive Director

4529 Society of Behavioral Sleep Medicine
1522 Player Drive
Lexington, KY 40511

859-312-8880
membership@behavioralsleep.org
www.behavioralsleep.org

Behavioral Sleep Medicine is the field of clinical practice and scientific inquiry that encompasses: the study of behavioral, psychological, and physiological factors underlying normal and disordered sleep across the life span; and, the development and application of evidence-based behavioral and psychological approaches to the prevention and treatment of sleep disorders and co-existing conditions.

Kathryn Hansen, Executive Director

State Agencies & Support Groups

4530 Center for Family Support
333 7th Avenue, #901
New York, NY 10001

212-629-7939
Fax: 212-239-2211
www.cfsny.org

The Center for Family (CFS) is a not-for-profit human service agency providing support and assistance to individuals with developmental disabilities and traumatic brain injuries throughout New York City, Long Island, the lower Hudson Valley region and New Jersey.

Steven Vernikoff, Executive Director
Linda Schellenberg, Director, Community Service
Barbara Greenwald, Associate Executive Director

Libraries & Resource Centers

4531 American Academy of Somnology
PO Box 27077
Las Vegas, NV 89126

702-371-0947
somnology@aol.com
www.hopperinstitute.com/aas_intro.html

Covers about 75 physicians, dentists, nurses, psychologists, technicians, and students and sponsoring organizations, including associations, institutions, and corporations, with a special interest in sleep.

David Hopper, Director

Web Sites

4532 CyberPsych
www.cyberpsych.org

www.cyberpsych.org

Nightmares / Book Publishers

CyberPsych presents information about psychoanalysis, psychotherapy, and special topics such as anxiety disorder, the problematic use of alcohol, homophobia, and the traumatic effects of racism. CyberPsych is a nonprofit network which offers free web hosting and technical support for internet communication, to non profit groups and individuals.

4533 NADD: National Association for the Dually Diagnosed
12 Hurley Avenue
Kingston, NY 12401
845-331-4336
800-331-5362
Fax: 845-331-4569
www.thenadd.org

Nonprofit organization designed to promote the interests of professional and care providers for individuals who have the coexistence of mental illness and intellectual disabilities. NADD provides conferences, educational services and training materials to professionals, parents, concerned citizens and service organizations.

Jeanne Farr, CEO
Michelle Jordan, Office Manager
Edward Seliger, Project Coordinator

4534 Psych Central
55 Pleasant St., Suite 207
Newburyport, MA 1950
talkback@psychcentral.com
www.psychcentral.com

Offers free informational and educational articles and resources on psychology, support and mental health online.

John M. Grohol, CEO & Founder

4535 Sleep Disorders
http://talhost.net/sleep/parasomnia.htm

http://talhost.net/sleep/parasomnia.htm

For those who have sleep disorders and have a problem sleeping.

4536 Sleepdisorders.com
www.sleepdisorders.com

www.sleepdisorders.com

Updated monthly and organized by sleep disorders with quality links.

Book Publishers

4537 Concise Guide to Evaluation and Management of Sleep Disorders
American Psychiatric Publishing
1000 Wilson Boulevard, Suite 1825
Arlington, VA 22209
703-907-7322
800-368-5777
Fax: 703-907-1091
appi@psych.org
www.appi.org

Overview of sleep disorders medicine, sleep physiology and pathology, insomnia complaints, excessive sleepiness disorders, parasomnias, medical and psychiatric disorders and sleep, medications with sedative-hypnotic properties, special problems and populations.

2002 296 pages Paper 3rd Ed
ISBN: 1-585620-45-6

Robert E. Hales, M.D., Editor-in-Chief
Rebecca D. Rinehart, Publisher
John McDuffie, Editorial Director

4538 Sleep Disorders and Psychiatry
Daniel J Buysse MD, author

American Psychiatric Publishing
1000 Wilson Boulevard, Ste 1825
Arlington, VA 22209
703-907-7322
800-368-5777
Fax: 703-907-1091
appi@psych.org
www.appi.org

Summarizes the major categories of sleep disorders including parasomnias and narcolepsy.

2005 256 pages Paperback
ISBN: 1-585622-29-0

Robert E. Hales, M.D., Editor-in-Chief
Rebecca D. Rinehart, Publisher
John McDuffie, Editorial Director

4539 Snoring From A to Zzzz
Spencer Press
2525 NW Lovejoy Street, Suite 402
Portland, OR 97210
503-223-4959
Fax: 503-223-1608
dereklipman@aol.com

Covers organizations, associations, support groups, and manufacturers of sleep-related medical products relevant to sleep disorders. Discussess every aspect of snoring abd sleep apnea from causes to cures.

256 pages Paperback
ISBN: 0-965070-81-6

Derek Lipman MD, Author/Editor

Description

4540 NIGHT TERRORS

Synonyms: Pavor nocturnus, Sleep-terror disorder

Involves the following Biologic System(s):

Developmental/Behavioral/Psychiatric Disorders

Night terrors is a sleep disorder characterized by episodes of sudden awakening from sleep in an extremely anxious or terrified state. This sleep disturbance occurs in from two to five children out of every hundred, and, in most cases, begins during the fourth to seventh year of life. Sleep-terror disorder more commonly affects boys than girls and often disappears before the onset of adolescence.

Episodes of night terrors usually take place during the third or fourth stage of the nonrapid eye movement or NREM phase of sleep. Each stage of NREM sleep is a successively deeper sleep leading up to rapid eye movement sleep or a deep REM during which dreams may occur. Typically, affected children awaken abruptly and may be screaming and extremely frightened. They may be in a semiconscious state and unaware of or unable to recognize people or surroundings. These children are generally inconsolable and may exhibit such physical symptoms as sweating; widening (dilation) of the pupils; elevated heart rate (tachycardia); abnormally deep, rapid breathing (hyperventilation); and violent thrashing. In about a third of patients, sleepwalking (somnambulism) may also occur. Children are usually able to fall back to sleep within minutes of these short-lived episodes and have no memory of the event when they awaken.

Night terrors are most often confused with nightmares, but unlike night terrors, a child having a nightmare is usually easily woken up and comforted. Sleep disorders such as night terrors often result from childhood fears or anxieties. For example, some young children may be apprehensive about going to bed because this actually represents a temporary separation from their parents (separation anxiety). In addition, any issues affecting the family or child (e.g., separation, divorce, death, school performance, social interactions, etc.) may translate into disturbances in normal sleep patterns. Other contributing factors may include the presence of a fever, depression, or other emotional disorders.

Although the administration of certain antianxiety and antidepressant drugs may, in some cases, be of benefit, treatment of night terrors is mainly supportive. If the precipitating cause can be determined, steps may then be taken to alleviate the fear or anxiety. In any case, parents or caregivers are encouraged to be supportive and firm, but nonjudgmental. Excitement before bedtime is discouraged; however, reading or other quiet, pleasurable activities may be beneficial.

Government Agencies

4541 Center for Mental Health Services
5600 Fishers Lane
Rockville, MD 20857

240-276-1310
www.samhsa.gov

Encourages a range of programs such as systems of care to respond to the increasing number of mental, emotional, and behavioral problems among children. Supports outreach and case management programs for the thousands of Americans who are homeless and the improvement of these services.

4542 NIH/National Institute of Mental Health
6001 Executive Blvd, Rm 6200, MSC 9663
Bethesda, MD 20892

866-615-6464
Fax: 301-443-4279
TTY: 301-443-8431
www.nimh.nih.gov

The mission of NIMH is to transform the understanding and treatment of mental illnesses through basic and clinical research, paving the way for prevention, recovery, and cure.

Joshua A. Gordon, MD, PhD, Director
Shelli Avenevoli, PhD, Deputy Director

National Associations & Support Groups

4543 American Academy of Pediatrics
345 Park Blvd
Itasca, IL 60143

847-434-4000
800-433-9016
Fax: 847-434-8000
csc@aap.org
www.aap.org

The American Academy of Pediatrics and its member pediatricians are committed to the attainment of optimal physical, mental and social health and well-being for all infants, children, adolescents, and young adults.

Kyle E. Yasuda, MD, FAAP, President
Mark Del Monte, JD, CEO/Executive VP
Vera Tait, MD, FAAP, Chief Medical Officer

4544 American Academy of Sleep Medicine
2510 N Frontage Road
Darien, IL 60561

630-737-9700
Fax: 630-737-9790
contact@aasm.org
aasm.org

As the leading voice in the sleep field, the AASM sets standards and promotes excellence in sleep medicine health care, education, and research. The AASM has a combined membership of 11,000 accredited member sleep centers and individual members, including physicians, scientists, and other health care professionals.

Steve Van Hout, Executive Director

4545 American Mental Health Foundation (AMHF)
P.O. Box 3
Riverdale, NY 10471
USA

212-737-9027
elomke@americanmentalhealthfoundation.or
www.americanmentalhealthfoundation.org

Dedicated to the extensive and intensive research in the theories and techniques of treatment of emotional illness and to the implementation of reforms in the mental health system. Efforts have resulted in development of better and less expensive treatment methods. Findings are disseminated in English and other major languages.

Sister Joan Curtin, Director
John P. Fowler, Treasurer
Eugene Gollogly, VP

4546 Center for Disabilities and Development
University of Iowa Stead Family Children's Hospita
100 Hawkins Drive
Iowa City, IA 52242

319-353-6900
877-686-0031
Fax: 319-356-7700
cdd-webmaster@uiowa.edu
www.medicine.uiowa.edu

A trusted resource for healthcare, training, research and information for people with disabilities that include: behavior disorders, brain injury, cerebral palsy, diabetes, down syndrome, learning disabilities, sleep disorders and spina bifida.

Dianne McBrien, MD, Medical Director

Night Terrors / State Agencies & Support Groups

4547 **NADD: National Association for the Dually Diagnosed**
12 Hurley Avenue
Kingston, NY 12401
845-331-4336
800-331-5362
Fax: 845-331-4569
info@thenadd.org
www.thenadd.org

Nonprofit organization designed to promote the interests of professional and parent development with resources for individuals who have the coexistence of mental illness and intellectual disabilities. Provides conferences, educational services and training materials to professionals, parents, concerned citizens and service organizations.

Jeanne Farr, CEO
Michelle Jordan, Office Manager
Edward Seliger, Project Coordinator

4548 **National Federation of Families**
15800 Crabbs Branch Way, Suite 300
Rockville, MD 20855
240-403-1901
ffcmh@ffcmh.org
www.ffcmh.org

The National family run organization is dedicated exclusively to helping children with mental health needs and their families achieve a better quality of life.

Lynda Gargan, PhD, Executive Director

4549 **National Mental Health Consumers' Self-Help Clearinghouse**
1211 Chestnut Street, Suite 1207
Philadelphia, PA 19107
267-507-3810
800-553-4539
Fax: 215-636-6312
selfhelpclearinghouse@gmail.com
www.mhselfhelp.org

Offers information, support and appropriate referrals; and promotes public and professional education. Provides networking for those with special interests related to albinism. Promotes and supports research and funding that will improve diagnosis and management of albinism and hypopigmentation.

Joseph Rogers, Founder/Executive Director
Susan Rogers, Director

4550 **National Sleep Foundation**
1414 NE 42nd St, Ste 400
Seattle, WA 98105
contact@sleepfoundation.org
www.sleepfoundation.org

Works to improve the quality of life for millions of Americans who suffer from sleep disorders, and to prevent the catastrophic accidents that are related to poor or disordered sleep through research, education and the dissemination of information towards the cause of the Narcolepsy Project. Seeks patients to aid new research project targeting the cause of the disorder.

Bill Fish, General Manager

State Agencies & Support Groups

4551 **Center for Family Support**
333 7th Avenue, #901
New York, NY 10001
212-629-7939
Fax: 212-239-2211
www.cfsny.org

The Center for Family (CFS) is a not-for-profit human service agency providing support and assistance to individuals with developmental disabilities and traumatic brain injuries throughout New York City, Long Island, the lower Hudson Valley region and New Jersey.

Steven Vernikoff, Executive Director
Linda Schellenberg, Director, Community Service
Barbara Greenwald, Associate Executive Director

Libraries & Resource Centers

4552 **American Academy of Somnology**
PO Box 27077
Las Vegas, NV 89126
702-371-0947
somnology@aol.com
www.hopperinstitute.com/aas_intro.html

Covers about 75 physicians, dentists, nurses, psychologists, technicians, and students and sponsoring organizations, including associations, institutions, and corporations, with a special interest in sleep.

David Hopper, Director

Research Centers

4553 **UC Berkeley School of Social Welfare**
Mental Health & Social Welfare Research Group
120 Haviland Hall #7400
Berkeley, CA 94720
510-642-4341
Fax: 510-643-6126
spsegal@berkeley.edu
www.socialwelfare.berkeley.edu

Steven P Segal, Director

Web Sites

4554 **About.com on Sleep Disorders**
www.sleepdisorders.about.com

www.sleepdisorders.about.com

Well-organized information including new developments and a chat room.

4555 **CyberPsych**
www.cyberpsych.org

www.cyberpsych.org

Presents information about psychoanalysis, psychtherapy and special topics such as anxiety disorder, the problamatic use of alcohol, homophobia, and the traumatic effects of racism.

4556 **NADD: National Association for the Dually Diagnosed**
12 Hurley Avenue
Kingston, NY 12401
845-331-4336
800-331-5362
Fax: 845-331-4569
www.thenadd.org

Nonprofit organization designed to promote the interests of professional and care providers for individuals who have the coexistence of mental illness and intellectual disabilities. NADD provides conferences, educational services and training materials to professionals, parents, concerned citizens and service organizations.

Jeanne Farr, CEO
Michelle Jordan, Office Manager
Edward Seliger, Project Coordinator

4557 **Psych Central**
55 Pleasant St., Suite 207
Newburyport, MA 1950
talkback@psychcentral.com
www.psychcentral.com

Offers free informational and educational articles and resources on psychology, support and mental health online.

John M. Grohol, CEO & Founder

4558 **Sleep Disorders**
http://talhost.net/sleep/parasomnia.htm

http://talhost.net/sleep/parasomnia.htm

For those who have sleep disorders and have a problem sleeping.

4559 **Sleepdisorders.com**
www.sleepdisorders.com

www.sleepdisorders.com

Updated monthly and organized by sleep disorders with quality links.

Book Publishers

4560 Concise Guide to Evaluation and Management of Sleep Disorders
American Psychiatric Publishing
1000 Wilson Boulevard, Suite 1825
Arlington, VA 22209
703-907-7322
800-368-5777
Fax: 703-907-1091
appi@psych.org
www.appi.org

Overview of sleep disorders medicine, sleep physiology and pathology, insomnia complaints, excessive sleepiness disorders, parasomnias, medical and psychiatric disorders and sleep, medications with sedative-hypnotic properties, special problems and populations.

2002 296 pages Paper 3rd Ed
ISBN: 1-585620-45-6

Robert E. Hales, M.D., Editor-in-Chief
Rebecca D. Rinehart, Publisher
John McDuffie, Editorial Director

4561 Principles and Practice of Sleep Medicine
Elsevier Health Sciences Division
1600 John F Kennedy Blvd, Suite 1800
Philadelphia, PA 19103
215-239-3900
800-523-1649
Fax: 215-239-3990
www.us.elsevierhealth.com

Covers the recent advances in basic sciences as well as sleep pathology in adults. Encompasses developments in this rapidly advancing field and also includes topics related to psychiatry, circadian rhythms, cardiovascualr diseases and sleep apnea diagnosis and treatment. Hardcover.

2005 1552 pages 4th Edition
ISBN: 0-721607-97-7

4562 Sleep Disorders and Psychiatry
Daniel J Buysse MD, author

American Psychiatric Publishing
1000 Wilson Boulevard, Ste 1825
Arlington, VA 22209
703-907-7322
800-368-5777
Fax: 703-907-1091
appi@psych.org
www.appi.org

Summarizes the major categories of sleep disorders including parasomnias and narcolepsy.

2005 256 pages Paperback
ISBN: 1-585622-29-0

Robert E. Hales, M.D., Editor-in-Chief
Rebecca D. Rinehart, Publisher
John McDuffie, Editorial Director

4563 Snoring From A to Zzzz
Spencer Press
2525 NW Lovejoy Street, Suite 402
Portland, OR 97210
503-223-4959
Fax: 503-223-1608
dereklipman@aol.com

Covers organizations, associations, support groups, and manufacturers of sleep-related medical products relevant to sleep disorders. Discusess every aspect of snoring abd sleep apnea from causes to cures.

256 pages Paperback
ISBN: 0-965070-81-6

Derek S Lipman, MD, Author/Editor

Nocturnal Enuresis / Description

Description

4564 **NOCTURNAL ENURESIS**

Synonym: Bed-wetting

Involves the following Biologic System(s):

Developmental/Behavioral/Psychiatric Disorders, Renal and Urologic Disorders

Nocturnal enuresis or bed-wetting refers to the discharge of urine during the night by children who have achieved urinary control during other periods of the day. It affects an estimated 5 to 7 million children in the United States. This type of bed-wetting is considered primary enuresis if nightly urinary incontinence has persisted since birth. Nocturnal enuresis that occurs in children who were previously continent during the night for a period of one year or more is considered secondary enuresis, a regressive form of this abnormality. Bed-wetting is a very common problem that occurs more often in boys than in girls and tends to run in families. In most cases, enuresis resolves spontaneously. The causes of nocturnal enuresis are varied and may include delayed maturation of certain functions of the nervous system that regulate bladder control, psychological influences, spinal abnormalities (e.g., spina bifida), structural abnormalities or defects, underlying disease (e.g., diabetes mellitus), urinary tract infection, or other physical causes. Secondary enuresis may be precipitated by stressful or traumatic events such as the birth of another child, death, divorce, or other situations that impact on the normal day-to-day routine.

Children with enuresis may undergo evaluation in order to determine if the condition is caused by neurological or physical problems. If this is the case, treatment is geared toward the underlying problem. Other treatment may include such supportive measures as establishing a reward system to give the child incentive to cooperate, charting the child's progress in order to offer positive reinforcement, limiting liquid intake before bedtime, having the child urinate directly before going to bed, and having affected older children take part in laundering soiled clothing and remaking the bed. Parents and caregivers are typically counseled to remain supportive and nonjudgmental. Additional treatment may include behavioral therapy and other counseling that involves both the parents or caregivers and the affected child. Bed-wetting alarms that detect small amounts of urine and certain types of medication (e.g., imipramine and desmopressin acetate nasal spray) may also be used to control enuresis. Imipramine is an antidepressant drug that is usually effective within two weeks; however, relapses are common after the drug is gradually stopped and, therefore, a longer course of administration may become necessary. Desmopressin acetate nasal spray reduces urine output in approximately 70 percent of affected children; however, its beneficial effect is temporary. Other treatment is supportive.

Government Agencies

4565 **NIH/National Institute of Mental Health**
6001 Executive Blvd, Rm 6200, MSC 9663
Bethesda, MD 20892

866-615-6464
Fax: 301-443-4279
TTY: 301-443-8431
nimhinfo@nih.gov
www.nimh.nih.gov

The mission of NIMH is to transform the understanding and treatment of mental illnesses through basic and clinical research, paving the way for prevention, recovery, and cure.

Joshua A. Gordon, MD, PhD, Director
Shelli Avenevoli, PhD, Deputy Director

4566 **National Institute of Diabetes and Digestive and Kidney Diseases - Urology**
9000 Rockville Pike
Bethesda, MD 20892

800-860-8747
TTY: 866-659-1162
healthinfo@niddk.nih.gov
www.urologic.niddk.nih.gov

To increase knowledge and understanding about diseases of the kidneys and urologic system among people with these conditions and their families, health care professionals and the general public.

National Associations & Support Groups

4567 **American Academy of Pediatrics**
345 Park Blvd
Itasca, IL 60143

847-434-4000
800-433-9016
Fax: 847-434-8000
csc@aap.org
www.aap.org

The American Academy of Pediatrics and its member pediatricians are committed to the attainment of optimal physical, mental and social health and well-being for all infants, children, adolescents, and young adults.

Kyle E. Yasuda, MD, FAAP, President
Mark Del Monte, JD, CEO/Executive VP
Vera Tait, MD, FAAP, Chief Medical Officer

4568 **Association for the Bladder Exstrophy Community**
505 Beachland Boulevard, Suite 1-#180
Vero Beach, FL 32963

425-941-1475
admin@bladderexstrophy.com
www.bladderexstrophy.com

The ABC is an international support network of individuals with bladder exstrophy (includes classic exstrophy, cloacal exstrophy, and epispadias), local parent-exstrophy support groups, and health care providers working with patients and families living with bladder exstrophy.

Pamela Artigas, President & Executive Director
Misty Blue Foster, Communications Manager
Jeffrey A. Niezgoda, Founder & President Emeritus

4569 **Mental Health America**
500 Montgomery Street, Ste 820
Alexandria, VA 22314

703-684-7722
800-969-6642
Fax: 703-684-5968
www.mentalhealthamerica.net

MHA, the leading advocacy organization addressing the full spectrum of mental and substance use conditions and their effects nationwide, works to inform, advocate and enable access to quality behavioral health services for all Americans.

Paul Gionfriddo, President/CEO
Whitney Ball, Assoc. Dir., Marketing/Outreach
Sachin Doshi, Sr. Dir, Finance/Operations

4570 **National Federation of Families**
15800 Crabbs Branch Way, Suite 300
Rockville, MD 20855

240-403-1901
ffcmh@ffcmh.org
www.ffcmh.org

The National family run organization is dedicated exclusively to helping children with mental health needs and their families achieve a better quality of life.

Lynda Gargan, PhD, Executive Director

4571 **National Mental Health Consumers' Self-Help Clearinghouse**
1211 Chestnut Street, Suite 1207
Philadelphia, PA 19107

215-751-1810
800-553-4539
Fax: 215-636-6312
selfhelpclearinghouse@gmail.com
www.mhselfhelp.org

Offers information, support and appropriate referrals; and promotes public and professional education. Provides networking for those with special interests related to albinism. Promotes and supports research and funding that will improve diagnosis and management of albinism and hypopigmentation.

Joseph Rogers, Founder/Executive Director
Susan Rogers, Director

4572 National Sleep Foundation
1414 NE 42nd St, Ste 400
Seattle, WA 98105

contact@sleepfoundation.org
www.sleepfoundation.org

Works to improve the quality of life for millions of Americans who suffer from sleep disorders, and to prevent the catastrophic accidents that are related to poor or disordered sleep through research, education and the dissemination of information towards the cause of the Narcolepsy Project. Seeks patients to aid new research project targeting the cause of the disorder.

Bill Fish, General Manager

Web Sites

4573 American Urological Association Foundation
1000 Corporate Boulevard
Linthicum, MD 21090

410-689-3700
800-828-7866
Fax: 410-689-3998
info@urologycarefoundation.org
www.urologyhealth.org

Provides information on enuresis as well as other pediatric disorders related to the kidneys and bladder.

Richard A. Memo, MD, Chair
Steven Schlossberg, MD, MBA, Secretary/Treasurer
Martin Dineen, Member-at-Large

4574 Bedwetting Online
www.bedwetting.ferring.ca

www.bedwetting.ferring.ca

Helps parents and children deal with Nocturnal Enuresis.

4575 Child Development Institute
500 State College, Suite 1100
Orange, CA 92868childdevelopmentinfo.com/disorders/bedwetting.shtml

Child development and parent information for learning, health and safety, as well as child disorders.

4576 Dr. Koop
750 Third Avenue, 6th Floor
New York, NY 10017

212-695-2223
Fax: 212-695-2936
www.healthcentral.com

Information on the condition, causes, symptoms, tests and treatment.

Michael Cunnion, Chief Executive Officer
Jim Curtis, Chief Revenue Officer
Rebecca Farwell, Chief Content Officer

Non-Hodgkin's Lymphoma / Description

Description

4577 NON-HODGKIN'S LYMPHOMA

Synonym: NHL

Covers these related disorders: Non-Hodgkin's lymphoma, large cell type, Non-Hodgkin's lymphoma, lymphoblastic type, Non-Hodgkin's lymphoma, small noncleaved cell(SNC)

Involves the following Biologic System(s):

Hematologic and Oncologic Disorders

Non-Hodgkin's lymphoma (NHL) consists of a group of cancers of the body's lymphatic system. This specialized system consists of the spleen, thymus gland, adenoids and tonsils, lymph nodes, and lymph ducts. Together these structures carry the clear fluid known as lymph and the white blood cells known as lymphocytes, and drain fluid and waste products from the body's organs and tissues. The lymph nodes act as tiny sieves that filter invading organisms and cancerous cells from the lymph that passes through the nodes, while lymphocytes in the nodes and elsewhere in the lymphatic system attack and destroy these hostile organisms and malignant cells. Besides its presence in these lymphatic structures, lymphatic tissue is present in the skin, stomach, and small intestine.

Non-Hodgkin lymphoma (NHL) is characterized by the proliferation of either T- or B-lymphocytes (white blood cells).T-lymphocytes act directly against infecting microorganisms and body cells that have turned cancerous by coming into contact with these hostile organisms or cells and secreting substances that either kill them directly or mark them for killing by other blood cells. B-cells combat infection by secreting antibodies that target alien microorganisms for killing by other cells. Types of NHL that occur among T-cells include the diseases known as mycosis fungoides, anaplastic large cell lymphoma, and precursor T-lymphoblastic lymphoma. Most NHLs occurring in the United States are B-cell lymphomas, whichinclude chronic lymphocytic leukemia/small lymphocytic lymphoma (CLL/SLL), diffuse large B-cell lymphoma, follicular lymphoma, Burkitt's lymphoma, immunoblastic large cell lymphoma, precursor B-lymphoblastic lymphoma, and mantle cell lymphoma, as well as the condition named hairy-cell leukemia because of the hair-like projections that extend from the abnormal B-lymphocytes in this disease.

Most types of NHL arise from lymph nodes in the head and neck, the chest cavity, or the abdomen. Some types may develop in lymph nodes at other sites in the body or affect other structures of the lymphoid system or other tissues, and a close association exists between specific types of NHL and the sites at which these diseases initially occur. For example, lymphoblastic NHL, which affects the immature cells that become lymphocytes, tends to arise in the head and neck or in the front of the chest cavity (anterior mediastinum).

Besides consisting of these different diseases, NHL is classified as being either aggressive, where lymphocytes multiply rapidly, or indolent, where cells proliferate slowly. Every individual case is further classified into one of four stages, based on the degree of progression. NHL symbolized by "E" indicates that the disease exists in lymphatic structures or tissues besides or beyond the lymph nodes; "S" indicates that it exists in the spleen.

Although lymphomas can occur at any age, they are the third most common kinds of childhood cancers in the United States, affecting about 13 of every 1 million children annually. While all lymphomas originate with a genetic defect in white cells or their immature precursor cells, other factors may instigate these lymphoid cancers or increase susceptibility to them. Thus, NHL particularly affects children with impaired immune systems. These include patients with acquired immune deficiency syndrome (AIDS) or certain genetic immunodeficiency disorders that are present at birth (primary immunodeficiencies), such as Wiskott-Aldrich syndrome, a condition marked by deficiencies in the numbers of platelet cells in the blood and in the body's immune system; X-linked lymphoproliferative syndrome; or ataxia-telangiectasia. Other sources of increased risk of developing NHL include infection with Epstein-Barr virus, which causes infectious mononucleosis; a high dietary meat or fat intake; and exposure to various pesticides and other toxic substances.

The diagnosis of NHL is based on physical examination, which may reveal swelling of the lymph nodes and other telltale signs of the disease; a complete blood count (CBC) that reveals increased numbers of either T- or B-lymphocytes and possibly decreased numbers of other kinds of blood cells; a decreased content of the oxygen-carrying substance known as hemoglobin in the body's red blood cells; abnormalities in tissue specimens taken from lymph nodes or other structures of the lymphatic system or in the bone marrow where lymphocyte progenitor cells originate. Procedures used to determine the stage of NHL in a particular patient include chest X-rays, computed tomography (CT), positron emission tomography (PET), magnetic resonance imaging (MRI), and the technique known as gallium scanning, in which a minuscule quantity of the element known as gallium is injected into the body and accumulates at sites where cancerous cells are proliferating, providing images of such disease activity.

In children with NHL, initial symptoms and findings vary and depend upon the specific type of the disease, its location, and its stage, or level of involvement. Findings often include painless swelling of lymph nodes in the neck, groin, or deep within the abdominal or chest region. Tumor growth in the chest cavity area may result in abnormal accumulations of fluid (pleural effusion) between layers of the lung lining (pleura), as well as difficulty in breathing and abnormal swelling of tissues of the face, neck, and arms, causing difficulty in swallowing. Other symptoms can include nausea, vomiting, lack of appetite (anorexia), abdominal pain and swelling (distension), severe constipation, or other digestive symptoms. Some cases of NHL affect the skin, resulting in dark, thickened, itchy patches. Tumors in the bone marrow may result in decreased numbers of red blood cells (anemia) or platelets (thrombocytopenia). In advanced cases of NHL, involvement of the brain may cause increased fluid pressure around the brain, severe headache, and p aralysis of certain nerves. As it progresses, NHL may also increasingly cripple the body's immune system and impair its infection-fighting ability, leading to potentially severe or life-threatening infections.

NHL is classified into different stages, based upon the number and location of tumors, the degree that the disease has spread, and other factors. Both the prognosis or outlook for patients with NHL and their treatment depend on the stage and type of their disease.

Treatment typically involves the use of drugs that kill cancerous cells known as cytotoxic drugs; radiation therapy, in which X-rays are directed at lymph nodes and other body sites affected by disease; immunotherapy, in which substances that bolster the immune system are given to help restore its infection-fighting and other capabilities; and biotherapy, in which a drug named rituximab, belonging to a highly cell- and tissue-specific group of newer drugs known as monoclonal antibodies, is used to hone in on cancerous cells and assist the immune system in destroying them. Treatment may also include the use of bone marrow transplantation to help restore the ability of the bone marrow to generate new lymphocytes and other blood cells to replace those affected by NHL or destroyed by the drugs or radiation used to treat it. In many cases, two or more of these treatment methods are combined with one another to combat NHL. In the recent technique known as radioimmunotherapy, monoclonal antibodies that specifically hone in on cancerous cells are linked to radioactive substances that carry these substances directly to such cells and kill them.

Both chemotherapy and radiation therapy for NHL can have side effects, including nausea and vomiting, diarrhea, weight loss, hair loss, and fatigue. Some children also experience psychological depression. Most of these effects are transitory, and gradually disappear after treatment is completed. More potentially serious side effects are declines in the numbers of infection-fighting cells. Severe neutrophil deficiency, or neutropenia, can open the way to infection, and may require treatment with granulocyte colony-stimulating factor (G-CSF), which promotes the proliferation of neutrophils and thus reduces the risk of infection. In some cases, antibiotics are used to prevent and treat infection occurring in patients with NHL. Serious but infrequent complications of treatment for NHL include sterility, from radiation therapy; osteoporosis, from treatment-related damage to bone cells; and damage to the heart by some drugs used in chemotherapy for NHL.

Government Agencies

4578 **NIH/National Cancer Institute**
Bethesda, MD 20892

800-422-6237
NCIinfo@nih.gov
www.cancer.gov

The National Cancer Institute coordinates the National Cancer Program, which conducts and supports research, training, health information dissemination, and other programs with respect to the cause, diagnosis, prevention, and treatment of cancer, rehabilitation from cancer, and the continuing care of cancer patients and the families of cancer patients.

Norman E. Sharpless, MD, Director
Douglas R. Lowy, MD, Principal Deputy Director

National Associations & Support Groups

4579 **American Academy of Pediatrics**
345 Park Blvd
Itasca, IL 60143

847-434-4000
800-433-9016
Fax: 847-434-8000
csc@aap.org
www.aap.org

The American Academy of Pediatrics and its member pediatricians are committed to the attainment of optimal physical, mental and social health and well-being for all infants, children, adolescents, and young adults.

Kyle E. Yasuda, MD, FAAP, President
Mark Del Monte, JD, CEO/Executive VP
Vera Tait, MD, FAAP, Chief Medical Officer

4580 **American Childhood Cancer Organization**
P.O. Box 498
Kensington, MD 20895

301-962-3520
855-858-2226
Fax: 310-962-3521
staff@acco.org
www.acco.org

The American Childhood Cancer Organization (ACCO) was founded in 1970 by a group of parents whose children had been diagnosed with cancer. Today ACCO is one of the largest grassroots, national organizations dedicated to improving the lives of children and adolescents with cancer and their families.

Ruth I. Hoffman, MPH, CEO
Krista Novak, Programs Manager
Blair Scroggs, Public Relations Coordinator

4581 **CancerCare**
275 7th Avenue
New York, NY 10001

212-712-8400
800-813-4673
Fax: 212-712-8495
info@cancercare.org
www.cancercare.org

Dedicated to providing emotional support, information, and practical help to people with cancer and their loved ones. CancerCare is the oldest, largest, nonprofit agency devoted to offering professional services.

Patricia J Goldsmith, CEO
Christine Verini, RPh, COO

4582 **Childhood Leukemia Foundation**
807 Mantoloking Road
Brick, NJ 08723

732-920-8860
888-253-7109
www.clf4kids.org

Childhood Leukemia Foundation proudly promotes patient education, advocacy and self-esteem.

4583 **CureSearch for Children's Cancer**
P.O. Box 45781
Baltimore, MD 21297

800-458-6223
Fax: 301-718-0047
info@curesearch.org
www.curesearch.org

CureSearch for Children's Cancer is a national non-profit foundation that accelerates the cure for children's cancer by driving innovation, eliminating research barriers and solving the field's most challenging problems.

Kay Koehler, CEO
Katharine A. Burke, COO & VP, Financing
Caitlyn W. Barrett, National Director, Research & Prgms

4584 **Leukemia & Lymphoma Society**
3 International Drive, Ste 200
Rye Brook, NY 10573

888-557-7177
www.lls.org

Large voluntary health organization dedicated to funding blood cancer research, education and patient services.

Louis J. DeGennaro, PhD, President & CEO
Troy Dunmire, COO
Gwen Nichols, MD, Chief Medical Officer

4585 **Lymphoma Research Foundation**
88 Pine Street, Suite 2400
New York, NY 10005

212-349-2910
800-500-9976
helpline@lymphoma.org
lymphoma.org

National nonprofit organization dedicated to eradicating lymphoma and serving those touched by this disease. LRF funds research to develop safer, more effective treatments and ultimately, a cure for lymphoma. LRF delivers a comprehensive slate of educational and support programs, services, and publications for lymphoma patients and their loved ones.

Meghan Gutierrez, Chief Executive Officer
Kyle Haines, Chief Information Officer
Sarah Quinlan, Chief Program Officer

Web Sites

4586 CancerCare
275 7th Avenue
New York, NY 10001
212-712-8400
800-813-4673
Fax: 212-712-8495
www.cancercare.org

Dedicated to providing emotional support, information, and practical help to people with cancer and their loved ones. CancerCare is the oldest, largest, nonprofit agency devoted to offering professional services.

Patricia J Goldsmith, CEO
Christine Verini, RPh, COO

4587 Children's Cancer Web
www.cancerindex.org/ccw

www.cancerindex.org/ccw

An independent nonprofit site, established to provide a directory of childhood cancer resources.

4588 Leukemia & Lymphoma Society
3 International Drive, Suite 200
Rye Brook, NY 10573
888-557-7177
www.lls.org

Large voluntary health organization dedicated to funding blood cancer research, education and patient services.

Louis J. DeGennaro, PhD, President & CEO
Troy Dunmire, COO
Gwen Nichols, MD, Chief Medical Officer

4589 Lymphoma Innovations
www.lymphomainnovations.com

www.lymphomainnovations.com

Targeted information for people with Non Hodgkins Lymphoma.

Book Publishers

4590 Cancer Information for Teens, 4th Edition
Omnigraphics
615 Griswold Street, Ste 520
Detroit, MI 48226
610-461-3548
800-234-1340
Fax: 800-875-1340
contact@omnigraphics.com
www.omnigraphics.com

Updated information and facts about cancer causes, diagnosis, prevention and treatment especially for teens.

480 pages
ISBN: 0-780816-15-2

4591 Cancer Sourcebook

Angela L. Williams, author

Omnigraphics
615 Griswold Street, Ste 520
Detroit, MI 48226
610-461-3548
800-234-1340
Fax: 800-875-1340
contact@omnigraphics.com
www.omnigraphics.com

Updated information and facts about cancer causes, diagnosis, prevention and treatment. Nearly 1.5 million people in the US are diagnosed with cancer every year.

1224 pages 8th Edition
ISBN: 0-780816-22-0

4592 Childhood Diseases and Disorders Sourcebook, 4th Edition
Omnigraphics
615 Griswold Street, Ste 520
Detroit, MI 48226
610-461-3548
800-234-1340
Fax: 800-875-1340
contact@omnigraphics.com
www.omnigraphics.com

Basic and up to date consumer health information about common disorders that affect the physical, mental, and developmental health of school-age children.

792 pages
ISBN: 0-780815-38-4

4593 Let's Talk About Going to the Hospital
Rosen Publishing Group's PowerKids Press
29 E 21st Street
New York, NY 10010
212-777-3017
800-237-9932
Fax: 888-436-4643
rosenpub@tribeca.ios.com
www.rosenpublishing.com

If a child has to check into the hospital, chances are he or she is already upset about being ill. Knowing how a hospital functions and what the procedures are, such as when family members can visit, will help in what is already a stressful situation. Grades K-5.

24 pages
ISBN: 0-823950-36-0

Roger Rosen, President

4594 Let's Talk About When Kids Have Cancer

Melanie Apel Gordon, author

Rosen Publishing Group's PowerKids Press
29 E 21st Street
New York, NY 10010
212-777-3017
800-237-9932
Fax: 888-436-4643
customerservice@rosenpub.com
www.rosenpublishing.com

In a straightforward yet comforting way, this book explains what cancer is, what kinds of treatments surround the disease and how to cope if a child or the friend of a child has cancer. K-5.

24 pages Paperback
ISBN: 0-823951-95-6

Roger Rosen, President

4595 Surviving Childhood Cancer: A Guide for Families
New Harbinger Publications
5674 Shattuck Avenue
Oakland, CA 94609
510-652-0215
800-748-6273
Fax: 800-652-1613
customerservice@newharbinger.com
www.newharbinger.com

Cancer in a child is an overwhelming experience for a family. This book explains common medical procedures and offers readers practical advice about how to cope with emotions and stress during this time.

215 pages Paperback
ISBN: 1-572241-02-0

Camps

4596 Arizona Camp Sunrise & Sidekicks
PO Box 27872
Tempe, AZ 85285
480-382-8564
928-478-4564
melissa@azcampsunrise.org
www.azcampsunrise.org

The camp is dedicated to provide an exciting, medically safe camp program for children whose families have been affected by cancer.

Melissa Lee, Camp Director

4597 Camp Catch-A-Rainbow
American Cancer Society
One Children's Plaza
Dayton, OH 45404

937-641-3000
800-228-4055
kwilson@ymcastorercamps.org
www.childrensdayton.org

Open to any child (age 7 thru 15) who has, or has had, cancer.

Katie Wilson, Coordinator

4598 Camp Sunshine Dreams
PO Box 28232
Fresno, CA 93729

contact@campsunshinedreams.com
www.campsunshinedreams.com

Summer camp for children with cancer.

Anthony Aiello, Board Member

4599 Okizu Foundation Camps
16 Digital Drive, Suite 130
Novato, CA 94949

415-382-9083
Fax: 415-382-8384
info@okizu.org
www.okizu.org

This foundation runs family camp programs for children who have cancer and their families, and for children who have or had a parent with cancer.

Lori Sparrow, Executive Director
Heather Ferrier, Camp Director of Operations

Noonan Syndrome / Description

Description

4600 NOONAN SYNDROME

Synonyms: Female Pseudo-Turner syndrome, Male Turner syndrome, NS

Involves the following Biologic System(s):
Cardiovascular Disorders,
Genetic/Chromosomal/Syndrome/Metabolic Disorders

Noonan syndrome is a genetic disorder that is usually apparent at birth (congenital) and interferes with the normal development of various body structures and organs. The symptoms and findings associated with the disorder may be extremely variable, differing in range and severity from case to case. However, children with Noonan syndrome often have short stature, webbing of the neck (pterygium colli), and characteristic abnormalities of the head and facial (craniofacial) area, such as downwardly slanting eyelid folds (palpebral fissures), drooping of the upper eyelids (ptosis), a small jaw (micrognathia), and prominent, low-set ears that are rotated toward the back of the head. In addition, in many males with Noonan syndrome, the testes fail to descend into the scrotum (cryptorchidism) before birth or during the first year of life. Therefore, in some cases, the male reproductive cells (sperm) may fail to develop appropriately within the testes, potentially causing infertility.

The genetic mutations responsible for Noonan syndrome chiefly affect four genes, which may be inherited from a parent, or result spontaneously from mutations occurring in the embryo. Most estimates indicate that this syndrome affects one in 1,000 to 2,500 newborns, but it may be difficult to determine the true frequency of Noonan syndrome because of the wide variation in its effects.

Many children with Noonan syndrome have distinctive skeletal malformations, such as abnormal depression of the lower portion of the breastbone (pectus excavatum) and protrusion of the upper portion of the breastbone (pectus carinatum); outward deviation of the elbows upon extension (cubitus valgus); sideways curvature of the spine (scoliosis); or front-to-back curvature of the spine (kyphosis). Affected children may also have structural abnormalities of the heart that are present at birth (congenital heart defects). These include obstruction of normal blood flow from the lower right pumping chamber (ventricle) of the heart to the lungs (pulmonary valvular stenosis). During infancy, there may also be an abnormal accumulation of lymph fluid in body tissues and a consequent swelling of these tissues (lymphedema) as the result of malformations in the body's lymphatic system. Additional symptoms and findings in Noonan syndrome may include deficient functioning of the blood cells known as platelets, which play an essential role in preventing or stopping bleeding; abnormally small numbers of platelets in circulating blood (thrombocytopenia); or defects in blood clotting (coagulation factor), potentially causing abnormal bleeding and susceptibility to bruising. In some cases, children with Noonan syndrome may have intellectual disabilities or experience delays in acquiring certain skills that require the coordination of physical and mental activities.

The diagnosis of Noonan syndrome is based on its physical effects, such as distortions in the chest, neck, ears, or eyelids, together with ultrasound or computed tomographic (CT) scans that reveal congenital heart, or other internal organ, defects, and tests that reveal disorders in blood clotting. The severity of Noonan syndrome in an infant or child is assessed through physical, neurological, and optical examinations; studies of heart function and body development; studies of the brain, spine, and rib cage done with X-ray images and the technique known as magnetic resonance imaging (MRI); ultrasound examination of the kidneys and urinalyses to assess kidney function; hearing tests; and blood and genetic testing.

The treatment of children with Noonan syndrome depends upon its severity and may include drugs, surgery to manage or correct congenital heart defects or to move undescended testes into the scrotum (orchiopexy) in males with cryptorchidism; hormone therapy (i.e., human growth hormone therapy); administration of platelets, blood-clotting factors, and other appropriate measures for treating thrombocytopenia, platelet dysfunction, and abnormalities in blood clotting, special education; and other treatment measures as required. Genetic counseling is recommended if there is a family history of Noonan syndrome.

National Associations & Support Groups

4601 American Academy of Pediatrics
345 Park Blvd
Itasca, IL 60143

847-434-4000
800-433-9016
Fax: 847-434-8000
csc@aap.org
www.aap.org

The American Academy of Pediatrics and its member pediatricians are committed to the attainment of optimal physical, mental and social health and well-being for all infants, children, adolescents, and young adults.

Kyle E. Yasuda, MD, FAAP, President
Mark Del Monte, JD, CEO/Executive VP
Vera Tait, MD, FAAP, Chief Medical Officer

4602 Genetic Alliance
426400 Woodfield Road, Ste 189
Damascus, MD 20872

202-966-5557
Fax: 202-966-8553
info@geneticalliance.org
www.geneticalliance.org

World's leading nonprofit health advocacy organization committed to transforming health through genetics and promoting an environment of openness centered on the health of individuals, families, and communities.

Sharon Terry, CEO
Ruth Child, CFO
Natasha Bonhomme, Chief Strategy Officer

4603 Human Growth Foundation
997 Glen Cove Avenue, Suite 5
Glen Head, NY 11545

800-451-6434
Fax: 516-671-4055
hgfl@hgfound.org
www.hgfound.org

A voluntary, nonprofit organization whose mission is to help children and adults with disorders of growth and growth hormones through research, education, support and advocacy. The foundation is dedicated to helping medical science to better understand the process of growth. It is composed of concerned parents and friends of children and adults with growth problems; and interested health professionals.

Joel Steelman, MD, President
Emily Germain-Lee, MD, Vice President

4604 MAGIC Foundation: Major Aspects of Growth in Children
4200 Cantera Drive, #106
Warrenville, IL 60555

630-836-8200
800-362-4423
Fax: 630-836-8181
contactus@magicfoundation.org
www.magicfoundation.org

A national nonprofit organization providing support and education regarding growth disorders in children and related adult disorders. Provides educational information, networking, a national conference, a kids' program and an extensive medical library.

Dianne Kremidas, Executive Director
Mary Andrews, CEO
Teresa Tucker, Patient Advocacy

4605 March of Dimes Foundation
1550 Crystal Drive, Ste 1300
Arlington, VA 22202

888-663-4637
www.marchofdimes.org

March of Dimes help moms have full-term pregnancies and research the problems that threaten the health of babies. The March of Dimes also acts globally: sharing best practices in perinatal health and helping improve birth outcomes where the needs are the most urgent.

Stacey D. Stewart, President
Alan Brogdon, SVP/COO/Board Officer
Rahul Gupta, MD, SVP & Chief Medical/Health Officer

4606 Noonan Syndrome Foundation
605 SW US Hwy 20, Suite 277
Blue Springs, MO 64014

info@teamnoonan.org
www.teamnoonan.org

The Noonan Syndrome Foundation is a nonprofit that was created to help support, educate, and advocate for and on behalf of all those who have been affected by Noonan Syndrome.

Web Sites

4607 Online Mendelian Inheritance in Man
McKusick-Nathans Institue of Genetic Medicine-JHU
Baltimore, MD 21205

www.omim.org

This database is a catalog of human genes and genetic disorders.

Ada Hamosh, MD, Scientific Director

Book Publishers

4608 Let's Talk About Going to the Hospital
Rosen Publishing Group's PowerKids Press
29 E 21st Street
New York, NY 10010

212-777-3017
800-237-9932
Fax: 888-436-4643
rosenpub@tribeca.ios.com
www.rosenpublishing.com

If a child has to check into the hospital, chances are he or she is already upset about being ill. Knowing how a hospital functions and what the procedures are, such as when family members can visit, will help in what is already a stressful situation. Grades K-5.

24 pages
ISBN: 0-823950-36-0

Roger Rosen, President

Newsletters

4609 Noonan Connection
Noonan Syndrome Support Group
PO Box 145
Upperco, MD 21155

410-374-5245
888-686-2224
www.noonansydrome.org

Provides basic information on Noonan syndrome and related current news and events.

Nystagmus / Description

Description

4610 NYSTAGMUS
Covers these related disorders: Jerky nystagmus, Pendular nystagmus
Involves the following Biologic System(s):
Neurologic Disorders, Ophthalmologic Disorders

Nystagmus is a condition characterized by involuntary, rhythmic movements of the eyes. These movements may be vertical, horizontal, circular, or a mixture of two varieties (mixed). Nystagmus may be present at birth (congenital) or develop later in life (acquired). There are two general categories or types of nystagmus: jerky nystagmus and pendular nystagmus.

Jerky nystagmus is the most common form of the condition. It is characterized by relatively slow movements of the eyes in one direction followed by rapid, corrective movements or jerks in the opposite direction. In many patients with jerky nystagmus, head movements accompany the eye movements. These unusual head movements are thought to represent so-called compensatory posturing, that is, turning of the head to bring the eyes to a position in which the nystagmus lessens and vision is best (null positioning) In pendular nystagmus, movements of the eyes are approximately equal in rate in both directions. The different forms of nystagmus result due to abnormalities in certain mechanisms that regulate the movements and positioning of the eyes. These include conjugate gaze, fixation, and vestibular mechanisms. Conjugate gaze is the normal movement of both eyes in the same direction to bring objects into view. Fixation describes the direction of the gaze so that visual images fall on a certain area of the retina, which is the nerve-rich membrane at the back of the eye (fovea centralis). The vestibular mechanism is the balancing mechanism of the inner ear.

In some affected individuals, pendular or jerky nystagmus is present at birth or develops during early infancy or childhood. Pendular nystagmus often occurs in association with eye and visual defects (e.g., congenital glaucoma, congenital cataract, albinism, etc.). In other patients, pendular nystagmus may be an isolated finding that occurs in the absence of such conditions. Jerky nystagmus is usually unassociated with other eye or visual defects, and its cause is unknown. Familial cases of isolated pendular or jerky nystagmus are reported in which the condition appears to be transmitted as an autosomal dominant, autosomal recessive, or X-linked trait.

A specific, acquired form of pendular nystagmus, known as spasmus nutans, may also affect some infants or children. This condition typically develops at approximately four months to two years of age. In spasmus nutans, nystagmus is accompanied by head nodding and, in some children, abnormal tightness or contractions of the neck muscles, resulting in twisting of the neck and abnormal positioning of the head (torticollis). In most children with spasmus nutans, pendular nystagmus is limited to or more pronounced in one eye. Symptoms usually spontaneously resolve within months or a few years.

Some infants or children may also have a form of nystagmus in which there is repetitive jerking of the eyes toward each other or backward into the eye sockets (convergent nystagmus). This form of nystagmus often occurs with impaired vertical gaze in association with certain underlying syndromes (e.g., Parinaud syndrome, sylvian aqueduct syndrome, etc.).

The development of persistent nystagmus later in life may occur in association with certain disorders of the nervous system (e.g., brain tumors, multiple sclerosis) or disorders affecting the balancing (vestibular) mechanism of the inner ear (labyrinthine-vestibular disease). Individuals with acquired nystagmus should receive immediate, thorough evaluations to diagnose the underlying cause and ensure prompt, appropriate treatment. Medications can cause nystagmus. Causes include excessive drinking of alcohol or use of medications such as those given for seizure control.

In infants and children with nystagmus, diagnostic evaluations typically include the use of a specialized imaging technique (electronystagmography) that records eye movements and helps to determine or confirm the type of nystagmus present. Treatment of patients with nystagmus includes appropriate therapies for any diagnosed, underlying causes of the condition. Other treatment includes symptomatic and supportive measures.

Government Agencies

4611 NIH/National Eye Institute
31 Center Drive MSC 2510
Bethesda, MD 20892
301-496-5248
2020@nei.nih.gov
www.nei.nih.gov

Conducts and supports research that helps prevent and treat eye diseases and other disorders of vision. This research leads to sight-saving treatments, reduces visual impairment and blindness, and improves the quality of life for people of all ages. NEI-supported research has advanced our knowledge of how the eye functions in health and disease.

Michael F. Chiang, MD, Director
Santa Tumminia, Deputy Director

National Associations & Support Groups

4612 American Academy of Pediatrics
345 Park Blvd
Itasca, IL 60143
847-434-4000
800-433-9016
Fax: 847-434-8000
csc@aap.org
www.aap.org

The American Academy of Pediatrics and its member pediatricians are committed to the attainment of optimal physical, mental and social health and well-being for all infants, children, adolescents, and young adults.

Kyle E. Yasuda, MD, FAAP, President
Mark Del Monte, JD, CEO/Executive VP
Vera Tait, MD, FAAP, Chief Medical Officer

4613 American Nystagmus Network
303-D Beltline Place, Suite 321
Decatur, AL 35603
info@nystagmus.org
www.nystagmus.org

A nonprofit organization founded in 1999 to serve the needs and interests of those affected by nystagmus, and to provide information to health care providers, educators and researchers.

4614 Genetic Alliance
426400 Woodfield Road, Ste 189
Damascus, MD 20872
202-966-5557
Fax: 202-966-8553
info@geneticalliance.org
www.geneticalliance.org

World's leading nonprofit health advocacy organization committed to transforming health through genetics and promoting an environment of openness centered on the health of individuals, families, and communities.

Sharon Terry, CEO
Ruth Child, CFO
Natasha Bonhomme, Chief Strategy Officer

4615 Lighthouse Guild
250 West 64th Street
New York, NY 10023
800-284-4422
info@lighthouseguild.org
www.lighthouseguild.org

Lighthouse Guild is dedicated to providing exceptional services that inspire people who are visually impaired to attain their goals.

James M. Dubin, Chair
Calvin W. Roberts, President & CEO
Maura J. Sweeney, SVP, Programs & Services

4616 March of Dimes Foundation
1550 Crystal Drive, Ste 1300
Arlington, VA 22202
888-663-4637
www.marchofdimes.org

March of Dimes help moms have full-term pregnancies and research the problems that threaten the health of babies. The March of Dimes also acts globally: sharing best practices in perinatal health and helping improve birth outcomes where the needs are the most urgent.

Stacey D. Stewart, President
Alan Brogdon, SVP/COO/Board Officer
Rahul Gupta, MD, SVP & Chief Medical/Health Officer

State Agencies & Support Groups

Alabama

4617 Alabama Institute for the Deaf & Blind
205 East South Street
Talladega, AL 35160
256-761-3200
Fax: 256-761-3344
www.aidb.org

Services include central directory, representatives of agencies, service providers, families, and coordinators of infant, toddler, and preschool special education programs.

John Mascia, President
Frieda Meacham, VP
Mike Hubbard, Director

Ohio

4618 Region 2 of the National Association for Parents of the Visually Impaired
3910 Pocahontas Avenue
Cincinnati, OH 45227
513-561-8542
Victoria Gorman Miller

Pennsylvania

4619 East Central Region-Helen Keller National Center
141 Middle Neck Road
Sands Point, NY 11050
516-944-8900
Fax: 516-944-7302
HKNCinfo@hknc.org
www.helenkeller.org

Christopher D. Maher, Chairman
Richard T. Arkwright, Vice-Chairman
John R. Caughey, Treasurer

South Carolina

4620 Region 4 of the National Association for Parents of the Visually Impaired
1032 Trail Road
Belton, SC 29627
864-338-9593

Washington

4621 Northwestern Region-Helen Keller National Center
1620 18th Ave., Ste 201
Seattle, WA 98112
206-324-9120
Fax: 206-324-9159
TTY: 206-324-1133
dorothy.walt@hknc.org
www.khnc.org

Dorothy Walt, Regional Rep.
Taryn Hill, Administrative Assistant

Libraries & Resource Centers

Alabama

4622 Mobile Association for the Blind
2440 Gordon Smith Drive
Mobile, AL 36617
251-473-3585
Fax: 251-470-8622
www.mobileblind.org

Offers work adjustment training, activities of daily living, mobility, communication skills and sheltered employment for adults and children who are visually impaired.

Jim Bullock, Executive Director

Arizona

4623 Educational Services for the Visually Impaired
2402 Wildwood Avenue Suite 112
Sherwood, AR 72120
501-835-5448
Fax: 501-835-6840
www.esvi.org

Offers textbooks, Braille books and more to the visually impaired grades K-12 in the Arkansas area.

Angyln Young, State Coordinator
Cindy Lester, Data Management Specialist/Preschoo

Arkansas

4624 Arkansas Regional Library for the Blind and Physically Handicapped
900 W. Capitol, Suite 100
Little Rock, AR 72201
501-682-2053
Fax: 501-682-1533
TDD: 501-682-1002
nlsbooks@asl.lib.ar.us
www.library.arkansas.gov

Public library books in recorded or Braille format. Popular fiction and nonfiction books for all ages, books and players are on free loan, sent to patrons by mail and may be returned postage free. Anyone who cannot see well enough to read regular print with glasses on or who has a disability that makes it difficult to hold a book or turn the pages is eligible.

Linda Bennett, Director
Dwain Gordon, Deputy Director
Danny Koonce, Public Information Specialist

California

4625 American Action Fund for Blind Children and Adults
18440 Oxnard Street
Tarzana, CA 91356
818-343-2022
Fax: 818-343-3219
lucyabba@aol.com
www.actinfund.org

A lending library for the visually impaired. We send out a weekly Braille newspaper for the deaf-blind (worldwide), we also send out pocket-sized Braille calendars. Our lending library is for pre-school thru high school. All of our services are free.

Lucille Abbazia, Manager

4626 Blind Children's Center
4120 Marathon Street
Los Angeles, CA 90029
323-664-2153
Fax: 323-665-3828
www.blindchildrenscenter.org

Offers support and informational groups.

Scott E. Schaldenbrand, President, Executive Committee
Danette M. Jones, Vice President
Lisa D. Hansen, Secretary

4627 Braille Institute Desert Center
70-251 Ramon Road
Rancho Mirage, CA 92270
760-321-1111
Fax: 760-321-9715
dc@brailleinstitute.org
www.brailleinstitute.org

Dedicated to providing blind and visually impaired men, women and children with the training, programs and services they need to enjoy productive lives. Services offered include child development, youth programs, library services and adult education.

Lester M Sussman, Chairman
James B. Boyle Jr., Director
Thomas K. Callister, Director

4628 Braille Institute Sight Center
741 N Vermont Avenue
Los Angeles, CA 90029
323-663-1111
Fax: 323-663-0867
la@brailleinstitute.org
www.brailleinstitute.org

Offers help, programs, services and information to the blind and visually impaired children and adults.

Lester M Sussman, Chairman
James B. Boyle Jr., Director
Thomas K. Callister, Director

4629 Braille Institute Youth Center
741 N Vermont Avenue
Los Angeles, CA 90029
323-663-1111
Fax: 323-663-0867
la@brailleinstitute.org
www.brailleinstitute.org

Offers various youth programs and services for the blind and visually impaired youngster.

Lester M Sussman, Chairman
James B. Boyle Jr., Director
Thomas K. Callister, Director

4630 New Beginnings - Blind Children's Center
4120 Marathon, Street
Los Angeles, CA 90029
323-664-2153
800-222-3566
Fax: 323-665-3828

Helps children and their families become independent by creating a climate of safety and trust. Services include an infant stimulation program, educational preschool, interdisciplinary assessment services, family services, correspondence program, toll-free national hotline and a publication and research service.

4631 San Francisco Public Library for the Blind and Print Disabled
100 Larkin Street
San Francisco, CA 94102
415-557-4253
Fax: 415-557-4252
lbpd@sfpl.org
www.sfpl.org/index.php?pg=0200002301

Foreign-language books on cassette, children's books on cassettes and more.

Luis Herrera, Manager

4632 Variety Audio
PO Box 5731
San Jose, CA 95150
408-277-4839

Summer reading programs, Braille writer, magnifiers, closed-circuit TV, large-print photocopier, cassette books and magazines, children's books on cassette, home visits and other reference materials on blindness and other handicaps.

Louisa Griehshammer

Florida

4633 Florida Bureau of Braille and Talking Book Library Services
1185 Dunn Avenue
Daytona Beach, FL 32114
386-254-3800
800-329-3801
Fax: 386-239-6107
TDD: 800-226-6079
James.Woolyhand@dbs.fldoe.org
www.dbs.myflorida.com/library/

Discs, cassettes, closed-circuit TV, large-print photocopier, films, children's books on cassettes and more.

Michael Gunde, Librarian
Jim Woolyhand, District Administrator

4634 Talking Book Library, Jacksonville Public Library
303 North Laura St
Jacksonville, FL 32202
904-630-1999
Fax: 904-768-7404
TDD: 904-630-2740
JPLTBSpecialNeeds@coj.net
www.jaxpubliclibrary.org/lib/talkingbooks.html

Discs, cassettes and reference materials on blindness and other disabilities.

Jerry Reynolds, Librarian Senior

4635 Talking Book Service - Manatee County Central Library
6081 26th Street W
Bradenton, FL 34207
941-742-5914
Fax: 941-751-7089
TDD: 941-742-5951
patricia.schubert@co.manatee.fl.us
www.co.manatee.fl.us

Offers children's books on disc and cassette and more reference materials for the blind and physically handicapped.

Patricia Schubert, Librarian

Georgia

4636 Albany Library for the Blind and Physical Handicapped
300 Pine Avenue
Albany, GA 31701
229-420-3220
Fax: 229-420-3215
sinquefk@mail.dougherty.public.lib.ga.us
www.docolib.org/LBPH/index.html

Offers discs, cassettes, reference materials on blindness and other handicaps, large-print photocopiers, summer reading programs, cassette books and more.

Katy Sinquefield, Manager

4637 Bainbridge Subregional Library for the Blind and Physically Handicapped
301 S Monroe Street
Bainbridge, GA 39819
229-248-2665
800-795-2680
Fax: 229-248-2670
TDD: 912-248-2665
lbph@mail.deccatur.public.lib.ga.us
www.swgrl.org

Discs, cassettes, summer reading programs, closed-circuit TV, magnifiers and more.

Kathy Hutchins, Librarian

Nystagmus / Libraries & Resource Centers

4638 CEL Subregional Library for the Blind and Physically Handicapped
2708 Mechanics
Savannah, GA 31404
912-354-5864
Fax: 912-354-5534
TDD: 912-652-3635
stokesl@cel.co.chatman.ga.us

Summer reading programs, Braille writer, magnifiers, closed-circuit TV, large-print photocopier, cassette books and magazines, children's books on cassette, home visits and other reference materials on blindness and other handicaps.

Linda Stokes, Librarian

Idaho

4639 Idaho State Talking Book Library
325 W State Street
Boise, ID 83702
208-334-2150
Fax: 208-334-4016
TDD: 800-377-1363
tblbooks@isl.state.id.us
www.lili.org/isl/tblinfo.htm

Summer reading programs, Braille writer, magnifiers, closed-circuit TV, large-print photocopier, cassette books and magazines, children's books on cassette, home visits and other reference materials on blindness and other handicaps.

Sue Walker, Manager

Illinois

4640 Chicago Library Service for the Blind
1055 W Roosevelt Road
Chicago, IL 60608
312-746-9210

Summer reading programs, Braille writer, magnifiers, closed-circuit TV, large-print photocopier, cassette books and magazines, children's books on cassette, home visits and other reference materials on blindness and other handicaps.

Carol Pellish, Librarian

4641 Illinois State Library, Talkng Book and Braille Service
213 State Capitol
Springfield, IL 62756
217-785-3000
Fax: 217-558-4723
TDD: 800-665-5576
isltbbs@ilsos.net
www.cyberdriveillinois.com

Summer reading programs, Braille writer, magnifiers, closed-circuit TV, large-print photocopier, cassette books and magazines, descriptive videos, children's books on cassette, home visits and other reference materials on blindness and other handicaps.

Anne Craig, Executive Director

4642 Mid Illinois Talking Book System
515 York Street
Quincy, IL 62301
217-224-6619
Fax: 217-224-9818

Summer reading programs, Braille writer, magnifiers, closed-circuit TV, large-print photocopier, cassette books and magazines, children's books on cassette, home visits and other reference materials on blindness and other handicaps.

4643 Mid-Illinois Talking Book Center
600 High Point Lane #2
East Peoria, IL 61611
309-694-9200
800-426-0709
Fax: 309-799-7916
hitbc@darkstar.rsa.lib.il.us
www.mitbc.org

Summer reading programs, Braille writer, magnifiers, closed-circuit TV, large-print photocopier, cassette books and magazines, children's books on cassette, home visits and other reference materials on blindness and other handicaps.

Eileen Sheppard, Librarian
Rose Chenoweth, Director
Valerie Brandon, Administrator

4644 Talking Book Center of Northwest Illinois
600 High Point Lane #2
East Peoria, IL 61611
309-694-9200
Fax: 309-799-7916
www.rbls.lib.il.us

Summer reading programs, Braille writer, magnifiers, closed-circuit TV, large-print photocopier, cassette books and magazines, children's books on cassette, home visits and other reference materials on blindness and other handicaps.

Indiana

4645 Northwest Indiana Subregional Library for Blind and Physically Handicapped
1919 W 81st Street
Merrillville, IN 46410
219-769-3541
Fax: 219-756-9358

Summer reading programs, Braille writer, magnifiers, closed-circuit TV, large-print photocopier, cassette books and magazines, children's books on cassette, home visits and other reference materials on blindness and other handicaps.

Renee Lewis

Iowa

4646 Iowa Library for the Blind and Physically Handicapped
Iowa Department for the Blind
524 4th Street
Des Moines, IA 50309
515-281-1333
800-362-2587
Fax: 515-281-1263
TDD: 515-281-1355
www.blind.state.ia.us

Summer reading programs, magnifiers, closed-circuit TV, large-print photocopier, children's books on cassette, children's books in Braille and Print Braille, cassette magazines, home visits and reference materials on blindness and other handicaps.

Karen Keninger, Program Manager/Librarian

Kansas

4647 CKLS Headquarters
PO Box 515
Northampton, MA 01061
316-792-2393
888-622-8527
Fax: 316-792-5495
cenks@ink.org
www.macular.org

Summer reading programs, Braille writer, magnifiers, closed-circuit TV, large-print photocopier, cassette books and magazines, children's books on cassette, home visits and other reference materials on blindness and other handicaps.

Chip Goehring, President
Mark E. Torrey, Vice President
Paul F. Gariepy, Secretary

4648 Services for the Visually Disabled
629 Poyntz Avenue
Manhattan, KS 66502
785-776-4741
Fax: 785-776-1545
marionr@manhattan.lib.ks.us

Summer reading programs, Braille writer, magnifiers, closed-circuit TV, large-print photocopier, cassette books and magazines, children's books on cassette, home visits and other reference materials on blindness and other handicaps.

Marion Rice, Librarian

Kentucky

4649 Kentucky Library for the Blind and Physically Handicapped
300 Coffee Tree Road PO Box 537
Frankfort, KY 40602
502-564-8300
800-372-2968
Fax: 502-564-5773
richard.feindel@kdla.net
www.kdla.net/libserv/ktbl.htm

Large-print photocopier, cassette books and magazines, children's books on cassette, and other reference materials on blindness and other handicaps.

5,200 members

Richard Feindel, Librarian

Maryland

4650 Maryland State Library for the Blind and Physically Handicapped
415 Park Avenue
Baltimore, MD 21201
410-230-2424
Fax: 410-333-2095
TTY: 800-934-2541
TDD: 410-333-8679
recept@lbta.lib.md.us
www.lbph.lib.md.us

Summer reading programs, Braille writer, magnifiers, large-print photocopier, cassette books and magazines, children's books on cassette, and other reference materials on blindness and other handicaps.

Jill Lewis, Manager

4651 Prince George's County Memorial Library Talking Book Center
6532 Adelphi Road
Hyattsville, MD 20782
301-699-3500

Summer reading programs, Braille writer, magnifiers, closed-circuit TV, large-print photocopier, cassette books and magazines, children's books on cassette, home visits and other reference materials on blindness and other handicaps.

Shirley Tuthill, Librarian

Massachusetts

4652 Braille and Talking Book Library Perkins School for the Blind
175 N Beacon Street
Watertown, MA 02472
617-924-3434
Fax: 617-972-7315
info@perkins.org
www.perkins.org

Patricia Kirk

4653 Carroll Center for the Blind
770 Centre Street
Newton, MA 02458
617-969-6200
800-852-3131
Fax: 617-969-6204
www.carroll.org

Assists blind and visually impaired adults and adolescents to adjust to loss of vision. The goal of this dynamic program is to help the person become more independent, to restore self-confidence, prepare for employment and improve the quality of life. Programs of individual counseling are offered as part of the program.

Rachel Rosenbaum, President

Michigan

4654 Downtown Detroit Subregional Library for the Blind and Handicapped
121 Gratiot Avenue
Detroit, MI 48226
313-224-0580
Fax: 313-965-1977
TDD: 313-224-0584
deveans@cms.xx.wayne.edu
www.detroit.lib.mi.us

Summer reading programs, Braille writer, magnifiers, closed-circuit TV, large-print photocopier, cassette books and magazines, children's books on cassette, home visits and other reference materials on blindness and other handicaps.

Deborah Evans, Librarian

4655 Kent County Library for the Blind
775 Ball Avenue NE
Grand Rapids, MI 49503
616-336-3250
Fax: 616-336-3201
kdlem@lakeland.lib.mi.us

Summer reading programs, Braille writer, magnifiers, closed-circuit TV, large-print photocopier, cassette books and magazines, children's books on cassette, home visits and other reference materials on blindness and other handicaps.

Claudya Muller, Librarian

4656 Library of Michigan Service for the Blind
PO Box 30007
Lansing, MI 48909
517-373-5614
Fax: 517-373-5865
BTBL@michigan.gov

Summer reading programs, Braille writer, magnifiers, closed-circuit TV, large-print photocopier, cassette books and magazines, children's books on cassette, home visits and other reference materials on blindness and other handicaps.

Nancy Robertson, Manager

4657 Macomb Library for the Blind and Physically Handicapped
40900 Romeo Plank
Clinton Township, MI 48038
586-226-5020
Fax: 586-286-0634
TDD: 810-869-40
macbld@libcoop.net
www.cmpl.org/MLBPH/

Summer reading programs, Braille writer, closed-circuit TV, cassette books and magazines, children's books on cassette, reference materials on blindness and other handicaps.

Larry Neal, Library Director
Juliane Morian, Associate Director
Debbie Prykucki, Head of Circulation

4658 Mideastern Michigan Library Co-op
503 S Saginaw Street Suite 711
Flint, MI 48502
810-232-7119
800-641-6639
Fax: 810-232-6639
dhooks@mmlc.info
www.mmlc.info/

Summer reading programs, Braille writer, magnifiers, closed-circuit TV, large-print photocopier, cassette books and magazines, children's books on cassette, home visits and other reference materials on blindness and other handicaps.

Carolyn Nash, Librarian
Denise Hooks, Director
Irene Bancroft, Admin. Assistant

4659 Muskegon County Library for the Blind
4845 Airline Road
Muskegon, MI 49444
231-737-6310
Fax: 231-724-6675
TDD: 231-722-4103
www.muskcolib.org

Nystagmus / Libraries & Resource Centers

Summer reading programs, Braille typewriter, magnifiers, closed-circuit TV, large-print photocopier, cassette books and magazines, children's books on cassette, home visits and other reference materials on blindness and other handicaps, The Reading Edge. Perkins Braille and large print books.

Linda Clapp, Librarian

4660 Upper Peninsula Library for the Blind Physically Handicapped
1615 Presque Isle Avenue
Marquette, MI 49855
906-228-7697
Fax: 906-228-5627
rruff@uproc.lib.mi.us
www.upesc.lib.mi.us/uplbph

Summer reading programs, Braille writer, magnifiers, closed-circuit TV, large-print photocopier, cassette books and magazines, children's books on cassette, home visits and other reference materials on blindness and other handicaps.

Suzanne Dees, Executive Director

4661 Washtenaw County Library
PO Box 8645
Ann Arbor, MI 48107
734-222-6850
Fax: 734-222-6715
mcdaniev@ewashtenaw.org
www.ewashtenaw.org

Summer reading programs, Braille writer, magnifiers, closed-circuit TV, large-print photocopier, cassette books and magazines, children's books on cassette, home visits and other reference materials on blindness and other handicaps.

Verna J. Mcdaniel, Administrator

4662 Washtenaw County Library for the Blind and Physically Disabled
PO Box 8645
Ann Arbor, MI 48107
734-973-4600
Fax: 734-663-2430
www.ewashtenaw.org

Book lovers club. adaptive technology, cassette equipment, cassette books and magazines, described videos, low vision aids reference and referral services.

Kyeena Slater, Executive Director

Minnesota

4663 Minnesota Library for the Blind & Physically Handicapped
Highway 298, PO Box 68
Fairbault, MN 55021
507-333-4828
800-722-0550
Fax: 507-333-4832
libblnd@state.mn.us

Summer reading programs, Braille writer, magnifiers, closed-circuit TV, large-print photocopier, cassette, large print, Braille books and magazines, children's books on cassette, and other reference materials on blindness and other handicaps.

Catherine A Durivage, Program Director

Missouri

4664 Adriene Resource Center for Blind Children
1445 Boonville Avenue
Springfield, MO 65802
417-831-8000
800-641-4310
Fax: 800-328-0294
blind@ag.org
www.gospelpublishing.com

Offers Braille and cassette lending library, Braille and cassette Sunday school materials for all ages, Braille and cassette periodicals and resource assistance, and resources for blind children and children of blind parents.

Paul Weingariner, Director

4665 Assemblies of God National Center for the Blind
1445 Boonville Avenue
Springfield, MO 65802
417-831-1964
Fax: 417-862-5120
blind@ag.org
www.radiantlife.org

Offers Braille and cassette lending library, Braille and cassette Sunday school materials for all ages, Braille and cassette periodicals and resource assistance, and resources for blind children and children of blind parents.

Thomas Trask, Manager

4666 Wolfner Memorial Library for the Blind
PO Box 387
Jefferson City, MO 65102
573-751-8720
Fax: 573-526-2985
TDD: 800-347-1379
wolfner@sos.mo.gov

Summer reading programs, Braille writer, magnifiers, closed-circuit TV, large-print photocopier, cassette books and magazines, children's books on cassette, home visits and other reference materials on blindness and other handicaps.

Richard J Smith, Executive Director

Nebraska

4667 Nebraska Library Commission Talking Book & Braille Services
1200 N Street
Lincoln, NE 68508
402-471-2045
800-307-2665
Fax: 402-471-2083
TDD: 402-471-4038
doertli@nlc.state.ne.us
www.nlc.state.ne.us

Free loan of books and magazines on cassette and in Braille, including children's materials, along with specially designed playback equipment. Summer reading program for children, Braille embossing, closed circuit TV, large-print copier. Reference materials on blindness and other disabilities.

David Oerti, Librarian

New Jersey

4668 New Jersey State Library Talking Book and Braille Center
185 West State Street
Trenton, NJ 08625
609-278-2640
800-792-8322
Fax: 609-278-2647
TDD: 877-882-5593
njlbh@njstatelib.org
www.njstatelib.org

Free home delivery of large-print, audio, and Braille books and magazines, children's books on cassettes in Braille and other reference materials on blindness and other handicaps. Services are for New Jersey residents with print disabilities.

Adanrah Szczepaniak, Director
Anne McArthur, Head of Outreach and Audiovision

New Mexico

4669 New Mexico State Library for the Blind and Physically Handicapped
1209 Camino Carlos Ray
Santa Fe, NM 87507
505-476-9700
Fax: 505-476-9761
jbrewstr@stlib.state.nm.us
www.stlib.state.nm.us

Summer reading programs, Braille writer, magnifiers, closed-circuit TV, large-print photocopier, cassette books and magazines, children's books on cassette, home visits and other reference materials on blindness and other handicaps.

Susan Overland, Manager

New York

4670 New York State Talking Book & Braille Library
Empire State Plaza, CEC
Albany, NY 12230
518-474-5935
Fax: 518-486-1957
TDD: 518-474-7121
tbbl@mail.nysed.gov
www.suffolk.lib.ny.us

Books on audio cassette, cassette players, Braille books, summer reading programs, Braille writer, magnifiers, closed-circuit TV, large-print photocopier, cassette books and magazines, children's books on cassette, reference materials on blindness and other handicaps.

Jane Somers, Director

North Carolina

4671 North Carolina Library for the Blind
1841 Capital Boulevard
Raleigh, NC 27635
919-733-4376
Fax: 919-733-6910
TDD: 919-733-1462
nclbph@ncder.gov

Summer reading programs, Braille writer, magnifiers, closed-circuit TV, large-print photocopier, cassette books and magazines, children's books on cassette, home visits and other reference materials on blindness and other handicaps.

Francine Martin, Manager

Ohio

4672 American Council of Blind Parents
34400 Cedar Road, Apartment 108
University Heights, OH 44121
800-424-8666

Members are sighted parents of blind or visually impaired children. Offers a forum for support and outreach, sharing of experiences in parent-child relationships, and educational and cultural information about child development. Monitors developments in technical and legislative arenas.

Nola Webb, President

Oregon

4673 Oregon State Library, Talking Book and Braille Services
250 Winter Street NE
Salem, OR 97301
503-378-5389
800-452-0292
Fax: 503-585-8059
TTY: 503-378-4334
TDD: 503-378-4276
www.tbabs.org

Cassette books and magazines, children's books on cassette, home visits and other reference materials on blindness and other handicaps.

Susan Westin, Manager

Virginia

4674 Alexandria Library Talking Book Service
5005 Duke Street
Alexandria, VA 22304
703-746-1760
Fax: 703-519-5916
TDD: 703-838-4568
emccaffr@lea.eda
www.alexandria.lib.va.us

Summer reading programs, Braille writer, magnifiers, closed-circuit TV, large-print photocopier, cassette books and magazines, children's books on cassette, home visits and other reference materials on blindness and other handicaps.

Karen Russell, Manager

4675 Division for the Visually Handicapped
1920 Association Drive
Reston, VA 20191
703-620-3660

Members are teachers, college faculty members, administrators, supervisors and others concerned with the education and welfare of visually handicapped and blind children and youth. This is a division of the Council For Exceptional Children.

Dr. Kay Ferrell, President

4676 Division on Visual Impairments
Council for Exceptional Children
1110 North Glebe Road, Suite 300
Arlington, VA 22201
800-224-6830
Fax: 703-264-9494
TTY: 866-915-5000
www.ed.arizona.edu/dvi/welcome.htm; www.cec.sped.org

A division within the CEC, it handles concerns for Federal, state and local issues and policies related to education of youths, children and infants with visual impairments.

Ellyn Ross, President
Shirley J Wilson, Secretary
Phyllis T Simmons, President Elect

4677 Virginia State Library for the Visually and Physically Handicapped
1901 Roane Street
Richmond, VA 23222
804-367-0014

Summer reading programs, Braille writer, magnifiers, closed-circuit TV, large-print photocopier, cassette books and magazines, children's books on cassette, home visits and other reference materials on blindness and other handicaps.

Mary Ruth Halapatz, Librarian

Washington

4678 Washington Library for the Blind and Physically Handicapped
1000 Fourth Ave.
Seattle, WA 98104
206-386-4636
Fax: 206-386-4685
wtbbl@spl.lib.wa.us
www.spl.lib.wa.us

Summer reading programs, Braille writer, magnifiers, closed-circuit TV, large-print photocopier, cassette books and magazines, children's books on cassette, home visits and other reference materials on blindness and other handicaps.

Marcellus Turner, Librarian

West Virginia

4679 West Virginia School for the Blind
301 E Main Street
Romney, WV 26757
304-822-4801
Fax: 304-822-3370
cjohn@access.mountain.net

Summer reading programs, Braille writer, magnifiers, closed-circuit TV, large-print photocopier, cassette books and magazines, children's books on cassette, home visits and other reference materials on blindness and other handicaps.

Patsy Shank, Administrator

Research Centers

4680 Center for the Partially Sighted
6101 W Centinela Ave, Suite 150
Culver City, CA 90230
310-988-1970
Fax: 310-988-1980
info@low-vision.org
www.low-vision.org

Provides professional, comprehensive vision rehabilitation services to visually impaired people of all ages. For those whose sight is severely limited due to macular degeneration, diabetic retinopathy, glaucoma, retinal detachment, stroke or other conditions not correctable medically or surgically.

La Donna S.Ringering, President

4681 Mobile Association for the Blind
2440 Gordon Smith Drive
Mobile, AL 36617
251-473-3585
877-292-5463
Fax: 251-470-8622
sales@mobileblind.org
www.mobileblind.org

Offers work adjustment training, activities of daily living, mobility, communication skills and sheltered employment for adults and children who are visually impaired.

James Bullock, Executive Director

4682 New Beginnings - The Blind Children's Center
4120 Marathon Street
Los Angeles, CA 90029
323-664-2153
Fax: 323-665-3828
www.blindchildrenscenter.org

The purpose of the Center is to turn initial fears into hope. Helps children and their families become independent by creating a climate of safety and trust. Children learn to develop self confidence and to master a wide range of skills. Services include an infant stimulation program, educational preschool, interdisciplinary assessment services, family services, correspondence program, toll free national hotline and a publication and research service.

4683 Research to Prevent Blindness
645 Madison Avenue
New York, NY 10022
212-752-4333
800-621-0026
Fax: 212-688-6231
www.rpbusa.org

Provides research grants to scientists interested in eye disease and vision disorders.

Jules Stein, Founder
David F. Weeks, Chairman
Diane Swift, President

Audio Video

4684 Heart to Heart
Blind Children's Center
4120 Marathon Street
Los Angeles, CA 90029
323-644-2153
Fax: 323-665-3828
www.blindcntr.org

Parents of blind and partially sighted children talk about their feelings.

Videotape

4685 Let's Eat
Blind Children's Center
4120 Marathon Street
Los Angeles, CA 90029
213-664-2153
Fax: 213-665-3828

Teaches competent feeding skills to children with visual impairments.

Videotape

4686 See What I Feel
Britannica Film Co.
345 4th Street
San Francisco, CA 94107
415-597-5555

A blind child tells her friends about her trip to the zoo. Each experience was explained as a blind child would experience it. A teacher's guide comes with this video.

Films

Web Sites

4687 American Nystagmus Network
303-D Beltline Place, Suite 321
Decatur, AL 35603
info@nystagmus.org
www.nystagmus.org

Is a nonprofit organization established to serve the needs and interests of those affected by Nystagmus.

4688 Lighthouse Guild
250 West 64th Street
New York, NY 10023
800-284-4422
info@lighthouseguild.org
www.lighthouseguild.org

Lighthouse Guild is dedicated to providing exceptional services that inspire people who are visually impaired to attain their goals.

James M. Dubin, Chair
Calvin W. Roberts, President & CEO
Maura J. Sweeney, SVP, Programs & Services

4689 Nystagmus Network
25 Eden Way
Beckenham, KT BR3 3
29 -045-4242
shop@nystagmusnet.org
www.nystagmusnet.org

A UK-based self-help group set up to provide support for adults and children with nystagmus, their parents and teachers and foster research into the condition.

4690 Online Mendelian Inheritance in Man
McKusick-Nathans Institue of Genetic Medicine-JHU
Baltimore, MD 21205
www.omim.org

This database is a catalog of human genes and genetic disorders.

Ada Hamosh, MD, Scientific Director

4691 Royal National Institute of Blind People
105 Judd Street
London, WC1H
303-123-9999
helpline@rnib.org.uk
www.rnib.org.uk

A leading UK charity offering information, support and advice to over two million people with sight problems.

Matt Stringer, Chief Executive
Keith Valentine, Director of Development
David Clarke, Director of Services

Magazines

4692 Journal of Visual Impairment and Blindness
American Foundation for the Blind
2 Penn Plaza, Suite 1102
New York, NY 10121
212-502-7600
Fax: 212-502-7777
afbinfo@afb.net
www.afb.org

Published in braille, regular print and on cassette this journal contains a wide variety of subjects including rehabilitation, psychology, education, legislation, medicine, technology, employment, sensory aids and childhood development as they relate to visual impairments.

10x Year

Carl Augusto, President and CEO
Rick Bozeman, Chief Financial Officer
Kelly Bleach, Chief Administrative Officer

4693 Reaching, Crawling, Walking - Let's Get Moving
Blind Children's Center
4120 Marathon Street
Los Angeles, CA 90029
323-664-2153
Fax: 323-665-3828
info@blindchildrencenter.org
www.blindchildrenscenter.org

Orientation and mobility for visually impaired preschool children.

24 pages

4694 **Tactic**
Clovernook Home and School for the Blind
400 Continental Blvd., Suite 600
El Segundo, CA 90245
310-426-2236
Fax: 513-728-3950
contact@southpawtech.com
www.southpawtech.com/tactic/

Quarterly

Newsletters

4695 **National Library Service for the Blind & Physically Handicapped**
Library of Congress
1291 Taylor Street NW
Washington, DC 20542
202-707-5100
800-424-8567
Fax: 202-707-0712
nls@loc.gov
www.loc.gov/nls

Provides information and advocacy resources for families and professionals, including listings of organizations focusing on more specific areas of concern to families and young adults who have disabilities. Administers a natural library service that provides recorded and braille reading materials to eligible children and adults who cannot read standard print.

12 pages Quarterly
ISSN: 1046-1663

4696 **Talking Book Topics**
National Library Services for the Blind
1291 Taylor Street NW
Washington, DC 20542
202-707-5100
Fax: 202-707-0712
TDD: 202-707-0744
www.loc.gov/nls

Offers hundreds of listings of books, fiction and nonfiction, for adults and children who cannot read regular print material. Also offers foreign language books, talking magazines and reviews.

Bimonthly

Pamphlets

4697 **Dancing Cheek to Cheek**
Blind Children's Center
4120 Marathon Street
Los Angeles, CA 90029
323-664-2153
Fax: 323-665-3828
www.blindchildrenscenter.org

Discusses beginning social, play and language interactions.

33 pages

4698 **Family Guide - Growth and Development of the Partially Seeing Child**
Lighthouse Guild
250 West 64th Street
New York, NY 10023
800-284-4422
info@lighthouseguild.org
www.lighthouseguild.org

Offers information for parents and guidelines in raising a partially seeing child.

4699 **Family Guide to Vision Care**
American Optometric Association
243 N Lindbergh Boulevard
Saint Louis, MO 63141
314-991-4100
Fax: 314-991-4101
www.aoanet.org

Offers information on the early developmental years of your vision, finding a family optometrist and how to take care of your eyesight through the learning years, the working years and the mature years.

4700 **Heart to Heart**
Blind Children's Center
4120 Marathon Street
Los Angeles, CA 90029
323-664-2153
Fax: 323-665-3828
www.blindchildrenscenter.org

Parents of blind and partially sighted children talk about their feelings.

12 pages

4701 **Learning to Play**
Blind Children's Center
4120 Marathon Street
Los Angeles, CA 90029
323-664-2153
Fax: 323-665-3828
www.blindchildrenscenter.org

Discusses how to present play activities to the visually impaired pre-school child.

12 pages

4702 **Let's Eat**
Blind Children's Center
4120 Marathon Street
Los Angeles, CA 90029
323-664-2153
Fax: 323-665-3828
www.blindchildrenscenter.org

Teaches competent feeding skills to children with visual impairments.

28 pages

4703 **Move with Me**
Blind Children's Center
4120 Marathon Street
Los Angeles, CA 90029
323-664-2153
Fax: 323-665-3828
www.blindchildrenscenter.org

A parent's guide to movement development for visually impaired babies.

12 pages

4704 **Selecting a Program**
Blind Children's Center
4120 Marathon Street
Los Angeles, CA 90029
323-664-2153
Fax: 323-665-3828
www.blindchildrenscenter.org

A guide for parents of infants and preschoolers with visual impairments.

28 pages

4705 **Standing on My Own Two Feet**
Blind Children's Center
4120 Marathon Street
Los Angeles, CA 90029
323-664-2153
Fax: 323-665-3828
info@blindchildrenscenter.org
www.blindchildrenscenter.org

A step-by-step guide to designing and constructing simple, individually tailored adaptive mobility devices for preschool-age children who are visually impaired.

36 pages

4706 **Talk to Me**
Blind Children's Center
4120 Marathon Street
Los Angeles, CA 90029
323-664-2153
Fax: 323-665-3828
www.blindchildrenscenter.org

A language guide for parents of deaf children.

11 pages

4707 Talk to Me II
Blind Children's Center
4120 Marathon Street
Los Angeles, CA 90029

323-664-2153
Fax: 323-665-3828
www.blindchildrenscenter.org

A sequel to Talk To Me, available in English and Spanish.

15 pages

Camps

4708 Bloomfield
35375 Mullholland Highway
Malibu, CA 90065

310-457-5330
800-352-2290
Fax: 310-457-3952
smarning@juniorblind.org
www.juniorblind.org

This camp is dedicated to serving blind and developmentally disabled children and adults.

Shirley Manning, Director of Recreation
Joan Marason, Director

4709 Florida School-Deaf and Blind Summer Camp
207 N. San Marco Avenue
Saint Augustine, FL 32084

904-827-2200
800-344-3732
Fax: 904-245-1022
info@fsdb.k12.fl.us
www.fsdb.k12.fl.us

The Florida School for the Deaf and the Blind hosts summer campers from all over teh state of Florida for a week of fun and adventure. FSDB's 80 acre campus is where campers participate in a variety of activities including rock climbing, archery, swimming, kayaking, team games, arts and crafts, dance music, and much more.

L Daniel Hutto, President
Cindy Day, Executive Director of Parent Svcs
Terri Wiseman, Administrator of Business Services

4710 National Camps for Blind Children
Christian Record
4444 S 52nd Street
Lincoln, NE 68516

402-488-0981
Fax: 402-488-7582
info@christianrecord.org
www.christianrecord.org

Camps throughout the US and Canada are offered at no cost to the legally blind, ages 9-65. Activities include archery, beeper basketball, water sports, hiking and rock climbing and horseback riding.

Peggy Hansen, Director
Larry Pitcher, President

4711 VISIONS/Vacation Camp for the Blind
500 Greenwich Street, 3rd Floor
New York, NY 10013

212-625-1616
888-245-8333
Fax: 212-219-4078
info@visionsvcb.org
www.visionsvcb.org

Family programs at Vacation Camp for the Blind in Rockland County, NY for children who are blind, severely visually impaired or multi-handicapped. Parent or guardian must attend winter weekends and summer session.

Nancy T. Jones, President
Richard P. Simon, Vice President
Burton M. Strauss, Jr., Treasurer

Obesity / Description

Description

4712 OBESITY

Involves the following Biologic System(s):

Developmental/Behavioral/Psychiatric Disorders, Endocrinologic Disorders

Obesity refers to a condition in which there is an excessive accumulation of fat in subcutaneous (below the skin) and other tissues of the body. Being obese and being overweight are not necessarily synonymous, as people who are overweight may have an increased body size as a result of increased muscle or skeletal tissue mass. Obesity in children may develop at any age, but peak development periods occur during the first 12 months of life, between the ages of five and six years, and during the adolescent years. The obesity epidemic is especially evident in industrialized nations where many people live sedentary lives and eat more convenience foods, which are typically high in calories and low in nutritional value, and is becoming an epidemic in the western hemisphere. Obesity may result from an increase in the actual number of fat cells or from an increase in the size of the individual fat cells. Researchers believe that fat cells increase in number in proportion to caloric intake increase and that this increase is particularly evident in the first 12 months of life. As children grow, increases in fat cell populations continue at a slower rate. Because the number of fat cells cannot be decreased, except surgically, later weight loss must result from the reduction of fat in individual cells.

Obesity usually results when caloric intake exceeds the energy demands of the body, thus increasing the storage of body fat. Fat accumulation is usually a progressive process, resulting from repeated episodes of food intake exceeding the body's demand for energy (calories). Many factors may influence appetite or obesity. Such factors may include environmental influences; psychologic disturbances that may be induced by stress or emotional upset or trauma; brain lesions that may involve certain areas of the brain such as the hypothalamus or the pituitary gland (both essential to hormone production); an overabundance of insulin in the body (hyperinsulinism); and genetic influences. In addition, in rare instances, obesity may be a feature of certain genetic disorders.

Complications of childhood obesity may include respiratory difficulties such as shortness of breath and increased cardiovascular risk factors such as high blood pressure, elevated total cholesterol levels as well as increased bad or LDL cholesterol and decreased good or HDL cholesterol, and increased levels of fatty acid and glycerol compounds (triglycerides). In addition, childhood obesity may be associated with a resistance to the hormone insulin that aids in the metabolism of glucose, fats, carbohydrates, and proteins. This resistance may lead to excessive levels of circulating insulin in the body (hyperinsulinism); however, the body is not able to appropriately use insulin and Type 2 Diabetes Mellitus results. The symptoms associated with insulin resistance may include hunger, weight loss, sweating, and tremor.

The diagnosis of obesity in children and adolescents is usually determined through the use of certain screening methods such as measurement of the body mass index (BMI) as well as the triceps skinfold thickness. In addition, special consideration may be given to certain criteria in determining differential diagnosis and possible treatment. These criteria may include elevated blood pressure; high total cholesterol levels; regular and consecutive increases in annual body mass index screenings; psychologic or emotional weight concerns; and a family history of heart disease, elevated cholesterol levels, and diabetes.

Patterns of behavior that may lead to obesity may be established as early as infancy. For example, if parents or caregivers persistently use a bottle to pacify a crying baby, the baby may learn that food is equivalent to relief of stress. Treatment for childhood and adolescent obesity should include the cooperation and support of the entire family and may be directed toward psychologic considerations, as well as proper exercise and nutrition to avoid complications. Treatment for psychologic and emotional needs may include behavior modification, as well as individual and family counseling.

For more information on binge eating, see chapter on Eating Disorders.

National Associations & Support Groups

4713 Action for Healthy Kids
www.actionforhealthykids.org

Action for Healthy Kidsr fights childhood obesity, undernourishment and physical inactivity by helping schools become healthier places so kids can live healthier lives.

Rob Bisceglie, Chief Executive Officer
Sara Honaker, Program Coordinator
Roxanne Martinez, Senior Marketing Manager

4714 Alliance for a Healthier Generation
Water Avenue Community Center
1028 SE Water Avenue, Suite 215
Portland, OR 97214

888-KID-HLTH
give@healthiergeneration.org
www.healthiergeneration.org

The Alliance for a Healthier Generation is a catalyst for children's health. They work with schools, companies, community organizations, healthcare professionals and families to transform the conditions and systems that lead to healthier kids.

Kathy Higgins, Chief Executive Officer

4715 American Academy of Pediatrics
345 Park Blvd
Itasca, IL 60143

847-434-4000
800-433-9016
Fax: 847-434-8000
csc@aap.org
www.aap.org

The American Academy of Pediatrics and its member pediatricians are committed to the attainment of optimal physical, mental and social health and well-being for all infants, children, adolescents, and young adults.

Kyle E. Yasuda, MD, FAAP, President
Mark Del Monte, JD, CEO/Executive VP
Vera Tait, MD, FAAP, Chief Medical Officer

4716 American Beverage Association
1275 Pennsylvania Avenue NW, Suite 1100
Washington, DC 20004

202-463-6732
Fax: 202-463-6774
info@americanbeverage.org
www.americanbeverage.org

The American Beverage Association (ABA) is the trade association that represents America's non-alcoholic beverage industry.

Katherine Lugar, President & CEO
Robb Micek, EVP & CFO
Marie Franco, VP, Finance & Administration

4717 American Medical Association
AMA Plaza, 330 North Wabash Ave., Suite 39300
Chicago, IL 60611

312-464-4782
800-262-3211
www.ama-assn.org

AMA is dedicated to ensuring sustainable physician practices that result in better health outcomes for patients.

Obesity / National Associations & Support Groups

James L. Madara, MD, CEO/EVP
Bernard L. Hengesbaugh, Chief Operating Officer
Kenneth J. Sharigian, SVP

4718 American Obesity Foundation
PO Box 310468
Queens, NY 11431

800-684-3263
info@americanobesityfdn.org
americanobesityfdn.org

The American Obesity Foundation ("AOF") is at the forefront of the fight against an obesity epidemic that has impacted our country, especially in under-served and most vulnerable neighborhoods. AOF seeks to promote healthy nutritional options at home, school, work, houses of worship, and the community as a whole by breaking down mental, emotional, social and physical challenges in under-served communities.

Afi Okon, Founder & Executive Director

4719 American Psychological Association
750 First St. NE
Washington, DC 20002

202-336-5500
800-374-2721
TTY: 202-336-6123
www.apa.org

The mission is to advance the creation, communication and application of psychological knowledge to benefit society and improve people's lives.

Arthur C. Evans Jr, PhD, CEO/EVP

4720 American School Counselor Association
1101 King Street, Ste 310
Alexandria, VA 22314

703-683-2722
asca@schoolcounselor.org
www.schoolcounselor.org

The mission of ASCA is to represent professional school counselors and to promote professionalism and ethical practices.

Jill Cook, Executive Director
Amanda Fitzgerald, Assistant Deputy Executive Director
Kathleen M Rakestraw, Director of Communications

4721 American Society for Metabolic and Bariatric Surgery
14407 SW 2nd Place, Suite F-3
Newberry, FL 32669

352-331-4900
info@asmbs.org
asmbs.org

The vision of the Society is to improve public health and well being by lessening the burden of the disease of obesity and related diseases throughout the world.

Kristie Kaufman, Interim Executive Director
Jennifer Wynn, Deputy Executive Director
Cindy Chambers, Programs & Compliance Manager

4722 American Society for Nutrition
9211 Corporate Boulevard, Suite 300
Rockville, MD 20850

240-428-3650
www.nutrition.org

The American Society for Nutrition (ASN) is a non-profit organization dedicated to bringing together the world's top researchers, clinical nutritionists and industry to advance our knowledge and application of nutrition for the sake of humans and animals.

John Courtney, Chief Executive Officer

4723 American Society of Clinical Oncology
2318 Mill Road, Suite 800
Alexandria, VA 22314

703-299-0158
888-282-2552
Fax: 703-299-0255
customerservice@asco.org
www.asco.org

Founded in 1964, the American Society of Clinical Oncology is the world's leading professional organization for physicians and oncology professionals caring for people with cancer.

4724 American Thoracic Society
25 Broadway
New York, NY 10004

212-315-8600
Fax: 212-315-6498
ATSInfo@Thoracic.org
www.thoracic.org

The American Thoracic Society improves global health by advancing research, patient care, and public health in pulmonary disease, critical illness, and sleep disorders. Founded in 1905 to combat TB, the ATS has grown to tackle asthma, COPD, lung cancer, sepsis, acute respiratory distress, and sleep apnea, among other diseases.

Karen J. Collishaw, MPP, CEO
Stephen Altobelli, COO

4725 Child Care Aware of America
www.childcareaware.org

703-341-4100
learnmore@usa.childcareaware.org
www.childcareaware.org

They work with state and local Child Care Resource and Referral agencies (CCR&Rs) and other community partners to ensure that all families have access to quality, affordable child care.

Michelle McCready, Interim CEO
Elizabeth Goodman, Chief Financial Officer
Matthew Henry, Chief Information Officer

4726 Children's Hospital Association
600 13th Street, NW, Suite 500
Washington, DC 20005

202-753-5500
www.childrenshospitals.net

Representing more than 220 children's hospitals, the Association is the voice of children's hospitals nationally. The Association champions public policies that enable hospitals to better serve children and is the premier resource for pediatric data and analytics, driving improved clinical and operational performance of member hospitals.

Mark Wietecha, Chief Executive Officer
Amy Wimpey Knight, President

4727 Compulsive Eaters Anonymous
3371 Glendale Boulevard, Suite 104
Los Angeles, CA 90039

323-660-4333
Fax: 323-660-4334
gso@ceahow.org
www.ceahow.org

A twelve-step program, with the primary purpose of, to stop eating compulsively.

4728 Food Research and Action Center
1200 18th Street NW, Suite 400
Washington, DC 20036

202-986-2200
Fax: 202-986-2525
shayward@frac.org
frac.org

RAC works with hundreds of national, state and local nonprofit organizations, public agencies, corporations and labor organizations to address hunger, food insecurity, and their root cause, poverty.

Luis Guardia, President
Barbara Western, Chief Operating Officer
Colleen Barton Sutton, Communications Director

4729 National Collaborative on Childhood Obesity Research
nccor.org

nccor@fhi360.org
nccor.org

NCCOR focuses on efforts that have the potential to benefit children, teens, and their families, and the communities in which they live.

4730 National Eating Disorders Association (NEDA)
333 Mamaroneck Avenue, Suite 214
White Plains, NY 10605

212-575-6200
info@NationalEatingDisorders.org
www.nationaleatingdisorders.org

Obesity / Libraries & Resource Centers

The National Eating Disorders Association (NEDA) is the largest not-for-profit organization in the United States working to prevent eating disorders and provide treatment referrals to those suffering from anorexia, bulimia and binge eating disorder and those concerned with body image and weight issues.

Elizabeth Thompson, Chief Executive Officer
Sarah Chase, VP, Communications & Marketing
Lauren Smolar, VP, Mission & Education

4731 National Resource Center for Health & Safety in Child Care & Early Education
nrckids.org

888-227-5125
health@ecetta.info
nrckids.org

Works to improve the quality of child care and early education programs by supporting child care providers and early educators, families, health professionals, early childhood comprehensive systems, state child care regulatory agencies, state and local health departments, and policy makers in their efforts to identify and promote healthy and safe child care and early education programs.

4732 Obesity Action Coalition
4511 North Himes Avenue, Suite 250
Tampa, FL 33614

800-717-3117
www.obesityaction.org

The Obesity Action Coalition (OAC) is a nearly 50,000 member-strong 501(c)(3) National non-profit organization dedicated to giving a voice to the individual affected by the disease of obesity and helping individuals along their journey toward better health through education, advocacy and support.

Joseph Nadglowski, President & CEO
James Zervios, VP & Chief of Staff
Lisa Gresco-White, Senior Membership/Operation Manager

4733 Partnership for a Healthier America
PO Box 1200
Prince Frederick, MD 20678

202-842-9001
info@ahealthieramerica.org
ahealthieramerica.org

The Partnership for a Healthier America (PHA) is devoted to working with the private sector to ensure the health of our nation's youth by solving the childhood obesity crisis.

Noreen Springstead, President & CEO

4734 Rudd Center for Food Policy & Health
University of Connecticut
One Constitution Plaza, Suite 600
Hartford, CT 06103

959-200-3520
uconnruddcenter.org

The Rudd Center for Food Policy and Health promotes solutions to food insecurity, poor diet quality, and weight bias through research and policy.

Marlene Schwartz, PhD, Director
Rebecca M. Puhl, PhD, Deputy Director
Carson Hardee, Director of Communications

4735 SHAPE America: Society of Health and Physical Educators
PO Box 225
Annapolis Junction, MD 20701

800-213-7193
Fax: 703-476-9527
www.shapeamerica.org

SHAPE America Society of Health and Physical Educators serves as the voice for 200,000+ health and physical education professionals across the United States. The organization's extensive community includes a diverse membership of health and physical educators, as well as advocates, supporters, and 50+ state affiliate organizations.

Stephanie A. Morris, Chief Executive Director

4736 The Obesity Society
9211 Corporate Boulevard, Suite 300
Rockville, MD 20850

301-563-6526
contact@obesity.org
www.obesity.org

The Obesity Society is the leading professional society dedicated to better understanding, preventing and treating obesity.

Anthony Comuzzie, Chief Executive Officer
Christe A. Turner, Director, Finance & Operations
Anita Wiler, Sr. Director, Education & Meetings

Libraries & Resource Centers

4737 National Digestive Diseases Information Clearinghouse (NDDIC)
NIH
2 Information Way
Bethesda, MD 20892

301-654-3810
800-891-5389
Fax: 703-738-4929
nddic@info.niddk.nih.gov
www.digestive.niddk.nih.gov

The National Institute of Diabetes and Digestive and Kidney Diseases conducts and supports research on many of the most serious diseases affecting public health. The Institute supports much of the clinical research on the diseases of internal medicine and related subspecialty fields as well as many basic science disciplines.

Griffin P. Rodgers, MD, Director
Gregory G. Germino, MD, Deputy Director
Kathy Kranzfelder, Communications Director

Research Centers

4738 New York Obesity Research Center
Saint Luke's-Roosevelt Hospital Center
1111 Amsterdam Avenue, 14th Floor, Babcock 10
New York, NY 10025

212-523-4161
Fax: 212-523-4830
www.nyorc.org

Dr F Xavier Pi-Sunyer, Co-Director
Dr. Rudolph Leibel, Co-Director
Rudolf L. Leibel, Core Director

4739 University of Chicago-Department of Psychiatry
5841 S Maryland Avenue. MC 3077, Rm W-413
Chicago, IL 60637

773-834-1007
Fax: 773-702-9929
www.psychiatry.uchicago.edu

Emil F. Coccaro, Chairman
Jean Harris, Secretary
Robert Naclerio, Research Administrator

Conferences

4740 American School Counselor Association Annual Conference
1101 King Street, Suite 310
Alexandria, VA 22314

703-683-2722
800-306-4722
Fax: 703-997-7572
asca@schoolcounselor.org
www.schoolcounselor.org

The mission of ASCA is to represent professional school counselors and to promote professionalism and ethical practices.

3,000 Attendees

Richard Wong, Executive Director
Jennifer Walsh, Director, Education & Training
Kathleen M Rakestraw, Director of Communications

Audio Video

4741 Reality Matters - Obesity & Nutrition
Discovery Education
PO Box 2284
South Burlington, VT 5407

888-892-3484
education_info@discovery.com
store.discoveryeduction.com

Teenagers have always been drawn to junk food, but more than ever, today's teens are suffering at the hands of less active lifestyles and unhealthy eating habits. Explore America's culture of obesity and its contributing factors-along with ways to help kids make healthy choices.

DVD/VHS 30 minutes

Web Sites

4742 **American Anorexia Bulimia Association of Philadelphia**
PO Box 27156
Philadelphia, PA 19118
www.aabaphila.org

Support for sufferers friends and family.

4743 **Gurze Books**
5145 B Avenida Encinas
Carlsbad, CA 92008
800-756-7533
www.gurze.com

Specializes in information about eating disorders including anorexia nervosa, bulimia nervosa, and binge eating, plus related topics such as body image and obesity. Books are offered at discounted prices, many free articles about eating disorders, newsletters, links to treatment facilities, organizations, other websites and much more.

4744 **Obesity Online**
www.obesity-online.com/

www.obesity-online.com/

Is a multi-disciplinary forum for research and treatment of massive obesity, including plastics, psychiatry, endocrinology nutrition, nursing, dietetics and allied health.

Book Publishers

4745 **Feed Your Kids Well: How to Help Your Child Lose Weight and Get Healthy**
Fred Pescatore MD, author

Wiley Publishing, Inc
10475 Crosspoint Boulevard
Indianapolis, IN 46256
317-572-3000
877-762-2974
Fax: 800-597-3299
consumer@wiley.com
www.wiley.com

Aimed toward parents, this book offers advice and tips to help their children lose excess weight. It also examines the popular fat-free diet fads and advises diets containing the small amounts of fat that are crucial to human growth.

1999 304 pages Paperback
ISBN: 0-471349-63-1

Peter B. Wiley, Chairman
Stephen M. Smith, President & CEO
Ellis E. Cousens, Executive Vice President, Chief Fin

4746 **Let's Talk About Being Overweight**
Melanie Apel Gordon, author

Rosen Publishing Group's PowerKids Press
29 E 21st Street
New York, NY 10010
212-777-3017
800-237-9932
Fax: 888-436-4643
rosenpub@tribeca.ios.com
www.rosenpublishing.com

Reminds kids that everyone's body is different and assures them that it is okay. Readers will also learn that they will feel better if they eat right and get regular exercise. Grades K-5.

2000 24 pages
ISBN: 0-823954-13-7

Roger Rosen, President

4747 **Making Peace with Food**
Gurze Books
5145 B Avenida Encinas, PO Box 2238
Carlsbad, CA 92208
760-434-7533
800-756-7533
Fax: 760-434-5476
leigh@gurze.net
www.gurze.com

Filled with ideas, workbook pages, exercises, and resources, an excellent aid to clarifying and overcoming your personal diet/weight struggle.

224 pages Paperback

Suan Kano, Author

4748 **Obesity Sourcebook**
Omnigraphics
615 Griswold Street, Ste 520
Detroit, MI 48226
610-461-3548
800-234-1340
Fax: 800-875-1340
contact@omnigraphics.com
www.omnigraphics.com

Basic consumer health information about diseases and other problems associated with obesity, including risk factors, prevention and management.

376 pages
ISBN: 0-780803-33-7

4749 **Overeaters Anonymous Lifeline Sampler**
World Service Office
6075 Zenith Court NE, PO Box 44020
Rio Rancho, NM 87144
505-891-2664
Fax: 505-891-4320
info@overeatersanonymous.org
www.overeatersanonymous.org

A selection of articles from Lifeline magazine. Issues and topics include: relationships in recovery, food and weight, relapse, spiritual insights, abstinent living and traditions and steps.

448 pages

4750 **Twelve Steps and Twelve Traditions of Over eaters Anonymous**
World Service Office
6075 Zenith Court NE, PO Box 44020
Rio Rancho, NM 87144
505-891-2664
Fax: 505-891-4320
www.overeatersanonymous.org

Provides a detailed exploration of how the 12 traditions help members recover and how the Fellowship functions as a whole.

240 pages Softcover

4751 **Understanding Childhood Obesity**
J Clinton Smith MD, author

University Press of Mississippi
3825 Ridgewood Road
Jackson, MS 39211
601-432-6205
800-737-7788
Fax: 601-432-6217
press@ihl.state.ms.us
www.upress.state.ms.us

A clear explanation of causes, diagnosis, and treatment of childhood obesity. A comprehensive guide that covers nearly every field of obesity research.

120 pages Paper
ISBN: 1-578061-34-2

4752 When Food is Love
Geneen Roth, author

Gurze Books
PO Box 2238
Carlsbad, CA 92018

760-434-7533
800-756-7533
Fax: 760-434-5467
mylo@gurze.net
www.gurze.com

Drawing on her own personal experience, Roth explores similarities between eating and loving such as fantasizing, wanting the forbidden, creating drama, control issues, and the experience of relationship.

1991 205 pages Paperback
ISBN: 0-452268-18-4

Leigh Cohn, Publisher & Marketing
Lindsey Hall Cohn, Editor-in-Chief

Pamphlets

4753 Media-Smart Youth: Eat, Think, and Active Fact Sheet
Natl Institute of Child Health & Human Development
P.O. Box 3006
Rockville, MD 20852

301-496-5133
800-370-2943
Fax: 866-760-5947
TTY: 888-320-6942
NICHDInformationResourceCenter@mail.nih.
www.nichd.nih.gov

Free government information on an interactive after-school education program that helps young people between the ages of 11 and 13 understand how physical activity and nutrition can influence their health.

2005 2 pages

Alan E. Guttmacher, Director

Camps

4754 Camp Shane
302 Harris Road
Ferndale, NY 12734

845-292-4644
Fax: 845-292-8636
office@campshane.com
www.campshane.com

Camp dedicated to weight loss.

David Ettenberg, Director

4755 Camp Shane Arizona
1000 Orme Road
Mayer, AZ 86333

928-227-3883
office@campshanearizona.com
www.campshanearizona.com

Camp dedicated to weight loss.

Vanessa Stiller, Director
Jessica Gray, Nutritionist
Andrea Crandell, Sports and Crafts

4756 Camp Shane California
60 W Olsen Rd
Thousand Oaks, CA 91360

805-259-3366
office@campshanecalifornia.com
www.campshanecalifornia.com

Camp dedicated to weight loss.

David Ruales, Camp Director
Camryn Kruger, Assistant Director
Erika Smith, Program Guru

4757 Camp Shining Stars
Barton College
Wilson, NC 27893

919-246-4865
866-644-2709
www.campshiningstars.org

Camp Shining Stars will help children lose weight, raise their self esteem, and learn the tools and habits necessary to lead a healthy lifestyle and reduce their risks for developing chronic diseases later in life.

Ira Green, Director

4758 Kingsmont
893 West Street
Amherst, MA 1002

703-288-0047
877-348-2267
Fax: 703-288-0075
www.campkingsmont.com

A non-profit organization dedicated to eliminating childhood obesity by promoting proper nutrition, physical activity and emotional well-being. The camp is dedicated to providing children with the tools needed to make fundamental changes in their lives.

Meghan Roman, Director
Danny Heisler, Programming Director
Katie Roman, Administrative Director

4759 New Image Camps
PO Box 417
Norwood, NJ 7648

201-750-1557
800-365-0556
tsparber@aol.com
www.newimagecamp.com

Weight loss camp that features private lakefronts at 2 outstanding camps where kids, ages 7-19, have fun, lose weight & gain self-esteem. With separate facilities for boys and girls including two swimming pools, about 30 kids in a given age group, and roughly a 4 to 1 counselor-to-camper ratio, your child will form healthy, age-appropriate friendships, with a guidance they need for a fun and successful summer.

Tony Sparber, Owner
Dale Sparber, Owner

4760 Wellspring Camps
42675 Road 44
Reedley, CA 93654

866-364-0808
www.wellspringcamps.com

Wellspring is the leading organization of weight loss camps for kids, teens, young adults and women. The scientific Wellspring Plan trains campers on the self-regulatory skills they need to return to a healthy weight, and ofers families a simple and sustainable solution to supporting their child at home. Locations in La Jolla, Texas, New York, North Carolina, Wisconsin, Pennsylvania, and Florida.

Eliza Kingsford, MA, Executive Director
Jessie Dean, Director of Operations
Michaela Clinton, Director of Admissions

Description

4761 OBSESSIVE-COMPULSIVE DISORDER

Synonyms: Obsessive-compulsive neurosis, OCD

Involves the following Biologic System(s):

Developmental/Behavioral/Psychiatric Disorders

Obsessive-compulsive disorder (OCD) is characterized by the performance of repetitive actions, rituals, or compulsions in response to recurrent, persistent thoughts or obsessions. These actions and thoughts may cause significant anxiety and interfere with personal, social, or occupational functioning. OCD may affect approximately two to three percent of the general population worldwide. In most cases, the onset of OCD is gradual and typically becomes apparent during adolescence or early adulthood. However, onset of the disorder during childhood is not rare. Males and females are thought to be affected equally.

Many children have minor compulsions that result in little or no distress, such as avoiding cracks while walking on the sidewalk. Most such compulsions typically subside later in life. However, some rituals may continue through adulthood, such as repeatedly checking that the stove is turned off. Children who develop obsessive-compulsive disorder may initially have repetitive, persistent thoughts that constantly invade their consciousness. They may conduct a repetitive action or a series of actions during certain situations, particularly during times of stress, such as preparing to go to school. Performing compulsive actions or rituals may temporarily relieve a feeling of anxiety, whereas resisting such compulsions may serve to increase their tension. Obsessions may consist of certain ideas, phrases, or strong images; impulses to perform objectionable acts; or impulses to perform objectionable acts; or impulses to repeatedly analyze certain acts before carrying them out. Some obsessions may concern bodily secretions or wastes or a need for routine or sameness. Compulsions often include repetitive hand washing, touching certain objects in a particular sequence, or checking and rechecking door locks. Attempts may be made to involve parents or other family members in the performance of certain compulsive actions or rituals. Children with OCD are usually aware of the irrationality of their obsessive thoughts and compulsive behaviors but are unable to control them. The symptoms associated with OCD often periodically decrease or increase in intensity over time. However, in some patients, a progressive worsening of the condition may result in gradual deterioration of personal and social functioning. First-line treatment of OCD may include antidepressant medications, such as fluoxetine, fluvoxamine, or clomipramine.Behavioral therapy, including gradually increased exposure to situations that typically trigger compulsive behaviors, may be helpful. Relaxation therapy has also demonstrated some benefit.

OCD may occur as an isolated condition or in association with other underlying disorders or conditions, such as Tourette syndrome, epilepsy, or anorexia nervosa. Although the exact cause of obsessive-compulsive disorder is not known, studies suggest that the disorder may result from biochemical abnormalities affecting particular areas of the brain. There are also reports of multiple cases of isolated OCD in a multigenerational family (kindred), suggesting autosomal dominant inheritance in these patients. In addition, the occurrence of OCD in several kindreds affected by Tourette syndrome also indicates that changes (mutations) of certain genes may result in or contribute to OCD.

Government Agencies

4762 Center for Mental Health Services
5600 Fishers Lane
Rockville, MD 20857

240-276-1310
www.samhsa.gov

Encourages a range of programs such as systems of care to respond to the increasing number of mental, emotional, and behavioral problems among children. Supports outreach and case management programs for the thousands of Americans who are homeless and the improvement of these services.

Anita Everett, MD, Director

4763 NIH/National Institute of Mental Health
6001 Executive Blvd, Rm 6200, MSC 9663
Bethesda, MD 20892

866-615-6464
Fax: 301-443-4279
TTY: 301-443-8431
nimhinfo@nih.gov
www.nimh.nih.gov

The mission of NIMH is to transform the understanding and treatment of mental illnesses through basic and clinical research, paving the way for prevention, recovery, and cure.

Joshua A. Gordon, MD, PhD, Director
Shelli Avenevoli, PhD, Deputy Director

National Associations & Support Groups

4764 American Academy of Pediatrics
345 Park Blvd
Itasca, IL 60143

847-434-4000
800-433-9016
Fax: 847-434-8000
csc@aap.org
www.aap.org

The American Academy of Pediatrics and its member pediatricians are committed to the attainment of optimal physical, mental and social health and well-being for all infants, children, adolescents, and young adults.

Kyle E. Yasuda, MD, FAAP, President
Mark Del Monte, JD, CEO/Executive VP
Vera Tait, MD, FAAP, Chief Medical Officer

4765 Anxiety and Depression Association of America
8701 Georgia Avenue, Suite 412
Silver Spring, MD 20910

240-485-1018
information@adaa.org
www.adaa.org

ADAA is a national non-profit organization dedicated to the prevention, treatment, and cure of anxiety, depression, OCD, PTSD, and related disorders and to improving the lives of all people who suffer from them through education, practice, and research.

Susan K Gurley, Executive Director
Lise Bram, Deputy Executive Director
Katie Russo, Senior Director, Operations

4766 Genetic Alliance
426400 Woodfield Road, Ste 189
Damascus, MD 20872

202-966-5557
Fax: 202-966-8553
info@geneticalliance.org
www.geneticalliance.org

World's leading nonprofit health advocacy organization committed to transforming health through genetics and promoting an environment of openness centered on the health of individuals, families, and communities.

Sharon Terry, CEO
Ruth Child, CFO
Natasha Bonhomme, Chief Strategy Officer

4767 International OCD Foundation
PO Box 961029
Boston, MA 02196

617-973-5801
Fax: 617-973-5801
iocdf.org

Obsessive-Compulsive Disorder / State Agencies & Support Groups

The Foundation aims to improve outcomes for individuals with OCD and related disorders by providing resources and support for those affected by OCD, including individuals with OCD and related disorders, and increasing access to effective treatment through educating mental health professionals about evidence-based treatments, providing a forum for professional collaboration and networking, and supporting research into the causes of and treatments for OCD and related disorders.

Matthew Antonelli, Interim Executive Director
Stephanie Cogen, Program Director
Fran Harrington, Director of Media & Technology

4768 **Mental Health America**
500 Montgomery Street, Ste 820
Alexandria, VA 22314
703-684-7722
800-969-6642
Fax: 703-684-5968
www.mentalhealthamerica.net

MHA, the leading advocacy organization addressing the full spectrum of mental and substance use conditions and their effects nationwide, works to inform, advocate and enable access to quality behavioral health services for all Americans.

Paul Gionfriddo, President/CEO
Whitney Ball, Assoc. Dir., Marketing/Outreach
Sachin Doshi, Sr. Dir, Finance/Operations

4769 **NADD: National Association for the Dually Diagnosed**
12 Hurley Avenue
Kingston, NY 12401
845-331-4336
800-331-5362
Fax: 845-331-4569
info@thenadd.org
www.thenadd.org

Nonprofit organization designed to promote the interests of professional and parent development with resources for individuals who have the coexistence of mental illness and intellectual disabilities. Provides conferences, educational services and training materials to professionals, parents, concerned citizens and service organizations.

Jeanne Farr, CEO
Michelle Jordan, Office Manager
Edward Seliger, Project Coordinator

4770 **National Alliance on Mental Illness (NAMI)**
4301 Wilson Blvd., Suite 300
Arlington, VA 22203
703-524-7600
888-999-6264
info@nami.org
www.nami.org

NAMI provides advocacy, education, support and public awareness so that all individuals and families affected by mental illness can build better lives.

Daniel H. Gillison, CEO
David Levy, CFO
Ken Duckworth, Chief Medical Officer

4771 **National Anxiety Foundation**
3135 Custer Drive
Lexington, KY 40517
859-281-0003
www.nationalanxietyfoundation.org

A volunteer nonprofit organization. Its goal is to educate the public and health professionals about anxiety and anxiety disorders (such as panic disorder and obsessive-compulsive disorder) through printed materials and electronic media.

Stephen Cox, MD, President & Medical Director
Linda Vernon Blair, VP
C. Todd Strecker, Secretary-Treasurer

4772 **National Federation of Families**
15800 Crabbs Branch Way, Suite 300
Rockville, MD 20855
240-403-1901
ffcmh@ffcmh.org
www.ffcmh.org

The National family run organization is dedicated exclusively to helping children with mental health needs and their families achieve a better quality of life.

Lynda Gargan, PhD, Executive Director

4773 **National Mental Health Consumers' Self-Help Clearinghouse**
1211 Chestnut Street, Suite 1207
Philadelphia, PA 19107
267-507-3810
800-553-4539
Fax: 215-636-6312
selfhelpclearinghouse@gmail.com
www.mhselfhelp.org

Offers information, support and appropriate referrals; and promotes public and professional education. Provides networking for those with special interests related to albinism. Promotes and supports research and funding that will improve diagnosis and management of albinism and hypopigmentation.

Joseph Rogers, Founder/Executive Director
Susan Rogers, Director

4774 **Obsessive Compulsive Anonymous**
PO Box 215
New Hyde Park, NY 11040
677-770-1523
www.obsessivecompulsiveanonymous.org

A fellowship of individuals dedicated to sharing their experience, strength and hope with one another to enable them to solve their common problems and help others recover from OCD. The Twelve Steps are adapted for OCA, to help obtain relief from obsessions and compulsions. Consisting of approximately 1,000 members and 50 chapters, OCA is not allied with any sect, denomination or organization.

4775 **Suncoast Residential Training Center/Developmental Services Program**
Goodwill Industries-Suncoast
www.goodwill-suncoast.org

727-523-1512
888-279-1988
www.goodwill-suncoast.org

A large group home which serves individuals with intellectual disabilities with a secondary diagnosis of psychiatric difficulties as evidenced by problem behavior. Providing residential, behavioral and instructional support and services that will promote the development of adaptive, socially appropriate behavior, each individual is assessed to determine socialization, basic academics and recreation. The primary intervention strategy is applied behavior analysis.

Deborah A. Passerini, President & CEO

State Agencies & Support Groups

4776 **Center for Family Support**
333 7th Avenue, #901
New York, NY 10001
212-629-7939
Fax: 212-239-2211
www.cfsny.org

The Center for Family (CFS) is a not-for-profit human service agency providing support and assistance to individuals with developmental disabilities and traumatic brain injuries throughout New York City, Long Island, the lower Hudson Valley region and New Jersey.

Steven Vernikoff, Executive Director
Linda Schellenberg, Director, Community Service
Barbara Greenwald, Associate Executive Director

4777 **Obsessive Compulsive Foundation of Metropolitan Chicago**
2300 Lincoln Park West
Chicago, IL 60614
773-661-9530
Fax: 773-661-9535
www.ocdchicago.org

Serves adults and children with OCD, their families, and the mental health professionals who treat them. The only Chicago area organization dedicated to OCD.

Ellen Sawyer, Executive Director

Research Centers

4778 **Brain & Behavior Research Foundation**
747 Third Avenue, 33rd Floor
New York, NY 10017
646-681-4888
800-829-8289
info@bbrfoundation.org
www.bbrfoundation.org

The Brain & Behavior Research Foundation is committed to alleviating the suffering caused by mental illness by awarding grants that will lead to advances and breakthroughs in scientific research.

Jeffrey Borenstein, MD, President & CEO

Audio Video

4779 **Hope and Solutions for OCD**
ADD WareHouse
300 NW 70th Avenue, Suite 102
Plantation, FL 33317
954-792-8100
800-233-9273
Fax: 954-792-8545
sales@addwarehouse.com
www.addwarehouse.com

A video series about obsessive compulsive disorder with some straight forward solutions and advice for individuals with OCD, their families, doctors, and school personnel. Viewers will learn what OCD is and how to treat it. Discusses how OCD can affect students in school and the impact on the family life.

85 Minutes
ISBN: 1-886941-37-8

4780 **It's Not Me...It's My OCD: A Look at Behavioral Therapy**
Aquarius Health Care Videos
3435 Main Street, Bldg. 28
Buffalo, NY 14214
716-829-5744
888-440-2963
Fax: 508-650-1665
emro.lib.buffalo.edu

1997 28 Minutes
ISBN: 1-581403-38-0

Lori Widzinski, Editor
Oksana Dykyj, Associate Editor
Angela Davis, Social Network Coordinator

4781 **Touching Tree**
Awareness Films, author

Pyramid Media
3200 Airport Ave, Ste 19
Santa Monica, CA 90405
310-398-6149
800-421-2304
Fax: 310-398-7869
info@pyramidmedia.com
www.pyramidmedia.com

Chronicles of a young boy trapped in the pain of OCD; how he faces his fears and begins the slow recovery with professional help. A film ideal for teaching the need for sensitivity when dealing with special children and their differences.

38 Minutes

Web Sites

4782 **Anxiety Disorders Association of America**
NOP-ONE-

Offers resources and information for persons with anxiety and stress-related disorders.

4783 **CyberPsych**
www.cyberpsych.org

www.cyberpsych.org

CyberPsych presents information about psychoanalysis, psychotherapy, and special topics such as anxiety disorder, the problematic use of alcohol, homophobia, and the traumatic effects of racism. CyberPsych is a nonprofit network which offers free web hosting and technical support for internet communication, to nonprofit groups and individuals.

4784 **Guidelines for Families Coping with OCD**
4901 NW 17th Way, Suite 101
Fort Lauderdale, FL 33309
954-962-6662
Fax: 954-962-6164
www.ocdhope.com/gdlines.htm

Offers 19 guidelines for families coping with OCD.

Dr. Bruce Hyman, Founder & Director
Dr. Stacy Sanders Shaup, Associate
Dr. Jennifer Hochman, Associate

4785 **International OCD Foundation**
PO Box 961029
Boston, MA 02196
617-973-5801
Fax: 617-973-5801
iocdf.org

The Foundation aims to improve outcomes for individuals with OCD and related disorders by providing resources and support for those affected by OCD, including individuals with OCD and related disorders, and increasing access to effective treatment through educating mental health professionals about evidence-based treatments, providing a forum for professional collaboration and networking, and supporting research into the causes of and treatments for OCD and related disorders.

4786 **NADD: National Association for the Dually Diagnosed**
12 Hurley Avenue
Kingston, NY 12401
845-331-4336
800-331-5362
Fax: 845-331-4569
www.thenadd.org

Nonprofit organization designed to promote the interests of professional and care providers for individuals who have the coexistence of mental illness and intellectual disabilities. NADD provides conferences, educational services and training materials to professionals, parents, concerned citizens and service organizations.

Jeanne Farr, CEO
Michelle Jordan, Office Manager
Edward Seliger, Project Coordinator

4787 **National Anxiety Foundation**
www.nationalanxietyfoundation.org

www.nationalanxietyfoundation.org

Nonprofit organization that provides education to the public and professionals about anxiety through printed and electronic media.

Stephen Cox, MD, President & Medical Director
Linda Vernon Blair, VP
C. Todd Strecker, Secretary-Treasurer

4788 **National Mental Health Consumers' Self-Help Clearinghouse**
www.mhselfhelp.org

selfhelpclearinghouse@gmail.com
www.mhselfhelp.org

A consumer run national technical assistance center serving the mental health consumer movement. We help connect individuals to self-help and advocacy resources, and we offer expertise to self-help groups, and other peer-run services for mental health consumers.

Joseph Rogers, Founder/Executive Director
Susan Rogers, Director

4789 **Obsessive Compulsive Disorder (OCD)**
6001 Executive Boulevard
Rockville, MD 20852
NIMHinfo@mail.nih.gov
www.nimh.nih.gov/healthinformation/ocdmenu.cfm

Discusses the diagnosis of obsessive-compulsive disorder, its prevalence among both children and adults. Descibes types of treatment including pharmacotherapy. Gives sources of information for both the individual who has OCD and the family.

Obsessive-Compulsive Disorder / Book Publishers

4790 **Psych Central**
55 Pleasant St., Suite 207
Newburyport, MA 1950

talkback@psychcentral.com
www.psychcentral.com

Offers free informational and educational articles and resources on psychology, support and mental health online.

John M. Grohol, CEO & Founder

Book Publishers

4791 **Boy Who Couldn't Stop Washing: The Experience and Treatment of OCD**

Judith L Rapoport, author

Penguin Group
375 Hudson Street
New York, NY 10014

212-366-2372
Fax: 212-366-2933
online@us.penguingroup.com
us.penguingroup.com

A comprehensive treatment of obsessive-compulsive disorder that summarizes evidence that the disorder is neurobiological. It also describes the effect of medication combined with behavioral therapy.

1991 304 pages Paperback
ISBN: 0-451172-02-0

John Makinson, CHAIRMAN
Coram Williams, CFO
David Shanks, CEO

4792 **Brain Lock: Free Yourself from Obsessive Compulsive Behavior**

Jeffrey M Schwartz, author

Harper Collins
10 E 53rd Street
New York, NY 10022

212-207-7000
800-242-7737
Fax: 212-207-7901
feedback2@harpercollins.com
www.harpercollins.com

A simple four-step method for overcoming OCD that is so effective, it's now used in academic treatment centers throughout the world. Proven by brain-imaging tests to actually alter the brain's chemistry, this method doesn't rely on psychopharmaceuticals but cognitive self-therapy and behavior modification to develop new patterns of response. Offers real-life stories of actual patients.

1997 256 pages Paperback
ISBN: 0-060987-11-1

4793 **Brief Strategic Solution-Oriented Therapy of Phobic and Obsessive Disorders**

Giorgio Nardone, author

Jason Aronson Publishers
4501 Forbes Boulevard, Suite 200
Lanham, MD 20706

301-459-3366
800-462-6420
Fax: 301-429-5748
www.aronson.com

1996 188 pages Cloth
ISBN: 1-568218-04-4

4794 **Childhood Obsessive Compulsive Disorder**

Greta Francis, author

Sage Publications
2455 Teller Road
Thousand Oaks, CA 91320

800-818-7243
800-818-7243
Fax: 800-583-2665
www.sagepub.com

1996 120 pages
ISBN: 0-803959-22-2

Sara Miller McCune, Chairman
Blaise R. Simqu, President & CEO
Chris Hickok, Senior Vice President & Chief Finan

4795 **Freeing Your Child from Obsessive-Compulsive Disorder**

Tamar E Chansky PhD, author

Crown Publishing Group/Random House
280 Park Avenue
New York, NY 10017

212-940-7381
800-733-3000
www.crownpublishing.com

ISBN: 0-812931-17-4

4796 **It's Nobody's Fault-New Hope and Help for Difficult Children and Their Parents**

ADD WareHouse
300 NW 70th Avenue, Suite 102
Plantation, FL 33317

954-792-8100
800-233-9273
Fax: 954-792-8545
www.addwarehouse.com

This book explains that neither the parents nor children are causes of mental disorders and related problems.

1997 320 pages Paperback
ISBN: 0-812929-21-7

4797 **Obsessive Compulsive Disorder: Helping Children and Adolescents**

Mitzi Waltz, author

O'Reilly Media
1005 Gravenstein Highway N
Sebastopol, CA 95472

707-827-7019
800-889-8969
Fax: 707-829-0104
www.oreilly.com

This book helps parents secure an accurate and complete diagnosis, and live with OCD children using effective parenting techniques. Offers support systems, medical interventions and explores therapeutic and other interventions, such as cognitive therapy; helps to secure care with an existing health plan even with no coverage of mental disorders, navigate the special education system and find resources.

2000 404 pages
ISBN: 1-565927-58-3

Tim O'Reilly, Founder & CEO

4798 **Obsessive-Compulsive Disorder in Children and Adolescents**

American Psychiatric Publishing
1000 Wilson Boulevard, Suite 1825
Arlington, VA 22209

703-907-7322
800-368-5777
Fax: 703-907-1091
appi@psych.org
www.appi.org

Examines the early development of obsessive-compulsive disorder and describes effective treatments.

1989 368 pages Hardcover
ISBN: 0-880482-82-0

Robert E. Hales, M.D, Editor-in-Chief
Rebecca D. Rinehart, Publisher
John McDuffie, Editorial Director

4799 **School Personnel: A Critical Link in the Identification and Management of OCD**

Gail B Adams, author

Obsessive Compulsive Foundation
18 Tremont Street, Suite 903
Boston, MA 02108

617-973-5801
Fax: 617-973-5803
info@ocfoundation.org
www.ocfoundation.org

Recognizing OCD in the school setting, current treatments, the role of school personnel in identification, assessment, and educational interventions are thoroughly covered in this brief, but informative booklet especially targeted to educators and guidance counselors.

2003 32 pages Booklet

Denise Egan Stack, President
Susan B. Dailey, Vice President
Diane Davey, Secretary

4800 Talking Back to OCD: The Program That Help Kids & Teens Say No Way
John March W/ Christine Benton, author

Guilford Publications
72 Spring Street
New York, NY 10012
212-431-9800
800-365-7006
Fax: 212-966-6708
info@guilford.com
www.guilford.com

Dr March's 8-step program to empower young people overcome OCD. Each chapter begins with a section that helps young readers zero in on specific problems and develop skills they can use to tune out the obsessions and resist compulsions. Filled with tips for parents to seperate the disorder from the child and to encourage their child in recovery. Hard- or paperback.

2007 276 pages Paperback
ISBN: 1-593853-55-6

Bob Matloff, President
Seymour Weingarten, Editor-in-Chief

4801 Teaching the Tiger
Hope Press
PO Box 188
Duarte, CA 91009
800-321-4039
Fax: 626-358-3520
dcomings@earthlink.net
www.hopepress.com

A handbook for individuals involved in the education of students with Attention Deficit Disorder, Tourette Syndrome, or Obsessive Compulsive Disorder.

ISBN: 1-878267-34-5

David E Comings MD, Presenter

Newsletters

4802 Key Update
National Mental Health Consumer's Self-Help Clrhs.
1211 Chestnut Street, Suite 1207
Philadelphia, PA 19107
215-751-1810
800-553-4539
Fax: 215-636-6312
selfhelpclearinghouse@gmail.com
www.mhselfhelp.org

A monthly e-newsletter that provides timely news and notes on important mental health issues, details on upcoming events, and recent publications on policy issues. Topics addressed in the newsletter include self-advocacy, self-care, community integration, human rights and mental health treatments and services.

Monthly

Joseph Rogers, Founder/Executive Director
Susan Rogers, Director

Pamphlets

4803 Children and Adolescents
Madison Institute of Medicine
7617 Mineral Point Road, Suite 300
Madison, WI 53717
608-827-2470
Fax: 608-827-2479
mim@miminc.org
www.miminc.org

Literature packet: diagnosis, treatment and other information on OCD in young children and adolescents.

4804 Obsessive Compulsive Disorder General Packet
Madison Institute of Medicine
7617 Mineral Point Road, Suite 300
Madison, WI 53717
608-827-2470
Fax: 608-827-2479
www.miminc.org

Literature packet: overview of OCD, including information on prevalence, diagnosis and treatment.

4805 Obsessive-Compulsive Disorder, A Real Illness
National Institute of Mental Health
Public Info, 6001 Executive Blvd, Rm 8184
Rockville, MD 20852
301-443-4513
866-615-6464
Fax: 301-443-4279
TTY: 301-443-8431
NIMHinfo@mail.nih.gov
www.nimh.nih.gov

Easy-to read booklet on OCD, explaining what it is, when it starts, how long it lasts and how to get help. The booklet also includes a self-test.

Camps

4806 Tourette Syndrome Camp Organization
6933 N Kedzie, #816
Chicago, IL 60640
773-465-7536
info@tourettecamp.com
www.tourettecamp.com

Dedicated to promoting camping opportunities for children with Tourette Syndrome and its assocaited disorders, Obsessive Compulsive Disorder (OCD) and Attention Deficit/Hyperactivity Disorder (ADD/ADHD).

Monica Newman, Camp Director
Marleen Martinez, Assistant Director
Sarah Matchen, Director

Omphalocele / Description

Description

4807 OMPHALOCELE

Involves the following Biologic System(s):

Gastrointestinal Disorders, Neonatal and Infant Disorders

An omphalocele is a birth defect characterized by bulging or protrusion of a portion of the intestines through an abnormal opening in the abdominal wall near the navel, the region where the umbilical cord meets the abdomen during fetal growth and development. The bulging area of the intestines is covered by a thin, membrane-like sac consisting of part of the amnion and peritoneum. The amnion is the inner layer of membrane that forms the amniotic sac, the fluid-filled sac within which a fetus grows and develops. The peritoneum is the thin membrane that lines the abdominal cavity and covers the internal abdominal organs.

Depending upon the size of the abdominal wall defect in an affected newborn, varying amounts of intestine or, in severe cases, other abdominal organs, may protrude through the navel. Associated complications may include rupture of the protruding, membranous sac, damage to body tissues due to drying, or onset of infection. Because these complications may be life-threatening, an omphalocele is usually surgically repaired immediately after birth.

An omphalocele is thought to affect approximately one in 4,000 newborns. Prenatal ultrasounds often identify infants with an omphalocele before birth. Otherwise, physical examination of the infant is sufficient to diagnose this condition. In many infants, omphaloceles occur in association with other birth defects, such as abnormalities of the urinary and reproductive systems, central nervous system, or cardiovascular system. This condition may also occur in association with certain rare malformation syndromes that are apparent at birth. These include Beckwith-Wiedemann syndrome, also known as exomphalos-macroglossia-gigantism, and Shprintzen omphalocele syndrome, also called pharynx and larynx hypoplasia with omphalocele.

In other cases, omphaloceles may occur as isolated findings for unknown reasons. Omphaloceles are repaired with surgery, although not always immediately; complete recovery is expected. There have been reports of multiple cases of isolated omphaloceles within certain families (kindreds). In these families, the condition may be caused by abnormal changes (mutations) in a gene or genes that may be inherited as an autosomal recessive or X-linked trait. It is also possible that the interaction of several different genes in association with certain environmental factors (multifactorial inheritance) may play a role in the development of some omphaloceles.

Government Agencies

4808 Division of Birth Defects & Developmental Disabilities
1600 Clifton Road
Atlanta, GA 30333
800-232-4636
TTY: 888-232-6348
www.cdc.gov/ncbddd

Information and advocacy resources for families and professionals dealing with children with birth defects and developmental disabilities.

Karen Remley, MD, Director
Stephanie Dulin, Deputy Director

National Associations & Support Groups

4809 American Academy of Pediatrics
345 Park Blvd
Itasca, IL 60143
847-434-4000
800-433-9016
Fax: 847-434-8000
csc@aap.org
www.aap.org

The American Academy of Pediatrics and its member pediatricians are committed to the attainment of optimal physical, mental and social health and well-being for all infants, children, adolescents, and young adults.

Kyle E. Yasuda, MD, FAAP, President
Mark Del Monte, JD, CEO/Executive VP
Vera Tait, MD, FAAP, Chief Medical Officer

4810 American College of Gastroenterology
6400 Goldsboro Road
Bethesda, MD 20817
301-263-9000
www.gi.org

The American College of Gastroenterology was founded in 1932 to advance the scientific study and medical practice of diseases of the GI tract.

13,000 members

4811 March of Dimes Foundation
1550 Crystal Drive, Ste 1300
Arlington, VA 22202
888-663-4637
www.marchofdimes.org

March of Dimes help moms have full-term pregnancies and research the problems that threaten the health of babies. The March of Dimes also acts globally: sharing best practices in perinatal health and helping improve birth outcomes where the needs are the most urgent.

Stacey D. Stewart, President
Alan Brogdon, SVP/COO/Board Officer
Rahul Gupta, MD, SVP & Chief Medical/Health Officer

4812 North American Society for Pediatric Gastroenterology/Hepatology/Nutrition
714 N Bethlehem Pike, Suite 300
Ambler, PA 19002
215-641-9800
Fax: 215-641-1995
www.naspghan.org

Strives to improve the care of infants, children and adolescents with digestive disorders by promoting advances in clinical care of children with chronic abdominal pain, diarrhea, constipation, vomiting, bleeding from the GI tract, inflammatory bowel disease, liver diseases, diseases of the pancreas, poor weight gain and nutritional problems.

Margaret K Stallings, Executive Director
Kim Rose, Associate Director
Gina Brown, Membership

Libraries & Resource Centers

4813 National Digestive Diseases Information Clearinghouse (NDDIC)
NIH
2 Information Way
Bethesda, MD 20892
301-654-3810
800-891-5389
Fax: 703-738-4929
nddic@info.niddk.nih.gov
www.digestive.niddk.nih.gov

The National Institute of Diabetes and Digestive and Kidney Diseases conducts and supports research on many of the most serious diseases affecting public health. The Institute supports much of the clinical research on the diseases of internal medicine and related subspecialty fields as well as many basic science disciplines.

Griffin P. Rodgers, MD, Director
Gregory G. Germino, MD, Deputy Director
Kathy Kranzfelder, Communications Director

Web Sites

4814 **Mothers of Omphaloceles**
www.omphalocele.com

www.omphalocele.com

Support and Webring.

4815 **National Digestive Diseases Information Clearinghouse (NDDIC)**
NIH
2 Information Way
Bethesda, MD 20892

301-654-3810
800-891-5389
nddic@info.niddk.nih.gov
www.digestive.niddk.nih.gov

The National Institute of Diabetes and Digestive and Kidney Diseases conducts and supports research on many of the most serious diseases affecting public health. The Institute supports much of the clinical research on the diseases of internal medicine and related subspecialty fields as well as many basic science disciplines.

Griffin P. Rodgers, MD, Director
Gregory G. Germino, MD, Deputy Director
Kathy Kranzfelder, Communications Director

4816 **Online Mendelian Inheritance in Man**
McKusick-Nathans Institue of Genetic Medicine-JHU
Baltimore, MD 21205

www.omim.org

This database is a catalog of human genes and genetic disorders.

Ada Hamosh, MD, Scientific Director

4817 **Pediatric Surgery Update**
P.O. Box 10426
San Juan, PR 922

home.coqui.net/titolugo/PSU11.htm#1152

An online handbook about many differnt diseases and disablilies.

Journals

4818 **Journal of Pediatric Gastroenterology and Nutrition**

NASPGHAN, author

Lippincott Williams & Wilkins
2700 Lake Cook Road
Riverwoods, IL 60015

847-580-5000
Fax: 215-521-8902
www.lww.com

Publication of the North American Society for Pediatric Gastroenterolgy, Hepatology and Nutrition, which strives to improve the care of infants, children and adolescents with digestive disorders by promoting advances in clinical care of children with chronic abdominal pain, diarrhea, constipation, vomiting, bleeding from the GI tract, inflammatory bowel disease, liver diseases, diseases of the pancreas, poor weight gain and nutritional problems.

Newsletters

4819 **NASPGHAN News**
714 N. Bethlehem Pike, Ste 300
Ambler, PA 19002

215-641-9800
Fax: 215-641-1995
www.naspghan.org

Publication of the North American Society for Pediatric Gastroenterolgy, Hepatology and Nutrition, which strives to improve the care of infants, children and adolescents with digestive disorders by promoting advances in clinical care of children with chronic abdominal pain, diarrhea, constipation, vomiting, bleeding from the GI tract, inflammatory bowel disease, liver diseases, diseases of the pancreas, poor weight gain and nutritional problems.

Margaret K Stallings, Executive Director
Kim Rose, Associate Director
Gina Brown, Membership

Oppositional Defiant Disorder / Description

Description

4820 OPPOSITIONAL DEFIANT DISORDER

Synonym: ODD

Involves the following Biologic System(s):

Developmental/Behavioral/Psychiatric Disorders

Oppositional Defiant Disorder (ODD) is a disruptive behavioral disorder along with conduct disorder. It is marked by an ongoing pattern of negativistic, argumentative, and hostile behaviors when interacting with some or all authority figures. The symptoms are usually seen in multiple settings, but may be more noticeable at home or at school. Five to fifteen percent of all school-age children have ODD. This disorder is usually apparent before age eight. Although it is more common in boys in the pre-pubertal years, the sex ratio evens out post puberty. The causes of ODD are unknown, but many parents report that their child with ODD was more rigid and demanding than the child's siblings from an early age. Biological and environmental factors may have a role. ODD can also be a precursor to conduct disorder later in life. Children with ODD also have a higher risk of other conditions, including ADHD (attention deficit hyperactivity disorder), anxiety and depression.

ODD is diagnosed by the presence of at least six months of hostile, negative and defiant behavior that is more frequent and intense than expected for a child's age. The behavior must cause significant functional impairment, either socially, academically or occupationally. ODD can not be diagnosed in patients who are actively psychotic or who meet criteria for conduct disorder or antisocial personality disorder.

Treatment for ODD centers upon evaluating the child's physical and psychosocial environment, ruling out or treating co-morbid conditions and assisting parents in anticipating and modifying behavior. Problems in the family or environment that may be driving the behaviors also need to be addressed. Many children with ODD will respond to the positive parenting techniques. A child with ODD can be very difficult for parents who need support and understanding. Older school age children and adolescents with ODD are more likely to benefit from an intensive intervention program.

National Associations & Support Groups

4821 American Academy of Child and Adolescent Psychiatry
3615 Wisconsin Avenue NW
Washington, DC 20016
202-966-7300
Fax: 202-464-0131
www.aacap.org

The AACAP (American Academy of Child and Adolescent Psychiatry) is the leading national professional medical association dedicated to the promotion of healthy development for children, adolescents, and families.

Heidi B. Fordi, Executive Director

4822 American Academy of Pediatrics
345 Park Blvd
Itasca, IL 60143
847-434-4000
800-433-9016
Fax: 847-434-8000
csc@aap.org
www.aap.org

The American Academy of Pediatrics and its member pediatricians are committed to the attainment of optimal physical, mental and social health and well-being for all infants, children, adolescents, and young adults.

Kyle E. Yasuda, MD, FAAP, President
Mark Del Monte, JD, CEO/Executive VP
Vera Tait, MD, FAAP, Chief Medical Officer

Audio Video

4823 Explosive Child
Ross W Greene PhD, author

HarperCollins Publishers
1350 Avenue of the Americas
New York, NY 10019
212-261-6500
800-242-7737
www.harpercollins.com

A new approach for understanding and parenting easily frustrated, cronically inflexible children. Dr Greene offers help for you and your child. Now updated with new practical information, The Explosive Child lays out a sensitive, practical approach to helping your child at home and school.

1999 Audio Cassette
ISBN: 0-694521-90-6

Brian Murray, President and CEO
Chantal Restivo-Alessi, Chief Digital Officer
Janet Gervasio, SVP & CFO

Web Sites

4824 American Academy of Child and Adolescent Pyschiatry
3615 Wisconsin Avenue NW
Washington, DC 20016
202-966-7300
Fax: 202-464-0131
www.aacap.org

The AACAP (American Academy of Child and Adolescent Psychiatry) is the leading national professional medical association dedicated to the promotion of healthy development for children, adolescents, and families.

Heidi B. Fordi, Executive Director

Book Publishers

4825 Disruptive Behavior Disorders in Children and Adolescents
Robert L Hendren, DO, author

American Psychiatric Publishing
1000 Wilson Boulevard, Suite 1825
Arlington, VA 22209
703-907-7322
800-368-5777
Fax: 703-907-1091
appi@psych.org
www.appi.org

Comprehensively reviews current research and clinical observations on this timely topic. The authors look at three subtypes of attention-deficit/hyperactivity disorder (ADHD), conduct disorder, and oppositional defiant disorder, all of which are common among youths and often share similar symptoms of impulse control problems.

1999 216 pages Paperback
ISBN: 0-880489-60-7

Robert E. Hales, M.D, Editor-in-Chief
Rebecca D. Rinehart, Publisher
John McDuffie, Editorial Director

4826 Explosive Child
Ross W Greene PhD, author

HarperCollins Publishers
10 East 53rd Street
New York, NY 10022
212-207-7000
800-242-7737
Fax: 212-207-7901
feedback2@harpercollins.com
www.harpercollins.com

A new approach for understanding and parenting easily frustrated, cronically inflexible children. Dr Greene offers help for you and your child. Now updated with new practical information, The Explosive Child lays out a sensitive, practical approach to helping your child at home and school.

2005 334 pages Paperbcak
ISBN: 0-060931-02-7

4827 Helping the Noncompliant Child

Robert McMahon, Rex Forehand, author

Guilford Press
72 Spring Street
New York, NY 10012
212-431-9800
800-365-7006
Fax: 212-966-6708
info@guilford.com
www.guilford.com

An empirically proven program for teaching parents to manage non-compliance in 3- to 8- year olds. Practitioners are provided step-by-step guidelines for child and family assessment, detailed descriptions of parent training procedures, effective adjunctive treatment strategies, and complete protocols for conducting the program. Hard- or soft-cover.

2005 264 pages Paperback
ISBN: 1-593852-41-2

Bob Matloff, President
Seymour Weingarten, Editor-in-Chief

4828 New Strong-Willed Child

James C Dobson, author

Tyndale House Publishers
351 Executive Drive
Carol Stream, IL 60188
800-323-9400
Fax: 800-684-0247
www.tyndale.com

A complete update of The Strong-Willed Child for a new generation of parents and teachers. It offers practical advice on raising difficult-to-handle children and incorporates the latest research.

2004 270 pages Hardcover
ISBN: 0-842336-22-2

Magazines

4829 EHealth

UAB Health System
1802 6th Avenue South
Birmingham, AL 35233
205-934-4011
800-822-8816
Fax: 205-934-9991
www.uabmedicine.org

A health and fitness publication packed with all the latest news and health tips from the UAB Health System.

Quarterly

Journals

4830 Official Journal of the American Academy of Child and Adolescent Psychiatry

Lippincott Williams & Wilkins
351 West Camden Street
Baltimore, MD 21201
410-528-4200
800-638-3030
Fax: 410-528-8557
www.jaacap.com

The journal is recognized as THE major journal focusing exclusively on today's psychiatric research and treatment of the child and adolescent.

12x a year

Mina K Dulcan MD, Editor
Sara Tiner, Editorial Coordinator

Osteogenesis Imperfecta / Description

Description

4831 OSTEOGENESIS IMPERFECTA

Synonyms: Brittle bone disease, OI

Covers these related disorders: Osteogenesis imperfecta Type I (OI Type I), Osteogenesis imperfecta Type II (OI Type II), Osteogenesis imperfecta Type III (OI Type III), Osteogenesis imperfecta Type IV (OI Type IV)

Involves the following Biologic System(s):

Genetic/Chromosomal/Syndrome/Metabolic Disorders, Orthopedic and Muscle Disorders

Osteogenesis imperfecta (OI) is an inherited genetic disorder characterized by abnormally brittle, fragile bones that are prone to fracture. The genetic abnormality responsible for OI produces defects in collagen, a protein that forms connective tissue such as bone, and is essential to normal bone growth and development.

Eight types of OI have been recognized, with each type having specific characteristics. The most common forms of OI are Types I through VI. Types VII and VIII of OI are recently recognized forms of the disease, of which only a few cases have so far been identified. Symptoms of OI, and how the disease is acquired, vary according to Type.

Of the eight types of OI, Type I is the least severe and most frequent. It occurs in approximately one in every 30,000 live births, and is inherited in an autosomal dominant manner, meaning that the defective gene that causes it can be inherited from only one parent, who will also have OI because of its dominant nature. Although the bones of infants and children with Type I are fragile and easily broken, and their teeth may be predisposed to cavities and breakage, there is little deformity of the bones. Other characteristics associated with Type I include flat feet, short stature, and a blue, purple, or gray coloration of the whites of the eyes. As children with this type of OI reach adolescence, they may experience bone fractures much less often than when they were younger.

OI Type II is the most severe form of the disease. Infants with Type II typically have a low birth weight, skeletal abnormalities of the limbs, ribs, and face, and frequent breakage of bones in prenatal fetuses. As many as half of births with OI of Type II are stillbirths, and many infants born with Type II die soon after birth from defects in the rib cage, resulting respiratory problems. Approximately one in 60,000 infants is affected with OI Type II. Both Types I and II are inherited as an autosomal dominant trait, or an recessive trait. The disease can also be caused by a genetic mutation, occurring only in the individual in whom the disease develops.

OI Type III is inherited as an autosomal recessive trait or as the result of a new mutation in affected offspring. It is a progressive form of the condition, characterized by multiple fractures and severely fragile bones in newborns, followed by deformity of the skeleton and skull. Other features of children with this type of OI include a triangular-shaped face, curvature of the spine, a barrel-shaped rib cage, diminished muscle development in the arms and legs, and short stature. Although many children with this type of OI reach adolescence, most do not reach adulthood.

OI Type IV, inherited as an autosomal dominant trait, is characterized by a reduced density of bones (osteoporosis) that causes them to be easily broken, and by shortness of stature. Bone fractures may be present at birth or at any time up to adulthood. As in Type I, curvature of thespine is likely to occur in Type IV, as is a barrel-shaped rib cage and triangular shape of the face, as well as brittleness of the teeth.

Type V is inherited in an autosomal dominant manner, and resembles Type IV, with the added symptom of calluses that develop at sites of bone fractures or surgical procedures. In many cases, the characteristics and symptoms of Type VI resemble those of Type IV, but it is not yet known whether this type of OI is inherited in a dominant or recessive manner. Type VII has so far been identified in only a small number of cases, some similar to Type IV, while others resembling the severe Type II, with surviving infants having short arm and leg bones, a short stature, a round face, and a small head. Type VIII OI resembles Type II or Type III, but surviving infants have seriously deficient growth and bones with a deficient mineral content.

OI is often detected as the result of a bone fracture, which then prompts further studies of an infant or child. Because of its effects on bone structure, OI can often be detected before birth by ultrasound examination, in which high-frequency sound waves are reflected by the bones and organs of a fetus in such a way as to permit a detailed examination of their structure. In some cases, laboratory tests can reveal the specific genetic defects responsible for OI.

OI cannot be completely cured or corrected. Treatment for most types and cases of the disease is medical and orthopedic, involving the use of drugs that reduce bone loss and others that promote growth of the body; casts and splints to repair fractures; and either braces or spinal fusion, in which bones of the spine are joined or fused to one another, to ease curvature of the spine and improve its supportive strength. Depending on the type and severity of OI, surgery may be done to treat fractures or to insert metal rods into the long bones of the arms and legs to strengthen and straighten them during growth. Physical therapy and exercise, including swimming, are used to build muscle, aid bone development, and strengthen the body.

Government Agencies

4832 NIH/ Eunice Kennedy Shriver National Institute of Child Health & Human Development
P.O. Box 3006
Rockville, MD 20847
800-370-2943
Fax: 866-760-5947
www.nichd.nih.gov

Conducts and supports laboratory research, clinical trials, and epidemiological studies that explore health processes; examines the impact of disabilities, diseases, and variations on the lives of individuals; and sponsors training programs for scientists, health care providers, and researchers to ensure that NICHD research can continue.

Diana W. Bianchi, Director
Alison Cernich, PhD, Depuy Director

4833 NIH/Osteoporosis and Related Bone Diseases National Resource Center
2 AMS Circle
Bethesda, MD 20892
202-223-0344
800-624-2663
Fax: 202-293-2356
TTY: 202-466-4315
NIHBoneInfo@mail.nih.gov
www.bones.nih.gov

The National Resource Center is an information service that provides general information on metabolic bone conditions.

Osteogenesis Imperfecta / State Agencies & Support Groups

National Associations & Support Groups

4834 **American Academy of Pediatrics**
345 Park Blvd
Itasca, IL 60143
847-434-4000
800-433-9016
Fax: 847-434-8000
csc@aap.org
www.aap.org

The American Academy of Pediatrics and its member pediatricians are committed to the attainment of optimal physical, mental and social health and well-being for all infants, children, adolescents, and young adults.

Kyle E. Yasuda, MD, FAAP, President
Mark Del Monte, JD, CEO/Executive VP
Vera Tait, MD, FAAP, Chief Medical Officer

4835 **Center for Parent Information and Resources (CPIR)**
c/o SPAN, 35 Halsey Street, 4th Floor
Newark, NJ 07102
973-642-8100
malizo@spanadvocacy.org
www.parentcenterhub.org

Family-friendly information and research-based materials on key topics for Parent Centers. Private workspaces for Parent Centers to exchange resources, discuss high-priority topics, and solve mutual challenges. Coordination of parent training efforts throughout the network.

Myriam Alizo, Project Assistant

4836 **Genetic Alliance**
426400 Woodfield Road, Ste 189
Damascus, MD 20872
202-966-5557
Fax: 202-966-8553
info@geneticalliance.org
www.geneticalliance.org

World's leading nonprofit health advocacy organization committed to transforming health through genetics and promoting an environment of openness centered on the health of individuals, families, and communities.

Sharon Terry, CEO
Ruth Child, CFO
Natasha Bonhomme, Chief Strategy Officer

4837 **Little People of America**
617 Broadway #518
Sonoma, CA 95476
714-368-3689
888-572-2001
Fax: 707-721-1896
info@lpaonline.org
www.lpaonline.org

A nonprofit organization that provides support and information to people of short stature and their families.

Deb Himsel, Executive Director
Mark Povinelli, President

4838 **March of Dimes Foundation**
1550 Crystal Drive, Ste 1300
Arlington, VA 22202
888-663-4637
www.marchofdimes.org

March of Dimes help moms have full-term pregnancies and research the problems that threaten the health of babies. The March of Dimes also acts globally: sharing best practices in perinatal health and helping improve birth outcomes where the needs are the most urgent.

Stacey D. Stewart, President
Alan Brogdon, SVP/COO/Board Officer
Rahul Gupta, MD, SVP & Chief Medical/Health Officer

4839 **Osteogenesis Imperfecta Foundation**
565 Quince Orchard Road, Suite 650
Gaithersburg, MD 20878
301-947-0083
844-889-7579
Fax: 301-947-0456
bonelink@oif.org
www.oif.org

The mission of the OI Foundation is to improve the quality of life for those living with osteogenesis imperfecta through research, education, awareness, and mutual support.

Tracy Smith Hart, Chief Executive Officer
Erika Carter, Chief Program Officer
Michael Stewart, Director of Education

State Agencies & Support Groups

Arkansas

4840 **Little People of America - District 7**
National Headquarters
617 Broadway #518
Sonoma, CA 95476
714-368-3689
888-572-2001
Fax: 707-721-1896
info@lpaonline.org
www.lpaonline.org

District 7 of the Little People of America represents short stature individuals from the states of Arkansas, Kansas, Missouri and Oklahoma.

Deb Himsel, Executive Director
Mark Povinelli, President
Cuquis Robledo, Public Relations Director

California

4841 **Little People of America - San Francisco Bay Area Chapter**
National Headquarters
250 El Camino Real, Suite 218
Tustin, CA 92780
714-368-3689
888-572-2001
Fax: 714-368-3367
info@lpaonline.org
www.lpabayarea.org

A nonprofit organization that provides support and information to people of short stature and their families.

Lee Uniacke, President
Keren Stronach, Co-Vice President
Caroline Jones, Co-Vice President

Colorado

4842 **Little People of America - Front Range Chapter**
7117 E Euclid Drive
Englewood, CO 80111
303-740-8555
ebennettebennett@netscape.net
http://frontrangelpa26.org

Little People of America, Inc. (LPA), will assist dwarfs with their physical and developmental concerns resulting from short stature. By providing medical, environmental, educational, vocational, and parental guidance, short-stature individuals and their families may enhance their lives and lifestyles with minimal limitations. Through peer support and personal example, members will be supportive of all those who reach out to LPA.

Chris & Bob Kotzian, President
Souda Bell, Vice President
Brandi VanAnne, Treasurer

Kansas

4843 **Little People of America - District 7**
National Headquarters
617 Broadway #518
Sonoma, CA 95476
714-368-3689
888-572-2001
Fax: 707-721-1896
info@lpaonline.org
www.lpaonline.org

District 7 of the Little People of America represents short stature individuals from the states of Arkansas, Kansas, Missouri and Oklahoma.

Deb Himsel, Executive Director
Mark Povinelli, President
Cuquis Robledo, Public Relations Director

Missouri

4844 Little People of America - District 7
National Headquarters
617 Broadway #518
Sonoma, CA 95476

714-368-3689
888-572-2001
Fax: 707-721-1896
info@lpaonline.org
www.lpaonline.org

District 7 of the Little People of America represents short stature individuals from the states of Arkansas, Kansas, Missouri and Oklahoma.

Deb Himsel, Executive Director
Mark Povinelli, President
Cuquis Robledo, Public Relations Director

New Jersey

4845 Little People of America - District 2
National Headquarters
617 Broadway #518
Sonoma, CA 95476

714-368-3689
888-572-2001
Fax: 707-721-1896
info@lpaonline.org
www.lpaonline.org

A nonprofit organization that provides support and information to people of short stature and their families.

Deb Himsel, Executive Director
Mark Povinelli, President
Cuquis Robledo, Public Relations Director

New York

4846 Little People of America - District 2
National Headquarters
617 Broadway #518
Sonoma, CA 95476

714-368-3689
888-572-2001
Fax: 707-721-1896
info@lpaonline.org
www.lpaonline.org

A nonprofit organization that provides support and information to people of short stature and their families.

Deb Himsel, Executive Director
Mark Povinelli, President
Cuquis Robledo, Public Relations Director

Oklahoma

4847 Little People of America - District 7
National Headquarters
617 Broadway #518
Sonoma, CA 95476

714-368-3689
888-572-2001
Fax: 707-721-1896
info@lpaonline.org
www.lpaonline.org

District 7 of the Little People of America represents short stature individuals from the states of Arkansas, Kansas, Missouri and Oklahoma.

Deb Himsel, Executive Director
Mark Povinelli, President
Cuquis Robledo, Public Relations Director

Pennsylvania

4848 Little People of America - District 2
National Headquarters
617 Broadway #518
Sonoma, CA 95476

714-368-3689
888-572-2001
Fax: 707-721-1896
info@lpaonline.org
www.lpaonline.org

A nonprofit organization that provides support and information to people of short stature and their families.

Deb Himsel, Executive Director
Mark Povinelli, President
Cuquis Robledo, Public Relations Director

Utah

4849 Little People of America - Utah Seagulls
National Headquarters
250 El Camino Real, Suite 218
Tustin, CA 92780

714-368-3689
888-572-2001
Fax: 714-368-3367
info@lpaonline.org
www.utahlittlepeople.org

A nonprofit organization that provides support and information to people of short stature and their families.

Steve Hatch, President

Libraries & Resource Centers

4850 NIH/Osteoporosis and Related Bone Diseases National Resource Center
2 AMS Circle
Bethesda, MD 20892

202-223-0344
800-624-2663
Fax: 202-293-2356
TTY: 202-466-4315
NIHBoneInfo@mail.nih.gov
www.bones.nih.gov

The National Resource Center is an information service that provides general information on metabolic bone conditions.

Conferences

4851 LPA National Conference
Little People of America
617 Broadway #518
Sonoma, CA 95476

714-368-3689
888-572-2001
Fax: 707-721-1896
info@lpaonline.org
www.lpaonline.org

July

Deb Himsel, Executive Director
Mark Povinelli, President
Cuquis Robledo, Public Relations Director

4852 National Conference on OI
Osteogenesis Imperfecta Foundation
565 Quince Orchard Road, Suite 650
Gaithersburg, MD 20878

301-947-0083
844-889-7579
Fax: 301-947-0456
bonelink@oif.org
www.oif.org

The OIF's biennial National Conference is the largest informational and social event for families and individuals living with osteogenesis imperfecta, bringing together more than 600 members of the OI community. Over the course of three days, OI families attend medical information sessions led by experts in OI from around the world and participate in networking activities that help build support systems that last long after the conference has ended.

Tracy Smith Hart, Chief Executive Officer
Erika Carter, Chief Program Officer
Michael Stewart, Director of Education

Web Sites

4853 **Little People of America**
617 Broadway #518
Sonoma, CA 95476
714-368-3689
888-572-2001
Fax: 707-721-1896
info@lpaonline.org
www.lpaonline.org

A nonprofit organization that provides support and information to people of short stature and their families.

Deb Himsel, Executive Director
Mark Povinelli, President

4854 **Online Mendelian Inheritance in Man**
McKusick-Nathans Institue of Genetic Medicine-JHU
Baltimore, MD 21205
www.omim.org

This database is a catalog of human genes and genetic disorders.

Ada Hamosh, MD, Scientific Director

4855 **Osteogenesis Imperfecta Foundation**
565 Quince Orchard Road, Suite 650
Gaithersburg, MD 20878
301-947-0083
844-889-7579
Fax: 301-947-0456
bonelink@oif.org
www.oif.org

The mission of the OI Foundation is to improve the quality of life for those living with osteogenesis imperfecta through research, education, awareness, and mutual support.

4856 **Osteoporosis and Related Bone Diseases - National Resource Center**
2 AMS Circle
Bethesda, DC
202-223-0344
800-624-2663
Fax: 202-293-2356
TTY: 202-466-4315
NIHBoneInfo@mail.nih.gov
www.niams.nih.gov/bone/

The National Resource Center is dedicated to increasing the awareness, knowledge and understanding of physicians, health professionals, patients, underserves and at-risk populations and the general public about the prevention, early detection and treatment of osteoperosis and related bone diseases.

4857 **Shriner's Hospital Research Study Report**
www.shrinershq.org

www.shrinershq.org

Provides patients, health professionals, and the public with an important link to resources and information on metabolic bone disease, including osteoporosis, Paget's disease of the bone, osteogenesis imperfecta, and hyperparathyroidism. It is dedicated to increasing the underserved and at-risk populations and the general public about the prevention, early detection and treatment of osteoporosis and related bone disease.

4858 **Wheeless' Textbook of Orthopaedics**
www.wheelessonline.com

www.wheelessonline.com

Derives from a variety of sources, including journals, articles, national meetings lectures and other textbooks.

Clifford R. Wheeless III, MD, Editor-in-Chief
James A. Nunley, II, MD, Managing Editor
James R. Urbaniak, MD, Managing Editor

Book Publishers

4859 **Let's Talk About Going to the Hospital**
Rosen Publishing Group's PowerKids Press
29 E 21st Street
New York, NY 10010
212-777-3017
800-237-9932
Fax: 888-436-4643
rosenpub@tribeca.ios.com
www.rosenpublishing.com

If a child has to check into the hospital, chances are he or she is already upset about being ill. Knowing how a hospital functions and what the procedures are, such as when family members can visit, will help in what is already a stressful situation. Grades K-5.

24 pages
ISBN: 0-823950-36-0

Roger Rosen, President

Otitis Media / Description

Description

4860 OTITIS MEDIA

Synonym: Tympanitis

Covers these related disorders: Acute otitis media, Chronic otitis media, Secretory otitis media

Involves the following Biologic System(s):

Infectious Disorders

Otitis media refers to an infection or inflammation of the middle ear, the irregularly-shaped cavity that lies in the temporal bone on each side of the skull, and contains structures essential to hearing. Otitis media is one of the most common disorders of childhood, especially in children from the ages of 6 months to 3 years.

Acute otitis media usually occurs in conjunction with or as a complication of upper respiratory tract infections such as the common cold. Infections of the respiratory tract can extend to the middle ear and cause otitis media by way of the eustachian tube, a narrow canal that extends from the rear of the nasal area to the middle ear and helps to maintain normal air pressure in the middle ear. Infants and young children are especially vulnerable to otitis media because they have a short and narrow eustachian tube that is positioned somewhat horizontally, making them more susceptible to the backward flow of infectious secretions from the nasal area and into the middle ear. Further increasing the risk of otitis media during colds and other respiratory infections in infants and young children is swelling of the lymph nodes known as the adenoids, which are located at the back of the throat, near the opening of the eustachian tube that extends to each ear, and which can block these tubes and limit their ability to drain infected secretions out of the middle ear.

Symptoms of acute otitis media often develop soon after the onset of a respiratory tract infection, and include sudden and severe ear pain (otalgia), ringing in the ears (tinnitus), fever, temporary hearing loss, and discomfort. Infants and young children with otitis media may exhibit the following symptoms: irritability; pulling at the infected ear; fluid draining from the infected ear; nausea; vomiting; and diarrhea. The eardrum (tympanic membrane) of the infected ear may rupture, thus releasing fluid, which usually relieves the pain in an infected ear. The eardrum may then heal within a short period, but if healing does not occur, this rupture can result in a permanent impairment of hearing, leading to difficulties in speech. Symptoms such as dizziness, headache, sudden and significant hearing loss or deafness, chills, and fever may suggest complications that may result from otitis media or which may occur in conjunction with it, including inflammation of the membranes surrounding the brain and spinal cord (meningitis), infection of the inner ear canals (labyrinthitis), or infection in the mastoid bone behind the ear (mastoiditis).

Otitis media can be detected with an otoscope, an instrument that allows examination of the eardrum to see whether it is inflamed or swollen, thus reflecting an infection of the middle ear, located behind the eardrum. A pneumatic otoscope is used to deliver a puff of air onto the eardrum to check for flexibility or swelling. A microphone can also be used to hear the sound that the air makes.

Treatment of acute otitis media depends upon its cause. If the infection causing an episode of otitis media is bacterial, antibiotics may be given. Some children may require a surgical procedure known as myringotomy, in which an incision is made in the eardrum to relieve pressure and allow the release of pus and other secretions, or through tympanocentesis, a procedure in which the eardrum is surgically punctured to release fluid. Other treatment of otitis media is symptomatic and supportive, with pain relievers, antihistamines, nasal decongestants, and other medications.

Some children with otitis media develop secretory otitis media, which sometimes follows blockage of the eustachian tube, or the successful treatment of acute otitis media. This is characterized by the escape of thin (serous), thick (mucoid), or pus-like fluid from the ear. Symptoms associated with secretory otitis media may include dizziness and tinnitus. Although this condition may resolve spontaneously, its treatment is often indicated to prevent possible hearing loss and subsequent difficulties in the acquisition of speech and language. This may be accomplished through surgical incision and the insertion of tubes into the eardrum to allow the drainage of fluid. Children who do not respond to such treatment may benefit by having their adenoids removed surgically (adenoidectomy) to drain fluids from the eustachian tubes and allow a normal flow of air through them.

An infection of the middle ear that persists beyond the usually course of acute otitis media is known as chronic otitis media Such infection is much less common than acute otitis media, but its symptoms, being less severe, may persist for varying periods without being noticed. This can impair hearing, learning, and speech. Chronic otitis media may, for example, result in small growths (polyps) in the ear and damage to the small bones (ossicles) of the middle ear, impairing the ability of the ear to conduct sound. Chronic otitis media may be treated by the continued administration of antibiotics for a longer period than for the acute condition, as well as by drainage of the ear and the other procedures used in acute otitis media, and by the surgical repair of a ruptured eardrum (tympanoplasty). Tympanoplasty may also be used to restore the mechanism by which the middle ear transmits sound, which involves three small bones known as the malleus, incus, and stapes. The incus transmits vibrations it receives from the malleus to the stapes, which in turn sends the vibrations through a membrane and into the fluid-filled canal of the inner ear, where the vibrations are transformed into nerve signals that travel to the hearing centers of the brain for sensing and comprehension.

Government Agencies

4861 NIH/National Institute of Allergy and Infectious Diseases
5601 Fishers Lane, MSC 9806
Bethesda, MD 20892

301-496-5717
866-284-4107
Fax: 301-402-3573
TDD: 800-877-8339
ocpostoffice@niaid.nih.gov
www.niaid.nih.gov

The principal advisory board of the NIAID. The council is composed of physicians, scientists and representatives of the public and advises on the conduct and support or research, training and dissemination of health information regarding allergies and infectious diseases.

Anthony S. Fauci, MD, Director

National Associations & Support Groups

4862 American Academy of Audiology
11480 Commerce Park Drive, Suite 220
Reston, VA 20191

703-790-8466
Fax: 703-790-8631
info@audiology.org
www.audiology.org

A professional organization dedicated to providing high quality and balanced hearing care to the public. Provides professional development, education and research and provides increased public awareness of hearing disorders and audiologic services.
ISSN: 1050-0545

Patrick E. Gallagher, Executive Director
Anne Poodiak, VP, Meetings & Education
Glenn Feder, Senior Director, Sales

4863　American Academy of Pediatrics
345 Park Blvd
Itasca, IL 60143
847-434-4000
800-433-9016
Fax: 847-434-8000
csc@aap.org
www.aap.org

The American Academy of Pediatrics and its member pediatricians are committed to the attainment of optimal physical, mental and social health and well-being for all infants, children, adolescents, and young adults.

Kyle E. Yasuda, MD, FAAP, President
Mark Del Monte, JD, CEO/Executive VP
Vera Tait, MD, FAAP, Chief Medical Officer

4864　American Hearing Research Foundation
154 W Park Avenue, Suite 586
Elmhurst, IL 60126
630-617-5079
ahrf@american-hearing.org
www.american-hearing.org

Funds medical research and education into the causes, prevention, and cures of hearing losses, and balance disorders. Also keeps physicians and the public informed of the latest developments in hearing research and education.

Richard G. Muench, Chair
Alan G. Micco, President
David J. Wuertz, Treasurer

4865　March of Dimes Foundation
1550 Crystal Drive, Ste 1300
Arlington, VA 22202
888-663-4637
www.marchofdimes.org

March of Dimes help moms have full-term pregnancies and research the problems that threaten the health of babies. The March of Dimes also acts globally: sharing best practices in perinatal health and helping improve birth outcomes where the needs are the most urgent.

Stacey D. Stewart, President
Alan Brogdon, SVP/COO/Board Officer
Rahul Gupta, MD, SVP & Chief Medical/Health Officer

4866　World Health Organization
Avenue Appia 20
1202 Geneva,
Switzerland
www.who.int

WHO is the directing and coordinating authority for health within the United Nations system. WHO operates in more than 150 countries around the world.

Dr. Tedros Adhanom Ghebreyesus, Director General
Dr. Zsuzsanna Jakab, Deputy Director General
Stewart Simonson, Asst Director General, UN NYC

Web Sites

4867　Baylor College of Medicine-Pathology & Pathogenesis of Otitis Media
One Baylor Plaza
Houston, TX 77030
713-798-4951
www.bcm.edu

Paul Klotman, M.D., President/ CEO & Executive Dean
William T. Butler, M.D., Chancellor Emeritus
Alicia Monroe, M.D., Provost/ SVP

4868　Indiana State University School of Medicine
340 West 10th Street, Suite 6200
Indianapolis, IN 46202
317-274-8157
medicine.iu.edu

Provides a presentation of the disease including signs, symptoms and illustrations.

Jay L. Hess, M.D., Vice President
Stephen P. Bogdewic, PhD, Executive Vice Dean
Diane Iseminger, Chief of Staff

4869　PDR.net
5 Paragon Drive
Montvale, NJ 7645
888-227-6469
PDRnet@pdr.net
www.pdr.net

Offers integrated medical information and education tools. Updated frequently, this site contains the drug information resources needed daily by its prescriber user base arranged together in one site for convenience and ease-of-use.

4870　University of Texas Medical Branch
301 University Boulevard
Galveston, TX 77555
www.utmb.edu/oto/

David L. Callender, President
Danny O. Jacobs, MD, Executive Vice President
Carolee King, JD, Senior Vice President

Book Publishers

4871　Let's Talk About Going to the Hospital
Rosen Publishing Group's PowerKids Press
29 E 21st Street
New York, NY 10010
212-777-3017
800-237-9932
Fax: 888-436-4643
rosenpub@tribeca.ios.com
www.rosenpublishing.com

If a child has to check into the hospital, chances are he or she is already upset about being ill. Knowing how a hospital functions and what the procedures are, such as when family members can visit, will help in what is already a stressful situation. Grades K-5.

24 pages
ISBN: 0-823950-36-0

Roger Rosen, President

4872　Living with Hearing Loss
Marcia B Dugan, author

Gallaudet University Press
800 Florida Avenue NE
Washington, DC 20002
202-651-5488
Fax: 202-651-5489
TTY: 888-630-9347
gupress@gallaudet.edu
gupress.gallaudet.edu

192 pages
ISBN: 1-563681-34-0

4873　Screening for Hearing Loss and Other Otitis Media
Jackson Roush PhD, author

AGB Association for the Deaf and Hard of Hearing
3417 Volta Place NW
Washington, DC 20007
202-337-5220
800-432-7543
Fax: 202-337-8314
TTY: 202-337-5221
info@agbell.org
www.listeningandspokenlanguage.org

2001 245 pages Softcover
ISBN: 0-769300-00-6

Donald M. Goldberg, President
Alexander T. Graham, Executive Director/CEO
Ted A. Meyer, MD, Ph.D. (SC), Secretary-Treasurer

Passive-Aggressive Behavior / Description

Description

4874 PASSIVE-AGGRESSIVE BEHAVIOR
Involves the following Biologic System(s):
Developmental/Behavioral/Psychiatric Disorders

Passive-aggressive behavior refers to a type of disruptive conduct that is apparent in approximately 20 percent of children and adolescents. Although seemingly compliant, affected individuals usually harbor negative, aggressive, or hostile feelings, but are unable to directly express them. These negative, hostile feelings are typically manifested indirectly and nonviolently through procrastination, forgetfulness, inefficiency, pouting or sullenness, stubbornness, obstructionism, and resistance to requests or demands. When infants and toddlers, passive-aggressive children and adolescents may have manifested their negativistic personalities through difficulties with feeding and toilet training.

Passive-aggressive individuals may be unaware that they are using their behavior to counteract or offset certain frustrations (e.g., feelings of inadequacy). They may persist in these behaviors in an attempt to regain control of a situation or to punish and retaliate. These stubbornly compliant behaviors are apparent in other situations that typically provoke direct displays of assertiveness, hostility, or other forms of aggression. Parents may be overly, but inconsistently, demanding and critical; conversely, affected individuals may, in some cases, be reared by parents or caregivers who are overly permissive and tolerant.

Treatment for passive-aggressive behavior includes the cooperation of parents or caregivers who are often in the best position to provide motivation for children to learn to appropriately express their assertiveness. Such motivation may be further supported by the establishment of firm rules and guidelines, the setting of realistic goals, and the prioritizing of responsibilities. Some parents or caregivers may benefit from direct management training that teaches the necessary skills to facilitate proper behavior and other social skills. Individual, group, and family psychotherapy may also be indicated. Other treatment is supportive.

Government Agencies

4875 NIH/National Institute of Mental Health
6001 Executive Blvd, Rm 6200, MSC 9663
Bethesda, MD 20892
866-615-6464
Fax: 301-443-4279
TTY: 301-443-8431
nimhinfo@nih.gov
www.nimh.nih.gov

The mission of NIMH is to transform the understanding and treatment of mental illnesses through basic and clinical research, paving the way for prevention, recovery, and cure.

Joshua A. Gordon, MD, PhD, Director
Shelli Avenevoli, PhD, Deputy Director

National Associations & Support Groups

4876 American Academy of Pediatrics
345 Park Blvd
Itasca, IL 60143
847-434-4000
800-433-9016
Fax: 847-434-8000
csc@aap.org
www.aap.org

The American Academy of Pediatrics and its member pediatricians are committed to the attainment of optimal physical, mental and social health and well-being for all infants, children, adolescents, and young adults.

Kyle E. Yasuda, MD, FAAP, President
Mark Del Monte, JD, CEO/Executive VP
Vera Tait, MD, FAAP, Chief Medical Officer

4877 American Mental Health Foundation (AMHF)
PO Box 3
Riverdale, NY 10471
USA
212-737-9027
elomke@americanmentalhealthfoundation.or
americanmentalhealthfoudnation.org

Dedicated to the extensive and intensive research in the theories and techniques of treatment of emotional illness and to the implementation of reforms in the mental health system. Efforts have resulted in development of better and less expensive treatment methods. Findings are disseminated in English and other major languages.

Evander Lomke, President/Executive Director

4878 Mental Health America
500 Montgomery Street, Ste 820
Alexandria, VA 22314
703-684-7722
800-969-6642
Fax: 703-684-5968
www.mentalhealthamerica.net

MHA, the leading advocacy organization addressing the full spectrum of mental and substance use conditions and their effects nationwide, works to inform, advocate and enable access to quality behavioral health services for all Americans.

Paul Gionfriddo, President/CEO
Whitney Ball, Assoc. Dir., Marketing/Outreach
Sachin Doshi, Sr. Dir, Finance Operations

4879 NADD: National Association for the Dually Diagnosed
12 Hurley Avenue
Kingston, NY 12401
845-331-4336
800-331-5362
Fax: 845-331-4569
info@thenadd.org
www.thenadd.org

Nonprofit organization designed to promote the interests of professional and parent development with resources for individuals who have the coexistence of mental illness and intellectual disabilities. Provides conferences, educational services and training materials to professionals, parents, concerned citizens and service organizations.

Jeanne Farr, CEO
Michelle Jordan, Office Manager
Edward Seliger, Project Coordinator

4880 National Alliance on Mental Illness (NAMI)
4301 Wilson Blvd., Suite 300
Arlington, VA 22203
703-524-7600
888-999-6264
info@nami.org
www.nami.org

NAMI provides advocacy, education, support and public awareness so that all individuals and families affected by mental illness can build better lives.

Daniel H. Gillison, CEO
David Levy, CFO
Ken Duckworth, Chief Medical Officer

4881 National Federation of Families
15800 Crabbs Branch Way, Wuite 300
Rockville, MD 20855
240-403-1901
ffcmh@ffcmh.org
www.ffcmh.org

The National family run organization is dedicated exclusively to helping children with mental health needs and their families achieve a better quality of life.

Lynda Gargan, PhD, Executive Director

4882 National Mental Health Consumers' Self-Help Clearinghouse
1211 Chestnut Street, Suite 1207
Philadelphia, PA 19107
215-751-1810
800-553-4539
Fax: 215-636-6312
selfhelpclearinghouse@gmail.com
www.mhselfhelp.org

Offers information, support and appropriate referrals; and promotes public and professional education. Provides networking for those with special interests related to albinism. Promotes and supports research and funding that will improve diagnosis and management of albinism and hypopigmentation.

Joseph Rogers, Founder/Executive Director
Susan Rogers, Director

State Agencies & Support Groups

4883 Center for Family Support
2811 Zuletteÿ Avenue
Bronx, NY 10461
718-518-1500
Fax: 718-518-8200
svernikoff@cfsny.org
www.cfsny.org

The Center for Family (CFS) is a not-for-profit human service agency providing support and assistance to individuals with developmental disabilities and traumatic brain injuries throughout New York City, Long Island, the lower Hudson Valley region and New Jersey.

Steven Vernikoff, Executive Director
Barbara Greenwald, Associate Executive Director

Web Sites

4884 Borderline Personality Disorder Sanctuary
borderlinepersonality.ca/bpdlinks.htm

borderlinepersonality.ca/bpdlinks.htm

Offers a bookstore, resources, articles, hotlines and answers questions about mental health.

4885 CyberPsych
www.cyberpsych.org

www.cyberpsych.org

CyberPsych presents information about psychoanalysis, psychotherapy, and special topics such as anxiety disorder, the problematic use of alcohol, homophobia, and the traumatic effects of racism. CyberPsych is a nonprofit network which offers free web hosting and technical support for internet communicatios, to nonprofit groups and individuals.

4886 Dual Diagnosis
1050 Hull Street
Baltimore, MD 21230
410-209-6799
877-438-8623
Fax: 410-244-5042
www.toad.net/~arcturus/dd/papd.htm

Review of personality disorders including PAPD.

4887 El Rolphe Center
members.aol.com/elrolphe/PassiveAggressive.html

members.aol.com/elrolphe/PassiveAggressive.html

Description and overview of the Passive/Aggressive Personality by Dr Sidney Langston.

4888 I.D. Weeks Library
414 E. Clark St.
Vermillion, SD 57069
www.usd.edu/library/

4889 NADD: National Association for the Dually Diagnosed
12 Hurley Avenue
Kingston, NY 12401
845-331-4336
800-331-5362
Fax: 845-331-4569
www.thenadd.org

Nonprofit organization designed to promote the interests of professional and care providers for individuals who have the coexistence of mental illness and intellectual disabilities. NADD provides conferences, educational services and training materials to professionals, parents, concerned citizens and service organizations.

Jeanne Farr, CEO
Michelle Jordan, Office Manager
Edward Seliger, Project Coordinator

4890 National Anxiety Foundation
www.nationalanxietyfoundation.org

www.nationalanxietyfoundation.org

Offers information and help to persons with panic disorders, manic and depressive disorders and mental illness.

Stephen Cox, MD, President & Medical Director
Linda Vernon Blair, VP
C. Todd Strecker, Secretary-Treasurer

4891 New York Online Access to Health
National Library of Medicine Building 38A
Bethesda, MD 20894
888-346-3656
info@ncbi.nlm.nih.gov
www.ncbi.nlm.nih.gov

Provides access to high quality full-text consumer health information that is accurate, timely, relevant and unbiased.

4892 Psych Central
55 Pleasant St., Suite 207
Newburyport, MA 1950
talkback@psychcentral.com
www.psychcentral.com

Offers free informational and educational articles and resources on psychology, support and mental health online.

John M. Grohol, CEO & Founder

Book Publishers

4893 Challenging Behaviour

Eric Emerson, author

Cambridge University Press
32 Avenue of the Americas
New York, NY 10013
212-924-3900
800-872-7423
Fax: 212-691-3239
information@cup.org
www.cup.org

Analysis and intervention in people with severe intellectual disabilities
2nd Edition 232 pages Paperback
ISBN: 0-521794-44-7

4894 Clinical Assessment and Management of Severe Personality Disorders
American Psychiatric Press
1000 Wilson Boulevard, Suite 1825
Arlington, VA 22209
703-907-7322
800-368-5777
Fax: 703-907-1091
appi@psych.org
www.appi.org

Focuses on issues relevant to the clinician in private practice, including the diagnosis of a wide range of personality disorders and alternative management approaches.

1996 250 pages Hardcover
ISBN: 0-880484-88-6

Robert E. Hales, M.D, Editor-in-Chief
Rebecca D. Rinehart, Publisher
John McDuffie, Editorial Director

4895 Personality and Psychopathology
American Psychiatric Press
1000 Wilson Boulevard, Suite 1825
Arlington, VA 22209

703-907-7322
800-368-5777
Fax: 703-907-1091
appi@psych.org
www.appi.org

Compiles the most recent findings from more than 30 internationally recognized experts. Analyzes the association between personality and psychopathology from several interlocking perspectives: descriptive, developmental, etiological, and theraputic.

1999 544 pages Hardcover
ISBN: 0-880489-23-2

Robert E. Hales, M.D, Editor-in-Chief
Rebecca D. Rinehart, Publisher
John McDuffie, Editorial Director

Description

4896 PATENT DUCTUS ARTERIOSUS
Synonym: PDA
Involves the following Biologic System(s):
Cardiovascular Disorders

Patent ductus arteriosus is characterized by the persistence of a fetal vessel that maintains a passageway between the major artery that carries oxygen-rich blood to the tissues of the body (descending aorta) and the artery that carries deoxygenated blood to the lungs (pulmonary artery). Before birth, fetal blood receives oxygen from the mother's blood rather than from its own lungs, making it unnecessary for fetal blood to pass from the right side of the heart to the lungs to be oxygenated. To accommodate this fetal blood flow, blood passes through an opening (foramen ovale) in the wall (septum) between the two upper chambers of the heart (atria). Fetal blood is diverted away from the lungs through a vessel known as the ductus arteriosus that connects the pulmonary artery and the aorta. Normally, both the foramen ovale and ductus arteriosus close soon after birth. The persistence of the opening (patency) of the ductus arteriosus causes some blood from the aorta to flow into the pulmonary artery to the lungs instead of moving away from the heart to nourish the tissues of the body.

Symptoms and physical findings associated with patent ductus arteriosus depend upon the size of the opening and the volume of the diverted blood. A small defect may result in no symptoms while a larger opening may result in difficulty in breathing (dyspnea), rapid heartbeat (tachycardia), failure to gain weight, inflammation of the lining of the heart (bacterial endocarditis), and inefficient pumping by the heart (heart failure). Physical findings may include enlargement of the heart (cardiomegaly); characteristic heart sounds; a machinery-like heart murmur; and, if left untreated, abnormally high pressure in the lung's circulatory system (pulmonary hypertension).

Premature infants may require early intervention through restriction of fluid intake, certain drug therapy, or surgery to prevent malfunctioning of the heart or lungs. However, if no immediate surgical or medicinal intervention is required or administered, this defect may spontaneously close in many premature newborns.

In full-term infants and children, a patent ductus arteriosus may require intervention (surgical or catheter closure). Such treatment may be helpful in preventing or alleviating associated complications. The exact cause of patent ductus arteriosus in the full-term infant is unknown. It is thought to result from different genetic and environmental factors (multifactorial). For example, this irregularity may be associated with maternal German measles (rubella) infection. In addition, patent ductus arteriosus is often accompanied by other congenital heart defects. This defect appears in approximately 60 of 100,000 births and is more prevalent in females than males by a ratio of about two to one. The patent ductus arteriosus is non routinely closed in a non-surgical, outpatient catheter procedure in otherwise healthy children.

Government Agencies

4897 NIH/ Eunice Kennedy Shriver National Institute of Child Health & Human Development
P.O. Box 3006
Rockville, MD 20847

800-370-2943
Fax: 866-760-5947
www.nichd.nih.gov

Conducts and supports research on topics related to the health of children, adults, families and populations. Some of these topics include: developmental disabilities, growth and development, infant death, reproductive health and birth defects.
Diana W. Bianchi, Director
Alison Cernich, PhD, Deputy Director

4898 NIH/National Heart, Lung and Blood Institute
31 Center Drive, Bldg 31
Bethesda, MD 20892

877-645-2448
www.nhlbi.nih.gov

Primary responsibility of this organization is the scientific investigation of heart, blood vessel, lung and blood disorders. Oversees research, demonstration, prevention, education, control and training activities in these fields and emphasizes the prevention and control of heart diseases.
Gary H. Gibbons, MD, Director
Kate O'Sullivan, Executive Officer

National Associations & Support Groups

4899 American Academy of Pediatrics
345 Park Blvd
Itasca, IL 60143

847-434-4000
800-433-9016
Fax: 847-434-8000
csc@aap.org
www.aap.org

The American Academy of Pediatrics and its member pediatricians are committed to the attainment of optimal physical, mental and social health and well-being for all infants, children, adolescents, and young adults.
Kyle E. Yasuda, MD, FAAP, President
Mark Del Monte, JD, CEO/Executive VP
Vera Tait, MD, FAAP, Chief Medical Officer

4900 American Heart Association
7272 Greenville Avenue
Dallas, TX 75231

214-570-5978
800-242-8721
www.heart.org

The mission of the American Heart Associate is to build healthier lives, free of cardiovascular diseases and stroke.
Nancy Brown, CEO
Mitchell S.V. Elkind, President
Suzie Upton, Chief Operating Officer

4901 Genetic Alliance
426400 Woodfield Road, Ste 189
Damascus, MD 20872

202-966-5557
Fax: 202-966-8553
info@geneticalliance.org
www.geneticalliance.org

World's leading nonprofit health advocacy organization committed to transforming health through genetics and promoting an environment of openness centered on the health of individuals, families, and communities.
Sharon Terry, CEO
Ruth Child, CFO
Natasha Bonhomme, Chief Strategy Officer

4902 March of Dimes Foundation
1550 Crystal Drive, Ste 1300
Arlington, VA 22202

888-663-4637
www.marchofdimes.org

March of Dimes help moms have full-term pregnancies and research the problems that threaten the health of babies. The March of Dimes also acts globally: sharing best practices in perinatal health and helping improve birth outcomes where the needs are the most urgent.
Stacey D. Stewart, President
Alan Brogdon, SVP/COO/Board Officer
Rahul Gupta, MD, SVP & Chief Medical/Health Officer

Patent Ductus Arteriosus / Web Sites

Web Sites

4903 Southern Illinois University School of Medicine
P.O.Box 19658
Springfield, IL 62794   217-545-8000
www.siumed.edu/peds/index.htm

Mission is to assist the people of central and southern Illinois in meeting their present and future health care needs through education, clinical service and research.

4904 Yale University School of Medicine
333 Cedar Street
New Haven, CT 6510   203-737-1770
medicine.yale.edu

A helpful site that explains the causes, symptoms and treatments for Patent Ductus Arteriosus.

Peter Salovey, President
Richard Belitsky, Deputy Dean
Benjamin Polak, Provost

Book Publishers

4905 Congenital Disorders Sourcebook

Greg Mullin, author

Omnigraphics
615 Griswold Street, Ste 520
Detroit, MI 48226   610-461-3548
800-234-1340
Fax: 800-875-1340
contact@omnigraphics.com
www.omnigraphics.com

Basic consumer health information on disorders aquired during gestation, including spina bifida, hydrocephalus, cerebral palsy, heart defects, craniofacial abnormalities and fetal alcohol syndrome.

664 pages
ISBN: 0-780816-13-8

Description

4906 PEMPHIGUS

Involves the following Biologic System(s):

Dermatologic Disorders

Pemphigus refers to a group of chronic skin disorders that are characterized by the appearance of blisters on the skin and delicate mucous membranes that line the mouth, for example. Pemphigus most often occurs among the adult population, but may appear at any age. Associated findings include a phenomenon known as Nikolsky's sign, characterized by the tendency of the upper layer of the skin to separate or slough off from the lower layer upon rubbing or other minor trauma. Pemphigus is thought to result from an autoimmune reaction during which the body mistakenly attacks healthy cells. In this case, antibodies attack the cells that glue skin together, resulting in disruptions in contact between the cells.

Benign familial pemphigus is a relatively mild form of this disorder that is inherited as an autosomal dominant trait and is characterized by the persistent and recurrent formation of blisters mainly in the groin area, the armpit (axillary) region, the sides of the neck, and on the bending surfaces of the arms and legs. These localized or widespread lesions rupture, erode, and then crust over and heal. This form of pemphigus is also known as Hailey-Hailey disease.

Pemphigus foliaceus is a rare, usually mild form of the disorder that is characterized by small blisters that are usually localized and rupture easily, erode, and then heal by crusting over or scaling. These lesions most commonly appear on the scalp, neck, face, and trunk. The blisters may cause itching, pain, or burning in the affected areas. Affected individuals may also experience the sloughing off of the upper skin layer (Nikolsky's sign). Some affected individuals may develop a more generalized pattern of eruptions characterized by excessive shedding or peeling of the skin. Treatment for pemphigus foliaceus may include therapy with corticosteriod drugs. In some cases, topical application of corticosteroid ointments, salves, or creams proves beneficial.

Pemphigus vulgaris is a very severe form of disease that is manifested by eruptions of painful, ulcerative lesions in the delicate mucous membranes that line the mouth. Later findings include the appearance of large blisters on previously unaffected areas of the face, chest, abdomen, armpit region, groin area, and the various pressure points of the body. These lesions enlarge and rupture, leaving raw areas that may partially crust over, but have little or no tendency to heal. These raw or denuded areas sometimes give rise to wart-like granulations that emit a strong, offensive odor. This stage of pemphigus vulgaris is sometimes referred to as pemphigus vegetans. The folds of the skin are particularly susceptible to the development of these wart-like lesions. Individuals with pemphigus vulgaris also exhibit Nikolsky's sign. Life-threatening complications associated with pemphigus vulgaris may include secondary bacterial infections such as sepsis or debilitating conditions such as malnutrition and the loss of essential elements, known as electrolytes, in the fluid portion of the blood (e.g., sodium, potassium, and calcium). For this reason, early diagnosis and treatment of pemphigus vulgaris is essential to its successful management. Positive diagnosis may be determined through microscopic examination of a skin sample, obtained through biopsy, that indicates the presence of certain antibody deposits. Initial treatment may include high-dose corticosteroid therapy, followed by long-term administration of corticosteroid or other immunosuppressive drugs to control the disease. Antibiotic therapy may be indicated for treatment of skin or secondary bacterial infections.

Neonatal pemphigus vulgaris develops in the unborn fetus of an affected mother by transmission of the mother's antibodies through the placenta. In most cases, the severity of disease in the fetus is related to the severity of the mother's disease. If the mother is severely affected, the placental transmission of antibodies may potentially threaten the life of the unborn child.

Government Agencies

4907 NIH/ Eunice Kennedy Shriver National Institute of Child Health & Human Development
P.O. Box 3006
Rockville, MD 20847

800-370-2943
Fax: 866-760-5947
www.nichd.nih.gov

Conducts and supports research on topics related to the health of children, adults, families and populations. Some of these topics include: developmental disabilities, growth and development, infant death, reproductive health and birth defects.

Diana W. Bianchi, Director
Alison Cernich, PhD, Deputy Director

4908 NIH/National Institute of Arthritis and Musculoskeletal and Skin Diseases
1 AMS Circle
Bethesda, MD 20892

301-495-4484
877-226-4267
Fax: 301-718-6366
TDD: 301-565-2966
niamsinfo@mail.nih.gov
www.niams.nih.gov

The mission of the NIAMS, a part of the NIH, is to support research into the causes, treatment and prevention of arthritis and musculoskeletal and skin diseases, the training of basic and clinical scientists to carry out this research, and the dissemination of information on research progress in these diseases.

Lindsey A. Criswell, MD, Director
Rick Phillips, Executive Officer

National Associations & Support Groups

4909 American Academy of Pediatrics
345 Park Blvd
Itasca, IL 60143

847-434-4000
800-433-9016
Fax: 847-434-8000
csc@aap.org
www.aap.org

The American Academy of Pediatrics and its member pediatricians are committed to the attainment of optimal physical, mental and social health and well-being for all infants, children, adolescents, and young adults.

Kyle E. Yasuda, MD, FAAP, President
Mark Del Monte, JD, CEO/Executive VP
Vera Tait, MD, FAAP, Chief Medical Officer

4910 American Autoimmune Related Diseases Association
19176 Hall Road, Suite 130
Clinton, MI 48038

586-776-3900
aarda@aarda.org
www.aarda.org

The American Autoimmune Related Diseases Association is dedicated to the eradication of autoimmune diseases and the alleviation of suffering and the socioeconomic impact of autoimmunity through fostering and facilitating collaboration in the areas of education, public awareness, research, and patient services in an effective, ethical and efficient manner.

Lilly Stairs, Interim President/CEO
Laura Simpson, COO

Pemphigus / State Agencies & Support Groups

4911 Genetic Alliance
426400 Woodfield Road, Ste 189
Damascus, MD 20872
202-966-5557
Fax: 202-966-8553
info@geneticalliance.org
www.geneticalliance.org

World's leading nonprofit health advocacy organization committed to transforming health through genetics and promoting an environment of openness centered on the health of individuals, families, and communities.

Sharon Terry, CEO
Ruth Child, CFO
Natasha Bonhomme, Chief Strategy Officer

4912 International Pemphigus Foundation
915 Highland Pointe Drive, Suite 250
Roseville, CA 59678
916-922-1298
855-473-6744
info@pemphigus.org
www.pemphigus.org

A nonprofit organization with these goals: to increase awareness of pemphigus and pemphigold among the public and the medical community; to provide information and emotional support to pemphigus and pemphigold patients and caregivers; to provide referrals to specialists and to support research into advanced treatments and a cure.

Patrick Dunn, Executive Director
Marc Yale, Advocavy & Research Coordinator
Becky Strong, Outreach Director

4913 March of Dimes Foundation
1550 Crystal Drive, Ste 1300
Arlington, VA 22202
888-663-4637
www.marchofdimes.org

March of Dimes help moms have full-term pregnancies and research the problems that threaten the health of babies. The March of Dimes also acts globally: sharing best practices in perinatal health and helping improve birth outcomes where the needs are the most urgent.

Stacey D. Stewart, President
Alan Brogdon, SVP/COO/Board Officer
Rahul Gupta, MD, SVP & Chief Medical/Health Officer

4914 Society for Pediatric Dermatology
8365 Keystone Crossing, Ste 107
Indianapolis, IN 46240
317-202-0224
Fax: 317-205-9481
info@pedsderm.net
www.pedsderm.net

The objective of the Society is to promote, develop and advance education, research and care of skin disease in all pediatric age groups.

Kent Lindeman, Executive Director

State Agencies & Support Groups

California

4915 International Pemphigus Foundation: Southern California Support Group
310-559-5462
lynntg@prodigy.net

Lynn Glick

Maryland

4916 International Pemphigus Foundation: Baltimore Support Group
410-750-1618
byrnete@comcast.net

Erica Byrne

Massachusetts

4917 International Pemphigus Foundation: Massachusetts Support Group
978-463-0965
alppy@comcast.net

Alan Papert

New York

4918 International Pemphigus Foundation: New York Support Group
Valley Stream, NY
516-825-4594
mayykoe@aol.com

Matt Koenig

South Carolina

4919 International Pemphigus Foundation: South Carolina Support Group
Gray Court, SC 29645
864-386-1620

Cheryl Jordan

Texas

4920 International Pemphigus Foundation Dallas Support Group
817-557-9642

Angela Vickers

4921 International Pemphigus Foundation: Houston Support Group
5231 Kinglet Street
Houston, TX 77035
713-723-5647
Fax: 713-726-0286

Richard M Schwartz

Web Sites

4922 American Autoimmune Related Diseases Association
www.aarda.org
586-776-3900
aarda@aarda.org
www.aarda.org

The American Autoimmune Related Diseases Association is dedicated to the eradication of autoimmune diseases and the alleviation of suffering and the socioeconomic impact of autoimmunity through fostering and facilitating collaboration in the areas of education, public awareness, research, and patient services in an effective, ethical and efficient manner.

Journals

4923 Pediatric Dermatology Journal
Society for Pediatric Dermatology
8365 Keystone Crossing, Suite 107
Indianapolis, IN 46240
317-202-0224
Fax: 317-205-9481
info@pedsderm.net
www.pedsderm.net

Answers the need for new ideas and strategies for today's pediatrician or dermatologist.

6 issues/yr

Kent Lindeman, Executive Director

Description

4924 PHENYLKETONURIA (PKU)

Synonyms: Classic phenylketonuria, PKU

Involves the following Biologic System(s):

Genetic/Chromosomal/Syndrome/Metabolic Disorders

Phenylketonuria (PKU) is an inherited metabolic disorder characterized by the absence or deficiency of phenylalanine hydroxylase (PAH), an enzyme that assists in processing or metabolizing the amino acid known as phenylalanine — which is present in almost all foods — so that cells can use it for various purposes. The role of PAH is to convert phenylalanine into another amino acid named tyrosine. An absence or deficiency of PAH results in the accumulation of excessive phenylalanine in the blood. This may lead to severe intellectual disabilities that is frequently accompanied by seizures and other neurologic problems.

Phenylketonuria gets its name from the appearance in the urine of abnormally large quantities of byproducts of phenylalanine known as phenylketones, which give an unpleasant odor to the sweat and urine of infants and children with PKU.

Phenylketonuria is transmitted as an autosomal recessive trait, meaning that both parents must carry and transmit the mutated genes for their child develop PKU. The mutations that cause the disease occur in the genes that carry instructions for making PAH. In the United States, approximately one in 16,000 infants is affected by PKU. All infants born in hospitals in the United States are now routinely screened for PKU. This procedure, known as the Guthrie or PKU test, takes a small sample of blood from an infant's heel and examining it for phenylalanine.

Initially, most newborns with PKU have no symptoms. Early symptoms may include severe vomiting and poor eating. As they increase in age, children with untreated PKU may have an abnormally small head, irregularities of the teeth and upper jaw (maxilla), abnormalities in the structure and function of the heart, and intellectual disabilities that develops slowly but progressively and may become apparent within the first few months of life. Other effects of untreated PKU include unusual paleness of the skin, accompanied by skin disorders such as eczema, behavioral abnormalities, and neuromuscular irregularities such as involuntary, continuous, slow movements of the arms and legs (athetosis). Other findings may include seizures and hyperactivity, sometimes accompanied by rhythmic behaviors such as rocking; light-colored skin, blonde hair, and blue eyes and an eczema-type rash that disappears with age.

Treatment for PKU is aimed toward reducing dietary intake of phenylalanine in order to prevent or reduce damage to the brain. The most effective treatment consists of a special diet of foods that help control the amount of PAH consumed (some PAH is needed for normal growth and development). The diet is begun as soon after birth as PKU is identified, and is monitored under close supervision. It consists of fruits and vegetables, breads, pastas, and cereals with a low protein content, since proteins contain relatively large quantities of phenylalanine. The diet does not contain high-protein foods such as eggs, cheeses, meat, milk, or nuts. People with PKU who are on this diet from birth or shortly thereafter develop normally and often have no symptoms of PKU. It is recommended that pregnant women with PKU or affected women who are planning to become pregnant maintain a low phenylalanine diet to avoid the risk of miscarriage. Infants born to women with PKU and are not on a special diet are at high risk of experiencing serious effects of the disease.

National Associations & Support Groups

4925 American Academy of Pediatrics
345 Park Blvd
Itasca, IL 60143

847-434-4000
800-433-9016
Fax: 847-434-8000
csc@aap.org
www.aap.org

The American Academy of Pediatrics and its member pediatricians are committed to the attainment of optimal physical, mental and social health and well-being for all infants, children, adolescents, and young adults.

Kyle E. Yasuda, MD, FAAP, President
Mark Del Monte, JD, CEO/Executive VP
Vera Tait, MD, FAAP, Chief Medical Officer

4926 March of Dimes Foundation
1550 Crystal Drive, Ste 1300
Arlington, VA 22202

888-663-4637
www.marchofdimes.org

March of Dimes help moms have full-term pregnancies and research the problems that threaten the health of babies. The March of Dimes also acts globally: sharing best practices in perinatal health and helping improve birth outcomes where the needs are the most urgent.

Stacey D. Stewart, President
Alan Brogdon, SVP/COO/Board Officer
Rahul Gupta, MD, SVP & Chief Medical/Health Officer

4927 National PKU Alliance
954 Lexington Avenue, Suite 269
New York, NY 10021

715-495-4008
Fax: 715-713-0138
www.npkua.org

The National PKU Alliance works to improve the lives of families and individuals associated with PKU through research, support, education and advocacy, while ultimately seeking a cure.

Lisa Milberg, Executive Director

State Agencies & Support Groups

4928 PKU Organization of Illinois
PO Box 102
Palatine, IL 60078

630-415-2219
Fax: 208-978-8963
www.pkuil.org

Resource for families in Illinois and around the world dealing with phenylketonuria. Founded in 1969 for the benefit of patients and families.

Joseph Annunzio, President
Lisa Irgang, VP
Christine Davis, Treasurer

Web Sites

4929 NIH/National Human Genome Research Institute (NHGRI)
www.genome.gov

www.genome.gov

Supports the NIH component of the Human Genome Project, a worldwide research effort designed to analyze the structure of human DNA and determine the location of the estimated 30,000 to 40,000 human genes. The NHGRI Intramural Research Program develops and implements understanding, diagnosing, and treating of genetic diseases.

Eric Green, MD, PhD, Director

4930 National Society for Phenylketonuria (UK)
PO Box 3143
Purley, CR 89DD

303-040-1090
Fax: 845-004-8341
info@nspku.org
www.nspku.org

Phenylketonuria (PKU) / Newsletters

Helps and supports people with PKU, their families and caregivers. The NSPKU actively promotes the care and treatment of PKU and works closely with medical professionals in the UK.

Eric Lange, Chair
Iain Williamson, Secretary
Lisa Lee, Treasurer

4931 Online Mendelian Inheritance in Man
McKusick-Nathans Institue of Genetic Medicine-JHU
Baltimore, MD 21205
www.omim.org

This database is a catalog of human genes and genetic disorders.

Ada Hamosh, MD, Scientific Director

4932 PKU Kid Zone
www.pkuil.org/kidzone.htm

www.pkuil.org/kidzone.htm

Provides activities for chidren to have fun online.

4933 PKU Mailing List
PO Box 3143
Purley, CR 89DD
303-040-1090
Fax: 845-004-8341
info@nspku.org
www.nspku.org/listserve

Worldwide mailing list making communication between families dealing with PKU easier.

Eric Lange, Chair
Iain Williamson, Secretary
Lisa Lee, Treasurer

4934 PKU Organization of Illinois
PO Box 102
Palatine, IL 60078
630-344-9758
pkuillinois@gmail.com
www.pkuil.org

Committed to the support of appropriate research initiatives to better understand PKU and eventually find a cure. Support services include: get togethers for kids and parents to express their concerns and share ways of coping with the disease, annual picnics throughout the state and family camp to get to know other PKU families, and activities on both state and national levels in protecting the interests of PKU families.

4935 Star-G: Screening, Technology and Research in Genetics
741 Sunset Avenue
Honolulu, HI 96816
808-733-9039
Fax: 808-733-9068
www.newbornscreening.info

General and newborn screening information for amino acid disorders including PKU.

Newsletters

4936 National PKU News
6869 Woodland Avenue NE, Suite 116
Seattle, WA 98115
206-525-8140
Fax: 206-525-5023
schuett@pkunews.org
www.pkunews.org

Nonprofit organization dedicated to providing up-to-date, accurate news and information to families and professionals dealing with phenylketonuria through this newsletter.

2000+ 3 issues/year

Virginia Schuett, Director/Editor

4937 PKU Press
PKU Organization of Illinois
PO Box 102
Palatine, IL 60078
630-344-9758
Fax: 208-978-8963
pkuillinois@gmail.com
www.pkuil.org

Provides information, support, and highlights achievements for the benefit of the PKU community.

20 pages 3x/year

Joseph Annunzio, President
Lisa Irgang, VP
Christine Davis, Treasurer

Pamphlets

4938 Phenylketonuria (PKU) Information Sheet
March of Dimes Resource Center
1550 Crystal Drive, Ste 1300
Arlington, VA 22202
914-997-4488
Fax: 914-997-4763
answers@marchofdimes.org
www.marchofdimes.org

Defines and discusses the implications and causes of PKU, as well as testing, treatment, prevention and research.

Description

4939 PHOBIAS

Involves the following Biologic System(s):

Developmental/Behavioral/Psychiatric Disorders

A phobia is a persistent, exaggerated, unreasonable fear or dread of certain activities, situations, objects, or events. Exposure to the activity, situation, or object that arouses fear typically elicits signs of anxiety or panic reaction. Such symptoms may include nausea, abdominal pain, irregular pulsation or racing of the heart (palpitations), sweating, and dizziness. In contrast to adults, children, especially younger one, don't see their fear as excessive or unreasonable. Most children are fearful of particular things as they reach certain age plateaus. For example, young children are often afraid of monsters or of being alone in the dark. Older children may be fearful of death or other distressing situations. Children may become fearful of events or situations that they view on television. Others may have fear or dread related to conflicts in the home. These fears are not unusual and may often be alleviated by reassurances and comforting by parents and caregivers. However, a fear or phobia that interferes with normal, day-to-day functioning is considered pathologic.

Simple or specific phobias include fear of certain animals and insects or particular situations (e.g., fear of flying, etc.). Social phobias, often appearing in late childhood or adolescence, include fear and avoidance of certain social situations such as using public bathroom facilities or eating, speaking, performing, or writing in public. Researchers believe that some simple phobias may result from an associated, traumatic childhood experience or from the existence of a similar fear in a parent or caregiver. More complicated specific phobias (e.g., fear of attending school, etc.) may be associated with such conflicts as a hostile-dependent relationship between the parent or caregiver and the child.

Treatment for phobias is dependent upon the specific fear, the extent of the fear, and the effect of the phobias on day-to-day living. Parents or caregivers are counseled to remain calm and patient when confronted with a phobic episode. Behavioral therapy, including relaxation therapy for older children, may be indicated and may include the training of parents or caregivers in the use of supportive measures and techniques. Slow and orderly exposure to the activity, situation, or object of fear (desensitization) may help to alleviate the fear. Older children and adolescents with social phobias may learn to overcome their particular fear through social skills training. Other treatment is symptomatic and supportive.

Government Agencies

4940 Center for Mental Health Services
5600 Fishers Lane
Rockville, MD 20857

240-276-1310
www.samhsa.gov

Encourages a range of programs such as systems of care to respond to the increasing number of mental, emotional, and behavioral problems among children. Supports outreach and case management programs for the thousands of Americans who are homeless and the improvement of these services.

Anita Everett, MD, Director

4941 NIH/National Institute of Mental Health
6001 Executive Blvd, Rm 6200, MSC 9663
Bethesda, MD 20892

866-615-6464
Fax: 301-443-4279
TTY: 301-443-8431
nimhinfo@nih.gov
www.nimh.nih.gov

The mission of NIMH is to transform the understanding and treatment of mental illnesses through basic and clinical research, paving the way for prevention, recovery, and cure.

Joshua A. Gordon, MD, PhD, Director
Shelli Avenevoli, PhD, Deputy Director

National Associations & Support Groups

4942 Agoraphobics in Motion
7636 Emerson
Washington, MI 40894

248-710-5719
aimforrecovery@gmail.com
www.aimforrecovery.com

A.I.M. has been helping people with anxiety disorders since 1983.

James Fortune, President
Robert Diedrich, VP & Secretary
Harley Sherman, Treasurer

4943 American Academy of Pediatrics
345 Park Blvd
Itasca, IL 60143

847-434-4000
800-433-9016
Fax: 847-434-8000
csc@aap.org
www.aap.org

The American Academy of Pediatrics and its member pediatricians are committed to the attainment of optimal physical, mental and social health and well-being for all infants, children, adolescents, and young adults.

Kyle E. Yasuda, MD, FAAP, President
Mark Del Monte, JD, CEO/Executive VP
Vera Tait, MD, FAAP, Chief Medical Officer

4944 American Counseling Association
PO Box 31110
Alexandria, VA 22310

800-347-6647
Fax: 800-473-2329
ACAMemberServices@counseling.org
www.counseling.org

Represents professional counselors in various practice settings, and stands ready to serve more than 55,000 members with the resources they need to make a difference. From webinars, publications, and journals to Conference education sessions and legislative action alerts, ACA is where counseling professionals turn for powerful, credible content and support.

Shawn Boynes, Chief Executive Director

4945 American Mental Health Foundation (AMHF)
PO Box 3
Riverdale, NY 10028

212-737-9027
elomke@americanmentalhealthfoundation.or
americanmentalhealthfoudnation.org

Dedicated to the extensive and intensive research in the theories and techniques of treatment of emotional illness and to the implementation of reforms in the mental health system. Efforts have resulted in development of better and less expensive treatment methods. Findings are disseminated in English and other major languages.

Monroe W Spero, MD
Evander Lomke, Executive Director

4946 American Psychiatric Association
800 Maine Avenue SW, Suite 900
Washington, DC 20024

202-559-3900
apa@psych.org
www.psychiatry.org

It is a medical specialty society representing growing membership of more than 36,000 psychiatrists.

Phobias / State Agencies & Support Groups

Saul Levin, MD, CEO & Medical Director

4947 American Psychological Association
750 First St. NE
Washington, DC 20002
202-336-5500
800-374-2721
TTY: 202-336-6123
www.apa.org

The mission is to advance the creation, communication and application of psychological knowledge to benefit society and improve people's lives.

Arthur C. Evans Jr, PhD, CEO/EVP

4948 American School Counselor Association
1101 King Street, Ste 310
Alexandria, VA 22314
703-683-2722
asca@schoolcounselor.org
www.schoolcounselor.org

The mission of ASCA is to represent professional school counselors and to promote professionalism and ethical practices.

Jill Cook, Executive Director
Amanda Fitzgerald, Assistant Deputy Executive Director
Kathleen M Rakestraw, Director of Communications

4949 Anxiety and Depression Association of America
8701 Georgia Ave., Suite 412
Silver Spring, MD 20910
240-485-1018
information@adaa.org
www.adaa.org

ADAA is a national nonprofit organization dedicated to the prevention, treatment, and cure of anxiety, depression, OCD, PTSD, and related disorders and to improving the lives of all people who suffer from them through education, practice, and research.

Susan K Gurley, Executive Director
Lise Bram, Deputy Executive Director
Katie Russo, Senior Director, Operations

4950 Mental Health America
500 Montgomery Street, Ste 820
Alexandria, VA 22314
703-684-7722
800-969-6642
Fax: 703-684-5968
www.mentalhealthamerica.net

MHA, the leading advocacy organization addressing the full spectrum of mental and substance use conditions and their effects nationwide, works to inform, advocate and enable access to quality behavioral health services for all Americans.

Paul Gionfriddo, President/CEO
Whitney Ball, Assoc. Dir., Marketing/Outreach
Sachin Doshi, Sr. Dir., Finance/Operations

4951 National Alliance on Mental Illness (NAMI)
4301 Wilson Blvd., Suite 300
Arlington, VA 22203
703-524-7600
888-999-6264
info@nami.org
www.nami.org

NAMI provides advocacy, education, support and public awareness so that all individuals and families affected by mental illness can build better lives.

Daniel H. Gillison, CEO
David Levy, CFO
Ken Duckworth, Chief Medical Officer

4952 National Anxiety Foundation
3135 Custer Drive
Lexington, KY 40517
859-281-0003
www.nationalanxietyfoundation.org

Nonprofit organization that provides education to the public and professionals about anxiety through printed and electronic media.

Stephen Cox, MD, President & Medical Director
Linda Vernon Blair, VP
C. Todd Strecker, Secretary-Treasurer

4953 National Federation of Families
15800 Crabbs Branch Way, Suite 300
Rockville, MD 20855
240-403-1901
ffcmh@ffcmh.org
www.ffcmh.org

The National family run organization is dedicated exclusively to helping children with mental health needs and their families achieve a better quality of life.

Lynda Gargan, PhD, Executive Director

4954 National Mental Health Consumers' Self-Help Clearinghouse
1211 Chestnut Street, Suite 1207
Philadelphia, PA 19107
215-751-1810
800-553-4539
Fax: 215-636-6312
selfhelpclearinghouse@gmail.com
www.mhselfhelp.org

Offers information, support and appropriate referrals; and promotes public and professional education. Provides networking for those with special interests related to albinism. Promotes and supports research and funding that will improve diagnosis and management of albinism and hypopigmentation.

Joseph Rogers, Founder/Executive Director
Susan Rogers, Director

4955 Phobics Anonymous
Rancho Mirage, CA
760-770-0462
rosemaryjane@dc.rr.com

Twelve-step program for panic disorders and anxiety. Publications available.

Rosemary Hartmann, Contact

4956 Selective Mutism Association
3152 Little Road, Suite 184
New Port Richey, FL 34655
www.selectivemutism.org

The Selective Mutism Association (SMA) works to increase public awareness of selective mutism and co-occurring disorders and to promote a greater understanding of these disorders by supporting research initiatives and providing educational resources. SMA provides scientific research-based support to professionals, affected individuals, and their families so that more people with SM can find their voices.

Lisa Kovac, Executive Director
Kristin Carey Leos, Director of Memberships

State Agencies & Support Groups

4957 Center for Family Support
333 7th Avenue, #901
New York, NY 10001
212-629-7939
Fax: 212-239-2211
www.cfsny.org

The Center for Family (CFS) is a not-for-profit human service agency providing support and assistance to individuals with developmental disabilities and traumatic brain injuries throughout New York City, Long Island, the lower Hudson Valley region and New Jersey.

Steven Vernikoff, Executive Director
Linda Schellenberg, Director, Community Service
Barbara Greenwald, Associate Executive Director

Research Centers

4958 UC Berkeley School of Social Welfare
Mental Health & Social Welfare Research Group
120 Haviland Hall #7400
Berkeley, CA 94720
510-642-4341
spsegal@berkeley.edu
socialwelfare.berkeley.edu/mhswrg/mhswrg.html

Steven P Segal, Director

Phobias / Web Sites

Conferences

4959 American School Counselor Association Annual Conference
1101 King Street, Suite 310
Alexandria, VA 22314
703-683-2722
800-306-4722
Fax: 703-997-7572
asca@schoolcounselor.org
www.schoolcounselor.org

The mission of ASCA is to represent professional school counselors and to promote professionalism and ethical practices.

3,000 Attendees

Richard Wong, Executive Director
Jennifer Walsh, Director, Education & Training
Kathleen M Rakestraw, Director of Communications

Audio Video

4960 Acquiring Courage: Audio Cassette Program for the Rapid Treatment of Phobias
New Harbinger Publications
5674 Shattuck Avenue
Oakland, CA 94609
510-652-2002
800-748-6273
Fax: 510-652-5472
customerservice@newharbinger.com
newharbinger.com

ISBN: 1-879237-03-2

4961 Anxiety Disorders
American Counseling Association
6101 Stevenson Ave.
Alexandria, VA 22304
703-823-9800
800-347-6647
Fax: 703-823-0252
webmaster@counseling.org
counseling.org

Increase your awareness of anxiety disorders, their symptoms, and effective treatments. Learn the effect these disorders can have on life and how treatment can change the quality of life for people presently suffering from these disorders. Includes 6 audiotapes and a study guide.

Robert L. Smith, Ph.D., NCC, FPPR, President
Brain Canfield, Treasurer
Richard Yep, Chief Executive Officer

4962 Fear of Illness
New Harbinger Publications
5674 Shattuck Avenue
Oakland, CA 94609
510-652-2002
800-748-6273
Fax: 510-652-5472
customerservice@newharbinger.com
newharbinger.com

120 minute videotape that reduces fears arising from unexplained pain or symptoms; learn to relax while you desensitize to strange body sensations.

ISBN: 1-572240-15-6

4963 Flying
New Harbinger Publications
5674 Shattuck Avenue
Oakland, CA 94609
510-652-2002
800-748-6273
Fax: 510-652-5472
customerservice@newharbinger.com
newharbinger.com

120 minute videotape that reduces fear to the point where you can take longer and longer flights; desensitize to the sensations of flying.

ISBN: 1-879237-90-3

4964 Heights
New Harbinger Publications
5674 Shattuck Avenue
Oakland, CA 94609
510-652-2002
800-748-6273
Fax: 510-652-5472
customerservice@newharbinger.com
newharbinger.com

120 minute videotape that makes you feel more comfortable in high - rise buildings, on bridges, and on mountain roads.

ISBN: 1-879237-91-1

Web Sites

4965 Answers to Your Questions about Panic Disorder
750 First St. NE
Washington, DC 20002
202-336-5500
800-374-2721
www.apa.org/pubinfo/panic.html

The objects of the APA shall be to advance psychology as a science and profession and as a means of promoting health, education, and human welfare by: encouragement of psychology in all its branches in the broadest and most liberal manner, the promotion of research in psychology and the improvement fo research methods and conditions, and the improvement of the qualifications and usefulness of psychologists through high standards of ethics, conduct, education, and achievement.

Barry S. Anton, PhD, President
Bonnie Markham, Treasurer
Norman B. Anderson, CEO & VP

4966 Anxiety Disorders Association of America
NOP-ONE-

Offers resources and information for persons with anxiety and stress-related disorders.

4967 Anxiety Panic Internet Resource
www.algy.com/anxiety/

www.algy.com/anxiety/

It is the web's first and still best self-help resource for those with anxiety disorders, Panic attacks, phobias, extreme shyness, obsessive-compulsive behaviors, and generalized anxiety disrupt the lives of an estimated 15% of the population. It is a free grass-root website dedicated to providing information, relief, and support for those recovering from debilitating anxiety.

4968 Basic Guided Relaxation: Advanced Technique
1258 Eagle Crest Dr.
Oak Harbor, WA 98277
360-593-3833
wellness@dstress.com
www.dstress.com/guided.htm

A guide to relaxation.

L. John Mason, Founder

4969 Causes of Anxiety and Panic Attacks
www.algy.com/anxiety/files/barlow.html

www.algy.com/anxiety/files/barlow.html

Provides information concerning phobias, what they are, the symptoms, and the effects of phobias.

4970 CyberPsych
www.cyberpsych.org

www.cyberpsych.org

CyberPsych presents information about psychoanalysis, psychotherapy, and special topics such as anxiety disorder, the problematic use of alcohol, homophobia, and the traumatic effects of racism. CyberPsych is a nonprofit network which offers free web hosting and technical support for internet communication, to nonprofit groups and individuals.

4971 National Anxiety Foundation
3135 Custer Dr.
Lexington, KY 40517
www.nationalanxietyfoundation.org

Endeavours to educate the public and professionals about anxiety through printed and electronic media. A volunteer, nonprofit entity.

Stephen Cox, MD, President & Medical Director
Linda Vernon Blair, VP
C. Todd Strecker, Secretary-Treasurer

4972 National Panic/Anxiety Disorder Newsletter
www.npadnews.com

editor@npadnews.com
www.npadnews.com

We provide the most up to date material which is gathered from many resourced and contributors form all corners of the globe.

4973 Panic Disorder, Separation, Anxiety Disorder
www.klis.com/chandler/pamphlet/panic

www.klis.com/chandler/pamphlet/panic

Provides information about panic attacks and more, about what can be done and what medican treatments there are.

4974 Recovery Panic Anxiety
www.alt.recovery.panic.anxiety.self-help

www.alt.recovery.panic.anxiety.self-help

An online support group t talk about anxiety recovery.

Book Publishers

4975 An End to Panic: Breakthrough Techniques for Overcoming Panic Disorder

Elke Zuercher-White, author

New Harbinger Publications
5674 Shattuck Avenue
Oakland, CA 94609
510-652-2002
800-748-6273
Fax: 510-652-5472
TTY: 800-652-1613
customerservice@newharbinger.com
www.newharbinger.com

A state of the art treatment program covers breathing retraining, taking charge of fear-fueling thoughts, overcoming the fear of physical symptoms, coping with phobic situations, avoiding relapse, and living in the here and now.

232 pages Paperback
ISBN: 1-572241-13-6

4976 Anxiety & Phobia Workbook

Edmund J Bourne, author

New Harbinger Publications
5674 Shattuck Avenue
Oakland, CA 94609
510-652-2002
800-748-6273
Fax: 510-652-5472
TTY: 800-652-1613
customerservice@newharbinger.com
www.newharbinger.com

This comprehensive guide is recommended to those struggling with anxiety disorders. Includes step-by-step instructions for the crucial cognitive-behavioral techniques that have given real help to hundreds of thousands of readers struggling with anxiety disorders.

448 pages 4th Edition
ISBN: 1-572244-13-5

4977 Anxiety Cure: An Eight-Step Program for Getting Well
John Wiley & Sons
10475 Crosspoint Boulevard
Indianapolis, IN 46256
877-762-2974
Fax: 800-597-3299
www.wiley.com

A practical guide, written by a father and his two daughters, featuring a step-by-step program for curing the six main kinds of anxiety.

272 pages 2nd Edition
ISBN: 0-471464-87-2

Peter B. Wiley, Chairman
Stephen M. Smith, President & CEO
Ellis E. Cousens, Executive Vice President, Chief Fin

4978 Anxiety Disorders
Cambridge University Press
40 W 20th Street
New York, NY 10011
212-924-3900
800-872-7423
Fax: 914-937-4712
marketing@cup.org
cup.org

This comprehensive text covers all the anxiety disorders found in the latest DSM and ICD classifications. Provides detailed information about seven principal disorders, including anxiety in the medically ill. For each disorder, the book covers diagnosis criteria, epidemiology, etiology and pathogenesis, clinical features, natural history and different diagnoses. Describes treatment approaches, both psychological and pharmacological.

354 pages

4979 Anxiety Disorders: Practioner's Guide
John Wiley & Sons
605 3rd Avenue
New York, NY 10058
212-850-6000
Fax: 212-850-6008
info@wiley.com
wiley.com

210 pages
ISBN: 0-471931-12-8

Peter B. Wiley, Chairman
Stephen M. Smith, President & CEO
Ellis E. Cousens, Executive Vice President, Chief Fin

4980 Encyclopedia of Phobias, Fears, and Anxieties
Facts on File
11 Penn Plaza, Room M274
New York, NY 10001
212-290-8090
800-322-8755

500 pages

4981 Helping Your Anxious Child
New Harbinger Publications
5674 Shattuck Avenue
Oakland, CA 94609
510-652-2002
800-748-6273
Fax: 510-652-5472
TTY: 800-652-1613
customerservice@newharbinger.com
www.newharbinger.com

Step-by-step guide for parents of anxious children to help them overcome their fears and anxieties. Detailed strategies and techniques.

168 pages Paperback
ISBN: 1-572241-91-8

4982 It's Nobody's Fault: New Hope and Help for Difficult Children and Their Parents
ADD WareHouse
300 NW 70th Avenue
Plantation, FL 33317
954-792-8944
800-233-9273
Fax: 954-792-8545
addwarehouse.com

This book explains that neither the parents nor children are causes of mental disorders and related problems.

184 pages

4983 Perfectionism: What's Bad About Being Too Good
Free Spirit Pub

NOP-ONE-

With help for superkids, workaholics, type A's, straight A's, procrastinators, overacheivers, and caring adults, this book explains the differance between healthy ambition and unhealthy perfectionism and gives straight strategies for getting out of the perfectionist trap- from recognizing the symptoms to rewarding yourself for who you are, not what you do. It explains why some people become perfectionists, what it does to the body, and why girls are more prone to it, and more.

1999 144 pages

Miriam Adderholt, PhD, Author
Miriam Elliot, Author
Judy Galbraith, Author

4984 Psychological Trauma
American Psychiatric Press
1400 K Street, NW
Washington, DC 20005

202-682-6262
800-368-5777
Fax: 202-789-2648
order@appi.org
www.appi.org

Epidemiology of trauma and post-tramatic stress disorder. Evaluation, neuroimaging, neuroendocrinology and pharmacology.

1998 206 pages

Robert E. Hales M.D, Editor-in-Chief
Rebecca D. Rinehart, Publisher
John McDuffie, Editorial Director

4985 Shy Children, Phobic Adults: Nature and Treatment of Social Phobia
American Psychological Press
1400 K Street, NW
Washington, DC 20005

202-682-6262
800-368-5777
Fax: 202-789-2648
orders@appi.org
www.appi.org

Describes the simuliarities and differences in the syndrome across all ages. Draws from the clinical, social and developmental literatures, as well as from extensive clinical experience. Illustrates the impact of developmental stage on phenomenology, diagnosis and assessment and treatment of social phobia.

1998 321 pages

Robert E. Hales M.D, Editor-in-Chief
Rebecca D. Rinehart, Publisher
John McDuffie, Editorial Director

Pamphlets

4986 5 Smart Steps to Less Stress
ETR Associates
PO Box 1830
Santa Cruz, CA 95061

831-438-4060
800-321-4407
Fax: 800-435-8433

Steps to managing stress include: know what stresses you, manage your stress, take care of your body, take care of your feelings, ask for help.

4987 Anxiety Disorders
National Institute of Mental Health
6001 Executive Boulevard, Room 6200
Bethesda, MD 20892

301-443-4513
866-615-6464
Fax: 301-443-4279
TTY: 301-443-8431
nimhinfo@nih.gov
www.nimh.nih.gov

This brochure helps to identify the symptoms of anxiety disorders, explains the role of research in understanding the causes of these conditions, describes effective treatments, helps you learn how to obtain treatment and work with a doctor or therapist, and suggests ways to make treatment more effective.

Francis Collins, M.D., Director
Tom Insel, Director

4988 Anxiety Disorders Fact Sheet
Center for Mental Health Services
PO Box 42490
Washington, DC 20015

800-789-2647
Fax: 301-984-8796
ken@mentalhealth.org
mentalhealth.org

This fact sheet presents basic information on the symptoms, formal diagnosis, and treatment for generalized anxiety disorder, panic disorders, phobias, and post traumatic stress disorder.

3 pages

4989 Anxiety Disorders in Children and Adolescents
Center for Mental Health Services
PO Box 42490
Washington, DC 20015

800-789-2647
Fax: 301-984-8796
ken@mentalhealth.org
mentalhealth.org

This fact sheet defines anxiety disorders, identifies warning signs, discusses risk factors, describes types of help available, and suggests what parents or other caregivers can do.

3 pages

4990 Families Can Help Children Cope with Fear, Anxiety
Center for Mental Health Services
PO Box 42490
Washington, DC 20015

800-789-2647
Fax: 301-984-8796
ken@mentalhealth.org
mentalhealth.org

This fact sheet defines conduct disorder, identifies risk factors, discusses types of help available, and suggests what parents or other caregivers responses should be to common signs of fear and anxiety.

4991 Panic Attacks
ETR Associates
PO Box 1830
Santa Cruz, CA 95061

831-438-4060
800-321-4407
Fax: 800-435-8433

Describes causes of panic attacks, including genetics, stress, and drug use; prevention and treatment, and how to stop a panic attack in its tracks.

Description

4992 PHOTOSENSITIVITY

Covers these related disorders: Photoallergic reaction, Phototoxic reaction

Involves the following Biologic System(s):
Dermatologic Disorders

Photosensitivity, sometimes referred to as sun allergy, is an abnormal reaction of the skin to sunlight or artificial light that is usually characterized by the rapid development of redness, swelling, tenderness, peeling, blistering, hives, or other skin irregularities. The skin reactions associated with photosensitivity are often induced by the interaction of light and certain substances known as photosensitizers that are ingested or applied directly to the skin. Such photosensitizers may include antibiotics, antifungal agents, and other drugs as well as some perfumes, soaps, dyes, and plants (e.g., buttercups, parsley, parsnips, mustard, etc.).

Particular wavelengths of light interact with photosensitizers to produce skin inflammations (dermatitis) that may be considered photoallergic or phototoxic. A photoallergic reaction is a delayed immune or allergic response of the skin that results from having been previously exposed to a photosensitizer and light. Such photosensitizers may include barbiturates, certain antibiotics such as tetracycline, and other medications as well as certain topical agents such as coal tar derivatives, perfume oils such as bergamot, etc. A phototoxic reaction is a nonimmune response to the accumulation of certain chemicals in the skin. This type of skin reaction may be similar in appearance to a severe sunburn; some individuals may develop hives or blisters. The initial inflammation is usually followed by abnormally increased skin pigmentation (hyperpigmentation). Phototoxic reactions result from high doses of certain photosensitizers that may cause photoallergic reactions in lower doses, as well as from additional chemical substances. Treatment includes the withdrawal of offending medications and other photosensitizers and sunlight avoidance. In addition, administration of antihistamines and topical corticosteroids may be effective in eliminating associated itching (pruritus).

Photosensitivity is also associated with certain disorders in children. Such disorders may include congenital erythropoietic porphyria (EPP), an autosomal recessive disorder that results from a deficiency of an enzyme. This particular enzyme is necessary for the synthesis of heme, which is the oxygen-carrying component of a certain protein (hemoprotein) found in the tissues of the body. Congenital erythropoietic porphyria develops within a few months of birth and is characterized by a severe sensitivity to light that may cause blistering eruptions on the skin, leading to severe scarring, abnormally increased skin pigmentation, and other skin irregularities. Children with this disorder may also have numerous other abnormalities. Erythropoietic protoporphyria is an autosomal dominant disorder that results from a deficiency of an enzyme that is also essential to the proper synthesis of heme. This disorder appears during early childhood and is characterized by pain, tingling, and a burning feeling upon exposure to sunlight. The skin may redden, swell, and form blisters or hives. In addition to having nail irregularities, children may develop fever and chills. Repeated exposure to sunlight may result in skin thickening and other chronic associated irregularities; however, some children experience improvement during their preadolescent years. Treatment for these types of disorders includes the avoidance of direct sunlight and the use of protective clothing and appropriate sunscreens. In addition, the administration of sufficient quantities of beta-carotene to cause a light yellowing of the skin may be effective in reducing sensitivity to sunlight. Photosensitivity is a feature of many other disorders that may include Cockayne syndrome, xeroderma pigmentosum, hydroa vacciniforme, Rothmund-Thomson syndrome, and other diseases.

Occasionally, some individuals experience an unusual photosensitive reaction to sunlight in the absence of any apparent photosensitizer or associated disease. This type of photosensitivity is called polymorphous light eruption and is one of the most common sun-related skin problems. It is characterized by the appearance of hives or other itchy, rash-type reactions on exposed areas. Polymorphous light eruption usually occurs after a prolonged initial sun exposure in the spring or summer. The eruption may occur within hours or days of the exposure and may remain for hours, days, or weeks. Treatment may include oral or topical corticosteroid therapy. In addition, susceptible people are counseled to avoid the sun, wear protective clothing, and use sunscreen.

Individuals with certain types of photosensitivity may benefit from the cautious administration of photosensitizing drugs that enhance pigmentation of the skin (psoralens). In addition, certain types of phototherapy may be effective. Other treatment is symptomatic and supportive.

Government Agencies

4993 NIH/ Eunice Kennedy Shriver National Institute of Child Health & Human Development
P.O. Box 3006
Rockville, MD 20847

800-370-2943
Fax: 866-760-5947
www.nichd.nih.gov

Conducts and supports research on topics related to the health of children, adults, families and populations. Some of these topics include: developmental disabilities, growth and development, infant death, reproductive health and birth defects.

Diana W. Bianchi, Director
Alison Cernich, PhD, Deputy Director

4994 NIH/National Eye Institute
31 Center Drive MSC 2510
Bethesda, MD 20892

301-496-5248
2020@nei.nih.gov
www.nei.nih.gov

Conducts and supports research that helps prevent and treat eye diseases and other disorders of vision. This research leads to sight-saving treatments, reduces visual impairment and blindness, and improves the quality of life for people of all ages. NEI-supported research has advanced our knowledge of how the eye functions in health and disease.

Michael F. Chiang, MD, Director
Santa Tumminia, Deputy Director

4995 NIH/National Institute of Arthritis and Musculoskeletal and Skin Diseases
1 AMS Circle
Bethesda, MD 20892

301-495-4484
877-226-4267
Fax: 301-718-6366
TDD: 301-565-2966
niamsinfo@mail.nih.gov
www.niams.nih.gov

The mission of the NIAMS, a part of the NIH, is to support research into the causes, treatment and prevention of arthritis and musculoskeletal and skin diseases, the training of basic and clinical scientists to carry out this research, and the dissemination of information on research progress in these diseases.

Lindsey A. Criswell, MD, Director
Rick Phillips, Executive Officer

Photosensitivity / Research Centers

National Associations & Support Groups

4996 American Academy of Pediatrics
345 Park Blvd
Itasca, IL 60143
847-434-4000
800-433-9016
Fax: 847-434-8000
csc@aap.org
www.aap.org

The American Academy of Pediatrics and its member pediatricians are committed to the attainment of optimal physical, mental and social health and well-being for all infants, children, adolescents, and young adults.

Kyle E. Yasuda, MD, FAAP, President
Mark Del Monte, JD, CEO/Executive VP
Vera Tait, MD, FAAP, Chief Medical Officer

4997 Genetic Alliance
426400 Woodfield Road, Ste 189
Damascus, MD 20872
202-966-5557
Fax: 202-966-8553
info@geneticalliance.org
www.geneticalliance.org

World's leading nonprofit health advocacy organization committed to transforming health through genetics and promoting an environment of openness centered on the health of individuals, families, and communities.

Sharon Terry, CEO
Ruth Child, CFO
Natasha Bonhomme, Chief Strategy Officer

4998 March of Dimes Foundation
1550 Crystal Drive, Ste 1300
Arlington, VA 22202
888-663-4637
www.marchofdimes.org

March of Dimes help moms have full-term pregnancies and research the problems that threaten the health of babies. The March of Dimes also acts globally: sharing best practices in perinatal health and helping improve birth outcomes where the needs are the most urgent.

Stacey D. Stewart, President
Alan Brogdon, SVP/COO/Board Officer
Rahul Gupta, MD, SVP & Chief Medical/Health Officer

4999 Society for Pediatric Dermatology
8365 Keystone Crossing, Ste 107
Indianapolis, IN 46240
317-202-0224
Fax: 317-205-9481
info@pedsderm.net
www.pedsderm.net

The objective of the Society is to promote, develop and advance education, research and care of skin disease in all pediatric age groups.

Kent Lindeman, Executive Director

Libraries & Resource Centers

California

5000 University of California, San Francisco Dermatology Drug Research
515 Spruce Street
San Francisco, CA 94115
415-476-4701
Fax: 415-502-4126
cc.ucsf.edu/people

Conducts clinical testing of new or existing pharmalogic agents used in the treatment of skin disorders.

John Koo, MD, Director

Delaware

5001 Delaware Division of Libraries for the Blind and Physically Handicapped
121 Duke of York Street
Dover, DE 19901
302-736-4748
800-282-8676
Fax: 302-736-6787
TDD: 302-739-4748
bedpg@lib.de.us

Braille readers receive service from Philadelphia and Pennsylvania, summer reading program, Braille writer and cassettes.

Beth Landon, Librarian

Illinois

5002 Dermatology Information Network (DERMINFONET)
American Academy of Dermatology
9500 W. Bryn Mawr Avenue, Ste 500
Rosemont, IL 60018
847-240-1737
888-462-3376
Fax: 847-240-1859
info@aad.org

Consists of a collection of dermatologic databases that are available to members on a subscription and/or purchase basis. These databases are designed to run on a wide variety of personal computers.

Irvin Bomberger, Interim Executive Director

5003 National Library of Dermatologic Teaching Slides
American Academy of Dermatology
9500 W. Bryn Mawr Avenue, Ste 500
Rosemont, IL 60018
847-240-1737
888-462-3376
Fax: 847-240-1859
info@aad.org
www.aad.org

A collection of dermatologic teaching slides offering the most comprehensive series ever assembled. Each set offers a realistic presentation of classic clinical skin conditions encountered by the dermatologist.

Irvin Bomberger, Interim Executive Director

New York

5004 Laboratory of Dermatology Research
Memorial Sloan-Kettering Cancer Center
1275 York Avenue
New York, NY 10065
212-639-2000
Fax: 212-639-3576
www.mskcc.org

Specific studies on the identification of skin disorders and dermatology.

Biijan Safai, MD, Head

5005 Rockefeller University Laboratory for Investigative Dermatology
1230 York Avenue
New York, NY 10065
212-327-8000
Fax: 212-327-7974

Research into skin disorders and the whole specialty of dermatology in general.

Barry Coller, Head

Research Centers

5006 University of California, San Francisco Dermatology Drug Research
515 Spruce Street
San Francisco, CA 94115
415-476-4701
Fax: 415-502-4126
cc.ucsf.edu/people

Conducts clinical testing of new or existing pharmalogic agents used in the treatment of skin disorders.

John Koo, MD, Director

Magazines

5007 International Journal of Dermatology
International Society of Dermatology
2323 North State Street #30
Bunnell, FL 32110
386-437-4405
Fax: 386-437-4427
info@intsocderm.org
www.intsocderm.org

Focuses on information for dermatologists and the whole specialty of dermatology research and education.

10 times a year

Evangeline˜ Handog, MD, President
Luca Borradori, Vice President
Paulo Rowilson Cunha, Vice President

5008 Journal of Dermatologic Surgery and Oncology
International Society for Dermatologic Surgery
930 N Meachan Road
Schaumburg, IL 60173
847-330-9830
Fax: 847-330-1135

Focuses on medical updates and information on dermatology.

Monthly

Journals

5009 Pediatric Dermatology Journal
Society for Pediatric Dermatology
8365 Keystone Crossing, Suite 107
Indianapolis, IN 46240
317-202-0224
Fax: 317-205-9481
info@pedsderm.net
www.pedsderm.net

Answers the need for new ideas and strategies for today's pediatrician or dermatologist.

6 issues/yr

Kent Lindeman, Executive Director

Newsletters

5010 DVH Quarterly
University of Arkansas at Little Rock
2801 S University Avenue
Little Rock, AR 72204
Fax: 501-663-3536

Offers information on upcoming events, conferences and workshops on and for visual disabilities. Book reviews, information on the newest resources and technology, educational programs, want ads and more.

Quarterly

Bob Brasher, Editor

5011 Dermatology Focus
Dermatology Foundation
1560 Sherman Avenue, Suite 870
Evanston, IL 60201
847-328-2256
Fax: 847-328-0509
dfgen@dermatologyfoundation.org
dermatologyfoundation.org

Includes membership activities, research articles and lists recipients of foundation awards.

Quarterly

Bruce U. Wintroub, Chairman
Michael D. Tharp, M.D., President
Staurt R. Lessin, M.D., Vice President

5012 Dermatology World
American Academy of Dermatology
9500 W. Bryn Mawr Avenue, Ste 500
Rosemont, IL 60018
847-240-1737
888-462-3376
Fax: 847-240-1859
info@aad.org
www.aad.org/dw

Offers Academy members information outside the clinical realm. It carries news of government actions, reports of socioeconomic issues, societal trends and other events which impinge on the practice of dermatology.

Monthly

Irvin Bomberger, Interim Executive Director

5013 Progress in Dermatology
Dermatology Foundation
1560 Sherman Avenue, Suite 870
Evanston, IL 60201
847-328-2256
Fax: 847-328-0509
dfgen@dermatologyfoundation.org
dermatologyfoundation.org

Bulletin offering information on research reports and clinical trials.

Quarterly

Bruce U. Wintroub, Chairman
Michael D. Tharp, M.D., President
Staurt R. Lessin, M.D., Vice President

Camps

5014 Camp Discovery
American Academy of Dermatology
9500 W. Bryn Mawr Avenue, Ste 500
Rosemont, IL 60018
847-240-1737
Fax: 847-240-1859
jmueller@aad.org
www.campdiscovery.org

A camp for young people with chronic skin conditions. There is no fee and transportation is provided. Five locations: Camp Victory in Millville, PA, Camp Knutson in Crosslake, MN, Camp For All in Burton, TX, Channel 3 Kids Camp in Andover, CT, and Camp Seymour in Gig harbor, WA.

J Mueller, Camp Contact
Irvin Bomberger, Interim Executive Director

Description

5015 PHYSICAL & SEXUAL ABUSE
Involves the following Biologic System(s):
Developmental/Behavioral/Psychiatric Disorders

Child abuse is a pervasive societal disease that has been gaining increasing recognition in the last 40 years. Maltreatment of children includes neglect, physical abuse and sexual abuse. In 1996, one million children were confirmed by protective US agencies as having been abused. Reporting figures since that time have been on the rise.

Neglect is the most common form of abuse, and covers a wide range of irresponsible behaviors that negatively impact the growth and well being of a child. Inadequate supervision may result in injury from falling, usage of a dangerous object such as a knife, scissors or other tools, or ingestion of toxic products and medications. Neglect may also include providing insufficient food, clothing and shelter for a child, which carries a high risk of malnutrition, illness, and poor emotional development. Parents or guardians who do not ensure proper medical care for their children are also negligent, particularly for children with chronic serious medical illnesses.

Physical abuse encompasses a wide range of symptoms but always involves purposeful injury inflicted on a child. Physical abuse can be difficult to identify, especially in toddlers, because children are prone to accidents and receive bruises and cuts as routine events. One key element in the diagnosis is ascertaining whether the injury could have happened the way it was reported. Another important clue is whether the child at a given developmental stage, could have performed the reported event. For example, a report of a six-month old who "fell" and broke his femur (thigh bone) should raise suspicion as a six-month old infant is too young to walk. Common abusive injuries include bruises from belts, hands or cords, burns from cigarettes or hot water immersion, fractures or brain injury from vigorous shaking and internal abdominal injuries from trauma to the back and abdomen. It is important for health care providers, or friends and family members, to record all injuries as a pattern may develop that will help diagnose the situation.

Sexual abuse occurs when a child is involved in sexual activities that he/she cannot fully comprehend, he/she cannot give consent to, or that violate societal norms. Common ages of abuse are between 9 and 12 years. Approximately 25 percent of women and 12 percent of men report histories of being sexually abused as children. Normal sexual play between children of similar age and developmental level can be distinguished from abuse by assessing disparity of age/development and the level of coercion involved. Abusive acts include fondling, intercourse, oral-genital and anal-genital contact, as well as voyeurism, exhibitionism and pornography. Perpetrators are more commonly male adults and adolescents, although women have been known to commit these crimes as well. This type of abuse is often very difficult to recognize because there are frequently no physical signs or symptoms and victims are reluctant and embarrassed to disclose the information. There is often a trusting and/or fearful relationship between the perpetrator and victim that binds the victim to secrecy. Certain telltale signs include inappropriate sexualized behaviors and language, and sexually transmitted diseases such as gonorrhea and chlamydia or symptoms such as discharge or bleeding. Physical evidence may include abrasions, hymenal tears, bruising, foul discharge or even pregnancy.

Professionals working with children, including teachers, social workers and health care providers are all mandated reporters, which means that if abuse is suspected they must report the family to the local protective service agency. It is critical to note that the burden of proof does not lie with the reporter, so even if there is a degree of uncertainty, one is required to act upon his or her concern.

Government Agencies

5016 Children's Bureau
Department of Health & Human Services
330 C Street SW
Washington, DC 20201   www.acf.hhs.gov/programs/cb

The Children's Bureau (CB) partners with federal, state, tribal and local agencies to improve the overall health and well-being of the nation's children and families. Provides support and guidance to programs that focus on preventing child abuse and neglect and protecting children when abuse or neglect has occurred.

Aysha E. Schomburg, Associate Commissioner

National Associations & Support Groups

5017 American Academy of Pediatrics
345 Park Blvd
Itasca, IL 60143
847-434-4000
800-433-9016
Fax: 847-434-8000
csc@aap.org
www.aap.org

The American Academy of Pediatrics and its member pediatricians are committed to the attainment of optimal physical, mental and social health and well-being for all infants, children, adolescents, and young adults.

Kyle E. Yasuda, MD, FAAP, President
Mark Del Monte, JD, CEO/Executive VP
Vera Tait, MD, FAAP, Chief Medical Officer

5018 American Professional Society on the Abuse of Children
590 Avenue of the Americas, 14th Floor
New York, NY 10011
877-402-7722
apsac@apsac.org
www.apsac.org

Dedicated to providing professional education which promotes effective, culturally sensitive and interdisciplinary approaches to the identification, intervention, treatment and prevention of child abuse and neglect.

Lorrie Brennan, Director
Hannah Gilbert, Operations Manager
Crystal Marks, Director of Publications

5019 Child Abuse Prevention Association
503 E 23rd Street
Independence, MO 64055
816-252-8388
info@capacares.org
capacares.org

Mission is to prevent and treat all forms of child abuse by creating changes in individuals, families and society which strengthen relationships and promote healing.

Rochelle Parker, President & CEO
Susan Ruddell, Manager of Administration
Kristina Jones, Vice President of Programs

5020 Child Welfare League of America
727 - 15th Street NW, Suite 1200
Washington, DC 20005
202-688-4200
cwla@cwla.org
www.cwla.org

National nonprofit organization dedicated to developing and promoting policies and programs to protect America's children from harm and strengthen America's families.

Christine James-Brown, President & CEO
Ray Bierria, Chief Financial Officer
Charlene Haskell, Executive Coordinator

Physical & Sexual Abuse / National Associations & Support Groups

5021 Childhelp
6730 N Scottdale Road, Suite 150
Scottsdale, AZ 85253
480-922-8212
800-422-4453
www.childhelp.org

Dedicated to meeting the physical, emotional and spiritual needs of abused and neglected children through focusing its efforts and resources upon treatment, prevention and research.

Chris Ruble, Chief Program Officer
Daphne Young, Chief Communications Officer
Denise Biben, Chief Administration Officer

5022 Children's Defense Fund
840 First Street NE, Suite 300
Washington, DC 20002
202-628-8787
cdfinfo@childrensdefense.org
www.childrensdefense.org

Mission is to ensure every child a healthy start, a head start, a fair start, a safe start and a moral start in life.

Rev. Dr. Starsky Wilson, President & CEO
Bob Farrace, National Director, Public Affairs
Sheri A. Brady, VP, Strategy & Program

5023 IVAT: Institute on Violence, Abuse and Tra uma
10065 Old Grove Road, Suite 101
San Diego, CA 92131
858-527-1860
Fax: 858-527-1743
www.ivatcenters.org

Formerly the Family Violence & Sexual Assault Institute. Shares and disseminates vital information, improves networking among professionals, and assists with program evaluation, consultation and training that promotes violence-free living.

Robert Geffner, President & Founder
Sandi Capuano Morrison, Chief Executive Officer

5024 KidsPeace
4085 Independence Drive
Schnecksville, PA 18078
800-257-3223
www.kidspeace.org

KidsPeace is a private charity dedicated to serving the behavioral and mental health needs of children, families and communities. Founded in 1882, KidsPeace provides a unique psychiatric hospital; a comprehensive range of residential treatment programs; accredited educational services; and a variety of foster care and community-based treatment programs to help people in need overcome challenges and transform their lives.

Michael Slack, President & CEO
Michael Callan, Chief Financial Officer
Matthew Koval, Chief Medical Officer

5025 National Center for Missing & Exploited Children
333 John Carlyle Street, Suite 125
Alexandria, VA 22314
703-224-2150
Fax: 703-224-2122
www.missingkids.com

Private, nonprofit organization, co-founded in 1984 by John Walsh, whose son Adam was abducted and murdered. NCMEC serves as a focal point in providing assistance to parents, children, law enforcement, schools and the community in recovering missing children and raising public awareness about ways to help prevent child abduction, molestation and sexual exploitation. NCMEC spends 94 cents of every dollar directly on programs and services.

Michelle C. DeLaune, President & CEO
Derrick Driscoll, Chief Operating Officer
Paul J. Beriault, Chief Financial Officer

5026 National Children's Advocacy Center
210 Pratt Avenue
Huntsville, AL 35801
256-533-5437
www.nationalcac.org

A nonprofit organization that provides training, prevention, intervention and treatment services to fight child abuse and neglect.

Chris Newlin, Executive Director
Jonathan Kingsford, Finance Director
Cynthia Parker, Development Director

5027 National Children's Alliance
921 Pennsylvania Avenue SE
Washington, DC 20003
202-548-0090
www.nationalchildrensalliance.org

Nationwide nonprofit membership organization which promotes and supports communities in providing a coordinated investigation and response to victims of severe child abuse.

Teresa Huizar, Chief Executive Director
Kim Day, Vice President, Programs
Dave Betz, Vice President, Operations

5028 National Exchange Club Foundation
3050 W Central Avenue
Toledo, OH 43606
419-535-3232
info@nationalexchangeclub.org
www.nationalexchangeclub.org

Committed to making a difference in the lives of children, families and communities through its national project, the prevention of child abuse.

5029 Prevent Child Abuse America
33 N Dearborn Street, Suite 2300
Chicago, IL 60602
312-663-3520
info@preventchildabuse.org
www.preventchildabuse.org

Mission is to prevent the abuse and neglect of the nation's children. Supports education and research.

Melissa T. Merrick, President & CEO

5030 Project Cuddle
2973 Harbor Boulevard, Suite 326
Costa Mesa, CA 92626
714-432-9681
888-628-3353
info@projectcuddle.org
www.projectcuddle.org

Safe infant abandonment, nationwide, 24-hour crisis line. All calls are confidential. Help in finding a safe, legal alternative to abandonment.

Debbe Magnusen, Founder

5031 RAINN (Rape, Abuse & Incest National Network)
www.rainn.org
202-544-3064
800-656-HOPE
www.rainn.org

Operates a 24 hour national sexual assault hotline and carries out programs to prevent sexual assault, help victims and ensure that rapists are brought to justice.

Scott Berkowitz, President & Founder
Sarah Glowa-Kollish, Consulting Services Operations
Caprecia Miller, Safe Helpline Vice President

5032 Stop It Now!
351 Pleasant Street, Suite B-319
Northampton, MA 01060
413-587-3500
888-PRE-VENT
www.stopitnow.org

Stop It Now! prevents the sexual abuse of children by mobilizing adults, families and communities to take actions that protect children before they are harmed. The nonprofit provides support, information and resources to keep children safe and create healthier communities.

Jenny Coleman, Director

5033 The Kempe Center: For the Prevention & Tre atment of Child Abuse and Neglect
13123 E 16th Avenue B390
Aurora, CO 80045
303-864-5300
kempe.center@ucdenver.edu
http://kempecenter.org

Provides education, clinical services and research on child abuse and neglect. Can provide referrals to local agencies.

Physical & Sexual Abuse / State Agencies & Support Groups

State Agencies & Support Groups

Alaska

5034 **Rid Alaska of Child Abuse**
PO Box 35595
Juneau, AK 99803
800-478-4444
www.ridalaskaofchildabuse.org

Nonprofit organization dedicated to providing resources and information, raising public awareness of the occurrence of child abuse, lessening the stigma placed on child sexual abuse victims/survivors, promoting child safety and abuse prevention programs, researching and posting safety tips and maintaining a website.

Debra Gerrish, President/State Coordinator
Tia M Holley, VP
Patti Fay Hickox, Treasurer/Secretary

Arizona

5035 **Crisis Nursery**
2334 East Polk Street
Phoenix, AZ 85006
602-273-7363
Fax: 602-244-1316
cninfo1@crisisnurseryphx.com
www.crisisnurseryphx.org

Offers hope and support, through prevention and protection, to children in our community threatened with abuse and neglect. Since 1977, over 13,000 children have found a safe refuge at Crisis Nursery. Its mission is to provide a last resort for parents and families who are simply overwhelmed, a safe and healthy place for children who can no longer remain with their families, a temporary home for children who haven't one to call their own and a transitional placement with follow up for services.

Marsha Porter, Executive Director

California

5036 **Child Sexual Abuse Treatment Program (Giar retto)**
EMQ Children & Family Services
232 E Gish Road
San Jose, CA 95112
408-453-7616
csc@emq.org
www.emq.org

Sexual abuse treatment center

F Jerome Doyle, CEO
Kristine Austin, Director Public Relations

Georgia

5037 **Prevent Child Abuse Georgia**
PO Box 3995
Atlanta, GA 30302
404-413-1281
800-244-5373
Fax: 404-413-1299
www.preventchildabusega.org

Private, statewide, community-based nonprofit organization with the sole mission of preventing child abuse and neglect.

Doug Middleton, Executive Director
Sonda Abernathy, College Facilities Manager
Frances Marine, Director of Communications

Illinois

5038 **Prevent Child Abuse Illinois**
528 S 5th Street, Suite 211
Springfield, IL 62701
217-522-1129
Fax: 217-522-0655
www.preventchildabuseillinois.org

Roy Harley, Executive Director

Indiana

5039 **Prevent Child Abuse Indiana**
3833 N Meridian Suite 101
Indianapolis, IN 46208
317-775-6439
888-542-7064
Fax: 317-775-6420
Generalinfo.pcain@villages.org
www.pcain.org

Sandy Runkle, Manager

Iowa

5040 **Prevent Child Abuse Iowa**
505 Fifth Avenue, Suite 900
Des Moines, IA 50309
515-244-2200
Fax: 515-280-7835
sscott@pcaiowa.org
www.pcaiowa.org

Stephen Scott, Executive Director

New York

5041 **Child Abuse Prevention Project: Be'ad HaYeled (For the Sake of the Child)**
Board of Jewish Education of Greater New York
135 West 50th Street
New York, NY 10020
212-582-9100
Fax: 646-472-5421
admin@jbfcs.org
www.bjeny.org

Be'ad HaYeled was created in 1995 specifically for the Jewish community by the Board of Jewish Education of Greater New York and the Jewish Board of Family and Children's Services. Training workshops give educators, parents and communal workers the skills needed to recognize signs of abuse and to intervene in an effective and appropriate manner Halachically, clinically and legally. Additional programs deal with parenting methods, communication skills and other relevant family issues.

Martin Haber, President

5042 **Prevent Child Abuse New York**
33 Elk Street Suite 201
Albany, NY 12207
518-445-1273
Fax: 518-436-5889
cdeyss@preventchildabuseny.org
www.preventchildabuseny.org

Not-for-profit agency whose singular mission is to prevent child abuse in all its forms. Prevent Child Abuse New York is a chartered state chapter of Prevent Child Abuse America.

Christine Deyss, Executive Director
Jennifer Matrazzo, Associate Executive Director

North Carolina

5043 **Prevent Child Abuse North Carolina**
3701 National Drive, Suite 211
Raleigh, NC 27612
919-829-8009
Fax: 919-832-0308
info@preventchildabusenc.org
www.prventchildabusenc.org

Statewide not-for-profit organization with the mission of ending child abuse in the state of North Carolina.

Rosie Allen, CEO

Physical & Sexual Abuse / Libraries & Resource Centers

Virginia

5044 **Childhelp Children's Center of Virginia**
11230 Waples Mill Road #105
Fairfax, VA 22030
703-208-1500
Fax: 703-208-1540
www.childhelpusa.org/regional/virginia2

Dedicated to meeting the physical, emotional and spiritual needs of abused and neglected children through focusing its efforts and resources upon treatment, prevention and research.

Stanley D Beder

Libraries & Resource Centers

5045 **Child Welfare Information Gateway**
Children's Burea/ACYF
1250 Maryland Avenue SW, 8th Floor
Washington, DC 20024
703-385-7565
800-394-3366
Fax: 703-385-3206
info@childwelfare.gov
www.childwelfare.gov

The National Clearinghouse on Child Abuse and Neglect Information and the National Adoption Information Clearinghouse have consolidated and expanded to create the Child Welfare Information Gateway. It is a service of the US DHHS and provides access to information and resources to help protect children and strengthen families.

Conferences

5046 **Annual New York State Child Abuse Prevention Conference**
33 Elk Street, Suite 201
Albany, NY 12207
518-445-1273
800-244-5373
Fax: 518-436-5889
www.preventchildabuseny.org/conf06/

Presented by Prevent Child Abuse New York, a not-for-profit agency whose singular mission is to prevent child abuse in all its forms. PCANY is a chartered state chapter of Prevent Child Abuse America. Conference attendees include those who work in home-based and center-based family support programs, child abuse prevention and child protective services, intervention and treatment, health care and mental health, schools, religious and civic organizations, and parents, themselves.

Christine Deyss, Executive Director
Robin Christenson, President
Dean Geesler, Vice President

Audio Video

5047 **Break the Silence: Kids Against Child Abuse**
The Health Connection
55 W Oak Ridge Drive
Hagerstown, MD 21740
301-393-3270
800-765-6955
Fax: 888-294-8405
www.adventistbookcenter.com/resources/health-connect

Jane Seymore explains physical abuse, sexual abuse and neglect. Animation illustrates each story. All the stories end happily, and the main point is that children should tell a trusted adult. 28 minutes. Grades 1-5.
1994

5048 **I Am the Boss of My Body: Preventing Child Sexual Abuse**
The Health Connection
55 W Oak Ridge Drive
Hagerstown, MD 21740
301-393-3270
800-765-6955
Fax: 888-294-8405
www.adventistbookcenter.com/resources/health-connect

Children feel empowered when they see this video and learn that they have the authority and the right to say no to any touch that makes them feel strange. Grades 1-4.
1999 18 Minutes

Web Sites

5049 **American Professional Society on the Abuse of Children**
590 Avenue of the Americas, 14th Floor
New York, NY 10011
877-402-7722
apsac@apsac.org
www.apsac.org

Dedicated to providing professional education which promotes effective, culturally sensitive and interdisciplinary approaches to the identification, intervention, treatment and prevention of child abuse and neglect.

Lorrie Brennan, Director

5050 **Bikers Against Child Abuse**
www.bacausa.com

www.bacausa.com

Has the intent to create a safer environment for abused children. An established, united body of bikers in a stand to empower children to not feel afraid of the world in which they live. They work in conjunction with local officials who are already in place to protect children.

Scootr , President
Pipes , Vice President

5051 **Child Abuse Legislation**
www.childabuse.com/legislat.htm

www.childabuse.com/legislat.htm

Prevention through education and awareness.

5052 **Child Abuse Prevention Network**
child-abuse.com

child-abuse.com

For professionals in the field of child abuse and neglect. Child maltreatment, physical abuse, psychological maltreatment, neglect, sexual abuse and emotional abuse and neglect are the key areas of concern. Provides unique and powerful tools for all workers to support the identification, investigation, treatment, adjudication and prevention of child abuse and neglect.

5053 **Child Abuse Quilts: Revealing and Healing the Pain of Child Abuse**
mbgoodman.tripod.com/caq/caq1.html

mbgoodman.tripod.com/caq/caq1.html

Site shows 28 quilts made dealing with the subject of child abuse, child abuse prevention and violence against children. Some of the quiltmakers knew the pain of abuse first hand, others knew it through the eyes of others, often close family members. Quilts are displayed in the hope that each person who sees them will leave re-awakened to the tragedy of child abuse and resolved to prevent it.

5054 **Child Abuse.com**
1231 W. Northern Lights Blvd, STE 458
Anchorage, AL 99503
www.childabuse.com

Comprehensive resource bringing awareness and education in preventing child abuse and related issues. The site was created to inform, support and encourage those dealing with any aspect of child abuse, in a positive non-threatening environment.

5055 **Child Trauma Academy**
www.childtraumaacademy.com

www.childtraumaacademy.com

Provides information on free online courses that offer creative and practical approaches to understanding and working with maltreated children.

Physical & Sexual Abuse / Book Publishers

5056 Children's Bureau
Department of Health & Human Services
330 C Street SW
Washington, DC 20201   www.acf.hhs.gov/programs/cb

The Children's Bureau (CB) partners with federal, state, tribal and local agencies to improve the overall health and well-being of the nation's children and families. Provides support and guidance to programs that focus on preventing child abuse and neglect and protecting children when abuse or neglect has occurred.

Aysha E. Schomburg, Associate Commissioner

5057 Children's House
child-abuse.com/childhouse/

child-abuse.com/childhouse/

An interactive resource center and meeting place for the exchange of information that serves the well-being of children.

5058 Connect for Kids
Benton Foundation
P.O. Box 45372
Westlake, OH 44145   440-250-5563
info@connectingforkids.org
www.connectforkids.org

Family-friendly politics and information on how to connect with hundreds of groups working on behalf of children.

Kathy Nash, President
Andrea Campesino, Secretary
Rebecca Baker, Treasurer

5059 Intrafamilial (Incest) Abuse Resources
www.vachss.com/help_text/incest.html

www.vachss.com/help_text/incest.html

Many resources on the subject of child abuse, both physical and sexual.

5060 KidsPeace
4085 Independence Drive
Schnecksville, PA 18078   800-257-3223
www.kidspeace.org

KidsPeace is a private charity dedicated to serving the behavioral and mental health needs of children, families and communities. Founded in 1882, KidsPeace provides a unique psychiatric hospital; a comprehensive range of residential treatment programs; accredited educational services; and a variety of foster care and community-based treatment programs to help people in need overcome challenges and transform their lives.

Michael Slack, President & CEO
Michael Callan, Chief Financial Officer
Matthew Koval, Chief Medical Officer

5061 Making Daughters Safe Again
mdsa-online.org

mdsa-online.org

Is the only organization in the world specializing in mother-daughter sexual abuse. We are also distinguished by the innovative online group experience we provide for survivors.

5062 National Council on Child Abuse & Family Violence
1025 Connecticut Avenue NW, Suite 1000
Washington, DC 20036   202-429-6695
Fax: 202-521-3479
info@nccafv.org
www.nccafv.org

Providing intergenerational violence prevention services since 1984.

5063 Pandora's Box
www.prevent-abuse-now.com

www.prevent-abuse-now.com

Offers more than 270 pages of resource information on child abuse prevention and child protection.

5064 Prevent Child Abuse America
33 N Dearborn Street, Suite 2300
Chicago, IL 60602   312-663-3520
info@preventchildabuse.org
www.preventchildabuse.org

Providing and inspiring hope to everyone involved in the effort to prevent the abuse and neglect of our nations children. Working with 40 statewide chapters to provide leadership in promoting and implementing prevention efforts at both the national and local levels.

Melissa T. Merrick, President & CEO

5065 Prevent Child Abuse California
P.O. Box 6400
Columbia, MD 21045   410-381-0911
Fax: 410-381-0924
www.pca.org

Mission is to prevent child abuse in all its forms by maximizing resources throughout the state of California.

Caren Cooper, President
Thomas Gorsuch, Vice President
Cindy Jacisin, Secretary

5066 RAINN (Rape, Abuse & Incest National Network)
www.rainn.org

202-544-3064
800-656-HOPE
www.rainn.org

Operates a 24 hour national sexual assault hotline and carries out programs to prevent sexual assault, help victims and ensure that rapists are brought to justice.

Scott Berkowitz, President & Founder
Sarah Glowa-Kollish, Consulting Services Operations
Caprecia Miller, Safe Helpline Vice President

5067 Sibling Abuse Survivors' Information & Advocacy Network
www.sasian.org

www.sasian.org

Provides information about problems associated with domestic sibling incest abuse.

5068 Stop Child Abuse Now
www.efn.org/~scan/scan.html

www.efn.org/~scan/scan.html

Is a nonprofit organization dedicated to stopping child abuse of all forms, and improving the lives of survivors of all types of abuse and loss. By speaking out about abuse, we increase the public's awareness of the prevalence of abuse. Our goal is to join with other organizations and individuals who wish to ultimately put a stop to child abuse.

Book Publishers

5069 A Child Called It: One Child's Courage to Survive
Dave Pelzer, author

Health Communications, Inc (HCI)
3201 SW 15th Street
Deerfield Beach, FL 33442   954-360-0909
800-441-5569
Fax: 954-360-0034
www.hci-online.com

The author's true story of abuse he suffered as a child.

Physical & Sexual Abuse / Pamphlets

ISBN: 1-558743-66-9

5070 Body Language of the Abused Child

Jacqueline A Rankin, author

Rankin File/Signature Book Printing
8041 Cessna Avenue
Gaithersburg, MD 20879

301-258-8353
Fax: 301-670-4147
book@sbpbooks.com
www.signaturebook.com/Books/rankin.htm

Uses body language to identify a suspected victim.

1999 271 pages Paperback
ISBN: 1-887711-06-6

5071 It's My Body

Lory Freeman, author

Parenting Press
PO Box 75267
Seattle, WA 98175

206-364-2900
800-992-6657
Fax: 206-364-0702
www.parentingpress.com

Helps adults and preschool children talk about sexual abuse together. Introduces touching codes children can use for their protection. Ages 3-8.

32 pages Paperback
ISBN: 1-403408-96-3

5072 My Body is Mine, My Feelings are Mine

Susan Hoke, author

YouthLight
714 Cove Trail, PO Box 115
Chapin, SC 29036

800-209-9774
Fax: 803-345-0888
yl@sc.rr.com
www.youthlightbooks.com

For K-5th grade. First part to be read to children, the second part teaches adults how to educate children about body safety. Sexual victimization can be prevented through explanation of how to identify inappropriate touching and what to do about it.

77 pages Paperback

5073 Out of Harm's Way: A Parent's Guide to Pro tecting Young Children from Sexual Abuse

Janie Hart-Rossi, author

Parenting Press
PO Box 75267
Seattle, WA 98175

206-364-2900
800-992-6657
Fax: 206-364-0702
www.parentingpress.com

An authoritative and objective look at child sexual abuse, which can be used at home and in school, or as a complement to existing school safety curricula. It describes how community members or extended family members might groom a child for abuse, as well as how to watch for such grooming and how to discuss it with children.

32 pages Paperback

Homer J Henderson, Operations Manager

5074 Something Happened and I'm Scared to Tell

Patricia Kehoe PhD, author

Parenting Press
PO Box 75267
Seattle, WA 98175

206-364-2900
800-992-6657
Fax: 206-364-0702
www.parentingpress.com

With the help of a friendly lion, a young sexual abuse victim is able to talk about sexual abuse and recover self-esteem. A gentle and positive approach to reassure children. Ages 3-7.

32 pages Paperback
ISBN: 0-943990-28-9

5075 Soul Murder Revisited

Leonard Shengold, author

Yale University Press
PO Box 209040
New Haven, CT 06520

203-432-0960
800-405-1619
Fax: 203-432-0948
marketing@yale.edu.
yalepress.yale.edu/yupbooks

Further reflections on how abuse occurs and its consequences. Discusses the psychopathology of soul murder and appropriate therapy for victims.

2000 336 pages Paperback
ISBN: 0-300086-99-7

John Donatich, Director

5076 Treating Abused and Traumatized Children

Eliana Gil, author

Guilford Press
72 Spring Street
New York, NY 10012

800-365-7006
Fax: 212-966-6708
info@guilford.com
www.guilford.com

The author presents a program combining play, art, and expressive therapies, with strategies from cognitave-behvior therapy and family therapy, as she demonstrates how to tailor the treatment to the needs of each child. Paperback or e-book.

2006 254 pages Paperback
ISBN: 1-593853-34-1

Bob Matloff, President
Seymour Weingarten, Editor-in-Chief

5077 Trouble with Secrets

Karen Johnson, author

Parenting Press
PO Box 75267
Seattle, WA 98175

206-364-2900
800-992-6657
Fax: 206-364-0702
www.parentingpress.com

Helps children distinguish between secrets that should be kept and those that shouldn't.

32 pages Paperback
ISBN: 0-943990-22-X

Pamphlets

5078 Understanding SBS/Shaken Impact Syndrome B rochure

National Center on Shaken Baby Syndrome
1433 N 1075 W Ste 110
Farmington, UT 84025

801-447-9360
888-273-0071
Fax: 801-447-9364
www.dontshake.com

Information brochure on shaken baby syndrome.

Jill Moore, Chairperson
Lori Frasier, Vice Chairperson
Ryan Steinbeigle, Executive Director

Description

5079 PICA

Involves the following Biologic System(s):
Developmental/Behavioral/Psychiatric Disorders

Pica is a type of eating disorder characterized by the recurrent or chronic ingestion of nonfood or nonnutritive substances such as dirt, flaking paint or plaster, clay, charcoal, ashes, wool, and other nonfoods. Although this psychological disorder usually commences during the first or second year of life, some children are affected during infancy. The pattern should last at least one month to fit the diagnosis of pica. Pica is often self-limiting with resolution occurring during the childhood years; however, sometimes it may persist into adolescence or adulthood. If the symptoms associated with pica occur initially in older children or adults (e.g., pregnant women), this is usually indicative of a nutritional deficiency, such as iron or zinc, rather than a psychological disorder.

Children who are intellectually disabled are particularly susceptible to development of this unusual disorder. Other factors that may influence the evolution of pica include environmental influences such as family discord, lack of or ineffective nurturing, and nutritional and emotional neglect. In addition, pica is sometimes associated with certain psychiatric disorders.

Children who eat nonfood or nonnutritive substances may be at risk of developing certain types of parasitic infections. For example, the ingestion of dirt (geophagia) may result in toxocariasis, an infection resulting from the spread of the larvae of the common roundworm (Toxocara canis) throughout the body. Symptoms of toxocariasis are often mild and may include fever, weakness, and discomfort. Other children may develop a cough, wheezing, enlarged liver (hepatomegaly), and eye lesions. In addition, another parasitic infection known as toxoplasmosis may develop from dirt ingestion. This common parasitic infection is caused by Toxoplasma gondii and may produce no symptoms or may sometimes be characterized by rash, fever, and other mononucleosis-type symptoms. In individuals with compromised immune systems, toxoplasmosis may result in more serious, widespread disease. Children who eat paint, paint dust, or paint flakes are at risk of developing lead poisoning that may damage the central nervous system, red blood cells, and digestive system.

Any nutritional deficiencies and other medical problems, such as lead toxicity, should be addressed. Treatment emphasizes psychosocial, environmental, and family education approaches. Nutritional supplements may be considered.

National Associations & Support Groups

5080 American Academy of Pediatrics
345 Park Blvd
Itasca, IL 60143
847-434-4000
800-433-9016
Fax: 847-434-8000
csc@aap.org
www.aap.org

The American Academy of Pediatrics and its member pediatricians are committed to the attainment of optimal physical, mental and social health and well-being for all infants, children, adolescents, and young adults.
Kyle E. Yasuda, MD, FAAP, President
Mark Del Monte, JD, CEO/Executive VP
Vera Tait, MD, FAAP, Chief Medical Officer

5081 International Association of Eating Disorders Professionals Foundation
PO Box 1295
Pekin, IL 61555
800-800-8126
iaedpmembers@earthlink.net
www.iaedp.com

The International Association of Eating Disorders Professionals provides first-quality education and high-level training standards to an international multidisciplinary group of various healthcare treatment providers and helping professions, who treat the full spectrum of eating disorder problems.
Bonnie Harken, Executive Director
Blanche Williams, Director, International Affairs
Marie Grover, Director, Events Manager

5082 Mental Health America
500 Montgomery Street, Ste 820
Alexandria, VA 22314
703-684-7722
800-969-6642
Fax: 703-684-5968
www.mentalhealthamerica.net

MHA, the leading advocacy organization addressing the full spectrum of mental and substance use conditions and their effects nationwide, works to inform, advocate and enable access to quality behavioral health services for all Americans.
Paul Gionfriddo, President/CEO
Whitney Ball, Assoc. Dir., Marketing/Outreach
Sachin Doshi, Sr. Dir, Finance/Operations

5083 NIH/National Institute of Mental Health Eating Disorders Program
6001 Executive Boulevard, Room 8184
Bethesda, MD 20892
301-443-4513
Fax: 301-443-4279

5084 National Alliance on Mental Illness (NAMI)
4301 Wilson Blvd., Suite 300
Arlington, VA 22203
703-524-7600
888-999-6264
info@nami.org
www.nami.org

NAMI provides advocacy, education, support and public awareness so that all individuals and families affected by mental illness can build better lives.
Daniel H. Gillison, CEO
David Levy, CFO
Ken Duckworth, Chief Medical Officer

5085 National Eating Disorders Association (NED A)
333 Mamaroneck Avenue, Suite 214
White Plains, NY 10605
212-575-6200
info@NationalEatingDisorders.org
www.nationaleatingdisorders.org

The National Eating Disorders Association (NEDA) is the largest not-for-profit organization in the United States working to prevent eating disorders and provide treatment referrals to those suffering from anorexia, bulimia and binge eating disorder and those concerned with body image and weight issues.
Elizabeth Thompson, Chief Executive Officer
Sarah Chase, VP, Communications & Marketing
Lauren Smolar, VP, Mission & Education

5086 National Mental Health Consumers' Self-Help Clearinghouse
1211 Chestnut Street, Suite 1207
Philadelphia, PA 19107
215-751-1810
800-553-4539
Fax: 215-636-6312
selfhelpclearinghouse@gmail.com
www.mhselfhelp.org

Offers information, support and appropriate referrals; and promotes public and professional education. Provides networking for those with special interests related to albinism. Promotes and supports research and funding that will improve diagnosis and management of albinism and hypopigmentation.
Joseph Rogers, Founder/Executive Director
Susan Rogers, Director

Web Sites

5087 Eating Disorder Referrals
www.eating-disorder-referral.com/pica.php

866-690-7238
www.eating-disorder-referral.com/pica.php

A free referral resource with listings across the nation. Can also access by phone, toll free at 866-323-5608

5088 KidsHealth for Parents
kidshealth.org/en/parents/pica.html

kidshealth.org/en/parents/pica.html

General overview of pica.
Neil Izenberg, MD, Editor-in-Chief & Founder

5089 Pica Information Page
archive.tobacco.org/resources/health/pica

archive.tobacco.org/resources/health/pica

A small group of citizens that seeks to alert the public about a new category of hazardous waste.

Description

5090 PINWORM (ENTEROBIUS VERMICULARIS)

Synonyms: Enterobiasis, Oxyuriasis, Threadworm

Involves the following Biologic System(s):

Infectious Disorders

Pinworm infection (enterobiasis) refers to a common condition in which small, white, parasitic worms (Enterobius vermicularis) infect the human intestinal tract. Such infection results from ingestion of parasitic eggs. The eggs hatch in the stomach, and the larvae then typically migrate to and grow within the upper part of the large intestine (cecum). On rare occasions, pinworms may migrate to the vagina of affected girls, potentially causing such symptoms as vaginal irritation or itching. Pinworms can also cause appendicitis, cystitis (infection of the urinary tract), and diverticulitis (inflammation from out-pouchings in the colon (large intestinal tract).

At night, pinworms migrate from the intestines to the anal region where they deposit their eggs, potentially causing itching (pruritus), irritation, and sleeplessness. Scratching often results in reinfestation from ingestion of eggs that become imbedded under the fingernails and are inadvertently deposited in the mouth. Parasitic eggs are also often deposited from the anal area onto clothing, bedding, furniture, or toys, where they may then be transferred from the fingers to the mouth, causing reinfection or infection of others. In addition, in some cases, eggs may be inhaled from the air and swallowed. Parasitic eggs may remain viable for up to three weeks at regular room temperature.

The diagnosis of enterobiasis is made by detecting parasitic eggs or pinworms. The eggs or worms may be obtained by pressing sticky tape against the perianal region of affected children during early morning hours before the children awaken. The tape is then examined under a microscope to verify the presence of pinworms or eggs. In addition, pinworms may sometimes be detected by the naked eye. Treatment may include the administration of drugs that destroy pinworms (anthelmintic drugs), such as pyrantel pamoate or mebendazole, and, in some patients, topical anti-itch ointments that help relieve itching and irritation. Anthelmintic medications should also be given to all other members of the household. Handwashing after going to the bathroom and before meals is critical. Linens should be washed thoroughly.

Enterobiasis is a very common infection that may occur in individuals of all ages. However, children between the ages of five to 14 years are most commonly affected.

Government Agencies

5091 NIH/ Eunice Kennedy Shriver National Institute of Child Health & Human Development
P.O. Box 3006
Rockville, MD 20847
800-370-2943
Fax: 866-760-5947
www.nichd.nih.gov

Conducts and supports research on topics related to the health of children, adults, families and populations. Some of these topics include: developmental disabilities, growth and development, infant death, reproductive health and birth defects.

Diana W. Bianchi, Director
Alison Cernich, PhD, Deputy Director

5092 NIH/National Institute of Allergy and Infectious Diseases
5601 Fishers Lane, MSC 9806
Bethesda, MD 20892
301-496-5717
866-284-4107
Fax: 301-402-3573
TDD: 800-877-8339
ocpostoffice@niaid.nih.gov
www.niaid.nih.gov

The principal advisory board of the NIAID. The council is composed of physicians, scientists and representatives of the public and advises on the conduct and support or research, training and dissemination of health information regarding allergies and infectious diseases.

Anthony S. Fauci, MD, Director

National Associations & Support Groups

5093 American Academy of Pediatrics
345 Park Blvd
Itasca, IL 60143
847-434-4000
800-433-9016
Fax: 847-434-8000
csc@aap.org
www.aap.org

The American Academy of Pediatrics and its member pediatricians are committed to the attainment of optimal physical, mental and social health and well-being for all infants, children, adolescents, and young adults.

Kyle E. Yasuda, MD, FAAP, President
Mark Del Monte, JD, CEO/Executive VP
Vera Tait, MD, FAAP, Chief Medical Officer

5094 World Health Organization
Avenue Appia 20
1202 Geneva,
Switzerland
www.who.int

WHO is the directing and coordinating authority for health within the United Nations system. WHO operates in more than 150 countries around the world.

Dr. Tedros Adhanom Ghebreyesus, Director General
Dr. Zsuzsanna Jakab, Deputy Director General
Stewart Simonson, Asst Director General, UN NYC

Web Sites

5095 KidsHealth for Parents
kidshealth.org

kidshealth.org

Signs, symptoms, doagnosis, and treatment of pinworms.
Neil Izenberg, MD, Editor-in-Chief & Founder

5096 MayoClinic.com
www.mayoclinic.com/health/pinworm/DS00687

www.mayoclinic.com/health/pinworm/DS00687

Introduction, risk factors, prevention and treatment of pinworms.

Pamphlets

5097 Pinworm Infection
CDC
13400 E. Shea Blvd.
Scottsdale, AZ 85259
480-301-8000
800-446-2279
www.mayoclinic.org/about-mayo-clinic

Pinworm infection factsheet provided by the CDC.

Pityriasis Rosea / Description

Description

5098 PITYRIASIS ROSEA
Involves the following Biologic System(s):
Dermatologic Disorders, Infectious Disorders

Pityriasis rosea is an inflammatory skin condition that may develop at any age but mostly commonly affects children and young adults. In some cases, the onset of the condition may be preceded by certain generalized symptoms, such as fever, inflammation of the throat (pharyngitis), and muscle and joint pain (myalgia and arthralgia). Pityriasis rosea typically begins with the development of a single oval or round patch known as a herald patch. This patch is usually red, pink, or light brown with a raised border and is covered with fine scales. A herald patch varies in diameter from one to 10 centimeters and may occur anywhere on the body. About five to 10 days after the appearance of the herald patch, there is a widespread eruption of similar, smaller patches (lesions), particularly on the torso and upper arms and thighs. These lesions, which are less than one centimeter in diameter, are usually slightly raised, oval or round, and red, pink, or light brown. In addition, they may be scaly and tend to peel. Lesions may continue to appear over several days and develop on other areas of the body, such as the forearms and calves, face, and scalp. The lesions are typically distributed along the subtle lines in the skin that indicate the direction of skin fibers (Langer's or cleavage lines). Some individuals with the condition may experience no associated symptoms (asymptomatic). Others may experience mild to severe itching (pruritus). Pityriasis rosea is a self-limited condition that has a duration of approximately two to 12 weeks, with an average of approximately four to five weeks. As skin lesions heal, affected areas may have abnormally increased or diminished pigmentation (postinflammatory hyperpigmentation or hypopigmentation) that gradually resolves after several weeks or months.

If individuals with pityriasis rosea experience no associated symptoms, treatment may not be necessary. Those with widespread lesions and scaling may benefit from using a cream that softens the skin (emollient). Associated itching may be relieved by lubricating lotions that contain the natural compounds camphor or menthol or medicated skin creams, such as a nonfluorinated topical corticosteroid. Certain medications taken by mouth such as oral antihistamines may help those who experience bothersome itching while attempting to sleep. Antihistamines, which are medications that often induce drowsiness, reduce the effects of histamine, a chemical that is released during allergic inflammatory reactions.

The cause of pityriasis rosea is unknown. However, many researchers speculate that the condition results from infection with a viral agent.

Government Agencies

5099 NIH/National Institute of Arthritis and Musculoskeletal and Skin Diseases
1 AMS Circle
Bethesda, MD 20892
301-495-4484
877-226-4267
Fax: 301-718-6366
TDD: 301-565-2966
niamsinfo@mail.nih.gov
www.niams.nih.gov

The mission of the NIAMS, a part of the NIH, is to support research into the causes, treatment and prevention of arthritis and musculoskeletal and skin diseases, the training of basic and clinical scientists to carry out this research, and the dissemination of information on research progress in these diseases.
Lindsey A. Criswell, MD, Director
Rick Phillips, Executive Officer

National Associations & Support Groups

5100 American Academy of Dermatology
P.O. Box 1968
Des Plaines, IL 60017
847-240-1280
888-462-3376
mrc@aad.org
www.aad.org

To promote and advance the art of medicine and surgery of the skin; promote the highest possible standards in clinical practice, education and research in dermatology and related disciplines.

5101 American Academy of Pediatrics
345 Park Blvd
Itasca, IL 60143
847-434-4000
800-433-9016
Fax: 847-434-8000
csc@aap.org
www.aap.org

The American Academy of Pediatrics and its member pediatricians are committed to the attainment of optimal physical, mental and social health and well-being for all infants, children, adolescents, and young adults.
Kyle E. Yasuda, MD, FAAP, President
Mark Del Monte, JD, CEO/Executive VP
Vera Tait, MD, FAAP, Chief Medical Officer

5102 Society for Pediatric Dermatology
8365 Keystone Crossing, Ste 107
Indianapolis, IN 46240
317-202-0224
Fax: 317-205-9481
info@pedsderm.net
www.pedsderm.net

The objective of the Society is to promote, develop and advance education, research and care of skin disease in all pediatric age groups.
Kent Lindeman, Executive Director

Web Sites

5103 DermNet NZ: The Dermatology Resource
www.dermnetnz.org

www.dermnetnz.org

Information about the skin from the New Zealand Dermatological Society.
Marius Rademaker, Chairperson
Anthony Young, Secretary
Sandra Winhoven, Treasurer

Journals

5104 Pediatric Dermatology Journal
Society for Pediatric Dermatology
8365 Keystone Crossing, Suite 107
Indianapolis, IN 46240
317-202-0224
Fax: 317-205-9481
info@pedsderm.net
www.pedsderm.net

Answers the need for new ideas and strategies for today's pediatrician or dermatologist.
6 issues/yr
Kent Lindeman, Executive Director

Pamphlets

5105 Pityriasis Rosea
American Academy of Dermatology
9500 W. Bryn Mawr Avenue, Ste 500
Rosemont, IL 60018

847-240-1737
888-462-3376
Fax: 847-240-1859
info@aad.org
www.aad.org

Discusses the appearance, symptoms, and causes of this common rash. Diagnosis and treatment are also explained.

Pkgs of 50

Irvin Bomberger, Interim Executive Director

Pneumonia / Description

Description

5106 PNEUMONIA
Involves the following Biologic System(s):
Infectious Disorders, Respiratory Disorders

Pneumonia refers to a group of disorders characterized by an acute inflammation of the lungs. The causes of pneumonia are many and may include infection by certain bacteria, viruses, bacteria-like organisms, fungi, yeasts, and protozoa. In addition, noninfectious causes include the inhalation (aspiration) of food or other substances into the airway and lungs, an abnormal response of the immune system to certain substances (hypersensitivity reaction), and an inflammatory response to radiation or certain drugs. Pneumonia may also result as a complication of surgery or injury, due to the impaired ability to cough, breathe deeply, or expel mucus.

Pneumonia in very young children is most commonly caused by certain respiratory viruses, such as RSV, or respiratory syncytial virus; influenza; parainfluenza (the virus that causes croup); and adenoviruses. Symptoms and findings associated with this type of pneumonia in infants and young children may include cough, nasal discharge, fever, rapid breathing (tachypnea), or a bluish color to the skin and mucous membranes (cyanosis). Antibiotics do not treat viral infections, though some viruses are susceptible to new antiviral therapies. Most infants and children recover from viral pneumonia with no complications. However, some may develop subsequent lung irregularities.

Although bacterial pneumonia is not common among children, certain conditions (e.g., viral respiratory illnesses, immune deficiency disorders, certain congenitaldefects, blood irregularities, etc.) may put them at increased risk for developing this type of pneumonia. The most common types of bacteria that cause pneumonia in children include Streptococcus pneumoniae (pneumococcus), Streptococcus pyogenes, Staphylococcus aureus, and Haemophilus influenzae type b. Symptoms associated with bacterial pneumonia vary according to age, type of bacteria involved, and other factors. Infants and young children may develop a stuffy nose and other signs of upper respiratory infection, loss of appetite, sudden onset of fever, restlessness, respiratory distress, and cyanosis. In addition, infants with Staphylococcus aureus infection, a more serious type of disease, may develop lethargy, increased irritability, difficulty breathing (dyspnea), vomiting, or diarrhea. Abscesses may form in the lungs and may lead to the development of air-containing cysts (pneumatoceles). Accumulation of pus, or empyema, may occur in the space surrounding the lungs. Older children and adolescents with bacterial pneumonia may develop symptoms commonly associated with mild upper respiratory tract infection followed by chills, shaking, fever, drowsiness, rapid breathing, coughing, or chest pain. Treatment for bacterial pneumonia includes the use of appropriate antibiotics. In the case of Staphylococcus aureus infection, drainage of pus accumulations may be indicated. Other treatment is symptomatic and supportive. Vaccination is important for preventing pneumonia in children. Vaccinations against Haemophilus influenzae and Streptococcus pneumoniae in the first year of life have greatly reduced their role in pneumonia in children.

Atypical pneumonias include those resulting from infection by bacteria-like microorganisms such as Mycoplasma pneumoniae and Chlamydia pneumoniae. Symptoms associated with these types of infections include fatigue, sore throat, cough, joint pain, or rash. Treatment may include the use of certain antibiotics.

Children with compromised immune systems are at risk for developing certain types of pneumonia infections caused by fungi (e.g., histoplasmosis, coccidioidomycosis, cryptococcosis, etc.) and other common organisms such as Pneumocystis carinii. Pneumocystis pneumonia is particularly prevalent among individuals with AIDS. Choice of drug therapy relates to the appropriate identification of the causative organism. Other treatment is symptomatic and supportive.

Government Agencies

5107 NIH/National Institute of Allergy and Infectious Diseases
5601 Fishers Lane, MSC 9806
Bethesda, MD 20892

301-496-5717
866-284-4107
Fax: 301-402-3573
TDD: 800-877-8339
ocpostoffice@niaid.nih.gov
www.niaid.nih.gov

The principal advisory board of the NIAID. The council is composed of physicians, scientists and representatives of the public and advises on the conduct and support or research, training and dissemination of health information regarding allergies and infectious diseases.

Anthony S. Fauci, MD, Director

National Associations & Support Groups

5108 American Academy of Pediatrics
345 Park Blvd
Itasca, IL 60143

847-434-4000
800-433-9016
Fax: 847-434-8000
csc@aap.org
www.aap.org

The American Academy of Pediatrics and its member pediatricians are committed to the attainment of optimal physical, mental and social health and well-being for all infants, children, adolescents, and young adults.

Kyle E. Yasuda, MD, FAAP, President
Mark Del Monte, JD, CEO/Executive VP
Vera Tait, MD, FAAP, Chief Medical Officer

5109 March of Dimes Foundation
1550 Crystal Drive, Ste 1300
Arlington, VA 22202

888-663-4637
www.marchofdimes.org

March of Dimes help moms have full-term pregnancies and research the problems that threaten the health of babies. The March of Dimes also acts globally: sharing best practices in perinatal health and helping improve birth outcomes where the needs are the most urgent.

Stacey D. Stewart, President
Alan Brogdon, SVP/COO/Board Officer
Rahul Gupta, MD, SVP & Chief Medical/Health Officer

5110 World Health Organization
Avenue Appia 20
1202 Geneva,
Switzerland

www.who.int

WHO is the directing and coordinating authority for health within the United Nations system. WHO operates in more than 150 countries around the world.

Dr. Tedros Adhanom Ghebreyesus, Director General
Dr. Zsuzsanna Jakab, Deputy Director General
Stewart Simonson, Asst Director General, UN NYC

Research Centers

5111 National Jewish Medical & Research Center
1400 Jackson Street
Denver, CO 80206

303-388-4461
877-225-5654
www.njc.org

National Jewish is a nonsectarian, nonprofit independent clinical research, medical center that focuses on respiratory, immunologic, allergic, and infectious diseases.

Russell P Bowler, President/CEO
J Verne Singleton, COO
Gary Cott MD, Medical & Clinical Services

Web Sites

5112 **American Lung Association**
55 W. Wacker Drive, Suite 1150
Chicago, IL 60601
800-586-4872
info@lung.org
www.lung.org

The American Lung Association fights lung disease in all its forms, with special emphasis on asthma, tobacco control and environmental health. The American Lung Association is funded with contributions from the public, along with gifts and grants from corporations, foundations and government agencies. The association achieves its many successes through the work of thousands of committed volunteers and staff.

Harold P. Wimmer, National President & CEO
Albert Rizzo, MD, Chief Medical Officer
Sue Swan, Chief Development Officer

5113 **Department of Health and Human Services**
5600 Fishers Lane
Rockville, MD 20857
301-427-1364
www.ahrq.gov

Pneumonia research findings for consumers.

5114 **Kid's Health**
kidshealth.org

kidshealth.org

KidsHealth provides doctor-approved health information about children from before birth through adolescense. Kids health provides families with accurate, up to date and jargon free health information they can use.

Neil Izenberg, MD, Editor-in-Chief & Founder

5115 **Mayo Clinic**
13400 E. Shea Blvd.
Scottsdale, AZ 85259
480-301-8000
800-446-2279
www.mayoclinic.com/health/pneumonia/DS00135

5116 **National Jewish Health**
1400 Jackson Street
Denver, CO 80206
877-225-5654
www.nationaljewish.org

National Jewish is a nonsectarian, nonprofit independent clinical research, medical center. Focusing on respiratory, immunologic, allergic, and infectious diseases. The Center's mission is to develop and provide innovative clinical programs for treating and rehabilitating patients of all ages and for preventing disease, discovering knowledge to enhance prevention, treatment and cures through an integrated program of basic and clinical research, and educating professionals and the public.

Michael Salem, MD, President & CEO
Richard Baer, Board Chair
Pamela L. Zeitlin, MD, PhD, Chair, Pediatrics Department

Book Publishers

5117 **Let's Talk About Going to the Hospital**
Rosen Publishing Group's PowerKids Press
29 E 21st Street
New York, NY 10010
212-777-3017
800-237-9932
Fax: 888-436-4643
rosenpub@tribeca.ios.com
www.rosenpublishing.com

If a child has to check into the hospital, chances are he or she is already upset about being ill. Knowing how a hospital functions and what the procedures are, such as when family members can visit, will help in what is already a stressful situation. Grades K-5.

24 pages
ISBN: 0-823950-36-0

Roger Rosen, President

Description

5118 POLYDACTYLY

Synonyms: Polydactylia, Polydactylism

Involves the following Biologic System(s):
Genetic/Chromosomal/Syndrome/Metabolic Disorders, Orthopedic and Muscle Disorders

Poldactyly refers to an abnormality that is present at birth (congenital) in which an infant has more than the usual number of fingers or toes. Defects associated with this abnormality may range from simple skin tags or stumps of flesh to extra fingers or toes that are completely developed. In some families polydactyly is passed from generation to generation.

Polydactyly involving the toes occurs in approximately two out of every 1,000 births. Although the fifth toe is the digit most often duplicated, polydactyly sometimes affects the great or big toe. Careful evaluation is indicated so that treatment of possible associated abnormalities may be appropriately coordinated. However, if the extra digit is small or rudimentary, it may be tied off (ligated) at birth or soon thereafter. This method allows for the digit to spontaneously detach itself after a period of time. In those cases where the digit is jointed, treatment usually involves surgical amputation of the extra digit and repair of other associated structures and tissues. Surgical intervention of this type is usually performed at approximately one year of age.

Duplication of a finger usually appears near the small finger (pinky) or thumb. As in polydactyly of the toes, small, rudimentary digits may be tied off, while more complex deformities typically require surgical intervention at about one year of age.

Polydactyly may also occur in association with several genetic disorders. These disorders include acrocephalopolysyndactyly type II (Carpenter's syndrome), characterized by intellectual disabilities and irregularities involving the head, hand, and genitalia; trisomy 13 syndrome (Patau's syndrome), characterized by cleft lip and palate, polydactyly, intellectual disabilities, and irregularities of the central nervous system, heart, genitalia, and internal organs; chondroectodermal dysplasia (Ellis-van Creveld syndrome), a bone growth disorder characterized by short stature, cardiac defects, polydactyly, and developmental defects of the teeth, and nails (hypoplastic). The efficacy of treating polydactyly associated with these and other disorders depends upon the exact nature of the disorder in question.

Government Agencies

5119 NIH/ Eunice Kennedy Shriver National Institute of Child Health & Human Development
P.O. Box 3006
Rockville, MD 20847
800-370-2943
Fax: 866-760-5947
www.nichd.nih.gov

Conducts and supports research on topics related to the health of children, adults, families and populations. Some of these topics include: developmental disabilities, growth and development, infant death, reproductive health and birth defects.

Diana W. Bianchi, Director
Alison Cernich, PhD, Deputy Director

5120 NIH/National Institute of Arthritis and Musculoskeletal and Skin Diseases
1 AMS Circle
Bethesda, MD 20892
301-495-4484
877-226-4267
Fax: 301-718-6366
TDD: 301-565-2966
niamsinfo@mail.nih.gov
www.niams.nih.gov

The mission of the NIAMS, a part of the NIH, is to support research into the causes, treatment and prevention of arthritis and musculoskeletal and skin diseases, the training of basic and clinical scientists to carry out this research, and the dissemination of information on research progress in these diseases.

Lindsey A. Criswell, MD, Director
Rick Phillips, Executive Officer

National Associations & Support Groups

5121 American Academy of Pediatrics
345 Park Blvd
Itasca, IL 60143
847-434-4000
800-433-9016
Fax: 847-434-8000
csc@aap.org
www.aap.org

The American Academy of Pediatrics and its member pediatricians are committed to the attainment of optimal physical, mental and social health and well-being for all infants, children, adolescents, and young adults.

Kyle E. Yasuda, MD, FAAP, President
Mark Del Monte, JD, CEO/Executive VP
Vera Tait, MD, FAAP, Chief Medical Officer

5122 Genetic Alliance
426400 Woodfield Road, Ste 189
Damascus, MD 20872
202-966-5557
Fax: 202-966-8553
info@geneticalliance.org
www.geneticalliance.org

World's leading nonprofit health advocacy organization committed to transforming health through genetics and promoting an environment of openness centered on the health of individuals, families, and communities.

Sharon Terry, CEO
Ruth Child, CFO
Natasha Bonhomme, Chief Strategy Officer

5123 March of Dimes Foundation
1550 Crystal Drive, Ste 1300
Arlington, VA 22202
888-663-4637
www.marchofdimes.org

March of Dimes help moms have full-term pregnancies and research the problems that threaten the health of babies. The March of Dimes also acts globally: sharing best practices in perinatal health and helping improve birth outcomes where the needs are the most urgent.

Stacey D. Stewart, President
Alan Brogdon, SVP/COO/Board Officer
Rahul Gupta, MD, SVP & Chief Medical/Health Officer

5124 Shriners Hospitals for Children
2900 N Rocky Point Drive
Tampa, FL 33607
800-237-5055
www.shrinerschildrens.org

Shriners Children's has been providing hope and healing to children for more than 100 years. Our compassionate, prestigious doctors and care teams are committed to excellence in pediatric care.

John McCabe, EVP & COO

Web Sites

5125 On The Other Hand
www.ontheotherhand.org

www.ontheotherhand.org

Provides information, support, and suggestions for parents, relatives. and friends of children with hand anomalies.

5126 Polydactyly
www.eatonhand.com/hw/hw024.htm

www.eatonhand.com/hw/hw024.htm

Explanation and general overview of the disorder.

Description

5127 PORPHYRIA

Synonyms: EPP, Erythrohepatic protoporphyria, Ferrochelatase deficiency, Protoporphyria

Involves the following Biologic System(s):
Hematologic and Oncologic Disorders

Porphyria is a rare group of hereditary metabolic disorders characterized by enzyme deficiencies that result in the abnormal accumulation of chemicals known as porphyrins in certain tissues of the body. Porphyrins are formed during the manufacture of heme, the pigmented, iron-containing component of hemoglobin, which is the oxygen-carrying protein in red blood cells. The porphyrias may be classified as erythropoietic or hepatic porphyrias. The erythropoietic porphyrias are characterized by overproduction of porphyrins in the blood-forming tissue of the bone marrow. In individuals with hepatic porphyrias, there is abnormally increased production of porphyrins in the liver. The range and severity of associated symptoms and the age at onset are variable and depend on the underlying enzyme deficiency and the form of porphyria present. Erythropoietic protoporphyria is the most common form of porphyria and is thought to affect approximately one in 5,000 to 10,000 individuals.

In patients with erythropoietic protoporphyria, also known as EPP, deficiency of the enzyme ferrochelatase results in excessive accumulation of protoporphyrin in red blood cells and the fluid portion of the blood (plasma). Excessive protoporphyrin is also concentrated in a liquid secreted by the liver (bile) and is eliminated in the feces. In some patients, abnormal accumulations of protoporphyrin also become deposited within the liver itself.

Symptoms associated with EPP usually begin in childhood before age 10. The most common symptom is an abnormal sensitivity of the skin to sunlight and certain forms of artificial light (photosensitivity). Affected children typically experience pain, burning, and itching of the skin within an hour of exposure to sunlight. Such symptoms are often followed hours later by redness and inflammation of the skin and abnormal accumulation of fluid (edema) beneath the skin in affected areas. However, abnormal burning sensations of the skin may occur in the absence of associated redness or fluid accumulation. Rarely, if sun exposure is prolonged, fluid-filled blisters (vesicles) may develop or there may be bleeding in the skin or mucous membranes, appearing as pinpoint purplish spots (petechiae) or small bluish-purple patches (purpura). Such blistering or bruising may persist for several days after exposure to the sun. In addition, prolonged, repeated sun exposure may cause mild scarring, abnormal thickening of the skin in certain areas, or an abnormality of the nails in which the nails become separated from the nail beds (onycholysis). Although symptoms associated with photosensitivity typically become apparent during infancy or early childhood, the condition sometimes does not occur until adolescence or adulthood.

Many patients with EPP may also develop lumps of solid matter in the gall bladder (gallstones or cholelithiasis) at an unusually early age. The gall bladder is a small, muscular sac under the liver that stores and concentrates bile from the liver. In addition, uncommonly, there may be mildly decreased levels of circulating red blood cells (anemia). Rarely, patients may develop progressive liver damage that may lead to liver failure.

EPP is caused by changes (mutations) in the gene that regulates the production of the enzyme ferrochelatase. This gene is located on the long arm of chromosome 18 (18q21.3). Several different mutations of the gene have been identified in individuals with the disorder. In most cases, EPP has autosomal dominant inheritance. However, there have been reports in which patients inherited two different mutations of the gene, one from each parent. In addition, some individuals who inherit one copy of the disease gene may have slightly elevated levels of protoporphyrin, yet do not experience symptoms associated with the disease.

Patients with EPP benefit from avoiding sunlight, using topical sunscreens, and wearing protective clothing, such as sunglasses, hats, long sleeves, and double layers. Administration of beta-carotene by mouth may help improve tolerance to sunlight. Therapy with cholestyramine, a medication that acts upon the liver's bile acids, may help to alleviate skin symptoms and liver disease. Additional treatment is symptomatic and supportive.

Government Agencies

5128 NIH/ Eunice Kennedy Shriver National Institute of Child Health & Human Development
P.O. Box 3006
Bethesda, MD 20847
800-370-2943
Fax: 866-760-5947
www.nichd.nih.gov

Conducts and supports research on topics related to the health of children, adults, families and populations. Some of these topics include: developmental disabilities, growth and development, infant death, reproductive health and birth defects.

Diana W. Bianchi, Director
Alison Cernich, PhD, Deputy Director

National Associations & Support Groups

5129 American Academy of Pediatrics
345 Park Blvd
Itasca, IL 60143
847-434-4000
800-433-9016
Fax: 847-434-8000
csc@aap.org
www.aap.org

The American Academy of Pediatrics and its member pediatricians are committed to the attainment of optimal physical, mental and social health and well-being for all infants, children, adolescents, and young adults.

Kyle E. Yasuda, MD, FAAP, President
Mark Del Monte, JD, CEO/Executive VP
Vera Tait, MD, FAAP, Chief Medical Officer

5130 American Porphyria Foundation
3475 Valley Road NW
Atlanta, GA 30305
301-347-7166
866-273-3635
general@porphyriafoundation.org
porphyriafoundation.org

Dedicated to improving the health and wellness of individuals and families affected by porphyria through enhanced public awareness; support of research; and development of educational programs and educational material.

Desiree Lyon, Executive Director

5131 Genetic Alliance
426400 Woodfield Road, Ste 189
Damascus, MD 20872
202-966-5557
Fax: 202-966-8553
info@geneticalliance.org
www.geneticalliance.org

World's leading nonprofit health advocacy organization committed to transforming health through genetics and promoting an environment of openness centered on the health of individuals, families, and communities.

Sharon Terry, CEO
Ruth Child, CFO
Natasha Bonhomme, Chief Strategy Officer

5132 **March of Dimes Foundation**
1550 Crystal Drive, Ste 1300
Arlington, VA 22202
888-663-4637
www.marchofdimes.org

March of Dimes help moms have full-term pregnancies and research the problems that threaten the health of babies. The March of Dimes also acts globally: sharing best practices in perinatal health and helping improve birth outcomes where the needs are the most urgent.

Stacey D. Stewart, President
Alan Brogdon, SVP/COO/Board Officer
Rahul Gupta, MD, SVP & Chief Medical/Health Officer

Libraries & Resource Centers

5133 **National Digestive Diseases Information Clearinghouse (NDDIC)**
NIH
2 Information Way
Bethesda, MD 20892
301-654-3810
800-891-5389
Fax: 703-738-4929
nddic@info.niddk.nih.gov
www.digestive.niddk.nih.gov

The National Institute of Diabetes and Digestive and Kidney Diseases conducts and supports research on many of the most serious diseases affecting public health. The Institute supports much of the clinical research on the diseases of internal medicine and related subspecialty fields as well as many basic science disciplines.

Griffin P. Rodgers, MD, Director
Gregory G. Germino, MD, Deputy Director
Kathy Kranzfelder, Communications Director

Newsletters

5134 **APF Newsletter**
American Porphyria Foundation
4900 Woodway, Suite 780
Houston, TX 77056
713-266-9617
866-APF-3635
Fax: 713-840-9552
porphyrus@aol.com
www.porphyriafoundation.com

The newsletter provides updates on treatment and reserach, as well as informative articles on patients and specialists who treat porphyria.

Quarterly

James V. Young, Chairman
Desiree H. Lyon, Executive Director
Dr. William McCutchen, Board Member

Pamphlets

5135 **Porphyria Fact Sheet**
Nat'l Digestive Diseases Information Clearinghouse
2 Information Way
Bethesda, MD 20892
301-496-3583
800-891-5389
Fax: 703-738-4929
nddic@info.niddk.nih.gov
www.niddk.nih.gov

Griffin P. Rodgers, M.D., Director

Post-Traumatic Stress Disorder / Description

Description

5136 POST-TRAUMATIC STRESS DISORDER
Synonym: PTSD
Involves the following Biologic System(s):
Developmental/Behavioral/Psychiatric Disorders

Traumatic events can stay with children for a long time. Such events can range from the rare and horrific, such as severe torture, to more common events such as an automobile accident or a violent crime. With immediate media coverage of violence in our world, children are often exposed to the violent acts of war and terror through the television. Moreover, children may be directly or indirectly affected by events of terror and violence that now pervade our society. Effects of some childhood experiences can last well into adulthood. When the after-effects of a traumatic event are so severe and so persistent that they impair normal childhood functioning, behavior or development, professional help should be considered.

Post-Traumatic Stress Disorder, or PTSD, is a diagnosis made to describe the psychological and physiological symptoms that arise from experiencing, witnessing or participating in a traumatic event. PTSD in a child may result from exposure to a traumatic event which the child experienced or witnessed. It may occur if the child was confronted by death or serious injury, or a threat to the physical integrity of self or others. Studies indicate that 15 to 43% of girls and 14 to 43% of boys have experienced at least one traumatic event in their lifetime. Of those children and adolescents who have experienced a trauma, 3 to 15% of girls and 1 to 6% of boys meet criteria for PTSD. Researchers and clinicians are beginning to recognize that PTSD may not present itself in children in the same way as it does in adults. The classical triad of symptoms includes re-experiencing, numbing of responsiveness, and hyperarousal. Other symptoms include regression, bedwetting, separation anxiety and new fears previously not expressed. Children are also more likely to exhibit their 're-experience' in play. Very young children may present with few PTSD symptoms. Instead, young children may report more generalized fears such as stranger or separation anxiety, avoidance of situations that may or may not be related to the trauma, sleep disturbances, and a preoccupation with words or symbols that may or may not be related to the trauma. Elementary school-aged children may be unable to recall the sequence of the events related to the trauma or believe that there were warning signs that predicted the trauma. PTSD in adolescents may begin to more closely resemble PTSD in adults. Adolescents are more likely to engage in traumatic reenactment in which they incorporate aspects of the trauma into their daily lives. In addition, adolescents are more likely than younger children or adults to exhibit impulsive and aggressive behaviors. Response to traumatic events can also vary from child to child. Some characteristics, however, are common among all children with PTSD. If a child has survived a life-threatening event, there may be a profound sense of guilt, particularly if others did not survive the event. These guilt feelings may be exacerbated if the child had to do extraordinary things to survive. In other cases, a child with PTSD may complain of physical symptoms that have no discernible anatomic or physiological explanation, but which are manifestations of psychic distress; these are known as somatic complaints. The child with PTSD is also liable to experience a range of feelings that make it difficult or impossible for him or her to carry on with life in a normal fashion. They may feel that the trauma they experienced damaged them permanently and irreparably. Children who suffer from PTSD may also experience depression, Obsessive-Compulsive Disorder, social phobia or in the adolescent population, substance abuse.

Therapies include medication and/or psychotherapy. Behavior therapy focuses on helping the child recognize the thought processes that result in traumatic stress reactions. Behavior therapy may involve exposing the patient in a safe and controlled environment to stimuli that prompt a stress reaction; through repeated exposures, the child slowly is desensitized and in time will be able to experience the stimuli without having a stress reaction. As with many psychiatric disorders, treatment often involves some combination of therapy and medication.

Early intervention with skilled providers is vital for successful treatment of children with PTSD.

Government Agencies

5137 National Center for PTSD
www.ptsd.va.gov

802-296-6300
ncptsd@va.gov
www.ptsd.va.gov

A special center within the US Department of Veterans Affairs, which advances clinical care and social welfare through research, education, training and diagnosis.

Paula Schnurr, PhD, Executive Director

National Associations & Support Groups

5138 American Academy of Pediatrics
345 Park Blvd
Itasca, IL 60143

847-434-4000
800-433-9016
Fax: 847-434-8000
csc@aap.org
www.aap.org

The American Academy of Pediatrics and its member pediatricians are committed to the attainment of optimal physical, mental and social health and well-being for all infants, children, adolescents, and young adults.

Kyle E. Yasuda, MD, FAAP, President
Mark Del Monte, JD, CEO/Executive VP
Vera Tait, MD, FAAP, Chief Medical Officer

5139 American Counseling Association
PO Box 31110
Alexandria, VA 22310

800-347-6647
Fax: 800-473-2329
ACAMemberServices@counseling.org
www.counseling.org

Represents professional counselors in various practice settings, and stands ready to serve more than 55,000 members with the resources they need to make a difference. From webinars, publications, and journals to Conference education sessions and legislative action alerts, ACA is where counseling professionals turn for powerful, credible content and support.

Shawn Boynes, Chief Executive Director

5140 American Psychological Association
750 First St. NE
Washington, DC 20002

202-336-5500
800-374-2721
TTY: 202-336-6123
www.apa.org

The mission is to advance the creation, communication and application of psychological knowledge to benefit society and improve people's lives.

Arthur C. Evans Jr, PhD, CEO/EVP

5141 Anxiety and Depression Association of America
8701 Georgia Avenue, Suite 412
Silver Spring, MD 20910
240-485-1018
information@adaa.org
www.adaa.org

ADAA is a national non-profit organization dedicated to the prevention, treatment, and cure of anxiety, depression, OCD, PTSD, and related disorders and to improving the lives of all people who suffer from them through education, practice, and research.

Susan K Gurley, Executive Director
Lise Bram, Deputy Executive Director
Katie Russo, Senior Director, Operations

5142 Association of Traumatic Stress Specialists
5052 Old Buncombe Road, Suite 1
Greenville, SC 29617
712-832-8330
www.atss.info

An international membership organization which develops standards of service and education for qualified individuals who provide services, intervention and treatment in the field of traumatic stress.

Jayne Crisp, Administrator

5143 International Critical Incident Stress Foundation
3290 Pine Orchard Lane, Suite 106
Ellicott City, MD 21042
410-750-9600
Fax: 410-750-9601
info@icisf.org
www.icisf.org

Nonprofit, open membership foundation dedicated to the prevention and mitigation of disabling stress by education, training and support services for all emergency service professionals; Continuing education and training in emergency mental health services for psychologists, psychiatrists, social workers and licensed professional counselors.

Richard Barton, Chief Executive Officer
Lisa Joubert, Chief Financial Officer
Victor Welzant, Education & Training Director

5144 National Child Traumatic Stress Network
11150 W Olympic Blvd., Suite 650
Los Angeles, CA 90064
310-235-2633
Fax: 310-235-2612
www.nctsnet.org

The mission is to raise the standard of care and improve access to services for traumatized children, their families and communities throughout the United States.

Research Centers

5145 International Society for Traumatic Stress Studies
111 Deer Lake Road Suite 100
Deerfield, IL 60015
847-480-9028
Fax: 847-480-9282
istss@istss.org
www.istss.org

Provides a forum for sharing research, clinical strategies, public policy concerns and theoretical formulation on trauma in the US and worldwide. Dedicated to discovery and dissemination of knowledge and to the stimulation of policy, program and service initiatives that seek to reduce traumatic stressors and their permanent and long-term consequences. Members include psychiatrists, psychologists, social workers, nurses, counselors, researchers, administrators, advocates, and others.

Marylene Cloitre PhD, President
Karestan C Koenen PhD, Vice President
Dean G Kilpatrick PhD, Treasurer

Audio Video

5146 Complex PTSD in Children
Sidran Institute
PO Box 436
Brooklandville, MD 21022
410-825-8888
888-825-8249
Fax: 410-560-0134
help@sidran.org
www.sidran.org

Tape I: Etiology, Assessment, Advocacy; Tape II: Therapeutic Interventions

VHS 41 Minutes

Esther Giller, President and Director
Sheila˜ Giller, Secretary/Treasurer
Tracy Howard, Book Sales/ Office Manager

5147 PTSD in Children: Move in the Rhythm of th e Child
Sidran Institute
PO Box 436
Brooklandville, MD 21022
410-825-8888
888-825-8249
Fax: 410-560-0134
help@sidran.org
www.sidran.org

Trauma experts explain the circumstances, symptoms and therapy techniques for PTSD in children and the effect on our communities. Primarily for use by mental health professionals, it is an excellent resource for any who work with children.

VHS 58 Minutes

Esther Giller, President and Director
Sheila˜ Giller, Secretary/Treasurer
Tracy Howard, Book Sales/ Office Manager

5148 Significant Event Childhood Trauma
Sidran Institute
PO Box 436
Brooklandville, MD 21022
410-825-8888
888-825-8249
Fax: 410-560-0134
help@sidran.org
www.sidran.org

Topics discussed inlude: effects; targeting resources; in the classroom; single parents; divorce; violence; addiction; and intervention.

DVD

Esther Giller, President and Director
Sheila˜ Giller, Secretary/Treasurer
Tracy Howard, Book Sales/ Office Manager

Web Sites

5149 Association of Traumatic Stress Specialists
5000 Old Buncombe Road, Suite 1
Greenville, SC 29617
712-832-8330
www.atss.info

An international membership organization which develops standards of service and education for qualified individuals who provide services, intervention and treatment in the field of traumatic stress.

Jayne Crisp, Administrator

5150 David Baldwin's Trauma Information Pages
www.trauma-pages.com

www.trauma-pages.com

Brief summary of what is known about traumatic symptoms and responses including PTSD and coping strategies. Pages include additional links to more detailed references, online articles and web resources.

5151 Facts for Health: PTSD
ptsd.factsforhealth.org

ptsd.factsforhealth.org

Post-Traumatic Stress Disorder / Book Publishers

5152 Helping Kids Cope With a New Threat
750 First St. NE
Washington, DC 20002
202-336-5500
800-374-2721
www.apa.org/monitor/apr02/helpingkids.html

An online article about the issues of traumatic stress in children in particular after the September 11 attacks.

Barry S. Anton, PhD, President
Bonnie Markham, Treasurer
Linda Frye Campbell, Member

5153 International Critical Incident Stress Foundation
3290 Pine Orchard Lane, Suite 106
Ellicott City, MD 21042
410-750-9600
Fax: 410-750-9601
info@icisf.org
www.icisf.org

Nonprofit, open membership foundation dedicated to the prevention and mitigation of disabling stress by education, training and support services for all emergency service professionals; Continuing education and training in emergency mental health services for psychologists, psychiatrists, social workers and licensed professional counselors.

Richard Barton, Chief Executive Officer
Lisa Joubert, Chief Financial Officer
Victor Welzant, Education & Training Director

5154 Madison Institute of Medicine
www.miminc.org

www.miminc.org

Disseminates innovative approaches to the education of professionals and the general public on many mental health topics such as PTSD, OCD, depression, SAD and others.

5155 PTSD Alliance
www.ptsdalliance.org

www.ptsdalliance.org

A group of professional and advocacy organizaions that have joined forces to provide educational resources to individuals diagnosed wth PTSD and their loves ones; those at risk for developing PTSD; and medical, healthcare and other frontline professionals.

5156 Sidran Institute - Traumatic Stress Education & Advocacy
PO Box 436
Brooklandville, MD 21022
410-825-8888
888-825-8249
Fax: 410-560-0134
help@sidran.org
www.sidran.org

Provides education, resources, information and advocacy, publications, training and consulting on traumatic stress.

Esther Giller, President and Director
Sheila˜ Giller, Secretary/Treasurer
Tracy Howard, Book Sales/ Office Manager

Book Publishers

5157 Coping with Post-Traumatic Stress Disorder
Rosen Publishing Group
29 E 21st Street
New York, NY 10010
800-237-9932
Fax: 888-436-4643
www.rosenpublishing.com

Revised 2002 192 pages
Roger Rosen, President

5158 Effective Treatments for PTSD, 2nd Ed
Foa, Keane, Friedman, & Cohen, author

Guilford Press
72 Spring Street
New York, NY 10012
800-365-7006
Fax: 212-966-6708
info@guilford.com
www.guilford.com

Represents the collaborative work of experts across a range of theoretical orientations and professional backgrounds. Addresses general treatment considerations and methodological issues, reviews and evaluates literature on treatment approaches for children, adolescents and adults.

2008 604 pages Paperback
ISBN: 1-606230-01-5
Bob Matloff, President
Seymour Weingarten, Editor-in-Chief

5159 Helping Kids Heal - 75 Activities to Help Children Recover from Trauma & Loss
Rebecca Carman CSW, author

Sidran Institute
PO Box 436
Brooklandville, MD 21022
410-825-8888
888-825-8249
Fax: 410-560-0134
info@sidran.org
www.sidran.org

75 activities to use with school-aged children after traumatic events. Broken down into 13 sections that follow the natural sequence of recovery.

117 pages Paperback
Esther Giller, President & Director
Sheila Giller, Secretary/Treasurer
Ruta Mazelis, Editor

5160 PTSD Workbook
Courage to Change
PO Box 486
Wilkes-Barre, PA 18703
800-440-4003
Fax: 800-772-6499
www.couragetochange.com

Outlines simple and effective techniques employed by PTSD experts for trauma survivors in order to conquer their most distressing symptoms. Readers learn to evaluate their type of trauma and then learn the most effective strategies to overcome them.

5161 Post Traumatic Stress Disorder Sourcebook
Glenn R Schiraldi, author

McGraw Hill Publishers
860 Taylor Station Road
Blacklick, 43004
877-833-5524
877-833-5524
Fax: 614-759-3823
www.mhprofessional.com

Offers help and hope for lasting recovery. A guide for sufferers and theor loved ones.

446 pages Paperback
ISBN: 0-737302-65-8
Lloyd G. Waterhouse, President & CEO
Patrick Milano, CFO
David Stafford, Senior Vice President

5162 Posttraumatic Stress Disorder in Children and Adolescents
Raul R Silva MD, author

Sidran Institute
PO Box 436
Brooklandville, MD 21022
410-825-8888
888-825-8249
Fax: 410-560-0134
info@sidran.org
www.sidran.org

An expert guide to the most importatnt issues pertaining to PTSD, trauma, stress and concurrent conditions. Includes 15 chapters that address different aspects of childhood and adolescent trauma.

384 pages Paperback

Esther Giller, President & Director
Sheila Giller, Secretary/Treasurer
Ruta Mazelis, Editor

5163 Treating Psychological Trauma and PTSD

John Wilson et al, author

Sidran Institute
PO Box 436
Brooklandville, MD 21022

410-825-8888
888-825-8249
Fax: 410-560-0134
info@sidran.org
www.sidran.org

Identifies 65 PTSD symptoms contained within five symptom clusters, and then addresses 80 target objectives for treatment, which can be treated by 11 different psychotherapeutic approaches.

443 pages Paperback

Esther Giller, President & Director
Sheila Giller, Secretary/Treasurer
Ruta Mazelis, Editor

5164 Treating Trauma & Traumatic Grief in Child ren and Adolescents

J Cohen, A Mannarino, E Deblinger, author

Guilford Press
72 Spring Street
New York, NY 10012

800-365-7006
Fax: 212-966-6708
info@guilford.com
www.guilford.com

The book presents a systematic treatment approach, grounded in CBT, for traumatized children and their families. Provides a comprehensive frameworkl for assessing PTSD, depression, anxiety, and other symptoms; assists in developing a flxible, patient-specific treatment plan to work with the children and parents in building core skills. Includes age and culture specific treatment components. Print or e-book.

2006 256 pages
ISBN: 1-593853-08-2

Bob Matloff, President
Seymour Weingarten, Editor-in-Chief

Pamphlets

5165 Helping Children and Adolescents Cope with Violence and Disasters

National Institute of Mental Health
6001 Executive Boulevard, Room 6200
Bethesda, MD 20892

301-443-4513
866-615-6464
Fax: 301-443-4279
TTY: 301-443-8431
nimhinfo@nih.gov
www.nimh.nih.gov

Booklet that discusses children and adolescents' reactions to violence and disasters, emphasizing the wide range of responses and the role that parents, teachers and therapists can play in the healing process.

Francis Collins, M.D., Director
Tom Insel, Director

5166 Post Traumatic Stress Disorder: A Guide

Madison Institute of Medicine
www.miminc.org/shop/store/

www.miminc.org/shop/store/

Comprehensive overview, diagnosis and treatment of PTSD.

2000 69 pages

5167 Post-Traumatic Stress Disorder, A Real Ill ness

National Institute of Mental Health
6001 Executive Boulevard, Room 6200
Bethesda, MD 20892

301-443-4513
866-615-6464
Fax: 301-443-4279
TTY: 301-443-8431
nimhinfo@nih.gov
www.nimh.nih.gov

An easy-to-read pamphlet of simple information about what it is, when it starts, how long it lasts and how to get help.

9 pages

Francis Collins, M.D., Director
Tom Insel, Director

5168 What Is Post Traumatic Stress Disorder?

Sidran Institute
PO Box 436
Brooklandville, MD 21022

410-825-8888
888-825-8249
Fax: 410-560-0134
help@sidran.org
www.sidran.org

Provides an introduction of PTSD as well as symptoms, possible treatment, and other helpful resources.

Esther Giller, President and Director
Sheila˜ Giller, Secretary/Treasurer
Tracy Howard, Book Sales/ Office Manager

Prader-Willi Syndrome / Description

Description

5169 PRADER-WILLI SYNDROME
Synonym: PWS
Involves the following Biologic System(s):
Endocrinologic Disorders,
Genetic/Chromosomal/Syndrome/Metabolic Disorders

Prader-Willi syndrome is a genetic disorder characterized by severely diminished muscle tone (hypotonia) during early infancy, short stature, unusually small hands and feet, obesity, genital abnormalities, and intellectual disabilities. The disorder is thought to affect approximately one in 15,000 individuals. In most cases of Prader-Willi syndrome, there is decreased fetal activity during the last months of pregnancy. After birth, most affected infants experience hypotonia, have feeding difficulties due to decreased swallowing and sucking reflexes, and fail to grow and gain weight at the expected rate (failure to thrive). Starting at approximately six months to six years of age, affected infants or children begin to have an excessive appetite (polyphagia), become obsessed with eating, or lack a sense of satisfaction after a meal and often engage in binge-type eating. As a result, patients develop an abnormally increased body weight (progressive obesity) due to an excessive accumulation of body fat, particularly over the thighs, buttocks, and lower abdomen.

Infants and children with Prader-Willi syndrome also may have characteristic abnormalities of the head and face (craniofacial area), such as almond-shaped eyes, upslanting eyelid folds (palpebral fissures), abnormal deviation of one eye in relation to the other (strabismus), a thin, tented upper lip, and full cheeks. In addition, affected males and females may have insufficient secretion of certain hormones that stimulate the gonads (hypogonadotropic hypogonadism). The gonads are the reproductive glands, such as the testes or ovaries, within which the reproductive cells (sperm or ova) are produced. Affected males typically have an abnormally small penis (micropenis) and undescended testes (cryptorchidism), potentially delayed or incomplete development of secondary sexual characteristics, insufficient production of the male sex hormone testosterone, decreased or absent sperm production, and infertility. Affected females often have abnormally small underdeveloped external genitalia (i.e., hypoplastic labia minor and clitoris), absence or abnormal cessation of menstrual cycles (primary or secondary amenorrhea), and infertility. Development of female secondary sexual characteristics may be normal or incomplete. Most children with Prader-Willi syndrome also have mild to moderate intellectual disabilities; however, in some cases, severe intellectual disabilities may be present. Many affected children experience difficulties with speech articulation and may have an abnormally high-pitched, nasal voice. Children with Prader-Willi syndrome may have behavioral problems that become apparent during later childhood, including outbursts of anger, rage-like episodes, and stubbornness.

Some individuals with Prader-Willi syndrome may develop diabetes mellitus during or soon after puberty. Diabetes mellitus is characterized by impaired fat, protein, and carbohydrate metabolism due to insufficient production of the hormone insulin or the body's inability to appropriately utilize insulin. Associated symptoms may include excessive thirst (polydipsia) and urination (polyuria). In addition, adolescents and young adults may be prone to experiencing cardiac insufficiency, potentially resulting in life-threatening complications during the second or third decade of life.

In children with Prader-Willi syndrome, treatment typically includes measures to help prevent progressive obesity or to ensure strict weight control, such as a low-calorie diet and a proper exercise program under a physician's direction. Nutritional behavioral modification methods may be implemented that require the cooperation and support of all family members, such as ensuring regular feeding habits (e.g., having meals at the same time and location on a daily basis) and the inaccessibility of food between meals. In young males with Prader-Willi syndrome, testosterone replacement therapy may result in enlargement of micropenis; in addition, testosterone therapy during adolescence or young adulthood may have beneficial effects on the development of secondary sexual characteristics. Treatment of children with Prader-Willi syndrome also may include special education and behavioral therapies to help manage behavioral problems.

Prader-Willi syndrome is caused by deletion or disruption of certain genes (contiguous gene syndrome) located on the long arm of chromos|ome 15 (15q11-13). Most affected individualshave missing genetic material or deletion of 15q11-13 that affects the chromosome received from the father (paternally derived chromosome).

Government Agencies

5170 NIH/ Eunice Kennedy Shriver National Insti tute of Child Health & Human Development
P.O. Box 3006
Rockville, MD 20847
800-370-2943
Fax: 866-760-5947
www.nichd.nih.gov

Conducts and supports laboratory research, clinical trials, and epidemiological studies that explore health processes; examines the impact of disabilities, diseases, and variations on the lives of individuals; and sponsors training programs for scientists, health care providers, and researchers to ensure that NICHD research can continue.

Diana W. Bianchi, Director
Alison Cernich, PhD, Deputy Director

National Associations & Support Groups

5171 American Academy of Pediatrics
345 Park Blvd
Itasca, IL 60143
847-434-4000
800-433-9016
Fax: 847-434-8000
csc@aap.org
www.aap.org

The American Academy of Pediatrics and its member pediatricians are committed to the attainment of optimal physical, mental and social health and well-being for all infants, children, adolescents, and young adults.

Kyle E. Yasuda, MD, FAAP, President
Mark Del Monte, JD, CEO/Executive VP
Vera Tait, MD, FAAP, Chief Medical Officer

5172 Foundation for Prader-Willi Research
440 N Barranca Avenue, Suite 3620
Covina, CA 91723
888-322-5487
info@fpwr.org
www.fpwr.org

Dedicated to the advancement of research on PWS. The Foundation chooses projects that are highly relevant for individuals with PWS and their families and that are scientifically sound.

Susan Hedstrom, Executive Director
Theresa Strong, Director of Research Programs
Jacqueline Mizon, Director of National Events

Prader-Willi Syndrome / State Agencies & Support Groups

5173 **Genetic Alliance**
426400 Woodfield Road, Ste 189
Damascus, MD 20872
202-966-5557
Fax: 202-966-8553
info@geneticalliance.org
www.geneticalliance.org

World's leading nonprofit health advocacy organization committed to transforming health through genetics and promoting an environment of openness centered on the health of individuals, families, and communities.

Sharon Terry, CEO
Ruth Child, CFO
Natasha Bonhomme, Chief Strategy Officer

5174 **March of Dimes Foundation**
1550 Crystal Drive, Ste 1300
Arlington, VA 22202
888-663-4637
www.marchofdimes.org

March of Dimes help moms have full-term pregnancies and research the problems that threaten the health of babies. The March of Dimes also acts globally: sharing best practices in perinatal health and helping improve birth outcomes where the needs are the most urgent.

Stacey D. Stewart, President
Alan Brogdon, SVP/COO/Board Officer
Rahul Gupta, MD, SVP & Chief Medical/Health Officer

5175 **Prader-Willi Syndrome Association**
1032 E Brandon Boulevard, Suite 4744
Brandon, FL 33511
941-312-0400
www.pwsausa.org

Provides educational materials, support, and advocacy for parents, caregivers, medical professionals, educators and all others involved with persons in PWS community.

Paige Rivard, Chief Executive Officer
Melanie McDonald, Director of Development
Stacy Ward, Director of Family Services

State Agencies & Support Groups

Alaska

5176 **Prader-Willi Northwest Association**
3706 29th Avenue W
Seattle, WA 98199
206-285-7679
jlunderwood@juno.com

Joane Underwood, Co-President

Arizona

5177 **Prader-Willi Syndrome Arizona Association**
13839 N Bentwater Drive
Tucson, AZ 85737
520-297-7025

Tammie Penta, President

California

5178 **Prader-Willi California Foundation**
514 N. Prospect Avenue, Ste 110, Lower Level
Redondo Beach, CA 90277
310-372-5053
800-400-9994
Fax: 310-316-3730
PWCF1@aol.com
www.pwcf.org

Willi Prader, Owner

Colorado

5179 **Prader-Willi Colorado Association**
PWSA
8290 South Yukon Way
Littleton, CO 80128
303-973-4780

Lynette Hosler, President

Connecticut

5180 **Prader-Willi Connecticut Association**
PWSA
35 Ansonia Drive
North Haven, CT 06473
860-204-9386
pwsactchapter@yahoo.com
www.angelfire.com/ct/pwsctchapter/

Eileen Fletcher
Vicki Knopf

Delaware

5181 **Prader-Willi Delaware Association**
PWSA
300 Bethel Circle Millwood
Middletown, DE 19709
302-378-7385
swede455@aol.com

Karen Swanson, President

Florida

5182 **PWSA Florida Chapter**
PWSA
694 SE Ashley Oak Way
Stuart, FL 34997
772-287-2587
pwfa2000@aol.com
http://members.aol.com/delchert/pwsa2.htm

Dan Krauer, President

Georgia

5183 **PWSA of Georgia**
562 Lakeland Plaza #327
Cumming, GA 30040
770-886-2334
877-886-2334
Fax: 770-886-2335
www.pwsaga.org

Debbie Lange, Executive Director

Hawaii

5184 **Prader-Willi Northwest Association**
3706 29th Avenue W
Seattle, WA 98199
206-285-7679
jlunderwood@juno.com

Joane Underwood, Co-President

Idaho

5185 **Prader-Willi Northwest Association-Idaho**
550 Lodgepole Road
Athol, ID 83801
208-683-2993
idaho4ts@aol.com

Gene Todhunter, Contact

Iowa

5186 **PWSA of Iowa**
15554 226th Street
Zwingle, IA 52079
319-686-4270
Ktcaedav@netins.net
www.pwsaiowa.org

Tammy Davis, President

Prader-Willi Syndrome / Research Centers

Kansas

5187 **Prader-Willi Syndrome Advocates**
14 NE Bayview Drive
Lees Summit, MO 64064   816-350-1375
Teri Douglas
Barry Douglas

Kentucky

5188 **PWSA of Kentucky**
Prader-Willi Syndrome Association
9213 Reigate Ct
Louisville,ÿ, KY 40222   502-339-7872
                                frankandannette@fuse.net

Frank Beck, President

Maine

5189 **Prader-Willi Association of New England (Maine, Mass, RI, NH, VT)**
2 Ernest Street
Webster, MA 01570   508-943-1400
                                sunsetrock@comcast.net
                                www.pwsane.org

Eileen Rullo, President
Mary Raymond, Vice President

Massachusetts

5190 **Prader-Willi Association of New England (Maine, Mass, RI, NH, VT)**
2 Ernest Street
Webster, MA 01570   508-943-1400
                                www.pwsane.org

Eileen Rullo, President
Mary Raymond, Vice President

Montana

5191 **Prader-Willi Northwest Association**
3706 29th Avenue W
Seattle, WA 98199   206-285-7679
Joane Underwood, Co-President

Nevada

5192 **PWSA Las Vegas/Nevada Support Group**
PWS NV S.H.A.R.E.
www.pwsnv.org

                                702-526-0630
                                pwsnv.org@gmail.com
                                www.pwsnv.org

New Mexico

5193 **PWS Project for New Mexico**

                                505-332-6700
                                claroque@arc-a.org

New York

5194 **Prader-Willi Alliance of New York**
PWSA NY Chapter
2224 Agnew Ter
The Villages, FL 32162   585-442-1655
                                800-442-1655
                                alliance@prader-willi.org
                                www.prader-willi.org

Hon. Daniel D Angiolillo, President
Rachel ÿÿÿÿ Johnson, Vice President

North Carolina

5195 **PWSA of North Carolina**
PWSA
4627 Mt Sinai Road
Durham, NC 27705   919-332-0621
Mary Jones Patterson

Ohio

5196 **PWSA of Ohio**
State Office
1087 Dover Drive
Medina, OH 44256   440-716-0552
                                pwsaohio@aol.com
                                www.pwsaohio.org

Jennifer Bolander, President

5197 **Prader-Willi Families of Ohio**
4075 West 226 Street
Fairview Park, OH ÿ4412   440-716-0552
                                pwfohio@aol.com
                                www.pwsaohio.org/

Johanna Costello, President

Research Centers

5198 **Foundation for Prader-Willi Research**
440 N Barranca Avenue, Suite 3620
Covina, CA 91723   888-322-5487
                                info@fpwr.org
                                www.fpwr.org

Dedicated to the advancement of research on PWS. The Foundation chooses projects that are highly relevant for individuals with PWS and their families and that are scientifically sound.

Susan Hedstrom, Executive Director
Theresa Strong, Director of Research Programs
Jacqueline Mizon, Director of National Events

Web Sites

5199 **International Prader-Willi Syndrome Organi zation (IPWSO)**
www.ipwso.org

                                info@ipwso.org
                                www.ipwso.org

5200 **Online Mendelian Inheritance in Man**
McKusick-Nathans Institue of Genetic Medicine-JHU
Baltimore, MD 21205   www.omim.org

This database is a catalog of human genes and genetic disorders.

Ada Hamosh, MD, Scientific Director

5201 **Prader-Willi Alliance of New York**
244 5th~Avenue, Suite D-110
New York, NY 10001   718-846-6606
                                800-442-1655
                                www.prader-willi.org

A chapter of the PWSA, it represents the interests of individuals in New York State with Prader-Willi Syndrome, their families, and the professionals who provide services to the Prader-Willi population.

Rachel Johnson, President
Nancy Finegold, Vice President
Tammy Reals, Vice President

5202 Prader-Willi Syndrome Association
1032 E Brandon Boulevard, Suite 4744
Brandon, FL 33511
941-312-0400
www.pwsausa.org

Provides educational materials, support, and advocacy for parents, caregivers, medical professionals, educators and all others involved with persons in PWS community.

Paige Rivard, Chief Executive Officer
Melanie McDonald, Director of Development
Stacy Ward, Director of Family Services

Precocious Puberty / Description

Description

5203 PRECOCIOUS PUBERTY
Synonym: Pubertas praecox
Covers these related disorders: Gonadotropin-dependent precocious puberty, Gonadotropin-independent precocious puberty
Involves the following Biologic System(s):
Endocrinologic Disorders

Precocious puberty refers to a condition in which the onset of sexual maturation occurs before the age of eight years in girls and nine years in boys. True precocious puberty refers to the premature sexual development of the sex glands (i.e., ovaries and testes) as well as the outward appearance of the child (secondary sexual characteristics). Precocious pseudopuberty refers to the early development of only the secondary sex characteristics with no involvement of the sex glands.

True precocious puberty results from the premature production and secretion by the pituitary gland of gonadotropin, a hormone that stimulates the ovaries and the testes. Because the release of hormones from the pituitary gland is controlled by another gland, the hypothalamus, functional abnormalities of or growth of a tumor in the pituitary or the hypothalamus may also result in premature sexual development. These abnormalities may include hormone-secreting tumors of the pituitary gland, brain lesions such as a hypothalamic hamartoma, and other lesions of the central nervous system that may activate the hypothalamus. True precocious puberty may also result from an underactive thyroid gland (hypothyroidism). However, for most children with precocious puberty, the exact cause is not known. More girls are affected by precocious puberty than boys. Although most cases appear sporadically, some patients have a family history of this condition. Sexual characteristics associated with true precocious puberty are always consistent with the sex of the affected child (isosexual characteristics). Such characteristics may include the early appearance of underarm and pubic hair, facial hair in boys, and breasts and menstrual cycles in girls. The penis, testes, and ovaries enlarge and acne may develop. Although height and weight may increase rapidly, advanced bone growth may result in premature closure of the growing ends of the bone (epiphyses) and, thus, slower linear growth leading to short stature.

Precocious pseudopuberty may be caused by a tumor of the ovary, testis, or adrenal gland. Such tumors may cause excessive production of sex hormones. This form of the disorder may also be inherited as an autosomal dominant trait. In addition, precocious pseudopuberty may be associated with other disorders such as McCune-Albright syndrome, which is a condition resulting from the overproduction of hormones of multiple glands. This syndrome is characterized by premature sexual development in girls, irregularities of skin color (pigmentation) and the skeletal system, and abnormalities of various glands. Physical characteristics associated with precocious pseudopuberty are similar to those of true precocious puberty, although the testes and ovaries are not usually involved. However, children affected with this form of the disorder may develop secondary sexual characteristics associated with those of the opposite sex (heterosexual characteristics). In addition, precocious pseudopuberty may prompt early maturation of the hormonal cycle that results in true precocious puberty.

Treatment for true precocious puberty may include the administration of gonadotropin-releasing hormones. These hormones work by diminishing the stimulatory response of the pituitary gland to the gonadotropin-releasing hormones produced naturally within the body until normal puberty begins. Treatment for precocious pseudopuberty may include the use of certain medications that reduce the levels of male and female sex hormones (i.e., testosterone and estrogen). In addition, surgery may be indicated in those patients who have precocious puberty as a result of certain types of tumors. Other treatment is symptomatic and supportive.

Government Agencies

5204 NIH/ Eunice Kennedy Shriver National Institute of Child Health & Human Development
P.O. Box 3006
Rockville, MD 20847
800-370-2943
Fax: 866-760-5947
www.nichd.nih.gov

Conducts and supports research on topics related to the health of children, adults, families and populations. Some of these topics include: developmental disabilities, growth and development, infant death, reproductive health and birth defects.

Diana W. Bianchi, Director
Alison Cernich, PhD, Deputy Director

National Associations & Support Groups

5205 American Academy of Pediatrics
345 Park Blvd
Itasca, IL 60143
847-434-4000
800-433-9016
Fax: 847-434-8000
csc@aap.org
www.aap.org

The American Academy of Pediatrics and its member pediatricians are committed to the attainment of optimal physical, mental and social health and well-being for all infants, children, adolescents, and young adults.

Kyle E. Yasuda, MD, FAAP, President
Mark Del Monte, JD, CEO/Executive VP
Vera Tait, MD, FAAP, Chief Medical Officer

5206 Genetic Alliance
426400 Woodfield Road, Ste 189
Damascus, MD 20872
202-966-5557
Fax: 202-966-8553
info@geneticalliance.org
www.geneticalliance.org

World's leading nonprofit health advocacy organization committed to transforming health through genetics and promoting an environment of openness centered on the health of individuals, families, and communities.

Sharon Terry, CEO
Ruth Child, CFO
Natasha Bonhomme, Chief Strategy Officer

5207 MAGIC Foundation: Major Aspects of Growth in Children
4200 Cantera Drive, #106
Warrenville, IL 60555
630-836-8200
800-362-4423
Fax: 630-836-8181
mary@magicfoundation.org
www.magicfoundation.org

A national nonprofit organization providing support and education regarding growth disorders in children and related adult disorders. Provides educational information, networking, a national conference, a kids' program and an extensive medical library.

Dianne Kremidas, Executive Director
Mary Andrews, CEO
Teresa Tucker, Patient Advocacy

5208 March of Dimes Foundation
1550 Crystal Drive, Ste 1300
Arlington, VA 22202
888-663-4637
www.marchofdimes.org

March of Dimes help moms have full-term pregnancies and research the problems that threaten the health of babies. The March of Dimes also acts globally: sharing best practices in perinatal health and helping improve birth outcomes where the needs are the most urgent.

Stacey D. Stewart, President
Alan Brogdon, SVP/COO/Board Officer
Rahul Gupta, MD, SVP & Chief Medical/Health Officer

Web Sites

5209 KidsHealth: Precocious Puberty
kidshealth.org/en/parents/precocious.html

kidshealth.org/en/parents/precocious.html

General overview of precocious puberty including signs, causes, diagnosis and treatment.

Neil Izenberg, MD, Editor-in-Chief & Founder

5210 Online Mendelian Inheritance in Man
McKusick-Nathans Institue of Genetic Medicine-JHU
Baltimore, MD 21205   www.omim.org

This database is a catalog of human genes and genetic disorders.

Ada Hamosh, MD, Scientific Director

5211 Society for Endocrinology
22 Apex Court, Woodlands
Bradley Stoke, BI BS32
                                        145-464-2200
                                   Fax: 145-464-2222
                                www.endocrinology.org

Aims to advance education and research in endocrinology for the benefit of the public. Lists resources such as journals, books, events, and training courses available.

5212 University of Michigan Health System
1500 E. Medical Center Drive
Ann Arbor, MI 48109   734-936-4000
                                    kylaboys@umich.edu
                         www.med.umich.edu/yourchild/topics/puberty

Information on early puberty or precocious puberty.

Pamphlets

5213 Precocious Puberty
Human Growth Foundation
997 Glen Cove Avenue, Suite 5
Glen Head, NY 11545   800-451-6434
                                   Fax: 516-671-4055
                                    hgf1@hgfound.org
                                    www.hgfound.org

Booklet

Pisit Pitukcheewanont, MD, President
Emily Germain-Lee, Vice President
Patricia D. Costa, Executive Director

Description

5214 PREMATURITY

Involves the following Biologic System(s):
Neonatal and Infant Disorders

Premature birth (also known as preterm birth) refers to the birth of an infant before the 37-week gestational period. Most pregnancies last for 40 weeks. About 12 percent of babies in the United States — or 1 in 8 — are born prematurely each year. Although at least 40 percent of premature births occur for unknown reasons, prematurity may result from many different factors including a condition in which the mother develops high blood pressure, large quantities of protein in the urine, and an abnormal accumulation of fluid in the body (preeclampsia); maternal heart disease, kidney disease, or diabetes; acute infection; trauma; uterine irregularities (e.g., bicornate uterus); and placental abnormalities (e.g., placenta previa). Other contributing factors may include multiple pregnancy, maternal drug use, and fetal distress. Poor nutrition and lack of appropriate prenatal care may also put the unborn child at risk for premature birth.

Premature infants usually have a characteristic appearance in addition to their small size. For example, their heads often appear too large for their bodies and their skin may be very pink, smooth, translucent, and covered with downy hair (lanugo). They may have sparse hair and very little subcutaneous fat. In girls, the genitals may be incompletely developed such that the labia majora do not cover the labia minora. In affected boys, the testes may not fully descend into the scrotum. Other findings may include the absence of the creases on the palms and soles, incomplete development of the ear, and other irregularities. In addition, the survival or health of a premature infant may be compromised as a result of the incomplete development of certain body systems. The earlier the delivery, the more immature the organs. Common irregularities associated with prematurity include inadequate development of the lungs and subsequent deficiency in the production of a substance that allows the air sacs in the lungs to remain open (surfactant). This condition may lead to respiratory distress syndrome (also called hyaline membrane disease) and associated life-threatening oxygen deficiency in the blood. Immature organ development may affect the brain, resulting in deficiencies in spontaneous breathing, inadequate sucking, and difficulty in swallowing. There is also an increased risk of bleeding in the brain (intraventricular hemorrhage). Premature infants are also particularly susceptible to serious infection resulting from incomplete placental transfer of maternal antibodies. Immature liver function may result in a temporary increase in blood levels of bilirubin causing yellowing of the eyes, skin, and mucous membranes (jaundice). Other complications of prematurity may include poor body temperature regulation, small stomach capacity, inadequacy of the intestinal tract that may result in injury or decreased blood flow to the intestines (necrotizing enterocolitis), immature kidney function, fluctuations in bloodsugar levels, reduced levels of calcium in the blood, and other irregularities related to underdevelopment of body systems. It has also been shown that premature babies are prone to developing depression as teenagers.

One of the most important steps to preventing prematurity is to receive prenatal care as early as possible in the pregnancy, and to continue such care until the baby is born. Statistics clearly show that early and good prenatal care reduces the chance of premature birth and related deaths. Two tactics are used to deal with a potential premature birth: delay the arrival of birth as much as possible, or prepare the premature fetus for arrival. Both of these tactics may be used simultaneously. Treatment for premature infants depends upon the maturity of the various organ systems at the time of birth. In many cases, these infants are cared for around the clock in a neonatal care unit where body temperature may be regulated in an incubator and respiration may be maintained through artificial ventilation, if necessary. Feeding may be accomplished through the use of intravenous feeding or through a feeding tube directly into the stomach. Nutritional supplementation may include the administration of iron and vitamins. In addition, liquids may be given to maintain fluid levels in the body. Antibiotics may be administered to help treat infection. Discharge from the hospital takes place once the infant has reached appropriate weight and certain functional criteria have been established. In addition, before discharge, parents or caregivers of these infants are given complete instructions in their proper care. Other treatment is symptomatic and supportive.

Government Agencies

5215 NIH/ Eunice Kennedy Shriver National Institute of Child Health & Human Development
P.O. Box 3006
Rockville, MD 20847
800-370-2943
Fax: 866-760-5947
www.nichd.nih.gov

Conducts and supports research on topics related to the health of children, adults, families and populations. Some of these topics include: developmental disabilities, growth and development, infant death, reproductive health and birth defects.

Diana W. Bianchi, Director
Alison Cernich, PhD, Deputy Director

National Associations & Support Groups

5216 American Academy of Pediatrics
345 Park Blvd
Itasca, IL 60143
847-434-4000
800-433-9016
Fax: 847-434-8000
csc@aap.org
www.aap.org

The American Academy of Pediatrics and its member pediatricians are committed to the attainment of optimal physical, mental and social health and well-being for all infants, children, adolescents, and young adults.

Kyle E. Yasuda, MD, FAAP, President
Mark Del Monte, JD, CEO/Executive VP
Vera Tait, MD, FAAP, Chief Medical Officer

5217 March of Dimes Foundation
1550 Crystal Drive, Ste 1300
Arlington, VA 22202
888-663-4637
www.marchofdimes.org

March of Dimes help moms have full-term pregnancies and research the problems that threaten the health of babies. The March of Dimes also acts globally: sharing best practices in perinatal health and helping improve birth outcomes where the needs are the most urgent.

Stacey D. Stewart, President
Alan Brogdon, SVP/COO/Board Officer
Rahul Gupta, MD, SVP & Chief Medical/Health Officer

5218 National Perinatal Association
PO Box 392
Lonedell, MO 63060
KLove@nationalperinatal.org
www.nationalperinatal.org

The National Perinatal Association promotes the health and well being of mothers and infants enriching families, communities and the world.

Kristy Love, Executive Director
Elizabeth Filipovich, Vice President, Programs
Jessica Restivo, Vice President, Development

Prematurity / Web Sites

5219 Sidelines
3167 Bern Drive
Laguna Beach, CA 92651
sidelines@sidelines.org
www.sidelines.org

Nonprofit organization that provides international support for women and their families experiencing premature births and complicated pregnancies.

Candace Hurley, Founder & Executive Director
Tracy Hoogenboom, Managing Director

State Agencies & Support Groups

Georgia

5220 Georgia Perinatal Association
c/o Terri Negron
5607 Walden Farm Drive
Powder Springs, GA 30127
www.georgiaperinatal.org

Works to promote perinatal health through education, collaboration and influence of state public policy. It collaborates with others to improve pregnancy and infant outcomes.

Bonnie Simmons, President
Diane Youmans, President
Margaret B. Hotz, Secretary

Texas

5221 Texas Perinatal Association
19 Cloister Parkway
Amarillo, TX 79121
lisaplat@aol.com
www.txpa.org

Committed to achieving continuous improvement in the quality of health care to mothers and infants in the state of Texas.

Laura Street

Wisconsin

5222 Wisconsin Association for Perinatal Care
McConnell Hall
211 S. Paterson St., ÿSuite 250
Madison, WI 53703
608-285-5858
Fax: 608-285-5004
wapc@perinatalweb.org
www.perinatalweb.org

Provides leadership and education for improved perinatal health outcomes of women, infants and their families through: increased public awareness; engaging the diverse community of perinatal health care advocates; and coordinating systems of perinatal care in Wisconsin.

Ann Conway, Executive Director
Kristine E Casto, Learning Coordinator

Libraries & Resource Centers

5223 National Center for Education in Maternal and Child Health
330 Whitehaven Street NW
Washington, DC 20007
MCHnavigator@ncemch.org
www.ncemch.org

Information and advocacy resources for families and professionals. Includes listings of organizations providing general information and organizations focusing on more specific areas of concern to families and young adults who have disabilities.

Rochelle Mayer, Director
John Richards, Executive Director

Research Centers

5224 NIH/ Eunice Kennedy Shriver National Institute of Child Health & Human Development
NICHD Clearinghouse
31 Center Drive, Building 31
Bethesda, MD 20892
301-496-5133
800-370-2943
Fax: 866-760-5947
nichdpress@mail.nih.gov
www.nichd.nih.gov

The National Institute for Child Health and Human Development conducts and supports laboratory, clinical and epidemiological research on the reproductive, neurobiologic, developmental, and behavioral processes that determine and maintain the health of children, adults, families, and populations.

Diana W. Bianchi, Director
Della M. Hann, PhD, Director, Extramural Research
Paul E. Williams, Communications

5225 NIH/National Institute of Mental Health Eating Disorders Program
6001 Executive Boulevard, Room 8184
Bethesda, MD 20892
301-443-4513
Fax: 301-443-4279

Web Sites

5226 Children's Medical Ventures
3000 Minuteman Road
Andover, MA 01810
www.healthcare.philips.com/

The company offers high quality products which meet the unique needs of these special babies, including appropriately sized items, safety equipment and specialty feeding and skin care products.

5227 Newborns in Need
3323 Transou Road
Pfafftown, NC 27040
www.newbornsinneed.org

Charity organization for the care of sick and needy babies and their families.

Sam Safrit, Chairman
Connie Edwards, President
Gayle McKeethan, Vice President

5228 PREBIC-International Preterm Birth Collaborative
www.prebic.org

www.prebic.org

Supports and enhances international networking among researchers in preterm birth.

Craig Pennell, President
Hanns Helmer, Vice President
Melanie White, Treasurer

5229 Preemie Ring
hub.familynhome.org/hub/preemie

hub.familynhome.org/hub/preemie

A collection of home pages about premature infants and premature infant care, etc.

5230 Preemie Twins
PO Box 12
Pierce, NE 68767
402-606-1820
Fax: 402-606-1820
www.preemietwins.com

Online resource for both parents of multiples and/or premature infants.

5231 Preemie World
preemie.info

preemie.info

A meeting place for family and friends of preemies.

Prematurity / Book Publishers

5232 Premature Baby-Premature Child
www.prematurity.org

www.prematurity.org

Preemie parent support for preemie special needs.

5233 Prematurely Yours
www.prematurelyyours.com

www.prematurelyyours.com

Special products for special babies.

Kim Bryant, RN, President
Becky Meloan, RN, VP
Curtis Bryant, Treasurer/Secretary

Book Publishers

5234 Prematurely Yours
6712 Townpoint Road
Suffolk, VA 23435

757-483-9879
Fax: 757-484-8267
www.prematurelyyours.com

Designed exclusively to record milestones for the premature infant, from birth to six years of age. Such milestones as maintaining their body temperature, nippling their feedings, and breathing without the aid of extra oxygen are, of course, taken for granted with a full term infant.

40 pages Hardcover

Kim Bryant, RN, President
Becky Meloan, RN, VP
Curtis Bryant, Treasurer/Secretary

Magazines

5235 Preemie Magazine
6412 Brandon Avenue, Suite 274
Springfield, VA 22150

703-468-1005
www.preemiemagazine.com

Started by five preemie parents, it provides free information and an on-line community for preemeie parents and professionals.

Deborah A Discenza, Founder & Publisher
Nicole Hutzul, Sales & Marketing
Alicia Michaels, Director Operations/Development

Pamphlets

5236 March of Dimes-Preterm Birth Fact Sheets
March of Dimes Foundation
1550 Crystal Drive, Ste 1300
Arlington, VA 22202

914-997-4488
888-663-4637
answers@marchofdimes.org
www.marchofdimes.org

Fact sheets discuss the possible causes of preterm birth, complications associated with, and current research.

Description

5237 PREVENTABLE CHILDHOOD INFECTIONS
Involves the following Biologic System(s):
Infectious Disorders

There are several infectious diseases that typically manifest in childhood, that are preventable with proper immunizations. This chapter will cover the following: Diphtheria; Tetanus; Pertussis; Rubella (German Measles); Measles; Mumps; Polio; Chickenpox; Influenza (flu); Meningococcal; Pneumococcal; Congenital Rubella; Genital Human Papillomavirus (HPV).

Diphtheria is an acute, contagious disease characterized at its onset by sore throat and painful swallowing. One to 4 days after exposure, infected individuals may also develop a low-grade fever, headache, nausea and vomiting, chills, and a rapid heart rate. Other symptoms may include signs associated with upper respiratory tract infection. Within a few days, a grayish-brown pseudomembrane may form over the tonsils, and the throat may swell. The lymph nodes in the neck may become swollen and enlarged. Damage to the heart or nervous system may occur. Diphtheria vaccine is usually combined with those for whooping cough (pertussis) and tetanus. This DPT combination is routinely given in a series in the first few months of life. Booster doses are required. In most cases, diphtheria is transmitted through coughed or exhaled droplets. Treatment is with antibiotics and an antitoxin.

Pertussis (whooping cough) is a highly contagious infectious disease in which inflammation of the respiratory tract results from a bacterial infection, transmitted through coughing or sneezing. Pertussis usually affects infants and children, but may occur at any age. Pertussis infection lasts about 6 weeks, occurring in 3 stages: moderate cold-like symptoms (catarrhal stage); severe coughing (paroxysmal stage); cessation of symptoms (convalescent stage). Treatment typically includes bed rest, proper nutrition and fluid intake. Erythromycin or other antibiotics may be given. Pertussis vaccine is usually combined with diptheria and tetanus.

Tetanus is an infectious disease of the central nervous system caused by a toxic bacteria that acts on nerves that control muscle activity. The bacterium typically enters puncture wounds caused by dirty objects such as nails, splinters or glass fragments, or via drug injection, surgical wounds, burns, animal bites or the umbilical cord stump. Symptoms usually appear from 2 to 14 days after infection, but could take months to appear. Tetanus may be classified into general or localized. Initial symptoms of generalized tetanus often include: prolonged spasms of the muscles of the jaw (trismus or lockjaw); difficulties in opening the mouth, chewing and swallowing (dysphagia); irritability, headaches and restlessness. Prolonged spasms of facial muscles, profuse sweating, a mild fever and rapid pulse may also occur. Progressed disease includes severe muscle contractions. Treatment includes human antibodies (tetanus immune globulin) and antibiotics, surgical cleaning of the wound site, and muscle relaxants. Children should receive the DPT (diptheria, pertussis, tetanus) vaccine and booster shots, which should also be given to anyone with wounds and unknown tetanus booster status.

German measles, or rubella, is a contagious viral disease characterized by swollen lymph nodes and a fine, reddish-pink rash that persists for 1 to 3 days. It is transmitted through inhalation of droplets coughed or exhaled by infected individuals. Early symptoms may include swollen lymph nodes, especially in the neck and back of the head; joint pain (arthralgia); low-grade fever; cold symptoms; and redness and discomfort of the throat. Within 1 or 2 days, a mildly itchy rash appears on the face, spreading to the trunk, arms and legs, accompanied by a spreading red flush. The rash usually subsides after 3 days. In some cases, enlargement of the spleen may occur. Measles symptoms range from slight to severe, the latter occuring primarily in older children and adults. Pregnant women with the disease are at risk of transmitting it to their newborn (congenital rubella, see below). Protection against infection is provided through rubella immunization, usually in combination with measles and mumps vaccine. Vaccines are recommended for women of child-bearing age who have not had German measles. Treatment for rubella is symptomatic.

Measles is a highly contagious infection caused by the measles virus. Infection is characterized by a spreading rash and other sypltoms. It typically infects the young, but may develop at any age. It is spread through airborne droplets from an infected individual. Infection usually results in lifelong immunity. Early symptoms develop 1 to 2 weeks after exposure and include low-grade fever; inflammation of the nasal mucous membranes; runny nose; hacking cough; conjunctivitis; and increased sensitivity to light. These symptoms are followed 2 to 3 days later by tiny, grayish-white specks surrounded by an irregular red ring (Koplik's spots), that appear on the inside of the cheeks, usually near the back teeth. A rash, accompanied by a high fever, may develop within 3 to 5 days after the onset of symptoms, characterized by faint, reddish flat spots that first appear behind the ears, at the hairline and on the neck, and then spread over the entire body. Certain lymph nodes and the spleen may become enlarged. Immunization, usually in combination with mumps and rubella vaccines provides protection; a second vaccine is usually given upon entering school. Treatment includes fever-recuding medication, antibiotics, increased fluid intake, and bed rest in a warm humidified room. Other treatment is symptomatic and supportive.

Congenital rubella is a condition caused by the German measles virus that is passed from an infected mother to the fetus. Likelihood for transmission and the potential for miscarriage, stillbirth or severe developmental abnormalities (stunted growth, heart defects, eye problems, microcephaly, skin lesions) is highest during the first trimester. Many infants with congenital rubella have inner ear and/or hearing problems. intellectual disabilities and motor delays may also occur, along with a risk of hepatitis, anemia, lowered blood platelets, pneumonia and bone irregularities. Prevention is directed toward immunization of women of child-bearing age via the measles vaccine.

Mumps is an acute, infectious viral disease caused by a paramyxovirus. It is characterized by enlargement of the salivary glands, particularly those that lie below and in front of the ears (parotid glands). Mumps usually affects children from 5 through 15 years. It is spread through airborne droplets or direct contact with saliva, or possibly, urine, from an infected individual. Outbreaks most often occur in late winter or early spring. Infection usually results in lifelong immunity. Symptoms appear in 14 to 24 days after exposure and include fever, neck pain, weakness, discomfort and headache. One or both parotid glands may become enlarged or tender to the touch. Chewing and swallowing may become difficult, and fever and swelling of other salivary glands and the throat may occur. Swelling of the parotid glands usually lasts 7 to 10 days. Possible complications include meningitis, and joint swelling. A vaccine to prevent the disease is given to children 12 to 15 months, and again before entering school. Treatment is symptomatic and supportive.

Preventable Childhood Infections / Government Agencies

Polio, or polimyelitis, is an acute infectious disease caused by one of three polio viruses transmitted through fecal contamination or, occasionally, through the air. It may produce no symptoms, but will grant immunity to those infected. In young children, it is usually accompanied by only mild symptoms that appear 3 to 5 days after infection — fever, headache, sore throat, vomiting, weakness and abdominal discomfort. Recovery often occurs in 1 to 3 days. In some cases, a brief recovery is followed by additional symptoms, including brain and spinal cord involvement with neck and back stiffness and skin sensitivity. This reappearance indicates major illness, and is more common in older children and adults, and may by paralytic or nonparalytic. Immunization to prevent polio is routinely administered. Treatment for the mild form includes bedrest and pain relievers. Paralysis requires physical therapy. Other treatment is symptomatic and supportive.

Chickenpox is a common, hightly contagious viral disease caused by the varicella zoster virus. Most cases occur before the age of 10. Those who do not contract the virus during childhood remain susceptible during adulthood, when symptoms are typically more severe. Chickenpox is spread by inhalation of airborne droplets or by direct contact with fluid from skin blisters. Older children particularly may experience fever,headache, mild abdominal pain, lack of appetite and malaise. A characteristic rash develops on the chest, abdomen, face or scalp, consisting of masses of small, red, extremely itchy spots that become fluid-filled blisters. As the first lesions dry, new ones form.Complication of chickenpox may include bacterial infection of the lesions, encephalitis, and impaired control of voluntary movements. Newborns may also experience a particularly severe, progressive form of chickenpox (neonatal chickenpox). Treatment of children with mild cases of chickenpox is symptomatic and supportive. In more severe cases, the antiviral drug acyclovir may be administered. A vaccine is available to help prevent chickenpox.

Influenza (flu) is a highly contagious viral infection of the nose, throat, and lungs. Spread easily through respiratory droplets of an infected person, influenza symptoms include sudden high fever, chills, dry cough, headache, runny nose, sore throat, muscle and joint pain, and extreme fatigue, which can last up to several weeks. Influenza can be prevented by the flu vaccine of thich there are two types: the flu shot is approved for children older than six months, inlcuding healthy children and those with chronic conditions. The nasal spray flu vaccine (LAIV) is approved for use in healthy individuals two to 49 years. Minor side effects of the flu shot include soreness, redness or swelling at the shot site, low-grade fever, and aches. These may occur soon after the shot and last one to two days. On rare occasions, flu vaccinations can cause severe allergic reactions. Side effects of the nasal spray can include runny nose, wheezing, headache, vomiting, muscle aches, and fever. A flu vaccine is needed every year to keep up with the changing flu virus. Also, studies show that the body's immunity to influenza viruses (either through infection or vaccination) declines over time.

Meningococcal disease is a leading cause of bacterial meningitis (infection of the covering of the brain and spinal cord) in children two to 18 years old, and can also cause blood infections. The bacteria that cause Meningococcal disease are spread through the exchange of nose and throat droplets through coughing, sneezing or kissing. Symptoms include nausea, vomiting, sensitivity to light, confusion and sleepiness. One of every 10 cases result in death. Meningococcal disease may leave patients limbless, with hearing and nervous system problems, developmental disabilities, and seizures or strokes. It is most common in infants less than one year, and in those 16 to 21 years. Children with certain medical conditions (i.e. no spleen), are at increased risk, as are college students living in dormitories. Meningococcal disease can be prevented by the MCV4 vaccine, which is recommended for those at risk, or who travel to countries where the disease is prevalant. The vaccine is given at age 11 to 12 years, and a booster dose at 16 years.

Genital human papillomavirus (HPV) is the most common sexually transmitted infection (STI) in the U.S. There are more than 40 types of HPV; some cause genital warts; some cause various cancers; some infect the mouth and throat. Aproximately 20 million Americans, including those 11-18 years, are currently infected with HPV, and about 6 million more are infected each year. The HPV virus can live for years in infected individuals, sometimes without symptoms. In rare cases, an infected pregnant woman can pass the HPV virus onto her newborn. HPV can be passed between straight and gay partners, even when the infected person has no symptoms. HPV can cause cervical cancer in women, and it is associated with other, less common cancers. HPV can be prevented by HPV vaccine which is given in three doses over six months. Children 11 to 12 years have the best protection from the vaccines. Two vaccines (Cervariz and Gardasil) are considered effective in protecting women against cancer and genital warts. Gardasil is considered effective in protecting men against genital warts and anal cancer; men at risk should receive the vaccine through 26 years. There is no cure for HPV.

Pneumococcal is an infection of the lungs that is caused by pneumococcus bacteria, which can also cause ear infections, sinus infections, meningitis, bacteremia and blood stream infection. In some cases pneumococcal disease can be fatal or result in brain damage, or hearing or limb loss. The bacteria is spread through infected respiratory droplets from the nose or mouth. It is common for children to carry the bacteria in their throats without becomming symptomatic. Children under two years, in group child care, or who have certain illnesses are at higher risk for pneumococcal disease, as are those with cochlear implants or cerebrospinal fluid (CSF) leaks. Pneumococcal disease is more common among certain ethnic groups, including Alaska Natives, American Indians, and African Americans. Meningitis is the most severe type of pneumococcal disease. Of children under five years with the disease, 5% will die from it, and others may have long-term effects, such as vision or hearing loss. Pneumococcal conjugate vaccine (PCV) prevents the infection. Treatment includes antibiotics which may slow or reverse emerging drug resistance found among pneumococcal infections. It is recommended that the vaccine be given to infants at two, four, and six months, followed by a booster dose at 12 to 15 months.

Hepatitis A and Hepatitis B also fall into the category of preventable childhood infections and are covered in depth in a separate chapter on Hepatitis.

Government Agencies

5238 Centers for Disease Control and Prevention Prevention
1600 Clifton Road
Atlanta, GA 30329
800-232-4636
TTY: 888-232-6348
www.cdc.gov

Federal agency that promotes America's health and safety, providing information to guide health decisions, and building strong partnerships to promote health and prevent disease.

Rochelle P. Walensky, MD, Director
Anne Schuchat, MD, Principal Deputy Director
Abbigail Tumpey, MPH, Associate Director, Communication

Preventable Childhood Infections / National Associations & Support Groups

5239 **Department of Health**
899 North Capitol St, NE
Washington, DC 20002
202-442-5955
Fax: 202-442-4795
doh@dc.gov
www.doh.dc.gov/page/vaccine-preventable-diseases

The DOH conducts investigations, tracking and reporting of vaccine preventable diseases.

LaQuandra Nesbitt, Director
Jacqueline Watson, Chief of Staff

5240 **NIH/National Institute of Allergy and Infectious Diseases**
5601 Fishers Lane, MSC 9806
Bethesda, MD 20892
301-496-5717
866-284-4107
Fax: 301-402-3573
TDD: 800-877-8339
ocpostoffice@niaid.nih.gov
www.niaid.nih.gov

The principal advisory board of the NIAID. The council is composed of physicians, scientists and representatives of the public and advises on the conduct and support or research, training and dissemination of health information regarding allergies and infectious diseases.

Anthony S. Fauci, MD, Director

National Associations & Support Groups

5241 **American Academy of Pediatrics**
345 Park Blvd
Itasca, IL 60143
847-434-4000
800-433-9016
Fax: 847-434-8000
csc@aap.org
www.aap.org

The American Academy of Pediatrics and its member pediatricians are committed to the attainment of optimal physical, mental and social health and well-being for all infants, children, adolescents, and young adults.

Kyle E. Yasuda, MD, FAAP, President
Mark Del Monte, JD, CEO/Executive VP
Vera Tait, MD, FAAP, Chief Medical Officer

5242 **American Association for Respiratory Care**
9425 N. MacArthur Blvd. Suite 100
Irving, TX 75063
972-243-2272
Fax: 972-484-2720
info@aarc.org
www.aarc.org

The AARC encourages and promotes professional excellence, advances the science and practice of respiratory care, and serves as an advocate for patients and their families, the public, the profession and the respiratory therapist.

Tom Kallstrom, Executive Director
Shawna Strickland, Associate Executive Director
Heather Willden, Communications Coordinator

5243 **American Association for Thoracic Surgery**
800 Cummings Center, Suite 350-V
Beverly, MA 01915
aats.org

The American Association for Thoracic Surgery is an international organization of over 1,300 of the world's foremost cardiothoracic surgeons representing 41 countries.

David R. Bobbitt, Chief Executive Officer
Adam Silva, Director of Administration
Jill Colsch, Program Manager

5244 **American Medical Association**
AMA Plaza, 330 North Wabash Ave., Suite 39300
Chicago, IL 60611
312-464-4782
800-262-3211
www.ama-assn.org

AMA is dedicated to ensuring sustainable physician practices that result in better health outcomes for patients.

James L. Madara, MD, CEO/EVP
Bernard L. Hengesbaugh, Chief Operating Officer
Kenneth J. Sharigian, SVP

5245 **American Nurses Association**
8515 Georgia Avenue, Suite 400
Silver Spring, MD 20910
800-284-2378
customerservice@ana.org
www.nursingworld.org

The American Nurses Association (ANA) is the only full-service professional organization representing the interests of the nation's 3.1 million registered nurses through its constituent and state nurses associations and its organizational affiliates.

Loressa Cole, Chief Executive Officer

5246 **American Pregnancy Association**
3007 Skyway Circle N., Ste 800
Irving, TX 75038
800-672-2296
info@americanpregnancy.org
americanpregnancy.org

The American Pregnancy Association is a 501(c)(3) nonprofit organization committed to promoting pregnancy wellness through education, advocacy and community awareness.

5247 **American Public Health Association**
800 I Street, NW
Washington, DC 20001
202-777-2742
Fax: 202-777-2534
TTY: 202-777-2500
www.apha.org

APHA champions the health of all people and all communities. They aim to strengthen the public health profession and speak out for public health issues and policies backed by science.

Georges C. Benjamin, MD, Executive Director
Kemi Oluwafemi, MBA, CPA, Chief Financial Officer
Susan Polan, PhD, Associate Executive Director

5248 **American Society for Microbiology**
1752 N Street NW
Washington, DC 20036
202-737-3600
service@asmusa.org
www.asm.org

The American Society for Microbiology is a life science membership organization. Members represent 26 disciplines of microbiological specialization plus a division for microbiology educators.

Jonathan Stevens-Garcia, Chief Operations Officer
Chris DeCasris, Chief Financial Officer
Catherine Ort-Mabry, Chief Marketing/Comm. Officer

5249 **American Thoracic Society**
25 Broadway
New York, NY 10004
212-315-8600
Fax: 212-315-6498
ATSInfo@Thoracic.org
www.thoracic.org

The American Thoracic Society improves global health by advancing research, patient care, and public health in pulmonary disease, critical illness, and sleep disorders. Founded in 1905 to combat TB, the ATS has grown to tackle asthma, COPD, lung cancer, sepsis, acute respiratory distress, and sleep apnea, among other diseases.

Karen J. Collishaw, MPP, CEO
Stephen Altobelli, COO

5250 **Association of Immunization Managers**
620 Hungerford Drive, Suite 29
Rockville, MD 20850
301-424-6080
Fax: 301-424-6081
www.immunizationmanagers.org

The Association of Immunization Managers (AIM) was created in 1999 to enable immunization managers to work together to effectively prevent and control vaccine-preventable diseases and improve immunization coverage in the United States and its territories.

Claire Hannan, Executive Director
Jennie Moss, Chief Financial Officer
Katelyn Wells, Research and Development Director

Preventable Childhood Infections / National Associations & Support Groups

5251 Healthy Mothers, Healthy Babies
1201 Eye Street NW, 10th Floor
Washington, DC 20005
HMHB@micronutrientforum.org
hmhbconsortium.org

The HMHB Consortium's mission is to improve maternal nutrition through collective action by Consortium members to accelerate availability and effective use of MMS in low- and middle-income countries.

5252 Immunization Action Coalition
2136 Ford Parkway, Suite 5011
Saint Paul, MN 55116
651-647-9009
Fax: 651-647-9131
admin@immunize.org
www.immunize.org

The Immunization Action Coalition (IAC) works to increase immunization rates and prevent disease by creating and distributing educational materials for health professionals and the public that enhance the delivery of safe and effective immunization services. The Coalition also facilitates communication about the safety, efficacy, and use of vaccines within the broad immunization community of patients, parents, health care organizations, and government health agencies.

Kelly L. Moore, President & CEO
Litjen Tan, Chief Policy Officer
David Sanders, Chief Health Informatics Officer

5253 Infectious Diseases Society of America
4040 Wilson Blvd, Suite 300
Arlington, VA 22203
703-299-0200
www.idsociety.org

The Infectious Diseases Society of America (IDSA) represents physicians, scientists and other health care professionals who specialize in infectious diseases. IDSA's purpose is to improve the health of individuals, communities, and society by promoting excellence in patient care, education, research, public health, and prevention relating to infectious diseases.

Carlos del Rio, President
Jeff Duchin, Secretary
Jeanne Marrazzo, Treasurer

5254 National Association of Pediatric Nurse Practitioners
5 Hanover Square, Suite 1401
New York, NY 10004
917-746-8300
877-662-7627
Fax: 212-785-1713
www.napnap.org

National Association of Pediatric Nurse Practitioners (NAPNAP) is the professional association for pediatric nurse practitioners (PNPs) and other advanced practice nurses who care for children.

James H. Wendroft, Executive Director
Laura Nelsen, Director, Education & Learning
Linda Young, Director, Finance & Administration

5255 National Association of School Nurses
1100 Wayne Avenue Suite 925
Silver Spring, MD 20910
240-821-1130
nasn@nasn.org
www.nasn.org

The mission is to advance school nurse practice to keep students healthy, safe and ready to learn.

Donna J. Mazyck, Executive Director
Nichole K. Bobo, Nursing Education Director
Jen McNally, Marketing/Communications Director

5256 National Foundation for Infectious Diseases
7201 Wisconsin Avenue, Suite 750
Bethesda, MD 20814
301-656-0003
www.nfid.org

The National Foundation for Infectious Diseases (NFID) is a non-profit, tax-exempt 501(c)(3) organization founded in 1973 dedicated to educating the public and healthcare professionals about the causes, treatment, and prevention of infectious diseases across the lifespan.

5257 National Tuberculosis Controllers Association
2452 Spring Road SE
Smyrna, GA 30080
678-503-0503
Fax: 678-503-0805
dhwegener@tbcontrollers.org
www.tbcontrollers.org

The NTCA was created in 1995 to bring together the leaders of tuberculosis control programs in all states and territories, as well as many counties and city health departments that organize their own TB control activities.

Donna Hope Wegener, Executive Director
Diana Fortune, Nurse Consultant
Sherry Brown, Conference Planner

5258 Pediatric Infectious Diseases Society
1300 Wilson Boulevard, Suite 300
Arlington, VA 22209
703-299-6764
Fax: 703-299-0473
pids@idsociety.org
www.pids.org

PIDS is the world's largest organization of professionals dedicated to the treatment, control and eradication of infectious diseases affecting children. Membership is comprised of physicians, doctoral-level scientists and others who have trained or are in training in infectious diseases or its related disciplines, and who are identified with the discipline of pediatric infectious diseases or related disciplines through clinical practice, research, teaching and/or administration activities.

Terri Christene Phillips, Executive Director
Winter Harris, Communications & Marketing Manager

5259 Polio Survivors Association
12720 La Reina Avenue
Downey, CA 90242
polio1953@gmail.com
www.polioassociation.org

Nonprofit organization dedicated to education, advocacy, and support to promote the well being and improve the quality of life for severely disabled polio survivors.

Richard Daggett, President

5260 Post-Polio Health International
50 Crestwood Executive Drive, Suite 440
St. Louis, MO 63126
314-534-0475
Fax: 314-534-5070
info@post-polio.org
www.post-polio.org

Provides information to Polio survivors, their families and the health care community and promotes networking among the post-polio community.

Brian M. Tiburzi, Executive Director

5261 Shot At Life
1750 Pennsylvania Avenue NW, Suite 300
Washington, DC 20006
202-419-6406
info@shotatlife.org
www.shotatlife.org

This organization aims to decrease vaccine-preventable childhood deaths and give every child a chance at a healthy life, by encouraging individuals to learn about, advocate for, and donate to vaccines to protect children worldwide.

Martha Rebour, Executive Director
Erinn Heffes, Campaign Coordinator
Roberta Plantak, Corporate Partnerships Officer

5262 World Health Organization
Avenue Appia 20
1202 Geneva,
Switzerland
www.who.int

WHO is the directing and coordinating authority for health within the United Nations system. WHO operates in more than 150 countries around the world.

Dr. Tedros Adhanom Ghebreyesus, Director General
Dr. Zsuzsanna Jakab, Deputy Director General
Stewart Simonson, Asst Director General, UN NYC

Preventable Childhood Infections / State Agencies & Support Groups

State Agencies & Support Groups

Arizona

5263 Maricopa Co Childhood Immunization Program
PO Box 44283
Phoenix, AZ 85064
602-262-2447
info@mcchip.org
www.mcchip.org

5264 The Arizona Partnership for Immunization
320 E. McDowell Rd
Phoenix, AZ 85004
602-253-0090
Fax: 602-262-2654
www.whyimmunize.org

Arkansas

5265 Arkansas Department of Health Div. of Comm Diseases/Immunizations
4815 West Markham St - Slot 48
Little Rock, AR 72205
501-661-2723
www.health.state.ar.us

California

5266 All Kids By Two Health Services Agency
1060 Emeline Ave - Bldg F
Santa Cruz, CA 95061
831-454-5477
Fax: 831-454-5049
www.santacruzhealth.org

5267 California Department of Health Services Immunization Branch
2151 Berkeley Way - Rm 712
Berkeley, CA 94704
510-540-2065
www.dhs.ca.gov

5268 Community Health Improvement Partners - Immunize San Diego (CHIP-ISD)
707 Broadway - Ste 905
San Diego, CA 92101
619-515-2858
Fax: 619-544-0888
tdanos@hasdic.org
www.sdchip.org

5269 Immunization Partnership of Alameda County
2000 Mowry Avenue
Fremont, CA 94538
510-494-7053
Fax: 510-791-3496
ruth_young@whhs.com
www.whhs.com

Colorado

5270 Colorado Dept. of Public Heand & Environment: Immunization Program, DCEED-IMM-A3
4300 Cherry Creek Drive South
Denver, CO 80222
303-692-2669
www.cdphe.state.co.us/health-h.asp

District of Columbia

5271 Commission of Public Health Immunization Program
1131 Spring Road, NW
Washington, DC 20010
202-576-7130

5272 Department of Health Division of Immunization
6323 Georgia Ave, NW - Ste 305
Washington, DC 20011
202-576-7130

Florida

5273 Florida Department of Health Immunization Program
2020 Capital Circle SE
Tallahassee, FL 32399
904-487-2755
www.doh.state.fl.us

Hawaii

5274 Hawaii Department of Health Immunization Program
1250 Punchbowl Street
Honolulu, HI 96813
808-586-4400
Fax: 808-586-4444
www.hawaii.gov/health

Idaho

5275 Idaho Dept. of Health & Welfare Immunizati on Program
PO Box 83720
Boise, ID 83720
208-334-5500
800-554-2922
Fax: 208-334-5942
www.healthandwelfare.idaho.gov

Indiana

5276 Indiana State Dept. of Health Immunization
2 North Meridian St
Indianapolis, IN 46204
317-233-1325
www.in.gov/isdh

Iowa

5277 Iowa Department of Public Health Bureau of Immunization
321 East 12th St - Lucas State Office Bldg
Des Moines, IA 50319
515-281-5787
www.idph.state.ia.us

Kansas

5278 Kansas Department of Health & Environment Immunization Program
109 SW 9th St - Ste 606
Topeka, KS 66612
785-296-5591
Fax: 785-296-6510
info@kdhe.state.ks.us
www.kdhe.state.ks.us/index.html

Maine

5279 Maine Dept. of Human Services: Bureau of Health Immunization Program
2 Bangor Street
Augusta, ME 04330   www.maine.gov/dhhs/boh/mip/index_home.htm

Maryland

5280 Dept. of Health & Mental Hygiene-Immunizat ion
201 West Preston St
Baltimore, MD 21201
410-767-6860
TDD: 800-735-2258
ww.dhmh.state.md.us

Preventable Childhood Infections / State Agencies & Support Groups

Mississippi

5281 Mississippi Dept. of Health Bureau of Preventative Health Immunization
2423 N State St - PO Box 1700
Jackson, MS 39215
601-576-7751
Fax: 601-576-7686
www.msdh.state.ms.us/msdhhome.htm

Nebraska

5282 Nebraska Dept. of Health Immunization Prog ram
PO Box 95044
Lincoln, NE 68509
402-471-3727
www.hhs.state.ne.us

Nevada

5283 Nevada State Health Division Bureau of Com munity Health - Immunization Program
4150 Technology Way
Carson City, NV 89706
775-684-5900
http://health.nv.gov/immunization.htm

New Hampshire

5284 NH Dept. of Health & Human Services Immunization Program
28 Hazen Drive
Concord, NH 03301
603-271-4482
800-852-3345
www.dhhs.state.nh.us/dhhs/immunization/default.htm

New Jersey

5285 New Jersey Department of Health Immunizations Program
PO Box 369
Trenton, NJ 08625
609-588-7512
Fax: 609-588-7431
www.state.nj.us/health

New Mexico

5286 New Mexico Department of Health Immunization Program
1190 St. Francis Dr - S1260
Santa Fe, NM 87505
505-827-2463
ww.health.state.nm.us/immunize

New York

5287 New York State Department of Health Immunization Program
Corning Tower Building - Rm 649
Albany, NY 12237
518-473-4437
www.health.state.ny.us

Ohio

5288 Ohio Department of Health Immunization Program
246 N High St, PO Box 118
Columbus, OH 43216
614-466-0302
www.odh.state.oh.us

Oklahoma

5289 Oklahoma State Department of Health Immunization Division
1000 North East 10th St
Oklahoma City, OK 73117
405-271-5600
www.health.state.ok.us

Rhode Island

5290 Rhode Island Department of Health Immunization Program
3 Capitol Hill
Providence, RI 02908
401-222-2231
Fax: 401-222-6548
TTY: 800-745-5555
www.health.state.ri.us

South Carolina

5291 SC Dept. of Health & Environmental Control Immunization Division
1751 Calhoun St
Columbia, SC 29201
803-898-3432
www.scdhec.gov/health/disease/immunization

South Dakota

5292 South Dakota Department of Health Office of Disease Prevention
Health Building, 600 E. Capitol
Pierre, SD 57501
605-773-3737
doh.info@state.sd.us
www.state.sd.us/state/executive/doh/doh.html

Tennessee

5293 Tennessee Department of Health Immunization
Cordell Hull Building, 425 5th Ave, North - 3rd Fl
Nashville, TN 37247
615-741-3111
Fax: 615-741-3491
www.state.tn.us/health

Texas

5294 Texas Department oF Health Immunization Division
1100 West 49th Street
Austin, TX 78756
512-458-7284
ww.tdh.state.tx.us

Utah

5295 Utah Department of Health
PO Box 1010
Salt Lake City, UT 84114
801-538-6101
http://hlunix.ex.state.ut.us

Vermont

5296 Vermont Department oF Health State Immunication Program
108 Cherry Street
Burlington, VT 05402
800-464-4343
TDD: 802-863-7200
www.healthyvermonters.info

Virginia

5297 Virginia Department of Health Bureau of Immunization
1500 East Main Street
Richmond, VA 23219
804-786-6246
www.vdh.state.va.us

Washington

5298 Washington State Department of Health Immunization Program
1112 SE Quince St, PO Box 47890
Olympia, WA 98504

360-236-4010
www.doh.wa.gov

Web Sites

5299 Canadian Task Force on Preventive Health Care
3280 Hospital Drive Northwest
Calgary, AL T2N 4

info@canadiantaskforce.ca
canadiantaskforce.ca

This website is designed to serve as a practical guide to health care providers, planners and consumers for determining the inclusion or exclusion, content and frequency of a wide variety of preventive health interventions, using the evidence based recommendations of the Canadian Task Force on Preventice Health Care.

Marcello Tonelli, Chair
Richard Birtwhistle, Vice Chair
C. Maria Bacchus, Board Member

5300 Centers for Disease Control and Prevention -Infection Control
1600 Clifton Rd
Atlanta, GA 30329

800-232-4636
www.cdc.gov/hai/

Promotes health and quality of life by preventing and controlling disease, injury, and disability.

5301 Health Research Program (HaRP)
www.harpnet.org

www.harpnet.org

A program by USAID, the project strives to improve the health status of infants, children, mothers and families through the development and research of new tools, technologies, policies and approaches.

5302 KidsHealth - Measles
kidshealth.org/en/parents/measles.html

kidshealth.org/en/parents/measles.html

KidsHealth provides doctor-approved health information about children from before birth through adolescence. KidsHealth provides families with accurate, up to date and jargon free health information they can use.

Neil Izenberg, MD, Editor-in-Chief & Founder

5303 KidsHealth - Rubella (German Measles)
kidshealth.org/en/parents/german-measles.html

kidshealth.org/en/parents/german-measles.html

KidsHealth provides doctor-approved health information about children from before birth through adolescence. KidsHealth provides families with accurate, up to date and jargon free health information they can use.

Neil Izenberg, MD, Editor-in-Chief & Founder

5304 KidsHealth - Tetanus
kidshealth.org/en/parents/tetanus.html

kidshealth.org/en/parents/tetanus.html

KidsHealth provides doctor-approved health information about children from before birth through adolescence. KidsHealth provides families with accurate, up to date and jargon free health information they can use.

Neil Izenberg, MD, Editor-in-Chief & Founder

5305 Pan American Health Organization (PAHO)
525 23rd Street, NW
Washington, DC 20037

202-974-3000
Fax: 202-974-3663
www.paho.org

The mission is to strengthen national and local health systems and improve the health of the peoples of the Americas, in collaboraton with Ministries of Health, other government and international agencies, nongovernmental organizations, universities, social security agencies, community groups, and many others. Health topics include measles, mumps, rubella and diptheria.

Dr. Carissa F. Etienne, Director
Dr. Isabella Danel, Deputy Director
Gerald Anderson, Director of Administration

5306 Polio Connection of America
www.geocities.com/w1066w/

www.geocities.com/w1066w/

For survivors of the Polio Survivors to chat and the site offers links to other polio sites.

5307 Polio Experience Network
825 Sherbrook Street
Winnipeg, MB R3A 1

204-975-3037
Fax: 204-975-3027
postpolionetwork@gmail.com
www.postpolionetwork.ca/pps

Offers information, inspiration, ideas and resources to help patients understand polio and post-poli syndrome, and to confidently manage life with it. Also helps loved ones cope with the effects of polio. Resources are also offered for students doing research on the disease as well as general resources available.

Cheryl Currie, President
Kathryn Harper, Vice President
Estelle Boissonneault, Secretary

5308 Post Polio Awareness & Support Society of British Columbia
#102-9775-4th Street
Sidney, BC V8L 2

250-665-8849
Fax: 250-665-8859
www.ppassbc.com

A non profit society formed as a network for polio survivors, those affected by polio, and any interested in polio.

Joan Toone, President

5309 Slack Incorporated
6900 Grove Road
Thorofare, NJ 8086

856-848-1000
Fax: 856-848-6091
email@slackinc.com
www.slackinc.com

A leading provider of healthcare information, educational programs, and meeting and exhibit management services worldwide.

5310 Virtual Pediatric Hospital
www.virtualpediatrichospital.org

www.virtualpediatrichospital.org

A digital library of pediatric information including resources for patients and health care professionals.

Book Publishers

5311 Everything You Need to Know About Measles and Rubella
Trisha Hawkins, author

Rosen Publishing/PowerKids Press
29 E 21st Street
New York, NY 10010

212-777-3017
800-237-9932
Fax: 888-436-4643
rosenpub@tribeca.ios.com
www.rosenpublishing.com

Examines the continuing threat of these highly infectious respiratory diseases. Grades 7-12.

2001 64 pages
ISBN: 0-823933-22-9

Roger Rosen, President

Preventable Childhood Infections / Newsletters

5312 IVUN Resource Directory
50 Crestwood Executive Drive, Suite 440
St. Louis, MO 63126
314-534-0475
Fax: 314-534-5070
info@post-polio.org
www.post-polio.org

A networking tool for health professionals and both long-term and new ventilator users. Sections include health professionals, ventilator users, equipment and aids, manufacturers, service and repair, organizations, etc.

Brian M. Tiburzi, Executive Director

5313 Let's Talk About Having Chicken Pox
Elizabeth Weitzman, author

Rosen Publishing/PowerKids Press
29 E 21st Street
New York, NY 10010
212-777-3017
800-237-9932
Fax: 888-436-4643
rosenpub@tribeca.ios.com
www.rosenpublishing.com

Highly contagious chicken pox is one of the childhood illnesses that few kids escape. This book tells kids how to handle the illness, where it comes from and how long it will take to recover. Grades K-5.

24 pages
ISBN: 0-823950-31-X

Roger Roger, President

5314 Measles
Maxine Rosaler, author

Rosen Publishing/PowerKids Press
29 E 21st Street
New York, NY 10010
212-777-3017
800-237-9932
Fax: 888-436-4643
rosenpub@tribeca.ios.com
www.rosenpublishing.com

An examination of the history of this once thought to be harmless disease, from its ancient origins to near eradication.

2005 64 pages
ISBN: 1-404202-56-0

Roger Roger, President

Newsletters

5315 Infectious Diseases in Children
Slack Incorporated
6900 Grove Road
Thorofare, NJ 08086
856-848-1000
800-257-8290
editor@healio.com
www.healio.com/footer/healio-dot-com

Pediatric news source.
Monthly
Philip A Brunell MD, Chief Medical Editor

Pamphlets

5316 Tetanus and Diptheria Vaccine
Centers for Disease Control & Prevention
1600 Clifton Road
Atlanta, GA 30333
404-639-3311
800-232-4636
www.cdc.gov/vaccines/pubs/vis/downloads/vis-td.pdf

Factsheet about the diseases and the vaccines.

Description

5317 PROTEIN C DEFICIENCY

Synonyms: PC deficiency, PROC deficiency

Covers these related disorders: Protein C deficiency Type I, Protein C deficiency Type II

Involves the following Biologic System(s):
Hematologic and Oncologic Disorders

Protein C deficiency is a blood clotting (thrombotic) disorder characterized by the recurrent formation of blood clots within the veins of the body (venous thrombosis). Protein C, which is formed in the liver, is a specialized protein that helps to prevent the formation of blood clots. When activated, protein C helps to dissolve fibrin, the semisolid portion of blood clots, thus inhibiting the formation of a clot. A deficiency of this protein, therefore, results in abnormal clot formation. Some signs of this disorder may become apparent during adolescence. Associated symptoms depend upon the organ or tissue affected by clot formation that leads to reduced or absent blood flow. Affected individuals may develop blood clots and inflammation in the veins of the legs (thrombophlebitis). This can occur when the blood moves slowly in the veins, such as from prolonged bed rest during an illness, surgery, or hospital stay. In some patients, these clots may dislodge from the vein and travel through the blood stream (embolus) to different parts of the body including the heart, lungs, or brain, potentially leading to life-threatening complications. However, not all patients with protein C deficiency experience all the signs associated with this disorder.

In the event of a blood clotting episode, the antithrombin factor heparin may be administered through injection into a vein (intravenous) or under the skin (subcutaneous). Other treatment may include continuing oral administration of the anti-coagulant drug warfarin to prevent a recurrence of thrombotic activity

Two types of protein C deficiency have been described in the general population. The more common form is Type I in which both protein C levels and activity are deficient. In the less common Type II, the amount of protein is normal but its activity or performance is impaired. The inherited form of protein C deficiency may be transmitted as an autosomal dominant trait. The gene for this disorder is located on the long arm of chromosome 2 (2q13-14). Protein C deficiency may also be acquired in connection with infection.

Government Agencies

5318 NIH/National Heart, Lung and Blood Institute
31 Center Drive, Bldg 31
Bethesda, MD 20892

877-645-2448
www.nhlbi.nih.gov

Primary responsibility of this organization is the scientific investigation of heart, blood vessel, lung and blood disorders. Oversees research, demonstration, prevention, education, control and training activities in these fields and emphasizes the prevention and control of heart diseases.

Gary H. Gibbons, MD, Director
Kate O'Sullivan, Executive Officer

National Associations & Support Groups

5319 American Academy of Pediatrics
345 Park Blvd
Itasca, IL 60143

847-434-4000
800-433-9016
Fax: 847-434-8000
csc@aap.org
www.aap.org

The American Academy of Pediatrics and its member pediatricians are committed to the attainment of optimal physical, mental and social health and well-being for all infants, children, adolescents, and young adults.

Kyle E. Yasuda, MD, FAAP, President
Mark Del Monte, JD, CEO/Executive VP
Vera Tait, MD, FAAP, Chief Medical Officer

5320 Genetic Alliance
426400 Woodfield Road, Ste 189
Damascus, MD 20872

202-966-5557
Fax: 202-966-8553
info@geneticalliance.org
www.geneticalliance.org

World's leading nonprofit health advocacy organization committed to transforming health through genetics and promoting an environment of openness centered on the health of individuals, families, and communities.

Sharon Terry, CEO
Ruth Child, CFO
Natasha Bonhomme, Chief Strategy Officer

5321 March of Dimes Foundation
1550 Crystal Drive, Ste 1300
Arlington, VA 22202

888-663-4637
www.marchofdimes.org

March of Dimes help moms have full-term pregnancies and research the problems that threaten the health of babies. The March of Dimes also acts globally: sharing best practices in perinatal health and helping improve birth outcomes where the needs are the most urgent.

Stacey D. Stewart, President
Alan Brogdon, SVP/COO/Board Officer
Rahul Gupta, MD, SVP & Chief Medical/Health Officer

State Agencies & Support Groups

5322 Vitamin C Foundation
24W500 Maple Avenue, Ste 107
Naperville, IL

630-983-6707
800-849-9025
Fax: 630-416-1309
vitamincfoundation@gmail.com
www.vitamincfoundation.org

A Texas nonprofit organization devoted to preserving and distributing knowledge about ascorbic acid and its vital role in the life process.

Owen R Fonorow, Co-Founder
M S Till Sr, Co-Founder

Web Sites

5323 Factor V Leiden: Thrombophilia Support Page
www.fvleiden.org

www.fvleiden.org

Factor V Leiden is the most common hereditary blood coagulation disorder in the US. It is present in 3-7% of the population in Europe and America. It is associated with Venous thrombosis, DVT, unexplained miscarriage, blood clots in the lungs, gall bladder dysfunction, preeclampsia and/or eclapsia, stroke and/or heart attack.

5324 HealthCentral.com
750 Third Avenue, 6th Floor
New York, NY 10017

212-695-2223
Fax: 212-695-2936
www.healthcentral.com

Offering information on health issues for children, women, men and seniors. Information on Protein C Deficiency includes a description, causes, symptoms, diagnosis, treatment and questions that can be asked of the doctor.

Micheael Cunnion, Chief Executive Officer
Jim Curtis, Chief Revenue Officer
Rebecca Farwell, Chief Content Officer

5325 MedicineNet
www.medicinenet.com

www.medicinenet.com

An online, healthcare media publishing company. It provides easy to read, in-depth, authoritative medical information for consumers via an interactive web site.

5326 Merck
2000 Galloping Hill Road
Kenilworth, NJ 7033
908-740-4000
www.merck.com

A site that offers research driven pharmaceutical products and services to improve human and animal health, directly and through its joint ventures.

Kenneth C.˜ Frazier, Chairman & CEO
Robert M. Davis, EVP & CFO
Willie A. Deese, EVP & President

5327 Online Mendelian Inheritance in Man
McKusick-Nathans Institue of Genetic Medicine-JHU
Baltimore, MD 21205
www.omim.org

This database is a catalog of human genes and genetic disorders.

Ada Hamosh, MD, Scientific Director

Book Publishers

5328 Merck Manual of Diagnosis and Therapy
Merck Publishing Group
PO Box 2000 RY84-15
Rahway, NJ 07065
732-594-4600
Fax: 732-388-3610
www.merckbooks.com

Since it was first published in 1899, The Merck Manual has set the standard for excellence in the medical community for current, complete, and comprehensive information for all healthcare professionals. Written by more than 300 medical experts in all fields of medicine from around the world.

2006 18th Ed 2832 pages Hardcover
ISBN: 0-911910-18-2

Mark H Beers MD, Editor-in-Chief
Robert S Porter MD, Editor

5329 Protein Deficiency and Pesticide Toxicity
Eldon M Boyd, author

Charles C Thomas
2600 South First Street
Springfield, IL 62704
217-789-8980
800-258-8980
Fax: 217-789-9130
books@ccthomas.com
www.ccthomas.com

Discusses the approaches for analyzing Protein Deficiency and Pesticide Toxicity.

468 pages Hardcover
ISBN: 0-398024-76-6

Description

5330 PSORIASIS

Involves the following Biologic System(s):
Dermatologic Disorders

Psoriasis is a common, chronic skin disease characterized by red patches of skin that are covered by dry, thick, silvery scales. This disorder may occur at any age, but most commonly appears from the ages of 10 to 40 years. Although males and females are affected equally, females are more prone to development of this disorder when it appears during childhood. In addition, approximately half of those individuals who develop psoriasis in childhood have a family history of the disorder, but the pattern of transmission has not been determined. Individuals with psoriasis appear to produce new skin cells at a greatly accelerated rate while shedding their old cells at a normal rate. The subsequent buildup of new cells produces thickened areas of new skin that are covered by old skin, thus forming the characteristic dry, thickened, silvery patches associated with psoriasis.

Psoriatic lesions may appear anywhere on the body, but most commonly form on the scalp, elbows, knees, back, buttocks, navel area, and genitalia. In addition, relatively smaller lesions may appear on the face and pitting may develop on the nails. Peeling away a scale produces specks of bleeding from the capillaries (Auspitz's sign). Itching of the skin (pruritus) is common and scratching leads to more lesions (Koebner's phenomenon). On rare occasions, severe psoriasis may develop in newborns, accompanied by lesion formation in the diaper area.

There are different types of psoriasis. The most common form is called discoid psoriasis and is characterized by patches that form mainly on the elbows, knees, scalp, and other areas of the arms, legs, and trunk. Other findings may include nail irregularities such as pitting, thickening, and separation from the nail beds. In addition, psoriasis is sometimes accompanied by painful swelling of the joints (arthritis). Guttate psoriasis occurs primarily in children and young adults and is characterized by the sudden appearance of small, oval, drop-like lesions on the trunk and upper portions of the arms and legs. Guttate psoriasis often develops following a streptococcal infection, viral infection, or sunburn. In addition, this form of the disorder sometimes follows the conclusion or withdrawal of corticosteroid treatment. Pustular psoriasis may be localized or generalized. In its localized form, eruptions of pustules develop over individual reddish patches that are present, usually, on the palms of the hands and the soles of the feet. Psoriasis is usually apparent on other parts of the body. Affected individuals may also experience localized discomfort. Generalized pustular psoriasis is an acute, severe, sometimes life-threatening form of the disorder that is characterized by the widespread eruption of small pustules in individuals with mild, moderate, or other types of psoriasis. Generalized pustular psoriasis is sometimes accompanied by high fever, pain in the joints, elevated levels of white blood cells (leukocytosis), low levels of blood calcium (hypocalcemia), and other irregularties.

Treatment of psoriasis is dependent upon age, area of involvement, and the type and severity of the disease. Many treatment protocols that are effective for adults may be too toxic for children; therefore, most treatment for children with psoriasis is conservative and mainly directed toward comfort and alleviation of pain. Such treatment may include the use of tar preparations in the form of gels, ointments, or bath emulsions. Additional topical treatments may include the cautious use of corticosteroid preparations, vitamin D analogs, and other ointments. Treatment for scalp lesions may include the use of a phenol and saline solution followed by tar shampoo and, when lesions are reduced, the application of a corticosteroid preparation. Severe psoriasis in children may indicate the use of various drugs such as methotrexate and certain oral retinoids; however, this therapy may be accompanied by severe side effects. Other treatment is symptomatic and supportive.

National Associations & Support Groups

5331 American Academy of Pediatrics
345 Park Blvd
Itasca, IL 60143
847-434-4000
800-433-9016
Fax: 847-434-8000
csc@aap.org
www.aap.org

The American Academy of Pediatrics and its member pediatricians are committed to the attainment of optimal physical, mental and social health and well-being for all infants, children, adolescents, and young adults.

Kyle E. Yasuda, MD, FAAP, President
Mark Del Monte, JD, CEO/Executive VP
Vera Tait, MD, FAAP, Chief Medical Officer

5332 National Psoriasis Foundation
6600 SW 92nd Avenue, Suite 300
Portland, OR 97223
503-244-7404
800-723-9166
Fax: 503-245-0626
getinfo@psoriasis.org
www.psoriasis.org

Promotes awareness and understanding of psoriasis and psoriatic arthritis through education and advocacy. The foundation also ensures access to treatment and supports research that leads to effective management of the condition.

Randy Beranek, President & CEO
Leah McCormick Howard, COO
Kris Bockmier, Director, Field Operations

Research Centers

5333 University of California, San Francisco Dermatology Drug Research
515 Spruce Street
San Francisco, CA 94115
415-476-4701
Fax: 415-502-4126
ycommunications@cc.ucsf.edu
cc.ucsf.edu/people

Conducts clinical testing of new or existing pharmalogic agents used in the treatment of skin disorders.

John Koo, MD, Director

Audio Video

5334 National Library of Dermatologic Teaching Slides
American Academy Of Dermatology
PO Box 94020
Palatine, IL 60094
847-330-0230
Fax: 847-330-0050
www.aad.org/store/product/

A collection of dermatologic teaching slides offering the most comprehensive series ever assembled. Each set offers a realistic presentation of classic clinical skin conditions encountered by the dermatologist.

Brett M. Coldiron, President
Elise A. Olsen, MD, Vice President
Suzanne M. Olbricht, Secretary-Treasurer

Psoriasis / Web Sites

Web Sites

5335 American Academy of Dermatology (AAD)
www.aad.org

info@aad.org
www.aad.org

The American Academy of Dermatoloy is dedicated to achieving the highest quality of dermatologic care for everyone. Acheivement of this vision requires a dynamic organization whose mission embodies: Excellence in patient care, education and research, adherence to eithical conduct, respinsiveness to its members and to the public unification and representation of the specialty.

Irvin Bomberger, Interim Executive Director

5336 National Psoriasis Foundation
6600 SW 92nd Avenue, Ste 300
Portland, OR 97223

800-723-9166
getinfo@psoriasis.org
www.psoriasis.org

Promotes awareness and understanding of psoriasis and psoriatic arthritis through education and advocacy. The foundation also ensures access to treatment and supports research that leads to effective management of the condition.

Randy Beranek, President & CEO
Leah McCormick Howard, COO
Kris Bockmier, Director, Field Operations

5337 Psoriasis Association
Dick Coles House, 2 Queensbridge
Northampton, NN4 7

845-676-0076
Fax: 160-425-1621
mail@psoriasis-association.org.uk
www.psoriasis-association.org.uk

Formed with these aims in view: to raise awareness of psoriasis; support those who have psoriasis; and fund research into the causes of and treatments for psoriasis.

4000 members

Ray Jobling, MBE, Chairman
Jonathan Swift, Vice Chairman
John Ford, MBE, Treasurer

5338 Psoriasis Connections
Thousand Oaks, CA 91320

www.psoriasisconnect.com

Connects people with medical experts on psoriasis, those affected by the condition, family and friends, and other relevant resources.

5339 Skin Page
pinch.com/skin/

skinpage-0907-admin@pinch.com
pinch.com/skin/

Noncommercial site that provides shortcuts to search past messages in the skin diseases newsgroups and other databases. Includes a psoriasis information page and other resources.

Book Publishers

5340 Handbook of Psoriasis
Charles Camisa, author

Blackwell Publishing
Commerce Place, 350 Main Street
Malden, MA 02148

781-388-8200
800-216-2522
Fax: 781-388-8210
www.wiley.com

Reference for health care professionals, easy to read, yet detailed information.

2005 2nd Ed Paperback
ISBN: 1-405109-27-7

Peter B. Wiley, Chairman
Stephen M. Smith, President & CEO
Ellis E. Cousens, Executive Vice President, Chief Fin

5341 Psychological Approaches to Dermatology
Linda Papadopoulos, author

Blackwell Publishing
Commerce Place, 350 Main Street
Malden, MA 02148

781-388-8200
800-216-2522
Fax: 781-388-8210
www.wiley.com

References all the main skin conditions - psoriasis, eczema, vitiligo, dermatitis, alopecia, and others. The book blends theory and practical experience, making it a highly recommended read.

1999 176 pages Paperback
ISBN: 1-854332-92-9

Peter B. Wiley, Chairman
Stephen M. Smith, President & CEO
Ellis E. Cousens, Executive Vice President, Chief Fin

5342 Textbook of Psoriasis
Peter Van de Kerkhof, author

Blackwell Publishing
Commerce Place, 350 Main Street
Malden, MA 02148

781-388-8200
800-216-2522
Fax: 781-388-8210
www.wiley.com

Written for dermatologists, it is a concise and clinical account of psoriasis, divided into three sections: morphology of the skin, etiology and pathogenesis, and current treatments.

2003 2nd Ed Hardback
ISBN: 1-405107-17-4

Peter B. Wiley, Chairman
Stephen M. Smith, President & CEO
Ellis E. Cousens, Executive Vice President, Chief Fin

Magazines

5343 International Journal of Dermatology
International Society of Dermatology
2323 North State Street #30
Bunnell, FL 32110

386-437-4405
Fax: 386-437-4427
info@intsocderm.org
www.intsocderm.org

Focuses on information for dermatologists and the whole specialty of dermatology research and education.

10 times a year

Evangeline˜ Handog, MD, President
Luca Borradori, Vice President
Paulo Rowilson Cunha, Vice President

5344 Journal of Dermatologic Surgery and Oncology
International Society for Dermatologic Surgery
930 N Meachan Road
Schaumburg, IL 60173

847-330-9830
Fax: 847-330-1135

Focuses on medical updates and information on dermatology.
Monthly

5345 Psoriasis Advance
National Psoriasis Foundation
6600 SW 92nd Avenue, Suite 300
Portland, OR 97223

503-244-7404
800-723-9166
Fax: 503-245-0626
getinfo@psoriasis.org
www.psoriasis.org

Member magazine that evolved from two formerly published newsletters (Bulletin & Psoriasis Resource) connecting the psoriasis community.

Psoriasis / Pamphlets

36 pages Bi-monthly
Randy Beranek, President & CEO
Stace Bell, PhD, VP, Research & Clinical Affairs
Denice Bradbury, Director, Marketing/Communication

Journals

5346 Journal of Psoriasis and Psoriatic Arthritis (JPPA)
National Psoriasis Foundation
6600 SW 92nd Avenue, Suite 300
Portland, OR 97223
503-244-7404
800-723-9166
Fax: 503-245-0626
getinfo@psoriasis.org
www.psoriasis.org

Journal for professional members of the foundation. It is dedicated to providing up-to-date, practical information to health care providers on the front line of psoriasis treatment.

Krista Kellogg, Chair
Pete Redding, Vice Chair
Randy Beranek, President/ CEO

Newsletters

5347 Bulletin
National Psoriasis Foundation
6600 SW 92nd Avenue, Suite 300
Portland, OR 97223
503-244-7404
800-723-9166
Fax: 503-245-0626
getinfo@psoriasis.org
www.psoriasis.org

Published for 35 years by the National Psoriasis Foundation, past issues are available online in pdf form. It covered both traditional and alternative treatments, self-help techniques, research and a wide variety of human-interest topics. Please refer to the foundation's magazine Psoriasis Advance for updated information and resources.

Krista Kellogg, Chair
Pete Redding, Vice Chair
Randy Beranek, President/ CEO

5348 DVH Quarterly
University of Arkansas at Little Rock
2801 S University Avenue
Little Rock, AR 72204
Fax: 501-663-3536

Offers information on upcoming events, conferences and workshops on and for visual disabilities. Book reviews, information on the newest resources and technology, educational programs, want ads and more.

Quarterly

Bob Brasher, Editor

5349 Dermatology Focus
Dermatology Foundation
1560 Sherman Avenue, Suite 870
Evanston, IL 60201
847-328-2256
Fax: 847-328-0509
dfgen@dermatologyfoundation.org
dermatologyfoundation.org

Includes membership activities, research articles and lists recipients of foundation awards.

Quarterly

Bruce U. Wintroub, Chairman
Michael D. Tharp, M.D., President
Staurt R. Lessin, M.D., Vice President

5350 Dermatology World
American Academy of Dermatology
9500 W. Bryn Mawr Avenue, Ste 500
Rosemont, IL 60018
847-240-1737
888-462-3376
Fax: 847-240-1859
info@aad.org
www.aad.org

Offers Academy members information outside the clinical realm. It carries news of government actions, reports of socioeconomic issues, societal trends and other events which impinge on the practice of dermatology.

Monthly

Irvin Bomberger, Interim Executive Director

5351 Progress in Dermatology
Dermatology Foundation
1560 Sherman Avenue, Suite 870
Evanston, IL 60201
847-328-2256
Fax: 847-328-0509
dfgen@dermatologyfoundation.org
dermatologyfoundation.org

Bulletin offering information on research reports and clinical trials.

Quarterly

Bruce U. Wintroub, Chairman
Michael D. Tharp, M.D., President
Staurt R. Lessin, M.D., Vice President

5352 Psoriasis Resource
National Psoriasis Foundation
6600 SW 92nd Avenue, Suite 300
Portland, OR 97223
503-244-7404
800-723-9166
Fax: 503-245-0626
getinfo@psoriasis.org
www.psoriasis.org

Published from 1999 to 2002, three times a year, by the National Psoriasis Foundation, past issues are available online in pdf form. It helped people make educated decisions about medication, therapy and product choices available for skin and joints. Please refer to the foundation's magazine Psoriasis Advance for updated information and resources.

Krista Kellogg, Chair
Pete Redding, Vice Chair
Randy Beranek, President/ CEO

Pamphlets

5353 Alternative Approaches
National Psoriasis Foundation
6600 SW 92nd Avenue, Suite 300
Portland, OR 97223
503-244-7404
800-723-9166
Fax: 503-245-0626
getinfo@psoriasis.org
www.psoriasis.org

Non-traditional therapies and treatments for both psoriasis and psoriatic arthritis including stress management, topical preparations and Chinese medicine.

2005 13 pages

Randy Beranek, President & CEO
Stace Bell, PhD, VP, Research & Clinical Affairs
Denice Bradbury, Director, Marketing/Communication

5354 Conception, Pregnancy and Psoriasis
National Psoriasis Foundation
6600 SW 92nd Avenue, Suite 300
Portland, OR 97223
503-244-7404
800-723-9166
Fax: 503-245-0626
getinfo@psoriasis.org
www.psoriasis.org

Overview of the effect of pregnancy on psoriasis and treatment, risks and other considerations during conception.

2006 9 pages

Randy Beranek, President & CEO
Stace Bell, PhD, VP, Research & Clinical Affairs
Denice Bradbury, Director, Marketing/Communication

Psoriasis / Pamphlets

5355 Phototherapy: Light Treatment for Psoriasis
National Psoriasis Foundation
6600 SW 92nd Avenue, Suite 300
Portland, OR 97223
503-244-7404
800-723-9166
Fax: 503-245-0626
getinfo@psoriasis.org
www.psoriasis.org

Light treatment options: PUVA, lasers, broad-band UVB, and narrow-band UVB.

2006 13 pages

Randy Beranek, President & CEO
Stace Bell, PhD, VP, Research & Clinical Affairs
Denice Bradbury, Director, Marketing/Communication

5356 Psoriasis 101: Learning to Live in the Skin You're In
National Psoriasis Foundation
6600 SW 92nd Avenue, Suite 300
Portland, OR 97223
503-244-7404
800-723-9166
Fax: 503-245-0626
getinfo@psoriasis.org
www.psoriasis.org

Designed to educate young people, teens and college-age young adults about psoriasis. It is written from a young person's standpoint with bytes of information.

2006 12 pages

Randy Beranek, President & CEO
Stace Bell, PhD, VP, Research & Clinical Affairs
Denice Bradbury, Director, Marketing/Communication

5357 Psoriasis Research: Progress & Promise
National Psoriasis Foundation
6600 SW 92nd Avenue, Suite 300
Portland, OR 97223
503-244-7404
800-723-9166
Fax: 503-245-0626
getinfo@psoriasis.org
www.psoriasis.org

Overview of present research and the foundation's role in supporting it. Includes new treatments and progress being made in genetics.

2004 11 pages

Randy Beranek, President & CEO
Stace Bell, PhD, VP, Research & Clinical Affairs
Denice Bradbury, Director, Marketing/Communication

5358 Psoriasis on Specific Skin Sites
National Psoriasis Foundation
6600 SW 92nd Avenue, Suite 300
Portland, OR 97223
503-244-7404
800-723-9166
Fax: 503-245-0626
getinfo@psoriasis.org
www.psoriasis.org

Information on the disease affecting nails, ears, eyelids, face, mouth and lips, hands, feet and skin folds.

2005 9 pages

Randy Beranek, President & CEO
Stace Bell, PhD, VP, Research & Clinical Affairs
Denice Bradbury, Director, Marketing/Communication

5359 Psoriasis: How it Makes You Feel
National Psoriasis Foundation
6600 SW 92nd Avenue, Suite 300
Portland, OR 97223
503-244-7404
800-723-9166
Fax: 503-245-0626
getinfo@psoriasis.org
www.psoriasis.org

Living with psoriasis and the emotional impact.

Randy Beranek, President & CEO
Stace Bell, PhD, VP, Research & Clinical Affairs
Denice Bradbury, Director, Marketing/Communication

5360 Psoriatic Arthritis
National Psoriasis Foundation
6600 SW 92nd Avenue, Suite 300
Portland, OR 97223
503-244-7404
800-723-9166
Fax: 503-245-0626
getinfo@psoriasis.org
www.psoriasis.org

Overview of the joint disease that affects about 10-30% of psoriasis sufferers. Includes diagnosis and treatment details.

2005 11 pages

Randy Beranek, President & CEO
Stace Bell, PhD, VP, Research & Clinical Affairs
Denice Bradbury, Director, Marketing/Communication

5361 Questions and Answers About Psoriasis
NAMSIC, National Institutes of Health
1 AMS Circle
Bethesda, MD 20892
301-495-4484
877-226-4267
Fax: 301-718-6366
TTY: 301-565-2966
NIAMSinfo@mail.nih.gov
www.niams.nih.gov

Offers various information for the psoriasis patient and their family regarding treatments, risks, nutrition and more.

2003 22 pages

Robert H. Carter, MD, Acting Director

5362 Scalp Psoriasis
National Psoriasis Foundation
6600 SW 92nd Avenue, Suite 300
Portland, OR 97223
503-244-7404
800-723-9166
Fax: 503-245-0626
getinfo@psoriasis.org
www.psoriasis.org

Possible treatment, tips and regimens for psoriasis of the scalp.

2005 9 pages

Randy Beranek, President & CEO
Stace Bell, PhD, VP, Research & Clinical Affairs
Denice Bradbury, Director, Marketing/Communication

5363 Specific Forms of Psoriasis
National Psoriasis Foundation
6600 SW 92nd Avenue, Suite 300
Portland, OR 97223
503-244-7404
800-723-9166
Fax: 503-245-0626
getinfo@psoriasis.org
www.psoriasis.org

Plaque, Pustular, guttate, inverse, and erythrodermic: overview and treatment considerations for each type of the disease.

2006 7 pages

Randy Beranek, President & CEO
Stace Bell, PhD, VP, Research & Clinical Affairs
Denice Bradbury, Director, Marketing/Communication

5364 Sun and Water Therapy
National Psoriasis Foundation
6600 SW 92nd Avenue, Suite 300
Portland, OR 97223
503-244-7404
800-723-9166
Fax: 503-245-0626
getinfo@psoriasis.org
www.psoriasis.org

Provides information on climatotherapy sites as well as an overview of natural sunlight and water treatment options.

2005 11 pages

Randy Beranek, President & CEO
Stace Bell, PhD, VP, Research & Clinical Affairs
Denice Bradbury, Director, Marketing/Communication

5365 Things to Consider
National Psoriasis Foundation
6600 SW 92nd Avenue, Suite 300
Portland, OR 97223

503-244-7404
800-723-9166
Fax: 503-245-0626
getinfo@psoriasis.org
www.psoriasis.org

Discusses making treatment decisions, talking with your physician and knowing your rights.

Randy Beranek, President & CEO
Stace Bell, PhD, VP, Research & Clinical Affairs
Denice Bradbury, Director, Marketing/Communication

5366 Your Diet & Psoriasis
National Psoriasis Foundation
6600 SW 92nd Avenue, Suite 300
Portland, OR 97223

503-244-7404
800-723-9166
Fax: 503-245-0626
getinfo@psoriasis.org
www.psoriasis.org

An overview of diet-related research and therapies.

2005 9 pages

Randy Beranek, President & CEO
Stace Bell, PhD, VP, Research & Clinical Affairs
Denice Bradbury, Director, Marketing/Communication

Camps

5367 Camp Discovery
American Academy of Dermatology
9500 W. Bryn Mawr Avenue, Ste 500
Rosemont, IL 60018

847-240-1737
Fax: 847-240-1859
jmueller@aad.org
www.campdiscovery.org

A camp for young people with chronic skin conditions. There is no fee and transportation is provided. Five locations: Camp Victory in Millville, PA, Camp Knutson in Crosslake, MN, Camp For All in Burton, TX, Channel 3 Kids Camp in Andover, CT, and Camp Seymour in Gig harbor, WA.

J Mueller, Camp Contact
Irvin Bomberger, Interim Executive Director

Ptosis / Description

Description

5368 PTOSIS

Synonym: Blepharoptosis

Covers these related disorders: Acquired ptosis, Congenital ptosis

Involves the following Biologic System(s):

Neurologic Disorders, Ophthalmologic Disorders

Ptosis, or blepharoptosis, refers to a condition in which one or both of the upper eyelids droop or sag as a result of an irregularity that is present at birth or an acquired weakness in the muscles of the upper eyelid that are responsible for movement. This condition may also be the result of irregularities of the nerve response for regulating muscle movements of the upper eyelids (third cranial nerve or oculomotor nerve). Congenital ptosis varies in severity; therefore, treatment depends upon the extent of the defect. If the eyelid droop is sufficient to cover the pupil, the ability to see is impaired. In some infants and children, the development of the affected eye may be slowed, resulting in reduced or lost vision (amblyopia) in that eye. In such cases, early intervention through surgery may aid in preventing the development of impaired vision. However, surgery to correct ptosis strictly for cosmetic reasons is often postponed until the affected child reaches the age of three or four years.

In some cases, ptosis is accompanied by an abnormality of certain eye muscles, resulting in irregular movements of the eyes. Other ocular irregularities often associated with congenital ptosis include misalignment of the eyes in relation to each other (strabismus) or an imbalance in the way each eye deflects light (anisometropia). Medical specialists recommended early treatment of any accompanying abnormalities to avert complications. Ptosis may also occur as a characteristic feature of several syndromes including congenital fibrosis syndrome, Horner syndrome, or Sturge-Weber syndrome. Congenital ptosis is transmitted as an autosomal dominant trait.

Acquired ptosis may develop secondary to several disorders or conditions including myasthenia gravis, a muscular disorder; botulism, a severe type of food poisoning; progressive lesions within the skull that impact on the third cranial nerve; inflammation or growths that impact the eye orbit or lid. Treatment for acquired ptosis depends upon and may be directed toward the underlying cause.

Government Agencies

5369 NIH/National Eye Institute
31 Center Drive MSC 2510
Bethesda, MD 20892

301-496-5248
2020@nei.nih.gov
www.nei.nih.gov

Conducts and supports research that helps prevent and treat eye diseases and other disorders of vision. This research leads to sight-saving treatments, reduces visual impairment and blindness, and improves the quality of life for people of all ages. NEI-supported research has advanced our knowledge of how the eye functions in health and disease.

Michael F. Chiang, MD, Director
Santa Tumminia, Deputy Director

National Associations & Support Groups

5370 American Academy of Pediatrics
345 Park Blvd
Itasca, IL 60143

847-434-4000
800-433-9016
Fax: 847-434-8000
csc@aap.org
www.aap.org

The American Academy of Pediatrics and its member pediatricians are committed to the attainment of optimal physical, mental and social health and well-being for all infants, children, adolescents, and young adults.

Kyle E. Yasuda, MD, FAAP, President
Mark Del Monte, JD, CEO/Executive VP
Vera Tait, MD, FAAP, Chief Medical Officer

5371 Genetic Alliance
426400 Woodfield Road, Ste 189
Damascus, MD 20872

202-966-5557
Fax: 202-966-8553
info@geneticalliance.org
www.geneticalliance.org

World's leading nonprofit health advocacy organization committed to transforming health through genetics and promoting an environment of openness centered on the health of individuals, families, and communities.

Sharon Terry, CEO
Ruth Child, CFO
Natasha Bonhomme, Chief Strategy Officer

5372 Lighthouse Guild
250 West 64th Street
New York, NY 10023

800-284-4422
info@lighthouseguild.org
www.lighthouseguild.org

Lighthouse Guild is dedicated to providing exceptional services that inspire people who are visually impaired to attain their goals.

James M. Dubin, Chair
Calvin W. Roberts, President & CEO
Maura J. Sweeney, SVP, Programs & Services

5373 March of Dimes Foundation
1550 Crystal Drive, Ste 1300
Arlington, VA 22202

888-663-4637
www.marchofdimes.org

March of Dimes help moms have full-term pregnancies and research the problems that threaten the health of babies. The March of Dimes also acts globally: sharing best practices in perinatal health and helping improve birth outcomes where the needs are the most urgent.

Stacey D. Stewart, President
Alan Brogdon, SVP/COO/Board Officer
Rahul Gupta, MD, SVP & Chief Medical/Health Officer

Web Sites

5374 Lighthouse Guild
250 West 64th Street
New York, NY 10023

800-284-4422
info@lighthouseguild.org
www.lighthouseguild.org

Lighthouse Guild is dedicated to providing exceptional services that inspire people who are visually impaired to attain their goals.

5375 Online Mendelian Inheritance in Man
McKusick-Nathans Institue of Genetic Medicine-JHU
Baltimore, MD 21205

www.omim.org

This database is a catalog of human genes and genetic disorders.

Ada Hamosh, MD, Scientific Director

5376 **Royal National Institute of Blind People**
105 Judd Street
London, WC1H

303-123-9999
helpline@rnib.org.uk
www.rnib.org.uk

A leading UK charity offering information, support and advice to over two million people with sight problems.

Matt Stringer, Chief Executive
Keith Valentine, Director of Development
David Clarke, Director of Services

Pulmonary Hypertension / Description

Description

5377 PULMONARY HYPERTENSION
Covers these related disorders: Persistent fetal circulation (PFC)
Involves the following Biologic System(s):
Cardiovascular Disorders, Respiratory Disorders

Primary pulmonary hypertension is a condition in which the blood pressure within the pulmonary artery is abnormally high (hypertension). The pulmonary artery arises from the base of the lower right chamber of the heart (ventricle) and carries oxygen-poor blood to the lungs, where the exchange of oxygen and carbon dioxide occurs. When this occurs in newborn infants, it is known as persistent fetal circulation or more appropriately, persistent pulmonary hypertension in the newborn (PPHN).

PPHN is a condition in newborns in which blood continues to circulate through certain fetal openings or channels which usually close shortly after birth. These include the fetal opening between the left and right upper chambers of the heart (foramen ovale) and the fetal channel that joins the major artery of the body (aorta) and the pulmonary artery (ductus arteriosus). PPHN may occur in newborns for unknown reasons (idiopathic) or may result from a lack of oxygen during the birth process (birth asphyxia); certain abnormalities during pregnancy (e.g., amniotic fluid leak); certain birth defects (e.g., underdevelopment of the lungs seen in a diaphragmatic hernia); or other conditions, such as meconium aspiration, polycythemia (excess number of red blood cells, etc. PPHN affects approximately one in 500 t0 700 newborns.

Newborns with PPHN often experience symptoms immediately after birth or within the first 12 hours of life. Some may have bluish discoloration of the skin and mucous membranes (cyanosis) and increasing difficulties breathing (respiratory distress). Symptoms associated with respiratory distress may include rapid breathing (tachypnea), grunting upon exhalation, drawing in of the chest wall during inhalation, and a rapid heart rate (tachycardia).

In newborns with PPHN, immediate measures may be necessary to prevent or treat potentially life-threatening complications. Additional therapy is directed toward treating the underlying cause of the condition and providing ongoing supportive measures to increase the supply of oxygen to bodily tissues. Oxygen therapies may include the use of measures to mechanically assist breathing (mechanical ventilation), administration of certain medications (e.g., surfactant therapy; inhalation of nitric oxide to help widen pulmonary blood vessels), or use of a device known as an extracorporeal membrane oxygenator (ECMO). This device delivers oxygen to an infant's blood as it is circulated outside of the body and then returns the oxygenated blood to the body.

In contrast to PPHN, primary pulmonary hypertension is a progressive condition that often becomes apparent between the ages of 10 to 20 years. Females appear to be slightly more affected than males. Researchers suspect that th|e condition may be the result of the interactions of different genes, possibly in association with the involvement of certain environmental factors (multifactorial inheritance).

In patients with primary pulmonary hypertension, abnormal thickening and loss of elasticity of pulmonary arterial walls may cause abnormal obstruction and increased resistance of the blood flow from the right ventricle to the lungs. Consequently, the heart muscle must pump harder and at a higher pressure to adequately propel blood through the pulmonary artery, leading to enlargement of the right ventricle. Affected individuals may experience exercise intolerance (inability to do physical exercise at the level that would be expected of someone in his or her general physical condition), easy fatigability, and, in some cases, dizziness, fainting episodes (syncope), headaches, and chest pain. In addition, as the right ventricle begins to weaken in its ability to pump blood efficiently (right ventricular failure), patients may experience cyanosis, coldness of the affected limbs, enlargement of the liver (hepatomegaly), and an abnormal accumulation of fluid in body tissues (edema). Patients with severe pulmonary hypertension may experience sudden abnormalities in the rhythm or rate of the heartbeat (arrhythmias), resulting in life-threatening complications. Supportive therapies for the treatment of primary pulmonary hypertension may include intravenous administration of the medication prostacyclin to help widen pulmonary arteries (vasodilation) and increase blood flow. In addition, in some patients, the administration of calcium channel blocking agents by mouth may be beneficial. In many patients with severe primary pulmonary hypertension, heart-lung or lung transplantation may be required.

Government Agencies

5378 NIH/ Eunice Kennedy Shriver National Insti tute of Child Health & Human Development
P.O. Box 3006
Rockville, MD 20847
800-370-2943
Fax: 866-760-5947
www.nichd.nih.gov

Conducts and supports research on topics related to the health of children, adults, families and populations. Some of these topics include: developmental disabilities, growth and development, infant death, reproductive health and birth defects.
Diana W. Bianchi, Director
Alison Cernich, PhD, Deputy Director

5379 NIH/National Heart, Lung and Blood Institute
31 Center Drive, Bldg 31
Bethesda, MD 20824
877-645-2448
www.nhlbi.nih.gov

Primary responsibility of this organization is the scientific investigation of heart, blood vessel, lung and blood disorders. Oversees research, demonstration, prevention, education, control and training activities in these fields and emphasizes the prevention and control of heart diseases.
Gary H. Gibbons, MD, Director
Kate O'Sullivan, Executive Officer

National Associations & Support Groups

5380 American Academy of Pediatrics
345 Park Blvd
Itasca, IL 60143
847-434-4000
800-433-9016
Fax: 847-434-8000
csc@aap.org
www.aap.org

The American Academy of Pediatrics and its member pediatricians are committed to the attainment of optimal physical, mental and social health and well-being for all infants, children, adolescents, and young adults.
Kyle E. Yasuda, MD, FAAP, President
Mark Del Monte, JD, CEO/Executive VP
Vera Tait, MD, FAAP, Chief Medical Officer

5381 American Heart Association
7272 Greenville Avenue
Dallas, TX 75231
214-570-5978
800-242-8721
www.heart.org

The mission of the American Heart Associate is to build healthier lives, free of cardiovascular diseases and stroke.

Nancy Brown, CEO
Mitchell S.V. Elkind, President
Suzie Upton, Chief Operating Officer

5382 American Lung Association
55 W. Wacker Drive, Suite 1150
Chicago, IL 60601
800-586-4872
info@lung.org
www.lung.org

The American Lung Association fights lung disease in all its forms, with special emphasis on asthma, tobacco control and environmental health. The American Lung Association is funded with contributions from the public, along with gifts and grants from corporations, foundations and government agencies. The association achieves its many successes through the work of thousands of committed volunteers and staff.

Harold P. Wimmer, National President & CEO
Albert Rizzo, MD, Chief Medical Officer
Sue Swan, Chief Development Officer

5383 Genetic Alliance
426400 Woodfield Road, Ste 189
Damascus, MD 20872
202-966-5557
Fax: 202-966-8553
info@geneticalliance.org
www.geneticalliance.org

World's leading nonprofit health advocacy organization committed to transforming health through genetics and promoting an environment of openness centered on the health of individuals, families, and communities.

Sharon Terry, CEO
Ruth Child, CFO
Natasha Bonhomme, Chief Strategy Officer

5384 March of Dimes Foundation
1550 Crystal Drive, Ste 1300
Arlington, VA 22202
888-663-4637
www.marchofdimes.org

March of Dimes help moms have full-term pregnancies and research the problems that threaten the health of babies. The March of Dimes also acts globally: sharing best practices in perinatal health and helping improve birth outcomes where the needs are the most urgent.

Stacey D. Stewart, President
Alan Brogdon, SVP/COO/Board Officer
Rahul Gupta, MD, SVP & Chief Medical/Health Officer

5385 Pulmonary Hypertension Association
8401 Colesville Road, Suite 200
Silver Spring, MD 20910
301-565-3004
800-748-7274
www.phassociation.org

PHA's mission is to seek a cure; provide hope, support and education; promote awareness, and advocate for the pulmonary hypertension community.

Matt Granato, President & CEO
Elizabeth Joseloff, VP of Quality Care & Research
Karen Smaalders, VP of Communications & Marketing

Web Sites

5386 MayoClinic.com - Pulmonary Hypertension
13400 E. Shea Blvd.
Scottsdale, AZ 85259
480-301-8000
800-446-2279
mayoclinic.com/health/pulmonary-hypertension/DS00430

Introduction to the disorder, signs, symptoms, treatment, etc.

Samuel A. Di Piazza, Jr., Chairman
John H. Noseworthy, M.D., CEO and President
Jeffrey W. Bolton, CAO and Vice President

Pulmonary Valve Stenosis / Description

Description

5387 PULMONARY VALVE STENOSIS
Covers these related disorders: Critical pulmonic stenosis
Involves the following Biologic System(s):
Cardiovascular Disorders

Pulmonary valve stenosis is a congenital heart defect characterized by abnormal narrowing (stenosis) of the valve between the lower right-sided, pumping chamber of the heart (right ventricle) and the pulmonary artery. Situated where the pulmonary artery arises from the base of the right ventricle, the pulmonary valve enables blood to flow from the right ventricle to the lungs while preventing the backward flow of blood. The pulmonary artery carries oxygen-depleted (deoxygenated) blood to the lungs, where the exchange of oxygen and carbon dioxide occurs. In infants and children with pulmonary valve stenosis, narrowing of the pulmonary valve opening increases resistance of the blood flow from the right ventricle to the pulmonary artery. As a result, the heart muscle must pump harder and at a higher pressure to propel blood to the pulmonary artery, potentially leading to thickening of the heart muscle (hypertrophy) of the right ventricle. Pulmonary valve stenosis affects approximately one in 1,250 individuals in the general population, comprising approximately 10 percent of all heart defects that are present at birth (congenital heart defects). Less commonly, pulmonary stenosis may be due to structural abnormalities other than a restricted valvular opening, such as narrowing within the upper region of the right ventricle or a portion of the pulmonary artery (e.g., isolated infundibular stenosis, branch pulmonary artery stenosis).

In infants and children with pulmonary valve stenosis, the severity of associated symptoms may vary, depending on the size of the restricted valvular opening and, in some patients, the presence of additional heart defects. For example, some affected children may also have relatively small septal defects, such as an abnormal opening in the fibrous partition (septum) that divides the ventricles or the two upper chambers (atria) of the heart (ventricular or atrial septal defects). Infants and children with mild pulmonary valve stenosis usually have no associated symptoms (asymptomatic), do not experience hypertrophy of heart muscle, and have normal growth and development. In such patients, the condition is usually initially suspected due to detection of characteristic, abnormal heart sounds (heart murmurs) during a physician's examination with a stethoscope. In patients with moderate pulmonary valve stenosis, the right ventricle may be of normal size or mildly thickened. Although such patients are usually asymptomatic, others may experience some symptoms, such as easy fatigability and exercise intolerance.

In newborns or young infants with severe pulmonary valve stenosis, the right ventricle may be unable to pump blood adequately (right ventricular failure) and become moderately or severely enlarged. Findings associated with right ventricular failure may include poor feeding, enlargement of the liver (hepatomegaly), an abnormal accumulation of fluid in body tissues (edema) or other abnormalities. In addition, blood may begin to circulate through a previously closed fetal opening in the heart (foramen ovale) between the left and right atria that closes shortly after birth. Abnormal opening of the foramen ovale in those with pulmonary valve stenosis may cause oxygen-depleted blood to pass from the right to the left side of the atria (right-to-left shunting), into the left ventricle and into the aorta for transport to the body's tissues. Because this oxygen-depleted blood bypasses the lungs and instead recirculates throughout the body, bodily tissues receive less oxygenated blood (hypoxia). In such cases, affected newborns or infants are said to have critical pulmonic stenosis. In addition, in some infants, certain associated heart (cardiac) defects, such as atrial or ventricular septal defects, may also allow some mixing of oxygen-poor and oxygen-rich blood. Due to recirculation of oxygen-poor blood to the body's tissues, affected newborns or infants may experience mild to moderate bluish discoloration of the skin and mucous membranes (cyanosis), shortness of breath (dyspnea), and other serious symptoms and findings.

In these newborns or infants, emergency procedures are performed to widen the restricted valvular opening. Such procedures may include inflation of a balloon-tipped cathet|er (valvuloplasty) or surgical correction or resection of the valve (valvotomy). Although corrective measures may not be required in those with mild stenosis, such patients should receive regular follow-up evaluations. Such monitoring is necessary to ensure appropriate intervention for patients who may potentially experience increasing obstruction across the pulmonary valve or increasing hypertrophy of the right ventricle requiring surgical intervention. Other treatment is symptomatic and supportive.

Pulmonary valve stenosis may occur as a spontaneous, isolated finding; with other congenital heart defects; or in association with certain underlying disorders (e.g., Noonan syndrome). In some patients, the condition is thought to be determined by the interactions of several different genes, possibly in association with the involvement of certain environmental factors (multifactorial inheritance).

Government Agencies

5388 NIH/ Eunice Kennedy Shriver National Institute of Child Health & Human Development
P.O. Box 3006
Rockville, MD 20847

800-370-2943
Fax: 866-760-5947
www.nichd.nih.gov

Conducts and supports research on topics related to the health of children, adults, families and populations. Some of these topics include: developmental disabilities, growth and development, infant death, reproductive health and birth defects.

Diana W. Bianchi, Director
Alison Cernich, PhD, Deputy Director

5389 NIH/National Heart, Lung and Blood Institute
31 Center Drive, Bldg 31
Bethesda, MD 20892

877-645-2448
www.nhlbi.nih.gov

Primary responsibility of this organization is the scientific investigation of heart, blood vessel, lung and blood disorders. Oversees research, demonstration, prevention, education, control and training activities in these fields and emphasizes the prevention and control of heart diseases.

Gary H. Gibbons, MD, Director
Kate O'Sullivan, Executive Officer

National Associations & Support Groups

5390 American Academy of Pediatrics
345 Park Blvd
Itasca, IL 60143

847-434-4000
800-433-9016
Fax: 847-434-8000
csc@aap.org
www.aap.org

The American Academy of Pediatrics and its member pediatricians are committed to the attainment of optimal physical, mental and social health and well-being for all infants, children, adolescents, and young adults.

Kyle E. Yasuda, MD, FAAP, President
Mark Del Monte, JD, CEO/Executive VP
Vera Tait, MD, FAAP, Chief Medical Officer

5391 American Heart Association
7272 Greenville Avenue
Dallas, TX 75231
214-570-5978
800-242-8721
www.heart.org

The mission of the American Heart Associate is to build healthier lives, free of cardiovascular diseases and stroke.

Nancy Brown, CEO
Mitchell S.V. Elkind, President
Suzie Upton, Chief Operating Officer

5392 Division of Pediatric Pulmonology
New York Medical College
40 Sunshine Cottage Road
Valhalla, NY 10595
914-493-7585
Fax: 914-594-2350
www.nymc.edu

The Division of Pediatric Pulmonology, Allergy, Immunology, and Sleep Medicine provides comprehensive inpatient and outpatient consultation and management for children suffering from a broad variety of respiratory problems. We are the only accredited Cystic Fibrosis center in the Hudson Valley. The division is dedicated to teaching, research and patient care.

5393 Genetic Alliance
426400 Woodfield Road, Ste 189
Damascus, MD 20872
202-966-5557
Fax: 202-966-8553
info@geneticalliance.org
www.geneticalliance.org

World's leading nonprofit health advocacy organization committed to transforming health through genetics and promoting an environment of openness centered on the health of individuals, families, and communities.

Sharon Terry, CEO
Ruth Child, CFO
Natasha Bonhomme, Chief Strategy Officer

5394 March of Dimes Foundation
1550 Crystal Drive, Ste 1300
Arlington, VA 22202
888-663-4637
www.marchofdimes.org

March of Dimes help moms have full-term pregnancies and research the problems that threaten the health of babies. The March of Dimes also acts globally: sharing best practices in perinatal health and helping improve birth outcomes where the needs are the most urgent.

Stacey D. Stewart, President
Alan Brogdon, SVP/COO/Board Officer
Rahul Gupta, MD, SVP & Chief Medical/Health Officer

Web Sites

5395 Southern Illinois University School of Medicine
PO Box 19658
Springfield, IL 62794
217-545-8000
800-342-5748
www.siumed.edu/peds/index.htm

The mission of SUI School of Medicine is to assist the people of central and southern Illinois in meeting their present and future health care needs through education, clinical service and research.

Book Publishers

5396 Congenital Disorders Sourcebook
Greg Mullin, author

Omnigraphics
615 Griswold Street, Ste 520
Detroit, MI 48226
610-461-3548
800-234-1340
Fax: 800-875-1340
contact@omnigraphics.com
www.omnigraphics.com

Basic consumer health information on disorders aquired during gestation, including spina bifida, hydrocephalus, cerebral palsy, heart defects, craniofacial abnormalities and fetal alcohol syndrome.

664 pages
ISBN: 0-780816-13-8

Pyloric Stenosis / Description

Description

5397 PYLORIC STENOSIS

Synonym: Infantile pyloric stenosis

Involves the following Biologic System(s):

Gastrointestinal Disorders

Pyloric stenosis refers to a condition in which the passageway (pyloric canal) that leads from the stomach to the first part of the small intestine known as the duodenum is narrowed or obstructed due to the thickening of the muscle that surrounds this opening (pyloric sphincter). Although the specific cause for this thickening is not known, many factors may be responsible, including breast-feeding, irregularities in nerve distribution to the muscle, and certain disorders such as Turner syndrome, Cornelia de Lange syndrome, trisomy 18 syndrome, and eosinophilic gastroenteritis. Pyloric stenosis is also commonly associated with certain birth defects of the gastrointestinal tract such as tracheoesophageal fistula.

Symptoms and findings associated with this disorder may develop as early as the first week of life; however, in some infants, this abnormality does not cause noticeable symptoms until the fourth or fifth month. At about the third week of life, episodes of forceful and explosive vomiting (projectile vomiting) may occur. After eating, rhythmic, wave-like movements (peristalsis) may be visible in the infant's abdominal area. Prolonged vomiting may result in excessive fluid loss (dehydration) and loss of essential elements known as electrolytes in the fluid portion of the blood (e.g., sodium, potassium, and calcium).

Treatment for infantile pyloric stenosis includes the administration of fluids to counteract the effects of dehydration. Once body fluids and electrolytes stabilize, a surgical procedure known as a pyloromyotomy may be performed. During this procedure, a lengthwise incision is made along the thickened pyloric muscle to correct the defect.

Pyloric stenosis affects approximately three in every 1,000 infants in the United States. Boys are more often affected than girls by a ratio of four to one. Children of parents who had pyloric stenosis are approximately 10 to 20 percent more likely to be affected. Infants with types B or O blood develop this defect more often than those with other blood types.

National Associations & Support Groups

5398 American Academy of Pediatrics
345 Park Blvd
Itasca, IL 60143
847-434-4000
800-433-9016
Fax: 847-434-8000
csc@aap.org
www.aap.org

The American Academy of Pediatrics and its member pediatricians are committed to the attainment of optimal physical, mental and social health and well-being for all infants, children, adolescents, and young adults.

Kyle E. Yasuda, MD, FAAP, President
Mark Del Monte, JD, CEO/Executive VP
Vera Tait, MD, FAAP, Chief Medical Officer

5399 American College of Gastroenterology
6400 Goldsboro Road
Bethesda, MD 20817
301-263-9000
www.gi.org

The American College of Gastroenterology was founded in 1932 to advance the scientific study and medical practice of diseases of the GI tract.

13,000 members

5400 Cyclic Vomiting Syndrome Association
PO Box 270341
Milwaukee, WI 53227
414-342-7880
cvsa@cvsaonline.org
www.cvsaonline.org

A volunteer organization serving the needs of CVS patients, their families around the world and the growing medical community studying CVS. The network has grown to over 37 medical advisors and over 90 volunteers in over 32 countries.

$75/year

Blynda Killian, President

5401 Digestive Disease National Coalition
507 Capitol Court NE, Suite 200
Washington, DC 20002
202-544-7497
Fax: 202-546-7105
www.ddnc.org

Advocacy organization comprised of over 30 voluntary and professional societies concerned with the many diseases of the digestive tract and liver.

Ceciel Rooker, Chairperson
Bryan Green, MD, President
Cathy Griffith, Vice Chairperson

5402 International Foundation for Functional Gastrointestinal Disorders (IFFGD)
3015 Dunes W Boulevard, Suite 512
Mount Pleasant, SC 29466
414-964-1799
www.iffgd.org

The organization offers responses to those commonly asked questions for families and individuals whose lives have been touched by gastrointestinal disorders.

Nancy J. Norton, Founder
Ceciel T. Rooker, President

5403 March of Dimes Foundation
1550 Crystal Drive, Ste 1300
Arlington, VA 22202
888-663-4637
www.marchofdimes.org

March of Dimes help moms have full-term pregnancies and research the problems that threaten the health of babies. The March of Dimes also acts globally: sharing best practices in perinatal health and helping improve birth outcomes where the needs are the most urgent.

Stacey D. Stewart, President
Alan Brogdon, SVP/COO/Board Officer
Rahul Gupta, MD, SVP & Chief Medical/Health Officer

5404 North American Society for Pediatric Gastroenterology/Hepatology/Nutrition
714 N Bethlehem Pike, Suite 300
Ambler, PA 19002
215-641-9800
Fax: 215-641-1995
www.naspghan.org

Strives to improve the care of infants, children and adolescents with digestive disorders by promoting advances in clinical care of children with chronic abdominal pain, diarrhea, constipation, vomiting, bleeding from the GI tract, inflammatory bowel disease, liver diseases, diseases of the pancreas, poor weight gain and nutritional problems.

Margaret K Stallings, Executive Director
Kim Rose, Associate Director
Gina Brown, Membership

Libraries & Resource Centers

5405 **National Digestive Diseases Information Clearinghouse (NDDIC)**
NIH
2 Information Way
Bethesda, MD 20892
301-654-3810
800-891-5389
Fax: 703-738-4929
nddic@info.niddk.nih.gov
www.digestive.niddk.nih.gov

The National Institute of Diabetes and Digestive and Kidney Diseases conducts and supports research on many of the most serious diseases affecting public health. The Institute supports much of the clinical research on the diseases of internal medicine and related subspecialty fields as well as many basic science disciplines.

Griffin P. Rodgers, MD, Director
Gregory G. Germino, MD, Deputy Director
Kathy Kranzfelder, Communications Director

Web Sites

5406 **American Pediatric Surgical Association**
111 Deer Lake Road, Suite 100
Deerfield, IL 60015
847-480-9576
Fax: 847-480-9282
www.eapsa.org/parents/pyloric.htm

For parents: an overview of Pyloric Stenosis including symptoms, treatment and complications.

Michael D. Klein, President
Mary L. Brandt, Secretary
Daniel von Almen, Treasurer

5407 **Dr. Koop**
750 Third Avenue, 6th Floor
New York, NY 10017
212-695-2223
Fax: 212-695-2936
www.healthcentral.com

Information on the condition, causes, symptoms, tests and treatment.

Micheael Cunnion, Chief Executive Officer
Jim Curtis, Chief Revenue Officer
Rebecca Farwell, Chief Content Officer

5408 **KidsHealth-Pyloric Stenosis**
kidshealth.org/en/parents/pyloric-stenosis.html

kidshealth.org/en/parents/pyloric-stenosis.html

Definition, causes, symptoms, treatment and complications.

Neil Izenberg, MD, Editor-in-Chief & Founder

5409 **MEDLINEplus Medical Encyclopedia: Pyloric Stenosis**
8600 Rockville Pike
Bethesda, MD 20894
nlm.nih.gov/medlineplus/ency/article/000970.htm

Definitions, causes, symptoms, treatment, prognosis and complications.

Donald A.B. Lindberg, Director

5410 **National Digestive Diseases Information Clearinghouse (NDDIC)**
NIH
2 Information Way
Bethesda, MD 20892
301-654-3810
800-891-5389
nddic@info.niddk.nih.gov
www.digestive.niddk.nih.gov

The National Institute of Diabetes and Digestive and Kidney Diseases conducts and supports research on many of the most serious diseases affecting public health. The Institute supports much of the clinical research on the diseases of internal medicine and related subspecialty fields as well as many basic science disciplines.

Griffin P. Rodgers, MD, Director
Gregory G. Germino, MD, Deputy Director
Kathy Kranzfelder, Communications Director

5411 **Online Mendelian Inheritance in Man**
McKusick-Nathans Institue of Genetic Medicine-JHU
Baltimore, MD 21205
www.omim.org

This database is a catalog of human genes and genetic disorders.

Ada Hamosh, MD, Scientific Director

5412 **Southern Illinois University School of Medicine**
PO Box 19658
Springfield, IL 62794
217-545-8000
800-342-5748
www.siumed.edu/peds/index.htm

The mission of SUI School of Medicine is to assist the people of central and southern Illinois in meeting their present and future health care needs through education, clinical service and research.

Journals

5413 **Journal of Pediatric Gastroenterology and Nutrition**
NASPGHAN, author

Lippincott Williams & Wilkins
530 Walnut Street
Philadelphia, PA 19106
215-521-8300
Fax: 215-521-8902
www.lww.com

Publication of the North American Society for Pediatric Gastroenterolgy, Hepatology and Nutrition, which strives to improve the care of infants, children and adolescents with digestive disorders by promoting advances in clinical care of children with chronic abdominal pain, diarrhea, constipation, vomiting, bleeding from the GI tract, inflammatory bowel disease, liver diseases, diseases of the pancreas, poor weight gain and nutritional problems.

Newsletters

5414 **NASPGHAN News**
714 N. Bethlehem Pike, Ste 300
Ambler, PA 19002
215-641-9800
Fax: 215-641-1995
www.naspghan.org

Publication of the North American Society for Pediatric Gastroenterolgy, Hepatology and Nutrition, which strives to improve the care of infants, children and adolescents with digestive disorders by promoting advances in clinical care of children with chronic abdominal pain, diarrhea, constipation, vomiting, bleeding from the GI tract, inflammatory bowel disease, liver diseases, diseases of the pancreas, poor weight gain and nutritional problems.

Margaret K Stallings, Executive Director
Kim Rose, Associate Director
Gina Brown, Membership

Description

5415 REFRACTION DISTURBANCES

Synonym: Ametropia

Disorder Type: Vision

Covers these related disorders: Anisometropia, Astigmatism, Hyperopia (Farsightedness), Myopia (Nearsightedness)

Involves the following Biologic System(s):

Ophthalmologic Disorders

Refraction abnormalities are defects in the cornea and the lens of the eye to focus visual images appropriately on the nerve-rich membrane at the back of the eye (retina). The cornea is the convex, transparent area in front of the eye. The lens, which is located behind the pupil, is held in place by a circular muscle that changes the shape of the lens to make appropriate adjustments in focus (ciliary muscle). As light passes through the cornea and the lens, it is bent (refracted) so that it is properly focused on the retina, which contains millions of tiny nerve cells that respond to light (photoreceptors). However, in individuals with refraction defects, light rays are not properly focused on the retina (ametropia) due to abnormalities of the cornea, the lens, or the size of the eye. These refraction defects lead to visual abnormalities.

There are three primary types of refraction abnormalities: namely, farsightedness (hyperopia), nearsightedness (myopia), and astigmatism. In farsightedness, parallel light rays come to focus behind rather that on the retina. This may be due to shortness of the eyeball from front to back, abnormally reduced refractive power of the cornea or lens, or backward displacement of the lens. If farsightedness is mild or moderate, affected children may be able to clearly visualize near and far objects due to accommodation, a process by which the shape of the lens changes and brings the area of focus forward. The range and extent of accommodation is highest durign childhood and gradually decreases with age. With greater degrees of farsightedness, affected children may experience blurring of vision, eyestrain, fatigue, and recurrent headaches. They may also engage in repeated eye rubbing and squinting and appear uninterested in reading or schoolwork. Children with farsightedness may achieve clear vision with glasses or contact lenses with convex lenses.

In children with nearsightedness (myopia), parallel light rays come to focus in front of the retina due to increased length of the eyeball from front to back, abnormally increased refractive power of the cornea or lens, or forward displacement of the lens. Affected children experience blurring of vision when focusing on distant objects, tend to hold reading material and other objects close to their face, and often squint in an effort to improve clearness and clarity of vision. Nearsightedness usually becomes apparent during school age, particularly in the years prior to and up to adolescence. The degree of nearsightedness typically becomes more severe until early adulthood, when it tends to stabilize. Many affected children have a hereditary predisposition for nearsightedness; in addition, the condition may occur in association with the other eye abnormalities (e.g., glaucoma, keratoconus) or other underlying disorders. Clear vision may be attained with glasses or contact lenses with concave lenses. Until the degree of nearsightedness stabilizes, prescriptions may need to be periodically increased in strength (e.g., varying from every few months to once every one or two years).

In children with astigmatism, parallel light rays are not clearly focused in a point on the retina due to unequal curvature of refractive surfaces of the eye. Astigmatism may result from irregularities in curvature of the cornea or, in some cases, abnormalities of the lens. Many individuals have minor degrees of astigmatism and have no associated symptoms. With more severe degrees of astigmatism, affected children may experience blurring and distortion of vision, fatigue, eyestrain, and recurrent headaches. In many cases, they may also engage in frequent eye rubbing, squint in an attempt to improve clearness and clarity of vision, hold reading materials and other objects close, and appear uninterested in schoolwork. In children with astigmatism, visual correction may be achieved with the part-time or ongoing use of glasses with cylindric or spherocylindric lenses. In some cases, contact lenses may be used to help correct vision.

Some children may also have a visual condition known as anisometropia in which the refractive or focusing ability of one eye significantly differs from the other. For example, one eye may have normal focusing ability, whereas the other may be affected by nearsightedness, farsightedness, and astigmatism. For proper vision to develop during infancy and early childhood, corresponding visual images mustform on both retinas to ensure the transmission of compatible nerve impulses (via the optic nerves) to the brain. If the images from one eye differ dramatically from the other, one may be suppressed, causing impaired visual development in one eye (amblyopia). Therefore, in infants and children with anisometropia, prompt detection and appropriate visual correction is essential to ensure proper visual development in both eyes.

Government Agencies

5416 NIH/National Eye Institute
31 Center Drive MSC 2510
Bethesda, MD 20892

301-496-5248
2020@nei.nih.gov
www.nei.nih.gov

Conducts and supports research that helps prevent and treat eye diseases and other disorders of vision. This research leads to sight-saving treatments, reduces visual impairment and blindness, and improves the quality of life for people of all ages. NEI-supported research has advanced our knowledge of how the eye functions in health and disease.

Michael J. Chiang, MD, Director
Santa Tumminia, Deputy Director

National Associations & Support Groups

5417 American Academy of Pediatrics
345 Park Blvd
Itasca, IL 60143

847-434-4000
800-433-9016
Fax: 847-434-8000
csc@aap.org
www.aap.org

The American Academy of Pediatrics and its member pediatricians are committed to the attainment of optimal physical, mental and social health and well-being for all infants, children, adolescents, and young adults.

Kyle E. Yasuda, MD, FAAP, President
Mark Del Monte, JD, CEO/Executive VP
Vera Tait, MD, FAAP, Chief Medical Officer

5418 Lighthouse Guild
250 West 64th Street
New York, NY 10023

800-284-4422
info@lighthouseguild.org
www.lighthouseguild.org

Lighthouse Guild is dedicated to providing exceptional services that inspire people who are visually impaired to attain their goals.

Refraction Disturbances / State Agencies & Support Groups

James M. Dubin, Chair
Calvin W. Robert, President & CEO
Maura J. Sweeney, SVP, Programs & Services

5419 National Association of Blind Students
200 East Wells Street, Jernigan Place
Baltimore, MD 21230
410-659-9314
nfb@nfb.org
nabslink.org

For over 50 years, the National Association of Blind Students has worked, as an integral part of the National Federation of the Blind, to promote the equality of the blind by serving as a source of information, forum for networking and vehicle for collective action for blind students. Our work on the local, state, and national levels is firmly rooted in the conviction that blindness need not prevent one from excelling in a chosen field of study or living a full and productive life.

State Agencies & Support Groups

Alabama

5420 Alabama Institute for the Deaf & Blind
PO Box 698
Talladega, AL 35161
256-761-3331
Fax: 256-761-3344
www.aidb.org

Services include central directory, representatives of agencies, service providers, families, and coordinators of infant, toddler, and preschool special education programs.

Terry Graham, President

California

5421 Blind Childrens Center
4120 Marathon Street
Los Angeles, CA 90029
323-664-2153
Fax: 323-665-3828
www.blindchildrenscenter.org

Family-centered agency that serves children with visual impairments from birth to school age. The center-based programs and services help the children acquire skills and build their independence.

Midge Horton, Executive Director

Connecticut

5422 Region 1 of the National Association for Parents of the Visually Impaired
252 Rye Street
Broad Brook, CT 06016
860-623-4129
Susan Ellsworth

Georgia

5423 Southeastern Region-Helen Keller National Center
1003 Virginia Avenue, Suite 104
Atlanta, GA 30354
404-766-9625
Fax: 404-766-3447
TTY: 404-766-2820

Susan Lascek, Supervisor of Reg Representatives

Illinois

5424 Region 3 of the National Association for Parents of the Visually Impaired
16 Thornfield Lane
Hawthorn Woods, IL 60047
847-438-0705
Kevin O'Connor

Kansas

5425 Great Plains Region-Helen Keller National Center
4330 Shawhee Mission Parkway, suite 108
Shawnee, KS 66205
913-677-4562
Fax: 913-677-1544
beth.jordan@hknc.org
www.helenkeller.org

Services are free and offer client advocacy, consultation and technical assistance to schools and agencies; assistance in developing local services information and referral; public education and awareness; maintenance of the National Registry.

Beth Jordan, Regional Representative

Maryland

5426 National Organization of Parents of Blind Children
350 Ignacio Blvd., Suite 200
Novato,, CA 94949
415-382-2530
Fax: 410-685-5653
www.nfh.org

Informational and emotional support to parents who have a child, adolescent, or adult family member with blindness or visual impairment.

Massachusetts

5427 New England Region-Helen Keller National Center
313 Washington Street
Newton, MA 02458
617-630-1580
Fax: 617-630-1579
hkncmeb@aol.com

New Mexico

5428 Region 5 of the National Association for Parents of the Visually Impaired
PO Box 1337
Alamogordo, NM 88311
505-682-2693

Ohio

5429 Region 2 of the National Association for Parents of the Visually Impaired
3910 Pocahontas Avenue
Cincinnati, OH 45227
513-561-8542
Victoria Gorman Miller

Pennsylvania

5430 East Central Region-Helen Keller National Center
4351 Garden City Drive
New Carrollton, MD 20785
301-459-5474
Fax: 301-459-5070
hkncreg3cl@aol.com
www.helenkeller.org

South Carolina

5431 Region 4 of the National Association for Parents of the Visually Impaired
1032 Trail Road
Belton, SC 29627
864-338-9593

Refraction Disturbances / Libraries & Resource Centers

Washington

5432 Northwestern Region-Helen Keller National Center
2366 Eastlake Avenue E
Seattle, WA 98102
206-324-9120

Libraries & Resource Centers

Alabama

5433 Mobile Association for the Blind
2440 Gordon Smith Drive
Mobile, AL 36617
251-473-3585
Fax: 251-470-8622
www.mobileblind.org

Offers work adjustment training, activities of daily living, mobility, communication skills and sheltered employment for adults and children who are visually impaired.

Jim Bullock, Executive Director

Arizona

5434 Educational Services for the Visually Impaired
2402 Wildwood Avenue Suite 112
Sherwood, AR 72120
501-371-5448

Offers textbooks, Braille books and more to the visually impaired grades K-12 in the Arkansas area.

David Beavers, Director

Arkansas

5435 Arkansas Regional Library for the Blind and Physically Handicapped
1 Capitol Mall
Little Rock, AR 72201
501-682-1527
Fax: 501-682-1533
TDD: 501-682-1002
www.asl.lib.ar.us/ASL_LBPH.htm

Public library books in recorded or Braille format. Popular fiction and nonfiction books for all ages, books and players are on free loan, sent to patrons by mail and may be returned postage free. Anyone who cannot see well enough to read regular print with glasses on or who has a disability that makes it difficult to hold a book or turn the pages is eligible.

John D Hall, Director

California

5436 American Action Fund for Blind Children and Adults
18440 Oxnard Street
Tarzana, CA 91356
818-343-2022
Fax: 818-343-3219
lucyabba@aol.com
www.actinfund.org

A lending library for the visually impaired. We send out a weekly Braille newspaper for the deaf-blind (worldwide), we also send out pocket-sized Braille calendars. Our lending library is for pre-school thru high school. All of our services are free.

Lucille Abbazia, Manager

5437 Blind Children's Center
4120 Marathon Street
Los Angeles, CA 90029
323-664-2153
Fax: 323-665-3828
www.blindchildrenscenter.org

Offers support and informational groups.

Scott E. Schaldenbrand, President, Executive Committee
Danette M. Jones, Vice President
Lisa D. Hansen, Secretary

5438 Braille Institute Desert Center
70-251 Ramon Road
Rancho Mirage, CA 92270
760-321-1111
Fax: 760-321-9715
dc@brailleinstitute.org
www.brailleinstitute.org

Dedicated to providing blind and visually impaired men, women and children with the training, programs and services they need to enjoy productive lives. Services offered include child development, youth programs, library services and adult education.

Lester M Sussman, Chairman
James B. Boyle Jr., Director
Thomas K. Callister, Director

5439 Braille Institute Sight Center
741 N Vermont Avenue
Los Angeles, CA 90029
323-663-1111
Fax: 323-663-0867
la@brailleinstitute.org
www.brailleinstitute.org

Offers help, programs, services and information to the blind and visually impaired children and adults.

Lester M Sussman, Chairman
James B. Boyle Jr., Director
Thomas K. Callister, Director

5440 Braille Institute Youth Center
741 N Vermont Avenue
Los Angeles, CA 90029
323-663-1111
Fax: 323-663-0867
la@brailleinstitute.org
www.brailleinstitute.org

Offers various youth programs and services for the blind and visually impaired youngster.

Lester M Sussman, Chairman
James B. Boyle Jr., Director
Thomas K. Callister, Director

5441 New Beginnings - Blind Children's Center
4120 Marathon, Street
Los Angeles, CA 90029
323-664-2153
800-222-3566
Fax: 323-665-3828

Helps children and their families become independent by creating a climate of safety and trust. Services include an infant stimulation program, educational preschool, interdisciplinary assessment services, family services, correspondence program, toll-free national hotline and a publication and research service.

5442 San Francisco Public Library for the Blind and Print Disabled
100 Larkin Street
San Francisco, CA 94102
415-557-4400
Fax: 415-557-4252
www.library.ca.us

Foreign-language books on cassette, children's books on cassettes and more.

Luis Herrera, Manager

5443 Variety Audio
PO Box 5731
San Jose, CA 95150
408-277-4839

Summer reading programs, Braille writer, magnifiers, closed-circuit TV, large-print photocopier, cassette books and magazines, children's books on cassette, home visits and other reference materials on blindness and other handicaps.

Louisa Griehshammer

Florida

5444 **Florida Bureau of Braille and Talking Book Library Services**
1185 Dunn Avenue
Daytona Beach, FL 32114
386-254-3800
Fax: 386-239-6069
TDD: 800-226-6079
www.state.fl.us/dbs/lswel.html

Discs, cassettes, closed-circuit TV, large-print photocopier, films, children's books on cassettes and more.

Michael Gunde, Librarian

5445 **Talking Book Library, Jacksonville Public Library**
2233 Park Avenue, Suite 402
Orange Park, FL 32073
904-278-5620
Fax: 904-278-5625
TDD: 904-768-7822
office@neflin.org
www.neflin.org

Discs, cassettes and reference materials on blindness and other disabilities.

Elizabeth Curry, President
Julie Sieg, Vice-President
Janet Loveless, Secretary

5446 **Talking Book Service - Manatee County Central Library**
6081 26th Street W
Bradenton, FL 34207
941-742-5914
Fax: 941-751-7089
TDD: 941-742-5951
www.co.manatee.fl.us

Offers children's books on disc and cassette and more reference materials for the blind and physically handicapped.

Patricia Schubert, Librarian

Georgia

5447 **Albany Library for the Blind and Physical Handicapped**
300 Pine Avenue
Albany, GA 31701
229-420-3220
Fax: 229-420-3215
www.docolib.org/LBPH/index.html

Offers discs, cassettes, reference materials on blindness and other handicaps, large-print photocopiers, summer reading programs, cassette books and more.

Katy Sinquefield, Manager

5448 **Bainbridge Subregional Library for the Blind and Physically Handicapped**
301 S Monroe Street
Bainbridge, GA 39819
229-248-2665
800-795-2680
Fax: 229-248-2670
TDD: 912-248-2665
www.swgrl.org

Discs, cassettes, summer reading programs, closed-circuit TV, magnifiers and more.

Shelley Sudderth, Branch Manager
Susan Whittle, Director
Debbie Worthington, Administrative Secretary

5449 **CEL Subregional Library for the Blind and Physically Handicapped**
2708 Mechanics
Savannah, GA 31404
912-354-5864
Fax: 912-354-5534
TDD: 912-652-3635

Summer reading programs, Braille writer, magnifiers, closed-circuit TV, large-print photocopier, cassette books and magazines, children's books on cassette, home visits and other reference materials on blindness and other handicaps.

Linda Stokes, Librarian

Idaho

5450 **Idaho State Talking Book Library**
325 W State Street
Boise, ID 83702
208-334-2150
Fax: 208-334-4016
TDD: 800-377-1363
www.lili.org/isl/tblinfo.htm

Summer reading programs, Braille writer, magnifiers, closed-circuit TV, large-print photocopier, cassette books and magazines, children's books on cassette, home visits and other reference materials on blindness and other handicaps.

Sue Walker, Manager

Illinois

5451 **Chicago Library Service for the Blind**
400 S State Street
Chicago, IL 60605
312-747-4300

Summer reading programs, Braille writer, magnifiers, closed-circuit TV, large-print photocopier, cassette books and magazines, children's books on cassette, home visits and other reference materials on blindness and other handicaps.

Carol Pellish, Librarian

5452 **Illinois State Library, Talkng Book and Braille Service**
213 State Capitol
Springfield, IL 62756
217-785-3000
Fax: 217-558-4723
TDD: 800-665-5576
isltbbs@ilsos.net
www.cyberdriveillinois.com

Summer reading programs, Braille writer, magnifiers, closed-circuit TV, large-print photocopier, cassette books and magazines, descriptive videos, children's books on cassette, home visits and other reference materials on blindness and other handicaps.

Anne Craig, Executive Director

5453 **Mid Illinois Talking Book System**
515 York Street
Quincy, IL 62301
217-224-6619
Fax: 217-224-9818

Summer reading programs, Braille writer, magnifiers, closed-circuit TV, large-print photocopier, cassette books and magazines, children's books on cassette, home visits and other reference materials on blindness and other handicaps.

5454 **Mid-Illinois Talking Book Center**
600 High Point Lane #2
East Peoria, IL 61611
309-694-9200
800-426-0709
Fax: 309-799-7916
hitbc@darkstar.rsa.lib.il.us
www.mitbc.org

Summer reading programs, Braille writer, magnifiers, closed-circuit TV, large-print photocopier, cassette books and magazines, children's books on cassette, home visits and other reference materials on blindness and other handicaps.

Rose Chenoweth, Director
Valerie Brandon, Administrator

5455 **Talking Book Center of Northwest Illinois**
601 High Point Lane #2
East Peoria, IL 61612
309-694-9201
800-426-0710
Fax: 309-799-7917
www.mitbc.org

Summer reading programs, Braille writer, magnifiers, closed-circuit TV, large-print photocopier, cassette books and magazines, children's books on cassette, home visits and other reference materials on blindness and other handicaps.

Rose Chenoweth, Director
Valerie Brandon, Administrator

Refraction Disturbances / Libraries & Resource Centers

Indiana

5456 Northwest Indiana Subregional Library for Blind and Physically Handicapped
1919 W 81st Street
Merrillville, IN 46410
219-769-3541
Fax: 219-756-9358

Summer reading programs, Braille writer, magnifiers, closed-circuit TV, large-print photocopier, cassette books and magazines, children's books on cassette, home visits and other reference materials on blindness and other handicaps.

Renee Lewis

Iowa

5457 Iowa Library for the Blind and Physically Handicapped
Iowa Department for the Blind
524 4th Street
Des Moines, IA 50309
515-281-1333
800-362-2587
Fax: 515-281-1263
TTY: 515-281-1355
www.blind.state.ia.us

Summer reading programs, magnifiers, closed-circuit TV, large-print photocopier, children's books on cassette, children's books in Braille and Print Braille, cassette magazines, home visits and reference materials on blindness and other handicaps.

Richard Sorey, Director
Bruce Snethen, Deputy Director

Kansas

5458 CKLS Headquarters
PO Box 515
Northampton, MA 01061
316-792-2393
888-622-8527
Fax: 316-792-5495
www.macular.org

Summer reading programs, Braille writer, magnifiers, closed-circuit TV, large-print photocopier, cassette books and magazines, children's books on cassette, home visits and other reference materials on blindness and other handicaps.

Chip Goehring, President
Mark E. Torrey, Vice President
Paul F. Gariepy, Secretary

5459 Services for the Visually Disabled
629 Poyntz Avenue
Manhattan, KS 66502
785-776-4741
Fax: 785-776-1545

Summer reading programs, Braille writer, magnifiers, closed-circuit TV, large-print photocopier, cassette books and magazines, children's books on cassette, home visits and other reference materials on blindness and other handicaps.

Marion Rice, Librarian

Kentucky

5460 Kentucky Library for the Blind and Physically Handicapped
PO Box 818
Frankfort, KY 40602
502-564-8300
800-372-2968
Fax: 502-564-5773
www.kdla.net/libserv/ktbl.htm

Large-print photocopier, cassette books and magazines, children's books on cassette, and other reference materials on blindness and other handicaps.

5,200 members

Richard Feindel, Librarian

Maryland

5461 Maryland State Library for the Blind and Physically Handicapped
415 Park Avenue
Baltimore, MD 21201
410-230-2424
Fax: 410-333-2095
TTY: 800-934-2541
TDD: 410-333-8679
www.lbph.lib.md.us

Summer reading programs, Braille writer, magnifiers, large-print photocopier, cassette books and magazines, children's books on cassette, and other reference materials on blindness and other handicaps.

Jill Lewis, Manager

5462 Prince George's County Memorial Library Talking Book Center
6532 Adelphi Road
Hyattsville, MD 20782
301-699-3500

Summer reading programs, Braille writer, magnifiers, closed-circuit TV, large-print photocopier, cassette books and magazines, children's books on cassette, home visits and other reference materials on blindness and other handicaps.

Shirley Tuthill, Librarian

Massachusetts

5463 Braille and Talking Book Library Perkins School for the Blind
175 N Beacon Street
Watertown, MA 02472
617-924-3434
Fax: 617-972-7315
info@perkins.org
www.perkins.org

C. Richard Carlson, Chairman
Leslie Nordin, Vice Chairman
Michael Schnitman, Secretary

5464 Carroll Center for the Blind
770 Centre Street
Newton, MA 02458
617-969-6200
800-852-3131
Fax: 617-969-6204
www.carroll.org

Assists blind and visually impaired adults and adolescents to adjust to loss of vision. The goal of this dynamic program is to help the person become more independent, to restore self-confidence, prepare for employment and improve the quality of life. Programs of individual counseling are offered as part of the program.

Rachel Rosenbaum, President

Michigan

5465 Downtown Detroit Subregional Library for the Blind and Handicapped
5201 Woodward Avenue
Detroit, MI 48202
313-481-1300
Fax: 313-965-1977
TDD: 313-224-0584
www.detroit.lib.mi.us

Summer reading programs, Braille writer, magnifiers, closed-circuit TV, large-print photocopier, cassette books and magazines, children's books on cassette, home visits and other reference materials on blindness and other handicaps.

Russell Bellant, President
Gregory Hicks, vice President
Jonathan C. Kinloch, Secretary

5466 Kent County Library for the Blind
775 Ball Avenue NE
Grand Rapids, MI 49503
616-336-3250
Fax: 616-336-3201

Summer reading programs, Braille writer, magnifiers, closed-circuit TV, large-print photocopier, cassette books and magazines, children's books on cassette, home visits and other reference materials on blindness and other handicaps.

Claudya Muller, Librarian

5467 Library of Michigan Service for the Blind
PO Box 30007
Lansing, MI 48909
517-373-5614
Fax: 517-373-5865
BTBL@michigan.gov

Summer reading programs, Braille writer, magnifiers, closed-circuit TV, large-print photocopier, cassette books and magazines, children's books on cassette, home visits and other reference materials on blindness and other handicaps.

Nancy Robertson, Manager

5468 Macomb Library for the Blind and Physically Handicapped
16480 Hall Road
Clinton Township, MI 48038
586-286-1580
Fax: 586-286-0634
TDD: 810-869-40
www.macomb.lib.mi.us/macspe/

Summer reading programs, Braille writer, closed-circuit TV, cassette books and magazines, children's books on cassette, reference materials on blindness and other handicaps.

Beverlee Babcock, Executive Director

5469 Mideastern Michigan Library Co-op
503 S Saginaw Street Suite 711
Flint, MI 48502
810-232-7119
Fax: 810-232-6639
www.fakon.edu/gdl/talking.htm

Summer reading programs, Braille writer, magnifiers, closed-circuit TV, large-print photocopier, cassette books and magazines, children's books on cassette, home visits and other reference materials on blindness and other handicaps.

Carolyn Nash, Librarian

5470 Muskegon County Library for the Blind
4845 Airline Road
Muskegon, MI 49444
231-737-6310
Fax: 231-724-6675
TDD: 231-722-4103
www.muskcolib.org

Summer reading programs, Braille typewriter, magnifiers, closed-circuit TV, large-print photocopier, cassette books and magazines, children's books on cassette, home visits and other reference materials on blindness and other handicaps, The Reading Edge, Perkins Braille and large print books.

Linda Clapp, Librarian

5471 Upper Peninsula Library for the Blind Physically Handicapped
1615 Presque Isle Avenue
Marquette, MI 49855
906-228-7697
Fax: 906-228-5627
rruff@uproc.lib.mi.us
www.upesc.lib.mi.us/uplbph

Summer reading programs, Braille writer, magnifiers, closed-circuit TV, large-print photocopier, cassette books and magazines, children's books on cassette, home visits and other reference materials on blindness and other handicaps.

Suzanne Dees, Executive Director

5472 Washtenaw County Library
PO Box 8645
Ann Arbor, MI 48107
734-222-6850
Fax: 734-222-6715
mcdaniev@ewashtenaw.org
www.ewashtenaw.org

Summer reading programs, Braille writer, magnifiers, closed-circuit TV, large-print photocopier, cassette books and magazines, children's books on cassette, home visits and other reference materials on blindness and other handicaps.

Verna J. Mcdaniel, Administrator

5473 Washtenaw County Library for the Blind and Physically Disabled
PO Box 8645
Ann Arbor, MI 48107
734-222-6850
Fax: 734-222-6715
mcdaniev@ewashtenaw.org
www.ewashtenaw.org

Book lovers club. adaptive technology, cassette equipment, cassette books and magazines, described videos, low vision aids reference and referral services.

Verna J. Mcdaniel, Administrator

Minnesota

5474 Minnesota Library for the Blind & Physically Handicapped
Highway 298, PO Box 68
Fairbault, MN 55021
507-333-4828
800-722-0550
Fax: 507-333-4832
libblnd@state.mn.us

Summer reading programs, Braille writer, magnifiers, closed-circuit TV, large-print photocopier, cassette, large print, Braille books and magazines, children's books on cassette, and other reference materials on blindness and other handicaps.

Catherine A Durivage, Program Director

Missouri

5475 Adriene Resource Center for Blind Children
1445 Boonville Avenue
Springfield, MO 65802
417-831-8000
800-641-4310
Fax: 800-328-0294
blind@ag.org
www.gospelpublishing.com

Offers Braille and cassette lending library, Braille and cassette Sunday school materials for all ages, Braille and cassette periodicals and resource assistance, and resources for blind children and children of blind parents.

Paul Weingariner, Director

5476 Assemblies of God National Center for the Blind
1445 Boonville Avenue
Springfield, MO 65802
417-831-8001
800-641-4311
Fax: 800-328-0295
blind@ag.org
www.gospelpublishing.com

Offers Braille and cassette lending library, Braille and cassette Sunday school materials for all ages, Braille and cassette periodicals and resource assistance, and resources for blind children and children of blind parents.

Thomas Trask, Manager

5477 Wolfner Memorial Library for the Blind
PO Box 387
Jefferson City, MO 65102
573-751-8720
Fax: 573-526-2985
TDD: 800-347-1379
wolfner@sos.mo.gov

Summer reading programs, Braille writer, magnifiers, closed-circuit TV, large-print photocopier, cassette books and magazines, children's books on cassette, home visits and other reference materials on blindness and other handicaps.

Richard J Smith, Executive Director

Nebraska

5478 Nebraska Library Commission Talking Book & Braille Services
1200 N Street
Lincoln, NE 68508
402-471-2045
800-307-2665
Fax: 402-471-2083
TDD: 402-471-4038
doertli@nlc.state.ne.us
www.nlc.state.ne.us

Free loan of books and magazines on cassette and in Braille, including children's materials, along with specially designed playback equipment. Summer reading program for children, Braille embossing, closed circuit TV, large-print copier. Reference materials on blindness and other disabilities.

David Oerti, Librarian

New Jersey

5479 New Jersey State Library Talking Book and Braille Center
185 West State Street
Trenton, NJ 08625
609-278-2640
800-792-8322
Fax: 609-278-2647
TDD: 877-882-5593
njlbh@njstatelib.org
www.njstatelib.org

Free home delivery of large-print, audio, and Braille books and magazines, children's books on cassettes in Braille and other reference materials on blindness and other handicaps. Services are for New Jersey residents with print disabilities.

Adanrah Szczepaniak, Director
Anne McArthur, Head of Outreach and Audiovision

New Mexico

5480 New Mexico State Library for the Blind and Physically Handicapped
1209 Camino Carlos Ray
Santa Fe, NM 87507
505-476-9700
Fax: 505-476-9761
www.stlib.state.nm.us

Summer reading programs, Braille writer, magnifiers, closed-circuit TV, large-print photocopier, cassette books and magazines, children's books on cassette, home visits and other reference materials on blindness and other handicaps.

Susan Overland, Manager

New York

5481 New York State Talking Book & Braille Library
Empire State Plaza, CEC
Albany, NY 12230
518-474-5935
Fax: 518-486-1957
TDD: 518-474-7121
tbbl@mail.nysed.gov
www.suffolk.lib.ny.us

Books on audio cassette, cassette players, Braille books, summer reading programs, Braille writer, magnifiers, closed-circuit TV, large-print photocopier, cassette books and magazines, children's books on cassette, reference materials on blindness and other handicaps.

Jane Somers, Director

North Carolina

5482 North Carolina Library for the Blind
1841 Capital Boulevard
Raleigh, NC 27635
919-733-4376
Fax: 919-733-6910
TDD: 919-733-1462

Summer reading programs, Braille writer, magnifiers, closed-circuit TV, large-print photocopier, cassette books and magazines, children's books on cassette, home visits and other reference materials on blindness and other handicaps.

Francine Martin, Manager

Ohio

5483 American Council of Blind Parents
34400 Cedar Road, Apartment 108
University Heights, OH 44121
800-424-8666

Members are sighted parents of blind or visually impaired children. Offers a forum for support and outreach, sharing of experiences in parent-child relationships, and educational and cultural information about child development. Monitors developments in technical and legislative arenas.

Nola Webb, President

Oregon

5484 Oregon State Library, Talking Book and Braille Services
250 Winter Street NW
Salem, OR 97310
503-378-3849
Fax: 503-585-8059
TDD: 503-378-4276
www.tbabs.org

Cassette books and magazines, children's books on cassette, home visits and other reference materials on blindness and other handicaps.

Susan Westin, Manager

Virginia

5485 Alexandria Library Talking Book Service
5005 Duke Street
Alexandria, VA 22304
703-746-1760
Fax: 703-519-5916
TDD: 703-838-4568
www.alexandria.lib.va.us

Summer reading programs, Braille writer, magnifiers, closed-circuit TV, large-print photocopier, cassette books and magazines, children's books on cassette, home visits and other reference materials on blindness and other handicaps.

Karen Russell, Manager

5486 Division for the Visually Handicapped
1920 Association Drive
Reston, VA 20191
703-620-3660

Members are teachers, college faculty members, administrators, supervisors and others concerned with the education and welfare of visually handicapped and blind children and youth. This is a division of the Council For Exceptional Children.

Dr. Kay Ferrell, President

5487 Division on Visual Impairments
Council for Exceptional Children
1110 North Glebe Road, Suite 300
Arlington, VA 22201
800-224-6830
Fax: 703-264-9494
TTY: 866-915-5000
www.ed.arizona.edu/dvi/welcome.htm; www.cec.sped.org

A division within the CEC, it handles concerns for Federal, state and local issues and policies related to education of youths, children and infants with visual impairments.

Ellyn Ross, President
Shirley J Wilson, Secretary
Phyllis T Simmons, President Elect

5488 Virginia State Library for the Visually and Physically Handicapped
1901 Roane Street
Richmond, VA 23222
804-367-0014

Summer reading programs, Braille writer, magnifiers, closed-circuit TV, large-print photocopier, cassette books and magazines, children's books on cassette, home visits and other reference materials on blindness and other handicaps.

Mary Ruth Halapatz, Librarian

Washington

5489 Washington Library for the Blind and Physically Handicapped
1000 Fourth Ave.
Seattle, WA 98104
206-386-4636
Fax: 206-386-4685
wtbbl@spl.lib.wa.us
www.spl.lib.wa.us

Summer reading programs, Braille writer, magnifiers, closed-circuit TV, large-print photocopier, cassette books and magazines, children's books on cassette, home visits and other reference materials on blindness and other handicaps.

Marcellus Turner, Librarian

West Virginia

5490 West Virginia School for the Blind
301 E Main Street
Romney, WV 26757
304-822-4801
Fax: 304-822-3370
cjohn@access.mountain.net

Summer reading programs, Braille writer, magnifiers, closed-circuit TV, large-print photocopier, cassette books and magazines, children's books on cassette, home visits and other reference materials on blindness and other handicaps.

Patsy Shank, Administrator

Research Centers

5491 Arlene R Gordon Research Institute
Lighthouse International
111 E 59th Street
New York, NY 10022
212-821-9525
800-829-0500
Fax: 212-821-9707
TTY: 212-821-9713
www.lighthouse.org

The institute is the only research institute within a vision rehabilitation agency. Trainees can come and acquire research skills in both laboratory and field settings. It is comprised on these major divisions: Evaluation research; Vision research; and Psychosocial research.

Amy Horowitz, Director
Joann P Reinhardt PhD, Director Psychosocial Research

5492 Center for the Partially Sighted
6101 W Centinela Ave, Suite 150
Los Angeles, CA 90230
310-988-1970
Fax: 310-988-1980
www.low-vision.org

Provides professional, comprehensive vision rehabilitation services to visually impaired people of all ages. For those whose sight is severely limited due to macular degeneration, diabetic retinopathy, glaucoma, retinal detachment, stroke or other conditions not correctable medically or surgically.

La Donna Ringering, Executive Director
Herbert Ruderman, Psychiatrist
Marc Gerberick, IT Manager

5493 Mobile Association for the Blind
2440 Gordon Smith Drive
Mobile, AL 36617
251-473-3585
877-292-5463
Fax: 251-470-8622

Offers work adjustment training, activities of daily living, mobility, communication skills and sheltered employment for adults and children who are visually impaired.

Jim Bullock, Executive Director

5494 New Beginnings - The Blind Children's Center
4120 Marathon Street
Los Angeles, CA 90029
323-664-2153

The purpose of the Center is to turn initial fears into hope. Helps children and their families become independent by creating a climate of safety and trust. Children learn to develop self confidence and to master a wide range of skills. Services include an infant stimulation program, educational preschool, interdisciplinary assessment services, family services, correspondence program, toll free national hotline and a publication and research service.

5495 Research to Prevent Blindness
645 Madison Avenue
New York, NY 10022
212-752-4333
800-621-0026
Fax: 212-688-6231
www.rpbusa.org

Provides research grants to scientists interested in eye disease and vision disorders.

Diane Swift, President

Audio Video

5496 Heart to Heart
Blind Children's Center
4120 Marathon Street
Los Angeles, CA 90029
323-644-2153
Fax: 323-665-3828
www.blindcntr.org

Parents of blind and partially sighted children talk about their feelings.
Videotape

5497 Let's Eat
Blind Children's Center
4120 Marathon Street
Los Angeles, CA 90029
213-664-2153
Fax: 213-665-3828

Teaches competent feeding skills to children with visual impairments.
Videotape

5498 See What I Feel
Britannica Film Co.
345 4th Street
San Francisco, CA 94107
415-597-5555

A blind child tells her friends about her trip to the zoo. Each experience was explained as a blind child would experience it. A teacher's guide comes with this video.
Films

Web Sites

5499 Lighthouse Guild
250 West 64th Street
New York, NY 10023
800-284-4422
info@lighthouseguild.org
www.lighthouseguild.org

Lighthouse Guild is dedicated to providing exceptional services that inspire people who are visually impaired to attain their goals.

James M. Dubin, Chair
Calvin W. Roberts, President & CEO
Maura J. Sweeney, SVP, Programs & Services

5500 National Association of Blind Students
200 East Wells Street, Jernigan Place
Baltimore, MD 21230
410-659-9314
nfb@nfb.org
nabslink.org

For over 50 years, the National Association of Blind Students has worked, as an integral part of the National Federation of the Blind, to promote the equality of the blind by serving as a source of information, forum for networking and vehicle for collective action for blind students. Our work on the local, state, and national levels is firmly rooted in the conviction that blindness need not prevent one from excelling in a chosen field of study or living a full and productive life.

Book Publishers

5501 **Children with Visual Impairments: A Parents' Guide**
Peytral Publications
PO Box 1162
Minnetonka, MN 55345
952-949-8707
877-739-8725
Fax: 952-906-9777
help@peytral.com
www.peytral.com

Covers visual impairments ranging from low vision to total blindness. Offers authoritative information and empathy, parental insight on diagnosis and treatment, orientation and mobility, literacy, legal issues and more. Valuable to parents, educators and support staff.

395 pages
M Cay Holbrook PhD, Editor

5502 **Eye Care Sourcebook**
Omnigraphics
615 Griswold Street, Ste 520
Detroit, MI 48226
610-461-3548
800-234-1340
Fax: 800-875-1340
contact@omnigraphics.com
www.omnigraphics.com

Basic consumer information about glaucoma, cataracts, macular degeneration, strabismus, refractive disorders and more.

2017 656 pages
ISBN: 0-780815-32-2

Magazines

5503 **Journal of Visual Impairment and Blindness**
American Foundation for the Blind
2 Penn Plaza, Suite 1102
New York, NY 10121
212-502-7600
Fax: 212-502-7777
afbinfo@afb.net
www.afb.org

Published in braille, regular print and on cassette this journal contains a wide variety of subjects including rehabilitation, psychology, education, legislation, medicine, technology, employment, sensory aids and childhood development as they relate to visual impairments.

10x Year
Carl R. Augusto, President & CEO
Kelly Bleach, Chief Administrative Officer
Rick Bozeman, Chief Financial Officer

5504 **Reaching, Crawling, Walking - Let's Get Moving**
Blind Children's Center
4120 Marathon Street
Los Angeles, CA 90029
323-664-2153
Fax: 323-665-3828
info@blindchildrenscenter.org
www.blindchildrenscenter.org

Orientation and mobility for visually impaired preschool children.

24 pages

5505 **Tactic**
Clovernook Home and School for the Blind
7000 Hamilton Avenue
Cincinnati, OH 45231
513-522-3860
Fax: 513-728-3950
clovernook@aol.com

Quarterly

Newsletters

5506 **National Library Service for the Blind & Physically Handicapped**
Library of Congress
1291 Taylor Street NW
Washington, DC 20542
202-707-5100
800-424-8567
Fax: 202-707-0712
nls@loc.gov
www.loc.gov/nls

Provides information and advocacy resources for families and professionals, including listings of organizations focusing on more specific areas of concern to families and young adults who have disabilities. Administers a natural library service that provides recorded and braille reading materials to eligible children and adults who cannot read standard print.

12 pages Quarterly
ISSN: 1046-1663

5507 **Talking Book Topics**
National Library Services for the Blind
1291 Taylor Street NW
Washington, DC 20542
202-707-5100
Fax: 202-707-0712
nls@loc.gov
www.loc.gov/nls

Offers hundreds of listings of books, fiction and nonfiction, for adults and children who cannot read regular print material. Also offers foreign language books, talking magazines and reviews.

Bimonthly

Pamphlets

5508 **Dancing Cheek to Cheek**
Blind Children's Center
4120 Marathon Street
Los Angeles, CA 90029
213-664-2153
Fax: 213-665-3828
www.blindchildrenscenter.org

Discusses beginning social, play and language interactions.

33 pages

5509 **Family Guide - Growth and Development of the Partially Seeing Child**
Lighthouse Guild
250 West 64th Street
New York, NY 10023
800-284-4422
info@lighthouseguild.org
www.lighthouseguild.org

Offers information for parents and guidelines in raising a partially seeing child.

5510 **Family Guide to Vision Care**
American Optometric Association
243 N Lindbergh Boulevard
Saint Louis, MO 63141
314-991-4100
Fax: 314-991-4101
www.aoanet.org

Offers information on the early developmental years of your vision, finding a family optometrist and how to take care of your eyesight through the learning years, the working years and the mature years.

5511 **Heart to Heart**
Blind Children's Center
4120 Marathon Street
Los Angeles, CA 90029
213-664-2153
Fax: 213-665-3828
www.blindchildrenscenter.org

Parents of blind and partially sighted children talk about their feelings.

12 pages

5512 Learning to Play
Blind Children's Center
4120 Marathon Street
Los Angeles, CA 90029

213-664-2153
Fax: 213-665-3828
www.blindchildrenscenter.org

Discusses how to present play activities to the visually impaired preschool child.

12 pages

5513 Let's Eat
Blind Children's Center
4120 Marathon Street
Los Angeles, CA 90029

213-664-2153
Fax: 213-665-3828
www.blindchildrenscenter.org

Teaches competent feeding skills to children with visual impairments.

28 pages

5514 Move with Me
Blind Children's Center
4120 Marathon Street
Los Angeles, CA 90029

213-664-2153
Fax: 213-665-3828
www.blindchildrenscenter.org

A parent's guide to movement development for visually impaired babies.

12 pages

5515 Selecting a Program
Blind Children's Center
4120 Marathon Street
Los Angeles, CA 90029

213-664-2153
Fax: 213-665-3828
www.blindchildrenscenter.org

A guide for parents of infants and preschoolers with visual impairments.

28 pages

5516 Standing on My Own Two Feet
Blind Children's Center
4120 Marathon Street
Los Angeles, CA 90029

323-664-2153
Fax: 323-665-3828
info@blindchildrenscenter.org
www.blindchildrenscenter.org

A step-by-step guide to designing and constructing simple, individually tailored adaptive mobility devices for preschool-age children who are visually impaired.

36 pages

5517 Talk to Me
Blind Children's Center
4120 Marathon Street
Los Angeles, CA 90029

213-664-2153
Fax: 213-665-3828
www.blindchildrenscenter.org

A language guide for parents of deaf children.

11 pages

5518 Talk to Me II
Blind Children's Center
4120 Marathon Street
Los Angeles, CA 90029

213-664-2153
Fax: 213-665-3828
www.blindchildrenscenter.org

A sequel to Talk To Me, available in English and Spanish.

15 pages

Camps

5519 Bloomfield
5300 Angeles Vista Boulevard
Los Angeles, CA 90043

323-295-4555
800-352-2290
Fax: 323-296-0424
info@juniorblind.org
www.junoirblind.org

This camp is dedicated to serving blind and developmentally disabled children and adults.

5520 Florida School-Deaf and Blind Summer Camp
207 San Marco Avenue
Saint Augustine, FL 32084

904-827-2200
800-800-344
www.fsdb.k12.fl.us

The Florida School for the Deaf and the Blind hosts summer campers from all over teh state of Florida for a week of fun and adventure. FSDB's 80 acre campus is where campers participate in a variety of activities including rock climbing, archery, swimming, kayaking, team games, arts and crafts, dance music, and much more.

L Daniel Hutto, President
Cindy Day, Executive Director of Parent Svcs
Terri Wiseman, Administrator of Business Services

5521 National Camps for Blind Children
Christian Record
4444 S 52nd Street
Lincoln, NE 68516

402-488-0981
Fax: 402-488-7582
info@christianrecord.org
www.christianrecord.org

Camps throughout the US and Canada are offered at no cost to the legally blind, ages 9-65. Activities include archery, beeper basketball, water sports, hiking and rock climbing and horseback riding.

Dan Jackson, Chair
Tom Lemon, Vice Chair
Larry Pitcher, Secretary

5522 VISIONS/Vacation Camp for the Blind
500 Greenwich Street, 3rd Floor
New York, NY 10013

212-625-1616
888-245-8333
Fax: 212-219-4078
info@visionsvcb.org
www.visionvcb.org

Family programs at Vacation Camp for the Blind in Rockland County, NY for children who are blind, severely visually impaired or multi-handicapped. Parent or guardian must attend winter weekends and summer session.

Nancy T. Jones, President
Richard P. Simon, Vice President
Burton M. Strauss, Treasurer

Respiratory Distress Syndrome of the Newborn / Description

Description

5523 RESPIRATORY DISTRESS SYNDROME OF THE NEWBORN

Synonyms: Hyaline membrane disese (HMD), RDS
Covers these related disorders: Meconium aspiration syndrome
Involves the following Biologic System(s):
Neonatal and Infant Disorders, Respiratory Disorders

Respiratory distress syndrome of the newborn (RDS) is a breathing disorder characterized by insufficient production of surfactant, which consists of substances produced by certain cells in the lungs. Surfactant contributes to the elasticity of lung (pulmonary) tissue and enables the air sacs (alveoli) of the lungs to remain open between breaths. The exchange of oxygen and carbon dioxide takes place across the thin walls of the air sacs. Due to insufficient surfactant in newborns with RDS, greater pressure is required to expand the lungs' airways and air sacs. As a result, the air sacs may collapse and the lungs may become unable to properly provide oxygenated blood to the body.

Surfactant is produced as the lungs mature during fetal development. Sufficient levels of surfactant are often present after approximately 35 weeks of pregnancy (gestation). RDS primarily occurs in newborns who are born prior to 37 weeks of gestation (premature newborns), affecting up to 80 percent of those who are born before 28 weeks' gestation and up to 30 percent of infants born between 32 and 36 weeks' gestation. The condition also occurs with increased frequency in infants who are born to mothers with diabetes or those who are delivered by Cesarean section. In other newborns, RDS may occur in the absence of known predisposing factors or may be due to certain birth defects or other conditions, such as meconium aspiration syndrome.rome, or persistent fetal circulation. Respiratory distress syndrome of the newborn is sometimes referred to as hyaline membrane disease, because insufficient surfactant production may cause the formation of a fibrous membrane known as hyaline membrane lining the lungs' small airways (bronchioles), ducts (alveolar ducts), and air sacs (alveoli).

Symptoms associated with RDS usually occur within minutes of birth, although they may not be recognized for several hours. These symptoms may vary in severity, depending upon the degree of prematurity or other underlying causes responsible for the condition. Newborns may experience increasing difficulty breathing (dyspnea), characterized by rapid, labored, shallow breaths (tachypnea); grunting upon exhalation; drawing in of the chest wall during inhalation; and bluish discoloration of the skin and mucous membranes (cyanosis) due to lack of sufficient oxygen supply to bodily tissues (hypoxia). Air may leak into the chest cavity surrounding the lungs (pneumothorax), causing collapse of the lungs and further breathing difficulties. Without appropriate treatment, cyanosis and breathing difficulties may progressively worsen and body temperature and blood pressure may fall. As infants with severe RDS tire, grunting upon exhalation may subside, breathing becomes irregular, and life-threatening complications may result. Depending upon the severity of the condition, infants with RDS may begin to gradually improve in about three days or may experience life-threatening symptoms within approximately two to seven days after birth.

Meconium aspiration syndrome is characterized by blockage and irritation of the airways of the lungs due to passage of meconium before birth and inhalation of meconium before or during delivery. Meconium is the thick, sticky material that forms a newborn's first stools, and is typically passed during the first 24 to 48 hours after birth. In some cases, a fetus may pass meconium into the amniotic fluid before birth and then inhale this into the lungs before or right after birth. The skin of newborns with meconium aspiration is usually stained with meconium. In severe cases, symptoms include diminished muscle tone, an abnormally slow heartbeat, or absence of spontaneous respiration at birth.

In newborns with meconium aspiration syndrome, treatment may include immediate suctioning of an affected infant's mouth, throuat, and nose and placement of a tube into the windpipe to remove meconium from the airways. In most affected newborns, imporvement usually occurs in approximately three days.

If physicians suspect that a newborn may be born prematurely, steps may be taken to delay delivery in order to help decrease the risk of RDS. If delivery cannot be delayed, some women may be given certain corticosteroid medications (e.g., dexamethasone or betamethasone) approximately 48 to 72 hours before the delivery of premature newborns to help stimulate the production of surfactant before birth. In addition, an artificial surfactant may be administered into the windpipe of affected newborns immediately after birth or within 24 hours, to help reduce the severity of RDS and associated symptoms or complications. Additional treatment may include symptomatic and supportive measures, such as use of an oxygen hood or support with a ventilator.

Government Agencies

5524 NIH/ Eunice Kennedy Shriver National Institute of Child Health & Human Development
P.O. Box 3006
Rockville, MD 20847
800-370-2943
Fax: 866-760-5947
www.nichd.nih.gov

Conducts and supports research on topics related to the health of children, adults, families and populations. Some of these topics include: developmental disabilities, growth and development, infant death, reproductive health and birth defects.

Diana W. Bianchi, Director
Alison Cernich, PhD, Deputy Director

5525 NIH/National Heart, Lung and Blood Institute
31 Center Drive, Bldg 31
Bethesda, MD 20892
877-645-2448
www.nhlbi.nih.gov

Primary responsibility of this organization is the scientific investigation of heart, blood vessel, lung and blood disorders. Oversees research, demonstration, prevention, education, control and training activities in these fields and emphasizes the prevention and control of heart diseases.

Gary H. Gibbons, MD, Director
Kate O'Sullivan, Executive Officer

National Associations & Support Groups

5526 American Academy of Pediatrics
345 Park Blvd
Itasca, IL 60143
847-434-4000
800-433-9016
Fax: 847-434-8000
csc@aap.org
www.aap.org

The American Academy of Pediatrics and its member pediatricians are committed to the attainment of optimal physical, mental and social health and well-being for all infants, children, adolescents, and young adults.

Kyle E. Yasuda, MD, FAAP, President
Mark Del Monte, JD, CEO/Executive VP
Vera Tait, MD, FAAP, Chief Medical Officer

5527 **American Lung Association**
55 W. Wacker Drive, Suite 1150
Chicago, IL 60601

800-586-4872
info@lung.org
www.lung.org

The American Lung Association fights lung disease in all its forms, with special emphasis on asthma, tobacco control and environmental health. The American Lung Association is funded with contributions from the public, along with gifts and grants from corporations, foundations and government agencies. The association achieves its many successes through the work of thousands of committed volunteers and staff.

Harold P. Wimmer, National President & CEO
Albert Rizzo, MD, Chief Medical Officer
Sue Swan, Chief Development Officer

5528 **Genetic Alliance**
426400 Woodfield Road, Ste 189
Damascus, MD 20872

202-966-5557
Fax: 202-966-8553
info@geneticalliance.org
www.geneticalliance.org

World's leading nonprofit health advocacy organization committed to transforming health through genetics and promoting an environment of openness centered on the health of individuals, families, and communities.

Sharon Terry, CEO
Ruth Child, CFO
Natasha Bonhomme, Chief Strategy Officer

5529 **March of Dimes Foundation**
1550 Crystal Drive, Ste 1300
Arlington, VA 22202

888-663-4637
www.marchofdimes.org

March of Dimes help moms have full-term pregnancies and research the problems that threaten the health of babies. The March of Dimes also acts globally: sharing best practices in perinatal health and helping improve birth outcomes where the needs are the most urgent.

Stacey D. Stewart, President
Alan Brogdon, SVP/COO/Board Officer
Rahul Gupta, MD, SVP & Chief Medical/Health Officer

Web Sites

5530 **American Lung Association**
55 W. Wacker Drive, Suite 1150
Chicago, IL 60601

800-586-4872
info@lung.org
www.lung.org

The American Lung Association fights lung disease in all its forms, with special emphasis on asthma, tobacco control and environmental health. The American Lung Association is funded with contributions from the public, along with gifts and grants from corporations, foundations and government agencies. The association achieves its many successes through the work of thousands of committed volunteers and staff.

Harold P. Wimmer, National President & CEO
Albert Rizzo, MD, Chief Medical Officer
Sue Swan, Chief Development Officer

5531 **KidsHealth**
kidshealth.org

kidshealth.org

KidsHealth provides doctor-approved health information about children from before birth through adolescence.

Neil Izenberg, MD, Editor-in-Chief & Founder

5532 **RSV Info Center**
www.rsvinfo.com

www.rsvinfo.com

A comprehensive overview about the most common cause of lower respiratory tract infections in children.

Respiratory Syncytial Virus Infection / Description

Description

5533 RESPIRATORY SYNCYTIAL VIRUS INFECTION
Synonym: RSV infection
Involves the following Biologic System(s):
Infectious Disorders, Respiratory Disorders

The respiratory syncytial virus (RSV) is the most common cause of lower respiratory tract infections in infants and young children. RSV is primarily spread by the inhalation of virus-containing airborne droplets. The virus is present worldwide and causes annual epidemics of RSV infection in late autumn, winter, or as late as May or June. Such outbreaks typically peak from January through March. Nearly every child is affected by RSV infection by age two, and many experience recurrent reinfection throughout childhood.

In older children and adults, RSV infection may cause no apparent symptoms (asymptomatic) or may result in mild to moderate lung infection and associated cold-like symptoms. However, RSV infection may be severe in others, particularly infants, young children, children with heart or lung disease, or individuals with compromised immune systems. In such patients, RSV infection may lead to inflammation of the lungs' small airways (bronchiolitis), inflammation of the airways and lung tissue (bronchopneumonia), or, in extremely severe cases, potentially life-threatening complications. RSV infection is known to be the leading cause of bronchiolitis or bronchopneumonia in children younger than one year of age.

In infants and young children with RSV infection, symptoms typically begin approximately four days after infection. Initial symptoms include a runny nose (rhinorrhea) and sore throat (pharyngitis). Patients may then develop a low fever, begin to cough and sneeze, and soon experience wheezing, which is the production of a whistling sound during breathing due to inflammation and associated narrowing of the airways. If RSV infection progresses, patients may develop additional symptoms, including increasing wheezing and coughing, an abnormally rapid rate of breathing (tachypnea), drawing in of the chest wall during inhalation, and bluish discoloration of the skin and mucous membranes (cyanosis). Patients with extremely severe disease progression may develop increasingly rapid breathing, temporary cessation of breathing (apnea), listlessness, and potentially life-threatening complications. In other infants or young children with RSV infection, initial running of the nose and coughing may be followed by poor feeding, listlessness, and difficulties breathing (dyspnea) with little or no wheezing.

As mentioned above, many children experience reinfection with RSV. Reinfection usually causes less severe symptoms than those associated with initial disease. However, depending upon the age of patients and other factors, secondary infections may also sometimes be associated with severe lower respiratory tract infections. Older children who experience reinfection with RSV generally have more mild symptoms.

In children with mild or moderate RSV infection without associated bronchiolitis or bronchopneumonia, treatment typically includes symptomatic and supportive measures. Affected infants, young children, children with heart or lung disease, or those with compromised immune systems may require hospitalization. Treatment may include providing respiratory therapy with humidified air to help supply adequate oxygen to bodily tissues; ensuring an adequate intake of fluids; or administering certain medications to relax the smooth muscles of the small airways (bronchodilators).

Certain infants and children are at high risk for severe RSV disease, such as those with lung disease, congenital heart disease, or immunodeficiency. In these children, certain preventive or prophylactic therapies such as RSV-specific antibodies may be recommended to help reduce (or even prevent) the severity of RSV infection in these at-risk infants and young children.

Government Agencies

5534 NIH/ Eunice Kennedy Shriver National Institute of Child Health & Human Development
P.O. Box 3006
Rockville, MD 20847
800-370-2943
Fax: 866-760-5947
www.nichd.nih.gov

Conducts and supports research on topics related to the health of children, adults, families and populations. Some of these topics include: developmental disabilities, growth and development, infant death, reproductive health and birth defects.
Diana W. Bianchi, Director
Alison Cernich, PhD, Deputy Director

5535 NIH/National Institute of Allergy and Infectious Diseases
5601 Fishers Lane, MSC 9806
Bethesda, MD 20892
301-496-5717
866-284-4107
Fax: 301-402-3573
TDD: 800-877-8339
ocpostoffice@niaid.nih.gov
www.niaid.nih.gov

The principal advisory board of the NIAID. The council is composed of physicians, scientists and representatives of the public and advises on the conduct and support or research, training and dissemination of health information regarding allergies and infectious diseases.
Anthony S. Fauci, MD, Director

National Associations & Support Groups

5536 American Academy of Pediatrics
345 Park Blvd
Itasca, IL 60143
847-434-4000
800-433-9016
Fax: 847-434-8000
csc@aap.org
www.aap.org

The American Academy of Pediatrics and its member pediatricians are committed to the attainment of optimal physical, mental and social health and well-being for all infants, children, adolescents, and young adults.
Kyle E. Yasuda, MD, FAAP, President
Mark Del Monte, JD, CEO/Executive VP
Vera Tait, MD, FAAP, Chief Medical Officer

5537 American Lung Association
55 W. Wacker Drive, Suite 1150
Chicago, IL 60601
800-586-4872
info@lung.org
www.lung.org

The American Lung Association fights lung disease in all its forms, with special emphasis on asthma, tobacco control and environmental health. The American Lung Association is funded with contributions from the public, along with gifts and grants from corporations, foundations and government agencies. The association achieves its many successes through the work of thousands of committed volunteers and staff.
Harold P. Wimmer, National President & CEO
Albert Rizzo, MD, Chief Medical Officer
Sue Swan, Chief Development Officer

5538 World Health Organization
Avenue Appia 20
1202 Geneva,
Switzerland
www.who.int

WHO is the directing and coordinating authority for health within the United Nations system. WHO operates in more than 150 countries around the world.

Dr. Tedros Adhanom Ghebreyesus, Director General
Dr. Zsuzsanna Jakab, Deputy Director General
Stewart Simonson, Asst Director General, UN NYC

Web Sites

5539 American Lung Association
55 W. Wacker Drive, Suite 1150
Chicago, IL 60601

800-586-4872
info@lung.org
www.lung.org

The American Lung Association fights lung disease in all its forms, with special emphasis on asthma, tobacco control and environmental health. The American Lung Association is funded with contributions from the public, along with gifts and grants from corporations, foundations and government agencies. The association achieves its many successes through the work of thousands of committed volunteers and staff.

Harold P. Wimmer, National President & CEO
Albert Rizzo, MD, Chief Medical Officer
Sue Swan, Chief Development Officer

5540 KidsHealth
kidshealth.org/en/parents/rsv.html

kidshealth.org/en/parents/rsv.html

Provides an explanation of the disorder as well as treatment and prevention.

Neil Izenberg, MD, Editor-in-Chief & Founder

5541 RSV Info Center
www.rsvinfo.com

www.rsvinfo.com

An information center where anyone can find a comprehensive overview about the most common cause of lower respiratory tract infections in children.

Retinitis Pigmentosa / Description

Description

5542 RETINITIS PIGMENTOSA

Synonym: RP

Involves the following Biologic System(s):

Ophthalmologic Disorders

Retinitis pigmentosa (RP) refers to a group of inherited disorders in which changes occur in the light-sensitive, nerve-rich tissue membrane (retina) at the rear of the eye. This process is a slow, progressive degeneration leading to blindness. Changes in the retina include clumping (aggregation) or scattering (dispersion) of the retinal pigment, thinning or weakening of the vessels that supply the retina with oxygen-rich blood, and shrinking of the retina and the area where the optic nerve enters the retina (optic disk). Characteristic findings and symptoms of RP include difficulty in seeing at night or in dim light (night blindness; nyctalopia), a progressive reduction in the visual field with gradual loss of central vision, tunnel vision associated with loss of the peripheral visual field, and accompanying reduction of retinal function. Retinitis pigmentosa usually becomes apparent in childhood, progressing to blindness during middle age. However, the onset, severity, and rate of this progressive degeneration are widely variable.

Leber congenital retinal amaurosis (amaurosis congenita; congenital amaurosis) is a form of retinitis pigmentosa that occurs at birth or shortly thereafter and is characterized by shrinking of the optic disk (optic atrophy), thinning or weakening of the blood vessels of the retina, and widespread irregularities of retinal pigmentation. Leber congenital retinal amaurosis is transmitted as an autosomal recessive trait. In addition, retinitis pigmentosa-like degenerative changes may be associated with several metabolic, neurodegenerative, and multifold disorders.

Treatment for retinitis pigmentosa is supportive and may include the use of visual devices to enhance remaining vision. This disorder may appear as a sporadic occurrence or may be inherited, usually as an autosomal dominant disorder. There is also evidence of autosomal recessive and X-linked genetic transmission.

Government Agencies

5543 NIH/National Eye Institute
31 Center Drive MSC 2510
Bethesda, MD 20892
301-496-5248
2020@nei.nih.gov
www.nei.nih.gov

Conducts and supports research that helps prevent and treat eye diseases and other disorders of vision. This research leads to sight-saving treatments, reduces visual impairment and blindness, and improves the quality of life for people of all ages. NEI-supported research has advanced our knowledge of how the eye functions in health and disease.

Michael F. Chiang, MD, Director
Santa Tumminia, Deputy Director

National Associations & Support Groups

5544 American Academy of Pediatrics
345 Park Blvd
Itasca, IL 60143
847-434-4000
800-433-9016
Fax: 847-434-8000
csc@aap.org
www.aap.org

The American Academy of Pediatrics and its member pediatricians are committed to the attainment of optimal physical, mental and social health and well-being for all infants, children, adolescents, and young adults.

Kyle E. Yasuda, MD, FAAP, President
Mark Del Monte, JD, CEO/Executive VP
Vera Tait, MD, FAAP, Chief Medical Officer

5545 Lighthouse Guild
250 West 64th Street
New York, NY 10023
800-284-4422
Fax: 212-727-2931
info@lighthouseguild.org
www.lighthouseguild.org

Lighthouse Guild is dedicated to providing exceptional services that inspire people who are visually impaired to attain their goals.

James M. Dubin, Chair
Calvin W. Roberts, President & CEO
Maura J. Sweeney, SVP, Programs & Services

Research Centers

5546 UIC Eye Center
Department of Ophthalmology & Visual Sciences
1855 W Taylor Street
Chicago, IL 60612
312-996-4356
Fax: 312-996-7770
eyeweb@uic.edu
www.uic.edu/com/eye/department

Offers help, support, information and research for persons with vision problems, including retinitis pigmentosa.

Gerald A Fishman

Web Sites

5547 British Retinitis Pigmentosa Society
PO Box 350
Buckingham, MK18
128-082-1334
Fax: 128-081-5900
info@rpfightingblindness.org.uk
www.rpfightingblindness.org.uk

Website aims to provide a better understanding of the inherited retinal disorders. The content of this website has been written by people who have many years experience of living with RP and by very knowledgeable professionals in the field of opththalmology.

David Head, Chief Executive Officer

5548 Foundation Fighting Blindness
7168 Columbia Gateway Drive, Suite 100
Columbia, MD 21046
410-423-0600
800-683-5555
TDD: 800-683-5551
info@FightBlindness.org
www.blindness.org

Searches for treatments and cures for macular degeneration, retinitis pigmentosa (RP), usher syndrome and the entire spectrum of retinal degenerative diseases.

William T. Schmidt, Chief Executive Officer
Stephen M. Rose, Ph.D., Chief Research Officer
Annette Hinkle, CPA, Chief Financial Officer

5549 Lighthouse Guild
250 West 64th Street
New York, NY 10023
800-284-4422
info@lighthouseguild.org
www.lighthouseguild.org

Lighthouse Guild is dedicated to providing exceptional services that inspire people who are visually impaired to attain their goals.

5550 Retina South Africa - Fighting Blindness
www.rpsa.org.za/retinitis.htm

www.rpsa.org.za/retinitis.htm

Represents retinitis pigmentosa, macular degeneration, usher syndrome and over 200 other rare conditions. Offers supports, education and counseling to affected people and their families. Self employment skills are also provided by unemployed sufferers to encourage financial independence and self esteem.

5551 **Royal National Institute of Blind People**
105 Judd Street
London, WC1H
303-123-9999
www.rnib.org.uk

A leading UK charity offering information, support and advice to over two million people with sight problems.

Matt Stringer, Chief Executive
Keith Valentine, Director of Development
David Clarke, Director of Services

5552 **Texas Association of Retinitis Pigmentosa**
www.geocities.com/HotSprings/7815/front.htm

www.geocities.com/HotSprings/7815/front.htm

Nonprofit organization based in Texas serving as a national information-sharing center to provide human services to persons with progressive vision loss from retinitis pigmentosa and other retinal degenerative disorders.

Book Publishers

5553 **Children with Visual Impairments: A Parents' Guide**
Peytral Publications
PO Box 1162
Minnetonka, MN 55345
952-949-8707
877-739-8725
Fax: 952-906-9777
help@peytral.com
www.peytral.com

Covers visual impairments ranging from low vision to total blindness. Offers authoritative information and empathy, parental insight on diagnosis and treatment, orientation and mobility, literacy, legal issues and more. Valuable to parents, educators and support staff.

395 pages

M Cay Holbrook PhD, Editor

Newsletters

5554 **RP Messenger**
Texas Association of Retinitis Pigmentosa
PO Box 8388
Corpus Christi, TX 78468
512-852-8515
Fax: 361-852-8515
www.jwen.com/rp

A biannual newsletter offering information on retinitis pigmentosa.

Biannual

Description

5555 RETINOBLASTOMA
Involves the following Biologic System(s):
Hematologic and Oncologic Disorders, Ophthalmologic Disorders

Retinoblastoma is a malignant tumor of the nerve-rich membrane at the back of the eye known as the retina. This membrane converts light waves into nerve impulses and transmits them to the brain via the optic nerve (the second cranial nerve), resulting in vision. Retinoblastoma occurs in approximately one in 18,000 live births. In most cases, one eye is affected (unilateral). However, both eyes may be involved (bilateral) in about 30 percent of affected children. In some severe cases, the tumor may spread to other parts of the body (metastasize), particularly when there is tumor invasion of the middle layer of the eye (choroid) or the optic nerve. If tumor growth occurs along the optic nerve, the brain may be affected. However, in most children with retinoblastoma, metastasis rarely occurs before the tumor is detected.

Unilateral retinoblastoma is usually detected at approximately 21 months to two years of age, whereas bilateral retinoblastoma is typically diagnosed at about 11 to 12 months. Rarely, the tumor may be detected at birth, during later childhood or adolescence, or adulthood. In most cases, the first sign associated with retinoblastoma is the appearance of a yellowish-white mass in the pupil area (leukokoria) due to the presence of the tumor behind the lens of the eye and reflection of light off the tumor. Additional symptoms and findings often include abnormal deviation of the affected eye in relation to the other (strabismus) and impaired or absent vision. In some cases, affected children experience secondary complications, such as detachment of the retina or abnormally increased pressure of the fluid of the eye (glaucoma). Children who have more advanced retinoblastoma may also experience bleeding (hemorrhaging) within the chamber of the eye in front of the iris (hyphema), irregularities of the pupil, pain, or other symptoms. In cases of severely advanced disease or metastasis, associated findings may include protusion of the eye ball (proptosis) and abnormally increased pressure within the skull (intracranial pressure).

A gene responsible for retinoblastoma (RB gene) has been located on the long arm chromosome 13 (13q14). Many cases of unilateral retinoblastoma are thought to be due to deletions or abnormal changes (mutations) of the gene that occur randomly, for unknown reasons (sporadic). In familial cases, the exact mechanisms of inheritance are not understood. However, bilateral retinoblastoma and some cases of unilateral disease are thought to result from deletion of the gene from one chromosome and inheritance of one mutated disease gene (hemizygous state) or inheritance of two mutated RB genes (homozygous state of RB gene). Individuals with familial retinoblastoma may also have an increased risk for other malignancies. About one percent of children treated for familial retinoblastoma eventually develop a malignant bone tumor (osteosarcoma) by 10 years of age. In addition, estimates in medical literature indicate that about 30 percent of those with familial retinoblastoma are affected by a second malignancy within 30 years after their initial diagnosis.

In some rare cases, affected children may have retinoblastoma in association with an underlying chromosomal deletion syndrome (chromosome 13, monosomy 13q syndrome) that is characterized by deletion (monosomy) of a portion of chromosome 13q including the RB gene at band 13q14. Although associated symptoms and findings may vary, affected children may have characteristic abnormalities of the head and facial (craniofacial) area including a high forehead, prominent eyebrows, a rounded (bulbous) tip of the nose and broad nasal bridge, prominent earlobes, a large mouth, and a thin upper lip.

The treatment of children with retinoblastoma is directed toward preserving vision. In children with unilateral retinoblastoma, treatment typically includes surgical removal of the affected eye and a portion of the optic nerve. However, if the tumor is very small, other measures may be indicated, such as the use of radiation or extremely cold temperatures (cryotherapy) to destroy the tumor. In children with bilateral retinoblastoma, treatment is directed toward preserving useful vision in at least one eye. Therefore, initial therapy may include cryotherapy or radiotherapy of one or both eyes. Bilateral therapy may be recommended since there have been cases in which the more severely affected eye has responded more dramatically to such measures. When one eye has no remaining vision or is affected by painful complications, removal of the eye may be advised. If tumor growth has begun to extend beyond the eye, radiation therapy may also be conducted. Therapy with anticancer drugs, such as cyclophosphamide and doxorubicin, may be considered with radiation therapy. Children and adults who have been affected by familial retinoblastoma should be carefully monitored for secondary malignancies. In addition, family members of affected children should be examined by an eye specialist to detect or help rule out the presence of retinoblastoma.

Government Agencies

5556 NIH/National Cancer Institute
Bethesda, MD 20892
800-422-6237
NCIinfo@nih.gov
www.cancer.gov

The National Cancer Institute coordinates the National Cancer Program, which conducts and supports research, training, health information dissemination, and other programs with respect to the cause, diagnosis, prevention, and treatment of cancer, rehabilitation from cancer, and the continuing care of cancer patients and the families of cancer patients.

Norman E. Sharpless, MD, Director
Douglas R. Lowy, MD, Principal Deputy Director

National Associations & Support Groups

5557 American Academy of Pediatrics
345 Park Blvd
Itasca, IL 60143
847-434-4000
800-433-9016
Fax: 847-434-8000
csc@aap.org
www.aap.org

The American Academy of Pediatrics and its member pediatricians are committed to the attainment of optimal physical, mental and social health and well-being for all infants, children, adolescents, and young adults.

Kyle E. Yasuda, MD, FAAP, President
Mark Del Monte, JD, CEO/Executive VP
Vera Tait, MD, FAAP, Chief Medical Officer

5558 American Childhood Cancer Organization
P.O. Box 498
Kensington, MD 20895
301-962-3520
800-366-2223
Fax: 310-962-3521
staff@acco.org
www.acco.org

The American Childhood Cancer Organization (ACCO) was founded in 1970 by a group of parents whose children had been diagnosed with cancer. Today ACCO is one of the largest grassroots, national organizations dedicated to improving the lives of children and adolescents with cancer and their families.

Retinoblastoma / Book Publishers

Ruth I. Hoffman, MPH, CEO
Krista Novak, Programs Manager
Blair Scroggs, Public Relations Coordinator

5559 CureSearch for Children's Cancer
P.O. Box 45781
Baltimore, MD 21297
800-458-6223
Fax: 301-718-0047
info@curesearch.org
www.curesearch.org

CureSearch for Children's Cancer is a national non-profit foundation that accelerates the cure for children's cancer by driving innovation, eliminating research barriers and solving the field's most challenging problems.

Kay Koehler, CEO
Katharine A. Burke, COO & VP, Financing
Caitlyn W. Barrett, National Director, Research & Prgms

5560 Genetic Alliance
426400 Woodfield Road, Ste 189
Damascus, MD 20872
202-966-5557
Fax: 202-966-8553
info@geneticalliance.org
www.geneticalliance.org

World's leading nonprofit health advocacy organization committed to transforming health through genetics and promoting an environment of openness centered on the health of individuals, families, and communities.

Sharon Terry, CEO
Ruth Child, CFO
Natasha Bonhomme, Chief Strategy Officer

5561 Institute for Families
1300 N Vermont Avenue, Suite 1004
Los Angeles, CA 90027
www.instituteforfamilies.org

A non-profit organization providing free of charge support and services to professionals and families of visually impaired children.

5562 Lighthouse Guild
250 West 64th Street
New York, NY 10023
800-284-4422
info@lighthouseguild.org
www.lighthouseguild.org

Lighthouse Guild is dedicated to providing exceptional services that inspire people who are visually impaired to attain their goals.

James M. Dubin, Chair
Calvin W. Roberts, President & CEO
Maura J. Sweeney, SVP, Programs & Services

State Agencies & Support Groups

Florida

5563 Florida Families of Children with Visual Impairments
Ormond Beach, FL 32174
386-677-7760
ffcvi@yahoo.com

Sue Townsend, President

Massachusetts

5564 Massachusetts Association for Parents of the Visually Impaired (MAPVI)
Maynard, MA 01754
978-897-3005
www.mapvi.org

Anita Sullivan, President
Susan Rawlay, Regional Representative
Chris Pine, Treasurer

New Hampshire

5565 New England Retinoblastoma Support Group (NERSG)
Salem, NH 03079
603-893-3908
Tom Gelinas, Treasurer

Web Sites

5566 A Parent's Guide to Understanding Retinoblastoma
1275 York Avenue
New York, NY 10065
212-639-2000
800-525-2225
www.mskcc.org

Craig B. Thompson, President
John Gunn, Chief Operating Officer
Kerry Bessey, Senior Vice President

5567 Children's Cancer Web
www.cancerindex.org/ccw

www.cancerindex.org/ccw

An independent nonprofit site, established to provide a directory of childhood cancer resources.

5568 Life With Retinoblastoma
www.mrmegabyte.net/rb/retino.html

www.mrmegabyte.net/rb/retino.html

A support site written by the parent of a child with retinoblastoma.

5569 Online Mendelian Inheritance in Man
McKusick-Nathans Institue of Genetic Medicine-JHU
Baltimore, MD 21205
www.omim.org

This database is a catalog of human genes and genetic disorders.

Ada Hamosh, MD, Scientific Director

5570 Retinoblastoma Solutions
1100 Bennett Road - Unit 4
Bowmanville, ON L1C 3
647-478-4902
877-624-9769
Fax: 905-697-9786
info@impactgenetics.com
impactgenetics.com

Dedicated to advancing retinoblastoma research and making available molecular diagnostic tests to families that cannot afford it.

Franny Jewett, CEO
David McDonald, CTO
Diane Rushlow, Scientific Director

Book Publishers

5571 Children with Visual Impairments: A Parents' Guide
Peytral Publications
PO Box 1162
Minnetonka, MN 55345
952-949-8707
877-739-8725
Fax: 952-906-9777
help@peytral.com
www.peytral.com

Covers visual impairments ranging from low vision to total blindness. Offers authoritative information and empathy, parental insight on diagnosis and treatment, orientation and mobility, literacy, legal issues and more. Valuable to parents, educators and support staff.

395 pages

M Cay Holbrook PhD, Editor

5572 Let's Talk About Going to the Hospital
Rosen Publishing Group's PowerKids Press
29 E 21st Street
New York, NY 10010
212-777-3017
800-237-9932
Fax: 888-436-4643
rosenpub@tribeca.ios.com
www.rosenpublishing.com

If a child has to check into the hospital, chances are he or she is already upset about being ill. Knowing how a hospital functions and what the procedures are, such as when family members can visit, will help in what is already a stressful situation. Grades K-5.

24 pages
ISBN: 0-823950-36-0

Roger Rosen, President

5573 Let's Talk About When Kids Have Cancer

Melanie Apel Gordon, author

Rosen Publishing Group's PowerKids Press
29 E 21st Street
New York, NY 10010

212-777-3017
800-237-9932
Fax: 888-436-4643
customerservice@rosenpub.com
www.rosenpublishing.com

In a straightforward yet comforting way, this book explains what cancer is, what kinds of treatments surround the disease and how to cope if a child or the friend of a child has cancer. K-5.

24 pages Paperback
ISBN: 0-823951-95-6

Roger Rosen, President

5574 Surviving Childhood Cancer: A Guide for Families

New Harbinger Publications
5674 Shattuck Avenue
Oakland, CA 94609

510-652-0215
800-748-6273
Fax: 800-652-1613
customerservice@newharbinger.com
www.newharbinger.com

Cancer in a child is an overwhelming experience for a family. This book explains common medical procedures and offers readers practical advice about how to cope with emotions and stress during this time.

215 pages Paperback
ISBN: 1-572241-02-0

Newsletters

5575 DVI Quarterly

Division on Visual Impairments (CEC)
2900 Crystal Drive, Suite 1000
Arlington, VA 22202

888-232-7733
TTY: 866-915-5000
www.cec.sped.org/mb/

News on the Division of Visual Impairments, articles and announcements having to do with the education of students with visual impairmnets.

1000+ Quarterly

James P. Heiden, President
Sharon Raimondi, Treasurer
Joni L. Baldwin, Associate Professor

Pamphlets

5576 A Parent's Guide to Understanding Retinobl astoma

IRIS Medical Instruments/IRIDEX Corp
1275 York Avenue
New York, NY 10065

212-639-2000
800-525-2225
www.mskcc.org

Craig B. Thompson, President
John Gunn, Chief Operating Officer
Kerry Bessey, Senior Vice President

Description

5577 RETINOPATHY OF PREMATURITY
Synonym: ROP
Involves the following Biologic System(s):
Neonatal and Infant Disorders, Ophthalmologic Disorders

Retinopathy of prematurity (ROP) is a condition characterized by improper development of blood vessels within the retinas of both eyes. The retinas are the nerve-rich membranes at the back of the eyes that contain specialized, light-sensitive nerve cells (rods and cones). The rods and cones convert visual images into nerve impulses that are transmitted to the brain via the optic nerve (second cranial nerve). ROP primarily occurs in newborns of low birth weight who are born at less than 37 weeks after conception (premature newborns). Premature infants who weigh less than approximately three pounds, are delivered before 33 weeks of pregnancy, and develop abnormally high levels of oxygen in the blood (hyperoxia) as a result of oxygen therapy for breathing difficulties are considered to be particularly at risk for retinopathy of prematurity. Less commonly, other factors may play some role in contributing to the condition, such as heart disease, infection, abnormally low levels of circulating red blood cells (anemia), or other conditions. Generally, the lower an infant's birthweight and the greater the degree of prematurity, the higher the risk for the development of ROP.

During fetal development, the blood vessels that will supply the retinas grow from the center of the retinas, gradually extending to their outer edges shortly after birth. However, in premature newborns, the retinal blood vessels are incompletely developed, potentially causing abnormalities in subsequent retinal growth and function. In infants with ROP, associated findings may range from mild or temporary changes of the outer edges of the retina to severe abnormalities affecting the entire retina. During the active or acute stage of ROP, which typically occurs within the first month or so of life, associated findings may include abnormal narrowing of certain retinal blood vessels and subsequent widening or abnormal twisting of other retinal vessels. In addition, there is an apparent lack of blood vessel growth in certain areas of the retina, particularly of the outer rim. There may also be a gradual development of new blood vessels outside the normal area of retinal blood vessel growth, such as over the surface of the retina or into the jelly-like fluid behind the lens of the eye (vitreous humor). These vessels may tend to bleed (hemorrhage) into the retina, and some patients may develop retinal scarring as well as the formation of retinal folds or breaks or detachment of the outer portion of the retina. In severe cases, patients may undergo chronic disease progression, leading to complete retinal detachment and progressive retinal degeneration. The retina may eventually appear as an abnormal whitish membrane behind the lens of the eye (leukokoria). As the condition continues to progress, infants may develop increased fluid pressure within the eye (glaucoma), gradual degeneration and shrinkage of the eye (phthisis bulbi), and associated visual impairment leading to blindness.

In many infants with ROP, the condition spontaneously subsides and regresses. Such children may have an increased risk of progressive nearsightedness (myopia) or other eye abnormalities. However, in fewer than 10 percent, there may be ongoing disease progression, potentially causing total retinal detachment and severe visual impairment or blindness. In fact, it is retinal detachment that is the main cause of visual impairment and blindness in ROP.

The prevention of ROP depends upon proper prenatal care and other measures to help prevent premature births. In addition, infants who are born prematurely are monitored closely to ensure prompt detection of ROP and appropriate treatment as required. In severe cases of ROP, a technique that freezes affected areas of the retina (cryotherapy) may help to reduce potentially severe complications. Laser therapy can "burn away" the periphery of the retina, which has no normal blood vessels. Both laser treatment and cryotherapy, only used in infants with advanced ROP, destroy the peripheral areas of the retina, slowing or reversing the abnormal growth of blood vessels. Unfortunately, the treatments also destroy some side vision but saves central vision. In some patients with total retinal detachment, surgical techniques may be used to help reattach the retina.

Government Agencies

5578 NIH/ Eunice Kennedy Shriver National Institute of Child Health & Human Development
P.O. Box 3006
Rockville, MD 20847

800-370-2943
Fax: 866-760-5947
www.nichd.nih.gov

Conducts and supports research on topics related to the health of children, adults, families and populations. Some of these topics include: developmental disabilities, growth and development, infant death, reproductive health and birth defects.
Diana W. Bianchi, Director
Alison Cernich, PhD, Deputy Director

5579 NIH/National Eye Institute
31 Center Drive MSC 2510
Bethesda, MD 20892

301-496-5248
2020@nei.nih.gov
www.nei.nih.gov

Conducts and supports research that helps prevent and treat eye diseases and other disorders of vision. This research leads to sight-saving treatments, reduces visual impairment and blindness, and improves the quality of life for people of all ages. NEI-supported research has advanced our knowledge of how the eye functions in health and disease.
Michael F. Chiang, MD, Director
Santa Tumminia, Deputy Director

National Associations & Support Groups

5580 American Academy of Pediatrics
345 Park Blvd
Itasca, IL 60143

847-434-4000
800-433-9016
Fax: 847-434-8000
csc@aap.org
www.aap.org

The American Academy of Pediatrics and its member pediatricians are committed to the attainment of optimal physical, mental and social health and well-being for all infants, children, adolescents, and young adults.
Kyle E. Yasuda, MD, FAAP, President
Mark Del Monte, JD, CEO/Executive VP
Vera Tait, MD, FAAP, Chief Medical Officer

5581 Lighthouse Guild
250 West 64th Street
New York, NY 10023

800-284-4422
info@lighthouseguild.org
www.lighthouseguild.org

Lighthouse Guild is dedicated to providing exceptional services that inspire people who are visually impaired to attain their goals.
James M. Dubin, Chair
Calvin W. Roberts, President & CEO
Maura J. Sweeney, SVP, Programs & Services

Web Sites

5582 **Lighthouse Guild**
250 West 64th Street
New York, NY 10023

800-284-4422
info@lighthouseguild.org
www.lighthouseguild.org

Lighthouse Guild is dedicated to providing exceptional services that inspire people who are visually impaired to attain their goals.

Book Publishers

5583 **Children with Visual Impairments: A Parents' Guide**
Peytral Publications
PO Box 1162
Minnetonka, MN 55345

952-949-8707
877-739-8725
Fax: 952-906-9777
www.peytral.com

Covers visual impairments ranging from low vision to total blindness. Offers authoritative information and empathy, parental insight on diagnosis and treatment, orientation and mobility, literacy, legal issues and more. Valuable to parents, educators and support staff.

395 pages
M Cay Holbrook PhD, Editor

Description

5584 RHINITIS

Synonyms: Hay Fever, Allergic Rhinitis, Non-Allergic Rhinitis

Involves the following Biologic System(s):

Immunologic and Rheumatologic Disorders, Respiratory Disorders

Rhinitis is a condition in which plant pollens, chemicals, and certain other substances irritate the membranes that line the nose, throat, sinuses, and eyelids, causing them to become swollen and inflamed, with resulting nasal stuffiness and runniness (rhinorrhea), sneezing, burning and tearing of the eyes, and soreness of the throat. It falls into two categories — allergic and non-allergic rhinitis.

Allergic rhinitis is either seasonal (tending to recur in a particular season of every year), or perennial (likely to occur or persist regardless of season). It occurs when pollens, dust, animal dander, house dust mites, and other protein substances, known collectively as allergens, prompt the body cells named plasma cells to secrete an antibody named immunoglobulin E (IgE). The IgE secreted by these cells reacts with specialized structures known as IgE receptors, which exist both on the surfaces of the cells known as mast cells, in the mucous membranes of the nose, throat, and some other parts of the body, and also on the cells known as basophils, which circulate through the body in the blood and lymphatic fluid. The reaction between IgE and its receptors on mast cells and basophils causes these cells to release histamine, a substance that triggers inflammation and swelling in surrounding tissues. The reaction of IgE with its receptors also prompts mast cells and basophils to secrete other substances, known as inflammatory mediators, that promote inflammation in various ways. Allergic rhinitis often accompanies other disorders that affect the respiratory system, eyes, or ears, such as sinusitis, asthma, and inflammation of the ear (otitis), and its effects can interfere with sleep, alertness, and schoolwork. It typically begins from childhood through early adulthood, and in most cases develops by the age of 20 years.

Non-allergic rhinitis is typically caused by smoke, fumes, cold or heat, viral and other respiratory infections, and other sources of inflammation of the nose, throat, and eyes. Moreover, although the symptoms of non-allergic rhinitis often resemble those of allergic rhinitis, it is not triggered by IgE, as is allergic rhinitis, but rather by direct irritation of mucous membranes and other tissues, by effects of cold, heat, or other factors on the nervous system, and by other mechanisms. In the condition known as non-allergic rhinitis with eosinophilia syndrome (NARES), rhinitis and other symptoms of allergy recur without being traceable to any specific allergen, and nasal secretions contain the cells known as eosinophils, which are important members of the body's immune defense system.

Although it can be difficult to distinguish allergic from non-allergic rhinitis, the distinction can be important in terms of preventing and treating these conditions. The diagnosis of allergic rhinitis is based on symptoms that recur upon exposure to seasonal pollens and other specific substances, and by tests in which exposure of a small area of skin to various allergens results in reddening or swelling. A laboratory test known as the radioallergosorbent test (RAST), in which a small sample of blood is withdrawn and IgE in the blood serum is exposed to various allergens, can also show which specific allergens are responsible for a patient's rhinitis.

Because of its more generalized nature and lack of seasonality, non-allergic rhinitis can be difficult to diagnose. Its diagnosis is usually based on its particular symptoms and on linking its occurrence to a particular chemical or other causative agent.

A first step in controlling both allergic and non-allergic rhinitis is to prevent or avoid the allergens or other substances that cause these disorders. The medicines known as antihistamines, which block the inflammatory effects of histamine in the nose, eyes, and other parts of the body, are useful in preventing or easing the symptoms of allergic rhinitis, but are much less effective for non-allergic rhinitis. Although conventional antihistamines can cause drowsiness and other undesirable effects, such effects are often less severe with newer or second-generation antihistamines, which are in some cases also useful for non-allergic rhinitis. Nasal sprays containing corticosteroid drugs are sometimes prescribed for easing nasal swelling, stuffiness, rhinorrhea, and itching in rhinitis. Nasal decongestants, which reduces swelling in the mucous membranes of the nose, may also be effective.

National Associations & Support Groups

5585 American Academy of Allergy, Asthma & Immunology
555 East Wells Street, Suite 1100
Milwaukee, WI 53202
414-272-6071
Fax: 414-272-6070
www.aaaai.org

The American Academy of Allergy, Asthma & Immunology is the largest professional medical organization in the United States devoted to the allergy/immunology specialty.

David Lang, MD, President
Mary-Beth Fasano, MD, President-Elect
Giselle S. Mosnaim, MD, Secretary-Treasurer

5586 American Academy of Pediatrics
345 Park Blvd
Itasca, IL 60143
847-434-4000
800-433-9016
Fax: 847-434-8000
csc@aap.org
www.aap.org

The American Academy of Pediatrics and its member pediatricians are committed to the attainment of optimal physical, mental and social health and well-being for all infants, children, adolescents, and young adults.

Kyle E. Yasuda, MD, FAAP, President
Mark Del Monte, JD, CEO/Executive VP
Vera Tait, MD, FAAP, Chief Medical Officer

5587 American College of Allergy, Asthma & Immunology
85 West Algonquin Road, Suite 550
Arlington Heights, IL 60005
847-427-1200
Fax: 847-427-9656
mail@acaai.org
www.acaai.org

The American College of Allergy, Asthma & Immunology is a professional association of 6,000 allergists/immunologists and allied health professionals. Established in 1942, the College is dedicated to improving the quality of patient care in allergy and immunology through research, advocacy and professional and public education.

Rick Slawny, Executive Director
Nancy Ryan, Associate Executive Director
Hollis Heavenrich-Jones, Public Relations Manager

5588 Asthma and Allergy Foundation of America
8201 Corporate Drive, Suite 1000
Landover, MD 20785
800-727-8462
info@aafa.org
www.aafa.org

AAFA provides practical information, community based services and support to people through a network of regional chapters, educational support groups and other local partners throughout the United States.

Richard Murray, Chair
Mary Ellen Conley, RN, Chair, Governance
Colette Martin, Chair, Communications & Marketing

Rhinitis / State Agencies & Support Groups

5589 **World Allergy Organization**
555 East Wells Street, Ste 1100
Milwaukee, WI 53202
414-276-1791
Fax: 414-276-3349
info@worldallergy.org
www.worldallergy.org

A world-wide alliance of national and regional allergy and clinical immunology societies and organizations dedicated to raising awareness and advancing excellence in clinical education, research and training in the field of allergy and pediatric allergy.

State Agencies & Support Groups

Colorado

5590 **Parents of Asthmatic/Allergic Children, Inc.**
1024 S. Lemay Avenue
Fort Collins, CO 80524
970-495-8153
Fax: 970-495-7608
cmc@pvhs.org
www.coloradoallergy.com

Support group for parents and children ages 6 and older, focusing on asthma, and issues such as allergic and non-allergic rhinitis.

Cindy Coopersmith, Coordinator

Illinois

5591 **Mothers of Children with Allergies (MOCHA)**
Highland Park Hospital
777 Park Avenue West
Highland Park, IL 60035
847-735-8244
supportgroups@aafa.org
www.mochallergies.org

Support group serving Chicago & the Northern suburbs for parents and children having allergies associated with the environment, food, and Asthma.

Anne Thompson, Coordinator
Denise Bunning, Coordinator

New Jersey

5592 **Allergy and Asthma Support Group of Central New Jersey**
www.allergyfriendsnj.org

www.allergyfriendsnj.org

The support group is for adults and parents of children with food allergies, environmental allergies, asthma, or a combination. The Allergy & Asthma Support Group of Central New Jersey supports families and friends afflicted by life threatening food allergies and other conditions such as environmental and non-environmental allergies.

Allison Inserro, Co-Facilitator

Libraries & Resource Centers

5593 **The University of Iowa Libraries**
100 Main Library (LIB)
Iowa City, IA 52242
319-335-5299
www.guides.lib.uiowa.edu/allergyimmunology

The libraries at the University of Iowa contain a collection of clinical resources on allergy and immunology.

5594 **University of South Florida**
12901 Bruce B. Downs Boulevard
Tampa, FL 33612
727-553-3533
Fax: 727-553-1295
sborst@health.usf.edu
www.health.usf.edu

Available libraries include ACH Medical Library, Bayfront Medical Center Library, and several libraries at USF such as: Hinks and Elaine Shimberg Health Sciences Library, Tampa Campus Library and many others. All libraries have access to MEDLINE.

Stacy Borst, Training Program Coordinator

Research Centers

5595 **Allergy and Asthma Medical Group and Research Center**
9610 Granite Ridge Drive, Suite B
San Diego, CA 92123
858-268-2368
Fax: 858-268-5147
www.allergyandasthma.com

The Allergy and Asthma Medical Group and Research Center provide quality care given by a highly-trained team of physicians, nurse practitioners, nurses, medical assistants and office personnel with an understanding of the impact of these disorders on patients and their families.

5596 **Children's National Health System**
111 Michigan Avenue NW
Washington, DC 20010
202-476-5000
TTY: 800-855-1155
www.childrensnational.org

Children's National Medical Center's recognized staff of pediatric healthcare professionals deliver sophisticated care to thousands of families throughout the region and around the world.

George Zalzal, MD, Division Chief, Otolaryngology

5597 **Duke University School of Medicine Pediatric and Allergy Immunology**
T901/Children's Health Center
Durham, NC 27710
919-681-4080
Fax: 919-681-2714
http://pediatrics.duke.edu

Thd Division of Pediatric Allergy and Immunology and its faculty and staff ar committed to excellence in patient care, research, education and advocacy. Areas of expertise include all allergic diseases, anaphylaxis, primary immunodeficiency, asthma, rhinitis and others.

George Zalzal, MD, Division Chief, Otolaryngology

5598 **Johns Hopkins Division of Allergy and Clinical Immunology**
5501 Hopkins Bayview Circle
Baltimore, MD 21224
410-550-2300
jhuallergy@jhmi.edu
www.hopkinsmedicine.org/allergy

The faculty and staff at the Johns Hopkins Division of Allergy and Clinical Immunology are working to meet the demand for advances in the treatment of allergies, asthma, and related disorders.

5599 **The University of Chicago Comer Children's Hospital**
5271 S. Maryland Avenue
Chicago, IL 60637
773-702-1000
888-824-0200
www.uchicagokidshospital.org/allergy

Doctors at Chicago Comer Children's Hospital are experts on a wide variety of childhood allergies, and specialize in diagnosing and treating the full range of allergic and immune disorders of infancy and childhood.

Web Sites

5600 **American Academy of Pediatrics**
345 Park Blvd
Itasca, IL 60143
847-434-4000
800-433-9016
Fax: 847-434-8000
csc@aap.org
www.aap.org

The American Academy of Pediatrics and its member pediatricians are committed to the attainment of optimal physical, mental and social health and well-being for all infants, children, adolescents, and young adults.

Kyle E. Yasuda, MD, FAAP, President
Mark Del Monte, JD, CEO/Executive VP
Vera Tait, MD, FAAP, Chief Medical Officer

5601 http://children.webmd.com
WebMD
www.webmd.com/children

www.webmd.com/children

Includes comprehensive health information on pediatric allergic rhinitis, plus a variety of other pediatric health conditions. This site includes news, videos, FAQs, the opportunity to chat with other patients and parents, a glossary, and parenting topics. Users can search by condition, age, symptoms, and more.

Kristy Hammam, Senior Vice President
Denise Dym, Senior Director
Annie Jobin, Senior Director

5602 www.Nasal-Allergies.com
www.nasal-allergies.com/nasx

www.nasal-allergies.com/nasx

This web site offers education about pediatric and adult nasal allergies, inlcuding treatment and resources.

5603 www.aap.org
American Academy of Pediatrics
141 Northwest Point Boulevard
Elk Grove Village, IL 60007
847-434-4000
800-433-9016
Fax: 847-434-8000
webeditor@aap.org
www.aap.org

This site includes a variety of resources to help deal with allergic rhinitis, including a parenting corner, publications, advocacy, and recommendations on treatment.

Sandra Hassink, MD, FAAP, President
Benard P. Dreyer, MD, FAAP, President-Elect
Errol R. Alden, MD, FAAP, Executive Director/ CEO

5604 www.acaai.org
85 West Algonquin Road, Suite 550
Arlington Heights, IL 60005
847-427-1200
Fax: 847-427-1294
mail@acaai.org
acaai.org

The American College of Allergy, Asthma & Immunology is a professional association of 6,000 allergists/immunologists and allied health professionals. Established in 1942, the College is dedicated to improving the quality of patient care in allergy and immunology through research, advocacy and professional and public education.

Rick Slawny, Executive Director
Nancy Ryan, Associate Executive Director
Hollis Heavenrich-Jones, Public Relations Manager

5605 www.pediatriccareonline.org
American Academy of Pediatrics
pediatriccare.solutions.aap.org/Pediatric-Care

pediatriccare.solutions.aap.org/Pediatric-Care

This online publication includes definitions, clinical features, complications, laboratory findings, differential diagnosis, treatment, prognosis, tools, and references for a number of pediatric conditions, including allergic rhinitis. Users can also search for other relevant American Academy of Pediatrics publications.

5606 www.wrongdiagnosis.com
www.localhealth.com

www.localhealth.com

WrongDiagnosis.com provides a free health information service to help people understand their health better. The site offers factual health information that is otherwise difficult to find. Topics include allergic rhinitis and the signs and symptoms associated with the allergy.

Richard G Grower, MD, President

5607 yourtotalhealth.ivillage.com

NOP-ONE-

Contains information on numerous medical topics including pediatric allergies and asthma.

Richard G Grower, MD, President

Book Publishers

5608 Fast Facts: Rhinitis
Glenis K Scadding & Wytske J Fokkens, author

Health Press
30 Amberwood Parkway
Ashland, OH 44805
800-247-6553
Fax: 419-281-6883
info@atlasbooks.com
www.fastfacts.com

This short and very practical book has been written for the individuals who are not seen by specialists for treatment of rhinitis, so treatment can be optimized and referral decisions are made easier.

5609 Immunology and Allergy Clinics of North America
1600 John F Kennedy Boulevard, Suite 1800
Philadelphia, PA 19103
314-447-8871
800-654-2452
ElsevierClinics@elsevier.com
www.immunology.theclinics.com

Comprehensive, state-of-the-art reviews by experts in the field of allergy and pediatric allergy provide current, practical information on the diagnosis and treatment of conditions affecting the respiratory system. Each issue focuses on a single topic.

Journals

5610 AAP News
American Academy of Pediatrics
141 Northwest Point Boulevard
Elk Grove Village, IL 60007
847-434-4000
800-433-9016
Fax: 847-434-8000
webeditor@aap.org
www.aap.org

A resource of product recall alerts, pediatric medication warnings, and key advancements in pediatric medicine, including allergies and related conditions.

Sandra Hassink, MD, FAAP, President
Benard P. Dreyer, MD, FAAP, President-Elect
Errol R. Alden, MD, FAAP, Executive Director/ CEO

5611 Ear, Nose and Throat Journal
www.entjournal.com

www.entjournal.com

Monthly journal with articles on pediatric and adult conditions that affect the ear, nose and throat, including allergic rhinitis.

Robert T. Sataloff, MD, DMA, FACS, Editor-in-Chief
Linda Zinn, Managing Director
Mark C. Horn, Sales Manager

5612 Journal of Allergy and Clinical Immunology
www.elsevier.com

www.elsevier.com

Includes articles written by experts in the fields of allergy, pediatric allergy and immunology that discuss current research, causes, diagnosis, treatments, and clinical studies relating to pediatric rhinitis and a variety of other allergic conditions. Also includes listings of new health products and medical equipment.

Youngsuk Chi, Chairman
Ron Mobed, Chief Executive Officer
Stuart Whayman, Chief Financial Officer

Rhinitis / Newsletters

5613 Pediatrics
American Academy of Pediatrics
141 Northwest Point Boulevard
Elk Grove Village, IL 60007
847-434-4000
800-433-9016
Fax: 847-434-8000
webeditor@aap.org
www.aap.org

The flagship journal of the AAP, whose authoritative content has been recognized by medical experts for 60 years. Includes information on a variety of pediaric conditions, including allergic rhinitis.

Sandra Hassink, MD, FAAP, President
Benard P. Dreyer, MD, FAAP, President-Elect
Errol R. Alden, MD, FAAP, Executive Director/ CEO

5614 Pediatrics in Review
American Academy of Pediatrics
141 Northwest Point Boulevard
Elk Grove Village, IL 60007
847-434-4000
800-433-9016
Fax: 847-434-8000
webeditor@aap.org
www.aap.org

Features real-life cases, best practices, and review articles mapped to ABP content specifications for maintenance of certification-pediatrics. Conditions covered include pediatric allergy rhinitis and related conditions.

Sandra Hassink, MD, FAAP, President
Benard P. Dreyer, MD, FAAP, President-Elect
Errol R. Alden, MD, FAAP, Executive Director/ CEO

5615 World Allergy Organization Journal
236 Gray's Inn Road
London, WC1X
203-192-2009
Fax: 203-192-2010
waoj@worldallergy.org
www.waojournal.org

The official journal of the World Allergy Organization whose goals include to: be a premier journal of original scientific and clinically relevant information for practicing allergists/immunologists; to publish state-of-the-art review articles and editorials on translational and clincal medicine in the field of allergy, pediatric allergy and immunology; and to present a forum for scientific interaction between allergists, pediatric allergists and immunologists worldwide.

Alessandro Fiocchi, Editor-in-Chief
Johannes Ring, Executive Editor
Erika Jensen-Jarolim, Deputy Director

Newsletters

5616 AAAAI Impact
American Academy of Allergy Asthma & Immunology
555 E. Wells Street, Suite 1100
Milwaukee, WI 53202
414-272-6071
Fax: 414-272-6070
media@aaaai.org
www.aaaai.org

A quarterly member publication produced by the AAAAI.

5617 AAP Grand Rounds
American Academy of Pediatrics
141 Northwest Point Boulevard
Elk Grove Village, IL 60007
847-434-4000
800-433-9016
Fax: 847-434-8000
webeditor@aap.org
www.aap.org

Features evidence-based summaries of clinical content from 100 journals. A key feature, 'Weighing the Evidence,' provides medical literature interpretation assistance.

Sandra Hassink, MD, FAAP, President
Benard P. Dreyer, MD, FAAP, President-Elect
Errol R. Alden, MD, FAAP, Executive Director/ CEO

5618 ACAAI eNews
85 West Algonquin Road, Suite 550
Arlington Heights, IL 60005
847-427-1200
Fax: 847-427-1294
enews@acaai.org
acaai.org

The ACAAI eNews is a monthly aggregated news service provided by the American College of Allergy, Asthma & Immunology.

Rick Slawny, Executive Director

Description

5619 SARCOIDOSIS

Synonyms: Sarcoid of Boeck, Schaumann's disease

Involves the following Biologic System(s):

Connective Tissue Disorders

Sarcoidosis is a multisystem disorder that is characterized by the abnormal development of inflammatory growths or nodules (i.e., epithelioid granulomas) in various organs in the body. The cause of this inflammatory disorder is unknown; however, it is believed that granuloma formation associated with sarcoidosis may result from infection or an exaggerated immune response to specific agents (antigens). In addition, researchers believe that some people may be genetically predisposed to sarcoidosis and develop the disease only if triggered by environmental or other factors. Although this disorder most commonly occurs during young adulthood, it may occur in children and in the elderly. Symptoms and physical findings associated with sarcoidosis are dependent upon the organ(s) involved and, in children, the age of onset. Most affected children, however, share the common symptoms of fatigue, weight loss, cough, pain in the bones and joints, and abnormally low levels of circulating red blood cells (anemia).

The nodules or granulomas associated with sarcoidosis may develop in almost any organ of the body, but most commonly affect the lungs, upper respiratory tract, lymph nodes, skin, eyes, liver, bones, joints, bone marrow, skeletal muscles, heart, liver, spleen, or the central and peripheral nervous systems. In older children and adults, the lungs are most often affected (90 percent of patients), while younger children experience less lung involvement. Characteristic findings in older children may include swelling of the lymph nodes near the blood vessels that enter and exit the lungs (hilar lymphadenopathy) as well as the lymph nodes near the windpipe (paratracheal lymphadenopathy) and those under the skin (peripheral lymphadenopathy). In addition, nodule formation may cause inflammations in the eye (e.g., uveitis and iritis) and other eye lesions, skin lesions, and liver changes. Younger children may develop a reddish, combination-type rash consisting of waxy pimples and flat, discolored lesions (maculopapular erythematous rash) as well as inflammation of the joints (arthritis).

Diagnosis of sarcoidosis is usually a challenge as it is often difficult to distinguish from other disorders with similar symptoms and findings. Therefore, differential diagnosis often involves a physical examination, medical and environmental history, and the comprehensive evaluation of laboratory tests and chest x-rays, biopsy of tissue samples, and specialized testing. Laboratory findings may show excessive levels of calcium in the blood (hypercalcemia) and in the urine (hypercalciuria), abnormally high levels of protein in the blood (hyperproteinemia), excessive levels of certain granular white cells in the blood (eosinophilia), and other blood irregularities. For example, the cells of the nodules secrete a substance called angiotensin-converting enzyme, which, in some patients, is elevated to detectable levels in the blood. Testing for this enzyme may also be employed to measure disease activity. In addition, pulmonary function tests may be used to measure progress of the disease in those children with lung involvement, and repeat chest x-rays may also be indicated to monitor progress.

In some children, sarcoidosis may resolve spontaneously within a period of months or years; however, some children may have a more chronic form of the disease that may result in progressive lung involvement, eye disease that may cause blindness, and other prolonged symptoms and findings. Treatment for sarcoidosis may include the use of corticosteroid drops or ointments to alleviate eye inflammations and oral corticosteroids to alleviate acute symptoms such as resistant inflammatory lesions of the eyes, joint pain, fever, shortness of breath, and other symptoms. Approximately 90 percent of cases are responsive to corticosteroids and can be controlled with modest maintenance doses. If no symptoms are present, corticosteroid treatment is usually not advised. Other treatment is symptomatic and supportive.

National Associations & Support Groups

5620 American Academy of Pediatrics
345 Park Blvd
Itasca, IL 60143

847-434-4000
800-433-9016
Fax: 847-434-8000
csc@aap.org
www.aap.org

The American Academy of Pediatrics and its member pediatricians are committed to the attainment of optimal physical, mental and social health and well-being for all infants, children, adolescents, and young adults.

Kyle E. Yasuda, MD, FAAP, President
Mark Del Monte, JD, CEO/Executive VP
Vera Tait, MD, FAAP, Chief Medical Officer

5621 American Autoimmune Related Diseases Association
19176 Hall Road, Suite 130
Clinton, MI 48038

586-776-3900
aarda@aarda.org
www.aarda.org

The American Autoimmune Related Diseases Association is dedicated to the eradication of autoimmune diseases and the alleviation of suffering and the socioeconomic impact of autoimmunity through fostering and facilitating collaboration in the areas of education, public awareness, research, and patient services in an effective, ethical and efficient manner.

Lilly Stairs, Interim President/CEO
Laura Simpson, COO

5622 Child Neurology Foundation
601 W Short Street
Lexington, KY 40508

888-417-3435
info@childneurologyfoundation.org
childneurologyfoundation.org

The Child Neurology Foundation connects partners from all areas of the child neurology community so those navigating the journey of disease diagnosis, management, and care have the ongoing support from those dedicated to treatments and cures.

Amy Brin, Executive Director
Katie Hentges, Director, Programs
Brea McCormley, Director, Development

5623 FSR Patient Registry
320 W Ohio Street, Suite 300
Chicago, IL 60654

312-341-0500
www.stopsarcoidosis.org/fsr-patient-registry

The Foundation for Sarcoidosis Research (FSR) has created an IRB-approved Patient Registry of self-reported information by individuals with sarcoidosis or their caretakers.

5624 Foundation for Sarcoidosis Research
320 W Ohio Street, Suite 300
Chicago, IL 60654

312-341-0500
www.stopsarcoidosis.org

The Foundation for Sarcoidosis Research (FSR) is the leading international organization dedicated to finding a cure for sarcoidosis and improving care for sarcoidosis patients through research, education, and support. Since its establishment in 2000, FSR has fostered over $6 million in sarcoidosis-specific research efforts.

Mary McGowan, Chief Executive Officer
Mindy Buchanan, Director of Patient Programs
Diane Driscoll, Global Head of Clinical Engagement

Sarcoidosis / State Agencies & Support Groups

5625 Sarcoidosis Research Institute
www.sarcoidosisri.org

info@sarcoidosisRI.org
www.sarcoidosisri.org

Provides information that will educate patients, family members, caregivers, and anyone who may be interested in or is impacted directly or indirectly by sarcoidosis.

State Agencies & Support Groups

California

5626 REACH - Sarcoidosis Support
10843 Kenney St
Norwalk, CA 90650   714-739-4023
Ruth Jacobs

Colorado

5627 Denver Sarcoidosis Awareness Support Group
4351 Ireland St
Denver, CO 80249   303-375-9376
contacts@denversarcoidosisawareness.org
www.denversarcoidosisawareness.org

Provides support through sharing of experiences, discussing feeling and emotions, and sharing coping strategies.

Shirley R Holley, President

Georgia

5628 Sarcoidosis Support Group
St Joseph's/Chandler Health System
5353 Reynolds St
Savannah, GA 31405   912-819-8032
Cindy Balkstra RN

Indiana

5629 Central Indiana Sarcoidosis Support Group
Kindred Hospital
1700 W 10th St
Indianapolis, IN 46222   317-809-7011
cissg@usa.com
www.indysarcoid.org

The Central Indiana Sarcoidosis Support Group was started in 1998 to offer hope and support to those diagnosed with Sarcoidosis.

Gloria Hooks, President
Kelisa Walker, Vice President
Mary Wineglass, Secretary

Maryland

5630 Sarcoidosis Awareness Network
10313 Farrar Avenue
Cheltenham, MD 20623   301-372-2885
www.sarcoidosisnetwork.net

The Sarcoidosis Awareness Network is a nonprofit organization established to increase and expand the public awareness of sarcoidosis; enhance the quality of life of sarcoidosis survivors; develop and implement a sarcoidosis registry; and to disseminate current literature on the disease so the general public is better informed about sarcoidosis and its impact on the lives of those afflicted with the disease.

Linda D. Lanier, Founder

Michigan

5631 Sarcoidosis Awareness Foundation
14540 Whitcomb St
Detroit, MI 48227   SarcoidAwareness@aol.com
Janie L Chuney

North Carolina

5632 University of North Carolina Sarcoidosis Support Group
Div. of Pulmonary Medicine
130 Mason Farm Rd, CB# 7020
Chapel Hill, NC 27599   919-966-5296
juliem@med.unc.edu
www.unceye.org

Ricky Bass, Manager

South Carolina

5633 Sarcoidosis Support
MUSC Medical Center
171 Ashley Ave
Charleston, SC 29425   803-792-0280
Kathy Lanza

Tennessee

5634 Sarcoidosis Patient Forum
Sarcoidosis Research Institute-SRI
3475 Central Avenue
Memphis, TN 38111   901-219-6883
Fax: 901-774-7294

Paula Polite, President

Libraries & Resource Centers

5635 Sarcoidosis Center
Baptist Hospital East
6005 Park Avenue, Suite 501
Memphis, TN 38119   901-761-5877
Fax: 901-761-2280
www.sarcoidcenter.com

A nonprofit organization providing an exchange of information regarding sarcoidosis for patients and professionals.

Norman T Soskel MD

Research Centers

5636 National Jewish Health
1400 Jackson Street
Denver, CO 80206   303-388-4461
800-222-5864
www.nationaljewish.org/disease-info

Information on ongoing sarcoidosis research and available treatment programs at the center.

Michael Salem, MD, President & CEO
Richard Baer, Board Chair
Pamela L. Zeitlin, MD, PhD, Chair, Pediatrics Department

5637 Sarcoidosis Research Institute
www.sarcoidosisri.org

info@sarcoidosisRI.org
www.sarcoidosisri.org

Provides information that will educate patients, family members, caregivers, and anyone who may be interested in or is impacted directly or indirectly by sarcoidosis.

Audio Video

5638 Dialogue with Doris
PC Publications
PO Box 1593
Piscataway, NJ 8855
732-699-0733
Fax: 732-699-0882
www.webmd.com

Kristy Hammam, Senior Vice President
Denise Dym, Senior Director
Annic Jobin, Senior Director

5639 Help with a Hidden Disease Update
PC Publications
PO Box 1593
Piscataway, NJ 8855
732-699-0733
800-223-6429
Fax: 732-699-0882
www.webmd.com

Kristy Hammam, Senior Vice President
Denise Dym, Senior Director
Annic Jobin, Senior Director

5640 International World Conference on Sarcoidosis-Patient Symposium
PC Publications
PO Box 1593
Piscataway, NJ 8855
732-699-0733
Fax: 732-699-0882
www.webmd.com

Cassette.

Kristy Hammam, Senior Vice President
Denise Dym, Senior Director
Annic Jobin, Senior Director

5641 Of Their Own-Person To Person Show
PC Publications
PO Box 1593
Piscataway, NJ 8855
732-699-0733
Fax: 732-699-0882
www.webmd.com

Kristy Hammam, Senior Vice President
Denise Dym, Senior Director
Annic Jobin, Senior Director

5642 Sarcoidosis Conference 2
PC Publications
PO Box 1593
Piscataway, NJ 8855
732-699-0733
Fax: 732-699-0882
www.webmd.com

Kristy Hammam, Senior Vice President
Denise Dym, Senior Director
Annic Jobin, Senior Director

5643 Sarcoidosis Conference 3
PC Publications
PO Box 1593
Piscataway, NJ 8855
732-699-0733
Fax: 732-699-0882
www.webmd.com

Kristy Hammam, Senior Vice President
Denise Dym, Senior Director
Annic Jobin, Senior Director

5644 Sarcoidosis and Lyme Disease
PC Publications
PO Box 1593
Piscataway, NJ 8855
732-699-0733
Fax: 732-699-0882
www.webmd.com

Kristy Hammam, Senior Vice President
Denise Dym, Senior Director
Annic Jobin, Senior Director

5645 Sarcoidosis-What's That?
PC Publications
PO Box 1593
Piscataway, NJ 8855
732-699-0733
Fax: 732-699-0882
www.webmd.com

Kristy Hammam, Senior Vice President
Denise Dym, Senior Director
Annic Jobin, Senior Director

Web Sites

5646 American Autoimmune Related Diseases Association
www.aarda.org
586-776-3900
aarda@aarda.org
www.aarda.org

The American Autoimmune Related Diseases Association is dedicated to the eradication of autoimmune diseases and the alleviation of suffering and the socioeconomic impact of autoimmunity through fostering and facilitating collaboration in the areas of education, public awareness, research, and patient services in an effective, ethical and efficient manner.

5647 Foundation for Sarcoidosis Research
320 W Ohio Street, Suite 300
Chicago, IL 60654
312-341-0500
www.stopsarcoidosis.org

The Foundation for Sarcoidosis Research (FSR) is the leading international organization dedicated to finding a cure for sarcoidosis and improving care for sarcoidosis patients through research, education, and support. Since its establishment in 2000, FSR has fostered over $6 million in sarcoidosis-specific research efforts.

Mary McGowan, Chief Executive Officer
Mindy Buchanan, Director of Patient Programs
Diane Driscoll, Global Head of Clinical Engagement

5648 Health Answers Education Sudler-WPP Health Practice
700 Dresher Road
Horsham, PA 19044
215-442-9010
www.healthanswers.com

HealthAnswers offers a breadth of services in medical education, sales force training, patient support solutions, professional promotion and consumer solutions.

Mike Hudnall, CEO

5649 NIH/National Heart, Lung and Blood Institute
31 Center Drive, Bldg 31
Bethesda, MD 20824
877-645-2448
www.nhlbi.nih.gov

Primary responsibility of this organization is the scientific investigation of heart, blood vessel, lung and blood disorders. Oversees research, demonstration, prevention, education, control and training activities in these fields and emphasizes the prevention and control of heart diseases.

Gary H. Gibbons, MD, Director
Kate O'Sullivan, Executive Officer

5650 Online Mendelian Inheritance in Man
McKusick-Nathans Institue of Genetic Medicine-JHU
Baltimore, MD 21205
www.omim.org

This database is a catalog of human genes and genetic disorders.

Ada Hamosh, MD, Scientific Director

5651 Sarcoid Life
www.sarcoidlife.org
www.sarcoidlife.org

5652 Sarcoidosis
www.epler.com/wsarc.html
www.epler.com/wsarc.html

Sarcoidosis / Book Publishers

General information and answers to questions about Sarcoidosis.

5653 Sarcoidosis Center
www.sarcoidcenter.com

www.sarcoidcenter.com

A nonprofit corporation designed to provide information for patients and physicians regarding sarcoidosis. The site includes a list of sarcoidosis experts by country.

5654 Sarcoidosis Research Institute
www.sarcoidosisri.org

info@sarcoidosisRI.org
www.sarcoidosisri.org

Provides information that will educate patients, family members, caregivers, and anyone who may be interested in or is impacted directly or indirectly by sarcoidosis.

Book Publishers

5655 Sarcoidosis Resource Guide and Directory
PC Publications
PO Box 1593
Piscataway, NJ 08855
732-699-0733
Fax: 732-699-0882

1993 304 pages Paperback
ISBN: 0-963122-25-8

Newsletters

5656 Online Sarcoidosis Newsletter
National Sarcoidosis Resource Center
PO Box 1593
Piscataway, NJ 8855
732-699-0733
Fax: 732-699-0882

Offers information on the center's activities and events, medical and legislative updates for the patients and their families.
Quarterly

5657 Sarcoidosis Networking
Sarcoid Networking Association
6424 151st Avenue E
Sumner, WA 98390
253-891-6886
sarcoidosis_network@prodigy.net
www.sarcoidnetwork.org

Helps those affected by sarcoidosis network with one another and the medical community.
Quarterly
Dolores O'Leary, Executive Director

Pamphlets

5658 A Sarcoidosis Questionnaire: Demographics and Symptomatology-Patients Respond
PC Publications
PO Box 1593
Piscataway, NJ 8855
732-699-0733
800-223-6429
Fax: 732-699-0882

5659 Anemia of Sarcoidosis
PC Publications
PO Box 1593
Piscataway, NJ 8855
732-699-0733
Fax: 732-699-0882

5660 Bronchoalveolar Lymphocytes in Sarcoidosis
PC Publications
PO Box 1593
Piscataway, NJ 8855
732-699-0733
Fax: 732-699-0882

5661 Case Report-MR Imaging of Myocardial Sarcoidosis
PC Publications
PO Box 1593
Piscataway, NJ 8855
732-699-0733
Fax: 732-699-0882

5662 Case Report-Osseous Sarcoidosis and Chronic Polyarthritis
PC Publications
PO Box 1593
Piscataway, NJ 8855
732-699-0733
Fax: 732-699-0882

5663 Coping with Sarcoidosis
National Sarcoidosis Resource Center
PO Box 1593
Piscataway, NJ 8855
732-699-0733
Fax: 732-699-0882

A pamphlet offering information on how to manage and live with sarcoidosis.

5664 Drugs That Have Been Used for the Treatment of Sarcoidosis
PC Publications
PO Box 1593
Piscataway, NJ 8855
732-699-0733
Fax: 732-699-0882

5665 Effects of Sarcoid and Steroids on Angiotensin-Converting Enzyme
PC Publications
PO Box 1593
Piscataway, NJ 8855
732-699-0733
Fax: 732-699-0882

5666 Masqueraders of Sarcoidosis
PC Publications
PO Box 1593
Piscataway, NJ 8855
732-699-0733
Fax: 732-699-0882

5667 Multidisciplinary Clinico-Pathologic Conference
PC Publications
PO Box 1593
Piscataway, NJ 8855
732-699-0733
Fax: 732-699-0882

5668 Neurosarcoidosis
PC Publications
PO Box 1593
Piscataway, NJ 8855
732-699-0733
Fax: 732-699-0882

5669 Neurosarcoidosis or Multiple Sclerosis?
National Sarcoidosis Resource Center
PO Box 1593
Piscataway, NJ 8855
732-699-0733
Fax: 732-699-0882

5670 Paranoid Psychosis Due to Neurosarcoidosis
PC Publications
PO Box 1593
Piscataway, NJ 8855
732-699-0733
800-223-6429
Fax: 732-699-0882

5671 Patient Information Package
National Sarcoidosis Resource Center
PO Box 1593
Piscataway, NJ 8855
732-699-0733
Fax: 732-699-0882

Sarcoidosis / Pamphlets

Contains various brochures and pamphlets offering information about sarcoidosis.

5672 Presidential Proclamation-National Sarcoidosis Awareness Day
PC Publications
PO Box 1593
Piscataway, NJ 8855
732-699-0733
Fax: 732-699-0882

5673 Psychological Factors in Sarcoidosis
PC Publications
PO Box 1593
Piscataway, NJ 8855
732-699-0733
Fax: 732-699-0882

5674 Pulmonary Sarcoidosis: Evaluation with High Resolution
PC Publications
PO Box 1593
Piscataway, NJ 8855
732-699-0733
Fax: 732-699-0882

5675 Pulmonary Sarcoidosis: What We Are Learning
PC Publications
PO Box 1593
Piscataway, NJ 8855
732-699-0733
Fax: 732-699-0882

5676 Right & Left Ventricular Function At Rest In Patients with Sarcoidosis
PC Publications
PO Box 1593
Piscataway, NJ 8855
732-699-0733
Fax: 732-699-0882

5677 Sarcoidosis
PC Publications
PO Box 1593
Piscataway, NJ 8855
732-699-0733
Fax: 732-699-0882

Offers information on the illness, causes, symptoms and treatments.

5678 Sarcoidosis Questionnaire: Demographics and Symptomatology-The Patients Respond
PC Publications
PO Box 1593
Piscataway, NJ 8855
732-699-0733
Fax: 732-699-0882

5679 Sarcoidosis and Other Granulatomous
PC Publications
PO Box 1593
Piscataway, NJ 8855
732-699-0733
800-223-6429
Fax: 732-699-0882

5680 Sarcoidosis and You-A Listing of Possible Symptoms
PC Publications
PO Box 1593
Piscataway, NJ 8855
732-699-0733
Fax: 732-699-0882

5681 Sarcoidosis-International Review
PC Publications
PO Box 1593
Piscataway, NJ 8855
732-699-0733
Fax: 732-699-0882

5682 Sarcoidosis-Pleural Involvement Mimicking a Coin Lesson
PC Publications
PO Box 1593
Piscataway, NJ 8855
732-699-0733
Fax: 732-699-0882

5683 Sarcoidosis: A Multisystem Disease
PC Publications
PO Box 1593
Piscataway, NJ 8855
732-699-0733
Fax: 732-699-0882

Explains the effects of the illness on the lungs and joints.

5684 Sarcoidosis: Usual and Unusual Manifestations
PC Publications
PO Box 1593
Piscataway, NJ 8855
732-699-0733
Fax: 732-699-0882

5685 Seasonal Clustering of Sarcoidosis
National Sarcoidosis Resource Center
PO Box 1593
Piscataway, NJ 8855
732-699-0733
Fax: 732-699-0882

5686 Successful Treatment of Myocardial Sarcoidosis with Steriods
PC Publications
PO Box 1593
Piscataway, NJ 8855
732-699-0733
Fax: 732-699-0882

5687 Support Group Listing
PC Publications
PO Box 1593
Piscataway, NJ 8855
732-699-0733
Fax: 732-699-0882

5688 World Association Sarcoidosis Other Granulatomous
PC Publications
PO Box 1593
Piscataway, NJ 8855
732-699-0733
Fax: 732-699-0882

Scleroderma / Description

Description

5689 SCLERODERMA

Covers these related disorders: Linear scleroderma, Morphea, Systemic sclerosis

Involves the following Biologic System(s):

Connective Tissue Disorders

Scleroderma is a connective tissue disease characterized by the build up of collagen (connective tissue) resulting in thickening and hardening of the skin and underlying tissues or, in some forms of scleroderma, other organs of the body. In patients with morphea, a form of the disease that primarily affects the skin and its underlying (subcutaneous) tissues, lesions appear as limited or localized patches. In linear scleroderma, lesions appear in a band-like pattern. In other patients, particularly in adults, scleroderma may occur as a generalized, systemic disease affecting the skin and subcutaneous tissues, blood vessels, and internal organs, such as the heart, lungs, kidneys, and certain parts of the digestive tract. Although the underlying cause of scleroderma is not known, some researchers speculate that it may be an autoimmune disease in which there is an abnormal immune response against the body's own tissues. During childhood, scleroderma is more common in girls than boys.

Children with scleroderma are primarily affected by morphea or linear scleroderma. Associated symptoms and findings usually become apparent at age two or older. Patients initially develop patchy skin lesions that are dry, red or violet, and shiny in appearance. These lesions may cause associated pain or unusual sensations, such as prickling feelings in affected areas. In some children, the lesions may have a linear distribution and develop primarily on one side of the body. The lesions gradually become hard (indurated) and develop waxy, pale centers and elevated borders. As the disease continues to progress, the lesions become larger and merge, potentially involving a large area, such as an entire arm or leg. Affected areas may eventually develop deep scar tissue and firmly bind to underlying tissues, potentially resulting in pain and permanent bending of affected joints in fixed postures (joint contractures). In children with morphea or linear scleroderma, active disease may spontaneously subside over months or years or may slowly progress over many years.

Rarely, children may develop generalized, systemic scleroderma (systemic sclerosis). In such cases, associated symptoms and findings usually become apparent at age four or older. Children with systemic sclerosis often initially experience Raynaud's phenomenon, a condition characterized by sudden contraction of blood vessels supplying the fingers or toes, causing an interruption of blood flow and a subsequent excess of blood in affected areas following the restoration of blood flow (reactive hyperemia). Such episodes are usually triggered by exposure to cold temperatures and are characterized by numbness, tingling, and bluish or whitish discoloration of the fingers or toes (cyanosis) due to lack of blood flow and subsequent reddening and pain.

Children with systemic sclerosis also often develop skin lesions on the hands and feet and, in some cases, the torso and facial area. These lesions may include groups of permanently widened (dilated) blood vessels (telangiectasias). As the disease progresses, skin lesions typically become hard, develop unusually light or dark pigmentation, and gradually bind to underlying tissues and structures. Children may also experience joint swelling, discomfort, and inflammation (arthritis) as well as degenerative changes of various organs, including those of the digestive tract, particularly the esophagus; the heart; the lungs and the kidneys. Associated symptoms may be extremely variable, depending upon the rate of disease progression and the specific bodily tissues and organs affected. In some patients, such abnormalities may include difficulty swallowing (dysphagia); chronic inflammation of the lungs due to unintended inhalation of foreign matter into the airways (aspiration pneumonia); high blood pressure (hypertension); or respiratory, heart, or kidney failure. Active disease may be gradually progressive or include periods during which symptoms temporarily subside (remit).

The treatment of children with scleroderma is symptomatic and supportive. Such measures may include the use of steroids, such as cortisone or prednisone, to decrease inflammation in muscles, joints or rarely in the skin itself. Non-steroidal anti-inflammatory drugs (NSAIDs) such as ibuprofen and naproxen are sometimes used for children who have arthritis to decrease joint inflammation early physical therapy to help prevent or minimize the development of joint contractures; systemic therapy with methotrexate or other medications (e.g., cytotoxic drugs), if appropriate; careful control of high blood pressure in those with systemic disease; and other measures as required. In addition, patients with Raynaud's phenomenon should avoid cold temperatures whenever possible and dress warmly before such exposure. Scleroderma is a chronic and slowly progressive disease, lasting for months or years. The outlook depends on the type of scleroderma, where and how much skin is involved and whether or not internal organs are affected.

Government Agencies

5690 NIH/National Institute of Arthritis and Musculoskeletal and Skin Diseases
1 AMS Circle
Bethesda, MD 20892

301-495-4484
877-226-4267
Fax: 301-718-6366
TDD: 301-565-2966
niamsinfo@mail.nih.gov
www.niams.nih.gov

The mission of the NIAMS, a part of the NIH, is to support research into the causes, treatment and prevention of arthritis and musculoskeletal and skin diseases, the training of basic and clinical scientists to carry out this research, and the dissemination of information on research progress in these diseases.

Lindsey A. Criswell, MD, Director
Rick Phillips, Executive Officer

National Associations & Support Groups

5691 American Academy of Pediatrics
345 Park Blvd
Itasca, IL 60143

847-434-4000
800-433-9016
Fax: 847-434-8000
csc@aap.org
www.aap.org

The American Academy of Pediatrics and its member pediatricians are committed to the attainment of optimal physical, mental and social health and well-being for all infants, children, adolescents, and young adults.

Kyle E. Yasuda, MD, FAAP, President
Mark Del Monte, JD, CEO/Executive VP
Vera Tait, MD, FAAP, Chief Medical Officer

5692 American Autoimmune Related Diseases Association
19176 Hall Road, Suite 130
Clinton, MI 48038

586-776-3900
aarda@aarda.org
www.aarda.org

The American Autoimmune Related Diseases Association is dedicated to the eradication of autoimmune diseases and the alleviation of suffering and the socioeconomic impact of autoimmunity through fostering and facilitating collaboration in the areas of education, public awareness, research, and patient services in an effective, ethical and efficient manner.

Lilly Stairs, Interim President/CEO
Laura Simpson, COO

5693 Scleroderma Foundation
300 Rosewood Dr, Suite 105
Danvers, MA 01923
978-463-5843
800-722-4673
Fax: 978-777-1313
info@scleroderma.org
www.scleroderma.org

The National Scleroderma Foundation's mission is to advance medical research, promote disease awareness, and provide support and education to people with scleroderma, their families and support networks.

Mary J. Wheatley, Chief Executive Officer
Michael B. Hyde, Chief Operating & Finance Officer
Jess Haas Gr,us, Sr. Director, Development

State Agencies & Support Groups

New Jersey

5694 Scleroderma Foundation New Jersey Chapter
PO Box 285
Haddon Heights, NJ 08035
856-547-5010
866-675-5545
Fax: 856-547-5010
sfdv1@verizon.net

Liz Van Dzura, Executive Director

Rhode Island

5695 Rhode Island Scleroderma Support Group
Roger Williams Medical Ctr
825 Chalkstone Ave
Providence, RI 02908
401-781-5013
scleroderma@hotmail.com
www.ri.sclerodermasupportgroup.net

Carole Cowell, Contact
Frank L. Fitzpatrick, Webmaster

Research Centers

Alabama

5696 University of Alabama - Birmingham Arthrit is Clinical Intervention Program
1717 6th Avenue South SRC 076
Birmingham, AL 35249
205-934-7727
866-876-2247
Fax: 205-975-5554
rand1951@uab.edu
www.uab.edu/medicine/acip/

Since 1990, the Arthritis Clinical Intervention Program (ACIP) has conducted over 300 rheumatology trials (Phase I-IV). All our doctors are Board Certified Rheumatologists with many years of research experience. Dr. Jeffrey Curtis is our Medical Director.

Randall Parks, MBA, RN, Program Director
David J. Mackey, MPH, Regulatory Manager
Martha R. Sanderson, MSN, NP, Nurse Practitioner

Arizona

5697 Mayo Clinic Scleroderma Service
13400 E Shea Blvd
Scottsdale, AZ 85259
480-301-8000
Fax: 480-301-8673
www.mayoclinic.org/rheumatology-sct/

Heidi Garcia, Research Info

California

5698 Scleroderma Research Foundation
220 Montgomery St, Suite 1411
San Francisco, CA 94104
415-834-9444
800-441-2873
Fax: 415-834-9177
info@sclerodermaresearch.org
www.srfcure.org

The Scleroderma Research Foundation's mission is to find a cure for scleroderma, a life-threatening and degenerative illness, by funding and facilitating the most promising, highest quality research and placing the disease and its need for a cure in the public eye.

Luke Evnin, PhD, Chairman
Charles Spaulding, Vice President, Communications
Jill Wayne, Director, Cure Advocate Program

District of Columbia

5699 Georgetown University
Dept of Rheumatology
PHC Bldg, 3800 Reservoir Rd, 6th Fl
Washington, DC 20007
202-784-6671
Fax: 202-784-4332
memory@georgetown.edu
www.memory.georgetown.edu/

For adult and pediatric patients with localized and systemic scleroderma.

Raoul L Wientzen, President
R. Scott Turner, MD, PhD, Program Director
Carolyn Ward, MSPH, Program Coordinator

Pennsylvania

5700 National Registry for Childhood Onset Scleroderma (NRCOS)
University of Pittsburgh School of Medicine
M240 Scaife Hall, 3550 Terrace Street
Pittsburge, PA 15261
412-383-8674
800-603-8960
jablonj@msx.dept-med.pitt.edu
www.sctc-online.org/studies/nrcos.htm

This registry provides a unique opportunity for researchers to study a variety of aspects of scleroderma. The registry will include systemic sclerosis and various forms of localized scleroderma such as morphea, linear scleroderma, and eosinophilic fasciitis.

Jennifer Jablon, Research Coordinator
Thomas A Medsger Jr, MD, Principal Investigator

Web Sites

5701 American Autoimmune Related Diseases Association
www.aarda.org
586-776-3900
aarda@aarda.org
www.aarda.org

The American Autoimmune Related Diseases Association is dedicated to the eradication of autoimmune diseases and the alleviation of suffering and the socioeconomic impact of autoimmunity through fostering and facilitating collaboration in the areas of education, public awareness, research, and patient services in an effective, ethical and efficient manner.

Scleroderma / Book Publishers

5702 Health Answers Education Sudler-WPP Health Practice
700 Dresher Road
Horsham, PA 19044
215-442-9010
www.healthanswers.com

HealthAnswers offers a breadth of services in medical education, sales force training, patient support solutions, professional promotion and consumer solutions.

Mike Hudnall, CEO

5703 Online Mendelian Inheritance in Man
McKusick-Nathans Institue of Genetic Medicine-JHU
Baltimore, MD 21205
www.omim.org

This database is a catalog of human genes and genetic disorders.

Ada Hamosh, MD, Scientific Director

5704 Scleroderma A to Z
7455 France Ave So #266
Edina, MN 55435
952-831-3091
800-564-7099
isn@sclero.org
www.sclero.org

Presented by the International Scleroderma Network, it has over 1000 pages of scleroderma and scleroderma related information, resources, and links in over 20 languages.

Shelley Ensz, Founder and President
Sid Strong, Vice President
Gene Ensz, Treasurer

5705 Scleroderma Foundation
300 Rosewood Drive, Suite 105
Danvers, MA 01923
978-463-5843
800-722-4673
Fax: 978-777-1313
info@scleroderma.org
www.scleroderma.org

The National Scleroderma Foundation's mission is to advance medical research, promote disease awareness, and provide support and education to people with scleroderma, their families and support networks.

Mary J. Wheatley, Chief Executive Officer
Michael B. Hyde, Chief Operating & Finance Officer
Jess Haas Gr,us, Sr. Director, Development

5706 Scleroderma Message Board
disc.server.com/Indices/7571.html

disc.server.com/Indices/7571.html

An online message board about scleroderma and related conditions.

5707 Scleroderma Support
health.groups.yahoo.com/group/sclerodermasupport2/

health.groups.yahoo.com/group/sclerodermasupport2/

A place where people who live with scleroderma can talk online.

Book Publishers

5708 It's Not Just Growing Pains
Thomas J.A. Lehman, PhD, author

Oxford University Press
198 Madison Ave
New York, NY 10016
212-726-6000
800-445-9714
Fax: 919-677-1303
custserv.us@oup.com
www.oup.com/usa

2004 Hardback
ISBN: 0-195157-28-1

5709 Let's Talk About Going to the Hospital
Rosen Publishing Group's PowerKids Press
29 E 21st Street
New York, NY 10010
212-777-3017
800-237-9932
Fax: 888-436-4643
rosenpub@tribeca.ios.com
www.rosenpublishing.com

If a child has to check into the hospital, chances are he or she is already upset about being ill. Knowing how a hospital functions and what the procedures are, such as when family members can visit, will help in what is already a stressful situation. Grades K-5.

24 pages
ISBN: 0-823950-36-0

Roger Rosen, President

5710 Medifocus Guidebook on Scleroderma
Medifocus.com, Inc
11529 Daffodil Lane, Suite 200
Silver Spring, MD 20902
301-649-9300
800-965-3002
Fax: 301-649-7809
info@medifocus.com
www.medifocus.com

This guidebook has four sections: an overview for patients; a guide to medical literature; research centers; and a resource and organization guide. Updates are available online for a year with purchase of the book. Also available in electronic format.

105 pages

Ovadia Abulafia, Board Member
William I. Bensinger, M.D., Board Member
Glenn D. Braunstein, M.D., Board Member

5711 Scleroderma Book (The)
Maureen Mayes, MD, author

Oxford University Press
198 Madison Ave
New York, NY 10016
212-726-6000
800-445-9714
Fax: 919-677-1303
custserv.us@oup.com
www.oup.com/usa

2005 Hardback
ISBN: 0-195169-40-9

Journals

5712 Scleroderma Care and Research
Scleroderma Clinical Trials Consortium
715 Albany St, E-5
Boston, MA 2118
617-638-4486
www.sclero.org/medical/journals/scar/a-to-z.html

Published by a group of international scleroderma researchers, it covers topics of interest to rheumatologists and others involved in scleroderma care, worldwide.

Pamphlets

5713 Handout on Health: Scleroderma
NIAMS, National Institutes of Health
31 Center Dr, Bldg 31, Rm 4C02
Bethesda, MD 20892
301-496-8190
Fax: 301-480-2814
www.niams.nih.gov/hi

Information including current research efforts for scleroderma.

Revised 7/2006

Robert H. Carter, MD, Acting Director
Robert H. Carter, Deputy Director
Gahan Breithaupt, Ass Dir for Management & Operations

Camps

5714 Camp Discovery
American Academy of Dermatology
9500 W. Bryn Mawr Avenue, Ste 500
Rosemont, IL 60018
847-240-1737
Fax: 847-240-1859
jmueller@aad.org
www.campdiscovery.org

A camp for young people with chronic skin conditions. There is no fee and transportation is provided. Five locations: Camp Victory in Millville, PA, Camp Knutson in Crosslake, MN, Camp For All in Burton, TX, Channel 3 Kids Camp in Andover, CT, and Camp Seymour in Gig harbor, WA.

J Mueller, Camp Contact
Irvin Bomberger, Interim Executive Director

5715 Camp Wonder
Children's Skin Disease Foundation
712 Bancroft Rd, #511
Walnut Creek, CA 94598
925-947-3825
Fax: 866-236-6474
www.csdf.org

Established by the CSDF for young people who suffer from skin diseases. Medically staffed camps are free to children, ages 7-17 with skin diseases that are serious or life threatening.

Christine Tenconi, Vice-President
Christine Clakley, Executive Director

Scoliosis / Description

Description

5716 SCOLIOSIS

Synonym: Rachioscoliosis

Covers these related disorders: Compensatory scoliosis, Congenital scoliosis, Idiopathic kyphosis (Scheuermann's disease), Idiopathic scoliosis, Kyphosis, Neuromuscular scoliosis, Syndrome-associated scoliosis

Involves the following Biologic System(s):

Orthopedic and Muscle Disorders

The term scoliosis refers to a condition characterized by a sideward (lateral) curvature of the spine. Idiopathic scoliosis is the most common form of this disorder and occurs for no known reason in otherwise healthy individuals who range in age from infancy to adolescence. Adolescent scoliosis is the most common form and accounts for 80 percent of idiopathic scoliosis. Approximately 20 percent of people with scoliosis report at least one other affected family member. Therefore, in these cases, scoliosis is thought to have a genetic component. Idiopathic scoliosis that develops during infancy often corrects itself, but it may become progressive in older children. Treatment is dependent upon age and the degree of curvature progression. Mild curvatures may require little or no treatment, while more severe involvement may require surgery or the use of braces, etc. (orthotics). Although men and women are affected in about equal numbers, women are more at risk for more significant curvature progression. Girls between onset of puberty growth spurt and cessation of spinal growth are at the greatest risk for idiopathic scoliosis. Physical examination reveals asymmetry in the height of the shoulder and hip, with forward bending.

Congenital scoliosis, apparent at birth or soon thereafter, results from the improper or incomplete development of the vertebrae during the first trimester of pregnancy. This condition may appear singularly or in association with abnormalities of other systems of the body including the heart (i.e., congenital heart disease) and genitourinary tract (e.g., absence of one kidney, duplication of the tubes that carry urine, horseshoe kidney, and other malformations). Congenital scoliosis is often accompanied by other spinal cord defects (spinal dysraphism) that may range from mild to severe. In addition, children born with certain genetic disorders such as Klippel-Feil syndrome may experience associated scoliosis. The progression of the curvature is dependent upon the specific underlying vertebral malformation, its particular growth potential, and its location. About one quarter of affected children experience no progression of the curvature and, therefore, require no treatment. Approximately half of those remaining may require early treatment, such as spinal fusion of the affected area, to stop progression of the curvature.

Neuromuscular scoliosis is associated with certain childhood diseases (e.g., cerebral palsy, Duchenne muscular dystrophy, polio, and other disorders). This type of scoliosis tends to be progressive, with the degree of deformity dependent upon many factors. Those affected children who are unable to walk (nonambulatory) often develop additional skeletal irregularities involving the pelvis and spine. In severe cases, respiratory difficulties may develop. Early evaluation and intervention through surgery and other means help to alter the progression of the spinal deformity and its associated complications.

Kyphosis is characterized by an exaggerated backward curvature of the spine. Children with poor posture resulting in mild kyphosis who have no associated spinal irregularities may be treated by maintaining good posture. Congenital kyphosis, however, results from various malformations in the spinal column and may range from mild to severe deformity. Scoliosis also is present in one-third of patients with kyphosis. When several vertebrae are involved, there is a round back appearance; when only one vertebra is involved, there is an angular curve. As affected children grow, progression of the spinal abnormality may continue until growth is complete, possibly resulting in partial paralysis. Idiopathic kyphosis or Scheuermann's disease is common to both adolescent boys and girls; cause remains unknown. Examination and x-ray screening may determine whether kyphosis is postural or a result of a spinal malformation. Symptoms of Scheuermann's disease may include mild but chronic back pain and a round-shouldered appearance.

Children with mild kyphosis may be advised to refrain from strenuous activities, while those with more severe symptoms may benefit from sleeping on a very firm mattress, or using a brace or cast. Surgery is rarely indicated.

Certain syndromes (e.g., Marfan syndrome, neurofibromatosis) place affected children at risk for spinal irregularities such as scoliosis and kyphosis. Treatment for these children includes regular orthopedic examination and intervention to prevent progression of the irregularity.

Scoliosis sometimes results from unequal leg length resulting from an irregular tilt (obliquity) of the pelvis. Treatment for this compensatory scoliosis may include the use of special orthopedic shoes.

Government Agencies

5717 NIH/National Institute of Arthritis and Musculoskeletal and Skin Diseases
1 AMS Circle
Bethesda, MD 20892

301-495-4484
877-226-4267
Fax: 301-718-6366
TDD: 301-565-2966
niamsinfo@mail.nih.gov
www.niams.nih.gov

The mission of the NIAMS, a part of the NIH, is to support research into the causes, treatment and prevention of arthritis and musculosketal and skin diseases, the training of basic and clinical scientists to carry out this research, and the dissemination of information on research progress in these diseases.

Lindsey A. Criswell, MD, Director
Rick Phillips, Executive Officer

National Associations & Support Groups

5718 American Academy of Pediatrics
345 Park Blvd
Itasca, IL 60143

847-434-4000
800-433-9016
Fax: 847-434-8000
csc@aap.org
www.aap.org

The American Academy of Pediatrics and its member pediatricians are committed to the attainment of optimal physical, mental and social health and well-being for all infants, children, adolescents, and young adults.

Kyle E. Yasuda, MD, FAAP, President
Mark Del Monte, JD, CEO/Executive VP
Vera Tait, MD, FAAP, Chief Medical Officer

5719 **Center for Parent Information and Resources (CPIR)**
c/o SPAN, 35 Halsey Street, 4th Floor
Newark, NJ 07102
973-642-8100
malizo@spanadvocacy.org
www.parentcenterhub.org

Family-friendly information and research-based materials on key topics for Parent Centers. Private workspaces for Parent Centers to exchange resources, discuss high-priority topics, and solve mutual challenges. Coordination of parent training efforts throughout the network.

Myriam Alizo, Project Assistant

5720 **National Scoliosis Foundation**
5 Cabot Place
Stoughton, MA 02072
781-341-6333
800-673-6922
nsf@scoliosis.org
www.scoliosis.org

Promotes school screening, offers public awareness materials to promote public education, maintains a resource center for professional information, conducts scoliosis conferences, and offers support groups to people affected by the disease.

5721 **Scoliosis Research Society**
555 E Wells Street, Suite 1100
Milwaukee, WI 53202
414-289-9107
Fax: 414-276-3349
info@srs.org
www.srs.org

An international society that is committed to research and education for health care professionals in the field of spinal deformities. It is recognized as one of the world's premier spine societies. Current membership includes over 1000 of the world's leading spine surgeons as well as researchers, physician assistants and orthotists.

Libraries & Resource Centers

5722 **Johns Hopkins Department of Orthopaedics Surgery**
601 N Caroline Street
Baltimore, MD 21287
410-955-5000
Fax: 410-955-1719
www.hopkinsinteractive.com

Scoliosis is a three-dimensional curvature of the spine, best appreciated on an anteroposterior radiograph and physical examination. Many different causes have been identified. The most common type is idiopathic scoliosis.

Claudia L Thomas

Research Centers

5723 **Scoliosis Research Society**
555 E Wells Street, Suite 1100
Milwaukee, WI 53202
414-289-9107
Fax: 414-276-3349
info@srs.org
www.srs.org

An international society that is committed to research and education for health care professionals in the field of spinal deformities. It is recognized as one of the world's premier spine societies. Current membership includes over 1000 of the world's leading spine surgeons as well as researchers, physician assistants and orthotists.

5724 **Shriners Hospital for Children**
Headquarters
2900 Rocky Point Drive
Tampa, FL 33607
813-281-0300
800-237-5055
Fax: 813-281-8113
patientreferrals@shrinenet.org
www.shrinershospitalsforchildren.org/

Shrine's official philanthropy is Shriners Hospital for Children, a network of 22 hospitals that provide expert, no-cost orthopaedic and burn care to children under 18.

Alan W. Madsen, Chairman of the Board
John McCabe, Executive Vice President
Kenneth Guidera, M.D., Chief Medical Officer

Audio Video

5725 **Taking the Mystery Out of Spinal Deformities**
Children's Hospital of LA, Div. of Orthopaedics
4650 Sunset Boulevard
Los Angeles, CA 90027
323-660-2450
888-631-2452
www.childrenshospitalla.org

Answers questions most often asked by screeners, patients and parents.

Videotape

Richard D. Cordova, FACHE, President/ CEO
Rodney B. Hanners, SVP/ COO
Barry L. Mangels, MS, CPHRM, Chief Compliance & Privacy Officer

Web Sites

5726 **American Academy of Orthopaedic Surgeons**
9400 West Higgins Road
Rosemont, IL 60018
847-823-7186
Fax: 847-823-8125
custserv@aaos.org
www.aaos.org

Provides an informational fact sheet on scoliosis in children and adolescents.

Frederick M Azar, MD, President
Karen L. Hackett, FACHE, CAE, Chief Executive Officer
William Bruce, Chief Technology Officer

5727 **Health Answers Education Sudler-WPP Health Practice**
700 Dresher Road
Horsham, PA 19044
215-442-9010
www.healthanswers.com

HealthAnswers offers a breadth of services in medical education, sales force training, patient support solutions, professional promotion and consumer solutions.

Mike Hudnall, CEO

5728 **John Hopkins Department of Orthopaedics Surgery**
601 N. Caroline Street, JHOC #5215
Baltimore, MD 21287
443-997-2663
hopkinsortho@jhmi.edu
www.hopkinsmedicine.org/orthopedicsurgery/

The orthopaedics faculty works together as a team to provide optimum patient care, seeking out a role in patient care as both educators and treating physicians working together with you and your community health care providers to offer you the best possible medical and surgical care available.

5729 **Natalie's Brace**
www.nataliesbrace.com/scoliosis/

www.nataliesbrace.com/scoliosis/

Personal website offering personal details and photos on scoliosis braces, general information and support.

5730 **North Ameerican Spine Society**
7075 Veterans Blvd.
Burr Ridge, IL 60527
630-230-3600
www.spine.org

Provides information on adolescent idiopathic scoliosis, including a description of, common problems associated with the curvature, and possible treatments.

Heidi Prather, DO, President
Christopher Bono, MD, First Vice President
Eric Muehlbauer, Executive Director

5731 **Online Mendelian Inheritance in Man**
McKusick-Nathans Institue of Genetic Medicine-JHU
Baltimore, MD 21205
www.omim.org

Scoliosis / Book Publishers

This database is a catalog of human genes and genetic disorders.

Ada Hamosh, MD, Scientific Director

5732 Scoliosis Help
www.scoliosishelp.org

www.scoliosishelp.org

5733 Scoliosis Research Society
555 E Wells Street, Suite 1100
Milwaukee, WI 53202
414-289-9107
Fax: 414-276-3349
info@srs.org
www.srs.org

An international society that is committed to research and education for health care professionals in the field of spinal deformities. It is recognized as one of the world's premier spine societies. Current membership includes over 1000 of the world's leading spine surgeons as well as researchers, physician assistants and orthotists.

5734 Wheeless' Textbook of Orthopaedics
www.wheelessonline.com

www.wheelessonline.com

Derives from a variety of sources, including journals, articles, national meetings lectures and other textbooks.

Clifford R. Wheeless III, MD, Editor-in-Chief
James A. Nunley, II, MD, Managing Editor
James R. Urbaniak, MD, Managing Editor

Book Publishers

5735 Deenie
Simon & Schuster/Atheneum Books
100 Front Street
Riverside, NJ 08075
856-461-6500
800-488-4308
Fax: 800-943-9831
www.simonandschuster.com

Deenie, a beautiful thirteen-year-old girl, had a mother who was pushing her to become a model. The agency representatives told Deenie she had the looks but walked differently. Deenie's main wish was to become a cheerleader. Her close friend, Janet, made the cheerleading squad but Deenie didn't make the finalist list. After this her gym teacher noticed her posture and called her family. After seeing therapists, the diagnosis of adolescent idiopathic scoliosis was made.

159 pages Hardcover
ISBN: 0-689866-10-0

Carolyn Reidy, President/CEO
Liz Perl, Senior Vice President, Marketing
Dennis Eulau, Executive Vice President, Operation

5736 Handbook of Scoliosis
Scoliosis Research Society
555 East Wells Street, Suite 1100
Milwaukee, WI 53202
414-289-9107
Fax: 414-276-3349
info@srs.org
www.srs.org

Kamal N. Ibrahim, MD, President
John P. Dormans, MD, Vice President
Hubert Labelle, MD, Secretary

5737 Scoliosis: What Young People and Parents Need to Know
American Physical Therapy Association
1111 N Fairfax Street
Alexandria, VA 22314
703-684-2782
800-999-2782
Fax: 703-706-8556
TDD: 703-683-6748
www.apta.org

A physical therapist's perspective about what scoliosis is and what parents and young people should look for to detect scoliosis. Also available in Spanish.

12 pages Packet of 25
Paul Rocker, President
Sharon I. Dunn, Vice President
Laurita M. Hack, Secretary

5738 Twenty Years At Hull House
Jane Addams, author

New American Library/Penguin Group
375 Hudson Street
New York, NY 10014
212-366-2372
Fax: 212-366-2933
online@us.penguingroup.com
us.penguingroup.com

336 pages
ISBN: 0-451527-39-4
John Makinson, CHAIRMAN
Coram Williams, CFO
David Shanks, CEO

Pamphlets

5739 Questions and Answers About Scoliosis
Federal Citizen Information Center
Pueblo, CO 81009
719-295-2675
888-878-3256
pueblo@gpo.gov
publications.usa.gov/USAPubs.php

5740 Scoliosis and Kyphosis
Scoliosis Research Society
555 East Wells Street, Suite 1100
Milwaukee, WI 53202
414-289-9107
Fax: 414-276-3349
info@srs.org
www.srs.org

Information and advice from parents.

John P. Dormans, MD, President
Tressa Goulding, CAE, CMP, Executive Director
Ashtin Neuschaefer, Administrative Manager

Camps

5741 Hemlocks Easter Seals Recreation
85 Jones Street
Hebron, CT 6248
860-228-9496
800-832-4409
Fax: 860-228-2091
www.eastersealscamphemlocks.org

Accepts campers, ages 6 and under, whose major disability is orthopedic. First preference is given to Connecticut residents. A computer camp is also available.

Carl Larson

Description

5742 SEIZURES

Synonyms: Convulsions, Epilepsy

Covers these related disorders: Absence (petit mal) seizures, Complex partial seizures, Generalized (grand mal) tonic-clonic seizures, Simple partial seizures, Epilepsy

Involves the following Biologic System(s):

Neurologic Disorders

Seizures are a neurologic condition characterized by sudden episodes of uncontrolled electrical activity in the brain. These electrical disturbances may cause abnormal motor activities, lost or impaired consciousness, impaired control of certain involuntary functions (autonomic dysfunction), or sensory or behavioral abnormalities. Seizures are a common neurologic condition of childhood, affecting approximately six in 1,000 children. Approximately 70 percent of children who experience one seizure never experience another, whereas about 30 percent develop recurring seizures, which is referred to as epilepsy. Seizures may result from many different causes, including fever, head injury, infection or inflammation of the brain, insufficient oxygen supply to the brain, or certain metabolic imbalances. Seizures may also be caused by brain tumors, particular degenerative metabolic or neurological diseases, abnormal reactions to certain medications, or drug intoxication. There are also a number of syndromes and genetic disorders in which seizures are a primary feature. In many children, the exact underlying cause of recurrent seizures cannot be determined and the disorder is termed idiopathic epilepsy.

The specific form that a seizure takes and its associated symptoms may depend upon a number of factors, including the region of the brain in which the electrical disturbance arises and how widely it spreads from its point of origin. Epileptic seizures may be broadly classified into two groups: partial and generalized seizures. Partial seizures often result due to damage or impairment of a limited area of the brain, whereas generalized seizures may affect a wide area of the brain. In addition, some partial seizures may begin in a particular brain region but spread to affect most of the brain, ultimately becoming a generalized seizure. Because different seizure types may cause similar symptoms, specialized techniques that record brain wave activity (electroencephalography or EEG) and other neurologic imaging tests (such as MRI or CT scans) may play an important role in classifying certain seizure disorders.

Partial seizures, which may account for up to 40 percent of childhood seizures, may be subdivided into simple partial seizures, during which consciousness is retained, and complex partial seizures, during which consciousness is impaired. Simple partial seizures are characterized by abnormal, rhythmic muscle contractions and relaxations (clonic activity) and increased muscle tone and rigidity (tonic activity), particularly affecting muscles of the neck, face, arms, and legs. Simple partial seizures, which usually last about 10 to 20 seconds, are frequently associated with abnormal eye movements and head turning. In many children, simple partial seizures may be preceded by an aura consisting of headache, chest discomfort, and a feeling of anxiety, fear, or dread.

Complex partial seizures are characterized by a sudden pause in activity and a blank stare and may be preceded by an aura that consists of a vague feeling of fear or unpleasantness, headache, and chest discomfort. Most patients also perform certain involuntary actions following loss of consciousness. In infants, such actions may include lip smacking, swallowing, or chewing, whereas older children may conduct incoordinated, semipurposeful actions, such as rubbing objects or pulling at clothing. Such seizures may last approximately one to two minutes.

Generalized seizures may be subdivided into nonconvulsive (petit mal, absence) seizures and convulsive (grand mal or tonic-clonic) seizures. Absence seizures, which rarely occur before the age of five, usually last from a few seconds up to half a minute. During an episode, children experience a momentary loss of consciousness during which they cease speaking or performing other motor activities. They typically have a blank facial expression, their eyelids may flicker, and the head may fall forward. Patients typically have no awareness of the episode and resume the activity they were performing before the seizure.

Generalized tonic-clonic seizures may be preceded by an aura and occasionally begin with a shrill cry as patients lose consciousness. During an episode, the eyes roll back, muscles of the entire body stiffen, and all muscle groups begin to rhythmically contract and relax. If temporary cessation of breathing (apnea) occurs, patients may quickly develop an abnormal, bluish discoloration of the skin and mucous membranes (cyanosis). Bladder and bowel control may be temporarily lost. After an episode, patients are typically semiconscious and disoriented and may remain in a deep sleep for up to two hours (postictal state). During such a seizure episode, patients should be placed on one side, tight clothing around the neck should be loosened, and the jaw should be gently extended to enhance breathing. However, the mouth should not be forcibly opened nor should an object be placed between the teeth.

Generalized seizures also include a form of epilepsy known as infantile spasms, which typically begin between the ages of four and eight months and continue to approximately 18 months. Infantile spasms are characterized by sudden, brief, symmetric contractions of the arms and legs, neck, and torso. Spasms may occur for several minutes with brief intervals between each spasm. Episodes tend to occur when children are drowsy or immediately upon awakening. Depending upon the underlying cause, the condition may evolve into different forms of epilepsy later in life and may be associated with an increased risk of intellectual disabilities.

Seizures that occur in association with a rapidly rising fever, known as febrile seizures, are the most common seizure disorder of childhood. Febrile seizures most commonly occur between nine months to five years of age and may affect up to four percent of all children. This type of seizure rarely develops into epilepsy. In many cases, there is a history of such seizures among siblings and parents, indicating that genetic factors may play some causative role. Febrile seizures often occur in association with certain upper respiratory infections and acute inflammation of the middle ear (otitis media). However, because convulsions may result from serious infections of the brain (e.g., meningitis), a thorough medical evaluation must be conducted to determine the cause of the fever. Febrile seizures are typically characterized by muscle rigidity followed by abnormal, rhythmic contractions and relaxations of muscle groups (generalized tonic-clonic seizures). The seizure may last from seconds up to about 10 minutes and is often followed by a brief period of drowsiness.

Generalized or partial seizures that continue for more than 30 minutes without a return to consciousness are known as status epilepticus. Such seizures may occur due to underlying metabolic abnormalities, neurologic disorders, congenital brain malformations, or inflammation of the brain. They may also represent prolonged febrile seizures, develop due to sudden withdrawal of

Seizures / National Associations & Support Groups

antiseizure (anticonvulsant) medication, or result from unknown causes. Status epilepticus may result in life-threatening complications and is considered a medical emergency, requiring hospitalization. Treatment may include supplemental oxygen, intravenous fluids, physical and neurologic evaluations, intravenous medications including appropriate antiseizure drugs, and other measures as required. Children affected by the condition before one year of age are more likely to have intellectual disabilities and other long-term effects, secondary to an underlying CNS disorder.

The treatment of seizures depends on the underlying cause, the type of seizure present, and other factors. If a treatable condition or disorder is identified, such as a fever, abnormal blood sugar levels, or certain tumors, measures are taken as required to treat the underlying cause. For example, in the case of febrile seizures, thorough evaluations are conducted to determine the fever's cause and measures are then taken as necessary to control the fever. If an underlying cause cannot be identified or adequately treated or controlled, treatment typically includes the administration of antiseizure (anticonvulsant) medications to help prevent, reduce, or control seizures. The specific anticonvulsant medication prescribed may depend on several factors, including the classification of the seizure, patient history, and possible side effects. Anticonvulsant drugs used to treat certain types of seizures may include carbamazepine, phenobarbital, primidone, phenytoin, gabapentin, or valproate. In addition, adrenocorticotropic hormone (ACTH) is often used to treat children with infantile spasms. If seizure control is not obtained with a particular medication, other anticonvulsants may be substituted. In some patients, combination drug therapy may be necessary to adequately control seizures. If seizure control is not obtained with anticonvulsant medications, surgery may be considered. Additional treatment is symptomatic and supportive.

National Associations & Support Groups

5743 **American Academy of Pediatrics**
345 Park Blvd
Itasca, IL 60143
847-434-4000
800-433-9016
Fax: 847-434-8000
csc@aap.org
www.aap.org

The American Academy of Pediatrics and its member pediatricians are committed to the attainment of optimal physical, mental and social health and well-being for all infants, children, adolescents, and young adults.

Kyle E. Yasuda, MD, FAAP, President
Mark Del Monte, JD, CEO/Executive VP
Vera Tait, MD, FAAP, Chief Medical Officer

5744 **American Epilepsy Society**
135 S LaSalle Street, Suite 2850
Chicago, IL 60603
312-883-3800
Fax: 312-896-5784
info@aesnet.org
www.aesnet.org

A society of clinicians, researchers, and health care professionals which promotes education and research of epilepsy.

Eileen Murray, Executive Director

5745 **Child Neurology Foundation**
601 W Short Street
Lexington, KY 40508
888-417-3435
info@childneurologyfoundation.org
childneurologyfoundation.org

The Child Neurology Foundation connects partners from all areas of the child neurology community so those navigating the journey of disease diagnosis, management, and care have the ongoing support from those dedicated to treatments and cures.

Amy Brin, Executive Director
Katie Hentges, Director, Programs
Brea McCormley, Director, Development

5746 **Cleveland Clinic Children's Hospital & Epilepsy Center**
9500 Euclid Avenue
Cleveland, OH 44195
800-223-2273
cms.clevelandclinic.org/childrenshospital/

Provides innovative care for infants, children, and adolescents with complex medical problems. Includes medical, surgical, rehabilitation, psychiatric and intensive care, latest technology, including a computerized epilepsy monitoring unit, a consolidated pediatric intensive care unit and operating suites. Physicians are known for their expertise in treating major medical problems, such as cardiovascular disease, cancer, digestive disorders, musculoskeletal problems and neurosensory disorders.

5747 **Epilepsy Foundation**
8301 Professional Place West, Ste 230
Landover, MD 20785
301-459-3700
800-332-1000
Fax: 301-577-2684
ContactUs@efa.org
www.epilepsy.org

Nationwide organization dedicated to help those living with epilepsy pursue seizure freedom through community services, public education, advocacy and research funding.

Phil Gattone, President & CEO
Ellen Hobby, COO
Steve Owens, VP, Programs & Services

5748 **Genetic Alliance**
426400 Woodfield Road, Ste 189
Damascus, MD 20872
202-966-5557
Fax: 202-966-8553
info@geneticalliance.org
www.geneticalliance.org

World's leading nonprofit health advocacy organization committed to transforming health through genetics and promoting an environment of openness centered on the health of individuals, families, and communities.

Sharon Terry, CEO
Ruth Child, CFO
Natasha Bonhomme, Chief Strategy Officer

5749 **National Association of Epilepsy Centers**
1150 Connecticut Avenue NW, Suite 803
Washington, DC 20036
202-800-7074
Fax: 202-484-1244
info@naec-epilepsy.org
www.naec-epilepsy.org

A nonprofit organization that encourages and supports professional and technical education in the treatment of epilepsy. Over 120 centers nationwide are members of the trade association, which will make referrals to its member centers.

Ellen Riker, Executive Director
Johanna Gray, Deputy Director
Barbara Small, Programs Manager

State Agencies & Support Groups

Arkansas

5750 **Epilepsy Education Association of Arkansas**
2902 E Kiehl, Suite 1B
Sherwood, AR 72120
501-833-8680
www.epilepsyarkansas.com

A resource and provider of support and education in Arkansas for those with epilepsy.

Sharon Wingo McGinn, Director
Judy Hess RN, Co-Director

Seizures / Research Centers

California

5751 Epilepsy Foundation of Northern California
1736 Franklin Street, Ste 450
Oakland, CA 94612
510-922-8687
800-632-3532
Fax: 510-677-4190
miriam@epilepsynorcal.org
www.epilepsynorcal.org

Nonprofit center serving families affected by epilepsy since 1953.

Carlos Quesada, CEO
Miriam Swanson, Events & Programs Coordinator

Florida

5752 Epilepsy Association of the Big Bend
1215 Lee Ave, Suite M-4
Tallahassee, FL 32303
850-222-1777
866-778-4583
Fax: 850-222-7440
www.epilepsyassoc.org

Services include: case management, prevention education, counseling and advocacy, information and referral.

Scott Mehle, Executive Director

5753 Florida Epilepsy Services
11200 NW 8th Avenue
Gainesville, FL 32601
352-392-6449
800-330-9746
Fax: 352-392-5792
www.floridaepilepsy.org

A nonprofit membership organization of epilepsy services providers in the state of Florida, that serve the needs of those with epilepsy and their families. Local offices for services can be found for different regions and counties of Florida.

Jim Lyons, Program Director

New York

5754 Chrissy & Friends
930 Willowbrook Rd
Staten Island, NY 10302
718-698-1800
info@chrissyandfriends.org
www.chrissyandfriends.org

Offers children with epilepsy an opportunity to develop friendships through a variety of activities and tutoring programs.

RoseAnne DeRenzo, President
RoseAnne Zielechowski, VP
Joan DeRenzo, Secretary

5755 EPIC Long Island
1500 Hempstead Turnpike
East Meadow, NY 11554
516-739-7733
888-672-7154
Fax: 516-739-1860
www.efli.org

Founded in 1953 as the Epilepsy Foundation of Long Island-a small group of parents who were determined to see their children lead productive and satisfying lives. Our role has expanded to providing top notch treatment, care, education and support to those with epilepsy and emotional and intellectual challenges.

Thomas Hopkins, President & CEO
Paul Giotis, VP, Operations
Irene Rodgers, Director, Community Services

5756 Epilepsy Foundation of Metropolitan New York
65 Broadway, Ste 505
New York, NY 10006
212-677-8550
www.efmny.org

Provides vocational services, counseling, respite services, job placement, educational presentations

Blanca Vazquez, Chair
Fred Lado, Vice Chair

Pennsylvania

5757 Epilepsy Foundation Eastern Pennsylvania
919 Walnut Street, Suite 700
Philadelphia, PA 19107
215-629-5003
800-887-7165
Fax: 215-629-4997
efepa@efepa.org
www.efepa.org

The mission of the EPEA is to lead the fight to stop seizures, find a cure and overcome challenges created by epilepsy. They choose to fulfill the mission by meeting the non-medical needs for people affected by epilepsy/seizure disorder to enhance their lives and build supportive communities.

Elizabeth Beil, President & CEO
Missy Dolaway, Director of Development
Bintu Kabba, Youth & Young Adult Coordinator

Washington

5758 Epilepsy Foundation Washington
2311 N. 45th St., #134
Seattle, WA 98103
206-487-5251
800-332-1000
Fax: 206-400-1651
washington@efa.org
epilepsywashington.org

Serves all of Washington.

Sharon Cupp, Executive Director
Dalia Contreras, Program Coordinator
Jessica Veach, Communications Manager

Libraries & Resource Centers

5759 EFWCP Resource Library
Epilepsy Foundation Western/Central Pennsylvania
1501 Reedsdale Street, Suite 3002
Pittsburgh, PA 15233
412-322-5880
800-361-5585
Fax: 412-322-7885
staff@efwp.org
www.efwp.org

For people with epilepsy and their families, comprehensive information on the disorder is often a valuable, yet hard-to-find asset. Living with epilepsy often requires special services to help better understand what epilepsy is and to learn how to deal with it. EFWCP can provide information beyond what is available in physician offices and in most cases the public library. The EFWCP maintains an Epilepsy Resource Library of brochures, books, reference manuals, videos and professional articles.

Judith Painter, Executive Director
Peggy Beem, Associate Director
Colleen K Fulkerson, Special Events Coordinator

Research Centers

California

5760 EpiCenter
University of California, Irvine
Irvine, CA 92697
949-824-5011
www.ucihs.uci.edu/epilepsyresearch/index.htm

Researchers, scientists and physicians studying the mechanisms and consequences of epilepsies through a variety of scientific approaches and research.

Tallie Z Baram, Chair

Seizures / Audio Video

Illinois

5761 Citizens United for Research in Epilepsy (CURE)
223 W. Erie, Suite 2SW
Chicago, IL 60654
312-255-1801
800-765-7118
Fax: 312-255-1809
info@CUREepilepsy.org
www.cureepilepsy.org

Citizens United for Research in Epilepsy is a nonprofit organization dedicated to finding a cure for epilepsy by raising funds for research and by increasing awareness of the prevalence and devastation of this disease.

Susan Axelrod, Chair
Bogdan Ewendt, Executive Director
Samantha Kreindel, Director of Communications

Maryland

5762 Epilepsy Research Laboratory, Department of Neurology
Johns Hopkins University
Meyer 2-147, 600 N Wolfe St
Baltimore, MD 21287
410-276-8560
Fax: 410-563-0559
www.erl.neuro.jhmi.edu/

The Epilepsy Center evaluates and cares for seizure disorder patients from pediatric through adult.

Gregory K. Bergey, M.D., Professor/Director Epilepsy Center/
Christophe Jouny, Ph.D., Assistant Professor/Co-Director Epi
Joanne Barnett, Senior Medical Office Coordinator

Missouri

5763 Pediatric Epilepsy Center
St Louis Children's Hospital
One Children's Place, Suite 12E47
St Louis, MO 63110
314-454-6120
Fax: 314-454-4225
www.neuro.wustl.edu/

A comprehensive and one of the largest centers for epilepsy and seizure disorder care and research in the nation. It includes dedicated staff and an inpatient Epilepsy Monitoring Unit.

W. Edwin Dodson, M.D., Professor of Neurology & Pediatrics
Mary Bertrand, M.D., Associate Professor of Neurology
Christina Gurnett, M.D., Ph.D., Assistant Professor of Neurology an

New York

5764 Center for Neural Recovery & Rehabilitation Research
Helen Hayes Hospital
Route 9W
West Haverstraw, NY 10993
845-786-4225
888-707-3422
Fax: 845-947-3097
www.helenhayeshospital.org/research/
Helen E Scharfman PhD, Director

North Carolina

5765 Duke University Comprehensive Epilepsy Center
200 Trent Drive, Room 4517, Busse Building
Durham, NC 27710
919-416-3853
Fax: 919-681-7973
koeni002@mc.duke.edu
neuro.surgery.duke.edu

Evaluation of potential surgical candidates by epilepsy specialists.

Roger L Cothran, Director
Allan H. Friedman, MD, Division Chief
Karen Koenig, Division Administrator

Tennessee

5766 Neuroscience Institute, University of Tennessee Health Science Center
875 Monroe Ave, Suite 426
Memphis, TN 38163
901-448-5960
Fax: 901-448-4685
www.uthsc.edu/neuroscience

Epilepsy research and studies.

William E. Armstrong, Ph.D., Director
Anton J. Reiner, Ph.D., Co-Director
Shannon Guyot, Administrative Services Assistant

Texas

5767 Baylor Comprehensive Epilepsy Center
Baylor College of Medicine
Smith Tower, 18th Floor, 6550 Fannin, Suite 1801
Houston, TX 77030
713-798-8259
Fax: 713-798-7533
www.bcm.edu/neurology/epilepsy/

Individualized care for those with seizure disorders.

Richard A. Hrachovy, M.D., Director
David K. Chen, M.D., Epileptology and Neurophysiology
Alica M. Goldman, M.D., Ph.D., Epileptology and Neurophysiology

Wisconsin

5768 Regional Epilepsy Center
Aurora St. Luke's Medical Center
2801 W Kinnickic River Pkwy, Ste 570
Milwaukee, WI 53215
414-385-8780
www.aurorahealthcare.org/services/epilepsy/
Christopher Inglese, Director

Audio Video

5769 Because You Are My Friend
Epilepsy Foundation
8301 Professional Place East, Suite 200
Landover, MD 20785
866-330-2718
800-332-1000
Fax: 301-459-1569
ContactUs@efa.org
www.epilepsyfoundation.org

Video tape for children that provides a clear explanation of epilepsy, first aid and the importance of friendship. Cartoon slide presentation with child narration.

Warren Lammert, Chair
Phil Gattone, President/ CEO
Roger Heldman, Treasurer

5770 Epilepsy: The Untold Story
Fanflight Productions
32 Court Street, 21st Floor
Brooklyn, NY 11201
718-488-8900
800-876-1710
Fax: 718-488-8642
info@fanlight.com
www.fanlight.com

This video tells the story of six people with Temporal Lobe Epilepsy.
1993 Video - 27 mins
ISBN: 1-572951-37-0

Nicole Johnson, Publicity Coordinator

Seizures / Web Sites

5771 How to Recognize and Classify Seizures
Epilepsy Foundation
8301 Professional Place East, Suite 200
Landover, MD 20785
866-330-2718
800-332-1000
Fax: 301-459-1569
ContactUs@efa.org
www.epilepsyfoundation.org

Discusses the classification of seizures and epileptic syndromes.

25 minutes

Warren Lammert, Chair
Phil Gattone, President/ CEO
Roger Heldman, Treasurer

5772 Just Like You and Me
WellMe/State of the Art
2201 Wisconsin Ave NW, Ste 350
Washington, DC 20008
202-537-0818
Fax: 202-537-0828
contact@wellme.com
wellme.stateart.com/productions/health/epilepsy/

A video/patient info guide package on successfully living with epilepsy.

5773 Rest of the Family
Epilepsy Foundation
8301 Professional Place East, Suite 200
Landover, MD 20785
866-330-2718
800-332-1000
Fax: 301-459-1569
ContactUs@efa.org
www.epilepsyfoundation.org

Presents the feelings and concerns of other family members, including siblings, of children with epilepsy.

Videocassette

Warren Lammert, Chair
Phil Gattone, President/ CEO
Roger Heldman, Treasurer

5774 Seizure First Aid
Epilepsy Foundation
8301 Professional Place East, Suite 200
Landover, MD 20785
866-330-2718
800-332-1000
Fax: 301-459-1569
ContactUs@efa.org
www.epilepsyfoundation.org

This video combines footage of real seizures with reenactments to demonstrate proper first aid procedures. In addition, people with epilepsy talk about how they feel when they have a seizure, and discuss how they would like friends, family and the general public to react when a seizure occurs. 10 minutes.

Video & DVD

Warren Lammert, Chair
Phil Gattone, President/ CEO
Roger Heldman, Treasurer

5775 Understanding Seizures & Epilepsy
Epilepsy Foundation
8301 Professional Place East, Suite 200
Landover, MD 20785
866-330-2718
800-332-1000
Fax: 301-459-1569
ContactUs@efa.org
www.epilepsyfoundation.org

Provides an explanation of seizure disorders in everyday language and dispels many misconceptions about epilepsy with medically accurate information.

Videocassette

Warren Lammert, Chair
Phil Gattone, President/ CEO
Roger Heldman, Treasurer

Web Sites

5776 American Epilepsy Society
www.aesnet.org
312-883-3800
Fax: 312-896-5784
info@aesnet.org
www.aesnet.org

The society promotes research and education of professionals in the field of epilepsy and related disorders. The site includes a comprehensive listing of postgraduate training opportunities in the fields related to epilepsy.

Eileen Murray, Executive Director

5777 Curing Epilepsy: Focus on the Future/Bench marks for Epilepsy Research
P.O. Box 5801
Bethesda, MD 20824
301-496-5751
800-352-9424
www.ninds.nih.gov/funding/research/epilepsyweb/

Summary of March 2000, White House-initiated conference.

Walter J. Koroshetz, M.D., Acting Director
Alan L. Willard, Ph.D., Acting Deputy Director
Caroline Lewis, Executive Officer

5778 Epilepsy Foundation
8301 Professional Place West, Ste 23000
Landover, MD 20785
301-459-3700
800-332-1000
Fax: 301-577-2684
ContactUs@efa.org
www.epilepsy.org

Nationwide organization dedicated to help those living with epilepsy pursue seizure freedom through community services, public education, advocacy and research funding.

Philen Gattone, President & CEO
Ellen Hobby, COO
Steve Owens, VP, Programs & Services

5779 Epilepsy.com
8301 Professional Place East, Suite 200
Landover, MD 20785
866-330-2718
800-332-1000
Fax: 301-459-1569
ContactUs@efa.org
www.epilepsy.com

Epilepsy resources made available through an initiative by the Epilepsy Therapy Development Project.

Warren Lammert, Chair
Phil Gattone, President/ CEO
Roger Heldman, Treasurer

5780 HealingWell.com
www.healingwell.com/epilepsy/
admin@healingwell.com
www.healingwell.com/epilepsy/

Offers information and resources including books, newsletters, and videos on a variety of diseases and chronic illnesses including epilepsy.

Peter Waite, Founder/ CEO

5781 NIH/National Institute of Neurological Disorders and Stroke (NINDS)
PO Box 5801
Bethesda, MD 20824
301-496-5751
800-352-9424
www.ninds.nih.gov

The mission of NINDS is to reduce the burden of neurological disease - a burden borne by every age group, by every segment of society, by people all over the world.

Walter J. Koroshetz, MD, Director

5782 North Pacific Epilepsy Research
The Northrup Center, 2311 NW Northrup Street, Suit
Portland, OR 97210
503-291-5300
Fax: 503-291-5303
www.seizures.net/

Provides information to the public and health care professionals.

Dr. Mark Yerby, Founder

Book Publishers

5783 Brainstorms Companion: Epilepsy in Our View

Steven C Schachter MD, author

Epilepsy Foundation
8301 Professional Place
Landover, MD 20785
301-459-3700
800-332-1000
Fax: 301-577-2684
www.epilepsyfoundation.org

Family members, friends and coworkers of those with seizure disorders describe their feelings and observations.

1994 160 pages Paperback
ISBN: 0-781702-30-5

Phil Gattone, President & CEO
Michele Dawson, Manager of Executive operations
Sandy Finucane, Senior Advisor

5784 Brainstorms: Epilepsy in Our Words

Steven C Schachter MD, author

Epilepsy Foundation
8301 Professional Place
Landover, MD 20785
301-459-3700
800-662-6922
Fax: 301-577-2684
www.epilepsyfoundation.org

Patients describe their experiences with seizures. Sixty-eight in-depth personal accounts of actual seizures are followed by a short section on how epilepsy affects the lives of the patients.

1993 197 pages Paperback
ISBN: 0-802774-65-2

Phil Gattone, President & CEO
Michele Dawson, Manager of Executive operations
Sandy Finucane, Senior Advisor

5785 Children with Seizures: A Guide For Parents, Teachers and Other Professionals

Epilepsy Foundation
8301 Professional Place
Landover, MD 20785
301-459-3700
800-332-1000
Fax: 301-577-2684
www.epilepsyfoundation.org

Phil Gattone, President & CEO
Michele Dawson, Manager of Executive operations
Sandy Finucane, Senior Advisor

5786 Dotty the Dalmatian Has Epilepsy

Tim Peters & Company, Inc
87 Main St, PO Box 370
Peapack, NJ 07977
908-234-2050
800-543-2230
Fax: 908-234-1961
info@timpetersandcompany.com
www.timpetersandcompany.com

Part of the Dr. Wellbook® series, this is the story of Dotty the Dalmatian who discovers she has epilepsy.

16 pages Softcover
ISBN: 1-879874-35-0

5787 Embrace the Dawn

Andrea Davidson, author

Epilepsy Foundation
8301 Professional Place
Landover, MD 20785
301-459-3700
800-332-1000
Fax: 301-577-2684
www.epilepsyfoundation.org

A moving biographical account of one person's lifelong experience with epilepsy.

127 pages Softcover

Phil Gattone, President & CEO
Michele Dawson, Manager of Executive operations
Sandy Finucane, Senior Advisor

5788 Epilepsy A to Z

Demos Medical Publishing
11 West 42nd Street, 15th Floor
New York, NY 10036
212-683-0072
800-532-8663
Fax: 212-683-0118
orderdept@demosmedpub.com
www.demosmedpub.com

Easy reference in finding brief answers to questions regarding epilepsy terminology.

1995 322 pages Softcover
ISBN: 0-939957-75-0

Kathy Gonzalez, Order Dept/Fulfillment Coordinator
Paul Choi, Vice-President of Finance and Opera
Richard Winters, Executive Editor

5789 Epilepsy, A Guide to Balancing Your Life

Ilo E Leppik MD, author

Demos Medical Publishing
11 West 42nd Street, 15th Floor
New York, NY 10036
212-683-0072
800-532-8663
Fax: 212-683-0118
orderdept@demosmedpub.com
www.demosmedpub.com

Part of the Quality of Life Guide Series from the American Academy of Neurology Press. Provides reliable and practical information for those diagnosed with epilepsy and seizure disorders.

2006 192 pages Softcover
ISBN: 1-932603-20-0

Kathy Gonzalez, Order Dept/Fulfillment Coordinator
Paul Choi, Vice-President of Finance and Opera
Richard Winters, Executive Editor

5790 Epilepsy: 199 Answers

Andrew N Wilner MD, author

Demos Medical Publishing
11 West 42nd Street, 15th Floor
New York, NY 10036
212-683-0072
800-532-8663
Fax: 212-683-0118
orderdept@demosmedpub.com
www.demosmedpub.com

Helps to better understand conversations with the doctor and empowers the patient/caregiver to ask the right questions, resulting in optimal care.

2003 180 pages Softcover
ISBN: 1-888799-70-5

Kathy Gonzalez, Order Dept/Fulfillment Coordinator
Paul Choi, Vice-President of Finance and Opera
Richard Winters, Executive Editor

Seizures / Book Publishers

5791 Epilepsy: Frequency, Causes and Consequences
Epilepsy Foundation
8301 Professional Place
Landover, MD 20785
301-459-3700
800-332-1000
Fax: 301-577-2684
www.epilepsyfoundation.org

Statistical study that addresses the causes, natural history, prevalence and risk factors of epilepsy in certain populations and the impact on the community.

1990

Phil Gattone, President & CEO
Michele Dawson, Manager of Executive operations
Sandy Finucane, Senior Advisor

5792 Epilepsy: I Can Live with That
Sue Goss, author

Epilepsy Foundation
8301 Professional Place
Landover, MD 20785
301-459-3700
800-332-1000
Fax: 301-577-2684
www.epilepsyfoundation.org

The experience of epilepsy as recorded by a group of ordinary men and women living in Australia. Each story focuses on personal growth, triumph over disability and emphasizes individual courage and hope.

1995 Softcover

Phil Gattone, President & CEO
Michele Dawson, Manager of Executive operations
Sandy Finucane, Senior Advisor

5793 Growing Up With Epilepsy
Lynn Bennett Blackburn MD, author

Demos Medical Publishing
11 West 42nd Street, 15th Floor
New York, NY 10036
212-683-0072
800-532-8663
Fax: 212-683-0118
orderdept@demosmedpub.com
www.demosmedpub.com

Guidance in raising a child with epilepsy, including navigating the educational system, discipline, and social development.

2003 168 pages Softcover
ISBN: 1-888799-74-3

Kathy Gonzalez, Order Dept/Fulfillment Coordinator
Paul Choi, Vice-President of Finance and Opera
Richard Winters, Executive Editor

5794 Keto Kid, Helping Your Child to Succeed on the Ketogenic Diet
Deborah Ann Snyder DO, author

Demos Medical Publishing
11 West 42nd Street, 15th Floor
New York, NY 10036
212-683-0072
800-532-8663
Fax: 212-683-0118
orderdept@demosmedpub.com
www.demosmedpub.com

2006 176 pages Softcover
ISBN: 1-932603-29-3

Kathy Gonzalez, Order Dept/Fulfillment Coordinator
Paul Choi, Vice-President of Finance and Opera
Richard Winters, Executive Editor

5795 Lee the Rabbit with Epilepsy
Deborah M. Moss, author

Epilepsy Foundation
8301 Professional Place
Landover, MD 20785
301-459-3700
800-332-1000
Fax: 301-459-1569
www.epilepsyfoundation.org

Written for children ages three to six, this illustrated picture book follows the adventures of a small rabbit who has seizures. It follows her journey from the first seizure, the initial doctors visit through to treatment.

1989 21 pages Hardcover

Phil Gattone, President & CEO
Michele Dawson, Manager of Executive operations
Sandy Finucane, Senior Advisor

5796 Living Well with Epilepsy
Robert Gumnit MD, author

Demos Medical Publishing
11 West 42nd Street, 15th Floor
New York, NY 10036
212-683-0072
800-532-8663
Fax: 212-683-0118
orederdept@demosmedpub.com
www.demosmedpub.com

Designed to help both health-care professionals and patients to understand all aspects of diagnosis and management; to enable patients to participate more knowledgeably in interactions with their health care team and to help steer them toward a more normal, fulfilling life.

1997 249 pages Soft / 2nd Ed
ISBN: 1-888799-11-0

Kathy Gonzalez, Order Dept/Fulfillment Coordinator
Paul Choi, Vice-President of Finance and Opera
Richard Winters, Executive Editor

5797 Missing Michael - A Mother's Story of Love
Epilepsy Foundation
8301 Professional Place
Landover, MD 20785
301-459-3700
800-332-1000
Fax: 301-459-1569
www.epilepsyfoundation.org

A mother's story of her struggle with raising her son with epilepsy. Deatils in dealing with the health care system, the school system, and the complications of medication.

Paperback

Phil Gattone, President & CEO
Michele Dawson, Manager of Executive operations
Sandy Finucane, Senior Advisor

5798 Mom I Have a Staring Problem
Epilepsy Foundation
8301 Professional Place
Landover, MD 20785
301-459-3700
800-332-1000
Fax: 301-459-1570
www.epilepsyfoundation.org

Tiffany, a seven-year old, describes her experiences with petit mal seizures; her feelings, wishes and fears. Written to help adults recognize a hidden problem that could be occuring with a child who has learning problems.

1994 24 pages Softcover
ISBN: 0-802774-65-2

Phil Gattone, President & CEO
Michele Dawson, Manager of Executive operations
Sandy Finucane, Senior Advisor

5799 My Friend Matty: A Story About Living with Epilepsy
Epilepsy Foundation
8301 Professional Place
Landover, MD 20785
301-459-3700
800-332-1000
Fax: 301-459-1571
www.epilepsyfoundation.org

A comic-book style publication for educating children written by parents whose 5-year old boy passed away.

Paperback

Phil Gattone, President & CEO
Michele Dawson, Manager of Executive operations
Sandy Finucane, Senior Advisor

Seizures / Magazines

5800 Pediatric Epilepsy
Demos Medical Publishing
11 West 42nd Street, 15th Floor
New York, NY 10036
212-683-0072
800-532-8663
Fax: 212-683-0118
orderdept@demosmedpub.com
www.demosmedpub.com

Covers the diagnosis, treatment, classification and management of childhood epilepsies.

2001 666 pages Hardcover
ISBN: 1-888799-30-9

Kathy Gonzalez, Order Dept/Fulfillment Coordinator
Paul Choi, Vice-President of Finance and Opera
Richard Winters, Executive Editor

5801 Pediatric Epilepsy Resource Handbook
FACES/NYU Medical Center
223 East 34th Street
New York, NY 10016
646-558-0900
Fax: 646-385-7163
FACESinfo@nyumc.org
www.faces.med.nyu.edu

3rd Edition

Pamela Mohr, Executive Director
Nako Ishii, Project Co-ordinator
Luis L. Valero, Associate Director of Special Event

5802 School Planning
Epilepsy Foundation
8301 Professional Place
Landover, MD 20785
301-459-3700
800-332-1000
Fax: 301-577-2684
TDD: 800-332-2070
www.epilepsyfoundation.org

This guide describes some epilepsy-related problems that children and youth may face in the areas of academics, school achievement and social development. Suggests ways parents can take a proactive approach to ensure appropriate testing, placement and achievement of educational goals for their children.

125 pages Hardcover
ISBN: 0-802774-65-2

Phil Gattone, President & CEO
Michele Dawson, Manager of Executive operations
Sandy Finucane, Senior Advisor

5803 Seizures and Epilepsy In Childhood: A Guide
Johns Hopkins University Press
2715 N Charles Street
Baltimore, MD 21218
410-516-6900
800-537-5487
Fax: 410-516-6968
www.press.jhu.edu

A standard resource for parents in need of comprehensive medical information about their child with epilepsy.

2002 432 pages 3rd Ed / Hard
ISBN: 0-801870-50-x

Kathleen Keane, Director
Timothy D. Fuller, Chief Information Officer
Erik A. Smist, Director, Finance and Administratio

5804 Your Child and Epilepsy
Roger J Gumnit MD, author

Demos Medical Publishing
11 West 42nd Street, 15th Floor
New York, NY 10036
212-683-0072
800-532-8663
Fax: 212-683-0118
www.demosmedpub.com

Provides information to help parents understand their child's epilepsy, suggestions on how to evaluate health care, to find better care if necessary and advice on how to help children with epilepsy to develop self-confidence and self-motivation.

1995 256 pages Softcover
ISBN: 0-939957-76-0

Kathy Gonzalez, Order Dept/Fulfillment Coordinator
Paul Choi, Vice-President of Finance and Opera
Richard Winters, Executive Editor

Magazines

5805 Epilepsy Foundation
Epilepsy Foundation
8301 Professional Place West, Ste 23000
Landover, MD 20785
301-459-3700
800-332-1000
Fax: 301-577-2684
ContactUs@efa.org
www.epilepsy.org

Nationwide organization dedicated to help those living with epilepsy pursue seizure freedom through community services, public education, advocacy and research funding.

Philen Gattone, President & CEO
Ellen Hobby, COO
Steve Owens, VP, Programs & Services

5806 EpilepsyUSA
Epilepsy Foundation
8301 Professional Place East, Suite 200
Landover, MD 20785
866-330-2718
800-332-1000
Fax: 301-459-1569
TDD: 800-332-2070
ContactUs@efa.org
www.epilepsyfoundation.org

Information on concerns about seizure disorders and epilepsy and new developments in treatment.

24 pages 6 issues/yr

Warren Lammert, Chair
Phil Gattone, President/ CEO
Roger Heldman, Treasurer

Journals

5807 Epilepsy & Behavior
Elsevier
Marquis One, 245 Peachtree Center Avenue, Suite 19
Atlanta, GA 30303
404-669-9400
800-999-6274
Fax: 404-669-9339
usjcs@elsevier.com
www.journals.elsevier.com/epilepsy-and-behavior/

An international journal that offers current information on the behavioral aspects of seizures and epilepsy.

Bi-monthly
ISSN: 1525-5050

Ron Mobed, Chief Executive Officer
Stuart Whayman, Chief Financial Officer
Gavin Howe, EVP, Human Resources

Newsletters

5808 Epilepsia: Journal of the International League Against Epilepsy
Blackwell Publishing
350 Main Street, Commerce Place
Malden, MA 2148
781-388-8200
888-661-5800
Fax: 781-388-8210
www.blackwellpublishing.com

A leading international journal on the epilepsies for more than 30 years, Epilepsia provides comprehensive coverage of current clinical and research results.

12 per year
ISSN: 0013-9580
Philip A Schwartzkroin, Co-Editor
Simon Shorvon, Co-Editor

Pamphlets

5809 Child with Epilepsy at Camp
Epilepsy Foundation
8301 Professional Place East, Suite 200
Landover, MD 20785
866-330-2718
800-332-1000
Fax: 301-459-1569
ContactUs@efa.org
www.epilepsyfoundation.org

Written for camp counselors, it helps parents explain to them the specific needs of children with epilepsy at camp to ensure a safe camping experience.

14 pages Pamphlet

Warren Lammert, Chair
Phil Gattone, President/ CEO
Roger Heldman, Treasurer

5810 Child's Guide To Seizure Disorders
Epilepsy Foundation
8301 Professional Place East, Suite 200
Landover, MD 20785
866-330-2718
800-332-1000
Fax: 301-459-1569
ContactUs@efa.org
www.epilepsyfoundation.org

A pamphlet for children, brightly-colored and explains seizures, why medication should be taken, etc.

Warren Lammert, Chair
Phil Gattone, President/ CEO
Roger Heldman, Treasurer

5811 Epilepsy in Children: The Teacher's Role
Epilepsy Foundation
8301 Professional Place East, Suite 200
Landover, MD 20785
866-330-2718
800-332-1000
Fax: 301-459-1569
ContactUs@efa.org
www.epilepsyfoundation.org

Provides an explanation for teachers on handling seizures in the classroom, the need for good communication between students and first aid procedures.

Warren Lammert, Chair
Phil Gattone, President/ CEO
Roger Heldman, Treasurer

5812 Epilepsy: You and Your Child
Epilepsy Foundation
8301 Professional Place East, Suite 200
Landover, MD 20785
866-330-2718
800-332-1000
Fax: 301-459-1569
ContactUs@efa.org
www.epilepsyfoundation.org

This instructional booklet offers information on emotional aspects of epilepsy, how to handle seizures, medication, diet and nutrition, and offers referral organizations for parents.

Warren Lammert, Chair
Phil Gattone, President/ CEO
Roger Heldman, Treasurer

5813 Febrile Seizures Fact Sheet
NINDS/NIH Neurological Institute
Office of Communications and Public Liaison, NINDS
Bethesda, MD 20892
301-496-5751
800-352-9424
TTY: 301-468-5981
www.ninds.nih.gov/disorders/febrile_seizures/

Also available in Spanish.

Walter J. Koroshetz, M.D., Acting Director
Alan L. Willard, Ph.D., Acting Deputy Director
Caroline Lewis, Executive Officer

5814 Finding Out About Seizures: A Guide to Medical Tests
Epilepsy Foundation
8301 Professional Place East, Suite 200
Landover, MD 20785
866-330-2718
800-332-1000
Fax: 301-459-1569
ContactUs@efa.org
www.epilepsyfoundation.org

Introduces adults and children with epilepsy to the types of tests they may have to undergo.

Warren Lammert, Chair
Phil Gattone, President/ CEO
Roger Heldman, Treasurer

5815 H.O.P.E. Series: Seizures in Childhood
Epilepsy Foundation
8301 Professional Place East, Suite 200
Landover, MD 20785
866-330-2718
800-332-1000
Fax: 301-459-1569
ContactUs@efa.org
www.epilepsyfoundation.org

Provides an overview of the challenges associated with living with epilepsy and other seizure disorders, including potential hazards, first aid procedures, and overall help in daily living.

Warren Lammert, Chair
Phil Gattone, President/ CEO
Roger Heldman, Treasurer

5816 H.O.P.E. Series: Seizures in the Teen Year s
Epilepsy Foundation
8301 Professional Place East, Suite 200
Landover, MD 20785
866-330-2718
800-332-1000
Fax: 301-459-1569
ContactUs@efa.org
www.epilepsyfoundation.org

Provides general information specifically for teens with epilepsy and seizure disorders.

Warren Lammert, Chair
Phil Gattone, President/ CEO
Roger Heldman, Treasurer

5817 Infantile Spasms
NINDS/NIH Neurological Institute
Office of Communications and Public Liaison, NINDS
Bethesda, MD 20892
301-496-5751
800-352-9424
TTY: 301-468-5981
www.ninds.nih.gov/disorders/infantilespasms/

Information sheet on infantile spasms (West Syndrome).

Walter J. Koroshetz, M.D., Acting Director
Alan L. Willard, Ph.D., Acting Deputy Director
Caroline Lewis, Executive Officer

5818 Kids and Seizures: Know the Hidden Signs
Epilepsy Foundation
8301 Professional Place East, Suite 200
Landover, MD 20785
866-330-2718
800-332-1000
Fax: 301-459-1569
ContactUs@efa.org
www.epilepsyfoundation.org

Written for camp counselors, it helps parents explain to them the specific needs of children with epilepsy at camp to ensure a safe camping experience.

Warren Lammert, Chair
Phil Gattone, President/ CEO
Roger Heldman, Treasurer

Seizures / Pamphlets

5819 Managing Seizures, Information for Caregivers
Epilepsy Foundation
8301 Professional Place East, Suite 200
Landover, MD 20785
866-330-2718
800-332-1000
Fax: 301-459-1569
ContactUs@efa.org
www.epilepsyfoundation.org

Explains seizures, routine and special care, emergency aid and first aid for caregivers. Includes a poster size chart for medicines and general guidance in handling a seizure.

Warren Lammert, Chair
Phil Gattone, President/ CEO
Roger Heldman, Treasurer

5820 Me and My World Storybook
Epilepsy Foundation
8301 Professional Place East, Suite 200
Landover, MD 20785
866-330-2718
800-332-1000
Fax: 301-459-1569
TDD: 800-332-2070
ContactUs@efa.org
www.epilepsyfoundation.org

An excellent pamphlet for explaining epilepsy to children and their friends. It also discusses various types of epilepsy and its effects on family members. Ages 4-8.

Warren Lammert, Chair
Phil Gattone, President/ CEO
Roger Heldman, Treasurer

5821 Medicines for Epilepsy
Epilepsy Foundation
8301 Professional Place East, Suite 200
Landover, MD 20785
866-330-2718
800-332-1000
Fax: 301-459-1569
ContactUs@efa.org
www.epilepsyfoundation.org

Offers information on medication and treatments, generic drugs, side effects, drug abuse and more. Contains a color chart with pictures of the most common medications for epilepsy.

Warren Lammert, Chair
Phil Gattone, President/ CEO
Roger Heldman, Treasurer

5822 Safety and Seizures
Epilepsy Foundation
8301 Professional Place East, Suite 200
Landover, MD 20785
866-330-2718
800-332-1000
Fax: 301-459-1569
ContactUs@efa.org
www.epilepsyfoundation.org

Warren Lammert, Chair
Phil Gattone, President/ CEO
Roger Heldman, Treasurer

5823 Seizures and Epilepsy: Hope Through Research
NINDS/NIH Neurological Institute
Office of Communications and Public Liaison, NINDS
Bethesda, MD 20892
301-496-5751
800-352-9424
TTY: 301-468-5981
www.ninds.nih.gov/disorders/epilepsy/

Also available in Spanish.

Walter J. Koroshetz, M.D., Acting Director
Alan L. Willard, Ph.D., Acting Deputy Director
Caroline Lewis, Executive Officer

5824 Seizures, Epilepsy and Your Child
Epilepsy Foundation
8301 Professional Place East, Suite 200
Landover, MD 20785
866-330-2718
800-332-1000
Fax: 301-459-1569
ContactUs@efa.org
www.epilepsyfoundation.org

A pamphlet for parents, providing guidance on daily life, first aid and treatment for children with epilepsy.

Warren Lammert, Chair
Phil Gattone, President/ CEO
Roger Heldman, Treasurer

5825 Surgery for Epilepsy
Epilepsy Foundation
8301 Professional Place East, Suite 200
Landover, MD 20785
866-330-2718
800-332-1000
Fax: 301-459-1569
ContactUs@efa.org
www.epilepsyfoundation.org

Describes current surgical treatment and the testing that precedes it.

12 pages

Warren Lammert, Chair
Phil Gattone, President/ CEO
Roger Heldman, Treasurer

5826 Talking to Your Doctor About Seizure Disorders
Epilepsy Foundation
8301 Professional Place East, Suite 200
Landover, MD 20785
866-330-2718
800-332-1000
Fax: 301-459-1569
ContactUs@efa.org
www.epilepsyfoundation.org

Designed to help the patient talk with medical personnel about treatment of epilepsy.

Warren Lammert, Chair
Phil Gattone, President/ CEO
Roger Heldman, Treasurer

5827 The ADA: Questions and Answers
Epilepsy Foundation
8301 Professional Place East, Suite 200
Landover, MD 20785
866-330-2718
800-332-1000
Fax: 301-459-1569
ContactUs@efa.org
www.epilepsyfoundation.org

Offers a brief overview of the Americans with Disabilities Act and how it covers those with epilepsy.

Warren Lammert, Chair
Phil Gattone, President/ CEO
Roger Heldman, Treasurer

5828 What Everyone Should Know About Epilepsy
Epilepsy Foundation
8301 Professional Place East, Suite 200
Landover, MD 20785
866-330-2718
800-332-1000
Fax: 301-459-1569
ContactUs@efa.org
www.epilepsyfoundation.org

Warren Lammert, Chair
Phil Gattone, President/ CEO
Roger Heldman, Treasurer

5829 When Seizures Don't Look Like Seizures
Epilepsy Foundation
8301 Professional Place East, Suite 200
Landover, MD 20785
866-330-2718
800-332-1000
Fax: 301-459-1569
ContactUs@efa.org
www.epilepsyfoundation.org

Describes and helps with the subtle signs of a seizure for parents, child care providers and school personnel.

ISBN: 0-802774-65-2

Warren Lammert, Chair
Phil Gattone, President/ CEO
Roger Heldman, Treasurer

Camps

5830 Camp Achieve
Epilepsy Foundation Eastern Pennsylvania
919 Walnut Street, Suite 700
Philadelphia, PA 19107
215-629-5003
800-887-7165
Fax: 215-629-4997
camp@efepa.org
www.efepa.org/programs-and-resources/camp-achieve

Camp Achieve is a week long, overnight, summer camp for youth with a primary diagnosis of epilepsy/seizure disorder that is held every year in August. Camp Achieve is a unique opportunity for the children ages 8-17 to connect with other individuals coping with the same day to day challenges. Many individuals with epilepsy/seizure disorder face isolation, bullying, and discrimination from their classmates, their neighbors, and the general public.

Frank Kotulka, Board President
Allison McCartin, Executive Director
Sue Livingston, Education Coordinator

5831 Camp Frog
Epilepsy Foundation Western/Central Pennsylvania
1501 Reedsdale Street, Suite 3002
Pittsburgh, PA 15233
412-261-5880
800-316-5585
Fax: 412-322-7885
astein@efwp.org
www.efwp.org/programs/ProgramsCampFrog.xml

The EFWCP sponsors two-week long, overnight summer camping programs called Camp Frog. This nationally recognized activity allows kids with epilepsy/seizure disorders to be integrated into a typical camping experience with hundreds of other children. The overnight program is available to boys and girls with epilepsy/seizure disorders from grades 4 to 11. Campers enjoy a host of activities such as arts and crafts, campfire sing-alongs, swimming, team games, sailing, archery and horseback riding.

Peggy Beem, President/ CEO
Francine Reyher, Adult Services Coordinator
Colleen K Fulkerson, Special Events Coordinator

5832 Camp Ramah in New England Tikvah Program
39 Bennett Street
Palmer, MA 01609
413-283-9771
Fax: 413-283-6661
info@campramahne.org
www.campramahne.org

The Tikvah program is one of the first summer programs for Jewish children with special needs. It continues to grow and evolve as it strives to serve campers with a wide range of special needs including, but not limited to, congitive impairments, autism, cerebral palsy and seizure disorder.

Howard Blas, Tikvah Program Director
Talya Kalender, Director, Camper Care
Benjamin Greene, Director of Education

5833 Camp Roehr
140 Iowa Ave # A
Belleville, IL 62220
618-236-2181
866-848-0472
Fax: 618-236-3654
www.epilepsyfoundation.org/local/swillinois/camp.cfm

Seven day residential camp for children designed to meet the special needs of children diagnosed with epilepsy, providing a safe and fun camp experience.

Ellen Becker, Executive Director
Trudy Baxter, Director of Programs and Services
Jan Conder, Development Coordinator

5834 Crotched Mountain School & Rehabilitation Center
1 Verney Drive
Greenfield, NH 3047
603-547-3311
800-800-966
Fax: 603-547-3232
info@crotchedmountain.org
www.cmf.org

Currently serves children ages 6-22 with multiple-handicaps including: Cerebral Palsy, Spina Bifida, visual and hearing impairments and neurological disabilities, developmental disorders, autism, behavioral and emotional disorders, seizure disorders, spinal cord and head injuries. Member of the National Association of Independent Schools and accredited with the NE Association of Schools and Colleges, Independent Schools of Northern NE.

Donald L. Shumway, President/ CEO
Kathleen C. Brittan, VP, Development
Frederick R. Bruch, Jr., Medical Director

Sickle Cell Disease / Description

Description

5835 SICKLE CELL DISEASE

Synonyms: Homozygous Hb S, Sickle cell anemia

Involves the following Biologic System(s):

Hematologic and Oncologic Disorders

Sickle cell disease is an inherited blood disorder that primarily affects African Americans and is characterized by the presence of crescent or sickle-shaped red cells in the blood and the chronic premature destruction of red blood cells (hemolytic anemia). In this disorder, the red blood cells contain an abnormal form of the oxygen-carrying protein (hemoglobin) called hemoglobin S (Hgb S). This abnormality reduces the level of available oxygen (ischemia) in the blood cells and results in their characteristic sickle shape. These irregular cells tend to block the tiny blood vessels of various tissues and organs; they may cause restricted or obstructed blood flow resulting in tissue or organ damage (infarction). In addition, their unusual shape renders them fragile, leading to their premature destruction and thus anemia.

The symptoms of sickle cell disease tend to appear at or around six months of age and may include headaches; shortness of breath (dyspnea); paleness; fatigue; and a yellowish hue of the eyes, skin, and mucous membranes (jaundice). Any activity that would normally reduce the blood oxygen levels (e.g., exercise, exertion, illness, or high-altitude flying) may induce a sickle cell crisis or sudden worsening of the anemic condition accompanied by abdominal and bone pain, dyspnea, and vomiting. Infarction or a blocked blood vessel (vaso-occlusion) may also result in sickle cell crisis with the affected child experiencing chest pain and increased dyspnea. By adolescence most of those affected develop an enlarged spleen (splenomegaly) that is no longer capable of assisting in fighting certain infections, leaving the body more vulnerable to certain types of infections (encapsulated organisms, notably pneumococcal pneumonia). Other symptoms may include skin changes resulting from poor circulation, stroke resulting from insufficient oxygen reaching the brain, or blood in the urine (hematuria) resulting from kidney damage. As the affected child grows to adulthood, the liver and heart may enlarge (hepatosplenomegaly) and a heart murmur may develop. The lungs, intestines, and gall bladder may also be affected. In addition, affected children may develop such distinct characteristics as a short torso with long extremities, fingers, and toes.

Because there is no known cure for sickle cell disease, treatment is geared toward prevention, control, and pain management. Such treatment may include the avoidance of activities that reduce blood oxygen levels, a full immunization regimen, and prompt medical intervention for any illness or viral infection. Other treatment may include folic acid supplementation, antibiotic medication for treatment and prevention of infection, oxygen therapy to improve the level of oxygen in the blood, and acetaminophen or other medication to relieve pain. To manage a sickle cell crisis, as well as the pain associated with it, affected children may be given intravenous fluids, pain-relieving drugs,and possibly blood transfusions. Other treatments being studied include certain drugs, gene therapy, and bone marrow transplantation.

Sickle cell disease is inherited as an autosomal recessive trait. In this case, the defective gene for hemoglobin S is transmitted by both parents. If a child inherits this gene from only one parent (and one normal gene from the other parent, that child will usually be symptom-free, but will be a carrier of the sickle cell trait. The incidence of this disorder in the United States is approximately 150 African American children in 100,000; however, approximately one in 12 black children carries the sickle cell trait.

Government Agencies

5836 NIH/ Eunice Kennedy Shriver National Institute of Child Health & Human Development
P.O. Box 3006
Rockville, MD 20847

800-370-2943
Fax: 866-760-5947
www.nichd.nih.gov

Conducts and supports research on topics related to the health of children, adults, families and populations. Some of these topics include: developmental disabilities, growth and development, infant death, reproductive health and birth defects.

Diana W. Bianchi, Director
Alison Cernich, PhD, Deputy Director

5837 NIH/National Heart, Lung and Blood Institute
31 Center Drive, Bldg 31
Bethesda, MD 20892

877-645-2448
www.nhlbi.nih.gov

Primary responsibility of this organization is the scientific investigation of heart, blood vessel, lung and blood disorders. Oversees research, demonstration, prevention, education, control and training activities in these fields and emphasizes the prevention and control of heart diseases.

Gary H. Gibbons, MD, Director
Kate O'Sullivan, Executive Officer

National Associations & Support Groups

5838 American Academy of Pediatrics
345 Park Blvd
Itasca, IL 60143

847-434-4000
800-433-9016
Fax: 847-434-8000
csc@aap.org
www.aap.org

The American Academy of Pediatrics and its member pediatricians are committed to the attainment of optimal physical, mental and social health and well-being for all infants, children, adolescents, and young adults.

Kyle E. Yasuda, MD, FAAP, President
Mark Del Monte, JD, CEO/Executive VP
Vera Tait, MD, FAAP, Chief Medical Officer

5839 American Sickle Cell Anemia Association
2390 E 79th Street
Cleveland, OH 44104

216-229-8600
Fax: 216-229-4500
irabragg@ascaa.org
www.ascaa.org

Provides education, testing, counseling, supportive services to the population at risk for sickle cell anemia and its hemoglobin variants. Bilingual educator on staff, educational materials and distribution of literature is provided by ASCAA. Referrals for children and families with special needs.

Ira Bragg-Grant, Executive Director

5840 Genetic Alliance
426400 Woodfield Road, Ste 189
Damascus, MD 20872

202-966-5557
Fax: 202-966-8553
info@geneticalliance.org
www.geneticalliance.org

World's leading nonprofit health advocacy organization committed to transforming health through genetics and promoting an environment of openness centered on the health of individuals, families, and communities.

Sharon Terry, CEO
Ruth Child, CFO
Natasha Bonhomme, Chief Strategy Officer

Sickle Cell Disease / State Agencies & Support Groups

5841 **Sickle Cell Disease Association of America**
3700 Koppers Street, #570
Baltimore, MD 21227
410-528-1555
800-421-8453
Fax: 410-528-1495
admin@sicklecelldisease.org
www.sicklecelldisease.org

Promotes the finding of a universal cure for sickle cell disease while improving the quality of life for individuals and families where sickle cell related conditions exists. It also assists in the crganization and development of local chapters.

Beverley Francis-Gibson, President & CEO
Leroy Hughes, Jr., VP, Operations
Carole Bernard, Director, Marketing/Communications

5842 **Sickle Cell Information Center**
Emory Center for Digital Scholarship
201 Dowman Drive
Atlanta, GA 30322
404-727-7857
Fax: 404-727-7880
aplatt@emory.edu
www.scinfo.org

Sickle cell resources, education, news and research updates for caregivers, patients and professionals.

Allan Platt, Director

State Agencies & Support Groups

Alabama

5843 **Sickle Cell Foundation of Greater Montgomery**
3180 US Highway 80 W
Montgomery, AL 36108
334-286-9122
800-742-5534
Fax: 334-286-4804
sickle2@aol.com
www.scfgm.org

Willie Owens, Executive Director

California

5844 **Sickle Cell Disease Foundation of California**
5777 W. Century Blvd. Suite 1230
Los Angeles, CA 90045
310-693-0247
877-288-2873
Fax: 310-216-0307
info@scdfc.org
www.scdfc.org

Educates, screens and offers counsel to those at risk for having children with sickle cell disease and other hemoglobin disorders.

Mary E Brown, President
Roger Brown, Director Development/Public Affairs

Connecticut

5845 **Sickle Cell Disease Association of America - Connecticut Chapter**
Hartford Regional Office
231 E Baltimore St, Suite 800
Baltimore, MD 21202
410-528-1555
800-421-8453
Fax: 410-528-1495
scdaa@sicklecelldisease.org
www.sicklecelldisease.org

Regional office loactions in Hartford, New Haven and New London.

Georgia

5846 **Sickle Cell Foundation of Georgia**
2391 Benjamin E Mays Drive
Atlanta, GA 30311
404-755-1641
800-326-5287
Fax: 404-755-7955
info@sicklecellga.org
www.sicklecellga.org/

Provides education, screening, and counseling programs for sickle cell and other abnormal hemoglobins. The Foundation has a deep-rooted commitment to making strides in monitoring the occurrence of sickle cell, improving the quality of life for those with the disease and cooperating with individuals conducting research.

Jean Brannan, Executive Director
Harold Dobbs, Outreach Coordinator
Nesby Gibson, Project Director

Louisiana

5847 **NE Louisiana Sickle Cell Anemia Foundation**
PO Box 1165
Monroe, LA 71210
318-322-0896
Fax: 318-387-4740
sickle@bayou.com
www.sicklecelldisease.org/index.cfm?page=chapter&id=

The Northeast Louisiana Sickle Cell Anemia Foundation is a community based tax exempt organization that assists victims with the inherited blood disease sickle cell anemia.

Christopher Hollins, Chair
Sonja L. Banks, President/Chief Operating Officer
Francis Aofolaju, Chief Financial Officer

Massachusetts

5848 **Community Sickle Cell Support Group**
1542 Tremont St
Roxbury, MA 02120
617-427-4100
cscsginc@aol.com
www.cscsginc.org

Jackie Rodriguez, Executive Director

New Mexico

5849 **Sickle Cell Council of New Mexico, Inc.**
1300 San Pedro NE
Albuquerque, NM 87108
505-254-9550
Fax: 505-254-9642
www.sicklecellnm.org

Blood screening, education, and genetic counseling.

Victoria A Jones, Executive Director

North Carolina

5850 **Eastern North Carolina Chapter (SCDAA)**
PO Box 5253
Jacksonville, NC 28540
910-346-2510
800-826-1314
Fax: 910-346-2614
sickle@bizec.rr.com
www.sicklecelleasternnc.org/index.php?pr=Home_Page

The North Carolina Sickle Cell Program was established in 1973. It provides services to persons with sickle cell disease, a lifelong red blood cell disorder that is passed from parents to children through genes. The program focuses on early detection and treatment, which can prevent many serious health prblems. It also offers education and genetic counseling for the general public.

Marcia M Wright, Executive Director

Sickle Cell Disease / Libraries & Resource Centers

5851 Sickle Cell Disease Association of the Piedmont
231 E Baltimore St, Suite 800
Baltimore, MD 21202
410-528-1555
800-421-8453
Fax: 410-528-1495
scdaa@sicklecelldisease.org
www.sicklecelldisease.org/index.cfm?page=chapter&id=

Dedicated to educating the public and providing support to people affected by sickle cell disease. Serving the following counties: Alamance, Forsyth, Caswell, Guilford, Randolph, and Rockingham.

Gladys A Robinson, Executive Director

5852 Sickle Cell Regional Network
Ste 404
Charlotte, NC 28202
704-332-4184
800-435-6004
Fax: 704-332-2246

Patricia Lambright, Executive Director

Pennsylvania

5853 Lehigh Valley Sickle Cell Support Group
PO Box 1711
Allentown, PA 18105
610-706-0636
SororW@aol.com
www.members.aol.com/SororW/index.html

For anyone affected/effected by Sickle Cell and all interested persons. Learn more about sickle cell disease and how you can help.

5854 Sickle Cell Disease Association of America,
Philadelphia/Delaware Valley Chapter
5070 Parkside Avenue- Suite 1404
Philadelphia, PA 19139
215-471-8686
Fax: 215-471-7441
scdaa.pdvc@verizon.net
www.sicklecelldisorder.com

A support group for parents of a child or children with sickle cell disease.

Stanley A Simpkins, Executive Director

South Carolina

5855 James R Clark Memorial Sickle Cell Foundation
1420 Gregg Street
Columbia, SC 29201
803-765-9916
800-506-1273
Fax: 803-799-6471
office@jamesrclarksicklecell.org
www.jamesrclarksicklecell.org/?

The mission of the foundation is to optimize the social and psychological well being of residents with sickle cell disease within the fifteen county area of South Carolina. This mission is accomplished through the provision of comprehensive services to individuals, families, and communities and is further enhanced by collaboration with appropriate federal, state, and local resources and through the involvement of volunteers and contributors.

Melodie Helms-Desilet, Executive Director

Texas

5856 Sickle Cell Association of Austin - Marc Thomas Chapter
1 Highland Ctr, 314 E Highland Mall Blvd, Ste 108
Austin, TX 78752
512-458-9767
Fax: 512-458-9714
sicklecellaustin@sbcglobal.net
www.sicklecellaustin.org/

To raise awareness, resources and support for clients with sickle cell disease.

Linda Thomas, Manager
Nora Bouie-Burleson, Office Manager

5857 Sickle Cell Association of the Texas Gulf Coast
501 S. Main St.
Galena Park, TX 77547
713-921-1400
888-908-2355
Fax: 713-921-4525
mbruce@steelassociates.net
www.steelassociates.net

Michael Bruce
Zachary Kitchens
Jaime Lozano

Libraries & Resource Centers

5858 Children's Center for Cancer and Blood Disorders
University of South Carolina School of Medicine
5 Richland Memorial Park
Columbia, SC 29203
803-434-3533

Joint clinical and basic research of juvenile cancer and blood disorders.

Fauni Lowe, Manager

Research Centers

California

5859 Northern California Comprehensive Sickle Cell Center
Children's Hospital at Oakland
747 52nd St
Oakland, CA 94609
510-450-5647
evichinsky@mail.cho.org

Sickle cell disease research.

Elliott Vichinsky MD, Director

5860 University of Southern California Comprehensive Sickle Cell Center
2025 Zonal Avenue, Room 304
Los Angeles, CA 90033
323-442-1259
Fax: 323-442-1255

Cage S Johnson MD, Director

District of Columbia

5861 Howard University Center for Sickle Cell Disease
1840 7th Street NW
Washington, DC 20000
202-865-8292
Fax: 202-806-4517
www.sicklecell.howard.edu

Okay H Odocha, Director

Georgia

5862 Comprehensive Sickle Cell Center
Medical College of Georgia
1521 Pope Ave
Augusta, GA 30904
706-721-0174
Fax: 706-721-2643
www.mcg.edu/center/sicklecell/

New York

5863 Bronx Comprehensive Sickle Cell Center
Albert Einstein College of Medicine
Ullman Bldg, 1300 Morris Park Ave
Bronx, NY 10461
718-430-2088
Fax: 718-824-3153

Ronald L Nagel MD, Director

Sickle Cell Disease / Book Publishers

North Carolina

5864 **Duke University Comprehensive Sickle Cell Center**
Medical Center
Box 2615
Durham, NC 27710
919-684-5378
Fax: 919-681-7688
telen002@mc.duke.edu
www.sicklecell.mc.duke.edu

Research into sickle cell disease including molecular and organ studies.

Marilyn Telen MD, Director

Ohio

5865 **Comprehensive Sickle Cell Center**
Cincinnati Children's Hospital Medical Ctr
3333 Burnet Avenue, MLC 7015
Cincinnati, OH 45229
513-636-4200
800-344-2462
Fax: 513-636-5562
TTY: 513-636-4900
blood@cchmc.org
www.cincinnatichildrens.org

Offers research and statistical information in the area of sickle cell disease.

Russell E. Ware, MD, PhD, Director, Hematology Division
Cindi Tillman, RN, Center Contact

Texas

5866 **Center for Cancer and Blood Disorders**
Children Medical Center Dallas
1935 Medical District Dr.
Dallas, TX 75235
214-456-7000
Fax: 214-456-6133
ccbdinfo@childrens.com
www.childrens.com/ccbd/

A comprehensive program for diagnosis, patient/family education and management of sickle cell diseases in childhood and adolesance. Offers access to state-of-the art research projects and clinical management.

George R Buchanan, Medical Director
Zora R Rogers, MD, Associate Medical Director
Shirley Miller, Community Relations

5867 **Southwestern Comprehensive Sickle Cell Center**
UT Southwestern Medical Ctr/Pediatrics Dept
5323 Harry Hines Blvd
Dallas, TX 75390
214-648-3111
Fax: 214-648-3122
George.Buchanan@UTsouthwestern.edu

State-of-the-art patient care, clinical and basic lab research, education and advocacy programs.

Chen Shi, Director

Web Sites

5868 **American Sickle Cell Anemia Association**
2390 E 79th Street
Cleveland, OH 44104
216-229-8600
Fax: 216-229-4500
irabragg@ascaa.org
www.ascaa.org

The mission of the American Sickle Cell Anemia Association is to ensure the availability and accessibility of quality, comprehensive sickle cell services, and promote the public professional awareness about sickle cell anemis an it's hemoglobin diseases ad trait variants.

Ira Bragg-Grant, Executive Director

5869 **Information Center for Sickle Cell and Thalassemic Disorders**
sickle.bwh.harvard.edu

sickle.bwh.harvard.edu

Free online information to the biomedical community, health care personnel and patients. The information can be of particular help to patients in enabling them to have a fuller and more knowledgeable role in their care.

5870 **International Association of Sickle Cell Nurses and Physician Assistants**
www.iascnapa.org

www.iascnapa.org

The association is made up of over 300 sickle cell nurses and physician assistants worldwide. It recognizes its responsibility to maintain high standards in the provision of quality and accessible health care services for individuals with sickle cell disease.

Coretta Jenerette, RN, PhD, President
Pat Corley, RN, Vice-President
Bonita Conley, MSN, RN, PNP-BC, Secretary

5871 **Online Mendelian Inheritance in Man**
McKusick-Nathans Institue of Genetic Medicine-JHU
Baltimore, MD 21205
www.omim.org

This database is a catalog of human genes and genetic disorders.

Ada Hamosh, MD, Scientific Director

5872 **Sickle Cell Disease Association of America**
3700 Koppers Street, #570
Baltimore, MD 21227
410-528-1555
800-421-8453
Fax: 410-528-1495
admin@sicklecelldisease.org
www.sicklecelldisease.org

Promotes the finding of a universal cure for sickle cell disease while improving the quality of life for individuals and families where sickle cell related conditions exists.

Beverley Francis-Gibson, President & CEO
Leroy Hughes, Jr., VP, Operations
Carole Bernard, Director, Marketing/Communications

5873 **Sickle Cell Disease Forum**
www.sicklecelldisease.org/forum/

www.sicklecelldisease.org/forum/

Online forum for sickle cell disease discussion/chat sponsored by the Sickle Cell Disease Association of America.

5874 **Sickle Cell Kids**
www.sicklecellkids.org

www.sicklecellkids.org

Teaches children how to stay healthy and answers questions about sickle cell disease. A joint venture of the Georgia Comprehensive Sickle Cell Center at Grady Health System and Cynthia Gentry, artist.

Book Publishers

5875 **Blood & Circulatory Disorders Sourcebook 4th Edition**
Omnigraphics
615 Griswold Street, Ste 520
Detroit, MI 48226
610-461-3548
800-234-1340
Fax: 800-875-1340
contact@omnigraphics.com
www.omnigraphics.com

Basic consumer health information on blood and its components, anemias, leukemias, bleeding disorders, and circulatory disorders, including sickle cell disease, aplastic anemia, thrombophilia, RH disease and hemophilia.

Sickle Cell Disease / Pamphlets

664 pages 2nd Edition
ISBN: 0-780814-76-9

5876 Let's Talk About Going to the Hospital
Rosen Publishing Group's PowerKids Press
29 E 21st Street
New York, NY 10010
212-777-3017
800-237-9932
Fax: 888-436-4643
rosenpub@tribeca.ios.com
www.rosenpublishing.com

If a child has to check into the hospital, chances are he or she is already upset about being ill. Knowing how a hospital functions and what the procedures are, such as when family members can visit, will help in what is already a stressful situation. Grades K-5.

24 pages
ISBN: 0-823950-36-0

Roger Rosen, President

5877 Let's Talk About Sickle Cell Anemia
Melanie Apel Gordon, author

Rosen Publishing Group's PowerKids Press
29 E 21st Street
New York, NY 10010
212-777-3017
800-237-9932
Fax: 888-436-4643
rosenpub@tribeca.ios.com
www.rosenpublishing.com

Explains why sickle cell anemia is a disease that strikes more African Americans than any other people in the country. Describes symptoms and explains how a kid can help take care of himself during a pain crisis. Grades K-5.

24 pages
ISBN: 0-823954-17-X

Roger Rosen, President

5878 Understanding Sickle Cell Disease
Miriam Bloom PhD, author

University Press of Mississippi
3825 Ridgewood Road
Jackson, MS 39211
601-432-6205
800-737-7788
Fax: 601-432-6217
press@ihl.state.ms.us
www.upress.state.ms.us

Part of the Understanding Health and Sickness Series. For general readers, a guide to understanding a debilitating genetic disease that affects tens of thousands who are of African heritage.

128 pages Paperback
ISBN: 0-878057-45-5

Leila W. Salisbury, Director
Cynthia Foster, Administrative Assistant
Tracey Curtis, Assistant For Development

Pamphlets

5879 Sickle Cell Disease
March of Dimes Resource Center
1550 Crystal Drive, Ste 1300
Arlington, VA 22202
914-997-4488
Fax: 914-997-4763
TTY: 914-977-4764
answers@marchofdimes.org
www.marchofdimes.org

Online Fact Sheets on the condition.

Camps

5880 Camp Crescent Moon
Sickle Cell Disease Foundation of California
6133 Bristol Parkway, Suite 240
Culver City, CA 90230
310-693-0247
877-288-2873
Fax: 310-693-0266
info@scdfc.org
www.campcrescentmoon.org

A specialized camp for children with sickle cell disease between the ages of 8 and 14 in southern & central California.

Mary E Brown, Camp Director
Deborah Green, Assistant Camp Director
Cage Johnson MD, Medical Director

5881 Camp Good Days & Special Times
1332 Pittsford-Mendon Rd, P.O. Box 665
Mendon, NY 14506
585-624-5555
800-785-2135
Fax: 585-624-5799
www.campgooddays.org

Camp for children ages 8 to 17 with sickle cell anemia. The camp is dedicated to improving the quality of life for children, adults and families whose lives have been touched by cancer and other life challenges.

Gary Mervis, Chairman/ Founder
Wendy Bleier-Mervis, Executive Director
Lisa Booz, Western New York Regional Director

5882 Camp Vacamas
256 Macopin Road
West Milford, NJ
973-838-1394
Fax: 973-838-7534
www.vacamas.org

Disadvantaged children with asthma or sickle cell anemia, ages 8-16, are offered special programs in canoeing, backpacking, camping, music and leadership training. Sliding scale tuition. Year round programs for groups.

Michael Friedman, Executive Director
Philip Smith, Camp Director

Description

5883 SLEEP APNEA

Involves the following Biologic System(s):
Respiratory Disorders

Obstructive sleep apnea (OSA) is a breathing disorder that is commonly seen in the pediatric population. Specifically, it is when normal ventilation during sleep is disrupted because of upper airway obstruction. This process occurs intermittently throughout sleep and causes significant disruptions in normal sleep patterns. Although in adults this can result in excessive daytime sleepiness, children typically manifest changes in behavior or deficits in attention, thus affecting school performance.

Studies indicate that roughly 2% of children between the ages of 2-18 years are affected by this disorder. Girls and boys are equally likely to have OSA and African American children are more commonly affected than children of other ethnicities. OSA is also more common in children with obesity, craniofacial abnormalities and/or neurologic disorders. Children with Down syndrome are at especially increased risk.

The cause of obstructive sleep apnea is not well understood. Adenotonsillar (adenoids and tonsils) hypertrophy (increase in size) seems to be part of the process but even after tonsillectomy and adenoidectomy (removal of these tissues) many patients relapse, implying other processes involved.

The clinical features commonly seem with OSA include noisy breathing during sleep, prominent snoring often in a crescendo pattern that ends with a pause in respirations for performance, nocturnal enuresis (bed wetting) and frequent daytime napping. Complications of OSA can be failure to thrive or gain weight appropriately, pulmonary hypertension which cause stress on the right side of the heart and neurological sequelae.

Diagnosis should not be based solely on a history of snoring. Many children snore who do not suffer from OSA, however, a careful history focusing on some of the clinical features mentioned above should raise the suspicion of OSA and further evaluation can be considered. The physical exam of tonsillar hypertrophy may help support the diagnosis but often a polysomnography test, commonly called sleep study, is the most accurate way to diagnose OSA. The sleep study is a comprehensive diagnostic tool involving monitoring a patient during sleep using multiple parameters including the visual surveillance, monitoring of the heart rate and rhythm, monitoring of the respiratory rate, measurement of expired lung gases, oxygen saturation in the blood, chest wall rise with breathing and others. While the necessity of this study in children may be debated, it is considered a definitive way to establish the diagnosis of OSA.

In general, nonsurgical therapy is very limited for the typical patient with OSA. Treatment of childhood OSA is primarily surgical. Removal of the tonsils and adenoids are often the first line of treatment as well as targeting weight reduction when relevant. Most children respond well to tonsillectomy and adenoidectomy, but for those who do not improve, nasal continued positive airway pressure (NCPAP) is another effective option which enhances the infant's respiratory function.

OSA is an important cause of health, emotional and behavioral problems in school aged children and effective and timely treatment can significantly improve school performance, and productivity and well-being of these children.

National Associations & Support Groups

5884 American Academy of Pediatrics
345 Park Blvd
Itasca, IL 60143

847-434-4000
800-433-9016
Fax: 847-434-8000
csc@aap.org
www.aap.org

The American Academy of Pediatrics and its member pediatricians are committed to the attainment of optimal physical, mental and social health and well-being for all infants, children, adolescents, and young adults.

Kyle E. Yasuda, MD, FAAP, President
Mark Del Monte, JD, CEO/Executive VP
Vera Tait, MD, FAAP, Chief Medical Officer

5885 American Academy of Sleep Medicine
2510 N Frontage Road
Darien, IL 60561

630-737-9700
Fax: 630-737-9790
contact@aasm.org
aasm.org

As the leading voice in the sleep field, the AASM sets standards and promotes excellence in sleep medicine health care, education, and research. The AASM has a combined membership of 11,000 accredited member sleep centers and individual members, including physicians, scientists, and other health care professionals.

Steve Van Hout, Executive Director

5886 American Sleep Apnea Association
1250 Connecticut Ave NW, Ste 700
Washington, DC 20036

888-293-3650
Fax: 888-293-3650
asaa@sleepapnea.org
www.sleepapnea.org

Dedicated to reducing injury, disability and death from sleep apnea and to enhancing the well-being of those affected by this common disorder. They promote education and awareness. Network of voluntary mutual support groups, research, and continuous improvement of care.

Will Headapohl, Chair (Emeritus)
Justine Amdur, Program Coordinator, AWAKE
Valerie Danielson, Program Coordinator, CPAP

5887 Center for Disabilities and Development
University of Iowa Stead Family Children's Hospita
100 Hawkins Drive
Iowa City, IA 52242

319-353-6900
877-686-0031
Fax: 319-356-7700
cdd-scheduling@uiowa.edu
www.uichildrens.org/cdd

A trusted resource for healthcare, training, research and information for people with disabilities that include: behavior disorders, brain injury, cerebral palsy, diabetes, down syndrome, learning disabilities, sleep disorders and spina bifida.

Dianne McBrien, MD, Medical Director

5888 National Sleep Foundation
1414 NE 42nd St, Ste 400
Seattle, WA 98105

contact@sleepfoundation.org
www.sleepfoundation.org

Works to improve the quality of life for millions of Americans who suffer from sleep disorders, and to prevent the catastrophic accidents that are related to poor or disordered sleep through research, education and the dissemination of information towards the cause of the Narcolepsy Project. Seeks patients to aid new research project targeting the cause of the disorder.

Bill Fish, General Manager

Sleep Apnea / Libraries & Resource Centers

Libraries & Resource Centers

5889 **American Academy of Somnology**
PO Box 27077
Las Vegas, NV 89126
702-371-0947
somnology@aol.com
www.hopperinstitute.com/aas_intro.html

Covers about 75 physicians, dentists, nurses, psychologists, technicians, and students and sponsoring organizations, including associations, institutions, and corporations, with a special interest in sleep. Newsletter, published yearly.

David Hopper, Director

Research Centers

5890 **Sleep Disorders Center**
Beth Israel Deaconess Medical Ctr
330 Brookline Avenue
Boston, MA 02215
617-667-7000
Fax: 617-975-5506
www.bidmc.harvard.edu

Provides testing and treatment for those with sleep disorders and offers educational workshops, plus support for their families.

Jean K Matheson, MD, Division Chief

Web Sites

5891 **About.com on Sleep Disorders**
www.sleepdisorders.about.com

www.sleepdisorders.about.com

Well-organized information including new developments and a chat room.

5892 **American Academy of Sleep Medicine**
2510 N Frontage Road
Darien, IL 60561
630-737-9700
Fax: 630-737-9790
contact@aasm.org
aasm.org

As the leading voice in the sleep field, the AASM sets standards and promotes excellence in sleep medicine health care, education, and research. The AASM has a combined membership of 11,000 accredited member sleep centers and individual members, including physicians, scientists, and other health care professionals.

Steve Van Hout, Executive Director

5893 **American Sleep Apnea Association**
1250 Connecticut Ave NW, Ste 700
Washington, DC 20036
888-293-3650
Fax: 888-293-3650
asaa@sleepapnea.org
www.sleepapnea.org

Dedicated to reducing injury, disability and death from sleep apnea and to enhancing the well-being of those affected by this common disorder. They promote education and awareness. Network of voluntary mutual support groups, research, and continuous improvement of care.

Will Headapohl, Chair (Emeritus)
Justine Amdur, AWAKE Program Coordinator
Valerie Danielson, CPAP Program Coordinator

5894 **MEDLINEplus on Sleep Apnea**
8600 Rockville Pike
Bethesda, MD 20894
custserv@nlm.nih.gov
www.nlm.nih.gov/medlineplus/sleepapnea.html

Offers information about Sleep Apnea.

Dr. Donald A.B. Lindberg, Director

5895 **NIH/National Center on Sleep Disorders Research**
www.nhlbi.nih.gov/about/org/ncsdr/

www.nhlbi.nih.gov/about/org/ncsdr/

Coordinates sleep research, training and education supported by the government.

5896 **National Sleep Foundation**
1414 NE 42nd St, Ste 400
Seattle, WA 98105
www.sleepfoundation.org

Works to improve the quality of life for millions of Americans who suffer from sleep disorders, and to prevent the catastrophic accidents that are related to poor or disordered sleep through research, education and the dissemination of information towards the cause of the Narcolepsy Project. Seeks patients to aid new research project targeting the cause of the disorder.

Bill Fish, General Manager

5897 **Sleepdisorders.com**
www.sleepdisorders.com

www.sleepdisorders.com

Provides a full range of internet communications and technology solutions from strategic consulting to concept design, content development, software engineering, and ongoing enhancements and maintenance. Our projects have encompassed direct-to-consumer marketing, direct-to-patient education, healthcare professional training, corporate intranets and database management systems, dynamic database-driven websites and hospital training.

John Douglas Hudson, M.D., Medical Director

5898 **Sleepnet.com**
www.sleepnet.com/sleeapnea2000.html

www.sleepnet.com/sleeapnea2000.html

Categorizes sleep disorders for research, forums are up-dated frequently and posts are thoughtful and insightful.

Book Publishers

5899 **Concise Guide to Evaluation and Management of Sleep Disorders**
American Psychiatric Publishing
1000 Wilson Boulevard, Suite 1825
Arlington, VA 22209
703-907-7322
800-368-5777
Fax: 703-907-1091
appi@psych.org
www.appi.org

Overview of sleep disorders medicine, sleep physiology and pathology, insomnia complaints, excessive sleepiness disorders, parasomnias, medical and psychiatric disorders and sleep, medications with sedative - hypnotic properties, special problems and populations.

2002 296 pages Paper 3rd Ed
ISBN: 1-585620-45-6

Robert E. Hales, M.D., Editor-in-Chief
Rebecca D. Rinehart, Publisher
John McDuffie, Editorial Director

5900 **Let's Talk About Going to the Hospital**
Rosen Publishing Group's PowerKids Press
29 E 21st Street
New York, NY 10010
212-777-3017
800-237-9932
Fax: 888-436-4643
rosenpub@tribeca.ios.com
www.rosenpublishing.com

If a child has to check into the hospital, chances are he or she is already upset about being ill. Knowing how a hospital functions and what the procedures are, such as when family members can visit, will help in what is already a stressful situation. Grades K-5.

24 pages
ISBN: 0-823950-36-0

Roger Rosen, President

Sleep Apnea / Book Publishers

5901 Principles and Practice of Sleep Medicine
Elsevier Health Sciences Division
1600 John F Kennedy Blvd, Suite 1800
Philadelphia, PA 19103
215-239-3900
800-523-1649
Fax: 215-239-3990
www.us.elsevierhealth.com

Covers the recent advances in basic sciences as well as sleep pathology in adults. Encompasses developments in this rapidly advancing field and also includes topics related to psychiatry, circadian rhythms, cardiovascualr diseases and sleep apnea diagnosis and treatment. Hardcover.

2005 1552 pages 4th Edition
ISBN: 0-721607-97-7

5902 Restless Nights
Yale University Press
PO Box 209040
New Haven, CT 06520
203-432-0960
800-405-1619
Fax: 203-432-0948
marketing@yale.edu.
yalepress.yale.edu/yupbooks

This book provides an explanation of sleep apnea symptoms, risk-factors, advice on diagnosis and consultation, and current available treatments.

2003 288 pages
ISBN: 0-300085-44-0

John Donatich, Director

5903 Sleep Disorders Sourcebook
Omnigraphics
615 Griswold Street, Ste 520
Detroit, MI 48226
610-461-3548
800-234-1340
Fax: 800-875-1340
contact@omnigraphics.com
www.omnigraphics.com

Basic consumer health information about sleep and its disorders, including sleep apnea, insomnia, sleepwalking, restless leg syndrome and narcolepsy.

504 pages 4th Ed.
ISBN: 0-780814-74-5

5904 Sleeping Like a Baby

Avi Sadeh, author

Yale University Press
PO Box 209040
New Haven, CT 06520
203-432-0960
800-405-1619
Fax: 203-432-0948
yalepress.yale.edu/yupbooks

A practical and sensitive guide to solving your child's sleep problems.

2001 224 pages
ISBN: 0-300088-24-3

John Donatich, Director

5905 Snoring From A to Zzzz
Spencer Press
2525 NW Lovejoy Street, Suite 402
Portland, OR 97210
503-223-4959
Fax: 503-223-1608
dereklipman@aol.com

Covers organizations, associations, support groups, and manufatorers of sleep-related medical products relevant to sleep disorders. Discussess every aspect of snoring and sleep apnea from causes to cures.

256 pages Paperback
ISBN: 0-965070-81-6

Derek S Lipman, MD, Author/Editor

5906 Snoring and Sleep Apnea
Demos Medical Publishing
386 Park Avenue S
New York, NY 10016
212-683-0072
800-532-8663
Fax: 212-683-0118
orderdept@demosmedpub.com
www.demosmedpub.com

A straightforward, jargon-free approach to dealing with snoring and sleep problems.

286 pages 3rd Ed/Soft
ISBN: 1-888799-29-3

Kathy Gonzalez, Order Dept/Fulfillment Coordinator
Paul Choi, Vice-President of Finance and Opera
Richard Winters, Executive Editor

Sleepwalking / Description

Description

5907 SLEEPWALKING

Synonym: Somnambulism

Involves the following Biologic System(s):

Developmental/Behavioral/Psychiatric Disorders

Sleepwalking, also known as somnambulism, is a condition where the child engages in activities that are normally associated with wakefulness while asleep or in a sleeplike state. It occurs most commonly in children, particularly those from approximately four to six years of age. About 10 to 15 percent of children experience at least one episode of sleepwalking during childhood. In addition, approximately one in five children who sleepwalk has a family history of the condition. In many patients, sleepwalking occurs in association with bed-wetting (nocturnal enuresis) or night terrors (sleep disturbances that typically occur shortly after the onset of sleep). In some cases, a stressful event may lead to an episode of sleepwalking.

In children, sleepwalking occurs during stage four of NREM (nonrapid eye movement) sleep. NREM sleep consists of four progressively deeper stages of sleep that are typically characterized by slow, deep brain waves, muscle relaxation and slowed breathing rate, slowed heart rate, and lowered blood pressure. In contrast, REM (rapid eye movement) sleep, which is associated with dreaming, is characterized by increased levels of brain activity, rapid eye movements, and involuntary muscle jerks.

During an episode of sleepwalking, affected children may simply sit up in bed or move to the edge of the bed, without engaging in actual sleepwalking. In other cases, however, children may get out of bed and walk through their home. They may also perform certain routine acts, such as turning on a hallway light. Unless children are simultaneously experiencing night terrors, they usually do not have associated anxiety. During an episode, most children have their eyes open and are guided by their vision. Therefore, they typically move around familiar obstacles; however, some children may make no effort to avoid certain objects in their path, potentially resulting in injury. In addition, some children may mumble simple words or phrases or repeatedly perform certain acts, such as turning a doorknob back and forth. If children are urged to return to bed during such an episode, they may sometimes follow such instruction; however, they usually must be gently steered back to their beds. Sleepwalking episodes typically last only a few minutes, and children usually have little or no memory of the experience. In children, sleepwalking is rarely associated with psychologic abnormalities, and the number of episodes usually decreases by early adolescence. However, the persistence of sleepwalking episodes into adulthood is thought to be associated with a significant risk of psychiatric disease. Parents or caregivers of children who sleepwalk should take precautions to help protect them against injury. Possible obstacles or breakable objects should be removed from their paths. It may be advisable to block staircases and to have children sleep on the ground floor of the house, if possible.

Government Agencies

5908 NIH/National Institute of Mental Health
6001 Executive Blvd, Rm 6200, MSC 9663
Bethesda, MD 20892

866-615-6464
Fax: 301-443-4279
TTY: 301-443-8431
nimhinfo@nih.gov
www.nimh.nih.gov

The mission of NIMH is to transform the understanding and treatment of mental illnesses through basic and clinical research, paving the way for prevention, recovery, and cure.

Joshua A. Gordon, MD, PhD, Director
Shelli Avenevoli, PhD, Deputy Director

National Associations & Support Groups

5909 American Academy of Pediatrics
345 Park Blvd
Itasca, IL 60143

847-434-4000
800-433-9016
Fax: 847-434-8000
csc@aap.org
www.aap.org

The American Academy of Pediatrics and its member pediatricians are committed to the attainment of optimal physical, mental and social health and well-being for all infants, children, adolescents, and young adults.

Kyle E. Yasuda, MD, FAAP, President
Mark Del Monte, JD, CEO/Executive VP
Vera Tait, MD, FAAP, Chief Medical Officer

5910 American Academy of Sleep Medicine
2510 N Frontage Road
Darien, IL 60561

630-737-9700
Fax: 630-737-9790
contact@aasm.org
aasm.org

As the leading voice in the sleep field, the AASM sets standards and promotes excellence in sleep medicine health care, education, and research. The AASM has a combined membership of 11,000 accredited member sleep centers and individual members, including physicians, scientists, and other health care professionals.

Steve Van Hout, Executive Director

5911 Center for Disabilities and Development
University of Iowa Stead Family Children's Hospita
100 Hawkins Drive
Iowa City, IA 52242

319-353-6900
877-686-0031
Fax: 319-356-7700
cdd-scheduling@uiowa.edu
www.uichildrens.org/cdd

A trusted resource for healthcare, training, research and information for people with disabilities that include: behavior disorders, brain injury, cerebral palsy, diabetes, down syndrome, learning disabilities, sleep disorders and spina bifida.

Dianne McBrien, MD, Medical Director

5912 National Federation of Families
15800 Crabbs Branch Way, Wuite 300
Rockville, MD 20855

240-403-1901
ffcmh@ffcmh.org
www.ffcmh.org

The National family run organization is dedicated exclusively to helping children with mental health needs and their families achieve a better quality of life.

Lynda Gargan, PhD, Executive Director

5913 **National Mental Health Consumers' Self-Help Clearinghouse**
1211 Chestnut Street, Suite 1207
Philadelphia, PA 19107
215-751-1810
800-553-4539
Fax: 215-636-6312
selfhelpclearinghouse@gmail.com
www.mhselfhelp.org

Offers information, support and appropriate referrals; and promotes public and professional education. Provides networking for those with special interests related to albinism. Promotes and supports research and funding that will improve diagnosis and management of albinism and hypopigmentation.

Joseph Rogers, Founder/Executive Director
Susan Rogers, Director

5914 **National Sleep Foundation**
1414 NE 42nd St, Se 400
Seattle, WA 98105
contact@sleepfoundation.org
www.sleepfoundation.org

Works to improve the quality of life for millions of Americans who suffer from sleep disorders, and to prevent the catastrophic accidents that are related to poor or disordered sleep through research, education and the dissemination of information towards the cause of the Narcolepsy Project. Seeks patients to aid new research project targeting the cause of the disorder.

Bill Fish, General Manager

Libraries & Resource Centers

5915 **American Academy of Somnology**
PO Box 27077
Las Vegas, NV 89126
702-371-0947
somnology@aol.com
www.hopperinstitute.com/aas_intro.html

Covers about 75 physicians, dentists, nurses, psychologists, technicians, and students and sponsoring organizations, including associations, institutions, and corporations, with a special interest in sleep.

David Hopper, Director

Web Sites

5916 **About.com on Sleep Disorders**
www.sleepdisorders.about.com

www.sleepdisorders.about.com

Well-organized information including new developments and a chat room.

5917 **National Sleep Foundation**
1414 NE 42nd St, Ste 400
Seattle, WA 98105
contact@sleepfoundation.org
www.sleepfoundation.org

Works to improve the quality of life for millions of Americans who suffer from sleep disorders, and to prevent the catastrophic accidents that are related to poor or disordered sleep through research, education and the dissemination of information towards the cause of the Narcolepsy Project. Seeks patients to aid new research project targeting the cause of the disorder.

Bill Fish, General Manager

5918 **Online Mendelian Inheritance in Man**
McKusick-Nathans Institue of Genetic Medicine-JHU
Baltimore, MD 21205
www.omim.org

This database is a catalog of human genes and genetic disorders.

Ada Hamosh, MD, Scientific Director

5919 **Sleep Walking in Children**
familydoctor.org/160.xml

familydoctor.org/160.xml

Brief overview of possible parental concerns of sleep walking in children.

5920 **SleepEducation.com**
2510 North Frontage Road
Darien, IL 60561
630-737-9700
Fax: 630-737-9790
www.sleepeducation.com

Online resources on sleep related topics and sleep disorders including sleepwalking.

5921 **Sleepdisorders.com**
www.sleepdisorders.com

www.sleepdisorders.com

Provides a full range of internet communications and technology solutions from strategic consulting to concept design, content development, software engineering, and ongoing enhancements and maintenance. Our projects have encompassed direct-to-customer marketing, direct-to-patient education, healthcare professional training, corporate intranets and database management systems, dynamic database-driven web sites and hospital training.

John Douglas Hudson, M.D., Medical Director

Book Publishers

5922 **Concise Guide to Evaluation and Management of Sleep Disorders**
American Psychiatric Publishing
1000 Wilson Boulevard, Suite 1825
Arlington, VA 22209
703-907-7322
800-368-5777
Fax: 703-907-1091
appi@psych.org
www.appi.org

Over view of sleep disorders medicine, sleep physiology and pathology, insomnia complaints, excessive sleepiness disorders, parasomnias, medical and psychiatric disorders and sleep, medications with sedative-hypnotic properties, special problems and populations.

2002 296 pages Paper 3rd Ed
ISBN: 1-585620-45-6

Robert E. Hales, M.D., Editor-in-Chief
Rebecca D. Rinehart, Publisher
John McDuffie, Editorial Director

5923 **Sleep Disorders Sourcebook**
Omnigraphics
615 Griswold Street, Ste 520
Detroit, MI 48226
610-461-3548
800-234-1340
Fax: 800-875-1340
contact@omnigraphics.com
www.omnigraphics.com

Basic consumer health information about sleep and its disorders, including insomnia, sleepwalking, sleep apnea, restless leg syndrome and narcolepsy.

504 pages 4th Ed.
ISBN: 0-780814-74-5

5924 **Sleep: The Brazelton Way**

T Berry Brazelton; Joshua D Sparrow, author

Perseus Books Group-Da Capo Press
250 West 57th Street, 15th Floor
New York, NY 10107
617-252-5200
www.perseusbooksgroup.com

Pediatrician provide highly effective and affordable guides to lead parents through struggles of getting babies and toddlers to sleep.

2003 Paperback
ISBN: 0-738207-82-9

David Steinberger, President & CEO

5925 **Snoring From A to Zzzz**
Spencer Press
2525 NW Lovejoy Street, Suite 402
Portland, OR 97210
503-223-4959
Fax: 503-223-1608
dereklipman@aol.com

Covers organizations, associations, support groups, and manufactorers of sleep-related medical products relevant to sleep disorders. Discussess every aspect of snoring and sleep apnea from causes to cures.

256 pages Paperback
ISBN: 0-965070-81-6

Derek S Lipman, MD, Author/Editor

Description

5926 SOCIAL ANXIETY DISORDER
Synonym: Social phobia
Involves the following Biologic System(s):
Neurologic Disorders

Social Anxiety Disorder (also called social phobia) is diagnosed in individuals who are overwhelmingly anxious and excessively self-conscious in everyday social situations. Children with social anxiety disorder are usually diagnosed once they reach school age, but symptoms have been seen in children as young as two years. Symptoms include an intense, chronic fear of being watched and judged by others, and fear of doing things that will embarrass them. This fear causes anxiety for days or weeks before a dreaded situation, and may become so severe that it interferes with school and other ordinary activities, often making it difficult to make and keep friends.

Social anxiety disorder is a fear reaction to a danger that isn't actually dangerous—although the body and mind react as if the danger is real. The physical responses to fear—fast heartbeat, quick breathing actually occur as adrenaline and other chemicals prepare the body to either fight or flee the danger (fight-flight). This biological mechanism kicks in when we feel afraid, alerting us to danger so we can protect ourselves. Those with the disorder experience this response too frequently, too strongly, and in situations where it's not appropriate (dangerous). Because the physcial sensations are real, however, the danger seems real, too.

Indivduals with social anxiety disorder are often unable to do common things in front of other people, like signing a check in front of a cashier, eating or drinking in a resta urant, or using a public restroom. Most people with the disorder know they shouldn't be afraid, but can't control their fear. They usually interact easily only with their family and a few close friends. Physical symptoms often accompany the anxiety, including blushing, profuse sweating, trembling, nausea, and difficulty speaking. These symptoms increase the feeling of being watched, which intensifies the anxiety.

Like many other anxiety-based disorders, social anxiety disorder usually results from the combination of three factors: genetics; learned behaviors; and life experiences. Those who constantly receive criticism may grow to expect that reaction from everyone they meet. Children who are teased or bullied are more likely to retreat into themselves. They will be paranoid of making a mistake or disappointing someone, and be overly sensitive to criticism.

Social anxiety disorder can increase feelings of loneliness or disappointment over missed opportunities for friendship, getting the most out of school, sharing talents, and learning new skills. Some children and teens are so shy and fearful about talking to others that they exhibit selective mutism—not speaking at all to certain people (i.e. teachers or students they don't know) or in certain places (i.e. at someone else's house). These individuals have normal conversations with people and places they are comfortable with, and their selective silence is sometimes mistaken for a stuck-up attitude or rudeness. Instead, selective mutism stems from feeling uncomfortable and afraid.

Psychotherapy is a successful treatment for social anxiety disorder, and is used sometimes in combination with certain medications. A physical examination will rule out physical reasons for the symptoms being exhibited. Cognitive behavior therapy is especially useful for treating social anxiety. It teaches different ways of thinking, behaving, and reacting to situations that help reduce the feelings of anxiousness and fear. It can also help people learn and practice social skills. Sometimes anti-anxiety or anti-depressant medications are prescribed. Although safe and effective for many people, they may be risky for some, especially children, teens, and young adults. Those taking anti-depressants should be monitored closely, especially at the start of their treatment.

Family and other supportive adults are especially important to children with social anxiety disorder. It is often a supportive environment that gives those with the disorder the courage to go outside their comfort zone.

Government Agencies

5927 Center for Mental Health Services
5600 Fishers Lane
Rockville, MD 20857
240-276-1310
www.samhsa.gov

Encourages a range of programs such as systems of care to respond to the increasing number of mental, emotional, and behavioral problems among children. Supports outreach and case management programs for the thousands of Americans who are homeless and the improvement of these services.

Anita Everett, MD, Director

5928 NIH/National Institute of Mental Health
6001 Executive Blvd, Rm 6200, MSC 9663
Bethesda, MD 20892
866-615-6464
Fax: 301-443-4279
TTY: 301-443-8431
nimhinfo@nih.gov
www.nimh.nih.gov

The mission of NIMH is to transform the understanding and treatment of mental illnesses through basic and clinical research, paving the way for prevention, recovery, and cure.

Joshua A. Gordon, MD, PhD, Director
Shelli Avenevoli, PhD, Deputy Director

National Associations & Support Groups

5929 American Academy of Pediatrics
345 Park Blvd
Itasca, IL 60143
847-434-4000
800-433-9016
Fax: 847-434-8000
csc@aap.org
www.aap.org

The American Academy of Pediatrics and its member pediatricians are committed to the attainment of optimal physical, mental and social health and well-being for all infants, children, adolescents, and young adults.

Kyle E. Yasuda, MD, FAAP, President
Mark Del Monte, JD, CEO/Executive VP
Vera Tait, MD, FAAP, Chief Medical Officer

5930 American Counseling Association
PO Box 31110
Alexandria, VA 22310
800-347-6647
Fax: 800-473-2329
ACAMemberServices@counseling.org
www.counseling.org

Represents professional counselors in various practice settings, and stands ready to serve more than 55,000 members with the resources they need to make a difference. From webinars, publications, and journals to Conference education sessions and legislative action alerts, ACA is where counseling professionals turn for powerful, credible content and support.

Shawn Boynes, Chief Executive Officer

Social Anxiety Disorder / Conferences

5931 American Mental Health Foundation (AMHF)
PO Box 3
Riverdale, NY 10028
212-737-9027
elomke@americanmentalhealthfoundation.or
americanmentalhealthfoundation.org

Dedicated to the extensive and intensive research in the theories and techniques of treatment of emotional illness and to the implementation of reforms in the mental health system. Efforts have resulted in development of better and less expensive treatment methods. Findings are disseminated in English and other major languages.

Monroe W Spero, MD
Evander Lomke, Executive Director

5932 American Psychiatric Association
800 Maine Avenue SW, Suite 900
Washington, DC 20024
202-559-3900
apa@psych.org
www.psychiatry.org

It is a medical specialty society representing growing membership of more than 36,000 psychiatrists.

Saul Levin, MD, CEO & Medical Director

5933 American Psychological Association
750 First St. NE
Washington, DC 20002
202-336-5500
800-374-2721
TTY: 202-336-6123
www.apa.org

The mission is to advance the creation, communication and application of psychological knowledge to benefit society and improve people's lives.

Arthur C. Evans Jr, PhD, CEO/EVP

5934 American School Counselor Association
1101 King Street, Ste 310
Alexandria, VA 22314
703-683-2722
asca@schoolcounselor.org
www.schoolcounselor.org

The mission of ASCA is to represent professional school counselors and to promote professionalism and ethical practices.

Jill Cook, Executive Director
Amanda Fitzgerald, Assistant Deputy Executive Director
Kathleen M Rakestraw, Director of Communications

5935 Anxiety and Depression Association of Ameria
8701 Georgia Avenue, Suite 412
Silver Spring, MD 20910
240-485-1018
information@adaa.org
www.adaa.org

ADAA is a national non-profit organization dedicated to the prevention, treatment, and cure of anxiety, depression, OCD, PTSD, and related disorders and to improving the lives of all people who suffer from them through education, practice, and research.

Susan K Gurley, Executive Director
Lise Bram, Deputy Executive Director
Katie Russo, Senior Director, Operations

5936 National Anxiety Foundation
3135 Custer Drive
Lexington, KY 40517
859-281-0003
www.nationalanxietyfoundation.org

Nonprofit organization that provides education to the public and professionals about anxiety through printed and electronic media.

Stephen Cox, MD, President & Medical Director
Linda Vernon Blair, VP
C. Todd Strecker, Secretary-Treasurer

5937 National Federation of Families
15800 Crabbs Branch Way, Suite 300
Rockville, MD 20855
240-403-1901
ffcmh@ffcmh.org
www.ffcmh.org

The National family run organization is dedicated exclusively to helping children with mental health needs and their families achieve a better quality of life.

Lynda Gargan, PhD, Executive Director

5938 Selective Mutism Association
3152 Little Road, Suite 184
New Port Richey, FL 34655
www.selectivemutism.org

The Selective Mutism Association (SMA) works to increase public awareness of selective mutism and co-occurring disorders and to promote a greater understanding of these disorders by supporting research initiatives and providing educational resources. SMA provides scientific research-based support to professionals, affected individuals, and their families so that more people with SM can find their voices.

Lisa Kovac, Executive Director
Kristin Carey Leos, Director of Memberships

5939 Social Anxiety Association
socialphobia.org

The Social Anxiety Association is a non-profit organization founded in 1997 to meet the growing needs of people with social anxiety.

Thomas A. Richards, Ph.D., President

Conferences

5940 American School Counselor Association Annual Conference
1101 King Street, Suite 310
Alexandria, VA 22314
703-683-2722
800-306-4722
Fax: 703-997-7572
asca@schoolcounselor.org
www.schoolcounselor.org

The mission of ASCA is to represent professional school counselors and to promote professionalism and ethical practices.

3,000 Attendees

Richard Wong, Executive Director
Jennifer Walsh, Director, Education & Training
Kathleen M Rakestraw, Director of Communications

Audio Video

5941 Acquiring Courage: Audio Cassette Program for the Rapid Treatment of Phobias
New Harbinger Publications
5674 Shattuck Avenue
Oakland, CA 94609
510-652-2002
800-748-6273
Fax: 800-652-1613
customerservice@newharbinger.com
newharbinger.com

ISBN: 1-879237-03-2

5942 Anxiety Disorders
American Counseling Association
6101 Stevenson Ave, Suite 600
Alexandria, VA 22304
703-823-9800
800-347-6647
Fax: 800-473-2329
webmaster@counseling.org
counseling.org

Increase your awareness of anxiety disorders, their symptoms, and effective treatments. Learn the effect these disorders can have on life and how treatment can change the quality of life for people presently suffering from these disorders. Includes 6 audiotapes and a study guide.

Robert L. Smith, President

Social Anxiety Disorder / Pamphlets

Book Publishers

5943 Anxiety & Phobia Workbook
Edmund J Bourne, author
New Harbinger Publications
5674 Shattuck Avenue
Oakland, CA 94609
510-652-2002
800-748-6273
Fax: 510-652-5472
TTY: 800-652-1613
customerservice@newharbinger.com
www.newharbinger.com

This comprehensive guide is recommended to those struggling with anxiety disorders. Includes step-by-step instructions for the crucial cognitive-behavioral techniques that have given real help to hundreds of thousands of readers struggling with anxiety disorders.

448 pages 4th Edition
ISBN: 1-572244-13-5

5944 Anxiety Cure: An Eight-Step Program for Getting Well
John Wiley & Sons
10475 Crosspoint Boulevard
Indianapolis, IN 46256
877-762-2974
Fax: 800-597-3299
www.wiley.com

A practical guide, written by a father and his two daughters, featuring a step-by-step program for curing the six main kinds of anxiety.

272 pages 2nd Edition
ISBN: 0-471464-87-2

Peter B. Wiley, Chairman
Stephen M. Smith, President & CEO
Ellis E. Cousens, Executive Vice President, Chief Fin

5945 Anxiety Disorders
Cambridge University Press
40 W 20th Street
New York, NY 10011
212-924-3900
800-872-7423
Fax: 914-937-4712
marketing@cup.org
cup.org

This comprehensive text covers all the anxiety disorders found in the latest DSM and ICD classifications. Provides detailed information about seven principal disorders, including anxiety in the medically ill. For each disorder, the book covers diagnosis criteria, epidemiology, etiology and pathogenesis, clinical features, natural history and different diagnoses. Describes treatment approaches, both psychological and pharmacological.

354 pages

5946 Anxiety Disorders: Practioner's Guide
John Wiley & Sons
111 River Street
Hoboken, NJ 7030-
212-850-6000
Fax: 212-850-6008
info@wiley.com
wiley.com

210 pages
ISBN: 0-471931-12-8

Stephen M. Smith, President/ CEO
John Kritzmacher, EVP/ CFO
MJ O'Leary, EVO, Human Resources

5947 Encyclopedia of Phobias, Fears, and Anxieties
Facts on File
11 Penn Plaza, Room M274
New York, NY 10001
212-290-8090
800-322-8755

500 pages

5948 Helping Your Anxious Child
New Harbinger Publications
5674 Shattuck Avenue
Oakland, CA 94609
510-652-2002
800-748-6273
Fax: 510-652-5472
TTY: 800-652-1613
customerservice@newharbinger.com
www.newharbinger.com

Step-by-step guide for parents of anxious children to help them overcome their fears and anxieties. Detailed strategies and techniques.

168 pages Paperback
ISBN: 1-572241-91-8

5949 Psychological Trauma
American Psychiatric Press
1400 K Street, NW
Washington, DC 20005
202-682-6262
800-368-5777
Fax: 202-789-2648
www.appi.org

Epidemiology of trauma and post-tramatic stress disorder. Evaluation, neuroimaging, neuroendocrinology and pharmacology.

1998 206 pages

Robert E. Hales M.D, Editor-in-Chief
Rebecca D. Rinehart, Publisher
John McDuffie, Editorial Director

5950 Shy Children, Phobic Adults: Nature and Treatment of Social Phobia
American Psychological Press
1400 K Street, NW
Washington, DC 20005
202-682-6262
800-368-5777
Fax: 202-789-2648
www.appi.org

Describes the simularities and differences in the syndrome across all ages. Draws from the clinical, social and developmental literatures, as well as from extensive clinical experience. Illustrates the impact of developmental stage on phenomenology, diagnosis and assessment and treatment of social phobia.

1998 321 pages

Robert E. Hales M.D, Editor-in-Chief
Rebecca D. Rinehart, Publisher
John McDuffie, Editorial Director

Pamphlets

5951 Anxiety Disorders
National Institute of Mental Health
6001 Executive Boulevard, Room 6200, MSC 9663
Bethesda, MD 20892
301-443-4536
866-615-6464
Fax: 301-443-4279
TTY: 301-443-8431
NIMHpress@mail.nih.gov
www.nimh.nih.gov

This brochure helps to identify the symptoms of anxiety disorders, explains the role of research in understanding the causes of these conditions, describes effective treatments, helps you learn how to obtain treatment and work with a doctor or therapist, and suggests ways to make treatment more effective.

5952 Anxiety Disorders Fact Sheet
Center for Mental Health Services
PO Box 42490
Washington, DC 20015
800-789-2647
Fax: 301-984-8796
ken@mentalhealth.org
mentalhealth.org

This fact sheet presents basic information on the symptoms, formal diagnosis, and treatment for generalized anxiety disorder, panic disorders, phobias, and post traumatic stress disorder.

Social Anxiety Disorder / Pamphlets

3 pages

5953 Anxiety Disorders in Children and Adolescents
Center for Mental Health Services
PO Box 42490
Washington, DC 20015

800-789-2647
Fax: 301-984-8796
ken@mentalhealth.org
mentalhealth.org

This fact sheet defines anxiety disorders, identifies warning signs, discusses risk factors, describes types of help available, and suggests what parents or other caregivers can do.

3 pages

5954 Families Can Help Children Cope with Fear, Anxiety
Center for Mental Health Services
PO Box 42490
Washington, DC 20015

800-789-2647
Fax: 301-984-8796
ken@mentalhealth.org
mentalhealth.org

This fact sheet defines conduct disorder, identifies risk factors, discusses types of help available, and suggests what parents or other caregivers responses should be to common signs of fear and anxiety.

Speech Impairment / National Associations & Support Groups

Description

5955 SPEECH IMPAIRMENT
Synonym: Speech dysfunction
Involves the following Biologic System(s):
Neurologic Disorders

Speech impairment refers to the decreased ability or inability to effectively communicate through vocalizations or uttered sounds. Difficulty speaking or more profound dysfunctions of speech may result from many different factors that include neurologic influences; muscular defects, injuries, or paralysis; structural irregularities of the vocal cords; psychologic influences; intellectual disabilities; and other factors.

In some children, speech impairment may be classified as a dysfunction of articulation characterized by the inability to articulate or produce words properly (dysarthria) as a result of damage to the part of the brain responsible for regulation of the muscles that control the speech apparatus (e.g., mouth, lips, and voice box or larynx). Such damage may result from head or brain injuries, tumors, strokes, and certain diseases. Characteristic speech patterns of children with dysarthria are varied and may be described as unintelligible, slow, slurred, halting, tremulous, hoarse, or possessing a nasal quality. Additional causes of articulation dysfunction or delay include structural defects such as cleft lip or palate, hearing impairment or deafness, and other nervous system irregularities. In addition, speech impairment may result from irregularities directly related to the vocal cords that may affect the quality of the voice.

Impaired ability to communicate (aphasia or dysphasia) may also result from injury to the part of the brain responsible for language comprehension, resulting in the reduced ability or inability to express, write, or understand language. Such injury may be caused by head trauma, brain lesions, infection, or other factors. This type of impairment may be present in many different variations such as garbled sentences, extremely slow and difficult speech, absence of speech (mutism), and other irregularities. In addition, children with behavioral, emotional, or psychologic irregularities as well as those with hearing impairment may also experience delays in language comprehension and development.

It is important to identify the underlying cause of any dysfunction of speech or delay in speech development in order to allow for the most favorable educational and social outcome. Specialists in the diagnosis and treatment of these types of disorders (e.g., otolaryngologists and speech therapists) may base their treatment plans on the evaluation of family and medical histories, physical examination of essential speech structures, and specialized testing that may include speech, language, and hearing assessments. Treatment is directed toward the specific cause of impairment and may include exercises tailored to the specific patient's needs, as well as the cooperation of parents or caregivers, pediatricians, educators, and others to provide a supportive environment.

Government Agencies

5956 NIH/National Institute on Deafness and Other Communication Disorders (NIDCD)
31 Center Drive, MSC 2320
Bethesda, MD 20892

800-241-1044
TTY: 800-241-1055
nidcdinfo@nidcd.nih.gov
www.nidcd.nih.gov

Conducts and supports biomedical research and research training on normal mechanisms, as well as diseases and disorders of hearing, balance, smell, taste, voice, speech and language.

Debara L. Tucci, MD, Director
Judith A. Cooper, PhD, Deputy Director
Timothy J. Wheeles, Executive Officer

National Associations & Support Groups

5957 American Academy of Pediatrics
345 Park Blvd
Itasca, IL 60143

847-434-4000
800-433-9016
Fax: 847-434-8000
csc@aap.org
www.aap.org

The American Academy of Pediatrics and its member pediatricians are committed to the attainment of optimal physical, mental and social health and well-being for all infants, children, adolescents, and young adults.

Kyle E. Yasuda, MD, FAAP, President
Mark Del Monte, JD, CEO/Executive VP
Vera Tait, MD, FAAP, Chief Medical Officer

5958 American Board of Fluency and Fluency Disorders
563 Carter Court, Suite B
Kimberly, WI 54136

920-750-7720
Fax: 920-882-3655
info@stutteringspecialists.org
www.stutteringspecialists.org

The mission is to promote among speech-language pathologists the highest standards for training and service delivery to impact positively the communication skills and thereby the lives of those who demonstrate fluency disorders.

5959 American Laryngological Association
PO Box 941
Antioch, TN 37013

615-812-6170
www.alahns.org

Founded in 1878, the ALA is a scholarly organization of physicians and scientists who have made significant contributions to the care of patients with disorders of the larynx and upper aerodigestive tract. The ALA recognizes the accomplishments of these individuals through membership, seeks to encourage research in laryngology and elevate the standards of the fundamental teaching of laryngology in medical schools and postgraduate medical education.

Maxine Cunningham, Administrator

5960 American School Counselor Association
1101 King Street, Ste 310
Alexandria, VA 22314

703-683-2722
asca@schoolcounselor.org
www.schoolcounselor.org

The mission of ASCA is to represent professional school counselors and to promote professionalism and ethical practices.

Jill Cook, Executive Director
Amanda Fitzgerald, Assistant Deputy Executive Director
Kathleen M Rakestraw, Director of Communications

5961 American Speech Language Hearing Association (ASHA)
2200 Research Blvd
Rockville, MD 20852

301-296-5700
800-638-8255
Fax: 301-296-8580
pr@asha.org
www.asha.org

A professional and credentialing association made up of more than 123,000 international pathologists, audiologists and scientists. The association promotes the interests of and provides services for those in the hearing, speech, and language field, and advocates for people with communication disorders.

Shari B. Robertson, President
Theresa H. Rodgers, President-Elect

Speech Impairment / National Associations & Support Groups

5962 Apraxia Kids
1501 Reedsdale Street, Suite 202
Pittsburgh, PA 15233
412-785-7072
info@apraxia-kids.org
apraxia-kids.org

Apraxia Kids is the leading nonprofit that strengthens the support systems in the lives of children with apraxia of speech.

Angela Grimm, Executive Director

5963 Association for Research in Otolaryngology
5034A Thoroughbred Lane
Brentwood, TN 37027
615-432-0100
headquarters@aro.org
www.aro.org

ARO Midwinter Meetings bring together over 1500 investigators from around the world to present current results in hearing, vestibular function, and related fields, as well as representatives of funding agencies, publishers, and scientific vendors.

5964 Association of Academic Physiatrists
10461 Mill Run Circle, Suite 730
Owings Mills, MD 21117
410-654-1000
Fax: 410-654-1001
aap@physiatry.org
www.physiatry.org

The Association of Academic Physiatrists (AAP) is the only academic association dedicated to the specialty of physical medicine and rehabilitation (PM&R) in the world. AAP is a community of leading physicians, researchers, in-training physiatrists, and others involved or interested in leadership, mentorship, and discovery in PM&R.

Tiffany Knowlton, JD, MBA, Executive Director
Bernadette M. Rensing, External Affairs Manager
Amy Schnappinger, Member Services Manager

5965 Association of University Centers on Disabilities
1100 Wayne Ave., Suite 1000
Silver Spring, MD 20910
301-588-8252
Fax: 301-588-2842
aucdinfo@aucd.org
www.aucd.org

The Association of University Centers on Disabilities (AUCD) is a membership organization that supports and promotes a national network of university-based interdisciplinary programs.

John Tschida, Executive Director
Jeannette Cordova, Program Manager
Chevelle Glymph, Senior Director of Public Health

5966 Center for Parent Information and Resources (CPIR)
35 Halsey Street, 4th Floor
Newark, NJ 07102
973-642-8100
malizo@spanadvocacy.org
www.parentcenterhub.org

Family-friendly information and research-based materials on key topics for Parent Centers. Private workspaces for Parent Centers to exchange resources, discuss high-priority topics, and solve mutual challenges. Coordination of parent training efforts throughout the network.

Myriam Alizo, Project Assistant

5967 Child Neurology Foundation
601 W Short Street
Lexington, KY 40508
888-417-3435
info@childneurologyfoundation.org
childneurologyfoundation.org

The Child Neurology Foundation connects partners from all areas of the child neurology community so those navigating the journey of disease diagnosis, management, and care have the ongoing support from those dedicated to treatments and cures.

Amy Brin, Executive Director
Katie Hentges, Director, Programs
Brea McCormley, Director, Development

5968 Council of Academic Programs in Communication
5490 Parmalee Gulch Road
Indian Hills, CO 80454
303-835-9089
admin@capcsd.org
www.capcsd.org

CAPCSD is dedicated to promoting academic excellence, visionary leadership and collaboration among communication sciences and disorders academic programs.

Deborah Ortiz, Executive Director
Michelle Reyes, Membership Manager

5969 Dysphonia International
300 Park Boulevard, Suite 175
Itasca, IL 60143
630-250-4504
800-272-4622
voice@dysphonia.org
www.dysphonia.org

The Dysphonia International, formerly the National Spasmodic Dysphonia Association is a nonprofit 501c(3) organization dedicated to improving the lives of people affected by spasmodic dysphonia and related voice conditions through research, education, awareness and support.

Kimberly Kuman, Executive Director

5970 Educational Audiology Association
24123 Peachland Boulevard, Suite C4 #349
Port Charlotte, FL 33954
800-460-7322
admin@edaud.org
edaud.org

The Educational Audiology Association is an international organization of audiologists and related professionals who deliver a full spectrum of hearing services to all children, particularly those in educational settings.

Krista Yuskow, AuD, President
Cassie Thomas, AuD, F-AAA, Vice President of Publications
Kathleen Riley, AuD, CCC-A, F-AAA, Vice President of Advocacy

5971 National Aphasia Association
PO Box 87
Scarsdale, NY 10583
naa@aphasia.org
www.aphasia.org

The National Aphasia Association (NAA) is a non-profit organization founded in 1987 by Martha Taylor Sarno, MA, MD,(hon) as the 1st National organization dedicated to advocating for persons with aphasia and their families. Several of our board members, including the President, are people with Aphasia or family members.

5972 National Black Association for Speech-Language and Hearing
701 Exposition Place, Suite 206
Raleigh, NC 27615
919-661-0820
nbaslh@nbaslh.org
www.nbaslh.org

The Association was incorporated in Washington D.C., June 30, 1978. The committee wanted to establish a viable mechanism through which the professional needs of the Black professionals, students, and the communicatively handicapped community could be met.

5973 The Cherab Foundation
2301 NE Savannah Road, Suite 1771
Jensen Beach, FL 34957
772-335-5135
cherabfoundation.org

The Cherab Foundation is a worldwide nonprofit organization working to improve the communication skills, education, and advocacy of children on the neurological spectrum; with an emphasis on autism and verbal apraxia, a severe, neurologically-based communication disorder that used to be rare in pediatrics but has been on the rise within the past two decades.

Lisa Geng, President & Founder

5974 Voice Foundation (The)
219 N. Broad Street, 10th Floor
Philadelphia, PA 19107
215-735-7999
voicefoundation.org

The Voice Foundation was founded in 1969 by the internationally celebrated voice specialist Wilbur James Gould, M.D.. At that time interdisciplinary care of the human voice was non-existent. Dr. Gould's groundbreaking foresight brought together physicians, scientists, speech-language pathologists, performers, and teachers to share their knowledge and expertise in the care of the professional voice user.

Robert Thayer Sataloff, Chairman
Stuart Orsher, MD, President
Michael S. Benninger, MD, Vice President

Speech Impairment / State Agencies & Support Groups

5975 **Voice Health Institute**
1 Bowdoin Square, 11th Floor
Boston, MA 02114
617-720-5000
Fax: 617-720-5001
info@voicehealth.org
www.voicehealth.org

Since its inception and qualification as a federally-approved non-profit public charity (501-C-3), the VHI has funded educational and award-wining pioneering research programs.

Julie Andrews, Honorary Chair
John E. Lichtenstein, President

State Agencies & Support Groups

New York

5976 **Brooklyn College Speech and Hearing Center**
2900 Bedford Ave, 4400 Boylan Hall
Brooklyn, NY 11210
718-951-5186
Fax: 718-951-4363
mbergen@brooklyn.cuny.edu
www.brooklyn.cuny.edu/bc/spot.ite/news/110804.htm

Provides diagnostic and rehabilitative services to children and adults with speech, language, hearing and voice impairments.

Christopher Kimmich, President
Susan Bohne, Assistant Director

North Carolina

5977 **North Carolina Speech, Hearing and Language Association**
PO Box 28359
Raleigh, NC 27611
919-833-3984
Fax: 919-832-0445
info@ncshla.org
www.ncshla.org

Promotes the professional practice of speech, language and hearing sciences and works to enhance the lives of those who are communicatively impaired, through a variety of programs and opportunities.

Louise Raleigh, President
Tracie Rice, President-Elect
Kathleen Cox, Ph.D., CCC-SLP, Past President

Ohio

5978 **Cleveland Hearing and Speech Center**
11635 Euclid Avenue
Cleveland, OH 44106
216-231-0787
Fax: 216-795-2135
www.chsc.org

A nonprofit organization in Northeast Ohio dedicated to serving the needs of those with special communication needs.

Hilary Beatrez, Director of Finance and Administrat
Susan M. Bungard, CCDHH Program Director
Michelle L. Burnett, Director of Clinical Services

5979 **Speech and Hearing Clinic**
Kent State University
A104 Music & Speech Bldg, PO Box 5190
Kent, OH 44242
330-672-2672
Fax: 330-672-2643
www.kent.edu/spa

Services provided include: full-service clinic diagnoses, therapy, treatment and hearing aid repair.

Lynn Rowan, Executive Director

Oklahoma

5980 **Oklahoma Speech Language Hearing Association**
1741 S Cleveland Ave, Suite 301
Sioux Falls, SD 57103
405-802-1630
Fax: 405-271-3360
office@oslha.org
www.oslha.org

Deborah Earley, President
Sarah Baker, President Elect
Tracy Grammer, Past President

Oregon

5981 **Reading and Speech Clinic**
Unit 9
Bend, OR 97701
541-389-3302
800-283-0818
www.readingandspeechclinic.com

Provides alternate therapies for improving speech, language, spelling and reading difficulties.

Ellen Jacobs PhD, Director

Tennessee

5982 **Memphis State University, Center for the Communicatively Impaired**
807 Jefferson Avenue
Memphis, TN 38105
901-678-2009
Fax: 901-525-1282
www.memphis.edu/csd/crisci.htm

Offers research into hearing loss, deafness, and speech impairments.

Maurice I Mendel, Director

Texas

5983 **Callier Center for Communication Disorders**
University of Texas at Dallas
1966 Inwood Road
Dallas, TX 75235
214-905-3000
Fax: 214-905-3022
TDD: 214-905-3012
barbara.ember@utdallas.edu
www.callier.utdallas.edu

Multidisciplinary center serving infants through adults with all types of communication disorders: diagnostic and treatment; hearing aid services; cochlear implant evaluation and follow-up; N Texas Cochlear Implant Summer Listening Camp; aural rehabilitation services; assistive listening device program; tinnitus and hyperacusis clinic; speech-language pathology and psychological diagnostic and therapy services; research.

Thomas Campbell, Executive Director
Christine A Dollaghan, Child Language Development
Robert Stillman PhD, Communication Disorders

Washington

5984 **Scottish Rite Centers for Childhood Language Disorders**
2800 16th Street, NW
Washington, DC 20009
202-232-8155
Fax: 202-483-8169
www.dcsr.org/clinic.php

Association offering speech-language evaluations and treatment, hearing screening and consultation and referrals to children ages birth to 18 years with hearing or speech disorders. Seven locations/clinincs are offered throughout the state of Washington.

Tommie L. Robinson, Jr., Ph.D, Director

Speech Impairment / Research Centers

5985 **University of Washington Department of Speech & Hearing Sciences**
1417 NE 42nd Street
Seattle, WA 98105
206-685-7400
Fax: 206-543-1093
www.depts.washington.edu/sphsc/

Committed to understanding the basic processes and mechanisms involved in human speech, hearing, language, their disorders and to improving the quality of life for individuals affected by communication disorders across the life span.

Stacy Betz, Child Language Disorders

Research Centers

Arizona

5986 **National Center for Neurogenic Communication Disorders**
University of Arizona
Speech & Hearing Sciences Bldg, Rm 500
Tucson, AZ 85721
520-621-1472
cnet.shs.arizona.edu

The center is supported by a grant from the NIDCD, a National Institute of Health, and is staffed by scientists, educators and students who are concerned with speech and language disorders caused by diseases of the nervous system.

Thomas J Hixon PhD, Director
Kathryn A Bayles PhD, Associate Director

Colorado

5987 **Speech, Language, and Hearing Center**
University of Colorado, Boulder
2501 Kittregde Loop Rd
Boulder, CO 80309
303-492-5375
slhs.colorado.edu/clinical-services?

Focuses on communication disorders including speech and hearing impairments.

Susan M Moore, Director

Michigan

5988 **University Center for the Development of Language & Literacy**
University of Michigan
1111 E Catherine Street
Ann Arbor, MI 48109
734-764-8440
Fax: 734-647-2489
www.languageexperts.org/research/

Focuses on communicative disorders including hearing impairments and speech disorders. Provides intensive language intervention for adults with aphasia as well as children with language disorders. Clinic offers residential program for adults and school liason for children.

Carol C. Persad, PhD., ABPP, Director of the University Center f
Mimi Block, MS, CCC-SLP, Clinical Services Manager

Nebraska

5989 **Boys Town National Research Hospital**
555 N 30th Street
Omaha, NE 68131
402-498-6511
Fax: 402-498-6638
TTY: 402-498-6543
www.boystownhospital.org

An internationally recognized center for state-of-the-art research, diagnosis, treatment of patients with ear diseases, hearing and balance disorders, cleft lip and palate, and speech/language problems.

Patrick E Brookhouser, President

Nevada

5990 **University of Nevada - Department of Speech-Language Pathology**
School of Medicine
Redfield Bldg, MS 152
Reno, NV 89557
775-784-4887
Fax: 775-784-4095
lgoldberg@medicine.nevada.edu
www.medicine.nevada.edu/spa/

The department includes an active clinic and nine faculty for research in language, speech and hearing.

Thomas Watterson, Chair
Leslie Goldberg, Clinical Director

New York

5991 **Henry Youngerman Center for Communication Disorders**
SUNY Fredonia/Dept of Comm Disorders/Sciences
Thompson Hall W123
Fredonia, NY 14063
716-673-3202
Fax: 716-673-3235

Studies communications disorders including hearing and speech. It features a newly constructed research labs and an in-house clinic that serves as a training ground for graduate clinicians. The clinic provides speech/language and hearing services to members of the college, student, and local community.

Melissa A Sidor MS, CCC/SLP Clinic Director
Dr Kim Tillery PhD, CCC/Aud-Chair, Professor

North Carolina

5992 **Communications Disorders Clinic**
Reich College of Education
400 University Hall Drive, PO Box 32041
Boone, NC 28608
828-262-2185
Fax: 828-262-6766
www.cdclinic.appstate.edu

The clinic provides prevention, assessment, and treatment of speech, language and hearing disorders for all ages. It also provides several outreach programs.

Mary Ruth Sizer, Director

Washington

5993 **University of Washington Speech and Hearing Clinic**
1417 N.E. 42nd St
Seattle, WA 98105
206-685-7400
Fax: 206-616-1185
shclinic@u.washington.edu
depts.washington.edu/sphsc/

A center for education and research serving speech, language, and hearing needs within the university and the community. Serves as a teaching facility in the fields of speech-language pathology and audiology, with state of the art technology, innovative diagnostic and treatment methods, and internationally and nationally recognized areas of research.

Nancy Alarcon MS, CCC-SLP, Director
Joan Hanson, Manager

Wisconsin

5994 **Waisman Center - Auditory Physiology Research Laboratory**
University of Wisconsin, Madison
1500 Highland Ave
Madison, WI 53705
608-263-1656
www.physiology.wisc.edu/brugge/bruggelab.html?

The research laboratory is part of the Waisman Center which is dedicated to advancing the knowledge about human development, developmental disabilities, and neurodegenerative disorders.

James S Malter, Director

Conferences

5995 American School Counselor Association Annual Conference
1101 King Street, Suite 310
Alexandria, VA 22314
703-683-2722
800-306-4722
Fax: 703-997-7572
asca@schoolcounselor.org
www.schoolcounselor.org

The mission of ASCA is to represent professional school counselors and to promote professionalism and ethical practices.

3,000 Attendees

Richard Wong, Executive Director
Jennifer Walsh, Director, Education & Training
Kathleen M Rakestraw, Director of Communications

Web Sites

5996 Parent Pals
parentpals.com/gossamer/pages/Speech_and_Language

parentpals.com/gossamer/pages/Speech_and_Language

Their goal is to provide special education and gifted information, continuing education, support, weekly tips, games, book resources, and news and views for parents and professionals.

Book Publishers

5997 Listen Little Star
Auditory-Verbal Learning Institute
7205 North Habana Ave
Tampa, FL 33614
813-227-8766
Fax: 813-932-9583
info@avli.org
www.avli.org

A family activity kit for parents designed to help their babies develop listening and speaking skills. It includes 12 activities, a workbook, checklist, plush toy, and note-taking section.

5998 Management of Motor Speech Disorders in Children and Adults
Pro-Ed
8700 Shoal Creek Boulevard
Austin, TX 78757
512-451-3246
800-897-3202
Fax: 800-397-7633
general@proedinc.com
www.proedinc.com

Second edition of this popular text incorporates information about both dysarthria and apraxia of speech in children and adults and reviews techniques for physical and motor speech examination and treatment techniques.

618 pages Hardcover
ISBN: 0-890797-84-6

5999 Preschool Motor Speech Evaluation & Intervention
Pro-Ed
8700 Shoal Creek Boulevard
Austin, TX 78757
512-451-3246
800-897-3202
Fax: 800-397-7633
general@proedinc.com
www.proedinc.com

Comprehensive resource manual for evaluating and treating oral motor and motor speech disorders in children 18 months to six years of age.

Journals

6000 American Journal of Speech-Language Pathology
American Speech Language Hearing Association
2200 Research Blvd
Rockville, MD 20850
301-296-5700
800-478-2071
Fax: 301-296-8580
TTY: 301-296-5650
TDD: 301-296-5650
www.asha.org

Pertains to all aspects of clinical practice in speech-language pathology.

Quarterly

Julie Barkmeier-Kraemer, Editor in Chief

6001 Communication Disorders Quarterly
Hammill Institute on Disabilities/Sage Publication
2455 Teller Road
Thousand Oaks, CA 91320
800-818-7243
Fax: 800-583-2665
journals@sagepub.com
www.sagepub.com

Presents cutting-edge information on typical and atypical communication disorders across the continuum-from oral language development to literacy. CDQ is the official journal of the Division for Communicaative Disabilities and Deafness of the CEC. ISSN: Print: 1525-722; Electronic: 1538-4837; Subscriptions available: Institutional - Print Only $141, Insitutional - Print & E-access $144, Personal $57.

Quarterly
ISSN: 1528-7401

Judy K Montgomery, PhD, Editor

6002 Journal of Speech, Language, and Hearing Research
American Speech Language Hearing Association
2200 Research Blvd
Rockville, MD 20850
301-296-5700
800-478-2071
Fax: 301-296-8580
TTY: 301-296-5650
TDD: 301-296-5650
www.asha.org

Pertains broadly to studies of the processes and disorders of hearing, language, and speech and to the diagnosis and treatment of such disorders.

Bi-monthly

Bharath Chandrasekaran, Editor in Chief, Speech
Sean Richmond, Editor in Chief, Language
Frederick Gallun, Editor in Chief, Hearing

6003 Language, Speech, and Hearing in Schools
American Speech Language Hearing Association
2200 Research Blvd
Rockville, MD 20850
301-296-5700
800-478-2071
Fax: 301-296-8580
TTY: 301-296-5650
TDD: 301-296-5650
www.asha.org

An archival journal for research and practice in educational settings. Publishes studies and articles that pertain to speech, language, and hearing disorders and differences in children and adolescents, as well as to professional issues affecting service delivery in educational settings.

Quarterly

Dr Kenn Apel, Editor

Newsletters

6004 Callier Communications
Callier Center - University of Texas at Dallas
1966 Inwood Road
Dallas, TX 75235
214-905-3000
Fax: 214-905-3022
TDD: 214-905-3012
www.callier.utdallas.edu

Speech Impairment / Camps

W. Bennett Cullum, President
Jodelle Oakley, MS, Director, Education Division
Jan Lougeay, MA, CCC/SLP, Director of Clinical Education

6005 Communique
NCSHLA Publications
PO Box 28359
Raleigh, NC 27611

919-833-3984
Fax: 919-832-0445
info@ncshla.org
www.ncshla.org

The official newsletter of NCSHLA.

Quarterly

G Peyton Maynard, Executive VP
AJ Jacques, Executive Secretary
Cindy Davis Ling, President

Camps

6006 Central Michigan University Summer Clinics
444 Moore
Mount Pleasant, MI

517-774-3803

Designed for children, ages 6 and up, with speech, language and hearing disorders who can benefit from intensive clinical work. A wide range of recreational and social activities form part of the clinical program and promote the social use of skills learned in class.

6007 Meadowood Springs Speech and Hearing Camp
PO Box 1025
Pendleton, OR 97801

541-276-2752
Fax: 541-276-7227
info@meadowoodsprings.org
www.meadowoodsprings.org

On 143 acres in the Blue Mountains of Eastern Oregon, this camp is designed to help young people who have diagnosed clinical disorders of speech, hearing or language. A full range of activities in recreational and clinical areas is available. For cabin reservations 541-566-2191.

Rosemarie Atfield, Executive Director
Marie Story, Camp Manager
Cliff Story, Camp Manager

6008 University of Iowa - Wendell Johnson Speech and Hearing Clinic
Wendell Johnson Speech And Hearing Center
Iowa City, IA 52242

319-335-8718
Fax: 319-335-8851
speech-path-aud@uiowa.edu
clas.uiowa.edu/comsci/

The clinic offers assessment and remediation for disordered communication in adults and children. The clinic also offers an Intensive Summer Residential Clinic for school age children needing intervention services because of speech, language, hearing and/or reading problems.

Ruth Bentler, Professor / Department Chair
Dorothy Albright, Secretary
Vicki Jennings, Secretary

Description

6009 SPINA BIFIDA

Covers these related disorders: Encephalocele, Meningocele, Myelocele (Myelomeningocele, Meningomyelocele), Spina bifida occulta

Involves the following Biologic System(s):
Neurologic Disorders, Orthopedic and Muscle Disorders

Spina bifida, literally meaning "cleft spine," is a congenital abnormality, known as a neural tube defect, which is characterized by the failure during embryonic development of one or more of the developing vertebrae to develop completely or fuse. This frequently results in the exposure of part of the spinal cord. It is the most common neural tube defect in the United States—affecting 1,500 to 2,000 of the more than 4 million babies born in the country each year. Spina bifida occulta, the most common and least severe form of this defect, is characterized by a dimpling, dark tufts of hair, spider-like fine lines (telangiectasia), or a benign fatty tumor (lipoma) on the lower back or lumbosacral area. There is no protrusion or exposure of the spinal cord and it rarely involves problems with the nervous system. Some affected children, however, may experience weakness in the legs and feet and difficulty in bladder and bowel control resulting from an adhesion of the spinal cord to the area of the abnormality.

Meningocele occurs when the three membranes surrounding the spinal cord (meninges) protrude through the vertebral defect. Most meningoceles are covered by skin and contain cerebrospinal fluid. Although most affected children have no apparent neurologic involvement, some children may experience nerve dysfunction and associated irregularities (e.g., tethered spinal cord, diastematomyelia, and syringomyelia). If cerebrospinal fluid is leaking from the meningocele, immediate surgery is usually required to avoid infection or inflammation of the meninges (meningitis). Surgery to correct the meningocele may be performed at a later date in those children who are not at risk for such infection.

Myelocele is a severe form of spina bifida that affects one in 1,000 newborns. This form of the disorder is characterized by a protrusion of the spinal cord and meninges through the vertebral canal, covered by a raw swelling. Most myeloceles are located in the lumbosacral region. This abnormality may result in impaired function of the skeletal system, the skin, the genitourinary tract, and the peripheral and central nervous systems. Physical findings associated with myelocele are widely variable and depend upon the portion of the spinal cord affected and may include the inability to control the bladder and bowel functions, lack of muscle tone in the legs, and other irregularities of the lower extremities. Some children with myelocele develop an unusual accumulation of cerebrospinal fluid in the skull, resulting in enlargement of the head (hydrocephalus) and associated symptoms that may include choking and difficulty in feeding and breathing. The insertion of a tube or shunt is often indicated to relieve fluid buildup. Treatment of myelocele often involves a team of medical specialists working closely to manage care for the affected child. This care usually involves surgery to repair the myelocele. Other approaches to treatment are geared toward correction, alleviation, or management of symptoms. For example, training children or their parents how to empty the bladder through catheterization may help to avoid urinary tract infections and kidney disease. Also, laxatives or enemas may be used to relieve the constipation often associated with this abnormality. Other treatment may include the use of braces and canes or crutches and physical therapy to maintain joint mobility and to strengthen muscular function. Further treatment is supportive. The exact cause of myelocele is unknown; however, it is thought that environmental and nutritional influences may be contributing factors.

Encephalocele, a very severe and rare type of spina bifida, is characterized by the protrusion of the brain through a defect in the cranium. Affected children often experience visual difficulties, intellectual disabilities, and seizures.

A common screening method used to look for spina bifida during pregnancy is a second trimester maternal serum alpha fetoprotein (MSAFP) screening. The MSAFP screen measures the level of a protein called alpha-fetoprotein (AFP), which is made naturally by the fetus and placenta. During pregnancy, a small amount of AFP normally crosses the placenta and enters the mother's bloodstream. But if abnormally high levels of this protein appear in the mother's bloodstream it may indicate that the fetus has a neural tube defect. Amniocentesis, an exam in which a sample of fluid is obtained from the amniotic sac that surrounds the fetus, may also be used to diagnose spina bifida. Research has shown that supplementation with folic acid, starting before pregnancy, reduces the risk of neural tube defects. It is recommended that all women of childbearing age consume 400 micrograms of folic acid daily.

Government Agencies

6010 NIH/National Institute of Arthritis and Musculoskeletal and Skin Diseases
1 AMS Circle
Bethesda, MD 20892

301-495-4484
877-226-4267
Fax: 301-718-6366
TDD: 301-565-2966
niamsinfo@mail.nih.gov
www.niams.nih.gov

The mission of the NIAMS, a part of the NIH, is to support research into the causes, treatment and prevention of arthritis and musculoskeletal and skin diseases, the training of basic and clinical scientists to carry out this research, and the dissemination of information on research progress in these diseases.

Lindsey A. Criswell, MD, Director
Rick Phillips, Executive Officer

National Associations & Support Groups

6011 American Academy of Pediatrics
345 Park Blvd
Itasca, IL 60143

847-434-4000
800-433-9016
Fax: 847-434-8000
csc@aap.org
www.aap.org

The American Academy of Pediatrics and its member pediatricians are committed to the attainment of optimal physical, mental and social health and well-being for all infants, children, adolescents, and young adults.

Kyle E. Yasuda, MD, FAAP, President
Mark Del Monte, JD, CEO/Executive VP
Vera Tait, MD, FAAP, Chief Medical Officer

6012 Center for Disabilities and Development
University of Iowa Stead Family Children's Hospita
100 Hawkins Drive
Iowa City, IA 52242

319-353-6900
877-686-0031
Fax: 319-356-7700
cdd-scheduling@uiowa.edu
www.uichildrens.org/cdd

Spina Bifida / State Agencies & Support Groups

A trusted resource for healthcare, training, research and information for people with disabilities that include: behavior disorders, brain injury, cerebral palsy, diabetes, down syndrome, learning disabilities, sleep disorders and spina bifida.

Dianne McBrien, MD, Medical Director

6013 Center for Parent Information and Resources (CPIR)
c/o SPAN, 35 Halsey Street, 4th Floor
Newark, NJ 07102
973-642-8100
malizo@spanadvocacy.org
www.parentcenterhub.org

Family-friendly information and research-based materials on key topics for Parent Centers. Private workspaces for Parent Centers to exchange resources, discuss high-priority topics, and solve mutual challenges. Coordination of parent training efforts throughout the network.

Myriam Alizo, Project Assistant

6014 Easter Seals
141 W Jackson Boulevard, Suite 1400A
Chicago, IL 60604
312-726-6200
800-221-6827
Fax: 312-726-1494
info@easterseals.com
www.easterseals.com

Easter Seals' mission is to create solutions that change lives for children and adults with disabilities and to provide appropriate developmental and rehabilitation services. Services provided include early intervention, after-school programs, preschool, tutoring, medical rehabilitation, vocational services, adult and senior day services, respite and in home care, camping and recreation, residential housing, support services, support groups, transportation, and referrals.

Kendra Davenport, President & CEO

6015 Genetic Alliance
426400 Woodfield Road, Ste 189
Damascus, MD 20872
202-966-5557
Fax: 202-966-8553
info@geneticalliance.org
www.geneticalliance.org

World's leading nonprofit health advocacy organization committed to transforming health through genetics and promoting an environment of openness centered on the health of individuals, families, and communities.

Sharon Terry, CEO
Ruth Child, CFO
Natasha Bonhomme, Chief Strategy Officer

6016 March of Dimes Foundation
1550 Crystal Drive, Ste 1300
Arlington, VA 22202
888-663-4637
www.marchofdimes.org

March of Dimes help moms have full-term pregnancies and research the problems that threaten the health of babies. The March of Dimes also acts globally: sharing best practices in perinatal health and helping improve birth outcomes where the needs are the most urgent.

Stacey D. Stewart, President
Alan Brogdon, SVP/COO/Board Officer
Rahul Gupta, MD, SVP & Chief Medical/Health Officer

6017 National Center for Education in Maternal and Child Health
3300 Whitehaven Street NW
Washington, DC 20007
MCHnavigator@ncemch.org
www.ncemch.org

Information and advocacy resources for families and professionals. Includes listings of organizations providing general information and organizations focusing on more specific areas of concern to families and young adults who have disabilities.

Rochelle Mayer, Director
Olivia Pickett, Director Library Services

6018 National Rehabilitation Information Center
8400 Corporate Drive, Suite 500
Landover, MD 20785
800-346-2742
Fax: 301-459-4263
TTY: 301-459-5984
naricinfo@heitechservices.com
www.naric.com

Committed to providing direct, personal and information services to anyone interested in disability rehabilitation issues; Committed to serving consumers, researchers, family members, health professionals, educators, counselors, students, librarians and the administrators.

Mark X. Odum, Project Director
Jessica H. Chaiken, Media/Information Services Manager
Natalie J. Collier, Library and Acquisitions Manager

6019 Spina Bifida Association
1600 Wilson Boulevard, Suite 800
Arlington, VA 22209
800-621-3141
sbaa@sbaa.org
www.spinabifidaassociation.org

Serves as the national office representing approximately 60 chapters of parents and other members of families having children born with spina bifida, individuals with spina bifida, and health professionals who work with them. Operates a national information and referral service, periodic public awareness campaigns, scholarships and an annual meeting.

Sara Struwe, President & CEO
Michael Wood, Chief Operating Officer
GlenRae Brown, Chief Financial Officer

State Agencies & Support Groups

Alabama

6020 Spina Bifida Association of Alabama
PO Box 13254
Birmingham, AL 35202
256-325-8600
info@sbaofal.org
www.sbaofal.org

Providing medical, social, and financial support to those afflicted with spina bifida.

Betsy Hopson, President
Angie Pate, Executive Director
Jamie Martin, Field Service Coordinator

Arizona

6021 Arizona Spina Bifida Association
1001 E Fairmount Avenue
Phoenix, AZ 85014
602-274-3323
Fax: 602-274-7632
office@sbaaz.org
www.sbaaz.org/?

Arlene Plouff, Manager

Arkansas

6022 Spina Bifida Association of Arkansas
www.spinabifidaassociation.org

NWASBConnect@gmail.com
www.spinabifidaassociation.org

Providing medical, social, and financial support to those afflicted with spina bifida.

California

6023 Spina Bifida Association of Greater Bay Area
4590 MacArthur Blvd., NW, Suite 250
Washington, DC 20007
202-944-3285
Fax: 202-944-3295
sbaa@sbaa.org
www.spinabifidaassociation.org

Providing medical, social, and financial support to those afflicted with spina bifida.

Traci Whittemore, President

Spina Bifida / State Agencies & Support Groups

6024 Spina Bifida Association of Greater San Diego
4590 MacArthur Blvd., NW, Suite 250
Washington, DC 20007
202-944-3285
Fax: 202-944-3295
sbaa@sbaa.org
www.spinabifidaassociation.org

Providing medical, social, and financial support to those afflicted with spina bifida.

Mary Robbins Wade, President

Colorado

6025 Spina Bifida Association of Colorado
PO Box 22994
Denver, CO 80222
303-797-7870
sbacolorado@gmail.com
www.coloradospinabifida.org

Providing medical, social, and financial support to those afflicted with spina bifida.

Chris Mestas, Board Chair / SBACO Website
Rev. John Anderson, Immediate Past Chair
LaVon Birney, Executive Director

Connecticut

6026 Spina Bifida Association of Connecticut
370 Osgood Avenue Suite 106
New Britain, CT 06053
860-839-0115
800-574-6274
Fax: 860-832-6260
sbac@sbac.org
www.sbac.org

Providing medical, social, and financial support to those afflicted with spina bifida.

Carol Toomey, Chair
Rebecca Hajosy, Treasurer/Secretary
Kiley J Carlson, Executive Director

Florida

6027 Spina Bifida Association of Central Florida
100 W. Lucerne Circle, Suite 100-M
Orlando, FL 32801
407-248-9210
Fax: 407-248-9227
sbacentralflorida.org

Providing medical, social, and financial support to those afflicted with spina bifida.

Beccy Hosoda, President

6028 Spina Bifida Association of Jacksonville Nemours Childrens Clinic
807 Children's Way
Jacksonville, FL 32207
904-390-3686
800-722-6355
Fax: 904-390-3466
www.sbaj.org

Providing medical, social, and financial support to those afflicted with spina bifida.

Stephanie King, Executive Director
Margaret Quintana, Treasurer

6029 Spina Bifida Association of Southeast Florida
4590 MacArthur Blvd., NW, Suite 250
Washington, DC 20007
202-944-3285
Fax: 202-944-3295
sbaa@sbaa.org
www.spinabifidaassociation.org

Providing medical, social, and financial support to those afflicted with spina bifida.

Irene Ballart, President

6030 Spina Bifida Association of Tampa Bay
PO Box 16603
Tampa, FL 33687
813-933-4827
sbatampabay@aol.com
www.sbatampabay.org

Providing medical, social, and financial support to those afflicted with spina bifida.

Dianne Gore, President

Georgia

6031 Spina Bifida Association of Georgia
5072 Bristol Industrial Way, Suite F
Buford, GA 30518
770-939-1044
Fax: 770-939-1049
spinabifidaga.org

Jim Okula, Executive Director

Illinois

6032 Spina Bifida Association of Illinois
8765 W Higgins Rd, Suite 403
Chicago, IL 60631
773-444-0305
800-969-4722
Fax: 773-444-0327
www.sbail.org

The Illinois Spina Bifida Association is dedicated to improving the quality of life of people with spina bifida through direct services, information and referral and public awareness. Direct services include family outreach, education advocacy and more.

Amy Maggio, Executive Director

Indiana

6033 Spina Bifida Association of Central Indiana
PO Box 19814
Indianapolis, IN 46219
317-592-1630
membership@sbaci.org
www.sbaci.org

Providing medical, social, and financial support to those afflicted with spina bifida.

Lisa Jones, President

6034 Spina Bifida Association of Northern Indiana
4590 MacArthur Blvd., NW, Suite 250
Washington, DC 20007
202-944-3285
Fax: 202-944-3295
sbaa@sbaa.org
www.spinabifidaassociation.org

Providing medical, social, and financial support to those afflicted with spina bifida.

Tim Yoder, President

Iowa

6035 Spina Bifida Association of Iowa
8525 Douglas Avenue Suite 39
Urbandale, IA 50322
515-964-8810
contact@sbaia.org
www.sbaia.org

Providing support, a reimbursement program, quarterly newsletter and public awareness campaigns.

Maryanne Lorenz, Manager

Spina Bifida / State Agencies & Support Groups

Kentucky

6036 Spina Bifida Association of Kentucky
982 Eastern Parkway, Box 18
Louisville, KY 40217
502-637-7363
866-340-7225
Fax: 502-637-1010
sbak@sbak.org
www.spinabifidakentucky.org

Providing support to those afflicted with spina bifida.

Joe O'Bryan, Board Chair/President
Eddie Brown Jr., Incoming Chair
Cris Miller, Secretary

Louisiana

6037 Spina Bifida Association of Greater New Orleans
PO Box 1346
Kenner, LA 70063
504-737-5181
sbagno@sbagno.org
www.sbagno.org

Providing support to those afflicted with spina bifida.

Julie Johnston, Coordinator

Maryland

6038 Spina Bifida Association of Chesapeake-Pot omac
PO Box 1750
Annapolis, MD 21404
888-733-0988
Fax: 410-295-9744
www.chesapeakespinabifida.org

Providing support to those afflicted with spina bifida.

Toni Shumate, Executive Director

Massachusetts

6039 Spina Bifida Association of Massachusetts
25 Birch Street, Building B
Milford, MA 01757
888-479-1900
Fax: 504-482-5301
www.sbamass.org

SBA Mass is a community of support for a large group of Massachusetts residents who sometimes need an empathetic ear or a voice of advocacy. They are staffed entirely be volunteers dedicated to supporting their mission.

Ellen Heffernan-Dugan, LIOSOW, Operations Associate
Cara Packard, President
Matt Neal, Vice Chair and Treasurer

Michigan

6040 Spina Bifida Association of Upper Peninsula Michigan
1220 N 3rd Street
Ishpeming, MI 49849
906-485-5127
sba-up.8m.com

Providing support to those affected by spina bifida.

Lois Bengson, President

6041 Spina Bifida Association of West Michigan
235 Wealthy SE
Grand Rapids, MI 49503
616-949-3428
wmisbo@gmail.com
www.wmspinabifida.org/

Providing support to those afflicted with spina bifida.

Carol Carpenter, Interim President

Minnesota

6042 Spina Bifida Association of Minnesota
PO Box 29323
Brooklyn Center, MN 55429
651-222-6395
Fax: 651-228-0914
sbamn@hotmail.com
www.sbamn.org

Providing support to those afflicted with spina bifida.

James Thayer, Executive Director

Mississippi

6043 Spina Bifida Association of Mississippi
PO Box 180594
Richland, MS 39218
601-420-0030
Fax: 601-420-0300
sbafms@yahoo.com
www.spinabifidams.com

Providing support to those afflicted with spina bifida.

Amy Wilkinson, Executive Director

Missouri

6044 Spina Bifida Association of Greater Saint Louis
9201 Watson Road, Suite 125
Crestwood, MO 63126
314-843-2244
800-784-0983
Fax: 314-765-6246
www.sbstl.com

Providing support to those afflicted with spina bifida.

Mark Abbott, Chairman

Nebraska

6045 Spina Bifida Association of Nebraska
7612 Maple St
Omaha, NE 68134
402-572-3570
Fax: 402-572-3002
sbamom@cox.net
www.spinabifidanebraska.org

Providing support to those afflicted with spina bifida.

Megan Sorensen, President

New Jersey

6046 Spina Bifida Association of the Tri-State Region
84 Park Avenue
Flemington, NJ 08822
908-782-7475
Fax: 908-782-6102
www.sbatsr.org

Serves New Jersey, New York metro area and Southern Connecticut. Providing medical, social, and financial support to those afflicted with spina bifida.

Jane Horowitz, Executive Director
Haley Hopper, Director Development

New York

6047 Spina Bifida Association of Albany/Capital District
109 Spring Road
Scotia, NY 12302
518-399-9151
Sbaalbany102@aol.com
www.sbaalbany.org

Providing support to those afflicted with spina bifida.

Karen Wentworth, Director

Spina Bifida / State Agencies & Support Groups

6048 **Spina Bifida Association of Greater Rochester**
PO Box 3
Fairport, NY 14450
585-388-7450
pritch50@yahoo.com
www.sbaa.com

Providing support to those afflicted with spina bifida.

Mary Pritchard, Manager

6049 **Spina Bifida Association of Nassau County**
12 Hampton Rd
South Beach, NY 11789
631-821-9028
kid3418@optonline.net
www.sbancny.org

Providing support to those afflicted with spina bifida.

Leslieann Sussman, President

6050 **Spina Bifida Association of Western New York**
137 Warner Ave
N Tonawanda, NY 14120
716-446-5595
Fax: 716-735-7561
www.sbawny.org

Providing support to those living with spina bifida.

Cynthia Carlson, President

North Carolina

6051 **Spina Bifida Association of North Carolina**
3915 Grace Court
Indian Trail, NC 28079
800-847-2262
Fax: 800-847-2262
sbanc.home.mindspring.com

Providing support to those afflicted with spina bifida. There are five regional support groups in the state.

Kim Gates, Charlotte/Piedmont Contact
Jolyne Wagner, Raleigh Area Contact

Ohio

6052 **Spina Bifida Association of Canton**
PO Box 9024
Canton, OH 44711
330-863-2531
cmgriffin@neo.rr.com
www.sbacanton.org

Providing support to those afflicted with spina bifida.

Connie Griffin, President

6053 **Spina Bifida Association of Central Ohio**
7574 Danbridge Way
Westerville, OH 43082
614-818-3840
lauriedvm@sbcglobal.net
www.sbaco.blogspot.com

Providing support to those afflicted with spina bifida.

Laurie Schulze, President

6054 **Spina Bifida Association of Cincinnati**
644 Linn Street, Suite 635
Cincinnati, OH 45203
513-923-1378
sbacincy@excel.com
www.sbacincy.org

Providing support to those afflicted with spina bifida.

Diane Burns, President

6055 **Spina Bifida Association of Greater Dayton**
4801 Springfield St
Dayton, OH 45431
937-236-1122
Fax: 937-434-4899
sbadayton@yahoo.com
www.sbadayton.org

Providing support to those afflicted with spina bifida.

David Skinner, President

6056 **Spina Bifida Association of North West Ohio**
302 Conant St., Suite C
Maumee, OH 43537
419-794-0561
jobrien@sbanwo.org
www.sbaofnorthwestohio.org

Providing support to those afflicted with spina bifida.

Mindy Gallant, Chair
Christina Fulton, Vice Chair
Jennifer O'Brien, Executive Director

6057 **Spina Bifida Association of Tri-County Ohio**
PO Box 8701
Warren, OH 44484
330-793-8544
jchappel@sbcglobal.net
www.spaa.org

Providing support to those living with spina bifida, from youth into adulthood. Also places an emphasis on parent support groups.

Julie Solomon, President

Pennsylvania

6058 **Spina Bifida Association Pittsburgh**
4590 MacArthur Blvd., NW, Suite 250
Washington, DC 20007
202-944-3285
Fax: 202-944-3295
sbaa@sbaa.org
www.spinabifidaassociation.org

Providing medical, social, and financial support to those afflicted with spina bifida.

Shannon Williams, President

6059 **Spina Bifida Association of Delaware Valley**
PO Box 1235
Havertown, PA 19803
610-584-5530
800-223-0222
info@sbadv.org
www.sbadv.org

Providing medical, social, and financial support to those living with spina bifida.

Keri Mascaro, President

6060 **Spina Bifida Association of Greater Pennsylvania**
215 E State St, Suite D
Quarryville, PA 17566
717-786-9280
Fax: 717-786-8821
SBAofPA@aol.com
spinabifidaresource.weebly.com

Providing medical, social, and financial support to those afflicted with spina bifida.

Patricia Fulvio, Executive Director

Tennessee

6061 **Spina Bifida Association of Tennessee**
4590 MacArthur Blvd., NW, Suite 250
Washington, DC 20007
202-944-3285
Fax: 202-944-3295
sbaa@sbaa.org
www.spinabifidaassociation.org

Providing medical, social, and financial support to those living with spina bifida.

Lynn Hess, President

Texas

6062 **Spina Bifida Association of Houston-Gulf Coast**
440 Benmar Suite 3052
Houston, TX 77060
281-447-2707
Fax: 281-997-2378
www.sbahgc.org

Spina Bifida / Conferences

Providing medical, social, and financial support to those afflicted with spina bifida.

Jennifer Franklin, Vice President
Joan Peck, Treasurer
Michelle Lockstedt, Secretary, Fundraising

6063 Spina Bifida Association of North Texas
705 Ave B, Suite 204
Garland, TX 75040
972-238-8755
Fax: 214-703-1981
sbnorthtexas@aol.com
www.spinabifidant.org/?

Providing medical, social, and financial support to those living with spina bifida.

Carol Barrett, Contact

6064 Spina Bifida Association of Texas
1550 NE Loop 410, Suite 224
San Antonio, TX 78209
210-826-7289
866-597-2289
www.sbatx.org

Providing medical, social, and financial support to those afflicted with spina bifida.

Nora Oyler, Executive Director

Utah

6065 Spina Bifida Association of Utah
900 S 1500 East, Apt C124
Clearfield, UT 84015
801-214-8070
www.utahspinabifida.org/

Providing medical, social, and financial support to those living with spina bifida.

Ilene Hall, President

Virginia

6066 Spina Bifida Association of the Roanoke Valley
PO Box 7652
Roanoke, VA 24019
540-342-1231
Fax: 540-890-1244
sbaroanokevalley@yahoo.com
www.sbarv.org

Providing medical, social, and financial support to those living with spina bifida.

Millie Wilson, President

Washington

6067 Evergreen Spina Bifida Association
611 2nd street, Suite A
Snohomish, WA 98290
253-589-3700
sbaws@yahoo.com
www.sbaws.org/?

Providing medical, social, and financial support to those afflicted with spina bifida.

Ed Kennedy, President

Wisconsin

6068 Spina Bifida Association of Greater Fox Valley
4590 MacArthur Blvd., NW, Suite 250
Washington, DC 20007
202-944-3285
Fax: 202-944-3295
sbaa@sbaa.org
www.spinabifidaassociation.org

Providing support to those living with spina bifida.

Kelly Richard

6069 Spina Bifida Association of Northern Wisconsin
PO Box 421
Schofield, WI 54476
715-359-9674
dtackley@cheqnet.net

Providing medical, social, and financial support to those afflicted with spina bifida.

David Bouchard, President

6070 Spina Bifida Association of Wisconsin
830 N 109th Street, Suite 6
Wauwatosa, WI 53226
414-607-9061
Fax: 414-607-9602
www.sbawi.org

SBAWI is made up of those with spina bifida, as well as family, friends and health care providers. The association is dedicated to helping its membership emotionally, educationally, and financially.

Karen Drzewiecki, President
James B. Hanley, Secretary
Alexandria Sluis, Treasurer

Conferences

6071 SBA National Conference
Spina Bifida Association
4590 MacArthur Boulevard NW, Suite 250
Washington, DC 20007
202-944-3285
800-621-3141
Fax: 202-944-3295
sbaa@sbaa.org
www.spinabifidaassociation.org

Children and adults with Spina Bifida, their families, physicians, nurses, and other clinicians have the unique opportunity to gain information on the latest medical care and network on various issues which affect their lives and professions.

June

Cindy Brownstein, CEO

Audio Video

6072 Challenge
Spina Bifida Association
1600 Wilson Blvd., Suite 800
Arlington, VA 22209
202-944-3285
800-621-3141
Fax: 202-944-3295
sbaa@sbaa.org
www.spinabifidaassociation.org

A human look of how people come to grips with and overcome the challenges related to living with Spina Bifida.

1992 14 minutes

Sara Struwe, President/ CEO
Elizabeth Merck, Director of Development
Lisa Raman, Director

Web Sites

6073 Association for Spina Bifida and Hydrocephalus
www.asbah.org

www.asbah.org

A UK charity that provides information and advice to those with spina bifida and their families.

6074 Children with Spina Bifida: A Resource Page for Parents
www.waisman.wisc.edu/~rowley/sb-kids/

rowley@waisman.wisc.edu
www.waisman.wisc.edu/~rowley/sb-kids/

A resource page for parents with children with Spina Bifida.

Spina Bifida / Book Publishers

6075 **International Federation for Spina Bifida and Hydrocephalus**
Cellebroersstraat 16/Rue des Alexiens 16
Brussels, B-100
32-0 2-502
info@ifglobal.org
www.ifglobal.org

The world-wide umbrella organization for spina bifida and hydracephalus organizations. It's primary goal is prevention through the dissemination of information and education.

Margo Whiteford, President
Jackie Bland, Treasurer
Lieven Bauwens, Secretary General

6076 **LFSN: Lipomyelomeningecele Family Support Network**
www.lfsn.org

www.lfsn.org

A network of families providing support and information sharing to those affected by Occult Spinal Dysraphisms.

6077 **March of Dimes Foundation**
1550 Crystal Drive, Ste 1300
Arlington, VA 22202
888-663-4637
www.marchofdimes.org

March of Dimes help moms have full-term pregnancies and research the problems that threaten the health of babies. The March of Dimes also acts globally: sharing best practices in perinatal health and helping improve birth outcomes where the needs are the most urgent.

Stacey D. Stewart, President
Alan Brogdon, SVP/COO/Board Officer
Rahul Gupta, MD, SVP & Chief Medical/Health Officer

6078 **National Center for Biotechnology Information**
National Library of Medicine, 8600 Rockville Pike
Bethesda, MD 20894
888-346-3656
info@ncbi.nlm.nih.gov
www.ncbi.nlm.nih.gov

NCBI's mission is to develop new information technologoes to aid in the understanding of fundamental molecular and genetic processes that control health and disease.

Patricia Flatley Brennan, RN, PhD, Director
James Ostell, PhD, Executive Secretary

6079 **Online Mendelian Inheritance in Man**
McKusick-Nathans Institue of Genetic Medicine-JHU
Baltimore, MD 21205
www.omim.org

This database is a catalog of human genes and genetic disorders.

Ada Hamosh, MD, Scientific Director

6080 **Spina Bifida Association of America**
1600 Wilson Blvd., Suite 800
Arlington, VA 22209
202-944-3285
Fax: 202-944-3295
sbaa@sbaa.org
www.spinabifidaassociation.org

The mission is to promote the prevention os spina bifida and to enhance the lives of all affected. The association was founded to address the specific needs of the spina bifida community and serves as the national representative of almost 60 chapters. SBAA's efforts benefit thousands of infants, children, adults, parents and professionals each year.

Sara Struwe, President/ CEO
Elizabeth Merck, Director of Development
Lisa Raman, Director

6081 **Wheeless' Textbook of Orthopaedics**
www.wheelessonline.com

www.wheelessonline.com

Derives from a variety of sources, imcluding journals, articles, national meetings lectures and other textbooks.

Clifford R. Wheeless, III, M.D., Author

Book Publishers

6082 **All Kinds of Friends, Even Green!**
Ellen B Sensi, author

Spina Bifida Association
4590 MacArthur Boulevard NW, Suite 250
Washington, DC 20007
202-944-3285
800-621-3141
Fax: 202-944-3295
sbaa@sbaa.org
www.spinabifidaassociation.org

Moses has spina bifida and a lot of friends. Which one will he choose to write about for his school project?

Cindy Brownstein, President & CEO
Sara Struwe, Chief Operating Officer & Director
Christopher Vance, Director of Development

6083 **Answering Your Questions About Spina Bifida**
Spina Bifida Association
4590 MacArthur Boulevard NW, Suite 250
Washington, DC 20007
202-944-3285
800-621-3141
Fax: 202-944-3295
sbaa@sbaa.org
www.spinabifidaassociation.org

Provides information to help people understand the basic medical, educational and social issues which commonly affect people with Spina Bifida.

Cindy Brownstein, President & CEO
Sara Struwe, Chief Operating Officer & Director
Christopher Vance, Director of Development

6084 **Bowel Continence and Spina Bifida**
Spina Bifida Association
4590 MacArthur Boulevard NW, Suite 250
Washington, DC 20007
202-944-3285
800-621-3141
Fax: 202-944-3295
sbaa@sbaa.org
www.spinabifidaassociation.org

An excellent book aimed at anyone (infant or adult) trying to attain bowel continence. Focuses on continence programs, bowel management development and includes a chart and glossary of terms.

Cindy Brownstein, President & CEO
Sara Struwe, Chief Operating Officer & Director
Christopher Vance, Director of Development

6085 **Children with Spina Bifida: A Parent's Gui de**
Spina Bifida Association
4590 MacArthur Boulevard NW, Suite 250
Washington, DC 20007
202-944-3285
800-621-3141
Fax: 202-944-3295
sbaa@sbaa.org
www.spinabifidaassociation.org

Comprehensive publication provides easy-to-understand coverage of neurosurgery, physical therapy, emotional health, education, urological concerns, orthopedic concerns, childhood development and more. Valuable for parents, educators and libraries.

Cindy Brownstein, President & CEO
Sara Struwe, Chief Operating Officer & Director
Christopher Vance, Director of Development

6086 **Complete IEP Guide: How to Advocate for Your Special Ed Child**
Spina Bifida Association
4590 MacArthur Boulevard NW, Suite 250
Washington, DC 20007
202-944-3285
800-621-3141
Fax: 202-944-3295
sbaa@sbaa.org
www.spinabifidaassociation.org

This all-in-one guide will help you understand special education law, identify your child's needs, prepare for meetings, develop the IEP and resolve disputes.

Spina Bifida / Book Publishers

Cindy Brownstein, President & CEO
Sara Struwe, Chief Operating Officer & Director
Christopher Vance, Director of Development

6087 Confronting the Challenges of Spina Bifida
Spina Bifida Association
4590 MacArthur Boulevard NW, Suite 250
Washington, DC 20007
202-944-3285
800-621-3141
Fax: 202-944-3295
sbaa@sbaa.org
www.spinabifidaassociation.org

A group curriculum addressing self-care, self-esteem, and social skills in eight to 13 year olds.
Cindy Brownstein, President & CEO
Sara Struwe, Chief Operating Officer & Director
Christopher Vance, Director of Development

6088 Congenital Disorders Sourcebook
Greg Mullin, author

Omnigraphics
615 Griswold Street, Ste 520
Detroit, MI 48226
610-461-3548
800-234-1340
Fax: 800-875-1340
contact@omnigraphics.com
www.omnigraphics.com

Basic consumer health information on disorders aquired during gestation, including spina bifida, hydrocephalus, cerebral palsy, heart defects, craniofacial abnormalities and fetal alcohol syndrome.
664 pages
ISBN: 0-780816-13-8

6089 Featherless/Desplumado
Juan Felipe Herrera, author

Spina Bifida Association
4590 MacArthur Boulevard NW, Suite 250
Washington, DC 20007
202-944-3285
800-621-3141
Fax: 202-944-3295
sbaa@sbaa.org
www.spinabifidaassociation.org

Tomasito, although confined to a wheelchair, feels free when on the soccer field.
Cindy Brownstein, President & CEO
Sara Struwe, Chief Operating Officer & Director
Christopher Vance, Director of Development

6090 Friends No Matter What
Rose Blivins, author

Spina Bifida Association
4590 MacArthur Boulevard NW, Suite 250
Washington, DC 20007
202-944-3285
800-621-3141
Fax: 202-944-3295
sbaa@sbaa.org
www.spinabifidaassociation.org

The story of two boys, one in a wheelchair and one who loves to play basketball. How will it work out?
Cindy Brownstein, President & CEO
Sara Struwe, Chief Operating Officer & Director
Christopher Vance, Director of Development

6091 Guidelines for Spina Bifida and Health Car e Services Throughout Life
Spina Bifida Association
4590 MacArthur Boulevard NW, Suite 250
Washington, DC 20007
202-944-3285
800-621-3141
Fax: 202-944-3295
sbaa@sbaa.org
www.spinabifidaassociation.org

Guidelines designed to help spina bifida sufferers throughout their entire lives.

6092 Introduction to Spina Bifida
Spina Bifida Association
4590 MacArthur Boulevard NW, Suite 250
Washington, DC 20007
202-944-3285
800-621-3141
Fax: 202-944-3295
sbaa@sbaa.org
www.spinabifidaassociation.org

An aid and guide for those who care for someone with spina bifida, written in non-medical terms and language.
Cindy Brownstein, President & CEO
Sara Struwe, Chief Operating Officer & Director
Christopher Vance, Director of Development

6093 Looking for Goodwill
Patt & Scott Price, author

Spina Bifida Association
4590 MacArthur Boulevard NW, Suite 250
Washington, DC 20007
202-944-3285
800-621-3141
Fax: 202-944-3295
sbaa@sbaa.org
www.spinabifidaassociation.org

An inspirational read, the result of a trek across the US and random interviews showing the heart and attitude of America.
Cindy Brownstein, President & CEO
Sara Struwe, Chief Operating Officer & Director
Christopher Vance, Director of Development

6094 Negotiating the Special Education Maze: A Guide for Parents and Teachers
Spina Bifida Association
4590 MacArthur Boulevard NW, Suite 250
Washington, DC 20007
202-944-3285
800-621-3141
Fax: 202-944-3295
sbaa@sbaa.org
www.spinabifidaassociation.org

An excellent aid for the development of an effective special education program.
Cindy Brownstein, President & CEO
Sara Struwe, Chief Operating Officer & Director
Christopher Vance, Director of Development

6095 New Language of Toys: Teaching Communicati on Skills to Children with Special Needs
Spina Bifida Association
4590 MacArthur Boulevard NW, Suite 250
Washington, DC 20007
202-944-3285
800-621-3141
Fax: 202-944-3295
sbaa@sbaa.org
www.spinabifidaassociation.org

A guide for parents and teachers, this reader-friendly resource guide provides a wealth of information on how play activities affect a child's language development (with a focus on special needs) and where to get the toys and materials to use in these activities.
Cindy Brownstein, President & CEO
Sara Struwe, Chief Operating Officer & Director
Christopher Vance, Director of Development

6096 Nick Joins In
Joe Lasker, author

Spina Bifida Association
4590 MacArthur Boulevard NW, Suite 250
Washington, DC 20007
202-944-3285
800-621-3141
Fax: 202-944-3295
sbaa@sbaa.org
www.spinabifidaassociation.org

When Nick, who is in a wheelchair, enters a regular classroom, for the first time he realizes that he has much to contribute.

Cindy Brownstein, President & CEO
Sara Struwe, Chief Operating Officer & Director
Christopher Vance, Director of Development

6097 **Rolling Along with Goldilocks and the Three Bears**
Cindy Meyers, author
Spina Bifida Association
4590 MacArthur Boulevard NW, Suite 250
Washington, DC 20007
202-944-3285
800-621-3141
Fax: 202-944-3295
sbaa@sbaa.org
www.spinabifidaassociation.org

The familiar folktale with a special-needs twist.
Cindy Brownstein, President & CEO
Sara Struwe, Chief Operating Officer & Director
Christopher Vance, Director of Development

6098 **SPINAbilities: A Young Person's Guide to Spina Bifida**
Spina Bifida Association
4590 MacArthur Boulevard NW, Suite 250
Washington, DC 20007
202-944-3285
800-621-3141
Fax: 202-944-3295
sbaa@sbaa.org
www.spinabifidaassociation.org

Practical suggestions and tips for young people on becoming independent and managing their healthcare.
Cindy Brownstein, President & CEO
Sara Struwe, Chief Operating Officer & Director
Christopher Vance, Director of Development

6099 **Sexuality and the Person with Spinabifida**
Stephen Sloan PhD, author
Spina Bifida Association
4590 MacArthur Boulevard NW, Suite 250
Washington, DC 20007
202-944-3285
800-621-3141
Fax: 202-944-3295
sbaa@sbaa.org
www.spinabifidaassociation.org

Focuses on sexuality, sexual development, sexual activity, and other important issues.
Cindy Brownstein, President & CEO
Sara Struwe, Chief Operating Officer & Director
Christopher Vance, Director of Development

6100 **Steps to Independence: Teaching Everyday Skills to Children with Special Needs**
Spina Bifida Association
4590 MacArthur Boulevard NW, Suite 250
Washington, DC 20007
202-944-3285
800-621-3141
Fax: 202-944-3295
sbaa@sbaa.org
www.spinabifidaassociation.org

A guide to help parents teach life skills to their disabled child.
Cindy Brownstein, President & CEO
Sara Struwe, Chief Operating Officer & Director
Christopher Vance, Director of Development

6101 **Teaching Students with Spina Bifida**
BOSC Books-Books on Special Children
PO Box 3378
Amherst, MA 01004
413-256-8164
Fax: 413-256-8896
www.boscbooks.com

Explores the vital issues of concern to students with spina bifida including aspects of their social, personal and cognitive development. The book is sensitively written and abounds with useful tips covering such things as crutch storage, work space organization, etc.

460 pages Softcover

6102 **Unlocking Potential: College and Other Choices for People with LD and AD/HD**
Spina Bifida Association
4590 MacArthur Boulevard NW, Suite 250
Washington, DC 20007
202-944-3285
800-621-3141
Fax: 202-944-3295
sbaa@sbaa.org
www.spinabifidaassociation.org

An indispensible tool for high school students with learning disabilities and AD/HD. Includes a comprehensive listing of resources.
Cindy Brownstein, President & CEO
Sara Struwe, Chief Operating Officer & Director
Christopher Vance, Director of Development

6103 **Views from Our Shoes: Growing Up with a Brother or Sister with Special Needs**
Spina Bifida Association
4590 MacArthur Boulevard NW, Suite 250
Washington, DC 20007
202-944-3285
800-621-3141
Fax: 202-944-3295
sbaa@sbaa.org
www.spinabifidaassociation.org

A balanced view of the positives and negatives of living with a disabled sibling. Written for siblings ages nine and up.
Cindy Brownstein, President & CEO
Sara Struwe, Chief Operating Officer & Director
Christopher Vance, Director of Development

Newsletters

6104 **Insights into Spina Bifida**
Spina Bifida Association
1600 Wilson Blvd., Suite 800
Arlington, VA 22209
202-944-3285
800-621-3141
Fax: 202-944-3295
sbaa@sbaa.org
www.spinabifidaassociation.org

Includes articles on the latest research, legislation, features, emotional aspects, educational information, and information on the Association's national conference.

Bimonthly

Sara Struwe, President/ CEO
Elizabeth Merck, Director of Development
Lisa Raman, Director

Pamphlets

6105 **Educational Issues Among Children With Spina Bifida**
Spina Bifida Association
1600 Wilson Blvd., Suite 800
Arlington, VA 22209
202-944-3285
800-621-3141
Fax: 202-944-3295
sbaa@sbaa.org
www.spinabifidaassociation.org

Sara Struwe, President/ CEO
Elizabeth Merck, Director of Development
Lisa Raman, Director

6106 **Learning Among Children with Spina Bifida**
Spina Bifida Association
1600 Wilson Blvd., Suite 800
Arlington, VA 22209
202-944-3285
800-621-3141
Fax: 202-944-3295
sbaa@sbaa.org
www.spinabifidaassociation.org

Sara Struwe, President/ CEO
Elizabeth Merck, Director of Development
Lisa Raman, Director

Spina Bifida / Camps

6107 Monetary Allowance, Health Care and Vocational Training & Rehabilitation
National Veterans Services Fund
PO Box 2465
Darien, CT 06820

203-656-0003
800-521-0198
Fax: 203-656-1957
nvsf@NVSF.org
www.nvsf.org

Monetary allowance, health care, vocational training and rehabilitation for Vietnam Veterans' children with spine bifida.

Pamphlet

6108 SBAA General Information Brochure
Spina Bifida Association
1600 Wilson Blvd., Suite 800
Arlington, VA 22209

202-944-3285
800-621-3141
Fax: 202-944-3295
sbaa@sbaa.org
www.spinabifidaassociation.org

Sara Struwe, President/ CEO
Elizabeth Merck, Director of Development
Lisa Raman, Director

6109 SBAA General Information Packet
Spina Bifida Association
1600 Wilson Blvd., Suite 800
Arlington, VA 22209

202-944-3285
800-621-3141
Fax: 202-944-3295
sbaa@sbaa.org
www.spinabifidaassociation.org

Sara Struwe, President/ CEO
Elizabeth Merck, Director of Development
Lisa Raman, Director

6110 Social Development and the Person With Spina Bifida
Spina Bifida Association
1600 Wilson Blvd., Suite 800
Arlington, VA 22209

202-944-3285
800-621-3141
Fax: 202-944-3295
sbaa@sbaa.org
www.spinabifidaassociation.org

20 pages

Sara Struwe, President/ CEO
Elizabeth Merck, Director of Development
Lisa Raman, Director

6111 Urologic Care of the Child with Spina Bifida
David Joseph MD, author

Spina Bifida Association
1600 Wilson Blvd., Suite 800
Arlington, VA 22209

202-944-3285
800-621-3141
Fax: 202-944-3295
sbaa@sbaa.org
www.spinabifidaassociation.org

2001

Sara Struwe, President/ CEO
Elizabeth Merck, Director of Development
Lisa Raman, Director

Camps

6112 Camp Boggy Creek
30500 Brantley Branch Road
Eustis, FL 32736

352-483-4200
866-462-6449
Fax: 352-483-0589
info@campboggycreek.org
www.boggycreek.org

A year round camp serving seriously ill children throughout Florida. We offer week-long summer sessions for the children and family retreat weekends for the whole family.

June Clark, President/CEO
David Mann, Camp Director
Kimmy Lamborn, Assistant Camp Director

6113 Camp Oakhurst
111 Monmouth Road
Oakhurst, NJ 7755

732-531-0215
Fax: 732-531-0292
info@nysh.org
www.campoakhurst.com

A summer camp and year round respite program for children and adults with physical disabilities.

Robert Pacenza, Executive Director
Charles Sutherland, Camp Director

6114 Mountaineer Spina Bifida Camp
350 Capital Street
Charleston, WV 800-6

304-558-7098
800-800-642
Fax: 304-558-2866
www.kidscamps.com

The mission is to help children and teens to develop self-esteem, social skills, and self reliance while they participate in recreational and social activities.

Spinal Muscular Atrophies / National Associations & Support Groups

Description

6115 SPINAL MUSCULAR ATROPHIES
Synonym: SMA
Covers these related disorders: Fazio-Londe disease (Progressive bulbar palsy of childhood), SMA type I (Werdnig-Hoffmann disease; Acute SMA), SMA type II (Intermediate SMA), SMA type III (Kugelberg-Welander disease)
Involves the following Biologic System(s):
Neurologic Disorders, Orthopedic and Muscle Disorders

The spinal muscular atrophies (SMAs) refer to a group of progressive, inherited neuromuscular disorders characterized by the progressive degeneration of motor neurons. Motor neurons are nerves that originate in the spinal cord and stimulate and control muscle movement (motor neurons). Spinal muscular atrophy type I, also called Werdnig-Hoffmann disease, usually becomes apparent between the second and fourth month of life; however, some infants may have symptoms at birth, including difficult breathing and the inability to feed. Other characteristic symptoms and findings include lack of muscle tone (hypotonia), muscle weakness, the inability to control head movements, absence of tendon stretch reflexes, and uncontrollable twitching or small movements (fasciculations) of the tongue and possibly other muscles. Within two to three years of age, continued breathing and feeding difficulties, along with other progressive problems, may lead to life-threatening complications. Treatment is symptomatic and supportive.

Children with SMA type II usually show signs of progressive muscle weakness of the legs and, to a lesser degree, the arms during the first or second year of life. As the disease progresses, many affected children develop side-to-side curvature of the spine (scoliosis), difficulty swallowing, and a nasal quality to their speech. Children with SMA type II may be severely physically handicapped and are usually of average or above average intelligence. Affected chidren are prone to repeated respiratory infections and breathing difficulties. Life-threatening complications may occur during adolescence or early adulthood.

SMA type III or chronic spinal muscular atrophy may become apparent between the ages of two to 17 years. This is the mildest form of SMA. Progressive weakness associated with chronic SMA is most apparent in the trunk area of the body, especially in the muscles of the shoulder girdle area. There is muscle weakness and loss of muscle mass (atrophy). In addition, deep tendon reflexes may be decreased or absent and muscle twitching (fasciculations) may be present. Some affected children may also have a tremor when the hands are outstretched. Repeated respiratory infections are common.

Fazio-Londe disease, also called progressive bulbar palsy of childhood, is a rare type of spinal muscular atrophy that results from degeneration of motor neurons located, for the most part, in the brain stem. This rare disorder is characterized by progressive palsy or paralysis of the nerves that emerge from the skull (cranial nerves). Symptoms and physical findings associated with Fazio-Londe disease include progressive loss of muscle mass (atrophy) and paralysis of the muscles of the tongue, mouth, lips, throat (pharynx), and voice box (larynx).

A team approach involving specialists such as neurologists, orthopedists, and physical therapists, in cooperation with parents or caregivers, may be helpful in providing care for children with spinal muscular atrophies. Other treatment is symptomatic and supportive.

SMA is usually inherited as an autosomal recessive trait, although some cases of autosomal dominant transmission have been reported. This disorder occurs in approximately one out of every 25,000 births. The genes for SMA types I, II, and III seem to be related and are located on the long arm of chromosome 5 (5q11-13).

National Associations & Support Groups

6116 American Academy of Pediatrics
345 Park Blvd
Itasca, IL 60143
847-434-4000
800-433-9016
Fax: 847-434-8000
csc@aap.org
www.aap.org

The American Academy of Pediatrics and its member pediatricians are committed to the attainment of optimal physical, mental and social health and well-being for all infants, children, adolescents, and young adults.

Kyle E. Yasuda, MD, FAAP, President
Mark Del Monte, JD, CEO/Executive VP
Vera Tait, MD, FAAP, Chief Medical Officer

6117 Cure SMA
925 Busse Road
Elk Grove Village, IL 60007
800-886-1762
info@curesma.org
www.curesma.org

ure SMA leads the way to a world where everyone impacted by spinal muscular atrophy (SMA) is empowered to lead independent, successful, and fulfilling lives. Cure SMA provides practical support programs for our community and advocates for their needs. We fund and direct comprehensive research that drives breakthroughs in treatment and we advance access to high quality care.

Kenneth Hobby, President
Mary Schroth, Chief Medical Officer
Marline Pagan, Chief Operating Officer

6118 Genetic Alliance
426400 Woodfield Road, Ste 189
Damascus, MD 20872
202-966-5557
Fax: 202-966-8553
info@geneticalliance.org
www.geneticalliance.org

World's leading nonprofit health advocacy organization committed to transforming health through genetics and promoting an environment of openness centered on the health of individuals, families, and communities.

Sharon Terry, CEO
Ruth Child, CFO
Natasha Bonhomme, Chief Strategy Officer

6119 March of Dimes Foundation
1550 Crystal Drive, Ste 1300
Arlington, VA 22202
888-663-4637
www.marchofdimes.org

March of Dimes help moms have full-term pregnancies and research the problems that threaten the health of babies. The March of Dimes also acts globally: sharing best practices in perinatal health and helping improve birth outcomes where the needs are the most urgent.

Stacey D. Stewart, President
Alan Brogdon, SVP/COO/Board Officer
Rahul Gupta, MD, SVP & Chief Medical/Health Officer

6120 Muscular Dystrophy Association
16 N Clark, Ste 3550
Chicago, IL 60601
646-992-2908
800-572-1717
www.mda.org

Spinal Muscular Atrophies / State Agencies & Support Groups

Voluntary health agency aimed at conquering neuromuscular diseases. The diseases in MDA's program include muscular dystrophy, ALS and numerous related muscle-debilitating diseases. With almost 100 field offices and over 150 affiliated MDA Care Centers nationwide, MDA conducts research, provides medical and community services, clinics, support groups, summer camps for youngsters and much more.

R. Rodney Howell, MD, Chairman
Lynn O'Connor Vos, President & CEO
Mary Fiance, Director, PR & Communications

6121 Spinal Muscular Atrophy Foundation
970 W Broadway, Suite E
Jackson, WY 83001
646-253-7100
info@smafoundation.org
www.smafoundation.org

A group of nonprofit organizations that stand together to raise awareness and advocate for progress towards the treatment and cure of SMA.

Loren A. Eng, President

State Agencies & Support Groups

Arizona

6122 Families of SMA - Arizona Chapter
P.O. Box 43861 Phoenix
Phoenix, AZ 85080
602-314-4902
arizona@fsma.org
www.fsma.org

Angel Wolff, President

California

6123 Families of SMA - Northern California Chapter
PO Box 9014
Santa Rosa, CA 95405
707-571-8990
ncalif@fsma.org
www.fsma.org

David Sereni, President

Connecticut

6124 Families of SMA - Connecticut Chapter
PO Box 124
Rowayton, CT 06853
203-288-1488
800-866-1762
conn@fsma.org
www.fsma.org

Jonathan Goldsberry, President

Indiana

6125 SMA Support Inc
PO Box 6301
Kokomo, IN 46904
765-688-0247
Fax: 801-460-2813
www.smasupport.com

Laura Stants, Contact

New York

6126 Families of SMA - Long Island NY Chapter
PO Box 322
Rockville Center, NY 11571
516-214-0348
greaterny@fsma.org
www.fsma.org

Debbie Cuevas, President

Tennessee

6127 Families of SMA - Tennessee Chapter
PO Box 7025
Knoxville, TN 37921
865-945-7636
tennessee@fsma.org
www.fsma.org

Sarah Boggess, President

Research Centers

6128 SMA Research Group
Stanford University School of Medicine
300 Pasteur Dr, Rm A343
Stanford, CA 94305
650-723-6469
Fax: 650-320-9443
mitzine@stanford.edu
neurology.stanford.edu

SMA clinical trials.

Mitzine Wright, Resident & Fellowship Coordinator
Chris Hopkins, Clerkship & Grand Rounds Coordinato
Diane Madsen, Administrative Associate to the Cha

6129 Spinal Muscular Atrophy Clinic
Columbia Pediatric Neuromuscular Disease Ctr
180 Ft Washington Ave, Harkness Pavilion, Ste 525
New York, NY 10032
212-342-0263
Fax: 212-342-2893
kidsmda@columbia.edu
www.columbiasma.org

Dr Darryl De Vivo, Director
Dr Petra Kaufmann, Associate Director
Leslie Disla, Clinic Coordinator

6130 Spinal Muscular Atrophy Project
NINDS
PO Box 5801
Bethesda, MD 20824
301-496-5751
800-352-9424
smaproject-fd@saic.com
www.smaproject.org

Research program established by NINDS (National Institute of Neurological Disorders and Stroke) as a model of developing a safe and effective treatment for SMA. The program adopts the methods used by the pharmaceutical industry to carry out drug discovery according to accepted standards.

Audio Video

6131 Living with SMA
Families of SMA
925 Busse Rd
Elk Grove Village, IL 60007
847-367-7620
800-886-1762
Fax: 847-357-7623
info@curesma.org
www.curesma.org

Tapes 3 and 4 are available and are part of the Living with SMA video series. Overview of Type II and Type III/Kennedy's.

18 pages

Kenneth Hobby, President
Jill Jarecki, PhD, Research Director
Colleen McCarthy O'Toole, Family Support Director

Web Sites

6132 Families of Spinal Muscular Atrophy
925 Busse Rd
Elk Grove Village, IL 60007
800-886-1762
info@curesma.org
www.curesma.org

Families of SMA was founded for the purpose of encouraging support and raising funds to promote research into the causes and cure of spinal muscular atrophy.

Kenneth Hobby, President
Jill Jarecki, PhD, Research Director
Colleen McCarthy O'Toole, Family Support Director

6133 Online Mendelian Inheritance in Man
McKusick-Nathans Institue of Genetic Medicine-JHU
Baltimore, MD 21205
www.omim.org

This database is a catalog of human genes and genetic disorders.

Ada Hamosh, MD, Scientific Director

6134 Spinal Muscular Atrophy Information Page
Office of Communications and Public Liaison, NINDS
Bethesda, MD 20892
301-496-5751
800-352-9424
www.ninds.nih.gov/disorders/sma/

Walter J. Koroshetz, M.D., Acting Director
Alan L. Willard, Ph.D., Acting Deputy Director
Caroline Lewis, Executive Officer

6135 Spinal Muscular Atrophy Project
www.smaproject.org

www.smaproject.org

Research program established by NINDS (National Institute of Neurological Disorders and Stroke) as a model of developing a safe and effective treatment for SMA. The program adopts the methods used by the pharmaceutical industry to carry out drug discovery according to accepted standards.

Newsletters

6136 Compass
Families of SMA
925 Busse Rd
Elk Grove Village, IL 60007
847-367-7620
800-886-1762
Fax: 847-357-7623
info@curesma.org
www.curesma.org

Newsletter dedicated solely to SMA research updates and information.
42 pages Quarterly

Kenneth Hobby, President
Jill Jarecki, PhD, Research Director
Colleen McCarthy O'Toole, Family Support Director

6137 Directions
Families of SMA
925 Busse Rd
Elk Grove Village, IL 60007
847-367-7620
800-886-1762
Fax: 847-357-7623
info@curesma.org
www.curesma.org

32 pages Quarterly

Kenneth Hobby, President
Jill Jarecki, PhD, Research Director
Colleen McCarthy O'Toole, Family Support Director

6138 SMA Newsletter
Columbia Pediatric Neuromuscular Disease Ctr
Harkness Pavilion, Floor 5, 180 Fort Washington Av
New York, NY 10032
212-342-0263
Fax: 212-342-2893
kidsmda@columbia.edu
www.columbiasma.org

Research updates, upcoming events and conferences, news, and a kids page.

Jessica Rascoll DPT, Newsletter Contact
Dr. Darryl C. De Vivo, Director

Pamphlets

6139 Facts About Spinal Muscular Atrophy
Muscular Dystrophy Association
222 S. Riverside Plaza, Suite 1500
Chicago, IL 60606
520-529-2000
800-572-1717
Fax: 520-529-5300
publications@mdausa.org
mda.org/publications/facts-about-spinal-muscular-atr

Covers the four forms of the disease and outlines the characteristics and genetic patterns of the SMAs. Research efforts aimed at finding the causes, treatments, and cures are also described. Online and in Spanish.
2003

Kristine Welker, Interim President/CEO
Valerie A. Cwik, MD, EVP, Chief Medical & Scientific
Julie Faber, EVP, CFO

6140 Understanding SMA
Families of SMA
925 Busse Rd
Elk Grove Village, IL 60007
847-367-7620
800-886-1762
Fax: 847-357-7623
info@curesma.org
www.curesma.org

This booklet is for the educaton and support of those with SMA.
18 pages

Kenneth Hobby, President
Jill Jarecki, PhD, Research Director
Colleen McCarthy O'Toole, Family Support Director

Description

6141 STRABISMUS

Synonyms: Heterotropia, Manifest deviation, Squint

Covers these related disorders: Accommodation strabismus, Nonparalytic strabismus, Paralytic strabismus

Involves the following Biologic System(s):

Neurologic Disorders, Ophthalmologic Disorders, Orthopedic and Muscle Disorders

Strabismus refers to a condition in which the eyes are not aligned properly in relation to each other and are focused on different objects simultaneously. Approximately four percent of all children under six years of age are affected by some form of strabismus. The eye deviations associated with this condition are classified according to the direction of the deviation. An eye that is turned inward is considered esotropic or convergent; an eye turned outward is exotropic or divergent; an eye turned upward is hypertropic; and an eye turned downward is hypotropic. In normal vision, both eyes focus as a unit to produce a single, three-dimensional image. In children with strabismus, the divergent images sent to the brain from the eyes may produce double vision (diplopia). In many cases, the brain will compensate for this error by blocking the image from the deviated eye, often resulting in poor vision or loss of vision in that eye (suppression amblyopia).

The most common type of strabismus is nonparalytic, in which this often-inherited ocular deviation is constant and results from a defect in the actual positioning of the eyes. Approximately 50 percent of individuals with nonparalytic strabismus have one eye turned inward. These inward-turned or esotropic deviations that appear before six months of age are classified as congenital or infantile esotropia. Outward-turned or exotropic deviations, the second most common type of strabismus, usually occur in children between six months and four years of age. Some outward deviations may result from neurologic disorders and craniofacial abnormalities.

Paralytic strabismus results from dysfunction of an eye muscle as the result of ocular muscle paralysis or a deficit of the nerves that supply the muscles. This resultant muscular imbalance causes the degree of deviation in the affected eye to vary as the eyes move.

Farsighted children are at particular risk for developing accommodative strabismus (accommodative esotropia), in which the lens of the eye tries to compensate for blurred images received by the brain by focusing the eyes inward (converging). If the compensation or accommodation demands are too great, some children may develop this additional eye abnormality.

Strabismus may result from many different factors; therefore, medical specialists make every effort to determine and treat the underlying cause as soon as possible after diagnosis. Such factors may include hereditary influences; trauma; neurologic abnormalities resulting from intracranial tumors or weaknesses in the walls of blood vessels in the brain (aneurysms); infection; systemic disorders; blood vessel malformations; structural abnormalities; and association with certain syndromes such as Duane syndrome.

Permanent loss of vision can occur if strabismus and its attendant amblyopia are not treated before age 4 to 6 years. Interventions may include wearing a patch over the normal eye in order to compel the brain to receive images from the affected eye. Patching often improves the vision in the deviating eye. Upon improvement, surgery may be performed to equalize the pull of the eye muscles.

Children affected with paralytic strabismus may also benefit from wearing glasses with special lenses (prisms) that deflect light, thus altering positioning of objects seen through the lenses. In addition, children with paralytic strabismus with significant ocular deviation may benefit from eye muscle surgery to improve alignment. Farsighted children with accommodative strabismus may be treated with prescription glasses that lessen the need for ocular accommodation when focusing on objects that are far away. Certain medications in the form of eye drops may also aid in focusing on objects that are nearby. Other treatment is aimed toward the underlying cause of the ocular deviation.

Government Agencies

6142 NIH/National Eye Institute
31 Center Drive MSC 2510
Bethesda, MD 20892

301-496-5248
2020@nei.nih.gov
www.nei.nih.gov

Conducts and supports research that helps prevent and treat eye diseases and other disorders of vision. This research leads to sight-saving treatments, reduces visual impairment and blindness, and improves the quality of life for people of all ages. NEI-supported research has advanced our knowledge of how the eye functions in health and disease.

Michael F. Chiang, MD, Director
Santa Tumminia, Deputy Director

National Associations & Support Groups

6143 American Academy of Pediatrics
345 Park Blvd
Itasca, IL 60143

847-434-4000
800-433-9016
Fax: 847-434-8000
csc@aap.org
www.aap.org

The American Academy of Pediatrics and its member pediatricians are committed to the attainment of optimal physical, mental and social health and well-being for all infants, children, adolescents, and young adults.

Kyle E. Yasuda, MD, FAAP, President
Mark Del Monte, JD, CEO/Executive VP
Vera Tait, MD, FAAP, Chief Medical Officer

6144 Genetic Alliance
426400 Woodfield Road, Ste 189
Damascus, MD 20872

202-966-5557
Fax: 202-966-8553
info@geneticalliance.org
www.geneticalliance.org

World's leading nonprofit health advocacy organization committed to transforming health through genetics and promoting an environment of openness centered on the health of individuals, families, and communities.

Sharon Terry, CEO
Ruth Child, CFO
Natasha Bonhomme, Chief Strategy Officer

6145 Lighthouse Guild
250 West 64th Street
New York, NY 10023

800-284-4422
info@lighthouseguild.org
www.lighthouseguild.org

Lighthouse Guild is dedicated to providing exceptional services that inspire people who are visually impaired to attain their goals.

James M. Dubin, Chair
Calvin W. Roberts, President & CEO
Maura J. Sweeney, SVP, Programs & Services

Research Centers

6146 **Emory Eye Center - Strabismus Research**
1365B Clinton Rd NE
Atlanta, GA 30322   404-778-2020
www.eyecenter.emory.edu/clinical_specialties/strabis

Clinical strabismus research.

Anastasios Costarides
Amy K Hutchinson MD

Web Sites

6147 **Lighthouse Guild**
250 West 64th Street
New York, NY 10023   800-284-4422
info@lighthouseguild.org
www.lighthouseguild.org

Lighthouse Guild is dedicated to providing exceptional services that inspire people who are visually impaired to attain their goals.

6148 **Online Mendelian Inheritance in Man**
McKusick-Nathans Institue of Genetic Medicine-JHU
Baltimore, MD 21205   www.omim.org

This database is a catalog of human genes and genetic disorders.

Ada Hamosh, MD, Scientific Director

6149 **Royal National Institute of Blind People**
105 Judd Street
London, WC1H   303-123-9999
www.rnib.org.uk

A leading UK charity offering information, support and advice to over two million people with sight problems.

Matt Stringer, Chief Executive
Keith Valentine, Director of Development
David Clarke, Director of Services

Book Publishers

6150 **Eye Care Sourcebook**
Omnigraphics
615 Griswold Street, Ste 520
Detroit, MI 48226   610-461-3548
800-234-1340
Fax: 800-875-1340
contact@omnigraphics.com
www.omnigraphics.com

Basic consumer information about glaucoma, cataracts, macular degeneration, strabismus, refractive disorders and more

2017 656 pages
ISBN: 0-780815-32-2

Journals

6151 **Journal of AAPOS**
Elsevier
P.O. Box 193832
San Francisco, CA 94119   415-561-8505
Fax: 415-561-8531
aapos@aao.org
www.jaapos.org

Covers pediatric ophthalmology and strabismus as it affects all groups. Presenting important clinical information on everything from the fundamentals to the finer points of diagnostic problem-solving, the Journal provides a comprehensive view of the field.

6 issues/yr
ISSN: 1091-8531

David G Hunter MD, PhD, Editor-in-Chief
T D Kozachek PhD, Managing Editor

Stuttering / Description

Description

6152 STUTTERING

Involves the following Biologic System(s):

Developmental/Behavioral/Psychiatric Disorders, Neurologic Disorders

Stuttering refers to a type of speech dysfunction that interferes with the normal flow of speech (dysfluency). This dysfunction is characterized by difficulty in uttering certain sounds, letters, syllables, words, or phrases and is usually manifested by frequent hesitations, stumbling, or delay in enunciation, as well as prolongation of certain sounds. As young children develop language skills, they typically experience hesitations in speech as a result of still-developing muscle coordination and limited vocabulary. If excessive attention is given to these temporary speech deficiencies, some children may become self-conscious, anxious, and fearful of speaking. These types of emotional reactions may be manifested as persistent and compulsive movements of certain muscle groups that interfere with the normal flow of speech. Children who stutter may have difficulty with only particular letters, sounds, or words. In addition, the severity of the stutter is often related to the amount of stress evoked by the particular situation. Some affected children and adults may have associated tremors or tics. It is estimated that over three million Americans stutter. Stuttering affects individuals of all ages but occurs most frequently in young children between the ages of 2 and 6 who are developing language. Boys are three times more likely to stutter than girls.

Although most stuttering results from psychological causes, this speech dysfunction may sometimes occur as a result of certain disorders of the central nervous system, neuromuscular abnormalities, or injury to organs related to speech. Stuttering that results from behavioral influences is often self-limited and, in 80 percent of those affected, resolves during childhood.

There are a variety of treatments available for stuttering. Any of the methods may improve stuttering to some degree, but there is at present no cure for stuttering. Stuttering therapy, however, may help prevent developmental stuttering from becoming a life-long problem. In young children, treatment for stuttering is mainly supportive. Parents or caregivers are often counseled not to place undue emphasis on speech irregularities. Additional supportive care may include recognition of accomplishments and other gestures that will contribute to the development of self-worth. If stuttering persists beyond early childhood or into adulthood, speech therapy is usually indicated.

Government Agencies

6153 NIH/National Institute on Deafness and Other Communication Disorders (NIDCD)
31 Center Drive, MSC 2320
Bethesda, MD 20892
800-241-1044
TTY: 800-241-1055
nidcdinfo@nidcd.nih.gov
www.nidcd.nih.gov

Conducts and supports biomedical research and research training on normal mechanisms, as well as diseases and disorders of hearing, balance, smell, taste, voice, speech and language.

Debara L. Tucci, MD, Director
Judith A. Cooper, MD, Deputy Director
Timothy J. Wheeles, Executive Officer

National Associations & Support Groups

6154 American Academy of Pediatrics
345 Park Blvd
Itasca, IL 60143
847-434-4000
800-433-9016
Fax: 847-434-8000
csc@aap.org
www.aap.org

The American Academy of Pediatrics and its member pediatricians are committed to the attainment of optimal physical, mental and social health and well-being for all infants, children, adolescents, and young adults.

Kyle E. Yasuda, MD, FAAP, President
Mark Del Monte, JD, CEO/Executive VP
Vera Tait, MD, FAAP, Chief Medical Officer

6155 American School Counselor Association
1101 King Street, Ste 310
Alexandria, VA 22314
703-683-2722
asca@schoolcounselor.org
www.schoolcounselor.org

The mission of ASCA is to represent professional school counselors and to promote professionalism and ethical practices.

Jill Cook, Executive Director
Amanda Fitzgerald, Assistant Deputy
Kathleen M Rakestraw, Director of Communications

6156 American Speech Language Hearing Association (ASHA)
2200 Research Blvd
Rockville, MD 20852
301-296-5700
800-638-8255
Fax: 301-296-8580
pr@asha.org
www.asha.org

A professional and credentialing association made up of more than 123,000 international pathologists, audiologists and scientists. The association promotes the interests of and provides services for those in the hearing, speech, and language field, and advocates for people with communication disorders.

Shari B. Robertson, President
Theresa H. Rodgers, President-Elect

6157 Genetic Alliance
426400 Woodfield Road, Ste 189
Damascus, MD 20872
202-966-5557
Fax: 202-966-8553
info@geneticalliance.org
www.geneticalliance.org

World's leading nonprofit health advocacy organization committed to transforming health through genetics and promoting an environment of openness centered on the health of individuals, families, and communities.

Sharon Terry, CEO
Ruth Child, CFO
Natasha Bonhomme, Chief Strategy Officer

6158 National Stuttering Association
www.westutter.org

info@westutter.org
www.westutter.org

The National Stuttering Association is the largest non-profit organization in the world dedicated to bringing hope and empowerment to children and adults who stutter, their families, and professionals, through support, education, advocacy, and research.

Tammy Flores, Executive Director
Mandy Finstad, Projects Director
Stephanie Coppen, Outreach & Events Coordinator

6159 Stuttering Foundation of America
www.stutteringhelp.org

Provides free online resources, services and support to those who stutter and their families, as well as support for research into the causes of stuttering. Extensive educational programs on stuttering for professionals are also offered.

Stuttering / Camps

State Agencies & Support Groups

6160 **Speech, Language, & Hearing Center University of Colorado**
2501 Kittredge Loop Rd., Campus Box 409
Boulder, CO 80309
303-492-5375
Fax: 303-492-3274
susan.moore@colorado.edu
slhs.colorado.edu/clinical-services?

Informational and emotional support to parents who have a child, adolescent, or adult family member with special needs.

Conferences

6161 **American School Counselor Association Annual Conference**
1101 King Street, Suite 310
Alexandria, VA 22314
703-683-2722
800-306-4722
Fax: 703-997-7572
asca@schoolcounselor.org
www.schoolcounselor.org

The mission of ASCA is to represent professional school counselors and to promote professionalism and ethical practices.

3,000 Attendees

Richard Wong, Executive Director
Jennifer Walsh, Director, Education & Training
Kathleen M Rakestraw, Director of Communications

Web Sites

6162 **NIH/National Institute on Deafness and Other Communication Disorders (NIDCD)**
www.nidcd.nih.gov/health/stuttering

www.nidcd.nih.gov/health/stuttering

Fact sheet and information page on stuttering and other resources.

6163 **Online Mendelian Inheritance in Man**
McKusick-Nathans Institue of Genetic Medicine-JHU
Baltimore, MD 21205
www.omim.org

This database is a catalog of human genes and genetic disorders.

Ada Hamosh, MD, Scientific Director

6164 **Parent Pals**
parentpals.com/gossamer/pages/Speech_and_Language
specialed@parentpals.com
parentpals.com/gossamer/pages/Speech_and_Language

Their goal is to provide special education and gifted information, continuing education, support, weekly tips, games, book resources, and news and views for parents and professionals.

Book Publishers

6165 **Programmed Therapy for Stuttering in Children and Adults**
Charles C Thomas Publisher
2600 S 1st Street
Springfield, IL 62704
217-789-8980
800-258-8980
Fax: 217-789-9130
books@ccthomas.com
www.ccthomas.com

This book highlights the systematic scientific approach to studying and treating stuttering by way of learning theory, single-subject research design and operant conditioning.

2001 360 pages 2nd Edition
ISBN: 0-398071-07-3

6166 **Straight Talk on Stuttering: Information, Encouragement, and Counsel**
Lloyd M Hulit, author

Charles C Thomas Publisher
2600 S 1st Street
Springfield, IL 62704
217-789-8980
800-258-8980
Fax: 217-789-9130
books@ccthomas.com
www.ccthomas.com

Written for stutterers and those who interact with stutterers, including parents, caregivers, teachers, and speech-language pathologists. The author dispels myths, corrects the misperceptions and creates a message of hope for all people who have this fascinating communication disorder.

338 pages 2nd Ed/ Hard
ISBN: 0-398075-19-4

Camps

6167 **Meadowood Springs Speech and Hearing Camp**
PO Box 1025
Pendleton, OR 97801
541-276-2752
Fax: 541-276-7227
info@meadowoodsprings.org
www.meadowoodsprings.org

On 143 acres in the Blue Mountains of Eastern Oregon, this camp is designed to help young people who have diagnosed clinical disorders of speech, hearing or language. A full range of activities in recreational and clinical areas is available. For cabin reservations 541-566-2191.

Rosemarie Atfield, Executive Director
Marie Story, Camp Manager
Cliff Story, Camp Manager

6168 **University of Iowa - Wendell Johnson Speech and Hearing Clinic**
Wendell Johnson Speech And Hearing Center
Iowa City, IA 52242
319-335-8718
Fax: 319-335-8851
speech-path-aud@uiowa.edu
clas.uiowa.edu/comsci/

The clinic offers assessment and remediation for disordered communication in adults and children. The clinic also offers an Intensive Summer Residential Clinic for school age children needing intervention services because of speech, language, hearing and/or reading problems.

Ruth Bentler, Professor / Department Chair
Dorothy Albright, Secretary
Vicki Jennings, Secretary

Subacute Sclerosing Panencephalitis (SSPE) / Description

Description

6169 SUBACUTE SCLEROSING PANENCEPHALITIS (SSPE)
Synonyms: Dawson's encephalitis, Van Bogaert's encophalitis
Involves the following Biologic System(s):
Immunologic and Rheumatologic Disorders, Neurologic Disorders

Subacute sclerosing panencephalitis (SSPE) is a rare, life-threatening, slow viral infection of the brain caused by a measles-like virus. SSPE appears months or years after a typical mild or severe measles infection and occurs most frequently in children and adolescents between the ages of five and 15 years. This disease occurs more often in children who develop measles before 18 months of age and is twice as prevalent in boys as it is in girls. Symptoms develop gradually and may commence with subtle behavorial changes such as forgetfulness or outbursts of temper, deterioration in school performance, sleeplessness, and hallucinations. These symptoms are often followed by more bizarre behavior, seizures, repetitive muscular jerks (myoclonic jerks) and other abnormal movements, eye irregularities, and mental deterioration (dementia). Late findings may include muscular rigidity or, in some patients, weak muscles, difficulty swallowing, blindness, or coma. In addition, due to generalized weakness and impaired muscle control associated with SSPE, life-threatening complications such as pneumonia may occur. Subacute sclerosing panencephalitis is incompatible with life; its usual duration is from one to three years.

The diagnosis of SSPE may be confirmed through laboratory tests that detect the presence of antibodies to the measles virus in the cerebrospinal fluid and the presence of large numbers of measles antibodies in the serum. In most cases, subacute sclerosing pnencephalitis may be prevented by immunization with attenuated measles virus vaccine.

Treatment of SSPE is geared toward chronic care. Over the last decade, however, stabilization of disease and in clinical progression has been observed with medications that alter the body's immune system response to this virus (immunomodulators), such as interferon and certain antiviral drugs including ribavirin and isoprinosine. Studies of other therapeutic programs are ongoing. Other treatment is symptomatic and supportive.

Government Agencies

6170 NIH/National Institute of Allergy and Infectious Diseases
5601 Fishers Lane, MSC 9806
Bethesda, MD 20892
301-496-5717
866-284-4107
Fax: 301-402-3573
TDD: 800-877-8339
ocpostoffice@niaid.nih.gov
www.niaid.nih.gov

The principal advisory board of the NIAID. The council is composed of physicians, scientists and representatives of the public and advises on the conduct and support or research, training and dissemination of health information regarding allergies and infectious diseases.

Anthony S. Fauci, MD, Director

6171 NIH/National Institute of Neurological Disorders and Stroke (NINDS)
PO Box 5801
Bethesda, MD 20824
800-352-9424
www.ninds.nih.gov

Works to reduce the burden of neurological disease by conducting, fostering, coordinating and guiding research on the causes, prevention, diagnosis and treatment of neurological disorders and stroke, while supporting basic research in related scientific areas.

Walter J. Koroshetz, MD, Director

National Associations & Support Groups

6172 American Academy of Pediatrics
345 Park Blvd
Itasca, IL 60143
847-434-4000
800-433-9016
Fax: 847-434-8000
csc@aap.org
www.aap.org

The American Academy of Pediatrics and its member pediatricians are committed to the attainment of optimal physical, mental and social health and well-being for all infants, children, adolescents, and young adults.

Kyle E. Yasuda, MD, FAAP, President
Mark Del Monte, JD, CEO/Executive VP
Vera Tait, MD, FAAP, Chief Medical Officer

6173 Child Neurology Foundation
601 W Short Street
Lexington, KY 40508
888-417-3435
info@childneurologyfoundation.org
childneurologyfoundation.org

The Child Neurology Foundation connects partners from all areas of the child neurology community so those navigating the journey of disease diagnosis, management, and care have the ongoing support from those dedicated to treatments and cures.

Amy Brin, Executive Director
Katie Hentges, Director, Programs
Brea McCormley, Director, Development

6174 Genetic Alliance
426400 Woodfield Road, Ste 189
Damascus, MD 20872
202-966-5557
Fax: 202-966-8553
info@geneticalliance.org
www.geneticalliance.org

World's leading nonprofit health advocacy organization committed to transforming health through genetics and promoting an environment of openness centered on the health of individuals, families, and communities.

Sharon Terry, CEO
Ruth Child, CFO
Natasha Bonhomme, Chief Strategy Officer

6175 World Health Organization
Avenue Appia 20
1202 Geneva,
Switzerland
www.who.int

WHO is the directing and coordinating authority for health within the United Nations system. WHO operates in more than 150 countries around the world.

Dr. Tedros Adhanom Ghebreyesus, Director General
Dr. Zsuzsanna Jakab, Deputy Director General
Stewart Simonson, Asst Director General, UN NYC

Web Sites

6176 Encephalitis Information Resource
www.encepahlitis.info

www.encepahlitis.info

Site is provided by the Encephalitis Society

6177 MedlinePlus
www.nlm.nih.gov/medlineplus/aboutmedlineplus.html

custserv@nlm.nih.gov
www.nlm.nih.gov/medlineplus/aboutmedlineplus.html

Information on the condition, causes, symptoms, tests, and treatment.

Dr. Donald A.B. Lindberg, Director

6178 **NIH/National Institute of Neurological Disorders and Stroke (NINDS)**
Office of Communications and Public Liaison, NINDS
Bethesda, MD 20824
301-496-5751
800-352-9424
www.ninds.nih.gov/disorders/subacute_panencephalitis

Information fact sheet on the disorder.

Walter J. Koroshetz, MD, Director

Book Publishers

6179 **Let's Talk About Going to the Hospital**
Rosen Publishing Group's PowerKids Press
29 E 21st Street
New York, NY 10010
212-777-3017
800-237-9932
Fax: 888-436-4643
rosenpub@tribeca.ios.com
www.rosenpublishing.com

If a child has to check into the hospital, chances are he or she is already upset about being ill. Knowing how a hospital functions and what the procedures are, such as when family members can visit, will help in what is already a stressful situation. Grades K-5.

24 pages
ISBN: 0-823950-36-0

Roger Rosen, President

Sudden Infant Death Syndrome / Description

Description

6180 SUDDEN INFANT DEATH SYNDROME
Synonyms: Cot death, Crib death, SIDS
Involves the following Biologic System(s):
Neonatal and Infant Disorders

Sudden infant death syndrome (SIDS) refers to the sudden, unexpected, and unexplained death of an apparently healthy infant. This syndrome may occur from the ages of two weeks to one year, but most commonly occurs between the ages of two to four months. Approximately 75 to 95 percent of all deaths related to SIDS occur by the age of six months. Sudden infant death syndrome is responsible for approximately half of all infant deaths that occur between the ages of 1 month and one year and, in the United States, affects approximately 1.3 of every 1,000 infants in that age group. SIDS is somewhat more common in boys and in infants born to individuals of African-American or Native American descent. In addition, sudden infant death syndrome occurs more often during the winter months.

Very little is sure about the exact cause of SIDS, but researchers believe that certain brain stem abnormalities may be a contributing factor to its occurrence. Such irregularities may affect the regulation of body temperature, cardiorespiratory function, and associated sleep and arousal mechanisms. Although the relationship is not fully understood, brain stem abnormalities, especially sleep and arousal deficit, may interact with certain other influencing factors (epidemiologic risk factors) to put infants at risk for SIDS. Such epidemiologic risk factors may include prematurity, low birth weight, bottle feeding, exposure to smoking, recent illness with fever and previous near death episodes requiring resuscitation. Also, mothers with abnormally low levels of circulating red blood cells (anemia) or those who smoke or use drugs during pregnancy may be at increased risk for having an infant with SIDS. Other factors may include insufficient prenatal care and low socioeconomic status. In addition, recent studies have shown that putting infants to sleep on their stomachs is a significant risk factor, as is the use of soft bedding or extra linens and toys (e.g., comforters, quilts, stuffed animals, etc.) in the crib.

To alleviate certain risk factors, appropriate prenatal care is essential in the possible prevention of SIDS. Also, after birth, parents are counseled to be alert to any respiratory changes or distress and to closely observe infants during and after any illness. In addition, new guidelines recommend that infants be placed in the crib on their backs, as statistics have shown declines in SIDS rates among those who have complied with this recommendation. Sleeping on the back has been recommended for some time to avoid SIDS, with the catchphrase "Back To Bed" and "Back to Sleep." Other guidelines include the advice that crib mattresses should be firm and should fit tightly within the crib frame; that comforters, quilts, pillows, toys, etc. should be removed from the crib; that, if possible, sleeper-type pajamas be used instead of blankets; that if a blanket must be used, it should be thin, should reach no further than the infant's chest, and should be tucked around the infant's chest and mattress; and that the baby's head should be uncovered at all times during sleep. Infants who die from SIDS tend to have higher concentrations of nicotine and cotinine (a biological marker for secondhand smoke exposure) in their lungs than those who die from other causes. Parents who smoke can significantly reduce their children's risk of SIDS by either quitting or smoking only outside and leaving their house completely smoke-free. In the event of the death of an infant from SIDS, counseling by trained specialists is strongly advised for parents and remaining siblings. In addition, support groups composed of families who have been affected by SIDS may be comforting and helpful.

Government Agencies

6181 National Center for Health Statistics
www.cdc.gov/nchs

800-232-4636
www.cdc.gov/nchs

Provides statistical information that will guide actions and policies to improve the health of the American people.
Brian C. Moyer, PhD, Director

National Associations & Support Groups

6182 American Academy of Pediatrics
345 Park Blvd
Itasca, IL 60143

847-434-4000
800-433-9016
Fax: 847-434-8000
csc@aap.org
www.aap.org

The American Academy of Pediatrics and its member pediatricians are committed to the attainment of optimal physical, mental and social health and well-being for all infants, children, adolescents, and young adults.
Kyle E. Yasuda, MD, FAAP, President
Mark Del Monte, JD, CEO/Executive VP
Vera Tait, MD, FAAP, Chief Medical Officer

6183 American SIDS Institute
528 Raven Way
Naples, FL 34110

239-431-5425
Fax: 239-431-5536
www.sids.org

A national nonprofit organization dedicated to the prevention of sudden infant death syndrome and the promotion of infant health.

6184 Compassionate Friends
48660 Pontiac Trail, #930808
Wixom, MI 48393

877-969-0010
www.compassionatefriends.org

Compassionate Friends assists families toward the positive resolution of grief following the death of a child of any age and provides information to help others be supportive. A national nonprofit, self-help support organization that offers friendship, understanding, and hope to bereaved parents, grandparents and siblings.
Shari O'Loughlin, Chief Executive Officer

6185 First Candle
21 Locust Avenue, Suite 2B
New Canaan, CT 06840

203-966-1300
800-221-7437
www.firstcandle.org

First Candle is committed to the elimination of SIDS and other sleep-related infant deaths through education, while providing support for grieving families who have suffered a loss. First Candle works with local organizations throughout the country to educate new and expectant parents on the importance of providing a safe sleep environment for their baby. The program also offers bereavement support and counselling for families who have suffered the lost of a child.
Alison Jacobson, Executive Director
Abby Lundy, Director, Development & Outreach
Barb Himes, Director, Education & Services

6186 National Center for Education in Maternal and Child Health
3300 Whitehaven Street NW
Washington, DC 20007

MCHnavigator@ncemch.org
www.ncemch.org

Information and advocacy resources for families and professionals. Includes listings of organizations providing general information and organizations focusing on more specific areas of concern to families and young adults who have disabilities.

Sudden Infant Death Syndrome / State Agencies & Support Groups

6187 National Center for the Prevention of SIDS
www.cdc.gov/sids

800-232-4636
www.cdc.gov/sids

Offers medical updates and information on prevention of Offers medical updates and information on prevention of sudden infant death syndrome (SIDS) and other disorders to parents and professionals.

6188 Parents Helping Parents
1400 Parkmoor Avenue, Suite 100
San Jose, CA 95126

408-727-5775
855-727-5775
Fax: 408-286-1116
info@php.com
www.php.com

Parents Helping Parents supports, educates, and inspires families and the community to build bright futures for youth and adults with special needs.

Maria Daane, Executive Director
Janet Nunez, Director, Programs
Virginia Hildebrand, Director, Finance

6189 SUID/SIDS Gateway (Resource Center)
Maternal and Child Health Library
www.mchlibrary.org/collections/suid-sids

mchevidence@ncemch.org
www.mchlibrary.org/collections/suid-sids

The Sudden Unexpected Infant Death (SUID) & Sudden Infant Death Syndrome (SIDS) Gateway is an online platform to find resources for states, communities, professionals, and families to reduce sudden unexpected infant death (SUID) and Sudden Infant Death Syndrome (SIDS), promote healthy outcomes, and cope with grief when losses occur.

6190 Share Pregnancy & Infant Loss Support
402 Jackson Street
St. Charles, MO 63301

800-821-6819
info@nationalshare.org
nationalshare.org

Share is a national organization with over 75 chapters in 29 states. Our services include bed-side companions, phone support, face-to-face support group meetings, resource packets, private online communities, memorial events, training for caregivers, and so much more.

Sarah Lawrenz, Executive Director
Rose Carlson, Program Director
Sarah Purcell, Development Director

State Agencies & Support Groups

Alabama

6191 Bureau of Family Health Services-Alabama Child Death Review
Alabama Department of Public Health
43 Foundry Avenue
Waltham, MA 02453

617-618-2918
Fax: 334-206-2972
jallison@edc.org
www.childrenssafetynetwork.org

Jennifer Allison, CSN Assistant Director, State Partn

Arizona

6192 Office of Women's & Children's Health
Arizona Department of Health Services
150 N 18th Ave, Suite 320
Phoenix, AZ 85007

602-542-1025
Fax: 602-542-0883
newbers@azdhs.gov
www.azdhs.gov

The Unexplained Infant Death Council comes under the OWCH and assists the department to develop unexplained infant death training and educational programs.

Sheila Sjolander, Manager

California

6193 CorStone-Children & Loss Group
CorStone
250 Camino Alto
Mill Valley, CA 94941

415-331-6161
Fax: 415-388-6165
info@corstone.org
www.corstone.org

For children who have suffered the loss of a close loved one. Parent group meets separately at the same time.

Richard Cuadra MFT, Program Director
Melissa Mullin MFT, Program Coordinator

6194 Region IX Office Program Consultants for Maternal and Child Health
50 United Nations Plaza
San Francisco, CA 94102

415-437-8101
Fax: 415-437-8105
nrc.uchsc.edu

Lyn Headley, MD

Colorado

6195 Region VIII Office Program Consultants for Maternal and Child Health
1961 Stout Street
Denver, CO 80294

303-844-7854
Fax: 303-844-2019
laurie.konsella@hhs.gov

Laurie Konsella, M.P.A

District of Columbia

6196 Division of Community Health Nursing
825 N Capitol Street, NE
Washington, DC 20002

202-698-0705
Fax: 202-645-7030

Mary Breach, RN, MSN, Nursing Coordinator

Florida

6197 Children's Medical Services Program Florida SIDS Program
Bin A-13 4025 Bald Cypress Way
Tallahassee, FL 32399

850-245-4444
Fax: 850-245-4047
susann-arbor@doh.state.fl.us
www.doh.state.fl.us

Georgia

6198 Georgia Department of Human Resources Children's Health Services
2 Peach Tree Street NW
Atlanta, GA 30303

404-656-6750
dhs.georgia.gov

Linette Jackson Hunt, MD, MPH, Chief

6199 Georgia Department of Human Resources - Center for Family Resource Planning
2 Peach Tree Street NW
Atlanta, GA 30303

404-656-7660
www.dhs.georgia.gov

Provides grief support for parents.

Lee Hackel

Sudden Infant Death Syndrome / State Agencies & Support Groups

6200 Region IV Office Program Consultants For Maternal and Child Health
Atlanta Federal Center
61 Forsyth Street, SW, Suite 3M60
Atlanta, GA 30303
404-562-7980
Fax: 404-562-7974
nrc.uchsc.edu

Dorothy Redfern, RN, MSPH

Idaho

6201 Child Health Improvement Program Idaho Department of Health
211 Idaho CareLine, PO Box 83720
Boise, ID 83720
208-334-5945
800-926-2588
Fax: 208-334-5531
careline@dhw.idaho.gov
www.idahocareline.org

Simonne deGlee, MS, PNP, SIDS Coordinator

Illinois

6202 Region V Office Program Consultants for Maternal and Child Health
233 N Michigan Avenue
Chicago, IL 60601
312-353-4042
Fax: 312-886-3770

Kathryn Vedder, MD, MPH

Kansas

6203 Kansas Department of Health & Environment Bureau of Family Health
1000 SW Jackson Street, Suite 220
Topeka, KS 66612
785-296-1500
800-332-6262
Fax: 785-296-1562
www.kdheks.gov

Azzie N Young, PhD, Director

Kentucky

6204 Kentucky Department of Human Resources Bureau of Health Services
700 Capitol Avenue, Suite 100
Frankfort, KY 40601
502-564-2611
governor.ky.gov

Ida Lyons, RN, SIDS Coordinator

Louisiana

6205 Public Health Services of Louisiana
628 N 4th Street
Baton Rouge, LA 70802
225-342-9500
Fax: 225-342-5568
dhhwebinfo@la.gov
www.dhh.louisiana.gov/

Dorris Brown, Center Director
Myrra Lowe, Chief Financial Officer
Beth Scalso, Chief of Staff

Maine

6206 Department of Human Services
221 State Street
Augusta, ME 04333
207-287-3707
Fax: 207-287-3005
TTY: 800-606-0215
www.maine.gov/dhhs

Brenda Harvey, Manager
Mary Mayhew, Commisioner

Maryland

6207 Center for Infant & Child Loss
737 W. Lombard Street, Room 233
Baltimore, MD 21201
410-706-5062
800-808-7437
Fax: 410-328-4596
caring@infantandchildloss.org
www.infantandchildloss.org

Donna C Becker, RN, MSN, Director

Massachusetts

6208 Region I Office Program Consultants For Maternal and Child Health
John F Kennedy Building
Room 1826
Boston, MA 02203
617-565-1433
Fax: 617-565-3044
www.mchb.hrsa.gob

Shirley A Smith, RN, MS

Michigan

6209 Apnea Identification Program
Children's Hospital of Michigan
3901 Beaubien Street
Detroit, MI 48201
313-745-5437
888-DMC-2500
www.chmkids.org

Karen Braniff, RN, MSW, Nurse Specialist

6210 Genesee County Health Department
630 S Saginaw Street
Flint, MI 48502
810-257-3612
Fax: 810-257-3147
gchd-info@gchd.us
www.gchd.us

Robert Pestronk, Manager
Mark Valck, Health Director
Gary Johnson, Medical Director

6211 Kent County Health Department
300 Monroe Avenue NW
Grand Rapids, MI 49503
616-632-7590
Fax: 616-632-7083
www.accesskent.com

Cathy Raevsky, Executive Director

Minnesota

6212 Minnesota Sudden Infant Death Center
Minneapolis Children's Medical Center
2525 Chicago Avenue
Minneapolis, MN 55404
612-813-6285
TTY: 800-732-3812

Kathleen Farnbach, PHN, Project Coordinator

Mississippi

6213 Mississippi State Department of Health and Child Health Services
570 East Woodrow Wilson Drive
Jackson, MS 39216
601-576-7634
www.msdh.state.ms.us

Jenny Griffin, Manager

Sudden Infant Death Syndrome / State Agencies & Support Groups

Missouri

6214 Region VII Office Program Consultants for Maternal and Child Health
Federal Building
601 E 12th Street
Kansas City, MO 64106
816-426-5291
Fax: 816-426-3633

Bradley Appelbaum, MD, MPH

Montana

6215 Montana Department of Health & Environmental Sciences
Family & Maternal & Child Health Bureau
Cogswell Building
Helena, MT 59620
406-444-4740

Maxine Ferguson, RN, MN, Bureau Chief

Nevada

6216 Nevada State Division of Health, Maternal & Child Health
505 E King Street, Room 205
Carson City, NV 89701
702-687-4885
www.health.nv.gov/MCH.htm

Luana Ritch, Health Educator

New Jersey

6217 New Jersey Department of Health - Child Health Program
CN 364, 363 W State Street
Trenton, NJ 08625
609-292-5616

Judith Hall, BSN, RNC, Evaluator

New York

6218 New York City Information & Counseling Program for SIDS
520 1st Avenue, Room 506
New York, NY 10016
212-757-1051
800-522-5006

Judith Gaines, CSW, PhD, SIDS Program Director

6219 Region II Office Program Consultants for Maternal and Child Health
26 Federal Plaza
New York, NY 10278
212-264-2571
Fax: 212-264-2673

Margaret Lee, MD

Oklahoma

6220 Oklahoma State Department of Health - Maternal and Child Health Services
1000 NE 10th Street
Oklahoma City, OK 73117
405-271-5600
Fax: 405-271-3431
www.ok.gov/health

Mike Crutcher, Manager

Pennsylvania

6221 Region III Office Program Consultants for Maternal and Child Health
Public Ledger Building
150 S Independence Mall West, Suite 1172
Philadelphia, PA 19106
215-861-4379
Fax: 215-861-4338

Jane Coury, MSN, RN

Rhode Island

6222 Rhode Island Department of Health National SIDS Foundation
3 Capitol Hl
Providence, RI 02908
401-222-5960
Fax: 401-444-3422
www.health.ri.gov/

Anne M Roach, RN, SIDS Coordinator

South Carolina

6223 South Carolina Department of Health & Environmental Control - SIDS Information
2600 Bull Street
Columbia, SC 29201
803-898-3300
www.scdhec.gov/administration/hplhc/health.htm

Brenda Creswell, ACSW, LMSW, SIDS Coordinator

South Dakota

6224 South Dakota Department of Health
Health Building
500 East Capitol Avenue
Pierre, SD 57501
605-773-3361
800-738-2301
Fax: 605-773-5683
www.doh.sd.gov

Doneen Hollingsworth, Manager

Texas

6225 Harris County Health Department
2223 West Loop South
Houston, TX 77027
713-439-6000
www.hcphes.org

Kathleen Ingrando, RN, BSN, Program Coordinator

6226 Region VI Office Program Consultants For Maternal and Child Health
1301 Young Street 10th Floor
Dallas, TX 75202
214-767-3003
Fax: 214-767-3038

Marianne Davenport, CPNP, MPH

Utah

6227 Utah Department of Health
Child Health Bureau
PO Box 141010
Salt Lake City, UT 84114
801-538-6003
health.utah.gov

Judith Ahrano, SIDS Director

Washington

6228 Region X Office Program Consultants for Maternal and Child Health
2201 6th Avenue
Seattle, WA 98121
206-553-0215

Kay Girl, RNC, MN, Acting

West Virginia

6229 West Virginia Department of Health and Human Services
One Davis Square, Suite 100, East
Charleston, WV 25301
304-558-0684
Fax: 304-558-1130
www.wvdhhr.org

Joan R Kenny, RN, SIDS Director

Sudden Infant Death Syndrome / Libraries & Resource Centers

Wyoming

6230 Wyoming Department of Health
Division of Health and Medical Services
401 Hathaway Building
Cheyenne, WY 82002
307-777-7656
Fax: 307-777-7439
www.health.wyo.gov

J Richard Hillman, MD, PhD, Administrator

Libraries & Resource Centers

6231 National Sudden Infant Death Syndrome Resource Center
Circle Solutions, Inc
8280 Greensboro Drive, Suite 300
McLean, VA 22102
703-893-6383
Fax: 703-821-2098
marketing@circlesolutions.com
www.circlesolutions.com

Resource Center provides information on keeping children safe through their first year and beyond, about SIDS, and about handling the grief of losing a child to SIDS, and so much more.

Kristina Lewis, Chairman, Executive Committee
Louis Cartwright, jr., Vice President-Finance
Michael Collins, Vice President-IT

Research Centers

6232 American SIDS Institute
528 Raven Way
Naples, FL 34110
239-431-5425
800-232-7437
Fax: 239-431-5536
prevent@sids.org
www.sids.org

A national nonprofit organization dedicated to the promotion of infant health and the prevention of sudden infant death syndrome.

Marc Peterzell, Chairman
Betty McEntire PhD, Executive Director

6233 Division of Extramural Research
31 Center Drive, Building 31
Bethesda, MD 20892
301-496-5575
1 - -
Fax: 866-760-5947
NICHDInformationResourceCenter@mail.nih.
www.nichd.nih.gov

This division conducts and supports research on all stages of human development, from the preconception to adulthood, to better understand the health of children, adults, families, and communities.

6234 Massachusetts Sudden Infant Death Syndrome
Boston City Hospital
818 Harrison Avenue
Boston, MA 02118
617-638-8131

A joint program of Boston City Hospital and Children's Hospital. Services provided include around-the-clock availability for consultation to health professionals and families, counseling of families, parent group meetings and supportive home visits.

6235 National Sudden Infant Death Syndrome Research Center
Circle Solutions, Inc
8280 Greensboro Drive, Suite 300
McLean, VA 22102
703-821-8955
Fax: 703-821-2098
marketing@circlesolutions.com
www.circlesolutions.com

Provides information services and technical assistance concerning SIDS and related topics in order to promote understanding of SIDS and to comfort those affected by a SIDS loss. Offers its services to parents, family members, caregivers, counselors, medical and legal professionals, and the general public.

6236 Pediatric Pulmonary Unit
Massachusetts General Hospital
55 Fruit Street
Boston, MA 02114
617-726-2000
www.massgeneral.org

Sudden infant death syndrome and childhood disorders research.

Douglas R Johnson, Associate Director

6237 USC - Neonatology Research Units
1240 Mission Road
Los Angeles, CA 90033
323-266-3813
Fax: 323-266-5049
www.usc.edu

Focuses on clinical problems of the newborn and premature infant.

Paul YK Wu, MD, Director

Conferences

6238 National Sudden Infant Death Syndrome Alliance Conference
www.healthyplace.com
210-225-4388
800-221-7437
www.healthyplace.com

Unites parents, caregivers, and researchers with government, business, and community service groups in a nationwide movement to advance the support of SIDS families and hasten the elimination of SIDS through medical research. Funds medical research and offers emotional support nationally and locally.

Gary Koplin, President
Harry Croft, M.D, Medical Director
Patricia Avila, Editor

Audio Video

6239 7 Steps to Reducing the Risk of SIDS
InJoy Productions
7107 La Vista Place
Longmont, CO 80503
303-447-2082
800-326-2082
Fax: 303-449-8788
custserv@injoyvideos.com
www.injoyvideos.com

Shows how to dramatically lower infant's risk of using simple, important safety steps. Although SIDS is a frightening subject, this video's positive and compassionate tone will help ease parent's anxieties by showing them how to give their baby a healthy and happy first year.

14 minutes

Web Sites

6240 American SIDS Institute
528 Raven Way
Naples, FL 34110
239-431-5425
Fax: 239-431-5536
www.sids.org

A national nonprofit health care organization that is dedicated to the prevention of sudden infant death and the promotion of infant health through an aggresive, comprehensive nationwide program of: Research, Clinical Services, Education and Family Support.

Marc Peterzell, JD, Chairman
Betty McEntire, PhD, CEO/ Executive Director

6241 Compassionate Friends
www.compassionatefriends.org
877-969-0010
www.compassionatefriends.org

Assists families toward the positive resolution of grief following the death of a child of any age and provides information to help others be supportive.

Sudden Infant Death Syndrome / Book Publishers

6242 Division of Extramural Research
31 Center Drive, Building 31, Building 31, Room 2A
Bethesda, MD 20892
800-370-2943
Fax: 866-760-5947
TTY: 888-320-6942
www.nichd.nih.gov

Composed of several branches the principle NIH source of support for research and research training in maternal and child health, through grants, contracts, and cooperative agreements. Through this research, CRMC-supported scientists are advancing fundamental and clinical knowledge concerning maternal health and child development problems such as low birth wieght, intellectual and developmental disabilities, specific learning disabilities, congenital and genetic defects and others.

Alan E. Guttmacher, M.D., Director
Lisa Kaeser, Program Analyst
Lisa Williams Simons, Senior Research Assistant

6243 Health Answers Education Sudler-WPP Health Practice
700 Dresher Road
Horsham, PA 19044
215-442-9010
www.healthanswers.com

HealthAnswers offers a breadth of services in medical education, sales force training, patient support solutions, professional promotion and consumer solutions.

Mike Hudnall, CEO

6244 National Center for Education in Maternal and Child Health
www.ncemch.org

MCHnavigator@ncemch.org
www.ncemch.org

Information and advocacy resources for families and professionals. Includes listings of organizations providing general information and organizations focusing on more specific areas of concern to families and young adults who have disabilities.

Rochelle Mayer, Ed.D., Director

6245 Online Mendelian Inheritance in Man
McKusick-Nathans Institue of Genetic Medicine-JHU
Baltimore, MD 21205
www.omim.org

This database is a catalog of human genes and genetic disorders.

Ada Hamosh, MD, Scientific Director

6246 SID Network
PO Box 520
Ledyard, CT 6339
sids-network.org/net.htm

Nonprofit voluntary agency that is dedicated to eliminate sudden infant death syndrome through the support of SIDS research projects, provide support for those who have been touched by the tragedy of sudden Infant Death Syndrome and to raise public awareness of sudden infant death syndrome through education.

6247 SUID/SIDS Gateway (Resource Center)
Maternal and Child Health Library
www.mchlibrary.org/collections/suid-sids

mchevidence@ncemch.org
www.mchlibrary.org/collections/suid-sids

The Sudden Unexpected Infant Death (SUID) & Sudden Infant Death Syndrome (SIDS) Gateway is an online platform to find resources for states, communities, professionals, and families to reduce sudden unexpected infant death (SUID) and Sudden Infant Death Syndrome (SIDS), promote healthy outcomes, and cope with grief when losses occur.

Book Publishers

6248 Apparent Life - Threatening Event and Sudden Infant Death Syndrome
Circle Solutions, Inc
8280 Greensboro Drive, Suite 300
McLean, VA 22102
703-821-8955
866-866-7437
Fax: 703-821-2098
marketing@circlesolutions.com
www.circlesolution.com

Provides information about ALTE and its relationship to SIDS.

1992 29 pages

Kristina Lewis, Chairman, Executive Committee
Louis Cartwright, jr., Vice President-Finance
Michael Collins, Vice President-IT

6249 Crib Death: The Sudden Infant Death Syndrome
Futura Publishing Company
135 Bedford Road
Armonk, NY 10504
914-273-1014
Fax: 914-273-1015
www.growinghealthcare.com

A thorough book, that discusses the theories of SIDS and their implications. Athough it is aimed at the medical professional, lay people will also gain a clearer understanding of SIDS.

1995 456 pages Hardcover

6250 Death Investigations and Sudden Infant Death Syndrome
Circle Solutions, Inc
8280 Greensboro Drive, Suite 300
McLean, VA 22102
703-821-8955
Fax: 703-821-2098
marketing@circlesolutions.com
www.circlesolutions.com

Contains abstracts of articles on autopsies, death certification, and infant death scene investigation and SIDS.

1991 104 pages

Kristina Lewis, Chairman, Executive Committee
Louis Cartwright, jr., Vice President-Finance
Michael Collins, Vice President-IT

6251 Death of a Child, the Grief of the Parents A Lifetime Journey
Circle Solutions, Inc
8280 Greensboro Drive, Suite 300
McLean, VA 22102
703-821-8955
Fax: 703-821-2098
marketing@circlesolutions.com
www.circlesolutions.com

1997 38 pages

Kristina Lewis, Chairman, Executive Committee
Louis Cartwright, jr., Vice President-Finance
Michael Collins, Vice President-IT

6252 Grief, Bereavement and Sudden Infant Death Syndrome
Circle Solutions, Inc
8280 Greensboro Drive, Suite 300
McLean, VA 22102
703-821-8955
Fax: 703-821-2098
marketing@circlesolutions.com
www.circlesolutions.com

Contains abstracts of selected materials on the grief and bereavement process specific to the loss of a child to SIDS.

1991 28 pages

Kristina Lewis, Chairman, Executive Committee
Louis Cartwright, jr., Vice President-Finance
Michael Collins, Vice President-IT

6253 SIDS Research
Circle Solutions, Inc
8280 Greensboro Drive, Suite 300
McLean, VA 22102
703-821-8955
Fax: 703-821-2098
marketing@circlesolutions.com
www.circlesolutions.com

Sudden Infant Death Syndrome / Newsletters

Contains abstracts of relevant articles published during 1993.

1995 146 pages

Kristina Lewis, Chairman, Executive Committee
Louis Cartwright, jr., Vice President-Finance
Michael Collins, Vice President-IT

6254 SIDS Survival Guide
Independent Publishers Group
814 N Franklin Street
Chicago, IL 60610
312-337-0747
800-888-4741
Fax: 312-337-5985
frontdesk@ipgbook.com
www.ipgbook.com

Offers information and comfort for grieving family, friends and professionals who seek to help them.

1994 290 pages Paperback
ISBN: 0-964121-87-5

Curt Matthews, CEO

6255 SIDS: A Parents Guide to Understanding & Preventing SIDS
Hachette Book Group USA
322 South Enterprise Blvd
Lebanon, IN 46052
800-759-0190
Fax: 800-286-9471
customer.service@hbgusa.com
www.hachettebookgroup.biz

1995
ISBN: 0-316779-12-1

David Young, Chairman
Evan Schnittman, Executive Vice President
Jamie Raab, President & Publisher

6256 Smoking and Sudden Infant Death Syndrome
Circle Solutions, Inc
8280 Breensboro Drive, Suite 300
McLean, VA 22102
703-821-8955
Fax: 703-821-2098
TTY: 703-556-4831
marketing@circlesolutions.com
www.circlesolutions.com

Contains abstracts of materials about tobacco use, its relationship to SIDS, and the dangers to the unborn and the newly born from passive and secondary smoking.

1992 34 pages

Kristina Lewis, Chairman, Executive Committee
Louis Cartwright, jr., Vice President-Finance
Michael Collins, Vice President-IT

6257 Sudden Death in Infancy, Childhood & Adolescence
Cambridge University Press
32 Avenue Of The Americas
New York, NY 10013
212-924-3900
Fax: 212-691-3239
newyork@cambridge.org
www.cambridge.org/us

1994 400 pages
ISBN: 0-521420-31-8

6258 Sudden Infant Death Syndrome Risk Factors
Circle Solutions, Inc
8280 Greensboro Drive, Suite 300
McLean, VA 22102
703-821-8955
Fax: 703-821-2098
TTY: 703-556-4831
marketing@circlesolutions.com
www.circlesolutions.com

Contains selected articles published between 1989 and 1993 on the risk factors for SIDS.

1994 131 pages

Kristina Lewis, Chairman, Executive Committee
Louis Cartwright, jr., Vice President-Finance
Michael Collins, Vice President-IT

Newsletters

6259 Network
Parent Care
9041 Colgate Street
Indianapolis, IN 46268
317-872-9913
Fax: 317-872-0795

Offers information on support groups, meetings, organizations and resources for parents and professionals dealing with the chronically ill child.

6260 Newsletter: SIDS
Massachusetts Center For SIDS
1 Boston Medical Center Place
Boston, MA 2118
617-638-8000
www.bmc.org/program/sids/

Offers information on SIDS, articles pertaining to the latest information available on the mystery condition, latest research and fund-raising news and professional resources available.

Monthly

Pamphlets

6261 After Sudden Infant Death Syndrome
Circle Solution, Inc
8280 Greensboro Drive, Suite 300
McLean, VA 22102
703-821-8955
Fax: 703-821-2098
marketing@circlesolutions.com
www.circlesolutions.com

1993 16 pages

Kristina Lewis, President/ Chair
Louis Cartwright, Jr., Vice President of Finance
Laura Scherzer, CMP, PMP, Vice President of Operations

6262 Facts About Apnea and Other Apparent Life-Threatening Events
Circle Solution, Inc
8280 Greensboro Drive, Suite 300
McLean, VA 22102
703-821-8955
Fax: 703-821-2098
marketing@circlesolutions.com
www.circlesolutions.com

Explains apparent life-threatening events in infants, their relationship to SIDS and current views on home monitoring.

1987 2 pages

Kristina Lewis, President/ Chair
Louis Cartwright, Jr., Vice President of Finance
Laura Scherzer, CMP, PMP, Vice President of Operations

6263 Facts About SIDS
Sudden Infant Death Syndrome Alliance
1314 Bedford Avenue
Baltimore, MD 21208
410-653-8226
Fax: 410-653-8709

Offers information on basic facts, answers to the most frequently asked questions about SIDS and information on numbers to call and referral centers for more help.

6264 Infant Positioning and Sudden Infant Death Syndrome
Circle Solutions, Inc
8280 Greensboro Drive, Suite 300
McLean, VA 22102
703-821-8955
Fax: 703-821-2098
marketing@circlesolutions.com
www.circlesolutions.com

Contains abstracts of selected articles on the topic of sleep position and SIDS.

1994

Kristina Lewis, President/ Chair
Louis Cartwright, Jr., Vice President of Finance
Laura Scherzer, CMP, PMP, Vice President of Operations

6265 National SIDS Resource Center Brochure
Circle Solutions, Inc
8280 Greensboro Drive, Suite 300
McLean, VA 22102

703-821-8955
Fax: 703-821-2098
marketing@circlesolutions.com
www.circlesolutions.com

1994

Kristina Lewis, President/ Chair
Louis Cartwright, Jr., Vice President of Finance
Laura Scherzer, CMP, PMP, Vice President of Operations

6266 Nationwide Survey of Sudden Infant Death Syndrome (SIDS) Service
Circle Solutions, Inc
8280 Greensboro Drive, Suite 300
McLean, VA 22102

703-821-8955
Fax: 703-821-2098
marketing@circlesolutions.com
www.circlesolutions.com

Analysis of availability of SIDS services.

1994

Kristina Lewis, President/ Chair
Louis Cartwright, Jr., Vice President of Finance
Laura Scherzer, CMP, PMP, Vice President of Operations

6267 SIDS Prevention
Corporate Office
100 Enterprise Way, Suite G300
Scotts Valley, CA 95066

831-438-4060
800-620-8884
Fax: 831-438-4284
www.etr.org

Gives overview, risk factors, prevention of Sudden Infant Death Syndrome.

50 pamphlets

Dan McCormick, MHA, Chief Executive Officer
David Kitchen, MBA, Chief Financial Officer
Erin Cassidy-Eagle, PhD, Director, Research

6268 SIDS: Toward Prevention and Improved Infant Health
American SIDS Institute
528 Raven Way
Naples, FL 34110

239-431-5425
800-232-sids
Fax: 239-431-5536
prevent@sids.org
www.sids.org

Practical guide for those planning a pregnancy, for parents-to-be and for new parents.

Marc Peterzell, JD, Chairman
Betty McEntire, PhD, CEO/ Executive Director

Syncope / Description

Description

6269 SYNCOPE

Synonyms: Swoon, Faint

Involves the following Biologic System(s):

Cardiovascular Disorders

Syncope is a medical term describing a phenomenon more commonly known as fainting. Specifically, syncope is a brief loss of consciousness that resolves without intervention. In the pediatric population most episodes of syncope are uncomplicated without neurologic or cardiac after effects (sequelae).

The true incidence of syncope is difficult to ascertain since many episodes are not reported to a medical provider. Roughly 15-25% of all children experience at least one episode of syncope or near-syncope, although adolescents are are the most common segment of the pediatric population to experience syncope and the most likely to have recurrent episodes.

The most common cause of fainting in pediatrics is neurocardiogenic (related to a problem of the nervous system and the heart) syncope, also known as vasovagal or vasodepressor syncope. The other cases of syncope can be divided into neurologic, cardiac, metabolic, toxin (drug abuse), and psychogenic. While greater than 95% of syncopal episodes have a benign etiology (cause), such as the simple vasovagal syncope, there are several rare causes that are fatal, accounting for 4-5 deaths per 100,000 pediatric patients. The possibility of a fatal etiology necessitates the need for a thorough investigation into any syncopal episode.

An appropriate evaluation begins with a thorough history and physical exam. The history should focus on details around the event, change in position (from sitting to standing, for instance), exercise, trauma, and past history of similar events. Family history is critical when evaluating unexplained sudden deaths, hearing loss, cardiac disease, recurrent fainting, seizure disorders or arrhythmias. The physical exam should include a careful neurologic exam as well as a thorough cardiac exam looking for murmurs, clicks or gallops (unusual heart sounds) and careful blood pressure measurements including orthostatic measurements (when the patient is sitting and then stands up. In individuals who have fainted, the blood pressure can drop significantly upon standing, indicating at least one possible cause of the syncopal episode.

The diagnostic evaluation continues with an electrocardiogram looking at abnormal rhythms as well as signs of cardiomyopathy (heart disease). If the physical examination and ECG are normal and the history is consistent with a simple 'faint', no further workup may be necessary. If the history is inconsistent with vasovagal syncope or if there are any abnormalities on the physical or ECG, referral to a specialist, usually a pediatric cardiologist or adult cardiologist, is appropriate. Further testing may include a tilt table test, 24-hour holter monitor, echocardiography, exercise stress testing or electrophysiology testing.

Treatment for syncope varies depending on the etiology. For simple vasodepressor syncope, management is often focused on increasing fluid and salt intake in an effort to improve blood volume and pressure. Often discovering the triggers for these patients enables them to avoid them or anticipate their response more effectively (i.e. lying on the ground with feet up before syncope occurs). Medication is an option if the syncopal episodes are frequent and impacton the patient's lifestyle. The most widely used and successfully used medication class has been beta-blockers. More serious cardiac causes of syncope may need to be treated with antiarrhythmics, pacemakers or defibrillators. These interventions can be life-saving and allow patients to lead full productive lives.

National Associations & Support Groups

6270 American Academy of Pediatrics
345 Park Blvd
Itasca, IL 60143
847-434-4000
800-433-9016
Fax: 847-434-8000
csc@aap.org
www.aap.org

The American Academy of Pediatrics and its member pediatricians are committed to the attainment of optimal physical, mental and social health and well-being for all infants, children, adolescents, and young adults.

Kyle E. Yasuda, MD, FAAP, President
Mark Del Monte, JD, CEO/Executive VP
Vera Tait, MD, FAAP, Chief Medical Officer

6271 Child Neurology Foundation
601 W Short Street
Lexington, KY 40508
888-417-3435
info@childneurologyfoundation.org
childneurologyfoundation.org

The Child Neurology Foundation connects partners from all areas of the child neurology community so those navigating the journey of disease diagnosis, management, and care have the ongoing support from those dedicated to treatments and cures.

Amy Brin, Executive Director
Katie Hentges, Director, Programs
Brea McCormley, Director, Development

6272 NIH/National Heart, Lung and Blood Institute
31 Center Drive, Bldg 31
Bethesda, MD 20892
877-645-2448
www.nhlbi.nih.gov

Primary responsibility of this organization is the scientific investigation of heart, blood vessel, lung and blood disorders. Oversees research, demonstration, prevention, education, control and training activities in these fields and emphasizes the prevention and control of heart diseases.

Gary H. Gibbons, MD, Director
Kate O'Sullivan, Executive Officer

6273 NIH/National Institute of Neurological Disorders and Stroke (NINDS)
PO Box 5801
Bethesda, MD 20824
800-352-9424
www.ninds.nih.gov

Works to reduce the burden of neurological disease by conducting, fostering, coordinating and guiding research on the causes, prevention, diagnosis and treatment of neurological disorders and stroke, while supporting basic research in related scientific areas.

Walter J. Koroshetz, MD, Director

Web Sites

6274 EMedicine Journal: Syncope
www.emedicine.com/med/topic3385.htm

www.emedicine.com/med/topic3385.htm

Syncope information covering background, pathophysiology, frequency, mortality/morbidity, causes, lab studies and tests, diet, activity, drugs used in treatment, complications and patient education. Authored by Dr Jatin Dave and co-authored by Dr John Michael Gaziano.

6275 NINDS Syncope Information Page
Office of Communications and Public Liaison, NINDS
Bethesda, MD 20892
301-496-5751
800-352-9424
www.ninds.nih.gov/disorders/syncope/

Walter J. Koroshetz, M.D., Acting Director
Alan L. Willard, Ph.D., Acting Deputy Director
Caroline Lewis, Executive Officer

Syndactyly / Description

Description

6276 SYNDACTYLY

Synonyms: Syndactylia, Syndactylism

Involves the following Biologic System(s):

Orthopedic and Muscle Disorders

Syndactyly refers to an abnormality that is present at birth (congenital) and characterized by the joining together (fusing) of two or more fingers or toes. This relatively common abnormality seems to occur more frequently in boys than in girls. It is often inherited as an autosomal dominant trait. Syndactyly often results from incomplete or abnormal embryonic development of the fingers or toes. In some infants, it occurs spontaneously as the hands or feet of the developing fetus may be unnaturally constricted within the uterus. Classification of syndactyly is based on the severity of the clinical presentation. Defects associated with syndactyly may range from a simple or incomplete joining or webbing of the skin between two digits to fusion from the base to the tip of the digits, complete with fusion of the bones and nails.

Syndactyly of the foot may involve complete or incomplete webbing that usually affects the second and third toes. This simple condition is referred to as zygosyndactyly and often requires no treatment. Syndactyly may also involve webbing and bone fusion (synostosis) of the fourth and fifth toes with duplication of the fifth toe in a condition called syndactyly/polysyndactyly.

As in the foot, syndactyly of the hand may involve a simple webbing. However, in some cases, the fusion of certain fingers may be more complex and involve shared nerves and blood supply. Syndactyly of the fingers should be carefully evaluated to determine the best method of treatment, allowing for growth and dexterity of the fingers.

Syndactyly may also occur in association with several genetic disorders. Such disorders include acrocephalopolysyndactyly type II (Carpenter's syndrome), characterized by intellectual disabilities and irregularities involving the head, hand, and genitalia; acrocephalosyndactyly type I (Apert's syndrome), characterized by craniofacial irregularities and syndactyly of the hands and feet; trisomy 18 syndrome, a chromosomal abnormality characterized by multiple craniofacial abnormalities, irregularities of the hands and feet, and severe intellectual disabilities; and other inherited diseases. Treatment of syndactyly associated with these and other inherited disorders depends upon the nature of the underlying disorder. In itself, a minor incomplete syndactyly is not an indication for surgery if the only issue is its appearance. However, a syndactyly that prevents full range of motion in the involved fingers warrants surgical release to increase the fingers' ability to function. The timing of surgery is variable. However, as more fingers are involved and as the syndactyly becomes more complex, release should be performed earlier.

Government Agencies

6277 NIH/National Institute of Arthritis and Musculoskeletal and Skin Diseases
1 AMS Circle
Bethesda, MD 20892

301-495-4484
877-226-4267
Fax: 301-718-6366
TDD: 301-565-2966
niamsinfo@mail.nih.gov
www.niams.nih.gov

The mission of the NIAMS, a part of the NIH, is to support research into the causes, treatment and prevention of arthritis and musculoskeletal and skin diseases, the training of basic and clinical scientists to carry out this research, and the dissemination of information on research progress in these diseases.

Lindsey A. Criswell, MD, Director
Rick Phillips, Executive Officer

National Associations & Support Groups

6278 American Academy of Pediatrics
345 Park Blvd
Itasca, IL 60143

847-434-4000
800-433-9016
Fax: 847-434-8000
csc@aap.org
www.aap.org

The American Academy of Pediatrics and its member pediatricians are committed to the attainment of optimal physical, mental and social health and well-being for all infants, children, adolescents, and young adults.

Kyle E. Yasuda, MD, FAAP, President
Mark Del Monte, JD, CEO/Executive VP
Vera Tait, MD, FAAP, Chief Medical Officer

6279 Genetic Alliance
426400 Woodfield Road, Ste 189
Damascus, MD 20872

202-966-5557
Fax: 202-966-8553
info@geneticalliance.org
www.geneticalliance.org

World's leading nonprofit health advocacy organization committed to transforming health through genetics and promoting an environment of openness centered on the health of individuals, families, and communities.

Sharon Terry, CEO
Ruth Child, CFO
Natasha Bonhomme, Chief Strategy Officer

6280 March of Dimes Foundation
1550 Crystal Drive, Ste 1300
Arlington, VA 22202

888-663-4637
www.marchofdimes.org

March of Dimes help moms have full-term pregnancies and research the problems that threaten the health of babies. The March of Dimes also acts globally: sharing best practices in perinatal health and helping improve birth outcomes where the needs are the most urgent.

Stacey D. Stewart, President
Alan Brogdon, SVP/COO/Board Officer
Rahul Gupta, MD, SVP & Chief Medical/Health Officer

6281 Shriners Hospitals for Children
2900 N Rocky Point Drive
Tampa, FL 33607

800-237-5055
www.shrinerschildrens.org

Shriners Children's has been providing hope and healing to children for more than 100 years. Our compassionate, prestigious doctors and care teams are committed to excellence in pediatric care.

John McCabe, EVP & COO

Web Sites

6282 A-to-Z Health & Disease Information
www.hmc.psu.edu/healthinfo/pq/poly.htm

www.hmc.psu.edu/healthinfo/pq/poly.htm

Information page on polydactyly and syndactyly provided by Penn State Medical Center. Information includes a listing of physicians who treat the disorder, causes, symptoms, a general overview, diagnosis and treatment.

6283 Online Mendelian Inheritance in Man
McKusick-Nathans Institue of Genetic Medicine-JHU
Baltimore, MD 21205

www.omim.org

This database is a catalog of human genes and genetic disorders.

Ada Hamosh, MD, Scientific Director

6284 Pediatric Plastic Surgery
One Hospital Drive, MC504
Columbia, MO 65212
573-882-4158
Fax: 573-884-4585
mumedicine@missouri.edu
medicine.missouri.edu/surgery/

Answers to questions about syndactyly and surgery provided by the University of Missouri Children's Hospital.

6285 Syndactyly
www.pncl.co.uk/~belcher/information/Syndactyly.pdf

www.pncl.co.uk/~belcher/information/Syndactyly.pdf

Information sheet on syndactyly.

Systemic Lupus Erythematosus / Description

Description

6286 SYSTEMIC LUPUS ERYTHEMATOSUS
Synonyms: Lupus, SLE
Involves the following Biologic System(s):
Immunologic and Rheumatologic Disorders

Systemic lupus erythematosus (SLE) is a chronic, inflammatory, multisystem disorder of connective tissue that may affect many organ systems in the body including the skin, joints, membranes that line the walls of certain bodily cavities (serosal membranes), or kidneys. In children with the disorder, associated symptoms are often progressive and, without appropriate treatment, may result in life-threatening complications. However, in some patients, symptoms may spontaneously subside and periodically recur with varying levels of severity (relapsing-remitting). SLE usually becomes apparent during late adolescence or a patient's 20s or 30s. However, in up to 20 percent of patients, symptoms may begin during childhood, usually after the age of eight. Females are more commonly affected than males in all age groups.

The specific underlying cause of SLE is unknown. However, the disorder is thought to result from abnormalities in the regulating mechanisms of the immune system that normally prevent it from attacking the body's own cells and tissues. In addition, researchers speculate that certain microorganisms or other environmental factors may play some role in causing SLE. Familial cases have also been reported, suggesting potential genetic mechanisms. In some individuals, SLE-like symptoms may also occur after exposure to certain medications, such as particular antiseizure drugs or certain antibiotics known as sulfonamides. Drug-induced symptoms are usually relatively mild and subside when the responsible medication is removed.

The range and severity of associated symptoms and findings may vary. Although associated symptoms may begin suddenly or gradually, most children with SLE tend to have more acute, severe symptoms than adults. In some children, symptoms may tend to recur or worsen in association with certain infections. In addition, exposure to sunlight may worsen associated skin or other symptoms. Many children with SLE initially experience generalized symptoms, such as a fever, a general feeling of ill health (malaise), joint swelling and inflammation (arthritis) or pain (arthralgia), loss of appetite (anorexia), and weight loss. Most children also have associated skin abnormalities, including a scaly, reddish or bluish rash that is in a distinctive butterfly distribution across the cheeks and the bridge of the nose (butterfly rash). The affected area may be abnormally sensitive to sunlight (photosensitive), and the rash may gradually spread to other facial areas, the neck, scalp, chest, and arms. Additional skin symptoms may include flat, reddish, dot-like spots (punctate lesions) on the fingertips, palms, soles, arms, legs, and torso; abnormal changes of the tissues beneath the fingernails and toenails (nail beds); tender, reddish-purple swellings or nodules on the legs (erythema nodosum); and itchy, reddish, flat or raised lesions of the skin and mucous membranes (erythema multiforme). Patients may also develop painless sores of the mucous membranes of the mouth and nose. The hair may be abnormally coarse and dry, and some children may have patchy areas of baldness on the scalp (alopecia).

Many children with SLE may also experience joint stiffness; inflammation of muscles (myositis), causing muscle pain and weakness; abnormal changes and localized loss of bone in certain areas (aseptic necrosis), particularly the head of the thigh bone (femur); and Raynaud's phenomenon. This condition is characterized by sudden contraction of the relatively small blood vessels supplying the fingers and toes (digits), causing an interruption of blood flow to the digits and a subsequent excess of blood in affected areas following restoration of blood flow (reactive hyperemia). Such episodes are usually triggered by exposure to cold temperatures and are characterized by numbing, tingling, and bluish or whitish discoloration of the digits due to lack of blood flow and subsequent reddening and pain as blood flow is reestablished. Many children with SLE may also develop inflammation of the membranes that line the lungs and chest cavity (pleurisy), surround the heart (pericarditis), and line the wall of the abdomen and cover the abdominal organs (peritonitis). Additional heart abnormalities may also be present, such as abnormal heart murmurs, inflammation of heart muscle (myocarditis), enlargement of the heart (cardiomegaly), a decreased ability of the heart to pump blood effectively to the lungs and the rest of the body (heart failure), and, in some severe cases, heart attacks (myocardial infarctions), potentially causing life-threatening complications.

Kidney involvement is common among children with SLE and may be the only disease manifestation. Associated inflammation of the filtering units of the kidneys (glomerulonephritis) may be mild, moderate, or severe. Symptoms and findings may range from small amounts of blood in the urine (hematuria) of mildly increased levels of protein in the urine (proteinuria) to kidney failure that causes potentially life-threatening complications. Some children with SLE may also experience symptoms due to involvement of the brain and spinal cord (central nervous system). Associated neurologic abnormalities may include personality changes, episodes of abnormally increased electrical activity in the brain (seizures), or other findings. In addition, in some children, disease progression may also affect other tissues and organs, causing additional symptoms and findings.

The treatment of SLE is individualized and based upon the severity of the disease and the specific organ systems affected. Episodes of active disease should be considered emergencies that require immediate evaluation and aggressive treatment to help prevent damage to affected tissues and organs. In addition, careful follow-up and ongoing monitoring is required to detect worsening disease and to ensure prompt, appropriate treatment as required. Therapy may include the use of nonsteroidal antiinflammatory drugs (NSAIDs)s or salicylates (aspirin) to help alleviate joint pain and antimalarial agents or topical corticosteroid creams to treat skin symptoms. In severe cases, immunosuppressive drugs may also be administered; however, such agents must be used with great caution in children. Treatment of kidney inflammation may also include the use of certain corticosteroids, such as prednisone, and in some patients, the addition of immunosuppressive agents, such as azathioprine. Children with severe kidney disease may require regular dialysis or kidney transplantation. Dialysis is a medical procedure that removes excess fluid from the body and waste products from the blood. Additional treatment is symptomatic and supportive.

National Associations & Support Groups

6287 American Academy of Pediatrics
345 Park Blvd
Itasca, IL 60143

847-434-4000
800-433-9016
Fax: 847-434-8000
csc@aap.org
www.aap.org

The American Academy of Pediatrics and its member pediatricians are committed to the attainment of optimal physical, mental and social health and well-being for all infants, children, adolescents, and young adults.

Kyle E. Yasuda, MD, FAAP, President
Mark Del Monte, JD, CEO/Executive VP
Vera Tait, MD, FAAP, Chief Medical Officer

6288 American Autoimmune Related Diseases Association
19176 Hall Road, Suite 130
Clinton, MI 48038
586-776-3900
aarda@aarda.org
www.aarda.org

The American Autoimmune Related Diseases Association is dedicated to the eradication of autoimmune diseases and the alleviation of suffering and the socioeconomic impact of autoimmunity through fostering and facilitating collaboration in the areas of education, public awareness, research, and patient services in an effective, ethical and efficient manner.

Lilly Stairs, Interim President/CEO
Laura Simpson, COO

6289 Children's Hospital Boston
300 Longwood Avenue
Boston, MA 02115
617-355-6000
www.childrenshospital.org

Mission is to provide the highest quality care; be the leading source of research and discovery; educate the next generation of leaders in child health and enhance the health and well-being of the children and families in our local community.

Kevin B. Churchwell, President & CEO
Jessica Farnham, Chief Operating Officer

6290 Genetic Alliance
426400 Woodfield Road, Ste 189
Damascus, MD 20872
202-966-5557
Fax: 202-966-8553
info@geneticalliance.org
www.geneticalliance.org

World's leading nonprofit health advocacy organization committed to transforming health through genetics and promoting an environment of openness centered on the health of individuals, families, and communities.

Sharon Terry, CEO
Ruth Child, CFO
Natasha Bonhomme, Chief Strategy Officer

6291 Lupus Foundation of America
2121 K Street NW, Suite 200
Washington, DC 20037
202-349-1155
Fax: 202-349-1156
info@lupus.org
www.lupus.org

The LFA mission is to educate and support those affected by lupus. It supports research into the cause and cure of lupus. Information resources are available on request, including free pamphlets, brochures (English/Spanish), and articles for people seeking an understanding of lupus. Books and materials on lupus are also available through the LFA. There are nearly 300 chapters, branches, and support groups in 32 states throughout the US.

Mary T. Crimmings, Interim CEO & SVP, Marketing
Julie Tune, Chief Financial Officer
Mike Donnelly, VP, Communications

Research Centers

6292 Lupus Research Institute
330 Seventh Ave, Suite 1701
New York, NY 10001
212-812-9881
Fax: 212-545-1843
lupus@LupusNY.org
www.lupusresearchinstitute.org

Established exclusively for lupus research. It has invested almost $20 million in new research and has funded 73 studies in 22 states.

Robert J Ravitz, Co-Chair
John A Luke, Treasurer

6293 SLE Lupus Foundation
330 Seventh Ave, Suite 1701
New York, NY 10001
212-685-4118
800-745-8787
Fax: 212-545-1843
www.lupusny.org

Purpose is to raise funds for research grants, provide information and services to lupus patients, and educate the public about lupus. Patient services include self-help groups, orientation meetings, referrals, publications, and counseling on personal and financial problems related to the disease.

Richard K DeScherer, President
Margaret G Dowd, Executive Director

Web Sites

6294 American Autoimmune Related Diseases Association
www.aarda.org
586-776-3900
aarda@aarda.org
www.aarda.org

The American Autoimmune Related Diseases Association is dedicated to the eradication of autoimmune diseases and the alleviation of suffering and the socioeconomic impact of autoimmunity through fostering and facilitating collaboration in the areas of education, public awareness, research, and patient services in an effective, ethical and efficient manner.

6295 Children's Hospital Boston
300 Longwood Avenue
Boston, MA 02115
617-355-6000
www.childrenshospital.org

Mission is to provide the highest quality care; be the leading source of research and discovery; educate the next generation of leaders in child health and enhance the health and well-being of the children and families in our local community.

Kevin B. Churchwell, President & CEO
Jessica Farnham, Chief Operating Officer

Book Publishers

6296 Immune System Disorders Sourcebook 3rd Edition
Omnigraphics
615 Griswold Street, Ste 520
Detroit, MI 48226
610-461-3548
800-234-1340
Fax: 800-875-1340
contact@omnigraphics.com
www.omnigraphics.com

Basic information about lupus, multiple sclerosis, guillain-barre syndrome and other disorders of the immune system.

624 pages
ISBN: 0-780807-48-0

6297 Let's Talk About Going to the Hospital
Rosen Publishing Group's PowerKids Press
29 E 21st Street
New York, NY 10010
212-777-3017
800-237-9932
Fax: 888-436-4643
rosenpub@tribeca.ios.com
www.rosenpublishing.com

If a child has to check into the hospital, chances are he or she is already upset about being ill. Knowing how a hospital functions and what the procedures are, such as when family members can visit, will help in what is already a stressful situation. Grades K-5.

24 pages
ISBN: 0-823950-36-0

Roger Rosen, President

Tay-Sachs Disease / Description

Description

6298 TAY-SACHS DISEASE

Synonyms: GM2 gangliosidosis, type I, Hexa deficiency, Hexosaminidase A deficiency, Tay-Sachs disease, infantile type, TSD

Covers these related disorders: Tay-Sachs disease, juvenile type (GM2 gangliosidosis, type III)

Involves the following Biologic System(s):
Genetic/Chromosomal/Syndrome/Metabolic Disorders

Tay-Sachs disease, also known as GM2 gangliosidosis type I or infantile type, is a progressive degenerative metabolic disorder that occurs when two copies of the disease gene are inherited from the parents (autosomal recessive trait). The disorder, which belongs to a group of diseases known as lysosomal storage disorders, results from insufficient activity of the enzyme beta-hexosaminidase A. Enzymes within lysosomes, which are the major digestive units of cells, break down particles of nutrients such as certain fats and carbohydrates. In individuals with Tay-Sachs disease, insufficient activity of the enzyme hbeta-exosaminidase A causes an abnormal accumulation of particular fats (i.e., gangliosides) in certain tissues of the body, particularly nerve cells of the brain. Tay-Sachs disease affects approximately one in 3,500 to 4,000 newborns. The disease occurs predominantly in people of Ashkenazi Jewish (i.e., northeastern European Jewish) descent. About one in 30 individuals of Ashkenazi Jewish ancestry carries a single copy of the disease gene (heterozygous carrier).

Infants with Tay-Sachs disease appear to develop as expected until approximately four to six months of age, except for a marked startle reaction to sudden noises (hyperacusis) that may be apparent soon after birth. From four to six months of age, affected infants may begin to have decreased focusing and eye contact and appear listless and irritable. As the disease progresses, infants have delays in the acquisition of skills requiring the coordination of mental and physical activities (psychomotor delays) and lose previously acquired skills. By about one year of age, most affected children lose the ability to roll over, sit, stand, or vocalize sounds. In addition, muscle tone is severely diminished (hypotonia). With continuing disease progression, children experience increasing muscle rigidity and associated restrictions of movement (spasticity); uncontrolled electrical disturbances in the brain (seizures) that may be accompanied by prolonged contractions and relaxations of certain muscles (tonic-clonic convulsions); development of abnormal red circular areas of the middle layer of the eyes (cherry-red spots or Tay's sign); blindness; deafness; and loss of cognitive abilities (dementia). In many affected children, there is also enlargement of the brain (metabolic megalencephaly) due to abnormal accumulation of gangliosides in brain cells. Life-threatening complications often develop by approximately two to four years of age.

There are also variants of Tay-Sachs disease in which the onset of symptoms occurs later in life. For example, in children with the variant known as Tay-Sachs disease, juvenile type (GM2 gangliosidosis, type III), symptoms typically become apparent during mid-childhood although they may sometimes develop as early as the second year of life. This disease variant, which is characterized by varying levels of hexosaminidase deficiency, is also inherited as an autosomal recessive trait. Associated symptoms may include progressive impairment of voluntary movements (ataxia); involuntary movements characterized by rapid, jerking or slow, repetitive, writhing movements (choreoathetosis); loss of speech; seizures; and visual loss. Patients may experience life-threatening complications by approximately 15 years of age.

The disease gene responsible for Tay-Sachs disease is located on the long arm of chromosome 15 (15q23-24). Several distinct changes (mutations) in this disease gene have been identified in individuals with Tay-Sachs disease. In addition, different mutations are responsible for the infantile and juvenile forms of the disorder. Tests have been developed to help confirm carrier status in individuals who may carry a single copy of the disease gene (e.g., serum or leukocyte hexosaminidase A testing). It is recommended that individuals of Askenazi Jewish descent obtain testing prior to starting a family. In addition, genetic counseling is provided for those individuals who are heterozygous carriers and desire to start a family or have additional children. Specialized testing is also available that may confirm a diagnosis of Tay-Sachs disease before birth (e.g., chorionic villus sampling). The treatment of infants and children with Tay-Sachs disease includes symptomatic and supportive measures. Even with the best of care, children with Tay-Sachs disease usually die by age 4, from recurring infection.

Government Agencies

6299 NIH/ Eunice Kennedy Shriver National Institute of Child Health & Human Development
P.O. Box 3006
Rockville, MD 20847

800-370-2943
Fax: 866-760-5947
www.nichd.nih.gov

Conducts and supports research on topics related to the health of children, adults, families and populations. Some of these topics include: developmental disabilities, growth and development, infant death, reproductive health and birth defects.

Diana W. Bianchi, Director
Alison Cernich, PhD, Deputy Director

6300 NIH/National Institute of Neurological Disorders and Stroke (NINDS)
PO Box 5801
Bethesda, MD 20824

800-352-9424
www.ninds.nih.gov

Works to reduce the burden of neurological disease by conducting, fostering, coordinating and guiding research on the causes, prevention, diagnosis and treatment of neurological disorders and stroke, while supporting basic research in related scientific areas.

Walter J. Koroshetz, MD, Director

National Associations & Support Groups

6301 American Academy of Pediatrics
345 Park Blvd
Itasca, IL 60143

847-434-4000
800-433-9016
Fax: 847-434-8000
csc@aap.org
www.aap.org

The American Academy of Pediatrics and its member pediatricians are committed to the attainment of optimal physical, mental and social health and well-being for all infants, children, adolescents, and young adults.

Kyle E. Yasuda, MD, FAAP, President
Mark Del Monte, JD, CEO/Executive VP
Vera Tait, MD, FAAP, Chief Medical Officer

6302 Canadian Society for Mucopolysaccharide & Related Diseases Inc
218-2055 Commercial Drive
Vancouver, BC
Canada

604-924-5130
info@mpssociety.ca
www.mpssociety.ca

The Canadian Society for Mucopolysaccharide and Related Diseases Inc. (The Canadian MPS Society), founded in 1984, serves all Canadians affected by MPS and related diseases through support, education, advocacy and by advancing research.

Kim Angel, Executive Director

6303 **Chicago Center for Jewish Genetic Disorder**
Ben Gurion Way, One S Franklin Street, Suite 2910
Chicago, IL 60606
312-357-4718
jewishgeneticsctr@juf.org
www.jewishgeneticscenter.org

Provides public and professional education and to empower community members to seek out information and prevention strategies. Represents the blending of science with religious, cultural and historical sensitivity and awareness.

6304 **Child Neurology Foundation**
601 W Short Street
Lexington, KY 40508
888-417-3435
info@childneurologyfoundation.org
childneurologyfoundation.org

The Child Neurology Foundation connects partners from all areas of the child neurology community so those navigating the journey of disease diagnosis, management, and care have the ongoing support from those dedicated to treatments and cures.

Amy Brin, Executive Director
Katie Hentges, Director, Programs
Brea McCormley, Director, Development

6305 **Genetic Alliance**
426400 Woodfield Road, Ste 189
Damascus, MD 20872
202-966-5557
Fax: 202-966-8553
info@geneticalliance.org
www.geneticalliance.org

World's leading nonprofit health advocacy organization committed to transforming health through genetics and promoting an environment of openness centered on the health of individuals, families, and communities.

Sharon Terry, CEO
Ruth Child, CFO
Natasha Bonhomme, Chief Strategy Officer

6306 **Jewish Genetic Disease Consortium**
1515 Route 202 - suite 121
Pomona, NY 10970
855-642-6900
info@jewishgeneticdiseases.org
www.jewishgeneticdiseases.org

Created as a means by which a number of smaller, individual organizations could join together to heighten awareness of Jewish genetic diseases with a strong and unified voice.

6307 **March of Dimes Foundation**
1550 Crystal Drive, Ste 1300
Arlington, VA 22202
888-663-4637
www.marchofdimes.org

March of Dimes help moms have full-term pregnancies and research the problems that threaten the health of babies. The March of Dimes also acts globally: sharing best practices in perinatal health and helping improve birth outcomes where the needs are the most urgent.

Stacey D. Stewart, President
Alan Brogdon, SVP/COO/Board Officer
Rahul Gupta, MD, SVP & Chief Medical/Health Officer

6308 **NIH/National Institute of Neurological Disorders and Stroke (NINDS)**
PO Box 5801
Bethesda, MD 20824
800-352-9424
www.ninds.nih.gov

Works to reduce the burden of neurological disease by conducting, fostering, coordinating and guiding research on the causes, prevention, diagnosis and treatment of neurological disorders and stroke, while supporting basic research in related scientific areas.

Walter J. Koroshetz, MD, Director

6309 **National Tay-Sachs and Allied Diseases Association**
2001 Beacon Street, Suite 204
Boston, MA 02135
617-277-4463
info@ntsad.org
www.ntsad.org

Direct, fund and promote research to develop treatments and cures; provide comprehensive support services to affected families and individuals; guide prevention, education, awareness and screening through effective grassroots collaborations with chapters and affiliates; lead advocacy efforts as the recognized authority for this family of genetic diseases.

Kathleen Flynn, Chief Executive Officer
Valerie Greger, PhD, Director of Research
Diana Jussila, Director of Family Services

Web Sites

6310 **Canadian Society for Mucopolysaccharide & Related Diseases Inc**
218-2055 Commercial Drive
Vancouver, BC
Canada
604-924-5130
info@mpssociety.ca
www.mpssociety.ca

The Canadian Society for Mucopolysaccharide and Related Diseases Inc. (The Canadian MPS Society), founded in 1984, serves all Canadians affected by MPS and related diseases through support, education, advocacy and by advancing research.

Kim Angel, Executive Director

6311 **Chicago Center for Jewish Genetic Disorder**
www.jewishgeneticscenter.org
312-357-4718
jewishgeneticsctr@juf.org
www.jewishgeneticscenter.org

Provides public and professional education and to empower community members to seek out information and prevention strategies.Represents the blending of science with religious, cultural and historical sensitivity and awareness.

6312 **Health Answers Education Sudler-WPP Health Practice**
700 Dresher Road
Horsham, PA 19044
215-442-9010
www.healthanswers.com

HealthAnswers offers a breadth of services in medical education, sales force training, patient support solutions, professional promotion and consumer solutions.

Mike Hudnall, CEO

6313 **Healthfinder**
1101 Wootton Parkway
Rockville, MD 20852
healthfinder@hhs.gov
www.healthfinder.gov

A key resource for finding the best government and nonprofit health and human services information on the internet. Links to carefully selected information and web sites from over 1,500 health-related organizations.

6314 **Jewish Genetic Disease Consortium**
1515 Route 202, Suite 121
Pomona, NY 10970
855-642-6900
info@jewishgeneticdiseases.org
www.jewishgeneticdiseases.org

Created as a means by which a number of smaller, individual organizations could join together to heighten awareness of Jewish genetic diseases with a strong and unified voice.

6315 **March of Dimes Foundation**
1550 Crystal Drive, Ste 1300
Arlington, VA 22202
888-663-4637
www.marchofdimes.org

March of Dimes help moms have full-term pregnancies and research the problems that threaten the health of babies. The March of Dimes also acts globally: sharing best practices in perinatal health and helping improve birth outcomes where the needs are the most urgent.

Stacey D. Stewart, President
Alan Brogdon, SVP/COO/Board Officer
Rahul Gupta, MD, SVP & Chief Medical/Health Officer

6316 NIH/National Institute of Neurological Disorders and Stroke (NINDS)
PO Box 5801
Bethesda, MD 20824
301-496-5751
800-352-9424
www.ninds.nih.gov

Mission is to reduce the burden of neurological disease - a burden borne by every age group, by every segment of society, by people all over the world.

Walter J. Koroshetz, MD, Director

6317 Online Mendelian Inheritance in Man
McKusick-Nathans Institue of Genetic Medicine-JHU
Baltimore, MD 21205
www.omim.org

This database is a catalog of human genes and genetic disorders.

Ada Hamosh, MD, Scientific Director

Book Publishers

6318 Let's Talk About Going to the Hospital
Rosen Publishing Group's PowerKids Press
29 E 21st Street
New York, NY 10010
212-777-3017
800-237-9932
Fax: 888-436-4643
rosenpub@tribeca.ios.com
www.rosenpublishing.com

If a child has to check into the hospital, chances are he or she is already upset about being ill. Knowing how a hospital functions and what the procedures are, such as when family members can visit, will help in what is already a stressful situation. Grades K-5.

24 pages
ISBN: 0-823950-36-0

Roger Rosen, President

6319 Tay-Sachs Disease
Rosen Publishing
29 East 21st Street
New York, NY 10010
212-777-3017
800-237-9932
Fax: 888-436-4643
rosenpub@tribeca.ios.com
www.rosenpublishing.com

With colorful graphics and photographs, and a clear presentation of a tragic genetic disease, this title looks at gentic inheritance, dominant and recessive genes, and the carrier screening programs working to prevent Tay-Sachs.

6-12 64 pages 2007
ISBN: 1-404206-97-3

Roger Rosen, President

6320 Tay-Sachs Disease-A Bibliography, Medical Dictionary, & Annotated Research Guide
ICON Health Publications/ICON Group International
9606 Tierra Grande St., Suite 205
San Diego, CA 92126
Fax: 858-635-9414
orders@icongroupbooks.com
www.icongrouponline.com

A 3-in-1 reference book that provides a complete medical dictionary covering hundreds of terms and expressions relationg to Tay-Sachs disease. Also gives extensive lists of bibliographic citations. Provides information to users on how to update their knowledge using various internet resources.

132 pages

6321 The Official Parent's Sourcebook on Tay-Sachs Disease
ICON Health Publications/ICON Group International
9606 Tierra Grande St., Suite 205
San Diego, CA 92126
Fax: 858-635-9414
orders@icongroupbooks.com
www.icongrouponline.com

A comprehensive manual for anyone interested in self-directed research on tay-Sachs. Fully referenced with ample Internet listings and glossary.

128 pages

Description

6322 TELANGIECTASIA

Synonym: Telangiectasis

Covers these related disorders: Ataxia-telangiectasia (AT), Phlebectasia, Cutis marmorata, Hereditary hemorrhagic telangiectasia, Rendu-Osler-Weber disease, Spider Angioma

Involves the following Biologic System(s):

Dermatologic Disorders

Telangiectasia refers to the permanent widening or dilation of small blood vessels near the surface of the skin (superficial capillaries, arterioles, and venules). This results in the appearance of relatively small, red, well-defined skin lesions that have fine or coarse red lines or a spider-like network of red lesions that radiate from a central point (spider telangiectasia). Telangiectasias may develop as the result of an underlying disorder such as lupus erythematosus, dermatomyositis, rosacea, or psoriasis. These skin lesions may also result from exposure to sunlight, x-rays, or other forms of radiation.

Ataxia-telangiectasia (AT) is a rare, inherited, progressive disorder of the nervous system involving degenerative changes in the central nervous system along with defects in the immune system. AT is transmitted as an autosomal recessive trait and is characterized by the appearance during early childhood of telangiectasias involving the ears, face, the membranes that line the white outer coat of the eyes (bulbar conjunctiva), or other areas. Affected children are at risk for recurrent respiratory infections. Degeneration of the cerebellum, which is the part of the brain responsible for the regulation and coordination of voluntary movement and other vital functions, also occurs in children with AT.

Congenital generalized phlebectasia, sometimes called cutis marmorata telangiectatica congenita, is a benign telangiectasia that is apparent at birth and is characterized by red or purple-hued net-like lesions that may have a somewhat marbled appearance. These telangiectasias may be localized to an arm or leg or the trunk of the body; however, sometimes these skin lesions are more widely spread. In addition, the lesions may become more prominent with changes in outside temperature, crying, or exertion. This condition often resolves spontaneously by adolescence. Treatment is supportive.

Generalized essential telangiectasia is a rare condition that may affect children or adults and is characterized by the appearance of solitary or convergent patches of network-like telangiectasias. These lesions may appear on large but localized areas of the body such as the arms or legs or may sometimes involve or progress to the entire body. This disorder is limited to the skin with no health-associated irregularities. Treatment is supportive.

Hereditary benign telangiectasia is a rare, genetic disorder that is inherited as an autosomal dominant trait and is characterized by the appearance of telangiectasias on the skin of the face, arms, and upper portion of the trunk. This progressive disorder is limited to the skin.

Hereditary hemorrhagic telangiectasia, also called Rendu-Osler-Weber disease, is an inherited disorder that is transmitted as an autosomal dominant trait and is characterized by recurrent nosebleeds and the development of small telangiectasias of the skin and mucous membranes. These lesions range in color from red to purple and most often appear on the face, lips, and the membranes of the nose and mouth. In addition, the gastrointestinal tract, genitourinary tract, liver, brain, lungs, throat, voice box (larynx), and the membrane that lines the eyelids and whites of the eyes (conjunctiva) may be involved. Because the affected blood vessels may be fragile, they often break resulting in bleeding or hemorrhage from the gastrointestinal and genitourinary tracts, lungs, mouth, and nose.

Spider angioma, sometimes called spider nevus, is a telangiectasia characterized by the central, elevated, red lesion that is surrounded by a radiating, spider-like network of small blood vessels. Although these types of telangiectasias are often associated with conditions in which levels of circulating estrogen are elevated (e.g., pregnancy and liver disease), spider angiomas may also occur in preschool and school-age children. These lesions usually appear on the face, ears, forearms, and hands and often resolve on their own. Treatment is directed toward the removal of persistent angiomas and may include various methods such as freezing with liquid nitrogen (cryotherapy), the use of electric current to promote coagulation (electrocoagulation), or certain laser techniques such as intensed pulse light using a specially constructed flash lamp and focusing optics.

Telangiectasias can result in naevus flammeus (port-wine stain), which is a flat birthmark on the head or neck that spontaneously regresses. A port-wine stain, if present, will grow proportionately with the child. There is a high association with Sturge-Weber syndrome, a nevus formation in the skin and is associated with glaucoma, meningeal angiomas, and intellectual disabilities. Unilateral nevoid telangiectasia refers to the appearance of telangiectasias on one side of the body in conjunction with an increase in the levels of circulating estrogen. These lesions sometimes develop in adolescent girls when they begin menstruation. Pregnancy may also prompt their development. When apparent in men, telangiectasias are the result of circulating estrogen secondary to liver disease. If this condition results from pregnancy, the lesions often fade or resolve during the postpartum period. Chronic treatment with corticosteroids may also lead to telangiectasias.

Government Agencies

6323 NIH/National Institute of Arthritis and Musculoskeletal and Skin Diseases
1 AMS Circle
Bethesda, MD 20892

301-495-4484
877-226-4267
Fax: 301-718-6366
TTY: 301-565-2966
niamsinfo@mail.nih.gov
www.niams.nih.gov

The mission of the NIAMS, a part of the NIH, is to support research into the causes, treatment and prevention of arthritis and musculoskeletal and skin diseases, the training of basic and clinical scientists to carry out this research, and the dissemination of information on research progress in these diseases.

Lindsey A. Criswell, MD, Director
Rick Phillips, Executive Officer

National Associations & Support Groups

6324 American Academy of Dermatology
P.O. Box 1968
Des Plaines, IL 60017

847-240-1280
888-462-3376
mrc@aad.org
www.aad.org

Telangiectasia / Web Sites

To promote and advance the art of medicine and surgery of the skin; promote the highest possible standards in clinical practice, education and research in dermatology and related disciplines.

6325 American Academy of Pediatrics
345 Park Blvd
Itasca, IL 60143
847-434-4000
800-433-9016
Fax: 847-434-8000
csc@aap.org
www.aap.org

The American Academy of Pediatrics and its member pediatricians are committed to the attainment of optimal physical, mental and social health and well-being for all infants, children, adolescents, and young adults.

Kyle E. Yasuda, MD, FAAP, President
Mark Del Monte, JD, CEO/Executive VP
Vera Tait, MD, FAAP, Chief Medical Officer

6326 American Skin Association
335 Madison Avenue, 22nd Floor
New York, NY 10017
212-889-4858
info@americanskin.org
www.americanskin.org

The American Skin Association is the only volunteer led health organization dedicated through research, education and advocacy to saving lives and alleviating human suffering caused by the full spectrum of skin disorders.

Kathleen Reichert, Executive Vice President
Kristin Ludl, Operations Manager

6327 Ataxia-Telangiectasia Children's Project
6810 N State Road 7, Suite 125
Coconut Creek, FL 33073
954-481-6611
800-543-5728
www.atcp.org

A non-profit organization that raises funds to support and coordinate biomedical research projects, scientific conferences and a clinical center aimed at finding a cure for ataxia-telagiectasia, a lethal genetic disease that attacks children, causing progressive loss of muscle control, cancer and immune system problems.

Jennifer Thornton, Executive Director
Kimberly Beisner, Fundraising Manager
Sara Reiling, Project Manager

6328 Child Neurology Foundation
601 W Short Street
Lexington, KY 40508
888-417-3435
info@childneurologyfoundation.org
childneurologyfoundation.org

The Child Neurology Foundation connects partners from all areas of the child neurology community so those navigating the journey of disease diagnosis, management, and care have the ongoing support from those dedicated to treatments and cures.

Amy Brin, Executive Director
Katie Hentges, Director, Programs
Brea McCormley, Director, Development

6329 Children's Hospital Boston
300 Longwood Avenue
Boston, MA 02115
617-355-6000
www.childrenshospital.org

Mission is to provide the highest quality care; be the leading source of research and discovery; educate the next generation of leaders in child health and enhance the health and well-being of the children and families in our local community.

Kevin Churchwell, President & CEO
Jessica Farnham, Chief Operating Officer

6330 Hereditary Hemorrhagic Telangiectasia (HHT) Foundation International
PO Box 329
Monkton, MD 21111
410-357-9932
Fax: 410-472-5559
curehht.org

Dedicated to increasing public and professional awareness and understanding of hereditary hemorrhagic telangiectasia (HHT). Supports ongoing medical research into the cause, prevention, and treatment of HHT; and offers a variety of materials including informational brochures and a quarterly newsletter.

Marianne Clancy, Executive Director
Nicole Schaefer, Chief Operating Officer

6331 NIH/National Institute of Neurological Disorders and Stroke (NINDS)
PO Box 5801
Bethesda, MD 20824
800-352-9424
www.ninds.nih.gov

Works to reduce the burden of neurological disease by conducting, fostering, coordinating and guiding research on the causes, prevention, diagnosis and treatment of neurological disorders and stroke, while supporting basic research in related scientific areas.

Walter J. Koroshetz, MD, Director

6332 National Ataxia Foundation
600 Highway 169 South, Ste 1725
Minneapolis, MN 55426
763-553-0020
Fax: 763-553-0167
naf@ataxia.org
ataxia.org

Objectives of this organization are to make an early diagnosis of ataxia by locating all potential victims and encouraging them to have an examination, public information and professional education materials and basic research on the disease.

William P. Sweeney, Board President
Andrew Rosen, Executive Director
Lori Shogren, Community Program/Services Director

6333 Society for Pediatric Dermatology
8365 Keystone Crossing, Ste 107
Indianapolis, IN 46240
317-202-0224
Fax: 317-205-9481
info@pedsderm.net
www.pedsderm.net

The objective of the Society is to promote, develop and advance education, research and care of skin disease in all pediatric age groups.

Kent Lindeman, CMP, Executive Director

Web Sites

6334 American Academy of Dermatology (AAD)
9500 W. Bryn Mawr Avenue, Ste 500
Rosemont, IL 60018
847-240-1737
888-462-3376
Fax: 847-240-1859
info@aad.org
www.aad.org

Dedicated to achieving high quality dermatologic care for everyone which encompasses: responsiveness, unification and representation of the specialty, and excellence in pateint care, education and research.

Irvin Bomberger, Interim Executive Director

6335 American Skin Association
335 Madison Avenue, 22nd Floor
New York, NY 10017
212-889-4858
info@americanskin.org
www.americanskin.org

The American Skin Association is the only volunteer led health organization dedicated through research, education and advocacy to saving lives and alleviating human suffering caused by the full spectrum of skin disorders.

Kristin Ludl, Operations Manager
Kathleen Reichert, Executive Vice President

6336 Ataxia-Telangiectasia Children's Project
6810 N State Road 7, Suite 125
Coconut Creek, FL 33073
954-481-6611
800-543-5728
www.atcp.org

A non-profit organization that raises funds to support and coordinate biomedical research projects, scientific conferences and a clinical center aimed at finding a cure for ataxia-telagiectasia, a lethal genetic disease that attacks children, causing progressive loss of muscle control, cancer, and immune system problems.

Jennifer Thornton, Executive Director
Kimberly Beisner, Fundraising Manager
Sara Reiling, Project Manager

6337 **Children's Hospital Boston**
300 Longwood Avenue
Boston, MA 02115
617-355-6000
www.childrenshospital.org

Mission is to provide the highest quality care; be the leading source of research and discovery; educate the next generation of leaders in child health and enhance the health and well-being of the children and families in our local community.

Kevin Churchwell, President & CEO
Jessica Farnham, Chief Operating Officer

6338 **Hereditary Hemorrhagic Telangiectasia (HHT) Foundation International**
PO Box 329
Monkton, MD 21111
410-357-9932
Fax: 410-472-5559
curehht.org

Dedicated to increasing public and professional awareness and understanding of hereditary hemorrhagic telangiectasia (HHT). Supports ongoing medical research into the cause, prevention, and treatment of HHT; and offers a variety of materials including informational brochures and a quarterly newsletter.

6339 **NIH/National Institute of Neurological Disorders and Stroke (NINDS)**
PO Box 5801
Bethesda, MD 20824
301-496-5751
800-352-9424
www.ninds.nih.gov

Mission is to reduce the burden of neurological disease - a burden borne by every age group, by every segment of society, by people all over the world.

Walter J. Koroshetz, MD, Director

6340 **National Ataxia Foundation**
600 Highway 169 South, Ste 1725
Minneapolis, MN 55426
763-553-0020
Fax: 763-553-0167
naf@ataxia.org
ataxia.org

Objectives of this organization are to make an early diagnosis of ataxia by locating all potential victims and encouraging them to have an examination, public information and professional education materials and basic research on the disease.

William P. Sweeney, Board President
Andrew Rosen, Executive Director
Lori Shogren, Community Program/Services Director

6341 **Online Mendelian Inheritance in Man**
McKusick-Nathans Institue of Genetic Medicine-JHU
Baltimore, MD 21205
www.omim.org

This database is a catalog of human genes and genetic disorders.

Ada Hamosh, MD, Scientific Director

6342 **Society for Pediatric Dermatology**
8365 Keystone Crossing, Suite 107
Indianapolis, IN 46240
317-202-0224
Fax: 317-205-9481
info@pedsderm.net
www.pedsderm.net

Objective is to promote, develop and advance education, research and care of skin disease in all pediatric age groups.

Kent Lindeman, CMP, Executive Director
Stephanie Garwood, MTA, Meeting Manager
Barbara Case, Accounting Manager

Journals

6343 **Pediatric Dermatology Journal**
Society for Pediatric Dermatology
8365 Keystone Crossing, Suite 107
Indianapolis, IN 46240
317-202-0224
Fax: 317-205-9481
info@pedsderm.net
www.pedsderm.net

Answers the need for new ideas and strategies for today's pediatrician or dermatologist.

6 issues/yr

Kent Lindeman, Executive Director

Newsletters

6344 **Hereditary Hemorrhagic Telangiectasia Foundation International Newsletter**
PO Box 329
Monkton, MD 21111
410-357-9932
Fax: 410-472-5559
curehht.org

The Foundation is dedicated to increasing public and professional awareness and understanding of hereditary hemorrhagic telangiectasia (HHT). Supports ongoing medical research into the cause, prevention, and treatment of HHT.

Quarterly

Tetralogy of Fallot / Description

Description

6345 TETRALOGY OF FALLOT
Synonym: Fallot's syndrome
Involves the following Biologic System(s):
Cardiovascular Disorders

Tetralogy of Fallot is a combination of four specific heart malformations that are present at birth (congenital heart defects). Normally, oxygen-poor blood that returns from the body to the heart into the right upper chamber of the heart (right atrium), is pumped into the right lower chamber (right ventricle), and is then pumped into the pulmonary artery and on to the lungs, where the exchange of oxygen and carbon dioxide occurs. Oxygen-rich blood returns from the lungs to the heart via the left atrium, is pumped into the left ventricle, and is subsequently pumped into the major artery of the body (aorta) for circulation to the body's tissues. However, newborns with tetralogy of Fallot typically have four coexisting cardiac defects: i.e., (1) obstruction of the normal outflow of blood from the right ventricle due to abnormal narrowing (stenosis) of the opening between the right ventricle and the pulmonary artery (pulmonary stenosis); (2) an abnormal opening in the partition (septum) that separates the ventricles of the heart (ventricular septal defect or VSD); (3) displacement or override of the aorta, allowing oxygen-poor blood to flow directly from the right ventricle into the aorta; and (4) abnormal thickness of the right ventricle (right ventricular hypertrophy). Tetralogy of Fallot is thought to affect approximately one in 1,000 infants and children.

In patients with tetralogy of Fallot, the onset and severity of associated symptoms depend, in part, upon the degree of right ventricular outflow obstruction. Primary symptoms and findings in mild cases may be only a an unusual heart sound (murmur) heard through the stethoscope. In other cases, there may be a bluish discoloration of the skin and mucous membranes (cyanosis) due to decreased levels of oxygen in the blood; an insufficient supply of oxygen to bodily cells (hypoxia); and difficulties feeding. In infants with tetralogy of Fallot, cyanosis is typically most apparent in the nail beds of the fingers and toes and in the mucous membranes of the mouth and lips. In severe cases, cyanosis may be apparent soon after birth. In such newborns, pulmonary blood flow may primarily depend upon the fetal vascular channel that joins the pulmonary artery and the aorta (ductus arteriosus). Because this fetal vascular channel closes shortly after birth, severe cyanosis may develop within the first hours or days after birth. In other patients, cyanosis may not become apparent until later during the first year of life.

Some affected infants experience periodic attacks or spells during which cyanosis worsens (hypoxic or blue spells). During such hypoxic spells, patients may become restless and cyanotic; develop extreme shortness of breath; and potentially lose consciousness (syncope). Although the onset of these attacks is unpredictable, they may tend to occur after severe crying episodes or upon awakening (Tet spells). The duration of the spells may range from a few minutes to a few hours, and they should be considered life-threatening and an indication for surgical repair.

Tetralogy of Fallot may be diagnosed based upon a complete clinical examination and patient history, detection of distinctive heart murmurs, and various specialized tests (e.g., x-ray studies, echocardiogram, electrocardiogram, cardiac catheterization). Surgery is performed in the first year of life, and often in the first six months of life, depending upon the severity of right ventricular outflow obstruction. Corrective open-heart surgery patches the ventricular septal defect, and enlarges the opening between the pulmonary artery and right ventricle. In many cases, corrective open-heart surgery may be recommended during the neonatal or infant period to avoid the risk of cyanotic spells later in infancy. Before and after corrective open-heart surgery, patients may be susceptible to bacterial infection of certain areas of the heart (e.g., bacterial endocarditis). Therefore, patients should be provided with antibiotic medication (antibiotic prophylaxis) with dental visits and certain surgical procedures. Additional treatment is symptomatic and supportive.

Tetralogy of Fallot may occur as an isolated condition, with other congenital heart defects, or in some cases, in association with certain chromosomal abnormalities (e.g., DiGeorge syndrome — a partial gene deletion that results in heart defects, low calcium levels, and immune deficiency — and Down syndrome.) Prenatal factors associated with higher than normal risk for this condition include maternal rubella (German measles) or other viral illnesses during pregnancy, poor prenatal nutrition, maternal alcoholism, mother over 40 years old, and diabetes. Researchers indicate that, in some patients, tetralogy of Fallot may be due to the interaction of one or more genes v(22q11). As with patients that have undergone any heart surgery, antibiotic prophylaxis (prevention) is indicated during dental treatment in order to prevent infective endocarditis, inflammation of the heart's inner lining or the heart valves.

Government Agencies

6346 NIH/ Eunice Kennedy Shriver National Institute of Child Health & Human Development
P.O. Box 3006
Rockville, MD 20847
800-370-2943
Fax: 866-760-5947
www.nichd.nih.gov

Conducts and supports research on topics related to the health of children, adults, families and populations. Some of these topics include: developmental disabilities, growth and development, infant death, reproductive health and birth defects.

Diana W. Bianchi, Director
Alison Cernich, PhD, Deputy Director

6347 NIH/National Heart, Lung and Blood Institute
31 Center Drive, Bldg 31
Bethesda, MD 20892
877-645-2448
www.nhlbi.nih.gov

Primary responsibility of this organization is the scientific investigation of heart, blood vessel, lung and blood disorders. Oversees research, demonstration, prevention, education, control and training activities in these fields and emphasizes the prevention and control of heart diseases.

Gary H. Gibbons, MD, Director
Kate O'Sullivan, Executive Officer

National Associations & Support Groups

6348 American Academy of Pediatrics
345 Park Blvd
Itasca, IL 60143
847-434-4000
800-433-9016
Fax: 847-434-8000
csc@aap.org
www.aap.org

The American Academy of Pediatrics and its member pediatricians are committed to the attainment of optimal physical, mental and social health and well-being for all infants, children, adolescents, and young adults.

Kyle E. Yasuda, MD, FAAP, President
Mark Del Monte, JD, CEO/Executive VP
Vera Tait, MD, FAAP, Chief Medical Officer

Tetralogy of Fallot / Book Publishers

6349 American Heart Association
7272 Greenville Avenue
Dallas, TX 75231
214-570-5978
800-242-8721
www.heart.org

The mission of the American Heart Associate is to build healthier lives, free of cardiovascular diseases and stroke.

Nancy Brown, CEO
Mitchell S.V. Elkind, President
Suzie Upton, Chief Operating Officer

6350 Children's Hospital Boston
300 Longwood Avenue
Boston, MA 02115
617-355-6000
www.childrenshospital.org

Mission is to provide the highest quality care; be the leading source of research and discovery; educate the next generation of leaders in child health and enhance the health and well-being of the children and families in our local community.

Kevin Churchwell, President & CEO
Jessica Farnham, Chief Operating Officer

6351 Genetic Alliance
426400 Woodfield Road, Ste 189
Damascus, MD 20872
202-966-5557
Fax: 202-966-8553
info@geneticalliance.org
www.geneticalliance.org

World's leading nonprofit health advocacy organization committed to transforming health through genetics and promoting an environment of openness centered on the health of individuals, families, and communities.

Sharon Terry, CEO
Ruth Child, CFO
Natasha Bonhomme, Chief Strategy Officer

6352 Little Hearts
www.littlehearts.org

info@littlehearts.org
www.littlehearts.org

Provides support, resources, networking, and hope to families affected by congenital heart defects. Membership consists of families nationwide who have or are expecting a child with a congenital heart defect.

Web Sites

6353 American Heart Association
7272 Greenville Avenue
Dallas, TX 75231
800-242-8721
www.heart.org

The mission of the American Heart Associate is to build healthier lives, free of cardiovascular diseases and stroke.

Nancy Brown, CEO
Mitchell S.V. Elkind, President
Suzie Upton, Chief Operating Officer

6354 Children's Hospital Boston
300 Longwood Avenue
Boston, MA 02115
617-355-6000
www.childrenshospital.org

Mission is to provide the highest quality care; be the leading source of research and discovery; educate the next generation of leaders in child health and enhance the health and well-being of the children and families in our local community.

Kevin Churchwell, President & CEO
Jessica Farnham, Chief Operating Officer

6355 Southern Illinois University School of Medicine
PO Box 19639
Springfield, IL 62794
217-545-8000
800-342-5748
admin@siuhealthcare.org
www.siumed.edu/peds/index.htm

The mission of SUI School of Medicine is to assist the people of central and southern Illinois in meeting their present and future health care needs through education, clinical service and research.

Book Publishers

6356 Congenital Disorders Sourcebook
Greg Mullin, author

Omnigraphics
615 Griswold Street, Ste 520
Detroit, MI 48226
610-461-3548
800-234-1340
Fax: 800-875-1340
contact@omnigraphics.com
www.omnigraphics.com

Basic consumer health information on disorders aquired during gestation, including spina bifida, hydrocephalus, cerebral palsy, heart defects, craniofacial abnormalities and fetal alcohol syndrome.

664 pages
ISBN: 0-780816-13-8

Thalassemias / Description

Description

6357 THALASSEMIAS
Covers these related disorders: Alpha-thalassemia, Beta-thalassemia, Beta-thalassemia minor, Beta-thalassemia major
Involves the following Biologic System(s):
Genetic/Chromosomal/Syndrome/Metabolic Disorders, Hematologic and Oncologic Disorders

The term thalassemia refers to a group of inherited blood disorders that includes the alpha-thalassemias and the more common beta-thalassemias. The thalassemias are characterized by the faulty production of hemoglobin, the protein that carries oxygen within the red blood cells. Hemoglobin is composed of two pairs of amino acid chains (globins), the alpha chains and the beta chains. The improper synthesis of hemoglobin is caused by a defect within the globin genes and results in abnormal, fragile red blood cells. Beta-thalassemia minor, a less severe form of the disease, is inherited when the defective gene is transmitted by one parent, while beta-thalassemia major is inherited through the defective genes of both parents.

A mild anemia is usually present in individuals with beta-thalassemia minor; however, it is not unusual for affected individuals to be symptom-free. Symptoms of beta-thalassemia major include fatigue; shortness of breath (dyspnea); and yellowing of the skin, eyes, and mucous membranes (jaundice). Other symptoms, usually associated with the premature destruction of red blood cells (hemolytic anemia) and subsequent release of iron, may include bronzed or freckled skin and enlargement of the spleen (splenomegaly). In severe cases, iron that gets deposited in the heart, liver, and pancreas may eventually lead to impaired function. In addition, extreme activity of the bone marrow may result in thickened and enlarged bones in the skull and face, while normal growth may be stunted.

Alpha-thalassemia, far less common than beta-thalassemia, ranges in severity from a carrier state with no symptoms to the most severe form that is incompatible with life. The severity of symptoms is dependent upon the level of alpha-chain involvement. The most severe form of alpha-thalassemia involves the complete absence of alpha-chain production.

Thalassemia patients vary a lot in their treatment needs depending on the severity of their anemia. Treatment for symptomatic thalassemias includes blood transfusion therapy to ensure normal growth. However, repeated blood transfusions may exacerbate iron deposition into the internal organs (hemosiderosis), necessitating treatment with iron-chelating drugs that increase iron excretion. Other treatment may include bone marrow transplantation.

Thalassemia is inherited as an autosomal recessive trait and is most prevalent among people living in or originating from the Mediterranean, the Middle East, and Southeast Asia. As with other genetically acquired disorders, aggressive birth screening and genetic counseling is recommended.

Government Agencies

6358 NIH/ Eunice Kennedy Shriver National Institute of Child Health & Human Development
P.O. Box 3006
Rockville, MD 20847
800-370-2943
Fax: 866-760-5947
www.nichd.nih.gov

Conducts and supports research on topics related to the health of children, adults, families and populations. Some of these topics include: developmental disabilities, growth and development, infant death, reproductive health and birth defects.

Diana W. Bianchi, Director
Alison Cernich, PhD, Deputy Director

6359 NIH/National Heart, Lung and Blood Institute
31 Center Drive, Bldg 31
Bethesda, MD 20892
877-645-2448
www.nhlbi.nih.gov

Primary responsibility of this organization is the scientific investigation of heart, blood vessel, lung and blood disorders. Oversees research, demonstration, prevention, education, control and training activities in these fields and emphasizes the prevention and control of heart diseases.

Gary H. Gibbons, MD, Director
Kate O'Sullivan, Executive Officer

6360 NIH/National Institute of Arthritis and Musculoskeletal and Skin Diseases
1 AMS Circle
Bethesda, MD 20892
301-495-4484
877-226-4267
Fax: 301-718-6366
TDD: 301-565-2966
niamsinfo@mail.nih.gov
www.niams.nih.gov

The mission of the NIAMS, a part of the NIH, is to support research into the causes, treatment and prevention of arthritis and musculoskeletal and skin diseases, the training of basic and clinical scientists to carry out this research, and the dissemination of information on research progress in these diseases.

Lindsey A. Criswell, MD, Director
Rick Phillips, Executive Officer

National Associations & Support Groups

6361 American Academy of Dermatology
P.O. Box 1968
Des Plaines, IL 60017
847-240-1280
888-462-3376
mrc@aad.org
www.aad.org

To promote and advance the art of medicine and surgery of the skin; promote the highest possible standards in clinical practice, education and research in dermatology and related disciplines.

6362 American Academy of Pediatrics
345 Park Blvd
Itasca, IL 60143
847-434-4000
800-433-9016
Fax: 847-434-8000
csc@aap.org
www.aap.org

The American Academy of Pediatrics and its member pediatricians are committed to the attainment of optimal physical, mental and social health and well-being for all infants, children, adolescents, and young adults.

Kyle E. Yasuda, MD, FAAP, President
Mark Del Monte, JD, CEO/Executive VP
Vera Tait, MD, FAAP, Chief Medical Officer

6363 American Heart Association
7272 Greenville Avenue
Dallas, TX 75231
214-570-5978
800-242-8721
www.heart.org

The mission of the American Heart Associate is to build healthier lives, free of cardiovascular diseases and stroke.

Nancy Brown, CEO
Mitchell S.V. Elkind, President
Suzie Upton, Chief Operating Officer

Thalassemias / National Associations & Support Groups

6364 **American Skin Association**
335 Madison Avenue, 22nd Floor
New York, NY 10017
212-889-4858
info@americanskin.org
www.americanskin.org

The American Skin Association is the only volunteer led health organization dedicated through research, education and advocacy to saving lives and alleviating human suffering caused by the full spectrum of skin disorders.

Kathleen Reichert, Executive Vice President
Kristin Ludl, Operations Manager

6365 **Ataxia-Telangiectasia Children's Project**
6810 N State Road 7, Suite 125
Coconut Creek, FL 33073
954-481-6611
800-543-5728
www.atcp.org

A non-profit organization that raises funds to support and coordinate biomedical research projects, scientific conferences and a clinical center aimed at finding a cure for ataxia-telagiectasia, a lethal genetic disease that attacks children, causing progressive loss of muscle control, cancer and immune system problems.

Jennifer Thornton, Executive Director
Kimberly Beisner, Fundraising Manager
Sara Reiling, Project Manager

6366 **Child Neurology Foundation**
601 W Short Street
Lexington, KY 40508
888-417-3435
info@childneurologyfoundation.org
childneurologyfoundation.org

The Child Neurology Foundation connects partners from all areas of the child neurology community so those navigating the journey of disease diagnosis, management, and care have the ongoing support from those dedicated to treatments and cures.

Amy Brin, Executive Director
Katie Hentges, Director, Programs
Brea McCormley, Director, Development

6367 **Children's Cancer & Blood Foundation**
466 Lexington Avenue, 16th Floor
New York, NY 10017
info@childrenscbf.org
www.childrenscbf.org

The foundation's major emphasis is on blood diseases affecting children: leukemia, thalassemia, hemophilia, sickle cell anemia, platelet disorders, retinoblastoma and cancer.

Les J. Lieberman, Co-Chairman & Co-President
Ronald J. Iervolino, Co-Chairman & Co-President

6368 **Children's Hospital Boston**
300 Longwood Avenue
Boston, MA 02115
617-355-6000
www.childrenshospital.org

Mission is to provide the highest quality care; be the leading source of research and discovery; educate the next generation of leaders in child health and enhance the health and well-being of the children and families in our local community.

Kevin Churchwell, President & CEO
Jessica Farnham, Chief Operating Officer

6369 **Cooley's Anemia Foundation**
330 Seventh Avenue, Suite 200
New York, NY 10001
212-279-8090
www.thalassemia.org

Advancing the treatment and cure for this fatal blood disease, enhancing the quality of life of patients and educating the medical profession, trait carriers and the public about Cooley's anemia/thalassemia major.

Craig Butler, National Executive Director

6370 **Genetic Alliance**
426400 Woodfield Road, Ste 189
Damascus, MD 20872
202-966-5557
Fax: 202-966-8553
info@geneticalliance.org
www.geneticalliance.org

World's leading nonprofit health advocacy organization committed to transforming health through genetics and promoting an environment of openness centered on the health of individuals, families, and communities.

Sharon Terry, CEO
Ruth Child, CFO
Natasha Bonhomme, Chief Strategy Officer

6371 **Hereditary Hemorrhagic Telangiectasia (HHT) Foundation International**
PO Box 329
Monkton, MD 21111
410-357-9932
Fax: 410-472-5559
curehht.org

Dedicated to increasing public and professional awareness and understanding of hereditary hemorrhagic telangiectasia (HHT). Supports ongoing medical research into the cause, prevention, and treatment of HHT; and offers a variety of materials including informational brochures and a quarterly newsletter.

Marianne Clancy, Executive Director
Nicole Schaefer, Chief Operating Officer

6372 **Little Hearts**
www.littlehearts.org
info@littlehearts.org
www.littlehearts.org

Provides support, resources, networking, and hope to families affected by congenital heart defects. Membership consists of families nationwide who have or are expecting a child with a congenital heart defect.

6373 **March of Dimes Foundation**
1550 Crystal Drive, Ste 1300
Arlington, VA 22202
888-663-4637
www.marchofdimes.org

March of Dimes help moms have full-term pregnancies and research the problems that threaten the health of babies. The March of Dimes also acts globally: sharing best practices in perinatal health and helping improve birth outcomes where the needs are the most urgent.

Stacey D. Stewart, President
Alan Brogdon, SVP/COO/Board Officer
Rahul Gupta, MD, SVP & Chief Medical/Health Officer

6374 **NIH/National Institute of Neurological Disorders and Stroke (NINDS)**
PO Box 5801
Bethesda, MD 20824
800-352-9424
www.ninds.nih.gov

Works to reduce the burden of neurological disease by conducting, fostering, coordinating and guiding research on the causes, prevention, diagnosis and treatment of neurological disorders and stroke, while supporting basic research in related scientific areas.

Walter J. Koroshetz, MD, Director

6375 **National Ataxia Foundation**
600 Highway 169 South, Ste 1725
Minneapolis, MN 55426
763-553-0020
Fax: 763-553-0167
naf@ataxia.org
ataxia.org

Objectives of this organization are to make an early diagnosis of ataxia by locating all potential victims and encouraging them to have an examination, public information and professional education materials and basic research on the disease.

William P. Sweeney, Board President
Andrew Rosen, Executive Director
Lori Shogren, Community Program/Services Director

6376 **National Tay-Sachs and Allied Diseases Association**
2001 Beacon Street, Suite 204
Boston, MA 02135
617-277-4463
info@ntsad.org
www.ntsad.org

Thalassemias / Conferences

Direct, fund and promote research to develop treatments and cures; provide comprehensive support services to affected families and individuals; guide prevention, education, awareness and screening through effective grassroots collaborations with chapters and affiliates; lead advocacy efforts as the recognized authority for this family of genetic diseases.

Kathleen Flynn, Chief Executive Officer
Valerie Greger, PhD, Director of Research
Diana Jussila, Director of Family Services

6377 Society for Pediatric Dermatology
8365 Keystone Crossing, Ste 107
Indianapolis, IN 46240
317-202-0224
Fax: 317-205-9481
info@pedsderm.net
www.pedsderm.net

The objective of the Society is to promote, develop and advance education, research and care of skin disease in all pediatric age groups.

Kent Lindeman, Executive Director

Conferences

6378 TAG Conference
Thalassemia Action Group
330 Seventh Avenue, #900
New York, NY 10001
800-522-7222
Fax: 212-279-5999
info@cooleysanemia.org
www.cooleysanemia.org

Held annually around March-April, look at website for more information.

Anthony J. Viola, President
Gina Cioffi, Executive Director
Amy Celento, Vice President

Web Sites

6379 Children's Cancer & Blood Foundation
www.childrenscbf.org

www.childrenscbf.org

The foundation's major emphasis is on blood diseases affecting children: leukemia, thalassemia, hemophilia, sickle cell anemia, platelet disorders, retinoblastoma and cancer.

6380 Children's Hospital Boston
300 Longwood Avenue
Boston, MA 02115
617-355-6000
www.childrenshospital.org

Mission is to provide the highest quality care; be the leading source of research and discovery; educate the next generation of leaders in child health and enhance the health and well-being of the children and families in our local community.

Kevin Churchwell, President & CEO
Jessica Farnham, Chief Operating Officer

6381 Cooley's Anemia Foundation
330 Seventh Avenue, #200
New York, NY 10001
800-522-7222
Fax: 212-279-5999
www.cooleysanemia.org

The only US-based voluntary health organization that aids in patient services, medical research, education and public information to fight thalassemia, a blood disease also known as Cooley's anemia. Members of CAF work alongside the Thalassemia Action Group (TAG) to provide national support, encouragement and friendship to other patients and families.

Anthony J. Viola, President
Gina Cioffi, Esq., National Executive Director
Eileen Scott, Patient Services Manager

6382 March of Dimes Foundation
1550 Crystal Drive, Ste 1300
Arlington, VA 22202
888-663-4637
www.marchofdimes.org

March of Dimes help moms have full-term pregnancies and research the problems that threaten the health of babies. The March of Dimes also acts globally: sharing best practices in perinatal health and helping improve birth outcomes where the needs are the most urgent.

Stacey D. Stewart, President
Alan Brogdon, SVP/COO/Board Officer
Rahul Gupta, MD, SVP & Chief Medical/Health Officer

6383 NIH/National Heart, Lung and Blood Institute
31 Center Drive, Bldg 31
Bethesda, MD 20892
301-592-8573
NHLBIinfo@nhlbi.nih.gov
www.nhlbi.nih.gov

Primary responsibility of this organization is the scientific investigation of heart, blood vessel, lung and blood disorders. Oversees research, demonstration, prevention, education, control and training activities in these fields and emphasizes the prevention and control of heart diseases.

Gary H. Gibbons, MD, Director
Kate O'Sullivan, Executive Officer

6384 Online Mendelian Inheritance in Man
McKusick-Nathans Institue of Genetic Medicine-JHU
Baltimore, MD 21205
www.omim.org

This database is a catalog of human genes and genetic disorders.

Ada Hamosh, MD, Scientific Director

Book Publishers

6385 Blood & Circulatory Disorders Sourcebook 4th Edition
Omnigraphics
615 Griswold Street, Ste 520
Detroit, MI 48226
610-461-3548
800-234-1340
Fax: 800-875-1340
contact@omnigraphics.com
www.omnigraphics.com

Basic consumer health information on blood and its components, anemias, leukemias, bleeding disorders, and circulatory disorders, including aplastic anemia, thrombophilia, RH disease and hemophilia.

664 pages
ISBN: 0-780814-76-9

6386 Coloring Book on Thalassemia
Cooley's Anemia Foundation
330 Seventh Avenue, #200
New York, NY 10001
212-279-8090
800-522-7222
Fax: 212-279-5999
info@cooleysanemia.org
www.cooleysanemia.org

Available in English, Italian, Greek and Chinese.

Anthony J. Viola, President
Gina Cioffi, Executive Director
Amy Celento, Vice President

6387 Cooley's Anemia 7th Annual Symposium
Cooley's Anemia Foundation
330 Seventh Avenue, #200
New York, NY 10001
800-522-7222
Fax: 212-279-5999
info@cooleysanemia.org
www.cooleysanemia.org

Published by the New York Academy of Sources.
1997

Anthony J. Viola, President
Gina Cioffi, Executive Director
Amy Celento, Vice President

Thalassemias / Pamphlets

6388 Genes, Blood & Courage
Cooley's Anemia Foundation
330 Seventh Avenue, #200
New York, NY 10001
800-522-7222
Fax: 212-279-5999
info@cooleysanemia.org
www.cooleysanemia.org

Anthony J. Viola, President
Gina Cioffi, Executive Director
Amy Celento, Vice President

6389 Let's Talk About Going to the Hospital
Rosen Publishing Group's PowerKids Press
29 E 21st Street
New York, NY 10010
212-777-3017
800-237-9932
Fax: 888-436-4643
rosenpub@tribeca.ios.com
www.rosenpublishing.com

If a child has to check into the hospital, chances are he or she is already upset about being ill. Knowing how a hospital functions and what the procedures are, such as when family members can visit, will help in what is already a stressful situation. Grades K-5.

24 pages
ISBN: 0-823950-36-0

Roger Rosen, President

Journals

6390 Pediatric Dermatology Journal
Society for Pediatric Dermatology
8365 Keystone Crossing, Suite 107
Indianapolis, IN 46240
317-202-0224
Fax: 317-205-9481
info@pedsderm.net
www.pedsderm.net

Answers the need for new ideas and strategies for today's pediatrician or dermatologist.

6 issues/yr

Kent Lindeman, Executive Director

Newsletters

6391 CAF Medical Update
Cooley's Anemia Foundation
330 Seventh Avenue, #200
New York, NY 10001
800-522-7222
Fax: 212-279-5999
info@cooleysanemia.org
www.cooleysanemia.org

Medical information.
Biannual

Anthony J. Viola, President
Gina Cioffi, Esq., National Executive Director
Eileen Scott, Patient Services Manager

6392 Lifeline
Cooley's Anemia Foundation
330 Seventh Avenue, #200
New York, NY 10001
800-522-7222
Fax: 212-279-5999
info@cooleysanemia.org
www.cooleysanemia.org

Cooley's Anemia Foundation
Biannual

Anthony J. Viola, President
Gina Cioffi, Esq., National Executive Director
Eileen Scott, Patient Services Manager

6393 TAG Newsletter
Cooley's Anemia Foundation
330 Seventh Avenue, #200
New York, NY 10001
800-522-7222
Fax: 212-279-5999
info@cooleysanemia.org
www.cooleysanemia.org

Anthony J. Viola, President
Gina Cioffi, Esq., National Executive Director
Eileen Scott, Patient Services Manager

Pamphlets

6394 Cooley's Anemia Fact Cards
Cooley's Anemia Foundation
330 Seventh Avenue, #200
New York, NY 10001
800-522-7222
Fax: 212-279-5999
info@cooleysanemia.org
www.cooleysanemia.org

Anthony J. Viola, President
Gina Cioffi, Esq., National Executive Director
Eileen Scott, Patient Services Manager

6395 Cooley's Anemia Foundation (CAF) Pamphlet
Cooley's Anemia Foundation
330 Seventh Avenue, #200
New York, NY 10001
800-522-7222
Fax: 212-279-5999
info@cooleysanemia.org
www.cooleysanemia.org

Anthony J. Viola, President
Gina Cioffi, Esq., National Executive Director
Eileen Scott, Patient Services Manager

6396 Desferal Q & A
Cooley's Anemia Foundation
330 Seventh Avenue, #200
New York, NY 10001
800-522-7222
Fax: 212-279-5999
info@cooleysanemia.org
www.cooleysanemia.org

Guidelines for home infusion.

Anthony J. Viola, President
Gina Cioffi, Esq., National Executive Director
Eileen Scott, Patient Services Manager

6397 Sibling Donor Cord Blood Program Pamphlet
Cooley's Anemia Foundation
330 Seventh Avenue, #200
New York, NY 10001
800-522-7222
Fax: 212-279-5999
info@cooleysanemia.org
www.cooleysanemia.org

Anthony J. Viola, President
Gina Cioffi, Esq., National Executive Director
Eileen Scott, Patient Services Manager

6398 Thalassemia Action Group (TAG) Patient Support Group Brochure
Cooley's Anemia Foundation
330 Seventh Avenue, #200
New York, NY 10001
800-522-7222
Fax: 212-279-5999
info@cooleysanemia.org
www.cooleysanemia.org

Anthony J. Viola, President
Gina Cioffi, Esq., National Executive Director
Eileen Scott, Patient Services Manager

6399 What is Thalassemia Trait?
Cooley's Anemia Foundation
330 Seventh Avenue, #200
New York, NY 10001
800-522-7222
Fax: 212-279-5999
info@cooleysanemia.org
www.cooleysanemia.org

This booklet offers information on the thalassemia trait.
Anthony J. Viola, President
Gina Cioffi, Esq., National Executive Director
Eileen Scott, Patient Services Manager

Description

6400 THROMBOCYTOPENIAS

Covers these related disorders: Idiopathic thrombocytopenia purpura (ITP)

Involves the following Biologic System(s):
Hematologic and Oncologic Disorders

Thrombocytopenia is a term that describes a condition in which the level of circulating platelets in the blood is reduced, resulting in a tendency to bleed. By changing shape and adhering to each other and the walls of broken blood vessels, platelets, also known as thrombocytes, play an essential role in the clotting process. Normal blood levels usually demonstrate 150,000 to 350,000 platelets per microliter. When the platelet count is reduced to 30,000 per microliter or lower, abnormal bleeding under the skin may occur and result in purple bruising or spots (purpura). Nosebleeds (epistaxis), bleeding of the gums, and blood in the urine (hematuria) are also common. Often, low platelet levels do not lead to clinical problems; rather, they are picked up on a routine full blood count.

Thrombocytopenia may result from a slowdown in platelet production or the rapid destruction of these cells. Certain diseases such as anemia, leukemia, lymphoma, bone marrow disorders, or autoimmune diseases may cause thrombocytopenia. Other causes include enlargement of the spleen (splenomegaly), cirrhosis, certain drugs, viral infection, and x-ray or radiation exposure.

The treatment of thrombocytopenia is based upon its underlying cause. For example, if the low platelet count is caused by a specific underlying disease, treatment is geared toward that disease. Low platelet counts caused by a specific drug necessitate the withdrawal of that drug. If bleeding is severe, platelet transfusions may be administered.

Idiopathic thrombocytopenia purpura (ITP) is a term used to describe thrombocytopenia of unknown origin. This condition often follows a viral infection and, in children, usually disappears within a month or so with no treatment. The duration of ITP in adolescents and adults is often more prolonged, and close medical follow up and avoidance of contact sports and activities is essential.

Government Agencies

6401 NIH/National Heart, Lung and Blood Institute
31 Center Drive, Bldg 31
Bethesda, MD 20892
877-645-2448
www.nhlbi.nih.gov

Primary responsibility of this organization is the scientific investigation of heart, blood vessel, lung and blood disorders. Oversees research, demonstration, prevention, education, control and training activities in these fields and emphasizes the prevention and control of heart diseases.

Gary H. Gibbons, MD, Director
Kate O'Sullivan, Executive Officer

National Associations & Support Groups

6402 American Academy of Pediatrics
345 Park Blvd
Itasca, IL 60143
847-434-4000
800-433-9016
Fax: 847-434-8000
csc@aap.org
www.aap.org

The American Academy of Pediatrics and its member pediatricians are committed to the attainment of optimal physical, mental and social health and well-being for all infants, children, adolescents, and young adults.

Kyle E. Yasuda, MD, FAAP, President
Mark Del Monte, JD, CEO/Executive VP
Vera Tait, MD, FAAP, Chief Medical Officer

6403 American Heart Association
7272 Greenville Avenue
Dallas, TX 75231
214-570-5978
800-242-8721
www.heart.org

The mission of the American Heart Associate is to build healthier lives, free of cardiovascular diseases and stroke.

Nancy Brown, CEO
Mitchell S.V. Elkind, President
Suzie Upton, Chief Operating Officer

6404 Children's Cancer & Blood Foundation
466 Lexington Avenue, 16th Floor
New York, NY 10017
info@childrenscbf.org
www.childrenscbf.org

The foundation's major emphasis is on blood diseases affecting children: leukemia, thalassemia, hemophilia, sickle cell anemia, platelet disorders, retinoblastoma and cancer.

Les J. Lieberman, Co-Chairman & Co-President
Ronald J. Iervolino, Co-Chairman & Co-President

6405 Children's Hospital Boston
300 Longwood Avenue
Boston, MA 02115
617-355-6000
www.childrenshospital.org

Mission is to provide the highest quality care; be the leading source of research and discovery; educate the next generation of leaders in child health and enhance the health and well-being of the children and families in our local community.

Kevin Churchwell, President & CEO
Jessica Farnham, Chief Operating Officer

6406 Genetic Alliance
426400 Woodfield Road, Ste 189
Damascus, MD 20872
202-966-5557
Fax: 202-966-8553
info@geneticalliance.org
www.geneticalliance.org

World's leading nonprofit health advocacy organization committed to transforming health through genetics and promoting an environment of openness centered on the health of individuals, families, and communities.

Sharon Terry, CEO
Ruth Child, CFO
Natasha Bonhomme, Chief Strategy Officer

6407 Platelet Disorder Support Association
8751 Brecksville Road, Suite 150
Cleveland, OH 44141
440-746-9003
877-528-3538
pdsa@pdsa.org
www.pdsa.org

Our organization is devoted to bringing you the most timely, accurate and comprehensive information about ITP and assisting you in meeting others who share your interests.

Caroline Kruse, Executive Director
Jody Shy, Director, Programs & Events
Jennifer Jurcisek, Chief Financial Officer

Web Sites

6408 American Heart Association
7272 Greenville Avenue
Dallas, TX 75231
800-242-8721
www.heart.org

The mission of the American Heart Associate is to build healthier lives, free of cardiovascular diseases and stroke.

Nancy Brown, CEO
Mitchell S.V. Elkind, President
Suzie Upton, Chief Operating Officer

6409 Children's Cancer & Blood Foundation
www.childrenscbf.org

www.childrenscbf.org

The foundation's major emphasis is on blood diseases affecting children: leukemia, thalassemia, hemophilia, sickle cell anemia, platelet disorders, retinoblastoma and cancer.

6410 Children's Hospital Boston
300 Longwood Avenue
Boston, MA 02115

617-355-6000
www.childrenshospital.org

Mission is to provide the highest quality care; be the leading source of research and discovery; educate the next generation of leaders in child health and enhance the health and well-being of the children and families in our local community.

Kevin Churchwell, President & CEO
Jessica Farnham, Chief Operating Officer

6411 Online Mendelian Inheritance in Man
McKusick-Nathans Institue of Genetic Medicine-JHU
Baltimore, MD 21205

www.omim.org

This database is a catalog of human genes and genetic disorders.

Ada Hamosh, MD, Scientific Director

6412 Platelet Disorder Support Association
8751 Brecksville Road, Suite 150
Cleveland, OH 44141

440-746-9003
877-528-3538
pdsa@pdsa.org
www.pdsa.org

Our organization is devoted to bringing you the most timely, accurate and comprehensive information about ITP and assisting you in meeting others who share your interests.

Caroline Kruse, Executive Director
Jennifer Jercisek, Chief Financial Officer
Jody Shy, Director, Programs & Events

Book Publishers

6413 Harrison's Principles of Inernal Medicine 15th Edition
McGraw-Hill
PO Box 182605
Columbus, OH 43218

800-338-3987
Fax: 609-308-4480
customer.service@mheducation.com
www.mcgraw-hill.com

Raises the bar for internal medicine references. Features over 90 new chapters, Harrison's continues to provide authoritative record of internal medicine as practiced by the leading experts in the field.

Lloyd G. Waterhouse, President & CEO
Patrick Milano, CFO
David Stafford, Senior Vice President

6414 Let's Talk About Going to the Hospital
Rosen Publishing Group's PowerKids Press
29 E 21st Street
New York, NY 10010

212-777-3017
800-237-9932
Fax: 888-436-4643
rosenpub@tribeca.ios.com
www.rosenpublishing.com

If a child has to check into the hospital, chances are he or she is already upset about being ill. Knowing how a hospital functions and what the procedures are, such as when family members can visit, will help in what is already a stressful situation. Grades K-5.

24 pages
ISBN: 0-823950-36-0

Roger Rosen, President

Description

6415 THUMBSUCKING

Involves the following Biologic System(s):
Developmental/Behavioral/Psychiatric Disorders

Thumbsucking is a common habit that is prevalent among infants and young children. This behavior is usually used as a device for providing pleasure, amusement, comfort, oral gratification, and release of stress or tension. Sometimes a security object, such as a blanket, may become part of the thumbsucking habit. In most children, thumbsucking reaches a plateau between the ages of 18 months to two years and then slowly but steadily decreases until it disappears at about five to six years of age. One reason to encourage children to give up the habit before they enter school is to prevent the teasing they would otherwise receive. By adolescence, most normal children abandon thumbsucking because of peer pressure.

Although it is generally thought that thumbsucking does not cause any long-term developmental irregularities, thumbsucking that continues beyond age six may lead to acquired problems with the bones and tissues of the thumb and an abnormal bite or contact pattern between upper and lower teeth (malocclusion). The longer the habit persists, the more likely affected children are to develop these types of problems. Conversely, the earlier this habit comes to an end, the more likely that irregular positioning of the teeth will improve without intervention.

Many physicians agree that, as a general rule, the best treatment for thumbsucking is to ignore the behavior and wait patiently for the children to outgrow the habit or to discontinue the behavior on their own. Treatment is generally supportive as punishing or reprimanding often adds to stress levels, becomes a power struggle with the parent, and may actually worsen the problem. Other treatment may include the use of certain appliances that are fitted with small projections that alert children to their behavior when they attempt to suck their thumbs. Older children may require the use of orthodontic appliances to correct irregularities associated with malocclusion.

Government Agencies

6416 NIH/National Institute of Dental and Craniofacial Research (NIDCR)
National Institutes of Health
Bldg 31, Rm 2C39, 31 Center Drive, MSC 2560
Bethesda, MD 20892
866-232-4528
nidcrinfo@mail.nih.gov
www.nidcr.nih.gov

The Institute promotes the general health of the American people by improving their oral, dental and craniofacial health. The NIDCR aims to promote health, to prevent diseases and conditions, and to develop new diagnostics and therapeutics.

Rena D'Souza, DDS, PhD, Director
Jonathan Horsford, PhD, Acting Deputy Director

National Associations & Support Groups

6417 American Academy of Pediatrics
345 Park Blvd
Itasca, IL 60143
847-434-4000
800-433-9016
Fax: 847-434-8000
csc@aap.org
www.aap.org

The American Academy of Pediatrics and its member pediatricians are committed to the attainment of optimal physical, mental and social health and well-being for all infants, children, adolescents, and young adults.

Kyle E. Yasuda, MD, FAAP, President
Mark Del Monte, JD, CEO/Executive VP
Vera Tait, MD, FAAP, Chief Medical Officer

6418 American Dental Association
211 E Chicago Avenue
Chicago, IL 60610
312-440-2500
msc@ada.org
www.ada.org

Founded in 1859, the American Dental Association is the oldest and largest national dental society in the world. Since then, the ADA has grown to become the leading source of oral health related information for dentists and their patients.

Raymond A. Cohlmia, Executive Director

6419 Children's Hospital Boston
300 Longwood Avenue
Boston, MA 02115
617-355-6000
www.childrenshospital.org

Mission is to provide the highest quality care; be the leading source of research and discovery; educate the next generation of leaders in child health and enhance the health and well-being of the children and families in our local community.

Kevin Churchwell, President & CEO
Jessica Farnham, Chief Operating Officer

Web Sites

6420 American Dental Association
211 E Chicago Avenue
Chicago, IL 60610
312-440-2500
msc@ada.org
www.ada.org

Founded in 1859, the American Dental Association is the oldest and largest national dental society in the world. Since then, the ADA has grown to become the leading source of oral health related information for dentists and their patients.

Raymond A. Cohlmia, Executive Director

6421 Children's Hospital Boston
300 Longwood Avenue
Boston, MA 02115
617-355-6000
www.childrenshospital.org

Mission is to provide the highest quality care; be the leading source of research and discovery; educate the next generation of leaders in child health and enhance the health and well-being of the children and families in our local community.

Kevin Churchwell, President & CEO
Jessica Farnham, Chief Operating Officer

6422 NIH/National Institute of Dental and Craniofacial Research (NIDCR)
Bldg 31, Rm 2C39, 31 Center Drive, MSC 2560
Bethesda, MD 20892
301-496-4261
866-232-4528
Fax: 301-480-4098
nidcrinfo@mail.nih.gov
www.nidcr.nih.gov

The mission is to promote the general health of American people by improving their oral, dental and craniofacial health. Through the conduct and support of research and training of researchers, the NIDCR aims to promote health, prevent diseases and conditions, and develop new diagnostic and therapeutics.

Martha J. Somerman, DDS, PhD, Director
Douglas M. Sheeley, Deputy Director
Karina Boehm, Director, Communications/Health Ed.

Thumbsucking / Pamphlets

Pamphlets

6423 A Healthy Mouth for Your Baby
National Oral Health Information Clearinghouse
1 NOHIC Way
Bethesda, MD 20892

301-496-4261
866-232-4528
Fax: 301-480-4098
nidcrinfo@mail.nih.gov
www.nidcr.nih.gov

Martha J. Somerman, DDS, PhD, Director
Kathleen G. Stephan, Executive Officer
Michelle A. Culp, Director

6424 Seal Out Tooth Decay
National Oral Health Information Clearinghouse
1 NOHIC Way
Bethesda, MD 20892

301-496-4261
866-232-4528
Fax: 301-480-4098
nidcrinfo@mail.nih.gov
www.nidcr.nih.gov

Martha J. Somerman, DDS, PhD, Director

Description

6425 TICS

Covers these related disorders: Chronic motor tic disorder, Tourette syndrome, Transient tics of childhood

Involves the following Biologic System(s):

Neurologic Disorders

Tics are repetitive or stereotypical, compulsive, abrupt (spasmodic) movements of a muscle or muscle groups. Although any muscle may be affected, tics most commonly involve muscles of the eyes, face, neck, or shoulders. Movements may include blinking, sniffing, facial grimacing, lip smacking, tongue thrusting, or shoulder shrugging. Tics may begin as intentional movements to relieve perceived tension. However, they may rapidly become unintentional or involuntary in nature. Although tics are extremely difficult to suppress, most patients are able to do so for short periods. Tics are often worsened by stress or any perceived attention to the condition; in contrast, they typically disappear during sleep.

In most patients, tics become apparent between approximately five to 10 years of age. According to some estimates, as many as 25 percent of children may be affected. Most children may experience a spontaneous disappearance of tics within a few weeks or less than one year after onset. In such patients, the condition is referred to as transient tics of childhood. Supportive measures that may be helpful in alleviating transient tics include providing children with a tranquil environment as well as additional rest.

Some children may experience chronic motor tics that persist throughout adult life. In such patients, the condition is known as chronic motor tic disorder. Chronic motor tics may simultaneously affect muscles in up to three different muscle groups.

In contrast to transient tics of childhood and chronic motor tics, which are considered relatively benign, restricted tic disorders, a genetic, neurologic disorder known as Tourette syndrome is characterized by multiple, chronic, complex tics. Tourette syndrome usually becomes apparent in children between the ages of two to 14 years. Initial symptoms typically include motor tics of the face, eyelids, shoulders, and neck. Movements may include grimacing, excessive eye blinking, or stretching of the neck. Vocal (phonic) tics, such as involuntary coughing, grunting, barking, or throat clearing, are also common. Additional symptoms may include involuntary repetition of obscene words (coprolalia) or words spoken by other individuals (echolalia); aggressive behaviors; the performance of repetitive actions or impulses in response to recurrent, persistent thoughts (obsessive-compulsive behaviors); and secondary learning, emotional, or social difficulties. Researchers suggest that variable expression of the disease gene responsible for Tourette syndrome may cause transient tics of childhood or chronic motor tics in other individuals, indicating possible overlap between the conditions. Several studies have demonstrated that immediate (first-degree) relatives of patients with Tourette syndrome have an increased frequency of such tic conditions.

In some patients with severe chronic motor tic disorder, treatment may include therapy with certain medications (e.g., certain benzodiazepines or haloperidol). The treatment of Tourette syndrome is symptomatic and supportive and may include therapy with certain medications, such as haloperidol, pimozide, clonidine, clonazepam, or carbamazepine. In addition, for those with learning, behavioral, and social difficulties, multidisciplinary management and the provision of special social, academic, and vocational services may be important in helping patients achieve their potential. (Please refer to the section entitled Tourette Syndrome for further information on this disorder.)

Government Agencies

6426 NIH/National Institute of Neurological Disorders and Stroke (NINDS)
PO Box 5801
Bethesda, MD 20824

800-352-9424
www.ninds.nih.gov

Works to reduce the burden of neurological disease by conducting, fostering, coordinating and guiding research on the causes, prevention, diagnosis and treatment of neurological disorders and stroke, while supporting basic research in related scientific areas.

Walter J. Koroshetz, MD, Director

National Associations & Support Groups

6427 American Academy of Child and Adolescent Psychiatry
3615 Wisconsin Avenue NW
Washington, DC 20016

202-966-7300
Fax: 202-464-0131
www.aacap.org

The AACAP (American Academy of Child and Adolescent Psychiatry) is the leading national professional medical association dedicated to the promotion of healthy development for children, adolescents, and families.

Heidi B. Fordi, Executive Director

6428 American Academy of Pediatrics
345 Park Blvd
Itasca, IL 60143

847-434-4000
800-433-9016
Fax: 847-434-8000
csc@aap.org
www.aap.org

The American Academy of Pediatrics and its member pediatricians are committed to the attainment of optimal physical, mental and social health and well-being for all infants, children, adolescents, and young adults.

Kyle E. Yasuda, MD, FAAP, President
Mark Del Monte, JD, CEO/Executive VP
Vera Tait, MD, FAAP, Chief Medical Officer

6429 American School Counselor Association
1101 King Street, Ste 310
Alexandria, VA 22314

703-683-2722
asca@schoolcounselor.org
www.schoolcounselor.org

The mission of ASCA is to represent professional school counselors and to promote professionalism and ethical practices.

Jill Cook, Executive Director
Amanda Fitzgerald, Assistant Deputy Executive Director
Kathleen M Rakestraw, Director of Communications

6430 Child Neurology Foundation
601 W Short Street
Lexington, KY 40508

888-417-3435
info@childneurologyfoundation.org
childneurologyfoundation.org

The Child Neurology Foundation connects partners from all areas of the child neurology community so those navigating the journey of disease diagnosis, management, and care have the ongoing support from those dedicated to treatments and cures.

Amy Brin, Executive Director
Katie Hentges, Director, Programs
Brea McCormley, Director, Development

Tics / Conferences

6431 **Genetic Alliance**
426400 Woodfield Road, Ste 189
Damascus, MD 20872
202-966-5557
Fax: 202-966-8553
info@geneticalliance.org
www.geneticalliance.org

World's leading nonprofit health advocacy organization committed to transforming health through genetics and promoting an environment of openness centered on the health of individuals, families, and communities.

Sharon Terry, CEO
Ruth Child, CFO
Natasha Bonhomme, Chief Strategy Officer

6432 **NADD: National Association for the Dually Diagnosed**
12 Hurley Avenue
Kingston, NY 12401
845-331-4336
800-331-5362
Fax: 845-331-4569
info@thenadd.org
www.thenadd.org

Nonprofit organization designed to promote the interests of professional and parent development with resources for individuals who have the coexistence of mental illness and intellectual disabilities. Provides conferences, educational services and training materials to professionals, parents, concerned citizens and service organizations.

Jeanne Farr, CEO
Michelle Jordan, Office Manager
Edward Seliger, Project Coordinator

6433 **WE MOVE (Worldwide Education and Awareness of Movement Disorders)**
204 West 84th Street
New York, NY 10024
wemove@wemove.org

Provides movement disorder information and education materials to physicians, patients, the media and the public via its comprehensive web sites, training courses, and more. It's goal is to make early diagnosis, up-to-date treatment and patient support a reality for all people living with movement disorders.

Susan Bressman, MD, President

Conferences

6434 **American School Counselor Association Annual Conference**
1101 King Street, Suite 310
Alexandria, VA 22314
703-683-2722
800-306-4722
Fax: 703-997-7572
asca@schoolcounselor.org
www.schoolcounselor.org

The mission of ASCA is to represent professional school counselors and to promote professionalism and ethical practices.

3,000 Attendees

Richard Wong, Executive Director
Jennifer Walsh, Director, Education & Training
Kathleen M Rakestraw, Director of Communications

Audio Video

6435 **Dakota**
Tourette Syndrome Association
42-40 Bell Boulevard
Bayside, NY 11361
718-224-2999
888-486-8738
Fax: 718-279-9596
ts@tsa-usa.org
tsa-usa.org

A happy eleven year old baseball playing, video game whiz, Dakota is diagnosed with Tourette's Syndrome and ADHD.

7 minutes

6436 **Family Life with Tourette Syndrome... Personal Stories**
Tourette Syndrome Association
42-40 Bell Boulevard
Bayside, NY 11361
718-224-2999
888-486-8738
Fax: 718-279-9596
ts@tsa-usa.org
tsa-usa.org

In extended, in-depth interviews, all the people engagingly profiled in After the Diagnosis...The Next Steps, reveal the individual ways they developed to deal with TS. Each shows us that the key to leading a successful life in spite of having TS, is having a loving, supportive network of family and friends. Available in its entirety or as separate vignettes.

58 minutes

6437 **Ryan**
Tourette Syndrome Association
42-40 Bell Boulevard
Bayside, NY 11361
718-224-2999
888-486-8738
Fax: 718-279-9596
ts@tsa-usa.org
tsa-usa.org

Ryan's family first thought his behavior was a deliberate way to get attention, lateer educate themselves and others about Ryan's Tourette's Syndrome.

11 minutes

6438 **The Turners**
Tourette Syndrome Association
42-40 Bell Boulevard
Bayside, NY 11361
718-224-2999
888-486-8738
Fax: 718-279-9596
ts@tsa-usa.org
tsa-usa.org

Three of the four Turner daughters have Tourette's Syndrome in varying degress.

12 minutes

Web Sites

6439 **American Academy of Child and Adolescent Psychiatry**
3615 Wisconsin Avenue NW
Washington, DC 20016
202-966-7300
Fax: 202-464-0131
www.aacap.org

The AACAP (American Academy of Child and Adolescent Psychiatry) is the leading national professional medical association dedicated to the promotion of healthy development for children, adolescents, and families.

Heidi B. Fordi, Executive Director

6440 **NADD: National Association for the Dually Diagnosed**
12 Hurley Avenue
Kingston, NY 12401
845-331-4336
800-331-5362
Fax: 845-331-4569
info@thenadd.org
www.thenadd.org

Nonprofit organization designed to promote the interests of professional and care providers for individuals who have the coexistence of mental illness and intellectual disabilities. NADD provides conferences, educational services and training materials to professionals, parents, concerned citizens and service organizations.

Jeanne Farr, CEO
Michelle Jordan, Office Manager
Edward Seliger, Project Coordinator

6441 **NIH/National Institute of Neurological Disorders and Stroke (NINDS)**
PO Box 5801
Bethesda, MD 20824

301-496-5751
800-352-9424
www.ninds.nih.gov

Works to reduce the burden of neurological disease by conducting, fostering, coordinating and guiding research on the causes, prevention, diagnosis and treatment of neurological disorders and stroke, while supporting basic research in related scientific areas.

Walter J. Koroshetz, MD, Director

6442 **Online Mendelian Inheritance in Man**
McKusick-Nathans Institue of Genetic Medicine-JHU
Baltimore, MD 21205

www.omim.org

This database is a catalog of human genes and genetic disorders.

Ada Hamosh, MD, Scientific Director

6443 **Parents Helping Parents**
1400 Parkmoor Avenue, Suite 100
San Jose, CA 95126

408-727-5775
855-727-5775
Fax: 408-286-1116
info@php.com
www.php.com

Parents Helping Parents supports, educates, and inspires families and the community to build bright futures for youth and adults with special needs.

Maria Daane, Executive Director
Janet Nunez, Director, Programs
Virginia Hildebrand, Director, Finance

6444 **Tourette Syndrome Online**
www.tourette-syndrome.com

www.tourette-syndrome.com

Devoted to children and adults with Tourette syndrome disorder and their families, friends, teachers and medical professionals.

6445 **WE MOVE (Worldwide Education and Awareness of Movement Disorders)**
204 West 84th Street
New York, NY 10024

NOP-ONE-

Provides movement disorder information and education materials to physicians, patients, the media and the public via its comprehensive web sites, training courses, and more. It's goal is to make early diagnosis, up-to-date treatment and patient support a reality for all people living with movement disorders.

Book Publishers

6446 **Cognitive-Behavioral Management of Tic Disorders**
John Wiley & Sons
111 River Street
Hoboken, NJ 07030

201-748-6000
Fax: 201-748-6088
info@wiley.com
www.wiley.com

Provides a comprehensive review of what is known about the occurance and diagnosis of Tics.

2005 Paperback
ISBN: 0-470093-80-1

Peter B. Wiley, Chairman
Stephen M. Smith, President & CEO
Ellis E. Cousens, Executive Vice President, Chief Fin

6447 **Hi, I'm Adam**
Hope Press
PO Box 188
Duarte, CA 91009

800-321-4039
Fax: 626-358-3520
dcomings@earthlink.net
www.hopepress.com

Adam Buehrens is ten years old and has Tourette syndrome. Adam wrote and illustrated this book because he wants everyone to know he and other children with Tourette syndrome are not crazy. They just hava a common neurological disorder. If you know a child that has tics, temper tantrums, unreasonable fears, or problems dealing with school, you will find this a reassuring story.

6448 **Teaching the Tiger**
Hope Press
PO Box 188
Duarte, CA 91009

800-321-4039
Fax: 626-358-3520
dcomings@earthlink.net
www.hopepress.com

A handbook for individuals involved in the education of students with Attention Deficit Disorder, Tourette Syndrome, or Obsessive Compulsive Disorder.

ISBN: 1-878267-34-5

David E Comings MD, Presenter

6449 **Tourette's Syndrome - Tics, Obsession, Compulsions: Developmental Psychopathology**
John Wiley & Sons
111 River Street
Hoboken, NJ 07030

201-748-6000
Fax: 201-748-6088
info@wiley.com
www.wiley.com

Once thought to be rare, Tourette's Syndrome is now seen as a relatively common childhood disorder either in its complete or partial incarnations. Drawing on the work of contributors hailing from the prestigious Yale University Child Psychiatry Department, this edited volume explores the disorder from many perspectives, mapping out the diagnosis, genetics, phenomenology, natural history, and treatment of Tourette's syndrome.

1998 600 pages Hardcover
ISBN: 0-471160-37-7

Peter B. Wiley, Chairman
Stephen M. Smith, President & CEO
Ellis E. Cousens, Executive Vice President, Chief Fin

6450 **What Makes Ryan Tic?**
Hope Press
PO Box 188
Duarte, CA 91009

800-321-4039
Fax: 626-358-3520
dcomings@earthlink.net
www.hopepress.com

Covers Ryan's very difficult adolescent years-a period when his symptoms were so severe he had to be placed in a residential treatment facility-and the subsequent period of returning home and pursuing a virtually normal life following his excellent response to the right combination of medication, family and school support.

Susan Hughes, Author

Journals

6451 **Movement Disorders**
John Wiley & Sons
111 River Street
Hoboken, NJ 7030-

201-748-6000
Fax: 201-748-6088
info@wiley.com
www.wiley.com

Publishes reviews, viewpoints, full length articles, historical reports, brief reports, clinical/scientific notes, videotape briefs, patient/imaging briefs, and letters. ISSN: 0885-3185

Vol 22 13 Issues

Stephen M. Smith, President/ CEO
John Kritzmacher, EVP/ CFO
MJ O'Leary, EVO, Human Resources

Tics / Pamphlets

Pamphlets

6452 Matthew and Tics
Tourette Syndrome Association
42-40 Bell Boulevard
Bayside, NY 11361

718-224-2999
888-486-8738
Fax: 718-279-9596
ts@tsa-usa.org
tsa-usa.org

A story for young children with Tourette's Syndrome and their peers; promotes acceptance and understanding.

6453 Tics and Tourette's Syndrome Fact Sheet
Movement Disorder Resource Center - WE MOVE
204 E 84th Street
New York, NY 10024

212-241-8567
800-437-6682
Fax: 212-987-7363
www.life-in-motion.org

Provides overviews of both diseases.

Description

6454 TOURETTE SYNDROME
Synonyms: Gilles de la Tourette syndrome, GTS
Involves the following Biologic System(s):
Neurologic Disorders

Tourette syndrome is a neurologic disorder that typically becomes apparent in children between the ages of two to 14 years, with approximately 50 percent of cases occurring before seven years of age. The disorder, which is thought to affect about one in 2,000 individuals, is approximately three times more prevalent in males than females and is more common among Caucasians than other populations. In children with Tourette syndrome, associated symptoms and findings vary greatly in range and severity. Initial symptoms may include involuntary, repetitive (stereotypical) muscle movements (motor tics) of the face, eyelids, shoulders, and neck, such as grimacing, abrupt head turning, excessive eye blinking, or stretching of the neck. In some patients with severe symptoms, motor tics may evolve to include self-mutilating behaviors, such as nail biting, lip biting, or facial punching. Children with Tourette syndrome may also develop vocal tics, such as involuntary coughing, grunting, barking, sniffling, or throat clearing. As the disease progresses, additional symptoms may develop including involuntary repetition of obscene words (coprolalia), words spoken by other individuals (echolalia), or one's own words (palilalia) or imitation of other individuals' behaviors (echokinesis or echopraxia). The symptoms associated with Tourette syndrome may periodically decrease or increase in intensity; may subside during high levels of concentration, such as when reading or studying; and may worsen with stress. Tourette syndrome is considered a life-long disorder; however, in approximately 50 to 66 percent of patients, symptoms significantly decrease about 10 to 15 years after initial diagnosis and treatment.

Children with Tourette syndrome may also experience associated behavioral abnormalities, such as aggressive behavior or the performance of repetitive actions or impulses in response to recurrent, persistent thoughts (obsessive-compulsive behaviors). Obsessive-compulsive behaviors are typically performed to help neutralize obsessive thoughts and relieve anxieties. Many affected children may also develop learning, emotional, or social difficulties. The treatment of Tourette syndrome is symptomatic and supportive and may include therapy with certain medications, such as haloperidol, pimozide, clonidine, clonazepam, or carbamazepine. In addition, for those with learning, behavioral, and social difficulties, multidisciplinary management and the provision of special social, academic, and vocational services may be important in helping patients achieve their potential.

Although the exact cause of Tourette syndrome is unknown, studies suggest that the disorder may result due to abnormalities of neurotransmitter (dopamine) activity within a certain area of the brain (basal ganglia). In most cases, Tourette syndrome is thought to be inherited as an autosomal dominant trait that occurs as the result of changes (mutations) in a gene located on the long arm (q) of chromosome 18 (18q22.1). Some children with mutations of this disease gene may not have symptoms associated with the disorder (incomplete penetrance). In addition, in those children with the defective gene who do have symptoms associated with Tourette syndrome, such symptoms may vary in range and severity from case to case (variable expressivity). Such variability of gene expression and penetrance may be suggested by the fact that immediate (first-degree) relatives of patients have an increased frequency of Tourette syndrome, tic conditions, and obsessive-compulsive disorder. In addition, some researchers suspect that Tourette syndrome may result from inheritance of a disease gene in combination with certain environmental factors that may trigger the gene's expression (multifactorial inheritance). Research suggests that individuals who have two copies of a disease gene for Tourette syndrome (homozygotes) typically express the disorder, whereas some who inherit one disease gene (heterozygotes) may not develop the disorder unless particular environmental factors (e.g., infection, such as due to exposure to Group A beta-hemolytic streptococcus) trigger its expression. Tourette syndrome is associated with a vary of misconceptions, for instance, that people with Tourette syndrome are mentally disturbed and that they always exhibit coprolalia. Tourette's is a neurological condition that (according to the most recent research) is primarily genetic in nature. Although there may be learning disabilities associated with Tourette's, the brain is wholly undamaged in respect to intellectual functioning. Statistically, coprolalia is present in less than 5% of TS patients.

Government Agencies

6455 Centers for Disease Control and Prevention -TB Prevention
1600 Clifton Road
Atlanta, GA 30329
800-232-4636
TTY: 888-232-6348
www.cdc.gov/tb/

Provides health and quality of life by preventing, controlling, and eventually eliminating tuberculosis in the United States.
Philip LeBue, MD, Director

6456 NIH/ Eunice Kennedy Shriver National Institute of Child Health & Human Development
P.O. Box 3006
Rockville, MD 20847
800-370-2943
Fax: 866-760-5947
www.nichd.nih.gov

Conducts and supports research on topics related to the health of children, adults, families and populations. Some of these topics include: developmental disabilities, growth and development, infant death, reproductive health and birth defects.
Diana W. Bianchi, Director
Alison Cernich, PhD, Deputy Director

6457 NIH/National Heart, Lung and Blood Institute
31 Center Drive, Bldg 31
Bethesda, MD 20892
877-645-2448
www.nhlbi.nih.gov

Primary responsibility of this organization is the scientific investigation of heart, blood vessel, lung and blood disorders. Oversees research, demonstration, prevention, education, control and training activities in these fields and emphasizes the prevention and control of heart diseases.
Gary H. Gibbons, MD, Director
Kate O'Sullivan, Executive Officer

6458 NIH/National Institute of Allergy and Infectious Diseases
5601 Fishers Lane, MSC 9806
Bethesda, MD 20892
301-496-5717
866-284-4107
Fax: 301-402-3573
TDD: 800-877-8339
ocpostoffice@niaid.nih.gov
www.niaid.nih.gov

The principal advisory board of the NIAID. The council is composed of physicians, scientists and representatives of the public and advises on the conduct and support or research, training and dissemination of health information regarding allergies and infectious diseases.
Anthony S. Fauci, MD, Director

6459 New York City Department of Health Bureau of Tuberculosis Control
New York, NY 10013
www.nyc.gov

The department aims to prevent the spread of tuberculosis (TB) and eliminate it as a public health problem in NYC.

National Associations & Support Groups

6460 American Academy of Child and Adolescent Psychiatry
3615 Wisconsin Avenue NW
Washington, DC 20016
202-966-7300
Fax: 202-464-0131
www.aacap.org

The AACAP (American Academy of Child and Adolescent Psychiatry) is the leading national professional medical association dedicated to the promotion of healthy development for children, adolescents, and families.

Heidi B. Fordi, Executive Director

6461 American Academy of Pediatrics
345 Park Blvd
Itasca, IL 60143
847-434-4000
800-433-9016
Fax: 847-434-8000
csc@aap.org
www.aap.org

The American Academy of Pediatrics and its member pediatricians dedicate their efforts and resources to the health, safety and well-being of infants, children, adolescents and young adults.

Kyle E. Yasuda, MD, FAAP, President
Mark Del Monte, JD, CEO/Executive VP
Vera Tait, MD, FAAP, Chief Medical Officer

6462 American Heart Association
7272 Greenville Avenue
Dallas, TX 75231
214-570-5978
800-242-8721
www.heart.org

The mission of the American Heart Associate is to build healthier lives, free of cardiovascular diseases and stroke.

Nancy Brown, CEO
Mitchell S.V. Elkind, President
Suzie Upton, Chief Operating Officer

6463 American Lung Association
55 W. Wacker Drive, Suite 1150
Chicago, IL 60601
800-586-4872
info@lung.org
www.lung.org

The American Lung Association fights lung disease in all its forms, with special emphasis on asthma, tobacco control and environmental health. The American Lung Association is funded with contributions from the public, along with gifts and grants from corporations, foundations and government agencies. The association achieves its many successes through the work of thousands of committed volunteers and staff.

Harold P. Wimmer, National President & CEO
Albert Rizzo, MD, Chief Medical Officer
Sue Swan, Chief Development Officer

6464 American School Counselor Association
1101 King Street, Ste 310
Alexandria, VA 22314
703-683-2722
asca@schoolcounselor.org
www.schoolcounselor.org

The mission of ASCA is to represent professional school counselors and to promote professionalism and ethical practices.

Jill Cook, Executive Director
Amanda Fitzgerald, Assistant Deputy Executive Director
Kathleen M Rakestraw, Director of Communications

6465 American Society for Reproductive Medicine
1209 Montgomery Highway
Birmingham, AL 35216
205-978-5000
Fax: 205-978-5005
asrm@asrm.org
www.asrm.org

The American Society for Reproductive Medicine is an organization devoted to advancing knowledge and expertise in infertility, reproductive medicine and biology. The ASRM is a voluntary nonprofit organization.

Jared C. Robins, Chief Executive Director
Chevis N. Shannon, Chief Education & Science Officer
Lee Pearce, Chief Operating Officer

6466 Arc of the United States
1825 K Street NW, Ste 1200
Washington, DC 20006
202-534-3700
800-433-5255
Fax: 202-534-3731
info@thearc.org
www.thearc.org

The Arc of the United States advocates for the rights and full participation of all children and adults with intellectual and developmental disabilities. Together with a network of members and affiliated chapters, they improve systems of support and services; connect families; inspire communities and influence public policy.

Peter V. Berns, CEO

6467 Center for Parent Information and Resources (CPIR)
c/o SPAN, 35 Halsey Street, 4th Floor
Newark, NJ 07102
973-642-8100
malizo@spanadvocacy.org
www.parentcenterhub.org

Family-friendly information and research-based materials on key topics for Parent Centers. Private workspaces for Parent Centers to exchange resources, discuss high-priority topics, and solve mutual challenges. Coordination of parent training efforts throughout the network.

Myriam Alizo, Project Assistant

6468 Child Neurology Foundation
601 W Short Street
Lexington, KY 40508
888-417-3435
info@childneurologyfoundation.org
childneurologyfoundation.org

The Child Neurology Foundation connects partners from all areas of the child neurology community so those navigating the journey of disease diagnosis, management, and care have the ongoing support from those dedicated to treatments and cures.

Amy Brin, Executive Director
Katie Hentges, Director, Programs
Brea McCormley, Director, Development

6469 Children's Hospital Boston
300 Longwood Avenue
Boston, MA 02115
617-355-6000
www.childrenshospital.org

Mission is to provide the highest quality care; be the leading source of research and discovery; educate the next generation of leaders in child health and enhance the health and well-being of the children and families in our local community.

Kevin Churchwell, President & CEO
Jessica Farnham, Chief Operating Officer

6470 Chromosome 18 Registry & Research Society
7155 Oakridge Drive
San Antonio, TX 78229
210-657-4968
office@chromosome18.org
www.chromosome18.org

The purpose of the Chromosome 18 Registry & Research Society is to offer support to patients and families, to educate the public about different available treatments and to connect families and doctors to the research community.

Neale Parker, Chief Executive Officer
Amelie Simons, Director of Operations
Jessica Sanders, Programs & Events Coordinator

6471 Epilepsy Foundation
8301 Professional Place West, Ste 230
Landover, MD 20785
301-459-3700
800-332-1000
Fax: 301-577-2684
ContactUs@efa.org
www.epilepsy.org

Nationwide organization dedicated to help those living with epilepsy pursue seizure freedom through community services, public education, advocacy and research funding.

Phil Gattone, President & CEO
Ellen Hobby, COO
Steve Owens, VP, Programs & Services

6472 Family Support Network
29 N Gore Avenue
St. Louis, MO 63119
314-963-1450
Fax: 314-963-9571
info@familysupportnet.org
www.familysupportnet.org

The Support Network is an organized partnership of individuals whose lives have been affected by Tuberous Sclerosis. Across the nation, the Support Network is providing the latest medical information, education and support to those individuals who are seeking understanding about the genetic disease and offering them words of encouragement and empowerment.

Dorothy Heltibrand, Executive Director
Vincent Marino, Program Director
Lynn Frost, Public Relations Director

6473 Genetic Alliance
426400 Woodfield Road, Ste 189
Damascus, MD 20872
202-966-5557
Fax: 202-966-8553
info@geneticalliance.org
www.geneticalliance.org

World's leading nonprofit health advocacy organization committed to transforming health through genetics and promoting an environment of openness centered on the health of individuals, families, and communities.

Sharon Terry, CEO
Ruth Child, CFO
Natasha Bonhomme, Chief Strategy Officer

6474 Global Tuberculosis Institute
225 Warren Street, 2nd Floor, East Wing
Newark, NJ 07103
973-972-3270
Fax: 973-972-3268
globaltbinstitute@njms.rutgers.edu
globaltb.njms.rutgers.edu

The mission of the Global Tuberculosis Institute (GTBI), located at the International Center for Public Health, has always been to advance tuberculosis care through excellence in practice, research and teaching.

Alfred A. Lardizabal, Executive Director
Amee Patrawalla, Medical Director
Rajita Bhavaraju, Deputy Director

6475 Parent to Parent USA
PO Box 472
State College, PA 16804
484-272-7368
www.p2pusa.org

Parent to Parent USA supports a network of viable, sustainable, fully-functioning and effective Parent to Parent programs in all 50 states through hands-on support, training and technical assistance, and high quality tools and resources.

Aurelie "Lily" Brown, Co-Director
Marsha Quinn, Co-Director

6476 Support Organization for Trisomy 18, 13, and Related Disorders (SOFT)
2982 S Union Street
Rochester, NY 14624
www.trisomy.org

SOFT is a network of families and professional dedication to providing support and understanding to families involved in the issue and decision surrounding the diagnosis and care in related chromosome disorders. Support is provided throughout pre-natal diagnosis, the child's life and after their passing. It is committed to the support of families personal decision in alliance with a parent-professional partnership.

6477 Trisomy 18 Foundation
4491 Cheshire Station Plaza, Suite 157
Dale City, VA 22193
810-867-4211
t18info@trisomy18.org
www.trisomy18.org

The foundation's mission is to search for a cure and treatments; to educate and support medical professionals; and to create a worldwide caring community for those affected.

Victoria Miller, Executive Director
Sean Brown, Vice-President of Development
Kris Shaughnessy, M.A., Community Affairs Program Office

6478 United Network for Organ Sharing
700 N 4th Street
Richmond, VA 23219
804-782-4800
800-292-9548
www.unos.org

Our mission is to advance organ availability and transplantation by uniting and supporting our communities for the benefit of patients through education, technology and policy development.

Maureen McBride, Interim CEO
David Klassen, Chief Medical Officer
Dale E. Smith, Chief Financial Officer

6479 WE MOVE (Worldwide Education and Awareness of Movement Disorders)
204 West 84th Street
New York, NY 10024
wemove@wemove.org

A nonprofit organization dedicated to educating and informing patients, professionals and the public about the latest clinical advances, management and treatment options for neurologic movement disorders.

Susan Bressman, MD, President

6480 World Health Organization
Avenue Appia 20
1202 Geneva,
Switzerland
www.who.int

WHO is the directing and coordinating authority for health within the United Nations system. WHO operates in more than 150 countries around the world.

Dr. Tedros Adhanom Ghebreyesus, Director General
Dr. Zsuzsanna Jakab, Deputy Director General
Stewart Simonson, Asst Director General, UN NYC

State Agencies & Support Groups

Arizona

6481 Tourette Syndrome Association - Arizona Chapter
6501 E. Greenway Pkwy, PO Box 103-414
Scottsdale, AZ 85254
520-620-2288
800-203-7490
www.tsa-az.org

The Arizona chapter of the Tourette Syndrome Association was established to serve the community touched by Touretty Syndrome.

Kelly Medlyn, President
Marci Frantz, Vice President
Teri Mendenhall, Secretary

California

6482 Tourette Syndrome Association - Northern California/Hawaii Chapter
www.tsanorcal-hawaii.org
925-548-3605
gibsonohare@sbcglobal.net
www.tsanorcal-hawaii.org

A voluntary organization dedicated to providing assistance and support for individuals with Tourette Syndrome, their families, friends & loved ones.

Sandy Gibson-O'Hare, Chair
Sandra Brackett, Vice Chair
Samantha Phillips, Secretary

Tourette Syndrome / State Agencies & Support Groups

6483 Tourette Syndrome Association - Southern California Chapter
PO Box 3778
Cerritos, CA 90703
866-478-1935
bcourdy@ca.rr.com
www.tourettesyndrome-sca.org

The TSA of Southern California is an all volunteer, non-profit organization whose missions is to support the needs of families affected by Tourette Syndrome. The goal is to advocate for individuals with TS, educate the public and professionals about TS, and promote awareness.

Colorado

6484 Tourette Syndrome Association - Rocky Mountain Region
992 S 4th Avenue, Suite 100, PMB 198
Brighton, CO 80601
720-212-7535
support@tsa-rmr.org
www.tsa-rmr.org

The TSARMR serves Colorado, Montana, Wyoming, and Nevada.

Sally Mescher Allen, Chair
Donna Davies, Vice Chair
Lorraine Alcott, Secretary

Connecticut

6485 Tourette Syndrome Association - Connecticut Chapter
PO Box 185883
Hamden, CT 06518
203-980-4215
www.tsact.org

The mission of the Connecticut chapter of the Tourette Syndrome Association, Inc. is to educate the general public about Touretty Syndrome and further the acceptance of people with Tourette Syndrome in all settings.

Peter Tavolacci, Vice-Chairman
Paul Nazario, Treasurer
Jeanette Nazario, Board Member

Florida

6486 Tourette Syndrome Association of Florida
PO Box 411416
Melbourne, FL 32941
727-418-0240
support@tsa-fl.org
www.tsa-fl.org

The TSA of Florida is a voluntary organization dedicated to helping individuals with Tourette Syndrome and their families by gathering and distributing information, promoting local self-help and professional services, and providing local TS support groups and meetings.

Donna Sakuta, Executive Director

Hawaii

6487 Tourette Syndrome Association - Northern California/Hawaii Chapter
www.tsanorcal-hawaii.org
925-548-3605
gibsonohare@sbcglobal.net
www.tsanorcal-hawaii.org

A voluntary organization dedicated to providing assistance and support for individuals with Tourette Syndrome, their families, friends & loved ones.

Sandy Gibson-O'Hare, Chair
Sandra Brackett, Vice Chair
Samantha Phillips, Secretary

Illinois

6488 Tourette Syndrome Association of Illinois
800 Roosevelt Road, Suite A-10
Glen Ellyn, IL 60137
630-790-8083
877-TSA-IL55
Fax: 630-790-8084
tsaillinois@yahoo.com
www.tsa-illinois.org

TSA of Illinois' mission is to serve and support those whose lives are affected by Tourette Syndrome. TSA-IL promotes awareness, advocates, and educates the public, health care providers, and educators about Tourette Syndrome. TSA-IL supports medical and scientific research about Tourette Syndrome.

Sande S Shamash, President
Jen Johnson, Vice President, Membership
Joan Lindauer, Vice President, Government Relation

Indiana

6489 Tourette Syndrome Association of Indiana
PO Box 3797
West Lafayette, IN 47996
765-714-9880
tsaofindiana@gmail.com
www.tsaindiana.org

One of TSA of Indiana's many priorities is to establish access to current information and easy communication for its members. The leaders are committed to serving and supporting those whose lives are affected by Tourette Syndrome.

Michele Lehman, President
Brenda Leopold, Youth Ambassador Program Coordin.
John Leopold, Youth Ambassador Program Coordin.

Maine

6490 Tourette Syndrome Association - Maine/New Hampshire Chapter
www.tsa-maine.org
207-699-4258
www.tsa-maine.org

The Tourette Syndrome Association is a non-profit organization aimed at identifying the cause of, finding the cure for, and controlling the effects of this disorder. TSA also seeks to broaden awareness of Tourette Syndrome and provide support for families and individuals who deal with it.

Maryland

6491 Tourette Syndrome Association of Greater Washington
5851 Deale Churchton Road, Suite 4
Deale, MD 20751
410-867-1151
877-295-2148
Fax: 301-576-4527
www.tsagw.org

The TSA of Greater Washington is a non-profit organization comprised of an all volunteer Board of Directors, two paid Staff and numerous unaffiliated volunteers. The mission is to improve the quality of life in those affected by Tourette Syndrome through education, advocacy and awareness in Maryland, Virginia and Washington D.C.

Marla Shea Gabala, Chairman
Judy Krauthamer, Vice Chair/Treasurer
Mark Etzel, Secretary

Massachusetts

6492 Tourette Syndrome Association of Massachusetts
39 Godfrey Street
Taunton, MA 02780
617-277-7589
www.tsa-ma.org

Tourette Syndrome / State Agencies & Support Groups

The Tourette Syndrome Association of Massachusets is an all volunteer, non-profit organization whose mission is to support the needs of families affected by Tourette Syndrome. The goal is to advocate for individuals with TS, educate the public and professionals about TS, and promote awareness.

Chrissy Joyal, President
Liliane Larsen, Vice President/Treasurer
Judy Storeygard, Education Specialist

Minnesota

6493 Tourette Syndrome Association - Minnesota Chapter
2233 University Avenue, Suite 338
St. Paul, MN 55114
651-646-0099
Fax: 952-918-0350
www.tsa-mn.org

The mission is to assist Minnesotan's with Tourette syndrome in achieving their fullest potential through education, support and public awareness programs.

Lee Baker, Executive Director

Missouri

6494 Tourette Syndrome Association - Greater Missouri Chapter
6526 Parkwood Place
St. Louis, MO 63116
314-984-9019
lmchd52@gmail.com
www.missouritsa.org

Serves individuals and families in the St. Louis and Kansas City metropolitan areas and beyond. In concert with the national TSA, they provide information about Tourette Syndrome (TS) and the resources available to help affected families throughout the service area.

Lynn Dunlap, Chair
Pete Abel, Co-Chair/ Government Liaison
Marty Guise, Secretary

Montana

6495 Tourette Syndrome Association - Rocky Mountain Region
992 S 4th Avenue, Suite 100, PMB 198
Brighton, CO 80601
720-212-7535
support@tsa-rmr.org
www.tsa-rmr.org

The TSARMR serves Colorado, Montana, Wyoming, and Nevada.

Sally Mescher Allen, Chair
Donna Davies, Vice Chair
Lorraine Alcott, Secretary

Nevada

6496 Tourette Syndrome Association - Rocky Mountain Region
992 S 4th Avenue, Suite 100, PMB 198
Brighton, CO 80601
720-212-7535
www.tsa-rmr.org

The TSARMR serves Colorado, Montana, Wyoming, and Nevada.

Sally Mescher Allen, Chair
Donna Davies, Vice Chair
Lorraine Alcott, Secretary

New Jersey

6497 Tourette Syndrome Association of New Jersey
50 Division Street, Suite 205
Somerville, NJ 08876
732-972-4459
www.tsanj.org

The Tourette Syndrome Association of New Jersey, Inc., a chapter of the national Tourette Syndrome Association, is a non-profit organization whos membership includes individuals with Tourette Syndrome, their families and friends, and interested professionals.

New Mexico

6498 Tourette Syndrome Association - New Mexico Chapter
42-40 Bell Boulevard
Bayside, NY 11361
718-224-2999
www.tsanm.org

The purpose is to provide information, support, and assistance to adults, children, and families affected by Tourette Syndrome. The hope is to provide education and to encourage an understanding and acceptance of this disorder.

Jennifer Johns, President
Helen Gutierrez, Secretary
Tanya Mueller, Treasurer

New York

6499 Tourette Syndrome Association - Greater Rochester and Finger Lakes Area
92 Windmere Road
Rochester, NY 14617
585-752-6190
info@rochestertourette.org
www.rochestertourette.org

The TSA of Greater Rochester and the Finger Lakes, Inc. is a non-profit organization whose mission is to provide support, information and advocacy to people with TS and their families in friends. The chapter serves the community at large with support groups, in-services, and public awareness programs to the local, educational, and medical communities.

Diana Pratt, Chair
Patrick Scanlon, Vice Chair
Bob Gleason, Treasurer

6500 Tourette Syndrome Association - Greater New York State Chapter
20 Thomas Jefferson Lane
Synder, NY 14226
716-839-4430
Fax: 716-839-1956
info@tsa-gnys.org
www.tsa-gnys.org

The Tourette Syndrome Association of Greater New York State is an affiliate chapter of the TSA, Inc. The chapter serves an area from Buffalo to the Pennsylvania border to the south. There is a Greater Rochester TSA chapter that serves greater Rochester, NY. TSA-GNYS then picks up from Rochester and continues east to serve Syracuse and all of the central NY area.

Susan Conners, President
Marge Henning, Co-Chair
John Silverwood, Co-Chair

6501 Tourette Syndrome Association - Hudson Valley Chapter
PO Box 517
Ardsley, NY 10502
914-378-5025
info@tsa-nyhv.org
www.tsa-nyhv.org

The mission of the Hudson Valley Chapter is; to provide service, information, and support to people with TS and their families; to educate medical and educational professionals in order to increase their understanding of TS; and to promote a greater understanding of TS in the community at large.

Shelly Cooler, President
Marilyn Trichon, Vice President
Richard Yannetti, Executive Director

6502 Tourette Syndrome Association - Long Island Chapter
PO Box 615
Jericho, NY 11753
516-876-6947
longisland.tsa@gmail.com
www.li-tsa.org

The Long Island TSA's mission is to provide help (at the community level) to families affected by Tourette Syndrome by providing services to its members in Nassau and Suffolk counties.

Lisa Filippi, Co Chair
Kate Callan, Co-Vice Chair
Jane Zwilling, 1st Vice Chair and Chair, Education

Tourette Syndrome / Research Centers

6503 Tourette Syndrome Association - New York City Chapter
www.tsa-nyc.org

646-395-0162
chapter@tsa-nyc.org
www.tsa-nyc.org

The New York city chapter offers a variety of services to people with Tourette Syndrome, their families, educators, and professionals.

Chelsea White, Chairperson
Linda McAndrew, Secretary
Jonathan Marks, Treasurer

Ohio

6504 Tourette Syndrome Association of Ohio
PO Box 40163
Cincinnatti, OH 45240

513-320-7161
800-543-2675
www.tsaohio.org

The Tourette Syndrome Association of Ohio is a nonprofit organization whose membership includes individuals with Tourette Syndrome, their families, friends, and interested professionals.

Coreen Brown, Chair of the Board
Joleah Dean, Executive Director of the Board

Oregon

6505 Tourette Syndrome Association - Washington and Oregon Chapter
318 West Galer Street
Seattle, WA 98119

718-224-2999
tsawashingtonchapter@yahoo.com
www.tsa-waor.org

This chapter exists to offer information, support and resources regarding Tourette Syndrome and its related conditions. They work together with the medical community, the schools and families whose lives are touched by TS.

Todd Henry, Chair
Erin Farrar, Vice Chair
Bernadette Witty, Secretary

Pennsylvania

6506 PA Tourette Syndrome Alliance
PO Box 148
McSherrystown, PA 17344

717-337-1134
800-990-3300
Fax: 717-698-1420
info@patsainc.org
www.patsainc.org

The services provided by PA-TSA are focused on increasing understanding of the disorder and providing proven accommodations and strategies so the child or adult can succeed.

Melinda Bowling, President
Lesley Geye, Vice-President
Susan Lutz, Treasurer

Rhode Island

6507 Tourette Syndrome Association of Rhode Island
6946 Post Road, Suite 402
North Kingstown, RI 00285

401-886-0887
info@oshean.org
www.ri.net/tsari

TSARI tries to define the needs of Rhode Islanders with TS and their families and design services for them. They offer support and education to families with TS.

Susan Cerrone Abely, Chair
John Smithers, Vice-Chair
Michael Pickett, Treasurer

Utah

6508 Tourette Syndrome Association - Utah Chapter
PO Box 701312
West Valley City, UT 84170

801-967-2125
866-274-0700
www.tsa-utah.org

The local chapter of the national TSA organization, serving as a resource for individuals who have Tourette Syndrome and their families. Membership is open to anyone who is interested in Tourette Syndrome.

Kelsey Brown, Chairman
Adam Westwood, Treasurer
Gerri Harper, Secretary

Washington

6509 Tourette Syndrome Association - Washington and Oregon Chapter
318 West Galer Street
Seattle, WA 98119

718-224-2999
tsawashingtonchapter@yahoo.com
www.tsa-waor.org

This chapter exists to offer information, support and resources regarding Tourette Syndrome and its related conditions. They work together with the medical community, the schools and families whose lives are touched by TS.

Todd Henry, Chair
Erin Farrar, Vice Chair
Bernadette Witty, Secretary

Wyoming

6510 Tourette Syndrome Association - Rocky Mountain Region
992 S 4th Avenue, Suite 100, PMB 198
Brighton, CO 80601

720-212-7535
tsarmr@att.net
www.tsa-rmr.org

The TSARMR serves Colorado, Montana, Wyoming, and Nevada.

Sally Mescher Allen, Chair
Donna Davies, Vice Chair
Lorraine Alcott, Secretary

Research Centers

6511 Tourette Syndrome and Tic Disorder Clinic
Cincinnati Children's Hospital Medical Center
3333 Burnet Avenue
Cincinnati, OH 45229

513-636-4200
800-344-2462
TTY: 513-636-4900
tics@cchmc.org
www.cincinnatichildrens.org

Clinic that specializes in evaluating, diagnosing and treating kids, adolescents and adults with Tourette's Syndrome symptoms, including tics, hyperactivity, attention deficits, obsessive compulsive behaviors and other symptoms of Tourette Syndrome.

Donald L Gilbert, MD, MS, Director
Steve W. Wu, MD, Medical Director

6512 Trisomy 18 Foundation
4491 Cheshire Station Plaza, Suite 157
Dale City, VA 22193

810-867-4211
t18info@trisomy18.org
www.trisomy18.org

The foundation's mission is to search for a cure and treatments; to educate and support medical professionals; and to create a worldwide caring community for those affected.

Victoria Miller, Executive Director
Sean Brown, Vice-President of Development
Kris Shaughnessy, M.A., Community Affairs Program Office

6513 University of Illinois at Chicago Institute for Tuberculosis Research
904 W Adams Street
Chicago, IL 60607
202-318-2476
www.uic.edu

Michael J Groves, PhD, Director
Paula Allen-Meares, Chancellor
Lon S. Kaufman, Vice Chancellor for Academic Affair

Conferences

6514 American School Counselor Association Annual Conference
1101 King Street, Suite 310
Alexandria, VA 22314
703-683-2722
800-306-4722
Fax: 703-997-7572
asca@schoolcounselor.org
www.schoolcounselor.org

The mission of ASCA is to represent professional school counselors and to promote professionalism and ethical practices.

3,000 Attendees

Richard Wong, Executive Director
Jennifer Walsh, Director, Education & Training
Kathleen M Rakestraw, Director of Communications

Audio Video

6515 After the Diagnosis...The Next Steps
Tourette Syndrome Association
42-40 Bell Boulevard, Suite 205
Bayside, NY 11361
718-224-2999
888-486-8738
Fax: 718-279-9596
ts@tsa-usa.org
www.tsa-usa.org

When the diagnosis is Tourette syndrome, what do you do first? How do you sort out the complexities of the disorder? Whose advice do you follow? What steps do you take to lead a normal life? Six people with TS—as different as any six people can be—relate the sometimes difficult, but finally triumphant path each took to lead the rich, fulfilling life they now enjoy. Narrated by Academy Award-winning actor, Richard Dreyfuss, the stories are refreshing blends of poignancy, fact and inspiration.

35 Minutes

6516 Clinical Counseling: Toward a Better Understanding of TS
Tourette Syndrome Association
42-40 Bell Boulevard, Suite 205
Bayside, NY 11361
718-224-2999
888-486-8738
Fax: 718-279-9596
ts@tsa-usa.org
www.tsa-usa.org

Certain key issues often surface during the counseling sessions of people with TS and their families. These important areas of concern are explored for counselors, social workers, educators, psychologists and other allied professionals. Expert clinical practitioners offer invaluable insights for those working with people affected by Tourette syndrome.

14 Minutes

6517 Complexities of TS Treatment: A Physician's Roundtable
Tourette Syndrome Association
42-40 Bell Boulevard, Suite 205
Bayside, NY 11361
718-224-2999
888-486-8738
Fax: 718-279-9596
ts@tsa-usa.org
www.tsa-usa.org

Three of the most highly regarded experts in the diagnosis and treatment of Tourette syndrome offer insight, advice and treatment strategies to fellow physicians and other healthcare professionals.

15 Minutes

6518 Dakota
Tourette Syndrome Association
42-40 Bell Boulevard
Bayside, NY 11361
718-224-2999
888-486-8738
Fax: 718-279-9596
ts@tsa-usa.org
www.tsa-usa.org

A happy eleven year old baseball playing, video game whiz, Dakota is diagnosed with Tourette's Syndrome and ADHD.

7 minutes

6519 Echolalia
Hope Press
PO Box 188
Duarte, CA 91009
800-321-4039
Fax: 626-358-3520
dcomings@earthlink.net
www.hopepress.com

A story about a best selling writer who is diagnosed at age 35 with having Tourette syndrome.

David E Comings, MD, Presenter

6520 Family Life with Tourette Syndrome
Tourette Syndrome Association
42-40 Bell Boulevard, Suite 205
Bayside, NY 11361
718-224-2999
888-486-8738
Fax: 718-279-9596
ts@tsa-usa.org
www.tsa-usa.org

In extended, in-depth interviews, all the people engagingly profiled in After the Diagnosis...The Next Steps, reveal the individual ways they developed to deal with TS. Each shows us that the key to leading a successful life in spite of having TS, is having a loving, supportive network of family and friends.

6521 Family Life with Tourette Syndrome... Personal Stories
Tourette Syndrome Association
42-40 Bell Boulevard
Bayside, NY 11361
718-224-2999
888-486-8738
Fax: 718-279-9596
ts@tsa-usa.org
tsa-usa.org

In extended, in-depth interviews, all the people engagingly profiled in After the Diagnosis...The Next Steps, reveal the individual ways they developed to deal with TS. Each shows us that the key to leading a successful life in spite of having TS, is having a loving, supportive network of family and friends. Available in its entirety or as separate vignettes.

58 minutes

6522 Gift of Hope
Tourette Syndrome Association
42-40 Bell Boulevard, Suite 205
Bayside, NY 11361
718-224-2999
Fax: 718-279-9596
www.tsa-usa.org

The cause of Tourette syndrome lies in the brain. This video offers five people who have TS explaining their reasons for agreeing to register with TSA's Brain Bank Program.

14 minutes

6523 Kevin and Me
Hope Press
PO Box 188
Duarte, CA 91009
800-321-4039
Fax: 626-358-3520
dcomings@earthlink.net
www.hopepress.com

A memoir of a single moter who struggled with her son's Tourette syndrome and discovered music therapy as a magincal influence on him and their relationship.

Tourette Syndrome / Web Sites

David E Comings, MD, Presenter

6524 Ryan
Tourette Syndrome Association
42-40 Bell Boulevard
Bayside, NY 11361

718-224-2999
888-486-8738
Fax: 718-279-9596
ts@tsa-usa.org
tsa-usa.org

Ryan's family first thought his behavior was a deliberate way to get attention, lateer educate themselves and others about Ryan's Tourette's Syndrome.

11 minutes

6525 The Turners
Tourette Syndrome Association
42-40 Bell Boulevard
Bayside, NY 11361

718-224-2999
888-486-8738
Fax: 718-279-9596
ts@tsa-usa.org
tsa-usa.org

Three of the four Turner daughters have Tourette's Syndrome in varying degress.

12 minutes

Web Sites

6526 American Academy of Child and Adolescent Psychiatry
3615 Wisconsin Avenue NW
Washington, DC 20016

202-966-7300
Fax: 202-464-0131
www.aacap.org

The AACAP (American Academy of Child and Adolescent Psychiatry) is the leading national professional medical association dedicated to the promotion of healthy development for children, adolescents, and families.

Heidi B. Fordi, Executive Director

6527 American Academy of Neurology
201 Chicago Avenue
Minneapolis, MN 55415

612-928-6000
800-879-1960
Fax: 612-454-2746
memberservices@aan.com
www.aan.com

Medical society established to advance the art and science of neurology, and thereby promote the best possible care for patients with neurological disorders by: ensuring appropriate access to neurological care, supporting, and advocating for an environment which ensures ethical, high quality neurological care and supporting clinical and basic research in the neurosciences and related fields.

Mary E. Post, Chief Executive Officer
Kelly Ricker, Chief Learning Officer
Kevin C. Myren, Chief Financial Officer

6528 Children's Hospital Boston
300 Longwood Avenue
Boston, MA 02115

617-355-6000
www.childrenshospital.org

Mission is to provide the highest quality care; be the leading source of research and discovery; educate the next generation of leaders in child health and enhance the health and well-being of the children and families in our local community.

Kevin Churchwell, President & CEO
Jessica Farnham, Chief Operating Officer

6529 Health Answers Education Sudler-WPP Health Practice
700 Dresher Road
Horsham, PA 19044

215-442-9010
www.healthanswers.com

HealthAnswers offers a breadth of services in medical education, sales force training, patient support solutions, professional promotion and consumer solutions.

Mike Hudnall, CEO

6530 NIH/National Institute of Neurological Disorders and Stroke (NINDS)
PO Box 5801
Bethesda, MD 20824

301-496-5751
800-352-9424
www.ninds.nih.gov

The mission of NINDS is to reduce the burden of neurological disease - a burden borne by every age group, by every segment of society, by people all over the world.

Walter J. Koroshetz, MD, Director

6531 Online Mendelian Inheritance in Man
McKusick-Nathans Institue of Genetic Medicine-JHU
Baltimore, MD 21205

www.omim.org

This database is a catalog of human genes and genetic disorders.

Ada Hamosh, MD, Scientific Director

6532 Parents Helping Parents
1400 Parkmoor Avenue, Suite 100
San Jose, CA 95126

408-727-5775
855-727-5775
Fax: 408-286-1116
info@php.com
www.php.com

Parents Helping Parents supports, educates, and inspires families and the community to build bright futures for youth and adults with special needs.

Maria Daane, Executive Director
Janet Nunez, Director, Programs
Virginia Hildebrand, Director, Finance

6533 Tourette Syndrome Association
42-40 Bell Boulevard
Bayside, NY 11361

718-224-2999
Fax: 718-279-9596
www.tsa-usa.org

Is the only voluntary nonprofit membership organization in this field. Its mission is to identify the cause of, find the cure for and control the effects of this disorder.

6534 Tourettes Syndrome Online
www.tourettes-syndrome.com

www.tourettes-syndrome.com

Devoted to children and adults with Tourette Syndrome disorder and their families, friends, teachers and medical professionals.

Book Publishers

6535 Adam and the Magic Marble
Hope Press
PO Box 188
Duarte, CA 91009

800-321-4039
Fax: 626-358-3520
dcomings@earthlink.net
www.hopepress.com

Constantly taunted by bullies, the boys find a marble full of magic powers that are nearly impossible to control. Humorous and delightful, this fantasy will take you from laughter to tears and happily back to laughter again every time you read it.

Adam Buehrens, Author
Carol Buehrens, Author

6536 Children with Tourette Syndrome: A Parent's Guide-2nd Edition
ADD WareHouse
300 NW 70th Avenue, Suite 102
Plantation, FL 33317

954-792-8100
800-233-9273
Fax: 954-792-8545
www.addwarehouse.com

The first guide written specifically for parents and other family members is a collaboration by a team of medical specialists, therapists, people with TS, and parents. It provides a complete introduction to TS and how it's diagnosed and treated. Also, chapters on family life, emotions, education and legal rights

2007 361 pages

6537 Don't Think About Monkeys: Extraordinary Stories Written by People with Tourette
Hope Press
PO Box 188
Duarte, CA 91009

800-321-4039
Fax: 626-358-3520
dcomings@earthlink.net
www.hopepress.com

A collection of stories written by fourteen people who live with Tourette syndrome. Ranging from three teenagers learning to come to grips with treatment to adults encountering discrimination, the collection represents the incredible diversity of a disorder as diverse as life itself.

200 pages
ISBN: 1-878267-33-7

Adam Seligman, Author
John Hilkevich, Author

6538 Hi! I'm Adam!
Hope Press
PO Box 188
Duarte, CA 91009

800-321-4039
Fax: 626-358-3520
www.hopepress.com

Adam Buehrens is ten years old and has Tourette syndrome. Adam wrote and illustrated this book because he wants everyone to know he and other children with Tourette syndrome are not crazy. They just have a common neurological disorder. If you know a child that has tics, temper tantrums, unresonable fears, or problems dealing with school, you will find this a reassuring story.

Adam Buehrens, Author

6539 Matthew and the Tics
Tourette Syndrome Association
42-40 Bell Boulevard, Suite 205
Bayside, NY 11361

718-224-2999
Fax: 718-279-9596
ts@tsa-usa.org
www.tsa-usa.org

A story for young children with TS and their peers.

2 pages

6540 RYAN: A Mother's Story of Her Hyperactive/ Tourette Syndrome Child
Hope Press
PO Box 188
Duarte, CA 91009

800-321-4039
Fax: 626-358-3520
dcomings@earthlink.net
www.hopepress.com

Tells of the struggles with understanding Ryan's unusual behaviors, of getting a diagnosis, and of struggling with her own feelings of guilt. The message is written in the ultimately understandable language of parent to parent. It is written so others need not feel alone or struggle through so many years of uncertainty.

Susan Hughes, Author

6541 Raising Joshua
Hope Press
PO Box 188
Duarte, CA 91009

800-321-4039
Fax: 626-358-3520
dcomings@earthlink.net
www.hopepress.com

The harrowing and heartwarming story of Josh, a boy caught in Tourette Syndrome, and Attention Deficit Hyperactivity Disorder, as told by his mother. The true story of two souls caught in a modern jungle of medical ignorance, powerful drugs, and the ravaging behavior of a mysterious condition.

Sheryl Johnson Hamer RN, Author

6542 Teaching the Tiger
Hope Press
PO Box 188
Duarte, CA 91009

800-321-4039
Fax: 626-358-3520
dcomings@earthlink.net
www.hopepress.com

A handbook for individuals involved in the education of students with Attention Deficit Disorder, Tourette Syndrome, or Obsessive Compulsive Disorder.

ISBN: 1-878267-34-5

David E Comings MD, Presenter

6543 Tourette Syndrome and Human Behavior
Hope Press
PO Box 188
Duarte, CA 91009

800-321-4039
Fax: 626-358-3520
dcomings@earthlink.net
www.hopepress.com

Packed with information on all aspects of Tourette syndrome, the diagnosis; chapters on ADHD, obsessive-compulsive behaviors, conduct disorder, learning disorders and dyslexia, sexual problems, phobias, anxiety attacks, depression, mood swings, addictive behaviors, sleep and other problems; genetics; structure and chemistry of the brain, role of dopamine and serotonin in behvior; detailed chapters on all the medications used and their side effects; psychological treatment and school problems.

828 pages

David E Comings MD, Author

6544 Tourette Syndrome: The Facts
Oxford University Press
2001 Evans Road
Cary, NC 27513

212-726-6000
800-445-9714
Fax: 919-677-1303
custserv.us@oup.com
www.oup-usa.org

A guide for clinicians, general practitioners, school teachers, and anyone seeking an accsible introduction the disorder.

1998 122 pages
ISBN: 0-198523-98-X

6545 Tourette's Syndrome
ADD WareHouse
300 NW 70th Avenue, Suite 102
Plantation, FL 33317

954-792-8100
800-233-9273
Fax: 954-792-8545
www.addwarehouse.com

Provides any information needed on Torette's Syndrome.

2001 400 pages
ISBN: 0-596500-07-6

6546 What Makes Ryan Tic?
Hope Press
PO Box 188
Duarte, CA 91009

800-321-4039
Fax: 626-358-3520
dcomings@earthlink.net
www.hopepress.com

Covers Ryan's very difficult adolescent years-a period when his symptoms were so severe he had to be placed in a residential treatment facility-and the subsequent period of returning home and pursuing a virtually normal life following his excellent response to the right combination of medication, family and school support

Susan Hughes, Author

Tourette Syndrome / Pamphlets

Pamphlets

6547 Coping with Tourette Syndrome, A Parent's Viewpoint
Tourette Syndrome Association
42-40 Bell Boulevard, Suite 205
Bayside, NY 11361
718-224-2999
Fax: 718-279-9596

An acclaimed medical writer and mother of three children with TS, the author sensitively addresses common concerns and feelings of parents.

6548 Development of Behavioral and Emotional Problems in Tourette Syndrome
Tourette Syndrome Association
National Library of Medicine, Building 38A
Bethesda, MD 20894
718-224-2999
888-346-3656
Fax: 718-279-9596
info@ncbi.nlm.nih.gov
www.ncbi.nlm.nih.gov/pubmed/

Using the Child Behavior Checklist, 78 male children were assessed for a variety of behavioral problems. Relation to tic severity covered.
Christine E. Seidman, M.D., Chair
David J. Lipman, M.D., Executive Secretary

6549 Discipline and the Child with Tourette Syndrome
Tourette Syndrome Association
42-40 Bell Boulevard, Suite 205
Bayside, NY 11361
718-224-2999
Fax: 718-279-9596

Helps children redirect impulses and compulsions through teaching cause and effect relationships.

6550 Georges Gilles de la Tourette-The Man and His Times
Tourette Syndrome Association
National Library of Medicine, Building 38A
Bethesda, MD 20894
718-224-2999
888-346-3656
Fax: 718-279-9596
info@ncbi.nlm.nih.gov
www.ncbi.nlm.nih.gov/pubmed/

Rare historical biography of the famous French neurologist G. Gilles De La Tourette.
Christine E. Seidman, M.D., Chair
David J. Lipman, M.D., Executive Secretary

6551 Getting Into College: Strategies for the Student with Tourette Syndrome
Tourette Syndrome Association
42-40 Bell Boulevard, Suite 205
Bayside, NY 11361
718-224-2999
Fax: 718-279-9596

6552 Guide to Diagnosis & Treatment
Tourette Syndrome Association
42-40 Bell Boulevard, Suite 205
Bayside, NY 11361
718-224-2999
Fax: 718-279-9596

Covers symptoms, pharmacology and clinical assessments.

6553 Health Insurance Issues and Solutions for People with Torette Syndrome
Tourette Syndrome Association
42-40 Bell Boulevard, Suite 205
Bayside, NY 11361
718-224-2999
Fax: 718-279-9596

Detailed, up-to-date packet of medical information for obtaining health insurance as well as information for submission to insurance carriers.

6554 Learning Problems & the Student with Tourette Syndrome
Tourette Syndrome Association
42-40 Bell Boulevard, Suite 205
Bayside, NY 11361
718-224-2999
Fax: 718-279-9596

Report on learning problems identified through a study of 200 children with TS.

6555 NINDS Seeks Patients with Tourette Syndrome
National Inst. of Neurological Disorders/Stroke
PO Box 5801
Bethesda, MD 20824
301-496-5751
800-352-9424
www.ninds.nih.gov

New program announcements and requests for applications.
Walter J. Koroshetz, M.D., Acting Director
Alan L. Willard, Ph.D., Acting Deputy Director
Caroline Lewis, Executive Officer

6556 Need to Know
Tourette Syndrome Association
42-40 Bell Boulevard, Suite 205
Bayside, NY 11361
718-224-2999
Fax: 718-279-9596

Recollections of a young woman who was diagnosed with TS in her 20s.

6557 Peer Problems in Tourette's Disorder
Tourette Syndrome Association
National Library of Medicine, Building 38A
Bethesda, MD 20894
718-224-2999
888-346-3656
Fax: 718-279-9596
info@ncbi.nlm.nih.gov
www.ncbi.nlm.nih.gov/pubmed/

Detailed research findings of peer problems in children with TS. Includes statistical results obtained from these studies.
Christine E. Seidman, M.D., Chair
David J. Lipman, M.D., Executive Secretary

6558 Problem Behaviors & Tourette Syndrome
Tourette Syndrome Association
42-40 Bell Boulevard, Suite 205
Bayside, NY 11361
718-224-2999
Fax: 718-279-9596

Describes recent research and what is now known about the relationship of a variety of behaviors and TS.

6559 Specific Classroom Strategies and Techniqu es for Students with TS-2nd Edition
Tourette Syndrome Association
42-40 Bell Boulevard, Suite 205
Bayside, NY 11361
718-224-2999
Fax: 718-279-9596

An educator with TS spells out concrete methods for managing students with TS. She outlines many valuable classroom interventions to help youngsters deal with tic symptons, ADHD, visual motor and fine motor integration, and behavioral difficulties.

6560 TS: A Look at the Interface Between Tourette Syndrome and the Law
Tourette Syndrome Association
42-40 Bell Boulevard, Suite 205
Bayside, NY 11361
718-224-2999
Fax: 718-279-9596

Summarizes important legislation protecting the rights of students with TS. Also covers resources and hints about how to prepare for dealing successfully with educators and school systems.

6561 Teens and Tourette Syndrome
Tourette Syndrome Association
42-40 Bell Boulevard, Suite 205
Bayside, NY 11361
718-224-2999
Fax: 718-279-9596
ts@tsa-usa.org
tsa-usa.org

Covers self esteem, friends, dating, drugs and alcohol, stress, depression, academic and vocational planning, sibling relationships and medication.

6562 Tourette Syndrome and the School Psychologist
Tourette Syndrome Association
42-40 Bell Boulevard, Suite 205
Bayside, NY 11361
718-224-2999
Fax: 718-279-9596

The role of the school psychologist is covered including testing procedures, counseling strategies and social implications.

6563 Tourette Syndrome and the School Nurse
Tourette Syndrome Association
42-40 Bell Boulevard, Suite 205
Bayside, NY 11361
718-224-2999
Fax: 718-279-9596

Comprehensive professional guide to educational, social and medical implications.

6564 What School Bus Drivers Need to Know About Students with Tourette Syndrome
Tourette Syndrome Association
42-40 Bell Boulevard, Suite 205
Bayside, NY 11361
718-224-2999
Fax: 718-279-9596
ts@tsa-usa.org
tsa-usa.org

Includes a description of the disorder, as well as related disorders and suggestions as to what school bus drivers can do for students with TS.

Camps

6565 Tourette Syndrome Camp Organization
6933 N Kedzie, #816
Chicago, IL 60640
773-465-7536
info@tourettecamp.com
www.tourettecamp.com

Dedicated to promoting camping opportunities for children with Tourette Syndrome and its associated disorders, Obsessive Compulsive Disorder (OCD) and Attention Deficit/Hyperactivity Disorder (ADD/ADHD).

Scott Loeff, President
Monica Newman, Camp Director

Description

6566 TOXOPLASMOSIS
Covers these related disorders: Congenital toxoplasmosis
Involves the following Biologic System(s):
Infectious Disorders

Toxoplasmosis is a common infection caused by the single-celled parasite Toxoplasma gondii. This parasite multiplies in the intestines of cats, and its eggs (oocysts) are shed in cat feces. Humans may acquire toxoplasmosis due to contact with cat feces (e.g., in litter boxes), from exposure to contaminated soil, or by eating undercooked or raw meat (lamb, pork, and beef) that contains a form of the parasite (tissue cysts). In addition, if a woman acquires toxoplasmosis during pregnancy, the developing fetus may be affected (congenital toxoplasmosis) due to transmission via the placenta.

Most children who acquire toxoplasmosis after birth and have normally functioning immune systems do not have any apparent symptoms (asymptomatic). However, some children may experience enlargement of one or more lymph nodes (lymphadenopathy). More rarely, such patients may also have other, variable symptoms and findings, such as fever; joint or muscle pain; enlargement of the liver (hepatomegaly); or inflammation of the lungs (pneumonia), the liver (hepatitis), or the middle layer of and the nerve-rich membrane at the back of the eyes (chorioretinitis). Most children with normal immune systems who acquire toxoplasmosis after birth recover spontaneously. However, others may require treatment with certain medications.

Toxoplasmosis is typically more severe in children who acquire the disease during fetal development or who have compromised immune systems. When the infection is transmitted via the placenta during pregnancy (or, in some cases, during vaginal delivery), patients are said to have congenital toxoplasmosis. The disease is typically more severe if the infection is acquired during early pregnancy (first trimester), but the risk of disease transmission is greatest during later pregnancy (third trimester). Approximately 50 percent of women who acquire toxoplasmosis during pregnancy and do not receive treatment transmit the infection to the developing fetus. In the United States, congenital toxoplasmosis affects approximately one in 1,000 newborns.

Without treatment, almost all patients demonstrate certain findings associated with toxoplasmosis by adolescence, particularly chorioretinitis. Chorioretinitis may cause blurred vision, abnormal sensitivity to light (photophobia), and possible visual impairment. In some affected infants, findings may include short height and low weight at birth (intrauterine stunted growth); persistent yellowish discoloration of the skin, whites of the eyes, and mucous membranes (jaundice); retinal scarring; skin rash; lymphadenopathy; decreased levels of circulating blood platelets (thrombocytopenia); hepatitis; hearing loss; or other findings. Severely affected infants may have an abnormally small head (microcephaly), an abnormal accumulation of cerebrospinal fluid around the brain (hydrocephalus), chorioretinitis, episodes of abnormally increased electrical activity in the brain (seizures), delays in the acquisition of skills requiring the coordination of physical and mental activities, and calcium deposits in the brain. Life-threatening complications may occur shortly after birth.

In children who have compromised immune systems, such as those with acquired immunodeficiency syndrome (AIDS), toxoplasmosis often occurs suddenly and is extremely severe (fulminant). In such patients, infection may rapidly affect the lungs, heart, and brain. In fulminant toxoplasmosis, the most common symptoms are often neurological and may include headache, impaired cognition (thinking), seizures, and impaired control of voluntary movement (ataxia). Without treatment, life-threatening complications result.

The treatment of newborns with congenital toxoplasmosis, affected children with compromised immune systems, and other patients with acquired toxoplasmosis may include the use of combination drug therapies with such medications as pyrimethamine, folinic acid, sulfadiazine or triple sulfonamides, leukovorin, or spiramycin. Additional treatment is symptomatic and supportive. It is important to note that all newborns with congenital toxoplasmosis should receive appropriate drug therapy, regardless of whether they have severe, mild, or no associated symptoms. Appropriate drug therapy for women who contract toxoplasmosis any time during pregnancy may reduce the risk of congenital toxoplasmosis by approximately 60 percent. Such therapy may includeclindamycin and pyrimethamine combined trimethoprim-sulfamethoxasole or sulfadiazine. Pyrimethamine is not given during early pregnancy since it may increase the risk of birth defects during early fetal development. Treatment in AIDS patients is continued as long as the immune system is weak, to prevent reactivation of the disease.In addition, certain measures may be helpful in preventing toxoplasmosis, such as thoroughly cooking all meat, washing hands after handling raw meat, and avoiding direct contact with cat feces.

Government Agencies

6567 Centers for Disease Control and Prevention
1600 Clifton Road
Atlanta, GA 30329
800-232-4636
TTY: 888-232-6348
www.cdc.gov

Federal agency that promotes America's health and safety, providing information to guide health decisions, and building strong partnerships to promote health and prevent disease.
Rochelle P. Walensky, MD, Director
Anne Schuchat, MD, Principal Deputy Director
Abbigail Tumpey, MPH, Associate Director, Communication

6568 NIH/National Institute of Allergy and Infectious Diseases
5601 Fishers Lane, MSC 9806
Bethesda, MD 20892
301-496-5717
866-284-4107
Fax: 301-402-3573
TDD: 800-877-8339
ocpostoffice@niaid.nih.gov
www.niaid.nih.gov

The principal advisory board of the NIAID. The council is composed of physicians, scientists and representatives of the public and advises on the conduct and support or research, training and dissemination of health information regarding allergies and infectious diseases.
Anthony S. Fauci, MD, Director

National Associations & Support Groups

6569 American Academy of Pediatrics
345 Park Blvd
Itasca, IL 60143
847-434-4000
800-433-9016
Fax: 847-434-8000
csc@aap.org
www.aap.org

The American Academy of Pediatrics and its member pediatricians are committed to the attainment of optimal physical, mental and social health and well-being for all infants, children, adolescents, and young adults.

Kyle E. Yasuda, MD, FAAP, President
Mark Del Monte, JD, CEO/Executive VP
Vera Tait, MD, FAAP, Chief Medical Officer

6570 Arc of the United States
1825 K Street NW, Ste 1200
Washington, DC 20006

202-534-3700
800-433-5255
Fax: 202-534-3731
info@thearc.org
www.thearc.org

The Arc of the United States advocates for the rights and full participation of all children and adults with intellectual and developmental disabilities. Together with a network of members and affiliated chapters, they improve systems of support and services; connect families; inspire communities and influence public policy.

Peter V. Berns, CEO

6571 Children's Hospital Boston
300 Longwood Avenue
Boston, MA 02115

617-355-6000
www.childrenshospital.org

Mission is to provide the highest quality care; be the leading source of research and discovery; educate the next generation of leaders in child health and enhance the health and well-being of the children and families in our local community.

Kevin Churchwell, President & CEO
Jessica Farnham, Chief Operating Officer

6572 World Health Organization
Avenue Appia 20
1202 Geneva,
Switzerland

www.who.int

WHO is the directing and coordinating authority for health within the United Nations system. WHO operates in more than 150 countries around the world.

Dr. Tedros Adhanom Ghebreyesus, Director General
Dr. Zsuzsanna Jakab, Deputy Director General
Stewart Simonson, Asst Director General, UN NYC

Web Sites

6573 Children's Hospital Boston
300 Longwood Avenue
Boston, MA 02115

617-355-6000
www.childrenshospital.org

Mission is to provide the highest quality care; be the leading source of research and discovery; educate the next generation of leaders in child health and enhance the health and well-being of the children and families in our local community.

Kevin Churchwell, President & CEO
Jessica Farnham, Chief Operating Officer

6574 Toxoplasmosis Fact Sheet
750 3rd Avenue, 6th Floor
New York, NY 10017

212-541-8500
www.thebody.com/treat/toxo.html

Offers information about what the disease is, how to treat it, what treatments to use, and if it can be prevented.

Myles Helfand, Editorial Director
Julie Davids, Managing Editor
Mathew Rodriguez, Community Editor

Pamphlets

6575 Toxoplasmosis Fact Sheet
Division of Parasitic Diseases
1600 Clifton Road
Atlanta, GA 30329

404-639-3534
800-232-4636
TTY: 888-232-6348
www.cdc.gov

Dr. Tom Frieden, Director
Ileana Arias, PhD, Principal Deputy Director
John M. Auerbach, MBA, Associate Director of Policy

Transposition of the Great Arteries / Description

Description

6576 TRANSPOSITION OF THE GREAT ARTERIES
Synonym: Transposition of the great vessels
Involves the following Biologic System(s):
Cardiovascular Disorders

Transposition of the great arteries is a heart defect that is present at birth (congenital) in which the major blood vessels that transport blood away from the heart (aorta and pulmonary artery) are switched (transposed) from their normal position. The pulmonary artery normally arises from the base of the lower right-sided pumping chamber (right ventricle) of the heart and carries oxygen-poor blood to the lungs, where the exchange of oxygen and carbon dioxide occurs. The aorta, the main artery of the body, normally arises from the base of the left ventricle and carries oxygen-rich (oxygenated) blood to the body's tissues. However, in infants with transposition of the great arteries, the aorta arises from the right ventricle and the pulmonary artery arises from the left ventricle. As a result, oxygenated blood recirculates to the lungs, while the oxygen-poor blood recirculates throughout the body, and bodily tissues receive insufficient levels of oxygenated blood (hypoxia).

Transpositon of the great arteries is not compatible with life unless there is some communication between the pulmonary and systemic circulation, thus allowing for some mixing of deoxygenated and oxygenated blood. Certain fetal shunts may provide such mixing. These include persistence of the fetal channel that joins the pulmonary artery and the aorta (ductus arteriosus), an opening in the fibrous partition (septum) between the upper chambers (atria) of the heart (patent foramen ovale). Some patients with transposition have mixing of blood through openings in the septum between the ventricles (ventricular septal defect, VSD) or atria (atrial septal defects, ASD)

In newborns with transposition of the great arteries, symptoms are primarily cyanosis (bluish discoloration of fingers and toes and mucous membranes). Shortly after birth, affected infants may experience abnormally rapid and deep breathing (tachypnea, hyperpnea) and cyanosis. Without treatment, life-threatening complications will result. Medical treatment includes a medication called prostaglandin E to open the ductus arteriosus and allow mixing. A cardiac catheterization to place a balloon catheter across the atrial septum (balloon septostomy) may be necessary to allow for mixing of blood. Permanent treatment of infants with transposition of the great arteries includes surgery to switch the aorta and coronary arteries and pulmonary artery back to their normal positions (arterial switch operation). This operation is done in the first weeks of life.

Transposition of the great arteries is more common in males than females and affects approximately one in 2,000 newborns. Infants are most often normal sized, full term, and otherwise healthy. The condition is thought to result from the interactions of several different genes, possibly in association with the involvement of environmental factors (multifactorial inheritance). Although the exact underlying cause of this heart defect is unknown, rese archers suggest that it may result from an error during the development of an embryonic structure that later divides the aorta and pulmonary artery.

Government Agencies

6577 NIH/ Eunice Kennedy Shriver National Insti tute of Child Health & Human Development
P.O. Box 3006
Rockville, MD 20847
800-370-2943
Fax: 866-760-5947
www.nichd.nih.gov

Conducts and supports research on topics related to the health of children, adults, families and populations. Some of these topics include: developmental disabilities, growth and development, infant death, reproductive health and birth defects.

Diana W. Bianchi, Director
Alison Cernich, PhD, Deputy Director

6578 NIH/National Heart, Lung and Blood Institute
31 Center Drive, Bldg 31
Bethesda, MD 20892
877-645-2448
www.nhlbi.nih.gov

Primary responsibility of this organization is the scientific investigation of heart, blood vessel, lung and blood disorders. Oversees research, demonstration, prevention, education, control and training activities in these fields and emphasizes the prevention and control of heart diseases.

Gary H. Gibbons, MD, Director
Kate O'Sullivan, Executive Officer

National Associations & Support Groups

6579 American Academy of Pediatrics
345 Park Blvd
Itasca, IL 60143
847-434-4000
800-433-9016
Fax: 847-434-8000
csc@aap.org
www.aap.org

The American Academy of Pediatrics and its member pediatricians dedicate their efforts and resources to the health, safety and well-being of infants, children, adolescents and young adults.

Kyle E. Yasuda, MD, FAAP, President
Mark Del Monte, JD, CEO/Executive VP
Vera Tait, MD, FAAP, Chief Medical Officer

6580 American Heart Association
7272 Greenville Avenue
Dallas, TX 75231
214-570-5978
800-242-8721
www.heart.org

The mission of the American Heart Associate is to build healthier lives, free of cardiovascular diseases and stroke.

Nancy Brown, CEO
Mitchell S.V. Elkind, President
Suzie Upton, Chief Operating Officer

6581 Genetic Alliance
426400 Woodfield Road, Ste 189
Damascus, MD 20872
202-966-5557
Fax: 202-966-8553
info@geneticalliance.org
www.geneticalliance.org

World's leading nonprofit health advocacy organization committed to transforming health through genetics and promoting an environment of openness centered on the health of individuals, families, and communities.

Sharon Terry, CEO
Ruth Child, CFO
Natasha Bonhomme, Chief Strategy Officer

6582 United Network for Organ Sharing
700 N 4th Street
Richmond, VA 23219
804-782-4800
800-292-9548
www.unos.org

Our mission is to advance organ availability and transplantation by uniting and supporting our communities for the benefit of patients through education, technology and policy development.

Maureen McBride, Interim CEO
David Klassen, Chief Medical Officer
Dale E. Smith, Chief Financial Officer

Web Sites

6583 **American Academy of Pediatrics**
345 Park Blvd
Itasca, IL 60143
847-434-4000
800-433-9016
Fax: 847-434-8000
csc@aap.org
www.aap.org

The American Academy of Pediatrics and its member pediatricians are committed to the attainment of optimal physical, mental and social health and well-being for all infants, children, adolescents, and young adults.

Kyle E. Yasuda, MD, FAAP, President
Mark Del Monte, JD, CEO/Executive VP
Vera Tait, MD, FAAP, Chief Medical Officer

6584 **American Heart Association**
7272 Greenville Avenue
Dallas, TX 75231
800-242-8721
www.heart.org

The mission of the American Heart Associate is to build healthier lives, free of cardiovascular diseases and stroke.

Nancy Brown, CEO
Mitchell S.V. Elkind, President
Suzie Upton, Chief Operating Officer

6585 **NIH/National Heart, Lung and Blood Institute**
31 Center Drive, Bldg 31
Bethesda, MD 20892
301-592-8573
NHLBIinfo@nhlbi.nih.gov
www.nhlbi.nih.gov

Provides leadership for a national program in diseases of the heart, blood vessels, lungs, and blood; blood resources; and sleep disorders.

Gary H. Gibbons, MD, Director
Kate O'Sullivan, Executive Officer

6586 **Southern Illinois University School of Medicine**
PO Box 19639
Springfield, IL 62794
217-545-8000
800-342-5748
admin@siuhealthcare.org
www.siumed.edu/peds/index.htm

The mission of SUI School of Medicine is to assist the people if Central and Southern Illinois in meeting thier present and future health care needs through education, clinical service and research.

6587 **United Network for Organ Sharing**
700 North 4th Street
Richmond, VA 23219
804-782-4800
800-292-9548
www.unos.org

Our mission is to advance organ availability and transplantation by uniting and supporting our communities for the benefit of patients through education, technology and policy development.

6588 **Yale University School of Medicine**
333 Cedar Street
New Haven, CT 6510
203-432-4771
www.info.med.yale.edu/intmed/cardio/chd

A site that offers information on Transposition of the Great Arteries and other congenital heart conditions.

Peter Salovey, President of the University
Richard Belitsky M.D., Deputy Dean for Education
Benjamin Polak, B.A., M.A., Ph.D., Provost of the University

Trisomy 18 Syndrome / Description

Description

6589 TRISOMY 18 SYNDROME

Synonyms: Chromosome 18, trisomy 18, Edwards syndrome

Covers these related disorders: Trisomy 18 mosaicism

Involves the following Biologic System(s):

Genetic/Chromosomal/Syndrome/Metabolic Disorders

Trisomy 18 syndrome is a chromosomal disorder that affects about one in 300 newborns. With the exception of reproductive cells, cells of the body normally have 23 pairs of chromosomes that are numbered from 1 to 22 (with a 23rd pair consisting of one X chromosome from the mother and an X or a Y chromosome from the father). However, in infants with trisomy 18 syndrome, all or a portion of chromosome 18 is present three times (trisomy) rather than twice in cells of the body. In some affected infants, only a percentage of cells may contain the trisomy 18 chromosomal abnormality (mosaicism).

The symptoms and physical findings associated with trisomy 18 syndrome are variable and depend upon the exact location, and percentage, of body cells containing the additional chromosomal material from chromosome 18. However, infants with trisomy 18 syndrome experience development delays, usually severe intellectual disabilities, low birth weight, difficulties feeding and breathing, and a failure to gain weight and grow at the expected rate (failure to thrive). In addition, almost all infants with trisomy 18 have complex structural heart defects, failure of one or both testes to descend into the scrotum (cryptorchidism) in affected males, malformations of the hands and feet, additional skeletal abnormalities, and characteristic malformations of the head and facial (craniofacial) area.

In infants with trisomy 18 syndrome, defects of the hands and feet often include closed fists with overlapping, abnormally bent fingers; underdeveloped or absent thumbs; and webbing between certain fingers or toes (syndactyly). Affected infants also often have additional skeletal abnormalities, such as a small pelvis, narrow hips with limited movements, fusion of certain bones of the spinal column (vertebrae), or sideways curvature of the spine (scoliosis). Characteristic craniofacial abnormalities associated with trisomy 18 syndrome typically include an abnormally small head (microcephaly); a prominent back portion of the head (occiput); a small mouth (microstomia) and a small jaw (micrognathia); malformed, low-set ears; and short, narrow eyelid folds (palpebral fissures). Additional craniofacial malformations may be present, such as incomplete closure of the roof of the mouth (cleft palate), an abnormal groove in the upper lip (cleft lip), and drooping of the upper eyelids (ptosis). Some infants may have kidney defects. The abnormalities of trisomy 18 are generally not compatible with more than a few months of life. Fifty percent of the affected infants do not survive beyond the first week of life. Although the exact cause of trisomy 18 syndrome is unknown, it is thought to result from errors during division of a parent's reproductive cells (meiosis) and, in some cases of mosaicism, errors during cellular division after fertilization (e.g., postzygotic nondisjunction). Parents who have a child with translocational trisomy 18 and want additional children should have chromosome studies, because they are at increased risk to have another child with trisomy 18.

Government Agencies

6590 NIH/ Eunice Kennedy Shriver National Institute of Child Health & Human Development
P.O. Box 3006
Rockville, MD 20847

800-370-2943
Fax: 866-760-5947
www.nichd.nih.gov

Conducts and supports research on topics related to the health of children, adults, families and populations. Some of these topics include: developmental disabilities, growth and development, infant death, reproductive health and birth defects.

Diana W. Bianchi, Director
Alison Cernich, PhD, Deputy Director

National Associations & Support Groups

6591 American Academy of Pediatrics
345 Park Blvd
Itasca, IL 60143

847-434-4000
800-433-9016
Fax: 847-434-8000
csc@aap.org
www.aap.org

The American Academy of Pediatrics and its member pediatricians are committed to the attainment of optimal physical, mental and social health and well-being for all infants, children, adolescents, and young adults.

Kyle E. Yasuda, MD, FAAP, President
Mark Del Monte, JD, CEO/Executive VP
Vera Tait, MD, FAAP, Chief Medical Officer

6592 Chromosome 18 Registry & Research Society
7155 Oakridge Drive
San Antonio, TX 78229

210-657-4968
office@chromosome18.org
www.chromosome18.org

The purpose of the Chromosome 18 Registry & Research Society is to offer support to patients and families, to educate the public about different available treatments and to connect families and doctors to the research community.

Neale Parker, Chief Executive Officer
Amelie Simons, Director of Operations
Jessica Sanders, Programs & Events Coordinator

6593 Genetic Alliance
426400 Woodfield Road, Ste 189
Damascus, MD 20872

202-966-5557
Fax: 202-966-8553
info@geneticalliance.org
www.geneticalliance.org

World's leading nonprofit health advocacy organization committed to transforming health through genetics and promoting an environment of openness centered on the health of individuals, families, and communities.

Sharon Terry, CEO
Ruth Child, CFO
Natasha Bonhomme, Chief Strategy Officer

6594 Parent to Parent USA
PO Box 472
State College, PA 16804

484-272-7368
www.p2pusa.org

Parent to Parent USA supports a network of viable, sustainable, fully-functioning, and effective Parent to Parent programs in all 50 states through hands-on support, training and technical assistance, and high-quality tools and resources.

Aurelie "Lily" Brown, Co-Director
Marsha Quinn, Co-Director

6595 Support Organization for Trisomy 18, 13, and Related Disorders (SOFT)
2982 S Union Street
Rochester, NY 14624

www.trisomy.org

SOFT is a network of families and professional dedication to provide support and understanding to families involved in the issue and decision surrounding the diagnosis and care related to chromosome disorders. Support is provided throughout prenatal diagnosis, the child's life and after their passing. It is committed to the support of families and personal decisions in alliance with a parent-professional partnership.

6596 Trisomy 18 Foundation
4491 Cheshire Station Plaza, Suite 157
Dale City, VA 22193

810-867-4211
t18info@trisomy18.org
www.trisomy18.org

The foundation's mission is to search for a cure and treatments; to educate and support medical professionals; and to create a worldwide caring community for those affected.

Victoria J. Miller, M.A., Executive Director/ President
Kris Shaughnessy, M.A., Community Affairs Program Office
Cathy Howard, Administration and Finance Office

Research Centers

6597 Trisomy 18 Foundation
4491 Cheshire Station Plaza, Suite 157
Dale City, VA 22193

t18info@trisomy18.org
www.trisomy18.org

The foundation's mission is to search for a cure and treatments; to educate and support medical professionals; and to create a worldwide caring community for those affected.

Victoria J. Miller, M.A., Executive Director/ President
Kris Shaughnessy, M.A., Community Affairs Program Office
Cathy Howard, Administration and Finance Office

Trisomy 13 Syndrome / Description

Description

6598 TRISOMY 13 SYNDROME

Synonyms: Chromosome 13, trisomy 13, D1 trisomy syndrome, Patau syndrome

Covers these related disorders: Trisomy 13 mosaicism

Involves the following Biologic System(s):

Genetic/Chromosomal/Syndrome/Metabolic Disorders

Trisomy 13 syndrome is a chromosomal disorder that is thought to affect approximately one in 5,000 newborns. With the exception of reproductive cells, cells of the body normally have 23 pairs of chromosomes that are numbered from 1 to 22. The 23rd pair includes one X chromosome from the mother and an X or a Y chromosome from the father. In infants with trisomy 13 syndrome, all or a portion of chromosome 13 is present three times (trisomy) rather than twice. In some affected infants, a certain percentage of cells contain the extra chromosome 13, whereas other cells have the normal two. This finding is known as chromosomal mosaicism.

In infants with trisomy 13 syndrome, associated symptoms and physical findings are pronounced and depend upon the specific length and location of the duplicated portion of chromosome 13 as well as the percentage of the body cells containing the defect.

Abnormalities associated with trisomy 13 syndrome include severe developmental delays, profound intellectual disabilities, incomplete closure of the roof of the mouth (cleft palate), an abnormal groove in the upper lip (cleft lip), and unusually small eyes (microphthalmia). Additional characteristic symptoms and findings include abnormal bending of the fingers, the presence of extra fingers and toes (polydactyly), failure of the testes to descend into the scrotum (cryptorchidis in affected males, and malformation of the uterus in affected females, i.e., bicornuate uterus). Many infants have severe feeding difficulties, abnormally diminished muscle tone (hypotonia), and episodes of temporary cessation of breathing (apnea).

Defects in the brain can result in seizure activity and deafness. Most infants with trisomy 13 syndrome also have additional physical malformations, including an abnormally small head (microcephaly) with a sloping forehead; widely set eyes (ocular hypertelorism); a broad, flat nose; low-set, malformed ears; and a small jaw (micrognthia). Reddish, purplish benign growths (hemangiomas) may be present on the forehead or other areas due to an abnormal distribution of minute blood vessels (capillaries). Many affected infants may also have additional skeletal abnormalities, heart defects, and brain malformations. More than 80% of children with trisomy 13 die in the first month.. Because of the severity of congenital defects, life-sustaining procedures are generally not attempted. Parents of infants with trisomy 13 caused by a translocation should have genetic testing and counseling, which may help them prevent recurrence. The exact cause of trisomy 13 syndrome is unknown.

Government Agencies

6599 NIH/ Eunice Kennedy Shriver National Institute of Child Health & Human Development
P.O. Box 3006
Rockville, MD 20847

800-370-2943
Fax: 866-760-5947
www.nichd.nih.gov

Conducts and supports research on topics related to the health of children, adults, families and populations. Some of these topics include: developmental disabilities, growth and development, infant death, reproductive health and birth defects.

Diana W. Bianchi, Director
Alison Cernich, PhD, Deputy Director

National Associations & Support Groups

6600 American Academy of Pediatrics
345 Park Blvd
Itasca, IL 60143

847-434-4000
800-433-9016
Fax: 847-434-8000
csc@aap.org
www.aap.org

The American Academy of Pediatrics and its member pediatricians are committed to the attainment of optimal physical, mental and social health and well-being for all infants, children, adolescents, and young adults.

Kyle E. Yasuda, MD, FAAP, President
Mark Del Monte, JD, CEO/Executive VP
Vera Tait, MD, FAAP, Chief Medical Officer

6601 Center for Parent Information and Resources (CPIR)
c/o SPAN, 35 Halsey Street, 4th Floor
Newark, NJ 07102

973-642-8100
malizo@spanadvocacy.org
www.parentcenterhub.org

Family-friendly information and research-based materials on key topics for Parent Centers. Private workspaces for Parent Centers to exchange resources, discuss high-priority topics, and solve mutual challenges. Coordination of parent training efforts throughout the network.

Myriam Alizo, Project Assistant

6602 Genetic Alliance
426400 Woodfield Road, Ste 189
Damascus, MD 20872

202-966-5557
Fax: 202-966-8553
info@geneticalliance.org
www.geneticalliance.org

World's leading nonprofit health advocacy organization committed to transforming health through genetics and promoting an environment of openness centered on the health of individuals, families, and communities.

Sharon Terry, CEO
Ruth Child, CFO
Natasha Bonhomme, Chief Strategy Officer

6603 Support Organization for Trisomy 18, 13, and Related Disorders (SOFT)
2982 S Union Street
Rochester, NY 14624

www.trisomy.org

SOFT is a network of families and professional dedication to providing support and understanding to families involved in the issue and decision surrounding the diagnosis and care in related chromosome disorders. Support is provided throughout pre-natal diagnosis, the child's life and after their passing. It is committed to the support of families personal decision in alliance with a parent-professional partnership.

Description

6604 TUBERCULOSIS
Synonym: TB
Involves the following Biologic System(s):
Infectious Disorders, Respiratory Disorders

Tuberculosis (TB) is an infectious disease that is most often caused by the bacterium Mycobacterium tuberculosis, but may sometimes result from infection with Mycobacterium bovis or Mycobacterium africanum. As a result of improvements in living conditions, the number of people in the United States infected with this disease declined dramatically throughout most of the twentieth century. However, tuberculosis rates once again began to rise in the mid-1980s in association with such factors as immigration of individuals from countries that had high incidence rates of TB, poverty, poor access to health care among groups at high risk, the increase in AIDS infections, overcrowded and sometimes unsanitary conditions in certain institutional settings, and the development of antibiotic-resistant strains of tuberculosis bacteria. The neglect of TB control programs has also contributed to the resurgence of TB. This disease is most prevalent among the elderly, people with compromised immune systems, and those of low socioeconomic status.

Tuberculosis is usually transmitted through airborne droplets coughed or sneezed into the air by an infected person. The droplets are inhaled into the lungs where the bacteria multiply and travel to the lymph nodes that are responsible for draining the lungs; however, in the vast majority of cases, the immune system either destroys or seals off the bacteria. If this primary pulmonary tuberculosis infection is not completely resolved, the bacteria may become dormant within certain white blood cells called macrophages and be later reactivated. This reemergence of symptoms at a later date may be due to influences such as an impaired immune system, corticosteroid drug usage, or advancing age. In addition to the lungs, the tuberculosis bacteria may sometimes spread throughout the body via the bloodstream and affect other parts of the body (extrapulmonary tuberculosis). This type of disseminated disease may infect the lymph nodes, upper respiratory tract, skin, liver, spleen, kidneys, gastrointestinal tract, bones, joints, brain, spine, the sac surrounding the heart (pericardium), and other organs.

Symptoms and physical findings associated with primary pulmonary tuberculosis in children may include enlargement of the lymph nodes and the subsequent compression and obstruction of the large air passages of the lungs (bronchial tubes). This obstruction may result in lung collapse, cough, and less commonly wheezing, rapid breathing (tachypnea), and respiratory distress. Other symptoms may be absent or mild, but more pronounced in infants, and may include moderate difficulty in breathing (dyspnea), a nonproductive cough, and occasionally fever, loss of appetite (anorexia), and night sweats. In addition, some infants may have failure to thrive, a condition in which the current weight or rate of weight gain is significantly below that of other children of similar age and sex. Pneumonia may develop and, in rare instances, blister-type lesions may develop in the lungs that sometimes rupture, resulting in the presence of air between the lungs and the chest wall (pneumothorax) and possible associated lung collapse.

On rare occasions, tuberculosis may be transmitted from mother to fetus through a placental lesion or by the inhalation or swallowing of infected amniotic fluid by the baby before or during birth. Congenital tuberculosis is rare and more commonly occurs soon after birth, usually through inhalation of airborne droplets from an infected person. Symptoms and findings associated with congenital tuberculosis may not develop for two or three weeks and may include drowsiness, fever, difficulty in breathing, poor feeding, drainage from the ears, enlarged lymph glands, enlarged liver and spleen (hepatosplenomegaly), abdominal swelling, skin lesions, and failure to thrive.

Diagnosis of tuberculosis may be established through evaluation of family and medical history, physical examination, skin and sputum testing, chest x-ray, and sometimes testing of cerebrospinal and other fluids as well as microscopic examination of tissue samples (biopsy).

Treatment for tuberculosis includes the prolonged administration of at least two different types of antibiotics to assure that all bacteria are destroyed. The antibiotics most often used for children with this disease include combinations of isoniazid, rifampin, pyrazinamide as well as streptomycin, and ethionamide that are especially effective for drug-resistant disease. The primary difference between treatment of TB in adults and children is ethambutol since one of the side effects is impaired vision. Because this effect is difficult to monitor in young children, ethambutol is not routinely recommended for children less then five years old. Corticosteroids may also be administered, especially in children with associated inflammatory irregularities that adversely affect organ function. In addition, the medication isoniazid may sometimes be preventively administered to those at high risk of tuberculosis infection, such as other members of the household, or to those with positive skin test results but no symptomatic or x-ray evidence of disease. The best method to prevent cases of pediatric tuberculosis is to find, diagnose, and treat cases of active tuberculosis among adults. Routine testing for TB with a tuberculin skin test is now only recommended in children who are at high risk for having the illness.

Government Agencies

6605 Centers for Disease Control and Prevention -TB Prevention
1600 Clifton Road
Atlanta, GA 30329
800-232-4636
TTY: 888-232-6348
www.cdc.gov/tb

Provides health and quality of life by preventing, controlling, and eventually eliminating tuberculosis in the United States.
Philip LeBue, MD, Director

6606 NIH/National Institute of Allergy and Infectious Diseases
5601 Fishers Lane, MSC 9806
Bethesda, MD 20892
301-496-5717
866-284-4107
Fax: 301-402-3573
TDD: 800-877-8339
ocpostoffice@niaid.nih.gov
www.niaid.nih.gov

The principal advisory board of the NIAID. The council is composed of physicians, scientists and representatives of the public and advises on the conduct and support or research, training and dissemination of health information regarding allergies and infectious diseases.
Anthony S. Fauci, MD, Director

6607 New York City Department of Health Bureau of Tuberculosis Control
New York, NY 10013
www.nyc.gov

The department aims to prevent the spread of tuberculosis (TB) and eliminate it as a public health problem in NYC.

Tuberculosis / National Associations & Support Groups

National Associations & Support Groups

6608 **American Academy of Pediatrics**
345 Park Blvd
Itasca, IL 60143
847-434-4000
800-433-9016
Fax: 847-434-8000
csc@aap.org
www.aap.org

The American Academy of Pediatrics and its member pediatricians are committed to the attainment of optimal physical, mental and social health and well-being for all infants, children, adolescents, and young adults.

Kyle E. Yasuda, MD, FAAP, President
Mark Del Monte, JD, CEO/Executive VP
Vera Tait, MD, FAAP, Chief Medical Officer

6609 **American Lung Association**
55 W. Wacker Drive, Suite 1150
Chicago, IL 60601
800-586-4872
info@lung.org
www.lung.org

The American Lung Association fights lung disease in all its forms, with special emphasis on asthma, tobacco control and environmental health. The American Lung Association is funded with contributions from the public, along with gifts and grants from corporations, foundations and government agencies. The association achieves its many successes through the work of thousands of committed volunteers and staff.

Harold P. Wimmer, National President & CEO
Albert Rizzo, MD, Chief Medical Officer
Sue Swan, Chief Development Officer

6610 **Global Tuberculosis Institute**
225 Warren Street, 2nd Floor, East Wing
Newark, NJ 07103
973-972-3270
Fax: 973-972-3268
globaltbinstitute@njms.rutgers.edu
globaltb.njms.rutgers.edu

The mission of the Global Tuberculosis Institute (GTBI), located at the International Center for Public Health, has always been to advance tuberculosis care through excellence in practice, research and teaching.

Alfred A. Lardizabal, Executive Director
Amee Patrawalla, Medical Director
Rajita Bhavaraju, Deputy Director

6611 **World Health Organization**
Avenue Appia 20
1202 Geneva,
Switzerland
www.who.int

WHO is the directing and coordinating authority for health within the United Nations system. WHO operates in more than 150 countries around the world.

Dr. Tedros Adhanom Ghebreyesus, Director General
Dr. Zsuzsanna Jakab, Deputy Director General
Stewart Simonson, Asst Director General, UN NYC

Research Centers

6612 **Francis J. Curry National Tuberculosis Center**
300 Frank H. Ogawa Plaza, Suite 520
Oakland, CA 94612
510-238-5100
877-390-6682
Fax: 415-861-7888
CurryTBcenter@ucsf.edu
www.currytbcenter.ucsf.edu

The Curry International Tuberculosis Center (CITC) creates, enhances and disseminates state-of-the-art resources and models of excellence and performs research to control and eliminate tuberculosis in the United States and internationally.

Francis Ho, President
Lisa Chen, MD, Medical Director, Principal Investi
James Sederberg, Deputy Director

6613 **University of Illinois at Chicago Institute for Tuberculosis Research**
904 W Adams Street
Chicago, IL 60607
202-318-2476
Michael J Groves, PhD, Director

Web Sites

6614 **American Lung Association**
55 W. Wacker Drive, Suite 1150
Chicago, IL 60601
800-586-4872
info@lung.org
www.lung.org

The American Lung Association fights lung disease in all its forms, with special emphasis on asthma, tobacco control and environmental health. The American Lung Association is funded with contributions from the public, along with gifts and grants from corporations, foundations and government agencies. The association achieves its many successes through the work of thousands of committed volunteers and staff.

Harold P. Wimmer, National President & CEO
Albert Rizzo, MD, Chief Medical Officer
Sue Swan, Chief Development Officer

6615 **Centers for Disease Control and Prevention**
1600 Clifton Road
Atlanta, GA 30329
800-232-4636
TTY: 888-232-6348
www.cdc.gov

Federal agency that promotes America's health and safety, providing information to guide health decisions, and building strong partnerships to promote health and prevent disease.

Rochelle P. Walensky, MD, Director
Anne Schuchat, MD, Principal Deputy Director
Abbigail Tumpey, MPH, Associate Director, Communication

6616 **Columbia University**
630 West 168th St.
New York, NY 10032
212-305-CUMC
www.cpmc.columbia.edu

Provides what you need to know about tuberculosis, and what kind of treatment to prevent tuberculosis.

Joanne M. J. Quan, SVP/ CFO
Mark McDougle, MPH, SVP/ COO
Amelia J. Alverson, SVP, Development

6617 **Health Answers Education Sudler-WPP Health Practice**
700 Dresher Road
Horsham, PA 19044
215-442-9010
www.healthanswers.com

HealthAnswers offers a breadth of services in medical education, sales force training, patient support solutions, professional promotion and consumer solutions.

Mike Hudnall, CEO

Book Publishers

6618 **Forgotten Plague: How the Battle Against Tuberculosis Was Won & Lost**
Hachette Book Group USA
1271 Avenue Of The Americans
New York, NY 10020
617-227-0730
Fax: 617-227-4633
www.hachettebookgroupusa.com

1994 Paperback
ISBN: 0-316763-81-0

Alison Lindsay, Director Of Marketing

6619 Respiratory Disorders Sourcebook, 4th Edition
Omnigraphics
615 Griswold Street, Ste 520
Detroit, MI 48226

610-461-3548
800-234-1340
Fax: 800-875-1340
contact@omnigraphics.com
www.omnigraphics.com

Basic consumer health information on lung disorders including tuberculosis, asthma and cystic fibrosis.

720 pages
ISBN: 0-780815-36-0

Pamphlets

6620 Global Epidemic Multi-Drug Resistant Tuberculosis
American Lung Association
55 W. Wacker Drive, Suite 1150
Chicago, IL 60601

312-801-7630
800-548-8252
Fax: 202-452-1805
www.lungusa.org

Kathryn A. Forbes, CPA, Chair
John F. Emanuel, JD, Vice Chair
Harold Wimmer, President/ CEO

6621 TB Skin Test
American Lung Association
1740 Broadway
New York, NY 10019

212-315-8700

Primary public information leaflet on the TB skin test.

8 pages

6622 TB: What You Should Know
American Lung Association
55 W. Wacker Drive, Suite 1150
Chicago, IL 60601

312-801-7630
800-548-8252
Fax: 202-452-1805
www.lungusa.org

Offers a brief overview of tuberculosis, how transmission is possible, and TB skin testing.

Kathryn A. Forbes, CPA, Chair
John F. Emanuel, JD, Vice Chair
Harold Wimmer, President/ CEO

6623 This Is Mr. TB Germ
American Lung Association
1740 Broadway
New York, NY 10019

212-315-8700

Lively booklet of drawings and very brief text giving a basic description of TB and its treatments.

20 pages

Tuberous Sclerosis / Description

Description

6624 TUBEROUS SCLEROSIS
Synonyms: Epiloia, TS
Involves the following Biologic System(s):
Dermatologic Disorders, Neurologic Disorders

Tuberous sclerosis (TS) is a hereditary multisystem disorder that is one of a group of diseases described as neuro-cutaneous syndromes, because of large involvement of both the skin and the central nervous system (brain and/or spinal cord). It is characterized by multiple, wart-like, raised areas (papules) on the skin of the face (adenoma sebaceum); benign, tumor-like nodules (hamartomas) of the brain, the heart, the kidneys, the nerve-rich membrane at the back of the eyes (retinas), or other organs; episodes of abnormally increased, uncontrolled electrical activity in the brain (seizures); and intellectual disabilities. Associated symptoms and findings may vary greatly from patient to patient, including among members of the same family. TS is caused by abnormal changes (mutations) in a gene or genes. These mutations may occur randomly for unknown reasons (sporadically) or may be inherited as an autosomal dominant trait. At least two genes have been identified that may cause TS. One disease gene, known as TSC1 gene, is located on the long arm (q) of chromosome 9 (9q34). A second gene, called the TSC2 gene, is on the short arm (p) of chromosome 16 (16p13.3). Tuberous sclerosis affects approximately one in 30,000 individuals.

TS is often apparent shortly after birth and presents as distinctive skin abnormalities and the development of either infantile spasms (hypsarrhythmia) or partial seizures characterized by sudden, repeated flexion or extension of the muscles of the neck, torso, arms, and legs. Seizures may later take the form of myoclonic epilepsy, in which there are sudden, shock-like contractions of a muscle or muscle groups. As many as 90 percent of infants with TS also have sharply defined areas of abnormally diminished skin coloration (hypopigmentation) on the torso, face, arms, or legs. These areas typically have an ashleaf-like appearance.

Seizures that begin during later childhood are often characterized by prolonged muscle contractions and alternating relaxation and contraction of muscles (generalized tonic-clonic seizures). Seizures tend to become progressively more severe and are often difficult to treat. In addition, approximately 60 to 70 percent of children with TS experience intellectual disabilities, almost all of whom also have seizure disorders. However, seizures also occur in most of those without intellectual disabilities. Generally, the younger a patient experiences symptoms associated with TS, the greater the risk for intellectual disabilities.

Beginning at about age two to six, about 80 percent of children with TS also develop red, shiny nodules (lesions) over the cheeks and nose. These nodules gradually become larger and assume a wart-like, fleshy appearance (adenoma sebaceum). Similar nodules may also develop on the forehead. Many children have additional, distinctive skin lesions. These may include raised, knobby, skin-colored lesions with an orange-peel consistency (shagreen patches) primarily located onthe lower back; firm, skin-colored nodules that develop around the nails of the fingers and toes during puberty, and rarely, coffee-colored discolorations of the skin (cafe-au-lait spots).

In patients with TS, the characteristic tumor-like nodules that develop in the brain are known as tubers. These growths often become hardened due to an abnormal accumulation of calcium salts (calcification). In addition, depending upon their size and location, tubers may block the normal flow of cerebrospinal fluid (CSF), causing an abnormal accumulation of CSF in the brain (hydrocephalus). The severity of neurologic impairment typically increases with the number of tubers within the brain. Rarely, a tuber may differentiate into a malignant brain tumor (astrocytoma).

Approximately 50 percent of affected children also have benign tumors of the heart muscle (rhabdomyoma). Although rhabdomyomas may disrupt the normal rhythm or rate of the heartbeat (arrythmias), these tumors tend to gradually resolve on their own. Benign, tumor-like nodules or multiple cysts may also develop in the kidneys, causing blood in the urine (hematuria), pain, or, in severe cases, kidney failure. Hamartomas may also develop in other tissues and organs of the body, such as the retinas and the lungs. In patients with severe TS, life-threatening complications may occur by adulthood.

The management of patients with TS is symptomatic and supportive, including therapy with anticonvulsant medications to help control seizures. In addition, physicians may regularly monitor patients to detect certain serious conditions potentially associated with TS, such as abnormal accumulations of cerebrospinal fluid or malignant transformation of hamartomas in the brain. If such conditions are confirmed, immediate surgical intervention or other measures are performed as required. Medications are required for controlling seizures, which is often difficult. The need for special schooling or care is determined by the severity of intellectual disabilities.

National Associations & Support Groups

6625 American Academy of Pediatrics
345 Park Blvd
Itasca, IL 60143
847-434-4000
800-433-9016
Fax: 847-434-8000
csc@aap.org
www.aap.org

The American Academy of Pediatrics and its member pediatricians are committed to the attainment of optimal physical, mental and social health and well-being for all infants, children, adolescents, and young adults.

Kyle E. Yasuda, MD, FAAP, President
Mark Del Monte, JD, CEO/Executive VP
Vera Tait, MD, FAAP, Chief Medical Officer

6626 Epilepsy Foundation
8301 Professional Place West, Ste 23000
Landover, MD 20785
301-459-3700
800-332-1000
Fax: 301-577-2684
ContactUs@efa.org
www.epilepsy.org

Nationwide organization dedicated to help those living with epilepsy pursue seizure freedom through community services, public education, advocacy and research funding.

Philen Gattone, President & CEO
Ellen Hobby, COO
Steve Owens, VP, Programs & Services

6627 Family Support Network
29 N Gore Avenue
St. Louis, MO 63119
314-963-1450
Fax: 314-963-9571
info@familysupportnet.org
www.familysupportnet.org

The Support Network is an organized partnership of individuals whose lives have been affected by Tuberous Sclerosis. Across the nation, the Support Network is providing the latest medical information, education and support to those individuals who are seeking understanding about the genetic disease and offering them words of encouragement and empowerment.

Dorothy Heltibrand, Executive Director
Vincent Marino, Program Director
Lynn Frost, Public Relations Director

6628 Genetic Alliance
426400 Woodfield Road, Ste 189
Damascus, MD 20872
202-966-5557
Fax: 202-966-8553
info@geneticalliance.org
www.geneticalliance.org

World's leading nonprofit health advocacy organization committed to transforming health through genetics and promoting an environment of openness centered on the health of individuals, families, and communities.

Sharon Terry, CEO
Ruth Child, CFO
Natasha Bonhomme, Chief Strategy Officer

6629 National Tuberous Sclerosis Association
8737 Colesville Road, Suite 400
Silver Spring, MD 20910
301-562-9890
800-225-6872
info@tsalliance.org
www.tsalliance.org

The TSC Alliance is an internationally recognized nonprofit that does everything it takes to improve the lives of people with TSC. We drive research, improve quality care and access and advocate for all affected by the disease.

Kari Luther Rosbeck, President & CEO

Web Sites

6630 Health Answers Education Sudler-WPP Health Practice
700 Dresher Road
Horsham, PA 19044
215-442-9010
www.healthanswers.com

HealthAnswers offers a breadth of services in medical education, sales force training, patient support solutions, professional promotion and ocnsumer solutions.

Mike Hudnall, CEO

6631 Online Mendelian Inheritance in Man
McKusick-Nathans Institue of Genetic Medicine-JHU
Baltimore, MD 21205
www.omim.org

This database is a catalog of human genes and genetic disorders.

Ada Hamosh, MD, Scientific Director

6632 TS International
www.stsn.nl/tsi/tsi.htm

www.stsn.nl/tsi/tsi.htm

Goals and objectives are to increase the knowledge of TS throughout the world, to stimulate, co-ordinate and originate research on TS, to interest statutory international organizations in the welfare of TS sufferers, to support national TS associations in the work, to initiate the realistation of new TS associatons, to exchange information of mutual interest between TS associations.

Book Publishers

6633 Tuberous Sclerosis: 3rd Edition
Oxford University Press
2001 Evans Road
Cary, NC 27513
Fax: 919-677-1303
www.oup-usa.org

A revision offering up-to-date medical information to families, researchers, and professionals on TS.

ISBN: 0-195122-10-0

Newsletters

6634 Perspective
National Tuberous Sclerosis Association
801 Roeder Road, Suite 750
Silver Spring, MD 20910
301-562-9890
800-225-6872
Fax: 301-562-9870
info@tsalliance.org
www.ntsa.org

Offers the latest research and medical information on tuberous sclerosis to physicians and health care professionals.

Bimonthly

Holly Knorr, Managing Editor

Pamphlets

6635 Living with Tuberous Sclerosis
National Tuberous Sclerosis Association
801 Roeder Road, Suite 750
Silver Spring, MD 20910
301-562-9890
800-225-6872
Fax: 301-562-9870
info@tsalliance.org
www.ntsa.org

True stories of people living with Tuberous Sclerosis.

Softcover

6636 Tuberous Sclerosis: Fact Sheet
National Inst. of Neurological Disorders/Stroke
P.O. Box 5801
Bethesda, MD 20824
301-496-5751
800-352-9424
www.ninds.nih.gov

Walter J. Koroshetz, M.D., Acting Director
Alan L. Willard, Ph.D., Acting Deputy Director
Caroline Lewis, Executive Officer

Turner Syndrome / Description

Description

6637 TURNER SYNDROME

Synonyms: Chromosome 45,X syndrome, XO syndrome

Involves the following Biologic System(s):
Genetic/Chromosomal/Syndrome/Metabolic Disorders

Turner syndrome is a chromosomal disorder that affects only females. In most cases, females have two X chromosomes and males have one X and one Y chromosome in cells of the body. However, in females with Turner syndrome, one of the X chromosomes is deleted (missing) from cells or is functionally defective; some cells have the normal pair of X chromosomes whereas others do not (mosaicism). Although associated symptoms and findings may be variable, the most consistent abnormalities associated with the disorder include short stature and defective development of the ovaries (gonadal dysgenesis).

Many newborns with Turner syndrome have an abnormal accumulation of fluid in and associated swelling of the backs of the hands and the tops of the feet (peripheral lymphedema). Additional features that may be apparent at birth include an abnormally short, webbed neck (pterygium colli) with a low hairline; a narrow roof of the mouth (palate) or a small jaw (micrognathia); abnormal outward deviation of the elbows upon extension (cubitus valgus); a broad chest with widely spaced, underdeveloped, and/or inverted nipples; or deeply set, narrow, and/or outwardly curved (convex) nails. In most cases, females with Turner syndrome also have kidney (renal) malformations (e.g., horseshoe kidney and/or cleft or double renal pelvis). In addition, in some cases, heart (cardiac) defects may be present, such as abnormalities affecting the major artery (aorta) that arises from the lower left chamber (ventricle) of the heart (e.g., bicuspid aortic valve, coarctation of the aorta). In almost all affected females, there is also defective development of the ovaries (ovarian dysgenesis), i.e., the paired glands within which the female reproductive cells are produced (ova or eggs) and from which certain female hormones are secreted. Consequently, in most cases, female secondary sexual characteristics fail to develop (e.g., breast development, appearance of hair in the pubic area and under the arms, menstruation) and most affected females are infertile. In addition, although intelligence is typically normal, some females with Turner syndrome may experience learning disabilities (e.g., difficulty with visual-spatial relationships) and may have poor coordination. The treatment of children with Turner syndrome may include hormone replacement therapy (e.g., estrogen therapy, human growth hormone therapy); surgical intervention for congenital heart defects, renal malformations, webbing of the neck, or other abnormalities; special education for those with learning disabilities; and other treatment measures as required. Turner syndrome is thought to result from errors during the division of a parent's reproductive cells (meiosis). According to estimates in the medical literature, the disorder may affect from approximately one in 2,000 to one in 4,000 female newborns.

Government Agencies

6638 NIH/ Eunice Kennedy Shriver National Institute of Child Health & Human Development
P.O. Box 3006
Rockville, MD 20847

800-370-2943
Fax: 866-760-5947
www.nichd.nih.gov

Conducts and supports research on topics related to the health of children, adults, families and populations. Some of these topics include: developmental disabilities, growth and development, infant death, reproductive health and birth defects.

Diana W. Bianchi, Director
Alison Cernich, PhD, Deputy Director

National Associations & Support Groups

6639 American Academy of Pediatrics
345 Park Blvd
Itasca, IL 60143

847-434-4000
800-433-9016
Fax: 847-434-8000
csc@aap.org
www.aap.org

The American Academy of Pediatrics and its member pediatricians are committed to the attainment of optimal physical, mental and social health and well-being for all infants, children, adolescents, and young adults.

Kyle E. Yasuda, MD, FAAP, President
Mark Del Monte, JD, CEO/Executive VP
Vera Tait, MD, FAAP, Chief Medical Officer

6640 American Society for Reproductive Medicine
1209 Montgomery Highway
Birmingham, AL 35216

205-978-5000
Fax: 205-978-5005
asrm@asrm.org
www.asrm.org

The American Society for Reproductive Medicine is an organization devoted to advancing knowledge and expertise in infertility, reproductive medicine and biology. The ASRM is a voluntary nonprofit organization.

Jared C. Robins, Chief Executive Officer
Lee Pearce, Chief Operating Officer
Chevis N. Shannon, Chief Education & Science Officer

6641 Endocrine Society
2055 L Street NW, Suite 600
Washington, DC 20036

202-971-3636
888-363-6274
Fax: 202-736-9705
info@endocrine.org
www.endocrine.org

The Endocrine Society is devoted to advancing hormone research, excellence in the clinical practice of endocrinology, broadening understanding of the critical role hormones play in health, and advocating on behalf of the global endocrinology community.

Kate Fryer, Chief Executive Officer
Mila Baker, Chief Policy Officer
Zerihun Haile-Selassie, Chief Financial Officer

6642 Genetic Alliance
426400 Woodfield Road, Ste 189
Damascus, MD 20872

202-966-5557
Fax: 202-966-8553
info@geneticalliance.org
www.geneticalliance.org

World's leading nonprofit health advocacy organization committed to transforming health through genetics and promoting an environment of openness centered on the health of individuals, families, and communities.

Sharon Terry, CEO
Ruth Child, CFO
Natasha Bonhomme, Chief Strategy Officer

6643 Human Growth Foundation
997 Glen Cove Avenue, Suite 5
Glen Head, NY 11545

800-451-6434
Fax: 516-671-4055
hgfl@hgfound.org
www.hgfound.org

A voluntary, nonprofit organization whose mission is to help children and adults with disorders of growth and growth hormones through research, education, support and advocacy. The foundation is dedicated to helping medical science to better understand the process of growth. It is composed of concerned parents and friends of children and adults with growth problems and interested health professionals.

Joel Steelman, MD, President
Emily Germain-Lee, MD, Vice President

6644 **MAGIC Foundation: Major Aspects of Growth in Children: Turner's Syndrome Division**
4200 Cantera Drive, #106
Warrenville, IL 60555
630-836-8200
800-362-4423
Fax: 630-836-8181
contactus@magicfoundation.org
www.magicfoundation.org

A national nonprofit organization providing support and education regarding growth disorders in children and related adult disorders. Provides educational information, networking, a national conference, a kids' program and an extensive medical library.

Dianne Kremidas, Executive Director
Mary Andrews, CEO
Teresa Tucker, Patient Advocacy

6645 **Turner's Syndrome Society of the US**
11250 West Road, Suite G
Houston, TX 77065
800-365-9944
info@turnersyndrome.org
www.turnersyndrome.org

More than 38 chapters across the country. Goals are to promote public awareness of the disease, support those affected by the condition and aid in continuing research. Membership dues for a single person are $40, a family, $60, and for professionals, $60.

2,500 members

Cindy Scurlock, President & CEO
Deborah Rios, National Director, Member Services
Becky Brown, National Director, Development

State Agencies & Support Groups

Alaska

6646 **Turner's Syndrome Society of Alaska**
1334 N Street
Anchorage, AK 99501
907-279-3202
marytullius@hotmail.com
www.turnersyndrome.org

Mary Tullius

Arizona

6647 **Turner's Syndrome Society of Arizona**
2215 Wickenburg Road
Ponopah, AZ 85354
602-443-3805
www.turnersyndrome.org

Tracie Holley

California

6648 **Turner's Syndrome Society Central And Northern**
Bay Point, CA 94565
925-299-7729
www.turnersyndrome.org

Rosemary Morris

6649 **Turner's Syndrome Society of Southern California**
8902 Heil Avenue #24
Westminster, CA 92683
714-749-7313
colleencurby1@gmail.com
www.turnersyndrome.org

Colleen Curby, President

Colorado

6650 **Turner's Syndrome Society of Rocky Mountain**
4972 S Garland
Littleton, CO 80123
720-981-2632
www.turnersyndrome.org

Donna Landrum

Connecticut

6651 **Turner's Syndrome Society of Connecticut**
57 Cianci Drive
Southington, CT 06489
860-329-2990
dmj_lewis@sbcglobal.net
www.turnersyndrome.org

Jessica Fitzgibbon Lewis, Contact

Florida

6652 **Turner's Syndrome Society - Tampa Support Group**
3202 W Fair Oaks Avenue
Tampa, FL 33611
813-837-0582
heddyb@gateway.net
www.turnersyndrome.org

Heddy Brown

6653 **Turner's Syndrome Society of Northern Florida**
6447 Cooper Lane
Jacksonville, FL 32210
407-859-3131
elrcook3@bellsouth.net
www.turnersyndrome.org

Kim Brown
Randy Cook, Contact

6654 **Turner's Syndrome Society of South Florida**
235 NE 23rd Street #204
Ft. Lauderdale, FL 33305
407-859-3131
elrcook3@bellsouth.net
www.turnersyndrome.org

Rachel Nowak
Randy Cook, Contact

Iowa

6655 **Turner's Syndrome Society of Iowa/New Found Friends**
2615 Meadow Glen Road
Ames, IA 50014
515-321-6021
ashley.artzer@yahoo.com
www.turnersyndrome.org

Ashley Artzer, Contact

Kentucky

6656 **Turner's Syndrome Society of Kentucky**
380 Bob-O-Link Drive
Lexington, KY 40503
502-292-2742
timrhon@insightbb.com
www.turnersyndrome.org

Rhonda Curtis, Contact

Louisiana

6657 **Turner's Syndrome Society of Gulf Coast**
7731 Butterfield Road
New Orleans, LA 70126
334-476-7940
www.turnersyndrome.org

Donna Baudier

Turner Syndrome / State Agencies & Support Groups

Maryland

6658 Turner's Syndrome Society of Maryland
2206 229th Street
Pasadena, MD 21122
410-360-5571
www.turnersyndrome.org

Kathy Mattson

Massachusetts

6659 Turner's Syndrome Society of New England
60 Joy Street, Apartment 303
Boston, MA 02114
617-557-4837
Fax: 617-636-6131
www.turnersyndrome.org

Geralyn Dwyer

Michigan

6660 Turner's Syndrome Society of Southeastern Michigan
7490 Drew Circle, Apartment 8
Westland, MI 48185
248-921-6298
hahoey@comcast.net
www.turnersyndrome.org

Heather Hoey, Contact

6661 Turner's Syndrome Society of West Michigan
1569 Sibley Street NW
Grand Rapids, MI 49504
517-85-959
maohler@att.net
www.turnersyndrome.org

Mary Ohler, Contact

Minnesota

6662 Turner's Syndrome Society of Minnesota
7109 Autumn Terrace
Eden Prairie, MN 55346
952-854-1224
jleon101@hotmail.com
www.tssminnesota.org

Julie Leon, Contact

Missouri

6663 Turner's Syndrome Society of St. Louis/ West Illinois
1514 Azalia Drive
Saint Louis, MO 63119
314-892-2635
www.turnersyndrome.org

Cheryl Jost

Nevada

6664 Turner's Syndrome Society of Nevada
1003 Mylert St
Jessup, PA 18434
702-731-3452
www.turnersyndrome.org

Joelle Barnes

New Hampshire

6665 Turner's Syndrome Society of Northern New England
1261 Old North Main Street
Laconia, NH 03246
603-528-3510
www.turnersyndrome.org

Lori Ann Pawlowski
Dawn And Matt Dragon

New Jersey

6666 Turner's Syndrome Society of New Jersey
238 Hempstead Drive
Somerset, NJ 08873
732-249-3727
www.turnersyndrome.org

Linda Kalb

New York

6667 Turner's Syndrome Society of Central New York
Apt 18
Owego, NY 13827
607-223-4124
tlkwwjd@gmail.com
www.turnersyndrome.org

Tammy Kozak, Contact

6668 Turner's Syndrome Society of Upstate New York
115 Union Avenue #205
Saratoga Springs, NY 12866
518-209-1793
saratogatif@aol.com
www.turnersyndrome.org

Tiffany Festo

North Carolina

6669 Turner's Syndrome Society of North Carolina
1223 Pine Springs Drive
Hendersonville, NC 28739
919-387-7974
denise.culin@gmail.com
www.turnersyndromenc.com

Denise Culin, Chapter President
Barbara Flink, Vice President
Megan Edwards, Secretary

Ohio

6670 Turner's Syndrome Society of Southwestern Ohio
8530 Gateview Court
Dayton, OH 45424
513-697-0941
lisa_lorigan@hotmail.com
www.swohioturnersyndrome.com

Lisa Lorigan, Chapter President

Oklahoma

6671 Turner's Syndrome Society of Oklahoma
5904 East Lattimer
Tulsa, OK 74115
405-271-6764
www.turnersyndrome.org

Traci Schaeffer, Contact

Pennsylvania

6672 Turner's Syndrome Society of Philadelphia
2322 Taggart Court
Wilmington, DE 19810
302-475-5780
jmkurze@aol.com
www.turnersyndrome.org

Joann Kurzeknabe

Rhode Island

6673 Turner's Syndrome Society of Rhode Island
24 Turner Street, Unit 3
Warwick, RI 02886
401-732-2136
www.turnersyndrome.org

South Carolina

6674 Turner's Syndrome Society of South Carolina
153 Gannet Point Road
Beaufort, SC 29907
843-522-8508
www.turnersyndrome.org
Robin Butler

Tennessee

6675 Turner's Syndrome Society of Mid-South
2541 Clydes Place Cove
Memphis, TN 38133
901-385-1720
hmschlmom3@yahoo.com
www.turnersyndrome.org
Penny Williams

6676 Turner's Syndrome Society of Tennessee
9202 Shady Bend Lane
Knoxville, TN 37922
423-539-2210
www.turnersyndrome.org
Kathy Blackbourne

Texas

6677 Turner's Syndrome Society of Houston
11602 Bexhil
Houston, TX 77065
832-689-3901
www.turnersupport.org
Heather DeRousse, Contact

6678 Turner's Syndrome Society of North Texas
3211 W Division #28
Arlington, TX 76012
832-689-3901
www.turnersyndrome.org
Patricia Burton

6679 Turner's Syndrome Society of San Antonio
923 Escalon Avenue
San Antonio, TX 78221
210-647-8981
xpictinaki@hotmail.com
www.turnersyndrome.org
Christine Ashenfelter, Contact

Utah

6680 Turner's Syndrome Society of Salt Lake City
2337 Chateau Drive
Roy, UT 84067
801-825-4118
kristyne70@hotmail.com
www.turnersyndrome.org
Kristyne Rudolph

Virginia

6681 Turner's Syndrome Society of National Capitol Area
6200 Westchester Park Drive #406
College Park, MD 20740
301-345-3136
www.turnersyndrome.org
Deb Shoup

Washington

6682 Turner's Syndrome Society of Inland Northwest
5317 N Washington Street
Spokane, WA 99205
509-326-3703
www.turnersyndrome.org
Nancy Owen

Wisconsin

6683 Turner's Syndrome Society of Southeastern Wisconsin
10122 63rd Street
Kenosha, WI 53142
608-385-5910
www.turnersyndrome.org
Melissa Caulum

Web Sites

6684 Health Answers Education Sudler-WPP Health Practice
700 Dresher Road
Horsham, PA 19044
215-442-9010
www.healthanswers.com

HealthAnswers offers a breadth of services in medical education, sales force training, patient support solutions, professional promotion and consumer solutions.

Mike Hudnall, CEO

6685 Human Growth Foundation
997 Glen Cove Avenue, Suite 5
Glen Head, NY 11545
800-451-6434
Fax: 516-671-4055
hgf1@hgfound.org
www.hgfound.org

A voluntary, nonprofit organization whose mission is to help children and adults with disorders of growth and growth hormones through research, education, support and advocacy. The foundation is dedicated to helping medical science to better understand the process of growth. It is composed of concerned parents and friends of children and adults with growth problems; and interested health professionals.

Joel Steelman, MD, President
Emily Germain-Lee, MD, Vice President

6686 MAGIC Foundation: Major Aspects of Growth in Children: Turner's Syndrome Division
4200 Cantera Drive, #106
Warrenville, IL 60555
630-836-8200
800-362-4423
Fax: 630-836-8181
ContactUs@magicfoundation.org
www.magicfoundation.org

Is a national nonprofit organization created to provide support services for the families of children afflicted with a wide variety of chronic and or critical disorders, syndromes and diseases that affected a child's growth.

Dianne Kremidas, Executive Director
Mary Andrews, CEO
Teresa Tucker, Patient Advocacy

6687 Online Mendelian Inheritance in Man
McKusick-Nathans Instiute of Genetic Medicine-JHU
Baltimore, MD 21205
www.omim.org

This database is a catalog of human genes and genetic disorders.

Ada Hamosh, MD, Scientific Director

6688 Turner's Syndrome Society of the US
11250 West Road, Suite G
Houston, TX 77065
800-365-9944
info@turnersyndrome.org
www.turnersyndrome.org

A nonprofit organization that provides assistance, support, and education to girls and women with turner syndrome, their families, physicians, and the interested public.

Cindy Scurlock, President & CEO
Deborah Rios, National Director, Member Services
Becky Brown, National Director, Development

Turner Syndrome / Pamphlets

Pamphlets

6689 Answers to Some Commonly Asked Questions
Turner Syndrome Society of the United States
11250 West Road, Suite G
Houston, TX 77065
832-912-6006
800-365-9944
Fax: 832-912-6446
www.turnersyndrome.org

Offers information on the Society's activities and the role they play in supporting people with Turner Syndrome.

Trudy McCarthy, President
Cindy Scurlock, Executive Director
Shawn Wier, Conference Coordinator

6690 Facing the Challenges of Turner Syndrome Together
Turner Syndrome Society of the United States
11250 West Road, Suite G
Houston, TX 77065
832-912-6006
800-365-9944
Fax: 832-912-6446
www.turnersyndrome.org

Brochure offering information on Turner's syndrome, statistics on how widespread the disease is and the Society's role in conquering this disease and supporting its members.

Trudy McCarthy, President
Cindy Scurlock, Executive Director
Shawn Wier, Conference Coordinator

6691 Facts About Turner Syndrome
Turner Syndrome Society of the United States
11250 West Road, Suite G
Houston, TX 77065
832-912-6006
800-365-9944
Fax: 832-912-6446
www.turnersyndrome.org

Offers statistical and factual information on the disease of Turner Syndrome, causes, symptoms, prevention and treatment.

Trudy McCarthy, President
Cindy Scurlock, Executive Director
Shawn Wier, Conference Coordinator

6692 How to Start a Turner Syndrome Support Group
Turner Syndrome Society of the United States
11250 West Road, Suite G
Houston, TX 77065
832-912-6006
800-365-9944
Fax: 832-912-6446
www.turnersyndrome.org

Offers information to the lay person on how to obtain material from medical professionals, and publicity aspects and funding aspects in pertaining to starting a support group.

Trudy McCarthy, President
Cindy Scurlock, Executive Director
Shawn Wier, Conference Coordinator

6693 Turner's Syndrome
Human Growth Foundation
11250 West Road, Suite G
Houston, TX 77065
832-912-6006
800-365-9944
Fax: 832-912-6446
www.turnersyndrome.org

Background of a tremendous need for further information about Turner's Syndrome.

Trudy McCarthy, President
Cindy Scurlock, Executive Director
Shawn Wier, Conference Coordinator

6694 Turner's Syndrome Society Resource Bibliographies
Turner's Syndrome Society of the United States
11250 West Road, Suite G
Houston, TX 77065
832-912-6006
800-365-9944
Fax: 832-912-6446
www.turnersyndrome.org

These fact sheets offer information on books, videos and other resources available on Turner Syndrome.

Trudy McCarthy, President
Cindy Scurlock, Executive Director
Shawn Wier, Conference Coordinator

6695 Turner's Syndrome: A Personal Perspective
Turner's Syndrome Society of the United States
11250 West Road, Suite G
Houston, TX 77065
832-912-6006
800-365-9944
Fax: 832-912-6446
www.turnersyndrome.org

A reprint from the Adolescent and Pediatric Gynecology Journal offering a personal account of a woman with Turner Syndrome and her experiences.

Trudy McCarthy, President
Cindy Scurlock, Executive Director
Shawn Wier, Conference Coordinator

6696 Turner's Syndrome: Guide for Families
Turner's Syndrome Society of the United States
11250 West Road, Suite G
Houston, TX 77065
832-912-6006
800-365-9944
Fax: 832-912-6446
www.turnersyndrome.org

Offers information to parents on the causes, symptoms, diagnosis and prognosis of Turner's syndrome, includes resources of where to go for help and support.

Trudy McCarthy, President
Cindy Scurlock, Executive Director
Shawn Wier, Conference Coordinator

6697 Turner's Syndrome: The Hows and Whys of the Missing X Chromosome
Human Growth Foundation
11250 West Road, Suite G
Houston, TX 77065
832-912-6006
800-365-9944
Fax: 832-912-6446
www.turnersyndrome.org

Women with Turner's Syndrome lack one of the X chromosomes. This carries genes for conditions relating to the development of ovaries, sex hormone production, and physical development in general.

Trudy McCarthy, President
Cindy Scurlock, Executive Director
Shawn Wier, Conference Coordinator

Description

6698 ULCERATIVE COLITIS
Involves the following Biologic System(s):
Gastrointestinal Disorders

Ulcerative colitis is an inflammatory bowel disease (IBD) characterized by chronic inflammation and ulceration of the lining of the colon, the major part of the large intestine. The disease initially affects the lowest region of the large intestine (rectum) and gradually progresses to involve varying lengths or all of the colon. The range and severity of associated symptoms is extremely variable and may depend in part on the amount of the colon that is affected. Ulcerative colitis usually becomes apparent during adolescence or young adulthood. However, in some patients, associated symptoms may occur as early as the first year of life. The frequency of the disorder varies greatly in different countries and is thought to be higher in urban areas. In the United States and northern Europe, ulcerative colitis affects approximately 100 to 200 per 100,000 individuals in the general population. In developed countries, inflammatory bowel disease, including ulcerative colitis, is the most common cause of chronic intestinal inflammation during mid-childhood. The exact cause of ulcerative colitis is unknown. However genetic, immune, and environmental factors are thought to be contributing factors.

In patients with ulcerative colitis, the onset of symptoms may be gradual (insidious) or sudden, rapid, and severe (fulminant). Most patients experience episodes of watery diarrhea with varying amounts of blood, mucus, or pus. Associated findings may include abdominal cramping and pain; persistant, inability or difficulty emptying the bowel at defecation (tenesmus); and an urgent, compelling urge to defecate. Fulminant colitis is characterized by over six daily bowel movements, a high fever, chills, abnormally low levels of iron or the protein albumin in the blood, an increase in certain circulating white blood cells (leukocytosis), and other findings. In some children, additional findings include failure to grow and gain weight at the expected rate and lack of appetite (anorexia). The frequency of episodes may vary greatly. Most patients experience periods of remission during which symptoms subside and eventual, periodic recurrences (exacerbations). However, some patients may have infrequent episodes and others may experience severe, ongoing symptoms.

Certain complications may occur in association with ulcerative colitis. For example, because of blood loss during episodes, there may be inadequate levels of iron and abnormally reduced levels of the oxygen-carrying protein of the blood (iron-deficiency anemia). Some individuals with ulcerative colitis may develop sudden massive enlargement of the colon (toxic megacolon). Without prompt, appropriate treatment, toxic megacolon may result in tearing or perforation of the colon, potentially causing life-threatening complications. In addition, patients who have ulcerative colitis for more than 10 years have an increased risk of colon cancer. Regular examination of the colon (colonoscopies) and biopsies are recommended beginning at 8 to 10 years after disease onset to help ensure prompt detection and treatment. During a colonoscopy, tissue inside the colon is examined using a flexible viewing instrument. To obtain a biopsy, small samples of tissue are removed from the colon for examination under a microscope.

Many patients with ulcerative colitis may also eventually experience more generalized, systemic symptoms. By the third decade of life, some patients may develop ankylosing spondylitis (AS), a chronic, progressive, inflammatory disease that affects joints of the spine and results in pain, stiffness, and possible loss of spinal mobility. In patients with ulcerative colitis, AS most commonly affects joints of the back and the hips and may cause lower back pain and stiffness, particularly in the morning. Some patients with ulcerative colitis may also develop a chronic skin condition characterized by irregular, bluish-red skin sores (pyoderma gangrenosum); chronic inflammation of the liver (chronic active hepatitis); and inflammation of the bile ducts (primary sclerosing cholangitis).

Since ulcerative colitis cannot be cured, the goals of treatment with medication are to induce remissions, maintain remissions, minimize side effects of treatment, and improve the quality of life. In patients with mild colitis, treatment often includes administration of anti-inflammatory drugs, such sulfasalazine, which may alleviate symptoms and potentially prevent recurrences. Patients with moderate to severe colitis who do not respond to such treatment may receive corticosteroid therapy, such as with the drug prednisone or immunomodulators that suppress the body's immune system, thus reducing inflammation. If affected individuals have fulminant colitis or colitis that is unresponsive to drug therapy, treatment may include surgical removal of the colon (colectomy). Additional treatment is symptomatic and supportive. An interesting new treatment uses nicotine. It has long been observed that the risk of ulcerative colitis appears to be higher in nonsmokers and in ex-smokers. In certain circumstances, patients improve when treated with nicotine where other medications have not been effective.

Government Agencies

6699 NIH/National Institute of Diabetes and Digestive and Kidney Diseases
9000 Rockville Pike
Bethesda, MD 20892

800-860-8747
TTY: 866-569-1162
healthinfo@niddk.nih.gov
www.niddk.nih.gov

Conducts and supports basic and applied research and provides leadership for a national program in diabetes, endocrinology, and metabolic diseases; digestive diseases and nutrition and kidney, urologic and hematologic diseases.

Griffin P. Rodgers, MD, Director
Gregory G. Germino, MD, Deputy Director

National Associations & Support Groups

6700 American Academy of Pediatrics
345 Park Blvd
Itasca, IL 60143

847-434-4000
800-433-9016
Fax: 847-434-8000
csc@aap.org
www.aap.org

The American Academy of Pediatrics and its member pediatricians are committed to the attainment of optimal physical, mental and social health and well-being for all infants, children, adolescents, and young adults.

Kyle E. Yasuda, MD, FAAP, President
Mark Del Monte, JD, CEO/Executive VP
Vera Tait, MD, FAAP, Chief Medical Officer

6701 Crohn's & Colitis Foundation
733 Third Avenue, Ste 510
New York, NY 10017

800-932-2423
info@crohnscolitisfoundation.org
www.crohnscolitisfoundation.org

The mission of the Crohn's & Colitis Foundation is to cure and prevent Crohn's disease and ulcerative colitis through research and improve the quality of life of children and adults affected by these digestive diseases through education and support.

Ulcerative Colitis / Libraries & Resource Centers

John Crosson, Chair
Michael Osso, President & CEO
Robert Territo, COO/CFO

6702 Digestive Disease National Coalition
507 Capitol Court NE, Suite 200
Washington, DC 20002
202-544-7497
Fax: 202-546-7105
www.ddnc.org

Advocacy organization comprised of over 30 voluntary and professional societies concerned with the many diseases of the digestive tract and liver.

Ceciel Rooker, Chairperson
Bryan Green, MD, President
Cathy Griffith, Vice Chairperson

6703 Genetic Alliance
426400 Woodfield Road, Ste 189
Damascus, MD 20872
202-966-5557
Fax: 202-966-8553
info@geneticalliance.org
www.geneticalliance.org

World's leading nonprofit health advocacy organization committed to transforming health through genetics and promoting an environment of openness centered on the health of individuals, families, and communities.

Sharon Terry, CEO
Ruth Child, CFO
Natasha Bonhomme, Chief Strategy Officer

6704 International Foundation for Functional Gastrointestinal Disorders (IFFGD)
3015 Dunes W Boulevard, Suite 512
Mount Pleasant, SC 29466
414-964-1799
www.iffgd.org

The organization offers responses to those commonly asked questions for families and individuals whose lives have been touched by gastrointestinal disorders.

Nancy J. Norton, Founder
Ceciel T. Rooker, President

6705 United Ostomy Association
PO Box 525
Kennebunk, MN 04043
800-826-0826
www.ostomy.org

An advocate for ostomy and alternative procedure patients answering questions from employment issues to insurability practices. Also publishes magazines, patient care guides, conducts conferences and youth rally summer camps. We sponsor networks and resources for children, teens young adults, and parents.

Christine Ryan, Executive Director

Libraries & Resource Centers

6706 National Digestive Diseases Information Clearinghouse (NDDIC)
NIH
2 Information Way
Bethesda, MD 20892
301-654-3810
800-891-5389
Fax: 301-907-8906
nddic@info.niddk.nih.gov
www.digestive.niddk.nih.gov

The National Institute of Diabetes and Digestive and Kidney Diseases conducts and supports research on many of the most serious diseases affecting public health. The Institute supports much of the clinical research on the diseases of internal medicine and related subspecialty fields as well as many basic science disciplines.

Griffin P. Rodgers, MD, Director
Gregory G. Germino, MD, Deputy Director
Kathy Kranzfelder, Communications Director

Research Centers

6707 Center for Digestive Disorders
Central Dupage Hospital
One Boston Medical Center Place
Boston, MA 02118
617-638-8000
Fax: 617-638-7448
TTY: 800-439-2370
www.bmc.org/digestivedisorders

Kate Walsh, President/CEO

Web Sites

6708 Ask NOAH About: Stomach and Intestinal (Gastrointestinal) Disorders
noah-health.org/english/illness/gastro/gastro.html

noah-health.org/english/illness/gastro/gastro.html

Provides access to high quality full-text consumer health information in English and Spanish that is accurate, timely, relevant and unbiased.

6709 Colitis Cookbook
www.colitiscookbook.com/

www.colitiscookbook.com/

A cookbook for people with colitis and other diseases.

Denise Weale, Co-Author
Ross Weale, Co-Author

6710 Crohn's & Colitis Foundation
733 Third Avenue, Ste 510
New York, NY 10017
800-932-2423
info@crohnscolitisfoundation.org
www.crohnscolitisfoundation.org

The mission of the Crohn's & Colitis Foundation is to cure and prevent Crohn's disease and ulcerative colitis through research and improve the quality of life of children and adults affected by these digestive diseases through education and support.

John Crosson, Chair
Michael Osso, President & CEO
Robert Territo, COO/CFO

6711 Health Answers Education Sudler-WPP Health Practice
700 Dresher Road
Horsham, PA 19044
215-442-9010
www.healthanswers.com

HealthAnswers offers a breadth of services in medical education, sales force training, patient support solutions, professional promotion and consumer solutions.

Mike Hudnall, CEO

6712 IBS Self-help group
www.ibsgroup.org/

www.ibsgroup.org/

Works to educate those who are living with IBS and to increase awareness about his and other functional gastrointesinal disorders. The group was founded in support for those who suffer from IBS, those who are looking for support for someone who has IBS, and medical professionals who want to learn more about IBS.

Jeffrey D. Roberts, MSEd, B.Sc., Founder

6713 National Digestive Diseases Information Clearinghouse (NDDIC)
NIH
2 Information Way
Bethesda, MD 20892
301-654-3810
800-891-5389
nddic@info.niddk.nih.gov
www.digestive.niddk.nih.gov

The National Institute of Diabetes and Digestive and Kidney Diseases conducts and supports research on many of the most serious diseases affecting public health. The Institute supports much of the clinical research on the diseases of internal medicine and related subspecialty fields as well as many basic science disciplines.

Griffin P. Rodgers, MD, Director
Gregory G. Germino, MD, Deputy Director
Kathy Kranzfelder, Communications Director

6714 Online Mendelian Inheritance in Man
McKusick-Nathans Institue of Genetic Medicine-JHU
Baltimore, MD 21205   www.omim.org

This database is a catalog of human genes and genetic disorders.

Ada Hamosh, MD, Scientific Director

6715 Pediatric Crohn's & Colitis Association
PO Box 188
Newton, MA 2468   617-489-5854
pcca.hypermart.net

We are committed to helping children with IBD and their families better understand the Crohn's disease and ulcerative colitis.

Book Publishers

6716 Angry Gut, The: Coping with Colitis and Crohn's Disease
Plenum Publishing Corporation
10 E 53 Street
New York, NY 10022   212-207-7600
Fax: 212-463-0742
onlineservice@springer.com
www.link.springer.com

Overview of the symptoms, diagnosis, complications, and treatment of IBD.
1993 364 pages
ISBN: 0-306444-70-4

6717 Ask Audrey
7466 Pebble Lane
West Bloomfield, MI 48322   248-626-6960

A compilation of material and the personal story of a medical psychotherapist who has inflammatory bowel disease. Includes practical tips on issues such as handling diarrhea, sexuality, relationships, traveling, coping with hospital stays, ostomies, and TPN.

6718 Gastrointestinal Diseases and Disorders Sourcebook, 4th Edition
Omnigraphics
615 Griswold Street, Ste 520
Detroit, MI 48226   610-461-3548
800-234-1340
Fax: 800-875-1340
contact@omnigraphics.com
www.omnigraphics.com

Basic consumer health information including celiac disease, crohn's disease, diarrhea, hernias, irritable bowel syndrome and ulcers.
816 pages
ISBN: 0-780816-50-3

6719 IBD Nutrition Book
John Wiley & Sons
432 Elizabeth Avenue
Somerset, NJ 08875   800-225-5945
Fax: 732-302-2300
custserv@wiley.com
www.wiley.com

Clinical dietitian/nutritionist's overview of the role of diet in IBD, including recipes and meal plans.

Peter B. Wiley, Chairman
Stephen M. Smith, President & CEO
Ellis E. Cousens, Executive Vice President, Chief Fin

6720 Inflammatory Bowel Disease
Lippincott Williams & Wilkins
351 W Camden Street
Baltimore, MD 21201   410-528-4000
800-638-3030
www.lww.com

Detailed information on every aspect of IBD. Topics include medical and surgical management, epidemiology, fertility and pregnancy, psychosocial factors, and diagnostic techniques. Written for medical professionals and laypersons who are comfortable with medical terminology.

Edward B. Hutton Jr., Chief Executive Officer, President
E. Passano Jr., Vice Chairman of the Board and Secr

6721 Inflammatory Bowel Disease - From Bench to Bedside
Williams & Wilkins
351 W Camden Street
Baltimore, MD 21201   301-528-4000
www.lww.com

Offers in-depth information on the impact of basic research developments on the management of Crohn's disease and ulcerative colities. Written for medical professionals and laypersons who are comfortable with medical terminology.

Edward B. Hutton Jr., Chief Executive Officer, President
E. Passano Jr., Vice Chairman of the Board and Secr

6722 New People Not Patients: A Source Book for Living with IBD
Crohn's and Colitis Foundation of America
4930 Del Ray Avenue
Bethesda, MD 20814   301-654-2055
Fax: 301-654-5920
member@gastro.org
www.gastro.org/public/ibd.html

Anil K. Rustgi, President
Michael Camiller, Vice President
J. Sumner Bell III, Secretary/Treasurer

6723 Ostomy Book: Living Comfortably with Colostomies, Ileostomies and Urostomies
United Ostomy Association
P.O. Box 512
Northfield, MN 55057   949-660-8624
800-826-0826
Fax: 949-660-9262
info@ostomy.org
www.ostomy.org

An in-depth resource on how to adapt to an ostomy.

Dave Ruzdin, President
Diane Miterko, Advocacy Chair
Joan McGorry, Director of Administrative Services

6724 Treating IBD: A Patient's Guide to the Medical and Surgical Management
Crohn's & Colitis Foundation
733 Third Avenue, Ste 510
New York, NY 10017   212-685-3440
info@crohnscolitisfoundation.org
www.crohnscolitisfoundation.org

John Crosson, Chair
Michael Osso, President & CEO
Robert Territo, COO/CFO

6725 You're Bigger than It
Hotel Dieu Hospital
Ontario, Canada,   613-544-3310

This cartoon book offers a lively, brief introduction to the basics of living with IBD. Contact can be reached at extension 2400.

Newsletters

6726 Inner Circle
Reach Out for Youth with Ileitis and Colitis
15 Chemung Place
Jericho, NY 11753   516-822-8010
www.reachoutforyouth.org

Ulcerative Colitis / Pamphlets

Newsletter for youth with ileitis and colitis.

Pamphlets

6727 Bleeding in the Digestive Tract
Nat'l Digestive Diseases Information Clearinghouse
9000 Rockville Pike
Bethesda, MD 20892
301-496-3583
www.niddk.nih.gov

Informational fact sheet.
Griffin P. Rodgers, M.D., M.A.C.P., Director
Kevin Abbott, Program Director
Kristin Abraham, Program Director

6728 Crohn's Disease, Ulcerative Colitis, and Your Child
Crohn's & Colitis Foundation
733 Third Avenue, Ste 510
New York, NY 10017
800-932-2423
info@crohnscolitisfoundation.org
www.crohnscolitisfoundation.org

John Crosson, Chair
Michael Osso, President & CEO
Robert Territo, COO/CFO

6729 Guide for Children & Teenagers
Crohn's & Colitis Foundation
733 Third Avenue, Ste 510
New York, NY 10017
212-685-3440
800-932-2423
info@crohnscolitisfoundation.org
www.crohnscolitisfoundation.org

John Crosson, Chair
Michael Osso, President & CEO
Robert Territo, COO/CFO

6730 Inside Story
Reach Out for Youth with Illeitis and Colitis
15 Chemung Place
Jericho, NY 11753
516-822-8010

Educational brochure for youth with illeitis and colitis.

6731 Living with IBD: A Guide for Teenagers
Crohn's & Colitis Foundation
733 Third Avenue, Ste 510
New York, NY 10017
212-685-3440
800-932-2423
info@crohnscolitisfoundation.org
www.crohnscolitisfoundation.org

John Crosson, Chair
Michael Osso, President & CEO
Robert Territo, COO/CFO

6732 Questions and Answers About Ulcerative Colitis
Crohn's & Colitis Foundation
733 Third Avenue, Ste 510
New York, NY 10017
212-685-3440
800-932-2423
info@crohnscolitisfoundation.org
www.crohnscolitisfoundation.org

John Crosson, Chair
Michael Osso, President & CEO
Robert Territo, COO/CFO

6733 Teacher's Guide to Crohn's Disease & Ulcerative Colitis
Crohn's & Colitis Foundation
733 Third Avenue, Ste 510
New York, NY 10017
212-665-3440
800-932-2423
Fax: 212-779-4098
info@crohnscolitisfoundation.org
www.crohnscolitisfoundation.org

John Crosson, Chair
Michael Osso, President & CEO
Robert Territo, COO/CFO

6734 Ulcerative Colitis
National Organization for Rare Disorders
55 Kenosia Avenue
Danbury, CT 6810
203-744-0100
800-999-6673
Fax: 203-798-2291
orphan@rarediseases.org
www.rarediseases.org

Informational fact sheet.
Sheldon M. Schuster, Acting Chair
Peter L. Saltonstall, President & CEO
Pamela Gravin, COO

Description

6735 URTICARIA

Synonym: Hives

Involves the following Biologic System(s):

Dermatologic Disorders

Urticaria, more commonly known as hives, is a skin condition characterized by the development of raised, usually itchy (pruritic), white or reddish lesions (wheals). The wheals associated with urticaria vary in size and may sometimes blend together to form large, patchy skin lesions. Although individual lesions may disappear within minutes, hours, or days, new eruptions may continue to appear for weeks. Urticaria is considered to be a chronic skin disorder if wheals continue to appear for 6 weeks or longer.

Although the cause of urticaria is sometimes unknown, it is often the result of an immune or allergic response in which cells in the skin release various substances that create the effects of this condition. One of these substances is histamine, a protein produced by nerve cells and certain specialized blood and tissue cells. Released into the skin by these cells in response to an allergen or other triggering factor, histamine allows fluid to escape from small blood vessels into surrounding tissues to create the characteristic blister-like wheals associated with hives. The triggers for urticaria include allergic reactions caused by the ingestion of certain foods such as shellfish, strawberries, nuts, and eggs; drugs such as aspirin, penicillin, or codeine; and food dyes or other additives. Urticarial reactions may also be triggered by contact with pollens or other plant substances, insects, animals; chemicals or drugs that come into contact with the skin; certain drugs that are taken orally or by injection; blood transfusions; and insect bites or stings; well as by viral, bacterial, fungal, and parasitic infections; and by cold or heat, pressure on the skin, sunlight, and exercise.

Beyond this, hives may develop in conjunction with the swelling of certain areas of soft tissue (angioedema or angioneurotic edema) in deeper layers of the skin or in the upper respiratory tract, gastrointestinal tract, face and neck, hands and feet, and genitalia. A distinct disorder that may develop during early childhood is urticaria pigmentosa which is characterized by reddish-brown skin lesions occurring across the body, which change into hive-like lesions when stroked, rubbed, or scratched. Hives may also be associated with other systemic disorders and with certain inherited disorders such as amyloidosis; familial cold urticaria, a hereditary disorder characterized by urticaria occurring in response to coldness; and hereditary angioedema, a severe and potentially life-threatening form of angioedema.

The rash derived from poison ivy is commonly mistaken for urticaria, but is instead what is known as a contact dermatitis, caused by a toxin named urushiol that is present in this plant.

Hives often disappear rapidly and spontaneously, without treatment, but in some cases may be part of a more severe reaction known as an anaphylactic reaction, that may affect the heart and respiratory system as well as other organs and systems of the body. Consequently, children with acute, severe urticaria or those who experience difficulty in breathing or swallowing should be given immediate medical attention. Other treatment for urticaria depends upon its underlying cause. In most instances, treatment of urticaria is directed at alleviating its symptoms. This may be accomplished with the drugs known as antihistamines, which block the effects of histamine; with oral steroids, which can be safely given over a short period to relieve inflammation and swelling; and by topical ointments or creams than relieve itching and swelling when applied directly to the skin. Avoidance to the agents or factors that trigger urticaria is often the best defense. Reducing or avoiding stress is often effective in preventing or limiting this condition. Other treatment is symptomatic and supportive.

Government Agencies

6736 NIH/ Eunice Kennedy Shriver National Institute of Child Health & Human Development
P.O. Box 3006
Rockville, MD 20847

800-370-2943
Fax: 866-760-5947
www.nichd.nih.gov

Conducts and supports research on topics related to the health of children, adults, families and populations. Some of these topics include: developmental disabilities, growth and development, infant death, reproductive health and birth defects.

Diana W. Bianchi, Director
Alison Cernich, PhD, Deputy Director

6737 NIH/National Institute of Allergy and Infectious Diseases
5601 Fishers Lane, MSC 9806
Bethesda, MD 20892

301-496-5717
866-284-4107
Fax: 301-402-3573
TDD: 800-877-8339
ocpostoffice@niaid.nih.gov
www.niaid.nih.gov

The principal advisory board of the NIAID. The council is composed of physicians, scientists and representatives of the public and advises on the conduct and support or research, training and dissemination of health information regarding allergies and infectious diseases.

Anthony S. Fauci, MD, Director

6738 NIH/National Institute of Arthritis and Musculoskeletal and Skin Diseases
1 AMS Circle
Bethesda, MD 20892

301-495-4484
877-226-4267
Fax: 301-718-6366
TTY: 301-565-2966
niamsinfo@mail.nih.gov
www.niams.nih.gov

The mission of the NIAMS, a part of the NIH, is to support research into the causes, treatment and prevention of arthritis and musculoskeletal and skin diseases, the training of basic and clinical scientists to carry out this research, and the dissemination of information on research progress in these diseases.

Lindsey A. Criswell, MD, Director
Rick Phillips, Executive Officer

National Associations & Support Groups

6739 American Academy of Pediatrics
345 Park Blvd
Itasca, IL 60143

847-434-4000
800-433-9016
Fax: 847-434-8000
csc@aap.org
www.aap.org

The American Academy of Pediatrics and its member pediatricians are committed to the attainment of optimal physical, mental and social health and well-being for all infants, children, adolescents, and young adults.

Kyle E. Yasuda, MD, FAAP, President
Mark Del Monte, JD, CEO/Executive VP
Vera Tait, MD, FAAP, Chief Medical Officer

6740 **Genetic Alliance**
426400 Woodfield Road, Ste 189
Damascus, MD 20872

202-966-5557
Fax: 202-966-8553
info@geneticalliance.org
www.geneticalliance.org

World's leading nonprofit health advocacy organization committed to transforming health through genetics and promoting an environment of openness centered on the health of individuals, families, and communities.

Sharon Terry, CEO
Ruth Child, CFO
Natasha Bonhomme, Chief Strategy Officer

6741 **Society for Pediatric Dermatology**
8365 Keystone Crossing, Ste 107
Indianapolis, IN 46240

317-202-0224
Fax: 317-205-9481
info@pedsderm.net
www.pedsderm.net

The objective of the Society is to promote, develop and advance education, research and care of skin disease in all pediatric age groups.

Kent Lindeman, Executive Director

Web Sites

6742 **Allergy Web**
Asthma & Allergy Associates of Florida
7800 SW 87th Avenue, Suite C-340
Miami, FL 33173

305-595-0109
Fax: 305-595-7092
www.allergyweb.com

Provides information that may help you learn more about allergies and asthma.

Dr. Morris Beck, Founder
Mark Young, MD, Physician
Elena Ubals, MD, Physician

Journals

6743 **Pediatric Dermatology Journal**
Society for Pediatric Dermatology
8365 Keystone Crossing, Suite 107
Indianapolis, IN 46240

317-202-0224
Fax: 317-205-9481
info@pedsderm.net
www.pedsderm.net

Answers the need for new ideas and strategies for today's pediatrician or dermatologist.

6 issues/yr

Kent Lindeman, Executive Director

Ventricular Septal Defects / Web Sites

Description

6744 VENTRICULAR SEPTAL DEFECTS
Synonym: VSDs
Involves the following Biologic System(s):
Cardiovascular Disorders

Ventricular septal defects (VSDs) are considered the most common structural heart malformations, comprising up to 20 percent of all heart defects that are present at birth (congenital). VSDs are characterized by the presence of an abnormal opening in the fibrous muscular partition (septum) that separates the two lower pumping chambers (ventricles) of the heart. The ventricles are the chambers that pump blood out of the heart via large blood vessels (arteries). The pulmonary artery arises from the base of the right ventricle and carries oxygen-poor (deoxygenated) blood to the lungs, where the exchange of oxygen and carbon dioxide occurs. The aorta, the main artery of the body, arises from the base of the left ventricle and carries oxygen-rich (oxygenated) blood to the body's tissues.

In infants with ventricular septal defects, the abnormal opening in the septum between the two ventricles allows oxygenated blood in the left ventricle to flow into the right ventricle and recirculate to the lungs rather than to the rest of the body's tissues. Symptoms and findings may vary, depending upon the size and location of the ventricular septal defect and the associated effects on pulmonary blood pressure and flow. If the VSD is large, it may result in significantly increased blood flow through the lungs' blood vessels.

Small VSDs usually cause no associated symptoms and, in up to 50 percent of patients, may close spontaneously before school age. Small ventricular septal defects may be detected during a routine physical examination based upon a characteristic heart sound (heart murmur) heard with a stethoscope. In infants with larger VSDs, too much blood is pumped to the lungs. This may result in persistent elevation of blood pressure in the pulmonary circulation (pulmonary hypertension), enlargement of the heart (cardiomegaly), and abnormally rapid breathing (tachypnea). Additional symptoms and findings may include difficulty with lower respiratory tract infections, increased sweating, difficulties feeding, and failure to grow and gain weight at the expected rate (failure to thrive). When these symptoms and findings occur, the infant is said to have congestive heart failure (CHF). Large VSDs may be diagnosed upon a complete clinical examination and various specialized tests, such as x-ray studies, echocardiogram (ultrasound of the heart), electrocardiogram, or cardiac catheterization.

Children and adolescents with unclosed VSDs may be at an increased risk of bacterial infection of the lining of the heart (endocarditis). Such infection is rare before the age of two years. Due to the increased risk of bacterial endocarditis, affected individuals are cautioned to take antibiotic medication before dental visits and surgical procedures. After the VSD is successfully closed, preventive treatment is needed only during a six-month healing period. Closing small ventricular septal defects may not be needed. They often close on their own in childhood or adolescence. But if the opening is large, even in patients with few symptoms, closing the hole in the first two years of life is recommended to prevent serious problems later.

In some patients, VSDs may occur in association with certain underlying genetic syndromes, chromosomal abnormalities, or malformation syndromes that are caused by exposure to certain infectious agents, medications, or other environmental factors (teratogenic syndromes).

National Associations & Support Groups

6745 American Academy of Pediatrics
345 Park Blvd
Itasca, IL 60143

847-434-4000
800-433-9016
Fax: 847-434-8000
csc@aap.org
www.aap.org

The American Academy of Pediatrics and its member pediatricians are committed to the attainment of optimal physical, mental and social health and well-being for all infants, children, adolescents, and young adults.

Kyle E. Yasuda, MD, FAAP, President
Mark Del Monte, JD, CEO/Executive VP
Vera Tait, MD, FAAP, Chief Medical Officer

6746 American Heart Association
7272 Greenville Avenue
Dallas, TX 75231

214-570-5978
800-242-8721
www.heart.org

The mission of the American Heart Associate is to build healthier lives, free of cardiovascular diseases and stroke.

Nancy Brown, CEO
Mitchell S.V. Elkind, President
Suzie Upton, Chief Operating Officer

Web Sites

6747 Southern Illinois University School of Medicine
PO Box 19639
Springfield, IL 62794

217-545-8000
800-342-5748
admin@siuhealthcare.org
www.siumed.edu

The mission of SUI School of Medicine is to assist the people of central and southern Illinois in meeting their present and future needs through education, clinical service and research.

6748 Yale University School of Medicine
www.info.med.yale.edu

www.info.med.yale.edu

A site that offers information on Ventricular Septal Defects and other congenital heart conditions.

Description

6749 VIOLENCE BY CHILDREN & TEENAGERS
Involves the following Biologic System(s):
Behavioral/Developmental/Psychiatric Disorders

Some children and teenagers prey on vulnerable people, exhibiting antisocial behavior, neurological dysfunctions, and mental illnesses. These youths may assault other children or adults for a variety of reasons, ranging from invoking fear as a form of entertainment to causing bodily harm as retribution for perceived wrongs such as social ostracism.

Criminal behavior by children and teenagers doubled during the late 1980s and early 1990s. Although homicide rates for teenage perpetrators began to decline in the United States by 1997, youth violence remained an urgent issue. By the beginning of the twenty-first century, violent youths were committing callous acts at increasingly younger ages. They also behaved more extremely with regard to weapons used or number of victims attacked during violent sprees. Crimes such as school shootings targeted individuals both known and unfamiliar to perpetrators. The fatal school shooting at Columbine High School in 1999 prompted many studies of why teenagers become violent.

Violent youths represent varying social classes and ethnicities, living in both rural and urban areas. Young males are twice as likely to act violently outside the home than are young females, but both genders are equally likely to be violent toward their families.

Violent tendencies sometimes emerge when children are toddlers. Aggressive children may fight with other youngsters, act up in class, challenge authority figures, or steal. Some sadistically abuse animals. Such aberrant behaviors can intensify during adolescence.

Researchers offer contrasting theories about why some youths become violent. Violent youths may suffer from severe mental illnesses, display disruptive behavior disorders or antisocial personalities, or have experienced brain damage. Some researchers suggest that brain circuits containing the neurotransmitter serotonin have malfunctioned in violent youths. A few researchers speculate that some infants have innate repressed violent characteristics that develop when the child encounters biological or psychological triggers, such as sexual or physical abuse, illegal substances, or peer pressure.

Authorities agree that many violent children and teenagers have been exposed to violence in their homes or communities. Inadequate or abusive parenting can prevent children from learning appropriate values of right and wrong. Neglected or abused children can feel emotionally abandoned and become self-centered. Egocentric youths are more likely to lack consciences and to be incapable of feeling empathy or compassion for others. Emotions such as depression, frustration, rage, and shame can intensify a child's perceived inadequacies. Many violent youths are alienated from emotional support systems and feel isolated and discriminated against. They may become desensitized to violence or emotionally numb and seek excitement through violence. Some are suicidal and resigned to accepting and participating in violence.

Youth violence can be categorized into four major types. **Situational violence**, one of the most common types of violence committed by children and teenagers, is sparked by an event that upsets or enrages the victimizer. For example, a student might assault a teacher who gave a failing grade. **Relational violence** occurs when a child or teenager is violent toward a relative or friend with whom he or she has a personal dispute. **Dating violence** is one of the most prevalent forms of this type of violence, as when a teenage boy attacks a girl who terminates their relationship. **Predatory violence** describes thefts and muggings involving violence or violent activities carried out to prove loyalty and ensure acceptance by a group. Violence connected to competition, drug dealing, riots, and gang fights and the use of concealed weapons with intent to maim or murder is considered predatory. Less than 1 percent of juvenile cases involve psychopathological violence, which involves perpetrators who probably are neurologically damaged or mentally ill and who commit extremely violent acts. These individuals require pharmaceutical and management therapy. Other violent acts that may be committed by youths include hate crimes, vandalism, bombings, or activism such as ecoterrorism. Some violent youths are attention seekers who believe that they will become celebrities through their acts.

While engaged in violent acts, youths may be dissociated from what they are doing and may feel as if they are experiencing a dreamlike or fantastical state instead of reality. Violent youths may verbally antagonize and ridicule their victims, who are often people whom the perpetrators view as weak, such as young children, the elderly, and handicapped individuals. Sometimes, groups of youths plan assaults to surround and attack one person. Preteens have raped or murdered children their own age or younger. Some children who commit violent acts are not sufficiently mature, intellectually and morally, to realize that their actions can hurt other people. In 2000, a six-year-old who shot a classmate at a Michigan school expressed confusion when she died.

Mental health professionals stress that children who display violent behaviors should be identified as young as possible so that intervention measures can be implemented to prevent them from harming other youths. Facilities that treat violent juvenile offenders include boot camps, detention centers, wilderness programs, and group or private psychotherapy sessions. Both public and private schools attempt to identify emotionally disturbed students who might interfere with the learning process of other students by disrupting classes and challenging faculty members.

Violent youths who are mentally ill should receive counseling and medication. Other options are available to those whose behavior has social and emotional roots. These youths may be enrolled in programs that promote self-esteem, emotional resilience, and self-control. Parents can teach their children appropriate coping techniques to prevent violence. Communities and churches can provide children with supervised recreational activities during afternoons, which are the hours when youths are most likely to act violently. Mentoring programs can demonstrate alternatives to destructive behavior. Peer counseling has been shown to be an effective deterrent to violence. Violence-prevention curricula can teach children to resolve conflicts creatively and help them develop skills to control emotional outbursts.

Government Agencies

6750 NIH/National Institute of Mental Health
6001 Executive Blvd, Rm 6200, MSC 9663
Bethesda, MD 20892
866-615-6464
Fax: 301-443-4279
TTY: 301-443-8431
nimhinfo@nih.gov
www.nimh.nih.gov

The mission of NIMH is to transform the understanding and treatment of mental illnesses through basic and clinical research, paving the way for prevention, recovery, and cure.

Joshua A. Gordon, MD, PhD, Director
Shelli Avenevoli, PhD, Deputy Director

National Associations & Support Groups

6751 American Academy of Child and Adolescent Psychiatry
3615 Wisconsin Avenue NW
Washington, DC 20016
202-966-7300
Fax: 202-464-0131
www.aacap.org

The AACAP (American Academy of Child and Adolescent Psychiatry) is the leading national professional medical association dedicated to the promotion of healthy development for children, adolescents, and families.

Heidi B. Fordi, Executive Director

6752 American Academy of Family Physicians
11400 Tomahawk Creek Parkway
Leawood, KS 66211
800-274-2237
aafp@aafp.org
www.aafp.org

The mission of the AAFP is to improve the health of patients, families, and communities by serving the needs of members with professionalism and creativity.

R. Shawn Martin, EVP & Executive Director
Shannon M. Scott, Deputy EVP & Chief Strategy Officer
Charlotte Kerner, Chief Financial Officer

6753 American Academy of Pediatrics
345 Park Blvd
Itasca, IL 60143
847-434-4000
800-433-9016
Fax: 847-434-8000
csc@aap.org
www.aap.org

The organization is committed to the optimal physical, mental, and social health and well-being for all infants, children, adolescents, and young adults.

Kyle E. Yasuda, MD, FAAP, President
Mark Del Monte, JD, CEO/Executive VP
Vera Tait, MD, FAAP, Chief Medical Officer

6754 American College of Neuropsychopharmacology
5034-A Thoroughbred Lane
Brentwood, TN 37027
615-324-2360
Fax: 615-523-1715
acnp@acnp.org
www.acnp.org

The American College of Neuropsychopharmacology (ACNP), founded in 1961, is a professional society in brain, behavior, and psychopharmacology research. The field of neuropsychopharmacology involves the evaluation of the effects of natural and synthetic compounds upon the brain, mind, and human behavior.

Sarah Timm, Executive Director

6755 American Congress of Obstetricians and Gynecologists
409 12th Street SW
Washington, DC 20024
202-638-5577
800-673-8444
www.acog.org

Founded in 1951 in Chicago, Illinois, The College has over 58,000 members and is the nation's leading group of professionals providing health care for women. Based in Washington, DC, it is a private, voluntary, nonprofit membership organization.

Maureen G. Phipps, Chief Executive Officer
Rob Batarla, Chief Financial Officer
AnnaMarie Connolly, Chief of Education/Academic Affairs

6756 American Counseling Association
PO Box 31110
Alexandria, VA 22310
800-347-6647
Fax: 800-473-2329
ACAMemberServices@counseling.org
www.counseling.org

Represents professional counselors in various practice settings, and stands ready to serve more than 55,000 members with the resources they need to make a difference. From webinars, publications, and journals to Conference education sessions and legislative action alerts, ACA is where counseling professionals turn for powerful, credible content and support.

Shawn Boynes, Chief Executive Officer

6757 American Medical Association
AMA Plaza, 330 North Wabash Ave., Suite 39300
Chicago, IL 60611
312-464-4782
800-262-3211
www.ama-assn.org

AMA is dedicated to ensuring sustainable physician practices that result in better health outcomes for patients.

James L. Madara, MD, CEO/EVP
Bernard L. Hengesbaugh, Chief Operating Officer
Kenneth J. Sharigian, SVP

6758 American Mental Health Foundation (AMHF)
PO Box 3
Riverdale, NY 10471
USA
212-737-9027
americanmentalhealthfoundation.org

Dedicated to the extensive and intensive research in the theories and techniques of treatment of emotional illness and to the implementation of reforms in the mental health system. Efforts have resulted in development of better and less expensive treatment methods. Findings are disseminated in English and other major languages.

Sister Joan Curtin. CND, Director
Evander Lomke, President/Executive Director
Eugene Gollogly, Vice President

6759 American Psychiatric Association
800 Maine Avenue SW, Suite 900
Washington, DC 20024
202-559-3900
apa@psych.org
www.psychiatry.org

It is a medical specialty society representing growing membership of more than 36,000 psychiatrists.

6760 American Psychological Association
750 First St. NE
Washington, DC 20002
202-336-5500
800-374-2721
TTY: 202-336-6123
www.apa.org

The mission is to advance the creation, communication and application of psychological knowledge to benefit society and improve people's lives.

Arthur C. Evans Jr, PhD, CEO/EVP

6761 American Public Health Association
800 I Street, NW
Washington, DC 20001
202-777-2742
Fax: 202-777-2534
TTY: 202-777-2500
www.apha.org

APHA champions the health of all people and all communities. They aim to strengthen the public health profession and speak out for public health issues and policies backed by science.

Georges C. Benjamin, MD, Executive Director
Kemi Oluwafemi, MBA, CPA, Chief Financial Officer
Susan Polan, PhD, Associate Executive Director

6762 American School Counselor Association
1101 King Street, Ste 310
Alexandria, VA 22314
703-683-2722
asca@schoolcounselor.org
www.schoolcounselor.org

Violence by Children & Teenagers / National Associations & Support Groups

The mission of ASCA is to represent professional school counselors and to promote professionalism and ethical practices.

Jill Cook, Executive Director
Amanda Fitzgerald, Assistant Deputy Executive Director
Kathleen M Rakestraw, Director of Communications

6763 Association for Behavioral and Cognitive Therapies
305 7th Avenue, 16th Floor
New York, NY 10001
212-647-1890
Fax: 212-647-1865
www.abct.org

Formerly known as the Association for Advancement of Behavior Therapy; this organization is concerned with the application of behavioral and cognitive sciences to understanding human behavior, developing interventions to enhance the human condition, and promoting the appropriate utilization of these interventions.

Mary Jane Eimer, CAE, Executive Director
Rachel Lamb, Membership & Marketing Manager
Ewan Johnson, Senior Communications Manager

6764 Center for Disabilities and Development
University of Iowa Stead Family Children's Hospita
100 Hawkins Drive
Iowa City, IA 52242
319-353-6900
877-686-0031
Fax: 319-356-7700
cdd-webmaster@uiowa.edu
www.uichildrens.org/cdd/

A trusted resource for healthcare, training, research and information for people with disabilities that include: behavior disorders, brain injury, cerebral palsy, diabetes, down syndrome, learning disabilities, sleep disorders and spina bifida.

Dianne McBrien, MD, Medical Director

6765 Center for Mental Health Services
5600 Fishers Lane
Rockville, MD 20857
240-276-1310
www.samhsa.gov

Encourages a range of programs such as systems of care to respond to the increasing number of mental, emotional, and behavioral problems among children. Supports outreach and case management programs for the thousands of Americans who are homeless and the improvement of these services.

Anita Everett, MD, Director

6766 Child Trends
7315 Wisconsin Avenue, Suite 1200
Bethesda, MD 20814
240-223-9200
www.childtrends.org

Child Trends is a nonprofit, nonpartisan research center that provides valuable information and insights on the well-being of children and youth.

Carol Emig, President
Natalia E. Pane, Chief Operating Officer

6767 Digital Wellness Lab
Boston Children's Hospital
300 Longwood Avenue
Boston, MA 02115
617-355-5420
Fax: 617-730-0004
dwl@childrens.harvard.edu
digitalwellnesslab.org

Digital Wellness Lab at Boston Children's Hospital and Harvard Medical School is on a mission to understand and promote positive and healthy digital media experiences for young people, from birth through young adulthood.

Michael Rich, MPH, Director, Founder
David S. Bickham, PhD, Research Scientist Lead
Cori Scott, MBA, EdM, Administrative Director

6768 Family Online Safety Institute
www.fosi.org
202-775-0158
www.fosi.org

The Family Online Safety Institute brings a unique, international perspective to the potential risks, harms as well as the rewards of our online lives.

Stephen Balkam, Founder & CEO
Emily Mulder, Program Director
Maria Conticelli, Chief of Staff

6769 Foundation for Child Development
475 Riverside Drive, Suite 248
New York, NY 10115
212-867-5777
info@fcd-us.org
fcd-us.org

There mission is to harness the power of research to ensure that all children benefit from early learning experiences that affirm their individual, family, and community assets, fortify them against harmful consequences arising from economic instability and social exclusion, and that strengthen their developmental potential.

Vivian Tseng, President and CEO
Sherice Brammer, Communications Officer
Andrea Kent, Program Officer

6770 International Society for Research in Child and Adolescent Psychopathology
University of British Columbia, Psychology Dept.
2136 W Mall
Vancouver, BC
Canada
ISRCAP@gmail.com
isrcap.org

The International Society for Research in Child and Adolescent Psychopathology (ISRCAP) was founded in 1988 by Herbert C. Quay, so that mental health professionals interested in child psychopathology would have a forum to exchange ideas concerning the nature and treatment of childhood mental disorders.

6771 Mental Health America
500 Montgomery Street, Ste 820
Alexandria, VA 22314
703-684-7722
800-969-6642
Fax: 703-684-5968
www.mentalhealthamerica.net

MHA, the leading advocacy organization addressing the full spectrum of mental and substance use conditions and their effects nationwide, works to inform, advocate and enable access to quality behavioral health services for all Americans.

Paul Gionfriddo, President/CEO
Whitney Ball, Assoc. Dir., Marketing/Outreach
Sachin Doshi, Sr. Dir, Finance/Operations

6772 NADD: National Association for the Dually Diagnosed
12 Hurley Avenue
Kingston, NY 12401
845-331-4336
800-331-5362
Fax: 845-331-4569
info@thenadd.org
www.thenadd.org

Nonprofit organization designed to promote the interests of professional and care providers for individuals who have the coexistence of mental illness and intellectual disabilities. NADD provides conferences, educational services and training materials to professionals, parents, concerned citizens and service organizations.

Jeanne Farr, CEO
Michelle Jordan, Office Manager
Edward Seliger, Project Coordinator

6773 NIH/National Institute of Mental Health
6001 Executive Blvd, Rm 6200, MSC 9663
Bethesda, MD 20892
866-615-6464
Fax: 301-443-4279
TTY: 301-443-8431
NIMHinfo@mail.nih.gov
www.nimh.nih.gov

The mission of NIMH is to transform the understanding and treatment of mental illnesses through basic and clinical research, paving the way for prevention, recovery, and cure.

Joshua A. Gordon, MD, PhD, Director
Shelli Avenevoli, PhD, Deputy Director

Violence by Children & Teenagers / Research Centers

6774 National Alliance on Mental Illness (NAMI)
4301 Wilson Blvd., Suite 300
Arlington, VA 22203
703-525-7600
800-999-6264
info@nami.org
www.nami.org

NAMI provides advocacy, education, support and public awareness so that all individuals and families affected by mental illness can build better lives.

Daniel H. Gillison, CEO
David Levy, CFO
Ken Duckworth, Chief Medical Officer

6775 National Association for the Education of Young Children
1401 H Street NW, Suite 600
Washington, DC 20005
202-232-8777
800-424-2460
www.naeyc.org

NAEYC promotes high-quality early learning for all children, birth through age 8, by connecting practice, policy, and research. We advance a diverse, dynamic early childhood profession and support all who care for, educate, and work on behalf of young children.

Michelle Kang, Chief Executive Officer
Treva Bustow, Sr Director, Membership & Marketing
Susan Friedman, Sr Director, Publishing & Content

6776 National Association of School Psychologists
4340 East West Highway, Suite 402
Bethesda, MD 20814
301-657-0270
866-331-NASP
Fax: 301-657-0275
www.nasponline.org

NASP empowers school psychologists by advancing effective practices to improve students' learning, behavior, and mental health.

Kathleen Minke, Executive Director
Pavel Obgolz, Chief Operating Officer

6777 National Center for Injury Prevention and Control
1600 Clifton Road
Atlanta, GA 30329
800-232-4636
TTY: 888-232-6348
www.cdc.gov/injury

CDC works to protect America from health, safety and security threats, both foreign and in the U.S. Whether diseases start at home or abroad, are chronic or acute, curable or preventable, human error or deliberate attack, CDC fights disease and supports communities and citizens to do the same.

6778 National Federation of Families
15800 Crabbs Branch Way, Suite 300
Rockville, MD 20855
240-403-1901
ffcmh@ffcmh.org
www.ffcmh.org

The National family run organization is dedicated exclusively to helping children with mental health needs and their families achieve a better quality of life.

Lynda Gargan, PhD, Executive Director

6779 National Medical Association
8403 Colesville Road, Suite 820
Silver Spring, MD 20910
202-347-1895
www.nmanet.org

The National Medical Association (NMA) is the collective voice of African American physicians and the leading force for parity and justice in medicine and the elimination of disparities in health.

Martin Hamlette, JD, MHA, Executive Director

Research Centers

6780 Menninger Child & Family Program
Menninger Clinic
2801 Gessner Drive, PO Box 809045
Houston, TX 77280
713-275-5000
800-351-9058
Fax: 713-275-5117
www.menninger.edu

Menninger's research strategies are developed through the Menninger Child & Family Program. Projects are designed to develop a better understanding of the mind in order to more effectively treat mental disorders.

Ian Aitken, Ceo

6781 National Technical Assistance Center for Children's Mental Health
Georgetown University
Center for Child and Human Development Georgetown
Washington, DC 20057
202-687-5000
Fax: 202-687-8899
TDD: 202-687-5503
gucdc@georgetown.edu
www.gucchd.georgetown.edu/67211.html

Devoted to helping states, tribes, territories, and communities discover, apply, and sustain innovative and collaborative solutions that improve the social, emotional, and behavioral well being of children and families.

James Wotring MSW, Director

6782 Research & Training Center for Children's Mental Health at University of South FL
Louis de la Parte Florida Mental Health Institute
13301 Bruce B. Downs Boulevard
Tampa, FL 33612
813-974-3154
Fax: 813-974-3078
friedman@fmhi.usf.edu
www.rtckids.fmhi.usf.edu/default.cfm

Working towards increasing the effectiveness of service systems by strengthening the empirical base for such systems through research and dissemination to key audiences. With its new, five-year research program, the Center expands its mission with an integrated research, training, and dissemination program targeted specifically at implementation issues for developing effective systems of care.

Robert M. Friedman, Ph.D, Center Director
Albert Duchnowski, Ph.D, Deputy Director
Krista Kutash, Ph.D, Deputy Director

6783 Research and Training Center on Family Support and Children's Mental Health
1600 SW 4th Avenue, Suite 900
Portland, OR 97201
503-725-4040
Fax: 503-725-4180
flemingd@pdx.edu
www.rtc.pdx.edu

Funded to pursue an integrated set of research, training, technical assistance, and dissemination activities. The center's work will focus on two related themes; community integration for children and adolescents with emotional and behavioral disorders and their families; and strengthening family and youth participation in child and adolescent mental health services.

Donna Flemming, Information Director

6784 Technical Assistance Partnership for Child and Family Mental Health
1000 Thomas Jefferson Street NW, Suite 400
Washington, DC 20007
202-403-6827
Fax: 202-342-5007
tapartnership@air.org
www.tapartnership.org

A staff of family members and professionals with extensive practice experience, grounded in an organization with vast research experience in children with serious emotional disturbance and their families.

Sharon Hunt, Deputy Director of Operations
Jeffrey Poirier, Continuous Quality Improvement
Regenia Hicks, Project Director Continuous Quality

Violence by Children & Teenagers / Conferences

Conferences

6785 **American School Counselor Association Annual Conference**
1101 King Street, Suite 310
Alexandria, VA 22314
703-683-2722
800-306-4722
Fax: 703-997-7572
asca@schoolcounselor.org
www.schoolcounselor.org

The mission of ASCA is to represent professional school counselors and to promote professionalism and ethical practices.

3,000 Attendees

Richard Wong, Executive Director
Jennifer Walsh, Director, Education & Training
Kathleen M Rakestraw, Director of Communications

6786 **FFCMH Annual Conference**
National Federation of Families
15800 Crabbs Branch Way, Suite 300
Rockville, MD 20855
240-403-1901
ffcmh@ffcmh.org
www.ffcmh.org

The only national conference dedicated solely to supporting families whose children - of any age - experience mental health and/or substance use challenges during their lifetime.

November

Lynda Gargan, PhD, Executive Director

6787 **NADD Annual Conference & Exhibit Show**
National Association for the Dually Diagnosed
12 Hurley Avenue
Kingston, NY 12401
845-331-4336
800-331-5362
Fax: 845-331-4569
info@thenadd.org
www.thenadd.org

Educating professionals, families and clients of services on standard and state-of-the-art information across many specialties; Enhancing specific skills required to provide maximum benefit to individuals with special or specific cognitive and/or developmental needs; Providing a forum for an exchange of ideas and information among professionals, families and those who may receive services.

Fall

Jeanne Farr, CEO
Michelle Jordan, Office Manager
Edward Seliger, Project Coordinator

6788 **NAMI Convention**
National Alliance on Mental Illness
3803 N Fairfax Drive, Suite 100
Arlington, VA 22203
703-524-7600
888-999-6264
Fax: 703-524-9094
TDD: 703-516-7227
info@nami.org
www.nami.org

The NAMI Convention is packed with information, chances to network, leadership development opportunities, and lots more.

Summer

Richele Keas, Senior Mgr, Media Relations

Audio Video

6789 **Managing the Defiant Child**
Courage To Change Publishing
PO Box 486
Wilkes-Barres, PA 18703
800-440-4003
Fax: 800-772-6499
www.couragetochange.com

An information-packed video brings to life a proven approach to behavior management. Shows clinicians, school practitioners, teachers, parents and students how enhanced parenting skills can dramatically improve the parent-child relationship.

Russell A Barkley, Editor

6790 **Understanding and Treating the Hereditary Psychiatric Spectrum Disorders**
Hope Press
PO Box 188
Duarte, CA 91009
818-303-0644
800-321-4039
Fax: 818-358-3520
hopepress.com

Learn with ten hours of audio tapes from a two day seminar given in May 1997 by David E Comings MD. Tapes cover: ADHD, Tourette syndrome, Obsessive-Compulsive Disorder, Conduct Disorder, Oppositional Defiant Disorder, Autism and other Hereditary Psychiatric Spectrum Disorders. Eight audio tapes.

David E Comings, MD, Presenter

6791 **Understanding the Defiant Child**
Courage To Change
PO Box 486
Wilkes-Barres, PA 18703
800-440-4003
Fax: 800-772-6499
www.couragetochange.com

Provides a vivid picture of what we know about Oppositional Defiant Disorder and presents real-life scenes of family interactions and commentary from parents. Illuminates the nature and causes of ODD, why it should be dealt with early, and what can be done. Ideal viewing for school practitioners, clinical child psychologists, counselors and parents coping with a defiant child.

Russell A Barkley, Editor

Web Sites

6792 **ADDitude**
108 W 39th Street, Suite 805
New Work, NY 10018
646-366-0830
customerservice@additudemag.com
www.additudemag.com

Founded in 1998 by Ellen Kingsley, an award-winning journalist with a unique ability to convey credible information with empathy and inspiration, ADDitude magazine has provided clear, accurate, user-friendly information and advice from the leading experts and practitioners in mental health.

Susan Caughman, Publisher
Wayne Kalyn, Editor

6793 **BookRags**
www.bookrags.com

www.bookrags.com

BookRags was founded in 1999 by two recent college graduates interested in providing on-demand educational resources to students around the world. Launched with just 40 book notes, BookRags has expanded over the past seven years into one of the largest, most respected student education websites, with over 4 million unique pages of content.

6794 **Child Welfare Information Gateway**
www.childwelfare.gov

www.childwelfare.gov

Child Welfare Information Gateway promotes the safety, permanency, and well-being of children, youth, and families by connecting child welfare, adoption, and related professionals as well as the public to information, resources, and tools covering topics on child welfare, child abuse and neglect, out-of-home care, adoption, and more.

6795 **Circle of Parents**
www.circleofparents.org

www.circleofparents.org

Circle of Parents provides a friendly, supportive environment led by parents and other caregivers. It's a place where anyone in a parenting role can openly discuss the successes and challenges of raising children. Where they can find and share support.

Julie Rivnak-McAdam, CEO

6796 **Conductdisorders.com**
www.conductdisorders.com

www.conductdisorders.com

Site for parents, teachers, and family members who deal with a child with one of the defined behavioral disorders.

6797 **Empowering Parents**
www.empoweringparents.com

www.empoweringparents.com

Empowering Parents has been giving the readers straight talk and real results since 2007. They are committed to providing parents and caregivers with sound advice using the same Cognitive Behavioral Therapy principles that The Total Transformation and there other programs are based upon.

Elisabeth Wilkins, Editor

6798 **Enough Is Enough**
www.enough.org

www.enough.org

The Enough Is Enoughr mission is to Make the Internet Safer for Children and Families. EIE is dedicated to continuing to raise public awareness about online dangers, specifically the dangers of Internet pornography and sexual predators.

Dee Jepsen, President Emeritus
Donna Rice Hughes, President and CEO

6799 **FRIENDS**
friendsnrc.org

friendsnrc.org

FRIENDS, the National Center for Community-Based Child Abuse Prevention (CBCAP), provides training and technical assistance to Federally funded CBCAP Programs. This site serves as a resource to those programs and to the rest of the Child Abuse Prevention community.

Linda Baker, Program Director
Dr. Valerie Spiva Collins, Training/ Technical Assis Sup.
Casandra Firman, Technical Assistance Coordinator

6800 **Find Counseling.com**
www.findcounseling.com

www.findcounseling.com

Since inception in 1996, the Find Counseling.com Network is a resource for those in need of mental health services. They enable users to find the therapist who is right for them.

6801 **FindYouthInfo.gov**
www.findyouthinfo.gov

www.findyouthinfo.gov

FindYouthInfo.gov is the U.S. government Web site that helps you create, maintain, and strengthen effective youth programs.

6802 **Guide to Psychology and its Practice (A)**
www.guidetopsychology.com

www.guidetopsychology.com

This website provides freewill information about the practice of Clinical Psychology, especially in regard to psychotherapy, counseling, self-growth, and mental health in general.

Raymond Lloyd Richmond, Ph.D., Author

6803 **Helpguide.org**
www.helpguide.org

www.helpguide.org

Guide for improving mental and emotional health.

Robert Segal, M.A., Publisher/ Managing Director
Jeanne Segal, Ph.D., Publisher/ Editorial Director
Melinda Smith, M.A., Senior Editor

6804 **Internet Mental Health**
www.mentalhealth.com

www.mentalhealth.com

Our goal is to improve understanding, diagnosis, and treatment of mental illness throughout the world.

Phillip W. Long, M.D., Psychiatrist

6805 **NADD: National Association for the Dually Diagnosed**
12 Hurley Avenue
Kingston, NY 12401

845-331-4336
800-331-5362
Fax: 845-331-4569
info@thenadd.org
www.thenadd.org

Nonprofit organization designed to promote the interests of professional and care providers for individuals who have the coexistence of mental illness and intellectual disabilities. NADD provides conferences, educational services and training materials to professionals, parents, concerned citizens and service organizations.

Jeanne Farr, CEO
Michelle Jordan, Office Manager
Edward Seliger, Project Coordinator

6806 **Online Mendelian Inheritance in Man**
McKusick-Nathans Institue of Genetic Medicine-JHU
Baltimore, MD 21205

www.omim.org

This database is a catalog of human genes and genetic disorders.

Ada Hamosh, MD, Scientific Director

6807 **Online Parenting Coach**
www.onlineparentingcoach.com

www.onlineparentingcoach.com

A resource for children, parents, teachers, mental health professionals, and others who deal with the challenges of Oppositional Defiant Disorder, Conduct Disorder, ADHD and other childhood disorders.

6808 **ParentsMedGuide.org**
www.parentsmedguide.org

www.parentsmedguide.org

Resources for parents developed by the American Psychiatric Association and the American Academy of Child and Adolescent Psychiatry.

6809 **Psych Central**
www.psychcentral.com

talkback@psychcentral.com
www.psychcentral.com

Since 1995, an award-winning website has been run by mental health professionals offering reliable, trusted information and over 200 support groups to consumers.

John M. Grohol, CEO & Founder

6810 **PsychAlive**
www.psychalive.org

www.psychalive.org

PsychAlive draws on the contribution of leading psychology experts who specialize in a broad spectrum of subjects related to our emotional well-being.

6811 **StopBullying.gov**
www.stopbullying.gov

www.stopbullying.gov

StopBullying.gov provides information from various government agencies on what bullying is, what cyberbullying is, who is at risk, and how you can prevent and respond to bullying.

6812 **The Successful Parent**
www.thesuccessfulparent.com

www.thesuccessfulparent.com

The impetus for The Successful Parent comes from 60 years of combined experience in providing psychotherapy for parents, children, and families.

6813 Violence Prevention Works
www.violencepreventionworks.org

www.violencepreventionworks.org

6814 Violentkids.com
www.violentkids.com

www.violentkids.com

Dr. Helen Smith

6815 domesticshelters.org
www.domesticshelters.org

www.domesticshelters.org

A searchable directory of domestic violence service providers in the United States providing users the ability to find services best suited to their needs and providing domestic violence providers with invaluable online resources.

Book Publishers

6816 Aggression and Violence Throughout the Life Span
Sage Publications
2455 Teller Road
Thousand Oaks, CA 91320

800-818-7243
Fax: 800-583-2665
info@sagepub.com
www.sagepub.com

A unique life span developmental perspective on some of society's most perplexing and pernicious problems, aggressive and violent behaviors. Examines issues in the development of aggressive behaviors in young children, the progression of these behaviors to older children and adolescents and cause, effect and treatment of aggressive and violent behaviors in adults. Integrates empirical research with clinical applications.

360 pages Softcover
ISBN: 0-803945-51-5

Sara Miller McCune, Founder/Chairman
Blaise R Simqu, President/CEO
Chris Hickok, Senior Vice President/CFO

6817 Antisocial Behavior by Young People
Cambridge University Press
32 Avenue of the Americas
New York, NY 10013

617-264-2300
Fax: 617-264-2323
www.cambridge.org

Written by a child psychiatrist, a criminologist and a social psychologist, this book is a major international review of research evidence on anti-social behavior. Covers all aspects of the field, including descriptions of different types of delinquency and time trends, the state of knowledge on the individuals, social-psychological and cultural factors involved and recent advances in prevention and intervention.

490 pages Paperback
ISBN: 0-521646-08-1

Michael Rutter, Editor
Ann Hagell, Editor
Henri Giller, Editor

6818 Conduct Disorders in Childhood and Adolescence (Developmental Clinical)
Sage Publications
2455 Teller Road
Thousand Oaks, CA 91320

800-818-7243
800-818-7243
Fax: 800-583-2665
info@sagepub.com
www.sagepub.com

Conduct disorder is a clinical problem among children and adolescents that includes aggressive acts, theft, vandalism, firesetting, running away, truancy, defying authority and other antisocial behaviors. This book describes the nature of conduct disorder and what is currently known from research and clinical work. Topics include psychiatric diagnosis, parent psychopathology and child-rearing processes.

192 pages Hardcover
ISBN: 0-803971-81-8

Sara Miller McCune, Founder/Chairman
Blaise R Simqu, President/CEO
Chris Hickok, Senior Vice President/CFO

6819 Conduct Disorders in Children and Adolescents
American Psychiatric Publishing
1000 Wilson Boulevard, Suite 1825
Arlington, VA 22009

703-907-7322
800-368-5777
Fax: 703-907-1091
appi@psych.org
www.appi.org

Examines the phenomenology, etiology, and diagnosis of conduct disorders, and describes therapeutic and preventive interventions. Includes the range of treatments now available, including individual, family, group, and behavior therapy; hospitalization; and residential treatment.

1995 414 pages Hardcover
ISBN: 0-880485-17-5

G Pirooz Sholevar, MD, Editor

6820 Conduct Problem/Emotional Problem Interventions: A Holistic Perspective
Slosson Educational Publications
PO Box 544
East Aurora, NY 14052

716-625-0930
888-756-7766
Fax: 800-655-3840
slosson@slosson.com
www.slosson.com

This innovative book is broad in scope and addresses the now what sensation that many professionals get when charged with the education or treatment of individuals with conduct disorders or emotional disturbance. Distinct intervention and screening strategies and patient involvement strategies are offered in clear and practical terms.

Edward J Kelly, Editor

6821 Disruptive Behavior Disorders in Children and Adolescents
Robert L Hendren, DO, author

American Psychiatric Publishing
1000 Wilson Boulevard, Suite 1825
Arlington, VA 22209

703-907-7322
800-368-5777
Fax: 703-907-1091
appi@psych.org
www.appi.org

Discusses attention deficit hyperactivity disorder, conduct disorder, substance abuse and disruptive behavior disorders. Examines the relationship between violence and mental illness in adolescence.

1999 216 pages Paperback
ISBN: 0-880489-60-7

6822 Preventing Antisocial Behavior: Interventions
Guilford Press
72 Spring Street
New York, NY 10012

212-431-9800
800-365-7006
Fax: 212-966-6708
info@guilford.com
www.guilford.com

Establishes the crucial link between theory, measurement and intervention. Brings together a collection of studies that utilize experimental approaches for evaluating intervention programs, both the feasibility, and necessity of independent evaluation. Also shows how the information obtained in such studies can be used to test and refine prevailing theories about human behavior in general, and behavior changes in particular.

1992 391 pages
ISBN: 0-898628-82-1
Joan McCord, Editor
Richard Tremblay, Editor

6823 Skills Training for Children with Behavior Disorders
Courage To Change
PO Box 486
Wilkes-Barres, PA 18703
800-440-4003
Fax: 800-772-6499
www.couragetochange.com

Designed for use by both parents and therapists, provides background information, step-by-step instructions and many useful, reproducible worksheets. Techniques offered help children with anger management, compliance and following rules, academic success, emotional well-being and self-esteem and much more.

272 pages
Michael L Bloomquist, Editor

Journals

6824 Best Practices of Youth Violence Prevention
4770 Buford Hwy, NE Mail Stop MS F-63
Atlanta, GA 30341
800-232-4636
TTY: 888-232-6348
www.cdc.gov/injury

Timothy N. Thornton, M.P.A., Editor
Carole A. Craft, Editor
Linda L. Dahlberg, Ph.D., Editor

6825 Children, Adolescents, and Media Violence
2455 Teller Road
Thousand Oaks, CA 91320
800-818-7243
Fax: 800-583-2665
marketingservices@sagepub.com
www.sagepub.com

This revised text provides updates that reflect new findings in the field of media violence research during childhood and adolescence

Steven J. Kirsh, Author

6826 Disruptive Behavior Disorders in Children
1000 Wilson Boulevard, Suite 1825
Arlington, VA 22209
703-907-7322
800-368-5777
Fax: 703-907-1091
appi@psych.org
www.appi.org

The authors look at three subtypes of attention-deficit/hyperactivity disorder (ADHD), conduct disorder, and oppositional defiant disorder, all of which are common among youths and often share similar symptoms of impulse control problems.

John M. Oldham, M.D., M.S., Series Editor
Michelle B. Riba, M.D., M.S., Series Editor
Robert L. Hendren, D.O., Editor

6827 Electronic Media and Youth Violence - A CDC Issue Brief
4770 Buford Hwy, NE Mail Stop MS F-63
Atlanta, GA 30341
800-232-4636
TTY: 888-232-6348
www.cdc.gov/injury

Electronic Media and Youth Violence: A CDC Issue Brief for Educators and Caregivers focuses on the phenomena of electronic aggression.

Marci Feldman Hertz, M.S, Co-Author
Corinne David-Ferdon, Ph.D., Co-Author

6828 Handbook of Children and the Media
2455 Teller Road
Thousand Oaks, CA 91320
800-818-7243
Fax: 800-583-2665
marketingservices@sagepub.com
www.sagepub.com

Cyber-bullying, sexting, and the effects that violent video games have on children are widely discussed and debated.

Dorothy G. Singer, Co-Author
Jerome L. Singer, Co-Author

6829 Helping Kids in Crisis: Managing Emergencies in Children & Adolescents
1000 Wilson Boulevard, Suite 1825
Arlington, VA 22209
703-907-7322
800-368-5777
Fax: 703-907-1091
appi@psych.org
www.appi.org

6830 Measuring Bullying Victimization, Perpetration and Bystander Experiences
4770 Buford Hwy, NE Mail Stop MS F-63
Atlanta, GA 30341
800-232-4636
TTY: 888-232-6348
www.cdc.gov/injury

This compendium provides researchers, prevention specialists, and health educators with tools to measure a range of bullying experiences: bully perpetration, bully victimization, bully-victim experiences, and bystander experiences.

Merle E. Hamburger, PhD, Editor
Kathleen C. Basile, PhD, Editor
Alana M. Vivolo, MPH, CHES, Editor

6831 Measuring Violence-Related Attitudes, Behaviors and Influences
4770 Buford Hwy, NE Mail Stop MS F-63
Atlanta, GA 30341
800-232-4636
TTY: 888-232-6348
www.cdc.gov/injury

This compendium provides researchers and prevention specialists with a set of tools to assess violence-related beliefs, behaviors, and influences, as well as to evaluate programs to prevent youth violence.

Linda L. Dahlberg, PhD, Editor
Susan B. Toal, MPH, Editor
Monica H. Swahn, PhD, Editor

6832 Media Violence and Children: A Complete Guide
130 Cremona Drive
Santa Barbara, CA 93117
805-968-1911
800-368-6868
Fax: 866-270-3856
CustomerService@abc-clio.com
www.abc-clio.com

Stripping away the hype, this book describes how, when, and why media violence can influence children of different ages, giving parents and teachers the power to maximize the media's benefits and minimize its harm.

Douglas A. Gentile, Editor

6833 Media and Youth: A Developmental Perspective
111 River Street
Hoboken, NJ 07030
201-748-6000
Fax: 201-748-6088
www.wiley.com

Media & Youth: A Developmental Perspective provides a comprehensive review and critique of the research and theoretical literature related to media effects on infants, children, and adolescents, with a unique emphasis on development.

Steven J. Kirsh, Author

6834 Research on Child and Adolescent Psychopathology
ISRCAP
University of British Columbia, 2136 W Mall
Vancouver, BC
Canada
ISRCAP@gmail.com
isrcap.org

Research on Child and Adolescent Psychopathology is the official publication of the International Society for Research in Child and Adolescent Psychopathology (ISRCAP) that brings together the latest innovative research that advances knowledge of psychopathology from infancy through adolescence. Studies focus on the epidemiology, etiology, assessment, treatment, prognosis, and developmental course of these forms of psychopathology. Prevention and treatment methods are also featured.

Violence by Children & Teenagers / Pamphlets

6835 Technology and Youth - Protecting Your Child
4770 Buford Hwy, NE Mail Stop MS F-63
Atlanta, GA 30341
800-232-4636
TTY: 888-232-6348
www.cdc.gov/injury

This tipsheet provides an overview of electronic aggression, any type of harassment or bullying that occurs through e-mail, a chat room, instant messaging, a website (including blogs), or text messaging. It provides parents and caregivers with strategies for protecting children from this type of violence.

6836 Violence in the Media: A Reference Handbook
130 Cremona Drive
Santa Barbara, CA 93117
805-968-1911
800-368-6868
Fax: 866-270-3856
CustomerService@abc-clio.com
www.abc-clio.com

From the popular video game Mortal Kombat to reality TV, this book offers a candid compilation of the history, problems, impacts, and solutions relating to media violence.

Nancy Signorielli, PhD, Author

Pamphlets

6837 Conduct Disorder in Children and Adolescents
National Mental Health Information Center
PO Box 42557
Washington, DC 20015
800-789-2647
Fax: 240-747-5470
TDD: 866-889-2647
ken@mentalhealth.org
www.mentalhealth.samhsa.gov

This fact sheet defines conduct disorder, identifies risk factors, discusses types of help available, and suggests what parents or other caregivers can do.

1997 2 pages

6838 Mental, Emotional, and Behavior Disorders in Children and Adolescents
National Mental Health Information
PO Box 42557
Washington, DC 20015
240-747-5484
800-789-2647
Fax: 240-747-5470
mentalhealth.samhsa.gov

This fact sheet describes mental, emotional, and behavioral problems that can occur during childhood and adolescence and discusses related treatment, support services, and research.

4 pages

6839 Treatment of Children with Mental Disorder
National Institute of Mental Health
PO Box 5801
Bethesda, MD 20824
301-496-5751
800-352-9424
Fax: 301-443-4279
TTY: 301-443-8431
nimhinfo@nih.gov
www.nimh.nih.gov

A short booklet that contains questions and answers about therapy for children with mental disorders. Includes a chart of mental disorders and medications used.

Walter J. Koroshetz, M.D., Acting Director
Alan L. Willard, Ph.D., Acting Deputy Director
Caroline Lewis, Executive Officer

6840 Understanding Bullying - Fact Sheet
4770 Buford Hwy, NE Mail Stop MS F-63
Atlanta, GA 30341
800-232-4636
TTY: 888-232-6348
www.cdc.gov/injury

6841 Understanding School Violence Fact Sheet
4770 Buford Hwy, NE Mail Stop MS F-63
Atlanta, GA 30341
800-232-4636
TTY: 888-232-6348
www.cdc.gov/injury

This fact sheet provides an overview of school violence.

6842 Understanding Youth Violence: Fact Sheet
4770 Buford Hwy, NE Mail Stop MS F-63
Atlanta, GA 30341
800-232-4636
TTY: 888-232-6348
www.cdc.gov/injury

This 2-page fact sheet provides a basic overview of youth violence. It is intended for the general public.

Camps

6843 Adventure Learning Center Camp Programs
Eagle Village
4507 170th Avenue
Hersey, MI 49639
231-832-2234
800-748-0061
Fax: 231-832-1468
summercamp@eaglevillage.org
www.eaglevillage.org

Offers a variety of fun camp experiences for children, including those with emotional and/or behavioral impairments. A low staff-to-camper ratio and exciting, challenging activities make the camps rewarding experiences. As funding is available, we will offer camp scholarships to eligible participants.

Sara Kofal, Camp Director

6844 Life Adventure Center
Life Adventure Center of the Bluegrass
PO Box 447
Versailles, KY 40383
859-873-3271
Fax: 859-873-2410
www.lifeadventurecamp.org

A unique experience of discovery and development where lifelong lessons are learned. Through purposeful play, using a combination of physical and mental problem-solving exercises, participants engage in opportunities to make positive choices, gain self-confidence, improve decision making, build on group strengths and much more.

6845 Talisman Summer Camps
Talisman Schools
64 Gap Creek Road
Zirconia, NC 28790
855-588-8254
Fax: 828-669-2521
www.talismansummercamp.com/

Camps for children ages 6 to 17 and young adults 18-21 with LD, ADD and ADHD, Asperger's Syndrome, and high functioning autism. Talisman has been offering such experiences since 1980 and is ACA accredited. The unique summer camps specialize in creating camps that offer not only adventure, but learning experiences, for children and teenagers with learning disabilities, attention deficit hyperactivity disorder, Asperger's syndrome and high-functioning autism.

Linda Tatsapaugh, Director
Aaron McGinley, Base Camp Program Manager

Williams Syndrome / National Associations & Support Groups

Description

6846 WILLIAMS SYNDROME
Synonyms: WBS, Williams-Beuren syndrome, WMS, WS
Involves the following Biologic System(s):
Cardiovascular Disorders,
Genetic/Chromosomal/Syndrome/Metabolic Disorders

Williams syndrome is a genetic disorder characterized by mild growth delays before birth (prenatal stunted growth); growth delays after birth (postnatal stunted growth); mild short stature; characteristic abnormalities of the head and face (craniofacial area); and variable levels of mental deficiency. Unusual features of the head and face may result in a distinctive appearance that becomes more pronounced with advancing age. Characteristic features include a rounded face with full cheeks; full, thick lips and a large mouth that is typically in an open position, prominent ears; flared eyebrows; short eyelid folds (palpebral fissures); and a broad nasal bridge with a wide tip and nostrils that flare forward (anteverted). Dental abnormalities are often present, such as small teeth (hypodontia) with underdeveloped (hypoplastic) tooth enamel. Distinctive abnormalities of the eyes may also occur, including divergence of one eye in relation to the other (strabismus) and an unusual star-like (stellate) pattern in the colored portions of the eyes (irides).

Most children and adults with Williams syndrome also have mild to moderate intellectual disabilities. Affected individuals may have an intelligence quotient (I.Q.) ranging from 80, which is considered the low end of average, to 40, which is considered moderate intellectual disabilities. The average I.Q. is approximately 56, which is considered at the lower end of the range for mild intellectual disabilities. Other findings associated with Williams syndrome may include a short attention span, easy distractibility, a poor relationship between visual stimuli and resultant movements (motor-visual integration skills), and strong general language skills as opposed to general cognitive abilities. Most affected children and adults have a friendly personality and a talkative, outgoing manner of speech.

Some infants and children with Williams syndrome may also have additional physical abnormalities, such as heart defects, musculoskeletal abnormalities, or unusually increased blood calcium levels during infancy (transient infantile hypercalcemia). For example, affected infants may develop narrowing (stenosis) in the area above the valve leading from the lower left-sided pumping chamber (ventricle) of the heart to the main artery (aorta) of the body (supravalvular aortic stenosis); obstruction of normal blood flow from the right ventricle of the heart to the lungs (branch pulmonary stenosis); high blood pressure (hypertension); or other cardiovascular abnormalities including narrowing of the blood vessels to the head and abdominal organs. Musculoskeletal defects may include limited movements of certain joints; abnormal curvature of the spine (e.g., scoliosis, kyphosis, lordosis); and an awkward gait. Some individuals with Williams syndrome also have abnormalities affecting the urinary tract, such as the return flow of urine from the urinary bladder back into a ureter (vesicoureteral reflux), recurrent urinary tract infections, and other findings (e.g., nephrocalcinosis, bladder diverticula). Digestive problems may also occur, including chronic constipation. Depending upon the specific abnormalities present, treatment may include limitation of calcium in and elimination of vitamin D from the diet in those with high levels of calcium in the blood; heart surgery for those with certain structural cardiac defects; and special educational and supportive services, such as physical therapy, individualized educational programs, speech therapy, and occupational therapy. Other treatment is symptomatic and supportive.

Most cases of Williams syndrome appear to occur randomly (sporadically) for unknown reasons; however, some familial cases have been reported. Sporadic and inherited cases of the disorder appear to occur due to missing genetic material (deletion) from genes located next to one another (contiguous genes) on the long arm (q) of chromosome 7 (7q11.23). The syndrome is thought to affect approximately one in 10,000 newborns.

Government Agencies

6847 NIH/ Eunice Kennedy Shriver National Institute of Child Health & Human Development
P.O. Box 3006
Rockville, MD 20847
800-370-2943
Fax: 866-760-5947
www.nichd.nih.gov

Conducts and supports research on topics related to the health of children, adults, families and populations. Some of these topics include: developmental disabilities, growth and development, infant death, reproductive health and birth defects.

Diana W. Bianchi, Director
Alison Cernich, PhD, Deputy Director

National Associations & Support Groups

6848 American Academy of Pediatrics
345 Park Blvd
Itasca, IL 60143
847-434-4000
800-433-9016
Fax: 847-434-8000
csc@aap.org
www.aap.org

The American Academy of Pediatrics and its member pediatricians are committed to the attainment of optimal physical, mental and social health and well-being for all infants, children, adolescents, and young adults.

Kyle E. Yasuda, MD, FAAP, President
Mark Del Monte, JD, CEO/Executive VP
Vera Tait, MD, FAAP, Chief Medical Officer

6849 Cincinnati Center for Developmental & Behavioral Pediatrics
Cincinnati Children's Hospital Medical Center
3333 Burnet Avenue, MLC 4002
Cincinnati, OH 45229
513-636-4200
800-344-2462
Fax: 513-636-7361
TTY: 513-636-4900
tics@cchmc.org
www.cincinnatichildrens.org

Cincinnati Center for Developmental Disorders provides diagnosis, evaluation, treatment, training and education for infants, children and adolescents with a variety of developmental disorders.

Patricia M. Manning-Courtney, MD, Co-Director
Susan E. Wiley, MD, Co-Director

6850 Genetic Alliance
426400 Woodfield Road, Ste 189
Damascus, MD 20872
202-966-5557
Fax: 202-966-8553
info@geneticalliance.org
www.geneticalliance.org

World's leading nonprofit health advocacy organization committed to transforming health through genetics and promoting an environment of openness centered on the health of individuals, families, and communities.

Sharon Terry, CEO
Ruth Child, CFO
Natasha Bonhomme, Chief Strategy Officer

Williams Syndrome / Research Centers

6851 Williams Syndrome Association
560 Kirts Blvd, Suite 116
Troy, MI 48084
284-244-2229
800-806-1871
Fax: 248-244-2230
info@williams-syndrome.org
www.williams-syndrome.org

Devoted to improving the lives of individuals with Williams Syndrome and their families. The WSA supports research into all facets of the syndrome, and the development of the most up to date educational materials regarding Williams Syndrome.

Mary Van Haneghan, Executive Director
Sarah Giddings, Vice President, Programs & Services
Lacie Stiewing, Communications Director

Research Centers

6852 Patient Recruitment & Public Liaison Office Clinical Center
10 Cloister Court, Building 61
Bethesda, MD 20892
800-411-1222
Fax: 301-480-9793
TTY: 866-411-1010
prpl@mail.cc.nih.gov
www.cc.nih.gov

The NIH Clinical Center is a federally funded biomedical research facility that supports clinical investigations conducted by the institutes of the National Institute of Health.

Martin Blaser, MD, Chair
Peter Markell, Vice Chair
Robert S. Balaban, PhD, Vice Chair

Web Sites

6853 Clinical Genetic Services-Department of Pediatrics
Hassenfeld Children's Hospital at NYU Langone
424 East 34th Street
New York, NY 10016
212-263-7300
Fax: 646-754-2250
nyulangone.org

Offers evaluations, genetic counseling and testing. Clinical services include carrier testing, prenatal counseling, and complete genetic evaluations for children and adults.

John G. Pappas, MD, Pediatric Genetic Associate
Naomi Yachelevich, MD, Pediatric Genetic Associate

6854 Healthfinder
1101 Wootton Parkway
Rockville, MD 20852
healthfinder@hhs.gov
www.healthfinder.gov

A guide for health information.
Dr. Wright, Chief Medical Advisor

6855 Kansas University Medical Center
3901 Rainbow Boulevard
Kansas City, KS 66160
913-588-5000
dgirod@kumc.edu
www.kumc.edu

A nationally recognized biomedical research center, offers educational programs through its Schools of Allied Health, Medicine, Nursing, Pharmacy and Graduate Studies.

Doug Girod, MD, Executive Vice Chancellor
Richard J. Barohn, MD, Vice Chancellor for Research
Natalie Lutz, Communications Director

6856 Lili Claire Foundation
3540 West Sahara Ave., #182
Las Vegas, NV 89102
702-862-8141
www.liliclairefoundation.org/

Helps to ease the challenges families face by providing a unique and comprehensive blend of programs and support services.

Leslie Litt, Founder
Keith Resnick, Co-Founder
Lydia Murphy, Board Member

6857 Online Mendelian Inheritance in Man
McKusick-Nathans Institue of Genetic Medicine-JHU
Baltimore, MD 21205
www.omim.org

This database is a catalog of human genes and genetic disorders.

Ada Hamosh, MD, Scientific Director

6858 Williams Syndrome Monthly Medline Alert
www.geocities.com/HotSprings/8172/

www.geocities.com/HotSprings/8172/

Camps

6859 ACM Lifting Lives Music Camp
110 Magnolia Circle
Nashville, TN 37203
615-322-8240
www.acmliftinglives.org

A week-long residential camp designed for people with Williams syndrome and other developmental disabilities who are at least 16 years-old.

Bill Mayne, Chairman of the Board
Lori Badgett, President
Ed Warm, Vice President

6860 Eden Wood Center
Friendship Ventures
6350 Indian Chief Road
Eden Prairie, MN
952-852-0101
800-450-8376
Fax: 952-852-0123
fv@friendshipventures.org
truefriends.org

Offers resident camp programs for children, teenagers and adults with developmental, physical or multiple disabilities, Down Syndrome, special medical conditions, Williams Syndrome, autism and/or other conditions. Fishing, creative arts, golf, sports and other activities are available. Creative Options Respite Care offers weekend camps year round for children, teenagers and adults. Ventures Travel offers guided vacations for teens and adults with developmental disabilities or other unique needs.

Jon Salmon, Director of Programs and Services
Mel Kloek, Program Director
Dawn Brenner, Director of Health Care

Description

6861 WILMS TUMOR

Synonyms: Nephroblastoma, Renal Tumor, Kidney Tumor

Involves the following Biologic System(s):
Hematologic and Oncologic Disorders

Wilms tumor (also known as nephroblastoma) is a rare malignant tumor of the kidney that accounts for about 8% of childhood cancers. It typically develops at about the age of 3 years and rarely after age 8, and occurs with equal frequency among males and females. Wilms tumor may develop in any region of either kidney. In most cases the tumor develops in only one kidney (unilateral). However, both kidneys may be involved (bilateral) in about 5-10% of affected children. In some severe cases the tumor may spread from the kidney to other parts of the body (metastasize), particularly the lungs.

Wilms tumor typically becomes apparent by approximately 3 to 5 years of age. The most common sign of its presence is a smooth, firm mass in the abdominal area. About 50% of children with Wilms tumor experience associated abdominal pain or vomiting (emesis), and about 10-25% have blood in their urine (microscopic or gross hematuria). Up to 60% of children with Wilms tumor also have high blood pressure (hypertension) caused by pressure exerted by the tumor on the major artery that carries blood to the kidney (renal artery). In severe cases, long-term hypertension may impair the ability of the heart to pump blood effectively through the body (cardiac failure). Other indicators of Wilms tumor may be loss of appetite, weight loss, constipation, and blood in the urine

The exact cause of Wilms tumor is unknown but the tumor is thought to be caused by mutations in genes that normally prevent cells from becoming cancerous and multiplying. These mutations either occur in a seemingly random manner, for unknown reasons (sporadic) in children who develop Wilms tumor, or can be inherited in an autosomal dominant manner, which means from only one parent.. In most instances, Wilms tumor begins to develop before birth, in cells destined to develop into normal kidney tissue.

Treatment for Wilms tumor is based on the stage of this cancer, or degree to which it has progressed, and whether its histology (appearance of the tumor tissue under the microscope) indicates a likelihood of rapid tumor growth or less aggressive growth. Treatment typically begins with surgical removal of the affected kidney (nephrectomy). During surgery, the remaining kidney is examined to determine whether it too contains any tumor. Treatment after surgery for Wilms tumor may consist of chemotherapy, in which drugs are used to destroy any residual tumor that may not have been removed surgically, and radiation therapy, in which X-rays or other sources of radioactivity are used to destroy residual tumor.In children with Wilms tumor in both kidneys, chemotherapy and radiation therapy may be given before surgical removal of their tumors. Children in whom both kidneys must be removed to eliminate Wilms tumors will require periodic, intermittent kidney dialysis to rid their bodies of toxic wastes, a need that usually continues for life.

Government Agencies

6862 NIH/National Cancer Institute
Bethesda, MD 20892

800-422-6237
NCIinfo@nih.gov
www.cancer.gov

The National Cancer Institute coordinates the National Cancer Program, which conducts and supports research, training, health information dissemination, and other programs with respect to the cause, diagnosis, prevention, and treatment of cancer, rehabilitation from cancer, and the continuing care of cancer patients and the families of cancer patients.

Norman E. Sharpless, MD, Director
Douglas R. Lowy, MD, Principal Deputy Director

National Associations & Support Groups

6863 American Academy of Pediatrics
345 Park Blvd
Itasca, IL 60143

847-434-4000
800-433-9016
Fax: 847-434-8000
csc@aap.org
www.aap.org

The American Academy of Pediatrics and its member pediatricians are committed to the attainment of optimal physical, mental and social health and well-being for all infants, children, adolescents, and young adults.

Kyle E. Yasuda, MD, FAAP, President
Mark Del Monte, JD, CEO/Executive VP
Vera Tait, MD, FAAP, Chief Medical Officer

6864 American Cancer Society
3380 Chastain Meadows Parkway NW, Suite 200
Kennesaw, GA 30144

800-227-2345
www.cancer.org

The American Cancer Society is the leading cancer-fighting organization with a vision of ending cancer as we know it, for everyone. We are the only organization working to improve the lives of people with cancer and their families through advocacy, research, and patient support, to ensure everyone has an opportunity to prevent, detect, treat, and survive cancer.

Karen E Knudsen, Chief Executive Officer
William L Dahut, MD, Chief Scientific Officer
Kymm Martinez, Chief Marketing Officer

6865 American Childhood Cancer Organization
P.O. Box 498
Kensington, MD 20895

301-962-3520
800-366-2226
Fax: 310-962-3521
staff@acco.org
www.acco.org

The American Childhood Cancer Organization (ACCO) was founded in 1970 by a group of parents whose children had been diagnosed with cancer. Today ACCO is one of the largest grassroots, national organizations dedicated to improving the lives of children and adolescents with cancer and their families.

Ruth I. Hoffman, MPH, CEO
Krista Novak, Programs Manager
Blair Scroggs, Public Relations Coordinator

6866 CancerCare
275 7th Avenue
New York, NY 10001

212-712-8400
800-813-4673
Fax: 212-712-8495
info@cancercare.org
www.cancercare.org

Dedicated to providing emotional support, information, and practical help to people with cancer and their loved ones. CancerCare is the oldest, largest, nonprofit agency devoted to offering professional services.

Patricia J Goldsmith, CEO
Christine Verini, RPh, COO

6867 Children's Cancer Research Fund
7301 Ohms Lane, Suite 355
Minneapolis, MN 55439

952-893-9355
888-422-7348
Fax: 952-893-9366
contact@childrenscancer.org
childrenscancer.org

Children's Cancer Research Fund is a national nonprofit dedicated to ending childhood cancer. Our main focus is to support the research of bright scientists across the country whose ideas can make the greatest impact for children fighting cancer. We also fund resources and programs that help kids and families as they navigate the difficult experience of cancer treatment and survivorship.

Jean Machart, Chief Executive Officer

6868 Children's Wish Foundation International
8615 Roswell Road
Atlanta, GA 30350
800-323-9474
info@childrenswish.org
www.childrenswish.org

Children's Wish Foundation International is dedicated to bringing joy and hope to seriously ill children and their families world wide by involving the public in putting children first with opportunities to experience the enhanced value and quality of life through the magic of a fulfilled wish.

Linda Dozoretz, Founder

6869 CureSearch for Children's Cancer
P.O. Box 45781
Baltimore, MD 21297
800-458-6223
Fax: 301-718-0047
info@curesearch.org
www.curesearch.org

CureSearch for Children's Cancer is a national non-profit foundation that accelerates the cure for children's cancer by driving innovation, eliminating research barriers and solving the field's most challenging problems.

Kay Koehler, CEO
Katharine A. Burke, COO & VP, Financing
Caitlyn W. Barrett, National Director, Research & Prgms

Research Centers

6870 Children's Cancer Research Fund
7301 Ohms Lane, Suite 355
Minneapolis, MN 55439
952-893-9355
888-422-7348
Fax: 952-893-9366
contact@childrenscancer.org
childrenscancer.org

Children's Cancer Research Fund is a national nonprofit dedicated to ending childhood cancer. Our main focus is to support the research of bright scientists across the country whose ideas can make the greatest impact for children fighting cancer. We also fund resources and programs that help kids and families as they navigate the difficult experience of cancer treatment and survivorship.

Jean Machart, Chief Executive Officer

6871 National Wilms Tumor Study
Fred Hutchinson Cancer Research Center
1100 Fairview Ave. N, M2-A876, PO Box 19024
Seattle, WA 98109
206-667-4842
800-553-4878
Fax: 206-667-6623
nwtsg@fhcrc.org
www.nwtsg.org

To improve the survival of children with Wilms tumor and other renal tumors, to study the long-term outcome of children with successfully treated by identifying adverse effects of treatment, to study the epidemiology and biology of Wilms tumor and to make information regarding successful treatment strategies for Wilms tumor available to physicians around the world.

Web Sites

6872 CancerCare
275 7th Avenue
New York, NY 10001
800-813-4673
info@cancercare.org
www.cancercare.org

Dedicated to providing emotional support, information, and practical help to people with cancer and their loved ones. CancerCare is the oldest, largest, nonprofit agency devoted to offering professional services.

Patricia J Goldsmith, CEO
Christine Verini, RPh, COO

6873 Children's Cancer Web
www.cancerindex.org/ccw

www.cancerindex.org/ccw

An independent nonprofit site, established to provide a directory of childhood cancer resources.

6874 OncoLink: The University of Pennsylvania Cancer Center Resource
www.oncolink.upenn.edu/about/index

www.oncolink.upenn.edu/about/index

Mission to help cancer patients, families, health care professionals, and the general public get accurate cancer-related information at no charge.

6875 Online Mendelian Inheritance in Man
McKusick-Nathans Institue of Genetic Medicine-JHU
Baltimore, MD 21205
www.omim.org

This database is a catalog of human genes and genetic disorders.

Ada Hamosh, MD, Scientific Director

Book Publishers

6876 Let's Talk About Going to the Hospital
Rosen Publishing Group's PowerKids Press
29 E 21st Street
New York, NY 10010
212-777-3017
800-237-9932
Fax: 888-436-4643
rosenpub@tribeca.ios.com
www.rosenpublishing.com

If a child has to check into the hospital, chances are he or she is already upset about being ill. Knowing how a hospital functions and what the procedures are, such as when family members can visit, will help in what is already a stressful situation. Grades K-5.

24 pages
ISBN: 0-823950-36-0

Roger Rosen, President

6877 Let's Talk About When Kids Have Cancer
Melanie Apel Gordon, author

Rosen Publishing Group's PowerKids Press
29 E 21st Street
New York, NY 10010
212-777-3017
800-237-9932
Fax: 888-436-4643
customerservice@rosenpub.com
www.rosenpublishing.com

In a straightforward yet comforting way, this book explains what cancer is, what kinds of treatments surround the disease and how to cope if a child or the friend of a child has cancer. K-5.

24 pages Paperback
ISBN: 0-823951-95-6

Roger Rosen, President

6878 Surviving Childhood Cancer: A Guide for Families
New Harbinger Publications
5674 Shattuck Avenue
Oakland, CA 94609
510-652-0215
800-748-6273
Fax: 800-652-1613
customerservice@newharbinger.com
www.newharbinger.com

Cancer in a child is an overwhelming experience for a family. This book explains common medical procedures and offers readers practical advice about how to cope with emotions and stress during this time.

215 pages Paperback
ISBN: 1-572241-02-0

Camps

6879 Arizona Camp Sunrise & Sidekicks
PO Box 27872
Tempe, AZ 85285
480-382-8564
928-478-4564
melissa@azcampsunrise.org
www.azcampsunrise.org

The camp is dedicated to provide an exciting, medically safe camp program for children whose families have been affected by cancer.

Melissa Lee, Camp Director

6880 Camp Catch-A-Rainbow
American Cancer Society
1205 E Saginaw Street
Lansing, MI 800-A
517-371-2920
www.ymcastorercamps.org/ccar/camp-catch-a-rainbow/

Open to any child (age 7 thru 15) who has, or has had, cancer.

Becky Spencer, Vice President of Camping
Angela Hayner, Program Director
Katie Wilson, Coordinator

6881 Camp Sunshine Dreams
PO Box 28232
Fresno, CA 93729
contact@campsunshinedreams.com
www.campsunshinedreams.com

Summer camp for children with cancer.

Anthony Aiello, Board Member
Jeff Clem, Board Member
Pam Aiello, Board Member

6882 Okizu Foundation Camps
16 Digital Drive, Suite 130
Novato, CA 94949
415-382-9083
Fax: 415-382-8384
info@okizu.org
www.okizu.org

This foundation runs family camp programs for children who have cancer and their families, and for children who have or had a parent with cancer.

Lori Sparrow, Executive Director
Heather Ferrier, Camp Director of Operations

Wilson Disease / Description

Description

6883 WILSON DISEASE
Synonyms: Hepatolenticular degeneration, WD, WND
Involves the following Biologic System(s):
Gastrointestinal Disorders

Wilson disease is a genetic disorder in which a defect in copper metabolism causes an abnormal accumulation of copper in the liver, brain, kidneys, corneas of the eyes, and other tissues of the body. The disorder is often characterized by progressive liver disease, degenerative changes in the brain, kidney failure, and characteristic grayish-green or reddish-gold rings (Kayser-Fleischer rings) at the outer margins of the corneas. Wilson disease is a progressive disorder, and if untreated can cause severe brain damage, liver failure, and death.

The age at which Wilson disease begins may vary from one patient to another. Symptoms and findings may not become apparent until 5 or 6 years of age and most commonly originate during mid-adolescence. In some patients, however, the disease may not become apparent until adulthood. Wilson disease is thought to occur in about 1 in 30,000 individuals worldwide. Wilson disease that results from alteration (mutation) in a gene that regulates the body's metabolism and handling of copper, with the result that copper accumulates excessively in the liver. Genetically, the disease is defined as an autosomal recessive disorder, meaning that it cannot occur unless the gene that causes it is inherited from both parents.

In Wilson disease, copper progressively collects in the liver and is released into other organs and tissues of the body, particularly the brain, corneas of the eyes, and kidneys. Associated symptoms and findings may be variable, but similar characteristics of the disease are typically observed in members of different generations of families within which the disease tends to occur with a greater than usual frequency.

In Wilson disease, the liver is typically enlarged (hepatomegaly) and may be acutely or chronically inflamed, and this may or may not be accompanied by enlargement of the spleen (splenomegaly). Internal scarring of the liver, as well as the condition known as cirrhosis and abnormalities in liver function, are uncommon in children under 10 years of age with Wilson disease, but do tend to occur in young adults with the disease.

Persons in whom Wilson disease causes cirrhosis may have yellowish discoloration of the skin, mucous membranes, and whites of the eyes (jaundice); unusually high blood pressure (hypertension) the veins that carry blood from the liver (portal hypertension); an abnormal accumulation of fluid in certain body tissues (edema) and in the abdominal cavity (ascites); and enlargement of blood vessels in the wall of the esophagus (esophageal varices), potentially causing them to rupture and bleed. In severe cases, affected individuals may develop fulminant hepatitis, a severe form of liver disease characterized by localized loss of liver tissue (necrosis), defects of blood clotting (coagulation), coma (hepatic encephalopathy), and other potentially life-threatening complications.

Neurologic symptoms associated with Wilson disease occur in about a third of all cases, and can develop suddenly or may occur gradually, but are rare in children under 10 years of age. Many such symptoms are thought to result from progressive involvement of a region of the brain (basal ganglia) that assists in regulating muscular movements. Neurologic symptoms often initially include abnormalities of muscle tone (progressive dystonia), muscle stiffness, and rigidity. In addition, persons with Wilson disease may experience involuntary, rhythmic, quivering movements of the extremities on one side of the body (unilateral) that may eventually become generalized. Other neurologic symptoms include difficulties in speech (dysphonia), drooling, a fixed smile caused by involuntary drawing back of the upper lip, and involuntary, rapid, jerky movements in association with slow, writhing movements of the limbs, head, and neck (choreoathetosis). Wilson disease may also result in the premature breakdown of red blood cells (hemolysis), which may progress to the chronic condition known as hemolytic anemia. In this type of anemia, premature destruction of red blood cells reduces these cells' transport of oxygen to all of the body's other cells. Wilson disease may also cause the condition known as progressive renal failure, by damaging the ability of the kidneys to maintain a proper balance between the body's water and salt contents, as well as their ability to filter waste products from the blood and excrete these wastes in urine, and to perform other vital functions. In addition to these effects, Wilson's disease can produce sudden changes in personality and behavior, which can interfere with a child's social development and performance in school, and are sometimes mistaken for other kinds of psychological problems.

The goal in treating Wilson disease is twofold: to remove excess copper and to prevent the mineral from building up again. This treatment often consists of giving penicillamine, a medication that binds with copper (chelation) and enables it to be excreted from the body. This is accompanied by vitamin B6 to supplement the quantity of this vitamin present in foods. For persons who cannot tolerate penicillamine, the medications trientine and zinc acetate may be appropriate substitutes. Physicians and other health care professionals may also recommend a diet that provides the body with only a small daily quantity of copper (less than 1 mg/day), and may recommend the avoidance of such foods that contain copper, such as chocolate, liver, and nuts. Liver transplantation may be considered for persons with Wilson disease who develop severe, fulminant hepatitis, since this can be life-threatening. Other treatment for Wilson disease is symptomatic and supportive.

National Associations & Support Groups

6884 American Academy of Pediatrics
345 Park Blvd
Itasca, IL 60143
847-434-4000
800-433-9016
Fax: 847-434-8000
csc@aap.org
www.aap.org

The American Academy of Pediatrics and its member pediatricians are committed to the attainment of optimal physical, mental and social health and well-being for all infants, children, adolescents, and young adults.

Kyle E. Yasuda, MD, FAAP, President
Mark Del Monte, JD, CEO/Executive VP
Vera Tait, MD, FAAP, Chief Medical Officer

6885 American Liver Foundation
P.O. Box 299
West Orange, NJ 07052
800-465-4837
www.liverfoundation.org

The American Liver Foundation is the nation leading nonprofit organization promoting liver health and disease prevention. ALF provides research, education and advocacy for those affected by liver-related diseases, including hepatitis.

Lorraine Stiehl, CEO
David Ticker, Executive VP & CFO

Wilson Disease / Pamphlets

6886 Children's Liver Association for Support Services
PO Box 186
Monaca, PA 15061
724-581-5527
classkidscares@gmail.com
www.classkids.org

CLASS is an all volunteer, nonprofit organization dedicated to serving the emotional, educational and financial needs of families coping with childhood liver disease and transplantation. Its goal is to be both a service to families and a valuable resource for the medical community.

Stephan Circle, Co-President
Tamara Circle, Co-President

6887 Community Liver Alliance
100 W Station Square Drive, Suite 212
Pittsburgh, PA 15219
412-501-3CLA
support@communityliveralliance.org
communityliveralliance.org

The CLA is dedicated to supporting the community through liver disease awareness, prevention, education, advocacy and research. Supported by a network of patients, caregivers, health care professionals and community leaders, CLA develops and runs educational workshops, coordinates support groups, facilities linkage to medical care and provides education to health care professionals, patients and caregivers.

Suzanna Masartis, Chief Executive Director
Johanna Murock, Director of Operations
Jill Harlan, Program Director

6888 Genetic Alliance
426400 Woodfield Road, Ste 189
Damascus, MD 20872
202-966-5557
Fax: 202-966-8553
info@geneticalliance.org
www.geneticalliance.org

World's leading nonprofit health advocacy organization committed to transforming health through genetics and promoting an environment of openness centered on the health of individuals, families, and communities.

Sharon Terry, CEO
Ruth Child, CFO
Natasha Bonhomme, Chief Strategy Officer

6889 Wilson's Disease Association
21 Pulaski Road, Unit 235
Kings Park, NY 11754
414-961-0533
866-961-0533
info@wilsondisease.org
www.wilsonsdisease.org

Provides patients and their families with a membership list, e-mail correspondence, meetings for support and education, and a newsletter. Supports patients with financial assistance for medication and travel, and develops centers of excellence.

Judi Keller, Executive Director

Libraries & Resource Centers

6890 National Digestive Diseases Information Clearinghouse (NDDIC)
NIH
2 Information Way
Bethesda, MD 20892
301-654-3810
800-891-5389
Fax: 703-738-4929
TTY: 866-569-1162
nddic@info.niddk.nih.gov
www.digestive.niddk.nih.gov

The National Institute of Diabetes and Digestive and Kidney Diseases conducts and supports research on many of the most serious diseases affecting public health. The Institute supports much of the clinical research on the diseases of internal medicine and related subspecialty fields as well as many basic science disciplines.

Griffin P. Rodgers, MD, Director
Gregory G. Germino, MD, Deputy Director
Kathy Kranzfelder, Communications Director

Research Centers

6891 National Center for the Study of Wilson's Disease
5572 North Diversey Blvd
Milwaukee, WI 53217
414-961-0533
866-961-0533
Fax: 330-264-0974
www.wilsonsdisease.org

Mary L. Graper, President
Stefanie F. Kaplan, Vice President
Jean P. Perog, Treasurer

Web Sites

6892 Children's Liver Alliance
www.livertx.org

www.livertx.org

Offers a fact sheet on liver conditions.

6893 Children's Liver Association for Support Services
www.classkids.org
724-581-5527
classkidscares@gmail.com
www.classkids.org

CLASS is an all volunteer, nonprofit organization dedicated to serving the emotional, educational and financial needs of families coping with childhood liver disease and transplantation. Its goal is to be both a service to families and a valuable resource for the medical community.

6894 Wilson's Disease Association
21 Pulaski Road, Uni 235
Kings Park, NY 11754
414-961-0533
866-961-0533
info@wilsonsdisease.org
www.wilsonsdisease.org

Funds research and facilitates and promotes the identification, education, treatment, and support of patients and other individuals affected by Wilson's Disease.

Judi Keller, Executive Director

6895 Wilson's Disease Patient Information Exchange
www.gourmandizer.com/wilsons/indexx.html

www.gourmandizer.com/wilsons/indexx.html

Pages provide Wilson's Disease patients and their families a forum to share and compare their symptoms, treatments and to tell how the disease has affected thier lives.

Newsletters

6896 Children's Liver Alliance Newsletter
University of Michigan Transplant Center, 3868 Tau
Ann Arbor, MI 48109
734-232-1113
Fax: 734-232-1111
www.transweb.org

Aids in easing the physical and emotional strains that the child is experiencing, so they can better deal with the disorder through different media resources that are also available to both friends and family.

4-12 pages

Kathie DeLuca, Office Manager

Pamphlets

6897 Wilson's Disease
Nat'l Digestive Diseases Information Clearinghouse
9000 Rockville Pike
Bethesda, MD 20892
301-496-3583
Fax: 301-907-8906
nddic@info.niddk.nih.gov
www.niddk.nih.gov

Wilson Disease / Pamphlets

Griffin P. Rodgers, M.D., M.A.C.P., Director
Kevin Abbott, Program Director
Kristin Abraham, Program Director

Section II
General Resources

General Resources / Government Agencies

Government Agencies

6898 Agency for Healthcare Research & Quality
5600 Fishers Lane
Rockville, MD 20857
301-427-1364
howard.holland@ahrq.hhs.gov
www.ahrq.gov

The Agency for Healthcare Research and Quality(AHRQ) mission is to produce evidence to make health care safer, higher quality, more accessible, equitable, and affordable, and to work within the U.S. Department of Health and Human Services and with other partners to make sure that the evidence is understood and used.

David Meyers, Acting Director
Howard E. Holland, Communications Director

6899 BeMedWise
NeedyMeds
50 Whittmore Street
Gloucester, MA 01931
978-281-6666
info@bemedwise.org
www.bemedwise.org

Working to promote the wise use of medicines through trusted communication for better health.

Rich Sagall, MD, President
Carla Dellaporta, Director of User Engagement

6900 Center for Mental Health Services
5600 Fishers Lane
Rockville, MD 20857
240-276-1310
www.samhsa.gov

Encourages a range of programs such as systems of care to respond to the increasing number of mental, emotional, and behavioral problems among children. Supports outreach and case management programs for the thousands of Americans who are homeless and the improvement of these services.

Anita Everett, MD, Director

6901 Centers for Disease Control and Prevention
1600 Clifton Road
Atlanta, GA 30329
800-232-4636
TTY: 888-232-6348
www.cdc.gov

Federal agency that promotes America's health and safety, providing information to guide health decisions, and building strong partnerships to promote health and prevent disease.

Rochelle P. Walensky, MD, Director
Anne Schuchat, MD, Principal Deputy Director
Abbigail Tumpey, MPH, Associate Director, Communication

6902 Early Childhood Development
330 C Street SW
Washington, DC 20201
www.acf.hhs.gov/ecd/

Promotes a joint federal approach to improve early childhood education and development.

Katie Hamm, Director

6903 HEATH Resource Center
George Washington University
2134 G Street NW
Washington, DC 20052
AskHEATH@gwu.edu
www.heath.gwu.edu

The HEATH Resource Center is a web-based clearinghouse that serves as an information exchange of educational resources, support services and opportunities. The HEATH Resource Center gathers, develops and disseminates information in the form of resource papers, fact sheets, website directories, newsletters, and resource materials.

Christopher Nace, Research Assistant

6904 NIH/ Eunice Kennedy Shriver National Institute of Child Health & Human Development
P.O. Box 3006
Rockville, MD 20847
800-370-2943
Fax: 866-760-5947
www.nichd.nih.gov

Conducts and supports laboratory, clinical and epidemiological research on the reproductive, neurobiologic, developmental, and behavioral processes that determine and maintain the health of children, adults, families, and populations.

Diana W. Bianchi, Director
Alison Cernich, PhD, Deputy Director

6905 NIH/National Cancer Institute
Bethesda, MD 20892
800-422-6237
NCIinfo@nih.gov
www.cancer.gov

The National Cancer Institute coordinates the National Cancer Program, which conducts and supports research, training, health information dissemination, and other programs with respect to the cause, diagnosis, prevention, and treatment of cancer, rehabilitation from cancer, and the continuing care of cancer patients and the families of cancer patients.

Norman E. Sharpless, MD, Director
Douglas R. Lowy, MD, Principal Deputy Director

6906 NIH/National Eye Institute
31 Center Drive MSC 2510
Bethesda, MD 20892
301-496-5248
2020@nei.nih.gov
www.nei.nih.gov

Conducts and supports research that helps prevent and treat eye diseases and other disorders of vision. This research leads to sight-saving treatments, reduces visual impairment and blindness, and improves the quality of life for people of all ages. NEI-supported research has advanced our knowledge of how the eye functions in health and disease.

Michael F. Chiang, MD, Director
Santa Tumminia, Deputy Director

6907 NIH/National Heart, Lung and Blood Institute
31 Center Drive, Bldg 31
Bethesda, MD 20892
877-645-2448
www.nhlbi.nih.gov

Provides leadership for a national research program in diseases of the heart, blood vessels, lungs, and blood and in transfusion medicine through support of innovative basic, clinical, population-based and health education research. NHLBI also maintains an information clearinghouse.

Gary H. Gibbons, MD, Director
Kate O'Sullivan, Executive Officer

6908 NIH/National Human Genome Research Institute (NHGRI)
31 Center Drive, Building 31, Room 4B09
Bethesda, MD 20892
301-402-0911
Fax: 301-402-2218
www.genome.gov

Supports the NIH component of the Human Genome Project, a worldwide research effort designed to analyze the structure of human DNA and determine the location of the estimated 30,000 to 40,000 human genes. The NHGRI Intramural Research Program develops and implements understanding, diagnosing, and treating of genetic diseases.

Eric Green, MD, PhD, Director
Adebowale A. Adeyemo, MD, Deputy Director

6909 NIH/National Instiues of Health-Genetic & Rare Diseases Information Ctr (GARD)
PO Box 8126
Gaithersburg, MD 20898
301-251-4925
888-205-2311
Fax: 301-251-4911
TTY: 888-205-3223
anne.pariser@nih.gov
rarediseases.info.nih.gov

Information and advocacy resources for families and professionals. Includes information that is current, reliable and easy to understand in both English and Spanish, focusing on more specific areas of concern to families and young adults with rare and genetic diseases.

Anne Pariser, MD, Director

General Resources / Government Agencies

6910 **NIH/National Institute of Allergy and Infectious Diseases**
5601 Fishers Lane, MSC 9806
Bethesda, MD 20892
301-496-5717
866-284-4107
Fax: 301-402-3573
TDD: 800-877-8339
ocpostoffice@niaid.nih.gov
www.niaid.nih.gov

The principal advisory board of the NIAID. The council is composed of physicians, scientists and representatives of the public and advises on the conduct and support or research, training and dissemination of health information regarding allergies and infectious diseases.

Anthony S. Fauci, MD, Director

6911 **NIH/National Institute of Arthritis and Musculoskeletal and Skin Diseases**
1 AMS Circle
Bethesda, MD 20892
301-495-4484
877-226-4267
Fax: 301-718-6366
TTY: 301-565-2966
niamsinfo@mail.nih.gov
www.niams.nih.gov

The mission of the NIAMS, a part of the NIH, is to support research into the causes, treatment and prevention of arthritis and musculosketal and skin diseases, the training of basic and clinical scientists to carry out this research, and the dissemination of information on research progress in these diseases.

Lindsey A. Criswell, MD, Director
Rick Phillips, Executive Officer

6912 **NIH/National Institute of Dental and Craniofacial Research (NIDCR)**
National Institutes of Health
Bldg 31, Rm 2C39, 31 Center Drive, MSC 2560
Bethesda, MD 20892
866-232-4528
nidcrinfo@mail.nih.gov
www.nidcr.nih.gov

The Institute promotes the general health of the American people by improving their oral, dental and craniofacial health. The NIDCR aims to promote health, to prevent diseases and conditions, and to develop new diagnostics and therapeutics.

Rena D'Souza, DDS, PhD, Director
Jonathan Horsford, PhD, Acting Deputy Director

6913 **NIH/National Institute of Diabetes and Digestive and Kidney Diseases**
9000 Rockville Pike
Bethesda, MD 20892
800-860-8747
TTY: 866-569-1162
healthinfo@niddk.nih.gov
www.niddk.nih.gov

Conducts and supports basic and applied research and provides leadership for a national program in diabetes, endocrinology, and metabolic diseases; digestive diseases and nutrition and kidney, urologic and hematologic diseases.

Griffin P. Rodgers, MD, Director
Gregory G. Germino, MD, Deputy Director

6914 **NIH/National Institute of Environmental Health Sciences (NIEHS)**
PO Box 12233
Durham, NC 27709
984-287-3815
www.niehs.nih.gov

NIEHS reduces the burden of human illness and dysfunction from environmental causes by defining how environmental exposures, genetics and age interact to affect an individual's health.

Chris Long, MPA, Executive Officer
Mitch Williams, Deputy Executive Officer

6915 **NIH/National Institute of Mental Health**
6001 Executive Blvd, Rm 6200, MSC 9663
Bethesda, MD 20892
866-615-6464
Fax: 301-443-4279
TTY: 301-443-8431
www.nimh.nih.gov

The mission of NIMH is to transform the understanding and treatment of mental illnesses through basic and clinical research, paving the way for prevention, recovery, and cure.

Joshua A. Gordon, MD, PhD, Director
Shelli Avenevoli, PhD, Deputy Director

6916 **NIH/National Institute of Neurological Disorders and Stroke (NINDS)**
PO Box 5801
Bethesda, MD 20824
800-352-9424
www.ninds.nih.gov

Works to reduce the burden of neurological disease by conducting, fostering, coordinating and guiding research on the causes, prevention, diagnosis and treatment of neurological disorders and stroke, while supporting basic research in related scientific areas.

Walter J. Koroshetz, MD, Director

6917 **NIH/National Institute on Alcohol Abuse an d Alcoholism (NIAAA)**
5635 Fishers Lane
Bethesda, MD 20892
301-443-3860
877-266-4267
niaaaweb-r@exchange.nih.gov
www.niaaa.nih.gov

NIAAA conducts research focused on improving the treatment and prevention of alcoholism and alcohol-related problems to reduce the enormous social and economic consequences of this disease.

George F. Koob, PhD, Director

6918 **NIH/National Institute on Deafness and Other Communication Disorders (NIDCD)**
31 Center Drive, MSC 2320
Bethesda, MD 20892
800-241-1044
TTY: 800-241-1055
nidcdinfo@nidcd.nih.gov
www.nidcd.nih.gov

Conducts and supports biomedical research and research training on normal mechanisms, as well as diseases and disorders of hearing, balance, smell, taste, voice, speech and language.

Debara L. Tucci, MD, Director
Judith A. Cooper, PhD, Deputy Director
Timothy J. Wheeles, Executive Officer

6919 **NIH/National Institute on Drug Abuse (NIDA)**
301 N Stonestreet Avenue
Bethesda, MD 20892
301-443-1124
www.drugabuse.gov

NIDA leads the nation in bringing the power of science to bear on drug abuse and addiction through support and conduct of research across all disciplines and rapid and effective dissemination of results of that research to improve drug abuse and addiction prevention and treatment.

Nora D. Volkow MD, Director
Wilson Compton, MD, MPE, Deputy Director
Joellen Austin, MP, Associate Director for Management

6920 **National Center for Education in Maternal and Child Health**
3300 Whitehaven Street NW
Washington, DC 20007
MCHnavigator@ncemch.org
www.ncemch.org

Information and advocacy resources for families and professionals. Includes listings of organizations providing general information and organizations focusing on more specific areas of concern to families and young adults who have disabilities.

Rochelle Mayor, Director
John Richards, Exectuive Director

6921 **National Center for Health Statistics**
www.cdc.gov/nchs

800-232-4636
TTY: 888-232-6348
www.cdc.gov/nchs

Provides statistical information that will guide actions and policies to improve the health of American people.

Brian C. Moyer, PhD, Director

General Resources / National Associations & Support Groups

6922 National Council on Disability
1331 F Street NW, Suite 850
Washington, DC 20004
202-272-2004
Fax: 202-272-2022
ncd@ncd.gov
www.ncd.gov

Information and advocacy resources for families and professionals. Includes listings of organizations providing general information and organizations focusing on more specific areas of concern to families and young adults who have disabilities.

Anne Sommers McIntosh, Executive Director

6923 National Health Council
1730 M Street NW, Ste 500
Washington, DC 20036
202-785-3910
Fax: 202-785-5923
www.nationalhealthcouncil.org

Their mission to provide a unified voice for those with chronic diseases and disabilities and their family caregivers.

Randall L. Rutta, Chief Executive Officer
Silke Schoch, Research & Programs Manager

6924 National Library Service for the Blind and Physically Handicapped
Library of Congress
1291 Taylor Street NW
Washington, DC 20542
202-707-5100
800-424-8567
Fax: 202-707-0712
nls@loc.gov
www.loc.gov/nls

Provides information and advocacy resources for families and professionals, including listings of organizations focusing on more specific areas of concern to families and young adults who have disabilities. Administers a natural library service that provides recorded and braille reading materials to eligible children and adults who cannot read standard print.

6925 National Prevention Information Network
Center for Disease Control
PO Box 6003
Rockville, MD 20849
NPIN-Info@cdc.gov
npin.cdc.gov

Facilitates program collaboration in sharing information, resources, published material, research, and trends among the four diseases.

6926 National Recreation and Park Association
22377 Belmont Ridge Road
Ashburn, VA 20148
800-626-6772
www.nrpa.org

Information on adaptive sports and recreation activities for people of many abilities. Includes local chapters, referrals, fun and social interaction and support groups.

Michael P. Kelly, Chair
Kristine Stratton, President/Chief Executive Officer

6927 National Rehabilitation Information Center
8400 Corporate Drive, Suite 500
Landover, MD 20785
800-346-2742
Fax: 301-459-4263
TTY: 301-459-5984
naricinfo@heitechservices.com
www.naric.com

Committed to providing direct, personal and information services to anyone interested in disability rehabilitation issues; Committed to serving consumers, researchers, family members, health professionals, educators, counselors, students, librarians and the administrators.

Mark X. Odum, Project Director
Jessica H. Chaiken, Media/Information Services Manager
Natalie J. Collier, Library and Acquisitions Manager

6928 Office for Fair Housing & Equal Opportunity
U.S. Department of Housing & Urban Development
451 7th Street SW
Washington, DC 20410
202-708-1112
TTY: 202-708-1455
www.hud.gov/program_offices/fair_housing_equal_opp

Information and advocacy resources for families and professionals. Includes listings of organizations providing general information and organizations focusing on more specific areas of concern to families and young adults who have disabilities.

Jeanine Worden, Acting Assistant Secretary
David Enzel, General Deputy Assistant Secretary

6929 Office of Special Education and Rehabilitation Services
400 Maryland Avenue, SW
Washington, DC 20202
202-245-7468
www.ed.gov

Information and advocacy resources for families and professionals. Includes listings of organizations providing general information and organizations focusing on more specific areas of concern to families and young adults who have disabilities.

David Cantrell, Assistant Secretary
Paul Steenen, Director, Communications

National Associations & Support Groups

6930 ABLEDATA
103 W. Broad Street, Suite 400
Falls Church, VA 22046
800-227-0216
Fax: 703-356-8314
TTY: 703-992-8313
www.abledata.com

ABLEDATA provides objective information on assistive technology and rehabilitation equipment available from domestic and international source to consumers, organizations, professionals, and caregivers within the United States. We serve the nation's disability, and senior communities.

David Johnson, Publications Director
Katherine Belknap, Project Director
Steve Lowe, Associate Project Manager

6931 AHRC New York City
83 Maiden Lane
New York, NY 10038
212-780-2500
www.ahrcnyc.org

Developmentally disabled children and adults, their families, and interested individuals. Provides support services, training programs, clinics, schools and residential facilities to the developmentally disabled.

Marco Damiani, Chief Executive Officer
Amy West, EVP & CFO
Elizabeth Lynam, EVP & Chief Program Officer

6932 AIM for the Handicapped Adventures in Movement
945 Danbury Road
Dayton, OH 45420
937-294-4611
800-332-8210
Fax: 937-294-3783
www.aimforthehandicapped.org

To help individuals achieve their highest potential through the AIM Method of Specialized Movement Education.

Jo Geiger, Founder & National Executive Direct
J. Voss, President
Nancy Lopez, National Ambassadors

6933 Academic Pediatric Association
6728 Old McLean Village Drive
McLean, VA 22101
703-556-9222
Fax: 703-556-8729
info@ambpeds.org
www.ambpeds.org

The Ambulstory Pediatric Association fosters the health of children, adolescents, and families by promoting generalism in academic pediatrics and academics in general pediatrics.

General Resources / National Associations & Support Groups

Jessica K. O'Hara, Executive Director
Stephanie Blyskal, Association Manager
Holly Tyrrell, Research/Network Coordinator

6934 Academy for Guided Imagery
30765 Pacific Coast Highway, Suite 355
Malibu, CA 90265
424-242-6369
800-726-2070
Fax: 310-589-9523
info@acadgi.com
www.acadgi.com

The Academy for Guided Imagery is dedicated to educating and supporting practicing clinicians in their uses of imagery and imagery related approaches to therapy and healing. The Academy is an accredited Post-graduate training provider for health professionals, and a source of self-care products and programs for those struggling with a chronic, difficult, or painful illness.

David E. Bresler PhD,LAc, President
Jeanne Achterberg, PhD, Conference Faculty
Mark Atkinson, MBBS, Conference Faculty

6935 Academy of Rehabilitative Audiology
www.audrehab.org

ara@audrehab.org
www.audrehab.org

The primary purpose of ARA is to promote excellence in hearing care through the provision of comprehensive rehabilitative and habilitative services.

6936 Access Board
1331 F Street NW, Suite 1000
Washington, DC 20004
202-272-0080
800-872-2253
Fax: 202-272-0081
TTY: 800-993-2822
info@access-board.gov
www.access-board.gov

The Access Board is an independent Federal agency devoted to accessibility for people with disabilities. Created in 1973 to ensure access to federally funded facilities, the Board is now a leading source of information on accessible design. The Board develops and maintains design criteria for the built environment, transit vehicles, telecommunications equipment, and for electronic and information technology.

Deborah A. Ryan, Chairman
David M. Capozzi, Executive Director
James J. Raggio, General Counsel

6937 Adoptive Families
108 West 39th Street, Suite 805
New York, NY 10018
646-366-0830
800-372-3300
Fax: 646-366-0842
letters@adoptivefamilies.com
www.adoptivefamilies.com

Information and advocacy resources for families and professionals interested in adoption.

Susan Caughman, Editor/Publisher
Eve Gilman, Editor

6938 Alexander Graham Bell Association for the Deaf and Hard of Hearing
3417 Volta Place NW
Washington, DC 20007
202-337-5220
Fax: 202-337-8314
TTY: 202-337-5221
info@agbell.org
www.agbell.org

The Alexander Graham Bell Association for the Deaf and Hard of Hearing (AG Bell) is a lifelong resource, support network and advocate for listening, learning, talking, and living independently with hearing loss. Through publications, advocacy, training, scholarships, and financial aid, AG Bell promotes the use of spoken language and hearing technology.

Emilio Alonso-Mendoza, Chief Executive Officer

6939 American Academy of Audiology
11480 Commerce Park Drive, Suite 220
Reston, VA 20191
703-790-8466
Fax: 703-790-8631
info@audiology.org
www.audiology.org

A professional organization dedicated to providing high quality and balanced hearing care to the public. Provides professional development, education and research and provides increased public awareness of hearing disorders and audiologic services.

Patrick E. Gallagher, Executive Director
Anne Poodiak, VP, Meetings & Education
Glenn Feder, Senior Director, Sales

6940 American Academy of Child and Adolescent Psychiatry
3615 Wisconsin Avenue NW
Washington, DC 20016
202-966-7300
Fax: 202-464-0131
www.aacap.org

The AACAP (American Academy of Child and Adolescent Psychiatry) is the leading national professional medical association dedicated to the promotion of healthy development for children, adolescents, and families.

Heidi B. Fordi, Executive Director

6941 American Academy of Dermatology
P.O. Box 1968
Des Plaines, IL 60017
847-240-1280
888-462-3376
mrc@aad.org
www.aad.org

To promote and advance the art of medicine and surgery of the skin; promote the highest possible standards in clinical practice, education and research in dermatology and related disciplines.

6942 American Academy of Pediatrics
345 Park Blvd
Itasca, IL 60143
847-434-4000
800-433-9016
Fax: 847-434-8000
csc@aap.org
www.aap.org

The American Academy of Pediatrics and its member pediatricians dedicate their efforts and resources to the health, safety and well-being of infants, children, adolescents and young adults.

Kyle E. Yasuda, MD, FAAP, President
Mark Del Monte, JD, CEO/Executive VP
Vera Tait, MD, FAAP, Chief Medical Officer

6943 American Association of Children's Residential Centers (AACRC)
11700 W. Lake Park Drive
Milwaukee, WI 53224
877-332-2272
877-332-2272
Fax: 877-332-2272
info@aacrc-dc.org
www.aacrc-dc.org

The American Association of Children's Residential Centers brings professionals together to advance the frontiers of knowledge pertaining to the spectrum of therapeutic living environments for children and adolescents with behavioral health disorders.

Richard Altman, MSW, ACSW, Chief Executive Officer
William Powers, Chief Executive Officer
Christopher Bellonci, President

6944 American Association on Intellectual and Developmental Disabilities
8403 Colesville Road, Ste 900
Silver Spring, MD 20910
202-387-1968
800-424-3688
Fax: 202-387-2193
www.aamr.org

American Association on Intellectual and Developmental Disabilities' mission is to promote progressive policies, sound research, effective practices, and universal human rights for people with intellectual disabilities.

General Resources / National Associations & Support Groups

Margaret A. Nygren, Executive Director & CEO
Maria Alfaro, Manager, Meetings & Website
Laura Thorn, Manager, Membership/Communications

6945 **American Auditory Society**
PO Box 779
Pennsville, NJ 08070

877-746-8315
Fax: 650-763-9185
amaudsoc@comcast.net
www.amauditorysoc.org

The primary aims of the Society are to increase knowledge and understanding of the ear, hearing and balance; disorders of the ear, hearing and balance, and preventions of these disorders; and habilitation and rehabilitation of individuals with hearing and balance dysfunction.

Darla M. Eastlack, Executive Director

6946 **American Autoimmune Related Diseases Association**
19176 Hall Road, Suite 130
Clinton, MI 48038

586-776-3900
aarda@aarda.org
www.aarda.org

The American Autoimmune Related Diseases Association is dedicated to the eradication of autoimmune diseases and the alleviation of suffering and the socioeconomic impact of autoimmunity through fostering and facilitating collaboration in the areas of education, public awareness, research, and patient services in an effective, ethical and efficient manner.

Lilly Stairs, Interim President/CEO
Laura Simpson, COO

6947 **American Blind Bowling Association**
7232 South Ridgeland
Chicago, IL 60649

773-255-3121
Fax: ica-go -
www.abba1951.org

Information on adaptive bowling activities for people who are blind.

Robert McDonald, President
Rozella Campbell, Secretary/Treasurer
Wilbert Turner, Public Relations Committee Chair

6948 **American Blind Skiing Foundation**
609 Crandell Lane
Schaumburg, IL 60193

312-409-1605
www.absf.org

ABSF is committed to serving visually impaired children and adults, giving them the opportunities and experiences that build confidence and independence.

Michelle Hulscher, President
Beth Zange, Vice President
William Kopp, Treasurer

6949 **American Board of Dermatology**
2 Wells Avenue
Newton, MA 02459

617-910-6400
abderm@hfhs.org
www.abderm.org

Sole mission is to ensure competence for patients with cutaneous diseases through board representation.

Stanley J. Miller, President
Karen E. Warschaw, Vice President
Thomas D. Horn, Executive Director

6950 **American Board of Pediatrics**
111 Silver Cedar Court
Chapel Hill, NC 27514

919-929-0461
Fax: 919-929-9255
abpeds@abpeds.org
www.abp.org

The American Board is Pediatrics certifies general pediatricians and pediatric subspecialists based on standards of excellence that lead to high quality health care for infants, children and adolescents.

Dr. David G. Nichols, President/CEO

6951 **American Camp Association**
5000 State Road, 67 North
Martinsville, IN 46151

765-342-8456
800-428-2267
www.acacamps.org

The American Camp Association is a community of camp professionals who, for nearly 100 years, have joined together to share our knowledge and experience and to ensure the quality of camp program.

Tom Rosenberg, President & CEO

6952 **American Cancer Society**
3380 Chastain Meadows Parkway NW, Suite 200
Kennedaw, GA 30144

800-227-2345
www.cancer.org

The American Cancer Society is the leading cancer-fighting organization with a vision of ending cancer as we know it, for everyone. We are the only organization working to improve the lives of people with cancer and their families through advocacy, research, and patient support, to ensure everyone has an opportunity to prevent, detect, treat, and survive cancer.

Karen E Knudsen, Chief Executive Officer
William L Dehut, MD, Chief Scientific Officer
Kymm Martinez, Chief Marketing Officer

6953 **American Canoe Association**
PO Box 7996
Fredricksburg, VA 22404

540-907-4460
www.americancanoe.org

The American Canoe Association was founded in 1880 and is a national 501(c)(3) nonprofit organization that serves the broader paddling public by providing educational programs, supporting stewardship initiatives that affect paddlers, and offering competition opportunities to athletes of all abilities.

6954 **American Childhood Cancer Organization**
P.O. Box 498
Kensington, MD 20895

301-962-3520
800-366-2226
Fax: 301-962-3521
staff@acco.org
www.acco.org

The American Childhood Cancer Organization (ACCO) was founded in 1970 by a group of parents whose children had been diagnosed with cancer. Today ACCO is one of the largest grassroots, national organizations dedicated to improving the lives of children and adolescents with cancer and their families.

Ruth I. Hoffman, MPH, CEO
Krista Novak, Programs Manager
Blair Scroggs, Public Relations Coordinator

6955 **American Deafness and Rehabilitation Association (ADARA)**
PO Box 675
Lakeville, MN 55044

info@adara.org
www.adara.org

The mission of the ADARA is to facilitate excellence in human service delivery with individuals who are Deaf or Hard of Hearing. This mission is accomplished by enhancing the professional competencies of the membership, expanding opportunities for networking among ADARA colleagues and supporting positive public policies for individuals who are Deaf or Hard of Hearing.

6956 **American Dermatological Association**
531 N Ocean Boulevard, Suite 1907
Pompano Beach, FL 33062

305-804-1150
Fax: 954-252-2093
ameriderm1930@gmail.com
ada1.org

Professional society of physicians specializing in dermatology. Promotes teaching, practice, public education and research into dermatology.

6957 **American Epilepsy Society**
135 S LaSalle Street, Suite 2850
Chicago, IL 60603

312-883-3800
Fax: 312-896-5784
info@aesnet.org
www.aesnet.org

837

General Resources / National Associations & Support Groups

A society of clinicians, researchers, and health care professionals which promotes education and research of epilepsy.

Eileen Murray, Executive Director

6958 **American Hearing Research Foundation**
154 W Park Avenue, Suite 586
Elmhurst, IL 60126
630-617-5079
ahrf@american-hearing.org
www.american-hearing.org

Funds medical research and education into the causes, prevention, and cures of hearing losses, and balance disorders. Also keeps physicians and the public informed of the latest developments in hearing research and education.

Richard G. Muench, Chair
Alan G. Micco, President
David J. Wuertz, Treasurer

6959 **American Heart Association**
7272 Greenville Avenue
Dallas, TX 75231
214-570-5978
800-242-8721
www.heart.org

The mission of the American Heart Associate is to build healthier lives, free of cardiovascular diseases and stroke.

Nancy Brown, CEO
Mitchell S.V. Elkind, President
Suzie Upton, Chief Operating Officer

6960 **American Liver Foundation**
P.O. Box 299
West Orange, NJ 07052
800-465-4837
www.liverfoundation.org

The American Liver Foundation is the nationleading nonprofit organization promoting liver health and disease prevention. ALF provides research, education and advocacy for those affected by liver-related diseases, including hepatitis.

Lorraine Stiehl, CEO
David Ticker, Executive VP & CFO

6961 **American Lung Association**
55 W. Wacker Drive, Suite 1150
Chicago, IL 60601
800-586-4872
info@lung.org
www.lung.org

The American Lung Association fights lung disease in all its forms, with special emphasis on asthma, tobacco control and environmental health. The American Lung Association is funded with contributions from the public, along with gifts and grants from corporations, foundations and government agencies. The association achieves its many successes through the work of thousands of committed volunteers and staff.

Harold P. Wimmer, National President & CEO
Albert Rizzo, MD, Chief Medical Officer
Sue Swan, Chief Development Officer

6962 **American Pediatrics Society**
9303 New Trails Drive, Suite 350
The Woodlands, TX 77381
346-980-9707
info@aps1888.org
info@aps1888.org

American Pediatrics Society works to shape the future of academic pediatrics through engagement of distinguished child health leaders to represent the full diversity within the field. The Society's mission to advance child and adolescent health and well-being through an engaged, diverse, inclusive, and impactful community of pediatric thought leaders.

6963 **American Red Cross**
Washington, DC 20006
202-303-5214
800-733-2767
www.redcross.org

The American Red Cross has been the nation's premier emergency response organization. As part of a worldwide movement that offers neutral humanitarian care to the victims of war, the American Red Cross distinguished itself by also aiding victims of devastating natural disasters.

Bonnie McElveen-Hunter, Chair
Gail J. McGovern, President and CEO
Carmel Darcy, Chief Financial Officer

6964 **American Skin Association**
335 Madison Avenue, 22nd Floor
New York, NY 10017
212-889-4858
info@americanskin.org
www.americanskin.org

The American Skin Association is the only volunteer led health organization dedicated through research, education and advocacy to saving lives and alleviating human suffering caused by the full spectrum of skin disorders.

Kathleen Reichert, Executive Vice President
Kristin Ludl, Operations Manager

6965 **American Society for Deaf Children**
PO Box 23
Woodbine, MD 21791
800-942-2732
info@deafchildren.org
deafchildren.org

A nonprofit parent-helping-parent organization promoting a positive attitude toward signing and deaf culture. Also provides support, encouragement, and current information about deafness to families with deaf and hard of hearing children.

6966 **American Speech Language Hearing Association (ASHA)**
2200 Research Blvd
Rockville, MD 20852
301-296-5700
800-638-8255
Fax: 301-296-8580
TTY: 301-296-5650
actioncenter@asha.org
www.asha.org

A professional organization made up of over 123,000 hearing, speech and language professionals. It is a credentialing organization as well promotes the interests of provides services and information for those with communication disorders.

Shari B. Robertson, President
Theresa H. Rodgers, President-Elect

6967 **Amputee Coalition**
9303 Center Street, Ste 100
Manassas, VA 20110
888-267-5669
info@amputee-coalition.org
www.amputee-coalition.org

Empowering and reaching out to people affected by limb loss to achieve their full potentional through education, advocacy and support, as well as promoting limb loss prevention.

Jack Richmond, President & CEO
Dan Ignaszewski, Chief Policy & Programs Officer
Tonya Osborne-Simpson, Director, Support & Outreach

6968 **Arc of the United States**
1825 K Street NW, Ste 1200
Washington, DC 20006
202-534-3700
800-433-5255
Fax: 202-534-3731
info@thearc.org
www.thearc.org

The Arc of the United States advocates for the rights and full participation of all children and adults with intellectual and developmental disabilities. Together with a network of members and affiliated chapters, they improve systems of support and services; connect families; inspire communities and influence public policy.

Peter V. Berns, CEO

6969 **Association for Children's Mental Health**
6017 W. St. Joseph Hwy., Suite 200
Lansing, MI 48917
517-372-4016
888-226-4543
Fax: 517-372-4032
www.acmh-mi.org

General Resources / National Associations & Support Groups

ACMH is a family organization with statewide staff and membership who support activities to enhance the system or services which address the needs of children with serious emotional disorders and their families. ACMH is a statewide chapter of the national Federation of families for Children's Mental Health and our membership of over 1200 individuals is comprised of family members, professionals and concerned.

Jane Shank, Executive Director
Mary Porter, Business Manager
Terri Henrizi, Education Coordinator

6970 Association for Education & Rehabilitation of the Blind & Visually Impaired
5680 King Centre Drive, Suite 600
Alexandria, VA 22215
703-671-4500
aer@aerbvi.org
www.aerbvi.org

This association is the only international membership organization dedicated to rendering all possible support and assistance to the professionals who work in all phases of education and rehabilitation of blind and visually impaired children and adults.

Lee Sonnenberg, Executive Director
Michele Basham, Membership & Community Engagement
Elly du Pre, Manager, Accreditation Program

6971 Association of Blind Athletes
1 Olympic Plaza
Colorado Springs, CO 80909
719-866-3224
www.usaba.org

The mission of the United States Association of Blind Athletes is to increase the number and quality of grassroots through competitive, world-class athletic opportunities for Americans who are blind or visually impaired. We value the life enhancing aspects of sports and the opportunity to demonstrate the abilities of people who are blind and visually impaired.

Molly Quinn, Chief Executive Officer
Bill Kellick, Communications Manager
Catherine Raney Norman, Grants Manager

6972 Association of Children's Prosthetic/ Orthotic Clinics
403 W St. Charles Road, Suite 403B
Lombard, IL 60148
acpoc@affinity-strategies.com
www.acpoc.org

The Association of Children's Prosthetic-Orthotic Clinics (ACPOC) provides a comprehensive resource of treatment options provided by professionals who serve children, adolescents, and young adults with various musculoskeletal differences.

6973 Association of University Centers on Disabilities
1100 Wayne Ave., Suite 1000
Silver Spring, MD 20910
301-588-8252
Fax: 301-588-2842
aucdinfo@aucd.org
www.aucd.org

The Association of University Centers on Disabilities (AUCD) is a membership organization that supports and promotes a national network of university-based interdisciplinary programs.

John Tschida, Executive Director
Jeannette Cordova, Program Manager
Chevelle Glymph, Senior Director of Public Health

6974 Beneficial Designs
2325 P51 Ct., Suite 402
Minden, NV 89423
775-783-8822
Fax: 775-783-0813
mail@beneficialdesigns.com
www.beneficialdesigns.com

Beneficial Designs works towards universal access through research, design, and education. We believe all individuals should have access to the physical, intellectual, and spiritual aspects of life. We seek to enhance the quality of life for people of all abilities, and work to achieve this aim by developing and marketing technology for daily living, vocational, and leisure activities.

Peter Axelson, Founder, Director of R&D

6975 Benetech
3790 El Camino Real, Suite 1072
Palo Alto, CA 94306
650-644-3400
Fax: 650-475-1066
www.benetech.org

Benetech is a nonprofit venture that combines the impact of technological solutions with the social entrepreneurship business model to help disadvantaged communities in our society and across the world.

Ayan Kishore, Chief Executive Officer
Kathie Lee, Chief Financial Officer
Lisa Wadors, Vice President, Programs

6976 Birth Defect Research for Children
976 Lake Baldwin Lane, Suite 104
Orlando, FL 32814
407-895-0802
staff@birthdefects.org
www.birthdefects.org

Birth Defect Research for Children is a non-profit organization that provides parents and expectant parents with information about birth defects and support services for their children.

Betty Mekdeci, Executive Director

6977 Boy Scouts of America National Council
9190 Rockville Pike
Bethseda, MD 20814
301-530-9360
Fax: 301-564-9513
www.boyscouts-ncac.org

The mission of the Boy Scouts of America is to prepare young people to make ethical and moral choices over their lifetimes by instilling in them the values of the values of the Scouts Oath and Law.

6978 Braille Revival League
20330 NE 20th Court
Miami, FL 33179
305-692-9206
Fax: 305-984-0909
edwards.paul955@gmail.com
www.braillerevivalleague.org

Encourages blind people to read and write in Braille, advocates for mandatory Braille instruction in educational facilities for the blind, strives to make available a supply of Braille materials from libraries and printing houses and more.

Paul Edwards, President
Ralph Smitherman, Secretary
Jane Carona, Treasurer

6979 Breckenridge Outdoor Education Center
PO Box 697
Breckenridge, CO 80424
970-453-6422
800-383-2632
Fax: 970-453-4676
boec@boec.org
www.boec.org

The Breckenridge outdoor Education Center is a non-profit organization whose mission is to expand the potential of people with disabilities and special needs through meaningful, educational, and inspiring outdoor experiences.

6980 C.S. Mott Children's Hospital
1540 East Hospital Drive
Ann Arbor, MI 48109
734-936-4000
www.mottchildren.org

Since 1903, the University of Michigan has led the way in providing comprehensive, specialized health care for children. Our mission is to integrate clinical care, education, research and advocacy to advance the health status of children, women, and their families and communities statewide.

6981 CW HOG
Idaho State University
921 South 8th Avenue
Pocatello, ID 83209
208-282-3912
outdoor@isu.edu
www.isu.edu/outdoor

General Resources / National Associations & Support Groups

The Cooperative Wilderness Handicapped Outdoor Group, otherwise known as CW HOG, is a regional self-help group that was formed in 1981 to provide recreational opportunities for people of all abilities. CW HOG provides challenging outdoor adventure activities in a supportive environment, helps establish a supportive social network for people with and without disabilities, and furthers societal integration by building ties between individuals with disabilities and other community members.

Justin Dayley, Director
Bob Ellis, Outdoor Recreation Coordinator

6982 Caregiver Action Network
1150 Connecticut Avenue NW, Suite 501
Washington, DC 20036
202-454-3970
855-227-3640
info@caregiveraction.org
www.caregiveraction.org

Caregiver Action Network (CAN) is the nation's leading family caregiver organization working to improve the quality of life for the more than 90 million Americans who care for loved ones with chronic conditions, disabilities, disease, or the frailties of old age. CAN serves a broad spectrum of family caregivers including parents of children with significant health needs.

Lisa Winstel, Interim CEO
Mae-Beth LeGeyt, Chief of Staff
Nichole Goble, Director of Community Initiatives

6983 Center for Best Practices in Early Childhood
Western Illinois University
1 University Circle
Macomb, IL 61455
309-298-1634
Fax: 309-298-2305
jk-johanson@wiu.edu
www.wiu.edu/thecenter

The mission of the Center for Best Practices in Early Childhood Education is to promote family-centered, research-based practices designed to improve educational opportunities for all young children. The Center promotes inclusion, transition, and other research-based practices which lead to improved child outcomes. The Center also offers professional development and training events, networking opportunities, technical assistance, and consultation services.

Joyce Johanson, Associate Director

6984 Center for Literacy and Disability Studies
University of North Carolina
321 S Columbia Street, Suite 1100 Bondurant Hall
Chaple Hill, NC 27599
919-966-8566
Fax: 919-843-3250
clds@unc.edu
www.med.unc.edu/healthsciences/clds

The Center's mission is to promote literacy and communication for individuals of all ages with disabilities. It is the belief of the CLDS that disabilities are only one of many factors that influence an individuals ability to learn to read and write and to use print throughout their life and across their living environments.

Karen Erickson, Director

6985 Center for Mental Health Services
5600 Fishers Lane
Rockville, MD 20857
240-276-1310
www.samhsa.gov

Encourages a range of programs such as systems of care to respond to the increasing number of mental, emotional, and behavioral problems among children. Supports outreach and case management programs for the thousands of Americans who are homeless and the improvement of these services.

Anita Everett, MD, Director

6986 Center for Parent Information and Resources (CPIR)
c/o SPAN, 35 Halsey Street, 4th Floor
Newark, NJ 07102
973-642-8100
malizo@spanadvocacy.org
www.parentcenterhub.org

Family-friendly information and research-based materials on key topics for Parent Centers. Private workspaces for Parent Centers to exchange resources, discuss high-priority topics, and solve mutual challenges. Coordination of parent training efforts throughout the network.

Myriam Alizo, Project Assistant

6987 Chai Lifeline
151 W 30th Street
New York, NY 10001
212-465-1300
Fax: 212-465-0949
www.chailifeline.org

Chai Lifeline is an international support network, providing social, emotional, and practical assistance to children, families, and communities impacted by medical crises and trauma through a variety of year-round programs and services.

Rabbi Simcha Scholar, Chief Executive Officer
Rabbi Abraham Cohen, Executive Director
Esther Bergman, Chief Financial Officer

6988 Child Abuse Prevention Association
503 E 23rd Street
Independence, MO 64055
816-252-8388
info@capacares.org
capacares.org

Mission is to prevent and treat all forms of child abuse by creating changes in individuals, families and society which strengthen relationships and promote healing.

Rochelle Parker, President & CEO
Susan Ruddell, Manager of Administration
Kristina Jones, Vice President of Programs

6989 Child Neurology Foundation
601 W Short Street
Lexington, KY 40508
888-417-3435
info@childneurologyfoundation.org
childneurologyfoundation.org

The Child Neurology Foundation connects partners from all areas of the child neurology community so those navigating the journey of disease diagnosis, management, and care have the ongoing support from those dedicated to treatments and cures.

Amy Brin, Executive Director
Katie Hentges, Director, Programs
Brea McCormley, Director, Development

6990 Children's Defense Fund
840 First Street NE, Suite 300
Washington, DC 20002
202-628-8787
cdfinfo@childrensdefense.org
www.childrensdefense.org

Information and advocacy resources for families and professionals. Includes listings of organizations providing general information and organizations focusing on more specific areas of concern to families and young adults who have disabilities.

Rev. Dr. Starsky Wilson, President & CEO
Bob Farrace, National Director, Public Affairs
Sheri A. Brady, VP, Strategy & Program

6991 Children's Hospice International
1800 Diagonal Road, Suite 600
Alexandria, VA 22314
703-684-0330
info@chionline.org
www.chionline.org

This nonprofit organization works to improve hospice care for children. Free services include information and referral service for child care, counseling, support groups, pain management, professional education, and research. This is a membership group, with a membership fee for other services.

6992 Children's Hospital Boston
300 Longwood Avenue
Boston, MA 02115
617-355-6000
www.childrenshospital.org

Mission is to provide the highest quality care; be the leading source of research and discovery; educate the next generation of leaders in child health and enhance the health and well-being of the children and families in our local community.

Kevin Churchwell, President & CEO
Jessica Farnham, Chief Operating Officer

General Resources / National Associations & Support Groups

6993 Children's Organ Transplant Association
2501 West Cota Drive
Bloomington, IN 47403
800-366-2682
Fax: 812-336-8885
cota@cota.org
www.cota.org

The association provides fundraising assistance for children needing life-saving transplants and promotes organ, marrow and tissue donation.

Rick Lofgren, President & CEO
Lisa Fulkerson, VP & CFO
Kristy Brown, Chief Development Officer

6994 Children's Wish Foundation International
8615 Roswell Road
Atlanta, GA 30350
800-323-9474
info@childrenswish.org
www.childrenswish.org

Children's Wish Foundation International is dedicated to bringing joy and hope to seriously ill children and their families world wide by involving the public in putting children first with opportunities to experience the enhanced value and quality of life through the magic of a fulfilled wish.

Linda Dozoretz, Founder

6995 Childswork/Childsplay
40 Aero Road, Suite 2
Bohemia, NY 11716
800-962-1141
Fax: 800-262-1886
www.childswork.com

Childswork/Childsplay uses a prevention and intervention model when creating its high-quality products. These programs focus on the behavioral, social, and emotional issues children deal with at home and at school. Through the use of games, print materials and visual media, counselors and educators have a superior array of counseling tools at their disposal.

6996 Compassionate Friends
48660 Pontiac Trail, #930808
Wixom, MI 48393
877-969-0010
www.compassionatefriends.org

Compassionate Friends assists families toward the positive resolution of grief following the death of a child of any age and provides information to help others be supportive. A national nonprofit, self-help support organization that offers friendship, understanding, and hope to bereaved parents, grandparents and siblings.

Shari O'Loughlin, Chief Executive Officer

6997 Council for Exceptional Children
3100 Clarendon Blvd, Suite 600
Arlington, VA 22201
888-232-7733
service@exceptionalchildren.org
exceptionalchildren.org

Advocates appropriate policies, standards and development for students with special needs.

Chad Rummel, Executive Director

6998 Council of Administrators of Special Education (CASE)
1736 E Sunshine Street, Suite 501
Springfield, MO 65804
417-427-7720
office@casecec.org
www.casecec.org

CASE provides leadership to advance the field of special education through professional learning, policy, and advocacy.

Phyllis Wolfram, Executive Director
Brigid Bright, Director, Communications/Membership
Vicki McNamara, Director, Professional Development

6999 CureSearch for Children's Cancer
P.O. Box 45781
Baltimore, MD 21297
800-458-6223
Fax: 301-718-0047
info@curesearch.org
www.curesearch.org

CureSearch for Children's Cancer is a national non-profit foundation that accelerates the cure for children's cancer by driving innovation, eliminating research barriers and solving the field's most challenging problems.

Kay Koehler, CEO
Katharine A. Burke, COO & VP, Financing
Caitlyn W. Barrett, National Director, Research & Prgms

7000 Developmental Delay Resources
5801 Beacon Street
Pittsburgh, PA 15217
800-497-0944
Fax: 412-422-1374
www.devdelay.org

A nonprofit organization dedicated to meeting the needs of those working with children who have developmental delays in sensory motor, language, social, and emotional areas. DDR provides a network for parents and professionals and current information after the diagnosis to support children with special needs.

Patricia S. Lemer, Executive Director

7001 Developmental Disabilities Nurses Association
1501 South Loop 288, Suite 104 - 381
Denton, TX 76205
800-888-6733
Fax: 844-336-2329
www.ddna.org

Developmental Disabilities Nurses Association (DDNA) is a 501(c)(3) not-for-profit nursing specialty organization that is committed to advocacy, education, and support for nurses who provide services to persons with intellectual and developmental disabilities (IDD).

7002 Disability Rights Education & Defense Fund
3075 Adeline Street, Suite 210
Berkeley, CA 94703
510-644-2555
Fax: 510-841-8645
info@dredf.org
www.dredf.org

Nonprofit law and public policy center that specializes in laws affecting more than 45 million Americans with disabilities. DREDF was founded 16 years ago to challenge the barriers that exclude people with disabilities from participating in all aspects of society.

Susan Henderson, Executive Director
Diana Vega, Operations Director
Claudia Center, Legal Director

7003 Disabled Shooting Services
National Rifle Association of America
11250 Waples Mill Road
Fairfax, VA 22030
703-267-1495
Fax: 703-267-3941
explore.nra.org

Information on adaptive shooting activities for people of many abilities.

David Baskin, Department Head

7004 Disabled Sports USA
451 Hungerford Drive, Suite 100
Rockville, MD 20850
jray@dsusa.org
www.teamusa.org

A national nonprofit, organization established in 1967 by disabled Vietnam veterans to serve the war injured. DS/USA now offers nationwide sports rehabilitation programs to anyone with a permanent disability.

Julia Ray, Program Manager

7005 Division for Early Childhood
PO Box 660289
Los Angeles, CA 90066
310-428-7209
Fax: 855-678-1989
dec@dec-sped.org
www.dec-sped.org

This division is one of seventeen divisions of the Council for Exceptional Children, the largest international professional organization dedicated to improving educational outcomes for individuals with exceptionalities, students with disabilities, and/or the gifted.

Peggy Kemp, Executive Director
Britt Clark, Operations & Communications Manager

General Resources / National Associations & Support Groups

7006 Division of Birth Defects & Developmental Disabilities
1600 Clifton Road NE
Atlanta, GA 30333
800-232-4636
TTY: 888-232-6348
www.cdc.gov/ncbddd

Information and advocacy resources for families and professionals dealing with children with birth defects and developmental disabilities.

Karen Remley, MD, Director
Stephanie Dulin, Deputy Director

7007 Division on Career Development and Transition
Council for Exceptional Children
217 Saint Charles Place
Pittsburgh, PA 15215
412-874-3111
sdojonovic@ku.edu
www.dcdt.org

Focuses on the career development of individuals with disabilities and their transition from school to adult life.

Stacie Dojonovic, Executive Director

7008 Easter Seals
141 W Jackson Boulevard, Suite 1400A
Chicago, IL 60604
312-726-6200
800-221-6827
Fax: 312-726-1494
info@easterseals.com
www.easterseals.com

Easter Seals' mission is to create solutions that change lives for children and adults with disabilities and to provide appropriate developmental and rehabilitation services. Services provided include early intervention, after-school programs, preschool, tutoring, medical rehabilitation, vocational services, adult and senior day services, respite and in home care, camping and recreation, residential housing, support services, support groups, transportation, and referrals.

Kendra Davenport, President & CEO

7009 Endocrine Society
2055 L Street NW, Suit 600
Washington, DC 20036
202-971-3636
888-363-6274
Fax: 202-736-9705
info@endocrine.org
www.endocrine.org

The Endocrine Society is devoted to advancing hormone research, excellence in the clinical practice of endocrinology, broadening understanding of the critical role hormones play in health, and advocating on behalf of the global endocrinology community.

Kate Fryer, Chief Executive Officer
Mila Baker, Chief Policy Officer
Zerihun Haile-Selassie, Chief Financial Officer

7010 Exceptional Children Foundation
5350 Machado Road
Culver City, CA 90230
310-204-3300
info@ecf.net
www.ecf.net

To improve the well-being of children and families by providing theapeutic, social and educational services.

Veronica Arteaga, President & CEO

7011 Family Voices
561 Virginia Road, Building 4, Suite 300
Concord, MA 01742
781-674-7224
888-835-5669
www.familyvoices.org

Family Voices, a national grassroots network of families and friends, advocates for health care services that are famliy-centered, community-based, comprehensive. coordinated and culturally competent for all children and youth with special health care needs; promotes the inclusion of all families as decision makers at all levels of health care; and supports essential partnerships between families and professionals.

Nora Wells, Executive Director

7012 Federation for Children with Special Needs Center
529 Main Street, Suite 1M3
Boston, MA 02129
617-236-7210
800-331-0688
Fax: 617-241-0330
info@fcsn.org
www.fcsn.org

The mission of the Federation for Children with Special Needs provides information, support, and assistance to parents of children with disabilities, and encouraging full participation in community life by all people, especially those with disabilities.

Pam Nourse, Executive Director

7013 Friends' Health Connection
www.friendshealthconnection.org

admin@friendshealthconnection.org
www.friendshealthconnection.org

Organization Mission Friends' Health Connection is a nonprofit organization that connects people who are currently experiencing or who have overcome the same disease, illness, handicap or injury in order to communicate for mutual support.

Roxanne Black-Weisheit, FHC Founder and Executive Director

7014 Genetic Alliance
426400 Woodfield Road, Ste 189
Damascus, MD 20872
202-966-5557
Fax: 202-966-8553
info@geneticalliance.org
www.geneticalliance.org

World's leading nonprofit health advocacy organization committed to transforming health through genetics and promoting an environment of openness centered on the health of individuals, families, and communities.

Sharon Terry, CEO
Ruth Child, CFO
Natasha Bonhomme, Chief Strategy Officer

7015 Girl Scouts of the USA
420 5th Avenue
New York, NY 10018
www.girlscouts.org

Girl Scout of the USA is the world's preeminent organization dedicated solely to girls-all girls-where, in an accepting and nurturing environment, girls build character and skills for success in the real world.

Bonnie Barczykowski, CEO

7016 Handicapped Scuba Association
1104 El Prado
San Clemente, CA 92672
949-498-4540
www.hsascuba.com

Information on adaptive scuba diving activities for people of many abilities. Includes local chapters, referrals, fun and social interaction and support groups.

7017 Handle with Care
184 McKinstry Road
Gardnier, NY 12525
845-255-4031
Fax: 845-256-0094
info@handlewithcare.com
www.handlewithcare.com

Information and advocacy resources for families and professionals. Includes listings of organizations providing general information and organizations focusing on more specific areas of concern to families and young adults who have disabilities.

Bruce Chapman, Founder/President

7018 Hearing Health Foundation
PO Box 1397
New York, NY 10018
212-257-6140
info@hhf.org
hearinghealthfoundation.org

Hearing Health Foundation (HHF) is the largest private funder of hearing research, with a mission to prevent and cure hearing loss and tinnitus through groundbreaking research.

General Resources / National Associations & Support Groups

Timothy Higdon, President & CEO
Noemi Disla, Director, Finance/Operations/Admin
Christopher Geissler, Director, Programs/Research Support

7019 Heriditary Disease Foundation
601 W 168th Street, Suite 54
New York, NY 10032
212-928-2121
cures@hdfoundation.org
www.hdfoundation.org

Conducts interdisciplinary workshop program that recruits scientists to develop and apply new technologies, supports basic research on genetic illness through grant and postdoctoral fellowship programs at major universities, and provides research tissue to medical investigators.

Meghan Donaldson, Chief Executive Officer
Nancy Wexler, President
Travis Carey, Chief Financial Officer

7020 Human Growth Foundation
997 Glen Cove Avenue, Suite 5
Glen Head, NY 11545
800-451-6434
Fax: 516-671-4055
www.hgfound.org

A voluntary, nonprofit organization whose mission is to help children and adults with disorders of growth and growth hormones through research, education, support and advocacy. The foundation is dedicated to helping medical science to better understand the process of growth. It is composed of concerned parents and friends of children and adults with growth problems; and interested health professionals.

Joel Steelman, MD, President
Emily Germain-Lee, MD, Vice President

7021 Independent Living Research Utilization Program
1333 Mournsund
Houston, TX 77030
713-520-0232
Fax: 713-520-5785
TTY: 713-520-0232
ilru@ilru.org
www.ilru.org

Information and advocacy resources for families and professionals on independent living for people with disabilities.

Lex Frieden, Director, ILRU
Richard Petty, Co-Director

7022 Institute for Families
1300 N Vermont Avenue, Suite 1004
Los Angeles, CA 90027
www.instituteforfamilies.org

A non-profit organization providing free of charge support and services to professionals and families of visually impaired children.

7023 International Society of Dermatology
7041 Canal Boulevard, Suite 175
New Orleans, LA 70124
386-437-4405
info@IntSocDermatol.org
www.intsocderm.org

Promotes interest, education and research in dermatology.

7024 Jewish Children's Adoption Network
PO Box 237
Brooklandville, MD 21022
720-260-5864
jcan613@gmail.com
jewishchildrensadoption.org

Our primary goal is to find Jewish homes for Jewish children. We have worked on over 2,000 cases since 1990, and charge no fees for any of our services, which include helping a birth family parent a child, locating resources for help with personal problems or coping with a child's limitations, helping an adoptive family find resources for adoption or parenting, helping families negotiate adoption subsidies, and helping biological and adoptive triad members in starting a search.

7025 Learning Disabilities Association of America
PO Box 10369, 4156 Library Road
Pittsburgh, PA 15234
412-341-1515
888-300-6710
Fax: 412-344-0224
info@LDAAmerica.org
www.ldaamerica.org

Helps families of the affected individual through information and referral to professionals in their area. A membership organization with affiliates across the country.

Stephanie Fedro-Byrom, Operations Manager
Maureen Swanson, Director, Healthy Children Project
Ericka Pardun, Communications Coordinator

7026 Lifespire (A.C.R.M.D.)
1 Whitehall Street, 9th Floor
New York, NY 10004
212-741-0100
Fax: 212-320-0407
info@lifespire.org
www.lifespire.org

Life is committees to the principle that all individuals with a development disability are able to become contributing members of their family and community. It is Lifespire's aim to provide these individuals with the assistance and support necessary so that they can attain the skills necessary to maintain themselves in their community in the most integrated and independent manner possible.

Mark Van Voorst, CEO/President
Tom Lydon, COO
Keith Lee, CFO

7027 March of Dimes Foundation
1550 Crystal Drive, Ste 1300
Arlington, VA 22202
888-663-4637
www.marchofdimes.org

March of Dimes help moms have full-term pregnancies and research the problems that threaten the health of babies. The March of Dimes also acts globally: sharing best practices in perinatal health and helping improve birth outcomes where the needs are the most urgent.

Stacey D. Stewart, President
Alan Brogdon, SVP/COO/Board Officer
Rahul Gupta, MD, SVP & Chief Medical/Health Officer

7028 NADD: National Association for the Dually Diagnosed
12 Hurley Avenue
Kingston, NY 12401
845-331-4336
800-331-5362
Fax: 845-331-4569
info@thenadd.org
www.thenadd.org

Nonprofit organization designed to promote the interests of professional and parent development with resources for individuals who have the coexistence of mental illness and intellectual disabilities. Provides conferences, educational services and training materials to professionals, parents, concerned citizens, and service organizations.

Jeanne Farr, CEO
Michelle Jordan, Office Manager
Edward Seliger, Project Coordinator

7029 NAMI DuPage
Linda A. Kurzawa Community Center
115 North Country Farm Road
Wheaton, IL 60187
630-752-0066
Fax: 630-752-1064
www.namidupage.org

NAMI DuPage was founded by a group of parents in 1985 as an affiliate of the National Alliance on Mental Illness, a nationwide mental health advocacy organization who were dedicated to improving the quality of lives of people affected by mental illnesses.

Geri Kerger, Executive Director
Meredith Kober, Director of Programs
Nancy Leguizamon, Director of Family Support Services

7030 National Ability Center
1000 Ability Way
Park City, UT 84060
435-649-3991
hello@discovernac.org
new.discovernac.org

The National Ability Center empowers individuals of all abilities by building self-esteem, confidence and lifetime skills through sport, recreation and educational programs.

General Resources / National Associations & Support Groups

7031 National Academy for Child Development (NACD)
5492 S 500 E
Washington Terrace, UT 84405
801-621-8606
www.nacd.org

International organization of parents and professionals dedicated to helping children and adults reach their full potential.

7032 National Adoption Center
1735 Market Street, Suite 441A
Philadelphia, PA 19103
215-735-9988
ac@adopt.org
www.adopt.org

Information and advocacy resources for families and professionals interested in or dealing with adoption. Includes listings of organizations providing general information and organizations focusing on specific areas of concern.

Dominique McFadden, Interim Executive Director
Dana Brady, Director of Development
Alexandra Buczek, Operations Manager

7033 National Alliance on Mental Illness (NAMI)
4301 Wilson Blvd., Suite 300
Arlington, VA 22203
703-524-7600
800-999-6264
info@nami.org
www.nami.org

NAMI provides advocacy, education, support and public awareness so that all individuals and families affected by mental illness can build better lives.

Daniel H. Gillison, CEO
David Levy, CFO
Ken Duckworth, Chief Medical Officer

7034 National Amputee Golf Association
701 Orkney Court
Smyrna, TN 37167
615-415-9518
800-633-6242
webmaster@nagagolf.org
www.nagagolf.org

Information on adaptive golf activities for people of many abilities. Includes regional chapters, referrals, fun and social interaction and support groups.

Adam Benza, Co-Executive Director
Tracy Ramin, Co-Executive Director
Chris Osborne, Public Relations Director

7035 National Arts and Disability Center
Semel Institute For Neuroscience & Human Behavior
760 Westwood Plaza
Los Angeles, CA 90095
www.semel.ucla.edu/nadc

The mission of the National Arts and Disability Center (NADC) is to promote the inclusion of audiences and artists with disabilities into all facets of the arts community. The NADC is a project of the UCLA Tarjan Center.

7036 National Association for the Education of Young Children
1401 H Street NW, Suite 600
Washington, DC 20005
202-232-8777
800-424-2460
www.naeyc.org

NAEYC promotes high-quality early learning for all young children, birth through age 8, by connecting early childhood practice, policy, and research. We advance a diverse, dynamic early childhood profession and support all who care for, educate, and work on behalf of young children.

Michelle Kang, Chief Executive Officer
Treva Bustow, Sr Director, Membership & Marketing
Susan Friedman, Sr Director, Publishing & Content

7037 National Association of Blind Students
200 East Wells Street, Jernigan Place
Baltimore, MD 21230
410-659-9314
nfb@nfb.org
nabslink.org

For over 50 years, the National Association of Blind Students has worked, as an integral part of the National Federation of the Blind, to promote the equality of the blind by serving as a source of information, forum for networking and vehicle for collective action for blind students. Our work on the local, state, and national levels is firmly rooted in the conviction that blindness need not prevent one from excelling in a chosen field of study or living a full and productive life.

7038 National Center for Learning Disabilities
1 Thomas Circle NW, #700
Washington, DC 20005
212-545-7510
888-575-7373
Fax: 212-545-9665
www.ncld.org

Works to ensure that the nation's 15 million children, adolescents and adults with learning disabilities have every opportunity to succeed in school, work and life. NCLD provides essential information to parents, professionals and individuals with learning disabilities, promotes research and programs to foster effective learning and advocates for policies to protect and strengthen educational rights and opportunities.

Lindsay E. Jones, Esq., CEO
Quinn Bradlee, Youth Engagement Associate
Meghan Whittaker, Esq., Director of Policy

7039 National Center on Accessbility
University of Indiana
2805 E 10th Street, Suite 170
Bloomington, IN 47408
812-855-3095
nca@indiana.edu
www.ncaonline.org

The National Center for Accessibility (NCA), is a program of the Eppley Institute for Parks and Public Lands, offering training, assessments, research, planning, and technical assistance on accessibility design, infrastructure, and best practices for parks.

7040 National Children's Cancer Society
500 North Broadway, Suite 1850
St Louis, MO 63102
314-241-1600
800-532-6459
Fax: 314-241-1996
www.thenccs.org

NCCS offers a multifaceted outreach program, which includes financial assistance, education, information, and emotional support. They provide financial assistance for bone marrow transplantation, donor harvest, donor search, donor recruitment, and family emergency expenses (such as travel, hotel, food). They also have an active advocacy program to help families with insurance companies and hospitals.

Mark Stolze, President & CEO
Julie Komanetsky, VP Patient & Family Services

7041 National Early Childhood Technical Assistance Center
517 S Greenboro Street
Carrboro, NC 27510
ectacenter.org

Supports the national implementation of the early childhood provisions of the Individuals with Disabilities Education Act (IDEA). The mission is to strengthen systems at all levels to ensure that children (birth through five) with disabilities and their families receive and benefit from high quality, culturally appropriate and family centered supports and services.

Christina Kasprzak, Co-Director
Megan Vinh, Co-Director

7042 National Federation of Families
15800 Crabbs Branch Way, Suite 300
Rockville, MD 20855
240-403-1901
ffcmh@ffcmh.org
www.ffcmh.org

The National family run organization is dedicated exclusively to helping children with mental health needs and their families achieve a better quality of life.

Lynda Gargan, PhD, Executive Director

General Resources / National Associations & Support Groups

7043 National Foundation for Transplants
3249 W. Sarazen's Cir, Suite 100
Memphis, TN 38125
901-684-1697
800-489-3863
Fax: 901-684-1128
info@transplants.org
www.transplants.org

Nonprofit organization that assists transplant candidates and recipients nationwide when public or private insurance does not cover all their transplant-related costs. Offers a fund raising program for patients who need to raise $10,000 or more, and grant program that helps patients with smaller, one-time needs.

7044 National Industries for the Blind
1310 Braddock Place
Alexandria, VA 22314
703-310-0500
Fax: 703-998-8268
communications@nib.org
www.nib.org

A nonprofit organization that represents over 100 associated industries serving people who are blind in thirty-six states. These agencies serve people who are blind or visually impaired and help them to reach their full potential. Services include job and family counseling, job skills training, instruction in Braille and other communication skills, children's programs and more.

Gary J. Krump, Chairperson
Kevin A. Lynch, President and Chief Executive Offic
Claudia Knott, Chief Operating Officer

7045 National Mental Health Consumers' Self-Help Clearinghouse
1211 Chestnut Street, Suite 1207
Philadelphia, PA 19107
267-507-3810
800-553-4539
Fax: 215-636-6312
selfhelpclearinghouse@gmail.com
www.mhselfhelp.org

Offers information, support, and appropriate referrals and promotes public and professional education. Provides networking for those with special interest related to albinism and management of albinism and hypopigmentation.

Joseph Rogers, Founder/Executive Director
Susan Rogers, Director

7046 National Organization for Rare Disorders
55 Kenosia Avenue, PO Box 1968
Danbury, CT 06810
203-744-0100
800-999-6673
Fax: 203-798-2291
TDD: 203-797-9590
orphan@rarediseases.org
www.rarediseases.org

The National Organization for Rare Disorders (NORD), a 501(c)(3) organization, is a unique federation of voluntary health organization dedicated to helping with rare 'orphan' diseases and assisting the organization that serve them. NORD is committed to the identification, treatment, and cure of rare disorders through programs of education, advocacy, research, and service.

Peter L Saltonstall, President & CEO
Pamela Gavin, Chief Operating Officer
Mary Cobb, SVP Membership & Organiz. Strategy

7047 National Organization on Disability
77 Water Street, Suite 204
New York, NY 10005
646-505-1191
Fax: 646-505-1184
TDD: 202-293-5968
info@nod.org
www.nod.org

The mission of the National Organization on Disability (N.O.D.) is to expand the participation and contribution of America's 54 million men, women and children with disabilities in all aspects of life, by raising awareness through programs and information.

Thomas J. Ridge, Chairman
Cory Olicker Henkel, Chief Operating Officer
Miranda Pax, Chief of Staff

7048 National Parent Resource Center
Federation for Children with Special Needs
95 Berkeley Street, Suite 104
Boston, MA 02116
617-482-2915
800-695-2939
Fax: 617-572-2094
fcsninfo@fcsn.org
www.fcsn.org

A parent-run resource system designed to further the needs and goals of family-centered, community-based coordinated care for children with special health needs and their families. Offers written materials, training packages, workshops and presentations for parents and professionals on special education, health care financing and other topics.

7049 National Perinatal Association
PO Box 392
Lonedell, MO 63060
KLove@nationalperinatal.org
www.nationalperinatal.org

Information and advocacy resources for families and professionals. Includes listings of organizations providing general information and organizations focusing on more specific areas of concern to families and young adults who have disabilities.

Kristy Love, Executive Director
Elizabeth Filipovich, Vice President, Programs
Jessica Restivo, Vice President, Development

7050 National Rehabilitation Information Center
8400 Corporate Drive, Suite 500
Landover, MD 20785
800-346-2742
Fax: 301-459-4263
TTY: 301-459-5984
naricinfo@heitechservices.com
www.naric.com

Committed to providing direct, personal and information services to anyone interested in disability rehabilitation issues; Committed to serving consumers, researchers, family members, health professionals, educators, counselors, students, librarians and the administrators.

Mark X. Odum, Project Director
Jessica H. Chaiken, Media/Information Services Manager
Natalie J. Collier, Library and Acquisitions Manager

7051 National Sleep Foundation
1414 NE 42nd St, Ste 400
Seattle, WA 98105
contact@sleepfoundation.org
www.sleepfoundation.org

Works to improve the quality of life for millions of Americans who suffer from sleep disorders, and to prevent the catastrophic accidents that are related to poor or disordered sleep through research, education and the dissemination of information towards the cause of the Narcolepsy Project. Seeks patients to aid new research project targeting the cause of the disorder.

Bill Fish, General Manager

7052 National Vaccines Information Center
407 Church Street, Suite H
Vienna, VA 22180
703-938-0342
Fax: 703-938-5768
contactNVIC@gmail.com
www.nvic.org

Information and advocacy resources for families and professionals. Includes listings of organizations providing general information and organizations focusing on more specific areas of concern to families and young adults who have disabilities.

Barbara Loe Fisher, Co-Founder and President
Kathi Williams, Co-Founder and Vice President
Paul Arhtur, Director of Operations

7053 National Wheelchair Softball Association
13414 Paul Street
Omaha, NE 68145
402-305-5020
Fax: 612-437-3889
bfroendt@cox.net
www.wheelchairsoftball.org

Information on adaptive softball activities for people of many abilities.

General Resources / National Associations & Support Groups

Brian Chavez, President
Bruce Froendt, Commissioner
Thomas Dodd, 1st Director at Large

7054 New England Center for Children
33 Turnpike Road
Southborough, MA 01772
508-481-1015
Fax: 508-485-3421
www.necc.org

Serving students between the ages of 3 and 22 diagnosed with autism, learning disabilities, language delays, behavior disorders and related disabilities; educational curriculum encompasses both the teaching of functional life skills and traditional academics; communication skills are taught throughout all activities in the school, residence, and community. Tuition and fees are set by the state. Consulting services also available.

Vincent Strully, Jr, President & CEO
Michael S Downey, EVP & CFO
Susan Langer, Chief Program Officer

7055 North American Riding for the Handicapped
7475 Dakin Street, Suite 600
Denver, CO 80223
303-452-1212
800-369-7433
Fax: 303-252-4610
www.pathintl.org

Information on adaptive riding activities for people of many abilities. Includes local chapters, referrals, fun and social interaction and support groups. NARHA is a membership organization that promotes and supports equine activities for the disabled. Membership dues are $50 - $150.

Kay Green, Chief Executive Officer
Carolyn Malcheski, Director of Human Resource and Fina
Kaye Marks, Director of Marketing and Communica

7056 Oak-Leyden Developmental Services
411 Chicago Avenue
Oak Park, IL 60302
708-524-1050
Fax: 708-524-2469
info@oak-leyden.org
www.oak-leyden.org

The mission of Oak-Leyden Developmental Services is to serve people with developmental disabilities and their families in a manner which recognizes their dignity, is supportive of their personal choices and promotes their inclusion in the larger community.

R.J. McMahon, CEO
Nancy Thomas, Director of Human Resources
Melissa Ehmann, Director of Children's Services

7057 Pan American Health Organization (PAHO)
525 23rd Street, NW
Washington, DC 20037
202-974-3000
Fax: 202-974-3663
postmaster@paho.org
www.paho.org

Acts as the directing and co-ordinating authority on international health work; aids in the prevention and control of epidemic, endemic and other diseases; promotes the improvement of nutrition, housing, sanitation, recreation, economic or working conditions; promotes improved standards of teaching and training in the health, medical and related professions; and fosters activities in the field of mental health.

Dr. Carissa F. Etienne, Director
Dr. Isabella Danel, Deputy Director
Gerald Anderson, Director of Administration

7058 Parent to Parent USA
PO Box 472
State College, PA 16804
484-272-7368
www.p2pusa.org

Parent to Parent USA supports a network of viable, sustainable, fully-functioning, and effective Parent to Parent programs in all 50 states through hands-on support, training and technical assistance, and high-quality tools and resources.

Aurelie "Lily" Brown, Co-Director
Marsha Quinn, Co-Director

7059 Pathways.org
355 E Erie Street
Chicago, IL 60611
friends@pathways.org
pathways.org

Provides free tools to maximize all children's motor, sensory, and communication development. Seeks to empower parents to understand and encourage their baby's development to keep them on track or catch potential delays early. Ensures every child is screened for motor, sensory, and communication development by 4 months of age, taking advantage of baby's neuroplasticity.

7060 Pioneers Division of CEC
Council for Exceptional Children
2900 Crystal Drive, Suite 1000
Arlington, VA 22202
703-620-3660
888-232-7733
Fax: 703-264-9474
TTY: 866-915-5000
exceptionalchildren.org

Promotes activities and programs to increase awareness of the educational needs of children with disabilities and/or who are gifted, and the services that are available to them.

Lynda Van Kuren, Contact

7061 Prevent Blindness America
225 West Wacker Drive, Suite 400
Chicago, IL 60606
800-331-2020
info@preventblindness.org
www.preventblindness.org

A volunteer eye health and safety organization dedicated to fighting blindness and saving sight. Focused on promoting a continuum of vision care, Prevent Blindness America touches the lives of millions of people each year through public and professional education, advocacy, certified vision screening training, community and patient service programs and research.

Jeff Todd, President & CEO
Karen Hartman, Vice President & COO
Kay Nottingham Chaplin, Education & Outreach Director

7062 Ronald McDonald Houses
One Kroc Drive
Oak Brook, IL 60523
603-623-7048
Fax: 630-623-7488
info@rmhc.org
www.rmhc.org

Provides national programs, funding and other support to network of 150 local Ronald McDonald Houses, homes-away-from-homes for families of seriously ill children

Martin J Coyne Jr, President and CEO
Aggie Dentice, Friends of Ronald McDonals House Ch
Linda Dunham, Ronald McDonald House Charities Boa

7063 Rural Institute on Disabilities
University of Montana
52 Corbin Hall
Missoula, MT 59812
406-243-5467
800-732-0323
Fax: 406-243-4730
TTY: 403-243-5467
rural@ruralinstitute.umt.edu
www.ruralinstitute.umt.edu

Information and advocacy resources for families and professionals. Includes listings of organizations providing general information and organizations focusing on more specific areas of concern to families and young adults who have disabilities.

7064 Sexuality Information and Education Council of the US (SIECUS)
90 John Street, Suite 402
New York, NY 10038
212-819-9770
Fax: 212-819-9776
siecus@siecus.org
www.siecus.org/

Information and advocacy resources for families and professionals. Includes listings of organizations providing general information and organizations focusing on more specific areas of concern to families and young adults who have disabilities.

General Resources / National Associations & Support Groups

Monica Rodriguez, President/CEO
Jason I. Osher, Chief Operating Officer
Kurt Conklin, MPH, MCHES, Program Director

7065 **Sibling Support Project**
Children's Hospital and Regional Medical Center
4800 Sand Point Way NE
Seattle, WA 98105
206-987-2000
Fax: 206-527-5705
TTY: 206-987-2280
www.seattlechildrens.org

Information and advocacy resources for families and professionals. Includes listings of organizations providing general information and organizations focusing on more specific areas of concern to families and young adults who have disabilities.

7066 **Ski for Light**
1455 West Lake Street
Minneapolis, MN 55408
612-827-3232
info@sfl.org
www.sfl.org

Nonprofit organization founded in 1975 to promote the physical fitness of visually and mobility impaired adults.

7067 **Society for Pediatric Dermatology**
8365 Keystone Crossing, Ste 107
Indianapolis, IN 46240
317-202-0224
Fax: 317-205-9481
info@pedsderm.net
www.pedsderm.net

The objective of the Society is to promote, develop and advance education, research and care of skin disease in all pediatric age groups.

Kent Lindeman, Executive Director

7068 **Spaulding for Children**
16250 Northland Drive, Suite 100
Southfield, MI 48075
248-443-7080
Fax: 248-443-7099
sfc@spaulding.org
www.spaulding.org

Information and advocacy resources for families and professionals. Includes listings of organizations providing general information and organizations focusing on more specific areas of concern to families and young adults who have disabilities.

7069 **Special Olympics**
1133 19th Street, NW
Washington, DC 20036
202-628-3630
800-700-8585
Fax: 202-824-0200
info@specialolympics.org
www.specialolympics.org

Information on adaptive sports and recreation activities and related health issues for people of many abilities. Including local chapters, referrals, fun and social interaction and support groups.

Timothy P. Shriver, Ph.D., Chairman/Board of Directors/Chief E
J. Brady Lum, President & Chief Operating Officer
Peter Wheeler, Chief Strategic Properties

7070 **TASH**
1825 K Street NW, Suite 1250
Washington, DC 20006
202-817-3264
www.tash.org

TASH is an international leader in disability advocacy. Founded in 1975, TASH advocates for human rights and inclusion for people with significant disabilities and support needs those most vulnerable to segregation, abuse, neglect and institutionalization. TASH works to advance inclusive communities through advocacy, research, professional development, policy, and information and resources for parents, families and self-advocates.

Michael Brogioli, Executive Director
DeVonne Parks, Director of Membership & Meetings
Chernet Weldeab, Project Coordinator

7071 **Technology Assistance for Special Consumers**
1856 Keats Drive
Huntsville, AL 35810
256-859-8300
Fax: 256-859-4332
TDD: 256-532-5996
ucphuntsville.org/at-consultations-trainings/

Technology group of parents, consumers and professionals; provides resources to help children and adults who have disabilities gain access to the benefits of technology. Includes nationwide network of community-based assistive technology, resource centers, hands on consultants and product demonstrations.

Cheryl Smith, CEO
Tracy Cieniewicz, Sustainability Dirtector

7072 **US Paralympics**
U.S. Olympic Committee
1 Olympic Plaza, 30 Cimino Drive
Colorado Springs, CO 80903
719-866-2030
Fax: 719-866-2029
alison.nicholas@usoc.org
www.teamusa.org

A division of the United States Olympic Committee, we focus our efforts on enhancing programs, funding and opportunities for persons with physical disabilities to participate in Paralympic sport. The Paralympic Games are the second largest sporting event in the world, conceding top honors only to the Olympics. The multi-sport competition showcases the talents and abilities of the world's most elite athletes with physical disabilities.

Alison Nicholas, Program Coordinator
Beth Bason, Communications Coordinator
Joe Walsh, Director

7073 **Vision of Children Foundation**
4310 Genesee Ave, Suite 101
San Diego, CA 92117
858-560-5181
Fax: 858-560-1926
www.familyvisioncaresd.com

Provides information, promotes research and assists the families of blind and visually impaired children, including those with ocular albinism, in locating organizations and service providers who can give support.

Gary Sneag, Manager

7074 **WE MOVE (Worldwide Education and Awareness of Movement Disorders)**
204 West 84th Street
New York, NY 10024
NOP-ONE-

WE MOVE provides movement disorder information and educational materials to physicians, patients, the media, and the public via its comprehensive web site, training courses, patient support group and more. Its goal is to make early diagnosis, up-to-date treatment and patient support a reality for all people living with movement disorders.

Susan Bressman, MD, President

7075 **World Institute on Disability**
3075 Adeline Street, Suite 280
Berkeley, CA 94703
510-225-6400
Fax: 510-225-0477
TTY: 510-225-0478
wid@wid.org
www.wid.org

Information and advocacy resources for families and professionals. Includes listings of organizations providing general information and organizations focusing on more specific areas of concern to families and young adults who have disabilities.

Stanley K Yarnell MD, Chairman
Martin B Schulter, Vice Chair

7076 **World Research Foundation**
41 Bell Rock Plaza
Sedona, AZ 86351
928-284-3300
Fax: 928-248-3530
info@wrf.org
www.wrf.org

Nonprofit organization. Your global source of information on illnesses and therapies used around the world.

General Resources / State Agencies & Support Groups

LaVerne Ross, Co-Founder
Steven Ross

7077 Young Adult Institute
460 West 34th St.
New York, NY 2382
212-273-6100
TDD: 212-290-2787
www.yai.org

A nonprofit professional organizations serving developmentally disabled children and adults in many programs throughout the New York metropolitan area. Provides over 50 program sites for thousands of participants.

Stephen E. Freeman, L.C.S.W., Chief Executive Officer
Thomas A. Dern, L.C.S.W., Chief Operating Officer
Sanjay Dutt, Chief Financial Officer

7078 Zero to Three
1255 23rd Street, NW, Suite 350
Washington, DC 20037
202-638-1144
800-899-4301
Fax: 202-638-0851
webhelp@zerotothree.org
zerotothree.org

The mission is to promote the healthy development of our nation's infants and toddlers by supporting and strengthening families, communities and those who work on their behalf. We are dedicated to advancing current knowledge, promoting beneficial policies and practices and providing training, technical assistance, and leadership development. A nonprofit organization.

Janice Im, Chief Program Officer
Laura Shiflett, Chief Financial/Administrative Offi
Matthew E Melmed, Executive Director

State Agencies & Support Groups

Alabama

7079 Arc of Morgan County
2234 Graham Avenue SW
Decatur, AL 35601
256-355-6192
www.arcofmorgancounty.org

Informational and emotional support to parents who have a child, adolescent, or adult family member with special needs.

Lisa English, President
Sherry Stephenson, Vice President
Ireta Hogan, Secretary

7080 Early Intervention Program
2129 East South Blvd
Montgomery, AL 36111
334-281-8780
800-441-7607
Fax: 334-281-1973
www.rehab.state.al.us

Services include central directory, representatives of agencies, service providers, families, and coordinators of infant, toddler, and preschool special education programs.

Stephen G. Kayes, Board of Director
Jimmie Varnado, Board of Director

7081 Friends for Life Auburn United Methodist Church
99 South Street
Auburn, NY 13021
315-253-6295
www.auburnunitedmethodist.org

Informational and emotional support to parents who have a child, adolescent, or adult family member with special needs.

Richelle Duchaner, Pastor
Geri Jackson, Administrative Assisstant
Mary Howard, Coordinator of Congregational Life

7082 Special Education Action Committee Huntsville Outreach Office
3322 S Memorial Parkway, Suite 25
Huntsville, AL 35801
256-882-3911
Fax: 256-882-3974
www.hsv.tis.net/~seachsv

Informational and emotional support to parents who have a child, adolescent, or adult family member with special needs.

7083 Special Education Services
Department of Education
PO Box 302101
Montgomery, AL 36130
334-242-8114
800-392-8020
Fax: 334-242-9192
www.alsde.edu

Services include central directory, representatives of agencies, service providers, families, and coordinators of infant, toddler, and preschool special education programs.

Robert J. Bentley, President
Thomas R. Bice, Ed.D., Secretary/Executive Officer
Stephanie Bell, Vice President

7084 Statewide Technology Access & Response System for Alabamians with Disabilities
2125 E South Boulevard, PO Box 20752
Montgomery, AL 36120
334-613-3480
800-782-7656
Fax: 334-613-3485
TDD: 334-613-3519
www.mindspring.com/alstar/

State assisted programs and support group information for people of many abilities. Includes local chapters, referrals, fun and social interaction and support groups.

Alaska

7085 Alaska Department of Education
801 W 10th Street, Suite 200, PO Box 110500
Juneau, AK 99811
907-465-2800
Fax: 907-465-4156
TTY: 907-465-2815
eed.webmaster@alaska.gov
www.eed.state.ak.us

Individuals with Disabilities Education Act requires early intervention and preschool special education for children with disabilities and special health care needs. Services include central directory, representatives of agencies, service providers, families, and coordinators of infant, toddler, and preschool special education programs.

Steven J. Hostetter, President

7086 Assistive Technologies of Alaska
3330 Arctic Blvd., Suite 101
Anchorage, AK 99503
907-563-2599
800-723-2852
Fax: 907-563-0699
TTY: 907-561-2592
TDD: 907-269-3569
mystie@atlaak.org
www.atlaak.org

State assisted programs and support group information for people of many abilities. Includes local chapters, referrals, fun and social interaction and support groups.

7087 Leukemia & Lymphoma Society - Washington/ Alaska Chapter
Leukemia & Lymphoma Society
5601 6th Avenue, Ste 182
Seattle, WA 98108
206-628-0777
anne.gillingham@lls.org
www.lls.org/washingtonalaska

Dedicated to finding cures for leukemia and related cancers and to improving the quality of life for patients and their families.

Anne Gillingham, Executive Director
Courtney Hale, Operations Director
Victoria Wenick, Senior Campaign Director

General Resources / State Agencies & Support Groups

7088 Maternal, Child & Family Health, Early Intervention/Infant Learning Program
State of Alaska Department of Health
1231 Gambell Street
Anchorage, AK 99501
907-269-3419
Fax: 907-269-3465
jbatuk@health.state.ak.us

Early intervention and preschool special education for children with disabilities and special health care needs. Services include administration of statewide early intervention programs for infants and toddlers with developmental delays or disabilities and their families.

Jane Atuk, Part C Coordinator
Karen Martinek, Special Needs Services Unit

7089 PARENTS
4743 E Northern Lights Boulevard
Anchorage, AK 99508
907-337-7678
800-478-7678
Fax: 907-337-7671
TDD: 907-337-7678
parentsss@alaska.com
www.parentsinc.org

Parent Training and Information (PTI) programs help parents to understand their children's specific needs, communicate more effectively with professionals, participate in the educational planning process, and obtain information about relevant programs, services and resources.

Arizona

7090 Arizona Early Intervention Program/ Department of Economic Security
3839 N. 3rd St, Suite 304 Site Code No. 801 A-6
Phoenix, AZ 85012
602-532-9960
888-439-5609
Fax: 602-200-9820
allazeip2@azdes.gov
www.azdes.gov/azeip

Early intervention and preschool special education for children with disabilities and special health care needs. Services include central directory, representatives of agencies, service providers, families, and coordinators of infant, toddler, and preschool special education programs.

7091 Arizona Technology Access Program Institute for Human Development
2400 N. Central Avenue, Suite 300
Pheonix, AZ 85004
602-728-9534
800-477-9921
Fax: 602-728-9353
TTY: 602-728-9536
www.nau.edu/ihd/aztap

State assisted programs and support group information for people of many abilities. Includes local chapters, referrals, fun and social interaction and support groups.

7092 Blake Foundation Children's Achievement Center
3825 E 2nd Street
Tucson, AZ 85716
520-325-0611
Fax: 520-327-5414
www.nectas.unc.edu

Services include central directory, representatives of agencies, service providers, families, and coordinators of infant, toddler, and preschool special education programs.

Annabell Rose, Interagency Coordinating Council

7093 Division of Special Education State Department of Education
1535 W Jefferson
Phoenix, AZ 85007
602-542-3852
Fax: 602-542-5404
www.nectas.unc.edu

Individuals with Disabilities Education Act requires all states and territories to provide early intervention and preschool special education for children with disabilities and special health care needs. Services include central directory, representatives of agencies, service providers, families, and coordinators of infant, toddler, and preschool special education programs.

Lynn Busenbark, Preschool Special Ed. Coordinator

7094 Pilot Parents of Southern Arizona
2600 N Wyatt Drive
Tucson, AZ 85712
520-324-3150
877-365-7220
Fax: 520-324-3152
ppsa@pilotparents.org
www.pilotparents.org

Parent Training and Information (PTI) programs help parents to understand their children's specific needs, communicate more effectively with professionals, participate in the educational planning process, and obtain information about relevant programs, services and resources.

Lynn Kallis, Executive Director
Robert Snyder, Director of Education & Training
Cheryl McKenzie, Administrative Assistant

7095 Raising Special Kids
5025 E Washington Street, Suite 204
Phoenix, AZ 85034
602-242-4366
800-237-3007
Fax: 602-242-4306
www.raisingspecialkids.org

Provides support and training to families of children who have disabilities and special health needs, helps parents communicate more effectively with professionals, participate in the educational planning process and obtain information about programs and resources available to them. Offers training to professionals in health, education and social services.

Paula Banahan, President
Joyce Millard-Hoie, Executive Director
Janna Murrell, Director of Family Support and Educ

7096 Southwest Human Development
PO BOX 28487
Austin, TX 78755
512-467-7916
800-369-9082
Fax: 512-467-1453
TTY: 888-467-1455
info@swhuman.org
www.swhuman.org

Services include central directory, representatives of agencies, service providers, families, and coordinators of infant, toddler, and preschool special education programs.

Blake Stanford, President/CEO

Arkansas

7097 Arkansas Disability Coalition
1501 N. University Avenue, Suite 268
Little Rock, AR 72207
501-614-7020
800-223-1330
Fax: 501-614-9082
TDD: 501-614-7020
adc@alltel.net
www.adcpti.org

Parent Training and Information (PTI) programs help parents to understand their children's specific needs, communicate more effectively with professionals, participate in the educational planning process, and obtain information about relevant programs, services and resources.

Wanda Horton, Executive Director
Karen Lutrick, Parent Educator
Bryan Cozart, Project Director

7098 Arkansas Disability Coalition Parent Train ing and Information Center
1501 N. University Avenue, Suite 268
Little Rock, AR 72207
501-614-7020
800-223-1330
Fax: 501-614-9082
TDD: 501-614-7020
adc@alltel.net
www.adcpti.org

General Resources / State Agencies & Support Groups

The Arkansas Parent Training and Information Center (PTI) is a project of the Arkansas Disability Coalition. It is funded through a federal grant from the US Department of Education that serves families of children ages birth through 26 years of age who have a disability, but not yet diagnosed.

Wanda Horton, Executive Director
Karen Lutrick, Parent Educator
Bryan Cozart, Project Director

7099 FOCUS
305 W Jefferson Avenue
Jonesboro, AR 72401
870-935-2750
Fax: 870-931-3755
www.taalliance.org

Parent Training and Information (PTI) programs help parents to understand their children's specific needs, communicate more effectively with professionals, participate in the educational planning process, and obtain information about relevant programs, services and resources.

7100 Family-2-Family Health Information Center of Arkansas
1501 N. University Avenue, Suite 268
Little Rock, AR 72207
501-614-7020
800-223-1330
Fax: 501-614-9082
TDD: 501-614-7020
www.adcpti.org

The Family-2-Family Health Information Center of Arkansas (F2F HIC) is a nonprofit family-run organization that assists families of children and youth with special health care needs and the professionals who serve them. They provide health-related support, information, resources and training.

Bryan Cozart, Project Director
Karen Lutrick, Parent Educator
Wanda Horton, Executive Director

7101 Increasing Capabilities Access Network
Dept of Education/Arkansas Rehabilitation Services
525 W. Capitol
Little Rock, AR 72201
501-666-8868
800-828-2799
Fax: 501-666-5319
TTY: 501-666-8868
TDD: 800-828-2799
www.ar-ican.org

State assisted programs and support group information for people of many abilities. Includes local chapters, referrals, fun and social interaction and support groups.

Barry Vuletich, Program Administrator

7102 Parent to Parent Arc of Arkansas
2004 South Main Street
Little Rock, AR 72206
501-375-7770
Fax: 501-372-4621

Informational and emotional support to parents who have a child, adolescent, or adult family member with special needs.

7103 Special Education Section State Department of Education
4 Capitol Mall, Room 105-C
Little Rock, AR 72201
501-682-4225
Fax: 501-682-4313
sreifeiss@arkedu.k12.ar.us
www.unc.edu

Individuals with Disabilities Education Act requires all states and territories to provide early intervention and preschool special education for children with disabilities and special health care needs. Services include central directory, representatives of agencies, service providers, families, and coordinators of infant, toddler, and preschool special education programs.

Sandra Reifeissk, Preschool Special Ed. Coordinator

California

7104 Arc Family Resource Project
2421 Lomitas Avenue, PO Box 219
Santa Rosa, CA 95402
877-694-4335
Fax: 707-578-8601

Parent Training and Information (PTI) programs help parents to understand their children's specific needs, communicate more effectively with professionals, participate in the educational planning process, and obtain information about relevant programs, services and resources.

Traci N Turner, Program Coordinator
Elvis Bozarth, President

7105 CARE Family Resource Center
1350 Arnold Drive, Suite 203
Martinez, CA 94553
925-313-0999
800-281-3023
Fax: 925-370-8651

Informational and emotional support to parents who have a child, adolescent, or adult family member with special needs.

7106 Carolyn Kordich Family Resource Center
1135 W. 257th Street
Harbor City, CA 90710
310-325-7288
Fax: 310-325-7288
ckfrc@worldnet.att.net

Informational and emotional support to parents who have a child, adolescent, or adult family member with special needs.

7107 Challenged Family Resource Center
827 West 20th Street
Merced, CA 95340
209-385-5314
Fax: 209-385-5317
dkuneck@aol.com
www.challengedfrc.org

Informational and emotional support to parents who have a child, adolescent, or adult family member with special needs.

7108 Children Living with Illness
The Center for Attitudinal Healing
33 Buchanan Drive
Sausalito, CA 94965
415-331-6161
Fax: 415-331-4545

For children who are ill, have an ill sibling, or an ill parent. Parent group meets separately at the same time.

Jimmy Pete

7109 Comfort Connection Family Resource Center
12361 Lewis Street, Suite 101
Garden Grove, CA 92840
714-748-7491
Fax: 714-748-8149

Informational and emotional support to parents who have a child, adolescent, or adult family member with special needs.

7110 Department of Developmental Services of Early Start Program
1600 9th Street, PO Box 944202
Sacramento, CA 94244
916-654-1690
800-515-2229
Fax: 916-654-2054
TTY: 916-654-2054
TDD: 916-654-2054
earlystart@dds.ca.gov
www.dds.ca.gov

Individuals with Disabilities Education Act requires all states and territories to provide early intervention and preschool special education for children with disabilities and special health care needs. Services include central directory, representatives of agencies, service providers, families, and coordinators of infant, toddler, and preschool special education programs.

Mark Hutchinson, Chief Deputy Director
Terri Delgadillo, Director
Rick Ingraham, Quality Management/Development Bran

7111 Early Start Family Resource Network
1425 S. Waterman Ave.
San Bernadino, CA 92408
909-890-4794
800-974-5553
Fax: 909-890-4709
www.esfrn.org

Informational and emotional support to parents who have a child, adolescent, or adult family member with special needs.

General Resources / State Agencies & Support Groups

7112 Exceptional Family Resource Center
9245 Sky Park Court, Suite 130
San Diego, CA 92123
619-594-7416
800-281-8252
Fax: 858-268-4275
www.efrconline.org

Informational and emotional support to parents who have a child, adolescent, or adult family member with special needs.

Sherry Torok, Executive Director
Susan Carlton-Bahm, Manager
Joyce Clark, Manager

7113 Exceptional Family Support, Education and Advocacy Center
6402 Skyway
Paradise, CA 95969
530-876-8321
Fax: 530-876-0346
sea@sunset.net
www.taalliance.org

Parent Training and Information (PTI) programs help parents to understand their children's specific needs, communicate more effectively with professionals, participate in the educational planning process, and obtain information about relevant programs, services and resources.

7114 Exceptional Parents
Family Resource Center
4440 N 1st Street
Fresno, CA 93726
559-229-2000
Fax: 559-229-2956
TTY: 559-225-6059
www.exceptionalparents.org

Informational and emotional support to parents who have a child, adolescent, or adult family member with special needs.

Suzanne Ellis, Chief Financial Officer
Kyle Loreto, President
Marion Karian, Executive Director

7115 Families Caring for Families
Family Resource Center
113 W Pillsbury Street, Suite A1
Lancaster, CA 93534
661-949-1746
Fax: 661-948-7266

Informational and emotional support to parents who have a child, adolescent, or adult family member with special needs.

7116 Family First Program Alpha Resource Center
4501 Cathedral Oaks Road, Suite A1
Santa Barbara, CA 93110
805-683-2145
Fax: 805-967-3647

Informational and emotional support to parents who have a child, adolescent, or adult family member with special needs.

7117 Family Focus Resource Center
18111 Nordhoff Street
Northridge, CA 91330
818-677-6854
Fax: 818-677-5574
family.focus@csun.edu
www.familyfocusresourcecenter.org

Informational and emotional support to parents who have a child, adolescent, or adult family member with special needs.

Ivor Weiner, Principal Investigator
Victoria Berrey, Program Manager
Stacie Anderle, PRRS, Coordinator

7118 Family Resource Center
5828 North Clark Street
Chicago, IL 60660
773-334-2300
800-676-2229
Fax: 773-334-8228
www.f-r-c.org

Informational and emotional support to parents who have a child, adolescent, or adult family member with special needs.

Debbie Frisch, Board President
Richard Pearlman, Executive Director
Jane Turner, Associate Director

7119 H.E.A.R.T.S. Connection Family Resource Center
3101 N Sillect Avenue, Suite 115
Bakersfield, CA 93308
661-328-9055
800-210-7633
Fax: 661-328-9940
www.heartsfrc.org

Informational and emotional support to parents who have a child, adolescent, or adult family member with special needs.

Susan Graham, Director
Ana Gomez, Family Resource Specialist
Ana Gomez, Family Resource Specialist

7120 Harbor Regional Center Family and Professional Resource Center
21231 Hawthorne Boulevard
Torrance, CA 90503
310-543-0691
Fax: 310-316-8843
familyresourcecntr@hddf.com
www.harborrc.org

Informational and emotional support to parents who have a child, adolescent, or adult family member with special needs.

7121 MATRIX: Parent Network and Family Resource Center
94 Galli Drive, Suite C
Novato, CA 94949
415-884-3535
800-578-2592
Fax: 415-884-3555
info@matrixparents.org
www.matrixparents.org

Informational and emotional support to parents who have a child, adolescent, or adult family member with special needs.

Lee Cox, Chief Financial Officer
Rhanda Dunn, Board President
Nora Thompson, Executive Director

7122 Matrix Parents Network and Resource Center
94 Galli Drive, Suite C
Novato, CA 94949
415-884-3535
800-578-2592
Fax: 415-884-3555
info@matrixparents.org
www.matrixparents.org

Matrix is a nonprofit agency that serves families of children with special needs and disabilities. Provides information and referral, individual support, technical assistance, support groups, training about special education and services, and direction to appropriate early start services.

Lee Cox, Chief Financial Officer
Rhanda Dunn, Board President
Nora Thompson, Executive Director

7123 Peaks and Valleys Family Resource Center
20 Sherwood Place No. 4
Salinas, CA 93906
831-755-1450
800-400-2937
Fax: 831-755-1470

Informational and emotional support to parents who have a child, adolescent, or adult family member with special needs.

7124 San Gabriel/Pomona Parents' Place
1500 S Hyacinth Avenue # B
West Covina, CA 91791
626-919-1091
800-422-2022
Fax: 626-337-2736
empower@gte.net
www.parentsplacefrc.com

Family Resource Center committed to supporting, promoting and enhancing family focused services in a parent driven atmosphere for families who have children with special needs. Family Resource Centers are part of the California Early Start Program which addresses the unique and individual needs of families raising a child with a disability. The Parent's Place is dedicated to empowering families through information/education, referrals and parent to parent support.

Sona Baghdassarian, Director
Judy Kyne, Administrative Secretary
Elena Sanchez, Parent Resource Specialist

General Resources / State Agencies & Support Groups

7125 South Central Los Angeles Regional Center for Devlopmentally Disabled Persons
6500 W Adams Boulevard
Los Angeles, CA 90007
213-744-7000
Fax: 213-744-8494
TTY: 213-763-5634

Informational and emotional support to parents who have a child, adolescent, or adult family member with special needs.

7126 Special Connections Family Resource Center
400 Encinal Street
Santa Cruz, CA 95060
831-464-0669
Fax: 831-465-9177
frcedp@aol.com

Informational and emotional support to parents who have an infant or toddler (birth to 36 months) with special needs.

Leslie Burnham, Program Supervisor

7127 Special Education Division State Department of Education
PO Box 944272
Sacramento, CA 94244
916-327-3696
Fax: 916-327-8878
www.nectas.unc.edu

Individuals with Disabilities Education Act requires all states and territories to provide early intervention and preschool special education for children with disabilities and special health care needs. Services include central directory, representatives of agencies, service providers, families, and coordinators of infant, toddler, and preschool special education programs.

Constance J Bourne, Preschool Special Ed. Coordinator

7128 Starlight Children's Foundation
2049 Century Park East. Suite 4320
Los Angeles, CA 90067
310-479-1212
800-274-7827
Fax: 323-634-0090
Jenny@starlight.org
www.starlight.org

International nonprofit organization dedicated to improving the quality of life for seriously ill children and their families. Working with more than 850 hospitals worldwide, the Foundation provides an impressive menu of both in-hospital and outpatient programs and services. A leader in delivering distractive entertainment therapies, over 85,000 children benefit from Starlight's programs each month.

Jacqueline Hart-Ibrahim, Chief Executive Officer
Clifford R. Ball, CFO/CTO
Denise Muniz, Development Director

7129 Support for Families of Children with Disabilities
1663 Mission Street, 7th Floor
San Francisco, CA 94103
415-282-7494
Fax: 415-282-1226
TTY: 415-920-5040
info@supportforfamilies.org
www.supportforfamilies.org

Parent Training and Information (PTI) programs help parents to understand their children's specific needs, communicate more effectively with professionals, participate in the educational planning process, and obtain information about relevant programs, services and resources.

Christian Dauer, SFCD, Board President
Laura Lanzone, SFCD, Vice President
Juno Duenas, SFCD, Executive Director

7130 Team Advocates for Special Kids, Anaheim
100 W. Cerritos Ave
Anaheim, CA 92805
714-533-8275
866-828-8275
Fax: 714-533-2533
taskca@yahoo.com
www.taskca.org

Programs help parents to understand their children's specific needs, communicate more effectively with professionals, participate in the educational planning process, and obtain information about relevant programs, services and resources.

Marta Anchondo, Executive Director/CEO

7131 Team Advocates for Special Kids, San Diego
4550 Kearney Villa Road, #102
San Diego, CA 92123
858-874-2386
Fax: 858-874-2375

Programs help parents to understand their children's specific needs, communicate more effectively with professionals, participate in the educational planning process, and obtain information about relevant programs, services and resources.

7132 Warmline Family Resource Center
6960 Destiny Dr., Suite 106
Rocklin, CA 95677
916-632-2100
800-660-7995
Fax: 916-632-2103
www.warmlinefrc.org

Informational and emotional support to parents who have a child, adolescent, or adult family member with special needs.

Heather Green, Contact
Amber Johnson, Contact

Colorado

7133 Assistive Technology Partners
601 E 18th Avenue, Suite 130
Denver, CO 80203
303-315-1280
800-255-3477
Fax: 303-837-1208
TTY: 303-837-8964
www.ucdenver.edu

State assisted programs and support group information for people of many abilities. Focuses on assistive technology devices and services for persons with disabilities, training and technical assistance available.

7134 Colorado Consortium of Intensive Care Nurseries United Parents (UP)
1056 E 19th Avenue, B535
Denver, CO 80218
303-861-6557
Fax: 303-764-8092

Informational and emotional support to parents who have a child, adolescent, or adult family member with special needs.

7135 Delta/Montrose Parent to Parent
2091 E Locust Road
Montrose, CO 81401
970-249-2878
Fax: 970-252-0544
children@gi.net

Informational and emotional support to parents who have a child, adolescent, or adult family member with special needs.

7136 Denver Early Childhood Connections
2727 W 92nd Avenue
Denver, CO 80204
303-458-0852
Fax: 303-744-9502

Provides resource coordination for children eligible for Part C services and referrals to other agencies for children with needs outside of the Part C realm. Parent to parent support, parent education and community playgroups are some of the services that are conducted. Forums are hosted on varied topics relevant to parents of young children as well as in-service and pre-service workshops on child development. IFSP development, parent's rights under IDEA, and other resource packets are available

Newsletter

Judith Persoff, Executive Director

7137 Disability Connection and RAFT, Larimer County's Early Childhood Connection
PO Box 270714
Fort Collins, CO 80527
970-229-0224
Fax: 970-229-0242

Informational and emotional support to parents who have a child, adolescent, or adult family member with special needs.

General Resources / State Agencies & Support Groups

7138 **Effective Parent Project**
255 Main Street
Grand Junction, CO 81501
970-241-4068
Fax: 970-241-3725

Informational and emotional support to parents who have a child, adolescent, or adult family member with special needs.

7139 **El Groupo Vida**
P.O. Box 11096
Denver, CO 80211
303-904-6073
Fax: 303-296-4105
info@elgrupovida.org
www.elgrupovida.org

Informational and emotional support to parents who have a child, adolescent, or adult family member with special needs.

Gabriela Perez, Board President
Italia Cortes-Santillan, Vice President
Gabriela Perez, Interim (Volunteer) Executive Direc

7140 **Help Parent Support Group Hope & Education for Loving Parents**
378 S Falcon
Pueblo West, CO 81007
719-545-2282
Fax: 719-547-1282
fastgram@aol.com

Informational and emotional support to parents who have a child, adolescent, or adult family member with special needs

7141 **Oasis**
1120 N Circle Drive, Suite 19
Colorado Springs, CO 80909
719-635-8722
Fax: 719-577-9482

Informational and emotional support to parents who have a child, adolescent, or adult family member with special needs.

7142 **PEAK Parent Center**
611 N Weber, Suite 200
Colorado Springs, CO 80903
719-531-9400
800-284-0251
Fax: 719-531-9452
TDD: 719-531-9403
info@peakparent.org
www.peakparent.org

Parent Training and Information (PTI) programs help parents to understand their children's specific needs, communicate more effectively with professionals, participate in the educational planning process, and obtain information about relevant programs, services and resources.

Kent Willis, President
Sarah Billerbeck, Vice President
Barbara Buswell, Executive Director

7143 **Parent Support Group of Littleton & Auora**
7600 E Arapahoe, Suite 219
Englewood, CO 80112
303-773-0044
Fax: 303-773-8780

Informational and emotional support to parents who have a child, adolescent, or adult family member with special needs.

7144 **Parents Supporting Parents of Eagle County**
PO Box 2656
Vail, CO 81658
970-926-6015
Fax: 970-926-6015

Informational and emotional support to parents who have a child, adolescent, or adult family member with special needs.

7145 **Parents Supporting Parents of Garfield and Pitkin County**
PO Box 784
Silt, CO 81652
970-876-5768
Fax: 970-876-5204

Informational and emotional support to parents who have a child, adolescent, or adult family member with special needs.

7146 **Prevention Initiatives State Department of Education**
210 E Colfax, Room 301
Denver, CO 80203
303-866-6600
Fax: 303-866-0793
smith_s@cde.state.co.us
www.cde.state.co.us

Provides early intervention and preschool special education for children with disabilities and special health care needs. Services include central directory, representatives of agencies, service providers, families, and coordinators of infant, toddler, and preschool special education programs.

Susan Smith, Infant/Toddler Program Coordinator
Marie Huchton, Senior Consultant
Dan Jorgensen, Principal Consultant

7147 **Resources for Young Children and Families**
1120 N Circle Drive, Suite 19
Colorado Springs, CO 80909
719-577-9190
Fax: 719-577-9482

Informational and emotional support to parents who have a child, adolescent, or adult family member with special needs.

7148 **Wilderness on Wheels Foundation**
PO Box 1007
Wheat Ridge, CO 80034
303-403-1110
www.wildernessonwheels.org

State assisted programs and support group information for people of many abilities. Includes local chapters, referrals, fun and social interaction and support groups.

Connecticut

7149 **A.J. Pappanikou Center for Developmental Disabilities**
263 Farmington Avenue, MC 6222
Farmington, CT 06030
860-679-1500
866-623-1315
Fax: 860-679-1571
TTY: 860-679-1502
contact.us.ucedd@uchc.edu
www.uconnucedd.org

Individuals with Disabilities Education Act requires all states and territories to provide early intervention and preschool special education for children with disabilities and special health care needs. Services include central directory, representatives of agencies, service providers, families, and coordinators of infant, toddler, and preschool special education programs.

Mary Beth Bruder, Director
Tierney Giannotti, Associate Director
Linda Procko, Program Coordinator

7150 **Assistive Technology Project**
Department of Social Services, BRS
25 Sigourney Street, 11th Floor
Hartford, CT 06106
860-424-4881
800-537-2549
Fax: 860-424-4850
TDD: 860-424-4850
www.tachact.uconn.edu

State assisted programs and support group information for people of many abilities. Includes local chapters, referrals, fun and social interaction and support groups.

7151 **CPAC**
338 Main Street
Niantic, CT 06357
860-739-3089
Fax: 860-739-7460
cpac@cpacinc.org
www.cpacinc.org

Programs help parents to understand their children's specific needs, communicate more effectively with professionals, participate in the educational planning process, and obtain information about relevant programs, services and resources.

General Resources / State Agencies & Support Groups

7152 Connecticut Birth to Three-Office of Early Childhood
450 Columbus Blvd, Ste 205
Hartford, CT 06103
860-500-4408
800-500-7000
Fax: 860-326-0559
ctbirth23@ct.gov
www.birth23.org

Individuals with Disabilities Education Act requires all states and territories to provide early intervention and preschool special education for children with disabilities and special health care needs. Services include central directory, representatives of agencies, service providers, families, and coordinators of infant, toddler, and preschool special education programs.

Linda Bamonte, Part C Director
Alice Ridgeway, System Manager

7153 Parent to Parent Network of Connecticut the Family Center
Dept. of Connecticut Children's Medical Center
282 Washington
Hartford, CT 06106
860-545-9021
Fax: 860-545-9201
TTY: 860-545-9002
www.ccmkids.org

Informational and emotional support to parents who have a child, adolescent, or adult family member with special needs.

7154 State Department of Education
25 Industrial Park Road
Middletown, CT 06457
860-632-1485
Fax: 860-807-2062
www.unc.edu

Individuals with Disabilities Education Act requires all states and territories to provide early intervention and preschool special education for children with disabilities and special health care needs. Services include central directory, representatives of agencies, service providers, families, and coordinators of infant, toddler, and preschool special education programs.

Leslie Averna, Acting Bureau Chief

Delaware

7155 Delaware Assisstive Technology Initiative (DATI)
University of Delaware
461 Wyoming Road
Newark, DE 19716
302-831-0354
800-870-3284
Fax: 302-831-4690
TDD: 302-651-6794
dati@asel.udel.edu
www.dati.org

The Delaware Assistive Technology Initiative (DATI) connects Delawareans who have disabilities with the tools they need in order to learn, work, play and participate in community life safely and independently. DATI services include: Equipment demonstration center in each county; no-cost, short-term equipment loans that let you try before you buy; Equipment Exchange Program; AT workshops and other training sessions; advocacy for improved AT access policies and funding and several more.

Beth Mineo, Director
Bob Piech, Project Coordinator
Ron Sibert, Funding Specialist

7156 Department of Public Instruction
PO Box 1402
Dover, DE 19903
302-739-5471
Fax: 302-739-2388
mbrooks@state.de.us
www.unc.edu

Individuals with Disabilities Education Act requires all states and territories to provide early intervention and preschool special education for children with disabilities and special health care needs. Services include central directory, representatives of agencies, service providers, families, and coordinators of infant, toddler, and preschool special education programs.

Martha Brooks, Director

7157 Parent Information Center of Delaware
6 Larch Avenue, Suite 404, Larch Corporate Center
Wilmington, DE 19804
302-999-7394
888-547-4412
Fax: 302-999-7637
PEP700@aol.com
www.picofdel.org

Programs help parents to understand their children's specific needs, communicate more effectively with professionals, participate in the educational planning process, and obtain information about relevant programs, services and resources.

Verna Hensley, President
Marie-Anne Aghazadian, Executive Director
Mindy Cox, Office Manager

District of Columbia

7158 Advocates for Justice and Education
1012 Pennsylvania Ave SE
Washington, DC 20020
202-678-8060
888-327-8060
Fax: 202-678-8062
www.aje-dc.org

Programs help parents to understand their children's specific needs, communicate more effectively with professionals, participate in the educational planning process, and obtain information about relevant programs, services and resources.

Tracey Davis, Board Chair
Kim Y. Jones, Executive Director & Member
Antoinette C. Bush, Board Secretary

7159 DC Arc
900 Vamum Street, NE
Washington, DC 20017
202-636-2950
Fax: 202-636-2996
www.taalliance.org

Programs help parents to understand their children's specific needs, communicate more effectively with professionals, participate in the educational planning process, and obtain information about relevant programs, services and resources.

7160 Georgetown University Child Development Center
National Early Childhood Technical Assistance Ctr
3700 O St., N.W.
Washington, DC 20057
202-687-0100
Fax: 202-687-8899
www.georgetown.edu

Individuals with Disabilities Education Act requires all states and territories to provide early intervention and preschool special education for children with disabilities and special health care needs. Services include central directory, representatives of agencies, service providers, families, and coordinators of infant, toddler, and preschool special education programs.

Paul Tagliabue, Chair
Chris Augostini, Senior Vice President and Chief Ope
John J. DeGioia, Ph.D., President

7161 Giddings School Special Education Division
National Early Childhood Technical Assistance Ctr
Campus Box 8040 Unc-Ch
Chapel Hill, NC 27599
919-962-2001
Fax: 919-966-7463
TDD: 919-843-3269
www.nectas.unc.edu

Services include central directory, representatives of agencies, service providers, families, and coordinators of infant, toddler, and preschool special education programs.

Ann Palmore, Preschool Special Ed. Coordinator

7162 Partnership for Assistive Technology
220 I Street NE, Suite 202
Washington, DC 20002
202-547-0198
Fax: 202-547-2662
TDD: 202-547-2657

General Resources / State Agencies & Support Groups

State assisted programs and support group information for people of many abilities. Includes local chapters, referrals, fun and social interaction and support groups.

Florida

7163 Alliance for Assistive Service and Technology (FAAST)
325 John Knox Road, Building 400, Suite 402
Tallahassee, FL 32301
850-487-3278
888-788-9216
Fax: 850-487-2805
TDD: 850-922-5951
www.faast.org

State assisted programs and support group information for people of many abilities. Includes local chapters, referrals, fun and social interaction and support groups.

2-8 pages Newsletter

Gayle Miller, Esq., Chair
Karen M. Clay, Chair-Elect
Lisa Taylor, Treasurer

7164 Early Intervention Unit, Division of Children's Medical Services
1309 Winewood Boulevard
Tallahassee, FL 32399
850-488-6005
Fax: 850-921-5241
Fran_L_Wilber@dcf.state.fl.us
www.nectas.unc.edu

Individuals with Disabilities Education Act requires all states and territories to provide early intervention and preschool special education for children with disabilities and special health care needs. Services include central directory, representatives of agencies, service providers, families, and coordinators of infant, toddler, and preschool special education programs.

Fran Wilber, Infant/Toddler Program Coordinator

7165 Family Network on Disabilities
2735 Whitney Road
Clearwater, FL 33760
727-523-1130
800-825-5736
Fax: 727-523-8687
TDD: 727-523-1130
www.fndfl.org

Parent Training and Information (PTI) programs help parents to understand their children's specific needs, communicate more effectively with professionals, participate in the educational planning process, and obtain information about relevant programs, services and resources.

Richard La Belle, Executive Director
Christine Goulbourne, Director of Programs
Joseph Hecker, Director of Finance

7166 Florida Department of Education
325 W Gaines Street
Tallahassee, FL 32399
850-245-0505
Fax: 850-245-9667
www.fldoe.org

Individuals with Disabilities Education Act requires all states and territories to provide early intervention and preschool special education for children with disabilities and special health care needs. Services include central directory, representatives of agencies, service providers, families, and coordinators of infant, toddler, and preschool special education programs.

Carale Chu, Chief of Staff
Will Krebs, Deputy Chief of Staff
Dr. Tony Bennett, Commissioner, Florida Department of

7167 Florida's Collaboration for Young Children and their Families Head State
1310 Cross Creek Circle, Suite A
Tallahassee, FL 32301
850-487-8871
Fax: 850-487-0045
www.nectas.unc.edu

Provides early intervention and preschool special education for children with disabilities and special health care needs. Services include central directory, representatives of agencies, service providers, families, and coordinators of infant, toddler, and preschool special education programs.

Katherine Kamiya, Interagency Coordinator

7168 US Blind Golfers Association
3093 Shamrock Street N
Tallahassee, FL 32308
904-893-4511
Fax: 904-893-4511
www.usblindgolf.com

State assisted programs and support group information for people of many abilities. Includes local chapters, referrals, fun and social interaction and support groups.

David Meador, President
Phil Hubbard, Vice President
Bill McMahon, Board Members

Georgia

7169 DHR/Division of Public Health - Babies Can t Wait Program
2 Peachtree Street NE, Room 7-315
Atlanta, GA 30303
404-657-2700
888-651-8224
Fax: 404-657-2763
www.health.state.ga.us/programs/bcw

Babies Can't Wait (BCW) Program is Georgia's Part C Early Intervention Program under Part C of the federal Individuals with Disabilities Education Improvement Act (IDEA). Services include a comprehensive, coordinated, multidisciplinary, interagency system of early intervention supports for infants and toddlers with disabilities from birth to age 3 and their families.

Janie Brodnax, Chief Operating Officer DHP
Brenda Fitzgerald, M.D., Commissioner, Georgia Department of
Russell Crutchfield, Deputy Chief of Staff

7170 Department for Exceptional Students Georgia Department of Education
205 Jessie Hill Jr. Drive, SE, Suite 1870
Atlanta, GA 30334
404-657-9965
Fax: 404-651-6457
www.nectas.unc.edu

Provides early intervention and preschool special education for children with disabilities and special health care needs. Services include central directory, representatives of agencies, service providers, families, and coordinators of infant, toddler, and preschool special education programs.

Toni Waylor Bowen, Preschool Special Ed. Coordinator

7171 Department of Counseling and Educational Leadership-Columbus State University
4225 University Avenue, Suite 754
Columbus, GA 31907
706-568-2222
Fax: 706-569-3134
www.nectas.unc.edu

Individuals with Disabilities Education Act requires all states and territories to provide early intervention and preschool special education for children with disabilities and special health care needs. Services include central directory, representatives of agencies, service providers, families, and coordinators of infant, toddler, and preschool special education programs.

Katherine McCormick, Interagency Coordinating Council

7172 Parent to Parent of Georgia
3070 Presidential Parkway, Suite 130
Atlanta, GA 30340
770-451-5484
800-229-2038
Fax: 770-458-4091
www.p2pga.org

Statewide informational and emotional support to families and individuals affected by disability.

General Resources / State Agencies & Support Groups

7173 Parents Educating Parents and Professional for All Children (PEPPAC)
8318 Durelee Lane, Suite 101
Douglasville, GA 30134
770-577-7771
Fax: 770-577-7774
peppac@bellsouth.net
www.taalliance.org

Parent Training and Information (PTI) programs help parents to understand their children's specific needs, communicate more effectively with professionals, participate in the educational planning process, and obtain information about relevant programs, services and resources.

7174 Tools for Life Division of Rehabilitation Services
1700 Century Circle B-4
Atlanta, GA 30345
404-894-4960
800-578-8665
Fax: 404-894-9320
TDD: 404-657-3085
102476.1737@compuserve.com
www.gatfl.org

State assisted programs and support group information for people of many abilities. Includes local chapters, referrals, fun and social interaction and support groups.

Hawaii

7175 AWARE
200 N Vineyard Boulevard, Suite 310
Honolulu, HI 96817
808-536-9684
Fax: 808-537-6780
LDAH@gte.net
www.taalliance.org

Parent Training and Information (PTI) programs help parents to understand their children's specific needs, communicate more effectively with professionals, participate in the educational planning process, and obtain information about relevant programs services, and resources.

7176 Assistive Technology Resource Centers of Hawaii (ATRC)
414 Kuiwii Street, Suite 104
Honolulu, HI 96817
808-532-7110
800-645-3007
Fax: 808-532-7120
atrc-info@atrc.org
www.atrc.org

State assisted programs and support group information for people of many abilities. Includes local chapters, referrals, fun and social interaction and support groups.

7177 Parents and Children Together (PACT) Honolulu, HI 96819
808-847-3285
Fax: 808-841-1485
admin@pacthawaii.org
www.pacthawaii.org

Individuals with Disabilities Education Act requires all states and territories to provide early intervention and preschool special education for children with disabilities and special health care needs. Services include central directory, representatives of agencies, service providers, families, and coordinators of infant, toddler, and preschool special education programs.

David Shibata, Chair
Dana Ann Takushi, Vice Chair
Lowell Kalapa, Treasurer

7178 Special Needs Branch Department of Education
637 18th Avenue, Building C, Room 101
Honolulu, HI 96816
808-733-4900
Fax: 808-733-4841
michael_fahley@notes.k12.hi.us
www.unc.edu

Individuals with Disabilities Education Act requires all states and territories to provide early intervention and preschool special education for children with disabilities and special health care needs. Services include central directory, representatives of agencies, service providers, families, and coordinators of infant, toddler, and preschool special education programs.

Michael Fahey, Preschool Special Ed. Coordinator

Idaho

7179 Assistive Technology Project
1 West Old State Capitol Plaza, Suite 100
Springfield, ID 62701
217-522-7985
800-852-5110
Fax: 217-522-8067
TTY: 217-522-9966
TDD: 208-855-3559
www.iltech.org

State assisted programs and support group information for people of many abilities. Includes local chapters, referrals, fun and social interaction and support groups.

7180 Department of Education
PO Box 83720
Boise, ID 83720
208-332-6917
Fax: 208-334-4664
www.unc.edu

Individuals with Disabilities Education Act requires all states and territories to provide early intervention and preschool special education for children with disabilities and special health care needs. Services include central directory, representatives of agencies, service providers, families, and coordinators of infant, toddler, and preschool special education programs.

Nolene Weaver, Supervisor

7181 Idaho Parents Unlimited
500 S 8th Street
Boise, ID 83702
208-342-5884
800-242-4785
Fax: 208-342-1408
TDD: 208-342-5884
parents@ipulidaho.org
www.ipulidaho.org

Parent Training and Information (PTI) programs help parents to understand their children's specific needs, communicate more effectively with professionals, participate in the educational planning process, and obtain information about relevant programs services, and resources.

Angela Lindig, Executive Director

7182 Infant/Toddler Program
PO Box 83720
Boise, ID 83720
208-334-5523
Fax: 208-334-6664
www.idahochild.org

Services include central directory, representatives of agencies, service providers, families, and coordinators of infant, toddler, and preschool special education programs.

Mary Jones, Infant/Toddler Program Coordinator

7183 Palouse Area Parent To Parent
317 17th Avenue
Lewiston, ID 83501
208-746-8599
TTY: 208-746-8599

Informational and emotional support to parents who have a child, adolescent, or adult family member with special needs.

7184 Parent Reaching Out to Parents
2195 Ironwood Court
Coeur d'Alene, ID 83814
208-769-1409
Fax: 208-769-1430
parentsreachingout.com

Informational and emotional support to parents who have a child, adolescent, or adult family member with special needs.

Lorena Freund, Coordinator
Kathy Dalberg, Secretary/Treasurer

General Resources / State Agencies & Support Groups

Illinois

7185 Archway
PO Box 1180, 2751 W Main
Carbondale, IL 62903
618-549-4442
Fax: 618-549-0231

Informational and emotional support to parents who have a child, adolescent, or adult family member with special needs.

7186 Assistive Technology Project
1 W Old State Capitol Plaza, Suite 100
Springfield, IL 62701
217-522-7985
800-852-5110
Fax: 217-522-8067
TTY: 217-522-9966
TDD: 217-522-9966
iatp@iltech.org
www.ittech.org

State assisted programs and support group information for people of many abilities. Includes local chapters, referrals, fun and social interaction and support groups.

Wilhelmina Gunther, Executive Director
Shelly Lowe, Finance/Personnel Manager
Theresa Ganci, Finance/Personnel Assistant

7187 Child and Family Connections
PO Box 741280
Boynton Beach, FL 33474
773-233-1799
800-554-1802
Fax: 773-233-2011
www.cfcpbc.org

Informational and emotional support to parents who have a child, adolescent, or adult family member with special needs.

7188 Developmental Services Center
1304 W Bradley
Champaign, IL 61821
217-356-9176
Fax: 217-356-9851
jmcateer@dsc-illinois.org
www.dsc-illinois.org

Informational and emotional support to parents who have a child, adolescent, or adult family member with special needs.

Dale Morrissey, Chief Executive Officer
Danielle Matthews, Executive Vice President of Support
Patty Walters, Executive Vice President of Consume

7189 Family Resource Center on Disabilities
11 E. Adams St. Suite 1002
Chicago, IL 60603
312-939-3513
800-952-4199
Fax: 312-854-8980
TTY: 312-939-3519
TDD: 312-939-3519
info@frcd.org
www.frcd.org

Parent Training and Information (PTI) programs help parents to understand their children's specific needs, communicate more effectively with professionals, participate in the educational planning process, and obtain information about relevant programs, services and resources.

Karen Aguilar, Coalition Director
Melody Musgrove, Director, Special Education Program

7190 Family T.I.E.S. Network
830 S Spring Street
Springfield, IL 62704
217-544-5809
800-865-7842
Fax: 217-544-6018
FTIESN@aol.com
www.taalliance.org

Parent Training and Information (PTI) programs help parents to understand their children's specific needs, communicate more effectively with professionals, participate in the educational planning process, and obtain information about relevant programs, services and resources.

7191 Greater Interagency Council Parent to Parent Support Network
925 W 175th Street
Homewood, IL 60430
708-799-2718
Fax: 708-799-7974

Informational and emotional support to parents who have a child, adolescent, or adult family member with special needs.

7192 Leukemia Research Foundation
3520 Lake Avenue, Suite #202
Wilmette, IL 60091
847-424-0600
888-558-5385
Fax: 847-424-0606
info@lrfmail.org
www.allbloodcancers.org

Founded to conquer leukemia by funding research into the causes and cures of the disease and to enrich the quality of life by those touched by leukemia.

Kevin Radelet, Executive Director
Cindy Kane, Senior Director of Development
Carl Alston, Director of Communications

7193 National Center for Latinos with Disabilities
1921 S Blue Island Avenue
Chicago, IL 60608
312-666-3393
800-532-3393
Fax: 312-666-1787
TTY: 312-666-1788
ncld@ncld.com
homepage.interaccess.com/~ncld/

Parent Training and Information (PTI) programs help parents to understand their children's specific needs, communicate more effectively with professionals, participate in the educational planning process, and obtain information about relevant programs, services and resources.

Everardo Franco, Executive Director
Nancy Perez, Coordinator Info and Referral

7194 Next Steps - Parents Reaching Parents
100 W Randolph, Suite 8-100
Chicago, IL 60601
312-814-4042
Fax: 708-799-7974
TTY: 312-814-4042
caroldors@aol.com

Informational and emotional support to parents who have a child, adolescent, or adult family member with special needs.

7195 Office of Community Health and Prevention Bureau of Early Intervention, DHR
222 South College, 2nd Floor
Springfield, IL 62704
217-782-9260
Fax: 217-782-7849
www.dhs.state.il.us/ei

Provides early intervention and preschool special education for children with disabilities and special health care needs. Services include central directory, representatives of agencies, service providers, families, and coordinators of infant, toddler, and preschool special education programs.

Mary Miller, Infant/Toddler Program Coordinator
Brian Bond, Contact

7196 Parent to Parent Network
1530 Lincoln Avenue
Charleston, IL 61920
217-348-0127
Fax: 217-348-0740

Informational and emotional support to parents who have a child, adolescent, or adult family member with special needs.

7197 Southern IL Child and Family Connections
2751 W Main Street
Carbondale, IL 62903
888-340-6702
Fax: 618-549-8137

Informational and emotional support to parents who have a child, adolescent, or adult family member with special needs.

General Resources / State Agencies & Support Groups

7198 **State Board of Education Department of Special Education**
National Early Childhood Technical Assistance Ctr
100 N 1st Street, Suite 233
Springfield, IL 62777
217-782-5589
Fax: 217-782-7849
www.unc.edu

Individuals with Disabilities Education Act requires all states and territories to provide early intervention and preschool special education for children with disabilities and special health care needs. Services include central directory, representatives of agencies, service providers, families, and coordinators of infant, toddler, and preschool special education programs.

Jack Shook, Division Administrator

Indiana

7199 **ATTAIN: Assistive Technology Through Action in Indiana**
32 E Washington Street, Suite 1400
Indianapolis, IN 46204
317-486-8808
800-527-8246
Fax: 317-486-8809
TDD: 800-743-3333
attaininfo@attaininc.org
www.attanic.org

State assisted programs and support group information for people of many abilities. Includes local chapters, referrals, fun and social interaction and support groups.

7200 **About Special Kids (ASK)**
7172 Graham Road, Suite 100
Indianapolis, IN 46250
317-257-8683
800-964-4746
Fax: 317-251-7488
familynetw@aboutspecialkids.org
www.aboutspecialkids.org

Helping children with special needs live better lives by education, empowering and connecting their families.

Cindy Robinson, Director of Education and Informati
Jane Scott, Director of Family Support
Joe Brubaker, Executive Director

7201 **Assistive Technology Training and Information Center**
3354 Pine Hill Drive, PO Box 2441
Vincennes, IN 47591
812-886-0575
800-962-8842
Fax: 812-886-1128
inattic1@aol.com
www.theattic.org

Technology group of parents, consumers and professionals that provides resources to help children and adults who have disabilities gain access to the benefits of technology. Includes nationwide network of community-based assistive technology, resource centers, hands on consultants and product demonstrations.

7202 **Division of Exceptional Learners Indiana Department of Education**
State House, Room 229
Indianapolis, IN 46204
317-232-0570
Fax: 317-232-0589
www.doe.state.in.us/exceptional

Individuals with Disabilities Education Act requires all states and territories to provide preschool special education for children with disabilities. Special Education and related services are provided through the public schools.

Sheron Cochran, Preschool Special Ed Coordinator

7203 **Down Syndrome Association of Central Indiana**
10792 Downing Street
Carmel, IN 46033
317-574-9757
Fax: 317-574-9757
MKaye62801@aol.com

Provides informational and emotional support to parents who have a child, adolescent, or adult family member with special needs. Program offers an important connection for a parent who is seeking support for a special disability issue, by matching him or her with a trained veteran parent.

7204 **Family Resource Center of Southeast Indiana**
4101 Timberview Road
West Harrison, IN 47060
812-637-1445

Informational and emotional support to parents who have a child, adolescent, or adult family member with special needs.

7205 **First Direction**
PO Box 4234
Lafayette, IN 47903
765-423-1460

Informational and emotional support to parents who have a child, adolescent, or adult family member with special needs.

7206 **First Steps for Families**
500 8th Avenue
Terre Haute, IN 47804
812-231-8419
Fax: 812-231-8208
famnetwork@aol.com

Informational and emotional support to parents who have a child, adolescent, or adult family member with special needs.

7207 **First Steps, Early Interventions, New Horizons Rehabilitation**
PO Box 98
Batesville, IN 47006
812-934-4528
Fax: 812-934-2522
TTY: 812-934-4528

Informational and emotional support to parents who have a child, adolescent, or adult family member with special needs.

7208 **Future Choices**
309 N High Street
Muncie, IN 47305
765-741-3494
Fax: 765-741-8333
futurechoicesinc@aol.com

Informational and emotional support to parents who have a child, adolescent, or adult family member with special needs.

7209 **Knox County Advocates**
1805 Indiana Avenue
Vincennes, IN 47591
812-882-0375
Fax: 812-886-1128
INATTIC1@aol.com

Informational and emotional support to parents who have a child, adolescent, or adult family member with special needs.

7210 **NEO Fight**
PO Box 17715
Indianapolis, IN 46217
317-446-3013
info@neofight.org
www.neofight.org

Informational and emotional support to parents who have a child, adolescent, or adult family member with special needs.

Michie Sebree, R.N., President
Kathleen Smith, Secretary
Amanda Blann, Board Member

7211 **Project Special Care**
4755 Kinsway Drive, Suite 105
Indianapolis, IN 46205
317-257-8683
Fax: 317-251-7488
www.ipin.org

Informational and emotional support to parents who have a child, adolescent, or adult family member with special needs.

General Resources / State Agencies & Support Groups

7212 US Rowing Assocation
2 Wall Street
Princeton, NJ 08540
609-751-0700
800-314-4769
Fax: 609-924-1578
members@usrowing.org
www.usrowing.org

State assisted programs and support group information for people of many abilities. Includes local chapters, referrals, fun and social interaction and support groups.

Brian Klausner, Chief Financial Officer
Glenn Merry, Chief Executive Officer
Beth Kohl, Chief Marketing Officer

Iowa

7213 Arc of East Central Iowa
680 2nd Street SE, Suite 200
Cedar Rapids, IA 52401
319-365-0487
800-843-0272
Fax: 319-365-9938
www.arceci.org

Informational and emotional support to parents who have a child, adolescent, or adult family member with special needs.

Anne Armknecht, Executive Director
Jody Bridgewater, Director, Services & Supports

7214 Family & Educator Connection - Cedar Falls /Waterloo Region
3706 Cedar Heights Drive
Cedar Falls, IA 50613
219-273-8265
800-542-8375
Fax: 319-273-8275
TTY: 319-273-8291
www.aea267.k12.ia.us

The Family & Educator Connection is part of the Parent & Educator Connection, a statewide network of families and educators working together to serve children and young adults with special needs. They work together in positive ways to improve educational programs for children and youth with disabilities.

Rod Ball, Administrator
Edie Penno, Special Education Coordinator and T
Sandy Lichty, Consultant for Challenging Behavior

7215 Family & Educator Connection - Clear Lake/ Mason City Region
Mason City Airport Grounds, 9184 B 265th Street
Clear Lake, IA 50428
641-357-6125
800-392-6640
www.aea267.k12.ia.us

The Family & Educator Connection is part of the Parent & Educator Connection, a statewide network of families and educators working together to serve children and young adults with special needs. They work together in positive ways to improve educational programs for children and youth with disabilities.

Roberta Kraft-Abrahamson, Director District 1 - Vice Presiden
Sandy Kraschel, Administrator

7216 Family & Educator Connection - Marshalltow n Region
909 South 12th Street
Marshalltown, IA 50158
641-844-2469
800-735-1539
Fax: 641-752-0075
www.aea267.k12.ia.us

The Family & Educator Connection is part of the Parent & Educator Connection, a statewide network of families and educators working together to serve children and young adults with special needs. They work together in positive ways to improve educational programs for children and youth with disabilities.

Andy Lawler, Administrator
David Giese, Director District 5

7217 Iowa Program for Assistive Technology
University Hospital School
303A CDD, 100 Hawkins Drive
Iowa City, IA 52242
319-353-6108
800-331-3027
Fax: 319-356-8284
TDD: 800-331-3027
jane_gay@uiowa.edu
www.uiowa.edu

State assisted programs and support group information for people of many abilities. Includeslocal chapters, referrals, fun and social interaction and support groups.

Linda Monroe, Contact

7218 Parent Educator Connection
Grimews State Office Bldg
Des Moines, IA 50318
515-242-5295
800-572-5073
Fax: 712-722-1643

Informational and emotional support to parents who have a child, adolescent, or adult family member with special needs.

7219 Parent Educator Connection Program
Heartland AEA 11, 6500 Corporate Drive
Johnston, IA 50131
515-270-9030
800-362-2720
Fax: 515-270-5383
www.aea11.k12.ia.us/parents/PEC/

Provides informational and emotional support to parents who have a child, adolescent, or adult family member with special needs. Program offers an important connection for a parent who is seeking support for special disability issue, by matching him or her with a trained veteran parent.

Paula Vincent, Chief Administrator
David King, Chief Financial Officer
Kevin Fangman, Director of District Services

Kansas

7220 Assistive Technology for Kansas Project
2601 Gabriel, PO Box 738
Parsons, KS 67357
316-421-8367
800-526-3648
Fax: 620-421-8367
TDD: 316-421-0954
www.atk.ku.edu/kansas/

State assisted programs and support group information for people of many abilities. Includes local chapters, referrals, fun and social interaction and support groups.

Sara Sack, ATK Director
Sheila Simmons, ATK Coordinator
Sarah Walters, Kansas Infant Toddler Services

7221 Department of Health & Environment
1000 Sw Jackson
Topeka, KS 66612
785-296-1500
Fax: 785-368-6368
info@kdheks.gov
www.kdheks.gov

Individuals with Disabilities Education Act requires all states and territories to provide early intervention and preschool special education for children with disabilities and special health care needs. Services include central directory, representatives of agencies, service providers, families, and coordinators of infant, toddler, and preschool special education programs.

Nathan Bainbridge, Senior Executive Policy Analyst
Tim Keck, Deputy Chief Counsel
Glen Yancey, Information Technology Director

7222 Families Together
3033 West 2nd, Suite 106
Wichita, KS 67203
316-945-7747
888-815-6364
Fax: 316-945-7795
wichita@familiestogetherinc.org
www.familiestogetherinc.org

General Resources / State Agencies & Support Groups

Parent Training and Information (PTI) programs help parents to understand their children's specific needs, communicate more effectively with professionals, participate in the educational planning process, and obtain information about relevant programs, services and resources.

Linda Peterson, President
Eric Morrison, Vice President
Jill Elkins, Secretary

7223 Families Together/Parent to Parent of KS
501 Jackson, Suite 400
Topeka, KS 66603
785-233-4777
800-264-6343
Fax: 756-233-4787
TTY: 785-233-4777

Informational and emotional support to parents who have a child, adolescent, or adult family member with special needs.

7224 Special Education Administration Kansas St ate Department of Education
120 E 10th Avenue
Topeka, KS 66612
785-296-3201
Fax: 785-296-7933
tsmith@ksde.org
www.ksde.org/Default.aspx?tabid=4745

Individuals with Disabilities Education Act requires all states and territories to provide early intervention and preschool special education for children with disabilities and special health care needs. Services include central directory, representatives of agencies, service providers, families, and coordinators of infant, toddler, and preschool special education programs.

Tiffany Smith, Consultant
Colleen Riley, Team Director
Gayle Stuber, Early Learning & Preschool Coord.

Kentucky

7225 Assistive Technology Services Network
8412 Westport Road
Louisville, KY 40242
502-429-4484
800-327-5287
Fax: 502-429-7114
TDD: 502-327-9855
www.katsnet.org

State assisted programs and support group information for people of many abilities. Includes local chapters, referrals, fun and social interaction and support groups.

Stephen M. Johnson, Executive Director

7226 College of Education - Western Kentucky University
Interdisciplinary Early Childhood Education
#1 Big Red Way, Western Kentucky University
Bowling Green, KY 42101
270-745-5414
Fax: 270-745-6474
vicki.stayton@wku.edu
www.nectas.unc.edu

Individuals with Disabilities Education Act requires all states and territories to provide early intervention and preschool special education for children with disabilities and special health care needs. Services include central directory, representatives of agencies, service providers, families, and coordinators of infant, toddler, and preschool special education programs.

Vicki Stayton, Interagency Coordinating Council

7227 Division of Preschool Services
1711 Capotol Plaza Tower
Frankfort, KY 40601
502-564-7056
Fax: 502-564-6771
www.nectas.unc.edu

Provides early intervention and preschool special education for children with disabilities and special health care needs. Services include central directory, representatives of agencies, service providers, families, and coordinators of infant, toddler, and preschool special education programs.

Barbara Singleton, Preschool Special Ed. Coordinator

7228 Special Parent Involvement Network
10301-B Deering Road
Louisville, KY 40272
502-937-6894
800-525-7746
Fax: 502-937-6464
spininc@kyspin.com
www.kyspin.com

Parent Training and Information (PTI) programs help parents to understand their children's specific needs, communicate more effectively with professionals, participate in the educational planning process, and obtain information about relevant programs, services and resources.

Crump Caroline, Director

Louisiana

7229 Division of Special Populations
PO Box 94064
Baton Rouge, LA 70804
225-342-3633
800-737-2958
Fax: 225-342-5880
Vberidon@mail.doe.state.la.us
www.doe.state.la.us

Individuals with Disabilities Education Act requires all states and territories to provide early intervention and preschool special education for children with disabilities and special health care needs. Services include central directory, representatives of agencies, service providers, families, and coordinators of infant, toddler, and preschool special education programs.

Evelyn Johnson, Infant/Toddler Program Coordinator
Virginia C. Beridon, Director

7230 Families Helping Families of Greater New Orleans
1323 Division Street, Suite 110
Metairie, LA 70002
504-888-9111
800-766-7736
Fax: 504-888-0246
www.fhfgno.org

Informational and emotional support to parents who have a child, adolescent, or adult family member with special needs.

7231 Louisiana Assistive Technology Access Network
3042 Old Forge Drive, Suite D
Baton Rouge, LA 70898
225-925-9500
800-270-6185
Fax: 225-925-9560
TDD: 225-925-9500
latanstate@aol.com
www.latan.org

State assisted programs and support group information for people of many abilities. Includes local chapters, referrals, fun and social interaction and support groups.

Charles Tate, Board Chair
Jim Parks, Vice Chair
Julie Nesbit, ATP, President/CEO

7232 Preschool Programs - Division of Special Populations
PO Box 94064
Baton Rouge, LA 70804
225-342-3633
800-737-2958
Fax: 225-342-5880
www.doe.state.la.us

Individuals with Disabilities Education Act requires all states and territories to provide early intervention and preschool special education for children with disabilities and special health care needs. Services include central directory, representatives of agencies, service providers, families, and coordinators of infant, toddler, and preschool special education programs.

Evelyn Johnson, Infant/Toddler Program Coordinator
Virginia C. Beridon, Director

7233 Project PROMPT
4323 Division Street, Suite 110
Metairie, LA 70002
504-888-9111
800-766-7736
Fax: 504-888-0246
www.taalliance.org

General Resources / State Agencies & Support Groups

Parent Training and Information (PTI) programs help parents to understand their children's specific needs, communicate more effectively with professionals, participate in the educational planning process, and obtain information about relevant programs, services and resources.

Maine

7234 CDC Lincoln County
PO Box 1114
Damariscotta, ME 04543
207-563-1411
Fax: 207-563-6312
www.nectas.unc.edu

Individuals with Disabilities Education Act requires all states and territories to provide early intervention and preschool special education for children with disabilities and special health care needs. Services include central directory, representatives of agencies, service providers, families, and coordinators of infant, toddler, and preschool special education programs.

Jean Eaton, Interagency Coordinating Council

7235 Child Department Services
146 State House Station
Augusta, ME 04333
207-287-3272
Fax: 207-287-5900

Provides early intervention and preschool special education for children with disabilities and special health care needs. Services include central directory, representatives of agencies, service providers, families, and coordinators of infant, toddler, and preschool special education programs.

Joanne C Holmes, Infant/Toddler Program Coordinator

7236 Child Department Services, Department of Education
23 State House Station
Augusta, ME 04333
207-287-5950
Fax: 207-287-2550
www.unc.edu

Provides early intervention and preschool special education for children with disabilities and special health care needs. Services include central directory, representatives of agencies, service providers, families, and coordinators of infant, toddler, and preschool special education programs.

Joanne C Holmes, Preschool Special Ed. Coordiantor

7237 Consumer Information and Technology Training Exchange (Maine CITE)
46 University Drive
Augusta, ME 04330
207-621-3195
Fax: 207-629-5429
TDD: 207-621-3195
powers@maine.maine.edu
www.mainecite.org

State assisted programs and support group information for people of many abilities. Includes local chapters, referrals, fun and social interaction and support groups.

Kathleen Powers, Program Director
Kathy Adams, OTR/L, ATP, Training Coordinator
Darcy York, Administrative Assistant

7238 Special Needs Parent Info Network
PO Box 2067
Augusta, ME 04338
207-623-2144
800-870-7746
Fax: 207-623-2148
parentconnect@mpf.org
www.startingpointsforme.org

Parent Training and Information (PTI) programs help parents to understand their children's specific needs, communicate more effectively with professionals, participate in the educational planning process, and obtain information about relevant programs, services and resources.

Lorraine Christensen, President
Steve Ocean, Vice President/Treasurer
Janice LaChance, Executive Director

7239 York County Parent Awareness
150 Main Street, Midtown Mall
Sanford, ME 04027
207-324-2337
Fax: 207-324-5621
ycpa@mmp.org

Informational and emotional support to parents who have a child, adolescent, or adult family member with special needs.

Maryland

7240 Arc Family Connection Parent to Parent Program
11600 Nebel Street
Rockville, MD 20852
301-984-5777
Fax: 301-816-2429

Informational and emotional support to parents who have a child, adolescent, or adult family member with special needs.

7241 Developmental Pediatrics School of Medicine, University of Maryland
630 W Fayette Street, Room 5686
Baltimore, MD 21201
410-706-3542
Fax: 410-706-0835
www.nectas.unc.edu

Individuals with Disabilities Education Act requires all states and territories to provide early intervention and preschool special education for children with disabilities and special health care needs. Services include central directory, representatives of agencies, service providers, families, and coordinators of infant, toddler, and preschool special education programs.

Renee Wachtel, Interagency Coordinating Council

7242 MD Infant/Toddler/Preschool Services Division
200 W Baltimore Street
Baltimore, MD 21201
410-767-0238
800-535-0182
Fax: 410-333-2661
TDD: 410-333-0781
cbaglin@msde.state.md.us
www.msde.state.md.us

Individuals with Disabilities Education Act requires all states and territories to provide early intervention and preschool special education for children with disabilities and special health care needs. Services include central directory, representatives of agencies, service providers, families, and coordinators of infant, toddler, and preschool special education programs.

Carol Ann Baglin, Assstant State Superintendent

7243 Maryland Infant and Toddlers Program Family Support Network
200 W Baltimore, 4th Floor
Baltimore, MD 21201
410-767-0652
Fax: 410-333-8165

Informational and emotional support to parents who have a child, adolescent, or adult family member with special needs.

7244 Parents Place of Maryland
801 Cromwell Park Drive, Suite 103
Glen Burnie, MD 21061
410-768-9100
Fax: 410-768-0830
TDD: 410-768-9100
www.ppmd.org

Parent Training and Information (PTI) programs help parents to understand their children's specific needs, communicate more effectively with professionals, participate in the educational planning process, and obtain information about relevant programs, services and resources.

Josie Thomas, Executive Director
Suzie Shannon, Administration
Mary Baskar, Health Projects Coordinator

7245 Partners in Intensive Care
PO Box 41043
Bethesda, MD 20824
301-681-2708
Fax: 301-681-2707

General Resources / State Agencies & Support Groups

Informational and emotional support to parents who have a child, adolescent, or adult family member with special needs.

7246 Technology Assistance Program Maryland Rehabilitation Center
2301 Argonne Drive, Room T-17
Baltimore, MD 21218
410-554-9230
800-832-4827
Fax: 410-554-9237
TTY: 866-881-7488
www.mdtap.org

State assisted programs and support group information for people of many abilities. Includes local chapters, referrals, fun and social interaction and support groups.

Tony Rice, Loan Program Director
Tanya Goodman, Loan Program Assistant Director
Lori Markland, Director of Communications, Outreac

Massachusetts

7247 Arc of Massachusetts
217 South Street
Waltham, MA 02453
781-891-6270
Fax: 781-891-6271
arcmass@arcmass.org
thearcofmass.org

Serving children and adults with intellectual and developmental disabilities.

Leo V. Sarkissian, Executive Director
Judy Zacek, Community Relations Manager
Kerry Mahoney, Director of Outreach & Education

7248 Bureau of Early Childhood Programs
350 Main Street
Malden, MA 02148
781-388-3300
Fax: 781-388-3394
eschaefer@doe.mass.edu
www.doe.mass.edu

Individuals with Disabilities Education Act requires all states and territories to provide early intervention and preschool special education for children with disabilities and special health care needs. Services include central directory, representatives of agencies, service providers, families, and coordinators of infant, toddler, and preschool special education programs.

David P. Driscoll, Commissioner

7249 Children's Happiness Foundation
PO Box 266
Marshfield, MA 02050
781-837-9609
Fax: 781-837-5229
rsvpmktg@aol.com

Serves New England children ages three to eighteen with life-threatening or chronic degenerative diseases.

7250 Early Intervention Services
250 Washington Street
Boston, MA 02108
617-624-5969
Fax: 617-624-5990
Ron.Benham@state.ma.us

Individuals with Disabilities Education Act requires all states and territories to provide early intervention and preschool special education for children with disabilities and special health care needs. Services include central directory, representatives of agencies, service providers, families, and coordinators of infant, toddler, and preschool special education programs.

Ron Benham, Infant/Toddler Program Coordinator

7251 Education Development Center - EDC
43 Foundry Avenue
Waltham, MA 02453
617-969-7100
800-225-4276
Fax: 617-969-5979
TTY: 617-964-5448
www.edc.org

One of the largest nonprofit education and health organizations. With programs for children and families combining research and practice, promoting professional development and systematic change, forging community links, and influencing the policies and legislation that affect the lives of children. The New England RAP incorporates proven strategies to enhance the efforts of organizations servicing children with disabilities and their families.

Luther Luedtke, President and Chief Executive Offic
Cheryl Hoffman-Bray, Vice President/Chief Financial Offi
Robert Spielvogel, Vice President/Chief Technology Off

7252 Family Ties at Massachusetts Department of Public Health
5 Randolph Street
Canton, MA 02021
781-774-6736
Fax: 781-774-6618
TTY: 781-774-6619
TDD: 508-947-0977
mcsummers@fcsn.org
www.massfamilyties.org

Informational and emotional support to parents who have a child, adolescent, or adult family member with special needs.

Mary Castro Summers, Program Director

7253 Federation for Children with Special Needs
1135 Tremont Street Suite 420
Boston, MA 02120
617-236-7210
800-331-0688
Fax: 617-572-2094
TDD: 617-482-2915
fcsninfo@fcsn.org
www.fcsn.org/

Parent Training and Information (PTI) programs help parents to understand their children's specific needs, communicate more effectively with professionals, participate in the educational planning process, and obtain information about relevant programs, services and resources.

James F. Whalen, President
Maureen Jerz, Director of Development
Tom Hamel, Director of Finance

7254 Massachusetts Assistive Technology Partnership
1295 Boylston Street, Suite 310
Boston, MA 02215
617-355-7153
Fax: 617-355-6345
TDD: 617-355-7301
www.matp.org

State assisted programs and support group information for people of many abilities. Includes local chapters, referrals, fun and social interaction and support groups.

7255 National Birth Defects Center
40 2nd Avenue, Suite 520
Waltham, MA 02451
781-466-9555
Fax: 781-487-2361

Treats patients with birth defects, intellectual disabilities and genetic diseases.

Michigan

7256 CAUSE
2365 Woodlake Frive, Suite 100
Okemos, MI 48864
517-347-2283
800-221-9105
Fax: 517-886-9366
TTY: 517-347-2283
TDD: 517-886-9167
www.causeonline.org

Parent Training and Information (PTI) programs help parents to understand their children's specific needs, communicate more effectively with professionals, participate in the educational planning process, and obtain information about relevant programs, services and resources.

7257 Early on Michigan
PO Box 30008
Lansing, MI 48909
517-335-4865
Fax: 517-373-7504
www.1800earlyon.org

General Resources / State Agencies & Support Groups

Provides early intervention and preschool special education for children with disabilities and special health care needs. Services include central directory, representatives of agencies, service providers, families, and coordinators of infant, toddler, and preschool special education programs.

Julie Banfield, Infant/Toddler Program Coordinator

7258 Family Support Network of Michigan Parent Participation Program-MDCH
200 6th Street, 3rd Fl., S Tower, Suite 315
Detroit, MI 48226
517-373-3740
Fax: 313-256-2605
TDD: 517-373-3573

Informational and emotional support to parents who have a child, adolescent, or adult family member with special needs.

7259 Livingston County CMH Services
2280 East Grand River
Howell, MI 48843
517-546-4126
Fax: 517-546-1300
www.nectas.unc.edu

Provides early intervention and preschool special education for children with disabilities and special health care needs. Services include central directory, representatives of agencies, service providers, families, and coordinators of infant, toddler, and preschool special education programs.

Mac Miller, Interagency Coordinating Council

7260 Office of Special Education
608 W. Allegan Street, PO Box 30008
Lansing, MI 48909
517-373-9433
Fax: 517-373-7504
webmaster@oses.mde.state.mi.us
www.michigan.gov

Individuals with Disabilities Education Act requires all states and territories to provide early intervention and preschool special education for children with disabilities and special health care needs. Services include central directory, representatives of agencies, service providers, families, and coordinators of infant, toddler, and preschool special education programs.

Sally Vaughn, Deputy Superintendent, Chief Academ
Jacqueline Thompson, Director
Mike P. Flanagan, Superintendent of Public Instructio

7261 Parents are Experts
23077 Greenfield Road, Suite 205
Southfield, MI 48075
248-557-5070
800-827-4843
Fax: 248-557-4456
TDD: 248-557-5070
ucp@ameritech.net
www.taalliance.org

Parent Training and Information (PTI) programs help parents to understand their children's specific needs, communicate more effectively with professionals, participate in the educational planning process, and obtain information about relevant programs, services and resources.

7262 TECH 2000 Project-Michigan Disability Rights Coalition
740 W Lake Lansing Road, Suite 400
East Lansing, MI 48823
517-333-2477
800-760-4600
Fax: 517-333-2677
TDD: 517-333-2477
www.discoalition.org

State assisted programs and support group information for people of many abilities. Includes local chapters, referrals, fun and social interaction and support groups.

Minnesota

7263 Arc Suburban
1526 E 122nd Street
Burnsville, MN 56337
612-890-3057
Fax: 612-890-3527

Informational and emotional support to parents who have a child, adolescent, or adult family member with special needs.

7264 Department of Children, Family, & Learning
1500 Highway 36 W
Roseville, MN 55113
651-582-8200
Fax: 651-582-8872
michael.eastman@state.mn.us

Individuals with Disabilities Education Act requires all states and territories to provide early intervention and preschool special education for children with disabilities and special health care needs. Services include central directory, representatives of agencies, service providers, families, and coordinators of infant, toddler, and preschool special education programs.

Michael Eastman, Preschool Special Ed. Coordinator

7265 Family to Family Network ARC of Hennepin County
4301 Highway 7, Suite 104
Minneapolis, MN 55416
612-920-0855
Fax: 612-920-1480

Informational and emotional support to parents who have a child, adolescent, or adult family member with special needs.

7266 Interagency Early Intervention Project
550 Cedar Street
Saint Paul, MN 55101
612-296-7032
Fax: 612-296-5076
jan.rubenstein@state.mn.us
www.pediatricservices.com

Individuals with Disabilities Education Act requires all states and territories to provide early intervention and preschool special education for children with disabilities and special health care needs. Services include central directory, representatives of agencies, service providers, families, and coordinators of infant, toddler, and preschool special education programs.

Jan Rubenstein, Infant/Toddler Program Coordinator

7267 Parents for Parents
345 N Smith Avenue, MS 70-403
Saint Paul, MN 55102
651-220-6731
Fax: 651-220-6125

Informational and emotional one-to-one support to parents who have a child or adolescent with special needs.

Pat Schaffner, Parent to Parent Specialist

7268 Pilot Parents in Anoka and Ramsey Counties
1201 89th Avenue NE, Suite 305
Blaine, MN 55434
612-783-4958
Fax: 612-783-4900

Informational and emotional support to parents who have a child, adolescent, or adult family member with special needs.

7269 Pilot Parents of Northeast Minnesota
201 Ordean Building
Duluth, MN 55802
218-726-4725
Fax: 218-726-4722

Informational and emotional support to parents who have a child, adolescent, or adult family member with special needs.

7270 Vinland Center
PO Box 308
Loretto, MN 55357
763-479-3555
Fax: 763-479-2605
www.vinlandcenter.org

State assisted programs and support group information for people of many abilities. Includes local chapters, referrals, fun and social interaction and support groups.

Gerald Seck, President
Mary Roehl, Executive Director
Duane Reynolds, Associate Director

7271 Voyageur Outward Bound School
101 E Chapman, Suite 120
St. Ely, MN 55731
218-365-7790
800-321-4453
Fax: 218-365-7079
www.vobs.com

General Resources / State Agencies & Support Groups

State assisted programs and support group information for people of many abilities. Includes local chapters, referrals, fun and social interaction and support groups.

Jack Lee, Executive Director
Suellen Sack, Program Director
Poppy Potter, Director of Operations

7272 Wilderness Inquiry
808 14th Avenue SE
Minneapolis, MN 55414

612-676-9400
800-728-0719
Fax: 612-676-9475
TTY: 800-728-0719
info@wildernessinquiry.org
www.wildernessinquiry.org

State assisted programs and support group information for people of many abilities. Includes local chapters, referrals, fun and social interaction and support groups.

Tom Nelson, Chair
Greg Lais, Executive Director
Beth Dooley, Communications Director

Mississippi

7273 First Steps Program
570 East Woodrow Wilson
Jackson, MS 39215

601-576-7816
Fax: 601-576-7540
www.nectas.unc.edu

Individuals with Disabilities Education Act requires all states and territories to provide early intervention and preschool special education for children with disabilities and special health care needs. Services include central directory, representatives of agencies, service providers, families, and coordinators of infant, toddler, and preschool special education programs.

Roy Hart, Infant/Toddler Program Coordinator

7274 Office of Special Education
359 NW Street, Suite 337, PO Box 771
Jackson, MS 39205

601-359-3498
Fax: 601-359-2078
www.nectas.unc.edu

Individuals with Disabilities Education Act requires all states and territories to provide early intervention and preschool special education for children with disabilities and special health care needs. Services include central directory, representatives of agencies, service providers, families, and coordinators of infant, toddler, and preschool special education programs.

Dot Bowman, Preschool Special Ed. Coordinator

7275 Parent Partners
5 Old River Place, Suite 101
Jackson, MS 39202

601-354-3302
800-366-5707
Fax: 601-354-2426
ptiofms@misnet.com
www.parentpartners.org

Parent Training and Information (PTI) programs help parents to understand their children's specific needs, communicate more effectively with professionals, participate in the educational planning process, and obtain information about relevant programs, services and resources.

7276 Project Start
PO Box 1698
Jackson, MS 39215

601-987-4872
800-852-8328
Fax: 601-364-2349
dyoung@mdrs.ms.gov
www.msprojectstart.org

State assisted programs and support group information for people of many abilities. Includes local chapters, referrals, fun and social interaction and support groups.

Dorothy Young, Project Director
Kacee Mott, Administrative Assistant

Missouri

7277 Assistance Technology Project
4731 S Cochise, Suite 114
Independence, MO 64055

816-373-5193
Fax: 816-373-9314
TTY: 816-373-9315
www.doir.state.mo.us/matp/

State assisted programs and support group information for people of many abilities. Includes local chapters, referrals, fun and social interaction and support groups.

7278 Children's Therapy Center
600 E 14th Street
Sedalia, MO 65301

660-826-4400
Fax: 660-826-4420
www.nectas.unc.edu

Services include central directory, representatives of agencies, service providers, families, and coordinators of infant, toddler, and preschool special education programs.

Roger Garlich, Interagency Coordinating Council

7279 Department of Elementary and Secondary Education
PO Box 480
Jefferson City, MO 65102

573-751-2965
Fax: 573-526-4404
www.unc.edu

Individuals with Disabilities Education Act requires all states and territories to provide early intervention and preschool special education for children with disabilities and special health care needs. Services include central directory, representatives of agencies, service providers, families, and coordinators of infant, toddler, and preschool special education programs.

Melodie Friedebach, Coordinator

7280 Disabilities Advocacy & Support Network
PO Box 4067
Parker, CO 80134

417-895-7464
Fax: 417-895-7412
TTY: 417-895-7430
sdasn@aol.com
www.invisibledisabilities.org

Informational and emotional support to parents who have a child, adolescent, or adult family member with special needs.

Wayne Connell, Founder & President
Steve Tonkin, Vice-President
Rob Germundson, Treasurer

7281 Family Resource Network
Park A Plaza
601 Business Loop 70 W, Suite 2161
Columbia, MO 65203

573-449-8663

Informational and emotional support to parents who have a child, adolescent, or adult family member with special needs.

7282 Missouri Parents Act
8301 State Line Road, Suite 204
Kansas City, MO 64114

816-531-7070
800-743-7634
Fax: 816-531-4777
info@ptimpact.org
www.ptimpact.org

Parent Training and Information (PTI) programs help parents to understand their children's specific needs, communicate more effectively with professionals, participate in the educational planning process, and obtain information about relevant programs, services and resources.

Mary Kay Savage, Executive Director
Diana Biere, Associate Director

7283 Parent Act
1 W Armour Boulevard, Suite 301
Kansas City, MO 64111

816-531-7070
Fax: 816-531-4777
www.taalliance.org

General Resources / State Agencies & Support Groups

Parent Training and Information (PTI) programs help parents to understand their children's specific needs, communicate more effectively with professionals, participate in the educational planning process, and obtain information about relevant programs, services and resources.

7284 Positive Solutions for Life Challenges
Route 3, Box 441
Warswaw, MO 65355
660-438-6990

Informational and emotional support to parents who have a child, adolescent, or adult family member with special needs.

7285 United Services
4140 Old Mill Parkway
Saint Peters, MO 63376
636-926-2700
Fax: 636-447-4919
ssalmo@unitedsrvcs.org
www.unitedsrvcs.org

Provides services to children ages infant to five-years-old with special needs. Preschool and daycare onsite. We also offer support groups for siblings and family members, parent library available.

Denise Liebel, President/CEO
Windy Spalding, Chief Operating Officer
Dick Frizzell, CFO

Montana

7286 CO-TEACH/Division of Educational Research and Service
School of Education
University of Montana
Missoula, MT 59812
406-243-5344
Fax: 406-243-2797

Informational and emotional support to parents who have a child, adolescent, or adult family member with special needs.

7287 Developmental Disabilities Program
PO Box 4210
Helena, MT 59604
406-444-5647
Fax: 406-444-0230
www.nectas.unc.edu

Individuals with Disabilities Education Act requires all states and territories to provide early intervention and preschool special education for children with disabilities and special health care needs. Services include central directory, representatives of agencies, service providers, families, and coordinators of infant, toddler, and preschool special education programs.

Jan Spiegle, Infant/Toddler Program Coordinator

7288 Division of Special Education
PO Box 202501
Helena, MT 59620
406-444-4429
Fax: 406-444-3924
drmccarthy@opi.mt.gov
www.unc.edu

Individuals with Disabilities Education Act requires all states and territories to provide early intervention and preschool special education for children with disabilities and special health care needs. Services include central directory, representatives of agencies, service providers, families, and coordinators of infant, toddler, and preschool special education programs.

Robert Runkel, Director

7289 MonTECH
634 Eddy Avenue, Rural Inst on Disab
Missoula, MT 59812
406-243-5676
800-732-0323
Fax: 406-243-4730
TDD: 800-732-0323
www.rudi.montech.umt.edu/

State assisted programs and support group information for people of many abilities. Includes local chapters, referrals, fun and social interaction and support groups.

7290 Parents Let's Unite for Kids
516 N 32nd Street
Billings, MT 59101
406-255-0540
800-222-7585
Fax: 406-255-0523
info@pluk.org
www.pluk.org

Parent Training and Information (PTI) programs help parents to understand their children's specific needs, communicate more effectively with professionals, participate in the educational planning process, and obtain information about relevant programs, services and resources.

7291 Quality Life Concepts
215 Smelter Ave. N.E. PO Box 250
Great Falls, MT 59403
406-452-9531
800-761-2680
Fax: 406-453-5930
www.qlc-gtf.org

Informational and emotional support to parents who have a child, adolescent, or adult family member with special needs.

Priscilla Halcro, Chief Executive Officer
Tracy Lane, Business Services Director
Lynn Morley, Community Support Services Director

Nebraska

7292 Assistive Technology Partnership
3901 N 27th Street, Suite 5
Lincoln, NE 68521
402-471-0734
888-806-6287
Fax: 402-471-6052
TDD: 402-471-0734
atp@nebraska.gov
www.atp.ne.gov

State assisted programs and support group information for people of many abilities. Includes local chapters, referrals, fun and social interaction and support groups.

David Altman, Technology Specialist
Lauren Rock, Program Director
Leslie Novacek, Director

7293 Individual and Family Support Arc of Lincoln & Lancaster County
645 M Street, Suite 19
Lincoln, NE 68508
402-477-6925
Fax: 402-477-6927

Informational and emotional support to parents who have a child, adolescent, or adult family member with special needs.

7294 PTI Nebraska (Parent, Training & Information
1941 S 42nd Street, Suite 205
Omaha, NE 68105
402-346-0525
800-284-8520
Fax: 402-934-1479
TDD: 402-346-0525
reception@pti-nebraska.org
pti-nebraska.org

Parent Training and Information (PTI) programs help parents to understand their children's specific needs, communicate more effectively with professionals, participate in the educational planning process, and obtain information about relevant programs, services and resources. The Nebrask Parent Center services families statewide. There is no fee for services. Call for additional information.

Mike Tufte, Executive Director
Heidi Sommer, Special Education Outreach Coord.
Nina Baker, Health Information Coordinator

7295 Parent Assistance Network
310 W 24th
Kearney, NE 68847
308-237-6025
Fax: 308-237-6014

Informational and emotional support to parents who have a child, adolescent, or adult family member with special needs.

General Resources / State Agencies & Support Groups

7296 Parent Support Group
123 S Webb Road
Grand Island, NE 68802
308-385-5925
Fax: 308-385-5797

Informational and emotional support to parents who have a child, adolescent, or adult family member with special needs.

7297 Parents Encouraging Parents
NE Department of Education
301 Centennial Mall Street, PO Box 94987
Lincoln, NE 68509
402-471-2471
Fax: 402-471-0117
TTY: 402-471-2471

Informational and emotional support to parents who have a child, adolescent, or adult family member with special needs.

Nevada

7298 Assistive Technology Collaborative
711 S Stewart Street, Rehab Division
Carson City, NV 89701
775-687-4452
Fax: 775-687-3292
TTY: 702-687-3388
www.state.nv.us.80

State assisted programs and support group information for people of many abilities. Includes local chapters, referrals, fun and social interaction and support groups.

7299 Early Intervention Services Division of Child & Family Services
3987 S McCarren Boulevard
Reno, NV 89502
775-688-2284
Fax: 775-688-2558
www.nectas.unc.edu

Provides early intervention and preschool special education for children with disabilities and special health care needs. Services include central directory, representatives of agencies, service providers, families, and coordinators of infant, toddler, and preschool special education programs.

Marilyn K Walter, Infant/Toddler Program Coordinator

7300 Educational Equity, Special Education Branch
700 E 5th Street, Suite 113
Carson City, NV 89701
775-687-9171
800-992-0900
Fax: 775-687-9123
www.unc.edu

Individuals with Disabilities Education Act requires all states and territories to provide early intervention and preschool special education for children with disabilities and special health care needs. Services include central directory, representatives of agencies, service providers, families, and coordinators of infant, toddler, and preschool special education programs.

Gloria Dopf, Preschool Special Ed. Coordinator

7301 Nevada Parent Network
University of Nevada-Reno
COE, REPC/285
Reno, NV 89557
702-784-4921
800-216-7988
Fax: 702-702-4997
www.iser.com/npn-NV.html

Informational and emotional support to parents who have a child, adolescent, or adult family member with special needs.

Cheryl Dinnell, Program Coordinator

7302 Nevada Parents Encouraging Parents (PEP)
2101 S. Jones Blvd., Suite 120
Las Vegas, NV 89146
702-388-8899
800-216-5188
Fax: 702-388-2966
pepinfo@nvpep.org
www.nvpep.org

Parent Training and Information (PTI) programs help parents to understand their children's specific needs, communicate more effectively with professionals, participate in the educational planning process, and obtain information about relevant programs, services and resources.

Karen Taycher, Executive Director
Stephanie Vrsnik, Community Development Director
Natalie Filipic, Director of Operations

7303 Parents Encouraging Parents
2101 S. Jones Blvd., Suite 120
Las Vegas, NV 89146
702-388-8899
800-216-5188
Fax: 702-388-2966
pepinfo@nvpep.org
www.nvpep.org

Informational and emotional support to parents who have a child, adolescent, or adult family member with special needs.

Karen Taycher, Executive Director
Stephanie Vrsnik, Community Development Director
Natalie Filipic, Director of Operations

New Hampshire

7304 Bureau of Early Learning
101 Pleasant Street
Concord, NH 03301
603-271-3791
Fax: 603-271-1953
www.education.nh.gov

Individuals with Disabilities Education Act requires all states and territories to provide early intervention and preschool special education for children with disabilities and special health care needs. Services include central directory, representatives of agencies, service providers, families, and coordinators of infant, toddler, and preschool special education programs.

Ruth Littlefield, Preschool Special Ed. Coordinator

7305 Dartmouth-Hitchcock Sleep Disorders Center Dartmouth Medical Center
One Medical Center Drive
Lebanon, NH 03756
603-650-7534
Fax: 603-650-7820
www.dartmouth-hitchcock.org

Rocco R Addante, Director
Glen Greenough MD, Fellowship Director
Joanne MacQuarrie, BS,RPSGT,RRT, Administrator

7306 Division of Special Education
101 Pleasant Street
Concord, NH 03301
603-271-3791
Fax: 603-271-1953
www.education.nh.gov

Individuals with Disabilities Education Act requires all states and territories to provide early intervention and preschool special education for children with disabilities and special health care needs. Services include central directory, representatives of agencies, service providers, families, and coordinators of infant, toddler, and preschool special education programs.

Ruth Littlefield, Preschool Special Ed. Coordinator

7307 High Hopes Foundation of New Hampshire
301 Daniel Webster Hwy., Suite 6
Merrimack, NH 03054
603-529-1010
800-639-6804
Fax: 603-529-0037
HighHopeNH@aol.com
www.highhopesfoundation.org

Volunteer organization dedicated to granting wishes of seriously ill New Hampshire children from three through 18 years old.

60+ members

Shaunae Nolet, President
Tom Perkins, Vice President
Dana Wallace, Treasurer

General Resources / State Agencies & Support Groups

7308 Parent Information Center
PO Box 2405
Concord, NH 03302
603-224-7005
Fax: 603-224-4365
TDD: 603-224-7005
mlewis@picnh.org
www.picnh.org

Parent Training and Information (PTI) programs help parents to understand their children's specific needs, communicate more effectively with professionals, participate in the educational planning process, and obtain information about relevant programs, services and resources.

Michelle Lewis, Executive Director
Sylvia Abbott, Administrative Supervisor
Jennifer Cunha, Project Staff

7309 Parent to Parent of New Hampshire
12 Flynn Street
Lebanon, NH 03766
603-448-6393
800-698-5465
Fax: 603-448-6311
www.p2pnh.org

Informational and emotional support to parents who have a child, adolescent, or adult family member with special needs.

Richard Cohen, Executive Director
Judith Iaconianni, Director/Co-founder

7310 Technology Partnership Project Institute on Disability/UAP
The Concord Center
10 West Edge Drive, Suite 101
Durham, NH 03824
603-862-4320
Fax: 603-862-0555
TDD: 603-224-0630
institute.disability@unh.edu
iod.unh.edu

State assistive programs funded by the National Institute on Disability and Rehabilitation Research. Includes directories, support group information, training and project information.

New Jersey

7311 Division of Student Services
Riverview Executive Plaza, Building 100
Trenton, NJ 08625
609-633-6833
Fax: 609-984-8422
www.unc.edu

Individuals with Disabilities Education Act requires all states and territories to provide early intervention and preschool special education for children with disabilities and special health care needs. Services include central directory, representatives of agencies, service providers, families, and coordinators of infant, toddler, and preschool special education programs.

Barbara Tkach, Preschool Special Ed. Coordinator

7312 Early Intervention System
PO Box 364
Trenton, NJ 08625
609-777-7734
Fax: 609-292-3580
www.state.nj-us/health/8hs/eiphome.htm

Individuals with Disabilities Education Act requires all states and territories to provide early intervention and preschool special education for children with disabilities and special health care needs. Services include central directory, representatives of agencies, service providers, families, and coordinators of infant, toddler, and preschool special education programs.

Charles E. Drum, Director & Professor
Jennifer Donahue, Director of Finance
Matthew Gianino, Director of Communications

7313 Family Support Center of New Jersey
Lion's Head Office Park
1 AAA Drive, Suite 203
Trenton, NJ 08691
732-262-8020
800-336-5843
Fax: 609-392-5621
FSCNJ@aol.com
www.efnj.com

Informational and emotional support to parents who have a child, adolescent, or adult family member with special needs.

Michael P. Rinaldo, Chairman
Robert L. D'Avanzo, President
Eric B. Geller, M.D., Vice President

7314 New Jersey Self-Help Clearinghouse
375 East McFarlan Street
Dover, NJ 07801
973-989-1122
800-367-6274
Fax: 973-989-1159
TTY: 973-625-9053
www.njgroups.org

The NJ Self-Help Group Clearinghouse provides contacts for over 4,500 New Jersey support groups and over 1,100 national support networks for most illnesses, addictions, disabilities, bereavement, parenting and other stressful life situations. The organization also helps individuals wanting to start a group.

7315 New Jersey Statewide Parent to Parent
2150 Highway 35, Suite 207C
Sea Girt, NJ 08750
800-372-6510
Fax: 973-642-8080
www.spannj.org

Informational and emotional support to parents who have a child, adolescent, or adult family member with special needs.

Malia Corde, Program Coordinator
Malia Corde, Coordinator
Jeannette Mejias, Bilingual (Spanish) Associate

7316 Statewide Parent Advocacy Network
35 Halsey Street, 4th Floor
Newark, NJ 07102
973-642-8100
800-654-SPAN
Fax: 973-642-8080
www.spanadvocacy.org

Parent Training and Information (PTI) programs help parents to understand their children's specific needs, communicate more effectively with professionals, participate in the educational planning process, and obtain information about relevant programs, services and resources.

Diana Autin, Co-Director
Maria Docherty, Co-Director
Carolyn Hayer, Co-Director

New Mexico

7317 EPICS Project-SW Communication Resources
PO Box 788, 2000 Camino del Pueblo
Bernalilo, NM 87004
505-867-3396
800-765-7320
Fax: 505-867-3398
TDD: 505-867-3396
www.disabilityrights.org

Parent Training and Information (PTI) programs help parents to understand their children's specific needs, communicate more effectively with professionals, participate in the educational planning process, and obtain information about relevant programs, services and resources.

7318 Long Term Services Division
PO Box 26110
Santa Fe, NM 87502
505-827-0103
Fax: 505-827-2455
www.nectas.unc.edu

Individuals with Disabilities Education Act requires all states and territories to provide early intervention and preschool special education for children with disabilities and special health care needs. Services include central directory, representatives of agencies, service providers, families, and coordinators of infant, toddler, and preschool special education programs.

Cathy Stevenson, Infant/Toddler Program Coordiantor

General Resources / State Agencies & Support Groups

7319 Parents Reaching Out
1920 B Columbia Drive SE
Albuquerque, NM 87106
505-247-0192
800-524-5176
Fax: 505-247-1345
TDD: 505-865-3700
info@parentsreachingout.org
www.parentsreachingout.org

Provides peer support, technical assistance and information statewide to families in New Mexico who have family member with unique or special needs and professionals who care for them.

Renata Witte, President
Johnny Wilson, Executive Director
Leon Emplit, Director of Operations

7320 Special Education Unit
300 Don Gaspar Avenue
Santa Fe, NM 87501
505-827-6541
Fax: 505-827-6791
www.unc.edu

Individuals with Disabilities Education Act requires all states and territories to provide early intervention and preschool special education for children with disabilities and special health care needs. Services include central directory, representatives of agencies, service providers, families, and coordinators of infant, toddler, and preschool special education programs.

Maria Landazuri, Preschool Special Ed. Coordinator

7321 Technology Assistance Program
435 St Michael's Drive, Building D
Santa Fe, NM 87505
505-954-8539
800-866-2253
Fax: 505-954-8562
TDD: 800-866-2253
nmdvrtap@aol.com
www.tap.gcd.state.nm.us

State assisted programs for people of many abilities. Includes local chapters, referrals, fun and social interaction and support groups.

New York

7322 Advocacy Center
590 South Avenue
Rochester, NY 14620
716-546-1700
800-650-4967
Fax: 716-546-7069
advocacy@frontiernet.net
www.advocacycenter.com

Parent Training and Information (PTI) programs help parents to understand their children's specific needs, communicate more effectively with professionals, participate in the educational planning process, and obtain information about relevant programs, services and resources.

Stephen G. Schwarz, President
Adam Anolik, Vice President
Paul Visca, Treasurer

7323 Advocates for Children of New York
151 W 30th Street, 5th Floor
New York, NY 10001
212-947-9779
Fax: 212-947-9790
info@advocatesforchildren.org
www.advocatesforchildren.org

Parent Training and Information (PTI) programs help parents to understand their children's specific needs, communicate more effectively with professionals, participate in the educational planning process, and obtain information about relevant programs, services and resources.

Jamie A. Levitt, President
Kim Sweet, Executive Director
Matthew Lenaghan, Deputy Director

7324 Aurora of Central New York
518 James Street, Suite 100
Syracuse, NY 13203
315-422-7263
Fax: 315-422-4792
TTY: 315-422-9746
TDD: 315-422-9746
auroracny@auroraofcny.org
www.auroraofcny.org

Professional counseling services to assist individuals and their families deal with the trauma of hearing or vision loss.

John McCormick, President
Scott Gucciardi, 1st Vice President
Robert C. Haege, Assistant Treasurer

7325 Early Intervention Program
Corning Tower Room 208, Empire Street Plaza
Albany, NY 12237
518-473-7016
Fax: 518-473-8673
dmn02@health.state.ny.us
www.nectas.unc.edu

Individuals with Disabilities Education Act requires all states and territories to provide early intervention and preschool special education for children with disabilities and special health care needs. Services include a central directory, representatives of agencies, service providers, families, and coordinators of infant, toddler, and preschool special education programs.

Donna Noyes, Infant/Toddler Program Coordinator

7326 Friends of Karen
118 Titicus Road, PO Box 190
Purdys, NY 10560
845-277-4547
800-637-2774
www.friendsofkaren.org

Dedicated to helping terminally and catastrophically ill children and their families in the New York metropolitan area only. They provide assistance with payments for physicians, hospitals and medications, help with extra expenses beyond medical bills, provide home nursing services and equipment, supplies for loans, and offers emotional support.

Pam Hervey, President
Bob Goldberg, Vice President
David Rosenberg, Vice President

7327 Marty Lyons Foundation
326 W 48th Street
New York, NY 10036
212-977-9474
877-560-9474
Fax: 212-977-1752
mlf_hq@martylyonsfoundation.org
www.martylyonsfoundation.org

Chapters in New Jersey, New York, Massachussets, Connecticut, Maryland, North Carolina, South Carolina, Georgia, Texas, Pennsylvania and Florida provide a special wish to children ages three to seventeen who are terminally ill or have a life-threatening disease.

300 volunteers

Marty Lyons, Chairman
Ken Schroy, Vice Chairman
Richard A. Miller, President

7328 New York Department of Education
1 Commerce Plaza
Albany, NY 12234
518-473-4823
Fax: 518-486-4154

Individuals with Disabilities Education Act requires all states and territories to provide early intervention and preschool special education for children with disabilities and special health care needs. Services include central directory, representatives of agencies, service providers, families, and coordinators of infant, toddler, and preschool special education programs.

Michael Plotzker Vesid, Preschool Special Ed. Coordinator

7329 Parent Network Center
250 Delaware Avenue, Suite 3
Buffalo, NY 14202
716-853-1570
800-724-7408
Fax: 716-853-1574
TDD: 716-853-1573
www.taalliance.org

General Resources / State Agencies & Support Groups

Parent Training and Information (PTI) programs help parents to understand their children's specific needs, communicate more effectively with professionals, participate in the educational planning process, and obtain information about relevant programs, services and resources.

7330 Parent to Parent of New York State
500 Balltown Road
Schenectady, NY 12304
518-381-4350
800-305-8817
Fax: 518-382-1959
parent2par@aol.com
www.parenttoparentnys.org

Informational and emotional support to parents who have a child, adolescent, or adult family member with special needs.

1500 Members

Linda Coull, Vice President
Holly Bartczak, Coordinator
Tina Beauparlant, Parent Advocate

7331 Resources for Children with Special Needs
116 East 16th Street, 5th Floor
New York City, NY 10003
212-667-4650
Fax: 212-254-4070
info@resourcesnyc.org
www.resourcesnyc.org

Parent Training and Information (PTI) programs help parents to understand their children's specific needs, communicate more effectively with professionals, participate in the educational planning process, and obtain information about relevant programs, services and resources.

Ellen Miller-Wachtel, Chair
Shon E. Glusky, President
Stephen Stern, Director of Finance and Administrat

7332 Saint Mary's Healthcare System for Children
One Penn Plaza Suite 2420
New York, NY 10119
212-586-8723
Fax: 212-586-5170
www.nycharities.org

Information and advocacy resources for families and professionals. Includes listings of organizations providing general information and organizations focusing on more specific areas of concern to families and young adults who have disabilities.

7333 Sinergia/Metropolitan Parent Center
15 W 65th Street, 6th Floor
New York, NY 10023
212-496-1300
Fax: 212-496-5608
www.panic.com/~sinergia

Parent Training and Information (PTI) programs help parents to understand their children's specific needs, communicate more effectively with professionals, participate in the educational planning process, and obtain information about relevant programs, services and resources.

7334 TRIAD Project-Advocates for Persons with Disabilities
One Empire State Plaza, Suite 1001
Albany, NY 12223
518-474-2825
800-522-4369
Fax: 518-473-6005
TTY: 518-473-4231

State assisted programs and support group information for people of many abilities. Includes local chapters, referrals, fun and social interaction and support groups.

7335 Ulster County Social Services
1061 Development Court
Kingston, NY 12401
845-334-5000
Fax: 845-255-3202
www.co.ulster.ny.us

Individuals with Disabilities Education Act requires all states and territories to provide early intervention and preschool special education for children with disabilities and special health care needs. Services include central directory, representatives of agencies, service providers, families, and coordinators of infant, toddler, and preschool special education programs.

Thomas Roach, Interagency Coordinating Council
Michael Iapoce, Commissioner

North Carolina

7336 Assistive Technology Project, Human Resources, Voc. and Rehab. Services
1110 Navaho Drive, Suite 101
Raleigh, NC 27609
919-850-2787
800-852-0042
Fax: 919-850-2792
TTY: 919-850-2787
www.ncatp.org

State assisted programs and support group information for people of many abilities. Includes local chapters, referrals, fun and social interaction and support groups.

7337 ECAC NC PTI
907 Barra Row, Suites 102/103
Davidson, NC 28036
704-892-1321
800-962-6817
Fax: 704-892-5028
TDD: 704-892-1321
ecac@ecacmail.org
www.ecac-parentcenter.org

Parent Training and Information (PTI) programs help parents to understand their children's specific needs, communicate more effectively with professionals, participate in the educational planning process, and obtain information about relevant programs, services and resources.

Laura J. Weber, PhD, Executive Director
Cache Owens, PTI Manager

7338 Exceptional Children Division
301 N Wilmington Street
Raleigh, NC 27601
919-807-3300
Fax: 919-807-3482
kbaars@state.nc.us
www.mcpublicschools.org

Individuals with Disabilities Education Act requires all states and territories to provide early intervention and preschool special education for children with disabilities and special health care needs. Services include central directory, representatives of agencies, service providers, families, and coordinators of infant, toddler, and preschool special education programs.

Kathy Baars, Preschool Special Ed. Coordinator

7339 Family Support Network of North Carolina
University of North carolina
200 N Greensboro St, Carr Mill Mall, 2nd Fl Ste D9
Carrboro, NC 27510
919-966-2841
800-852-0042
Fax: 919-966-2916
cdr@med.unc.edu
www.fsnnc.org

Family Support Network of North Carolina promotes and provides support for families with children who have special needs. Families are in a unique position to offer information and support to other families. An experienced family member can share the most practical advice and help a parent navigate the complex service systems. Having support can make it easier for families to experience the joy and satisfaction that can come from parenting a child with special needs.

Laura Curtis, Education & Outreach Coordinator
Irene Nathan Zipper, Director

7340 Partnerships for Inclusion
2415 W Vernon Avenue
Kingston, NC 28501
919-559-5156
www.nectas.unc.edu

Individuals with Disabilities Education Act requires all states and territories to provide early intervention and preschool special education for children with disabilities and special health care needs. Services include central directory, representatives of agencies, service providers, families, and coordinators of infant, toddler, and preschool special education programs.

Sandy Steele, Interagency Coordinating Council

General Resources / State Agencies & Support Groups

7341 Rockingham County Schools
511 Harrington Highway
Eden, NC 27288
336-627-2615
Fax: 336-627-2660
www.ncpublicschools.org/success/regionalcontacts

Individuals with Disabilities Education Act requires all states and territories to provide early intervention and preschool special education for children with disabilities and special health care needs. Services include central directory, representatives of agencies, service providers, families, and coordinators of infant, toddler, and preschool special education programs.

Susan Peele, Interagency Coordinating Council

North Dakota

7342 Developmental Disabilities Unit
1237 W Divide Avenue, Suite 1A
Bismarck, ND 58501
701-328-8936
800-755-8529
Fax: 701-328-8969
www.nectas.unc.edu

Individuals with Disabilities Education Act requires all states and territories to provide early intervention and preschool special education for children with disabilities and special health care needs. Services include central directory, representatives of agencies, service providers, families, and coordinators of infant, toddler, and preschool special education programs.

Debra Balsdon, Infant/Toddler Program Coordinator

7343 Interagency Program Assistive Technology
3240-15th Street South, Suite B
Fargo, ND 58104
701-365-4728
800-895-4728
Fax: 701-365-6242
TDD: 701-265-4807
lee@pioneer.state.nd.us
www.ndipat.org

State assisted programs and support group information for people of many abilities. Includes local chapters, referrals, fun and social interaction and support groups.

7344 Special Education Division
600 E Boulevard
Bismarck, ND 58505
701-328-2277
Fax: 701-328-4149
TTY: 701-328-4920
dpi@nd.gov
www.dpi.state.nd.us

Individuals with Disabilities Education Act requires all states and territories to provide early intervention and preschool special education for children with disabilities and special health care needs. Services include central directory, representatives of agencies, service providers, families, and coordinators of infant, toddler, and preschool special education programs.

Ann Chase, Child Nutrition, Grant Manager
Jerry Coleman, School Finance, Director
Jim Bosch, Maintenance/Clerk

Ohio

7345 Bureau of EI Services
246 N High Strees, PO Box 118
Columbus, OH 43215
614-644-8389
Fax: 614-728-9163
www.ohiohelpmegrow.org

Individuals with Disabilities Education Act requires all states and territories to provide early intervention and preschool special education for children with disabilities and special health care needs. Services include central directory, representatives of agencies, service providers, families, and coordinators of infant, toddler, and preschool special education programs.

Cindy Oser, Infant/Toddler Program Coordinator

7346 Celebrating Families of Children & Adults with Special Needs
16 Vassar Drive
Dayton, OH 45406
937-275-0990
800-432-2199
Fax: 937-275-0277
families@erinet.com
www.eparent.com

Informational and emotional support to parents who have a child, adolescent, or adult family member with special needs.

Joseph M Valenzano, Jr., President, CEO & Publisher
James P. McGinnis, VP of Operations/CFO
Rick Rader, MD, Editor-in-Chief

7347 East Central Regional Office
170 W High Avenue
New Philadelphia, OH 44663
330-364-5567
Fax: 330-343-3038
www.nectas.unc.edu

Individuals with Disabilities Education Act requires all states and territories to provide early intervention and preschool special education for children with disabilities and special health care needs. Services include central directory, representatives of agencies, service providers, families, and coordinators of infant, toddler, and preschool special education programs.

Edith Greer, Preschool Special Ed. Coordinator

7348 Family Information Network
143 NW Avenue, Building A
Tallmadge, OH 44278
330-633-2055
Fax: 330-633-2658

Informational and emotional support to parents who have a child, adolescent, or adult family member with special needs.

7349 OCECD
165 W Center Street, Suite 302
Marion, OH 43302
614-382-5452
800-374-2806
Fax: 614-383-6421
www.ocecd.org

Parent Training and Information (PTI) programs help parents to understand their children's specific needs, communicate more effectively with professionals, participate in the educational planning process, and obtain information about relevant programs, services and resources.

Margaret M. Burley, Director

7350 Ohio Protection and Advocacy Organization
5350 Brookpark Avenue
Cleveland, OH 44134
216-398-5501
800-672-1220
Fax: 216-398-5505

Informational and emotional support to parents who have a child, adolescent, or adult family member with special needs.

7351 Operation Liftoff of Ohio
PO Box 1094
Gallipolis, OH 45631
NOP-ONE-

Fulfills a dream for children in Ohio and surrounding states who have a life-threatening illness.

7352 Society for Rehabilitation
9521 Lake Shore Boulevard
Mentor, OH 44060
440-352-8993
Fax: 440-352-6632
www.societyhelps.org

Individuals with Disabilities Education Act requires all states and territories to provide early intervention and preschool special education for children with disabilities and special health care needs. Disability therapy is provided for children and adults.

Richard J Kessler, Executive Director

General Resources / State Agencies & Support Groups

7353 Train-Ohio Super Computer Center
1224 Kinnear Road
Columbus, OH 43212
614-292-9248
Fax: 614-292-7168
TDD: 614-292-2426
www.osc.edu

State assisted programs and support group information for people of many abilities. Includes local chapters, referrals, fun and social interaction and support groups.

Pankaj Shah, Executive Director
Kevin Wohlever, Director of Supercomputing Operatio
Brian Guilfoos, Client and Technology Support Manag

Oklahoma

7354 Oklahoma ABLE Tech-Wellness Center
1514 W Hall of Fame
Stillwater, OK 74078
405-744-9748
800-257-1705
Fax: 405-744-7670
TTY: 800-257-1705
www.okabletech.okstate.edu

State assisted programs and support group information for people of many abilities. Includes local chapters, referrals, fun and social interaction and support groups.

Linda Jaco, Director of Sponsored Programs
Milissa Gofourth, Program Manager
Diana Sargent, Staff Assistant

7355 Parents Reaching Out in Oklahoma
1917 S Harvard Avenue
Oklahoma City, OK 73128
405-681-9710
Fax: 405-685-4006
TDD: 405-681-9710
prook@aol.com
www.ucp.org/probase.htm

Parent Training and Information (PTI) programs help parents to understand their children's specific needs, communicate more effectively with professionals, participate in the educational planning process, and obtain information about relevant programs, services and resources.

7356 Special Education Office
2500 N Lincoln Boulevard
Oklahoma City, OK 73105
405-521-3351
Fax: 405-522-2066
TDD: 405-521-4875
mark_sharp@mail.sde.state.ok.us
www.ok.gov

Individuals with Disabilities Education Act requires all states and territories to provide early intervention and preschool special education for children with disabilities and special health care needs. Services include central directory, representatives of agencies, service providers, families, and coordinators of infant, toddler, and preschool special education programs.

Joel Robison, Chief of Staff
Mark Sharp, Associate Director
Janet Barresi, State Superintendent of Public Inst

Oregon

7357 Early Childhood CARES Program
1895 E 15th Avenue
Eugene, OR 97403
541-346-2639
Fax: 541-343-5650

Individuals with Disabilities Education Act requires all states and territories to provide early intervention and preschool special education for children with disabilities and special health care needs. Services include central directory, representatives of agencies, service providers, families, and coordinators of infant, toddler, and preschool special education programs.

Judy Newman, Interagency Coordinating Council

7358 Early Intervention Programs
255 Capitol Street NE
Salem, OR 97301
503-378-3598
Fax: 503-373-7968
TDD: 503-378-2892
www.unc.edu

Individuals with Disabilities Education Act requires all states and territories to provide early intervention and preschool special education for children with disabilities and special health care needs. Services include central directory, representatives of agencies, service providers, families, and coordinators of infant, toddler, and preschool special education programs.

Steven B. Johnson, Associate Superintendent

7359 Oregon Department of Education
255 Capitol Street NE
Salem, OR 97301
503-947-5747
Fax: 503-378-5156
www.ode.state.or.us

Provides early intervention and preschool special education for children with disabilities. Services include central directory, representatives of agencies, service providers, families, and coordinators of infant, toddler, and preschool special education programs.

Nancy Johnson-Dorn, Early Childhood Director
Susan Castillo, State Superintendent of Public Inst

7360 Oregon Parent Training and Information Center
2295 Liberty Street NE
Salem, OR 97303
503-581-8156
888-505-2673
Fax: 503-391-0429
orpti@orpti.org
www.orpti.org

Informational and emotional support to parents who have a child, adolescent, or adult family member with special needs.

7361 Technology Access for Life Needs Project
1257 Ferry Street, Se
Salem, OR 97310
503-361-1201
Fax: 503-370-4530
TDD: 503-361-1201

State assisted programs and support group information for people of many abilities. Includes local chapters, referrals, fun and social interaction and support groups.

Pennsylvania

7362 Bureau of Special Education
333 Market Street, 7th Floor
Harrisburg, PA 17126
717-783-6788
800-874-2301
Fax: 717-783-6139
TTY: 717-783-8445
TDD: 717-787-7367
ebeck@state.pa.us
www.portal.state.pa.us

Services include central directory, representatives of agencies, service providers, families, and coordinators of infant, toddler, and preschool special education programs.

Esther Beck, Educational Supervisor
Rick Price, Division Chief
Patti Skunta, Preschool Spcl.Education Supervisor

7363 Division of Early Intervention Services
PO Box 2675
Harrisburg, PA 17105
717-783-7213
Fax: 717-772-0012
www.unc.edu

Individuals with Disabilities Education Act requires all states and territories to provide early intervention and preschool special education for children with disabilities and special health care needs. Services include central directory, representatives of agencies, service providers, families, and coordinators of infant, toddler, and preschool special education programs.

Jacqueline Epstein, Infant/Toddler Program Coordinator

871

General Resources / State Agencies & Support Groups

7364 Montgomery County Intermediate Unit #23
1605 B W Main Street
Norristown, PA 19403
610-539-8550
Fax: 610-539-5973
www.mciu.org

Services include a central directory, representatives of agencies, service providers, families, and coordinators of infant, toddler, and preschool special education programs.

Burunda Prince-Jones, President
Louis A. Polaneczky, Vice President
Nancy Landes, Secretary

7365 Parent Education Network
2107 Industrial Highway
York, PA 17402
717-600-0100
800-441-5028
Fax: 717-600-8101
TTY: 717-600-0100
TDD: 717-600-0100
www.parentednet.org

Parent Training and Information (PTI) programs help parents to understand their children's specific needs, communicate more effectively with professionals, participate in the educational planning process, and obtain information about relevant programs, services and resources.

Kay Lipsitz, PEN Director
Jane Erdo, Parent Support Coordinator
Jackie Hines, Technology & Parent Support Coordin

7366 Parent to Parent ARC Allegheny
711 Bingham Street
Pittsburgh, PA 15203
412-995-5001
www.arcallegheny.org

Informational and emotional support to parents who have a child, adolescent, or adult family member with special needs.

7367 Parent to Parent of Pennsylvania
150 S Progress Avenue
Harrisburg, PA 17109
717-540-4722
Fax: 717-540-7603
bril1134@cdc.gov
www.parenttoparent.org

Informational and emotional support to parents who have a child, adolescent, or adult family member with special needs.

Fiona Patrick, Program Director
Janice Forosisky, Statewide Supervisor
Kim Huff, Database Coordinator

7368 Parents Union for Public Schools
1315 Walnut Street, Suite 1124
Philadelphia, PA 19107
215-546-1166
Fax: 215-731-1688
Parents@aol.com
www.nyfac.org

Parent Training and Information (PTI) programs help parents to understand their children's specific needs, communicate more effectively with professionals, participate in the educational planning process, and obtain information about relevant programs, services and resources.

7369 Pennsylvania's Initiative on Assistive Technology, Institute on Disabilities
University Affiliated Program
423 Ritter Annex, Temple University
Philadelphia, PA 19122
215-204-5966
800-204-7428
Fax: 215-204-9371
TTY: 800-750-7428
www.temple.edu/inst_disabilities

Most of PAIT's activities are free to Pennsylvania residents, and are focused on the provision of public awareness of the benefit and scope of assistive technology (AT), information and referral, advocacy and funding, and training. PAIT is the state's contractor for the implementation of Pennsylvania's Assistive Technology Lending library.

7370 US Wheelchair Weightlifting Association
39 Michael Place
Levittown, PA 19057
215-945-1964

State assisted programs and support group information for people of many abilities. Includes local chapters, referrals, fun and social interaction and support groups.

Rhode Island

7371 Assistive Technology Access Partnership
40 Fountain Street
Providence, RI 02903
401-421-7005
Fax: 401-222-3574
TTY: 401-421-7016
www.atap.state.ri.us

State assisted programs and support group information for people of many abilities. Includes local chapters, referrals, fun and social interaction and support groups.

7372 Central Region Early Intervention Program
J Arthur Trudeau Memorial Center
250 Commonwealth Avenue
Warwick, RI 02886
401-823-1731
Fax: 401-823-1849

Informational and emotional support to parents who have a child, adolescent, or adult family member with special needs.

7373 Office Integrated Social Services
255 Westminister Road
Providence, RI 02903
401-222-4600
Fax: 401-222-6030
ride0032@ride.ri.net
www.unc.edu

Individuals with Disabilities Education Act requires all states and territories to provide early intervention and preschool special education for children with disabilities and special health care needs. Services include central directory, representatives of agencies, service providers, families, and coordinators of infant, toddler, and preschool special education programs.

Robert M. Pryhoda, Director

7374 Rhode Island Arc
99 Bald Hill Road
Cranston, RI 02920
401-463-9191
Fax: 401-463-9244
www.nectas.unc.edu

Individuals with Disabilities Education Act requires all states and territories to provide early intervention and preschool special education for children with disabilities and special health care needs. Services include central directory, representatives of agencies, service providers, families, and coordinators of infant, toddler, and preschool special education programs.

James Healey, Interagency Coordinating Council

7375 Rhode Island Department of Health
600 New London Avenue
Cranston, RI 02920
401-462-0318
Fax: 401-462-6253
www.nectas.unc.edu

Individuals with Disabilities Education Act requires all states and territories to provide early intervention and preschool special education for children with disabilities and special health care needs. Services include central directory, representatives of agencies, service providers, families, and coordinators of infant, toddler, and preschool special education programs.

Ron Caldarone, Infant/Toddler Program Coordinator

7376 Rhode Island Parent Information Network
1210 Pontiac Avenue
Cranston, RI 02920
401-270-0101
800-464-3399
Fax: 401-270-7049
info@ripin.org
www.ripin.org

Nonprofit organization providing information, training, support and advocacy to parents.

Kathleen DiChiara, Chair
Rebecca Kislak, Esq, Vice Chair
Louis J. Simon, CPA, MST, Treasurer

General Resources / State Agencies & Support Groups

South Carolina

7377 Assistive Technology Project
Center for Developmental Disabilities
USC School of Medicine
Columbia, SC 29208
Fax: 803-935-5342
TDD: 803-935-5263
www.scsn.net/users/scatp

State assisted programs and support group information for people of many abilities. Includes local chapters, referrals, fun and social interaction and support groups.

7378 BabyNet
1751 Calhoun Street
Columbia, SC 29201
803-898-0784
Fax: 803-898-0613
strickll@dhec.sc.gov
www.scdhec.net/babynet

Individuals with Disabilities Education Act requires all states and territories to provide early intervention and preschool special education for children with disabilities and special health care needs. Services include central directory, representatives of agencies, service providers, families, and coordinators of infant, toddler, and preschool special education programs.

Kathy Hart, Infant/Toddler Program Coordinator

7379 Office of Exceptional Children South Carolina Department of Education
1429 Senate Street, Room 808
Columbia, SC 29201
803-734-8811
Fax: 803-734-4824
www.myschools.com/offices/ec

Individuals with Disabilities Education Act requires all states and territories to provide early intervention and preschool special education for children with disabilities and special health care needs. Services include central directory, representatives of agencies, service providers, families, and coordinators of infant, toddler, and preschool special education programs.

Norma Donaldson-Jenkins, Preschool Special Ed. Coordinator
Susan Duranti, Director

7380 PRO-Parents
652 Bush River Road
Columbia, SC 29210
803-772-5688
800-759-4776
Fax: 803-772-5341
proparents@proparents.org
www.proparents.org

Parent Training and Information (PTI) programs help parents to understand their children's specific needs, communicate more effectively with professionals, participate in the educational planning process, and obtain information about relevant programs, services and resources.

3500 Members

Dana C. Reed, President
Melina Lee, Vice President
Erik Norton, Treasurer

South Dakota

7381 DakotaLink
P.O. Box 218
Sturgis, SD 57785
605-347-4476
605-394-1876
Fax: 605-394-5315
TTY: 800-645-0673
www.dakotalink.tie.net

State assisted programs and support group information for people of many abilities. Includes local chapters, referrals, fun and social interaction and support groups.

7382 Office of Special Education
700 Governors Drive
Pierre, SD 57501
605-773-3678
Fax: 605-773-6846
TTY: 605-773-6302
www.sd.gov

Individuals with Disabilities Education Act requires all states and territories to provide early intervention and preschool special education for children with disabilities and special health care needs. Services include central directory, representatives of agencies, service providers, families, and coordinators of infant, toddler, and preschool special education programs.

Barb Hemmelman, Education Program Assistant Manager

7383 South Dakota Parent Connection
3701 W 49th, Suite 102
Souix Falls, SD 57106
605-361-3171
Fax: 605-361-2928
www.sdparent.org

Parent Training and Information (PTI) programs help parents to understand their children's specific needs, communicate more effectively with professionals, participate in the educational planning process, and obtain information about relevant programs, services and resources.

Elaine Roberts, Executive Director
Mary Pat Jones, Finance Director
Nykki Sutton, Office Coordinator

7384 University Affiliated Program, School of Medicine
414 E Clark Street
Vermillion, SD 57069
605-677-5311
Fax: 605-677-6274
www.nectas.unc.edu

Individuals with Disabilities Education Act requires all states and territories to provide early intervention and preschool special education for children with disabilities and special health care needs. Services include central directory, representatives of agencies, service providers, families, and coordinators of infant, toddler, and preschool special education programs.

Joanne Wounded Head, Interagency Coordinating Council

Tennessee

7385 Center for Early Childhood
E Tennessee State University, Box 70434
Johnson City, TN 37614
423-439-7555
Fax: 423-439-7561
doylel@etsu.edu
child.etsu.edu

Individuals with Disabilities Education Act requires all states and territories to provide early intervention and preschool special education for children with disabilities and special health care needs. Services include central directory, representatives of agencies, service providers, families, and coordinators of infant, toddler, and preschool special education programs.

Wesley Brown, Interagency Coordinating Council

7386 Office of Special Education, State Department of Education
710 James Robertson Parkway
Nashville, TN 37243
615-741-2851
Fax: 615-532-9412
dmattraw@mail.state.tn.us
www.state.tn.us

Individuals with Disabilities Education Act requires all states and territories to provide early intervention and preschool special education for children with disabilities and special health care needs. Services include central directory, representatives of agencies, service providers, families, and coordinators of infant, toddler, and preschool special education programs.

Joseph Fisher, Executive Director

General Resources / State Agencies & Support Groups

7387 STEP (Support & Training for Exceptional Parents)
712 Professional Plaza
Greenvilles, TN 37745
800-975-2919
800-280-7837
Fax: 423-636-8217
TTY: 423-639-8802
TDD: 423-639-8802
information@tnstep.org
www.tnstep.org

STEP is the Parent Training and Information Center (PTI) for TN. The purpose of STEP is to support families by providing free information, advocacy training, and support services to parents of children in special education or that might need special education. STEP serves parents of children eligible to receive special education services under the Individuals with Disabilities Education Act (IDEA) who reside in Tennessee (birth through age 22).

Sally Ottinger, Information Coordinator
Karen Harrison, Executive Director
Donna Jennings, Business and Personnel Manager

Texas

7388 Department of Assistive and Rehabilitation Services
4900 N Lamar Boulevard
Austin, TX 78751
512-424-6754
800-250-2246
Fax: 512-424-6749
www.eci.state.tx.us

Individuals with Disabilities Education Act part C requires all states and territories to provide early intervention to infants and toddlers with disabilities. Services include a full array of infant intervention fields and disciplines.

MaryBeth O'Hanlon, Assistant Commissioner

7389 Office of Special Education and Rehabilitation Services
400 Maryland Avenue SW
Washington, DC 20202
202-245-7468
www.ed.gov

Information and advocacy resources for families and professionals. Includes listings of organizations providing general information and organizations focusing on more specific areas of concern to families and young adults who have disabilities.

David Cantrell, Assistant Secretary
Paul Steenen, Director, Communications

7390 Office of the Dean, University of Texas at Austin
College of Education, EBB 210
Austin, TX 78712
512-471-7255
Fax: 512-471-0846
www.nectas.unc.edu

Individuals with Disabilities Education Act requires all states and territories to provide early intervention and preschool special education for children with disabilities and special health care needs. Services include central directory, representatives of agencies, service providers, families, and coordinators of infant, toddler, and preschool special education programs.

Alba Ortiz, Interagency Coordinating Council

7391 Parent Case Management
4601 Hartford
Abilene, TX 79605
915-691-7232
Fax: 915-793-3549

Support network for parents of children with disabilities and/or chronic illness. Veteran parents offer support to parents who are just learning of their child's diagnosis. Offers support and insight into parenting a child with special needs, as well as referrals to trained veteran parents.

7392 Partners Resource Network
1090 Longfellow Drive, Suite B
Beaumont, TX 77706
409-898-4684
800-866-4726
Fax: 409-898-4869
TTY: 409-898-4816
partnersresource@sbcglobal.net
www.partnerstx.org

Support network for parents of children with disabilities and/or chronic illness. Veteran parents offer support to parents who are just learning of their child's diagnosis. Offers support and insight into parenting a child with special needs, as well as referrals to trained veteran parents.

Janice Meyer, M. Ed., Executive Director
Alva Adkins, Business Manager
Shene St. Simone, Administrative Assistant

7393 Project PODER
1017 N Main Avenue, Suite 207
San Antonio, TX 78212
210-222-2637
Fax: 210-475-9283
TDD: 800-682-9747
www.tfepoder.org/poder

Parent Training and Information (PTI) programs help parents to understand their children's specific needs, communicate more effectively with professionals, participate in the educational planning process, and obtain information about relevant programs, services and resources.

7394 South Central Region-Helen Keller National Center
4230 Lyndon B Johnson
Dallas, TX 75244
972-490-9677
Fax: 972-490-6042
ccfutbol@aol.com

7395 Texas Assistive Technology Partnership
Texas University Affiliated Program
10100 Burnet Road
Austin, TX 78758
512-232-0740
800-828-7839
Fax: 512-232-0761
TTY: 512-232-0762
www.tcds.edb.utexas.edu

State assisted programs and support group information for people of many abilities. Includes local chapters, referrals, fun and social interaction and support groups.

Penny Seay, Ph.D., Executive Director
Laura Buckner, M.Ed., L.P.C., Community Education Specialist, TCD
Karen Fonken, Office Manager, TCDS

Utah

7396 Baby Watch Early Intervention Program
288 North 1460 West
Salt Lake City, UT 84116
801-538-6003
Fax: 801-584-8496
www.utahbabywatch.org

Individuals with Disabilities Education Act requires all states and territories to provide early intervention and preschool special education for children with disabilities and special health care needs. Services include central directory, representatives of agencies, service providers, families, and coordinators of infant, toddler, and preschool special education programs.

W. David Patton, Ph.D., Executive Director
Michael Hales, Director, Medicaid and Health Finan
Barry Nangle, Ph.D, Director, Center for Health Data

7397 Computer Center for Citizens with Disabilities
UT Center for Assistive Technology
1595 W 500 Street
Salt Lake City, UT 84104
801-887-9533
888-866-5550
Fax: 801-887-9382
cboogaar@usoe.k12.ut.us
www.usor.utah.gov/ucat/computers

Technology group of parents, consumers and professionals; provides resources to help children and adults who have disabilities gain access to the benefits of technology. Includes nationwide network of community-based assistive technology, resource centers, hands on consultants and product demonstrations.

General Resources / State Agencies & Support Groups

7398 Special Education Services Unit
250 E 500 S
Salt Lake City, UT 84111
801-538-7706
Fax: 801-538-7991
TTY: 801-538-7876
mtaylor@usoe.k12.ut.us
www.unc.edu

Individuals with Disabilities Education Act requires all states and territories to provide early intervention and preschool special education for children with disabilities and special health care needs. Services include central directory, representatives of agencies, service providers, families, and coordinators of infant, toddler, and preschool special education programs.

Mae Taylor, Director

7399 US Disabled Ski Team
Box 100
Park City, UT 84060
435-649-9090
Fax: 435-649-3613
info@usaa.org

State assisted programs and support group information for people of many abilities. Includes local chapters, referrals, fun and social interaction and support groups.

7400 Utah Center for Assistive Technology
Center for Persons with Disabilities
Judy Ann Buffmire Building, 1595 West 500 South
Salt Lake City, UT 84104
801-887-9380
Fax: 801-887-9382
TDD: 801-797-2096
www.ucat.usor.utah.gov

State assisted programs and support group information for people of many abilities. Includes local chapters, referrals, fun and social interaction and support groups.

Kent Remund, Director
Lynn Marcoux, Executive Secretary
Michael Offutt, Assistive Technology Specialist

7401 Utah Parent Center
230 West 200 South, Suite 1101
Salt Lake City, UT 84101
801-272-1051
800-468-1160
Fax: 801-272-8907
utahparentcenter.org

Parent Training and Information (PTI) programs help parents to understand their children's specific needs, communicate more effectively with professionals, participate in the educational planning process, and obtain information about relevant programs, services and resources. Offers free written materials, workshops, individual consultations, newsletter, statewide volunteer network, parent to parent support.

Jaey Hanna, Executive Director
Gina Pola-Money, Associate Director
Sherrie Wignall, Fiscal Manager

Vermont

7402 Assistive Technology Project
103 S Main Street, Weeks Building, 1st Floor
Waterbury, VT 05671
Fax: 802-241-2174
TTY: 802-241-2620
TDD: 801-797-2096
www.uvm.edu/uapvt/cats.html

State assisted programs and support group information for people of many abilities. Includes local chapters, referrals, fun and social interaction and support groups.

7403 Center on Disabilities and Community Inclusion
101 Cherry Street, Suite 450
Burlington, VT 05401
802-656-4031
Fax: 802-656-1357
TDD: 802-656-4031
ccloning@zoo.uvm.edu
www.uvm.edu/~cdci

In collaboration with individuals with disabilities, their families and communities, will promote the independence, inclusion, participation and personal choice of individuals with disabilities of all ages in all environments through the development and enhancement of culturally sensitive, responsive services and supports, interdisiplinary training, technical assistance, exemplary service models, research, dissemination of information and advocacy for the legal and civil rights of the disabled.

Rachel Cronin, Human Resources, CDCI Core Project
Michael Coleman, CDCI Alliliated Faculty Researcher:
Michaella Collins, Dissemination Coordinato

7404 Family, Infant, and Toddler Project
208 Colchester Avenue
Burlington, VT 05405
802-656-8112
Fax: 802-656-1357
www.nectas.unc.edu

Individuals with Disabilities Education Act requires all states and territories to provide early intervention and preschool special education for children with disabilities and special health care needs. Services include central directory, representatives of agencies, service providers, families, and coordinators of infant, toddler, and preschool special education programs.

Beverly MacCarty, Infant/Toddler Program Coordinator

7405 Special Education Unit
120 State Street
Montpelier, VT 05620
802-828-2755
Fax: 802-828-3140
www.vermont.gov

Individuals with Disabilities Education Act requires all states and territories to provide early intervention and preschool special education for children with disabilities and special health care needs. Services include central directory, representatives of agencies, service providers, families, and coordinators of infant, toddler, and preschool special education programs.

Dennis Kane, Director

7406 Vermont Parent Information Center
1 Mill Street, Suite 310
Burlington, VT 05401
802-658-5315
800-639-7170
Fax: 802-658-5395
TDD: 802-658-5315
www.allthebuzzmarketing.com/Vermont

Dedicated to increasing and expanding educational and developmental opportunities that improve the quality of life for children with special needs and their families. We believe that we can achieve this goal only when we provide families with the chance to build on their own strengths, and to feel respected for their values and beliefs.

Connie Curtain, Executive Director

Virginia

7407 Infant & Toddler Program
PO Box 1797
Richmond, VA 23218
804-371-6592
Fax: 804-371-7959
www.nectas.unc.edu

Provides early intervention and preschool special education for children with disabilities and special health care needs. Services include central directory, representatives of agencies, service providers, families, and coordinators of infant, toddler, and preschool special education programs.

Anne Lucas, Infant/Toddler Program Coordinator

7408 Office of Special Education, Virginia
101 N 14th Street
Richmond, VA 23219
804-225-2675
Fax: 804-371-8796
www.doe.virginia.gov

Individuals with Disabilities Education Act requires all states and territories to provide early intervention and preschool special education for children with disabilities and special health care needs. Services include central directory, representatives of agencies and coordinators preschool special education programs.

General Resources / State Agencies & Support Groups

Thomas Broyles, Director, Business & Risk Managemen
Marie G. Williams, Director, Office of Accounting
June F. Eanes, Director, Office of Support Service

7409 Parent Educational Advocacy Training Cente r
100 N Washington Street, Suite 234
Falls Church, VA 22046
703-923-0010
800-869-6782
Fax: 800-693-3514
TTY: 703-923-0010
TDD: 703-923-0010
partners@peatc.org
www.peatc.org

Parent Training and Information (PTI) programs help parents to understand their children's specific needs, communicate more effectively with professionals, participate in the educational planning process, and obtain information about relevant programs, services and resources.

Cathy Healy, Chief Executive Officer
Francisco R. Ramirez, President
Suzanne Bowers, Executive Director

7410 Virginia Assistive Technology System
8004 Franklin Farms Drive
8004 Franklin Farms Drive
Richmond, VA 23229
804-662-9990
800-552-5019
Fax: 804-662-9478
TTY: 757-662-9990
vatskhk@aol.com
www.vats.org

State assisted programs and support group information for people of many abilities. Includes local chapters, referrals, fun and social interaction and support groups.

Barclay Shepard, Manager, VATS
Robert W. Krollman, AT Specialist-Aging Coordinator
Elin Glass, Administrative Office Specialist, V

Washington

7411 Infant Toddler Early Intervention Program
640 Woodland Square Loop, SE
Olympia, WA 98504
360-725-3516
Fax: 360-725-3523
www.nectas.unc.edu

Early intervention and preschool special education for children with disabilities and special health care needs. Services include central directory, representatives of agencies, service providers, families, and coordinators of infant, toddler, and preschool special education programs.

Sandy Loerch, Infant/Toddler Program Coordinator

7412 Leukemia & Lymphoma Society - Washington/ Alaska Chapter
Leukemia & Lymphoma Society
5601 6th Avenue, Ste 182
Seattle, WA 98108
206-628-0777
anne.gillingham@lls.org
www.lls.org/washingtonalaska

Dedicated to finding cures for leukemia and related cancers and to improving the quality of life for patients and their families.

Anne Gillingham, Executive Director
Courtney Hale, Operations Director
Victoria Wenick, Senior Campaign Director

7413 Office of the Superintendent of Public Instruction
PO Box 47200
Olympia, WA 98504
360-753-6733
Fax: 360-586-0247
TTY: 360-586-0126
www.unc.edu

Services include central directory, representatives of agencies, service providers, families, and coordinators of infant, toddler, and preschool special education programs.

Anne Shureen, Preschool Special Ed. Coordinator

7414 Washington PAVE
6316 S 12th Street
Tacoma, WA 98465
253-565-2266
800-572-7368
Fax: 253-566-8052
TTY: 800-572-7368
pave@wapave.org
www.washingtonpave.org

Parent Training and Information (PTI) programs help parents to understand their children's specific needs, communicate more effectively with professionals, participate in the educational planning process, and obtain information about relevant programs, services and resources.

Joanna S Butts, Executive Director

West Virginia

7415 Early Intervention Program
350 Capitol Street, Room 427
Charleston, WV 25301
304-558-6311
Fax: 304-558-4984
www.unc.edu

Individuals with Disabilities Education Act requires all states and territories to provide early intervention and preschool special education for children with disabilities and special health care needs. Services include central directory, representatives of agencies, service providers, families, and coordinators of infant, toddler, and preschool special education programs.

Pam Roush, Part C Coordinator

7416 Office of Special Education Administration
1900 Kawanha Boulevard E
Charleston, WV 25305
304-558-2696
800-642-8541
Fax: 304-558-3741
www.unc.edu

Individuals with Disabilities Education Act requires all states and territories to provide early intervention and preschool special education for children with disabilities and special health care needs. Services include central directory, representatives of agencies, service providers, families, and coordinators of infant, toddler, and preschool special education programs.

Liza Cordeiro, Executive Director, Office of Commu
Dee Bodkins, Director
Allison Barker, Coordinator

7417 West Virginia Assistive Technology System
Airport Research and Office Park
959 Hartman Run Road
Morgantown, WV 26505
304-293-4692
888-829-9426
Fax: 304-293-7294
TTY: 800-518-1448
TDD: 304-293-4692
www.wvats.cedwvu.org

State assisted programs and support group information for people of many abilities. Includes local chapters, referrals, fun and social interaction and support groups.

Martha Ankney, Accountant
Donna J. Brewer, Database Manager
Lashanna Brunson, Research Coordinator

7418 West Virginia Parent Training and Information
1701 Hamill Ave.
Clarksburg, WV 26301
304-624-1436
800-281-1436
Fax: 304-624-1438
WVPTI@aol.com
www.wvpti.org

Parent Training and Information (PTI) programs help parents to understand their children's specific needs, communicate more effectively with professionals, participate in the educational planning process, and obtain information about relevant programs, services and resources.

General Resources / Libraries & Resource Centers

Wisconsin

7419 Birth to 3 Program
1 West Wilson St, Room 418, PO Box 7851
Madisonton, WI 53370
608-267-3270
Fax: 608-261-6752
www.nectas.unc.edu

Early intervention and preschool special education for children with disabilities and special health care needs. Services include central directory, representatives of agencies, service providers, families, and coordinators of infant, toddler, and preschool special education programs.

Mitchell Kremer, Infant/Toddler Program Coordinator

7420 Development and Training Center
2125 3rd Street
Eau Circle, WI 54703
715-833-7755
Fax: 715-833-7757
www.nectas.unc.edu

Individuals with Disabilities Education Act requires all states and territories to provide early intervention and preschool special education for children with disabilities and special health care needs. Services include central directory, representatives of agencies, service providers, families, and coordinators of infant, toddler, and preschool special education programs.

Stacy H Wigfield, Interagency Coordinating Council

7421 Division of Community Services
1 Wilson Street, Room 418, PO Box 7851
Madison, WI 53707
608-267-3270
Fax: 608-267-6752
dhfs.wisconsin.gov/bdds/birthto3

Individuals with Disabilities Education Act requires all states and territories to provide early intervention and preschool special education for children with disabilities and special health care needs. Services include central directory, representatives of agencies, service providers, families, and coordinators of infant, toddler, and preschool special education programs.

Beth Wroblewski, Preschool Special Ed. Coordinator

7422 Early Childhood Handicapped Prgrams
125 S. Webster St., PO Box 7841
Madison, WI 53707
608-266-1649
800-441-4563
Fax: 608-267-3746
www.dpi.state.wi.us

Services include central directory, representatives of agencies, service providers, families, and coordinators of infant, toddler, and preschool special education programs.

Juanita S. Pawlisch, Ph. D.,, Assistant State Superintendent

7423 Parent Education Project of Wisconsin
2192 S 60th Street
West Allis, WI 53219
414-328-5520
Fax: 414-328-5530
TDD: 414-328-5520
pmcolletti@aol.com
www.members.aol.com/pepofwi

Parent Training and Information (PTI) programs help parents to understand their children's specific needs, communicate more effectively with professionals, participate in the educational planning process, and obtain information about relevant programs, services and resources.

7424 WisTech
1 W. Wilson Street, Room 527
Madison, WI 53703
608-266-7974
Fax: 608-266-3386
TTY: 608-267-9880
sarah.lincoln@DHS.wisconsin.gov
www.dhs.wisconsin.gov/disabilities/wistech/

State assisted programs and support group information for people of many abilities. Includes local chapters, referrals, fun and social interaction and support groups.

Sarah Lincoln, Contact

Wyoming

7425 Division of Developmental Disabilities
6101 Yellowstone Road
Cheyenne, WY 82002
307-777-7115
Fax: 307-777-3337
www.nectas.unc.edu

Provides early intervention and preschool special education for children with disabilities and special health care needs. Services include central directory, representatives of agencies, service providers, families, and coordinators of infant, toddler, and preschool special education programs.

Mitch Brauchie, Interagency Coordinating Council

7426 Parent Information Center
500 W. Lott St Suite A
Buffalo, WY 82834
307-684-2277
Fax: 307-684-5314
TDD: 307-684-2277
tdawson@wpic.org
www.wpic.org

Parent Training and Information (PTI) programs help parents to understand their children's specific needs, communicate more effectively with professionals, participate in the educational planning process, and obtain information about relevant programs, services and resources.

Terri Dawson, Executive Director
Betty Carmon, Outreach Parent Liaison
Janet Kinstetter, Outreach Parent Liaison

7427 Special Education Unit
2300 Cheyenne Avenue, 2nd Floor
Cheyenne, WY 82002
307-777-7414
Fax: 307-777-6234
www.edu.wyoming.gov

Individuals with Disabilities Education Act requires all states and territories to provide early intervention and preschool special education for children with disabilities and special health care needs. Services include central directory, representatives of agencies, service providers, families, and coordinators of infant, toddler, and preschool special education programs.

Ron Micheli, Chairman

7428 Wyoming's New Options in Technology (WYNOT)
University of Wyoming
1000 East University Avenue
Laramie, WY 82072
307-766-2084
Fax: 307-721-2084
TTY: 800-861-4312
wynot.uw@uwyo.edu
www.uwyo.edu/wynot

State assisted programs and support group information for people of many abilities. Includes local chapters, referrals, fun and social interaction and support groups.

Libraries & Resource Centers

Arizona

7429 Special Needs Center/Phoenix Public Library
12 E McDowell Road
Phoenix, AZ 85004
602-261-8690
www.ci.phoinx.az.us

Offers talking books and records, braille books and magazines, large print books, video print enlarger, video magnifier and VersaBraille software with synthetic speech for the blind, visually handicapped, physically/mentally handicapped and speech and hearing impaired children and adults.

Mary Roatch, Supervisor

General Resources / Libraries & Resource Centers

7430 Technology Access Center of Tucson
PO Box 13178
Tucson, AZ 85732
520-638-2733
Fax: 520-519-7954
tact1@qwestoffice.net
www.uacoe.arizona.edu/tact/

Technology group of parents, consumers and professionals; provides resources to help children and adults who have disabilities gain access to the benefits of technology. Includes nationwide network of community-based assistive technology, resource centers, hands on consultants and product demonstrations.

Arkansas

7431 Arkansas Easter Seals Technology Resource Center
3920 Woodland Heights Road
Little Rock, AR 72212
501-227-3602
Fax: 501-227-3601
atrce@aol.com
www.arkeasterseals.org

Technology group of parents, consumers and professionals; provides resources to help children and adults who have disabilities gain access to the benefits of technology. Includes nationwide network of community-based assistive technology, resource centers, hands on consultants and product demonstrations.

7432 Crowley Ridge Regional Library
315 W Oak
Jonesboro, AR 72401
870-935-5133
reference@libraryinjonesboro.org
www.libraryinjonesboro.org

Offers a children's summer reading program, large print and books on cassette.

James Dunivan, Chairman
Mary Norris, Vice-Chairman

7433 Educational Services for the Visually Impaired
2402 Wildwood Avenue, Suite 112
Sherwood, AR 72120
501-835-5448
Fax: 501-835-6840
www.esvi.org

Offers textbooks, braille books and more to the visually impaired grades K-12 in the Arizona area.

Angyln Young, State Coordinator
Cindy Lester, Data Management Specialist/Preschoo
Cynthia Kelly, ESVI Office Manager

7434 Library for the Blind and Handicapped, Southwest
PO Box 668
Magnolia, AR 71754
870-234-0399
Fax: 870-234-5077
lbph@hotmail.com

Offers a children's summer reading program and a book collection featuring discs and casettes.

Susan Walker, Librarian

California

7435 Assistive Technology Center Simi Valley Hospital
Rehabilatation Unit North
PO Box 1325
Simi Valley, CA 93062
805-582-1881
Fax: 805-582-2855
dssacca@aol.com

Technology group of parents, consumers and professionals; provides resources to help children and adults who have disabilities gain access to the benefits of technology. Includes nationwide network of community-based assistive technology, resource centers, hands on consultants and product demonstrations.

7436 Center for Accessible Technology
3075 Adeline Street, Suite 220
Berkeley, CA 94703
510-841-3224
Fax: 510-841-3224
TDD: 510-841-5621
info@cforat.org
www.cforat.org

Provides resources to help children and adults who have disabilities gain access to the benefits of technology. Clients are seen by appointment only.

Guy Thomas, Board President
Sara Armstrong Ph.D., Board Treasure
Carol Cody, Executive Director

7437 Clearinghouse for Specialized Media and Technology (CSMT)
California Department of Education
1430 N Street, Suite 3207
Sacramento, CA 95814
916-445-5103
Fax: 916-323-9732
rbrawley@cde.ca.gov
http://csmt.cde.ca.gov

Assists California schools and students in the identification and acquisition of textbooks, reference books and study materials in aural media, braille, large print and electronic media access technology.

Rod Brawley, Manager

7438 Sacramento Center for Assistive Technology
701 Howe Avenue, Suite E-5
Sacramento, CA 95825
916-927-7228
www.quicknet.com/~scat

Technology group of parents, consumers and professionals; provides resources to help children and adults who have disabilities gain access to the benefits of technology. Includes nationwide network of community-based assistive technology, resource centers, hands on consultants and product demonstrations.

District of Columbia

7439 Georgetown University Child Development Center
3300 Whitehaven Street, NW, Suite 3300
Washington, DC 20007
202-687-5000
Fax: 202-687-8899
gucdc@georgetown.edu
www.gucchd.georgetown.edu

7440 HEATH Resource Center
George Washington University
2134 G Street NW
Washington, DC 20052
www.heath.gwu.edu

The HEATH Resource Center is a web-based clearinghouse that serves as an information exchange of educational resources, support services and opportunities. The HEATH Resource Center gathers, develops and disseminates information in the form of resource papers, fact sheets, website directories, newsletters, and resource materials.

Christopher Nace, Research Assistant

Florida

7441 Center for Independence Technology and Education, (CITE)
215 E New Hampshire Street
Orlando, FL 32804
407-898-2483
Fax: 407-895-5255
comcite@aol.com

Technology group of parents, consumers and professionals; provides resources to help children and adults who have disabilities gain access to the benefits of technology. Includes nationwide network of community-based assistive technology, resource centers, hands on consultants and product demonstrations.

7442 University of Miami, Mailman Center for Child Development
1601 NW 12th Avenue
Miami, FL 33136
305-243-6631
Fax: 305-284-4911
pediatrics.med.miani.edu/mccd1

General Resources / Libraries & Resource Centers

Focuses on birth defects and children's illnesses.

Dr. Robert Stempfel, Jr, Director

7443 West Florida Regional Library
239 North Spring Street
Pensacola, FL 32502
850-436-5060
Fax: 850-436-5039
TDD: 850-435-1763
tlambert@ci.pensacola.fl.us
www.mywfpl.com/

Offers children's print/braille books.

Tamatha Lambert, Librarian

Georgia

7444 Augusta-Richmond County Public Library
425 9th Street
Augusta, GA 30901
706-821-2625
Fax: 706-724-5403
www.scescape.net/~ecgrl/lbph.htm

Discs, cassettes, braille writer, films, large print books, summer reading program, magnifiers and reference materials on blindness and other handicaps.

Gary Swint, Librarian

7445 Gainesville Subregional LBPH Hall County Public Library
2434 Old Cornelia Highway
Gainesville, GA 30507
770-531-2500
Fax: 770-531-2502
TDD: 770-531-2530
www.hall.public.lib.ga.us/ehmap.htm#program

Summer reading programs, braille writer, magnifiers, closed-circuit TV, large-print photocopier, cassette books and magazines, children's books on cassette, home visits and other reference materials on blindness and other handicaps.

Kathy Evans, Librarian

7446 La Fayette Subregional Library for the Blind and Physically Disabled
305 S Duke Street
La Fayette, GA 30728
706-638-2992
Fax: 706-638-4028
chelseak@chrl.org
www.chrl.org/

Summer reading programs, braille writer, magnifiers, closed-circuit TV, large-print photocopier, cassette books and magazines, children's books on cassette, home visits and other reference materials on blindness and other handicaps.

Chelsea Kovalevskiy, Youth Education Coordinator
Marilyn Southerland, Library Assistant
Carol Smith, Genealogy Librarian

7447 Macon Subregional Library for the Blind and Handicapped, Washington Memorial
1180 Washington Avenue
Macon, GA 31201
912-744-0877
800-805-7613
Fax: 912-742-3161
TDD: 912-744-0877

Summer reading programs, braille writer, magnifiers, closed-circuit TV, large-print photocopier, cassette books and magazines, children's books on cassette, home visits and other reference materials on blindness and other handicaps.

Rebecca Sherrill, Librarian

7448 Oconee Regional Library, Library for the Blind and Physically Handicapped
801 Bellevue Avenue, PO Box 100
Dublin, GA 31040
478-272-5710
Fax: 478-275-5381
TDD: 478-275-3821
heritage@ocrl.org
www.ocrl.org/

Summer reading programs, braille writer, magnifiers, closed-circuit TV, large-print photocopier, cassette books and magazines, children's books on cassette, home visits and other reference materials on blindness and other handicaps.

Betty Schlid, Librarian

7449 Rome Subregional Library for the Blind and Physically Handicapped
205 Riverside Parkway NE
Rome, GA 30161
706-236-4618
Fax: 706-236-4631
TDD: 706-236-4618
www.rome-lpd.org/romsub.htm

Summer reading programs, braille writer, magnifiers, closed-circuit TV, large-print photocopier, cassette books and magazines, children's books on cassette, home visits and other reference materials on blindness and other handicaps.

Diana Mills, Librarian

7450 Special Needs Library of NE Georgia Athens-Clarke County Regional Library
2025 Baxter Street
Athens, GA 30606
706-613-3655
Fax: 706-613-3660
TDD: 706-613-3655
www.clarke.public.lib.ga.us/tbc.htm

Discs, cassettes, large print books, reference materials on blindness, films, closed-circuit TV, magnifiers, braille writer, summer reading programs, cassette books and magazines and more.

Paige Burns, Librarian

7451 Subregional Library for the Blind and Physically Handicapped
1120 Bradley Drive
Columbus, GA 31906
706-649-0780
Fax: 706-649-1914
TDD: 706-649-0974

Braille writer, magnifiers, closed-circuit TV, large-print photocopier, cassette books and magazines, children's books on cassette, home visits and other reference materials on blindness and other handicaps.

Suzanne Barnes, Librarian

7452 Tech-Able
1112A Brett Drive
Conyers, GA 30094
770-922-6768
Fax: 770-922-6769
www.gatfl.org

Technology group of parents, consumers and professionals; provides resources to help children and adults who have disabilities gain access to the benefits of technology. Includes nationwide network of community-based assistive technology, resource centers, hands on consultants and product demonstrations.

Hawaii

7453 Aloha Special Technology Access Center
710 Green Street
Honolulu, HI 96813
808-523-5547
Fax: 808-536-3765
gstachi@yahoo.com
www.geocities.com/astachi/index.html

Technology group of parents, consumers and professionals; provides resources to help children and adults who have disabilities gain access to the benefits of technology. Member of nationwide network of community-based assistive technology, resource centers, hands on consultants and product demonstrations.

7454 Library for the Blind and Physically Handicapped, Hawaii State Library
402 Kapahulu Avenue
Honolulu, HI 96815
808-733-8444
Fax: 808-733-8449
TDD: 808-733-8444
www.hcc.hawaii.edu/hspls/oahu/lbph.html

General Resources / Libraries & Resource Centers

Summer reading programs, braille writer, magnifiers, closed-circuit TV, large-print photocopier, cassette books and magazines, children's books on cassette, home visits and other reference materials on blindness and other handicaps.

Fusako Miyashiro, Librarian

Illinois

7455 Parents Alliance Employment Project
Illinois Employment and Training Center
2525 Cabot Drive, Suite 302
Lisle, IL 60532
630-955-2075
Fax: 630-955-2080
TTY: 630-955-2098
TDD: 630-495-6055
ktribe@parents-alliance.org
www.parents-alliance.org

Information and advocacy resources for families and professionals. Includes listings of organizations providing general information and organizations focusing on more specific areas of concern to families and young adults who have disabilities.

Kristen Tribe, M.A., CRC, Executive Director
Roger Joseph B. Cave, Employment Coordinator
Paul Engman, Employment Specialist II

7456 Professional Assistance Center for Education (PACE)
National-Louis University
2840 Sheridan Road
Evanston, IL 60201
847-475-1100
Fax: 847-256-5190

A two-year, noncredit certification program servicing students with learning disabilities. The program provides a rare opportunity for students from all parts of the country to continue their education in an age appropriate environment. Committed to an instructional approach that integrates both group and individual teaching for career preparation, academics, life skills, and socialization. Transitional program offered to qualified graduates.

Carol Burns, Director

7457 Shawnee Library System
607 S Greenbriar Road
Carterville, IL 62918
618-985-3711
800-445-2665
Fax: 618-985-4211
dbrawley@shawls.lib.il.us
www.shawls.lib.il.us

Lends recorded books and magazines, descriptive videos, and braille to adults and children unable to read standard print due to blindness, visual impairment, physical disablity and reading disability. Information on blindness and disabilities. Public presentations.

Karen Bounds, President
Thomas Turner, Vice-President
Sarah Doerner, Secretary

7458 Suburban Audio Visual Service
920 Barnsdale Road
La Grange Park, IL 60526
630-352-7671

Summer reading programs, braille writer, magnifiers, closed-circuit TV, large-print photocopier, cassette books and magazines, children's books on cassette, home visits and other reference materials on blindness and other handicaps.

Leon Drolet, Jr, Librarian

Indiana

7459 Allen County Public Library
900 Library Plaza
Fort Wayne, IN 46802
260-421-1200
Fax: 260-421-1386
webmaster@acpl.lib.in.us
www.acpl.lib.in.us

Summer reading programs, braille writer, magnifiers, closed-circuit TV, large-print photocopier, cassette books and magazines, children's books on cassette, home visits and other reference materials on blindness and other handicaps.

Gloria Shamanof, President
Martin E. Seifert, Vice-President
John Gerni, Secretary

7460 Assistive Technology Training and Information Center
3354 Pine Hill Drive
Vincennes, IN 47591
812-886-0575
800-962-8842
Fax: 812-886-1128
TTY: 800-962-8842
inattic2@aol.com

Informational and emotional support to parents who have a child, adolescent, or adult family member with special needs.

7461 Bartholomew County Public Library
536 Fifth Street
Columbus, IN 47201
812-379-1255
Fax: 812-379-1275
library@barth.lib.in.us
www.barth.lib.in.us

Summer reading programs, braille writer, magnifiers, closed-circuit TV, large-print photocopier, cassette books and magazines, children's books on cassette, home visits and other reference materials on blindness and other handicaps.

Wilma Perry, Librarian

7462 Elkhart Public Library
300 S 2nd Street
Elkhart, IN 46516
574-522-5669
www.myepl.org

Summer reading programs, braille writer, magnifiers, closed-circuit TV, large-print photocopier, cassette books and magazines, children's books on cassette, home visits and other reference materials on blindness and other handicaps.

Barbara G. Anderson, President
Janice E. Dean, Vice-President
Krystal Anderson, Secretary

7463 Special Services Division - Indiana State Library
140 N Senate Avenue
Indianapolis, IN 46204
317-232-3684
800-622-4970
Fax: 317-232-3728

Summer reading programs, braille writer, magnifiers, closed-circuit TV, braille and large print books and magazines, children's books on cassette and in braille, and other reference materials on blindness and other handicaps.

Lissa Shanahan, Librarian
Carole Rose, Childrens/Braille Services

Kansas

7464 Kansas State Library
State Capitol Building
Topeka, KS 66612
785-296-3296
800-432-3919
Fax: 785-296-6650
TDD: 785-256-0733
www.kslib.info/

Summer reading programs, braille writer, magnifiers, closed-circuit TV, large-print photocopier, cassette books and magazines, children's books on cassette, home visits and other reference materials on blindness and other handicaps.

Jo Budler, State Librarian
Daniel Eells, Production/Network/Technical Assist
Lianne Flax, Online Services and Programming Lib

7465 Manhattan Public Library
629 Poyntz Avenue
Manhattan, KS 66502
785-776-4741
Fax: 785-776-1545
refstaff@manhattan.lib.ks.us
www.manhattan.lib.ks.us/

General Resources / Libraries & Resource Centers

Summer reading programs, braille writer, magnifiers, closed-circuit TV, large-print photocopier, cassette books and magazines, children's books on cassette, home visits and other reference materials on blindness and other handicaps.

Linda Knupp, Director
John Pecoraro, Assistant Director
Teri Belin, Admistrative Assistant

7466 Prenatal Diagnostic and Genetic Center
HCA Wesley Medical Center
550 N Hillside
Wichita, KS 67214
Sechin Cho, MD

316-688-2362

7467 Solution Outreach Center at OCCK, Inc.
2941 Centennial
Salina, KS 67401

785-827-9383
800-526-9731
Fax: 785-452-9374
TTY: 785-827-7051
TDD: 785-827-9383
www.occk.com

Technology group of parents, customers and professionals; provides resources to help children and adults who have disabilities gain access to the benefits of technology. Includes nationwide network of community-based assistive technology, resource centers, hands on consultants and product demonstrations.

Kathy Reed, Director
Sidney Gray, Coordinator

7468 South Central Kansas Library System
321 North Main Street
South Hutchinson, KS 67505

620-336-5441
800-234-0529
Fax: 620-663-9797
sharon@sckls.info
skyways.lib.ks.us/sckls/

Summer reading programs, braille writer, magnifiers, closed-circuit TV, large-print photocopier, cassette books and magazines, children's books on cassette, home visits and other reference materials on blindness and other handicaps.

Paul Hawkins, Director
Katherine Goodenberger, Library Support Specialist
Sharon Barnes, Technology Consultant

7469 Wesley Medical Research Institutes
3306 E Central
Wichita, KS 67208

316-686-7172
Fax: 316-687-0033
tjones@wichitamedicalresearch.org
www.wichitamedicalresearch.org/

Respiratory and birth defects disorders research.

Peggy L Johnson, Executive Director/COO
William Hendry, PhD, President
Thomas R Kluzak, MD, MMM, President Elect

7470 Wichita Public Library
223 S Main Street
Wichita, KS 67202

316-261-8500
Fax: 316-262-4540
admin@wichita.lib.ks.us
www.wichita.lib.ks.us/

Summer reading programs, braille writer, magnifiers, closed-circuit TV, large-print photocopier, cassette books and magazines, children's books on cassette, home visits and other reference materials on blindness and other handicaps.

Brad Reha, Librarian

Kentucky

7471 Bluegrass Technology Center
409 Southland Drive
Lexington, KY 40505

859-294-4343
800-209-7767
Fax: 866-576-9625
office@bluegrass.org
www.bluegrass-tech.org

Technology group of parents, consumers and professionals; provides resources to help children and adults who have disabilities gain access to the benefits of technology. Includes nationwide network of community-based assistive technology, resource centers, hands on consultants and product demonstrations.

Vicki Cooper, President
Bruce W. Turley, Treasurer
Jeanna Richardson, Secretary

7472 EnTech: Enabling Technologies of Kentuckiana
301 York Street
Louisville, KY 40203

502-574-1637

Technology group of parents, consumers and professionals; provides resources to help children and adults who have disabilities gain access to the benefits of technology. Includes nationwide network of community-based assistive technology, resource centers, hands on consultants and product demonstrations.

7473 Louisville Talking Book Library
301 York Street
Louisville, KY 40203

502-574-1611
Fax: 502-574-1657
www.lfpl.org/

Summer reading programs, braille writer, magnifiers, closed-circuit TV, large-print photocopier, cassette books and magazines, children's books on cassette, home visits and other reference materials on blindness and other handicaps.

Tad Thomas, Chair
Deborah Williams, Vice-chair

7474 Northern Kentucky Talking Book Library
502 Scott Boulevard
Covington, KY 41011

859-962-4095
Fax: 859-962-4096
www.kenton.lib.ky.us/information/talking

Summer reading programs, braille writer, magnifiers, closed-circuit TV, large-print photocopier, cassette books and magazines, children's books on cassette, home visits and other reference materials on blindness and other handicaps.

Jama Rooney, Librarian

7475 Western Kentucky Assistive Technology Consortium
607 Poplar Street, Suite 211, PO Box 266
Murray, KY 42071

270-759-4233
Fax: 270-759-4208

Technology group of parents, consumers and professionals; provides resources to help children and adults who have disabilities gain access to the benefits of technology. Includes nationwide network of community-based assistive technology, resource centers, hands on consultants and product demonstrations.

Louisiana

7476 Louisiana State Library
701 N 4th Street
Baton Rouge, LA 70802

225-342-4923
Fax: 225-219-8404
admin@state.lib.la.us
www.state.lib.la.us/

Summer reading programs, braille writer, magnifiers, closed-circuit TV, large-print photocopier, cassette books and magazines, children's books on cassette, home visits and other reference materials on blindness and other handicaps.

General Resources / Libraries & Resource Centers

Rebecca Hamilton, State Librarian
Beverly Dugas, Business Manager
Tabitha Tabitha Pimlott, Executive Assistant

7477 Louisiana State University Genetics Section of Pediatrics
1501 Kings Highway
Shreveport, LA 71130   318-675-5681
TF Thurman, MD, Director

Maine

7478 Bangor Public Library
145 Harlow Street
Bangor, ME 04401   207-947-8336
Fax: 207-945-6694
bplill@bpl.lib.me.us
www.bpl.lib.me.us/

Summer reading programs, braille writer, magnifiers, closed-circuit TV, large-print photocopier, cassette books and magazines, children's books on cassette, home visits and other reference materials on blindness and other handicaps.

Barbara McDade, Director
Matt Brown, Network Administrator
Caroline Hammond, Business Manager

7479 Cary Library
107 Main Street
Houlton, ME 04730   207-532-1302
Fax: 207-532-4350
faucherl@cary.lib.me.us
www.cary.lib.me.us

Summer reading programs, braille writer, magnifiers, closed-circuit TV, large-print photocopier, cassette books and magazines, children's books on cassette, home visits and other reference materials on blindness and other handicaps.

Leigh Cummings Jr., President
Forrest Barnes, Treasurer
Gary Hagan, Secretary

7480 Lewiston Public Library
200 Lisbon Street
Lewiston, ME 04240   207-513-3004
Fax: 207-784-3011
rspeer@LewistonMaine.gov
www.lplonline.org/

Summer reading programs, braille writer, magnifiers, closed-circuit TV, large-print photocopier, cassette books and magazines, children's books on cassette, home visits and other reference materials on blindness and other handicaps.

Rick Speer, Director
Beth Martel, Circulation Supervisor
David Moorhead, Children's Librarian

7481 Maine State Library
64 State House Station
Augusta, ME 04333   207-287-5650
Fax: 207-287-5615
TTY: 888-577-6690
reference.desk@maine.gov
www.state.me.us/

Summer reading programs, braille writer, magnifiers, closed-circuit TV, large-print photocopier, cassette books and magazines, children's books on cassette, home visits and other reference materials on blindness and other handicaps.

Linda H. Lord, State Librarian
Janet McKenney, Director of Library Development
James Ritter, Director of Reader & Information S

7482 New England Regional Genetics Group
PO Box 920288
Needham, MA 02492   781-444-0126
Fax: 781-444-0127
mfgnergg@verizon.net
www.nergg.org

Human genetic services and educational planning pertaining to birth defects.

Mary-Frances Garber, Executive Director
Lisa Demers, MS, CGC, President
Marinell Newton, MSW, President Elect

7483 Portland Public Library
5 Monument Square
Portland, ME 04101   207-871-1700
Fax: 207-871-1703
reference@portland.lib.me.us
www.portlandlibrary.com/

Summer reading programs, braille writer, magnifiers, closed-circuit TV, large-print photocopier, cassette books and magazines, children's books on cassette, home visits and other reference materials on blindness and other handicaps.

Janice Littlefield, Librarian
Steve Podgajny, Executive Director

7484 Waterville Public Library
73 Elm Street
Waterville, ME 04901   207-872-5433
Fax: 207-873-4779
www.watervillelibrary.org/

Summer reading programs, braille writer, magnifiers, closed-circuit TV, large-print photocopier, cassette books and magazines, children's books on cassette, home visits and other reference materials on blindness and other handicaps.

Meta Vigue, Librarian

Maryland

7485 Learning Independence Through Computers
1001 Eastern Avenue, 3rd Floor
Baltimore, MD 21202   410-659-5462
Fax: 410-659-5472
lincmd@aol.com

Technology group of parents, consumers and professionals; provides resources to help children and adults who have disabilities gain access to the benefits of technology. Includes nationwide network of community-based assistive technology, resource centers, hands on consultants and product demonstrations.

Massachusetts

7486 Resources for Rehabilitation
22 Bonad Road
Winchester, MA 01890   781-368-9080
800-621-0026
Fax: 781-368-9096
info@rfr.org
www.rfr.org

Provides training and information to professionals who serve individuals with vision loss and other disabilities. Publishes a variety of resource guides on coping with visual impairment.

7487 Talking Book Library at Worcester Public Library
3 Salem Square
Worcester, MA 01608   508-799-1730
800-762-0085
Fax: 508-799-1656
TDD: 508-799-1731
www.worcpublib.org/talkingbook

Massachusetts subregional library within the Library of Congress National Library Service for the Blind and Physically Handicapped network. Provides audiocassette books, large print books, described videos and print/braille books to registered partons. Has adapted computers and other assistive technology for on-site use. Offers reference and referral service.

James L Izatt, Librarian

7488 Worcester Public Library
3 Salem Square
Worcester, MA 01608   508-799-1655
Fax: 508-799-1652
www.worcpublib.org/

General Resources / Libraries & Resource Centers

Summer reading programs, braille writer, magnifiers, closed-circuit TV, large-print photocopier, cassette books and magazines, children's books on cassette, home visits and other reference materials on blindness and other handicaps.

Susan Gately, President
James Kersten, Vice-President
Jyoti Datta, Secretary

Michigan

7489 Frederick Douglas Branch for Specialized Services and Physically Handicapped
3666 Grand River/Trumbull
Detroit, MI 48226

313-883-9414
Fax: 313-833-9717
TDD: 313-833-5492
www.detroit.lib.mi.us

Summer reading programs, braille writer, magnifiers, closed-circuit TV, large-print photocopier, cassette books and magazines, children's books on cassette, home visits and other reference materials on blindness and other handicaps.

Deborah Evans, Librarian

Minnesota

7490 PACER Center
8161 Normandale Blvd.
Minneapolis, MN 55437

952-838-9000
888-248-0822
Fax: 952-838-0199
TTY: 952-838-0190
pacer@pacer.org
www.pacer.org

Parent Training and Information (PTI) programs help parents to understand their children's specific needs, communicate more effectively with professionals, participate in the educational planning process, and obtain information about relevant programs, services and resources.

Paula F. Goldberg, Executive Director
Mary Schrock, Chief Operating and Development Off
Alicia Kunin-Batson, Board Vice-President

7491 Star Center for Family Health
University of Minnesota Gateway
200 Oak Street SE, Suite 160
Minneapolis, MN 55455

612-626-4260
Fax: 612-626-2134
www.peds.umn.edu/peds-adol/

Helps children, youth, and families develop new and enhanced ways of coping with stress, learn strategies for adjusting to living with a chronic illness, and discover new ways of finding health, balance and well-being.

Elizabeth Latts, MSW, Resource Coordinator

Missouri

7492 Technology Access Center
475 Metroplex Drive, Suite 301
Nashville, TN 37211

615-248-6733
800-368-4651
Fax: 615-259-2536
TTY: 314-569-8446
TDD: 615-248-6733
www.tacnashville.org/

Technology group of parents, consumers and professionals; provides resources to help children and adults who have disabilities gain access to the benefits of technology. Includes nationwide network of community-based assistive technology, resource centers, hands on consultants and product demonstrations.

Kenyatta Lovett, President
J P Williams, Vice President
Jeffery A. Betzler, Treasurer

7493 Whitney Library for the Blind
1445 Boonville Avenue
Springfield, MO 65802

417-862-2781
Fax: 417-862-7566
blind@ag.org
www.gospelpublishing.com

Offers braille and cassette lending library, braille and cassette Sunday school materials for all ages, braille and cassette periodicals and resource assistance, and resources for blind children and children of blind parents.

Paul Weingariner, Director

Montana

7494 Montana State Library
1515 E 6th Avenue, PO Box 201800
Helena, MT 59601

406-444-3009
Fax: 406-444-0266
TDD: 406-444-4799
jstapp2@mt.gov
www.apps.msl.mt.gov/

Summer reading programs, braille writer, magnifiers, closed-circuit TV, large-print photocopier, cassette books and magazines, children's books on cassette, home visits and other reference materials on blindness and other handicaps.

Jennie Stapp, State Librarian
Sarah McHugh, Director of Statewide Library Resou
Cara Orban, Statewide Projects Librarian

Nebraska

7495 North Platte Public Library
120 W 4th Street
North Platte, NE 69101

308-535-8036
Fax: 308-535-8296
library@ci.north-platte.ne.us
www.ci.north-platte.ne.us/library/

Summer reading programs, braille writer, magnifiers, closed-circuit TV, large-print photocopier, cassette books and magazines, children's books on cassette, home visits and other reference materials on blindness and other handicaps.

Brenda Behsman, Librarian
Cecelia Lawrence, Library Director

Nevada

7496 Las Vegas-Clark County Library District
7060 W. Windmill Lane
Las Vegas, NV 89113

702-507-3400
Fax: 702-507-3482
www.lvccld.org/

Summer reading programs, braille writer, magnifiers, closed-circuit TV, large-print photocopier, cassette books and magazines, children's books on cassette, home visits and other reference materials on blindness and other handicaps.

Jeanne Goodrich, Executive Director

7497 Nevada State Library and Archives
100 N Stewart Street
Carson City, NV 89701

775-684-3360
800-922-2880
Fax: 775-684-3330
TDD: 775-687-8338
www.nsla.nevadaculture.org/

Summer reading programs, braille writer, magnifiers, closed-circuit TV, large-print photocopier, cassette books and magazines, children's books on cassette, home visits and other reference materials on blindness and other handicaps.

Kevin E Putnam, Librarian

General Resources / Libraries & Resource Centers

New Hampshire

7498 **New Hampshire State Library**
117 Pleasant Street
Concord, NH 03301
603-271-3429
800-491-4200
michael.york@dcr.nh.gov
www.nh.gov/nhsl/about/index.html

Summer reading programs, braille writer, magnifiers, closed-circuit TV, large-print photocopier, cassette books and magazines, children's books on cassette, home visits and other reference materials on blindness and other handicaps.

Michael Yorks, State Librarian
Janet Eklund, Administrator of Library Operations
Donna Gilbreth, Supervisor

New Jersey

7499 **Center for Enabling Technology**
622 Route 10 W, Suite 22B
Whippany, NJ 07981
973-428-1455
Fax: 973-560-9751
TTY: 973-428-1450
cetnj@aol.com

Technology group of parents, consumers and professionals; provides resources to help children and adults who have disabilities gain access to the benefits of technology. Includes nationwide network of community-based assistive technology, resource centers, hands on consultants and product demonstrations.

New York

7500 **Institute for Basic Research in Developmental Disabilities**
1050 Forest Hill Road
Staten Island, NY 10314
718-494-0600
Fax: 718-494-0837
ibr@opwdd.ny.gov
www.opwdd.ny.gov/

Conducts research into neurodegenerative diseases, Alzheimer's disease, developmental disabilities, fragile X syndrome, Down syndrome, autism, epilepsy and basic science issues underlying all developmental disabilities.

Dr. Krystyna Wisniewski

7501 **JGB Cassette Library International**
Jewish Guild for the Blind
15 W 65th Street
New York, NY 10023
212-769-6331

Summer reading programs, braille writer, magnifiers, closed-circuit TV, large-print photocopier, cassette books and magazines, children's books on cassette, home visits and other reference materials on blindness and other handicaps.

Bruce Massis

7502 **Keren-Or Jerusalem Center for Multi- Handicapped Blind Children**
350 7th Avenue, Suite 200
New York, NY 10010
212-279-4070
Fax: 212-279-4043
info@keren-or.org
www.keren-or.org

Center houses and cares for over 85 resident and day students who in addition to blindness or very low vision suffer from other severe physical and or mental disabilities. Provides training in daily living skills, as well as therapy, rehabilitation and education. Funds aquired through government stipends, contributions, bequests and legacies. Keren-OR is an IRS 501(C)(3) tax exempt organization.

Dr. Edward L Steinburg, Chairman
Dr. Albert Hornblass, President
Madelyn Cohen, Executive Director

7503 **Nassau Library System**
900 Jerusalem Avenue
Uniondale, NY 11553
516-292-8920
Fax: 516-565-0950
www.nassaulibrary.org/

Summer reading programs, braille writer, magnifiers, closed-circuit TV, large-print photocopier, cassette books and magazines, children's books on cassette, home visits and other reference materials on blindness and other handicaps.

Dorothy Pruyear, Librarian

7504 **Techspress Resource Center for Independent Living**
401-409 Columbia Street, PO Box 210
Utica, NY 13503
315-797-4642
Fax: 315-797-4747

Technology group of parents, consumers and professionals; provides resources to help children and adults who have disabilities gain access to the benefits of technology. Includes nationwide network of community-based assistive technology, resource centers, hands on consultants and product demonstrations.

Ohio

7505 **Blick Clinic for Developmental Disabilities**
640 W Market Street
Akron, OH 44303
330-762-5425
Fax: 330-762-4019
blickclinic@blickclinic.com
www.blickclinic.org/

Blick Clinic began providing services in 1969 during the philosophical era when warehousing individuals with intellectual disabilities in state institutions were commonplace and considered appropriate treatment.

Karin Lopper, Executive Director
Tami Mastrojohn, Kevin
Kelly Director of Finance

7506 **Cleveland Public Library**
325 Superior Avenue N.E.
Cleveland, OH 44114
216-623-2800
Fax: 216-623-7015
www.cpl.org

Summer reading programs, braille writer, magnifiers, closed-circuit TV, large-print photocopier, cassette books and magazines, children's books on cassette, home visits and other reference materials on blindness and other handicaps.

Barbara Mates, Librarian

7507 **Ohio Regional Library for the Blind and Physically Handicapped**
800 Vine Street, Library Square
Cincinnati, OH 45202
513-369-6999
Fax: 513-369-3111
TDD: 513-369-6072

Summer reading programs, braille writer, magnifiers, closed-circuit TV, large-print photocopier, cassette books and magazines, children's books on cassette, home visits and other reference materials on blindness and other handicaps.

Donna Foust, Librarian

7508 **Technology Resource Center**
1133 Edwin C. Moses Boulevard, #370
Dayton, OH 45408
937-461-3305
Fax: 937-461-6304
TDD: 937-236-6110
trcdoh@aol.com
www.trcd.org

Technology group of parents, consumers and professionals; provides resources to help children and adults who have disabilities gain access to the benefits of technology. Includes nationwide network of community-based assistive technology, resource centers, hands on consultants and product demonstrations.

Kevin Leonard, Coordinator
Judy Havens, Community Based Rehab Technologist

General Resources / Libraries & Resource Centers

Oklahoma

7509 Oklahoma Library for the Blind & Physically Handicapped
300 NE 18th Street
Oklahoma City, OK 73105
405-521-3514
800-523-0288
Fax: 405-521-4582
TTY: 405-521-4672
olbph@oltn.odl.state.ok.us
www.library.state.ok.us/

Summer reading programs, braille writer, magnifiers, closed-circuit TV, large-print photocopier, cassette books and magazines, children's books on cassette, home visits and other reference materials on blindness and other handicaps.

Geraldine Adams, Director

7510 Tulsa City-County Library System
400 Civic Center
Tulsa, OK 74103
918-549-7323
www.tulsalibrary.org

Summer reading programs, braille writer, magnifiers, closed-circuit TV, large-print photocopier, cassette books and magazines, children's books on cassette, home visits and other reference materials on blindness and other handicaps.

Ellen Ontko, Librarian

Oregon

7511 Oregon State Library
250 Winter Street NW
Salem, OR 97310
503-378-4243
Fax: 503-585-8059
TDD: 503-378-4276
library.help@state.or.us

Summer reading programs, braille writer, magnifiers, closed-circuit TV, large-print photocopier, cassette books and magazines, children's books on cassette, home visits and other reference materials on blindness and other handicaps.

Mary Mohr, Librarian

Pennsylvania

7512 Free Library of Philadelphia
1901 Vine Street
Philadelphia, PA
215-686-5322
www.library.phila.gov

Summer reading programs, braille writer, magnifiers, closed-circuit TV, large-print photocopier, cassette books and magazines, children's books on cassette, home visits and other reference materials on blindness and other handicaps.

Tobey Gordon Dichter, Chair
Leslie Anne Miller, First Vice Chair
Siobhan A. Reardon, President/Director

7513 Library for the Blind & Physically Handicapped, Leonard C Staisey Building
Carnegie Library of Pittsburgh
4724 Baum Boulevard
Pittsburgh, PA 15213
412-687-2440
800-242-0586
Fax: 412-687-2442
lbph@carnegielibrary.org
www.clpgh.org/clp/lbph

Provides on loan recorded books and magazines, large print books, and described videos to Western Pennsylvania residents unable to use standard printed materials due to visual, physically-based reading disabilities. Also loans special cassette and disc machines; does not loan equipment to play described videos. Information about disabilities and related agencies is also available.

Lou Testoni, Chair, Carnegie Library of Pittsbur
Mary Frances Cooper, President/Director
Susan Banks, Deputy Director

Rhode Island

7514 TechACCESS of Rhode Island
100 Jefferson Boulevard
Warwick, RI 02888
401-463-0202
800-916-8324
Fax: 401-463-3433
TTY: 401-273-0202
techaccess@techaccess-ri.org
www.techaccess-ri.org/

Technology group of parents, consumers and professionals; provides resources to help children and adults who have disabilities gain access to the benefits of technology. Includes nationwide network of community-based assistive technology, resource centers, hands on consultants and product demonstrations.

Judith Hammerlind Carlson, M.S., Executive Director
Kelly Charlebois, ATP, Clinical Manager/AT Consultant
Matthew Provost, M.S., CCC-SLP, Augmentative Communication Consulta

South Carolina

7515 Family Connection of South Carolina
2712 Middleburg Dr., Suite 103
Columbia, SC 29204
803-252-0914
800-578-8750
Fax: 866-420-4082
info@FamilyConnectionSC.org
www.familyconnectionsc.org/

Support network for parents of children with disabilities and/or chronic illness. Veteran parents offer support to parents who are just learning of their child's diagnosis. Offers support and insight into parenting a child with special needs, as well as referrals to trained veteran parents.

Esther Dennis, President
McIver Williamson, Vice President
Jackie Richards, Executive Director

7516 South Carolina State Library
P.O. Box 11469
Columbia, SC 29211
803-734-8666
888-221-4643
Fax: 803-734-8676
TDD: 803-734-7298
reference@statelibrary.sc.gov
www.statelibrary.sc.gov/

Summer reading programs, braille writer, magnifiers, closed-circuit TV, large-print photocopier, cassette books and magazines, children's books on cassette, home visits and other reference materials on blindness and other handicaps.

Deborah P. Anderson, Administrative Coordinator
Leesa Benggio, Deputy Director
Paula James, Finance Director

South Dakota

7517 South Dakota State Library
800 Governors Drive
Pierre, SD 57501
605-773-3131
800-423-6665
Fax: 605-773-6962
TDD: 605-773-4950
www.library.sd.gov/

Summer reading programs, braille writer, magnifiers, closed-circuit TV, large-print photocopier, cassette books and magazines, children's books on cassette, home visits and other reference materials on blindness and other handicaps.

Lesta Turchen, President
Monte Loos, Vice President
Daria Bossman, State Librarian

General Resources / Libraries & Resource Centers

Tennessee

7518 East Tennessee Technology Access Center
116 Childress Street
Knoxville, TN 37920
865-219-0130
Fax: 865-219-0137
ettacmain@gmail.com
www.ettac.org/

Assistive technology group of parents, consumers and professionals; provides resources to help children and adults who have disabilities gain access to the benefits of technology. Includes nationwide network of community-based assistive technology, resource centers, hands on consultants and product demonstrations.

Lois M. Symington, Executive Director
Bedros Bozdogan, President/Board of Directors
Mat Jones, Coordinator, Technology Support Ser

7519 Saint Jude Children's Research Hospital
262 Danny Thomas Place
Memphis, TN 38105
901-495-3300
www.stjude.org

Mike Canarios, SVP/Chief Financial Officer
Camille Sarrouf, Jr., Chair / President
Pam Dotson, SVP Patient Care Services/Chief Nur

Texas

7520 Baylor College of Medicine Birth Defects Center
One Baylor Plaza
Houston, TX 77030
713-798-4951
president@bcm.edu
www.bcm.tmc.edu

Baylor College of Medicine in Houston, the only private medical school in the Greater Southwest, is recognized as a premier academic health science center and is known for excellence in education, research and patient care.

Paul Klotman, M.D., President/CEO
Claire M. Bassett, Vice President, Communications and
Kristi Cooper, Vice President, Development

7521 Texas State Library
1201 Brazos St.
Austin, TX 78701
512-463-5455
Fax: 512-463-5436
TDD: 512-463-5449
info@tsl.state.tx.us
www.tsl.state.tx.us

Summer reading programs, braille writer, magnifiers, closed-circuit TV, large-print photocopier, cassette books and magazines, children's books on cassette, home visits and other reference materials on blindness and other handicaps.

Edward Seidenberg, Interim Director and Librarian
Donna Osborne, Administrative Services
Jelain Chubb, Archives & Information Services

Utah

7522 Utah State Library Commission
2150 S 300 W
Salt Lake City, UT 84115
801-468-6789

Summer reading programs, braille writer, magnifiers, closed-circuit TV, large-print photocopier, cassette books and magazines, children's books on cassette, home visits and other reference materials on blindness and other handicaps.

Gerald Buttars, Librarian

Vermont

7523 Vermont Department of Libraries Special Service Unit
109 State Street, Pavilion Office Building
Montpelier, VT 05609
802-828-3261
800-479-1711
Fax: 802-828-2199
libraries.vermont.gov

Summer reading programs, braille writer, magnifiers, closed-circuit TV, large-print photocopier, cassette books and magazines, children's books on cassette, home visits and other reference materials on blindness and other handicaps.

Martha Reid, State Librarian
Christine Friese, Assistant State Librarian
Brittney Wilson, Executive Asst. to the State Librar

Virginia

7524 Arlington County Department of Libraries
1015 N Quincy Street
Arlington, VA 22201
703-228-5990
Fax: 703-228-5962
TDD: 703-358-6320
www.co.arlington.va.us/lib/

Summer reading programs, braille writer, magnifiers, closed-circuit TV, large-print photocopier, cassette books and magazines, children's books on cassette, home visits and other reference materials on blindness and other handicaps.

Roxanne Barnes, Librarian

7525 Fairfax County Public Library
12000 Government Center Parkway
Fairfax, VA 22035
703-324-3100
Fax: 703-222-5921
TDD: 703-660-8524
www.co.fairfax.va.us/library/defaylt

Summer reading programs, braille writer, magnifiers, closed-circuit TV, large-print photocopier, cassette books and magazines, children's books on cassette, home visits and other reference materials on blindness and other handicaps.

Jeanette Studley, Librarian

7526 Newport News Public Library System
110 Main Street
Newport News, VA 23601
757-597-2917
Fax: 757-591-7425
www.nnpls.libguides.com/

Summer reading programs, braille writer, magnifiers, closed-circuit TV, large-print photocopier, cassette books and magazines, children's books on cassette, home visits and other reference materials on blindness and other handicaps.

Sue Balswin, Librarian

7527 Roanoke City Public Library System
2607 Salem Turnpike NW
Roanoke, VA 24017
540-853-2648
Fax: 540-853-1030

Summer reading programs, braille writer, magnifiers, closed-circuit TV, large-print photocopier, cassette books and magazines, children's books on cassette, home visits and other reference materials on blindness and other handicaps.

Rebecca Cooper, Librarian

7528 Virginia Beach Public Library
930 Independence Boulevard
Virginia Beach, VA 23455
757-385-0150
Fax: 757-523-9452
library@vbgov.com

Summer reading programs, braille writer, magnifiers, closed-circuit TV, large-print photocopier, cassette books and magazines, children's books on cassette, home visits and other reference materials on blindness and other handicaps.

Susan Head, Librarian

General Resources / Research Centers

West Virginia

7529 Cabell County Public Library
455 Ninth Street Plaza
Huntington, WV 25701
304-528-5700
Fax: 304-528-5701
www.cabell.lib.wv.us/

Summer reading programs, braille writer, magnifiers, Arkenstone reader/scanner, cassette books and magazines, children's books on cassette, home visits and other reference materials on blindness and other handicaps.

Judy K. Rule, Director
Angela Strait, Assistant Director
Mary Lou Pratt, Adult Services Coordinator

7530 Kanawha County Public Library
123 Capitol Street
Charleston, WV 25301
304-343-4646
Fax: 304-348-6530
www.kanawhalibrary.org/

Summer reading programs, braille writer, magnifiers, closed-circuit TV, large-print photocopier, cassette books and magazines, children's books on cassette, home visits and other reference materials on blindness and other handicaps.

Michael Albert, President
Elizabeth O. Lord, First Vice President
Cheryl Morgan, Second Vice President

7531 West Virginia Library Commission
1900 Kanawha Boulevard E
Charleston, WV 25305
304-340-2041
800-642-9021
Fax: 304-558-2044
karen.e.goff@wv.gov
www.librarycommission.wv.gov/

Summer reading programs, braille writer, magnifiers, closed-circuit TV, large-print photocopier, cassette books and magazines, children's books on cassette, home visits and other reference materials on blindness and other handicaps.

Karen Goff, Secretary
Denise Seabolt, Library Administrative Services Dir
Deborah McNeal, Personnel Officer

Wisconsin

7532 Brown County Library
515 Pine Street
Green Bay, WI 54301
920-448-4400
Fax: 920-448-4376
www.co.brown.wi.us

Summer reading programs, braille writer, magnifiers, closed-circuit TV, large-print photocopier, cassette books and magazines, children's books on cassette, home visits and other reference materials on blindness and other handicaps.

Angela Basten, Librarian

Research Centers

7533 Association for Research of Childhood Cancer
PO Box 251
Buffalo, NY 14225
716-681-4433
www.arocc.org

A nonprofit organization staffed by volunteers and formed in 1971 by parents who had lost children to pediatric cancer. Chapter members raise funds by various projects in order to provide seed money to various pediatric research centers in order to find a cure and, ultimately, prevent the types of cancers that attack children.

Anne O'Donnell, President
Larry Lorenz, 1st Vice President
Phyllis Winkle, Treasurer

7534 Baylor College of Medicine Birth Defects Center
6621 Fannin Street
Houston, TX 77030
713-770-3013
Fax: 713-770-4294

Frank Greenberg, MD, Director

7535 Computer Access Center
PO Box 12464
Albuquerque, NM 87195
505-242-9588
Fax: 310-338-9318
www.cac.org

Includes nationwide network of community-based assistive technology, resource centers, hands on consultants and product demonstrations.

7536 Division for Research (CEC-DR)
Council for Exceptional Children
1920 Association Drive
Reston, VA 20191
703-620-3660
Fax: 703-264-9474
TTY: 703-264-9446
www.cecdr.org

Devoted to the advancement of research related to the education of individuals with disabilities and/or who are gifted. Members include university, public, and private school teachers, researchers, administrators, psychologists, speech/language clinicians, parents of children with special learning needs.

Kathleen Lane, President
David Houchins, Vice President
Tanya Santangelo, Treasurer

7537 Division of Birth Defects and Genetic Diseases
4770 Buford Highway
Chamblee, GA 30341
770-488-7150
Fax: 770-488-7156

Muin J Khoury, MD

7538 Early Intervention Research Institute, Developmental Center
Utah State University
9510 Old Main Hill
Logan, UT 84322
435-750-1172

7539 Georgetown University Child Development Center
3307 Main Street, NW
Washington, DC 20007
202-687-8899
Fax: 202-687-5000
gucdc@georgetown.edu
gucdc.georgetown.edu

7540 Institute for Basic Research in Developmental Disabilities
1050 Forest Hill Road
Staten Island, NY 10314
718-494-0600
Fax: 718-494-0837

Conducts research into neurodegenerative diseases, Alzheimer's disease, developmental disabilities, fragile X syndrome, Down's syndrome, autism, epilepsy and basic science issues underlying all developmental disabilities.

7541 Keren-Or Jerusalem Center for Multi- Handicapped Blind Children
350 7th Avenue, Suite 200
New York, NY 10001
212-279-4070
Fax: 212-279-4043
info@keren-or.org
www.karen-or.org

Center houses and cares for over 85 resident and day students who in addition to blindness or very low vision, suffer from other severe physical and or mental disabilities. Provides training in daily living skills, as well as therapy, rehabilitation and education. Funds aquired through government stipends, government contributions, grants, bequests and legacies. Keren-Or is an IRS 501 (C)(3) tax exempt organization.

Dr. Edward L Steinburg, Chairman
Dr. Albert Hornblass, President
Madelyn Cohen, Executive Director

General Resources / Research Centers

7542 Louisiana State University Genetics Section of Pediatrics
1501 Kings Highway
Shreveport, LA 71103   318-675-5681
TF Thurman, MD, Director

7543 New England Regional Genetics Group
PO Box 920288
Needham, MA 02492   781-444-0126
Fax: 781-444-0127
mfgnergg@verizon.net
www.nergg.org

Human genetic services and educational planning pertaining to birth defects.

Lisa Demers, MS, CGC, President
Mary-Frances Garber, Coordinator
Lisa Demers, MS, CGC, Officer

7544 Parent and Information Center
5 N Lobban
Buffalo, WY 82834   307-684-2277
800-660-9742
Fax: 307-684-5314
tdawsonpic@vcn.com

Support network for parents of children with disabilities and/or chronic illness. Veteran parents offer support to parents who are just learning of their child's diagnosis. Offers support and insight into parenting a child with special needs, as well as referrals to trained veteran parents.

7545 Prenatal Diagnostic and Genetic Center
HCA Wesley Medical Center
550 N Hillside Street
Wichita, KS 67214   316-962-2000
Fax: 316-962-7076
www.wesleymc.com

Sechin Cho, MD

7546 Primary Children's Medical Center
Graduate Parents
100 North Mario Capecchi Drive
Salt Lake City, UT 84113   801-662-1000
Fax: 801-588-3869
www.intermountainhealthcare.org

7547 Research and Training Center for Children' Mental Health
Univerity of South Florida
13303 Bruce B Downs Boulevard
Tampa, FL 33612   813-974-4661
Fax: 813-974-6257
www.rtckids.fmhi.usf.edu

Dedicated to promoting effective community based culturally competent family centered services for familes and thier children who are affeed by mental, emotional or behavoiral disorders.

Bob Frieman, PhD, Center Director
Albert Duchnowski, Ph.D., Deputy Director
Krista Kutash, Ph.D., Deputy Director

7548 Research and Training Center on Family Support and Children's Mental Health
Portland State University/Regional Research Instit
PO Box 751
Portland, OR 97207   503-725-4040
Fax: 503-725-4180
rtc.pdx.edu

Dedicated to promoting effective community based, culturally competent, family centered services for families and their children who are or may be affected by mental, emotional or behavioral disorders. This goal is accomplished through collaborative research partnerships with family members, service providers, policy makers, and other concerned persons. Major efforts in dissemination and training include an annual conference and comprehensive web site.

Rachel Elizabeth, Public Information/Outreach

7549 Rusk Institute of Rehabilitation Medicine
NYU Langone Medical Center
301 East 17th Street, at Second Avenue
New York, NY 10003   212-263-7300
Fax: 212-263-5499
www.rusk.med.nyu.edu

The world's first university-affiliated facility devoted entirely to rehabilitation medicine, Rusk is among the most renowned center of its kind for the treatment of adults and children with disabilities-home to innovations and advances that have set the standard in rehabilitation care for every stage of life and for every stage of recovery.

Dr. Steven Flanagan, Professor & Chairman
Marilyn Shoo, Pediatrics Director

7550 TIES, The Children's Hospital
1056 E 19th Avenue
Denver, CO 80218   303-861-6395
800-332-2082
Fax: 303-861-3992

Karen Prescott, MS

7551 Team of Advocates for Special Kids
100 W Cerritos Avenue
Anaheim, CA 92805   714-533-8275
866-828-8275
Fax: 714-533-2533
taskca@aol.com
www.taskca.org

Technology group of parents, consumers and professionals; provides resources to help children and adults who have disabilities gain access to the benefits of technology. Includes nationwide network of community-based assistive technology, resource centers, hands on consultants and product demonstrations.

Marta Anchondo, Executive Director/CEO

7552 Teratogen and Birth Defects Information Project
University of South Dakota
414 E Clark Street
Vermillion, SD 57069   605-677-5011
www.usd.edu

7553 UC Berkeley School of Social Welfare
Mental Health & Social Welfare Research Group
303 Haviland Hall
Berkeley, CA 94720   510-642-3949
spsegal@berkeley.edu
www.socialwelfare.berkeley.edu

Steven P Segal, Director

7554 University of Alaska, Fairbanks
College of Rural Alaska
PO Box 7565000
Fairbanks, AK   907-474-7143
www.uaf.edu/rural/

Bernice Joseph, Vice Chancellor/Executive Dean
Pete Pinney, Associate Executive Dean
Cecelia Chamberlain, CRCD Executive Officer

7555 University of Iowa Birth Defects and Genetic Disorders Unit
2614 JCP
Iowa City, IA 52242   319-335-9901
val-sheffield@uiowa.edu
www.uiowa.edu

James M Smith, Director

7556 University of Miami, Mailman Center for Child Development
PO Box 16820
Miami, FL 33101   305-585-2703
Fax: 305-547-6309
www.pediatrics.med.miami.edu/mailman-center/

Focuses on birth defects and children's illnesses.

Dr. Robert Stempfel Jr, Director

7557 Wesley Medical Research Institutes
3306 E Central Avenue
Wichita, KS 67208   316-686-7172
www.wesleymc.com

General Resources / Audio Video

Respiratory and birth defects disorders research.
Dr. Sechin Cho, MD, Director

Conferences

7558 ACLP Annual Conference
Association of Child Life Professionals
1820 N Fort Myer Drive, Ste 520
Arlington, MD 22209
501-483-4500
800-252-4515
Fax: 501-483-4482
aclpadmin@childlife.org
www.childlife.org

The premier educational experience for child life professionals. The largest gathering of child life specialists of the year, offers ample opportunities for both formal and informal networking with peers.

1,000 May

Bailey Kasten, COO & Interim CEO
Yvonne Kassimatis, Marketing & Communications
Ramona Spencer, Director, Professional Development

7559 ADAA Annual Conference
Anxiety Disorders Association of America
8701 Georgia Avenue, Suite 412
Silver Spring, MD 20910
240-485-1018
information@adaa.org
www.adaa.org

ADAA is a national non-profit organization dedicated to the prevention, treatment, and cure of anxiety, depression, OCD, PTSD, and related disorders and to improving the lives of all people who suffer from them through education, practice, and research.

April

Susan K Gurley, Executive Director
Lise Bram, Deputy Executive Director
Katie Russo, Senior Director, Operations

7560 Arc Annual National Convention
Arc of the United States
1825 K Street NW, Ste 1200
Washington, DC 20006
202-534-3700
800-433-5255
Fax: 202-534-3731
mckiernan@thearc.org
www.thearc.org

Held in cities throughout the U.S. each fall which attracts nearly 1000 people for educational sessions, business meetings and social events.

Peter V. Berns, CEO
Kristen McKiernan, Sr Exec. Offcr, Comms & Marketing
Liz Mahar, Director, Family/Sibling Initiative

7561 CEC Convention & Expo
Council for Exceptional Children
2900 Crystal Drive, Suite 1000
Arlington, VA 22201
703-243-0446
888-232-7733
Fax: 703-264-9494
TTY: 866-915-5000
service@cec.sped.org
www.cec.sped.org

April

Bruce Ramirez, Executive Director
Krista Barnes, Assistant Executive Director
Karen Niles, Assistant Executive Director

7562 FFCMH Annual Conference
National Federation of Families
15800 Crabbs Branch Way, Suite 300
Rockville, MD 20855
240-403-1901
ffcmh@ffcmh.org
www.ffcmh.org

The only national conference dedicated solely to supporting families whose children - of any age - experience mental health and/or substance use challenges during their lifetime.

November

Lynda Gargan, PhD, Executive Director

7563 NADD Annual Conference & Exhibit Show
National Association for the Dually Diagnosed
12 Hurley Avenue
Kingston, NY 12401
845-331-4336
800-331-5362
Fax: 845-331-4569
info@thenadd.org
www.thenadd.org

Fall

Jeanne Farr, CEO
Michelle Jordan, Office Manager
Edward Seliger, Project Coordinator

7564 NAMI Convention
National Alliance on Mental Illness
3803 N. Fairfax Dr., Ste. 100
Arlington, VA 22203
703-524-7600
800-950-6264
Fax: 703-524-9094
TDD: 703-516-7227
info@nami.org
www.nami.org

The NAMI Convention is packed with information, chances to network, leadership development opportunities, and lots more

Summer

Richele Keas, Senior Mgr, Media Relations

Audio Video

7565 A Mind of Your Own
Fanlight Productions
32 Court Street, 21st Floor
Brooklyn, NY 11201
718-488-8900
800-876-1710
Fax: 718-488-8642
info@fanlight.com
www.fanlight.com

Learning disabilities can make children feel lonely, confused, hopeless and worthless, even if they know they are smart, but it doesn't have to feel that way. Meet Henry, Matthew, Max and Stephanie, four incredible kids who don't let learning differences hold them back or get them down.

38 minutes DVD or VHS

Nicole Johnson, Publicity Coordinator

7566 Assisting Parents Through the Mourning Process
Hope
55 E 100 N
Logan, UT 84321
435-752-9533
Fax: 435-752-9533

Describes the mourning process experienced by some parents of children with disabilities and ways in which the professional can help them through the process.

20 minutes

7567 CANCER
Rosen Publishing Group
29 E 21st Street
New York, NY 10010
800-237-9932
Fax: 888-436-4643
www.rosenpublishing.com

Interviews with experts and cancer patients reveal the many types, causes, and treatments for cancer. Recommended for grades seven-twelve.

General Resources / Audio Video

30 Minutes
ISBN: 0-823921-76-0

7568 Disability Awareness
Active Parenting Publishers
1220 Kennestone Circle, Suite 130
Marietta, GA 30066
770-429-0565
Fax: 770-429-0334
cservice@activeparenting.com
www.activeparenting.com

Helps viewers think about how they feel when confronted by people with disabilities. Close-captioned with study guide.

19 minutes

Michael H. Popkin, PhD, Founder & President
Virginia Murray, Marketing Manager
Melody Popkin, Manager of Christian Resources

7569 Kid's Health: TV Late Breaking News Video About Broken Bones and Cast Care
Aquarius Health Care Videos
5 Powderhouse Lane, PO Box 1159
Sherborn, MA 1770
508-651-2963
888-440-2963
Fax: 508-650-4216
info@aquariusproductions.com
www.aquariusproductions.com

You probably have lots of questions. How do doctors know if a bone is really broken? What are casts and what do they do? What are some ways to take good care of your cast so you won't need a new one? The Kids Health TV News Tem answer these questions and more in an entertaining format.

Donna Kaufman

7570 Laughter Therapy
PO Box 827
Monterey, CA 93942
408-625-3788

These people can supply tapes of old Candid Camera movies to patients. Maintains a library of 50 topics.

7571 Meeting the Challenge: Parenting Children with Disabilities
Active Parenting Publishers
1220 Kennestone Circle, Suite 130
Marietta, GA 30066
770-429-0565
800-825-0060

Award-winning video for parents of special-needs children. Other parents share their stories.

94 minutes

7572 My Body Is Not Who I Am
Aquarius Health Care Videos
5 Powderhouse Lane, PO Box 1159
Sherborn, MA 1770
508-651-2963
888-440-2963
Fax: 508-650-4216
info@aquariusproductions.com
www.aquariusproductions.com

Children host this video and educate themselves and the viewer about disabilities. While profiling adults and children who talk candidly about their disabilites, they learn that people are more alike than different. This video is crafted to foster senitivity toward others and acceptance of people with disabilities. It provides general disability etiquette guidelines that both children and adults can benefit from. The video is fast paced and designed to keep children's attention. Closed caption.

K - 12 25 Minutes

Donna Kaufman

7573 No Fears, No Tears
Fanlight Productions
32 Court Street, 21st Floor
Brooklyn, NY 11201
718-488-8900
800-876-1710
Fax: 718-488-8642
info@fanlight.com
www.fanlight.com

Dr. Leora Kuttner explores the pioneer pain management project for children with cancer. The film proves the strenth of the human spirit and mind's ability to ease away excruciating pain. See No Fears, No Tears - 13 Years Later.

28 minutes DVD
ISBN: 1-572958-73-1

7574 No Fears, No Tears - 13 Years Later
Fanlight Productions
32 Court Street, 21st Floor
Brooklyn, NY 11201
718-488-8900
800-876-1710
Fax: 718-488-8642
info@fanlight.com
www.fanlight.com

Dr. Leora Kuttner explore the effects of children's pain management therapies 13 years after use. See original No Fears, No Tears. ISBN: DVD: 1-57295-874-X; VHS: 1-572952-77-6

47 minutes DVD or VHS

7575 Not Just a Cancer Patient
Fanlight Productions
32 Court Street, 21st Floor
Brooklyn, NY 11201
718-488-8900
800-876-1710
Fax: 718-488-8642
info@fanlight.com
www.fanlight.com

Focuses on several articulate teenagers who are undergoing cancer treatment to help caregivers understand the needs and feelings of this very special population.

23 minutes VHS
ISBN: 1-572950-86-2

Nicole Johnson, Publicity Coordinator

7576 Operation Sneek-a-Peek
Aquarius Health Care Videos
5 Powderhouse Lane, PO Box 1159
Sherborn, MA 1770
508-651-2963
888-440-2963
Fax: 508-650-4216
info@aquariusproductions.com
www.aquariusproductions.com

Helps children feel more comfortable and safe in a hospital envirnoment. The puppets in the video take the children on an educational, comforting and at times, humorous tour of the hospital operating and recovery rooms. This video eases children's concerns and fears with factual information and truthful demonstrations. Closed captioned.

20 Minutes

Donna Kaufman

7577 Recognizing Children with Special Needs
Aquarius Health Care Videos
5 Powderhouse Lane, PO Box 1159
Sherborn, MA 1770
508-651-2963
888-440-2963
Fax: 508-650-4216
info@aquariusproductions.com
www.aquariusproductions.com

A great overview for caregivers of children on how to recognize special needs. Often times it is the little things children do everyday to compensate for, or express, a disability that can be observed by their caregiver. All types of disabilities are addressed, emotional, physical, psychological, and chonic illness. A wonderful tool for teachers, childcare staff, and students who play a vital role in our children's development. Closed captioned.

18 Minutes

Donna Kaufman

7578 Stress Reduction Tapes, Stress Reduction Clinic
University Massachusetts Medical
PO Box 547
Lexington, MA 2420
508-856-2656
mindfulness@umassmed.edu
www.mindfulnesstapes.com

There are two tapes sold separately that are appropriate for preteens or adolescents. Tapes may be ordered from the website

Jon Kabat-Zinn, PhD, Author

7579 They're Just Kids
Aquarius Health Care Videos
5 Powderhouse Lane, PO Box 1159
Sherborn, MA 1770

508-651-2963
888-440-2963
Fax: 508-650-4216
www.aquariusproductions.com

This documentary explores the advantages of the inclusion of disabled children in the classroom, Cub Scouts and other extracurricular activities. Unfortunately, there is a great deal of fear, apprehension and concern regarding mainstreaming. This film is an excellent tool to expedite and ease that integration of children and adults into the community as well as into recreational, social and educational programs. Closed captioned, for schools, parents and those working with disabled children.

27 Minutes

Donna Kaufman

7580 When Parents Can't Fix It
Fanlight Productions
32 Court Street, 21st Floor
Brooklyn, NY 11201

718-488-8900
800-876-1710
Fax: 718-488-8642
info@fanlight.com
www.fanlight.com

Looks at the stresses and rewards in the lives of five families who are raising children with disabilities. Offers a realistic look and different family strengths and coping styles. ISBN: DVD: 1-57295-876-6; VHS: 1-572952-55-5

58 minutes DVD or VHS

Nicole Johnson, Publicity Coordinator

Web Sites

7581 Adoptive Families
108 West 39th Street, Suite 805
New York, NY 10018

646-366-0830
800-372-3300
Fax: 646-366-0842
letters@adoptivefamilies.com
www.adoptivefamilies.com

Information and advocacy resources for families and professionals interested in adoption.

Susan Caughman, Editor/Publisher
Eve Gilman, Editor

7582 American Academy of Pediatrics
345 Park Blvd
Itasca, IL 60143

847-434-4000
800-433-9016
Fax: 847-434-8000
csc@aap.org
www.aap.org

The American Academy of Pediatrics and its member pediatricians are committed to the attainment of optimal physical, mental and social health and well-being for all infants, children, adolescents, and young adults.

Kyle E. Yasuda, MD, FAAP, President
Mark Del Monte, JD, CEO/Executive VP
Vera Tait, MD, FAAP, Chief Medical Officer

7583 American Autoimmune Related Diseases Association
www.aarda.org

586-776-3900
aarda@aarda.org
www.aarda.org

The American Autoimmune Related Diseases Association is dedicated to the eradication of autoimmune diseases and the alleviation of suffering and the socioeconomic impact of autoimmunity through fostering and facilitating collaboration in the areas of education, public awareness, research, and patient services in an effective, ethical and efficient manner.

7584 American Board of Pediatrics
111 Silver Cedar Court
Chapel Hill, NC 27514

919-929-0461
Fax: 919-929-9255
abpeds@abpeds.org, ite@abpeds.org

Is an independent, nonprofit organization whose certificate is recognized throughout the world signifying a high level of physician competence. It consists of distinguished pediatricians in education, research, and clinical practice, as well as one or more nonphysicians who have a professional interest in the health and welfare of children and adolescents.

7585 American College of Medical Genetics
7220 Wisconsin Avenue, Suite 300
Bethesda, MD 20814

301-718-9603
Fax: 301-718-9604
acmg@acmg.net
www.acmg.net

Provides education, resources and a voice for the medical genetics profession. To make genetic services available to and improve the health of the public, the ACMG promoted the development and implementation of methods to diagnose, treat and prevent genetic disease.

7586 American Society of Pediatric Neurosurgeons
www.aspn.org

aspnhelp@aspn.org
www.aspn.org

The society is dedicated to the advancement of the subspecialty of Pediatric Neurosugery and to assure superlative care for children with neurosurgical disorders. It holds an annual meeting where recent advances in clinical and basic research into pediatric neurosurgical disorders are presented and discussed, and sponsors a journal, Pediatric Neurosurgery.

Alan R. St. Geme III, MD, President
James M. Drake, Secretary
John Ragheb, MD, Treasurer

7587 Archives of Pediatric and Adolescent Medicine
333 Seventh Avenue, 20th Floor
New York, NY 10001

646-674-6300
800-950-2035
Fax: 646-674-6301
sales@ovid.com
www.ovid.com/site/cataloge/journal

It provides a forum for dialogue on a range of scientific, clinical, and humanistic issues relevant to the care of pediatric patients, from infancy to young adulthood. The journal's core articles are original clinical studies and reviews by experts.

7588 Association for Children with Hand or Arm Deficiency (REACH)
Pearl Assurance House, Brook Street   NOP-ONE-

Provides the means by which parents and professionals share experiences, information, and support.

7589 Birth Defect Research for Children
976 Lake Baldwin Lane, Suite 104
Orlando, FL 32814

407-895-0802
staff@birthdefects.org
www.birthdefects.org

Birth Defect Research for Children is a non-profit organization that provides parents and expectant parents with information about birth defects and support services for their children.

Betty Mekdeci, Executive Director

General Resources / Web Sites

7590 Cedars-Sinai Medical Center
8700 Beverly Road
Los Angeles, CA 90048
310-423-3277
800-233-2771
cedars-sinai.edu

Focused on providing the finest healthcare available, resulting in advances in all areas of healthcare for both children and adult disorders.

Vera S. Guerin, Chair
Marc H. Rapaport, Vice Chair
Thomas M. Priselac, President & CEO

7591 CenterWatch Clinical Trials Listings
10 Winthrop Square, Fifth Floor
Boston, MA 2110
617-948-5100
866-219-3440
Fax: 617-948-5101
customerservice@centerwatch.com
www.centerwatch.com

CenterWatch is a Boston-based publishing and information services company. We provide information services used by patients, pharmaceutical, biotechnology and medical device companies, CRO's and research centers involved in clinical research around the world.

Kenneth A. Getz, Founder & Owner
Joan A. Chambers, COO
Cheryl Appel Rosenfeld, Editor-in-Chief

7592 Clinical Genetic Services-Department of Pediatrics
Hassenfeld Children's Hospital at NYU Langone
424 East 34th Street
New York, NY 10016
212-263-7300
Fax: 646-754-2250
nyulangone.org

Offers evaluations, genetic counseling and testing. Clinical services include carrier testing, prenatal counseling, and complete genetic evaluations for children and adults.

John G. Pappas, MD, Pediatric Genetic Associate
Naomi Yachelevich, MD, Pediatric Genetic Associate

7593 Council for Exceptional Children
3100 Clarendon Blvd, Suite 600
Arlington, VA 22201
888-232-7733
service@exceptionalchildren.org
exceptionalchildren.org

Advocates appropriate policies, standards and development for students with special needs.

Chad Rummel, Executive Director

7594 CyberPsych
www.cyberpsych.org

www.cyberpsych.org

CyberPsych presents information about psychoanalysis, psychotherapy, and special topics such as anxiety disorder, the problematic use of alcohol, homophobia, and the traumatic effects of racism. CyberPsych is a nonprofit network which offers free web hosting and technical support for internet communication, to nonprofit groups and individuals.

Carol Lindemann, PHD, Webmaster

7595 Dermatology Foundation
1560 Sherman Ave., Suite 870
Evanston, IL 60201
847-328-2256
Fax: 847-328-0509
dermatologyfoundation.org

Committed to advancing dermatologic through research and education. The foundation is a charitable organization that has the primary service to fund research in skin cancer and other diseases of the skin, hair, and nails.

Bruce U. Wintroub, MD, Chair
Michael D. Tharp, MD, President
Stuart R. Lessin, MD, Vice President

7596 Easter Seals
141 W Jackson Boulevard, Suite 1400A
Chicago, IL 60604
312-726-6200
800-221-6827
Fax: 312-726-1494
info@easterseals.com
www.easterseals.com

Easter Seals' mission is to create solutions that change lives for children and adults with disabilities and to provide appropriate developmental and rehabilitation services. Services provided include early intervention, after-school programs, preschool, tutoring, medical rehabilitation, vocational services, adult and senior day services, respite and in home care, camping and recreation, residential housing, support services, support groups, transportation, and referrals.

Kendra Davenport, President & CEO

7597 European Society for Pediatric Urology
www.espu.org

www.espu.org

Is a nonprofit society whose main purpose is to promote pediatric urology, appropriate practice, education as well as exchanges between practitioners involved in the treatment of genitourinary disorders in children.

Gianantonio Manzoni, President
Guy Bogaert, President-Elect
Serdar Tekgul, Secretary

7598 Federation for Children with Special Needs
529 Main Street, Suite 1M3
Boston, MA 2129
617-236-7210
800-331-0688
Fax: 617-241-0330
fcsninfo@fcsn.org
fcsn.org

Mission is to provide information, support, and assistance to parents of children with disabilites, their professional partners, and their communities. We are committed to listening to and learning from families and encouraging full participation in community life by all people, especially those with disabilities.

James F. Whalen, President
Rich Robison, Executive Director
Michael Weiner, Treasurer

7599 GeneTest
481B Edward H. Ross Drive
Elmwood Park, NJ 7407
888-729-1204
Fax: 202-212-6457
www.geneclinics.org

By providing current, authoritative information on genetic testing and its use in diagnosis, management, and genetic couseling, GeneTests promotes the appropriate use of genetic services in patient care and personal decision making.

Roberta A. Pagon, MD, Founder & Medical Director
Amar Kamath, Commercial Director
Deb Eunpu, MS, CGC, Program Manager

7600 ICAN (International Child Amputee Network)
PO Box 13812
Tuscon, AZ 85732
jcb525@att.net
child-amputee.net

Is an internet mailing list to provide information and support contacts to children with absent or underdeveloped limbs and their parents.

Sami Madden, President
Mike Holmes, Vice President
Joyce Baughn, Director

7601 International Foundation for Functional Gastrointestinal Disorders (IFFGD)
www.iffgd.org

414-964-1799
www.iffgd.org

The organization offers responses to those commonly asked questions for families and individuals whose lives have been touched by gastrointestinal disorders.

General Resources / Web Sites

Nancy J. Norton, Founder
Ceciel T. Rooker, President

7602 LSUMC Family Medicine Patient Education
lib-sh.lsumc.edu

lib-sh.lsumc.edu

Offers databases, E-journals, E-books, and a library catalog.

7603 Learning Disabilities Association of America
PO Box 10369, 4156 Library Road
Pittsburgh, PA 15234
412-341-1515
888-300-6710
Fax: 412-344-0224
info@LDAAmerica.org
www.ldaamerica.org

Helps families of the affected individual through information and referral to professionals in their area. A membership organization with affiliates across the country.

Stephanie Fedro-Byrom, Operations Manager
Maureen Swanson, Director, Healthy Children Project
Ericka Pardun, Communications Coordinator

7604 Lighthouse Guild
250 West 64th Street
New York, NY 10023
800-284-4422
info@lighthouseguild.org
www.lighthouseguild.org

Lighthouse Guild is dedicated to providing exceptional services that inspire people who are visually impaired to attain their goals.

7605 Low Vision Gateway
www.lowvision.org

www.lowvision.org

Devoted to issues of vision loss, low vision aids, vision rehabilitation and the role of the doctor.

7606 March of Dimes Foundation
1550 Crystal Drive, Ste 1300
Arlington, VA 22202
888-663-4637
www.marchofdimes.org

March of Dimes help moms have full-term pregnancies and research the problems that threaten the health of babies. The March of Dimes also acts globally: sharing best practices in perinatal health and helping improve birth outcomes where the needs are the most urgent.

Stacey D. Stewart, President
Alan Brogdon, SVP/COO/Board Officer
Rahul Gupta, MD, SVP & Chief Medical/Health Officer

7607 Medical Economics Company
24950 Country Club Drive, Suite 200
North Olmsted, OH 44070
www.medec.com

Full text for non-prescription drugs and the PDR Guide to Drug Interactions.

Georgiann DeCenzo, Executive Vice President
Ken Sylvia, Vice President
Don Berman, Director, Business Development

7608 Medical Matrix: Pediatrics
medmatrix.org/_SPages/Pediatrics.asp

medmatrix.org/_SPages/Pediatrics.asp

Christoph U. Lehman, MD, Assoc. Professor
Andy Spooner, MD, Pediatrics Dept.

7609 Mental Help Net
P.O. Box 20709
Columbus, OH 43220
614-448-4055
800-232-TALK
mentalhelp.net

Seeks to advance the state of online mental health communications. We wish to provide the following: to discuss, develop and debate in an open forum the future of the mental health field in America and throughout the world, to help coordinate various componenets of the mental health field.

7610 NADD: National Association for the Dually Diagnosed
12 Hurley Avenue
Kingston, NY 12401
845-331-4336
800-331-5362
Fax: 845-331-4569
info@thenadd.org
www.thenadd.org

Nonprofit organization designed to promote the interests of professional and care providers for individuals who have the coexistence of mental illness and intellectual disabilities. NADD provides conferences, educational services and training materials to professionals, parents, concerned citizens and service organizations.

Jeanne Farr, CEO
Michelle Jordan, Office Manager
Edward Seliger, Project Coordinator

7611 National Arthritis and Musculoskeletal & Skin Disease Info. Clearinghouse
NIAMS Information Clearinghouse
1 AMS Circle
Bethesda, MD 20892
301-495-4484
877-226-4267
Fax: 301-718-6366
TTY: 301-565-2966
NIAMSinfo@mail.nih.gov
www.niams.nih.gov

Supports and provides clinical and public information and research to increase understanding of the many skin diseases and related disorders. Also provides lists and order forms for their resources and materials.

Robert H. Carter, MD, Acting Director
Robert H. Carter, MD, Deputy Director
Gahan Breithaupt, Assoc. Dir. For Management

7612 National Center for Biotechnology Information
National Library of Medicine, 8600 Rockville Pike
Bethesda, MD 20894
888-346-3656
info@ncbi.nlm.nih.gov
www.ncbi.nlm.nih.gov

NCBI's mission is to develop new information technologoes to aid in the understanding of fundamental molecular and genetic processes that control health and disease.

Patricia Flatley Brennan, RN, PhD, Director
James Ostell, PhD, Executive Secretary

7613 National Dissemination Center for Children with Disabilities
c/o Statewide Parent Advocacy Network, 35 Halsey S NOP-ONE-

Provides information to the nation on: disabilities in children and youth; programs and services for infants, children, and youth with disabilities; IDEA, the nation's special education law; No Child Left Behind, the nation's general education law; and research-based information on effective practices for children with disabilities.

7614 National Institute on Disability, Indepen dent Living & Rehabilitation Research
U.S. DHHS
330 C Street SW, Room 1304
Washington, DC 20201
202-795-7398
Fax: 202-205-0392
nidilrr-mailbox@acl.hhs.gov
acl.gov/Programs/NIDILRR/

Is committed to improving results and outcomes for people with dsiabilities of all ages. It supports programs that serve millions of children, youth and adults with disablties.

Kristi Hill, Acting Deputy Director
Ruth Brannon, Director, Research Sciences

7615 National Library Service for the Blind and Physically Handicapped
Library of Congress
1291 Taylor Street NW
Washington, DC 20542
202-707-5100
800-424-8567
Fax: 202-707-0712
nls@loc.gov
www.loc.gov/nls

General Resources / Web Sites

Provides information and advocacy resources for families and professionals, including listings of organizations focusing on more specific areas of concern to families and young adults who have disabilities. Administers a natural library service that provides recorded and braille reading materials to eligible children and adults who cannot read standard print.

7616 National Newborn Screening and Genetic Resources Center
3907 Galacia Drive
Austin, TX 78759
512-345-5685
therrell@uthscsa.edu
genes-r-us.uthscsa.edu

The mission is to provide a forum for interaction between consumers, health care professionals, researchers, organizations, and policy-makers in-refining and developing public health, newborn screening and geneting programs, and to serve as a national resource center for information and education in the areas of newborn screening and genetics.

Bradford L. Therrell, Jr., Ph.D., Director
Celia Kaye, MD, PhD, Professor & Senior Associate Dean
Louis Bartoshesky, MD, MPH, Pediatrician & Clinical Geneticist

7617 National Organization of Parents of Blind Children
200 East Wells Street at Jernigan Place
NOP-ONE-

Is a national membership organization of parents and friends of blind chilren reaching out to each other to give support, encouragement and information. We believe the real problem of blindness is not the loss of eyesight, but the misunderstanding and lack of information which exists. With proper training opportunity, blindness can be reduced to a physical nuisance.

7618 National Resource Library on Youth With Disabilities
3 Morrill Hall, 100 Church St. SE
Minneapolis, MN 55455
www.cyfc.umn.edu/NRL/

Brings together comprehensive sources of information related to youth with chronic or disabling conditions and their families. Topics include psychosocial issues, disability awareness, developmental processes, family, sexuality, education, employment, independent living, cultural issues, gender issues, service delivery, professional issues, advocacy and legal issues, and health issues.

Eric W. Kaler, President
Karen Hanson, Provost
Scott Studham, VP & CIO

7619 Nuclear Medicine at Children's Hospital, Boston
www.jpnm.org/contentch.html

www.jpnm.org/contentch.html

7620 Office of Special Education and Rehabilitative Services
www2.ed.gov/about/offices/list/osers/

www2.ed.gov/about/offices/list/osers/

Mission is to strengthen the federal commitment to assuring access to equal opportunity for every individual; to supplement and complement the efforts of states, the local school systems and other instrumentalities of the states, the private nonprofit educational research institutions, community-based organizations, parents, and students to improve the quality of education; and to encourage the increased involvement of the public, parents, and students in federal education programs.

7621 Online Mendelian Inheritance in Man
McKusick-Nathans Institue of Genetic Medicine-JHU
Baltimore, MD 21205
www.omim.org

This database is a catalog of human genes and genetic disorders.

Ada Hamosh, MD, Scientific Director

7622 PDR - Physicians' Desk Reference
5 Paragon Drive
Montvale, NJ 7645
888-227-6469
PDRnet@pdr.net
www.pdr.net

Robert Carmignani, Sales & Marketing
Kim Marich, Sr. Director, Marketing

7623 PEDINFO: An index of the Pediatric Internet
www.pedinfo.org

www.pedinfo.org

Collection of links to pediatric information.

7624 Parent to Parent USA
PO Box 472
State College, PA 16804
484-272-7368
www.p2pusa.org

Parent to Parent USA supports a network of viable, sustainable, fully-functioning, and effective Parent to Parent programs in all 50 states through hands-on support, training and technical assistance, and high-quality tools and resources.

Aurelie "Lily" Brown, Co-Director
Marsha Quinn, Co-Director

7625 Pathways.org
355 E Erie Street
Chicago, IL 60611
friends@pathways.org
pathways.org

Provides free tools to maximize all children's motor, sensory, and communication development. Seeks to empower parents to understand and encourage their baby's development to keep them on track or catch potential delays early. Ensures every child is screened for motor, sensory, and communication development by 4 months of age, taking advantage of baby's neuroplasticity.

7626 Pediatric Behavior and Development
www.dbpeds.org

www.dbpeds.org

Is an independent web site created to promote better care and outcomes for children and families affected by developmental, learning, and behavioral problems by providing access to clinically relevant information and educational materials for physicians, fellows, resident physicians, and students. The site may also be of interest to psychologists, nurses, nurse practitioners, social workers, therapists, educators, and parents.

7627 Pediatric Points of Interest
www.pslgroup.com/dg/20112

www.pslgroup.com/dg/20112

Are a collection of updated links for pediatricians, parents and children to medical sources on the internet.

7628 Pregnancy and Child Health Resource Center from Mayo Health Oasis
13400 E. Shea Blvd.
Scottsdale, AZ 85259
480-301-8000
800-446-2279
www.mayohealth.org

Our mission is to empower people to manage their health. We accomplish this by providing useful and up-to-date information and tools that reflect the expertise and standard of excellence of Mayo Clinic.

Roger W. Harms, MD, Medical Director, Content
Brooks S. Edwards, MD, Founding Medical Director
Philip T. Hagen, Senior Medical Editor

7629 Psych Central
55 Pleasant St., Suite 207
Newburyport, MA 1950
talkback@psychcentral.com
www.psychcentral.com

Offers free informational and educational articles and resources on psychological support and mental health online.

John M. Grohol, CEO & Founder

7630 PubMed
National Library of Medicine, Building 38A
Bethesda, MD 20894
888-346-3656
info@ncbi.nlm.nih.gov
www.ncbi.nlm.nih.gov/pubmed/

Creates public databases, conducts research in computational biology, develops software tools for analyzing genome data, and disseminates biomedical information - all for better understanding molecular processes affecting human health and disease.

General Resources / Magazines

Christine E. Seidman, M.D., Chair
David J. Lipman, M.D., Executive Secretary

7631 Save Babies Through Screening Foundation
PO Box 2313
Palm Harbor, FL 34682
888-454-3383
www.savebabies.org

Is a national nonprofit public charity run by volunteers. Its mission is to improve the lives of babies by working to prevent disabilities and early death resulting from disorders detectable through newborn screening.

Jill Levy-Fisch, President
Sarah Wilkerson, Vice President
Anne Rugari, Treasurer

7632 Society for Adolescent Medicine
111 Deer Lake Road, Suite 100
Deerfield, IL 60015
847-753-5226
Fax: 847-480-9282
info@adolescenthealth.org
www.adolescenthealth.org

A multidisciplinary organization of professionals committed to improving the physical and psychosocial health and well-being of all adolescents.

Carol Ford, President
Paula Braverman, Secretary-Treasurer
Michael Resnick, President Elect

7633 Southern Illinois University School of Medicine
PO Box 19639
Springfield, IL 62794
217-545-8000
800-342-5748
www.siumed.edu/peds/index.htm

The mission of SUI School of Medicine is to assist the people of central and southern Illinois in meeting their present and future health care needs through education, clinical service and research.

Paul Castillo, CPA, CFO
Denise A. Gray-Felder, APR, Chief Communication Officer
Quinta Vreede, Chief Administrative Officer

7634 TRIP Database
www.tripdatabase.com
734-615-0863
800-211-8181
contact@tripdatabase.com
www.tripdatabase.com

The TRIP Database allows users to rapidly and easily identify high quality medical literature from a wide range of sources.

7635 TransWeb
www.transweb.org

www.transweb.org

Mission is to provide information about donation and transplantation to the general public in order to improve organ and tissue procurement efforts worldwide, to provide transplant patients and families world wide with information specifically dealing with transplant-related issues and concerns and to provide and index sources for transplant-related information available through the internet and otherwise.

7636 Virtual Childrens Hosptial
www.virtualpediatrichospital.org

www.virtualpediatrichospital.org

Is dedicated to helping patients find the highest quality medical information in the world today. We offer patients the tools necessary to make informed treatment decisions within the short timlines dictated by their illness or disease.

7637 WebMD Community Services
my.webmd.com

my.webmd.com

Provides valuable health information, tools for managing youth health, and support to those who seek information.

Michael Smith, MD, MBA, CPT, Chief Medical Officer
Brunilda Nazario, MD, BC-ADM, Lead Medical Editor
Hansa Bhargava, MD, Medical Editor

Book Publishers

7638 March of Dimes Nursing Modules
1550 Crystal Drive, Ste 1300
Arlington, VA 22202
914-997-4488
888-663-4637
Fax: 914-428-8203
productquestions@marchofdimes.org
www.marchofdimes.com/catalog

Nursing modules are self-directed learning monographs designed for registered nurses and nurse-midwives. Created to help nurses meet the challenges posed by a rapidly changing world of technological advances, evolving demographics and greater cultural diversity, they focus on effective care delivery during the pre-conceptional, prenatal, intrapartum, postpartum and inter-conceptional periods.

7639 Parental Alienation, DSM-5, and ICD-11
William Bernet, author

Charles C Thomas Publisher
2600 S 1st Street
Springfield, IL 62704
217-789-8980
800-258-8980
Fax: 217-789-9130
books@ccthomas.com
www.ccthomas.com

264 pages
ISBN: 0-398079-44-4

Sue F V Rakow, Co-Author
Carol B Carpenter, Co-Author

Magazines

7640 Adoptive Families
108 West 39th Street, Suite 805
New York, NY 10018
646-366-0830
800-372-3300
Fax: 646-366-0842
letters@adoptivefamilies.com
www.adoptivefamilies.com

Information and advocacy resources for families and professionals interested in adoption.

Susan Caughman, Editor/Publisher
Eve Gilman, Editor

7641 Exceptional Parent
209 Harvard Street, Suite 303
Brookline, MA 2146
617-730-5800
Fax: 617-730-8742
www.eparent.com

Provides information and support for families, parents, physicians and professionals in the special needs community. Published 11 times monthly plus a special January issue.

Monthly
ISSN: 0046-9157

Joseph M. Valenzano, Jr., President, CEO & Publisher
Rick Rader MD, Editor-in-Chief
Vanessa B. Ira, Contributing Writer / Editor

7642 Future Reflections
National Federation of the Blind
200 East Wells Street at Jernigan Place
NOP-ONE-

National magazine written specifically for parents and educators of blind children. Each issue addresses various topics important to blind children, their families and to school personnel.

General Resources / Journals

Quarterly

7643 Journal of the Academy of Dermatology
American Academy of Dermatology
9500 W. Bryn Mawr Avenue, Ste 500
Rosemont, IL 60018
847-240-1737
888-462-3376
Fax: 847-240-1859
info@aad.org

A scientific publication serving the clinical needs of the specialty and providing a wide selection of articles on various topics important to continuing medical education of Academy members and the international dermatologic community.

Monthly

Irvin Bomberger, Interim Executive Director

Journals

7644 International Journal of Nursing in Intellectual & Developmental Disabilities
Developmental Disabilities Nurses Association
1501 South Loop 288, Suite 104-PMB 381
Denton, TX 76205
800-888-6733
Fax: 844-336-2329
ddnahq@aol.com
www.ddna.org

Electronic journal for nurses, individuals, families and others interested in promoting health and nursing supports for individuals with intellectual and developmental disabilities. Provides information and resources, educational strategies and policy development on a variety of clinical topics.

Karen Green McGowan, RN, CDDN, President
Wendy Herbers, RN, CDDN, QDDP, Vice President
Linda Coley, RN, CDDN, Secretary

7645 Pediatric Dermatology Journal
Society for Pediatric Dermatology
8365 Keystone Crossing, Suite 107
Indianapolis, IN 46240
317-202-0224
Fax: 317-205-9481
info@pedsderm.net
www.pedsderm.net

Answers the need for new ideas and strategies for today's pediatrician or dermatologist.

6 issues/yr

Kent Lindeman, Executive Director

Newsletters

7646 ABDC Newsletter
Birth Defect Research for Children
976 Lake Baldwin Lane, Suite 104
Orlando, FL 32814
407-895-0802
Fax: 407-566-8341
staff@birthdefects.org
www.birthdefects.org

Offers updated information on the association activities, events and medical updates. Back issues available.

8 pages Quarterly

7647 ACLP Bulletin Newsletter
Association of Child Life Professionals
1820 N Fort Myer Drive, Ste 520
Arlington, MD 22209
501-483-4500
800-252-4515
Fax: 501-483-4482
aclpadmin@childlife.org
www.childlife.org

The Association of Child Life Professionals (formerly Child Life Council) newsletter provides information to promote the well-being of children and families in health care settings. Newsletter is provided to members only.

12 pages Quarterly

Bailey Kasten, COO & Interim CEO
Yvonne Kassimatis, Marketing & Communications
Ramona Spencer, Director, Professional Development

7648 BDRC Newsletter
Birth Defect Research for Children
976 Lake Baldwin Lane, Suite 104
Orlando, FL 32814
407-895-0802
Fax: 407-566-8341
staff@birthdefects.org
www.birthdefects.org

Offers updated information on the association activities, events and medical updates.

8 pages Quarterly

7649 Children's Hopes and Dreams
Wish Fulfillment Foundation
280 Route 46
Dover, NJ 7801
973-361-7366
Fax: 973-361-6627
childrenscharities.org/childrens_wisheso

Dream Newsletter (describes dreams recently fulfilled, events, request and info about programs) available upon request; at no cost. 4 times per year.

10,000 Members

7650 Connecting
5025 E Washington Street, Suite 204
Phoenix, AZ 85034
602-242-4366
800-237-3007
Fax: 602-242-4306
TDD: 602-242-4366
info@raisingspecialkids.org
www.raisingspecialkids.org

Presenting informational and personal articles, calendar of events and news relevant to Arizona families of children with special needs. Subscription is free to families.

Bimonthly

Paula Banahan, President
Blanca Esparza-Pap, Vice President
Joyce Millard Hoie, Executive Director

7651 For Siblings Only
Family Resource Associates
35 Haddon Avenue
Shrewsbury, NJ 7702
732-747-5310
Fax: 732-747-1896

Quarterly newsletter for siblings of children with disabilities, aged four through 10.

S Levine, Editor

7652 Newsline
Federation for Children with Special Needs
529 Main Street, Suite 1M3
Boston, MA 2129
617-236-7210
800-331-0688
Fax: 617-241-0330
TDD: 800-331-0688
fcsninfo@fcsn.org
www.fcsn.org

Carolyn Romano, Editor
Janet Vohs, Editor
Rich Robison, Executive Director

7653 Orphan Disease Update
National Organization for Rare Disorders
55 Kenosia Avenue
Danbry, CT 6810
203-744-0100
800-999-6673
Fax: 203-798-2291
orphan@rarediseases.org
www.rarediseases.org

It provides updates on research, advocacy, and special events, as well as advice and sources of help for caregivers, Web sites of interest, current clinical trials, and funding opportunities.

General Resources / Pamphlets

16 pages 3/year
Sheldon M. Schuster, Chair
Peter L Saltonstall, President & CEO
Pamela Gavin, COO

7654 PAL News
Parent Professional Advocacy League
529 Main Street, Suite 1M3
Boston, MA 2129
617-236-7210
800-331-0688
Fax: 617-241-0330
fcsninfo@fcsn.org
www.fcsn.org

Offers information on medical and technological updates in the area of research on birth defects, support groups and family resources for persons with disabled children.

Quarterly
Rich Robison, Executive Director
Sara Miranda, Associate Executive Director
John Sullivan, Associate Executive Director

7655 Sibling Forum
Family Resource Associates
35 Haddon Avenue
Shrewsbury, NJ 7702
732-747-5310
Fax: 732-747-1896
info@frainc.org
www.frainc.org

Quarterly newsletter for siblings of children with disabilities, aged 10 and up.
Allan Proske, President
Bill Sheeser, Vice President
Sue Levine, Editor

Pamphlets

7656 AAP Education Resource Guide
American Academy of Pediatrics
141 NW Point Boulevard
Elk Grove Village, IL 60007
847-434-4000
800-433-9016
Fax: 847-434-8000
cme@aap.org
www.aap.org

Sandra Hassink, MD, FAAP, President
Benard P. Dreyer, MD, FAAP, President-Elect
?Errol R. Alden, MD, FAAP, Executive Director/CEO

7657 About Children's Eyes
Lighthouse Guild
250 West 64th Street
New York, NY 10023
800-284-4422
info@lighthouseguild.org
www.lighthouseguild.org

How to identify the child with a visual problem.

7658 About Children's Vision: A Guide for Parents
Lighthouse Guild
250 West 64th Street
New York, NY 10023
800-284-4422
info@lighthouseguild.org
www.lighthouseguild.org

Offers a better understanding of the normal and possible abnormal development of a child's eyesight.

7659 Advanced Cancer: Coping with Advanced Cancer
National Cancer Institute
6116 Executive Blvd, Room 3036A
Bethesda, MD 20892
800-422-6237
800-422-6237
TTY: 800-332-8615

Booklet delving into all aspects of everyday living with cancer. Offers information on coping, how children react, facing the unknown, living wills, additional resources and making treatment decisions.

30 pages

7660 Amyloidosis and Kidney Disease
Information Clearinghouse
9000 Rockville Pike
Bethesda, MD 20892
301-496-3583
Fax: 301-907-8906
nddic@info.niddk.nih.gov
www.niddk.nih.gov

Griffin P. Rodgers, M.D., M.A.C.P., Director
Kevin Abbott, Program Director
Kristin Abraham, Program Director

7661 Birth Defects: A Brighter Future
March of Dimes Resource Center
1550 Crystal Drive, Ste 1300
Arlington, VA 22202
914-997-4488
Fax: 914-997-4763
www.marchofdimes.org

7662 Heart Disease, High Blood Pressure, Stroke and Diabetes
Information Clearinghouse
9000 Rockville Pike
Bethesda, MD 20892
301-496-3583
Fax: 301-907-8906
nddic@info.niddk.nih.gov
www.niddk.nih.gov

Griffin P. Rodgers, M.D., M.A.C.P., Director
Kevin Abbott, Program Director
Kristin Abraham, Program Director

7663 How to Find Out More About Your Child's Birth Defect or Disability
Birth Defect Research for Children
976 Lake Baldwin Lane, Suite 104
Orlando, FL 32814
407-895-0802
Fax: 407-895-0824
staff@birthdefects.org
www.birthdefects.org

An informational fact sheet that encourages parents who have a child with a birth defect or disability to become the expert on the child's disability with some suggestions on how to educate themselves.

7664 Interstitial Cyctitis
Information Clearinghouse
9000 Rockville Pike
Bethesda, MD 20892
301-496-3583
Fax: 301-907-8906
ndoc@info.niddk.nih.gov
www.niddk.nih.gov

Griffin P. Rodgers, M.D., M.A.C.P., Director
Kevin Abbott, Program Director
Kristin Abraham, Program Director

7665 Liver Transplantation
American Liver Foundation
1425 Pompton Avenue
Cedar Grove, NJ 7009
973-857-2626
800-223-0179

7666 NPF Benefits of Membership Pamphlets
National Psoriasis Foundation
6600 SW 92nd Avenue, Ste. 300
Portland, OR 97223
503-244-7404
800-723-9166
Fax: 503-245-0626
getinfo@psoriasis.org
www.psoriasis.org

Offers all the pamphlets that are published through the foundation for members. Includes NPF 800 number and reply tear-off card.
Randy Beranek, President & CEO
Stace Bell, PhD, VP, Research & Clinical Affairs
Denice Bradbury, Director, Marketing/Communication

General Resources / Camps

7667 New Challenge: Responding to Families
Federation for Children with Special Needs
529 Main Street, Suite 1M3
Boston, MA 2129
617-236-7210
800-331-0688
Fax: 617-241-0330
fcsninfo@fcsn.org
www.fcsn.org

Addresses the needs of children with emotional, behavioral and mental disorders and their families.

Rich Robison, Executive Director
Sara Miranda, Associate Executive Director
John Sullivan, Associate Executive Director

7668 Nutrition for Early Chronic Kidney Disease
Information Clearing House
9000 Rockville Pike
Bethesda, MD 20892
301-496-3583
Fax: 301-907-8906
nddic@info.niddk.nih.gov
www.niddk.nih.gov

Griffin P. Rodgers, M.D., M.A.C.P., Director
Kevin Abbott, Program Director
Kristin Abraham, Program Director

7669 Nutrition for Later Chronic Disease
Information Clearinghouse
9000 Rockville Pike
Bethesda, MD 20892
301-496-3583
Fax: 301-907-8906
nddic@info.niddk.nih.gov
www.niddk.nih.gov

Griffin P. Rodgers, M.D., M.A.C.P., Director
Kevin Abbott, Program Director
Kristin Abraham, Program Director

7670 Pain, Pain Go Away: Helping Children with Pain
Association for the Care of Children's Health
7910 Woodmont Avenue, Suite 300
Bethesda, MD 20814
301-654-6549
800-808-2224
Fax: 301-986-4553

This booklet teaches parents about pain in children.
1993

7671 Proteinuria
Information Clearinghouse
9000 Rockville Pike
Bethesda, MD 20892
301-496-3583
Fax: 301-907-8906
nddic@info.niddk.nih.gov
www.niddk.nih.gov

Griffin P. Rodgers, M.D., M.A.C.P., Director
Kevin Abbott, Program Director
Kristin Abraham, Program Director

7672 Renal Tubular Acidosis
Information Clearinghouse
9000 Rockville Pike
Bethesda, MD 20892
301-496-3583
Fax: 301-907-8906
nddic@info.niddk.nih.gov
www.niddk.nih.gov

Griffin P. Rodgers, M.D., M.A.C.P., Director
Kevin Abbott, Program Director
Kristin Abraham, Program Director

7673 When Your Child Has a Life-Threatening Illness
Association for the Care of Children's Health
7910 Woodmont Avenue
Bethesda, MD 20814
301-654-6549
Fax: 301-986-4553

A concise, supportive booklet for parents. Sections include initial reactions, hope, communication, other children, impact on marriage, and single parent families.

1983

7674 Wish Fulfillment Organizations
Candlelighters' Childhood Cancer Foundation
7910 Woodmont Avenue, Suite 460
Bethesda, MD 20814
301-657-8401
800-366-2223

A list of groups granting wishes of children with life-threatening, chronic or terminal illnesses, with criteria and contacts.

7675 Young People with Cancer: A Handbook for Parents
National Cancer Institute
BG 9609 MSC 9760, 9609 Medical Center Drive
Bethesda, MD 20892
800-422-6237
TTY: 800-332-8615
www.cancer.gov

Discusses the most common types of childhood cancer, treatments, and side effects and issues that may arise when a child is diagnosed with cancer.

86 pages

7676 Your Kidneys and How They Work
Information Clearinghouse
9000 Rockville Pike
Bethesda, MD 20892
301-496-3583
Fax: 301-907-8906
ndoc@info.niddk.nih.gov
www.niddk.nih.gov

Griffin P. Rodgers, M.D., M.A.C.P., Director
Kevin Abbott, Program Director
Kristin Abraham, Program Director

Camps

7677 Camp Brave Eagle
8326 Nabb Rd.
Indianapolis, IN 46260
317-871-0000
www.campbraveeagle.org

Summer camp for children with bleeding disorders and their siblings.

Angel Couch, Program Director
Jennifer Maahs, Pediatric Nurse Practitioner

7678 Camp Horizon
930 E Woodfield Road
Schaumburg, IL 60173
847-240-1280
866-503-7546
Fax: 847-240-1859
president@aad.org
www.campdiscovery.org

Camp for children with chronic dermatologic conditions. The camp offers the opportunity to experience summer camp and support each other in a setting of acceptance, love and fun.

Brett M. Coldiron, MD, President
Elise A. Olsen, MD, Vice President
Suzanne M. Olbricht, MD, Secretary-Treasurer

7679 Crotched Mountain School & Rehabilitation Center
One Verney Drive
Greenfield, NH 03047
603-547-3311
Fax: 603-547-3232
info@cmf.org
www.cmf.org

Crotched Mountain is a charitable organization with a mission to serve individuals with disabilities and their families, embracing personal choice and development and building communities of mutual support.

William Cossaboon, MS, Director of Education
Jerry Hunter, VP Information Services
Lorrie Rudis, Director of Human Resources

General Resources / Camps

Alabama

7680 Camp ASCCA/Easter Seals
PO Box 21, 5278 Camp Ascca Dr
Jackson's Gap, AL 36861
256-825-9226
800-THE-CAMP
Fax: 256-825-8332
info@campascca.org
www.campascca.org

Camp for children and adults with disabilities, ages 6+.

Matt Rickman, Camp Director
John Stephenson, Administrator
Jocelyn Jones, Secretary

7681 Camp Merrimack
3320 Triana Boulevard
Huntsville, AL 35805
256-534-6455
www.merrimackhall.com

A unique arts half-day camp for children ages 3 through 12; open to children with special needs including Cerebral Palsy, Down Syndrome, autism and others.

Debra Jenkins, Executive Director, Founder
Melissa Reynolds, Program & Operations Dir.
Claire Lindsay, Marketing Manager

7682 Camp Rap A Hope
2701 Airport Blvd
Mobile, AL 36606
251-476-9880
Fax: 251-476-9495
info@camprapahope.org
www.camprapahope.org

A week-long summer camp in Alabama that is open to children between the ages of 7 and 17 who have and have ever had cancer.

Sandy Blount, President
Melissa McNichol, Executive Director
Roz Dorsett, Asst. Director

7683 Camp Smile-A-Mile
PO Box 550155
Birmingham, AL 35255
205-323-8427
888-500-7920
jennifer.amundsen@campsam.org
www.campsam.org

Camp for children who have or have had cancer. Year round programs are provided for the campers and their family at no cost.

Sam Heide, President
Ryan M. Weiss, Vice President
Fred Elliott, Vice President

Arizona

7684 Camp Abilities Tucson
PO Box 86838
Tucson, AZ 85754
520-770-3204
campabilitiestucson@gmail.com
www.campabilitiestucson.org

Comprehensive developmental sports camp for children in middle and high school who are blind, deaf-blind or multiply disabled.

Murry Everson, Camp Director

7685 Camp Civitan
12635 North 42nd Street
Phoenix, AZ 85032
602-953-2944
Fax: 602-953-2946
info@campcivitan.org
www.campcivitan.org

A 501c3 non-profit organization, that has been providing multiple ever-changing programs to meet the needs of children and adults who are developmentally disabled.

Jane Armstrong, Director
Rob Adams, Camp Director
Mary Kellogg, Operations

Arkansas

7686 Camp Aldersgate
Med Camps Coordinator
2000 Aldersgate Road
Little Rock, AR 72205
501-225-1444
Fax: 501-225-2019
info@campaldersgate.net
www.campaldersgate.net

The camps allow children and youth, ages 6-16, who have various medical conditions and physical disabilities to enjoy traditional camping experiences adapted to their abilities.

Sarah C. Wacaster, CEO
Bill Faggard, COO
Kerri Daniels, Dir. Of Development

California

7687 Ability First
1300 E Green Street
Pasadena, CA 91106
626-396-1010
877-768-4600
Fax: 626-396-1021
www.abilityfirst.org

Services include residential camping programs, aquatics, lifespan programs and housing.

Steve Brockmeyer, Chair
John Kelly, Vice Chair
Lori Gangemi, President & CEO

7688 Ability First, Camp Paivika
600 Playground Drive
Cedarpines Park, CA 92332
909-338-1102
Fax: 909-338-2502
jane.garcia@abilityfirst.org
camppaivika.org

Nonprofit camp owned and operated by Ability First to provide outdoor, recreational camping services for children and adults with physical and/or developmental disabilities. Located in the San Bernadino mountains, the camp has a dining lodge and rec room, four cabins, infirmary, program building and pool that are all fully accessible. Camp is available to rent during winter/spring for up to 80 people.

Kelly Kunsek, Camp Director
Ievgeniia (Jade) Garcia, Camper Services Coordinator
Sonia Ramirez, Marketing Manager

7689 All Nations Camp
1908 Grand Avenue
Nashville, TN 37212
760-249-3822
877-899-2780
Fax: 760-249-4492
info@gbod.org
www.gbod.org

Camp for children with disabilities, ages 8 to 18.

Bishop Elaine Stanovsky, President
Eric Park, Vice President
Tim Bias, General Secretary

7690 Camp Alex A. Krem
Camping Unlimited
102 Brook Lane
Boulder Creek, CA 95006
510-222-6662
Fax: 510-223-3046
campkrem@campingunlimited.com
www.campingunlimited.com

Camp serves people of all ages and all disabilities. Summer Program: six one- and two-week sessions of residential or outdoor adventure camps. Year-round: weekend outings throughout the year. Vendorized by the California Regional Centers; camperships are available. Member of the American Camping Association.

Mary Farfaglia, Executive Director
Leon Wong, Program Director

General Resources / Camps

7691 Camp Joan Mier
Ability First
11677 E Pacific Coast Highway
Malibu, CA
310-457-9863
Fax: 310-457-6374
www.kidscamps.com

7692 Camp Ronald McDonald at Eagle Lake
1250 Lyman Place
Los Angeles, CA 90029
310-268-8488
Fax: 310-473-3338
rmhcsc.org/camp/

Camp dedicated to creating a positive long-lasting impact on children with cancer and their families by providing, fun-filled, medically supervised year-round camp program.

Edward Lodgen, President
Jodie Lesh, Vice President
Martin Breidsprecher, Chief Executive Officer

7693 Camp Rubber Soul
325A East Redwood Avenue
Fort Bragg, CA 95437
707-962-0906
www.camprubbersoul.org

Summer camp for children and young adults with special needs that is not affiliated with any church, School District or state program.

Rachel Miller, Director
Sayre Statham, Director

7694 Camp-A-Lot
3030 Market Street
San Diego, CA 92102
619-685-1175
800-800-748
Fax: 619-234-3759
info@arc-sd.com
www.arc-sd.com

Residential camping program for children and adults, ages 7 and up. San Diego locals offered transportation.

David W. Schneider, President/ CEO
Anthony J. DeSalis, Esq., EVP & COO
Rich Coppa, VP of Infra & Facilities/ CIO

7695 Christian Berets
1317 Oakdale Road, Suite 340
Modesto, CA 95355
209-524-7993
Fax: 209-524-7979
www.christianberets.org

A community-based program for children and adults with developmental disabilities.

James Woodhead, President
Carletta Evans Steele, Treasurer
Kelly Luth, Secretary

7696 Dream Street Foundation
324 South Beverly Drive, Suite 500
Beverly Hills, CA 90212
424-333-1371
Fax: 310-388-0302
dreamstreatca@gmail.com
www.dreamstreetfoundation.org

A customized camping program for children with terminal, chronic, and life threatening infirmities. Over 600 children with cancer, AIDS, cystic fibrosis, leukemia, blood disorders and other serious diseases are given the opportunity to enjoy activities.

Patty Grubman, Director

7697 Easter Seal Summer Camp Programs
2645 Pleasant Hill Road
Pleasant Hill, CA
925-689-1777

Offers education, adventure and the experience and enjoyment of living-out-of-doors in a striking and challenging wilderness environment. Serves ages 6 to 60, male and female.

Beverly Mayhall

7698 Gloriana Opera Company
210 N. Corry Street, PO Box 273
Fort Bragg, CA 95437
707-964-7469
Fax: 707-965-9653
info@gloriana.org
www.gloriana.org

Since 1977 superlative music theater productions all year long, plus concerts, childrens workshops and classes.

Diane Larson, President
Ana Lucas, Artistic Director

7699 Junior Wheelchair Sports Camp
Santa Barbara Parks and Recreation Department
1819 Farnam St Suite 701
Omaha, NE 68183
402-444-5900
Fax: 402-444-4921
www.ci.omaha.ne.us/parks

This five-day camp is for children 5-19 years old that are physically disabled. Sports instruction in aquatics, tennis, track and field, basketball, archery and new sports activities introduced each year. The camp counselors and instructors are also physically disabled to provide the children with a role model. Fee based on fundraising efforts.

Colorado

7700 Magic of Music and Dance
PO Box M
Aspen, CO 800-5
970-923-0578
Fax: 970-923-7338
www.kidscamps.com

Connecticut

7701 Mansfield's Holiday Hill
41 Chaffeeville Road
Mansfield Center, CT 6250
860-423-1375
Fax: 860-456-2444
info@holidayrecreation.com
www.holidayrecreation.com/camp

A home not far from home where beautiful fields, forests, facilities and a caring staff support the activities and relationships of our camp families. The camp offers many programs such as: Outdoor Adventure; Tumbling; Dance; Adventure Ropes Course; Swimming; Arts & Crafts; Archery; Tennis and more to thirty boys and girls.

Dudley Hamlin

Florida

7702 Camp Thunderbird
500 E. Colonial Drive
Orlando, FL 32803
407-218-4300
Fax: 407-218-4301
campthunderbird@questinc.org
www.questinc.org

Residential summer camping program for children and adults with a developmental disability. Campers enjoy swimming, sports, nature hikes, canoeing, etc. In short, a real summer camp experience provided by people who understand the physical, and behavioral challenges associated with Down syndrome, autism, Cerebral Palsy, and other developmental disabilities. Camp provides the chance to try new things, learn new skills, and focus on can-do with new friends. 6- & 12-day overnights.

Rosa Figueroa, Camp Coordinator

7703 Easter Seals Camp Challenge
31600 Camp Challenge Road
Sorrento, FL
352-383-4711
Fax: 352-383-0744
www.kidscamps.com

Micheal Currence, Director Camping/Recreation
Melissa Guinta, Summer Camp Director

General Resources / Camps

Hawaii

7704 Camp Erdman YMCA
69-385 Farrington Highway
Waialua, HI
808-637-4615
Fax: 808-637-8874
www.camperdman.net

A specialized youth camp serving the needs of the disabled.

Lance Wihelm, Chair
Steven C. Ai, Vice Chair
Michael A. Pietsch, President & CEO

Illinois

7705 Camp Discovery
American Academy of Dermatology
9500 W. Bryn Mawr Avenue, Ste 500
Rosemont, IL 60018
847-240-1737
Fax: 847-240-1859
jmueller@aad.org
www.campdiscovery.org

A camp for young people with chronic skin conditions. There is no fee and transportation is provided. Five locations: Camp Victory in Millville, PA, Camp Knutson in Crosslake, MN, Camp For All in Burton, TX, Channel 3 Kids Camp in Andover, CT, and Camp Seymour in Gig harbor, WA.

J Mueller, Camp Contact
Irvin Bomberger, Interim Executive Director

7706 Jewish Council for Youth Services
JCYS Camp Red Leaf
180 W. Washington Street, Suite 1100
Chicago, IL 60602
312-726-8891
Fax: 312-726-7920
jthomason@jcys.org
jcys.org

Overnight summer camp for youth and adults with developmental disabilites. Family Camps, respite weekends, trips, and other special events are offered throughout the year.

Jeffery Heftman, President
Adam Tarantur, President Elect
Jennifer Gartenberg, VP, Programming

7707 Olympia
Southern Illinois University
Mail Code 6519
Carbondale, IL
618-453-1423
Fax: 618-453-1445

Located on 6,500 acres of forests and meadows on the shores of Little Grassy Lake, Olympia Camp is for mentally and physically handicapped children and adults. Among the activities offered are arts and crafts, hay wagon rides, canoeing and swimming.

Craig Dittmar

7708 Summer Wheelchair Sports Camp
University of Illinois
1207 S Oak Street, Division of Rehab Education
Champaign, IL
217-333-4606
Fax: 217-333-0248
TTY: 217-333-1970
www.kidscamps.com

7709 Touch of Nature Environmental Center
Southern Illinois University
Carbondale, IL 62901
618-453-6793
Fax: 618-453-1188
webdev@pso.siu.edu
www.pso.siu.edu

Providing a traditional camping experience for non-traditional campers, including recreational and outdoor programs for adults and children with various developmental, mental and physical disabilities as well as learning and behavioral disorders.

Phil Gatton, Director
Dawn Wilson, Administrative Assistant
Tammy Baumharte, Customer Service Specialist

Indiana

7710 Camp Isanogel
7601 W Isanogel Road
Muncie, IN
765-288-1073
Fax: 765-288-3103
isanogel@iquest.net
www.isanogelcenter.og

Thirty-two years of programs for special needs of children through adults.

Karen Kovacn, Executive Director
Monica Sauter, Recreation Director

7711 Camp Millhouse
25600 Kelly Road
South Bend, IN
219-287-9833
Fax: 812-358-4381
www.kidscamps.com

7712 Easter Seal Society
4251 S 600 E
Columbus, IN
812-342-0134
www.kidscamps.com

7713 Happiness Bag Incorporated
3833 Union Road
Terre Haute, IN 47802
812-234-8867
Fax: 812-238-0728
www.happinessbag.org

Serves developmentally disabled age 5-adult; day and residential camp program; after school program; scouting; Special Olympic anticipation (basketball, athletics, bowling, softball and aquatics); and a bowling league.

Trudy Rupska, President
Caren Elrod, Vice President
Jodi Moan, Executive Director

7714 Happy Hollow Children's Camp
3049 Happy Hollow Road
Nashville, IN
812-988-4900
Fax: 812-988-7505
hhcdir@aol.com
www.happyhollowcamp.net

Accepts disabled campers.

Bernard Schrader, Executive Director

7715 Kiwanis Twin Lakes Camp
15543 12th Road
Plymouth, IN
219-941-2750

Serving the orthopedically handicapped children and young adults.

Iowa

7716 Camp Courageous
PO Box 418
Monticello, IA 52310
319-465-5916
info@campcourageous.org
www.campcourageous.org

Over 3,500 disabled campers have attended this recreational and respite care facility. The camp is open 24 hours a day, 365 days a year and operates entirely on donations.

Aly Jonson, Dietary Director
Amanda Brenneman, Assistant Nursing
Amatullah Richard, Communications Director

7717 Camp Courageous of Iowa
PO Box 418
Monticello, IA 52310
319-465-5916
Fax: 319-465-5919
info@campcourageous.org
www.campcourageous.com

General Resources / Camps

A year round residential and respite care facility for individuals with special needs. Campers range in age from 3-80 years old. Activities include traditional activities like canoeing, hiking, swimming, nature and crafts plus adventure activities like caving, rock climbing, etc. Campers with disabilities have opportunities to succeed at challenging activities. This feeling of self-worth can transfer to home, work or school environments.

Aly Jonson, Dietary Director
Amanda Brenneman, Assistant Nursing
Amatullah Richard, Communications Director

7718 Camp Tanager
1614 W Mount Vernon Road
Mount Vernon, IA 52314

319-363-0681
Fax: 319-365-6411
www.camptanager.org

Nonprofit camp for children with disabilities.
Robin Butler

Kentucky

7719 Bethel Mennonite Camp
2773 Bethel Church Road
Clayhole, KY 41317

606-666-4911
Fax: 606-666-4911
grow@bethelcamp.org
www.bethelcamp.org

Roger Voth, Camp Director

7720 Easter Seal Kysoc
2050 Versailles Road
Lexington, KY 40504

859-254-5701
800-233-3260
Fax: 502-732-0783
ek1@cardinalhill.org
www.cardinalhill.org

Designed for the fullest camping experience for children or adults with physical disabilities, blind, deaf, behavior disorders, diabetes and multiple handicaps, ages 7 and up.

Gary Payne, President/ CEO
Heide Miller, CCD, CTRS, Director

Louisiana

7721 Camp Bon Coeur
405 W. Main St.
Lafayette, LA 70501

337-233-8437
Fax: 337-233-4160
www.heartcamp.com

7722 Louisiana Lions Camp for Crippled Children
292 L. Beauford Dr.
Anacoco, LA 71403

337-239-0782
800-348-6567
Fax: 337-239-9975
lalions@lionscamp.org
www.lionscamp.org

Camp for disabled children.
Raymond Cecil III

7723 Med-Camps of Louisiana
102 Thomas Road Suite 615
West Monroe, LA 71291

318-329-8405
Fax: 318-329-8407
info@medcamps.com
www.medcamps.com

Maine

7724 Camp Waban
Waban Projects, Inc.
5 Dunaway Drive
Sanford, ME

207-324-7955
Fax: 207-324-6050
www.kidscamps.com

7725 Pine Tree Camp Children - Adults
149 Front Street
Bath, ME 4530

207-443-3341
Fax: 207-443-1070
ptcamp@pinetreesociety.org
www.pinetreesociety.org

Paul Jacques, Chair
Dean Paterson, 1st Vice Chair
Penny Plourde, 2nd Vice Chair

Maryland

7726 Easter Seals Camp Fairlee Manor
22242 Bay Shore Road
Chestertown, MD

410-778-0566
Fax: 410-778-0567
www.kidscamps.com

7727 Kamp-A-Kom-Plish
9035 Ironsides Road
Nanjemoy, MD 20662

301-870-3226
Fax: 301-870-2620
www.kampakomplish.org

7728 The League at Camp Greentop and The Therapeutic Recreation
League: Serving People with Disabilities
1111 E Cold Spring Lane
Baltimore, MD 21239

410-323-0500
Fax: 410-323-3298
TTY: 410-435-4298
jrondeau@leagueforpeople.org
www.campgreentop.org

Summer residential camp located in the Catoctin Mountain National Park. Since 1937, Greentop has been serving children and adults with physical, cognitive, emotional and multiple disabilities in a completely accessible camp setting. Campers enjoy a traditional camping program. Medical facilities, staffed with registered nurses 24 hours a day. ACA/MD Youth Camp. Year round travel programs also offered.

Jonathon Rondeau, Director
Katrina Johnson, Executive Director

Massachusetts

7729 Camp Ramah in New England Tikvah Program
39 Bennett Street
Palmer, MA 01609

413-283-9771
Fax: 413-283-6661
info@campramahne.org
www.campramahne.org

The Tikvah program is one of the first summer programs for Jewish children with special needs. It continues to grow and evolve as it strives to serve campers with a wide range of special needs including, but not limited to, congitive impairments, autism, cerebral palsy and seizure disorder.

Howard Blas, Tikvah Program Director
Talya Kalender, Director, Camper Care
Benjamin Greene, Director of Education

7730 Camp Ramah in New England (Summer)
39 Bennett Street
Palmer, MA 1069

413-283-9771
Fax: 413-283-6661
www.campramahane.org

8 week sleep-away camp for Jewish adolescents with developmental disabilities. Full camping program includes swimming, Hebrew singing and dancing, sports, arts and crafts, daily services, Kosher food, and Jewish studies classes.

Howard Blas, Director

7731 Camp Ramah in New England (Winter)
35 Highland Circle
Needham Heights, MA

701-449-7090
Fax: 413-283-6661
www.campramahane.org

8 week sleep-away camp for Jewish adolescents with developmental disabilities. Full camping program includes swimming, Hebrew singing and dancing, sports, arts and crafts, daily services, Kosher food, and Jewish studies classes.

Howard Blas, Director

7732 Carroll School Summer Programs
25 Baker Bridge Road
Lincoln, MA 1773

989-879-5199
Fax: 781-259-8852
admissions@carrollschool.org
www.carrollschool.org

Academic and recreational programs designed to improve learning skills and build self-confidence. The school is a tutorial program for students not achieving their potential due to poor skills in reading, writing and math. The summer camp complements the summer school offering outdoor activities in a supportive, non-competitive environment.

Sam Foster, Chair
Josh Levy, Co-Vice Chair
Laura Rehnert, Co-Vice Chair

7733 Handi-Kids/King Solomon Foundation
470 Pine Street
Bridgewater, MA

508-697-7557
Fax: 508-697-1529
handi7557@aol.com
www.handikids.com

A therapeutic recreational facility in Bridgewater, Massachusetts offering after-school programs, special events, school vacation full-week and summer day camp programs. Every individual is welcome regardless of the severity of a child's disability.

Mary L Gallant, Program Director

7734 Massachusetts Easter Seals Camping Program
484 Main Street
Worcester, MA 1608

800-922-8290
Fax: 508-831-9768
TTY: 800-564-9700
www.kidscamps.com

Michigan

7735 Camp Barakel
PO Box 159
Fairview, MI 48621

989-848-2279
Fax: 979-848-2280
info@CampBarakel.org
www.campbarakel.org

Five-day Christian camp experience in mid-August for campers ages 13-55 who are physically disabled, visually impaired, upper trainable mentally impaired or educable mentally impaired, bus transportation provided from locations in Lansing, Flint, Bay City, and Marshall, Michigan.

Lee Brown, Program Director
Mike Alchin, Resident Missionary Staff
Teresa Alchin, Resident Missionary Staff

7736 Camp Fish Tales
2177 Erickson Road
Pinconning, MI 48650

989-879-5199
www.campfishtales.org

Larry Hammond, Chair
Lara Beth Sullivan, Executive Director
Brad Sullivan, Assistant Director

7737 Eric RicStar Winter Music Therapy Summer Camp
4930 S. Hagadorn Rd.
East Lansing, MI 48823

517-353-7661
Fax: 517-355-3292
commusic@msu.edu
www.cms.msu.edu

The purpose of this camp is to provide opportunities for musical expression, enjoyment and interaction for all people with special needs and their siblings.

Cindy Edgerton, Director
Judy Winter, Co-Chair

7738 Indian Trails Camp
0-1859 Lake Michigan Drive NW
Grand Rapids, MI

616-677-5251
Fax: 616-677-2955
www.indiantrails-camp.org

Year round residential camping program for children and adults with physical disabilities.

Lynn Gust, Executive Director

Minnesota

7739 Camp Friendship
Friendship Ventures
10509 108th Street NW
Annandale, MN 55302

952-852-0101
800-450-8376
Fax: 952-852-0123
fv@friendshipventures.org
truefriends.org

Camp Friendship offers kids, teens, and adults the chance to have the time of their lives. The program focuses on building self-esteem and independence, and practicing social skills; and we nurture each person's strengths and abilities and encourage participation in activies at their own pace. Specially designed for persons with developmental, physical or multiple disabilities, special medical conditions, Down syndrome, autism or other conditions. Weekend camps and longer available.

Jon Salmon, Director of Programs and Services
Mel Kloek, Program Director
Dawn Brenner, Director of Health Care

7740 Camp New Hope
Friendship Ventures
53035 Lake Avenue
McGregor, MN 55760

952-852-0101
800-450-8376
Fax: 952-852-0123
fv@friendshipventures.org
truefriends.org

Camp New Hope is a great place for children, teens, and adults to have the time of their lives. The program provides a unique opportunity for having fun, learning skills, boosting confidence, and making friends. Services are specifically designed for persons with developmental, phyisical or multiple disabilities, special medical needs, Down syndrome, autism, or other conditions. Weekend camps and longer available. Other services available throughout the year.

Jon Salmon, Director of Programs and Services
Mel Kloek, Program Director
Dawn Brenner, Director of Health Care

7741 Camp Winnebago
19708 Camp Winnebago Road
Caledonia, MN 55921

507-724-2351
Fax: 507-724-3786
www.campwinnebago.org

We offer one week summer sessions for children and adults with developmental disabilities. We also do integrated youth sessions to allow friends and siblings to attend with our traditional campers. Respite week-ends are offered monthly throughout the year. Travel vacations are also offered as an option. We also have a campground open to the public.

General Resources / Camps

8-12 pages
Terry Chiglo, President
Eileen Loken, Vice President
Jane Palen, Secretary

7742 Courage Camps
Courage Center
3915 Golden Valley Road
Golden Valley, MN 55422
952-852-0101
800-450-8376
Fax: 952-852-0123
truefriends.org

Summer resident camp serving children and adults who have physical or sensory disabilities. Also for children who need the help of a speech clinician. Special sessions include those for children who have been burned, children who have cancer and their siblings, and children who have hemophilia or sickle cell anemia. Offers special outdoor education or leadership sessions for deaf, or physically disabled teens and a sports camp for physically disabled and blind teens.

Jon Salmon, Director of Programs and Services
Mel Kloek, Program Director
Dawn Brenner, Director of Health Care

7743 Courage North
PO Box 1626
Lake George, MN 56458
952-852-0101
800-450-8376
Fax: 952-852-0123
truefriends.org

Jon Salmon, Director of Programs and Services
Mel Kloek, Program Director
Dawn Brenner, Director of Health Care

7744 Eden Wood Center
Friendship Ventures
6350 Indian Chief Road
Eden Prairie, MN
952-852-0101
800-450-8376
Fax: 952-852-0123
fv@friendshipventures.org
truefriends.org

Offers resident camp programs for children, teenagers and adults with developmental, physical or multiple disabilities, Down Syndrome, special medical conditions, Williams Syndrome, autism and/or other conditions. Fishing, creative arts, golf, sports and other activities are available. Creative Options Respite Care offers weekend camps year round for children, teenagers and adults. Ventures Travel offers guided vacations for teens and adults with developmental disabilities or other unique needs.

Jon Salmon, Director of Programs and Services
Mel Kloek, Program Director
Dawn Brenner, Director of Health Care

7745 Knutson
523 N 3rd Street
Brainerd, MN
218-828-7610

Provides a camping program for mentally and physically disabled and emotionally disturbed children and adults. Campers must come with an established group that brings its own counselors. Swimming, sailing, archery, nature study and hiking are among the non-competitive activities.

Robert Larson

7746 Search Beyond Adventures
400 S Cedar Lake Road
Minneapolis, MN 800-8
612-374-4845
800-800-800
www.kidscamps.com

Mississippi

7747 Tik-A-Witha
PO Box 126
Van Vleet, MS
662-844-7577
Fax: 662-680-3164
www.kidscamps.com

Missouri

7748 Sidney R. Baer Day Camp
2 Millstone Drive
Saint Louis, MO
NOP-ONE-

Co-ed day camp serving campers ages 5-12 years old.

Astrid Balzer, Special Needs
Andy Brown, Camp Director

Nebraska

7749 Camp Easter Seals
609 N 60th Road
Nebraska City, NE 800-6
402-578-3992
800-800-650
www.kidscamps.com

New Hampshire

7750 Camp Allen
56 Camp Allen Road
Bedford, NH 03110
603-622-8471
Fax: 603-626-4295
mary@campallennh.org
www.campallennh.org

A summer camp for individuals with disabilities.

Sebastian Grasso, Chair
Bret Cote, Vice Chair
Mary Constance, Executive Director

7751 Camp Dartmouth-Hitchcock
1 Medical Center Drive
Lebanon, NH
603-650-5597
Fax: 603-650-8980
www.kidscamps.com

7752 Crotched Mountain School & Rehabilitation Center
1 Verney Drive
Greenfield, NH 3047
603-547-3311
800-800-966
Fax: 603-547-3232
info@crotchedmountain.org
www.cmf.org

Currently serves children ages 6-22 with multiple-handicaps including: Cerebral Palsy, Spina Bifida, visual and hearing impairments and neurological disabilities, developmental disorders, autism, behavioral and emotional disorders, seizure disorders, spinal cord and head injuries. Member of the National Association of Independent Schools and accredited with the NE Association of Schools and Colleges, Independent Schools of Northern NE.

James W. Varnum, Chair
Donald L. Shumway, President & CEO
Tom Zubricki, CFO

New Jersey

7753 Bancroft Camp
1255 Caldwell Road
Cherry Hill, NJ 8034
856-429-0010
800-774-5516
Fax: 207-729-1603
TTY: 856-428-2697
lynn.tomaio@bancroft.org
www.bancroft.org

Has served as a summer camp for children and adults enrolled in Bancroft programs. The camp recognizes the need for individuals with developmental disabilities to vacation with their families. The camp offers a resort program for people wishing to explore the fascinating coast of Maine or to relax in the clean New England air. Accommodations include accessible rustic cabins and bayfront cottages.

General Resources / Camps

Toni Pergolin, MA, CPA, President & CEO
Charles McLister, COO
Thomas J. Burke, MBA, CFO

7754 Camp Chatterbox
200 Portland Rd A-20
Highlands, NJ 7732

908-301-5451
campchatterbox@gmail.com
www.campchatterbox.org

Joan Bruno, Ph.D., Director

7755 Camp Oakhurst
111 Monmouth Road
Oakhurst, NJ

908-531-0215
www.kidscamps.com

7756 Cross Roads Outdoor Ministries
29 Pleasant Grove Road
Port Murray, NJ 7865

908-832-7264
Fax: 908-832-6593
officemanager@crossroadsretreat.com
www.crossroadsretreat.com

Program for ages 6-15 offers Bible study, worship, swimming, crafts, hiking, canoeing and campfires. Special education program for those with developmental disabilities.

Anthony P. Briggs, Executive Director
Kathy Felch, Office Manager
Kathryn Schaefer, Program Director

New Mexico

7757 Santa Fe Mountain Center
PO Box 449
Tesuque, NM

505-983-6158
Fax: 505-983-0460
sky@santafemc.org
www.sf-mc.com

Camp sessions offered to disabled campers from the ages of 1-20.

Juanita Thorne-Connerty, Vice Chair
Seth R. Fullerton, President
Skye Gray, MS, Executive Director

New York

7758 Advocates for Children of New York
151 W 30th Street, 5th Floor
New York, NY 10001

212-947-9779
Fax: 212-947-9790
info@advocatesforchildren.org
www.advocatesforchildren.org

Mental Health

Eric F. Grossman, President
Jamie A. Levitt, Vice President
Kim Sweet, Executive Director

7759 Camp Sun 'N Fun
Routes 322 & 555
Williamstown, NJ

856-629-4502
Fax: 856-875-1499
www.kidscamps.com

7760 Freedom Camp
Carr Bldg, 188 Genesee St, Suite 109
Auburn, NY 13021

315-253-5465

A summer day camp for youths with disabilities sponsored by Freedom Recreational Services. Freedom Camp is offered in two-week sessions at Casey Park in Auburn, New York.

Mary Ellen Perry, Executive Director

7761 Gow School Summer Programs
2491 Emery Road, PO Box 85
South Wales, NY 14139

716-652-3450
Fax: 716-652-3457
summer@gow.org
www.gow.org

Co-ed summer programs for ages 8-16, offer a balanced blend of morning academics, afternoon/evening traditional camp activities and weekend overnight trips (teen-tours). The primary purpose of these programs is to provide a positive experience while balancing these three elements. Committed to the creation of a positive and enjoyable experience for each participant, by defining and merging the goals of the camp and the school, with those of camper students, their families and educators.

M. Bradley Rogers, Jr., Headmaster
Bekah D Atkinson, Admissions Director

7762 Marist Brothers Mid-Hudson Valley Camp Marist Brothers
1455 Broadway, 9W
Esopus, NY 12429

845-384-6620
Fax: 845-384-6479
kids2@esopuscamps.com
www.esopuscamps.com

Individual camps serve different special people: Special Children Camps 1 & 2; Deaf Camp; Young Adult Camp; Sacred Heart Camp; Sr. Pat's Camp; Camp Hope; Molloy Freshman Camp; and Adult Vacation. Cost varies.

Brother Don Nugent, President
Frances Rurley, Coordinator

7763 Oakhurst
853 Broadway
New York, NY

212-253-8680

Accepts children and young adults who are physically handicapped, ages 8-18. The program includes physical therapy, recreational activities and a work program for teenagers.

Marvin Raps

7764 Programs for Children with Special Health Care Needs
Tower Building
Albany, NY

518-474-2084

Claudia Lee, Acting Director

7765 Programs for Infants and Toddlers with Disabilities: Ages Birth Through 2
Box 2000
Albany, NY 12220

518-473-7016
800-698-4543
TTY: 877-898-5849
dmn02@health.state.ny.us
www.autismgateway.com/resources_NY.html

Donna M Noyes, PhD, Director

7766 Ramapo Anchorage Camp
PO Box 266, Rt. 52/Salisbury Turnpike

NOP-ONE-

Residential program which serves children, ages 4-16, with a wide range of emotional, behavoral, and learning problems. A one-to-one ratio of counselors-to-campers enables children to build healthy relationships, increase self-esteem and improve learning skills. Character values such as honesty, concern for others, responsibility, and the courage to do one's best are encouraged. Campers demonstrate significant gains in their ability to maintain relationships, control impulses and adjust.

North Carolina

7767 Camp Winding Gap
Rural Route 1, Box 56
Lake Toxaway, NC

828-966-4520
Fax: 828-883-8720
www.campwindinggap.com

For boys and girls ages 8-16, with facilities for up to 75 campers. A high staff-camper ratio (less than 1 to 3) of carefully selected counselors provides a nurturing family atmosphere. A few children with disabilities are mainstreamed each session. Must be able to handle horseback riding and rugged terrain, this is a ranch type camp in a farm setting with many animals. Program includes regular camp activities.

Ann Hertzberg, Director

General Resources / Camps

7768 Talisman Programs
64 Gap Creek Road
Zirconia, NC 28790
828-669-8639
888-458-8226
Fax: 828-669-2521
summer@stonemountainschool.com
www.talismansummercamp.com

Talisman Programs offers summer programs for kids ages 8-17 with ADHD, learning disabilities, high functioning autism, or Aspergers Syndrome. Our high-adventure programs include paddling, hiking, rock climbing, an Alpine Tower, swimming, arts and crafts, and many other activities designed to promote communication and cooperation skills. We focus on building social skills and self esteem in 2 and 3 week programs. One session of academics.

Linda Tatsapaugh, Director

Ohio

7769 Camp Allyn
1414 Lake Allyn Road
Batavia, OH
513-732-0240
Fax: 513-735-1461
www.steppingstonecenter.org

A camp for children and adults with disabilities.

Dennis Carter, Associated Director

7770 Highbrook Lodge Camp
12944 Aquilla Road
Chardon, OH
216-791-8118
Fax: 216-791-1101
mmullin@clevelandsightcenter.org
www.clevelandsightcenter.org

A summer residential camp for blind and disabled children, adults and families.

Mike Mullin, Director

Oregon

7771 Easter Seals Oregon Camping Program
5757 SW Macadam Avenue
Portland, OR 800-5
503-228-5108
Fax: 503-228-1352
www.kidscamps.com

7772 Mt Hood Kiwanis Camp
9320 SW Barbur Blvd, Suite 165
Portland, OR 97219
503-272-3288
Fax: 503-452-0062
www.kidscamps.com

Pennsylvania

7773 Briarwood Day Camp
1380 Creek Road
Furlong, PA 18925
215-598-7143
Fax: 215-598-9813
info@briarwood-camp.com
www.briarwood-camp.com

A comprehensive day camp providing lunch and transportation for children with disabilities.

Ted Levin

7774 Camp Lee Mar
450 Route 590
Lackawaxen, PA
570-685-7188
Fax: 570-685-7590
gtour400@aol.com
www.leemar.com

A camp for children with developmental challenges, ages 5-21. Offers a program of academics, speech therapy, vocational training and recreation. The academic program is designed to help each child develop skills in the areas of communication, reading and math. Activities include swimming, boating, team sports, tennis and perceptual motor training.

Ari Segal, MSW, Director
Lynsey Trohoske, BA, Asst. Dir./ Admissions Director
Laura Leibowitz, BA, M.Ed, Asst. Dir./ Academic Coordinator

7775 Camp Yomeca Upper Perkiomen Valley YMCA
476 Pottstown Avenue
Pennsburg, PA 18073
215-679-9622
www.fvymca.org/youth/

The YMCA day camp for children ages 4-18. Small group and camp-wide activities are offered. Streams, woods and trails to explore. Children ages 10-12 also have several overnights offered to them during the summer. Children continue to build upon established skills from earlier years, take on more leadership, challenge and responsibility and strengthen past friendships.

Debbie Rothensberger, Camp Contact; School Age Care Dir

7776 Keystone Community Resources
100 Abington Executive Park
Carks Summit, PA 18411
570-702-8000
Fax: 570-702-8093
LCunningham@keycommres.com
www.keycommres.com

Keystone serves both children and adults with developmental disabilities in a variety of residential settings. Support services include 24 hour supervision, on site nursing services, special and therapeutic recreation programs and psychological and psychiatric services.

Robert Fleese, President
Lisa Cunningham, Director Admissions
Ignatz Deutsch, Founder

7777 Variety Club Camp & Development Center
Variety Club
PO Box 609, 2950 Potshop Road
NOP-ONE-

Year-round camping and recreation facility for children with special needs and their families. Includes summer camping, aquatics, weekend retreats and other specialty programs.

South Carolina

7778 Burnt Gin Camp
SC Department of Health and Environmental Control
Box 101106
Columbia, SC
803-898-0455
Fax: 803-898-0613
www.scdhec.net/hs/mch/burntgin/hsbgin5.htm

A residential camp for children who have physical disabilities and/or chronic illnesses. Camper/staff ratio is 2:1. Four seven-day sessions for 7-15 year olds and two six-day sesssions for 16-19 year olds. Limited to residents of South Carolina.

Marie I Aimone, Camp Director

Tennessee

7779 Camp Easter Seal
750 Old Hickory Blvd, #2-260
Brentwood, TN 37027
615-292-6640
Fax: 615-251-0994
www.tn.easter-seals.org

John Pfeiffer, Chair
Chuck Mataya, Vice Chair
Rita Baumgartner, President & CEO

General Resources / Camps

Texas

7780 Children's Association for Maxiumum Potential CAMP
PO Box 27086
San Antonio, TX 78227
210-671-5411
Fax: 210-671-5225
campmail@campcamp.org
www.campcamp.org

Overnight camping, day-care, respite and rehabilitation to children with severe medical, physical or mental disabilities. Large medical staff enables nationwide acceptance of children with severe problems.

Mike Zerda, Chair
Susan Osborne, Executive Director
Ben Elble, Camp Director

7781 Hughen Center
2849 9th Avenue
Port Arthur, TX 77642
409-983-6659
Fax: 409-983-6408
www.hughencenter.org/contact_us

The Center provides a therapeutic, educational, and recreational program for children with physical disabilities. Physical and occupational therapy are featured. Day and residential.

Jeff Kuchar, Executive Director

7782 Texas Lions Camp
Lions Clubs of Texas
PO Box 290247
Kerrville, TX 78029
830-896-8500
830-896-8500
Fax: 830-896-3666
www.lionscamp.com

The primary purpose of Texas Lions camp is to provide, without charge, a camp for physically disabled, hearing/vision impaired and diabetic children from the State of Texas, regardless of race, religion, or national origin. Our goal is to create an atmosphere wherein campers will learn the can do philosophy and be allowed to achieve maximum personal growth and self esteem. The camp welcomes boys and girls ages 7-16.

Stephen Mabry, Executive Director
Doug Parker, Business Manager
Steven King, Program/Client Service Director

Utah

7783 Camp Kostopulos
4180 Emigration Canyon Road
Salt Lake City, UT 84108
801-582-0700
Fax: 801-583-5176
www.campk.org

One of only a few camps in the Intermountain region that provides recreational opportunities for individuals of all ages with mental or physical disabilities. Activities include fifteen days of swimming, fishing, fieldtrips, nature study, arts and crafts and traditional outdoor adventure games. Five year-round programs offered.

John Miller, Chairman
Rick Lifferth, Vice Chairman
Layne Smith, Vice Chairman

Vermont

7784 Farm and Wilderness Camps
HCR 70, Box 27
Plymouth, VT
802-422-3761
802-422-3761
Fax: 802-422-8660
www.kidscamps.com

Virginia

7785 Camp Baker Services
7600 Beach Road
Chesterfield, VA
804-748-4789
Fax: 804-796-6889
www.veryspecialcamps.com/summer-camps/Camp-Baker-Ser

Year round support services for children and adults with disabilities. Operated by the Richmond Area ARC, programs include: an 8-week summer camp program; weekend congregate respite services; summer day camp (8 wks); spring fling (spring break).

Melissa Wahers, Director
Jolene Loving, Assistant Director
Heather Elliot, Administrative Assistant

7786 Camp Easter Seal East, Camp Easter Seal West
201 E Main Street
Salem, VA 800-3
540-362-1656
Fax: 540-563-8928
www.campeasterseal-va.org

Six and 12 day summer camp sessions for children and adults ages 5 and older with physical disabilities, cognitive disabilities, sensory impairments. Therapeutic recreation activities including swimming, fishing, sports, horseback riding, rock climbing, and more. 26 speech therapy camp children with disabilities ages 8-16. 12 day Spina Bifida Self Help Skills Camp.

Deborah Duerk, Director
Devin Brown, Director

7787 Camp Holiday Trails
400 Holiday Trails Lane
Charlottesville, VA 22903
434-977-3781
Fax: 434-977-8814
www.campholidaytrails.org

A nonprofit camp for children with special health needs, various chronic illnesses. Residential, 1 and 2 week sessions are open June - August; camperships are available. Coed 5-17, nationwide and international. Canoeing, swimming, horseback riding, arts and crafts, drama, ropes course, etc. 24-hr. medical supervision by doctor and nursing staff. Air conditioned cabins.

Tina LaRoche, Executive Director

7788 Makemie Woods Camp Conference Center
PO Box 39
Barhamsville, VA 23011
757-566-1496
800-566-1496
Fax: 757-566-8803
www.makwoods.org

Counselors serve as teachers, friends and activity leaders. The individual is important within the small group. No camper is lost in the crowd, but is an integral partner in the group process. Residential Christian Camp and conference center. Summer camp for children 8-18 special camp for children with diabetes.

Michelle Burcher, Director
Beth Martin, Office Assistant

7789 Overlook
RR 1, Box 203
Keezletown, VA
540-269-2267

A Christian life experience for youth and children, located at the base of the scenic Massanutten Mountains.

Ronald Robey

7790 Triangle D Camp for Children
1701 North Beauregard Street
Alexandria, VA 22311
414-248-1330
800-342-2383

Disabled campers.

Marilyn Caras

907

General Resources / Grant a Wish Foundations

West Virginia

7791 Mountain Milestones Stepping Stones
15 Cottage Street
Morgantown, WV 800-9
304-296-0150
800-800-982
Fax: 304-296-0194
stepping@westco.net
www.kidscamps.com

A nonprofit organization.
Missy Weimex, Recreation Coordinator

Wisconsin

7792 Camp Joy
W7725 Kettle Moraine Drive
Whitewater, WI 53190
262-473-3132
Fax: 262-473-0941
www.campjoy.org

A year round residential camping program for children and adults with intellectual and physical disabilities. Brochure, video, and application available upon request.
Charlie Hatchett, Camp Director
Todd Hatchett, Program & Promotion
Dannett Smith, JBCF Secretary & Promotion

7793 Timbertop Nature Adventure Camp
Stevens Point Area YMCA-Glacier Hollow
1000 Division Street
Stevens Point, WI 54481
715-342-2980
Fax: 715-342-2987
www.glacierhollow.com/timbertop-camp/

For children who can benefit from an individualized program of learning in a non-competitive outdoor setting under the skilled leadership of people who understand the environment and the unique potential of these children.
Pete Matthai, Camp Director

Grant a Wish Foundations

7794 Children's Dream Factory of Maine
400 US Route 1, ATTN: Doris Simard
Falmouth, ME 04105
207-781-3406
800-639-1492

Grants wishes for chronically or seriously ill children from Maine.

7795 Children's Wish Foundation International
8615 Roswell Road
Atlanta, GA 30350
800-323-9474
info@childrenswish.org
www.childrenswish.org

Children's Wish Foundation International is dedicated to bringing joy and hope to seriously ill children and their families world wide by involving the public in putting children first with opportunities to experience the enhanced value and quality of life through the magic of a fulfilled wish.
Linda Dozoretz, Founder

7796 Dream Factory
120 W Broadway, Suite 300
Louisville, KY 40202
502-561-3001
800-456-7556
Fax: 502-561-3004
dfinfo@dreamfactoryinc.org
www.dreamfactoryinc.org

The Dream Factory grants dreams to children disgnosed with critical or chronic illnesses who are 3 through 18 years of age.
David Zukowski, Director of Program Services
Janice Harris, President
Ralph Coldiron, Vice President

7797 Famous Fone Friends
9101 Sawyer Street
Los Angeles, CA 90035
310-204-5683
fonefriends@aol.com
www.famousfonefriends.org

Offers the ability for a sick child's doctor or nurse to arrange for a well-known actor, athlete or other celebrity to call the child.

7798 Freedom's Wings International
324 Charles Street
Coopersberg, PA 18036
800-382-1197
www.freedomswings.org

Freedom's Wings International (FWI) is a non-profit organization run by and for people with physical disabilities. We provide the opportunity for those who are physically challenged to fly in specially adapted sailplanes, either as a passenger or as a member of the flight training program.

7799 Give Kids the World
210 S Bass Road
Kissimmee, FL 34746
407-396-1114
800-995-5437
Fax: 407-396-1207
dream@gktw.org
www.gktw.org

Makes dreams come true for children with life-threatening illnesses and their families with a week-long, cost-free fantasy vacation to our 'story book' village located near central Florida's most beloved attractions.
Sarah Jones, Communications Manager

7800 Magic Moments- Children's Hospital of Alabama
2112 11th Aves., Ste 219
Birmingham, AL 35205
205-939-9372
Fax: 205-939-6717
info@magicmoments.org
www.magicmoments.org

Grants wishes to children four to nineteen living or being treated in Alabama, who have chronic, life-threatening diseases, or who have severe trauma (burns, spinal cord, head trauma).

7801 Make A Wish Foundation of America
4742 N 24th St, Ste 400
Pheonix, AZ 85016
602-279-9474
800-722-9474
Fax: 602-279-0855
www.wish.org

Information and advocacy resources for families and professionals. Includes listings of organizations providing general information and organizations focusing on more specific areas of concern to families and young adults who have disabilities.

7802 Sunshine Foundation
1041 Mill Creek Drive
Feasterville, PA 19053
215-396-4770
800-767-1976
Fax: 215-396-4774
philly@sunshinefoundation.org
www.sunshinefoundation.org

Grants dreams of seriously ill, physically challenged and abused children ages 3-18 whose parents cannot fulfill their request due to the financial strain caused by the child's illness.
Diane Mazzeo, Admin Assistant

7803 Teddi Project
Camp Good Days and Special Times
356 North Midler Avenue
Syracuse, NY 13206
315-434-9477
Fax: 315-434-9590
www.campgooddays.org

Priority given to children from Central Florida and the upstate New York area, especially Buffalo, Rochester, Syracuse, Albany, and Binghamton. Services chronically or terminally ill children ages seven to seventeen.

General Resources / Grant a Wish Foundations

7804 Thursday's Child
PO Box 95
Mt. Hope, WI 53816

608-988-4234
dorothyf@chorus.net

Grants wishes to seriously ill children who live in or are being treated in southwest and south central Wisconsin.

7805 Wish Upon a Star
California Law Enforcement
PO Box 4000
Visalia, CA 93278

559-733-7753
Fax: 559-733-0962
www.wishuponastar.org

Serves children in the state of California. Nonprofit, law enforcement effort designed to grant wishes of children afflicted with high-risk and terminal illnesses.

Carmen Perez, Executive Director

7806 Wish with Wings
3817 Alamo Ave
Ft. Worth, TX 76107

817-469-9474
Fax: 817-275-6005
wish@awishwithwings.org
www.awishwithwings.org

Founded in 1982, grants wishes for children ages three-eighteen years of age who have life threatening diseases. The organization serves children who reside in or are receiving treatment in the state of Texas.

Kim Christian, Executive Director

7807 Wishing Star Foundation
139 S Sherman
Spokane, WA 99202

509-744-3411
Fax: 509-744-3414
info@wishingstar.org
www.wishingstar.org

Serves Idaho, eastern and western Washington. Grants wishes to children ages three to twenty-one with life-threatening diseases.

Paula Nordgaarden, Executive Director

7808 Wishing Well Foundation
3000 West Esplanade Ave, Ste 100
Metaine, LA 70002

888-663-9474
www.wishingwellusa.org

Grants wishes to children in the St. Louis area only who are chronically or terminally ill.

Section III
The Human Body

Cardiovascular System

The cardiovascular system, also known as the circulatory system, consists of the heart and the blood vessels. The functions of the cardiovascular system include the following:

- To maintain the continual flow of blood throughout the body to provide cells with oxygen and vital nutrients

- To assist in the removal of carbon dioxide and other waste products from cells

The Heart

Anatomy
The heart, a hollow, muscular organ the approximate size and shape of a clenched fist, is an efficient pump that maintains the continuous flow of blood through the vessels to all areas of the body. It is located between the lungs in approximately the center of the chest, with its right margin located under the right side of the breastbone (sternum) and the remaining areas pointing toward the left. The "tip" or the lowest point of the heart, known as the apex, rests on the diaphragm and is situated beneath the left nipple.

The heart consists of four chambers and is divided into left and right sides by a thick, fibrous, central partition known as the septum. The upper chambers of the heart are known as atria, and the lower chambers are called ventricles. Each chamber is referred to by its location: i.e., the left and right atria and the left and right ventricles. The atria are smaller and have thinner walls than the ventricles. The walls of the chambers of the heart are composed of specialized cardiac muscle known as the myocardium, and their internal surfaces are lined with a thin layer of smooth membrane tissue called the endocardium.

The heart and the roots of its major blood vessels are surrounded by a membrane (pericardium) that consists of two fibrous layers. The pericardium has a tough outer layer (fibrous pericardium) that surrounds the heart like a loose-fitting bag, providing space for the heart to beat. The inner layer (serous pericardium) consists of an innermost "sheet" (visceral layer) that is attached to the heart and an outer most layer (parietal layer) that lines the inside of the fibrous pericardium. A space between the inner layers contains a thin film of fluid that lubricates the opposing surfaces of the inner membranes, enabling the heart to beat without friction.

Cardiac Function
Contraction of the heart muscle is termed systole, whereas relaxation is known as diastole. The atria and ventricles beat in a precise rhythmic pattern. One cycle of this pattern is known as a heartbeat. As the atria contract, they force blood into the ventricles. Once the ventricles fill with blood, they contract, pumping blood either to the lungs or out to the rest of the body.

The pumping action of the heart also involves the heart valves at the entrance to and exit from the ventricles. These valves control and direct the flow of blood through the heart. Two heart valves separate the atria from the ventricles (atrioventricular valves), preventing the backward flow of blood into the atria during ventricular contraction. The valves include the mitral or bicuspid valve, situated between the left atrium and left ventricle, and the tricuspid valve, located between the right atrium and right ventricle. In addition, two heart valves (semilunar valves) are situated between the two ventricles and the large blood vessels that transport blood away from the heart during ventricular contractions. The aortic semilunar valve, located where the major artery of the body (aorta) arises from the base of the left ventricle, enables blood to flow from the left ventricle into the aorta while preventing the backward flow of blood into the ventricle. The pulmonary semilunar valve, situated where the pulmonary artery arises from the base of the right ventricle, enables blood to flow from the right ventricle to the lungs while preventing the backward flow of blood.

"Oxygen-poor" or deoxygenated blood that has circulated through the body enters the right side of the heart into the right atrium through two large veins (the superior and inferior vena cava). The blood is then pumped through the tricuspid valve into the right ventricle. When the ventricle contracts, blood is pumped through the pulmonary semilunar valve into the pulmonary artery and on to the lungs, where the exchange of oxygen and carbon dioxide occurs. Oxygen-rich blood is returned to the left atrium by way of four pulmonary veins and is pumped through the bicuspid valve into the left ventricle. When the ventricle contracts, blood is pumped through the aortic semilunar valve into the aorta for circulation to the body's tissues.

The heart muscle or myocardium requires an ongoing supply of oxygen and other nutrients to function efficiently; thus, the coronary circulation transports vital oxygen-rich (oxygenated) and nutrient-rich arterial blood to the heart muscle and returns deoxygenated, nutrient-poor blood back to the venous system. Blood is transported to the myocardium by way of the left and right coronary arteries, which are the first branches of the aorta. Once blood is circulated to the myocardium, supplying the heart with oxygen and other nutrients, it passes into the cardiac veins, which then empty into the coronary sinus and into the right atrium.

Each heartbeat, also known as a cardiac cycle, consists of the contraction (systole) and relaxation (diastole) of the atria and ventricles. In order for the heart to pump efficiently, the different areas of the heart and the cardiac muscle fibers must work together in an exact sequence. Precise coordination is achieved through the transmission of electrical impulses originating from the heart's "pacemaker" (the sinoatrial node at the apex of the right atrium). These signals are then relayed to the various areas of the heart via a complex system of fibers (atrioventricular node, bundle of His, and Purkinje fibers). The electrical transmissions are delivered with precision timing to various areas of the heart, resulting in a rhythmic beat.

The Blood Vessels

Blood vessels are like a system of complex tubing of different sizes through which blood flows to various parts of the body. Different types of blood vessels have different purposes. For example:

- Some vessels ensure the movement of blood from one part of the body to another.

- Other much smaller vessels (i.e., the capillaries) facilitate the exchange of certain nutrients and waste products between the blood and the fluid surrounding cells within bodily tissues.

Cardiovascular System

Function

There are several types of blood vessels including arteries, arterioles, capillaries, venules, and veins. The arteries, which carry blood away from the heart, progressively subdivide into smaller and smaller vessels known as arterioles, which control blood flow into the minute vessels known as capillaries. The arterioles help to regulate proper arterial blood distribution and pressure by constricting or expanding as necessary. The thin walls of microscopic capillaries facilitate the exchange of nutrients and waste products between the blood and tissue fluid surrounding the cells. For example, oxygen and glucose move from the blood in the capillaries to the fluid surrounding cells and then into the cells themselves; in contrast, carbon dioxide and other waste products move from the cells into the blood within the capillaries. The oxygen-poor blood then flows from the capillaries into the small blood vessels known as venules. The venules join with other venules and progressively increase in size, becoming larger veins that transport the blood toward the heart.

The systemic circulation also includes a specialized group of vessels known as the hepatic portal circulation, within which blood flow follows a somewhat different route. Veins from certain organs, such as the stomach, intestines, spleen, pancreas, and gallbladder, do not transport blood directly into the inferior vena cava but, rather, into the hepatic portal vein, which carries blood to veins, venules, and capillaries within the liver. Nutrients pass from the blood in the capillaries into liver cells where various toxic substances are filtered from the blood. Hepatic veins carry blood from the liver and rejoin the systemic circulation via the inferior vena cava.

Structure

Arteries and veins consist of three layers including an outermost layer (tunica adventitia), a middle layer of smooth muscle (involuntary muscle) tissue (tunica media), and an inner lining (tunica intima or endothelium). The middle layer of arteries is thicker than that of veins, enabling the arteries to withstand the pressure of ventricular contractions. In contrast, blood returning to the heart via the veins remains at a relatively low pressure. The passage of blood through the veins is assisted by involuntary muscle that compresses the walls of the veins; in addition, veins have one-way valves that prevent the backward flow of blood.

Capillaries have extremely thin walls and cannot be seen by the naked eye. They consist of only one layer (tunica in tima), enabling oxygen and certain wastes to easily pass through them.

Fetal Blood Circulation

Because the developing fetus must obtain nutrients and oxygen from the mother's blood, the fetal circulation differs somewhat from the circulation after birth. During pregnancy, blood vessels carry fetal blood to the placenta, where oxygen and nutrients are exchanged between the fetal and maternal blood supply, and then return blood to the fetus. Two relatively small umbilical arteries carry deoxygenated blood, whereas a larger umbilical vein carries oxygen-rich blood. The fetal circulation also includes vascular channels or openings (e.g., ductus venosus, ductus arteriosus, foramen ovale), enabling most blood to bypass the developing liver and lungs. In most cases, once an infant is born and the pulmonary circulation is established, such vascular channels close and the umbilical blood vessels collapse soon after birth.

Cells

The human body consists of literally trillions of atoms, molecules, and cells that are organized in several "structural levels."

Atoms and molecules. Atoms of oxygen, sodium, nitrogen, and carbon, for example, are the infinitesimal components of the most basic level of living matter of the body. Atoms link to one another to form molecules.

Cells. These are the smallest structural units that are able to live independently. The human body has billions of cells that are functionally integrated to perform the complex, vital tasks necessary for sustaining life. Cells are organized in the following ways:

- Tissues. Bodily tissues are organizations of structurally similar, specialized cells that carry out a common function.

- Organs. The organs of the body are groupings of two or more different types of tissues incorporated into a functional, structural unit to perform certain, specialized functions.

- Bodily systems. These comprise the final level of structural organization within the body. Bodily systems consist of several, interdependent organs that work together to perform integrated functions.

Certain mechanisms enable cells of the body to conduct activities that are vital for ongoing growth and survival. These include the processes of metabolism and homeostasis.

Metabolism

Metabolism refers to all the physical and chemical processes occurring within the body's tissues and includes catabolism and anabolism. Catabolism refers to the breakdown of large, complex substances into simpler, smaller substances, usually resulting in the release of energy. During anabolism, complex substances are built up from simpler substances, usually resulting in consumption of energy. The processes of respiration, circulation, digestion, and excretion, for example, collectively enable the body to provide those substances required for metabolism and remove the byproducts or waste products of metabolism. Abnormal changes in genetic material (mutations) or inherited defective genes may cause inborn errors of metabolism, affecting the body's ability to function properly.

Homeostasis

Homeostasis refers to the processes by which the body maintains a balanced internal environment (equilibrium). In order to maintain homeostasis, the body requires oxygen, water, other nutrients, and regulated atmospheric pressure and body temperature, for example. Because disturbances from the external environment as well as cellular activity continually challenge internal equilibrium, the body has ongoing self-regulating systems (feedback systems) that induce the responses necessary to maintain or restore homeostasis. For example, abnormally decreased levels of oxygen in the blood are counteracted by increased breathing rates that restore normal blood oxygen levels.

Cells

Cells are extremely complex, containing several subcellular structures vital to life. Human cells vary greatly in size and shape and are adapted for their specific functions. However, most cells are similar in structure. They contain fluid material known as cytoplasm surrounded by a thin, outer membrane (plasma membrane). The plasma membrane separates the fluid and specialized structures (organelles) within each cell from the fluid that surrounds and bathes the cells of the body. The cytoplasm of most human cells contains a circular, membrane-bound structure known as the nucleus.

Plasma Membrane

The plasma membrane serves to keep cells intact. In addition, it regulates the entry of oxygen and certain vital nutrients into cells and enables the passage of carbon dioxide and other waste materials out of cells. Certain protein molecules on the surface of the plasma membrane also bind with other protein molecules, activating particular cellular functions.

Cytoplasm

The cytoplasm is essentially the "living matter" of the cell, containing the fluid that comprises the cell's inner environment and the specialized parts known as organelles. The organelles include the following:

- Ribosomes are relatively tiny particles that function as "protein factories." They produce proteins, which are large molecules consisting of combinations of certain chemical "building blocks" (amino acids). Proteins play an essential role in the body. Particular proteins serve as the source of "building materials" for certain tissues and organs of the body (e.g., muscle, skin, blood, etc.). Other protein compounds known as enzymes accelerate the rate of chemical reactions in the body. Proteins also play an essential role in the elimination of waste materials and have many other functions.

- Endoplasmic reticulum (ER) is a complex network of small tubular membranes arranged in complex folds. This network winds throughout the cytoplasm of a cell. Passageways within the endoplasmic reticulum transport proteins and other substances to different areas within a cell. Rough ER has a rough texture due to the presence of ribosomes attached to its outer surface. Carbohydrates, fats, and certain types of proteins are manufactured within smooth ER.

- The Golgi apparatus, which is located near the nucleus, is a system of microscopic, stacked membranous sacs and spaces. Small "bubbles" or sacs (vesicles) from the smooth ER transport newly produced proteins to the Golgi apparatus, where they fuse with the Golgi sacs. The Golgi apparatus then processes and modifies the proteins and packages them into small vesicles. These vesicles break away and eventually fuse with the plasma membrane, at which point they break open and release their contents outside of the cell for transport to other cells.

- Centrioles are typically paired rod-like structures that participate in cell division.

- Mitochondria are tiny organelles that have double membranes and sacs with inner, folded partitions. Known as the "power plants" of the cells, the mitochondria serve as the major source of cellular energy production due to their complex, ongoing chemical reactions.

Cells

- Lysosomes are the major digestive units of cells. Enzymes within lysosomes break down (digest) particles of nutrients as well as certain invading particles such as bacteria.

- Cilia are hair-like projections on the surfaces of certain cells that move together in a wave-like manner. For example, cilia within the mucous membranes of the respiratory tract (respiratory mucosa) propel mucus upward and out of the tract.

Nucleus

The nucleus regulates cellular activities by controlling the functions of the organelles and cell reproduction. It is surrounded by a nuclear envelope that encloses a cellular material within the nucleus known as nucleoplasm. Pores within the nuclear envelope's membranes enable the interior of the nucleus to "communicate" with the cell's cytoplasm. The nucleoplasm of the nucleus contains several structures including the nucleolus and chromatin.

The nucleolus regulates the formation of ribosomes within the nucleus. Ribosomes then move through the nuclear envelope to the cell's cytoplasm where they engage in protein production.

Chromatin, the material within the nucleus from which chromosomes are created, consists of thread-like structures comprised of protein and deoxyribonucleic acid (DNA). DNA is the carrier of the genetic code and is described as a "double helix" because of its relatively long, spiraling, ladder-like structure. It consists of strands of certain chemical groups that are linked by pairs of substances known as "bases." There are four types of bases including adenine, which always pairs with thymine, and the base cytosine, which always pairs with guanine. Therefore, the sequence of bases on one strand of the helix coincides with the sequence on the other strand, enabling DNA molecules to duplicate before cell division.

Chromosomes

During the division and reproduction of cells, DNA condenses and gradually forms into the rod-like structures known as chromosomes. The DNA of the chromosomes carries the genetic information that controls the ultimate growth, development, and functioning of the body and determines the expression of certain inherited traits, such as blood groups, various physical characteristics (e.g., hair color, eye color, height, etc.).

The cell that is produced when an egg (ovum) is fertilized by a sperm is known as a zygote. With the first and each subsequent division of the zygote, chromosomes within the zygote's nucleus are duplicated. Therefore, in most cases, all cells in the human body contain the same chromosomal material. In rare cases, some individuals may have some cells that contain differences in certain genetic material (mosaicism) due to an error in cellular division.

The nuclei of cells (except for ova and sperm) normally contain 46 individual chromosomes, one of each pair from the mother and the other from the father. Chromosome pairs are numbered from 1 to 22 with a 23rd pair consisting of one X chromosome from the mother and an X or a Y chromosome from the father. Males have an X and a Y chromosome and females have two X chromosomes within the 23rd pair. Each chromosome has a long arm designated "q" and a short arm designated "p." Both arms are further divided into numbered bands. Every individual chromosome contains thousands of genes, which are the hereditary units that contain segments of DNA. Genes function within cells by regulating the production of proteins. The 46 human chromosomes collectively contain approximately 100,000 genes that, together, are referred to as the "human genome."

Chromosomal Disorders

In some cases, due to certain abnormalities during cellular division (meiosis or mitosis), individuals may have abnormalities in the structure or number of chromosomes in the nuclei of cells of the body. There may be extra or missing whole chromosomes or chromosomal material within all or some of the body's cells. Because chromosomes contain many genes, the range and severity of associated symptoms and physical findings may vary greatly, depending upon the exact nature and location of the chromosomal abnormality.

RNA

Genes, which are sections of DNA, regulate the production of certain proteins. Ribonucleic acid or RNA is essential in "decoding" the inherited instructions within genes. RNA is similar in structure to one strand of DNA, with some differences-e.g., replacement of the base thymine with uracil. During the formation of RNA, a strand of DNA "unwinds" and a duplicate copy of a gene sequence is created. This copy is known as messenger RNA or mRNA. The mRNA migrates from the nucleus to the cytoplasm, promoting protein production in the ribosomes and endoplasmic reticulum. The ribosomes use information within the mRNA molecule to translate chemical "building blocks" known as amino acids into a properly sequenced protein strand.

Cellular Reproduction: Mitosis

Most cells of the body are replicated or reproduced during a complex process known as mitosis. During mitosis, a single cell divides in order to form two "daughter cells" with chromosomes identical to those within the original cell. The process of mitosis enables the body to produce new cells, to replace cells that have been damaged or lost due to injury or disease, and to replace cells that have aged and no longer function efficiently.

Sometimes mitosis may become uncontrolled, resulting in the development of an abnormal mass of replicating cells known as a neoplasm. Such growths may be noncancerous (benign tumors) or cancerous (malignant).

Cellular Reproduction: Meiosis

Reproductive cells in the male and female sex glands (gonads, including the testes and ovaries) carry out a different form of cell division known as meiosis. During mitosis, one cell division occurs, creating two daughter cells-each of which contains 46 chromosomes. Unlike mitosis, two cellular divisions occur during meiosis, resulting in four daughter cells-each of which contains half of the chromosomes (i.e., 23 chromosomes).

Genetic Mutations

During the processes of mitosis and meiosis, the chromosomes within an original cell and thus its genetic material (DNA) are replicated and passed along to its daughter cells. Sometimes, errors may occur during this replication process, resulting in small changes or mutations in genetic composition. Such genetic mutations are passed along with every subsequent division of the daughter cell. For example, a genetic mutation may occur during the production of a reproductive cell (ovum or sperm). If that cell is eventually involved in fertilization, the resultant zygote and all of its reproduced cells will contain the same genetic error. Thus, every cell of the developing embryo and fetus will contain the identical mutant gene.

Genes function within cells by directing the manufacture of a particular protein. Therefore, mutations of a particular gene may impair the appropriate production of its protein. The effects of a particular gene mutation depend upon the function of its protein within the body. Disorders that result due to such mutations are termed genetic disorders.

Genetic Disorders

Human traits are the result of the interaction of two genes, one received from the mother and one received from the father. There are typically two genes engaged in the regulation of a particular protein. If one such gene changes or mutates and "overrides" the instructions of the normal gene on the other chromosome, the abnormal gene is said to be dominant. If the mutated gene is not expressed and is "masked" by the normal gene on the other chromosome, the mutated gene is termed recessive. In such cases, two copies of the mutated gene are required for possible expression of the disease trait.

Genetic disorders may be classified into unifactorial and multifactorial defects. Unifactorial genetic disorders result due to abnormalities of a single gene or gene pair. Such disorders may be autosomal or X-linked.

In autosomal dominant disorders, the presence of a single copy of the disease gene results in the disorder. The mutated gene "overrides" or dominates the other normal gene. An affected individual may have inherited the disease gene from one of his or her parents, or the disease may arise as a result of an abnormal change (mutation) that occurred randomly, for unknown reasons (sporadically). If an individual with an autosomal dominant disorder has children, all offspring have a 50 percent risk of inheriting the defective gene.

In autosomal recessive disorders, two copies of the same disease gene are necessary for an individual to potentially develop the disorder. If both parents carry a single copy of the disease gene, all offspring have a 25 percent risk of inheriting both disease genes and expressing the disorder. Fifty percent of their children risk being carriers, and 25 percent may receive both normal genes for that trait.

In X-linked disorders, the disease gene is located on the X chromosome. As discussed earlier, females have two X chromosomes, whereas males have one X chromosome from the mother and one Y chromosome from the father. In females, certain disease traits on the X chromosome may be "masked" by the presence of a normal gene on the other X chromosome. In other cases, certain disease traits may not be fully masked by the normal gene; as a result, some females who carry a single copy of such a disease gene (heterozygous carriers) may express some of the symptoms associated with the disorder. In such cases, heterozygous females often have more variable, less severe symptoms than affected males. Because males have only one X chromosome, if they inherit such a disease gene, they generally express the physical characteristics or other findings associated with the disease and are typically more severely affected than females. Males with X-linked disorders transmit the disease gene to their daughters but not to their sons. Females with one copy of such a disease gene have a 50 percent risk of transmitting the gene to their daughters and their sons.

In multifactorial disorders, susceptibility to a disorder is determined by the interaction of several different genes, possibly in association with the involvement of certain environmental factors.

Tissues

As mentioned above, tissues are groups of structurally similar cells that perform a common function. Different tissues within the human body may vary greatly in terms of the size, shape, and specific functioning of their cells.

There are four main types of tissue in the human body including epithelial tissue, connective tissue, muscle tissue, and nervous tissue.

Epithelial tissue or epithelium covers the surfaces of the body, lines most of its hollow structures or cavities, and serves to provide protection and support. In addition, some epithelial tissues permit the absorption of certain nutrients (e.g., oxygen into the blood); help to protect the body against invading microorganisms; or produce and release certain secretions. The cells within epithelial tissue are tightly packed together and contain no blood vessels; however, blood vessels within underlying connective tissue provide epithelial cells with nutrients. Different types of epithelial tissue are categorized based upon cellular shape and thickness.

Connective Tissue

The purpose of connective tissue, the most widely distributed tissue of the body, is to bind together and, along with the skeleton, provide a supporting framework to bodily tissues and organs. The shape and arrangement of connective tissue cells and the intercellular substance between such cells differ depending upon the type of connective tissue. There are several major forms of connective tissue in the body including the following:

- Areolar tissue, which consists of cells embedded in webs of loosely arranged fibers, supports and provides form to most internal organs of the body.

- Adipose tissue, which consists of fat cells within a mesh of areolar tissue, serves to insulate the body against heat loss, protect and cushion certain areas of the body, and store fat as a future energy source.

- Fibrous connective tissue, which consists primarily of parallel rows of white collagen fibers, are the cords of strong, dense, flexible tissue that connect muscle to bone (tendons). Collagen is the major structural protein of the body.

- Bone, the hardest connective tissue of the body, provides a supportive framework, assists in movement, and houses bone marrow.

- Cartilage, which has the consistency of firm or gel-like plastic, helps to absorb shock and provides flexibility.

- Blood, interestingly, is considered to be a type of connective tissue. Even though it has a different function in comparison to other connective tissues, it does have an extracellular liquid matrix (plasma). Plasma has several functions including providing a defense against invading microorganisms, repairing damage to blood vessels and tissues through blood clotting, and transporting oxygen, vital nutrients, and waste products.

The purpose of the body's muscle tissue is to enable movement through muscle contraction and relaxation. The nervous tissue of the body includes specialized cells that ensure ongoing, rapid communication between structures of the body and the control of bodily functions necessary to maintain life.

Dermatologic System

The dermatologic system includes the skin, the largest organ of the body, and its derivatives, such as the skin glands, the hair, and the nails. The skin, the sheet-like, outermost covering of body tissue, has several vital functions:

- To serve as a sensory organ. The skin's millions of sensory nerve endings (receptors) serve as somatic sense organs, enabling the body to respond to pain, variations in temperature, pressure or touch sensations, and other important changes in the surrounding environment.

- To help protect the human body from the harmful effects of the sun, chemicals, invading microorganisms, injuries, fluid loss, and other hazards.

- To assist in normalizing the body's temperature through the regulation of blood flow close to the body's surface and sweat secretion. For example, when the body is too cold, blood vessels within the skin constrict to help conserve body heat. When the body is too hot, blood vessels within the inner layer of the skin (dermis) widen (dilate) and the sweat glands secrete perspiration to cool the body.

The skin comprises several tissue layers including a thin, outermost layer (epidermis); a thicker, inner layer (dermis); and a thick underlying layer of subcutaneous tissue, which is a loose layer of connective tissue and fat. The subcutaneous tissue helps to insulate the body from extremes in temperature, protects underlying tissues from injury, and serves as a stored energy source.

Epidermis

The epidermis, which serves as the protective outer layer of skin, is made up of tightly packed cells (epithelial cells) that are arranged in layers. The thickness of the epidermis is variable, depending on its function; for example, it is relatively thick on the palms of the hands, yet comparatively thin on the eyelids.

The outermost layer of the epidermis (stratum corneum epidermidis) consists of dead cells that create a tough, protective covering. As the dead cells are sloughed off, they are replaced by new cells that are produced by rapidly dividing cells within the innermost layer of the epidermis (stratum germinativum). As new cells rise upward though cellular layers (strata) and approach the surface, their cytoplasm i.e., the inner substance of cells other than the nucleus is replaced by the tough protein keratin. In addition, specialized cells (melanocytes) within the deepest layer of the epidermis produce melanin, a pigment that gives coloration to the skin.

Dermis

The dermis, the innermost layer of skin, consists of connective tissue; lymph vessels, blood vessels, sensory nerve endings (skin receptors), and muscle fibers; as well as other specialized structures, including sweat glands, sebaceous glands, and hair follicles.

The uppermost portion of the dermis contains rows of peg-like projections (dermal papillae) that help bind together the dermal and epidermal layers (dermal-epidermal junction) and form the characteristic grooves and ridges (dermatoglyphic patterns) on the skin of the palms and tips of the fingers. Such ridges, which are unique to each individual, develop before birth.

The deeper portion of the dermis contains a network of fibers including those that provide the skin with the necessary toughness (collagen fibers) as well as elasticity and the ability to stretch (elastic fibers). The number of elastic fibers decreases with advancing age and the level of fat stored within the subcutaneous tissue is also reduced. Consequently, the skin loses its elasticity.

Skin Glands

The sweat glands within the dermis are classified according to their location and type of secretion. These glands include the eccrine and apocrine glands.

The eccrine glands are the most widespread sweat glands in the body. Their function is to produce sweat or perspiration, which helps to eliminate certain waste products (e.g., uric acid, etc.) and to maintain a constant body temperature.

The apocrine glands, larger glands that produce a thicker secretion than that of the eccrine glands, are primarily located under the arms (axilla) and around the genitals. Such glands begin to function during puberty.

The dermis also contains sebaceous glands, tiny glands that open into hair follicles. They produce an oily secretion known as sebum that helps to lubricate the hair and skin and protect the skin from drying. Sebum secretion increases during adolescence (due to increased levels of certain sex hormones); however, it decreases during later adulthood, contributing to skin wrinkling and cracking.

Hair

When epidermal cells grow into the dermis, a small tube called a hair follicle may be formed. The growth of a hair begins from a tiny cluster of cells (hair papilla) at the base of the follicle. New hair replaces any that has been cut or plucked, for example, as long as the hair papilla is alive. The hair itself is a threadlike structure consisting of dead cells filled with keratin. The root is that portion of the hair that remains hidden within the follicle, whereas the shaft is the visible portion of the hair. A particular hair color results from the amount and specific form of the pigment melanin that has been produced by melanocytes at the base of the hair follicle. The straightness or curliness of the hair depends upon the shape of the hair follicle.

A few areas of the body are hairless, including the palms of the hands, the soles of the feet, and the lips. Most hair on the body is fine and barely visible, with the most visible hair typically including that on the scalp, the eyebrows, and the eyelashes. Coarse hair also typically develops under the arms and in the pubic area during puberty (i.e., in response to the secretion of certain hormones). In addition, most males also develop coarser hair in the facial area, on the trunk, and on the arms and legs.

Skin Receptors

The dermis also has sensory nerve endings (skin receptors) that function as sense organs (i.e., somatic sense organs), transmitting messages to the brain concerning temperature, touch, pressure, and pain. For example, Pacini's corpuscle receptors, which are located deep within the dermis, detect pressure on the surface of the skin. Meissner's corpuscle receptors, which are usually close to the skin's surface, detect light touch sensations. Other skin receptors include those that detect other touch sensations, cold, heat, vibration, or pain.

Nails

The nails are produced when epidermal cells on the ends of the fingers and toes fill with the tough protein keratin. The nail body is the visible portion of the nail, whereas the remainder of the nail, known as the nail root, is hidden by a fold of skin (cuticle). A portion of the nail body that is closest to the root has a white, crescent-shaped area called the lunula. Tissue underneath the nail, known as the nail bed, contains many blood vessels, causing it to appear pinkish in color.

Digestive System

The digestive system consists of organs that break down food into small chemical components that ultimately may be used by cells of the body for energy (metabolism), growth, and repair. It includes the alimentary canal or gastrointestinal (GI) tract, which is the long, hollow passageway through which food passes, as well as associated organs, such as glands whose secreted juices help to break down (digest) food. Organs that comprise the GI tract include the mouth, pharynx, esophagus, stomach, small intestine, large intestine, and anus. Associated organs include the tongue, teeth, gallbladder, and digestive glands, such as the salivary glands, pancreas, and liver.

Nutrients

The foods of an individual's diet primarily include water as well as other nutrients necessary for growth and development. These include proteins, which play an essential role in cell repair and replacement; vitamins; carbohydrates, which serve as the primary energy source and assist in the breakdown and metabolism of other nutrients; fats; and minerals. Most minerals and vitamins may be absorbed into the blood circulation from the digestive system with no change in structure. However, other nutrients must be broken down into smaller, simpler (less complex) food molecules. Food is broken down (digested) through physical and chemical processes. Physical breakdown of food materials is performed by the chewing and grinding actions of the teeth, for example. The actions of certain digestive enzymes (i.e., substances that act as catalysts in the breakdown of proteins and other nutrients) as well as other substances (e.g., acids) chemically break down food as it travels through the GI tract. Thus, the nutrients are reduced into smaller molecules that may be absorbed through the lining of the intestinal wall for distribution to body cells.

Layers of the GI Tract

The hollow internal space within the alimentary canal or GI tract is known as the lumen. The walls of the GI tract consist of four layers of tissue, including an outermost covering (serosa); the mucous membrane (mucosa), which produces the mucus that lines the canal; the submucosa, a layer of connective tissue beneath the mucosa; and underlying layers of muscle tissue (muscularis). Regular, rhythmic contractions of involuntary (smooth) muscle within these layers of underlying muscle tissue propel food through the GI tract in a process known as peristalsis.

Mouth

Digestion begins in the mouth. The roof of the mouth, known as the palate, has a hard, bony, front portion (hard palate) and a soft, fleshy area (soft palate) that consists primarily of muscle. The tongue, which forms most of the floor of the mouth, is a flexible, muscular organ that helps manipulate food during chewing. It also contains the microscopic chemical receptors (taste receptors) that produce the nerve impulses necessary for taste (taste buds).

The teeth, which assist in the chewing and grinding of food, are firmly attached to the upper and lower jaws. The gums (gingiva), which consist of a mucous membrane and supporting fibrous tissues, surround the teeth, serving as "shock absorbers" and keeping the teeth tightly set into the jaws. Enclosing the oral cavity are the cheeks and the upper and lower lip. In addition, as with all of the GI tract, the mouth is lined by a mucous membrane. Saliva, a thin, watery fluid that is secreted by the salivary glands and the mucosa of the mouth, assists in the process of swallowing by moistening the oral mucosa; lubricating food; initiating the breakdown of certain food products through its digestive enzymes; and promoting the sense of taste.

Teeth

The teeth are essential for the chewing, tearing, and grinding of food (mastication) as it mixes with saliva. Humans typically have two sets of teeth including the primary (deciduous) teeth and the permanent (secondary) teeth. There are usually 20 primary teeth that erupt between the ages of six months and two to three years. The primary teeth are gradually replaced by the permanent teeth beginning at about six years of age. Adults typically have 32 permanent teeth.

There are four major types of teeth that are classified based upon their shape and location:

- Incisors are chisel shaped and have sharp edges for cutting during mastication. The incisors are the eight front teeth (i.e., four in the upper jaw and four in the lower jaw).

- Canines or cuspids are sharp, pointed teeth that tear or pierce food. The four canines (i.e., two in the upper jaw and two in the lower jaw) are situated next to the incisors.

- Premolars or bicuspids have large, flat surfaces with two grinding "cusps" to assist in the breakdown of food during mastication. The eight premolars are situated next to and in back of the canines. The primary teeth include no premolars.

- Molars or tricuspids also have large, flat surfaces, yet have three grinding "cusps." The 12 molars are located in back of the premolars. The primary teeth typically include only four molars in the upper jaw and four in the lower jaw. Wisdom teeth are typically known as third molars. They usually erupt in the late teens and early twenties.

The interior of each tooth contains living pulp, which includes connective tissue, sensory nerves, and blood and lymphatic vessels. The pulp is surrounded by the dental tissue known as dentin. In addition, each tooth is divided into a crown, neck, and root. The crown, the exposed portion of a tooth, is covered by enamel, the hardest tissue in the human body. The neck, which is the narrow portion of the tooth surrounded by the gums, and the root, which fits into the bony socket of the lower or upper jaw, are covered by the sensitive dental tissue cementum. A fibrous membrane (periodontal membrane) connects the cementum to the jaw and gums.

Salivary Glands

The salivary glands are the three pairs of glands that secrete saliva. Their secretions are released into ducts that empty into the mouth. Because the salivary glands release their secretions into ducts, they are exocrine glands. The salivary glands include the parotid, submandibular, and sublingual. The parotid glands, the largest of the salivary glands, are located below and in front of the ears at the angle of the jaws. Their ducts open inside the cheeks. The submandibular glands are located toward the back of the mouth, and their ducts open under the tongue. The ducts of the sublingual glands secrete saliva onto the floor of the mouth. Saliva contains digestive enzymes (salivary amylase) that initiate the chemical digestion of certain foods (e.g., carbohydrates).

Digestive System

Pharynx

The pharynx, also known as the throat, is a muscular tube lined with mucous membranes and is part of the digestive and respiratory systems. Food and fluids enter the throat from the mouth and exit via the esophagus. However, air normally enters the pharynx from the nasal cavities and exits via the larynx. (For more information, please see the section entitled The Respiratory System.)

Esophagus

The esophagus is a muscular tube that transports food from the pharynx to the stomach. It is also lined with mucous membrane. The upper portion of the esophagus is encircled by a ring-shaped muscle (sphincter) that opens to allow the passage of food products. A similar muscle (cardiac sphincter) is located where the esophagus joins the stomach. The walls of the esophagus contain strong smooth muscles fibers, and rhythmic wavelike contractions of these involuntary muscles (peristalsis) propel food toward the stomach.

Stomach

The stomach is a hollow, pouch-like organ located in the upper portion of the abdominal cavity. It continues the breakdown of food that began in the mouth. Once food passes through the cardiac sphincter from the esophagus, it is contained in the stomach by contraction of the ring-shaped muscle at the end of the stomach (pyloric sphincter).

The walls of the stomach consist of three layers of smooth muscle and are lined with mucous membrane containing specialized cells that secrete gastric juices. These juices contain hydrochloric acid and digestive enzymes (e.g., rennin, pepsin) that are necessary for the breakdown of proteins. Rhythmic contractions of the stomach's smooth muscle layers mix digesting food with gastric juices, forming a semiliquid mixture known as chyme. Once partially digested food has been mixed into the chyme, relaxation of the pyloric sphincter and contractions of the stomach propel the chyme into the duodenum of the small intestine.

Small Intestine

The small intestine has three sections: the duodenum, jejunum, and the ileum. The function of the small intestine is to continue the breakdown of food products as they travel through the GI tract and to promote the absorption of nutrients into the bloodstream.

As rhythmic contractions of smooth muscles (peristalsis) propel food through the small intestine, digestive juices from the pancreas and bile from the liver are added to partially digested food within the duodenum. In addition, the mucus lining of the small intestine contains tiny glands that secrete intestinal digestive juice. Mucus, the enzymes within the intestinal digestive juice (e.g., maltase, sucrase, lactase, peptidase), and the secretions from the pancreas and liver serve to further break down food into smaller food molecules that may be more easily absorbed.

The mucosa of the small intestine is organized into several circular folds (plicae) covered with minute projections known as villi. Each villus contains finger-like lymphatic vessels (lacteals that absorb fat soluble nutrients (lipids) from the small intestine for transport to the blood circulation. Such fats are absorbed in the form of chyle, a cloudy milky substance containing products of digestion. The villi also contain blood capillaries that absorb certain products of digestion (e.g., amino acids, sugars).

Pancreas

The pancreas, an elongated gland located across the back of the abdomen, functions as both an exocrine and endocrine gland. It primarily consists of exocrine tissues that secrete pancreatic juice into ducts entering the duodenum. Pancreatic juice is an essential digestive juice that contains enzymes (e.g., trypsin, lipase, amylase) necessary for the breakdown of proteins, fats, carbohydrates, and certain acids. The pancreas also contains tiny clumps of endocrine cells (pancreatic islets) that secrete certain hormones, directly into the bloodstream.

The exocrine cells of the pancreas secrete their enzymes into several ducts that combine to form the main pancreatic duct. This duct joins with the common bile duct, which conveys bile from the gallbladder, and then opens into the duodenum. Most of the digestive enzymes secreted by the exocrine cells are activated by enzymes within the duodenum. In addition, exocrine cells of the pancreas secrete sodium bicarbonate, a substance that neutralizes the hydrochloric acid within the stomach's gastric juice as it enters the duodenum.

Liver, Bile Ducts, and Gallbladder

The liver, one of the largest organs of the body, is located within the upper right abdominal cavity. As part of the digestive system, the liver functions as an exocrine gland whose cells secrete the substance known as bile into a network of ducts (bile ducts). Bile, a liquid that consists of waste products, cholesterol, and bile salts, carries waste products from the liver and assists in the digestion and absorption of fats within the small intestine. The bile ducts transport bile from the liver to the gallbladder and on to the uppermost region of the small intestine (duodenum). The gallbladder, a small, muscular sac located under the liver, stores and concentrates bile from the liver. When chyme that contains fats (lipids) enters the duodenum from the stomach, the fats stimulate the secretion of a hormone (cholecystokinin) from the mucous membrane of the duodenum; in turn, the hormone stimulates contraction of the gallbladder, forcing bile into the small intestine.

The liver also has several additional essential functions in the body. These include regulating the blood levels of amino acids, the building blocks of proteins; helping to filter toxic substances from the blood; and producing certain proteins within the fluid portion of the blood (plasma). Such proteins include certain components that play a role in blood clotting (coagulation factors); particular blood proteins (complement system) that, when activated, destroy invading microorganisms; and the protein albumin, which helps to regulate the exchange of water between the bloodstream and bodily tissues. In addition, the liver produces cholesterol and certain proteins that transport fats in the bloodstream to cells throughout the body and processes hemoglobin for use of its iron content. Hemoglobin is the protein that enables red blood cells to transport large amounts of oxygen to cells.

Large Intestine

The large intestine is the organ that forms the lower portion of the GI tract. This organ, which has a larger diameter than the small intestine, consists of several areas. These include a pouch-like area (cecum); the ascending, transverse, descending, and sigmoid colons, the latter of which descends into the pelvic area and terminates in the rectum; and the end of the rectum known as the anal canal, which terminates at the external opening known as the anus. In addition, the appendix, a small, tubular structure, hangs from the cecum. Because the appendix contains lymphatic tissue, it may play a small role in helping to protect the body against infection; however, it has no known role in the body's digestive system.

Digestive System

As food matter that has not been broken down or absorbed moves through the lower region of the small intestine (ileum), it passes into the large intestine through the ileocecal valve. Bacteria within the large intestine act upon the undigested material, potentially resulting in the release and absorption of additional nutrients. Water, vitamins, fats and minerals are absorbed into the bloodstream through the lining of the large intestine. Remaining undigested material is expelled through the rectum, anal canal, and anus as feces.

Swelling (distension) of the rectum typically stimulates the desire to defecate, i.e., empty feces from the rectum. Two ring-shaped muscles (sphincters) usually remain contracted to keep the anus closed except during the process of defecation. The inner anal sphincter consists of involuntary (smooth) muscle, where the outer anal sphincter is composed of voluntary muscle.

Endocrine System

The term "endocrine system" is used to describe a group of specialized tissues, glands, and other structures that have the ability to produce and secrete certain complex chemical substances (hormones) into the bloodstream or lymphatic circulation for transport to particular tissues or organs. These hormones have specific effects on certain bodily functions. Hormones assist in regulating the body's growth; controlling the rate of chemical processes in the body (metabolism); promoting the maturation and function of reproductive organs and the development of secondary sexual characteristics (puberty); and regulating many other bodily activities. Each hormone molecule may eventually combine with (or bind to) a specific area (receptor) on the surface of a cell within its "target organ," triggering the appropriate response. In contrast, exocrine glands are "outwardly secreting glands"—i.e., they secrete certain substances into ducts for emptying into a particular cavity or onto a bodily surface. (For example, the salivary glands of the digestive system secrete saliva via ducts that empty into the mouth.)

The endocrine glands include the pituitary gland, gonads (ovaries and testes), thyroid gland, parathyroid glands, adrenal glands, pancreatic islets, thymus, pineal gland, and placenta.

Pituitary Gland

The pituitary gland, also known as the "master gland," is a relatively small structure located deep in a saddle-shaped cavity in the skull (sella turcica). The gland is connected to a region of the brain known as the hypothalamus by a stalk of nerve fibers (pituitary stalk). The hypothalamus controls the functioning of the pituitary gland through direct nerve stimulation as well as through the actions of certain nerve cells that secrete hormones (hormone-releasing and hormone-inhibiting factors) into the bloodstream for transport directly to the pituitary. Hormone-releasing factors cause the secretion of certain hormones by the pituitary gland, whereas hormone-inhibiting factors inhibit the production and release of such hormones.

The pituitary gland is divided into two main regions: i.e., the anterior pituitary gland (adenohypophysis) and the posterior pituitary gland (neurohypophysis). Each region is responsible for producing different hormones. The anterior lobe of the pituitary gland produces the following hormones, most of which are considered tropic hormones, i.e., hormones that stimulate the growth of another endocrine gland and the secretion of its hormones.

- Prolactin stimulates the growth of the female breasts (mammary glands) during pregnancy and the secretion of milk by the mammary glands after birth.

- Growth hormone serves to stimulate body development.

- Melanocyte-stimulating hormone (MSH) controls the amount of dark brown or black pigment (melanin) produced by certain specialized skin cells (melanocytes).

- Thyroid-stimulating hormone (TSH) stimulates the production of thyroid hormones.

- Adrenocorticotropic hormone (ACTH) stimulates the growth of the outer regions of the adrenal glands (adrenal cortex) and their production of hormones.

- Follicle-stimulating hormone (FSH) and luteinizing hormone (LH), which are known as gonadotropins, stimulate the gonads, i.e., the sex glands (ovaries and testes) within which the reproductive cells (ova and sperm) are produced.

In addition, the posterior region of the pituitary gland releases two hormones:

- Antidiuretic hormone (ADH) decreases urine production by increasing the reabsorption of water from urine into the blood.

- Oxytocin stimulates powerful contractions of involuntary (smooth) muscle within the uterus during labor. This hormone also stimulates the secretion of milk (lactation) by the female mammary glands during breast-feeding.

Gonads

In females, the paired glands, known as the ovaries, produce the female sex cells (ova or eggs), and, in males, the paired structures, called the testes, produce the male sex cells (spermatozoa or sperm). Follicle-stimulating hormone produced by the pituitary gland promotes the growth and maturation of the cavities in the ovaries (follicles) within which the ova develop and mature; in addition, it stimulates the ovarian follicles' production of the female hormone estrogen. In males, FSH promotes the growth and maturation of and production of sperm by the long, coiled tubules (seminiferous tubules) that form the bulk of the testes. In addition, in females, luteinizing hormone produced by the pituitary gland stimulates the maturation of ovarian follicles and their eggs, the follicles' secretion of estrogen, and the monthly release of ova from the follicles (ovulation). LH stimulates the formation of glandular structures (corpus luteum) within the ruptured follicles that secrete the female hormones progesterone and estrogen. In males, LH stimulates the cells located between the seminiferous tubules in the testes to produce and secrete the male sex hormone testosterone.

Thyroid Gland

The horseshoe-shaped thyroid gland consists of two lobes on either side of the windpipe (trachea) that are joined by a narrow region of tissue (isthmus). Tissue within the thyroid gland consists of follicular cells and parafollicular cells. The follicular cells, which comprise most of the thyroid gland, secrete the thyroid hormones thyroxine (T4) and triiodothyronine (T3). Certain amounts of the thyroid hormones are stored as a semifluid material within the follicular cells, from which they are released into the bloodstream as required. The parafollicular cells secrete the hormone calcitonin.

Secretion of the thyroid hormones T4 and T3 is controlled by the pituitary gland. These hormones assist in regulation of the metabolic rate, i.e., chemical activities within cells that release energy from nutrients or consume energy to create certain substances. The thyroid hormones also play a vital role in the normal mental and physical development and growth of infants and children.

Release of the hormone calcitonin occurs independently of the pituitary gland and hypothalamus. This hormone-in coordination with parathyroid hormone released by the parathyroid glands-helps to regulate the concentrations of calcium in the body. Calcium is a mineral that is important for proper functioning of the cells, blood clotting, muscle contraction, nerve impulse transmission, and other vital functions. Most calcium in the body is stored in bones of the

Endocrine System

skeleton. Calcitonin has the ability to decrease blood levels of calcium. It suppresses resorption of bone by inhibiting the activity of cells that "digests" bone matrix (osteoclasts), releasing calcium and phosphorus into blood.

Parathyroid Glands

The parathyroid glands are the two pairs of small, oval glands on the back of both lobes of the thyroid gland. These glands produce parathyroid hormone, which serves to increase levels of calcium in the blood by stimulating osteoclasts to reabsorb bone mineral, thus liberating calcium into blood.

Adrenal Glands

The adrenal glands are small, triangular organs that curve over the top of each kidney. The outer region (adrenal cortex) and inner region (adrenal medulla) of the glands have different functions.

The secretion of hormones by the adrenal cortex is regulated by hormones produced by the pituitary gland (e.g., adrenocorticotropic hormone [ACTH]). The adrenal cortex consists of three distinct zones of cells. The outer zone secretes hormones known as mineralocorticoids that help to regulate the levels of certain mineral salts (e.g., sodium) in the blood. The main mineralocorticoid, known as aldosterone, assists in maintaining the delicate balance between sodium and potassium-ultimately helping to regulate blood pressure and blood volume.

The middle and inner zones of the adrenal cortex together secrete hormones known as glucocorticoids, such as hydrocortisone. Glucocorticoids help to regulate the body's use of carbohydrates, fats, and proteins; maintain normal blood pressure; produce certain anti-inflammatory effects; and decrease the production of certain white blood cells that produce antibodies (anti-allergic effect). The middle and inner zones of the adrenal cortex also secrete small amounts of sex hormones (androgens) that stimulate the development of male secondary sexual characteristics and the female sexual drive.

The adrenal medulla or inner region of the adrenal glands releases the hormones epinephrine and norepinephrine in response to nerve impulses from sympathetic nerve fibers. The release of such hormones into the bloodstream serves to increase the heart rate, widen the air passages of the lungs, and dilate blood vessels that supply the skeletal muscles of the body.

Pancreatic Islets

The pancreas, an elongated gland that is located across the back of the abdomen, is divided into a head, body, and tail. It primarily consists of exocrine tissue that secretes digestive enzymes necessary for the breakdown of proteins, fats, carbohydrates, and certain acids.

The endocrine tissue of the pancreas, known as pancreatic islets or islets of Langerhans, consists of tiny clumps of cells among the exocrine cells. The alpha cells of the pancreatic islets secrete glucagon, whereas the beta cells secrete insulin. Glucagon promotes a chemical process (glycogenolysis) during which glycogen, a carbohydrate that is stored in the liver, is broken down into glucose and released into the bloodstream. Insulin serves to regulate and stabilize blood glucose levels by promoting the movement of energy-rich glucose into the cells of the body. The secretion of glucagon increases blood glucose levels. In contrast, secretion of insulin decreases levels of glucose in the blood.

Thymus

The thymus, a small lymphoid organ located behind the breastbone (sternum) in the upper portion of the chest, consists of two lobes that join in front of the windpipe (trachea). This organ functions as an essential part of the immune system, beginning its functions at approximately the twelfth week of fetal development until puberty. The thymus serves as a source of certain white blood cells (lymphocytes) before birth. In addition, the organ secretes hormones (e.g., thymosin) that promote the development of specialized lymphocytes, known as T lymphocytes, which defend the body against certain microorganisms (i.e., during cell-mediated immunity.)

Pineal Gland

The pineal gland is a small, cone-shaped gland that is located deep in the brain. It secretes the hormone melatonin, which is thought to play a role in regulating puberty, ovarian cycles, mood, sleep, and the body's "internal clock" (e.g., 24-hour circadian cycle).

Placenta

The placenta, the organ that develops in the uterus during pregnancy, serves to connect the blood supplies of the mother and the developing fetus. It develops from the chorion, i.e., the outermost layer of cells from the fertilized egg (zygote). The placenta produces chorionic gonadotropin hormone, which stimulates the ovaries to produce the female sex hormones estrogen and progesterone. Both of these hormones are necessary for the functioning of the placenta during pregnancy.

Growth and Development

Human growth and development may be encompassed in two broad categories: namely, prenatal growth and postnatal growth.

Prenatal Growth

The prenatal period, which means the "period before birth," begins when the male reproductive cell (sperm) fertilizes the female reproductive cell (egg or ovum). The fertilized egg (zygote) is a single cell containing all the genetic information (DNA) necessary for the growth and development of a human being. Half of the genetic information (in the form of 23 chromosomes) comes from the egg and half is from the sperm (for a total of 46 chromosomes).

As the zygote begins to travel down the mother's fallopian tube, its single cell immediately begins to divide (in the process called mitosis). (Please see the section entitled Cells for more information.) In approximately three days, the zygote has become a solid mass of cells known as a morula. About a week to 10 days after fertilization, what has become a hollow cellular "ball" (blastocyst) becomes implanted in the lining of the mother's uterus. During the zygote's journey to the uterus for implantation, the ovum supplies nutrients necessary for development of the embryo. The "embryonic phase" of development extends from fertilization until the end of the eighth week of pregnancy (gestation).

As the blastocyst continues to develop, its walls form an outer layer of membranes (chorion) that surround and protect the embryo. In addition, an inner layer of membranes (amnion) forms the amniotic sac, the fluid-filled sac within which the embryo grows and develops, protecting it from injury.

The chorion develops into the placenta, the organ attached to the lining of the uterus that serves to connect the blood supplies of the mother and the developing embryo, enabling the exchange of vital nutrients (including oxygen) and waste products. Blood from the embryo flows through a cord-like structure (umbilical cord) to the placenta and passes into tiny, finger-like blood vessels (chorionic villi) surrounded by maternal blood. The umbilical cord contains three blood vessels: two umbilical arteries that carry oxygen-poor (deoxygenated) blood and a larger umbilical vein that carries oxygen-rich (oxygenated) blood.

Teratogens and Birth Defects

A thin layer of tissue separates the developing embryo's blood and the mother's blood, thus providing protection from certain harmful substances that may circulate in the mother's bloodstream. However, in some cases, particular substances, such as certain infectious agents or drugs (teratogens), may cross this barrier, potentially interfering with prenatal growth and causing developmental abnormalities. The specific abnormalities that may result depend upon a number of factors, including the stage of developppment during which such exposure occurred, certain genetic influences, the specific teratogen in question, and other ennvironmental factors. Birth defects are abnormalities that are apparent at birth (congenital) or early infancy. Such malforrmations may occur due to prenatal exposure to teratogens, genetic factors, or a combination of both (multifactorial).

As mentioned above, the embryonic stage of development takes place from fertilization until the end of the eighth week of gestation. The fetal stage of development extends from the ninth week of gestation until birth. Pregnancy is usually approximately 39 weeks in duration and is divided into three phases known as trimesters, each of which is about three months in length.

By approximately the third week of gestation, the head of the developing embryo begins to form and the region that will later become the brain and spinal cord (neural crest) starts to develop. At about four weeks, "buds" of tissue have begun to form that will later develop into certain orrgans (e.g., liver, lungs, pancreas, etc.) and into the arms, hands, legs, and feet (limb buds); the neural tube continues to develop; and rudimentary eyes form. By approximately five weeks, all internal organs have begun to develop, the jaws form, and the limb buds continue to grow. And by six weeks, the nose, mouth, and ears are beginning to develop and fingers and toes are becoming apparent.

Early during the first trimester, the growing embryo develops three layers of cells known as primary germ layers: an inner layer (endoderm), a middle layer (mesoderm), and an outer layer (ectoderm). Specific tissues and organs develop from each of these layers. For example, the lining of the lungs, gastrointestinal tract, and thyroid arise from the endoderm; the dermis of the skin, the muscles, most bones, the kidneys, and the circulatory system arise from the mesoderm; and the facial bones, the brain and spinal cord, the sensory organs such as the eyes and ears, and the epidermis of the skin arise from the ectoderm. By approximately the fourth month of gestation, the internal organs and organ systems are formed and almost mature. Growth and development continue until approximately nine months' gestation, when birth typically occurs.

Labor and Birth

Birth is the process during which the fetus moves from the uterus down through the cervix and passes out through the vagina. During the end of pregnancy, the uterus begins to contract in preparation for birth. The process known as laabor begins when contractions become regular and occur at progressively shorter intervals. In addition, strong uterine muscular contractions cause the cervix to open and widen (dilate), and the membranes surrounding the amniotic fluid rupture, resulting in the release of the amniotic fluid through the vagina ("breaking of the waters"). The process of labor includes the following stages:

- First stage, which begins with the onset of contractions and ends with full dilation of the cervix

- Second stage, during which the baby exits through the vagina

- Third stage, during which the placenta is expelled through the vagina

Postnatal Growth and Development

The postnatal period, which means "the period after birth," begins at birth and extends until death. The most rapid rate of growth during one's development occurs prenatally in embryonic and fetal development. Although the rate of growth decreases after birth, it remains high during childhood, particularly during the first year of life. Individuals also experience a "growth spurt" at the onset of puberty that progresses until their adult height is obtained.

During the first five months of life, infants grow approximately 30 percent in height and their weight usually doubles. By the age of one year, their height has increased by about 50 percent from birth

Growth and Development

and their weight has typically tripled. Height and weight are carefully measured and recorded during regular visits to pediatricians to ensure that growth is progressing at a predictable, steady rate. Physicians use measurements known as percentiles to compare the height and weight of infants who are of the same age. If an infant is said to be at the "fiftieth percentile" for weight, 50% of infants weigh more and 50% weigh less. If an infant is at the "tenth percentile" for height, 90% of infants have a higher height and 10% have a lower height. When assessing growth and development, physicians consider the actual percentile as well as changes in percentiles between visits.

Between birth and adolescence, the relative proportions of the head, limbs, and trunk change dramatically. For example, an infant's head tends to be about one quarter of the height of the body; however, an adult's head is approximately one eighth that of the height of the body. In addition, from childhood to adulthood, the trunk tends to become proportionally shorter and the legs proportionally longer.

Different organs have varying rates of growth. For example, the human brain is about one quarter of its adult size at birth. The brain grows primarily during the first year of life and is typically three quarters of its adult size by the age of one year. In contrast, the small lymphoid organ known as the thymus gradually enlarges until puberty, at which time it begins to decrease in size (involution).

Developmental Milestones
Infants and children develop mental, physical, and behavioral skills in certain stages known as developmental milestones. Although the particular rate of development may vary from child to child, most children typically acquire such skills at certain ages. The development of these skills depends upon a number of factors including the following:

Genetic factors-e.g., certain developmental patterns, such as developing the ability to speak earlier than otherwise expected, may be present in particular families.

Physical factors-e.g., visual or hearing impairment may innerfere with the ability to learn certain skills, potentially necessitating the use of special supportive techniques or services to ensure that children have the best chance to reach their developmental potential.

Environmental factors-e.g., appropriate levels of stimulation are important in helping children to develop certain skills, such as receiving regular verbal stimulation to promote language development.

When infants are born, they primarily communicate any needs (e.g., hunger, thirst, etc.) by crying. In addition, certain essential reflex reactions are typically present at birth. For example, when any objects touch newborns' lips, they usually respond by sucking (sucking reflex). When a side of the mouth is touched, newborns typically move their head toward that side, enabling them to locate the mother's nipple for breast-feeding (rooting reflex). And when newborns are startled, they stretch their arms and legs forward and out and extend their fingers (startle or Moro's reflex). These reflex reactions gradually fade as infants develop muscle strength and the ability to conduct and coordinate certain voluntary movements. For example, hand-eye coordination skills include watching objects, developing the ability to focus, tracking moving objects, and forming an association between seeing and performing certain actions by focusing on hand movements.

Development is typically assessed by evaluating the acquisition of skills in the areas of vision and fine movement, hearing and speech, locomotion, and social behavior. The following is a description of developmental milestones that are generally acquired during the first year of life:

By approximately one month of age, infants are usually able to:
- Focus on faces
- Bring their hands toward the face (e.g., mouth, eyes)
- Look at objects directly in front of them
- Turn toward familiar voices and respond to other sounds
- Move their head from side to side while lying on their stomach

At about three months, infants are usually able to:
- Track objects that move approximately 180 degrees
- Grasp objects placed in their hands
- Smile at familiar voices (e.g., mother's or father's)
- Make sounds that begin to resemble speech
- Raise their head 45 degrees when lying on their stomach

At approximately five months, infants are usually able to:
- Reach for objects
- Listen carefully to certain voices
- Hold their head steady while upright
- Roll from the stomach to the back
- Spontaneously smile

At about six months, infants are usually able to:
- Reach out for and move objects from one hand to another
- Turn their head to locate sounds
- Laugh, make certain vowel sounds, and babble to toys
- Roll from back to front and vice versa
- Sit with support
- Bear weight on their legs with support

At the age of nine months, infants are usually able to:
- Look for toys that have been hidden
- Grasp for toys that are out of reach
- Manipulate objects with both hands
- Listen to and comprehend certain sounds
- Occasionally utter strings of syllables (e.g., "mama" or "dada")
- Attempt to crawl, sit without support, and pull themselves to a sitting or standing position
- Step on alternative feet with support

By 12 months of age, infants are usually able to:
- Grasp and release objects
- Say several words
- Respond when they hear their names
- Wave good-bye
- Move from their stomach to a sitting position
- Crawl on their hands and knees
- Walk by holding furniture
- Walk without support for a few steps or with one hand held

Hematologic System

The blood is a circulating tissue composed of fluid and other formed elements such as red blood cells, white cells, and platelets. The study of the blood, its components, and blood-forming tissues is known as hematology. Blood is pumped by the heart through the body's arteries, veins, and capillaries. The noncellular, fluid portion of the blood is a pale, yellowish liquid known as plasma. The blood has several functions including:

- To serve as a transport system, carrying oxygen and other vital nutrients to body tissues and promoting the exchange and removal of carbon dioxide and other waste products from cells

- To help provide a defense against invading microorganisms, foreign tissue cells, and certain abnormal cells

- To help repair damage to blood vessels and tissues through the process of blood clotting

Blood Plasma

Approximately half of the blood's volume consists of plasma. This liquid, noncellular portion of the blood is approximately 95 percent water. In addition, the blood plasma also contains dissolved sugars (e.g., glucose, etc.), fats, salts, vitamins and minerals, amino acids necessary for the production of cellular proteins, and chemical messengers (such as hormones) that regulate specific cellular activities. Plasma also contains certain plasma proteins including globulins (e.g., antibodies, which are produced in response to a particular foreign protein [antigen]); albumin, which plays an important role in maintaining the balance of pressure from inside and outside the cell; and fibrinogen, a protein that is essential for blood clotting. In addition, certain waste products are dissolved in plasma and transported to the kidneys for excretion.

Formed Elements

The formed elements of the blood include red blood cells (erythrocytes), white blood cells (leukocytes), and platelets (thrombocytes). Red blood cells, platelets, and some white blood cells are produced in the bone marrow. However, most white blood cells are produced by lymphatic tissue (e.g., lymph nodes, spleen, thymus).

Red Blood Cells

The red blood cells (RBCs) are mostly rounded, double concave cells with thin centers and thicker edges. A cubic millimeter of blood contains approximately five million red blood cells. The relatively large surface area of the red blood cells because they are concave allows them to absorb and release oxygen molecules, and their shape facilitates their movement through narrow blood vessels. As mentioned above, red blood cells are produced in the bone marrow, where the rate of their formation is regulated by erythropoietin, a hormone produced by the kidneys. They typically circulate in the blood for approximately four months, at which time they break apart and are removed from the blood by the liver.

The red blood cells perform several essential functions. For example, RBCs transport carbon dioxide from the body's cells to the lungs for release into the environment. Carbon dioxide is a harmful waste product that is generated by normal cellular activities. The red blood cells also carry hemoglobin, an essential protein that contains iron. This red pigmented protein chemically combines (binds) with oxygen, producing oxyhemoglobin, which enables the red blood cells to transport oxygen to cells.

The various blood groups, such as blood types A, B, AB, and O, are classified based upon the presence or absence of certain antigens (or "marker proteins"). Antigens are proteins that stimulate the body to produce antibodies. The red blood cells may have two types of antigens: namely, A and/or B. The different A or B blood types are classified according to whether the red blood cells have both, one or the other, or neither antigen. In individuals with type B blood, for example, the body does not produce antibodies to inactivate or destroy the type B antigen; however, the blood plasma contains anti-A antibodies. In individuals with type A blood, the red blood cells contain type A antigen and the blood plasma has anti-B antibodies. In type O blood, the red blood cells contain neither type A nor type B antigens, whereas the blood plasma has both anti-A and anti-B antibodies. In contrast, in individuals with type AB blood, the red blood cells have both type A and type B antigens, and the blood plasma contains neither anti-A nor anti-B antibodies.

In approximately 85 percent of individuals, red blood cells also contain an antigen called Rh factor. Those with this antigen are said to have Rh-positive blood, whereas those without the antigen have Rh-negative blood.

White Blood Cells

White blood cells (WBCs) are larger than red blood cells; however, they are present in the blood in lower quantities. A cubic millimeter of blood contains approximately 7,500 white blood cells.

The white blood cells include two major categories: granular leukocytes, which have granules in the substance of the cell outside the nucleus (cytoplasm), and nongranular leukocytes. Granular leukocytes include neutrophils, eosinophils, and basophils, and nongranular leukocytes include lymphocytes and monocytes.

Neutrophils and monocytes, which are also known as phagocytes, are responsible for isolating, engulfing, and destroying microorganisms that have invaded the bloodstream. These cells engulf the microorganisms and digest them in a process known as phagocytosis.

Lymphocytes originate in the bone marrow and mature in lymphatic tissue. They become active immune cells in response to the presence of invading microorganisms. Lymphocytes known as B lymphocytes produce specific antibodies to inhibit certain microorganisms, whereas those known as T lymphocytes may actively destroy microorganisms or assist in the functions of the B lymphocytes.

Eosinophils help protect the body from various irritants that may cause allergies and are able to participate in phagocytosis. In addition, white blood cells known as basophils also play a role in allergic reactions and secrete certain chemicals such as heparin, which assists in the prevention of clotting as the blood circulates through the blood vessels (intravascular clotting).

Although granular leukocytes may have a lifespan of only a few days, nongranular leukocytes may survive for over six months. In fact, in some cases, certain individual lymphocytes may remain in the bloodstream for years.

Hematologic System

Platelets

Platelets, which are the smallest blood cells, are produced in the bone marrow by specialized cells known as megakaryocytes and typically survive for approximately nine days. A cubic millimeter of blood contains approximately 250,000 platelets.

Platelets usually circulate in the bloodstream in an inactive state. However, when a blood vessel wall is injured, platelets respond through a complex process by clumping at the injury site and sticking to one another. The platelets and damaged tissue cells also release certain chemicals that stimulate blood clotting (coagulation) factors in the blood plasma. Due to a series of complex reactions, known as a cascade, long filaments of fibrin, a fibrous gel, are produced that capture circulating platelets, red blood cells, and white blood cells. Once the damaged blood vessel is "plugged," the filaments contract, forming a solid blood clot.

In some cases, blood clots may form in undamaged blood vessels, potentially blocking vital blood supply to certain tissues and organs. A stationary blood clot is called a thrombus. If a portion of such a clot dislodges and circulates in the bloodstream, it is known as an embolus. Healthy blood vessel walls secrete the chemical prostacyclin, which helps to prevent the unnecessary activation of platelets and clot formation. However, under certain circumstances, emboli travel from their origin to other parts of the body, notably the lungs, heart, and brain.

Measurement of Blood Components

The complete blood count (CBC) is a calculation of the cellular (formed elements) of blood. These calculations are generally determined by specially designed machines that analyze the different components of blood in less than a minute. A major portion of the complete blood count is the measure of the concentration of white blood cells, red blood cells, and platelets in the blood. The complete blood count (also called CBC) is generated by testing a simple blood sample.

White Blood Count (WBC), also called leukocyte count. Normal range varies slightly between laboratories but is generally between 4,300 and 10,800 cells per cubic millimeter (cmm).

Automated white cell differential. A machine generated percentage of the different types of white blood cells, usually split into granulocytes, lymphocytes, monocytes, eosinophils, and basophils.

Red cell count (RBC), also called erythrocyte count. Normal range varies slightly between laboratories but is generally between 4.2 -5.9 million cells/cmm.

Hemoglobin (Hb). Hemoglobin is the protein molecule within red blood cells that carries oxygen and gives blood its red color. Normal range for hemoglobin is different between the sexes and is approximately 13 -18 grams per deciliter (g/dl) for men and 12 -16 g/dl for women.

Platelet count, also called thrombocyte count. Normal range varies slightly between laboratories but is in the range of 150,000 -400,000/cmm.

Immune System

The body's immune system consists of specialized proteins, cells, and tissues that function to protect the body against...

- Invading microorganisms (e.g., bacteria, viruses, etc.) that may cause disease

- Foreign tissue cells (such as those that may have been transplanted from a donor)

- Toxins (such as harmful chemicals)

- Cells that have become cancerous

Nonspecific Immunity
Certain mechanisms provide the body with general protection from invading cells and toxins, maintaining "nonspecific immunity." For example, nonspecific immunity is provided by the presence of certain physical barriers that may prevent the entry of invading cells or toxins or expel them-as well as chemical barriers that may destroy invading cells or toxins. Such barriers include certain enzymes within the saliva of the mouth, tears, and sweat; the protective barrier of the skin; the cough reflex; hairs within the nose and the sneeze reflex; the presence of harmless bacteria within the intestines that help to control harmful microorganisms; and secretion of mucus by cells lining certain organs of the respiratory tract.

In addition, tissue injury results in an inflammatory response, which consists of a series of nonspecific immune reactions. During an inflammatory response-which produces characteristic swelling, discomfort, and redness-the blood vessels widen (dilate), increasing the blood supply and enabling certain white blood cells to move from the vessels to the site of injury. For example, invading microorganisms typically encounter white blood cells known as phagocytes, which contain the infection by engulfing and destroying the microbes (phagocytosis). Invading microorganisms may also encounter certain naturally produced substances, such as a group of blood proteins (complement system) that, when activated, serve to destroy such microbes, or interferon, proteins that are produced in response to viral infection.

Specific Immunity
Specific immunity consists of particular defenses against certain invading microorganisms or toxins and includes inborn and acquired immunity. From birth, individuals are immune to certain diseases that affect other animals (inborn immunity). Acquired immunity is obtained when certain protective proteins known as antibodies are passed to a developing fetus via the mother's placenta or to an infant via the mother's breast milk. Acquired immunity also results from casual exposure to certain disease-causing agents and immunization (stimulation of the immune system to provide protection against a particular disease, such as through vaccination).

Humoral or Cellular Immune Responses
Specific immunity, which relies on the actions of the white blood cells known as lymphocytes, includes the humoral and cell-mediated immune responses.

Humoral Response
A humoral-mediated immune response, also known as an antibody-mediated response, primarily consists of the production of antibodies by cells called B lymphocytes or B cells. B lymphocytes initially arise from primitive cells in the bone marrow known as stem cells. Shortly before and after birth, certain stem cells develop into immature B cells.

When immature B cells recognize a disease-causing agent as foreign (antigen), they develop into activated B cells. Activated B cells rapidly divide into two lines of cells (clones): plasma cells, which secrete large amounts of antibodies into the blood, and memory cells, which are stored within the lymph nodes until they are stimulated by the same antigen that prompted their formation. They then also develop into plasma cells, secreting antibodies into the blood in response to the recognized antigen.

When antibodies are secreted into the blood, they bind to their specific antigens (antibody-antigen complex), making the antigens or the cells on which they are located harmless. Phagocytes then engulf and destroy large numbers of such antibody-antigen complexes. The binding of antibodies and antigens may stimulate the complement system, thereby improving the efficiency of phagocytosis.

Cellular Response
Cell-mediated immunity defends the body against certain microorganisms and possibly cancerous cells through the actions of particular white blood cells known as T lymphocytes or T cells. These cells initially develop within the thymus before birth. They arise from stem cells that migrate from the bone marrow to the thymus, where their development is facilitated by certain hormones. Newly formed T cells then migrate from the thymus to other lymphatic tissues, primarily the lymph nodes.

There are two main types of T lymphocytes involved in cell-mediated immunity including the helper cells and killer cells. Helper cells assist in the recognition of certain antigens and help to activate killer cells. The killer cells bind to cells invaded by viruses or other microbes and destroy them. It is thought that killer cells may function similarly against cancerous cells or foreign tissue cells.

Allergies and Autoimmune Disease
In some cases, humoral-or cell-mediated immune responses may inappropriately occur against the body's own tissues. Such "autoimmunity" may result in hypersensitivity or autoimmune diseases. A hypersensitivity reaction is characterized by an excessive immune response to a substance that the body perceives as foreign (sensitizing antigen). For example, an allergic reaction is a hypersensitive response that occurs upon exposure to previously encountered, usually environmental substances (allergens), such as pollen, dust, or certain foods. Autoimmune diseases may be caused by the production of antibodies against the body's own cells (autoantibodies) and inappropriate cell-mediated immune responses against self antigens (autoantigens). One proposed theory suggests that certain viruses or bacteria may play some role in provoking an abnormal autoimmune reaction. For example, when a foreign protein from an invading bacterium or virus is very similar to one of the body's proteins, the immune system may be unable to distinguish between the invading and the "self" protein, potentially triggering an autoimmune response. It is not known what role genetic, hormonal, or other environmental factors may play in contributing to such a response. Autoimmune diseases may be localized, affecting a particular tissue, or may involve many tissues and organs of the body (systemic).

Infectious Diseases and Vaccination

The purpose of immunization is to induce immunity to provide protection against a certain disease. In response to a vaccine, the body's immune system produces certain immune defenses, such as antibodies or particular white blood cells that should protect against infection upon exposure to the disease-causing organism.

There are two major types of vaccination. In passive vaccination, antibodies obtained from a donor who was previously exposed to the microorganism are introduced into the body, thereby providing short-term protection against the disease-causing organism. In active vaccination, noninfectious portions of bacteria or viruses are introduced into the body, stimulating the production of antibodies against the foreign protein, resulting in longer-term immunity.

Some vaccines are intended for the general population, particularly infants and young children, such as immunization against the infectious diseases diphtheria, pertussis (whooping cough), and tetanus (DPT); measles, mumps, and rubella (German measles); hepatitis B; and polio. The recommended ages for immunization may vary from case to case. A child's pediatrician can recommend an appropriate immunization schedule.

Other vaccines are available for individuals who are at risk for certain infectious diseases due to their work situations (e.g., health care workers); their living situations or age groups (e.g., students living in dormitories, elderly individuals in nursing homes); local outbreaks of dangerous infectious diseases; or travel in certain countries.

Some individuals should not receive certain vaccinations, such as people with deficient immune systems. In individuals who have a fever or a preexisting infection, immunizations should be delayed. In addition, particular vaccines should not be given to young children or pregnant women.

Musculoskeletal System

Neuromuscular Activities

The muscles of the body, collectively referred to as the muscular system, consist of bundles of specialized cells that, unlike other cells, have the ability to contract and relax, resulting in movement of body parts and organs. There are two main types of muscles: namely, skeletal muscle and smooth muscle. In addition, the cardiac muscle is a highly specialized muscle that is sometimes referred to as a third muscle type.

Skeletal Muscle

The skeletal muscles, so named because they attach to bones of the skeleton, are the most prominent muscles in the body and typically contribute to approximately 40 to 45 percent of an individual's body weight. These muscles may also be referred to as striated ("cross striped") muscles or called voluntary muscles because their movements are under voluntary control.

Each skeletal muscle consists of groups of threadlike muscle cells, known as muscle fibers, in a highly organized arrangement. Each muscle fiber is made up of slender, striated strands called myofibrils that, in turn, are composed of bunches of microscopic, threadlike structures known as myofilaments. The myofilaments contain minute fibers or threads of proteins known as myosin and actin. The interactions of these proteins are essential for muscle contraction. During voluntary movement, skeletal muscle contracts and the bone to which it is attached (via tendons) moves in response to the contraction.

Neuromuscular Activities and Voluntary Movement

The brain regulates voluntary movements of skeletal muscles by sending impulses to the nerve fibers that supply the muscle fibers (motor neurons). The area where nerve endings and muscle fibers join is known as the neuromuscular junction. When the brain sends such impulses, nerve endings release a specialized chemical (the neurotransmitter acetylcholine) that serves to stimulate the muscle fibers. A complex series of electrical and chemical processes is initiated resulting in muscle contraction.

When voluntary movements occur, there are coordinated contractions and simultaneous relaxations of several muscles. In other words, as several muscles contract, one muscle is primarily responsible for producing the particular movement (prime mover or agonist) and the others (synergists) contract in order to assist the prime mover in making the movement in question. While such muscles contract, other muscles known as antagonists simultaneously relax, producing movements that oppose those of the prime mover and synergists. Such coordination of skeletal muscle movements helps to ensure smooth rather than jerky motions.

In addition to producing movement, the skeletal muscles also function to maintain posture and to produce body heat. For example, skeletal muscles are typically maintained at a level of slight, continuous contraction (muscle tone). Such muscle tone helps the body to maintain proper posture—i.e., the specific positioning of body parts to support their optimum function, place the least strain on different areas of the body, and maintain proper weight distribution. In addition, muscle fiber contraction creates most of the heat that the body needs to maintain its proper temperature.

Smooth Muscle

Smooth muscle cells have a smooth appearance when viewed under a microscope, lacking the striations of skeletal muscle cells. Rather, they consist of elongated, "spindle-shaped" cells that are typically organized parallel to one another. Also known as involuntary muscles since their movements are not under voluntary control, the smooth muscles help to regulate certain functional movements of internal organs. For example, in the process known as peristalsis, the rhythmic contractions of smooth muscle propel food forward through the digestive tract. Smooth muscle is also located within the blood vessel walls and several other areas of the body.

The actions of the smooth muscles are regulated by the autonomic nervous system, the portion of the nervous system that controls involuntary activities of blood vessels, organs, and other tissues and organ systems. Neurotransmitters released at nerve endings contribute to the series of events that lead to contraction of smooth muscles. As with the skeletal muscles, smooth muscle contractions rely upon the interactions between the myosin and actin filaments. In addition, smooth muscle cell activities may be affected by changes in the chemical composition of the fluid surrounding the cells as well as the release of certain hormones.

Cardiac Muscle

Cardiac muscle, also known as the myocardium, is a special type of striated muscle that is located only in the heart. Like the cells within the skeletal muscles, cardiac muscle cells also have cross striations. In addition, there are dark bands or disks (intercalated disks) at the junctures of adjacent cardiac fibers. These disks enable the fibers to contract as a unit, thereby ensuring the heart's efficiency in pumping blood throughout the circulatory system.

As with the smooth muscles, contraction of cardiac muscle is regulated by the autonomic nervous system. Cardiac muscle activities may also be affected by the release of specific hormones. Electrical impulses that stimulate a regulated, coordinated sequence of contractions originate from the heart's "pacemaker" (sinoatrial node), an area within the upper right chamber of the heart (right atrium).

Nervous System

The nervous system is a complex network of structures that function to:

- obtain information about the body's internal environment and the external environment

- relay and analyze such "data"

- initiate, integrate, and control appropriate responses to this information

The nervous system includes the brain and spinal cord, known as the central nervous system; nerves that extend from the brain and spinal cord to all areas of the body, referred to as the peripheral nervous system; somatic sense organs, which are distributed in almost every area of the body but concentrated primarily in the skin; and special sensory organs, such as the eyes. In addition, the peripheral nervous system is further subdivided into the autonomic nervous system, which includes structures that regulate involuntary functions of the body.

Nervous System Cells

Cells of the nervous system ensure ongoing, rapid communications between different structures of the body and the control of bodily functions necessary to maintain life. There are two main types of cells within the nervous system:

- Nerve cells, also known as neurons, which conduct (transmit) impulses

- Glia, which are the connective tissue cells of the nervous system

Neurons contain a cell body, one or more slender, branching projections (dendrites) that transmit impulses toward the cell body, and a slender extension (axon or nerve fiber) that carries nerve impulses away from the cell body. A whitish, fatty substance known as myelin forms a protective "wrapping" or insulating sheath around certain axons, serving as an electrical insulator and ensuring the efficient conduction of nerve impulses.

There are three types of neurons:

- Sensory neurons (afferent ["toward"] neurons) carry impulses to the brain and spinal cord from all areas of the body.

- Motor neurons (efferent ["away from"] neurons) transmit impulses away from the brain and spinal cord to certain tissues (e.g., muscle or glandular tissues).

- Interneurons (connecting or central neurons) carry impulses from sensory neurons to motor neurons.

Glia hold together and protect neurons. The different types of glia include the following:

- Astrocytes are relatively large cells with thread-like projections. These "branches" connect with blood capillaries and neurons, holding them in proximity to one another. The walls of the capillaries and the projections of the astrocytes are said to form the "blood-brain barrier," which functions to separate systemic blood circulation from the central nervous system. This barrier prevents or slows the passage of certain toxic substances or infectious agents from the blood to the central nervous system.

- Oligodendroglia produce myelin and hold together nerve fibers.

- Microglia are relatively small cells with slender projections. When brain tissue becomes inflamed, these cells migrate toward the affected tissue, surround invading microorganisms or waste products, and digest them (phagocytosis).

Nerves and Nerve Impulses

Nerves consist of one or more bundles of impulse-carrying fibers known as axons that extend from the brain and spinal cord to all areas of the body. Certain nerves transmit impulses from particular receptor organs to the brain and spinal cord (afferent impulses) or from the CNS to certain specialized tissues (efferent impulses). White matter within the central nervous system and peripheral nervous system consists of bundles of axons that are myelinated; in contrast, gray matter of the nervous system primarily includes neuron cell bodies, dendrites, and unmyelinated axons.

The pathways by which nerve impulses are transmitted by neurons are known as neuron pathways. Nerve signals are electrical impulses or waves of electrical disturbances that result due to complex electrochemical changes in a neuron's environment. Such nerve impulses travel from the axon of one neuron (presynaptic neuron) to the dendrite of another neuron (postsynaptic neuron). The junction between two neurons is known as a synapse. As an electrical impulse reaches a synapse, the presynaptic neuron's axon releases small amounts of chemical substances known as neurotransmitters, which bind to certain areas (receptors) of the postsynaptic neuron. Consequently, the electrical impulse is conducted across the synapse to the postsynaptic neuron's dendrite. Thus, neurotransmitters are the chemical substances that enable neurons to communicate with one another.

Central Nervous System

The central nervous system includes the brain and the spinal cord. Bones of the skull enclose the brain, and bones of the spinal column (vertebrae) surround the spinal cord. In addition, a three-layered membrane (meninges) provides additional protection for the brain and spinal cord. The tough, fibrous outermost layer is known as the dura mater. The delicate middle layer, called the arachnoid mater, is separated from the elastic innermost layer (pia mater) by a space (subarachnoid space) that contains cerebrospinal fluid (CSF). This fluid, which acts as a protective "shock absorber," flows through the cavity within the vertebrae containing the spinal cord (spinal canal), the four cavities of the brain (ventricles), and the subarachnoid space.

Brain

The brain controls and regulates the many functions of the central nervous system including muscle control and coordination, sensory reception and response, and speech production as well as elaboration of thought and emotions. It consists of several major regions including the brain stem, diencephalon, cerebellum, and cerebrum.

Nervous System

Brain Stem
The brain stem consists of three structures: the medulla oblongata, pons, and midbrain. All regions of the brain stem serve as "two-lane" conduction "highways," with motor fibers relaying impulses from the brain to the spinal cord, and sensory fibers conducting messages from the spinal cord to other areas of the brain.

The medulla oblongata, a thick extension of the spinal cord, is located above the large opening (foramen magnum) in the bone that forms the back of the skull (occipital bone). It primarily consists of white matter mixed with bits of gray matter (reticular formation). The medulla contains groups of nerve cells (nuclei) of the ninth, eleventh, and twelfth cranial nerves (see below), thereby receiving and sending impulses involved in the sensation of taste and sending messages to muscles involved in swallowing, speech, and movements of the neck, shoulders, and tongue, for example. This region of the brain stem also contains nuclei of the tenth cranial nerve (vagus nerve) and thus receives and relays information concerning the regulation of blood vessel diameter (thus affecting blood pressure), beating of the heart, breathing, and digestion.

The pons and the midbrain both also contain white matter mixed with bits of gray matter. The pons has bundles of nerve fibers that connect with the region of the brain known as the cerebellum. In addition, it contains nuclei of the fifth, sixth, seventh, and eighth cranial nerves, thus relaying messages involved in movement of the eyes, jaws, and muscles of facial expression as well as receiving and transmitting sensory impulses from the face and ears. The midbrain contains nuclei of the third and fourth cranial nerves and therefore relays messages to muscles involved in controlling the reactions of the pupils of the eyes as well as five of the six muscles that move the eyes.

Diencephalon
The diencephalon is the region of the brain located between the midbrain and the cerebrum. It includes the hypothalamus and the thalamus.

The hypothalamus, a relatively small area of the brain, is situated under the thalamus and above the pituitary gland. One of its functions is to regulate the sympathetic nervous system, a division of the autonomic nervous system. The sympathetic nervous system controls certain involuntary activities during times of stress, such as raising blood pressure, increasing the heart rate and the breathing rate, and widening (dilating) the pupils. The hypothalamus is also involved in regulating body temperature, appetite, moods and emotions (such as anger, fear, etc.), and the sleep cycle.

Sleep and the Brain
Sleep is a natural state characterized by reduced consciousness and metabolic activity. During sleep, the brain typically engages in two main cycles, known as REM (rapid eye movement) and NREM (nonrapid eye movement) sleep. NREM sleep, which makes up approximately 80 percent of sleep in adults (and about 50 percent of sleep in infants), consists of four progressively deeper stages of sleep characterized by slow, deep brain waves, muscle relaxation; and regular, reduced autonomic activities (e.g., slowed breathing and heart rate; lowered blood pressure; etc.). Episodes of REM sleep periodically alternate with NREM sleep. REM sleep, which is associated with dreaming, includes increased levels of brain activity, irregular autonomic activities, rapid eye movements, and involuntary muscle jerks. A complete sleep cycle is usually approximately 90 minutes. Most individuals experience approximately four or five sleep cycles each night. It is not completely understood why sleep is a necessity, although most scientists agree that the brain requires regular rest to ensure optimum functioning-and that dreaming may help the brain to sort, manipulate, and store information obtained during waking activities. Many different areas of the brain, including the hypothalamus, are thought to play a role in regulating sleep.

The hypothalamus also controls the functions of the pituitary gland, an endocrine gland also known as the "master gland." The hypothalamus is attached to the pituitary gland by a stalk of nerve fibers known as the pituitary stalk. It regulates the gland's activities through direct nerve stimulation as well as through the actions of certain nerve cells whose axons secrete chemicals (hormone-releasing and hormone-inhibiting factors) into the bloodstream for transport directly to the pituitary. Hormone-releasing factors cause the secretion of certain hormones by the pituitary gland, whereas hormone-inhibiting factors halt the production and release of such hormones. The balance of these factors, via a feedback mechanism, is crucial in maintaining effective function of many of the body's activities.

The thalamus consists of two masses of gray matter located above the hypothalamus. The neurons within the thalamus relay impulses from sense organs of the body to the outer region of the cerebrum (cerebral cortex); transmit motor impulses from the cerebral cortex toward the spinal cord; associate certain sensations with emotions (e.g., unpleasant or pleasant feelings); and play a role in the body's state of responsiveness to sensory stimulation (arousal or alerting mechanisms).

Cerebellum
The cerebellum, a two-lobed, rounded region of the brain, has a "wrinkled" surface and is located under the back portion of the cerebrum and behind the brain stem. The surface (cortex) of the cerebellum contains parallel ridges that are separated by deep fissures. Three stalks of nerve fibers (peduncles) that arise from the inner side of each cerebellar hemisphere link to different areas of the brain stem. Messages between the cerebellum and other regions of the brain travel along these nerve stalks. Through messages transmitted via the brain stem, the cerebellum receives information concerning muscle contraction and relaxation and posture. The cerebellum works in conjunction with the basal ganglia and the thalamus, adjusting messages relayed to muscle groups from a certain area of the cerebrum (motor cortex) in order to maintain normal postures, sustain balance, and produce smooth and coordinated movements.

Cerebrum
The cerebrum is the largest area of the brain and is responsible for voluntary movements, sensory perception, emotions, memory, and comprehensive thought. The cerebrum contains several ridges (gyri) and grooves (sulci or fissures) and one deep groove known as the longitudinal fissure that divides the cerebrum into two halves (cerebral hemispheres). The left cerebral hemisphere controls the right side of the body, whereas the right hemisphere controls the left side of the body due to crossing of nerve fibers in the medulla of the brain stem. A thick band of myelinated nerve fibers known as the corpus callosum joins the lower midportions of and carries messages between the cerebral hemispheres. In addition, each hemisphere contains a fluid-filled cavity known as a ventricle (first and second or lateral ventricles). These ventricles communicate with a third ventricle in the center of the brain, and a fourth ventricle is located between the brain stem and the cerebellum.

Two sulci divide each hemisphere into four lobes that are designated by the bones over them: i.e., frontal, temporal, parietal, and occipital lobes. The surface of the cerebrum, called the cerebral cortex, consists of a thin layer of gray matter, whereas most of the interior of the cerebrum contains bundles of myelinated nerve fibers (white matter) known as tracts. In addition, deep within the white matter of the cerebrum are paired nerve cell clusters of gray matter known as the basal ganglia. Their function includes assisting in the regulation of muscular actions as well as initiating and ceasing movements.

The cerebrum has various areas that are responsible for particular complex functions. These areas include the following:

- Sensory areas, which receive sensory information from somatic sense organs (e.g., in the skin, muscles, internal organs) and special sense organs (e.g., ears, eyes, etc.) and analyze and sort such information

- Motor areas, which transmit messages that control muscles, resulting in movement

- Association areas, which link sensory and motor areas, integrate information received from the various sense organs, and engage in memory storage, recall, recognition, decision making, judgment, comprehensive thought, and the experience of emotions.

Spinal Cord
The spinal cord is housed inside a central canal within the spinal column and extends from the foramen magnum at the base of the skull to the bottom of the first vertebra of the lower back. It is a long, cylindrical structure of nerve tissue and is an extension of the medulla oblongata of the brain stem. As mentioned above, the spinal cord is enclosed and protected by a three-layered membrane (meninges) and is bathed by cerebrospinal fluid.

The inner core of the spinal cord consists of gray matter (i.e., primarily containing nerve cell bodies and dendrites). Its outer portion is composed of columns of white matter that contain bundles of myelinated nerve fibers (spinal tracts). These pathways transmit sensory impulses from the spinal cord to the brain (ascending tracts) and motor impulses from the brain to the spinal cord (descending tracts). Certain ascending tracts transmit impulses that produce sensations of temperature and pain, and certain descending tracts convey impulses that control specific voluntary movements.

Peripheral Nervous System

The peripheral nervous system refers to those nerves outside the central nervous system. This part of the nervous system establishes communications between the brain and spinal cord and outlying (peripheral) parts of the body, such as muscles, glands, and internal organs. Nerves of the peripheral nervous system include the cranial nerves and the spinal nerves.

The cranial nerves are the 12 nerve pairs that arise directly from the brain and emerge through various openings in the skull (foramen). The cranial nerve pairs...

- Carry sensory impulses to the brain that are analyzed, sorted, and integrated, resulting in vision, smell, taste, hearing, and/or balance.

- Transmit motor and/or sensory information to particular areas of the head and neck.

- Convey impulses to glands and organs, resulting in certain involuntary (autonomic) activities.

The cranial nerve pairs include the...
- First cranial nerves or olfactory nerves
- Second cranial nerves or optic nerves
- Third cranial nerves or oculomotor nerves
- Fourth cranial nerves or trochlear nerves
- Fifth cranial nerves or trigeminal nerves
- Sixth cranial nerve or abducens nerves
- Seventh cranial nerves or facial nerves
- Eighth cranial nerves or vestibulocochlear nerves
- Ninth cranial nerves or glossopharyngeal nerves
- Tenth cranial nerves or vagus nerves
- Eleventh cranial nerves or accessory nerves
- Twelfth cranial nerves or hypoglossal nerves

The spinal nerves are the 31 pairs of nerves that emerge from either side of the spinal cord through gaps between adjacent bones (vertebrae) in the spinal column. The nerves are assigned a specific letter and number based upon the level of the spinal column from which they emerge. Eight pairs of spinal nerves are attached to the cervical segments; 12 pairs to the thoracic segments; five pairs to the lumber segments; five pairs to the sacrospinal segments; and one pair to the coccygeal segment. The designation "C2," for example, refers to the pair of spinal nerves attached to the second segment of the cervical region of the spinal cord. The spinal nerves that emerge from the spinal cord branch to form many of the nerves supplying the trunk and limbs. The function of the spinal nerves is to transmit sensory and motor impulses between the spinal cord to those areas of the body that are not supplied (innervated) by the cranial nerve pairs. More specifically, the sensory nerve fibers of the spinal nerves transmit impulses from sensory receptors in muscles, internal organs, and the skin to the spinal cord, whereas the motor nerve fibers convey motor impulses from the spinal cord to glands and muscles.

Autonomic Nervous System

The autonomic nervous system (ANS) is that portion of the peripheral nervous system responsible for regulation of the involuntary functioning of certain tissues and organs. The ANS includes specialized motor neurons that transmit impulses from the brain stem or the spinal cord to involuntary muscle tissue, cardiac muscle tissue, and specialized glandular cells that produce and secrete certain chemical substances (e.g., hormones, enzymes).

The autonomic nervous system includes two groups of motor neurons (preganglionic and postganglionic neurons) and a group of nerve cell bodies (ganglia) located between them. The cell bodies and dendrites of preganglionic neurons are located in gray matter of the brain stem or spinal cord, and their axons extend to a set of ganglia in the peripheral nervous system. Within the ganglia, the endings of preganglionic neuron axons join with cell bodies or dendrites of postganglionic neurons, which, in turn, convey nerve impulses from ganglia to smooth muscle, cardiac muscle, or glandular tissue. The tissues to which postganglionic neurons transmit impulses are known as visceral effectors.

Autonomic Nervous System Neurotransmitters
There are four distinct types of nerve fibers (axons) in the autonomic nervous system that release certain neurotransmitters (i.e.,

acetylcholine or norepinephrine). The sympathetic and parasympathetic nervous systems work somewhat, although not completely, in opposition to each other (antagonistic), since each division may inhibit certain visceral effectors and activate others.

The autonomic nervous system is further subdivided into the sympathetic and the parasympathetic nervous systems.

Sympathetic Nervous System

The sympathetic nervous system functions to prepare the body for an emergency. When the body is affected by stress, such as occurs during strong emotions (fear, anger) or exercise, sympathetic nerve impulses increase to many of the body's visceral effectors, resulting in what is sometimes called the "fright-or-flight response." During this response, the heart and breathing rates increase; the pupils of the eyes widen (dilate); and secretions of certain glands increase, while those of other glands decrease. In addition, most blood vessels constrict, resulting in raised blood pressure; blood vessels that supply skeletal muscle widen, supplying additional blood; and the digestive process slows due to a reduction in the rate of the wave-like contractions of smooth muscle within the GI tract.

Parasympathetic Nervous System

The parasympathetic nervous system controls most visceral nerve transmission under normal circumstances, thus slowing and steadying certain bodily activities. For example, impulses conducted by parasympathetic neurons tend to increase peristalsis, speeding the digestive process; slow the heart and breathing rates; contract the pupils; and stimulate the salivary glands.

Reproductive System

The female reproductive system includes those organs that enable females to produce the specialized reproductive or sex cells (gametes) known as eggs (ova); engage in reproductive activity; provide nourishment to a fertilized ovum (zygote) during embryonic and fetal development; and give birth. The male reproductive system consists of those organs that enable males to produce and store the reproductive cells (gametes) known as sperm, engage in reproductive activity, and fertilize ova with sperm. The production and secretion of certain chemical substances (hormones) by glands of the endocrine system promote the maturation and normal functioning of reproductive organs and the development of secondary sexual characteristics (puberty) in males and females.

Female Reproductive System

The female reproductive system includes several organs, including the ovaries, fallopian tubes, uterus, vagina, and vulva. With the exception of the vulva (external genitalia), the female reproductive organs are located within the pelvic cavity. In addition, the female breasts (mammary glands) are supportive glands of the female reproductive system.

Ovaries

The female reproductive cells are produced in the paired structures known as the ovaries. These small, egg-shaped glands contain cavities known as follicles in which the female sex cells develop and mature (oogenesis). As females reach puberty (i.e., which typically has an onset between approximately nine to 13 years of age), the follicles begin to release eggs (ovulation) on a regular monthly cycle. This cycle is regulated by female sex hormones (estrogen and progesterone) that are also secreted by the ovaries.

The hormone estrogen promotes the development of female secondary sexual characteristics and normal functioning of reproductive organs (i.e., puberty). It promotes the development and maturation of female reproductive organs; development of the breasts; development of female body contours caused by fat deposition in the breasts and hip area, for example; and initiation (menarche) and regulation of the menstrual cycle. The menstrual cycle is the recurring monthly cycle during which the mucous membrane lining of the uterus (endometrium) is shed; begins to regrow, becoming thick and supplied with blood; is maintained in the uterus, and is again shed. The thickening of the endometrium is stimulated by the hormone progesterone in preparation for implantation of a fertilized egg (zygote). If such fertilization does not occur, progesterone and estrogen production decrease, causing the uterine lining and the unfertilized egg to be shed (menstruation). Progesterone also plays an essential role in the normal functioning of the placenta, the organ that nourishes the developing embryo and fetus during pregnancy.

Fallopian Tubes

A funnel-shaped duct, known as a fallopian tube, uterine tube, or oviduct, extends from each ovary to the uterus. Each tube ends in a structure shaped like a funnel whose edge has finger-like projections. When an egg is released from an ovary, it enters the fallopian tube with the assistance of the beating motions of these projections and microscopic hairs (cilia) on their surfaces. These motions help to propel the egg toward the uterus. In addition, the fallopian tubes serve as the passageways within which the male sex cells (sperm) move toward the ovaries.

Uterus

The uterus, a hollow, pear-shaped organ composed almost entirely of muscle (myometrium), is the organ within which a fertilized egg (zygote) becomes implanted and the developing embryo and fetus is nourished and grows during pregnancy. The organ consists of a lower narrow section known as the cervix and an upper portion called the body. The uterus usually lies in the pelvic cavity behind the bladder. However, during pregnancy, the uterus expands in size as the developing fetus grows and may eventually extend to the top of the abdominal cavity. During the end of pregnancy, strong uterine muscular contractions cause the cervix to open and widen (dilate) and expel the fetus through the vagina.

Other Components of the Female Reproductive System

The vagina is the muscular passage that connects the cervix and the external genitalia and is the portion of the female reproductive tract that opens to the exterior of the body. The vulva is the external, visible portion of the external genitalia.

Breasts

The female breasts, which are supportive glands of the female reproductive system, produce milk to nourish infants after birth (lactation). The female breast consists of approximately 15 to 20 divisions or lobes embedded within fatty tissue. Each lobe is comprised of smaller lobules of milk-secreting glandular cells that are organized in grape-like clusters (alveoli). The small ducts that drain the alveoli have their outlet within the nipple. The circular, colored (pigmented) area of skin surrounding the nipple is known as the areola. Due to secretion of the hormones progesterone and estrogen by the placenta and the ovaries during pregnancy, the milk-secreting glandular cells become active, causing the nipple to become enlarged. Before and after birth, the glands initially produce a thin, watery fluid (colostrum) containing antibodies and proteins that help to protect the newborn from certain infections. Another hormone known as prolactin is responsible for the secretion of milk.

Male Reproductive System

The male reproductive system also includes several organs, including the testes, reproductive ducts, seminal vesicles, bulbourethral glands, prostate gland, and penis.

Testes

In males, the gonads, i.e., the sex glands within which the reproductive cells are produced, are the paired oval-shaped structures known as the testes. The male sex cells produced by the testes, known as spermatozoa or sperm, are responsible for fertilizing the female ova. The testes are located in pouch-like structures called the scrotum.

Each testis is surrounded by a tough, fibrous membrane (tunica albuginea) and contains a long, narrow, coiled structure known as a seminiferous tubule. Sperm develop within the walls of the tubules in a process known as spermatogenesis. In addition, cells located between the tubules produce the male sex hormone testosterone. This male hormone and certain hormones produced in the pituitary gland (gonadotropin hormones) are responsible for the development and production of sperm.

As males reach puberty (i.e., which typically has an onset between approximately 12 to 14 years of age), increased secretion of testos-

Reproductive System

terone promotes muscle and bone growth, stimulates the development of male secondary sexual characteristics, and promotes the normal functioning of the reproductive organs. More specifically, it stimulates sperm production; the development and maturation of male reproductive organs (e.g., seminal vesicles, prostate gland); and the development of male characteristics (e.g., deepening of the voice due to enlargement of the larynx and the vocal cords, growth of facial and body hair, etc.).

Reproductive Ducts
Sperm develop within the walls of the seminiferous tubules of the testes and pass through several reproductive ducts: i.e., the epididymis, ductus (vas) deferens, ejaculatory duct, and urethra. The first of these is the epididymis, a tightly coiled tube that runs along the top and behind the testes. The ductus or vas deferens is the muscular, movable tube that enables sperm to pass from the testes and the epididymis. The ductus deferens joins the duct from the seminal vesicles to form the ejaculatory duct. This duct enables sperm to empty into the urethra, the tube that passes along the length of the penis and carries sperm to the exterior of the body. In males, the urethra also serves as the passageway through which urine is excreted from the body.

Other Components of the Male Reproductive System
Semen (seminal fluid) is a fluid consisting of sperm as well as the secretions of certain supportive sex glands of the male reproductive tract. Such glands include the seminal vesicles, the prostate gland, and the bulbourethral glands.

Semen serves to protect sperm from the acidic environment within the female reproductive tract.

The seminal vesicles, a pair of pouch-like glands, produce the largest portion of the semen's volume. The secretions of the seminal vesicles contain the sugar fructose, which provides a source of energy promoting the mobility of the sperm. The prostate gland, the chestnut-shaped organ under the bladder and in front of the rectum, secretes a thin fluid that forms a portion of the semen's volume and helps sperm to maintain their mobility. The bulbourethral glands, also known as Cowper's glands, are two relatively small, pea-shaped organs located below the prostate gland. The glands produce mucus-like fluids that form a small portion of the semen's volume. In addition, such secretions help to lubricate the end of the urethra. The penis is the portion of the male genitalia through which semen and urine pass.

Respiratory System

The respiratory system, comprising the air passages from the nose, throat, bronchial tubes, and lungs, is responsible for filtering the air that enters the body, supplying oxygen to the body, and removing carbon dioxide from the blood. This process is known as respiration. Certain organs of the respiratory (pulmonary) system also influence speech and help to produce the sense of smell (olfaction).

The organs of the respiratory system are often classified into the upper and lower respiratory tract. The upper respiratory tract, which consists of organs that are located outside the actual chest cavity (thorax), includes the nose, pharynx, and larynx. The organs within the lower respiratory tract are located primarily within the thorax and include the trachea, the bronchial tree, and the lungs.

Nose

The nose functions as the uppermost portion of the respiratory tract. This hollow passage, which connects the naval cavities and the upper portion of the throat (nasopharynx), serves to filter, warm, and moisten the air entering the respiratory tract. Mucous membranes (respiratory mucosa) covered by microscopic hairs (cilia) line the entire nasal passage-as well as most passageways of the respiratory tract. Located within the nasal mucosa are specialized nerve receptors necessary for the sense of smell.

During inspiration, air enters the respiratory tract through the nostrils (external nares). Small hairs within the nostrils trap foreign particles, such as dust, pollen, or microorganisms, thus protecting against infection and allergic responses. Filtered air passes into the nasal cavities, which have moist surfaces due to mucus production. The nasal cavities are divided by a structure made of cartilage (nasal septum). Bones surrounding the nose contain hollow, air-filled cavities (paranasal sinuses) that affect the resonance of sound (e.g., during speech). In addition, these mucous-membrane lined cavities, which drain into the nasal cavities, assist in producing mucus for the respiratory tract.

As air passes through the nasal cavities, it is warmed, humidified, and filtered by three thin, mucosa-covered structures (conchae). Mucus on the surface of the conchae and other organs of the respiratory tract flows toward the nasopharynx due to the beating action of the cilia, thereby helping to move trapped foreign particles out of the respiratory tract.

Pharynx

The pharynx, also known as the throat, is a muscular tube lined with mucous membranes. The throat is part of both the respiratory and digestive systems and is divided into three regions: an uppermost portion (nasopharynx) that serves as an air passage; an area of the throat behind the mouth (oropharynx) that is a passage for food and air; and a lower segment (laryngopharynx) that functions as a passage for food only. Air normally enters the pharynx from the nasal cavities (although it may sometimes enter through the mouth) and exits via the larynx. However, food enters the pharynx from the mouth and continues through the digestive system via the esophagus.

The eustachian or auditory tubes also open into the nasopharynx, connecting the middle ears and the throat. In addition, the masses of lymphoid tissue that serve as the "front line" against invading microorganisms (tonsils) are located under the mucous membranes at the back of the pharynx.

Larynx

The larynx, also known as the voice box, connects the pharynx with the trachea. It consists of several areas of fibrous, flexible connective tissue (cartilage) and is also lined with mucous membranes. The larynx is responsible for producing the voice and preventing food from entering the airway during swallowing.

The opening of the larynx is partially covered by a "lid-like" flap of cartilage known as the epiglottis. This structure normally remains open, maintaining the larynx as part of the airway. However, when swallowing occurs, the epiglottis closes, sealing off the opening of the larynx and preventing food from passing into the larynx and the trachea. In addition, two strong, fibrous sheets of tissue known as the vocal cords stretch across the interior of the larynx. Passage of air over the vocal cords results in vibrations that help to create speech.

Trachea

The trachea, also known as the windpipe, extends from the larynx to an area behind the upper breastbone (sternum), where it then divides to form the two bronchi. The windpipe is a tube-like structure composed of elastic and fibrous tissues, smooth (involuntary) muscle, and rings of cartilage that help to keep the trachea open (patent). As with other organs of the respiratory tract, the trachea is also lined with mucous membranes (respiratory mucosa) covered by cilia. The secreted mucus helps to trap tiny foreign particles remaining in the inhaled air of the trachea, and the beating action of the cilia propels the mucus upward toward the pharynx and out of the respiratory tract.

Bronchial Tree

Because the numerous air passages of the lungs resemble an upside-down, tree-like structure, the bronchi and their branching airways are known as the bronchial tree. The trachea branches to form the main bronchi (primary bronchi) of the left and right lungs. Both of the primary bronchi then branch into smaller bronchi (secondary bronchi). The bronchi walls consist of three layers including an outer layer of fibrous, dense tissue; a middle layer of smooth muscle; and an inner layer of mucous membranes. In addition, the walls of the primary and secondary bronchi, like the trachea, are kept open by rings of cartilage, allowing the passage of air.

The bronchi divide into progressively smaller airways that eventually branch into tiny passages known as bronchioles. The walls of the bronchioles include only smooth muscle. The bronchioles then branch into microscopic tubes known as alveolar ducts that lead to the alveolar sacs. The walls of the alveolar sacs consist of many microscopic, grape-like structures called alveoli. The alveoli lie in contact with microscopic blood vessels (capillaries). The exchange of oxygen and carbon dioxide takes place across the thin walls of the alveoli, i.e., oxygen moves from the alveoli to the blood while carbon dioxide moves from the blood to the alveoli.

Lungs

The lungs, which are spongy, elastic organs located in the chest cavity, are divided into lobes: the left lung has two lobes, whereas the right lung has three. The narrow, rounded, upper area of each lung is known as the apex, and the broad, concave, lower portion of each lung that rests on the diaphragm is referred to as the base. In addition, a thin, moist, two-layered membrane known as the pleura lines the outside of the lungs and the inside of the chest cavity. A small amount of fluid separates the two layers of the pleura, serving as a lubricant as the lungs contract and expand during respiration.

The act of breathing (pulmonary ventilation) consists of two phases: inspiration and expiration. During inspiration, the chest and lungs expand, and air is drawn into the lungs During expiration, the chest and lungs contract and air is forced out of the lungs.

Pulmonary Circulation
Pulmonary circulation refers to the movement of blood through vessels between the heart and the lungs for the removal of carbon dioxide and the addition of oxygen (oxygenation) to the blood. When the right lower chamber of the heart (ventricle) contracts, "oxygen-poor" (deoxygenated) blood is pumped to the lungs via the pulmonary artery. From there, the blood flows through the capillaries that lie in contact with the air-filled alveoli. Oxygen moves across the thin walls of the alveoli into the blood, whereas carbon dioxide is transported by the blood to the alveoli. Carbon dioxide exits the lungs during expiration. Oxygenated blood is returned to the left upper chamber of the heart (atrium) via four pulmonary veins and is propelled into the left ventricle. When the left ventricle contracts, the blood is pumped into the major artery of the body (aorta) for circulation to the body's tissues. In addition, the blood that nourishes the lungs themselves is supplied by the bronchial arteries.

Sensory Organs

Certain specialized components of the nervous system, known as sense organs, are able to recognize specific stimuli in the external environment that affect the body, such as light, sound, temperature, or pressure. When the specialized microscopic structures that comprise the sensory organs (sensory receptors) recognize certain stimuli, they produce nervous impulses that are sent to the brain, the spinal cord, or both. The sense organs may be classified into two general categories: the somatic sense organs and the special sense organs.

Special Sense Organs
Sensory receptors for the special senses of hearing, vision, smell, and taste, are collected in the special sense organs, including the eyes (i.e., in the retinas), the ears (within the hearing apparatus), the nose (smell receptors), and the tongue (taste receptors). Sensory information received by these special sense organs travels to the brain via the cranial nerves, the 12 nerve pairs that arise from the brain and emerge through various openings in the skull. Most sensory information is transmitted to the sensory cortex of the brain.

Ears, Hearing, and Balance

The ear is the special sensory organ involved in hearing and balance. It consists of three major parts including:
- external ear
- middle ear
- inner ear

The External Ear
The external ear includes the visible portion of the ear (pinna or auricle) and the external auditory canal. The pinna consists of folds of cartilage and skin surrounding the opening of the auditory canal, which is the tube that extends into the lower cranium bone (temporal bone) and ends at the partition between the external and middle ear (eardrum or tympanic membrane). The skin of the auditory canal contains specialized glands (ceruminous glands) that produce cerumen, a waxy substance that traps dust and other foreign bodies. Sound waves pass through the auditory canal and strike the eardrum, causing it to vibrate.

The Middle Ear
The middle ear, a tiny cavity between the eardrum and the inner ear, contains three minute, movable bones (ossicles) that conduct sound to the inner ear. The names of the bones essentially describe their shapes: i.e., the malleus (hammer), incus (anvil), and stapes (stirrup). When the eardrum vibrates in response to sound waves, the vibrations are transmitted and amplified by the three ear bones. The stapes' movement against a membrane-covered opening to the inner ear results in movement of the fluid within the inner ear.

The eustachian or auditory tube connects the middle ear to the uppermost region of the throat (nasopharynx). Although the eustachian tube is usually closed at rest, it opens due to muscle contractions associated with swallowing or yawning. The eustachian tube is shorter in infants and young children than in older children and adults. As a result, when an upper respiratory tract infection occurs, infants and young children have an increased likelihood of experiencing the backward flow of secretions from the nasopharynx into the middle ear space and associated infection of the middle ear (otitis media).

The Inner Ear
The inner ear contains a maze of complex, winding passages (known as the labyrinth) deep within the temporal bone. The major parts of the inner ear include the organ of hearing, known as the cochlea, and the organ of balance, the semicircular canals.

The cochlea, a hollow, coiled passage that resembles a snail's shell, contains the organ of Corti and thick fluid. The organ of Corti has tiny cells with hair-like extensions projecting into the fluid. Vibrations transmitted to the inner ear cause the fluid and the hair-like extensions to vibrate. As a result, the hair cells are stimulated to generate nerve impulses that are transmitted by the vestibulocochlear nerve (acoustic nerve or eighth cranial nerve) to the brain.

The three semicircular canals are fluid-filled tubes containing specialized hair cells that respond to movement of the fluid. When movements of the head cause fluid movement within a canal, the cells initiate nerve impulses to the brain via the vestibulocochlear nerve, resulting in necessary adjustments to maintain balance.

The Eyes and Vision

The eye is a specialized sensory organ that is actually part of the central nervous system. It focuses light waves to create an image on the nerve-rich membrane at the back of the eye (retina). The retina, in turn, converts the image into nerve impulses that are transmitted to the brain via the optic nerve (second cranial nerve).

Anatomy and Function of the Eye
The eye is embedded in pads of fat within the bony socket in the skull. Movements of the eye are regulated by a network of six muscles, each of which moves the eye in a particular direction or directions.

The outermost layer of the eye, known as the sclera, is a tough, fibrous tissue that includes the "white" of the eye and the cornea, which is the front, circular, transparent area that serves as the eye's primary lens. A flexible mucous membrane, the conjunctiva, covers the sclera and lines the eyelid; in addition, the conjunctiva contains several glands that secrete tears and mucus. The eyelid consists of a thin layer of skin over muscle that covers a thin plate of connective tissue (tarsal plate). The edge of the eyelid contains a row of strong protective hairs known as eyelashes as well as several glands (meibomian glands) that produce an oily secretion known as sebum. The combined actions of the tear-secreting and mucus-producing glands of the conjunctiva and the meibomian glands of the eyelid produce an essential tear film that protects the conjunctiva and cornea from damage due to drying. The eyelid spreads the tear film over the cornea during the blink reflex, helping to ensure clear vision. Moreover, the eyelid further protects the eye by closing quickly as an involuntary reaction (reflex action) to the approach of any foreign object.

The middle layer of the eye, known as the choroid, includes two involuntary muscles: the iris and the ciliary muscle. The iris, the pigmented area visible through the cornea, is a circular muscle with a hole in its center known as the pupil, which controls the amount of light entering the eye. When certain fibers in the iris contract, the pupil widens, allowing in additional light; in contrast, when other iris fibers contract, the pupil constricts, allowing in less light. The lens of the eye, which is behind the pupil, is held in place by the ciliary muscle, a circular muscle that changes the shape of the lens to make appropriate adjustments in focus. For example, the ciliary muscle contracts when the eye focuses on near objects and relaxes when the eye views distant objects.

The hollow main cavity of the eye is filled with fluids that help to ensure the proper shape of the eyeball and assist in bending light rays that fall on the retina. The fluids include the thin, watery fluid in front of the lens (aqueous humor) and the jelly-like fluid behind the lens (vitreous humor).

The retina, the innermost layer of the eye, is a complex nerve-rich membrane upon which images created by the cornea and the lens fall. More specifically, as light passes through the cornea, the pupil, the aqueous humor, the lens, and the vitreous humor, it is bent (refracted) so that it is properly focused on the retina, which contains millions of tiny nerve cells that respond to light (photoreceptors). Such nerve cells are named based upon their shapes: i.e., rods and cones. Rods are stimulated by dim light and are necessary for night vision. Cones are stimulated by brighter light and are the receptors for daytime vision. Three different types of cones respond to the colors red, blue, or green. The rods and cones convert images formed on the retina into nerve impulses that are transmitted by the optic nerve (second cranial nerve) to the brain.

The Nose and the Smell Receptors

In addition to serving as the uppermost region of the respiratory tract, the nose also functions as the special sensory organ involved in the sense of smell (olfaction). The chemical receptors necessary for olfaction are specialized nerve cell endings located in a small area of mucous membrane (nasal mucosa) lining the nasal cavities. The olfactory cells have specialized, microscopic hairs (cilia) that are stimulated by different chemicals. In response to such chemicals, the cilia generate nerve impulses that pass through the olfactory nerve (first cranial nerve) to the smell centers of the brain.

The Tongue and the Taste Receptors

The tongue is the muscular, flexible organ in the floor of the mouth. This organ-which also plays an essential role in producing speech, breaking down food during chewing (mastication), and swallowing -functions as a specialized sensory organ involved in taste.

There are approximately 10,000 microscopic chemical receptors known as taste buds that produce the nerve impulses required for taste. Although most are located on the tongue, there are also some taste buds on the roof of the mouth (palate) and the back of the throat. The taste buds surround the bases of nipple-shaped elevations (papillae) that cover the surface of the tone and other tissues. Specialized cells within the taste buds (gustatory cells) generate nerve impulses in response to dissolved chemicals within saliva. Most of these impulses pass through the facial nerve (seventh cranial nerve) and the glossopharyngeal nerve (ninth cranial nerve) to the taste center of the brain. Stimulation of the taste buds results in four types of taste sensations including sour, sweet, bitter, and salty. Other taste sensations or "flavors" result due to the combined stimulation of taste and olfactory receptors.

Urologic System

The urinary system, which consists of the two kidneys, the ureters, the bladder, and the urethra, filters waste products from the blood, returns essential nutrients back into the blood, and produces and excretes urine.

The Kidneys

The kidneys, which are located at the back of the abdominal cavity, are situated on either side of the spinal column above the waistline. The right kidney lies beneath the liver. The left kidney, which is usually slightly higher than the right, is located below the spleen.

The primary functions of the kidneys are to regulate the delicate balance of electrolytes including sodium and potassium; control the acid-base balance of the body (i.e., ensuring that the blood and other bodily fluids are neither too acidic nor alkaline); and filter soluble wastes from the blood and eliminate these waste products. More specifically, the purpose of the kidneys includes the following:

- To filter certain waste products (e.g., urea, ammonia) and excessive sodium and water from the blood

- To reabsorb particular substances and return them to the blood

- To regulate the levels of certain substances in the blood and maintain the appropriate balance between water and salt content in the body (i.e., by filtration, reabsorption, and secretion)

- To regulate blood pressure and the production and release of red blood cells. For example, cells of the juxtaglomerular apparatus of the kidneys secrete a hormone (renin) that results in the constriction of blood vessels, thereby raising blood pressure. In addition, the kidneys produce erythropoietin, a hormone that assists in stimulating and regulating the production and release of red blood cells (erythrocytes) from the bone marrow. An increase in the number of circulating red blood cells boosts the body's capacity to carry oxygen to its tissues and organs.

Urine Production and Excretion

The kidneys each contain approximately one million nephrons, the filtering units of the kidneys. Each nephron consists of two primary components, the renal corpuscle and the renal tubule, both of which are further divided into additional regions.

The top of each nephron consists of a cup-shaped structure known as Bowman's capsule. Within Bowman's capsule is a network of tiny capillaries known as a glomerulus. Together, the two structures are known as the renal corpuscle.

As blood flows through the kidneys, the fluid portion of the blood is filtered by minute pores in the blood vessels of the glomerulus and the inner layer of Bowman's capsule. The fluid then moves into the region between the inner and outer layers of Bowman's capsule and enters into the first portion of the renal tubule (proximal convoluted tubule), where most filtered substances (e.g., most of the water, glucose, and sodium) are reabsorbed into the blood via capillaries around the tubules (peritubular capillaries). Next, as fluid moves into the loop of Henle, sodium and other electrolytes are pumped out. As the fluid passes through the next portion of the renal tubule (distal convoluted tubule), additional sodium is removed in exchange for potassium. Diluted fluid from distal convoluted tubules then passes into a collecting tubule, where fluid may continue to pass through the urinary tract as dilute urine or be returned to the blood to ensure appropriate water content in the body.

Urine then drains from the collecting tubules into central collecting areas (renal pelvis) of each kidney, which are the upper portions of the ureters. The ureters are narrow muscular tubes lined by mucous membranes. Contractions of the ureters' muscular walls move small quantities of urine into the bladder, a hollow organ that gradually expands as the volume of urine increases. As the bladder nears its capacity, nerve signals are transmitted to the brain to signal that urination is necessary. When urination occurs, the circular muscle (sphincter) between the bladder and the urethra opens, allowing urine to pass out of the body. Contractions of the bladder create pressure that forces urine into the urethra and out its external opening (urinary meatus).

Section IV
Indexes

Entry Name Index

A

A-TMRF Newsletter, 544
A-to-Z Health & Disease Information, 6282
A.J. Pappanikou Center for Developmental Disabilities, 7149
AAAAI Annual Meeting, 430
AAAAI Impact, 434, 5616
AABA Newsletter, 2663
AAIDD Texas Chapter, 2409
AAP Education Resource Guide, 7656
AAP Grand Rounds, 5617
AAP News, 5610
AASCEND, 339
ABA Program Companion, 847
Abbott Northwestern Brain Tumor Support Group at Abbott Northwestern Hospital, 1084
ABC Stories DVD, 3190
ABC's of Finger Spelling, 3319
ABCs of AVT: Analyzing Auditory-Verbal Therapy, 3320
ABCs of AVT: Analyzing Auditory-Verbal Therapy, 3191
ABDC Newsletter, 7646
Ability Connection Oklahoma, 1306
Ability First, 7687
Ability First, Camp Paivika, 7688
ABLEDATA, 6930
AbleData, 3147
About Brain Tumors: A Primer for Patients & Caregivers, 1152
About Children's Eyes, 7657
About Children's Vision: A Guide for Parents, 7658
About Hydrocephalus - Book for Families, 3799
About Meningioma, 1153
About Metastatic Tumors to the Brain and Spine, 1154
About Pituitary Tumors, 1155
About Special Kids (ASK), 7200
About the American Brain Tumor Association, 1156
About.com on Sleep Disorders, 4554, 5891, 5916
AboutFace USA, 1502
ACAAI Annual Meeting, 431
ACAAI eNews, 5618
Academic Pediatric Association, 6933
Academy for Eating Disorders (AED), 2584
Academy for Guided Imagery, 6934
Academy for Sports Dentistry, 2145
Academy of General Dentistry, 2146
Academy of Nutrition and Dietetics, 1204, 2551
Academy of Operative Dentistry, 2147
Academy of Osseointegration, 2148
Academy of Rehabilitative Audiology, 3103, 6935
Access Board, 6936
Accidents of Nature, 1325
Achieve Beyond, 681
Achondroplasia, 2, 21
Achondroplasia UK, 13
ACLP Annual Conference, 99, 7558
ACLP Bulletin Newsletter, 7647
ACM Lifting Lives Music Camp, 6859
Acoustic Neuroma Association, 2997
Acoustical Society of America, 3104
Acoustics, Audition and Speech Reception, 3195
Acquiring Courage: Audio Cassette Program for the Rapid Treatment of Phobias, 4960, 5941
Action for Healthy Kids, 4713
Activity Schedules for Children with Autism, 848
Acute Gastrointestinal Infections, 22
Acute Lymphoblastic Leukemia, 63
Acute Lymphocytic Leukemia, 170
Acute Myeloid Leukemia, 124
The ADA: Questions and Answers, 5827
ADAA Annual Conference, 2222, 7559
Adam and the Magic Marble, 6535
ADAPT Community Network, 1297

ADD & Learning Disabilities, 610
ADD From A To Z-Understanding The Diagnosis & Treatment of ADD in Children & Adult, 592
ADD: Helping Your Child, 611
ADDitude, 6792
ADHD, 657
The ADHD Book of Lists, 652
ADHD in Schools: Assessment and Intervention Strategies, 614
ADHD in the Young Child, 615
ADHD Parenting Handbook: Practical Advice for Parents from Parents, 612
ADHD Report, 655
ADHD Survival Guide for Parents and Teachers, 613
ADHD: Handbook for Diagnosis & Treatment, 616
ADHD: What Can We Do?, 593
ADHD: What Do We Know?, 594
Adolescents with Down Syndrome, 2459
Adoptive Families, 6937, 7581, 7640
Adriene Resource Center for Blind Children, 1670, 1799, 4664, 5475
Adult Brain Tumor Support Group, 1133
Adult Down Syndrome Center of Lutheran General Hospital, 2415
Adult Endocrine Disorders/GHD Educational Convention, 11, 330, 1612
Advanced Cancer: Coping with Advanced Cancer, 7659
Adventure Learning Center Camp Programs, 1603, 6843
Adventures of Maxx, 3624
Advocacy Center, 7322
Advocate Lutheran General Children's Hospital, Pediatric Research, 2416
Advocates for Children of New York, 7323, 7758
Advocates for Justice and Education, 7158
AEGIS, 2966
After Sudden Infant Death Syndrome, 6261
After the Diagnosis...The Next Steps, 6515
After the Tears: Parents Talk About Raising a Child with a Disability, 1338
AG Bell Biennial Convention, 3181
Agency for Healthcare Research & Quality, 2190, 6898
Aggression and Violence Throughout the Life Span, 1591, 6816
Agoraphobics in Motion, 4942
AHRC New York City, 3897, 6931
AIDS and the Education of Our Children, 2980
AIDS Awareness Library, 2979
AIDS Healthcare Foundation, 2931
AIDS Knowledge Base, 2967
AIDS United, 2932
AIM for the Handicapped Adventures in Movement, 6932
AJAO Newsletter, 3967
Al Capone Does My Shirts: A Novel, 849
Alabama Department of Rehabilitation Services, 3558
Alabama Head Injury Foundation, 3004
Alabama Institute for the Deaf & Blind, 1626, 1753, 3153, 4617, 5420
Alabama/Northwest Florida Chapter of Crohns Colitis Foundation of America, 1904
Alandra's Lilacs, 3324
Alaska Chapter of Asthma and Allergy Foundation of America, 414
Alaska Department of Education, 7085
Albany Library for the Blind and Physical Handicapped, 1643, 1772, 4636, 5447
Albany Medical College Pediatric Pulmonary & Cystic Fibrosis Center, 2061
Albany New York Regional Comprehensive Hemophilia Treatment Center, 3561
Albinism, 177
Alcohol, Tobacco and Other Drugs May Harm the Unborn, 2820
Alert, 545
Alex's Journey: The Story of a Child with a Brain Tumor, 1146
Alex: The Life of a Child Rutledge Press, 2113
Alexander Graham Bell Association for the Deaf and Hard of Hearing, 3105, 6938
Alexandria Library Talking Book Service, 1678, 1808, 4674, 5485
All About Amblyopia (Lazy Eye), 4026
All About Vision, 4027
All About Vision.Com, 4028

Entry Name Index

All Ages Support Group, 1059
All Children Have Different Eyes, 4038
ALL Kids, 101
All Kids By TwoHealth Services Agency, 5266
All Kinds of Friends, Even Green!, 6082
All Kinds of Minds, 617
All Nations Camp, 7689
All of Us Together, 3325
Alleghenies United Cerebral Palsy, 1308
Allen County Public Library, 7459
Allergy & Asthma Network Mothers of Asthmatics, 393, 443
Allergy & Asthma Today, 460
Allergy and Asthma Medical Group and Research Center, 5595
Allergy and Asthma Support Group of Central New Jersey, 5592
Allergy and Pulmonary Medicine, 418
Allergy Control Begins at Home: House Dust Allergy, 435
Allergy Web, 6742
Alliance Brochure, 550
Alliance for a Healthier Generation, 4714
Alliance for Assistive Service andTechnology (FAAST), 7163
Alliance of Genetic Support Groups, 2903
Aloha Special Technology Access Center, 7453
Alone in the Mainstream: A Deaf Women Remembers Public School, 3326
Alopecia Areata, 200
Alpha Omega International Dental Society, 2149
Alpha-1-Antitrypsin Deficiency, 212
Alphabet of Animal Signs, 3327
Alphabet Soup: A Recipe for Understanding& Treating ADD, 618
AlphaNet, Inc., 213
Alternative Approaches, 5353
Amblyopia, 4045
America's Special Kidz, 340
American Academy for Cerebral Palsy andDevelopmental Medicine, 1231, 1323, 1327
American Academy of Allergy, Asthma &Immunology, 394, 444, 5585
American Academy of Audiology, 3106, 4862, 6939
American Academy of Child and Adolescent Psychiatry, 1482, 2232, 4821, 4824, 6427, 6439, 6460, 6526, 6751, 6940
American Academy of Cosmetic Dentistry, 2150
American Academy of Dental Hygiene, 2151
American Academy of Dental Practice Administration, 2152
American Academy of Dermatology, 201, 3500, 3982, 5100, 6324, 6361, 6941
American Academy of Dermatology (AAD), 5335, 6334
American Academy of Esthetic Dentistry, 2153
American Academy of Family Physicians, 6752
American Academy of HIV Medicine, 2933
American Academy of Neurology, 4228, 4234, 6527
American Academy of Orthopaedic Surgeons, 5726
American Academy of Otolaryngology-Headand Neck Surgery, 940, 945
American Academy of Pediatric DentistryFoundation, 2154, 2184
American Academy of Pediatrics, 6, 24, 66, 127, 179, 202, 214, 226, 237, 249, 259, 283, 293, 301, 309, 325, 341, 395, 475, 563, 573
American Academy of Periodontology, 2156
American Academy of Sleep Medicine, 4342, 4517, 4544, 5885, 5892, 5910
American Academy of Somnology, 4531, 4552, 5889, 5915
American Action Fund for Blind Childrenand Adults, 1632, 1761, 3155, 4625, 5436
American Annals of the Deaf, 3452
American Anorexia Bulimia Association of Philadelphia, 4742
American Association for Cancer Research, 1008
American Association for Dental, Oral, and Craniofacial Research, 2157
American Association for Klinefelter Syndrome Information & Support (AAKSIS), 4002
American Association for Marriage and Family Therapy, 342
American Association for Pediatric Opthalmology and Strabismus, 2372, 2812
American Association for Respiratory Care, 396, 5242
American Association for the Study ofLiver Diseases, 951
American Association for Thoracic Surgery, 5243
American Association of Children'sResidential Centers (AACRC), 6943
American Association of ClinicalEndocrinologists, 1984, 3876, 3881
American Association of Diabetes Educators, 2288
American Association of Endodontists, 2158
American Association of Neurological Surgeons, 1009
American Association of Oral and Maxillofacial Surgeons, 2159
American Association of Orthodontists, 2160
American Association of People with Disabilities, 3899
American Association Of Psychiatric Pharmacists, 966
American Association of Public Health Dentistry, 2161
American Association of Sleep Technologists, 4518
American Association of Suicidology, 2192
American Association on Health and Disabilities, 3900
American Association on Intellectual andDevelopmental Disabilities, 3930, 6944
American Auditory Society, 6945
American Autoimmune Related DiseasesAssociation, 203, 250, 255, 1206, 1393, 1407, 1898, 2289, 2923, 2925, 3513, 3514, 4505, 4509, 4910, 4922, 5621, 5646, 5692, 5701, 6288
American Beverage Association, 4716
American Blind Bowling Association, 6947
American Blind Skiing Foundation, 6948
American Board of Dermatology, 6949
American Board of Fluency and Fluency Disorders, 5958
American Board of Pediatrics, 6950, 7584
American Board of Sleep Medicine, 4519
American Brain Tumor Association, 1010, 1141
American Camp Association, 4142, 6951
American Cancer Society, 1011, 2778, 6864, 6952
American Canoe Association, 6953
American Celiac Disease Alliance, 1207
American Childhood Cancer Organization, 67, 128, 1012, 2779, 3737, 4484, 4500, 4580, 5558, 6865, 6954
American Cleft Palate Craniofacial Association, 1497, 2162
American Cochlear Implant Alliance, 3108
American College Counseling Association, 2193
American College Health Association, 2194
American College of Allergy, Asthma & Immunology, 5587
American College of Allergy, Asthma andImmunology, 397
American College of Cardiology, 310
American College of Dentists, 2163
American College of Gastroenterology, 25, 260, 1548, 2764, 3683, 3689, 4432, 4810, 5399
American College of Medical Genetics, 2850, 7585
American College of Preventive Medicine, 2935
American College ofNeuropsychopharmacology, 6754
American Congress of Obstetricians andGynecologists, 6755
American Council of Blind Parents, 1676, 1806, 4672, 5483
American Council of the Blind, 180, 1621
American Counseling Association, 967, 4944, 5139, 5930, 6756
American Deaf Culture: An Anthology, 3328
American Deafness and Rehabilitation Association (ADARA), 3109, 6955
American Dental Assistants Association, 2164
American Dental Association, 2165, 2672, 2679, 4222, 4223, 6418, 6420
American Dental Education Association, 2166
American Dental Hygienists Association, 2167
American Dental Society of Anesthesiology, 2168
American Dermatological Association, 2688, 6956
American Diabetes Association, 2290, 2339
American Epilepsy Society, 5744, 5776, 6957
American Foundation for Children with AIDS, 2936
American Foundation for Suicide Prevention, 2195
American Foundation for the Blind, 181, 4019
American Gastroenterological Association, 26, 37
American Group Psychotherapy Association, 968
American Hair Loss Association, 204
American Headache Society, 4230
American Hearing Impaired Hockey Association, 3110
American Hearing Research Foundation, 3111, 4864, 6958

Entry Name Index

American Heart Association, 284, 311, 564, 1539, 3826, 3830, 4900, 5381, 5391, 6349, 6353, 6363, 6403, 6408, 6462, 6580, 6584, 6746, 6959
American Institute for Preventive Medicine, 1865
American Journal of Gastroenterology, 45
American Journal of Speech-LanguagePathology, 6000
American Journal on IntellectualDisabilities, 3933
American Kidney Fund, 4446, 4449
American Laryngological Association, 5959
American Liver Foundation, 215, 2857, 2862, 3658, 3663, 3672, 3991, 4433, 4439, 6885, 6960
American Lung Association, 216, 398, 445, 1178, 1181, 1994, 5112, 5382, 5527, 5530, 5537, 5539, 6463, 6609, 6614, 6961
American Lung Association of the City ofNew York, 2107
American Lyme Disease Foundation, 4143, 4154
American Medical Association, 399, 1549, 4717, 5244, 6757
American Mental Health Counselors Association, 969
American Mental Health Foundation (AMHF), 1427, 1567, 3901, 4520, 4545, 4877, 4945, 5931, 6758
American Network of Community Options & Resources, 3902
American Nurses Association, 2937, 5245
American Nystagmus Network, 4613, 4687
American Obesity Foundation, 4718
American Occupational Therapy Association, 3903
American Osteopathic College of Dermatology, 1394, 1408, 3984
American Pediatric Surgical Association, 5406
American Pediatrics Society, 6962
American Porphyria Foundation, 5130
American Pregnancy Association, 1550, 2813, 5246
American Professional Society on the Abuse of Children, 5018, 5049
American Psychiatric Association, 970, 2196, 2553, 2938, 4946, 5932, 6759
American Psychiatric Nurses Association, 971
The American Psychiatric Publishing Textbook of Schizophrenia, 1471
American Psychoanalytic Association, 972
American Psychological Association, 683, 973, 2197, 2554, 2939, 4719, 4947, 5140, 5933, 6760
American Public Health Association, 2198, 2555, 2940, 3904, 5247, 6761
American Red Cross, 6963
American School Counselor Association Annual Conference, 182, 190, 343, 363, 400, 432, 684, 812, 1233, 1324, 2199, 2223, 2373, 2439, 2491, 2501, 2556, 2607, 4054, 4069, 4720
American Sexual Health Association, 2941, 2968, 3702, 4420, 4421
American Sickle Cell Anemia Association, 5839, 5868
American SIDS Institute, 6183, 6232, 6240
American Sign Language Dictionary Third Edition, 3329
American Sign Language Handshape Dictionary DVD, 3196
American Sign Language V2.0, 3284
American Sign Language Video Series, 3197
American Sign Language Vocabulary, 3285
American Sign Language: A Student Text;Units 10-18, 3330
American Sign Language: A Student Text; Units 19-27, 3332
American Sign Language: A Student Text;Units 1-9, 3331
American Sign Language: Green Books Text and Tapes, 3198
American Skin Association, 3502, 3985, 6326, 6335, 6364, 6964
American Sleep Apnea Association, 294, 5886, 5893
American Sleep Medicine Foundation, 4521
American Social Health Association, 3699
American Society for Deaf Children, 3112, 6965
American Society for Dental Aesthetics, 2169
American Society for Gastrointestinal Endoscopy, 1208
American Society for Metabolic and Bariatric Surgery, 4721
American Society for Microbiology, 2942, 5248
American Society for Nutrition, 4722
American Society for Reproductive Medicine, 6465, 6640
American Society of Clinical Oncology, 2943, 4723
American Society of Clinical Psychopharmacology, 2200
American Society of Forensic Odontology, 2170
American Society of PediatricNeurosurgeons, 7586
American Speech Language HearingAssociation (ASHA), 2492, 2505, 2523, 2535, 3113, 4055, 5961, 6156, 6966

American Student Dental Association, 2171
American Thoracic Society, 401, 4724, 5249
American Thyroid Association, 3877
American Tinnitus Association, 3114
American Urological Association, 1551
American Urological Association Foundation, 4573
AmeriFace, 1495, 1881, 2718, 4125
AMOR - A Cancer Support Group forPatients & Their Families, 1090
Amputee Coalition, 6967
Amyloidosis and Kidney Disease, 7660
An End to Panic: Breakthrough Techniquesfor Overcoming Panic Disorder, 4975
An Introduction to Cystic Fibrosis forPatients and Families, 2124
An Introduction to Your Child Who HasCerebral Palsy, 1339
Ancient Greece, 3199
Anemia of Sarcoidosis, 5659
Anencephaly, 224
anfAR, 2962
Angels in the Sun Brain Tumor SupportGroup, 1056
Angels of Hope, 1096
Angry Gut, The: Coping with Colitis andCrohn's Disease, 6716
Animal Signs: A First Book of Sign Language, 3333
Animals, Insects, School, Colors Spanish/English Videos, 3200
Aniridia, 235
Aniridia Network, 241
Aniridia Web Site, 242
Ankylosing Spondylitis, 247, 257
Ann Whitehill Down Syndrome Program, 2418
Annual International Conference on ADHD, 588
Annual Meeting & OTO Experience, 944
Annual New York State Child AbusePrevention Conference, 5046
Annual World Symposium on Ocular Albinism, 191
Anorectal Malformations, 258
Anorexia Nervosa & Recovery: A Hunger forMeaning, 2625
Answering Your Questions About SpinaBifida, 6083
Answers to Some Commonly Asked Questions, 6689
Answers to Your Questions about PanicDisorder, 4965
Antisocial Behavior by Young People, 1592, 6817
Anxiety & Depression In Adults & Children, 2242
Anxiety & Phobia Workbook, 4976, 5943
Anxiety and Depression Association of Ameria, 974, 2201, 4765, 4949, 5141, 5935
Anxiety Cure: An Eight-Step Program for Getting Well, 4977, 5944
Anxiety Disorders, 4961, 4978, 4987, 5942, 5945, 5951
Anxiety Disorders Association of America, 2233, 4782, 4966
Anxiety Disorders Fact Sheet, 4988, 5952
Anxiety Disorders in Children andAdolescents, 4989, 5953
Anxiety Disorders: Practioner's Guide, 4979, 5946
Anxiety Panic Internet Resource, 4967
Aortic Stenosis, 280
APF Newsletter, 5134
Apnea Identification Program, 6209
Apnea of Prematurity, 290, 297
Apparent Life - Threatening Event andSudden Infant Death Syndrome, 6248
Applying New Attitudes & Directions, 2666
Approaching Equality, 3334
Apraxia Kids, 5962
Arc Annual National Convention, 589, 2440, 2819, 2849, 3754, 7560
Arc Family Connection Parent to ParentProgram, 7240
Arc Family Resource Project, 7104
Arc of East Central Iowa, 7213
Arc of Massachusetts, 7247
Arc of Montgomery County, 2374
Arc of Morgan County, 7079
Arc of New York, 3923
Arc of the United States, 574, 2375, 2450, 2814, 2842, 2851, 2871, 2875, 3751, 3755, 3905, 4167, 4174, 4210, 6466, 6570, 6968
Arc Suburban, 7263
Archives of Pediatric and AdolescentMedicine, 7587
Archway, 7185
Arizona Ataxia Support Group, 479

943

Entry Name Index

Arizona Camp Sunrise & Sidekicks, 117, 171, 1168, 2796, 4596, 6879
Arizona Chapter of Crohn's & Colitis Foundation of America, 1905
Arizona Early Intervention Program/Department of Economic Security, 7090
Arizona HeartLight, 3841
The Arizona Partnership for Immunization, 5264
Arizona Sleep Disorders Center, 4348
Arizona Spina Bifida Association, 6021
Arizona Technology Access Program Institute for Human Development, 7091
Arkansas Department of Health Div. of CommDiseases/Immunizations, 5265
Arkansas Disability Coalition, 7097
Arkansas Disability Coalition Parent Training and Information Center, 7098
Arkansas Easter Seals Technology Resource Center, 7431
Arkansas Regional Library for the Blind and Physically Handicapped, 1631, 1760, 4624, 5435
Arkansas Rehabilitation Research and Training Center for Deaf Persons, 3169
Arlene R Gordon Research Institute, 5491
Arlington County Department of Libraries, 7524
Armond V. Mascia CF Center, 2062
Arnold-Chiari Malformation, 299
Arrhythmias, 308
Art Show, 3201
Artery, 3635
Arthritis, 3958
Arthritis Foundation, 251, 1395, 1409, 3953
Arthritis in Children, 1420
Arthritis in Children and La Artritis Infantojuvenil, 3968
Arthritis in Children: Resources for Children, Parents and Teachers, 3969
Arthritis Sourcebook 5th Edition, 3959
Arthrogryposis Multiplex Congenita, 323
Articles on Legg-Calve-Perthes, 4109
As You Get Older, 1509
ASCD Biennial Conference, 3182
ASHA Convention, 2500, 2533, 3183
ASHFoundation, 3102
Ask Audrey, 6717
Ask NOAH About: Stomach and Intestinal (Gastrointestinal) Disorders, 6708
Ask the Doctor: Depression, 2243
ASL Babies: First Signs, 3321
ASL Babies: Let's Eat, 3322
ASL Clip and Create Version 3, 3278
ASL Songs for Kids, 3279
ASL Stories: Christmas Stories, 3192
ASL Stories: Fairy Tales I, 3193
ASL Stories: Fairy Tales II, 3194
ASL Tales and Games for Kids, 3280
ASL Tales and Games for Kids 2, 3281
ASL Tales and Songs for Kids CD-1, 3282
ASL Tales and Songs for Kids CD-2, 3283
Aspects of Lyme Borreliosis, 4157
ASPEN Annual Spring Conference, 362
Asperger Autism Spectrum Education Network (ASPEN), 344, 835
Asperger Syndrome, 335, 370, 380
Asperger Syndrome and Your Child: A Parent's Guide, 371
Asperger Syndrome: A Practical Guide for Teachers, 372
Asperger Syndrome: Guide for Educators and Parents, Second Edition, 373
Asperger's Network Support for Well-being Education and Research, 345
Asperger's Syndrome: A Guide for Parents and Professionals, 374
Asperger's Syndrome: Autism and Obsessive Behavior, 365
Asperger/Autism Network, 346, 685
Aspergers Women's Association, 347
Aspire of WNY, 1298
Assemblies of God National Center for the Blind, 1671, 1800, 4665, 5476
Assistance Technology Project, 7277
Assisting Parents Through the Mourning Process, 7566
Assistive Media, 195
Assistive Technologies of Alaska, 7086
Assistive Technology Access Partnership, 7371
Assistive Technology Center Simi Valley Hospital, 7435
Assistive Technology Collaborative, 7298
Assistive Technology for Kansas Project, 7220
Assistive Technology Partners, 7133
Assistive Technology Partnership, 7292
Assistive Technology Project, 7150, 7179, 7186, 7377, 7402
Assistive Technology Project, Human Resources, Voc. and Rehab. Services, 7336
Assistive Technology Resource Centers of Hawaii (ATRC), 7176
Assistive Technology Services Network, 7225
Assistive Technology Training and Information Center, 7201, 7460
Association for Behavioral and Cognitive Therapies, 1568, 6763
Association for Children with Down Syndrome, 2376, 2451
Association for Children with Hand or Arm Deficiency (REACH), 7588
Association for Children's Mental Health, 6969
Association for Education & Rehabilitation of the Blind & Visually Impaired, 1622, 6970
Association for Psychological Science, 975
Association for Research in Otolaryngology, 5963
Association for Research of Childhood Cancer, 7533
Association for Science in Autism Treatment, 686
Association for Size Diversity and Health, 2557
Association for Spina Bifida and Hydrocephalus, 6073
Association for the Bladder Exstrophy Community, 4568
Association For X And Y Chromosome Variations (AXYS), 4003
Association of Academic Physiatrists, 5964
Association of Asthma Educators, 402
Association of Blind Athletes, 6971
Association of Child Life Professionals, 68, 129
Association of Children's Prosthetic/Orthotic Clinics, 2833, 2836, 6972
Association of Developmental Disabilities, 3906
Association of Gastrointestinal Motility Disorders, 1209, 2600
Association of Immunization Managers, 5250
Association of Nurses in AIDS Care, 2944
Association of Professional Developmental Disabilities Administrators, 3907
Association of State and Territorial Health Officials, 2945
Association of Traumatic Stress Specialists, 5142, 5149
Association of University Centers on Disabilities, 3908, 5965, 6973
Asthma, 389, 451
Asthma & Allergy Foundation of America, 416, 1210
Asthma - Understanding and Control, 436
Asthma and Allergy Answers: Patient Education Library, 463
Asthma and Allergy FAQs, 446
Asthma and Allergy Foundation of America, 403, 419, 447, 5588
Asthma Self Help Book, 452
Ataxia, 473
Ataxia Fact Sheet, 551
Ataxia Telangiectasia Medical Research Foundation, 528
Ataxia Telangiectasia Project, 529
Ataxia-Telangiectasia Children's Project, 6327, 6336, 6365
Atrial Septal Defects, 560
ATTAIN: Assistive Technology Through Action in Indiana, 7199
Attention Deficit Disorder and Learning Disabilities, 619
Attention Deficit Disorder and Parenting Site, 604
Attention Deficit Disorder Association, 575, 603
Attention Deficit Disorder: Concise Source of Information for Parents, 620
Attention Deficit Disorders and Hyperactivity, 658
Attention Deficit Hyperactivity Disorder, 570
Attention Deficit Hyperactivity Disorder: What Every Parent Wants to Know, 621
Attention Deficit-Hyperactivity Disorder: Is it a Learning Disability?, 659
Attention Disorders and Eyesight, 4029
Auditory - Verbal International, 3447
Auditory-Verbal Therapy and Practice, 3335
Augusta-Richmond County Public Library, 7444
Aurora of Central New York, 7324

Entry Name Index

AUSPLAN Auditory Speech and Language, 3323
Autism, 817
Autism Acceptance Book: Being A Friend to Someone With Autism, 850
Autism and Asperger Syndrome, 375
Autism and Learning, 852
Autism and the Family: Problems, Prospects and Coping with the Disorder, 853
Autism as an Executive Director, 854
The Autism Community in Action, 719
Autism Fact Sheet, 381, 911
Autism Is a World, 818
Autism National Committee, 687
Autism National Committee Conference, 813
Autism Network for Dietary Intervention, 836
Autism New Jersey, 348
Autism Research Foundation, 688, 805
Autism Resources, 367, 837
Autism Science Foundation, 689
Autism Services Center, 690, 803
Autism Society National Conference & Expo, 814
Autism Society National Conference and Exposition, 364
Autism Society of Alabama, 726
Autism Society of America, 349, 691, 838
Autism Society of America Baltimore Chesapeake Chapter, 768
Autism Society of America Bluegrass Chapter, 765
Autism Society of America Broward Chapter, 750
Autism Society of America Coachella Valley, 730
Autism Society of America Connecticut Chapter, 747
Autism Society of America District of Columbia Chapter, 749
Autism Society of America East Tennessee Chapter, 789
Autism Society of America Emerald Coast Chapter, 751
Autism Society of America Florida Chapter, 752
Autism Society of America Gateway Chapter, 773
Autism Society of America Greater Austin Chapter, 790
Autism Society of America Greater Georgia Chapter, 757
Autism Society of America Greater Long Beach/San Gabriel Valley, 731
Autism Society of America Greater Phoenix Chapter, 728
Autism Society of America Greater Harrisburg Area Chapter, 785
Autism Society of America Inland Empire Chapter, 732
Autism Society of America Jacksonville Chapter, 753
Autism Society of America Larimer County Chapter, 743
Autism Society of America Los Angeles Chapter, 733
Autism Society of America Manasota Chapter, 754
Autism Society of America Massachusetts Chapter, 769
Autism Society of America North San Diego County Chapter, 734
Autism Society of America Northern Virginia Chapter, 792
Autism Society of America Orange County Chapter, 735
Autism Society of America Panhandle Chapter, 755
Autism Society of America Pikes Peak Chapter, 744
Autism Society of America San Diego Chapter, 736
Autism Society of America San Francisco Bay Chapter, 737
Autism Society of America San Gabriel Valley Chapter, 738
Autism Society of America Santa Barbara Chapter, 739
Autism Society of America Southern Arizona Chapter, 729
Autism Society of America Treasure Valley Chapter, 759
Autism Society of America Tulare County Chapter, 740
Autism Society of America: Colorado Chapter, 745
Autism Society of American Boulder County Chapter, 746
Autism Society of California, 741
Autism Society of Delaware, 748
Autism Society of Greater Cincinnatti, 781
Autism Society of Greater Orlando, 756
Autism Society of Hawaii, 758
Autism Society of Illinois, 760
Autism Society of Indiana, 761
Autism Society of Iowa, 762
Autism Society of Louisiana, 766
Autism Society of Maine, 767
Autism Society of Michigan, 770
Autism Society of Minnesota, 771
Autism Society of Mississippi, 772
Autism Society of Nebraska, 774
Autism Society of New Hampshire, 776
Autism Society of North Alabama, 727
Autism Society of North Carolina, 780, 802
Autism Society of Northern Nevada Chapter, 775
Autism Society of Ohio Tri-County Chapter, 782
Autism Society of Oklahoma, 783
Autism Society of Oregon, 784
Autism Society of Rhode Island, 786
Autism Society of South Carolina, 787
Autism Society of South Dakota Black Hills Chapter, 788
Autism Society of the Heartland, 764
Autism Society of Vermont, 791
Autism Society of Washington, 793
Autism Society of West Virginia, 794
Autism Society of Wisconsin, 795
Autism Speaks, 692, 806, 839
Autism Spectrum Connection, 350, 368, 693
Autism Spectrum Disorders: The Complete Guide, 851
Autism Training Center, 804
Autism Treatment Center of America, 694
Autism: A Strange, Silent World, 819
Autism: A World Apart, 820
Autism: Being Friends, 821
Autism: Effective Biomedical Treatments, 855
Autism: From Tragedy to Triumph, 856
Autism: Mind and Brain, 857
Autism: The Child Who Couldn't Play, 822
Autism: The Facts, 858
Autism: The Unfolding Mystery, 823
Autistic Disorder, 678
Autistic Services, 695
AWARE, 7175
Awareness, 4044

B

B.A.S.E. Camp Children's Cancer Foundation, 69, 130, 2780
Babies with Down Syndrome, 2460
Baby Breaths: How to Get Babies to Sit Still During Nebulizer Treatments, 437
Baby Center, 38, 273
Baby See 'n Sign, 3202
Baby See 'n Sign II, 3203
Baby Sign Language Basics, 3336
Baby Signing Time, 3204
Baby Signing Time DVD 2, 3205
Baby Watch Early Intervention Program, 7396
Baby's First Book of Signs: An ASL Word Book (Volume 1-3), 3286
Baby's First Book of Signs: Volumes I-III, 3287
Baby's First Signs, 3337
BabyNet, 7378
Bachelor Father, 3206
Bainbridge Subregional Library for the Blind and Physically Handicapped, 1644, 1773, 4637, 5448
A Balancing Act: Living with Spinal Cerebellar Ataxia, 539
Bancroft Camp, 7753
Bangor Public Library, 7478
Bartholomew County Public Library, 7461
BASH Magazine, 2660
Basic Course in American Sign Language Videotape Package, 3207
A Basic Course in American Sign Lanugage, Second Edition, 3315
Basic Guided Relaxation: Advanced Technique, 4968
A Basic Vocabulary: American Sign Language for Parents and Children, 3316
Baxter Healthcare Hyland Division, 3519
Bay Community Support Services, 1285
Baylor College of Medicine, 4298
Baylor College of Medicine Birth Defects Center, 7520, 7534
Baylor College of Medicine-Pathology & Pathogenesis of Otitis Media, 4867
Baylor Comprehensive Epilepsy Center, 5767
Baylor Sleep Wellness Center, 4403

Entry Name Index

Baystate Medical Center, 2040
BDRC Newsletter, 7648
Be Careful, 3338
Be Happy Not Sad, 3339
Because You Are My Friend, 5769
Bedwetting Online, 4574
Beech Brook, 914, 4083
Beginning Level Curriculum Tapes CompleteSet, 3208
Beginning Reading and Sign Language Video, 3209
Behavioral and Developmental PediatricsDivision, University of Maryland, 2419
Believe In Tomorrow Children's Foundation, 131
Believe In Tomorrow Children'sFoundation, 70, 2781
Bell's Palsy, 938
Bell's Palsy Network, 946
Bell's Palsy Research Foundation, 947
Belonging, 3340
BeMedWise, 6899
Ben and Catherine Ivy Foundation, 1013
Bend Support Group, 1118
Beneficial Designs, 6974
Benetech, 6975
Benign Essential Blepharospasm ResearchFoundation Newsletter, 2531, 2542
Berkshire Center, 4066
Best of Superstuff Activity Booklet, 453
Best Practices of Youth ViolencePrevention, 6824
Beth Israel Medical Center-Hydrocephalus, 3785
Bethel Mennonite Camp, 7719
Bethesda Oak Hospital, Sleep DisordersCenter, 4376
Better Hearing Industries Association, 3115
Beyond Celiac, 1211
Beyond Ritalin: Facts About Medication andOther Strategies for Helping Children, 622
Beyond the Autism Diagnosis: A Professional's Guide to Helping Families, 859
BeyondHunger, 2558
Big Crystal Camp, 915
Big Hearts for Little Hearts, 3855
Big Red Factor, 3636
Big Sky Kids Cancer Camp, 118
The Big Test, 3266
Bikers Against Child Abuse, 5050
Biliary Atresia, 949, 960
Bill Wilkerson Center, 3179
Bioengineering Center of Wayne StateUniversity, 3061
Biology of Schizophrenia and AffectiveDisease, 1455
Biomedical Concerns in Persons with Down'sSyndrome, 2461
Bipolar Disorder, 962, 1001
Bipolar Disorders: A Guide to HelpingChildren & Adolescents, 997
Bipolar Puzzle Solutions, 998
Bipolar World, 993
Birmingham Support Group, 478
Birth Defect Research for Children, 227, 2377, 2452, 2720, 3766, 3786, 4127, 4168, 4213, 6976, 7589
Birth Defects: A Brighter Future, 7661
Birth to 3 Program, 7419
Black AIDS Institute, 2946
Blake Foundation Children's AchievementCenter, 7092
Blank Children's Hospital: Department of Pulmonology, 2030
Bleeding Disorders Association of Northeastern New York, 3539
Bleeding Disorders Foundation ofWashington, 3555
Bleeding in the Digestive Tract, 49, 6727
Blick Clinic for DevelopmentalDisabilities, 7505
Blind Children's Center, 1633, 1762, 4626, 5437
Blind Childrens Center, 5421
Blood, 7810
Blood & Circulatory Disorders Sourcebook4th Edition, 105, 163, 5875, 6385
Blood Research Institute of SaintMichael's Medical Center, 3562
Bloodlines, 3637
Bloodstone Magazine, 3633

Bloomfield, 1715, 1852, 4708, 5519
Blue's Clues: All Kinds of Signs, 3210
Blueberry Eyes, 4039
Bluegrass Technology Center, 7471
Body Betrayed, 2626
Body Image, 2667
Body Language of the Abused Child, 5070
The Body Positive, 2580
Bold as Brianna, 3211
Bonnie Tapes, 1440
The Book of Choice, 3431
A Book of Colors: Baby's First Sign Book, 3317
BookRags, 6793
Books for Parents of Deaf and Hard-of-Hearing Children, 3463
Borderline Personality Disorder Sanctuary, 4884
Boston Children's HospitalDept. of Otolaryngology & Communication, 3168
Boston Hemophilia Center, 3563
Bowel Continence and Spina Bifida, 6084
Boy in the World, 2444
The Boy Inside, 366
Boy Scouts of America National Council, 6977
Boy Who Couldn't Stop Washing: TheExperience and Treatment of OCD, 4791
Boys Town National Research Hospital, 5989
Brady Institute for Traumatic BrainInjury, 3063
Braille and Talking Book LibraryPerkins School for the Blind, 1660, 1789, 4652, 5463
Braille Institute Desert Center, 1634, 1763, 4627, 5438
Braille Institute Sight Center, 1635, 1764, 4628, 5439
Braille Institute Youth Center, 1636, 1765, 4629, 5440
Braille Revival League, 6978
Brain & Behavior Research Foundation, 976, 1428, 4778
Brain and Spinal Injury Center (BASIC)Research at University of California, 3058
Brain Cancer Support Group at Mid-AmericaCancer Center, 1091
Brain Center Brain Tumor Support Group, 1072
Brain Disorders Sourcebook, 3082
Brain Imaging Center at the University ofCalifornia, Irvine, 3056
Brain Injury Association, 3075
Brain Injury Association of America, 2999
Brain Injury Association of Arizona, 3005
Brain Injury Association of Arkansas, 3006
Brain Injury Association of Colorado, 3009
Brain Injury Association of Connecticut, 3010
Brain Injury Association of Florida, 3013
Brain Injury Association of Idaho, 3018
Brain Injury Association of Illinois, 3019
Brain Injury Association of Indiana, 3020
Brain Injury Association of Iowa, 3021
Brain Injury Association of Kansas &Greater Kansas City, 3022
Brain Injury Association of Kentucky, 3023
Brain Injury Association of Louisiana, 3024
Brain Injury Association of Maine, 3025
Brain Injury Association of Maryland, 3026
Brain Injury Association of Massachusetts, 3027
Brain Injury Association of Minnesota, 3029
Brain Injury Association of Mississippi, 3030
Brain Injury Association of Missouri, 3031
Brain Injury Association of Montana, 3032
Brain Injury Association of New Hampshire, 3033
Brain Injury Association of New Jersey, 3034
Brain Injury Association of New Mexico, 3035
Brain Injury Association of New York State, 3036
Brain Injury Association of North Carolina, 3039
Brain Injury Association of North Dakota, 3040
Brain Injury Association of Ohio, 3041
Brain Injury Association of Oklahoma, 3042
Brain Injury Association of Oregon, 3043
Brain Injury Association of Tennessee, 3046
Brain Injury Association of Texas, 3047
Brain Injury Association of Utah, 3048

Entry Name Index

Brain Injury Association of Vermont, 3049
Brain Injury Association of Virginia, 3050
Brain Injury Association of Washington, 3051
Brain Injury Association of Washington DC, 3012
Brain Injury Association of West Virginia, 3052
Brain Injury Association of Wisconsin, 3053
Brain Injury Association of Wyoming, 3054
Brain Injury Glossary, 3094
Brain Injury Research Center of theInstitute for Rehabilitation & Research, 3071
Brain Injury Resource Foundation, 3016
Brain Injury Support And Education Group, 1066
Brain Injury Support Group, 1065, 1067
Brain Injury Support Group at AbbottNorthwestern Hospital, 1085
Brain Injury Update, 3095
Brain Lock: Free Yourself from ObsessiveCompulsive Behavior, 4792
Brain Research Center, 1139
Brain Research Foundation, 1140
Brain Research Institute, 3057
Brain Research Institute (BRI) School ofMedicine University of California LA, 3076
Brain Trauma Foundation, 3000
Brain Tumor Dictionary, 1157
Brain Tumor Education & Support Group, 1119
Brain Tumor Foundation for Children, 1060
Brain Tumor Networking Club, 1078
Brain Tumor Networking Group, 1070
Brain Tumor Patient & Family Support Group, 1041
Brain Tumor Support Group, 1073, 1079, 1092, 1097, 1101, 1113, 1132, 1134, 1135
Brain Tumor Support Group at Ann Arbor, 1080
Brain Tumor Support Group at Burlington, 1074
Brain Tumor Support Group at Dallas, 1127
Brain Tumor Support Group at Duluth, 1086
Brain Tumor Support Group at Milwaukee, 1136
Brain Tumor Support Group at Newport Beach, 1042
Brain Tumor Support Group at NovaCareRehabilitation Institute of Tucson, 1039
Brain Tumor Support Group at Philadelphia, 1121
Brain Tumor Support Group at Phoenix, 1040
Brain Tumor Support Group at Pittsburgh, 1122
Brain Tumor Support Group at PlainfieldMuhlenberg Medical Center, Neuroscience, 1098
Brain Tumor Support Group at Plano, 1128
Brain Tumor Support Group at Providence, 1124
Brain Tumor Support Group at Robbinside, 1087
Brain Tumor Support Group at San Diego, 1043
Brain Tumor Support Group at San LuisObispo, 1044
Brain Tumor Support Group at Santa Monica, 1045
Brain Tumor Support Group at South NassauCommunity Hospital, 1102
Brain Tumor Support Group at the NebraskaMedical Center, 1094
Brain Tumor Support Group at UnitedHospital, 1088
Brain Tumor Support Group at WauwatosaFroederdt Memorial Lutheran Hospital, 1137
Brain Tumor Support Group at Worcester, 1075
Brain Tumor Support Group for Patients & Families: University of Michigan Med Ctr, 1081
Brain Tumor Support Group of Greater StLouis, 1093
Brain Tumor Support Group of the Carolinasand Virginia Cancer Services, 1109
Brain Tumor Support Program Cedars-SinaiNeurosurgical Inst. & Wellness Communit, 1046
Brain Tumor Survivor Support Group, 1076
Brain Tumors, 1004
Brainstorms Companion: Epilepsy in Our View, 5783
Brainstorms: Epilepsy in Our Words, 5784
Break the Silence: Kids Against ChildAbuse, 5047
Breaking Ground: Ten Families BuildingOpportunities Through Integration, 1340
Breathe Easy: Respiratory Care in Neuromuscular Disorders, 4313
Breathing Association (The), 404
Breckenridge Outdoor Education Center, 6979

Brian Wesley Ray Cystic Fibrosis Center, 2002
Briarwood Day Camp, 7773
Bridges4Kids, 351
Brief Strategic Solution-Oriented Therapyof Phobic and Obsessive Disorders, 4793
Brigham and Women's Hospital, Asthma andAllergic Disease Research Center, 422
British Dyslexia Association, 2506
British Retinitis Pigmentosa Society, 5547
Broadscope Disability Services, 1317
Bronchoalveolar Lymphocytes in Sarcoidosis, 5660
Bronchopulmonary Dysplasia, 1174
Bronx Comprehensive Sickle Cell Center, 5863
Brooklyn College Speech and Hearing Center, 5976
Broward County Support Group, 489
Brown County Library, 7532
Building Cue Reading, 3212
Bulimia, 2613
Bulimia Nervosa & Binge Eating: A Guide toRecovery, 2627
Bulimia: A Guide to Recovery, 2628
Bulletin, 5347
Bureau of Early Childhood Programs, 7248
Bureau of Early Learning, 7304
Bureau of EI Services, 7345
Bureau of Family Health Services-AlabamaChild Death Review, 6191
Bureau of Special Education, 7362
Burger School for the Autistic, 798
Burn Injuries, 1183
Burn Institute, 1185, 1192
Burn Prevention Foundation, 1186, 1193
Burn Survivors Throughout the World, 1187, 1194
Burnt Gin Camp, 7778
Butterworth Hospital, Cystic FibrosisCenter, 2044

C

C.S. Mott Children's Hospital, 6980
Cabell County Public Library, 7529
CAF Medical Update, 6391
California Brain Injury Association, 3007
California Department of Health ServicesImmunization Branch, 5267
Callier Center for Communication Disorders, 5983
Callier Communications, 6004
Camelot For Children, 1123
Camp Abilities Tucson, 7684
Camp About Face, 1895
Camp Achieve, 5830
Camp Akeela, 382
Camp Aldersgate, 7686
Camp Alex A. Krem, 7690
Camp Allen, 7750
Camp Allyn, 7769
Camp ASCCA/Easter Seals, 7680
Camp Baker Services, 7785
Camp Barakel, 7735
Camp Boggy Creek, 6112
Camp Bon Coeur, 7721
Camp Brave Eagle, 7677
Camp Buckskin, 667, 916, 4084
Camp Catch-A-Rainbow, 119, 172, 1169, 2797, 4597, 6880
Camp Chatterbox, 7754
Camp Civitan, 1716, 1853, 3480, 7685
Camp Courageous, 7716
Camp Courageous of Iowa, 7717
Camp Crescent Moon, 5880
Camp Dartmouth-Hitchcock, 7751
Camp de los Ninos - Diabetes Society, 2345
Camp Discovery, 199, 1422, 2708, 5014, 5367, 5714, 7705
Camp Discovery American Diabetes Association, 2340
Camp Dunnabeck at Kildonan, 2517
Camp Easter Seal, 7779
Camp Easter Seal East, Camp Easter Seal West, 7786

947

Entry Name Index

Camp Easter Seals, 7749
Camp Emanuel, 3481
Camp Erdman YMCA, 7704
Camp Fantastic, 120, 173, 1170
Camp Fish Tales, 7736
Camp Friendship, 917, 2481, 7739
Camp Frog, 5831
Camp Funshine, 2131
Camp Good Days & Special Times, 5881
Camp Grizzly, 3482
Camp Hawkins, 2482
Camp Heartland, 2991
Camp Hickory Wood, 3096
Camp Hodia, 2341
Camp Holiday Trails, 7787
Camp Horizon, 7678
Camp Huntington, 2483, 3936, 4085
Camp Isanogel, 7710
Camp Joan Mier, 7691
Camp Joslin, 2342
Camp Joy, 7792
Camp Juliena, 3483
Camp Kindle, 2992
Camp Kindle- Project Kindle, 2993
Camp Kostopulos, 7783
Camp Krem, 918
Camp Kudzu, 2343
Camp Kushtaka, 2344
Camp Lee Mar, 7774
Camp Lotsafun, 919
Camp Merrimack, 920, 1362, 2484, 7681
Camp Millhouse, 7711
Camp New Friends, 4480
Camp New Hope, 921, 2485, 7740
Camp Northwood, 383
Camp Nuhop, 668, 922, 4086
Camp O' Fair Winds, 4087
Camp Oakhurst, 6113, 7755
Camp PALS, 2486
Camp Ramah in New England (Summer), 7730
Camp Ramah in New England (Winter), 7731
Camp Ramah in New England Tikvah Program, 923, 1363, 5832, 7729
Camp Rap A Hope, 7682
Camp Roehr, 5833
Camp Ronald McDonald at Eagle Lake, 7692
Camp Rubber Soul, 7693
Camp Shane, 4754
Camp Shane Arizona, 4755
Camp Shane California, 4756
Camp Shining Stars, 4757
Camp Shocco for the Deaf, 3484
Camp Smile-A-Mile, 7683
Camp Sun 'N Fun, 7759
Camp Sunshine Dreams, 121, 174, 1171, 2798, 4598, 6881
Camp Tanager, 7718
Camp Thunderbird, 7702
Camp Tushmehata, 1717
Camp Vacamas, 470, 5882
Camp Waban, 7724
Camp Winding Gap, 7767
Camp Winnebago, 7741
Camp Wonder, 5715
Camp Yomeca Upper Perkiomen Valley YMCA, 7775
Camp-A-Lot, 7694
Can I Tell You About Asperger Syndrome?: A Guide for Friends and Family, 376
Can Your Baby Hear?, 3464
Can't You be Still?, 1341
Canadian Society for Mucopolysaccharide & Related Diseases Inc, 4278, 6302, 6310
Canadian Task Force on Preventive Health Care, 5299
CANCER, 7567

Cancer & Blood Diseases Institute, 3564
Cancer Information for Teens, 4th Edition, 106, 164, 1147, 2791, 4493, 4590
Cancer Sourcebook, 107, 165, 1148, 2792, 4494, 4591
Cancer Support Group for Children, 1057
CancerCare, 71, 102, 132, 159, 1015, 1142, 2782, 2787, 4485, 4490, 4581, 4586, 6866, 6872
Capital Regional Sleep-Wake Disorders Center, 4365
Cardeza Foundation Hemophilia Center, 3565
Cardiac Kids, 3856
Cardiac Kids/Association of Volunteers, 3842
Cardiovascular Research Foundation, 315
Cardiovascular System, 7811
CARE Family Resource Center, 7105
Caregiver Action Network, 6982
Caregiver Brain Tumor Support Group, 1145
CARES Foundation, 1608, 1613
CARES Foundation Newsletter, 1616
Carolinas Chapter of Crohn's & Colitis Foundation of America, 1936
Carolinas Support Group, 523
Carolyn Kordich Family Resource Center, 7106
Carroll Center for the Blind, 1790, 4067, 4653, 5464
Carroll School Summer Programs, 7732
Cary Library, 7479
Case Report-MR Imaging of Myocardial Sarcoidosis, 5661
Case Report-Osseous Sarcoidosis and Chronic Polyarthritis, 5662
Case Western Research University, Bolton Brush Growth Study Center, 2898
Case Western Reserve University Cystic Fibrosis Center, 2074
CAUSE, 7256
Causes of Anxiety and Panic Attacks, 4969
CDC Lincoln County, 7234
CDH International, 1728
CdLS Biennial Conference, 1878
CEA-HOW Annual Global Convention, 2608
CEC Convention & Expo, 590, 7561
Cedars-Sinai Medical Center, 7590
CEL Subregional Library for the Blind and Physically Handicapped, 1645, 1774, 4638, 5449
Celebrating Families of Children & Adults with Special Needs, 7346
Celiac Disease, 1203
Celiac Disease Foundation, 1212, 1219
Celiac Support Page, 1220
Cells and Tissues, 7809
Center for Accessible Technology, 7436
Center for Auditory and Speech Sciences-Gallaudet University, 3157
Center for Autism and Related Disorders, 352, 696
Center for Best Practices in Early Childhood, 6983
Center for Cancer and Blood Disorders, 5866
Center for Cancer and Blood Disorders at Children's Medical Center in Dallas, 3566
Center for Digestive Disorders, 6707
Center for Disabilities and Development, 1234, 1569, 2291, 2378, 2493, 3001, 3909, 4546, 5887, 5911, 6012, 6764
Center for Disability Services, 1277, 1299
Center for Early Childhood, 7385
Center for Early Intervention of Deafness (CEID), 3116
Center for Eating Disorders, 2585
Center for Enabling Technology, 7499
Center for Family Support, 778, 988, 1435, 2406, 3924, 4530, 4551, 4776, 4883, 4957
Center for Hearing and Communication, 3148
Center for Independence Technology and Education, (CITE), 7441
Center for Infant & Child Loss, 6207
Center for Interdisciplinary Research on Immunologic Diseases, 423
Center for Literacy and Disability Studies, 6984
Center for Mental Health Services, 963, 1424, 1570, 4514, 4541, 4762, 4940, 5927, 6765, 6900, 6985
Center for Narcolepsy Research at the University of Illinois at Chicago, 4398
Center for Neural Recovery & Rehabilitation Research, 5764

Entry Name Index

Center for Parent Information and Resources (CPIR), 228, 261, 697, 1235, 1328, 1738, 2379, 4056, 4071, 4128, 4169, 4214, 4835, 5719, 5966, 6013, 6467, 6601, 6986
Center for Peripheral Neuropathy, 4144
Center for Psychiatric Rehabilitation, 977
Center for Sleep & Wake Disorders, Miami Valley Hospital, 4377
Center for Sleep Diagnostics, 4361
Center for Sleep Medicine of the Mount Sinai Medical Center, 4366
Center for Sleep Science at University of Michigan, 4360
Center for the Partially Sighted, 1684, 1814, 2295, 4680, 5492
Center for the Research and Treatment of Anorexia Nervosa, 2603
Center for the Study of Anorexia and Bulimia, 2604
Center for the Study of Autism, 840
Center for the Study of Bioethics, 2438
Center on Disabilities and Community Inclusion, 7403
Center on Disability and Inclusion, 698
Centers for Disease Control and Prevention, 5238, 5300, 6455, 6567, 6605, 6615, 6901
Centers for Disease Control and Prevention, 3664
CenterWatch Clinical Trials Listings, 7591
Central Brain Tumor Registry of the United States, 1016
Central Connecticut Chapter of Crohn's & Colitis Foundation of America, 1910
Central DuPage Hospital Center for Digestive Disorders, 1558
Central Indiana Sarcoidosis Support Group, 5629
Central Indiana Support Group, 498
Central Institute for the Deaf, 3172
Central Maine Medical Center, 2036
Central Michigan University Summer Clinics, 3485, 6006
Central Missouri Area Support Group, 509
Central New York Chapter of Crohn's & Colitis Foundation of America, 1929
Central Ohio Brain Tumor Support Group, 1114
Central Ohio Chapter of Crohn's & Colitis Foundation of America, 1937
Central Ohio Chapter of the National Hemophilia Foundation, 3543
Central Pennsylvania Area Support Group, 520
Central Region Early Intervention Program, 7372
Central Texas Brain Tumor Support Group, 1129
Centre for Neuro Skills, 3077
Cephalic Disorders Fact Sheet, 3800
Cerebral Palsy, 1228
Cerebral Palsy Associations of New York State, 1300
Cerebral Palsy Center Summer Program, 1364
Cerebral Palsy of Nassau County, 1301
Cerebral Palsy Research Foundation, 1281
Cerebral Palsy-Facts & Figures, 1361
Cerebral Palsy: What Every Parent Should Know, 1326
Cerebrospinal Fluid Shunt Systems for the Management of Hydrocephalus, 3801
CERN Foundation, 1014
CF & Pediatric Pulmonary Care Center, 2063
CF & Pediatric Pulmonary Disease Center, 2017
CF Center at The Children's Hospital of Philadelphia, 2081
CF Center, Pulmonary Section, 2090
CF Center/Medical University of South Carolina, 2086
CF Index of Online Resources, 2108
CF Web, 2109
CF, Pediatric Pulmonary & GI Center, 2064
CHADD: Children and Adults with Attention Deficit Disorders, 576, 605
Chadder, 656
Chai Lifeline, 6987
Challenge, 6072
Challenged Family Resource Center, 7107
Challenging Behaviour, 4893
Charcot-Marie-Tooth Association, 1375
Charcot-Marie-Tooth Disease, 1369
Charcot-Marie-Tooth Disorders: A Guide about Genetics for Patients, 1388
Charcot-Marie-Tooth Disorders: A Handbook for Primary Care Physicians, 1378
CHARGE Syndrome Foundation, 952
Charis Hills, 384
Charles Campbell Children's Camp, 1365
Chemotherapy, 1158
The Cherab Foundation, 5973
Chesapeake Chapter, 504
Chicago Center for Jewish Genetic Disorder, 6303, 6311
Chicago Library Service for the Blind, 1647, 1776, 4640, 5451
Chicago, IL Area Ataxia Support Group, 497
Child Abuse Legislation, 5051
Child Abuse Prevention Association, 5019, 6988
Child Abuse Prevention Network, 5052
Child Abuse Prevention Project: Be'adHaYeled (For the Sake of the Child), 5041
Child Abuse Quilts: Revealing and Healing the Pain of Child Abuse, 5053
Child Abuse.com, 5054
Child and Adolescent Bipolar Disorder, 1002
Child and Family Connections, 7187
A Child Called It: One Child's Courage to Survive, 5069
Child Care Aware of America, 4725
Child Department Services, 7235
Child Department Services, Department of Education, 7236
Child Development Clinical Services, 2426
Child Development Institute, 4575
Child Health Improvement Program Idaho Department of Health, 6201
Child Neurology Foundation, 295, 353, 476, 577, 699, 942, 1017, 1236, 1429, 1484, 2292, 2380, 2524, 3002, 3767, 4145, 4231, 4286, 4343, 4459, 4486
Child Sexual Abuse Treatment Program (Giarretto), 5036
Child Trauma Academy, 5055
Child Trends, 6766
Child Welfare Information Gateway, 5045, 6794
Child Welfare League of America, 5020
Child With A Bleeding Disorder: First Aid For School Personnel, 3646
Child with Epilepsy at Camp, 5809
Child's Guide To Seizure Disorders, 5810
Childhelp, 5021
Childhelp Children's Center of Virginia, 5044
Childhood Asthma, 438
Childhood Asthma: A Matter of Control, 464
Childhood Cancer Canada Foundation, 72
Childhood Dermatomyositis, 1391
Childhood Diseases and Disorders Sourcebook, 4th Edition, 108, 166, 1149, 2793, 4495, 4592
Childhood Leukemia Foundation, 73, 133, 3738, 4582
Childhood Leukemia: A Guide for Families, Friends & Caregivers, 109
Childhood Nephrotic Syndrome, 4454
Childhood Obsessive Compulsive Disorder, 4794
Childhood Schizophrenia, 1423
Children and Adolescents, 4803
Children and Autism: Time is Brain, 824
Children Living with Illness, 7108
Children of the Stars, 825
Children Special Needs-Pediatric Eye Care, 4030
Children with ADD: A Shared Responsibility, 661
Children with AIDS Project, 2969
Children with Autism and Asperger Syndrome A Guide for Practitioners and Carers, 861
Children with Autism: A Developmental Perspective, 862
Children With Autism: A Parents Guide, 860
Children With Cerebral Palsy: A Parents Guide, 1342
Children with Diabetes, 2325
Children With Fragile X Syndrome, 2854
Children with Hearing Difficulties, 3341
Children with Seizures: A Guide For Parents, Teachers and Other Professionals, 5785
Children with Spina Bifida: A Parent's Guide, 6085
Children with Spina Bifida: A Resource Page for Parents, 6074
Children with Starving Brains, 863
Children with Talipes (Clubfoot), 1527
Children with Tourette Syndrome: A Parent's Guide-2nd Edition, 6536
Children with Traumatic Brain Injury, 3083

949

Entry Name Index

Children with Visual Impairments: AParents' Guide, 245, 1696, 1832, 5501, 5553, 5571, 5583
Children's Alopecia Project, 205, 209
Children's Association for Maxiumum Potential CAMP, 7780
Children's Beach House, 3486
Children's Brain Tumor Foundation, 1018
Children's Bureau, 5016, 5056
Children's Cancer & Blood Foundation, 74, 134, 3520, 6367, 6379, 6404, 6409
Children's Cancer Research Fund, 6867, 6870
Children's Cancer Web, 103, 160, 2788, 3743, 4491, 4587, 5567, 6873
Children's Center for Cancer and BloodDisorders, 3505, 3567, 5858
Children's Center for NeurodevelopmentalStudies, 807
Children's Clinical Research Center, 2963
Children's Craniofacial Association, 1873, 1883, 2721, 4129
Children's Defense Fund, 5022, 6990
Children's Dream Factory of Maine, 7794
Children's Gaucher Research Fund, 2876
Children's Glaucoma Foundation, 1747
Children's Happiness Foundation, 7249
Children's Heart Society, 3869
Children's Hemiplegia & Stroke Association, 3003
Children's Hopes and Dreams, 7649
Children's Hospice International, 6991
Children's Hospital & Research Center ofOakland, 2412
Children's Hospital Association, 4726
Children's Hospital at Montefiore, 3944, 3947
Children's Hospital Boston, 2041, 6289, 6295, 6329, 6337, 6350, 6354, 6368, 6380, 6405, 6410, 6419, 6421, 6469, 6528, 6571, 6573, 6992
Children's Hospital Merit Care DownSyndrome Service, 2427
Children's Hospital of Los Angeles, 2003
Children's Hospital of Michigan CysticFibrosis Care, Teaching & Resource, 2045
Children's Hospital of New York Presbyterian, 3948, 4072
Children's Hospital of Orange County: Department of Pulmonology - Cystic Fibrosis, 2004
Children's Hospital of PhiladelphiaHemophilia Program, 3568
Children's Hospital of Pittsburgh GeneralClinical Research Center, 2431
Children's Hospital: Academic PediatricSurgery Department, 1542
Children's Hospital: Pediatric PulmonaryCenter, 2005
Children's House, 5057
Children's Leukemia ResearchAssociation, 75, 135
Children's Liver Alliance, 6892
Children's Liver Alliance Newsletter, 6896
Children's Liver Association for Support Services, 217, 220, 953, 957, 6886, 6893
Children's Lung and Cystic FibrosisCenter, 2065
Children's Lung Specialists, 2056
Children's Lyme Disease Network, 4146
Children's Medical Services ProgramFlorida SIDS Program, 6197
Children's Medical Ventures, 5226
Children's Mercy Hospital, Down SyndromeClinic, 2423
Children's Mercy Hospital, University ofMissouri, 2051
Children's National Health System, 97, 157, 1213, 5596
Children's Neurodevelopment Center atHasbro Children's Hospital, 2435
Children's Organ Transplant Association, 6993
Children's Seashore House, 2432
Children's Therapy Center, 7278
Children's Tumor Foundation, 4460, 4475
Children's Tumor Foundation - Indiana Affiliate, 4468
Children's Tumor Foundation-Arkansas Inforwww.php.com, 4465
Children's Wish Foundation International, 4487, 6868, 6994, 7795
Children, Adolescents, and Media Violence, 6825
Childswork/Childsplay, 6995
Chilren's Heart Services, 3846
Chorea, 1480
Chris Gets Ear Tubes, 3342
Chris Gets Ear Tubes: Spanish Edition, 3343
Chrissy & Friends, 5754
Christian Berets, 7695
Christian Dental Society, 2172
Christian Medical & Dental Associations, 2173
Chromosome 18 Registry & Research Society, 6470, 6592
Chronic Viral Hepatitis Backgrounder, 3673
Cincinnati Center for Developmental &Behavioral Pediatrics, 6849
Cincinnati Children's Hospital Medical Center, 3870
Cincinnati Digestive Health Center, 1559
Circle of Parents, 6795
Citizens United for Research in Epilepsy(CURE), 5761
CKLS Headquarters, 1655, 1784, 4647, 5458
Clara Barton Camp, 2346
Classroom GOALS, 3344
Classroom Notetaker, 3345
Clearinghouse for Specialized Media andTechnology (CSMT), 7437
Clearwater, FL Support Group, 490
Cleft Lip & Palate, 1511
Cleft Lip and Cleft Palate, 1494
Cleft Palate/Craniofacial Birth Defects:Cleft Palate Foundation, 1503
Cleft Surgery, 1512
Cleveland Brain Tumor Patient Network -Adult and Pediatric, 1115
Cleveland Clinic, 3779
Cleveland Clinic Children's Hospital & Epilepsy Center, 5746
Cleveland Clinic Foundation, SleepDisorders Center, 4378
Cleveland Hearing and Speech Center, 5978
Cleveland Public Library, 7506
CLIMB: Children Living with InheritedMetabolic Disorders, 3756
Clinical Assessment and Management ofSevere Personality Disorders, 4894
Clinical Counseling: Toward a BetterUnderstanding of TS, 6516
Clinical Diabetes, 2320
Clinical Genetic Services-Department ofPediatrics, 232, 304, 2726, 2863, 2877, 3690, 3757, 3787, 3995, 4013, 4134, 6853, 7592
Clinical Research Center, Pediatrics, 955
CLIPS: Clubfoot Information and ParentalSupport, 1526
Club Foot & Other Physical Deformities, 1533
Club Foot and Other Foot Deformities, 1534
Clubfoot, 1521
CMT Brochure, 1382
CMT Facts I, 1383
CMT Facts II, 1384
CMT Facts III, 1385
CMT Facts IV, 1386
CMT Facts V, 1387
CMT Net, 1374
CMTA Chapter - New York (Greater), 1371
CMTA Chapter - Ohio, 1372
CMTA Chapter - Pennsylvania, 1373
CMTA Report, 1381
CO-TEACH/Division of Educational Researchand Service, 7286
Coalition for Global Hearing Health, 3117
Coarctation of the Aorta, 1535
Cochlear Impant Auditory Training Guide, 3288
Cochlear Implant Auditory TrainingGuidebook, 3346
Cochlear Implant Awareness Foundation, 3118
Cochlear Implants for Kids, 3347
Cochlear Implants in Children, 3348
Cochlear Implants in Children: Ethics andChoices, 3349
Coconut Creek Eating Disorders SupportGroup, 2582
Cognition, Eduction, and Deafness: Directions for Research and Instruction, 3350
Cognitive Effects of Early Brain Injury, 3084
Cognitive Rehabilitation for Persons withTraumatic Brain Injury, 3085
Cognitive-Behavioral Management of Tic Disorders, 6446
COGREHAB, 660
Colic, 1546
Colitis Cookbook, 6709
College of Education - Western KentuckyUniversity, 7226
Colorado Consortium of Intensive CareNurseries United Parents (UP), 7134
Colorado Dept. of Public Heand & Environment: Immunization Program, DCEED-IMM-A3, 5270
Colorado Support Group, 487
Coloring Book on Thalassemia, 6386

Colors, 3351

Columbia Presbyterian Medical Center, 4294
Columbia Presbyterian Medical Center SleepDisorders Center, 4367
Columbia University, 6616
Columbus Children's Hospital, CysticFibrosis Center, 2075
Come Sign With Us: Sign Language Activities for Children, 3352
Come Sign with UsSign Language Activities for Children, 3353
Comfort Connection Family Resource Center, 7109
Commission of Public HealthImmunization Program, 5271
Commitment, 2123
Communicating Together, 2480
Communicating with People who Have aHearing Loss, 3465
Communication Disorders Quarterly, 6001
Communication Service for the Deaf, Inc., 3149
Communication Skills in Children withDown Syndrome: A Guide for Parents, 2462
Communications Disorders Clinic, 5992
Communique, 6005
Community Health Improvement Partners -Immunize San Diego (CHIP-ISD), 5268
Community Liver Alliance, 6887
Community Medical Center, Sleep DisordersClinic, 4384
Community Outreach for Prevention of Eating Disorders, 2559
Community Services for Autistic Adults & Children (CSAAC), 700, 841
Community Sickle Cell Support Group, 5848
Compass, 6136
Compassionate Friends, 6184, 6241, 6996
Complementary and Alternative Therapiesfor Diabetes Treatment, 2326
The Complete Family Guide to Schizophrenia, 1472
Complete IEP Guide: How to Advocate forYour Special Ed Child, 6086
Complex PTSD in Children, 5146
Complexities of TS Treatment: APhysician's Roundtable, 6517
Comprehensive Bleeding Disorder Center, 3569
Comprehensive Pediatric HemophiliaTreatment Center, 3570
Comprehensive Sickle Cell Center, 5862, 5865
Compulsive Eaters Anonymous, 2560, 4727
Computer Access Center, 7535
Computer Center for Citizens withDisabilities, 7397
Concentration Video, 595
Conception, Pregnancy and Psoriasis, 5354
Concise Guide to Evaluation and Managementof Sleep Disorders, 4560, 5899
Concise Guide to Evaluation andManagement of Sleep Disorders, 4537, 5922
Conduct Disorder, 1564
Conduct Disorder in Children andAdolescents, 1600, 6837
Conduct Disorders in Childhood andAdolescence (Developmental Clinical), 1593, 6818
Conduct Disorders in Children andAdolescents, 1594, 6819
Conduct Problem/Emotional ProblemInterventions: A Holistic Perspective, 1595, 6820
Conductdisorders.com, 1587, 6796
Conference on the Cause and Treatment ofFacioscapulohumeral Muscular Dystrophy, 4314
Confronting the Challenges of SpinaBifida, 6087
Congenital Adrenal Hyperplasia, 1606
Congenital Cataracts, 1618
Congenital Diaphragmatic Hernia, 1725
Congenital Disorders Sourcebook, 289, 569, 1343, 1545, 1894, 2728, 2821, 3794, 4905, 5396, 6088, 6356
Congenital Disorders Sourcebook 2nd Edit., 4138
Congenital Dysplasia of the Hip, 1734
Congenital Glaucoma, 1744
Congratulations? An Introduction to DownSyndrome for Parents/Family/Friends, 2445
Congressional Testimony on MuscularDystrophy, 4315
Conjunctivitis, 1861
Connect for Kids, 5058
Connecticut Birth to Three-Office of EarlyChildhood, 7152
Connecticut Down Syndrome Congress, 2396
Connecticut Lead Poisoning PreventionProgram, 4048

Connecting, 7650
Connecting Students: A Guide to ThoughtfulFriendship Facilitation, 1344
Connections Conference, 1501
Constipation, 2737
Constipation in Children, 2738
Consumer Fact Sheet, 2125
Consumer Indicators of Quality Genetic Services, 552
Consumer Information and TechnologyTraining Exchange (Maine CITE), 7237
Consumer Product Safety Commission Hotline, 4049
Consumer Products Safety Commission, 1195
Contemporary Issues in the Treatment ofSchizophrenia, 1456
Controlling Asthma, 461
Conventional Radiation Therapy, 1159
Convergence Insufficiency, 4031
Conversation with Anorexics: ACompassionate & Hopeful Journey, 2629
Cook-Ft. Worth Medical Center, CF Center, 2091
Cool the Burn, 1196
Cooley's Anemia 7th Annual Symposium, 6387
Cooley's Anemia Fact Cards, 6394
Cooley's Anemia Foundation, 6369, 6381
Cooley's Anemia Foundation (CAF) Pamphlet, 6395
Coping with Allergies and Asthma, 462
Coping with Cancer Magazine, 115
Coping with Childhood Cancer, 100, 158
Coping with Crohn's and Colitis is Tough, 1964
Coping with Depression, 2227, 2244
Coping with Eating Disorders, 2630
Coping with Post-Traumatic Stress Disorder, 5157
Coping with Sarcoidosis, 5663
Coping with Tourette Syndrome, A Parent'sViewpoint, 6547
Coping with Your Inattentive Child, 662
Cornelia de Lange Syndrome, 1871
Cornelia de Lange Syndrome Foundation, 1874
CorStone-Children & Loss Group, 6193
Cosmo Gets An Ear, 3354
COTT Washington Update, 3638
Council for Exceptional Children, 6997, 7593
The Council For Exceptional Children, 587
Council for Learning Disabilities, 4057
Council of Academic Programs in Communication, 5968
Council of Administrators of Special Education (CASE), 6998
Council of the American Instructors of the Deaf, 3119
Council on Education of the Deaf, 3120
Council on Quality and Leadership, 3910
Council on Size and Weight Discrimination(CSWD), 2561
Count Us In: Growing up with Down Syndrome, 2463
Countdown, 2314
Courage Camps, 7742
Courage North, 7743
Covert Modeling and Reinforcement, 999
Cowden Preautism Observation Inventory, 864
CPAC, 7151
CPF Teddy Bears, 1510
Craniofacial Center at University of Illinois, Chicago, 1891
Craniosynostosis, 1880
Craniosynostosis and PositionalPlagiocephaly Support, 1884
CRI Worldwide Pediatric Center forExcellence, 1557
Crib Death: The Sudden Infant DeathSyndrome, 6249
Crisis Nursery, 5035
Crohn's & Colitis Foundation, 1899, 1950, 1953, 6701, 6710
Crohn's & Colitis Foundation Carol FisherChapter, 1915
Crohn's Disaese and Ulcerative Colitis:Emotional Factors Q & A, 1965
Crohn's Disease, 1896
Crohn's Disease & Ulcerative Colitis: AGuide for Parents, 1967
Crohn's Disease & Ulcerative Colitis:A Guide for Teachers & Other Personnel, 1966
Crohn's Disease and Ulcerative ColitisFact Book, 1955
Crohn's Disease, Ulcerative Colitis, andYour Child, 6728
Cross Roads Outdoor Ministries, 7756

Entry Name Index

Crotched Mountain School & Rehabilitation Center, 924, 1366, 3097, 3937, 5834, 7679, 7752
Crowley Ridge Regional Library, 7432
Crozer-Chester Medical Center, 4385
Cry for Help - How to Help a Friend Who isDepressed or Suicidal, 2228
Cryptorchidism, 1973
Cued Speech Resource Book, 3355
Cult of Thinness, 2631
Cure SMA, 6117
CureSearch for Children's Cancer, 76, 1019, 2783, 3739, 4583, 5559, 6869, 6999
Curing Epilepsy: Focus on the Future/Benchmarks for Epilepsy Research, 5777
Current Approaches to Down's Syndrome, 2464
Cushing's Support and Research Foundation, 1020, 1985, 1988
Cushing's Syndrome, 1982
CW HOG, 6981
CyberPsych, 994, 1444, 4532, 4555, 4783, 4885, 4970, 7594
Cyclic Vomiting Syndrome, 50
Cyclic Vomiting Syndrome Association, 5400
Cystic Fibrosis, 1992, 2114
Cystic Fibrosis and Chronic PulmonaryDisease Clinic, 2028
Cystic Fibrosis and Pediatric RespiratoryDiseases Center, 2009
Cystic Fibrosis Care, Teaching andResearch Center, 2092
Cystic Fibrosis Center - All Children'sHospital, 2018
Cystic Fibrosis Center at PolyclinicMedical Center, 2082
Cystic Fibrosis Center/Pediatric Pulmonaryand Sleep Medicine, 2046
Cystic Fibrosis Center/University ofVirginia Health System, 2097
Cystic Fibrosis Center: Cedars-SinaiMedical Center, 2006
Cystic Fibrosis Center: Children's Memorial Hospital, 2023
Cystic Fibrosis Center: Phoenix Children'sHospital, 2001
Cystic Fibrosis Center: University ofCalifornia at San Francisco, 2007
Cystic Fibrosis Foundation, 1995
Cystic Fibrosis Program of the MedicalCollege of Virginia, 2098
Cystic Fibrosis Research, Inc., 1996, 2008
Cystic Fibrosis, Pediatric Pulmonary andPediatric Gastrointestinal Center, 2052
Cystic Fibrosis-Lung Disease CenterSanta Rosa Children's Hospital, 2093
Cystic Fibrosis: A Guide for Patient andFamily, 2115
Cystic Fibrosis: Guide for Parents, 2126
Cystic Fibrosis: The Facts, 2116
Cytomegalovirus, 2134

D

Dad and Me in the Morning, 3356
Daddy's Girl, 2446
Dakota, 6435, 6518
DakotaLink, 7381
Dallas Academy, 669, 925, 4088
Dana Alliance for Brain Initiatives, 3064, 3078
Dancing Cheek to Cheek, 1704, 1839, 4697, 5508
Dangerous DecibelsOregon Health & Science University, 3150
The Daniel Jordan Fiddle Foundation, 720
Dartmouth-Hitchcock Sleep Disorders CenterDartmouth Medical Center, 4362, 7305
David Baldwin's Trauma InformationPages, 5150
Davis Dyslexia Association InternationalDyslexia: The Gift, 2494, 2507
Day for Night: Recognizing TeenageDepression, 2229
DC Arc, 7159
Deadly Diet: Recovering From Anorexia andBulimia, 2632
Deaf Children in China, 3357
Deaf Children in Public Schools: Placement, Context, and Consequences, 3358
Deaf Children Signers, 3213
Deaf Counseling, Advocacy & Referral Agency, 3121
Deaf Daughter, Hearing Fahter, 3359
Deaf Life, 3448
Deaf REACH, 3122
Deaf Side Story: Deaf Sharks, Hearing Jets, and a Classic American Musical, 3360

Deaf Students Can Be Great Readers, 3361
Deaf USA, 3449
Deafness: A Fact Sheet, 3466
Dealing with Depression: Five Ways to Help, 2245
Death Investigations and Sudden InfantDeath Syndrome, 6250
Death of a Child, the Grief of the ParentsA Lifetime Journey, 6251
DebRA: Dystrophic Epidermolysis BullosaResearch Association of America, 2743
Deenie, 5735
Delaware Assisstive Technology Initiative(DATI), 7155
Delaware Division of Libraries for theBlind and Physically Handicapped, 1399, 5001
Delaware Valley Chapter of the NationalHemophilia Foundation, 3548
Delightful as Derek, 3214
Delta/Montrose Parent to Parent, 7135
Dental Conditions, 2142
Dental Consumer Advisory, 2185, 4224
Dental Problems with Growth HormoneDeficiency, 2916
Dental Resources on the Web, 2186, 2680, 4225
Denver Children's Hospital, 2014
Denver Early Childhood Connections, 7136
Denver Sarcoidosis Awareness Support Group, 5627
Department for Exceptional StudentsGeorgia Department of Education, 7170
Department of Assistive and RehabilitationServices, 7388
Department of Children, Family, & Learning, 7264
Department of Counseling and EducationalLeadership-Columbus State University, 7171
Department of Developmental Services ofEarly Start Program, 7110
Department of Education, 7180
Department of Elementary and SecondaryEducation, 7279
Department of Health & Environment, 7221
Department of Health and Human Services, 5113
Department of HealthDivision of Immunization, 5239, 5272
Department of Human Services, 6206
Department of Pediatrics, Medical Collegeof Georgia, 2021
Department of Public Instruction, 7156
Depressed Anonymous, 2202
Depression, 2188
Depression and Bipolar Support Alliance, 978, 2203
Depression and Its Treatment, 2246
Depression in Children and Adolescents: AFact Sheet for Physicians, 2275
Depression Is a Treatable Illness: APatients Guide, 2274
Depression, the Mood Disease, 2247
Depressive and Manic-DepressiveAssocation of Mount Sinai, 989, 2217
Depressive Illnesses: Treatments Bring NewHope, 2248
Dept. of Health & Mental Hygiene-Immunization, 5280
Dermatologic System, 7812
Dermatology Focus, 1417, 2703, 5011, 5349
Dermatology Foundation, 7595
Dermatology Information Network(DERMINFONET), 1400, 2692, 5002
Dermatology World, 1418, 2704, 5012, 5350
DermNet NZ: The Dermatology Resource, 5103
Des Moines YMCA Camp, 122, 175, 471, 1172, 2132, 2347, 3487
Described and Captioned Media Program, 3167
Desferal Q & A, 6396
Detroit Michigan Ataxia Support Group, 506
Developing and Writing IEPs Under the New IDEA, 827
Developing Cognition in Young Children Whoare Deaf, 3467
Developing Friendships: Wonderful People to Get to Know, 826
Developing Good Speech, 1513
Development and Training Center, 7420
Development of Behavioral and EmotionalProblems in Tourette Syndrome, 6548
The Development of Deaf Children: AcademicAchievement Levels and Social Processes, 3432
Developmental Center, 670, 926, 4089
Developmental Delay Resources, 701, 7000
Developmental Disabilities Nurses Association, 3911, 7001
Developmental Disabilities Program, 7287
Developmental Disabilities Unit, 7342

Entry Name Index

Developmental Medicine Center, 2964
Developmental Pediatrics School of Medicine, University of Maryland, 7241
Developmental Services Center, 7188
DHR/Division of Public Health - Babies Cant Wait Program, 7169
Diabetes, 2317
Diabetes 101, 2300
Diabetes Advisor, 2321
Diabetes Care, 2318
Diabetes Dateline, 2322
Diabetes Dictionary, 2301
Diabetes Educator, 2323
Diabetes Forecast, 2315
Diabetes in African Americans, 2329
Diabetes in Hispanic Americans, 2330
Diabetes Insipidus, 2327
Diabetes Medical Nutrition Therapy, 2302
Diabetes Mellitus, 2286
Diabetes Overview, 2328
Diabetes Spectrum: From Research to Practice, 2319
Diabetes Teaching Guide for People Who Use Insulin, 2303
Diabetic Neuropathy: the Nerve Damage of Diabetes, 2331
Diabetics Control and Complications Trial, 2332
Diagnosing and Managing IBD, 1968
Diagnosis Autism: Now What? 10 Steps to Improve Treatment Outcomes, 865
Diagnosis Schizophrenia: A Comprehensive Resource, 1457
Diagnostic and Statistical Manual of Mental Disorders, 1490
Diagnostic Approach to the Dysmorphic Patient, 531
Diagnostic Tests, 51
Dialogue with Doris, 5638
Diarrhea, 52
Diet Instruction, 1225
Different Like Me: My Book of Autism Heroes, 866
Difficult Child, 1596
DiGeorge Syndrome, 2356
Digestive Disease National Coalition, 27, 262, 1552, 1729, 1900, 2765, 4434, 5401, 6702
Digestive Diseases Dictionary, 44
Digestive Diseases Self-Education Program (DDSEP 9), 36
Digestive System, 7813
Digital Wellness Lab, 6767
Directions, 6137
Directory of National Genetic Voluntary Organizations, 540
Directory of Pediatric Neurosurgeons, 3802
Disabilities Advocacy & Support Network, 7280
Disability Awareness, 7568
Disability Connection and RAFT, Larimer County's Early Childhood Connection, 7137
Disability Information and Resource Center, 2864
Disability Rights Education & Defense Fund, 7002
Disabled Shooting Services, 7003
Disabled Sports USA, 7004
Discipline and the Child with Tourette Syndrome, 6549
Discovering Cued Speech, 3215
Discovery Book, 1345
Disruptive Behavior Disorders in Children, 1597, 4825, 6821, 6826
Distant Drums, Different Drummers: A Guide for Young People with ADHD, 623
District of Columbia Public Library/Librarian for the Deaf Community, 3158
Diverticular Disease, 53
Division for Early Childhood, 7005
Division for Learning Disabilities, 4058, 4073
Division for Research (CEC-DR), 7536
Division for the Visually Handicapped, 1679, 1809, 4675, 5486
Division of Birth Defects & Developmental Disabilities, 7006
Division of Birth Defects & Developmental Disabilities, 4808
Division of Birth Defects and Genetic Diseases, 7537
Division of Community Health Nursing, 6196
Division of Community Services, 7421
Division of Developmental Disabilities, 7425
Division of Early Intervention Services, 7363
Division of Exceptional Learners Indiana Department of Education, 7202
Division of Extramural Research, 6233, 6242
Division of Pediatric Pulmonology, 5392
Division of Preschool Services, 7227
Division of Special Education, 7288, 7306
Division of Special Education State Department of Education, 7093
Division of Special Populations, 7229
Division of Student Services, 7311
Division on Career Development and Transition, 7007
Division on Visual Impairments, 1680, 1810, 4676, 5487
DMRF/NINDS Dystonia Workshop: From Gene to Function in Dystonia, 2543
Do I Look Fat in This?: Life Doesn't Begin Five Pounds From Now, 2633
Does My Child Have Autism?, 867
domesticshelters.org, 6815
Don't Give Up Kid, 624
Don't Think About Monkeys: Extraordinary Stories Written by People with Tourette, 6537
Dotty the Dalmatian Has Epilepsy, 5786
The Doug Flutie, Jr. Foundation for Autism, 721
Down Sydrome: Living and Learning in the Community, 2465
Down Syndrome, 2369
Down Syndrome Affiliates in Action, 2381
Down Syndrome Association of Atlanta, 2399
Down Syndrome Association of Central Indiana, 7203
Down Syndrome Association of Los Angeles, 2394
Down Syndrome Association of Middle Tennessee, 2408
Down Syndrome Association of Minnesota, 2405
Down Syndrome Association of NWI, 2401
Down Syndrome Clinic of Minneapolis Children's Medical Center, 2422
Down Syndrome Clinic, Children's Hospital of Alabama, 2411
Down Syndrome Clinic, Rainbow Babies and Children's Hospital, 2428
Down Syndrome Guild, 2453
Down Syndrome Guild of Dallas, 2410
Down Syndrome Information Alliance, 2382
Down Syndrome Innovations, 2383
Down Syndrome Program, Children's Hospital Boston, 2421
Down Syndrome Specialty Clinic, 2436
Down Syndrome Support Association of Southern Indiana (DSSASI), 2402
Down Syndrome: Birth to Adulthood: Giving Families an Edge, 2466
Down Syndrome: The Facts, 2467
Down's Syndrome Medical Clinic, 2424
Downtown Detroit Subregional Library for the Blind and Handicapped, 1661, 1791, 4654, 5465
Dr. Gertrude A. Barber National Institute, 2433
Dr. Ivan's Depression Central, 2234
Dr. Koop, 1742, 1867, 4576, 5407
Draw Me a Picture, 110
Dream Factory, 7796
Dream Street Foundation, 7696
The Driving Test, 3267
Drugs and Pregnancy: It's Not Worth The Risk, 2822
Drugs That Have Been Used for the Treatment of Sarcoidosis, 5664
Dual Diagnosis, 4886
Duke Brain Tumor Support Group, 1110
Duke Pediatric Brain Tumor Family Support Program, 1111
Duke University Comprehensive Epilepsy Center, 5765
Duke University Comprehensive Sickle Cell Center, 5864
Duke University Medical Center/ CF Center, 2071
Duke University School of Medicine Pediatric and Allergy Immunology, 5597
Durable Power of Attorney for Health Care Decisions, 3803
DVH Quarterly, 1416, 2702, 5010, 5348
DVI Quarterly, 5575
Dyslexia, 2488, 2504
Dyslexia Research Institute, 4059
Dysphonia International, 5969
Dystonia, 2520
Dystonia Medical Research Foundation, 2525, 2532, 2536

953

Entry Name Index

Dytonias: Fact Sheet, 2544

E

EA Message, 2272
Each of Us Remembers: Parents of Children With Cerebral Palsy, 1346
Eagle Eyes A Child's View od Attention Deficit Disorder, 625
Eagle Eyes: A Child's View of Attention Deficit Disorder, 626
Eagle Hill School - Summer Program, 671, 927, 4090
Ear, Nose and Throat Journal, 5611
Early Childhood CARES Program, 7357
Early Childhood Development, 6902
Early Childhood Handicapped Prgrams, 7422
Early Intervention Program, 7080, 7325, 7415
Early Intervention Programs, 7358
Early Intervention Research Institute, Developmental Center, 7538
Early Intervention Services, 7250
Early Intervention Services Division of Child & Family Services, 7299
Early Intervention System, 7312
Early Intervention Unit, Division of Children's Medical Services, 7164
Early on Michigan, 7257
The Early Stages of Schizophrenia, 1473
Early Start Family Resource Network, 7111
East Central Region-Helen Keller National Center, 1627, 1755, 4619, 5430
East Central Regional Office, 7347
East Tennessee Comprehensive Hemophilia Center, 3571
East Tennessee Technology Access Center, 7518
Easter Seal Kysoc, 2349, 3488, 3938, 7720
Easter Seal Society, 7712
Easter Seal Summer Camp Programs, 7697
Easter Seals, 1237, 1329, 6014, 7008, 7596
Easter Seals Camp Challenge, 7703
Easter Seals Camp Fairlee Manor, 7726
Easter Seals of Greater Houston, 1315
Easter Seals Oregon Camping Program, 7771
Easter Seals Wisconsin Camp Respite, 1367
Eastern Maine Medical Center: Cystic Fibrosis Center, 2037
Eastern Michigan Hemophilia Center, 3572
Eastern North Carolina Chapter (SCDAA), 5850
Eastern Virginia Medical Center, 2099
Eating Disorder Anonymous EDA, Inc., 2562
Eating Disorder Hope, 2563
Eating Disorder Recovery Support, 2564
Eating Disorder Referrals, 5087
Eating Disorder Sourcebook, 2634
Eating Disorder Video, 2614
Eating Disorders, 2547, 2635
Eating Disorders & Obesity, 2nd Ed., 2636
Eating Disorders Association of New Jersey, 2587
Eating Disorders Coalition, 2565
Eating Disorders Information Network, 2566
Eating Disorders Online.com: 15 Styles of Distorted Thinking, 2617
Eating Disorders Research and Treatment Program, 2605
Eating Disorders Research Society, 2567
Eating Disorders Resource Catalogue, 2637
Eating Disorders Review, 2664
Eating Disorders: When Food Turns Against You, 2638
Eaton-Peabody Laboratory of Auditory Physiology, 3163
EB Medical Research Foundation, 2746
ECACNC PTI, 7337
Echolalia, 6519
Ecology and Enviromental Management of Lyme Disease, 4158
Economic Glitch, 3216
Ectodermal Dysplasias, 2668
Eczema, 2684
Eczema/Atopic Dermatitis, 2706
Eden Wood Center, 2487, 6860, 7744
EDI, 2348
Educating Deaf Children: An Introduction, 3468
Educating Deaf Students: Global Perspectives, 3362
Educating Inattentive Children, 596

Educating Peter, 2447
Educating Students with Autism: Implementation of Applied Bahavior Analysis, 828
Education and Care for Adolescents and Adults with Autism, 868
Education Development Center - EDC, 7251
Educational and Development Aspects of Deafness, 3365
Educational and Developmental Aspects of Deafness, 3366
Educational Audiology Association, 3123, 5970
Educational Audiology for the Limited-Hearing Infant and Preschooler, 3363
Educational Equity, Special Education Branch, 7300
Educational Interpreting: How It Can Succeed, 3364
Educational Issues Among Children With Spina Bifida, 6105
Educational Rights for Children With Arthritis: Parents Manual, 3960
Educational Services for the Visually Impaired, 1630, 1759, 4623, 5434, 7433
Effective Parent Project, 7138
Effective Treatments for PTSD, 2nd Ed, 5158
Effects of Alcohol on Pregnancy National Clearinghouse for Alcohol Information, 2825
Effects of Sarcoid and Steroids on Angiotensin-Converting Enzyme, 5665
EFWCP Resource Library, 5759
Egleston Cystic Fibrosis Center: Department of Pediatrics, 2022
EHealth, 4829
The Ehlers-Danlos Society, 2714
Ehlers-Danlos Syndrome, 2709
El Groupo Vida, 7139
El Rolphe Center, 4887
Electronic Media and Youth Violence - ACDC Issue Brief, 6827
Elf on a Shelf for Minimal Pairs: Giant CD Print Program, 3289
Elizabeth Glazer Pediatric AIDS Foundation, 2947, 2970
Elkhart Public Library, 7462
Embrace the Dawn, 5787
EMedicine Journal: Syncope, 6274
Emory Autism Resource Center, 796
Emory Eye Center - Strabismus Research, 6146
Empowering Parents, 6797
Encephalitis Information Resource, 6176
Encephalocele, 2716
Enchanted Hills Camp, 1718, 1854, 3489
Encopresis, 2729
Encyclopedia of Depression, 2249
Encyclopedia of Obesity and Eating Disorders, 2639
Encyclopedia of Phobias, Fears, and Anxieties, 4980, 5947
Encyclopedia of Schizophrenia and the Psychotic Disorders, 1458
Endeavor, 3455
Endocrine & Metabolic Disorders Sourcebook 3rd Edition, 1989, 2304, 2911, 3884
Endocrine Society, 6641, 7009
Endocrine System, 7814
Endorphins: Eating Disorders & Other Addictive Behavior, 2640
Endoscopic Third Ventriculoscopy, 3804
Enough Is Enough, 6798
EnTech: Enabling Technologies of Kentuckiana, 7472
Environmental Protection Agency, 405
Ependymoma, 1160
EPIC Long Island, 5755
EpiCenter, 5760
EPICS Project-SW Communication Resources, 7317
Epidermolysis Bullosa, 2740
Epilepsia: Journal of the International League Against Epilepsy, 5808
Epilepsy & Behavior, 5807
Epilepsy A to Z, 5788
Epilepsy Association of the Big Bend, 5752
Epilepsy Education Association of Arkansas, 5750
Epilepsy Foundation, 1238, 5747, 5778, 5805, 6471, 6626
Epilepsy Foundation Eastern Pennsylvania, 5757
Epilepsy Foundation of Metropolitan New York, 5756
Epilepsy Foundation of Northern California, 5751
Epilepsy Foundation Washington, 5758
Epilepsy in Children: The Teacher's Role, 5811
Epilepsy Research Laboratory, Department of Neurology, 5762

Entry Name Index

Epilepsy, A Guide to Balancing Your Life, 5789
Epilepsy.com, 5779
Epilepsy: 199 Answers, 5790
Epilepsy: Frequency, Causes and Consequences, 5791
Epilepsy: I Can Live with That, 5792
Epilepsy: The Untold Story, 5770
Epilepsy: You and Your Child, 5812
EpilepsyUSA, 5806
Episcopal Conference of the Deaf, 3124
Erb's Palsy, 2748
Eric RicStar Winter Music Therapy Summer Camp, 1368, 7737
Erythema Infectiosum, 2754
Esophageal Atresia, 2762
Essential Guide to Psychiatric Drugs, 2250
Eukee the Jumpy, Jumpy Elephant, 627
European Society for Pediatric Urology, 1979, 7597
Even Little Kids Get Diabetes, 2305
Evergreen Spina Bifida Association, 6067
Everybody is Different: A Book for Young People, 869
Everybody's Different, Nobody's Perfect, 4316
Everyday Solutions: A Practical Guide for Families of Children with Autism, 870
Everyone Likes to Eat, 2306
Everything You Need to Know About Measles and Rubella, 5311
Everything You Need To Know About Depression, 2251
Ewing's Sarcoma, 2775
Ewing's Sarcoma Support Group Resources Page, 2789
Exceptional Children Division, 7338
Exceptional Children Foundation, 7010
Exceptional Family Resource Center, 7112
Exceptional Family Support, Education and Advocacy Center, 7113
Exceptional Parent, 7641
Exceptional Parents, 7114
Explosive Child, 4823, 4826
Eye Care Sourcebook, 1697, 1833, 5502, 6150
Eye on NEI, 4042
Eye Problems Associated with Hydrocephalus in Children, 3805
EyeWorld, 4043

F

FAA World Convention, 2609
Face First, 1892, 2183, 3073
FACES: National Craniofacial Association, 1498, 1504, 1875, 1885, 2722, 4130
Facilitated Communication Institute at Syracuse University, 808
Facing the Challenges of Turner Syndrome Together, 6690
Facioscapulohumeral Dystrophy Society, 4287
Fact Sheet: Guillain-Barre Syndrome, 2928
Fact Sheet: Hydrocephalus, 3806
Fact Sheet: Syringomyelia, 3807
Factor Nine News, 3639
Factor V Leiden: Thrombophilia Support Page, 5323
Facts & Fallacies About Digestive Diseases, 54
Facts About Apnea and Other Apparent Life-Threatening Events, 6262
Facts About Autism, 912
Facts About Charcot-Marie-Tooth Disease and Dejerine-Sottas, 1389
Facts About Duchenne and Becker Muscular Dystrophies, 4317
Facts About Facioscapulohumeral Muscular Dystrophy, 4318
Facts About Friedreich's Ataxia, 553
Facts About Inflammatory Bowel Disease, 1969
Facts About Inflammatory Myopathies-DM, PM and IBM, 4319
Facts About Limb-Girdle Muscular Dystrophy, 4320
Facts About Metabolic Diseases of Muscle, 4321
Facts About Mitochondrial Myopathies, 4322
Facts About Muscular Dystrophy, 4323
Facts About Myasthenia Gravis (MG, LEMS, &CMS), 4324
Facts About Myopathies, 4325
Facts About Myotonic Muscular Dystrophy, 4326
Facts About Plasmapheresis, 4327
Facts About Rare Muscular Dystrophies, 4328
Facts About SIDS, 6263
Facts About Spinal Muscular Atrophy, 6139
Facts About Turner Syndrome, 6691
Facts for Health: PTSD, 5151
Facts on Liver Transplantation, 961
Fairfax County Public Library, 7525
Fairfield/Westchester Chapter of Crohn's &Colitis Foundation of America, 1911, 1930
Familial Dysautonomia, 2800
Familial Dysautonomia Foundation, 2802
Families at Heart, 3850
Families Can Help Children Cope with Fear, Anxiety, 4990, 5954
Families Caring for Families, 7115
Families Coping with Mental Illness, 992, 1441
Families Empowered and Supporting Treatment of Eating Disorders, 2601
Families for Depression Awareness, 979, 2204
Families for Early Autism Treatment, 702, 842
Families Helping Families of Greater New Orleans, 7230
Families of SMA - Arizona Chapter, 6122
Families of SMA - Connecticut Chapter, 6124
Families of SMA - Long Island NY Chapter, 6126
Families of SMA - Northern California Chapter, 6123
Families of SMA - Tennessee Chapter, 6127
Families of Spinal Muscular Atrophy, 6132
Families Together, 7222
Families Together/Parent to Parent of KS, 7223
Families with Heart, 3853
Family & Educator Connection - Cedar Falls/Waterloo Region, 7214
Family & Educator Connection - Clear Lake/Mason City Region, 7215
Family & Educator Connection - Marshalltown Region, 7216
Family Connection of South Carolina, 7515
Family First Program Alpha Resource Center, 7116
Family Focus Resource Center, 7117
Family Guide - Growth and Development of the Partially Seeing Child, 1705, 1840, 4698, 5509
Family Guide to Vision Care, 1706, 1841, 4699, 5510
Family Information Network, 7348
Family Life with Tourette Syndrome, 6520
Family Life with Tourette Syndrome...Personal Stories, 6436, 6521
Family Network on Disabilities, 7165
Family Online Safety Institute, 6768
Family Resource Center, 7118
Family Resource Center at Lucile Packard Children's Hospital, 1555
Family Resource Center of Southeast Indiana, 7204
Family Resource Center on Disabilities, 7189
Family Resource Network, 7281
Family Support Bulletin, 1357
Family Support Center of New Jersey, 7313
Family Support Network, 6472, 6627
Family Support Network of Michigan Parent Participation Program-MDCH, 7258
Family Support Network of North Carolina, 7339
Family T.I.E.S. Network, 7190
Family Ties at Massachusetts Department of Public Health, 7252
Family to Family Network ARC of Hennepin County, 7265
Family Traditions, 3217
Family Voices, 7011
Family, Infant, and Toddler Project, 7404
Family-2-Family Health Information Center of Arkansas, 7100
Family/Community Support Group of the Brain Injury Association of Florida, 3014
FamilyConnect, 4032
Famous Fone Friends, 7797
Fantastic Videos: Colonial Times, Chocolate, and Cars, 3218
Fantastic Videos: Dogs at Work and Play, 3219
Fantastic Videos: Exciting People, Places and Things!, 3220
Fantastic Videos: From Post Offices to Dairy Goats!, 3221
Fantastic Videos: Imagination, Actors, and 'Deaf Way!', 3222
Fantastic Videos: Roller Coasters, Maps, and Ice Cream!, 3223
Fantastic Videos: Skiing, Factories, and Race Horses, 3224
Fantastic Videos: The Wonderful Worlds of Sports and Travel, 3225
Farm and Wilderness Camps, 7784

Entry Name Index

Fast Facts: Rhinitis, 5608
Fear of Being Fat, 2641
Fear of Illness, 4962
Featherless/Desplumado, 6089
Febrile Seizures Fact Sheet, 5813
Fecal Incontinence, 2739
Federal Hemophilia Treatment Center of Hawaii, 3574
Federal Hemophilia Treatment Center Program of Los Angeles, 3573
Federation for Children with Special Needs, 4060, 7012, 7253, 7598
Feed Your Kids Well: How to Help Your Child Lose Weight and Get Healthy, 4745
Feeding Your Baby, 1514
Feingold Association of the US, 578, 606
Fetal Alcohol Syndrome, 2807, 2826
Fetal Health Foundation, 229
Fetal Retinoid Syndrome, 2830
A Few Errands, 3186
FFCMH Annual Conference, 815, 990, 1438, 1581, 2224, 6786, 7562
Fight Drug Abuse at Home, Work, School and in the Community, 2827
Financial Assistance and Insurance for People with Kidney Disease, 4455
Financial Help for Diabetics Care, 2333
Find Counseling.com, 6800
Finding Out About Seizures: A Guide to Medical Tests, 5814
FindYouthInfo.gov, 6801
Fingerspelling: Expressive and Receptive Fluency, 3226
Fire Fighter Brown, 3367
Firefighters Kids Camp Camp Concord, 1202
First Candle, 6185
First Direction, 7205
First Regional Hemophilia Center, 3575
First Signs at Home, 3368
First Signs at Play, 3369
First Steps for Families, 7206
First Steps Program, 7273
First Steps, Early Interventions, New Horizons Rehabilitation, 7207
The First Year, 1518
FIRST: Foundation for Ichthyosis and Related Skin Types, 3890
5 Smart Steps to Less Stress, 4986
50 Freqeuntly Asked Questions About Auditory-Verbal Therapy, 3314
50th Anniversary Collection, 3185
Florida Bureau of Braille and Talking Book Library Services, 1640, 1769, 4633, 5444
Florida Camp for Children and Youth, 2350
Florida Chapter of Crohn's & Colitis Foundation of America, 1913
Florida Department of Education, 7166
Florida Department of Health Immunization Program, 5273
Florida Epilepsy Services, 5753
Florida Families of Children with Visual Impairments, 5563
Florida Ophthalmic Institute, 1815
Florida School-Deaf and Blind Summer Camp, 1719, 1855, 3490, 4709, 5520
Florida's Collaboration for Young Children and their Families Head State, 7167
Floyd Rogers, 2351
Flying, 4963
FOCUS, 7099
Focus on Autism and Other Developmental Disabilities, 907
Fontan Friends, 3859
Food Addicts Anonymous, 2568
Food Allergy Research & Education, 1214, 2618
Food and Drug Administration, 2971
Food for Recovery, 2642
Food Research and Action Center, 4728
Foods to Avoid or Limit During Pregnancy, 2828
For Siblings Only, 7651
Forgotten Plague: How the Battle Against Tuberculosis Was Won & Lost, 6618
Foundation Fighting Blindness, 5548
Foundation for Child Development, 6769
Foundation for Prader-Willi Research, 5172, 5198
Foundation for Sarcoidosis Research, 5624, 5647
Foundations of Spoken Language for Hearing-Impaired Children, 3370

Four for You! Fables and Fairy Tales Series, 3227
Fragile X Alliance of Ohio, 2848
Fragile X Association of Southern California, 2846
Fragile X Center of San Diego, 2847
Fragile X Syndrome, 2839
Francis J. Curry National Tuberculosis Center, 6612
FRAXA Research Foundation, 2843, 2852
Frederick Douglas Branch for Specialized Services and Physically Handicapped, 7489
Free Hand: Enfranchising the Education of Deaf Children, 3371
Free Library of Philadelphia, 7512
Freedom Camp, 7760
Freedom From Headaches, 4236
Freedom's Wings International, 7798
Freeing Your Child from Obsessive-Compulsive Disorder, 4795
Friedrich's Ataxia, 554
FRIENDS, 6799
Friends for Life Auburn United Methodist Church, 7081
Friends No Matter What, 6090
Friends of Karen, 7326
Friends' Health Connection, 7013
From Gesture to Language in Hearing and Deaf Children, 3372
From Mime to Sign, 3228
Frontier Travel Camp, 385
FSR Patient Registry, 5623
Functional Behavior Assessment for People with Autism, 871
Future Choices, 7208
Future Reflections, 7642

G

G. Advocacy, 3796
Gainesville Subregional LBPH Hall County Public Library, 7445
Galactosemia, 2855
Galactosemia Foundation, 2858, 4253, 4256
Galactosemia Resources and Information, 2865
Gallaudet Today, 3456
Gallstones, 55
Gas in the Digestive Tract, 56
Gastoparesis in Diabetes, 2334
Gastroesophageal Reflux Disease in Children, 57
Gastrointestinal Diseases and Disorders Sourcebook, 4th Edition, 1223, 1733, 1956, 6718
Gaucher Registry, 2878
Gaucher's Disease, 2869
Gaylord Hospital Sleep Medicine, 4351
Gazoontite, 448
GBS Support Group of the UK, 2926
GBS/CIDP Foundation International, 2924
Geisinger Wyoming Valley Medical Center, Sleep Disorders Center, 4386
Gemma B Publishing, 1347
Gene Clinics, 535
Gene Testing for Ataxia, 555
Generating Business, 3229
Generations, 546
Genes, Blood & Courage, 6388
Genesee County Health Department, 6210
GeneTest, 7599
Genetic Alliance, 183, 218, 230, 238, 285, 302, 326, 406, 565, 579, 703, 954, 1179, 1485, 1499, 1524, 1540, 1623, 1730, 1739, 1748
Genetic Network of the Empire State, 512
Genetics and Neuromuscular Diseases, 4329
Genetics and You, 1515
Genetics Coloring Book, 3625
Genetics, Disability and Deafness, 3373
Georges Gilles de la Tourette-The Man and His Times, 6550
Georgetown University, 5699
Georgetown University Child Development Center, 7160, 7439, 7539
Georgetown University Sleep Disorders Center, 4352
Georgia Ataxia Support Group, 493
Georgia Chapter of Crohn's & Colitis Foundation of America, 1914

Entry Name Index

Georgia Department of Human Resources -Center for Family Resource Planning, 6199
Georgia Department of Human ResourcesChildren's Health Services, 6198
Georgia Perinatal Association, 5220
Get a Grip on Asthma Programs, 407
Get Ready to Read!, 4077
Getting a Grip on ADD: A Kid's Guide toUnderstanding & Coping with ADD, 628
Getting Better Bit(e) by Bit(e), 2643
Getting Into College: Strategies for theStudent with Tourette Syndrome, 6551
Getting Ready for the Big Date, 3230
Getting Started with Facilitated Communication, 829
Getting Your Life Back Together When YouHave Schizophrenia, 1459
Ghost Investigation, 3231
Giddings School Special Education Division, 7161
Gift of Hope, 6522
Girl Scouts of the USA, 7015
Give Kids the World, 7799
Give Me One Wish, 2117
Give Your ADD Teen a Chance: A Guide forParents of Teenagers with ADD, 629
Glaucoma, 1842
Glaucoma Laser Trabeculoplasty Study, 1816
Glaucoma Research Foundation, 1749, 1817, 1826
Glaucoma: The Sneak Thief of Sight, 1843
GLC Annual Education Conference, 1217
Gleams, 1701
Glenn Garcelon Foundation, 1021
Glioblastoma and Anaplastic Astrocytoma, 1161
Global Advocacy for HIV Prevention, 2948
Global and Regional Asperger Syndrome Partnership, 354, 704
Global Down Syndrome Foundation, 2385
Global EpidemicMulti-Drug Resistant Tuberculosis, 6620
Global Lyme Alliance, 4147
Global Tuberculosis Institute, 6474, 6610
Gloriana Opera Company, 7698
Gluten Intolerance Group of North America(GIG), 1215
Gluten-Free Page, 1221
Go Togethers, 3374
Gold Coast Down Syndrome Organization, 2397
The Golden Fund for Autism, 722
Goldilocks and the Three Bears Told in Signed English, 3375
Good Morning Me!Hand and Voices, 3376
Goodwill Industries-Suncoast, 2398
Goodwill Industries-Suncoast: Choices forWork Program, 3015
The Gossip, 3268
Governor's Campaign, 3232
Gow School Summer Programs, 7761
Graduate School, 3233
Grandfather Moose!, 3377
Great Lakes Hemophilia Foundation, 3557
Great Plains Region-Helen Keller NationalCenter, 5425
Greater Atlanta Area Support Group, 494
Greater Interagency Council Parent toParent Support Network, 7191
Greater Los Angeles/Orange County Chapterof Chron's & Colitis Foundation, 1906
Greater New York Chapter of Crohn's &Colitis Foundation of America, 1931
Greater North Valley California SupportGroup, 480
Greater San Diego/Desert Chapter of Crohn's & Colitis Foundation of America, 1907
Gregory Fleming James Cystic Fibrosis Center, 2000
Grief, Bereavement and Sudden InfantDeath Syndrome, 6252
Grilled Cheese, 2307
The Grocer and the Cook, 3269
Group Psychotherapy for Eating Disorders, 2644
Groupworks West, 705
Groves Academy, 672, 928, 4091
Growing Children: A Parent's Guide, 2912
Growing Up With Epilepsy, 5793

Growth Hormone Deficiency, 2881, 2917
Growth Hormone Testing, 2918
Guardians of Hydrocephalus ResearchFoundation, 3788
Guide for Children & Teenagers, 6729
Guide to Diagnosis & Treatment, 6552
Guide to Insurance Coverage for PeopleWith Hemophilia, 3626
Guide to Psychology and its Practice (A), 6802
Guidelines for Families Coping with OCD, 4784
Guidelines for Spina Bifida and Health Care Services Throughout Life, 6091
Guillain-Barre Syndrome, 2921
Gurze Books, 4743
Gurze Bookstore, 2619

H

H.E.A.R.T.S. Connection Family ResourceCenter, 7119
H.O.P.E. Series: Seizures in Childhood, 5815
H.O.P.E. Series: Seizures in the Teen Years, 5816
HairClub, 77, 136, 2784
Hand Eczema, 2707
Handbook of Autism and Pervasive Developmental Disorders, 872
Handbook of Children and the Media, 6828
Handbook of Head Truma: Acute Care toRecovery, 3086
Handbook of Headache, 4237
The Handbook of Pediatric Audiology, 3433
Handbook of Psoriasis, 5340
Handbook of School-Based Interventions, 2252
Handbook of Scoliosis, 5736
Handi-Kids/King Solomon Foundation, 7733
Handicapped Scuba Association, 7016
Handle with Care, 7017
Handling the Young Cerebral Palsied Childat Home, 1348
Handout on Health: Scleroderma, 5713
Hands & Voices National, 3125
Happiness Bag Incorporated, 7713
Happy Hollow Children's Camp, 7714
Harbor Regional Center Family andProfessional Resource Center, 7120
Hard of Hearing Advocates, 3151
Harold Goodglass Aphasia Research Center, 3060
Harold Talks About How He InheritedHemophilia, 3627
Harold's Secret: A Boy with Hemophilia, 3628
Harris County Health Department, 6225
Harrison's Principles of Inernal Medicine15th Edition, 6413
Having Leukemia Isn't So Bad, of Course,It Wouldn't Be My First Choice, 111
Hawaii Department of Health ImmunizationProgram, 5274
Hawaii Down Syndrome Congress, 2400
Head Injuries, 2995
Head Injury in Children and Adolescents: AResource and Review for School, 3087
Headache, 4244
Headache Book: Prevention & Treatmentfor All Types of Headaches, 4238
Headache Facts-What Everyone Should Know, 4245
Headaches and Hydrocephalus, 3808
Headline News, 3640
The Headliner, 3093
Headlines, 3091
Headway, 3092
Healing Exchange Brain Trust, 1022
Healing Hearts, 3858
Healing Well, 2110
HealingWell.com, 5780
Health Answers EducationSudler-WPP Health Practice, 536, 607, 1222, 1330, 1376, 1954, 2454, 2620, 2879, 2904, 3621, 5648, 5702, 5727, 6243, 6312, 6529, 6617, 6630, 6684, 6711
Health Insurance Issues and Solutions forPeople with Torette Syndrome, 6553
Health Research Program (HaRP), 39, 274, 3703, 4422, 5301
Healthcare for Children on the AutismSpectrum, 873
HealthCentral.com, 5324

Entry Name Index

Healthfinder, 4269, 4279, 6313, 6854
Healthy Mothers, Healthy Babies, 5251
A Healthy Mouth for Your Baby, 6423
Hear, 3457
Hear & Listen! Talk & Sing!, 3290
Hear Center, 3156
The Hearing Aid Handbook: Clinician's Guide to Client Orientation, 3434
Hearing Alert Informational Brochures, 3469
Hearing Education & Awareness for Rockers, 3152
Hearing Health Foundation, 3126, 7018
Hearing Impairment/Deafness, 3099
Hearing is Believing, Volume One, 3291
Hearing is Believing, Volume Three, 3292
Hearing is Believing, Volume Two, 3293
Hearing Loss Association of America, 3127
Heart Burn, Hiatal Hernia, and Gastroesophageal Reflux Disease, 58
Heart Center Online, 317
Heart Disease, High Blood Pressure, Stroke and Diabetes, 7662
Heart Failure Society Newsletter, 322
Heart Failure Society of America, 312
The Heart Institute, 3840
Heart of the Matter, 3847
Heart to Heart, 1689, 1707, 1823, 1844, 3844, 3862, 3864, 3866, 4684, 4700, 5496, 5511
Heart to Heart - St. Louis, 3852
Heart to Heart Fund, 3849
Hearts and Homes For Youth, 3128
HEATH Resource Center, 6903, 7440
Heights, 4964
The Help Group, 723
Help Me, I'm Sad, 2253
Help Parent Support Group Hope & Education for Loving Parents, 7140
Help with a Hidden Disease Update, 5639
Helpguide.org, 6803
Helping Children and Adolescents Cope with Violence and Disasters, 5165
Helping Children with Autism Learn, 874
Helping Hearts, 3857
Helping Kids Cope With a New Threat, 5152
Helping Kids Heal - 75 Activities to Help Children Recover from Trauma & Loss, 5159
Helping Kids in Crisis: Managing Emergencies in Children & Adolescents, 6829
Helping the Noncompliant Child, 4827
Helping with Hearing, 1516
Helping Your Anxious Child, 4981, 5948
Helping Your Child Cope with Depression and Suicidal Thoughts, 2254
Helping Your Depressed Child, 2255
Helping Your Hard-of-Hearing Child Succeed, 3470
HEMALOG, 3634
Hemangiomas and Lymphangiomas, 3498
Hemlocks Easter Seals Recreation, 5741
Hemochromatosis, 59
Hemolytic Disease of the Newborn, 3509
Hemophila Foundation of North Carolina, 3542
Hemophilia, 3517
Hemophilia & Thrombosis Program at Children's National Health System, 3576
Hemophilia and Coagulation Programs, 3582
Hemophilia and Mild Hemophilia What To Expect, 3647
Hemophilia and Thrombosis Center at the University of Minnesota Medical Center, 3583
Hemophilia and Thrombosis Center of Nevada, 3584
Hemophilia Association of San Diego County, 3523
Hemophilia Association of South Carolina, 3550
Hemophilia Association of the Capital Area, 3554
Hemophilia Center of Arkansas, 3522, 3577
Hemophilia Center of the New England Medical Center, 3580
Hemophilia Center of Western New York, 3540, 3578
Hemophilia Center of Western Pennsylvania, 3579
Hemophilia Diseases and People, 3629

Hemophilia Federation of America, 2950
Hemophilia Foundation of Georgia, 3528
Hemophilia Foundation of Greater Florida, 3527
Hemophilia Foundation of Hawaii, 3529
Hemophilia Foundation of Idaho, 3530
Hemophilia Foundation of Illinois, 3531
Hemophilia Foundation of Indiana, 3532
Hemophilia Foundation of Maryland, 3534
Hemophilia Foundation of Michigan, 3535
Hemophilia Foundation of Minnesota and the Dakotas, 3536
Hemophilia Foundation of Northern California, 3524
Hemophilia Foundation of Oregon, 3547
Hemophilia Foundation of Southern California, 3525
Hemophilia Foundation of Washington, 3556
Hemophilia Handbook, 3630
Hemophilia Headlines, 3641
Hemophilia Outreach Center, 3560
Hemophilia Society of Colorado, 3526
Hemophilia Treatment Center at the University of Iowa, 3581
Hemophilia, Sports, and Exercise, 3648
Hemophilia: Current Medical Management, 3649
Henry Youngerman Center for Communication Disorders, 5991
Hepatitis, 3655, 3674
Hepatitis A, 40
Hepatitis B, 41
Hepatitis B Foundation, 3659, 3665
Hepatitis B Prevention: A Resource Guide, 3668
Hepatitis B: Your Child at Risk, 3675
Hepatitis C, 42
Hepatitis C: An Information Resource, 3669
Hepatitis Education Project, 3660, 3666
Hepatitis Fact Sheet, 3676
Hepatitis International Foundation, 3667
Here's Everything You'll Need to Save Money with the CFF Health Services, 2127
Here's Everything You'll Need to Start Saving Money with the CFF Pharmacy, 2128
Here's What I Mean to Say, 1349
Hereditary Ataxia: A Guidebook for Managing Speech & Swallowing, 541
Hereditary Ataxia: The Facts, 556
Hereditary Fructose Intolerance, 3681
Hereditary Hemorrhagic Telangiectasia (HHT) Foundation International, 6330, 6338, 6344, 6371
Heriditary Disease Foundation, 7019
Hermansky-Pudlak Syndrome Network Annual Family Conference, 192
Hermansky-Pudlak Syndrome Network Newsletter, 184, 198
Heroes Against AIDS, 2981
Herpes Simplex, 3696
Herpes.com, 3705, 4424
HerpeSite, 3704, 4423
Hey! I'm Here, Too!, 4330
HFSA Annual Scientific Meeting, 316
Hi! I'm Adam!, 6538
Hi, I'm Adam, 6447
Hickory Hill, 2352
High Five! Fables and Fairy Tales, 3234
High Hopes Foundation of New Hampshire, 7307
Highbrook Lodge Camp, 1720, 1856, 7770
Hill School of Fort Worth, 673, 929, 4092
Hirschsprung Disease, 3710, 3723
Hispanic Dental Association, 2174
Histicytosis Association, 3730
Histiocytosis, 3724
Histiocytosis Association, 3728
HIV Infection, 2929
HIV Medicine Association, 2949
Hodgkin's Disease, 3734
Hodgkin's Disease and Non-Hodgkin's Lymphomas, 3748
Hole in the Wall Gang Camp, 2994, 3654
Holidays CD-ROM, 3294
Holidays: An ASL Word Book, 3295

Entry Name Index

Holistic Dental Association, 2175
Home Line, 2129
Homocystinuria, 3749
HOPE (Helping Oncology Parents Endure)Brain Tumor Foundation of the Southwest, 1130
Hope and Recovery: A Mother-Daughter StoryAbout Anorexia Nervosa & Bulimia, 2645
Hope and Solutions for OCD, 4779
Hope for Children with AIDS, 2990
Hope for Hypothalamic Hamartomas, 1023
Hospitalization Tips, 3809
House Guests, 3235
The House Institute Foundation, 3146
Houston Area Brain Tumor Network, 1131
Houston Ear Research Foundation, 3180
Houston Support Group, 524
Houston-Gulf Coast/South Texas Chapter ofCrohn's & Colitis Foundation of America, 1945
How Children Learn Language, 3378
How Does Your Child Hear and Talk?, 3471
How I Am (Wie Ich Bin), 830
How Many Times a Day Do You Risk BeingInfected with Hepatitis B?, 3677
How to be an Assertive Member of theTreatment Team, 3810
How to Find Out More About Your Child's Birth Defect or Disability, 7663
How to get Your Kid to Eat..., 2646
How to Help Your Child Succeed in School, 597, 4070
How to Recognize and Classify Seizures, 5771
How to Start a Turner Syndrome SupportGroup, 6692
How to Take Care of Your Baby Before Birth, 2829
Howard University Center for Sickle CellDisease, 5861
Hughen Center, 7781
Human Growth Foundation, 7, 14, 327, 1986, 2885, 2905, 4199, 4603, 6643, 6685, 7020
Hungry Caterpillar and Goodnight Moon, 3236
Hy Feinstein Clubhouse, 3037
HYCEPH-L, 3789
Hydrocephalus, 3764
Hydrocephalus Association, 2723, 3769
Hydrocephalus Association of N Texas, 3781
Hydrocephalus Association of Rhode Island, 3780
Hydrocephalus Family Support Group ofCentral Florida, 3774
Hydrocephalus Group - Children's Hospitalof New Jersey, 3776
Hydrocephalus, a Neglected Disease, 3784
Hydrocephalus: A Guide for Patients,Families, and Friends, 3795
Hydrocephalus: Fact Sheet, 3811
Hydrohaven Chat Room, 3790
Hyperactive Child, Adolescent, and Adult:ADD Through the Lifespan, 630
Hyperactivity: Why Won't My Child PayAttention?, 631
Hypertrophic Cardiomyopathy, 3824
Hypertrophic Cardiomyopathy Association, 3827, 3831
Hypertrophic Cardiomyopathy Program atSt. Luke's-Roosevelt Hospital Center, 3829
Hypertrophic Cardiomyopathy: Heart CenterOnline for Patients, 3832
Hypoplastic Left Heart Syndrome, 3838
Hypothyroidism, 3874

I

I Am the Boss of My Body: PreventingChild Sexual Abuse, 5048
I Can Sign my ABCs, 3379
I Can't Hear You in the Dark: How to Learnand Teach Lipreading, 3380
I Cue, U Cue, 3296
I Have Diabetes: How Much Should I Eat?, 2335
I Have Diabetes: What Should I Eat?, 2336
I Have Diabetes: When Should I Eat?, 2337
I Love You Story, 3381
I Remember it Well, 3237
I Was a Fifteen-Year-Old Blimp, 2647
I'M Deaf and It's Okay, 3382

I.D. Weeks Library, 4888
IAEDP Symposium, 2610
Ian's Walk: A Story About Autism, 875
IBD & Me: Activity Book for Kids!, 1970
IBD Nutrition Book, 6719
IBS Self-help group, 6712
ICAN (International Child Amputee Network), 7600
iCanShine, 725
ICARE, 137
Ichthyosis, 3885
Ichthyosis Information, 3894
ICPA, 1553
ID Card for Third VentriculostomyPatients, 3812
Idaho Dept. of Health & Welfare Immunization Program, 5275
Idaho Parents Unlimited, 7181
Idaho State Talking Book Library, 1646, 1775, 4639, 5450
Identification and Treatment of Attention Deficit Disorders, 663
If Your Child Has Diabetes: An Answer Bookfor Parents, 2308
IFFGD Professional Symposia, 33, 269, 1952, 2734, 2769
Illinois State Library, Talkng Book andBraille Service, 1648, 1777, 4641, 5452
Illustrated Dictionary - 3D ASL, 3297
Immune Deficiency Foundation, 2360, 2951, 2972
Immune Deficiency Foundation NationalConference, 2362, 2965
Immune System, 7815
Immune System Disorders Sourcebook3rd Edition, 2927, 6296
Immunization Action Coalition, 5252
Immunization Partnership of Alameda County, 5269
Immunology and Allergy Clinics of North America, 5609
Impact of Migraine-A Disabling and CostlyCondition, 4246
Implantable Defibrillators in PreventingSudden Death, 3833
In Control: Guide for Teens with Diabetes, 2309
In Our House, 3383
In Silence: Growing Up Hearing in a Deaf World, 3384
Incorporating Consumers into Regional Genetics Networks, 557
Increasing Capabilities Access Network, 7101
Incredible 5-Point Scale, 876
Independent Holoprosencephaly SupportSite, 4135
Independent Living Research UtilizationProgram, 7021
Indian Trails Camp, 7738
Indiana Chapter of Crohn's & Colitis Foundation of America, 1916
Indiana Deaf Camp, 3491
Indiana Hemophilia and Thrombosis Center, 3585
Indiana Resource Center for Autism, 797
Indiana State Dept. of Health Immunization, 5276
Indiana State University School of Medicine, 4868
Individual and Family SupportArc of Lincoln & Lancaster County, 7293
Individualized Education Program (IEP) -Communication Skills for Parents, 3813
Infant & Toddler Program, 7407
Infant Behavior, Cry and Sleep Clinic, 1560
Infant Motor Development: A Look at thePhases, 2448
Infant Positioning and Sudden Infant DeathSyndrome, 6264
Infant Toddler Early Intervention Program, 7411
Infant/Toddler Program, 7182
Infantile Spasms, 5817
Infectious Diseases in Children, 4425, 5315
Infectious Diseases Society of America, 2952, 5253
Infinitec, 1331
Inflammatory Bowel Disease, 6720
Inflammatory Bowel Disease - From Bench toBedside, 6721
Infocus Newsletter, 211
Information Center for Sickle Cell and Thalassemic Disorders, 5869
Information for Adults, 1517
Informed Consent: Participation in Genetic Research Studies, 558
Infusions, 3642
Inheritance of Hemophilia, 3650
Initiatives, 3643
Injury Prevention Center, 3773
Inland Empire Brain Tumor Support Group, 1047
Inner Circle, 6726
Inner Lives of Deaf Children: Interviews and Analysis, 3385

Entry Name Index

Inside Out: Stories of Bulimia, 2615
Inside Story, 6730
Insights in the Dynamic Psychotherapy of Anorexia And Bulimia, 2648
Insights into Spina Bifida, 6104
Inspire - Cerebral Palsy Center, 1302
Institute for Basic Research in Developmental Disabilities, 800, 7500, 7540
Institute for Families, 5561, 7022
Institute on Communication and Inclusion, 809, 843
Institute on Community Integration, 3912
Institutes for Achievement of Human Potential, 3068
Intellectual Disabilities, 3896
Intellectual Disability, 3934
Interagency Early Intervention Project, 7266
Interagency Program Assistive Technology, 7343
Internal Journal of Eating Disorders, 2661
International Albinism Center, 196
International Antiviral Society-USA, 2953
International Association for Orthodontics, 2176
International Association of Dental Research, 2177
International Association of Eating Disorders Professionals Foundation, 2569, 5081
International Association of Providers of AIDS Care, 2954
International Association of Sickle Cell Nurses and Physician Assistants, 5870
International Bone Marrow Transplant Registry, 98
International Center for Skeletal Dysplasia Registry, 2677
International Critical Incident Stress Foundation, 5143, 5153
International Deaf Education Association, 3129
International Dyslexia Association, 2496, 2502, 2508, 4061
International Federation for Spina Bifida and Hydrocephalus, 6075
International Foundation for Functional Gastrointestinal Disorders (IFFGD), 28, 263, 1902, 2732, 2766, 4254, 4257, 4435, 5402, 6704, 7601
International Foundation for Genetic Research/Michael Fund, 2434
International Foundation for Research and Education on Depression (IFred), 2205
International Hearing Society, 3130
International Herpes Alliance, 4426
International Herpes Management Forum, 3706
International Journal of Dermatology, 1413, 2699, 5007, 5343
International Journal of Nursing in Intellectual & Developmental Disabilities, 7644
International Mosaic Down Syndrome Association, 2386
International Network of Ataxia Friends, 537
International OCD Foundation, 4767, 4785
International Patient Organization for Primary Immunodeficiencies, 2363
International Pemphigus Foundation, 4912
International Pemphigus Foundation Dallas Support Group, 4920
International Pemphigus Foundation: Baltimore Support Group, 4916
International Pemphigus Foundation: Houston Support Group, 4921
International Pemphigus Foundation: Massachusetts Support Group, 4917
International Pemphigus Foundation: New York Support Group, 4918
International Pemphigus Foundation: South Carolina Support Group, 4919
International Pemphigus Foundation: Southern California Support Group, 4915
International Prader-Willi Syndrome Organization (IPWSO), 5199
International Skeletal Dysplasia Registry, 4196
International Society for Burn Injuries, 1188, 1197
International Society for Research in Child and Adolescent Psychopathology, 6770
International Society for Traumatic Stress Studies, 5145
International Society of Dermatology, 7023
International World Conference on Sarcoidosis-Patient Symposium, 5640
Internet Mental Health, 995, 1445, 1588, 2235, 6804
Interstitial Cyctitis, 7664
Intestinal Complications, 1971
Intrafamilial (Incest) Abuse Resources, 5059
Intrauterine Growth Restriction, 2919
Intraventricular Hemorrhage, 3942

Introduction to Spina Bifida, 6092
Introductory Packet Brochure, 1226
Iowa Chapter of Crohn's Colitis Foundation of America, 1917
Iowa Department of Public Health Bureau of Immunization, 5277
Iowa Library for the Blind and Physically Handicapped, 1653, 1782, 4646, 5457
Iowa Program for Assistive Technology, 7217
Irritable Bowel Syndrome, 60
A is for Access: Creating Full & Interactive Access for Students, 3189
It Only Takes One Bite: Food Allergy and Anaphylaxis, 2616
It's My Body, 5071
It's Nobody's Fault-New Hope and Help for Difficult Children and Their Parents, 4796
It's Nobody's Fault: New Hope and Help for Difficult Children and Their Parents, 4982
It's Not Just Growing Pains, 5708
It's Not Me...It's My OCD: A Look at Behavioral Therapy, 4780
It's So Much Work to Be Your Friend, 632
IVAT: Institute on Violence, Abuse and Trauma, 5023
IVUN Resource Directory, 5312

J

Jackson Laboratory, 2899
Jake's Ride for Dystonia Research, 2534
James R Clark Memorial Sickle Cell Foundation, 5855
James S. McDonnell Foundation, 1024
Jane and Richard Thomas Center for Down Syndrome, 2429
The Jed Foundation, 986
Jeffrey Modell Foundation, 2364
Jewish Children's Adoption Network, 7024
Jewish Council for Youth Services, 7706
Jewish Genetic Disease Consortium, 6306, 6314
JGB Cassette Library International, 7501
Jodi House, 3008
John Hopkins Arthritis Center, 254, 3955, 4153
John Hopkins Children's Hospital, 2039
John Hopkins Department of Orthopaedics Surgery, 5728
John Sierzant Brain Tumor Support Group, 1138
John Tracy Clinic, 3131
John Warvel, 2353
Johnny Rock's Christmas, 3298
Johns Hopkins Brain Tumor Education Group, 1071
Johns Hopkins Department of Orthopaedics Surgery, 5722
Johns Hopkins Department of Orthopaedic Surgery, 1528
Johns Hopkins Division of Allergy and Clinical Immunology, 5598
Johns Hopkins University Sleep Disorders Center, 4358
Joslin Diabetes Center, 2296
Journal of AAPOS, 6151
Journal of Allergy and Clinical Immunology, 5612
Journal of Cardiac Failure, 320
Journal of Dermatologic Surgery and Oncology, 1414, 2700, 5008, 5344
Journal of Head Trauma Rehabilitation, 3090
Journal of Learning Disabilities, 4081
Journal of Pediatric Gastroenterology and Nutrition, 46, 276, 1562, 2772, 3694, 4442, 4818, 5413
The Journal of Positive Behavior Interventions, 908
Journal of Psoriasis and Psoriatic Arthritis (JPPA), 5346
The Journal of Special Education, 909
Journal of Speech, Language, and Hearing Research, 3453, 6002
Journal of Spirochetal and Tick-borne Diseases, 4162
Journal of the Academy of Dermatology, 7643
Journal of the American Dietetic Association, 2662
Journal of the American Medical Association, 4163
Journal of Visual Impairment and Blindness, 1698, 1834, 4692, 5503
Journey of Love: Parent's Guide to Duchenne Muscular Dystrophy, 4304
The Joy of Signing Second Edition, 3435
JRA and Me, 3961
Judevine Center for Autism, 799
Judge David L. Bazelon Center for Mental Health, 3913
Jumpin' Johnny Get Back to Work! A Child's Guide to ADHD/Hyperactivity, 633

Entry Name Index

Junior National Association of the Deaf, 3132
Junior Wheelchair Sports Camp, 7699
Just In Time, 78, 138, 2785
Just Like You and Me, 5772
Just Take a Bite: Easy, Effective Answers to Food Aversions and Eating Challenges, 877
Juvenile Arthritis, 3970
Juvenile Arthritis: A Teacher's Guide, 3971
Juvenile Bipolar Research Foundation, 980
Juvenile Dermatomyositis, 1421
Juvenile Diabetes Foundation International, 2293
Juvenile Rheumatoid Arthritis, 3950

K

Kaiser Permanente Medical Center, 2010
Kalamazoo Center for Medical Studies, 2047
Kalamazoo Comprehensive Hemophilia Treatment Center, 3586
Kamp-A-Kom-Plish, 7727
Kanawha County Public Library, 7530
Kansas City, Missouri Support Group, 510
Kansas Department of Health & Environment Bureau of Family Health, 5278, 6203
Kansas State Library, 7464
Kansas University Medical Center, 2365, 6855
Kansas University Medical Center: Department of Pulmonology, 2032
Kardiac Kids, 3845
Kathy's Hats: A Story of Hope, 112
Kawasaki Disease, 3973
Kawasaki Disease Foundation, 3978
Kawasaki Kids Foundation, 3979
Keloids, 3980
The Kempe Center: For the Prevention & Treatment of Child Abuse and Neglect, 5033
KenCrest Services, 3925
Kennedy Krieger Institute, 4233
Kennedy Krieger Institute, Down Syndrome Clinic, 2420
Kent County Health Department, 6211
Kent County Library for the Blind, 1662, 1792, 4655, 5466
Kentucky Chapter of Crohn's & Colitis Foundation of America, 1919
Kentucky Department of Human Resources Bureau of Health Services, 6204
Kentucky Hemophilia Foundation, 3533
Kentucky Library for the Blind and Physically Handicapped, 1657, 1786, 4649, 5460
Keren-Or Jerusalem Center for Multi-Handicapped Blind Children, 7502, 7541
Kern Autism Network, 742
Kernicterus, 3988
Keto Kid, Helping Your Child to Succeed on the Ketogenic Diet, 5794
Kettering Medical Center, Sleep Disorders Center, 4379
Kevin and Me, 6523
Key Update, 4802
Keystone Community Resources, 7776
Kid's Corner, 2324
Kid's Health, 2140, 2759, 5114
Kid's Health: TV Late Breaking News Video About Broken Bones and Cast Care, 7569
Kid-Friendly Parenting with Deaf and Hard of Hearing Children, 3386
Kidney Disease of Diabetes, 2338, 4456
Kids and Seizures: Know the Hidden Signs, 5818
Kids In the Syndrome Mix, 878
Kids with AIDS, 2982
Kids with Food Allergies, 1216
Kids With Heart, 3867
Kids with Incredible Potential Leader's Guide, 635
Kids With Incredible Potential Parent's Guide, 634
KidsHealth, 5531, 5540
KidsHealth - Measles, 5302
KidsHealth - Rubella (German Measles), 5303
KidsHealth - Tetanus, 5304
KidsHealth for Parents, 5088, 5095
KidsHealth-Pyloric Stenosis, 5408
KidsHealth: Precocious Puberty, 5209
KidsPeace, 5024, 5060
King Midas, 3387
Kingsmont, 4758
Kiss the Candy Days Good-Bye, 2310
Kiwanis Twin Lakes Camp, 7715
Klaman Eating Disorders Center at McLean Hospital, 2570
Klamath Falls Support Group, 1120
Klinefelter Syndrome, 3999
Klinefelter Syndrome Support Group, 4005
Klippel-Feil Syndrome, 4007
Knox County Advocates, 7209
Knutson, 7745
Kranser Center for Inflammatory Bowel Disease Research, 1951
Kris' Camp, 930
Kudos to Kuualoha, 3238

L

La Fayette Subregional Library for the Blind and Physically Disabled, 7446
LA Lions Camp Pelican, 2133
Lab School of Washington Summer Program, 674, 931, 4093
Laboratory of Dermatology Research, 1402, 2694, 5004
Lactose Intolerance, 4263
Landmark School, 2518
Language, Speech, and Hearing in Schools, 3454, 6003
Lankenau Hospital, Sleep Disorders Center, 4387
LaRabida Children's Hospital, Down Syndrome Clinic, 2417
Las Vegas-Clark County Library District, 7496
Laughter Therapy, 7570
Laurent Clerc National Deaf Education Center-Gallaudet Universty, 3159
Lazy Eye, 4016
Lazy Eye Discussion Group, 4033
LD Advocate, 4078
The LD Child and the ADHD Child: Ways Parents and Professionals Can Help, 653
LD News, 4079
LDA Annual Conference, 2503
Lead Poisoning, 4046
Leading National Publications of and for Deaf People, 3472
The League at Camp Greentop and The Therapeutic Recreation, 7728
Learning Among Children with Spina Bifida, 6106
Learning Disabilities and Challenging Behaviors, 4076
Learning Disabilities Association of America, 580, 608, 2497, 2509, 4062, 4074, 7025, 7603
Learning Disabilities in Children with Hydrocephalus, 3815
Learning Disability/Reading Dyslexia, 4052
Learning Independence Through Computers, 7485
Learning Ladder: Assessing and Teaching Text Comprehension, 3388
Learning Problems & the Student with Tourette Syndrome, 6554
Learning to Live with Neuromuscular Disease: A Message for Parents, 4331
Learning to Play, 1708, 1845, 4701, 5512
Learning to See: American Sign Language as a Second Language, 3389
Learning To Slow Down and Pay Attention, 636
Lee the Rabbit with Epilepsy, 5795
Left Hearts, 3868
Legacy Good Samaritan Hospital & Medical Center, 4471
Legal Rights: The Guide for Deaf and Hard of Hearing People - Fifth Edition, 3390
Legg-Calve-Perthes Disease, 4103
Lehigh Valley Sickle Cell Support Group, 5853
A Lesson With Heart, 3187
Let's Eat, 1690, 1709, 1824, 1846, 3239, 4685, 4702, 5497, 5513
Let's Talk About Being Overweight, 4746
Let's Talk About Depression, 2276
Let's Talk About Diabetes, 2311
Let's Talk About Down Syndrome, 2468
Let's Talk About Dyslexia, 2513

Entry Name Index

Let's Talk About Going to the Hospital, 113, 167, 223, 246, 307, 334, 454, 1150, 1379, 1412, 1743, 1957, 1990, 2118, 2141, 2368, 2794, 2983, 3088, 3631, 3670
Let's Talk About Having Asthma, 455
Let's Talk About Having Chicken Pox, 5313
Let's Talk About Having Lyme Disease, 4159
Let's Talk About Sickle Cell Anemia, 5877
Let's Talk About When Kids Have Cancer, 168, 1151, 2795, 3745, 4497, 4594, 5573, 6877
Let's Talk Facts About Childhood Disorders, 2277
Leukemia & Lymphoma Society - North Texas Chapter, 91
Leukemia & Lymphoma Society, 79, 104, 139, 161, 3740, 4584, 4588
Leukemia & Lymphoma Society - Central OhioChapter, 84, 145
Leukemia & Lymphoma Society - NationalCapital Area Chapter, 94, 155
Leukemia & Lymphoma Society - North TexasChapter, 152
Leukemia & Lymphoma Society - NorthCarolina Chapter, 83, 144
Leukemia & Lymphoma Society - NorthernOhio Chapter, 85, 146
Leukemia & Lymphoma Society - OklahomaChapter, 87, 148
Leukemia & Lymphoma Society - OregonChapter, 88, 149
Leukemia & Lymphoma Society - SouthCentral Texas - San Antonio Chapter, 92, 153
Leukemia & Lymphoma Society - Texas GulfCoast Chapter, 93, 154
Leukemia & Lymphoma Society - Tri-StateSouthern Ohio Chapter, 86, 147
Leukemia & Lymphoma Society - Washington/Alaska Chapter, 82, 95, 7087, 7412
Leukemia & Lymphoma Society - Westchester/Connecticut/Hudson Valley Chapter, 142
Leukemia & Lymphoma Society - Western &Central New York Chapter, 143
Leukemia & Lymphoma Society - WesternPennsylvania/West Virginia Chapter, 89, 150
Leukemia & Lymphoma Society - WisconsinChapter, 96, 156
Leukemia & Lymphoma Society, TennesseeChapter, 90, 151
Leukemia Research Foundation, 7192
Leukodystrophies, 4112
Lewis H. Walker, MD, Cystic FibrosisCenter, 2076
Lewiston Public Library, 7480
LFSN: Lipomyelomeningecele Family SupportNetwork, 6076
Library for the Blind & PhysicallyHandicapped, Leonard C Staisey Building, 7513
Library for the Blind and Handicapped,Southwest, 7434
Library for the Blind and PhysicallyHandicapped, Hawaii State Library, 7454
Library of Michigan Service for the Blind, 1663, 4656, 5467
Lied Learning and Technology Center for Childhood Deafness and Vision Disorders, 3173
Life Adventure Center, 1604, 6844
Life Beyond Your Eating Disorder, 2649
Life in the Country, 3240
Life with Diabetes: A Series of TeachingOutlines, 2312
Life With Retinoblastoma, 5568
Lifeline, 6392
LifelineLetter, 47, 277
Lifespire (A.C.R.M.D.), 7026
Lighthouse Guild, 239, 243, 1624, 1692, 1750, 1827, 4020, 4615, 4688, 5372, 5374, 5418, 5499, 5545, 5549, 5562, 5581, 5582, 6145, 6147, 7604
Lili Claire Foundation, 6856
Ling Series, 3299
LINK, 3797
The Link, 763
LINK Directory Information, 3814
Linking Factor, 3644
Lipomyelomeningocele Family Support, 3778
Lissencephaly, 4123
Listen - Hear for Parents of HearingImpaired Children, 3473
Listen Learn and Talk, 3241
Listen Little Star, 3391, 5997
Listen to This, Volume One, 3242
Listen to This, Volume Two, 3243
The Listener, 3436

Literacy and Your Deaf Child: What Every Parent Should Know, 3392
Literacy, Classroom Amplification and the Brain, 3245
Literacy, Classroom Amplification and the Brain DVD, 3244
Little Hearts, 6352, 6372
Little People of America, 8, 15, 2886, 2906, 4837, 4853
Little People of America - District 2, 2893, 2894, 2896, 4845, 4846, 4848
Little People of America - District 7, 2889, 2891, 2892, 2895, 4840, 4843, 4844, 4847
Little People of America - Front RangeChapter, 4842
Little People of America - San FranciscoBay Area Chapter, 2890, 4841
Little People of America - Utah Seagulls, 2897, 4849
Little Read Riding Hood: Told in Signed Enlish, 3393
Liver Disease in Children, 959, 3671
Liver Transplantation, 7665
Living in a World with AIDS, 2984
Living Well with Epilepsy, 5796
Living with Arthritis, 3962
Living with Asthma, 456
Living with Asthma and Allergies Brochure Series, 465
Living with Ataxia, 542
Living with Childhood Cancer: A PracticalGuide to Help Families Cope, 3746
Living with Cystic Fibrosis, 2106
Living with Depression and ManicDepression, 2230
Living with Hearing Loss, 3394, 4872
Living with HIV: Talking With Your Child, 3651
Living with IBD: A Guide for Teenagers, 6731
Living with Narcolepsy, 4415
Living with Schizophrenia, 1442
Living with SMA, 6131
Living with Tuberous Sclerosis, 6635
Living Without Depression & ManicDepression: A Workbook, 2278
Livingston County CMH Services, 7259
LIVITUP, Inc., 1313
Loma Linda University Sleep Disorders Center, 4349
Long Island Adult Brain Tumor SupportGroup, 1103
Long Island Chapter of Crohn's & ColitisFoundation of America, 1932
Long Island College Hospital, 2066
Long Term Services Division, 7318
Looking After Louis, 879
Looking for Goodwill, 6093
Los Angeles Ataxia Support Group, 481
Loss & FoundHands & Voices, 3246
Louisiana Assistive Technology AccessNetwork, 7231
Louisiana Chapter, 500
Louisiana Comprehensive Hemophilia CareCenter, 3587
Louisiana Lions Camp for Crippled Children, 7722
Louisiana State Library, 7476
Louisiana State University GeneticsSection of Pediatrics, 7477, 7542
Louisiana State University Health SciencesCenter, 2035
Louisiana Support Group, 501
Louisiana/Mississippi Chapter of Crohn's &Colitis Foundation of America, 1920
Louisiana/Mississippi Chapter of Crohn's& Colitis Foundation of America, 1925
Louisville Talking Book Library, 7473
Lovaas Institute, 706
Low Vision Gateway, 7605
Loyola University Medical Center/Department of Pediatrics, 2024
Loyola University of Children, ParmlyHearing Institute, 3161
LPA National Conference, 12, 2902, 4851
LSU Health Sciences Center, 1868
LSUMC Family Medicine Patient Education, 7602
Lucile Packard Children's Hospital, 3945
Lucky Lou Gets Game, 1350
Lupus Foundation of America, 6291
Lupus Research Institute, 6292
Lydia's Lessons, 3247
Lyme Disease, 4140, 4160
Lyme Disease (Deadly Diseases andEpidemics), 4161
Lyme Disease Association, Inc. (LDA), 4148, 4155
Lyme Disease Foundation, 4149, 4156

Entry Name Index

Lyme Disease Research Foundation, 4150
Lymphatic System, 7816
Lymphoma Innovations, 4589
Lymphoma Research Foundation, 3741, 4585

M

MAAP Newsletter, 910
Macomb Library for the Blind andPhysically Handicapped, 1664, 1793, 4657, 5468
Macon Subregional Library for the Blindand Handicapped, Washington Memorial, 7447
Macon Support Group, 495
Macrocephaly, 4164
Madison Institute of Medicine, 5154
MAGIC Foundation: Major Aspects of Growthin Children: Turner's Syndrome Division, 9, 16, 328, 1609, 1614, 2887, 2914, 4197, 4604, 5207, 6644, 6686
Magic Moments- Children's Hospital of Alabama, 7800
Magic of Music and Dance, 7700
Maine Dept. of Human Services:Bureau of Health Immunization Program, 5279
Maine Hemophilia and Thrombosis Center, 3588
Maine State Library, 7481
Maine Support, 502
Major Depression in Children andAdolescents, 2279
Make A Wish Foundation of America, 7801
Makemie Woods Camp Conference Center, 2354, 7788
Making Daughters Safe Again, 5061
Making Headway Foundation-Family SupportProgram, 1104
Making Peace with Food, 2650, 4747
Management of Eating Disorders and Obesity, 2651
Management of Headache & HeadacheMedications, 4239
Management of Motor Speech Disordersin Children and Adults, 5998
Managing Attention Deficit HyperactivityDisorder in Children, 637
Managing Childhood Asthma, 439
Managing Food Allergy and Intolerance, 4261
Managing Inflammatory Bowel Disease as aYoung Adult, 1972
Managing Seizures, Information for Caregivers, 5819
Managing the Defiant Child, 1584, 6789
Managing Your Child's Crohn's Disease orUlcerative Colitis, 1958
Mandy, 3395
Manhattan Public Library, 7465
Mansfield's Holiday Hill, 7701
Maple Syrup Urine Disease, 4172
Maplebrook School, 675, 932, 4094
March of Dimes Foundation, 219, 231, 240, 252, 264, 286, 303, 329, 566, 581, 707, 943, 1180, 1239, 1486, 1500, 1505, 1525, 1541, 1740, 1877
March of Dimes Nursing Modules, 7638
March of Dimes-Preterm Birth Fact Sheets, 5236
Marfan Syndrome, 4181, 4190
Maricopa Co Childhood Immunization Program, 5263
Marist Brothers Mid-Hudson Valley Camp Marist Brothers, 7762
Marty Lyons Foundation, 7327
Marvelwood Summer, 2519
Marvin Teaches Fingerspelling, 3300
Mary M Gooley Hemophilia Center of theNational Hemophilia Foundation, 3541
Maryland Department of Health, 3760, 4207
Maryland Infant and Toddlers ProgramFamily Support Network, 7243
Maryland State Library for the Blindand Physically Handicapped, 1658, 1787, 4650, 5461
Maryland/South Delaware Chapter of Crohn's& Colitis Foundation of America, 1921
Masqueraders of Sarcoidosis, 5666
Massachusetts Assistive TechnologyPartnership, 7254
Massachusetts Association for Parents of the Visually Impaired (MAPVI), 5564
Massachusetts Down Syndrome Congress(MDSC), 2404
Massachusetts Easter Seals Camping Program, 7734
Massachusetts Eating Disorder Association(MEDA), 2586
Massachusetts General Hospital, 2042
Massachusetts Sudden Infant Death Syndrome, 6234
Mastering Asthma, 440
Maternal, Child & Family Health, EarlyIntervention/Infant Learning Program, 7088
Matrix Parents Network and Resource Center, 7122
MATRIX: Parent Network and Family ResourceCenter, 7121
Matthew and the Tics, 6539
Matthew and Tics, 6452
Maybe You Know My Kid: A Parent's Guide toIdentifying ADHD, 638
Mayo Clinic, 5115
Mayo Clinic and Foundation, 4293
Mayo Clinic Scleroderma Service, 5697
Mayo Comprehensive Hemophilia Center, 3589
MayoClinic.com, 5096
MayoClinic.com - Pulmonary Hypertension, 5386
McCallum Place, 2571
McCune-Albright Syndrome, 4191
MD Infant/Toddler/Preschool ServicesDivision, 7242
MDA Fact Sheet, 1390, 4332
MDA Services for the Individual, Familyand Community, 4333
MDA Summer Camp, 4338
MDA Summer Camp Brochure, 4334
MDA/ALS Newsmagazine, 4311
Me and My World Storybook, 5820
Meadowood Springs Speech and Hearing Camp, 3492, 6007, 6167
Meals Without Squeals Sense, 2652
Measles, 5314
Measuring Bullying Victimization,Perpetration and Bystander Experiences, 6830
Measuring Violence-Related Attitudes,Behaviors and Influences, 6831
Med Help International, 2760
Med-Camps of Louisiana, 7723
Media and Youth: A DevelopmentalPerspective, 6833
Media Violence and Children: A CompleteGuide, 6832
Media-Smart Youth: Eat, Think, and Be Active Fact Sheet, 4753
Medical and Surgical Care for Childrenwith Down Syndrome, 2469
Medical Center Hospital of Vermont, 2096
Medical College of Pennsylvania, SleepDisorders Center, 4388
Medical College of Wisconsin, 17, 4118
Medical College of Wisconsin CysticFibrosis Center, 2103
Medical Economics Company, 7607
Medical Genetics Clinic, 2425
Medical Illness and Schizophrenia, 1460
Medical Matrix: Pediatrics, 7608
Medical Sign Language: Easily Understood Definitions of Commonly Used Medical Term, 3396
Medication for ADHD, 598
MedicineNet, 5325
MedicineNet.com, 1869
Medicines for Epilepsy, 5821
Mediconsult, 162, 2298
Medifocus Guidebook On Reflex SympatheticDystrophy, 4306
Medifocus Guidebook on Scleroderma, 5710
MEDLINEplus, 3834
MedlinePlus, 6177
MEDLINEplus Medical Encyclopedia:Pyloric Stenosis, 5409
MEDLINEplus on Sleep Apnea, 5894
Medulloblastoma, 1162
Meeting the Challenge: Parenting Childrenwith Disabilities, 7571
The Memo, 3270
Memorial Miller Children's HospitalCystic Fibrosis Center, 2011
Memphis Cystic Fibrosis Center, 2088
Memphis Regional Brain Tumor SurvivorsGroup, 1126
Memphis State University, Center for theCommunicatively Impaired, 5982
Meningitis, 4202
Meningitis Foundation of America, 4206
Menninger Child & Family Program, 1576, 6780
Mental Fitness, Inc., 2572
Mental Health America, 582, 708, 981, 1430, 1571, 2816, 4522, 4569, 4768, 4878, 4950, 5082, 6771

963

Entry Name Index

Mental Health Net, 996, 1446, 2236, 2510
Mental Help Net, 2735, 7609
Mental Help Net- Eating Disorders, 2621
Mental Wellness, 1447
Mental, Emotional, and Behavior Disorders in Children and Adolescents, 1601, 6838
Mercer Mayer Frog Stories, 3248
Merck, 5326
Merck Manual of Diagnosis and Therapy, 1491, 5328
Mercy Hospital of Johnstown, SleepDisorders Center, 4389
Mercy Sleep Laboratory, 4399
Messy Monsters Jungle Joggers and Bubble Baths, 3397
Methodist Hospital Sleep Disorders Center, 4353
Metro Intergroup of Overeaters Anonymous, 2589
Miami Children's Hospital, Division ofPulmonology, 2019
Miami Comprehensive Hemophilia Center, 3590
Miami Valley Downs Syndrome Association, 2407
Michigan Chapter of Allergy and AsthmaFoundation of America, 417
Michigan Chapter of Crohn's & ColitisFoundation of America, 1923
Michigan State University ComprehensiveCenter for Bleeding Disorders, 3591
Microcephaly, 4209
Microdontia, 4218
Mid Illinois Talking Book System, 1649, 1778, 4642, 5453
Mid-America Chapter of Crohn's & Colitis Foundation of America, 1918
Mid-Atlantic ADA Center, 1240
Mid-Atlantic Regional Human GeneticsNetwork, 521
Mid-Illinois Talking Book Center, 1650, 1779, 4643, 5454
Mideastern Michigan Library Co-op, 1665, 1794, 4658, 5469
MidWest Medical Center - Sleep DisordersCenter, 4354
Migraine and Coexisting Conditions-OtherIllnesses That May Affect Migraine, 4247
Migraine and Other Headaches: VascularMechanisms, 4240
Migraine Headaches, 4226
Mile High Down Syndrome Association, 2395
Milk Protein Allergy/Lactose Intolerance, 4251
A Mind of Your Own, 7565
Mindblindness: An Essay on Autism & Theoryof Mind, 880
Minneapolis, MN Support Group, 507
Minnesota Cystic Fibrosis Center, 2049
Minnesota Library for the Blind &Physically Handicapped, 4663, 5474
Minnesota Sudden Infant Death Center, 6212
Minnesota/Dakotas Chapter of Crohn's &Colitis Foundation of America, 1924
Miracle to Believe In, 881
Mirror, Mirror, 2622
Missing Michael - A Mother's Story of Love, 5797
Mississippi Chapter, 508
Mississippi Dept. of Health Bureau ofPreventative Health Immunization, 5281
Mississippi Hemophilia Foundation, 3537
Mississippi State Department of Health andChild Health Services, 6213
Missouri Parents Act, 7282
Misunderstood Child, 2514
Mobile Association for the Blind, 1685, 1758, 1818, 4622, 4681, 5433, 5493
Mom I Have a Staring Problem, 5798
Monetary Allowance, Health Care andVocational Training & Rehabilitation, 6107
Monmouth Medical Center, Cystic Fibrosis& Pediatric Pulmonary Center, 2058
Montana Department of Health &Environmental Sciences, 6215
Montana State Library, 7494
MonTECH, 7289
Montgomery County Intermediate Unit #23, 7364
Montifiore Medical Center, 3174
Mood Apart, 2256
Mood Disorders, 1003
Mosaic, 3914
Most Frequently Asked Questions withGrowth Hormone Deficiency, 2920
A Mother's Persepctive on the IEP Process, 3188

A Mother's Touch: The Tiffany Callo Story, 1337
Mothers of Children with Allergies (MOCHA), 5591
Mothers of Omphaloceles, 4814
Mount Sinai Traumatic Brain Injury, 3038
Mountain Milestones Stepping Stones, 7791
Mountain States Regional Genetics ServicesNetwork, 488
Mountaineer Spina Bifida Camp, 6114
Move with Me, 1710, 1847, 4703, 5514
Movement Disorders, 6451
MSRGSN Newsletter, 547
MSUD Newsletter, 4180
MSUD:(Maple Syrup Urine Disease) FamilySupport Group, 4176
Mt Hood Kiwanis Camp, 7772
Mucolipidoses, 4264
Mucolipidosis IV Foundation, 4267, 4270
Mucopolysaccharidoses, 4274
Multidisciplinary Clinico-PathologicConference, 5667
Muscular Dystrophies, 4284
Muscular Dystrophy, 4300
Muscular Dystrophy and Allied Diseases: Impacts on Patients, Family, and Staff, 4307
Muscular Dystrophy and OtherNeuromuscular Diseases, 4308
Muscular Dystrophy Association, 1377, 1487, 2528, 2537, 4288, 4301, 6120
Muscular Dystrophy Family Foundation, 4289, 4302
Muscular System, 7817
Musella Foundation for Brain Tumor Research and Information, 1025
Muskegon County Library for the Blind, 1666, 1795, 4659, 5470
My Baby Can Talk: First Signs, 3249
My Body is Mine, My Feelings are Mine, 5072
My Body Is Not Who I Am, 7572
My Brother Sammy, 882
My Brother's a World Class Pain: ASibling's Guide To ADHD/Hyperactivity, 639
My Child Without Limits, 1332
My Child Without Limits Newsletter, 1358
My Friend Matty: A Story About Living withEpilepsy, 5799
My Friend With Autism, 883
My Social Stories Book, 884
My Surprise, 3250
My Travelin' Eye, 4040
MyFace, 1888, 3771
Myositis Association, 1396, 1410
Myths and Facts About AIDS, 2985
MyTTY for Windows 95, 98, ME, 2000, XP, 3302
MyTTY Phone Messenger Software for Windows, 3301

N

NAAFA Annual Convention, 2611
NAD Biennial Conference, 3184
NAD Youth Leadership Camp, 3493
NADD Annual Conference & Exhibit Show, 1582, 2225, 6787, 7563
NADD Bulletin, 1476, 3935
NADD: National Association for the DuallyDiagnosed, 1431, 1448, 1572, 1589, 2206, 2237, 3915, 3931, 4523, 4533, 4547, 4556, 4769, 4786, 4879, 4889, 6432, 6440, 6772, 6805, 7028
NADF News, 1617, 1991
NAMI Convention, 591, 991, 1439, 1583, 2226, 6788, 7564
NAMI DuPage, 7029
NAQ, 3916
Narcolepsy, 4339, 4405, 4416
Narcolepsy Network, 4346
Narcolepsy Primer, 4411
Narcolepsy: Evaluation and Treatment, 4406
NASPGHAN, 4258
NASPGHAN Annual Meeting, 34, 270, 1561, 2770, 3688
NASPGHAN News, 48, 278, 1563, 2773, 3695, 4262, 4443, 4819, 5414
Nassau Library System, 7503
Natalie's Brace, 5729
National Ability Center, 7030
National Academy for Child Development(NACD), 7031

Entry Name Index

National Adoption Center, 7032
National Adrenal Diseases Foundation, 1610, 1615, 1987
National Advisory Allergic and Infectious Disease Council, 392
National Alliance for Eating Disorders, 2573
National Alliance for Research onSchizophrenia and Depression, 1436
National Alliance of State & Territorial AIDS Directors, 2956
National Alliance on Mental Illness (NAMI), 357, 583, 982, 1432, 1573, 2207, 2817, 3917, 4524, 4770, 4880, 4951, 5084, 6774, 7033
National Alopecia Areata Foundation, 206
National Alopecia Areata Foundation AnnualConference, 208
National Amputee Golf Association, 7034
National Anxiety Foundation, 2208, 4771, 4787, 4890, 4952, 4971, 5936
National Aphasia Association, 5971
National Arthritis and Musculoskeletal &Skin Disease Info. Clearinghouse, 7611
National Arts and Disability Center, 7035
National Association for Anorexia Nervosaand Associated Disorders (ANAD), 2623
National Association for Down Syndrome(NADS), 2388, 2455
National Association for Hearing andSpeech Action, 3134
National Association for Proton Therapy, 1026
National Association for the Education ofYoung Children, 6775
National Association for theEducation of Young Children, 7036
National Association of Addiction Treatmemt Providers, 2574
National Association of Anorexia Nervosaand Associated Disorders (ANAD), 2575
National Association of Blind Students, 1625, 1693, 1751, 1828, 5419, 5500, 7037
National Association of Community Health Centers, 2957
National Association of Councils on Developmental Disabilities, 3918
National Association of Epilepsy Centers, 5749
National Association of Pediatric Nurse Practitioners, 5254
National Association of School Nurses, 409, 5255
National Association of School Psychologists, 3135, 6776
National Association of Special Education Teachers, 358, 709
National Association of State Directors of Developmental Disabilities Services, 3919
National Association of State Mental Health Program Directors, 983, 3920
National Association of the Deaf (NAD), 3136
National Association to Advance FatAcceptance (NAAFA), 2576
National Asthma Educator Certification Board, 410
National Ataxia Foundation, 477, 538, 6332, 6340, 6375
National Ataxia Foundation AnnualMembership Meeting, 530
National Autism Association, 359, 710
National Birth Defects Center, 7255
National Black Association for Speech-Language and Hearing, 5972
National Black Deaf Advocates, 3137
National Black Leadership Commission on Health, Inc., 2958
National Bone Marrow Transplant Link, 80, 140
National Brain Tumor Society, 1027
National Camps for Blind Children, 1721, 1857, 4710, 5521
National Capital Lyme Disease Association, 4152
National Captioning Institute, 3138
National Catholic Office for the Deaf, 3139
National Center for BiotechnologyInformation, 18, 221, 233, 331, 844, 1980, 2366, 2681, 2907, 3761, 4407, 6078, 7612
National Center for Education in Maternaland Child Health, 5223, 6017, 6186, 6244, 6920
National Center for Environmental Health, 1522
National Center for Health Statistics, 6181, 6921
National Center for Injury Prevention andControl, 6777
National Center for Latinos withDisabilities, 7193
National Center for Learning Disabilities, 584, 609, 4063, 7038
National Center for Missing & ExploitedChildren, 5025
National Center for Neurogenic Communication Disorders, 5986
National Center for PTSD, 5137
National Center for the Prevention of SIDS, 6187
National Center for the Study of Wilson'sDisease, 6891
National Center on Accessbility, 7039
National Center On Deaf-Blindness, 3140
National Child Traumatic Stress Network, 5144

National Children's Advocacy Center, 5026
National Children's Alliance, 5027
National Children's Cancer Society, 1028, 7040
National Coalition for Cancer Survivorship, 81, 141, 2786
National Collaborative on Childhood Obesity Research, 4729
National Comprehensive Cancer Network, 1029
National Conference of State Legislatures, 4050
National Conference on OI, 4852
National Congenital CMV Disease Registry, 2139
National Council for Behavioral Health, 984
National Council on Child Abuse & FamilyViolence, 5062
National Council on Disability, 6922
National Cued Speech Association, 3141
National Cystic Fibrosis EducationConference, 2105
National Deaf Center, 4108
National Dental Association, 2178
National Diabetes InformationClearinghouse, 2294, 2299
National Digestive Diseases InformationClearinghouse (NDDIC), 32, 43, 268, 275, 1556, 1731, 1949, 1999, 2768, 2771, 2861, 3687, 3691, 3716, 3880, 3994, 4178, 4438, 4440, 4737, 4813
National Directory of HydrocephalusSupport Groups, 3816
National Disability Rights Network, 3921
National Dissemination Center for Children with Disabilities, 7613
National Down Syndrome Adoption Network, 2389
National Down Syndrome Coalition, 2390
National Down Syndrome Congress, 2391, 2456
National Down Syndrome Society, 2392, 2457
National Down Syndrome Society AnnualNational Conference, 2442
National Early Childhood TechnicalAssistance Center, 2393, 7041
National Eating Disorder Association of Long Island (NEDA-LI), 2602
National Eating Disorders Association (NEDA), 2577, 4730, 5085
National Eating Disorders Association-LongIsland (NEDA-LI), 2590
National Eczema Association, 2689
National Education Alliance for Borderline Personality Disorder, 2209
National Environmental Education Foundation, 411
National Exchange Club Foundation, 5028
National Eye Research Foundation, 1819
National Family Association for Deaf-Blind, 3142
National Federation of Families, 711, 985, 1433, 1574, 2210, 4525, 4548, 4570, 4772, 4881, 4953, 5912, 5937, 6778, 7042
National Fire Protection Association, 1189, 1198
National Foundation for Cancer Research, 3742
National Foundation for Depressive Illness, 2273
National Foundation for EctodermalDysplasias, 2675
National Foundation for Infectious Diseases, 5256
National Foundation for Transplants, 7043
National Fragile X Foundation, 2845, 2853
National Gaucher Foundation, 2873, 2880
National Headache Foundation, 4232, 4235
National Health Council, 6923
National Hemophilia Foundation, 3521, 3622
National Hydrocephalus Foundation, 1889, 1893, 2725, 2727, 3772, 3791, 4132, 4136
National Industries for the Blind, 7044
National Institute of Diabetes andDigestive and Kidney Diseases - Urology, 4566
National Institute of Health NINDSInformation Page, 305
National Institute on Disability, Independent Living & Rehabilitation Research, 7614
National Jewish Health, 420, 424, 5116, 5636
National Jewish Medical & Research Center, 5111
National Kidney Foundation, 4447, 4450
National Library of Dermatologic TeachingSlides, 1401, 2693, 2698, 5003, 5334
National Library Service for the Blind &Physically Handicapped, 1702, 1837, 4695, 5506
National Library Service for the Blind andPhysically Handicapped, 6924, 7615
National Marfan Foundation, 4186, 4187
National Medical Association, 412, 2959, 6779

965

Entry Name Index

National Mental Health Consumers' Self-Help Clearinghouse, 185, 360, 585, 712, 1434, 1575, 2818, 4526, 4549, 4571, 4773, 4788, 4882, 4954, 5086, 5913, 7045
National MPS Society, 4268, 4271, 4277, 4280
National Multiple Sclerosis Society, 2211
National Network of Depression Centers, 2212
National Neutropenia Network, 4510
National Newborn Screening and Genetic Resources Center, 7616
National Ophthalmic Research Institute, 1820
National Organization for Albinism and Hypopigmentation, 186
National Organization for Rare Disorders, 7046
National Organization of Parents of Blind Children, 4021, 5426, 7617
National Organization on Disability, 7047
National Panic/Anxiety Disorder Newsletter, 4972
National Parent Resource Center, 7048
National Pediatric & Family HIV Resource Center, 2973
National Pediatric AIDS Network, 2974
National Perinatal Association, 5218, 7049
National PKU Alliance, 4927
National PKU News, 4936
National Prevention Information Network, 6925
National Psoriasis Foundation, 5332, 5336
National Recreation and Park Association, 6926
National Registry for Childhood Onset Scleroderma (NRCOS), 5700
National Rehabilitation Information Center, 1320, 2752, 2835, 2838, 3143, 6018, 6927, 7050
National Resource Center for Health & Safety in Child Care & Early Education, 4731
National Resource Library on Youth With Disabilities, 7618
National Scoliosis Foundation, 5720
National SIDS Resource Center Brochure, 6265
National Sleep Foundation, 296, 4347, 4527, 4550, 4572, 5888, 5896, 5914, 5917, 7051
National Society for Phenylketonuria (UK), 4930
National Spasmodic Torticollis Association, 2539
National Spasmodic Torticollis Association, 2529
National Stuttering Association, 6158
National Sudden Infant Death Syndrome Alliance Conference, 6231, 6235, 6238
National Tay-Sachs and Allied Diseases Association, 2874, 4116, 6309, 6376
National Technical Assistance Center for Children's Mental Health, 1577, 6781
National Technical Institute for the Deaf, 3144
National Temporal Bone, Hearing and Balance Pathology Resource Registry, 3170
National Tuberculosis Controllers Association, 5257
National Tuberous Sclerosis Association, 6629
National Vaccines Information Center, 7052
National Wheelchair Softball Association, 7053
National Wilms Tumor Study, 6871
The National Women's Health Information Center, 2550
Nationwide Survey of Sudden Infant Death Syndrome (SIDS) Service, 6266
The Natural History of Mania, Depression, and Schizophrenia, 1474
Natural Supports in School/Work/Community for the Severely Disabled, 1351
NC BEGINNINGS, 3133
NDSC Annual Convention, 2441
NE Florida Support Group, 491
NE Indiana Support Group, 499
NE Louisiana Sickle Cell Anemia Foundation, 5847
Nebraska Chapter of the National Hemophilia Foundation, 3538
Nebraska Dept. of Health Immunization Program, 5282
Nebraska Library Commission Talking Book & Braille Services, 1672, 1801, 4667, 5478
Nebraska Regional Hemophilia Center, 3592
NEDA Annual Conference, 2612
Need to Know, 6556
Negative Symptom and Cognitive Deficit Treatment Response in Schizophrenia, 1461

Negotiating the Special Education Maze: A Guide for Parents and Teachers, 6094
NEO Fight, 7210
Neonatal Herpes Simplex, 4417
Neonatal Jaundice, 4429
NephCure Foundation, 4448, 4451
NephCure Now, 4453
Nephrotic Syndrome, 4444
NERG News, 548
Nervous System, 7818
Network, 6259
Networker, 1359
Neuroanatomy: Text and Atlas 3rd Edition, 1492
Neurobiology of Autism, 885
Neuroblastoma, 4481
Neuroblastoma Children's Cancer Society, 4489
Neurofibromatosis, 4457
Neurofibromatosis Center at North Broward Medical Center, 4473
Neurofibromatosis Ink, 4479
Neurofibromatosis, Inc, 4463, 4476
Neurofibromatosis, Inc - Arizona Chapter, 4464
Neurofibromatosis, Inc - California Chapter, 4466
Neurofibromatosis, Inc - Illinois/Midwest, 4467
Neurofibromatosis, Inc - Kansas & Central Plains, 4469
Neurofibromatosis, Inc - MidAtlantic, 4470
The Neurology of Autism, 900
Neuromuscular Disease Guidebooks & Pamphlets, 4335
Neurosarcoidosis, 5668
Neurosarcoidosis or Multiple Sclerosis?, 5669
Neuroscience Institute at Mercy Hospital, 4474
Neuroscience Institute Brain Tumor Support Group, 1048
Neuroscience Institute, University of Tennessee Health Science Center, 5766
Neutropenia, 4501
Nevada Parent Network, 7301
Nevada Parents Encouraging Parents (PEP), 7302
Nevada State Division of Health, Maternal & Child Health, 6216
Nevada State Health Division Bureau of Community Health - Immunization Program, 5283
Nevada State Library and Archives, 7497
Nevus Outreach, 1030
New Beginnings - Blind Children's Center, 1637, 1766, 4630, 5441
New Beginnings - The Blind Children's Center, 1686, 1821, 4682, 5494
New Challenge: Responding to Families, 7667
New England Center for Children, 713, 4064, 7054
New England Chapter of Crohn's & Colitis Foundation of America, 1922
New England Region-Helen Keller National Center, 5427
New England Regional Genetics Group, 503, 7482, 7543
New England Retinoblastoma Support Group (NERSG), 5565
New England Support Group, 505
New Expectations, 2449
New Hampshire Cystic Fibrosis Care and Teaching Center, 2057
New Hampshire State Library, 7498
New Image Camps, 4759
New Jersey Camp Jaycee, 3939
New Jersey Chapter of Crohn's & Colitis Foundation of America, 1927
New Jersey Department of Health - Child Health Program, 6217
New Jersey Department of Health Immunizations Program, 5285
New Jersey Institute of Technology Center for Biomedical Engineering, 2900
New Jersey Medical School, 2059
New Jersey Self-Help Clearinghouse, 7314
New Jersey State Library Talking Book and Braille Center, 1673, 1802, 4668, 5479
New Jersey Statewide Parent to Parent, 7315
New Language of Toys: Teaching Communication Skills to Children with Special Needs, 6095
New Mexico Autism Society, 777
New Mexico Department of Health Immunization Program, 5286
New Mexico State Library for the Blind and Physically Handicapped, 1674, 1803, 4669, 5480
New Neighbors, 3251

Entry Name Index

New People Not Patients: A Source Book for Living with IBD, 6722
New People...Not Patients: a Source Book for Living with Bowel Disease, 1959
New Pharmacotherapy of Schizophrenia, 1462
New Strong-Willed Child, 4828
New York Autism Network, 779
New York Brain Tumor Support Group, 1105
New York City Area Support Group, 513
New York City Department of Health Bureau of Tuberculosis Control, 6459, 6607
New York City Information & Counseling Program for SIDS, 6218
New York Department of Education, 7328
New York Glaucoma Research Institute, 1829
New York Obesity Research Center, 2606, 4738
New York Online Access to Health, 4891
New York Presbyterian Morgan Stanley Children's Hospital, 3946
New York State Department of Health Immunization Program, 2761, 5287
New York State Talking Book & Braille Library, 1675, 1804, 4670, 5481
New York Support Group, 514
New York University Langone Medical Center Auxiliary of Tisch Hospital, 3777
New York University Medical Center Auxillary of Tisch Hospital, 3782
Newark Sleep Disorders Center, 4364
Newberry County Memorial Hospital Brain Tumor Support Group, 1125
Newborns in Need, 5227
Newport News Public Library System, 7526
Newsletter: SIDS, 6260
Newsline, 3458, 7652
Newsline Eight & Nine, 3645
Newslink, 906
Next Steps - Parents Reaching Parents, 7194
NF Clinic - University of Pittsburgh Children's Hospital, 4472
NFB National Convention, 193
NH Dept. of Health & Human Services Immunization Program, 5284
Nick Joins In, 6096
The Night Before Christmas told in Signed english, 3437
Night Terrors, 4540
Nightmares, 4513
NIH News Advisory, 3717
NIH/ Eunice Kennedy Shriver National Institute of Child Health & Human Development, 178, 225, 281, 291, 300, 355, 561, 1175, 1229, 1536, 1726, 1735, 1974, 2135, 2143, 2370, 2489, 2511, 2717, 2730, 2808
NIH/National Cancer Institute, 64, 125, 1005, 2776, 3725, 3735, 4482, 4578, 5556, 6862, 6905
NIH/National Center on Sleep Disorders Research, 5895
NIH/National Eye Institute, 236, 1619, 1745, 1862, 4017, 4227, 4611, 4994, 5369, 5416, 5543, 5579, 6142, 6906
NIH/National Heart, Lung and Blood Institute, 65, 126, 282, 390, 562, 1176, 1537, 3511, 3975, 4503, 4898, 5318, 5379, 5389, 5525, 5649, 5837, 6272, 6347, 6359, 6383
NIH/National Human Genome Research Institute (NHGRI), 4929, 6908
NIH/National Institues of Health-Genetic & Rare Diseases Information Ctr (GARD), 6909
NIH/National Institute of Allergy and Infectious Diseases, 391, 449, 1863, 2136, 2685, 2755, 2930, 3656, 3697, 3887, 3976, 4203, 4418, 4861, 5092, 5107, 5240, 5535, 6170, 6458, 6568
NIH/National Institute of Arthritis and Musculoskeletal and Skin Diseases, 3, 248, 324, 1736, 2669, 2686, 2710, 2741, 3499, 3888, 3951, 3981, 4009, 4105, 4151, 4182, 4193, 4908, 4995, 5099, 5120
NIH/National Institute of Dental and Craniofacial Research (NIDCR), 2144, 2670, 4220, 6416, 6422, 6912
NIH/National Institute of Diabetes and Digestive and Kidney Diseases, 23, 6699, 6913
NIH/National Institute of Environmental Health Sciences (NIEHS), 4, 356, 408, 6914
NIH/National Institute of Mental Health, 336, 571, 964, 1425, 1565, 1978, 2189, 2548, 2809, 4006, 4515, 4542, 4565, 4763, 4875, 4941, 5083, 5225, 5908, 5928, 6750

NIH/National Institute of Neurological Disorders and Stroke (NINDS), 292, 337, 474, 572, 679, 939, 948, 1006, 1230, 1481, 2521, 2538, 2996, 3079, 4340, 4345, 5781, 6171, 6178, 6273, 6300
NIH/National Institute on Alcohol Abuse and Alcoholism (NIAAA), 2810, 6917
NIH/National Institute on Deafness and Other Communication Disorders (NIDCD), 338, 680, 3100, 5956, 6153, 6162, 6918
NIH/National Institute on Drug Abuse (NIDA), 5, 6919
NIH/National Institutes of Health-Genetic & Rare Diseases Information Ctr (GARD), 3515
NIH/National Library of Medicine (NLM), 10
NIH/Osteoporosis and Related Bone Diseases National Resource Center, 4010, 4833, 4850
NINDS Seeks Patients with Generalized Dystonia, 2545
NINDS Seeks Patients with Tourette Syndrome, 6555
NINDS Syncope Information Page, 6275
NM Alliance for the Neurologically Impaired, 1099
NMAC, 2955
No Fears, No Tears, 7573
No Fears, No Tears - 13 Years Later, 7574
No Time for Jello: One Family's Experience, 1352
Nobody Knows, 1353
Nocturnal Enuresis, 4564
Non-Hodgkin's Lymphoma, 4577
Non-Malignant Brain Tumor Support Group, 1089
Nonverbal Learning Disorder Syndrome, 3817
Noonan Connection, 4609
Noonan Syndrome, 4600
Noonan Syndrome Foundation, 4606
North Ameerican Spine Society, 5730
North American Riding for the Handicapped, 7055
North American Society for Pediatric Gastroenterology/Hepatology/Nutrition, 29, 265, 1554, 2767, 3686, 3692, 4255, 4437, 4812, 5404
North Carolina Library for the Blind, 1805, 4671, 5482
North Carolina Speech, Hearing and Language Association, 5977
North Central Oklahoma Support Group, 517
North Dakota Comprehensive Hemophilia and Thrombosis Treatment Center, 3593
North Pacific Epilepsy Research, 5782
North Platte Public Library, 7495
North Texas Chapter of Crohn's & Colitis Foundation of America, 1946
North Texas Support Group, 525
Northeast Ohio Chapter of Crohn's & Colitis Foundation of America, 1938
Northeast Rehabilitation Health Network, 3080
Northern California Chapter of Crohn's and Colitis Foundation, 1908
Northern California Comprehensive Sickle Cell Center, 5859
Northern California Support Group, 482
Northern Connecticut Affiliate Chapter of Crohn's & Colitis Foundation of America, 1912
Northern Kentucky Talking Book Library, 7474
Northern Ohio Chapter of the National Hemophilia Foundation, 3544
Northern Regional Bleeding Disorder Center, 3594
Northridge Hospital: Leavey Cancer Center, 1049
Northwest Indiana Subregional Library for Blind and Physically Handicapped, 1652, 1781, 4645, 5456
Northwest Ohio Hemophilia Treatment Center, 3595
Northwestern Region-Helen Keller National Center, 1629, 1757, 4621, 5432
Northwestern University Asthma and Allergy Disease Center, 425
Not Just a Cancer Patient, 7575
Not So Sweet: Living With Diabetes, 2297
Now We Can Successfully Treat the Illness Called Depression, 2280
NPF Benefits of Membership Pamphlets, 7666
Nuclear Medicine at Children's Hospital, Boston, 7619
Number Signs for Everyone: Numbering in American Sign Language, 3252
Nursery Rhymes from Mother Goose: Told in Signed English, 3398
Nutrition for Early Chronic Kidney Disease, 7668
Nutrition for Later Chronic Disease, 7669
NW Ohio Sleep Disorders Center, 4380

Entry Name Index

Nystagmus, 4610
Nystagmus Network, 4689
NYU, 2805, 4119
NYU Rusk Institute, 4295

O

Oak-Leyden Developmental Services, 714, 7056
Oakhurst, 7763
Oakland School & Camp, 4095
Oasis, 7141
Oasis Guide to Asperger Syndrome, 377
Obesity, 4712
Obesity Action Coalition, 4732
Obesity Online, 4744
The Obesity Society, 4736
Obesity Sourcebook, 4748
Obsessive Compulsive Anonymous, 4774
Obsessive Compulsive Disorder (OCD), 4789
Obsessive Compulsive Disorder General Packet, 4804
Obsessive Compulsive Disorder: Helping Children and Adolescents, 4797
Obsessive Compulsive Foundation of Metropolitan Chicago, 4777
Obsessive-Compulsive Disorder, 4761
Obsessive-Compulsive Disorder in Children and Adolescents, 4798
Obsessive-Compulsive Disorder, A Real Illness, 4805
OCECD, 7349
Oconee Regional Library, Library for the Blind and Physically Handicapped, 7448
Of Their Own-Person To Person Show, 5641
Office for Fair Housing & Equal Opportunity, 6928
Office Integrated Social Services, 7373
Office of Community Health and Prevention Bureau of Early Intervention, DHR, 7195
Office of Exceptional Children South Carolina Department of Education, 7379
Office of Special Education, 7260, 7274, 7382
Office of Special Education Administration, 7416
Office of Special Education and Rehabilitation Services, 3101
Office of Special Education and Rehabilitative Services, 6929, 7389, 7620
Office of Special Education, State Department of Education, 7386
Office of Special Education, Virginia, 7408
Office of the Dean, University of Texas at Austin, 7390
Office of the Superintendent of Public Instruction, 7413
Office of Women's & Children's Health, 6192
Official Journal of the American Academy of Child and Adolescent Psychiatry, 4830
The Official Parent's Sourcebook on Tay-Sachs Disease, 6321
The Official Parent's Sourcebook on Childhood Nephrotic Syndrome, 4452
Ohio Department of Health Immunization Program, 5288
Ohio Protection and Advocacy Organization, 7350
Ohio Regional Library for the Blind and Physically Handicapped, 7507
Ohio Sleep Medicine Institute, 4381
Ohio State University Hospitals, Sleep Disorders Center, 4382
Ohio State University Laboratory of Psychobiology, 3067
Ohio Support Group, 516
OHSU Homepage Search, 2908
Okizu Foundation Camps, 123, 176, 1173, 2799, 4599, 6882
Oklahoma ABLE Tech-Wellness Center, 7354
Oklahoma Brain Injury Camp, 3098
Oklahoma Chapter of Crohn's & Colitis Foundation of America, 1940
Oklahoma Library for the Blind & Physically Handicapped, 7509
Oklahoma Speech Language Hearing Association, 5980
Oklahoma State Department of Health - Maternal and Child Health Services, 6220
Oklahoma State Department of Health Immunization Division, 5289
Oley Foundation, 30, 266
Oley Foundation Annual Conference, 35, 271
Oligodendrogliomas and Oligoastrocytomas, 1163
Olympia, 7707
Omphalocele, 4807

On The Other Hand, 5125
On the Threshold of a Cure...You Can Make the Difference!, 2130
OncoLink: The University of Pennslyvania Cancer Center Resource, 2790, 6874
Onhealth, 2111
Online Mendelian Inheritance in Man, 19, 222, 234, 244, 256, 306, 332, 450, 845, 958, 1143, 1449, 1489, 1506, 1590, 1694, 1830, 1879, 1981, 2112, 2238
Online Parenting Coach, 6807
Online Pediatric Surgery Handbook, 3720
Online Sarcoidosis Newsletter, 5656
Online Support Group, 4110
Open Support Group-All Kinds of Cancer Care of Maine, 1069
Opening Doors: Strategies for Including All Students in Regular Education, 1354
Operation Liftoff of Ohio, 7351
Operation Sneek-a-Peek, 7576
Opinion Section, 3253
Opposites, 3399
Oppositional Defiant Disorder, 4820
Option Institute: Son Rise Program, 586, 715, 2499, 2512
Optometrists Network, 4034
Oral Cancer Foundation, 2179
Orange County Support Group, 483
Oregon Brain Injury Resource Network, 3044
Oregon Department of Education, 7359
Oregon Health Sciences Unit, 2080
Oregon Health Sciences University Research Center, 3177
Oregon Parent Training and Information Center, 7360
Oregon State Library, 7511
Oregon State Library, Talking Book and Braille Services, 1677, 1807, 4673, 5484
Organization for Autism Research, 716
Organizing and Facilitating a Support Group, 1164
Orphan Disease Update, 2915, 7653
Orthopaedic Biomechanics Laboratory, 1321
Orthopaedic Hospital's Hemophilia Treatment Center, 3596
Orthoseek, 1529
Osteogenesis Imperfecta, 4831
Osteogenesis Imperfecta Foundation, 4839, 4855
Osteoporosis and Related Bone Diseases -National Resource Center, 4856
Ostomy Book: Living Comfortably with Colostomies, Ileostomies and Urostomies, 6723
Otitis Media, 4860
Otto Learns About His Medicine A Story About Medication for Hyperative Children, 640
Our Brother Has Down's Syndrome: An Introduction for Children, 2470
Our Hearts, 3848
Our World, 4080
Out for a Walk: Baby's First Sign Book, 3400
Out of Darkness, 664
Out of Harm's Way: A Parent's Guide to Protecting Young Children from Sexual Abuse, 5073
Out-of-Sync Child: Recognizing and Coping with Sensory Processing Disorder, 378
Overcoming Depression, 2257
Overcoming Dyslexia in Children, Adolescents, and Adults, 2515
Overcoming Headaches & Migraines, 4241
Overeaters Anonymous Lifeline Sampler, 4749
Overeaters Anonymous Support Group, 2591
Overeaters Anonymous, World Service Office, 2578
Overlook, 7789

P

PA Tourette Syndrome Alliance, 6506
PACER Center, 7490
Pacific Northwest Regional Genetics Group, 518
Pacific Southwest Regional Genetics Group, 484
Pain Sourcebook, 1200
Pain, Pain Go Away: Helping Children with Pain, 7670

Entry Name Index

PAL News, 7654
Palo Alto Brain Tumor Support Group, 1050
Palouse Area Parent To Parent, 7183
Pan American Health Organization (PAHO), 5305, 7057
Pandora's Box, 5063
Panic Attacks, 4991
Panic Disorder, 2281
Panic Disorder in the Medical Setting, 2258
Panic Disorder, Separation, AnxietyDisorder, 4973
Paranoid Psychosis Due to Neurosarcoidosis, 5670
Parent Act, 7283
Parent and Information Center, 7544
Parent Assistance Network, 7295
Parent Case Management, 7391
Parent Education Network, 7365
Parent Education Project of Wisconsin, 7423
Parent Education/Support Group, 1077
Parent Educational Advocacy Training Center, 7409
The Parent Educational Advocacy Training Center, 4075
Parent Educator Connection, 7218
Parent Educator Connection Program, 7219
Parent Information Center, 7308, 7426
Parent Information Center of Delaware, 7157
Parent Network Center, 7329
Parent Packets, 3474
Parent Pals, 5996, 6164
Parent Partners, 7275
Parent Project for Muscular Dystrophy, 4290, 4296, 4303
Parent Reaching Out to Parents, 7184
Parent Sign Series, 3254
Parent Support Group, 7296
Parent Support Group of Littleton & Auora, 7143
Parent to Parent ARC Allegheny, 7366
Parent to Parent Arc of Arkansas, 7102
Parent to Parent Network, 7196
Parent to Parent Network of Connecticutthe Family Center, 7153
Parent to Parent of Georgia, 7172
Parent to Parent of New Hampshire, 7309
Parent to Parent of New York State, 7330
Parent to Parent of Pennsylvania, 7367
Parent to Parent USA, 6475, 6594, 7058, 7624
Parent's Guide to Children's CongenitalHeart Defects, 3872
Parent's Guide to Chochlear Implants, 3401
Parent's Guide to Down Syndrome: Towarda Brighter Future, 2471
A Parent's Guide to Understanding Retinoblastoma, 5566, 5576
Parental Alienation, DSM-5, and ICD-11, 7639
Parenting Across the Autism Spectrum, 886
Parenting Attention Deficit Disordered Teens, 665
Parenting Children with ADHD: LessonsThat Medicine Cannot Teach, 641
PARENTS, 7089
Parents Alliance Employment Project, 7455
Parents and Children Together (PACT), 7177
Parents and Their Deaf Children: The Early Years, 3402
Parents are Experts, 7261
Parents Educating Parents and Professionalfor All Children (PEPPAC), 7173
Parents Encouraging Parents, 7297, 7303
Parents For Heart of Minnesota, 3851
Parents for Parents, 7267
Parents Helping Parents, 2975, 4065, 6188, 6443, 6532
Parents Let's Unite for Kids, 7290
Parents of Asthmatic/Allergic Children,Inc., 415, 5590
Parents of Children with Brain Tumors(PCBT), 1063
Parents of Children with Down SyndromeArc of Montgomery County, 2403
Parents of Galactosemic Children, 2867
Parents of Infants and Children withKernicterus, 3997
Parents Place of Maryland, 7244
Parents Reaching Out, 7319
Parents Reaching Out in Oklahoma, 7355
Parents Supporting Parents of Eagle County, 7144
Parents Supporting Parents of Garfield andPitkin County, 7145
Parents Union for Public Schools, 7368
Parents' Hyperactivity Handbook: Helpingthe Fidgety Child, 642
ParentsMedGuide.org, 6808
Park Ridge, Cystic Fibrosis Center, 2025
Partners in Intensive Care, 7245
Partners Resource Network, 7392
Partnership for a Healthier America, 4733
Partnership for Assistive Technology, 7162
Partnerships for Inclusion, 7340
Passive-Aggressive Behavior, 4874
Passport: Global Treatment CentreDirectory, 3632
The Patch, 4041
Patent Ductus Arteriosus, 4896
Pathways.org, 7059, 7625
Patient Information Package, 5671
Patient Packets For Celiac Disease, 1227
Patient Recruitment & Public LiaisonOffice Clinical Center, 6852
Patients with Cervical or Focal HandDystonia Sought, 2546
Paws Sign Stories, 3303
PDR - Physicians' Desk Reference, 7622
PDR.net, 4869
PEAK Parent Center, 7142
Peaks and Valleys Family Resource Center, 7123
Pearls of Dysmorphology, 532
Pediatric AIDS Clinical Trials Group, 2976
Pediatric Behavior and Development, 7626
Pediatric Brain Foundation, 1241, 1333
Pediatric Brain Tumor Foundation, 1031
Pediatric Brain Tumor Support Group, 1038
Pediatric Clinical Trials International, 2430
Pediatric Crohn's & Colitis Association, 6715
Pediatric Cystic Fibrosis Center, 2038
Pediatric Dermatology Journal, 197, 210, 1201, 1415, 2683, 2701, 3508, 3895, 3987, 4923, 5009, 5104, 6343, 6390, 6743, 7645
Pediatric Disabilities Clinic, DownSyndrome Clinic, 2413
Pediatric Epilepsy, 5800
Pediatric Epilepsy Center, 5763
Pediatric Epilepsy Resource Handbook, 5801
Pediatric Heart Foundation, 3843
Pediatric Hemophilia Program ofPennsylvania, 3597
Pediatric Infectious Diseases Society, 5258
Pediatric Neurodevelopmental Center atMarcus Institute, 2414
Pediatric Neurosurgery-Hydrocephalus, 3793
Pediatric Ophathalmology and Adult Strabismus Service Research, 1687
Pediatric Plastic Surgery, 6284
Pediatric Points of Interest, 7627
Pediatric Pulmonary and Cystic FibrosisCenter, 2083
Pediatric Pulmonary Center, 2067, 2077
Pediatric Pulmonary Medicine, 2089
Pediatric Pulmonary Unit, 6236
Pediatric Rheumatoid Clinic, 3956
Pediatric Surgery Update, 3722, 4817
Pediatrics, 5613
Pediatrics in Review, 5614
PEDINFO: An index of the PediatricInternet, 7623
Peer Problems in Tourette's Disorder, 6557
Pemphigus, 4906
Pen-Pal Directory, 559
Peninsula Support & Education Group forParents of Children with Brain Tumors, 1051
Penn Center for Sleep Disorders, Hospitalof the University of Pennsylvania, 4390
Penn Neurological Institute, 4297
Pennsylvania Chapter of the AmericanAnorexia Bulimia Association, 2595
Pennsylvania Educational Network forEating Disorders (PENED), 2596
Pennsylvania's Initiative on AssistiveTechnology, Institute on Disabilities, 7369
Pennsylvania/Delaware Valley Chapter ofCrohn's & Colitis Foundation of America, 1941
People First International, 3932

969

Entry Name Index

People First of California, 3926
People First of Missouri, 3927
People First of Ohio, 3928
People First-West Virginia, 3929
People Living Through Cancer, 1100
People Treated for Brain Tumors and TheirCaregivers, 1106
Perceptual-Motor Behavior in DownSyndrome, 2472
Perfectionism: What's Bad About Being TooGood, 4983
Personality and Psychopathology, 4895
Perspective, 6634
Perspectives Folio: Parent-Child, 3475
Perspectives in Education and Deafness, 3450
Perspectives on Language and Literacy, 4082
Pervasive Developmental Disorders, 913
The Pet Show, 3271
Pharmacologic Therapy of Pediatric Asthma, 441
Pharmacotherapy of Schizophrenia, 1443
Phelps School, 4096
Phenylketonuria (PKU), 4924
Phenylketonuria (PKU) Information Sheet, 4938
Phobias, 4939
Phobics Anonymous, 4955
Phoenix Center for Cancer and BloodDisorders, 3598
Photosensitivity, 4992
Phototherapy: Light Treatment for Psoriasis, 5355
Physical & Sexual Abuse, 5015
Physician Referral and Information Line, 421
Physician's Research Network, 2960
PICA, 5079
Pica Information Page, 5089
Pilot Parents in Anoka and Ramsey Counties, 7268
Pilot Parents of Northeast Minnesota, 7269
Pilot Parents of Southern Arizona, 7094
Pine Tree Camp Children - Adults, 7725
Pinworm (Enterobius Vermicularis), 5090
Pinworm Infection, 5097
Pioneers Division of CEC, 7060
Pittsburgh Area Brain Injury Alliance, 3045
Pituitary Network Association, 1032
Pityriasis Rosea, 5098, 5105
PKU Kid Zone, 4932
PKU Mailing List, 4933
PKU Organization of Illinois, 4928, 4934
PKU Press, 4937
Plain Talk About Depression, 2282
Plasma Homovanillic Asid in Schhizophrenia, 1463
Platelet Disorder Support Association, 6407, 6412
Pneumonia, 5106
Police Officer Jones, 3403
Polio Connection of America, 5306
Polio Experience Network, 5307
Polio Survivors Association, 5259
Polydactyly, 5118, 5126
Porphyria, 5127
Porphyria Fact Sheet, 5135
Portland Public Library, 7483
Positive Behavioral Strategies to SupportChildren & Young People with Autism, 887
Positive Exposure, 187
Positive Solutions for Life Challenges, 7284
Post Polio Awareness & Support Society ofBritish Columbia, 5308
Post Traumatic Stress Disorder Sourcebook, 5161
Post Traumatic Stress Disorder: A Guide, 5166
Post-Polio Health International, 5260
Post-Traumatic Stress Disorder, 5136
Post-Traumatic Stress Disorder, A Real Illness, 5167
Postpartum Support International, 2213
Posttraumatic Stress Disorder in Childrenand Adolescents, 5162
Practice Guidelines for Eating Disorders, 2653
Prader-Willi Alliance of New York, 5194, 5201
Prader-Willi Association of New England(Maine, Mass, RI, NH, VT), 5189, 5190

Prader-Willi California Foundation, 5178
Prader-Willi Colorado Association, 5179
Prader-Willi Connecticut Association, 5180
Prader-Willi Delaware Association, 5181
Prader-Willi Families of Ohio, 5197
Prader-Willi Northwest Association, 5176, 5184, 5191
Prader-Willi Northwest Association-Idaho, 5185
Prader-Willi Syndrome, 5169
Prader-Willi Syndrome Advocates, 5187
Prader-Willi Syndrome Arizona Association, 5177
Prader-Willi Syndrome Association, 5175, 5202
PREBIC-International Preterm Birth Collaborative, 5228
Precious Hearts, 3865
Precocious Puberty, 5203, 5213
Preemie Magazine, 5235
Preemie Ring, 5229
Preemie Twins, 5230
Preemie World, 5231
Pregnancy and Child Health Resource Centerfrom Mayo Health Oasis, 7628
Pregnancy and Exposure to Alcohol andOther Drug Use, 2823
Premature Baby-Premature Child, 5232
Prematurely Yours, 5233, 5234
Prematurity, 5214
Prenatal and Postnatal Growth and Development, 7824
Prenatal Diagnostic and Genetic Center, 7466, 7545
Prenatal Exposures in Schizophrenia, 1464
Prenatal Hydrocephalus-Book for Parents, 3818
Presbyterian-University Hospital,Pulmonary Sleep Evaluation Center, 4391
Preschool Issues in Autism, 888
Preschool Motor Speech Evaluation & Intervention, 5999
Preschool Programs - Division of SpecialPopulations, 7232
Prescription for Success, 889
Prescription Parents, 1507
Presidential Proclamation-NationalSarcoidosis Awareness Day, 5672
Preuss Foundation, 1033
Prevent Blindness America, 1752, 7061
Prevent Child Abuse America, 5029, 5064
Prevent Child Abuse California, 5065
Prevent Child Abuse Georgia, 5037
Prevent Child Abuse Illinois, 5038
Prevent Child Abuse Indiana, 5039
Prevent Child Abuse Iowa, 5040
Prevent Child Abuse New York, 5042
Prevent Child Abuse North Carolina, 5043
Preventable Childhood Infections, 5237
Preventing Antisocial Behavior:Interventions, 1598, 6822
Prevention Initiatives State Department ofEducation, 7146
Prevention Resource Guide: Pregnant,Postpartum Women and Their Infants, 2824
Primary Brain Cancer Support Group, 1064
Primary Care Needs of Children withHydrocephalus, 3819
Primary Children's Medical Center, 7546
Prince George's County Memorial LibraryTalking Book Center, 1659, 1788, 4651, 5462
Principles and Practice of Sleep Medicine, 4561, 5901
PRO-Parents, 7380
Problem Behaviors & Tourette Syndrome, 6558
Professional Assistance Center forEducation (PACE), 7456
Programmed Therapy for Stuttering in Children and Adults, 6165
Programs for Children with Special Health Care Needs, 7764
Programs for Infants and Toddlers with Disabilities: Ages Birth Through 2, 7765
Progress in Dermatology, 1419, 2705, 5013, 5351
Project Cuddle, 5030
Project PODER, 7393
Project PROMPT, 7233
Project Special Care, 7211
Project Start, 7276
Protein C Deficiency, 5317
Protein Deficiency and Pesticide Toxicity, 5329

Entry Name Index

Proteinuria, 7671
Prozac Nation: Young & Depressed inAmerica, A Memoir, 2259
Psoriasis, 5330
Psoriasis 101: Learning to Live in the Skin You're In, 5356
Psoriasis Advance, 5345
Psoriasis Association, 5337
Psoriasis Connections, 5338
Psoriasis on Specific Skin Sites, 5358
Psoriasis Research: Progress & Promise, 5357
Psoriasis Resource, 5352
Psoriasis: How it Makes You Feel, 5359
Psoriatic Arthritis, 5360
Psych Central, 1450, 4534, 4557, 4790, 4892, 6809, 7629
PsychAlive, 6810
Psychological Approaches to Dermatology, 5341
Psychological Factors in Sarcoidosis, 5673
Psychological Trauma, 4984, 5949
Psychosocial Aspects of Narcolepsy, 4412
Psychotherapy of Severe and MildDepression, 2260
PTI Nebraska (Parent, Training &Information, 7294
PTN National Conference, 272
PTN News, 279, 3721
Ptosis, 5368
PTSD Alliance, 5155
PTSD in Children: Move in the Rhythm of the Child, 5147
PTSD Workbook, 5160
Public Health Services of Louisiana, 6205
Publications From the National InformationCenter on Deafness, 3476
PubMed, 7630
Puget Sound Blood Center, 3599
Pull-Thru Network, 267, 3719
PullThrough, 3714
Pulmonary Care and Cystic Fibrosis Center, 2012
Pulmonary Hypertension, 5377
Pulmonary Hypertension Association, 5385
Pulmonary Sarcoidosis: Evaluation withHigh Resolution, 5674
Pulmonary Sarcoidosis: What We AreLearning, 5675
Pulmonary Valve Stenosis, 5387
Pulmonary Wellness Program, 2020
Putting on the Brakes, 644
Putting On The Brakes - Young People'sGuide To Understanding ADHD, 643
PWS Project for New Mexico, 5193
PWSA Florida Chapter, 5182
PWSA Las Vegas/Nevada Support Group, 5192
PWSA of Georgia, 5183
PWSA of Iowa, 5186
PWSA of Kentucky, 5188
PWSA of North Carolina, 5195
PWSA of Ohio, 5196
Pyloric Stenosis, 5397

Q

Q and A: Hepatitis B Prevention, 3678
Quality Life Concepts, 7291
Quest Magazine, 1380, 4312
Questions and Answers About Psoriasis, 5361
Questions and Answers About Scoliosis, 5739
Questions and Answers About UlcerativeColitis, 6732

T

The Race, 3272
Rainbow's End, 3255
RAINN (Rape, Abuse & Incest National Network), 5031, 5066
Rainrock Treatment Center, 2594
Raising a Child With Arthritis, 3963
Raising a Child with Diabetes: A Guide forParents, 2313
Raising Joshua, 6541
Raising Special Kids, 7095

Raising Your Child Without Milk:Reassuring Advice and Recipes For Parent, 4259
Raleigh TEACCH Center, 717
Ramapo Anchorage Camp, 4097, 7766
Rather Strange Stories, 3256
Raven Rock Lutheran Camp, 3940
REACH - Sarcoidosis Support, 5626
Reaching the Autistic Child: A ParentTraining Program, 890
Reaching, Crawling, Walking - Let's GetMoving, 1699, 1835, 4693, 5504
Reading and Speech Clinic, 5981
Ready! Set! Sign!, 3304
Realities in Coping with ProgressiveNeuromuscular Diseases, 4309
Reality Matters - Obesity & Nutrition, 4741
Recognizing Children with Special Needs, 7577
Recovery Panic Anxiety, 4974
Reflex Sympathetic Dystrophy SyndromeAssociation, 4291
Refraction Disturbances, 5415
Region 1 of the National Association forParents of the Visually Impaired, 5422
Region 2 of the National Association forParents of the Visually Impaired, 1754, 4618, 5429
Region 3 of the National Association forParents of the Visually Impaired, 5424
Region 4 of the National Association forParents of the Visually Impaired, 1628, 1756, 4620, 5431
Region 5 of the National Association forParents of the Visually Impaired, 5428
Region I Office Program Consultants ForMaternal and Child Health, 6208
Region II Office Program Consultants forMaternal and Child Health, 6219
Region III Office Program Consultants forMaternal and Child Health, 6221
Region IV Office Program Consultants ForMaternal and Child Health, 6200
Region IX Office Program Consultants forMaternal and Child Health, 6194
Region V Office Program Consultants forMaternal and Child Health, 6202
Region VI Office Program Consultants ForMaternal and Child Health, 6226
Region VII Office Program Consultants forMaternal and Child Health, 6214
Region VIII Office Program Consultants forMaternal and Child Health, 6195
Region X Office Program Consultants forMaternal and Child Health, 6228
Regional Epilepsy Center, 5768
Regional Hemophilia Program, 3600
Regional Resource Center on Deafness, 3166
A Regular Kid, 433
Rehabilitation Institute of Michigan, 3028, 3062
Rehabilitation Research and TrainingCenter on Traumatic Brain Injury, 3065
Religious Signing: A Comprehensive Guide for All Faiths, 3404
Renal Tubular Acidosis, 7672
Renfrew Center of Bryn Mawr, 2597
Renfrew Center of Connecticut, 2581
Renfrew Center of Miami, 2583
Renfrew Center of New York City, 2592
Renfrew Center of Northern New Jersey, 2588
Renfrew Center of Philadelphia, 2598
Report of the Secretary's Task Force onYouth Suicide, 2261
Reproductive Systems, 7819
Research & Training Center for Children'sMental Health at University of South FL, 1578, 6782
Research and Training Center for Children'Mental Health, 7547
Research and Training Center on FamilySupport and Children's Mental Health, 1579, 6783, 7548
Research at BloodCenter of Wisconsin, 3601
Research on Child and Adolescent Psychopathology, 6834

Entry Name Index

Research to Prevent Blindness, 1688, 1822, 4683, 5495
Resource Center for the American Alliance of Cancer - Pain Initiatives, 116
Resource Guide, 3820
Resource Survival Handbook, 4498
Resources for Children with Special Needs, 7331
Resources for Rehabilitation, 7486
Resources for Young Children and Families, 7147
Respiratory Disorders Sourcebook, 4thEdition, 457, 2119, 6619
Respiratory Distress Syndrome of the Newborn, 5523
Respiratory Health Association, 413
Respiratory Syncytial Virus Infection, 5533
Respiratory System, 7820
Rest of the Family, 5773
Restless Nights, 5902
Restricted Growth Association, 20
Rethink autism, 718
Rethinking Attention Deficit Disorders, 645
Retina South Africa - Fighting Blindness, 5550
Retinitis Pigmentosa, 5542
Retinoblastoma, 5555
Retinoblastoma Solutions, 5570
Retinopathy of Prematurity, 5577
Rheumatoid Arthritis, 3972
Rhinitis, 5584
Rhode Island Arc, 7374
Rhode Island Department of Health, 5290, 6222, 7375
Rhode Island Hemostasis and ThrombosisCenter, 3602
Rhode Island Hospital, Cystic FibrosisCenter, 2085
Rhode Island Parent Information Network, 7376
Rhode Island Scleroderma Support Group, 5695
Rhode Island Test of Language StructureRITLS, 3405
Rid Alaska of Child Abuse, 5034
Riddle of Autism: A Psychological Analysis, 891
Right & Left Ventricular Function At RestIn Patients with Sarcoidosis, 5676
Riley Cystic Fibrosis Center, 2029
Riley Hemophilia and Thrombophilia Center, 3559
The Rising of Lotus Flowers: Self-Educating Deaf Children in Thai Boarding Schools, 3438
Ritalin is Not the Answer, 646
Roanoke City Public Library System, 7527
Robyn's Book: A True Diary, 2120
Rochester Chapter of Crohn's & ColitisFoundation of America, 1933
Rockefeller University Laboratory forInvestigative Dermatology, 1403, 2695, 5005
Rockingham County Schools, 7341
Rocky Mountain Chapter of Crohn's &Colitis Foundation of America, 1909
Rolling Along with Goldilocks and theThree Bears, 6097
Rome Subregional Library for the Blindand Physically Handicapped, 7449
Ronald McDonald Houses, 7062
Round Lake Camp, 676, 933, 4098
Royal National Institute of Blind People, 1695, 1831, 4691, 5376, 5551, 6149
RP Messenger, 5554
RSV Info Center, 5532, 5541
Rudd Center for Food Policy & Health, 4734
Rural Institute on Disabilities, 7063
Rush Children's Heart Center, 313, 318
Rusk Institute of Rehabilitation Medicine, 4292, 7549
Russian Soldier, 3257
Ryan, 6437, 6524
The Ryan Licht Sang Bipolar Foundation, 987
RYAN: A Mother's Story of Her Hyperactive/Tourette Syndrome Child, 6540

S

Sacramento Area Brain Tumor Support GroupLawrence J Ellison Ambulatory Care Ctr, 1052
Sacramento Center for Assistive Technology, 7438
Sad Days, Glad Days, 2262
Safe Drinking Water Hotline, 4051
Safety and Seizures, 5822
Saint Alexius Medical Center/CF Center, 2073
Saint Francis Medical Center SpecialtyClinics, CF Center, 2026
Saint Joseph's Hospital Health CenterSleep Laboratory, 4368
Saint Jude Children's Research Hospital, 7519
Saint Louis Chapter of Crohn's & ColitisFoundation of America, 1926
Saint Mary's Healthcare System forChildren, 7332
Saint Vincent Medical Center, SleepDisorders Center, 4383
San Diego Support Group, 485
San Fernando Valley Support Group, 486
San Francisco Brain Tumor Support Group, 1053
San Francisco Public Library for the Blindand Print Disabled, 1638, 1767, 4631, 5442
San Gabriel/Pomona Parents' Place, 7124
Santa Fe Mountain Center, 7757
Sarcoid Life, 5651
Sarcoidosis, 5619, 5652, 5677
Sarcoidosis and Lyme Disease, 5644
Sarcoidosis and Other Granulatomous, 5679
Sarcoidosis and You-A Listing ofPossible Symptoms, 5680
Sarcoidosis Awareness Foundation, 5631
Sarcoidosis Awareness Network, 5630
Sarcoidosis Center, 5635, 5653
Sarcoidosis Conference 2, 5642
Sarcoidosis Conference 3, 5643
Sarcoidosis Networking, 5657
Sarcoidosis Patient Forum, 5634
A Sarcoidosis Questionnaire: Demographicsand Symptomatology-Patients Respond, 5658
Sarcoidosis Questionnaire: Demographicsand Symptomatology-The Patients Respond, 5678
Sarcoidosis Research Institute, 5625, 5637, 5654
Sarcoidosis Resource Guide and Directory, 5655
Sarcoidosis Support, 5633
Sarcoidosis Support Group, 5628
Sarcoidosis-International Review, 5681
Sarcoidosis-Pleural InvolvementMimicking a Coin Lesson, 5682
Sarcoidosis-What's That?, 5645
Sarcoidosis: A Multisystem Disease, 5683
Sarcoidosis: Usual and UnusualManifestations, 5684
Save Babies Through Screening Foundation, 2868, 3763, 3998, 7631
SBA National Conference, 6071
SBAA General Information Brochure, 6108
SBAA General Information Packet, 6109
SC Dept. of Health & Environmental ControlImmunization Division, 5291
Scalp Psoriasis, 5362
Schedules of Development for HearingImpaired Infants and Their Parents, 3406
Schizophrenia, 1465, 1477
Schizophrenia and Comorbid ConditionsDiagnosis and Treatment, 1468
Schizophrenia Fact Sheet, 1478
Schizophrenia Into Later Life: Treatment,Research, and Policy, 1466
Schizophrenia Revealed: From Neurons toSocial Interactions, 1467
Schizophrenia Support Organizations, 1451
Schizophrenia.com, 1452
Schizophrenia.com Home Page, 1453
Schizophrenia: Handbook for Families, 1454
Schneider Children's Hospital of LongIsland, 2068
School Based Assessment of Attention Deficit Disorders, 666
School Days, 3305
School Days: An ASL Word Book, 3306
School Personnel: A Critical Link in theIdentification and Management of OCD, 4799
School Planning, 5802
The School-Aged Child, 1519
Science, Math, 3258
Scizophrenia in a Molecular Age, 1469
Scleroderma, 5689

Entry Name Index

Scleroderma A to Z, 5704
Scleroderma Book (The), 5711
Scleroderma Care and Research, 5712
Scleroderma Foundation, 5693, 5705
Scleroderma Foundation New Jersey Chapter, 5694
Scleroderma Message Board, 5706
Scleroderma Research Foundation, 5698
Scleroderma Support, 5707
Scoliosis, 5716
Scoliosis and Kyphosis, 5740
Scoliosis Help, 5732
Scoliosis Research Society, 5721, 5723, 5733
Scoliosis: What Young People and Parents Need to Know, 5737
Scope (UK), 1334
Scottish Rite Centers for Childhood Language Disorders, 5984
Screening for Down Syndrome, 2473
Screening for Hearing Loss and Other Otitis Media, 4873
Screening for Hearing Loss and Otitis Media in Children, 3407
Seal Out Tooth Decay, 6424
Search Beyond Adventures, 7746
A Season of Change, 3318
Seasonal Affective Disorder, 2239
Seasonal Clustering of Sarcoidosis, 5685
Seattle Area Support Group, 527
See What I Feel, 1691, 1825, 4686, 5498
Seeking Techniques Advancing Research inShunts (STARS), 3783
Seizure First Aid, 5774
Seizures, 5742
Seizures and Epilepsy In Childhood: A Guide, 5803
Seizures and Epilepsy: Hope Through Research, 5823
Seizures, Epilepsy and Your Child, 5824
Selecting a Program, 1711, 1848, 4704, 5515
Selective Mutism Association, 4956, 5938
Self-Control Games & Workbook, 647
Self-Starvation: from Individual to FamilyTherapy in the Treatment of Anorexia Ne, 2654
A Sense of Belonging: Including Students with Autism in their School Community, 816
Sense of Belonging: Including Students with Autism in Their School Community, 831
Sensory Organs, 7821
SERGG Regional News, 549
Services for the Visually Disabled, 1656, 1785, 4648, 5459
7 Steps to Reducing the Risk of SIDS, 6239
Severe Chronic Neutropenia InternationalRegistry (SCNIR), 4508
Sexuality and the Person with Spinabifida, 6099
Sexuality Information and EducationCouncil of the US (SIECUS), 7064
SHAPE America: Society of Health andPhysical Educators, 4735
Share Pregnancy & Infant Loss Support, 6190
Shattered Dreams - Lonely Choices: BirthParents of Babies with Disabilities, 2474
Shawnee Library System, 7457
Shelley The Hyperactive Turtle, 648
Short and OK, 2913
Shot At Life, 5261
Show Me No Mercy: Compelling Story ofRemarkable Courage, 2475
Shriner's Hospital Research Study Report, 4857
Shriners Hospital for Children, 5724
Shriners Hospitals for Children, 5124, 6281
Shy Children, Phobic Adults: Nature andTreatment of Social Phobia, 4985, 5950
Sibling Abuse Survivors' Information & Advocacy Network, 5067
Sibling Donor Cord Blood Program Pamphlet, 6397
Sibling Forum, 7655
Sibling Support Project, 7065
Sickle Cell Association of Austin - MarcThomas Chapter, 5856
Sickle Cell Association of the Texas GulfCoast, 5857
Sickle Cell Council of New Mexico, Inc., 5849
Sickle Cell Disease, 5835, 5879
Sickle Cell Disease Association of America, 5841, 5845, 5854, 5872
Sickle Cell Disease Association of thePiedmont, 5851
Sickle Cell Disease Forum, 5873

Sickle Cell Disease Foundation ofCalifornia, 5844
Sickle Cell Foundation of Georgia, 5846
Sickle Cell Foundation of GreaterMontgomery, 5843
Sickle Cell Information Center, 5842
Sickle Cell Kids, 5874
Sickle Cell Regional Network, 5852
SID Network, 6246
Sidelines, 5219
Sidney R. Baer Day Camp, 7748
Sidran Institute - Traumatic Stress Education & Advocacy, 5156
SIDS Prevention, 6267
SIDS Research, 6253
SIDS Survival Guide, 6254
SIDS: A Parents Guide to Understanding &Preventing SIDS, 6255
SIDS: Toward Prevention and ImprovedInfant Health, 6268
Sign Fine - Vacations, 3307
Sign Language for Babies, 3408
Sign Numbers, 3409
Sign Songs: Fun Songs to Sign and Sing, 3259
Sign With Kids Supplement, 3410
Sign With Your Baby-Complete Learning Kit, 3260
Sign-Me-Fine, 3411
Significant Event Childhood Trauma, 5148
Signing Exact English Using Affixes, 3412
Signing Family: What Every Parent Should Know About Sign Communication, 3413
Signing Fun: American Sign Language Vocabulary, Phrases, Games and Activities, 3414
Signing Naturally, 3261
Signing: How to Speak With Your Hands, Second Edition, 3415
Signs for Me, 3416
Signs for Me: Basic Sign Vocabulary for Children, Parents and Teachers, 3417
Signs for Me: Basic Sign Vocabulary forChildren, Parents, & Teachers, 3459, 3477
Signs of Sharing: An Elementary SignLanguage and Deaf Awareness Curriculum, 3418
Silent Garden, 3419
Silent Observer, 3420
Simple Signs, 3421
Simser Series, 3308
Since Owen, 2476
Sinergia/Metropolitan Parent Center, 7333
Sioux Valley Hospital, South DakotaCystic Fibrosis Center, 2087
Six-Sound Song, 3422
Skeletal System, 7822
Ski for Light, 7066
Skills Training for Children with BehaviorDisorders, 1599, 6823
Skin Page, 5339
Slack, 3707
Slack Incorporated, 5309
SLE Lupus Foundation, 6293
Sleep Apnea, 5883
Sleep Center, Community General Hospital, 4369
Sleep Disorder Center, St Elizabeth Medical Center, 4355
Sleep Disorders, 4409, 4535, 4558
Sleep Disorders and Psychiatry, 4414, 4538, 4562
Sleep Disorders Center, 5890
Sleep Disorders Center for Children, 4395
Sleep Disorders Center of Lifespan Hospitals, 4394
Sleep Disorders Center of Western New YorkMillard Fillmore Hospital, 4370
Sleep Disorders Center, UniversityHospital, 4371
Sleep Disorders Center-Good SamaritanHospital, 4356
Sleep Disorders Sourcebook, 4413, 5903, 5923
Sleep Disorders Unit, Beth Israel Hospital, 4359
Sleep Laboratory, Maine Medical Center, 4400
Sleep Medicine Associates of Texas, 4396
Sleep Research Society, 4528
Sleep Walking in Children, 5919
Sleep-Wake Disorders Center, MontefioreSleep Disorders Center, 4372
Sleep-Wake Disorders Center, New YorkPresbyterian Hospital, 4373

Entry Name Index

Sleep/Wake Disorders Center, Hampstead Hospital, 4363
Sleep/Wake Disorders Center-Community Health Network, 4357
Sleep: The Brazelton Way, 5924
Sleepdisorders.com, 4536, 4559, 5897, 5921
SleepEducation.com, 5920
Sleeping Beauty, 3262
Sleeping Like a Baby, 5904
Sleepnet.com, 5898
Sleepwalking, 5907
SMA Newsletter, 6138
SMA Research Group, 6128
SMA Support Inc, 6125
Smile, 3309
Smoking and Sudden Infant Death Syndrome, 6256
Snap! Kids American Sign Language, 3310
Snoring and Sleep Apnea, 5906
Snoring From A to Zzzz, 4539, 4563, 5905, 5925
The Snowman, 3273
Social Anxiety Association, 5939
Social Anxiety Disorder, 5926
Social Development and the Person With Spina Bifida, 6110
Social Skills Development in Children with Hydrocephalus, 3821
Social Skills Picture Book, 892
Society for Adolescent Medicine, 7632
Society for Endocrinology, 2910, 5211
Society for Mucopolysaccharide Diseases, 4282
Society for NeuroOncology, 1034
Society for Pediatric Dermatology, 188, 207, 1190, 1199, 1397, 1411, 2676, 2690, 3503, 3893, 3986, 4914, 4999, 5102, 6333, 6342, 6377, 6741, 7067
Society for Pediatric Dermatology Annual Meeting, 194, 1191, 1405, 2678, 2697
Society for Rehabilitation, 7352
Society of Behavioral Sleep Medicine, 4529
Solution Outreach Center at OCCK, Inc., 7467
Solving Behavior Problems in Autism, 893
Something Fishy, 2624
Something Happened and I'm Scared to Tell, 5074
Son-Rise: The Miracle Continues, 894
Songs for Listening! Songs for Life!, 3311
Songs in Sign, 3423
Sontag Foundation, 1035
Soul Murder Revisited, 5075
Sound & Fury, 3263
Sound and Fury: Six Years Later, 3264
South Carolina Chapter of Crohn's & Colitis Foundation of America, 1943
South Carolina Department of Health & Environmental Control - SIDS Information, 6223
South Carolina State Library, 7516
South Central Kansas Library System, 7468
South Central Los Angeles Regional Center for Devlopmentally Disabled Persons, 7125
South Central Region-Helen Keller National Center, 7394
South Dakota Center For Bleeding Disorders, 3604
South Dakota Department of Health, 5292, 6224
South Dakota Parent Connection, 7383
South Dakota State Library, 7517
South Florida Brain Tumor Association Lynn Regional Cancer Center, 1058
South Texas Comprehensive Hemophilia and Thrombophilia Treatment Center, 3605
Southeast Pennsylvania Support Group, 522
Southeast Regional Genetics Group, 496
Southeastern Brain Tumor Foundation Brain Tumor Support Group, 1061
Southeastern Region-Helen Keller National Center, 5423
Southern IL Child and Family Connections, 7197
Southern Illinois University School of Medicine, 287, 567, 1543, 4903, 5395, 5412, 6355, 6586, 6747, 7633
Southern Nevada 'Grey Matters' Valley Hospital Medical Center, 1095
Southwest Chapter of Crohn's & Colitis Foundation of America, 1928
Southwest Human Development, 7096

Southwest Ohio Brain Tumor Support Group, 1116
Southwest Ohio Chapter of Crohn's & Colitis Foundation of America, 1939
Southwestern Comprehensive Sickle Cell Center, 5867
Southwestern Ohio Chapter of the National Hemophilia Foundation, 3545
Spaulding for Children, 7068
Speak to Me (Second Edition), 3424
Special Care Dentistry Association, 2180
Special Connections Family Resource Center, 7126
Special Education Action Committee Huntsville Outreach Office, 7082
Special Education Administration Kansas State Department of Education, 7224
Special Education Center of Hawaii, 3017
Special Education Division, 7344
Special Education Division State Department of Education, 7127
Special Education Office, 7356
Special Education Section State Department of Education, 7103
Special Education Services, 7083
Special Education Services Unit, 7398
Special Education Unit, 7320, 7405, 7427
A Special Love, 2443
Special Needs Branch Department of Education, 7178
Special Needs Center/Phoenix Public Library, 7429
Special Needs Library of NE Georgia Athens-Clarke County Regional Library, 7450
Special Needs Parent Info Network, 7238
Special Olympics, 7069
Special Parent Involvement Network, 7228
Special Services Division - Indiana State Library, 7463
Specific Classroom Strategies and Techniques for Students with TS-2nd Edition, 6559
Specific Forms of Psoriasis, 5363
Spectrum Brain Tumor Support Group, 1082
Spectrum Health Research, 3606
Speech and Deafness Newsletter, 3460
Speech and Hearing Clinic, 5979
Speech and the Hearing Impaired Child (Second Edition), 3425
Speech Impairment, 5955
Speech, Language, & Hearing Center University of Colorado, 6160
Speech, Language, and Hearing Center, 5987
Speechreading: A Way to Improve Understanding, 3426
Spina Bifida, 6009
Spina Bifida Association, 6019
Spina Bifida Association of Alabama, 6020
Spina Bifida Association of Albany/Capital District, 6047
Spina Bifida Association of America, 608
Spina Bifida Association of Arkansas, 6022
Spina Bifida Association of Canton, 6052
Spina Bifida Association of Central Florida, 6027
Spina Bifida Association of Central Indiana, 6033
Spina Bifida Association of Central Ohio, 6053
Spina Bifida Association of Chesapeake-Potomac, 6038
Spina Bifida Association of Cincinnati, 6054
Spina Bifida Association of Colorado, 6025
Spina Bifida Association of Connecticut, 6026
Spina Bifida Association of Delaware Valley, 6059
Spina Bifida Association of Georgia, 6031
Spina Bifida Association of Greater Bay Area, 6023
Spina Bifida Association of Greater Dayton, 6055
Spina Bifida Association of Greater Fox Valley, 6068
Spina Bifida Association of Greater New Orleans, 6037
Spina Bifida Association of Greater Pennsylvania, 6060
Spina Bifida Association of Greater Rochester, 6048
Spina Bifida Association of Greater Saint Louis, 6044
Spina Bifida Association of Greater San Diego, 6024
Spina Bifida Association of Houston-Gulf Coast, 6062
Spina Bifida Association of Illinois, 6032
Spina Bifida Association of Iowa, 6035
Spina Bifida Association of Jacksonville Nemours Childrens Clinic, 6028
Spina Bifida Association of Kentucky, 6036
Spina Bifida Association of Massachusetts, 6039

Entry Name Index

Spina Bifida Association of Minnesota, 6042
Spina Bifida Association of Mississippi, 6043
Spina Bifida Association of Nassau County, 6049
Spina Bifida Association of Nebraska, 6045
Spina Bifida Association of North Carolina, 6051
Spina Bifida Association of North Texas, 6063
Spina Bifida Association of North WestOhio, 6056
Spina Bifida Association of NorthernWisconsin, 6034, 6069
Spina Bifida Association of SoutheastFlorida, 6029
Spina Bifida Association of Tampa Bay, 6030
Spina Bifida Association of Tennessee, 6061
Spina Bifida Association of Texas, 6064
Spina Bifida Association of the RoanokeValley, 6066
Spina Bifida Association of the Tri-StateRegion, 6046
Spina Bifida Association of Tri-CountyOhio, 6057
Spina Bifida Association of UpperPeninsula Michigan, 6040
Spina Bifida Association of Utah, 6065
Spina Bifida Association of West Michigan, 6041
Spina Bifida Association of Western NewYork, 6050
Spina Bifida Association of Wisconsin, 6070
Spina Bifida Association Pittsburgh, 6058
SPINAbilities: A Young Person's Guide toSpina Bifida, 6098
Spinal Muscular Atrophies, 6115
Spinal Muscular Atrophy Clinic, 6129
Spinal Muscular Atrophy Foundation, 6121
Spinal Muscular Atrophy Information Page, 6134
Spinal Muscular Atrophy Project, 6130, 6135
Spondylitis Association of America, 253
Springfield Area Support Group, 511
Squirrel Hollow, 934, 4099
Standing on My Own Two Feet, 1712, 1849, 4705, 5516
Stanford CF Center, 2013
Stanford University Center for Narcolepsy, 4350
The Stanley Medical Research Institute, 2216
Star Center for Family Health, 7491
Star-G: Screening, Technology and Research in Genetics, 4935
Starlight Children's Foundation, 7128
Starting Point: To Connect with Resources Related to Pediatric Neuro-oncology, 1144
Starving to Death in a Sea of Objects, 2655
State Board of Education Department ofSpecial Education, 7198
State Department of Education, 7154
State University College at PlattsburghAuditory Research Laboratory, 3175
State University Hospital/Upstate MedicalUniversity, 2069
State University of New York HealthSciences Center, 801, 810
Statewide Parent Advocacy Network, 7316
Statewide Services for Deaf and Hard ofHearing People, 3478
Statewide Technology Access & ResponseSystem for Alabamians with Disabilities, 7084
Steele Children's Research Center, 3607
STEP (Support & Training for ExceptionalParents), 7387
Steps to Independence: Teaching EverydaySkills to Children with Special Needs, 6100
Stereotactic Radiosurgery, 1165
Stop Child Abuse Now, 5068
Stop It Now!, 5032
StopBullying.gov, 6811
Stories About Growing Up, 3265
Strabismus, 4035, 6141
Straight Talk about Psychological Testingfor Kids, 2516
Straight Talk on Stuttering: Information,Encouragement, and Counsel, 6166
Stress and Coping in Autism, 895
Stress Reduction Tapes, Stress ReductionClinic, 7578
Stroke Rehabilitation & Traumatic BrainInjury Research, 3066
Student Study Guide to A Basic Course in American Sign Language, 3427
Students Supporting Brain Tumor Research, 1036
Sturge-Weber Syndrome: A Resource Guidefor a Reason, a Season and a Lifetime, 3507
Stuttering, 6152

Stuttering Foundation of America, 6159
Subacute Sclerosing Panencephalitis (SSPE), 6169
Subregional Library for the Blind andPhysically Handicapped, 7451
Substance Abuse and Mental Health ServicesAdministration, 2549
Suburban Audio Visual Service, 7458
The Successful Parent, 6812
Successful Treatment of MyocardialSarcoidosis with Steriods, 5686
Sudden Arrhythmia Death SyndromesFoundation, 314
Sudden Death in Infancy, Childhood &Adolescence, 6257
Sudden Death of Young Athletes Can BePrevented (Hypertrophic Cardiomyopathy), 3836
Sudden Infant Death Syndrome, 6180
Sudden Infant Death Syndrome Risk Factors, 6258
Suicide Awareness Voices of Education, 2214
Suicide Prevention Resource Center, 2215
Suicide, Why?, 2263
SUID/SIDS Gateway (Resource Center), 6189, 6247
Summer Experience, 386, 935, 4100
Summer Wheelchair Sports Camp, 7708
Summit Camp, 387
Sun and Water Therapy, 5364
Suncoast Residential TrainingCenter/Developmental Services Program, 1437, 4775
Sunshine for HIV Kids, 2977
Sunshine Foundation, 7802
SUNY Upstate Medical University ResearchDevelopment, 3603
Superstuff, 466
Support for Families of Children withDisabilities, 7129
Support for Parents of Children with BrainTumors, Siblings and Young Adults, 1107
Support Group for Parents of Childrenwith a Brain Tumor, 1117
Support Group Listing, 5687
Support Organization for Trisomy 18, 13,and Related Disorders (SOFT), 6476, 6595, 6603
Surgery for Epilepsy, 5825
Surprising Truth About Depression: MedicalBreakthroughs That Can Work, 2264
Survival Skills for the Family Unit, 3822
Surviving an Eating Disorder, 2656
Surviving Childhood Cancer: A Guide forFamilies, 114, 169, 3747, 4499, 4595, 5574, 6878
Surviving Coma: the Journey Back, 3074
Surviving Schizophrenia: A Manual forFamilies, Consumers and Providers, 1470
SW Michican Spina Bifida & HydrocephalusAssociation, 3775
Sweeney, 2355
Sydenham Chorea Information Page, 1493
Syncope, 6269
Syndactyly, 6276, 6285
Syndromes Associated with Multiple Congenital Anomalies, 533
Syracuse University, Institute for SensoryResearch, 3176
Systemic Lupus Erythematosus, 6286

T

Tactic, 1700, 1836, 4694, 5505
TAG Conference, 6378
TAG Newsletter, 6393
Take Charge, 1962
Taking Autism to School, 896
Taking Charge of ADHD: The Complete,Authoritative Guide for Parents, 649
Taking the Mystery Out of SpinalDeformities, 5725
Talisman Programs, 7768
Talisman Summer Camps, 1605, 6845
Talk About Sleep, 4410
Talk to Me, 1713, 1850, 4706, 5517
Talk to Me II, 1714, 1851, 4707, 5518
Talking Back to OCD: The Program That HelpKids & Teens Say No Way, 4800
Talking Book Center of NorthwestIllinois, 1651, 1780, 4644, 5455
Talking Book Library at Worcester PublicLibrary, 7487

Entry Name Index

Talking Book Library, Jacksonville Public Library, 1641, 1770, 4634, 5445
Talking Book Service - Manatee County Central Library, 1642, 1771, 4635, 5446
Talking Book Topics, 1703, 1838, 4696, 5507
Talking Books - National Library Service, 4023
Talking Finger Series - At Grandma's House, 3428
Talking Finger Series - Little Green Monster, 3429
Talking to Your Doctor About Seizure Disorders, 5826
Tampa Support Group, 492
TASH, 7070
Tay-Sachs Disease, 6298, 6319
Tay-Sachs Disease-A Bibliography, Medical Dictionary, & Annotated Research Guide, 6320
TB Skin Test, 6621
TB: What You Should Know, 6622
TBI Support Group for Families & Survivors, 3011
Teach Your Tot to Sign, 3430
Teacher's Guide to Crohn's Disease & Ulcerative Colitis, 6733
Teacher's Guide to Neuromuscular Disease, 4336
Teaching Children with Autism to Mind-Read A Pratical Guide for Teachers & Parents, 897
Teaching Coversations to Children With Autism: Scripts and Script Fading, 898
Teaching Motor Skills to Children with Cerebral Palsy & Similar Movement Disorders, 1355
Teaching Students with Spina Bifida, 6101
Teaching the Tiger, 650, 4801, 6448, 6542
Team Advocates for Special Kids, Anaheim, 7130
Team Advocates for Special Kids, San Diego, 7131
Team of Advocates for Special Kids, 7551
TECH 2000 Project-Michigan Disability Rights Coalition, 7262
Tech-Able, 7452
TechACCESS of Rhode Island, 7514
Technical Assistance Partnership for Child and Family Mental Health, 1580, 6784
Technology Access Center, 7492
Technology Access Center of Tucson, 7430
Technology Access for Life Needs Project, 7361
Technology and Youth - Protecting Your Child, 6835
Technology Assistance for Special Consumers, 7071
Technology Assistance Program, 7246, 7321
Technology Partnership Project Institute on Disability/UAP, 7310
Technology Resource Center, 7508
Techspress Resource Center for Independent Living, 7504
Ted R. Montoya Hemophilia Program, 3608
Teddi Project, 7803
Teens and Tourette Syndrome, 6561
Teens Talk to Teens About Asthma, 467
TEF/VATER International Support Network, 2774
Telangiectasia, 6322
Telecommunications for the Deaf and Hard of Hearing, 3145
Temple University, Section of Auditory Research, 3178
Ten Things Every Child With Autism Wishes You Know, 899
Ten Years to Live, 543
Tender Love and Care PPEC and Early Learning Center, 1270
Tennese Hemophilia & Bleeding Disorders Foundation, 3551
Tennessee Chapter of Crohn's & Colitis Foundation of America, 1944
Tennessee Department of Health Immunization, 5293
Tennessee Saving Little Hearts, 3861
Teratogen and Birth Defects Information Project, 7552
Tetanus and Diptheria Vaccine, 5316
Tetralogy of Fallot, 6345
Texas Assistive Technology Partnership, 7395
Texas Association of Retinitis Pigmentosa, 5552
Texas Central Chapter of the National Hemophilia Foundation, 3552
Texas Children's Cancer Center, 3732
Texas Children's Hospital, 2753
Texas Department oF Health Immunization Division, 5294
Texas Heart Institute Journal, 321
Texas Heart to Heart, 3863
Texas Lions Camp, 1722, 1858, 3494, 7782

Texas Perinatal Association, 5221
Texas State Library, 7521
Textbook of Psoriasis, 5342
Thalassemia Action Group (TAG) Patient Support Group Brochure, 6398
Thalassemias, 6357
There are Solutions for the Student with Asthma, 468
They're Just Kids, 7579
Things to Consider, 5365
This Is Mr. TB Germ, 6623
Thomas Jefferson University Brain Injury Rehabilitation Program, 3069
Thomas Jefferson University Sleep Disorders Center, 4392
Thorpe Camp, 3941
3D Vision, 4025
Thrombocytopenias, 6400
Thumbsucking, 6415
Thumpers, 3860
Thursday's Child, 7804
Thyroid Federation International, 3883
Tics, 6425
Tics and Tourette's Syndrome Fact Sheet, 6453
TIES, The Children's Hospital, 7550
Tik-A-Witha, 7747
Timbertop Nature Adventure Camp, 7793
TIPS: Talipes Information and Parental Support, 1530
Tlane Cancer Center, 1068
TMA Annual Patient Conference, 1406
To Be Me: Understanding What It's Like to Have Asperger's Syndrome, 379
To Give An Edge: A Guide for New Parents of Children with Down's Syndrome, 2477
Toddlers and Preschoolers, 1520
Together...There Is Hope, 534
Toilet Training for Individuals with Autism and Related Disorders, 901
Tools for Life Division of Rehabilitation Services, 7174
Toothpick, 2121
TOPS Club, 2579
Touch of Nature Environmental Center, 7709
Touched with Fire-Manic Depressive Illness & the Artistic Temperament, 1000
Touching Tree, 4781
Tourette Syndrome, 6454
Tourette Syndrome and Human Behavior, 6543
Tourette Syndrome and the School Nurse, 6563
Tourette Syndrome and the School Psychologist, 6562
Tourette Syndrome and Tic Disorder Clinic, 6511
Tourette Syndrome Association, 6533
Tourette Syndrome Association - Arizona Chapter, 6481
Tourette Syndrome Association - Greater New York State Chapter, 6494, 6500
Tourette Syndrome Association - Hudson Valley Chapter, 6501
Tourette Syndrome Association - Long Island Chapter, 6502
Tourette Syndrome Association - Maine/New Hampshire Chapter, 6490
Tourette Syndrome Association - Minnesota Chapter, 6493
Tourette Syndrome Association - New Mexico Chapter, 6498
Tourette Syndrome Association - New York City Chapter, 6503
Tourette Syndrome Association - Northern California/Hawaii Chapter, 6482, 6487
Tourette Syndrome Association - Rocky Mountain Region, 6484, 6495, 6496, 6510
Tourette Syndrome Association - Southern California Chapter, 6483
Tourette Syndrome Association - Utah Chapter, 6508
Tourette Syndrome Association - Washington and Oregon Chapter, 6505, 6509
Tourette Syndrome Association -Greater Rochester and Finger Lakes Area, 6485, 6499
Tourette Syndrome Association of Florida, 6486
Tourette Syndrome Association of Greater Washington, 6491
Tourette Syndrome Association of Illinois, 6488
Tourette Syndrome Association of Indiana, 6489
Tourette Syndrome Association of New Jersey, 6497
Tourette Syndrome Association of Ohio, 6504
Tourette Syndrome Association of Rhode Island, 6507

Entry Name Index

Tourette Syndrome Association of Massachusetts, 6492
Tourette Syndrome Camp Organization, 677, 4806, 6565
Tourette Syndrome Online, 6444
Tourette Syndrome: The Facts, 6544
Tourette's Syndrome, 6545
Tourette's Syndrome - Tics, Obsession, Compulsions: Developmental Psychopathology, 6449
Tourettes Syndrome Online, 6534
Toxoplasmosis, 6566
Toxoplasmosis Fact Sheet, 6574, 6575
Train-Ohio Super Computer Center, 7353
Transposition of the Great Arteries, 6576
TransWeb, 7635
Traumatic Brain Injury Model Systems National Data and Statistical Center, 3081
Travis: I Got Lots of Neat Stuff Children Living with Muscular Dystrophy, 4310
The Treasure Chest, 3274
Treasure Chest of Behavioral Strategies for Individuals with Autism, 902
Treasure Valley Brain Injury Support Group, 1062
Treating Abused and Traumatized Children, 5076
Treating Bulimia: A Psychoeducational Approach, 2657
Treating Depressed Children, 2265
Treating Depression, 2266
Treating IBD, 1960
Treating IBD: A Patient's Guide to the Medical and Surgical Management, 6724
Treating Psychological Trauma and PTSD, 5163
Treating the Headache Patient, 4242
Treating Trauma & Traumatic Grief in Children and Adolescents, 5164
Treatment of Children with Mental Disorder, 1602, 6839
Tri-Services Military CF Center, 2094
Tri-State Bleeding Disorders Chapter of the National Hemophilia Foundation, 3546
Tri-State Sleep Disorders Center Center for Research in Sleep Disorders, 4402
Tri-State Support Group, 515
TRIAD Project-Advocates for Persons with Disabilities, 7334
Triangle D Camp for Children, 7790
TRIP Database, 7634
Trisomy 13 Syndrome, 6598
Trisomy 18 Foundation, 6477, 6512, 6596, 6597
Trisomy 18 Syndrome, 6589
Troll In A Bowl: Games and Card Print Factory, 3313
Trouble with Secrets, 5077
TS International, 6632
TS: A Look at the Interface Between Tourette Syndrome and the Law, 6560
TSC Alliance, 1242
Tuberculosis, 6604
Tuberous Sclerosis, 6624
Tuberous Sclerosis: 3rd Edition, 6633
Tuberous Sclerosis: Fact Sheet, 6636
Tufts New England Medical Center Floating Hospital for Children, 2043
Tug McGraw Foundation, 1037
Tulane University Clinical Immunology Section, 426
Tulane University, US-Japan Biomedical Research Laboratories, 3059
Tulsa City-County Library System, 7510
Turner Syndrome, 6637
Turner's Syndrome, 6693
Turner's Syndrome Society - Tampa Support Group, 6652
Turner's Syndrome Society of Alaska, 6646
Turner's Syndrome Society of Arizona, 6647
Turner's Syndrome Society of Central New York, 6667
Turner's Syndrome Society of Connecticut, 6651
Turner's Syndrome Society of Gulf Coast, 6657
Turner's Syndrome Society of Houston, 6677
Turner's Syndrome Society of Inland Northwest, 6682
Turner's Syndrome Society of Iowa/New Found Friends, 6655
Turner's Syndrome Society of Kentucky, 6656
Turner's Syndrome Society of Maryland, 6658
Turner's Syndrome Society of Mid-South, 6675
Turner's Syndrome Society of Minnesota, 6662
Turner's Syndrome Society of National Capitol Area, 6681
Turner's Syndrome Society of Nevada, 6664
Turner's Syndrome Society of New England, 6659
Turner's Syndrome Society of New Jersey, 6666
Turner's Syndrome Society of North Texas, 6678
Turner's Syndrome Society of North Carolina, 6669
Turner's Syndrome Society of Northern New England, 6665
Turner's Syndrome Society of Northern Florida, 6653
Turner's Syndrome Society of Oklahoma, 6671
Turner's Syndrome Society of Philadelphia, 6672
Turner's Syndrome Society of Rhode Island, 6673
Turner's Syndrome Society of Rocky Mountain, 6650
Turner's Syndrome Society of Salt Lake City, 6680
Turner's Syndrome Society of San Antonio, 6679
Turner's Syndrome Society of South Florida, 6654
Turner's Syndrome Society of South Carolina, 6674
Turner's Syndrome Society of Southeastern Wisconsin, 6660, 6683
Turner's Syndrome Society of Southern California, 6649
Turner's Syndrome Society of Southwestern Ohio, 6670
Turner's Syndrome Society of St. Louis/West Illinois, 6663
Turner's Syndrome Society of Tennessee, 6676
Turner's Syndrome Society of the US, 6645, 6688
Turner's Syndrome Society of Upstate New York, 6668
Turner's Syndrome Society of West Michigan, 6661
Turner's Syndrome Society Resource Bibliographies, 6694
Turner's Syndrome Society Central And Northern, 6648
Turner's Syndrome: A Personal Perspective, 6695
Turner's Syndrome: Guide for Families, 6696
Turner's Syndrome: The Hows and Whys of the Missing X Chromosome, 6697
The Turners, 6438, 6525
Twelve Steps and Twelve Traditions of Overeaters Anonymous, 4750
Twenty Years At Hull House, 5738
Two Worlds - One Planet, 832
22Q and You Center, 2357
25 Ways to Promote Spoken Language in Your Child with a Hearing Loss, 3462

U

UC Berkeley School of Social Welfare, 4553, 4958, 7553
UCD Hemophilia Treatment Center, 3609
UCP Norwood Stepping Stones, 1304
UCP of Long Island, 1303
UCP Seguin of Greater Chicago, 1278
UCP Washington Wire, 1360
UCSD Hemophilia Treatment Center, 3610
UIC Eye Center, 5546
Ulcerative Colitis, 61, 6698, 6734
Ulster County Social Services, 7335
The Ultimate ASL Dictionary, 3312
Un Curso Basico de Lenguaje Americano de Senas, 3440
UNC CF Center, 2072
Under the Microscope, 1963
Understanding and Treating Children with Autism, 903
Understanding and Treating Depression, 2240
Understanding and Treating the Hereditary Psychiatric Spectrum Disorders, 1585, 6790
Understanding Asthma, 458
Understanding Attention Deficit Disorder, 599
Understanding Autism, 833
Understanding Bullying - Fact Sheet, 6840
Understanding Childhood Obesity, 4751
Understanding Crohn Disease and Ulcerative Colitis, 1961
Understanding Cystic Fibrosis, 2122
Understanding Dental Health, 2187
Understanding Depression, 2267
Understanding Down Syndrome, 2478
Understanding Herpes, 3709, 4428
Understanding Hyperactivity, 600
Understanding Juvenile Rheumatoid Arthritis, 3964

Entry Name Index

Understanding Panic Disorder, 2283
Understanding SBS/Shaken Impact Syndrome Brochure, 5078
Understanding Schizophrenia, 1479
Understanding School Violence Fact Sheet, 6841
Understanding Seizures & Epilepsy, 5775
Understanding Sickle Cell Disease, 5878
Understanding SMA, 6140
Understanding the Defiant Child, 1586, 6791
Understanding Your Child's Education Needs/Individualized Education Program Packet, 3823
Understanding Your Teenager's Depression, 2268
Understanding Youth Violence: Fact Sheet, 6842
Unified Community Connections, 1286
United Ability, 1245
United Brachial Plexus Network, 2751
United Cerebral Palsy (UCP), 1243, 1335
United Cerebral Palsy Central Pennsylvania, 1309
United Cerebral Palsy Detroit, 1289
United Cerebral Palsy Heartland, 1293
United Cerebral Palsy Land of Lincoln, 1279
United Cerebral Palsy Michigan, 1290
United Cerebral Palsy of Alabama, 1246
United Cerebral Palsy of Alaska/PARENTS, 1251
United Cerebral Palsy of Baton Rouge McMains Children's Developmental Center, 1282
United Cerebral Palsy of Berkshire County, 1287
United Cerebral Palsy of Central Arizona, 1252
United Cerebral Palsy of Central Arkansas, 1254
United Cerebral Palsy of Central California, 1255
United Cerebral Palsy of Central Florida, 1271
United Cerebral Palsy of Central Minnesota, 1291
United Cerebral Palsy of Delaware, 1268
United Cerebral Palsy of Eastern Connecticut, 1266
United Cerebral Palsy of Georgia, 1275
United Cerebral Palsy of Greater Cleveland, 1305
United Cerebral Palsy of Greater Dane County, 1318
United Cerebral Palsy of Greater Hartford, 1267
United Cerebral Palsy of Greater Indiana, 1280
United Cerebral Palsy of Greater New Orleans, 1283
United Cerebral Palsy of Greater Sacramento & Northern California, 1256
United Cerebral Palsy of Hawaii, 1276
United Cerebral Palsy of Hudson County, 1296
United Cerebral Palsy of Huntsville & Tennessee Valley, 1247
United Cerebral Palsy of Los Angeles, Ventura and Santa Barbara Counties, 1257
United Cerebral Palsy of Maine, 1284
United Cerebral Palsy of MetroBoston, 1288
United Cerebral Palsy of Middle Tennessee, 1314
United Cerebral Palsy of Minnesota, 1292
United Cerebral Palsy of Mobile, 1248
United Cerebral Palsy of Nebraska, 1295
United Cerebral Palsy of Northeastern Pennsylvania, 1310
United Cerebral Palsy of Northwest Alabama, 1249
United Cerebral Palsy of Northwest Missouri, 1294
United Cerebral Palsy of Orange County, 1258
United Cerebral Palsy of Rhode Island, 1311
United Cerebral Palsy of San Diego County, 1259
United Cerebral Palsy of San Joaquin, Calaveras & Amador Counties, 1260
United Cerebral Palsy of San Luis Obispo, 1261
United Cerebral Palsy of South Carolina, 1312
United Cerebral Palsy of Southern Arizona, 1253
United Cerebral Palsy of Southwest Florida, 1272
United Cerebral Palsy of Stanislaus County, 1262
United Cerebral Palsy of Tampa Bay, 1273
United Cerebral Palsy of the Golden Gate, 1263
United Cerebral Palsy of the Inland Empire, 1264
United Cerebral Palsy of the North Bay, 1265
United Cerebral Palsy of Washington DC & Northern Virginia, 1269
United Cerebral Palsy of Washington DC & Northern Virginia, 1316
United Cerebral Palsy of West Alabama, 1250
United Cerebral Palsy of West Central Wisconsin, 1319
United Cerebral Palsy Oregon, 1307
United Cerebral Palsy Research and Educational Foundation, 1322
United Community Options of South Florida, 1274
United Health Services Blood Disorder Center, 3612
United Leukodystrophy Foundation, 4117
United Network for Organ Sharing, 6478, 6582, 6587
United Ostomy Association, 3715, 6705
United Services, 7285
Unity Sleep Disorders Clinic Unity Health System, 4374
Univ. of Texas-Southwestern Med. Ctr. at Dallas - Clinical Ctr. for Liver Disease, 956
University Affiliated Program, School of Medicine, 7384
University Alabama Birmingham, 4200
University Center for the Development of Language & Literacy, 5988
University of Alabama - Birmingham Arthritis Clinical Intervention Program, 5696
University of Alabama Speech and Hearing Center, 3154
University of Alaska, Fairbanks, 7554
University of California, San Francisco Dermatology Drug Research, 1398, 1404, 2691, 2696, 5000, 5006, 5333
University of Chicago Children's Hospital, Department of Pediatrics, 2027
The University of Chicago Comer Children's Hospital, 5599
University of Chicago-Department of Psychiatry, 4739
University of Cincinnati Adult Hemophilia Program, 3613
University of Cincinnati College of Medicine/Division of Pediatrics, 2078
University of Connecticut Health Center, 2015
University of Illinois at Chicago, Craniofacial Center, 1890, 2181, 3055
University of Illinois at Chicago Institute for Tuberculosis Research, 6513, 6613
University of Iowa - Wendell Johnson Speech and Hearing Clinic, 3495, 6008, 6168
University of Iowa Birth Defects and Genetic Disorders Unit, 1611, 1654, 1732, 1741, 1783, 7555
University of Iowa Hospitals & Clinics, 2031
The University of Iowa Libraries, 5593
University of Kansas Center for Research on Learning, 4068
University of Kentucky: Pediatric Pulmonary Medicine, 2034
University of Maine, Conley Speech and Hearing Center, 3162
University of Maryland Medical Center, 4401
University of Memphis Neuropsychology Lab, 3070
University of Miami, Mailman Center for Child Development, 7442
University of Miami, Mailman Center for Child Development, 7556
University of Michigan Adult Hemophilia and Cougulation Disorders Program, 3614
University of Michigan Health System, 5212
University of Michigan, Cystic Fibrosis Center, 2048
University of Michigan, Kresge Hearing Research Institute, 3171
University of Mississippi Medical Center, 2050, 2182
University of Missouri-Columbia Cystic Fibrosis Center, 2053
University of Nebraska at Omaha Pediatric Pulmonary/Cystic Fibrosis Center, 2055
University of Nebraska, Lincoln Barkley Memorial Center, 3164
University of Nevada - Department of Speech-Language Pathology, 5990
University of New Mexico School of Medicine, 2060
University of North Carolina at Chapel Hill, Brain Research Center, 811
University of North Carolina Sarcoidosis Support Group, 5632
University of Oklahoma Cystic Fibrosis Center, 2079
University of Pennsylvania Weight and Education Program, 2599
University of Pennsylvania, Depression Research Unit, 2218
University of Pittsburgh Cystic Fibrosis Center/Children's Hospital, 2084
University of Rochester Medical Center, 2070
University of South Florida, 5594
University of Southern California Comprehensive Sickle Cell Center, 5860
University of Tennessee Hemophilia Clinic, 3615
University of Texas Department of Hematology Research, 3616
University of Texas Medical Branch, 4870
University of Texas Medical Branch at Galveston, Clinical Research Center, 4404
University of Texas Sleep/Wake Disorders Center, 4397

Entry Name Index

University of Texas Southwestern MedicalCenter/Asthma & Allergic Diseases, 427
University of Texas, Mental HealthClinical Research Center, 2219
University of Utah, 4299
University of Utah Intermountain CysticFibrosis Center, 2095
University of Virginia General ClinicalResearch Center, 428
University of Washington CF Center, 2100
University of Washington Department of Speech & Hearing Sciences, 5985
University of Washington Speech and Hearing Clinic, 5993
University of Washington: ExperimentalEducation Unit, 2437
University of Wisconsin Asthma andAllergic Disease Center, 429
University of Wisconsin-Madison CysticFibrosis/Pulmonary Center, 2104
University Professor, 3276
University Students with Autism and Asperger's Syndrome Web Site, 369, 846
Unlocking Potential: College and OtherChoices for People with LD and AD/HD, 6102
Unmarking Celiac Disease, 1218
Update, 3798
Upper Peninsula Library for the BlindPhysically Handicapped, 1667, 1796, 4660, 5471
Upstate/Northeast New York Chapter of Crohn's & Colitis Foundation of America, 1934
Urinary System, 7823
Urologic Care of the Child with SpinaBifida, 6111
Urticaria, 6735
US Autism Association, 361, 724
US Blind Golfers Association, 7168
US Disabled Ski Team, 7399
US Paralympics, 7072
US Rowing Assocation, 7212
US Wheelchair Weightlifting Association, 7370
USC - Neonatology Research Units, 6237
Useful Information on Phobias and Panic, 2284
UT Southwestern Medical Center at Dallas:Hematology-Oncology Research, 3611
Utah Center for Assistive Technology, 7400
Utah Chapter of the National HemophiliaFoundation, 3553
Utah Department of Health, 5295, 6227
Utah Parent Center, 7401
Utah State Library Commission, 7522
Utah Support GroupNational Ataxia Foundation, 526

V

VACC Camp, 298, 472, 1182
Vanderbilt Hemostasis-Thrombosis Clinic, 3617
Variety Audio, 1639, 1768, 4632, 5443
Variety Club Camp & Development Center, 7777
Vascular Anomalies Center, 3506
Vascular Birthmarks Foundation, 3504
Ventricular Septal Defects, 6744
Vermont Department of HealthState Immunication Program, 5296
Vermont Department of LibrariesSpecial Service Unit, 7523
Vermont Parent Information Center, 7406
Vermont Regional Hemophilia Center, 3618
Via Christi Specialty Clinics: Cystic Fibrosis, Adult and Pediatrics, 2033
Views from Our Shoes: Growing Up with aBrother or Sister with Special Needs, 6103
Vinland Center, 7270
Violence by Children & Teenagers, 6749
Violence in the Media: A ReferenceHandbook, 6836
Violence Prevention Works, 6813
Violentkids.com, 6814
Viral Hepatitis: Everybody's Problem?, 3679
Virginia Assistive Technology System, 7410
Virginia Beach Public Library, 7528
Virginia Commonwealth UniversityDepartment of Neurosurgery Research, 3072
Virginia Department of HealthBureau of Immunization, 5297

Virginia State Library for the Visuallyand Physically Handicapped, 1681, 1811, 4677, 5488
Virtual Children's Hospital, 1870
Virtual Children's Hospital: Treatment ofCongenital Clubfoot, 1531
Virtual Childrens Hosptial, 7636
Virtual Pediatric Hospital, 3708, 4121, 4427, 5310
Vision of Children Foundation, 189, 7073
Vision Service Plan, 4022
Vision Therapy, 4036
Vision Therapy Success Stories, 4037
VISIONS/Vacation Camp for the Blind, 1723, 1859, 4711, 5522
Visual Strategies for Improving Communication, 904
Visual Systems Research Group, 4024
Vital Options, 1054
Vitamin C Foundation, 5322
Voice Foundation (The), 5974
Voice Health Institute, 5975
Voice of the Diabetic, 2316
Volta Bureau Library, 3160
Volta Review, 3461
Volta Voices, 3451
VOR, 3922
Voyageur Outward Bound School, 7271

W

W.M. Krogman Center for Research In ChildGrowth and Development, 2901
Waisman Center - Auditory Physiology Research Laboratory, 5994
Walk with Me, 1356
Wallace Memorial Library, 3165
Warmline Family Resource Center, 7132
Washington Library for the Blind andPhysically Handicapped, 1682, 1812, 4678, 5489
Washington PAVE, 7414
Washington State Chapter of Crohn's &Colitis Foundation of America, 1947
Washington State Department of HealthImmunization Program, 5298
Washington University Cystic FibrosisCenter, 2054
Washtenaw County Library, 1668, 1797, 4661, 5472
Washtenaw County Library for the Blind andPhysically Disabled, 1669, 1798, 4662, 5473
Water Balance in Schizophrenia, 1475
Waterville Public Library, 7484
Wayne State University, 2978
We Can Hear and Speak, 3441
We Can: Guide for Parents of Childrenwith Arthritis, 3965
WE MOVE (Worldwide Education and Awarenessof Movement Disorders), 1244, 1336, 1488, 2530, 2541, 6433, 6445, 6479, 7074
We've Climbed Mountains: Increasing Our Understanding of Autism Spectrum Disorders, 834
WebMD Community Services, 7637
Wellness Community San Francisco/East Bay, 1055
Wellspring Camps, 4760
Wesley Medical Research Institutes, 7469, 7557
Wesley Woods, 388, 936, 4101
West Central Ohio Hemophilia Center, 3619
West Florida Regional Library, 7443
West Michigan Cancer Center Support Group, 1083
West Virginia Assistive Technology System, 7417
West Virginia Department of Health andHuman Services, 6229
West Virginia Library Commission, 7531
West Virginia Parent Training andInformation, 7418
West Virginia School for the Blind, 1683, 1813, 4679, 5490
West Virginia University Cystic FibrosisCenter, 2101
West Virginia University Mountain StateCystic Fibrosis Center, 2102
Westchester Center for Eating Disorders, 2593
Western Kentucky Assistive TechnologyConsortium, 7475
Western New York Chapter ofCrohn's & Colitis Foundation of America, 1935
Western North Carolina Brain Tumor SupportGroup, 1112

Entry Name Index

Western Pennsylvania Chapter of Crohn's & Colitis Foundation of America, 1942
Western Pennsylvania Chapter of The National Hemophilia Foundation, 3549
Western Psychiatric Institute & Clinic, Sleep Evaluation Center, 4393
What Everyone Should Know About Epilepsy, 5828
What Health Care Workers Should Know About Hepatitis B, 3680
What I Need to Know About Constipation, 2736
What Is AIDS?, 2986
What Is Hemophilia?, 3652
What Is Post Traumatic Stress Disorder?, 5168
What is Thalassemia Trait?, 6399
What Makes Ryan Tic?, 6450, 6546
What School Bus Drivers Need to Know About Students with Tourette Syndrome, 6564
What School Personnel Should Know About Asthma, 442
What To Do About Your Brain Injured Child, 3089
What to Do When a Friend Is Depressed: Guide for Students, 2285
What You Can Do About AIDS, 2987
What You Need to Know About Brain Tumors, 1166
What You Need To Know About Lactose Intolerance, 4260
What You Should Know About Bleeding Disorders, 3653
What's the Best Medicine for My Headaches?, 4248
Wheeless' Textbook of Orthopaedics, 333, 1532, 2715, 4015, 4111, 4188, 4858, 5734, 6081
When Are Opioid (Narcotic) Drugs Appropriate for Headache?, 4249
When Food is Love, 2658, 4752
When Nothing Matters Anymore: A Survival Guide for Depressed Teens, 2269
When Parents Can't Fix It, 7580
When Seizures Don't Look Like Seizures, 5829
When Someone You Know Has AIDS, 2988
When Your Child Has a Life-Threatening Illness, 7673
When Your Child is Ready to Return to School, 1167
Where Did AIDS Come From?, 2989
Where's Chimpy?, 2479
Whitney Library for the Blind, 7493
Whoo's Report, 1224
Why Can't Michael Pay Attention?, 601
Why Isn't My Child Happy? A Video Guide About Childhood Depression, 2231
Why We Can Hear And Speak, 3277
Why Won't My Child Pay Attention?, 602
Wichita Public Library, 7470
Wide Smiles, 1508
Wilderness Inquiry, 7272
Wilderness on Wheels Foundation, 7148
Willamette Valley Ataxia Support Group, 519
Williams Syndrome, 6846
Williams Syndrome Association, 6851
Williams Syndrome Monthly Medline Alert, 6858
Wilms Tumor, 6861
Wilson Disease, 6883
Wilson's Disease, 6897
Wilson's Disease Association, 6889, 6894
Wilson's Disease Patient Information Exchange, 6895
Windsor Mountain Camp, 3496
Wing of Madness: A Depression Guide, 2241
Winnie-the-Pooh's ABCs, 3442
Winthrop-University Hospital Sleep Disorders Center, 4375
Wisconsin Association for Perinatal Care, 5222
Wisconsin Chapter of Crohn's & Colitis Foundation of America, 1948
Wisconsin Lions Camp, 1724, 1860, 3497
Wish Fulfillment Organizations, 7674
Wish Upon a Star, 7805
Wish with Wings, 7806
Wishing Star Foundation, 7807
Wishing Well Foundation, 7808
WisTech, 7424
Withering Child, 2659
WNY Brain Tumor Support Group, 1108
Wolff's Headaches & Other Head Pain, 4243
Wolfner Memorial Library for the Blind, 4666, 5477
Women and Headache, 4250
Worcester Public Library, 7488
Word Signs: A First Book of Sign Language, 3443
Working Together, 2665
Working with Children and Adolescents in Groups, 2270
Workshop on Therapeutic Approaches for Duchenne Muscular Dystrophy, 4337
The World According to Pat: Reflections of Residential School Days, 3275
World Allergy Organization, 5589
World Allergy Organization Journal, 5615
World Association Sarcoidosis Other Granulatomous, 5688
World Craniofacial Foundation, 4133
World Health Organization, 31, 1866, 2758, 2961, 3662, 3701, 4866, 5094, 5110, 5262, 5538, 6175, 6480, 6572, 6611
World Institute on Disability, 7075
World of Sound, 3479
World of the Autistic Child, 905
World Research Foundation, 7076
Worthmore Academy, 937, 4102
Wyoming Department of Health, 6230
Wyoming's New Options in Technology (WYNOT), 7428

Y

Yale Pediatric Hematology/Oncology Research Center, 3620
Yale University Cystic Fibrosis Research Center, 2016
Yale University School of Medicine, 288, 319, 568, 1544, 3871, 3949, 4904, 6588, 6748
Yale University, Behavioral Medicine Clinic, 2220
Yale University, Ribicoff Research Facilities, 2221
Yard Sale Coloring Book, 3966
Yesterday's Tomorrow, 2271
York County Parent Awareness, 7239
You and Your ADD Child, 654
You and Your Deaf Child, 3444
You and Your Deaf Child: A Self-Help Guide for Parents of Deaf and Hard of Hearing, 3445
You Can Control Asthma - Books for the Family & Kids, 459
You're Bigger than It, 6725
Young Adult Institute, 7077
The Young Deaf Child, 3439
Young Deaf Child, 3446
Young Hearts, 3854
Young People and Chronic Illness: True Stories, Help and Hope, 3873
Young People with Cancer: A Handbook for Parents, 7675
Your Child and Asthma, 469
Your Child and Epilepsy, 5804
Your Diet & Psoriasis, 5366
Your Digestive System & How it Works, 62
Your Kidneys and How They Work, 7676
yourtotalhealth.ivillage.com, 5607

Z

Zero to Three, 7078

Geographic Index

Alabama

Alabama Department of Rehabilitation Services, 3558
Alabama Head Injury Foundation, 3004
Alabama Institute for the Deaf & Blind, 1626, 1753, 3153, 4617, 5420
Alabama/Northwest Florida Chapter of Crohn s Colitis Foundation of America, 1904
Arc of Morgan County, 7079
Autism Society of Alabama, 726
Autism Society of North Alabama, 727
Birmingham Support Group, 478
Camp ASCCA/Easter Seals, 7680
Camp Merrimack, 920, 1362, 2484, 7681
Camp Rap A Hope, 7682
Camp Shocco for the Deaf, 3484
Camp Smile-A-Mile, 7683
Down Syndrome Clinic, Children's Hospital of Alabama, 2411
Early Intervention Program, 7080
Gregory Fleming James Cystic Fibrosis Center, 2000
Mobile Association for the Blind, 1685, 1758, 1818, 4622, 4681, 5433
Pediatric Brain Tumor Support Group, 1038
Sickle Cell Foundation of Greater Montgomery, 5843
Special Education Action Committee Huntsville Outreach Office, 7082
Special Education Services, 7083
Spina Bifida Association of Alabama, 6020
Statewide Technology Access & Response System for Alabamians with Disabilities, 7084
United Ability, 1245
United Cerebral Palsy of Alabama, 1246
United Cerebral Palsy of Huntsville & Tennessee Valley, 1247
United Cerebral Palsy of Mobile, 1248
United Cerebral Palsy of Northwest Alabama, 1249
United Cerebral Palsy of West Alabama, 1250
University of Alabama - Birmingham Arthritis Clinical Intervention Program, 5696
University of Alabama Speech and Hearing Center, 3154

Alaska

Alaska Chapter of Asthma and Allergy Foundation of America, 414
Alaska Department of Education, 7085
Assistive Technologies of Alaska, 7086
Camp Kushtaka, 2344
Maternal, Child & Family Health, Early Intervention/Infant Learning Program, 7088
PARENTS, 7089
Rid Alaska of Child Abuse, 5034
Turner's Syndrome Society of Alaska, 6646
United Cerebral Palsy of Alaska/PARENTS, 1251
University of Alaska, Fairbanks, 7554

Arizona

Arizona Ataxia Support Group, 479
Arizona Camp Sunrise & Sidekicks, 117, 171, 1168, 2796, 4596, 6879
Arizona Chapter of Crohn's & Colitis Foundation of America, 1905
Arizona Early Intervention Program/ Department of Economic Security, 7090
Arizona Sleep Disorders Center, 4348
Arizona Spina Bifida Association, 6021
Arizona Technology Access Program Institute for Human Development, 7091
Autism Society of America Greater Phoenix Chapter, 728
Autism Society of America Southern Arizona Chapter, 729
Blake Foundation Children's Achievement Center, 7092
Brain Injury Association of Arizona, 3005
Brain Tumor Support Group at NovaCare Rehabilitation Institute of Tucson, 1039
Brain Tumor Support Group at Phoenix, 1040
Camp Abilities Tucson, 7684
Camp Civitan, 1716, 1853, 3480, 7685
Camp Shane Arizona, 4755
Children's Center for Neurodevelopmental Studies, 807
Crisis Nursery, 5035
Cystic Fibrosis Center: Phoenix Children's Hospital, 2001
Division of Special Education State Department of Education, 7093
Families of SMA - Arizona Chapter, 6122
Injury Prevention Center, 3773
Maricopa Co Childhood Immunization Program, 5263
Mayo Clinic Scleroderma Service, 5697
Mayo Comprehensive Hemophilia Center, 3589
National Center for Neurogenic Communication Disorders, 5986
Neurofibromatosis, Inc - Arizona Chapter, 4464
Office of Women's & Children's Health, 6192
Phoenix Center for Cancer and Blood Disorders, 3598
Pilot Parents of Southern Arizona, 7094
Prader-Willi Syndrome Arizona Association, 5177
Raising Special Kids, 7095
Southwest Chapter of Crohn's & Colitis Foundation of America, 1928
Special Needs Center/Phoenix Public Library, 7429
Steele Children's Research Center, 3607
Technology Access Center of Tucson, 7430
The Arizona Partnership for Immunization, 5264
Tourette Syndrome Association - Arizona Chapter, 6481
Turner's Syndrome Society of Arizona, 6647
United Cerebral Palsy of Central Arizona, 1252
United Cerebral Palsy of Southern Arizona, 1253

Arkansas

Arkansas Department of Health Div. of Comm Diseases/Immunizations, 5265
Arkansas Disability Coalition, 7097
Arkansas Disability Coalition Parent Training and Information Center, 7098
Arkansas Easter Seals Technology Resource Center, 7431
Arkansas Regional Library for the Blind and Physically Handicapped, 1631, 1760, 4624, 5435
Arkansas Rehabilitation Research and Training Center for Deaf Persons, 3169
Brain Injury Association of Arkansas, 3006
Camp Aldersgate, 7686
Camp Funshine, 2131
Children's Tumor Foundation-Arkansas Infor www.php.com, 4465
Crowley Ridge Regional Library, 7432
Educational Services for the Visually Impaired, 1630, 1759, 4623, 5434, 7433
Epilepsy Education Association of Arkansas, 5750
FOCUS, 7099
Family-2-Family Health Information Center of Arkansas, 7100
Hemophilia Center of Arkansas, 3522, 3577
Increasing Capabilities Access Network, 7101
Library for the Blind and Handicapped, Southwest, 7434
Parent to Parent Arc of Arkansas, 7102
Special Education Section State Department of Education, 7103
United Cerebral Palsy of Central Arkansas, 1254

California

Ability First, 7687
Ability First, Camp Paivika, 7688
All Kids By Two Health Services Agency, 5266
Allergy and Asthma Medical Group and Research Center, 5595
American Action Fund for Blind Children and Adults, 1761, 3155, 4625, 5436
Arc Family Resource Project, 7104
Assistive Technology Center Simi Valley Hospital, 7435
Ataxia Telangiectasia Medical Research Foundation, 528
Autism Society of America Coachella Valley, 730
Autism Society of America Greater Long Beach/San Gabriel Valley, 731
Autism Society of America Inland Empire Chapter, 732

Geographic Index

Autism Society of America Los Angeles Chapter, 733
Autism Society of America North San Diego County Chapter, 734
Autism Society of America Orange County Chapter, 735
Autism Society of America San Diego Chapter, 736
Autism Society of America San Francisco Bay Chapter, 737
Autism Society of America San Gabriel Valley Chapter, 738
Autism Society of America Santa Barbara Chapter, 739
Autism Society of America Tulare County Chapter, 740
Autism Society of California, 741
Blind Children's Center, 1633, 1762, 4626, 5437
Blind Childrens Center, 5421
Bloomfield, 1715, 1852, 4708, 5519
Braille Institute Desert Center, 1634, 1763, 4627, 5438
Braille Institute Sight Center, 1635, 1764, 4628, 5439
Braille Institute Youth Center, 1636, 1765, 4629, 5440
Brain Imaging Center at the University of California, Irvine, 3056
Brain Research Institute, 3057
Brain Tumor Patient & Family Support Group, 1041
Brain Tumor Support Group at Newport Beach, 1042
Brain Tumor Support Group at San Diego, 1043
Brain Tumor Support Group at San Luis Obispo, 1044
Brain Tumor Support Group at Santa Monica, 1045
Brain Tumor Support Program Cedars-Sinai Neurosurgical Inst. & Wellness Communit, 1046
Brain and Spinal Injury Center (BASIC) Research at University of California, 3058
Brian Wesley Ray Cystic Fibrosis Center, 2002
CARE Family Resource Center, 7105
California Brain Injury Association, 3007
California Department of Health Services Immunization Branch, 5267
Camp Alex A. Krem, 7690
Camp Crescent Moon, 5880
Camp Grizzly, 3482
Camp Joan Mier, 7691
Camp Kindle- Project Kindle, 2993
Camp Krem, 918
Camp Ronald McDonald at Eagle Lake, 7692
Camp Rubber Soul, 7693
Camp Shane California, 4756
Camp Sunshine Dreams, 121, 174, 1171, 2798, 4598, 6881
Camp Wonder, 5715
Camp de los Ninos - Diabetes Society, 2345
Camp-A-Lot, 7694
Carolyn Kordich Family Resource Center, 7106
Center for Accessible Technology, 7436
Center for the Partially Sighted, 1684, 1814, 2295, 4680, 5492
Center for the Research and Treatment of Anorexia Nervosa, 2603
Challenged Family Resource Center, 7107
Child Sexual Abuse Treatment Program (Giar retto), 5036
Children Living with Illness, 7108
Children's Hospital & Research Center of Oakland, 2412
Children's Hospital of Los Angeles, 2003
Children's Hospital of Orange County: Depa rtment of Pulmonology - Cystic Fibrosis, 2004
Children's Hospital: Pediatric Pulmonary Center, 2005
Christian Berets, 7695
Clearinghouse for Specialized Media and Technology (CSMT), 7437
Comfort Connection Family Resource Center, 7109
Community Health Improvement Partners - Immunize San Diego (CHIP-ISD), 5268
CorStone-Children & Loss Group, 6193
Cystic Fibrosis Center: Cedars-Sinai Medical Center, 2006
Cystic Fibrosis Center: University of California at San Francisco, 2007
Cystic Fibrosis Research, Inc., 2008
Cystic Fibrosis and Pediatric Respiratory Diseases Center, 2009
Department of Developmental Services of Early Start Program, 7110
Down Syndrome Association of Los Angeles, 2394
Dream Street Foundation, 7696
Early Start Family Resource Network, 7111
Easter Seal Summer Camp Programs, 7697
Eating Disorders Research and Treatment Program, 2605
Enchanted Hills Camp, 1718, 1854, 3489

EpiCenter, 5760
Epilepsy Foundation of Northern California, 5751
Exceptional Family Resource Center, 7112
Exceptional Family Support, Education and Advocacy Center, 7113
Exceptional Parents, 7114
Families Caring for Families, 7115
Families of SMA - Northern California Chap ter, 6123
Family First Program Alpha Resource Center, 7116
Family Focus Resource Center, 7117
Family Resource Center at Lucile Packard Children's Hospital, 1555
Federal Hemophilia Treatment Center Program of Los Angeles, 3573
Firefighters Kids Camp Camp Concord, 1202
Foundation for Prader-Willi Research, 5198
Fragile X Association of Southern California, 2846
Fragile X Center of San Diego, 2847
Francis J. Curry National Tuberculosis Center, 6612
Glaucoma Research Foundation, 1817
Gloriana Opera Company, 7698
Greater Los Angeles/Orange County Chapter of Chron's & Colitis Foundation, 1906
Greater North Valley California Support Group, 480
Greater San Diego/Desert Chapter of Crohn' s & Colitis Foundation of America, 1907
H.E.A.R.T.S. Connection Family Resource Center, 7119
Harbor Regional Center Family and Professional Resource Center, 7120
Hear Center, 3156
Hearing Education & Awareness for Rockers, 3152
Hemophilia Association of San Diego County, 3523
Hemophilia Foundation of Northern California, 3524
Hemophilia Foundation of Southern California, 3525
Immunization Partnership of Alameda County, 5269
Inland Empire Brain Tumor Support Group, 1047
Jodi House, 3008
Kaiser Permanente Medical Center, 2010
Kern Autism Network, 742
Little People of America - District 2, 2893, 2894, 2896, 4845, 4846, 4848
Little People of America - District 7, 2889, 2891, 2892, 2895, 4840, 4843
Little People of America - San Francisco Bay Area Chapter, 2890, 4841
Little People of America - Utah Seagulls, 2897, 4849
Loma Linda University Sleep Disorders Cent er, 4349
Los Angeles Ataxia Support Group, 481
MATRIX: Parent Network and Family Resource Center, 7121
Matrix Parents Network and Resource Center, 7122
Memorial Miller Children's Hospital Cystic Fibrosis Center, 2011
National Organization of Parents of Blind Children, 5426
Neurofibromatosis, Inc - California Chapte r, 4466
Neuroscience Institute Brain Tumor Support Group, 1048
New Beginnings - Blind Children's Center, 1637, 1766, 4630, 5441
New Beginnings - The Blind Children's Center, 1686, 1821, 4682, 5494
Northern California Chapter of Crohn's and Colitis Foundation, 1908
Northern California Comprehensive Sickle C ell Center, 5859
Northern California Support Group, 482
Northridge Hospital: Leavey Cancer Center, 1049
Okizu Foundation Camps, 123, 176, 1173, 2799, 4599, 6882
Orange County Support Group, 483
Orthopaedic Biomechanics Laboratory, 1321
Orthopaedic Hospital's Hemophilia Treatment Center, 3596
Pacific Southwest Regional Genetics Group, 484
Palo Alto Brain Tumor Support Group, 1050
Peaks and Valleys Family Resource Center, 7123
Pediatric Disabilities Clinic, Down Syndrome Clinic, 2413
Peninsula Support & Education Group for Parents of Children with Brain Tumors, 1051
People First of California, 3926
Prader-Willi California Foundation, 5178
Pulmonary Care and Cystic Fibrosis Center, 2012
REACH - Sarcoidosis Support, 5626
Region IX Office Program Consultants for Maternal and Child Health, 6194
SMA Research Group, 6128
Sacramento Area Brain Tumor Support Group Lawrence J Ellison Ambulatory Care Ctr, 1052

Geographic Index

Sacramento Center for Assistive Technology, 7438
San Diego Support Group, 485
San Fernando Valley Support Group, 486
San Francisco Brain Tumor Support Group, 1053
San Francisco Public Library for the Blind and Print Disabled, 1638, 1767, 4631, 5442
San Gabriel/Pomona Parents' Place, 7124
Scleroderma Research Foundation, 5698
Sickle Cell Disease Foundation of California, 5844
South Central Los Angeles Regional Center for Devlopmentally Disabled Persons, 7125
Special Connections Family Resource Center, 7126
Special Education Division State Department of Education, 7127
Stanford CF Center, 2013
Stanford University Center for Narcolepsy, 4350
Starlight Children's Foundation, 7128
Support for Families of Children with Disabilities, 7129
Team Advocates for Special Kids, Anaheim, 7130
Team Advocates for Special Kids, San Diego, 7131
Team of Advocates for Special Kids, 7551
Tourette Syndrome Association - Southern California Chapter, 6483
Turner's Syndrome Society Central And Northern, 6548
Turner's Syndrome Society of Southern California, 6649
UC Berkeley School of Social Welfare, 4553, 4958, 7553
UCD Hemophilia Treatment Center, 3609
UCSD Hemophilia Treatment Center, 3610
USC - Neonatology Research Units, 6237
United Cerebral Palsy of Central California, 1255
United Cerebral Palsy of Greater Sacramento & Northern California, 1256
United Cerebral Palsy of Los Angeles, Ventura and Santa Barbara Counties, 1257
United Cerebral Palsy of Orange County, 1258
United Cerebral Palsy of San Diego County, 1259
United Cerebral Palsy of San Joaquin, Calaveras & Amador Counties, 1260
United Cerebral Palsy of San Luis Obispo, 1261
United Cerebral Palsy of Stanislaus County, 1262
United Cerebral Palsy of the Golden Gate, 1263
United Cerebral Palsy of the Inland Empire, 1264
United Cerebral Palsy of the North Bay, 1265
University of California, San Francisco Dermatology Drug Research, 1398, 1404, 2691, 2696, 5000, 5006
University of Southern California Comprehensive Sickle Cell Center, 5860
Variety Audio, 1639, 1768, 4632, 5443
Vital Options, 1054
Warmline Family Resource Center, 7132
Wellness Community San Francisco/East Bay, 1055
Wellspring Camps, 4760

Colorado

Assistive Technology Partners, 7133
Autism Society of America Larimer County Chapter, 743
Autism Society of America Pikes Peak Chapter, 744
Autism Society of America: Colorado Chapter, 745
Autism Society of American Boulder County Chapter, 746
Brain Injury Association of Colorado, 3009
Cardiac Kids/Association of Volunteers, 3842
Children's Hospital: Academic Pediatric Surgery Department, 1542
Colorado Consortium of Intensive Care Nurseries United Parents (UP), 7134
Colorado Dept. of Public Heand & Environme nt: Immunization Program, DCEED-IMM-A3, 5270
Colorado Support Group, 487
Delta/Montrose Parent to Parent, 7135
Denver Children's Hospital, 2014
Denver Early Childhood Connections, 7136
Denver Sarcoidosis Awareness Support Group, 5627
Disabilities Advocacy & Support Network, 7280
Disability Connection and RAFT, Larimer County's Early Childhood Connection, 7137
Effective Parent Project, 7138
El Groupo Vida, 7139
Help Parent Support Group Hope & Education for Loving Parents, 7140
Hemophilia Society of Colorado, 3526
Little People of America - Front Range Chapter, 4842
Magic of Music and Dance, 7700
Mile High Down Syndrome Association, 2395
Mountain States Regional Genetics Services Network, 488
National Jewish Health, 420, 424, 5636
National Jewish Medical & Research Center, 5111
Oasis, 7141
PEAK Parent Center, 7142
Parent Support Group of Littleton & Auora, 7143
Parents Supporting Parents of Eagle County, 7144
Parents Supporting Parents of Garfield and Pitkin County, 7145
Parents of Asthmatic/Allergic Children, Inc., 415, 5590
Prader-Willi Colorado Association, 5179
Prevention Initiatives State Department of Education, 7146
Region VIII Office Program Consultants for Maternal and Child Health, 6195
Resources for Young Children and Families, 7147
Rocky Mountain Chapter of Crohn's & Colitis Foundation of America, 1909
Speech, Language, & Hearing Center University of Colorado, 6160
Speech, Language, and Hearing Center, 5987
Spina Bifida Association of Colorado, 6025
TIES, The Children's Hospital, 7550
Tourette Syndrome Association - Rocky Mountain Region, 6484, 6495, 6496, 6510
Turner's Syndrome Society of Rocky Mountain, 6650
Wilderness on Wheels Foundation, 7148

Connecticut

A.J. Pappanikou Center for Developmental Disabilities, 7149
Assistive Technology Project, 7150
Autism Society of America Connecticut Chapter, 747
Brain Injury Association of Connecticut, 3010
CPAC, 7151
Central Connecticut Chapter of Crohn's & Colitis Foundation of America, 1910
Connecticut Birth to Three-Office of Early Childhood, 7152
Connecticut Down Syndrome Congress, 2396
Connecticut Lead Poisoning Prevention Program, 4048
Families of SMA - Connecticut Chapter, 6124
Gaylord Hospital Sleep Medicine, 4351
Hemlocks Easter Seals Recreation, 5741
Hole in the Wall Gang Camp, 2994, 3654
Leukemia & Lymphoma Society - Westchester/ Connecticut/Hudson Valley Chapter, 142
Mansfield's Holiday Hill, 7701
Marvelwood Summer, 2519
Northern Connecticut Affiliate Chapter of Crohn's & Colitis Foundation of America, 1912
Parent to Parent Network of Connecticut the Family Center, 7153
Prader-Willi Connecticut Association, 5180
Region 1 of the National Association for Parents of the Visually Impaired, 5422
Spina Bifida Association of Connecticut, 6026
State Department of Education, 7154
TBI Support Group for Families & Survivors, 3011
Tourette Syndrome Association - Connecticut Chapter, 6485
Turner's Syndrome Society of Connecticut, 6651
United Cerebral Palsy of Eastern Connecticut, 1266
United Cerebral Palsy of Greater Hartford, 1267
University of Connecticut Health Center, 2015
Yale Pediatric Hematology/Oncology Research Center, 3620
Yale University Cystic Fibrosis Research Center, 2016
Yale University, Behavioral Medicine Clinic, 2220
Yale University, Ribicoff Research Facilities, 2221

Geographic Index

Delaware

Autism Society of Delaware, 748
Children's Beach House, 3486
Delaware Assisstive Technology Initiative (DATI), 7155
Delaware Division of Libraries for the Blind and Physically Handicapped, 1399, 5001
Department of Public Instruction, 7156
Parent Information Center of Delaware, 7157
Prader-Willi Delaware Association, 5181
Turner's Syndrome Society of Philadelphia, 6672
United Cerebral Palsy of Delaware, 1268

District of Columbia

Advocates for Justice and Education, 7158
Autism Society of America District of Columbia Chapter, 749
Brain Injury Association of Washington DC, 3012
Brain Research Center, 1139
Center for Auditory and Speech Sciences-Gallaudet University, 3157
Child Welfare Information Gateway, 5045
Children's National Health System, 97, 157, 5596
Commission of Public Health Immunization Program, 5271
DC Arc, 7159
Department of Health Division of Immunization, 5272
District of Columbia Public Library/ Librarian for the Deaf Community, 3158
Division of Community Health Nursing, 6196
Georgetown University, 5699
Georgetown University Child Development Center, 7160, 7439, 7539
Georgetown University Sleep Disorders Center, 4352
HEATH Resource Center, 7440
Hemophilia & Thrombosis Program at Children's National Health System, 3576
Howard University Center for Sickle Cell Disease, 5861
Lab School of Washington Summer Program, 674, 931, 4093
Laurent Clerc National Deaf Education Center-Gallaudet Universty, 3159
National Center for Education in Maternal and Child Health, 5223
National Technical Assistance Center for Children's Mental Health, 1577, 6781
Office of Special Education and Rehabilitation Services, 7389
Parent Project for Muscular Dystrophy, 4296
Partnership for Assistive Technology, 7162
Scottish Rite Centers for Childhood Langua ge Disorders, 5984
Spina Bifida Association Pittsburgh, 6058
Spina Bifida Association of Greater Bay Ar ea, 6023
Spina Bifida Association of Greater Fox Valley, 6068
Spina Bifida Association of Greater San Di ego, 6024
Spina Bifida Association of Northern Indiana, 6034
Spina Bifida Association of Southeast Florida, 6029
Spina Bifida Association of Tennessee, 6061
Talking Books - National Library Service, 4023
Technical Assistance Partnership for Child and Family Mental Health, 1580, 6784
United Cerebral Palsy of Washington DC & Northern Virginia, 1269
United Cerebral Palsy of Washington DC & Northern Virginia, 1316
Volta Bureau Library, 3160

Florida

Alliance for Assistive Service and Technology (FAAST), 7163
American SIDS Institute, 6232
Angels in the Sun Brain Tumor Support Group, 1056
Autism Society of America Broward Chapter, 750
Autism Society of America Emerald Coast Chapter, 751
Autism Society of America Florida Chapter, 752
Autism Society of America Jacksonville Chapter, 753
Autism Society of America Panhandle Chapter, 755
Autism Society of Greater Orlando, 756
Brain Injury Association of Florida, 3013
Broward County Support Group, 489
CF & Pediatric Pulmonary Disease Center, 2017
Camp Boggy Creek, 6112
Camp Thunderbird, 7702
Cancer Support Group for Children, 1057
Center for Independence Technology and Education, (CITE), 7441
Child and Family Connections, 7187
Children's Medical Services Program Florida SIDS Program, 6197
Clearwater, FL Support Group, 490
Coconut Creek Eating Disorders Support Group, 2582
Comprehensive Pediatric Hemophilia Treatment Center, 3570
Cystic Fibrosis Center - All Children's Hospital, 2018
Developmental Center, 670, 926, 4089
Early Intervention Unit, Division of Children's Medical Services, 7164
Easter Seals Camp Challenge, 7703
Epilepsy Association of the Big Bend, 5752
Family Network on Disabilities, 7165
Family/Community Support Group of the Brain Injury Association of Florida, 3014
Florida Bureau of Braille and Talking Book Library Services, 1640, 1769, 4633, 5444
Florida Camp for Children and Youth, 2350
Florida Chapter of Crohn's & Colitis Found ation of America, 1913
Florida Department of Education, 7166
Florida Department of Health Immunization Program, 5273
Florida Epilepsy Services, 5753
Florida Families of Children with Visual I mpairments, 5563
Florida Ophthalmic Institute, 1815
Florida School-Deaf and Blind Summer Camp, 1719, 1855, 3490, 4709, 5520
Florida's Collaboration for Young Children and their Families Head State, 7167
Frontier Travel Camp, 385
Gold Coast Down Syndrome Organization, 2397
Goodwill Industries-Suncoast, 2398
Goodwill Industries-Suncoast: Choices for Work Program, 3015
Hemophilia Foundation of Greater Florida, 3527
Hydrocephalus Family Support Group of Central Florida, 3774
Kris' Camp, 930
Miami Children's Hospital, Division of Pulmonology, 2019
Miami Comprehensive Hemophilia Center, 3590
NE Florida Support Group, 491
National Ophthalmic Research Institute, 1820
Neurofibromatosis Center at North Broward Medical Center, 4473
PWSA Florida Chapter, 5182
Pediatric Heart Foundation, 3843
Prader-Willi Alliance of New York, 5194
Pulmonary Wellness Program, 2020
Renfrew Center of Miami, 2583
Research & Training Center for Children's Mental Health at University of South FL, 1578, 6782
Research and Training Center for Children' Mental Health, 7547
Shriners Hospital for Children, 5724
South Florida Brain Tumor Association Lynn Regional Cancer Center, 1058
Spina Bifida Association of Central Florid a, 6027
Spina Bifida Association of Jacksonville N emours Childrens Clinic, 6028
Spina Bifida Association of Tampa Bay, 6030
Suncoast Residential Training Center/Developmental Services Program, 1437
Talking Book Library, Jacksonville Public Library, 1641, 1770, 4634, 5445
Talking Book Service - Manatee County Central Library, 1642, 1771, 4635, 5446
Tampa Support Group, 492
Tender Love and Care PPEC and Early Learning Center, 1270
Tourette Syndrome Association of Florida, 6486
Turner's Syndrome Society - Tampa Support Group, 6652
Turner's Syndrome Society of Northern Florida, 6653
Turner's Syndrome Society of South Florida, 6654
US Blind Golfers Association, 7168

Geographic Index

United Cerebral Palsy of Central Florida, 1271
United Cerebral Palsy of Southwest Florida, 1272
United Cerebral Palsy of Tampa Bay, 1273
United Community Options of South Florida, 1274
University of Miami, Mailman Center for Child Development, 7442
University of Miami, Mailman Center for Child Development, 7556
University of South Florida, 5594
VACC Camp, 298, 472, 1182
West Florida Regional Library, 7443

Georgia

Albany Library for the Blind and Physical Handicapped, 1643, 1772, 4636, 5447
All Ages Support Group, 1059
Augusta-Richmond County Public Library, 7444
Autism Society of America Greater Georgia Chapter, 757
Bainbridge Subregional Library for the Blind and Physically Handicapped, 1644, 1773, 4637, 5448
Brain Injury Resource Foundation, 3016
Brain Tumor Foundation for Children, 1060
CEL Subregional Library for the Blind and Physically Handicapped, 1645, 1774, 4638, 5449
Camp Hawkins, 2482
Camp Juliena, 3483
Camp Kudzu, 2343
Comprehensive Sickle Cell Center, 5862
DHR/Division of Public Health - Babies Can t Wait Program, 7169
Department for Exceptional Students Georgia Department of Education, 7170
Department of Counseling and Educational Leadership-Columbus State University, 7171
Department of Pediatrics, Medical College of Georgia, 2021
Division of Birth Defects and Genetic Diseases, 7537
Down Syndrome Association of Atlanta, 2399
Egleston Cystic Fibrosis Center: Departmen t of Pediatrics, 2022
Emory Autism Resource Center, 796
Emory Eye Center - Strabismus Research, 6146
Gainesville Subregional LBPH Hall County Public Library, 7445
Georgia Ataxia Support Group, 493
Georgia Chapter of Crohn's & Colitis Foundation of America, 1914
Georgia Department of Human Resources - Center for Family Resource Planning, 6199
Georgia Department of Human Resources Children's Health Services, 6198
Georgia Perinatal Association, 5220
Greater Atlanta Area Support Group, 494
Hemophilia Foundation of Georgia, 3528
La Fayette Subregional Library for the Blind and Physically Disabled, 7446
Macon Subregional Library for the Blind and Handicapped, Washington Memorial, 7447
Macon Support Group, 495
Oconee Regional Library, Library for the Blind and Physically Handicapped, 7448
PWSA of Georgia, 5183
Parent to Parent of Georgia, 7172
Parents Educating Parents and Professional for All Children (PEPPAC), 7173
Pediatric Neurodevelopmental Center at Marcus Institute, 2414
Prevent Child Abuse Georgia, 5037
Region IV Office Program Consultants For Maternal and Child Health, 6200
Rome Subregional Library for the Blind and Physically Handicapped, 7449
Sarcoidosis Support Group, 5628
Sickle Cell Foundation of Georgia, 5846
Southeast Regional Genetics Group, 496
Southeastern Brain Tumor Foundation Brain Tumor Support Group, 1061
Southeastern Region-Helen Keller National Center, 5423
Special Needs Library of NE Georgia Athens-Clarke County Regional Library, 7450
Spina Bifida Association of Georgia, 6031
Squirrel Hollow, 934, 4099
Subregional Library for the Blind and Physically Handicapped, 7451
Tech-Able, 7452
Tools for Life Division of Rehabilitation Services, 7174
United Cerebral Palsy of Georgia, 1275

Hawaii

AWARE, 7175
Aloha Special Technology Access Center, 7453
Assistive Technology Resource Centers of H awaii (ATRC), 7176
Autism Society of Hawaii, 758
Camp Erdman YMCA, 7704
Federal Hemophilia Treatment Center of Hawaii, 3574
Hawaii Department of Health Immunization Program, 5274
Hawaii Down Syndrome Congress, 2400
Hemophilia Foundation of Hawaii, 3529
Kardiac Kids, 3845
Library for the Blind and Physically Handicapped, Hawaii State Library, 7454
Parents and Children Together (PACT), 7177
Special Education Center of Hawaii, 3017
Special Needs Branch Department of Education, 7178
United Cerebral Palsy of Hawaii, 1276

Idaho

Assistive Technology Project, 7179
Autism Society of America Treasure Valley Chapter, 759
Brain Injury Association of Idaho, 3018
Camp Hodia, 2341
Child Health Improvement Program Idaho Department of Health, 6201
Department of Education, 7180
Hemophilia Foundation of Idaho, 3530
Idaho Dept. of Health & Welfare Immunizati on Program, 5275
Idaho Parents Unlimited, 7181
Idaho State Talking Book Library, 1646, 1775, 4639, 5450
Infant/Toddler Program, 7182
Palouse Area Parent To Parent, 7183
Parent Reaching Out to Parents, 7184
Prader-Willi Northwest Association-Idaho, 5185
Treasure Valley Brain Injury Support Group, 1062

Illinois

Academy for Eating Disorders (AED), 2584
Adult Down Syndrome Center of Lutheran General Hospital, 2415
Advocate Lutheran General Children's Hospital, Pediatric Research, 2416
Archway, 7185
Assistive Technology Project, 7186
Autism Society of Illinois, 760
Brain Injury Association of Illinois, 3019
Brain Research Foundation, 1140
Camp Discovery, 199, 1422, 2708, 5014, 5367, 5714
Camp Horizon, 7678
Camp New Friends, 4480
Camp Roehr, 5833
Center for Disability Services, 1277
Center for Narcolepsy Research at the University of Illinois at Chicago, 4398
Central DuPage Hospital Center for Digestive Disorders, 1558
Chicago Library Service for the Blind, 1647, 1776, 4640, 5451
Chicago, IL Area Ataxia Support Group, 497
Chilren's Heart Services, 3846
Citizens United for Research in Epilepsy (CURE), 5761
Comprehensive Bleeding Disorder Center, 3569
Craniofacial Center at University of Illin ois, Chicago, 1891

Geographic Index

Crohn's & Colitis Foundation Carol Fisher Chapter, 1915
Cystic Fibrosis Center: Children's Memoria l Hospital, 2023
Dermatology Information Network (DERMINFONET), 1400, 2692, 5002
Developmental Services Center, 7188
Dystonia Medical Research Foundation, 2532
Family Resource Center, 7118
Family Resource Center on Disabilities, 7189
Family T.I.E.S. Network, 7190
Greater Interagency Council Parent to Parent Support Network, 7191
Hemophilia Foundation of Illinois, 3531
Illinois State Library, Talkng Book and Braille Service, 1648, 1777, 4641, 5452
International Society for Traumatic Stress Studies, 5145
Jewish Council for Youth Services, 7706
LaRabida Children's Hospital, Down Syndrome Clinic, 2417
Leukemia Research Foundation, 7192
Loyola University Medical Center/ Department of Pediatrics, 2024
Loyola University of Children, Parmly Hearing Institute, 3161
MDA Summer Camp, 4338
Mid Illinois Talking Book System, 1649, 1778, 4642, 5453
Mid-Illinois Talking Book Center, 1650, 1779, 4643, 5454
Mothers of Children with Allergies (MOCHA), 5591
National Center for Latinos with Disabilities, 7193
National Eye Research Foundation, 1819
National Library of Dermatologic Teaching Slides, 1401, 2693, 5003
Neurofibromatosis, Inc - Illinois/Midwest, 4467
Next Steps - Parents Reaching Parents, 7194
Northwestern University Asthma and Allergy Disease Center, 425
Obsessive Compulsive Foundation of Metropo litan Chicago, 4777
Office of Community Health and Prevention Bureau of Early Intervention, DHR, 7195
Olympia, 7707
PKU Organization of Illinois, 4928
Parent to Parent Network, 7196
Parents Alliance Employment Project, 7455
Parents of Children with Brain Tumors (PCBT), 1063
Park Ridge, Cystic Fibrosis Center, 2025
Prevent Child Abuse Illinois, 5038
Professional Assistance Center for Education (PACE), 7456
Region 3 of the National Association for Parents of the Visually Impaired, 5424
Region V Office Program Consultants for Maternal and Child Health, 6202
Saint Francis Medical Center Specialty Clinics, CF Center, 2026
Shawnee Library System, 7457
Southern IL Child and Family Connections, 7197
Spina Bifida Association of Illinois, 6032
State Board of Education Department of Special Education, 7198
Suburban Audio Visual Service, 7458
Summer Wheelchair Sports Camp, 7708
Talking Book Center of Northwest Illinois, 1651, 1780, 4644, 5455
The University of Chicago Comer Children's Hospital, 5599
Touch of Nature Environmental Center, 7709
Tourette Syndrome Association of Illinois, 6488
Tourette Syndrome Camp Organization, 677, 4806, 6565
UCP Seguin of Greater Chicago, 1278
UIC Eye Center, 5546
United Cerebral Palsy Land of Lincoln, 1279
University of Chicago Children's Hospital, Department of Pediatrics, 2027
University of Chicago-Department of Psychi atry, 4739
University of Illinois at Chicago Institute for Tuberculosis Research, 6513, 6613
University of Illinois at Chicago, Craniofacial Center, 1890, 2181, 3055
Vitamin C Foundation, 5322

Indiana

ATTAIN: Assistive Technology Through Action in Indiana, 7199
About Special Kids (ASK), 7200
Allen County Public Library, 7459
Ann Whitehill Down Syndrome Program, 2418
Assistive Technology Training and Information Center, 7201, 7460
Autism Society of Indiana, 761
Bartholomew County Public Library, 7461
Brain Injury Association of Indiana, 3020
Camp About Face, 1895
Camp Brave Eagle, 7677
Camp Isanogel, 7710
Camp Millhouse, 7711
Central Indiana Sarcoidosis Support Group, 5629
Central Indiana Support Group, 498
Children's Tumor Foundation - Indiana Affi liate, 4468
Cystic Fibrosis and Chronic Pulmonary Disease Clinic, 2028
Division of Exceptional Learners Indiana Department of Education, 7202
Down Syndrome Association of Central Indiana, 7203
Down Syndrome Association of NWI, 2401
Down Syndrome Support Association of Southern Indiana (DSSASI), 2402
Easter Seal Society, 7712
Elkhart Public Library, 7462
Family Resource Center of Southeast Indiana, 7204
First Direction, 7205
First Steps for Families, 7206
First Steps, Early Interventions, New Horizons Rehabilitation, 7207
Future Choices, 7208
Happiness Bag Incorporated, 7713
Happy Hollow Children's Camp, 7714
Hemophilia Foundation of Indiana, 3532
Indiana Chapter of Crohn's & Colitis Found ation of America, 1916
Indiana Deaf Camp, 3491
Indiana Hemophilia and Thrombosis Center, 3585
Indiana Resource Center for Autism, 797
Indiana State Dept. of Health Immunization, 5276
John Warvel, 2353
Kiwanis Twin Lakes Camp, 7715
Knox County Advocates, 7209
Methodist Hospital Sleep Disorders Center, 4353
MidWest Medical Center - Sleep Disorders Center, 4354
NE Indiana Support Group, 499
NEO Fight, 7210
Northwest Indiana Subregional Library for Blind and Physically Handicapped, 1652, 1781, 4645, 5456
Our Hearts, 3848
Pediatric Ophathalmology and Adult Strabis mus Service Research, 1687
Prevent Child Abuse Indiana, 5039
Primary Brain Cancer Support Group, 1064
Project Special Care, 7211
Riley Cystic Fibrosis Center, 2029
Riley Hemophilia and Thrombophilia Center, 3559
SMA Support Inc, 6125
Sleep Disorder Center, St Elizabeth Medica l Center, 4355
Sleep Disorders Center-Good Samaritan Hospital, 4356
Sleep/Wake Disorders Center-Community Heal th Network, 4357
Special Services Division - Indiana State Library, 7463
Spina Bifida Association of Central Indian a, 6033
Tourette Syndrome Association of Indiana, 6489
United Cerebral Palsy of Greater Indiana, 1280
Worthmore Academy, 937, 4102

Iowa

Arc of East Central Iowa, 7213
Blank Children's Hospital: Department of P ulmonology, 2030
Brain Injury Association of Iowa, 3021
Camp Courageous, 7716
Camp Courageous of Iowa, 7717
Camp Tanager, 7718
Des Moines YMCA Camp, 122, 175, 471, 1172, 2132, 2347
Family & Educator Connection - Cedar Falls /Waterloo Region, 7214
Family & Educator Connection - Clear Lake/ Mason City Region, 7215
Family & Educator Connection - Marshalltow n Region, 7216
Hemophilia Treatment Center at the University of Iowa, 3581

Geographic Index

Iowa Department of Public Health Bureau of Immunization, 5277
Iowa Library for the Blind and Physically Handicapped, 1653, 1782, 4646, 5457
Iowa Program for Assistive Technology, 7217
Mercy Sleep Laboratory, 4399
PWSA of Iowa, 5186
Parent Educator Connection, 7218
Parent Educator Connection Program, 7219
Prevent Child Abuse Iowa, 5040
Spina Bifida Association of Iowa, 6035
The Link, 763
The University of Iowa Libraries, 5593
Turner's Syndrome Society of Iowa/New Found Friends, 6655
University of Iowa - Wendell Johnson Speech and Hearing Clinic, 3495, 6008, 6168
University of Iowa Birth Defects and Genetic Disorders Unit, 1611, 1654, 1732, 1741, 1783, 7555
University of Iowa Hospitals & Clinics, 2031

Kansas

Assistive Technology for Kansas Project, 7220
Autism Society of the Heartland, 764
Brain Injury Association of Kansas & Greater Kansas City, 3022
CKLS Headquarters, 1784
Camp Discovery American Diabetes Association, 2340
Cerebral Palsy Research Foundation, 1281
Department of Health & Environment, 7221
Families Together, 7222
Families Together/Parent to Parent of KS, 7223
Great Plains Region-Helen Keller National Center, 5425
Heart to Heart, 3844, 3862, 3864, 3866
Kansas Department of Health & Environment Bureau of Family Health, 6203
Kansas Department of Health & Environment Immunization Program, 5278
Kansas State Library, 7464
Kansas University Medical Center: Department of Pulmonology, 2032
Manhattan Public Library, 7465
Neurofibromatosis, Inc - Kansas & Central Plains, 4469
Prenatal Diagnostic and Genetic Center, 7466, 7545
Services for the Visually Disabled, 1656, 1785, 4648, 5459
Solution Outreach Center at OCCK, Inc., 7467
South Central Kansas Library System, 7468
Special Education Administration Kansas State Department of Education, 7224
University of Kansas Center for Research on Learning, 4068
Via Christi Specialty Clinics: Cystic Fibrosis, Adult and Pediatrics, 2033
Wesley Medical Research Institutes, 7469, 7557
Wichita Public Library, 7470

Kentucky

AbleData, 3147
Assistive Technology Services Network, 7225
Autism Society of America Bluegrass Chapter, 765
Bethel Mennonite Camp, 7719
Bluegrass Technology Center, 7471
Brain Injury Association of Kentucky, 3023
Brain Injury Support Group, 1065
College of Education - Western Kentucky University, 7226
Division of Preschool Services, 7227
Easter Seal Kysoc, 2349, 3488, 3938, 7720
EnTech: Enabling Technologies of Kentuckiana, 7472
Kentucky Chapter of Crohn's & Colitis Foundation of America, 1919
Kentucky Department of Human Resources Bureau of Health Services, 6204
Kentucky Hemophilia Foundation, 3533
Kentucky Library for the Blind and Physically Handicapped, 1657, 1786, 4649, 5460
Life Adventure Center, 1604, 6844
Louisville Talking Book Library, 7473
Northern Kentucky Talking Book Library, 7474
PWSA of Kentucky, 5188
Special Parent Involvement Network, 7228
Spina Bifida Association of Kentucky, 6036
Turner's Syndrome Society of Kentucky, 6656
University of Kentucky: Pediatric Pulmonary Medicine, 2034
Western Kentucky Assistive Technology Consortium, 7475

Louisiana

Autism Society of Louisiana, 766
Brain Injury Association of Louisiana, 3024
Brain Injury Support And Education Group, 1066
Brain Injury Support Group, 1067
Camp Bon Coeur, 7721
Division of Special Populations, 7229
Families Helping Families of Greater New Orleans, 7230
LA Lions Camp Pelican, 2133
Louisiana Assistive Technology Access Network, 7231
Louisiana Chapter, 500
Louisiana Comprehensive Hemophilia Care Center, 3587
Louisiana Lions Camp for Crippled Children, 7722
Louisiana State Library, 7476
Louisiana State University Genetics Section of Pediatrics, 7477, 7542
Louisiana State University Health Sciences Center, 2035
Louisiana Support Group, 501
Louisiana/Mississippi Chapter of Crohn's & Colitis Foundation of America, 1920
Louisiana/Mississippi Chapter of Crohn's & Colitis Foundation of America, 1925
Med-Camps of Louisiana, 7723
NE Louisiana Sickle Cell Anemia Foundation, 5847
Preschool Programs - Division of Special Populations, 7232
Project PROMPT, 7233
Public Health Services of Louisiana, 6205
Spina Bifida Association of Greater New Orleans, 6037
Tlane Cancer Center, 1068
Tulane University Clinical Immunology Section, 426
Tulane University, US-Japan Biomedical Research Laboratories, 3059
Turner's Syndrome Society of Gulf Coast, 6657
United Cerebral Palsy of Baton Rouge McMains Children's Developmental Center, 1282
United Cerebral Palsy of Greater New Orleans, 1283

Maine

Autism Society of Maine, 767
Bangor Public Library, 7478
CDC Lincoln County, 7234
Camp Waban, 7724
Cary Library, 7479
Central Maine Medical Center, 2036
Child Department Services, 7235
Child Department Services, Department of Education, 7236
Consumer Information and Technology Training Exchange (Maine CITE), 7237
Department of Human Services, 6206
Eastern Maine Medical Center: Cystic Fibrosis Center, 2037
Jackson Laboratory, 2899
Lewiston Public Library, 7480
Maine Dept. of Human Services: Bureau of Health Immunization Program, 5279
Maine Hemophilia and Thrombosis Center, 3588
Maine State Library, 7481
Maine Support, 502
Open Support Group-All Kinds of Cancer Care of Maine, 1069
Pediatric Cystic Fibrosis Center, 2038
Pine Tree Camp Children - Adults, 7725
Portland Public Library, 7483
Sleep Laboratory, Maine Medical Center, 4400

Geographic Index

Special Needs Parent Info Network, 7238
United Cerebral Palsy of Maine, 1284
University of Maine, Conley Speech and Hearing Center, 3162
Waterville Public Library, 7484
York County Parent Awareness, 7239

Maryland

American Action Fund for Blind Children and Adults, 1632
Arc Family Connection Parent to Parent Program, 7240
Autism Society of America Baltimore Chesapeake Chapter, 768
Bay Community Support Services, 1285
Behavioral and Developmental Pediatrics Division, University of Maryland, 2419
Brain Injury Association of Maryland, 3026
Center for Eating Disorders, 2585
Center for Infant & Child Loss, 6207
Chesapeake Chapter, 504
Dept. of Health & Mental Hygiene-Immunizat ion, 5280
Developmental Pediatrics School of Medicine, University of Maryland, 7241
Division of Extramural Research, 6233
East Central Region-Helen Keller National Center, 1627, 5430
Easter Seals Camp Fairlee Manor, 7726
Epilepsy Research Laboratory, Department o f Neurology, 5762
Hemophilia Foundation of Maryland, 3534
International Center for Skeletal Dysplasia Registry, 2677
John Hopkins Arthritis Center, 254, 3955, 4153
John Hopkins Children's Hospital, 2039
Johns Hopkins Brain Tumor Education Group, 1071
Johns Hopkins Department of Orthopaedics Surgery, 5722
Johns Hopkins Division of Allergy and Clin ical Immunology, 5598
Johns Hopkins University Sleep Disorders Center, 4358
Kamp-A-Kom-Plish, 7727
Kennedy Krieger Institute, 4233
Kennedy Krieger Institute, Down Syndrome Clinic, 2420
Learning Independence Through Computers, 7485
MD Infant/Toddler/Preschool Services Division, 7242
Maryland Infant and Toddlers Program Family Support Network, 7243
Maryland State Library for the Blind and Physically Handicapped, 1658, 1787, 4650, 5461
Maryland/South Delaware Chapter of Crohn's & Colitis Foundation of America, 1921
NAD Youth Leadership Camp, 3493
NIH/ Eunice Kennedy Shriver National Insti tute of Child Health & Human Development, 5224
NIH/National Institute of Mental Health Eating Disorders Program, 5225
NIH/National Library of Medicine (NLM), 10
NIH/Osteoporosis and Related Bone Diseases National Resource Center, 4850
National Diabetes Information Clearinghouse, 2294
National Digestive Diseases Information Clearinghouse (NDDIC), 32, 268, 1556, 1731, 1949, 1999
National Rehabilitation Information Center, 1320, 2752
Neurofibromatosis, Inc - MidAtlantic, 4470
Parents Place of Maryland, 7244
Parents of Children with Down Syndrome Arc of Montgomery County, 2403
Partners in Intensive Care, 7245
Patient Recruitment & Public Liaison Office Clinical Center, 6852
Prince George's County Memorial Library Talking Book Center, 1659, 1788, 4651, 5462
Raven Rock Lutheran Camp, 3940
Sarcoidosis Awareness Network, 5630
Sickle Cell Disease Association of America - Connecticut Chapter, 5845
Sickle Cell Disease Association of the Piedmont, 5851
Spina Bifida Association of Chesapeake-Pot omac, 6038
Spinal Muscular Atrophy Project, 6130
Technology Assistance Program Maryland Rehabilitation Center, 7246
The League at Camp Greentop and The Therapeutic Recreation, 7728
Tourette Syndrome Association of Greater Washington, 6491
Turner's Syndrome Society of Maryland, 6658
Turner's Syndrome Society of National Capitol Area, 6681
Unified Community Connections, 1286
University of Maryland Medical Center, 4401

Massachusetts

Arc of Massachusetts, 7247
Association of Gastrointestinal Motility Disorders, 2600
Asthma & Allergy Foundation of America New England Chapter, 416
Autism Research Foundation, 805
Autism Society of America Massachusetts Chapter, 769
Baystate Medical Center, 2040
Berkshire Center, 4066
Boston Children's Hospital Dept. of Otolaryngology & Communication, 3168
Boston Hemophilia Center, 3563
Braille and Talking Book Library Perkins School for the Blind, 1660, 1789, 4652, 5463
Brain Center Brain Tumor Support Group, 1072
Brain Injury Association of Massachusetts, 3027
Brain Tumor Support Group, 1073
Brain Tumor Support Group at Burlington, 1074
Brain Tumor Support Group at Worcester, 1075
Brain Tumor Survivor Support Group, 1076
Brigham and Women's Hospital, Asthma and Allergic Disease Research Center, 422
Bureau of Early Childhood Programs, 7248
Bureau of Family Health Services-Alabama Child Death Review, 6191
CKLS Headquarters, 1655, 4647, 5458
Camp Joslin, 2342
Camp Ramah in New England (Summer), 7730
Camp Ramah in New England (Winter), 7731
Camp Ramah in New England Tikvah Program, 923, 1363, 5832, 7729
Carroll Center for the Blind, 1790, 4067, 4653, 5464
Carroll School Summer Programs, 7732
Center for Digestive Disorders, 6707
Center for Interdisciplinary Research on Immunologic Diseases, 423
Children's Happiness Foundation, 7249
Children's Hospital Boston, 2041
Clara Barton Camp, 2346
Community Sickle Cell Support Group, 5848
Developmental Medicine Center, 2964
Down Syndrome Program, Children's Hospital Boston, 2421
Eagle Hill School - Summer Program, 671, 927, 4090
Early Intervention Services, 7250
Eaton-Peabody Laboratory of Auditory Physiology, 3163
Education Development Center - EDC, 7251
Family Ties at Massachusetts Department of Public Health, 7252
Federation for Children with Special Needs, 7253
Handi-Kids/King Solomon Foundation, 7733
Hard of Hearing Advocates, 3151
Harold Goodglass Aphasia Research Center, 3060
Heart to Heart Fund, 3849
Hemophilia Center of the New England Medical Center, 3580
Joslin Diabetes Center, 2296
Kingsmont, 4758
Landmark School, 2518
Massachusetts Assistive Technology Partnership, 7254
Massachusetts Association for Parents of t he Visually Impaired (MAPVI), 5564
Massachusetts Down Syndrome Congress (MDSC), 2404
Massachusetts Easter Seals Camping Program, 7734
Massachusetts Eating Disorder Association (MEDA), 2586
Massachusetts General Hospital, 2042
Massachusetts Sudden Infant Death Syndrome, 6234
National Birth Defects Center, 7255
National Temporal Bone, Hearing and Balanc e Pathology Resource Registry, 3170
New England Chapter of Crohn's & Colitis Foundation of America, 1922
New England Region-Helen Keller National Center, 5427
New England Regional Genetics Group, 503, 7482, 7543
New England Support Group, 505

Geographic Index

Parent Education/Support Group, 1077
Pediatric Clinical Trials International, 2430
Pediatric Pulmonary Unit, 6236
Prader-Willi Association of New England (Maine, Mass, RI, NH, VT), 5189, 5190
Region I Office Program Consultants For Maternal and Child Health, 6208
Resources for Rehabilitation, 7486
Sleep Disorders Center, 5890
Sleep Disorders Unit, Beth Israel Hospital, 4359
Spina Bifida Association of Massachusetts, 6039
Talking Book Library at Worcester Public Library, 7487
Tourette Syndrome Association of Massachusetts, 6492
Tufts New England Medical Center Floating Hospital for Children, 2043
Turner's Syndrome Society of New England, 6659
United Cerebral Palsy of Berkshire County, 1287
United Cerebral Palsy of MetroBoston, 1288
Worcester Public Library, 7488

Michigan

Adventure Learning Center Camp Programs, 1603, 6843
Apnea Identification Program, 6209
Autism Society of Michigan, 770
Big Crystal Camp, 915
Bioengineering Center of Wayne State University, 3061
Brain Tumor Networking Club, 1078
Brain Tumor Support Group at Ann Arbor, 1080
Brain Tumor Support Group for Patients & Families: University of Michigan Med Ctr, 1081
Burger School for the Autistic, 798
Butterworth Hospital, Cystic Fibrosis Center, 2044
CAUSE, 7256
Camp Barakel, 7735
Camp Catch-A-Rainbow, 119, 172, 1169, 2797, 6880
Camp Fish Tales, 7736
Camp O' Fair Winds, 4087
Camp Tushmehata, 1717
Center for Sleep Science at University of Michigan, 4360
Central Michigan University Summer Clinics, 3485, 6006
Children's Hospital of Michigan Cystic Fibrosis Care, Teaching & Resource, 2045
Cystic Fibrosis Center/Pediatric Pulmonary and Sleep Medicine, 2046
Detroit Michigian Ataxia Support Group, 506
Downtown Detroit Subregional Library for the Blind and Handicapped, 1661, 1791, 4654, 5465
Early on Michigan, 7257
Eastern Michigan Hemophilia Center, 3572
Eric RicStar Winter Music Therapy Summer Camp, 1368, 7737
Families at Heart, 3850
Family Support Network of Michigan Parent Participation Program-MDCH, 7258
Frederick Douglas Branch for Specialized Services and Physically Handicapped, 7489
Genesee County Health Department, 6210
Glaucoma Laser Trabeculoplasty Study, 1816
Hemophilia Foundation of Michigan, 3535
Indian Trails Camp, 7738
Kalamazoo Center for Medical Studies, 2047
Kalamazoo Comprehensive Hemophilia Treatment Center, 3586
Kent County Health Department, 6211
Kent County Library for the Blind, 1662, 1792, 4655, 5466
Library of Michigan Service for the Blind, 1663, 4656, 5467
Livingston County CMH Services, 7259
Macomb Library for the Blind and Physically Handicapped, 1664, 1793, 4657, 5468
Michigan Chapter of Allergy and Asthma Foundation of America, 417
Michigan Chapter of Crohn's & Colitis Foundation of America, 1923
Michigan State University Comprehensive Center for Bleeding Disorders, 3591
Mideastern Michigan Library Co-op, 1665, 1794, 4658, 5469
Muskegon County Library for the Blind, 1666, 1795, 4659, 5470

Northern Regional Bleeding Disorder Center, 3594
Parents are Experts, 7261
Regional Hemophilia Program, 3600
Rehabilitation Institute of Michigan, 3028, 3062
SW Michican Spina Bifida & Hydrocephalus Association, 3775
Sarcoidosis Awareness Foundation, 5631
Seeking Techniques Advancing Research in Shunts (STARS), 3783
Spectrum Brain Tumor Support Group, 1082
Spectrum Health Research, 3606
Spina Bifida Association of Upper Peninsula Michigan, 6040
Spina Bifida Association of West Michigan, 6041
TECH 2000 Project-Michigan Disability Rights Coalition, 7262
Turner's Syndrome Society of Southeastern Michigan, 6660
Turner's Syndrome Society of West Michigan, 6661
United Cerebral Palsy Detroit, 1289
United Cerebral Palsy Michigan, 1290
University Center for the Development of L anguage & Literacy, 5988
University of Michigan Adult Hemophilia and Cougulation Disorders Program, 3614
University of Michigan, Cystic Fibrosis Center, 2048
University of Michigan, Kresge Hearing Research Institute, 3171
Upper Peninsula Library for the Blind Physically Handicapped, 1667, 1796, 4660, 5471
Washtenaw County Library, 1668, 1797, 4661, 5472
Washtenaw County Library for the Blind and Physically Disabled, 1669, 1798, 4662, 5473
West Michigan Cancer Center Support Group, 1083

Minnesota

Abbott Northwestern Brain Tumor Support Group at Abbott Northwestern Hospital, 1084
Arc Suburban, 7263
Autism Society of America Manasota Chapter, 754
Autism Society of Minnesota, 771
Brain Injury Association of Minnesota, 3029
Brain Injury Support Group at Abbott Northwestern Hospital, 1085
Brain Tumor Support Group at Duluth, 1086
Brain Tumor Support Group at Robbinside, 1087
Brain Tumor Support Group at United Hospital, 1088
Camp Buckskin, 667, 916, 4084
Camp Friendship, 917, 2481, 7739
Camp New Hope, 921, 2485, 7740
Camp Winnebago, 7741
Center for Sleep Diagnostics, 4361
Children's Cancer Research Fund, 6870
Courage Camps, 7742
Courage North, 7743
Department of Children, Family, & Learning, 7264
Down Syndrome Association of Minnesota, 2405
Down Syndrome Clinic of Minneapolis Children's Medical Center, 2422
Eden Wood Center, 2487, 6860, 7744
Family to Family Network ARC of Hennepin County, 7265
Groves Academy, 672, 928, 4091
Hemophilia Foundation of Minnesota and the Dakotas, 3536
Hemophilia and Thrombosis Center at the University of Minnesota Medical Center, 3583
Interagency Early Intervention Project, 7266
Knutson, 7745
Mayo Clinic and Foundation, 4293
Minneapolis, MN Support Group, 507
Minnesota Cystic Fibrosis Center, 2049
Minnesota Library for the Blind & Physically Handicapped, 4663, 5474
Minnesota Sudden Infant Death Center, 6212
Minnesota/Dakotas Chapter of Crohn's & Colitis Foundation of America, 1924
Non-Malignant Brain Tumor Support Group, 1089
PACER Center, 7490
Parents For Heart of Minnesota, 3851
Parents for Parents, 7267
Pilot Parents in Anoka and Ramsey Counties, 7268
Pilot Parents of Northeast Minnesota, 7269

Geographic Index

Search Beyond Adventures, 7746
Spina Bifida Association of Minnesota, 6042
Star Center for Family Health, 7491
Tourette Syndrome Association - Minnesota Chapter, 6493
Turner's Syndrome Society of Minnesota, 6662
United Cerebral Palsy of Central Minnesota, 1291
United Cerebral Palsy of Minnesota, 1292
Vinland Center, 7270
Voyageur Outward Bound School, 7271
Wilderness Inquiry, 7272

Mississippi

Autism Society of Mississippi, 772
Brain Injury Association of Mississippi, 3030
First Steps Program, 7273
Mississippi Chapter, 508
Mississippi Dept. of Health Bureau of Preventative Health Immunization, 5281
Mississippi Hemophilia Foundation, 3537
Mississippi State Department of Health and Child Health Services, 6213
Office of Special Education, 7260, 7274
Parent Partners, 7275
Project Start, 7276
Spina Bifida Association of Mississippi, 6043
Tik-A-Witha, 7747
University of Mississippi Medical Center, 2050, 2182

Missouri

AMOR - A Cancer Support Group for Patients & Their Families, 1090
Adriene Resource Center for Blind Children, 1670, 1799, 4664, 5475
Allergy and Pulmonary Medicine, 418
Assemblies of God National Center for the Blind, 1671, 1800, 4665, 5476
Assistance Technology Project, 7277
Asthma and Allergy Foundation of America St Louis Chapter, 419
Autism Society of America Gateway Chapter, 773
Brain Cancer Support Group at Mid-America Cancer Center, 1091
Brain Injury Association of Missouri, 3031
Brain Tumor Support Group, 1079, 1092
Brain Tumor Support Group of Greater St Louis, 1093
Central Institute for the Deaf, 3172
Central Missouri Area Support Group, 509
Children's Mercy Hospital, Down Syndrome Clinic, 2423
Children's Mercy Hospital, University of Missouri, 2051
Children's Therapy Center, 7278
Cystic Fibrosis, Pediatric Pulmonary and Pediatric Gastrointestinal Center, 2052
Department of Elementary and Secondary Education, 7279
Down's Syndrome Medical Clinic, 2424
EDI, 2348
Family Resource Network, 7281
Heart to Heart - St. Louis, 3852
Hickory Hill, 2352
Judevine Center for Autism, 799
Kansas City, Missouri Support Group, 510
Mid-America Chapter of Crohn's & Colitis Foundation of America, 1918
Missouri Parents Act, 7282
Parent Act, 7283
Pediatric Epilepsy Center, 5763
People First of Missouri, 3927
Positive Solutions for Life Challenges, 7284
Prader-Willi Syndrome Advocates, 5187
Region VII Office Program Consultants for Maternal and Child Health, 6214
Saint Louis Chapter of Crohn's & Colitis Foundation of America, 1926
Sidney R. Baer Day Camp, 7748
Spina Bifida Association of Greater Saint Louis, 6044
Springfield Area Support Group, 511
Tourette Syndrome Association - Greater Missouri Chapter, 6494
Turner's Syndrome Society of St. Louis/ West Illinois, 6663
United Cerebral Palsy Heartland, 1293
United Cerebral Palsy of Northwest Missouri, 1294
United Services, 7285
University of Missouri-Columbia Cystic Fibrosis Center, 2053
Washington University Cystic Fibrosis Center, 2054
Whitney Library for the Blind, 7493
Wolfner Memorial Library for the Blind, 4666, 5477

Montana

Big Sky Kids Cancer Camp, 118
Brain Injury Association of Montana, 3032
CO-TEACH/Division of Educational Research and Service, 7286
Charles Campbell Children's Camp, 1365
Developmental Disabilities Program, 7287
Division of Special Education, 7288
MonTECH, 7289
Montana Department of Health & Environmental Sciences, 6215
Montana State Library, 7494
Parents Let's Unite for Kids, 7290
Quality Life Concepts, 7291

Nebraska

Assistive Technology Partnership, 7292
Autism Society of Nebraska, 774
Boys Town National Research Hospital, 5989
Brain Tumor Support Group at the Nebraska Medical Center, 1094
Camp Easter Seals, 7749
Camp Kindle, 2992
Floyd Rogers, 2351
Individual and Family Support Arc of Lincoln & Lancaster County, 7293
Iowa Chapter of Crohn's Colitis Foundation of America, 1917
Junior Wheelchair Sports Camp, 7699
Lied Learning and Technology Center for Childhood Deafness and Vision Disorders, 3173
National Camps for Blind Children, 1721, 1857, 4710, 5521
Nebraska Chapter of the National Hemophilia Foundation, 3538
Nebraska Dept. of Health Immunization Program, 5282
Nebraska Library Commission Talking Book & Braille Services, 1672, 1801, 4667, 5478
Nebraska Regional Hemophilia Center, 3592
North Platte Public Library, 7495
PTI Nebraska (Parent, Training & Information, 7294
Parent Assistance Network, 7295
Parent Support Group, 7296
Spina Bifida Association of Nebraska, 6045
United Cerebral Palsy of Nebraska, 1295
University of Nebraska at Omaha Pediatric Pulmonary/Cystic Fibrosis Center, 2055
University of Nebraska, Lincoln Barkley Memorial Center, 3164

Nevada

American Academy of Somnology, 4531, 4552, 5889, 5915
Assistive Technology Collaborative, 7298
Autism Society of Northern Nevada Chapter, 775
Camp Lotsafun, 919
Children's Lung Specialists, 2056
Early Intervention Services Division of Child & Family Services, 7299
Educational Equity, Special Education Branch, 7300
Hemophilia and Thrombosis Center of Nevada, 3584
Las Vegas-Clark County Library District, 7496
Nevada Parent Network, 7301
Nevada Parents Encouraging Parents (PEP), 7302
Nevada State Division of Health, Maternal & Child Health, 6216
Nevada State Health Division Bureau of Community Health - Immunization Program, 5283
Nevada State Library and Archives, 7497

Geographic Index

Parents Encouraging Parents, 7297, 7303
Southern Nevada 'Grey Matters' Valley Hospital Medical Center, 1095
University of Nevada - Department of Speech-Language Pathology, 5990

New Hampshire

Angels of Hope, 1096
Autism Society of New Hampshire, 776
Brain Injury Association of Maine, 3025
Brain Injury Association of New Hampshire, 3033
Bureau of Early Learning, 7304
Camp Allen, 7750
Camp Dartmouth-Hitchcock, 7751
Crotched Mountain School & Rehabilitation Center, 924, 1366, 3097, 3937, 5834, 7679
Dartmouth-Hitchcock Sleep Disorders Center Dartmouth Medical Center, 4362, 7305
Division of Special Education, 7306
Families with Heart, 3853
Hemophilia and Coagulation Programs, 3582
High Hopes Foundation of New Hampshire, 7307
Medical Genetics Clinic, 2425
NH Dept. of Health & Human Services Immunization Program, 5284
New England Retinoblastoma Support Group (NERSG), 5565
New Hampshire Cystic Fibrosis Care and Teaching Center, 2057
New Hampshire State Library, 7498
Parent Information Center, 7308
Parent to Parent of New Hampshire, 7309
Sleep/Wake Disorders Center, Hampstead Hospital, 4363
Technology Partnership Project Institute on Disability/UAP, 7310
Turner's Syndrome Society of Northern New England, 6665
Windsor Mountain Camp, 3496

New Jersey

Bancroft Camp, 7753
Blood Research Institute of Saint Michael's Medical Center, 3562
Brain Injury Association of New Jersey, 3034
Brain Tumor Support Group at Plainfield Muhlenberg Medical Center, Neuroscience, 1098
CRI Worldwide Pediatric Center for Excellence, 1557
Camp Chatterbox, 7754
Camp Oakhurst, 6113, 7755
Camp Sun 'N Fun, 7759
Camp Vacamas, 470, 5882
Center for Enabling Technology, 7499
Cerebral Palsy Center Summer Program, 1364
Cross Roads Outdoor Ministries, 7756
Division of Student Services, 7311
Early Intervention System, 7312
Eating Disorders Association of New Jersey, 2587
Family Support Center of New Jersey, 7313
Hydrocephalus Group - Children's Hospital of New Jersey, 3776
Monmouth Medical Center, Cystic Fibrosis & Pediatric Pulmonary Center, 2058
New Image Camps, 4759
New Jersey Camp Jaycee, 3939
New Jersey Chapter of Crohn's & Colitis Foundation of America, 1927
New Jersey Department of Health - Child Health Program, 6217
New Jersey Department of Health Immunizations Program, 5285
New Jersey Institute of Technology Center for Biomedical Engineering, 2900
New Jersey Medical School, 2059
New Jersey Self-Help Clearinghouse, 7314
New Jersey State Library Talking Book and Braille Center, 1673, 1802, 4668, 5479
New Jersey Statewide Parent to Parent, 7315
Newark Sleep Disorders Center, 4364
Renfrew Center of Northern New Jersey, 2588
Round Lake Camp, 676, 933
Scleroderma Foundation New Jersey Chapter, 5694
Spina Bifida Association of the Tri-State Region, 6046
Statewide Parent Advocacy Network, 7316
Tourette Syndrome Association of New Jersey, 6497
Turner's Syndrome Society of New Jersey, 6666
US Rowing Assocation, 7212
United Cerebral Palsy Research and Educational Foundation, 1322
United Cerebral Palsy of Hudson County, 1296
Young Hearts, 3854

New Mexico

Brain Injury Association of New Mexico, 3035
Computer Access Center, 7535
EPICS Project-SW Communication Resources, 7317
Long Term Services Division, 7318
NM Alliance for the Neurologically Impaired, 1099
New Mexico Autism Society, 777
New Mexico Department of Health Immunization Program, 5286
New Mexico State Library for the Blind and Physically Handicapped, 1674, 1803, 4669, 5480
Parents Reaching Out, 7319
People Living Through Cancer, 1100
Region 5 of the National Association for Parents of the Visually Impaired, 5428
Santa Fe Mountain Center, 7757
Sickle Cell Council of New Mexico, Inc., 5849
Special Education Unit, 7320
Technology Assistance Program, 7321
Ted R. Montoya Hemophilia Program, 3608
University of New Mexico School of Medicine, 2060

New York

ADAPT Community Network, 1297
Advocacy Center, 7322
Advocates for Children of New York, 7323, 7758
Albany Medical College Pediatric Pulmonary & Cystic Fibrosis Center, 2061
Albany New York Regional Comprehensive Hemophilia Treatment Center, 3561
Arc of New York, 3923
Arlene R Gordon Research Institute, 5491
Armond V. Mascia CF Center, 2062
Aspire of WNY, 1298
Association for Research of Childhood Cancer, 7533
Aurora of Central New York, 7324
Autism Speaks, 806
Big Hearts for Little Hearts, 3855
Bleeding Disorders Association of Northeastern New York, 3539
Brady Institute for Traumatic Brain Injury, 3063
Brain & Behavior Research Foundation, 4778
Brain Injury Association of New York State, 3036
Brain Tumor Support Group, 1097, 1101
Brain Tumor Support Group at South Nassau Community Hospital, 1102
Bronx Comprehensive Sickle Cell Center, 5863
Brooklyn College Speech and Hearing Center, 5976
CF & Pediatric Pulmonary Care Center, 2063
CF, Pediatric Pulmonary & GI Center, 2064
CMTA Chapter - New York (Greater), 1371
Camp Dunnabeck at Kildonan, 2517
Camp Good Days & Special Times, 5881
Camp Huntington, 2483, 3936, 4085
Camp Northwood, 383
Camp Shane, 4754
Capital Regional Sleep-Wake Disorders Center, 4365
Cardiac Kids, 3856
Cardiovascular Research Foundation, 315
Center for Disability Services, 1299
Center for Family Support, 778, 988, 1435, 2406, 3924, 4530
Center for Hearing and Communication, 3148

991

Geographic Index

Center for Neural Recovery & Rehabilitatio n Research, 5764
Center for Sleep Medicine of the Mount Sinai Medical Center, 4366
Center for the Study of Anorexia and Bulimia, 2604
Central New York Chapter of Crohn's & Colitis Foundation of America, 1929
Cerebral Palsy Associations of New York State, 1300
Cerebral Palsy of Nassau County, 1301
Child Abuse Prevention Project: Be'ad HaYeled (For the Sake of the Child), 5041
Child Development Clinical Services, 2426
Children's Clinical Research Center, 2963
Children's Lung and Cystic Fibrosis Center, 2065
Chrissy & Friends, 5754
Columbia Presbyterian Medical Center, 4294
Columbia Presbyterian Medical Center Sleep Disorders Center, 4367
Crohn's & Colitis Foundation, 1950
Dana Alliance for Brain Initiatives, 3064
Depressive and Manic-Depressive Assocation of Mount Sinai, 989, 2217
EPIC Long Island, 5755
Early Intervention Program, 7325
East Central Region-Helen Keller National Center, 1755, 4619
Epilepsy Foundation of Metropolitan New York, 5756
Facilitated Communication Institute at Syracuse University, 808
Fairfield/Westchester Chapter of Crohn's & Colitis Foundation of America, 1911, 1930
Families of SMA - Long Island NY Chapter, 6126
Freedom Camp, 7760
Friends for Life Auburn United Methodist Church, 7081
Friends of Karen, 7326
Genetic Network of the Empire State, 512
Gow School Summer Programs, 7761
Greater New York Chapter of Crohn's & Colitis Foundation of America, 1931
Helping Hearts, 3857
Hemophilia Center of Western New York, 3540, 3578
Henry Youngerman Center for Communication Disorders, 5991
Hy Feinstein Clubhouse, 3037
Hypertrophic Cardiomyopathy Program at St. Luke's-Roosevelt Hospital Center, 3829
Inspire - Cerebral Palsy Center, 1302
Institute for Basic Research in Developmental Disabilities, 800, 7500, 7540
Institute on Communication and Inclusion, 809
International Pemphigus Foundation: New Yo rk Support Group, 4918
JGB Cassette Library International, 7501
Keren-Or Jerusalem Center for Multi- Handicapped Blind Children, 7502, 7541
Laboratory of Dermatology Research, 1402, 2694, 5004
Leukemia & Lymphoma Society - Western & Central New York Chapter, 143
Long Island Adult Brain Tumor Support Group, 1103
Long Island Chapter of Crohn's & Colitis Foundation of America, 1932
Long Island College Hospital, 2066
Lupus Research Institute, 6292
Making Headway Foundation-Family Support Program, 1104
Maplebrook School, 675, 932, 4094
Marist Brothers Mid-Hudson Valley Camp Marist Brothers, 7762
Marty Lyons Foundation, 7327
Mary M Gooley Hemophilia Center of the National Hemophilia Foundation, 3541
Metro Intergroup of Overeaters Anonymous, 2589
Montifiore Medical Center, 3174
Mount Sinai Traumatic Brain Injury, 3038
NYU Rusk Institute, 4295
Nassau Library System, 7503
National Alliance for Research on Schizophrenia and Depression, 1436
National Eating Disorder Association of Lo ng Island (NEDA-LI), 2602
National Eating Disorders Association-Long Island (NEDA-LI), 2590
New York Autism Network, 779
New York Brain Tumor Support Group, 1105
New York City Area Support Group, 513
New York City Information & Counseling Program for SIDS, 6218
New York Department of Education, 7328
New York Obesity Research Center, 2606, 4738
New York State Department of Health Immunization Program, 5287
New York State Talking Book & Braille Library, 1675, 1804, 4670, 5481
New York Support Group, 514
New York University Langone Medical Center Auxillary of Tisch Hospital, 3777
New York University Medical Center Auxillary of Tisch Hospital, 3782
Northwestern Region-Helen Keller National Center, 1757
Oakhurst, 7763
Overeaters Anonymous Support Group, 2591
Parent Network Center, 7329
Parent to Parent of New York State, 7330
Pediatric Pulmonary Center, 2067
People Treated for Brain Tumors and Their Caregivers, 1106
Prevent Child Abuse New York, 5042
Programs for Children with Special Health Care Needs, 7764
Programs for Infants and Toddlers with Disabilities: Ages Birth Through 2, 7765
Ramapo Anchorage Camp, 4097
Region II Office Program Consultants for Maternal and Child Health, 6219
Rehabilitation Research and Training Center on Traumatic Brain Injury, 3065
Renfrew Center of New York City, 2592
Research to Prevent Blindness, 1688, 1822, 4683, 5495
Resources for Children with Special Needs, 7331
Rochester Chapter of Crohn's & Colitis Foundation of America, 1933
Rockefeller University Laboratory for Investigative Dermatology, 1403, 2695, 5005
Rusk Institute of Rehabilitation Medicine, 4292, 7549
SLE Lupus Foundation, 6293
SUNY Upstate Medical University Research Development, 3603
Saint Joseph's Hospital Health Center Sleep Laboratory, 4368
Saint Mary's Healthcare System for Children, 7332
Schneider Children's Hospital of Long Island, 2068
Sinergia/Metropolitan Parent Center, 7333
Sleep Center, Community General Hospital, 4369
Sleep Disorders Center of Western New York Millard Fillmore Hospital, 4370
Sleep Disorders Center, University Hospital, 4371
Sleep-Wake Disorders Center, Montefiore Sleep Disorders Center, 4372
Sleep-Wake Disorders Center, New York Presbyterian Hospital, 4373
Spina Bifida Association of Albany/Capital District, 6047
Spina Bifida Association of Greater Roches ter, 6048
Spina Bifida Association of Nassau County, 6049
Spina Bifida Association of Western New York, 6050
Spinal Muscular Atrophy Clinic, 6129
State University College at Plattsburgh Auditory Research Laboratory, 3175
State University Hospital/Upstate Medical University, 2069
State University of New York Health Sciences Center, 801, 810
Stroke Rehabilitation & Traumatic Brain Injury Research, 3066
Support for Parents of Children with Brain Tumors, Siblings and Young Adults, 1107
Syracuse University, Institute for Sensory Research, 3176
TRIAD Project-Advocates for Persons with Disabilities, 7334
Techspress Resource Center for Independent Living, 7504
Tourette Syndrome Association - Greater New York State Chapter, 6500
Tourette Syndrome Association - Greater Rochester and Finger Lakes Area, 6499
Tourette Syndrome Association - Hudson Valley Chapter, 6501
Tourette Syndrome Association - Long Island Chapter, 6502
Tourette Syndrome Association - New Mexico Chapter, 6498
Tri-State Support Group, 515
Turner's Syndrome Society of Central New York, 6667
Turner's Syndrome Society of Upstate New York, 6668
UCP of Long Island, 1303
Ulster County Social Services, 7335
United Health Services Blood Disorder Center, 3612
Unity Sleep Disorders Clinic Unity Health System, 4374
University of Rochester Medical Center, 2070

Geographic Index

Upstate/Northeast New York Chapter of Crohn's & Colitis Foundation of America, 1934
VISIONS/Vacation Camp for the Blind, 1723, 1859, 4711, 5522
WNY Brain Tumor Support Group, 1108
Wallace Memorial Library, 3165
Westchester Center for Eating Disorders, 2593
Western New York Chapter of Crohn's & Colitis Foundation of America, 1935
Winthrop-University Hospital Sleep Disorders Center, 4375

North Carolina

Assistive Technology Project, Human Resources, Voc. and Rehab. Services, 7336
Autism Society of North Carolina, 780, 802
Brain Injury Association of North Carolina, 3039
Brain Tumor Support Group of the Carolinas and Virginia Cancer Services, 1109
Camp Shining Stars, 4757
Camp Winding Gap, 7767
Carolinas Chapter of Crohn's & Colitis Foundation of America, 1936
Communications Disorders Clinic, 5992
Duke Brain Tumor Support Group, 1110
Duke Pediatric Brain Tumor Family Support Program, 1111
Duke University Comprehensive Epilepsy Center, 5765
Duke University Comprehensive Sickle Cell Center, 5864
Duke University Medical Center/ CF Center, 2071
Duke University School of Medicine Pediatric and Allergy Immunology, 5597
ECAC NC PTI, 7337
Eastern North Carolina Chapter (SCDAA), 5850
Exceptional Children Division, 7338
Family Support Network of North Carolina, 7339
Giddings School Special Education Division, 7161
Hemophila Foundation of North Carolina, 3542
Leukemia & Lymphoma Society - North Carolina Chapter, 83, 144
Lipomyelomeningocele Family Support, 3778
North Carolina Library for the Blind, 1805, 4671, 5482
North Carolina Speech, Hearing and Language Association, 5977
PWSA of North Carolina, 5195
Partnerships for Inclusion, 7340
Pediatric Rheumatoid Clinic, 3956
Prevent Child Abuse North Carolina, 5043
Rockingham County Schools, 7341
Sickle Cell Regional Network, 5852
South Carolina Chapter of Crohn's & Colitis Foundation of America, 1943
Spina Bifida Association of North Carolina, 6051
Talisman Programs, 7768
Talisman Summer Camps, 1605, 6845
Turner's Syndrome Society of North Carolina, 6669
UNC CF Center, 2072
University of North Carolina Sarcoidosis Support Group, 5632
University of North Carolina at Chapel Hill, Brain Research Center, 811
Western North Carolina Brain Tumor Support Group, 1112

North Dakota

Brain Injury Association of North Dakota, 3040
Children's Hospital Merit Care Down Syndrome Service, 2427
Developmental Disabilities Unit, 7342
Interagency Program Assistive Technology, 7343
North Dakota Comprehensive Hemophilia and Thrombosis Treatment Center, 3593
Saint Alexius Medical Center/CF Center, 2073
Special Education Division, 7344

Ohio

American Council of Blind Parents, 1676, 1806, 4672, 5483
Autism Society of Greater Cincinnatti, 781
Autism Society of Ohio Tri-County Chapter, 782
Beech Brook, 914, 4083
Bethesda Oak Hospital, Sleep Disorders Center, 4376
Blick Clinic for Developmental Disabilities, 7505
Brain Injury Association of Ohio, 3041
Brain Tumor Support Group, 1113
Bureau of EI Services, 7345
CMTA Chapter - Ohio, 1372
Camp Allyn, 7769
Camp Catch-A-Rainbow, 4597
Camp Emanuel, 3481
Camp Nuhop, 668, 922, 4086
Cancer & Blood Diseases Institute, 3564
Case Western Research University, Bolton Brush Growth Study Center, 2898
Case Western Reserve University Cystic Fibrosis Center, 2074
Celebrating Families of Children & Adults with Special Needs, 7346
Center for Sleep & Wake Disorders, Miami Valley Hospital, 4377
Central Ohio Brain Tumor Support Group, 1114
Central Ohio Chapter of Crohn's & Colitis Foundation of America, 1937
Central Ohio Chapter of the National Hemophilia Foundation, 3543
Cincinnati Digestive Health Center, 1559
Cleveland Brain Tumor Patient Network - Adult and Pediatric, 1115
Cleveland Clinic, 3779
Cleveland Clinic Foundation, Sleep Disorders Center, 4378
Cleveland Hearing and Speech Center, 5978
Cleveland Public Library, 7506
Clinical Research Center, Pediatrics, 955
Columbus Children's Hospital, Cystic Fibrosis Center, 2075
Comprehensive Sickle Cell Center, 5865
Down Syndrome Clinic, Rainbow Babies and Children's Hospital, 2428
East Central Regional Office, 7347
Family Information Network, 7348
Fragile X Alliance of Ohio, 2848
Highbrook Lodge Camp, 1720, 1856, 7770
Jane and Richard Thomas Center for Down Syndrome, 2429
Kettering Medical Center, Sleep Disorders Center, 4379
Leukemia & Lymphoma Society - Central Ohio Chapter, 84, 145
Leukemia & Lymphoma Society - Northern Ohio Chapter, 85, 146
Leukemia & Lymphoma Society - Tri-State Southern Ohio Chapter, 86, 147
Lewis H. Walker, MD, Cystic Fibrosis Center, 2076
Miami Valley Downs Syndrome Association, 2407
NW Ohio Sleep Disorders Center, 4380
Northeast Ohio Chapter of Crohn's & Colitis Foundation of America, 1938
Northern Ohio Chapter of the National Hemophilia Foundation, 3544
Northwest Ohio Hemophilia Treatment Center, 3595
OCECD, 7349
Ohio Department of Health Immunization Program, 5288
Ohio Protection and Advocacy Organization, 7350
Ohio Regional Library for the Blind and Physically Handicapped, 7507
Ohio Sleep Medicine Institute, 4381
Ohio State University Hospitals, Sleep Disorders Center, 4382
Ohio State University Laboratory of Psychobiology, 3067
Ohio Support Group, 516
Operation Liftoff of Ohio, 7351
PWSA of Ohio, 5196
Pediatric Pulmonary Center, 2077
People First of Ohio, 3928
Prader-Willi Families of Ohio, 5197
Region 2 of the National Association for Parents of the Visually Impaired, 1754, 4618, 5429
Saint Vincent Medical Center, Sleep Disorders Center, 4383
Society for Rehabilitation, 7352
Southwest Ohio Brain Tumor Support Group, 1116
Southwest Ohio Chapter of Crohn's & Colitis Foundation of America, 1939
Southwestern Ohio Chapter of the National Hemophilia Foundation, 3545
Speech and Hearing Clinic, 5979
Spina Bifida Association of Canton, 6052

Geographic Index

Spina Bifida Association of Central Ohio, 6053
Spina Bifida Association of Cincinnati, 6054
Spina Bifida Association of Greater Dayton, 6055
Spina Bifida Association of North West Ohio, 6056
Spina Bifida Association of Tri-County Ohio, 6057
Support Group for Parents of Children with a Brain Tumor, 1117
Technology Resource Center, 7508
Tourette Syndrome Association of Ohio, 6504
Tourette Syndrome and Tic Disorder Clinic, 6511
Train-Ohio Super Computer Center, 7353
Tri-State Bleeding Disorders Chapter of the National Hemophilia Foundation, 3546
Tri-State Sleep Disorders Center Center for Research in Sleep Disorders, 4402
Turner's Syndrome Society of Southwestern Ohio, 6670
UCP Norwood Stepping Stones, 1304
United Cerebral Palsy of Greater Cleveland, 1305
University of Cincinnati Adult Hemophilia Program, 3613
University of Cincinnati College of Medicine/Division of Pediatrics, 2078
Visual Systems Research Group, 4024
West Central Ohio Hemophilia Center, 3619

Oklahoma

Ability Connection Oklahoma, 1306
Autism Society of Oklahoma, 783
Brain Injury Association of Oklahoma, 3042
Leukemia & Lymphoma Society - Oklahoma Chapter, 87, 148
Neuroscience Institute at Mercy Hospital, 4474
North Central Oklahoma Support Group, 517
Oklahoma ABLE Tech-Wellness Center, 7354
Oklahoma Brain Injury Camp, 3098
Oklahoma Chapter of Crohn's & Colitis Foundation of America, 1940
Oklahoma Library for the Blind & Physically Handicapped, 7509
Oklahoma State Department of Health - Maternal and Child Health Services, 6220
Oklahoma State Department of Health Immunization Division, 5289
Parents Reaching Out in Oklahoma, 7355
Special Education Office, 7356
Tulsa City-County Library System, 7510
Turner's Syndrome Society of Oklahoma, 6671
University of Oklahoma Cystic Fibrosis Center, 2079

Oregon

Autism Society of Oregon, 784
Bend Support Group, 1118
Brain Injury Association of Oregon, 3043
Brain Tumor Education & Support Group, 1119
Dangerous Decibels Oregon Health & Science University, 3150
Early Childhood CARES Program, 7357
Early Intervention Programs, 7358
Easter Seals Oregon Camping Program, 7771
Hemophilia Foundation of Oregon, 3547
Klamath Falls Support Group, 1120
Legacy Good Samaritan Hospital & Medical Center, 4471
Leukemia & Lymphoma Society - Oregon Chapter, 88, 149
Meadowood Springs Speech and Hearing Camp, 3492, 6007, 6167
Mt Hood Kiwanis Camp, 7772
Oregon Brain Injury Resource Network, 3044
Oregon Department of Education, 7359
Oregon Health Sciences Unit, 2080
Oregon Health Sciences University Research Center, 3177
Oregon Parent Training and Information Center, 7360
Oregon State Library, 7511
Oregon State Library, Talking Book and Braille Services, 1677, 1807, 4673, 5484
Pacific Northwest Regional Genetics Group, 518
Rainrock Treatment Center, 2594
Reading and Speech Clinic, 5981
Regional Resource Center on Deafness, 3166
Research and Training Center on Family Support and Children's Mental Health, 1579, 6783, 7548
Technology Access for Life Needs Project, 7361
United Cerebral Palsy Oregon, 1307
Willamette Valley Ataxia Support Group, 519

Pennsylvania

Alleghenies United Cerebral Palsy, 1308
Autism Society of America Greater Harrisburg Area Chapter, 785
Brain Tumor Support Group at Philadelphia, 1121
Brain Tumor Support Group at Pittsburgh, 1122
Briarwood Day Camp, 7773
Bureau of Special Education, 7362
CF Center at The Children's Hospital of Philadelphia, 2081
CMTA Chapter - Pennsylvania, 1373
Camelot For Children, 1123
Camp Achieve, 5830
Camp Frog, 5831
Camp Lee Mar, 7774
Camp PALS, 2486
Camp Yomeca Upper Perkiomen Valley YMCA, 7775
Cardeza Foundation Hemophilia Center, 3565
Central Pennsylvania Area Support Group, 520
Children's Hospital of Philadelphia Hemophilia Program, 3568
Children's Hospital of Pittsburgh General Clinical Research Center, 2431
Children's Seashore House, 2432
Community Medical Center, Sleep Disorders Clinic, 4384
Crozer-Chester Medical Center, 4385
Cystic Fibrosis Center at Polyclinic Medical Center, 2082
Delaware Valley Chapter of the National Hemophilia Foundation, 3548
Division of Early Intervention Services, 7363
Dr. Gertrude A. Barber National Institute, 2433
EFWCP Resource Library, 5759
Epilepsy Foundation Eastern Pennsylvania, 5757
Fontan Friends, 3859
Free Library of Philadelphia, 7512
Geisinger Wyoming Valley Medical Center, Sleep Disorders Center, 4386
Hemophilia Center of Western Pennsylvania, 3579
Institutes for Achievement of Human Potential, 3068
International Foundation for Genetic Research/Michael Fund, 2434
KenCrest Services, 3925
Keystone Community Resources, 7776
Kranser Center for Inflammatory Bowel Disease Research, 1951
Lankenau Hospital, Sleep Disorders Center, 4387
Lehigh Valley Sickle Cell Support Group, 5853
Leukemia & Lymphoma Society - Western Pennsylvania/West Virginia Chapter, 89, 150
Library for the Blind & Physically Handicapped, Leonard C Staisey Building, 7513
Medical College of Pennsylvania, Sleep Disorders Center, 4388
Mercy Hospital of Johnstown, Sleep Disorders Center, 4389
Mid-Atlantic Regional Human Genetics Network, 521
Montgomery County Intermediate Unit #23, 7364
NF Clinic - University of Pittsburgh Children's Hospital, 4472
National Registry for Childhood Onset Scleroderma (NRCOS), 5700
PA Tourette Syndrome Alliance, 6506
Parent Education Network, 7365
Parent to Parent ARC Allegheny, 7366
Parent to Parent of Pennsylvania, 7367
Parents Union for Public Schools, 7368
Pediatric Hemophilia Program of Pennsylvania, 3597
Pediatric Pulmonary and Cystic Fibrosis Center, 2083
Penn Center for Sleep Disorders, Hospital of the University of Pennsylvania, 4390
Penn Neurological Institute, 4297
Pennsylvania Chapter of the American Anorexia Bulimia Association, 2595
Pennsylvania Educational Network for Eating Disorders (PENED), 2596

Geographic Index

Pennsylvania's Initiative on Assistive Technology, Institute on Disabilities, 7369
Pennsylvania/Delaware Valley Chapter of Crohn's & Colitis Foundation of America, 1941
Phelps School, 4096
Pittsburgh Area Brain Injury Alliance, 3045
Presbyterian-University Hospital, Pulmonary Sleep Evaluation Center, 4391
Region III Office Program Consultants for Maternal and Child Health, 6221
Renfrew Center of Bryn Mawr, 2597
Renfrew Center of Connecticut, 2581
Renfrew Center of Philadelphia, 2598
Round Lake Camp, 4098
Sickle Cell Disease Association of America, Philadelphia/Delaware Valley Chapter, 5854
Southeast Pennsylvania Support Group, 522
Spina Bifida Association of Delaware Valley, 6059
Spina Bifida Association of Greater Pennsylvania, 6060
Summer Experience, 386, 935, 4100
Summit Camp, 387
Temple University, Section of Auditory Research, 3178
Thomas Jefferson University Brain Injury Rehabilitation Program, 3069
Thomas Jefferson University Sleep Disorders Center, 4392
Turner's Syndrome Society of Nevada, 6664
US Wheelchair Weightlifting Association, 7370
United Cerebral Palsy Central Pennsylvania, 1309
United Cerebral Palsy of Northeastern Pennsylvania, 1310
University of Pennsylvania Weight and Education Program, 2599
University of Pennsylvania, Depression Research Unit, 2218
University of Pittsburgh Cystic Fibrosis Center/Children's Hospital, 2084
W.M. Krogman Center for Research In Child Growth and Development, 2901
Wesley Woods, 388, 936, 4101
Western Pennsylvania Chapter of Crohn's & Colitis Foundation of America, 1942
Western Pennsylvania Chapter of The National Hemophilia Foundation, 3549
Western Psychiatric Institute & Clinic, Sleep Evaluation Center, 4393

Rhode Island

Assistive Technology Access Partnership, 7371
Autism Society of Rhode Island, 786
Brain Tumor Support Group at Providence, 1124
Central Region Early Intervention Program, 7372
Children's Neurodevelopment Center at Hasbro Children's Hospital, 2435
Hydrocephalus Association of Rhode Island, 3780
Infant Behavior, Cry and Sleep Clinic, 1560
Office Integrated Social Services, 7373
Rhode Island Arc, 7374
Rhode Island Department of Health, 7375
Rhode Island Department of Health Immunization Program, 5290
Rhode Island Department of Health National SIDS Foundation, 6222
Rhode Island Hemostasis and Thrombosis Center, 3602
Rhode Island Hospital, Cystic Fibrosis Center, 2085
Rhode Island Parent Information Network, 7376
Rhode Island Scleroderma Support Group, 5695
Sleep Disorders Center of Lifespan Hospitals, 4394
TechACCESS of Rhode Island, 7514
Tourette Syndrome Association of Rhode Island, 6507
Turner's Syndrome Society of Rhode Island, 6673
United Cerebral Palsy of Rhode Island, 1311

South Carolina

Assistive Technology Project, 7377
Autism Society of South Carolina, 787
BabyNet, 7378
Burnt Gin Camp, 7778
CF Center/Medical University of South Carolina, 2086
Carolinas Support Group, 523
Children's Center for Cancer and Blood Disorders, 3505, 3567, 5858
Described and Captioned Media Program, 3167
Family Connection of South Carolina, 7515
Hemophilia Association of South Carolina, 3550
International Pemphigus Foundation: South Carolina Support Group, 4919
James R Clark Memorial Sickle Cell Foundation, 5855
Newberry County Memorial Hospital Brain Tumor Support Group, 1125
Office of Exceptional Children South Carolina Department of Education, 7379
PRO-Parents, 7380
Region 4 of the National Association for Parents of the Visually Impaired, 1628, 1756, 4620, 5431
SC Dept. of Health & Environmental Control Immunization Division, 5291
Sarcoidosis Support, 5633
South Carolina Department of Health & Environmental Control - SIDS Information, 6223
South Carolina State Library, 7516
Turner's Syndrome Society of South Carolina, 6674
United Cerebral Palsy of South Carolina, 1312

South Dakota

Autism Society of South Dakota Black Hills Chapter, 788
Communication Service for the Deaf, Inc., 3149
DakotaLink, 7381
Office of Special Education, 7382
Oklahoma Speech Language Hearing Association, 5980
Sioux Valley Hospital, South Dakota Cystic Fibrosis Center, 2087
South Dakota Center For Bleeding Disorders, 3604
South Dakota Department of Health, 6224
South Dakota Department of Health Office of Disease Prevention, 5292
South Dakota Parent Connection, 7383
South Dakota State Library, 7517
Teratogen and Birth Defects Information Project, 7552
Thumpers, 3860
University Affiliated Program, School of Medicine, 7384

Tennessee

ACM Lifting Lives Music Camp, 6859
All Nations Camp, 7689
Autism Society of America East Tennessee Chapter, 789
Bill Wilkerson Center, 3179
Brain Injury Association of Tennessee, 3046
Camp Easter Seal, 7779
Camp Hickory Wood, 3096
Center for Early Childhood, 7385
Down Syndrome Association of Middle Tennessee, 2408
East Tennessee Comprehensive Hemophilia Center, 3571
East Tennessee Technology Access Center, 7518
Families of SMA - Tennessee Chapter, 6127
First Regional Hemophilia Center, 3575
LIVITUP, Inc., 1313
Leukemia & Lymphoma Society, Tennessee Chapter, 90, 151
Memphis Cystic Fibrosis Center, 2088
Memphis Regional Brain Tumor Survivors Group, 1126
Memphis State University, Center for the Communicatively Impaired, 5982
Neuroscience Institute, University of Tennessee Health Science Center, 5766
Office of Special Education, State Department of Education, 7386
Pediatric Pulmonary Medicine, 2089
STEP (Support & Training for Exceptional Parents), 7387
Saint Jude Children's Research Hospital, 7519
Sarcoidosis Center, 5635
Sarcoidosis Patient Forum, 5634

Geographic Index

Technology Access Center, 7492
Tennesse Hemophilia & Bleeding Disorders Foundation, 3551
Tennessee Chapter of Crohn's & Colitis Foundation of America, 1944
Tennessee Department of Health Immunization, 5293
Tennessee Saving Little Hearts, 3861
Turner's Syndrome Society of Mid-South, 6675
Turner's Syndrome Society of Tennessee, 6676
United Cerebral Palsy of Middle Tennessee, 1314
University of Memphis Neuropsychology Lab, 3070
University of Tennessee Hemophilia Clinic, 3615
Vanderbilt Hemostasis-Thrombosis Clinic, 3617

Texas

AAIDD Texas Chapter, 2409
Arizona HeartLight, 3841
Ataxia Telangiectasia Project, 529
Autism Society of America Greater Austin Chapter, 790
Baylor College of Medicine, 4298
Baylor College of Medicine Birth Defects Center, 7520, 7534
Baylor Comprehensive Epilepsy Center, 5767
Baylor Sleep Wellness Center, 4403
Benign Essential Blepharospasm Research Foundation, 2531
Brain Injury Association of Texas, 3047
Brain Injury Research Center of the Institute for Rehabilitation & Research, 3071
Brain Tumor Support Group at Dallas, 1127
Brain Tumor Support Group at Plano, 1128
CF Center, Pulmonary Section, 2090
Callier Center for Communication Disorders, 5983
Center for Cancer and Blood Disorders, 5866
Center for Cancer and Blood Disorders at Children's Medical Center in Dallas, 3566
Central Texas Brain Tumor Support Group, 1129
Charis Hills, 384
Children's Association for Maxiumum Potential CAMP, 7780
Cook-Ft. Worth Medical Center, CF Center, 2091
Cystic Fibrosis Care, Teaching and Research Center, 2092
Cystic Fibrosis-Lung Disease Center Santa Rosa Children's Hospital, 2093
Dallas Academy, 669, 925, 4088
Department of Assistive and Rehabilitation Services, 7388
Down Syndrome Guild of Dallas, 2410
Down Syndrome Specialty Clinic, 2436
Easter Seals of Greater Houston, 1315
HOPE (Helping Oncology Parents Endure) Brain Tumor Foundation of the Southwest, 1130
Harris County Health Department, 6225
Hill School of Fort Worth, 673, 929, 4092
Houston Area Brain Tumor Network, 1131
Houston Ear Research Foundation, 3180
Houston Support Group, 524
Houston-Gulf Coast/South Texas Chapter of Crohn's & Colitis Foundation of America, 1945
Hughen Center, 7781
Hydrocephalus Association of N Texas, 3781
International Pemphigus Foundation: Houston Support Group, 4921
Leukemia & Lymphoma Society - North Texas Chapter, 91
Leukemia & Lymphoma Society - North Texas Chapter, 152
Leukemia & Lymphoma Society - South Central Texas - San Antonio Chapter, 92, 153
Leukemia & Lymphoma Society - Texas Gulf Coast Chapter, 93, 154
Menninger Child & Family Program, 1576, 6780
North Texas Chapter of Crohn's & Colitis Foundation of America, 1946
North Texas Support Group, 525
Office of the Dean, University of Texas at Austin, 7390
Parent Case Management, 7391
Partners Resource Network, 7392
Project PODER, 7393
Region VI Office Program Consultants For Maternal and Child Health, 6226
Sickle Cell Association of Austin - Marc Thomas Chapter, 5856
Sickle Cell Association of the Texas Gulf Coast, 5857
Sleep Disorders Center for Children, 4395
Sleep Medicine Associates of Texas, 4396
South Central Region-Helen Keller National Center, 7394
South Texas Comprehensive Hemophilia and Thrombophilia Treatment Center, 3605
Southwest Human Development, 7096
Southwestern Comprehensive Sickle Cell Center, 5867
Spina Bifida Association of Houston-Gulf Coast, 6062
Spina Bifida Association of North Texas, 6063
Spina Bifida Association of Texas, 6064
Sweeney, 2355
Texas Assistive Technology Partnership, 7395
Texas Central Chapter of the National Hemophilia Foundation, 3552
Texas Department of Health Immunization Division, 5294
Texas Heart to Heart, 3863
Texas Lions Camp, 1722, 1858, 3494, 7782
Texas Perinatal Association, 5221
Texas State Library, 7521
Tri-Services Military CF Center, 2094
Turner's Syndrome Society of Houston, 6677
Turner's Syndrome Society of North Texas, 6678
Turner's Syndrome Society of San Antonio, 6679
UT Southwestern Medical Center at Dallas: Hematology-Oncology Research, 3611
Univ. of Texas-Southwestern Med. Ctr. at Dallas - Clinical Ctr. for Liver Disease, 956
University of Texas Department of Hematology Research, 3616
University of Texas Medical Branch at Galveston, Clinical Research Center, 4404
University of Texas Sleep/Wake Disorders Center, 4397
University of Texas Southwestern Medical Center/Asthma & Allergic Diseases, 427
University of Texas, Mental Health Clinical Research Center, 2219

Utah

Baby Watch Early Intervention Program, 7396
Brain Injury Association of Utah, 3048
Camp Kostopulos, 7783
Computer Center for Citizens with Disabilities, 7397
Early Intervention Research Institute, Developmental Center, 7538
Heart of the Matter, 3847
Primary Children's Medical Center, 7546
Special Education Services Unit, 7398
Spina Bifida Association of Utah, 6065
Tourette Syndrome Association - Utah Chapter, 6508
Turner's Syndrome Society of Salt Lake City, 6680
US Disabled Ski Team, 7399
University of Utah, 4299
University of Utah Intermountain Cystic Fibrosis Center, 2095
Utah Center for Assistive Technology, 7400
Utah Chapter of the National Hemophilia Foundation, 3553
Utah Department of Health, 5295, 6227
Utah Parent Center, 7401
Utah State Library Commission, 7522
Utah Support Group National Ataxia Foundation, 526

Vermont

Assistive Technology Project, 7402
Autism Society of Vermont, 791
Brain Injury Association of Vermont, 3049
Camp Akeela, 382
Center on Disabilities and Community Inclusion, 7403
Family, Infant, and Toddler Project, 7404
Farm and Wilderness Camps, 7784
Medical Center Hospital of Vermont, 2096
Special Education Unit, 7405
Thorpe Camp, 3941
Vermont Department of Health State Immunization Program, 5296

Geographic Index

Vermont Department of Libraries Special Service Unit, 7523
Vermont Parent Information Center, 7406
Vermont Regional Hemophilia Center, 3618

Virginia

Alexandria Library Talking Book Service, 1678, 1808, 4674, 5485
American Diabetes Association, 2339
Arlington County Department of Libraries, 7524
Autism Society of America Northern Virginia Chapter, 792
Brain Injury Association of Virginia, 3050
Brain Tumor Support Group, 1132
Camp Baker Services, 7785
Camp Easter Seal East, Camp Easter Seal West, 7786
Camp Fantastic, 120, 173, 1170
Camp Holiday Trails, 7787
Childhelp Children's Center of Virginia, 5044
Cystic Fibrosis Center/University of Virginia Health System, 2097
Cystic Fibrosis Program of the Medical College of Virginia, 2098
Division for Research (CEC-DR), 7536
Division for the Visually Handicapped, 1679, 1809, 4675, 5486
Division on Visual Impairments, 1680, 1810, 4676, 5487
Eastern Virginia Medical Center, 2099
Fairfax County Public Library, 7525
Families Empowered and Supporting Treatment of Eating Disorders, 2601
Hemophilia Association of the Capital Area, 3554
Infant & Toddler Program, 7407
Leukemia & Lymphoma Society - National Capital Area Chapter, 94, 155
Makemie Woods Camp Conference Center, 2354, 7788
National Sudden Infant Death Syndrome Research Center, 6235
National Sudden Infant Death Syndrome Resource Center, 6231
Newport News Public Library System, 7526
Oakland School & Camp, 4095
Office of Special Education, Virginia, 7408
Overlook, 7789
Parent Educational Advocacy Training Center, 7409
Precious Hearts, 3865
Roanoke City Public Library System, 7527
Spina Bifida Association of the Roanoke Valley, 6066
Triangle D Camp for Children, 7790
Trisomy 18 Foundation, 6512, 6597
University of Virginia General Clinical Research Center, 428
Virginia Assistive Technology System, 7410
Virginia Beach Public Library, 7528
Virginia Commonwealth University Department of Neurosurgery Research, 3072
Virginia Department of Health Bureau of Immunization, 5297
Virginia State Library for the Visually and Physically Handicapped, 1681, 1811, 4677, 5488

Washington

Adult Brain Tumor Support Group, 1133
Autism Society of Washington, 793
Bleeding Disorders Foundation of Washington, 3555
Brain Injury Association of Washington, 3051
Brain Tumor Support Group University of Washington Medical Center, 1134
Epilepsy Foundation Washington, 5758
Evergreen Spina Bifida Association, 6067
Healing Hearts, 3858
Hemophilia Foundation of Washington, 3556
Infant Toddler Early Intervention Program, 7411
Leukemia & Lymphoma Society - Washington/Alaska Chapter, 82, 95, 7087, 7412
National Wilms Tumor Study, 6871
Northwestern Region-Helen Keller National Center, 1629, 4621, 5432
Office of the Superintendent of Public Instruction, 7413
Prader-Willi Northwest Association, 5176, 5184, 5191
Puget Sound Blood Center, 3599
Region X Office Program Consultants for Maternal and Child Health, 6228
Seattle Area Support Group, 527
Tourette Syndrome Association - Washington and Oregon Chapter, 6505, 6509
Turner's Syndrome Society of Inland Northwest, 6682
University of Washington CF Center, 2100
University of Washington Department of Speech & Hearing Sciences, 5985
University of Washington Speech and Hearing Clinic, 5993
University of Washington: Experimental Education Unit, 2437
Washington Library for the Blind and Physically Handicapped, 1682, 1812, 4678, 5489
Washington PAVE, 7414
Washington State Chapter of Crohn's & Colitis Foundation of America, 1947
Washington State Department of Health Immunization Program, 5298

West Virginia

Autism Services Center, 803
Autism Society of West Virginia, 794
Autism Training Center, 804
Brain Injury Association of West Virginia, 3052
Cabell County Public Library, 7529
Early Intervention Program, 7415
Kanawha County Public Library, 7530
Mountain Milestones Stepping Stones, 7791
Mountaineer Spina Bifida Camp, 6114
Office of Special Education Administration, 7416
People First-West Virginia, 3929
West Virginia Assistive Technology System, 7417
West Virginia Department of Health and Human Services, 6229
West Virginia Library Commission, 7531
West Virginia Parent Training and Information, 7418
West Virginia School for the Blind, 1683, 1813, 4679, 5490
West Virginia University Cystic Fibrosis Center, 2101
West Virginia University Mountain State Cystic Fibrosis Center, 2102

Wisconsin

Autism Society of Wisconsin, 795
Birth to 3 Program, 7419
Brain Injury Association of Wisconsin, 3053
Brain Tumor Support Group, 1135
Brain Tumor Support Group at Milwaukee, 1136
Brain Tumor Support Group at Wauwatosa Froederdt Memorial Lutheran Hospital, 1137
Broadscope Disability Services, 1317
Brown County Library, 7532
Camp Heartland, 2991
Camp Joy, 7792
Center for the Study of Bioethics, 2438
Development and Training Center, 7420
Division of Community Services, 7421
Early Childhood Handicapped Prgrams, 7422
Easter Seals Wisconsin Camp Respite, 1367
Great Lakes Hemophilia Foundation, 3557
Hemophilia Outreach Center, 3560
International Bone Marrow Transplant Registry, 98
John Sierzant Brain Tumor Support Group, 1138
Kids With Heart, 3867
Left Hearts, 3868
Leukemia & Lymphoma Society - Wisconsin Chapter, 96, 156
Medical College of Wisconsin Cystic Fibrosis Center, 2103
National Center for the Study of Wilson's Disease, 6891
Parent Education Project of Wisconsin, 7423
Physician Referral and Information Line, 421
Regional Epilepsy Center, 5768
Research at BloodCenter of Wisconsin, 3601

Geographic Index

Scoliosis Research Society, 5723
Spina Bifida Association of Northern Wisconsin, 6069
Spina Bifida Association of Wisconsin, 6070
Timbertop Nature Adventure Camp, 7793
Turner's Syndrome Society of Southeastern Wisconsin, 6683
United Cerebral Palsy of Greater Dane County, 1318
United Cerebral Palsy of West Central Wisconsin, 1319
University of Wisconsin Asthma and Allergic Disease Center, 429
University of Wisconsin-Madison Cystic Fibrosis/Pulmonary Center, 2104
Waisman Center - Auditory Physiology Research Laboratory, 5994
WisTech, 7424
Wisconsin Association for Perinatal Care, 5222
Wisconsin Chapter of Crohn's & Colitis Foundation of America, 1948
Wisconsin Lions Camp, 1724, 1860, 3497

Wyoming

Brain Injury Association of Wyoming, 3054
Division of Developmental Disabilities, 7425
Parent Information Center, 7426
Parent and Information Center, 7544
Special Education Unit, 7427
Wyoming Department of Health, 6230
Wyoming's New Options in Technology (WYNOT), 7428

Disorder & Related Term Index

A

Accommodation strabismus, 6141
ACM, 299
Acquired hypothyroidism, 3874
Acquired Immune Deficiency Syndrome, 2929
Acquired ptosis, 5368
Acrocephaly, 1880
Acute ascending polyneuritis, 2921
Acute febrile polyneuritis, 2921
Acute gastrointestinal infection, 22
Acute granulocytic leukemia, 124
Acute hepatitis, 3655
Acute idiopathic polyneuritis, 2921
Acute infectious diarrhea, 22
Acute lymphoblastic leukemia, 63
Acute lymphocytic leukemia, 63
Acute myeloblastic leukemia, 124
Acute myelocytic leukemia, 124
Acute myelogenous leukemia, 124
Acute myeloid leukemia, 124
Acute myelomonocytic leukemia, 124
Acute otitis media, 4860
Acute postinfectious polyneuropathy, 2921
ADHD, 570
Adrenoleukodystrophy (ALD), 4112
Adrenomyeloneuropathy, 4112
Adult Gaucher's disease, 2869
Agranulocytosis, genetic infantile, 4501
Agyria, 4123
AHF, 3517
AIDS, 2929
Albinism, 177
Albino, 177
Albright syndrome, 4191
ALL, 63
Allergic reaction, 5584
Allergic rhinitis, 5584
Alopecia areata, 200
Alopecia circumscripta, 200
Alopecia totalis, 200
Alopecia universalis, 200
Alpha-1-antitrypsin deficiency, 212
Alpha-thalassemia, 6357
Amaurosis congenita, 5542
Amaurosis fugax, 4226
Amblyopia, 4016, 5415
AMC, 323
AML, 124
Amyoplasia, 323
Anaclitic depression of infancy, 2188
Anal atresia, 258
Anal fistula, 258
Anal stenosis, 258
Androgenetic alopecia, 200
Anencephaly, 224
Angioedema, 6735
Angioneurotic edema, 6735
Anhidrotic ectodermal dysplasia, 2668
Aniridia, 235
Aniridia-cerebellar ataxia, 235
Anisometropia, 5415
Ankylosing spondylitis, 247
Anorectal malformations, 258
Anorexia nervosa, 2547, 4761
Antihemophilic factor deficiency, 3517
Anus, ectopic, 258
Anus, imperforate, 258
Aortic arch obstruction, 1535
Aortic coarctation, 1535
Aortic stenosis, 280

Aortic valve stenosis, 280
Aphasia, 5955
Apnea of prematurity, 290
Apnea of prematurity, idiopathic, 290
Apnea, central, 290
Apnea, obstructive, 290
Arnold-Chiari deformity, 299
Arnold-Chiari malformation, 299, 3764
Arnold-Chiari malformation type I, 299
Arnold-Chiari malformation type II, 299
Arnold-Chiari syndrome, 299
Arrhythmias, 308
Arthrogryposis multiplex congenita, 323
Articulation, 5955
AS, 247
ASD, 560
Asperger syndrome, 335
Aspiration pneumonia, 5106
Asthma, 389
Asthma, bronchial, 389
Astigmatism, 5415
AT, 473
Ataxia, 473
Ataxia-telangiectasia, 473, 6322
Ataxias, hereditary, 473
Ataxias, spinocerebellar, 473
Ataxic cerebral palsy, 1228
Athetosis, 1480
Atrial septal defects, 560
Atrioseptal defects, 560
Attention deficit disorder, 570
Attention deficit hyperactivity disorder, 570
Atypical pneumonia, 5106
Autism, 335
Autism, infantile, 678
Autistic disorder, 678

B

Baby bottle tooth decay, 2142
Bacterial gastroenteritis, 22
Bacterial pneumonia, 5106
Baldness, 200
Basilar migraine, 4226
BDLS, 1871
Becker muscular dystrophy, 4284
Beckwith-Wiedemann syndrome, 4807
Bed-wetting, 4564
Behavioral abnormalities, 2729
Bell's palsy, 938, 4140
Benign familial pemphigus, 4906
Beta-thalassemia, 6357
Beta-thalassemia major, 6357
Beta-thalassemia minor, 6357
Bicuspid aortic valve, 280
Biliary Atresia, 949
Bilirubin, 4429
Bilirubin encephalopathy, 3988
Binge eating, 2547
Bipolar disorder, 962
Blepharoptosis, 5368
Blepharospasm, 2520
Blood cancer, 63, 124
Bone tumor, 2775
BPD, 1174
Brain infection, 4202
Brain injuries, 2995
Brain trauma, 2995
Brain tumors, 1004
Branched chain ketoaciduria, 4172
Bretonneau's disease, 5237
Brittle bone disease, 4831

Disorder & Related Term Index

Bronchiolitis, 5533
Bronchopulmonary dysplasia, 1174
Bruxism, 2142
Bulimia nervosa, 2547
Burn injuries, 1183

C

CAH, 1606
Cataplexy, 4339
Cataracts, 1618
Cavernous hemangiomas, 3498
CD, 1203
CDH, 1725, 1734
CdLS, 1871
Celiac disease, 1203
Celiac sprue, 1203
Central precocious puberty, 5203
Cerebellar astrocytoma, 1004
Cerebral diseases, 4112
Cerebral infections, 4202
Cerebral palsy, 1228
Cerebral trauma, 2995
CF, 1992
Chelation, 4046
Cheloids, 3980
Chiari malformation, 299
Chickenpox, 5237
Child abuse, 5015
Child care virus, 2134
Childhood dermatomyositis, 1391
Cholestasis, Neonatal, 212
Chorea, 1480
Chorea, benign familial, 1480
Chorea, drug-induced, 1480
Choreoathetoid cerebral palsy, 1228
Christ-Siemens-Touraine syndrome, 2668
Christmas disease, 3517
Chromosome 13, monosomy 13q syndrome, 5555
Chromosome 13, trisomy 13, 6598
Chromosome 18, trisomy 18, 6589
Chromosome 21, trisomy 21, 2369
Chromosome 45,X syndrome, 6637
Chromosome XXY, 3999
Chronic Gaucher's disease, 2869
Chronic hepatitis, 3655
Chronic otitis media, 4860
Chronic relapsing polyradiculoneuropathy, 2921
Chronic unremit'g polyradiculoneuropathy, 2921
Class I histiocytoses, 3724
Class I malocclusion, 2142
Class II malocclusion, 2142
Class III malocclusion, 2142
Classic galactosemia, 2855
Classic Gaucher's disease, 2869
Classic hemophilia, 3517
Classic homocystinuria, 3749
Classic migraine, 4226
Classic MSUD, 4172
Classic phenylketonuria, 4924
Cleft lip, 1494
Cleft lip with cleft palate, 1494
Cleft palate, 1494
Closed-head injury, 2995
Clouston's syndrome, 2668
Clubfoot, 1521
CMV, 2134
Coarctation of the aorta, 1535
Cold Sore, 3696
Colic, 1546
Collodion baby, 3885
Common migraine, 4226

Communicating hydrocephalus, 3764
Compensatory scoliosis, 5716
Concussion, 2995
Conduct disorder, 1564
Conductive deafness, 3099
Conductive hearing loss, 3099
Congenital adrenal hyperplasia, 1606
Congenital amaurosis, 5542
Congenital biliary obstruction, 949
Congenital cataracts, 1618
Congenital diaphragmatic hernia, 1725
Congenital dislocation of the hip, 1734
Congenital dysplasia of the hip, 1734
Congenital generalized phlebectasia, 6322
Congenital glaucoma, 1744
Congenital heart disease, 280
Congenital herpes, 3696, 4417
Congenital hip dysplasia, 1734
Congenital hypothyroidism, 3874
Congenital kyphosis, 5716
Congenital liver disease, 949
Congenital malformation of palate/lip, 1494
Congenital oculocutaneous albinism, 177
Congenital ptosis, 5368
Congenital scoliosis, 5716
Congenital synostosis, 4007
Congenital talipes equinovarus, 1521
Congenital toxoplasmosis, 6566
Conjunctivitis, 1861
Constipation, 2729
Convulsions, 5742
Cornelia de Lange syndrome, 1871
Cot death, 6180
CP, 1228
Cradle cap, 2684
Craniopharyngioma, 1004
Craniostenosis, 1880
Craniostosis, 1880
Craniosynostosis, 1880
Crib death, 6180
Crohn's disease, 1896
Cryptorchidism, 1973
Cryptorchidy, 1973
Cryptorchism, 1973
Cushing's basophilism, 1982
Cushing's syndrome, 1982
Cutaneous diphtheria, 5237
Cutis marmorata telangiectatica, 6322
Cystathionine synthase deficiency, 3749
Cystic fibrosis, 1992
Cystic hygromas, 3498
Cytomegalic inclusion disease, 2134
Cytomegalovirus, 2134

D

D1 trisomy syndrome, 6598
Dawson's encephalitis, 6169
DDH, 1734
De Lange syndrome, 1871
Deafness, 3099
Deer tick disease, 4140
Deficiency of fructose-1,6-bisphosphate, 3681
Deficiency of phosphofructaldolase, 3681
Deficiency of uridyl diphosphogalactose, 2855
Dental caries, 2142
Dental mottling, 2142
Denys-Drash syndrome, 6861
Depression, 2188
Depth perception, 4016
Dermatitis, allergic contact, 2684
Dermatitis, atopic, 2684

Disorder & Related Term Index

Dermatitis, contact, 2684
Dermatitis, eczematous, 2684
Dermatitis, irritant contact, 2684
Dermatitis, seborrheic, 2684
Dermatomyositis, childhood, 1391
Dermatomyositis, juvenile, 1391
Developmental dysplasia of the hip, 1734
Diabetes, 2286
Diabetes mellitus, 2286
Diaphragmatic hernia, congenital, 1725
Diarrhea, 22
DiGeorge sequence, 2356
DiGeorge syndrome, 2356
Diphtheria, 5237
Distomolar, 2142
DMD, 2520
Dopa-responsive dystonia, 2520
Down syndrome, 2369
DRD, 2520
Drooping eyelid, 5368
Duchenne muscular dystrophy, 4284
Dysarthria, 5955
Dyscalculia, 4052
Dysgraphia, 4052
Dyshidrosis, 2684
Dyslexia, 2488, 4052
Dysphasia, 5955
Dystonia, 2520
Dystonia musculorum deformans, 2520
Dystonia, buccomandibular, 2520
Dystonia, cervical, 2520
Dystonia, dopa-responsive, 2520
Dystonia, drug-induced, 2520
Dystonia, focal, 2520
Dystonia, torsion, 2520

E

Eating disorders, 2547
Ectodermal dysplasias, 2142, 2668
Ectrodactyly-ectodermal dysplasia, 2668
Eczema, 2684
Eczema herpeticum, 3696
Eczema, infantile, 2684
Edwards syndrome, 6589
EEC syndrome, 2668
Ehlers-Danlos syndrome, 2709
EI, 2754
Embryopathy, etretinate, 2830
Embryopathy, isotretinoin, 2830
Embryopathy, retinol, 2830
Encephalocele, 2716, 6009
Encopresis, 2729
Enteritis, regional, 1896
Enterobiasis, 5090
Enterobius vermicularis, 5090
Enuresis, 4564
Enuresis, nocturnal, 5907
Eosinophelia syndrome (NARES), 5584
Eosinophilic granuloma, 3724
Epidemic parotitis, 5237
Epidermolysis bullosa, 2740
Epidermolysis bullosa dystrophica, 2740
Epidermolysis bullosa simplex, 2740
Epidermolytic hyperkeratosis, 3885
Epidural hematoma, 2995
Epilepsy, 4761, 5742
Epilepsy, idiopathic, 5742
EPP, 5127
Erb's palsy, 2748
Erb-Duchenne paralysis, 2748
Erythema infectiosum, 2754

Erythema migrans, 4140
Erythroblastosis fetalis, 3509
Erythroblastosis neonatorum, 3509
Erythrohepatic protoporphyria, 5127
Erythropoietic protoporphyria, 5127
Esophageal atresia, 2762
Ewing's sarcoma, 2775
Ewing's tumor, 2775
Exomphalos-macroglossia-gigantism, 4807
Extrapulmonary tuberculosis, 6604

F

Facial nerve paralysis, 938
Facioscapulohumeral muscular dystrophy, 4284
Factor IX deficiency, 3517
Factor VIII deficiency, 3517
Factor VIIIR deficiency, 3517
FAE, 2807
Fainting, 6269
Fallot's syndrome, 6345
Familial dysautonomia, 2800
Farsightedness, 5415
FAS, 2807
Fazio-Londe disease, 6115
FD, 2800
Fecal incontinence, 2729
Female Pseudo-Turner syndrome, 4600
Ferrochelatase deficiency, 5127
Fetal acquired immune deficiency, 2929
Fetal AIDS, 2929
Fetal alcohol effect, 2807
Fetal alcohol syndrome, 2807
Fetal retinoid syndrome, 2830
Fifth disease, 2754
First degree burns, 1183
Food poisoning, 22
45,X/46,XY/47,XXY mosaicism, 3999
46,XX/47,XXY mosaicism, 3999
46,XY/47,XXY mosaicism, 3999
46,XY/48,XXYY mosaicism, 3999
48,XXXY, 3999
49,XXXYY, 3999
Fragile X syndrome, 2839
Friedereich's ataxia, 473
Fungal pneumonia, 5106

G

Galactokinase deficiency, 2855
Galactose epimerase deficiency, 2855
Galactosemia, 2855
Gastroenteritis, 22
Gaucher disease, 2869
GBS, 2921
Gelineau's syndrome, 4339
Generalized essential telangiectasia, 6322
Generalized tetanus, 5237
Genital herpes, 3696
Geophagia, 5079
German measles, 5237
Germinal matrix hemorrhage, 3942
GH deficiency, 2881
Gilles de la Tourette syndrome, 6454
Globoid cell leukodystrophy, 4112
Glucosyl cerebroside lipidosis, 2869
Glucosylceramide lipidosis, 2869
Gluten-sensitive enteropathy, 1203
GM2 gangliosidosis, type I, 6298
GM2 gangliosidosis, type III, 6298
GMH, 3942

Disorder & Related Term Index

Group conduct disorder, 1564
Growth hormone deficiency, 2881
Growth hormone deficiency, isolated, 2881
GSE, 1203
GTS, 6454
Guillain-Barre syndrome, 2921

H

Hailey-Hailey disease, 4906
Hallervorden-Spatz disease, 2520
Hand-Schüller-Christian disease, 3724
Harlequin fetus, 3885
Hashimoto's disease, 3874
Hay fever, 5584
Head injuries, 2995
Head trauma, 2995
Hearing impairment, 3099
Hearing loss, 3099
Hemangiomas, 3498
Hemangiomas, capillary, 3498
Hemangiomas, mixed, 3498
Hemangiomatosis, disseminated, 3498
Hemiplegic migraine, 4226
Hemolytic anemia, 5835
Hemolytic disease of the newborn, 3509
Hemophilia, 3517
Hemophilia A, 3517
Hemophilia B, 3517
Hepatitis, 3655
Hepatitis A, 3655
Hepatitis B, 3655
Hepatitis C, 3655
Hepatitis D, 3655
Hepatitis E, 3655
Hepatolenticular degeneration, 6883
Hepatotropic virus, 3655
Hereditary benign telangiectasia, 6322
Hereditary fructose intolerance, 3681
Hereditary hemorrhagic telangiectasia, 6322
Hereditary sensory and autonomic neuropa, 2800
Herpes labialis, 3696
Herpes simplex, 3696, 4417
Herpes simplex virus, 3696, 4417
Herpetic gingivostomatitis, 3696
Herpetic whitlow, 3696
Heterotropia, 6141
Hexa deficiency, 6298
Hexosaminidase A deficiency, 6298
Hidrotic ectodermal dysplasia, 2668
Hip dislocation, 1734
Hip dysplasia, 1734
Hirschsprung disease, 3710
Histiocytosis, 3724
Histiocytosis X, 3724
HIV, 2929
Hives, 6735
HLHS, 3838
HMD, 5523
Hodgkin's disease, 3734
Hodgkin's disease, lymphocyte depletion, 3734
Hodgkin's disease, lymphocyte predominan, 3734
Homocystinuria Type I, 3749
Homocystinuria Type II, 3749
Homocystinuria Type III, 3749
Homozygous Hb S, 5835
HSAN-III, 2800
HSV-1, 3696, 4417
HSV-2, 3696, 4417
Human immunodeficiency virus infection, 2929
Hunter syndrome, 4274
Hurler syndrome, 4274

Hyaline membrane disease, 1174, 5523
Hydrocephalus, 3764
Hydrocephalus, acute, 3764
Hydrocephalus, occult tension, 3764
Hydrocephalus, overt tension, 3764
Hydrocephaly, 3764
Hyperactive child syndrome, 570
Hyperadrenocorticism, 1982
Hyperbilirubinemia, 3988, 4429
Hyperkinetic syndrome, 570
Hyperopia, 5415
Hyperphenylalaninemia, 4924
Hypertrophic cardiomyopathy, 3824
Hypertrophy, 3824
Hypnagogic hallucinations, 4339
Hypnolepsy, 4339
Hypohidrotic ectodermal dysplasia, 2668
Hypopituitarism, 2881
Hypoplasia of thymus and parathyroids, 2356
Hypoplastic Left Heart Syndrome, 3838
Hypothyroidism, 3874

I

IBD, 1896, 6698
Ichthyosiform erythroderma, bullous, 3885
Ichthyosiform erythroderma, congenital, 3885
Ichthyosiform erythroderma, nonbullous, 3885
Ichthyosis, 3885
Ichthyosis simplex, 3885
Ichthyosis vulgaris, 3885
Ichthyosis, lamellar, 3885
Ichthyosis, X-linked, 3885
Icterus neonatorum, 4429
Idiopathic kyphosis, 5716
Idiopathic scoliosis, 5716
Idiopathic thrombocytopenia purpura, 6400
IGHD, 2881
Immunodeficiency, thymic agenesis, 2356
Imperforate anus, 258
Infant respiratory distress syndrome, 5523
Infantile colic, 1546
Infantile glaucoma, 1744
Infantile hypertrophic pyloric stenosis, 5397
Infantile pyloric stenosis, 5397
Infantile spasms, 5742
Infectious conjunctivitis, 1861
Infectious gastroenteritis, 22
Infectious parotitis, 5237
Inflammatory bowel disease, 1896, 6698
Inherited absence of skin pigment, 177
Insulin-dependent diabetes, 2286
Intellectual Disabilities, 3896
Intermediate MSUD, 4172
Intermittent MSUD, 4172
Intraventricular hemorrhage, 3942
Iris, hypoplasia of, 235
Isolated lissencephaly sequence, 4123
ITP, 6400
IVH, 3942

J

Jaundice, 4429
JDMS, 1391
JRA, 3950
Junctional epidermolysis bullosa, 2740
Juvenile rheumatoid arthritis, 3950

Disorder & Related Term Index

K

Kanner's syndrome, 678
Kawasaki disease, 3973
Keloids, 3980
Kernicterus, 3988
KFS, 4007
Kidney tumor, 6861
Kleeblattschadel deformity, 1880
Klinefelter syndrome, 3999
Klippel-Feil syndrome, 4007
Klippel-Feil syndrome Type I, 4007
Klippel-Feil syndrome Type II, 4007
Klippel-Feil syndrome Type III, 4007
Kostmann's disease, 4501
Krabbe disease, 4112
Kugelberg-Welander disease, 6115
Kyphosis, 5716

L

Lactose intolerance, 4251
Landouzy-Dejerine disease, 4284
Landry's paralysis, 2921
Langerhans cell histiocytosis, 3724
Language, 5955
Laron syndrome, 2881
Lazy eye, 4016
LCH, 3724
LCPD, 4103
LDD, 4052
Lead exposure, 4046
Lead poisoning, 4046
Lead toxicity, 4046
Learning disability, 2488, 4052
Learning disorder, 4052
Leber congenital retinal amaurosis, 5542
Left heart obstruction, 280
Legg-Calve-Perthes disease, 4103
Lens opacities, 1618
Letterer-Siwe disease, 3724
Leukemia, 63
Leukodystrophies, 4112
Limb-girdle muscular dystrophy, 4284
Lissencephaly, 4123
Liver, inflammation of, 3655
Localized tetanus, 5237
Loss of hair, 200
Lupus, 6286
Lyme disease, 4140
Lymphangiomas, 3498
Lymphatic malformations, 3498
Lymphoma, Hodgkin's, 3734
Lysosomal storage disorders, 4264

M

Macrocephalia, 4164
Macrocephaly, 3764, 4164
Macrocephaly, benign familial, 4164
Major depressive disorder, 2188
Male Turner syndrome, 4600
Manic-depressive disorder, 962
Manic-depressive illness, 962
Manic-depressive psychosis, 962
Manifest deviation, 6141
Maple syrup urine disease, 4172
Marfan syndrome, 4181
Marfan syndrome, infantile, 4181
Marfan syndrome, neonatal, 4181
Marie-Strumpell spondylitis, 247

Marker X syndrome, 2839
Martin-Bell syndrome, 2839
MAS, 4191
Maternal phenylketonuria, 4924
McCune-Albright syndrome, 4191
MCNS, 4444
Measles, 5237, 6169
Meckel-Gruber syndrome, 2716
Meconium aspiration syndrome, 5523
Medulloblastoma, 1004
Megacolon, aganglionic, 3710
Megacolon, congenital aganglionic, 3710
Megalocephaly, 4164
Meningitis, 4202
Meningitis, bacterial, 4202
Meningitis, chronic, 4202
Meningitis, neonatal, 4202
Meningitis, viral, 4202
Meningocele, 6009
Meningomyelocele, 6009
Mesiodens, 2142
Metachromatic leukodystrophy, 4112
Methionine, 3749
Methylcobalamin defect, 3749
Methylenetetrahydrofolate reductase, 3749
MFS, 4181
Microcephalia, 4209
Microcephalism, 4209
Microcephaly, 4209
Microdontia, 4218
Microdontism, 4218
Middle ear, inflammation of, 4860
Migraine headaches, 4226
Migraine with aura, 4226
Migraine without aura, 4226
Mild MSUD, 4172
Milk protein allergy, 4251
Miller-Dieker lissencephaly syndrome, 4123
Miller-Fisher syndrome, 2921
Minimal change nephrotic syndrome, 4444
Mixed cerebral palsy, 1228
Mixed hearing loss, 3099
ML, 4264
MLNS, 3973
Mood disturbance, 2188
Morbilli, 5237
Morphea, 5689
Movement disorders, 1480, 2520
MPS, 4274
MSUD, 4172
Mucocutaneous lymph node syndrome, 3973
Mucolipidoses, 4264
Mucopolysaccharidoses, 4274
Mucoviscidosis, 1992
Mumps, 5237
Muscular dystrophy, 4284
Mycobacterium africanum, 6604
Mycobacterium bovis, 6604
Mycobacterium tuberculosis, 6604
Myelocele, 6009
Myelomeningocele, 299, 6009
Myopia, 5415

N

Narcolepsy, 4339
Natal teeth, 2142
NB, 4481
Nearsightedness, 5415
Neonatal conjunctivitis, 1861
Neonatal herpes simplex, 4417
Neonatal jaundice, 4429

Disorder & Related Term Index

Neonatal opthalmia, 1861
Neonatal pemphigus vulgaris, 4906
Neonatal tetanus, 5237
Nephroblastoma, 6861
Nephrotic syndrome, 4444
Neural tube defect, 224, 2716
Neuroblastoma, 4481
Neurocardiogenic syncope, 6269
Neurofibromatosis, 4457
Neurofibromatosis type I, 4457
Neurofibromatosis type II, 4457
Neuromuscular scoliosis, 5716
Neutropenia, 4501
Neutropenia, chronic, 4501
Neutropenia, cyclic, 4501
Neutropenia, transient, 4501
Nevi, strawberry, 3498
Newborn respiratory distress, 5523
NF1, 4457
NF2, 4457
NHL, 4577
Night terrors, 4540, 5907
Nightmares, 4513
Nine-day measles, 5237
Nocturnal enuresis, 4564
Non-allergic rhinitis, 5584
Non-communicating hydrocephalus, 3764
Non-Hodgkin's lymphoma, 4577
Non-Hodgkin's lymphoma, Burkitt's type, 4577
Non-Hodgkin's lymphoma, large cell type, 4577
Non-Hodgkin's lymphoma, small noncleaved, 4577
Non-Hodgkin's lymphoma, SNCC type, 4577
Noninfectious conjunctivitis, 1861
Nonparalytic strabismus, 6141
Nontropical sprue, 1203
Noonan syndrome, 4600
Norman-Roberts lissencephaly syndrome, 4123
NS, 4600
Nystagmus, 4610
Nystagmus, acquired, 4610
Nystagmus, congenital, 4610
Nystagmus, convergent, 4610
Nystagmus, jerky, 4610
Nystagmus, pendular, 4610

O

Obesity, 4712
Obsessive-compulsive disorder, 4761
Obsessive-compulsive neurosis, 4761
Obstructive sleep apnea, 5883
OCD, 4761
Ocular albinism, 177
Ocular herpes, 3696
Oculocutaneous albinism, 177
Oculocutaneous albinism, type I, 177
Oculocutaneous albinism, type II, 177
ODD, 4820
OI, 4831
Olivopontocerebellar atrophy, 473
Omphalocele, 4807
OPCA, 473
OPCA of neonatal onset, 473
Open-head injury, 2995
Ophiasis, 200
Ophthalmia neonatorum, 1861
Ophthalmoplegic migraine, 4226
Oppositional Defiant Disorder, 4820
Oral herpes, 3696
OSA, 5883
Osteochondroses, 4103
Osteogenesis imperfecta, 4831

Otitis, 5584
Otitis media, 4860
Otitis media with effusion, 4860
Oxycephaly, 1880
Oxyuriasis, 5090

P

Paralytic strabismus, 6141
Paramolar, 2142
Parasitic gastroenteritis, 22
Paroxysmal sleep, 4339
Paroxysmal SVT, 308
Partial albinism, 177
Parvovirus B19, 2754
Passive-aggressive behavior, 4874
Patau syndrome, 6598
Patent ductus arteriosus, 4896
Pauciarticular JRA, 3950
Pavor nocturnus, 4540
PC deficiency, 5317
PDA, 4896
Pediatric AIDS, 2929
Pelade, 200
Pelizaeus-Merzbacher disease, 4112
Pemphigus, 4906
Pemphigus foliaceus, 4906
Pemphigus vegetans, 4906
Pemphigus vulgaris, 4906
Peridens, 2142
Peripheral precocious puberty, 5203
Periventricular hemorrhage, 3942
Permanent discoloration of the teeth, 2142
Persistent fetal circulation, 5377
Perthes disease, 4103
Pertussis, 5237
Pervasive developmental disorder, 335
PFC, 5377
PFD, 4191
Pharynx and larynx hypoplasia, 4807
Phenylalanine hydroxylase deficiency, 4924
Phenylketonuria, 4924
Phobias, 4939
Phobic disorder, 4939
Photoallergic reaction, 4992
Photosensitivity, 4992
Phototoxic reaction, 4992
Physical abuse, 5015
PICA, 5079
Piebaldism, 177
Pinkeye, 1861
Pinworm, 5090
Pituitary basophilism, 1982
Pituitary dwarfism, 2881
Pityriasis rosea, 5098
PKU, 4924
Plagiocephaly, frontal, 1880
Pneumocystis pneumonia, 5106
Pneumonia, 5106
POFD, 4191
Polio, 5237
Polyarticular JRA, 3950
Polydactylia, 5118
Polydactylism, 5118
Polydactyly, 5118
Polydontia, 2142
Polymorphous light eruption, 4992
Polyostotic fibrous dysplasia, 4191
Polysyndactyly, 6276
Pompholyx, 2684
Porphyrias, 5127
Port-wine stains, 3498

Disorder & Related Term Index

Post traumatic stress disorder, 5136
Postural kyphosis, 5716
Prader-Willi syndrome, 5169
Precocious pseudopuberty, 5203
Precocious puberty, 5203
Prematurity, 5214
Primary glaucoma, 1744
PROC deficiency, 5317
Prognathism, 2142
Progressive bulbar palsy of childhood, 6115
Progressive obliterative cholangiopathy, 949
Protein C deficiency, 5317
Protoporphyria, 5127
Psoriasis, 5330
Ptosis, 5368
PTSD, 5136
Pubertas praecox, 5203
Pulmonary hypertension, primary, 5377
Pulmonary tuberculosis, 6604
Pulmonary valve stenosis, 5387
Pulmonic stenosis, critical, 5387
PVH, 3942
PWS, 5169
Pyloric stenosis, 5397

R

Rachioscoliosis, 5716
RDS, 5523
Reactive airway disease, 389
Reading problems, 4052
Refraction abnormalities, 5415
Refraction errors, 5415
Renal tumor, 6861
Rendu-Osler-Weber disease, 6322
Respiratory distress syndrome, 1174, 5523
Respiratory syncytial virus infection, 5533
Respiratory tract diphtheria, 5237
Retinitis pigmentosa, 5542
Retinoblastoma, 5555
Retinopathy of prematurity, 5577
Retrognathis, 2142
Retromolar, 2142
Rheumatic fever, 1480
Rhinitis, 5584
Rhinorrhea, 5584
Riley-Day syndrome, 2800
ROP, 5577
Roussy-Levy syndrome, 473
RP, 5542
RSV infection, 5533
Rubella, 5237
Rubeola, 5237

S

Salmon stains, 3498
Sanfilippo syndrome, 4274
Sarcoid of Boeck, 5619
Sarcoidosis, 5619
Scaphocephaly, 1880
Schaumann's disease, 5619
Scheuermann's disease, 5716
Schizophrenia, childhood, 1423
Scleroderma, 5689
Scleroderma, linear, 5689
Scoliosis, 5716
Second degree burns, 1183
Secondary glaucoma, 1744
Secretory otitis media, 4860
Segawa syndrome, 2520

Seizures, 5742
Seizures, absence, 5742
Seizures, complex partial, 5742
Seizures, febrile, 5742
Seizures, generalized, 5742
Seizures, generalized tonic-clonic, 5742
Seizures, grand mal, 5742
Seizures, partial, 5742
Seizures, petit mal, 5742
Seizures, simple partial, 5742
Sensorineural deafness, 3099
Sensorineural hearing loss, 3099
Sexual abuse, 5015
Sheie syndrome, 4274
Shprintzen omphalocele syndrome, 4807
Sickle cell anemia, 5835
Sickle cell disease, 5835
Sickle cell trait, 5835
SIDS, 6180
Simple phobias, 4939
Skull fracture, 2995
Slapped cheek, 2754
SLE, 6286
Sleep apnea, 5883
Sleep disturbances, 4513, 4540
Sleep paralysis, 4339
Sleep-terror disorder, 4540
Sleepwalking, 5907
SMA, 6115
SMA type I, 6115
SMA type II, 6115
SMA type III, 6115
Social phobias, 4939
Soiling, 2729
Solitary aggressive conduct disorder, 1564
Somnambulism, 5907
Spasmodic torticollis, 2520
Spasmus nutans, 4610
Spastic cerebral palsy, 1228
Speech, 5955
Speech dysfunction, 5955
Speech impairment, 5955
Spider angioma, 6322
Spider nevus, 6322
Spider telangiectasia, 6322
Spina bifida, 2716, 6009
Spina bifida occulta, 6009
Spinal muscular atrophies, 6115
Squint, 6141
SSPE, 6169
Stammering, 6152
Status epilepticus, 5742
Sticker's disease, 2754
Still's Disease, 3950
Strabismus, 6141
Strawberry hemangioma, 3498
Stuttering, 6152
Subacute sclerosing leukoencephalopathy, 6169
Subacute sclerosing panencephalitis, 6169
Subdural hematoma, 2995
Sudden infant death syndrome, 6180
Supplementary teeth, 2142
Supraventricular tachycardia, 308
Surfactant deficiency, 1174
SVT, 308
Swallowing abnormality in the newborn, 2762
Sydenham's chorea, 1480
Syncope, 6269
Syndactylia, 6276
Syndactylism, 6276
Syndactyly, 6276
Syndrome-associated scoliosis, 5716

Disorder & Related Term Index

Synostosis, 4007
Systemic lupus erythematosus, 6286
Systemic sclerosis, 5689
Systemic-onset JRA, 3950

T

Talipes, 1521
Tay-Sachs disease, 6298
Tay-Sachs disease, infantile type, 6298
Tay-Sachs disease, juvenile type, 6298
TB, 6604
TED, 5317
Teeth, 4218
Teeth, Absence of, 2142
Temporary discoloration of the teeth, 2142
Teratologic congenital dysplasia of the, 1734
Testes, ectopic, 1973
Testes, maldescended, 1973
Testes, true undescended, 1973
Tetanus, 5237
Tetralogy of Fallot, 6345
Thalassemia, 6357
Thiamine-responsive MSUD, 4172
Third and fourth pharyngeal pouch, 2356
Third degree burns, 1183
Threadworm, 5090
Three-day measles, 5237
Three-month colic, 1546
Thrombocytopenia, 6400
Thromboembolic disease, 5317
Thrombotic disorder, 5317
Thumbsucking, 6415
Tic disorder, chronic motor, 6425
Tics, 6425, 6454
Tics of childhood, transient, 6425
Tooth decay, 2142
Tourette syndrome, 4761, 6425, 6454
Toxoplasmosis, 6566
Tracheoesophageal fistula, 2762
Transposition of the great arteries, 6576
Transposition of the great vessels, 6576
Traumatic brain injury, 2995
Trigonocephaly, 1880
Trisomy 13 syndrome, 6598
Trisomy 18 mosaicism, 6589
Trisomy 18 syndrome, 6589
Trisomy 21 mosaicism, 2369
Trisomy 21 syndrome, 2369
Trisomy 21 translocation, 2369
True precocious puberty, 5203
TS, 6624
TSD, 6298
Tuberculosis, 6604
Tuberous sclerosis, 6624
Tumor, benign, 1004
Tumor, malignant, 1004
Turner phenotype with normal chromosomes, 4600
Turner syndrome, 6637
Turricephaly, 1880
Tympanitis, 4860
Tyrosinase neg.oculocutaneous albinism, 177
Tyrosinase pos.oculocutaneous albinism, 177

U

Ulcerative colitis, 6698
Uncoordinated movements, 473
Undescended testes, 1973
Undifferentiated conduct disorder, 1564
Unilateral neviod telangiectasia, 6322
Unstable gait, 473
Urticaria pigmentosa, 6735

V

VACTERL association, 258
Van Bogaert's encephalitis, 6169
Vasodepressor syncope, 6269
Ventricular septal defects, 6744
Vertebrae, fused, 4007
Viral gastroenteritis, 22
Viral infections of childhood, 2754
Viral pneumonia, 5106
Vision, 4016
Visual disturbances, 5415
Visual impairment, 4016
Von Recklinghausen disease, 4457
Von Willebrand's disease, 3517
VSDs, 6744

W

Waardenburg syndrome, 177
WAGR syndrome, 235, 6861
Walker-Warburg syndrome, 4123
WBC, 6846
WD, 6883
Weber-Cockayne syndrome, 2740
Werdnig-Hoffmann disease, 6115
White matter diseases, 4112
Whooping cough, 5237
Williams syndrome, 6846
Williams-Beuren syndrome, 6846
Wilms tumor, 6861
Wilson disease, 2520, 6883
WMS, 6846
WND, 6883
Wohlfart-Kugelberg-Welander disease, 6115
Wolff-parkinson-white syndrome, 308
WPW, 308
Writer's cramp, 2520
WS, 6846

X

X-linked lissencephaly, 4123
XO syndrome, 6637
XXY syndrome, 3999

Z

Zygosyndactyly, 6276

Titles from Grey House

Visit www.GreyHouse.com for Product Information, Table of Contents, and Sample Pages.

Opinions Throughout History
Opinions Throughout History: Church & State
Opinions Throughout History: Conspiracy Theories
Opinions Throughout History: The Death Penalty
Opinions Throughout History: Diseases & Epidemics
Opinions Throughout History: Drug Use & Abuse
Opinions Throughout History: The Environment
Opinions Throughout History: Free Speech & Censorship
Opinions Throughout History: Gender: Roles & Rights
Opinions Throughout History: Globalization
Opinions Throughout History: Guns in America
Opinions Throughout History: Immigration
Opinions Throughout History: Law Enforcement in America
Opinions Throughout History: Mental Health
Opinions Throughout History: Nat'l Security vs. Civil & Privacy Rights
Opinions Throughout History: Presidential Authority
Opinions Throughout History: Robotics & Artificial Intelligence
Opinions Throughout History: Social Media Issues
Opinions Throughout History: The Supreme Court
Opinions Throughout History: Voters' Rights
Opinions Throughout History: War & the Military
Opinions Throughout History: Workers Rights & Wages

This is Who We Were
This is Who We Were: Colonial America (1492-1775)
This is Who We Were: 1880-1899
This is Who We Were: In the 1900s
This is Who We Were: In the 1910s
This is Who We Were: In the 1920s
This is Who We Were: A Companion to the 1940 Census
This is Who We Were: In the 1940s (1940-1949)
This is Who We Were: In the 1950s
This is Who We Were: In the 1960s
This is Who We Were: In the 1970s
This is Who We Were: In the 1980s
This is Who We Were: In the 1990s
This is Who We Were: In the 2000s
This is Who We Were: In the 2010s

Working Americans
Working Americans—Vol. 1: The Working Class
Working Americans—Vol. 2: The Middle Class
Working Americans—Vol. 3: The Upper Class
Working Americans—Vol. 4: Children
Working Americans—Vol. 5: At War
Working Americans—Vol. 6: Working Women
Working Americans—Vol. 7: Social Movements
Working Americans—Vol. 8: Immigrants
Working Americans—Vol. 9: Revolutionary War to the Civil War
Working Americans—Vol. 10: Sports & Recreation
Working Americans—Vol. 11: Inventors & Entrepreneurs
Working Americans—Vol. 12: Our History through Music
Working Americans—Vol. 13: Education & Educators
Working Americans—Vol. 14: African Americans
Working Americans—Vol. 15: Politics & Politicians
Working Americans—Vol. 16: Farming & Ranching
Working Americans—Vol. 17: Teens in America
Working Americans—Vol. 18: Health Care Workers
Working Americans—Vol. 19: The Performing Arts

Grey House Health & Wellness Guides
Addiction Handbook & Resource Guide
The Autism Spectrum Handbook & Resource Guide
Autoimmune Disorders Handbook & Resource Guide
Cardiovascular Disease Handbook & Resource Guide
Dementia Handbook & Resource Guide
Depression Handbook & Resource Guide
Diabetes Handbook & Resource Guide
Nutrition, Obesity & Eating Disorders Handbook & Resource Guide

Consumer Health
Complete Mental Health Resource Guide
Complete Resource Guide for Pediatric Disorders
Complete Resource Guide for People with Chronic Illness
Complete Resource Guide for People with Disabilities
Older Americans Information Resource
Parenting: Styles & Strategies
Teens: Growing Up, Skills & Strategies

General Reference
American Environmental Leaders
Constitutional Amendments
Encyclopedia of African-American Writing
Encyclopedia of Invasions & Conquests
Encyclopedia of Prisoners of War & Internment
Encyclopedia of the Continental Congresses
Encyclopedia of the United States Cabinet
Encyclopedia of War Journalism
The Environmental Debate
Financial Literacy Starter Kit
From Suffrage to the Senate
The Gun Debate: Gun Rights & Gun Control in the U.S.
Historical Warrior Peoples & Modern Fighting Groups
Human Rights and the United States
Political Corruption in America
Privacy Rights in the Digital Age
The Religious Right and American Politics
Speakers of the House of Representatives, 1789-2021
US Land & Natural Resources Policy
The Value of a Dollar 1600-1865 Colonial to Civil War
The Value of a Dollar 1860-2019

Business Information
Business Information Resources
Complete Broadcasting Industry Guide: TV, Radio, Cable & Streaming
Directory of Mail Order Catalogs
Environmental Resource Handbook
Food & Beverage Market Place
The Grey House Guide to Homeland Security Resources
The Grey House Performing Arts Industry Guide
Guide to Healthcare Group Purchasing Organizations
Guide to U.S. HMOs and PPOs
Guide to Venture Capital & Private Equity Firms
Hudson's Washington News Media Contacts Guide
New York State Directory
Sports Market Place

Grey House Publishing | Salem Press | H.W. Wilson | 4919 Route, 22 PO Box 56, Amenia NY 12501-0056

Grey House Imprints

Visit www.GreyHouse.com for Product Information, Table of Contents, and Sample Pages.

Grey House Titles, continued

Education
Complete Learning Disabilities Resource Guide
Digital Literacy: Skills & Strategies
Educators Resource Guide
The Comparative Guide to Elem. & Secondary Schools
Special Education: Policy & Curriculum Development

Statistics & Demographics
America's Top-Rated Cities
America's Top-Rated Smaller Cities
The Comparative Guide to American Suburbs
Profiles of America
Profiles of California
Profiles of Florida
Profiles of Illinois
Profiles of Indiana
Profiles of Massachusetts
Profiles of Michigan
Profiles of New Jersey
Profiles of New York
Profiles of North Carolina & South Carolina
Profiles of Ohio
Profiles of Pennsylvania
Profiles of Texas
Profiles of Virginia
Profiles of Wisconsin

Canadian Resources
Associations Canada
Canadian Almanac & Directory
Canadian Environmental Resource Guide
Canadian Parliamentary Guide
Canadian Venture Capital & Private Equity Firms
Canadian Who's Who
Cannabis Canada
Careers & Employment Canada
Financial Post: Directory of Directors
Financial Services Canada
FP Bonds: Corporate
FP Bonds: Government
FP Equities: Preferreds & Derivatives
FP Survey: Industrials
FP Survey: Mines & Energy
FP Survey: Predecessor & Defunct
Health Guide Canada
Libraries Canada

Weiss Financial Ratings
Financial Literacy Basics
Financial Literacy: How to Become an Investor
Financial Literacy: Planning for the Future
Weiss Ratings Consumer Guides
Weiss Ratings Guide to Banks
Weiss Ratings Guide to Credit Unions
Weiss Ratings Guide to Health Insurers
Weiss Ratings Guide to Life & Annuity Insurers
Weiss Ratings Guide to Property & Casualty Insurers
Weiss Ratings Investment Research Guide to Bond & Money Market
  Mutual Funds
Weiss Ratings Investment Research Guide to Exchange-Traded Funds
Weiss Ratings Investment Research Guide to Stock Mutual Funds
Weiss Ratings Investment Research Guide to Stocks

Books in Print Series
American Book Publishing Record® Annual
American Book Publishing Record® Monthly
Books In Print®
Books In Print® Supplement
Books Out Loud™
Bowker's Complete Video Directory™
Children's Books In Print®
El-Hi Textbooks & Serials In Print®
Forthcoming Books®
Law Books & Serials In Print™
Medical & Health Care Books In Print™
Publishers, Distributors & Wholesalers of the US™
Subject Guide to Books In Print®
Subject Guide to Children's Books In Print®

Grey House Publishing | Salem Press | H.W. Wilson | 4919 Route, 22 PO Box 56, Amenia NY 12501-0056

Titles from Salem Press

SALEM PRESS

Visit www.SalemPress.com for Product Information, Table of Contents, and Sample Pages.

LITERATURE

Critical Insights: Authors

- Louisa May Alcott
- Sherman Alexie
- Isabel Allende
- Maya Angelou
- Isaac Asimov
- Margaret Atwood
- Jane Austen
- James Baldwin
- Saul Bellow
- Roberto Bolano
- Ray Bradbury
- The Brontë Sisters
- Gwendolyn Brooks
- Albert Camus
- Raymond Carver
- Willa Cather
- Geoffrey Chaucer
- John Cheever
- Joseph Conrad
- Charles Dickens
- Emily Dickinson
- Frederick Douglass
- T. S. Eliot
- George Eliot
- Harlan Ellison
- Ralph Waldo Emerson
- Louise Erdrich
- William Faulkner
- F. Scott Fitzgerald
- Gustave Flaubert
- Horton Foote
- Benjamin Franklin
- Robert Frost
- Neil Gaiman
- Gabriel Garcia Marquez
- Thomas Hardy
- Nathaniel Hawthorne
- Robert A. Heinlein
- Lillian Hellman
- Ernest Hemingway
- Langston Hughes
- Zora Neale Hurston
- Henry James
- Thomas Jefferson
- James Joyce
- Jamaica Kincaid
- Stephen King
- Martin Luther King, Jr.
- Barbara Kingsolver
- Abraham Lincoln
- C.S. Lewis
- Mario Vargas Llosa
- Jack London
- James McBride
- Cormac McCarthy
- Herman Melville
- Arthur Miller
- Toni Morrison
- Alice Munro
- Tim O'Brien
- Flannery O'Connor
- Eugene O'Neill
- George Orwell
- Sylvia Plath
- Edgar Allan Poe
- Philip Roth
- Salman Rushdie
- J.D. Salinger
- Mary Shelley
- John Steinbeck
- Amy Tan
- Leo Tolstoy
- Mark Twain
- John Updike
- Kurt Vonnegut
- Alice Walker
- David Foster Wallace
- Edith Wharton
- Walt Whitman
- Oscar Wilde
- Tennessee Williams
- Virginia Woolf
- Richard Wright
- Malcolm X

Critical Insights: Works

- Absalom, Absalom!
- Adventures of Huckleberry Finn
- The Adventures of Tom Sawyer
- Aeneid
- All Quiet on the Western Front
- All the Pretty Horses
- Animal Farm
- Anna Karenina
- The Awakening
- The Bell Jar
- Beloved
- Billy Budd, Sailor
- The Book Thief
- Brave New World
- The Canterbury Tales
- Catch-22
- The Catcher in the Rye
- The Color Purple
- The Crucible
- Death of a Salesman
- The Diary of a Young Girl
- Dracula
- Fahrenheit 451
- The Grapes of Wrath
- Great Expectations
- The Great Gatsby
- Hamlet
- The Handmaid's Tale
- Harry Potter Series
- Heart of Darkness
- The Hobbit
- The House on Mango Street
- How the Garcia Girls Lost Their Accents
- The Hunger Games Trilogy
- I Know Why the Caged Bird Sings
- In Cold Blood
- The Inferno
- Invisible Man
- Jane Eyre
- The Joy Luck Club
- Julius Caesar
- King Lear
- The Kite Runner
- Life of Pi
- Little Women
- Lolita
- Lord of the Flies
- The Lord of the Rings
- Macbeth
- The Merchant of Venice
- The Metamorphosis
- Midnight's Children
- A Midsummer Night's Dream
- Moby-Dick
- Mrs. Dalloway
- Nineteen Eighty-Four
- The Odyssey
- Of Mice and Men
- The Old Man and the Sea
- On the Road
- One Flew Over the Cuckoo's Nest
- One Hundred Years of Solitude
- Othello
- The Outsiders
- Paradise Lost
- The Pearl
- The Plague
- The Poetry of Baudelaire
- The Poetry of Edgar Allan Poe
- A Portrait of the Artist as a Young Man
- Pride and Prejudice
- A Raisin in the Sun
- The Red Badge of Courage
- Romeo and Juliet
- The Scarlet Letter
- Sense and Sensibility
- Short Fiction of Flannery O'Connor
- Slaughterhouse-Five
- The Sound and the Fury
- A Streetcar Named Desire
- The Sun Also Rises
- A Tale of Two Cities
- The Tales of Edgar Allan Poe
- Their Eyes Were Watching God
- Things Fall Apart
- To Kill a Mockingbird
- War and Peace
- The Woman Warrior

Critical Insights: Themes

- The American Comic Book
- American Creative Non-Fiction
- The American Dream
- American Multicultural Identity
- American Road Literature
- American Short Story
- American Sports Fiction
- The American Thriller
- American Writers in Exile
- Censored & Banned Literature
- Civil Rights Literature, Past & Present
- Coming of Age
- Conspiracies
- Contemporary Canadian Fiction
- Contemporary Immigrant Short Fiction
- Contemporary Latin American Fiction
- Contemporary Speculative Fiction

Grey House Publishing | Salem Press | H.W. Wilson | 4919 Route, 22 PO Box 56, Amenia NY 12501-0056

Titles from Salem Press

Visit www.SalemPress.com for Product Information, Table of Contents, and Sample Pages.

Crime and Detective Fiction
Crisis of Faith
Cultural Encounters
Dystopia
Family
The Fantastic
Feminism Flash Fiction
Gender, Sex and Sexuality
Good & Evil
The Graphic Novel
Greed
Harlem Renaissance
The Hero's Quest
Historical Fiction
Holocaust Literature
The Immigrant Experience
Inequality
LGBTQ Literature
Literature in Times of Crisis
Literature of Protest
Love
Magical Realism
Midwestern Literature
Modern Japanese Literature
Nature & the Environment
Paranoia, Fear & Alienation
Patriotism
Political Fiction
Postcolonial Literature
Power & Corruption
Pulp Fiction of the '20s and '30s
Rebellion
Russia's Golden Age
Satire
The Slave Narrative
Social Justice and American Literature
Southern Gothic Literature
Southwestern Literature
Survival
Technology & Humanity
Truth & Lies
Violence in Literature
Virginia Woolf & 20th Century Women Writers
War

Critical Insights: Film

Bonnie & Clyde
Casablanca
Alfred Hitchcock
Stanley Kubrick

Critical Approaches to Literature

Critical Approaches to Literature: Feminist
Critical Approaches to Literature: Moral
Critical Approaches to Literature: Multicultural
Critical Approaches to Literature: Psychological

Literary Classics

Recommended Reading: 600 Classics Reviewed

Novels into Film

Novels into Film: Adaptations & Interpretation
Novels into Film: Adaptations & Interpretation, Volume 2

Critical Surveys of Literature

Critical Survey of American Literature
Critical Survey of Drama
Critical Survey of Long Fiction
Critical Survey of Mystery and Detective Fiction
Critical Survey of Poetry
Critical Survey of Poetry: Contemporary Poets
Critical Survey of Science Fiction & Fantasy Literature
Critical Survey of Shakespeare's Plays
Critical Survey of Shakespeare's Sonnets
Critical Survey of Short Fiction
Critical Survey of World Literature
Critical Survey of Young Adult Literature

Critical Surveys of Graphic Novels

Heroes & Superheroes
History, Theme, and Technique
Independents & Underground Classics
Manga

Critical Surveys of Mythology & Folklore

Creation Myths
Deadly Battles & Warring Enemies
Gods & Goddesses
Heroes and Heroines
Love, Sexuality, and Desire
World Mythology

Cyclopedia of Literary Characters & Places

Cyclopedia of Literary Characters
Cyclopedia of Literary Places

Introduction to Literary Context

American Poetry of the 20th Century
American Post-Modernist Novels
American Short Fiction
English Literature
Plays
World Literature

Magill's Literary Annual

Magill's Literary Annual, 2023
Magill's Literary Annual, 2022
Magill's Literary Annual, 2021
Magill's Literary Annual (Backlist Issues 2020-1977)

Masterplots

Masterplots, Fourth Edition
Masterplots, 2010-2018 Supplement

Notable Writers

Notable African American Writers
Notable American Women Writers
Notable Mystery & Detective Fiction Writers
Notable Writers of the American West & the Native American Experience
Notable Writers of LGBTQ+ Literature

Grey House Publishing | Salem Press | H.W. Wilson | 4919 Route, 22 PO Box 56, Amenia NY 12501-0056

Titles from Salem Press

Visit www.SalemPress.com for Product Information, Table of Contents, and Sample Pages.

HISTORY

The Decades
The 1910s in America
The Twenties in America
The Thirties in America
The Forties in America
The Fifties in America
The Sixties in America
The Seventies in America
The Eighties in America
The Nineties in America
The 2000s in America
The 2010s in America

Defining Documents in American History
Defining Documents: The 1900s
Defining Documents: The 1910s
Defining Documents: The 1920s
Defining Documents: The 1930s
Defining Documents: The 1950s
Defining Documents: The 1960s
Defining Documents: The 1970s
Defining Documents: The 1980s
Defining Documents: American Citizenship
Defining Documents: The American Economy
Defining Documents: The American Revolution
Defining Documents: The American West
Defining Documents: Business Ethics
Defining Documents: Capital Punishment
Defining Documents: Civil Rights
Defining Documents: Civil War
Defining Documents: The Constitution
Defining Documents: The Cold War
Defining Documents: Dissent & Protest
Defining Documents: Domestic Terrorism & Extremism
Defining Documents: Drug Policy
Defining Documents: The Emergence of Modern America
Defining Documents: Environment & Conservation
Defining Documents: Espionage & Intrigue
Defining Documents: Exploration and Colonial America
Defining Documents: The First Amendment
Defining Documents: The Free Press
Defining Documents: The Great Depression
Defining Documents: The Great Migration
Defining Documents: The Gun Debate
Defining Documents: Immigration & Immigrant Communities
Defining Documents: The Legacy of 9/11
Defining Documents: LGBTQ+
Defining Documents: Manifest Destiny and the New Nation
Defining Documents: Native Americans
Defining Documents: Political Campaigns, Candidates & Discourse
Defining Documents: Postwar 1940s
Defining Documents: Prison Reform
Defining Documents: Secrets, Leaks & Scandals
Defining Documents: Slavery
Defining Documents: Supreme Court Decisions
Defining Documents: Reconstruction Era
Defining Documents: The Vietnam War
Defining Documents: U.S. Involvement in the Middle East
Defining Documents: Workers' Rights
Defining Documents: World War I
Defining Documents: World War II

Defining Documents in World History
Defining Documents: The 17th Century
Defining Documents: The 18th Century
Defining Documents: The 19th Century
Defining Documents: The 20th Century (1900-1950)
Defining Documents: The Ancient World
Defining Documents: Asia
Defining Documents: Genocide & the Holocaust
Defining Documents: Human Rights
Defining Documents: The Middle Ages
Defining Documents: The Middle East
Defining Documents: Nationalism & Populism
Defining Documents: The Nuclear Age
Defining Documents: Pandemics, Plagues & Public Health
Defining Documents: Renaissance & Early Modern Era
Defining Documents: Revolutions
Defining Documents: Women's Rights

Great Events from History
Great Events from History: American History, Exploration to the Colonial Era, 1492-1775
Great Events from History: The Ancient World
Great Events from History: The Middle Ages
Great Events from History: The Renaissance & Early Modern Era
Great Events from History: The 17th Century
Great Events from History: The 18th Century
Great Events from History: The 19th Century
Great Events from History: The 20th Century, 1901-1940
Great Events from History: The 20th Century, 1941-1970
Great Events from History: The 20th Century, 1971-2000
Great Events from History: Modern Scandals
Great Events from History: African American History
Great Events from History: The 21st Century, 2000-2016
Great Events from History: LGBTQ Events
Great Events from History: Human Rights
Great Events from History: Women's History

Great Lives from History
Great Athletes
Great Athletes of the Twenty-First Century
Great Lives from History: The 17th Century
Great Lives from History: The 18th Century
Great Lives from History: The 19th Century
Great Lives from History: The 20th Century
Great Lives from History: The 21st Century, 2000-2017
Great Lives from History: African Americans
Great Lives from History: The Ancient World
Great Lives from History: American Heroes
Great Lives from History: American Women
Great Lives from History: Asian and Pacific Islander Americans
Great Lives from History: Autocrats & Dictators
Great Lives from History: The Incredibly Wealthy
Great Lives from History: Inventors & Inventions
Great Lives from History: Jewish Americans
Great Lives from History: Latinos
Great Lives from History: The Middle Ages
Great Lives from History: The Renaissance & Early Modern Era
Great Lives from History: Scientists and Science

Grey House Publishing | Salem Press | H.W. Wilson | 4919 Route, 22 PO Box 56, Amenia NY 12501-0056

Titles from Salem Press

Visit www.SalemPress.com for Product Information, Table of Contents, and Sample Pages.

History & Government
American First Ladies
American Presidents
The 50 States
The Ancient World: Extraordinary People in Extraordinary Societies
The Bill of Rights
The Criminal Justice System
The U.S. Supreme Court

Innovators
Computer Technology Innovators
Fashion Innovators
Human Rights Innovators
Internet Innovators
Music Innovators
Musicians and Composers of the 20th Century
World Political Innovators

SOCIAL SCIENCES
Civil Rights Movements: Past & Present
Countries, Peoples and Cultures
Countries: Their Wars & Conflicts: A World Survey
Education Today: Issues, Policies & Practices
Encyclopedia of American Immigration
Ethics: Questions & Morality of Human Actions
Issues in U.S. Immigration
Principles of Sociology: Group Relationships & Behavior
Principles of Sociology: Personal Relationships & Behavior
Principles of Sociology: Societal Issues & Behavior
Racial & Ethnic Relations in America
Weapons, Warfare & Military Technology
World Geography

HEALTH
Addictions, Substance Abuse & Alcoholism
Adolescent Health & Wellness
Aging
Cancer
Community & Family Health Issues
Integrative, Alternative & Complementary Medicine
Genetics and Inherited Conditions
Infectious Diseases and Conditions
Magill's Medical Guide
Nutrition
Parenting: Styles & Strategies
Psychology & Behavioral Health
Teens: Growing Up, Skills & Strategies
Women's Health

Principles of Health
Principles of Health: Allergies & Immune Disorders
Principles of Health: Anxiety & Stress
Principles of Health: Depression
Principles of Health: Diabetes
Principles of Health: Nursing
Principles of Health: Obesity
Principles of Health: Occupational Therapy & Physical Therapy
Principles of Health: Pain Management
Principles of Health: Prescription Drug Abuse

SCIENCE
Ancient Creatures
Applied Science
Applied Science: Engineering & Mathematics
Applied Science: Science & Medicine
Applied Science: Technology
Biomes and Ecosystems
Digital Literacy: Skills & Strategies
Earth Science: Earth Materials and Resources
Earth Science: Earth's Surface and History
Earth Science: Earth's Weather, Water and Atmosphere
Earth Science: Physics and Chemistry of the Earth
Encyclopedia of Climate Change
Encyclopedia of Energy
Encyclopedia of Environmental Issues
Encyclopedia of Global Resources
Encyclopedia of Mathematics and Society
Forensic Science
Notable Natural Disasters
The Solar System
USA in Space

Principles of Science
Principles of Aeronautics
Principles of Anatomy
Principles of Astronomy
Principles of Behavioral Science
Principles of Biology
Principles of Biotechnology
Principles of Botany
Principles of Chemistry
Principles of Climatology
Principles of Computer-aided Design
Principles of Computer Science
Principles of Digital Arts & Multimedia
Principles of Ecology
Principles of Energy
Principles of Fire Science
Principles of Forestry & Conservation
Principles of Geology
Principles of Information Technology
Principles of Marine Science
Principles of Mathematics
Principles of Mechanics
Principles of Microbiology
Principles of Modern Agriculture
Principles of Pharmacology
Principles of Physical Science
Principles of Physics
Principles of Programming & Coding
Principles of Robotics & Artificial Intelligence
Principles of Scientific Research
Principles of Sports Medicine & Exercise Science
Principles of Sustainability
Principles of Zoology

Titles from Salem Press

Visit www.SalemPress.com for Product Information, Table of Contents, and Sample Pages.

CAREERS

Careers: Paths to Entrepreneurship
Careers in Archaeology & Museum Services
Careers in Artificial Intelligence
Careers in the Arts: Fine, Performing & Visual
Careers in the Automotive Industry
Careers in Biology
Careers in Biotechnology
Careers in Building Construction
Careers in Business
Careers in Chemistry
Careers in Communications & Media
Careers in Cybersecurity
Careers in Education & Training
Careers in Engineering
Careers in Environment & Conservation
Careers in Financial Services
Careers in Fish & Wildlife
Careers in Forensic Science
Careers in Gaming
Careers in Green Energy
Careers in Healthcare
Careers in Hospitality & Tourism
Careers in Human Services
Careers in Information Technology
Careers in Law, Criminal Justice & Emergency Services
Careers in the Music Industry
Careers in Manufacturing & Production
Careers in Nursing
Careers in Physics
Careers in Protective Services
Careers in Psychology & Behavioral Health
Careers in Public Administration
Careers in Sales, Insurance & Real Estate
Careers in Science & Engineering
Careers in Social Media
Careers in Sports & Fitness
Careers in Sports Medicine & Training
Careers in Technical Services & Equipment Repair
Careers in Transportation
Careers in Writing & Editing
Careers Outdoors
Careers Overseas
Careers Working with Infants & Children
Careers Working with Animals

BUSINESS

Principles of Business: Accounting
Principles of Business: Economics
Principles of Business: Entrepreneurship
Principles of Business: Finance
Principles of Business: Globalization
Principles of Business: Leadership
Principles of Business: Management
Principles of Business: Marketing

Grey House Publishing | Salem Press | H.W. Wilson | 4919 Route, 22 PO Box 56, Amenia NY 12501-0056

Titles from H.W. Wilson

Visit www.HWWilsonInPrint.com for Product Information, Table of Contents, and Sample Pages.

The Reference Shelf

Affordable Housing
Aging in America
Alternative Facts, Post-Truth and the Information War
The American Dream
Artificial Intelligence
The Business of Food
Campaign Trends & Election Law
College Sports
Democracy Evolving
The Digital Age
Embracing New Paradigms in Education
Food Insecurity & Hunger in the United States
Future of U.S. Economic Relations: Mexico, Cuba, & Venezuela
Gene Editing & Genetic Engineering
Global Climate Change
Guns in America
Hacktivism
Hate Crimes
Immigration
Income Inequality
Internet Abuses & Privacy Rights
Internet Law
LGBTQ in the 21st Century
Marijuana Reform
Mental Health Awareness
Money in Politics
National Debate Topic 2014/2015: The Ocean
National Debate Topic 2015/2016: Surveillance
National Debate Topic 2016/2017: US/China Relations
National Debate Topic 2017/2018: Education Reform
National Debate Topic 2018/2019: Immigration
National Debate Topic 2019/2021: Arms Sales
National Debate Topic 2020/2021: Criminal Justice Reform
National Debate Topic 2021/2022: Water Resources
National Debate Topic 2022/2023: Emerging Technologies & International Security
National Debate Topic 2023/2024: Economic Inequality
New Frontiers in Space
Policing in 2020
Pollution
Prescription Drug Abuse
Propaganda and Misinformation
Racial Tension in a Postracial Age
Reality Television
Renewable Energy
Representative American Speeches, Annual Editions
Rethinking Work
Revisiting Gender
The South China Sea Conflict
Sports in America
The Supreme Court
The Transformation of American Cities
The Two Koreas
UFOs
Vaccinations
Voting Rights
Whistleblowers

Core Collections

Children's Core Collection
Fiction Core Collection
Graphic Novels Core Collection
Middle & Junior High School Core
Public Library Core Collection: Nonfiction
Senior High Core Collection
Young Adult Fiction Core Collection

Current Biography

Current Biography Cumulative Index 1946-2021
Current Biography Monthly Magazine
Current Biography Yearbook

Readers' Guide to Periodical Literature

Abridged Readers' Guide to Periodical Literature
Readers' Guide to Periodical Literature

Indexes

Index to Legal Periodicals & Books
Short Story Index
Book Review Digest

Sears List

Sears List of Subject Headings
Sears List of Subject Headings, Online Database
Sears: Lista de Encabezamientos de Materia

History

American Game Changers: Invention, Innovation & Transformation
American Reformers
Speeches of the American Presidents

Facts About Series

Facts About the 20th Century
Facts About American Immigration
Facts About China
Facts About the Presidents
Facts About the World's Languages

Nobel Prize Winners

Nobel Prize Winners: 1901-1986
Nobel Prize Winners: 1987-1991
Nobel Prize Winners: 1992-1996
Nobel Prize Winners: 1997-2001
Nobel Prize Winners: 2002-2018

Famous First Facts

Famous First Facts
Famous First Facts About American Politics
Famous First Facts About Sports
Famous First Facts About the Environment
Famous First Facts: International Edition

American Book of Days

The American Book of Days
The International Book of Days

Grey House Publishing | Salem Press | H.W. Wilson | 4919 Route, 22 PO Box 56, Amenia NY 12501-0056